AMERICAN INDIAN LAW: NATIVE NATIONS AND THE FEDERAL SYSTEM

AMERICAN INDIAN LAW: NATIVE NATIONS AND THE FEDERAL SYSTEM

CASES AND MATERIALS

Seventh Edition

Carole E. Goldberg
Jonathan D. Varat Professor of Law
UCLA School of Law

Rebecca Tsosie
Regent's Professor of Law
Sandra Day O'Connor College of Law
Arizona State University

Robert N. Clinton
Foundation Professor of Law
Sandra Day O'Connor College of Law
Arizona State University

Angela R. Riley
Professor of Law
UCLA School of Law

CAROLINA ACADEMIC PRESS

Durham, North Carolina

ISBN: 978-1-63280-967-4 (Print)
ISBN: 978-1-63280-969-8 (eBook)

Library of Congress Cataloging-in-Publication Data

American Indian law : native nations and the federal system : cases and materials / Carole E. Goldberg, Jonathan D. Varat Professor of Law, UCLA School of Law, Rebecca Tsosie, Regent's Professor of Law, Sandra Day O'Connor College of Law, Arizona State University, Robert N. Clinton, Foundation Professor of Law, Sandra Day O'Connor College of Law, Arizona State University, Angela R. Riley, Professor of Law, UCLA School of Law. — 7th ed.

p. cm.

Includes index.

ISBN 978-1-63280-967-4 (hardbound)

1. Indians of North America—Legal status, laws, etc.—Cases. I. Goldberg, Carole E., author. II. Tsosie, Rebecca, author. III. Clinton, Robert N., author.

KF8205.C55 2015
342.7308'72—dc23

2015027942

Carolina Academic Press, LLC
700 Kent Street
Durham, North Carolina 27701
Telephone (919) 489-7486
Fax (919) 493-5668
www.caplaw.com

Printed in the United States of America

Dedications

To my loving parents, Joseph and Ida Goldberg, my partner and husband,
Professor Duane Champagne, and my dearest daughter, Andrea.

Carole E. Goldberg

To my beloved children, Daniel and Lisa Tsosie, and to the wonderful
students I have had, who continually inspire and motivate me.

Rebecca Tsosie

For my parents, Fred & Phyllis Clinton, whose love and suppport
made my contributions to this work possible.
"Honor thy father and thy mother."
Exodus 20:12a

Robert N. Clinton

For Avah and Oona.

Angela R. Riley

Acknowledgements

Preparation of this edition took several years. The authors are deeply indebted to many people who assisted either directly or indirectly in the preparation of this book. We are pleased to welcome Professor Angela R. Riley, Professor of Law at the UCLA School of Law, as our newest co-author on this casebook. We congratulate Kevin Washburn on his appointment as Assistant Secretary for Indian Affairs and thank Kevin and Libby Washburn for their contributions to the previous edition of the casebook. We also extend a particular note of gratitude to Adeleene Rockwell (UCLA '14) for her assistance in bringing this latest edition to completion.

We greatly appreciate the support of Dean Rachel Moran, UCLA School of Law. This edition benefited greatly from research grant support from UCLA School of Law, the UCLA American Indian Studies Center, and the Office of the Chancellor, UCLA. Professor Rebecca Tsosie is very grateful to Professor Goldberg and Professor Riley for sharing the staff and research support of UCLA to enable her contributions to this casebook.

Many of the cases included in this book were downloaded through LexisNexis's LEXIS electronic information retrieval services or West Publishing Company's WESTLAW service. We acknowledge the kind cooperation of these firms in making these services available. As requested by West Publishing Company, we also note that insofar as this volume contains any work in which West Publishing Company can claim a valid copyright, they have asked us to include for those portions the following notice: Copyright © 2007–2015 West Publishing Company.

A note about the reproduced case opinions: In order to not encumber the page with dots, omissions have not always been indicated with ellipses. In addition, some footnotes have been removed from the cases; those included have the original footnote numbers retained in brackets at the beginning of the footnote text. Occasionally in the text we discuss an important footnote from an excerpted court opinion. We reference it by its original footnote number, which is the number appearing in brackets.

We also deeply appreciate the kind cooperation of the many authors, law reviews, and publishers who have graciously agreed to permit us to use or reproduce their work in this volume. Their permissions are acknowledged below.

In particular, Professor Carole Goldberg offers her deepest appreciation to UCLA law student Scott Satkin for his assistance with research for this new edition. The entire staff of the UCLA Law Library, especially Linda Karr O'Connor and Amy Atchison, did a fabulous job of overseeing the law student work and carrying out additional research. Finally, her husband Duane Champagne, UCLA Professor of Sociology and American Indian Studies, supplied countless research leads, primary resources, and conceptual tools that have enabled this casebook to incorporate Native perspectives more fully and effectively. His patience, constructive criticism, and never-ending encouragement were essential sustenance for the demanding work of producing this casebook.

Professor Rebecca Tsosie also gratefully acknowledges the support of her research assistant, Kristyne Schaff-Olson (ASU '15). She also expresses her heartfelt thanks to Beth Difelice, David Gay, and Tara Mospan, librarians at the Ross-Blakely Law Library, at the Sandra Day O'Connor College of Law, for their consistent and excellent support

Acknowledgements

with the Indian law research necessary to complete the annual updates to this text and this revision. Finally, Professor Tsosie acknowledges, with appreciation, the many outstanding colleagues in the field of Federal Indian Law who have informed her thinking about the compelling issues presented by these materials and the best ways in which to present these issues to students. In addition to those colleagues who teach Indian law in the classroom, there are some very important colleagues who teach the subject in the public arena. Professor Rebecca Tsosie is very grateful to Philip S. Deloria, Director of the American Indian Graduate Center, John Echohawk, Executive Director of the Native American Rights Fund, the staff attorneys, and board members of NARF, for their vision, their dedication to justice for Native people, and the generous ways in which they shared their time and thoughts as we worked to develop and revise this text.

Angela Riley would like to thank her co-authors, first and foremost, for inviting her to join them on this exciting endeavor, and for being outstanding mentors, colleagues, and friends in this project and in so many others. A special thanks goes to Adeleene Rockwell, who dedicated herself to moving this edition to completion as manager of the project. She also deeply appreciates extensive feedback and insights from Professors William Wood and Addie Rolnick, both of whom shared insights and experiences around teaching with this casebook. Thanks goes to the entire staff of the UCLA American Indian Studies Center, but particularly Jamie Chan, Pamela Grieman, and Ken Wade, all of whom supported and contributed to this project in various ways. Finally, she thanks current and former UCLA students who have worked on this project and continue to inspire her.

For all of us, this has been a wonderfully rewarding collaboration, both personally and professionally. We have benefited enormously from the spirited exchanges and integration of diverse ideas that have marked this project. We hope to carry on the commitment to deep and critical examination of federal Indian law that has always marked the work of Professor Robert N. Clinton, who has inspired us as a longtime co-author of this casebook.

The authors gratefully acknowledge permission to reprint from the following copyrighted material:

Robert T. Anderson, *Indian Water Rights: Litigation and Settlements*, 42 TULSA L. REV. 23 (2006). Copyright © 2006. All rights reserved.

Barbara Atwood, *Flashpoints Under the Indian Child Welfare Act: Toward a New Understanding of State Court Resistance*, 51 EMORY L.J. 587, 639–41 (2002).

Milner S. Ball, *Constitution, Courts, Indian Tribes*, 1987 A.B.F. RES. J. 1, 63 (1987).

LESLIE BENDER & DAAN BRAVEMAN, POWER, PRIVILEGE AND LAW 139–141 (1995).

THOMAS BERGER, VILLAGE JOURNEY: THE REPORT OF THE ALASKA NATIVE REVIEW COMMISSION 142 (1985). Copyright © 1985. All rights reserved.

Michael C. Blumm, David H. Becker, & Joshua D. Smith, *The Mirage of Indian Reserved Water Rights and Western Streamflow Restoration in the McCarran Amendment Era: A Promise Unfulfilled*, 36 ENVTL. L. 1157, 1169–1170 (2006). Copyright © 2006. All rights reserved.

Kenneth H. Bobroff, *Retelling Allotment: Indian Property Rights and the Myth of Common Ownership*, 54 VAND. L. REV. 1559, 1590 (2001). Copyright © 2001. All rights reserved.

Acknowledgements

JACK CAMPISI, THE MASHPEE INDIANS: TRIBE ON TRIAL (1991).

Nancy Carol Carter, *Race and Power Politics as Aspects of Federal Guardianship over American Indians: Land-Related Cases, 1887–1924*, 4 AM. INDIAN L. REV. 197, 227 (1976).

Reid Peyton Chambers, *Judicial Enforcement of the Federal Trust Responsibility to Indians*, 27 STAN. L. REV. 1213, 1213–48 (1975).

Eric T. Cheyfitz, *Theory and Practice: The Case of the Navajo-Hopi Land Dispute*, 10 AM. U. J. GENDER SOC. POL'Y & L. 619, 629 (2002).

Chief John Ross's Petition to Congress (1837), 1 The Papers of Chief John Ross, 1807–1839, 470–74 (Gary E. Moulton ed., 1985).

Robert N. Clinton, *Criminal Jurisdiction Over Indian Lands*, 18 ARIZ. L. REV. 503, 507–513, 520–52 (1976).

Robert N. Clinton, *The Dormant Indian Commerce Clause*, 27 CONN. L. REV. 1055, 1155–1164 (1995). Copyright © 1995. All rights reserved.

Robert N. Clinton, *There is No Federal Supremacy Clause for Indian Tribes*, 34 ARIZ. ST. L.J. 113, 232 (2002).

George Cameron Coggins & William Modrcin, *Native American Indians and Federal Wildlife Law*, 31 STAN. L. REV. 375, 415–19 (1979).

FELIX S. COHEN, HANDBOOK OF FEDERAL INDIAN LAW xxvii–xxviii, 122 (1942).

Richard Collins, *Indian Allotment Water Rights*, 20 LAND & WATER L. REV. 421–57 (1985).

Comment, *Tribal Self Government and the Indian Reorganization Act of 1934*, 70 MICH. L. REV. 955 (1972).

Vine Deloria Jr., *The Size and Status of Nations*, in NATIVE AMERICAN VOICES: A READER 457, 465 (S. Lobo & S. Talbot eds., 1998). Copyright © 1998. All rights reserved.

P.S. Deloria and Robert Laurence, *What's an Indian? A Conversation About Law School Admissions, Indian Tribal Sovereignty, and Affirmative Action*, 44 ARK. L. REV. 1107 (1991).

Allison M. Dussias, *Science, Sovereignty, and the Sacred Text: Paleontological Resources and Native American Rights*, 55 MD. L. REV. 84, 158 (1996). Copyright © 1985. All rights reserved.

John Echohawk, *We are Sovereign Peoples*, in L. CROZIER-HOGLE & D. BABE WILSON, SURVIVING IN TWO WORLDS: CONTEMPORARY NATIVE AMERICAN VOICES 67–68 (Jay Leibold ed., 1997).

William J. Eskridge & Philip P. Frickey, *Statutory Interpretation as Practical Reasoning*, 42 STAN. L. REV. 321, 371, 374–75 (1990).

Arthur Foerster, *Divisiveness and Delusion: Public Law 280 and the Evasive Criminal/Regulatory Distinction*, 46 UCLA L. REV. 1333, 1358 (1999).

David Getches, *Water Rights on Indian Allotments*, 26 S.D. L REV. 405, 422 (1981).

Carole Goldberg, *American Indians and "Preferential" Treatment*, 49 UCLA L. REV. 943, 971–72 (2002).

Acknowledgements

Carole Goldberg, *Descent into Race*, 49 UCLA L. REV. 1373, 1383–84 (2002).

Carole Goldberg-Ambrose, *Heeding the "Voice" of Tribal Law in Indian Child Welfare Proceedings*, 7 LAW & ANTHROPOLOGY 1, 3–4 (1994). Copyright © 1994. All rights reserved.

Carole E. Goldberg, *Individual Rights and Tribal Revitalization*, 35 ARIZ. ST. L.J. 889, 933–34 (2003).

Carole E. Goldberg, *Public Law 280: The Limits of State Jurisdiction over Reservation Indians*, 22 UCLA L. REV. 535, 537–47, 549–52, 558–59 (1975).

Carole Goldberg & Duane Champagne, *Ramona Redeemed? The Rise of Tribal Political Power in California*, 17 WICAZO SA REV. 43, 47–56 (2001). Copyright © 2001. All rights reserved.

Kevin Gover & Robert Laurence, *Avoiding* Santa Clara Pueblo v. Martinez: *The Litigation in Federal Court of Civil Actions Under the Indian Civil Rights Act*, 8 HAMLINE L. REV. 497, 522 (1985).

GREAT DOCUMENTS IN AMERICAN INDIAN HISTORY, 152, 239, 297–98, 307 (Wayne Moquin & Charles L. Van Doren eds., 1973).

Margaret Howard, *Transracial Adoption: Analysis of the Best Interests Standard*, 59 NOTRE DAME L. REV. 503, 544 (1984)).

I HAVE SPOKEN: AMERICAN HISTORY THROUGH THE VOICES OF THE INDIANS 34 (V. Armstrong ed., 1971).

FRANCIS JENNINGS, THE INVASION OF AMERICA: INDIANS, COLONIALISM, AND THE CANT OF CONQUEST 15, 32 (1975). Copyright © 1975. All rights reserved.

Ralph Johnson, *The States Versus Indian Off-Reservation Fishing: A United States Supreme Court Error*, 47 WASH. L. REV. 207, 208–09 (1972).

Poka Laenui, *The Rediscovery of Hawaiian Sovereignty*, 17 AM. IND. CULTURE & RES. J. 79, 96 (1993).

Nancy O. Lurie, *Epilogue*, *in* IRREDEEMABLE AMERICA: THE INDIANS' ESTATE AND LAND CLAIMS 363, 372 (I. Sutton ed., 1985).

Avishai Margalit & Joseph Raz, *National Self-Determination*, THE RIGHTS OF MINORITY CULTURES (W. Kymlicka ed., 1995).

Mohawk Nation Council of Chiefs, Letter from Mohawk Nation Council of Chiefs of the Assembly of the First Nations of Canada (July 1996).

NATIONAL CONGRESS OF AMERICAN INDIANS & NATIONAL CONFERENCE OF STATE LEGISLATURES, GOVERNMENT TO GOVERNMENT: MODELS OF COOPERATION BETWEEN STATES AND TRIBES 3–5, 32–33 (2002).

Nell Jessup Newton, *At the Whim of the Sovereign: Aboriginal Title Reconsidered*, 31 HASTINGS L. J. 1215, 1241–53 (1980).

Nell Jessup Newton, *Federal Power over Indians: Its Sources, Scope, and Limitations*, 132 U. PA. L. REV. 195, 213–14 (1984).

Caroline Orlando, *Aboriginal Title Claims in the Indian Claims Commission*: United States v. Dann *and Its Due Process Implications*, 13 B.C. ENVTL. AFF. L. REV. 241, 261 (1986). Copyright © 1986. All rights reserved.

Acknowledgements

Sean Paige, *Rewriting Tribal Law*, 16 INSIGHT MAGAZINE No. 20 (May 29, 2000).

Robert Pelcyger, *Indian Water Rights: Some Emerging Frontiers*, 21 ROCKY MT. MIN. L. INST. 743, 769–70 (1976). Copyright © 1976. All rights reserved.

INDIAN SELF RULE: FIRST-HAND ACCOUNTS OF INDIAN-WHITE RELATIONS FROM ROOSEVELT TO REAGAN 48 (K. Philp ed., 1986).

Frank Pommersheim, *The Crucible of Sovereignty: Analyzing Issues of Tribal Jurisdiction*, 31 ARIZ. L. REV. 329, 360–61 (1989).

Robert B. Porter, *A Proposal to the Hanodaganyas to Decolonize Federal Indian Control Law*, 31 U. MICH. J.L. REFORM 899, 955–56 (1998).

Robert B. Porter, Lone Wolf v. Hitchcock *in the Supreme Court of the American Indian Nations*, 8 KAN. J.L. & PUB. POL'Y 174, 185 (1999).

Angela R. Riley, *"Straight-Stealing": Towards an Indigenous System of Cultural Property Protection*, 80 WASH. L. REV. 69, 70–71 (2005). Copyright © 2005. All rights reserved.

Joseph William Singer, *Well-Settled?: The Increasing Weight of History in American Indian Land Claims*, 28 GA. L. REV. 481, 530–31 (1994).

Scott Taylor, *An Introduction and Overview of Taxation and Indian Gaming*, 29 ARIZ. ST. L.J. 251, 263 (1997).

Dagmar Thorpe, *Sovereignty, A State of Mind: A Thakiwa Citizen's Viewpoint*, 23 AM. INDIAN L. REV. 481, 481–84 (1998–99).

Rebecca Tsosie, *Reclaiming Native Stories: An Essay on Cultural Appropriation and Cultural Rights*, 34 ARIZ. ST. L. J. 299, 311–12 (2002). Copyright © 2002. All rights reserved.

Rebecca Tsosie, *Tribal Environmental Policy in an Era of Self-Determination: The Role of Ethics, Economics, and Traditional Ecological Knowledge*, 21 VT. L. REV. 225, 286–87 (1996).

Laura S. Underkuffler-Freund, *Property: A Special Right*, 71 NOTRE DAME L. REV. 1033, 1046 (1996). Reprinted with permission © 1996 by *Notre Dame Law Review*, University of Notre Dame.

Kevin K. Washburn, *Recurring Problems in Indian Gaming*, 1 WYO. L. REV. 427, 428–30, 435–36, 440–41 (2001).

Hollis A. Whitson, *A Policy Review of the Federal Government's Relocation of Navajo Indians Under P.L. 93-531 and P.L. 96-305*, 27 ARIZ. L. REV. 371, 373–74 (1985).

Robert A. Williams, Jr., *The Algebra of Federal Indian Law: The Hard Trail of Decolonizing and Americanizing the White Man's Indian Jurisprudence*, 1986 WIS. L. REV. 219. Copyright © 1986. All rights reserved.

Preface

Since its inception in 1973, this casebook has surveyed the tribal-federal relationship. It therefore has historically been and remains primarily devoted to the study of federal Indian law, *i.e.*, the federal law developed to regulate the tribal-federal relationship. The separate subject of tribal law, *i.e.* the law by which any particular tribe governs its people and its lands, is equally deserving of scholarly attention. While the authors frequently reference the subject of tribal law in this work, the primary focus of this book has been and continues to be federal Indian law.

This volume represents the Seventh Edition of the first casebook developed to teach federal Indian law, initially published by Monroe E. Price in 1973. Over time, significant changes have occurred both in federal Indian law and in the authors and approaches adopted by this casebook. When the First Edition of the casebook was published in 1973, fewer than a dozen instructors focused their scholarly or teaching attention on federal Indian law. At latest count, the number was well over 100. Additionally, the 37-year lifespan of this casebook has witnessed significant changes in federal Indian law, as reflected in the successive editions. In the Second Edition, published in 1983, Robert N. Clinton joined the book, and the authors reorganized the casebook to recognize the explosive growth in legal attention to federal Indian law during the prior decade, including 32 new decisions of the United States Supreme Court, many, perhaps most, favoring tribal interests. In the Third Edition, published in 1991, Nell Jessup Newton joined as a co-author, and the Preface noted that "the rising expectations created by the previous legislative and judicial successes only represented a prelude to a more bumpy roller coaster ride for the resolution of many Indian issues, particularly in federal and state courts."

Following publication of the Third Edition, that "bumpy roller coaster ride" continued for Indian nations. Indian law cases have occupied a large and disproportionate amount of the Supreme Court's docket. Indians may be around 1.5% of the total United States population, but their cases often consume as much as 5% of the Court's caseload. Between 1994 and 2009, tribal interests have found themselves losing far more cases than they were winning. Of 38 cases involving Native interests over that fifteen-year period (including two that address Native Hawaiians), tribes have prevailed in seven, won partly in one, and had lower court decisions vacated and remanded in three. The other 27 were losses.[1]

Yet, the picture was not as bleak for tribal interests as their win-loss record in the Supreme Court might have suggested. To appropriate Charles Dickens's well-worn phrase from *A Tale of Two Cities*, for Indian tribes, "It was the best of times, it was the worst of times." Tribal governments and their legal systems expanded in size and sophistication, and their business enterprises — particularly in the gaming industry — exploded. Tribes became increasingly self-sufficient and far less reliant on the federal government both for funding and technical assistance. They also became more adept at promoting and defending their positions in federal and state legislative and administrative settings. Furthermore, international attention to the rights of indigenous peoples

---

[1] *See* Carole Goldberg, *Finding the Way to Indian Country: Justice Ruth Bader Ginsburg's Decisions in Indian Law Cases*, 70 Ohio St. L.J. 1003, 1013–14 (2009).

Preface

worldwide has opened rhetorical space for criticism of Supreme Court decisions as well as new venues for asserting Indian rights.

Such changing times required adaptation from this casebook, and change it did. The Fourth Edition, published in 2003, and the Fifth Edition, published three years later, included a new set of authors, with Carole E. Goldberg and Rebecca Tsosie joining the work. Nevertheless, while no longer named as authors, prior contributors Monroe E. Price and Nell Jessup Newton greatly enhanced the vision still reflected in this casebook, and their significant contributions are gratefully acknowledged. In addition to these changes in personnel, the recent divergence of federal Indian law decisions of the United States Supreme Court from its historic legacy rendered it even more imperative that the authors honor, acknowledge, teach, and publicize the tribal voice and views on the appropriate relationship that should exist between Native nations and the United States. Thus, far greater attention was paid in the Fourth Edition to Indian perspectives and voices on the tribal-federal relationship and to tribal reactions to Supreme Court decisions. The authors' point in undertaking that effort has been to highlight the fact that the tribal-federal relationship has always been and remains a bilateral arrangement in which the federal courts' role in unilaterally finding solutions traditionally has been quite limited. By focusing far greater attention on tribal perspectives in the tribal-federal relationship, the authors also have invited readers to consider precisely how much of the relationship the federal courts and Congress can unilaterally dictate. Ultimately, the authors have asked readers to consider for themselves the appropriate model for tribal-federal relations by focusing on international developments, historic models and understandings, legal treaty and other commitments, and contemporary events, and to further consider how the most appropriate model can be pursued and legally implemented.

The Fifth Edition, coming only three years after its predecessor, maintained considerable continuity with the Fourth Edition, both in the continued collaboration of Professors Clinton, Goldberg, and Tsosie, and in the focus on tribal as well as non-Indian perspectives on Native nations in the federal system. Benefiting from the authors' experience teaching from the Fourth Edition as well as feedback from colleagues in the field, the Fifth edition mainly updated material, reduced the heft of the volume, and reorganized some of the topics to eliminate duplication and enhance "teachability."

The Sixth Edition saw the inclusion of two new co-authors, Kevin K. Washburn and Elizabeth (Libby) Rodke Washburn, who added significant perspectives borne of their deep experience in Indian law scholarship, practice, and advocacy. Their approaches to the material enhanced the casebook by emphasizing political realities in both federal and tribal settings.

This Seventh edition builds on previous work, and is also influenced by the addition of its newest co-author, Angela R. Riley, of the UCLA School of Law. It also marks the departure of now-Secretary for Indian Affairs, Kevin Washburn, and Elizabeth Rodke Washburn, who have rotated off the casebook.

While casebooks obviously tend to focus on reported appellate cases to search for predictably stable decisional patterns, from its inception, this book has pursued a far broader perspective, merging jurisprudence, history, comparative law, ethnology, and sociology to bring meaning to the tribal-federal relationship. The authors of this volume, like the authors of prior editions, have never been interested in merely presenting the "black letter" law as is, without providing the historical, cultural, and jurisprudential tools for a reader to critically analyze the current state of legal doctrine in federal Indian law and also providing some historical perspective on how it emerged and some tools for its improvement going forward. We seek to provide a wide-ranging inquiry into the role of law and legal processes, both domestic and international, in protecting or frustrating the desires for political and cultural autonomy of various racial, cultural, religious, or national subgroups within a society.

To carry out this broader mission for the casebook, we have incorporated insights from an array of new intellectual developments in law and related fields, including critical race theory, the new legal realism of the law and society movement, empirical approaches to law, law and economics, indigenous methodology, legal pluralism, and neoinstitutionalism. As federal Indian law doctrine has become increasingly hostile to tribal claims to sovereignty and property, Indian law scholars and practitioners have turned to these intellectual tools to explain doctrinal developments (*e.g.*, as reflections of institutional racism or the pursuit of economic gains) to refute the empirical premises of adverse decisions (*e.g.*, assertions that tribal courts are unfair to outsiders), and to suggest ways tribes might avoid harmful rulings (*e.g.*, through cooperative agreements or political advocacy). Our own approach, while eclectic, benefits especially from the conceptual apparatus of legal pluralism and institutionalism. Legal pluralism emphasizes the interplay of multiple legal systems that may possess authority over the same territory and people. Institutionalism examines the ways in which the legal entities administering law affect legal actors, including governments as well as individuals. Federal Indian law is especially rich in opportunities for the interaction of legal systems and institutions. Federal, tribal, state, and international legal regimes are all implicated in the governance of Native nations, their territories, and their people. These multiple institutional settings create opportunities for different normative visions of tribal-federal relations, as well as alternative legal routes for pursuing Indian and non-Indian objectives. We have sought to highlight these opportunities and to suggest how Indian law may enhance or inhibit these pursuits at the federal and tribal levels. Our aim is to inform future practitioners and advocates about pragmatic, political possibilities, and constraints, complementing theoretical and critical perspectives that may challenge the current state of affairs. Thus at several points in the casebook (see especially Chapters 5 and 7), we emphasize intergovernmental relations through cooperative agreements and institutional innovation.

The cross-currents and inconsistencies of such legislative developments, case decisions, and intellectual ferment present formidable challenges to anyone who sets out in a casebook format to capture the depth and richness of the intellectual efforts of tribal people and others, including judges, legislators, lawyers, and academics, to build a coherent body of Indian law. From its inception in Professor Monroe E. Price's hands, this book always sought to present a broad jurisprudential and comparative perspective that transcended mere efforts to accurately portray existing federal Indian law doctrine. The book has not only repeatedly questioned and challenged those doctrines, but also aspired to place federal Indian law in a larger historical and global context and to tie federal legal doctrines affecting indigenous peoples to other similar problems of preserving autonomous cultures and nationalities in South America, Africa, Canada, New Zealand, and Australia, to name but a few. Editors of a book in such a rich field are faced with an exacting task. They can ignore the breadth and richness of the field and devote extended attention to a small part of the panorama of Indian law — such as federal court doctrine — or they can attempt to survey the various cross-currents and expose the reader to a broad, but not necessarily in-depth, treatment of the major issues and perspectives in the field. We deliberately have chosen the second approach. Since the Fourth Edition, we have added a third and long overdue objective: to accurately portray Indian tribal perspectives and voices on questions of federal Indian law. Thus, we continue to hold to a broad vision for this casebook, although the increasingly diverse directions of the scholarship, decisions, and legislation in Indian law have made it ever more difficult to devote equal attention to all three of our objectives.

In addition, while this casebook was developed primarily as a teaching tool, its authors are deeply committed to providing a sufficiently rich set of legal and other sources, such that the book also serves double-duty as a research sourcebook in the field of federal Indian law. The need for such a sourcebook was greater during the period 1982–2005, when there were no updated editions of the major treatise in the field of Indian law, originally published by Felix Cohen in 1941 and revised by a group of legal scholars, including Professors Clinton and Goldberg, in 1982. With the publication in 2005 of a new edition of this treatise, in which Dean Washburn and Professor Goldberg participated, an invaluable research sourcebook has become available to scholars, students, judges, and practitioners in the field. Furthermore, the authors and editors of the 2005 edition have produced biannual updates to the treatise. Thus, where appropriate, we have referred readers of the casebook to *Cohen's Handbook*, rather than repeat the research it presents. Nevertheless, where illuminating historical analyses and background material are unavailable in other sources, we have included them in the casebook to enrich students' understanding. We have aimed for a casebook that will serve as a resource for students long after graduation.

Chapter 1 of this edition introduces the basic problem of federal Indian law, establishing an appropriate model for the tribal-federal relationship. By examining historical materials, the views of tribal leaders, and early case decisions, including the famous benchmarks of federal Indian law, the Marshall trilogy (*Johnson v. M'Intosh, Cherokee Nation v. Georgia*, and *Worcester v. Georgia*), the first chapter seeks to introduce varying conceptions of how Native nations fit with or in the federal union, and how those conceptions have evolved over time. To facilitate a fuller understanding of that evolution, Chapter 1 also provides a mini-history of the evolution of federal Indian policy. Finally, this chapter offers an introduction to international legal protections and comparative models of the treatment of indigenous peoples, designed to encourage those attracted to reformative visions of federal Indian law to challenge their ideas from a global perspective.

Chapter 2 focuses attention on some cross-cutting themes in federal Indian law, including examining the legal definitions applied to some basic questions such as who is an Indian or tribal member, what is an Indian tribe, and what land constitutes Indian country. It also examines critical equal protection and due process constitutional questions that surround having a body of law addressing Indians. Finally, the chapter introduces the idea that special canons of interpretation affect the judicial interpretation of Indian treaties and statutes in important ways, often benefiting Indian tribes.

Chapters 3 through 5 focus attention on the competition for legal authority and power in Indian country among the three sovereign authorities, each of which asserts claims to political dominion and sovereignty over Indian country and its people — the tribal government, the federal government, and the state government. These chapters examine in that order the history and legal doctrines surrounding each respective government's claim to exercise legitimate political power and authority over the people and resources of Indian country, culminating in a separate chapter (Chapter 5) devoted to jurisdiction under special statutory schemes addressing matters such as child welfare, gaming, and environmental protection. These chapters explore the historical evolution of each sovereign's claim to authority and the prevailing legal doctrines that shape those claims. These materials also question the historical or political legitimacy of some of those claims to political authority. In short, these chapters explore the limits of sovereignty. They provide a test of the extent to which the original self-government and political authority of the aboriginal tribes of the North American continent have been eroded by the dominant colonial power, and they examine how sovereignty and jurisdictional issues have shaped the underlying model applied to the tribal-federal relationship.

Sovereignty and political authority are not ends unto themselves, however. One cannot eat jurisdiction, and sovereignty alone does not support the needs of Indian families. Rather, sovereignty is a tool to be used to support or suppress the destiny and future of Native peoples. Allocating political authority or sovereignty also delegates decision-making responsibilities, and thereby determines whether the political, economic, or cultural destinies of Native American peoples and those who enter onto their reservations will be decided by Native Americans or by non-Indian federal or state governments. To give meaning to such decision-making, however, the very existence of Indian resources, goods, and services must be assured by legal protections.

Chapters 6 and 7 focus attention on the legal protections afforded to Indian property and resource rights, and the manner in which the law facilitates or frustrates the development of those resources. Chapter 6 focuses primary attention on the legal protection of the one resource that simultaneously is often the tribe's most valued cultural resource and sometimes its only major remaining economic resource — tribal land and resources appurtenant thereto, such as oil and gas, minerals, or timber. It also explores issues associated with a special kind of tribal property — cultural property.

Chapter 7 focuses on important hunting and fishing, food gathering, and water rights. The protection and enforcement of such Indian rights are critical to Indian survival in the harsh terrains that characterize some reservations. This chapter illustrates the manner in which the political, cultural, and economic facets of Indian autonomy are interwoven into a complex legal fabric governing how Indians and Euro-Americans compete in the legal system for control of the same scarce resources, and how they may also cooperate to achieve their material and cultural needs for those resources. It will illustrate how federal Indian law and its concepts of property and sovereignty have been used to protect or frustrate tribal concerns central to Indian survival.

By choosing to survey some of the broad currents in federal Indian law and provide a rich set of research sources, we have been forced to make certain basic decisions about the organization and structure of this book. First, we have concluded that the richness and diversity of the cases and scholarship relating to Native Americans called for a book that was larger and deeper than would be possible to teach in any single two- or three-hour Native American law course or seminar. Rather, we chose to present an organized body of source material from which any instructor could select the ingredients to craft his or her own course to suit individual objectives. Thus, teachers and students most interested in questions of political authority, sovereignty, legitimacy, and jurisdiction may focus the primary attention of their courses on Chapters 1 through 5. Those primarily interested in the protection of Indian property and natural resources may find their time most profitably spent concentrating mainly on Chapters 1 and 6–7. A two-hour course focused mostly on jurisdiction might consider covering Chapters 1, 2, and portions of 3, 4, and 5. Some schools, including those of the authors, offer more than one course in federal Indian law. The first course could cover jurisdiction issues, and the second could focus on resource issues, perhaps including some of the special jurisdictional regimes (such as Alaska, Hawaii, and federal environmental laws) covered in Chapter 5. Thus, the authors see the casebook as a flexible tool, readily adaptable to various course configurations.

A further problem for the creation of this volume was imposed by size constraints dictated by both our publisher and the concessions that unfortunately must be made to the length of the academic calendar. As the decisions from the courts grow longer and more ponderous, and the richness, depth, and diversity of the literature increases, casebook editors are forced to make very difficult editing decisions — decisions about issues we did not always agree upon even among ourselves. Significant problems emerge in paring down extensive, sometimes convoluted, often carefully integrated opinions from the Supreme Court into a few pages manageable for a class session. The Fourth and Fifth Editions sometimes paraphrased long significant cases while giving them separate treatment that prevented the lesser attention that students frequently afford to note cases. In the Sixth Edition and in this Seventh Edition, we have maintained some use of this device, but have employed it for fewer cases, to ensure that students read as much of the most important text as possible. Similarly, the historical, political, and legal arguments found in the secondary literature often do not lend themselves to brief encapsulation, either by way of paraphrased description or through inclusion of a carefully pruned snippet or two. Nevertheless, employing these techniques, we have sought to present very complicated material in a more condensed form, while attempting to do justice to the complexity of analysis in the original.

The authors have chosen to leave statutory and regulatory language out of the casebook text, relying on the relatively easy access that today's students have to online sources. That decision was made both to decrease the size of the book and to promote greater readability of the casebook text. Editing of cases and source materials, of course, poses its own technical problems. Specifically, how is a reader to know where editing in a text has occurred? On the other hand, if every editing change is appropriately flagged, the text becomes far less readable. On this question, the authors deliberately opted for visual readability, rather than detailed technical cues. Thus, we have liberally deleted citations and footnotes from both primary cases and secondary works without any indication in text of the omission. Similarly, in new cases, we have used ellipses sparingly, preferring instead when possible to use brackets to indicate where minor editing was necessary to smooth transitions required by omissions. Parallel citations, pinpoint citations, footnotes, and other references have been liberally removed from published cases and other sources, without any flag or indication. Furthermore, in an effort to increase readability, we have chosen not to indicate each deletion of interstitial paragraphs by indented hanging ellipses, relying instead primarily on brackets that begin or end a paragraph to indicate that some editing was done with the intervening material. That editing may represent a short phrase or many paragraphs omitted from the original source. Some deletions are not noted at all. Additionally, in the interest of space, the authors have not consistently noted denials of review by the United States Supreme Court or other non-significant subsequent histories of cases. We believe that this casebook, while intended to have some utility as a research source, should be designed primarily as an instructional volume in which readability represents the most important asset. Those interested in the details of the complete opinion or source should consult the original rather than relying on our abridged version of those materials, and for case opinions should also employ electronic databases to assure the complete citation to the materials in question.

Carole E. Goldberg
Jonathan D. Varat Professor of Law
UCLA School of Law
Associate Justice, Hualapai Court of Appeals

Rebecca Tsosie
Regent's Professor of Law
Sandra Day O'Connor College of Law, Arizona State University
Associate Justice, Fort McDowell Yavapai Nation Supreme Court
Associate Judge, San Carlos Apache Court of Appeals

Robert Clinton
Foundation Professor of Law
Sandra Day O'Connor College of Law, Arizona State University
Chief Justice, Winnebago Supreme Court
Associate Justice, Colorado River Indian Tribes Court of Appeals
Associate Justice, Hualapai Court of Appeals
Associate Justice, Hopi Appellate Court

Angela R. Riley
Professor of Law, UCLA School of Law
Co-Director, Native Nations Law and Policy Center
Director, Joint Degree Program in Law and American Indian Studies
Chief Justice, Citizen Potawatomi Nation of Oklahoma

Table of Contents

Table of Contents

Table of Contents

Table of Contents

Table of Contents

Table of Contents

Table of Contents

Table of Contents

Table of Contents

Table of Contents

Table of Contents

Table of Contents

Table of Contents

Chapter 1

HISTORIC AND MODERN CONCEPTIONS OF THE TRIBAL-FEDERAL RELATIONSHIP

A. HISTORIC MODELS OF TRIBAL-FEDERAL RELATIONS

1. Introduction

Mohawk Treaty Propositions, September 6, 1659: They say we have been here before and made an alliance. The Dutch, indeed, say we are brothers and are joined together with chains, but that lasts only as long as we have beavers. After that we are no longer thought of, but much will depend upon it when we shall need each other. [They thereupon gave two beavers.]

They say, the alliance which was made in this country, who can break it? Let us always maintain this alliance which was once made. [Give thereupon two beavers.][1]

From first contact, Native nations dealt with Euro-American colonial powers on political and economic terms through diplomatic alliance. Both sides brought their worldviews to the diplomatic bargaining table to work out new and changing sets of political relationships. As scholars have noted, frequently the outcome of such diplomacy produced a new set of political realities, neither entirely Native nor entirely European in origin. *See generally* RICHARD WHITE, THE MIDDLE GROUND: INDIANS, EMPIRES, AND REPUBLICS IN THE GREAT LAKES REGION 1650–1815 (1991).

Traditionally organized horizontally around kinship, clan, and extended family relationships, the tribal nations had long understood and described such political alliances, whether with other tribes or with European colonizing powers, as metaphorical extensions of kinship obligations. As reflected by the language of diplomatic discourse found in the Mohawk Treaty Propositions set forth above, trade and diplomatic relations were mediated through the metaphor of family. Alliance partners became brothers and political protectors or sources of economic support became fathers. Euro-American negotiators were quick to adopt the Native *lingua franca* of political discourse and eventually the colonial head of state, later the President of the United States, became known as the Great Father in diplomatic discussions. For Indians, the Great Father metaphor did not symbolize a position of political superiority, but, rather, a protector with obligations of familial protection and economic support, a position accurately describing that which the tribal nations

---

[1] Quoted in FRANCIS JENNINGS, THE AMBIGUOUS IROQUOIS EMPIRE 47 (1984).

sometimes sought from Great Britain, or, later, the United States, through diplomatic alliance.

The European colonizing powers, however, had a very different political tradition. Derived from the feudal monarchies of Europe, European notions of political organization were vertical with commands and laws flowing downward from the sovereign at the top, sometimes mediated through intermediate feudal lords. Hierarchy in power relationships therefore constituted an integral part of the European worldview. For European colonizers, the Great Father metaphor constituted one of superiority and command, with authority to demand obedience from a subservient child.

These divergent worldviews collided in the colonial cauldron that resulted from contact between Western Euro-American colonists and the indigenous occupants of the Americas. The working out of the political, economic, and social relationships that emerged from such contact constitutes the subject of this book. The noted contact historian Francis Jennings nicely captured the essence of the problem of colonial contact when he wrote, "[The Europeans] did not settle a virgin land. They invaded and displaced a resident population." He continued:

> [Initially, the European's] intention was to exploit rather than to settle. Among the early European visitors residence was merely a means of increasing the efficiency of exploitation. A taste for permanent habitation came later. Regularly the first Europeans were welcomed by natives with gifts of food and tokens of honor until the moment came when the gifts were demanded as tribute and the honors were commanded as homage — a moment that sometimes came very rapidly. At the outset native hostility was never directed against European settlement as such; what made trouble was the European purpose of settling on top.

FRANCIS JENNINGS, THE INVASION OF AMERICA: INDIANS, COLONIALISM, AND THE CANT OF CONQUEST 15, 32 (1975).

The body of jurisprudence in the United States surrounding the legal rights of Native Americans emerges from this process and represents the effort to process in legal doctrine the continuing contours of this diplomatic relationship. Thus, federal Indian law recognizes and sometimes protects the unique political status of Indian tribes within the American legal structure. In short, Indian tribes are sovereign governments, whose inherent right to govern themselves and their lands predated contact between Euro-American peoples and the indigenous occupants of the Americas. Most rights that American Indians have under federal Indian law derive, not from their ethnological ancestry, but from their citizenship, or, as it is more commonly put, membership, in an Indian tribe. The rights usually are tribal, not individual, rights.

Unlike other minority groups, whose primary legal protections arise from laws prohibiting discrimination designed to facilitate their complete integration into the social, political, and economic fabric of the country, Indians have long enjoyed a legal status that, from the outset, was sought and designed primarily to protect their cultural separateness and political autonomy. Protecting Indian tribal sovereignty and the rights that flow from the Indian tribal relationship with the United

States often involves protecting Indian separatism, special tribal property and cultural rights, and other rights that facilitate Indian cultural and economic survival or their group autonomy.

In a nation composed of immigrants that has prided itself on its role as a melting pot of diverse cultural traditions, Indian separatism, political authority, and legal autonomy initially appear to some non-Indians to be a political aberration. Many conservatives and liberals alike ask why should the law protect Indian autonomy? How can the special legal protection of Indians be squared with the equal protection and due process clauses of the Fifth and Fourteenth Amendments? Should not the Indians be forced to assimilate into the economic, social, and political structure of the larger society and abandon their tribal traditions and autonomy as have many immigrants to North America?

Perhaps, one simple answer is that Native Nations and their members are not immigrants. They were here first. But that answer is far too simple (or perhaps far too troubling) for many critics of Indian tribal sovereignty. Many Indians and their legal supporters question whether legal efforts to force such assimilation on non-consenting Indian peoples constitutes a form of colonialism. Does forced assimilation violate current domestic and international legal protections of human rights? Does it constitute a form of genocide or, at least, cultural ethnocide?

This chapter is devoted to consideration of these issues and the history from which they arise. It also introduces varying alternative models of the political relationships between tribal nations and the federal government and explores the way in which legal doctrine processes these models into policy and enforceable law. In the course of doing so it presents diverse voices offering political and legal perspectives on the proper scope and nature of the political relationship between tribal nations and the federal government.

By way of introduction, it should be noted that much of this book deals primarily with *federal* Indian law, rather than *tribal* law. Unlike tribal law (both written and customary), federal Indian law was developed by the federal government to regulate *its* relationship with tribes, which sometimes (and only recently) involved regulating the Indians themselves. Federal Indian law constitutes a doctrinal, historical vestige of the legal regime that tried to rationalize, legitimate, and regulate American colonialism over Indian tribes. Tribes often had little voice in that development beyond their resistance to its implementation. They frequently constituted the objects of federal regulation with little agency in its development.

By contrast, true "Indian law" is tribal law, the body of written norms or tribal customs under which tribes have chosen to govern themselves and their lands. While this volume will periodically present tribal law readings, such issues do not constitute the primary focus of the volume. That choice does not reflect any hierarchy of importance, but rather a clear recognition that federal Indian law and tribal law constitute separate, discrete subjects each equally worthy of separate attention. The primary objective of this particular work is to describe the law that mediates tribal relations with the remainder of the federal union.

Where the Indian voice was perhaps most clearly heard and recorded in the early development of federal Indian law was in the negotiations that produced bilaterally negotiated Indian treaties with the United States government, albeit sometimes resulting from grossly unequal bargaining power, fraud, or duress. While not all United States tribes have treaties with the federal government, the Indian voice in the creation of such documents explains why Indian treaties loom so large in the development of federal Indian law. The prominence of Indian voices in the negotiations of these treaties also helps to explain why Indians tend to focus extraordinary attention both on the terms and on the spirit in which such treaty relationships were established. The treaties therefore form a sort of baseline against which one can measure tribal-federal relations.

2. Treaty Models of the Political Relationship Between Indian Tribes and the Federal Government

Over time, at least three models have been employed in Indian treaties to characterize the political relationship between Indian tribes and the United States government. Each of these models rests on a distinctive conception of tribal sovereignty or political authority. Importantly, throughout the nineteenth century, Indian nations were viewed as separate governments which were not formally incorporated into the United States' political structure and whose members were not entitled to United States citizenship. Although not all Indian nations entered into treaties with the United States, the treaties represent a political template of the various political relationships that have emerged between Indian nations and the United States.

a. International Self-Determination Model

The fact that the United States regularly made treaties with Indian tribes, ratifying more than 400 such documents before the practice was formally discontinued in 1871, suggests an international model of self-determination. Within a self-determination model, each sovereign has complete control over its territory, its citizens, and its destiny. Under this model, sovereigns negotiate their political relationships with other sovereigns on the basis of mutual respect, equality, comity, and consent. Today, this model characterizes the relationship between nation-states at the international level. For Indian nations, the paradigmatic example of this model emerges from the United States' treaty with the Delaware Nation, which is the first ratified treaty between the United States and an Indian tribe.

Treaty of Fort Pitt with the Delaware Nation
Sept. 17, 1778, 7 Stat. 13

ARTICLE 3. And whereas the United States are engaged in a just and necessary war, in defence [sic] and support of life, liberty and independence, against the King of England and his adherents, and as said King is yet possessed of several posts and forts on the lakes and other places, the reduction of which is of great importance to the peace and security of the contracting parties, and as the most practicable way for the troops of the United States to some of the posts and forts is by passing through the country of the Delaware nation, the aforesaid deputies, on behalf of themselves and their nation, do hereby stipulate and agree to give a free passage through their country to the troops aforesaid, and the same to conduct by the nearest and best ways to the posts, forts or towns of the enemies of the United States, affording to said troops such supplies of corn, meat, horses, or whatever may be in their power for the accommodation of such troops, on the commanding officer's, &c. paying, or engaging to pay, the full value of whatever they can supply them with. And the said deputies, on the behalf of their nation, engage to join the troops of the United States aforesaid, with such a number of their best and most expert warriors as they can spare. . . . .

For the better security of the peace and friendship now entered into by the contracting parties, against all infractions of the same by the citizens of either party, to the prejudice of the other, neither party shall proceed to the infliction of punishments on the citizens of the other, otherwise than by securing the offender or offenders by imprisonment, or any other competent means, till a fair and impartial trial can be had by judges or juries of both parties, as near as can be to the laws, customs and usages of the contracting parties and natural justice: The mode of such trials to be hereafter fixed by the wise men of the United States in Congress assembled, with the assistance of such deputies of the Delaware nation, as may be appointed to act in concert with them in adjusting this matter to their mutual liking. And it is further agreed between the parties aforesaid, that neither shall entertain or give countenance to the enemies of the other, or protect in their respective states, criminal fugitives, servants or slaves, but the same to apprehend, and secure and deliver to the State or States, to which such enemies, criminals, servants or slaves respectively belong.

. . . .

ARTICLE 6. Whereas the enemies of the United States have endeavored, by every artifice in their power, to possess the Indians in general with an opinion, that it is the design of the States aforesaid, to extirpate the Indians and take possession of their country: to obviate such false suggestion, the United States do engage to guarantee to the aforesaid nation of Delawares, and their heirs, all their territorial rights in the fullest and most ample manner, as it hath been bounded by former treaties, as long as they the said Delaware nation shall abide by, and hold fast the chain of friendship now entered into. And it is further agreed on between the contracting parties should it for the future be found conducive for the mutual interest of both parties to invite any other tribes who have been friends to the interest of the United States, to join the present confederation, and to form a state whereof the Delaware nation shall be the head, and have a representation in Congress: Provided, nothing contained in this article to be considered as conclusive until it meets with the approbation of Congress. . . . .

b. Treaty Federalism Model

To the extent that treaties place an Indian nation under the exclusive "protection of the United States" or offer Indian nations the option, at some future point in time, to join the federal Union, this might be described as a model of "treaty federalism." Under this model, the political autonomy and sovereignty of the Indian nation is recognized and protected, although the tribe may possess a "right" to join the federal union, at some future point in time, and have formal representation in the United States Congress. The treaty federalism model requires tribal consent as a precondition to any change in political status, but it also envisions an exclusive relationship between the Indian nation and the United States, potentially limiting the ability of Indian nations to engage in international relations with multiple nation-states.

As illustrated by the following treaties with the Cherokee Nation, the transition in treaty language from international self-determination to treaty federalism was often gradual, foreshadowing the eventual application of federal law and at least a partial political incorporation of the Indian nation into the United States federal system.

Treaty of Hopewell with the Cherokee Nation
Nov. 28, 1785, 7 Stat. 18

ARTICLE 3. The said Indians for themselves and their respective tribes and towns do acknowledge all the Cherokees to be under the protection of the United States of America, and of no other sovereign whosoever.

. . . .

ARTICLE 5. If any citizen of the United States, or other person not being an Indian shall attempt to settle on any of the lands westward or southward of the said boundary which are hereby allotted to the Indians for their hunting grounds, or having already settled and will not remove from the same within six months after the ratification of this treaty, such person shall forfeit the protection of the United States, and the Indians may punish him or not as they please. . . .

ARTICLE 6. If any Indian or Indians, or person residing among them, or who shall take refuge in their nation, shall commit a robbery, or murder, or other capital crime, on any citizen of the United States, or person under their protection, the nation, or the tribe to which such offender or offenders may belong, shall be bound to deliver him or them up to be punished according to the ordinances of the United States; Provided, that the punishment shall not be greater than if the robbery or murder, or other capital crime had been committed by a citizen on a citizen.

ARTICLE 7. If any citizen of the United States, or person under their protection, shall commit a robbery or murder, or other capital crime, on any Indian, such offender or offenders shall be punished in the same manner as if the murder or robbery, or other capital crime, had been committed on a citizen of the United States; and the punishment shall be in presence of some of the Cherokees, if any shall attend at the time and place, and that they may have an opportunity so to do, due notice of the time of such intended punishment shall be sent to some one of the tribes.

. . . .

ARTICLE 12. That the Indians may have full confidence in the justice of the United States, respecting their interests, they shall have the right to send a deputy of their choice, whenever they think fit, to Congress.

Treaty of New Echota with the Cherokee Nation
Dec. 29, 1835, 7 Stat. 478

WHEREAS the Cherokees are anxious to make some arrangements with the Government of the United States whereby the difficulties they have experienced by a residence within the settled parts of the United States under the jurisdiction and laws of the State Governments may be terminated and adjusted; and with a view to reuniting their people in one body and securing a permanent home for themselves and their posterity in the country selected by their forefathers without the territorial limits of the State sovereignties, and where they can establish and enjoy a government of their choice and perpetuate such a state of society as may be most consonant with their views, habits and condition; and as may tend to their individual comfort and their advancement in civilization. . . .

. . . .

ARTICLE 5. The United States hereby covenant and agree that the lands ceded to the Cherokee nation in the forgoing article shall, in no future time without their consent, be included within the territorial limits or jurisdiction of any State or Territory. But they shall secure to the Cherokee nation the right by their national councils to make and carry into effect all such laws as they may deem necessary for the government and protection of the persons and property within their own country belonging to their people or such persons as have connected themselves with them: provided always that they shall not be inconsistent with the constitution of the United States and such acts of Congress as have been or may be passed regulating trade and intercourse with the Indians; and also, that they shall not be considered as extending to such citizens and army of the United States as may travel or reside in the Indian country by permission according to the laws and regulations established by the Government of the same.

. . . .

ARTICLE 7. The Cherokee nation having already made great progress in civilization and deeming it important that every proper and laudable inducement should be offered to their people to improve their condition as well as to guard and secure in the most effectual manner the rights guarantied to them in this treaty, and with a view to illustrate the liberal and enlarged policy of the Government of the United States towards the Indians in their removal beyond the territorial limits of the States, it is stipulated that they shall be entitled to a delegate in the House of Representatives of the United States whenever Congress shall make provision for the same.

c. Colonial Federalism Model

Some provisions within Indian treaties, particularly those negotiated during the latter half of the nineteenth century, contain language assigning a governance role to federal officials on the reservation, and inserting language authorizing the "civilization" of "the Indians entering the treaty," through Anglo-American forms of private property ownership and education. Although the form of the instrument is based on political consent, like the treaty federalism model, the actual provisions of the treaty impose some forms of political domination upon tribal governments, in an effort to "assimilate" them to Western norms. The Navajo Nation's 1868 Treaty, for example, confirms the sovereignty of the Navajo Nation over its reservation, but contains various provisions authorizing federal control over matters that were formerly under the political autonomy of the Navajo people. In this sense, the colonial federalism model instantiates a notion of "federal supremacy," which is inconsistent with true treaty federalism.

Treaty of Fort Sumner with the Navajo Nation
June 1, 1868, 15 Stat. 667

ARTICLE 4. The United States agrees that the agent for the Navajos shall make his home at the agency building; that he shall reside among them, and shall keep an office open at all times for the purpose of prompt and diligent inquiry into such matters of complaint by or against the Indians as may be presented for investigation, as also for the faithful discharge of other duties enjoined by law. In all cases of depredation on person or property he shall cause the evidence to be taken in writing and forwarded, together with his finding, to the Commissioner of Indian Affairs, whose decision shall be binding on the parties to this treaty.

ARTICLE 5. If any individual belonging to said tribe, or legally incorporated with it, being the head of a family, shall desire to commence farming, he shall have the privilege to select, in the presence and with the assistance of the agent then in charge, a tract of land within said reservation, not exceeding one hundred and sixty acres in extent, which tract, when so selected, certified, and recorded in the "land-book" as herein described, shall cease to be held in common, but the same may be occupied and held in the exclusive possession of the person selecting it, and of his family, so long as he or they may continue to cultivate it.

ARTICLE 6. In order to insure the civilization of the Indians entering into this treaty, the necessity of education is admitted, especially of such of them as may be settled on said agricultural parts of this reservation, and they therefore pledge themselves to compel their children, male and female, between the ages of six and sixteen years, to attend school; and it is hereby made the duty of the agent for said Indians to see that this stipulation is strictly complied with; and the United States agrees that, for every thirty children between said ages who can be induced or compelled to attend school, a house shall be provided, and a teacher competent to teach the elementary branches of an English education shall be furnished, who will reside among said Indians, and faithfully discharge his or her duties as a teacher.

The provisions of this article to continue for not less than ten years.

NOTES ON MODELS OF TRIBAL-FEDERAL RELATIONS

1. **Tribal Political Organization and Treaty-Based Conceptions of Tribal Sovereignty:** During the treaty period, European notions of sovereignty dictated the negotiations between tribal leaders and Europeans. At that time, the European conception of sovereignty was heavily reliant upon the notion of the Crown's centralized authority over territory, and the writ of the crown (*i.e.*, government) ran to all persons and property within the sovereign's realm irrespective of nationality (except foreign emissaries with diplomatic immunity). This model of centralized

authority was not commonly found among Indian nations, which often were comprised of relatively autonomous and dispersed bands. However, one result of treaty-making was to define the political leadership of Indian nations with respect to relations with the European sovereigns, and to allocate sovereignty among the Indian tribes, the federal government, and the states. Notice, for example, that the Treaty of Hopewell describes the allocation of criminal jurisdiction between the Cherokee Nation and the United States for various categories of crimes, and the Treaty of New Echota disclaims the reach of state sovereignty into the Cherokee Nation's territory.

In fact, the study of Indian treaties provides insight into the actual nature of Indian political organization and tribal conceptions of sovereignty. In the United States, treaties are memorialized in writing and in the English language. As legal instruments, they are often analogized to "contracts" between sovereigns. However, given the language differences between Indians and Europeans, the treaties were often negotiated in the native language, and through the use of interpreters, translated into English terms, which were then recorded and transmitted to Congress. Thus, for Indians, the treaty is often memorialized through the oral tradition of the Indian nation, and the treaty is often perceived to represent an on-going and dynamic relationship, rather than a static set of promises written in English upon a piece of paper.

In addition, the treaty process illustrates the procedural differences between Indian nations and the United States with respect to entering binding political agreements. The treaties employed a limited number of treaty commissioners, charged by the United States to negotiate the treaty, while the ultimate legal effect of the treaty depended upon the constitutional requirement that all treaties be ratified by a two-thirds vote of the Senate. U.S. CONST. Art. II, § 2, par. 2. In comparison, most of the Indian treaties are signed by a large number of Indian signatories, almost always male, some of whom are designated as chiefs. This reflects the commonly-held belief of Europeans that sovereignty is hierarchical and that those designated as "chiefs" have the right to speak for the entire Indian nation. In reality, customary norms of tribal governance were often much more integrated, representing differentiated authority between different clans and societies, and designed to prevent imbalances of power or the exercise of coercive authority. In many tribal communities, norms of reciprocity, kinship, duty, and obligation operated to constrain or promote certain behavior for the good of the entire community. Thus, as a matter of tribal customary law, it was not always the case that individuals named by the United States in a treaty as the "chief" of an entire Indian nation had the political authority to permanently cede traditional territories in the possession of clans, families, and individuals.

2. The Impact of U.S. Citizenship: At the time the Indian treaties were negotiated, the tribes and their members were not considered to be part of the federal union in any respect. The legal rights of Native peoples were a product of the political relationship between Indian nations and the U.S. government and were not tied to the citizenship status of tribal members. In fact, citizenship was not uniformly extended to Indians until 1924, when Congress enacted the Indian Citizenship Act of 1924, Pub. L. No. 68-175, ch. 233, 43 Stat. 253 (codified as amended at 8 U.S.C. § 1401(b)), which granted citizenship to all Indians born within the United States, thereby naturalizing all Indians who previously lacked citizenship and assuring that all Indians subsequently born in the United States would be treated as natural born citizens. The Indian Citizenship Act expressly indicated that Indian treaty rights, *i.e.*, *group* rights held by the tribe and enjoyed by virtue of tribal membership, were not affected by the grant of U.S. citizenship. Thus, under contemporary U.S. law, Indians are entitled to all of the rights of any U.S. citizen, and, in addition, are entitled to certain rights that stem from their political status as members of federally recognized Indian tribes. If Indians are now incorporated into the United States as U.S. citizens, with political access to the state and federal legislatures, can Indian nations still make a claim for full rights to self-determination under the International Self-Determination Model?

3.   **The Importance of History:** The treaties set forth above were negotiated at very different times in the history of federal Indian policy. The historical context affected the nature and terms of the treaties, the federal and tribal objectives sought to be furthered by the treaties, and the leverage of each party in the negotiation. When the Fort Pitt Treaty with the Delaware was negotiated, the United States was conducting the Revolution and its very survival was at stake, reflecting the relative bargaining strength of Indian nations at the time when the United States was still in a fledgling and emergent state. At this time, the United States was primarily focused on negotiating a treaty of "peace and friendship" and securing a military alliance with the Delaware. The United States also sought permission to pass through "the country of the Delaware Nation," acknowledging the territorial sovereignty of the Delawares.

In comparison, when the Treaty of Hopewell was negotiated in 1785, the Revolution was over and the federal government sought to place the Cherokee Nation in a subordinate political position, deeming them to be "under the protection of the United States of America, and of no sovereign whatsoever." This Treaty continues to recognize the territorial sovereignty of the Cherokee Nation within its aboriginal territory, as illustrated by the extradition provision. By 1835, when the United States negotiated the Treaty of New Echota with the Cherokee Nation, the power balance had shifted further. This Treaty secured the consent of the Cherokee Nation for its removal to the Oklahoma Indian Territory. In this treaty, the United States agrees that the Cherokee Nation shall not be "included within the territorial limits or jurisdiction of any State or Territory" without its prior consent, and secures the Cherokee Nation's rights of self-government, provided that this is not "inconsistent with the constitution of the United States" or "acts of Congress."

The 1868 Treaty of Fort Sumner with the Navajo Nation was negotiated when the Navajo people were being held as prisoners of war at Bosque Redondo, following a U.S. army campaign led by Kit Carson, which burned Navajo fields and homes, rounded up Navajo families, and marched them over 300 miles to a desolate military camp in New Mexico. The Treaty is notable because the Navajo Nation succeeded in its petition to return to its traditional territory in between the four sacred mountains that define the Navajo universe. However, the diminished bargaining position of the Navajo Nation is apparent in the provisions that assign a dominant governance role to the United States' Indian agent assigned to the reservation, and provide for the compulsory education of Navajo children in federally-operated schools.

4. Colonial Domination and the Push for Assimilation: As the next section of this chapter demonstrates, Federal policymakers exercised the most extreme forms of colonial domination during the nineteenth and early twentieth centuries in an effort to break down the structure of the traditional tribal governments and assimilate tribal members to Western norms. At this time, policymakers denounced "tribalism" as incompatible with civilized norms of governance and posited that individual Indians would benefit from assimilating into the dominant society. Although federal policy ultimately shifted later in the twentieth century to encourage tribal self-governance, a small minority of American society has always opposed any model of tribal-federal relations, preferring that Indians be totally assimilated as individuals and tribes eliminated. The more modern language of opposition has been variously couched in arguments for "equal citizenship" or arguments against "racial preferences." *See* Ch. 2, Sec. B.

5. Modern Tribal Governments and Sovereignty: As you will see in Chapter 3, modern tribal governments differ in their structures and forms of governance. Some operate according to tribal constitutions, and some do not. Some tribal constitutions formally acknowledge the overarching role of the federal government and federal law, and some do not. Consider these excerpts from the 2002 Constitution of the Crow Tribe of Indians.

Preamble

We, the adult members of the Crow Tribe of Indians located on the Crow Indian Reservation as established by the Fort Laramie Treaties of 1851 and 1866, in an effort to exercise our treaty rights, our inherent sovereign rights . . . to secure certain privileges and retain inherent powers do hereby adopt this Constitution to create a governing body to represent the members of the Crow Tribe of Indians, to promote the general welfare of the Crow Tribe and to provide for the lawful operation of government.

Article I — Governing Body

The traditional name of the government of the Crow Tribe of Indians of the Crow Indian Reservation shall be the Apsaalooke Nation Tribal General Council hereinafter known formally as the Crow Tribal General Council. The Crow Tribal General Council . . . [shall be comprised of] three branches of government, the Executive, Legislative and Judicial Branches, which shall exercise a separation of powers. . . .

Article II — Territory

The jurisdiction of the Crow Tribal General Council shall extend to all lands within the exterior boundaries of the Crow Indian Reservation including those lands within the original boundaries of the Crow Indian Reservation as determined by federal statutes and case law and to such other lands as may hereafter be acquired by or for the Crow Tribe of Indians.

Article XV — Approval

I, Secretary of Interior, or designee, do hereby approve this Constitution of the Crow Tribe of Indians in accordance with Article XV of this Constitution. It is effective as of July 14, 2001, provided, that nothing in this approval shall be construed as authorizing any action under this document that would be contrary to federal law.

[Signed by Assistant Secretary Neal A. McCaleb, Designee of the Secretary of Interior.]

To what extent must contemporary tribal forms of government follow Western models (through, for example, the creation of tribal legislative bodies and court systems) in an effort to secure legal protection for tribal autonomy? If a tribal constitution maintains the requirement that it be validated by the signature of a United States official, is this equivalent to treaty federalism or does this reflect some measure of continuing colonial domination?

6.   The Dynamic Nature of Tribal-Federal Relations: Just as the three models identified above gradually evolved over time, so the evolution of tribal-federal relations continues and is ever-changing, inspiring the possibility of alternative models. On both an international and a domestic law level, the political and legal relationships between indigenous peoples and the colonial governments which have encompassed them continue to be reconsidered and reconfigured. For example, as demonstrated by the last section of this chapter, the United Nations General Assembly formally adopted the Declaration on the Rights of Indigenous Peoples in 2007. This instrument crafts a norm of self-determination to guide the continuing relationship between indigenous peoples and nation-states. Similarly, many domestic governments, including Canada and New Zealand, are actively engaged in negotiating new political relationships to confirm indigenous rights to self-governance, as well as rights to land and resources. In the United States, Indian nations such as the Crow Tribe and the Navajo Nation, continue to draw upon the nineteenth century treaties that they negotiated with the United States as a basis for the expression of their inherent sovereignty and the continuing obligation of the federal government to protect their lands and resources. Thus, the three models of tribal-federal relations identified in this introduction should not be seen as a static or an exhaustive classification, but rather, as baseline tools for measuring evolving legal, political, and cultural developments.

B.   HISTORY OF TRIBAL-FEDERAL RELATIONS

1.   Introductory Perspectives

Cornplanter (Seneca), Speech Delivered to President George Washington at Fort Stanwix, 1790

in I HAVE SPOKEN: AMERICAN HISTORY THROUGH THE VOICES OF THE INDIANS
34 (V. Armstrong ed., 1971)

When your army entered the country of the Six Nations, we called you *Caunotaucarius*, the Town Destroyer; and to this day when that name is heard, our women look behind them and turn pale, and our children cling to the knees of their mothers. Our councilors and warriors are men and cannot be afraid; but their hearts are grieved with the fears of their women and children, and desire that it may be buried so deep as to be heard no more. When you gave us peace, we called you Father, because you promised to secure us in possession of our lands. Do this, and so long as the lands shall remain, the beloved name will remain in the heart of every Seneca.

Tecumseh (Shawnee), Speech Delivered at Vincennes, Indiana, August 12, 1810

in ANNETTE ROSENSTIEL, RED & WHITE: INDIAN VIEWS OF THE WHITE MAN
1492–1982, 114 (1983)

[U]ntil lately, there was no white man on this continent. That it then all belonged to red men, children of the same parents, placed on it by the Great Spirit that made them, to keep it, to traverse it, to enjoy its productions, and to fill it with the same race, once a happy race. Since made miserable by the white people, who are never contented, but always encroaching. The way, and the only way to check and stop this evil, is, for all the red men to unite in claiming a common and equal right to the land, as it was at first, and should be yet; for it never was divided, but belongs to all, for the use of each. That no part has a right to sell, even to each other, much less to strangers, those who want all, and will not do with less. The white people have no right to take the land from the Indians, because they had it first; it is theirs. They may sell, but all must join. Any sale not made by all is not valid. . . . All red men have equal rights to the unoccupied land. The right of occupancy is as good in one place as in another. There cannot be two occupations in the same place. The first excludes all others. It is not so in hunting or traveling; for there the same ground will serve many, as they may follow each other all day; but the camp is stationary, and that is occupancy. It belongs to the first who sits down on his blanket or skins, which he has thrown down upon the ground and till he leaves it no other had a right [to it].

2. The Uneven History of Federal Indian Policy: Politics, Assimilation, and Autonomy

Federal Indian law necessarily constitutes a reflection of the policies Congress, the President, and, more recently, the federal judiciary have from time to time adopted to deal with Indian affairs. The objectives of those policies have not always been consistent either within any given period or over a broader time perspective. Furthermore, shifting federal objectives and the oscillation of federal policy often have created situations that complicate and frustrate efforts to achieve later policy objectives. Thus, any attempt to understand federal Indian law must be grounded in a full appreciation of the history of federal Indian policy. That story, of course, represents only half the equation. When the federal government acted in bilateral treaty cooperation with tribes, the outcome was obviously a partnership, a treaty federalism of equal sovereigns. When, however, the federal government unilaterally asserted power over Indian tribes and their members without their consent through legislative or other policies, their claims to authority often emerged from colonialist impulses that have strongly shaped the history of Indian law. In such circumstances, the mere fact that the federal government adopted a policy did not mean that they could always implement it. For example, while the Removal Act of 1830 forced the signing of coerced removal treaties with members of the Haudenosaunee of the Iroquois Confederation of upstate New York or the Menominee Tribe of Wisconsin, those tribes today substantially remain in diminished portions of their aboriginal domains in great part because of the initiatives of tribal members in resisting removal.

In the introduction to Felix S. Cohen, Handbook of Federal Indian Law xxvii–xxviii (1942), then-solicitor of the Department of the Interior Nathan R. Margold wrote:

> . . . Federal Indian law is a subject that cannot be understood if the historical dimension of existing law is ignored. As I have elsewhere observed, the groups of human beings with whom Federal Indian law is immediately concerned have undergone, in the century and a half of our national existence, changes in living habits, institutions, needs and aspirations far greater than the changes that separate from our own age the ages for which Hammurabi, Moses, Lycurgus, or Justinian legislated. Telescoped into a century and a half, one may find changes in social, political, and property relations which stretch over more than 30 centuries of European civilization. The toughness of law which keeps it from changing as rapidly as social conditions change in our national life is, of course, much more serious where the rate of social change is 20 times as rapid. Thus, if the laws governing Indian affairs are viewed as lawyers generally view existing law, without reference to the varying times in which particular provisions are enacted, the body of the law thus viewed is a mystifying collection of inconsistencies and anachronisms. To recognize the different dates at which various provisions were enacted is the first step towards order and sanity in this field.

Not only is it important to recognize the temporal "depth" of existing legislation, it is also important to appreciate the past existence of legislation which has, technically, ceased to exist. For there is a very real sense in which it can be said that no provision of law is ever completely wiped out. This is particularly true in the field of Indian law. At every session of the Supreme Court, there arise cases in which the validity of a present claim depends upon the question: "What was the law on such and such a point in some earlier period?" Laws long repealed have served to create legal rights which endure and which can be understood only by reference to the repealed legislation. Thus, in seeking a complete answer to various questions of Indian law, one finds that he cannot rest with a collection of laws "still in force," but must constantly recur to legislation that has been repealed, amended, or superseded.

The study of the history of federal Indian policy is a subject that could easily fill several volumes. *See generally* NELL JESSUP NEWTON ET AL., COHEN'S HANDBOOK OF FEDERAL INDIAN LAW ch. 1 (2005 ed.); HISTORY OF INDIAN-WHITE RELATIONS, VOL. 4, HANDBOOK OF NORTH AMERICAN INDIANS (W. Washburn, ed., 1988); FRANCIS PAUL PRUCHA, THE GREAT FATHER (1984); S. LYMAN TYLER, A HISTORY OF INDIAN POLICY (1973); ANGIE DEBO, A HISTORY OF THE INDIANS OF THE UNITED STATES (1970). For excellent general bibliographies, see FRANCIS PAUL PRUCHA, A BIBLIOGRAPHICAL GUIDE TO THE HISTORY OF INDIAN-WHITE RELATIONS IN THE UNITED STATES (1977); FRANCIS PAUL PRUCHA, UNITED STATES INDIAN POLICY: A CRITICAL BIBLIOGRAPHY (1977); FRANCIS PAUL PRUCHA, INDIAN-WHITE RELATIONS IN THE UNITED STATES: A BIBLIOGRAPHY OF WORKS PUBLISHED 1975–1980 (1982).

The following material is presented to provide a sufficient introduction to the history of federal Indian policy to facilitate understanding of modern federal Indian law. As you will see, the history often suggests major cyclical swings between federal willingness to protect and foster tribal sovereignty and autonomy and other periods where forced assimilation and the breakdown of Indian autonomy constituted the primary objective. For each period of federal policy set forth below, consider whether the goals of federal policy were designed to promote Native American assimilation into the broader society or to protect and foster Indian autonomy from the American society. Finally, assess how the changes in federal Indian policy over time have complicated the resolution of legal questions in the field of Indian law.

a.   The Colonial Period (1492–1776)

The European nations that colonized America generally operated on the presumption that discovery vested certain rights to acquire land in the sovereign of the discovering nation. This theory, however, recognized the Indian right of occupancy to land held from time immemorial and merely limited the Indians' right to dispose of their lands to whomever they chose. Thus, the fact of discovery was seen as vesting certain preemption rights in the discovering nation as compared with other European countries and the subjects of the discovering power, but discovery did not extinguish the Indian right of occupancy.

The doctrines of the rights of discovery and the protection of aboriginal possession were profoundly shaped by papers presented by Francisco de Vitoria in Spain in 1532. Responding to those in Spain who then argued that the natives inhabiting the Americas were not Christian (and, according to some, not human) and therefore had no legitimate property rights in the lands that they occupied, Vitoria urged that "aborigines undoubtedly had true dominion in both public and private matters, just like Christians and that neither their princes nor private persons could be despoiled of their property on the ground of their not being true owners." Francisco de Vitoria, De Indis et de Iure Belli Relectiones 128 (E. Nys ed., J. Bate trans., 1917).

In the British colonies the Crown set general policies but the management of Indian affairs initially was left primarily to the separate colonies. Some of the colonies, such as Massachusetts Bay, Virginia, and Connecticut, pursued policies of land expropriation followed by conquest when the Indians resisted. Thus, Indian wars in 1622 in Virginia and in 1675 in Virginia and New England resulted in a decimation and subjugation of some of the tribes of the eastern seaboard in the affected colonies. *See generally* Francis Jennings, The Invasion of America (1975). New York dealt with the Six Nations Iroquois Confederation through diplomatic means and treaty. Similarly, in the Southeast, Georgia treated with the Creeks and the Carolinas and Virginia dealt with the Cherokees as separate sovereign polities, using trade and diplomacy to manage relations with the affected tribes. Nevertheless, Indian dissatisfaction over land frauds, unauthorized encroachment by non-Indian settlers, and improprieties in the Indian trade produced periodic disruptions in Indian affairs. French and Spanish traders also fueled such disruptions and sought trade advantages, as well as military and diplomatic alliances for themselves. *See generally* Allen W. Trelease, Indian Affairs in Colonial New York: The Seventeenth Century (1960); Georgiana C. Nammack, Fraud, Politics and the Dispossession of the Indians (1969); John Phillip Reid, A Better Kind of Hatchet (1976).

During the colonial period most colonies tried extensively to regulate Indian trade and land cessions. The colonial authorities were torn, however, between the conflicting demands posed by the profits to be made from Indian trade and lands on the one hand and the need to placate and pacify the Indians on the other. As a result, the separate management of Indian affairs by the colonies proved uneven, inconsistent, and unsuccessful. When certain Indian tribes either threatened to remain neutral or sided with the French during a series of French and Indian wars in the middle of the eighteenth century, the stage was set for a structural change in the management of Indian affairs. The colonial authorities led by Benjamin Franklin proposed a union of colonies at the Albany Congress of 1754. This proposed union was principally designed to assure centralized control over Indian affairs. Beginning in 1755 the Crown, acting independently, started to centralize the management of Indian affairs through the appointment of Indian agents directly responsible to London. The Proclamation of 1763 forbade further cessions of Indian land in the Indian territory roughly westward of the crest of the Appalachians. It also centralized in the Crown the process of licensing and approving all Indian land cessions eastward of that line, thereby revoking the earlier authority exercised by the colonies over this subject. And in 1764 the Crown proposed a plan to centralize the management of Indian trade in British Crown agents and divesting authority from the colonial government. The trade plan was never formally approved, only partially implemented, and finally abandoned in 1768.

b. The Confederation Period (1776–1789)

During the Revolution the principal objective of United States Indian policy was to secure the neutrality of the Indian tribes. This policy produced one of the first treaties between the United States and the Indians — the Treaty with the Delaware, Sept. 17, 1778, 7 Stat. 13. As noted above, among other things this treaty guaranteed the territorial integrity of the Delaware Nation and expressly contemplated the possibility that the United States might invite the Delaware Nation to form a state and join the Confederation with other tribes allied to the national government. This treaty also provided that the punishment of crimes by citizens of either party to the prejudice of the other would be by judges or juries of both parties.

Even though the United States never engaged in battle with many of the Indian tribes, and others, like the Oneida and parts of the Seneca, supported the Americans during the Revolution, the American negotiating position with the tribes in a series of treaties at Fort Stanwix and Fort Hopewell in 1783 and 1784 was that the tribes were conquered peoples to whom it could dictate terms. Thus, the United States began its post-Revolutionary relations with tribes by attempting to impose a colonial federalism model of relationship. Indian resistance to this position ultimately led the federal government to formally abandon it in negotiations after 1790 and to embrace in its negotiation posture a full international self-determination model. Nevertheless, the myth of conquest continued to have profound implications both for popular American perceptions of Indian tribes and for federal Indian law.

In 1781 the nation approved the Articles of Confederation, in which Article IX vested the Continental Congress with "the sole and exclusive right and power of . . . regulating the trade and managing all affairs with Indians not members of any of the states; provided, that the legislative right of any state within its own limits be not infringed or violated. . . . " This ambiguous commitment of Indian affairs power to the national government — hedged, as it was, with two clauses purporting to reserve some ill-defined, residual state authority over Indian affairs — plagued the national government during the pre-Constitution period. During the Confederation period New York, North Carolina, and Georgia, states containing some of the largest and most powerful tribal groups and confederacies of the day, repeatedly protested federal initiatives regarding tribes located within their borders. When the Continental Congress sought to guarantee Indian occupancy of land against encroachment of white settlers, it could secure approval only for a proclamation restraining alienation of Indian lands "without the limits or jurisdiction of any particular state." 25 JOURNALS OF THE CONTINENTAL CONGRESS 602 (1783).

The conflict between national and state governments over the management of Indian affairs came to a head when Georgia negotiated certain state treaties involving substantial lands with a rump delegation of the Creeks after national treaty commissioners had refused to deal with the group, deeming it unrepresentative of the Creek Nation. This action on the part of the State of Georgia spawned an Indian war on the eve of the convening of the Constitutional Convention in 1787. When Georgia requested the assistance of the Continental Congress, a committee appointed to look into the matter reported:

> An avaricious disposition in some of our people to acquire large tracts of land and often by unfair means, appears to be the principal source of difficulties with the Indians. [The members of this] committee conceive that it has been long the opinion of the country, supported by Justice and humanity, that the Indians have just claims to all lands occupied by and not fairly purchased from them. [Therefore] it cannot be supposed, the state has the powers [to make war with Indians or buy land from them] without making [the Indian affairs clause of article IX] useless and [thus] no particular state can have an exclusive interest in the management of Affairs with any of the tribes, except in some uncommon cases.

33 JOURNALS OF THE CONTINENTAL CONGRESS 457–59 (1787).

c.   The Trade and Intercourse Act Era (1789–1835)

The adoption of the Constitution ushered in a new era in the national management of Indian affairs. Specifically, the Indian commerce clause of Article 1, section 8, clause 3, authorized Congress to regulate "Commerce . . . with the Indian Tribes" and enumerated the Indian tribes with two other sovereign entities, "foreign Nations" and "the several States." Article 1, section 2, also excluded "Indians not taxed" from the enumeration of state citizens for purposes of congressional apportionment, thereby suggesting that they were not part of the polity. In THE FEDERALIST No. 42, Madison wrote of the advantages of the Indian commerce clause over the Articles:

> The regulation of commerce with the Indian tribes is very properly unfettered from two limitations in the articles of confederation, which render the provision obscure and contradictory. The power is there restrained to Indians, not members of any of the States, and is not to violate or infringe the legislative right of any State within its own limits. What description of Indians are to be deemed members of a State, is not yet settled, and has been a question of frequent perplexity and contention in the federal Councils. And how the trade with Indians, though not members of a State, yet residing within its legislative jurisdiction, can be regulated by an external authority, without so far intruding on the internal rights of legislation, is absolutely incomprehensible.

Scholar Gregory Ablavsky provides an in-depth discussion of the role that Indian affairs played in the drafting of the Constitution, highlighting how federalist and anti-federalist narratives structured the debates and ultimately informed the final document. *See* Gregory Ablavsky, *The Savage Constitution*, 63 DUKE L.J. 999, 1000 (2014).

The first Congress promptly acted to assert the national government's exclusive control over Indian affairs by enacting the Trade and Intercourse Act of 1790, ch. 33, 1 Stat. 137. The breadth of congressional assertion of authority is indicated by the restraint on alienation of Indian lands contained in section 4 of the Act (now codified as amended at 25 U.S.C. § 177), which prohibits sale of Indian lands to any person or state unless authorized by the United States. When compared with the limited proclamation of 1783, which only restrained alienation of Indian lands "without the limits or jurisdiction of any particular State," the Trade and Intercourse Act of 1790 represented a new effort to place the exclusive management of trade, diplomatic relations, and land cessions involving the Indians exclusively in the hands of the federal government. This effort was, however, sometimes resisted by the states, and the constitutional tension created during this period is responsible for late twentieth century claims of eastern tribes to possessory interests in land in several eastern states.

While the federal government during this period sought to implement its Indian policy in a series of bilaterally negotiated treaties made with the Indian tribes, the broad outlines of the policy were established in this series of federal laws "to regulate trade and intercourse with the Indian tribes, and to preserve peace on the frontier." The first of these laws, the Trade and Intercourse Act of 1790, was by its terms temporary and was later succeeded by new temporary statutes in 1793, 1796, and 1799 and later by permanent Trade and Intercourse Acts in 1802 and 1834. *See generally* Francis Paul Prucha, American Indian Policy in the Formative Years (1962). The Trade and Intercourse Acts established definite geographically described boundaries for Indian country that tried to replicate the then prevailing treaty boundaries, prohibited private or state negotiated cessions of Indian lands without congressional approval, regulated and licensed non-Indians who entered into Indian trade or sought entry into Indian country, regulated, and later, prohibited liquor trafficking in Indian country, provided for federal punishment of offenders who committed crimes against Indians in Indian country in order to remove the occasions for private retaliation that contributed to frontier hostilities, and promoted the "civilization and education" of the Indians in contemplation of their ultimate incorporation into the mainstream of American economic and political society. The ultimate goal of the effort was to preserve an orderly and economically efficient advance of the frontier of American settlement in Indian country without costly warfare.

Unlike the restraint against alienation of Indian lands, the trade licensing, liquor control, criminal, and certain other provisions of the Trade and Intercourse Acts applied only in "Indian country." Considerable effort was made in the treaties of the time to establish clear lines of demarcation separating protected Indian country enclaves from other lands claimed by the states. *See, e.g.*, Treaty with the Cherokees, July 2, 1791, 7 Stat. 39. Beginning in 1796 the Trade and Intercourse Act codified the Indian country lines established by these various treaties, but the lines were continually changing as new treaties with the United States ceded more Indian land. The statutory revisions were only partially able to keep up with the process of treaty making.

The defeat of Tecumseh's forces allied with the British and the hostile Muscogee (Creek) villages in the Red Sticks War, all part of the general conflict popularly known as the War of 1812, dramatically changed federal Indian law. As reflected by the Treaty of Fort Pitt with the Delaware, despite initial posturing to the contrary, the central model for most of the early relations between the tribes and the federal government was the international model of arms length negotiation between equals, an international self-determination model. This model was the logical outgrowth of the fact that both Indian tribes and European colonial powers on the North American continent had long used diplomacy and alliance in a complex geopolitical balance of power chess match. Until that time, Indian law had been thought of by both the United States and the Indians a species of international diplomacy. Indians had been adept at playing a balance of power geopolitical game, pitting first the French and the English against one another and, later, the British and the Americans, always in pursuit of their own tribal objectives. The War of 1812, however, dramatically changed the geopolitical alignment in North America. With the defeat of the British as their last significant ally on the North American continent, the Indians were left to confront American encroachment directly. For the Americans, after the War of 1812, Indian affairs increasingly came to be seen as a matter of domestic policy, and less a species of international diplomacy. Gradually, the federal government, but not the tribes, tried to steer Indian law away from international models of self-determination and toward other relationships, first treaty federalism, then colonial federalism, and finally by the late nineteenth century toward colonial domination.

At least until 1817, consistent with notions of tribal self-determination, no federal statutes specifically applied to individual Indians in Indian country.[2] In that year, however, Congress passed the first statute providing for the exercise of federal criminal jurisdiction over tribal Indians who committed serious crimes against non-Indians in Indian country. Act of Mar. 3, 1817, ch. 92, 3 Stat. 383. This Act was later modified in 1834 and 1854 and forms the basis of the statute now codified at 18 U.S.C. § 1152.

During this period, Congress extensively managed the trade with Indian tribes. During most of the early nineteenth century until 1822 that regulation involved the establishment of federally sanctioned monopolies under the so-called factory system to handle trade with the Indians.

d.   The Removal Period (1835–1861)

The governments of the states became increasingly dissatisfied with the continued existence of Indian tribal enclaves within their boundaries. As early as 1802 the State of Georgia had ceded to the United States certain lands it formerly claimed in exchange for a promise to promptly extinguish Indian title and remove the Indians from the state. Until the War of 1812 the federal government did little to further the removal of the Indians, in part because the Indian tribes, particularly those on the western frontiers, held an important balance of power on the North American continent. Therefore, placating Native American tribes and preventing their alliance with the English against the American interests remained the dominant theme in federal Indian policy. The outcome of the War of 1812, however, ended this threat and set the stage for removal of the Indians.

The removal process began slowly with the federal government encouraging Indian tribes voluntarily to remove westward, ultimately accepting their agreements to do so by treaty. Thus, in the Treaty with the Cherokee, July 8, 1817, 7 Stat. 156, the federal government accepted a cession of land from some of the leaders of

---

[2] Indians who left their territory and committed crimes against non-Indians on lands over which the states or territories exercised jurisdiction were apparently subject to state or territorial law. The 1796 Trade and Intercourse Act explicitly provides for the apprehension and arrest of such Indians in Indian country. Act of May 19, 1796, ch. 30, § 14, 1 Stat. 472–73.

the lower Cherokee towns so that the Indians could remove westward of the Mississippi River to public lands on the Arkansas and White rivers. The leaders of the lower towns purportedly agreed to the removal in order "to continue the hunter life, and also [because of] the scarcity of game where they then lived." The remaining Cherokees "proposed to begin the establishment of fixed laws and a regular government. . . . " This treaty created a schism in the Cherokee Nation between "western Cherokee" or Old Settler Faction who moved westward and the bulk of the tribe who remained to defend their ancestral homelands. Efforts to secure voluntary tribal removal continued throughout the 1820s but met with only limited success.

Toward the end of the 1820s matters reached crisis proportions. In 1827 the Cherokee Nation, making good on its earlier treaty promise, organized a tribal constitution loosely patterned on the federal constitution and asserted complete territorial sovereignty over its lands. Almost simultaneously gold was discovered in Cherokee country and non-Indian settlement pressures on the Cherokee lands increased. In 1828 the presidential election of Andrew Jackson, an ardent supporter of Indian removal, galvanized the states to take action. In 1828 and 1829 Georgia passed two statutes appropriating most of the lands of the Cherokee Nation, extending state law to these areas, and providing that all laws, ordinances, or regulations of the Cherokee Nation were null and void. These acts also outlawed the Cherokee tribal government and required that all white persons residing in the Cherokee nation secure a license from the governor and take an oath of allegiance to the state. Other statutes in 1830 also rendered Creek and Cherokee Indians incompetent to testify in cases in which a white person was a party. Similar statutes were enacted for the Creeks and Choctaws in Alabama and Mississippi and the Cherokees in Tennessee. As discussed elsewhere in this chapter, the Cherokees tried to resist these state statutes through federal court litigation. *See Cherokee Nation v. Georgia*, 30 U.S. (5 Pet.) 1 (1831); *Worcester v. Georgia*, 31 U.S. (6 Pet.) 515 (1832). In *Worcester* the Georgia laws were declared unconstitutional and the sovereignty of the Cherokees was reaffirmed.

Despite this litigation victory, the Cherokees, like most of the other tribes in the southeastern states, were removed from the states and resettled on the west side of the Mississippi River in the Indian Territory, now eastern Oklahoma. While undertaken pursuant to the federal Removal Act of 1830, the forced relocation policy called removal nevertheless was thought to require tribal consent in the form of individually negotiated treaties with tribes. *E.g.*, Act of May 28, 1830, 4 Stat. 411; Treaty with the Cherokee, Dec. 29, 1835, 7 Stat. 478; Treaty with the Chickasaw, May 24, 1834, 7 Stat. 450; Treaty with the Creeks, Feb. 14, 1833, 7 Stat. 417; Treaty with the Shawnee, Aug. 8, 1831, 7 Stat. 355; Treaty with the Choctaw, Sept. 27, 1830, 7 Stat. 333. The federal government did not simply impose the policy. Thus, the model adopted by the federal government during the period looked quite a bit like treaty federalism. The forced Cherokee removal in the dead of winter produced the infamous Trail of Tears on which almost a quarter of the removed Indians died. Even with removal, approximately one-fourth of the population of the tribes of the southeastern United States were never successfully removed and now form newly recognized tribes in their aboriginal territory, such as the Eastern Band of

Cherokee Indians, the Mississippi Band of Choctaws, and the Poarch Band of Creeks.

Removal was also contemplated for tribes elsewhere. For example, members of the Six Nations Iroquois Confederation of upstate New York, the Menominee and Winnebago tribes of Wisconsin, all signed removal treaties. *E.g.*, Treaty with the Tonawanda Band of the Seneca Indians, Nov. 5, 1857, 11 Stat. 735, 12 Stat. 991; Treaty with the New York Indians, Jan. 15, 1838, 7 Stat. 550. *See also* Treaty with the Menominee, May 12, 1854, 10 Stat. 1064; Treaty with the Menominee, Oct. 18, 1848, 9 Stat. 952. Since considerably less support for removal existed in the northeast and the old Northwest Territory and comparatively far less pressure was being exerted by whites on their remaining lands, removal treaties for these and other tribes were never fully implemented, leaving most of these tribes in portions of their aboriginal homelands. Partial implementation of these treaties, however, explains why an Oneida Tribe can be found in Wisconsin while the remainder of the Oneida Nation forms a separate tribe in upstate New York, or why the Winnebago Tribe now occupies lands in Nebraska, while the remainder of the tribe, the Ho-Chunk Nation, remains on aboriginal homelands in Wisconsin.

Thereafter until at least 1861 a central theme in federal Indian policy was the removal of the tribes beyond state boundary lines, often as a prelude to the admission of new states into the Union. *See, e.g.*, Treaty with the Sac and Fox Indians, Oct. 11, 1842, 7 Stat. 596. The political and jurisdictional importance of this process to the tribes was captured in the guarantees made in Articles 4 and 5 of the Treaty of Dancing Rabbit Creek with the Choctaw Nation and Article 5 of the Treaty of New Echota with the Cherokee Nation, the latter of which is set forth at the start of this chapter. In light of their experiences with the states in which they formerly resided, the tribes sought and received through these provisions federal guarantees of complete territorial sovereignty over the lands to which they were removed.

e.   The Reservation Policy (1861–1887)

Like the prior effort at establishing clear lines of demarcation for Indian country under the Trade and Intercourse Acts, the federal removal policy was hampered by the speed of westward expansion of non-Indian settlement and the logistics of removing and relocating large Native communities. It was also impeded by the limited remaining unoccupied areas outside of the states and territories for removal of Indian tribes and, of course, by the resistance of the tribes. Once westward American settlement leap-frogged the Indian Territory to California, the effort to remove and relocate Indian tribes outside of newly formed states was doomed. Thus, in California during the early 1850s, federal agents experimented with the creation of smaller reservations *within* the state that might become permanent. Eighteen treaties were negotiated with California tribes during this period and several reservations were established. The Senate, however, refused to ratify these treaties, in part because they departed from the declared removal policy of clearing resident Native American tribes from the states. This history left a large Indian population in California landless and without treaty protections for their rights.

Despite this inauspicious beginning, the reservation policy rapidly was adopted for other states and territories west of the Mississippi River. Thus, in a series of early experiments with reservations in Kansas and Wisconsin, a number of treaties in the 1850s explicitly reserved land for permanent tribal occupancy. *E.g.*, Treaty with the Kansas, Oct. 5, 1859, 12 Stat. 1111; Treaty with the Winnebago, Apr. 15, 1859, 12 Stat. 1101; Treaty with the Menominee, May 12, 1854, 10 Stat. 1064. The first clear congressional recognition that such reservations were intended as permanent jurisdictional enclaves *within the states* is found in the Enabling Act for the Kansas Territory. This Act, which authorized the formation of the State of Kansas, explicitly stated that the establishment of the state would not be construed to extend state jurisdiction over Indians of the Kansas territory or to impair the rights of Indians on their property in the territory. Act of Jan. 29, 1861, ch. 20, § 1, 12 Stat. 127. This disclaimer of jurisdiction established a pattern, and the enabling acts and constitutions of many states admitted to the Union after 1861 therefore contain such disclaimers of jurisdiction. *See, e.g.*, Act of July 7, 1958, Pub. L. No. 85-508, § 4, 72 Stat. 339 (Alaska); Act of June 20, 1910, ch. 310, §§ 2, 20, 36 Stat. 558–59, 569–70 (Arizona and New Mexico); Act of Feb. 22, 1889, ch. 180, § 4, 25 Stat. 677 (North Dakota, South Dakota, Montana, and Washington). Thus, the clear understanding at the time of the formation of the reservations was that the states lacked any inherent authority in Indian country. These enclaves remained territory subject to the exclusive control of the tribes and, to a lesser extent, the federal government.

Often the reservation policy was a form of relocation by another name. Instead of removing Indians from within the limits of the states, the reservation policy contemplated moving them out of the way of non-Indian settlement by fencing them into small reservations, which freed their former subsistence areas for homesteading. Thus, at core, the reservation policy simply continued the prior effort to geographically move Indians off valuable lands demanded by white settlers and to move them out of the way of encroaching Americans. The major difference is that the reservation policy largely recognized the geographic constraints on pushing Indians totally out of states and tried to fence them into small areas within states. The only virtue of that policy over removal was that sometimes the remaining reservation was at least located in a diminished portion of the tribe's aboriginal homeland.

The reservation policy remained the cornerstone of the federal approach throughout the remainder of the nineteenth century, accelerating dramatically as the emergence of the transcontinental railroad after the Civil War facilitated western American settlement in the traditional aboriginal domains of many of the western tribes. Most of the famous Indian wars of the last half of the century, including the unsuccessful flight of Chief Joseph and his band of Nez Perce Indians to Canada, the flight of the Northern Cheyenne, General Custer's Last Stand at the Battle of Greasy Grass (or the Little Big Horn, as it is commonly known by non-Indians) in 1876, and the military's long and relatively unsuccessful search for Geronimo a decade later, were caused by federal military efforts to force Indian tribes onto reservations or, in the cases of Geronimo, Sitting Bull, and Crazy Horse, forcibly to keep them there. Thus, the reservation was not only a means of keeping non-Indian settlers off Indian lands; during the late nineteenth century, it also was a device to keep the Indians forcibly fenced within geographic and political lines of demarcation. While Indians and non-Indians might not agree on the appropriate size and boundaries for a reservation, they shared a common view at that time that mutual isolation of the two cultures and communities from one another was essential.

This period also constituted a very productive time for the making of Indian treaties, since the massive relocation of Indians required by the reservation policy necessitated coming to terms with the affected tribes. Excerpts from one of the most famous such treaties commenced this chapter — the Treaty of Fort Sumner of 1868 with the Navajo, which reversed Kit Carson's forced removal and incarceration of the Navajo at a barren reservation Bosque Redondo in New Mexico and permitted them to return to their sacred lands in the four corners region.

Throughout this period, the tribes of the Indian Territory — as well as certain other tribes east of the frontier like the Menominees, the Eastern Band of Cherokees in North Carolina, or the New York Indians — were at peace and engaged in the work of strengthening and adapting their tribal institutions and their social and economic condition to confront the colonialist pressures that surrounded them. In the Indian Territory, Western style tribal governments with written laws and constitutions and courts of record emerged among the Cherokees, Choctaws, Chickasaws, Muscogee (Creeks), and Seminoles, then lumped together as the so-called Five Civilized Tribes. Proposals were even heard for the formation of an Indian state of the Union out of the tribes comprising the Indian Territory, an idea that later died when Oklahoma was admitted to the Union as a multiracial state in the early twentieth century. Thus, while a time of tremendous relocation and dislocation for Indian tribes, the reservation period nevertheless was characterized from a federal perspective first in treaty federalism models and, later, in colonial federalism approaches. From the Native perspective, however, the treaties that were negotiated were always seen as assuring self-determination as separate nations.

f.   The Allotment Period and Forced Assimilation (1871–1934)

The late-nineteenth century ushered in a new model of colonial domination of Native peoples. With Indian tribes moved onto reservations, there was both a massive transfer of the remaining Indian lands to non-Indian ownership and a corresponding increase in federal claims of legal power to govern Indian country and the persons and property of Indian tribes. This development was perhaps a reflection of the general imperialist impulse of the United States during this period, which included the federal government assuming colonial authority over Cuba, Puerto Rico, and the Philippines, and overthrowing the internationally recognized, indigenous monarchy of the Kingdom of Hawaii. *See* Ch. 2, Sec. B.3; Ch. 5, Sec. B.2. Until this period, Western colonialism had focused exclusively on exploiting resources, leaving the Indian tribes largely to govern themselves as autonomous states. Thus, from colonial contact until the very late nineteenth century, the first wave of American colonialism was fundamentally about the exploitation of resources that were once in Indian hands. But in the late nineteenth century, the federal government asserted greater control over Indian peoples, without Indian consent. For the first time, the federal government sought to govern Indians directly, rather than leaving such matters to the tribes.

The period from 1871 to 1887 represented a transition period in federal Indian policy. While implementation of the reservation policy continued during this period, various events signaled significant structural changes in federal Indian policy. First, in 1871, Congress ended formal treaty making with the Indian tribes. The Appropriations Act of Mar. 3, 1871, ch. 120, 16 Stat. 544, 566, codified at 25 U.S.C. § 71, provided that Indian nations shall not be dealt with as independent nations through treaties.

This Act grew out of a long-standing dispute between the Senate and the House of Representatives over control of Indian affairs. The House of Representatives, dissatisfied with the preeminent role in Indian affairs that the treaty ratification process gave to the Senate, had cut off funds for treaty negotiations as early as 1867. *See* Act of Mar. 29, 1867, ch. 13, § 6, 15 Stat. 9; *see also* Act of Apr. 10, 1869, ch. 16, § 5, 16 Stat. 40. After 1871 agreements with Indian tribes continued to be negotiated into the early twentieth century, but they were approved by statutory enactment. *E.g.*, Act of Mar. 1, 1901, ch. 675, 31 Stat. 848 (Cherokees); Act of July 10, 1882, ch. 284, 22 Stat. 157 (Crows). In addition to ending treaty making, section 3 of the Act of Mar. 3, 1871 required that contracts involving the payment of funds for services related to Indian lands or claims against the United States had to be approved by the Commissioner of Indian Affairs and the Secretary of the Interior. *See also* Act of May 21, 1872, ch. 177, 17 Stat. 136, now codified at 25 U.S.C. § 81.

Stunned by the 1883 Supreme Court decision in *Ex parte Crow Dog*, discussed in Sec. D.1, this chapter, Congress appended a section to the Appropriations Act of Mar. 3, 1885, ch. 341, 23 Stat. 362, 385, providing for the exercise of federal court jurisdiction over seven major crimes committed by Indians on Indian reservations in the states or territories against the person or property of an "Indian or other person." This statute provided federal court jurisdiction for the first time over intratribal affairs. Such matters had previously been left exclusively to tribal authorities. The Major Crimes Act has been amended and expanded to cover more than sixteen enumerated crimes and presently is codified at 18 U.S.C. § 1153.

Another major departure in federal Indian policy was brought about by the Dawes General Allotment Act of 1887, ch. 119, 24 Stat. 388, codified as amended at 25 U.S.C. § 331 et seq. (General Allotment Act). This statute has had long-lasting implications for Indian country since it all but ended the collective nature of tribal land tenure on affected reservations and opened some, but not all, reservations to non-Indian settlement. For the first time, non-Indians were permitted to live in Indian country in large numbers without being federally licensed traders. As early as the Treaty with the Oto and Missouri, Mar. 15, 1854, 10 Stat. 1038, the federal government had experimented in Kansas and the Indian Territory with a policy of allotting tribally held lands into separate lots or parcels that were assigned to tribal members for a permanent home and to encourage agricultural pursuits. The roots of such allotment experiments can be traced back to the colonial period. The goal behind the nineteenth-century federal allotment policy was to lure the nomadic hunting tribes away from their mobile, communal village existence and to encourage a sedentary, rural agricultural life on separate allotments, replicating the residential pattern of non-Indian rural America. *See also* Treaty with the Omaha, Mar. 16, 1854, 10 Stat. 1043; Treaty with the Shawnee, May 10, 1854, 10 Stat. 1053; Treaty with the Sacs and Foxes of Missouri, May 18, 1854, 10 Stat. 1074; Treaty with the Kickapoo, May 18, 1854, 10 Stat. 1078. All of these early efforts involved voluntary tribal consent to the allotment process.

While the Civil War and Reconstruction temporarily interrupted the implementation of the allotment policy, Congress returned to allotment as a model for federal Indian policy in the 1887 statute. This time, however, Congress forced the Indians to accept allotment, and coupled its allotment policy with provisions that likely anticipated (but did not direct) the ultimate dissolution of the Indian tribe and its reservation after expiration of an interim 25-year trust period. The central theme of federal policy during this period was the detribalization and individualization of property holding and federal-Indian relationships. *See generally* Delos Sacket Otis, *History of the Allotment Policy*, Hearings on H.R. 7902 Before the House Committee on Indian Affairs, 73d Cong., 2d Sess., pt. 9, at 428 (1934). The primary provisions of the General Allotment Act of 1887 included granting each family head 160 acres of land, 80 acres to each single person over 18 years of age and to each orphan under 18, and granting all other single persons under eighteen 40 acres of land. Generally, the land was held in trust title for 25 years by the United States, with an unencumbered patent in fee issuing at the close of the trust period. During the trust period the land generally was not subject to alienation or taxation. The General Allotment Act provided that citizenship would be conferred on the allottees at the conclusion of the trust process. Section 6 of the General Allotment Act, codified as amended at 25 U.S.C. § 349, contemplated that the Indian allottees would be subjected to state law and jurisdiction at the expiration of the restraint on alienation or, as later amended, the completion of the allotment program on any particular reservation. Whether this authorization for state jurisdiction extended to the allottees' lands and successors in interest has been the subject of litigation. *See* Ch. 4, Sec. B.3. Section 5 of the Act also contemplated that "surplus" land, not needed for the fixed-acreage allotments to tribal members, would be ceded to the federal government for compensation through negotiations with the tribe. Such lands were thereafter opened to non-Indian settlement under the public lands program; thus, Indian reservations were opened to non-Indian settlement for the first time.

Like the Trade and Intercourse Acts and the Removal Act of 1830 that preceded it, the General Allotment Act only stated and authorized a general policy. Implementation of the policy was left to the discretion of the President and his designated Indian agents. Thus, allotment was not implemented on all reservations. Further, even on reservations on which it was implemented, the degree of penetration of the policy into the traditional tribal land holding arrangements varied considerably. Consequently, the remaining modern effects of the allotment policy are uneven across Indian country. Some tribes, including many southwestern tribes, like the Hopi and New Mexico pueblos, and most of the tribes east of the Mississippi, were untouched by allotment. The land bases of many other Plains, Midwest, and Pacific Northwest tribes, however, were ravaged by allotment. Due to the variation in application, allotment has produced a legacy of geographical and jurisdictional complexities for many Indian nations. The checkerboard land ownership patterns produced by the policy, created by interspersing Indian and non-Indian parcels, made rational land management and governance much more difficult. An illustrative map of the current land ownership pattern of the Lac Courte Oreilles Reservation in Wisconsin is set forth below to demonstrate the point.

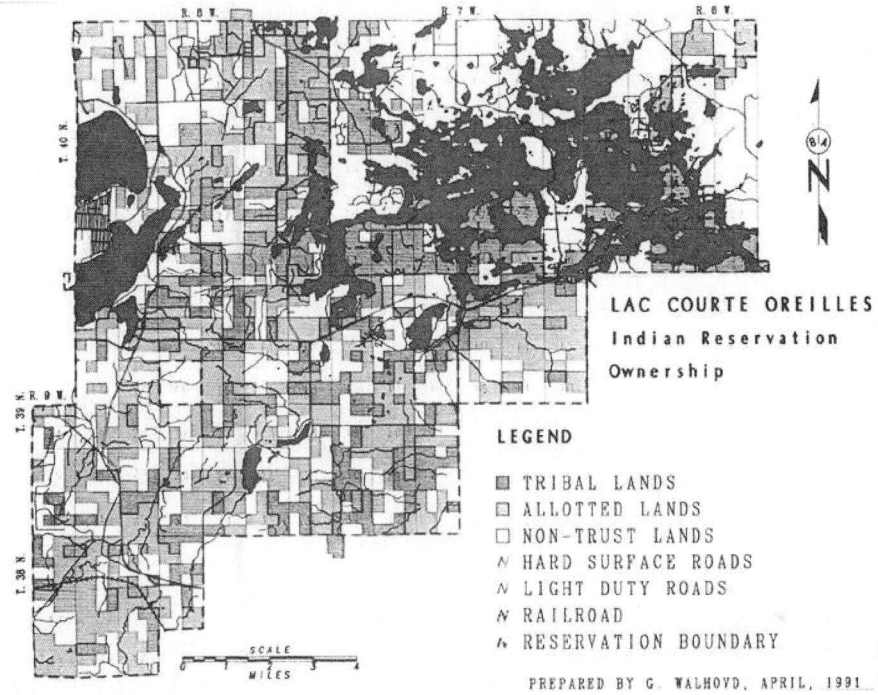

LAC COURTE OREILLES
Indian Reservation
Ownership

LEGEND

■ TRIBAL LANDS
☐ ALLOTTED LANDS
☐ NON-TRUST LANDS
∧ HARD SURFACE ROADS
∧ LIGHT DUTY ROADS
∧ RAILROAD
∧ RESERVATION BOUNDARY

SCALE
MILES

PREPARED BY G. WALHOVD, APRIL, 1991

Many of those in Congress who supported allotment favored opening Indian lands to non-Indian development. Indian agents and Indian rights associations throughout the country also supported the policy. The backing of the program by eastern Indian rights advocates was evident at the Lake Mohonk Conference in 1889. These Indian rights supporters sought to protect the Indian in his land holding. They believed that an Indian holding a patent from the federal government, restricted against alienation, enjoyed greater security for his land tenure than the protection afforded by tribal possession, and that individual ownership would promote industry by creating an incentive for greed. Additionally, the program held forth the vision that the Indian would acquire the benefits of civilization through the pursuit of sedentary agricultural life and would, therefore, abandon his "uncivilized," nomadic, hunting tribal culture. Of course, these paradigm extremes rarely existed in practice. Despite the fact that agriculture already formed an important ingredient of many tribal cultures, Congress approved the allotment program, over significant tribal opposition, based on these cultural stereotypes. Indeed, the uncritical manner in which the General Allotment Act treated Indian lands, for example by allotting large units suitable for grazing into small farming plots for which it was not suited, often frustrated, rather than facilitated, Indian agricultural development.

During consideration of the General Allotment Act, Senator Teller warned the Senate that, within 30 or 40 years, the Indians would be dispossessed of their lands and would curse those who professedly spoke in their defense. The Creeks, Choctaws, and Cherokees warned that a change from communal title to individual title would concentrate ownership of Indian land, within a few years, in the hands of a few persons. Despite these predictions, the allotment program authorized by the General Allotment Act was implemented by a series of agreements and statutes specifying the allotment process and ceding surplus lands on particular reservations. While the 1887 General Allotment Act restrained alienation of allotted land for a 25-year period, later legislation authorized the Secretary of the Interior to shorten this period, to make sales of allotted land, to approve the issuance of a patent upon the death of the allottee, or to otherwise remove the restraints on alienation and authorize sale on a finding that the Indian allottee was competent to manage his own affairs. *E.g.*, Act of May 29, 1908, ch. 216, 35 Stat. 444, codified at 25 U.S.C. § 404; Act of Mar. 1, 1907, ch. 2285, 34 Stat. 1018, codified at 25 U.S.C. § 405. The Act of Mar. 2, 1907, ch. 2523, 34 Stat. 1221, codified at 25 U.S.C. §§ 119, 121, applied the allotment concept to tribal trust funds, authorizing the allotment of pro rata shares in tribal trust funds to Indians deemed competent to manage their own affairs. Other statutes authorized allottees to dispose of their restricted property by will, requiring secretarial approval for such distributions, and provided a plan for the administration of allottees' estates. Act of June 25, 1910, ch. 431, 36 Stat. 855, codified in various sections of 25 U.S.C.

The individualization of Indian land tenure caused by allotment required provisions for the productive use of property when the allottee was unable to work the allotment. Thus, the Act of Feb. 28, 1891, ch. 383, 26 Stat. 794, authorized the leasing of allotted land whenever the Secretary found that the allottee, by reason of age or other disability, could not personally occupy and improve the allotment. The same statute authorized the leasing of tribal lands under authority of the tribal council, subject to approval by the Secretary of the Interior. This Act began the surface-leasing program for Indian lands, frequently administered by federal agents for the benefit of non-Indian lessees. The Act was later supplemented by a host of statutes governing the leasing of tribal and allotted lands both for surface occupancy and for mineral, oil, and gas development. *See* 25 U.S.C. § 415; Act of May 11, 1938, ch. 198, 52 Stat. 347, codified at 25 U.S.C. §§ 396a–396g; Act of Mar. 3, 1927, ch. 299, 44 Stat. 1347, codified at 25 U.S.C. §§ 398a–398d. Most such later leasing legislation was not limited to allotted lands held by minors or incompetents.

Ultimately, the surface and mineral leasing programs expanded to cover the remaining tribally held lands. Act of May 11, 1938, ch. 198, 52 Stat. 347, codified at 25 U.S.C. §§ 396a–396g; Act of Mar. 3, 1927, ch. 299, 44 Stat. 1347, codified as amended at 25 U.S.C. §§ 398a–398e; Act of July 3, 1926, ch. 787, 44 Stat. 894, codified as amended at 25 U.S.C. § 402a; Act of May 29, 1924, ch. 210, 43 Stat. 244, codified at 25 U.S.C. § 398; Act of June 30, 1919, ch. 4, 41 Stat. 31, codified as amended at 25 U.S.C. § 399. Other federal legislation enacted during this period authorized for the first time the sale of timber on Indian lands. *E.g.*, Act of June 25, 1910, ch. 431, 36 Stat. 857, codified as amended at 25 U.S.C. §§ 406–07. Collectively, these leasing and timber statutes of the allotment period partially restored to the American marketplace the Indian real estate interests that the restraints on alienation contained in the early Trade and Intercourse Acts had removed from market dealings. As individual Indian lands became more fractionated in ownership through inheritance, the difficulty of securing agreement and coordination among partial owners meant that the actual active management of the Indian parcels increasingly fell to the federal Bureau of Indian Affairs (BIA), which discharged that task poorly, at best.

As originally adopted, the General Allotment Act of 1887 did not apply to the tribes of the Indian Territory. Later legislation and agreements extended the act or special allotment provisions to these tribes and suspended the laws of the tribal governments in the Indian Territory as a prelude to the admission of the State of Oklahoma into the Union. *See, e.g.*, Act of Apr. 26, 1906, ch. 1876, 34 Stat. 137; *see also Cherokee Nation v. Hitchcock*, 187 U.S. 294 (1902); *Stephens v. Cherokee Nation*, 174 U.S. 445 (1899).

During the allotment period, the federal government implemented a number of other policies designed to forcibly assimilate Indians and destroy their culture and tribal institutions. The most dramatic of these efforts involved the formation by the Indian Service of the Indian Police and the Courts of Indian Offenses. The regulations they enforced are set forth later in this chapter. Amazingly, these institutions were created by federal regulations never explicitly authorized by statute, and they flagrantly denied tribal members' rights as protected by the U.S. Bill of Rights, including First Amendment guarantees of religious freedom. They involved the employment by the BIA of Indian tribal members to serve as police officers and judges for their reservations, thereby creating an alternative power structure to the traditional forms of governance followed by the tribe. The Code of Indian Offenses, the regulations implemented by the Indian Police and the Courts of Indian Offenses, initially proscribed many traditional Indian cultural and religious practices, including ceremonial dances, such as the sun dance, destruction of an Indian's personal property at death, the practices of medicine men, and the payment of compensation to a woman's family when she is married. At the height of this program, in 1900, Courts of Indian Offenses were established on two-thirds of the Indian reservations. The effort to enforce the prohibition on tribal dances against the Sioux in order to suppress the Ghost Dance, a messianic Native religious movement, produced the "Wounded Knee Massacre" in 1890, in which the Seventh Cavalry killed nearly 200 Indians.

During this period, the federal government also established a series of boarding schools deliberately designed to remove Indian children from tribally based child rearing and socialization and thereby stamp out all tribal influences, including language. The model for these schools was the Carlisle School, founded by Richard Henry Pratt, an army officer who first experimented with Indian education while a jailer for Indians at the Fort Marion prison in Florida, to which Geronimo would later be sent. These Indian boarding schools emphasized vocational training, and Indian children were severely punished for traditional dress, tribal ceremonial practices, or use of their Native language. The motto was that tribal traditions were the enemy of progress. Since these schools removed large numbers of Indian children from their homes for many years — during critical developmental and socialization periods — they account for a number of contemporary Native problems, including the diminishment or extinction of many Native languages, the loss of many Indian traditions and ceremonies, and the disruption of Indian family life and inappropriate child rearing techniques, sometimes traceable to instances of corporal punishments and sexual abuse in the boarding schools.

Another product of this assimilationist era of federal Indian policy was the Indian Citizenship Act of June 2, 1924, ch. 233, 43 Stat. 253, which conferred United States citizenship on "all noncitizen Indians born within the territorial limits of the United States." This Act simplified a plethora of provisions in the General Allotment Act and various special allotment statutes and treaties that originally contemplated that Indians would become citizens upon the completion of the allotment process or the expiration of the restraints on alienation of their allotments and some later statutes that gave citizenship to Indian veterans who had fought for the United States. The Indian Citizenship Act of 1924 nevertheless provided that it would not affect Indian treaty rights or their status. Nothing in the Act granted any Indian state citizenship.

As Senator Teller predicted in 1887, implementation of the allotment policy did result in the dispossession of the Indians. During the period from 1887 to 1934, allotment policies reduced Indian land holdings by two-thirds — from 138 million acres to 48 million acres. Most of the land was lost when it was declared "surplus" (*i.e.*, not needed for fixed acreage allotments to tribal members) and later opened to non-Indian settlement under the homesteading laws. Some of the Indian land base, however, fell out of federal trust restraints after the 25-year restrictions on alienation expired or when the land was taken, sometimes illegally, at state forced tax sales or in mortgage foreclosure proceedings, often from Indians whose primary language was not English and who never understood the tax bill or mortgage that they received.

g.   The Indian Reorganization Act Period (1934–1940)

If the General Allotment Act was the predominant piece of legislation representing the public attitude in the late nineteenth and early twentieth centuries, then the Indian Reorganization Act of 1934 (Wheeler-Howard Act), ch. 576, 48 Stat. 984, codified at 25 U.S.C. §§ 461–479, provides an important clue to the ripening consciousness of the twentieth century. By 1934, there was a sense that something very serious was wrong with the direction of federal policy based on the General Allotment Act and the principles that undergirded it. There was chaos where it had been implemented and uncertainty where it had not taken hold.

In 1928 the famous Meriam Report was issued, summarizing the failure of the federal policies followed since the late nineteenth century. The report, entitled "Problems of Indian Administration," scored the loss of land from Indian ownership that occurred partly as a consequence of implementing the General Allotment Act philosophy and called for many of the reforms that reached fruition in the Indian Reorganization Act. Federal policy generally, as expressed in the National Industrial Recovery Act, seemed to rely on the strengthening of private corporate institutions. Federal Indian policy reflected this trend. As the nineteenth century dream of homesteading as a general solution to economic problems faded, confidence in allotment as a technique for providing a secure economic basis for Indian families also diminished.

President Franklin Roosevelt's appointment of John Collier as Commissioner of Indian Affairs marked the emergence of a very different kind of consciousness, and a different way of using the land to produce what at the time was considered to be the road to civilization. *See Readjustment of Indian Affairs*, Hearings on H.R. 7902 Before the House Committee on Indian Affairs, 73d Cong., 2d Sess. (1934). Collier had a vision of new Native American governments emerging to take control of the destiny of Indian communities, thereby displacing the heavy hand of the Indian Service which, to Collier's thinking, had been responsible for the debacle of the allotment policy and which thereby had gained too large a role in the daily governance of Indian affairs. Collier's thinking put him at odds with both his own agency and with more conservative elements of Congress. He was therefore only able to get portions of his programs enacted into law in the form of the Indian Reorganization Act of 1934 (IRA). Cursory review of the provisions of the IRA reveals, however, that it marked a major departure from the Indian policies of the previous half-century.

Section 1 of the IRA, 25 U.S.C. § 461, ended further allotment by providing "No land of any Indian reservation, created or set apart by treaty or agreement with the Indians [shall] be allotted in severalty to any Indian." Section 2 of the Act indefinitely extended the existing periods of trust restrictions on Indian allotted land where such restrictions had not already expired. 25 U.S.C. § 462. Later legislation in 1948, however, did permit the Secretary of the Interior to authorize the issuance of patents in fee and the conveyance of Indian allotments on application of the Indian owners, thereby selectively removing the restrictions. Act of May 14, 1948, c. 293, 62 Stat. 236, codified at 25 U.S.C. § 483. In order to rebuild the tribal land base and make the remaining Indian lands more compact and governable, sections 4 and 5 of the IRA authorized the Secretary of the Interior to exchange lands of equal value and to acquire lands by gift or purchase at a cost of two million dollars a year (an authorization that has never been fully implemented). 25 U.S.C. §§ 464–465. Under section 7 of the Act, 25 U.S.C. § 467, the Secretary was authorized to proclaim any new lands so acquired as additions to existing reservations or as new reservations, provided that the "lands added to existing reservations shall be designated for the exclusive use of Indians entitled by enrollment or by tribal membership to residence at such reservations."

In order to facilitate the long-term productive management of Indian forests, section 6 of the IRA directed the Secretary to make rules for the operation of Indian forestry units "on the principle of sustained-yield management," rather than clear cutting, and to restrict the grazing of livestock on Indian grazing units to the estimated carrying capacity of such ranges. 25 U.S.C. § 466. Recognizing the impairment of economic development created by the inability of Indian tribes to mortgage their land, their most important asset, the IRA authorized grants for the creation of Indian business corporations or other business entities and established a revolving loan fund authorized, but not appropriated, at twenty million dollars. 25 U.S.C. §§ 469–470. The IRA also established educational grants and created an Indian preference for all positions in the Indian Office. 25 U.S.C. §§ 471–472.

By far the most important provisions of the IRA, however, were sections 16–18 of the Act, which authorized the Secretary to approve constitutions and corporate charters for Indian tribes seeking to organize under its provisions. 25 U.S.C.

§§ 476–478. These provisions were the heart of Collier's plan to displace the Indian Service with new indigenous tribal governments, reviving the sense of tribal self-government and control of their own destinies of which the Indian tribes had been robbed by the allotment policy. Section 16 specified that a tribe could adopt a written tribal constitution and required just a few basic powers be included in the constitution. The Bureau of Indian Affairs employees who assisted tribes in drafting constitutions, however, leveraged a whole new role for the BIA by including in many of them requirements for BIA approval of some or all tribal laws, even though the statute contained no such requirement. Reflecting the duality between the public and private sectors in non-Indian American society, section 17 of the Act, 25 U.S.C. § 477, also authorized the Secretary to recognize charters of incorporation of tribal business corporations, a separation of governmental and business functions of the tribal community that was and remains alien to most tribes.

Consistent with the democratic traditions of American society, section 18 of the IRA called for an election at which a majority of the adult members of the tribe would vote to take advantage of its provisions. 25 U.S.C. § 478. While this provision probably was originally intended only for purposes of the provisions of the Act dealing with the formation of constitutions and by-laws for tribal governments and charters of incorporation for tribal business entities, through a quirk of ill-considered draftsmanship this section applied to the entirety of the Act, including the provisions ending the allotment policy, an error rectified more than 50 years later by technical amendments to the IRA.

Finally, in order to define those eligible for the benefits provided under the Act, including the Indian preference for employment with the Indian Service, section 19 of the Act, 25 U.S.C. § 479, contained a comprehensive definition of the term "Indian" which was in part keyed to tribal membership requirements established by the tribes themselves. This section also defined an adult Indian eligible to vote in the elections provided for in section 18 as one who has attained the age of 21 years.

The Act of June 15, 1935, ch. 260, 49 Stat. 378, codified at 25 U.S.C. §§ 478a–478b, amended the IRA to provide that only a majority of those actually voting in an IRA election, rather than an absolute majority of the entire adult tribal membership rolls, was needed to approve acceptance of the IRA. A total of 258 tribal elections were held in which 181 tribes then comprising 129,750 Indians accepted the Act and 77 tribes encompassing 86,365 Indians rejected it (including the 45,000 member Navajo Nation). Another 14 groups did not hold elections to exclude themselves and became included. Within twelve years after the adoption of the Act, 161 tribal constitutions and 131 tribal corporate charters had been drafted and approved under the provisions of the IRA. Clearly, the BIA not only supplied technical assistance in the process and conducted the election, it also exerted considerable pressure and employed legally manipulative tactics to secure ratification for tribal constitutions and, therefore, the implementation of the IRA on each reservation. Many traditionalists claim the elections were not fair and that the BIA essentially forced the tribes to adopt the accouterments of Western democracy, including representative government and majority (rather than consensus) rules, both of which were alien to tribal democratic traditions. For tribes that voted to exclude themselves from the coverage of the Act, all provisions of the Act, including those extending the trust periods on allotments, were believed to be inapplicable.

However, later court decisions and congressional acts clarified that tribes that had not organized through the IRA were entitled to partake of its other benefits. The nation's geographically largest tribe, the Navajo, voted down the IRA and has since functioned, like Great Britain, New Zealand, or Israel, without a written constitution. Its government was later reorganized under the Navajo-Hopi Rehabilitation Act of 1950, ch. 92, 64 Stat. 44.

Since the provisions of section 16 of the IRA regarding tribal reorganization applied to "any Indian tribe, or tribes, residing on the same reservation," they were inapplicable to most of the tribes in Oklahoma, some of whose reservations in the eastern portion of the state had been extinguished near the turn of the century. As a result, Congress enacted the Oklahoma Indian Welfare Act of 1936, ch. 831, 49 Stat. 1967, codified at 25 U.S.C. § 501 et seq., which authorized the Oklahoma tribes to organize for their common welfare and to adopt business charters like the IRA tribes. Like the IRA, the Oklahoma Act also authorized the Secretary to acquire real property interests in trust for the tribes. Some of the so-called Five Civilized Tribes declined the invitation and continued to function more or less under their nineteenth century written constitutions.

During the Depression Indian tribes also benefited greatly from New Deal programs of general application that were aimed at economic rehabilitation. These programs caused a significant infusion of new resources and funds into Indian reservations. This fact ironically made the Depression years some of the most prosperous times reservation Indians had known.

Clearly federal policy shifted during the Indian Reorganization Act period away from a colonial domination paradigm bent on termination and ultimate assimilation. The more interesting question, and one hotly debated in Indian country, is precisely which model it shifted toward. Was it a model based on international self-determination or one based on some form of federalism? If it was a federalism model, was it more like treaty federalism (albeit without the formal treaty, the making of which was ended in 1871) or was it a form of colonial federalism?

h.   The Termination Era (1940–1962)

The explicit ideological nature of the Indian Reorganization Act provoked considerable debate, much of it after passage of the law. Hearings began during the 1940s which signaled a potential shift away from the protection of Indian autonomy sought by the IRA, even before the Act was fully implemented. The indictment leveled against the IRA can be found in Hearings on S. 2103 before the Committee on Indian Affairs, H.R. 76th Cong., 3d Sess. (1940), which suggested that by promoting tribal communal governance, the IRA diminished private initiative, inheritance, and private property and tended "to force the Indians back into a primitive state." Significant criticism was also voiced as to the manner in which the BIA had conducted the elections to approve the constitutions and accept the Act.

While the Indian Reorganization Act of 1934 survived such legislative attacks, almost all the reforming zeal promised by the Act quickly came to an end during the war years as a result of the hearings and the focus of the government elsewhere. These hearings therefore heralded a new and very different era in Indian relations begun during the 1940s. During this period the notion of tribal sovereignty and the separate jurisdictional status of the reservations again came under attack. The legislative output of this decade was, however, relatively modest. Various statutes were enacted throughout the decade subjecting certain specific tribes or tribes in designated states to state jurisdiction. *See, e.g.*, Act of June 30, 1948, ch. 759, 62 Stat. 1161 (Sac and Fox Reservation in Iowa); Act of June 8, 1940, ch. 276, 54 Stat. 249, codified at 18 U.S.C. § 3243 (all reservations in Kansas). The most pervasive of these statutes were enacted in 1948 and 1952 and granted criminal and civil jurisdiction, respectively, to the State of New York over all reservations within the state. Act of Sept. 13, 1950, ch. 947, § 1, 64 Stat. 845, codified at 25 U.S.C. § 233; Act of July 2, 1948, ch. 809, 62 Stat. 1224, codified at 25 U.S.C. § 232.

In 1949 the Hoover Commission, appointed to review executive branch reorganization as part of the post-war downsizing of the federal government, issued a report on Indian affairs. The report called for the total assimilation of the Indians "into the mass of the population as full, tax-paying citizens." COMMISSION ON ORGANIZATION OF THE EXECUTIVE BRANCH OF GOVERNMENT: INDIAN AFFAIRS: A REPORT TO CONGRESS 77–80 (1949). The report began a momentum toward a policy of federal termination that culminated in the 1950s, reaching its peak in 1953. In that year Congress passed House Concurrent Resolution 108, announcing the policy of Congress, "as rapidly as possible," to make all Indians "subject to the same laws and entitled to the same privileges and responsibilities as are applicable to other citizens of the United States, and to grant them all the rights and prerogatives pertaining to American citizenship," and declaring that the tribes in certain states and certain other tribes "at the earliest time possible . . . should be freed from Federal supervision and control and from all disabilities and limitations specially applicable to Indians." The Congress thereafter set about providing in separate statutes for the winding up of the affairs of various designated tribes and for their termination from federal supervision, from eligibility for federal benefits, and from coverage under federal Indian laws. At the end of this process the terminated tribes were to be fully subjected to state authority. *E.g.*, Act of Aug. 13, 1954, ch. 732, 68 Stat. 718, codified at 25 U.S.C. § 564 et seq. (Klamath).

In each case the termination statute mandated the preparation of a termination plan that frequently took some time. Thus, the last termination plan, that of the Ponca, did not take effect until 1966. All other affected tribes were terminated by 1962. In all, approximately 109 tribes and bands were terminated. Over 1,362,155 acres of reservation land were affected, as were 11,466 tribal members. It has been estimated that 3% of all federally managed Indians and 3.2% of the total trust land were involved in these termination statutes.

During the termination period Congress also adopted a statute, commonly known as Public Law 280, which operated for affected reservations to transfer the jurisdiction over crimes previously exercised by federal courts to state authorities. Act of August 15, 1953, ch. 505, 67 Stat. 588, codified in part at 18 U.S.C. § 1162 and 28 U.S.C. § 1360. It also opened state courts to civil lawsuits against Indians arising in Indian country. This statute was essentially a halfway measure short of termination for tribes not yet ready for or objecting to complete termination of federal supervision. As originally enacted it mandated the transfer of jurisdiction to the states over all reservations in California, Minnesota (except the Red Lake Reservation), Nebraska, Oregon (except the Warm Springs Reservation), and

Wisconsin (except the Menominee Reservation). It also authorized all other states to voluntarily assume complete or partial civil and criminal jurisdiction over other Indian reservations within the states. A number of major states, including Washington, Florida, and Iowa accepted that invitation for some or all of the reservations within their borders. Alaska was later added to the list of states affected by the mandatory provisions of the Act when it was admitted to statehood.

Also consistent with the shift to state jurisdiction then prevailing as federal Indian policy, the federal government transferred its trust responsibilities over Native Hawaiian peoples under the Hawaiian Homes Commission Act and other statutes to the State of Hawai'i when it was admitted to the Union during this period. Thus, the amended 1978 Constitution of the State of Hawai'i contains provisions establishing the Office of Hawaiian Affairs, charged in part with administering these trust obligations. *See* Ch. 5, Sec. C.

As part of the programs of the 1950s aimed at Indian assimilation, the Bureau of Indian Affairs set up a relocation program to encourage and assist reservation Indians to move to the cities. Once reservation Indians were relocated, however, the BIA's responsibility for the urban Indian ceased. This program greatly contributed to the growth of urban Indian communities in Los Angeles, Minneapolis, Seattle, Chicago, Phoenix, and elsewhere after World War II.

i.   The Self-Determination Era (1962–1980)

While many of the termination plans took effect in the early 1960s, this decade witnessed few new departures in federal Indian policy. On the other hand, during this period it was clear that the support for termination had waned. It was a period for regrouping and rethinking in the arena of Indian affairs. President Kennedy promised the Indians that "[t]here would be no change in treaty or contractual relationships without the consent of the tribes concerned. No steps would be taken to impair the cultural heritage of any group. [There also] would be protection for the Indian land base. . . . " Kennedy's Secretary of the Interior, Stewart L. Udall, said of HCR 108 that it had "died with the 83rd Congress and is of no legal effect at the present time." ANGIE DEBO, A HISTORY OF THE INDIANS OF THE UNITED STATES 405 (1970). *See generally* THOMAS CLARKIN, FEDERAL INDIAN POLICY IN THE KENNEDY AND JOHNSON ADMINISTRATIONS 1961–1969 (2001).

During the 1960s the long-unresolved problems of the Alaskan Natives and their aboriginal claims to substantial portions of the state surfaced. Secretary of the Interior Udall ordered a halt to state selections of the public domain under the Alaska Statehood Act and all other dispositions of federal land until Congress could resolve the Alaska Native claims to the affected property. *Id.* at 383–404. This action, coupled with the requirement of the nation for a pipeline from Prudhoe Bay, galvanized a bargaining process between the affected interests that led to the enactment of the Alaska Native Claims Settlement Act of 1971 (ANCSA), Pub. L. No. 92-203, 85 Stat. 688, codified at 43 U.S.C. § 1601 et seq.

ANCSA awarded the Alaska Natives fee title to over forty million acres of land, federal payments of $462.5 million over an 11-year period, and a royalty of 2% to a ceiling of $500 million on mineral development in Alaska in exchange for the extinguishment of their aboriginal claims to land in the state. The Act also organized the Alaska Natives into thirteen regional corporations, incorporated under state law, and various village corporations. It implemented the settlement "without establishing any permanent racially defined institutions, rights, privileges, or obligations, without creating a reservation system or lengthy wardship or trustee-ship, and without adding to the categories of property and institutions engaging special tax privileges. . . . " 43 U.S.C. § 1601(b). While ANCSA created a new business-oriented model of tribal autonomy that freed Alaska Natives from controls of the Bureau of Indian Affairs, it also stripped those Natives of many federal protections for tribal sovereignty and land. In the following decades, Alaska Natives fought, with limited success, to reinstate some of those protections. ANCSA is considered in detail in Ch. 5, Sec. B.

The 1960s was a period of often turbulent revitalization of tribal entities and improvement of conditions on Indian reservations. The Indian tribes benefited from many of the War on Poverty programs of the Johnson administration and new policy initiatives were frequently undertaken at the tribal level.

Two important pieces of Indian legislation were passed during the 1960s. In the Act of Oct. 10, 1966, Pub. L. No. 89-635, § 1, 80 Stat. 880, codified at 28 U.S.C. § 1362, Congress authorized any Indian tribe or band with a governing body duly recognized by the Secretary of the Interior to file suit in federal district court without reference to amount in controversy for cases arising under the Constitu-tion, laws, and treaties of the United States. By this simple statute Congress placed the standing of an Indian tribe to sue on a clear statutory footing and granted federal courts jurisdiction over the cases. Prior to that time Indians had to rely on the United States, as trustee, to protect their rights or secure a special statutory authorization to sue. This statute thereby set the stage for the commencement during the 1970s of many cases brought by tribes involving land, hunting and fishing rights, and other claims that previously had been overlooked or not aggressively enforced by the federal government.

In 1968 Congress enacted the Indian Civil Rights Act of 1968, Pub. L. No. 90-284, 82 Stat. 77, codified in part at 25 U.S.C. § 1301 et seq. This legislation was the culmination of nearly a decade of Senate hearings on the civil rights of Indians. Among other things, the Act: (1) required all Indian tribes in exercising their self-governing powers to observe and protect most, but not all, of the guarantees of the Bill of Rights, the Fourteenth Amendment, and Article 1, section 10 of the Constitution; (2) amended Public Law 280 to require tribal consent for all future state acquisitions of jurisdiction over an Indian reservation; (3) authorized the federal courts to exercise habeas corpus jurisdiction to review tribal convictions; (4) provided for state-initiated retrocession to the federal government of jurisdiction previously acquired by the states under Public Law 280; and (5) mandated the preparation of a model code governing courts of Indian offenses and the revision and updating of Felix S. Cohen's HANDBOOK OF FEDERAL INDIAN LAW[3] and other collections of primary Indian resource materials.

---

[3] After considerable delay by the Department of the Interior a group of academics and practicing attorneys ultimately revised this classic Indian law treatise. *See* FELIX S. COHEN, HANDBOOK OF FEDERAL INDIAN LAW (1982 ed.).

In 1970 President Nixon served notice in a message to Congress that he intended to steer a policy course designed to strengthen tribal sovereignty, transfer control of Indian programs from federal to tribal governments, restore and protect the Indian land base, and forever declare an end to involuntary tribal termination. Message from the President of the United States Transmitting Recommendations for Indian Policy, H.R. Doc. No. 363, 91st Cong., 2d Sess. (1970). This message represented the single strongest statement to date by the federal government supporting the strengthening of tribal sovereignty and control while advocating protection of the Indian land base and resources. The statement also advocated the encouragement of economic development of Indian lands, particularly the facilitation of leasing of Indian resources. The potential inconsistency between tribal sovereignty and control over the Indian reservation and the impacts caused by extensive leasing of Indian lands for non-Indian controlled economic development was not noted, although this tension became a major theme in Indian economic development during the decade.

The Nixon message set the legislative agenda for Congress in the field of Indian affairs for the entire decade. It thus ushered in one of the most productive periods for the enactment of statutes affecting Indian tribes. Some of this legislation affected only particular tribes. For example, the Menominee Tribe of Wisconsin, the Siletz tribe of Oregon, the Wyandotte, Peoria, Ottawa, and Modoc Tribes of Oklahoma, and others were restored to federal recognition and supervision in 1973, 1977, and 1978, respectively, after having been terminated by legislation in the 1950s. Pub. L. 95-281, 92 Stat. 246, codified at 25 U.S.C. § 861 et seq. (Wyandotte, Peoria, Ottawa, and Modoc Tribes); Siletz Indian Tribe Restoration Act, Pub. L. No. 95-195, 91 Stat. 1415, codified at 25 U.S.C. § 711 et seq.; Menominee Restoration Act, Pub. L. No. 93-197, 87 Stat. 770, codified at 25 U.S.C. § 903 et seq. The Alaska Native Claims Settlement Act was passed, as already noted, in 1971.

Indian title to submarginal lands first allocated to tribal use under various New Deal programs of the 1930s was perfected by the Act of Oct. 17, 1975, Pub. L. No. 94-114, 89 Stat. 577, codified at 25 U.S.C. § 459 et seq. The Taos Pueblo was restored to ownership of Blue Lake, a sacred site in tribal culture. Act of Dec. 15, 1970, Pub. L. No. 91-550, 84 Stat. 1437.

In the category of Indian laws of general application, the two most important pieces of legislation to emerge during the decade were the Indian Self-Determination and Education Assistance Act of 1975, Pub. L. No. 93-638, 88 Stat. 2203 (codified at 25 U.S.C. § 450a and elsewhere in titles 25, 42, and 50, U.S.C. app.), and the Indian Child Welfare Act of 1978, Pub. L. No. 95-608, 92 Stat. 3069 (codified at 25 U.S.C. § 1901 et seq.). The Indian Self-Determination Act was aimed at strengthening tribal governmental control over federally funded programs for Indians, including programs for educational assistance to local school districts. The heart of the statute is contained in two parallel provisions, 25 U.S.C. §§ 450f and 450g, authorizing the Secretary of the Interior and the Secretary of Health, Education, and Welfare (now Health and Human Services), under whose auspices the Indian Health Service and certain Indian educational programs were administered, to contract with Indian tribes for the formation, implementation, and administration of federally funded Indian programs. This legislation finally brought to fruition a proposal to turn federal programs over to tribal administration first made by John Collier when he proposed the Indian Reorganization Act four decades earlier. Other provisions of the 1975 Act, together with the Indian Education Act of 1972, Pub. L. No. 92-318, tit. IV, 86 Stat. 339 (found in its most recent form at 20 U.S.C. § 7401 et seq.) sought to increase Indian political control over federal programs of assistance for Indian education to public school systems.

The Indian Child Welfare Act of 1978, discussed in detail in Ch. 5, Sec. D, was designed to maximize tribal jurisdiction and to reduce the exercise of state jurisdiction in child custody or adoption proceedings involving Indian children who were tribal members or eligible for membership in a tribe. It also provided rigorous standards limiting state court intervention in such cases and requiring state authorities to attempt to place an Indian child needing placement in the home of an extended family member, the home of a tribal member, a tribal group home, or an Indian home before the child could be placed with a non-Indian family. The Act further provided for tribal intervention in such state custody proceedings and authorized federally funded programs to support tribal efforts to supervise and provide facilities for tribal children in need of placements.

In addition to these laws, the 1970s brought new federal legislation to strengthen and reorganize a federal revolving loan fund for Indian economic development and to provide federal loan guarantees for private-sector loans to support such development (25 U.S.C. § 1451 et seq.), to improve Indian health care services (25 U.S.C. § 1601 et seq.), to improve and increase tribal input into education programs of the BIA (25 U.S.C. § 2001 et seq.), and to establish and fund tribally controlled community colleges (25 U.S.C. § 1801 et seq.).

This rash of legislation — together with very visible Indian litigation initiatives and successes over fishing rights in the Pacific Northwest and the Great Lakes, water rights in the West, and tribal claims to land in the Northeast — generated some non-Indian resentment and new political efforts to alter federal Indian policy. The lack of consensus on the policy issue first emerged when the American Indian Policy Review Commission, established by Congress in 1975 (25 U.S.C. § 174), delivered its final report to Congress on May 17, 1977. AMERICAN INDIAN POLICY REVIEW COMMISSION, FINAL REPORT (1977). This report generally recommended a continuation of the federal policy of protecting and strengthening tribal governments as permanent governmental units in the federal system. It disparaged assimilationist policies and proposals and called for reevaluation of the federal commitment to over 132 terminated and nonrecognized Indian tribes. The report called for increased financial support for tribal economic development and social and economic programs for tribal members. This strong reaffirmation for a policy of federal protection of Indian self-determination, while approved by the other members of the Commission, was criticized by Congressman Lloyd Meeds of Washington, the Vice-Chair of the Commission and the former Chair of the House Indian Affairs Subcommittee. He dissented, arguing that the Commission had given too broad a scope to the concept of tribal government, fearing that tribal governments would "hold sway over the lives and fortunes of many who have no representation in the governing body which makes decisions affecting their lives." Unfortunately, Meeds's dissent appears to have established a theoretical approach for opposition to broad Indian sovereignty that emerged during the 1980s.

After 1977, the political momentum for a fundamental change in the direction of federal Indian policy became intense. Organized political groups, like Montanans Opposed to Discrimination and the Interstate Congress for Equal Rights and Responsibilities, unsuccessfully lobbied Congress to extinguish Indian rights and force Indian assimilation. Others in Congress sought to go beyond Representative Meeds's call for a limited reevaluation of Indian law and policy. In 1977 H.R.J. Res. 1 was proposed to limit Indian treaty hunting and fishing rights. Then Representative Cunningham of Washington introduced H.R. 13329, 95th Cong., 2d Sess. (1978), Orwellianly entitled the Native Americans Equal Opportunity Act. While not enacted, the bill would have, *inter alia*, directed the President within one year to abrogate all treaties entered into by the United States with Indians, terminated federal supervision over the property and rights of all Indian tribes, fully subjected all Indians to state jurisdiction, compelled Indian tribes to distribute certain tribal assets on a per capita basis to their members, eliminated the restraints on alienation and tax immunities enjoyed by tribal lands, and abrogated treaty-protected Indian hunting and fishing rights.

j. Government-to-Government Relations and Decreases in Federal Indian Program Funding (1980–present)

The 1980s marked an important transitional period both for federal Indian policy and for tribal self-sufficiency. Increasing focus on general federal budget deficits resulted in persistent, and often unsuccessful, executive efforts during President Reagan's administration to reduce the funding of many federal programs targeted for Indians, to merge such specialized federal Indian programs into more general, often state administered, social services and benefits programs, or to eliminate federal funding altogether. Such trends were most evident in proposals to curtail funding for Indian housing programs and other proposals to radically alter the administrative structure and funding for the provision of medical services previously provided through the Indian Health Service. Since many of the tribes had assumed some responsibility under the Indian Self-Determination Act of 1975 for the administration of many of the federally funded programs, some suggested that these trends represented a new age of creeping termination through the cessation of federal funding.

The federal budget reductions in Indian Service programs and the simultaneous growth and strengthening of many tribal governments during the 1980s increasingly directed focus on tribal economic development and self-sufficiency during the decade. In 1983, President Reagan issued a Statement on Indian Policy in which federal protection of Indian tribal self-government was reaffirmed and Indian tribes were called upon to assume a greater fiscal role in providing governmental services and programs to tribal members through economic development and taxation. The statement indicated that "[i]t is important to the concept of self-government that tribes reduce their dependence on Federal funds by providing a greater percentage of the cost of their self-government." 1 PUBLIC PAPERS OF THE PRESIDENTS OF THE UNITED STATES: RONALD REAGAN, 1983, at 96, 97 (1984). The policy statement called for extensive economic development of reservation economies to support such fiscal tribal self-sufficiency.

As part of this statement, President Reagan announced the formation of a Commission on Indian Reservation Economies. This commission issued its final report in November 1984. PRESIDENTIAL COMMISSION ON INDIAN RESERVATION ECONO-MIES, REPORT AND RECOMMENDATIONS TO THE PRESIDENT OF THE UNITED STATES (1984). While the report called for the formal rejection of the termination policy, it also contained many features that some tribal leaders viewed as a return to the thinking that produced the assimilationist allotment and termination policies. Chief among these features was a call for the privatization of reservation economies by removing the control of reservation economic development programs from tribal governments and enterprises and through the development of Indian reservation land by privately owned Indian corporations, partnerships, and sole proprietorships. The report was rejected by most tribal governmental leaders and did not directly result in any successful legislative changes.

The major Indian legislation enacted during the 1980s also generally reflected the prominent focus on economic development of Indian reservations during this period. In the Indian Tribal Government Tax Status Act of 1982, Pub. L. 97-473, 96 Stat. 2608, partially codified at 26 U.S.C. § 7871, Indian tribes were extended many of the tax advantages that were already enjoyed by state and local governments, including deductibility for charitable contributions for tribal government, various federal tax exemptions, and limited authority to issue tax exempt tribal bonds. The Indian Mineral Development Act of 1982, Pub. L. 97-382, codified at 25 U.S.C. §§ 2101–2108, authorized the Secretary of the Interior to approve various types of mineral development agreements involving Indian tribes and their lands, including joint ventures and operating, production sharing, and service agreements, thereby freeing Indian mineral development from the primary reliance on the leasing of Indian mineral resources to non-Indian development firms that had marked the preceding laws. The Indian Land Consolidation Act of 1982, Pub. L. 97-459, 96 Stat. 2517, codified at 25 U.S.C. §§ 2201–2211, sought to remedy some of the vestigial effects of allotment by authorizing tribes to establish plans for land consolidation on heavily allotted, checkerboarded reservations, by affording tribes some control over the descent and distribution of allotted land, and by providing an escheat mecha-nism, the initial version of which was later declared unconstitutional, by which small, unproductive interests in allotted land might escheat to the tribe. The Indian Gaming Regulatory Act of 1988, Pub. L. 100-497, 102 Stat. 2467, codified at 25 U.S.C. §§ 2701–2721, created the National Indian Gaming Commission to regulate the emerging Indian gaming operations that became a substantial source of tribal revenues during the 1980s, and required that most casino-style gaming be carried out pursuant to tribal-state compacts.

Apart from economic development, the most important federal Indian policy developments of the 1980s centered on tribal control of reservation environments. Amendments to the Clean Water Act (33 U.S.C. § 1377) the Clean Air Act (42 U.S.C. § 7601 (D)(2)), the Comprehensive Environmental Response, Compensation, and Liability Act (CERCLA) (42 U.S.C. § 9626), and the Safe Drinking Water Act (42 U.S.C. § 300h-le), among others, authorized the federal Environmental Protection Agency (EPA) to designate tribes as the government entities with program authority on reservation lands. In 1984, EPA issued its first statement of "Indian Policy," declaring that tribes, not states, should implement federal environmental statutes on Indian lands, and that tribes should receive federal assistance in assuming that authority. *See* Ch. 5, Sec. G.2.

As we shall see throughout this book, commencing around 1981, the Supreme Court and some of the lower federal courts began demonstrating a marked hostility toward tribal rights claims, particularly claims involving tribal sovereignty or authority over nonmember owned lands and activities within the reservation. While nominally cooperating with tribal courts, the federal courts evolved legal doctrines that permitted them to second-guess tribal court determinations of the reach of their jurisdiction, and therefore the tribe's sovereignty.

The Native American Graves Protection and Repatriation Act of 1990, Pub. L. 101-601, 104 Stat. 3048, codified at 25 U.S.C. § 3001 et seq., provided federal protection for Native American human remains, funerary objects, sacred objects, and objects of cultural patrimony. The statute imposes criminal prohibitions on commercial trafficking of Native American human remains and cultural objects, and provides protections for Native American burial sites that are excavated after 1990 on federal or tribal lands, establishing procedures to transfer possession of the items to the culturally affiliated tribal groups. In addition, the legislation requires federally funded museums and federal agencies to prepare inventories of Native American human remains and funerary objects in their possession as of 1990, and to prepare summaries of sacred objects and objects of cultural patrimony in their possession as of this date. The inventories and summaries provide notice to potential tribal claimants, and they are also used to assist in the cultural affiliation of the items to contemporary tribal groups, who are entitled to gain repatriation of the remains and objects upon request.

During the Clinton Administration of the 1990s, the federal government undertook both highly public formal efforts and low level support that renewed formal government-to-government relations between the federal government and the Indian tribes. President Clinton convened the first ever meeting between the President of the United States and the heads of the various tribal governments. Additionally, a new Office of Tribal Justice was created in the United States Department of Justice to serve as a liaison between federal law enforcement authorities and the tribes. President Clinton also issued numerous Executive Orders underscoring the government-to-government relationship between Indian nations and the United States, affording some protections for Indian sacred sites, and directing federal agencies to adhere to their trust responsibilities.

Nevertheless, the downsizing of the federal government continued and with it many Indian programs either simply disappeared or continued to witness massive reductions in federal support, just as need was often growing. Thus, the period from 1980 to the present might be seen as either a period of the strengthening of respect for tribal self-determination or as a period of termination by cessation of funding — termination of the expenditure responsibility for federal Indian programs (the original justification for the termination policy) without the termination of the formal federal governmental recognition of the tribe, which had been a hallmark of the termination policy.

A good illustration of the nature of current federal Indian policy is the Indian Tribal Justice Act of 1993, Pub. L. 103-176, 107 Stat. 2004, which authorized (but did not appropriate) large sums for the improvement of tribal judicial systems. The appropriations necessary to fund such assistance were never forthcoming from Congress and, accordingly, the promise of the statute was lost. Federal policy therefore often makes a great show of maintaining formal governmental relations with the Indian tribes, while delivering far less than promised.

As funds dwindled, tribes sought greater flexibility in their use. As a result Congress passed a block grant program under which tribes would apply to take most federal Indian program monies in one block grant and establish their own priorities for its use, *i.e.*, tribal priority allocation, rather than contracting for management of earmarked federal program funds under the original Indian Self-Determination Act. Pub. L. 100-472, Title III, 102 Stat. 2285 (1988); Pub. L. 103-413, Title IV, 108 Stat 4250 (1994), codified at 25 U.S.C. §§ 458aa–458hh. This approach was reminiscent of the Nixon administration's block grant program for revenue sharing with states. In *Cherokee Nation of Oklahoma v. Leavitt*, 543 U.S. 631 (2005) and *Salazar v. Ramah Navajo Chapter*, 132 S. Ct. 2181, 183 L. Ed. 2d 186 (2012), tribes prevailed in suits against the Secretary of Health and Human Services (HHS) under the Indian Self-Determination and Education Assistance Act, seeking to recover full contract support costs. For further discussion of the *Salazar* case, see Ch. 4, Sec. A.5.

While few significant general Indian legislative initiatives were passed during the Clinton administration, many tribally specific bills and technical amendments to existing legislation were enacted into law. As President Clinton left office in 2001, he advanced administrative proposals for tribal recognition and federal action taking land into trust that were promptly withdrawn by the Bush administration. The new President's administration also put forward controversial plans for reorganizing the Bureau of Indian Affairs in response to a massive class action challenging years of federal mismanagement of individual trust allottees' accounts. *See* Ch. 4, Sec. A.5.b. During the presidency of George W. Bush, Indian country initiatives were not a high priority, and several United States Attorneys who expressed an interest in Indian country justice issues were dismissed as part of a larger wave of politically inspired firings within the United States Department of Justice. *See* Emily Gurdon, *Minnesota U.S. Attorney Firings/Heffelfinger Defends Work*, ST. PAUL PIONEER PRESS (Minnesota), May 24, 2007.

President Barack Obama campaigned on a platform of commitment to "tribal nation building and enforcing the federal government's obligations to Indian people." Barack Obama's "Principles for Stronger Tribal Communities," *available at* http://my.barackobama.com/page/content/firstamissues. Apart from restoring the practice of high level meetings with tribal leaders, his administration's main accomplishments have been in two areas: trust administration and criminal justice. With support from Congress, President Obama's Justice Department finally settled the massive 1996 class action over trust mismanagement, with the public support of the named plaintiff, Eloise Cobell. The parties agreed to the settlement in 2009, Congress passed a bill in 2010 allocating a total of 3.4 billion dollars for distribution to the plaintiffs and for repurchase of land distributed under the Dawes act. Claims Resolution Act of 2010, Pub. L. No. 111-291, § 101, 124 Stat. 3064 (2010). *See* Ch. 4, Sec. A.5. As part of the settlement, Secretary of the Interior Ken Salazar established a Secretarial Commission on Indian Trust Administration and Reform, which issued a comprehensive report in December 2013, recommending a more robust definition of the federal trust responsibility as well as an independent commission housed within the Department of the Interior to carry out trust-related functions. This report is available at http://www.doi.gov/cobell/commission/upload/ Report-of-the-Commission-on-Indian-Trust-Administration-and-Reform_FINAL_ Approved-12-10-2013.pdf. The Obama administration has also accelerated the process of taking land into trust, with nearly 300,000 acres added to trust status (thereby becoming Indian country) as of early 2015, and regulations enacted allowing land to be taken into trust in Alaska. *See* Ch. 5, Sec. B.1. In 2012, Congress passed the HEARTH Act (Helping Expedite and Advance Responsible Tribal Homeownership Act, Pub. L. No. 112-151), which expedites the surface lease approval process by allowing tribal governments to approve trust land leases directly, rather than having to go through the lengthy BIA approval process. In addition, the Act removes existing bureaucratic obstacles to prospective Native American homebuyers wishing to purchase homes on tribal land.

Regarding Indian country criminal justice, President Obama supported and signed two major pieces of legislation, the Tribal Law and Order Act of 2010, and the 2013 Reauthorization of the Violence Against Women Act (VAWA 2013). Both measures strengthened the capacity of tribes to take control of justice within their communities and to engage more effectively with state and federal systems. The Tribal Law and Order Act also established a joint legislative/executive branch commission, the Indian Law and Order Commission, to investigate and recommend improvements in Indian country criminal justice. The Commission's report, issued in November 2013, recommended far-reaching changes in criminal jurisdiction, which would greatly expand the exclusive authority of tribes within their territory, subject to limited review by a newly established federal appellate court. *See* Ch. 4, Sec. A.3. The 2013 reauthorization of VAWA provided federal recognition of tribal criminal authority over some offenses committed by non-Indians, thereby overturning the Supreme Court's decision in *Oliphant v. Suquamish Indian Tribe*, 435 U.S. 191 (1978). *See* Ch. 3, Sec. C. The Obama Justice Department also initiated a major effort to address the needs of Native children exposed to violence. For that Task Force Report, see http://www.justice.gov/defendingchildhood/task-force-american-indian-and-alaska-native-children-exposed-violence.

k. History, Federal Indian Policy, and Statutory Interpretation

The rate of change in federal Indian policy objectives has accelerated greatly in the last half-century. The period of allotment gave way to renewed protection of tribal autonomy in the Indian Reorganization Act of 1934. Federal protection of Indian tribal self-government, however, was quickly replaced by efforts to assimilate Indians into the social and legal mainstream of American society during the 1940s and 1950s. These efforts included enactment of Public Law 280 and a host of statutes terminating federal supervision over certain Indian tribes. Termination soon yielded in the late 1960s and the 1970s to renewed efforts to foster Indian tribal government and autonomy, including the Indian Self-Determination and Education Assistance Act of 1975 and the Indian Child Welfare Act of 1978. As one federal policy gave way to another, statutes enacted during a prior period generally were not repealed. Rather, litigation regarding statutes enacted under a subsequently discarded Indian policy continued to crop up in the courts. How should the courts respond to such legal questions? Should they enforce the intent of the Congress that enacted the statute and ignore the subsequent shift in federal Indian policy or should they attempt to construe the statute in light of the subsequent changes in congressional policy?

This question repeatedly has arisen in construing Public Law 280 since most litigation over this termination-era statute has arisen after termination was abandoned in favor of renewed federal efforts to foster tribal autonomy. In *Bryan v. Itasca County*, 426 U.S. 373 (1976), set forth and discussed in Ch. 5, Sec. A.2, a unanimous Supreme Court narrowly construed the scope of civil jurisdiction committed to the states under Public Law 280, relying in part on congressional statements made in 1968 when the jurisdictional allocation schemes created by Public Law 280 were modified, consistent with then-prevailing federal policy of fostering tribal self-determination, to require tribal consent as a condition of further state assumptions of jurisdiction. *Cf. Menominee Tribe v. United States*, 391 U.S. 404 (1968). By contrast, in *Washington v. Confederated Bands & Tribes of Yakima Indian Nation*, 439 U.S. 463, 488 (1979), another case construing aspects of Public Law 280, the Court relied exclusively on the intent of the framers of the act: "Public Law 280 was the first jurisdictional bill of general applicability ever to be enacted by Congress. [It also was] without question reflective of the general assimilationist policy followed by Congress from the early 1950s through the late 1960s." While the Court noted that later congressional actions might be inconsistent with its construction, it paid them no heed in construing the statute. Which approach represents a sounder effort at statutory construction? Does the approach proposed in *Bryan* obfuscate the original intent of the framers of the legislation? Will the methodology advanced by the Court in *Confederated Bands & Tribes of Yakima Indian Nation* frustrate current congressional Indian policy? What role should a court assume in this context? The complexity of such legal questions, together with the oscillation of federal policy objectives in the field of Indian affairs, helps account for the intricacy of a number of issues in federal Indian law.

C. ORIGINS OF THE MODELS: FOUNDATIONAL UNITED STATES SUPREME COURT DECISIONS AND THE TRIBAL RESPONSE

The 1783 treaty of peace with Great Britain, which ended the American Revolution, left the Indians out of the equation even though they had been important players during the conflict. While the United States sought neutrality from the tribes and secured alliances with some, as in the Fort Pitt Treaty with the Delaware and the notable efforts of the Oneida and some Seneca to save Washington's army in upstate New York, the American negotiating posture at the close of the Revolution was to treat all tribes as conquered nations, subject to any terms the United States wished to impose. This policy was short-lived, however, as the United States realized that the Indians would resist militarily, burdening the fledgling nation at a time when it was saddled with war debt and vulnerable to continued British assaults. Accordingly, throughout the 1790s, the United States entered into Indian treaties that implemented land cessions while recognizing the Indians' reservation of some ancestral lands as protected homelands. The legal consequences of these treaties, and the broader contours of tribal status and relations with federal and state governments, remained to be elaborated in the context of American population growth and expanding appetite for Indian resources.

1.   Property, Sovereignty, and Claims of Conquest: The Case of *Johnson v. M'Intosh*

Speech of Corn Tassel (Cherokee at Hopewell Treaty Negotiations)
in Native American Testimony
122–23 (P. Nabokov ed., 1991)

[At the negotiations of the Treaty of Hopewell with the Cherokee in July 1785, federal treaty negotiators attempted to advance the conquered nation position. Corn Tassel, a then elderly Cherokee orator and statesman responded with the following speech.]

Suppose, in considering the nature of your claim (and in justice to my nation I shall and will do it freely), I were to ask one of you, my brother warriors, under what kind of authority, by what law, or on what pretense he makes this exorbitant demand of nearly all the lands we hold between your settlements and our towns, as the cement and consideration of our peace.

Would he tell me that it is by right of conquest? No! If he did, I should retort on him that *we* had last marched over his territory; even up to this very place which he has *fortified* so far within his former limits; nay, that some of our young warriors (whom we have not yet had an opportunity to recall or give notice to, of the general treaty) are still in the woods, and continue to keep his people in fear, and that it was but till lately that these identical walls were your strongholds, out of which you durst scarcely advance.

If, therefore, a bare march, or reconnoitering a country is sufficient reason to ground a claim to it, we shall insist upon transposing the demand, and your relinquishing your settlements on the western waters and removing one hundred miles back towards the east, whither some of our warriors advanced against you in the course of last year's campaign.

Let us examine the facts of your present eruption into our country, and we shall discover your pretensions on that ground. What did you do? You marched into our territories with a superior force; our vigilance gave us no timely notice of your maneuvers; your numbers far exceeded us, and we fled to the stronghold of our extensive woods, there to secure our women and children.

Thus you marched into our towns; they were left to your mercy; you killed a few scattered and defenseless individuals, spread fire and desolation wherever you pleased, and returned again to your own habitations. If you meant this, indeed, as a conquest you omitted the most essential point; you should have fortified the junction of the Holstein and Tennessee rivers, and have thereby conquered all the waters above you. But, as all are fair advantages during the existence of a state of war, it is now too late for us to suffer for your mishap of generalship!

Again, were we to inquire by what law or authority you set up a claim, I answer, *none!* Your laws extend not into our country, nor ever did. You talk of the law of nature and the law of nations, and they are both against you.

Indeed, much has been advanced on the want of what you term civilization among the Indians; and many proposals have been made to us to adopt your laws, your religion, your manners and your customs. But, we confess that we do not yet see the propriety or practicability of such a reformation, and should be better pleased with beholding the good effect of these doctrines in your own practices than with hearing you talk about them, or reading your papers to us upon such subjects.

JOHNSON v. M'INTOSH
United States Supreme Court
21 U.S. (8 Wheat.) 543 (1823)

Mr. Chief Justice Marshall delivered the opinion of the Court.

The plaintiffs in this cause claim the land in their declaration mentioned, under two grants, purporting to be made, the first in 1773, and the last in 1775, by the chiefs of certain Indian tribes, constituting the Illinois and the Piankeshaw nations; and the question is, whether this title can be recognized in the courts of the United States? The facts, as stated in the case agreed, show the authority of the chiefs who executed this conveyance, so far as it could be given by their own people; and likewise show, that the particular tribes for whom these chiefs acted were in rightful possession of the land they sold. The inquiry, therefore, is, in a great measure, confined to the power of Indians to give, and of private individuals to receive, a title, which can be sustained in the courts of this country.

As the right of society to prescribe those rules by which property may be acquired and preserved is not, and cannot, be drawn into question; as the title to lands, especially, is, and must be, admitted, to depend entirely on the law of the nation in which they lie; it will be necessary, in pursuing this inquiry, to examine, not simply those principles of abstract justice, which the Creator of all things has impressed on the mind of his creature man, and which are admitted to regulate, in a great degree, the rights of civilized nations, whose perfect independence is acknowledged; but those principles also which our own government has adopted in the particular case, and given us as the rule for our decision.

On the discovery of this immense continent, the great nations of Europe were eager to appropriate to themselves so much of it as they could respectively acquire. Its vast extent offered an ample field to the ambition and enterprise of all; and the character and religion of its inhabitants afforded an apology for considering them as a people over whom the superior genius of Europe might claim an ascendancy. The potentates of the old world found no difficulty in convincing themselves, that they made ample compensation to the inhabitants of the new, by bestowing on them civilization and Christianity, in exchange for unlimited independence. But as they were all in pursuit of nearly the same object, it was necessary, in order to avoid conflicting settlements, and consequent war with each other, to establish a principle, which all should acknowledge as the law by which the right of acquisition, which they all asserted, should be regulated, as between themselves. This principle was, that discovery gave title to the government by whose subjects, or by whose authority, it was made, against all other European governments, which title might be consummated by possession. The exclusion of all other Europeans, necessarily gave to the nation making the discovery the sole right of acquiring the soil from the natives, and establishing settlements upon it. It was a right with which no Europeans could interfere. It was a right which all asserted for themselves, and to the assertion of which, by others, all assented. Those relations which were to exist between the discoverer and the natives, were to be regulated by themselves. The rights thus acquired being exclusive, no other power could interpose between them.

In the establishment of these relations, the rights of the original inhabitants were, in no instance, entirely disregarded; but were, necessarily, to a considerable extent, impaired. They were admitted to be the rightful occupants of the soil, with a legal as well as just claim to retain possession of it, and to use it according to their own discretion; but their rights to complete sovereignty, as independent nations, were necessarily diminished, and their power to dispose of the soil, at their own will, to whomsoever they pleased, was denied by the original fundamental principle, that discovery gave exclusive title to those who made it. While the different nations of Europe respected the right of the natives, as occupants, they asserted the ultimate dominion to be in themselves; and claimed and exercised, as a consequence of this ultimate dominion, a power to grant the soil, while yet in possession of the natives. These grants have been understood by all, to convey a title to the grantees, subject only to the Indian right of occupancy. . . .

The United States, then, have unequivocally acceded to that great and broad rule by which its civilized inhabitants now hold this country. They hold, and assert in themselves, the title by which it was acquired. They maintain, as all others have maintained, that discovery gave an exclusive right to extinguish the Indian title of occupancy, either by purchase or by conquest; and gave also a right to such a degree of sovereignty, as the circumstances of the people would allow them to exercise. The power now possessed by the government of the United States to grant lands, resided, while we were colonies, in the crown or its grantees. The validity of the titles given by either has never been questioned in our courts. It has been exercised uniformly over territory in possession of the Indians. The existence of this power must negative the existence of any right which may conflict with and control it. An absolute title to lands cannot exist, at the same time, in different persons, or in different governments. An absolute, must be an exclusive title, or at least a title which excludes all others not compatible with it. All our institutions recognize the absolute title of the crown, subject only to the Indian right of occupancy, and recognize the absolute title of the crown to extinguish that right. This is incompatible with an absolute and complete title in the Indians.

We will not enter into the controversy, whether agriculturists, merchants and manufacturers, have a right, on abstract principles, to expel hunters from the territory they possess, or to contract their limits. Conquest gives a title which the courts of the conqueror cannot deny, whatever the private and speculative opinions of individuals may be, respecting the original justice of the claim which has been successfully asserted. The British government, which was then our government, and whose rights have passed to the United States, asserted a title to all the lands occupied by Indians, within the chartered limits of the British colonies. It asserted also a limited sovereignty over them, and the exclusive right of extinguishing the titles which occupancy gave to them. These claims have been maintained and established as far west as the river Mississippi, by the sword. The title to a vast portion of the lands we now hold, originates in them. It is not for the courts of this country to question the validity of this title, or to sustain one which is incompatible with it.

Although we do not mean to engage in the defense of those principles which Europeans have applied to Indian title, they may, we think, find some excuse, if not justification, in the character and habits of the people whose rights have been wrested from them. The title by conquest is acquired and maintained by force. The conqueror prescribes its limits. Humanity, however, acting on public opinion, has established, as a general rule, that the conquered shall not be wantonly oppressed, and that their condition shall remain as eligible as is compatible with the objects of the conquest. Most usually, they are incorporated with the victorious nation, and become subjects or citizens of the government with which they are connected. The new and old members of the society mingle with each other; the distinction between them is gradually lost, and they make one people. Where this incorporation is practicable, humanity demands, and a wise policy requires, that the rights of the conquered to property should remain unimpaired; that the new subjects should be governed as equitably as the old, and that confidence in their security should gradually banish the painful sense of being separated from their ancient connections, and united by force to strangers. When the conquest is complete, and the conquered inhabitants can be blended with the conquerors, or safely governed as a distinct people, public opinion, which not even the conqueror can disregard, imposes these restraints upon him; and he cannot neglect them, without injury to his fame, and hazard to his power.

But the tribes of Indians inhabiting this country were fierce savages, whose occupation was war, and whose subsistence was drawn chiefly from the forest. To leave them in possession of their country, was to leave the country a wilderness; to govern them as a distinct people, was impossible, because they were as brave and as high-spirited as they were fierce, and were ready to repel by arms every attempt on their independence. What was the inevitable consequence of this state of things? The Europeans were under the necessity either of abandoning the country, and relinquishing their pompous claims to it, or of enforcing those claims by the sword, and by the adoption of principles adapted to the condition of a people with whom it was impossible to mix, and who could not be governed as a distinct society, or of remaining in their neighborhood, and exposing themselves and their families to the perpetual hazard of being massacred. Frequent and bloody wars, in which the whites were not always the aggressors, unavoidably ensued. European policy, numbers and skill prevailed; as the white population advanced, that of the Indians necessarily receded; the country in the immediate neighborhood of agriculturists became unfit for them; the game fled into thicker and more unbroken forests, and the Indians followed. The soil, to which the crown originally claimed title, being no longer occupied by its ancient inhabitants, was parcelled out according to the will of the sovereign power, and taken possession of by persons who claimed immediately from the crown, or mediately, through its grantees or deputies.

That law which regulates, and ought to regulate in general, the relations between the conqueror and conquered, was incapable of application to a people under such circumstances. The resort to some new and different rule, better adapted to the actual state of things, was unavoidable. Every rule which can be suggested will be found to be attended with great difficulty. However extravagant the pretension of converting the discovery of an inhabited country into conquest may appear; if the principle has been asserted in the first instance, and afterwards sustained; if a country has been acquired and held under it; if the property of the great mass of the community originates in it, it becomes the law of the land, and cannot be questioned. So too, with respect to the concomitant principle, that the Indian inhabitants are to be considered merely as occupants, to be protected, indeed, while in peace, in the possession of their lands, but to be deemed incapable of transferring the absolute title to others. However this restriction may be opposed to natural right, and to the usages of civilized nations, yet, if it be indispensable to that system under which the country has been settled, and be adapted to the actual condition of the two people, it may, perhaps, be supported by reason, and certainly cannot be rejected by courts of justice.

This question is not entirely new in this court. The case of *Fletcher v. Peck*, grew out of a sale made by the State of Georgia, of a large tract of country within the limits of that state, the grant of which was afterwards resumed. The action was brought by a sub-purchaser, on the contract of sale, and one of the covenants in the deed was, that the State of Georgia was, at the time of sale, seised in fee of the premises. The real question presented by the issue was, whether the seisin in fee was in the State of Georgia, or in the United States. After stating, that this controversy between the several states and the United States had been compromised, the court thought it necessary to notice the Indian title, which, although entitled to the respect of all courts, until it should be legitimately extinguished, was declared not to be such as to be absolutely repugnant to a seisin in fee on the part of the state. This opinion conforms precisely to the principle which has been supposed to be recognised by all European governments, from the first settlement of America. The absolute ultimate title has been considered as acquired by discovery, subject only to the Indian title of occupancy, which title the discoverers possessed the exclusive right of acquiring. Such a right is no more incompatible with a seisin in fee, than a lease for years, and might as effectually bar an ejectment.

Another view has been taken of this question, which deserves to be considered. The title of the crown, whatever it might be, could be acquired only by a conveyance from the crown. If an individual might extinguish the Indian title, for his own benefit, or, in other words, might purchase it, still he could acquire only that title. Admitting their power to change their laws or usages, so far as to allow an individual to separate a portion of their lands from the common stock, and hold it in severalty, still it is a part of their territory, and is held under them, by a title dependent on their laws. The grant derives its efficacy from their will; and, if they choose to resume it, and make a different disposition of the land, the courts of the United States cannot interpose for the protection of the title. The person who purchases lands from the Indians, within their territory, incorporates himself with them, so far as respects the property purchased; holds their title under their protection, and subject to their laws. If they annul the grant, we know of no tribunal which can revise and set aside [their decision].

The acts of the several colonial assemblies, prohibiting purchases from the Indians, have also been relied on, as proving, that, independent of such prohibitions, Indian deeds would be valid. But, we think, this fact, at most, equivocal. While the existence of such purchases would justify their prohibition, even by colonies which considered Indian deeds as previously invalid, the fact that such acts have been generally passed, is strong evidence of the general opinion, that such purchases are opposed by the soundest principles of wisdom and national policy.

After bestowing on this subject a degree of attention which was more required by the magnitude of the interest in litigation, and the able and elaborate arguments of the bar, than by its intrinsic difficulty, the court is decidedly of opinion, that the plaintiffs do not exhibit a title which can be sustained in the courts of the United States; and that there is no error in the judgment which was rendered against them in the district court of Illinois.

Judgment affirmed, with costs.

NOTES ON *JOHNSON v. M'INTOSH*

1. **Stereotypes of "savagery" in Federal Indian Law:** In *M'Intosh* Chief Justice Marshall suggested that the reason for the policy of separate autonomous treatment of Indians was that the natives were "fierce savages, whose occupation was war, and whose subsistence was drawn chiefly from the forest" and therefore could not be subjected to the usual policy of assimilation of conquered peoples into the dominant population. History demonstrates that Indian nations engaged in active military resistance to European encroachment, as do all nations defending their territory. The stereotype of Indians as "fierce savages," however, rested upon a European mythology that perceived the indigenous peoples of the "New World" as living in an uncivilized "state of nature." Europeans drew on their own perceptions of "sovereignty" and the "law" to characterize Indians as living in an emergent state of social organization. This notion of human beings living in a "state of nature" serves as a starting point for Western political philosophers from Locke to Rawls, who have engaged the role of law in ordering the affairs of a "civil society" and who constructed the theoretical foundations for Western liberal democratic thought.

Chief Justice Marshall's opinion is almost contemporaneous with the appearance of important literary works by James Fenimore Cooper extolling and romanticizing savagism, such as THE LAST OF THE MOHICANS. These fictional depictions of Native peoples as "noble savages" doomed to extinction in the face of "civilization" illustrate the prevalent nineteenth century Eurocentric notions about the superiority of Western civilization. Not surprisingly, the Cooper novels emerged at the height of the national effort to generate a "removal policy" for Indian nations. Cooper's romantic and stereotypic depictions of Indians, however well-intended, reflected a truly anti-Indian message that generated popular support for Indian removal.

Contemporary scholars have documented that the Europeans relied upon these stereotypes to justify their exploitation of Native lands. For example, in FRANCIS JENNINGS, THE INVASION OF AMERICA: INDIANS, COLONIALISM AND THE CANT OF CONQUEST 15–16, 32 (1975), the author observes that:

> European explorers and invaders discovered an inhabited land. Had it been pristine wilderness then, it would possibly be so still today, for neither the technology nor the social organization of Europe in the sixteenth and seventeenth centuries had the capacity to maintain, of its own resources, outpost colonies thousands of miles from home. Incapable of conquering true wilderness, the Europeans were highly competent in the skill of conquering other people, and that is what they did. They did not settle a virgin land. They invaded and displaced a resident population.

> This is so simple a fact that it seems self-evident. All historians of the European colonies in America begin by describing the natives' reception of the newcomers. Yet, paradoxically, most of the same historians also repeat identical mythical phrases purporting that the land-starved people of Europe had found magnificent opportunity to pioneer in a savage wilderness and to bring civilization to it. As rationalization for the invasion and conquest of unoffending peoples, such phrases function to smother retroactive moral scruples that have been dismissed as irrelevant to objective history. Unfortunately, however, the price of repressing scruples has been the suppression of facts.

> The basic conquest myth postulates that America was virgin land, or wilderness, inhabited by nonpeople called savages; that these savages were creatures sometimes defined as demons, sometimes as beasts "in the shape of men"; that their mode of existence and cast of mind were such as to make them incapable of civilization and therefore of full humanity; that civilization was required by divine sanction or the imperative of progress to conquer the wilderness and make it a garden; that the savage creatures of the wilderness, being unable to adapt to any environment other than the wild, stubbornly and viciously resisted God or fate, and thereby incurred their suicidal extermination; that civilization and its bearers were refined and ennobled in their contest with the dark powers of the wilderness; and that it all was inevitable.

Jennings notes that contemporary historians have begun to "examine and analyze the origins of the myth," and its application to prevailing accounts of the encounters between the European and Native peoples. In particular, the common understanding that Europeans "settled" North America has at least three different implications. First, it "implies that preexisting populations did not classify as humanity," because the term does not "apply to Indians; only Europeans 'settle.'" Second, it "dismisses the Indians' ability to wrest a generally satisfactory living from the 'wilderness' and to travel over established trails to known destinations." Most importantly, the word provides "bland misdirection about the Europeans' intentions, for their common purpose was to exploit rather than to settle. Among the early European visitors, residence was merely a means of increasing the efficiency of exploitation. A taste for permanent habitation came later."

Rennard Strickland goes further, asserting that the history of contact between Indians and Euro-Americans best can be described as a struggle for human survival by Indians against genocidal extermination. Rennard Strickland, *Genocide-at-Law: An Historical and Contemporary View of the Native American Experience*, 34 U. KAN. L. REV. 713 (1986). The author asserts that the law has been an important instrument in this struggle "both as a factor in the genocidal extermination and as a weapon in the contemporary struggle for survival." Strickland maintains that for most of the nineteenth century, the law constituted both a formal and informal agent of genocide. As he put it, "I share de Tocqueville's conclusion that it would be impossible to destroy men with more respect for the law." As you read the next two opinions by Marshall regarding the Cherokee Nation, consider whether these cases are exceptions to this trend or whether they merely regularize the process of European appropriation and genocide.

2. **Other perspectives on the Doctrine of Discovery:** Several fascinating book-length studies of *M'Intosh* have been released in recent years. *See* LINDSAY G. ROBERTSON, CONQUEST BY LAW: HOW THE DISCOVERY OF AMERICA DISPOSSESSED INDIGENOUS PEOPLE OF THEIR LANDS (2005); STUART BANNER, HOW THE INDIANS LOST THEIR LAND (2005). In Eric Kades, *History and Interpretation of the Great Case of* Johnson v. M'Intosh, 19 LAW & HIST. REV. 67, 100 (2001), the author points out that while an important test case, the *M'Intosh* decision really did not constitute an actual case since the claims by Johnson and M'Intosh were not within 50 miles of one another, a fact previously unnoticed by the Supreme Court or other scholars studying the case. In another article, Kades employs an economic account to assert that *Johnson v. M'Intosh* created a monopsonistic buyer for Indian lands thereby establishing the most economically efficient mechanism for Euro-Americans to dispossess the Native peoples of their lands. Eric Kades, *The Dark Side of Efficiency:* Johnson v. M'Intosh *and the Expropriation of American Indian Lands*, 148 U. PA. L. REV. 1065 (2000). In Professor Kades' view the doctrine of discovery operated in conjunction with European military campaigns, rapidly expanding settlement, and the spread of European diseases to appropriate Native lands at the least expense possible to the colonizing power. Under the guise of "protecting Indians" from the alienation of their lands, the national government received an economic windfall as the exclusive purchaser of Native lands as well as an incentive to create conditions that would force Indians to sell. *See also*, Lindsay G. Robertson, *The Judicial Conquest of Native America: The Story of* Johnson v. M'Intosh, *in* INDIAN LAW STORIES (Carole Goldberg, Kevin K. Washburn, and Philip P. Frickey, eds., 2011).

Professor Robert A. Williams, Jr., characterizes the Doctrine of Discovery as a "discourse of conquest" founded upon the cultural racism of Europeans that legitimated their colonial expansion into the lands of many non-European peoples. In his classic article, *The Algebra of Federal Indian Law: The Hard Trail of Decolonizing and Americanizing the White Man's Indian Jurisprudence*, 1986 WIS. L. REV. 219, 255, Professor Williams notes that:

[O]nce a European nation firmly established its occupancy of territories discovered in the New World, relations with the indigenous inhabitants of that region became matters of exclusively domestic concern between the tribes and the particular invading European sovereign. Any independent rights of the tribes to their aboriginal lands or to sovereignty had been subsumed within the hierarchical, universalized conceptions centering European political and legal theory toward alien peoples.

Professor Williams asserts that a primary consequence of *Johnson v. M'Intosh* was that "[t]he Doctrine of Discovery's discourse of conquest was available to legitimate, energize, and constrain as needed white society's will to empire over the North American continent" because it "confirmed the superior rights of a European-derived nation to the lands occupied by 'infidels, heathens, and savages,' encouraged further efforts by white society to acquire the Indians' 'waste' lands, and vested authority in a centralized sovereign to regulate the Indians' dispossession according to national interest, security, and sometimes even honor." ROBERT A. WILLIAMS, JR., THE AMERICAN INDIAN IN WESTERN LEGAL THOUGHT: THE DISCOURSES OF CONQUEST 316–17 (1990).

What model of tribal-federal relations is embodied in *Johnson v. M'Intosh*? What paradigms of tribal-federal relations are used in the various scholarly critiques of the case? Notice that toward the end of the opinion, Marshall recognizes the tribes' "power to change their laws or usages, so far as to allow an individual to separate a portion of their lands from the common stock, and hold it in severalty, still it is a part of their territory, and is held under them, by a title dependent on their laws." If tribes possess the power to make such transfers, is this more consistent with a model of self-determination or colonial domination? Who would enforce such transfers of title?

Like so many Indian law decisions of the early nineteenth century, note that the parties to the *Johnson v. M'Intosh* case were *both* non-Indians. The Indian voice was therefore totally lacking in this important Indian law case and in the formulation of much of the early *federal* Indian law. Consider the role of the Cherokee Nation as a litigant in the case that follows, which deals with the efforts of the Cherokee Nation to defend its legal claim to its traditional and treaty-guaranteed lands, which had become encompassed within the State of Georgia.

2. Sovereignty Revisited: The Cherokee Cases

During the early nineteenth century and especially, after the War of 1812, the Cherokees experienced a national revitalization movement that profoundly affected Cherokee society. As early as 1802, President Jefferson had urged the Cherokee to adopt a republican form of government, and the then-prevailing federal Indian policy encouraged bringing the benefits of Euro-American civilization to the Indians. Western missionaries were also heavily involved in bringing Christianity to the Cherokee people and had an influence in transforming aspects of Cherokee customary law. In 1821, Sequoyah, also known as George Guess (or Gist), revealed a Cherokee syllabary that permitted the transcribing of Cherokee, thereby producing the first written Indian language in the United States and further accelerating Cherokee literacy. By 1828, a national newspaper, *The Cherokee*

Phoenix, was being published at the national capital of New Echota in both English and Cherokee. The first set of Cherokee written laws was published in 1821, and the Supreme Court of the Cherokee was created by the Cherokee legislature in 1822 and held its first sessions in 1823. Finally, in 1827, the Cherokee Nation created a written tribal constitution, patterned after the United States Constitution, which asserted exclusive "Sovereignty and Jurisdiction" over all lands of the Cherokee Nation. *See generally* HENRY T. MALONE, CHEROKEES OF THE OLD SOUTH: A PEOPLE IN TRANSITION (1956).

As the Cherokee Nation's government flourished, its relations with the State of Georgia deteriorated. As early as 1802 the United States entered into an agreement with the State of Georgia in which Georgia ceded her western land claims to the federal government in exchange for the promise that the United States would extinguish as soon as possible the Indian title to lands within the state on peaceable and reasonable terms. Although the United States made sporadic efforts in this direction, it was not until after the War of 1812 that the federal government began earnest attempts to encourage the southern tribes to remove westward to an area that would become known as the Indian Territory, and now encompasses eastern Oklahoma and portions of southern Kansas. Although some Cherokees agreed to remove and accept the incentives of United States citizenship and fee land ownership that were offered to them, most remained on their lands. The demands of white settlers for Cherokee lands were fueled by the discovery of gold in the Cherokee Nation in July 1829. By the summer of 1830, over 3000 miners had illegally entered the Cherokee Nation to dig for gold.

The State of Georgia lost patience with federal efforts to remove the Cherokee and enacted legislation on December 29, 1828 that annexed the lands of the Cherokee Nation to Georgia counties. The legislation attempted to annul all laws, ordinances, or orders enacted by the Cherokee Nation and made it illegal to enforce them. Drawing on the then-existing slave laws, the legislation also provided that no Indian "shall be deemed a competent witness in any court of this state to which a white person may be a party, except when such white person resides within the said nation." Conveniently, the legislation also opened Indian lands to settlement under the land lottery system. Later, the state established an entry permit system by which all whites residing in the Cherokee Nation were required to swear an oath to support Georgia law. State legislator Wilson Lumpkin, who later became Governor, justified this law by an appeal to state sovereignty and a claim to "entire and complete jurisdiction over soil and population, regardless of complexion." This set the stage for the first great constitutional conflict in United States history over Indian policy and the Cherokee Nation. *See generally,* Rennard Strickland, *The Story of the* Cherokee *Cases in* INDIAN LAW STORIES (Carole Goldberg, Kevin K. Washburn, and Philip P. Frickey, eds., 2011); *see also* LOUIS FILLER & ALLEN GUTTMAN, THE REMOVAL OF THE CHEROKEE: MANIFEST DESTINY OR NATIONAL DISHONOR (1962); William F. Swindler, *Politics as Law: The* Cherokee *Cases,* 3 AM. IND. L. REV. 7 (1975); Joseph C. Burke, *The* Cherokee *Cases, A Study in Law, Politics and Morality,* 21 STAN. L. REV. 500 (1969).

CHEROKEE NATION v. GEORGIA
United States Supreme Court
30 U.S. (5 Pet.) 1 (1831)

Mr. Chief Justice Marshall delivered the opinion of the Court.

This bill is brought by the Cherokee nation, praying an injunction to restrain the State of Georgia from the execution of certain laws of that state, which, as is alleged, go directly to annihilate the Cherokee as a political society, and to seize for the use of Georgia, the lands of the nation which have been assured to them by the United States, in solemn treaties repeatedly made and still in force.

If courts were permitted to indulge their sympathies, a case better calculated to excite them can scarcely be imagined. A people, once numerous, powerful, and truly independent, found by our ancestors in the quiet and uncontrolled possession of an ample domain, gradually sinking beneath our superior policy, our arts and our arms, have yielded their lands, by successive treaties, each of which contains a solemn guarantee of the residue, until they retain no more of their formerly extensive territory than is deemed necessary to their comfortable subsistence. To preserve this remnant, the present application is made.

Before we can look into the merits of the case, a preliminary inquiry presents itself. Has this court jurisdiction of the cause? The third article of the constitution describes the extent of the judicial power. The second section closes an enumeration of the cases to which it is extended, with "controversies" "between a state or citizens thereof, and foreign states, citizens or subjects." A subsequent clause of the same section gives the supreme court original jurisdiction, in all cases in which a state shall be a party. The party defendant may then unquestionably be sued in this court. May the plaintiff sue in it? Is the Cherokee nation a foreign state, in the sense in which that term is used in the constitution? The counsel for the plaintiffs have maintained the affirmative of this proposition with great earnestness and ability. So much of the argument as was intended to prove the character of the Cherokees as a state, as a distinct political society, separated from others, capable of managing its own affairs and governing itself, has, in the opinion of a majority of the judges, been completely successful. They have been uniformly treated as a state, from the settlement of our country. The numerous treaties made with them by the United States, recognise them as a people capable of maintaining the relations of peace and war, of being responsible in their political character for any violation of their engagements, or for any aggression committed on the citizens of the United States, by any individual of their community. Laws have been enacted in the spirit of these treaties. The acts of our government plainly recognise the Cherokee nation as a state, and the courts are bound by those acts.

A question of much more difficulty remains. Do the Cherokees constitute a *foreign* state in the sense of the constitution? The counsel have shown conclusively, that they are not a state of the Union, and have insisted that, individually, they are aliens, not owing allegiance to the United States. An aggregate of aliens composing a state must, they say, be a foreign state; each individual being foreign, the whole must be foreign.

This argument is imposing, but we must examine it more closely, before we yield to it. The condition of the Indians in relation to the United States is, perhaps, unlike that of any other two people in existence. In general, nations not owing a common allegiance, are foreign to each other. The term *foreign nation* is, with strict propriety, applicable by either to the other. But the relation of the Indians to the United States is marked by peculiar and cardinal distinctions which exist nowhere else. The Indian territory is admitted to compose a part of the United States. In all our maps, geographical treatises, histories and laws, it is so considered. In all our intercourse with foreign nations, in our commercial regulations, in any attempt at intercourse between Indians and foreign nations, they are considered as within the jurisdictional limits of the United States, subject to many of those restraints which are imposed upon our own citizens. They acknowledge themselves, in their treaties, to be under the protection of the United States; they admit, that the United States shall have the sole and exclusive right of regulating the trade with them, and managing all their affairs as they think proper; and the Cherokees in particular were allowed by the treaty of Hopewell, which preceded the constitution, "to send a deputy of their choice, whenever they think fit, to Congress." Treaties were made with some tribes, by the State of New York, under a then unsettled construction of the confederation, by which they ceded all their lands to that state, taking back a limited grant to themselves, in which they admit their dependence. Though the Indians are acknowledged to have an unquestionable, and, heretofore, unquestioned, right to the lands they occupy, until that right shall be extinguished by a voluntary cession to our government; yet it may well be doubted, whether those tribes which reside within the acknowledged boundaries of the United States can, with strict accuracy, be denominated foreign nations. They may, more correctly, perhaps, be denominated domestic dependent nations. They occupy a territory to which we assert a title independent of their will, which must take effect in point of possession, when their right of possession ceases. Meanwhile, they are in a state of pupilage. Their relation to the United States resembles that of a ward to his guardian. They look to our government for protection; rely upon its kindness and its power; appeal to it for relief to their wants; and address the president as their great father. They and their country are considered by foreign nations, as well as by ourselves, as being so completely under the sovereignty and dominion of the United States, that any attempt to acquire their lands, or to form a political connection with them, would be considered by all as an invasion of our territory and an act of hostility. These considerations go far to support the opinion, that the framers of our constitution had not the Indian tribes in view, when they opened the courts of the Union to controversies between a state or the citizens thereof and foreign states.

In considering this subject, the habits and usages of the Indians, in their intercourse with their white neighbors, ought not to be entirely disregarded. At the time the constitution was framed, the idea of appealing to an American court of justice for an assertion of right or a redress of wrong, had perhaps never entered the mind of an Indian or of his tribe. Their appeal was to the tomahawk, or to the government. This was well understood by the statesmen who framed the constitution of the United States, and might furnish some reason for omitting to enumerate them among the parties who might sue in the courts of the Union. Be this as it may, the peculiar relations between the United States and the Indians occupying our territory are such, that we should feel much difficulty in considering them as designated by the term *foreign state*, were there no other part of the constitution which might shed light on the meaning of these words. But we think that in construing them, considerable aid is furnished by the clause in the eighth section of the [first] article, which empowers congress to "regulate commerce with foreign nations, and among the several states, and with the Indian tribes." In this clause, they are as clearly contradistinguished, by a name appropriate to themselves, from foreign nations, as from the several states composing the Union. They are designated by a distinct appellation; and as this appellation can be applied to neither of the others, neither can the application distinguishing either of the others be, in fair construction, applied to them. The objects to which the power of regulating commerce might be directed, are divided into three distinct classes — foreign nations, the several states, and Indian tribes. When forming this article, the convention considered them as entirely distinct. We cannot assume that the distinction was lost, in framing a subsequent article, unless there be something in its language to authorize the assumption.

The counsel for the plaintiffs contend, that the words "Indian tribes" were introduced into the article, empowering congress to regulate commerce, for the purpose of removing those doubts in which the management of Indian affairs was involved by the language of the ninth article of the confederation. Intending to give the whole power of managing those affairs to the government about to be instituted, the convention conferred it explicitly; and omitted those qualifications which embarrassed the exercise of it as granted in the confederation. This may be admitted without weakening the construction which has been intimated. Had the Indian tribes been foreign nations, in the view of the convention, this exclusive power of regulating intercourse with them might have been, and most probably would have been, specifically given, in language indicating that idea, not in language contradistinguishing them from foreign nations. Congress might have been empowered "to regulate commerce with foreign nations, including the Indian tribes, and among the several states." This language would have suggested itself to statesmen who considered the Indian tribes as foreign nations, and were yet desirous of mentioning them [specifically].

If it be true that the Cherokee nation have rights, this is not the tribunal in which those rights are to be asserted. If it be true that wrongs have been inflicted, and that still greater are to be apprehended, this is not the tribunal which can redress the past or prevent the future.

The motion for an injunction is denied.

Mr. Justice Johnson. [Concurring opinion.]

I cannot but think that there are strong reasons for doubting the applicability of the epithet state, to a people so low in the grade of organized society as our Indian tribes most generally are. I would not here be understood as speaking of the Cherokees under their present form of government; which certainly must be classed among the most approved forms of civil government. Whether it can be yet said to have received the consistency which entitles that people to admission under the family of nations is, I conceive, yet to be determined by the executive of these states. Until then . . . we cannot recognize it as an existing state, under any other character than that which it has maintained hitherto as one of the Indian tribes or nations.

[The Treaty of Hopewell] . . . was intended to give them no other rights over the territory than what were needed by a race of hunters [and could not be read to support an effort to organize them as states]. . . .

Where is the rule to stop? Must every petty kraal of Indians designating themselves a tribe or nation, and having a few hundred acres of land to hunt on exclusively, be recognized as a state?

[The] condition [of the Indians] is something like that of the Israelites, when inhabiting the deserts. Though without land that they may call theirs in the sense of property, their right of personal self-government has never been taken from them; and such form of government may exist though the land occupied be in fact that of another. . . . [The right of tribal self-government] has never been questioned, nor any attempt made at subjugating them as a people, or restraining their personal liberty except as to land and trade. . . .

I think it very clear that the constitution neither speaks of them as states or foreign states, but as just what they were, Indian tribes; an anomaly unknown to the books that treat of states, and which the law of nations would regard as nothing more than wandering hordes, held together only by ties of blood and habit, and having neither laws or government, beyond what is required in a savage state.

[Concurring opinion of Mr. Justice Baldwin omitted.]

Mr. Justice Thompson, dissenting [joined by Justice Story].

The terms state and nation are used in the law of nations, as well as in common parlance, as importing the same thing; and imply a body of men, united together, to procure their mutual safety and advantage by means of their union. Such a society has its affairs and interests to manage; it deliberates, and takes resolutions in common, and thus becomes a moral person, having an understanding and a will peculiar to itself, and is susceptible of obligations and laws. . . . Every nation that governs itself, under what form soever, without any dependence on a foreign power, is a sovereign state. Its rights are naturally the same as those of any other state. Such are moral persons who live together in a natural society under the law of nations. It is sufficient if it be really sovereign and independent: that is, it must govern itself by its own authority and laws. . . . [A] weak state, that, in order to provide for its safety, places itself under the protection of a more powerful one, without stripping itself of the right of government and sovereignty, does not cease on this account to be placed among the sovereigns who acknowledge no other power. Tributary and feudatory states do not thereby cease to be sovereign and independent states, so long as self-government, and sovereign and independent authority is left in the administration of the state.

Testing the character and condition of the Cherokee Indians by these rules, it is not perceived how it is possible to escape the conclusion that they form a sovereign state.

[There] is a rule which has been repeatedly sanctioned by this court, that the judicial department is to consider as sovereign and independent states or nations those powers, that are recognized as such by the executive and legislative departments of the government; they being more particularly entrusted with our foreign relations.

If we look to the whole course of treatment by this country of the Indians, from the year 1775, to the present day, when dealing with them in their aggregate capacity as nations or tribes, and regarding the mode and manner in which all negotiations have been carried on and concluded with them; the conclusion appears to me irresistible, that they have been regarded, by the executive and legislative branches of the government, not only as sovereign and independent, but as foreign nations or tribes, not within the jurisdiction nor under the government of the states within which they were located. . . .

Upon the whole, I am of opinion:

1. That the Cherokees compose a foreign State, within the sense and meaning of the Constitution, and constitute a competent party to maintain a suit against the State of Georgia.

2. That the bill presents a case for judicial consideration, arising under the laws of the United States and treaties made under their authority with the Cherokee Nation, and which laws and treaties have been and are threatened to be still further violated by the laws of the State of Georgia referred to in this opinion.

3. That an injunction is a fit and proper writ to be issued to prevent the further execution of such laws, and ought therefore to be awarded.

NOTES

1. **The Federal Trusteeship over Indian Affairs:** While Chief Justice Marshall's opinion in *Cherokee Nation* never uses the term, that opinion is the origin in the Supreme Court of an important and controversial notion in federal Indian law, the federal trusteeship over Indian affairs, discussed in more detail in Ch. 4, Sec. A.5. What precisely did Marshall have in mind when he described the Indian tribes as "in a state of pupilage. Their relation to the United States resembles that of a ward to his guardian"? Did Marshall contemplate that the federal trusteeship over Indian affairs would constitute an independent source of federal authority over Indians, as it was later invoked in the cases of *United States v. Kagama*, 118 U.S. 375 (1886) and *Lone Wolf v. Hitchcock*, 187 U.S. 553 (1903), both discussed in this chapter, Sec. D? Did Marshall intend the trusteeship to limit the exercise of federal authority over Indian affairs? Why, then, did he describe the Indian commerce clause as "intending to give the whole power of managing those [Indian] affairs to the government about to be instituted"? Was Marshall's description of the guardian-ward relationship between the federal government and the Indian tribes conceived to create enforceable fiduciary obligations between the parties? Was Marshall merely attempting to explain that Indian allegiance and control of Indian affairs rested in the federal government, rather than the State of Georgia?

Fiduciary relationships generally are created to protect the ward or beneficiary in a described fashion and to marshal trust assets toward a designated objective.

From whom did the Indian tribes need protection? Toward what end did Chief Justice Marshall conceive that the federal trust responsibility was created?

   2.   **Origins of the Trusteeship Concept:** The concept of trust supervision over indigenous populations is not unique to the United States. Furthermore, the seeds of this legal status did not originate in Chief Justice Marshall's opinion in *Cherokee Nation*. Rather, Marshall only imparted into American law an idea that had been prevalent, if not uniformly accepted, since the sixteenth century. *See generally* Felix S. Cohen, *The Spanish Origin of Indian Rights in the Law of the United States*, 31 GEO. L.J. 1 (1942); Felix S. Cohen, *Original Indian Title*, 32 MINN. L. REV. 28, 44–45 (1947). In 1532, Francisco de Vitoria, a Spanish cleric and professor of theology at the University of Salamanca in Spain, delivered a series of dissertations responding to the then-prevalent argument that the Indians were heathens and heretics who did not enjoy the rights of other humans. Vitoria reasoned that "the aborigines in question" were "not wholly unintelligent, yet they are a little short of that condition, and so are unfit to found or administer a lawful State up to the standard required by human and civil claims." Because they lacked "proper laws" and "magistrates," it was fitting and "in their own interests" that "the sovereigns of Spain might undertake the administration of their country, providing them with prefects and governors for their towns . . . so long as this was clearly for their benefit." Vitoria concluded that the Indians were "of defective intelligence," comparable to "the wild beasts," and thus, "their governance should in the same way be entrusted to people of intelligence." *See* FRANCISCO DE VITORIA, DE INDIS ET DE IURE BELLI RELECTIONES 160–61 (E. Nys. ed., J. Bate trans., 1917).

   The conception of the Indians as ignorant savages without law or governance in need of supervision and protection had some popularity in America even prior to Chief Justice Marshall's ruling in *Cherokee Nation*. Ridiculing a ruling of an English tribunal that the Mohegan tribe of Connecticut was a sovereign state, William Samuel Johnson had written during the colonial period of the eighteenth century:

> When the English Treated with [the Indians] it was not with Independent States (for they had no such thing as a Civil Polity, nor hardly any one Circumstance essential to the existence of a state) but as with savages, whom they were to quiet and manage as well as they could, sometimes by flattery, but oftener by force. [Certainly], the English have taken Infinite Pains to Civilize and Christianize the Indians, and they sometimes flattered themselves with hopes of success, and that they should by degrees make them Men and Christians, but after all their Endeavours (except in a very few Instances) they remain but little superior in point of Civilization, to the Beasts of the Field. This notion of their being free States is perfectly ridiculous and absurd. Without Polity, Laws *etc.* there can be no such thing as a State. The Indian had neither in any proper sense of the words. It is also Inconsistent with their own Ideas that they were always under the Guardianship of the Mason's [trustees appointed by the Connecticut government to manage the affairs of the Indians].

Quoted in JOSEPH SMITH, APPEALS TO THE PRIVY COUNCIL FROM THE AMERICAN PLANTATION 434–35 n.109 (1965). For the story of the Mohegan Indians' case, *see*

Craig Yirush, *Claiming the New World: Empire, Law, and Indigenous Rights in the Mohegan Case, 1704–1743*, LAW AND HIST. REV. 333 (2011). Of course, this view of the Indians was the product of an ethnocentric conception of governance and laws on the part of the colonial powers. The Indian tribes did in fact have clear social, political, and legal institutions. *See, e.g.*, DONALD GRINDE & BRUCE JOHANSEN, EXEMPLAR OF LIBERTY: NATIVE AMERICA AND THE EVOLUTION OF DEMOCRACY (1991); RENNARD STRICKLAND, FIRE AND THE SPIRITS: CHEROKEE LAW FROM CLAN TO COURT (1975); KARL LLEWELLYN & E. ADAMSON HOEBEL, THE CHEYENNE WAY: CONFLICT AND CASE LAW IN PRIMITIVE JURISPRUDENCE (1941).

During the colonial period, Massachusetts Bay, Connecticut, and other colonies sometimes formally appointed non-Indian trustees to supervise Indian lands, particularly lands of tribes conquered during King Philip's War of 1675 and earlier Indian conflicts. Indeed, after similar Indian wars in Virginia, the Commonwealth entered into treaties that established the conquered tribes of that region, principally remnants of the Powhatan Confederation, as "tributary tribes," formally paying feudal tribute to the colonial government. Jefferson specifically referred to the Virginia tributary or feudatory tribes when he proposed the somewhat confused Indian affairs clause of the Articles of Confederation to the Continental Congress.

As Justice Thompson recognized in his dissenting opinion in *Cherokee Nation*, the Law of Nations recognized "tributary and feudatory" states as sovereign, albeit under the protection of a more powerful state. Today, perhaps the best and most well-known remaining European feudatory states are the Principality of Monaco, which relies on the protection of France, and Vatican City and San Marino, which rely primarily on Italy for defense and diplomacy. Marshall's opinion, on the other hand, designates Indian nations as having the character of "wards" in a domestic and "dependent" relationship to the federal "guardian." This relationship is also broadly applied to Indian nations as a class, rather than examining the particulars of the treaties that defined their relationship to the United States. What national concerns might have animated such pretentious claims?

Given the modern progress Indian nations in the United States have made toward governmental institutions structured along Anglo-American models (*see* Ch. 3), does the federal trusteeship over Indians have a continued viable role to play in the regulation of Indian affairs? Did it make sense at the time it was applied to the Cherokee Nation in 1830? What model of tribal-federal relations is represented by the trusteeship? Is it compatible with a model of international self-determination or with treaty federalism? Does it reflect norms of colonialism? For a contemporary effort to address these questions, see Mary Cristina Wood, *Indian Land and the Promise of Native Sovereignty: The Trust Doctrine Revisited*, UTAH L. REV. 1471 (1994), and *Protecting the Attributes of Native Sovereignty: A New Trust Paradigm for Federal Actions Affecting Tribal Land and Resources*, UTAH L. REV. 109 (1995). As you review the remainder of the materials in this book, analyze what role, if any, the federal trusteeship should play in Indian law.

    3. The Trusteeship as a Source of Rights: In light of the last paragraph of the opinion in *Cherokee Nation*, can it be said that Chief Justice Marshall intended the federal trusteeship over Indian affairs to create enforceable legal rights and obligations? By what agency could such legal rights and obligations be enforced? If the trusteeship creates no enforceable legal relationships, what role does it play in federal Indian law? For further discussion of the trust relationship in Indian law, see Ch. 4, Sec. A.5.

4.   **Indians as Litigants:** The *Cherokee Nation* decision marks an important constitutional milestone. In this case, an Indian tribe, a domestic dependent nation, had initially gone to court, relying upon American judicial processes to prevent white encroachment and preserve its culture and government. Only once before, in the *Mohegan Indians* case, a land title litigation carried on for 70 years before the Privy Council during the colonial period, had an Indian tribe or its allies resorted to litigation rather than war or diplomacy to protect its cultural and political heritage. Of course, the Supreme Court in *Cherokee Nation* does not respond directly to the claims of the Cherokee Nation. Rather, it suggested that "If it be true that the Cherokee nation have rights, this is not the tribunal in which those rights are to be asserted." Does this reluctance to intervene on the merits of the case suggest an international self-determination model of the relationship? If the United States Supreme Court is not the proper forum to adjudicate tribal treaty rights, then which branch of the federal government constitutes the appropriate forum? Suppose that Canada and the United States had a boundary dispute or a dispute over their respective sovereignty. Would that claim end up in federal court? If not, how would it be resolved? Notice how different the Supreme Court's approach is in the following case, involving only non-Indian parties.

WORCESTER v. GEORGIA
United States Supreme Court
31 U.S. (6 Pet.) 515 (1832)

[The *Worcester* case involved the criminal prosecution and conviction of a number of white missionaries to the Cherokees, including Samuel A. Worcester, for violating an 1830 law enacted by the legislature of the State of Georgia that required any person residing within the Cherokee Nation to have a license or permit from the Georgia governor and to take an oath of loyalty. Georgia law also purported to annex the Cherokee Nation to the state, extend state law over the Cherokees, and disqualify Indians from testifying in state court. Similar laws were passed in other southeastern states, including Mississippi and Tennessee. The appeal of Worcester's criminal conviction reached the Court after the Tribe failed in *Cherokee Nation* to establish original jurisdiction in the United States Supreme Court to contest the legality of Georgia's unilateral efforts to extend its laws to that portion of the Cherokee Nation located within its boundaries and to appropriate Cherokee lands.

[As a missionary, Worcester was in the Cherokee Nation expending federal "civilization" funds under the Indian Trade and Intercourse Act of 1802. He also was the United States postmaster at New Echota. When Worcester, other missionaries, and certain other whites living in the Cherokee Nation were again arrested for violating the Georgia laws, the local court dismissed the prosecution, believing that they were agents of the federal government since they were expending federal funds. After the Governor of Georgia consulted federal authorities, a ruling was issued that they were not federal agents and Worcester was further dismissed, at Georgia's request, from his position as federal postmaster in order to clear the way for his prosecution. After approximately 10 whites residing in the Cherokee Nation without entry permits from Georgia were arrested, all were offered pardons on condition of swearing an oath to uphold Georgia law and leaving the Cherokee Nation. All accepted the pardons except two missionaries — Worcester and Butler. They were convicted of violating the Georgia legislation and sentenced to four years in prison. They ultimately appealed their criminal convictions to the Supreme Court, claiming that the State of Georgia had no legitimate authority over the Cherokee Nation.

[Even before *Worcester* was decided, the Court had good reason to doubt that Georgia would comply with its mandate. Earlier, another Cherokee removal test case involving the murder conviction of a Cherokee named Corn, or George, Tassel had come before the Court. Notwithstanding a Supreme Court stay of execution, Georgia had hung Tassel, thereby mooting the case.]

MR. CHIEF JUSTICE MARSHALL delivered the opinion of the Court.

This cause, in every point of view in which it can be placed, is of the deepest interest. The defendant is a state, a member of the Union, which has exercised the powers of government over a people who deny its jurisdiction, and are under the protection of the United States. The plaintiff is a citizen of the State of Vermont, condemned to hard labour for four years in the penitentiary of Georgia; under colour of an act which he alleges to be repugnant to the Constitution, laws, and treaties of the United States. The legislative power of a state, the controlling power of the Constitution and laws of the United States, the rights, if they have any, the political existence of a once numerous and powerful people, the personal liberty of a citizen, are all involved in the subject now to be considered.

[It has been argued] that the acts of the Legislature of Georgia seize on the whole Cherokee country, parcel it out among the neighbouring counties of the state, extend her code over the whole country, abolish its institutions and its laws, and annihilate its political existence. [E]xtra-territorial power of every legislature being limited in its action to its own citizens or subjects, the very passage of this act is an assertion of jurisdiction over the Cherokee Nation, and of the rights and powers consequent on jurisdiction. The first step, then, in the inquiry which the Constitution and laws impose on this Court, is an examination of the rightfulness of this claim.

America, separated from Europe by a wide ocean, was inhabited by a distinct people, divided into separate nations, independent of each other and of the rest of the world, having institutions of their own, and governing themselves by their own laws. It is difficult to comprehend the proposition that the inhabitants of either quarter of the globe could have rightful original claims of dominion over the inhabitants of the other, or over the lands they occupied; or that the discovery of either by the other should give the discoverer rights in the country discovered which annulled the pre-existing rights of its ancient possessors. After lying concealed for a series of ages, the enterprise of Europe, guided by nautical science, conducted some of her adventurous sons into this western world. They found it in possession of a people who had made small progress in agriculture or manufactures, and whose general employment was war, hunting, and fishing. Did these adventurers, by sailing along the coast and occasionally landing on it, acquire for the several governments to whom they belonged, or by whom they were commissioned, a rightful property in the soil from the Atlantic to the Pacific; or rightful dominion over the numerous people who occupied it? Or has nature, or the great Creator of all things, conferred these rights over hunters and fishermen, on agriculturists and manufacturers? But power, war, conquest, give rights, which, after possession, are conceded by the world; and which can never be controverted by those on whom they descend. We proceed, then, to the actual state of things, having glanced at their origin, because holding it in our recollection might shed some light on existing pretensions. . . .

Certain it is, that our history furnishes no example, from the first settlement of our country, of any attempt on the part of the crown, to interfere with the internal affairs of the Indians, further than to keep out the agents of foreign powers, who, as traders or otherwise, might seduce them into foreign alliances. The king purchased their lands, when they were willing to sell, at a price they were willing to take, but never coerced a surrender of them. He also purchased their alliance and dependence by subsidies, but never intruded into the interior of their affairs, nor interfered with their self-government, so far as respected themselves only.

The general views of Great Britain, with regard to the Indians, were detailed by Mr. Stuart, superintendent of Indian affairs, in a speech delivered at Mobile, in presence of several persons of distinction, soon after the peace of 1763. Towards the conclusion he says, "Lastly, I inform you that it is the king's order to all his governors and subjects, to treat Indians with justice and humanity, and to forbear all encroachments on the territories allotted to them; accordingly, all individuals are prohibited from purchasing any of your lands; but as you know that, as your white brethren cannot feed you when you visit them, unless you give them ground to plant, it is expected that you will cede lands to the king for that purpose. But whenever you shall be pleased to surrender any of your territories to his majesty, it must be done, for the future, at a public meeting of your nation, when the governors of the provinces, or the superintendent shall be present, and obtain the consent of all your people. The boundaries of your hunting-grounds will be accurately fixed, and no settlement permitted to be made upon them. As you may be assured that all treaties with your people will be faithfully kept, so it is expected that you, also, will be careful strictly to observe them."

The proclamation issued by the King of Great Britain, in 1763, soon after the ratification of the articles of peace, forbids the governors of any of the colonies to grant warrants of survey, or pass patents upon any lands whatever, which, not having been ceded to, or purchased by, us (the king), as aforesaid, are reserved to the said Indians, or any of them. The proclamation proceeds: "And we do further declare it to be our royal will and pleasure, for the present, as aforesaid, to reserve, under our sovereignty, protection and dominion, for the use of the said Indians, all the lands and territories lying to the westward of the sources of the rivers which fall into the sea from the west and northwest as aforesaid; and we do hereby strictly forbid on pain of our displeasure, all our loving subjects from making any purchases or settlements whatever, or taking possession of any of the lands above reserved, without our special leave and license for that purpose first obtained. And we do further strictly enjoin and require all persons whatever, who have, either wilfully or inadvertently, seated themselves upon any lands within the countries above described, or upon any other lands which, not having been ceded to, or purchased by us, are still reserved to the said Indians, as aforesaid, forthwith to remove themselves from such settlements."

[In 1783 the Cherokee Nation and the United States concluded the Treaty of Hopewell.] The third article acknowledges the Cherokees to be under the protection of the United States of America, and of no other power.

This stipulation is found in Indian treaties, generally. It was introduced into their treaties with Great Britain; and may probably be found in those with other European powers. Its origin may be traced to the nature of their connexion with those powers; and its true meaning is discerned in their relative situation.

The general law of European sovereigns, respecting their claims in America, limited the intercourse of Indians, in a great degree, to the particular potentate whose ultimate right of domain was acknowledged by the others. This was the general state of things in time of peace. It was sometimes changed in war. The consequence was, that their supplies were derived chiefly from that nation, and their trade confined to it. Goods, indispensable to their comfort, in the shape of presents, were received from the same hand. What was of still more importance, the strong hand of government was interposed to restrain the disorderly and licentious from intrusions into their country, from encroachments on their lands, and from those acts of violence which were often attended by reciprocal murder. The Indians perceived in this protection only what was beneficial to themselves — an engagement to punish aggressions on them. It involved, practically, no claim to their lands, no dominion over their persons. It merely bound the nation to the British crown, as a dependent ally, claiming the protection of a powerful friend and neighbour, and receiving the advantages of that protection, without involving a surrender of their national character.

This is the true meaning of the stipulation, and is undoubtedly the sense in which it was made. Neither the British government, nor the Cherokees, ever understood it otherwise.

The same stipulation entered into with the United States, is undoubtedly to be construed in the same manner. They receive the Cherokee nation into their favor and protection. The Cherokees acknowledge themselves to be under the protection of the United States, and of no other power. Protection does not imply the destruction of the protected. The manner in which this stipulation was understood by the American government, is explained by the language and acts of our first president.

The fourth article draws the boundary between the Indians and the citizens of the United States. But, in describing this boundary, the term "allotted" and the term "hunting ground" are used.

Is it reasonable to suppose, that the Indians, who could not write, and most probably could not read, who certainly were not critical judges of our language, should distinguish the word "allotted" from the words "marked out." The actual subject of contract was the dividing line between the two nations, and their attention may very well be supposed to have been confined to that subject. When, in fact, they were ceding lands to the United States, and describing the extent of their cession, it may very well be supposed that they might not understand the term employed, as indicating that, instead of granting, they were receiving lands. If the term would admit of no other signification, which is not conceded, its being misunderstood is so apparent, results so necessarily from the whole transaction; that it must, we think, be taken in the sense in which it was most obviously used.

So with respect to the words "hunting grounds." Hunting was at that time the principal occupation of the Indians, and their land was more used for that purpose than for any other. It could not, however, be supposed, that any intention existed of restricting the full use of the lands they reserved.

To the United States, it could be a matter of no concern, whether their whole territory was devoted to hunting grounds, or whether an occasional village, and an occasional corn field, interrupted, and gave some variety to the scene.

These terms had been used in their treaties with Great Britain, and had never been misunderstood. They had never been supposed to imply a right in the British government to take their lands, or to interfere with their internal government.

The fifth article withdraws the protection of the United States from any citizen who has settled, or shall settle, on the lands allotted to the Indians, for their hunting grounds; and stipulates that if he shall not remove within six months the Indians may punish him.

The sixth and seventh articles stipulate for the punishment of the citizens of either country, who may commit offences on or against the citizens of the other. The only inference to be drawn from them is, that the United States considered the Cherokees as a nation.

The ninth article is in these words: "For the benefit and comfort of the Indians, and for the prevention of injuries or oppressions on the part of the citizens or Indians, the United States in Congress assembled, shall have the sole and exclusive right of regulating the trade with the Indians, and managing all their affairs, as they think proper."

To construe the expression "managing all their affairs," into a surrender of self-government, would be, we think, a perversion of their necessary meaning, and a departure from the construction which has been uniformly put on them. The great subject of the article is the Indian trade. The influence it gave, made it desirable that Congress should possess it. The commissioners brought forward the claim, with the profession that their motive was "the benefit and comfort of the Indians, and the prevention of injuries or oppressions." This may be true, as respects the regulation of their trade, and as respects the regulation of all affairs connected with their trade, but cannot be true, as respects the management of all their affairs. The most important of these, are the cession of their lands, and security against intruders. Is it credible, that they should have considered themselves as surrendering to the United States the right to dictate their future cessions, and the terms on which they should be made? or to compel their submission to the violence of disorderly and licentious intruders? It is equally inconceivable that they could have supposed themselves, by a phrase thus slipped into an article, on another and most interesting subject, to have divested themselves of the right of self-government on subjects not connected with trade. Such a measure could not be "for their benefit and comfort," or for "the prevention of injuries and oppression." Such a construction would be inconsistent with the spirit of this and of all subsequent treaties; especially of those articles which recognise the right of the Cherokees to declare hostilities, and to make war. It would convert a treaty of peace covertly into an act, annihilating the political existence of one of the parties. Had such a result been intended, it would have been openly avowed.

[Article 2 of the Treaty of Holston of July 1791] repeats the important acknowledgement, that the Cherokee nation is under the protection of the United States of America, and of no other sovereign whosoever.

The meaning of this has already been explained. The Indian nations were, from their situation, necessarily dependent on some foreign potentate for the supply of their essential wants, and for their protection from lawless and injurious intrusions into their country. That power was naturally termed their protector. They had been arranged under the protection of Great Britain: but the extinguishment of the British power in their neighborhood, and the establishment of that of the United States in its place, lead naturally to the declaration, on the part of the Cherokees, that they were under the protection of the United States, and no other power. They assumed the relation with the United States, which had before subsisted with Great Britain. This relation was that of a nation claiming and receiving the protection of one more powerful, not that of individuals abandoning their national character, and submitting as subjects to the laws of a master.

[The] treaty [of Holston], thus explicitly recognizing the national character of the Cherokees, and their right of self government; thus guarantying their lands; assuming the duty of protection, and of course pledging the faith of the United States for that protection; has been frequently renewed, and is now in full force.

To the general pledge of protection have been added several specific pledges, deemed valuable by the Indians. Some of these restrain the citizens of the United States from encroachments on the Cherokee country, and provide for the punishment of intruders.

From the commencement of our government, Congress has passed acts to regulate trade and intercourse with the Indians; which treat them as nations, respect their rights, and manifest a firm purpose to afford that protection which treaties stipulate. All these acts, and especially that of 1802, which is still in force, manifestly consider the several Indian nations as distinct political communities, having territorial boundaries, within which their authority is exclusive, and having a right to all the lands within those boundaries, which is not only acknowledged, but guarantied by the United States.

[These] treaties and the laws of the United States contemplate the Indian territory as completely separated from that of the states; and provide that all intercourse with them shall be carried on exclusively by the government of the Union. Is this the rightful exercise of power, or is it usurpation?

While these states were colonies, this power, in its utmost extent, was admitted to reside in the crown. When our revolutionary struggle commenced, Congress was composed of an assemblage of deputies acting under specific powers granted by the legislatures, or conventions of the several colonies. It was a great popular movement, not perfectly organized; nor were the respective powers of those who were intrusted with the management of affairs accurately defined. The necessities of our situation produced a general conviction that those measures which concerned all, must be transacted by a body in which the representatives of all were assembled, and which could command the confidence of all: Congress, therefore, was considered as invested with all the powers of war and peace, and Congress dissolved our connection with the mother country, and declared these United Colonies to be independent states. Without any written definition of powers, they employed diplomatic agents to represent the United States at the several courts of England; offered to negotiate treaties with them, and did actually negotiate treaties with France. From the same necessity, and on the same principles, Congress assumed the management of Indian affairs; first in the name of these United Colonies, and afterwards in the name of the United States. Early attempts were made at negotiation, and to regulate trade with them. These not proving successful, war was carried on under the direction, and with the forces of the United States, and the efforts to make peace by treaty were earnest and incessant. The confederation found Congress in the exercise of the same powers of peace and war, in our relations with Indian nations, as with those of Europe.

Such was the state of things when the confederation was adopted. That instrument surrendered the powers of peace and war to Congress and prohibited them to the states, respectively, unless a state be actually invaded, "or shall have received certain advice of a resolution being formed by some nation of Indians to invade such state, and the danger is so imminent as not to admit of delay till the United States in Congress assembled can be consulted." This instrument also gave the United States in Congress assembled the sole and exclusive right of "regulating the trade and managing all the affairs with the Indians, not members of any of the states: provided, that the legislative power of any state within its own limits be not infringed or violated."

The ambiguous phrases which follow the grant of power to the United States were so construed by the States of North Carolina and Georgia as to annul the power itself. The discontents and confusion resulting from these conflicting claims produced representations to Congress, which were referred to a committee, who made their report in 1787. The report does not assent to the construction of the two states, but recommends an accommodation, by liberal cessions of territory, or by an admission on their part of the powers claimed by Congress. The correct exposition of this article is rendered unnecessary by the adoption of our existing Constitution. That instrument confers on Congress the powers of war and peace; of making treaties, and of regulating commerce with foreign nations, and among the several states, and with the Indian tribes. These powers comprehend all that is required for the regulation of our intercourse with the Indians. They are not limited by any restrictions on their free actions. The shackles imposed on this power, in the confederation, are discarded.

The Indian nations had always been considered as distinct, independent political communities, retaining their original natural rights, as the undisputed possessors of the soil from time immemorial, with the single exception of that imposed by irresistible power, which excluded them from intercourse with any other European potentate than the first discoverer of the coast of the particular region claimed; and this was a restriction which those European potentates imposed on themselves, as well as on the Indians. The very term "nation," so generally applied to them, means "a people distinct from others." The Constitution, by declaring treaties already made, as well as those to be made, to be the supreme law of the land, has adopted and sanctioned the previous treaties with the Indian nations, and consequently admits their rank among those powers who are capable of making treaties. The words "treaty" and "nation" are words of our own language, selected in our diplomatic and legislative proceedings, by ourselves, having each a definite and well understood meaning. We have applied them to Indians, as we have applied them to the other nations of the earth. They are applied to all in the same sense.

[The articles repeated in treaties with the Cherokee Nation] are associated with others, recognizing their title to self government. The very fact of repeated treaties with them recognizes it; and the settled doctrine of the law of nations is, that a weaker power does not surrender its independence — its right to self government, by associating with a stronger, and taking its protection. A weak state, in order to provide for its safety, may place itself under the protection of one more powerful, without stripping itself of the right of government, and ceasing to be a state. Examples of this kind are not wanting in Europe. "Tributary and feudatory states," says Vattel, "do not thereby cease to be sovereign and independent states, so long as self government and sovereign and independent authority are left in the administration of the state." At the present day, more than one state may be considered as holding its right of self government under the guarantee and protection of one or more allies.

The Cherokee nation, then, is a distinct community, occupying its own territory, with boundaries accurately described, in which the laws of Georgia can have no force, and which the citizens of Georgia have no right to enter, but with the assent of the Cherokees themselves, or in conformity with treaties, and with the acts of Congress. The whole intercourse between the United States and this nation, is, by our Constitution and laws, vested in the government of the United States. The act of the State of Georgia, under which the plaintiff in error was prosecuted, is, consequently void, and the judgment a nullity. Can this court revise and reverse it?

If the objection to the system of legislation, lately adopted by the legislature of Georgia, in relation to the Cherokee nation, was confined to its extra-territorial operation, the objection, though complete, so far as respected mere right, would give this court no power over the subject. But it goes much further. If the view which has been taken be correct, and we think it is, the acts of Georgia are repugnant to the Constitution, laws and treaties of the United States. They interfere forcibly with the relations established between the United States and the Cherokee nation, the regulation of which, according to the settled principles of our Constitution, are committed exclusively to the government of the Union.

They are in direct hostility with treaties, repeated in a succession of years, which mark out the boundary that separates the Cherokee country from Georgia; guaranty to them all the land within their boundary; solemnly pledge the faith of the United States to restrain their citizens from trespassing on it; and recognize the pre-existing power of the nation to govern itself. They are in hostility with the acts of Congress for regulating this intercourse, and giving effect to the treaties. The forcible seizure and abduction of the plaintiff in error, who was residing in the nation, with its permission, and by authority of the President of the United States, is also a violation of the acts which authorize the chief magistrate to exercise this authority.

[T]he judgment of the superior court for the county of Gwinnett, in the State of Georgia, condemning Samuel A. Worcester to hard labor in the penitentiary of the State of Georgia, for four years, was pronounced by that court under color of a law which is void, as being repugnant to the Constitution, treaties and laws of the United States, and ought, therefore, to be reversed and annulled.

JUSTICE MCLEAN. [Concurring Opinion.]

As this case involves principles of the highest importance, and may lead to consequences which shall have an enduring influence on the institutions of this country; and as there are some points in the case on which I wish to state, distinctly, my opinion, I embrace the privilege of doing so. With the decision just given, I concur.

[T]he Indians sustain a peculiar relation to the United States. They do not constitute, as was decided at the last term, a foreign state, so as to claim the right to sue in the supreme court of the United States; and yet, having the right of self-government, they, in some sense, form a state. In the management of their internal concerns, they are dependent on no power. They punish offences, under their own laws, and in doing so, they are responsible to no earthly tribunal. They make war, and form treaties of peace. The exercise of these and other powers, gives to them a distinct character as a people, and constitutes them, in some respects, a state, although they may not be admitted to possess the right of soil.

By various treaties, the Cherokees have placed themselves under the protection of the United States; they have agreed to trade with no other people, nor to invoke the protection of any other sovereignty. But such engagements do not divest them of the right of self-government, nor destroy their capacity to enter into treaties or compacts. Every state is more or less dependent on those which surround it; but, unless this dependence shall extend so far as to merge the political existence of the protected people into that of their protectors, they may still constitute a state. They may exercise the powers not relinquished, and bind themselves as a distinct and separate community.

[No one would doubt] that, so far as the Indians, as distinct communities, have formed a connection with the federal government, by treaties; that such connection is political, and is equally binding on both parties. This cannot be questioned, except upon the ground, that in making these treaties, the federal government has transcended the treaty-making power. Such an objection, it is true, has been stated, but it is one of modern invention, which arises out of local circumstances; and is not only opposed to the uniform practice of the government, but also to the letter and spirit of the constitution.

But the inquiry may be made, is there no end to the exercise of this power over Indians, within the limits of a state, by the general government? The answer is, that, in its nature, it must be limited by circumstances. If a tribe of Indians shall become so degraded or reduced in numbers, as to lose the power of self-government, the protection of the local law, of necessity, must be extended over them. The point at which this exercise of power by a state would be proper, need not now be considered; if, indeed, it be a judicial question. Such a question does not seem to arise in this case. So long as treaties and laws remain in full force, and apply to Indian nations, exercising the right of self-government, within the limits of a state, the judicial power can exercise no discretion in refusing to give effect to those laws, when questions arise under them, unless they shall be deemed unconstitutional. The exercise of the power of self-government by the Indians, within a state, is undoubtedly contemplated to be temporary. This is shown by the settled policy of the government, in the extinguishment of their title, and especially, by the compact with the State of Georgia. It is a question, not of abstract right, but of public policy. I do not mean to say, that the same moral rule which should regulate the affairs of private life, should not be regarded by communities or nations. But a sound national policy does require, that the Indian tribes within our states should exchange their territories, upon equitable principles, or eventually consent to become amalgamated in our political communities. At best, they can enjoy a very limited independence within the boundaries of a state, and such a residence must always subject them to encroachments from the settlements around them; and their existence within a state, as a separate and independent community, may seriously embarrass or obstruct the operation of the state laws. If, therefore, it would be inconsistent with the political welfare of the states, and the social advance of their citizens, that an independent and permanent power should exist within their limits, this power must give way to the greater power which surrounds it, or seek its exercise beyond the sphere of state authority.

This state of things can only be produced by a co-operation of the state and federal governments. The latter has the exclusive regulation of intercourse with the Indians; and so long as this power shall be exercised, it cannot be obstructed by the state. It is a power given by the constitution, and sanctioned by the most solemn acts of both the federal and state governments; consequently, it cannot be abrogated at the will of a state. It is one of the powers parted with by the states, and vested in the federal government. But if a contingency shall occur, which shall render the Indians who reside in a state, incapable of self-government, either by moral degradation, or a reduction of their numbers, it would undoubtedly be in the power of a state government, to extend to them the *aegis* of its laws. Under such circumstances, the agency of the general government, of necessity, must cease. But if it shall be the policy of the government, to withdraw its protection from the Indians who reside within the limits of the respective states, and who not only claim the right of self-government, but have uniformly exercised it; the laws and treaties which impose duties and obligations on the general government should be abrogated by the powers competent to do so. So long as those laws and treaties exist, having been formed within the sphere of the federal powers, they must be respected and enforced by the appropriate organs of the federal government.

[Dissenting opinion of JUSTICE BALDWIN omitted.]

NOTES

1. **The *Worcester* Decision:** In *Worcester* what was it that rendered the state law invalid and unconstitutional? Was it merely the continued existence of Cherokee tribal sovereignty, or was it the federal law and policy protecting that tribal sovereignty? If the latter, what federal law controls the legal issue? Was the commitment to the federal government of the power over Indian affairs in the Indian commerce clause sufficient to control the issue of the scope of state authority? In the absence of affirmative congressional legislation or treaties, would the negative implications of the Indian commerce clause preclude state control over resident Indian tribal populations under Chief Justice Marshall's analysis? What about under Justice McLean's analysis?

What role did the treaties with the Cherokee play in the Marshall opinion? Did the treaties expressly purport to resolve the jurisdictional question with which the Court was confronted? How did Chief Justice Marshall approach the problem of construction of the treaties with the Cherokee for purposes of resolving the jurisdictional question?

What role did the Trade and Intercourse Acts play in the Marshall opinion? Did they explicitly resolve the jurisdictional question posed by the case? How, then, were they relevant to the final outcome of the litigation?

Are the three Marshall cases consistent? Do they envision the same model of tribal-federal relations? Some have suggested that *Johnson v. M'Intosh* and *Cherokee Nation* denied tribal sovereignty, but *Worcester* rejuvenated the notion of tribal political autonomy. Does a careful reading of all three opinions support that conclusion? While *Worcester* clearly recognizes and vindicates tribal sovereignty over Cherokee country, is the political autonomy envisioned one within a model of international self-determination or treaty federalism? Is some other model being articulated? Are there ambiguities in the model? For the narrative behind *Worcester*, see Rennard Strickland, *The Story of the* Cherokee *Cases in* INDIAN LAW STORIES (Carole Goldberg, Kevin K. Washburn, and Philip P. Frickey, eds., 2011)

2. **The Cherokee Removal Cases and the Constitutional Crisis:** Conflict between state and tribal governments was not, however, all that was involved in *Worcester*. The unilateral legislative action of the State of Georgia, and similar actions taken simultaneously by Mississippi, Tennessee, and other states, were in part attributable to the election of Andrew Jackson as President. Jackson was perceived as an avowed enemy of Indian interests in the affected states (despite his military alliances with some of the affected tribes), and these states properly perceived that the federal government under Jackson's stewardship would not interfere in their unilateral extension of state authority over the tribes. Indeed, at least one historian has attributed to Jackson the following famous retort to the *Worcester* decision: "John Marshall has made his decision; now let him enforce it." HORACE GREELEY, AMERICAN CONFLICT 106 (1884). While the story about the remark is probably apocryphal, the statement accurately captures the prevailing political climate and the conflict between the executive and judicial branches wrought by the *Worcester* case. *See* 2 CHARLES WARREN, THE SUPREME COURT IN UNITED STATES HISTORY 189–239 (1923); MARQUIS JAMES, THE LIFE OF ANDREW JACKSON 603–04 (1938). Indeed, writing in 1923, Professor Charles Warren called the Cherokee cases "the

most serious crises in the history of the Court." For several years the Supreme Court decision was simply ignored — an unprecedented constitutional phenomenon, then and now. Immediate constitutional crisis was averted, however, when the Court adjourned in 1832, a few days after issuing the opinion and special mandate in *Worcester*, without issuing the necessary order to a federal marshal to secure Worcester's release. During the interim, until the Court reconvened for its 1833 Term, successful efforts were made to secure a pardon from the Georgia governor in order to compromise the litigation and avert a constitutional confrontation. At the same time, the nation was also embroiled in the South Carolina tariff nullification controversy, and the Jackson administration sought to avoid constitutional confrontation on Cherokee removal.

While Worcester and the Cherokee Nation won the battle of legal doctrine, they ultimately lost the war of federal policy in the halls of Congress and in the White House. Despite Chief Justice Marshall's ringing rhetoric about the legally protected separate sovereign status of the Cherokee Nation, the Cherokees were finally forced to assent to removal when the federal government refused to protect the Tribe from political, cultural, and physical encroachment by the State of Georgia and its citizens. Treaty of New Echota with the Cherokees, Dec. 29, 1835, 7 Stat. 478. *See generally* Francis Prucha, American Indian Policy in the Formative Years 213–73 (1962); Rennard Strickland, Fire and the Spirits: Cherokee Law from Clan to Court 40–72 (1975).

Seeking to forestall removal, Chief John Ross, leading an official delegation of the Cherokee Nation, presented a petition to Congress in 1837, which denied the authority of those Cherokees who signed the 1835 removal treaty, and pleaded for protection by the United States. Noting the historic bonds of friendship between the Cherokee and the United States, the petition also emphasized Cherokee success in incorporating non-Indian ways:

> A smooth and beautiful prospect of future advancement was opened before us. Our people had abandoned the pursuits, the habits and the tastes of the savage, and had put on the vestments of civilization, of intelligence and of pure religion. The progress we had made furnished us with the most assured hopes of continued improvement, and we indulged in the anticipation that the time was not far distant when we should be recognized, on the footing of equality by the brethren from whom we had received all which we were now taught to prize.

> The promise of golden sunshine is now overspread. Clouds and darkness have obscured its brilliancy. The winds are beginning to mutter their awful forebodings, the tempest is gathering thick and heavy over our heads, and threatens to burst upon us with terrific energy and overwhelming ruin.

> In this season of calamity, where can we turn with hope or confidence? On all former occasions of peril or of doubt the Government of the United States spread over us its broad and paternal shield. It invited us to seek an asylum and a protection under its mighty arm. It assisted us with its encouragement and advice, it soothed us with its consoling assurances, it inspired us with hope and gave us a feeling of confidence and security.

But alas! This our long-cherished friend seems now to be alienated from us: this our father has raised his arm to inflict the hostile blow; this strength so long our protection is now exerted against us, and on the wide scene of existence no human aid is left us. Unless you avert your arm we are destroyed. Unless your feelings of affection and compassion are once more awakened towards your destitute and despairing children our annihilation is complete. . . .

Challenging the Congress to detail any Cherokee offenses against the United States that would justify removal, the petition continued its entreaty:

We will not and we cannot believe after the long connexion that has subsisted between us, after all that has been done and all that has been promised that our whole nation will be forcibly ejected from their native land and from their social hearths without pretence of crime, without charge, without evidence, without trial: that we shall be exiled from all that we hold dear and venerable and sacred, and driven into a remote, a strange and a sterile region, without even the imputation of guilt. We will not believe that this will be done by our ancient allies, our friends, our brethren. Yet between this and the abrogation to the pretended treaty there is no medium. Such an instrument so obtained, so contaminated cannot cover the real nature of the acts which it is invoked to sanction. If power is to be exerted let it come unveiled. We shall but submit and die.

The Cherokee delegation asked Congress to undertake an inquiry into the validity of the 1835 removal treaty, known as the Treaty of New Echota. Unwilling to do so, Congress allowed the forced removal to go forward, leading to the Cherokees' infamous Trail of Tears, during which many Cherokee died on the harsh winter road to the Indian Territory.

The last Cherokee party left on December 4, 1838, but some Cherokee literally headed for the hills in North Carolina to escape removal, and their descendants can still be found there — the Eastern Band of Cherokee. The racism of the Cherokee removal controversy is evidenced by the fate of Articles 12 and 13 of the Treaty of New Echota. Those provisions guaranteed that Cherokees in North Carolina, Tennessee, and Alabama who wished to remain and become citizens of the state could retain a farm of 160 acres, including their improvements, and become subject to state law and that similar reservations under prior treaties would be honored. President Jackson refused to accede even to these provisions, and they were abrogated in a supplemental agreement with the Cherokee dated March 1, 1836.

Review Article 5 of the Treaty of New Echota in Sec. A.2, this chapter, with its guarantees of Cherokee law-making authority over all individuals within Cherokee territory and its promises of freedom from state law. While the government of the Cherokee Nation, like the governments of most of the removed tribes in the Indian Territory, flourished and became quite westernized during the last half of the nineteenth century, this treaty promise was broken by the Curtis Act of 1898, ch. 517, 30 Stat. 495, which, as prelude to Oklahoma statehood, purported to suspend the Cherokee government and nullify the force of Cherokee law. It purported to do the same for the governments of the other four members of the so-called Five Civilized Tribes (Creek, Choctaw, Chickasaw, and Seminole).

3. Indian Islands and State Sovereignty: What significance should be attached to Justice McLean's suggestion that if "a tribe of Indians shall become so degraded or reduced in numbers, as to lose the power of self-government, the protection of the local law, of necessity, must be extended over them." Does this principle of state sovereignty by "necessity" make sense? If so, which government or branch of government has the responsibility of ascertaining the degraded status of the tribe and its loss of self-governing powers? Can the state legislatures or governors be trusted with final authority to ascertain the Indians' abandonment of tribal status? Is a finding of detribalization of an Indian society a proper function for the federal courts?

Not all jurists of Marshall's time perceived the Indian tribes as separate, autonomous, self-governing political groups. Justice McLean's ambivalent position doubted the long-term ability of Indian tribes to survive as separate sovereign entities when surrounded by the governments of non-Indian communities. While sitting as a circuit judge, Justice McLean later had an opportunity to implement his ideas partially. In *United States v. Cisna*, 25 F. Cas. 422 (C.C. Ohio 1835), he held that the federal courts lacked jurisdiction over an offense committed against an Indian on the Wyandot reserve in Ohio because the Wyandot reservation had become surrounded by and intermixed with white settlements and had become subject to state law, at least for white inhabitants, through the passage of a state statute. Thus, McLean held that the provisions of the 1802 Trade and Intercourse Act proscribing larceny of Indian property governed only non-Indians who committed crimes on remote Indian settlements and were therefore inoperative on the Wyandot reserve. Similarly, in *United States v. Bailey*, 24 F. Cas. 937 (C.C. Tenn. 1834), Justice McLean, sitting as a circuit judge, dismissed a murder indictment against a white person for the murder of another white person in Cherokee country, stating that the federal power to regulate commerce with the Indian tribes could not constitutionally reach such a crime. Significantly, in each of these cases the accused was a non-Indian. Note that in implementing his earlier dicta McLean was not holding that state laws could be extended to Indians within the states. Indeed, in *Bailey* McLean said, "The power of Congress is limited to the regulation of a commercial intercourse, with such tribes that exist, as a distinct community, governed by their own laws, and resting for their protection on the faith of treaties and laws of the Union."

While Justice McLean's efforts to extend state laws to Indian lands were limited to non-Indians, some of the state courts that sought to implement his views during the nineteenth century extended the principle to Indians as well. In *State v. Foreman*, 16 Tenn. 256 (1835), the court affirmed the jurisdiction of the state courts over a murder committed by a Cherokee Indian in Indian country, basing its decision primarily on the principle that the Cherokee Nation had been conquered and, under accepted principles of international law was thereby subjected to the laws of the conquering nation. Similarly, in *State v. Doxtater*, 2 N.W. 439 (Wis. 1879), the court affirmed the jurisdiction of state authorities to try an Oneida Indian for the crime of adultery occurring on the Oneida reservation.[4] Reasoning that the

---

[4] The Wisconsin Supreme Court later recognized the error of its decision in *Doxtater* and overruled that decision in State v. Rufus, 237 N.W. 67 (Wis. 1931).

power to punish Indians for crimes committed against white persons had been exercised by the Wisconsin territorial courts prior to statehood, the court concluded that these Indians were therefore not an independent tribe subject only to their own laws. Consequently, the court concluded that punishment of offenses committed by Indians in Indian country fell within the reserved rights of the states.

While these examples do not reflect the modern state of the law on state jurisdiction, they highlight the continuing debate during the early nineteenth century over the legal status of Indian tribes within the Union and the states and suggest that Chief Justice Marshall's assumptions about Indian legal autonomy were not uniformly shared.

4. Proposals for Indian Statehood: In light of Chief Justice Marshall's comments in *Johnson v. M'Intosh* and *Worcester* regarding the inability of the European colonists to absorb the Native population, consider the historical fact that proposals for the formation of an Indian state frequently were voiced in the late eighteenth and nineteenth centuries. The idea of an Indian state, while never fulfilled, is almost as old as the nation. Article VI of the Treaty of Sept. 17, 1778, with the Delawares, 7 Stat. 13, one of the first treaties the newly independent government of the United States entered into with an Indian nation, provided:

> And it is further agreed on between the contracting parties should it for the future be found conducive for the mutual interest of both parties to invite any other tribes who have been friends to the interest of the United States, to join the present confederation, and to form a state whereof the Delaware nation shall be the head, and have a representation in Congress.

Echoing this earlier treaty promise to the Delaware in 1778, article 7 of the Treaty of New Echota also contained the promise that the removed Cherokees "shall be entitled to a delegate in the House of Representatives of the United States whenever Congress shall make provision for the same." Like the similar promise made to the Delawares, this guarantee was never carried into force.

In Annie H. Abel, *Proposals for an Indian State 1778–1878*, ANNUAL REPORT OF THE AMERICAN HISTORICAL ASSOCIATION 89, 94–102 (1907), the author traces the later nineteenth century shift from the idea of an Indian territory or state under the governance of Indians to a territory of mixed populations. These debates for the most part centered on the history of unsuccessful late nineteenth century ideas for an organized territorial government and later an Indian state, proposed by some to be named for the Cherokee linguist Sequoyah, to be formed out of the former Indian Territory in what is now eastern Oklahoma. The admission of Oklahoma into the United States as a mixed, rather than Indian, state, over very strong tribal opposition, ended any plans for an Indian state.

Nevertheless, the 1778 treaty with the Delaware and the 1835 Treaty of New Echota with the Cherokee, the Cherokee removal treaty, both contain provisions promising representation of these tribes in Congress, which to this day remain unfulfilled. Could such treaty promises constitutionally be honored today? Could these tribes be afforded voting membership in Congress? In New Zealand the indigenous population, the Maori, automatically are granted four seats in Parliament, irrespective of population.

What political or social advantages would a separate Indian state have afforded to the Indians? What advantages, if any, would have accrued to the non-Indian portion of the nation from such proposals? Would a separate Indian state have been compatible with nineteenth-century American constitutional notions of federalism? Would it be compatible with twentieth-century concepts of federalism? Has acceptance of the doctrine that the due process clause of the Fourteenth Amendment incorporates the Bill of Rights and makes them applicable to the states and the revolution in federal-state relations since the New Deal undermined the value of statehood in protecting Indian autonomy? As you review the materials in this book, consider to what extent federal law now accomplishes the objectives behind these early proposals for an Indian state.

NOTE ON THE RHETORIC OF EXCLUSION

In Leslie Bender & Daan Braveman, POWER, PRIVILEGE AND LAW 139–141 (1995), the authors discuss what they call the "rhetoric of exclusion" used by courts to justify or rationalize the exclusion or subordination of various groups of peoples, including (1) "rhetoric of self/other" (stressing and assigning value to real or imaginary differences among groups); (2) using explicitly racist or demeaning language; (3) denying that discriminatory classifications have been made on the basis of race or gender; (4) using metaphors, such as those of family or citizenship, to sanction continued exclusion of groups; (5) blaming the targeted group for its own predicament; (6) comparing and ranking targeted groups; (7) suggesting that targeting the group is the intent of the "framers" of the Constitution; (8) relying on separation of powers or federalism concerns to shift responsibility away from the court; (9) explaining that the subordination of a group is "natural, or just part of the way things are . . . "; (10) using arguments to "convey the impression that the court's position is objective and neutral, not the product of a partial perspective"; (11) trivializing the harm to the subordinated group; (12) presenting the problem outside its social, historical, or political context; (13) suggesting that the issue in a case is a social rather than a legal problem; (14) arguing that descent down a slippery slope or parade of horribles will follow from adopting a particular legal position protecting the subordinated group; (15) denying responsibility by relying on earlier court decisions that used the techniques described above.

How many of these rhetorical devices did Chief Justice Marshall employ in the trilogy of cases you just read? Did the petition of Chief John Ross, quoted in Note 2 above, employ any of these rhetorical devices to minimize the claims of Georgia and the federal government to Cherokee lands? As you review the other materials in the book, consider whether these rhetorical devices occur with decreased or increased frequency as we approach the modern era. Remember that the Marshall trilogy and most federal and state court decisions dealing with Indian tribes come from legal institutions that derive their authority from the non-Indian settlement of North America. The story they tell is necessarily likely to be one-sided, too often ignoring the Indian version of history. The interests they see and privilege too often will be non-Indian interests. The devices identified by Bender and Braveman, therefore, will often be employed to mask the privileging of non-Indian over tribal interests. These concerns with the manner in which the rhetoric of federal and state courts hides the privileging of non-Indian over tribal interests represents one manner in which colonialism may still exist as an institutional part of a seemingly post-colonialist legal system.

D. PROCESSING MODELS OF TRIBAL-FEDERAL RELATIONS AS LEGAL DOCTRINE: NINETEENTH AND EARLY TWENTIETH CENTURY ILLUSTRATIONS

Throughout the nineteenth and early twentieth centuries, Native nations and the federal government struggled and negotiated over the terms of their relationship. During much of this period, the United States pressed for increased integration of individual Indians into the general polity and economy, as well as increased access for non-Indians to their resources. In doing so, the federal government sought support in constitutional authority and judge-made doctrine. Simultaneously, Native people demanded respect for their cultural and political autonomy, appealing to treaties, the Marshall trilogy of cases, tribal and international law, and their lack of participation in the compact that produced the United States in the first place.

The success of the United States or the Indian nations in implementing their respective models depended on a variety of circumstances, including the existence of serious political divisions among non-Indians that Native peoples could exploit; the prevailing international climate regarding colonialism; the capacity of Indian nations to mobilize general public sympathy on behalf of their cause; and the kinds of demographic and other pressures that affected non-Indian demand for tribal resources. Did United States law serve as a source of principle and stability through this turmoil, or did it swing from model to model with the political fortunes of the contenders? What were the roles of courts and the more political branches in crafting a legal framework for the tribal-federal relationship? The following sections examine the process by which each side in this ongoing conflict attempted to enlist law in support of its preferred version of their relationship, and the visions of that relationship reflected in the resulting United States legal regime.

1. Treaties Between Nations

In the 50 years following the Marshall trilogy, the non-Indian U.S. population swelled and non-Indian settlements forged westward into Indian territories, precipitating armed conflict with Indian nations. Non-Indians increasingly rejected the claim that Indian lands were off-limits, especially when valuable minerals, water, or other resources were located there; and they turned to the federal government for support and protection. In turn, these new political realities triggered federal reassessment of the old policy of separating Indians from non-Indians via treaty promises of tribal autonomy on reserved or granted lands remote from non-Indian outposts. The United States continued to negotiate treaties or legislatively confirmed agreements with Indian nations, usually because federal officials found it too costly, in both money and lives, to respond to the tribal insurgencies that greeted American expansion. At the same time, however, federal officials searched for policies and models that fit conditions of long-term proximity and coexistence between Native and non-Indian communities. For example, Congress abolished treaty-making with Indian nations (1871) and transferred the

Bureau of Indian Affairs from the War Department to the Department of the Interior (1849). These actions signaled departure from an international self-determination or other consensual model on the part of the United States. During this same period, the approach of non-Indians left Native communities vulnerable to deadly epidemics, declining food supplies, and conversion efforts of federally-supported Christian missionaries. Seeking to survive as distinct cultural and political entities, they fought, negotiated, and (if resources or volunteer attorneys could be found) litigated. *See, e.g.*, BLUE CLARK, *LONE WOLF V. HITCHCOCK*: TREATY RIGHTS AND INDIAN LAW AT THE END OF THE NINETEENTH CENTURY (1994).

In these conditions of geopolitical transformation, were treaties and agreements the only way the Constitution would allow the United States to regulate Indian affairs? Or did the Constitution grant Congress a unilateral power over the Indian tribes, their members, or their territory? As Professor Clinton has documented, the earliest understandings of the federal Indian affairs power, both in the Articles of Confederation and the United States Constitution, envisioned such power as extending only to relations *with* the Indians, not control *over* the tribes. *See* Robert N. Clinton, *There Is No Federal Supremacy Clause for Indian Tribes*, 34 ARIZ. ST. L.J. 113 (2002). He observes that for almost 100 years following adoption of Article I, section 8 of the Constitution, the Indian commerce clause, Congress enacted almost no statutes directly regulating tribes or their members in any fashion. As he notes, even the provisions of the Nonintercourse Act regulating tribal land transactions and crimes committed by Indians against non-Indians can be understood within this framework. The former only regulated the title that non-Indians could receive, not the actions of the tribes; and the latter fits within international frameworks allowing nations to protect their citizens while on foreign territory. Indeed, the removal acts themselves can be reconciled with this vision of limited federal power, because Congress would only activate the process after the Treaty of New Echota with the Cherokee.

The geopolitical forces described above generated political pressure to recast federal Indian affairs power as a unilateral power. Accordingly, the Supreme Court was presented with cases, like the ones that follow, requiring it to determine whether federal-Indian relations would continue along a consensual model, structured by treaties and agreements that largely left sovereignty and jurisdiction within Indian country to the tribes. The position of the executive and legislative branches of the United States government was that federal power over Indian affairs was so extensive that it allowed for unilateral federal control over tribal property and activities by tribal members in Indian country. Should geopolitical changes alter the scope of federal authority granted to the United States government in a constitution ratified in 1789? As you read the materials in this section, consider whether these changes have accomplished that result and how much of modern legal doctrine can be justified under any traditional legal analysis.

EX PARTE CROW DOG
United States Supreme Court
109 U.S. 556 (1883)

Mr. Justice Matthews delivered the opinion of the Court.

The petitioner is in the custody of the Marshal of the United States for the Territory of Dakota, imprisoned in the jail of Lawrence County in the First Judicial District of that Territory, under sentence of death, adjudged against him by the district court for that district, to be carried into execution January 14th, 1884. That judgment was rendered upon a conviction for the murder of an Indian of the Brule Sioux Band of the Sioux Nation of Indians by the name of Sin-ta-ge-le-Scka, or in English, Spotted Tail, the prisoner also being an Indian, of the same band and nation, and the homicide having occurred, as alleged in the indictment, in the Indian country, within a place and district of country under the exclusive jurisdiction of the United States and within the said judicial district. The judgment was affirmed, on a writ of error, by the Supreme Court of the Territory. It is claimed on behalf of the prisoner that the crime charged against him, and of which he stands convicted, is not an offense under the laws of the United States; that the district court had no jurisdiction to try him, and that its judgment and sentence are void. He, therefore, prays for a writ of habeas corpus, that he may be delivered from an imprisonment which he asserts to be illegal.

[Title 28] of the Revised Statutes relates to Indians, and the sub-title of chapter four is, Government of Indian Country. It embraces many provisions regulating the subject of intercourse and trade with the Indians in the Indian country, and imposes penalties and punishments for various violations of them. Section 2142 provides for the punishment of assaults with deadly weapons and intent, by Indians upon white persons, and by white persons upon Indians; section 2143, for the case of arson, in like cases; and section 2144 provides that "the general laws of the United States defining and prescribing punishments for forgery and depredations upon the mails shall extend to the Indian country."

The next two sections are as follows:

> Sec. 2145. Except as to crimes, the punishment of which is expressly provided for in this title, the general laws of the United States as to the punishment of crimes committed in any place within the sole and exclusive jurisdiction of the United States, except the District of Columbia, shall extend to the Indian country.

> Sec. 2146. The preceding section shall not be construed to extend to [crimes committed by one Indian against the person or property of another Indian, nor to] any Indian committing any offence in the Indian country who has been punished by the local law of the tribe, or to any case where by treaty stipulations the exclusive jurisdiction over such offences is or may be secured to the Indian tribes respectively.

[This] argument in support of the jurisdiction and conviction is, that the exception contained in § 2146 Rev. Stat. is repealed by the operation and legal effect of the treaty with the different tribes of the Sioux Indians of April 29th, 1868, 15 Stat. 635; and an act of Congress, approved February 28th, 1877, to ratify an agreement with certain bands of the Sioux Indians, &c., 19 Stat. 254.

The following provisions of the treaty of 1868 are relied on:

Article I. From this day forward all war between the parties to this agreement shall forever cease. The government of the United States desires peace, and its honor is hereby pledged to keep it. The Indians desire peace, and they now pledge their honor to maintain it.

If bad men among the whites, or among other people subject to the authority of the United States, shall commit any wrong upon the person or property of the Indians, the United States will, upon proof made to the agent and forwarded to the commissioner of Indian affairs at Washington City, proceed at once to cause the offender to be arrested and punished according to the laws of the United States, and also reimburse the injured person for the loss sustained.

If bad men among the Indians shall commit a wrong or depredation upon the person or property of any one, white, black, or Indian, subject to the authority of the United States and at peace therewith, the Indians herein named solemnly agree that they will, upon proof made to their agent and notice by him, deliver up the wrong-doer to the United States, to be tried and punished according to its laws; and in case they willfully refuse so to do, the person injured shall be reimbursed for his loss from the annuities or other moneys due or to become due to them under this or other treaties made with the United States. And the President, on advising with the commissioner of Indian affairs, shall prescribe such rules and regulations for ascertaining damages under the provisions of this article as in his judgment may be proper. But no one sustaining loss while violating the provisions of this treaty or the laws of the United States shall be reimbursed therefor.

[If these agreements] have the effect contended for, to support the conviction in the present case, it also makes punishable, when committed within the Indian country by one Indian against the person or property of another Indian, the following offences, defined by the general laws of the United States as to crimes committed in places within their exclusive jurisdiction, viz.: manslaughter, § 5341; attempt to commit murder or manslaughter, § 5342; rape, § 5345; mayhem, § 5348; bigamy, § 5352; larceny, § 5356; and receiving stolen goods, § 5357. That this legislation could constitutionally be extended to embrace Indians in the Indian country, by the mere force of a treaty, whenever it operates of itself, without the aid of any legislative provision, was decided by this court in the case of *The United States v. 43 Gallons of Whiskey*, 93 U.S. 188. *See Holden v. Joy*, 17 Wall. [83 U.S.] 211; *The Cherokee Tobacco*, 11 Wall. [78 U.S.] 616. It becomes necessary, therefore, to examine the particular provisions that are supposed to work this result.

The first of these is contained in the first article of the treaty of 1868, that "if bad men among the Indians shall commit a wrong or depredation upon the person or property of any one, white, black, or Indian, subject to the authority of the United

States and at peace therewith, the Indians herein named solemnly agree that they will, upon proof made to their agent and notice by him, deliver up the wrong-doer to the United States, to be tried and punished according to its laws."

But it is quite clear from the context that this does not cover the present case of an alleged wrong committed by one Indian upon the person of another of the same tribe. The provision must be construed with its counterpart, just preceding it, which provides for the punishment by the United States of any bad men among the whites, or among other people subject to their authority, who shall commit any wrong upon the person or property of the Indians. Here are two parties, among whom, respectively, there may be individuals guilty of a wrong against one of the other — one is the party of whites and their allies, the other is the tribe of Indians with whom the treaty is made. In each case, the guilty party is to be tried and punished by the United States, and in case the offender is one of the Indians who are parties to the treaty, the agreement is that he shall be delivered up. In case of refusal, deduction is to be made from the annuities payable to the tribe, for compensation to the injured person, a provision which points quite distinctly to the conclusion that the injured person cannot himself be one of the same tribe.

[The second provision used to] justify the jurisdiction asserted in the present case, is the eighth article of the agreement, embodied in the Act of 1877, in which it is declared:

> And Congress shall, by appropriate legislation, secure to them an orderly government; they shall be subject to the laws of the United States, and each individual shall be protected in his rights of property, person, and life.

It is equally clear, in our opinion, that the words can have no such effect as that claimed for them. The pledge to secure to these people, with whom the United States was contracting as a distinct political body, an orderly government, by appropriate legislation thereafter to be framed and enacted, necessarily implies, having regard to all the circumstances attending the transaction, that among the arts of civilized life, which it was the very purpose of all these arrangements to introduce and naturalize among them, was the highest and best of all, that of self-government, the regulation by themselves of their own domestic affairs, the maintenance of order and peace among their own members by the administration of their own laws and customs. They were nevertheless to be subject to the laws of the United States, not in the sense of citizens, but, as they had always been, as wards subject to a guardian; not as individuals, constituted members of the political community of the United States, with a voice in the selection of representatives and the framing of the laws, but as a dependent community who were in a state of pupilage, advancing from the condition of a savage tribe to that of a people who, through the discipline of labor and by education, it was hoped might become a self-supporting and self-governed society. . . .

The nature and circumstances of this case strongly reinforce this rule of interpretation in its present application. It is a case involving the judgment of a court of special and limited jurisdiction, not to be assumed without clear warrant of law. It is a case of life and death. It is a case where, against an express exception in the law itself, that law, by argument and inference only, is sought to be extended over aliens and strangers; over the members of a community separated by race, by tradition, by the instincts of a free though savage life, from the authority and power which seeks to impose upon them the restraints of an external and unknown code, and to subject them to the responsibilities of civil conduct, according to rules and penalties of which they could have no previous warning; which judges them by a standard made by others and not for them, which takes no account of the conditions which should except them from its exactions, and makes no allowance for their inability to understand it. It tries them, not by their peers, nor by the customs of their people, nor the law of their land, but by superiors of a different race, according to the law of a social state of which they have an imperfect conception, and which is opposed to the traditions of their history, to the habits of their lives, to the strongest prejudices of their savage nature; one which measures the red man's revenge by the maxims of the white man's morality. [As stated] by Mr. Justice Miller, delivering the opinion of the court in *United States v. Joseph*, 94 U.S. 614, 617:

> The tribes for whom the act of 1834 was made were those semi-independent tribes whom our government has always recognized as exempt from our laws, whether within or without the limits of an organized state or territory, and, in regard to their domestic government, left to their own rules and traditions, in whom we have recognized the capacity to make treaties, and with whom the governments, state and national, deal, with a few exceptions only, in their national or tribal character, and not as individuals.

[Thus], the First District Court of Dakota was without jurisdiction to find or try the indictment against the prisoner, that the conviction and sentence are void, and that his imprisonment is illegal.

The writs of habeas corpus and certiorari prayed for will accordingly be issued.

NOTES

1. **Indian Political Autonomy:** In *Ex parte Crow Dog*, an individual tribal member's criminal defense implicated the autonomy claims of his nation and, at least implicitly, of Native peoples nationwide. In arguing that Brule rather than federal criminal law applied to his acts, Crow Dog forced federal courts to decide whether they would become agents of assimilation or protectors of Indian autonomy. This choice could be framed exclusively as a policy decision for the U.S. to make regarding different groups within its own polity. After all, there are many groups within the United States, such as the Mormons in Utah, the Amish in Pennsylvania, and immigrant ethnic groups, which possess different cultural beliefs that may come into conflict with dominant norms. *See, e.g., Wisconsin v. Yoder*, 406 U.S. 205 (1972) (exempting Amish children from compulsory education laws); *Meyer v. Nebraska*, 262 U.S. 390 (1923) (upholding right to conduct private school education in foreign language). Sometimes those beliefs inspire practices, such as polygamy, that may in fact constitute criminal behavior under the dominant society's legal code. *See Reynolds v. United States*, 98 U.S. 145 (1878) (upholding prosecution of Mormon for bigamy). Because U.S. law is heavily weighted in favor of the rights of individuals, rather than groups, such claims of cultural autonomy are typically treated as a First Amendment right to speech, association, or free exercise of religion. In that sense, individual claims for cultural autonomy are balanced

against the interests of society to determine which should be given greater weight.

Should American constitutional norms be equally applicable to Indians? In *Ex parte Crow Dog*, the Court draws on language in *United States v. Joseph* to assert that the United States government recognizes Indians as largely "exempt from our laws" and, with respect "to their domestic government, left to their own rules and traditions." Thus, the policy of the United States was to engage with Indians "in their national or tribal character, and not as individuals." In this respect, Indian nations are markedly different from other cultural groups, such as the Mormons, Amish, and immigrant groups, which voluntarily incorporated themselves into the American political system and became subject to the individual rights framework of liberal constitutional theory.

The question for contemporary theorists is whether and to what extent Indian nations today ought to be free to engage in "illiberal practices." Should Indian nations be forced to adhere to the constitutional norms of a liberal democracy in their governance of tribal members? What about in their governance of non-members? Professor Angela Riley argues that the perception that tribal governments are prone to violate individual rights has triggered an expansion of federal law intended to limit the ability of tribal governments to engage in "illiberal practices." Professor Riley maintains that such intrusions on tribal sovereignty cannot be justified as a matter of federal Indian law and argues that this body of law requires that internal tribal decisions regarding Indian culture and tradition be left to Indian tribes, even when such decisions conflict with Western liberal ideals. *See* Angela R. Riley, *(Tribal) Sovereignty and Illiberalism*, 97 Cal. L. Rev. 799 (2007). Professor Riley's theory focuses on tribal governance of members, and she attempts to demonstrate that cultural difference is central to the expression of tribal political autonomy, and this difference ought to be protected by federal law. In another work, Professor Riley suggests that Indian nations ought to reject the notion that "good governance" is equivalent to the norms that structure a liberal democracy, and she argues instead that tribes ought to draw on their own cultural traditions of governance, as well as a set of baseline international human rights (*e.g.*, the right to dissent, the right to exit) intended to "restore and maintain fairness, balance, and inclusion in tribal communities." Angela R. Riley, *Good (Native) Governance*, 107 Colum. L. Rev. 1049 (2007).

What model of tribal-federal relations is represented by the Court's decision in *Ex parte Crow Dog*? What model underlies Professor Riley's argument for tribal governmental autonomy? Should the United States have a right to intervene in tribal governance if it believes that the tribe has violated international human rights norms?

2.   **Major Crimes Act and Non-Indian Responses to *Crow Dog*:** Even prior to the federal prosecution of Crow Dog, the Lakota families involved in the Spotted Tail killing reputedly had resolved the matter with an apology and an exchange of $600, eight horses, and blankets to Spotted Tail's kin as compensation for their lost relative pursuant to traditional Lakota concepts of restorative justice. Sidney L. Harring, Crow Dog's Case: American Indian Sovereignty, Tribal Law, and United States Law in the Nineteenth Century 1 (1994). The federal prosecution of Crow Dog was the result of pressure from white settlers who decried the lack of

punishment for the murder of a Lakota chief who had maintained relatively friendly relations with the white settlers. Thus, the federal prosecution of Crow Dog sought to vindicate non-Indian, rather than Lakota, interests. As a consequence of *Ex parte Crow Dog*, serious disputes among Indians in the Indian country could continue to be resolved according to tribal legal traditions.

This outcome of the *Crow Dog* case greatly distressed the agents of the Bureau of Indian Affairs, whose mission it was to pacify and assimilate the tribes that had been settled onto reservations. For almost a decade, these agents had been seeking authority for federal and state prosecution of serious offenses committed by one tribal member against another, despite the evident exclusion of such offenses from federal jurisdiction under the Nonintercourse Act (now 18 U.S.C. § 1152). A typical complaint is contained in this statement by the Commissioner of Indian Affairs in his annual report for 1884:

> I again desire to call attention to the necessity for legislation for the punishment of crimes on the Indian reservations. Since my last report the Supreme Court of the United States decided in the case of *Ex parte Crow Dog*, indicted for murder, that the District Court of Dakota was without jurisdiction, when the crime was committed on the reservation by one Indian against another. If offenses of this character cannot be tried in the courts of the United States, there is no tribunal in which the crime of murder can be punished. Minor offenses may be punished through the agency of the [federal administrative] "court of Indian offenses," but it will hardly do to leave the punishment of the crime of murder to a tribunal that exists only by the consent of the Indians of the reservation. If the murderer is left to be punished according to the old Indian custom, it becomes the duty of the next of kin to avenge the death of his relative by either killing the murderer or some one of his kinsmen. The laws of the state or territory wherein the reservation is situated ought to be extended over the reservation, and the Indians should be compelled to obey such laws and be allowed to claim the protection thereof.

Legal historian Sidney Harring has assembled considerable evidence that Indian agents actually whipped up non-Indian sentiment over the killing of Spotted Tail in order to advance their objective of passing a federal Major Crimes Act and giving themselves more leverage over their restive charges. SIDNEY L. HARRING, CROW DOG'S CASE, *supra*. According to Professor Harring, the agents' portrayal of Crow Dog as a "savage," freed by the United States Supreme Court, despite his murder of Spotted Tail, a "loyal and courageous chief," left Congress with no other choice but to "correct" the situation by statute.

Within two years of *Ex parte Crow Dog* the Congress enacted the Major Crimes Act (23 Stat. 362, 385, codified as amended at 18 U.S.C. § 1153), which was the first major declaration of federal authority over purely internal tribal offenses. Nothing in the language of the Act compels the conclusion that Indian nations lost concurrent jurisdiction over the enumerated offenses; and in fact, concurrent tribal jurisdiction over major crimes has been confirmed through Interior Department approval of tribal codes asserting such jurisdiction, and through the ruling of one federal circuit court. *Decision of the Assistant Secretary of Indian Affairs, Ross O.*

Swimmer, approving ordinance of the Washoe Tribe, April 18, 1987; *Wetsit v. Stafne*, 44 F.3d 823 (9th Cir. 1995); *see* Ch. 4, Sec. A.3.c. But the Indian Civil Rights Act of 1968, 25 U.S.C. § 1302(7), has precluded tribal courts from imposing sentences in excess of one year in prison and $5,000 for any one offense, leaving federal courts with responsibility for most serious offenses where Indians are both perpetrator and victim.

More important, concurrent jurisdiction does not satisfy the Indian nations' concern that they may choose to punish different offenses than those defined in the federal criminal code or may choose to achieve social control by means other than criminal punishment. For example, indigenous legal traditions regarding homicide have functioned within an intricately woven framework of spiritual beliefs and social institutions designed to maintain cosmic balance and social harmony. *See* RENNARD STRICKLAND, FIRE AND THE SPIRITS: CHEROKEE LAW FROM CLAN TO COURT (1975); KARL LLEWELLYN & E. ADAMSON HOEBEL, THE CHEYENNE WAY: CONFLICT AND CASE LAW IN PRIMITIVE JURISPRUDENCE (1944). Furthermore, traditional justice systems may carry out punishments that the federal government treats as criminal acts. In *United States v. Whaley*, 37 Fed. 145 (C.C.S.D. Cal. 1888), a tribal council had determined that a particular medicine man should be killed for poisoning several individuals under his care, including the tribal chief. The tribal members who carried out this sentence were subsequently prosecuted for homicide under the Major Crimes Act. For a detailed account of the *Whaley* case and its aftermath, see GELYA FRANK & CAROLE GOLDBERG, DEFYING THE ODDS: THE TULE RIVER TRIBE'S STRUGGLE FOR SOVEREIGNTY IN THREE CENTURIES (2010). As these examples illustrate, preempting tribal processes for addressing homicide and other serious offenses, the Major Crimes Act threatened to unravel central features of tribal cultures.

What is the non-Indian community's interest if the Navajo Nation, for example, considers certain homicides (such as euthanasia) not murder, or if it prefers to banish certain offenders rather than incarcerate them? Can the Major Crimes Act be understood as anything other than an attempt to obliterate cultural as well as political distinctions between Indians and the dominant society? Who are likely to serve as the decision-makers in cases heard under the Major Crimes Act? Not only does the Major Crimes Act present these normative questions, it also raises a profound question of constitutional law — whether Congress has the power to make laws regulating intratribal matters. That issue came before the United States Supreme Court shortly after the Major Crimes Act went into effect.

2.   The Rise of Federal Plenary Power

UNITED STATES v. KAGAMA
United States Supreme Court
118 U.S. 375 (1886)

[This case, which tests the constitutionality of the Major Crimes Act, arose when the accused, an Indian, demurred to an indictment charging him with the murder of another Indian on the Hoopa Valley Indian Reservation in California. The circuit and district judges divided on the demurrer, and the issue was certified to the Supreme Court.]

Mr. Justice Miller delivered the opinion of the Court.

[As originally adopted, the Major Crimes Act stated:]

§ 9. That immediately upon and after the date of the passage of this act all Indians committing against the person or property of another Indian or other person any of the following crimes, namely, murder, manslaughter, rape, assault with intent to kill, arson, burglary and larceny, within any Territory of the United States, and either within or without the Indian reservation, shall be subject therefor to the laws of said Territory relating to said crimes, and shall be tried therefor in the same courts and in the same manner, and shall be subject to the same penalties, as are all other persons charged with the commission of the said crimes, respectively; and the said courts are hereby given jurisdiction in all such cases; and all such Indians committing any of the above crimes against the person or property of another Indian or other person, within the boundaries of any State of the United States, and within the limits of any Indian reservation, shall be subject to the same laws, tried in the same courts and in the same manner, and subject to the same penalties, as are all other persons committing any of the above crimes within the exclusive jurisdiction of the United States. 23 Stat. ch. 341, 362; § 9, 385.

[T]he offence charged in this indictment was committed within a State and not within a Territory, [but] the considerations which are necessary to a solution of the problem in regard to the one must in a large degree affect the other.

The Constitution of the United States is almost silent in regard to the relations of the government which was established by it to the numerous tribes of Indians within its borders.

In declaring the basis on which representation in the lower branch of the Congress and direct taxation should be apportioned, it was fixed that it should be according to numbers, *excluding Indians not taxed*, which, of course, excluded nearly all of that race, but which meant that if there were such within a State as were taxed to support the government, they should be counted for representation, and in the computation for direct taxes levied by the United States. This expression, excluding Indians not taxed, is found in the XIVth amendment, where it deals with the same subject under the new conditions produced by the emancipation of the slaves. Neither of these shed much light on the power of Congress over the Indians in their existence as tribes, distinct from the ordinary citizens of a State or Territory.

The mention of Indians in the Constitution which has received most attention is that found in the clause which gives Congress "power to regulate commerce with foreign nations and among the several States, and with the Indian tribes."

This clause is relied on in the argument in the present case, the proposition being that the statute under consideration is a regulation of commerce with the Indian tribes. But we think it would be a very strained construction of this clause, that a system of criminal laws for Indians living peaceably in their reservations, which left out the entire code of trade and intercourse laws justly enacted under that provision, and established punishments for the common-law crimes of murder, manslaughter, arson, burglary, larceny, and the like, without any reference to their relation to any kind of commerce, was authorized by the grant of power to regulate commerce with the Indian tribes. While we are not able to see, in either of these clauses of the Constitution and its amendments, any delegation of power to enact a code of criminal law for the punishment of the worst class of crimes known to civilized life when committed by Indians, there is a suggestion in the manner in which the Indian tribes are introduced into that clause, which may have a bearing on the subject before us. The commerce with foreign nations is distinctly stated as submitted to the control of Congress. Were the Indian tribes foreign nations? If so, they came within the first of the three classes of commerce mentioned, and did not need to be repeated as Indian tribes. Were they nations, in the minds of the framers of the Constitution? If so, the natural phrase would have been "foreign nations and Indian nations," or, in the terseness of language uniformly used by the framers of the instrument, it would naturally have been "foreign and Indian nations." And so in [*Cherokee Nation v. Georgia*, set forth and discussed in this chapter,] brought in the Supreme Court of the United States, under the declaration that the judicial power extends to suits between a State and foreign States, and giving to the Supreme Court original jurisdiction where a State is a party, it was conceded that Georgia as a State came within the clause, but held that the Cherokees were not a State or nation within the meaning of the Constitution, so as to be able to maintain the suit.

But these Indians are within the geographical limits of the United States. The soil and the people within these limits are under the political control of the Government of the United States, or of the States of the Union. There exist within the broad domain of sovereignty but these two. There may be cities, counties, and other organized bodies with limited legislative functions, but they are all derived from, or exist in, subordination to one or the other of these. The territorial governments owe all their powers to the statutes of the United States conferring on them the powers which they exercise, and which are liable to be withdrawn, modified, or repealed at any time by Congress. What authority the State governments may have to enact criminal laws for the Indians will be presently considered. But this power of Congress to organize territorial governments, and make laws for their inhabitants, arises not so much from the clause in the Constitution in regard to disposing of and making rules and regulations concerning the Territory and other property of the United States, as from the ownership of the country in which the Territories are, and the right of exclusive sovereignty which must exist in the National Government, and can be found nowhere else.

[The Hoopa Valley reservation] is land bought by the United States from Mexico by the treaty of Guadaloupe Hidalgo, and the whole of California, with the allegiance of its inhabitants, many of whom were Indians, was transferred by that treaty to the United States.

The relation of the Indian tribes living within the borders of the United States, both before and since the Revolution, to the people of the United States has always been an anomalous one and of a complex character.

[Indians] were, and always have been, regarded as having a semi-independent position when they preserved their tribal relations; not as States, not as nations, not as possessed of the full attributes of sovereignty, but as a separate people, with the power of regulating their internal and social relations, and thus far not brought under the laws of the Union or of the State within whose limits they resided.

Perhaps the best statement of their position is found in the two opinions of this court by Chief Justice Marshall in [*Cherokee Nation v. Georgia*] and [*Worcester v. Georgia*]. In the first of the above cases it was held that these tribes were neither States nor nations, had only some of the attributes of sovereignty, and could not be so far recognized in that capacity as to sustain a suit in the Supreme Court of the United States. In the second case it was said that they were not subject to the jurisdiction asserted over them by the State of Georgia, which, because they were within its limits, where they had been for ages, had attempted to extend her laws and the jurisdiction of her courts over them.

In the opinions in these cases they are spoken of as "wards of the nation," "pupils," as local dependent communities. In this spirit the United States has conducted its relations to them from its organization to this time. But, after an experience of a hundred years of the treaty-making system of government, Congress has determined upon a new departure — to govern them by acts of Congress. This is seen in the act of March 3, 1871, embodied in § 2079 of the Revised Statutes:

> No Indian nation or tribe, within the territory of the United States shall be acknowledged or recognized as an independent nation, tribe, or power, with whom the United States may contract by treaty; but no obligation of any treaty lawfully made and ratified with any such Indian nation or tribe prior to March third, eighteen hundred and seventy one, shall be hereby invalidated or impaired.

The case of *Crow Dog*, 109 U.S. 556, in which an agreement with the Sioux Indians, ratified by an act of Congress, was supposed to extend over them the laws of the United States and the jurisdiction of its courts, covering murder and other grave crimes, shows the purpose of Congress in this new departure. The decision in that case admits that if the intention of Congress had been to punish, by the United States courts, the murder of one Indian by another, the law would have been valid. But the court could not see, in the agreement with the Indians sanctioned by Congress, a purpose to repeal § 2146 of the Revised Statutes, which expressly excludes from that jurisdiction the case of a crime committed by one Indian against another in the Indian country. The passage of the act now under consideration was designed to remove that objection, and to go further by including such crimes on reservations lying within a State.

Is this latter fact a fatal objection to the law? [Does federal] authority extend to this case?

It seems to us that this is within the competency of Congress. These Indian tribes *are* the wards of the nation. They are communities *dependent* on the United States. Dependent largely for their daily food. Dependent for their political rights. They owe no allegiance to the States, and receive from them no protection. Because of the local ill feeling, the people of the States where they are found are often their deadliest enemies. From their very weakness and helplessness, so largely due to the course of dealing of the federal government with them and the treaties in which it has been promised, there arises the duty of protection, and with it the power. This has always been recognized by the Executive and by Congress, and by this court, whenever the question has arisen [in past cases such as *Worcester v. Georgia*].

The power of the General Government over these remnants of a race once powerful, now weak and diminished in numbers, is necessary to their protection, as well as to the safety of those among whom they dwell. It must exist in that government, because it never has existed anywhere else, because the theatre of its exercise is within the geographical limits of the United States, because it has never been denied, and because it alone can enforce its laws on all the tribes.

[The law is constitutional; thus the district court has jurisdiction.]

NOTES ON *KAGAMA*

1. **"Deadliest Enemies":** When the *Kagama* Court referred to the states as the tribes' "deadliest enemies," it was not employing a mere figure of speech. In California, where the *Kagama* case arose, non-Indians had been hunting down and killing Indian men, women, and children in a systematic project of extermination. *See* EXTERMINATE THEM! WRITTEN ACCOUNTS OF THE MURDER, RAPE, AND ENSLAVEMENT OF NATIVE AMERICANS DURING THE GOLD RUSH (Clifford Trafzer & Joel Hyer eds., 1999).

2. **Historical Background of Federal Indian Country Criminal Laws:** As the Supreme Court's decision in *Ex parte Crow Dog* made clear, prior to the enactment of the Major Crimes Act, the federal government exercised almost no governing authority over tribal Indians for actions undertaken by them in Indian country. Their governance was left exclusively to the Indian tribes. The only exception to this statement was the General Crimes Act (sometimes also known as the Indian Country Crimes Act), first enacted in 1817, and now codified at 18 U.S.C. § 1152. This statute afforded the federal government jurisdiction to criminally try and punish Indians who committed crimes in Indian country against the person or property of non-Indian citizens of the United States, albeit only if they had not already been punished by the laws of the tribe. As noted earlier, this statute is not unlike modern statutes designed to protect United States citizens abroad that rely primarily on foreign governments for their protection but afford federal jurisdiction as a supplement or backstop to that protection. Thus, until the enactment of the Major Crimes Act in 1885, federal Indian policy and, perhaps, American constitutional law assumed that the governance of Indian country rested almost exclusively with the tribes, and the federal government could exercise almost no role in that arena without tribal consent. For a good survey of the history of the enactment of the Major Crimes Act and the background of the *Kagama* case, see SIDNEY L. HARRING, CROW DOG'S CASE: AMERICAN INDIAN SOVEREIGNTY, TRIBAL LAW, AND UNITED STATES LAW IN THE NINETEENTH CENTURY 142–74 (1994). *See also,* Sidney L. Harring, *The Distorted History That Gave Rise to the "So Called" Plenary Power Doctrine: The Story of* United States v. Kagama *in* INDIAN LAW STORIES (Carole Goldberg, Kevin K. Washburn, and Philip P. Frickey, eds., 2011). *Kagama*, therefore, marked a major turning point in American constitutional analysis. While the phrase is never employed in the opinion, the *Kagama* decision represented the origins of the idea

of federal plenary power over Indians, an idea that arose comparatively quite late in the history of contact between Indians and Euro-American settlers.

In analyzing the extraordinary expansion of national power over Indian tribes contemplated by the *Kagama* decision, consider that the United States in the second half of the nineteenth century was engaged in the same type of colonial rush that characterized the European nations in their efforts to involuntarily annex other countries. The American will to "empire" is perhaps represented by its acquisition of large portions of Mexico following the Mexican-American War and 1848 Treaty of Guadalupe Hidalgo, its annexation of Cuba and the Philippines as a result of the Spanish American War, the overthrow of the indigenous Hawaiian Monarchy by the American military in 1893 and the subsequent annexation of the "Republic of Hawaii," first as an American territory and then as a state of the Union. *Kagama* and the subsequent development of the "plenary power doctrine" within federal Indian law can be seen as part of this colonialist impulse. *See generally* Robert N. Clinton, *There Is No Federal Supremacy Clause for Indian Tribes*, 34 ARIZ. ST. L.J. 113, 162–205 (2002).

3. Doctrinal Basis for Federal Plenary Power: In her outstanding study of the roots of the notion of federal plenary power over Indian tribes, Dean Nell Jessup Newton offered the following:

> In seeking to justify this assertion of federal power, however, the Court [in *Kagama*] had, through its earlier decisions, painted itself into a corner. In the first place, congressional power to regulate activities within the territories [using the property clause of Article IV, § 2] could not be invoked, because the land was within the state of California. Nor could the power to regulate Indian commerce be used, since at that time, the Court required a direct nexus with commerce to sustain federal laws regulating interstate and Indian commerce. The power to enact a criminal code applicable within the states, although fairly well-established today, was beyond the grant of power to regulate commerce with Indian tribes in 1885. Finally, the congressional power to effectuate treaties with Indian tribes was similarly inapplicable, since no treaty was involved.

Nell Jessup Newton, *Federal Power over Indians: Its Sources, Scope, and Limitations*, 132 U. PA. L. REV. 195, 213–14 (1984). Did the *Kagama* Court's solution to the dilemma that Dean Newton raises comport with traditional notions of American constitutional law?

Basic American constitutional law requires that exercises of congressional power be rooted in a textual grant of power to Congress reflected in the text of the United States Constitution. As Chief Justice Marshall put it in *McCulloch v. Maryland*, "Let the end be legitimate, let it be within the scope of the constitution, and all means which are appropriate, which are plainly adopted to that end, which are not prohibited, but consistent with the letter and spirit of the constitution, are constitutional." Is the analysis employed in *Kagama* consistent with this conventional approach to determining the scope of federal legislative power? Is the federal trusteeship upon which *Kagama* relies a legitimate "end" within the scope of the Constitution, as Chief Justice Marshall employed that term?

Notice that the only textual grant of federal legislative authority implicating Indians in the United States Constitution is found in the Indian commerce clause of Article I, section 8, clause 3, granting Congress the power to regulate "Commerce . . . *with* the Indian Tribes." That phrase, of course, subsumes the commerce *with*, not *of*, the Indian tribes and employs precisely the same phrase used in the same clause to describe commerce "*with* Foreign nations." Did the *Kagama* opinion rely on the Indian commerce clause as the source of the broad federal power over Indian affairs that it sustained? If not, what did it rely upon? Was that reliance based on any textual grant of power found in the Constitution of the type *McCulloch* conventionally would require? If not, what should we make of the doctrinal analysis contained in the *Kagama* opinion?

In sustaining the congressional power to enact the Major Crimes Act, the *Kagama* Court relied quite heavily on the trusteeship relationship announced in *Cherokee Nation v. Georgia*, 30 U.S. (5 Pet.) 1 (1831), set forth and discussed in this chapter. It then proceeded to announce in a recently often quoted phrase: "But these Indians are within the geographical limits of the United States. The soil and the people within these limits are under the political control of the Government of the United States, or of the States of the Union. There exist within the broad domain of sovereignty but these two."

Is the quoted statement at all consistent with the tenor and holding of the *Cherokee Nation* decision? What sovereign power did *Cherokee Nation* recognize as within the geographic limits of the United States that is omitted from the quoted phrase? In *Worcester v. Georgia*, 31 U.S. (6 Pet.) 515, 552 (1832), Chief Justice Marshall, referring to the obligations of protection contained in the Cherokee treaties, wrote "The Cherokees acknowledge themselves to be under the protection of the United States, and of no other power. Protection does not imply the destruction of the protected." Is *Kagama* consistent with this maxim? How, if at all, had changes in the history of tribal-federal relations between the time *Cherokee Nation* was decided in 1831 and the time *Kagama* was decided in 1886 contributed to the doctrinal differences in these two cases? Should such changes have affected the scope of federal constitutional power over Indian tribes? Should federal legislative power expand through judicial interpretation to fill perceived federal needs in Indian affairs or should a constitutional amendment be required to supply such changes? Both *Cherokee Nation* and *Kagama* rely on a federal trusteeship over Indian tribes, but do they employ the concept in the same manner? In *Kagama* the trusteeship appears to be a source of federal power *over* the Indian tribes and their members. Did *Cherokee Nation* employ the trusteeship as a sword to be used against the Indian tribes? If not, did the *Kagama* opinion pervert the original understanding of the trusteeship? Indeed, might it be argued that *Kagama* turned the trusteeship notion advanced in *Cherokee Nation* on its head and used it in precisely the opposite of the manner in which Chief Justice Marshall employed it in *Cherokee Nation?* If so, how?

4. Native Responses to the Major Crimes Act: Calls for repeal or curtailment of the Major Crimes Act have been a staple of contemporary Native scholarship challenging the colonial domination model of federal Indian law. *See, e.g.*, Robert Porter, *A Proposal to the* Hanodaganyas *to Decolonize Federal Indian Control Law*, 31 U. MICH. J. L. REFORM 899, 994–95 (1998) (supporting exclusive tribal jurisdiction over all crimes committed by Indians who have been "punished in accordance with the laws of the Indian nation in which the crime occurred"); Kevin Washburn, *Federal Criminal Law and Tribal Self-Determination*, 84 N.C. L. REV. 779, 854 (2006) (describing the Major Crimes Act as an "unfortunate anachronism" in an era of federal policy supporting tribal self-determination). By the year 2000, many Indian nations had developed tribal court systems with criminal justice machinery that, at least outwardly, resembles the non-Indian criminal courts. Should the Major Crimes Act be treated as only a temporary measure — an intervention by Congress that was necessary only so long as the tribes did not develop adequate judicial machinery more in conformity with American traditions? Would repeal of the Major Crimes Act at that point merely demonstrate that the process of colonial domination has been complete?

United States v. Clapox, 35 F. 575 (D.C. Or. 1888): The United States prosecuted several Umatilla tribal members for aiding another tribal member to escape from a federal detention facility erected on the reservation. The escaped prisoner was being held pending trial for violation of a provision of the Code of Indian Offenses promulgated by the Secretary of the Interior, which included a prohibition on "living and cohabiting" on the reservation with a person other than one's spouse. It also penalized other activities such as ceremonial dances (including the sun dance), polygamy, "the usual practices of so-called medicine-men," destruction or theft of Indian property, and "misdemeanors committed by Indians belonging to the reservation." This same Code provided for a Court of Indian Offenses and an Indian police force, as well as the erection of a jail for purposes of punishment or examination. The officers of the Indian police force, acting under the direction of the BIA agent assigned to the reservation, had broad authority to arrest any Indian for alleged violation of the Code, and to commit that person to jail for examination or trial before the Court of Indian Offenses, a court that acted without written warrants or written records of its findings or judgments.

Defendants questioned whether the Department of the Interior had authority to define "Indian offenses," or establish courts for the punishment of Indian offenders, as set forth in the Secretary's rules. District Court Judge Deady ruled,

> By article 8 of the treaty of June 9, 1855 (12 St. 948) [with the Umatilla,] it is provided:
>
> > The confederate bands acknowledge their dependence on the government of the United States, . . . and engage to submit to and observe all laws, rules and regulations which may be prescribed by the United States for the government of said Indians.
>
> The Revised Statutes provide:
>
> > Sec. 441. The secretary of the interior is charged with the supervision of the public business relating to the . . . Indians.
>
> > Sec. 463. The commissioner of Indian affairs shall, under the direction of the secretary of the interior, and agreeably to such regulations as the President may prescribe, have the management of all Indian affairs, and of all matters arising out of the Indian relations.

Sec. 465. The President may prescribe such regulations as he may think fit for carrying into effect the various provisions of any act relating to Indian affairs.

By this treaty the Umatilla Indians engaged to submit to any rule that might be prescribed by the United States for their government. This obviously includes the power to organize and maintain this Indian court and police, and to specify the acts or conduct concerning which it shall have jurisdiction. This treaty is an "act" or law "relating to Indian affairs" — the affairs of these Indians; and by said section 465 the power to prescribe a rule for carrying the same into effect is given to the President, who has exercised the same in this case through the proper instrumentality — the Secretary of the Interior.

Then there is the general power given by said sections 441 and 463 to the President, acting through the Secretary of the Interior and the Commissioner of Indian Affairs, to make regulations for the "management of all Indian affairs, and of all matters arising out of the Indian relations."

These "courts of Indian offenses" are not the constitutional courts provided for in section I, art. 3, Const., which Congress only has the power to "ordain and establish," but mere educational and disciplinary instrumentalities, by which the government of the United States is endeavoring to improve and elevate the condition of these dependent tribes to whom it sustains the relation of guardian. In fact, the reservation itself is in the nature of a "school," and the Indians are gathered there, under the charge of an agent, for the purpose of acquiring the habits, ideas, and aspirations which distinguish the civilized from the uncivilized man.

[I]n conclusion, the act with which these defendants are charged is in flagrant opposition to the authority of the United States on this reservation, and directly subversive of this laudable effort to accustom and educate these Indians in the habit and knowledge of self-government. It is therefore appropriate and needful that the power and name of the government of the United States should be invoked to restrain and punish them. The case falls within the letter of the statute providing for the punishment of persons who are guilty of rescuing any one committed for an offense against the United States.

The demurrer is overruled.

NOTES

1.   **Federal Power and the Assimilative Goals of Reservations:** The federal government saw legal institutions as educational tools in the nineteenth-century reservation context. Self-governance was good not only because it enhanced the possibility of order, but also because it provided a special classroom for Indian wards, in the ideology of the times, to absorb the methods of the mainstream society. In this view, the reservation was a way station between the society prior to the advent of the European settlers and the society when reservations would no longer be needed.

If the rules on the reservation are designed to civilize, then to what extent is it deleterious for such rules to reflect Indian ways and customs? If the agent is the "teacher," should the agent or the federal government write the rules, or it is part of the lesson that the Indian nations themselves engage in legislative activity? Note that the Indian Reorganization Act of 1934, which appeared to empower Native nations to write their own constitutions and laws, was administered in such a way that BIA agents had considerable influence over such enactments. *See* Ch. 3, Sec. C.1.

In order to implement the Code and Courts of Indian Offenses, the United States not only had to assert the vaguely supported power identified in *Kagama*, it had to contend with Article III of the Constitution, which allows only certain types of courts (with judges enjoying lifetime tenure and irreducible salaries) to exercise federal "judicial power." Outside the Indian law context, the Supreme Court determined, nearly 100 years after *Clapox*, that Congress may employ non-Article III courts "to accommodate plenary grants of power to Congress to legislate with respect to specialized areas having particularized needs and warranting distinctive treatment." *Palmore v. United States*, 411 U.S. 389 (1973). Does that language sustain the result in *Clapox*?

2.   **Indian Resistance to Assimilation:** Tribal members confined on reservations under BIA supervision often did not make model pupils. Despite losing much of their land base and food supply, they carried out warfare and raids, protected their homelands, hid their children rather than send them to BIA boarding schools, and continued their sacred practices. As Salish scholar Luana Ross has shown, the high incidence of Natives arrested for offenses such as adultery, traditional dancing, and vagrancy indicates the persistence of a Native belief in their right to determine their own way of life. LUANA ROSS, INVENTING THE SAVAGE: THE SOCIAL CONSTRUCTION OF NATIVE AMERICAN CRIMINALITY 34–45 (1998). Traditional methods of governance and dispute resolution often went underground. *See* DUANE CHAMPAGNE, AMERICAN INDIAN SOCIETIES: STRATEGIES AND CONDITIONS OF POLITICAL AND CULTURAL SURVIVAL (2d ed. 1989). Spiritual revitalization movements, such as the Ghost Dance religion of the late nineteenth century, attracted many tribal members with the promise of cataclysmic events that would rid their territory of Euro-American intruders. As one Blackfeet Native stated regarding the ban on the Sun Dance,

> I do not understand why the white men desire to put an end to our religious ceremonials. What harm can they do to our people? If they deprive us of our religion, we will have nothing left, for we know of no other that can take its place. . . . We do not understand the white man's religion. The Black Robes (Catholic Priests) teach us one thing and the Men-with-white-neckties (Protestant Missionaries) teach us another; so we are confused.

Anonymous, quoted in NATIVE AMERICAN TESTIMONY 225 (P. Nabokov, ed., 1992).

LONE WOLF v. HITCHCOCK
United States Supreme Court
187 U.S. 553 (1903)

[Lone Wolf and other members of the Kiowa, Comanche, and Apache tribes brought a class suit seeking declaratory and injunctive relief to prevent the Secretary of the Interior from implementing a statute directing the sale of over 2 million acres of "surplus" Indian land (land not needed for allotment to tribal members) ceded by the Tribes to the federal government. The cession resulted from an agreement allegedly signed by three-fourths of the adult males of the Tribes as required by prior treaties. Tribal members claimed that the number of signatures was insufficient, that the signatures had been obtained by fraud and concealment, and that, therefore, the agreement had not been approved by the requisite three-quarters majority. Nevertheless Congress enacted the statute, which differed from the agreement in a number of respects. The plaintiffs claimed the statute was invalid because it violated the treaty requirement of approval by an extraordinary majority and because it took their property without due process of law. When relief was denied, this appeal followed.]

Mr. Justice White [delivered the opinion of the Court].

[The Treaty of Medicine Lodge, 15 Stat. 581, article 12] reads as follows:

> Article 12. No treaty for the cession of any portion or part of the reservation herein described, which may be held in common, shall be of any validity or force as against the said Indians, unless executed and signed by at least three fourths of all the adult male Indians occupying the same, and no cession by the tribe shall be understood or construed in such manner as to deprive, without his consent, any individual member of the tribe of his rights to any tract of land selected by him as provided in article III (VI) of this treaty.

The appellants base their right to relief on the proposition that by the effect of the article just quoted the confederated tribes of Kiowas, Comanches, and Apaches were vested with an interest in the lands held in common within the reservation, which interest could not be divested by Congress in any other mode than that specified in the said twelfth article, and that as a result of the said stipulation the interest of the Indians in the common lands fell within the protection of the fifth amendment to the Constitution of the United States, and such interest — indirectly at least — came under the control of the judicial branch of the government. We are unable to yield our assent to this view.

The contention in effect ignores the status of the contracting Indians and the relation of dependency they bore and continue to bear towards the government of the United States. To uphold the claim would be to adjudge that the indirect operation of the treaty was to materially limit and qualify the controlling authority of Congress in respect to the care and protection of the Indians, and to deprive Congress, in a possible emergency, when the necessity might be urgent for a partition and disposal of the tribal lands, of all power to act, if the assent of the Indians could not be obtained.

Now, it is true that in decisions of this court, the Indian right of occupancy of tribal lands, whether declared in a treaty or otherwise created, has been stated to be sacred, or, as sometimes expressed, as sacred as the fee of the United States in the same lands. [*E.g., Johnson v. M'Intosh; Cherokee Nation v. Georgia; Worcester v. Georgia.*] But in none of these cases was there involved a controversy between Indians and the government respecting the power of Congress to administer the property of the Indians. [These cases involved third parties who traced title to Indians. Only the United States has the power to interfere with Indian occupancy.] "It is to be presumed that in this matter the United States would be governed by such considerations of justice as would control a Christian people in their treatment of an ignorant and dependent race." [*Beecher v. Wetherby*, 95 U.S. 517, 525 (1877).]

Plenary authority over the tribal relations of the Indians has been exercised by Congress from the beginning, and the power has always been deemed a political one, not subject to be controlled by the judicial department of the government. Until the year 1871 the policy was pursued of dealing with the Indian tribes by means of treaties, and, of course, a moral obligation rested upon Congress to act in good faith in performing the stipulations entered into on its behalf. But, as with treaties made with foreign nations, *Chinese Exclusion Case*, 130 U.S. 581, 600, the legislative power might pass laws in conflict with treaties made with the Indians.

The power exists to abrogate the provisions of an Indian treaty, though presumably such power will be exercised only when circumstances arise which will not only justify the government in disregarding the stipulations of the treaty, but may demand, in the interest of the country and the Indians themselves, that it should do so. When, therefore, treaties were entered into between the United States and a tribe of Indians it was never doubted that the *power* to abrogate existed in Congress, and that in a contingency such power might be availed of from considerations of governmental policy, particularly if consistent with perfect good faith towards the Indians. In [*Kagama,*] speaking of the Indians, the court said:

> The power of the general government over these remnants of a race once powerful, now weak and diminished in numbers, is necessary to their protection, as well as to the safety of those among whom they dwell. It must exist in that government, because it never has existed anywhere else, because the theatre of its exercise is within the geographical limits of the United States, because it has never been denied, and because it alone can enforce its laws on all the tribes.

That Indians who had not been fully emancipated from the control and protection of the United States are subject, at least so far as the tribal lands were concerned, to be controlled by direct legislation of Congress, is also declared in *Choctaw Nation v. United States*, 119 U.S. 1, 27, and *Stephens v. Cherokee Nation*, 174 U.S. 445, 483.

In view of the legislative power possessed by Congress over treaties with the Indians and Indian tribal property, we may not specially consider the contentions pressed upon our notice that the signing by the Indians of the agreement of October 6, 1892, was obtained by fraudulent misrepresentations and concealment, that the requisite three fourths of adult male Indians had not signed, as required by the twelfth article of the treaty of 1867, and that the treaty as signed had been amended by Congress without submitting such amendments to the action of the Indians, since all these matters, in any event, were solely within the domain of the legislative authority and its action is conclusive upon the courts.

The act of June 6, 1900, which is complained of in the bill, was enacted at a time when the tribal relations between the confederated tribes of Kiowas, Comanches and Apaches still existed, and that statute and the statutes supplementary thereto dealt with the disposition of tribal property and purported to give an adequate consideration for the surplus lands not allotted among the Indians or reserved for their benefit. Indeed, the controversy which this case presents is concluded by the decision in *Cherokee Nation v. Hitchcock*, 187 U.S. 294, decided at this term, where it was held that full administrative power was possessed by Congress over Indian tribal property. In effect, the action of Congress now complained of was but an exercise of such power, a mere change in the form of investment of Indian tribal property, the property of those who, as we have held, were in substantial effect the wards of the government. We must presume that Congress acted in perfect good faith in the dealings with the Indians of which complaint is made, and that the legislative branch of the government exercised its best judgment in the premises. In any event, as Congress possessed full power in the matter, the judiciary cannot question or inquire into the motives which prompted the enactment of this legislation. If injury was occasioned, which we do not wish to be understood as implying, by the use made by Congress of its power, relief must be sought by an appeal to that body for redress and not to the courts. The legislation in question was constitutional, and the demurrer to the bill was therefore rightly sustained.

[*Affirmed.*]

NOTES ON *LONE WOLF*

1. **Historical Background:** The Major Crimes Act of 1885 and the Dawes General Allotment Act of 1887 together represented the first major federal assaults on the long-standing ability of the Indian tribes to govern themselves free from federal or state laws. The Dawes General Allotment Act sought to significantly diminish tribal authority by depriving the traditional leadership of control over communal resources. Thus, along with *Kagama, Lone Wolf* embodied the major federal judicial rationalization for the late nineteenth century expansion of colonial power over the tribes. For an excellent survey of the history of federal policies, pressure, and fraud that produced the *Lone Wolf* decision, see BLUE CLARK, LONE WOLF V. HITCHCOCK: TREATY RIGHTS AND INDIAN LAW AT THE END OF THE NINETEENTH CENTURY (1994). For a detailed accounting of the historical and legal background of the case, *see* Angela R. Riley, *The Apex of Congress' Plenary Power over Indian Affairs: The Story of* Lone Wolf v. Hitchcock *in* INDIAN LAW STORIES (Carole Goldberg, Kevin K. Washburn, and Philip P. Frickey, eds., 2011). One federal judge said, "[t]he day *Lone Wolf* was handed down, January 5, 1903, might be called one of the blackest days in the history of the American Indian, the Indians' Dred Scott decision." *Sioux Nation v. United States*, 601 F.2d 1157, 1173 (Ct. Cl. 1979) (Nichols, J., concurring), *aff'd*, 448 U.S. 371 (1980). Do you agree or did this comment constitute a gross overstatement?

Lone Wolf claims that "[p]lenary authority over the tribal relations of the Indians has been exercised by Congress from the beginning." Almost no statement in an Indian law case offered by the United States Supreme Court could be further from the truth. In reality, the term plenary power had only once, four years earlier, been previously employed by a majority of the United States Supreme Court to describe federal congressional authority over Indian affairs. *Stephens v. Cherokee Nation*, 174 U.S. 445 (1899) (sustaining the power of Congress to create a federal court to hear 174 tribal citizenship and enrollment appeals on issues governing allotment in the Indian Territory). Rather, until the enactment of the Major Crimes Act in 1885, the Indian tribes had near total control over both their members and their territory and almost no federal governing power ever previously existed for either. Thus, for example, until the 1890s, despite proposals to contrary, no federal court ever existed that had direct jurisdiction over the Indian Territory. Indeed, as recently as *Elk v. Wilkins*, 112 U.S. 94 (1884), the Court had held that Indians were not subject to the jurisdiction of the United States. What was happening in federal Indian policy that made the growth of the notion of a federal plenary power over Indians a convenient rationalization? Given the provisions on land cessions of the Medicine Lodge Treaty, which were also found in several other treaties, could the prevailing federal allotment and assimilation policies easily be implemented without a federal plenary power that afforded the national government the ability to ignore or sweep away its prior treaty commitments?

However dubious the historical lineage of the plenary power doctrine, since the late nineteenth century, the Court has often repeated the doctrine that Congress possesses plenary power to regulate Indian affairs. *See, e.g., Stephens v. Cherokee Nation*, 174 U.S. 445, 484–86, 491 (1899), *supra*; *Perrin v. United States*, 232 U.S. 478, 482 (1914) (liquor regulation); *United States v. Ramsey*, 271 U.S. 467, 471 (1926) (same).

2.   **Another View of the Treaty Abrogation Question:** In an interesting effort to reconsider the basic tenets of federal Indian law, Professor Robert Porter undertook a project to reargue some of the major landmark cases to a panel of tribal judges, which he called the American Indian Nations Supreme Court. These judges, of course, sat without any delegated legal authority, but served as a forum of public tribal conscience, not unlike some of the tribunals conducted during the Viet Nam War by the noted British philosopher Bertrand Russell. The American Indian Nations Supreme Court generated a very different response to the *Lone Wolf* treaty abrogation question, finding that:

> under the tribal laws, customs, and political understandings of most tribes in the United States, including the KCAs, no single party to a treaty has any authority to legally or morally unilaterally terminate, abrogate, or modify the agreement. To do so would be a gross breach of respect due to allied family members and bring great shame and moral approbation on the transgressor. Thus, under the laws of the tribes served by this Court, the Court is bound to hold that the United States has no power whatsoever to breach the Medicine Lodge Treaty by adopting the 1900 legislation. In order for the 1900 legislation to be valid, the United States would have needed to validly secure the knowing signatures of three-fourths of the

adult males of the KCA tribes, which it admittedly did not do. Therefore, the 1900 legislation cannot and will not be recognized as valid by any tribal court.

Lone Wolf v. Hitchcock, *In the Supreme Court of the American Indian Nations*, 8 KAN. J.L. & PUB. POL'Y 174, 185 (1999).

The American Indian Nations Supreme Court's opinion was based on tribal customary law and the documented fact that Indian tribes generally understood the diplomacy involved in treaty negotiations as a means of establishing kinship obligations to an extended "family" of political relationships. The "Great Father" metaphor was not an "icon of superiority," as many Europeans might assume, but rather a "political metaphor that captured the Indian understanding of the obligations that Euro-American governments assumed in the treaty process." Given the fact that the United States voluntarily adopted the metaphors of tribal kinship relationships in negotiating Indian treaties, should it also assume a duty to interpret those obligations as Native peoples would have understood them? Is *Lone Wolf* consistent with the canon of treaty construction first announced in *Worcester v. Georgia*, 31 U.S. (6 Pet.) 515 (1832), that Indian treaties should be interpreted as the Indian parties to the treaty would have understood them? For more on the canons of construction, *see* Ch. 2, Sec. C.

3. International and Indian Treaties: *Lone Wolf* correctly makes the point that the United States has the constitutional power to unilaterally abrogate its international treaties, a power it sometimes must exercise as a result of changed circumstances. That power continues today. *E.g., Goldwater v. Carter*, 444 U.S. 996 (1979) (treating as a political question the procedural issue of how the power of unilateral treaty abrogation should be exercised). Are the consequences of unilaterally abrogating a foreign treaty the same as unilaterally abrogating an Indian treaty? Does it make any difference that Indian tribes are geographically within the exterior boundaries of the United States and foreign nations are not? Does unilateral abrogation of a foreign treaty enlarge United States sovereignty over the foreign government, its lands, or people? Did abrogation of the Medicine Lodge Treaty do so in *Lone Wolf* to the Kiowa, Comanche, and Apache? Is this difference a sufficient reason to formulate a different rule for Indian treaties?

4. Another Application of the *Lone Wolf* Doctrine: The Fort Laramie Treaty of 1868 set apart the Great Sioux Reservation for the "absolute and undisturbed use and occupation" of the Sioux Nation. Treaty of Fort Laramie with the Sioux Nation and others, April 29, 1868, Art. 2, 15 Stat. 635. The Great Sioux Reservation included the *Paha Sapa*, the Black Hills, which represent the sacred center of the Lakota universe. After General George Armstrong Custer provoked a gold rush by white prospectors in the Black Hills by leading a well publicized military expedition into the Hills which found gold, Lakota raids on trespassing prospectors became common. The military's effort to stamp out Lakota resistance to the trespasses into their territory ultimately produced the fateful Battle of Greasy Grass (Little Big Horn) that led to the defeat of General Custer and his Seventh Cavalry when they attacked a huge Sioux encampment.

As retaliation for that defeat, the United States government sought to deprive the Sioux of ownership of the Black Hills. Apparently, not believing that it had unilateral authority to do so, the federal government sent the Manypenny Commission to Sioux country to secure agreement of the Sioux to the sale, threatening to cut off the federal rations of the Lakota, which had become their primary source of subsistence as the Plains buffalo had been all but exterminated by white hunters. The Fort Laramie Treaty included a provision in Article 12 worded almost identically to the provision of the Medicine Lodge Treaty of 1868 at issue in *Lone Wolf* that required three-quarters adult male signatures for approving any treaty ceding any portion of the Great Sioux Reservation. As in the facts of *Lone Wolf*, the Manypenny Commission attempted to secure from the Sioux the necessary three-quarters signatures. These examples suggest that in both cases the federal government's behavior indicated that it then thought it was bound by the prior treaty provisions and could not alter them unilaterally. Unlike the Kiowa situation, however, the federal government never secured more than 10% of the signatures of the adult male Sioux tribal members. Nevertheless, the so-called agreement was returned to Washington, D.C. and in 1877 the Congress enacted the agreement as a statute with some changes. Act of Feb. 28, 1877, 19 Stat. 254. *See generally* EDWARD LAZARUS, BLACK HILLS/WHITE JUSTICE: THE SIOUX NATION VERSUS THE UNITED STATES 1775 TO THE PRESENT 71–95 (1991); John LaVelle, *Rescuing Paha Sapa: Achieving Environmental Justice by Restoring the Great Grasslands and Returning the Sacred Black Hills to the Great Sioux Nation*, 5 GREAT PLAINS NAT. RES. J. 40 (2001).

The Sioux continue to insist that they lawfully own the Black Hills, relying on the Fort Laramie Treaty to support their claim. How, if at all, does *Lone Wolf* affect the legal vitality of the Sioux claim to the Black Hills? Is the Sioux argument one that relies primarily on federal Indian law or is it more grounded in tribal understandings of the nature of a treaty and appeals to natural law and the moral justness of their claim? How should these approaches be weighed? This case, and the issues it raises, are discussed in Ch. 6, Sec. A.2.

UNITED STATES v. SANDOVAL
United States Supreme Court
231 U.S. 28 (1913)

MR. JUSTICE VAN DEVANTER delivered the opinion of the Court.

This is a criminal prosecution for introducing [liquor] into Indian country, [the Santa Clara Pueblo. The district court dismissed the indictment, holding the underlying statute unconstitutional because it encroached on the state's police power.]

The question to be considered, then, is, whether the status of the Pueblo Indians and their lands is such that Congress competently can prohibit the introduction of intoxicating liquor into those lands notwithstanding the admission of New Mexico to statehood.

There are as many as twenty Indian pueblos scattered over the State, having an aggregate population of over 8,000. The lands belonging to the several pueblos vary in quantity, but usually embrace about 17,000 acres, held in communal, fee simple ownership under grants from the King of Spain made during the Spanish sovereignty and confirmed by Congress since the acquisition of that territory by the United States. As respects six of the pueblos, one being the Santa Clara, adjacent public lands have been reserved by executive orders for the use and occupancy of the Indians.

The people of the pueblos, although sedentary rather than nomadic in their inclinations, and disposed to peace and industry, are nevertheless Indians in race, customs, and domestic government. Always living in separate and isolated communities, adhering to primitive modes of life, largely influenced by superstition and fetishism, and chiefly governed according to the crude customs inherited from their ancestors, they are essentially a simple, uninformed and inferior people. Upon the termination of the Spanish sovereignty they were given enlarged political and civil rights by Mexico, but it remains an open question whether they have become citizens of the United States. Be this as it may, they have been regarded and treated by the United States as requiring special consideration and protection, like other Indian communities. Thus, public moneys have been expended in presenting them with farming implements and utensils, and in their civilization and instruction; agents and superintendents have been provided to guard their interests; central training schools and day schools at the pueblos have been established and maintained for the education of their children; dams and irrigation works have been constructed to encourage and enable them to cultivate their lands and sustain themselves; public lands, as before indicated, have been reserved for their use and occupancy where their own lands were deemed inadequate; a special attorney has been employed since 1898, at an annual cost of $2,000, to represent them and maintain their rights; and when latterly the Territory undertook to tax their lands and other property, Congress forbade such taxation, [in a statute stating their lands and other property "shall be free and exempt from taxation of any sort whatsoever . . . until Congress shall otherwise provide." 33 Stat. 1048, 1069, c. 1479.]

[T]he reports of the superintendents charged with guarding their interests show that they are dependent upon the fostering care and protection of the Government, like reservation Indians in general; that, although industrially superior, they are intellectually and morally inferior to many of them; and that they are easy victims to the evils and debasing influence of intoxicants. [Examples follow:]

Santa Fe, 1905: "Until the old customs and Indian practices are broken among this people we cannot hope for a great amount of progress. The secret dance, from which all whites are excluded is perhaps one of the greatest evils. What goes on at this time I will not attempt to say, but I firmly believe that it is little less than a ribald system of debauchery."

[Under the Spanish] the Indians of the pueblos were treated as wards requiring special protection, were subjected to restraints and official supervision in the alienation of their property, and were the beneficiaries of a law [prohibiting the sale of wine to them.] After the Mexican succession they were elevated to citizenship and civil rights not before enjoyed, but whether the prior tutelage and restrictions were wholly terminated has been the subject of differing opinions.

[I]t is not necessary to dwell specially upon the legal status of this people under either Spanish or Mexican rule, for whether Indian communities within the limits of the United States may be subjected to its guardianship and protection as dependent wards turns upon other considerations. Not only does the Constitution expressly authorize Congress to regulate commerce with the Indian tribes, but long continued legislative and executive usage and an unbroken current of judicial decisions have attributed to the United States as a superior and civilized nation the power and the duty of exercising a fostering care and protection over all dependent Indian communities within its borders, whether within its original territory or territory subsequently acquired, and whether within or without the limits of a State. As was said by this court in [*Kagama*]: "The power of the General Government over these remnants of a race once powerful, now weak and diminished in numbers, is necessary to their protection, as well as to the safety of those among whom they dwell. It must exist in that government, because it never has existed anywhere else, because the theatre of its exercise is within the geographical limits of the United States, because it has never been denied, and because it alone can enforce its laws on all the tribes." In *Tiger v. Western Investment Co.*, 221 U.S. 286, 315, prior decisions were carefully reviewed and it was further said: "Taking these decisions together, it may be taken as the settled doctrine of this court that Congress, in pursuance of the long-established policy of the Government, has a right to determine for itself when the guardianship which has been maintained over the Indian shall cease. It is for that body, and not for the courts, to determine when the true interests of the Indian require his release from such condition of tutelage."

Of course, it is not meant by this that Congress may bring a community or body of people within the range of this power by arbitrarily calling them an Indian tribe, but only that in respect of distinctly Indian communities the questions whether, to what extent, and for what time they shall be recognized and dealt with as dependent tribes requiring the guardianship and protection of the United States are to be determined by Congress, and not by the courts.

As before indicated, by an uniform course of action beginning as early as 1854 and continued up to the present time, the legislative and executive branches of the Government have regarded and treated the Pueblos of New Mexico as dependent communities entitled to its aid and protection, like other Indian tribes, and, considering their Indian lineage, isolated and communal life, primitive customs and limited civilization, this assertion of guardianship over them cannot be said to be arbitrary but must be regarded as both authorized and controlling.

[The defendant argues that the legislation cannot be applied to the Pueblo Indians because they are citizens.] As before stated, whether they are citizens is an open question, and we need not determine it now, because citizenship is not in itself an obstacle to the exercise by Congress of its power to enact laws for the benefit and protection of tribal Indians as a dependent people.

It also is said that such legislation cannot be made to include the lands of the Pueblos, because the Indians have a fee simple title. It is true that the Indians of each pueblo do have such a title to all the lands connected therewith, excepting such as are occupied under executive orders, but it is a communal title, no individual owning any separate tract. In other words, the lands are public lands of the pueblo, and so the situation is essentially the same as it was with the Five Civilized Tribes, whose lands, although owned in fee under patents from the United States, were adjudged subject to the legislation of Congress enacted in the exercise of the Government's guardianship over those tribes and their affairs.

[Because it is] a legitimate exercise of [federal] power, the legislation in question does not encroach upon the police power of the State or disturb the principle of equality among the States.

[*Reversed.*]

NOTES ON *SANDOVAL*

1. **Historical Background:** Almost four decades before the Supreme Court decided *Sandoval*, it ruled in *United States v. Joseph*, 94 U.S. 614 (1877), that the Pueblo of Taos was not covered by a provision of the Trade and Intercourse Act of 1834 creating a penalty for settling on lands belonging to an Indian tribe. The ostensible reason for the decision was that the Pueblo people constituted sedentary, civilized agricultural communities that bore no resemblance to the more nomadic Indian tribes and therefore should not be treated as such. In his opinion for the Court, Justice Miller wrote:

> The character and history of these people are not obscure, but occupy a well-known page in the story of Mexico, from the conquest of the country by Cortez to the cession of this part of it to the United States by the treaty of Guadaloupe Hidalgo. The subject is tempting and full of interest, but we have only space for a few well-considered sentences of the opinion of the chief justice of the court whose judgment we are reviewing.
>
> "For centuries," he says, "the pueblo Indians have lived in villages, in fixed communities, each having its own municipal or local government. As far as their history can be traced, they have been a pastoral and agricultural people, raising flocks and cultivating the soil. Since the introduction of the Spanish Catholic missionary into the country, they have adopted mainly not only the Spanish language, but the religion of a Christian church. In every pueblo is erected a church, dedicated to the worship of God, according to the form of the Roman Catholic religion, and in nearly all is to be found a priest of this church, who is recognized as their spiritual guide and adviser. They manufacture nearly all of their blankets, clothing, agricultural and culinary implements, &c. Integrity and virtue among them is fostered and encouraged. They are as intelligent as most nations or people deprived of means or facilities for education. Their names, their customs, their habits, are similar to those of the people in whose midst they reside, or in the midst of whom their pueblos are situated. The criminal records of the courts of the Territory scarcely contain the name of a pueblo Indian. In short, they are a peaceable, industrious, intelligent, honest, and virtuous people. They are Indians only in feature, complexion, and a few of their habits; in all other respects superior to all but a few of the civilized Indian tribes of the country, and the equal of the most civilized thereof. This description of the pueblo Indians, I think, will be deemed by all who know them as faithful and true in all respects. Such was their character at the time of the

acquisition of New Mexico by the United States; such is their character now."

At the time the act of 1834 was passed there were no such Indians as these in the United States, unless it be one or two reservations or tribes, such as the Senecas or Oneidas of New York, to whom, it is clear, the eleventh section of the statute could have no application. When it became necessary to extend the laws regulating intercourse with the Indians over our new acquisitions from Mexico, there was ample room for the exercise of those laws among the nomadic Apaches, Comanches, Navajoes, and other tribes whose incapacity for self-government required both for themselves and for the citizens of the country this guardian care of the general government.

The pueblo Indians, if, indeed, they can be called Indians, had nothing in common with this class. The degree of civilization which they had attained centuries before, their willing submission to all the laws of the Mexican government, the full recognition by that government of all their civil rights, including that of voting and holding office, and their absorption into the general mass of the population (except that they held their lands in common), all forbid the idea that they should be classed with the Indian tribes for whom the intercourse acts were made, or that in the intent of the act of 1851 its provisions were applicable to them. The tribes for whom the act of 1834 was made were those semi-independent tribes whom our government has always recognized as exempt from our laws, whether within or without the limits of an organized State or Territory, and, in regard to their domestic government, left to their own rules and traditions; in whom we have recognized the capacity to make treaties, and with whom the governments, state and national, deal, with a few exceptions only, in their national or tribal character, and not as individuals.

If the pueblo Indians differ from the other inhabitants of New Mexico in holding lands in common, and in a certain patriarchal form of domestic life, they only resemble in this regard the Shakers and other communistic societies in this country, and cannot for that reason be classed with the Indian tribes of whom we have been speaking.

94 U.S. at 616–18. Can this description of the Pueblo peoples be reconciled with the picture painted in *Sandoval*? Perhaps the only change in the Pueblo lifestyle between 1876 when *Joseph* was decided and 1913 when *Sandoval* was decided was an increase in income occasioned by Fred Harvey's creation and promotion of their pottery sales as passenger rail traffic increased through their territory. So why did the Supreme Court in *Sandoval* describe the Pueblos as "dependent upon the fostering care and protection of the Government" while the *Joseph* Court described the same people as "a peaceable, industrious, intelligent, honest, and virtuous people?" Could these differences have anything to do with the origins and doctrinal justification for federal plenary power and, of course, nothing whatsoever to do with the people of the Pueblos? Perhaps the only commonality in the decisions in *Joseph* and *Sandoval* is that the tribal interests lose in *both* cases. What does that suggest about the nature of federal plenary power? For more on Sandoval, *see* Gerald Torres, *Who Is an Indian? The Story of* United States v. Sandoval *in* INDIAN LAW

STORIES (Carole Goldberg, Kevin K. Washburn, and Philip P. Frickey, eds., 2011).

2.   A Doctrine Rooted in Racial Prejudice? "The narrow question decided in the *Sandoval* case was that the dependent status of the Pueblo Indians was such that Congress could expressly prohibit the introduction of intoxicating liquors into their lands under its power '[t]o regulate Commerce . . . with the Indian Tribes.'" *Mountain States Tel. & Tel. Co. v. Pueblo of Santa Ana*, 472 U.S. 237, 242 (1985) (Stevens, J.) Given the narrow breadth of the issue, why did the Court delve into the Pueblo Indians' cultural practices and religious beliefs? One author has commented:

> The undisguised contempt for the native culture was unrelieved by an open-minded assessment in any of the principal cases studied. Rather, the Indians were described as semi-barbarous, savage, primitive, degraded, and ignorant. The relationship between the federal government and the Indian was frequently termed as one between a superior and inferior. The white race was called more intelligent and highly developed. There was no question but that a higher civilization was thought to be justly replacing that of a passing race whose time was over and whose existence could no longer be justified. The very weakness of the Indians in resisting the tide seemed to be one of their greatest moral shortcomings, but not as serious as the Indian communal tradition. To the white observer, the lack of proprietary interest generally displayed by tribal members was repulsive and backward. Removing the "herd" instinct was deemed by some to be the key to civilizing the Indian.

Nancy Carter, *Race and Power Politics as Aspects of Federal Guardianship over American Indians: Land-Related Cases, 1887–1924*, 4 AM. INDIAN L. REV. 197, 227 (1976).

Many other commentators have also been struck by the openly ethnocentric tone of the opinions of the plenary power era. *See, e.g.*, ROBERT BERKHOFER, JR., THE WHITE MAN'S INDIAN (1978); Robert A. Williams, Jr., *Documents of Barbarism: The Contemporary Legacy of European Racism and Colonialism in the Narrative Traditions of Federal Indian Law*, 31 ARIZ. L. REV. 237 (1989); Note, *Constitutional Law: Congressional Plenary Power over Indian Affairs — A Doctrine Rooted in Prejudice*, 10 AM. INDIAN L. REV. 117 (1982).

3.   Citizenship and Federal Plenary Power: While resting on highly questionable factual grounds, *Sandoval* nevertheless is important to modern federal Indian law as a consequence of its holding that "citizenship is not in itself an obstacle to the exercise by Congress of its power to enact laws for the benefit and protection of tribal Indians as a dependent people." At the time *Sandoval* was decided, most Indians, other than the Pueblos and others granted citizenship through the treaty ending the Mexican-American War, were not citizens of the United States. Notice, therefore, that the plenary power doctrine originally developed to govern Indians who had absolutely no opportunity through the ballot box or holding elective office to influence the laws that governed them. As you will see in Ch. 3, Sec. A.3.a, the United States Supreme Court has become increasingly concerned about tribal governance over peoples who cannot vote in tribal elections. *E.g., Duro v. Reina*, 495 U.S. 676 (1990). Did it manifest the same concern over governance of Indian peoples as it developed the plenary power doctrine?

After *Sandoval* was decided, greater American citizenship rights were involuntarily conferred on Indians. After World War I, in recognition of the extraordinary participation of Indian soldiers in the war effort, Congress conferred United States citizenship on Indian veterans. Ch. 95, 41 Stat. 350 (1919). Shortly, thereafter, Congress partially overturned *Elk v. Wilkins*, 112 U.S. 94 (1884), and made all Indians born in the United States citizens of the United States, thereby making Indians one of the only, or perhaps the only, group of people in the United States naturalized as citizens without application and without their consent. Indian Citizenship Act of 1924, ch. 233, 43 Stat. 253 (1924) (codified at 8 U.S.C. § 1401(b)). The Indian Citizenship Act of 1924, however, provided "the granting of citizenship under this subsection shall not in any manner impair or otherwise affect the right of such person to tribal or other property." Did the Indian Citizenship Act itself constitute an exercise of federal plenary power? At least one scholar has questioned the constitutionality of the measure. Robert Porter, *The Demise of the Ongwehoweh and the Rise of the Native Americans: Redressing the Genocidal Act of Forcing American Citizenship upon Indigenous Peoples*, 15 HARV. BLACKLETTER L.J. 107, 135–38 (1999) (focusing on the lack of Indian consent). Significantly, the Act only expressly granted United States citizenship, it did not expressly confer state citizenship. What, if anything, therefore makes Indians citizens of the states in which they reside? While the cases considering the question uniformly assume the existence of Indian state citizenship, some scholars have questioned its legal justification. *E.g.*, Frank Pommersheim, *Coyote Paradox: Some Indian Law Reflections from the Edge of the Prairie*, 31 ARIZ. ST. L.J. 439, 472–73 (1999).

The granting of United States citizenship to Indians in 1924 meant that the broad federal plenary power over Indians thereafter would apply to peoples who were citizens of the United States. Nevertheless, *Sandoval* would come to stand for the proposition that the federal plenary power doctrine justified singling out such citizens for special legal treatment. The dividing line between the people who could be singled out for the exercise of such broad federal powers and those who could not was perplexing. Recall that *Sandoval* suggested

> it is not meant by this that Congress may bring a community or body of people within the range of this power by arbitrarily calling them an Indian tribe, but only that in respect of distinctly Indian communities the questions whether, to what extent, and for what time they shall be recognized and dealt with as dependent tribes requiring the guardianship and protection of the United States are to be determined by Congress, and not by the courts.

231 U.S. at 46. Is the only distinguishing characteristic of the people singled out for the exercise of this broader, nonreviewable, federal congressional power that they were all racially or culturally Indian? Is the federal plenary power doctrine, then, a direct product of late nineteenth century "white man's burden" arguments justifying colonialism?

4. The Role of the Political Question Doctrine and the Future of Plenary Power: In both *Lone Wolf* and *Sandoval*, the Court indicated that the exercise of power by Congress in the field of Indian affairs constituted a political question not cognizable by the judiciary. *See also United States v. Santa Fe Pac. R.R.*, 314 U.S.

339, 347 (1941); *Cherokee Tobacco*, 78 U.S. (11 Wall.) 616, 621 (1871) (statutory abrogation of treaty); *United States v. Holliday*, 70 U.S. (3 Wall.) 407 (1866). What do such pronouncements mean? Can the federal judiciary never call Congress to account when power over Indians is challenged? *See* Louis Henkin, *Is There a "Political Question" Doctrine?*, 85 YALE L.J. 597, 606, 622 (1976). What is the continued vitality of the plenary power and political question doctrines in twenty-first century Indian law? As you will see from studying *United States v. John*, 437 U.S. 634 (1978) and *Delaware Tribal Bus. Comm. v. Weeks*, 430 U.S. 73 (1977), both presented in Ch. 4, Sec. A.1, federal plenary power over Indian affairs was somewhat recast in the later twentieth century, as unlimited with respect to subject matter, but nonetheless subject to judicial oversight via the Bill of Rights. The courts' scrutiny has been quite minimal, however, and deference to Congress remains the rule. One noteworthy exception has been review of tribal claims that Congress has "taken" tribal property without providing the "just compensation" required under the Fifth Amendment. For the Supreme Court's treatment of the political question doctrine in a tribal takings case that openly challenged *Lone Wolf v. Hitchcock*, see *United States v. Sioux Nation*, 448 U.S. 371 (1980), set forth in Ch. 6, Sec. A.2.

E. INTERNATIONAL HUMAN RIGHTS LAW AND INDIGENOUS PEOPLES' RIGHTS

Indian law began as part of the Law of Nations. With the changed geopolitical realities following the War of 1812, there was a gradual nonconsensual domestication of federal Indian law. As a result, the legal terms and framework of federal Indian law — represented, for example, by concepts of federal "plenary power" and the "domestic dependent status" of Native nations — are products of a colonial system that sought to place Native nations in a subordinate position in order to facilitate the political domination by Europeans. Despite these efforts, Native nations have retained their separate political and cultural identities. Today, indigenous peoples throughout the world are challenging whether contemporary nation-states have the "right" to define indigenous peoples' political and cultural rights at all. The post-World War II global movement toward decolonization and "self-determination" for all "peoples" has provided a useful context for indigenous peoples' claims to self-determination. In their quest for self-determination, indigenous peoples have looked to international human rights law for normative standards to guide these efforts toward political and cultural self-realization. Additionally, indigenous peoples from every continent have increasingly mobilized as a political force to lobby for greater international protection from the incursions of domestic governments upon indigenous peoples' rights to their lands, cultural resources, and political autonomy. The United Nations Declaration on the Rights of Indigenous Peoples, which was adopted by the General Assembly on September 13, 2007, exemplifies that collective effort. *See generally* S. JAMES ANAYA, INTERNATIONAL HUMAN RIGHTS AND INDIGENOUS PEOPLES 55 (2009); United Nations Declaration on the Rights of Indigenous Peoples, Adopted by the U.N. General Assembly, Sept. 13, 2007, G.A. Res. 61/295.

As Professor Anaya notes, the Declaration's primary normative significance is to articulate a standard of "self-determination" to guide the relationship of nation-states to the indigenous peoples within their boundaries. S. JAMES ANAYA, INTERNATIONAL HUMAN RIGHTS AND INDIGENOUS PEOPLES 58 (2009). Article 3 of the Declaration asserts, "Indigenous peoples have the right to self-determination. By virtue of that right they freely determine their political status and freely pursue their economic, social and cultural development." What does the indigenous right to "self-determination" entail? It clearly encompasses the political, cultural, social, and economic dimensions important to the survival of Native peoples as autonomous groups. However, it is less clear what the right means in relationship to the power of nation-states to govern their territories and the inhabitants of those territories. Article 4 of the Declaration describes the political right of indigenous peoples as a "right to autonomy or self-government in matters relating to their internal and local affairs, as well as ways and means for financing their economic functions." This language suggests that different models might be negotiated between indigenous peoples and the nation-states that encompass them, which would allow indigenous peoples to freely exercise a right to "autonomy" or a right to "self-government" with respect to "internal and local affairs."

At this juncture, the Declaration on the Rights of Indigenous Peoples is purely prescriptive, and it will not be legally binding upon individual nation-states unless it is incorporated into a treaty to which individual states may choose to sign onto. However, the instrument is very important because, in its various articles, the Declaration summarizes the primary human rights norms that have been held to be central to the cultural and political survival of indigenous peoples as distinctive groups. Given the importance of international human rights norms to the articulation of indigenous rights, this section discusses the models of political governance that are represented within international law jurisprudence and highlights the intersection of those models with domestic jurisprudence in the countries colonized by Great Britain. This comparative exercise is intended to provide students a broader framework within which to evaluate domestic federal Indian law.

1. International Models of Political Self-Governance

Under contemporary international law, there are at least three different perspectives on the political status of indigenous peoples. Some argue that indigenous peoples ought to be recognized as having an equal status to the nation-states of the world, claiming that the nineteenth-century racism and colonial attitudes have no place in the modern world. Some see indigenous peoples as ethnic minority groups that have a claim to certain fundamental protections under international human rights law. And some would argue that "indigenous peoples" share a special "hybrid" status under international law that possesses aspects of national identity and aspects of minority group identity.

Professor James Anaya's work has highlighted the importance of international human rights law in generating a normative basis for recognition of Native peoples' rights to autonomy and cultural survival. *See, e.g.*, S. JAMES ANAYA, INDIGENOUS PEOPLES IN INTERNATIONAL LAW (1996); S. James Anaya, *Indigenous Rights Norms in Contemporary International Law*, 8 ARIZ. J. INT'L & COMP. L. 1 (1991). To understand how this jurisprudential movement operates, it is necessary to understand the institutional structures that govern global applications of human rights law, the primary documents that embody the relevant norms, and how concepts such as "self-determination" and "cultural integrity" inform notions of political and human rights for indigenous peoples. Although a detailed examination of these concepts and principles is beyond the scope of our study in this book, consider the position of many contemporary Native leaders that Indian nations are entitled to recognition among the family of nations in the international arena. *See, e.g.*, Oren Lyons, *When You Talk About Client Relationships, You Are Talking About the Future of Nations, in* NATIONAL LAWYERS GUILD COMMITTEE ON NATIVE AMERICAN STRUGGLES, RE-THINKING INDIAN LAW iv (1982); Vine Deloria Jr., *The Size and Status of Nations, in* NATIVE AMERICAN VOICES: A READER 457, 465 (S. Lobo & S. Talbot eds., 1998). Deloria states the case as follows:

> Having reviewed international law and practice where the concept of sovereignty is concerned, what conclusions can be drawn about the Indian demand for a sovereign status as a basis for their future relations with the United States? First, there is no reason for rejecting such a demand on the grounds of inadequate Indian land, since many geographically minuscule nations function with full sovereignty and international recognition in the contemporary world. Second, the fact that most Indian lands are almost totally landlocked by the United States is not a valid argument against Indian sovereignty, because the same precedent has been set through international practice. Third, the population size of many Indian tribes equals or exceeds those of some small nations of the world and is adequate for a sovereign status. Fourth, economic deficiencies should not discredit the Indian claim to sovereignty, given the low standard in the independent Third World and the fact that continuing U.S. assistance can be a formally negotiated part of any sovereignty agreement. Fifth, insufficient educational levels used as an argument to prove that Indians should not totally govern themselves will not withstand the test of international practice; indeed, American Indians have a higher literacy rate than many of the Third World countries. Finally, in the world today sovereignty permits an abundance of different forms of relative dependence or independence, any of which could be available as a model for a future U.S. Government-Indian relationship. Therefore, the proposal advanced in this book and by other Indian spokesmen for a return to the sovereign relationship of the early nineteenth century has every justification from an international point of view.

NOTES

1. The Conventions of the International Labour Organization: There are three foundational documents of international human rights law dealing with indigenous peoples' rights. Two were adopted by the International Labour Organization (ILO), a United Nations agency that brings together governments, employers, and workers of its member states to promote a decent work environment throughout the world. The third, and most recent, is the Declaration on the Rights of Indigenous Peoples, adopted by the United Nations General Assembly, which represents all of the member states.

ILO Convention 107, adopted in 1957, became the first instrument of international human rights law to focus on the rights of indigenous peoples. The Convention assumes a norm of assimilation and identifies the primary human rights problem as the denial of rights to fully participate in the "progress of the national community." Thus, the instrument is intended to articulate "general standards" to assure the "protection of the populations concerned, their progressive integration into their respective national communities, and the improvement of their living and working conditions." The Convention assigned to the national governments the primary responsibility to discharge these goals, and encouraged remedial actions such as guaranteeing indigenous peoples equal rights to other citizens, promoting the "social, economic and cultural development" of these populations, and "creating possibilities of national integration," so long as these policies do not demand the "artificial assimilation" of indigenous populations. Although ILO 107 contains provisions detailing the importance of land to indigenous populations, and counsels against their forcible removal from such lands, the Convention is largely silent on the political rights of indigenous peoples in any other capacity than as "equal citizens" within the nation-state. The focus is on the rights of individual group members to receive education and to participate as workers in the national economy. How is a norm of "integration" different from a governmental practice of "artificial assimilation"? Which model of tribal-federal relations is reflected in ILO 107?

ILO No. 107 was revised by the International Labour Organization in 1989. ILO No. 169, "Convention Concerning Indigenous and Tribal Peoples in Independent countries," went into force in 1991. ILO 169 overtly rejects the "assimilationist orientation of the earlier standards," and affirms the right of indigenous peoples "to live and develop their own designs as distinct communities." The Convention contemplates the continuing existence of indigenous peoples as separate groups with their own institutions and customary practices and counsels the nation-states to respect the integrity of the "values, practices, and institutions" of these peoples. Article 5(b). The Convention's focus is on empowering indigenous peoples to "decide their own priorities for the process of development" within the nations and regions that they inhabit, while participating in the national and local governance structures that affect them. Article 7. The Convention specifies that indigenous peoples "shall have the right to retain their own customs and institutions, where these are not incompatible with fundamental rights defined by the national legal system and with internationally recognized human rights." Article 8. Thus, the Convention supports only a qualified right to autonomy. Furthermore, although the Convention describes indigenous groups as "peoples," the instrument specifically states, "the use of the term peoples in this Convention shall not be construed as having any implications as regards the rights which may attach to the term under international law." Article 1(3). This description is, of course, a clear disclaimer of any right to "self-determination," which, under international law, is reserved to "peoples." What model of federal-tribal relations is reflected by ILO 169? Note that the United States is not a signatory to ILO No. 169. Why might the United States have declined to be bound by this Convention?

2. The U.N. Declaration on the Rights of Indigenous Peoples: The U.N. General Assembly's 2007 Declaration is the first international law instrument to provide that indigenous peoples have a right to self-determination. Article 3. The language is virtually identical to that of Article 1 of the International Covenant on Economic, Social and Cultural Rights, adopted by the U.N. General Assembly in 1966, which guarantees "all peoples" the right of self-determination and the right to freely pursue their economic, social, and cultural development. However, the Declaration on the Rights of Indigenous Peoples also includes provisions that appear to qualify the right. For example, Article 4 provides, "Indigenous peoples, in exercising their right to self-determination, have the right to autonomy or self-government in matters relating to their *internal and local affairs*" (emphasis added). Article 46 of the Declaration specifically states that the instrument shall not be construed in a way "which would dismember or impair, totally or in part, the territorial integrity or political unity of sovereign and independent States." In comparison, the international political right to self-determination for "peoples" as defined under Article 1 of the International Covenant on Economic, Social and Cultural Rights, may justify the remedy of secession for previously independent "peoples" that have been involuntarily subsumed by another national power. Professor Anaya has pointed out that the substance of the norm of self-determination — the principles that define the standard — must be distinguished from the remedial prescriptions that may follow a violation of the norm. S. JAMES ANAYA, INDIGENOUS PEOPLES IN INTERNATIONAL LAW 80 (1996). The essence of the norm of self-determination, according to Professor Anaya, is the right of a people to choose its own political status within its territory, free of external domination. In some circumstances, a "people" may be granted the right to form a new state; however, in many cases, this can be accomplished in cooperation with the existing political structure. Assuming that Indian nations were understood to have an unqualified right to "self-determination" under international law, would most Indian nations opt for independent statehood? Voluntary association with the United States as separate sovereigns? Incorporation into the United States with respect for local rights of self-governance and cultural rights?

The Declaration on the Rights of Indigenous Peoples takes the position "that indigenous peoples are equal to all other peoples, while recognizing the right of all peoples to be different, to consider themselves different, and to be respected as such." The Declaration endorses the equal citizenship of indigenous peoples in the national polity, while recognizing the collective rights of indigenous peoples to govern themselves; to their land, territory, and natural resources; to their cultural, religious, and spiritual practices; and to maintain their own political, social, and economic institutions. Which model or models of tribal-state relations would be consistent with the Declaration on the Rights of Indigenous Peoples?

When a vote was taken on the Declaration, 144 nations voted in favor of the Declaration and 11 abstained. Does it surprise you to learn that the United States was one of only four nation-states that voted against adopting the Declaration on the Rights of Indigenous Peoples? The other dissenters were Canada, Australia, and New Zealand. Since the vote, however, each nation has reversed course, with the United States being the last to do so, in 2010.

What motivations might countries have either to oppose or to support such a resolution? For an explanation of the status of the Declaration under international law and the meaning of self-determination as articulated in the Declaration, see Christopher J. Fromherz, *Indigenous Peoples' Courts: Egalitarian Juridical Pluralism, Self-Determination, and the United Nations Declaration on the Rights of Indigenous Peoples*, 156 U. Pa. L. Rev. 1341 (2008).

In 2012, Professor S. James Anaya, as Special Rapporteur on Indigenous Peoples to the United Nations Human Rights Council (HRC), visited the United States, compiling the first-of-its-kind comprehensive assessment of the human rights situation of indigenous peoples within the United States under modern international law standards. The Special Rapporteur found that, despite incredible resilience and dynamism, across almost every metric, indigenous peoples have lower indicators of education, health, income, and success of any group in the United States. The Special Rapporteur emphasized that the U.N. Declaration on the Rights of Indigenous Peoples, as part of a series of broader developments, serves as the normative frame for indigenous rights in the world today, including for the United States. The full report can be found at Human Rights Council, Report of the Special Rapporteur on the Rights of Indigenous Peoples: The Situation of Indigenous Peoples in the United States of America, S. James Anaya, 21st Sess., U.N., Doc. A/HRC/21/247/Add.1 (Aug. 30, 2012)

3.   Implementation of UNDRIP into Tribal Law: In their work, Professors Kristen Carpenter and Angela Riley describe the ways in which indigenous peoples today deploy international human rights norms and laws in their own legal systems and work to incorporate their own laws and legal epistemologies into tribal, national, and international law. The authors characterize this modern indigenous-driven approach and the resulting generation of law across "levels" of law making as a "jurisgenerative moment" in indigenous peoples' human rights. *See* Kristen A. Carpenter and Angela R. Riley, *Indigenous Peoples and the Jurisgenerative Moment in Human Rights*, 102 Cal L. Rev. 173 (2014).

4.   Moral Justifications for Self-Determination: Many scholars ground the legal entitlement of groups to "self-determination" upon the moral basis for such claims. As Avishai Margalit and Joseph Raz point out in their article, *National Self-Determination, in* The Rights of Minority Cultures (W. Kymlicka ed., 1995), many groups have argued for a right to self-determination, and it is thus important to distinguish the claims of "nations" and "peoples" from those of "tribes," "ethnic minorities," or "religious minorities." They suggest that the terminology is only of limited use. Margalit and Raz define "the core content of the claim" to self-determination as follows:

> [T]hat there is a right to determine whether a certain territory shall become, or remain, a separate state (and possibly also whether it should enjoy autonomy within a large state). The idea of national self-determination or (as we shall refer to it in order to avoid confusion) the idea of self-government encompasses much more. The value of national self-government is the value of entrusting the general political power over a group and its members to the group. . . . The idea of national self-government, in other words, speaks of groups determining the character of

their social and economic environment, their fortunes, the course of their development, and the fortunes of their members by their own actions. . . . Given the current international state system, in which political power rests, in the main, with sovereign states, the right to determine whether a territory should be an independent state is quite naturally regarded as the main instrument for realizing the ideal of self-determination. . . . But . . . the right of self-determination so understood is not ultimate, but is grounded in the wider value of national self-government.

Id. at 79–92. Margalit and Raz examine various moral justifications for the claim of self-determination and its root claim of national self-government, including instrumental justifications and those resting on intrinsic value. They assume that it is possible to distinguish groups that possess morally valid claims to self-determination from those who do not, based on a composite of characteristics that define the "tie between the individual and the collective" that is "at the heart of the case for self determination."

2. The Institutional Framework for International Human Rights Law

As Professor Anaya asserts, international human rights law provides a series of norms that might be used to more fairly adjudicate indigenous peoples' rights to self-determination, land and resources, and culture. However, what institutions are available to enforce these norms?

The United Nations International Covenant on Civil and Political Rights is one mechanism to adjudicate indigenous peoples' human rights. The International Covenant on Civil and Political Rights and the International Covenant on Economic, Social, and Cultural Rights transformed the values embodied in the United Nations Universal Declaration of Human Rights into binding legal norms. The General Assembly approved the Covenants in 1966, and the Covenant on Civil and Political Rights became legally binding in 1976. As international treaties, the Covenants are legally binding on all the nations that ratify them.

The Covenant on Civil and Political Rights establishes an 18-member Human Rights Committee to implement the Covenant. Member nations have the option to ratify the instrument, as well as a supplemental treaty, the Optional Protocol to the Covenant on Civil and Political Rights, which establishes procedures for implementing the Covenant. Thus far, the United States has not ratified the Covenant on Civil and Political Rights, raising the question of whether its provisions can be useful for the claims of Native nations in the United States. Under domestic law, international covenants are not automatically enforceable in American courts. At the first level, domestic law requires the Senate to ratify international covenants or treaties before they can become valid in the United States. In some cases, the ratification is contingent upon the "exception" of certain provisions that the Senate feels may violate other aspects of domestic law or policy. Even after ratification, however, domestic law generally requires further legislation to implement the treaty or convention. Thus, unlike some other countries, international law in the United States is not "self-executing."

Professor Anaya's argument in favor of reading international human rights law as "customary law" has considerable merit. International customary law is applicable in the United States courts. *See Paquete Habana*, 175 U.S. 677 (1900). On this theory, to the extent that international human rights covenants have become part of "customary international law," they could be given effect by United States courts. *See generally* Comment, *Toward Consent and Cooperation: Reconsidering the Political Status of Indian Nations*, 22 HARV. C.R.-C.L. L. REV. 509 (1987).

For nations that have chosen to ratify the Covenant and the Optional Protocol, the Human Rights Committee can receive individual complaints filed against state parties to the Covenant. Article 1 of the Covenant on Civil and Political Rights recognizes that "all peoples have a right of self-determination. By virtue of that right they freely determine their political status and freely pursue their economic, social and cultural development." Article 27 of the Covenant on Civil and Political Rights provides:

> In those States in which ethnic, religious or linguistic minorities exist, persons belonging to such minorities shall not be denied the right, in community with other members of their group to enjoy their own culture, to profess and practice their own religion, or to use their own language.

The Human Rights Committee has consistently used Article 27, rather than Article 1, as the basis for its decisions on indigenous peoples' rights. For example, in the *Case of Sandra Lovelace*, Communication No. R.6/24 (Dec. 1977), U.N. Doc. Supp. No. 40 at 166 (1981), the Committee considered the petition of a Maliseet woman who lost her Indian status and her right to live on her reserve under Canadian law when she married a non-Indian man. Ms. Lovelace later divorced her husband and wanted to move back to her reserve on a permanent basis and build a new house, but was denied this right because she had lost her Indian status, as defined by Canada's Indian Act. The Committee found that article 27 protected the right of Sandra Lovelace, as a member of an ethnic minority, to live "in community with other members" of her group. Thus, any statutory restriction on her right to live on her reserve must "have both a reasonable and objective justification and be consistent with the other provisions of the Covenant, read as a whole." Under the facts of this case, the Committee found that denial of Sandra Lovelace's right to reside on her reserve was not reasonable or necessary to preserve the identity of the tribe, and was an "unjustifiable denial of her rights under article 27 of the Covenant."

In *Kitok v. Sweden*, Communication No. 197/1985 (2 Dec. 1985) CCPR/C/33/D/197/1985, the Committee considered the petition of a Sami individual that he had been wrongfully denied the right to engage in reindeer breeding according to a Swedish law that conditioned the exercise of such rights upon maintenance of an active connection to the Sami community and traditional lifeways of the Village. In this case, the Committee found that Ivan Kitok did not have standing to raise a claim under Article 1 for denial of self-determination to the Sami people. Rather, his claim arose under Article 27 because it alleged that he was a victim of the state's violation of his right to enjoy the same rights enjoyed by other members of the Sami community. However, in this case, the Committee held that the Swedish law protected the collective survival of the Sami people, and permissibly distinguished membership rights on the basis of an individual's commitment to retain his or her traditional identity. In other words, the collective survival of the group could take a legitimate priority over the individual rights of a single member.

NOTES

1. **The Optional Protocol:** The enforceability of international covenants is conditioned upon the willingness of the nation-states to bind themselves to such processes. With respect to the International Covenant on Civil and Political Rights, of the 87 parties to the Covenant, only 44 had adopted the Protocol as of 1989. Even as to states that adopt the Protocol, the Committee's opinion represents only a non-binding recommendation. In other words, the effectiveness of such an opinion rests on persuasion and the public embarrassment of being labeled a human rights violator. Canada ultimately changed the offending provision in the *Case of Sandra Lovelace* in 1985. For a comprehensive review of the Optional Protocol decisions, see Alfred DeZayas, Jacob Moller & Torkel Opsahl, *Application of the International Covenant on Civil and Political Rights Under the Optional Protocol by the Human Rights Committee*, 26 COMP. JUD. REV. 3 (1989).

2. **The Equality Principle:** Under the challenged provision in the *Case of Sandra Lovelace*, Indian men not only did not lose their status when they married non-Indian women, but also their non-Indian wives actually gained Indian status. What rationale could the government have for granting Indian status to non-Indian wives? How does this case square with *Santa Clara Pueblo v. Martinez*, presented in Ch. 3, Sec. C.5? Suppose that the Santa Clara Pueblo signed onto the Covenant and Protocol. Would the Committee's recommendation be different?

In 1985, Canada amended the Indian Act to provide that individual bands can determine membership instead of the central government. R.S.C. c. 27. If a Band adopted a rigid patrilineal rule of membership, would such an action present any issue under the Covenant? Would your answer change if the Band's adoption of such a rule deviated from its traditional practice and was motivated by a perceived need to restrict eligibility for membership in order to keep down the members eligible for scarce national benefits? Why would the Committee decline to reach the question of whether the Indian Act violated the nondiscrimination norms of the Covenant? The Committee has expressed the view that state laws discriminating based on gender violate the Covenant. In a 1978 case, the Committee found that state immigration laws that subjected foreign husbands of nationals to restrictions not imposed on foreign wives violated both article 23's right to protection of the family and articles 2, 3, and 26 as a discrimination based on gender. *Aumeeruddy-Cziffra v. Mauritius, No. 35/1978*, 1981 Human Rights Committee Report, Annex VII.

3. **Cultural Versus Political Rights:** Does the Committee's decision in *Kitok* set up a dichotomy between the "cultural" rights of indigenous peoples and their "political" rights? Is such a distinction in tension with indigenous views on sovereignty?

4. **Art. 27 and the Organization of American States Inter-American Commission on Human Rights:** As Professor Anaya notes in *Indigenous Rights*

Norms in Contemporary International Law, 8 ARIZ. J. INT'L & COMP. L. 1 (1991), the cultural integrity norm embodied in Article 27 of the Covenant on Civil and Political Rights has also served as the basis for decisions favorable to indigenous peoples by other bodies, including the Inter-American Commission on Human Rights of the Organization of American States (OAS). The Inter-American Commission has treated the norm as generally binding upon the states regardless of any specific treaty obligation.

The Commission is chartered by the OAS in order to observe and protect human rights. The Commission does not have direct enforcement authority, but it has the ability to initiate proceedings in the Inter-American Court of Human Rights, which does have jurisdiction to adjudicate claims alleging violation of the American Convention on Human Rights and to issue decisions binding upon states that are parties to the Convention and that have formally submitted themselves to the Court's jurisdiction.

The Commission has issued several decisions concerning the land rights of indigenous peoples. In a 1985 decision concerning the Yanomami Indians of Brazil, the Commission interpreted Article 27 as protecting the Indians of Brazil, even though Brazil is not a party to the Covenant. *See* Res. No. 12/85, Case No. 7615 Inter-Am C.H.R. 24 (1985), in Annual Report of the Inter-American Commission on Human Rights 1984-85, OEA/Ser.L./V/II.66, Doc. 10, Rev. 1 (1985). The Commission found that the OAS and its member states are committed to the "preservation and strengthening" of indigenous cultural heritage as a "priority," and declared that Brazil's failure to protect the Yanomami from incursions by miners and others into their ancestral lands put the Indians in physical jeopardy as well as in danger of losing their cultures and traditions. The Commission recommended that the government secure the boundaries of a reserve for the Yanomami.

The OAS Inter-American Commission on Human Rights also relied on Article 27 in evaluating the claim of the Miskito Indians of Nicaragua that the Sandinista government had impaired the rights of the Miskito Indians to political autonomy. *See* OAS Inter-American Human Rights Report, OEA/Ser.L/V/II.62 doc. 10 rev. 3 (1983); OEA Ser.L/V/II.62, doc. 26 (1984). The Commission encouraged the Sandinista government to respond to these claims by establishing "an adequate institutional order as part of the structure of the Nicaraguan state." Ultimately, the government enacted a 1987 Autonomy statute, setting up regional governments for the Miskito and other Native communities along Nicaragua's Atlantic coast.

The Inter-American Commission on Human Rights considered the claim of the Western Shoshone Dann sisters for aboriginal title in Nevada, a claim the sisters had earlier presented in the United States courts. *See* Ch. 6, Sec. A.5.a; *Mary and Carrie Dann v. United States*, Case 11.140, Report No. 113/01, Inter-Am. C.H.R. (2001). The Dann sisters' petition alleged that the United States had violated several provisions of the American Declaration of the Rights and Duties of Man ("American Declaration"), including the provisions relating to rights of property, equality, cultural integrity, self-determination, and judicial protection and due process of law. The United States responded by asserting that the American Declaration had not been violated because the Dann's claims did not involve human rights violations at all, but rather involved lengthy litigation of land title and land use questions that have been and are still subject to careful consideration by all three branches of the U.S. government. The United States pointed out that the Danns have title to their ranch and distinguished the Dann's claims regarding grazing livestock (allegedly in violation of BLM policies) from their claims to aboriginal title in the extended area involved in the Indian Claims Commission's adjudication of the Western Shoshone land claim.

The Commission found that it had jurisdiction to hear the claim because the United States is a member of the Organization of American States, although not a signatory to the American Convention on Human Rights. The Commission found that in addressing violations of the American Declaration, it was necessary to consider these claims in light of the evolving rules and principles of human rights law in the Americas and in the international community more broadly, as reflected in treaties, custom, and other sources of international law. In particular, the Commission and other international authorities have recognized the collective aspect of indigenous rights, and the unique connection between indigenous peoples and their traditional lands and resources. The Commission commended the United States for enacting the Indian Claims Commission Act to redress indigenous claims, instead of asserting the bar of sovereign immunity. However, the Commission found that, with respect to the Dann's claim, the processes used were not sufficient to comply with contemporary international human rights norms governing the determination of indigenous property interests. The Commission expressed concern that the processes used did not depend upon "fully informed and mutual consent on the part of the indigenous community as a whole," and that the Indian Claims Commission had failed to conduct an independent review of the historical and other evidence to determine as a matter of fact whether the Western Shoshone had properly claimed title to some of their traditional lands. Thus, with respect to the Dann's claims to property rights in the Western Shoshone ancestral lands, they had been denied an "effective and fair process" in compliance with the norms of the American Declaration.

The Commission held that the United States had failed to ensure the Danns' right to property under conditions of equality contrary to Articles II, XVIII, and XXIII of the American Declaration in connection with their claims to property rights in the Western Shoshone ancestral lands. The Commission declined, however, to express any factual determination as to whether and to what extent the Danns may properly claim a subsisting right to property in these lands, claiming that this issue "involves complex issues of law and fact that are more appropriately left to the State for determination through those legal processes it may consider suitable for that purpose."

5.   The Inter-American Court of Human Rights and Native Land Claims: The Inter-American Court of Human Rights issued an important decision on indigenous land rights. The Court found Nicaragua to be in violation of the relevant provisions of the American Convention on Human Rights with respect to the rights of the Awas Tingni Community to their traditional lands and resources. *See* Inter-Am. C.H.R., *The Case of the Mayagna (Sumo) Awas Tingni Community v. Nicaragua*, Judgment of Aug. 31, 2001. In issuing its ruling, the Court relied upon the American Convention and other documents of international human rights law to find that the international human right of property embraces the communal property regimes of indigenous peoples as defined by their own customs and traditions, such that "possession of land should suffice for indigenous communities lacking real title to property of the land to obtain official recognition of that property." *See* S. James Anaya & Claudio Grossman, *The Case of the* Awas Tingni v. Nicaragua: *A New Step in the International Law of Indigenous Peoples*, 19 ARIZ. J. INT'L & COMP. L. 1 (2002). This ruling is of critical importance to the many indigenous communities of the region that, like the Awas Tingni, lack official government recognition of their traditional lands. In the case of the Awas Tingni, Nicaraguan authorities had treated these untitled indigenous lands as state lands, available to be leased out to logging companies and other commercial enterprises for development. The Court's decision orders "Nicaragua to demarcate and title Awas Tingni's traditional lands in accordance with its customary land and resource tenure patterns, to refrain from any action that might undermine the Community's interests in those lands, and to establish an adequate mechanism to secure the land rights of all indigenous communities of the country." As Professor Anaya and Dean Grossman observe, this is "the first legally binding decision by an international tribunal to uphold the collective land and resource rights of indigenous peoples in the face of a state's failure to do so. It strengthens a contemporary trend in the processes of international law that helps to empower indigenous peoples as they press their demands for self-determination as distinct groups with secure territorial rights."

6. The OAS Proposed Declaration: The OAS has also drafted a Proposed American Declaration on the Rights of Indigenous Peoples that was approved by the Inter-American Commission on Human Rights on February 26, 1997.

Chapter 2

RECURRING ISSUES IN TRIBAL-FEDERAL LEGAL RELATIONS

Legal questions concerning tribal-federal relations range broadly across criminal matters, family law, contracts, taxation, regulation of all kinds, land and water rights, as well as other natural and cultural resource claims. Regardless of the particular topic, however, three sets of issues almost invariably arise: first, basic definitional questions about what is an Indian tribe or nation, who is an Indian, and what is the extent of tribal territory, known as Indian country; second, when does a federal or state law addressing Indian affairs pose constitutional equal protection problems; and third, how should courts go about interpreting the plethora of federal treaties and statutes affecting tribes and Indians.

The three basic definitional questions of Indian law set the boundaries for the field, in terms of political units, individuals, and territory. Federal responses to these questions also embody a host of policy choices about allocation of resources and jurisdictional authority. That's because eligibility for many federal benefits, the operation of federal rather than state authority, and federal recognition of tribal governmental powers normally turn on these definitions. Moreover, opening the definitional questions immediately exposes conflicts between tribal and federal understandings. For example, an Indian tribe may have meaning and function for its members, but may lack recognition by the federal government. Or an individual may not be treated as a citizen of her tribe for purposes of tribal elections, but may nonetheless be treated as an Indian under federal criminal statutes or benefit programs. Finally, an Indian nation may consider its ancestral homeland to be its tribal territory, but the federal government may deem much of that land lost to the tribe by virtue of treaties, congressional acts, or land claims settlements, all of which the tribes may contest. The first part of this chapter will consider the fundamental definitions affecting tribal-federal legal relations from both tribal and federal perspectives.

Constitutional equal protection questions have been more prominent within Indian law since the Supreme Court's decision in the well-known school desegregation case, *Brown v. Board of Education*, 347 U.S. 483 (1954). Critics have raised questions about the constitutionality of federal and state legislation directed at Indians and tribes following *Brown*'s strong words condemning discrimination on the basis of race, framing such legislation as impermissible racial preferences in violation of the equal protection clause. The second part of this chapter focuses on whether these measures ought to be characterized as race and ancestry-based, or political in nature, and ultimately, whether they ought to be deemed unconstitutional.

Since their first involvement in disputes over tribal-federal relations, federal courts have applied special principles of interpretation, known as canons of construction, to the more than 400 treaties between Indian nations and the United States as well as to the volumes of congressional acts affecting Indian affairs. Under these canons, treaties are generally interpreted "as the Indians would have understood them," and ambiguities are resolved against the United States. Congressional acts are interpreted to preserve Indians' treaty rights, other property rights, and inherent tribal powers unless Congress is sufficiently clear in expressing its intention to override them. These judicially developed principles reflect federal concerns about the unfair circumstances of negotiation of treaties, and also the absence of tribal or Indian consent to incorporation into the United States. Thus, more or less explicit models of the federal-tribal relationship, as well as critiques of those models, undergird the canons of construction. The last part of this chapter examines the origins and application of these principles across a broad spectrum of Indian law cases.

A. FUNDAMENTAL DEFINITIONAL QUESTIONS

The key terms normally delineating jurisdictional authority, legal responsibilities, and property rights in federal Indian law are Indian tribe or nation, Indian, and Indian country. None of these terms has had a single, all-purpose definition that has operated consistently across time. Although these terms encompass most of federal Indian law, they do not comprehend the entire field. For example, a few federal services are provided to members of non-federally recognized as well as federally recognized tribes. Some federal statutes, such as the Indian Child Welfare Act of 1978, regulate Indian affairs outside as well as within Indian country. *See* Ch. 5, Sec. D. Nonetheless, appreciating the significance of these three terms, both from a federal and a tribal perspective, is key to understanding the complexities of the tribal-federal legal relationship.

1. What Is an Indian Tribe or Nation?

a. Tribal vs. Federal Definitions

The term "Indian tribe" has distinct and different meanings for Native people and for federal law. For Native people, existence as a nation or tribe turns on shared language, rituals, narratives, kinship or clan ties, and a shared relationship to specific land. Often the word that tribal members use to describe themselves collectively is a word signifying "the people." In contrast, for purposes of federal law, the term usually designates a group of Native people with whom the federal government has established some kind of political relationship or "recognition."

Thus, for example, a tribe that has been "terminated" by the federal government may continue to exist for the Native community that was the object of the legal action, but not for the purpose of interpreting a federal statute granting statutory benefits only to federally recognized tribes. Indeed, the successful efforts of some terminated tribes to be restored to federally recognized status illustrate tribal persistence apart from federal law.

On the other hand, some federally recognized tribes are legal entities only. A congressionally created confederated or consolidated tribe can be made up of different ethnological tribes presently occupying the same reservation because of federal policies, such as the Wind River Tribes (Shoshone and Arapaho). Or tribes may confederate for political purposes, forming governmental entities such as the Minnesota Chippewa Tribes or the Central Council of the Tlingit & Haida Indian Tribes, which have received federal recognition in addition to their constituent tribes. Under the Indian Reorganization Act of 1934, Indians living on any given reservation were allowed to organize into federally recognized tribes, regardless whether they were linguistically, culturally, or politically united. *See* 25 U.S.C. § 479. And because of the cultural disruption and destitution visited on California Indians, Congress appropriated funds in 1902 for the purchase of lands in southern California to be set aside for any "Mission Indians as may not be provided with suitable lands elsewhere," regardless whether they belonged to a single tribal community. 32 Stat. 245. The groups that organized under these statutes hold federal status as tribes, even though they may not have had meaningful social or political ties before European and American invasions. Other federally recognized entities represent fragments of previously unified peoples. Federal law divided the Great Sioux Nation, for example, into geographically separated and independently recognized tribes in order to weaken the Sioux militarily. Other groups, such as the Oneida, the Cherokee, and the Choctaw, are recognized as multiple separate nations because some members moved to new territories as part of the federal removal process and others refused to leave ancestral homelands. Over time, some Indian groups brought together under United States pressures have established new social and political formations, adapting to their changed circumstances. For others, the poor fit between federal definitions and their own understandings creates ongoing tensions in the operations of tribal politics. *See* Carole Goldberg-Ambrose, *Of Native Americans and Tribal Members: The Influence of Law on Indian Group Life*, 28 LAW & SOC'Y REV. 1123, 1131–33 (1994).

Should Congress have unlimited power to characterize a group as a federally recognized tribe, thereby triggering preemption of state power and acknowledging tribal governmental authority? In *United States v. Sandoval*, 231 U.S. 28, 46 (1913), discussed in Ch. 1, Sec. D.2, the Supreme Court held that so long as Congress has any reason for maintaining its guardian-ward relationship with a "distinctly Indian" community, the courts should not disturb Congress's decision to recognize and deal with the group as a tribe. At issue in that case was Congress's power to enact liquor regulations for the Pueblo Indians — settled, agricultural groups that had owned their communal lands in fee under Mexican law. The Court's analysis focused on the degree of "primitiveness" of the Pueblo Indians in order to support Congress's action. Does *Sandoval* mean that tribes with successful economic development should be stripped of their federal recognition, by the courts if not by Congress? Should courts fully defer to decisions by Congress or the Interior Department to recognize tribes, just as they defer to actions by the executive branch of the federal government regarding recognition of foreign nations? In the case of foreign nations, the Constitution specifically empowers the President to receive foreign ambassadors. For an interesting discussion of this comparison, see *Miami Nation of Indians of Indiana v. United States Department of the Interior*, 255 F.3d 342 (7th Cir. 2001).

b.   Definitions of "Tribe" Under Federal Statutes

Although Indian nations exist apart from federal law, federal law often imposes definitions of "Indian tribe" for purposes of administering statutes and regulations. Before 1934, few definitions were spelled out in statutory form. For example, the Indian Depredation Act of 1891, 26 Stat. 851, granted jurisdiction to the Court of Claims to compensate settlers whose property was "taken or destroyed by Indians belonging to any band, tribe, or nation, in amity with the United States." The statute has no "definitions" section in it, so courts had to figure out what the term "tribe" meant. In *Montoya v. United States*, 180 U.S. 261, 266 (1901), the Supreme Court established the following definitions of tribe and band for purposes of applying the Depredation Act:

> By a "tribe" we understand a body of Indians of the same or a similar race, united in a sometimes ill-defined territory; by a "band," a company of Indians not necessarily, though often of the same race or tribe, but united under the same leadership in a common design. While a "band" does not imply the separate racial origin characteristic of a tribe, of which it is usually an offshoot, it does imply a leadership and a concert of action.

This definition came to be used to determine whether a group was a tribe for purposes of the Nonintercourse Act, which invalidates transfers of lands "from any Indian nation or tribe of Indians" if made without federal approval. 25 U.S.C. § 177. In 1972, the Passamaquoddy Tribe sought to force the government to represent them in their claim that treaties the Tribe had made with Maine's predecessor, Massachusetts, were void because they violated the Nonintercourse Act. The government's sole reason for refusing to represent the Tribe was the argument that since the Tribe had never been federally recognized, the federal government had no obligations to the Tribe. The First Circuit Court of Appeals disagreed, holding that federal recognition was not necessary for Nonintercourse Act purposes, and that the Tribe met the definition developed in the *Montoya* case. *Joint Tribal Council of Passamaquoddy Tribe v. Morton*, 528 F.2d 370 (1st Cir. 1975). As discussed in the next section, the fact that courts must define "tribe" for purposes of Nonintercourse Act claims may make litigation a possible route to federal recognition for tribes that can prevail on such claims.

Today, Indian statutes normally offer some definition of "tribe." Typical is the definition in the Native American Graves Protection and Repatriation Act of 1990 (NAGPRA), 25 U.S.C. § 3001(7): "any tribe, band, nation, or other organized group or community of Indians, including any Alaska Native village . . . , which is recognized as eligible for the special programs and services provided by the United States to Indians because of their status as Indians." This language appears to tie tribal existence, for statutory purposes, to federal recognition. For discussion of the process of achieving federal recognition, see the next section.

The present trend to define the term "tribe" in particular statutes began with the Indian Reorganization Act of 1934 (IRA), which extended its benefits to "any Indian tribe, organized band, pueblo, or the Indians residing on a reservation." 25 U.S.C. § 479. Benefits available to tribes under the IRA included tribal government organization under federally-approved constitutions, and tribal land taken into trust by the federal government. *See* 25 U.S.C. §§ 476 and 465. The Department of the

Interior has interpreted the provision broadly. In allowing tribal government organization under IRA constitutions in the 1930s, Interior looked not only to formal federal recognition through treaties, statutes, or executive branch actions, but also to the history of tribal organization and operation. For example, a group's relations with non-federal actors such as states, other tribes, and private organizations, counted in favor of treatment as a tribe for purposes of forming an IRA government. In more recent decades, Interior has been willing to take land into trust for any federally recognized tribe, regardless of when or how that federal recognition occurred. *See* 25 C.F.R. §§ 151.2(b), (c)(1).

Beginning in the 1980s, Interior's broad definition of "Indian tribe" came under attack from states unhappy over the agency's land-into-trust decisions. States lose some jurisdiction and considerable taxing authority once land achieves trust status. So many states sought to prevent any more tribal land from going into trust. See Ch. 6, Sec. A.4 for a discussion of the administrative process for land-into-trust and the various challenges to Secretarial action. One line of attack came from states, such as Rhode Island, where the local tribes had only recently received formal federal recognition. Rhode Island argued that the term "Indian tribe" in the IRA must be interpreted in light of the definition of "Indian" in the same statute. 25 U.S.C. § 479. In the IRA, "Indian" is defined as "all persons of Indian descent who are members of *any recognized Indian tribe now under Federal jurisdiction*" (emphasis added). Thus, according to Rhode Island, only a "recognized Indian tribe now under Federal jurisdiction" could qualify as an "Indian tribe" for purposes of taking land into trust. And "now" must mean the date of enactment of the IRA (1934), not the time of taking the land into trust.

In *Carcieri v. Salazar*, 555 U.S. 379 (2009), presented in Ch. 6, Sec. A.4, the Court, in an opinion by Justice Thomas, agreed that land could be taken into trust only for tribes that are "now under Federal jurisdiction," with "now" meaning at the time of passage of the IRA in 1934. Justice Stevens dissented in *Carcieri*, contending that it made no sense, in light of the overall structure and provisions of the IRA, to read the definition of "Indian" back into the definition of "Indian tribe." *See* Heidi M. Staudenmaier & Ruth K. Khalsa, *Post-*Carcieri *Vocabulary Exercise: What if Now Really Means Then*, 1 UNLV GAMING L.J. 39 (2010) (providing a history of administrative interpretation of the phrase "now under federal jurisdiction" prior to *Carcieri* and discussing potential remedial measures following the case).

Because the *Carcieri* Court was not asked to determine what constitutes "under federal jurisdiction," it is unclear what that term means, especially as of 1934, when no definitive list existed of tribes "under federal jurisdiction." Could it mean simply having the qualities of tribal organization, regardless of federal recognition? Justice Breyer, concurring in *Carcieri*, suggested that might be the case, pointing out that some tribes were erroneously overlooked for recognition purposes during the early twentieth century, and later such errors were corrected. If federal recognition of a tribe today requires demonstration that the tribe continuously sustained political and social organization (see the next section of this chapter), wouldn't any current federally recognized tribe have been "under federal jurisdiction" in 1934 and much earlier?

On March 14, 2014, the Solicitor of the Department of the Interior, Hillary Tompkins, issued a Solicitor's Opinion, M-37029, explaining how the Department will interpret the phrase "under federal jurisdiction" for purposes of the 1934 date of the IRA. The Solicitor's detailed analysis of the legislative history of the IRA led her to conclude that the statute "does not unambiguously give meaning to the phrase 'under federal jurisdiction.' " Thus, the agency is entitled to make a "reasonable interpretation," to which courts must defer. Against the backdrop of the federal government's broad "plenary authority" over Indian affairs, Solicitor Tompkins determined that a tribe would be deemed "under federal jurisdiction" based on "evidence of a particular exercise of plenary authority, even where the United States did not otherwise believe that the tribe was under such jurisdiction." The Solicitor explained that the Department would engage in a two-part inquiry, first determining "whether the United States had, in 1934 or at some point in the tribe's history prior to 1934, taken an action or series of actions — through a course of dealings or other relevant acts for or on behalf of the tribe or in some instance tribal members — that are sufficient to establish, or that generally reflect federal obligations, duties, responsibility for or authority over the tribe by the Federal Government." Examples of such actions would include making treaties or contracts with the tribe, sending individual tribal member children to BIA schools, or BIA administration of tribal or individual Indian lands. The second part of the inquiry would be determining "whether the tribe's jurisdictional status remained intact in 1934." Any change in the tribe's jurisdictional status would have to be via congressional action. Administrative action would not suffice to remove a tribe from "under federal jurisdiction" status once that status was achieved before 1934 under the first part of the inquiry.

How onerous is Interior's two-part inquiry? Is it the same as a requirement that a tribe be federally recognized as of 1934 as well as at the time of taking the land into trust? In adopting its two-part approach, Interior rejected the alternative of treating any tribe as "under federal jurisdiction" if it were subject to the federal government's broad constitutional power over Indian affairs (*see* Ch. 4, Sec. A), without regard to any particular exercise of that power directed at the tribe in question. Can you imagine situations in which a tribe would not be able to satisfy the two-part inquiry but would meet the test of being subject to the federal government's "plenary authority" over tribes? Would the Indian law canons of construction (see section C, this chapter) support the constitutional power test over the two-part inquiry? For a federal trial court decision deferring to the Secretary's two-part test and upholding a trust acquisition on that basis, see *Confederated Tribes of the Grand Ronde Cmty. v. Jewell*, 2014 U.S. Dist. LEXIS 172111 (D.D.C. Dec. 12, 2014).

c.   Achieving Federal Recognition

Increasingly, statutory benefits and judge-made rules regarding tribal sovereignty are confined to tribes with the general status of federal recognition or acknowledgment, terms that are typically used interchangeably. Indian nations have come to depend on acknowledgment or recognition by the federal government to ascertain when the federal government will respect their inherent powers of self-government, and when the federal government will provide them with benefits and services. Federal recognition formally establishes a government-to-government relationship between tribes and the United States, and may trigger opportunities to carry on economic development such as gaming, greater control over child welfare matters, rights to employment preference under tribal law, rights to repatriation of ancestors and sacred objects, and, often more important, affirmation of identity. Occasionally, Congress has allowed members of unacknowledged or terminated tribes to participate in such programs. *See* 25 U.S.C. § 1679 (Indian Health Care Improvement Act Amendments affording benefits to some California Indians who are members of nonrecognized tribes). More often, however, Congress and the courts have limited application of federal Indian law to the class of tribes with which the federal government has formed some official intergovernmental relationship. Hence, knowing whether an Indian nation has attained this status matters greatly.

Congress made some effort to simplify these determinations by passing the Federally Recognized Indian Tribe List Act of 1994, Pub. L. 103-454, 108 Stat. 4791, which mandates the annual publication of "a list of all Indian tribes which the Secretary recognizes to be eligible for the special programs and services provided by the United States to Indians because of their status as Indians." 25 U.S.C. § 479a-1. For example, prior to the publication of this list, courts had labored over the question whether Alaskan Native villages constituted "tribes" for purposes of federal doctrines recognizing tribal sovereignty. *See, e.g.*, *Native Village of Venetie I.R.A. Council v. State of Alaska*, 944 F.2d 548, 557–560 (9th Cir. 1991). Publication of the list, which included the Native villages, obviated the need for continued agonizing.

For some Indian nations excluded from the list, publication has not ended their quest for federal recognition. They continue to believe that federal officials have overlooked or deliberately ignored their survival as a people. Failure to engage in warfare against the United States, bureaucratic ineptitude, accidents of timing that prevented treaty negotiations, and fragmentation of tribes due to the removal process are some of the many reasons they cite for nonrecognition. The pursuit of federal recognition is usually an arduous process, however. Federal interests in confining expenditures on Indian programs, coupled with resistance from some established Indian nations, have complicated and lengthened the process for tribes seeking federal recognition. *See* MARK EDWIN MILLER, FORGOTTEN TRIBES: UNRECOGNIZED INDIANS AND THE FEDERAL ACKNOWLEDGMENT PROCESS (2006); Mark D. Myers, *Federal Recognition of Indian Tribes in the United States*, 12 STAN. L. & POL'Y REV. 271 (2001).

In the Federally Recognized Indian Tribe List Act of 1994, *supra*, Congress affirmed that "Indian tribes presently may be recognized by Act of Congress; by the administrative procedures set forth in part 83 of the Code of Federal Regulations . . . ; or by a decision of a United States court; . . . " Legislative recognition may be implied, as when Congress creates a reservation, or express, as when Congress passes a law for that purpose. In recent years, express recognition has often occurred in connection with the settlement of land claims. *See, e.g.*, Massachusetts Indian Land Claims Settlement Act, 25 U.S.C. § 1771 et seq. (settling the claims of the Wampanoag Tribe of Gay Head). Some of these laws include provisions authorizing state jurisdiction and/or limiting tribal jurisdiction, suggesting a negotiation process in which the Indian nations had little leverage. *See, e.g.*, 25 U.S.C. §§ 1300b-11, 1300b-15 (recognizing the Texas Band of Kickapoo Indians and providing for state jurisdiction over the Band's trust lands).

Administrative recognition occurs through regulations first promulgated by the Secretary of the Interior in 1978, and later liberalized somewhat in 1994. *See* 25 C.F.R. Part 83. Administering these regulations is the Office of Federal Acknowledgment within the Bureau of Indian Affairs (OFA), previously known as the Branch of Acknowledgment and Research (BAR). From the time BAR/OFA was established until the end of 2013, 87 tribes have completed petitions for recognition. Of those, 34 have been denied administratively, and 17 have been granted. Another 19 tribes have been recognized by Congressional action or had their status confirmed by other administrative order. The remainder of the 87 petitions await resolution. To complete the picture, nearly 270 petitioners have not completed their applications.

The seven currently applicable "mandatory" criteria for administrative recognition, in 25 C.F.R. § 83.7, can be summarized as follows:

- Continuous identification as an "American Indian entity" since 1900 by federal, state, or tribal governments, by academics, or in publications;

- Existence as "a distinct community" from historical times to the present;

- Maintenance of political influence over the membership from historical times until the present;

- Maintenance of membership criteria and governing procedures;

- A membership that consists of individuals who descend from a historical Indian tribe "or from historical Indian tribes which combined and functioned as a single autonomous political entity;

- Members are not also members of some other federally acknowledged tribe;

- The tribe is not the object of Congressional termination.

These criteria have been criticized for placing unreasonable demands upon tribes seeking recognition. According to the Advisory Council on California Indian Policy, the OFA criteria require "tribes to prove their status as self-governing entities continuously throughout history, substantially without interruption," but ignore the fact that for decades "federal and state policies contributed to the destruction and repression of these very same Native peoples and cultures." Any gap in documentation of tribal actions for as few as 10 years can sink a recognition effort. Is it possible to modify the criteria to accommodate this concern without opening the door to endless claims by scattered descendants of long-defunct groups motivated by New Age religious beliefs or romanticized images of Indians? What kind of language would you suggest if you were drafting such modified criteria? *See* Indian Tribal Federal Recognition Administrative Procedures Act of 2009, H.R. 3690, 111th Cong., § 5 (b).

On May 29, 2014, Assistant Secretary of the Interior Kevin Washburn published proposed amendments to the Part 83 criteria, designed to make the federal recognition process less burdensome on tribes and more reflective of their actual experience. Among other things, the proposed amendments eliminate the requirement of "external identification" of the group as "Indian;" provide that the evidence of "community" and "political influence and authority" need only date from 1934 (rather than the previous requirement of 1789); specify that attendance of the group's children at an Indian boarding school counts as evidence of an "Indian community;" allow for an interruption of up to 20 years in the evidence of community and political authority; and require only 80% of the group's members to be descended from a pre-1900 tribe.

Do these proposed changes go far enough to account for the devastating effects of federal policies that dispossessed Native peoples and pressed them to hide their identities, ceremonies, and gatherings? One of the biggest hurdles facing petitioning groups is OFA's demand for written documentation, including agendas, minutes, and attendance lists of social and political gatherings. How can that demand be reconciled with the fact that most Native groups have oral traditions? *See* Duane Champagne, *Traditional Government and Federal Recognition Bids Don't Mix* (Indian Country Today, July 27, 2014), available at http://indiancountrytodaymedianetwork.com/2014/07/27/traditional-government-and-federal-recognition-bids-dont-mix-155954. The proposed regulations do not address the relative value of oral history evidence versus documentary evidence. Another obstacle to several tribes' federal recognition efforts, especially in California, has been OFA's distinction between federal interaction with tribes versus federal interaction with Indians as individuals. For example, although one non-federally recognized group, the Muwekma Ohlone, showed that many of its members had submitted claims in federal proceedings for lands taken from "the California Indians" (defined by ancestry), and that Muwekma children attended BIA schools in the 1930s and 1940s, OFA and the D.C. Circuit did not view the evidence as supporting federal recognition. According to the D.C. Circuit, "interaction between Muwekma *members* and the federal government does not equate to *tribal* interaction with the federal government on a government-to-government basis." *Muwekma Ohlone Tribe v. Salazar*, 708 F.3d 209, 216 (D.C. Cir. 2013). Would the proposed amendments to Part 83 support or repudiate such an analysis? How easy is it, in fact, to separate tribal from individual interactions for recognition purposes?

Tribal groups have also attacked the OFA *process* for inconsistent application of the criteria, staff reviews that go on endlessly, lack of transparency, and denial of a fair airing of their claims. The current OFA process requires tribes to spend hundreds of thousands of dollars for expert witnesses and documents in order to mount a plausible claim. For example, the Shinnecock Nation of New York spent 32 years and $33 million before finally achieving federal recognition through the OFA process. Opponents of recognition, often local citizen groups fearing loss of control over activities on tribal lands, complain that they are not afforded sufficient voice in the recognition process.

What kind of administrative process should be afforded to tribes seeking federal recognition? The original regulatory procedures for BAR lacked any provision for a hearing, cross-examination of witnesses, or inspection by the applicant tribe of the actual record on which the administrative decision was based. The Ninth Circuit described it as "[i]nformal decision-making, behind closed doors and with an undisclosed record. . . . " *Greene v. Babbitt*, 64 F.3d 1266, 1275 (9th Cir. 1995). In more recent years, tribes (and their opponents) have been afforded more opportunity to comment on proposed OFA findings regarding acknowledgment; but the process remains largely the same. Would it be preferable to establish an independent commission, separate from the Department of the Interior, to review petitions and to conduct adjudicatory hearings on any omissions or deficiencies that the commission's staff finds in the petition, including an opportunity for the petitioner to cross-examine the staff? For such a proposal, see the Indian Tribal Federal Recognition Administrative Procedures Act of 2009, H.R. 3690, 111th Cong. The May, 2014 proposed amendments to Part 83 are also intended to improve the process, by facilitating the timely issuance of decisions and allowing for an administrative judge designated by the Interior's Office of Hearings and Appeals to conduct a comprehensive hearing and review of a negative proposed finding, including questioning of OFA staff. However, promulgation of the new regulations has been delayed by actions of the House Committee on Natural Resources, Subcommittee on Indian, Insular and Alaska Native Affairs.

In addition to legislation and the OFA process, litigation is sometimes available as a means for achieving federal recognition. The process is somewhat indirect, as there does not appear to be any federal cause of action based on refusal of federal recognition. *But cf. Mashpee Tribe v. Secretary of the Interior*, 820 F.2d 480 (1st Cir. 1987). Rather, an unacknowledged group must bring a legal claim where one of the elements necessary for recovery is the existence of a treaty right (*e.g.*, *U.S. v. Washington*, 641 F.2d 1368 (9th Cir. 1981)), federal statutory protection directed at tribes (*Mashpee v. New Seabury Corp.*, 592 F.2d 575 (1st Cir. 1979)), or inherent tribal rights of self-government (*Native Village of Venetie I.R.A. Council v. State of Alaska*, 944 F.2d 548 (9th Cir. 1991)). If an Indian nation should win such a case, the victory can potentially serve as the predicate for federal recognition, especially if the United States was a party. Victory, however, requires persuading the fact-finder — which may be a jury if the desired remedy is legal rather than equitable — that the plaintiff satisfies the doctrinal criteria for tribal status.

The most notorious case to present this proof dilemma for federal recognition involved the Mashpee Wampanoag Tribe of Massachusetts. The Mashpee advanced their tribal status through a land claim under the Nonintercourse Act. In 1869, the Massachusetts General Court had authorized land sales from the Mashpee to non-Indians, despite the opposition of a majority of the Mashpee and without obtaining the necessary approval from the federal government under the Nonintercourse Act. Thus, the crucial question in the case was whether the Mashpee constituted a tribe in 1869, and if so, whether the currently claiming Mashpee represented that same tribe. Certain "facts" were undisputed. Prior to 1869, the tribal language ceased to be spoken, and the Mashpee were converted to Christianity. They regularly intermarried with outsiders, and governed themselves through a Massachusetts town government rather than a separate tribal organization. Yet their community had been continuously identified as an "Indian town" on Cape Cod, and leading Mashpee families were closely related. Many of the Mashpees' choices had been made in order to ensure their survival as a community. In this "borderline" case (*see* JAMES CLIFFORD, THE PREDICAMENT OF CULTURE: TWENTIETH CENTURY ETHNOGRAPHY, LITERATURE, AND ART 277–346 (1988)), anthropologists, historians, and other expert witnesses sparred in an unfamiliar adversarial setting over the question whether this type of community constituted an Indian tribe during the relevant time periods. For example, Sioux scholar Vine Deloria, Jr.

offered the definition of a tribe from a distinctly Native perspective:

> As I use [the term "tribe"] and as I understand other Indian people
> using it, it means a group of people living pretty much in the same place
> who know who their relatives are. . . . [Questions about the necessity of
> political organization are] getting increasingly difficult to respond to,
> because we don't make the distinctions that you do in the Anglican [Anglo]
> world, religious, political, and everything else. What you are talking about
> is a group of people who know where they are. They may have to respond
> to outside pressures and adopt political structures, religious structures, or
> economic structures to deal with that outside society. There is no question
> I can answer where I have to begin to divide that community up and say we
> have these identifiable structures, the same way you do in the white men's
> world, because it's not the way I look at it.

Trial Transcript in *Mashpee Tribe v. New Seabury Corp.*, 17:127–128, *quoted in* JACK
CAMPISI, THE MASHPEE INDIANS: TRIBE ON TRIAL (1991). After more than a month of
such testimony and intensely fought disputes over jury instructions, the jury found
against the Mashpee, pronouncing that the Mashpee had abandoned their tribal
relations before 1869. In the court's view, once tribal relations have been abandoned,
they cannot be reconstituted. The First Circuit affirmed, upholding the principle
that courts may determine when tribal status has ended through voluntary
abandonment. *Mashpee Tribe v. New Seabury Corp.*, 592 F.2d 575, 586–87 (1st Cir.
1979). Undaunted, the Mashpee turned their attention to their pending petition for
federal acknowledgment. Nearly 20 years later, on February 22, 2007, the Department of the Interior issued a notice announcing its final determination that the
Mashpee Indian Tribal Council, Inc. of Massachusetts was federally recognized,
based on the Tribe's satisfaction of all seven mandatory criteria. 72 Fed. Reg. 8007
(Feb. 22, 2007). At the specific request of the Massachusetts Attorney General, the
Department had reexamined the record in the federal litigation over Mashpee tribal
status, but had not found any evidence that would change its findings. Apparently
OFA and the Department did not believe themselves bound by the earlier judicial
finding that the Mashpee had abandoned their tribal status.

Should the OFA administrative process take precedence over legislative and
judicial means of achieving federal recognition? In 1989 Congressional testimony
regarding federal recognition of the Lumbee Tribe, Representative James Clarke of
North Carolina objected to recognition via federal statute, stating that "the proper
way to do this is through the established acknowledgement process that is carried
out by the Bureau of Indian Affairs. . . . I do not believe the way to solve the
problem [of protracted proceedings before BAR] is to circumvent the established
process." Hearing Before the House Committee on Interior and Insular Affairs, No.
101-57 (September 26, 1989). If the act of federal recognition is inescapably political,
how is it possible to deny the political branches an active role? Similarly, the Second
Circuit has held that courts presented with Nonintercourse Act claims should not
make critical findings about the plaintiff's tribal status until the administrative
recognition process has had a reasonable period of time to make its determinations.
Golden Hill Paugussett Tribe of Indians v. Weicker, 39 F.3d 51, 58–59 (2d Cir. 1994).
OFA's eventual decision denying their petition sent the Paugussetts back to federal
court, seeking to reopen their original complaint asserting tribal status. Judge

Arterton dismissed the suit, stating that the BIA's determination against tribal status would be given collateral estoppel effect. Given that Congress has identified legislation, the OFA process, and litigation as three alternative means of achieving federal recognition, is it proper for courts to accord OFA such a decisive role?

The experience of the Shinnecock Nation of New York offers a striking demonstration of how the administrative process for recognition through OFA has preempted other methods. In 2005, a federal district court found that the Shinnecock Nation was a tribe for Nonintercourse Act purposes, based on longstanding intergovernmental relations between the Nation and the State of New York. Nonetheless, the Department of the Interior took the position that it would not include the Shinnecock on the list of federally recognized tribes until it successfully traversed the administrative acknowledgment process. *See New York v. Shinnecock Indian Nation*, 400 F. Supp. 2d 486 (E.D.N.Y. 2005). The Shinnecocks then sued to force an expedited review by OFA, and Interior eventually agreed to provide a determination by the end of 2009. On October 1, 2010, the Department of the Interior finally ended the process with a finding that the Shinnecock met all the Part 83 criteria, and therefore were entitled to federal recognition as a tribe with a government-to-government relationship with the United States. Given that the federal judge had made specific findings about tribal existence based on an adversarial proceeding, should an administrative process have been required as well? Should it matter that the United States was initially brought into the federal litigation, and then left the lawsuit with no objection by the parties?

d.   The Politics of Federal Recognition

Complicating the law of federal recognition is an undeniable political dimension. When tribes began conducting high-stakes gaming within the framework of the Indian Gaming Regulatory Act of 1988 (IGRA), 25 U.S.C. § 2701 et seq., federal recognition took on new significance. Unless tribe-specific federal legislation provided otherwise, newly recognized tribes would have the same power as others to build casinos, under compacts with their respective states. See Ch. 5, Sec. D for a detailed discussion of IGRA. Perhaps most important, IGRA placed strict limitations on the location of tribal gaming facilities for tribes that were federally recognized as of 1988; but tribes recognized after 1988 were not bound by those limitations. Gaming is permissible under IGRA on "the initial reservation of an Indian tribe acknowledged by the Secretary under the Federal acknowledgment process, or the restoration of lands for an Indian tribe that is restored to Federal recognition." 25 U.S.C. § 2719 (b)(1)(B). Especially for non-federally recognized tribes located near strong markets for gaming, new financial backers for gaming petitions — and their lobbyists — presented themselves, promising fabulous results. Of course, gaming opponents also saw new urgency in repelling federal recognition. Suspicions arose that federal recognition decisions bore no relationship to the legal criteria set forth in CFR Part 83. In 2004, Kevin Gover, former Assistant Secretary for Indian Affairs in the Clinton administration, offered his astute assessment of the political issues surrounding federal acknowledgment.

Testimony of Kevin Gover, Professor of Law, Arizona State University College of Law

United States Senate Committee on Indian Affairs
Hearing on S. 297, Federal Acknowledgment Process Reform Act of 2003
(Apr. 21, 2004)

What I find in observing what has gone on both while I was in office and after is that there is a mythology that has grown around BAR [now OFA] and about the Federal recognition process. The first myth is that it seems to be understood that the process is about gaming, when of course we know that it is not. The process was established before any of us had thought of casinos, and yet because of the importance of the decision and the fact that a newly recognized tribe becomes eligible under the Indian Gaming Regulatory Act to conduct gaming in accordance with that act, it is understood to be about gaming. It really is not, and we have to work very hard in making policy to make that point and distinguish this process from gaming.

There are several other approvals that have to take place before a newly recognized tribe can engage in gaming, and at every one of those points — the process of compacting, the process of taking land into trust — both the local community and the affected States are deeply involved and their concerns weigh very heavily in that process in the Department.

The second, and it is closely related to the gaming idea, is the myth that some group of very powerful lobbyists have an extraordinary amount of influence over the program. I can only speak for myself, of course, but I suspect it is also true of [comparable officials in the Bush administration]. The truth is that I rarely if ever saw a lobbyist on these issues. If I did, it was also in the presence of tribal leadership from the petitioning tribes where it would be expected. What we do not get is any sort of backroom, underhanded, undue influence by anybody in the lobbying business.

The third is again related, and that is the idea that somehow the Branch of Acknowledgment and Research, or now the Office of Federal Acknowledgment, possesses some sort of superior and unassailable expertise about these matters. I do not want to be understood to be putting them down in any way. They are expert. They are professional. They are very good at what they do. But so are the police officers that an assistant secretary works with; so are the educators; so are the social workers; so are the many hundreds of other experts and professionals that are in the BIA, and yet no one suggests that an assistant secretary should not override a decision by any of those other experts and professionals. And yet for some reason, it seems that BAR's work is understood to be entitled to some sort of special deference.

Well, it is not. Assistant secretaries are also experts in Indian affairs, and we are asked to bring our expertise and our broader policy vision to bear on these petitions. That is why we are nominated by Presidents. That is why we are confirmed by the Senate. So it should come as no surprise that from time to time we find ourselves deciding to not follow the recommendations of the BAR.

2.   Who Is an Indian?

a.   Traditional Tribal Views of Status and Community Membership

Before contact with Europeans, Indians were organized in at least two thousand groups with divergent languages, rituals, social systems, and methods of subsistence. Membership (or citizenship) in any given community was a function of the system of social organization. The constituent social units of most Native communities were clans or extended kinship groups. Some of these social systems tied membership to one's mother's clan or kinship group (matrilineal), others to one's father's (patrilineal).

Notwithstanding this emphasis on descent, membership in the precontact period was relatively fluid, and ancestry within the group was not always essential. Individuals sometimes left their group to reside with one that was alien. The cause might be ritual banishment, personal disgrace, fear of revenge for a crime that one has committed, or intermarriage. Sometimes adoption, formal or informal, was available as a means of permanently integrating the newcomer into the group, especially when clan membership was essential to group participation. Furthermore, the rules of warfare among certain tribes dictated that prisoners of war might be taken as slaves or servants and eventually integrated into the victorious group. *See* Carole Goldberg-Ambrose, *Of Native Americans and Tribal Members: The Influence of Law on Indian Group Life*, 28 LAW & SOC'Y REV. 1123, 1140 (1994).

In the post-contact period, the social systems of Native communities often made it possible to integrate European newcomers as members. Thus, for example, when European traders settled in Cherokee country and married Cherokee women, their children were tribal members under the Nation's matrilineal clan system because they were members of their mother's clan. This system led to the rise of a "mixed-blood" group of Cherokee who often assumed positions of leadership within the Nation. *See* RENNARD STRICKLAND, FIRE AND THE SPIRITS: CHEROKEE LAW FROM CLAN TO COURT (1975). Alternatively, an outsider could be adopted under special circumstances, as when the individual married a tribal member. Thus, for example, an amendment in 1866 to section 5 of Article 3 of the Cherokee Constitution gave the following definition of citizenship: "All native-born Cherokees, all Indians and whites legally members of the Nation by adoption, . . . and their descendants, who reside within the limits of the Cherokee Nation, shall be taken and be deemed to be citizens of the Cherokee Nation." The Cherokee statutes likewise made it clear that all white men legally married to Cherokee women and residing within the Nation were adopted citizens. (Sections 659–663, 666 and 667, Laws of the Cherokee Nation, 1892, pp. 329, and following.) In order to solemnize such a marriage, a non-Indian had to present a certificate of good moral character, signed by at least10 respectable citizens of the Cherokee Nation, and had to take an oath of allegiance.

In *United States v. Rogers*, 45 U.S. (4 How.) 567 (1846), a white man who had married a Cherokee woman and had been adopted into the Nation was charged with the murder of another white man who had been adopted into the Nation under the same circumstances. The defendant challenged the authority of the United States to prosecute him, citing the language in the Nonintercourse Act providing that the federal criminal laws applicable within Indian Country "shall not extend to crimes committed by one Indian against the person or property of another Indian." The Supreme Court found that even though the Cherokee Nation might treat a non-Indian as one of its citizens, the exception in the Nonintercourse Act was limited to individuals who were Indians by race (*i.e.*, descent). According to the Court,

> . . . [W]e think it very clear, that a white man who at mature age is adopted in an Indian tribe does not thereby become an Indian, and was not intended to be embraced in the exception above mentioned. He may by such adoption become entitled to certain privileges in the tribe, and make himself amenable to their laws and usages. Yet he is not an Indian; and the exception is confined to those who by the usages and customs of the Indians are regarded as belonging to their race. It does not speak of members of a tribe, but of the race generally, — of the family of Indians; and it intended to leave them both, as regarded their own tribe, and other tribes also, to be governed by Indian usages and customs. And it would perhaps be found difficult to preserve peace among them, if white men of every description might at pleasure settle among them, and, by procuring an adoption by one of the tribes, throw off all responsibility to the laws of the United States, and claim to be treated by the government and its officers as if they were Indians born. It can hardly be supposed that Congress intended to grant such exemptions, especially to men of that class who are most likely to become Indians by adoption, and who will generally be found the most mischievous and dangerous inhabitants of the Indian country.

It may have been supposed, that the treaty of New Echota, made with the Cherokees in 1835, ought to have some influence upon the construction of this act of Congress, and extend the exception to all the adopted members of the tribe. But there is nothing in the treaty in conflict with the construction we have given to the law. The fifth article of the treaty stipulates, it is true, that the United States will secure to the Cherokee nation the right, by their national councils, to make and carry into effect such laws as they may deem necessary for the government and protection of the persons and property within their own country, belonging to their people, or such persons as have connected themselves with them. But a proviso immediately follows, that such laws shall not be inconsistent with the Constitution of the United States, and such acts of Congress as had been, or might be, passed, regulating trade and intercourse with the Indians. Now the act of Congress under which the prisoner is indicted had been passed but a few months before, and this proviso in the treaty shows that the stipulation above mentioned was not intended or understood to alter in any manner its provisions, or affect its construction. Whatever obligations the prisoner may have taken upon himself by becoming a Cherokee by adoption, his responsibility to the laws of the United States remained unchanged and undiminished. He was still a white man, of the white race, and therefore not within the exception in the act of Congress.

45 U.S. at 572–73.

United States v. Rogers treats "Indian" as a racial or ancestry-based classification rather than a political category. Is a purely racial definition consistent with the federalism or international self-determination models of tribal-federal relations? Could the United States be deemed to have special responsibilities to people of Native descent even if the governments to which they might have belonged were destroyed or suppressed by action of the United States or if they do not satisfy citizenship requirements of a contemporary tribe to which they are linked by ancestry? If so, would it make sense to extend federal statutes such as the Nonintercourse Act to Indians as defined by ancestry or descent as well as to Indians defined by political status? Is *United States v. Rogers* consistent with the rationale of *Morton v. Mancari*, set forth in Sec. B.1, this chapter?

The treaty with the Cherokee of July 19, 1866, 14 Stat. 799–803, prescribed a different approach from the one taken in *United States v. Rogers*. Article 13 of that treaty provided for a court of the United States in the Cherokee territory, but guaranteed "That the judicial tribunals of the [Cherokee] Nation shall be allowed to retain exclusive jurisdiction in all civil and criminal cases arising within their country in which members of the Nation, *by nativity or adoption*, shall be the only parties . . . " (emphasis added). Likewise, the federal statute organizing the Oklahoma Territory, 26 Stat. 81 (1890) stipulated in § 30 "that the judicial tribunals of the Indian Nations shall retain exclusive jurisdiction in all civil and criminal cases arising in the country in which members of the Nation, *by nativity or by adoption*, shall be the only parties;" and in § 31, that "nothing in this act shall be so construed as to deprive any of the courts of the civilized Nations of exclusive jurisdiction over all cases arising wherein members of said Nations, *whether by treaty, blood or adoption*, are the sole parties; nor so as to interfere with the right and power of said civilized Nations to punish said parties for violation of the statutes and laws enacted by their national councils, where such laws are not contrary to the treaties and laws of the United States (emphasis added)." *See Nofire v. United States*, 164 U.S. 657 (1897).

That same 1866 treaty with the Cherokee Nation provided in Article 9 that all former Cherokee slaves (known as Cherokee Freedmen) "who have been liberated by voluntary act of their former owners or by law, as well as all free colored persons who were in the country at the commencement of the rebellion, and are now residents therein, or who may return within six months, and their descendants, shall have all the rights of native Cherokees." Over the past decade, controversy has raged within the Cherokee Nation over whether the descendants of these Freedmen should be entitled to Cherokee citizenship. For further discussion of this controversy, as well as the federal government's reaction to various Cherokee actions on this subject, see Ch. 3, Sec. D.

Today, formal tribal membership or citizenship typically turns on descent from an individual on a base list or roll, possession of a specified degree of ancestry from such an individual (often referred to as blood quantum), domicile at the time of one's birth, or some combination of these criteria. Some Indian nations also permit naturalization or adoption of individuals with close but nonbiological ties to the community. *See, e.g.,* Const. and Bylaws of the Fort McDermitt Paiute and Shoshone Tribe, Art. II, 2 (b) (allowing adoption of spouses who are descended by at least one-half blood degree from any tribe); Const. of the Lower Brule Sioux

Tribe, Art. II, Sec. 2 (allowing adoption of individuals who live on the reservation). Should Indian nations liberalize their adoption provisions in order to underscore that tribal citizenship is not a racial category and to include all persons with cultural, linguistic, or other ties to the community? Are there reasons why an Indian nation, which might have welcomed adoptees in the pre-colonial period, might view the matter differently today? For a discussion of these questions, see Carole Goldberg, *Members Only? Designing Citizenship Requirements for Indian Nations*, 50 Kan. L. Rev. 437 (2002); Ch. 3, Sec. D; Matthew L.M. Fletcher, *Tribal Membership and Indian Nationhood*, 37 Am. Indian L. Rev. 1 (2012–2013).

b.   Federal Definitions

Today, characterizing an individual as an "Indian" has a wide range of consequences under federal law, including subjection to federal or tribal rather than state criminal jurisdiction; eligibility for federal benefits and employment preferences; exemption from state taxation, child welfare, and other civil authority; and entitlement to inherit certain trust or restricted lands. Indeed, an entire volume of the United States Code, Title 25, is devoted to laws that single out Indians for special treatment. In addition, federal (and state) nondiscrimination and affirmative action laws include Indians among the protected groups.

In view of federal constitutional and statutory provisions prohibiting discrimination on the basis of race, ancestry, and ethnicity, courts and policy makers have contended with the question whether laws singling out Indians for special treatment are making impermissible racial or ancestry-based distinctions. *See* Sec. B, this chapter. In answering this question, it may be important to consider the particular definition of "Indian" used for purposes of the federal law under examination. Some statutes use the term without definition, leaving the task of interpretation to the courts or agencies. Thus, for example, the Supreme Court has been required to define "Indian" for purposes of the criminal provisions of the Nonintercourse Act, 18 U.S.C. § 1152, and lower courts have labored to fashion a definition for the term in prosecutions under the Major Crimes Act, 18 U.S.C. § 1153. The common test that has evolved after *United States v. Rogers, supra,* considers both Indian descent and recognition as an Indian by a federally recognized tribe. There is no specific percentage of Indian ancestry required to satisfy the "descent" prong of this test. Furthermore, enrollment on a formal tribal membership list is not required in order to satisfy the "tribal recognition" component. Thus, for example, in *United States of America v. A.W.L.*, 117 F.3d 1423 (8th Cir. 1997), evidence adduced at the adjudication hearing established that the defendant was not an enrolled member of the Tribe at the time of the offenses. Nonetheless, because he had 15/32 Indian ancestry; he held himself out to be Indian; he lived on the reservation all of his life, attending reservation schools and receiving benefits of BIA schools; he was removed from the Tribe's enrollment only pending clarification of his paternity; and both of his parents — with whom he resided — lived and were respected as Indians, the Eighth Circuit found that he was an Indian for purposes of section 1153.

This manner of defining "Indian" under federal criminal statutes survived constitutional challenge under the "void for vagueness" doctrine in *United States v. Broncheau*, 597 F.2d 1260 (9th Cir. 1979). Should it? At the very least, outcomes can be highly contested and unpredictable. Consider the facts of *United States v. Cruz*, 554 F.3d 840 (9th Cir. 2009). There a person with 29/128 Blackfeet ancestry and 32/128 related Canadian Indian ancestry did not satisfy the "tribal recognition" portion of the definition, even though the Blackfeet Tribe had accorded him "descendant" status entitling him to many benefits of membership, he had been prosecuted earlier under Blackfeet criminal law, and he lived on the Blackfeet reservation. Chief Judge Kozinski sharply dissented from the panel majority's conclusion. Should it have made a difference that the defendant in *Cruz* was entitled to benefits as a "descendant," but had not actually received them? Then consider the facts of a case from another federal Circuit, *United States v. Stymiest*, 581 F.3d 759 (8th Cir. 2009), where a defendant of 3/32 Leech Lake Ojibwe descent, not enrolled in the Leech Lake Tribe, was found to be an Indian for purposes of federal prosecution. Stymiest had presented himself as a tribal member on the Rosebud Sioux Reservation, where he lived and worked, utilizing the Indian Health Service hospital there and submitting to tribal criminal jurisdiction on several occasions. Many members of the Rosebud community, including his longtime girlfriend, testified that they understood him to be Indian.

The different federal Circuits appear to be using different approaches to determine Indian descent and recognition by the tribe or federal government as an Indian. The Ninth Circuit focuses on a discrete set of criteria, whereas the Eighth Circuit applies a more flexible, holistic test. Which of these approaches is sounder? Should federal courts encourage federal prosecutions in Indian country by making it easier to prove a defendant is Indian? One commentator has argued that a broader definition is needed because it "allows the federal government to better fulfill its duties and strengthens the rule of law in Indian Country. The Eighth Circuit's test should be adopted to aid law enforcement, ameliorate conditions in Indian Country, and promote equal protection for Indians across the country." Brian Lewis, *Indian Status for the Purpose of Federal Criminal Jurisdiction and the Current Split in the Courts of Appeals*, 26 HARV. J. RACIAL & ETHNIC JUST. 241, 242 (2010). Should self-identity and social expression matter more than "objective" facts such as tribal enrollment or receipt of federal benefits? For an affirmative answer, as well as many useful practice pointers from experienced federal defense attorneys, see Daniel Donovan and John Rhodes, *To Be or Not to Be? Who Is an "Indian Person?,"* 73 MONT. L. REV. 61 (2012). Apart from difficulties applying the definition of "Indian" under federal criminal statutes, should the statutes relying on this definition survive scrutiny under the equal protection component of the Fifth Amendment due process clause? See *United States v. Antelope*, presented in Sec. B.1, this chapter.

Where they do exist, federal statutory definitions of who is an Indian vary considerably from statute to statute. Some emphasize membership or eligibility for membership in a federally recognized Indian nation. For example, under the Indian Child Welfare Act, 25 U.S.C. § 1901 et seq., which creates special procedural and substantive rules for child welfare proceedings involving Indian children, an "Indian child" is defined as "any unmarried person who is under age eighteen and is either (a) a member of an Indian tribe or (b) is eligible for membership in an Indian tribe and is the biological child of a member of an Indian tribe." § 1903(4). The term "member" is not defined. Should it be limited to officially enrolled members? Or should it also encompass individuals who are not formally enrolled but are recognized to be members of the tribal community? *See In re Adoption of C.D.*, 751 N.W.2d 236 (N.D. 2008) (for purposes of ICWA, enrollment is not required to establish membership, but evidence establishing Indian heritage, Indian blood quantum, acceptance in the Indian community, and receipt of Indian scholarships, awards, and benefits, but without a corresponding connection to tribal membership, was insufficient).

In contrast, other federal statutes, or parts of those statutes, define "Indian" based on ancestry alone. Thus, for example, the definitional section of the Indian Reorganization Act, 25 U.S.C. § 479, includes descendants of members of federally recognized tribes who were living on Indian reservations as of June 1, 1934, as well as "all other persons of one-half or more Indian blood." Similarly, the Indian Health Care Improvement Act of 1976, 25 U.S.C. § 1601 et seq., establishes programs to assist Indians in becoming health care professionals. 25 U.S.C. §§ 1611, 1612. For purposes of this portion of the statute, "Indian" includes individuals who are descendants of first or second degree of tribal members as well as members of terminated tribes. Certain 1988 amendments to the Indian Health Care Improvement Act also authorized provision of Indian Health Service care to California Indians who are members of federally non-recognized tribes, so long as those individuals can demonstrate their descent from tribal members resident in California as of 1852. 25 U.S.C. § 1679. Is it possible to characterize these ancestry-based definitions as "political" rather than racial? Is an ancestry-based definition consistent with one or more of the previously examined models of the tribal-federal relationship?

Sometimes federal definitions of who is an Indian do not coincide with the views of the Indian community to which the individual claims some affiliation. Problems most often arise when federal statutes referring to tribal membership are interpreted to require formal tribal enrollment. One Midwestern tribe, for example, has had as its tribal historian an individual who speaks the language, who participates in religious ceremonies, and whose mother is an enrolled member. Because the Tribe determines membership according to the father, however, the tribal historian is not eligible for formal enrollment. In fact, the concept of formal enrollment has no counterpart in traditional tribal views of membership. An Indian may be treated as a member of a tribal community even without formal enrollment, because that person fully participates in the social, religious, and cultural life of the tribe; yet a federal law that defines Indians solely as enrolled tribal members may exclude such an individual because she has no formal place in the community's political and economic processes.

Formal tribal enrollment first achieved prominence through the allotment policy of the late nineteenth century, which required official lists of tribal members entitled to participate in the anticipated per capita distributions of tribal property. In some instances, these rolls included previously adopted white tribal members as well as ex-slaves of certain southern tribes. *See generally* ANGIE DEBO, AND STILL THE WATERS RUN 3–60 (1940). Thus the General Allotment Act did not institute minimum blood quantum requirements, and the Act should not be considered the source of such requirements in tribal constitutions and membership ordinances. *See* John LaVelle, *The General Allotment Act "Eligibility" Hoax: Distortions of Law,*

Policy, and History in Derogation of Indian Tribes, 14 WICAZO SA REV. 251 (1999).

Should the requirement of formal tribal enrollment be introduced into all federal statutes and legal doctrines that allude to membership? The following dialogue regarding affirmative action, between Indian law scholar Robert Laurence and Sam Deloria, for many years director of the American Indian Law Program at the University of New Mexico, offers insight into that question. Among other things, the American Indian Law Program provides a summer program to prepare Indian students for admission and success in law school.

P.S. Deloria & Robert Laurence, *What's an Indian?* *A Conversation About Law School Admissions, Indian Tribal Sovereignty, and Affirmative Action*
44 ARK. L. REV. 1107 (1991)

LAURENCE: O.K., here's a hypothetical; not so hypothetical, really. A colleague on the Admissions Committee stops by my officer and says that the law school has received an application from someone claiming to be an Indian. How, she wants to know, does the Committee react, and, in particular, What's an Indian?

DELORIA: That question gets asked a lot and people are surprised to hear that our answer is not always to check for enrollment in a federally recognized Indian tribe.

LAURENCE: "Not always." The answer is sometimes "Yes?"

DELORIA: Sure. Various federal entitlements [such as Indian scholarship funds] are based on enrollment. . . . But if there is no connection between the question asked and a particular federal requirement, then there is no easy answer.

LAURENCE: Why not?

DELORIA: Because the answer to your question requires that one define exactly why the institution wants to have an Indian around. . . .

LAURENCE: Well, imagine a spectrum of "Indianness." On one end you have enrollment in a federally recognized Indian tribe. On the other end is anyone who self-identifies as an Indian.

DELORIA: That strikes me as less a spectrum of "Indianness" and more a classification of identifiers. In one case, it's a government who is doing the identification and in the other it's the individual. There is no reason to expect that those persons identified as "Indians" by a government — federal or tribal — will be more "Indian" that those who only identify themselves as "Indians." There may be some sort of attenuated correlation, but nothing one can count on. Think of Audrey Martinez.

[The authors discuss the case of *Santa Clara Pueblo v. Martinez*, 436 U.S. 49 (1978), involving a woman, Audrey Martinez, who was ineligible for tribal membership because her mother, a member of the tribe, had married an Indian of another tribe. Under tribal law, only individuals whose *fathers* are tribal members were eligible for membership. The *Martinez* case is presented in Ch. 3, Sec. C.5.]

LAURENCE: Audrey Martinez, while unenrolled is *surely* an Indian for some purposes. Like affirmative action?

DELORIA: As I said: that depends on exactly why the institution wants to have an Indian around.

LAURENCE: It's hard to imagine a reason for affirmative action that would not be satisfied by Audrey's presence: she speaks an Indian language, practices an Indian religion, has Indian parents and children, *looks* like an Indian, if that's important to you.

DELORIA: It's not hard at all to imagine an affirmative action program in which she would not be considered an Indian. [The Indian Reorganization Act's Indian preference provision, applicable to the Bureau of Indian Affairs, arguably is such a program. *See Morton v. Mancari*, discussed in Sec. B, this chapter.] Besides, a program that uses an objective criterion like membership will be easier to administer. . . .

LAURENCE: O.K. Suppose the law school asks your difficult "why-do-you-want-an-Indian" question and decides that it is to diversify the student body, to make it less white, less wealthy, less homogeneous. "Cultural pluralism" is the going phrase. . . .

DELORIA: Look. There are two basic reasons for affirmative action. One: a mostly white institution wishes to diversify itself. Two: pay-backs. [The former is mainly for the benefit of the white institutions, the latter mainly to make reparations for past wrongs.] Now here is what is, for me, a nearly fundamental principle: to the degree that an institution is taking affirmative action steps to service itself, *its* definition of "Indian" might control, but to the extent that it's trying to pay-back the Indians for past wrongs, then to that same extent the Indians have an important say in how the program is structured and whom it serves.

LAURENCE: O.K. Then . . .

DELORIA: . . . back to Audrey Martinez. She is not an Indian under *every* possible definition, but if the school's interest is in cultural pluralism, it would be crazy to exclude her because she isn't enrolled. . . .

[The authors consider whether rejecting enrollment as a requirement opens the door to self-identified "Indians" caught up in the myth of the "noble savage" or adhering to "new age" beliefs. Self-identification may be just too costless, and perhaps even too fashionable.]

LAURENCE: How can we go to Indian self-identification without opening the law school up to these charlatans?

DELORIA: I think that the applicant, especially if unenrolled, but maybe in any case, should be put to the proof of having been an Indian at some important time in the past.

LAURENCE: "Been an Indian" or "held oneself out as an Indian?"

DELORIA: *"Been."* One does not become an Indian just by declaring oneself an Indian. . . . I think we're talking here about some connection with Indian family or community.

LAURENCE: You mean *reservation* community, or would hanging around the Indian Center in downtown Cleveland do?

DELORIA: In theory, Cleveland will do, but given the last spot to fill and an applicant from Pine Ridge, South Dakota and one from Cleveland, I'd probably take the Pine Ridge resident, because I think that is what your institution is looking for. . . . It seems to me that for most purposes, the policy [of diversity] is better advanced by the unenrolled Audrey Martinez than by a card-carrying Cherokee member, 1/256th, from Orange County. . . . Tribal membership is a political definition by the tribe that serves a fixed tribal purpose and it is not usually fit for other purposes. In some tribes, many people are included in such a definition who would not meet the ordinary meaning of the word "Indian." And vice versa: Audrey Martinez is left out, as are many other very Indian people. Same issue as all along: diversity or pay-back? But there are very few issues for which tribal membership is the correct working definition. . . .

LAURENCE: Instead of diversity, how are the problems different when affirmative action is designed to right past wrongs? Do we agree that, if reparations are to be made, it makes sense to do it based on membership in a group, rather than on an individualized inspection of merit? . . .

DELORIA: When affirmative action is intended to accomplish pay-backs, then the Indians themselves necessarily must have a say in who participates. . . .

LAURENCE: So, in the end, we have this; Pluralistic driven affirmative action is sensible; just as surely, it is difficult to administer when it comes to Indians. "Indian" should not be defined for these purposes as based only on enrollment. Rather, both in addition to and instead of enrollment, some past identification with the American Indian community should be demonstrated. . . .

             With respect to reparations-based affirmative action, the institution is on solid historical grounds because of widespread abrogation of treaty provisions promising education to the Indians. This could, perhaps, lead to a narrower definition of "Indian" than used above for pluralism-based affirmative action [because not all tribes have treaties]. On the other hand, the definition above is broadly consistent with the treaty-based theory. Certainly, for an institution with both kinds of affirmative action in mind, our broad definition is appropriate.

NOTES ON DEFINING WHO IS AN "INDIAN"

1. **Tribal Enrollment and Tribal Control over Who Is an Indian:** The dialogue between Laurence and Deloria examines when it might be appropriate to expand the definition of "Indian," for purposes of federal law, beyond formal tribal enrollment or citizenship. Is the case for this broader definition so clear when a federal Indian statute is not seeking to achieve diversity, but to compensate for past deprivations or to support tribal self-determination? Deloria emphasizes the importance of the Indians having a say in who qualifies as Indian in these latter situations. But why does he think that an enrollment criterion offers tribes an insufficient voice in determining Indian status? What is the alternative to enrollment? Consider the federal criminal statutes discussed above, with their requirement of tribal "recognition." Is that what Deloria meant by the Indians having some control? How could the federal government administer benefit programs, such as preferences for "Indian" contractors, using some tribally-controlled criterion other than enrollment? At least one tribe, the Fort Peck Assiniboine and Sioux Tribes, has created a category of non-voting Associate Members, who have 1/8 ancestry, rather than the 1/4 required for voting membership, but are entitled to benefits other than distributions of tribal funds or property. Enrollment Ordinance No. 1 of the Assiniboine and Sioux Tribes of the Fort Peck Indian Reservation, § 1(e). Is this an effective way for tribes to separately identify citizenship and community recognition as an Indian?

2. **State Court Decisions Excluding Tribally Enrolled Indians from Federal Law:** State courts interpreting federal law sometimes have gone in the opposite direction — defining "Indian" in a way that excludes some enrolled members. For example, under the Indian Child Welfare Act (ICWA), 25 U.S.C. § 1901 et seq., some state courts have embellished the statutory definition of an "Indian child" to include requirements beyond enrollment or eligibility for enrollment. Because the Act enables Indian nations and Indian parents to prevent or undo the adoption of Indian children by non-Indian families, state courts have struggled to limit its application. Despite the Act's broad definition of an "Indian child," some state courts have insisted that its reach extends only to "existing Indian families." These rulings have generally involved a child who has never lived with an Indian parent, or whose Indian parents have had little or no contact with their tribal community. *See* Ch. 5, Sec. C.3. In California, one state appellate court went so far as to hold that ICWA violates a child's substantive due process rights if it is employed to sever the child's temporary placement with a non-Indian family, unless the biological parents "maintain a significant social, cultural or political relationship with their tribe." *In re Bridget R.*, 41 Cal. App. 4th 1483, 1492 (1996). Positing that ICWA was enacted to preserve tribal cultural traditions and affiliations, the court found that "mere formal enrollment in a tribe, or a self-serving after-the-fact tribal recognition" of the parents' membership would not suffice to supply a compelling government interest. Thus, the court put the burden of proof on the biological parents to demonstrate, as a matter of fact, that they maintained significant ties to the tribe, either privately or openly, through such acts as contributing to Indian charities or subscribing to tribal newsletters.

How viable is it for the courts of one culture to probe into the nature of belonging within a very different culture? For example, the Sitka Community Association

Court of Elders held in one child welfare proceeding,

> Traditional law holds "children of female members of a clan are children of the clan regardless of where or under what circumstances they may be found. Clan membership does not wash off, nor can such membership be removed by any force, or any distance, or over time. Even in death clan membership continues, and in rebirth is it renewed."

Finding of Traditional Law by the Sitka Community Association Court of Elders in *Hepler v. Perkins*, 13 Ind. L. Rep. 6011, 6016 (1986). Convinced of the unseemliness of involving state courts in sensitive determinations of community membership, the California legislature acted in 1999 to repeal the "existing Indian family" doctrine for the courts of that state. Under § 175 (c) of the California Family Code and § 224(c) of the Welfare and Institutions Code, a determination by a tribe that a child is a member of a tribe or eligible for membership "shall constitute a significant political affiliation with the tribe and shall require the application of the federal Indian Child Welfare Act to the proceedings." Increasingly, state courts are rejecting or repudiating their early acceptance of the "existing Indian family" doctrine. *See* Ch. 5, Sec. C.3.

3. What Is the Extent of Tribal Territory, or Indian Country?

a. Indian Nations' Relationships to the Land

For Indian people, land represents sacred gifts, the basis for individual and community survival, their sovereignty, and links to their ancestors. Testifying before Congress in 1933, Lakota author Luther Standing Bear tried to explain Indians' distinctive relationship to their land:

> The white man does not understand the Indian for the reason that he does not understand America. He is too far removed from its formative processes. The roots of the tree of his life have not yet grasped the rock and soil. The white man is still troubled with primitive fears; he still has in his consciousness the perils of this frontier continent. . . .

> But in the Indian the spirit of the land is still vested; it will be until other men are able to divine and meet its rhythm. Men must be born and reborn to belong. Their bodies must be formed of the dust of their forefathers' bones.

GREAT DOCUMENTS IN AMERICAN INDIAN HISTORY 307 (Wayne Moquin & Charles L. Van Doren eds., 1973). Sixty years later, also in Congressional testimony, Lakota medicine man Pete Catches offered his own statement of the significance of the Black Hills to the Lakota:

> To the Indian spiritual way of life, the Black Hills is the center of the Lakota people. There, ages ago, before Columbus came over the sea, seven spirits came to the Black Hills. They selected that area, the beginning of sacredness to the Lakota people. Each spirit brought a gift to the Lakota people.

[The first six spirits brought earth, fire, water, air, minerals, medicine, and animals.] The seventh spirit brought the Black Hills as a whole — brought it to give it to the Lakota forever, for all eternity, not only in this life, but in the life hereafter. The two are tied together. Our people that have passed on, their spirits are contained in the Black Hills. This is why it is the center of the universe, and this is why it is sacred to the Oglala Sioux. In this life and the life hereafter, the two are together.

Quoted in Mario Gonzales, *The Black Hills: The Sacred Land of the Lakota and Tsistsistas, in* NATIVE AMERICAN VOICES: A READER 125–26 (Susan Lobo & Steve Talbot eds., 1998).

Similarly, Alaskan Native villagers have explained why they chose land over cash settlement under the terms of the Alaska Native Claims Settlement Act of 1971:

When ANCSA was passed, the people of St. Lawrence Island chose the whole island instead of cash settlement, with the understanding that the survival of the people was from the land. They understand the land and the waters around it brought the people for thousands of years in which the land was their life-identity-as well as their habitation. They understand the close relationship with the land, the life-giving resources it brought. (Roger Silook, Gambell)

THOMAS BERGER, VILLAGE JOURNEY: THE REPORT OF THE ALASKA NATIVE REVIEW COMMISSION 142 (1985).

b.   Defining "Indian Country"

Since the inception of federal Indian law, efforts have been made to restrict the protected legal status of Indian tribes primarily to a defined geographic area. The long effort to demarcate jurisdictional boundaries for Indians dates back to the first treaties between Indian tribes and colonial authorities in the early seventeenth century. Use of the term "Indian country" to describe Indian enclaves dates at least to the Proclamation of 1763, by which the Crown tried to prevent unrestrained encroachment on Indian lands by designating the lands west of the crest of the Appalachians as Indian country protected from colonial settlement. Geographically based lines of demarcation for Indian country also were contained in the 1796, 1802, and 1834 Trade and Intercourse Acts. 1 Stat. 469, 2 Stat. 139, 4 Stat. 729. Another approach, in the 1834 Act, was essentially definition by creating a residue: Indian country was "that part of the United States west of the Mississippi" not within certain states, "to which Indian title has not been extinguished." *Bates v. Clark*, 95 U.S. 204 (1877). *But see* § 29, 1834 Act, 4 Stat. 734. With the westward expansion of non-Indian settlement, each of these lines became outmoded. Consequently, in the late nineteenth century, judicial decisions began to treat Indian country as a generic term encompassing land areas in which Indian autonomy was protected rather than an area subject to precise geographic description. *See, e.g., Ex parte Crow Dog*, 109 U.S. 556, 561–62 (1883).

Indian country has come to have important jurisdictional implications. Within Indian country, tribal autonomy and self-government are generally fostered and state law enforcement is frequently precluded. The scope of some federal Indian statutes, such as the criminal jurisdictional provisions of 18 U.S.C. §§ 1152 and 1153, is expressly limited to Indian country. On the other hand, federal Indian law does not operate solely in Indian country. Some statutes operate anywhere in the United States. The federal statutory restraints against the alienation of Indian land, for example, have been held to apply to all tribally held land regardless whether the tribe is federally recognized or its land constitutes Indian country. *See Passamaquoddy Tribe v. Morton*, 528 F.2d 370 (1st Cir. 1975). Similarly, nineteenth century federal statutes proscribing the sale of liquor to Indians outside of Indian country frequently were sustained. *E.g., United States v. Holliday*, 70 U.S. (3 Wall.) 407 (1865); *United States v. Forty-Three Gallons of Whiskey*, 93 U.S. 188 (1876). More recently, Congress included within the coverage of the Indian Child Welfare Act of 1978, child custody proceedings involving certain Indian children domiciled outside of Indian country. *See* Ch. 5, Sec. C.4. Thus, every statute must be carefully analyzed to determine the precise scope of its application. Nevertheless, despite these exceptions, many important legal issues affecting Indians turn on whether the area in question constitutes Indian country.

Since 1948, the accepted definition of Indian country has been provided in 18 U.S.C. § 1151. This statute largely codified existing case law, although it also supplied some clear statutory solutions to problems not fully resolved by the cases, especially problems spawned by the allotment acts. *See* Robert N. Clinton, *Criminal Jurisdiction over Indian Lands: A Journey Through a Jurisdictional Maze*, 18 ARIZ. L. REV. 503, 507–13 (1976). While the definition of Indian country is contained in the federal criminal jurisdiction statutes, the Supreme Court has held that it "generally applies as well to questions of civil jurisdiction." *DeCoteau v. District County Court*, 420 U.S. 425, 427 n.2 (1975). Thus, "Indian country" represents a term of art in Indian law, the meaning of which has important implications for jurisdiction and governance of the affected area.

The three categories of Indian country under section 1151 are reservations (including fee lands and rights-of-way), "dependent Indian communities," and trust allotments located within or outside reservations. As Professor Clinton notes,

> [T]he definition of Indian country set forth in section 1151 [therefore] is quite expansive. Once a reservation has been established, or a dependent Indian community shown to exist, it will remain Indian country until terminated by Congress, irrespective of the nature of the land ownership. Moreover, even if individual allotted parcels of land are not located within the reservation, they may still constitute Indian country if the Indian title thereto has not been extinguished. . . . [T]he expansiveness of the definition of Indian country is important in preserving policies of tribal self-government and the protective federal trusteeship over Indians.

Clinton, *Criminal Jurisdiction over Indian Lands, supra*, 18 ARIZ. L. REV. at 513.

i.   Formal and Informal Reservations

United States v. John, 437 U.S. 634 (1978): Smith John, a Choctaw Indian, was tried in federal court under the Major Crimes Act, 18 U.S.C. § 1153, for assault with intent to kill. The jury convicted him of the lesser included offense of simple assault. The actions in question had occurred on "lands within the area designated as a reservation for the Choctaw Indians residing in central Mississippi." Only if this land was "Indian country" would federal rather than state jurisdiction prevail. The Fifth Circuit determined that the territory in question was not "Indian country," and overturned the conviction. Later John was indicted and convicted for the same acts in state court. On appeal, the Mississippi Supreme Court found the state had jurisdiction, and the United States Supreme Court granted review.

Choctaw lands and self-government had been guaranteed by the Treaty of Hopewell in 1786. Within decades, Mississippi became a state and attempted to gain control over Choctaw lands for the benefit of non-Indians. When the federal government failed to protect the Choctaw, they entered into the Treaty of Dancing Rabbit Creek (7 Stat. 333, 1830), in which they ceded their lands in Mississippi in exchange for lands west of the Mississippi River. Each Choctaw "head of a family being desirous to remain and become a citizen of the States," could do so by signifying his intention within six months to the federal agent assigned to the area. Lands were to be reserved, at least 640 acres per household, to be held by the Indians in fee simple if they would remain upon the lands for five years. Various other lands were reserved to the chiefs and to others already residing on improved lands. Choctaws who remained, however, were not to "lose the privilege of a Choctaw citizen," although they were to receive no share of the annuity provided for those who chose to remove.

Even after removal, the United States continued to acknowledge, if not to fulfill, obligations to the Choctaws who remained in Mississippi. Until the early twentieth century, however, federal policy was to encourage these Choctaws to follow the others west to the Indian Territory. A change in policy occurred in 1917, when Congress began appropriating funds for federal services and land acquisition for the Choctaws remaining in Mississippi. These lands were to be acquired through contracts with individual Choctaw purchasers, who would hold them in fee. Congress repudiated its policy of individual Indian land ownership in the Indian Reorganization Act of 1934. The method of land acquisition specified for the Mississippi Choctaw was inconsistent with the new federal policy of encouraging the preservation of Indian communities with commonly held lands. Equally important, the land program for the Mississippi Choctaw was not providing them with the benefits intended. In 1939, Congress passed an Act providing that title to all the lands previously purchased for the Mississippi Choctaws would be "in the United States in trust for such Choctaw Indians of one-half or more Indian blood, resident in Mississippi, as shall be designated by the Secretary of the Interior." 53 Stat. 851. In December 1944, the Assistant Secretary of the Department of the Interior officially proclaimed all the lands then purchased in aid of the Choctaws in Mississippi, totaling at that time more than 15,000 acres, to be a reservation. 9 Fed. Reg. 14907. Shortly thereafter, the Mississippi Choctaw adopted a constitution in accordance with the Indian Reorganization Act, and the Secretary of Interior gave his approval.

After laying out this history, the United States Supreme Court considered whether the land on which John had allegedly committed the crime was "Indian country." Justice Blackmun wrote,

With certain exceptions not pertinent here, § 1151 includes within the term "Indian country" three categories of land. The first, with which we are here concerned, is "all land within the limits of any Indian reservation under the jurisdiction of the United States Government, notwithstanding the issuance of any patent." This language first appeared in the Code in 1948 as a part of the general revision of Title 18. The Reviser's notes indicate that this definition was based on several decisions of this Court interpreting the term as it was used in various criminal statutes relating to Indians. In one of these cases, *United States v. McGowan*, 302 U.S. 535 (1938), the Court held that the Reno Indian Colony, consisting of 28.38 acres within the State of Nevada, purchased out of federal funds appropriated in 1917 and 1926 and occupied by several hundred Indians theretofore scattered throughout Nevada, was "Indian country" for the purposes of what was then 25 U.S.C. § 247 [now 18 U.S.C. § 3669], providing for the forfeiture of a vehicle used to transport intoxicants into the Indian country. The Court noted that the "fundamental consideration of both Congress and the Department of the Interior in establishing this colony has been the protection of a dependent people." 302 U.S., at 538. The principal test applied was drawn from an earlier case, *United States v. Pelican*, 232 U.S. 442 (1914), and was whether the land in question "had been validly set apart for the use of the Indians as such, under the superintendence of the Government." 232 U.S., at 449.[1]

The Mississippi lands in question here were declared by Congress to be held in trust by the Federal Government for the benefit of the Mississippi Choctaw Indians who were at that time under federal supervision. There is no apparent reason why these lands, which had been purchased in previous years for the aid of those Indians, did not become a "reservation," at least for the purposes of federal criminal jurisdiction at that particular time. *See United States v. Celestine*, 215 U.S. 278, 285 (1909). But if there were any doubt about the matter in 1939 when, as hereinabove described, Congress declared that title to lands previously purchased for the Mississippi Choctaws would be held in trust, the situation was completely clarified by the proclamation in 1944 of a reservation and the subsequent approval of the constitution and bylaws adopted by the Mississippi Band.

Because John's alleged offense had occurred within Indian country, the state court lacked jurisdiction, and his state court conviction was reversed.

---

[1] [18] Some earlier cases had suggested a more technical and limited definition of "Indian country." *See, e.g.*, Bates v. Clark, 95 U.S. 204 (1877). Throughout most of the nineteenth century, apparently the only statutory definition was that in § 1 of the Act of June 30, 1834, 4 Stat. 729. But this definition was dropped in the compilation of the Revised Statutes. *See* Ex parte Crow Dog, 109 U.S. 556 (1883). This Court was left with little choice but to continue to apply the principles established under the earlier statutory language and to develop them according to changing conditions. *See, e.g.*, Donnelly v. United States, 228 U.S. 243 (1913). It is the more expansive scope of the term that was incorporated in the 1948 revision of Title 18.

NOTE

In the absence of the 1939 Act and the Proclamation of 1944, would the result have been the same in *United States v. John*? In *Youngbear v. Brewer*, 415 F. Supp. 807 (N.D. Iowa 1976), *aff'd*, 549 F.2d 74 (8th Cir. 1977), and *State v. Youngbear*, 229 N.W.2d 728 (Iowa 1975), the courts held that the Sac and Fox Reservation in Iowa (commonly known as the Mesquakie Settlement) was Indian country despite the lack of any federal statute or order declaring the land to be a reservation. This settlement, like the Choctaw Reservation in Mississippi, was created when Indians either refused to remove or returned to lands ceded in removal treaties during the early nineteenth century. Originally, land was purchased with tribal funds under authority of a state statute in 1856 and held in trust for the Indians by state officials. A federal Indian agent was assigned to the settlement in 1865 and title to the land was conveyed by the state to the United States to be held in trust for the tribe in 1896. Similarly, the Eastern Band of Cherokee Reservation in North Carolina was created by Indians who resisted removal during the early nineteenth century and has been treated as Indian country despite the absence of a specific statute or executive order proclaiming the Cherokee lands to be an Indian reservation. *See, e.g., United States v. Lossiah*, 537 F.2d 1250 (4th Cir. 1976); *United States v. Wright*, 53 F.2d 300 (4th Cir. 1931). Upon what basis could these lands be considered Indian country? *See Oklahoma Tax Comm'n v. Chickasaw Nation*, 515 U.S. 450, 453 n.2 (1995) (referring to "informal reservations"); *United States v. Azure*, 801 F.2d 336, 339 (8th Cir. 1986) (referring to a "de facto reservation, at least for purposes of federal criminal jurisdiction"). Other portions of the opinion in *United States v. John* are presented in connection with the discussion of federal power over Indian affairs in Ch. 4, Sec. A.1.

Can a "de facto reservation" be created whenever an Indian nation acquires land in fee subject to a restriction on alienation? The United Keetoowah Band of Cherokee Indians (UKB) located in Oklahoma has a federally approved tribal charter that includes a requirement that any sale of tribal land be approved by the Secretary of the Interior. The Tribe claimed that 25 U.S.C. § 177, the federal Nonintercourse Act, also imposed a restraint against alienation. That act invalidates any conveyance of land from an Indian nation that occurs without federal permission. *See* Ch. 6, Sec. A.5.b. UKB contended that these restrictions rendered their lands Indian country and therefore free from state taxation of tribal members. In *Buzzard v. Oklahoma Tax Commission*, 992 F.2d 1073 (10th Cir. 1993), the Tenth Circuit answered in the negative, finding that the federal government had never made a choice to assume responsibility for the land, nor had it considered the jurisdictional consequences of doing so. In contrast, when the United States takes land into trust, federal statutes and regulations require such consideration. According to the court:

> If the restriction against alienation were sufficient to make any land purchased by the UKB Indian country, the UKB could remove land from state jurisdiction and force the federal government to exert jurisdiction over that land without either sovereign having any voice in the matter. Nothing in . . . the cases concerning trust land indicates that the Supreme Court intended for Indian tribes to have such unilateral power to create Indian country.

Id. at 1077. Should it matter for purposes of determining restrictions against alienation (and hence "Indian country") whether the tribal fee land is within or outside a reservation? In 2009, the Solicitor of the Department of the Interior said the answer is "yes," but without much support from court decisions. Op. Sol. Interior, M-37023 (Jan. 18, 2009). As you read the United States Supreme Court's decision in the *Venetie* case, *infra*, recall the concerns expressed by the Tenth Circuit in *Buzzard.*

ii.   Dependent Indian Communities

The term "dependent Indian community" in section 1151(b) is derived from *United States v. Sandoval*, 231 U.S. 28 (1913), presented in Ch. 1, Sec. D.2, in which the Supreme Court applied the term to refer to the New Mexico pueblos — tribes that had long had relations with the federal government and for which agents had been appointed through the Indian Service, but whose land was not held in trust. Following codification of the term in 1948, courts considered a wide array of claims that nontrust lands constituted dependent Indian communities, including state reservations occupied by tribes and protected under the Nonintercourse Act (*State v. Dana*, 404 A.2d 551 (Me. 1979)), tribally owned housing developments located near but outside the reservation and developed with federal Department of Housing and Urban Development funds (*United States v. South Dakota*, 665 F.2d 837 (8th Cir. 1981)), and near-reservation communities with large Indian populations and federal facilities providing benefits to Indians (*Weddell v. Meierhenry*, 636 F.2d 211 (8th Cir. 1980); *United States v. Morgan*, 614 F.2d 166, 170 (8th Cir. 1980)). Lower federal courts developed various multifactored tests, which generally focused on "the nature of the area in question, the relationship of the inhabitants of the area to Indian Tribes and to the federal government, and the established practice of government agencies toward the area." *United States v. Martine*, 442 F.2d 1022, 1023 (10th Cir. 1971). The overall inquiry stressed the history of federal legislative and administrative treatment of the area, drawing upon the methodology of *Sandoval*. In a case with some unusual features, the United States Supreme Court finally tackled the question of the appropriate criteria for identifying a "dependent Indian community."

ALASKA v. NATIVE VILLAGE OF VENETIE
United States Supreme Court
522 U.S. 520 (1998)

Justice Thomas delivered the opinion for a unanimous Court.

In this case, we must decide whether approximately 1.8 million acres of land in northern Alaska, owned in fee simple by the Native Village of Venetie Tribal Government pursuant to the Alaska Native Claims Settlement Act, 43 U.S.C. § 1601 et seq., is "Indian country." We conclude that it is not, and we therefore reverse the judgment below.

I

The Village of Venetie, which is located in Alaska above the Arctic Circle, is home to the Neets'aii Gwich'in Indians. In 1943, the Secretary of the Interior created a reservation for the Neets'aii Gwich'in out of the land surrounding Venetie and another nearby tribal village, Arctic Village. This land, which is about the size of Delaware, remained a reservation until 1971, when Congress enacted the Alaska Native Claims Settlement Act (ANCSA), a comprehensive statute designed to settle all land claims by Alaska Natives. See 85 Stat. 688, as amended, 43 U.S.C. § 1601 et seq. In enacting ANCSA, Congress sought to end the sort of federal supervision over Indian affairs that had previously marked federal Indian policy. ANCSA's text states that the settlement of the land claims was to be accomplished "without litigation, with maximum participation by Natives in decisions affecting their rights and property, without establishing any permanent racially defined institutions, rights, privileges, or obligations, [and] *without creating a reservation system or lengthy wardship or trusteeship.*" § 1601(b) (emphasis added).

To this end, ANCSA revoked "the various reserves set aside . . . for Native use" by legislative or executive action, except for the Annette Island Reserve inhabited by the Metlakatla Indians, and completely extinguished all aboriginal claims to Alaska land. §§ 1603, 1618(a). In return, Congress authorized the transfer of $962.5 million in federal funds and approximately 44 million acres of Alaska land to state-chartered private business corporations that were to be formed pursuant to the statute; all of the shareholders of these corporations were required to be Alaska Natives. §§ 1605, 1607, 1613. The ANCSA corporations received title to the transferred land in fee simple, and no federal restrictions applied to subsequent land transfers by them.

Pursuant to ANCSA, two Native corporations were established for the Neets'aii Gwich'in, one in Venetie, and one in Arctic Village. In 1973, those corporations elected to make use of a provision in ANCSA allowing Native corporations to take title to former reservation lands set aside for Indians prior to 1971, in return for forgoing the statute's monetary payments and transfers of nonreservation land. See § 1618(b). The United States conveyed fee simple title to the land constituting the former Venetie Reservation to the two corporations as tenants in common; thereafter, the corporations transferred title to the land to the Native Village of Venetie Tribal Government (the Tribe).

In 1986, the State of Alaska entered into a joint venture agreement with a private contractor for the construction of a public school in Venetie, financed with state funds. In December 1986, the Tribe notified the contractor that it owed the Tribe approximately $ 161,000 in taxes for conducting business activities on the Tribe's land. When both the contractor and the State, which under the joint venture agreement was the party responsible for paying the tax, refused to pay, the Tribe attempted to collect the tax in tribal court from the State, the school district, and the contractor.

The State then filed suit in Federal District Court for the District of Alaska and sought to enjoin collection of the tax. The Tribe moved to dismiss the State's complaint, but the District Court denied the motion. It held that the Tribe's ANCSA lands were not Indian country within the meaning of 18 U.S.C. § 1151(b), which provides that Indian country includes all "dependent Indian communities within the borders of the United States"; as a result, "the Tribe [did] not have the power to impose a tax upon non-members of the tribe such as the plaintiffs." *Alaska ex rel. Yukon Flats School Dist. v. Native Village of Venetie Tribal Government*, No. F87-0051CV(HRH) (D. Alaska, Aug. 2, 1995).

The Court of Appeals for the Ninth Circuit reversed. 101 F.3d 1286 (1996). The Court held that a six-factor balancing test should be used to interpret the term "dependent Indian communities" in § 1151(b), see *id.*, at 1292–1293, and it summarized the requirements of that test as follows:

> [A] dependent Indian community requires a showing of federal set aside and federal superintendence. These requirements are to be construed broadly and should be informed in the particular case by a consideration of the following factors:
>
> > (1) the nature of the area; (2) the relationship of the area inhabitants to Indian tribes and the federal government; (3) the established practice of government agencies toward that area; (4) the degree of federal ownership of and control over the area; (5) the degree of cohesiveness of the area inhabitants; and (6) the extent to which the area was set aside for the use, occupancy, and protection of dependent Indian peoples.

Id., at 1294. Applying this test, the Court of Appeals concluded that the "federal set aside" and "federal superintendence" requirements were met and that the Tribe's land was therefore Indian country. *Id.*, at 1300–1302. . . .

II

A

. . . Because ANCSA revoked the Venetie Reservation, and because no Indian allotments are at issue, whether the Tribe's land is Indian country depends on whether it falls within the "dependent Indian communities" prong of the statute, § 1151(b). Since 18 U.S.C. § 1151 was enacted in 1948, we have not had an occasion to interpret the term "dependent Indian communities." We now hold that it refers to a limited category of Indian lands that are neither reservations nor allotments, and that satisfy two requirements — first, they must have been set aside by the federal government for the use of the Indians as Indian land; second, they must be under federal superintendence. Our holding is based on our conclusion that in enacting § 1151, Congress codified these two requirements, which previously we had held necessary for a finding of "Indian country" generally.

Before § 1151 was enacted, we held in three cases that Indian lands that were not reservations could be Indian country and that the federal government could therefore exercise jurisdiction over them. *See United States v. Sandoval*, 231 U.S. 28 (1913); *United States v. Pelican*, 232 U.S. 442 (1914); *United States v. McGowan*, 302 U.S. 535 (1938). The first of these cases, *United States v. Sandoval*, posed the question whether the federal government could constitutionally proscribe the introduction of "intoxicating liquor" into the lands of the Pueblo Indians. 231 U.S. at 36. We rejected the contention that federal power could not extend to the Pueblo lands because, unlike Indians living on reservations, the Pueblos owned their lands in fee simple. *Id.*, at 48. We indicated that the Pueblos' title was not fee simple title in the commonly understood sense of the term. Congress had recognized the Pueblos' title to their ancestral lands by statute, and Executive orders had reserved additional public lands "for the [Pueblos'] use and occupancy." *Id.*, at 39. In addition, Congress had enacted legislation with respect to the lands "in the exercise of the Government's guardianship over the [Indian] tribes and their affairs," *id.*, at 48, including federal restrictions on the lands' alienation.[2] Congress therefore could exercise jurisdiction over the Pueblo lands, under its general power over "all dependent Indian communities within its borders, whether within its original territory or territory subsequently acquired, and whether within or without the limits of a State." *Id.*, at 46.

In *United States v. Pelican*, we held that Indian allotments — parcels of land created out of a diminished Indian reservation and held in trust by the federal government for the benefit of individual Indians — were Indian country. 232 U.S. at 449. We stated that the original reservation was Indian country "simply because it had been validly set apart for the use of the Indians as such, under the superintendence of the Government." *Ibid.* After the reservation's diminishment, the allotments continued to be Indian country, as "the lands remained Indian lands set apart for Indians under governmental care; . . . we are unable to find ground for the conclusion that they became other than Indian country through the distribution into separate holdings, the Government retaining control." *Ibid.*

In *United States v. McGowan*, we held that the Reno Indian Colony in Reno, Nevada was Indian country even though it was not a reservation. 302 U.S. at 539. We reasoned that, like Indian reservations generally, the Colony had been " 'validly set apart for the use of the Indians . . . under the superintendence of the Government.' " Ibid. (quoting *United States v. Pelican*, supra, at 449) (emphasis deleted). We noted that the federal government had created the Colony by purchasing the land with "funds appropriated by Congress" and that the federal government held the Colony's land in trust for the benefit of the Indians residing there. 302 U.S. at 537, and n. 4. We also emphasized that the federal government possessed the authority to enact "regulations and protective laws respecting the [Colony's] territory," *id.*, at 539, which it had exercised in retaining title to the land and permitting the Indians to live there. For these reasons, a federal statute requiring the forfeiture of automobiles carrying "intoxicants" into the Indian country applied to the Colony; we noted that the law was an example of the protections that Congress had extended to all "dependent Indian communities" within the territory of the United States. *Id.*, at 538 (quoting *United States v. Sandoval*, supra, at 46) (emphasis deleted).

In each of these cases, therefore, we relied upon a finding of both a federal set-aside and federal superintendence in concluding that the Indian lands in

---

[2] [4] One such law was Rev. Stat. § 2116, 25 U.S.C. § 177, which rendered invalid any conveyance of Indian land not made by treaty or convention entered into pursuant to the Constitution, and which we later held applicable to the Pueblos. *See United States v. Candelaria*, 271 U.S. 432, 441–442 (1926).

question constituted Indian country and that it was permissible for the federal government to exercise jurisdiction over them. Section 1151 does not purport to alter this definition of Indian country, but merely lists the three different categories of Indian country mentioned in our prior cases. . . . The entire text of § 1151(b), and not just the term "dependent Indian communities," is taken virtually verbatim from *Sandoval*, which language we later quoted in *McGowan. See United States v. Sandoval, supra,* at 46; *United States v. McGowan, supra,* at 538. Moreover, the Historical and Revision Notes to the statute that enacted § 1151 state that § 1151's definition of Indian country is based "on [the] latest construction of the term by the United States Supreme Court in *U.S. v. McGowan* . . . following *U.S. v. Sandoval.* (*See also Donnelly v. U.S.*). . . .

We therefore must conclude that in enacting § 1151(b), Congress indicated that a federal set-aside and a federal superintendence requirement must be satisfied for a finding of a "dependent Indian community" — just as those requirements had to be met for a finding of Indian country before 18 U.S.C. § 1151 was enacted.[3] These requirements are reflected in the text of § 1151(b): The federal set-aside requirement ensures that the land in question is occupied by an "Indian community";[4] the federal superintendence requirement guarantees that the Indian community is sufficiently "dependent" on the federal government that the federal government and the Indians involved, rather than the States, are to exercise primary jurisdiction over the land in question.[5]

---

[3] [5] In attempting to defend the Court of Appeals's judgment, the Tribe asks us to adopt a different conception of the term "dependent Indian communities." Borrowing from Chief Justice Marshall's seminal opinions in *Cherokee Nation v. Georgia*, 5 Pet. 1 (1831), and *Worcester v. Georgia*, 6 Pet. 515 — (1832), the Tribe argues that the term refers to political dependence, and that Indian country exists wherever land is owned by a federally recognized tribe. Federally recognized tribes, the Tribe contends, are "dependent domestic nations," *Cherokee Nation v. Georgia, supra,* at 17, and thus ipso facto under the superintendence of the federal government. This argument ignores our Indian country precedents, which indicate both that the federal government must take some action setting apart the land for the use of the Indians "as such," and that it is the land in question, and not merely the Indian tribe inhabiting it, that must be under the superintendence of the federal government. *See, e.g., United States v. McGowan,* 302 U.S. 535 (1938) ("The Reno Colony has been validly set apart for the use of the Indians. It is under the superintendence of the Government. The Government retains title to the lands which it permits the Indians to occupy"); *United States v. Pelican,* 232 U.S. 442, 449 (1914) (noting that the federal government retained "ultimate control" over the allotments in question).

[4] [6] The federal set-aside requirement also reflects the fact that because Congress has plenary power over Indian affairs, see U.S. Const., Art. I, § 8, cl. 3, some explicit action by Congress (or the Executive, acting under delegated authority) must be taken to create or to recognize Indian country.

[5] [7] Although the Court of Appeals majority also reached the conclusion that § 1151(b) imposes federal set-aside and federal superintendence requirements, it defined those requirements far differently, by resort to its "textured" six-factor balancing test. *See* 101 F.3d 1286, 1293 (CA9 1996). Three of those factors, however, were extremely far removed from the requirements themselves: "the nature of the area"; "the relationship of the area inhabitants to Indian tribes and the federal government"; and "the degree of cohesiveness of the area inhabitants." *Id.*, at 1300–1301. The Court of Appeals majority, however, accorded those factors virtually the same weight as other, more relevant ones: "the degree of federal ownership of and control over the area," and "the extent to which the area was set aside for the use, occupancy, and protection of dependent Indian peoples." *Id.*, at 1301. By balancing these "factors" against one another, the Court of Appeals reduced the federal set-aside and superintendence requirements to mere considerations.

B

The Tribe's ANCSA lands do not satisfy either of these requirements. After the enactment of ANCSA, the Tribe's lands are neither "validly set apart for the use of the Indians as such," nor are they under the superintendence of the federal government.

With respect to the federal set-aside requirement, it is significant that ANCSA, far from designating Alaskan lands for Indian use, revoked the existing Venetie Reservation, and indeed revoked all existing reservations in Alaska "set aside by legislation or by Executive or Secretarial Order for Native use," save one. 43 U.S.C. § 1618(a). In no clearer fashion could Congress have departed from its traditional practice of setting aside Indian lands. *Cf. Hagen v. Utah*, 510 U.S. 399, 401 (1994) (holding that by diminishing a reservation and opening the diminished lands to settlement by non-Indians, Congress had extinguished Indian country on the diminished lands).

The Tribe argues — and the Court of Appeals majority agreed, see 101 F.3d at 1301–1302 — that the ANCSA lands were set apart for the use of the Neets'aii Gwich'in, "as such," because the Neets'aii Gwich'in acquired the lands pursuant to an ANCSA provision allowing Natives to take title to former reservation lands in return for forgoing all other ANCSA transfers. 43 U.S.C. § 1618(b). The difficulty with this contention is that ANCSA transferred reservation lands to private, state-chartered Native corporations, without any restraints on alienation or significant use restrictions, and with the goal of avoiding "any permanent racially defined institutions, rights, privileges, or obligations." § 1601(b); see also §§ 1607, 1613. By ANCSA's very design, Native corporations can immediately convey former reservation lands to non-Natives, and such corporations are not restricted to using those lands for Indian purposes. Because Congress contemplated that non-Natives could own the former Venetie Reservation, and because the Tribe is free to use it for non-Indian purposes, we must conclude that the federal set-aside requirement is not met. *Cf. United States v. McGowan*, 302 U.S. at 538 (noting that the land constituting the Reno Indian Colony was held in trust by the federal government for the benefit of the Indians); *see also United States v. Pelican*, 232 U.S. at 447 (noting federal restraints on the alienation of the allotments in question).

Equally clearly, ANCSA ended federal superintendence over the Tribe's lands. As noted above, ANCSA revoked the Venetie Reservation along with every other reservation in Alaska but one, see 43 U.S.C. § 1618(a), and Congress stated explicitly that ANCSA's settlement provisions were intended to avoid a "lengthy wardship or trusteeship." § 1601(b). After ANCSA, federal protection of the Tribe's land is essentially limited to a statutory declaration that the land is exempt from adverse possession claims, real property taxes, and certain judgments as long as it has not been sold, leased, or developed. See § 1636(d). These protections, if they can be called that, simply do not approach the level of superintendence over the Indians' land that existed in our prior cases. In each of those cases, the federal government actively controlled the lands in question, effectively acting as a guardian for the Indians. *See United States v. McGowan, supra*, 302 U.S. at 537–539 (emphasizing that the federal government had retained title to the land to protect the Indians living there); *United States v. Pelican, supra*, at 447 (stating that the allotments were "under the jurisdiction and control of Congress for all governmental purposes, relating to the guardianship and protection of the Indians"); *United States v. Sandoval*, 231 U.S. at 37, n. 1 (citing federal statute placing the Pueblos' land under the " 'absolute jurisdiction and control of the Congress of the United States' "). Finally, it is worth noting that Congress conveyed ANCSA lands to state-chartered and state-regulated private business corporations, hardly a choice that comports with a desire to retain federal superintendence over the land.

The Tribe contends that the requisite federal superintendence is present because the federal government provides "desperately needed health, social, welfare, and economic programs" to the Tribe. The Court of Appeals majority found this argument persuasive. 101 F.3d at 1301. Our Indian country precedents, however, do not suggest that the mere provision of "desperately needed" social programs can support a finding of Indian country. Such health, education, and welfare benefits are merely forms of general federal aid; considered either alone or in tandem with ANCSA's minimal land-related protections, they are not indicia of active federal control over the Tribe's land sufficient to support a finding of federal superintendence.

The Tribe's federal superintendence argument, moreover, is severely undercut by its view of ANCSA's primary purposes, namely, to effect Native self-determination and to end paternalism in federal Indian relations. The broad federal superintendence requirement for Indian country cuts against these objectives, but we are not free to ignore that requirement as codified in 18 U.S.C. § 1151. Whether the concept of Indian country should be modified is a question entirely for Congress.

The judgment of the Court of Appeals is reversed. It is so ordered.

NOTES ON *VENETIE* AND "DEPENDENT INDIAN COMMUNITIES"

1. **Indian Country and Tribal Authority in Alaska After *Venetie***: Despite *Venetie*, there is some Indian country remaining in Alaska, particularly the Metlakatla Reservation, individual trust allotments, and Alaska Native townsites. DAVID A. CASE & DAVID S. VOLUCK, ALASKA NATIVES AND AMERICAN LAWS 113–165 (3d ed. 2012). Furthermore, some tribal jurisdiction is not territorially based, such as jurisdiction over membership and the personal status of tribal members. Thus, for example, after *Venetie*, Alaska Native villages have continued to exercise jurisdiction over child welfare matters. *See, e.g., John v. Baker*, 982 P.2d 738 (Alaska 1999) and *Simmonds v. Parks*, 329 P.3d 995 (Alaska 2014) (discussed in Ch. 5, Sec. B.2). What other powers might Alaska Native villages wield after *Venetie*? Should criminal jurisdiction exist over tribal citizens who commit acts within the village's borders or even outside that territory? In the geographically isolated Native Village of Venetie, and many other similarly situated villages, the only way for state police to enforce state law is by expensive flights to and from the village. Would it be surprising if Native Villages were to fill this void, regardless of court decisions? For example, they might exclude individuals who fail to comply with community rules. Nonetheless, the absence of recognized Indian country has made it exceedingly

difficult for Native Alaskan communities to hold residents accountable for their conduct and to restore good relations. In 2013, the Indian Law and Order Commission, created by the Tribal Law and Order Act of 2010, 25 U.S.C. § 2812, issued a scathing critique of the delivery of justice services to Alaska Natives, pointing out rates of violence, especially sexual violence, far above national levels, and presenting enhanced tribal authority as the only workable solution. Among the Commission's recommendation are federal legislation overturning *Venetie*; federal administrative acknowledgment of the Indian country status of Alaska Native allotments and townsites; repeal of the federal regulation barring the Department of the Interior from taking land into trust in Alaska; and federal and state recognition that Alaska Native villages have criminal jurisdiction over their territory held in fee. *See* INDIAN LAW AND ORDER COMMISSION, A ROADMAP FOR MAKING NATIVE AMERICA SAFER 33–61 (2013), available at http://www.aisc.ucla.edu/iloc/report/. The Commission's recommendations were both bi-partisan and unanimous. What principles and considerations might unite left and right around expanded recognition of Indian country in Alaska? See also Ch. 5, Sec. B.1 for more information about the jurisdiction problems Alaska Native communities face.

2. ***Venetie*'s Construction of ANCSA:** In construing the Alaska Native Claims Settlement Act, does *Venetie* attend sufficiently to the canons of construction regarding interpretation of statutes that could adversely affect the exercise of tribal sovereignty? *See* Sec. C, this chapter. Should the Court have paid greater heed to more recent amendments to ANCSA that reflected a greater federal concern over protecting the land base of Alaska Native villages and that provided benefits to Alaska Natives on the same basis as Indian people elsewhere in the United States? Compare the approach taken in relation to another significantly altered federal statute in *Bryan v. Itasca County*, discussed in Ch. 5, Sec. A.2. Was it relevant to the issue in *Venetie* that in 1993, Alaska Native villages were confirmed as federally recognized Indian nations with a government-to-government relationship with the United States?

3. **The Reach of the *Venetie* Decision:** Does *Venetie* provide much guidance in ordinary situations, outside of ANCSA, where reservations have not been specifically abolished and federal controls over tribal lands have not been disclaimed? How should the situations described at the beginning of this subsection be resolved under the test established in *Venetie*? Is the presence of trust land now essential for a finding of a dependent Indian community? Wouldn't the presence of such land qualify the area as an "informal reservation" under section 1151(a)? If so, has *Venetie* rendered section 1151(b) redundant? Pueblo lands are still held in fee simple and not held by the federal government. Do they satisfy the *Venetie* federal superintendence requirement? If not, did *Venetie* overrule *Sandoval*, the very case Congress thought it was codifying in section 1151(b)?

Before *Venetie*, the federal Circuits felt compelled to demarcate the relevant "community of reference" before determining whether the land in question was part of a "dependent Indian community." Thus, pre-*Venetie*, if the entire community had the requisite Indian character and federal supervision, the specific parcel did not need to satisfy those criteria. Does *Venetie* dispense with this preliminary inquiry, focusing entirely on whether the particular parcel qualifies as Indian country? Consider the following facts: A non-Indian owned parcel of land, unoccupied but used for mining, is approximately six miles from the center of a Navajo unit of local government known as a Chapter. The Chapter is not within the boundaries of the Navajo Reservation, but in a checkerboard area to its southeast. Half of the Chapter's 55,000 acres of territory consists of tribal trust land; an additional one-quarter consists of allotments in trust for individual Indians; and 10% is land held by the federal Bureau of Land Management and subject to grazing leases granted to Navajos. The State of New Mexico owns about 4% the remaining land, and private interests own approximately 6%. The private interests pay property taxes to the local county, and the county provides road access and public services to the private property owners, but the Navajo Nation and federal government provide most of the services to occupants of the area. A divided Tenth Circuit, en banc, decided that *Venetie* had rejected the "community of reference" test, limiting the determination of a "dependent Indian community" to the particular parcels implicated in that inquiry. *Hydro Res., Inc. v. United States EPA*, 608 F.3d 1131 (10th Cir. 2010). Is the establishment of a "community of reference" a necessary first step if the word "community" is to have any significance in the determination of a "dependent Indian community" for purposes of § 1151? Alternatively, does the "community of reference" test introduce too much uncertainty and variability into the interpretation of a phrase that dictates the existence of federal and tribal vs. state jurisdiction in criminal matters?

4. **Venetie's Implicit Model of the Tribal-Federal Relationship:** What model of the tribal-federal relationship seems to guide Justice Thomas in his *Venetie* opinion? What does he mean when he describes federal prohibitions against the taxation and alienation of tribal lands as "protections, if they can be called that?"

iii.   Allotted Land Outside Reservations

Allotted Indian land still held in Indian trust title but located outside of Indian reservations is considered Indian country under the provisions of section 1151(c). Some of this land involves Indian allotments created out of the public domain for Indians overlooked during the allotment of their reservations. Other such land — for example, the land of the Eastern Navajo Agency — involves allotments created adjacent to, but outside of, the statutory boundaries of the reservation. Section 1151(c), however, has played a more important role with respect to Indian owned allotments that originally were within Indian reservations but ceased to be after the reservation was disestablished by Congress. In *DeCoteau v. District County Court*, 420 U.S. 425 (1975), for example, the Court held that Congress had disestablished the former Lake Traverse Reservation of the Sisseton-Wahpeton bands of the Sioux. Nevertheless, the Court carefully noted that since Indian owned allotments remained, "§ 1151(c) contemplates that isolated tracts of 'Indian country' may be scattered checkerboard fashion over a territory otherwise under state jurisdiction." 420 U.S. at 429 n.3.

In *Oklahoma Tax Comm'n v. Sac and Fox Nation*, 508 U.S. 114 (1993), the Supreme Court confirmed that trust allotments in Oklahoma were Indian country, even where reservations had been abolished. The issue in *Sac and Fox* was whether the State of Oklahoma could tax the income of Indians earned on either tribal land or the lands comprising Indian allotments. The Court held that to be exempt from state taxation the Indian must both earn the income in Indian country and reside in Indian country. The state argued that since the only remaining lands of the Sac and Fox Nation comprised 800 acres reserved in the allotment agreements that were used for the tribal office complex, the individual tribal members were not immune from tax. Rejecting that argument, Justice O'Connor's opinion for the Court noted "we ask only whether the land is Indian country. . . . " Later in the opinion, the Court stated that allotments still held in trust constitute Indian country, even if not within a remaining Indian reservation.

iv.   Determining the Boundaries of an Indian Reservation

Under the provisions of section 1151(a), whether land constitutes Indian country turns on whether it is located within the exterior boundaries of an Indian reservation. Thus, it is often important, as in *John*, to determine whether the land constitutes a reservation. Ascertaining the precise legal boundaries of an existing reservation may be equally significant. In many instances reservation boundaries have been changed since the treaty, statute, or executive order first created the reservation, either by adding to or subtracting from the original expanse.

Additions may have been made to the land area owned by the tribe through purchase, statute, or executive order. Whether the acquisition of additional land enlarges the boundaries of the reservation so as to render the additional tracts Indian country often turns on the manner in which the land was acquired. For example, section 5 of the Indian Reorganization Act of 1934 (IRA), 25 U.S.C. § 465, authorizes the Secretary of the Interior to acquire real property for Indians and tribes, including land located without existing reservations through purchase, exchange, gift, or assignment. Under section 7 of the Act, 25 U.S.C. § 467, the Secretary is authorized to proclaim any lands so acquired as new Indian reservations or as additions to existing reservations. In *Mescalero Apache Tribe v. Jones*, 411 U.S. 145 (1973), the Supreme Court considered the state tax status of a tribal ski enterprise operated on lands leased to the Tribe by the United States from national forest lands adjacent to the reservation. The lands had been acquired under section 5 of the IRA and had been leased rather than conveyed by actually transferring title in trust for the Tribe because "it would have been meaningless for the United States, which already had title to the forest, to convey title to itself for the use of the Tribe." Although no mention of this fact is made in the opinion, apparently no reservation proclamation was ever issued under section 7 of the IRA to cover the land so acquired. The Court treated the ski enterprise as a tribal activity conducted outside of the reservation, thereby upholding a nondiscriminatory state gross receipts tax on the tribal revenues from the enterprise. However, noting that section 5 of the IRA expressly exempted real estate acquired under its provision from state and local taxation, the Court did hold that the state could not impose a use tax on the fixtures (the ski lifts) purchased by the enterprise — a reminder that federal Indian statutes sometimes operate outside of Indian country.

In addition to the difficulty of ascertaining whether additions to tribal land have enlarged the boundaries of a reservation, problems have frequently arisen as to whether the cession of Indian land to non-Indian purchasers has diminished the boundaries of the reservation. Under section 1151(a), all land within the exterior boundaries of any Indian reservation constitutes Indian country "notwithstanding the issuance of any patent. . . . " This provision was intended to partially resolve some of the jurisdictional ambiguities created by the allotment policy. The allotment policy had substantially opened Indian reservations to non-Indian settlement, by two different means — through sale of allotments after the 25-year trust period expired, and through sale of the unallotted, or "surplus" lands that remained after each male head of household received his 160-acre parcel. According to section 1151(a), allotments leaving trust status are still Indian country so long as they remain within reservations. Congress plainly did not want "checkerboard" jurisdiction within reservations. The so-called "surplus" lands are more difficult to characterize. Often concentrated in one part of the reservation, these lands pose the difficult question whether Congress had severed the entire area from the reservation by putting it up for sale. If the answer is yes, a new kind of checkerboard jurisdiction can emerge. Picture some trust allotments remaining in the area opened for sale, while the area as a whole is deemed outside the reservation. Those trust allotments, still Indian country under section 1151(c), will be interspersed with fee lands no longer holding Indian country status. The result will be a mixed pattern of Indian and non-Indian jurisdiction in the area.

Tribes have a great interest in avoiding this situation. On the Yankton Sioux Reservation, for example, fragmentation of jurisdiction has meant that a non-Indian owning fee land has been able to develop a huge hog farm in close proximity to preexisting tribal headquarters and the preexisting site of the Tribe's Head Start program. The hog farm, which creates a severe stench and pollutes the water table, is outside the Tribe's jurisdiction because the fee land is no longer considered within the reservation. *See South Dakota v. Yankton Sioux Tribe*, 522 U.S. 329 (1998); *Yankton Sioux Tribe v. Podhradsky*, 529 F. Supp. 2d 1040 (D.S.D. 2007). Thus it is deeply important to tribes that older laws allotting reservations be read to maintain reservations intact, and not to slice off significant portions. Under what circumstances will such a severance or diminishment of a reservation be found? For purposes of section 1151, can the boundaries of a reservation be diminished or the reservation extinguished to reflect changing social conditions? At what point and through what mechanism can this change legally occur?

SOLEM v. BARTLETT
United States Supreme Court
465 U.S. 463 (1984)

MR. JUSTICE MARSHALL delivered the opinion of the Court.

On May 29, 1908, Congress authorized the Secretary of the Interior to open 1.6 million acres of the Cheyenne River Sioux Reservation for homesteading. Act of May 29, 1908, ch. 218, 35 Stat. 460 et seq. ("Act" or "Cheyenne River Act"). The question presented in this case is whether that Act of Congress diminished the boundaries of the Cheyenne River Sioux Reservation or simply permitted non-Indians to settle within existing Reservation boundaries.

I

In 1979, the State of South Dakota charged respondent John Bartlett, an enrolled member of the Cheyenne River Sioux Tribe, with attempted rape. Respondent pleaded guilty to the charge, and was sentenced to a ten-year term in the state penitentiary at Sioux Falls. After exhausting state remedies, respondent filed a pro se petition for a writ of habeas corpus in the United States District Court for the District of South Dakota. Respondent contended that the crime for which he had been convicted occurred within the Cheyenne River Sioux Reservation, established by Congress in the Act of March 2, 1889, ch. 405, § 4, 25 Stat. 889; that, although on May 29, 1908, Congress opened for settlement by non-Indians the portion of the Reservation on which respondent committed his crime, the opened portion nonetheless remained Indian country; and that the State therefore lacked criminal jurisdiction over respondent.[6]

Relying on previous decisions of the Eighth Circuit dealing with the Act of May 29, 1908,[7] the District Court accepted respondent's claim that the Act had not diminished the original Cheyenne River Sioux Reservation, and issued a writ of habeas corpus. On appeal, the Eighth Circuit, sitting en banc, affirmed, two judges dissenting. [Since] the Supreme Court of South Dakota has issued a pair of opinions offering a conflicting interpretation of the Act of May 29, 1908,[8] we granted certiorari [and] affirm.

II

In the latter half of the nineteenth century, large sections of the western States and Territories were set aside for Indian reservations. Towards the end of the century, however, Congress increasingly adhered to the view that the Indian tribes should abandon their nomadic lives on the communal reservations and settle into an agrarian economy on privately-owned parcels of land.[9] This shift was fueled in part by the belief that individualized farming would speed the Indians' assimilation into American society and in part by the continuing demand for new lands for the waves

---

[6] [2] 18 U.S.C. § 1153 provides: "Any Indian who commits against the person or property of another Indian or other person any of the following offenses, namely, ... assault with intent to commit rape . . . within the Indian country, shall be subject to the same laws and penalties as all other persons committing any of the above offenses, within the exclusive jurisdiction of the United States." Within Indian country, State jurisdiction is limited to crimes by non-Indians against non-Indians, *see New York ex rel. Ray v. Martin*, 326 U.S. 496 (1946), and victimless crimes by non-Indians. Tribes exercise concurrent jurisdiction over certain minor crimes by Indians, 18 U.S.C. §§ 1152, 1153, unless a State has assumed jurisdiction under *id.*, § 1162.

[7] [3] *United States v. Dupris*, 612 F.2d 319 (1979), *vacated and remanded on other grounds*, 446 U.S. 980 (1980); *United States v. Long Elk*, 565 F.2d 1032 (1977); *United States ex rel. Condon v. Erickson*, 478 F.2d 684 (1973).

[8] [4] *See State v. Janis*, 317 N.W.2d 133 (S.D. 1982); *Stankey v. Waddell*, 256 N.W.2d 117 (S.D. 1977).

[9] [5] An account of the movement and its effect on the Cheyenne River Sioux Tribe appears in F. HOXIE, JURISDICTION ON THE CHEYENNE RIVER INDIAN RESERVATION: AN ANALYSIS OF THE CAUSES AND CONSEQUENCES OF THE ACT OF MAY 29, 1908, at 1–30 (undated manuscript) (hereinafter HOXIE), which was prepared for presentation in *United States v. Dupris, supra,* and incorporated into the record of this case. *See also* Note, *Jurisdictional Confusion on the Cheyenne River Indian Reservation*, 25 S. D. L. REV. 355 (1980).

of homesteaders moving West.[10] As a result of these combined pressures, Congress passed a series of surplus land acts at the turn of the century to force Indians onto individual allotments carved out of reservations and to open up unallotted lands for non-Indian settlement. Initially, Congress legislated its Indian allotment program on a national scale,[11] but by the time of the Act of May 29, 1908, Congress was dealing with the surplus land question on a reservation-by-reservation basis, with each surplus land act employing its own statutory language, the product of a unique set of tribal negotiation and legislative compromise.

The modern legacy of the surplus land acts has been a spate of jurisdictional disputes between state and federal officials as to which sovereign has authority over lands that were opened by the acts and have since passed out of Indian ownership.[12] As a doctrinal matter, the States have jurisdiction over unalloted opened lands if the applicable surplus land act freed that land of its reservation status and thereby diminished the reservation boundaries. On the other hand, federal, state, and tribal authorities share jurisdiction over these lands if the relevant surplus land act did not diminish the existing Indian reservation because the entire opened area is Indian country under 18 U.S.C. § 1151(a).

Unfortunately, the surplus land acts themselves seldom detail whether opened lands retained reservation status or were divested of all Indian interests. When the surplus land acts were passed, the distinction seemed unimportant. The notion that reservation status of Indian lands might not be coextensive with Tribal ownership was unfamiliar at the turn of the century.

Indian lands were judicially defined to include only those lands in which the Indians held some form of property interest: trust lands, individual allotments, and, to a more limited degree, opened lands that had not yet been claimed by non-Indians. *See Bates v. Clark*, 95 U.S. 204 (1877); *Ash Sheep Co. v. United States*, 252 U.S. 159 (1920). Only in 1948 did Congress uncouple reservation status from Indian ownership, and statutorily define Indian country to include lands held in fee by non-Indians within reservation boundaries. See Act of June 25, 1948, ch. 645, § 1151, 62 Stat. 757 (codified at 18 U.S.C. § 1151).

Another reason why Congress did not concern itself with the effect of surplus land acts on reservation boundaries was the turn-of-the-century assumption that Indian reservations were a thing of the past. Consistent with prevailing wisdom,

---

[10] [6] *See* COHEN, HANDBOOK OF FEDERAL INDIAN LAW 127–134 (1982 ed.) (hereinafter COHEN). The amount of surplus lands freed up by moving Indians onto individual allotments was considerable. For instance, in 1908, the 2,626 members of the Cheyenne River Sioux Tribe had over 2.8 million acres of reservation land, or over 1,000 acres per Tribal member. Under the allotment program, the average allotment per member was under 500 acres. *See* S. Rep. 439, 60th Cong., 1st Sess., 4 (1908); HOXIE 38, 40.

[11] [7] *See, e.g.*, General Allotment Act of 1887, c. 119, 24 Stat. 388 et seq.

[12] [8] Regardless of whether the original reservation was diminished, federal and tribal courts have exclusive jurisdiction over those portions of the opened lands that were and have remained Indian allotments. *See* 18 U.S.C. § 1151(c). In addition, opened lands that have been restored to reservation status by subsequent act of Congress, *see, e.g.*, Indian Reorganization Act of 1934, ch. 576, 48 Stat. 984 (codified at 25 U.S.C. § 461 et seq. (1982)) (authorizing the return of opened lands to the original reservations), fall within the exclusive criminal jurisdiction of federal and tribal courts under 18 U.S.C. §§ 1152, 1153.

members of Congress voting on the surplus land acts believed to a man that within a short time — within a generation at most — the Indian tribes would enter traditional American society and the reservation system would cease to exist.[13] Given this expectation, Congress naturally failed to be meticulous in clarifying whether a particular piece of legislation formally sliced a certain parcel of land off one reservation.

Although the Congresses that passed the surplus land acts anticipated the imminent demise of the reservation and, in fact, passed the acts partially to facilitate the process, we have never been willing to extrapolate from this expectation a specific congressional purpose of diminishing reservations with the passage of every surplus land act. Rather, it is settled law that some surplus land acts diminished reservations, *see, e.g.*, *Rosebud Sioux Tribe v. Kneip*, 430 U.S. 584 (1977); *DeCoteau v. District County Court*, 420 U.S. 425 (1975), and other surplus land acts did not, *see, e.g.*, *Mattz v. Arnett*, 412 U.S. 481 (1973); *Seymour v. Superintendent*, 368 U.S. 351 (1962). The effect of any given surplus land act depends on the language of the act and the circumstances underlying its passage.[14]

Between these extremes was the case of the Rosebud Sioux Reservation. In 1901, the Rosebud Sioux Tribe voted in favor of an agreement to cede a portion of their land in Gregory County to the United States in exchange for a sum certain. Three years later, Congress passed the Act of April 23, 1904, ch. 1484, 33 Stat. 254–258, which incorporated the agreement's cession language, but replaced sum-certain payment with a provision guaranteeing the Tribe only the proceeds from the sale of the opened lands. Over the following years, Congress passed two more surplus land acts involving Rosebud Reservation land into other counties; each of the subsequent acts authorized the sale and disposal of additional lands and promised the tribes the proceeds of the sales. *See* Act of March 2, 1907, ch. 2536, 34 Stat. 1230–1232; Act of May 30, 1910, ch. 260, 36 Stat. 448–452. Although none of the Rosebud Acts clearly severed the Tribe from its interest in the unallotted opened lands and even though the last two Acts were strikingly similar to the 1906 Act found not to have diminished the Colville Reservation in *Seymour v. Superintendent, supra*, this Court held that the circumstances surrounding the passage of the three Rosebud Acts unequivocally demonstrated that Congress meant for each Act to diminish the Rosebud Reservation. *Rosebud Sioux Tribe v. Kneip, supra*.

---

[13] [9] *See Montana v. United States*, 450 U.S. 544, 559–560, n.9 (1981); HOXIE 1–20. Congress rejected the policy of allotment and surplus land sales in 1934. Indian Reorganization Act, 48 Stat. 984 et seq.

[14] [10] At one extreme, for example, the Act of March 3, 1891, ch. 543, 26 Stat. 1035 et seq., expressly stated that the Lake Traverse Indian Tribe agreed to "cede, sell, relinquish and convey" all interest in unallotted lands on the Lake Traverse Indian Reservation, and the Act further provided that the Tribe would receive full compensation in consideration for its loss. In *DeCoteau v. District County Court, supra*, we found that the Lake Traverse Act, with its express language of cession, diminished the Lake Traverse Indian Reservation. At the other extreme, the Act of March 22, 1906, ch. 1126, § 1, 34 Stat. 80, simply authorized the Secretary of Interior "to sell or dispose of" unallotted lands on a portion of the Colville Indian Reservation; under the Act, the Colville Tribe received whatever proceeds these sales generated, rather than a sum certain. *Id.*, § 9. 34 Stat., at 81. In *Seymour v. Superintendent*, [this Court] held that, because the Colville Act lacked an unconditional divestiture of Indian interest in the lands, the Act simply opened a portion of the Colville Reservation to non-Indian settlers and did not diminish the Reservation. *See also Mattz v. Arnett.* . . .

Our precedents in the area have established a fairly clean analytical structure for distinguishing those surplus land acts that diminished reservations from those acts that simply offered non-Indians the opportunity to purchase land within established reservation boundaries. The first and governing principle is that only Congress can divest a reservation of its land and diminish its boundaries. Once a block of land is set aside for an Indian reservation and no matter what happens to the title of individual plots within the area, the entire block retains its reservation status until Congress explicitly indicates otherwise. *See United States v. Celestine*, 215 U.S. 278, 285 (1909).[15]

Diminishment, moreover, will not be lightly inferred. Our analysis of surplus land acts requires that Congress clearly evince an "intent to change boundaries" before diminishment will be found. *Rosebud v. Kneip, supra*, 430 U.S., at 615. The most probative evidence of congressional intent is the statutory language used to open the Indian lands. Explicit reference to cession or other language evidencing the present and total surrender of all tribal interests strongly suggests that Congress meant to divest from the reservation all unalloted opened lands. *DeCoteau v. District County Court, supra*, 420 U.S., at 444–445; *Seymour v. Superintendent, supra*, 368 U.S., at 355. When such language of cession is buttressed by an unconditional commitment from Congress to compensate the Indian tribe for its opened land, there is an almost insurmountable presumption that Congress meant for the tribe's reservation to be diminished. *See DeCoteau v. District County Court, supra*, 420 U.S., at 447–448.

As our opinion in *Rosebud Sioux Tribe* demonstrates, . . . explicit language of cession and unconditional compensation are not prerequisites for a finding of diminishment. When events surrounding the passage of a surplus land act — particularly the manner in which the transaction was negotiated with the tribes involved and the tenor of legislative reports presented to Congress — unequivocally reveal a widely-held, contemporaneous understanding that the affected reservation would shrink as a result of the proposed legislation, we have been willing to infer that Congress shared the understanding that its action would diminish the reservation, notwithstanding the presence of statutory language that would otherwise suggest reservation boundaries remained unchanged. To a lesser extent, we have also looked to events that occurred after the passage of a surplus land act to decipher Congress's intentions. Congress's own treatment of the affected areas, particularly in the years immediately following the opening, has some evidentiary value, as does the manner in which the Bureau of Indian Affairs and local judicial authorities dealt with unalloted open lands. On a more pragmatic level, we have recognized that who actually moved onto opened reservation lands is also relevant to deciding whether a surplus land act diminished a reservation. Where non-Indian settlers flooded into the opened portion of a reservation and the area has long since lost its Indian character, we have acknowledged that de facto, if not de jure, diminishment may have occurred. *See Rosebud Sioux Tribe v. Kneip, supra*, at 588, n.3 and 604–605; *DeCoteau v. District County Court*, 420 U.S. at 428. In addition to

---

[15] [11] At one time, it was thought that Indian consent was needed to diminish a reservation, but in *Lone Wolf v. Hitchcock*, 187 U.S. 553 (1903), this Court decided that Congress could diminish reservations unilaterally.

the obvious practical advantages of acquiescing to de facto diminishment,[16] we look to the subsequent demographic history of opened lands as one additional clue as to what Congress expected would happen once land on a particular reservation was opened to non-Indian settlers.[17]

There are, of course, limits to how far we will go to decipher Congress's intention in any particular surplus land act. When both an act and its legislative history fail to provide substantial and compelling evidence of a congressional intention to diminish Indian lands, we are bound by our traditional solicitude for the Indian tribes to rule that diminishment did not take place and that the old reservation boundaries survived the opening. *Mattz v. Arnett*, 412 U.S. 481, 505 (1973); *Seymour v. Superintendent*, 368 U.S. 351 (1962).

III

A

We now turn to apply these principles to the Act of May 29, 1908. We begin with the Act's operative language, which reads:

> "[T]he Secretary of the Interior [hereby is authorized] and directed, as hereinafter provided, to sell and dispose of all that portion of the Cheyenne River and Standing Rock[18] Indian reservations in the States of South Dakota and North Dakota lying and being within the following described boundaries. . . .

> "[F]rom the proceeds arising from the sale and disposition of the lands aforesaid, exclusive of the customary fees and commissions, there shall be deposited in the Treasury of the United States, to the credit of the Indians belonging and having tribal rights on the reservation aforesaid in the States of South Dakota and North Dakota the sums to which the respective tribes may be entitled. . . ."

Ch. 218, §§ 1, 6, 35 Stat. 460–461, 463. These provisions stand in sharp contrast to the explicit language of cession employed in the Lake Traverse and 1904 Rosebud Acts discussed in our opinions in *DeCoteau* and *Rosebud Sioux Tribe*. [Instead of] reciting an Indian agreement to "cede, sell, relinquish and convey" the opened

---

[16] [12] When an area is predominately populated by non-Indians with only a few surviving pockets of Indian allotments, finding that the land remains Indian country seriously burdens the administration of state and local governments. *See Rosebud Sioux Tribe v. Kneip, supra; DeCoteau v. District County Court, supra.* Conversely, problems of an imbalanced checkerboard jurisdiction arise if a largely Indian opened area is found to be outside Indian country. *See Seymour v. Superintendent.* . . .

[17] [13] Resort to subsequent demographic history is, of course, an unorthodox and potentially unreliable method of statutory interpretation. However, in the area of surplus land acts, where various factors kept Congress from focusing on the diminishment issue, *see, supra,* at 1165, the technique is a necessary expedient.

[18] [14] As this language reveals, the Act dealt with land on two bordering Sioux reservations. Although for purposes of this case we are only concerned with the Act's effect on the Cheyenne River Reservation, nothing in the record leads us to suspect that Congress intended the Act to have a different effect on the Standing Rock Reservation.

lands, the Cheyenne River Act simply authorizes the Secretary to "sell and dispose" of certain lands. This reference to the sale of Indian lands, coupled with the creation of Indian accounts for proceeds, suggests that the Secretary of the Interior was simply being authorized to act as the Tribe's sales agent. Indeed, when faced with precisely the same language in *Seymour v. Superintendent*, [this Court] concluded that such provisions "did no more than to open the way for non-Indian settlers to own land on the reservation in a manner which the Federal Government, acting as guardian and trustee for the Indians, regarded as beneficial to the development of its wards."[19]

The balance of the Cheyenne River Act is largely consistent with the implication of the operative language that the Act opened but did not diminish the Cheyenne River Sioux Reservation. Nowhere else in the Act is there specific reference to the cession of Indian interests in the opened lands or any change in existing reservation boundaries. In fact, certain provisions of the Act strongly suggest that the unalloted opened lands would for the immediate future remain [an] integral part of the Cheyenne River Reservation. In § 1 of the Act, the Secretary was authorized to set aside portions of the opened lands "for agency, school, and religious purposes, to remain reserved as long as needed, and as long as agency, school, or religious institutions are maintained thereon for the benefit of said Indians." 35 Stat. 461. It is difficult to imagine why Congress would have reserved lands for such purposes if it did not anticipate that the opened area would remain part of the reservation. This interpretation is supported by § 2 of the Act, under which Cheyenne River Indians were given permission to continue to obtain individual allotments on the affected portion of the reservation before the land was officially opened to non-Indian settlers. [Further] in § 2, Congress instructed the Geological Survey to examine the opened area for "lands bearing coal" and exempted those sections from allotment or disposal, the apparent purpose being to reserve those mineral resources for the whole tribe. *Id.*, at 462; see S. Rep. 439, 60th Cong., 1st Sess., 6 (1908).

This case is made more difficult, however, by the presence of some language in the Cheyenne River Act that indirectly supports petitioner's view that the reservation was diminished. For instance, in a provision permitting Indians already holding allotment on the opened lands to obtain new allotments in the unopened territories, the Act refers to the unopened territories as "within the respective reservations thus diminished." C. 218, § 2, 35 Stat. 461. Elsewhere, the Act permits tribal members to harvest timber on certain parts of the opened lands, but conditions the grant for "only as long as the lands remain part of the public domain." *Id.*, § 9, 35 Stat. 464. On the assumption that Congress would refer to opened lands as being part of the public domain only if the lands had lost all vestiges of reservation status, petitioners and several amici point to the term "public domain" as well as the phrase "reservations thus diminished" as evidence that Congress understood the Cheyenne River Act to divest unalloted open lands of their

---

[19] [15] As Petitioner stresses, the operative language of the Cheyenne River Act is also similar to language in the 1907 and 1908 Rosebud Acts, which this Court held diminished the Rosebud Sioux Reservation. Our analysis of Rosebud acts, however, was strongly colored by the existence of a 1904 Rosebud act containing cession language "precisely suited" to disestablishment, and the admission of the Indians that the second two Rosebud acts must have diminished their reservation if the previous act did. [*Rosebud Sioux Tribe v. Kneip.*]

reservation status. Undisputedly, the references to the opened areas as being in "the public domain" and the unopened areas as comprising "the reservation thus diminished" support petitioner's view that the Cheyenne River Act diminished the reservation. These isolated phrases, however, are hardly dispositive.[20] And, when balanced against the Cheyenne River Act's stated and limited goal of opening up reservation lands for sale to non-Indian settlers, these two phrases cannot carry the burden of establishing an express congressional purpose to diminish. Cf. *Mattz v. Arnett*, 412 U.S., at 497–499.[21] The Act of May 29, 1908, read as a whole, does not present an explicit expression of congressional intent to diminish the Cheyenne River Sioux Reservation.[22]

B

The circumstances surrounding the passage of the Cheyenne River Act also fail to establish a clear congressional purpose to diminish the Reservation. In contrast to the Lake Traverse Act and 1904 Rosebud Act, the Cheyenne River Act did not begin with an agreement between the United States and the Indian Tribes, in which the Indians agreed to cede a portion of their territory to the federal government. The Cheyenne River Act had its origins in "A bill to authorize the sale and disposition of a portion of the surplus and unalloted lands in the Cheyenne River and Standing Rock reservations," introduced by Senator Gamble of South Dakota on December 9, 1907. S. 1385, 60th Cong., 1st Sess. (1907). Once the bill was under consideration, the Secretary of the Interior dispatched an Inspector McLaughlin to the two affected Reservations to consult with the Tribes about the bills.

During his meeting with members of the Cheyenne River Tribe, Inspector McLaughlin admittedly spoke in terms of cession and the relinquishment of Indian interests in the opened territories. However, it is impossible to say that the Tribe agreed to the terms that presented. Due to bad weather during McLaughlin's visit, only 63 members of the Tribe attended his meeting. At the close of McLaughlin's presentation, the president of the Cheyenne River Business Council said that he would have to discuss the matter with the entire Tribe before he could respond to the proposed bill. McLaughlin agreed to delay submission of his report to Congress

---

[20] [17] There is also considerable doubt as to what Congress meant in using these phrases. In 1908, "diminished" was not yet a term of art in Indian law. When Congress spoke of the "reservation thus diminished," it may well have been referring to diminishment in common lands and not diminishment of reservation boundaries. *See United States ex rel. Condon v. Erickson*, 478 F.2d at 687. Similarly, even without diminishment, unallotted opened lands could be conceived of as being in the "public domain" inasmuch as they were available for settlement.

[21] [18] Both the South Dakota Supreme Court and dissenting judges from the Eighth Circuit have found further support for diminishment in the so-called school lands provision and a subsequently enacted liquor prohibition for the opened lands. *Stankey v. Waddell*, 256 N.W.2d, at 121, 126; *United States v. Dupris*, 612 F.2d, at 334; *see* Act of May 29, 1908, ch. 218, § 7, 35 Stat. 463 (school land provision); Act of Feb. 17, 1910, ch. 40, 36 Stat. 196–197 (liquor prohibition act). Although we credited similar provisions as supportive of our holding in *Rosebud Sioux Tribe v. Kneip*, [any] inferences from these provisions were obviously of secondary importance to our decision, see nn. 10 and 15, *supra*. Moreover, as independent evidence of a congressional intention to diminish, such evidence is suspect. . . .

[22] [19] Read as authorizing the Secretary to serve as the Tribe's sales agent, the Act fulfills Congress's original plan that the surplus lands of the Cheyenne River Sioux Reservation could be sold off once members of the Tribe moved onto allotment lands. *See* Act of Mar. 2, 1889, ch. 405, § 12, 25 Stat. 892.

until he had received word from the Tribe, but, when the Tribe's vote had not reached Washington 14 days later, McLaughlin sent his report to Congress with the conclusion: "The general sentiment of the Indians in council with me at the agency was in favor of the relinquishment (of the opened lands.)" H.R. Rep. No. 1539, 60th Cong., 1st Sess., 7 (1908); see *id.*, at 23–24, 28. McLaughlin, however, also informed Congress of the low attendance at his meeting with the Cheyenne River Tribe and acknowledged that he had never received formal approval from the Tribe. *Id.*, at 8.

With a full report of Inspector McLaughlin's meeting with the Cheyenne River Tribe before it, Congress considered the Cheyenne River Act in April and May of 1908. In neither floor debates or legislative reports is there a clear statement that Congress interpreted Inspector McLaughlin's report to establish an agreement on the part of the Cheyenne River Indians to cede the opened areas.[23] Indeed, the most explicit statement of Congress's view of the Indian's position was: "The Indians upon both reservations are satisfied to have the surplus and unalloted lands disposed of under the provisions of the bill as amended." S. Rep. 439, 60th Cong., 1st Sess., 4 (1908), quoted in H.R. Rep. 1539, 60th Cong., 1st Sess., 3 (1908). For the most part, the legislative debate of the Cheyenne River Act centered on how much money the Indians would be paid for certain sections of the opened area that the United States was going to buy for school lands, and no mention was made of the Act's effect on the reservation's boundaries or whether State or Federal officials would have jurisdiction over the opened areas. See 42 Cong. Rec. 4753–4755 (Apr. 15, 1908) (Senate debate); 42 Cong. Rec. 7003–7007 (May 26, 1908) (House debate).

To be sure, there are a few phrases scattered through the legislative history of the Cheyenne River Act that support petitioner's position. Both the Senate and House Reports refer to the "reduced reservation" and state that "lands reserved for the use of the Indians upon both reservations as diminished . . . are ample . . . for the present and future needs of the respective tribes." S. Rep. 439, *supra*, at 4, quoted and adopted in H.R. Rep. 1539, *supra*, at 3. However, it is unclear whether Congress was alluding to the reduction in Indian-owned lands that would occur once some of the opened lands were sold to settlers or to the reduction that a complete cession of tribal interests in the opened area would precipitate. See also n.17, *supra*. Without evidence that Congress understood itself to be entering into an agreement under which the Tribe committed itself to cede and relinquish all interests in unallotted opened lands, and in the absence of some clear statement of congressional intent to alter reservation boundaries, it is impossible to infer from a few isolated and ambiguous phrases a congressional purpose to diminish the Cheyenne River Sioux Reservation.

C

The subsequent treatment of the Cheyenne River Sioux Reservation by Congress, courts, and the Executive is so rife with contradictions and inconsistencies as

---

[23] [21] One reason why Congress may not have interpreted the McLaughlin report as evidence of tribal agreement to cede the land is that a delegation from the Tribe followed McLaughlin back to Washington to urge Congress not to pass the proposed legislation. *See* HOXIE 55–56. The particulars of the delegation's trip [are] not known.

to be of no help to either side. For instance, two years after the Cheyenne River Act, Congress passed a bill to sell a portion of the opened lands and called the area "surplus and unallotted lands in the Cheyenne River Indian Reservation," suggesting that the opened area was still part of the reservation. Act of June 23, 1910, ch. 369, 36 Stat. 602 (emphasis added). But, twelve years after that, Congress passed another piece of legislation referring to the opened lands as "the former" Cheyenne River Sioux Reservation and suggesting that the reservation had been diminished. See Act of Apr. 25, 1922, ch. 140, 42 Stat. 499. Ample additional examples pointing in both directions leave one with the distinct impression that subsequent Congresses had no clear view whether the opened territories were or were not still part of the Cheyenne River Reservation. A similar state of confusion characterizes the Executive's treatment of the Cheyenne River Sioux Reservation's opened lands. Moreover, both parties have been able to cite instances in which state and federal courts exerted criminal jurisdiction over the disputed area in the years following opening.[24] Neither sovereign dominated the jurisdictional history of the opened lands in the decades immediately following 1908.

What is clear, however, is what happened to the Cheyenne River Sioux Tribe after the Act of May 29, 1908, was passed. Most of the members of the Tribe obtained individual allotments on the lands opened by the Act. Because most of the tribe lived on the opened territories, tribal authorities and Bureau of Indian Affairs personnel took primary responsibility for policing and supplying social services to the opened lands during the years following 1908. The strong tribal presence in the opened area has continued until the present day. Now roughly two-thirds of the Tribe's enrolled members live in the opened area. The seat of tribal government is now located in a town in the opened area, where most important tribal activities take place.

Also clear is the historical fact that the opening of the Cheyenne River Sioux Reservation was a failure. Few homesteaders perfected claims on the lands, due perhaps in part to the price of the land but probably more importantly to the fact that the opened area was much less fertile than the lands in southern South Dakota opened by other surplus land acts.[25] As a result of [the] small number of homesteaders who settled on the opened lands and the high percentage of tribal members who continue to live in the area, the population of the disputed area is now evenly divided between Indian and non-Indian residents. Under these circum-

---

[24] [23] According to one study, Federal, Tribal, and State courts shared jurisdiction over the opened areas in the decades following opening. HOXIE 100–128. Between 1910 and 1920, only two Indians were tried in state court for crimes committed on the opened lands. *Id.*, at 128. During this period, the Federal authorities were primarily responsible for Indian life on both opened and unopened portions of the reservation. In later years, however, the state courts came to assume that the opened areas fell within their general criminal jurisdiction. *See, e.g., State v. Barnes*, 81 S.D. 511, 137 N.W.2d 683 (1965). It was only in 1973 that the Eighth Circuit challenged this assumption in *United States ex rel. Condon v. Erickson, supra.*

[25] [26] During a debate on subsequent surplus land, Congressman Burke, a sponsor of the Cheyenne River Act, reported: "At the opening of the Cheyenne and the Standing Rock Reservations . . . there were not sufficient people to begin to take anywhere near the land that was to be disposed of, and the reason they did not take it was the price of the land, which was undoubtedly too high." 49 Cong. Rec. 1106 (1913). According to the Government's estimates, only half of the opened lands ever passed out of Indian ownership. . . .

stances, it is impossible to say that the opened areas of the Cheyenne River Sioux Reservation have lost their Indian character.

Neither the Act of May 29, 1908, the circumstances surrounding its passage, nor subsequent events clearly establish that the Act diminished the Cheyenne River Sioux Reservation. The presumption that Congress did not intend to diminish the reservation therefore stands, and the judgment of the Eighth Circuit is

Affirmed.

NOTES ON DETERMINING CONGRESSIONAL INTENT TO DIMINISH BOUNDARIES

1. **Historical Inquiry vs. Contemporary Demographics:** While the result in *Solem* was not surprising, the unanimity of the Court's decision was somewhat startling in light of the divided case law that preceded the decision. In *United States v. Celestine*, 215 U.S. 278, 285 (1909), the Court held that the Tulalip Reservation in Washington remained Indian country notwithstanding the allotment of Tulalip land, including the land on which the crime in question occurred, to members of the Tribe. Speaking for the Court, Justice Brewer wrote, "when Congress has once established a reservation all tracts included within it remain a reservation until separated therefrom by Congress." The Court reached a similar conclusion for the south half of the Colville Reservation, also in Washington, in *Seymour v. Superintendent*, 368 U.S. 351 (1962), and for the Klamath River Reservation in California in *Mattz v. Arnett*, 412 U.S. 481 (1973). *Seymour* and *Mattz* seemed to suggest that a finding of reservation diminishment could only be supported either by an express and unequivocal Congressional statement or by a showing of an unequivocal Congressional intent to terminate the reservation. Both cases involved reservations that had retained a distinctly Indian character notwithstanding the opening of the reservation to non-Indian settlement — Indians were the dominant population group living on reservation lands. The Court, however, was soon confronted with two cases involving land within heavily allotted reservation areas in which Indians no longer made up the dominant population group. In both, Indians made up only 10% of the total population. In *DeCoteau v. District County Court*, 420 U.S. 425 (1975), involving the Sisseton-Wahpeton Sioux Reservation and *Rosebud Sioux Tribe v. Kneip*, 430 U.S. 584 (1977), involving the Rosebud Sioux Reservation, both in South Dakota, the Court denied continued reservation status to lands that had been designated "surplus" as part of the allotment process, and opened for sale. In neither case had Congress expressly indicated an intention to sever the area in question from the reservation, as opposed to selling land that would remain within reservation boundaries. It had, however, established a "sum certain" as payment for the opened lands.

Solem is thus one of a group of conflicting cases tracing the level of congressional specificity required to support a finding of reservation diminishment or termination. Most of these cases involve interpreting the legal effect of allotment era statutes on the continued existence and the exterior boundaries of a reservation. As the *Solem* case suggests, however, the *immediate* impact of such allotment statutes and laws approving agreements with tribes on the continued existence or precise boundaries of the reservation was not then a salient question, since the allotment policy anticipated the ultimate dissolution of Indian reservations through termination of the trust restrictions on Indian land after 25 years. Thus, the interpretive question posed in such cases constitutes a uniquely historical issue since the legal problem only emerged as a result of the legal persistence of Indian reservations after the allotment policy — an event neither assumed nor foreseen by the designers of the statutes in question. Consequently, the more rigorously courts require the statutes authorizing the allotment of a reservation or the opening of the reservation to non-Indian settlement to demonstrate a clear, unequivocal congressional intent immediately to terminate or diminish a reservation, the less likely the test will be satisfied.

Were differences in *contemporary* demographic profiles of the reservations, particularly the current percentage of Indian population, influencing the outcomes of cases in which the legal test called solely for a historical inquiry? Should current demography play a role in the resolution of such questions? Does the opinion in the *Solem* case resolve any perceived inconsistency between reliance on contemporary demography and reliance on historical background to decide these important questions of reservation termination and diminishment? What if different parts of a ceded area have experienced different levels of non-Indian settlement and political domination? For example, in 2013 the EPA ruled that the boundaries of the Wind River Reservation of the Eastern Shoshone and Northern Arapaho, located in Wyoming, encompass the city of Riverton, which is 85% non-Indian. A 1905 statute had opened part of the reservation for sale and homesteading, but as of 2013, 75% of the opened area (nearly 1.5 million acres) was still held by the Tribes. Furthermore, the City of Riverton, within the opened area, occupies only 6,000 acres. The legal basis for the EPA's ruling, which references a detailed analysis by the Solicitor of the Department of the Interior, can be found at http://www2.epa. gov/sites/production/files/2013-12/documents/attachment2capabilitystatement.pdf. The State of Wyoming has brought suit, challenging the EPA's determination, and the Tribes are promoting mediation. Can you envision a mediated settlement to this dispute? If so, on what terms?

Note that in *Solem*, the Tribe had the benefit of intensive historical research conducted by an eminent historian, Fred Hoxie. Did the historical research the Court relied on in *Solem* resemble conventional legislative history, as produced by lawyers? Would such legislative history have been sufficient to support a finding of continued reservation status? Developing a strong factual record is important in persuading decision-makers in Indian law cases.

2. **Post-*Solem* Decisions:** In *Hagen v. Utah*, 510 U.S. 399 (1994), and *South Dakota v. Yankton Sioux Tribe*, 522 U.S. 329 (1998), the Court again returned to the question of reservation diminishment and termination. In *Hagen*, the Court held that the Uintah and Ouray Reservation of the Utes in Utah had been diminished by 1902 legislation that opened the reservation to allotment, as supplemented by later legislation in 1903 and 1905. This legislation also provided that when the deadline for allotments passed, "all the unallotted lands within said reservation shall be restored to the public domain" and subject to homesteading at $1.25 per acre. The proceeds from the sale of lands restored to the public domain were to be used for the benefit of the Indians. Justice O'Connor's opinion for the Court held that the

reservation had been diminished, relying heavily on language in the 1902 statute, which initially provided for allotment to be based on tribal consent. The later statutes provided for unilateral allotment in accordance with the 1902 Act, using such terms as "to carry out the purposes" of the 1902 Act. The Court reasoned:

> The operative language of the 1902 Act provided for allocations of reservation land to Indians, and that "all the unallotted lands within said reservation shall be restored to the public domain." 32 Stat. 263. The public domain was the land owned by the Government, mostly in the West, that was "available for sale, entry, and settlement under the homestead laws, or other disposition under the general body of land laws." E. Peffer, The Closing of the Public Domain 6 (1951). "From an early period in the history of the government it [was] the practice of the President to order, from time to time, . . . parcels of land belonging to the United States to be reserved from sale and set apart for public uses." This power of reservation was exercised for various purposes, including Indian settlement, bird preservation, and military installations, "when it appeared that the public interest would be served by withdrawing or reserving parts of the public domain."

> It follows that when lands so reserved were "restored" to the public domain — i.e., once again opened to sale or settlement — their previous public use was extinguished. *See Sioux Tribe v. United States*, 316 U.S. 317, 323 (1942) (President ordered lands previously reserved for Indian use " 'restored to the public domain[,] . . . the same being no longer needed for the purpose for which they were withdrawn from sale and settlement' "). Statutes of the period indicate that Congress considered Indian reservations as separate from the public domain. . . .

Id. at 412–13. After reviewing the reservation diminishment cases, the Court concluded that language in the surplus land Act restoring the unallotted reservation lands to the public domain indicates a congressional intent inconsistent with continued reservation status, and thus the reservation was terminated.

Yankton posed the diminishment question in the context of an 1894 statute and agreement that ceded all unalloted reservation lands to the United States for a sum certain, giving it some resemblance to *DeCoteau*. However, unlike *DeCoteau*, there was a savings clause in the agreement which stated that nothing in the agreement's terms "shall be construed to abrogate the treaty [of 1858, which established the reservation boundaries]" and that "all provisions of the said treaty . . . shall be in full force and effect, the same as though this agreement had not been made." Furthermore, there was mixed evidence from Interior Department documents about whether the United States had considered the reservation diminished by the cession of lands. After reciting the general principles relevant to such determinations, Justice O'Connor turned to the language in the savings clause, which strongly suggested maintenance of the original reservation boundaries:

> Such a literal construction of the saving clause . . . would "impugn the entire sale." The unconditional relinquishment of the Tribe's territory for settlement by non-Indian homesteaders can by no means be reconciled with the central provisions of the 1858 Treaty, which recognized the reservation as the Tribe's "permanent" home and prohibited white settle-

ment there. *See Oregon Dept. of Fish and Wildlife v. Klamath Tribe*, 473 U.S. 753, 770 (1985) (discounting a saving clause on the basis of a "glaring inconsistency" between the original treaty and the subsequent agreement). Moreover, the Government's contention that the Tribe intended to cede some property but maintain the entire reservation as its territory contradicts the common understanding of the time: that tribal ownership was a critical component of reservation status. See *Solem, supra*, at 468.

Rather than read the saving clause in a manner that eviscerates the agreement in which it appears, we give it a "sensible construction" that avoids this "absurd conclusion." See *United States v. Granderson*, 511 U.S. 39, 56 (1994). The most plausible interpretation of Article XVIII revolves around the annuities in the form of cash, guns, ammunition, food, and clothing that the Tribe was to receive in exchange for its aboriginal claims for 50 years after the 1858 Treaty. Along with the proposed sale price, these annuities and other unrealized Yankton claims dominated the 1892 negotiations between the Commissioners and the Tribe. The tribal historian testified, before the District Court, that the loss of their rations would have been "disastrous" to the Tribe, and members of the Tribe clearly perceived a threat to the annuities. . . . Given the Tribe's evident concern with reaffirmance of the Government's obligations under the 1858 Treaty, and the Commissioners' tendency to wield the payments as an inducement to sign the agreement, we conclude that the saving clause pertains to the continuance of annuities, not the 1858 borders.

522 U.S. at 345–46.

Do the results and analyses in the *Hagen* and *Yankton* cases evidence respect for the Court's consistent statement that "we resolve any ambiguities in favor of the Indians, and we will not lightly find diminishment?" *Hagen*, 510 U.S. at 411. *See* Sec. C, this chapter. Accepting that at the time of allotment, Congress did not foresee the persistence of tribal governments, should the tribe or the state have the burden of demonstrating that ambiguous language was designed to end reservation status?

3.   Avoiding Checkerboard Jurisdiction? In *Seymour v. Superintendent*, 368 U.S. 351, 358 (1962), the Court rejected the suggestion that only Indian owned parcels within an allotted Indian reservation constituted Indian country. Speaking for a unanimous Court, Justice Black said:

The State urges that we interpret the words "notwithstanding the issuance of any patent" to mean only notwithstanding the issuance of any patent to an Indian. But the State does not suggest, nor can we find, any adequate justification for such an interpretation. Quite the contrary, it seems to us that the strongest argument against the exclusion of patented lands from an Indian reservation applies with equal force to patents issued to non-Indians and Indians alike. For that argument rests upon the fact that where the existence or nonexistence of an Indian reservation, and therefore the existence or nonexistence of federal jurisdiction, depends upon the ownership of particular parcels of land, law enforcement officers operating in the area will find it necessary to search tract books in order to determine whether criminal jurisdiction over each particular offense, even though committed within the reservation, is in the State or Federal Government. Such an impractical pattern of checkerboard jurisdiction was avoided by the plain language of § 1151. . . .

Seymour indicates that within reservation boundaries, Indian country status exists without regard to land title or the identity of landowners, and that this interpretation of section 1151(a) is designed to prevent checkerboard jurisdiction. Does the approach to questions of reservation diminishment or termination reflected in *Solem* and subsequent cases take adequate account of this stated congressional policy? The rationale of preventing checkerboard jurisdiction rests on two assumptions: first, that tribal jurisdiction extends through Indian country without regard to land title or the identity of landowners, thereby enabling tribes to exert uniform jurisdiction; and second, that the reservation is an intact expanse with a continuous perimeter, thereby insuring uniform jurisdiction within a defined area.

The first of these assumptions has been undermined considerably by United States Supreme Court decisions limiting tribal civil jurisdiction over nonmember activities on nonmember-owned land within Indian country. *See* Ch. 3, Sec. C.1. The second assumption does not hold when a reservation is allotted, the allotments are scattered all over the reservation, and the surrounding "surplus" lands are ceded to the United States in a transaction which is deemed to sever the ceded lands from the reservation. Under those circumstances, the remaining reservation consists of many relatively small and disconnected parcels. *See South Dakota v. Yankton Sioux Tribe*, 522 U.S. 329 (1998). When these two assumptions are discarded, tribal jurisdiction over reservation Indian country has no continuous geographic sweep. As a result, should *Seymour*'s holding be reconsidered in some or all cases? Under these conditions, is there any way to avoid checkerboard jurisdiction, with its attendant confusions and uncertainties?

On remand in *Yankton*, the Eighth Circuit tackled the jurisdictional status of the *un*ceded lands within the original reservation boundaries. The court read the 1894 cession act as not disestablishing the original reservation altogether. Nonetheless, based on its understanding of the assimilative purposes of the 1894 Act, the court found that Congress "had intended to diminish the reservation by not only the ceded land, but also by the land which it foresaw would pass into the hands of the white settlers and homesteaders." *Yankton Sioux Tribe v. Gaffey*, 188 F.3d 1010, 1028 (1999). Subsequent jurisdictional treatment of nontrust lands in the unceded area — especially the federal government's enforcement of federal Indian country criminal laws solely on allotted lands — gave the court added confidence in its interpretation. Moreover, the court determined that the remaining reservation, consisting of disconnected allotments, was diminished in size whenever an allotment transferred to non-Indian ownership. The court concluded that any such lands that had been allotted and had since "passed out of Indian hands" were no longer part of the reservation. *Id.* at 1030. At another point, however, the court described the excluded parcels as all nonceded lands that had "passed out of trust," which presumably would cover Indian-owned fee lands.

In the wake of the Eighth Circuit's decision, the daunting task of delineating Yankton Indian country fell to United States District Court Judge Lawrence

Piersol. Judge Piersol affirmed that the Yankton Sioux Reservation is a "checkerboard reservation" that has been diminished, but not disestablished. After careful analysis, he ruled that parcels within the scope of the original 1858 treaty boundaries are reservation lands for purposes of 18 U.S.C. § 1151(a) if they have continuously remained trust allotments; if they earlier went out of trust but were later taken back into trust for the Tribe by the United States under the Indian Reorganization Act (IRA); and if they are allotments that went out of trust but have been continuously held by Indians in fee. *Yankton Sioux Tribe v. Podhradsky*, 529 F. Supp. 2d 1040 (D.S.D. 2007). The Eighth Circuit affirmed everything except Judge Piersol's ruling regarding the fee lands continuously owned by Indians, which the appellate court found to be unripe due to inadequate information regarding the history of those tracts. *Yankton Sioux Tribe v. Podhradsky*, 606 F.3d 994 (8th Cir. 2010). The Eighth Circuit's opinion notes the importance of finding reservation status for the trust allotments, as that means the land will remain Indian country even if the trust status ends, as through inheritance by a non-Indian. Should the tribal trust lands be treated as "reservation" under 18 U.S.C. § 1151(a) or as a "dependent Indian community" under 18 U.S.C. § 1151(b)? South Dakota argued that the tribal trust lands could not be deemed a "reservation" because there had been no proclamation to that effect under the IRA. Why would it matter which subdivision of section 1151 applied to establish "Indian country" status for those tribal trust lands? For purposes of addressing the state's argument, should it matter whether the tribal trust lands were within the boundaries of a former reservation? What about the former Indian allotments now and continuously held by Indians, which the Eighth Circuit chose not to address? The state's position is that those lands should lose reservation status once they go from trust to fee. According to the state, that outcome accords with the historical understanding during the allotment era. For a contrary historical analysis, contending that "federal officials and Congress understood during the allotment era that reservation lands allotted to Indians and then transferred into non-Indian hands would remain within reservation boundaries," see Marc Slonim, *Indian Country, Indian Reservations, and the Importance of History in Indian Law*, 45 GONZ. L. REV. 517, 529 (2010).

Commenting on the potential difficulties of law enforcement and administration under the checkerboard conditions resulting from the Yankton litigation, Judge Piersol observed that "[even if the checkerboarded reservation] as now diminished presented law enforcement problems, those problems would have to be countenanced for the Reservation as diminished is what varying federal Indian policies have created." At the same time, he commented that he thought the patchwork jurisdictional arrangement was "workable," as measured by his own "busy criminal docket" of cases arising at Yankton. It is noteworthy, however, that Charles Mix County, where the Yankton Sioux Reservation is located, has been the site of a successful race discrimination lawsuit by Indian plaintiffs under the Voting Rights Act of 1965. *See Blackmoon v. Charles Mix County*, 2005 U.S. Dist. LEXIS 27551 (D.S.D. Oct. 24, 2005). Furthermore, the Tribe and the County have been unable to arrive at a cross-deputization agreement. Under those circumstances, how easy can it be for law enforcement officers and courts to ascertain which cases are within their jurisdiction?

4. **Underlying Concern About Tribes Governing Non-Indians:** In the cases dealing with reservation diminishment, are the courts responding to anything other than the prospect of a small group of tribal members governing a territory in which a vastly greater number of non-Indians reside but cannot participate? Is the proper solution to this dilemma to limit Indian nations' governing authority to scattered tracts of allotted land? Is the Court in a position to craft a more satisfactory solution than either of these alternatives? *See* Ch. 3, Sec. C.1. To blunt the concern about non-participation by non-Indians, should tribes invite resident non-Indians to participate some way in governance? Does the United States allow resident aliens to vote? If Congress operated on an international self-determination model of tribal-federal relations, how might it legislate to improve the situation?

B. EQUAL PROTECTION QUESTIONS POSED BY INDIAN LEGISLATION

In the last several decades of the twentieth century, a backlash against race-based affirmative action has prompted litigation and policy initiatives to outlaw all classifications based on race and ethnicity. One spillover effect of these assaults on affirmative action has been an increase in challenges to federal and state laws addressing Indian affairs. Do these laws violate constitutional requirements of equal protection because they introduce race-based or ethnic classifications?

One possible answer is that the classifications are based on the political status of tribal members rather than on race, ancestry, or ethnicity, akin to an educational program aimed at foreign students or immunities offered to foreign diplomats. Another possible answer is that the classifications, though based partly on race or ancestry, are authorized under the federal trust responsibility and provisions of the United States Constitution such as the Indian commerce clause. Yet a third possible answer is that the classifications are race or ancestry based, but they are justified under equal protection doctrine by a sufficiently compelling set of governmental purposes and interests. This section separately highlights the legal issues surrounding each of these three possible responses. How does the material on traditional tribal conceptions of membership, *supra*, suggest the equal protection question should be answered for federal Indian laws? Should the various federal definitions of who is an Indian lead to different answers under different federal laws? For a discussion of these different doctrinal approaches, see Carole Goldberg, *American Indians and "Preferential" Treatment*, 49 UCLA L. REV. 943, 955–74 (2002).

Of course, it is difficult to conceive of a tribal-federal relationship at all if the federal government is constitutionally prohibited from affording separate treatment to Native people. Indeed, contemporary equal protection challenges to federal Indian legislation follow along on a trail blazed by earlier supporters of assimilation and termination. Often these earlier campaigns tried to strike a chord of benevolence — equal treatment would be a means to "emancipate" Indian people from oppressive BIA restrictions on their capacity to manage property and from "confinement" on reservations. Thus, for example, termination supporters of the 1950s harnessed the rhetoric of civil rights to advance their cause. H. Con. Res. 108, 83d Cong. (1953); "Statement of Gary Orfield" *in* INDIAN SELF-RULE: FIRST HAND ACCOUNTS OF INDIAN-WHITE RELATIONS FROM ROOSEVELT TO REAGAN 129 (Kenneth Philp ed., 1986). And the Alaska Native Claims Settlement Act of 1971 created Native corporations holding fee land rather than tribal governments with reservations in order to avoid creating "permanent racially defined institutions, rights, privileges, or obligations." 43 U.S.C. § 1601(b). *See* Sec. A.3.b.ii, this chapter. Likewise, contemporary opponents of Indian treaty rights to hunt and fish have marched under the banner of equal treatment. For example, in 1978 a federal bill was proposed, creatively entitled the "Native American Equal Opportunity Act," which was intended to abrogate all treaties entered into by the United States with Indian nations, to eliminate all separate or special legal protections of Indians, and to terminate federal supervision over the property and members of Indian tribes. H.R. 13,329, 95th Cong., 2d Sess. One of the major lobbying groups during the late 1970s fighting for the abrogation of the special legal status of Indians styled itself the Interstate Congress for Equal Rights and Responsibilities.

Given the widespread critiques of termination and ANCSA, should the equality rhetoric be taken at face value? Might *non*enforcement or differential enforcement of Indian property rights such as hunting and fishing rights raise as many equal protection problems as the existence of such rights? Does recognition of Native nations' governmental status violate principles of equal treatment of individuals when it is designed to take into account that Indian people never consented to inclusion within the American polity? According to Professor Bethany Berger, who has studied the history of racialization of Indians and tribes, "Modern backlash against tribes, which emphasizes the racial composition of Indian tribes and their adherence to insular traditions construed as inferior and unfair, is . . . not the product of a society committed to racial equality, but [a continuation of] the same old pattern of tribal oppression reshaped for modern ideology." She focuses on the fact that historically, claims about the racial inferiority of tribes have served the purpose of justifying non-Indian dispossession of tribal lands and other property. Bethany R. Berger, *Red: Racism and the American Indian*, 56 UCLA L. Rev. 591, 654 (2009).

As you read the cases and commentaries that follow, attend to the way the equal protection question is posed, the various answers that are offered, and the model(s) of the tribal-federal relationship that drive the analysis. In light of the following case, is the debate over affirmative action relevant to these issues affecting Indian peoples? Does the answer foment divisions between Indians and other historically disadvantaged groups seeking benefits through affirmative action?

1.   Indian Classifications as Political Rather than Racial

MORTON v. MANCARI
United States Supreme Court
417 U.S. 535 (1974)

Mr. Justice Blackmun delivered the opinion of the Court.

The Indian Reorganization Act of 1934, also known as the Wheeler-Howard Act, 48 Stat. 984, 25 U.S.C. § 461 *et seq.*, accords an employment preference for qualified Indians in the Bureau of Indian Affairs (BIA or Bureau). Appellees, non-Indian BIA employees, challenged this preference as contrary to the anti-discrimination provisions of the Equal Employment Opportunity Act of 1972, [and as a violation] of the Due Process Clause of the fifth amendment. A three-judge Federal District Court concluded that the Indian preference under the 1934 Act was impliedly repealed by the 1972 Act. [This Court] noted probable jurisdiction in order to examine the statutory and constitutional validity of this longstanding Indian preference. . . .

I

Section 12 of the Indian Reorganization Act, 48 Stat. 986, 25 U.S.C. § 472, provides:

> The Secretary of the Interior is directed to establish standards of health, age, character, experience, knowledge, and ability for Indians who may be appointed, without regard to civil-service laws, to the various positions maintained, now or hereafter, by the Indian Office, in the administration of functions or services affecting any Indian tribe. Such qualified Indians shall hereafter have the preference to appointment to vacancies in any such positions.

In June 1972, pursuant to this provision, the Commissioner of Indian Affairs, with the approval of the Secretary of the Interior, issued a directive (Personnel Management Letter No. 72–12) (App. 52) stating that the BIA's policy would be to grant a preference to qualified Indians not only, as before, in the initial hiring stage, but also in the situation where an Indian and a non-Indian, both already employed by the BIA, were competing for a promotion within the Bureau. The record indicates that this policy was implemented immediately.

Shortly thereafter, appellees, who are non-Indian employees of the BIA at Albuquerque, instituted this class action, on behalf of themselves and other non-Indian employees similarly situated, in the United States District Court for the District of New Mexico, claiming that the "so-called 'Indian Preference Statutes,' " [were repealed by Congress in] the 1972 Equal Employment Opportunity Act and deprived them of rights to property without due process of law, in violation of the fifth amendment. Named as defendants were the Secretary of the Interior, the Commissioner of Indian Affairs, and the BIA Directors for the Albuquerque and Navajo Area Offices. Appellees claimed that implementation and enforcement of the new preference policy "placed and will continue to place [appellees] at a distinct disadvantage in competing for promotion and training programs with Indian employees, all of which has and will continue to subject the [appellees] to discrimination and deny them equal employment opportunity."

[T]he District Court concluded that the Indian preference was implicitly repealed by § 11 of the Equal Employment Opportunity Act of 1972, Pub. L. 92–261, 86 Stat. 111, 42 U.S.C. § 2000e-16(a) (1970 ed., Supp. II), proscribing discrimination in most federal employment on the basis of race.[26] Having found that Congress

---

[26] [6] Section 2000e-16 (a) reads:

All personnel actions affecting employees or applicants for employment (except with regard to

repealed the preference, it was unnecessary for the District Court to pass on its constitutionality. The court permanently enjoined appellants "from implementing any policy in the Bureau of Indian Affairs which would hire, promote, or reassign any person in preference to another solely for the reason that such person is an Indian." The execution and enforcement of the judgment of the District Court was stayed by Mr. Justice Marshall on August 16, 1973, pending the disposition of this appeal.

II

The federal policy of according some hiring preference to Indians in the Indian service dates at least as far back as 1834.[27] Since that time, Congress repeatedly has enacted various preferences of the general type here at issue. The purpose of these preferences, as variously expressed in the legislative history, has been to give Indians a greater participation in their own self-government;[28] to further the Government's trust obligation toward the Indian tribes; and to reduce the negative effect of having non-Indians administer matters that affect Indian tribal life.

The preference directly at issue here was enacted as an important part of the sweeping Indian Reorganization Act of 1934. The overriding purpose of that particular Act was to establish machinery whereby Indian tribes would be able to assume a greater degree of self-government, both politically and economically. Congress was seeking to modify the then-existing situation whereby the primarily non-Indian-staffed BIA had plenary control, for all practical purposes, over the lives and destinies of the federally recognized Indian tribes. Initial congressional proposals would have diminished substantially the role of the BIA by turning over to federally chartered self-governing Indian communities many of the functions normally performed by the Bureau. Committee sentiment, however, ran against

---

aliens employed outside the limits of the United States) in military departments as defined in section 102 of Title 5, in executive agencies (other than the General Accounting Office) as defined in section 105 of Title 5 (including employees and applicants for employment who are paid from nonappropriated funds), in the United States Postal Service and the Postal Rate Commission, in those units of the Government of the District of Columbia having positions in the competitive service, and in those units of the legislative and judicial branches of the Federal Government having positions in the competitive service, and in the Library of Congress shall be made free from any discrimination based on race, color, religion, sex, or national origin.

[27]   [7] Act of June 30, 1834, § 9, 4 Stat. 737, 25 U.S.C. § 45:

[I]n all cases of the appointments of interpreters or other persons employed for the benefit of the Indians, a preference shall be given to persons of Indian descent, if such can be found, who are properly qualified for the execution of the duties.

[28]   [9] Senator Wheeler, cosponsor of the 1934 Act, explained the need for a preference as follows:

We are setting up in the United States a civil service rule which prevents Indians from managing their own property. It is an entirely different service from anything else in the United States, because these Indians own this property. It belongs to them. What the policy of this Government is and what it should be is to teach these Indians to manage their own business and control their own funds and to administer their own property, and the civil service has worked very poorly so far as the Indian Service is concerned. . . . Hearings on S. 2755 and S. 3645 before the Senate Committee on Indian Affairs, 73d Cong., 2d Sess., pt. 2, p. 256 (1934).

such a radical change in the role of the BIA. The solution ultimately adopted was to strengthen tribal government while continuing the active role of the BIA, with the understanding that the Bureau would be more responsive to the interests of the people it was created to serve.

One of the primary means by which self-government would be fostered and the Bureau made more responsive was to increase the participation of tribal Indians in the BIA operations.[29] In order to achieve this end, it was recognized that some kind of preference and exemption from otherwise prevailing civil service requirements was necessary.[30] Congressman Howard, the House sponsor, expressed the need for the preference:

> The Indians have not only been thus deprived of civic rights and powers, but they have been largely deprived of the opportunity to enter the more important positions in the service of the very bureau which manages their affairs. Theoretically, the Indians have the right to qualify for the Federal civil service. In actual practice there has been no adequate program of training to qualify Indians to compete in these examinations, especially for technical and higher positions; and even if there were such training, the Indians would have to compete under existing law, on equal terms with multitudes of white applicants. . . . The various services on the Indian reservations are actually local rather than Federal services and are comparable to local municipal and county services, since they are dealing with purely local Indian problems. It should be possible for Indians with the requisite vocational and professional training to enter the service of their own people without the necessity of competing with white applicants for these positions. This bill permits them to do so. 78 Cong. Rec. 11729 (1934).

Congress was well aware that the proposed preference would result in employment disadvantages within the BIA for non-Indians. Not only was this displacement unavoidable if room were to be made for Indians, but it was explicitly determined that gradual replacement of non-Indians with Indians within the Bureau was a desirable feature of the entire program for self-government. Since 1934, the BIA has implemented the preference with a fair degree of success. The percentage of Indians employed in the Bureau rose from 34% in 1934 to 57% in 1972. This reversed the former downward trend, [and this result] was due, clearly, to the presence of the 1934 Act. The Commissioner's extension of the preference in 1972 to promotions within the BIA was designed to bring more Indians into positions of responsibility and, in that regard, appears to be a logical extension of the congressional intent.

---

[29] [15] [Section 12] was intended to integrate the Indian into the government service connected with the administration of his affairs. Congress was anxious to promote economic and political self-determination for the Indian. *Mescalero Apache Tribe v. Hickel*, 432 F.2d at 960 (footnote omitted).

[30] [16] The bill admits qualified Indians to the position [*sic*] in their own service. Thirty-four years ago, in 1900, the number of Indians holding regular positions in the Indian Service, in proportion to the total of positions, was greater than it is today. The reason primarily is found in the application of the generalized civil service to the Indian Service, and the consequent exclusion of Indians from their own jobs. House Hearings 19 (memorandum dated Feb. 19, 1934, submitted by Commissioner Collier to the Senate and House Committees on Indian Affairs).

III

It is against this background that we encounter the first issue in the present case: whether the Indian preference was repealed by the Equal Employment Opportunity Act of 1972. Title VII of the Civil Rights Act of 1964, 78 Stat. 253, was the first major piece of federal legislation prohibiting discrimination in *private* employment on the basis of "race, color, religion, sex, or national origin." 42 U.S.C. § 2000e-2(a). Significantly, §§ 701(b) and 703(i) of that Act explicitly exempted from its coverage the preferential employment of Indians by Indian tribes or by industries located on or near Indian reservations. 42 U.S.C. §§ 2000e(b) and 2000e-2(i).[31] This exemption reveals a clear congressional recognition, within the framework of Title VII, of the unique legal status of tribal and reservation-based activities. The Senate sponsor, Senator Humphrey, stated on the floor by way of explanation:

> [T]his exemption is consistent with the Federal Government's policy of encouraging Indian employment and with the special legal position of Indians. 110 Cong. Rec. 12723 (1964).

The 1964 Act did not specifically outlaw employment discrimination by the federal government. Yet the mechanism for enforcing longstanding Executive Orders forbidding Government discrimination had proved ineffective for the most part. In order to remedy this, Congress, by the 1972 Act, amended the 1964 Act and proscribed discrimination in most areas of federal employment. [Generally,] the substantive anti-discrimination law embraced in Title VII was carried over and applied to the federal government. [Nowhere] in the legislative history of the 1972 Act, however, is there any mention of Indian preference.

Appellees assert, and the District Court held, that since the 1972 Act proscribed racial discrimination in Government employment, the Act necessarily, albeit *sub silentio*, repealed the provision of the 1934 Act that called for the preference in the BIA of one racial group, Indians, over non-Indians.

[W]e conclude that Congress did not intend to repeal the Indian preference and that the District Court erred in holding that it was repealed.

First: There are the above-mentioned affirmative provisions in the 1964 Act excluding coverage of tribal employment and of preferential treatment by a business or enterprise on or near a reservation. 42 U.S.C. §§ 2000e (b) and 2000e-2 (i). [The] 1964 exemptions as to private employment indicate Congress's recognition of the longstanding federal policy of providing a unique legal status to Indians in matters concerning tribal or "on or near" reservation employment. The exemptions reveal a clear congressional sentiment that an Indian preference in the narrow context of tribal or reservation-related employment did not constitute racial discrimination of the [proscribed type].

---

[31] [19] Section 701(b) excludes "an Indian Tribe" from the Act's definition of "employer." Section 703(i) states:

> Nothing contained in this subchapter shall apply to any business or enterprise on or near an Indian reservation with respect to any publicly announced employment practice of such business or enterprise under which a preferential treatment is given to any individual because he is an Indian living on or near a reservation.

Second: Three months after Congress passed the 1972 amendments, it enacted two *new* Indian preference laws. These were part of the Education Amendments of 1972, 86 Stat. 235, 20 U.S.C. §§ 887c (a) and (d), and § 1119a (1970 ed., Supp. II). The new laws explicitly require that Indians be given preference in Government programs for training teachers of Indian children. It is improbable, to say the least, that the same Congress which affirmatively approved and enacted these additional and similar Indian preferences was, at the same time, condemning the BIA preference as racially discriminatory. . . .

Third: Indian preferences, for many years, have been treated as exceptions to Executive Orders forbidding Government employment discrimination. The 1972 extension of the Civil Rights Act to Government employment is in large part merely a codification of prior anti-discrimination Executive Orders that had proved ineffective because of inadequate enforcement machinery. There certainly was no indication that the substantive proscription against discrimination was intended to be any broader than that which previously existed. By codifying the existing anti-discrimination provisions, and by providing enforcement machinery for them, there is no reason to presume that Congress affirmatively intended to erase the preferences that previously had co-existed with broad anti-discrimination provisions in Executive Orders.

Fourth: Appellees encounter head-on the "cardinal rule . . . that repeals by implication are not favored." . . .

This is a prototypical case where an adjudication of repeal by implication is not appropriate. The preference is a longstanding, important component of the Government's Indian program. The anti-discrimination provision, aimed at alleviating minority discrimination in employment, obviously is designed to deal with an entirely different and, indeed, opposite problem. Any perceived conflict is thus more apparent than real.

[In addition,] the Indian preference statute is a specific provision applying to a very specific situation. The 1972 Act, on the other hand, is of general application. Where there is no clear intention otherwise, a specific statute will not be controlled or nullified by a general one, regardless of the priority of enactment.

[Thus, we] hold that the District Court erred in ruling that the Indian preference was repealed by the 1972 Act.

IV

We still must decide whether, as the appellees contend, the preference constitutes invidious racial discrimination in violation of the Due Process Clause of the fifth amendment. *Bolling v. Sharpe*, 347 U.S. 497 (1954). The District Court, while pretermitting this issue, said: "[W]e could well hold that the statute must fail on constitutional grounds."

Resolution of the instant issue turns on the unique legal status of Indian tribes under federal law and upon the plenary power of Congress, based on a history of treaties and the assumption of a "guardian-ward" status, to legislate on behalf of federally recognized Indian tribes. The plenary power of Congress to deal with the special problems of Indians is drawn both explicitly and implicitly from the Constitution itself. Article I, § 8, cl. 3, provides Congress with the power to "regulate Commerce . . . with the Indian Tribes," and thus, to this extent, singles Indians out as a proper subject for separate legislation. Article II, § 2, cl. 2, gives the President the power, by and with the advice and consent of the Senate, to make treaties. This has often been the source of the Government's power to deal with the Indian tribes. The Court has described the origin and nature of the special relationship:

> In the exercise of the war and treaty powers, the United States overcame the Indians and took possession of their lands, sometimes by force, leaving them an uneducated, helpless and dependent people, needing protection against the selfishness of others and their own improvidence. Of necessity, the United States assumed the duty of furnishing that protection, and with it the authority to do all that was required to perform that obligation and to prepare the Indians to take their place as independent, qualified members of the modern body politic. . . . *Board of County Comm'rs v. Seber*, 318 U.S. 705, 715 (1943).

See also United States v. Kagama, 118 U.S. 375, 383–384 (1886).

Literally every piece of legislation dealing with Indian tribes and reservations, and certainly all legislation dealing with the BIA, single[s] out for special treatment a constituency of tribal Indians living on or near reservations. If these laws, derived from historical relationships and explicitly designed to help only Indians, were deemed invidious racial discrimination, an entire Title of the United States Code (25 U.S.C.) would be effectively erased and the solemn commitment of the Government toward the Indians would be jeopardized. *See Simmons v. Eagle Seelatsee*, 244 F. Supp. 808, 814 n.13 (ED Wash. 1965), *aff'd*, 384 U.S. 209 (1966).

It is in this historical and legal context that the constitutional validity of the Indian preference is to be determined. As discussed above, Congress in 1934 determined that proper fulfillment of its trust required turning over to the Indians a greater control of their own destinies. The overly paternalistic approach of prior years had proved both exploitative and destructive of Indian interests. Congress was united in the belief that institutional changes were required. An important part of the Indian Reorganization Act was the preference provision here at issue.

Contrary to the characterization made by appellees, this preference does not constitute "racial discrimination." Indeed, it is not even a "racial" preference.[32]

---

[32] [24] The preference is not directed towards a "racial" group consisting of "Indians"; instead, it applies only to members of "federally recognized" tribes. This operates to exclude many individuals who are racially to be classified as "Indians." In this sense, the preference is political rather than racial in nature. The eligibility criteria appear in 44 BIAM 335, 3.1:

> .1 Policy — An Indian has preference in appointment in the Bureau. To be eligible for preference in appointment, promotion, and training, an individual must be one-fourth or more degree Indian blood and be a member of a Federally-recognized tribe. It is the policy for promotional consideration that where two or more candidates who meet the established qualification requirements are available for filling a vacancy, if one of them is an Indian, he shall be given preference in filling the vacancy. In accordance with the policy statement approved by the Secretary, the Commissioner may grant exceptions to this policy by

Rather, it is an employment criterion reasonably designed to further the cause of Indian self-government and to make the BIA more responsive to the needs of its constituent groups. It is directed to participation by the governed in the governing agency. The preference is similar in kind to the constitutional requirement that a United States Senator, when elected, be "an Inhabitant of that State for which he shall be chosen," Art. I, § 3, cl. 3, or that a member of a city council reside within the city governed by the council. Congress has sought only to enable the BIA to draw more heavily from among the constituent group in staffing its projects, all of which, either directly or indirectly, affect the lives of tribal Indians. The preference, as applied, is granted to Indians not as a discrete racial group, but, rather, as members of quasi-sovereign tribal entities whose lives and activities are governed by the BIA in a unique fashion. *See* n.24, *supra.* In the sense that there is no other group of people favored in this manner, the legal status of the BIA is truly *sui generis.* Furthermore, the preference applies only to employment in the Indian service. The preference does not cover any other Government agency or activity, and we need not consider the obviously more difficult question that would be presented by a blanket exemption for Indians from all civil service examinations. Here, the preference is reasonably and directly related to a legitimate, nonracially based goal. This is the principal characteristic that generally is absent from proscribed forms of racial discrimination.

On numerous occasions this Court specifically has upheld legislation that singles out Indians for particular and special treatment. *See, e.g., Board of County Comm'rs v. Seber*, 318 U.S. 705 (1943) (federally granted tax immunity); *McClanahan v. Arizona State Tax Comm'n*, 411 U.S. 164 (1973) (same); *Simmons v. Eagle Seelatsee*, 384 U.S. 209 (1966), *aff'g* 244 F. Supp. 808 (ED Wash. 1965) (statutory definition of tribal membership, with resulting interest in trust estate); *Williams v. Lee*, 358 U.S. 217 (1959) (tribal courts and their jurisdiction over reservation affairs). Cf. *Morton v. Ruiz*, 415 U.S. 199 (1974) (federal welfare benefits for Indians "on or near" reservations). This unique legal status is of long standing, see *Cherokee Nation v. Georgia*, 5 Pet. 1 (1831); *Worcester v. Georgia*, 6 Pet. 515 (1832), and its sources are [varied and diverse]. As long as the special treatment can be tied rationally to the fulfillment of Congress's unique obligation toward the Indians, such legislative judgments will not be disturbed. Here, where the preference is reasonable and rationally designed to further Indian self-government, we cannot say that Congress's classification violates due process.

[*Reversed and remanded.*]

NOTES ON *MORTON v. MANCARI*

1. *Mancari* and Constitutional Standards of Review: For a full account of the litigation in *Morton v. Mancari*, including background on the parties and the attorneys who framed the issues, see Carole Goldberg, *What's Law Got to Do with*

---

approving the selection and appointment of non-Indians, when he considers it in the best interest of the Bureau.

This program does not restrict the right of management to fill positions by methods other than through promotion. Positions may be filled by transfers, reassignment, reinstatement, or initial appointment. App. 92.

It?: The Story of Morton v. Mancari, *in* INDIAN LAW STORIES (Carole Goldberg, Kevin K. Washburn & Philip P. Frickey eds., 2011). At issue in *Mancari* as well as other Indian equal protection cases is the standard of review courts should apply in evaluating the constitutionality of legislation. The Supreme Court has applied a "strict scrutiny" standard of review to legislative classifications based on race, ancestry, and national origin, inquiring whether the government has demonstrated that the classification is necessary to achieve a compelling government purpose. In practice, it has been nearly impossible for race-based laws to survive equal protection challenge. *But see Grutter v. Bollinger*, 539 U.S. 306 (2003) (upholding law school admission policy that took race into account). At the other extreme, the Court has applied a "rational basis" standard of review to most social and economic legislation, upholding such laws whenever there is a plausible justification for enactment. Between these extremes lies an intermediate standard of review, which has been applied most notably to gender discrimination. In applying this standard,

> the reviewing court must determine whether the proffered justification is "exceedingly persuasive." The burden of justification is demanding and it rests entirely on the State. The State must show "at least that the [challenged] classification serves 'important governmental objectives and that the discriminatory means employed' are 'substantially related to the achievement of those objectives.'" The justification must be genuine, not hypothesized or invented post hoc in response to litigation. And it must not rely on overbroad generalizations about the different talents, capacities, or preferences of males and females.

United States v. Virginia, 518 U.S. 515, 532–33 (1996) (citations omitted). How would you characterize the standard of review applied in *Mancari*? Does it match any of the standards described above?

2. Indian Preference After *Mancari*: Use of the Indian preference for reductions in force and reassignments within the Bureau of Indian Affairs and the Indian Health Service provoked some Congressional response. Under Pub. L. 96-135, § 2, 93 Stat. 1057, codified at 25 U.S.C. § 472a, certain reassignments within the Bureau, including those related to reductions in force, are exempted from the Indian preference. Furthermore, 25 U.S.C. § 472a(c)(1) authorizes any affected tribe to grant a waiver of Indian preference for employment. The same legislation also mandates the Office of Personnel Management to assist in placing non-Indian employees of the BIA and the Indian Health Service with other federal agencies.

In *Indian Educators Federation Local 4524 of the American Federation of Teachers v. Kempthorne*, 541 F. Supp. 2d 257 (D.D.C. 2008), Judge Hogan of the D.C. United States District Court considered whether the Indian Reorganization Act's employment preference extends to positions in the Interior Department outside the BIA. The statutory language refers only to employment within the "Indian Office." At issue in *Indian Educators* were jobs within the Office of Special Trustee for American Indians, an office established by the American Indian Trust Fund Management Reform Act of 1994 to improve the accountability and management of Indian funds held in trust by the federal government. *See Cobell v. Norton*, presented in Ch. 4, Sec. A.5.b. Reversing longstanding Interior Department policy, the Interior Solicitor in the administration of President Ronald Reagan had issued an opinion in 1988 stating that only BIA positions were subject to the preference. Judge Hogan rejected this reading of the statute, relying on the Indian law canons of construction, and found that the preference applies to "all positions in the Department [of the Interior] that directly and primarily relate to providing services to Indians. . . . " Should that ruling allay the concerns of some tribal leaders that the Department of the Interior might respond to Indian trust mismanagement claims by taking management of all trust assets outside the BIA? The United States voluntarily dismissed its appeal in the case. *Fed'n of Indian Serv. Emples., Local 4524 v. Salazar*, 2009 U.S. App. LEXIS 10987 (D.C. Cir. Mar. 31, 2009), and the Tenth Circuit agreed with Judge Hogan's decision in *Hester v. Jewell*, 2014 U.S. App. LEXIS 1081 (10th Cir. Jan. 21, 2014).

3.   *Mancari's* **Definition of Who Is an Indian:** How does the Indian Reorganization Act define the class of Indians eligible for employment preference within the BIA? See 25 U.S.C. § 479, discussed in Sec. A.2, this chapter. How did the Bureau define "Indians" for purposes of implementing the preference? Was this regulation consistent with the statute? Who might have challenged the regulation on that basis? In 1977, after *Mancari* was decided, the BIA amended its regulations on qualifications for the Indian employment preference to conform with the statutory definition of Indian contained in the IRA. 43 Fed. Reg. 2393 (1978), currently in amended form at 25 C.F.R. § 5.1.

Which definition, the statute's or the regulation's, did the Supreme Court incorporate into its analysis? Did the Court's decision to apply a form of "rational basis" review in *Mancari* turn on the particular definition of "Indian" in that case? Should the 1977 amendment to the BIA regulation call the result in *Mancari* into question? In *City of Richmond v. J.A. Croson Co.*, 488 U.S. 469 (1989), the Supreme Court indicated that strict scrutiny should be applied to an affirmative action program that advantaged members of a variety of racial and ethnic groups, including "American Eskimo, Aleut, [and] American Indian;" but the definitions of those groups were not specified, and the case did not involve a challenge to a preference given to a Native American. Should it matter that the affirmative action program challenged in *City of Richmond v. J.A. Croson Co.* did not specifically attempt to benefit Indian nations as opposed to individuals of Indian ancestry? *See* Carole Goldberg, *American Indians and "Preferential" Treatment*, 49 UCLA L. REV. 943, 973 (2002). The Supreme Court's most recent cases addressing affirmative action do not reexamine *Mancari. See Gratz v. Bollinger*, 539 U.S. 244 (2003); *Grutter v. Bollinger*, 539 U.S. 306 (2003); *Fisher v. Univ. of Tex.*, 133 S. Ct. 2411, 186 L. Ed. 2d 474 (2013).

4.   **Political or Racial/Ancestry-Based Classification?** How sound is the suggestion offered in the *Mancari* opinion that the Indian employment preference is not a racial preference, but rather a "political" preference or "an employment criterion reasonably designed to further the cause of Indian self-government and to make the BIA more responsive to the needs of its constituent groups?" Does it further Indian self-government to assign a Navajo BIA employee to a program that services the Pine Ridge Sioux Reservation? While the Court notes that it is not a sufficient condition for the employment preference that an applicant be racially identifiable as an Indian, is not Indian ancestry a necessary condition for the preference under the definition provided in the IRA? *Cf. Geduldig v. Aiello*, 417 U.S.

484 (1974) (exclusion of pregnant women from state disability insurance benefits did not constitute an impermissible gender classification since the distinction was based on pregnancy, not gender). Assuming that classifications involving Indians are political rather than racial or ancestry-based, should bans on race-based affirmative action apply to Indian preferences? For analyses emphasizing the political nature of the classification, see Sarah Krakoff, *Inextricably Political: Race, Membership, and Tribal Sovereignty*, 87 WASH. L. REV. 1041 (2012) (offering detailed illustrations of federally recognized tribes that are political amalgams of ethnically diverse groups); Eugene Volokh, *The California Civil Rights Initiative: An Interpretive Guide*, 44 UCLA L. REV. 1335, 1358–59 (1997) (contending that the state's anti-affirmative action initiative measure does not apply to classifications based on tribal membership); Addie C. Rolnick, *The Promise of* Mancari: *Political Rights as Racial Remedy*, 86 N.Y.U. L. REV. 958 (2011) (discussing the political classification doctrine's construction of race and positing a new framework for understanding Indian law that draws on both race and political status).

If classifications involving Indians are political rather than racial, shouldn't a "rational basis" standard of review be applied regardless whether a given Indian classification promotes "the fulfillment of Congress's unique obligation toward the Indians?" In other words, shouldn't it be sufficient that Congress is advancing a valid governmental purpose, whether or not that purpose involves recognition of intergovernmental relations with Indian nations or the exercise of a trust responsibility? To test this proposition, consider the following case, decided three years after *Mancari*.

United States v. Antelope, 430 U.S. 641 (1977): A Coeur d'Alene Indian was prosecuted for murder under the Major Crimes Act, 18 U.S.C. § 1153. Had a non-Indian been accused of the identical offense against the same victim, the non-Indian would have been subject only to state jurisdiction. The Indian defendant challenged this disparate treatment under the equal protection provision of the Fifth Amendment Due Process Clause, focusing on the fact that the Major Crimes Act incorporates a felony murder rule while state law does not. The Supreme Court upheld this scheme, stating:

> The decisions of this Court leave no doubt that federal legislation with respect to Indian tribes, although relating to Indians as such, is not based upon impermissible racial classifications. Quite the contrary, classifications expressly singling out Indian tribes as subjects of legislation are expressly provided for in the Constitution[33] and supported by the ensuing history of the Federal Government's relations with Indians.

> Indian tribes are unique aggregations possessing attributes of sovereignty over both their members and their territory, *Worcester v. Georgia*, 6 Pet. 515, 557 (1832); they are "a separate people" possessing "the power of regulating their internal and social relations. . . . " *United States v. Mazurie*, 419 U.S. 544, 557 (1975).

---

[33] [6] Article I, § 8, of the Constitution gives Congress power "[to] regulate Commerce with foreign Nations, and among the several States, and with the Indian tribes."

Legislation with respect to these "unique aggregations" has repeatedly been sustained by this Court against claims of unlawful racial discrimination [citing and quoting from *Morton v. Mancari*].

Last Term, in *Fisher v. District Court*, 424 U.S. 382 (1976), we held that members of the Northern Cheyenne Tribe could be denied access to Montana State courts in connection with an adoption proceeding arising on their reservation. Unlike *Mancari*, the Indian plaintiffs in *Fisher* were being denied a benefit or privilege available to non-Indians [access to state court for adoption proceedings involving on-reservation Indian children]; nevertheless, a unanimous Court dismissed the claim of racial discrimination:

[W]e reject the argument that denying [the Indian plaintiffs] access to the Montana courts constitutes impermissible racial discrimination. The exclusive jurisdiction of the Tribal Court does not derive from the race of the plaintiff but rather from the quasi-sovereign status of the Northern Cheyenne Tribe under federal law. 424 U.S., at 390.

The *Antelope* Court acknowledged that both *Mancari* and *Fisher* had involved preferences or disabilities directly promoting Indian interests in self-government, whereas *Antelope* addressed federal regulation of criminal conduct within Indian country implicating Indian interests. But according to the Court,

[T]he principles reaffirmed in *Mancari* and *Fisher* point more broadly to the conclusion that federal regulation of Indian affairs is not based upon impermissible classifications. Rather, such regulation is rooted in the unique status of Indians as "a separate people" with their own political institutions. Federal regulation of Indian tribes, therefore, is governance of once-sovereign political communities; it is not to be viewed as legislation of a " 'racial' group consisting of 'Indians'. . . . " *Morton v. Mancari*, supra, at 553 n. 24. Indeed, respondents were not subjected to federal criminal jurisdiction because they are of the Indian race but because they are enrolled members of the Coeur d'Alene Tribe.[34]

---

[34] [7] As was true in *Mancari*, federal jurisdiction under the Major Crimes Act does not apply to "many individuals who are racially to be classified as 'Indians.' " 417 U.S., at 553 n. 24. Thus, the prosecution in this case offered proof that respondents are enrolled members of the Coeur d'Alene Tribe and thus not emancipated from tribal relations. Moreover, members of tribes whose official status has been terminated by congressional enactment are no longer subject, by virtue of their status, to federal criminal jurisdiction under the Major Crimes Act. United States v. Heath, 509 F.2d 16, 19 (CA9 1974) ("While anthropologically a Klamath Indian even after the Termination Act obviously remains an Indian, his unique status vis-à-vis the Federal Government no longer exists"). In addition, as enrolled tribal members, respondents were subjected to federal jurisdiction only because their crimes were committed within the confines of Indian country, as defined in 18 U.S.C. § 1151. Crimes occurring elsewhere would not be subject to exclusive federal jurisdiction. Puyallup Tribe v. Department of Game, 391 U.S. 392, 397 n. 11 (1968). It should be noted, however, that enrollment in an official tribe has not been held to be an absolute requirement for federal jurisdiction, at least where the Indian defendant lived on the reservation and "maintained tribal relations with the Indians thereon." Ex parte Pero, 99 F.2d 28, 30 (CA7 1938). *See also* United States v. Ives, 504 F.2d 935, 953 (CA9 1974) (dicta). Since respondents are enrolled tribal members, we are not called on to decide whether nonenrolled Indians are subject to 18 U.S.C. § 1153, and we therefore intimate no views on the matter.

Thus, the Court concluded that the Major Crimes Act is "based neither in whole nor in part upon impermissible racial classifications."

Finally, the Court considered whether the difference between federal and Idaho law could establish an equal protection violation. The Court emphatically affirmed that federal criminal laws need not replicate the criminal laws of the states in which they are located. According to the Court, "[u]nder our federal system, the National Government does not violate equal protection when its own body of law is evenhanded,[35] regardless of the laws of States with respect to the same subject matter." Because the defendant in this case had been treated the same as all other persons subject to federal jurisdiction, and the regulatory scheme itself "did not erect impermissible racial classifications," the Court found no equal protection violation, and upheld the defendant's conviction.

NOTES ON TREATING INDIAN CLASSIFICATIONS AS POLITICAL RATHER THAN RACIAL

1.   Does Relaxed Equal Protection Review Invite Federal Classifications That Unfairly Burden Indians? What "unique obligations" of the federal government toward Indian nations and their members does the legal classification in *Antelope* seek to advance? Does the Court seem to care whether the classification advances any Indian interests? Or is it sufficient for the Court's purpose that separate federal governance of Indian nations and their citizens, preempting state jurisdiction, reflects federal treatment of Native communities as governments? Given the Court's failure to analyze the law in light of the trust responsibility or any other federal obligation to benefit tribes, does *Antelope* insulate classifications that burden or discriminate against Indian people from equal protection challenge? The federal homicide law involved in *Antelope* also applied to federal prosecutions for murder outside of Indian country. Did that fact negate any concerns that the Major Crimes Act singled out Indians for special harm? Would a law that deliberately targeted Indians for a racially discriminatory purpose survive equal protection analysis regardless whether the classification is treated as "political" or "racial"? One case that the Court relied on in *Antelope*, *Fisher v. District Court*, 424 U.S. 382 (1976), did invoke federal obligations to the tribes in analyzing a classification that apparently burdened Indians. Does *Fisher*'s effort to justify legal distinctions based on the federal obligations to benefit Indians suggest that something beyond ordinary "rational basis" review is at work? Is the standard of review beginning to approximate the "intermediate standard" applied in gender cases, discussed above? Assuming that the classification is political rather than racial, why would a justification based on "unique" federal obligations or the application of a higher standard of review be required at all?

---

[35]   [11] It should be noted, however, that this Court has consistently upheld federal regulations aimed solely at tribal Indians, as opposed to all persons subject to federal jurisdiction. See, e.g., United States v. Holliday, 3 Wall 407, 417–418 (1866); Perrin v. United States, 232 U.S. 478, 482 (1914). *See also Rosebud Sioux Tribe v. Kneip, ante*, at 613–615, n. 47. Indeed, the Constitution itself provides support for legislation directed specifically at the Indian tribes. *See* n. 6, supra. As the Court noted in Morton v. Mancari, the Constitution therefore "singles Indians out as a proper subject for separate legislation." 417 U.S., at 552.

2.   Relevance of Tribal Enrollment and Federal Recognition: Should the result in *Antelope* turn on the fact that Antelope himself was an enrolled tribal member? *See* fn. 7 of the opinion. Why might that fact matter, given the Court's analysis in *Morton v. Mancari*? Was the *U.S. v. A.W.L.* case, discussed in Sec. A.2 of this chapter, correctly decided in light of *Antelope*? Recall that *A.W.L.* and other cases defining "Indian" for purposes of federal Indian country criminal statutes do not require formal citizenship or enrollment in a tribe; recognition as an Indian by the tribal community will suffice. Do cases such as *A.W.L.* undermine the claim that Indian classifications are political in nature, or do they reinforce the notion that Indian nations, as distinct political communities, are free to define membership by informal means? Should equal protection doctrine as applied to Indian legislation demand that Indian nations incorporate and adhere to rigidly formal citizenship or enrollment requirements? In 1990 in the case of *Duro v. Reina*, set forth in Ch. 3, Sec. A.3.a, the Court held that tribal courts do not have criminal jurisdiction over nonmember Indians. Furthermore, in dicta the Court characterized congressional power as follows:

> That Indians are citizens does not alter the Federal Government's broad authority to legislate with respect to *enrolled* Indians as a class, whether to impose burdens or benefits.

495 U.S. 676, 692 (1990) (emphasis added). Does the inclusion of the word "enrolled" suggest that the Court may restrict the power of Congress to enrolled members of federally recognized tribes? Note that in the same year *Duro v. Reina* was decided, Secretary of the Interior Manuel Lujan noted that "nearly 40% of the Indian tribal entities we deal with do not have any formally approved governing document or, indeed, any written governing document at all which would define tribal membership." Letter to Richard Thornburgh, Attorney General, *quoted in* Margo S. Brownell, *Who Is an Indian? Searching for an Answer to the Question at the Core of Federal Indian Law*, 34 U. Mich. J. L. Reform 275, 297 n.161 (2000). Recall the dialogue between Robert Laurence and Sam Deloria, presented in Sec. A.2.b, this chapter.

3.   Applying the Political/Racial Distinction to Classifications Under State Law: If classifications involving Indian nations and their members are political rather than racial or ancestry-based, one would expect that state laws drawing these distinctions would face the same judicial analysis as federal laws. Yet the Supreme Court has insisted that state laws singling out Indians for separate treatment will be analyzed under the *Morton v. Mancari* rational basis test only if they further federal policies. In *Washington v. Confederated Bands & Tribes of the Yakima Nation*, 439 U.S. 463, 500–502 (1979), the Court briefly addressed the equal protection problems raised under the Fourteenth Amendment by such state legislation:

> It is settled that "the unique legal status of Indian tribes under federal law" permits the Federal Government to enact legislation singling out tribal Indians, legislation that might otherwise be constitutionally offensive. . . . States do not enjoy this same unique relationship with Indians.

The Court noted, however, that the state legislation it was reviewing had not been enacted unilaterally by the state, but rather "was enacted in response to a federal measure [Public Law 280] explicitly designed to readjust the allocation of jurisdiction over Indians."

In *Yakima*, the state law in question had been enacted pursuant to express federal authorization. Are there other circumstances when states may avail themselves of the more relaxed standard of review announced in *Mancari*? When does state legislation become sufficiently associated with federal policies for purposes of this type of equal protection analysis? Is it enough that the state law advances the same general objectives as some existing federal policy? In *Peyote Way Church of God, Inc. v. Thornburgh*, 922 F.2d 1210 (5th Cir. 1991), both federal and Texas law afforded Native American religious practitioners belonging to the Native American Church (NAC) a special exemption from laws outlawing use of peyote. After upholding the federal exemption under the principles of *Mancari*, the Fifth Circuit noted that "The similarity of language, date of passage, and legislative history of Texas' NAC exemption all indicate that the Texas legislature enacted the exemption to parallel the federal NAC exemption." Then it framed the issue as "whether states may enact laws beneficial to tribal Native Americans in exercise of the federal government's trust power pursuant to implied Congressional authorization." According to the court:

> Although Congress has not expressly authorized states to adopt the federal NAC exemption, we think that it would be preposterous to attribute any other intent to Congress. When the federal government entered the arena of drug control, it purposely left intact the states' enforcement structures. See 21 U.S.C. § 903 (states may regulate drugs concurrently with Congress unless there is a "positive conflict" between federal and state law). If the states are to enforce their own laws controlling peyote possession, they may . . . refuse all exemptions, exempt only NAC members, or exempt all bona fide religious peyote use. If Congress wanted states to prohibit NAC peyote use, there would be no reason for its members to tolerate the continued existence of the 25-year-old federal exemption. Just before the federal NAC exemption was first promulgated, Congress rejected the alternative . . . that all bona fide religious peyote use be allowed. Thus, we conclude that Congress would want states to exercise its trust power in exempting NAC members from their laws prohibiting peyote possession.

922 F.2d at 1218–19.

Under the rationale of the *Peyote Way* case, should a state policy giving preferences to Indians in admission to state universities survive an equal protection challenge, based on the fact that the federal government provides special higher education grants to Indian students? What about a state museum that permits only Indians to sell hand-made goods in an Indian arts and crafts market, part of a longstanding tradition at the museum? *See Livingston v. Ewing*, 455 F. Supp. 825 (D.N.M. 1978), *aff'd*, 601 F.2d 1100 (10th Cir. 1979).

For an argument that preemption law should be more widely deployed to invalidate state Indian laws, beneficial or otherwise, see Robert B. Porter, *Legalizing, Decolonizing, and Modernizing New York State's Indian Law*, 63 ALB. L. REV. 125 (1999). State classifications directed against Indians for a racially discriminatory purpose, such as those denying voting rights, access to education, or public utility services, routinely fail under equal protection's strict scrutiny. *See* NELL JESSUP NEWTON ET AL., COHEN'S HANDBOOK OF FEDERAL INDIAN LAW 932–43 (2012 ed.). Such classifications plainly cannot invoke any supportive federal policies. An example of a court applying strict scrutiny to tribal members' claim of race discrimination is *Pyke v. Cuomo*, 567 F.3d 74 (2d Cir. 2009). A class of Mohawk Indians alleged that New York law enforcement personnel violated their rights to equal protection through their inadequate and harmful response to widespread, violent unrest on the reservation. Among other things, plaintiffs claimed that the New York police deliberately ceased regular patrols inside the reservation, caving in to violent elements within. The Second Circuit noted that *Morton v. Mancari*'s standard of review was inapplicable, because New York was not carrying out any federal policies. 567 F.3d at 77, n.3. It then went on to find that even applying strict scrutiny, there was no basis for an equal protection claim because there was no evidence that the state officials' actions were directed at a racial group rather than a geographical area or social group.

2. Indians as a Constitutional Racial Classification?

The centrality of the federal trust responsibility in the federal and state law cases discussed above strongly suggests that courts are applying something other than ordinary "rational basis" review, though short of the "strict scrutiny" normally required in race discrimination cases. Yet even if one were to view Indian classifications as at least partly racial or ancestry-based, would strict scrutiny necessarily follow? Keep in mind that some federal classifications may add an Indian ancestry requirement to tribal membership, and federal classifications that rest on tribal membership typically incorporate membership requirements based on ancestry. Still other classifications affect Indians defined specifically by ancestry and recognition rather than tribal membership, as the federal criminal statute discussed in the *Antelope* case, above, demonstrates. The Indian commerce clause contained in Article 1, section 8, clause 3 of the Constitution expressly empowers Congress to "regulate Commerce . . . with the Indian tribes." To what extent does this provision expressly authorize Congress to draw racial or ethnic classifications in regulating Indian affairs?

AFGE v. United States, 330 F.3d 513 (D.C. Cir. 2003): A provision of the Defense Appropriations Act for fiscal year 2000 provided an outsourcing preference for firms "under 51 percent Native American ownership." After a joint venture formed by two Native Alaskan corporations received an Air Force contract through administration of the preference, a union sued to invalidate the provision, claiming it violates the Fifth Amendment Due Process Clause ban on race discrimination. Relying on a Supreme Court decision that applied strict scrutiny to a different contracting preference law, *Adarand Constructors, Inc. v. Pena*, 515 U.S. 200, 227, (1995), plaintiffs argued that "Native American" is an unconstitutional racial classification, subject to strict scrutiny.

At the outset, the D.C. Circuit panel narrowed its task, refusing to consider the constitutionality of the provision as applied to individual Native Americans who are not tribal members. Since the only contract actually made under the provision was directed at tribal entities, the court confined its analysis to tribal beneficiaries of the contracting preference. Launching into the analysis, Judge Randolph stated:

> With respect to the question properly before us, only a few general principles of federal Indian law need to be mentioned. Congress has the power "to regulate Commerce . . . with the Indian Tribes," U.S. Const. art. I, § 8, cl. 3. Congress thus has the authority, exclusive of the States, to determine which "distinctly Indian communities" should be recognized as Indian tribes. *United States v. Sandoval*, 231 U.S. 28, 46 (1913). . . . For these reasons, and others, the Supreme Court has sustained "legislation that singles out Indians for particular and special treatment." *Morton v. Mancari*, 417 U.S. 535, 554–55. The Court's decisions "leave no doubt that federal legislation with respect to Indian tribes, although relating to Indians as such, is not based on impermissible racial classifications." *United States v. Antelope*, 430 U.S. 641, 645 (1977).
>
> . . . In *Narragansett Indian Tribe v. National Indian Gaming Commission*, 158 F.3d 1335 (D.C. Cir. 1998), we summed up the state of the law this way: "ordinary rational basis scrutiny applies to Indian classifications just as it does to other non-suspect classifications under equal protection analysis." *Id.* at 1340.
>
> On the other hand, "all racial classifications, imposed by whatever federal, state, or local governmental actor, must be analyzed by a reviewing court under strict scrutiny. In other words, such classifications are constitutional only if they are narrowly tailored measures that further compelling governmental interests." *Adarand*, 515 U.S. at 227.
>
> These two lines of authority may be reconciled, plaintiffs argue, on the basis that the preference in *Mancari* was limited to members of federally recognized Indian tribes, while the preference in *Adarand* was not so limited, and thus constituted — in the Court's words in *Mancari* — a preference "granted to Indians . . . as a discrete racial group," 417 U.S. at 554. That distinction aside, the Supreme Court has made it clear enough that legislation for the benefit of recognized Indian tribes is not to be examined in terms applicable to suspect racial classifications. Not only in *Mancari*, but also in *Washington v. Confederated Bands & Tribes of Yakima Indian Nation*, 439 U.S. 463, 500–01 (1979), the Court held that "'the unique legal status of Indian tribes under federal law' permits the Federal Government to enact legislation singling out tribal Indians, legislation that might otherwise be constitutionally offensive" (quoting *Mancari*, 417 U.S. at 551–52).
>
> . . . The critical consideration is Congress' power to regulate commerce "with the Indian Tribes." While Congress may use this power to regulate tribal members, see *United States v. Holliday*, 70 U.S. 407, 417 (1865), regulation of commerce with tribes is at the heart of the Clause, particularly when the tribal commerce is with the federal government, as it is here. 2 The Founders' Constitution 530–31 (Philip B. Kurland & Ralph Lerner eds. 1987). When Congress exercises this constitutional power it necessarily must engage in classifications that deal with Indian tribes. Justice Scalia, when he was on our court, put the matter this way: "in a sense the

Constitution itself establishes the rationality of the . . . classification, by providing a separate federal power that reaches only the present group." *United States v. Cohen*, 733 F.2d 128, 139 (D.C. Cir. 1984) (en banc). He then quoted the following passage from *United States v. Antelope*, 430 U.S. at 649 n.11: the "Constitution itself provides support for legislation directed specifically at Indian tribes."

The court then found a rational basis for the preference in the need for tribal economic development and other means of overcoming "the socioeconomic hardships suffered by Native Americans." The Fourth Circuit agrees that *Adarand* has not changed the level of scrutiny applicable to Indian classifications. *United States v. Garrett*, 2005 U.S. App. LEXIS 2611, *6–*9 (4th Cir. Feb. 15, 2005).

NOTE ON INDIANS AS A CONSTITUTIONAL RACIAL CLASSIFICATION

Use of the Indian commerce clause to justify arguably race or ancestry-based Indian classifications has the advantage of explaining *Morton v. Mancari*'s requirement that federal Indian classifications conform with the federal government's "unique obligation" to the Indians. If one accepts the view that a federal trust responsibility attaches to the exercise of Indian commerce clause power, only such classifications would support that authority. *See* Ch. 4, Sec. A.2. This approach also explains why some but not all state classifications survive equal protection scrutiny under existing law. Only those state classifications that advance federal objectives articulated under the Indian commerce clause would be acceptable under the Indian commerce clause approach.

But invoking the Indian commerce clause to defend against equal protection challenges also presents some conceptual difficulties. First, does reliance on the Indian commerce clause to justify arguably race-based classifications produce general judicial insensitivity to the harm of race discrimination against other groups? Does it render Indian people too vulnerable to harmful forms of discrimination? For discussion of these issues, see the exchange of views in David Williams, *The Borders of the Equal Protection Clause: Indians as Peoples*, 38 UCLA L. Rev. 759, 780–85 (1991); Carole Goldberg, *Not "Strictly" Racial: A Response to "Indians as Peoples,"* 39 UCLA L. Rev. 169, 174–75 (1991).

The other major problem that comes from using the Indian commerce clause to defend against racial discrimination charges is that the scope of federal power under the clause should limit the types of federal laws that survive equal protection challenges. The language of the clause, for example, refers to "Indian tribes," not to individual Indians. Does that language suggest that the only federal classifications justified under the Indian commerce clause should be those directed at federally recognized tribes and their citizens? How well does the *AFGE* court deal with this question? Does it seriously have to engage the problem? Is there any way to separate those federal laws directed at individual Indians in order to benefit tribes as opposed to federal laws directed at individual Indians for unrelated purposes, such as the achievement of educational diversity? Professor Goldberg offers the following two possible alternative solutions to this dilemma:

One solution emerges from the Indian country federal criminal laws, which apply to individuals based upon a combination of descent and recognition. The descent prong does not require a specific percentage of Indian ancestry. The recognition prong refers not to federal recognition but to recognition as a member of the tribal community by the relevant tribe. This form of recognition does not require formal enrollment. These kinds of determinations are made on a case-by-case basis in federal criminal prosecutions and could be considerably more unwieldy as applied to larger-scale benefit programs. A second alternative solution derive from the Indian Arts and Crafts Act of 1990 [18 U.S.C. § 1159; 25 U.S.C. § 305], which penalizes any sale of goods in a manner that falsely suggests that the goods are Indian produced. For purposes of this Act, Indians are enrolled tribal members plus individuals who have been certified by the tribe from which they are descended as Indians. Thus, individuals ineligible for enrollment because of intermarriage or because their parents did not live on the reservation when they were born may still have sufficient connections with the tribe to constitute tribal affiliation, at least for limited purposes.

Carole Goldberg, *American Indians and "Preferential" Treatment*, 49 UCLA L. REV. 943, 971–72 (2002).

3.   When Might Equal Protection's "Strict Scrutiny" Invalidate Federal Indian Legislation?

Notwithstanding some of its language, should *Morton v. Mancari* be understood as a case where constitutional "strict scrutiny" was applied to a race- or ancestry-based classification, but the Court was able to find the necessary compelling governmental interest? Would that understanding make it easier to reconcile *Morton v. Mancari* with the Court's anti-affirmative action jurisprudence? If strict scrutiny were applied to Indian classifications, what potential would the equal protection clause have for limiting the possible scope of federal legislative protection for Indians? How closely would a federal classification have to relate to tribal interests in order to survive such scrutiny? For example, although the Snyder Act, 25 U.S.C. § 13, authorizes the Bureau of Indian Affairs to provide various services and programs "for the benefit, care and assistance of the Indians throughout the United States," federal programs have generally been limited to Indians living on or near reservations. Could Congress constitutionally extend Indian services and benefits to urban Indians under a strict scrutiny regime? *Cf.* Indian Health Care Improvement Act of 1976, 25 U.S.C. § 1601 et seq. (extending educational assistance for health care professionals and alcoholism treatment programs to many urban Indians, including members of terminated or state-recognized tribes).

In *St. Paul Intertribal Hous. Bd. v. Reynolds*, 564 F. Supp. 1408, 1411 (D. Minn. 1983), the federal government argued that granting HUD subsidies to a state agency for low-income rental units available to heads of households who were enrolled members of federally recognized tribes would violate Title VI of the Civil Rights Act of 1964 and Title VIII of the Civil Rights Act of 1968 because it constituted an impermissible racial preference. The government stressed that the project was far removed geographically from any Indian reservation and that the preference therefore had little, if anything, to do with the promotion of tribal self-government.

The district court rejected HUD's argument, stating that an Indian preference program is not racially discriminatory if "there is an expression of legislative intent to benefit Indians" as part of Congress's trust relationship. The court noted that the Housing Act of 1937 provides for funds for states and includes within the definition of "state" "Indian tribes, bands, and groups," 42 U.S.C. § 1437a(b)(6), and contains other provisions benefiting Indians. In addition, the court noted that the 1974 amendments to the Act set aside housing funds for low income Indian families "who are members of any Indian tribe, band, pueblo, group or community of Indians or Alaska natives which is recognized by the Federal Government," 42 U.S.C. § 1437c(c), without any limitation to on-reservation Indians. As a result, the court concluded that this statutory scheme was a manifestation of the federal-Indian trust responsibility and not a purely racial preference. One panel of the Ninth Circuit has taken a more restrictive view of the applicability of politically based preferences, as the following case indicates.

Babbitt v. Williams, 115 F.3d 657 (9th Cir. 1997): The Reindeer Act of 1937, 25 U.S.C. § 500 et seq. gives certain advantages and support to Alaska Natives in carrying on the business of reindeer herding, but does not expressly prohibit non-Natives from engaging in such activity. The Interior Department's Board of Indian Appeals (IBIA) construed the Act so as to bar non-Indians. Invoking judicial review under the APA, non-Indian herders raised two alternative equal protection challenges to this interpretation: first, that a Native monopoly could not satisfy the rational-basis standard articulated in *Morton v. Mancari*, and, second, that *Mancari*'s holding had in any event been overruled by the application of strict scrutiny to affirmative action programs in *City of Richmond v. J.A. Croson Co.*, 488 U.S. 469 (1989), and *Adarand Constructors, Inc. v. Pena*, 515 U.S. 200 (1995). Without ruling on these arguments, Judge Kozinski gave them credibility by advancing a narrow reading of *Mancari*:

> According to the IBIA, the Reindeer Act provides a preference in an industry that is not uniquely native, whether the beneficiaries live in a remote native village on the Seward Peninsula or in downtown Anchorage. The Act in no way relates to native land, tribal or communal status, or culture. Legislation that relates to Indian land, tribal status, self-government or culture passes *Mancari*'s rational relation test because "such regulation is rooted in the unique status of Indians as 'a separate people' with their own political institutions." *United States v. Antelope*, 430 U.S. 641 (1977). As "a separate people," Indians have a right to expect some special protection for their land, political institutions (whether tribes or native villages), and culture. . . .

> While *Mancari* is not necessarily limited to statutes that give special treatment to Indians on Indian land, we do read it as shielding only those statutes that affect uniquely Indian interests. *See, e.g., Antelope*, 430 U.S. at 646 ("Both *Mancari* and *Fisher* [*v. District Court*, 424 U.S. 382 (1976),]

involved preferences or disabilities directly promoting Indian interests in self-government, whereas in the present case we are dealing, not with matters of tribal self-regulation, but with federal regulation of criminal conduct within Indian country implicating Indian interests." (emphasis added)). For example, we seriously doubt that Congress could give Indians a complete monopoly on the casino industry or on Space Shuttle contracts. At oral argument, counsel for the government conceded that granting natives a monopoly on all Space Shuttle contracts would not pass *Mancari*'s rational-relation test. Counsel could only distinguish the Space Shuttle preference from a reindeer preference by noting that, in 1937, natives were heavily involved in the reindeer business whereas they aren't involved in the Space Program. The casino example defies this distinction, but is equally unrelated to "Congress' unique obligation toward the Indians." *Mancari*, 417 U.S. at 555.

Judge Kozinski's cramped reading of *Mancari* left him with "strict scrutiny" as the applicable legal standard. In his view, the IBIA's interpretation of the Reindeer Act could not survive strict scrutiny because the monopoly given to Alaska Natives is broader than necessary to provide economic assistance to Natives in their home communities. However, given the gravity of the constitutional questions and the implications for much of Title 25 of the United States Code, the panel declined to resolve the equal protection challenges. Rather, they interpreted the Reindeer Act so as to allow non-Indian hunting.

While the United States government has sometimes included Native Hawaiians within the reach of federal statutes intended to protect Indian tribes and individuals, the history and political status of indigenous Hawaiians is distinct from that of American Indians. These distinctions form the basis of the very different political treatment that the United States affords to Indian tribes and Native Hawaiians. This history of political treatment has generated questions about the constitutionality of federal laws treating Native Hawaiians differently from others. Prior to contact with Europeans, the indigenous peoples of Hawaii lived in independent kingdoms ruled by chiefs. Contact decimated the indigenous population. At the time of contact in 1778, about 400,000 people populated the islands. A century later, just over 11% of the indigenous population remained. In response to the tension that occurred after contact, the indigenous groups united as the Kingdom of Hawai'i and were recognized as an international sovereign by many different nations, including the United States.

However, American imperialists eventually overthrew the Kingdom in the last decade of the nineteenth century. Shortly following the overthrow, Americans with material interests began pushing Congress to annex the island, using rhetoric oft directed at justifying the colonization of indigenous peoples. As Erik K. Yamamoto and Catherine Corpus Betts write, "American military and plantation owners lobbied hard for annexation of the Hawaiian islands, racializing the indigenous people as either uncivilized or childlike — in either case, in need of American control. With a military base at Pearl Harbor and a hot commodity (sugar) at stake, the United States annexed Hawai'i in 1898. After the United States declared sovereignty over the islands, officials confiscated all former Hawaiian government and royal lands — two-thirds of Hawai'i's fertile territory." Erik K. Yamamoto and

Catharine Corpus Betts, *Disfiguring Civil Rights to Deny Indigenous Hawaiian Self-Determination: The Story of* Rice v. Cayetano *in* RACE LAW STORIES (Rachel F. Moran and Devon W. Carbado, eds., 2008). As Yamamoto and Betts explain, the U.S. annexed the islands despite vocal resistance from indigenous Hawaiians — former Queen Lili'uokalani and 27,000 indigenous Hawaiians petitioned Congress in protest against the annexation. After annexation, the Organic Act of 1900 created a government for the Territory of Hawai'i, which was later admitted into statehood in 1959. In 1993, Congress passed an Apology Resolution recognizing that the United States participated in an illicit "conspiracy" to overthrow the Kingdom of Hawai'i in 1893. *See* Ch. 5, Sec. B.2.

RICE v. CAYETANO
United States Supreme Court
528 U.S. 495 (2000)

[A law of the State of Hawaii allowed only descendants of indigenous Hawaiians to vote for the trustees of the state's Office of Hawaiian Affairs, which administers funds derived from certain state lands and other sources for the benefit of "Native Hawaiians" and "Hawaiians." For further description of this law, see Ch. 5, Sec. B.2. The District Court and Ninth Circuit both upheld the classification, acknowledging its racial character, but finding that there was a trust relationship between Hawaii and the Native Hawaiians that justified the special voting rules. After declining to address a host of related questions, including the constitutionality of the Hawaiian Homes Commission Act and its administrative structure; the constitutionality of federal or federally-mandated benefits for Native Hawaiians; and whether Congress may treat Native Hawaiians as it does Indian nations, the Supreme Court reversed.]

MR. JUSTICE KENNEDY delivered the opinion of the Court.

. . . Ancestry can be a proxy for race. It is that proxy here. Even if the residents of Hawaii in 1778 had been of more diverse ethnic backgrounds and cultures, it is far from clear that a voting test favoring their descendants would not be a race-based qualification. But that is not this case. For centuries Hawaii was isolated from migration. 1 Kuykendall 3. The inhabitants shared common physical characteristics, and by 1778 they had a common culture. . . . The provisions before us reflect the State's effort to preserve that commonality of people to the present day. In the interpretation of the Reconstruction era civil rights laws we have observed that "racial discrimination" is that which singles out "identifiable classes of persons . . . solely because of their ancestry or ethnic characteristics." *Saint Francis College v. Al-Khazraji*, 481 U.S. 604, 613 (1987). The very object of the statutory definition in question and of its earlier congressional counterpart in the Hawaiian Homes Commission Act is to treat the early Hawaiians as a distinct people, commanding their own recognition and respect. The State, in enacting the legislation before us, has used ancestry as a racial definition and for a racial purpose. . . .

As for the further argument that the restriction differentiates even among Polynesian people and is based simply on the date of an ancestor's residence in

Hawaii, this too is insufficient to prove the classification is nonracial in purpose and operation. Simply because a class defined by ancestry does not include all members of the race does not suffice to make the classification race neutral. Here, the State's argument is undermined by its express racial purpose and by its actual effects.

The ancestral inquiry mandated by the State implicates the same grave concerns as a classification specifying a particular race by name. One of the principal reasons race is treated as a forbidden classification is that it demeans the dignity and worth of a person to be judged by ancestry instead of by his or her own merit and essential qualities. An inquiry into ancestral lines is not consistent with respect based on the unique personality each of us possesses, a respect the Constitution itself secures in its concern for persons and citizens.

The ancestral inquiry mandated by the State is forbidden by the fifteenth amendment for the further reason that the use of racial classifications is corruptive of the whole legal order democratic elections seek to preserve. The law itself may not become the instrument for generating the prejudice and hostility all too often directed against persons whose particular ancestry is disclosed by their ethnic characteristics and cultural traditions. "Distinctions between citizens solely because of their ancestry are by their very nature odious to a free people whose institutions are founded upon the doctrine of equality." *Hirabayashi v. United States*, 320 U.S. 81 (1943). Ancestral tracing of this sort achieves its purpose by creating a legal category which employs the same mechanisms, and causes the same injuries, as laws or statutes that use race by name. The State's electoral restriction enacts a race-based voting qualification. . . .

The most far reaching of the State's arguments [in defense of the voting restriction] is that exclusion of non-Hawaiians from voting is permitted under our cases allowing the differential treatment of certain members of Indian tribes. The decisions of this Court, interpreting the effect of treaties and congressional enactments on the subject, have held that various tribes retained some elements of quasi-sovereign authority, even after cession of their lands to the United States. The retained tribal authority relates to self-governance. In reliance on that theory the Court has sustained a federal provision giving employment preferences to persons of tribal ancestry. *Mancari*, 417 U.S. at 553–555. The *Mancari* case, and the theory upon which it rests, are invoked by the State to defend its decision to restrict voting for the OHA trustees, who are charged so directly with protecting the interests of native Hawaiians.

If Hawaii's restriction were to be sustained under *Mancari* we would be required to accept some beginning premises not yet established in our case law. Among other postulates, it would be necessary to conclude that Congress, in reciting the purposes for the transfer of lands to the State — and in other enactments such as the Hawaiian Homes Commission Act and the Joint Resolution of 1993 — has determined that native Hawaiians have a status like that of Indians in organized tribes, and that it may, and has, delegated to the State a broad authority to preserve that status. These propositions would raise questions of considerable moment and difficulty. It is a matter of some dispute, for instance, whether Congress may treat the native Hawaiians as it does the Indian tribes. *Compare* Van Dyke, *The Political Status of the Hawaiian People*, 17 YALE L. & POL'Y REV. 95 (1998), *with* Benjamin,

Equal Protection and the Special Relationship: The Case of Native Hawaiians, 106 YALE L.J. 537 (1996). We can stay far off that difficult terrain, however.

The State's argument fails for a more basic reason. Even were we to take the substantial step of finding authority in Congress, delegated to the State, to treat Hawaiians or native Hawaiians as tribes, Congress may not authorize a State to create a voting scheme of this sort.

Of course, as we have established in a series of cases, Congress may fulfill its treaty obligations and its responsibilities to the Indian tribes by enacting legislation dedicated to their circumstances and needs [citing, among other cases, *United States v. Antelope* and *Fisher v. District Court*]. As we have observed, "every piece of legislation dealing with Indian tribes and reservations . . . singles out for special treatment a constituency of tribal Indians." *Mancari*, 417 U.S. at 552.

Mancari, upon which many of the above cases rely, presented the somewhat different issue of a preference in hiring and promoting at the federal Bureau of Indian Affairs (BIA), a preference which favored individuals who were " 'one-fourth or more degree Indian blood and . . . members of a Federally-recognized tribe.' " 417 U.S. at 553, n. 24 (quoting 44 BIAM 335, 3.1 (1972)). Although the classification had a racial component, the Court found it important that the preference was "not directed towards a 'racial' group consisting of 'Indians,' " but rather "only to members of 'federally recognized' tribes." 417 U.S. at 553, n.2 "In this sense," the Court held, "the preference [was] political rather than racial in nature." *Ibid.*; . . . The opinion was careful to note, however, that the case was confined to the authority of the BIA, an agency described as "sui generis." 417 U.S. at 554.

Hawaii would extend the limited exception of *Mancari* to a new and larger dimension. The State contends that "one of the very purposes of OHA — and the challenged voting provision — is to afford Hawaiians a measure of self-governance," and so it fits the model of *Mancari*. It does not follow from *Mancari*, however, that Congress may authorize a State to establish a voting scheme that limits the electorate for its public officials to a class of tribal Indians, to the exclusion of all non-Indian citizens.

The tribal elections established by the federal statutes the State cites illuminate its error. *See id.* at 22 (citing, *e.g.*, the Menominee Restoration Act, 25 U.S.C. § 903b, and the Indian Reorganization Act, 25 U.S.C. § 476). If a non-Indian lacks a right to vote in tribal elections, it is for the reason that such elections are the internal affair of a quasi-sovereign. The OHA elections, by contrast, are the affair of the State of Hawaii. OHA is a state agency, established by the State Constitution, responsible for the administration of state laws and obligations. *See* Haw. Const., Art. XII, §§ 5–6. The Hawaiian Legislature has declared that OHA exists to serve "as the principal public agency in the State responsible for the performance, development, and coordination of programs and activities relating to native Hawaiians and Hawaiians." Haw. Rev. Stat. § 10-3(3). . . . Although it is apparent that OHA has a unique position under state law, it is just as apparent that it remains an arm of the State.

. . . [T]he elections for OHA trustee are elections of the State, not of a separate quasi-sovereign, and they are elections to which the fifteenth amendment applies.

To extend *Mancari* to this context would be to permit a State, by racial classification, to fence out whole classes of its citizens from decisionmaking in critical state affairs. The fifteenth amendment forbids this result. . . .

When the culture and way of life of a people are all but engulfed by a history beyond their control, their sense of loss may extend down through generations; and their dismay may be shared by many members of the larger community. As the State of Hawaii attempts to address these realities, it must, as always, seek the political consensus that begins with a sense of shared purpose. One of the necessary beginning points is this principle: The Constitution of the United States, too, has become the heritage of all the citizens of Hawaii.

In this case the fifteenth amendment invalidates the electoral qualification based on ancestry. The judgment of the Court of Appeals for the Ninth Circuit is *reversed.*

[In a concurring opinion resting on both the fourteenth and fifteenth amendments, Justices Breyer and Souter located the constitutional defect in the very breadth of the group entitled to vote for trustees of the OHA. Although they were prepared to accept the general purpose of the voting restriction, they concluded that the absence of any limit on the degree of Native Hawaiian ancestry rendered the state law "unreasonable." According to these concurring Justices, voters with only 1/500th Native Hawaiian ancestry were included among the eligible voters; yet these individuals were so removed from indigenous Hawaiians as to be indistinguishable from those who were ineligible.

Finally, Justices Stevens and Ginsburg offered overlapping dissents, relying heavily on the reasoning of *Morton v. Mancari.* They both subscribed to the following position, articulated by Justice Stevens.]

Justice Stevens, dissenting.

[N]either the extent of Congress's sweeping power nor the character of the trust relationship with indigenous peoples has depended on the ancient racial origins of the people, the allotment of tribal lands, the coherence or existence of tribal self-government, or the varying definitions of "Indian" Congress has chosen to adopt. Rather, when it comes to the exercise of Congress's plenary power in Indian affairs, this Court has taken account of the "numerous occasions" on which "legislation that singles out Indians for particular and special treatment" has been upheld, and has concluded that as "long as the special treatment can be tied rationally to the fulfillment of Congress's unique obligation towards the Indians, such legislative judgments will not be disturbed." *Morton v. Mancari,* 417 U.S. 535, 554–555. . . .

The descendants of the native Hawaiians share with the descendants of the Native Americans on the mainland or in the Aleutian Islands not only a history of subjugation at the hands of colonial forces, but also a purposefully created and specialized "guardian-ward" relationship with the Government of the United States. It follows that legislation targeting the native Hawaiians must be evaluated according to the same understanding of equal protection that this Court has long applied to the Indians on the continental United States: that "special treatment . . .

be tied rationally to the fulfillment of Congress' unique obligation" toward the native peoples.

It is only by refusing to face this Court's entire body of Indian law, that the majority is able to hold that the OHA qualification denies non-"Hawaiians' the right to vote 'on account of race.' "

NOTES ON TREATING INDIANS AS A SUSPECT RACIAL CLASSIFICATION

1.   **Surviving Strict Scrutiny:** *Babbitt v. Williams* seems to invoke strict scrutiny for Indian classifications, only to conclude that federal laws focusing on core tribal activities can survive such examination. Is that a faithful rendition of strict scrutiny? Does the court's attempt to separate core tribal activities from others put the courts in the position of imposing a backward-looking and static understanding of tribal cultures? Are non-Indian courts well-equipped to make such judgments about core activities?

An illustration of the application of strict scrutiny to an Indian classification is *In the Interest of A.W. and S.W.*, 741 N.W.2d 793 (Iowa 2007). There, the Iowa Supreme Court used the "strict scrutiny" standard to evaluate a classification created by a state law affording tribes special intervention rights in child welfare proceedings. Under that statute, the tribal rights would arise in any case involving a child of an enrolled tribal member, whether or not the child herself was eligible for tribal membership. Viewing *Morton v. Mancari*'s relaxed standard of review applicable only to classifications directed at enrolled tribal members, the Iowa court concluded that strict scrutiny was compelled. According to the court, this particular classification could not survive strict scrutiny because it was not narrowly tailored to advance the compelling governmental interest of protecting essential tribal relations. If an Indian child is ineligible for membership in her or his own right, then special tribal rights are not necessary to allow the tribe "to protect its interests in those individuals who will perpetuate the next generation of the tribe's existence." Is this decision consistent with the more forgiving treatment of "strict scrutiny" in *Grutter v. Bollinger*? Does it read the concept of "narrow tailoring" too narrowly? The Winnebago Tribe of Nebraska, whose member was involved in *In the Interest of A.W. and S.W.*, had adopted a resolution stating that "[F]or purposes of determining the applicability of the Iowa ICWA, any child of an enrolled Winnebago tribal member shall be included as a child of the Winnebago tribal community." Why wasn't this affirmation by the Winnebago Tribe sufficient to indicate a tribal interest in such children and to trigger a federal trust obligation? What are the implications of the Iowa Supreme Court's decision for tribal choices regarding enrollment criteria or other indices of tribal membership? *See* Sec. A.1.b, this chapter, especially Note 1 following the Deloria-Laurence dialogue.

2.   **Reconciling *Rice v. Cayetano* and *Morton v. Mancari*:** How much does the outcome in *Rice* turn on the Court's judgment that Native Hawaiian "culture and way of life" are no longer viable? Has Justice Kennedy adopted the views of Justice McClean in his concurring opinion in *Worcester v. Georgia*, presented in Ch. 1, Sec. C.2? Is the Supreme Court competent to make a finding regarding tribal viability?

Can you square that finding with the activism of the Native Hawaiian sovereignty movement? *See* Ch. 5, Sec. B.2. What model of tribal-federal relations underlies Justice Kennedy's opinion in *Rice*? How does it compare with the models discussed in Chapter 1? Does one's choice of model depend on how one weighs the fact that Native Hawaiians never consented to American government?

How does the *Rice v. Cayetano* majority understand the Court's holding in *Morton v. Mancari*? Justice Kennedy indicates that the Court would reach the same result regardless whether Native Hawaiians may be treated the same as mainland tribal Indians. Does the Court's statement mean that after *Rice*, Congress may not enact a law creating a federal entity like the Office of Hawaiian Affairs for the benefit of Indians, with voting for its trustees limited to those Indians? Does *Rice v. Cayetano* jeopardize any other federal Indian laws? Consider the fact that *Rice v. Cayetano* involved the Fifteenth Amendment, with its specific language against racial discrimination, rather than the equal protection clause, which contains no such language. When the specific language of the Indian commerce clause authorizing special treatment of tribes encounters the more general language of the equal protection clause, it is possible to view the former as taking precedence. But when specific language of the Fifteenth Amendment meets equally specific language of the Indian commerce clause, the ban on discrimination may be entitled to more weight because it is more recent.

Outside the Fifteenth Amendment context, courts have had an easier time finding that Native Hawaiian classifications survive strict scrutiny. In *Doe v. Kamehameha Sch./Bernice Pauahi Bishop Estate*, 470 F.3d 827 (9th Cir. 2006), the Ninth Circuit, en banc, decided that a private school's admission policy preferring Native Hawaiians did not violate a federal statute barring race discrimination by private entities. The school had been established more than 100 years earlier with funds from the estate of the last member of the Hawaiian monarchy, on lands that were then monarchy lands. The opinion for the court, written by Judge Graeber, emphasized, "in the unique context of Native Hawaiian history, affirmative measures are needed to address present, severe inequalities in educational achievement." *Id.* at 845. That opinion also found the preference to impose only a limited hardship on non-Native Hawaiians, given historical expectations and actual admission practices. Judge William Fletcher, concurring, would have resolved the dispute by characterizing Native Hawaiians as a political group, and applying *Morton v. Mancari*. For him, *Rice v. Cayetano* was distinguishable as a voting rights case under the Fifteenth Amendment. *Id.* at 849–53. After canvassing the history of U.S. treatment of Native Hawaiians, Professor Bethany Berger concludes: "If the impact of racism for Native Hawaiians was to translate their governmental bonds into racial ones, then recognizing the claims of their descendants to political and property rights is the means to undo this racism. Recognizing sovereign rights in Native Hawaiians and providing them with financial support and governance rights on the lands of the former Kingdom of Hawaii, far from creating racial inequality, instead takes tentative steps toward correcting it." Bethany R. Berger, *Reconciling Equal Protection and Federal Indian Law*, 98 CALIF. L. REV. 1165, 1196 (2010). Is this argument sufficient to satisfy "strict scrutiny" for all Native Hawaiian classifications?

C. CANONS OF CONSTRUCTION FOR INTERPRETING THE TRIBAL-FEDERAL LEGAL RELATIONSHIP

In *Worcester v. Georgia*, 31 U.S. (6 Pet.) 515 (1832), presented in Ch. 1, Sec. C.2, Chief Justice John Marshall employed special rules of construction to interpret the Treaties of Hopewell and Holston involved in that case. The Chief Justice wrote:

> Is it reasonable to suppose, that the Indians, who could not write, and most probably could not read, who certainly were not critical judges of our language, should distinguish the word "allotted" from the words "marked out." The actual subject of contract was the dividing line between the two nations, and their attention may very well be supposed to have been confined to that subject. When, in fact, they were ceding lands to the United States, and describing the extent of their cession, it may very well be supposed that they might not understand the term employed, as indicating that, instead of granting, they were receiving lands. If the term would admit of no other signification, which is not conceded, its being misunderstood is so apparent, results so necessarily from the whole transaction; that it must, we think, be taken in the sense in which it was most obviously used.

Id. at 552–553. In a separate concurring opinion, Justice McLean wrote:

> The language used in treaties with the Indians should never be construed to their prejudice. If words be made use of which are susceptible of a more extended meaning than their plain import, as connected with the tenor of the treaty, they should be considered as used only in the latter sense. To contend that the word "allotted," in reference to the land guarantied to the Indians in certain treaties, indicates a favour conferred, rather than a right acknowledged, would, it would seem to me, do injustice to the understanding of the parties. How the words of the treaty were understood by this unlettered people, rather than their critical meaning, should form the rule of construction.

Id. at 582. The efforts in *Worcester* by Chief Justice Marshall and Justice McLean to arrive at "the understanding of the parties" by probing how the Indians would have understood the treaty language constitute the origins of a series of canons of construction, *i.e.*, special rules of interpretation, that have had profound influences on the development of federal Indian law. The quoted paragraphs demonstrate that the Chief Justice and other members of the Court properly understood Indian treaties to constitute grants of lands and other rights *from* the Indians to the United States, rather than the other way around. It also demonstrates that any effort to interpret those treaties requires a full appreciation of the Indian understanding of the deal if the bilateral nature of the agreement is to be properly enforced. Should the same rules be applied to statutes affecting Indians? What if the statute merely adopts and enacts an antecedent agreement with the Indian tribes, as is frequently true of older Indian statutes? Should any bright line be drawn between Indian treaties and federal Indian statutes for this purpose?

Consider the modern vitality of such canons of construction in light of the following materials. The first case involves an off-reservation fishing rights dispute of a type considered in more detail in Chapter 7.

MINNESOTA v. MILLE LACS BAND
OF CHIPPEWA INDIANS
United States Supreme Court
526 U.S. 172 (1999)

[An 1830 Removal Act authorized the President to convey land west of the Mississippi to Indian tribes "in exchange" for the land where they resided. Article V of the Treaty of Fort Snelling in 1837 guaranteed to the Chippewa:

> The privilege of hunting, fishing, and gathering the wild rice, upon the lands, the rivers and the lakes included in the territory ceded, is guarantied to the Indians, during the pleasure of the President of the United States.

7 Stat. 537. The Chippewa later negotiated an 1842 treaty with the United States which, while continuing to reserve use rights on the lands in that treaty, provided that the Chippewa would "be subject to removal therefrom at the pleasure of the President of the United States." 1842 Treaty with the Chippewa, Art. 6, 7 Stat. at 592. Minnesota questioned the survival of the Chippewa's rights to use ceded land for food-gathering purposes, known as usufructury rights, for two reasons. First, after settler pressure mounted on the federal government to remove the Chippewa, the territorial government adopted a resolution urging the President to do so, and President Zachary Taylor thereafter unilaterally issued a removal order in February 1850. Although this Executive Order was primarily understood as a removal order, it also specifically provided:

> The privileges granted temporarily to the Chippewa Indians of the Mississippi, by the Fifth Article of the Treaty made with them on the 29th of July 1837, "of hunting, fishing and gathering the wild rice, upon the lands, the rivers and the lakes included in the territory ceded" by that treaty to the United States; and the right granted to the Chippewa Indians of the Mississippi and Lake Superior, by the Second Article of the treaty with them of October 4th 1842, of hunting on the territory which they ceded by that treaty, "with the other usual privileges of occupancy until required to remove by the President of the United States," are hereby revoked; and all of the said Indians remaining on the lands ceded as aforesaid, are required to remove to their unceded lands.

Although the removal order was never fully implemented, and the Chippewa remained in Minnesota on later-established reservations, Minnesota argued that the President's express removal order revoking the 1837 treaty — which guaranteed off-reservation fishing and food-gathering rights — extinguished all such rights.

Second, Minnesota argued that by agreeing to the 1855 treaty provision relinquishing "all right, title, and interest, of whatsoever nature the same may be" in any lands in Minnesota, the Chippewa relinquished the off-reservation hunting, fishing, and food-gathering rights guaranteed in the 1837 treaty. Even though both circuits and all other federal and state courts that had considered these or like arguments had sustained the persistence of the Indian off-reservation fishing and food-gathering rights, see *Mille Lacs Band of Chippewa Indians v. Minnesota*, 124 F.3d 904 (8th Cir. 1997); *Lac Courte Oreilles Band of Lake Superior Chippewa*

Indians v. Voigt, 700 F.2d 341 (7th Cir. 1983); *see also, United States v. Michigan*, 471 F. Supp. 192 (W.D. Mich. 1979), *vacated on other grounds*, 623 F.2d 448 (6th Cir. 1980); *United States v. Michigan*, 508 F. Supp. 480 (W.D. Mich. 1980); *Grand Traverse Band of Ottawa and Chippewa Indians v. Michigan Dep't of Nat'l Res.*, 141 F.3d 635 (6th Cir. 1998); *People v. Le Blanc*, 248 N.W.2d 199, 202 (Mich. 1976); *People v. Jondreau*, 185 N.W.2d 375, 379 (Mich. Sup. Ct. 1971), the United States Supreme Court granted review on the question.]

JUSTICE O'CONNOR delivered the opinion of the Court.

II

We are first asked to decide whether President Taylor's Executive Order of February 6, 1850, terminated Chippewa Hunting, fishing, and gathering rights under the 1837 Treaty. The Court of Appeals began its analysis of this question with a statement of black letter law: " 'The President's power, if any, to issue the order must stem either from an act of Congress or from the Constitution itself.' " 124 F.3d at 915 (quoting *Youngstown Sheet & Tube Co. v. Sawyer*, 343 U.S. 579, 585 (1952)). The court considered whether the President had authority to issue the removal order under the 1830 Removal Act (hereinafter Removal Act), 4 Stat. 411. The Removal Act authorized the President to convey land west of the Mississippi to Indian tribes that chose to "exchange the lands where they now reside, and remove there." *Id.* at 412. According to the Court of Appeals, the Removal Act only allowed the removal of Indians who had consented to removal. 124 F.3d at 915–916. Because the Chippewa had not consented to removal, according to the court, the Removal Act could not provide authority for the President's 1850 removal order. 124 F.3d at 916–917.

. . . We agree that the Removal Act did not forbid the President's removal order, but as noted by the Court of Appeals, it also did not authorize that order.

Because the Removal Act did not authorize the 1850 removal order, we must look elsewhere for a constitutional or statutory authorization for the order. In this Court, only the [intervening] landowners argue for an alternative source of authority; they argue that the President's removal order was authorized by the 1837 Treaty itself. There is no support for this proposition, however. The Treaty makes no mention of removal, and there was no discussion of removal during the Treaty negotiations. Although the United States could have negotiated a treaty in 1837 providing for removal of the Chippewa — and it negotiated several such removal treaties with Indian tribes in 1837 — the 1837 Treaty with the Chippewa did not contain any provisions authorizing a removal order. The silence in the Treaty, in fact, is consistent with the United States' objectives in negotiating it. Commissioner of Indian Affairs Harris explained the United States' goals for the 1837 Treaty in a letter to Governor Dodge on May 13, 1837. In this letter, Harris explained that through this Treaty, the United States wanted to purchase Chippewa land for the pinewoods located on it; the letter contains no reference to removal of the Chippewa. Based on the record before us, the proposition that the 1837 Treaty authorized the President's 1850 removal order is unfounded. Because the parties have pointed to no colorable source of authority for the President's removal order, we agree with the Court of Appeals' conclusion that the 1850 removal order was unauthorized.

The State argues that even if the removal portion of the order was invalid, the 1837 Treaty privileges were nevertheless revoked because the invalid removal order was severable from the portion of the order revoking Chippewa usufructuary rights. Although this Court has often considered the severability of statutes, we have never addressed whether Executive Orders can be severed into valid and invalid parts, and if so, what standard should govern the inquiry. In this case, the Court of Appeals assumed that Executive Orders are severable, and that the standards applicable in statutory cases apply without modification in the context of Executive Orders. Because no party before this Court challenges the applicability of these standards, for purposes of this case we shall assume, arguendo, that the severability standard for statutes also applies to Executive Orders.

The inquiry into whether a statute is severable is essentially an inquiry into legislative intent. *Regan v. Time, Inc.*, 468 U.S. 641, 653 (1984) (plurality opinion). We stated the traditional test for severability over 65 years ago: "Unless it is evident that the legislature would not have enacted those provisions which are within its power, independently of that which is not, the invalid part may be dropped if what is left is fully operative as a law." *Champlin Refining Co. v. Corporation Comm'n of Okla.*, 286 U.S. 210, 234 (1932). Translated to the present context, we must determine whether the President would not have revoked the 1837 Treaty privileges if he could not issue the removal order.

We think it is clear that President Taylor intended the 1850 order to stand or fall as a whole. The 1850 order embodied a single, coherent policy, the predominant purpose of which was removal of the Chippewa from the lands that they had ceded to the United States. The federal officials charged with implementing the order certainly understood it as such. As soon as the Commissioner of Indian Affairs received a copy of the order, he sent it to Governor Ramsey and placed him in charge of its implementation. [The Commissioner's letter to Governor Ramsey, as well as Governor Ramsey's directive to the LaPointe subagent and the subagent's circular notifying the Wisconsin tribes, all mention the removal order, but say nothing about the Indian usufructuary rights.]

When the 1850 order is understood as announcing a removal policy, the portion of the order revoking Chippewa usufructuary rights is seen to perform an integral function in this policy. The order tells the Indians to "go," and also tells them not to return to the ceded lands to hunt and fish. The State suggests that President Taylor might also have revoked Chippewa usufructuary rights as a kind of "incentive program" to encourage the Indians to remove had he known that he could not order their removal directly. The State points to no evidence, however, that the President or his aides ever considered the abrogation of hunting and fishing rights as an "incentive program." Moreover, the State does not explain how this incentive was to operate. As the State characterizes Chippewa Treaty rights, the revocation of those rights would not have prevented the Chippewa from hunting, fishing, and gathering on the ceded territory; the revocation of treaty rights would merely have subjected Chippewa hunters, fishers, and gatherers to territorial, and, later, state regulation. The State does not explain how, if the Chippewa were still permitted to hunt, fish, and gather on the ceded territory, the revocation of the treaty rights would have encouraged the Chippewa to remove to their unceded lands.

There is also no evidence that the treaty privileges themselves — as opposed to the presence of the Indians — caused any problems necessitating the revocation of those privileges. In other words, there is little historical evidence that the treaty privileges would have been revoked for some other purpose. . . . [I]mportantly, Governor Ramsey and the Minnesota Territorial Legislature explicitly tied revocation of the treaty privileges to removal. Common sense explains the logic of this strategy: If the legislature was concerned with ensuring "the security and tranquility of the white settlements," this concern was not addressed by merely revoking Indian treaty rights; the Indians had to be removed.

We conclude that President Taylor's 1850 Executive Order was ineffective to terminate Chippewa usufructuary rights under the 1837 Treaty. The State has pointed to no statutory or constitutional authority for the President's removal order, and the Executive Order, embodying as it did one coherent policy, is inseverable. We do not mean to suggest that a President, now or in the future, cannot revoke Chippewa usufructuary rights in accordance with the terms of the 1837 Treaty. All we conclude today is that the President's 1850 Executive Order was insufficient to accomplish this revocation because it was not severable from the invalid removal order.

III

The State argues that the Mille Lacs Band of Chippewa Indians relinquished its usufructuary rights under the 1855 Treaty with the Chippewa. Specifically, the State argues that the Band unambiguously relinquished its usufructuary rights by agreeing to the second sentence of Article 1 in that Treaty:

> "And the said Indians do further fully and entirely relinquish and convey to the United States, any and all right, title, and interest, of whatsoever nature the same may be, which they may now have in, and to any other lands in the Territory of Minnesota or elsewhere." 10 Stat. 1166.

This sentence, however, does not mention the 1837 Treaty, and it does not mention hunting, fishing, and gathering rights. The entire 1855 Treaty, in fact, is devoid of any language expressly mentioning — much less abrogating — usufructuary rights. Similarly, the Treaty contains no language providing money for the abrogation of previously held rights. These omissions are telling because the United States treaty drafters had the sophistication and experience to use express language for the abrogation of treaty rights. In fact, just a few months after Commissioner Manypenny completed the 1855 Treaty, he negotiated a Treaty with the Chippewa of Sault Ste. Marie that expressly revoked fishing rights that had been reserved in an earlier Treaty. See Treaty with the Chippewa of Sault Ste. Marie, Art. 1, 11 Stat. 631 ("The said Chippewa Indians surrender to the United States the right of fishing at the falls of St. Mary's . . . secured to them by the treaty of June 16, 1820"). *See, e.g., Choctaw Nation v. Oklahoma*, 397 U.S. 620, 631 (1970) (rejecting argument that language in Treaty had special meaning when United States was competent to state that meaning more clearly).

The State argues that despite any explicit reference to the 1837 Treaty rights, or to usufructuary rights more generally, the second sentence of Article 1 nevertheless abrogates those rights. But to determine whether this language abrogates Chippewa Treaty rights, we look beyond the written words to the larger context that frames the Treaty, including "the history of the treaty, the negotiations, and the practical construction adopted by the parties." *Choctaw Nation v. United States*, 318 U.S. 423, 432 (1943). In this case, an examination of the historical record provides insight into how the parties to the Treaty understood the terms of the agreement. This insight is especially helpful to the extent that it sheds light on how the Chippewa signatories to the Treaty understood the agreement because we interpret Indian treaties to give effect to the terms as the Indians themselves would have understood them. *See Washington v. Washington State Commercial Passenger Fishing Vessel Ass'n*, 443 U.S. 658, 675–676 (1979); *United States v. Winans*, 198 U.S. 371, 380–381 (1905).

The 1855 Treaty was designed primarily to transfer Chippewa land to the United States, not to terminate Chippewa usufructuary rights. It was negotiated under the authority of the Act of December 19, 1854. This Act authorized treaty negotiations with the Chippewa "for the extinguishment of their title to all the lands owned and claimed by them in the Territory of Minnesota and State of Wisconsin." Ch. 7, 10 Stat. 598. The Act is silent with respect to authorizing agreements to terminate Indian usufructuary privileges, and this silence was likely not accidental. During Senate debate on the Act, Senator Sebastian, the chairman of the Committee on Indian Affairs, stated that the treaties to be negotiated under the Act would "reserv[e] to them [*i.e.*, the Chippewa] those rights which are secured by former treaties." Cong. Globe, 33d Cong., 1st Sess., 1404 (1854).

[After extensively surveying the historical record behind the 1855 Treaty, the Court concluded that the historical record failed to support the state's contention that the second sentence of Article I was intended to abrogate the Chippewa's usufructuary rights under the 1837 Treaty. "At the very least," Justice O'Connor noted, "the historical record refutes the State's assertion that the 1855 Treaty 'unambiguously' abrogated the 1837 hunting, fishing, and gathering privileges." Having found an ambiguity in the meaning of Article I of the 1855 Treaty, the Court looked to the canons of construction employed in Indian cases to resolve that ambiguity.]

Given this plausible ambiguity, we cannot agree with the State that the 1855 Treaty abrogated Chippewa usufructuary rights. We have held that Indian treaties are to be interpreted liberally in favor of the Indians, *Washington v. Washington State Commercial Passenger Fishing Vessel Assn.*, 443 U.S., at 675–676; *Choctaw Nation v. United States*, 318 U.S., at 432, and that any ambiguities are to be resolved in their favor, *Winters v. United States*, 207 U.S. 564, 576–577 (1908). *See also County of Yakima v. Confederated Tribes and Bands of Yakima Nation*, 502 U.S. 251, 269 (1992).

IV

Finally, the State argues that the Chippewa's usufructuary rights under the 1837 Treaty were extinguished when Minnesota was admitted to the Union in 1858. In making this argument, the State faces an uphill battle. Congress may abrogate Indian treaty rights, but it must clearly express its intent to do so. *United States v. Dion*, 476 U.S. 734, 738–740 (1986); *see also Washington v. Washington State Commercial Passenger Fishing Vessel Assn.*, 443 U.S., at 690; *Menominee Tribe v. United States*, 391 U.S. 404, 413 (1968). There must be "clear evidence that Congress actually considered the conflict between its intended action on the one hand and Indian treaty rights on the other, and chose to resolve that conflict by abrogating the treaty." *United States v. Dion, supra*, at 740. There is no such "clear evidence" of congressional intent to abrogate the Chippewa Treaty rights here. The relevant statute — Minnesota's enabling Act — provides in relevant part:

> "The State of Minnesota shall be one, and is hereby declared to be one, of the United States of America, and admitted into the Union on an equal footing with the original States in all respects whatever." Act of May 11, 1858, 11 Stat. 285.

This language, like the rest of the Act, makes no mention of Indian treaty rights; it provides no clue that Congress considered the reserved rights of the Chippewa and decided to abrogate those rights when it passed the Act. The State concedes that the Act is silent in this regard, Brief for Petitioners 36, and the State does not point to any legislative history describing the effect of the Act on Indian treaty rights.

With no direct support for its argument, the State relies principally on this Court's decision in *Ward v. Race Horse*, 163 U.S. 504 (1896). In *Race Horse*, we held that a Treaty reserving to a Tribe " 'the right to hunt on the unoccupied lands of the United States, so long as game may be found thereon, and so long as peace subsists among the whites and Indians on the borders of the hunting districts' " terminated when Wyoming became a State in 1890. Id. at 507 (quoting Art. 4 of the Treaty). This case does not bear the weight the State places on it, however, because it has been qualified by later decisions of this Court.

[The Court found that the *Race Horse* case rested on the false premise that tribal off-reservation food gathering rights were irreconcilable with state regulatory authority over wildlife located within its border. The Court noted that its decision sustaining the off-reservation fishing and food gathering rights of certain Pacific Northwest tribes in *Washington v. Washington State Commercial Passenger Fishing Vessel Assn.* demonstrated that "Indian treaty rights can coexist with state management of natural resources." The Court also noted that while states had important interests in regulating wildlife and natural resources within their borders, that authority constituted a power shared with the federal government. Thus, it found that "the 1837 Treaty gave the Chippewa the right to hunt, fish, and gather in the ceded territory free of territorial, and later state, regulation, a privilege that others did not enjoy" and that "this freedom from state regulation curtails the State's ability to regulate hunting, fishing, and gathering by the Chippewa in the ceded lands." Nevertheless, the Court noted that under existing cases, the Indian treaty-based usufructuary rights do not guarantee the Indians "absolute freedom" from state regulation. Rather, the Court noted that it had repeatedly "reaffirmed state authority to impose reasonable and necessary nondiscriminatory regulations on Indian hunting, fishing, and gathering rights in the interest of conservation."]

The focus of the *Race Horse* inquiry is whether Congress (more precisely, because this is a treaty, the Senate) intended the rights secured by the 1837 Treaty to survive statehood. 163 U.S. at 514–515. The 1837 Treaty itself defines the circumstances under which the rights would terminate: when the exercise of those rights was no longer the "pleasure of the President." There is no suggestion in the Treaty that the President would have to conclude that the privileges should end when a State was established in the area. Moreover, unlike the rights at issue in *Race Horse*, there is no fixed termination point to the 1837 Treaty rights. Finally, we note that there is nothing inherent in the nature of reserved treaty rights to suggest that they can be extinguished by implication at statehood. Treaty rights are not impliedly terminated upon statehood. *Wisconsin v. Hitchcock*, 201 U.S. 202, 213–214 (1906); *Johnson v. Gearlds*, 234 U.S. 422, 439–440 (1914). The *Race Horse* Court's decision to the contrary — that Indian treaty rights were impliedly repealed by Wyoming's statehood Act — was informed by that Court's conclusion that the Indian treaty rights were inconsistent with state sovereignty over natural resources and thus that Congress (the Senate) could not have intended the rights to survive statehood. But as we described above, Indian treaty-based usufructuary rights are not inconsistent with state sovereignty over natural resources. Thus, contrary to the State's contentions, *Race Horse* does not compel the conclusion that Minnesota's admission to the Union extinguished Chippewa usufructuary rights guaranteed by the 1837 Treaty.

Accordingly, the judgment of the United States Court of Appeals for the Eighth Circuit is *affirmed*.

CHIEF JUSTICE REHNQUIST, with whom JUSTICE SCALIA, JUSTICE KENNEDY, and JUSTICE THOMAS join, dissenting.

[T]here was some discussion during the treaty negotiations that the Chippewa wished to preserve some right to hunt in the ceded territory. The United States agreed to this request to some extent [in Article V of the Treaty, quoted at the beginning of the majority opinion].

As the Court also notes, the Chippewa were aware that their right to come onto the ceded land was not absolute — the Court quotes the statement of Governor Dodge to the Chippewa that he would "make known to your Great Father, your request to be permitted to make sugar, on the lands; and you will be allowed, during his pleasure, to hunt and fish on them."

Thus, the Treaty by its own plain terms provided for a quid pro quo: Land was ceded in exchange for a 20-year annuity of money and goods. Additionally, *the United States granted the Chippewa* a quite limited "privilege" to hunt and fish, "guarantied . . . during the pleasure of the President." Art. 5, 7 Stat. 537. [Emphasis added.]

[Attacking what he saw as the majority's flawed severability analysis, Chief Justice Rehnquist would have treated the 1850 Executive Order as a valid revocation of the Chippewa's treaty-guaranteed food gathering rights.] Pursuant to a Treaty, the President terminated the Indians' hunting and fishing privileges in an Executive Order which stated, in effect, that the privilege to come onto federal lands and hunt was terminated, and that the Indians move themselves from those lands.

[Furthermore, avoiding, or perhaps ignoring, the canons of construction relied upon by the majority opinion, Chief Justice Rehnquist's dissent also relied on the "plain meaning" of the 1855 Treaty cession to relinquish the usufructuary rights.] First, the language of the Treaty is so broad as to encompass "all" interests in land possessed or claimed by the Indians. Second, while it is important to the Court that the Treaty "is devoid of any language expressly mentioning — much less abrogating — usufructuary rights," the definition of "usufructuary rights" explains further why this is so. Usufructuary rights are "a real right of limited duration on the property of another." *See* Black's Law Dictionary 1544 (6th ed. 1990). It seems to me that such a right would fall clearly under the sweeping language of the Treaty under any reasonable interpretation, and that this is not a case where "even 'learned lawyers' of the day would probably have offered differing interpretations of the [treaty language]." And third, although the Court notes that in other treaties the United States sometimes expressly mentioned cessions of usufructuary rights, there was no need to do so in this case, because the settled expectation of the United States was that the 1850 Executive Order had terminated the hunting rights of the Chippewa. Thus, rather than applying the plain and unequivocal language of the 1855 Treaty, the Court holds that "all" does not in fact mean "all."

[Chief Justice Rehnquist's dissent also objected to the majority's "feat of jurisprudential legerdemain" in *sub silentio* overruling *Race Horse* through a "jurisprudential bait-and-switch." Justice Thomas wrote a separate dissent similarly relying on "plain language" approaches to the terms of the treaties. He also tried to draw a new distinction between treaty guaranteed rights and lesser reserved privileges contained in treaties, suggesting with little authority that some federal officials previously had drawn the same distinction, albeit not in connection with the pending case.]

SAN MANUEL INDIAN BINGO AND CASINO v. N.L.R.B.
United States Court of Appeals, District of Columbia Circuit
475 F.3d 1306 (2007)

BROWN, CIRCUIT JUDGE.

In this case, we consider whether the National Labor Relations Board (the "Board") may apply the National Labor Relations Act, 29 U.S.C. §§ 151et seq. (the "NLRA"), to employment at a casino the San Manuel Band of Serrano Mission Indians ("San Manuel" or the "Tribe") operates on its reservation. The casino employs many non-Indians and caters primarily to non-Indians. We hold the Board may apply the NLRA to employment at this casino, and therefore we deny the petition for review.

I

San Manuel owns and operates the San Manuel Indian Bingo and Casino (the "Casino") on its reservation in San Bernardino County, California. This proceeding arose out of a competition between the Communication Workers of America ("CWA") and the Hotel Employees & Restaurant Employees International Union ("HERE"), each seeking to organize the Casino's employees. According to HERE's evidence, the Casino is about an hour's drive from Los Angeles. It includes a 2300-seat bingo hall and over a thousand slot machines. It also offers live entertainment. HERE's evidence further suggests the Tribe actively directs its marketing efforts to non-Indians, and the Board found that "many, and perhaps the great majority, of the casino's patrons are nonmembers who come from outside the reservation." *San Manuel Indian Bingo & Casino*, 341 N.L.R.B. 1055, 1056 (2004). The Tribe does not contract with an independent management company to operate the Casino, and therefore many Tribe members hold key positions at the Casino. Nevertheless, given the Casino's size, the Tribe must employ a significant number of non-members to ensure effective operation. *Id.* at 1056, 1061.

The Casino was established by the San Manuel tribal government as a "tribal governmental economic development project," *id.* at 1055, and it operates pursuant to the Indian Gaming Regulatory Act of 1988 ("IGRA"), which authorized gaming on tribal lands expressly "as a means of promoting tribal economic development, self-sufficiency, and strong tribal governments," 25 U.S.C. § 2702(1). According to San Manuel's evidence, its tribal government consists of a "General Council," which elects from among its members a "Business Committee." The General Council includes all tribal members twenty-one years of age or older. The record is not specific in regards to the size of the Tribe, but the Tribe's "Articles of Association" call for monthly meetings of the General Council, suggesting the Tribe is relatively small. The record also does not indicate the Casino's gross annual revenues, but HERE submitted a declaration indicating that, as of February 8, 2000, the Casino's website was advertising in regard to its bingo operation "Over 1 BILLION Dollars in Cash and Prizes awarded since July 24th, 1986." Revenues from the Casino are used to fund various tribal government programs and to provide for the general welfare of Tribe members.

In the Tribe's case, IGRA appears to have fulfilled its purpose, as the Casino has markedly improved the Tribe's economic condition. The Tribe's evidence indicates its one-square-mile reservation consists primarily of steep, mountainous, arid land, most of it unsuitable to economic development. For many years, the Tribe had no resources, and many of its members depended on public assistance. As a result of the Casino, however, the Tribe can now boast full employment, complete medical coverage for all members, government funding for scholarships, improved housing, and significant infrastructure improvements to the reservation. In addition, according to the Tribe's evidence, the tribal government is authorized to make direct per capita payments of Casino revenues to Tribe members, suggesting that improved government services are not the only way Tribe members might benefit from the Casino.

II

On January 18, 1999, HERE filed an unfair labor practice charge with the Board. The charge asserted the Casino "has interfered with, coerced and restrained employees in the exercise of their [collective bargaining] rights, and has dominated and discriminatorily supported the [CWA] by allowing CWA representatives access to Casino property . . . , while denying the same — or any — right of access to representatives of the Charging Party. . . . " HERE filed a second charge on March 29, 1999, making similar allegations. On September 30, 1999, the Board's Regional Director for Region 31 issued an order consolidating the two cases, as well as a consolidated complaint. The complaint alleged the Casino had permitted CWA: (1) to place a trailer on Casino property for the purpose of organizing Casino employees; (2) to distribute leaflets from the trailer; and (3) to communicate with Casino employees on Casino property during working hours. The complaint further alleged the Casino's security guards denied HERE equal access to Casino employees.

The Tribe appeared specially, seeking dismissal for lack of jurisdiction. The Tribe asserted the NLRA does not apply to the actions of tribal governments on their reservations. *See Fort Apache Timber Co.*, 226 N.L.R.B. 503 (1976). On January 27, 2000, the matter was transferred to the Board in Washington, D.C., and on May 28, 2004, the Board issued a decision and order finding the NLRA applicable. [The Board cited the Supreme Court's statement in *Federal Power Commission v. Tuscarora Indian Nation*, 362 U.S. 99, 116, (1960), that "a general statute in terms applying to all persons includes Indians and their property interests," and found that none of the judicially-crafted exceptions to that rule applied. Specifically, the Board found that the law did not address "purely intramural matters," did not abrogate any treaty rights, and did not reflect a clear intent by Congress to exclude tribal Indians.]

Failing in its effort to obtain a dismissal of the complaint, the Tribe filed an amended answer, admitting the key factual allegations and again denying the applicability of the NLRA. The Board issued a cease-and-desist order requiring the Tribe to give HERE access to the Casino and also to post notices in the Casino describing the rights of employees under the NLRA. The Tribe petitioned for review, and the Board filed a cross-application for enforcement of its order.

III

Several factors make resolution of this case particularly difficult. We have before us conflicting Supreme Court canons of interpretation that are articulated at a fairly high level of generality. In addition, the NLRA was enacted by a Congress that in all likelihood never contemplated the statute's potential application to tribal employers, and probably no member of that Congress imagined a small Indian tribe might operate like a closely held corporation, employing hundreds, or even thousands, of non-Indians to produce a product it profitably marketed to non-Indians. Further, the casino at issue here, though certainly exhibiting characteristics that are strongly commercial (non-Indian employees and non-Indian patrons), is also in some sense governmental (the casino is the primary source of revenue for the tribal government). Finally, out-of-circuit precedent is inconsistent as to the applicability of general federal laws to Indian tribes.

The gravitational center of San Manuel's case is tribal sovereignty, but even if we accept the paramount significance of this factor, our resolution of the case depends on how the Supreme Court and Congress have defined the contours and limits of tribal sovereignty. Our central inquiry is whether the relation between the Tribe's sovereign interests and the NLRA is such that the ambiguity in the NLRA should be resolved against the Board's exercise of jurisdiction. By focusing on the sovereignty question and addressing it first, we find the statutory interpretation question resolves itself fairly simply. Thus, we analyze this case in two parts: (1) Would application of the NLRA to San Manuel's casino violate federal Indian law by impinging upon protected tribal sovereignty? and (2) Assuming the preceding question is answered in the negative, does the term "employer" in the NLRA reasonably encompass Indian tribal governments operating commercial enterprises?

A

When we begin to examine tribal sovereignty, we find the relevant principles to be, superficially at least, in conflict. First, we have the Supreme Court's statement in *Tuscarora* that "a general statute in terms applying to all persons includes Indians and their property interests." 362 U.S. at 116. In *Tuscarora*, the Court applied this principle to permit condemnation of private property owned by a tribal government, finding a general grant of eminent domain powers applicable to the tribe. Id. at 118. This *Tuscarora* statement is, however, in tension with the longstanding principles that (1) ambiguities in a federal statute must be resolved in favor of Indians, see [*e.g.*,] *County of Yakima v. Confederated Tribes & Bands of the Yakima Indian Nation*, 502 U.S. 251, 268–69, (1992), and (2) a clear expression of Congressional intent is necessary before a court may construe a federal statute so as to impair tribal sovereignty, see *White Mountain Apache Tribe v. Bracker*, 448 U.S. 136, 143–44 (1980); *Santa Clara Pueblo v. Martinez*, 436 U.S. 49, 59–60 (1978). Moreover, *Tuscarora*'s statement is of uncertain significance, and possibly dictum, given the particulars of that case. Unlike the NLRA, the Federal Power Act at issue in *Tuscarora* included a specific limitation on eminent domain on Indian reservations. *See* 362 U.S. at 107 (noting that lands within a reservation could not be taken by eminent domain unless the Federal Power Commission found that the taking would "not interfere or be inconsistent with the purpose for which such reservation was created or acquired" (internal quotation marks omitted)). This limitation supported the inference that Congress intended in other circumstances to include Indians within the Federal Power Act's eminent domain provision. See id. at 118 ("[The Federal Power Act] neither overlooks nor excludes Indians or lands owned or occupied by them. Instead, as has been shown, the Act specifically defines and treats with lands occupied by Indians. . . . The Act gives every indication that, within its comprehensive plan, Congress intended to include lands owned or occupied by any person or persons, including Indians.").

Each of the cases petitioners cite in support of the principle that statutory ambiguities must be construed in favor of Indians (as well as the cases we have found supporting the principle) involved construction of a statute or a provision of a statute Congress enacted specifically for the benefit of Indians or for the regulation of Indian affairs. We have found no case in which the Supreme Court applied this principle of pro-Indian construction when resolving an ambiguity in a statute of general application.

With regard to the alternative principle relied on by petitioners, that a clear statement of Congressional intent is necessary before a court can construe a statute to limit tribal sovereignty, we can reconcile this principle with *Tuscarora* by recognizing that, in some cases at least, a statute of general application can constrain the actions of a tribal government without at the same time impairing tribal sovereignty.

Tribal sovereignty is far from absolute, ... An examination of Supreme Court cases shows tribal sovereignty to be at its strongest when explicitly established by a treaty, see, e.g., *McClanahan*, 411 U.S. at 173–75, or when a tribal government acts within the borders of its reservation, in a matter of concern only to members of the tribe, see, e.g., *White Mountain Apache Tribe*, 448 U.S. at 144; *Moe v. Confederated Salish & Kootenai Tribes*, 425 U.S. 463, 480–81 (1976). Examples of such intramural matters include regulating the status of tribe members in relation to one another, see *Fisher v. District Court*, 424 U.S. 382, 387–88 (1976); *United States v. Quiver*, 241 U.S. 602, 605–06 (1916), and determining tribe membership, see *Santa Clara Pueblo*, 436 U.S. at 71. Conversely, when a tribal government goes beyond matters of internal self-governance and enters into off-reservation business transaction with non-Indians, its claim of sovereignty is at its weakest. *Mescalero Apache Tribe v. Jones*, 411 U.S. 145, 148–49 (1973). In the latter situation, courts recognize the capacity of a duly established tribal government to act as an unincorporated legal person, engaging in privately negotiated contractual affairs with non-Indians, but the tribal government does so subject to generally applicable laws. *See, e.g., Niagara Mohawk Power Corp. v. Tonawanda Band of Seneca Indians*, 94 F.3d 747, 753 (2d Cir. 1996); *Gila River Indian Cmty. v. Henningson, Durham & Richardson*, 626 F.2d 708, 715 (9th Cir. 1980). The primary qualification to this rule is that the tribal government may be immune from suit. *See Kiowa Tribe v. Mfg. Techs., Inc.*, 523 U.S. 751, 754 (1998).

Many activities of a tribal government fall somewhere between a purely intramural act of reservation governance and an off-reservation commercial enter-prise. In such a case, the "inquiry [as to whether a general law inappropriately impairs tribal sovereignty] is not dependent on mechanical or absolute conceptions of . . . tribal sovereignty, but has called for a particularized inquiry into the nature of the state, federal, and tribal interests at stake." *White Mountain Apache Tribe*, 448 U.S. at 145. The determinative consideration appears to be the extent to which application of the general law will constrain the tribe with respect to its govern-mental functions. If such constraint will occur, then tribal sovereignty is at risk and a clear expression of Congressional intent is necessary. Conversely, if the general law relates only to the extra-governmental activities of the tribe, and in particular activities involving non-Indians, see generally *Reich v. Mashantucket Sand & Gravel*, 95 F.3d 174, 180–81 (2d Cir. 1996) ("[E]mployment of non-Indians weighs heavily against [a] claim that . . . activities affect rights of self-governance in purely intramural matters."), then application of the law might not impinge on tribal sovereignty. Of course, it can be argued any activity of a tribal government is by definition "governmental," and even more so an activity aimed at raising revenue that will fund governmental functions. Here, though, we use the term "governmental" in a restrictive sense to distinguish between the traditional acts governments perform and collateral activities that, though perhaps in some way related to the foregoing, lie outside their scope.

In sum, the Supreme Court's decisions reflect an earnest concern for maintaining tribal sovereignty, but they also recognize that tribal governments engage in a varied range of activities many of which are not activities we normally associate with governance. These activities include off-reservation fishing, investments in non-residential private property, and commercial enterprises that tend to blur any distinction between the tribal government and a private corporation. The Supreme Court's concern for tribal sovereignty distinguishes among the different activities tribal governments pursue, focusing on acts of governance as the measure of tribal sovereignty. The principle of tribal sovereignty in American law exists as a matter of respect for Indian communities. It recognizes the independence of these communities as regards internal affairs, thereby giving them latitude to maintain traditional customs and practices. But tribal sovereignty is not absolute autonomy, permitting a tribe to operate in a commercial capacity without legal constraint.

Of course, in establishing and operating the Casino, San Manuel has not acted solely in a commercial capacity. Certainly its enactment of a tribal labor ordinance to govern relations with its employees was a governmental act, as was its act of negotiating and executing a gaming compact with the State of California, as required by IGRA. *See* 25 U.S.C. § 2710(d)(3). Moreover, application of the NLRA to employment at the Casino will impinge, to some extent, on these governmental activities. Nevertheless, impairment of tribal sovereignty is negligible in this context, as the Tribe's activity was primarily commercial and its enactment of labor legislation and its execution of a gaming compact were ancillary to that commercial activity. The total impact on tribal sovereignty at issue here amounts to some unpredictable, but probably modest, effect on tribal revenue and the displacement of legislative and executive authority that is secondary to a commercial undertaking. We do not think this limited impact is sufficient to demand a restrictive construction of the NLRA.

Therefore, we need not choose between *Tuscarora*'s statement that laws of general applicability apply also to Indian tribes and *Santa Clara Pueblo*'s statement that courts may not construe laws in a way that impinges upon tribal sovereignty absent a clear indication of Congressional intent. Even applying the more restrictive rule of *Santa Clara Pueblo*, the NLRA does not impinge on the Tribe's sovereignty enough to indicate a need to construe the statute narrowly against application to employment at the Casino. First, operation of a casino is not a traditional attribute of self-government. Rather, the casino at issue here is virtually identical to scores of purely commercial casinos across the country. Second, the vast majority of the Casino's employees and customers are not members of the Tribe, and they live off the reservation. For these reasons, the Tribe is not simply engaged in internal governance of its territory and members, and its sovereignty over such matters is not called into question. Because applying the NLRA to San Manuel's Casino would not impair tribal sovereignty, federal Indian law does not prevent the Board from exercising jurisdiction. . . .

B

The second question before us, whether the term "employer" in the NLRA encompasses Indian tribal governments operating commercial enterprises, requires a much briefer analysis. The Board concluded the NLRA's definition of employer extended to San Manuel's commercial activities. Neither the text of the NLRA, nor any other reliable indicator of Congressional intent, indicates whether or not Congress specifically intended to include the commercial enterprises of Indian tribes when it used the term "employer." Therefore, Congress has not "directly spoken to the precise question at issue," *Chevron U.S.A. Inc. v. Natural Resources Defense Council*, 467 U.S. 837, 842 (1984), and the question is therefore one Congress has implicitly delegated to the Board for determination. Under these circumstances, the scope of our review is limited, the matter falling under step two of Chevron's analytical diptych. Id. at 842–43; see also *Yukon-Kuskokwim Health Corp. v. NLRB*, 234 F.3d 714, 717 (D.C. Cir. 2000) (applying *Chevron's* step two to the Board's interpretation of the term "employer" in the NLRA). Specifically, if the Board's interpretation is "a permissible construction of the statute," *Chevron*, 467 U.S. at 843, we must give that interpretation "controlling weight," *id.* at 844.

. . . Black's Law Dictionary defines employer as "[a] person who controls and directs a worker under an express or implied contract of hire and who pays the worker's salary or wages." BLACK'S LAW DICTIONARY 565 (8th ed. 2004). Under this generic definition of the term employer, we have no doubt it was reasonable for the Board to conclude the Tribe is an employer of its Casino workers. The Tribe does not suggest that it lacks control over these workers, or that it has no contract of hire with these workers, or that these workers are unpaid. Certainly, then, the Tribe is an employer in the ordinary sense of that term; indeed, the Tribe calls its Casino workers "employees" in its briefs filed in this court. Thus, the Tribe does not seriously contend it is not an employer; rather it contends it falls within one of the NLRA's listed exceptions.

Section 2(2) states that "[t]he term 'employer' . . . shall not include the United States or any wholly owned Government corporation, or any Federal Reserve Bank, or any State or political subdivision thereof, or any person subject to the Railway Labor Act, as amended from time to time, or any labor organization." 29 U.S.C. § 152(2). The Tribe asserts it falls within the exception for "any State or political subdivision thereof," calling this exception a "governmental exemption." *Cf. NLRB v. Pueblo of San Juan*, 276 F.3d 1186 (10th Cir. 2002) (tribal governments come within NLRA provision allowing states to enact right-to-work laws); *Reich v. Great Lakes Indian Fish & Wildlife Comm'n*, 4 F.3d 490 (7th Cir. 1993) (tribal police come within FLSA exemption for the police of state and local governments). The Tribe's argument is certainly plausible, but we cannot say the Board's more restrictive reading of the NLRA's government exception is not "a permissible construction of the statute," *Chevron*, 467 U.S. at 843. The exception is limited by its terms to state governments (and their political subdivisions), and we can hardly call it impermissible for an agency to limit a statutory phrase to its ordinary and plain meaning. In short, the Board could reasonably conclude that Congress's decision not to include an express exception for Indian tribes in the NLRA was because no such exception was intended or exists.

San Manuel argues, however, that nothing in the legislative history or text of the NLRA indicates a Congressional intent to apply the NLRA to tribal governments. *See NLRB v. Catholic Bishop*, 440 U.S. 490, 500 (1979) (in light of the constitutional avoidance canon, finding church-operated schools exempt because there was no indication of Congressional intent to extend NLRA to such schools); *McCulloch v. Sociedad Nacional de Marineros de Honduras*, 372 U.S. 10, 20–22 (1963) (in light of the "highly charged international circumstances" surrounding the case, finding foreign-flag ships exempt from NLRA because "for us to sanction the exercise of local sovereignty under such conditions in this delicate field of international relations there must be present the affirmative intention of the Congress clearly expressed" (internal quotation marks omitted)). This point is irrelevant in light of our conclusion above that the NLRA does not impinge on the Tribe's sovereignty enough to warrant construing the statute as inapplicable. In the absence of a presumption against application of the NLRA, the legislative history need not expressly anticipate every category of employer that might fall within the NLRA's broad definition.

San Manuel also argues Congress intended, by enacting IGRA, to give tribes and states a primary role in regulating tribal gaming activities, including labor relations, and that Congress therefore, by implication, foreclosed application of the NLRA to tribal gaming. Among other things, IGRA requires tribes that engage or intend to engage in "class III gaming" (the broad category of gaming at issue here) to negotiate, enter into, and comply with a compact between the tribe and the state in which the gaming will occur. *See* 25 U.S.C. § 2710(d)(1)(C), (3)(A). [This tribal-state compact may include provisions relating to any subjects "that are directly related to the operation of gaming activities." 25 U.S.C. § 2710(d)(3)(C).] The compact San Manuel entered into with the State of California specifically addresses labor relations, requiring San Manuel to adopt "an agreement or other procedure acceptable to the State for addressing organizational and representational rights of Class III Gaming Employees." San Manuel satisfied this requirement by enacting a detailed labor relations ordinance, which differs substantively from the NLRA.

In addition, IGRA makes class III gaming activities lawful on Indian lands only if authorized by a tribal ordinance or resolution approved by the Chairman of the National Indian Gaming Commission. *Id.* § 2710(d)(1)(A). To gain this approval, the ordinance or resolution must include several provisions, one of which [limits the uses of gaming revenues to five specific purposes.] *Id.* § 2710(b)(2)(B). . . .

San Manuel argues that IGRA, by authorizing tribes and states to enter into compacts addressing labor-relations issues and by mandating a tribal ordinance or resolution regulating gaming activities, contemplates tribal and state control over gaming and therefore implicitly restricts the scope of the NLRA. *Cf. FDA v. Brown & Williamson Tobacco Corp.*, 529 U.S. 120, 144 (2000) (a later-enacted, specific statute can "effectively ratif[y]" a narrow construction of an earlier-enacted, general statute).

We think San Manuel reads too much into IGRA. IGRA certainly permits tribes and states to regulate gaming activities, but it is a considerable leap from that bare fact to the conclusion that Congress intended federal agencies to have no role in regulating employment issues that arise in the context of tribal gaming. This is not a case in which Congress enacted a comprehensive scheme governing labor relations at Indian casinos, and then the Board sought to expand its jurisdiction into that field. *See id.* at 126. We find no indication that Congress intended to limit the scope of the NLRA when it enacted IGRA, and certainly nothing strong enough to render the Board's interpretation of the NLRA impermissible. *See Chevron*, 467 U.S. at 843.

In sum, the Board has given the NLRA a natural interpretation that falls within the range of interpretations the NLRA permits, and regardless of whether we think the Board's decision wise, we are without authority to reject it. *Id.*

The petition for review is *denied*, and the cross-application for enforcement is *granted*. So ordered.

NOTES ON INDIAN LAW CANONS OF CONSTRUCTION

1.   **Applying Canons of Treaty Construction:** As *Worcester* and *Mille Lacs* demonstrate, the Court has developed a set of rules of interpretation, *i.e.*, canons of construction, to formulate meaning within and between various treaties and other documents in Indian law. When interpreting Indian treaties and agreements, the courts historically relied on a number of maxims of interpretation: "[W]e will construe a treaty with the Indians as 'that unlettered people' understood it, and 'as justice and reason demand in all cases where power is exerted by the strong over those to whom they owe care and protection,' and counterpoise the inequality 'by the superior justice which looks only to the substance of the right without regard to technical rules.'" *United States v. Winans*, 198 U.S. 371, 380–81 (1905); *accord Choctaw Nation v. Oklahoma*, 397 U.S. 620, 631 (1970); *United States v. Shoshone Tribe*, 304 U.S. 111, 116 (1938); "Doubtful expressions are to be resolved in favor of the weak and defenseless people who are wards of the nation, dependent upon its protection and good faith." *Carpenter v. Shaw*, 280 U.S. 363, 367 (1930); *accord Winters v. United States*, 207 U.S. 564, 576–77 (1908); "[A] treaty was not a grant of rights to the Indians, but a grant of rights from them — a reservation of those not granted." *Washington v. Washington State Com. Passenger Fishing Vessel Ass'n*, 443 U.S. 658, 680 (1979); *accord United States v. Winans*, 198 U.S. 371, 381 (1905). Can the majority opinion in *Mille Lacs* be explained primarily by resort to these canons of construction? Do such rules seem to play the same role, or any role, for the dissenters? Notice the difference between the majority opinion's treatment of Article V as a right reserved by the Chippewa and the dissent's assertion that it was "granted" to them by the United States. Which approach is most consistent with *Worcester*? Significantly, reference to the canons of construction of Indian treaties and statutes, relied upon repeatedly in the majority opinion, were almost totally absent from the two dissents in *Mille Lacs*. Does that fact suggest that four members of the Supreme Court have almost completely abandoned reliance on such rules of interpretation or did it merely signal that such rules have little or no role to play where the Justices think the "plain language" of an executive order, treaty, or statute resolves the issue posed? What is the proper role of such canons of construction? Are they mainly to bolster the position of weaker bargainers in the treaty-making process, or are they designed to compensate for fundamental deficiencies in the justification for any exercise of federal power at all over

nonconsenting tribes? Which of these justifications is more likely to continue supporting application of the canons to a tribe that has been successful in economic development?

What should happen when a canon of Indian treaty construction comes into conflict with another canon, such as the canon providing that waivers of federal sovereign immunity should be strictly construed? This conflict is likely to recur, because many tribes seek redress for lands taken by the federal government, and typically these claims must be authorized by federal statute. Consider the following facts, not involving a land claim, but recently presented to the Federal Circuit. Two members of the Oglala Sioux Tribe were killed by a non-Indian, white man who was driving while intoxicated on the Pine Ridge Reservation. A treaty with the Sioux provided, "If bad men among the whites, or among other people subject to the authority of the United States, shall commit any wrong upon the person or property of the Indians, the United States will, upon proof made to the agent and forwarded to the Commissioner of Indian Affairs at Washington city, proceed at once to . . . reimburse the injured person for the loss sustained." The United States took the position that the treaty applies only to "bad men among the whites" who were employees or agents of the federal government (and hence "subject to the authority of the United States"), while the plaintiffs contended that anyone subject to U.S. law should be considered "subject to the authority of the United States." The United States also invoked the canon of interpretation requiring strict construction of waivers of federal sovereign immunity. Historical documents suggested that depredations by settlers as well as violent acts by U.S. agents and soldiers had generated conflicts with the tribes at the time the treaty was made. However, in the preceding 100 years, the only claims that had been actually brought under the treaty had been cases against federal employees, agents, or military. *See Richard v. United States*, 677 F.3d 1141 (Fed. Cir. 2012). Should such a claim against the United States be accepted?

2.   Canons of Statutory Construction: Since statutorily-ratified agreements replaced Indian treaties after Congress ended Indian treaty-making by statute in 1871, the canons of construction originally developed to interpret Indian treaties quickly also became applicable to statutes affecting Indians, both those approving Indian agreements and those later adopted unilaterally by Congress without tribal consent. Thus, the Supreme Court applied the canon requiring interpretation of doubtful expressions in favor of the Indians to cases involving interpretation of statutes ratifying agreements between the government and Indian tribes. *See, e.g., Choate v. Trapp*, 224 U.S. 665, 675–76, 78 (1912), *citing Jones v. Meehan*, 175 U.S. 1 (1899); *see also Antoine v. Washington*, 420 U.S. 194, 199–200 (1975) (statute ratifying agreement) (collecting cases). Ultimately, the Court came to recognize that the policies underlying federal Indian law also justified the application of special rules in interpreting Indian statutes. For example, the Supreme Court stated in *County of Oneida v. Oneida Indian Nation*, 470 U.S. 226, 247 (1985), "The canons of construction applicable in Indian law are rooted in the unique trust relationship between the United States and the Indians." When the Court has determined that a federal statute affecting Indians contains an ambiguity, it has historically demanded that ambiguous language be resolved in favor of Indians in order to protect the unique federal trust relationship with the Indian tribes. *See*

Mattz v. Arnett, 412 U.S. 481, 504–05 (1973) (clear statutory language needed to terminate reservation status); *Squire v. Capoeman*, 351 U.S. 1, 6–7 (1956) (federal tax inapplicable). The Supreme Court has also indicated that federal laws affecting Indians tribes and their members should be interpreted so as to minimize infringement on inherent tribal sovereignty, by "tread[ing] lightly in the absence of clear indications of legislative intent." *Santa Clara Pueblo v. Martinez*, 436 U.S. 49, 60 (1978). The federal courts have also applied the same canons of construction developed for Indian statutes to the interpretation of federal regulations directed toward Indian tribes and their members. *Jicarilla Apache Tribe v. Andrus*, 687 F.2d 1324 (10th Cir. 1982) (Secretary violated BIA regulations in notice procedures for oil and gas leases; doubts in interpretation of regulations should be resolved in favor of the tribe). Professor Richard Collins contends that the best justification for the statutory canons is the "democratic deficit," meaning the systematic and relative lack of political power of Indian nations in the American democratic process. Can support for this theory be found in the Supreme Court's references over time to the weak and defenseless position of tribes in relation to the United States? *See* Richard Collins, *Never Construed to Their Prejudice: In Honor of David Getches*, 84 U. COLO. L. REV. 1, 25–28 (2013).

Canons of statutory construction constitute effective tools for Indian advocates but frequently will not, by themselves, dispose of the case. Scholars have demonstrated that the process of interpreting federal statutes constitutes a dynamic, multi-variate process, not one governed by any single factor, or even by one overarching theory. *See* William J. Eskridge & Philip P. Frickey, *Statutory Interpretation as Practical Reasoning*, 42 STAN. L. REV. 321 (1990). In any particular case, where canons of Indian statutory construction are invoked, the Court may find a number of reasons to avoid or evade application of the traditional rules. For example, the canon simply may not apply. In *Northern Cheyenne Tribe v. Hollowbreast*, 425 U.S. 649, 655 n.7 (1976), a canon favoring Indian rights was found to give no guidance where "the contesting parties are an Indian tribe and a class of individuals consisting primarily of tribal members." Sometimes the Court may find that competing canons of statutory construction requiring strict construction in favor of some other interest, often involving state claims, may outweigh or obscure the possibility of application of a canon favoring Indian tribes. *See, e.g., Montana v. United States*, 450 U.S. 544 (1981) (treaty language did not overcome strong presumption in favor of state ownership of beds of navigable water); *United States v. Mitchell*, 445 U.S. 535, 538 (1980) (traditional rule requiring strict construction against waiver of federal sovereign immunity applied to defeat jurisdiction in the Court of Claims for Indian tribal and individual trust claims against the United States). By contrast, in *Mille Lacs*, the Court rejected application of the countervailing equal footing doctrine as a reason for limiting Indian treaty rights in contravention of the canons of construction of Indian treaties and statutes.

In addition, since the canons of statutory construction are designed to resolve ambiguity in favor of Indians, such rules favoring Indian tribes may not be invoked where the Court finds the statutory language unambiguous. *See, e.g., Amoco Prod. Co. v. Village of Gambell*, 480 U.S. 531, 555 (1987) (no ambiguity, therefore special canons not applicable). Indeed, the important threshold question of whether statutory language is sufficiently ambiguous to require resort to a canon favoring Indian tribes is often hotly debated between the majority and dissent, as it was in *Mille Lacs*. Similarly, in *South Carolina v. Catawba Indian Tribe*, 476 U.S. 498, 506 (1986), Justice Stevens, writing for the majority applied a general canon, the plain meaning rule, stating: "The canon of construction regarding the resolution of ambiguities in favor of Indians, however, does not permit reliance on ambiguities that do not exist; nor does it permit disregard of the clearly expressed intent of Congress." In a footnote the Court collected a number of cases making the same point. Mr. Justice Blackmun's dissent collected an equally imposing list of competing cases. He suggested that "the distinction smacks of the kind of semantic trap that this Court consistently has attempted to avoid when construing . . . statutes ostensibly passed for the benefit of Indians."

As Eskridge and Frickey note, the recent opinions of the Supreme Court display a tendency to oversimplify the factors involved in interpretation. As they put it, "Too often the Court's statutory interpretations ignore opposing arguments or treat them in a dismissive, mechanical fashion, typically in footnotes, and too rarely do they engage in an open dialogue that notes the virtues of various positions and explains why one of them is preferable." Eskridge & Frickey, *supra* at 371. Does that explain how the majority in *Mille Lacs* could find ambiguity in treaties and executive orders from which the dissenters derive a "plain meaning?" If the Justices themselves cannot agree that the statute has only one meaning, is it not clearly ambiguous? Do the dissenters in *Mille Lacs* follow that approach?

Nevertheless, as *Mille Lacs* suggests, federal courts sometimes still do engage in treaty, statutory, and executive order interpretation with sensitivity toward the underlying policies of Indian law and the canons of construction of Indian treaties and statutes. Where, as in *Mille Lacs*, such attention is paid to traditional rules of construction of Indian treaties and statutes, these canons of construction operate as powerful tools protecting Indian rights and interests. As Professor Richard Collins points out, the statutory canon has had much more purchase in suits where tribes oppose states or private interests, rather than the federal government. Collins, *supra*, at 20–44. For an illustration of the use of statutory canons to favor the tribe in a suit involving a private party, see *Santa Clara Pueblo v. Martinez*, 436 U.S. 49, 60 (1978), presented in Ch. 3, Sec. D.1.

Since federal Indian policy has evolved over time, courts frequently find themselves construing a federal statute passed in some prior era long after Congress has formally abandoned the policy that provoked the statute, albeit without formal repeal of the earlier statutory provision. Should intervening changes in federal Indian policy affect the construction of the statute? Should a court interpret such a statute only as the enacting Congress meant it to apply or should it tailor its interpretation to take account of intervening statutory and policy changes that affect the purposes of the statute without changing its precise terms? In *Bryan v. Itasca County*, 426 U.S. 373, 392 (1976), presented in Ch. 5, Sec. A.2, Minnesota argued that it had power to tax Indians living on reservations under a 1953 federal statute (Public Law 280), granting it

> jurisdiction over civil causes of action between Indians or to which Indians are parties which arise in the areas of Indian country listed . . . to the same

extent that such State . . . has jurisdiction over other civil causes of action, and those civil laws of such State . . . that are of general application to private persons or private property shall have the same force and effect within such Indian country as they have elsewhere within the State. . . .

This language might have been read as delegating to covered states the authority to impose their civil taxing and regulatory laws on reservation Indians. Neverthe-less, the Court rejected that construction and read the statutory language as a grant of adjudicatory jurisdiction only. In reaching that decision, the Court looked not only to the 1953 legislative history when the statute was first enacted but also the later legislative history of 1968 amendments to the legislation that did not affect the precise language at issue in *Bryan*. Was such resort to later congressional pronouncements appropriate? Was it required? According to Eskridge and Frickey:

> *Bryan* is a useful illustration of the way in which evolutive considerations are often the decisive ones in statutory interpretation. On the face of the statute, Minnesota probably had the better argument. There was appar-ently nothing very specific in the legislative history, but if the enacting Congress had been asked about the *Bryan* issue while it was considering Public Law 280, one would guess that the answer would have supported Minnesota as well. Indeed, it would be difficult to find a Congress in this century that seemed more animated by the desire to destroy tribal sovereignty. For in addition to enacting Public Law 280, the 1953 Congress adopted a concurrent resolution that created the federal policy of termi-nating the unique federal legal status — and thus the sovereignty — of Native American tribes.
>
> A legal-process purpose inquiry might also support Minnesota, since the purpose of Public Law 280 was to extend state authority over certain tribal Indians. These legislative intentions and purpose, however, became obso-lete within about five years. By the time *Bryan* made its way to the Supreme Court, the firmly established federal policy was to promote tribal sovereignty.

Eskridge & Frickey, *supra*, at 374–75. For a comprehensive treatment of interpre-tive issues in Indian law, see Philip P. Frickey, *Congressional Intent, Practical Reasoning, and the Dynamic Nature of Federal Indian Law*, 78 CAL. L. REV. 1137 (1990). Another context in which such questions have arisen in the interpretation of Indian statutes involves the reservation diminishment and termination cases, such as *Solem v. Bartlett*, set forth and discussed earlier in this chapter. Do these cases take the same approach to interpreting earlier statutes as that taken in *Bryan*? Should they do so?

3.   Canons of Construction and the Applicability of General Federal Stat-utes: One area in which questions of congressional intent frequently arise involves the applicability to Indian tribes of general federal regulatory or taxing statutes that are otherwise silent as to their reach into Indian country, such as the National Labor Relations Act involved in *San Manuel*. The cases in this area tend to be confusing because courts and litigants fail to analyze whether the application of the federal statute infringes upon a specific right guaranteed to Indians by treaty, statute, or otherwise. The origin of the issue traces to the decision in *Federal Power*

Comm'n v. Tuscarora Indian Nation, 362 U.S. 99 (1960), discussed in *San Manuel*. In affirming the right of utilities, acting under license from the Federal Power Commission, to condemn lands held by the Tuscarora Tribe for a power project, the Supreme Court majority stated bluntly, "general Acts of Congress apply to Indians as well as to others in the absence of a clear expression to the contrary." While those advocating application of broad national statutes to Indian country frequently quote this language in isolation, the decision in the case was actually far narrower and turned on unique facts. The Federal Power Act, 16 U.S.C. § 797(e), expressly placed some restrictions on the condemnation of reservation lands. The Tuscarora Nation, however, held title to its lands in fee simple. Moreover, the lands were not technically denominated a reservation under the limited definition of reservation included in the Federal Power Act. Thus, the Court concluded that the statute's specific protections for reservation land did not apply, and treated the Tuscarora Tribe like any other fee simple property owner. Its property could therefore be condemned for public works projects. Later cases analyzing *Tuscarora* have stressed the absence of a treaty promise to give the tribe any greater rights than normal property owners and the legislative history of the Power Act indicating that all Indian-owned property was not intended to be automatically immune from its provisions. *See, e.g., Escondido Mut. Water Co. v. La Jolla Band of Mission Indians*, 466 U.S. 765, 787 (1984).

The statement in *Tuscarora* that general laws do apply remains good law, but only as a statement of a general rule serving as a starting point for analysis. For reasons that will become more evident in Chapter 4, while Congress claims unilateral constitutional authority to abrogate Indian treaty rights, the prevailing cases indicate that it can only do so through a clear congressional statement that reflects an understanding of the prior existence of those rights and a specific intent to abrogate them. *United States v. Dion*, 476 U.S. 734 (1986). The reservation termination and diminishment cases such as *Solem v. Bartlett*, covered in Sec. A.3.b.iv, this chapter, illustrate that point. Thus, in analyzing the applicability of general federal laws to Indian country, one must first look for infringement on specific Indian rights. Where a federal law would infringe or abrogate existing Indian rights, courts require a clear and specific congressional intent to limit such rights in the general federal statute or its legislative history. In the absence of such an indication, courts hold the federal statute inapplicable to Indian tribes. Labor and employment law disputes have become a focal point for such analyses. *See, e.g., National Labor Relations Board v. Pueblo of San Juan*, 276 F.3d 1186 (10th Cir. 2002) (National Labor Relations Act did not prevent the Pueblo of San Juan from adopting a right to work ordinance); *Florida Paraplegic, Ass'n, Inc. v. Miccosukee Tribe of Indians of Florida*, 166 F.3d 1126 (11th Cir. 1999) (Americans with Disabilities Act did not permit suit against Indian tribe over inaccessibility of tribal restaurant). *But see Menominee Tribal Enters. v. Solis*, 601 F.3d 669 (7th Cir. 2010) (Occupational Safety and Health Act (OSHA) applied to sawmill owned and operated by Indian tribe notwithstanding claim of contrary treaty right).

By contrast, where no prior Indian rights are abrogated, the *Tuscarora* rule is often applied and the federal statutes made applicable to Indian country. *See, e.g., Yukon-Kuskokwim Health Corp. v. N.L.R.B.*, 234 F.3d 714 (D.C. Cir. 2000) (non-profit intertribal health corporation in Alaska where no treaties existed was not exempt from the National Labor Relations Act). The federal circuits have disagreed about whether a treaty exemption must be express in order to preclude application of a general federal law to a tribal activity. *Compare Confederated Tribes of Warm Springs Reservation v. Kurtz*, 691 F.2d 878 (9th Cir. 1982) (general federal excise tax applies to tribal sawmill since treaty silent on federal taxation), *with Lazore v. Commissioner*, 11 F.3d 1180 (3d Cir. 1993) (rejecting the view that exemptions must be express, but finding no exemption from federal income tax in the applicable treaties).

Judge Janice Brown's opinion in *San Manuel* is notable for its narrow view of tribal sovereign interests. Once the panel determines that no "activities we normally associate with governance" are involved, and that San Manuel's casino is largely a "commercial" venture, it easily dismisses the canons, whose very purpose is to protect tribes' sovereign interests. Was the *San Manuel* court correct to dismiss as "non-governmental" the only significant revenue source for the tribal government? Should it matter whether other governments raise revenue in the same fashion? Of course, many states operate lotteries, and the country of Monaco derives a considerable portion of its revenue from its casino operations. Should the court have given greater weight to the fact that San Manuel had a labor ordinance? Review the court's description of the facts in the case, and see whether it reflects some view that tribal sovereignty deserves protection only so long as tribes fit the stereotype of poor communities operating in some "traditional" fashion outside the market economy.

For a thorough critique of the D.C. Circuit's opinion, see Bryan Wildenthal, *Federal Labor Law, Indian Sovereignty, and the Canons of Construction*, 86 OREGON L. REV. 413 (2007). Wildenthal contends that the United States Supreme Court has actually abandoned the statements from *Tuscarora* that formed the foundation for the *San Manuel* decision, and that lower federal courts have been departing from Supreme Court practice when they disregard the canons. He also argues that the Supreme Court has been affording states considerable leeway to experiment with government programs that some may disparage as non-"traditional," and that tribes deserve the same freedom. The Summer, 2008 issue of the Michigan State Law Review is devoted to a symposium on labor law in Indian country. Many of the articles analyze the *San Manuel* decision, and suggest ways tribes can respond effectively to its holding. For example, if a tribe is actively regulating labor and employment on the reservation, is there a stronger argument available to the tribe that application of the NLRA will interfere with government functions — namely the regulation of such activities as Indian preference and worker strikes? Professor Collins states that any "democratic deficit" rationale for the canons applies less powerfully where federal statutes of general applicability are involved. Why might that be so? *See* Collins, *supra*, at 26–28.

4. Statutory Abrogation of Treaty Rights: Under the holding of *Lone Wolf v. Hitchcock*, 187 U.S. 553 (1903), discussed in Ch. 1, Sec. D.2, the federal government claims power to unilaterally abrogate prior Indian treaty rights by subsequent federal statutory action. One important check on that awesome power is a series of canons of interpretation that require a showing of clear congressional intent to abrogate or modify an Indian treaty right before any such abrogation or modification will be found by the courts. The prevailing decision on this issue is *United*

States v. Dion, 476 U.S. 734, 738–740 (1986), cited and relied upon in *Mille Lacs*, and presented in Ch. 4, Sec. A.2.

Chapter 3

TRIBAL SOVEREIGNTY AND ITS EXERCISE

In July 1996 the Mohawk Nation Council of Chiefs, based in New York, composed a letter to the National Chief of the Assembly of First Nations of Canada. The letter addressed recent constitutional reform efforts in Canada, which included some overtures by the First Nations that could have been interpreted as requests for inclusion in the Canadian federation. The Mohawk Nation Council of Chiefs used this letter to restate its understanding of Mohawk sovereignty.

> Our sovereignty exists. It cannot be removed or given away. . . . [W]e need to remove the yoke of oppression that occupying governments have tried to make us wear for centuries now.

> For the Kanienkehaka [Mohawk people], our legitimacy as a people comes from our Creator. That legitimacy is articulated in the Kaswentah [two-row wampum, a treaty made with the Dutch, later renegotiated with the English]:

>> We will not be like father and son, but like sisters and brothers. These two rows will symbolize vessels, travelling down the same river together. One will be for the canoe of the Onkwehonwe and their laws, their customs. The other will be for the sailing ship of the European people and their laws and customs. We will each travel the river together, but each in our own boat, and neither of us will try to steer the other's vessel.

> The fundamental principle accentuated in the Kaswentah is that we, as a people, have the right to make our own laws for our own people in our own territories, free from outside interference. This is not to say that we can do as we please, without regard for our neighbours. We do have a law — it is a law of the mind. Our law is the Kaianerekowa (The Great Law of Peace). Our people are the Kanienkehaka (People of Flint) and we call our territory Kanienkeh (Land of Flint). The Kaswentah is a living extension of our Kaianerekowa.

>> You have surely seen the Kaswentah. We know you are familiar with its meaning and importance to us and the relationship we have with our neighbours. The two purple rows are separated by three rows of white beads. These three rows also represent peace, respect and friendship — the principles by which we are to co-exist. The tri-lateral beads serve to keep us at a respectful distance of one another, so that we do not accidentally trip over one another or otherwise cause distress. The Kaswentah acknowledges the fact that we are different, as well as our respective right to be so.

Dagmar Thorpe, Executive Director of the Thakiwa Foundation, and Citizen of the Sac and Fox Tribe, has written:

> . . . If we are to look for a Native understanding of sovereignty, this can be understood within the way of life from which each of us emerges. A Shawnee elder explained,
>
>> It was understood that we recognized all peoples' right to their own existence. We recognized the right of each nation to live according to the instructions given to them. Although we might be in conflict with one another, the right of a people to their own existence was never questioned. We recognized one sovereign — the Creator. He has give us life, and we live by the Creator's good will. If we are to survive, we must recognize and live within His law. Our laws were created to keep our people within the framework of the Creator's laws. They were principles of behavior toward each other and all of creation. . . .
>
> If we permit our existence to be solely defined by Euro-American law, we give the United States power to define who we are and who we are not. If we follow the original instructions given to our people, then no one has the right to seize, define, or diminish the sovereignty of our people because this sovereignty comes from a higher power. If we follow the Euro-American definition, we submit to the will of a government which was conceived with the intention to destroy our ways of life. . . .
>
> As Native American people, we view things in spiritual and physical dimensions. When we speak of sovereignty from a native perspective, this is not limited to the physical boundaries of our reservations. The concept of sovereignty encompasses all of those things which represent our lives as Thakiwaki — spiritual, emotional, mental, and physical. We can influence but cannot control those things external to us. They belong to the other world. However, we have the collective responsibility to manage the internal boundaries of our reservations. . . .
>
> If we are to strengthen and protect our sovereignty in the fullest sense of the word, then we must stand once again with the Creator's law. . . .

Dagmar Thorpe, *Sovereignty, A State of Mind: A Thakiwa Citizen's Viewpoint*, 23 Am. Indian L. Rev. 481, 481–84 (1998–99).

Note how the Mohawk Nation Council of Chiefs and Dagmar Thorpe describe the source of Native nations' sovereignty. Does that sovereignty depend for its existence on any act of the United States? How do these excerpts characterize the scope and operation of sovereign powers of Indian nations? Is it possible simultaneously to call Indian nations "sovereign" and to acknowledge that the United States can limit some tribal powers or exercise some independent authority within tribal territories? In what ways, if any, has the tribal-federal relationship affected how Indian nations express or act upon their sovereignty? These are the questions addressed in Chapter 3.

A. MODERN TRIBAL GOVERNMENTS

1. Tribal Constitutions and Courts

If we understand constitutions as setting forth a community's fundamental and stable rules regarding government organization and behavioral norms, then Indian nations have always had constitutions. These constitutions differ from the American constitution in being passed down orally or through pictographs such as wampum belts. They also trace their legitimacy to sacred narratives, often associated with creation or with hero figures, rather than to self-conscious "social compacts" among citizens. Nevertheless, they perform the same functions of establishing government order, identifying the responsibilities and rights of individuals, regulating external relations, and pronouncing basic social norms. Indeed, there is a lively debate among historians about the extent to which tribal constitutions influenced the shape of the Articles of Confederation and the United States Constitution. *See generally* DONALD A. GRINDE & BRUCE E. JOHANSEN, EXEMPLAR OF LIBERTY: NATIVE AMERICA AND THE EVOLUTION OF DEMOCRACY 22, 24, 27–32 (1991) (describing the governmental structure of the Haudenosaunee Confederacy and demonstrating its influence on the emergence of the United States confederated government).

As the newly formed United States established treaty relations with Indian nations and later attempted to assimilate Indian people into the American social, political, and economic system, federal policy-makers focused their attention on transforming the governmental systems of Indian nations. To extract treaty concessions and natural resources from Indian nations, federal officials needed tribal leaders who could control their people and make binding decisions. Consensus-based, decentralized tribal governments, such as the Iroquois, did not lend themselves to such dealings. In the early nineteenth century Thomas Jefferson urged Indian tribes to westernize their governments if they wanted to survive. During the nineteenth century, a small handful of tribes, such as the so-called Five Tribes (Cherokee, Choctaw, Chickasaw, Muscogee, and Seminole) and the Seneca Nation of New York, followed that advice and, without any coercion from the federal government, adopted western forms of government, usually including written tribal constitutions, written laws, police and courts of record. *See generally* RENNARD STRICKLAND, FIRE AND THE SPIRITS: CHEROKEE LAW FROM CLAN TO COURT (1982). Thus, an indigenous tradition of tribal constitutions and written law began to emerge in the nineteenth century.

To administer unpopular federal policies such as settlement onto reservations and compulsory boarding school attendance, federal officials needed simple, tractable decision-making bodies. Consensus decision-making and the complex system of checks and balances practiced by tribes such as the Iroquois only frustrated the implementation of such policies. And the traditional leadership chosen under the old constitutions did not usually support federal aims. After resistance to federal relocation and reservation policies had been quelled, the federal government first tried to displace traditional Indian tribal governance and to replace it with a colonial puppet government ostensibly responsible to the Bureau of Indian Affairs and, in particular, the reservation superintendent. Thus, commencing in 1883, the Bureau imposed the Court of Indian Offenses and the Indian Police on perhaps two-thirds of the reservations. This involved efforts to coopt tribal members to govern the reservation under the direction of *federal* personnel. In order to protect their members from this new effort by the federal government to control and punish Indian people, some tribal leaders, such as the Comanche leader (and alleged founder of the Native American Church) Quannah Parker, actually became judges of the Court of Indian Offenses, perhaps in order to subvert its colonial impact on their people. In any event for approximately a half-century between the formation of the Court of Indian Offenses and the emergence of the New Deal, federal policy sought to replace traditional Indian governance in favor of colonial institutions formally staffed by tribal members but actually controlled by Bureau of Indian Affairs officials. Thus, the goal, while retaining distinctive jurisdictional and governing structures for Indian country, was to substitute federal for tribal control of native institutions. During this half-century the federal Indian service increasingly came to see itself as the primary government in Indian country. Not all reservations were so affected, and perhaps the most notable exceptions to this policy were the Pueblos of New Mexico, which retained their traditional governing structures traceable to both Native and Spanish roots.

a.   Emergence of Modern Written Tribal Constitutions

Some tribes such as the Crow Nation and the Rosebud Sioux tried to respond to late nineteenth and early twentieth century federal usurpation of their governing authority by adopting their own written governing documents. Thus, even before the enactment of the Indian Reorganization Act of 1934, a small indigenous movement was underway in Indian country to take governing authority back from federal officials through the process of constitution making.

With the issuance of the 1928 Merriam Report by the Brookings Institution declaring the allotment policy a resounding failure, the stage was set for a major change in the nature of Indian governance. The election of the President Franklin Delano Roosevelt in 1932 and the initiation of the New Deal brought with it a new Indian Commissioner, John Collier, with new and radical ideas. Having worked with and on behalf of Pueblo people during the 1920s, Collier had seen effective Indian governing institutions. He was determined to bring economic development to Indian country and to return the primary governance of Indian country to hands of the Indians themselves. Furthermore, to facilitate intergovernmental relations and non-Indian business ventures on reservations, federal officials needed written documents with official standing. Oral traditions would not be accessible to the outside world. Consequently, remaking tribal constitutions became a deliberate federal policy, achieved most fully in the Indian Reorganization Act of 1934, 25 U.S.C. § 461 et seq., commonly known as the IRA.

As originally conceived by John Collier, the IRA would have tailored each tribal constitution to the culture and traditions of the tribe utilizing the services of an ethnology bureau proposed in the legislation; proposed turning over management of federally administered Indian programs to the tribes; contemplated tribally-created trial courts; and created a federally-created, pan-tribal Indian Court of Appeals to centrally hear appeals from the separate tribally created judiciaries.

Efforts to turn over the management of federal Indian programs to the tribes did not become part of the final legislation and did not come to fruition until Congress passed the Indian Self-Determination and Educational Assistance Act of 1975, Public Law 93-638, which first created such a process now commonly known as "638 contracting." The removal of both the Bureau of Ethnology and the Indian Court of Appeals from the bill during the legislative process had profound long-term impacts on tribal governance.

As finally enacted, the IRA contained a set of provisions designed to end allotment, rebuild the Indian landbase, facilitate Indian economic development, and rebuild tribal governmental and business institutions. For tribes which approved the legislation, section 1, codified in current form at 25 U.S.C. § 461, ended all future allotments for tribes that approved the Act. Section 2, codified in current form at 25 U.S.C. § 462, authorized (but did not require) restoration of unsold surplus land and section 5, codified in current form at 25 U.S.C. § 465, authorized the purchase (or in some cases, more accurately, repurchase) of lands to Indian tribes. Lands so acquired could be declared either new reservations or additions to existing reservations under section 7, codified in current form at 25 U.S.C. § 467. For present purposes, by far the most important parts of the IRA are sections 16 and 17, codified in current form at 25 U.S.C. §§ 476–477, which respectively authorize the Secretary of the Interior to approve for tribes that adopted the IRA tribal governmental constitutions and tribal articles of incorporation. The contemplated conceptual separation of tribal business into *separate* governmental and business entities, while reflecting western conceptions of expected business models, did not comport with most tribal notions of how to conduct business and therefore the expected separation of governmental and business affairs generally never occurred in Indian country even if the tribe adopted both a section 16 tribal constitution and a section 17 charter of incorporation. While tribes vary greatly, generally, in tribes that adopted the IRA, the tribal government, organized under section 16 of the IRA, rather than a tribal corporation organized under section 17, conducts most business affairs, including the operation of tribal gaming, mineral, or timber operations.

As originally enacted, the IRA expressly provided that none of its provisions would apply if a majority of adult Indians vote against its application. 25 U.S.C. § 478. Originally, this meant that for tribes which rejected the IRA, not only would there be no recognized tribal constitution or articles of incorporation, but also no economic development programs, no end to allotment, no land reacquisition programs, and the like. In 1935, that provision was amended to lower the requirement to a "majority of those actually voting," thereby effectively counting as "yes" votes any Indians who exercised common traditional prerogatives to vote with their feet, *i.e.*, intending to vote "no" by refusing to cooperate with the process and staying away from the polls.

The process of adopting written tribal constitutions quickly swung into high gear after enactment of the IRA, with the Bureau of Indian Affairs providing technical assistance to the tribes in the form of model IRA boiler-plate constitutions, many of which were adopted virtually verbatim with few, if any, changes. Review section 16 of the IRA, 25 U.S.C. § 476, and consider how much actual direction it supplies regarding the content of any tribal constitution and the structure of IRA governments. Are most of the constitutional structural questions dictated by federal law or choices made by tribal communities, albeit often at the urging of federal officials, ostensibly providing technical assistance? Does the IRA require any particular form of government beyond mandating democratic approval of the constitution?

According to one study:

> During the two-year period within which tribes could accept or reject the IRA, 258 elections were held. In these elections, 181 tribes (129,750 Indians) accepted the Act and 77 tribes (86,365 Indians, including 45,000 Navajos) rejected it. The IRA also applies to 14 groups of Indians who did not hold elections to exclude themselves. Within 12 years, 161 constitutions and 131 corporate charters had been adopted pursuant to the IRA.

Comment, *Tribal Self-Government and the Indian Reorganization Act of 1934*, 70 MICH. L. REV. 955 (1972). The nation's largest Indian tribe, the Navajo Nation, voted to reject the IRA for a variety of reasons, most notably perhaps because of then-prevailing hostility to federal Indian policy caused by recent stock reduction efforts that economically decimated and demoralized the Navajo population. To this day, the Navajo Nation operates without a written tribal constitution, like certain other nations without entrenched constitutional documents such as Great Britain, New Zealand and Israel. Some other tribes, like the traditional members of the Haudenosaunee Confederacy in upstate New York, operate with traditional constitutional structures without formalizing written constitutions. Several smaller but economically successful California Indian nations, such as the Viejas Band of Kumeyaay Indians, also lack written constitutions, describing themselves as "customs and traditions" tribes. Unlike the Navajo and the Haudenosaunee, most tribes in the continental United States today operate with written tribal constitutions, most approved under the IRA, but some, like the constitutions of the Cherokee or Crow Nations, adopted outside of the regime of the IRA. Since the IRA by its express terms did not apply to the Oklahoma tribes, *see* 25 U.S.C. § 473, many of the Oklahoma tribal constitutions were approved and adopted outside of the IRA structure. Many of the tribal constitutions can be found online at http://thorpe.ou.edu/const.html.

Today approximately 161 tribes have adopted IRA constitutions, and at least 75 tribes have non-IRA constitutions. Can an Indian nation that once "accepted" the IRA simply abandon its organization under that Act, and reconstitute itself with a non-IRA constitution or without any constitution at all? Several tribes, such as the Yankton Sioux, the Fallon Paiute Shoshone, and the Miccosukke of Florida, have done just that, substituting a non-IRA constitution for one adopted under its terms. What legal and/or practical difference does it make that a tribe is organized under the IRA? Do IRA tribes have more or less ability to govern themselves? Does organization under the IRA protect Indian nations against state efforts to assert concurrent jurisdiction over non-Indians on reservations? Does it enhance the case for tribal jurisdiction over non-Indians?

Current conflicts within one of the tribes of the Haudenosaunee Confederacy, the St. Regis Mohawk Tribe, illustrate the challenges facing Indian nations as they navigate between traditional forms of government and constitutional forms more closely resembling federal and state governments. *Tarbell v. DOI*, 307 F. Supp. 2d

409 (N.D.N.Y. 2004), addresses the question whether the Department of the Interior should recognize the results of a disputed St. Regis tribal referendum designed to replace the traditional three-chief system of governance with a constitution. The court found that the agency actions in question were not the product of a considered analysis of the leadership dispute, but instead resulted from a misconception that the agency had been ordered by another court to reject the plaintiff traditional chiefs' position, and thus granted plaintiffs' motion to vacate and remand the matter to the Department of the Interior for further proceedings consistent with its position. Notably, the court stated that "[t]he question of Indian governance is a matter properly entrusted to each particular tribe and, to the extent that they may exist, the tribal courts. Despite this indisputable core precept, however, the question of who the federal government should recognize for purposes of its dealings with a tribe as duly authorized leaders is properly within the province of the BIA."

While many assume that the IRA prescribed a particular form of governance since the tribal constitutions originally drafted with BIA assistance looked quite similar to one another, the IRA contained no such provisions. The defeat of Collier's proposal for a bureau of ethnologists to assist tribes in assuring that their constitutions were adapted to their cultures meant that little federal assistance was provided in assuring the cultural and historical relevance of the form of government selected in IRA constitutions. Instead, federal technical advisors relied upon model documents drafted in Washington, D.C. This fact tended to produce boilerplate tribal constitutions containing remarkable similarities. While very few of those similarities are required by the IRA or any other provisions of federal law, they nevertheless found their way into tribal constitutions. Felix S. Cohen, author of the seminal HANDBOOK OF FEDERAL INDIAN LAW (1942), was the attorney in the Interior Department responsible for implementation of the IRA. Professor David Wilkins has recently published Cohen's memorandum directing this effort, adding valuable commentary and context. ON THE DRAFTING OF TRIBAL CONSTITUTIONS BY FELIX S. COHEN (D. Wilkins, ed., 2007).

While it is fashionable to suggest that the IRA had supplanted traditional tribal governance in favor of models derived from federal and state constitutions, close analysis of both history and the original IRA constitutional documents suggests serious flaws with this assumption. First, for many tribes, traditional tribal governance had been at least driven underground if not ended as a result of the allotment era policies for the half-century preceding enactment of the IRA. Second, while some similarities exist, the structure of most of the original IRA constitutions differs markedly from the structure of most state and federal constitutions.

While the IRA certainly first introduced to many tribes the idea of representative tribal government with majority rule (displacing tribal direct participatory government, leadership by elders and consensus decision-making), most of the similarities between the original IRA constitutions and state and federal documents stop at that level of generality. Unlike state and federal constitutions, most of the original IRA constitutions had no separation of powers. All of the sovereign power of the tribe frequently was vested in an elected multimember tribal council. In most instances, the tribal counsel members were elected at large, although districted elections were chosen instead in some larger tribes. While the IRA constitutions invariably created some sort of legislative branch (often called the tribal or business council), the bicameralism found in federal and state constitutional models was totally lacking. In most IRA constitutions, the tribal chair was simply the presiding officer of the tribal council, selected by the council members, but in some tribes a separate election for tribal chair was prescribed. The tribal chair commonly was the presiding officer of the tribal council and, less commonly, was expressly granted some executive and administrative responsibilities. More commonly, tribes operating IRA constitutions administratively appointed a chief administrative officer thereby effectively creating a form of government more closely mirroring what is commonly called a city manager form of municipal government than anything found in federal or state constitutions. Unlike federal and state constitutions, many of the original IRA constitutions lacked any bill of rights. Perhaps reflecting the traditions of direct democracy of many tribes, the IRA constitutions relied far more heavily on provisions for referendum, initiative, and recall to keep government in check and protect rights than the federal or most state constitutions. Finally, while some of the original IRA constitutions expressly authorized the tribal council to create tribal courts, almost none of the original documents created a constitutionally separate judicial branch, as is found in federal and state constitutions. Thus, while the IRA introduced western ideas of representative majoritarian government to Indian country, in some, but not all, cases for the first time, the forms of government implemented under the IRA actually were not directly modeled on federal and state plans, as often claimed.

Not all of the original IRA tribal constitutions were boilerplate documents derived from model federal documents. A few tribes, like the Hopi Tribe, secured assistance of elders and ethnology experts and attempted to craft written tribal documents that reflected the cultural and historic realties of their tribal identity. In the case of the Hopi, a leading ethnologist named Oliver LaFarge assisted in the drafting of the 1936 Hopi Constitution. That document, unlike many of the IRA boilerplate constitutions, carefully tried to constitutionalize the federated nature of Hopi life, allocating powers between a central Hopi Tribal Council and the separate villages. The constitution tried to allocate authority between the central government and the villages, much like the United States Constitution does between the federal government and the states. Many of the villages were then and are now governed by traditional religious leaders, the Kikmongwi. Under Article III, section 3 of the 1936 Hopi Constitution, "Each village shall decide for itself how it shall be organized. Until a village shall decide to organize in another manner, it. shall be considered as being under the traditional Hopi organization and the Kikmongwi of such village shall be recognized as its leader." Furthermore, Article IV divided up representation in the Tribal Council among the nine Hopi villages and provided in section 4 that "[e]ach village shall decide for itself how it shall choose its representatives. . . . Representatives shall be recognized by the Council only if they are certified by the Kikmongwi of their respective villages. Certifications may be made in writing or in person." Despite the careful attention the Hopis and LaFarge lavished on crafting a culturally appropriate document, many of the Hopi traditional religious leaders originally rejected the document and voted with their feet, refusing the vote, participate, or certify winners. As a consequence, Hopi central governance gradually fell into the hands of nontraditional Hopis, some of whom eventually agreed in 1967 to a very controversial lease to strip mine for coal an area known as Black Mesa, which contained sacred sites for traditional Hopis. Eventually, many traditional Hopis recognized the importance of the IRA government and reclaimed their important role in it.

For surveys of the enactment and implementation of the IRA, see GRAHAM D. TAYLOR, THE NEW DEAL AND AMERICAN INDIAN TRIBALISM: THE ADMINISTRATION OF THE INDIAN REORGANIZATION ACT, 1934–45 (1980); INDIAN SELF RULE: FIRST-HAND ACCOUNTS OF INDIAN-WHITE RELATIONS FROM ROOSEVELT TO REAGAN (K. Philp ed., 1986). The IRA encountered opposition from both ends of the political spectrum. The right condemned it as collectivist legislation. *See, e.g.*, Hearings on S. 2103 Before the Committee on Indian Affairs, House of Representatives, 76th Cong., 3d Sess. (1940). The left attacked it for perpetuating federal domination. According to southern California Cahuilla leader Rupert Costo:

> The IRA was the last great drive to assimilate the American Indian. It was also a program to colonialize the Indian tribes. . . . Colonialization of the tribes was to be accomplished through communal enclaves subject to federal domination through the power of the secretary of the interior. . . .
>
> All one must do is to read and study the hearings held in the Congress, the testimony of Indian witnesses, the evidence of life itself, the statements of the Indian commissioner, and the practically identical tribal constitutions adopted by, or forced upon, the Indians under the IRA. In these constitutions the authority of the secretary of the interior is more powerful than it was before the so-called New Deal. No wonder the Indians called it the Indian Raw Deal. The IRA did not allow the Indians their independence, which was guaranteed in treaties and agreements and confirmed in court decisions. It did not protect their sovereignty. Collier did not invent self-government: the right of Indians to make their own decisions, to make their own mistakes, to control their own destiny. The IRA had within it, in its wording and in its instruments, such as the tribal constitutions, the destruction of the treaties and of Indian self-government.

Philip at 48. Notwithstanding these criticisms, others have defended the IRA as laying the foundation for rebuilding tribal governments after years of federal domination. *See, e.g.*, VINE DELORIA, JR. & CLIFFORD M. LYTLE, AMERICAN INDIANS, AMERICAN JUSTICE 101 (1983).

To outsiders, tribal constitutions seem to describe the governing systems for reservations, and tribal councils are the most visible power structures. But the flip side of the weak institutionalization of IRA and similar tribal governments is the strength of other social control mechanisms within Indian country. Religious organizations, age and kinship groups, and social clubs may all exert independent pressure on tribal members' conduct. In turn, a tribal member's standing in the community and participation in these cultural social control mechanisms is often an important factor in getting elected to political office.

Today, the major difference between IRA and non-IRA tribes is the requirement that IRA constitutions be ratified by a majority of tribal members at an election called by the Secretary of the Interior, and that the Secretary approve the constitutions, by-laws, and all amendments. 25 U.S.C. § 476. Although the Secretary claims the power under 25 U.S.C. § 2 to approve constitutions of non-IRA tribes as well, there is no requirement that the Secretary do so. *See* S. REP. No. 577, 100th Cong., 2d Sess. 35 (1988).

As originally enacted, the IRA offered certain benefits limited to tribes that organized under its terms, such as access to revolving loan funds (25 U.S.C. § 470), taking of land into trust (25 U.S.C. § 465), and formation of federally chartered business corporations (25 U.S.C. § 477). However, Congress and the courts have subsequently extended these benefits to non-IRA tribes as well. For example, Congress has consolidated several Indian revolving loan funds, including the fund authorized in the IRA, into a single fund available to all tribes. 25 U.S.C. § 1461. In 1990, Congress amended the IRA by adding section 478-1, which states that the power to form federally chartered business corporations shall extend to all Indian tribes. Other provisions were made applicable to non-IRA tribes by other legislation. Finally, Congress has adopted a general policy against differential treatment of Indian nations, directing that agencies of the United States shall not promulgate any regulation or make any decision or determination pursuant to the IRA or any other federal legislation with respect to a federally recognized tribe that "classifies, enhances, or diminishes the privileges and immunities available" to that tribe relative to others. 25 U.S.C. § 476(f).

The Secretarial approval power over tribal constitutions and amendments initially served to produce tribal constitutions in keeping with Secretarial rather than tribal visions of proper government. It also worked to maintain the regulatory duties of the Bureau. The following memorandum from the Solicitor for the Department of the Interior on the proposed constitution of the Puyallup Tribe, dating from 1936, illustrates these functions, and also reflects the Bureau's concern that tribal governments be organized so that they can work efficiently with the federal bureaucracy. The Puyallup Constitution, said the Solicitor,

> confers very large powers over tribal affairs and individual conduct on a small council of five members. . . . There is no provision in this constitution for general meetings . . . or for the submission to a referendum.
>
> It seems to me that this set-up is very likely to produce a council that is not truly representative of the reservation. If this should happen the Department would find itself in conflict either with the Indians of the reservation or with the council, with no way provided for ironing out differences between the council and the members of the tribe. This danger is likely to be serious since experience shows that one of the most serious weaknesses of Indian tribal government in the past has been the susceptibility of tribal authorities to improper outside influences in connection with the disposition of tribal property. Setting up a small body of five individuals with power to act in matters affecting tribal property without any consultation or review by the tribe at large, and granting to these five individuals three years' tenure of office without possibility of recall or removal except by a vote of four out of five of the council members themselves, all has the effect, I am afraid, of making the tribe and its property easy prey for hunters. . . .
>
> . . . In addition to the foregoing criticisms the suggested structure of local government is undemocratic and defective, I think, in that it permits a

minority of two members in the council of five to obstruct any action at all, without any possible recourse, merely by absenting themselves from a meeting. I would suggest that the provision requiring the presence of four members of the council for the transaction of business be replaced by the more usual provision recognizing a majority of the members as a quorum.

The foregoing impediments to a satisfactory relationship between the Department and the Puyallup Indians are aggravated by the provision that the council of five, with whom all departmental business must be transacted, is to meet regularly only four times a year. Many activities of the department in the future will have to be submitted to this council for comment or for approval and the three months' delay between council meetings will very definitely slow up the work of the Department in handling various pressing matters. On the large Sioux reservations, where it is difficult for representatives of scattered communities to come together and where most of the activities of the Indians along lines of self-government will be within the separate communities, quarterly meetings may be quite satisfactory. It is dangerous, I think, to transfer such a provision to a small unified reservation such as Puyallup. At least the Indians should be warned of the magnitude of the tasks they are undertaking and advised that this business can be transacted more efficiently, with fewer complaints, if the period between regular meetings is shortened.

Is the Solicitor demonstrating more concern for the needs of the Puyallup Tribe in light of its traditional methods of social-political organization, or for the expectations and needs of the federal government?

IRA constitutions were not the product of grass roots constitutional conventions that might have captured the knowledge and values of tribal people. In the early years of administration of the IRA, most tribes were unfamiliar with the format of written constitutions, and the Secretary took this opportunity to provide tribes with strongly worded recommendations and standard boilerplate documents. In a document entitled "Basic Memorandum on Drafting of Tribal Constitutions," which Felix Cohen wrote some time in 1934, he states that "For the present, the Indian Office will not furnish tribes with 'model constitutions.'" Cohen notes that even if a tribe adopted such a model, it "would be only an adopted child and not the natural offspring of Indian hearts and minds." But the same memorandum delivers detailed direction on constitutional design as well as draft provisions. For examples of what have been called "boilerplate" IRA constitutions, see COLORADO STATE COLLEGE, MUSEUM OF ANTHROPOLOGY, CHARTERS, CONSTITUTIONS, AND BY-LAWS OF THE INDIAN TRIBES OF NORTH AMERICA (Occasional Publications on Anthropology, Ethnology Series (G. Fay ed., 1967)). These nearly identical draft constitutions created simple one-branch governments amenable to Bureau control, and contained provisions requiring Secretarial approval of tribal laws and regulations. Such features of the standard IRA constitution have impeded tribal self-government and economic development. The lack of fit between constitutional structure and basic patterns of community decision-making and accountability has led one commentator to describe IRA governments as "poorly institutionalized," meaning that the governments are not the objects of peoples' political loyalties, tribal members lack internal commitments to the constitutional rules and procedures, and have not accepted the secular nature of constitutional governments. The consequences of such weakly internalized political systems have included political instability, abuse of power, and social conflict. Duane Champagne, *American Indian Values and the IRA Governments, in* AMERICAN INDIAN POLICY AND CULTURAL VALUES: CONFLICT AND ACCOMMODATION (J. Joe ed., 1986). In addition, the Secretarial veto power over ordinances, discussed below, has sapped tribal initiative and handed decision-making power to bureaucrats who have no stake in the decisions. As a result, Secretarial rather than tribal control is associated with reservation poverty and other social ills. Stephen Cornell & Joseph P. Kalt, *Sovereignty and Nation-Building: The Development Challenge in Indian Country Today*, 22:3 AM. IND. CULTURE & RESEARCH J. 187, 207–212 (1998).

In recent years, some IRA tribes have attempted to redesign their constitutional structures to match their community organization, to establish more effective checks and balances, and to eliminate the Secretary's approval power. See Ch. 1, Sec. A.2, presenting portions of the Crow Tribe's Constitution, and this section, *infra*. Is there any basis upon which the Secretary could refuse to approve a constitutional amendment that removed secretarial review of tribal ordinances or reconstituted the government in a more traditional way?

At first, the Secretary thwarted these efforts to revise IRA constitutions by delaying calls for tribal ratification elections until the Bureau carried out a pre-election clearance process. This same obstacle confronted newly recognized or "unterminated" tribes that wanted to adopt constitutions. In *Coyote Valley Band of Pomo Indians v. United States*, 639 F. Supp. 165 (E.D. Cal. 1986), the court found that the preclearance process was not authorized by the IRA and was thus arbitrary and capricious in violation of the Administrative Procedure Act. It also ordered the Secretary to call an election within a reasonable time after request from the Tribe. Two years later, Congress modified the IRA to facilitate and expedite the process for establishing and amending tribal constitutions. The new provision sets deadlines for ratification elections once the Secretary has received a tribal request, and requires the Secretary to hold the election even if the Secretary finds that the proposed provision is "contrary to applicable laws." 25 U.S.C. § 476(c). During the period preceding the tribal ratification election, the Secretary must provide technical assistance to the tribe, and must give the tribe at least 30 days' written notice of any grounds for finding the provision contrary to law. Once the constitution or amendment has been ratified, the Secretary must approve or disapprove within 45 days, and may only disapprove upon a finding "that the proposed constitution, and bylaws or any amendments are contrary to applicable laws." 25 U.S.C. § 476(d). Any finding by the Secretary as to the legality of a proposed tribal document may be challenged in federal court.

These new provisions of the IRA do not offer much guidance to the Secretary in deciding whether to approve a constitution, referring only to "applicable laws." Nonetheless, either because of the threat of litigation or because of a change in Secretarial policies regarding tribal constitutions, many Indian nations have been successful in revising their constitutions to delete the Secretary's veto power over tribal ordinances. The Interior Board of Indian Appeals within the Department of the Interior has concluded that "in reviewing IRA constitutions or amendments, BIA must . . . seek to avoid unnecessary interference with tribal self-government," and "where the tribe's constitutional amendment is subject to a construction which would avoid conflict with [a] Solicitor's memorandum, and where there is not at present a definitive ruling in federal court that the tribe lacks authority [to do what is specified in a proposed constitutional amendment, the] BIA's duty to respect tribal self-government requires that it approve the amendment." *Cheyenne River Sioux Tribe v. Aberdeen Area Director, Bureau of Indian Affairs*, IBIA 92-218-A (June 15, 1993), 20 IND. L. REP. 7065, 7068–69; *see also* Timothy W. Joranko & Mark C. Van Norman, *Indian Self-Determination at Bay: Secretarial Authority to Disapprove Tribal Constitutional Amendments*, 29 GONZ. L. REV. 81 (1993–94).

Would you advise a newly recognized tribe to organize under the IRA? Are there symbolic considerations as well as practical ones in making such a decision?

Drafting and amending constitutions is a high priority for Indian nations today. The increased economic development potential on reservations has created a need for greater stability and certainty in government. Furthermore, tribal governments need to accommodate the complexities of expanding jurisdiction, increased responsibilities under federal law, growing budgets and bureaucracies, new types of disputes, and community demands for more traditional governing forms.

Two modern constitutions by IRA tribes illustrate how Indian nations are breaking out from the old boilerplate documents: the 1986 constitution of the Tohono O'Odham Nation of Arizona (formerly known as the Papago Tribe) and the 1994 constitution of the Ho-Chunk Nation (formerly Winnebago Tribe of Wisconsin). Both constitutions assert broad tribal inherent powers over persons and land within reservation boundaries, including land that may be acquired in the future. The Tohono O'Odham also affirms jurisdiction over its members beyond reservation borders. Tohono O'Odham Nation Constitution, Art I; Ho-Chunk Constitution, Art. I. Provisions for tribal powers and legislative authority are broader than those found in Article VI of the Hopi Constitution and in most other IRA constitutions. Ho-Chunk Constitution, Art. V, § 2; Tohono O'Odham Nation Constitution, Art. VI.

Both constitutions incorporate more separation of powers than the IRA boilerplate documents. Each has a separate executive branch with power to appoint heads of departments, although the Ho-Chunk President presides over the Legislature, and only the Tohono O'Odham President can veto legislation. Tohono O'Odham Constitution, Arts. IV, VII; Ho-Chunk Constitution, Art. VI. An appointed judiciary and appellate review are present in both the Ho-Chunk and Tohono O'Odham documents, with both constitutions specifying that judges shall be appointed or elected for a term rather than for life. Although removing a judge from office is more difficult under the Ho-Chunk Constitution, both documents guarantee the independence of the judiciary and authorize appellate review of tribal legislation. Ho-Chunk Constitution, Art. III, § 3 and VII, § 3 ("No branch of the government shall exercise the powers or functions delegated to another branch" and the Supreme Court "shall have the power to interpret the Constitution and laws of the Ho-Chunk Nation"); Tohono O'Odham Constitution, Art. VIII § 10 (power to interpret and "declare the laws . . . void if such laws are not in agreement with this constitution"). Indeed, a general trend within recent tribal constitution-making is the creation of more independent judicial branches. *See, e.g.*, Constitution and

Bylaws of the Turtle Mountain Band of Chippewa Indians, Art. XIV (1992 amendment which provides for separately elected judges and court clerk, as well as an elected Judicial Board to oversee court policy and practice, including removal of judges).

The Ho-Chunk and Tohono O'Odham constitutions also differ in some significant ways. Under the Ho-Chunk Constitution, there is a fourth branch of government, the General Council consisting of all eligible voters, with power "to set policy for the Nation" and to veto legislation. The Ho-Chunks' eleven-person Legislature is elected partly by districts, partly at-large. Two districts are allotted three representatives each, and two districts have one apiece. Ho-Chunk Constitution, Arts. IV, V. The Tohono O'Odham Constitution, in contrast, has district elections with votes apportioned by population, so that each district has as many votes as there are members of the Tribe in that district, divided by 10.

Non-IRA tribes have been creative with their constitutions as well in the recent period, often incorporating traditional governing methods. For example, in its 1988 government organization ordinance (which functions as a constitution-equivalent), the Navajo Nation separated its President from the Tribal Council, designating instead a Speaker to preside over the Council meetings. As a consequence, the President now heads an independent branch of government. 2 NAVAJO NATION CODE §§ 281–287; 1001–1005. Even more innovative has been the Navajo Nation's Local Governance Act of 1998, which devolves considerable authority upon units of local government known as Chapters. This shift of authority over matters such as zoning and leasing, comports more fully with the Navajo social-political order, which consisted of relatively autonomous groups of families under the leadership of a wise and respected member of a local family. See OFFICE OF NAVAJO GOVERNMENT DEVELOPMENT, NAVAJO NATION GOVERNMENT (4th ed. 1998). The Mashantucket Pequot Tribe of Connecticut turned to traditional ways to establish some check on its Tribal Council. Included in its constitution is an Elders Council, comprised of all the elders of the Tribe, with responsibility to determine membership applications and exclusions from the reservation, monitor and advise the Tribal Council, hear matters referred by the Tribal Council, and propose constitutional amendments. Constitution and By-Laws of the Mashantucket (Western) Pequot Tribe, Art. XII.

Important design questions remain for tribal communities seeking to update and make their governments more legitimate and effective. Important questions that should be considered on any tribal constitutional reform agenda should include:

- Should they abandon their IRA-style single-branch governments in favor of more divided government, with true executive and judicial branches? Would transforming tribal governments this way simply bring Indian nations closer to mimicking American government, or might such changes enable tribal governments to reflect more faithfully traditions of division of authority (for example, between religious and secular leaders, peace and war leaders, or among clans) that functioned effectively before European contact?

- Do contemporary Indian nations require more powerful executives in order to compete effectively in an increasingly global economy? Or will creating such offices establish concentrations of power that are alien to the consensus-based decision-making systems of many traditional tribal communities?

- Would substituting family- or clan-based electoral systems for more at-large systems bring tribal governments more in line with traditional social-political organization, thereby reducing conflict over winner-take-all political spoils, or would such changes merely exacerbate conflict by underscoring tribal divisions? What about introducing cumulative voting systems, which enable voters to distribute all their votes to a single candidate?

- Should membership or citizenship requirements be relaxed in order to reflect patterns of intermarriage or to focus on community participation and recognition rather than on ancestry?

Unlike the period of the IRA, grassroots constitution-making is finally beginning to take place in Indian country. For a guidebook on the process of drafting a constitution, and a selection of constitutions from a variety of Native nations, *see* MELISSA J. TATUM ET AL., STRUCTURING SOVEREIGNTY: CONSTITUTIONS OF NATIVE NATIONS (UCLA American Indian Center Press, 2014).

b.   Types of Tribal Courts

Traditionally, tribal societies had detailed political organization and understood procedures for adjudicating and settling disputes, handling social misbehavior, and taking collective political action long before contact with Euro-American societies. Those procedures differed from tribe to tribe, but as one can tell from the Lakota excerpt, frequently involved councilors or peacemakers mediating private disputes and seeking restorative, compensatory resolutions and public officials enforcing public norms, although still often receiving restorative compensatory payments in lieu of punishment. Some of those traditions survive, others have been westernized, and still others reflect a middle ground between tribal and Euro-American methods for dispute resolution. Today, the methods for resolving both internal tribal disputes and disputes involving tribal members and others are centered on tribal courts.

Tribal courts roughly can be divided into four types. First, and oldest, are the *traditional courts*, the origins of which often predate the establishment of western-style tribal governmental institutions. Frequently, the role of traditional courts involves peacemaking, *i.e.*, healing the wounds to kinship groups and the community created by social misconduct within the community through a community-based process of mediation. Ada Pecos Melton, *Indigenous Justice Systems and Tribal Society*, 79 JUDICATURE 126 (1995). Tribal religious leaders or elders often are involved in such proceedings. As is also true of mediation processes, traditional courts usually are not courts of record in the western sense, where recorded testimony is received and a decision is rendered based on the record made in the trial proceedings. Furthermore, as with modern mediation, the proceedings of such courts in some instances are secret. While some aspects of traditional dispute resolution procedures may sometimes be found in the informal kinship relationships existing on many reservations, until recently few tribes maintained traditional courts as part of their formal governing structure. Nevertheless, long-standing traditional courts are common among the Pueblos and some other tribes of the southwest and they have played a major role in the adjudication of disputes, particularly internal tribal disputes.

The concept of peacemaking, *i.e.*, informal, community-based dispute resolution that was part of the traditional court structure, recently has had a major resurgence in tribal jurisprudence. A number of Native nations have sought to reintroduce the concept into their western court structures. A good example is the Navajo Nation, which established a Peacemaker Court, as part of its formal court structures. *See generally* Robert Yazzie, *Navajo Peacekeeping: Technology and Traditional Indian Law*, 10 St. Thomas L. Rev. 95 (1997). Names, however, can sometimes be misleading. Thus, the Peacemaker Court of the Seneca Nation of New York is merely the name long associated with the western style court that gradually has moved away from its peacemaking mission. *See* Robert B. Porter, *Strengthening Tribal Sovereignty Through Peacemaking: How the Anglo-American Legal Tradition Destroys Indigenous Societies*, 28 Colum. Hum. Rts. L. Rev. 235, 259–63 (1997).

Second, so-called "CFR Courts," or Courts of Indian Offenses as they were formerly known, still exist and serve perhaps a couple of dozen reservations and many tribes in Oklahoma. The tribes currently served by CFR Courts are listed in 25 C.F.R. § 11.100(a). These courts are direct descendants of the Courts of Indian Offenses established by the Bureau of Indian Affairs in the late nineteenth century. *See generally* William T. Hagan, Indian Police and Judges 104–125 (1966). They are the courts which the *Clapox* decision, set forth in Chapter 1, sustained against claims of illegality. More recently, the validity of modern CFR Courts was again unsuccessfully challenged in *Tillett v. Lujan*, 931 F.2d 636 (10th Cir. 1991). Originally designed by the Indian Service in the late nineteenth century to enforce a Code of Indian Offenses which attacked traditional Indian cultural practices, such as ceremonial dances, the potlach and other gift-giving ceremonies, the practices of medicine men, and polygamy and to break down traditional tribal governing institutions, today these courts enforce a code representing a less drastic intrusion into tribal culture. That code and the provisions establishing and governing the CFR Courts are set forth at 25 Code of Federal Regulations (CFR) Part 11. The CFR Courts therefore derive their acronym from the Code of Federal Regulations under the sole auspices of which they operate.

For the reservations served by CFR Courts, 25 C.F.R. § 11.200 provides that the CFR court shall consist of a trial division composed of at least one magistrate and an appellate division staffed with at least three magistrates who did not sit on the original trial of the case. Under 25 C.F.R. § 11.201(a), the magistrates of a CFR Court are "appointed by the Assistant Secretary — Indian Affairs or his or her designee subject to confirmation by a majority vote of the tribal governing body of the tribe occupying the Indian country over which the court has jurisdiction, or, in the case of multi-tribal courts, confirmation by a majority of the tribal governing bodies of the tribes under the jurisdiction of a Court of Indian Offenses." The judges of the CFR courts are therefore formally federal governmental employees, although frequently in fact selected in advance by the tribal council of the reservation served by the court. Federal confirmation of the appointment therefore often merely rubber-stamps tribal council decisions already made. Under 25 C.F.R. § 11.102, the criminal jurisdiction of the CFR Courts extends "over any action by an Indian (hereafter referred to as person) that is made a criminal offense under this part and that occurred within the Indian country subject to the court's jurisdiction." By contrast, the civil jurisdiction of the CFR Courts covers "any civil action arising within the territorial jurisdiction of the court in which the defendant is an Indian, and of all other suits between Indians and non-Indians which are brought before the court by stipulation of the parties." 25 C.F.R. § 11.103. If Indian nations possess inherent sovereignty, why should the jurisdiction of a CFR Court be limited as to non-Indians — there being no criminal jurisdiction over them and the civil jurisdiction over them requiring their consent or stipulation? Is it because these institutions are really federal, not tribal, institutions and in the federal system jurisdiction over such matters is lodged elsewhere, such as the federal courts? While originally clearly a federal imposition on resisting tribal communities, the contemporary CFR Courts no longer serve the colonizing purposes articulated in *Clapox*. Today, should they be seen more as tribal institutions? If so, should their jurisdiction be broadened?

CFR courts continue to exist in Indian country primarily at the sufferance of tribal councils, who also in fact, if not form, appoint the judges. As one court nicely put it, "CFR courts, however, also function as tribal courts, they constitute the judicial forum through which the tribe can exercise its jurisdiction until such time as the tribe adopts a formal law and order code. *See* 25 C.F.R. § 11.1(d) and (e). . . . " *Tillett v. Lujan*, 931 F.2d 636, 639 (10th Cir. 1991). Nevertheless, legal questions sometimes have arisen as to whether such institutions are formally arms of the tribal or federal government. *E.g.*, *United States v. Wheeler*, 435 U.S. 313, 326 n.26 (1978) (raising, but not resolving, the question for double jeopardy purposes); *Tillett v. Lujan*, *supra* (requiring exhaustion of remedies in a CFR Court under a rule requiring exhaustion of *tribal* remedies); *United States v. Red Lake Band of Chippewa Indians*, 827 F.2d 380 (8th Cir. 1987) (records of the Red Lake Band Court of Indian Offenses constituted federal, not tribal, records). Should the CFR Courts, unlike other tribal courts, be directly governed by all requirements of the Bill of Rights, including grand jury indictment and the right to appointed counsel? No CFR Court functions in that manner and no provisions are made for such procedures in 25 C.F.R. Part 11. As one can tell from these illustrations, the decisions on such questions are, at best, inconsistent. Under the provisions of 25 C.F.R. §§ 11.449 and 11.500, the CFR Courts not only enforce the federal Code of Indian Offenses set forth in the regulations, they also enforce any validly adopted tribal criminal ordinance and, in civil cases, tribal positive customary law. Whatever the appropriate legal answer to the question of whether CFR Courts are tribal or federal institutions, the tribes served by CFR courts tend to view them as arms and agencies of the tribal government, merely paid, as a matter of economy and convenience, by the federal government.

At their height in the 1920s, CFR Courts existed on perhaps two-thirds of the nation's Indian reservations. After Congress adopted the Indian Reorganization Act of 1934 to encourage displacing such federally imposed institutions with indigenous tribal ones, the regulations governing CFR courts were revised to permit tribes to replace CFR courts with their own institutions. *See* 25 C.F.R. § 11.100(c). CFR Courts, therefore, continue to operate in Indian country serving only those tribes that, for whatever reason, have chosen not to shoulder the financial and governmental responsibilities of operating their own courts and law enforcement system afforded by this provision.

As sovereign governments, Indian tribes have an inherent right to create and change their own governing structures, a right that 25 C.F.R. § 11.100(c) has recognized since the adoption of the IRA. Most have, indeed, used those powers to create their own courts of record, modeled loosely on western models of civil and criminal adjudication, rather than traditional peacemaking concepts. Nevertheless, the informality and restorative justice objectives of peacemaking may sometimes infuse the deliberations of such tribal courts. These courts commonly are called *tribal courts*, and constitute the third and most numerous type of court serving tribal communities. Tribal courts actually come in two varieties, reflecting the third and fourth types — *legislatively-created tribal courts* and *constitutional tribal courts*.

Historically, the creation of tribal courts occurred in two waves. First, a number of southeastern tribes, responding to the urgings of American leaders and missionaries, voluntarily began to adopt western political institutions in the first third of the nineteenth century immediately prior to removal, a tradition they continued in the Indian Territory following removal. Indeed, the name Five Civilized Tribes (today, more commonly referred to as the Five Tribes), found in old Indian statutes, referred to the Cherokee, Choctaw, Chickasaw, Muscogee (Creek), and Seminole who, during the early nineteenth century voluntarily adopted the so-called "civilized" traditions of western governance, including western-style tribal courts with written records enforcing written laws. The *Talton* case, Sec. B.1, this chapter, evidences the long-standing tradition of tribal courts among the Cherokee. *See generally* RENNARD STRICKLAND, FIRE AND THE SPIRITS: CHEROKEE LAW FROM CLAN TO COURT (1975). These tribes had written constitutions and tended to follow the federal governmental practice of creating their court structure in their tribal constitution.

The second great wave in the creation of tribal courts occurred in the aftermath of the Indian Reorganization Act of 1934 (IRA). Then Indian Commissioner John Collier envisioned replacing the federal governing institutions for Indian country orchestrated by the BIA with tribally run governing institutions. That policy naturally led to efforts to replace the Courts of Indian Offenses (CFR Courts) with tribal courts.

Unlike some of the earliest written tribal constitutions among the Five Tribes, many of the tribal constitutions *initially* adopted under the IRA lack any constitutional division of authority. While some tribal leaders occasionally suggest that the lack of separation of powers resulted from the lack of any such tradition in tribal customs (a claim that the materials that begin this section perhaps question), one commentator has suggested another reason for the lack of separation of powers in the IRA tribal constitutions:

> If you look at these IRA constitutions, they had built into them a lot of federal approval requirements which were designed to maintain the jobs of BIA bureaucrats and maintain colonial control," according to University of Iowa professor Robert Clinton. "I've long suspected, but can't prove, that

the IRA constitutions lack a separation of powers because it's easier to control one branch of tribal government than many."

Sean Paige, *Rewriting Tribal Law*, 16 INSIGHT MAGAZINE No. 20 (May 29, 2000). Thus, under these often boiler-plate, IRA tribal constitutions, all delegated governing power of the tribe usually was lodged in a single, elected, sometimes small tribal council. In a few cases, provisions were included in the tribal constitution contemplating tribal council creation of tribal courts, while in most other cases the tribal constitution was completely silent on the matter. Compare Article V, section 1(a) of the Cheyenne River Sioux's IRA-era By-Laws ("It shall be the duty of the council to provide through necessary by-laws and ordinances, for the establishment of a tribal court upon the reservation.") with the IRA-era Constitution and By-Laws of the Confederated Tribes of the Colville Reservation in Washington, which were entirely silent about the existence of tribal courts. Both Cheyenne River and Colville, however, amended their constitution, in 1981 and 1990 respectively, to include a separate judicial article, thereby creating constitutionally-established tribal judiciaries.

The judicial amendments to the Colville constitution reflect a growing trend in Indian country favoring greater separation of powers. This trend derives from dissatisfaction with the manner in which the old standard IRA constitutions concentrated power in the hands of a few elected tribal council members and the corruption or abuses of that power that sometimes accompanied such concentrations of authority.

What implications exist for judicial independence and separation of powers when a tribal constitution fails to create tribal courts or any separate branches of government or otherwise fails to provide checks on the tribal council? The Navajo Nation, for example, operates without a written constitution. Like the United Kingdom, Israel, or New Zealand, the governing structure of the Navajo Nation is spelled out in its statutes and alterable by normal legislative process. Could such a government have judicial independence and separation of powers? Canon 2 of the Navajo Nation Code of Judicial Conduct provides "A Navajo Nation judge shall promote and protect the independence of the courts." Former Navajo Chief Justice Tom Tso explains that this provision "recognizes that while the Navajo Nation uses the doctrine of separation of legislative, executive, and judicial powers, judicial independence will not be honored if judges do not promote it." Tom Tso, *Moral Principles, Traditions, and Fairness in the Navajo Nation Code of Judicial Conduct*, 76 JUDICATURE 15, 18 (1992). Does separation of powers exist in the United Kingdom, Israel, or New Zealand? Are the judiciaries in such countries normally considered subservient to their elected officials? From the standpoint of the customary values of many tribal communities, should separation of powers be viewed simply as a matter of respect, a highly prized traditional value? Might such traditional notions of respect explain how judicial independence can exist in a tribal court that lacks constitutional independence or a written constitutional tradition of separation of powers?

Despite the fact that constitutional separations of powers does not exist in many foreign nations, the courts of which are routinely recognized and respected by state and federal officials, the lack of constitutional separation of powers that exists in some, but not all, tribal courts has routinely become an excuse for denigrating tribal court authority among hostile federal judges. For example, in a concurring opinion in *Nevada v. Hicks*, 533 U.S. 353, 384–85 (2001), Justice Souter wrote:

> Tribal courts also differ from other American courts (and often from one another) in their structure, in the substantive law they apply, and in the *independence of their judges*. Although some modern tribal courts "mirror American courts" and "are guided by written codes, rules, procedures, and guidelines," tribal law is still frequently unwritten, being based instead "on the values, mores, and norms of a tribe and expressed in its customs, traditions, and practices," and is often "handed down orally or by example from one generation to another." Ada Pecos Melton, *Indigenous Justice Systems and Tribal Society*, 79 JUDICATURE 126, 130–131 (1995). The resulting law applicable in tribal courts is a complex "mix of tribal codes and federal, state, and traditional law," *National American Indian Court Judges Assn., Indian Courts and the Future* 43 (1978), which would be unusually difficult for an outsider to sort out.

(Emphasis added.) Are such criticisms fair? Is constitutional separation of powers a necessary precondition for judicial independence or, rather, does judicial independence constitute a judicial attitude which may exist with or without constitutional separation of powers?

In *Ninigret Development Corp. v. Narragansett Indian Wetuomuck Housing Authority*, 32 F. Supp. 2d 497 (D.R.I. 1999), *vacated for want of jurisdiction*, 207 F.3d 21 (1st Cir. 2000), a party sought to void a forum selection clause in a contract on the ground that the tribe fraudulently failed to disclose that the tribal court selected in the clause lacked constitutional separation of powers. The district court responded:

> Plaintiff does not allege that NIWHA or its agents described a fictional tribal judicial procedure. Nor does plaintiff allege that no Tribal Court has ever convened. It argues that the language of the Village Contract is fraudulent because it implies the existence of an independent Tribal Court or, rephrasing the argument, implies a separation of powers between the Tribal Council and the Tribal Court. Plaintiff's argument fails. . . .

> An Indian tribe is a sovereign, and it need not follow the American blueprint for a court system. Specifically, it does not need to adopt the separation of powers doctrine that rests as the bedrock of the federal system. The Supreme Court has been clear that "[n]onjudicial tribal institutions have also been recognized as competent law-applying bodies." *See Santa Clara Pueblo*, 436 U.S. at 66. This is part of the federal government's longstanding policy of encouraging tribal self-government. Therefore, an American Indian court system that is different from the American federal model cannot cause avoidance of either an arbitration or forum selection agreement as unreasonable. Similarly, plaintiff had no right to assume that the Narragansett Tribe's system for resolving disputes would mimic the federal court system, especially where the principal of plaintiff was a member of the Tribe himself. In short, there was no fraud which led to the execution of the Village Contract by plaintiff. Why did the

party challenging the choice of forum clause deem the lack of separation of powers a material non-disclosure? If operating in a state which elects its judges, would non-disclosure of that fact constitute a fraudulent failure to disclose?

Id. at 504–05.

2. Tribal Law Provisions on Jurisdiction

As the materials at the beginning of Chapter 1 suggest, Indian tribes appear to have negotiated treaties recognizing their complete territorial jurisdiction over their reservation. Article IV of the Treaty of Dancing Rabbit Creek with the Choctaw Nation perhaps most explicitly reflects that understanding:

> The Government and people of the United States are hereby obliged to secure to the said Choctaw Nation of Red People the *jurisdiction and government of all the persons and property that may be within their limits west*, so that no Territory or State shall ever have a right to pass laws for the government of the Choctaw Nation of Red People and their descendants; and that no part of the land granted them shall ever be embraced in any Territory or State. . . .

7 Stat. 333 (emphasis added). Notice that nothing in Article IV limits tribal authority solely to tribal members. It includes "all persons and property that may be within their limits," a very accurate legal description of the English idea of Crown sovereignty over the realm, the source of some of Anglo-American conceptions of sovereignty.

Having negotiated for complete jurisdiction over all persons and lands within their reservation, most tribes adopt tribal codes asserting complete jurisdiction in territorial terms, drawing few distinctions among the tribal affiliation or race of the parties. Two provisions of the Law and Order Code of the Cheyenne River Sioux Tribe illustrate the types of jurisdictional claims commonly made under tribal law:

Sec. 1-4-1 Jurisdiction-Tribal Policy

> It is hereby declared as a matter of Tribal policy, that the public interest and the interests of the Cheyenne River Sioux Tribe demand that the Tribe provide itself, its members, and other persons living within the territorial jurisdiction of the Tribe as set forth in Section 4 of the Act of March 2, 1889, (48 Stat. 888) with an effective means of redress in both civil and criminal cases against members and non-Tribal members who through either their residence, presence, business dealings, other actions or failures to act, or other significant minimum contacts with this Reservation and/or its residents commit criminal offenses against the Tribe or incur civil obligations to persons or entities entitled to the Tribes protection. This action is deemed necessary as a result of the confusion and conflicts caused by the increased contact and interaction between the Tribe, its members, and other residents of the Reservation and other persons and entities over which the Tribe has not previously elected to exercise jurisdiction. The jurisdictional provisions of this Code, to insure maximum protection for the

Tribe, its members and other residents of the Reservation, should be applied equally to all persons, members and non-members alike.

Sec. 1-4-2 Territorial Jurisdiction

The Jurisdiction of the Courts of the Cheyenne River Sioux Tribe shall extend to the territory within the exterior boundaries as set forth in Section 4 of the Act of March 2, 1889 (48 Stat. 888) and to such other lands without such boundaries as may hereafter be added to the Reservation or held in Trust for the Tribe under any law of the United States or otherwise.

Are such tribal law claims of the scope of jurisdiction of tribal courts any broader than the scope of jurisdiction frequently claimed by state courts? Given that all Indian reservations today are located within states, is there potential for conflict between such similar competing claims? How did the United States Supreme Court initially resolve such potential concerns in *Worcester v. Georgia*, 31 U.S. (6 Pet.) 515 (1832), discussed in Chapter 1? Do sections 1-4-1 through 1-4-2 of the Cheyenne River Sioux Tribal Law and Order Code assert any broader jurisdiction than *Worcester* recognized? Did the opening of western Indian reservations to allotment under the Dawes General Allotment of 1887 diminish the Tribe's jurisdiction and sovereignty over its reservation by the inclusion of non-Indian homesteaders within the reservation? There were no provisions within the allotment legislation that expressly purported to do so for lands that remained within the reservation. Do these tribal conceptions of the territorial nature and scope of their governmental authority comport with the more recent view announced by the United States Supreme Court in cases like *Strate v. A-1 Contractors*, 520 U.S. 438 (1997), and *Nevada v. Hicks*, 533 U.S. 353 (2001), discussed in Sec. C.1, this chapter.

3. Sources of Law in Tribal Courts

Litigation in tribal courts often raises important questions about the law to apply. Such questions sometimes pose difficult problems, not the least of which involve the relationship of tribal customary or traditional law to the emerging written law traditions of the tribe. Tribal code provisions governing applicable law, often found in tribal codes, restrict the discretion of tribal courts on such questions. The following provision from the Code of the Winnebago Tribe of Nebraska § 1-109 illustrates a common tribal provision specifying the law a tribal court should apply:

> The courts shall apply the tribal Constitution, and the provisions of all statutory law heretofore or hereafter adopted by the tribe. In matters not covered by tribal statute, the court shall apply traditional tribal customs and usages, which shall be called common law. When in doubt as to the tribal common law, the court may request the advice of counselors and tribal elders familiar with it. In any dispute not covered by the tribal Constitution, tribal statute, or tribal common law, the court may apply any rules of the United States or any state therein, and any regulation of the Department of the Interior which may be of general or specific applicability. Upon this code becoming effective, neither Part 11 of Title 25 of the Code of Federal Regulations, except those Sections thereof which are effective when the tribe receives certain funding from the Bureau of Indian

Affairs, nor state law shall be binding upon the court unless incorporated into tribal law by tribal statute or by decision of the tribal courts adopting some federal or state law as tribal common law.

Like many such tribal code provisions, the Winnebago ordinance inexplicably makes no reference to borrowing the law of other tribes when no controlling Winnebago authority exists. Does that mean that a Winnebago tribal court cannot look to the precedents of other tribes for guidance? In *Rave v. Reynolds*, 23 Ind. L. Rep. 6150 (Winn. Sup. Ct. 1996), the Winnebago Supreme Court interpreted section 1-109 to permit Winnebago courts to look for persuasive authority in other tribal jurisdictions when interpreting analogous provisions of the tribal code. It did not decide whether section 1-109 prevented the tribal courts from looking to the court decisions of other tribes where there was no governing tribal statutory authority. Should a tribal court be permitted to look to the decisions of other tribes in such circumstances?

Section 2-111(3) of the Winnebago Tribal Code provides "[w]here any doubt arises as to the customs and usages of the tribe, the court, either on its own motion or the motion of any party, may subpoena and request the advice of elders and counselors familiar with those customs and usages." Such authorization for *ex parte* communication with tribal elders or experts on questions of tribal customary law are common. *See, e.g.*, Colville Tribal Code, § 3.4.04. Would it be helpful to have the parties prove up tribal customary law as fact with witnesses at trial, a procedure followed by some states for proof of the law of other countries? Would the opportunities for a contest on such questions and for cross-examination help sharpen the court's understanding of the basis for and limitations of any tribal customary law relied upon by a party? Might subjecting tribal elders or other experts on tribal customary law to cross-examination be seen as disrespectful both to them and to the tribal customs and traditions?

In light of section 1-109, which is paramount in tribal court decision-making-positive written tribal law, such as the tribal constitution or tribal statutes, ordinances, or regulations, or tribal customary law? In *Winnebago Tribe v. Bigfire*, 25 Ind. L. Rep. 6229 (Winn. Sup. Ct. 1998), portions of which are discussed in Sec. D.2, this chapter, the Winnebago Supreme Court rejected an argument by the defendant that the Tribe's adoption of an equal protection clause in the tribal Bill of Rights imported into tribal law the protections against gender discrimination employed in federal and state courts under the equal protection clause of the Fourteenth Amendment. To reconcile the tribal customs and traditions of the Winnebago community with its written law, the Justices relied heavily on section 1-109, indicating that their challenge was to determine "when will the adoption of a new written tribal positive law, either in the form of a constitutional provision or a tribal code provision, be found to displace prior tribal customs and usages." Based on a reading of the broader purposes of Winnebago sovereignty, the Court concluded that all written tribal law should be interpreted in the context of evolving tribal custom and tradition. Applying this approach, the court found that equal protection concepts contained in the tribal constitution prohibited *non-traditional* forms of gender discrimination, since the customary respect owed the dignity of each individual under tribal tradition was compromised by gender discrimination. Thus, any gender classification that could be justified on the basis of tribal custom and tradition would be upheld as supported by a compelling governmental interest-preserving tribal culture. Consistent with its interpretation of section 1-109, the Winnebago Supreme Court declined to interpret adoption by the Tribal Council of a gender-neutral aggravated sexual assault provision covering underage sex as evidence of an intent to abandon and displace the customarily gendered tribal view of sexual misconduct.

NOTES ON CUSTOMARY LAW

1. **Proof of Customary Law:** Unlike statutory or case authority, tribal customary law cannot be researched in a law library beyond those reported cases that have already discussed it. How should a tribal court become informed about tribal customary law? If, as in *Bigfire*, the tribal court is staffed by one or more judges who are either members of the governing tribal community or of a culturally-related tribe, a tribal judge may have some inherent knowledge of the tribal customary law of which she can take judicial notice. Some tribal courts, however, employ nonmember Indians or non-Indians as tribal judges. Such judges must be informed about tribal customs and traditions by the lawyers or parties in the case or must look to some other source to inform their knowledge of customary tribal law. Do the tribal code provisions, discussed above, which authorize tribal judges to consult tribal elders, counselors, or experts in tribal customary law completely resolve the problem? Should all parties be notified of such *ex parte* inquires about tribal customary law and the results of the inquiry and, thereafter, have a right to respond? Most tribal codes provide no such opportunity.

As tribal customary law is determined and described in reported tribal court opinions, a body of written tribal common law decisions will emerge for any tribe grounded on its customary law. Western-trained lawyers might think that this common law process over time would ameliorate the research problems attendant to tribal customary law. Nevertheless, this process has its own pitfalls. In a tribal community, historically dependent on an oral tradition for the transmission of tribal customary law, traditional tribal law naturally evolved over time with the needs of the tribal community and the current generation's understanding of how its traditions applied to their present circumstances. Does the very process of writing down tribal customary law in court opinions pose dangers to the evolutionary nature and flexibility of tribal customary law? Might tribal customs become inelastic when they are captured as *written* tribal law in court opinions? Are those dangers increased where the tribal courts adhere to the Anglo-American legal tradition of *stare decisis*, or precedent, as most tribal courts do? Might the secrecy of some tribal customary practices be compromised by inclusion in written tribal judicial decisions? For an insightful account of the development of customary law within the Hopi Tribe, see Pat Sekaquaptewa, *Evolving the Hopi Common Law*, 9 KAN. J. L. & PUB. POL'Y 761 (2000). *See also* Pat Sekaquaptewa, *Key Concepts in the Finding, Definition, and Consideration of Custom Law in Tribal Law Making*, 32 AM. INDIAN L. REV. 319 (2007) (discussing the functional definition of customary law within tribal communities); Matthew L. M. Fletcher, *Rethinking Customary Law in Tribal Court Jurisprudence*, 13 MICH. J. RACE & L. 57 (2007) (postulating a methodology for tribal judges to find and apply customary law); Justice Raymond D. Austin, *American Indian Customary Law in the Modern Courts of American*

Indian Nations, 11 Wyo. L. Rev. 351 (2011).

In *Mexican v. Circle Bear*, 370 N.W.2d 737 (S.D. 1985), the South Dakota Supreme Court granted comity to and enforced a tribal judgment of the Cheyenne River Sioux tribal courts that had determined based on customary Lakota law the disposition of the body of and funeral arrangements for a deceased Lakota medicine man. A dispute had arisen between his widow and his sisters as to the appropriate place of burial, both claiming his body for that purpose. The tribal court based its ruling on Lakota customary law that "upon the death of a married person the surviving spouse, absent any showing that the parties were separated at the time of death, has the duty to bury the deceased spouse and the right to custody of the body for the limited purpose of burial." The words of the tribal judge, delivered orally from the bench, and quoted in a concurring opinion in the state court decision, reflect the sensitive and healing manner in which the tribal judiciary often employs tribal customary law:

> I do know a lot of things pursuant to history and custom regarding the custody of this body. First of all to the audience here, know that the Great Sioux Nation was before Pine Ridge; it was before Cheyenne River; it was before Ft. Yates and any of the other reservations. We were all one people at one time. The custom does not vary from one reservation to another today. You must understand that. And the thing that exists with the case we are talking about today — and that is — you've all heard the expression — the older ones in the crowd here know the expression that was used when a young lady married into another Tribe and she passed away. The same for the man marrying into another Tribe who chose to remain with that Tribe and died there. You know what that means. Those are the traditions and we are getting away from them. You are all completely against tradition and custom today, let me tell you. You are dealing with the spirit of a medicine man. That is dangerous. You don't know what spirit can do; his spirit will not rest in peace if this court is to grant the request of the relatives. That man chose to marry here, there was not a divorce here, he died while he was still married to this woman. I will now rule for Mabel Mexican on this issue here simply based on tradition and custom, but I do want to leave this word with all of you, being relatives. This is a sad time indeed for all of you no matter which side you are on. You must bring yourself to understand that to come together to respect the memory of a medicine man you must put your feelings aside and no matter where he will be buried come to that funeral. You've all expressed your desires. You've all expressed that you loved him. That's what you need to do — don't let the white man's law or any other law tear you apart. If you respect custom and tradition, then respect our tradition and come, all of you. That I will leave with you.

Id. at 743.

2. Customary Law and Confederated Tribes: The Winnebago, Navajo, and other tribal communities discussed in the preceding materials on customary law are fairly homogeneous cultural Indian nations, composed of people of like tribal cultural and linguistic ancestry. Many modern Indian tribes, however, are actually confederations of different cultural communities and historic tribal groups. Tribes like the Confederated Tribes & Bands of the Yakima Reservation or the Confederated Colville Tribes are composed of peoples from divergent cultural and tribal communities, many of whom historically had very distinct customary and traditional laws. The Flathead Reservation community is composed of three distinct tribal communities: the Salish, Kootenai and Pend d'Oreille. Federal Indian law treats these confederated tribes as a single nation with a single tribal court, and the consolidating effects of federal policy have significantly complicated tribes' enforcement of their customs and traditions. How is the tribal court on a confederated reservation supposed to employ tribal customary law, particularly if the customs and traditions of the various tribal communities on the reservation differ relative to any question before the court? Notice that tribal judges on the Colville Reservation are charged with enforcing tribal customary law without any attention being paid in the tribal code to the important question of which tribal band constitutes the source for the customary law to be applied. Intermarriage between cultural communities on such reservations further complicates the picture. Even in seemingly homogenous tribal communities, traditional practices and customary law sometimes might vary by extended family, clan, village or chapter. Thus, the process of finding tribal customary law is sometimes complicated by its diversity and requires great sensitivity from any tribal judge.

4. Tribal Restrictions on Tribal Governments

a. Tribal Provisions for Federal Approval

As indicated above, standard form IRA constitutions handed the Secretary of the Interior power to approve enactments, including "a veto power over such tribal actions as the assessment of dues, fees, and taxes against nonmembers, the removal of nonmembers from the Indian community, the control of private land sales by members, the enactment of criminal and civil codes, and the appointment of guardians for minors and incompetents." William H. Kelly, *Indian Adjustment and the History of Indian Affairs*, 10 ARIZ. L. REV. 559, 568 (1968). At one point, the Solicitor for the Department of the Interior took the position that these Secretarial approval provisions were mandatory under federal law. *See* Memorandum of the Solicitor to the Commissioner of Indian Affairs, *Proposed Constitution for Navajo Tribe*, June 21, 1954. Over the years, however, the Secretary's promotion of federal control over tribal lawmaking has also attracted considerable criticism. For example, the Senate Judiciary Committee "failed to uncover any Federal statute which specifically requires secretarial approval of tribal ordinances," and found that the Tribes' dependence on unreviewable Secretarial approval decisions "frustrates responsible tribal self-government." Summary Report of Hearings and Investigations by the Subcommittee on Constitutional Rights, Senate Committee on the Judiciary, 88th Cong., 2d Sess. 1–4 (1964). In its 1976 report, the American Indian Policy Review Commission concurred:

> It is ironic that this Act, which was intended to strengthen the governments of Indian tribes, is now generally regarded by the Indian people as an impediment to their governmental functions. . . .

[The constitutional provisions for Secretarial review of ordinances have] been generally condemned as perpetuating a paternalistic relationship between the Department of the Interior and the tribes. Paternalism aside, it has also impeded tribes in their efforts to assert authority within reservation boundaries. . . . Thus, for years, the Department denied that tribes could exercise any jurisdiction over non-Indians even though there was no clear statute and no judicial decision to affirm the Department's position. The efforts of the Colville Tribe to impose a water use code within the boundaries of their reservation was thwarted by the refusal of the Secretary to approve their proposed code. In a most extraordinary case, the Coeur d'Alene Tribe was denied permission to enact a code provision regulating the playing of an Indian stick game within their reservation even though a Federal court had held that the playing of the game was not within the purview of Federal law. In this case, Departmental veto of the tribal ordinance was instigated at the request of the Department of Justice.

AMERICAN INDIAN POLICY REVIEW COMMISSION, FINAL REPORT 188–89 (1976).

In view of the existence of a federal trust responsibility, what may the Secretary take into account in deciding whether to approve a tribal ordinance? Is it appropriate for the Secretary to balance the interests of the tribe against those of the surrounding non-Indian community as well as other federal policy interests such as those of other non-BIA agencies within the Department of the Interior? In *Moapa Band of Paiute Indians v. United States Dep't of Interior*, 747 F.2d 563 (9th Cir. 1984), the Secretary had invoked a general federal policy against prostitution in disapproving a tribal ordinance that permitted houses of prostitution on a Nevada reservation. In upholding the Secretary's action, the Ninth Circuit relied on the federal policy, but also emphasized a provision in the tribal constitution that allowed the Secretary to rescind tribal ordinances "for any cause."

Not all IRA constitutions afford such broad powers to the Secretary. The Blackfeet, for example, have no constitutional provision for Secretarial review of law and order ordinances. Conversely, some non-IRA tribal constitutions have incorporated secretarial approval. For instance, until recently, the Hoopa Valley Tribe, which had emphatically rejected the IRA, had a constitutional provision that required the Secretary of the Interior to approve ordinances regulating the conduct of non-Indians.

Many Indian nations are deploying the new, easier amendment provisions of the IRA to repeal Secretarial approval language in their constitutions. The Ho-Chunk and Tohono O'Odham constitutions discussed above do not provide for Secretarial approval, except, in the case of the Tohono O'Odham, for the transfer, encumbrance, or leasing of tribal land. Even as to the latter, the Tohono O'Odham Constitution requires approval "only to the extent and for so long as such approval is expressly required by federal statutes." Tohono O'Odham Constitution, Art. VI, § 2. Similarly, under the current Hoopa Valley Constitution, there is no Secretarial approval requirement for "ordinances governing the conduct of members and nonmembers of the Hoopa Valley Indian Tribe." Art. IX, § 1(k). In view of the Supreme Court's growing reliance on federal preemption as the basis for striking down state regulation of non-Indians on reservations, *see* Ch. 4, Sec. B.4, will Indian nations have to forego litigation advantages of federal approval if they eliminate the Secretarial review language in their constitutions? Interestingly, although the Navajo Nation does not have a written constitution and the federal government imposes no requirement that tribal ordinances be approved, the Navajos submitted their mineral severance tax ordinance to the Secretary for approval. Why would they have done so? The Secretary responded that he lacked authority either to approve or disapprove the ordinance, and the United States Supreme Court later held that the approval was unnecessary. *See Kerr-McGee v. Navajo Tribe*, Sec. C.3, this chapter.

B. TRIBAL GOVERNING AUTHORITY

1. Inherent Tribal Sovereignty

TALTON v. MAYES
United States Supreme Court
163 U.S. 376 (1896)

[Talton was indicted and convicted of murder in the tribal courts of the Cherokee Nation. Under then applicable Cherokee law, the grand jury which indicted Talton consisted of only five persons. Talton sought a writ of habeas corpus in federal district court and the judge refused to discharge the petitioner from custody. Talton appealed to the United States Supreme Court.]

MR. JUSTICE WHITE delivered the opinion of the Court.

Appellant and the person he was charged with having murdered were both Cherokee Indians, and the crime was committed within the Cherokee territory.

To bring himself within the statute, the appellant asserts, 1st, that the grand jury, consisting only of five persons, was not a grand jury within the contemplation of the fifth amendment to the Constitution, which it is asserted is operative upon the Cherokee nation in the exercise of its legislative authority as to purely local matters; 2d, that the indictment by a grand jury thus constituted was not due process of law within the intendment of the fourteenth amendment. [We must consider] the relation of the Cherokee nation to the United States, and of the operation of the constitutional provisions relied on upon the purely local legislation of that nation.

By treaties and statutes of the United States the right of the Cherokee nation to exist as an autonomous body, subject always to the paramount authority of the United States, has been recognized. And from this fact there has consequently been conceded to exist in that nation power to make laws defining offenses and providing for the trial and punishment of those who violate them when the offences are committed by one member of the tribe against another one of its members within the territory of the nation.

Thus, by the fifth article of the treaty of 1835, 7 Stat. 478, 481, it is provided:

The United States hereby covenant and agree that the lands ceded to the Cherokee nation in the foregoing article shall, in no future time without their consent, be included within the territorial limits or jurisdiction of any State or Territory. But they shall secure to the Cherokee nation the right by their national councils to make and carry into effect all such laws as they may deem necessary for the government and protection of the persons and property within their own country belonging to their people or such persons as have connected themselves with them: Provided always that they shall not be inconsistent with the Constitution of the United States and such acts of Congress as have been or may be passed regulating trade and intercourse with the Indians; and also, that they shall not be considered as extending to such citizens and army of the United States as may travel or reside in the Indian country by permission according to the laws and regulations established by the government of the same.

This guarantee of self government was reaffirmed in the treaty of 1868, 14 Stat. 799, 803, the thirteenth article of which reads as follows:

Art. XIII. The Cherokees also agree that a court or courts may be established by the United States in said territory, with such jurisdiction and organized in such manner as may be prescribed by law: *Provided*, That the judicial tribunals of the nation shall be allowed to retain exclusive jurisdiction in all civil and criminal cases arising within their country in which members of the nation, by nativity or adoption, shall be the only parties, or where the cause of action shall arise in the Cherokee nation, except as otherwise provided in this treaty.

[The crime of murder of one Cherokee Indian by another] within the jurisdiction of the Cherokee nation is, therefore, clearly not an offence against the United States, but an offence against the local laws of the Cherokee nation. Necessarily, the statutes of the United States which provide for an indictment by a grand jury, and the number of persons who shall constitute such a body, have no application, for such statutes relate only, if not otherwise specially provided, to grand juries empanelled for the courts of and under the laws of the United States.

The question, therefore, is, does the fifth amendment to the Constitution apply to the local legislation of the Cherokee nation so as to require all prosecutions for offences committed against the laws of that nation to be initiated by a grand jury organized in accordance with the provisions of that amendment. The solution of this question involves an inquiry as to the nature and origin of the power of local government exercised by the Cherokee nation and recognized to exist in it by the treaties and statutes above referred to. Since the case of *Barron v. Baltimore*, 7 Pet. 243, it has been settled that the fifth amendment to the Constitution of the United States is a limitation only upon the powers of the General Government, that is, that the amendment operates solely on the Constitution itself by qualifying the powers of the National Government which the Constitution called into being.

[The answer] depends upon whether the powers of local government exercised by the Cherokee nation are Federal powers created by and springing from the Constitution of the United States, and hence controlled by the fifth amendment to that Constitution, or whether they are local powers not created by the Constitution, although subject to its general provisions and the paramount authority of Congress. The repeated adjudications of this court have long since answered the former question in the negative. [*E.g., The Cherokee Cases.*]

True it is that in many adjudications of this court the fact has been fully recognized, that although possessed of these attributes of local self government, when exercising their tribal functions, all such rights are subject to the supreme legislative authority of the United States. *Cherokee Nation v. Kansas Railway Co.*, 135 U.S. 641, where the cases are fully reviewed. But the existence of the right in Congress to regulate the manner in which the local powers of the Cherokee nation shall be exercised does not render such local powers Federal powers arising from and created by the Constitution of the United States. It follows that as the powers of local self government enjoyed by the Cherokee nation existed prior to the Constitution, they are not operated upon by the fifth amendment, which, as we have said, had for its sole object to control the powers conferred by the Constitution on the National Government. The fact that the Indian tribes are subject to the dominant authority of Congress, and that their powers of local self government are also operated upon and restrained by the general provisions of the Constitution of the United States, completely answers the argument of inconvenience which was pressed in the discussion at bar. The claim that the finding of an indictment by a grand jury of less than thirteen violates the due process clause of the fourteenth amendment is conclusively answered by *Hurtado v. California*, 110 U.S. 516, and *McNulty v. California*, 149 U.S. 645. [T]he determination of what was the existing law of the Cherokee nation as to the constitution of the grand jury, were solely matters within the jurisdiction of the courts of that nation, and the decision of such a question in itself necessarily involves no infraction of the Constitution of the United States.

[*Affirmed.*]

MR. JUSTICE HARLAN dissented.

UNITED STATES v. WHEELER
United States Supreme Court
435 U.S. 313 (1978)

MR. JUSTICE STEWART delivered the opinion of the Court.

The question presented in this case is whether the Double Jeopardy Clause of the fifth amendment bars the prosecution of an Indian in a federal district court under the Major Crimes Act, 18 U.S.C. § 1153, when he has previously been convicted in a tribal court of a lesser included offense arising out of the same incident.

I

On October 16, 1974, the respondent, a member of the Navajo Tribe, was arrested by a tribal police officer at the Bureau of Indian Affairs High School in

Many Farms, Ariz., on the Navajo Indian Reservation. He was taken to the tribal jail in Chinle, Ariz., and charged with disorderly conduct, in violation of § 17-351 of the Navajo Tribal Code. On October 18, two days after his arrest, the respondent pleaded guilty to disorderly conduct and a further charge of contributing to the delinquency of a minor, in violation of § 17-321 of the Navajo Tribal Code. He was sentenced to 15 days in jail or a fine of $30 on the first charge and to 60 days in jail (to be served concurrently with the other jail term) or a fine of $120 on the second.

Over a year later, on November 19, 1975, an indictment charging the respondent with statutory rape was returned by a grand jury in the United States District Court for the District of Arizona. The respondent moved to dismiss this indictment, claiming that since the tribal offense of contributing to the delinquency of a minor was a lesser included offense of statutory rape, the proceedings that had taken place in the Tribal Court barred a subsequent federal prosecution. See *Brown v. Ohio*, 432 U.S. 161. The District Court, rejecting the prosecutor's argument that "there is not an identity of sovereignties between the Navajo Tribal Courts and the courts of the United States," dismissed the indictment. The Court of Appeals for the Ninth Circuit affirmed the judgment of dismissal, concluding that since "Indian tribal courts and United States district courts are not arms of separate sovereigns," the Double Jeopardy Clause barred the respondent's trial. We granted certiorari to resolve an intercircuit conflict.

II

In *Bartkus v. Illinois*, 359 U.S. 121, and *Abbate v. United States*, 359 U.S. 187, this Court reaffirmed the well-established principle that a federal prosecution does not bar a subsequent state prosecution of the same person for the same acts, and a state prosecution does not bar a federal one. The basis for this doctrine is that prosecutions under the laws of separate sovereigns do not, in the language of the fifth amendment, "subject [the defendant] for the same offence to be twice put in jeopardy." . . .

III

It is undisputed that Indian tribes have power to enforce their criminal laws against tribe members. Although physically within the territory of the United States and subject to ultimate federal control, they nonetheless remain "a separate people, with the power of regulating their internal and social relations." *United States v. Kagama*, [118 U.S. 375,] at 381–82; *Cherokee Nation v. Georgia*, 5 Pet. 1, 16. Their right to internal self-government includes the right to prescribe laws applicable to tribe members and to enforce those laws by criminal sanctions. [T]he controlling question in this case is the source of this power to punish tribal offenders: Is it a part of inherent tribal sovereignty, or an aspect of the sovereignty of the federal government which has been delegated to the tribes by Congress?

A

The powers of Indian tribes are, in general, "*Inherent powers of a limited sovereignty which has never been extinguished.*" F. Cohen, Handbook of Federal

Indian Law 122 (1941) (emphasis in original). Before the coming of the Europeans, the tribes were self-governing sovereign political communities. See *McClanahan v. Arizona State Tax Comm'n*, 411 U.S. 164, 172. Like all sovereign bodies, they then had the inherent power to prescribe laws for their members and to punish infractions of those laws.

Indian tribes are, of course, no longer "possessed of the full attributes of sovereignty." *United States v. Kagama, supra* at 381. Their incorporation within the territory of the United States, and their acceptance of its protection, necessarily divested them of some aspects of the sovereignty which they had previously exercised. By specific treaty provision they yielded up other sovereign powers; by statute, in the exercise of its plenary control, Congress has removed still others.

But our cases recognize that the Indian tribes have not given up their full sovereignty. We have recently said that "Indian tribes are unique aggregations possessing attributes of sovereignty over both their members and their territory. . . . [They] are a good deal more than 'private, voluntary organization.'" *United States v. Mazurie*, 419 U.S. 544, 557; [*see also Cherokee Nation v. Georgia*]. The sovereignty that the Indian tribes retain is of a unique and limited character. It exists only at the sufferance of Congress and is subject to complete defeasance. But until Congress acts, the tribes retain their existing sovereign powers. In sum, Indian tribes still possess those aspects of sovereignty not withdrawn by treaty or statute, or by implication as a necessary result of their dependent status. *See Oliphant v. Suquamish Indian Tribe*, [435 U.S., at] 191.

B

It is evident that the sovereign power to punish tribal offenders has never been given up by the Navajo Tribe and that tribal exercise of that power today is therefore the continued exercise of retained tribal sovereignty. Although both of the treaties executed by the Tribe with the United States provided for punishment by the United States of Navajos who commit crimes against non-Indians, nothing in either of them deprived the Tribe of its *own* jurisdiction to charge, try and punish members of the Tribe for violations of tribal law. On the contrary, we have said that "[i]mplicit in these treaty terms . . . was the understanding that the internal affairs of the Indians remained exclusively within the jurisdiction of whatever tribal government existed." *Williams v. Lee*, 358 U.S. 217, 221–222.

Similarly, statutes establishing federal criminal jurisdiction over crimes involving Indians have recognized an Indian tribe's jurisdiction over its members. The first Indian Trade and Intercourse Act, Act of July 22, 1790, § 5, 1 Stat. 138, provided only that the federal government would punish offenses committed *against* Indians by "any citizen or inhabitant of the United States"; it did not mention crimes committed *by* Indians. In 1817 federal criminal jurisdiction was extended to crimes committed within the Indian country by "any Indian, or other person or persons," but "any offense committed by one Indian against another, within any Indian boundary" was excluded. Act of March 3, 1817, ch. 92, 3 Stat. 383. In the Indian Trade and Intercourse Act of 1834, § 25, 4 Stat. 733, Congress enacted the direct progenitor of the General Crimes Act, now 18 U.S.C. § 1152, which makes federal enclave criminal law generally applicable to crimes in "Indian country." In this statute Congress carried forward the intra-Indian offense exception because "the tribes have exclusive jurisdiction" of such offenses and "we can [not] with any justice or propriety extend our laws to" them. H.R. Rep. No. 474, 23d Cong., 1st Sess., 13 (1834). And in 1854 Congress expressly recognized the jurisdiction of tribal courts when it added another exception to the General Crimes Act, providing that federal courts would not try an Indian "who has been punished by the local law of the Tribe." Act of March 27, 1854, § 3, 10 Stat. 270.[1] Thus, far from depriving Indian tribes of their sovereign power to punish offenses against tribal law by members of a tribe, Congress has repeatedly recognized that power and declined to disturb it.

Moreover, the sovereign power of a tribe to prosecute its members for tribal offenses clearly does not fall within that part of sovereignty which the Indians implicitly lost by virtue of their dependent status. The areas in which such implicit divestiture of sovereignty has been held to have occurred are those involving the relations between an Indian tribe and nonmembers of the tribe. Thus, Indian tribes can no longer freely alienate to non-Indians the land they occupy. *Oneida Indian Nation v. County of Oneida*, 414 U.S. 661, 667–668; *Johnson v. M'Intosh*, 8 Wheat. 543, 574. They cannot enter into direct commercial or governmental relations with foreign nations. *Worcester v. Georgia*, 6 Pet. 515, 559; *Cherokee Nation v. Georgia*, 5 Pet., at 17–18; *Fletcher v. Peck*, 6 Cranch 87, 147 (concurring opinion of Mr. Justice Johnson). And, as we have recently held, they cannot try nonmembers in tribal courts. *Oliphant v. Suquamish Indian Tribe*, [435 U.S., at] 191.

These limitations rest on the fact that the dependent status of Indian tribes within our territorial jurisdiction is necessarily inconsistent with their freedom independently to determine their external relations. But the powers of self-government, including the power to prescribe and enforce internal criminal laws, are of a different type. They involve only the relations among members of a tribe. Thus, they are not such powers as would necessarily be lost by virtue of a tribe's dependent status. "[T]he settled doctrine of the law of nations is, that a weaker power does not surrender its independence — its right to self government, by associating with a stronger, and taking its protection." *Worcester v. Georgia, supra,* at 560–561.

C

That the Navajo Tribe's power to punish offenses against tribal law committed by its members is an aspect of its retained sovereignty is further supported by the absence of any federal grant of such power. If Navajo self-government were merely the exercise of delegated federal sovereignty, such a delegation should logically appear somewhere. But no provision in the relevant treaties or statutes confers the

---

[1] [22] This statute is not applicable to the present case. The Major Crimes Act, under which instant prosecution was brought, was enacted in 1885. Act of March 3, 1885, § 9, 23 Stat. 385. It does not contain any exception for Indians punished under tribal law. We need not decide whether this "carefully limited intrusion of federal power into the otherwise exclusive jurisdiction of the Indian tribes to punish Indians for crimes committed on Indian land," *United States v. Antelope*, 430 U.S. 641, 643 n.1, deprives a tribal court of jurisdiction over the enumerated offenses, since the crimes to which the respondent pleaded guilty in the Navajo Tribal Court are not among those enumerated in the Major Crimes Act. *Cf. Oliphant v. Suquamish Indian Tribe*, [435 U.S.,] at 203–204, n. 14.

right of self-government in general, or the power to punish crimes in particular, upon the Tribe.

It is true that in the exercise of the powers of self-government, as in all other matters, the Navajo Tribe, like all Indian tribes, remains subject to ultimate federal control. Thus, before the Navajo Tribal Council created the present Tribal Code and Tribal Courts,[2] the Bureau of Indian Affairs established a Code of Indian Tribal Offenses and a Court of Indian Offenses for the reservation. *See* 25 CFR Part 11 (1977); *cf.* 25 U.S.C. § 1311.[3] Pursuant to federal regulations, the present Tribal Code was approved by the Secretary of the Interior before becoming effective. *See* 25 CFR § 11.1 (e) (1977). Moreover, the Indian Reorganization Act of 1934, § 16, 48 Stat. 987, 25 U.S.C. § 476, and the Act of April 19, 1950, § 6, 64 Stat. 46, 25 U.S.C. § 636, each authorized the Tribe to adopt a constitution for self-government. And the Indian Civil Rights Act of 1968, 82 Stat. 77, 25 U.S.C. § 1302, made most of the provisions of the Bill of Rights applicable to the Indian tribes and limited the punishment tribal courts could impose. . . .

But none of these laws *created* the Indians' power to govern themselves and their right to punish crimes committed by tribal offenders. Indeed, the Wheeler-Howard Act and the Navajo-Hopi Rehabilitation Act both recognized that Indian tribes already had such power under "existing law." See Powers of Indian Tribes, 55 I.D. 14 (1934). That Congress has in certain ways regulated the manner and extent of the tribal power of self-government does not mean that Congress is the source of that power.

In sum, the power to punish offenses against tribal law committed by Tribe members, which was part of the Navajos' primeval sovereignty, has never been taken away from them, either explicitly or implicitly, and is attributable in no way to any delegation to them of federal authority. It follows that when the Navajo Tribe exercises this power, it does so as part of its retained sovereignty and not as an arm of the federal government.

D

The conclusion that an Indian tribe's power to punish tribal offenders is part of its own retained sovereignty is clearly reflected in a case decided by this Court more than 80 years ago, *Talton v. Mayes*, 163 U.S. 376. [Its relevance] to the present case is clear. The Court there held that when an Indian tribe criminally punishes a tribe member for violating tribal law, the tribe acts as an independent sovereign, and not as an arm of the federal government. Since tribal and federal prosecutions are brought by separate sovereigns, they are not "for the same offence," and the Double

---

[2] [25] The Tribal Courts were established in 1958, and the law and order provisions of the Tribal Code in 1959, by resolution of the Navajo Tribal Council. See Titles 7 and 17 of the Navajo Tribal Code; *Oliver v. Udall*, 306 F.2d 819, 113 U.S. App. D.C. 212.

[3] [26] Such Courts of Indian Offenses, or "CFR Courts," still exist on approximately 30 reservations "in which traditional agencies for the enforcement of tribal law and custom have broken down [and] no adequate substitute has been provided." 25 CFR § 11.1 (b) (1977). We need not decide today whether such a court is an arm of the federal government or, like the Navajo Tribal Court, derives its powers from the inherent sovereignty of the tribe.

Jeopardy Clause thus does not bar one when the other has occurred.

IV

[T]ribal courts are important mechanisms for protecting significant tribal interests. Federal pre-emption of a tribe's jurisdiction to punish its members for infractions of tribal law would detract substantially from tribal self-government, just as federal pre-emption of state criminal jurisdiction would trench upon important state interests. Thus, just as in *Bartkus* and *Abbate*, there are persuasive reasons to reject the respondent's argument that we should arbitrarily ignore the settled "dual sovereignty" concept as it applies to successive tribal and federal prosecutions.

Accordingly, the judgment of the Court of Appeals is reversed, and the case is remanded for further proceedings consistent with this opinion.

NOTES

1. **Source of Tribal Sovereignty:** Professor Stephen Young writes, "[Like federal and state sovereignties], Indian tribes are . . . self-authenticating, because their will and integrity were created by and are sustained by no source other than their own internal beliefs and arrangements. Neither state nor federal governments ever put the breath of communal life into them." Stephan B. Young, *Indian Tribal Sovereignty and American Fiduciary Undertakings*, 8 Whittier L. Rev. 825, 827 (1987). To what extent do *Talton* and *Wheeler* support Young's claims? If the Cherokee Nation's governmental powers depended on a grant from the United States, would the *Talton* Court have been required to apply the Fifth Amendment right to grand jury indictment on the theory that Cherokee government action expressed federal power? If the Navajo Nation's governmental powers depended on a grant from the United States, could a Navajo criminal prosecution be treated as the act of a "separate sovereign" from the United States for purposes of applying the double jeopardy clause of the Fifth Amendment? For the competing view that tribal sovereignty is "illusory" because it enjoys no protection against the exercise of overriding federal power, see Note, *Sovereignty by Sufferance: The Illusion of Indian Tribal Sovereignty*, 79 Cornell L. Rev. 404 (1994). Scholars Rebecca Tsosie and Wallace Coffey advocate a vision of "cultural sovereignty," which offers a reexamination of the political sovereignty doctrine. *See* Wallace Coffey & Rebecca Tsosie, *Rethinking the Tribal Sovereignty Doctrine: Cultural Sovereignty and the Collective Future of Indian Nations,* 12 Stan. L. & Pol'y Rev. 191 (2001).

Examples of tribal exercises of sovereignty abound. One illustration is the increasingly frequent practice of Indian tribes establishing their own motor vehicle registration system and issuing tribal license plates, often at a fraction of the cost assessed by the states in which they are located. In *Prairie Band of Potawatomi Indians v. Wagnon*, 402 F.3d 1015 (10th Cir. 2005), the Tenth Circuit upheld an injunction requiring the state to recognize the Tribe's motor vehicle registrations and licenses and to refrain from enforcing state motor licensing laws against the vehicles of licensed tribal members. *See also Queets Band of Indians v. Wash.*, 765

F.2d 1399 (9th Cir. 1985); *Red Lake Band of Chippewa Indians v. State*, 248 N.W.2d 722 (Minn. 1976).

2. Treaty and Early Federal Statutory Recognition of Inherent Tribal Sovereignty: Many treaties and statutes acknowledge the existence and exercise of tribal sovereignty. For example, the 1856 treaty between the United States and the Creeks and Seminoles, August 7, 1856, 11 Stat. 699, 700 provides:

> [N]o State or Territory shall ever pass laws for the government of the Creek and Seminole tribes of Indians, and . . . no portion of either of the tracts of [their] country . . . shall ever be embraced or included within, or annexed to, any Territory or State, nor shall either, or any part of either, ever be erected into a Territory without the full and free consent of the legislative authority of the tribe owning the same.

Similarly, as noted in *Wheeler*, Congress excluded intra-Indian offenses from the early federal statutes addressing criminal conduct within Indian country out of respect for the Indian nations' authority. Does such federal recognition of tribal governmental powers enhance or detract from the conception of tribal sovereignty as "inherent" or "self-authenticating," in Young's words? One commentator claims that *Talton*'s references to treaties and statutes recognizing Cherokee sovereignty establish that "[t]he Cherokees' right to self-government had its origin in federal treaties and statutes." Frederick J. Martone, *American Indian Tribal Self-Government in the Federal System: Inherent Right or Congressional License?*, 51 Notre Dame L. Rev. 600, 624 (1976). How does the *Wheeler* Court address this kind of argument?

3. Tribal Governments and Federal Constitutional Rights: Most individual rights afforded by the United States Constitution operate through limitations on federal or state power. *Barron v. Baltimore*, 32 U.S. (7 Pet.) 243 (1833); *Civil Rights Cases*, 109 U.S. 3 (1883). As *Talton v. Mayes* affirms, tribal governments exist independent of federal or state authority, and thus are not subject to these constitutional limitations. The Court's reliance on *Talton* in *United States v. Wheeler* demonstrates the continued vitality of this proposition. *See also Barona Group of Capitan Grande Band of Mission Indians v. American Mgt. & Amusement, Inc.*, 840 F.2d 1394 (9th Cir. 1987) (no just compensation claim available for tribal voiding of bingo management contract); *Native American Church v. Navajo Tribal Council*, 272 F.2d 131 (10th Cir. 1959) (denying application of First Amendment to Navajo law prohibiting the sale, use, or possession of peyote). Recent Supreme Court decisions denying tribal court jurisdiction over nonmembers have expressed some concern that those courts need not protect litigants' federal constitutional rights. *See, e.g., Duro v. Reina*, 495 U.S. 676, 709 (1990). As the Court noted in *Nevada v. Hicks*, 533 U.S. 353, 383 (2001), a case denying tribal jurisdiction over a tort and civil rights action against state officers, " . . . [I]t has been understood for more than a century that the Bill of Rights and the fourteenth amendment do not of their own force apply to Indian tribes" (citing *Talton v. Mayes* and F. Cohen, Handbook of Federal Indian Law (1982 ed.)). The federal Indian Civil Rights Act of 1968 (*see* Sec. D.1, this chapter) and tribal bills of rights (*see* Sec. D.2, this chapter) do afford alternative sources of protection when federal constitutional guarantees are inapplicable.

In contrast, constitutional rights that exist as against *all* actors, not just state and federal governments, apply fully to Indian nations. A notable illustration is the Thirteenth Amendment's proscription against slavery. *United States v. Choctaw Nation*, 38 Ct. Cl. 558 (1903), *aff'd*, 193 U.S. 115 (1904); *In re Sah Quah*, 31 F. 327 (D. Alaska 1886). Likewise, federal civil rights statutes effectuating such constitutional provisions have been applied to tribes. *See Evans v. McKay*, 869 F.2d 1341 (9th Cir. 1989) (denying motion to dismiss claim alleging overt acts and racial remarks by Blackfeet tribal members acting in their official capacities in violation of 42 U.S.C. § 1981).

4. Tribal-Federal Entanglements: For purposes of constitutional rights affording protection only against federal or state action, how should courts view tribal actions receiving federal approval? Under the Indian Self-Determination Act of 1975, 25 U.S.C. §§ 450–450n, the Secretary of the Interior and the Secretary of Health and Human Services are authorized to contract with Indian nations to provide services and manage federal programs previously administered by their agencies. In 1994, Congress added the Indian Self-Governance Program, 25 U.S.C. § 458aa–hh, which allows tribes to enter into compacts through which tribes fund and administer a broad range of federal programs. Many tribes have chosen to operate tribal courts with federal funds under contract or compact with the Bureau of Indian Affairs. Does the Bill of Rights directly restrain the actions of such tribal courts? Consider this question as you read *United States v. Mazurie* in Sec. B.2, this chapter.

MERRION v. JICARILLA APACHE TRIBE
United States Supreme Court
455 U.S. 130 (1982)

Mr. Justice Marshall delivered the opinion of the Court.

Pursuant to long-term leases with the Jicarilla Apache Tribe, petitioners, 21 lessees, extract and produce oil and gas from the tribe's reservation lands. In these two consolidated cases, petitioners challenge an ordinance enacted by the Tribe imposing a severance tax on "any oil and natural gas severed, saved and removed from Tribal lands." *See* Oil and Gas Severance Tax No. 77-00-02, App. 38. We granted certiorari to determine whether the Tribe has the authority to impose this tax, and, if so, whether the tax imposed by the Tribe violates the Commerce Clause.

The Jicarilla Apache Tribe resides on a reservation in northwestern New Mexico. Established by Executive Order in 1887, the reservation [is inhabited by approximately 2,100 individuals and] contains 742,315 acres, all of which are held as tribal trust property. [T]he Tribe's sovereign power is not affected by the manner in which its reservation was created. The Tribe is organized under the [Indian Reorganization Act. The Tribe's Constitution has been revised and approved by the Secretary of the Interior and contains a provision requiring tribal ordinances to be approved by the Secretary.]

To develop tribal lands, the Tribe has executed mineral leases encompassing some 69% of the reservation land. Beginning in 1953, the petitioners entered into leases with the Tribe. The Commissioner of Indian Affairs, on behalf of the Secretary, approved these leases, as required by the Act of May 11, 1938, ch. 198, 52 Stat. 347, 25 U.S.C. §§ 396a–396g (1938 Act). In exchange for a cash bonus, royalties, and rents, the typical lease grants the lessee "the exclusive right and privilege to drill for, mine, extract, remove, and dispose of all the oil and natural gas deposits in or under" the leased land for as long as the minerals are produced in paying quantities. Petitioners may use oil and gas in developing the lease without incurring the royalty. In addition, the Tribe reserves the rights to use gas without charge for any of its buildings on the leased land, and to take its royalties in kind. Petitioner's activities on the leased land have been subject to taxes imposed by the State of New Mexico on oil and gas severance and on oil and gas production equipment. *See* Act of Mar. 3, 1927, ch. 299, § 3, 44 Stat. 1347, 25 U.S.C. § 398c (permitting state taxation of mineral production on Indian reservations (1927 Act)).

Pursuant to its Revised Constitution, the Tribal Council adopted an ordinance imposing a severance tax on oil and gas production on tribal land. The ordinance was approved by the Secretary, through the Acting Director of the Bureau of Indian Affairs, on December 23, 1976. The tax applies to "any oil and natural gas severed, saved and removed from Tribal lands. . . . "

In two separate actions, petitioners sought to enjoin enforcement of the tax by either the tribal authorities or the Secretary. The United States District Court for the District of New Mexico consolidated the cases, granted other lessees leave to intervene, and permanently enjoined enforcement of the tax. The District Court ruled that the Tribe lacked the authority to impose the tax, that only state and local authorities had the power to tax oil and gas production on Indian reservations, and that the tax violated the Commerce Clause.

The United States Court of Appeals for the Tenth Circuit, sitting en banc, reversed [reasoning] that the taxing power is an inherent attribute of tribal sovereignty that has not been divested by any treaty or Act of Congress, including the 1927 Act, 25 U.S.C. § 398c. The court also found no Commerce Clause violation. We granted certiorari, and we now affirm the decision of the Court of Appeals.

II

Petitioners argue, and the dissent agrees, that an Indian tribe's authority to tax non-Indians who do business on the reservation stems exclusively from its power to exclude such persons from tribal lands. Because the Tribe did not initially condition the leases upon the payment of a severance tax, petitioners assert that the Tribe is without authority to impose such a tax at a later time. We disagree with the premise that the power to tax derives only from the power to exclude. Even if that premise is accepted, however, we disagree with the conclusion that the Tribe lacks the power to impose the severance tax.

A

In *Washington v. Confederated Tribes of the Colville Indian Reservation*, [447 U.S. 134 (1980)] (Colville), we addressed the Indian tribes' authority to impose taxes on non-Indians doing business on the reservation. We held that "[t]he power to tax transactions occurring on trust lands and significantly involving a tribe or its members is a fundamental attribute of sovereignty which the tribes retain unless divested of it by federal law or necessary implication of their dependent status." *Id.*, at 152. The power to tax is an essential attribute of Indian sovereignty because it is a necessary instrument of self-government and territorial management. This power enables a tribal government to raise revenues for its essential services. The power does not derive solely from the Indian tribe's power to exclude non-Indians from tribal lands. Instead, it derives from the tribe's general authority, as sovereign, to control economic activity within its jurisdiction, and to defray the cost of providing governmental services by requiring contributions from persons or enterprises engaged in economic activities within that jurisdiction. *See, e.g., Gibbons v. Ogden*, [9 Wheat. 1, 199] (1824).

The petitioners avail themselves of the "substantial privilege of carrying on business" on the reservation. They benefit from the provision of police protection and other governmental services, as well as from " 'the advantages of a civilized society' " that are assured by the existence of tribal government. Numerous other governmental entities levy a general revenue tax similar to that imposed by the Jicarilla Tribe when they provide comparable services. Under these circumstances, there is nothing exceptional in requiring petitioners to contribute through taxes to the general cost of tribal government.[4]

As we observed in *Colville, supra*, the tribe's interest in levying taxes on nonmembers to raise "revenues for essential governmental programs . . . is strongest when the revenues are derived from value generated on the reservation by activities involving the Tribes and when the taxpayer is the recipient of tribal services." 447 U.S., at 156–57. This surely is the case here. The mere fact that the government imposing the tax also enjoys rents and royalties as the lessor of the mineral lands does not undermine the government's authority to impose the tax. The royalty payments from the mineral leases are paid to the Tribe in its role as partner in petitioners' commercial venture. The severance tax, in contrast, is petitioners' contribution "to the general cost of providing governmental services." State governments commonly receive both royalty payments and severance taxes from lessees of mineral lands within their borders.

Viewing the taxing power of Indian tribes as an essential instrument of self-government and territorial management has been a shared assumption of all three branches of the federal government. In *Colville*, the Court relied in part on a 1934 opinion of the Solicitor for the Department of the Interior. In this opinion, the Solicitor recognized that, in the absence of congressional action to the contrary, the tribes' sovereign power to tax " 'may be exercised over members of the tribe and over nonmembers, so far as such nonmembers may accept privileges of trade, residence, etc., to which taxes may be attached as conditions.' " 447 U.S., at 153 (quoting *Powers of Indian Tribes*, 55 I.D. 14, 46 (1934)). Congress has [also]

---

[4] [5] Through various Acts governing Indian tribes, Congress has expressed the purpose of "fostering tribal self-government." *Colville*, 447 U.S., at 155. We agree with Judge McKay's observation that "[i]t simply does not make sense to expect the tribes to carry out municipal functions approved and mandated by Congress without being able to exercise at least minimal taxing powers, whether they take the form of real estate taxes, leasehold taxes or severance taxes." (McKay, J., concurring).

acknowledged that the tribal power to tax is one of the tools necessary to self-government and territorial control. As early as 1879, the Senate Judiciary Committee acknowledged the validity of a tax imposed by the Chickasaw Nation on non-Indians legitimately within its territory. [T]he views of the three branches of government, as well as general principles of taxation, confirm that Indian tribes enjoy authority to finance their governmental services through taxation of non-Indians who benefit from those services. Indeed, the conception of Indian sovereignty that this Court has consistently reaffirmed permits no other conclusion. [*Mazurie*] Adhering to this understanding, we conclude that the Tribe's authority to tax non-Indians who conduct business on the reservation does not simply derive from the Tribe's power to exclude such persons, but is an inherent power necessary to tribal self-government and territorial management.

Of course, the Tribe's authority to tax nonmembers is subject to constraints not imposed on other governmental entities: the federal government can take away this power, and the Tribe must obtain the approval of the Secretary before any tax on nonmembers can take effect. These additional constraints minimize potential concern that Indian tribes will exercise the power to tax in an unfair or unprincipled manner, and ensure that any exercise of the tribal power to tax will be consistent with national policies.

We are not persuaded by the dissent's attempt to limit an Indian tribe's authority to tax non-Indians by asserting that its only source is the tribe's power to exclude such persons from tribal lands. Limiting the tribes' authority to tax in this manner contradicts the conception that Indian tribes are domestic, dependent nations, as well as the common understanding that the sovereign taxing power is a tool for raising revenue necessary to cover the costs of government.

Nor are we persuaded by the dissent that three early decisions upholding tribal power to tax nonmembers support this limitation. [T]here is a significant territorial component to tribal power: a tribe has no authority over a nonmember until the nonmember enters tribal lands or conducts business with the tribe. However, we do not believe that this territorial component to Indian taxing power, which is discussed in these early cases, means that the tribal authority to tax derives solely from the tribe's power to exclude nonmembers from tribal lands.

[Of the three decisions discussed by the dissent,] the decision in *Buster v. Wright* actually undermines the theory that the tribes' taxing authority derives solely from the power to exclude non-Indians from tribal lands. Under this theory, a non-Indian who establishes a lawful presence in Indian territory could avoid paying a tribal tax by claiming that no residual portion of the power to exclude supports the tax. This result was explicitly rejected in *Buster v. Wright*. In *Buster*, deeds to individual lots in Indian territory had been granted to non-Indian residents, and cities and towns had been incorporated. As a result, Congress had expressly prohibited the Tribe from removing these non-Indian residents. Even though the ownership of land and the creation of local governments by non-Indians established their legitimate presence on Indian land, the court held that the Tribe retained its power to tax. The court concluded that "[n]either the United States, nor a state, nor any other sovereignty loses the power to govern the people within its borders by the existence of towns and cities therein endowed with the usual powers of municipalities, *nor by the ownership nor occupancy of the land within its territorial jurisdiction by citizens or foreigners.*" 135 F., at 952 (emphasis added). This result confirms that the Tribe's authority to tax derives not from its power to exclude, but from its power to govern and to raise revenues to pay for the costs of government.

We choose not to embrace a new restriction on the extent of the tribal authority to tax, which is based on a questionable interpretation of three early cases. Instead, based on the views of each of the federal branches, general principles of taxation, and the conception of Indian tribes as domestic, dependent nations, we conclude that the Tribe has the authority to impose a severance tax on the mining activities of petitioners as part of its power to govern and to pay for the costs of self-government.

B

Alternatively, if we accept the argument, advanced by petitioners and the dissent, that the Tribe's authority to tax derives solely from its power to exclude non-Indians from the reservation, we conclude that the Tribe has the authority to impose the severance tax challenged here. Nonmembers who lawfully enter tribal lands remain subject to the tribe's *power* to exclude them. This power necessarily includes the lesser power to place conditions on entry, on continued presence, or on reservation conduct, such as a tax on business activities conducted on the reservation. When a tribe grants a non-Indian the right to be on Indian land, the tribe agrees not to exercise its *ultimate* power to oust the non-Indian as long as the non-Indian complies with the initial conditions of entry. However, it does not follow that the lawful property right to be on Indian land also immunizes the non-Indian from the tribe's exercise of its lesser-included power to tax or to place other conditions on the non-Indian's conduct or continued presence on the reservation. A nonmember who enters the jurisdiction of the tribe remains subject to the risk that the tribe will later exercise its sovereign power. The fact that the tribe chooses not to exercise its power to tax when it initially grants a non-Indian entry onto the reservation does not permanently divest the tribe of its authority to impose such a tax.[5]

Petitioners argue that their leaseholds entitle them to enter the reservation and exempt them from further exercises of the Tribe's sovereign authority. Similarly, the dissent asserts that the Tribe has lost the power to tax petitioners' mining activities because it has leased to them the use of the mineral lands and such rights of access to the reservation as might be necessary to enjoy the leases. [T]his conclusion is not compelled by linking the taxing power to the power to exclude. Instead, it is based on additional assumptions and confusions about the consequences of the commercial arrangement between petitioners and the Tribe.

Most important, petitioners and the dissent confuse the Tribe's role as commercial partner with its role as sovereign. This confusion relegates the powers of

---

[5] [10] Here, the leases extend for as long as minerals are produced in paying quantities, in other words, until the resources are depleted. Thus, under the dissent's approach, the Tribe would never have the power to tax petitioners regardless of the financial burden to the Tribe of providing and maintaining governmental services for the benefit of petitioners.

sovereignty to the bargaining process undertaken in each of the sovereign's commercial agreements. It is one thing to find that the Tribe has agreed to sell the right to use the land and take from it valuable minerals; it is quite another to find that the Tribe has abandoned its sovereign powers simply because it has not expressly reserved them through a contract.

Confusing these two results denigrates Indian sovereignty. Indeed, the dissent apparently views the tribal power to exclude, as well as the derivative authority to tax, as merely the power possessed by any individual landowner or any social group to attach conditions, including a "tax" or fee, to the entry by a stranger onto private land or into the social group, and not as a sovereign power. The dissent does pay lip service to the established views that Indian tribes retain those fundamental attributes of sovereignty, including the power to tax transactions that occur on tribal lands, which have not been divested by Congress or by necessary implication of the tribe's dependent status, [*Colville*] and that tribes "are a good deal more than 'private, voluntary organizations.' " [*Mazurie*] However, in arguing that the Tribe somehow "lost" its power to tax petitioners by not including a taxing provision in the original leases or otherwise notifying petitioners that the Tribe retained and might later exercise its sovereign right to tax them, the dissent attaches little significance to the sovereign nature of the tribal authority to tax, and it obviously views tribal authority as little more than a landowner's contractual right. [S]overeignty is not conditioned on the assent of a nonmember; to the contrary, the nonmember's presence and conduct on Indian lands are conditioned by the limitations the tribe may choose to impose.

Viewed in this light, the absence of a reference to the tax in the leases themselves hardly impairs the Tribe's authority to impose the tax. Contractual arrangements remain subject to subsequent legislation by the presiding sovereign. Even where the contract at issue requires payment of a royalty for a license or franchise issued by the governmental entity, the government's power to tax remains unless it "has been specifically surrendered in terms which admit of no other reasonable interpretation." *St. Louis v. United R. Co.*, 210 U.S. 266, 280 (1908).

[Petitioners do not claim] that petitioners' leases contain the clear and unmistakable surrender of taxing power required for its extinction. We could find a waiver of the Tribe's taxing power only if we inferred it from silence in the leases. To presume that a sovereign forever waives the right to exercise one of its sovereign powers unless it expressly reserves the right to exercise that power in a commercial agreement turns the concept of sovereignty on its head, and we do not adopt this analysis.

C

The Tribe has the inherent power to impose the severance tax on petitioners, whether this power derives from the Tribe's power of self-government or from its power to exclude. Because Congress may limit tribal sovereignty, we now review petitioners' argument that Congress, when it enacted two federal Acts governing Indians and various pieces of federal energy legislation, deprived the Tribe of its authority to impose the severance tax.

In *Colville*, we concluded that the "widely held understanding within the Federal Government has always been that *federal law to date has not worked a divestiture of Indian taxing power.*" 447 U.S., at 152 (emphasis added). Moreover, we noted that "[n]o federal statute cited to us shows any congressional departure from this view." *Id.*, at 153. Likewise, petitioners can cite to no statute that specifically divests the Tribe of its power to impose the severance tax on their mining activities. Instead, petitioners argue that Congress *implicitly* took away this power when it enacted the Acts and various pieces of legislation on which petitioners rely. Before reviewing this argument, we reiterate here our admonition in *Santa Clara Pueblo v. Martinez*, 436 U.S. 49, 60 (1978): "a proper respect both for tribal sovereignty itself and for the plenary authority of Congress in this area cautions that we treat lightly in the absence of clear indications of legislative intent."

[In the statutes cited by petitioners we] find no "clear indications" that Congress has implicitly deprived the Tribe of its power to impose the severance tax. In any event, if there were ambiguity on this point, the doubt would benefit the Tribe, for "[a]mbiguities in federal law have been construed generously in order to comport with . . . traditional notions of sovereignty and with the federal policy of encouraging tribal independence." *White Mountain Apache Tribe v. Bracker*, 448 U.S. 136, 143–144 (1980). Accordingly, we find that the federal government has not divested the Tribe of its inherent authority to tax mining activities on its land, whether this authority derives from the Tribe's power of self-government or from its power to exclude. . . .

IV

In *Worcester v. Georgia*, Chief Justice Marshall observed that Indian tribes had "always been considered as distinct, independent political communities, retaining their original natural rights." Although the tribes are subject to the authority of the federal government, the "weaker power does not surrender its independence — its right to self-government, by associating with a stronger, and taking its protection." *Id.*, at 561. Adhering to this understanding, we conclude that the Tribe did not surrender its authority to tax the mining activities of petitioners, whether this authority is deemed to arise from the Tribe's inherent power of self-government or from its inherent power to exclude nonmembers. Therefore, the Tribe may enforce its severance tax unless and until Congress divests this power, an action that Congress has not taken to date. Finally, the severance tax imposed by the Tribe cannot be invalidated on the ground that it violates the "negative implications" of the Commerce Clause.

Affirmed.

JUSTICE STEVENS, with whom THE CHIEF JUSTICE and JUSTICE REHNQUIST join, dissenting. . . .

II

The powers possessed by Indian tribes stem from three sources: federal statutes, treaties, and the tribe's inherent sovereignty. [There are no statutes or treaties on point.] Therefore, if the severance tax is valid, it must be as an exercise of the Tribe's inherent sovereignty. [Although] Indian tribes possess broad powers of self-governance over tribal members, [they] do not possess the same attributes of sovereignty that the federal government and the several States enjoy. In determining the extent of the sovereign powers that the tribes retained in submitting to the authority of the United States, this Court has recognized a fundamental distinction between the right of the tribes to govern their own internal affairs and the right to exercise powers affecting nonmembers of the tribe.

The Court has been careful to protect the tribes from interference with tribal control over their own members. [Nevertheless, in] sharp contrast to the tribes' broad powers over their own members, tribal powers over nonmembers have always been narrowly confined. The Court has emphasized that "exercise of tribal power beyond what is necessary to protect tribal self-government or to control internal relations is inconsistent with the dependent status of the tribes, and so cannot survive without express congressional delegation." *Montana v. United States*, 450 U.S. 544, 564.

[Tribal] authority to enact legislation affecting nonmembers is therefore of a different character than their broad power to control internal tribal affairs. This difference is consistent with the fundamental principle that "[i]n this Nation each sovereign governs only with the consent of the governed." *Nevada v. Hall*, 440 U.S. 410, 426. Since nonmembers are excluded from participation in tribal government, the powers that may be exercised over them are appropriately limited. Certainly, tribal authority over nonmembers — including the power to tax — is not unprecedented. An examination of cases that have upheld this power, however, demonstrates that the power to impose such a tax derives solely from the tribes' power to exclude nonmembers entirely from territory that has been reserved for the tribe. This "power to exclude" logically has been held to include the lesser power to attach conditions on a right of entry granted by the tribe to a nonmember to engage in particular activities within the reservation.

IV

[The Tribe granted petitioners the authority] to extract oil and gas from reservation lands. The Tribe now seeks to change retroactively the conditions of that authority. These petitioners happen to be prosperous oil companies. Moreover, it may be sound policy to find additional sources of revenue to better the economic conditions of many Indian tribes. If this retroactive imposition of a tax on oil companies is permissible, however, an Indian tribe may with equal legitimacy contract with outsiders for the construction of a school or a hospital, or for the rendition of medical or technical services, and then — after the contract is partially performed — change the terms of the bargain by imposing a gross receipts tax on the outsider. If the Court is willing to ignore the risk of such unfair treatment of a local contractor or a local doctor because the Secretary of the Interior has the power to veto a tribal tax, it must equate the unbridled discretion of a political appointee with the protection afforded by rules of law. That equation is unacceptable to me. Neither wealth, political opportunity, nor past transgressions can justify denying any person the protection of the law.

NOTES ON NONMEMBER EXCLUSION AND TRIBAL GOVERNING AUTHORITY

1. **Different Conceptions of Tribal Power in** *Merrion*: How do the majority and dissent differ in their views of tribal sovereignty? Do you think the majority would have been as willing to embrace inherent tribal taxing authority over nonmembers if the Jicarillas had not imposed "a general revenue tax similar to that imposed by [non-Indian governments] when they provide comparable services?" In other words, is the Court tying its recognition of inherent tribal sovereignty to the implicit requirement that tribal governments operate in the same fashion as state and local governments? *See* Robert A. Williams, Jr., *The Algebra of Federal Indian Law: The Hard Trail of Decolonizing and Americanizing the White Man's Indian Jurisprudence*, 1986 Wis. L. Rev. 219. If that is true, does tribal sovereignty lose its significance?

How critical to the result in *Merrion* was the fact that under the Jicarilla Constitution, the Secretary of the Interior had the power to approve the Tribe's taxing ordinances? In a subsequent case, the Court upheld a similar tax imposed by the Navajo Nation, a tribe which has no constitution at all, let alone one that requires Secretarial approval of tribal ordinances. *Kerr-McGee Corp. v. Navajo Tribe*, 471 U.S. 195 (1985).

By treating the power to exclude as an alternative basis for upholding tribal taxing power over non-Indians, does the majority's opinion diminish tribal sovereignty? Could the existence of a tribal power to exclude actually reinforce and support the exercise of tribal jurisdiction? See *Water Wheel Camp Recreational Area, Inc., v. Larance*, 642 F.3d 802 (9th Cir. 2011), discussed in Sec. C.1, this chapter. The dissent, in contrast, treats the power to exclude as the sole basis for the Jicarillas' taxing power. The dissenters claim that tribes "became part of the United States," thereby yielding "their status as independent nations." Are they suggesting that Indian nations voluntarily incorporated themselves into the United States, giving up their powers of self-government? If so, is the dissent's claim historically accurate? What models of tribal-federal relations prevail in the majority and dissenting opinions?

2. **Federal Law and the Power to Exclude:** Many Indian nations, such as the Navajo, entered into treaties that expressly protected the tribe's right to exclude persons from the reservation. *See, e.g.,* Treaty with the Navajo Tribe of 1868, 15 Stat. 667, § 2 ("no persons except those . . . authorized [by the government or the tribe] shall ever be permitted to pass over, settle upon, or reside in, the territory described in this article"). Indeed, the Lakota people fought the so-called Red Cloud's War in a successful effort to keep whites out of their territory and to close federal forts that had been opened in Sioux country without their consent. As a result, Article II of the Fort Laramie Treaty with the Sioux and other tribes, gave the Lakota "absolute and undisturbed use and occupation" of the Great Sioux Reservation described therein. Treaty with the Sioux Nation and Others, April 29, 1868, 15 Stat. 635. The Article further expressly provided that "the United States now solemnly agrees that no persons except those herein designated and authorized so to do, and except such officers, agents, and employees of the Government as may be authorized to enter upon Indian reservations in discharge of duties enjoined by

law, *shall ever be permitted to pass over, settle upon, or reside in the territory described in this article.*" (Emphasis supplied.) Conflict between the Lakota people and prospectors who had moved into the Black Hills with federal support in violation of this express provision of the Treaty constituted an important backdrop to the ultimate demise of General George Armstrong Custer's Seventh Cavalry at the hands of the Sioux in the Battle of Greasy Grass (commonly known as the Little Big Horn). *See generally* EDWARD LAZARUS, BLACK HILLS/WHITE JUSTICE 38–70 (1991). Of course, a treaty is not necessary to establish the power of exclusion because the power is inherent. *Quechan Tribe v. Rowe*, 531 F.2d 408, 410 (9th Cir. 1976) (suggesting the basis of the exclusion authority is inherent tribal power).

Later acts of Congress opening reservation land to non-Indian settlement have modified the right to exclude. The Supreme Court has said that federal allotment statutes prevent tribes from excluding nonmembers who own fee land within the boundaries of the reservation, at least so long as that land is not part of an area that has been closed to the general public. *Brendale v. Confederated Tribes and Bands of Yakima Indian Nation*, 492 U.S. 408 (1989). Does *Brendale* mean that the power to exclude derives exclusively from a tribe's status as landowner? What about allotted lands that are still held in trust or in fee by Indians? What about lands as to which the tribe has granted a right-of-way? *See Strate v. A-1 Contractors*; Sec. C.1, this chapter.

3. **Implementing the Power to Exclude Nonmembers:** Sometimes an Indian nation wants to enforce its standards of conduct, but the federal government is unwilling to acknowledge the tribe's inherent authority over the behavior in question. This problem most often arises with respect to non-Indians, who have been deemed beyond the bounds of most tribal criminal jurisdiction as a result of the "implicit divestment" of tribal authority. *See* C.1, this chapter. Because of the limitations placed on tribal jurisdiction over nonmembers by the federal government, civil exclusion can be an effective way of removing non-Indians who engage in unwanted conduct. In *Duro v. Reina*, 495 U.S. 676, 696–97 (1990), the Supreme Court gave its support to the exercise of such tribal power. According to the Court:

> The tribes . . . possess their traditional and undisputed power to exclude persons whom they deem to be undesirable from tribal lands. *See Brendale v. Confederated Tribes and Bands of Yakima Indian Nation*, 492 U.S., at 422. *New Mexico v. Mescalero Apache Tribe*, 462 U.S. 324, 333 (1983); *Worcester v. Georgia*, 6 Pet. 515, 561 (1832); . . . .

For example, the Omaha Tribe of Nebraska's tribal code includes the following provision: "In the event that any person who is not subject to the criminal jurisdiction of the Omaha Tribe commits any [class A or class B level offense] the Tribal Court shall make application to the Omaha Tribal Council to begin proceedings to expel, ban, or exclude such person from the exterior boundaries of the Omaha tribal reservation." Omaha Tribal Code, Domestic Violence, 11;3;12 (2013).

Tribal law enforcement authorities have the power to restrain those who disturb public order on the reservation, and if necessary, to eject them. Where jurisdiction to try and punish an offender rests outside the tribe, tribal officers may exercise their power to detain the offender and transport that person to the proper authorities. To carry out an exclusion order, tribal police might drive an excluded person to the reservation boundary and drop him or her off. What kind of notice or process, if any, must the tribe provide before carrying out such action? What if the tribe does not have a tribal court? Apart from tribal requirements, the only potentially applicable federal statute is the Indian Civil Rights Act, which allows access to federal courts solely through a petition for a writ of habeas corpus. 25 U.S.C. §§ 1301–03. In *Alire v. Jackson*, 65 F. Supp. 2d 1124 (D. Ore. 1999), the court refused to allow an excluded non-Indian to challenge the Tribe's order of exclusion via habeas corpus. The court indicated that exclusion should trigger a habeas corpus proceeding only when the exclusion constitutes the sentence in a criminal prosecution and gives rise to a severe restraint on the excluded person's liberty. In the court's view, excluding a nonmember from the reservation, even a nonmember Indian, does not impair the individual's life opportunities in any significant way. Under what circumstances might a nonmember successfully sustain a habeas petition? What if the nonmember owns land in fee on the reservation and has family or business ties? Could the inability to access those connections constitute "collateral consequences" severe enough to sustain a petition even after tribal police release the nonmember outside the boundaries of the reservation? Keep in mind that the United States routinely denies select noncitizens the right to enter the country despite any ties they may have to people or property inside the country.

Note that while some tribes have used exclusion to combat domestic violence by non-Indians against tribal members, the 2013 reauthorization of the Violence Against Women Act recognized tribal criminal jurisdiction over non-Indians who commit statutorily specified acts of domestic violence or dating violence, or violate restraining orders. 25. U.S.C § 1304.

Exclusion of members is discussed in Sec. D.3, this chapter.

2.   Federally Supported Tribal Authority

UNITED STATES v. MAZURIE
United States Supreme Court
419 U.S. 544 (1975)

[The defendants were convicted under 18 U.S.C. § 1154 for introducing alcoholic beverages into Indian country. Under 18 U.S.C. § 1161 the proscriptions of section 1154 do not apply to any act or transaction in conformity with the laws of the state "and with an ordinance duly adopted by the tribe having jurisdiction over such area of Indian country, certified by the Secretary of the Interior, and published in the Federal Register."

[The Mazuries owned and operated the Blue Bull bar on fee patent land within the Wind River Reservation in Wyoming that had passed out of Indian trust title as a result of the allotment policy. Until 1971 the tribe had authorized any liquor sale made on the reservation in accordance with state law and the Mazuries had operated the Blue Bull under state license. In 1971 the Wind River Tribes adopted a new tribal ordinance requiring both tribal and state licenses for retail liquor outlets within the reservation. The Mazuries applied for and were denied a tribal liquor license but nevertheless continued to operate the Blue Bull. The Tribes had denied the license after hearing the testimony of witnesses who complained of singing and shooting at late hours, disturbances of elderly residents of a nearby housing development, and unauthorized entry of Indian minors into the bar.]

Mr. Justice Rehnquist delivered the opinion of the Court.

III

The Court of Appeals expressed doubt that "the Government has the power to regulate a business on the land it granted in fee without restrictions." 487 F.2d, at 18. Because the Court went on to hold that even if Congress did possess such power, it could not be delegated to an Indian tribe, that Court did not find it necessary to resolve the issue of congressional power. We do, however, reach the issue, because we hereinafter conclude that federal authority was properly delegated to the Indian tribes. We conclude that federal authority is adequate, even though the lands were held in fee by non-Indians, and even though the persons regulated were non-Indians.

Article I, § 8, of the Constitution gives Congress power "[t]o regulate Commerce with foreign Nations, and among the several States, and with the Indian Tribes." This Court has repeatedly held that this clause affords Congress the power to prohibit or regulate the sale of alcoholic beverages to tribal Indians, wherever situated, and to prohibit or regulate the introduction of alcoholic beverages into Indian country. [*E.g.,*] *United States v. Holliday,* 3 Wall. 407, 417–418.

[N]either the Constitution nor our previous cases leave any room for doubt that Congress possesses the authority to regulate the distribution of alcoholic beverages by establishments such as the Blue Bull.

IV

The Court of Appeals said, however, that even if Congress possessed authority to regulate the Blue Bull, it could not delegate such authority to the Indian tribes. The court reasoned as follows:

> The tribal members are citizens of the United States. It is difficult to see how such an association of citizens could exercise any degree of governmental authority or sovereignty over other citizens who do not belong, and who cannot participate in any way in the tribal organization. The situation is in no way comparable to a city, county, or special district under state laws. There cannot be such a separate "nation" of United States citizens within the boundaries of the United States which has any authority, other than as landowners, over individuals who are excluded as members. . . .

> The purported delegation of authority to the tribal officials contained in 18 U.S.C. § 1161 is therefore invalid. Congress cannot delegate its authority to a private, voluntary organization, which is obviously not a governmental agency, to regulate a business on privately owned lands, no matter where located. It is obvious that the authority of Congress under the Constitution

to regulate commerce with Indian Tribes is broad, but it cannot encompass the relationships here concerned. 487 F.2d, at 19.

This Court has recognized limits on the authority of Congress to delegate its legislative power. *Panama Refining Co. v. Ryan*, 293 U.S. 388 (1935). Those limitations are, however, less stringent in cases where the entity exercising the delegated authority itself possesses independent authority over the subject matter. *United States v. Curtiss-Wright Export Corp.*, 299 U.S. 304, 319–322 (1936). Thus it is an important aspect of this case that Indian tribes are unique aggregations possessing attributes of sovereignty over both their members and their territory, *Worcester v. Georgia*, 6 Pet. 515, 557 (1832); they are "a separate people" possessing "the power of regulating their internal and social relations. . . . " *United States v. Kagama*, 118 U.S. 375 (1886); *McClanahan v. Arizona State Tax Comm'n*, 411 U.S. 164, 173 (1973).

Cases such as [*Worcester* and *Kagama*] surely establish the proposition that Indian tribes within "Indian country" are a good deal more than "private, voluntary organizations," and they thus undermine the rationale of the Court of Appeals' decision. These same cases, in addition make clear that when Congress delegated its authority to control the introduction of alcoholic beverages into Indian country, it did so to entities which possess a certain degree of independent authority over matters that affect the internal and social relations of tribal life. Clearly the distribution and use of intoxicants is just such a matter. We need not decide whether this independent authority is itself sufficient for the Tribes to impose Ordinance No. 26. It is necessary only to state that the independent tribal authority is quite sufficient to protect Congress's decision to vest in tribal councils this portion of its own authority "to regulate Commerce . . . with the Indian tribes." Cf. [*Curtiss-Wright, supra*].

The fact that the Mazuries could not become members of the tribe, and therefore could not participate in the tribal government, does not alter our conclusion. This claim, that because respondents are non-Indians Congress could not subject them to the authority of the Tribal Council with respect to the sale of liquor,[6] is answered by this Court's opinion in *Williams v. Lee*, 358 U.S. 217 (1959). In holding that the authority of tribal courts could extend over non-Indians, insofar as concerned their transactions on a reservation with Indians, we stated:

---

[6] [12] Respondents attempt to bolster this claim with the argument that "the basic rights and principles of equal protection and due process [are] currently not available to non-Indians within the tribal councils." Brief for Respondents 24. However, respondents make no claim that the tribal decision to deny them a license constituted a denial of equal protection or that it resulted from a hearing which lacked due process. Whether and to what extent the fifth amendment would be available to correct arbitrary or discriminatory exercise of its delegated federal authority must therefore await decision in a case in which the issue is squarely presented and appropriately briefed. This observation is also applicable with regard to 25 U.S.C. § 1302((8), which provides that, "[n]o Indian tribe in exercising powers of self-government shall . . . deny to any person within its jurisdiction the equal protection of its laws or deprive any person of liberty or property without due process of law." Quite apart from these potential sources of protection against arbitrary tribal action, such protection is to some extent assured by § 1161's requirement that delegated authority be exercised pursuant to a tribal ordinance which itself has been approved by the Secretary of the Interior.

It is immaterial that respondent is not an Indian. He was on the Reservation and the transaction with an Indian took place there. [Citations omitted.] The cases in this Court have consistently guarded the authority of Indian governments over their reservations. Congress recognized this authority in the Navajos in the Treaty of 1868, and has done so ever since. If this power is to be taken away from them, it is for Congress to do it.

For the foregoing reasons the judgment of the Court of Appeals must be reversed, and the convictions of the respondents reinstated.

Reversed.

NOTE ON VARIETIES OF CONGRESSIONAL SUPPORT FOR THE EXERCISE OF TRIBAL AUTHORITY

In *Mazurie,* Congress made it a federal offense to sell liquor in Indian country in violation of a tribal ordinance. Similarly, Congress has made it a federal crime for nonmembers to hunt and fish on reservations or trust land without tribal permission. 18 U.S.C. § 1165. In both instances, federal law has incorporated tribal exercise of authority into the definition of a federal offense. The entanglement of federal and tribal governments is significant in these situations because the offense and enforcement are federal. In other situations, Congress has simply provided its support for or announced its approval of tribal jurisdiction, without supplying the enforcement mechanism. For example, in a variety of environmental statutes, Congress has declared that Indian nations may petition the federal government for authority to regulate the reservation environment in accordance with minimum federal standards. Where federal approval is provided, enforcement of the ensuing regulations is tribal, not federal. Thus, for example, the 1990 amendments to the Clean Air Act provide that when a tribal plan for implementation of the Act is approved by EPA and becomes effective, that tribal plan shall be "applicable to all areas . . . located within the exterior boundaries of the reservation, notwithstanding the issuance of any patent and including rights-of-way running through the reservation." 42 U.S.C. § 7410(o). *See* Dean B. Suagee *Tribal Self-Determination and Environmental Federalism: Cultural Values as a Force for Sustainability,* 3 WIDENER L. SYMP. J. 229, 232–34 (1998). Yet another example of congressional support for tribal jurisdiction is the Indian Child Welfare Act, 25 U.S.C. § 1901 et seq., which establishes exclusive tribal jurisdiction over child welfare proceedings involving on-reservation Indian children, and directs state courts to transfer to tribal court certain child welfare proceedings involving off-reservation Indian children. 25 U.S.C. § 1911. *See* Ch. 5, Sec. D.2. The federal courts play no role in this scheme other than to serve as a forum when disputes arise about its application.

Federal statutes supporting tribal jurisdiction vary along another dimension as well. Some, such as the statute involving hunting and fishing without tribal permission, provide federal support for authority that the tribes could exercise independently. Others, such as the jurisdiction transfer provision of the Indian Child Welfare Act, allow for tribal jurisdiction where it might not otherwise exist under federal Indian law because the child is domiciled outside Indian country. *But see John v. Baker* (discussed in Ch. 5, Sec. B.2).

The latter situation has arisen more frequently in recent years because of United States Supreme Court decisions restricting the exercise of inherent tribal jurisdiction. *See* Sec. B, this chapter for a discussion of cases differentiating inherent powers *retained by tribes* from those *implicitly divested* by virtue of the dependent relationship between tribes and the United States. According to these decisions, this dependent relationship limited tribal powers to determine their "external relations," defined to include some relations with nonmembers on nonmember-owned land within Indian country. These cases also indicated, however, that Congress could act to restore tribal jurisdiction. For example, in *United States v. Montana*, 450 U.S. 544 (1981) (regulatory jurisdiction over non-Indians on non-Indian land) and *Oliphant v. Suquamish Indian Tribe*, 435 U.S. 191 (1978) (criminal jurisdiction over non-Indians), the Supreme Court both found tribal jurisdiction to have been implicitly divested, and acknowledged that tribal jurisdiction could become operative if Congress enacted an express "delegation." Thus, the EPA and the courts have interpreted the Clean Air Act to provide for tribal regulation of nonmember activities on nonmember-owned land, even though the Supreme Court has cast some doubt on tribes' authority to regulate such matters absent federal authorization. *See Arizona Public Service Co. v. EPA*, 211 F.3d 1280 (D.C. Cir. 2000).

The Supreme Court opinion in *Mazurie* does not bother to resolve the issue of inherent tribal authority over non-Indians on fee land, even though the bar in question was located on such land. Why do the Justices believe it's unnecessary to do so in order to uphold the law in question? Consider, however, the implications of resolving the question in the two alternative ways. If Indian nations do have "retained" inherent authority to regulate liquor sales by non-Indians on fee land, is it proper to speak of the federal legislation involved in *Mazurie* as a "delegation"? Would it be correct to call the legislation a delegation if Congress had not also provided for federal definition of the underlying offense and federal enforcement, and had merely expressed its approval for the exercise of tribal jurisdiction? Alternatively, if tribes had been implicitly divested of their power to regulate non-Indian liquor sales on fee land, is the federal liquor statute, 18 U.S.C. § 1161, then properly characterized as a delegation? What other characterization might be appropriate? Could you say that the federal government had merely lifted a previous (judicially announced) bar on tribal authority?

Bugenig v. Hoopa Valley Tribe, 266 F.3d 1201 (9th Cir. 2001) (en banc): Roberta Bugenig, a non-Indian living on fee land, filed suit in federal district court challenging the jurisdiction of the Hoopa Valley Tribe to restrict logging on her land. The trial court ruled for the Tribe on two alternative grounds: first, it agreed with the tribal court that the Tribe's justification for restricting logging by non-Indians on non-Indian fee land satisfied the first *Montana* exception, as further elaborated in *Brendale*; second, it held that the Hoopa-Yurok Settlement Act constituted a delegation of jurisdiction to the Tribe. Sitting en banc, the Ninth Circuit emphasized the latter ground of the decision, finding this the crucial language in the Act:

The existing govening [sic] documents of the Hoopa Valley Tribe and the governing body established and elected thereunder, as heretofore recognized by the Secretary, are hereby ratified and confirmed.

25 U.S.C. § 1300i-7.

The Tribe's position was that this language gave their 1972 Constitution, an "existing governing document," the force of federal law. And because of Articles III and IX(1)(l), quoted in the decision of the tribal court, when Congress ratified and confirmed the Tribe's Constitution, Congress delegated power to the Tribe to regulate the use of all nonmembers' land within the boundaries of the Reservation. In contrast, Bugenig argued that any delegation of regulatory power to the Tribe from Congress must be express, and the language in the Settlement Act ratifying and confirming the Tribe's Constitution did not constitute such an express delegation.

Examining first the statute's text, the court noted,

> Referring to the ordinary legal significance of the terms, when Congress "ratified and confirmed" the governing documents that were "heretofore recognized by the Secretary," Congress was authorizing, giving effect to, and formally approving the Tribe's 1972 Constitution. The phrase "ratified and confirmed" has additional significance because it is the same phrase that Congress historically has used to give legal recognition to agreements between Native Americans and the United States . . . .

> Furthermore, in 1988, Congress was well aware of the significance of the term "ratified," for the Supreme Court recently had held that an agreement with an Indian tribe is given the force of law when "ratified" by Congress. . . . We presume that Congress knew of this interpretation.

> In view of the usual meaning of the terms, their historic usage, and the Supreme Court's interpretation, the plain text of the Settlement Act establishes that, when Congress "ratified and confirmed" the Tribe's governing documents, it intended to give the Tribe's Constitution the force of law.

266 F.3d at 1212–13.

The court turned next to the legislative history of the Settlement Act, which revealed to the court that the Act was designed to alleviate confusion over who had the right to manage the lands and resources of the Reservation. The court concluded, "In sum, the natural reading of § 1300i-7 — confirmed by its context and history — is that Congress was giving legal force to the Tribe's governing body and governing documents, and that is the reading that we give it."

Likewise, having found the necessary delegation of power from Congress, the court determined that the Hoopa Constitution expresses the Tribe's intent to extend its authority over "all lands" within the borders of the Square, which the court found to include fee lands, even those of nonmembers.

Viewing the Settlement Act and the Tribal Constitution together, the court found that Congress had expressly delegated regulatory jurisdiction over nonmember-owned land to the Tribe. The court made this determination despite the fact that the "Settlement Act does not contain a detailed explanation, such as 'we hereby delegate to the Tribe the power to regulate all lands within the Reservation, notwithstanding any patent owned by non-Indians.'" Nevertheless, the court determined that such a statement was not required. 266 F.3d at 1216–18.

Finally, the court addressed whether Congress could delegate such authority to the Tribe, even if it meant to. Bugenig had argued that Congress could not effect such a delegation because Congress would be removing authority from the state. But the court pointed out that "the want of state regulatory jurisdiction over land is not a necessary condition for federal regulatory jurisdiction over the same land," citing Justice Stevens' statement in *Brendale*, 492 U.S. at 440 n.3: "The possibility that the county might have jurisdiction to prohibit certain land uses . . . does not suggest that the Tribe lacks similar authority." The court further pointed out that its concern was not with California's jurisdiction, but with "whether Congress, in order to protect sites of cultural or religious significance to a tribe, can regulate timber harvesting on private property that is located within a reservation and, if so, whether it can delegate that power to the Tribe. The answer to both questions is 'yes.'"

The only remaining potential obstacle to upholding the delegation was the possibility that the Tribe was not a permissible recipient of such jurisdiction. The en banc panel looked to *Mazurie* for an answer, especially the Court's statement that limits on Congress's power to delegate its legislative power are "less stringent in cases where the entity exercising the delegated authority itself possesses independent authority over the subject matter." *Mazurie* had approved of delegation in precisely the situation presented in *Bugenig*, regulation of a non-Indian's conduct on non-Indian owned land within a reservation, where the tribal ordinance affected internal and social relations of the tribe, "a subject as to which the Tribe retains at least some independent authority" (citing *Montana*, 450 U.S. at 566 for the proposition that tribes retain inherent power to exercise civil authority over the conduct of non-Indians on fee lands within the reservation "when that conduct threatens or has some direct effect on the . . . health or welfare of the tribe") . . . .

Concluding its analysis, the en banc panel wrote:

> Because the Tribe possesses unique "attributes of sovereignty," and because the Tribe has at least some "independent authority over the subject matter" at issue, we hold that the federal government could delegate to the Tribe its authority to protect cultural and historical resources of significance, "even though the lands were held in fee by non-Indians, and even though the persons regulated were non-Indian." *Mazurie*, 419 U.S. at 554, 557. . . .

> We hold that Congress expressly delegated authority to the Tribe to enact the ordinance in question and that Congress had the power to do so.

266 F.3d at 1223.

The three dissenting judges on the en banc panel found the "ratify and confirm" language of the Hoopa-Yurok Settlement Act inadequate to delegate jurisdiction to the Tribe because it did not specifically allude to the law's jurisdictional conse-quences. The dissent acknowledged that it was establishing a demanding standard for an effective delegation, but justified its position as necessary to protect non-Indians from subjection to tribal authority.

NOTE ON *BUGENIG*

Was there any doubt that Congress intended to put the authority of federal law behind the Hoopa Valley Tribe's constitution? Assuming that a delegation must be "express," why should the courts require that Congress make such delegations through a particular verbal formula, as the dissent suggests? Are the Indian law canons of construction relevant and helpful in resolving this question? In light of the Ninth Circuit's holding in this case, does the federal Bill of Rights now constrain exercises of zoning power by the Hoopa Valley Tribe? Do tribes (or states, for that matter), become arms to the federal government for purpose of applicable federal constitutional or statutory requirements when they exercise power delegated or confirmed to them by Congress or when Congress removes preexisting preemptive law that would have prevented them from exercising jurisdiction without the aid of such congressional legislation? Consider these questions in light of the *Lara* case set forth in the next section.

In light of *Bugenig*, will any provision in a tribal constitution authorizing the exercise of jurisdiction over nonmembers qualify as a federal confirmation of such authority? Must the tribal constitution be one approved under an Act of Congress, such as the legislation at issue in *Bugenig*? Will approval under the Indian Reorganization Act of 1934 suffice?

C. FEDERAL JUDICIAL AND LEGISLATIVE RESPONSES TO INHERENT TRIBAL SOVEREIGNTY

1. Federal Judicial Plenary Power Purporting to Preempt Tribal Sovereignty

In the nineteenth century, if the federal government sought to limit the exercise of tribal authority, federal officials generally would resort to treaty-making and, if unsuccessful, sometimes to warfare. For example, Lakota efforts to keep non-Indians out of their territory led to conflict when overland trails to Oregon were run through Lakota territory. Efforts to secure Lakota cooperation in providing safe passage for overland wagon trails through Lakota territory eventually led to Red Cloud's War and a Sioux victory and the negotiation of the Fort Laramie Treaty of 1868, 15 Stat. 635. Article II pushed overland routes south of the Great Sioux Reservation by protecting railroad development. The Sioux nevertheless agreed in Article I to refrain from exercising their sovereign power against non-Indian intruders and to turn over non-Indians who committed crimes against Indians to the BIA agent for federal prosecution. This clause is the famous "bad men among the whites" provision, the companion clause of which was at issue in the *Crow Dog* case set forth and discussed in Chapter 1.

Later, at the same time that the Court was developing the plenary power doctrine in Indian affairs (an issue discussed in the next chapter), Congress began to curtail the exercise of tribal power by statute. For example, the Curtis Act of 1898, as part of the breakup of the Oklahoma reservations and the allotment of portions of the Indian Territory, expressly made the civil laws of the Five Tribes (Cherokee, Choctaw, Chickasaw, Muscogee [Creek], and Seminole) unenforceable in federal courts and abolished the tribal courts of those Indian nations. Act of June 28, 1898, ch. 517, §§ 26, 28, 30 Stat. 495, 504. More recently, in the Indian Civil Rights Act of 1968, 25 U.S.C. §§ 1301–03, Congress limited the exercise of governing powers of the tribes by requiring that they provide all people with whom they deal many of the guarantees found in the Bill of Rights and the Fourteenth Amendment. Nevertheless, until the last quarter of the twentieth century the federal judiciary invariably assumed that if the power of Indian tribes was to be curtailed that decision had to originate with Congress, not the courts. In *The Kansas Indians*, 72 U.S. 737, 756–57 (1867), the Court wrote of the Shawnees in Kansas:

> This people have their own customs and laws by which they are governed. Because some of those customs have been abandoned, owing to the proximity of their white neighbors, may be an evidence of the superior influence of our race, but does not tend to prove that their tribal organization is not preserved. There is no evidence in the record to show that the Indians with separate estates have not the same rights in the tribe as those whose estates are held in common. Their machinery of government, though simple, is adapted to their intelligence and wants, and effective, with faithful agents to watch over them. If broken into, it is the natural result of Shawnees and whites owning adjoining plantations, and living and trafficking together as neighbors and friends. But the action of the political department of the government settles, beyond controversy, that the Shawnees are as yet a distinct people, with a perfect tribal organization. . . . While the general government has a superintending care over their interests, and continues to treat with them as a nation, the State of Kansas is estopped from denying their title to it. She accepted this status when she accepted the act admitting her into the Union. Conferring rights and privileges on these Indians cannot affect their situation, *which can only be changed by treaty stipulation, or a voluntary abandonment of their tribal organization.* As long as the United States recognizes their national character they are under the protection of treaties and the laws of Congress, and their property is withdrawn from the operation of State laws (emphasis added).

Over the past quarter century, the Supreme Court, at least in the field of Indian affairs, abandoned these traditions of relying on Congress and developed its own set of common law limitations on the exercise of tribal sovereignty. As you consider the cases that follow, carefully analyze the sources the Court relies upon to justify its limitations on the exercise of tribal sovereignty. Are they consistent with eighteenth and nineteenth century treaties? Are they consistent with federal statutes? What policy model does the Court appear to be advancing? What justifications does the Court advance for having power to address the scope of tribal governing power?

An important background to these cases was the final report of the congressionally created American Indian Policy Review Commission issued in 1976. American Indian Policy Review Comm'n, 95th Cong 1st Sess. Final Report (Comm. Print 1977). That final report sought to reaffirm the *Worcester* principle of tribal territorial jurisdiction and made sweeping proposals for tribal authority that greatly alarmed some commission members and many non-Indians living on or near Indian reservations. Vice-Chairman Lloyd Meeds, formerly a supporter of some Indian legislative initiatives, wrote a stinging dissent attempting to limit tribal authority to tribal members. Later, together with Congressman Glen Cunningham, he introduced a number of bills to define tribal jurisdiction in such limited ways. None of those bills ever passed. *See generally* P.S. Deloria, *The American Indian Law Center: An Informal History*, 24 N.M. L. REV. 285, 304 (1994). That debate was quite heated at the time the next case reached the United States Supreme Court. Should the congressional failure of the Meeds-Cunningham bills have played any role in the following cases?

OLIPHANT v. SUQUAMISH INDIAN TRIBE
United States Supreme Court
435 U.S. 191 (1978)

MR. JUSTICE REHNQUIST delivered the opinion of the Court.

[As a result of] the 1855 Treaty of Point Elliott, 12 Stat. 927, the Suquamish Indian Tribe relinquished all rights that it might have had in the lands of the State of Washington and agreed to settle on a 7,276-acre reservation near Port Madison, Wash. Located on Puget Sound across from the city of Seattle, the Port Madison Reservation is a checkerboard of tribal community land, allotted Indian lands, property held in fee simple by non-Indians, and various roads and public highways maintained by Kitsap County.[7]

The Suquamish Indians are governed by a tribal government which in 1973 adopted a Law and Order Code. The Code, which covers a variety of offenses from theft to rape, purports to extend the Tribe's criminal jurisdiction over both Indians

---

[7] [1] According to the District Court's findings of fact, "the Port Madison Indian Reservation consists of approximately 7,276 acres of which approximately 63% thereof is owned in fee simple absolute by non-Indians and the remaining 37% is Indian-owned lands subject to the trust status of the United States, consisting mostly of unimproved acreage upon which no persons reside. Residing on the reservation is an estimated population of approximately 2,928 non-Indians living in 976 dwelling units. There lives on the reservation approximately 50 members of the Suquamish Indian Tribe. Within the reservation are numerous public highways of the State of Washington, public schools, public utilities and other facilities in which neither the Suquamish Indian Tribe nor the United States has any ownership or interest."

The Suquamish Indian Tribe, unlike many other Indian tribes, did not consent to non-Indian homesteading of unallotted or "surplus" lands within their reservation pursuant to 25 U.S.C. § 348 and 43 U.S.C. §§ 1195–1197. Instead, the substantial non-Indian population on the Port Madison Reservation is primarily the result of the sale of Indian allotments to non-Indians by the Secretary of the Interior [and] of the lifting of various trust restrictions, which has enabled individual Indians to sell their allotments. *See* 25 U.S.C. §§ 349, 392.

and non-Indians.[8] Proceedings are held in the Suquamish Indian Provisional Court. Pursuant to the Indian Civil Rights Act of 1968, 25 U.S.C. § 1302, defendants are entitled to many of the due process protections accorded to defendants in federal or state criminal proceedings. However, the guarantees are not identical. Non-Indians, for example, are excluded from Suquamish tribal court juries.[9]

Both petitioners are non-Indian residents of the Port Madison Reservation. Petitioner Mark David Oliphant was arrested by tribal authorities during the Suquamish's annual Chief Seattle Days celebration and charged with assaulting a tribal officer and resisting arrest. After arraignment before the tribal court, Oliphant was released on his own recognizance. Petitioner Daniel B. Belgarde was arrested by tribal authorities after an alleged high-speed race along the Reservation highways that only ended when Belgarde collided with a tribal police vehicle. Belgarde posted bail and was released. Six days later he was arraigned and charged under the tribal code with "recklessly endangering another person" and injuring tribal property. Tribal court proceedings against both petitioners have been stayed pending a decision in this case.

Both petitioners applied for a writ of habeas corpus to the United States District Court for the Western District of Washington [arguing] that the Suquamish Indian Provisional Court does not have criminal jurisdiction over non-Indians. [T]he District Court denied the petitions [and] the Court of Appeals for the Ninth Circuit affirmed the denial of habeas corpus in the case of petitioner Oliphant. We granted certiorari to decide whether Indian tribal courts have criminal jurisdiction over non-Indians. We decide that they do not.

I

Respondents do not contend that their exercise of criminal jurisdiction over non-Indians stems from affirmative congressional authorization or treaty provision.[10] Instead, respondents urge that such jurisdiction flows automatically from the

---

[8] [2] Notices were placed in prominent places at the entrances to the Port Madison Reservation informing the public that entry onto the reservation would be deemed implied consent to the criminal jurisdiction of the Suquamish tribal court.

[9] [4] The Indian Civil Rights Act of 1968 provides for "a trial by jury of not less than six persons," 25 U.S.C. § 1302(10), but the tribal court is not explicitly prohibited from excluding non-Indians from the jury even where a non-Indian is being tried. In 1977, the Suquamish Tribe amended its Law and Order Code to provide that only Suquamish tribal members shall serve as jurors in tribal court.

[10] [6] Respondents do contend that Congress has "confirmed" the power of Indian tribes to try and punish non-Indians through the Indian Reorganization Act of 1934, 25 U.S.C. § 476, and the Indian Civil Rights Act of 1968, 25 U.S.C. § 1302. Neither Act, however, addresses, let alone "confirms," tribal criminal jurisdiction over non-Indians. The Indian Reorganization Act merely gives each Indian Tribe the right "to organize for its common welfare" and to "adopt an appropriate constitution and bylaws." With certain specific additions not relevant here, the tribal council is to have such powers as are vested "by existing law." The Indian Civil Rights Act merely extends to "any person" within the tribe's jurisdiction certain enumerated guarantees of the Bill of Rights of the Federal Constitution. As respondents note, an earlier version of the Indian Civil Rights Act extended its guarantees only to "American Indians," rather than to "any person." The purpose of the later modification was to extend the Act's guarantees to "all persons who may be subject to the jurisdiction of tribal governments, whether Indians or non-Indians." Summary Report on the Constitutional Rights of American Indians, Subcomm. on Const.

"Tribe's retained inherent powers of government over the Port Madison Indian Reservation." Seizing on language in our opinions describing Indian tribes as "quasi-sovereign entities," [*Morton v. Mancari*], the Court of Appeals agreed and held that Indian tribes, "though conquered and dependent, retain those powers of autonomous states that are neither inconsistent with their status nor expressly terminated by Congress." According to the Court of Appeals, criminal jurisdiction over anyone committing an offense on the reservation is a "sine qua non" of such powers.

The Suquamish Indian Tribe does not stand alone today in its assumption of criminal jurisdiction over non-Indians. Of the 127 reservation court systems that currently exercise criminal jurisdiction in the United States, 33 purport to extend that jurisdiction to non-Indians. Twelve other Indian tribes have enacted ordinances which would permit the assumption of criminal jurisdiction over non-Indians. Like the Suquamish these tribes claim authority to try non-Indians not on the basis of congressional statute or treaty provision but by reason of their retained national sovereignty.

The effort by Indian tribal courts to exercise criminal jurisdiction over non-Indians, however, is a relatively new phenomenon. And where the effort has been made in the past, it has been held that the jurisdiction did not exist. Until the middle of this century, few Indian tribes maintained any semblance of a formal court system. Offenses by one Indian against another were usually handled by social and religious pressure and not by formal judicial processes; emphasis was on restitution rather than on punishment. In 1834 the Commissioner of Indian Affairs described the then status of Indian criminal systems: "With the exception of two or three tribes, who have within a few years past attempted to establish some few laws and regulations amongst themselves, the Indian tribes are without laws, and the chiefs without much authority to exercise any restraint." H.R. Rep. No. 474, 23d Cong., 1st Sess., at 91 (1834).

It is therefore not surprising to find no specific discussion of the problem before us in the volumes of United States Reports. But the problem did not lie entirely dormant for two centuries. A few tribes during the nineteenth century did have formal criminal systems. From the earliest treaties with these tribes, it was apparently assumed that the tribes did not have criminal jurisdiction over non-Indians absent a congressional statute or treaty provision to that effect. For example, the 1830 Treaty with the Choctaw Indian Tribe, which had one of the most sophisticated of tribal structures, guaranteed to the Tribe "the jurisdiction and government of all the persons and property that may be within their limits." [7 Stat. 333, Art. IV] Despite the broad terms of this governmental guarantee, however, the Choctaws at the conclusion of this treaty provision "express *a wish* that Congress *may grant* to the Choctaws the right of punishing by their own laws any white man

---

Rights of the Senate Judiciary Comm., 89th Cong., 2d Sess., at 10 (1966). But this change was certainly not intended to give Indian tribes criminal jurisdiction over non-Indians. Nor can it be read to "confirm" respondents' argument that Indian tribes have inherent criminal jurisdiction over non-Indians. Instead, the modification merely demonstrates Congress's desire to extend the Act's guarantees to non-Indians if and where they come under a tribe's criminal or civil jurisdiction by either treaty provision or act of Congress.

who shall come into their nation, and infringe any of their national regulations."[11] Such a request for affirmative congressional authority is inconsistent with respondents' belief that criminal jurisdiction over non-Indians is inherent in tribal sovereignty. Faced by attempts of the Choctaw Tribe to try non-Indian offenders in the early-1800's, the United States Attorneys General also concluded that the Choctaws did not have criminal jurisdiction over non-Indians absent congressional authority. *See* 2 Opinions of the Attorney General 693 (1834); 7 Opinions of the Attorney General 174 (1855). According to the Attorney General in 1834, tribal criminal jurisdiction over non-Indians is *inter alia* inconsistent with treaty provisions recognizing the sovereignty of the United States over the territory assigned to the Indian nation and the dependence of the Indians on the United States.

At least one court has previously considered the power of Indian courts to try non-Indians and it also held against jurisdiction. In *Ex parte Kenyon*, 14 Fed. Cas. 7,720, p. 353 (W.D. Ark. 1878), Judge Isaac C. Parker, who as District Court Judge for the Western District of Arkansas was constantly exposed to the legal relationships between Indians and non-Indians, held that to give an Indian tribal court "jurisdiction of the person of an offender, such offender must be an Indian." *Id.*, at 355. The conclusion of Judge Parker was reaffirmed only recently in a 1970 Opinion of the Solicitor of the Department of the Interior. *See* 77 I.D. 113 (1970).[12]

---

[11] [8] The history of Indian treaties in the United States is consistent with the principle that Indian tribes may not assume criminal jurisdiction over non-Indians without the permission of Congress. The earliest treaties typically expressly provided that "any citizen of the United States, who shall do an injury to any Indian of the [tribal] nation, or to any other Indian or Indians residing in their towns, and under their protection, shall be punished according to the laws of the United States." *See, e.g.*, Treaty with the Shawnees, Art. III, 7 Stat. 26 (1786). While, as elaborated further below, these provisions were not necessary to remove criminal jurisdiction over non-Indians from the Indian tribes, they would naturally have served an important function in the developing stage of United States-Indian relations by clarifying jurisdictional limits of the Indian tribes. The same treaties generally provided that "[i]f any citizen of the United States . . . shall attempt to settle on any of the lands hereby allotted to the Indians to live and hunt on, such person shall forfeit the protection of the United States of America, and the Indians may punish him or not as they please." *See, e.g.*, Treaty with the Choctaws, Art. IV, 7 Stat. 21 (1786). Far from representing a recognition of any inherent Indian criminal jurisdiction over non-Indians settling on tribal lands, these provisions were instead intended as a means of discouraging non-Indian settlements on Indian territory, in contravention of treaty provisions to the contrary. *See* 5 Annals of Congress 903–904 (April 9, 1796). Later treaties dropped this provision and provided instead that non-Indian settlers would be removed by the United States upon complaint being lodged by the tribe. *See, e.g.*, Treaty with the Sacs and Foxes, 7 Stat. 84 (1804). As the relationship between Indian tribes and the United States developed over time, specific provisions for the punishment of non-Indians by the United States, rather than by the tribes, slowly disappeared from the treaties. . . . Only one treaty signed by the United States has ever provided for any form of tribal criminal jurisdiction over non-Indians (other than in the illegal settler context noted above). The first treaty signed by the United States with an Indian tribe, the 1778 Treaty with the Delawares, provided that neither party to the treaty could "proceed to the infliction of punishments on the citizens of the other, otherwise than by securing the offender or offenders by imprisonment, or any other competent means, till a fair and impartial trial can be had by judges or juries *of both parties*, as near as can be to the laws, customs and usages of the contracting parties and natural justice: *The mode of such trials to be hereafter fixed by the wise men of the United States in Congress assembled*, with the assistance of . . . deputies of the Delaware nation. . . . " Treaty with the Delawares, Art. IV, 7 Stat. 14 (1778) (emphasis added). While providing for Delaware participation in the trial of non-Indians, this treaty section established that non-Indians could only be tried under the auspices of the United States and in a manner fixed by the Continental Congress.

[12] [11] The 1970 Opinion of the Solicitor was withdrawn in 1974 but has not been replaced. No reason was given for the withdrawal.

While Congress was concerned almost from its beginning with the special problems of law enforcement on the Indian reservations, it did not initially address itself to the problem of tribal jurisdiction over non-Indians. For the reasons previously stated, there was little reason to be concerned with assertions of tribal court jurisdiction over non-Indians because of the absence of formal tribal judicial systems. Instead, Congress's concern was with providing effective protection for the Indians "from the violence of the lawless part of our frontier inhabitants." Seventh Annual Address of President George Washington, I Messages and Papers of the Presidents, 1789–1897, at 181, 185 (1897, J. Richardson, ed.). Without such protection, it was felt that "all the exertions of the Government to prevent destructive retaliations by the Indians will prove fruitless and all our present agreeable prospects illusory." *Ibid.* Beginning with the Trade and Intercourse Act of 1790, 1 Stat. 137, therefore, Congress assumed federal jurisdiction over offenses by non-Indians against Indians which "would be punishable by the laws of [the] state or district . . . if the offense had been committed against a citizen or white inhabitant thereof." In 1817, Congress went one step further and extended federal enclave law to the Indian country; the only exception was for "any offense committed by one Indian against another." 3 Stat. 383, as amended, 18 U.S.C. § 1152.

It was in 1834 that Congress was first directly faced with the prospect of Indians trying non-Indians. In the Western Territory Bill, Congress proposed to create an Indian territory beyond the western-directed destination of the settlers; the territory was to be governed by a confederation of Indian tribes and was expected ultimately to become a State of the Union. While the Bill would have created a political territory with broad governing powers, Congress was careful not to give the tribes of the territory criminal jurisdiction over United States officials and citizens traveling through the area. The reasons were quite practical:

> Officers, and persons in the service of the United States, and persons required to reside in the Indian country by treaty stipulations, must necessarily be placed under the protection, and subject to the laws of the United States. To persons merely travelling in the Indian country the same protection is extended. The want of fixed laws, of competent tribunals of justice, which must for some time continue in the Indian country, absolutely requires for the peace of both sides that this protection be extended. H.R. Rep. No. 474, 23d Cong., 1st Sess., at 18 (1834).

Congress's concern over criminal jurisdiction in this proposed Indian Territory contrasts markedly with its total failure to address criminal jurisdiction over non-Indians on other reservations, which frequently bordered non-Indian settlements. The contrast suggests that Congress shared the view of the Executive Branch and lower federal courts that Indian tribal courts were without jurisdiction to try non-Indians.

This unspoken assumption was also evident in other congressional actions during the nineteenth century. In 1854, for example, Congress amended the Trade and Intercourse Act to proscribe the prosecution in federal court of an Indian who has already been tried in tribal court. 10 Stat. 270, as amended, 18 U.S.C. § 1152. No similar provision, such as would have been required by parallel logic if tribal courts had jurisdiction over non-Indians, was enacted barring retrial of non-Indians. Similarly, in the Major Crimes Act of 1885, Congress placed under the jurisdiction of federal courts Indian offenders who commit certain specified major offenses. 23 Stat. 385, as amended, 18 U.S.C. § 1153. If tribal courts may try non-Indians, however, as respondents contend, those tribal courts are free to try non-Indians even for such major offenses as Congress may well have given the federal courts *exclusive* jurisdiction to try members of their own tribe committing the exact same offenses.[13]

[A 1960 report expressly confirmed the Senate's] assumption that Indian tribal courts are without inherent jurisdiction to try non-Indians, and must depend on the federal government for protection from intruders. In considering a statute that would prohibit unauthorized entry upon Indian land for the purpose of hunting or fishing, the Senate Report noted that

> The problem confronting Indian tribes with sizable reservations is that the United States provides no protection against trespassers comparable to the protection it gives to Federal property as exemplified by title 18, United States Code, section 1863 [trespass on national forest lands]. Indian property owners should have the same protection as other property owners. For example, a private hunting club may keep nonmembers off its game lands or it may issue a permit for a fee. One who comes on such lands without permission may be prosecuted under State law but a non-Indian trespasser on an Indian reservation enjoys immunity. *This is by reason of the fact that Indian tribal law is enforceable against Indians only; not against non-Indians.*
>
> . . . .
>
> *Non-Indians are not subject to the jurisdiction of Indian courts and cannot be tried in Indian courts on trespass charges.* Further, there are no Federal laws which can be invoked against trespassers.
>
> . . . .
>
> The committee has considered this bill and believes that the legislation is meritorious. The legislation will give to the Indian tribes and to individual Indian owners certain rights that now exist as to others, and fills a gap in the present law for the protection of their property. S. Rep. No. 1686, 86th Cong., 2d Sess., 2–3 (1960) (emphasis added).

---

[13] [14] The Major Crimes Act provides that Indians committing any of the enumerated offenses "shall be subject to the same laws and penalties as all other persons committing any of the above offenses, *within the exclusive jurisdiction of the United States.*" While the question has never been directly addressed by this Court, Courts of Appeals have read this language to exclude tribal jurisdiction over the Indian offender. *See, e.g., Sam v. United States*, 385 F.2d 213, 214 (10th Cir. 1967); *Felicia v. United States*, 495 F.2d 353, 354 (9th Cir. 1974). We have no reason to decide today whether jurisdiction under the Major Crimes Act is exclusive.

II

While not conclusive on the issue before us, the commonly shared presumption of Congress, the Executive Branch, and lower federal courts that tribal courts do not have the power to try non-Indians carries considerable weight. [Indian law is based primarily on treaties and statutes.] These instruments, which beyond their actual text form the backdrop for the intricate web of judicially made Indian law, cannot be interpreted in isolation but must be read in light of the common notions of the day and the assumptions of those who drafted them. *Ibid.*

While in isolation the Treaty of Point Elliott, 12 Stat. 927 (1855), would appear to be silent as to tribal criminal jurisdiction over non-Indians, the addition of historical perspective casts substantial doubt upon the existence of such jurisdiction. In the Ninth Article, for example, the Suquamish "acknowledge their dependence on the Government of the United States." As Chief Justice Marshall explained in *Worcester v. Georgia*, 8 L. Ed. 483, 6 Pet. 515, 551–552, 554 (1832), such an acknowledgement is not a mere abstract recognition of the United States' sovereignty. "The Indian nations were, from their situation, necessarily dependent on [the United States] for their protection from lawless and injurious intrusions into their country." *Id.*, at 555. By acknowledging their dependence on the United States, in the Treaty of Point Elliott, the Suquamish were in all probability recognizing that the United States would arrest and try non-Indian intruders who came within their reservation. Other provisions of the Treaty also point to the absence of tribal jurisdiction. Thus the tribe "agree[s] not to shelter or conceal offenders against the laws of the United States, but to deliver them up to the authorities for trial." Read in conjunction with 18 U.S.C. § 1152, which extends federal enclave law to non-Indian offenses on Indian reservations, this provision implies that the Suquamish are to promptly deliver up any non-Indian offender, rather than try and punish him themselves.

By themselves, these treaty provisions would probably not be sufficient to remove criminal jurisdiction over non-Indians if the Tribe otherwise retained such jurisdiction. But an examination of our earlier precedents satisfies us that, even ignoring treaty provisions and congressional policy, Indians do not have criminal jurisdiction over non-Indians absent affirmative delegation of such power by Congress. Indian tribes do retain elements of "quasi-sovereign" authority after ceding their lands to the United States and announcing their dependence on the federal government. *See The Cherokee Nation v. Georgia*, 5 Peters 1, 15 (1831). But the tribes' retained powers are not such that they are limited only by specific restrictions in treaties or congressional enactments. As the Court of Appeals recognized[,] Indian tribes are proscribed from exercising both those powers of autonomous states that are expressly terminated by Congress *and* those powers *"inconsistent with their status."* 544 F.2d, at 1009.

Indian reservations are "a part of the territory of the United States." *United States v. Rogers*, 4 How. 567, 571 (1846). Indian tribes "hold and occupy [the reservations] with the assent of the United States, and under their authority." *Id.*, at 572. Upon incorporation into the territory of the United States, the Indian tribes thereby come under the territorial sovereignty of the United States and their exercise of separate power is constrained so as not to conflict with the interests of this overriding sovereignty. "[T]heir rights to complete sovereignty, as independent nations, [are] necessarily diminished." *Johnson v. M'Intosh*, 8 Wheat. 543, 574 (1823).

We have already described some of the inherent limitations on tribal powers that stem from their incorporation into the United States. In *Johnson v. M'Intosh, supra*, we noted that the Indian tribes' "power to dispose of the soil at their own will, to whomever they pleased," was inherently lost to the overriding sovereignty of the United States. And in *The Cherokee Nation v. Georgia, supra*, the Chief Justice observed that since Indian tribes are "completely under the sovereignty and dominion of the United States, . . . any attempt [by foreign nations] to acquire their lands, or to form a political connexion with them, would be considered by all as an invasion of our territory, and an act of hostility."

[In] submitting to the overriding sovereignty of the United States, Indian tribes therefore necessarily give up their power to try non-Indian citizens of the United States except in a manner acceptable to Congress. This principle would have been obvious a century ago when most Indian tribes were characterized by a "want of fixed laws [and] of competent tribunals of justice." H.R. Rep. No. 474, 23d Cong., 1st Sess., at 18 (1834). It should be no less obvious today, even though present day Indian tribal courts embody dramatic advances over their historical antecedents.

In *Ex parte Crow Dog*, 109 U.S. 556 (1883), the Court was faced with almost the inverse of the issue before us here — whether, prior to the passage of the Major Crimes Act, federal courts had jurisdiction to try Indians who had offended against fellow Indians on reservation land. In concluding that criminal jurisdiction was exclusively in the tribe, it found particular guidance in the "nature and circumstances of the case." The United States was seeking to extend United States

> law, by argument and inference only, . . . over aliens and strangers; over the members of a community separated by race [and] tradition, . . . from the authority and power which seeks to impose upon them the restraints of an external and unknown code . . . ; which judges them by a standard made by others and not for them. . . . It tries them, not by their peers, nor by the customs of their people, nor the law of their land, but by . . . a different race, according to the law of a social state of which they have an imperfect conception. . . . *Id.*, at 571.

These considerations, applied here to the non-Indian rather than Indian offender, speak equally strongly against the validity of respondents' contention that Indian tribes, although fully subordinated to the sovereignty of the United States, retain the power to try non-Indians according to their own customs and procedure.

As previously noted, Congress extended the jurisdiction of federal courts, in the Trade and Intercourse Act of 1790, to offenses committed by non-Indians against Indians within Indian Country. In doing so, Congress was careful to extend to the non-Indian offender the basic criminal rights that would attach in non-Indian related cases. Under respondents' theory, however, Indian tribes would have been free to try the same non-Indians without these careful proceedings unless Congress affirmatively legislated to the contrary. Such an exercise of jurisdiction over non-Indian citizens of the United States would belie the tribes' forfeiture of full sovereignty in return for the protection of the United States.

In summary, respondents' position ignores that

> Indians are within the geographical limits of the United States. The soil and people within these limits are under the political control of the Government of the United States, or of the States of the Union. There exist in the broad domain of sovereignty but these two. There may be cities, counties, and other organized bodies with limited legislative functions, but they . . . exist in subordination to one or the other of these. *United States v. Kagama*, 118 U.S. 375, 379 (1886).

We recognize that some Indian tribal court systems have become increasingly sophisticated and resemble in many respects their state counterparts. We also acknowledge that with the passage of the Indian Civil Rights Act of 1968, which extends certain basic procedural rights to *anyone* tried in Indian tribal court, many of the dangers that might have accompanied the exercise by tribal courts of criminal jurisdiction over non-Indians only a few decades ago have disappeared. Finally, we are not unaware of the prevalence of non-Indian crime on today's reservations which the tribes forcefully argue requires the ability to try non-Indians. But these are considerations for Congress to weigh in deciding whether Indian tribes should finally be authorized to try non-Indians. They have little relevance to the principles which lead us to conclude that Indian tribes do not have inherent jurisdiction to try and punish non-Indians. The judgments below are therefore reversed.

Reversed.

MR. JUSTICE BRENNAN took no part in the consideration or decision of these cases.

MR. JUSTICE MARSHALL, with whom THE CHIEF JUSTICE joins, dissenting.

I agree with the court below that the "power to preserve order on the reservation . . . is a sine qua non of the sovereignty that the Suquamish originally possessed." 544 F.2d 1007, 1009 (CA9 1976). In the absence of affirmative withdrawal by treaty or statute, I am of the view that Indian tribes enjoy as a necessary aspect of their retained sovereignty the right to try and punish all persons who commit offenses against tribal law within the reservation. Accordingly, I dissent.

DURO v. REINA
United States Supreme Court
495 U.S. 676 (1990)

MR. JUSTICE KENNEDY delivered the opinion of the Court.

We address in this case whether an Indian tribe may assert criminal jurisdiction over a defendant who is an Indian but not a tribal member. We hold that the retained sovereignty of the tribe as a political and social organization to govern its own affairs does not include the authority to impose criminal sanctions against a citizen outside its own membership.

I

The events giving rise to this jurisdictional dispute occurred on the Salt River Indian Reservation [in Arizona, which is] the home of the Salt River Pima-Maricopa Indian Community, a recognized Tribe with an enrolled membership. The petitioner in this case, Albert Duro, is an enrolled member of another Indian Tribe, the Torres-Martinez Band of Cahuilla Mission Indians. Petitioner is not eligible for membership in the Pima-Maricopa Tribe. As a nonmember, he is not entitled to vote in Pima-Maricopa elections, to hold tribal office, or to serve on tribal juries.

Petitioner has lived most of his life in his native State of California, outside any Indian reservation. Between March and June 1984, he resided on the Salt River Reservation with a Pima-Maricopa woman friend. He worked for the PiCopa Construction Company, which is owned by the Tribe.

On June 15, 1984, petitioner allegedly shot and killed a 14-year-old boy within the Salt River Reservation boundaries. The victim was a member of the Gila River Indian Tribe of Arizona, a separate Tribe that occupies a separate reservation. [Duro was charged with murder in violation of the Major Crimes Act, 18 U.S.C. § 1153, but the indictment was later dismissed.][14]

Petitioner [was turned over to the tribal police,] was taken to stand trial in the Pima-Maricopa Indian Community Court [and] charged with the illegal firing of a weapon on the Reservation. [Petitioner sought a writ of habeas corpus after the tribal court denied his motion to dismiss for lack of jurisdiction.]

[After the] District Court granted the writ, [a] divided panel of the Court of Appeals for the Ninth Circuit reversed [and this appeal followed.]

II

[In *United States v. Wheeler*, 435 U.S. 313 (1978), we found] that jurisdiction over a Navajo defendant by a Navajo court was part of retained tribal sovereignty, not a delegation of authority from the federal government. [The] analysis of tribal power was directed to the tribes' status as limited sovereigns, necessarily subject to the overriding authority of the United States, yet retaining necessary powers of internal self-governance. We recognized that the "sovereignty that the Indian tribes retain is of a unique and limited character." *Id.*, at 323.

A basic attribute of full territorial sovereignty is the power to enforce laws against all who come within the sovereign's territory, whether citizens or aliens.

---

[14] [1] Jurisdiction in "Indian country," which is defined in 18 U.S.C. § 1151, is governed by a complex patchwork of federal, state, and tribal law. [The Court's discussion of 18 U.S.C. §§ 1152–1153 is omitted.] For Indian country crimes involving only non-Indians, longstanding precedents of this Court hold that state courts have exclusive jurisdiction despite the terms of § 1152. Certain states may also assume jurisdiction over Indian country crime with the consent of the affected Tribe pursuant to Public Law 280. The final source of criminal jurisdiction in Indian country is the retained sovereignty of the tribes themselves. It is undisputed that the tribes retain jurisdiction over their members, subject to the question of exclusive jurisdiction under § 1153 mentioned above. *See* [*United States v. Wheeler*]. The extent of tribal jurisdiction over nonmembers is at issue here. For a scholarly discussion of Indian country jurisdiction, see Clinton, *Criminal Jurisdiction Over Indian Lands: A Journey Through a Jurisdictional Maze*, 18 ARIZ. L. REV. 505 (1976).

Oliphant recognized that the tribes can no longer be described as sovereigns in this sense. Rather, as our discussion in *Wheeler* reveals, the retained sovereignty of the tribes is that needed to control their own internal relations, and to preserve their own unique customs and social order. The power of a tribe to prescribe and enforce rules of conduct for its own members "does not fall within that part of sovereignty which the Indians implicitly lost by virtue of their dependent status. The areas in which such implicit divestiture of sovereignty has been held to have occurred are those involving the relations between an Indian tribe and nonmembers of the tribe."

[The] finding that the tribal prosecution of the defendant in *Wheeler* was by a sovereign other than the United States rested on the premise that the prosecution was a part of the tribe's *internal* self-governance. Had the prosecution been a manifestation of external relations between the Tribe and outsiders, such power would have been inconsistent with the tribe's dependent status, and could only have come to the Tribe by delegation from Congress, subject to the constraints of the Constitution.

The distinction between members and nonmembers and its relation to self-governance is recognized in other areas of Indian law. Exemption from state taxation for residents of a reservation, for example, is determined by tribal membership, not by reference to Indians as a general class. We have held that States may not impose certain taxes on transactions of tribal members on the reservation because this would interfere with internal governance and self-determination. But this rationale does not apply to taxation of nonmembers, even where they are Indians:

> "Nor would the imposition of Washington's tax on these purchasers contravene the principle of tribal self-government, for the simple reasons that nonmembers are not constituents of the governing Tribe. For most practical purposes they stand on the same footing as non-Indians resident on the reservation. There is no evidence that nonmembers have a say in tribal affairs or significantly share in tribal disbursements." *Washington v. Confederated Tribes of Colville Indian Reservation*, 447 U.S. 134, 161 (1980).

Similarly, in [*Montana v. United States*], we held that the Crow Tribe could regulate hunting and fishing by nonmembers on land held by the Tribe or held in trust for the Tribe by the United States. But this power could not extend to nonmembers' activities on land they held in fee. Again we relied upon the view of tribal sovereignty set forth in *Oliphant*:

> "Though *Oliphant* only determined inherent tribal authority in criminal matters, the principles on which it relied support the general proposition that the inherent sovereign powers of an Indian tribe do not extend to the activities of nonmembers of the tribe." 450 U.S., at 565 (footnote omitted).

It is true that our decisions recognize broader retained tribal powers outside the criminal context. Tribal courts, for example, resolve civil disputes involving nonmembers, including non-Indians. *See, e.g.,* [*Santa Clara Pueblo v. Martinez*;] *Williams v. Lee*, 358 U.S. 217, 223 (1959). Civil authority may also be present in areas such as zoning where the exercise of tribal authority is vital to the maintenance of tribal integrity and self-determination. *See, e.g., Brendale v. Confederated Tribes and Bands of Yakima Indian Nation,* [492 U.S. 408 (1989)]. As distinct from criminal prosecution, this civil authority typically involves situations arising from property ownership within the reservation or "consensual relationships with the tribe or its members, through commercial dealing, contracts, leases, or other arrangements." [*Montana v. United States.*] The exercise of criminal jurisdiction subjects a person not only to the adjudicatory power of the tribunal, but also to the prosecuting power of the tribe, and involves a far more direct intrusion on personal liberties.

The tribes are, to be sure, "a good deal more than 'private voluntary organizations,'" and are aptly described as "unique aggregations possessing attributes of sovereignty over both their members and their territory." [*United States v. Mazurie.*] In the area of criminal enforcement, however, tribal power does not extend beyond internal relations among members. Petitioner is not a member of the Pima-Maricopa Tribe, and is not now eligible to become one. Neither he nor other members of his Tribe may vote, hold office, or serve on a jury under Pima-Maricopa authority. For purposes of criminal jurisdiction, petitioner's relations with this Tribe are the same as the non-Indian's in *Oliphant.* We hold that the Tribe's powers over him are subject to the same limitations.

III

[A] review of history [is] somewhat less illuminating than in *Oliphant*, but tends to support the conclusion we reach. Early evidence concerning tribal jurisdiction over nonmembers is lacking because "[u]ntil the middle of this century, few Indian tribes maintained any semblance of a formal court system. Offenses by one Indian against another were usually handled by social and religious pressure and not by formal judicial processes; emphasis was on restitution rather than punishment." [*Oliphant* at 197.] Cases challenging the jurisdiction of modern tribal courts are few, perhaps because "most parties acquiesce to tribal jurisdiction" where it is asserted. See National American Indian Court Judges Association, Indian Courts and the Future 48 (1978). We have no occasion in this case to address the effect of a formal acquiescence to tribal jurisdiction that might be made, for example, in return for a tribe's agreement not to exercise its power to exclude an offender from tribal lands.

Respondents rely for their historical argument upon evidence that definitions of "Indian" in federal statutes and programs apply to all Indians without respect to membership in a particular tribe. For example, the federal jurisdictional statutes applicable to Indian country use the general term "Indian." In construing [an 1834 statute using the term] this Court stated that it "does not speak to members of a tribe, but of the race generally — of the family of Indians." *United States v. Rogers,* 4 How. 567, 573 (1846). Respondents also emphasize that Courts of Indian Offenses, which were established by regulation in 1883 by the Department of the Interior and continue to operate today on reservations without tribal courts, possess jurisdiction over *all* Indian offenders within the relevant reservation. *See* 25 CFR § 11.2(a) (1989).

This evidence does not stand for the proposition respondents advance. Congressional and administrative provisions such as those cited above reflect the Government's treatment of Indians as a single large class with respect to *federal* jurisdiction and programs. Those references are not dispositive of a question of *tribal* power to treat Indians by the same broad classification. [F]or the novel and disputed issue in the case before us, the statutes reflect at most the tendency of past Indian policy to treat Indians as an undifferentiated class. The historical record prior to the creation of modern tribal courts shows little federal attention to the individual tribes' powers as between themselves or over one another's members. Scholars who do find treaties or other sources illuminating have only [been] divided in their conclusions.

The brief history of the tribal courts themselves provides somewhat clearer guidance. The tribal courts were established under the auspices of the [IRA,] which allowed the expression of retained tribal sovereignty by authorizing creation of new tribal governments, constitutions, and courts. The new tribal courts supplanted the federal Courts of Indian Offenses operated by the Bureau of Indian Affairs. Significantly, new law and order codes were required to be approved by the Secretary of the Interior. *See* 25 U.S.C. § 476. The opinions of the Solicitor of the Department of the Interior on the new tribal codes leave unquestioned the authority of the tribe over its members.

Evidence on criminal jurisdiction over nonmembers is less clear, but on balance supports the view that inherent tribal jurisdiction extends to tribe members only. [Early opinions by the Solicitor were divided; two] later opinions, however, give a strong indication that the new tribal courts were not understood to possess power over nonmembers. One mentions only adoption of nonmembers into the tribe or receipt of delegated authority as means of acquiring jurisdiction over nonmember Indians. 1 Op. Sol. 849 (Aug. 26, 1938). A final opinion states more forcefully that the only means by which a tribe could deal with interloping nonmember Indians were removal of the offenders from the reservation or acceptance of delegated authority. 1 Op. Sol. 872 (Feb. 17, 1939).

These opinions provide the most specific historical evidence on the question before us and, we think, support our conclusion. Taken together with the general history preceding the creation of modern tribal courts, they indicate that the tribal courts embody only the powers of *internal* self-governance we have described. We are not persuaded that external criminal jurisdiction is an accepted part of the courts' function.

IV

Whatever might be said of the historical record, we must view it in light of petitioner's status as a citizen of the United States. Many Indians became citizens during the era of allotment and tribal termination around the turn of the century, and all were made citizens in 1924. That Indians are citizens does not alter the federal government's broad authority to legislate with respect to enrolled Indians as a class, whether to impose burdens or benefits. *See United States v. Antelope*, 430 U.S. 641 (1977); *Morton v. Mancari*, 417 U.S. 535 (1974). In the absence of such legislation, however, Indians like other citizens are embraced within our Nation's "great solicitude that its citizens be protected . . . from unwarranted intrusions on their personal liberty." [*Oliphant* at 210.]

Criminal trial and punishment is so serious an intrusion on personal liberty that its exercise over non-Indian citizens was a power necessarily surrendered by the tribes in their submission to the overriding sovereignty of the United States. We hesitate to adopt a view of tribal sovereignty that would single out another group of citizens, nonmember Indians, for trial by political bodies that do not include them. As full citizens, Indians share in the territorial and political sovereignty of the United States. The retained sovereignty of the tribe is but a recognition of certain additional authority the tribes maintain over Indians who consent to be tribal members. Indians like all other citizens share allegiance to the overriding sovereign, the United States. A tribe's additional authority comes from the consent of its members, and so in the criminal sphere membership marks the bounds of tribal authority.

The special nature of the tribunals at issue makes a focus on consent and the protections of citizenship most appropriate. While modern tribal courts include many familiar features of the judicial process, they are influenced by the unique customs, languages, and usages of the tribes they serve. Tribal courts are often "subordinate to the political branches of tribal governments," and their legal methods may depend on "unspoken practices and norms." Cohen 334–335. It is significant that the Bill of Rights does not apply to Indian tribal governments. [*Talton v. Mayes.*] The Indian Civil Rights Act provides some statutory guarantees of fair procedure, but these guarantees are not equivalent to their constitutional counterparts. There is, for example, no right under the Act to appointed counsel for those unable to afford a lawyer.

Our cases suggest constitutional limitations even on the ability of Congress to subject American citizens to criminal proceedings before a tribunal that does not provide constitutional protections as a matter of right. *Cf. Reid v. Covert*, 354 U.S. 1 (1957). We have approved delegation to an Indian tribe of the authority to promulgate rules that may be enforced by criminal sanction in *federal* court, [*United States v. Mazurie,*] but no delegation of authority to a tribe has to date included the power to punish nonmembers in *tribal* court. We decline to produce such a result through recognition of inherent tribal authority.

Tribal authority over members, who are also citizens, is not subject to these objections. Retained criminal jurisdiction over members is accepted by our precedents and justified by the voluntary character of tribal membership and the concomitant right of participation in a tribal government, the authority of which rests on consent. This principle finds support in our cases decided under provisions that predate the present federal jurisdictional statutes. We held in *United States v. Rogers*, 4 How. 567 (1846), that a non-Indian could not, through his adoption into the Cherokee Tribe, bring himself within the federal definition of "Indian" for purposes of an exemption to a federal jurisdictional provision. But we recognized that a non-Indian could, by adoption, "become entitled to certain privileges in the tribe, and make himself amenable to their laws and usages." *Id.*, at 573.

With respect to such internal laws and usages, the tribes are left with broad freedom not enjoyed by any other governmental authority in this county. *See, e.g.,* [*Santa Clara Pueblo v. Martinez*]. This is all the more reason to reject an extension of tribal authority over those who have not given the consent of the governed that provides a fundamental basis for power within our constitutional system.

The United States suggests that Pima-Maricopa tribal jurisdiction is appropriate because petitioner's enrollment in the Torres-Martinez Band of Cahuilla Mission Indians "is a sufficient indication of his self-identification as an Indian, with traditional Indian cultural values, to make it reasonable to subject him to the tribal court system, which . . . implements traditional Indian values and customs." Brief for United States as *Amicus Curiae* 27. But the tribes are not mere fungible groups of homogenous persons among whom any Indian would feel at home. On the contrary, wide variations in customs, art, language, and physical characteristics separate the tribes, and their history has been marked by both intertribal alliances and animosities. Petitioner's general status as an Indian says little about his consent to the exercise of authority over him by a particular tribe.

The Court of Appeals sought to address some of these concerns by adopting a "contacts" test to determine which nonmember Indians might be subject to tribal jurisdiction. But the rationale of the test would apply to non-Indians on the reservation as readily as to Indian nonmembers. Many non-Indians reside on reservations, and have close ties to tribes through marriage or long employment. Indeed, the population of non-Indians on reservations generally is greater than the population of all Indians, both members and nonmembers, and non-Indians make up some 35% of the Salt River Reservation population. The contacts approach is little more than a variation of the argument that any person who enters an Indian community should be deemed to have given implied consent to tribal criminal jurisdiction over him. We have rejected this approach for non-Indians. It is a logical consequence of that decision that nonmembers, who share relevant jurisdictional characteristics of non-Indians, should share the same jurisdictional status.

V

Respondents and *amici* contend that without tribal jurisdiction over minor offenses committed by nonmember Indians, no authority will have jurisdiction over such offenders. They assert that unless we affirm jurisdiction in this case, the tribes will lack important power to preserve order on the reservation, and nonmember Indians will be able to violate the law with impunity. Although the jurisdiction at stake here is over relatively minor crime, we recognize that protection of the community from disturbances of the peace and other misdemeanors is a most serious matter. But this same interest in tribal law enforcement is applicable to non-Indian reservation residents, whose numbers are often greater. It was argued in *Oliphant* that the absence of tribal jurisdiction over non-Indians would leave a practical, if not legal, void in reservation law enforcement. The argument that only tribal jurisdiction could meet the need for effective law enforcement did not provide a basis for finding jurisdiction in *Oliphant;* neither is it sufficient here.

For felonies such as the murder alleged in this case at the outset, federal jurisdiction is in place under the Major Crimes Act, 18 U.S.C. § 1153. The tribes also possess their traditional and undisputed power to exclude persons whom they deem to be undesirable from tribal lands. Tribal law enforcement authorities have the power to restrain those who disturb public order on the reservation, and if necessary, to eject them. Where jurisdiction to try and punish an offender rests outside the tribe, tribal officers may exercise their power to detain the offender and transport him to the proper authorities.

Respondents' major objection to this last point is that, in the circumstances presented here, there may not be any lawful authority to punish the nonmember Indian. State authorities may lack the power, resources, or inclination to deal with reservation crime. Arizona, for example, specifically disclaims jurisdiction over Indian country crimes. Ariz. Const., Art. 20, para. 4. And federal authority over minor crime, otherwise provided by the Indian Country Crimes Act, 18 U.S.C. § 1152, may be lacking altogether in the case of crime committed by a nonmember Indian against another Indian, since § 1152 states that general federal jurisdiction over Indian country crime "shall not extend to offenses committed by one Indian against the person or property of another Indian."

Our decision today does not imply endorsement of the theory of a jurisdictional void presented by respondents and the court below. States may, with the consent of the tribes, assist in maintaining order on the reservation by punishing minor crime. Congress has provided a mechanism by which the States now without jurisdiction in Indian country may assume criminal jurisdiction through Public Law 280. Our decision here also does not address the ability of neighboring tribal governments that share law enforcement concerns to enter into reciprocal agreements giving each jurisdiction over the other's members. As to federal jurisdiction under § 1152, both academic commentators and the dissenting judge below have suggested that the statute could be construed to cover the conduct here. Others have disagreed. That statute is not before us and we express no views on the question.

If the present jurisdictional scheme proves insufficient to meet the practical needs of reservation law enforcement, then the proper body to address the problem is Congress, which has the ultimate authority over Indian affairs. We cannot, however, accept these arguments of policy as a basis for finding tribal jurisdiction that is inconsistent with precedent, history, and the equal treatment of Native American citizens.

[*Reversed.*]

JUSTICE BRENNAN with whom JUSTICE MARSHALL joins, dissenting.

The Court today holds that an Indian tribal court has no power to exercise criminal jurisdiction over a defendant who is an Indian but not a tribal member. The Court concedes that Indian tribes never expressly relinquished such power. Instead, the Court maintains that tribes *implicitly* surrendered the power to enforce their criminal laws against nonmember Indians when the tribes became dependent on the federal government. Because I do not share such a parsimonious view of the sovereignty retained by Indian tribes, I respectfully dissent.

I

The powers of Indian tribes are " '*inherent powers of a limited sovereignty which has never been extinguished.*' " [*United States v. Wheeler*] (emphasis in original).

When the tribes were incorporated into the territory of the United States [as] "domestic dependent nations," [they became] implicitly divested of powers to have external relations because they are *necessarily* inconsistent with the overriding interest of the greater sovereign.

By contrast, we have recognized that tribes did not "surrender [their] independence — [the] right to self-government, by associating with a stronger [power], and taking its protection." [*Worcester v. Georgia.*] [*Oliphant*] held that tribes did not have the power to exercise criminal jurisdiction over *non-Indians* because such power was inconsistent with the overriding national interest. But it does not follow that because tribes lost their power to exercise criminal jurisdiction over non-Indians, they also lost their power to enforce criminal laws against Indians who are not members of their tribe.

. . . .

II

This country has pursued contradictory policies with respect to the Indians. Since the passage of the [IRA] however, Congress has followed a policy of promoting the independence and self-government of the various tribes. The Court's decision today not only ignores the assumptions on which Congress originally legislated with respect to the jurisdiction over Indian crimes, but also stands in direct conflict with current congressional policy. I respectfully dissent.

NOTES

1. **The Judicial Role in Making Indian Policy:** In his classic work, the HANDBOOK OF FEDERAL INDIAN LAW, Felix Cohen offered the following formulation of tribal powers:

> Perhaps the most basic principle of all Indian law . . . is the principle that *those powers which are lawfully vested in an Indian tribe are not, in general, delegated powers granted by express acts of Congress, but rather inherent powers of a limited sovereignty which has never been extinguished.*

FELIX COHEN, HANDBOOK OF FEDERAL INDIAN LAW 122 (1942). The problem noted by several scholars with this formulation is that it unduly narrows tribal sovereignty by accepting federal power to extinguish it. *See, e.g.,* RUSSELL L. BARSH & JAMES Y. HENDERSON, THE ROAD, AMERICAN INDIAN TRIBES AND POLITICAL LIBERTY 59–60 (1980); Milner S. Ball, *Constitution, Court, Indian Tribes,* 1987 AM. B. FOUND. RES. J. 1, 43–44. For a critique of *Oliphant,* see Russell L. Barsh & James Y. Henderson, *The Betrayal:* Oliphant v. Suquamish Indian Tribe *and the Hunting of the Snark,* 63 MINN. L. REV. 609 (1979).

Not only does this formulation recognize federal authority to limit or extinguish tribal powers, it also takes no position regarding who has the power to extinguish that authority. If one compares two of the opinions in *Worcester v. Georgia,* 31 U.S. (6 Pet.) 515 (1832), set forth and discussed in Chapter 1, it is apparent that the early justices were not in full agreement on this question. Chief Justice Marshall's majority opinion deferred to treaties and federal statutes as recognizing the separate sovereign status of the Cherokee Nation, strongly suggesting that until Congress acted to withdraw its recognition of the Nation or expressly curtailed its powers the Cherokee Nation remained in complete governmental control of its territory. Thus, the congressional recognition and protection of that sovereignty not only preempted the state from governing Indian country, but also prevented the federal courts from taking any inconsistent position. Indeed, it is important to recall that Reverends Worcester and Butler, whose convictions were at issue in *Worcester*, were white, not Indian. Thus, when *Worcester* suggested that the Cherokees had exclusive criminal jurisdiction over crimes in their territory, the opinion included alleged crimes by non-Indians as well. By contrast, recall that Justice McLean questioned whether complete tribal control over its territory was meant to constitute a permanent legal reality. He wrote, "If a tribe of Indians shall become so degraded or reduced in numbers, as to lose the power of self-government, the protection of the local law, of necessity, must be extended over them. The point at which this exercise of power by a state would be proper, need not now be considered; if, indeed, it be a judicial question." The last point advanced by Justice McLean is telling since he expressed some doubt regarding the ability of the judiciary to curtail tribal authority without the benefit of federal treaty or statute approved by Congress. The classic modern formulation of the same point is found in *United States v. Wheeler*, 435 U.S. 313, 322–23 (1978). In that case Justice Stewart wrote:

> The powers of Indian tribes are, in general, "inherent powers of a limited sovereignty which has never been extinguished." F. Cohen, Handbook of Federal Indian Law 122 (1945). Before the coming of the Europeans, the tribes were self-governing sovereign political communities. *See McClanahan v. Arizona State Tax Comm'n*, 411 U.S. 164, 172. Like all sovereign bodies, they then had the inherent power to prescribe laws for their members and to punish infractions of those laws.

> Indian tribes are, of course, no longer "possessed of the full attributes of sovereignty." *United States v. Kagama, supra*, 118 U.S., at 381. Their incorporation within the territory of the United States, and their acceptance of its protection, necessarily divested them of some aspects of the sovereignty which they had previously exercised. *By specific treaty provision they yielded up other sovereign powers; by statute, in the exercise of its plenary control, Congress has removed still others.*

(Emphasis supplied.) Is *Oliphant* or *Duro* consistent with these traditions? Does the Supreme Court in either decision explain why it believes it has the authority to determine on its own the scope of power of a tribal government? Is there any satisfactory explanation?

2. **Inconsistent with Their Dependent Status and Historical Fidelity:** In *Oliphant*, Chief Justice Rehnquist relied on *Worcester* as the source of the idea that Indian tribes lost independent sovereign power as a result of their relationship with the federal government, particularly their dependent status. Unfortunately, the Chief Justice quotes *Worcester* out of context. Precisely what Chief Justice Marshall said was:

The Indian nations had always been considered as distinct, *independent political communities*, retaining their original natural rights, as the undisputed possessors of the soil, from time immemorial, *with the single exception of that imposed by irresistible power, which excluded them from intercourse with any other European potentate than the first discoverer of the coast of the particular region claimed: and this was a restriction which those European potentates imposed on themselves, as well as on the Indians.*

Worcester v. Georgia, 31 U.S. (6 Pet.) 515, 559 (1832) (emphasis supplied). Notice that the only limitation on the sovereignty of Indian tribes as "independent political communities" that *Worcester* recognized was the impairment of their foreign affairs power to deal "with any other European potentate." That limitation did not even exclude external diplomacy with other tribes. It is quite a leap from suggesting that dependent domestic nations impliedly lost a portion of their foreign affairs powers through their dependent status, as suggested in *Worcester*, to suggesting that they lost complete sovereign control over their lands, as suggested in *Oliphant*. Implied in the *Oliphant* holding is the assumption that the sovereignty of Native peoples over their territories as "independent political communities" is somehow less than the sovereignty of other nations and states over their territory. What, if anything, do the *Oliphant* and *Duro* opinions offer to justify their departure from the traditions of territoriality in measuring tribal sovereignty, jurisdiction, and governing authority? Noting that one of the frequent results of *Oliphant*, *Duro*, and their progeny is the enlargement of state authority in Indian country at the expense of the tribes (precisely the opposite of what *Worcester* sought to protect), Judge William C. Canby of the United States Court of Appeals for the Ninth Circuit has criticized the *Oliphant* line of cases, suggesting, "[i]t is not appropriate, however, to limit tribal power because of the tribe's dependent status when the power is lost to a state, upon whom the tribe is not dependent." William C. Canby, Jr., *The Status of Indian Tribes in American Law Today*, 62 WASH. L. REV. 1, 18 n.57 (1987). Is there any answer to this criticism?

An equally interesting question is whether *Oliphant* and *Duro* offer any consistent methodological approach for determining when exercise of a tribal power was inconsistent with the dependent status of Indian tribes. Did the Supreme Court in either case merely purport to interpret the intent of Congress in statutes and treaties or, rather, did the Court find the lessons derived from congressional sources to be inconclusive? If the Court is merely interpreting the intent of Congress, which possesses the only constitutionally delegated power related to Indian tribes, what do you think of the Court's method of statutory interpretation? *See* Richard B. Collins, *Implied Limitations on the Jurisdiction of Indian Tribes*, 54 WASH. L. REV. 479, 490–99 (1979).

Consider the accuracy of Chief Justice Rehnquist's reading of history in light of materials contained at the start of Chapter 1. Notice that the current version of 18 U.S.C. § 1152, which had roots in the earliest Trade and Intercourse Acts, contemplated federal jurisdiction over crimes by non-Indians against the person or property of Indians, except "where, by treaty stipulations, the exclusive jurisdiction over such offenses is or may be secured to the Indian tribes respectively." Consider the treaties referenced in footnote 8 of *Oliphant*. Are they not precisely the treaties in which Congress long ago recognized tribes did have jurisdiction over non-Indians in their territory?

The historical methodology of *Oliphant* poses another problem as a result of the history of federal Indian policy. Until the allotment policy of the late nineteenth century, federal policy closed Indian country to entry by non-Indians. Indeed, recall from the *Worcester* case that the Trade and Intercourse Acts required a federal permit for non-Indians to enter Indian country. Thus, until the twentieth century, there simply were not large numbers of non-Indians in Indian country other than illegal trespassers of the type referenced in the treaties mentioned in footnote 8 or like the gold prospectors that invaded the Black Hills and produced conflict with the Sioux in the 1870s. In light of these facts, was the historical methodology of *Oliphant* misguided? More importantly, could any "tacit assumption" about tribal jurisdiction over non-Indians arise in a context where the questions rarely would emerge?

Consider the sources upon which the Court relies in *Oliphant* to demonstrate that tacit assumption. Is the historical evidence that Justice Rehnquist marshals very relevant to the issue at hand? Most of the sources on which Justice Rehnquist relies, including the adoption of the predecessor of 18 U.S.C. § 1152, and the Western Territory Bill, arose before most Indian tribes had any type of formal court structure or written laws. Even though the Choctaw did have a formal court system at the time of the Choctaw treaty cited by the Court, in practice the system was then still relatively rudimentary. Could these early sources be read only to reflect a reluctance to relegate non-Indians to nonjudicial or rudimentary forms of tribal justice instead of demonstrating a lack of jurisdiction of even a sophisticated western style tribal court? Likewise, the treaties referred to by Justice Rehnquist provide even less support for his position. Promising to turn offenders over to the United States could just as well be read, as it was in the *Crow Dog* decision set forth and discussed in Chapter 1, as an extradition provision dealing with fugitives from United States justice, rather than a statement about tribal jurisdiction over crimes occurring in Indian country. Some of the evidence on which then Justice Rehnquist relies, such as *Ex parte Kenyon* and the 1960 legislation, certainly supports his argument, but it adds up to far less than an overwhelming historical case. Evaluate the strength of these sources, particularly in light of the countervailing evidence reflected in the treaties cited in footnote 8. In light of those treaties consider the language Justice Rehnquist employed in his dissent in *United States v. Sioux Nation*, 448 U.S. 371, 437 (1980), in which he criticized the majority for engaging in revisionist history and chided his fellow justices for overlooking that "in a Court opinion, as a historical and not a legal matter, both settler and Indian are entitled to the benefit of the Biblical adjuration: 'Judge not, that ye be not judged.' "

While *Oliphant* employed an historical analysis to determine whether the exercise of a sovereign power by a tribe was inconsistent with its dependent status, *Duro* demonstrably does not rely on the same historical inquiry. The reason for the Supreme Court's abandonment of history as a touchstone of inconsistency might perhaps be found buried in Part III of the *Duro* opinion. The Court of Indian Offenses, which many tribal courts displaced, defined their criminal jurisdiction as covering any Indian on the reservation, irrespective of tribal membership. Today that grant of jurisdiction is found in 25 C.F.R. 11.102. When tribal courts began to displace CFR courts after enactment of the Indian Reorganization Act of 1934, the criminal jurisdiction originally granted in most tribal law and orders codes paralleled that of the CFR courts and covered all Indians irrespective of enrollment in the governing tribe. The BIA repeatedly approved such ordinances. Does not this history show an almost continuous assumption that both CFR and tribal courts could exercise jurisdiction over all Indians irrespective of enrollment in the governing tribe? Since *Oliphant* suggested an historical methodology for determining the inconsistency of the exercise of a tribal power with its dependent status, would not this history almost conclusively show that the exercise of tribal inherent criminal jurisdiction over nonmember Indians was not inconsistent with their dependent status? Why did the Supreme Court not choose to defer to this history? What methodology did it suggest instead for ascertaining whether the exercise of a tribal power would be inconsistent with the dependent status of the tribe? Does its substitute approach provide any greater guidance? Does it make sense? Does it fully explain why tribes are entitled to less territorial sovereignty than any other sovereign? Does this difference between the methodological approaches in *Oliphant* and *Duro* suggest that the Supreme Court first reaches the result and then searches for a legal analysis to justify it?

One way to understand *Duro* is to note that the Court had to decide that nonmember Indians were outside the tribe's inherent criminal jurisdiction since any contrary decision would have made the line drawn by *Oliphant* transparently racial. Thus, the need for a particular result, rather than any line of inquiry, drove the outcome of the case. Would that explain why *Oliphant* and *Duro* do not appear to apply consistent analytical methodologies to determine whether the exercise of a power by an Indian tribe is inconsistent with its dependent status?

Note that the Ninth Circuit was willing in *Bugenig*, presented in Sec. B.2, this chapter, to uphold jurisdiction over nomembers if sanctioned by the federal government. What explains the current federal judicial reluctance to uphold tribal jurisdiction over non-Indians and nonmembers on inherent tribal sovereignty grounds but converse willingness to sustain such jurisdiction if federally authorized? Is this a new form of federal dependence for tribes? Might it stem from a recognition of nonrepresentation of affected interests in tribal governments but their greater political power over federal actions? Does this perverse position limit tribal authority to whatever the federal government is willing to permit? Is that position consistent with the idea of an inherent tribal sovereignty? Keep in mind that governments regularly apply their criminal laws to noncitizens and nonvoters, so long as the offense is committed within the government's territorial jurisdiction. Would Indian nations increase the likelihood of federal recognition of their criminal jurisdiction over non-Indians if they incorporated non-Indians into their juries or gave them greater standing within tribal governments? What risks would such actions pose for tribal governments? For discussion of some tribes' efforts to involve non-Indians in their systems of governance and law, see Note 3 on Tribal Regulatory Power, Sec. 6, this chapter.

3. Criminal Jurisdiction over Non-Indians in Indian Country Before *Oliphant* and *Duro*: The *Oliphant* and *Duro* decisions were extraordinarily unpopular in Indian country. As *Oliphant* indicates, despite the fact that the decision claims there was no historical tradition of recognizing inherent tribal criminal jurisdiction over non-Indians, at least 30 tribes had been asserting such at the time the case was decided, many of them relying on statutes that deemed entry onto the reservation as an implied consent to the exercise of criminal jurisdiction by the tribe. Such tribes had posted conspicuous signs at entry points to their reservations informing those who entered of the effect of such statutes. Before the decision in *Oliphant*, those statutes seemingly had an arguable theoretical justification as applied to outsiders entering the reservation, although it would certainly have been harder to justify the theory as applied to non-Indian residents of the reservation, like Oliphant and Belgarde. Could the rule of *Oliphant* be avoided by excluding a non-Indian committing an offense against the tribe rather than by exercising criminal jurisdiction? *See* Sec. B.1, this chapter. *Duro* was even more disruptive of existing jurisdictional practices of tribal courts. For historical reasons discussed above, almost all tribes exercising any inherent tribal criminal jurisdiction through tribal courts were exercising criminal jurisdiction over both member and nonmember Indians without distinction.

4. **The Factual Setting of *Oliphant*:** In the *Oliphant* case, the reservation was heavily allotted, as reflected by footnote 1 of the opinion, with Indians comprising far less than 1% of the resident population of the reservation. The persons accused of crimes in the tribal courts were residents of the reservation living on fee patent land no longer held in Indian trust title. Might the result in the case have been any different had the issue arisen on an unallotted, isolated reservation like that of the Hopi Tribe in Arizona? Could a case involving non-Indian outsiders who entered the reservation bent on disrupting tribal activities have yielded a different result? On the face of the *Oliphant* opinion is there any room to argue that its holding does not apply to unallotted or isolated Indian reservations that remain substantially Indian-held or to non-Indians who are outsiders, as opposed to residents, and who enter the reservation? Can or should the type of reservation and the number of non-Indians living there affect the rules of Indian law? *See* Robert N. Clinton, *Reservation Specificity and Indian Adjudication: An Essay on the Importance of Limited Contextualism in Indian Law*, 8 HAMLINE L. REV. 543 (1985) (criticizing the *Oliphant* "one rule fits all" approach to federal Indian law for not recognizing the great differences in the needs, context, demography and setting of Indian reservations); *see also* Indian Reservation Special Magistrate: Hearing on S.1177 Before the Senate Select Committee on Indian Affairs, 99th Cong., 2d Sess. 167–68 (1986) (Statement of Gerald Anton, President of the Salt River Pima-Maricopa Indian Community relating the Tribe's agreement with city, county, and state officials to pursue a federal law specific to the needs of that reservation, which lies within the Phoenix metropolitan area). For more information on the factual setting of the *Oliphant* case, *see generally,* Sarah Krakoff, *Mark the Plumber v. Tribal Empire, or Non-Indian Anxiety v. Tribal Sovereignty?: The Story of* Oliphant v. Suquamish Indian Tribe, *in* INDIAN LAW STORIES (Carole Goldberg, Kevin K. Washburn, and Philip P. Frickey, eds., 2011).

5. **Law Enforcement on the Reservation After *Oliphant* and *Duro*:** The Supreme Court held in *Oliphant v. Suquamish Indian Tribe* that tribes lacked inherent criminal jurisdiction over non-Indians. This holding has contributed to what has often been referred to as a "jurisdictional maze" in Indian Country — a complicated interplay of authority between federal, state, and tribal governments

that often leaves victims, offenders, and tribal communities with inefficient and unjust legal outcomes. A non-Indian who commits a crime against the person or property of an Indian victim must be tried in federal court generally under 18 U.S.C. § 1152 (unless a federal statute, such as Public Law 280, has granted the state jurisdiction over crimes occurring on reservations). Many such crimes may be lesser offenses, such as domestic abuse, assault, theft, poaching, larceny, forgery, or the like. Federal prosecutors' priorities frequently center on white-collar crime, drugs, and political corruption. Federal prosecutors and courts are understaffed and the federal system therefore is not geared or inclined toward prosecuting non-major crimes, most of which are misdemeanors. Consequently, crimes like domestic assault, other simple assaults, and burglaries are simply not prosecuted, which creates grave problems for tribes attempting to police their reservation and protect their members from crimes by non-Indians.

Prohibitions on exercises of tribal jurisdiction against non-Indians create a truly anomalous legal situation by dislocating the process of justice from the community in which the crimes occur. As a recent report by the Indian Law and Order Commission states, "Federal and State agencies can be invaluable in creating effective partnerships with Tribal governments, but there is no substitute for the effectiveness of locally controlled Tribal governmental institutions that are transparent and accountable. U.S. citizens rightly cherish the value of local control: that government closest to the people is best equipped to serve them." INDIAN LAW AND ORDER COMMISSION, A ROADMAP FOR MAKING NATIVE AMERICA SAFER: REPORT TO CONGRESS AND THE PRESIDENT OF THE UNITED STATES 3 (2013).

Given that national statistics (not limited to Indian country) show that Native women are 2–3 times more likely than other women to be victims of sexual assault, and that more than three-quarters of the perpetrators are non-Native, *Oliphant* precludes tribes from protecting a large, vulnerable population. *See* Jacqueline Actuga, *Beloved Women: Life Givers, Caretakers, Teachers of Future Generations in* SHARING OUR STORIES OF SURVIVAL: NATIVE WOMEN SURVIVING VIOLENCE 3–4 (S. Deer, B. Clairmont & C. Martell eds., 2007). Moreover, the distance between the federal courts and reservations often exacerbates the problem. The nearest federal courts and prosecutors to the Fort Peck Reservation in Montana are in Billings and Great Falls, over 250 miles from the reservation. Several bills designed to increase the number of federal prosecutors and place federal magistrates in Indian country have been unsuccessful, partly because of Indian opposition to the addition of another layer of federal law enforcement in Indian country in place of a solution that would strengthen tribal authority. *See, e.g.,* S. 1177, 99th Cong., 2d Sess. (1986). Other experiments with deputizing tribal prosecutors as special assistant United States Attorneys have been tried on the Cheyenne River Sioux Reservation and in Oregon, and ultimately formalized in the Tribal Law and Order Act of 2010. Pub. L. 111-211, 124 Stat. 2258, § 213. Nevertheless, *Oliphant* has created a practical law enforcement problem in Indian country that tribes have tried to address through civil means. Consider whether the contraction of tribal civil jurisdiction over non-Indians discussed in the cases that follow may interfere with those efforts as well.

The law enforcement problems created by *Oliphant* were "merely" practical because, in theory, any crime foreclosed from tribal jurisdiction by *Oliphant* could most often be heard in federal court under 18 U.S.C. section 1152 or in state courts for those jurisdictions covered by delegations of state criminal jurisdiction through Public Law 280 or otherwise. In contrast, as the dissent points out in *Duro*, that decision left an actual legal void in the jurisdictional arrangements for some lesser nonmember Indian crimes committed against other Indians. Lesser crimes between Indians (which had never been defined in terms of member of the governing tribe) not covered by the federal Major Crimes Act, 18 U.S.C. § 1153, and which are expressly excluded from the jurisdiction contained in 18 U.S.C. section 1152, had traditionally been left to tribal jurisdiction. The *Duro* holding left no available forum in which to handle some of those crimes. While the last portion of the *Duro* majority opinion briefly alludes to this problem, the actual effects of its decision on law enforcement in Indian country did not seem to affect the Supreme Court.

In addition to the jurisdictional void left by the *Duro* decision, the decision seemed oblivious to the different classes of Indians impacted by the decision. Basically, three different classes of Indians often reside on most reservations today: (1) members of the governing tribe; (2) enrolled members of other tribes who reside on the reservation either as a result of marriage, tribal, BIA, IHS, or other federal employment or for other reasons; and (3) tribal descendants who may have some ancestry of the governing tribe but for various reasons, whether blood quantum or the side of the family from which the ancestry derives, are ineligible for enrollment under prevailing tribal law or perhaps have refused to enroll. Notice that only two of these classes are enrolled and only two have some kinship or blood ties to reservation and they are not the same two classes. Sometimes traditionalists who object to the IRA government, as in the case of Hopi traditionalists, may refuse to enroll. This third class can be quite large. For example, 25% of the criminal defendants on the Ft. Belknap reservation in Montana in 1989 were nonmembers, and 31% of the defendants on the Wind River reservation in Wyoming were also nonmembers. How would the decision in *Duro* affect each of these categories?

Because Indians often live on reservations other than their own as a result of marriage or domestic partnership, might *Duro* seriously interfere with the ability of any tribe to prevent and punish domestic sexual and physical abuse? *See generally* Melissa L. Tatum, *A Jurisdictional Quandary: Challenges Facing Tribal Governments in Implementing the Full Faith and Credit Provisions of the Violence Against Women Acts*, 90 Ky. L.J. 123, 171 (2002). For illustrations of factors resulting in sizable numbers of nonmember Indians residing on present-day Indian reservations, see *Means v. District Court of the Chinle Judicial District*, 26 Ind. L. Rep. 6083 (Nav. Sup. Ct. 1999) (upholding tribal criminal jurisdiction over a nonmember Indian based on his having achieved the Navajo status of "hadane," or in-law, by marrying into the Tribe and assuming a clan relation); *Miller v. Crow Creek Sioux Tribe*, 12 Ind. L. Rep. 6008 (N. Plains Intertr. Ct. App. 1984) (upholding tribal court jurisdiction over a Sioux from one tribe prosecuted for malicious mischief in a tribal court of another Sioux tribe).

6. The *"Duro* Fix" Legislation and the 2013 VAWA Reauthorization's Limited *"Oliphant* Fix": Perhaps responding to the legal jurisdictional void left by the *Duro* decision, Congress attempted to overturn that decision by statute. Initially passed in 1990 as a rider to the Defense Appropriations Act, the legislation amended the definition section of the Indian Civil Rights Act, 25 U.S.C. § 1301. It added to the definition of "powers of self-government" language indicating it included "the inherent power of Indian Tribes, hereby recognized and affirmed, to exercise criminal jurisdiction over all Indians." Defense Appropriations Act for FY 91, Pub. L. No. 101-938, § 8077(b)–(d), (1990) (amending 25 U.S.C. § 1301(2)). The amendment also added a definition of the term "Indian," not previously defined in the ICRA:

> Indian means any person who would be subject to the jurisdiction of the United States as an Indian under section 1153, title 18, United States Code if that person were to commit an offense listed in that section in Indian country to which that section applies.

Id., § 8077(c) (amending 25 U.S.C. § 1301(4)). For an analysis of the *Duro* fix legislation, see Nell Jessup Newton, *Permanent Legislation to Correct* Duro v. Reina, 17 AM. INDIAN L. REV. 109, 112 (1992).

The *Duro* fix legislation generated a wave of litigation over whether the statute properly should be read and can be sustained as a federal delegation or as a confirmation of preexisting tribal jurisdiction. *Oliphant* and *Duro* dealt with criminal jurisdiction. In light of the next case, do they automatically apply to issues of civil adjudicative, regulatory, or taxing powers of tribes? If not, what test does apply? In which contexts?

Recently, Congress addressed the epidemic of violence against Native women by carving out a partial fix to *Oliphant* in the 2013 Reauthorization of the Violence Against Women Act. The VAWA recognizes inherent tribal sovereignty and jurisdiction over non-Indians who commit statutorily specified acts of domestic violence, dating violence, or violations of restraining orders directed at Indian victims. Importantly, the VAWA recognizes this power as inherent, rather than delegated by Congress. 25. U.S.C § 1304. Tribes may exercise this jurisdiction provided that they adopt federal law requirements protecting the rights of defendants. In 2014, the Department of Justice named three tribes to begin pilot projects wherein they may prosecute non-Indian domestic abusers. 79 Fed. Reg. 8487-02 (2014).

MONTANA v. UNITED STATES
United States Supreme Court
450 U.S. 544 (1981)

[By a tribal regulation, the Crow Tribe of Montana prohibited hunting and fishing within its reservation by anyone who was not a member of the Tribe. Relying on its ownership of the bed of the Big Horn River, on treaties which created its reservation, and on its inherent power as a sovereign, the Tribe claimed authority to prohibit hunting and fishing by nonmembers of the Tribe even on lands within the reservation owned by them in fee simple. Montana, however, continued to assert its authority to regulate hunting and fishing by non-Indians within the reservation. The First Treaty of Fort Laramie of 1851, in which the signatory tribes acknowledged various designated lands as their respective territories, specified that, by making the treaty, the tribes did not "surrender the privilege of hunting, fishing, or passing over" any of the lands in dispute. In 1868, the Second Treaty of Fort Laramie established the Crow Reservation, including land through which the Big Horn River flows, and provided that the reservation "shall be set apart for the absolute and undisturbed use and occupation" of the Tribe, and that no non-Indians except Government agents "shall ever be permitted to pass over, settle upon, or reside in" the reservation. To resolve the conflict between the Tribe and the State, the United States, proceeding in its own right and as fiduciary for the Tribe, filed an action seeking a declaratory judgment quieting title to the riverbed in the United States as trustee for the Tribe and establishing that the Tribe and the United States have sole authority to regulate hunting and fishing within the reservation, and an injunction requiring Montana to secure the Tribe's permission before issuing hunting or fishing licenses for use within the reservation. The District Court denied relief, but the Court of Appeals reversed. It held that the bed and banks of the river were held by the United States in trust for the Tribe; that the Tribe could regulate hunting and fishing within the reservation by nonmembers, except for hunting and fishing on fee lands by resident nonmember owners of those lands; and that nonmembers permitted by the Tribe to hunt or fish within the reservation remained subject to Montana's fish and game laws.

The Supreme Court opinion first addressed the ownership issue and held that title to the bed of the Big Horn River passed to Montana upon its admission into the Union, the United States not having conveyed beneficial ownership of the riverbed to the Crow Tribe by the treaties of 1851 or 1868. The Court held that as a general principle, the federal government holds lands under navigable waters in trust for future States, to be granted to such States when they enter the Union, and there is a strong presumption against conveyance of such lands by the United States. The 1851 treaty failed to overcome this presumption, since it did not by its terms formally convey any land to the Indians at all. And whatever property rights the 1868 treaty created, its language is not strong enough to overcome the presumption against the sovereign's conveyance of the riverbed. *Cf. United States v. Holt State Bank*, 270 U.S. 49. Moreover, the Court said that the situation of the Crow Indians at the time of the treaties presented no "public exigency" which would have required Congress to depart from its policy of reserving ownership of beds under navigable waters for the future States. By applying for the first time the general presumptive rule that the federal government holds title to navigable waters for future states to an Indian reservation created prior to statehood, the Supreme Court opinion abandoned on this issue the usual rules that Indian treaties are to be construed liberally in favor of the Indians and that Indian treaties are to be read as grants from, rather than to, the Indians.

Having addressed the ownership question, Justice STEWART's opinion for the majority then turned to the jurisdictional question in a context in which the State of Montana was found to own the beds of the streams in the reservation over which the Crow Tribe purported to assert exclusive jurisdiction. Furthermore, the major dispute in the case centered on fishing and the Court had found that the State of Montana effectively owned the entirety of the fish habitat.]

III

Though the parties in this case have raised broad questions about the power of the Tribe to regulate hunting and fishing by non-Indians on the reservation, the regulatory issue before us is a narrow one. The Court of Appeals held that the Tribe may prohibit nonmembers from hunting or fishing on land belonging to the Tribe or held by the United States in trust for the Tribe, and with this holding we can readily agree. We also agree with the Court of Appeals that if the Tribe permits nonmembers to fish or hunt on such lands, it may condition their entry by charging a fee or establishing bag and creel limits. What remains is the question of the power of the Tribe to regulate non-Indian fishing and hunting on reservation land owned in fee by nonmembers of the Tribe. The Court of Appeals held that, with respect to fee-patented lands, the Tribe may regulate, but may not prohibit, hunting and fishing by nonmember resident owners or by those, such as tenants or employees, whose occupancy is authorized by the owners. The court further held that the Tribe may totally prohibit hunting and fishing on lands within the reservation owned by non-Indians who do not occupy that land.

The Court of Appeals found two sources for this tribal regulatory power: the Crow treaties, "augmented" by 18 U.S.C. § 1165, and "inherent" Indian sovereignty. We believe that neither source supports the court's conclusion.

A

The purposes of the 1851 Treaty were to assure safe passage for settlers across the lands of various Indian tribes; to compensate the Tribes for the loss of buffalo, other game animals, timber and forage; to delineate tribal boundaries; to promote intertribal peace; and to establish a way of identifying Indians who committed depredations against non-Indians. As noted earlier, the treaty did not even create a reservation, although it did designate tribal lands. *See Crow Tribe v. United States*, 284 F.2d 361, 364, 366, 368 (Ct. Cl.). Only Article 5 of that treaty referred to hunting and fishing, and it merely provided that the eight signatory tribes "do not surrender the privilege of hunting, fishing, or passing over any of the tracts of country heretofore described." [11 Stat. 749.][15] The treaty nowhere suggested that Congress intended to grant authority to the Crow Tribe to regulate hunting and fishing by nonmembers on nonmember lands. Indeed, the Court of Appeals acknowledged that after the treaty was signed non-Indians, as well as members of other Indian tribes, undoubtedly hunted and fished within the treaty-designated territory of the Crows.

The 1868 Fort Laramie Treaty, 15 Stat. 649, reduced the size of the Crow territory designated by the 1851 Treaty. Article II of the Treaty established a reservation for the Crow Tribe, and provided that it be "set apart for the *absolute and undisturbed use and occupation* of the Indians herein named, and for such other friendly tribes or individual Indians as from time to time they may be willing, with the consent of the United States, to admit amongst them . . . ," (emphasis added) and that "the United States now solemnly agrees that no persons, except those herein designated and authorized so to do . . . shall ever be permitted to pass over, settle upon, or reside in the territory described in this article for the use of said Indians. . . . " The treaty, therefore, obligated the United States to prohibit most non-Indians from residing on or passing through reservation lands used and

---

[15] [6] The complaint in this case did not allege that non-Indian hunting and fishing on reservation lands has impaired this privilege.

occupied by the Tribe, and, thereby, arguably conferred upon the Tribe the authority to control fishing and hunting on those lands. But that authority could only extend to land on which the Tribe exercises "absolute and undisturbed use and occupation." And it is clear that the quantity of such land was substantially reduced by the allotment and alienation of tribal lands as a result of the passage of the [General Allotment Act] and the Crow Allotment Act of 1920, 41 Stat. 751. If the 1868 Treaty created tribal power to restrict or prohibit non-Indian hunting and fishing on the reservation, that power cannot apply to lands held in fee by non-Indians.[16]

In *Puyallup Tribe v. Washington Game Dep't*, 433 U.S. 165 (1977) (*Puyallup III*), the relevant treaty included language virtually identical to that in the 1868 Treaty of Fort Laramie. The Puyallup Reservation was to be "set apart, and, so far as necessary, surveyed and marked out for their exclusive use . . . [and no] white man [was to] be permitted to reside upon the same without permission of the tribe. . . . " *See id.*, at 174. The Puyallup Tribe argued that those words amounted to a grant of authority to fish free of state interference. But this Court rejected that argument, finding, in part, that it "clashe[d] with the subsequent history of the reservation . . . ," *ibid.*, notably two Acts of Congress under which the Puyallups alienated, in fee simple, the great majority of the lands in the reservation, including all the land abutting the Puyallup River. Thus, "[n]either the Tribe nor its members continue to hold Puyallup River fishing grounds for their 'exclusive use.' " *Ibid.* *Puyallup III* indicates, therefore, that treaty rights with respect to reservation lands must be read in light of the subsequent alienation of those lands. Accordingly, the language of the 1868 Treaty provides no support for tribal authority to regulate hunting and fishing on land owned by non-Indians. . . .

B

[T]he Court of Appeals also identified the power [to regulate non-Indian hunting and fishing on non-Indian lands] as an incident of the inherent sovereignty of the

---

[16] [9] [N]othing in the Allotment Acts supports the view of the Court of Appeals that the Tribe could nevertheless bar hunting and fishing by nonresident fee owners. The policy of the Acts was the eventual assimilation of the Indian population, *Organized Village of Kake v. Egan*, 369 U.S. 60, 72, and the "gradual extinction of Indian reservations and Indian titles." *Draper v. United States*, 164 U.S. 240, 246. The Secretary of the Interior and the Commissioner of Indian Affairs repeatedly emphasized that the allotment policy was designed to eventually eliminate tribal relations. [T]hroughout the Congressional debates on the subject of allotment, it was assumed that the "civilization" of the Indian population was to be accomplished, in part, by the dissolution of tribal relations. [Nothing] in the legislative history [suggests] that Congress intended that the non-Indians who would settle upon alienated allotted lands would be subject to tribal regulatory authority. Indeed, throughout the congressional debates, allotment of Indian land was consistently equated with the dissolution of tribal affairs and jurisdiction. . . . [Thus] Congress [did not] intend that non-Indians purchasing allotted lands would become subject to tribal jurisdiction when an avowed purpose of the allotment policy was the ultimate destruction of tribal government. And it is hardly likely that Congress could have imagined that the purpose of peaceful assimilation could be advanced if feeholders could be excluded from fishing or hunting on their acquired property. The policy of allotment and sale of surplus reservation land was, of course, repudiated in 1934 by the Indian Reorganization Act, 48 Stat. 984 (current version at 25 U.S.C. § 461 et seq.). But what is relevant in this case is the effect of the land alienation occasioned by that policy on Indian treaty rights tied to Indian use and occupation of reservation land.

Tribe over the entire Crow reservation. But "inherent sovereignty" is not so broad as to support the application of Resolution No. 74-05 to non-Indian lands.

This Court most recently reviewed the principles of inherent sovereignty in *United States v. Wheeler*, 435 U.S. 313. In that case, noting that Indian tribes are "unique aggregations possessing attributes of sovereignty over both their members and their territory," *id.*, at 323, the Court upheld the power of a tribe to punish tribal members who violate tribal criminal laws. But the Court was careful to note that, through their original incorporation into the United States as well as through specific treaties and statutes, the Indian tribes have lost many of the attributes of sovereignty. The Court distinguished between those inherent powers retained by the tribes and those divested:

> The areas in which such implicit divestiture of sovereignty has been held to have occurred are those involving *the relations between an Indian tribe and nonmembers of the tribe. . . .*

> These limitations rest on the fact that the dependent status of Indian tribes within our territorial jurisdiction is necessarily inconsistent with their freedom independently *to determine their external relations.* But the powers of self-government, including the power to prescribe and enforce internal criminal laws, are of a different type. They involve *only the relations among members of a tribe.* Thus, they are not such powers as would necessarily be lost by virtue of a tribe's dependent status. *Ibid.* (Emphasis added.)

Thus, in addition to the power to punish tribal offenders, the Indian tribes retain their inherent power to determine tribal membership, to regulate domestic relations among members, and to prescribe rules of inheritance for members. But exercise of tribal power beyond what is necessary to protect tribal self-government or to control internal relations is inconsistent with the dependent status of the tribes, and so cannot survive without express congressional delegation. Since regulation of hunting and fishing by nonmembers of a tribe on lands no longer owned by the tribe bears no clear relationship to tribal self-government or internal relations,[17] the general principles of retained inherent sovereignty did not authorize the Crow Tribe to adopt Resolution No. 74-05.

The Court recently applied these general principles in *Oliphant v. Suquamish Indian Tribe*. [Although] *Oliphant* only determined inherent tribal authority in criminal matters,[18] the principles on which it relied support the general proposition that the inherent sovereign powers of an Indian tribe do not extend to the activities

---

[17] [13] Any argument that Resolution No. 74-05 is necessary to Crow tribal self-government is refuted by the findings of the District Court that the State of Montana has traditionally exercised "near exclusive" jurisdiction over hunting and fishing on fee lands within the reservation, and that the parties to this case had accommodated themselves to the state regulation. The Court of Appeals left these findings unaltered and indeed implicitly reaffirmed them, adding that the record reveals no attempts by the Tribe at the time of the Crow Allotment Act to forbid non-Indian hunting and fishing on reservation lands.

[18] [14] By denying the Suquamish Tribe criminal jurisdiction over non-Indians, however, the *Oliphant* case would seriously restrict the ability of a tribe to enforce any purported regulation of non-Indian hunters and fishermen. . . .

of nonmembers of the tribe. To be sure, Indian tribes retain inherent sovereign power to exercise some forms of civil jurisdiction over non-Indians on their reservations, even on non-Indian fee lands. A tribe may regulate, through taxation, licensing, or other means, the activities of nonmembers who enter consensual relationships with the tribe or its members, through commercial dealing, contracts, leases, or other arrangements. [*E.g.,*] *Williams v. Lee*, 358 U.S. 217, 223. A tribe may also retain inherent power to exercise civil authority over the conduct of non-Indians on fee lands within its reservation when that conduct threatens or has some direct effect on the political integrity, the economic security, or the health or welfare of the tribe.

No such circumstances, however, are involved in this case. Non-Indian hunters and fishermen on non-Indian fee land do not enter any agreements or dealings with the Crow Tribe so as to subject themselves to tribal civil jurisdiction. And nothing in this case suggests that such non-Indian hunting and fishing so threaten the Tribe's political or economic security as to justify tribal regulation. The complaint in the District Court did not allege that non-Indian hunting and fishing on fee lands imperil the subsistence or welfare of the Tribe.[19] Furthermore, the District Court made express findings, left unaltered by the Court of Appeals, that the Crow Tribe has traditionally accommodated itself to the State's "near exclusive" regulation of hunting and fishing on fee lands within the reservation. And the District Court found that Montana's statutory and regulatory scheme does not prevent the Crow Tribe from limiting or forbidding non-Indian hunting and fishing on lands still owned by or held in trust for the Tribe or its members.

[*Reversed and remanded.*]

JUSTICE BLACKMUN, with whom JUSTICE BRENNAN and JUSTICE MARSHALL join, dissenting in part.

Only two years ago, this Court reaffirmed that the terms of a treaty between the United States and an Indian tribe must be construed " 'in the sense in which they would naturally be understood by the Indians.' " *Washington v. Fishing Vessel Assn.*, 443 U.S. 658, 676 (1979), quoting from *Jones v. Meehan*, 175 U.S. 1, 11 (1899). In holding today that the bed of the Big Horn River passed to the State of Montana upon its admission to the Union, the Court disregards this settled rule of statutory construction. Because I believe that the United States intended, and the Crow Nation understood, that the bed of the Big Horn was to belong to the Crow Indians, I dissent from so much of the Court's opinion as holds otherwise.[20]

---

[19] [16] Similarly, the complaint did not allege that the State has abdicated or abused its responsibility for protecting and managing wildlife, has established its season, bag, or creel limits in such a way as to impair the Crow Indians' treaty rights to fish or hunt, or has imposed less stringent hunting and fishing regulations within the reservation than in other parts of the State. *Cf. United States v. Washington*, 384 F. Supp. 312, 410–411 (W.D. Wash.), *aff'd*, 520 F.2d 676 (9th Cir. 1974).

[20] [1] I agree with the Court's resolution of the question of the power of the Tribe to regulate non-Indian fishing and hunting on reservation land owned in fee by nonmembers of the Tribe. I note only that nothing in the Court's disposition of that issue is inconsistent with the conclusion that the bed of the Big Horn River belongs to the Crow Indians. . . .

NOTES

1. ***Montana*'s Effect on Non-Allotted Reservations:** A few weeks after *Montana* was decided, the Supreme Court summarily vacated a Tenth Circuit decision and remanded it "for reconsideration in light of *Montana v. United States*." *New Mexico v. Mescalero Apache Tribe*, 462 U.S. 324, 330 (1983), *remanding*, 630 F.2d 724 (10th Cir. 1980). The Court of Appeals had held that the Tribe's exemplary record of wildlife management justified the district court's order declaring that the Tribe could regulate non-Indian hunting and fishing on its reservation and that the State of New Mexico could not apply or enforce its hunting and fishing laws against any person, Indian or non-Indian, within the boundaries of the reservation. In contrast to the Crow Reservation, where 28% of the reservation land was owned by non-Indians, the Mescalero Apache Reservation had never been allotted or other-wise opened to non-Indian settlement. In fact, non-Indians owned less than 4% of the reservation land. Upon reconsideration, the Tenth Circuit reinstated its prior opinion. 677 F.2d 55 (10th Cir. 1982). The Supreme Court affirmed in a unanimous opinion, stating "[o]ur decision in [*Montana*] does not resolve this question. Unlike this case, *Montana* concerned lands located within the reservation but *not* owned by the tribe or its members." *New Mexico v. Mescalero Apache Tribe*, 462 U.S. 324 (1983). This history would seem to demonstrate that the *Montana* case was originally conceived only as a limitation on tribal regulation of nonmember activity on non-Indian owned land within the reservation. The Court indicated, however, in *Nevada v. Hicks*, 533 U.S. 353 (2001), set forth and discussed later in this section, that the so-called *Montana* exceptions, *i.e.*, the test offered in *Montana* of when Indian tribes might exercise jurisdiction over nonmember activities on non-Indian owned lands within the reservation, applied to all exercises of tribal jurisdiction over nonmembers, irrespective of whether the Indian tribe or its members owned the land. The Court made no effort to reconcile that suggestion with its behavior in *New Mexico v. Mescalero Apache Tribe*.

While the state ownership of the bed of the Big Horn River did not derive from the General Allotment Act of 1887, but rather from the rules on streambed ownership first announced in that case, the Court's opinion is clearly focused on the consequences for tribal regulatory jurisdiction of the opening of Indian reservations caused by allotment. Indeed, footnote 9 is quite telling in that respect. While the Court seems to recognize that the policies of the General Allotment Act were expressly rejected by Congress in adopting the Indian Reorganization Act, the Court appears bent on working out the policies and implications of the allotment legislation for modern tribal authority. Indeed, one way to understand the hornets' nest of litigation seeking to curtail tribal regulatory, taxing, and civil adjudicatory jurisdiction spawned by *Montana* is that the Supreme Court has busily been implementing the congressional policies of allotment despite their subsequent rejection by Congress. *See* Judith Royster, *The Legacy of Allotment*, 27 Ariz. St. L. J. 1 (1995). Is that an appropriate legal or policy position for the Supreme Court to take? Since Congress sought to decouple land ownership from jurisdiction in 1948 when it enacted the definition of Indian country now found in 18 U.S.C. § 1151, did the Court's reliance on land ownership as a determinative legal factor affecting tribal jurisdiction arguably undermine the policies Congress sought to advance both in the IRA and its definition of Indian country? *See generally*, John P. LaVelle,

Beating a Path of Retreat from Treaty Rights and Tribal Sovereignty: The Story of Montana v. United States *in* INDIAN LAW STORIES (Carole Goldberg, Kevin K. Washburn, and Philip P. Frickey, eds., 2011).

2. ***Oliphant* and Civil Jurisdiction:** While the State of Montana sought to extend the *Oliphant* case to civil regulatory jurisdiction in order to create an automatic exclusion of tribal regulatory authority over non-Indians, the *Montana* Court declined to make any broad sweeping statements about the nonexistence of tribal regulatory jurisdiction over nonmembers or non-Indians. Rather, it relied on more limited grounds, resting primarily on the ownership of the land and required that a tribe make an exceptional showing of need or prior relationship to extend its conservation jurisdiction over fee land within its reservation.

3. **Domestic Dependent Nation Status as a Limitation on Tribal Power and the *Montana* Exceptions:** Unlike *Oliphant* which operates as a bright line prohibition on the exercise of criminal jurisdiction over non-Indians by tribes, the so-called *Montana* exceptions suggest the necessity of a more sensitive interest-based analysis of civil authority by indicating that:

> A tribe may regulate, through taxation, licensing, or other means, the activities of nonmembers who enter consensual relationships with the tribe or its members, through commercial dealing, contracts, leases, or other arrangements. A tribe may also retain inherent power to exercise civil authority over the conduct of non-Indians on fee lands within its reservation when that conduct threatens or has some direct effect on the political integrity, the economic security, or the health or welfare of the tribe.

Montana v. United States, 450 U.S. 544, 565 (1981). What guidance do *Oliphant* and *Montana* offer for determining in which other settings Native nations will be deprived of power to regulate non-Indians because of their dependent status?

Judge William Canby predicted that "*Montana* shows the potential open-endedness of the Court's new willingness to find limitations of tribal power arising from the tribe's domestic dependent status. *Montana* comes very close to placing the burden on the tribe of showing why its self-government interests are affected sufficiently to support the regulation." William C. Canby, Jr., *The Status of Indian Tribes in American Law Today*, 62 WASH. L. REV. 1, 16 (1987). This approach, of course, turns sovereignty on its head. Instead of presuming that a government has power within its exterior borders until a clear curtailment of its authority is demonstrated, the *Montana* approach requires the tribe to demonstrate a need for its sovereignty before it can be exercised. This inversion of presumptions about the scope of authority of a sovereign government obviously undermines considerably its territorial sovereignty. Insofar as Judge Canby anticipated that the open-ended *Montana* analysis would seriously impair the powers tribes need to protect their members and effectively govern, he proved to be correct.

As reflected by the *A-1 Contractors* decision set forth below, the Court has also expanded *Montana* from its original role in limiting the legislative regulatory power of a tribe to employing it to evaluate the adjudicative jurisdiction of tribal courts. Is the scope of a state's legislative power (*i.e.*, its power to regulate and tax) co-extensive with the scope of the adjudicative jurisdiction of its courts? For state court jurisdiction is there a difference between the reach of a state court's criminal jurisdiction and the reach of its civil adjudicative powers? What doctrines govern those differences? In light of *A-1 Contractors* set forth below, do those doctrines work the same way when Indian tribes are involved? If not, what if anything, justifies the unique rules applied to tribal court jurisdiction?

STRATE v. A-1 CONTRACTORS
United States Supreme Court
520 U.S. 438 (1997)

JUSTICE GINSBURG delivered the opinion of the Court.

This case concerns the adjudicatory authority of tribal courts over personal injury actions against defendants who are not tribal members. Specifically, we confront this question: When an accident occurs on a portion of a public highway maintained by the State under a federally granted right-of-way over Indian reservation land, may tribal courts entertain a civil action against an allegedly negligent driver and the driver's employer, neither of whom is a member of the tribe?

Such cases, we hold, fall within state or federal regulatory and adjudicatory governance; tribal courts may not entertain claims against nonmembers arising out of accidents on state highways, absent a statute or treaty authorizing the tribe to govern the conduct of nonmembers on the highway in question. We express no view on the governing law or proper forum when an accident occurs on a tribal road within a reservation.

I

In November 1990, petitioner Gisela Fredericks and respondent Lyle Stockert were involved in a traffic accident on a portion of a North Dakota state highway running through the Fort Berthold Indian Reservation. The highway strip crossing the reservation is a 6.59-mile stretch of road, open to the public, affording access to a federal water resource project. North Dakota maintains the road under a right-of-way granted by the United States to the State's Highway Department; the right-of-way lies on land held by the United States in trust for the Three Affiliated Tribes (Mandan, Hidatsa, and Arikara) and their members.

The accident occurred when Fredericks' automobile collided with a gravel truck driven by Stockert and owned by respondent A-1 Contractors, Stockert's employer. A-1 Contractors, a non-Indian-owned enterprise with its principal place of business outside the reservation, was at the time under a subcontract with LCM Corporation, a corporation wholly owned by the Tribes, to do landscaping work related to the construction of a tribal community building. A-1 Contractors performed all work under the subcontract within the boundaries of the reservation. The record does not show whether Stockert was engaged in subcontract work at the time of the accident. Neither Stockert nor Fredericks is a member of the Three Affiliated Tribes or an Indian. Fredericks, however, is the widow of a deceased member of the Tribes and has five adult children who are tribal members.[21]

Fredericks sustained serious injuries in the accident and was hospitalized for 24 days. In May 1991, she sued respondents A-1 Contractors and Stockert, as well as A-1 Contractors' insurer, in the Tribal Court for the Three Affiliated Tribes of the Fort Berthold Reservation. In the same lawsuit, Fredericks' five adult children filed a loss-of-consortium claim. Together, Fredericks and her children sought damages exceeding $13 million. App. 8–10.

Respondents and the insurer made a special appearance in the Tribal Court to contest that court's personal and subject-matter jurisdiction. The Tribal Court ruled that it had authority to adjudicate Gisela Fredericks' case, and therefore denied respondents' motion to dismiss the action.[22] Respondents appealed the Tribal Court's jurisdictional ruling to the Northern Plains Intertribal Court of Appeals, which affirmed. Thereafter, pursuant to the parties' stipulation, the Tribal Court dismissed the insurer from the suit. *See id.*, at 38–40.

Before Tribal Court proceedings resumed, respondents commenced this action in the United States District Court for the District of North Dakota. Naming as defendants Fredericks, her adult children, the Tribal Court, and Tribal Judge William Strate, respondents sought a declaratory judgment that, as a matter of federal law, the Tribal Court lacked jurisdiction to adjudicate Fredericks' claims. The respondents also sought an injunction against further proceedings in the Tribal Court.

Relying particularly on this Court's decisions in *National Farmers Union Ins. Cos. v. Crow Tribe*, 471 U.S. 845 (1985), and *Iowa Mut. Ins. Co. v. LaPlante*, 480 U.S. 9 (1987), the District Court determined that the Tribal Court had civil jurisdiction over Fredericks' complaint against A-1 Contractors and Stockert; accordingly, on cross-motions for summary judgment, the District Court dismissed the action. On appeal, a divided panel of the United States Court of Appeals for the Eighth Circuit affirmed. The Eighth Circuit granted rehearing en banc and, in an 8-to-4 decision, reversed the District Court's judgment. 76 F.3d 930 (1996). The Court of Appeals concluded that our decision in *Montana v. United States*, 450 U.S. 544 (1981), was the controlling precedent, and that, under *Montana*, the Tribal Court lacked subject-matter jurisdiction over the dispute.[23]

We granted certiorari and now affirm.

---

[21] [2] The Court of Appeals for the Eighth Circuit stated that petitioner Fredericks resides on the reservation. *See* 76 F.3d 930, 932 (1996) (en banc). Respondents assert, however, that there is an unresolved factual dispute regarding Fredericks's residence at the time of the accident. Under our disposition of the case, Fredericks's residence at the time of the accident is immaterial. [Mrs. Fredericks was actually married to a tribal member and was the mother of children who were other tribal members. She was hit turning left into her husband's allotment on the reservation.— Eds.]

[22] [3] Satisfied that it could adjudicate Gisela Fredericks's claims, the Tribal Court declined to address her adult children's consortium claim, thus, no ruling on that claim is here at issue.

[23] [4] Petitioner Fredericks has commenced a similar lawsuit in a North Dakota state court "to protect her rights against the running of the State's six-year statute of limitations." Reply Brief 6, n. 2. Respondents assert that they have answered the complaint and "are prepared to proceed in that forum." Respondents also note, without contradiction, that the state forum "is physically much closer by road to the accident scene . . . than [is] the tribal courthouse."

II

Our case law establishes that, absent express authorization by federal statute or treaty, tribal jurisdiction over the conduct of nonmembers exists only in limited circumstances. In *Oliphant v. Suquamish Tribe*, 435 U.S. 191 (1978), the Court held that Indian tribes lack criminal jurisdiction over non-Indians. *Montana v. United States*, decided three years later, is the pathmarking case concerning tribal civil authority over nonmembers. *Montana* concerned the authority of the Crow Tribe to regulate hunting and fishing by non-Indians on lands within the Tribe's reservation owned in fee simple by non-Indians. The Court said in *Montana* that the restriction on tribal criminal jurisdiction recognized in *Oliphant* rested on principles that support a more "general proposition." 450 U.S., at 565. In the main, the Court explained, "the inherent sovereign powers of an Indian tribe" — those powers a tribe enjoys apart from express provision by treaty or statute — "do not extend to the activities of nonmembers of the tribe." The *Montana* opinion added, however, that in certain circumstances, even where Congress has not expressly authorized it, tribal civil jurisdiction may encompass nonmembers:

> "To be sure, Indian tribes retain inherent sovereign power to exercise some forms of civil jurisdiction over non-Indians on their reservations, even on non-Indian fee lands. A tribe may regulate, through taxation, licensing, or other means, the activities of nonmembers who enter consensual relation-ships with the tribe or its members, through commercial dealing, contracts, leases, or other arrangements. A tribe may also retain inherent power to exercise civil authority over the conduct of non-Indians on fee lands within its reservation when that conduct threatens or has some direct effect on the political integrity, the economic security, or the health or welfare of the tribe." *Id.*, at 565–566, 101 S. Ct., at 1258–1259 (citations and footnote omitted).

The term "non-Indian fee lands," as used in this passage and throughout the *Montana* opinion, refers to reservation land acquired in fee simple by non-Indian owners.

Montana thus described a general rule that, absent a different congressional direction, Indian tribes lack civil authority over the conduct of nonmembers on non-Indian land within a reservation, subject to two exceptions: The first exception relates to nonmembers who enter consensual relationships with the tribe or its members; the second concerns activity that directly affects the tribe's political integrity, economic security, health, or welfare. The *Montana* Court recognized that the Crow Tribe retained power to limit or forbid hunting or fishing by nonmembers on land still owned by or held in trust for the Tribe. The Court held, however, that the Tribe lacked authority to regulate hunting and fishing by non-Indians on land within the Tribe's reservation owned in fee simple by non-Indians.[24]

---

24 [6] *Montana*'s statement of the governing law figured prominently in *Brendale v. Confederated Tribes and Bands of Yakima Nation*, 492 U.S. 408 (1989), and in *South Dakota v. Bourland*, 508 U.S. 679 (1993). The Court held in *Brendale*, 6 to 3, that the Yakima Indian Nation lacked authority to zone nonmembers' land within an area of the Tribe's reservation open to the general public; almost half the land in the area was owned in fee by nonmembers. The Court also held, 5 to 4, that the Tribe retained authority to zone fee land in an area of the reservation closed to the general public. No opinion garnered

Petitioners and the United States as *amicus curiae* urge that *Montana* does not control this case. They maintain that the guiding precedents are *National Farmers* and *Iowa Mutual*, and that those decisions establish a rule converse to *Montana*'s. Whatever *Montana* may instruct regarding *regulatory* authority, they insist, tribal courts retain *adjudicatory* authority in disputes over occurrences inside a reservation, even when the episode-in-suit involves nonmembers, unless a treaty or federal statute directs otherwise. Petitioners, further supported by the United States, argue, alternately, that *Montana* does not cover lands owned by, or held in trust for, a tribe or its members. *Montana* holds sway, petitioners say, only with respect to alienated reservation land owned in fee simple by non-Indians. We address these arguments in turn.

A

We begin with petitioners' contention that *National Farmers* and *Iowa Mutual* broadly confirm tribal-court civil jurisdiction over claims against nonmembers arising from occurrences on any land within a reservation. We read our precedent differently. *National Farmers* and *Iowa Mutual*, we conclude, are not at odds with, and do not displace, *Montana*. Both decisions describe an exhaustion rule allowing tribal courts initially to respond to an invocation of their jurisdiction; neither establishes tribal-court adjudicatory authority, even over the lawsuits involved in those cases. *Accord Brendale v. Confederated Tribes and Bands of Yakima Nation*, 492 U.S. 408, 427, n. 10 (1989) (opinion of White, J.).

National Farmers involved a federal-court challenge to a tribal court's jurisdiction over a personal injury action initiated on behalf of a Crow Indian minor against a Montana school district. The accident-in-suit occurred when the minor was struck by a motorcycle in an elementary school parking lot. The school occupied land owned by the State within the Crow Indian Reservation. The school district and its insurer sought a federal-court injunction to stop proceedings in the Crow Tribal Court. The District Court granted the injunction, but the Court of Appeals reversed, concluding that federal courts lacked subject-matter jurisdiction to entertain such a case.

We reversed the Court of Appeals' judgment and held that federal courts have authority to determine, as a matter "arising under" federal law, see 28 U.S.C. § 1331, whether a tribal court has exceeded the limits of its jurisdiction. We further held, however, that the federal suit was premature. Ordinarily, we explained, a federal court should stay its hand "until after the Tribal Court has had a full

---

a majority. Justice White, writing for four Members of the Court, concluded that, under *Montana*, the Tribe lacked authority to zone fee land in both the open and closed areas of the reservation. Justice Stevens, writing for two Justices, concluded that the Tribe retained zoning authority over nonmember land only in the closed area. Justice Blackmun, writing for three Justices, concluded that, under *Montana*'s second exception, the Tribe retained authority to zone fee land in both the open and the closed areas. In *Bourland*, the Court considered whether the Cheyenne River Sioux Tribe could regulate hunting and fishing by non-Indians in an area within the Tribe's reservation, but acquired by the United States for the operation of a dam and a reservoir. We determined, dominantly, that no treaty or statute reserved to the Tribe regulatory authority over the area, and we left for resolution on remand the question whether either *Montana* exception applied, see also 39 F.3d 868, 869–870 (C.A.8 1994) (decision of divided panel on remand that neither *Montana* exception justified regulation by the Tribe).

opportunity to determine its own jurisdiction." Finding no cause for immediate federal-court intervention,[25] we remanded the case, leaving initially to the District Court the question "[w]hether the federal action should be dismissed, or merely held in abeyance pending . . . further Tribal Court proceedings." *Ibid.*

Petitioners underscore the principal reason we gave in *National Farmers* for the exhaustion requirement there stated. Tribal-court jurisdiction over non-Indians in criminal cases is categorically restricted under *Oliphant*, we observed, while in civil matters "the existence and extent of a tribal court's jurisdiction will require a careful examination of tribal sovereignty, the extent to which that sovereignty has been altered, divested, or diminished, as well as a detailed study of relevant statutes, Executive Branch policy as embodied in treaties and elsewhere, and administrative or judicial decisions."

The Court's recognition in *National Farmers* that tribal courts have more extensive jurisdiction in civil cases than in criminal proceedings, and of the need to inspect relevant statutes, treaties, and other materials, does not limit *Montana*'s instruction. As the Court made plain in *Montana*, the general rule and exceptions there announced govern only in the absence of a delegation of tribal authority by treaty or statute. In *Montana* itself, the Court examined the treaties and legislation relied upon by the Tribe and explained why those measures did not aid the Tribe's case. Only after and in light of that examination did the Court address the Tribe's assertion of "inherent sovereignty," and formulate, in response to that assertion, *Montana*'s general rule and exceptions to it. In sum, we do not extract from *National Farmers* anything more than a prudential exhaustion rule, in deference to the capacity of tribal courts "to explain to the parties the precise basis for accepting [or rejecting] jurisdiction."

Iowa Mutual involved an accident in which a member of the Blackfeet Indian Tribe was injured while driving a cattle truck within the boundaries of the reservation. The injured member was employed by a Montana corporation that operated a ranch on reservation land owned by Blackfeet Indians residing on the reservation. See *ibid.* The driver and his wife, also a Tribe member, sued in the Blackfeet Tribal Court, naming several defendants: the Montana corporation that employed the driver; the individual owners of the ranch; the insurer of the ranch; and an independent insurance adjuster representing the insurer. *See ibid.* Over the objection of the insurer and the insurance adjuster — both companies not owned by members of the Tribe — the Tribal Court determined that it had jurisdiction to adjudicate the case.

Thereafter, the insurer commenced a federal-court action against the driver, his wife, the Montana corporation, and the ranch owners. Invoking federal jurisdiction based on the parties' diverse citizenship, see 28 U.S.C. § 1332, the insurer alleged that it had no duty to defend or indemnify the Montana corporation or the ranch

---

[25] [7] The Court indicated in *National Farmers* that exhaustion is not an unyielding requirement:

"We do not suggest that exhaustion would be required where an assertion of tribal jurisdiction " 'is motivated by a desire to harass or is conducted in bad faith,' " or where the action is patently violative of express jurisdictional prohibitions, or where exhaustion would be futile because of the lack of an adequate opportunity to challenge the court's jurisdiction." 471 U.S., at 856, n. 21, 105 S. Ct., at 2454, n. 21 (citation omitted).

owners because the injuries asserted by the driver and his wife fell outside the coverage of the applicable insurance policies. The Federal District Court dismissed the insurer's action for lack of subject-matter jurisdiction, and the Court of Appeals affirmed.

We reversed. Holding that the District Court had diversity-of-citizenship jurisdiction over the insurer's complaint, we remanded, as in *National Farmers*, for a determination whether "the federal action should be stayed pending further Tribal Court proceedings or dismissed." The Court recognized in *Iowa Mutual* that the exhaustion rule stated in *National Farmers* was "prudential," not jurisdictional. 480 U.S., at 20, n. 14 (stating that "[e]xhaustion is required as a matter of comity, not as a jurisdictional prerequisite"). Respect for tribal self-government made it appropriate "to give the tribal court a 'full opportunity to determine its own jurisdiction.' That respect, the Court reasoned, was equally in order whether federal-court jurisdiction rested on § 1331 (federal question) or on § 1332 (diversity of citizenship). Elaborating on the point, the Court stated:

> "Tribal authority over the activities of non-Indians on reservation lands is an important part of tribal sovereignty. *See Montana v. United States*, 450 U.S. 544, 565–566 (1981); *Washington v. Confederated Tribes of Colville Indian Reservation*, 447 U.S. 134, 152–153 (1980); *Fisher v. District Court [of Sixteenth Judicial Dist. of Mont.]*, 424 U.S. [382,] 387–389. Civil jurisdiction over such activities presumptively lies in the tribal courts unless affirmatively limited by a specific treaty provision or federal statute. . . . In the absence of any indication that Congress intended the diversity statute to limit the jurisdiction of the tribal courts, we decline petitioner's invitation to hold that tribal sovereignty can be impaired in this fashion." *Id.*, at 18.

Petitioners and the United States fasten upon the Court's statement that "[c]ivil jurisdiction over such activities presumptively lies in the tribal courts." Read in context, however, this language scarcely supports the view that the *Montana* rule does not bear on tribal-court adjudicatory authority in cases involving nonmember defendants.

The statement stressed by petitioners and the United States was made in refutation of the argument that "Congress intended the diversity statute to limit the jurisdiction of the tribal courts." The statement is preceded by three informative citations. The first citation points to the passage in *Montana* in which the Court advanced "the general proposition that the inherent sovereign powers of an Indian tribe do not extend to the activities of nonmembers of the tribe," with two prime exceptions. The case cited second is *Washington v. Confederated Tribes of Colville Reservation*, 447 U.S. 134 (1980) a decision the *Montana* Court listed as illustrative of the first *Montana* exception, applicable to "nonmembers who enter consensual relationships with the tribe or its members," 450 U.S., at 565–566; the Court in *Colville* acknowledged inherent tribal authority to tax "non- Indians entering the reservation to engage in economic activity," 447 U.S., at 153. The third case noted in conjunction with the *Iowa Mutual* statement is *Fisher v. District Court of Sixteenth Judicial Dist. of Mont.*, 424 U.S. 382 (1976) (*per curiam*), a decision the *Montana* Court cited in support of the second *Montana* exception, covering on-reservation activity of nonmembers bearing directly "on the political integrity, the economic security, or the health or welfare of the tribe." The Court held in *Fisher* that a tribal court had exclusive jurisdiction over an adoption proceeding when all parties were members of the tribe and resided on its reservation. State-court jurisdiction over such matters, the Court said, "plainly would interfere with the powers of self-government conferred upon the . . . Tribe and exercised through the Tribal Court." The Court observed in *Fisher* that state courts may not exercise jurisdiction over disputes arising out of on-reservation conduct — even over matters involving non-Indians — if doing so would " 'infring[e] on the right of reservation Indians to make their own laws and be ruled by them.' "

In light of the citation of *Montana, Colville,* and *Fisher,* the *Iowa Mutual* statement emphasized by petitioners does not limit the *Montana* rule. In keeping with the precedent to which *Iowa Mutual* refers, the statement stands for nothing more than the unremarkable proposition that, where tribes possess authority to regulate the activities of nonmembers, "[c]ivil jurisdiction over [disputes arising out of] such activities presumptively lies in the tribal courts."

Recognizing that our precedent has been variously interpreted, we reiterate that *National Farmers* and *Iowa Mutual* enunciate only an exhaustion requirement, a "prudential rule." These decisions do not expand or stand apart from *Montana*'s instruction on "the inherent sovereign powers of an Indian tribe." While *Montana* immediately involved regulatory authority, the Court broadly addressed the concept of "inherent sovereignty." Regarding activity on non-Indian fee land within a reservation, *Montana* delineated — in a main rule and exceptions — the bounds of the power tribes retain to exercise "forms of civil jurisdiction over non-Indians." As to nonmembers, we hold, a tribe's adjudicative jurisdiction does not exceed its legislative jurisdiction. Absent congressional direction enlarging tribal-court jurisdiction, we adhere to that understanding. Subject to controlling provisions in treaties and statutes, and the two exceptions identified in *Montana,* the civil authority of Indian tribes and their courts with respect to non-Indian fee lands generally "do[es] not extend to the activities of nonmembers of the tribe." *Ibid.*

B

We consider next the argument that *Montana* does not govern this case because the land underlying the scene of the accident is held in trust for the Three Affiliated Tribes and their members. Petitioners and the United States point out that in *Montana,* as in later cases following *Montana*'s instruction — *Brendale v. Confederated Tribes and Bands of Yakima Nation,* 492 U.S. 408 (1989), and *South Dakota v. Bourland,* 508 U.S. 679 (1993) — the challenged tribal authority related to nonmember activity on alienated, non-Indian reservation land. We "can readily agree," in accord with *Montana* that tribes retain considerable control over nonmember conduct on tribal land. On the particular matter before us, however, we agree with respondents: The right-of-way North Dakota acquired for the State's highway renders the 6.59-mile stretch equivalent, for nonmember governance purposes,[26] to alienated, non-Indian land.

---

[26] [9] For contextual treatment of rights-of-way over Indian land, compare 18 U.S.C. § 1151 (defining

Congress authorized grants of rights-of-way over Indian lands in 1948 legislation. Act of Feb. 5, 1948, ch. 45, 62 Stat. 17, 25 U.S.C. §§ 323–328. A grant over land belonging to a tribe requires "consent of the proper tribal officials," § 324, and the payment of just compensation, § 325.[27]

The grant involved in this case was made, pursuant to the federal statute, in 1970. Its purpose was to facilitate public access to Lake Sakakawea, a federal water resource project under the control of the Army Corps of Engineers.

In the granting instrument, the United States conveyed to North Dakota "an easement for a right-of-way for the realignment and improvement of North Dakota State Highway No. 8 over, across and upon [specified] lands." The grant provides that the State's "easement is subject to any valid existing right or adverse claim and is without limitation as to tenure, so long as said easement shall be actually used for the purpose . . . specified." *Id.*, at 3. The granting instrument details only one specific reservation to Indian landowners:

> "The right is reserved to the Indian land owners, their lessees, successors, and assigns to construct crossings of the right-of-way at all points reasonably necessary to the undisturbed use and occupan[cy] of the premises affected by the right-of-way; such crossings to be constructed and maintained by the owners or lawful occupants and users of said lands at their own risk and said occupants and users to assume full responsibility for avoiding, or repairing any damage to the right-of-way, which may be occasioned by such crossings." *Id.*, at 3–4.

Apart from this specification, the Three Affiliated Tribes expressly reserved no right to exercise dominion or control over the right-of-way.

Forming part of the State's highway, the right-of-way is open to the public, and traffic on it is subject to the State's control.[28] The Tribes have consented to, and received payment for, the State's use of the 6.59-mile stretch for a public highway. They have retained no gatekeeping right. So long as the stretch is maintained as part of the State's highway, the Tribes cannot assert a landowner's right to occupy and exclude. *Cf. Bourland*, 508 U.S., at 689, 113 S. Ct., at 2316–2317 (regarding reservation land acquired by the United States for operation of a dam and a reservoir, Tribe's loss of "right of absolute and exclusive use and occupation . . . implies the loss of regulatory jurisdiction over the use of the land by others"). We therefore align the right-of-way, for the purpose at hand, with land alienated to

---

"Indian country" in criminal law chapter generally to include "rights-of-way running through [a] reservation") with §§ 1154(c) and 1156 (term "Indian country," as used in sections on dispensation and possession of intoxicants, "does not include . . . rights-of-way through Indian reservations").

[27] [10] Rights-of-way granted over lands of individual Indians also require payment of compensation, 25 U.S.C. § 325, and ordinarily require consent of the individual owners, see § 324 (describing circumstances in which rights-of-way may be granted without the consent of owners).

[28] [11] We do not here question the authority of tribal police to patrol roads within a reservation, including rights-of-way made part of a state highway, and to detain and turn over to state officers nonmembers stopped on the highway for conduct violating state law. *Cf. State v. Schmuck*, 121 Wash. 2d 373, 390, 850 P.2d 1332, 1341 (1993) (en banc) (recognizing that a limited tribal power "to stop and detain alleged offenders in no way confers an *unlimited* authority to regulate the right of the public to travel on the Reservation's roads").

non-Indians. Our decision in *Montana*, accordingly, governs this case.

III

Petitioners and the United States refer to no treaty or statute authorizing the Three Affiliated Tribes to entertain highway-accident tort suits of the kind Fredericks commenced against A-1 Contractors and Stockert. Rather, petitioners and the United States ground their defense of tribal-court jurisdiction exclusively on the concept of retained or inherent sovereignty. *Montana*, we have explained, is the controlling decision for this case. To prevail here, petitioners must show that Fredericks' tribal-court action against nonmembers qualifies under one of *Montana*'s two exceptions.

The first exception to the *Montana* rule covers "activities of nonmembers who enter consensual relationships with the tribe or its members, through commercial dealing, contracts, leases, or other arrangements." The tortious conduct alleged in Fredericks' complaint does not fit that description. The dispute, as the Court of Appeals said, is "distinctly non-tribal in nature." It "arose between two non-Indians involved in [a] run-of-the-mill [highway] accident." Although A-1 was engaged in subcontract work on the Fort Berthold Reservation, and therefore had a "consensual relationship" with the Tribes, "Gisela Fredericks was not a party to the subcontract, and the [T]ribes were strangers to the accident."

Montana's list of cases fitting within the first exception indicates the type of activities the Court had in mind: *Williams v. Lee*, 358 U.S. 217, 223 (1959) (declaring tribal jurisdiction exclusive over lawsuit arising out of on-reservation sales transaction between nonmember plaintiff and member defendants); *Morris v. Hitchcock*, 194 U.S. 384 (1904) (upholding tribal permit tax on nonmember-owned livestock within boundaries of the Chickasaw Nation); *Buster v. Wright*, 135 F. 947, 950 (8th Cir. 1905) (upholding Tribe's permit tax on nonmembers for the privilege of conducting business within Tribe's borders; court characterized as "inherent" the Tribe's "authority . . . to prescribe the terms upon which noncitizens may transact business within its borders"); *Colville*, 447 U.S., at 152–154 (tribal authority to tax on-reservation cigarette sales to nonmembers "is a fundamental attribute of sovereignty which the tribes retain unless divested of it by federal law or necessary implication of their dependent status"). Measured against these cases, the Fredericks-Stockert highway accident presents no "consensual relationship" of the qualifying kind.

The second exception to *Montana*'s general rule concerns conduct that "threatens or has some direct effect on the political integrity, the economic security, or the health or welfare of the tribe." Undoubtedly, those who drive carelessly on a public highway running through a reservation endanger all in the vicinity, and surely jeopardize the safety of tribal members. But if *Montana*'s second exception requires no more, the exception would severely shrink the rule. Again, cases cited in *Montana* indicate the character of the tribal interest the Court envisioned.

. . . .

Read in isolation, the *Montana* rule's second exception can be misperceived. Key to its proper application, however, is the Court's preface: "Indian tribes retain their inherent power [to punish tribal offenders,] to determine tribal membership, to regulate domestic relations among members, and to prescribe rules of inheritance for members. . . . But [a tribe's inherent power does not reach] beyond what is necessary to protect tribal self-government or to control internal relations." 450 U.S., at 564. Neither regulatory nor adjudicatory authority over the state highway accident at issue is needed to preserve "the right of reservation Indians to make their own laws and be ruled by them." *Williams*, 358 U.S., at 220. The *Montana* rule, therefore, and not its exceptions, applies to this case.

Gisela Fredericks may pursue her case against A-1 Contractors and Stockert in the state forum open to all who sustain injuries on North Dakota's highway. Opening the Tribal Court for her optional use is not necessary to protect tribal self-government; and requiring A-1 and Stockert to defend against this common-place state highway accident claim in an unfamiliar court[29] is not crucial to "the political integrity, the economic security, or the health or welfare of the [Three Affiliated Tribes]." *Montana*, 450 U.S., at 566, 101 S. Ct., at 1258.[30]

For the reasons stated, the judgment of the Court of Appeals for the Eighth Circuit is

Affirmed.

NOTES

1. **Personal or Subject Matter Jurisdiction?** As understood by the federal courts the *Oliphant* limitation on tribal criminal jurisdiction and the *Strate* limitation on tribal civil adjudicative jurisdiction are generally understood to constitute *subject matter* limitations imposed by the federal courts on the exercise of tribal court jurisdiction. Precisely why these decisions are thought to curtail the subject matter jurisdiction of the tribal court is less clear. Many tribes have tribal codes that extend the jurisdiction of their tribal courts to cover all crimes and civil causes of action arising on or causing injury on their reservation. Those codes often also create their tribal courts and vest them with jurisdiction coextensive with this limit. *See generally* Robert N. Clinton, *There Is No Federal Supremacy Clause for Indian Tribes*, 34 ARIZ. ST. L. J. 113, 235 (2002). Thus, as a matter of *tribal law*, the tribes often choose to vest their courts with the very subject matter jurisdiction that *Oliphant* and *Strate* deny to them. In both cases the problem with exercise of tribal court jurisdiction involves a matter personal to the defendant, *i.e.*, they are non-Indian. Conventionally such matters more often affect personal, rather than subject matter jurisdiction. *But see* 28 U.S.C. § 1332 (federal diversity subject

---

[29] [13] Within the federal system, when nonresidents are the sole defendants in a suit filed in state court, the defendants ordinarily may remove the case to federal court. *See* 28 U.S.C. § 1441.

[30] [14] When, as in this case, it is plain that no federal grant provides for tribal governance of nonmembers' conduct on land covered by *Montana*'s main rule, it will be equally evident that tribal courts lack adjudicatory authority over disputes arising from such conduct. As in criminal proceedings, state or federal courts will be the only forums competent to adjudicate those disputes. *See National Farmers Union Ins. Cos. v. Crow Tribe*, 471 U.S. 845, 854 (1985). Therefore, when tribal-court jurisdiction over an action such as this one is challenged in federal court, the otherwise applicable exhaustion requirement, must give way, for it would serve no purpose other than delay. *Cf. National Farmers*, 471 U.S., at 856, n. 21.

matter jurisdiction determined by citizenship). Even more significantly, state and federal courts generally have broad civil adjudicative jurisdiction over any transitory cause of action, irrespective of whether it arose within the state where the forum court sits, so long as there are sufficient minimum contacts to justify the exercise of personal jurisdiction over the defendant. *Burger King Corp. v. Rudzewicz*, 471 U.S. 462, 474 (1985). This point appears to be underlying the Tribe's reliance on *National Farmers Union Ins. Cos.* and *Iowa Mutual* in *Strate*. Does *Strate* conceive tribal courts as having jurisdiction that parallels their state and federal counterparts? Why not?

2. **The Role of the Court in Making Law:** As the judicial plenary power limitations on tribal authority demonstrate, not all federal laws affecting Indians or limiting their rights can be directly traced to treaties or federal statutes. Over the past quarter-century the federal judiciary has assumed a far broader role in defining the outer contours and limitations on tribal sovereignty, often pursuing an agenda that conflicts with Congress's professed policy of tribal self-determination. *See* Ch. 1, Secs. B.2.i, j. While the Court has often played an activist role in Indian affairs, as it did in the days of *Worcester v. Georgia*, rarely before has it charted its own Indian policy without any guidance from treaties or federal statutes. Today, the Supreme Court increasingly undertakes such a role by creating federal common law defining and often delimiting tribal rights and powers. *Compare, e.g., National Farmers Union Ins. Cos. v. Crow Tribe*, 471 U.S. 845 (1985) (finding jurisdiction over a claim asserting federal common law limitations over Indian tribal court jurisdiction over non-Indians), *with County of Oneida v. Oneida Indian Nation*, 470 U.S. 226, 231–32 (1985) (sustaining federal jurisdiction over tribal land claim since federal common law creates tribal cause of action to challenge allegedly illegal land sales to states in violation of federal law).

What should be the source and scope of the Court's authority to make federal common law affecting Indians? Indian law is one of several enclaves of federal common law. Professor Martha Field argues that when it creates federal common law, the federal judiciary "must point to a federal enactment, constitutional or statutory, that it interprets as authorizing the federal common law rule." Martha A. Field, *Sources of Law: The Scope of Federal Common Law*, 99 HARV. L. REV. 883, 887, 927 (1986). Can the Court do so in cases like *Oliphant, Montana*, and *Strate*? In other fields of federal regulation where federal common law is frequently announced, the federal courts conceive their role as filling in the interstices of a complex regulatory scheme. *See, e.g., Textile Workers Union v. Lincoln Mills*, 353 U.S. 448 (1957). Can *Oliphant, Montana*, and *Strate* be justified on these grounds? Can the federal treaties affecting Indians, both the treaties with the tribes and American treaties with Great Britain and Mexico implicating tribes, perform that task for Indian law? Does it make any difference that many tribes do not have treaties? Professor Field argues that since Indian law is based on treaties it satisfies her formulation of federal common law. Relying on *Worcester v. Georgia*, she argues that in Indian law "courts sometimes fail to address authority for federal common law simply because the existence of such authority is well-established." *Id.* at 948. Do you agree with her characterization and justification for these cases? Is the Supreme Court performing a legitimate role in cases like *Oliphant, Montana*, and *Strate* or engaging in unprincipled and unjustified judicial activism?

3. Tribal Law Approaches to Scope of Tribal Civil Adjudicative Authority:
Tribal courts have approached the questions of subject matter jurisdiction and
personal jurisdiction in varying ways. In *Coeur d'Alene Tribe v. AT&T Corp.*, 23
Ind. L Rep. 6060 (Coeur d'Alene Tr. Ct. 1996), the Tribal Court looked primarily to
the tribal code to ascertain the scope of its subject matter jurisdiction, which
defined the reach of the Tribe's civil jurisdiction to extend to all persons and
property located on the reservation and to all causes of action arising on the
reservation. Questions regarding the level of contact were treated primarily as
questions of personal jurisdiction. Other than where preempted by exclusive federal
jurisdiction, the only federal limitations on the subject matter jurisdiction of state
courts generally involve local action rules affecting litigation about property and
some rules related to the granting of divorces. Most other civil causes of action are
thought transitory and can be litigated anywhere so long as the forum court has
proper jurisdiction over the person or property before the court. Should this
approach also be applied to tribal courts?

Courts of Indian Offenses traditionally have limited the exercise of their civil
jurisdiction to cases arising in Indian country in which the defendant is Indian and
to "all other suits between Indians and non-Indians which are brought before the
court by stipulation of the parties." 25 C.F.R. § 11.103(a). Most tribes, however, have
amended their tribal codes to adopt territorially based definitions of their tribal civil
jurisdiction.

Some tribes, however, have created special courts of limited jurisdiction. The
Cheyenne River Sioux Tribe, for example, has a special Juvenile Court. CRST Law
& Order Code § 1-2-1(3). Many tribes, like the Navajo Nation, have established
Peacemaker Courts to offer traditional peacemaking mediation services, particu-
larly in cases involving only tribal members. *See* Howard L. Brown, *The Navajo
Nation's Peacemaker Division: An Integrated, Community-Based Dispute Reso-
lution Forum*, 24 AM. INDIAN L. REV. 297 (1999–2000); Donna Coker, *Enhancing
Autonomy for Battered Women: Lessons from Navajo Peacemaking*, 47 UCLA L.
REV. 1 (1999). Sometimes these courts operate as adjunct to the tribal court process
and in other cases as a separate and independent procedure. Other tribes, like Taos
Pueblo, maintain traditional courts operating independently of their western style
courts of record and a tribal member may file a claim in either court. While tribal
courts of record are governed by tribal constitutions, codes, and precedents, their
proceedings, reflecting the peacemaking traditions of most tribes, sometimes reflect
a greater mediative objective than might be found in federal or state courts.
Nevertheless, if the parties cannot reach agreement, tribal courts generally proceed
in an adversarial manner, which, while sometimes less formal, resembles that found
in federal or state courts. Just as common law plays a role in state adjudication,
customary law is sometimes employed in tribal courts, particularly where no
positive tribal law exists on a matter under adjudication. Gloria Valencia-Weber,
Tribal Courts: Custom and Innovative Law, 24 N.M. L. REV. 225 (1994); Elizabeth
E. Joh, *Custom, Tribal Court Practice and Popular Justice*, 25 AM. INDIAN L. REV.
117 (2000–2001); Christine Zuni Cruz, *Tribal Law as Indigenous Social Reality
and Separate Consciousness — [Re]Incorporating Customs and Traditions into
Tribal Law*, 1 N.M. TRIBAL L.J. (Fall 2000), available at http://tlj.unm.edu/tribal-
law-journal/articles/volume_1/zuni_cruz/index.php.

4. Federal Law Approaches to Scope of Tribal Civil Adjudicative Authority: Over the past decade federal courts have unilaterally claimed a power to limit the exercise of tribal subject matter jurisdiction. That claim was facilitated by the holdings in *National Farmers Union* and *Iowa Mutual.* Having ruled that limitations on tribal civil jurisdiction were governed by federal common law, the Court created an implied right of action derived from that federal common law facilitating suits to be brought in federal court to *collaterally attack* the exercise of jurisdiction by the tribal courts even when undertaken in conformity with tribal law. One might reasonably ask where the federal courts have obtained such a power since no federal statute limits the civil subject matter jurisdiction of tribal courts and no federal statute authorizes any federal court, including the United States Supreme Court, to review the final decisions of tribal courts. Nevertheless, whatever the source of such power, federal courts have routinely been involved in exercising such authority since *National Farmers Union* recognized such review power.

The federal view of the scope of tribal civil adjudicative authority frequently conflicts with and is far narrower than the scope of subject matter jurisdiction the tribe has conferred on its court. Most tribal courts exercise jurisdiction over transitory causes of action so long as they can establish personal jurisdiction over the defendant(s) through sufficient contacts with the forum. However, in *Strate,* the United States Supreme Court held for the first time that Indian tribes had no inherent civil adjudicative power over lands to which they had no present possessory right unless they could satisfy the *Montana* tests. Recall that the case held that the Fort Berthold Tribal Court had no subject matter jurisdiction over a claim arising from a motor vehicle accident that occurred on a state highway right-of-way within the reservation where both parties were non-Indians, although the plaintiff was married to a tribal member, lived on the reservation on a trust allotment, and was the mother of other members of the Tribe. By holding that the subject matter jurisdiction of tribal courts was limited by the *Montana* tests, the Court impliedly held that the civil jurisdiction of tribal courts is far more limited than that of state courts of general jurisdiction. While a state generally cannot regulate matters occurring outside its borders, its courts can hear transitory civil causes of action arising outside the state so long as they can establish *in personam* jurisdiction over the defendant(s) to the action. By purporting to limit tribal court civil jurisdiction to the *Montana* tests, the Supreme Court held without much discussion that the civil adjudicative power of a tribal court, at least under federal common law, was no broader than its regulatory authority. Is there any justification that can be offered as to why this limitation has been uniquely applied to tribal courts and not state courts? While some lower courts took *Strate* as a signal to enforce increasingly narrow restrictions on the exercise of tribal court civil subject matter jurisdiction, *see, e.g., Wilson v. Marchington,* 127 F.3d 805 (9th Cir. 1997) (set forth and discussed in Sec. E, this chapter), the full implications of *Strate* were not apparent until the Court decided *Nevada v. Hicks,* which follows.

NEVADA v. HICKS
United States Supreme Court
533 U.S. 353 (2001)

Justice Scalia delivered the opinion of the Court.

This case presents the question whether a tribal court may assert jurisdiction over civil claims against state officials who entered tribal land to execute a search warrant against a tribe member suspected of having violated state law outside the reservation.

I

Respondent Hicks is one of about 900 members of the Fallon Paiute-Shoshone Tribes of western Nevada. He resides on the Tribes' reservation of approximately 8,000 acres, established by federal statute in 1908, ch. 53, 35 Stat. 85. In 1990 Hicks came under suspicion of having killed, off the reservation, a California bighorn sheep, a gross misdemeanor under Nevada law, see Nev. Rev. Stat. § 501.376 (1999). A state game warden obtained from state court a search warrant "SUBJECT TO OBTAINING APPROVAL FROM THE FALLON TRIBAL COURT IN AND FOR THE FALLON PAIUTE-SHOSHONE TRIBES." According to the issuing judge, this tribal-court authorization was necessary because "this Court has no jurisdiction on the Fallon Paiute-Shoshone Indian Reservation." A search warrant was obtained from the tribal court, and the warden, accompanied by a tribal police officer, searched respondent's yard, uncovering only the head of a Rocky Mountain bighorn, a different (and unprotected) species of sheep.

Approximately one year later, a tribal police officer reported to the warden that he had observed two mounted bighorn sheep heads in respondent's home. The warden again obtained a search warrant from state court; though this warrant did not explicitly require permission from the Tribes, see App. F to Pet. for Cert. 2, a tribal-court warrant was nonetheless secured, and respondent's home was again (unsuccessfully) searched by three wardens and additional tribal officers.

Respondent, claiming that his sheep-heads had been damaged, and that the second search exceeded the bounds of the warrant, brought suit against the Tribal Judge, the tribal officers, the state wardens in their individual and official capacities, and the State of Nevada in the Tribal Court in and for the Fallon Paiute-Shoshone Tribes. (His claims against all defendants except the state wardens and the State of Nevada were dismissed by directed verdict and are not at issue here.) Respondent's causes of action included trespass to land and chattels, abuse of process, and violation of civil rights — specifically, denial of equal protection, denial of due process, and unreasonable search and seizure, each remediable under 42 U.S.C. § 1983. Respondent later voluntarily dismissed his case against the State and against the state officials in their official capacities, leaving only his suit against those officials in their individual capacities.

The Tribal Court held that it had jurisdiction over the claims, a holding affirmed by the Tribal Appeals Court. The state officials and Nevada then filed an action in federal district court seeking a declaratory judgment that the Tribal Court lacked jurisdiction. The District Court granted summary judgment to respondent on the issue of jurisdiction, and also held that the state officials would have to exhaust any claims of qualified immunity in the tribal court. The Ninth Circuit affirmed, concluding that the fact that respondent's home is located on tribe-owned land within the reservation is sufficient to support tribal jurisdiction over civil claims against nonmembers arising from their activities on that land. We granted certiorari.

II

In this case, which involves claims brought under both tribal and federal law, it is necessary to determine, as to the former, whether the Tribal Court in and for the Fallon Paiute-Shoshone Tribes has jurisdiction to adjudicate the alleged tortious conduct of state wardens executing a search warrant for evidence of an off-reservation crime; and, as to the latter, whether the Tribal Court has jurisdiction over claims brought under 42 U.S.C. § 1983. We address the former question first.

A

The principle of Indian law central to this aspect of the case is our holding in *Strate v. A-1 Contractors*, 520 U.S. 438, 453 (1997): "As to nonmembers . . . a tribe's adjudicative jurisdiction does not exceed its legislative jurisdiction. . . . " That formulation leaves open the question whether a tribe's adjudicative jurisdiction over nonmember defendants *equals* its legislative jurisdiction.[31] We will not have to answer that open question if we determine that the Tribes in any event lack legislative jurisdiction in this case. We first inquire, therefore, whether the Fallon Paiute-Shoshone Tribes — either as an exercise of their inherent sovereignty, or under grant of federal authority — can regulate state wardens executing a search warrant for evidence of an off-reservation crime.

Indian tribes' regulatory authority over nonmembers is governed by the principles set forth in *Montana v. United States*, 450 U.S. 544 (1981) . . . , which we have called the "pathmarking case" on the subject. In deciding whether the Crow Tribe could regulate hunting and fishing by nonmembers on land held in fee simple by nonmembers, *Montana* observed that, under our decision in *Oliphant v. Suquamish Tribe*, 435 U.S. 191 (1978), tribes lack criminal jurisdiction over nonmembers. Although, it continued, "*Oliphant* only determined inherent tribal

---

[31] [2] In *National Farmers Union Ins. Cos. v. Crow Tribe*, 471 U.S. 845, 855–856(1985), we avoided the question whether tribes may generally adjudicate against nonmembers claims arising from on-reservation transactions, and we have never held that a tribal court had jurisdiction over a nonmember defendant. Typically, our cases have involved claims brought against tribal defendants. See, e.g., *Williams v. Lee*, 358 U.S. 217 (1959). In *Strate v. A-1 Contractors*, 520 U.S. 438, 453 (1997), however, we assumed that "where tribes possess authority to regulate the activities of nonmembers, civil jurisdiction over disputes arising out of such activities presumably lies in the tribal courts," without distinguishing between nonmember plaintiffs and nonmember defendants. See also *Iowa Mut. Ins. Co. v. LaPlante*, 480 U.S. 9, 18 (1987). Our holding in this case is limited to the question of tribal-court jurisdiction over state officers enforcing state law. We leave open the question of tribal-court jurisdiction over nonmember defendants in general.

authority in criminal matters, the principles on which it relied support the general proposition that the inherent sovereign powers of an Indian tribe do not extend to the activities of nonmembers of the tribe." Where nonmembers are concerned, the "exercise of tribal power *beyond what is necessary to protect tribal self-government or to control internal relations* is inconsistent with the dependent status of the tribes, and so cannot survive without express congressional delegation." (emphasis added).[32]

Both *Montana* and *Strate* rejected tribal authority to regulate nonmembers' activities on land over which the tribe could not "assert a landowner's right to occupy and exclude." Respondents and the United States argue that since Hicks's home and yard *are* on tribe-owned land within the reservation, the Tribe may make its exercise of regulatory authority over nonmembers a condition of nonmembers' entry. Not necessarily. . . . While it is certainly true that the non-Indian ownership status of the land was central to the analysis in both *Montana* and *Strate*, the reason that was so was *not* that Indian ownership suspends the "general proposition" derived from *Oliphant* that "the inherent sovereign powers of an Indian tribe do not extend to the activities of nonmembers of the tribe," except to the extent "necessary to protect tribal self-government or to control internal relations." *Oliphant* itself drew no distinctions based on the status of land. And *Montana*, after announcing the general rule of no jurisdiction over nonmembers, cautioned that "to be sure, Indian tribes retain inherent sovereign power to exercise some forms of civil jurisdiction over non-Indians on their reservations, even on non-Indian fee lands," — clearly implying that the general rule of *Montana* applies to both Indian and non-Indian land. The ownership status of land, in other words, is only one factor to consider in determining whether regulation of the activities of nonmembers is "necessary to protect tribal self-government or to control internal relations . . . . " It may sometimes be a dispositive factor. Hitherto, the absence of tribal ownership has been virtually conclusive of the absence of tribal civil jurisdiction; with one minor exception, we have never upheld under *Montana* the extension of tribal civil authority over nonmembers on non-Indian land. . . . But the existence of tribal ownership is not alone enough to support regulatory jurisdiction over nonmembers.

We proceed to consider, successively, the following questions: whether regulatory jurisdiction over state officers in the present context is "necessary to protect tribal self-government or to control internal relations," and, if not, whether such regulatory jurisdiction has been congressionally conferred.

B

In *Strate*, we explained that what is necessary to protect tribal self-government and control internal relations can be understood by looking at the examples of tribal

---

[32] [3] *Montana* recognized an exception to this rule for tribal regulation of "the activities of nonmembers who enter consensual relationships with the tribe or its members, through commercial dealing, contracts, leases, or other arrangements." Though the wardens in this case "consensually" obtained a warrant from the Tribal Court before searching respondent's home and yard, we do not think this qualifies as an "other arrangement" within the meaning of this passage. Read in context, an "other arrangement" is clearly another *private consensual* relationship, from which the official actions at issue in this case are far removed.

power to which *Montana* referred: tribes have authority "[to punish tribal offenders,] to determine tribal membership, to regulate domestic relations among members, and to prescribe rules of inheritance for members," These examples show, we said, that Indians have "the right . . . to make their own laws and be ruled by them . . . ."

[However s]tate sovereignty does not end at a reservation's border. Though tribes are often referred to as "sovereign" entities, it was "long ago" that "the Court departed from Chief Justice Marshall's view that 'the laws of [a State] can have no force' within reservation boundaries. *Worcester v. Georgia*, 6 Peters 515, 561 (1832)," *White Mountain Apache Tribe v. Bracker*, 448 U.S. 136, 141 (1980).[33] "Ordinarily," it is now clear, "an Indian reservation is considered part of the territory of the State." U.S. Dept. of Interior, Federal Indian Law 510, and n. 1 (1958), citing *Utah & Northern R. Co. v. Fisher*, 116 U.S. 28 (1885); see also *Organized Village of Kake v. Egan*, 369 U.S. 60, 72 (1962).

That is not to say that States may exert the same degree of regulatory authority within a reservation as they do without. To the contrary, the principle that Indians have the right to make their own laws and be governed by them requires "an accommodation between the interests of the Tribes and the Federal Government, on the one hand, and those of the State, on the other." *Washington v. Confederated Tribes of Colville Reservation*, 447 U.S. 134, 156 (1980) "When on-reservation conduct involving only Indians is at issue, state law is generally inapplicable, for the State's regulatory interest is likely to be minimal and the federal interest in encouraging tribal self-government is at its strongest." *Bracker, supra*, at 144. When, however, state interests outside the reservation are implicated, States may regulate the activities even of tribe members on tribal land, as exemplified by our decision in *Confederated Tribes*. In that case, Indians were selling cigarettes on their reservation to nonmembers from off-reservation, without collecting the state cigarette tax. We held that the State could require the Tribes to collect the tax from nonmembers, and could "impose at least 'minimal' burdens on the Indian retailer to aid in enforcing and collecting the tax." It is also well established in our precedent that States have criminal jurisdiction over reservation Indians for crimes committed (as was the alleged poaching in this case) off the reservation. *See Mescalero Apache Tribe v. Jones*, 411 U.S. 145, 148–149 (1973).

While it is not entirely clear from our precedent whether the last mentioned authority entails the corollary right to enter a reservation (including Indian-fee lands) for enforcement purposes, several of our opinions point in that direction. In *Confederated Tribes*, we explicitly reserved the question whether state officials could seize cigarettes held for sale to nonmembers in order to recover the taxes due. In *Utah & Northern R. Co.*, however, we observed that "it has . . . been held that process of [state] courts may run into an Indian reservation of this kind, where the subject-matter or controversy is otherwise within their cognizance," 116 U.S. at

---

[33] [4] Our holding in *Worcester* must be considered in light of the fact that "the 1828 treaty with the Cherokee nation . . . guaranteed the Indians their lands would never be subjected to the jurisdiction of any State or Territory." *Organized Village of Kake v. Egan*, 369 U.S. 60, 71 (1962); *cf. Williams v. Lee*, 358 U.S. 217, 221–222 (1959) (comparing Navajo treaty to the Cherokee treaty in *Worcester*).

31.[34] Shortly thereafter, we considered, in *United States v. Kagama*, 118 U.S. 375 (1886), whether Congress could enact a law giving federal courts jurisdiction over various common-law, violent crimes committed by Indians on a reservation within a State. We expressed skepticism that the Indian Commerce Clause could justify this assertion of authority in derogation of state jurisdiction, but ultimately accepted the argument that the law

> does not interfere with the process of the State courts within the reservation, nor with the operation of State laws upon white people found there. Its effect is confined to the acts of an Indian of some tribe, of a criminal character, committed within the limits of the reservation.

It seems to us that this is within the competency of Congress. *Id.* at 383.

The Court's references to "process" in *Utah & Northern R. Co.* and *Kagama*, and the Court's concern in *Kagama* over possible federal encroachment on state prerogatives, suggest state authority to issue search warrants in cases such as the one before us. ("Process" is defined as "any means used by a court to acquire or exercise its jurisdiction over a person or over specific property," Black's Law Dictionary 1084 (5th ed. 1979), and is equated in criminal cases with a warrant. It is noteworthy that *Kagama* recognized the right of state *laws* to "operate . . . upon [non-Indians] found" within a reservation, but did not similarly limit to non-Indians or the property of non-Indians the scope of the *process* of state courts. This makes perfect sense, since, as we explained in the context of federal enclaves, the reservation of state authority to serve process is necessary to "prevent [such areas] from becoming an asylum for fugitives from justice." *Fort Leavenworth R. Co. v. Lowe*, 114 U.S. 525, 533 (1885).[35]

We conclude today, in accordance with these prior statements, that tribal authority to regulate state officers in executing process related to the violation, off reservation, of state laws is not essential to tribal self-government or internal relations — to "the right to make laws and be ruled by them." The State's interest in execution of process is considerable, and even when it relates to Indian-fee lands it no more impairs the tribe's self-government than federal enforcement of federal law impairs state government. Respondents argue that, even conceding the State's general interest in enforcing its off-reservation poaching law on the reservation, Nevada's interest in *this suit* is minimal, because it is a suit against state officials in their *individual* capacities. We think, however, that the distinction between individual and official capacity suits is irrelevant. To paraphrase our opinion in *Tennessee v. Davis*, 100 U.S. 257, 263 (1880), which upheld a federal statute permitting federal officers to remove to federal court state criminal proceedings

---

[34] [5] Though *Utah & Northern R. Co.* did not state what it meant by a "reservation of this kind," the context makes clear that it meant a reservation not excluded from the territory of a State by treaty. *See, e.g., Harkness v. Hyde*, 98 U.S. 476, 478 (1879); *The Kansas Indians*, 72 U.S. 737, 5 Wall. 737, 739–741 (1867).

[35] [6] That this risk is not purely hypothetical is demonstrated by *Arizona ex rel. Merrill v. Turtle*, 413 F.2d 683 (9th Cir. 1969), a case in which the Navajo Tribal Court refused to extradite a member to Oklahoma because tribal law forbade extradition except to three neighboring States. The Ninth Circuit held that Arizona (where the reservation was located) could not enter the reservation to seize the suspect for extradition since (among other reasons) this would interfere with tribal self-government.

brought against them for their official actions, a State "can act only through its officers and agents," and if a tribe can "affix penalties to acts done under the immediate direction of the [state] government, and in obedience to its laws," "the operations of the [state] government may at any time be arrested at the will of the [tribe]." . . .

III

We turn next to the contention of respondent and the Government that the tribal court, as a court of general jurisdiction, has authority to entertain federal claims under § 1983. It is certainly true that state courts of "general jurisdiction" can adjudicate cases invoking federal statutes, such as § 1983, absent congressional specification to the contrary. "Under [our] system of dual sovereignty, we have consistently held that state courts have inherent authority, and are thus presumptively competent, to adjudicate claims arising under the laws of the United States," *Tafflin v. Levitt*, 493 U.S. 455, 458 (1990). That this would be the case was assumed by the Framers, see The Federalist No. 82, pp. 492–493 (C. Rossiter ed. 1961). Indeed, that state courts could enforce federal law is presumed by Article III of the Constitution, which leaves to Congress the decision whether to create lower federal courts at all. This historical and constitutional assumption of concurrent state-court jurisdiction over federal-law cases is completely missing with respect to tribal courts.

Respondents' contention that tribal courts are courts of "general jurisdiction" is also quite wrong. A state court's jurisdiction is general, in that it "lays hold of all subjects of litigation between parties within its jurisdiction, though the causes of dispute are relative to the laws of the most distant part of the globe." Tribal courts, it should be clear, cannot be courts of general jurisdiction in this sense, for a tribe's inherent adjudicative jurisdiction over nonmembers is at most only as broad as its legislative jurisdiction. . . . It is true that some statutes proclaim tribal-court jurisdiction over certain questions of federal law. *See, e.g.,* 25 U.S.C. § 1911(a) (authority to adjudicate child custody disputes under the Indian Child Welfare Act of 1978); 12 U.S.C. § 1715z-13(g)(5) (jurisdiction over mortgage foreclosure actions brought by the Secretary of Housing and Urban Development against reservation homeowners). But no provision in federal law provides for tribal-court jurisdiction over § 1983 actions.

Furthermore, tribal-court jurisdiction would create serious anomalies, as the Government recognizes, because the general federal-question removal statute refers only to removal from *state* court, see 28 U.S.C. § 1441. Were § 1983 claims cognizable in tribal court, defendants would inexplicably lack the right available to state-court § 1983 defendants to seek a federal forum. The Government thinks the omission of reference to tribal courts in § 1441 unproblematic. Since, it argues, "it is doubtful . . . that Congress intended to deny tribal court defendants the right given state court defendants to elect a federal forum for the adjudication of causes of action under federal law," we should feel free to create that right by permitting the tribal-court defendant to obtain a federal-court injunction against the action, effectively forcing it to be refiled in federal court. Brief for United States as *Amicus Curiae* 25–26. . . . Not only are there missing here any distinctive federal-court procedures, but in order even to *confront* the question whether an unspecified removal power exists, we must first attribute to tribal courts jurisdiction that is not apparent. Surely the simpler way to avoid the removal problem is to conclude (as other indications suggest anyway) that tribal courts cannot entertain § 1983 suits.

IV

The last question before us is whether petitioners were required to exhaust their jurisdictional claims in Tribal Court before bringing them in Federal District Court. *See National Farmers Union Ins. Cos. v. Crow Tribe*, 471 U.S. 845, 856 (1985). In *National Farmers Union* we recognized exceptions to the exhaustion requirement, where "an assertion of tribal jurisdiction is motivated by a desire to harass or is conducted in bad faith, . . . or where the action is patently violative of express jurisdictional prohibitions, or where exhaustion would be futile because of the lack of an adequate opportunity to challenge the court's jurisdiction." None of these exceptions seems applicable to this case, but we added a broader exception in *Strate:* "when . . . it is plain that no federal grant provides for tribal governance of nonmembers' conduct on land covered by *Montana*'s main rule," so the exhaustion requirement "would serve no purpose other than delay." Though this exception too is technically inapplicable, the reasoning behind it is not. Since it is clear, as we have discussed, that tribal courts lack jurisdiction over state officials for causes of action relating to their performance of official duties, adherence to the tribal exhaustion requirement in such cases "would serve no purpose other than delay," and is therefore unnecessary.

V

Finally, a few words in response to the concurring opinion of JUSTICE O'CONNOR, which is in large part a dissent from the views expressed in this opinion.[36]

The principal point of the concurrence is that our reasoning "gives only passing consideration to the fact that the state officials' activities in this case occurred on land owned and controlled by the Tribe." According to JUSTICE O'CONNOR, "that factor is not prominent in the Court's analysis." Even a cursory reading of our opinion demonstrates that this is not so. To the contrary, we acknowledge that tribal ownership is a factor in the *Montana* analysis, and a factor significant enough that it "may sometimes be . . . dispositive." We simply do not find it dispositive in the present case, when weighed against the State's interest in pursuing off-reservation violations of its laws. *See supra*, at 10 (concluding that "the State's interest in execution of process is considerable" enough to outweigh the tribal interest in

---

[36] [9] JUSTICE O'CONNOR claims we have gone beyond the scope of the Questions Presented in this case by determining whether the tribe could *regulate* the state game warden's actions on tribal land, because this is a case about tribal "civil *adjudicatory*" authority." But the third Question Presented, see Petn. for Writ of Certiorari i, is as follows: "Is the rule of *[Montana]*, creating a presumption against tribal court jurisdiction over nonmembers, limited to cases in which a cause of action against a nonmember arises on lands within a reservation which are not controlled by the tribe?" *Montana* dealt only with regulatory authority, and is tied to adjudicatory authority by *Strate*, which held that the latter at best *tracks* the former. As is made clear in the merits briefing, petitioners' argument is that the Tribes lacked adjudicatory authority *because* they lacked regulatory authority over the game wardens.

self-government "even when it relates to Indian-fee lands").

The concurrence is of course free to disagree with this judgment; but to say that failure to give tribal ownership determinative effect "fails to consider adequately the Tribe's inherent sovereign interests in activities on their land," is an exaggeration. . . . *Self*-government and *internal* relations are not directly at issue here, since the issue is whether the Tribes' law will apply, not to their own members, but to a narrow category of outsiders. And the concurrence does not try to explain how allowing state officers to pursue off-reservation violation of state law "threatens or has some direct effect on the political integrity, the economic security, or the health or welfare of the tribe. . . . "

We must comment upon the final paragraphs of Part II of the concurrence's opinion — which bring on stage, in classic fashion, a *deus ex machina* to extract, from the seemingly insoluble difficulties that the prior writing has created, a happy ending. The concurrence manages to have its cake and eat it too — to hand over state law-enforcement officers to the jurisdiction of tribal courts and yet still assure that the officers' traditional immunity (and hence the State's law-enforcement interest) will be protected — by simply announcing "that in order to protect government officials, immunity defenses should be considered in reviewing tribal court jurisdiction." What wonderful magic. Without so much as a citation (none is available), the concurrence declares the qualified immunity inquiry to be part of the jurisdictional inquiry, thus bringing it within the ken of the federal court at the outset of the case. There are two problems with this declaration. The first is that it is not true. There is no authority whatever for the proposition that absolute- and qualified-immunity defenses pertain to the court's jurisdiction — much less to the tribe's *regulatory* jurisdiction, which is what is at issue here. (If they did pertain to the court's jurisdiction, they would presumably be nonwaivable. *Cf. Idaho v. Coeur d'Alene Tribe of Idaho*, 521 U.S. 261, 267 (1997)). And the second problem is, that without *first* determining whether the tribe has regulatory jurisdiction, it is impossible to know which "immunity defenses" the federal court is supposed to consider. The tribe's law on this subject need not be the same as the State's; indeed, the tribe may decide (as did the common law until relatively recently) that there is no immunity defense whatever without a warrant. See *California v. Acevedo*, 500 U.S. 565, 581 (1991) (SCALIA, J., concurring in judgment). One wonders whether, deprived of its *deus ex machina*, the concurrence would not alter the conclusion it reached in Part I of its opinion, and agree with us that a proper balancing of state and tribal interests would give the Tribes no jurisdiction over state officers pursuing off-reservation violations of state law.

Finally, it is worth observing that the concurrence's resolution would, for the first time, hold a non-Indian subject to the jurisdiction of a tribal court. The question (which we have avoided) whether tribal regulatory and adjudicatory jurisdiction are coextensive is simply answered by the concurrence in the affirmative. As JUSTICE SOUTER's separate opinion demonstrates, it surely deserves more considered analysis.

Because the Fallon Paiute-Shoshone Tribes lacked legislative authority to restrict, condition, or otherwise regulate the ability of state officials to investigate off-reservation violations of state law, they also lacked adjudicative authority to hear respondent's claim that those officials violated tribal law in the performance of their duties. Nor can the Tribes identify any authority to adjudicate respondent's § 1983 claim. And since the lack of authority is clear, there is no need to exhaust the jurisdictional dispute in tribal court. State officials operating on a reservation to investigate off-reservation violations of state law are properly held accountable for tortious conduct and civil rights violations in either state or federal court, but not in tribal court.

The judgment of the Court of Appeals is reversed, and the case remanded for further proceedings consistent with our opinion.

It is so ordered.

JUSTICE SOUTER, with whom JUSTICES KENNEDY and THOMAS join, concurring.

I agree that the Fallon Paiute-Shoshone Tribal Court had no jurisdiction to entertain Hicks's claims against the petitioning state officers here, and I join the Court's opinion. While I agree with the Court's analysis as well as its conclusion, I would reach that point by a different route. Like the Court, I take *Montana v. United States*, 450 U.S. 544 (1981), to be the source of the first principle on tribal-court civil jurisdiction, see *Atkinson Trading Co. v. Shirley*, 532 U.S. 645 (2001) (SOUTER, J., concurring). But while the Court gives emphasis to measuring tribal authority here in light of the State's interest in executing its own legal process to enforce state law governing off-reservation conduct, I would go right to *Montana*'s rule that a tribe's civil jurisdiction generally stops short of nonmember defendants, subject only to two exceptions, one turning on "consensual relationships," the other on respect for "the political integrity, the economic security, or the health or welfare of the tribe."[37]

Montana applied this presumption against tribal jurisdiction to nonmember conduct on fee land within a reservation; I would also apply it where, as here, a nonmember acts on tribal or trust land, and I would thus make it explicit that land status within a reservation is not a primary jurisdictional fact, but is relevant only insofar as it bears on the application of one of *Montana*'s exceptions to a particular case. Insofar as I rest my conclusion on the general jurisdictional presumption, it follows for me that, although the holding in this case is "limited to the question of tribal-court jurisdiction over state officers enforcing state law," one rule independently supporting that holding (that as a general matter "the inherent sovereign powers of an Indian tribe do not extend to the activities of nonmembers of the tribe") is not so confined . . . .

. . . [W]e confirmed in *Strate* what we had indicated in *Montana*: that as a general matter, a tribe's civil jurisdiction does not extend to the "activities of non-Indians on reservation lands," and that the only such activities that trigger civil jurisdiction are those that fit within one of *Montana*'s two exceptions.

After *Strate*, it is undeniable that a tribe's remaining inherent civil jurisdiction to

---

[37] [1] The virtue of the Court's approach is in laying down a rule that would be unquestionably applicable even if in a future case the state officials issuing and executing state process happened to be tribal members (which they apparently are not here).

adjudicate civil claims arising out of acts committed on a reservation depends in the first instance on the character of the individual over whom jurisdiction is claimed, not on the title to the soil on which he acted. The principle on which *Montana* and *Strate* were decided (like *Oliphant* before them) looks first to human relationships, not land records, and it should make no difference *per se* whether acts committed on a reservation occurred on tribal land or on land owned by a nonmember individual in fee. It is the membership status of the unconsenting party, not the status of real property, that counts as the primary jurisdictional fact.[38]

JUSTICE O'CONNOR, with whom JUSTICE STEVENS and JUSTICE BREYER join, concurring in part and concurring in the judgment.

The Court holds that a tribe has no power to regulate the activities of state officials enforcing state law on land owned and controlled by the tribe. The majority's sweeping opinion, without cause, undermines the authority of tribes to "make their own laws and be ruled by them." *Strate v. A-1 Contractors*, 520 U.S. 438, 459 (1997) (quoting *Williams v. Lee*, 358 U.S. 217, 220 (1959)). I write separately because Part II of the Court's decision is unmoored from our precedents.

I

A

Today, the Court finally resolves that *Montana v. United States*, 450 U.S. 544 (1981), governs a tribe's civil jurisdiction over nonmembers regardless of land ownership. This is done with little fanfare, but the holding is significant because we have equivocated on this question in the past . . . .

B

Montana and our other cases concerning tribal civil jurisdiction over nonmembers occupy a middle ground between our cases that provide for nearly absolute tribal sovereignty over tribe members, see generally *Williams v. Lee*, 358 U.S. 217, 218–223 (1959), and our rule that tribes have no inherent criminal jurisdiction over nonmembers, see *Oliphant v. Suquamish Tribe*, 435 U.S. 191 (1978). *Montana* recognizes that tribes retain sovereign interests in activities that occur on land owned and controlled by the tribe, and provides principles that guide our determination of whether particular activities by nonmembers implicate these sovereign interests to a degree that tribal civil jurisdiction is appropriate . . . .

---

[38] [4] Thus, it is not that land status is irrelevant to a proper *Montana* calculus, only that it is not determinative in the first instance. Land status, for instance might well have an impact under one (or perhaps both) of the *Montana* exceptions. *See Atkinson Trading Co. v. Shirley*, 532 U.S. 645, 659–660 (2001) (SOUTER, J., concurring); cf. *White Mountain Apache Tribe v. Bracker*, 448 U.S. 136, 151 (1980) ("[T]here is a significant geographic component to tribal sovereignty").

C

In this case, the Court purports to apply *Montana* . . . to determine whether a tribe, "as an exercise of [its] inherent sovereignty . . . can regulate state wardens executing a search warrant for evidence of an off-reservation crime." The Court's reasoning suffers from two serious flaws: It gives only passing consideration to the fact that the state officials' activities in this case occurred on land owned and controlled by the Tribes, and it treats as dispositive the fact that the nonmembers in this case are state officials. . . .

The majority's rule undermining tribal interests is all the more perplexing because the conduct in this case occurred on land owned and controlled by the Tribes. Although the majority gives a passing nod to land status at the outset of its opinion, that factor is not prominent in the Court's analysis. This oversight is significant. *Montana* recognizes that tribes may retain inherent power to exercise civil jurisdiction when the nonmember conduct "threatens or has some direct effect on the political integrity, the economic security, or the health or welfare of the tribe." These interests are far more likely to be implicated where, as here, the nonmember activity takes place on land owned and controlled by the tribe. If *Montana* is to bring coherence to our case law, we must apply it with due consideration to land status, which has always figured prominently in our analysis of tribal jurisdiction. . . .

The Court's reasoning does not reflect a faithful application of *Montana* and its progeny. Our case law does not support a broad *per se* rule prohibiting tribal jurisdiction over nonmembers on tribal land whenever the nonmembers are state officials. If the Court were to remain true to the principles that have governed in prior cases, the Court would reverse and remand the case to the Court of Appeals for a proper application of *Montana* to determine whether there is tribal jurisdiction.

II

The Court's sweeping analysis gives the impression that this case involves a conflict of great magnitude between the State of Nevada and the Fallon Paiute-Shoshone Tribes. That is not so. At no point did the Tribes attempt to exclude the State from the reservation. At no point did the Tribes attempt to obstruct state officials' efforts to secure or execute the search warrants. Quite the contrary, the record demonstrates that judicial and law enforcement officials from the State and the Tribes acted in full cooperation to investigate an off-reservation crime. . . .

To resolve this case, it suffices to answer the questions presented, which concern the civil adjudicatory jurisdiction of tribal courts. Petitioners contend that tribal court jurisdiction over state officials should be determined with reference to officials' claims of immunity. I agree and would resolve this case by applying basic principles of official and qualified immunity. . . .

The Court issues a broad holding that significantly alters the principles that govern determinations of tribal adjudicatory and regulatory jurisdiction. While I agree that *Montana* guides our analysis, I do not believe that the Court has properly applied *Montana*. I would not adopt a *per se* rule of tribal jurisdiction that fails to consider adequately the Tribes' inherent sovereign interests in activities on their land, nor would I give nonmembers freedom to act with impunity on tribal land based solely on their status as state law enforcement officials. I would hold that *Montana* governs a tribe's civil jurisdiction over nonmembers, and that in order to protect government officials, immunity claims should be considered in reviewing tribal court jurisdiction. Accordingly, I would reverse the judgment of the United States Court of Appeals for the Ninth Circuit and remand the case for further proceedings consistent with this opinion.

JUSTICE STEVENS, with whom JUSTICE BREYER joins, concurring in the judgment.

While I join the Court's disposition of the case for the reasons stated by JUSTICE O'CONNOR, I do not agree with the Court's conclusion that tribal courts may not exercise their jurisdiction over claims seeking the relief authorized by 42 U.S.C. § 1983. I agree instead with the Solicitor General's submission that a tribal court may entertain such a claim unless enjoined from doing so by a federal court.

NOTES ON *HICKS*

1. **Holding and Dicta in *Hicks*:** What precisely constitutes the holding of *Hicks*? Is the holding of the case limited to the exercise of tribal court civil subject matter jurisdiction over state officials or does the holding reach all jurisdiction over non-Indians? Justice Souter's separate opinion nicely raises this question in his footnote 1 by seeking the outcome of *Hicks* if applied to a state law enforcement official who happens to be a member of the governing tribe, which was not the actual fact in that case. By noting that he believes the majority's opinion holds that the tribal court would not have jurisdiction, Justice Souter raises important questions as to whether the Court's opinion resolved questions of civil adjudicatory power over nonmembers who are not officers of the state. Does it purport to do so? Consider Justice Ginsburg's separate opinion.

While the Court seemed to be relatively agreed that the *Montana* test should be extended beyond the original context in which it was adopted and should be employed to govern all exercises of tribal power within Indian country, whether on Indian owned land or otherwise, all members of the Court also agreed that the fact that lands are held by an Indian tribe constitutes a factor to be applied in considering the *Montana* tests. Do they all agree how large a factor Indian land ownership should constitute? Given the language and structure of the *Montana* test, do any of the members of the Court even bother to explain how to factor Indian land ownership into the precise language of the *Montana* tests? How should one accomplish that feat?

Since the litigation in *Hicks* was brought under the jurisdiction afforded in *National Farmers Union* to consider the scope of tribal court jurisdiction, why is the majority opinion purporting to decide the scope of *state* power to serve criminal process, including the search warrant on a tribal member on Indian land within the reservation? Is any of its discussion of this issue holding or is it all dicta? If dicta, why did the Court discuss the question at all? Notice that even the state trial court that issued the initial warrants understood that conventional Indian law had not permitted state officials to serve process, even for off-reservation crimes over which the state had subject matter jurisdiction, on the reservation. Given that settled understanding, why did the Supreme Court unsettle it by the discussion of *state* power in *Hicks*? Is the discussion of state power necessary or even helpful to its resolution of the question of tribal court jurisdiction pending before it? Is the Court's decision of the scope of state power consistent with the conception of the tribal-federal relationship established in *Worcester v. Georgia*, 31 U.S. (6 Pet.) 515 (1832)? How does the *Hicks* case deal with this seemingly inconsistent precedent? Does the Court's handling of *Worcester* and its approach to this question suggest that it, and it alone, has charted an entirely new course for the tribal-federal relationship? Is that a proper role for the United States Supreme Court? What new relationship does it envision?

With few exceptions, the scholarly commentary on *Hicks* has been highly critical. *See, e.g.*, Joseph William Singer, *Canons of Conquest: The Supreme Court's Attack on Tribal Sovereignty*, 37 NEW ENG. L. REV. 641 (2003); Catherine T. Struve, *How Bad Law Made a Hard Case Easy*, Nevada v. Hicks *and the Subject Matter Jurisdiction of Tribal Courts*, 5 U. PA. J. CONST. L. 288 (2003); Gloria Valencia-Weber, *The Supreme Court's Indian Law Decisions: Deviations from Constitutional Principles and the Crafting of Judicial Smallpox Blankets*, 5 U. PA. J. CONST. L. 405 (2003); Daan Braveman, *Tribal Sovereignty: Them and Us*, 82 ORE. L. REV. 75 (2003); Dean B. Suagee, *The Supreme Court's "Whack-a-Mole" Game Theory in Federal Indian Law, A Theory That Has No Place in the Realm of Environmental Law*, 7 GREAT PLAINS NAT. RESOURCES J. 90 (2002).

The most forceful defender of *Hicks*, Professor Gould, has opined that after *Hicks*, "*Montana* has replaced *Worcester* as the paradigm of tribal sovereignty." L. Scott Gould, *The Role of Jurisdiction in the Quest for Sovereignty: Tough Love for Tribes: Rethinking Sovereignty After* Atkinson *and* Hicks, 37 NEW ENG. L. REV. 669, 692 (2003). His statement suggests that as a result of *Hicks*, issues of state jurisdiction (the question addressed in *Worcester*) as well as tribal jurisdiction will be governed by *Montana*'s analytic framework, and that jurisdiction on trust lands will receive the same treatment as jurisdiction on nonmember-owned fee lands. Do the post-*Hicks* state and federal court decisions bear out this reading of the case? For a case addressing the application of *Hicks* to state jurisdiction, see *State v. Cummings*, discussed in Ch. 4, Sec. A.3.d.

A case finding *Hicks* inapplicable to tribal jurisdiction over a suit against a nonmember that arose on a tribal road is *McDonald v. Means*, 309 F.3d 530 (9th Cir. 2002). More recently, however, another panel of the Ninth Circuit, over a vigorous dissent by Judge William Fletcher, has ignored *McDonald v. Means* in denying the courts of the Navajo Nation jurisdiction over a products liability claim by parents of a tribal member who was killed when her vehicle rolled over on a tribal road. *Ford Motor Co. v. Todecheene*, 394 F.3d 1170 (9th Cir. 2005). The court proceeded to apply the *Montana* test, finding none of the exceptions satisfied. As one commentator has noted, *Hicks* itself espoused a balancing test to determine whether tribal interests in activities on tribal land warrant application of the general *Worcester* principles favoring tribal sovereignty as opposed to the more restrictive *Montana* test. Yet the *Ford Motor Co.* panel did not even bother to make that threshold determination. *Recent Cases: American Indian Law — Tribal Court Civil Jurisdiction — Ninth*

Circuit Holds That Tribal Courts Lack Subject Matter Jurisdiction over Products Liability Suits Arising on Tribal Land, 118 HARV. L. REV. 2469 (2005). More fundamentally, given that *Montana* justified the formulation of its test based on congressional intent reflected in the allotment acts, which had resulted in the shift of tribal land to non-Indian fee ownership, how can the Ninth Circuit explain the application of that test to land still owned in trust for the tribe?

Another Ninth Circuit decision provided further support for Professor Gould's prediction, applying the *Montana* test to a suit brought *against* a tribal college by a nonmember, where the suit arose on a state right of way road on the reservation. *Smith v. Salish Kootenai College,* 434 F.3d 1127 (9th Cir. 2006). In this case the nature of the land resembles the facts of *Strate,* but the tribal court plaintiff, unlike the defendant in *Strate,* was a tribal member, albeit of the Umatilla Tribe and not of the Confederated Salish and Kootenai Tribes, whose tribal college sued him in the courts of the Confederated Salish and Kootenai Tribes. Specifically, the Umatilla plaintiff was a student at the college and initially sued the college in tribal court over an automobile accident. After the tribal jury returned a verdict in favor of the college, the student sought to enjoin the verdict in federal court based on lack of jurisdiction since he was a nonmember. In one of the rare federal cases *approving* tribal court jurisdiction under the *Montana* tests since *Strate* and *Hicks,* an en banc panel of the Ninth Circuit found the *Montana* test satisfied, noting: "even though his claims did not arise from contracts or leases with the Tribes, Smith could and did consent to the civil jurisdiction of the Tribes' courts. And in this case, the exercise of tribal jurisdiction is consistent with the limited sovereignty of the Tribes." The court also began its analysis with a reference to *Williams v. Lee,* presented in Ch. 4, Sec. B.4.a, which contained an identical alignment of parties. Perhaps the lesson of *Smith* and *Williams v. Lee* is that a nonmember who files suit in tribal court always consents to tribal court jurisdiction within the meaning of the *Montana* tests.

2.   ***Hicks* and Intergovernmental Agreements:** As Justice O'Connor's opinion notes many tribes and states (or local governments), recognizing the limits of each other's jurisdiction, have entered into cooperative agreements to handle matters of mutual concern. *See* Ch. 5, Sec. H. These arrangements may include cross-deputization agreements for their police forces, arrangements for housing of prisoners, provisions for handling protective orders, cooperative agreements on child welfare services, or arrangements for service of process such as subpoenas or warrants. Does *Hicks* encourage or discourage such cooperative agreements? Does *Hicks* have any potential to unsettle existing agreements?

3.   **Excluding Agents of Federal and State Governments:** In *United States v. White Mountain Apache Tribe,* 784 F.2d 917 (9th Cir. 1986), the Ninth Circuit Court of Appeals invalidated a tribal court order prohibiting United States agents from entry onto the reservation. The court held that the power to exclude does not extend to United States agents conducting official business on the reservation. On what basis can such a curtailment of the tribal power of exclusion be explained? Consider the great lengths to which the Lakota people went to exclude federal military personnel when they successfully defeated the United States military in Red Cloud's war and forced the removal of federal forts and overland trails. Does that history suggest that the tribal power of exclusion should extend to federal officials

not covered by a treaty right to enter the reservation? Could a private landowner exclude federal officials acting without a warrant from his private property? If so, why is a tribe prevented from doing the same thing?

In *Hicks*, the Supreme Court addressed the question of tribal power to exclude state law enforcement officers carrying out official business. Recall that the officer was seeking to serve a search warrant on a tribal member for an off-reservation offense, and the tribal court had given the officer permission to enter the reservation for that limited purpose. The Court found that Indian nations could not use their landowner status to exclude or regulate the service of state process against Indians on tribal lands, including tribal fee lands. In reaching that conclusion, was the Court simply saying that properly authorized state law enforcement activities are analogous to state rights-of-way, where there is no right to exclude, and hence no presumptive tribal right to regulate conduct? Could a private landowner off the reservation exclude a police officer serving a properly authorized warrant?

PLAINS COMMERCE BANK v. LONG FAMILY LAND & CATTLE CO., INC.
United States Supreme Court
554 U.S. 316 (2008)

CHIEF JUSTICE ROBERTS delivered the opinion of the Court.

This case concerns the sale of fee land on a tribal reservation by a non-Indian bank to non-Indian individuals. The question presented is whether the tribal court had jurisdiction to adjudicate a discrimination claim concerning the non-Indian bank's sale of fee land it owned.

I

The Long Family Land and Cattle Company, Inc., is a family-run ranching and farming operation incorporated under the laws of South Dakota. Its lands are located on the Cheyenne River Sioux Indian Reservation. Once a massive, 60-million acre affair, the reservation was appreciably diminished by Congress in the 1880s and at present consists of roughly 11 million acres located in Dewey and Ziebach Counties in north-central South Dakota. The Long Company is a respondent here, along with Ronnie and Lila Long, husband and wife, who together own at least 51 percent of the Company's shares. Ronnie and Lila Long are both enrolled members of the Cheyenne River Sioux Indian Tribe.

The Longs and their Company have been customers for many years at Plains Commerce Bank (Bank), located some 25 miles off the reservation as the crow flies in Hoven, South Dakota. The Bank, like the Long Company, is a South Dakota corporation, but has no ties to the reservation other than its business dealings with tribal members. The Bank made its first commercial loan to the Long Company in 1989, and a series of agreements followed. As part of those agreements, Kenneth Long-Ronnie Long's father and a non-Indian-mortgaged to the Bank 2,230 acres of fee land he owned inside the reservation. At the time of Kenneth Long's death in the summer of 1995, Kenneth and the Long Company owed the Bank $750,000.

In the spring of 1996, Ronnie and Lila Long began negotiating a new loan contract with the Bank in an effort to shore up their Company's flagging financial fortunes and come to terms with their outstanding debts. After several months of back-and-forth, the parties finally reached an agreement in December of that year-two agreements, to be precise. The Company and the Bank signed a fresh loan contract, according to which Kenneth Long's estate deeded over the previously mortgaged fee acreage to the Bank in lieu of foreclosure. App. 104. In return, the Bank agreed to cancel some of the Company's debt and to make additional operating loans. The parties also agreed to a lease arrangement: The Company received a two-year lease on the 2,230 acres, deeded over to the Bank, with an option to purchase the land at the end of the term for $468,000. *Id.*, at 96–103.

It is at this point, the Longs claim, that the Bank began treating them badly. The Longs say the Bank initially offered more favorable purchase terms in the lease agreement, allegedly proposing to sell the land back to the Longs with a 20-year contract for deed. The Bank eventually rescinded that offer, the Longs claim, citing "possible jurisdictional problems" that might have been caused by the Bank financing an "Indian owned entity on the reservation." 491 F.3d 878, 882 (C.A.8 2007) (case below).

Then came the punishing winter of 1996–1997. The Longs lost over 500 head of cattle in the blizzards that season, with the result that the Long Company was unable to exercise its option to purchase the leased acreage when the lease contract expired in 1998. Nevertheless, the Longs refused to vacate the property, prompting the Bank to initiate eviction proceedings in state court and to petition the Cheyenne River Sioux Tribal Court to serve the Longs with a notice to quit. In the meantime, the Bank sold 320 acres of the fee land it owned to a non-Indian couple. In June 1999, while the Longs continued to occupy a 960-acre parcel of the land, the Bank sold the remaining 1,910 acres to two other nonmembers.

In July 1999, the Longs and the Long Company filed suit against the Bank in the Tribal Court, seeking an injunction to prevent their eviction from the property and to reverse the sale of the land. They asserted a variety of claims, including breach of contract, bad faith, violation of tribal-law self-help remedies, and discrimination. The discrimination claim alleged that the Bank sold the land to nonmembers on terms more favorable than those offered the Company. The Bank asserted in its answer that the court lacked jurisdiction and also stated a counterclaim. The Tribal Court found that it had jurisdiction, denied the Bank's motion for summary judgment on its counterclaim, and proceeded to trial. Four causes of action were submitted to the seven-member jury: breach of contract, bad faith, violation of self-help remedies, and discrimination.

The jury found for the Longs on three of the four causes, including the discrimination claim, and awarded a $750,000 general verdict. After denying the Bank's post-trial motion for judgment notwithstanding the verdict by finding again that it had jurisdiction to adjudicate the Longs' claims, the Tribal Court entered judgment awarding the Longs $750,000 plus interest. A later supplemental judgment further awarded the Longs an option to purchase the 960 acres of the land they still occupied on the terms offered in the original purchase option, effectively nullifying the Bank's previous sale of that land to non-Indians.

The Bank appealed to the Cheyenne River Sioux Tribal Court of Appeals, which affirmed the judgment of the trial court. The Bank then filed the instant action in the United States District Court for the District of South Dakota, seeking a declaration that the tribal judgment was null and void because, as relevant here, the Tribal Court lacked jurisdiction over the Longs' discrimination claim. The District Court granted summary judgment to the Longs. The court found tribal court jurisdiction proper because the Bank had entered into a consensual relationship with the Longs and the Long Company. 440 F. Supp. 2d 1070, 1077–1078, 1080–1081 (D.S.D. 2006). According to the District Court, this relationship brought the Bank within the first category of tribal civil jurisdiction over nonmembers outlined in *Montana v. United States*, 450 U.S. 544 (1981).

. . . .

III

A

. . . .

As part of their residual sovereignty, tribes retain power to legislate and to tax activities on the reservation, including certain activities by nonmembers to determine tribal membership and to regulate domestic relations among members. They may also exclude outsiders from entering tribal land. See *Duro v. Reina*, 495 U.S. 676, 696–697 (1990). But tribes do not, as a general matter, possess authority over non-Indians who come within their borders[.] . . . As we explained in *Oliphant v. Suquamish Tribe*, 435 U.S. 191 (1978), the tribes have, by virtue of their incorporation into the American republic, lost "the right of governing . . . person[s] within their limits except themselves." *Id.*, at 209 (emphasis and internal quotation marks omitted).

This general rule restricts tribal authority over nonmember activities taking place on the reservation, and is particularly strong when the nonmember's activity occurs on land owned in fee simple by non-Indians — what we have called "non-Indian fee land." *Strate v. A-1 Contractors*, 520 U.S. 438, 446 (1997). Thanks to the Indian General Allotment Act of 1887, 24 Stat. 388, as amended, 25 U.S.C. § 331 et seq., there are millions of acres of non-Indian fee land located within the contiguous borders of Indian tribes. The history of the General Allotment Act and its successor statutes has been well rehearsed in our precedents. *See, e.g., Montana*, supra, at 558–563; *County of Yakima v. Confederated Tribes and Bands of Yakima Nation*, 502 U.S. 251, 254–255 (1992). Suffice it to say here that the effect of the Act was to convert millions of acres of formerly tribal land into fee simple parcels, "fully alienable," *id.*, at 264 and "free of all charge or encumbrance whatsoever," 25 U.S.C. § 348 (2000 ed., Supp. V).

Our cases have made clear that once tribal land is converted into fee simple, the tribe loses plenary jurisdiction over it. . . . Among the powers lost is the authority to prevent the land's sale, see *County of Yakima*, supra, at 263 (General Allotment

Act granted fee holders power of voluntary sale) — not surprisingly, as "free alienability" by the holder is a core attribute of the fee simple, C. Moynihan, Introduction to Law of Real Property § 3, p. 32 (2d ed. 1988). Moreover, when the tribe or tribal members convey a parcel of fee land "to non-Indians, [the tribe] loses any former right of absolute and exclusive use and occupation of the conveyed lands." *South Dakota v. Bourland*, 508 U.S. 679, 689 (1993) (emphasis added). This necessarily entails the "the loss of regulatory jurisdiction over the use of the land by others." Ibid. As a general rule, then, "the tribe has no authority itself, by way of tribal ordinance or actions in the tribal courts, to regulate the use of fee land." *Brendale v. Confederated Tribes and Bands of Yakima Nation*, 492 U.S. 408, 430 (1989) (opinion of White, J.).

. . . .

Given *Montana*'s "general proposition that the inherent sovereign powers of an Indian tribe do not extend to the activities of nonmembers of the tribe," *Atkinson*, supra, at 651 (quoting *Montana*, supra, at 565), efforts by a tribe to regulate nonmembers, especially on non-Indian fee land, are "presumptively invalid," *Atkinson*, supra, at 659. The burden rests on the tribe to establish one of the exceptions to *Montana*'s general rule that would allow an extension of tribal authority to regulate nonmembers on non-Indian fee land. The Bank contends that neither exception authorizes tribal courts to exercise jurisdiction over the Longs' discrimination claim at issue in this case. We agree.

B

According to our precedents, "a tribe's adjudicative jurisdiction does not exceed its legislative jurisdiction." *Strate*, at 453. We reaffirm that principle today and hold that the Tribal Court lacks jurisdiction to hear the Longs' discrimination claim because the Tribe lacks the civil authority to regulate the Bank's sale of its fee land.

The Longs' discrimination claim challenges a non-Indian's sale of non-Indian fee land. . . . That discrimination claim concerned the sale of a 2,230-acre fee parcel that the Bank had acquired from the estate of a non-Indian.

The status of the land is relevant "insofar as it bears on the application of . . . *Montana*'s exceptions to [this] case." *Hicks*, 533 U.S., at 376 (SOUTER, J., concurring). The acres at issue here were alienated from the Cheyenne River Sioux's tribal trust and converted into fee simple parcels as part of the Act of May 27, 1908, 35 Stat. 312, commonly called the 1908 Allotment Act. While the General Allotment Act provided for the division of tribal land into fee simple parcels owned by individual tribal members, that Act also mandated that such allotments would be held in trust for their owners by the United States for a period of 25 years — or longer, at the President's discretion — during which time the parcel owners had no authority to sell or convey the land. *See* 25 U.S.C. § 348. The 1908 Act released particular Indian owners from these restrictions ahead of schedule, vesting in them full fee ownership. In 1934, Congress passed the Indian Reorganization Act, 48 Stat. 984, 25 U.S.C. § 461 et seq., which "pu[t] an end to further allotment of reservation land," but did not "return allotted land to pre-General Allotment status, leaving it fully alienable by the allottees, their heirs, and assigns." *County of Yakima*, 502 U.S., at 264.

The tribal tort law the Longs are attempting to enforce, however, operates as a restraint on alienation. It "set[s] limits on how nonmembers may engage in commercial transactions," 491 F.3d, at 887 — and not just any transactions, but specifically nonmembers' sale of fee lands they own. It regulates the substantive terms on which the Bank is able to offer its fee land for sale. Respondents and their principal amicus, the United States, acknowledge that the tribal tort at issue here is a form of regulation. They argue the regulation is fully authorized by the first *Montana* exception. They are mistaken.

Montana does not permit Indian tribes to regulate the sale of non-Indian fee land. *Montana* and its progeny permit tribal regulation of nonmember conduct inside the reservation that implicates the tribe's sovereign interests. *Montana* expressly limits its first exception to the "activities of nonmembers," 450 U.S., at 565, allowing these to be regulated to the extent necessary "to protect tribal self-government [and] to control internal relations," *id.*, at 564.

We cited four cases in explanation of *Montana's* first exception. Each involved regulation of non-Indian activities on the reservation that had a discernable effect on the tribe or its members. . . .

Our cases since *Montana* have [permitted] regulation of certain forms of nonmember conduct on tribal land. We have upheld as within the tribe's sovereign authority the imposition of a severance tax on natural resources removed by nonmembers from tribal land. *See Merrion v. Jicarilla Apache Tribe*, 455 U.S. 130 (1982). We have approved tribal taxes imposed on leasehold interests held in tribal lands, as well as sales taxes imposed on nonmember businesses within the reservation. *See Kerr-McGee*, 471 U.S., at 196–197. We have similarly approved licensing requirements for hunting and fishing on tribal land. See *New Mexico v. Mescalero Apache Tribe*, 462 U.S. 324, 337 (1983).

Tellingly, with only "one minor exception, we have never upheld under *Montana* the extension of tribal civil authority over nonmembers on non-Indian land." *Hicks*, supra, at 360 (emphasis added). The exception is *Brendale v. Confederated Tribes and Bands of Yakima Nation*, 492 U.S. 408, and even it fits the general rubric noted above: In that case, we permitted a tribe to restrain particular uses of non-Indian fee land through zoning regulations. . . .

But again, whether or not we have permitted regulation of nonmember activity on non-Indian fee land in a given case, in no case have we found that *Montana* authorized a tribe to regulate the sale of such land. Rather, our *Montana* cases have always concerned nonmember conduct on the land. . . .[39]

The distinction between sale of the land and conduct on it is well-established in

---

[39] [1] JUSTICE GINSBURG questions this distinction between sales and activities on the ground that "[s]ales of land-and related conduct-are surely 'activities' within the ordinary sense of the word." Post, at 2729–2730. We think the distinction is readily understandable. In any event, the question is not whether a sale is, in some generic sense, an action. The question is whether land ownership and sale are "activities" within the meaning of *Montana* and the other cited precedents.

our precedent, as the foregoing cases demonstrate, and entirely logical given the limited nature of tribal sovereignty and the liberty interests of nonmembers. By virtue of their incorporation into the United States, the tribe's sovereign interests are now confined to managing tribal land, see *Worcester*, 6 Pet., at 561 (persons are allowed to enter Indian land only "with the assent of the [tribal members] themselves"), "protect[ing] tribal self-government," and "control[ling] internal relations," see *Montana*, supra, at 564. The logic of *Montana* is that certain activities on non-Indian fee land (say, a business enterprise employing tribal members) or certain uses (say, commercial development) may intrude on the internal relations of the tribe or threaten tribal self-rule. To the extent they do, such activities or land uses may be regulated. Put another way, certain forms of nonmember behavior, even on non-Indian fee land, may sufficiently affect the tribe as to justify tribal oversight. While tribes generally have no interest in regulating the conduct of nonmembers, then, they may regulate nonmember behavior that implicates tribal governance and internal relations.

The regulations we have approved under *Montana* all flow directly from these limited sovereign interests. The tribe's "traditional and undisputed power to exclude persons" from tribal land, *Duro*, 495 U.S., at 696, for example, gives it the power to set conditions on entry to that land via licensing requirements and hunting regulations. Much taxation can be justified on a similar basis. The power to tax certain nonmember activity can also be justified as "a necessary instrument of self-government and territorial management," *Merrion*, 455 U.S., at 137, insofar as taxation "enables a tribal government to raise revenues for its essential services," to pay its employees, to provide police protection, and in general to carry out the functions that keep peace and order, ibid.

JUSTICE GINSBURG wonders why these sorts of regulations are permissible under *Montana* but regulating the sale of fee land is not. The reason is that regulation of the sale of non-Indian fee land, unlike the above, cannot be justified by reference to the tribe's sovereign interests. By definition, fee land owned by nonmembers has already been removed from the tribe's immediate control. It has already been alienated from the tribal trust. The tribe cannot justify regulation of such land's sale by reference to its power to superintend tribal land, then, because non-Indian fee parcels have ceased to be tribal land.

Nor can regulation of fee land sales be justified by the tribe's interests in protecting internal relations and self-government. Any direct harm to its political integrity that the tribe sustains as a result of fee land sale is sustained at the point the land passes from Indian to non-Indian hands. It is at that point the tribe and its members lose the ability to use the land for their purposes. Once the land has been sold in fee simple to non-Indians and passed beyond the tribe's immediate control, the mere resale of that land works no additional intrusion on tribal relations or self-government. Resale, by itself, causes no additional damage.

This is not to suggest that the sale of the land will have no impact on the tribe. The uses to which the land is put may very well change from owner to owner, and those uses may well affect the tribe and its members. As our cases bear out, the tribe may quite legitimately seek to protect its members from noxious uses that threaten tribal welfare or security, or from nonmember conduct on the land that does the same. But the key point is that any threat to the tribe's sovereign interests flows from changed uses or nonmember activities, rather than from the mere fact of resale. The tribe is able fully to vindicate its sovereign interests in protecting its members and preserving tribal self-government by regulating nonmember activity on the land, within the limits set forth in our cases. The tribe has no independent interest in restraining alienation of the land itself, and thus, no authority to do so.

Not only is regulation of fee land sale beyond the tribe's sovereign powers, it runs the risk of subjecting nonmembers to tribal regulatory authority without commensurate consent. Tribal sovereignty, it should be remembered, is "a sovereignty outside the basic structure of the Constitution." *United States v. Lara*, 541 U.S. 193, 212 (2004) (KENNEDY, J., concurring in judgment). The Bill of Rights does not apply to Indian tribes. *See Talton v. Mayes*, 163 U.S. 376, 382–385 (1896). Indian courts "differ from traditional American courts in a number of significant respects." *Hicks*, 533 U.S., at 383 (SOUTER, J., concurring). And nonmembers have no part in tribal government — they have no say in the laws and regulations that govern tribal territory. Consequently, those laws and regulations may be fairly imposed on nonmembers only if the nonmember has consented, either expressly or by his actions. Even then, the regulation must stem from the tribe's inherent sovereign authority to set conditions on entry, preserve tribal self-government, or control internal relations. *See Montana*, 450 U.S., at 564.

. . . .

The Longs point out that the Bank in this case could hardly have been surprised by the Tribe's assertion of regulatory power over the parties' business dealings. The Bank, after all, had "lengthy on-reservation commercial relationships with the Long Company." But as we have emphasized repeatedly in this context, when it comes to tribal regulatory authority, it is not "in for a penny, in for a Pound." *Atkinson*, 532 U.S., at 656 (internal quotation marks omitted). The Bank may reasonably have anticipated that its various commercial dealings with the Longs could trigger tribal authority to regulate those transactions — a question we need not and do not decide. But there is no reason the Bank should have anticipated that its general business dealings with respondents would permit the Tribe to regulate the Bank's sale of land it owned in fee simple.

Even the courts below recognized that the Longs' discrimination claim was a "novel" one. It arose "directly from Lakota tradition as embedded in Cheyenne River Sioux tradition and custom," including the Lakota "sense of justice, fair play and decency to others." The upshot was to require the Bank to offer the same terms of sale to a prospective buyer who had defaulted in several previous transactions with the Bank as it offered to a different buyer without such a history of default. This is surely not a typical regulation. But whatever the Bank anticipated, whatever "consensual relationship" may have been established through the Bank's dealing with the Longs, the jurisdictional consequences of that relationship cannot extend to the Bank's subsequent sale of its fee land.

The Longs acknowledge, if obliquely, the critical importance of land status. They emphasize that the Long Company "operated on reservation fee and trust lands," and note that "the fee land at issue in the lease-repurchase agreement" had previously belonged to a tribal member. These facts, however, do not change the status of the land at the time of the challenged sale. Regardless of where the Long Company operated, the fee land whose sale the Longs seek to restrain was owned by the Bank at the relevant time. And indeed, before that, it was owned by Kenneth Long, a non-Indian.

The Longs attempt to salvage their position by arguing that the discrimination claim is best read to challenge the Bank's whole course of commercial dealings with the Longs stretching back over a decade — not just the sale of the fee land. That argument is unavailing. The Longs are the first to point out that their breach-of-contract and bad-faith claims, which do involve the Bank's course of dealings, are not before this Court. *Ibid.* Only the discrimination claim is before us and that claim is tied specifically to the sale of the fee land. As relief, the Longs claimed they "should get possession and title to their land back." The Longs' discrimination claim, in short, is an attempt to regulate the terms on which the Bank may sell the land it owns.

. . . .

Montana provides that, in certain circumstances, tribes may exercise authority over the conduct of nonmembers, even if that conduct takes place on non-Indian fee land. But conduct taking place on the land and the sale of the land are two very different things. The Cheyenne River Sioux Tribe lost the authority to restrain the sale of fee simple parcels inside their borders when the land was sold as part of the 1908 Allotment Act. Nothing in *Montana* gives it back.

C

Neither the District Court nor the Court of Appeals relied for its decision on the second *Montana* exception. . . . The second *Montana* exception stems from the same sovereign interests that give rise to the first, interests that do not reach to regulating the sale of non-Indian fee land.

The second exception authorizes the tribe to exercise civil jurisdiction when non-Indians' "conduct" menaces the "political integrity, the economic security, or the health or welfare of the tribe." The conduct must do more than injure the tribe, it must "imperil the subsistence" of the tribal community. *Ibid.* One commentator has noted that "th[e] elevated threshold for application of the second *Montana* exception suggests that tribal power must be necessary to avert catastrophic consequences." Cohen § 4.02[3][c], at 232, n. 220.

The sale of formerly Indian-owned fee land to a third party is quite possibly disappointing to the tribe, but cannot fairly be called "catastrophic" for tribal self-government. The land in question here has been owned by a non-Indian party for at least 50 years, during which time the project of tribal self-government has proceeded without interruption. The land's resale to another non-Indian hardly "imperil[s] the subsistence or welfare of the tribe." *Montana*, supra, at 566. Accordingly, we hold the second *Montana* exception inapplicable in this case.

D

Finally, we address the Longs' argument that the Bank consented to tribal court jurisdiction over the discrimination claim by seeking the assistance of tribal courts in serving a notice to quit. When the Longs refused to vacate the land, the Bank initiated eviction proceedings in South Dakota state court. The Bank then asked the Tribal Court to appoint a process server able to reach the Longs. Seeking the Tribal Court's aid in serving process on tribal members for a pending state-court action does not, we think, constitute consent to future litigation in the Tribal Court. Notably, when the Longs did file their complaint against the Bank in Tribal Court, the Bank promptly contended in its answer that the court lacked jurisdiction. Under these circumstances, we find that the Bank did not consent by its litigation conduct to tribal court jurisdiction over the Longs' discrimination claim.

The judgment of the Court of Appeals for the Eighth Circuit is reversed. It is so ordered.

JUSTICE GINSBURG, with whom JUSTICE STEVENS, JUSTICE SOUTER, and JUSTICE BREYER join, concurring in part, concurring in the judgment in part, and dissenting in part.

. . . .

I dissent from the Court's decision to the extent that it overturns the Tribal Court's principal judgment awarding the Longs damages in the amount of $750,000 plus interest. That judgment did not disturb the Bank's sale of fee land to non-Indians. It simply responded to the claim that the Bank, in its on-reservation commercial dealings with the Longs, treated them disadvantageously because of their tribal affiliation and racial identity. A claim of that genre, I would hold, is one the Tribal Court is competent to adjudicate. As the Court of Appeals correctly understood, the Longs' case, at heart, is not about "the sale of fee land on a tribal reservation by a non-Indian bank to non-Indian individuals." "Rather, this case is about the power of the Tribe to hold nonmembers like the bank to a minimum standard of fairness when they voluntarily deal with tribal members."

As the basis for their discrimination claim, the Longs essentially asserted that the Bank offered them terms and conditions on land-financing transactions less favorable than the terms and conditions offered to non-Indians. Although the Tribal Court could not reinstate the Longs as owners of the ranch lands that had been in their family for decades, that court could hold the Bank answerable in damages, the law's traditional remedy for the tortious injury the Longs experienced.

I

. . . .

Ronnie and Lila Long, husband and wife and owners of the Long Family Land and Cattle Company (Long Company), are enrolled members of the Cheyenne River Sioux Tribe. Although the Long Company was incorporated in South Dakota, the enterprise "was overwhelmingly tribal in character, as were its interactions with the bank." 491 F.3d, at 886. All Long Company property was situated — and all operations of the enterprise occurred — within the Cheyenne River Sioux Indian

Reservation. The Long Company's articles of incorporation required Indian ownership of a majority of the corporation's shares. This requirement reflected the Long Company's status as an Indian-owned business entity eligible for Bureau of Indian Affairs (BIA) loan guarantees. *See* 25 CFR § 103.25 (2007) (requiring at least 51% Indian ownership). Loan guarantees are among the incentives the BIA offers to promote the development of on-reservation Indian enterprises. The Long Company "was formed to take advantage of [the] BIA incentives."

The history of the Bank's commercial dealings with the Long Company and the Long family is lengthy and complex. The business relationship dates from 1988, when Ronnie Long's parents — one of them a member of the Tribe — mortgaged some 2,230 acres of land to the Bank to gain working capital for the ranch. As security for the Bank's loans over the years, the Longs mortgaged both their land and their personal property. The Bank benefited significantly from the Long Company's status as an Indian-owned business entity, for the BIA loan guarantees "allowed [it] to greatly reduce its lending risk." Ibid. Eventually, the Bank collected from the BIA almost $400,000, more than 80% of the net losses resulting from its loans to the Longs.

The discrimination claim here at issue rests on the allegedly unfair conditions the Bank exacted from the Longs when they sought loans to sustain the operation of their ranch. Following the death of Ronnie's father, the Bank and the Longs entered into an agreement under which the mortgaged land would be deeded over to the Bank in exchange for the Bank's canceling some debt and making additional loans to keep the ranch in business. The Longs were given a two-year lease on the property with an option to buy the land back when the lease term expired. Negotiating sessions for these arrangements were held at the Tribe's on-reservation offices and were facilitated by tribal officers and BIA employees.

Viewing the deal they were given in comparative light, the Longs charged that the Bank offered to resell ranch land to them on terms less advantageous than those the Bank offered in similar dealings with non-Indians. Their claim, all courts prior to this one found, fit within the *Montana* exception for "activities of nonmembers who enter [into] . . . commercial dealing, contracts, leases, or other arrangements" with tribal members. 450 U.S., at 565. I am convinced that the courts below got it right.

This case, it bears emphasis, involves no unwitting outsider forced to litigate under unfamiliar rules and procedures in tribal court. Hardly a stranger to the tribal court system, the Bank regularly filed suit in that forum. The Bank enlisted tribal-court aid to serve notice to quit on the Longs in connection with state-court eviction proceedings. The Bank later filed a counterclaim for eviction and motion for summary judgment in the case the Longs commenced in the Tribal Court. In its summary judgment motion, the Bank stated, without qualification, that the Tribal Court "ha[d] jurisdiction over the subject matter of this action." Had the Bank wanted to avoid responding in tribal court or the application of tribal law, the means were readily at hand: The Bank could have included forum selection, choice-of-law, or arbitration clauses in its agreements with the Longs, which the Bank drafted.

II

Resolving this case on a ground neither argued nor addressed below, the Court holds that a tribe may not impose any regulation — not even a nondiscrimination requirement — on a bank's dealings with tribal members regarding on-reservation fee lands. I do not read *Montana* or any other case so to instruct, and find the Court's position perplexing.

First, I question the Court's separation of land sales tied to lending activities from other "activities of nonmembers who enter consensual relationships with the tribe or its members," *Montana*, 450 U.S., at 565. Sales of land — and related conduct — are surely "activities" within the ordinary sense of the word.

Second, the Court notes the absence of any case "f[i]nd[ing] that *Montana* authorized a tribe to regulate the sale of [non-Indian fee] land." But neither have we held that *Montana* prohibits all such regulation. If the Court in *Montana*, or later cases, had intended to remove land sales resulting from loan transactions entirely from tribal governance, it could have spoken plainly to that effect. Instead, *Montana* listed as examples of consensual relationships that tribes might have authority to regulate "commercial dealing, contracts, [and] leases." 450 U.S., at 565. Presumably, the reference to "leases" includes leases of fee land. But why should a nonmember's lease of fee land to a member be differentiated, for *Montana* exception purposes, from a sale of the same land? And why would the enforcement of an antidiscrimination command be less important to tribal self-rule and dignity when the command relates to land sales than when it relates to other commercial relationships between nonmembers and members?

. . . .

For the reasons stated, I would leave undisturbed the Tribal Court's initial judgment, see App. 194–196, awarding the Longs damages, prejudgment interest, and costs as redress for the Bank's breach of contract, bad faith, and discrimination. Accordingly, I would affirm in large part the judgment of the Court of Appeals.

NOTES

1. **Case Commentary:** Commentary on the *Plains Commerce Bank* opinion has been critical. One of the critics is Professor Frank Pommersheim, who also sits as a Justice of the Cheyenne River Sioux Tribal Court, and wrote the unanimous decision for that court that the Supreme Court effectively set aside. As Pommersheim has noted, the rule of *Plains Commerce Bank* was narrow, holding that *Montana* does not authorize tribes to exercise jurisdiction over the sale of non-Indian fee land. Frank Pommersheim, Plains Commerce Bank v. Long Family Land and Cattle Company, Inc.: *An Introduction with Questions*, 54 S.D. L. Rev. 365 (2009). In the first Indian law case to be decided after Chief Justice Roberts and Justice Alito joined the Court, Pommersheim sees troubling signs, concluding: "The Court, it would seem remains adrift from both law and equity, as well as the reality of economic development in Indian country, which requires certainty, predictability, and respect for tribal institutions." *Id.* at 373–74. Both *Hicks* and *Plains Commerce Bank* have narrowed the role of tribal courts on Indian reservations. Can they

continue to play an important role on Indian reservations? What role?

Despite the Court's decision in *Plains Commerce*, the dispute seemingly remains unsettled. Four years after Supreme Court ruled on the case, Long Family Land and Cattle Company, Inc., and the Longs filed another action in the Cheyenne River Sioux Tribal Court against Plains Commerce Bank, seeking to collect on the appeal bond executed by the tribal court in its original 2003 holding. The Longs asserted that because the Bank did not appeal from the tribal court jury verdict, the Bank still owes the entire amount awarded, plus interest. The Bank appealed to the United States District Court for the District of South Dakota, seeking to enjoin any tribal court action for lack of jurisdiction.

The District Court deferred to the tribal court, citing the doctrine of tribal court exhaustion and comity interests, but cautioned: "If the Tribal Court somehow were to determine that, notwithstanding the apparent contemplation of the Supreme Court, [that the original verdict was valid, but based on other claims], this Court could foresee an action similar to this one being started anew. If, however, the Tribal Court . . . conducts a new jury trial on the damages to which the Longs are entitled on the breach of contract and contractual bad faith claims, then there may be no more proceedings in this Court." *Plains Commerce Bank v. Long Family Land and Cattle Co., Inc.*, 910 F. Supp. 2d 1188, 1199 (D.S.D. 2012). Why might the District Court holding urge the Tribal Court to adopt federal approaches to determining the validity of damages claims? Is this something that the Supreme Court's holding in *Plains Commerce Bank* implicitly encourages?

Water Wheel Camp Recreational Area, Inc. v. LaRance, 642 F.3d 802 (9th Cir. 2011): In 1975, the Colorado River Indian Tribes (CRIT) and Water Wheel Camp Recreational Area, Inc. (Water Wheel) entered into a 32-year business lease of 26 acres of CRIT reservation trust land along the Colorado River. A closely held corporation controlled by Robert Johnson (a non-Indian), Water Wheel operated a resort on the leased land, collecting rent from subtenants and paying rent to CRIT. When negotiations for renewal of the lease failed in 2001, Water Wheel stopped making payments as required under the lease; and when the lease expired in July 2007, Water Wheel refused to vacate or pay further rent to CRIT, but continued collecting funds from the resort patrons. CRIT therefore brought an action for unlawful detainer, breach of lease, and trespass in tribal court. The tribal court found it had jurisdiction over Water Wheel and Johnson and entered judgment in favor of the Tribe. For Water Wheel, the tribal court relied on *Montana's* first exception — that the resort company had entered into a consensual relationship with the Tribe through commercial dealings. For Johnson, the tribal court relied on *Montana's* first exception, combined with the fact that Johnson had "minimum contacts" with CRIT and its territory. While the case was still pending before the tribal court, Johnson and Water Wheel sued in federal court, challenging both the Tribe's right to evict them and the jurisdiction of the CRIT tribal courts. The federal district court rejected the Tribe's argument that its inherent power to exclude provides a basis for jurisdiction over Johnson independent of *Montana*, and therefore upheld tribal civil jurisdiction over Water Wheel, but not Johnson.

On appeal, the Ninth Circuit affirmed as to Water Wheel, but reversed the decision denying tribal civil jurisdiction over Johnson. The Ninth Circuit opined:

In considering the extent of a tribe's civil authority over non-Indians on tribal land, we first acknowledge the long-standing rule that Indian tribes possess inherent sovereign powers, including the authority to exclude, *New Mexico v. Mescalero Apache Tribe*, 462 U.S. 324, 333 (1983). . . . From a tribe's inherent sovereign powers flow lesser powers, including the power to regulate non-Indians on tribal land. . . .

The CRIT and the United States, through its amicus brief, argue that *Montana* does not apply to this case. Their position is that the CRIT's inherent authority to exclude provides regulatory jurisdiction over Water Wheel and Johnson and that there are no competing state interests at play that might otherwise trigger *Montana's* application. They further suggest that because regulatory jurisdiction exists and neither Congress nor the Supreme Court have said otherwise, the tribal court may also exercise adjudicative jurisdiction. We agree.

[T]he Supreme Court has recognized that a tribe's power to exclude exists independently of its general jurisdictional authority. *See Duro v. Reina*, 495 U.S. 676, 696–97 (1990). *Montana* limited the tribe's ability to exercise its power to exclude only as applied to the regulation of non-Indians on non-Indian land, not on tribal land. *See Merrion v. Jicarilla Apache Tribe*, 455 U.S. 130, 144–45 (1982). Here, through its sovereign authority over tribal land, the CRIT had power to exclude Water Wheel and Johnson, who were trespassers on the tribe's land and had violated the conditions of their entry. Having established that the tribe had the power to exclude, we next consider whether it had the power to regulate them unless Congress has said otherwise, or unless the Supreme Court has recognized that such power conflicts with federal interests promoting tribal self-government. *Iowa Mut. Ins. Co.*, 480 U.S. at 18 . . . .

In this instance, where the non-Indian activity in question occurred on tribal land, the activity interfered directly with the tribe's inherent powers to exclude and manage its own lands, and there are no competing state interests at play, the tribe's status as landowner is enough to support regulatory jurisdiction without considering *Montana*. Finding otherwise would contradict Supreme Court precedent establishing that land ownership may sometimes be dispositive and would improperly limit tribal sovereignty without clear direction from Congress.

2. Civil Jurisdiction over Non-Members: The Tenth Circuit Court of Appeals also addressed the issue of tribal court jurisdiction over a nonmember in *Crowe & Dunlevy, P.C. v. Stidham*, 640 F.3d 1140 (10th Cir. 2011). The Court affirmed the district court's ruling and found that a nonmember attorney had not entered a "consensual relationship" with the Muscogee (Creek) Nation by enrolling in its bar association and practicing before its courts, where there was no "nexus" between that relationship and the exertion of tribal authority, which concerned an order to return attorney's fees already paid pursuant to a contract with another federally-recognized Indian tribe. The Court noted that the Tribe in question (the Thlopth-locco Tribe) did not want Crowe to return the funds, and found that "[f]or ancillary jurisdiction over Crowe as a nonmember of the tribe to be appropriate under the consensual relationship exception to *Montana*, the dispute before the tribal court must arise directly out of that consensual relationship." In this case, Crowe's consensual relationship with the Thlopthlocco tribal government had "nothing to do with Crowe attorneys' consensual relationship with the Creek Nation based on their Bar membership."

In *Dolgencorp v. Mississippi Band of Choctaw Indians*, 746 F.3d 167, 173 (5th Cir. 2014), the employee of a non-Indian store operator sexually assaulted a tribal member child who was interning at the store. The Fifth Circuit Court of Appeals, upholding the tribal court's exercise of jurisdiction over the store operator, wrote that *Plains Commerce Bank* did not narrow *Montana's* consensual relationship exception to limit tribal regulation of nonmembers to only reach conduct that implicated tribal government and internal relations. As the Court noted in *Dolgencorp*, no court has interpreted *Plains Commerce* to limit the consensual relationship exception in this manner. In two recent cases from Arizona, the federal district court relied upon the *Montana*, *Strate*, and *Plains Commerce* decisions to find that tribal courts lacked civil jurisdiction over nonmembers.

In *Rolling Frito-Lay Sales LP v. Stover*, a nonmember was injured in a slip and fall accident in a store owned by a tribal member on the Salt River Pima-Maricopa Indian Reservation. 2012 U.S. Dist. LEXIS 9555 (D. Ariz. Jan. 26, 2012). Stover initially filed her claim against the tribal member, the store, and Rolling Frito-Lay Sales, a non-Indian limited partnership that provided products to the store, in state court. The state court dismissed the claims against the tribal member and store for lack of jurisdiction and then dismissed the claim against Rolling Frito-Lay Sales, due to lack of prosecution. Stover then brought an action in Salt River Tribal Court against plaintiff, Rolling Frito-Lay Sales. In turn, Rolling Frito-Lay Sales filed an action in federal district court to enjoin Stover from proceeding in tribal court. Judge Martone granted the motion, finding that Plaintiff could not be sued in tribal court because neither of the *Montana* exceptions applied and she had adequate remedies in state court. The court ruled that the location of the store on tribal land was not relevant to this case because the tribal court presumptively lacks jurisdiction over nonmembers unless one of the exceptions is met. Judge Martone also ruled that Stover could assert her claim against the tribal member and store in the tribal court.

In *EXC, Inc. v. Jensen*, a tour bus chartered by EXC, Inc. was traveling within the boundaries of the Navajo Nation as part of a 12-day tour when the bus collided with a passenger vehicle, killing the driver of the vehicle and causing substantial injury to the other two passengers, one of whom was pregnant, but suffered a miscarriage. 2012 U.S. Dist. LEXIS 112153 (D. Ariz. Aug. 9, 2012). All three victims were members of the Navajo Nation and the accident occurred within the boundaries of the Navajo reservation on a state highway right-of-way granted by the federal government over Navajo Nation land. Navajo emergency and law enforcement personnel tended to the accident victims and conducted the investigation in cooperation with the Arizona Department of Public Safety. The *Jensen* Defendants filed claims against Plaintiff EXC, Inc. in Kayenta District Court, and the Navajo Nation Supreme Court upheld the Kayenta District Court's ruling that it had jurisdiction over the company.

Plaintiffs then filed in federal district court to enjoin the tribal court proceeding for lack of jurisdiction. Defendants moved to dismiss for failure to exhaust remedies, but the court held that exhaustion of remedies would be futile, leading both Plaintiffs and Defendants to move for summary judgment on the jurisdictional issue. Judge Teilborg granted summary judgment to EXC, Inc., finding that the Navajo Nation had not reserved any right to exercise dominion or control over the state highway, and thus the case fell squarely within the *Montana* analysis. The court found that the Navajo Nation's treaty did not "grant" jurisdiction over a tort action arising on a highway under these circumstances, and further ruled that neither of the *Montana* exceptions supported a finding of jurisdiction over Plaintiff. The court acknowledged that Plaintiff had violated Navajo law by its failure to apply to the Navajo Nation for a tour permit, provide proof of liability insurance, and comply with the other provisions of the Navajo Nation Tour and Guide Services Act. Under the terms of the Act, the permit process specifically requires applicants to consent to the jurisdiction of the Navajo Nation courts for all activities undertaken on the Navajo Nation. The court conflated the Navajo Nation's right to exclude, as a landowner, with its inherent sovereign authority, finding that the permit application could not give rise to a "consensual relationship" under *Montana* because the land in question belonged to the state. The court further found the Navajo Nation's interest in traffic safety to be too general to justify a finding, under *Montana's* second exception, of a serious intrusion on the political integrity or health and welfare of the tribe.

3. The Exhaustion Requirement: The federal circuit courts have upheld the exhaustion requirement in several notable recent cases. In *Grand Canyon Skywalk Dev., LLC v. 'Sa'Nyu Wa Inc.*, 715 F.3d 1196 (9th Cir. 2013), the Ninth Circuit Court of Appeals upheld the district court's ruling requiring a Nevada development corporation to exhaust its remedies in the Hualapai Tribal Court before seeking a declaratory judgment from the federal courts that the Hualapai Tribe lacked the authority to condemn the Nevada corporation's intangible property rights under a revenue sharing contract with the tribe. The Circuit Court rejected the corporation's argument that the tribal court would be politically influenced by the tribal council and held that the case did not justify applying the exceptions to the exhaustion requirement that pertain in cases where "bad faith" exists or the requirement would be "futile." The Court further ruled that the "tribal court did not plainly lack jurisdiction" so as to excuse the exhaustion requirement.

In *DISH Network v. Laducer*, 725 F.3d 877 (8th Cir. 2013), a member of the Turtle Mountain Chippewa Tribe brought suit in tribal court against DISH network for abuse of process after the company charged his daughter's credit card for his alleged breach of a satellite TV contract and then brought a federal court action to enforce its remedies. The company moved to dismiss the tribal court action, but the Eighth Circuit Court of Appeals held that DISH Network must first exhaust all remedies in the Turtle Mountain Tribal Court, finding that it is "not 'plain' that a tribal court lacks authority to exercise jurisdiction over tort claims closely related to contractual relationships between Indians and non-Indians on matters occurring on tribal lands."

DISH Network has also challenged the Hopi Tribe's attempt to impose its business license requirement on the company in connection with satellite TV services provided to tribal members on the Hopi reservation. The company asserted that the tax is preempted by the federal Communications Act of 1934, which regulates the provision of such services throughout the country. Without ruling on the merits of the preemption issue, the federal district court in Arizona held that the company was required to exhaust its remedies in tribal court before bringing the jurisdictional challenge in federal court. *DISH Network v. Tewa*, 2012 U.S. Dist. LEXIS 156631 (D. Ariz. Nov. 1, 2012).

However, in *Evans v. Shoshone-Bannock* 736 F.3d 1298 (9th Cir. 2013), a non-Indian who owned property in fee within the boundaries of the reservation, and was building a home on his land, refused to obtain requisite tribal building permits and licenses or pay permitting fees. The Ninth Circuit held that it was not necessary for him to exhaust remedies in tribal court, stating that because he was a non-Indian owner on fee land, the tribe's efforts to regulate his conduct were "presumptively invalid."

2. Congressional Acknowledgment of Inherent Tribal Sovereignty

UNITED STATES v. LARA
United States Supreme Court
541 U.S. 193 (2004)

JUSTICE BREYER delivered the opinion of the Court.

This case concerns a congressional statute "recogniz[ing] and affirm[ing]" the "inherent" authority of a tribe to bring a criminal misdemeanor prosecution against an Indian who is not a member of that tribe-authority that this Court previously held a tribe did not possess. Compare 25 U.S.C. § 1301(2) with *Duro v. Reina*, 495 U.S. 676 (1990). We must decide whether Congress has the constitutional power to relax restrictions that the political branches have, over time, placed on the exercise of a tribe's inherent legal authority. We conclude that Congress does possess this power.

I

Respondent Billy Jo Lara is an enrolled member of the Turtle Mountain Band of Chippewa Indians in north-central North Dakota. He married a member of a different tribe, the Spirit Lake Tribe, and lived with his wife and children on the Spirit Lake Reservation, also located in North Dakota. After several incidents of serious misconduct, the Spirit Lake Tribe issued an order excluding him from the reservation. Lara ignored the order; federal officers stopped him; and he struck one of the arresting officers.

The Spirit Lake Tribe subsequently prosecuted Lara in the Spirit Lake Tribal Court for "violence to a policeman." Lara pleaded guilty and, in respect to that crime, served 90 days in jail.

After Lara's tribal conviction, the federal government charged Lara in the

Federal District Court for the District of North Dakota with the federal crime of assaulting a federal officer. 18 U.S.C. § 111(a)(1). Key elements of this federal crime mirror elements of the tribal crime of "violence to a policeman." And this similarity between the two crimes would ordinarily have brought Lara within the protective reach of the Double Jeopardy Clause. U.S. Const., Amdt. 5 (the Government may not "subject" any person "for the same offense to be twice put in jeopardy of life or limb"). But the Government, responding to Lara's claim of double jeopardy, pointed out that the Double Jeopardy Clause does not bar successive prosecutions brought by separate sovereigns, and it argued that this "dual sovereignty" doctrine determined the outcome here. *See Heath v. Alabama*, 474 U.S. 82, 88 (1985) (the Double Jeopardy Clause reflects the "common-law conception of crime as an offense against the sovereignty of the government"; when "a defendant in a single act violates the 'peace and dignity' of two sovereigns by breaking the laws of each, he has committed two distinct 'offenses' ").

. . . .

II

We assume, as do the parties, that Lara's double jeopardy claim turns on the answer to the "dual sovereignty" question. What is "the source of [the] power to punish" nonmember Indian offenders, "inherent tribal sovereignty" or delegated federal authority?

We also believe that Congress intended the former answer. The statute says that it "recognize[s] and affirm[s]" in each tribe the "inherent" tribal power (not delegated federal power) to prosecute nonmember Indians for misdemeanors.

Thus the statute seeks to adjust the tribes' status. It relaxes the restrictions, recognized in Duro, that the political branches had imposed on the tribes' exercise of inherent prosecutorial power. The question before us is whether the Constitution authorizes Congress to do so. Several considerations lead us to the conclusion that Congress does possess the constitutional power to lift the restrictions on the tribes' criminal jurisdiction over nonmember Indians as the statute seeks to do.

First, the Constitution grants Congress broad general powers to legislate in respect to Indian tribes, powers that we have consistently described as "plenary and exclusive." *E.g., Washington v. Confederated Bands and Tribes of Yakima Nation*, 439 U.S. 463, 470–471 (1979); *Negonsott v. Samuels*, 507 U.S. 99, 103, (1993); see *Wheeler*, 435 U.S., at 323; *see also* W. Canby, American Indian Law 2 (3d ed. 1998) (hereinafter Canby) ("[T]he independence of the tribes is subject to exceptionally great powers of Congress to regulate and modify the status of the tribes").

This Court has traditionally identified the Indian Commerce Clause, U.S. Const., Art. I, § 8, cl. 3, and the Treaty Clause, Art. II, § 2, cl. 2, as sources of that power. E.g., *Morton v. Mancari*, 417 U.S. 535, 552 (1974); *McClanahan v. Arizona Tax Comm'n*, 411 U.S. 164, 172, n. 7 (1973); see also Canby 11–12; F. Cohen, Handbook of Federal Indian Law 209–210 (1982 ed.) (hereinafter Cohen) (also mentioning, inter alia, the Property Clause). The "central function of the Indian Commerce Clause," we have said, "is to provide Congress with plenary power to legislate in the field of Indian affairs." *Cotton Petroleum Corp. v. New Mexico*, 490 U.S. 163, 192

(1989); *see also, e.g., Ramah Navajo School Bd., Inc. v. Bureau of Revenue of N.M.*, 458 U.S. 832, 837 (1982) ("broad power" under the Indian Commerce Clause); *White Mountain Apache Tribe v. Bracker*, 448 U.S. 136, 142(1980) (same, and citing *Wheeler, supra*, at 322–323).

The treaty power does not literally authorize Congress to act legislatively, for it is an Article II power authorizing the President, not Congress, "to make Treaties." U.S. Const., Art. II, § 2, cl. 2. But, as Justice Holmes pointed out, treaties made pursuant to that power can authorize Congress to deal with "matters" with which otherwise "Congress could not deal." *Missouri v. Holland*, 252 U.S. 416, 433 (1920); see also L. Henkin, Foreign Affairs and the U.S. Constitution 72 (2d ed.1996). And for much of the Nation's history, treaties, and legislation made pursuant to those treaties, governed relations between the federal government and the Indian tribes. *See, e.g.*, Cohen 109–111; F. Prucha, American Indian Policy in the Formative Years 44–49 (1962).

We recognize that in 1871 Congress ended the practice of entering into treaties with the Indian tribes. 25 U.S.C. § 71 (stating that tribes are not entities "with whom the United States may contract by treaty"). But the statute saved existing treaties from being "invalidated or impaired," and this Court has explicitly stated that the statute "in no way affected Congress' plenary powers to legislate on problems of Indians." *Antoine v. Washington*, 420 U.S. 194 (1975) (emphasis deleted).

Moreover, "at least during the first century of America's national existence . . . Indian affairs were more an aspect of military and foreign policy than a subject of domestic or municipal law." Cohen 208 (footnotes omitted). Insofar as that is so, Congress's legislative authority would rest in part, not upon "affirmative grants of the Constitution," but upon the Constitution's adoption of preconstitutional powers necessarily inherent in any federal government, namely powers that this Court has described as "necessary concomitants of nationality." *cf.* 2 J. Continental Cong. 174–175 (1775) (W. Ford ed. 1905) (creating departments of Indian affairs, appointing Indian commissioners, and noting the great importance of "securing and preserving the friendship of the Indian Nations"); *Worcester v. Georgia*, 6 Pet. 515, 557 (1832) ("The treaties and laws of the United States contemplate . . . that all intercourse with [Indians] shall be carried on exclusively by the government of the union").

Second, Congress, with this Court's approval, has interpreted the Constitution's "plenary" grants of power as authorizing it to enact legislation that both restricts and, in turn, relaxes those restrictions on tribal sovereign authority. From the Nation's beginning, Congress's need for such legislative power would have seemed obvious. After all, the Government's Indian policies, applicable to numerous tribes with diverse cultures, affecting billions of acres of land, of necessity would fluctuate dramatically as the needs of the Nation and those of the tribes changed over time. *See, e.g.*, Cohen 48. And Congress has in fact authorized at different times very different Indian policies (some with beneficial results but many with tragic consequences). Congressional policy, for example, initially favored "Indian removal," then "assimilation" and the break-up of tribal lands, then protection of the tribal land base (interrupted by a movement toward greater state involvement and "termination" of recognized tribes); and it now seeks greater tribal autonomy within the framework of a "government-to-government relationship" with federal agencies. 59 Fed. Reg. 22951 (1994); see also 19 Weekly Comp. of Pres. Doc. 98 (1983) (President Reagan reaffirming the rejection of termination as a policy and announcing the goal of decreasing tribal dependence on the federal government); see 25 U.S.C. § 450a(b) (congressional commitment to "the development of strong and stable tribal governments"). See generally, Cohen 78–202 (describing this history); Canby 13–32 (same).

Such major policy changes inevitably involve major changes in the metes and bounds of tribal sovereignty. The 1871 statute, for example, changed the status of an Indian tribe from a "powe[r] . . . capable of making treaties" to a "power with whom the United States may [not] contract by treaty." *Compare Worcester, supra*, at 559, *with* 25 U.S.C. § 71.

One can readily find examples in congressional decisions to recognize, or to terminate, the existence of individual tribes. *See United States v. Holliday*, 3 Wall. 407, 419 (1866) ("If by [the political branches] those Indians are recognized as a tribe, this court must do the same"); *Menominee Tribe v. United States*, 391 U.S. 404 (1968) (examining the rights of Menominee Indians following the termination of their Tribe). Indeed, Congress has restored previously extinguished tribal status — by re-recognizing a Tribe whose tribal existence it previously had terminated. 25 U.S.C. §§ 903–903f (restoring the Menominee Tribe); *cf. United States v. Long*, 324 F.3d 475 (8th Cir.) (upholding against double jeopardy challenge successive prosecutions by the restored Menominee Tribe and the federal government), cert. denied, 540 U.S. 822. Congress has advanced policies of integration by conferring United States citizenship upon all Indians. 8 U.S.C. § 1401(b). Congress has also granted tribes greater autonomy in their inherent law enforcement authority (in respect to tribal members) by increasing the maximum criminal penalties tribal courts may impose. § 4217, 100 Stat. 3207-146, codified at 25 U.S.C. § 1302(7) (raising the maximum from "a term of six months and a fine of $500" to "a term of one year and a fine of $5,000").

Third, Congress's statutory goal — to modify the degree of autonomy enjoyed by a dependent sovereign that is not a State — is not an unusual legislative objective. The political branches, drawing upon analogous constitutional authority, have made adjustments to the autonomous status of other such dependent entities — sometimes making far more radical adjustments than those at issue here. *See, e.g.*, Hawai'i — *Hawaii v. Mankichi*, 190 U.S. 197, 209–210 (1903) (describing annexation of Hawai'i by joint resolution of Congress and the maintenance of a "Republic of Hawaii" until formal incorporation by Congress); Northern Mariana Islands — note following 48 U.S.C. § 1801 ("in accordance with the [United Nations] trusteeship agreement . . . [establishing] a self-governing commonwealth . . . in political union with and under the sovereignty of the United States"); the Philippines — 22 U.S.C. § 1394 (congressional authorization for the president to "withdraw and surrender all right of . . . sovereignty" and to "recognize the independence of the Philippine Islands as a separate and self-governing nation"); Presidential Proclamation No. 2695, 60 Stat. 1352 (so proclaiming); Puerto Rico — Act of July 3, 1950, 64 Stat. 319 ("[T]his Act is now adopted in the nature of a compact so that people of Puerto Rico may organize a government pursuant to a constitution of their own adoption"); P.R.

Const., Art. I, § 1 ("Estado Libre Asociado de Puerto Rico"); see also *Cordova & Simonpietri Ins. Agency Inc. v. Chase Manhattan Bank N.A.*, 649 F.2d 36, 39–41 (C.A. 1 1981) (describing various adjustments to Puerto Rican autonomy through congressional legislation since 1898).

Fourth, Lara points to no explicit language in the Constitution suggesting a limitation on Congress's institutional authority to relax restrictions on tribal sovereignty previously imposed by the political branches.

Fifth, the change at issue here is a limited one. It concerns a power similar in some respects to the power to prosecute a tribe's own members — a power that this Court has called "inherent." *Wheeler*, 435 U.S., at 322–323. In large part it concerns a tribe's authority to control events that occur upon the tribe's own land. See *United States v. Mazurie*, 419 U.S. 544, 557 (1975) ("Indian tribes are unique aggregations possessing attributes of sovereignty over both their members and their territory" (emphasis added)); see also, e.g., S. Rep. No. 102-168, at 21. And the tribes' possession of this additional criminal jurisdiction is consistent with our traditional understanding of the tribes' status as "domestic dependent nations." See *Cherokee Nation v. Georgia*, 5 Pet. 1, 16, 17 (1831) (describing tribe as "a distinct political society, separated from others, capable of managing its own affairs and governing itself") . . . In particular, this case involves no interference with the power or authority of any State. Nor do we now consider the question whether the Constitution's Due Process or Equal Protection Clauses prohibit tribes from prosecuting a nonmember citizen of the United States.

Sixth, our conclusion that Congress has the power to relax the restrictions imposed by the political branches on the tribes' inherent prosecutorial authority is consistent with our earlier cases . . .

To the contrary, *Oliphant* and *Duro* make clear that the Constitution does not dictate the metes and bounds of tribal autonomy, nor do they suggest that the Court should second-guess the political branches' own determinations. In *Oliphant*, the Court rested its conclusion about inherent tribal authority to prosecute tribe members in large part upon "the commonly shared presumption of Congress, the Executive Branch, and lower federal courts," a presumption which, "[w]hile not conclusive . . . [,] carries considerable weight." The Court pointed out that " 'Indian law' draws principally upon the treaties drawn and executed by the Executive Branch and legislation passed by Congress." It added that those "instruments, . . . form the backdrop for the intricate web of judicially made Indian law."

Similarly, in *Duro*, the Court drew upon a host of different sources in order to reach its conclusion that a tribe does not possess the inherent power to prosecute a nonmember. The Court referred to historic practices, the views of experts, the experience of forerunners of modern tribal courts, and the published opinions of the Solicitor of the Department of the Interior. *See also, e.g., Nevada v. Hicks*, 533 U.S. 353, 361, n. 4 (2001) ("Our holding in *Worcester* must be considered in light of . . . the 1828 treaty" (internal alterations and quotation marks omitted)); *South Dakota v. Bourland*, 508 U.S. 679, 695 (1993) ("Having concluded that Congress clearly abrogated the Tribe's pre-existing regulatory control over non-Indian hunting and fishing, we find no evidence in the relevant treaties or statutes that Congress intended to allow the Tribes to assert regulatory jurisdiction over these lands pursuant to inherent sovereignty" (emphasis added)); *National Farmers Union Ins. Cos. v. Crow Tribe*, 471 U.S. 845, 855–856 (1985) ("[T]he existence and extent of a tribal court's jurisdiction will require [inter alia] a detailed study of relevant statutes, Executive Branch policy as embodied in treaties and elsewhere, and administrative or judicial decisions"); *United States v. Kagama*, 118 U.S. 375, 383 (1886) (characterizing *Ex parte Crow Dog*, 109 U.S. 556, 570 (1883) as resting on extant treaties and statutes and recognizing congressional overruling of *Crow Dog*).

Thus, the Court in these cases based its descriptions of inherent tribal authority upon the sources as they existed at the time the Court issued its decisions. Congressional legislation constituted one such important source. And that source was subject to change. Indeed *Duro* itself anticipated change by inviting interested parties to "address the problem [to] Congress."

We concede that *Duro*, like several other cases, referred only to the need to obtain a congressional statute that "delegated" power to the tribes. But in so stating, *Duro* (like the other cases) simply did not consider whether a statute, like the present one, could constitutionally achieve the same end by removing restrictions on the tribes' inherent authority. Consequently we do not read any of these cases as holding that the Constitution forbids Congress to change "judicially made" federal Indian law through this kind of legislation. Cf. *County of Oneida v. Oneida Indian Nation of N.Y.*, 470 U.S. 226, 233–237 (1985) (recognizing the "federal common law" component of Indian rights, which "common law" federal courts develop as "a 'necessary expedient' when Congress has not 'spoken to a particular issue.' ")

Wheeler, *Oliphant*, and *Duro*, then, are not determinative because Congress has enacted a new statute, relaxing restrictions on the bounds of the inherent tribal authority that the United States recognizes. And that fact makes all the difference.

III

Lara makes several additional arguments. First, he points out that the Indian Civil Rights Act of 1968, 82 Stat. 77, lacks certain constitutional protections for criminal defendants, in particular the right of an indigent defendant to counsel. See 25 U.S.C. § 1302. And he argues that the Due Process Clause forbids Congress to permit a tribe to prosecute a nonmember Indian citizen of the United States in a forum that lacks this protection. *See Argersinger v. Hamlin*, 407 U.S. 25 (1972) (Constitution guarantees indigents counsel where imprisonment possible).

Lara's due process argument, however, suffers from a critical structural defect. . . . That argument (if valid) would show that any prosecution of a nonmember Indian under the statute is invalid; so Lara's tribal prosecution would be invalid, too. Showing Lara's tribal prosecution was invalid, however, does not show that the source of that tribal prosecution was federal power (showing that a state prosecution violated the Due Process Clause does not make that prosecution federal). But without that "federal power" showing, Lara cannot win his double jeopardy claim here. Hence, we need not, and we shall not, consider the merits of Lara's due process claim. . . .

Second, Lara argues that Congress's use of the words "all Indians," in the statutory phrase "inherent power . . . to exercise criminal jurisdiction over all Indians," violates the Equal Protection Clause. He says that insofar as the words include nonmember Indians within the statute's scope (while excluding all non-Indians) the statute is race-based and without justification. Like the due process argument, however, this equal protection argument is simply beside the point, therefore we do not address it. At best for Lara, the argument (if valid) would show, not that Lara's first conviction was federal, but that it was constitutionally defective. And that showing cannot help Lara win his double jeopardy claim.

Third, Lara points out that the *Duro* Court found the absence of certain constitutional safeguards, for example, the guarantee of an indigent's right to counsel, as an important reason for concluding that tribes lacked the "inherent power" to try a "group of citizens" (namely nonmember Indians) who were not "include[d]" in those "political bodies." In fact, *Duro* says the following: "We hesitate to adopt a view of tribal sovereignty that would single out another group of citizens, nonmember Indians, for trial by political bodies that do not include them." But this argument simply repeats the due process and equal protection arguments rejected above in a somewhat different form. Since precisely the same problem would exist were we to treat the congressional statute as delegating federal power, this argument helps Lara no more than the others.

IV

For these reasons, we hold, with the reservations set forth in Part III, *supra*, that the Constitution authorizes Congress to permit tribes, as an exercise of their inherent tribal authority, to prosecute nonmember Indians. We hold that Congress exercised that authority in writing this statute. That being so, the Spirit Lake Tribe's prosecution of Lara did not amount to an exercise of federal power, and the Tribe acted in its capacity of a separate sovereign. Consequently, the Double Jeopardy Clause does not prohibit the federal government from proceeding with the present prosecution for a discrete federal offense. *Heath*, 474 U.S., at 88.

The contrary judgment of the Eighth Circuit is Reversed.

[Justices Stevens, Kennedy, and Thomas concurred in the judgment while Justices Souter and Scalia dissented. Justice Stevens wrote to emphasize the history of tribal sovereignty, pointing out that states, unlike tribes, were never independent sovereigns. Justice Kennedy concurred with the judgment but indicated his discomfort with the constitutionality of the *Duro*-fix legislation, stating: "It is a most troubling proposition to say that Congress can relax the restrictions on inherent tribal sovereignty in a way that extends that sovereignty beyond those historical limits. To conclude that a tribe's inherent sovereignty allows it to exercise jurisdiction over a nonmember in a criminal case is to enlarge the 'unique and limited character' of the inherent sovereignty that *Wheeler* recognized. . . . Lara, after all, is a citizen of the United States. To hold that Congress can subject him, within our domestic borders, to a sovereignty outside the basic structure of the Constitution is a serious step." Justice Thomas went further, questioning the validity of the tribal sovereignty doctrine, while acknowledging that he believed that the Court's precedents required his concurrence. "Federal Indian policy is, to say the least, schizophrenic," he wrote. "And this confusion continues to infuse federal

Indian law and our cases. Nevertheless, if I accept *Wheeler*, I also must accept that the tribes do retain inherent sovereignty (at least to enforce their criminal laws against their own members) and the logical consequences of this fact."

Justice Souter, joined by Justice Scalia, dissented from the majority opinion, expressing his belief that Congress could not "reinvest tribal courts with inherent criminal jurisdiction over nonmember Indians." In his estimation, the "dependent position" of tribal nations in relation to the federal government, along with treaty and congressionally imposed limits on tribal jurisdiction "[strip] the tribes of any power to exercise criminal jurisdiction over those outside their own memberships." He wrote " . . . [T]here are only two ways that a tribe's inherent sovereignty could be restored so as to alter application of the dual sovereignty rule: either Congress could grant the same independence to the tribes that it did to the Philippines, or this Court could repudiate its existing doctrine of dependent sovereignty." Ultimately, he would have decided that the exercise of tribal power was delegated, not inherent, meaning Lara's prosecution was barred by double jeopardy.]

NOTES ON *LARA*

1. **The *"Duro* Fix" Legislation:** After the Supreme Court ruled in *Duro v. Reina* that tribal courts had no inherent criminal jurisdiction over nonmember Indians, Congress promptly passed the *"Duro* fix" legislation to amend the Indian Civil Rights Act of 1968, 25 U.S.C. § 1301(2) to indicate that tribes had such inherent power. The legislation clearly was not framed as a delegation, but, rather, as a recognition of such inherent tribal authority. That legislation established a decade long debate in the lower federal courts over whether the legislation was a delegation or a confirmation and the implications of each approach for constitutional double jeopardy guarantees. *Lara* takes Congress at its word, the majority (but not the dissent), treating the legislation as a recognition of tribal inherent power. Should it, however, have made any difference to double jeopardy principles whether Congress delegated or confirmed tribal authority? For example, as discussed in Ch. 5, Sec. A.1, in 1953, Congress removed the preemption of state jurisdiction over certain specified areas of Indian country affected by so-called Public Law 280 legislation. While that legislation expressly prohibited concurrent federal prosecutions in the designated states, 18 U.S.C. § 1162(c), this did not totally resolve analogous problems. For example, the United States Constitution guarantees federal grand jury indictment for federal, but not state, criminal prosecutions. U.S. Const. Amend. 5. Must states prosecuting Indians under Public Law 280 employ a grand jury even if they do not otherwise do so as part of their normal criminal charging procedures? None do! Does Justice Souter's dissent provide any explanation for this result and his conclusion that tribal prosecution of nonmember Indians must be pursuant to delegated federal authority with attendant double jeopardy consequences? Should it make any difference to the application of the double jeopardy clause whether the source of tribal authority to prosecute nonmember Indians is inherent or delegated? Why? Can these two different results (state prosecutorial authority under Public Law 280 and tribal authority under the *Duro* fix legislation) be harmonized? Might the majority of the Court been influenced by these analytical problems, which were raised in some of the amicus briefs in *Lara*?

2.   Federal Plenary Power and Tribal Sovereignty: The *Lara* litigation not only called into question the source of tribal authority to prosecute nonmember Indians after enactment of the *Duro* fix legislation, it also raised fundamental issues about the source and scope of Congressional power to enact legislation affecting tribal sovereignty and its scope. Careful attention should be paid to the positions of the various members of the Court on the sources in the text of the Constitution for the claimed authority to alter tribal sovereignty. The majority assumes the existence of a broad constitutional "plenary power" of Congress to curtail, or enlarge, tribal authority, although its textual source is sometimes a bit obscure. This so-called plenary power of Congress, which arose originally from nontextual sources in the late nineteenth and early twentieth centuries, has been a cornerstone of federal Indian law doctrine at the same time it has been widely criticized by Indians and academics. *See* Robert N. Clinton, *There Is No Federal Supremacy Clause for Indian Tribes*, 34 ARIZ. ST. L.J. 113 (2002) (tracing the history of the emergence of the federal plenary power doctrine in Indian affairs). Justice Thomas's concurring opinion in *Lara* raises profound questions about the co-existence of doctrines of inherent tribal sovereignty and the Plenary Power Doctrine in Indian affairs. Is Justice Thomas correct when he says that much of the confusion of Indian law comes from the existence of two incompatible ideas — inherent tribal sovereignty and federal plenary power over Indians? Are those two ideas necessarily incompatible? Consider Justice Thomas' definition of sovereignty upon which his argument is centrally based: "The sovereign is, by definition, the entity 'in which independent and supreme authority is vested.' Black's Law Dictionary 1395 (6th ed. 1990). It is quite arguably the essence of sovereignty not to exist merely at the whim of an external government." Under that definition are states of the Union sovereign? Does Justice Thomas answer that conundrum? Why does he think that tribes are different than states? Does Justice Thomas believe that the treaty power or the Indian commerce clause authorizes broad federal plenary power over Indian affairs? What precisely did Justice Thomas mean when he asked whether "Congress (*as opposed to the President*) has this power" (emphasis added)? Was Justice Thomas questioning the existence of a plenary power to curtail tribal sovereignty in the federal government, or only in Congress? Would the logic of the remainder of his opinion suggest that it could reside with the President? Contrast *Minnesota v. Mille Lacs Band of Chippewa Indians*, 526 U.S. 172 (1999) (Presidential removal order invalidated by restrictions contained in the Indian Removal Act of 1830), presented in Ch. 2, Sec. C.

Notice that the majority of the Court declined to resolve Lara's Fifth Amendment due process and equal protection claims in the course of resolving his double jeopardy defense. Does the line drawn in the *"Duro* fix" amendment pose any significant Fifth Amendment issues?

The *Lara* Court declined to address two important questions that Lara raised. First, since the *Duro* fix legislation overturns *Duro* but not *Oliphant*, making nonmember Indians subject to tribal criminal jurisdiction but leaving non-Indians outside tribal criminal authority, does it draw an illegal racial line that violates the due process clause of the Fifth Amendment? Second, in subjecting nonmember Indians to prosecution in tribal courts that are not bound by all provisions of the Bill of Rights under the Indian Civil Rights Act of 1968, 25 U.S.C. § 1302, did Congress violate the due process rights of such individuals? Justice Breyer pointed out that these questions did not affect Lara's federal prosecution, which afforded all Bill of Rights protections and did not differentiate between non-Indians and nonmember Indians. Any nonmember Indian who wishes to raise these questions in a federal court, he noted, can present them as a challenge to the tribal court prosecution, and bring a petition for a writ of habeas corpus under the Indian Civil Rights Act.

In *Means v. Navajo Nation*, 432 F.3d 924 (9th Cir. 2005), the Ninth Circuit upheld the constitutionality of the "*Duro* fix" legislation when it was attacked by former AIM leader and Oglalla Sioux leader Russell Means. Means unsuccessfully challenged the jurisdiction of the Navajo Nation in both tribal and federal courts to prosecute him for allegedly threatening and battering his then father-in-law, who is an Omaha Indian, and for allegedly threatening another man on the Navajo Nation where he then lived with his Navajo wife. The Ninth Circuit responded to the equal protection claims by noting:

> We conclude that a law subjecting nonmember Indians to tribal criminal jurisdiction in "Indian country" passes the "rational tie" standard of *Mancari*. First, recognizing criminal jurisdiction of tribal courts over nonmember Indians furthers Indian self-government. The Navajo reservation, larger than many states and countries, has to be able to maintain order within its boundaries. The 1990 Amendments to the Indian Civil Rights Act were meant to protect Indians and others who reside in or visit Indian country against lawlessness by nonmember Indians who might not otherwise be subject to any criminal jurisdiction. As the Navajo Supreme Court notes, there are a significant number of Indians who are not Navajos but live on the Navajo reservation because of intermarriage. It is a matter of ordinary experience that many people are not at their best when their marriages break up, so misdemeanor jurisdiction over nonmember Indians is rationally related to Indian self-government in an area where rapid and effective tribal responses may be needed. The Navajo Nation has a sophisticated body of published laws, and an experienced court system in which trained trial and appellate judges adjudicate thousands of cases per year. If Means was not subject to prosecution in the Navajo courts, he could not be prosecuted in any court. The state of Arizona, like the majority of states, does not have jurisdiction to try Indians for offenses committed on a reservation, and there is no federal court jurisdiction because Means's alleged offenses do not fall within the Major Crimes Act.

Id. at 933. When these issues are properly presented, how should the Court resolve them? With regard to equal protection, review the various approaches presented in Ch. 2, Sec. B. *See also Morris v. Tanner*, 288 F. Supp. 2d 1133 (D. Mont. 2003) (upholding constitutionality); Alex Tallchief Skibine, Duro v. Reina *and the Legislation that Overturned It: A Power Play of Constitutional Dimensions*, 66 S. Cal. L. Rev. 767 (1993); (supporting constitutionality); L. Scott Gould, *The Congressional Response to* Duro v. Reina: *Compromising Sovereignty and the Constitution*, 28 U.C. Davis L. Rev. 53 (1994) (arguing against constitutionality).

On the question of violation of the Bill of Rights, is it sufficient to respond that Congress did not create the tribe's jurisdiction over nonmembers, but merely lifted a restraint on its operation, *i.e.* removed a preemption? If Congress's action is the "but-for cause" of tribal power to prosecute nonmember Indians, should Bill of Rights protection necessarily follow in tribal court, regardless of some omissions of those protections in the Indian Civil Rights Act? What about analogous situations where Congress lifts a restraint on state jurisdiction under the interstate or Indian commerce clauses? Keep in mind that not all provisions of the Bill of Rights have been incorporated into the Fourteenth Amendment.

3. **Implications of *Lara* for Tribal Civil Jurisdiction over Nonmember Indians:** As you saw in the preceding section, the Supreme Court has rendered federal common law decisions restricting Indian nations' civil jurisdiction over nonmembers. Although the earliest decision in this line, *Montana v. United States*, 450 U.S. 544 (1981), suggested that the limitations on tribal civil jurisdiction applied only to jurisdiction over non-Indians, a later case, *Strate v. A-1 Contractors*, 520 U.S. 438 (1997), indicated in dictum that the limitations applied to civil jurisdiction over nonmember Indians as well. Does *Lara* spell the end to this notion? If so, on what basis? Or could one argue that the *Duro* fix applied only to criminal jurisdiction, and therefore the courts should wait for Congress to weigh in similarly on tribal civil jurisdiction?

4. **Commentary on *Lara*:** *Lara* has inspired two symposia, one in volume 40 of the Tulsa Law Review (Fall 2004) and one in volume 28 of the American Indian Law Review (2003/2004). *See also* Terrill Pollman, *Double Jeopardy and Nonmember Indians in Indian Country*, 82 NEB. L. REV. 889 (2004).

3. Federal Conceptions of Tribal Taxing and Regulatory Power

KERR-McGEE v. NAVAJO TRIBE
United States Supreme Court
471 U.S. 195 (1985)

CHIEF JUSTICE BURGER delivered the opinion of the Court.

We granted certiorari to decide whether the Navajo Tribe of Indians may tax business activities conducted on its land without first obtaining the approval of the Secretary of the Interior.

I

In 1978, the Navajo Tribal Council, the governing body of the Navajo Tribe of Indians, enacted two ordinances imposing taxes known as the Possessory Interest Tax and the Business Activity Tax. The Possessory Interest Tax is measured by the value of leasehold interests in tribal lands; the tax rate is 3% of the value of those interests. The Business Activity Tax is assessed on receipts from the sale of services within the Nation; a tax rate of 5% is applied after subtracting a standard deduction and specified expenses. The tax laws apply to both Navajo and non-Indian businesses, with dissatisfied taxpayers enjoying the right of appeal to the Navajo

Tax Commission and the Navajo Court of Appeals.

The Navajo Tribe, uncertain whether federal approval was required, submitted the two tax laws to the Bureau of Indian Affairs of the Department of the Interior. The Bureau informed the Tribe that no federal statute or regulation required the Department of the Interior to approve or disapprove the taxes.

Before any taxes were collected, petitioner, a substantial mineral lessee on the Navajo Reservation, brought this action seeking to invalidate the taxes. Petitioner claimed in the United States District Court for the District of Arizona that the Navajo taxes were invalid without approval of the Secretary of the Interior. The District Court agreed and permanently enjoined the Tribe from enforcing its tax laws against petitioner.

The United States Court of Appeals for the Ninth Circuit reversed. Relying on *Southland Royalty Co. v. Navajo Tribe of Indians*, 715 F.2d 486 (CA10 1983), it held that no federal statute or principle of law mandated Secretarial approval.

We granted certiorari [and] affirm.

II

In [*Merrion v. Jicarilla Apache Tribe*], we held that the "power to tax is an essential attribute of Indian sovereignty because it is a necessary instrument of self-government and territorial management." Congress, of course, may erect "checkpoints that must be cleared before a tribal tax can take effect." The issue in this case is whether Congress has enacted legislation requiring Secretarial approval of Navajo tax laws.

Petitioner suggests that the Indian Reorganization Act is such a law. Section 16 of the IRA authorizes any tribe on a reservation to adopt a constitution and bylaws, subject to the approval of the Secretary of the Interior. 25 U.S.C. § 476. The Act, however, does not provide that a tribal constitution must condition the power to tax on Secretarial approval. Indeed, the terms of the IRA do not govern tribes, like the Navajo, which declined to accept its provisions. 25 U.S.C. § 478.

Many tribal constitutions written under the IRA in the 1930's called for Secretarial approval of tax laws affecting non-Indians. See, e.g., Constitution and Bylaws of the Rosebud Sioux Tribe of South Dakota, Art. 4, § 1(h) (1935). But there were exceptions to this practice. For example, the 1937 Constitution and By-laws of the Saginaw Chippewa Indian Tribe of Michigan authorized the Tribal Council, without Secretarial approval, to "create and maintain a tribal council fund by . . . levying taxes or assessments against members or non-members." Art. 4, § 1(g). Thus the most that can be said about this period of constitution writing is that the Bureau of Indian Affairs, in assisting the drafting of tribal constitutions, had a policy of including provisions for Secretarial approval; but that policy was not mandated by Congress.

Nor do we agree that Congress intended to recognize as legitimate only those tribal taxes authorized by constitutions written under the IRA. Long before the IRA was enacted, the Senate Judiciary Committee acknowledged the validity of a tax imposed by the Chickasaw nation on non-Indians. *See* S. Rep. No. 698, 45th

Cong., 3d Sess., 1–2 (1879). And in 1934, the Solicitor of the Department of the Interior published a formal opinion stating that a tribe possesses "the power of taxation [which] may be exercised over members of the tribe and over nonmembers." *Powers of Indian Tribes*, 55 I.D. 14, 46. The 73rd Congress, in passing the IRA to advance tribal self-government, *see Williams v. Lee*, 358 U.S. 217, 220 (1959), did nothing to limit the established, pre-existing power of the Navajos to levy taxes.

Some tribes that adopted constitutions in the early years of the IRA may be dependent on the Government in a way that the Navajos are not. However, such tribes are free, with the backing of the Interior Department, to amend their constitutions to remove the requirement of Secretarial approval. *See, e.g.*, Revised Constitution and Bylaws of the Mississippi Band of Choctaw Indians, Art. 8, § 1(r) (1975).

Petitioner also argues that the Indian Mineral Leasing Act of 1938, 52 Stat. 347, 25 U.S.C. § 396a et seq., requires Secretarial approval of Navajo tax laws. Sections 1 through 3 of the 1938 Act establish procedures for leasing oil and gas interests on tribal lands. And § 4 provides that "[a]ll operations under any oil, gas, or other mineral lease issued pursuant to the [Act] shall be subject to the rules and regulations promulgated by the Secretary of the Interior." 25 U.S.C. § 396d. Under this grant of authority, the Secretary has issued comprehensive regulations governing the operation of oil and gas leases. *See* 25 CFR pt. 211 (1984). The Secretary, however, does not demand that tribal laws taxing mineral production be submitted for his approval.

Petitioner contends that the Secretary's decision not to review such tax laws is inconsistent with the statute. In *Merrion*, we emphasized the difference between a tribe's "role as commercial partner," and its "role as sovereign." The tribe acts as a commercial partner when it agrees to sell the right to the use of its land for mineral production, but the tribe acts as a sovereign when it imposes a tax on economic activities within its jurisdiction. Plainly Congress, in passing § 4 of the 1938 Act, could make this same distinction.

Even assuming that the Secretary could review tribal laws taxing mineral production, it does not follow that he must do so. We are not inclined to impose upon the Secretary a duty that he has determined is not needed to satisfy the 1938 Act's basic purpose — maximizing tribal revenues from reservation lands. *See* S. Rep. No. 985, 75th Cong., 1st Sess., 2–3 (1937). Thus, in light of our obligation to "tread lightly in the absence of clear indications of legislative intent," [*Santa Clara Pueblo v. Martinez*,] we will not interpret a grant of authority to regulate leasing operations as a command to the Secretary to review every tribal tax relating to mineral production.

[T]he federal government is "firmly committed to the goal of promoting tribal self-government." [*New Mexico v. Mescalero Apache Tribe*, 462 U.S. 324, 334–335 (1983).] The power to tax members and non-Indians alike is surely an essential attribute of such self-government; the Navajos can gain independence from the federal government only by financing their own police force, schools, and social programs.

III

The Navajo government has been called "probably the most elaborate" among tribes. H.R. Rep. No. 78, 91st Cong., 1st Sess., 8 (1969). The legitimacy of the Navajo Tribal Council, the freely elected governing body of the Navajos, is beyond question.[40]

We agree with the Court of Appeals that neither Congress nor the Navajos have found it necessary to subject the Tribal Council's tax laws to review by the Secretary of the Interior.

[*Affirmed.*]

ATKINSON TRADING COMPANY, INC. v. SHIRLEY
United States Supreme Court
532 U.S. 645 (2001)

CHIEF JUSTICE REHNQUIST delivered the opinion of the Court.

In *Montana v. United States*, 450 U.S. 544 (1981), we held that, with limited exceptions, Indian tribes lack civil authority over the conduct of nonmembers on non-Indian fee land within a reservation. The question with which we are presented is whether this general rule applies to tribal attempts to tax nonmember activity occurring on non-Indian fee land. We hold that it does and that neither of *Montana*'s exceptions obtains here.

In 1916, Hubert Richardson, lured by the possibility of trading with wealthy Gray Mountain Navajo cattlemen, built the Cameron Trading Post just south of the Little Colorado River near Cameron, Arizona. G. Richardson, Navajo Trader, pp. 136–137 (1986). Richardson purchased the land directly from the United States, but the Navajo Nation Reservation, which had been established in 1868, see 15 Stat. 667, was later extended eight miles south so that the Cameron Trading Post fell within its exterior boundaries. *See* Act of June 14, 1934, ch. 521, 48 Stat. 960–962. This 1934 enlargement of the Navajo Reservation — which today stretches across northeast Arizona, northwest New Mexico, and southeast Utah — did not alter the status of the property: It is, like millions of acres throughout the United States, non-Indian fee land within a tribal reservation.

Richardson's "drafty, wooden store building and four small, one-room-shack cabins overlooking the bare river canyon," Richardson, *supra*, at 135, have since evolved into a business complex consisting of a hotel, restaurant, cafeteria, gallery, curio shop, retail store, and recreational vehicle facility. The current owner, petitioner Atkinson Trading Company, Inc., benefits from the Cameron Trading Post's location near the intersection of Arizona Highway 64 (which leads west to the Grand Canyon) and United States Highway 89 (which connects Flagstaff on the south with Glen Canyon Dam to the north). A significant portion of petitioner's hotel

---

[40] [4] The Tribal Council has 88 members who are elected every four years. There are approximately 79,000 registered tribal voters, and 69% of these persons voted in the last tribal election in 1982.

business stems from tourists on their way to or from the Grand Canyon National Park.

In 1992, the Navajo Nation enacted a hotel occupancy tax, which imposes an 8 percent tax upon any hotel room located within the exterior boundaries of the Navajo Nation Reservation. *See* 24 Navajo Nation Code §§ 101–142 (1995), App. to Pet. for Cert. 102a-124a. Although the legal incidence of the tax falls directly upon the guests, the owner or operator of the hotel must collect and remit it to respondents, members of the Navajo Tax Commission. §§ 104, 107. The nonmember guests at the Cameron Trading Post pay approximately $ 84,000 in taxes to respondents annually.

Petitioner's challenge under *Montana* to the Navajo Nation's authority to impose the hotel occupancy tax was rejected by both the Navajo Tax Commission and the Navajo Supreme Court. Petitioner then sought relief in the United States District Court for the District of New Mexico, which also upheld the tax. A divided panel of the Court of Appeals for the Tenth Circuit affirmed. . . .

We granted certiorari, . . . and now reverse.

Tribal jurisdiction is limited: For powers not expressly conferred them by federal statute or treaty, Indian tribes must rely upon their retained or inherent sovereignty. In *Montana*, the most exhaustively reasoned of our modern cases addressing this latter authority, we observed that Indian tribe power over nonmembers on non-Indian fee land is sharply circumscribed. At issue in *Montana* was the Crow Tribe's attempt to regulate nonmember fishing and hunting on non-Indian fee land within the reservation. Although we "readily agreed" that the 1868 Fort Laramie Treaty authorized the Crow Tribe to prohibit nonmembers from hunting or fishing on tribal land, we held that such "power cannot apply to lands held in fee by non-Indians." This delineation of members and nonmembers, tribal land and non-Indian fee land, stemmed from the dependent nature of tribal sovereignty. Surveying our cases in this area dating back to 1810, *see Fletcher v. Peck*, 10 U.S. 87 (1810) (Johnson, J., concurring) (stating that Indian tribes have lost any "right of governing every person within their limits except themselves"), we noted that "through their original incorporation into the United States as well as through specific treaties and statutes, Indian tribes have lost many of the attributes of sovereignty." We concluded that the inherent sovereignty of Indian tribes was limited to "their members and their territory": "Exercise of tribal power beyond what is necessary to protect tribal self-government or to control internal relations is inconsistent with the dependent status of the tribes." [*Montana*] (citing *United States v. Wheeler*, 435 U.S. 313 (1978) ("The dependent status of Indian tribes . . . is necessarily inconsistent with their freedom to determine their external relations" (emphasis deleted))).

Although we extracted from our precedents "the general proposition that the inherent sovereign powers of an Indian tribe do not extend to the activities of nonmembers of the tribe," we nonetheless noted in *Montana* two possible bases for tribal jurisdiction over non-Indian fee land. First, "[a] tribe may regulate, through taxation, licensing, or other means, the activities of nonmembers who enter consensual relationships with the tribe or its members, through commercial dealings, contracts, leases, or other arrangements." Second, "[a] tribe may . . .

exercise civil authority over the conduct of non-Indians on fee lands within its reservation when that conduct threatens or has some direct effect on the political integrity, the economic security, or the health or welfare of the tribe." Applying these precepts, we found that the nonmembers at issue there had not subjected themselves to "tribal civil jurisdiction" through any agreements or dealings with the Tribe and that hunting and fishing on non-Indian fee land did not "imperil the subsistence or welfare of the Tribe." We therefore held that the Crow Tribe's regulations could not be enforced.

The framework set forth in *Montana* "broadly addressed the concept of 'inherent sovereignty.' " *Strate v. A-1 Contractors*, 520 U.S. 438, 453 (1997) (quoting *Montana, supra*, at 563). In *Strate*, we . . . held that *Montana* governed tribal assertions of adjudicatory authority over non-Indian fee land within a reservation. ("Subject to controlling provisions in treaties and statutes, and the two exceptions identified in *Montana*, the *civil authority* of Indian tribes and their courts with respect to non-Indian fee lands generally 'does not extend to the activities of nonmembers of the tribe' " (emphasis added) (quoting *Montana, supra*, at 565)).

Citing our decision in *Merrion*, respondents submit that *Montana* and *Strate* do not restrict an Indian tribe's power to impose revenue-raising taxes.[41] In *Merrion*, just one year after our decision in *Montana*, we upheld a severance tax imposed by the Jicarilla Apache Tribe upon non-Indian lessees authorized to extract oil and gas from tribal land. In so doing, we noted that the power to tax derives not solely from an Indian tribe's power to exclude non-Indians from tribal land, but also from an Indian tribe's "general authority, as sovereign, to control economic activity within its jurisdiction." Such authority, we held, was incident to the benefits conferred upon nonmembers: "They benefit from the provision of police protection and other governmental services, as well as from " 'the advantages of a civilized society' " that are assured by the existence of tribal government." . . .

Merrion, however, was careful to note that an Indian tribe's inherent power to tax only extended to " 'transactions occurring on *trust lands* and significantly involving a tribe or its members.' " 455 U.S. at 137 (emphasis added) (quoting *Washington v. Confederated Tribes of Colville Reservation*, 447 U.S. 134, 152 (1980)). There are undoubtedly parts of the *Merrion* opinion that suggest a broader scope for tribal taxing authority than the quoted language above.[42] But *Merrion* involved a tax that only applied to activity occurring on the reservation, and its holding is therefore easily reconcilable with the *Montana-Strate* line of authority, which we deem to be controlling. *See Merrion, supra*, at 142 ("[A] tribe has no authority over a nonmember until the nonmember enters tribal lands or conducts business with the tribe"). An Indian tribe's sovereign power to tax — whatever its

---

[41] [3] Respondents concede that regulatory taxes fall under the *Montana* framework. *See* 450 U.S. at 565 ("A tribe may regulate, through taxation . . . the activities of nonmembers").

[42] [4] *Merrion v. Jicarilla Apache Tribe*, 455 U.S. 130 (1982), for example, referenced the decision of the Court of Appeals for the Eighth Circuit in *Buster v. Wright*, 135 F. 947 (1905). But we have never endorsed *Buster*'s statement that an Indian tribe's "jurisdiction to govern the inhabitants of a country is not conditioned or limited by the title to the land which they occupy in it." Accordingly, beyond any guidance it might provide as to the type of consensual relationship contemplated by the first exception of [*Montana*], *Buster* is not an authoritative precedent.

derivation — reaches no further than tribal land.[43]

We therefore do not read *Merrion* to exempt taxation from *Montana*'s general rule that Indian tribes lack civil authority over nonmembers on non-Indian fee land. Accordingly, as in *Strate*, we apply *Montana* straight up. Because Congress has not authorized the Navajo Nation's hotel occupancy tax through treaty or statute, and because the incidence of the tax falls upon nonmembers on non-Indian fee land, it is incumbent upon the Navajo Nation to establish the existence of one of *Montana*'s exceptions.

Respondents argue that both petitioner and its hotel guests have entered into a consensual relationship with the Navajo Nation justifying the imposition of the hotel occupancy tax. Echoing the reasoning of the Court of Appeals, respondents note that the Cameron Trading Post benefits from the numerous services provided by the Navajo Nation. The record reflects that the Arizona State Police and the Navajo Tribal Police patrol the portions of United States Highway 89 and Arizona Highway 64 traversing the reservation; that the Navajo Tribal Police and the Navajo Tribal Emergency Medical Services Department will respond to an emergency call from the Cameron Trading Post; and that local Arizona Fire Departments and the Navajo Tribal Fire Department provide fire protection to the area.[44] Although we do not question the Navajo Nation's ability to charge an appropriate fee for a particular service actually rendered,[45] we think the generalized availability of tribal services patently insufficient to sustain the Tribe's civil authority over nonmembers on non-Indian fee land.

The consensual relationship must stem from "commercial dealing, contracts, leases, or other arrangements," *Montana*, 450 U.S. at 565 and a nonmember's actual or potential receipt of tribal police, fire, and medical services does not create the requisite connection. If it did, the exception would swallow the rule: All non-Indian fee lands within a reservation benefit, to some extent, from the "advantages of a civilized society" offered by the Indian tribe. Such a result does not square with our

---

[43] [5] We find misplaced the Court of Appeals's reliance upon 18 U.S.C. § 1151, a statute conferring upon Indian tribes jurisdiction over certain criminal acts occurring in "Indian country," or "all land within the limits of any Indian reservation under the jurisdiction of the United States Government, notwithstanding the issuance of any patent, and, including rights-of-way running through the reservation." . . . Although § 1151 has been relied upon to demarcate state, federal, and tribal jurisdiction over criminal and civil matters, *see DeCoteau v. District County Court for Tenth Judicial Dist.*, 420 U.S. 425, 427 n.2 (1975) ("While § 1151 is concerned, on its face, only with criminal jurisdiction, the Court has recognized that it generally applies as well to questions of civil jurisdiction [citing cases]"), we do not here deal with a claim of statutorily conferred power. Section 1151 simply does not address an Indian tribe's inherent or retained sovereignty over nonmembers on non-Indian fee land.

At least in the context of non-Indian fee land, we also find inapt the Court of Appeals's analogy to state taxing authority. Our reference in *Merrion* to a State's ability to tax activities with which it has a substantial nexus was made in the context of describing an Indian tribe's authority over *tribal land*. . . . Only full territorial sovereigns enjoy the "power to enforce laws against all who come within the sovereign's territory, whether citizens or aliens," and Indian tribes "can no longer be described as sovereigns in this sense." *Duro v. Reina, supra*, at 685.

[44] [7] The Navajo Tribal Fire Department has responded to a fire at the Cameron Trading Post. *See* App. to Pet. for Cert. 57a.

[45] [8] The Navajo Nation charges for its emergency medical services (a flat call-out fee of $300 and a mileage fee of $6.25 per mile). *See* App. 127–129.

precedents; indeed, we implicitly rejected this argument in *Strate*, where we held that the nonmembers had not consented to the Tribes' adjudicatory authority by availing themselves of the benefit of tribal police protection while traveling within the reservation. We therefore reject respondents' broad reading of *Montana*'s first exception, which ignores the dependent status of Indian tribes and subverts the territorial restriction upon tribal power.

Respondents and their principal *amicus*, the United States, also argue that petitioner consented to the tax by becoming an "Indian trader." Congress has authorized the Commissioner of Indian Affairs "to appoint traders to the Indian tribes and to make such rules and regulations as he may deem just and proper specifying the kind and quantity of goods and the prices at which such goods shall be sold to the Indians." 25 U.S.C. § 261. Petitioner has acquired the requisite license to transact business with the Navajo Nation and therefore is subject to the regulatory strictures promulgated by the Indian Affairs Commissioner. *See* 25 CFR pt. 141 (2000). But whether or not the Navajo Nation could impose a tax on activities arising out of this relationship, an issue not before us, it is clear that petitioner's "Indian trader" status by itself cannot support the imposition of the hotel occupancy tax.

Montana's consensual relationship exception requires that the tax or regulation imposed by the Indian tribe have a nexus to the consensual relationship itself. In *Strate*, for example, even though respondent A-1 Contractors was on the reservation to perform landscaping work for the Three Affiliated Tribes at the time of the accident, we nonetheless held that the Tribes lacked adjudicatory authority because the other nonmember "was not a party to the subcontract, and the Tribes were strangers to the accident." A nonmember's consensual relationship in one area thus does not trigger tribal civil authority in another — it is not "in for a penny, in for a Pound." E. Ravenscroft, *The Canterbury Guests; Or A Bargain Broken*, act v, sc. 1. The hotel occupancy tax at issue here is grounded in petitioner's relationship with its nonmember hotel guests, who can reach the Cameron Trading Post on United States Highway 89 and Arizona Highway 64, non-Indian public rights-of-way. Petitioner cannot be said to have consented to such a tax by virtue of its status as an "Indian trader."

Although the Court of Appeals did not reach *Montana*'s second exception, both respondents and the United States argue that the hotel occupancy tax is warranted in light of the direct effects the Cameron Trading Post has upon the Navajo Nation. Again noting the Navajo Nation's provision of tribal services and petitioner's status as an "Indian trader," respondents emphasize that petitioner employs almost 100 Navajo Indians; that the Cameron Trading Post derives business from tourists visiting the reservation; and that large amounts of tribal land surround petitioner's isolated property.[46] Although we have no cause to doubt respondents' assertion that the Cameron Chapter of the Navajo Nation possesses an "overwhelming Indian

---

[46] [11] The record does not reflect the amount of non-Indian fee land within the Navajo Nation. A 1995 study commissioned by the United States Department of Commerce states that 96.3% of the Navajo Nation's 16,224,896 acres is tribally owned, with allotted land comprising 762,749 acres, or 4.7%, of the reservation. *See* Economic Development Administration V. Tiller, American Indian Reservations and Indian Trust Areas, p. 214 (1995). The 1990 Census reports that that 96.6% of residents on the Navajo

character," we fail to see how petitioner's operation of a hotel on non-Indian fee land "threatens or has some direct effect on the political integrity, the economic security, or the health or welfare of the tribe." *Montana*, 450 U.S. at 566.[47]

We find unpersuasive respondents' attempt to augment this claim by reference to *Brendale v. Confederated Tribes and Bands of Yakima Nation*, 492 U.S. 408, 440 (1989) (opinion of STEVENS, J.). In this portion of *Brendale*, per the reasoning of two Justices, we held that the Yakima Nation had the authority to zone a small, non-Indian parcel located "in the heart" of over 800,000 acres of closed and largely uninhabited tribal land. *Ibid.* Respondents extrapolate from this holding that Indian tribes enjoy broad authority over nonmembers wherever the acreage of non-Indian fee land is miniscule in relation to the surrounding tribal land. But we think it plain that the judgment in *Brendale* turned on both the closed nature of the non-Indian fee land[48] and the fact that its development would place the entire area "in jeopardy." Irrespective of the percentage of non-Indian fee land within a reservation, *Montana*'s second exception grants Indian tribes nothing " 'beyond what is necessary to protect tribal self-government or to control internal relations.' " Whatever effect petitioner's operation of the Cameron Trading Post might have upon surrounding Navajo land, it does not endanger the Navajo Nation's political integrity. *See Brendale*, *supra*, at 431 (opinion of White, J.) (holding that the impact of the nonmember's conduct "must be demonstrably serious and must imperil the political integrity, the economic security, or the health and welfare of the tribe").

Indian tribes are "unique aggregations possessing attributes of sovereignty over both their members and their territory," but their dependent status generally precludes extension of tribal civil authority beyond these limits. *United States v. Mazurie*, 419 U.S. 544, 557 (1975). The Navajo Nation's imposition of a tax upon nonmembers on non-Indian fee land within the reservation is, therefore, presumptively invalid. Because respondents have failed to establish that the hotel occupancy tax is commensurately related to any consensual relationship with petitioner or is necessary to vindicate the Navajo Nation's political integrity, the presumption

---

Nation are Indian. Joint Lodging 182. The Cameron Chapter of the Navajo Nation, in which petitioner's land lies, has a non-Indian population of 2.3%.

47 [12] Although language in *Merrion* referred to taxation as "necessary to tribal self-government and territorial management," 455 U.S. at 141, it did not address assertions of tribal jurisdiction over non-Indian fee land. Just as with *Montana*'s first exception, incorporating *Merrion*'s reasoning here would be tantamount to rejecting *Montana*'s general rule. In *Strate v. A-1 Contractors*, 520 U.S. 438, 459 (1997), we stated that *Montana*'s second exception "can be misperceived." The exception is only triggered by *nonmember conduct* that threatens the Indian tribe, it does not broadly permit the exercise of civil authority wherever it might be considered "necessary" to self-government. Thus, unless the drain of the nonmember's conduct upon tribal services and resources is so severe that it actually "imperils" the political integrity of the Indian tribe, there can be no assertion of civil authority beyond tribal lands. *Montana*, 450 U.S. at 566. Petitioner's hotel has no such adverse effect upon the Navajo Nation.

48 [13] JUSTICE STEVENS's opinion in *Brendale* sets out in some detail the restrictive nature of "closed area" surrounding the non-Indian fee land. Pursuant to the powers reserved it in an 1855 treaty with the United States, the Yakima Nation closed this forested area to the public and severely limited the activities of those who entered the land through a "courtesy permit system." The record here establishes that, save a few natural areas and parks not at issue, the Navajo reservation is open to the general public.

ripens into a holding. The judgment of the Court of Appeals for the Tenth Circuit is accordingly

Reversed.

JUSTICE SOUTER, with whom JUSTICES KENNEDY and THOMAS join, concurring.

If we are to see coherence in the various manifestations of the general law of tribal jurisdiction over non-Indians, the source of doctrine must be *Montana v. United States*, 450 U.S. 544 (1981), and it is in light of that case that I join the Court's opinion. Under *Montana*, the status of territory within a reservation's boundaries as tribal or fee land may have much to do (as it does here) with the likelihood (or not) that facts will exist that are relevant under the exceptions to *Montana*'s "general proposition" that "the inherent sovereign powers of an Indian tribe do not extend to the activities of nonmembers of the tribe." That general proposition is, however, the first principle, regardless of whether the land at issue is fee land, or land owned by or held in trust for an Indian tribe.

NOTES ON TRIBAL TAXING JURISDICTION

1.   **Taxation as a Source of Revenue:** In the past, Indian nations have refrained from imposing taxes on their own members, largely because of reservation poverty and the members' objection to taxes. Today, however, tribal members as well as nonmembers may encounter a variety of taxes, including those on fuel, motor vehicles, beer, employees, cigarettes, and beverages. For some examples of tribal taxes, see Richard J. Ansson, Jr., *State Taxation of Non-Indians Who Do Business with Indian Tribes: Why Several Recent Ninth Circuit Holdings Reemphasize the Need for Indian Tribes to Enter into Taxation Compacts with Their Respective States*, 78 OR. L. REV. 501, 512–14 (1999).

Revenue from taxation of nonmembers' activity and property within reservations could assist Indian nations in providing public services and supporting tribal initiatives. Especially if tribes were able to set taxes lower than surrounding non-Indian communities, businesses and consumers would have an incentive to come to Indian country. As a practical matter, have Indian nations been able to capture this potential advantage? In *Washington v. Confederated Tribes of the Colville Indian Reservation*, 447 U.S. 134 (1980) (presented in Ch. 4, Sec. B.4.b), the Supreme Court held that a tribal tax on nonmember purchases of cigarettes from a tribal retail outlet did not preclude a state tax on the same purchases. Before this ruling, the Tribe's lower tax rate had attracted large numbers of off-reservation consumers, raising considerable revenue for the Tribes.

Colville, Atkinson, and other Supreme Court decisions presented later in this section suggest the Court's discomfort with tribes shifting their tax burden to outsiders. Is this discomfort warranted? By definition, outsiders are unable to participate in the tribe's political process. And after *Kerr-McGee*, tribes may impose taxes without prior approval of the Secretary of the Interior, absent tribal constitution provisions to the contrary. Are tribes then likely to exact onerous taxes on those who come to the reservation to transact business? The wish to shift tax burdens to nonresidents is hardly unique to Indian nations. When municipalities impose hotel taxes or car rental taxes, or set up auto sales malls, they are looking to bring in revenue from outsiders. For an excellent discussion of the economic limits on such taxation, see Kirk J. Stark, *The Right to Vote on Taxes*, 96 Nw. U. L. Rev. 191, 223–26 (2001). Problems associated with dual taxation within Indian country are discussed further in Ch. 4, Sec. B.4.b.

In addition to excise-type taxes, tribes have also attempted to secure revenue from outsiders by taxing nonmember-owned property within reservations. One attractive target has been utilities with rights-of-way through tribal lands, especially those providing services to tribal members and potentially imposing costs on the tribal community as a result of environmental or other problems. Before *Strate* equated rights-of-way with nonmember fee land for jurisdiction purposes, the Ninth Circuit upheld such a tax. *See Burlington Northern R. R. Co. v. Blackfeet Tribe*, 924 F.2d 899, 904 (9th Cir. 1991). Following *Strate*, the Ninth Circuit overruled that decision in *Big Horn County Electric Coop. v. Adams*, 219 F.3d 944 (9th Cir. 2000), and the later decision in *Atkinson* only confirmed the switch in outcomes.

Interestingly, however, the Ninth Circuit has not ruled out such taxes altogether on reservation rights-of-way. In a case involving a railroad with such a right-of-way through the Fort Peck Reservation, the Ninth Circuit left open the possibility that the Assiniboine and Sioux Tribes of that Reservation could demonstrate that the railroad posed a sufficient health or safety threat to the tribal community to satisfy the second *Montana* exception. The Tribes were seeking discovery from the Burlington Northern Santa Fe Railroad (BN) regarding such threats when BN made a summary judgment motion. In reversing the trial judge's order granting the motion, the Ninth Circuit acknowledged that *Atkinson* had given a "narrow" reading to the second *Montana* exception. Nonetheless, the panel noted that

> in the year 2000, more than 1,695 freight cars crossed the Reservation each day. The Tribes are aware that hazardous materials are carried on BN's cars because BN has asked the Tribes to work with the Company on emergency contingency plans. The Tribes know of derailment incidents and, in their own words, "have gathered evidence of numerous fires and accidents with attendant property damage and sometimes fatalities . . . but discovery of Burlington's own files [is] necessary for a complete record on application of *Montana*'s second exception."

The court held that the Tribes were entitled to obtain such discovery before any ruling on its taxing jurisdiction.

In her penetrating study of the Navajo Nation's enactment of its sovereignty over the past 50 years, Sarah Krakoff includes an illuminating account of *Atkinson* and the consequences of its categorical limitations on the inherent power to tax. *See* Sarah Krakoff, *A Narrative of Sovereignty: Illuminating the Paradox of the Domestic Dependent Nation*, 83 Ore. L. Rev. 1109, 1174–80 (2004). According to Krakoff, the amount of hotel tax revenue lost to the Nation as a result of *Atkinson* (approximately $500,000 per year) is "not enormous," but it is also "not likely to be recouped." Because hotel tax revenues are used to fund tourism-related services provided by the Navajo government, "[t]he loss of this income . . . hurts the Navajo Nation's ability to engage further in this relatively non-exploitative form of economic development." The Nation could conceivably withdraw its police, fire, and other services to the areas with hotels owned by non-Indians, and agree to provide them only on condition that the hotels consent to tribal taxing jurisdiction. But this type of confrontational strategy does not appear likely. What the Nation has done is to include consent-to-taxation provisions in all of its agreements for state rights of way and other limited interests in land across Navajo Indian country.

2. **The Court's Shift from *Kerr-McGee* to *Atkinson*:** How well does *Atkinson* distinguish *Kerr-McGee* and its direct progenitor, *Merrion v. Jicarilla Apache Tribe* (presented in Sec. C.3, this chapter)? Do *Kerr-McGee* and *Atkinson* rest on similar or different understandings of the tribal-federal relationship? Between the Court's 1983 decision in *Kerr-McGee* and its 2001 decision in *Atkinson*, did anything take place within federal Indian policy to redirect that relationship away from one emphasizing tribal autonomy? Note that during that period, Congress passed legislation authorizing tribal regulatory jurisdiction over many environmental matters involving nonmembers on reservation fee lands, as well as tribal criminal jurisdiction over nonmember Indians. *See, e.g.,* Clean Water Act, 33 U.S.C. § 1377. Congress also passed laws enabling tribes to take far greater control over budgets for their federally funded services, and encouraging tribal economic development. *See, e.g.,* Tribal Self-Governance Act of 1994, 25 U.S.C. § 458aa et seq. Federal Executive Orders reaffirmed the "government-to-government relationship" between Indian nations and the United States. *See, e.g.,* Executive Order 13175, November 6, 2000. Should congressional and Executive Branch support for tribal jurisdiction lead the Court to uphold tribal taxation of nonmembers, or should the Court view congressional action in some areas as an indication that Congress wishes to go no farther?

3. ***Atkinson's* Use of *Montana*:** Justice Rehnquist presents *Atkinson* as a straightforward application of the *Montana* test for tribal jurisdiction over nonmembers on nonmember-owned land. Yet *Montana* rested in part on an interpretation of the General Allotment Act, particularly Congress's intent in dividing tribal lands and permitting sale of those allotted lands to nonmembers. According to the *Montana* Court

> . . . Congress [did not] intend that non-Indians purchasing allotted lands would become subject to tribal jurisdiction when an avowed purpose of the allotment policy was the ultimate destruction of tribal government. And it is hardly likely that Congress could have imagined that the purpose of peaceful assimilation could be advanced if feeholders could be excluded from fishing or hunting on their acquired property. *Montana v. United States,* 450 U.S. 544, 559 n.9 (1981).

In contrast, the nonmember-owned land in *Atkinson* had been land that was initially outside Navajo reservation boundaries, and became part of Indian country when Congress expanded the reservation around it. Act of Congress on June 14, 1934, Ch. 521, 48 Stat. 960–62. At the time this expansion took place, Atkinson's predecessor in interest and other non-Indian landowners within the newly expanded reservation were offered the option to exchange their lands for lands outside the reservation. Atkinson's predecessor declined the offer, and proceeded to market his trading post for tourists interested in Navajo culture. Brief for

Respondent Navajo Nation, 2000 U.S. Briefs 454. Should *Montana*'s presumption against tribal jurisdiction attach under such circumstances?

As Justice Stewart's opinion in *Montana* acknowledged, "A tribe may regulate, through taxation, licensing, or other means, the activities of nonmembers who enter consensual relationships with the tribe or its members, through commercial dealing, contracts, leases, or other arrangements." 450 U.S. at 565. Clearly Atkinson Trading Co. had made agreements with the Navajo tribal members it hired to work at its hotel. Why wasn't that sufficient to trigger tribal taxing authority under the language just quoted? Why wasn't Atkinson's acceptance of tribal services sufficient for that purpose? What more could the Navajo Nation do to support its taxing authority on the basis of "consensual relationships" Could it condition Atkinson's receipt of emergency medical and fire protection services on its agreement to submit to taxing jurisdiction? If Atkinson or any other company wanted to do business with the Navajo Nation, could the Nation establish a prequalification requirement for bidding on such business that included acceptance of tribal taxing jurisdiction? Would either of these possibilities be practically feasible?

Montana also approved of tribal jurisdiction over nonmembers on fee land "when that conduct threatens or has some direct effect on the political integrity, the economic security, or the health or welfare of the tribe." 450 U.S. at 565. Why wasn't the Navajo Nation's need for tax revenue to support services to travelers and tourists on the reservation a sufficient "direct effect" to justify tribal taxing jurisdiction? What would have to happen before the drain of such services could be deemed to "imperil" the political integrity of the Nation, as the Court seems to require in footnote 12 of the opinion? Note that in supporting state taxation of nonmembers on tribal land, the Court has taken into account the state's provision of services to those nonmembers, but has never required that the value of state services provided equal the amount of tax sought to be collected, let alone required that the value of such services greatly exceed the amount of tax revenue. *See Cotton Petroleum Corp. v. New Mexico*, 490 U.S. 163 (1989), *infra*.

4.   **Justice Souter's Concurring Opinion in *Atkinson*:** Three Justices concurring in *Atkinson* indicate that they would apply *Montana*'s presumption against tribal jurisdiction over nonmembers to tribal trust land as well as to nonmember-owned fee land. Their brief opinion acknowledges that the circumstances surrounding nonmember activities on tribal trust land may lend themselves more readily to application of the two "exceptions" to *Montana*. But how can the Justices jettison precedents such as *Merrion* and *Kerr-McGee*, both decided after *Montana*, without so much as an explanation? Neither of these cases even hinted that *Montana*'s framework applied to tribal jurisdiction over activities on trust lands. Is it sufficient for Justice Souter to hold up *Montana* as the only source of "coherence" in the doctrine addressing tribal jurisdiction over nonmembers? Is it "coherent" to apply *Montana* to trust land when the *Montana* opinion itself relied on Congress's intent in opening up tribal land for sale to nonmembers?

Brendale v. Confederated Tribes & Bands of the Yakima Indian Nation, 492 U.S. 408 (1989): The Yakima reservation, located in southeastern Washington, encompasses 1.3 million acres, approximately 20% of which are former allotments held in fee by nonmembers. Nearly all of these fee lands are found in the one-third of the reservation that is used for agricultural, dairy, and residential purposes (the "open area"). Indeed, almost half the land in this open area is fee land owned by nonmembers. The remaining few parcels of fee land held by nonmembers are widely scattered throughout the remainder of the reservation, an area to which the general public had restricted access (the "closed area"). There are no permanent inhabitants in the closed area, and the state provides no substantial services to that area.

Both the County of Yakima and the Yakima Nation enacted zoning ordinances applicable to the fee land within the reservation. The County's ordinance allowed a wider variety of uses than the Yakima Nation's ordinance, both in the open and closed areas. The conflicting requirements precipitated litigation when two non-Indian owners of fee land within the reservation — one in the open area, one in the closed — received permission from the county to develop their land in ways outlawed under the tribal zoning ordinance. In the closed area, the fee owner wanted to subdivide his lot for cabins, but the tribal ordinance prohibited construction of cabins, motels, stores, or similar structures. In the open area, the fee owner wanted to subdivide his land for single family homes, but the tribal ordinance designated the area as agricultural.

The Yakima Nation sued for a declaratory judgment barring enforcement of the county zoning ordinance, and affirming the Nation's exclusive jurisdiction to zone the entire reservation, including non-Indian-owned fee land. The federal district court ruled for the Nation with respect to the closed area, finding that the non-Indian development would damage the surrounding area, for example, by diminishing water quality and disrupting wildlife habitats. The court also took account of the important religious and cultural sites in the closed area and the fact that timber harvesting was an important source of revenue for the tribe. According to the district court, "To allow development in this unique and undeveloped area would drastically diminish [the area's cultural and spiritual] values." With respect to the open area, the district court found no comparable threat to tribal interests, and upheld the county ordinance. The Ninth Circuit affirmed the decision regarding the closed area, but reversed as to the open area, holding that the Yakima Nation had exclusive jurisdiction to zone the entire reservation. According to the appellate court, zoning ordinances exist "to protect against the damage caused by uncontrolled development, which can affect all of the residents and land of the reservation." *Confederated Tribes & Bands of the Yakima Indian Nation v. Whiteside*, 828 F.2d 529, 534 (9th Cir. 1987).

Fracturing into three opinions with no majority, the Supreme Court ruled in favor of state zoning authority over nonmember-owned fee land in the open area, and in favor of tribal zoning authority over such land in the closed area. Writing for four Justices, Justice White opined that the state should be able to zone all nonmember-owned fee land throughout the reservation. Relying on *Montana v. United States*, he noted that allotment had deprived the Nation of the right to exclude nonmembers from fee land, making exclusion power unavailable as a basis for tribal zoning authority. Turning to the tribe's claim of inherent sovereignty, White purported to apply *Montana*'s test for determining inherent tribal power over nonmembers on fee land. According to this test, a tribe can exercise such jurisdiction only when it can demonstrate either a consensual relationship between the nonmember and the tribe or its members or alternatively, that the nonmember's conduct "threatens or has some direct effect on the political integrity, the economic security, or the health or welfare of the tribe." Focusing on the second alternative, White first denied that tribal jurisdiction *must* be recognized under these circumstances, and refused to equate this alternative with a general tribal police power. He expressed concern that making tribal authority turn on specific impacts would create the possibility of zoning authority over the same property varying over time. Instead, he announced, "The governing principle is that the tribe has no authority itself . . . to regulate the use of fee land. The inquiry thus becomes whether and to what extent the tribe has a protectable interest in what activities are taking place on fee land within the reservation and, if it has such an interest, how it may be protected." In the context of a checkerboard reservation (alternating tribal and nonmember lands), White found that the tribe has a federally protected interest in avoiding impacts on its political integrity, economic security, or health and welfare, but only if those impacts are "demonstrably serious" and actually "imperil" tribal well-being. Even when this tribal interest exists, White insisted that the state retains zoning jurisdiction and the tribe must present its concerns to the local zoning authority. The county could be enjoined from proceeding "only if it failed to respect the rights of the Tribe under federal law." In White's view, this approach "will sufficiently protect Indian tribes while at the same time avoiding undue interference with state sovereignty and providing the certainty needed by property owners."

Writing for three dissenting Justices, Justice Blackmun maintained that Justice White had read *Montana* too broadly, encroaching on inherent tribal civil jurisdiction over nonmembers that had long been recognized. According to Blackmun, *Montana* should be read "to recognize that tribes may regulate the on-reservation conduct of non-Indians whenever a significant tribal interest is threatened or directly affected." On this view, tribal zoning authority necessarily extends to all reservation fee land as well as trust land because Indians "enjoy a unique historical and cultural connection to the land," and because "a tribe's inability to zone substantial tracts of fee land within its own reservation . . . would destroy the tribe's ability to engage in the systematic and coordinated utilization of land that is the very essence of zoning authority[.]" For Justice Blackmun, affirmation of state power to zone nonmember fee land, coupled with the tribe's unquestioned power to zone trust land, creates "nothing short of a nightmare, nullifying the efforts of both sovereigns to segregate incompatible land uses and exacerbating the already considerable tensions that exist between local and tribal governments in many parts of the Nation about the best use of reservation lands." Blackmun dismissed White's concern about varying zoning authorities over time for the same property as a problem of White's "own creation," noting that the tribe's interest is in comprehensive zoning authority, not in parcel-by-parcel determinations of impacts. Furthermore, Blackmun characterized the opportunity for tribes to question state zoning determinations in federal court as "legal tokenism: the opportunity to sue in court has replaced the opportunity to exercise sovereign authority. This substitution is without sound basis in law, and without practical value" because of the tribe's inability to use such an action to achieve comprehensive land use planning.

The decisive votes in the case came from Justices Stevens and O'Connor, who rested their analysis on the Nation's right to exclude nonmembers from territory reserved for the tribe, which power necessarily includes the lesser power "to require that nonmembers, as a condition of entry, not disturb the traditional character of the reserved area." Thus, according to the opinion by Justice Stevens, "proper resolution of these cases depends on the extent to which the Tribe's virtually absolute power to exclude has been either diminished by federal statute or voluntarily surrendered." Not only did the General Allotment Act prevent the tribe from denying a fee owner access to his or her own parcel, "to the extent that large portions of reservation land were sold in fee, such that the Tribe could no longer determine the essential character of the region by setting conditions on entry to those parcels, the Tribe's legitimate interest in land use regulation was also diminished." As to the area of the reservation generally closed to public access, Stevens found that the Yakima Nation retained zoning power over the isolated parcels of nonmember-owned fee land because it "has preserved the power to define the essential character of that area." Just as the Allotment Act entailed an access easement for the nonmember owner of allotted parcels, so that Act reasonably should be construed to establish a kind of "equitable servitude" requiring fee owners to comply with tribal zoning rules. Stevens reconciled this holding with *Montana* by noting that in the case of the closed area, the tribe's zoning rule "is neutrally applied, is necessary to protect the welfare of the Tribe, and does not interfere with any significant state or county interest."

As to the "open area," Justice Stevens joined Justice White's opinion, finding that the alienation of about half the property in fee "has produced an integrated community that is not economically or culturally delimited by reservation boundaries," and also destroyed the tribe's power "to define the essential character of the territory." Stevens emphasized the considerable amount of services that the county supplies to all residents of the open area, and the fact that all reservation residents can vote in county (but not tribal) elections. He also underscored the district court's findings "that the county has a substantial interest in regulating land use in the open area — and in particular in protecting 'the county's valuable agricultural land' — and that the open area lacks 'a unique religious or spiritual significance to the members of the Yakima Nation.'" Stevens concluded that whatever equitable servitude-like claim the tribe may have possessed to zone allotted land vanished when the area "lost its character as an exclusive tribal resource" and became "as a practical matter, an integrated portion of the county." While acknowledging that his distinction between the two areas of the reservation created a difficult problem of line-drawing, Stevens pointed out that "line-drawing is inherent in the continuum that exists between those reservations that still maintain their status as distinct social structures and those that have become integrated in other local polities."

NOTES ON TRIBAL REGULATORY POWER

1. **The Opinions in *Brendale*:** While the opinion of Justice White would deny tribes the right to zone any nonmember-owned fee land within their reservations, Justice Stevens' crucial opinion distinguishes between fee land in "open" versus "closed" parts of the reservation. As to the former, he agrees with Justice White. But as to the "closed" parts, he joins with the dissenting Justices, who support

tribal jurisdiction to zone *all* fee lands. Can tribes with allotted reservations carry out coherent land use planning under the resulting legal regime? Can counties do any better on such reservations?

What conceptions of tribal sovereignty and the tribal-federal relationship animate the opinions of Justices White and Stevens? Both seem to acknowledge that the tribe might have a federally protected interest in particular uses of all fee lands on the reservation, even where they have lost an interest in conducting comprehensive land use planning. This interest would be in the nature of preventing serious threats to nearby Indian lands. Is this interest anything more than a property interest, analogous to an equitable servitude? Is Justice Stevens embracing the position, rejected in the *Merrion* case (Sec. B.1, this chapter), that inherent tribal power over non-Indians derives entirely from the power to exclude? Even accepting this view, why wasn't the county's zoning law therefore preempted under the Indian commerce clause, and the tribe left with exclusive jurisdiction? Could the tribe's interest be satisfied by having the opportunity to present its concerns in the local county zoning process? Does Justice Stevens' association of tribal interests with maintaining social distinctiveness prevent tribes from adapting to contemporary social and economic conditions and falsely characterize them as static societies?

Scholarly opinion of the *Brendale* case has been very critical. *See, e.g.*, Joseph William Singer, *Legal Theory: Sovereignty and Property*, 86 Nw. U. L. Rev. 1 (1991).

2.   Applying the "Open/Closed" Distinction in *Brendale*: The consequence of *Brendale* is that "opened" reservations with mixed trust, Indian fee, and nonmember fee land will be zoned by two different authorities — state or local government for the non-Indian fee land, tribal government for the remainder. Yet how will tribal and county governments know how to characterize particular areas of each reservation? Is the percentage of fee land alone determinative? Stevens also emphasizes the character of the open area, citing the amount of development, the existence of three incorporated townships, and its placement adjacent to off-reservation lands, including a municipal airport. What if the fee land were more evenly scattered throughout the entire reservation? Would Justice Stevens say that the tribe retained its zoning authority? Recall the Court's refusal to apply *Brendale*'s approach in the *Atkinson* case, despite the fact that the fee land there was entirely surrounded by reservation land. What does the Court's reasoning in that case tell you about which facts influenced Justice Stevens' opinion in *Brendale*?

3.   MOUs, Non-Indian Appointees, and Environmental Regulation as Practical Responses to *Brendale*: There are several ways Native nations and counties may try to overcome the planning uncertainty spawned by *Brendale*. One is for the two governments to enter into agreements or memoranda of understanding (MOUs) to establish a system of coordinated land use planning and regulatory activities for the reservation. The Swinomish Tribe in Washington State has made such an agreement with Skagit County, in which the governments resolve to set jurisdictional conflicts aside and create a joint comprehensive land use plan together with implementing ordinances and administrative procedures.

A second solution may be to work with on-reservation non-Indian communities to reduce the likelihood of a challenge to tribal zoning or perhaps even to secure nonmembers' consent to tribal jurisdiction. For example, the Colville Tribe has provided for the appointment of two non-Indian residents of that Reservation to the seven-member Land Use Review Board that administers the Tribe's zoning ordinance. The Colville assert zoning jurisdiction over all lands within their Reservation, regardless of trust status or non-Indian ownership. Should Indian nations have to resort to such measures in order to achieve coherent land use for their homelands?

A third solution to the planning dilemma created by *Brendale* is for tribes to invoke their environmental regulatory powers rather than their zoning powers to control land use. Most land uses require some type of environmental permit or review as well as zoning permission. Note that federal environmental laws, regulations, and Environmental Protection Agency (EPA) policies promote unitary controls over reservation lands, largely because spillover effects preclude effective application of environmental laws on a checkerboard basis. Several federal environmental regimes allow the EPA to designate tribes as having "primacy" over environmental regulation reservation-wide (known as "treatment in the same manner as a state" or TAS), so long as the EPA concludes that the tribe possesses adequate jurisdiction. *See* Ch. 5, Sec. G.

For example, under the Clean Water Act, 33 U.S.C. § 1377(e) (also referred to as section 518), Congress authorized EPA to treat Indian tribes as states for purposes of establishing water quality standards within their boundaries, certifying compliance with those standards, and issuing and enforcing discharge permits. At one point in his opinion in *Brendale*, Justice White accompanied his statement that Congress had not expressly delegated authority to zone to the Yakima Nation with a citation to this provision in the Clean Water Act, implying his belief that this part of the Act did establish an express delegation. The EPA disagrees with Justice White on this point, having concluded that the issue of whether section 1377(e) grants tribal authority is not resolved. Nevertheless, the agency has determined that tribes may be the appropriate authorities to administer the requirements of the Clean Water Act on fee as well as trust land within reservations. Disagreeing with commenters who had urged the EPA to adopt a blanket rule that tribes had no authority over fee land after *Brendale*, the agency stated that "the ultimate decision regarding Tribal authority must be made on a Tribe-by-Tribe basis. . . . " 58 FR 67966, 67975 (1993). In 1991, the EPA concluded a formal rule-making process designed to specify the requirements tribes would have to meet in order to demonstrate authority over the activities of nonmembers on non-Indian fee land and receive TAS status. Under these rules, EPA requires a tribe to show that the regulated activities affect "the political integrity, the economic security, or the health or welfare of the tribe." Final Rule, 56 FR 64,877 (quoting *Montana*). According to the agency, there is no reason, in light of *Brendale*, to assume that tribes "would be per se unable to demonstrate authority over water resource management on fee land within reservation borders for purposes of administering" various water quality programs. 58 FR 67966, 67976 (1993). In fact, EPA announced that it would be disposed to find such tribal authority in many instances through the following process:

> Operationally, EPA's generalized findings regarding the relationship of water quality to tribal health and welfare will affect the legal analysis of a

tribal submission by, in effect, supplementing the factual showing a tribe makes in applying for treatment as a State. Thus, a tribal submission meeting the requirements of § 131.8 of this regulation will need to make a relatively simple showing of facts that there are waters within the reservation used by the Tribe or tribal members, (and thus that the Tribe or tribal members could be subject to exposure to pollutants present in, or introduced into, those waters) and that the waters and critical habitat are subject to protection under the Clean Water Act. The Tribe must also explicitly assert that impairment of such waters by the activities of non-Indians, would have a serious and substantial effect on the health and welfare of the Tribe. Once the Tribe meets this initial burden, EPA will, in light of the facts presented by the tribe and the generalized statutory and factual findings regarding the importance of reservation water quality discussed above, presume that there has been an adequate showing of tribal jurisdiction of fee lands, unless an appropriate governmental entity (e.g., an adjacent Tribe or State) demonstrates a lack of jurisdiction on the part of the Tribe.

In *Montana v. EPA*, 137 F.3d 1135 (9th Cir. 1998), and *Wisconsin v. EPA*, 266 F.3d 741 (7th Cir. 2001), federal circuit courts upheld EPA's method of reviewing tribal claims of inherent authority over nonmember-owned fee land. The Ninth Circuit in particular praised EPA for taking "a cautious view by incorporating both Justice White's and Justice Stevens' admonitions in *Brendale* that, to support the exercise of inherent authority, the potential impact of regulated activities must be serious and substantial." It also emphasized that "due to the mobile nature of pollutants in surface water it [is in practice] very difficult to separate the effects of water quality impairment on non-Indian fee land from impairment on the tribal portions of the reservation." The Confederated Salish and Kootenai Tribes, recipients of TAS status in that case, were thereby empowered to regulate discharges by a wide range of reservation-based non-Indian landowners, including feedlots, dairies, auto wrecking yards and dumps, construction contractors, landfills, slaughterhouses, hydroelectric facilities, and wood processing plants. Is this power an adequate substitute for zoning authority?

D. INDIVIDUAL RIGHTS AND TRIBAL AUTHORITY

1. Federal Restrictions on Tribal Governments: The Indian Civil Rights Act of 1968

Tribes as well as the federal government may impose limitations on the exercise of tribal power. Recall that *Talton v. Mayes*, 163 U.S. 376, 382–83 (1896), discussed at the beginning of this chapter, held that since tribal authority derived from inherent aboriginal sovereignty, not from the United States, the Fifth Amendment, and inferentially other provisions of the Bill of Rights, did not apply to the operation of Indian tribal governments. The Indian Civil Rights Act of 1968 (ICRA), Pub. L. No. 90-284, 82 Stat. 77, sought to change that situation. *See generally* Donald L. Burnett, *An Historical Analysis of the 1968 "Indian Civil Rights" Act*, 9 HARV. J. ON LEGIS. 557 (1972); Comment, *The Indian Bill of Rights and the Constitutional Status of Tribal Governments*, 82 HARV. L. REV. 1343 (1969). The ICRA was the first major federal legislation regarding the operation of tribal government since Congress enacted the Indian Reorganization Act in 1934 (IRA). Unlike the IRA, however, which contained no provisions purporting to limit the operation of tribal government beyond the need for approval of the Act and tribal constitutions or charters in votes conducted by the Secretary, the ICRA expressly purported to limit the operation of tribal governments in important ways. Title II of the ICRA, codified as amended at 25 U.S.C. §§ 1301–1303, applied many, but not all, provisions of the Bill of Rights to Indian tribes.

While the tribes did not enthusiastically embrace the ICRA during the debates, some only offered mild opposition. Others, including the Pueblos of the southwest, were adamantly opposed to the ICRA. They argued that imposing western style rights guarantees would fundamentally alter their traditional theocratic way of life. According to Burnett: "American Indian tribes were many and various, and each had its unique problems; they were not equally prepared or willing to accommodate themselves to the structures of the Constitution." Burnett, *supra*, at 590.

In its final form, the ICRA imposed most, but not all, of the Bill of Rights on the tribes through federal *statutory* limitations on the exercise of their powers. Specifically omitted were the establishment clause, any right to appointed counsel, the requirement of grand jury indictment, and civil jury trial. Notice that the last two rights have never been made applicable to the states as well. Why do you suspect Congress omitted the establishment clause from the ICRA? Why do you think it failed to include any right to appointed, as opposed to retained, counsel in criminal cases? Review the provisions of the ICRA carefully to understand how it operates and what it contains.

The only remedy expressly afforded in the ICRA for violation of rights it guarantees is a grant of authority to the federal district courts to entertain applications for writ of habeas corpus for those held in tribal "detention" in violation of the rights set forth in the ICRA. Nevertheless, almost immediately after its enactment federal courts began enforcing the ICRA in civil, as well as criminal, cases often employing the general federal question and civil rights jurisdictional grants set forth in 28 U.S.C. §§ 1331, 1343. Most of these decisions required exhaustion of tribal remedies before seeking federal review. *See, e.g., O'Neal v. Cheyenne River Sioux Tribe*, 482 F.2d 1140 (8th Cir. 1973). Many, perhaps most, federal cases decided during this period applied the due process, equal protection, and even the bill of attainder clauses to intrude substantially into tribal decision-making, particularly in matters having little to do with criminal process, such as the conduct of tribal elections. *See, e.g., Wounded Head v. Tribal Council of Oglala Sioux Tribe*, 507 F.2d 1079 (8th Cir. 1975) (election procedures); *Brown v. United States*, 486 F.2d 658 (8th Cir. 1973) (tribal apportionment); *Johnson v. Lower Elwha Tribal Community*, 484 F.2d 200 (9th Cir. 1973) (due process complaints in tribal land assignments); *Slattery v. Arapahoe Tribal Council*, 453 F.2d 278 (10th Cir. 1971) (tribal membership criteria); *Dodge v. Nakai*, 298 F. Supp. 26 (D. Ariz. 1969) (legislative exclusion of legal services lawyer from reservation a bill of attainder). In all of these cases, the federal courts simply assumed, frequently without discussion, both that the ICRA created a claim to sue a tribe that violated any of its provisions and that the ICRA waived tribal sovereign immunity from suit. The next case put an end to both those assumptions. For a collection of essays on the Indian Civil Rights Act, reflecting on the legislation on its fortieth anniversary, *see* THE INDIAN CIVIL RIGHTS ACT AT FORTY (Kristen A. Carpenter, Matthew L. M. Fletcher & Angela R. Riley eds., 2012).

SANTA CLARA PUEBLO v. MARTINEZ
United States Supreme Court
436 U.S. 49 (1978)

MR. JUSTICE MARSHALL delivered the opinion of the Court.

This case requires us to decide whether a federal court may pass on the validity of an Indian tribe's ordinance denying membership to the children of certain female tribal members.

Petitioner Santa Clara Pueblo is an Indian tribe that has been in existence for over 600 years. Respondents, a female member of the tribe and her daughter, brought suit in federal court against the tribe and its Governor, petitioner Lucario Padilla, seeking declaratory and injunctive relief against enforcement of a tribal ordinance denying membership in the tribe to children of female members who marry outside the tribe, while extending membership to children of male members who marry outside the tribe. Respondents claimed that this rule discriminates on the basis of both sex and ancestry in violation of Title I of [ICRA], which provides in relevant part that "[n]o Indian tribe in exercising powers of self-government shall deny to any person within its jurisdiction the equal protection of its laws." *Id.*, § 1302(8).

Title I of the ICRA does not expressly authorize the bringing of civil actions for declaratory or injunctive relief to enforce its substantive provisions. The threshold issue in this case is thus whether the Act may be interpreted to impliedly authorize such actions, against a tribe or its officers, in the federal courts. For the reasons set forth below, we hold that the Act cannot be so read.

I

Respondent Julia Martinez is a full-blooded member of the Santa Clara Pueblo, and resides on the Santa Clara Reservation in Northern New Mexico. In 1941 she married a Navajo Indian with whom she has since had several children, including respondent Audrey Martinez. Two years before this marriage, the Pueblo passed the membership ordinance here at issue, which bars admission of the Martinez children to the tribe because their father is not a Santa Claran.[49] Although the

---

[49] [2] The ordinance, enacted by the Santa Clara Pueblo Council pursuant to its legislative authority under the Constitution of the Pueblo, establishes the following membership rules:

1. All children born of marriages between members of the Santa Clara Pueblo shall be members of the Santa Clara Pueblo.
2. That children born of marriages between male members of the Santa Clara Pueblo and non-members shall be members of the Santa Clara Pueblo.

children were raised on the reservation and continue to reside there now that they are adults, as a result of their exclusion from membership they may not vote in tribal elections or hold secular office in the tribe; moreover, they have no right to remain on the reservation in the event of their mother's death, or to inherit their mother's home or her possessory interests in the communal lands.

After unsuccessful efforts to persuade the tribe to change the membership rule, respondents filed this lawsuit in the United States District Court for the District of New Mexico, on behalf of themselves and others similarly situated. Petitioners moved to dismiss the complaint on the ground that the court lacked jurisdiction to decide intratribal controversies affecting matters of tribal self-government and sovereignty. The District Court rejected petitioners' contention, finding that jurisdiction was conferred by 28 U.S.C. § 1343 (4) and 25 U.S.C. § 1302 (8). The court apparently concluded, first, that the substantive provisions of Title I impliedly authorized civil actions for declaratory and injunctive relief, and second, that the tribe was not immune from such suit. Accordingly, the motion to dismiss was denied.

Following a full trial, the District Court found for petitioners on the merits. While acknowledging the relatively recent origin of the disputed rule, the District Court nevertheless found it to reflect traditional values of patriarchy still significant in tribal life. The court recognized the vital importance of respondents' interests,[50] but also determined that membership rules were "no more or less than a mechanism of social self-definition," and as such were basic to the tribe's survival as a cultural and economic entity. In sustaining the ordinance's validity under the "equal protection clause" of the ICRA, 25 U.S.C. § 1302(8), the District Court concluded that the balance to be struck between these competing interests was better left to the judgment of the Pueblo:

> [T]he equal protection guarantee of the Indian Civil Rights Act should not be construed in a manner which would require or authorize this Court to determine which traditional values will promote cultural survival and should therefore be preserved. Such a determination should be made by the people of Santa Clara; not only because they can best decide what values are important, but also because they must live with the decision every day. . . .
>
> . . . To abrogate tribal decisions, particularly in the delicate area of membership, for whatever "good" reasons, is to destroy cultural identity under the guise of saving it. 402 F. Supp., at 18–19.

On respondents' appeal, the Court of Appeals for the Tenth Circuit upheld the

---

3. Children born of marriages between female members of the Santa Clara Pueblo and non-members shall not be members of the Santa Clara Pueblo.

4. Persons shall not be naturalized as members of the Santa Clara Pueblo under any circumstances.

Respondents challenged only subparagraphs (2) and (3). By virtue of subparagraph (4), Julia Martinez's husband is precluded from joining the Pueblo and thereby assuring the children's membership pursuant to subparagraph (1).

[50] [5] The court found that "Audrey Martinez and many other children similarly situated have been brought up on the Pueblo, speak the Tewa language, participate in its life, and are, culturally, for all practical purposes, Santa Claran Indians." 402 F. Supp., at 18.

District Court's determination [on the issue of jurisdiction, but not] on the merits. While recognizing that standards of analysis developed under the fourteenth amendment's Equal Protection Clause were not necessarily controlling in the interpretation of this statute, the Court of Appeals apparently concluded that because the classification was one based upon sex it was presumptively invidious and could be sustained only if justified by a compelling tribal interest. Because of the ordinance's recent vintage, and because in the court's view the rule did not rationally identify those persons who were emotionally and culturally Santa Clarans, the court held that the tribe's interest in the ordinance was not substantial enough to justify its discriminatory effect.

We granted certiorari [and] now reverse.

II

Indian tribes are "distinct, independent political communities, retaining their original natural rights" in matters of local self-government. [*Worcester v. Georgia; Mazurie*]; F. Cohen, Handbook of Federal Indian Law 122–123 (1941). Although no longer "possessed of the full attributes of sovereignty," they remain a "separate people, with the power of regulating their internal and social relations." *United States v. Kagama*, 118 U.S. 375, 381–382 (1886). They have power to make their own substantive law in internal matters, see *Roff v. Burney*, 168 U.S. 218 (1897) (membership); *Jones v. Meehan*, 175 U.S. 1, 29 (1899) (inheritance rules); *United States v. Quiver*, 241 U.S. 602 (1916) (domestic relations), and to enforce that law in their own forums, see, *e.g., Williams v. Lee*, 358 U.S. 217 (1959).

As separate sovereigns pre-existing the Constitution, tribes have historically been regarded as unconstrained by those constitutional provisions framed specifically as limitations on federal or state authority. Thus, in [*Talton v. Mayes,*] this Court held that the fifth amendment did not "operat[e] upon" "the powers of local self-government enjoyed" by the tribes. In ensuing years the lower federal courts have extended the holding of *Talton* to other provisions of the Bill of Rights, as well as to the fourteenth amendment.

As the Court in *Talton* recognized, however, Congress has plenary authority to limit, modify or eliminate the powers of local self-government which the tribes otherwise possess. 163 U.S., at 384. Title I of ICRA, 25 U.S.C. §§ 1301–1303, represents an exercise of that authority. In 25 U.S.C. § 1302, Congress acted to modify the effect of *Talton* and its progeny by imposing certain restrictions upon tribal governments similar, but not identical, to those contained in the Bill of Rights and the fourteenth amendment. In 25 U.S.C. § 1303, the only remedial provision expressly supplied by Congress, the "privilege of the writ of habeas corpus" is made "available to any person, in a court of the United States, to test the legality of his detention by order of an Indian tribe."

III

Indian tribes have long been recognized as possessing the common-law immunity from suit traditionally enjoyed by sovereign powers. This aspect of tribal sovereignty, like all others, is subject to the superior and plenary control of Congress.

But "without congressional authorization," the "Indian Nations are exempt from suit." *United States v. United States Fidelity & Guaranty Co.*, [309 U.S. 506, 512 (1940)].

It is settled that a waiver of sovereign immunity " 'cannot be implied but must be unequivocally expressed.' " *United States v. Testan*, 424 U.S. 392, 399 (1976), quoting *United States v. King*, 395 U.S. 1, 4 (1969). Nothing on the face of Title I of the ICRA purports to subject tribes to the jurisdiction of the federal courts in civil actions for injunctive or declaratory relief. Moreover, since the respondent in a habeas corpus action is the individual custodian of the prisoner, see, *e.g.*, 28 U.S.C. § 2243, the provisions of § 1303 can hardly be read as a general waiver of the tribe's sovereign immunity. In the absence here of any unequivocal expression of contrary legislative intent, we conclude that suits against the tribe under the ICRA are barred by its sovereign immunity from suit.

IV

As an officer of the Pueblo, petitioner Lucario Padilla is not protected by the tribe's immunity from suit. See *Puyallup Tribe, Inc. v. Washington Dept. of Game, supra*, 433 U.S., at 171–172; cf. *Ex parte Young*, 209 U.S. 123 (1908). We must therefore determine whether the cause of action for declaratory and injunctive relief asserted here by respondents, though not expressly authorized by the statute, is nonetheless implicit in its terms.

In addressing this inquiry, we must bear in mind that providing a federal forum for issues arising under § 1302 constitutes an interference with tribal autonomy and self-government beyond that created by the change in substantive law itself. Even in matters involving commercial and domestic relations, we have recognized that "subject[ing] a dispute arising on the reservation among reservation Indians to a forum other than the one they have established for themselves," *Fisher v. District Court*, 424 U.S. 382, 387–388 (1976), may "undermine the authority of the tribal court . . . and hence . . . infringe on the right of the Indians to govern themselves." *Williams v. Lee, supra*, 358 U.S., at 223. *A fortiori*, resolution in a foreign forum of intratribal disputes of a more "public" character, such as the one in this case, cannot help but unsettle a tribal government's ability to maintain authority. Although Congress clearly has power to authorize civil actions against tribal officers, and has done so with respect to habeas corpus relief in § 1303, a proper respect both for tribal sovereignty itself and for the plenary authority of Congress in this area cautions that we tread lightly in the absence of clear indications of legislative intent. Cf. *Antoine v. Washington*, 420 U.S. 194, 199–200 (1975); *Choate v. Trapp*, 224 U.S. 665, 675 (1912).

With these considerations of "Indian sovereignty . . . [as] a backdrop against which the applicable . . . federal statut[e] must be read," *McClanahan v. Arizona State Tax Commission*, 411 U.S. 164, 172 (1973), we turn now to those factors of more general relevance in determining whether a cause of action is implicit in a statute not expressly providing one. See *Cort v. Ash*, 422 U.S. 66 (1975). We note at the outset that a central purpose of the ICRA and in particular of Title I was to "secur[e] for the American Indian the broad constitutional rights afforded to other Americans," and thereby to "protect individual Indians from arbitrary and unjust actions of tribal governments." S. Rep. No. 841, 90th Cong., 1st Sess., 5–6 (1967). There is thus no doubt that respondents, American Indians living on the Santa Clara reservation, are among the class for whose especial benefit this legislation was enacted. Moreover, we have frequently recognized the propriety of inferring a federal cause of action for the enforcement of civil rights, even when Congress has spoken in purely declarative terms. See, *e.g.*, *Jones v. Alfred H. Mayer Co.*, 392 U.S. 409, 414 n.13 (1968). These precedents, however, are simply not dispositive here. Not only are we unpersuaded that a judicially sanctioned intrusion into tribal sovereignty is required to fulfill the purposes of the ICRA, but to the contrary, the structure of the statutory scheme and the legislative history of Title I suggest that Congress's failure to provide remedies other than habeas corpus was a deliberate one.

A

Two distinct and competing purposes are manifest in the provisions of the ICRA: In addition to its objective of strengthening the position of individual tribal members *vis-à-vis* the tribe, Congress also intended to promote the well-established federal "policy of furthering Indian self-government." *Morton v. Mancari*, 417 U.S. 535, 551 (1974). This commitment to the goal of tribal self-determination is demonstrated by the provisions of Title I itself. Section 1302, rather than providing in wholesale fashion for the extension of constitutional requirements to tribal governments, as had been initially proposed, selectively incorporated and in some instances modified the safeguards of the Bill of Rights to fit the unique political, cultural, and economic needs of tribal governments. [F]or example, the statute does not prohibit the establishment of religion, nor does it require jury trials in civil cases, or appointment of counsel for indigents in criminal cases, cf. *Argersinger v. Hamlin*, 407 U.S. 25 (1972).[51]

[When] Congress seeks to promote dual objectives in a single statute, courts must be more than usually hesitant to infer from its silence a cause of action that, while serving one legislative purpose, will disserve the other. Creation of a federal cause of action for the enforcement of rights created in Title I, however useful it might be in securing compliance with § 1302, plainly would be at odds with the congressional goal of protecting tribal self-government. Not only would it undermine the authority of tribal forums, . . . but it would also impose serious financial burdens on already "financially disadvantaged" tribes. Subcommittee on Constitutional Rights, Senate Judiciary Committee, Constitutional Rights of the American

---

[51] [14] The provisions of § 1302 . . . differ in language and in substance in many other respects from those contained in the constitutional provisions on which they were modeled. The provisions of the second and third amendments, in addition to those of the seventh amendment, were omitted entirely. The provision here at issue, § 1302(8), differs from the constitutional Equal Protection Clause in that it guarantees "the equal protection of *its* [the tribe's] laws," rather than of "*the* laws." Moreover, § 1302(7), which prohibits cruel or unusual punishments and excessive bails, sets an absolute limit of six months imprisonment and a $500 fine on penalties which a tribe may impose. Finally, while most of the guarantees of the fifth amendment were extended to tribal actions, it is interesting to note that § 1302 does not require tribal criminal prosecutions to be initiated by grand jury indictment, which was the requirement of the fifth amendment specifically at issue and found inapplicable to tribes in *Talton v. Mayes*. . . .

Indian: Summary Report of Hearings and Investigations Pursuant to S. Res. 194, 89th Cong., 2d Sess., 12 (Comm. Print 1966) (hereinafter cited as Summary Report).

Moreover, contrary to the reasoning of the court below, implication of a federal remedy in addition to habeas corpus is not plainly required to give effect to Congress's objective of extending constitutional norms to tribal self-government. Tribal forums are available to vindicate rights created by the ICRA, and § 1302 has the substantial and intended effect of changing the law which these forums are obliged to apply. Tribal courts have repeatedly been recognized as appropriate forums for the exclusive adjudication of disputes affecting important personal and property interests of both Indians and non-Indians. See, *e.g.*, *Fisher v. District Court*, 424 U.S. 382 (1976); *Williams v. Lee*, 358 U.S. 217 (1959). See also *Ex parte Crow Dog*, 109 U.S. 556 (1883). Nonjudicial tribal institutions have also been recognized as competent law-applying bodies. See [*Mazurie*].[52]

Under these circumstances, we are reluctant to disturb the balance between the dual statutory objectives which Congress apparently struck in providing only for habeas corpus relief.

B

Our reluctance is strongly reinforced by the specific legislative history underlying 25 U.S.C. § 1303. This history, extending over more than three years, indicates that Congress's provision for habeas corpus relief, and nothing more, reflected a considered accommodation of the competing goals of "preventing injustices perpetrated by tribal governments, on the one hand, and, on the other, avoiding undue or precipitous interference in the affairs of the Indian people." Summary Report, *supra*, at 11.

In settling on habeas corpus as the exclusive means for federal-court review of tribal criminal proceedings, Congress opted for a less intrusive review mechanism than had been initially proposed. Originally, the legislation would have authorized *de novo* review in federal court of all convictions obtained in tribal courts. At hearings held on the proposed legislation in 1965, however, it became clear that even those in agreement with the general thrust of the review provision — to provide some form of judicial review of criminal proceedings in tribal courts — believed that *de novo* review would impose unmanageable financial burdens on tribal governments and needlessly displace tribal courts. [Thus, a]fter considering numerous alternatives for review of tribal convictions, Congress apparently decided that review by way of habeas corpus would adequately protect the individual interests at stake while avoiding unnecessary intrusions on tribal governments.

[In light of] this history, it is highly unlikely that Congress would have intended

---

[52] [22] By the terms of its Constitution, adopted in 1935 and approved by the Secretary of the Interior in accordance with the Indian Reorganization Act of 1934, 25 U.S.C. § 476, judicial authority in the Santa Clara Pueblo is vested in its tribal council.

Many tribal constitutions adopted pursuant to [the IRA], though not that of the Santa Clara Pueblo, include provisions requiring that tribal ordinances not be given effect until the Department of Interior gives its approval. In these instances, persons aggrieved by tribal laws may, in addition to pursuing tribal remedies, be able to seek relief from the Department of the Interior.

a private cause of action for injunctive and declaratory relief to be available in the federal courts to secure enforcement of § 1302. Although the only committee report on the ICRA in its final form, S. Rep. No. 841, 90th Cong., 1st Sess. (1967), sheds little additional light on this question, it would hardly support a contrary conclusion. Indeed, its description of the purpose of Title I, as well as the floor debates on the bill, indicates that the ICRA was generally understood [as limiting judicial review to the habeas corpus mechanism under § 1303].

V

As the bill's chief sponsor, Senator Ervin, commented in urging its passage, the ICRA "should not be considered as the final solution to the many serious constitutional problems confronting the American Indian." 113 Cong. Rec. 13473 (1967). Although Congress explored the extent to which tribes were adhering to constitutional norms in both civil and criminal contexts, its legislative investigation revealed that the most serious abuses of tribal power had occurred in the administration of criminal justice. [Because] of this finding, and given Congress's desire not to intrude needlessly on tribal self-government, it is not surprising that Congress chose at this stage to provide for federal review only [by means of habeas corpus.][53]

As we have repeatedly emphasized, Congress's authority over Indian matters is extraordinarily broad, and the role of courts in adjusting relations between and among tribes and their members correspondingly restrained. See *Lone Wolf v. Hitchcock*, 187 U.S. 553, 565 (1903). Congress retains authority expressly to authorize civil actions for injunctive or other relief to redress violations of § 1302, in the event that the tribes themselves prove deficient in applying and enforcing its substantive provisions. But unless and until Congress makes clear its intention to permit the additional intrusion on tribal sovereignty that adjudication of such actions in a federal forum would represent, we are constrained to find that § 1302 does not impliedly authorize actions for declaratory or injunctive relief against either the tribe or its officers.

[*Reversed.*]

MR. JUSTICE BLACKMUN took no part in the consideration or decision of this case.

MR. JUSTICE WHITE, dissenting.

The declared purpose of the [ICRA] is "to insure that the American Indian is afforded the broad constitutional rights secured to other Americans." S. Rep. No. 841, 90th Cong., 1st Sess., 6 (1967) (hereinafter Senate Report). The Court today, by denying a federal forum to Indians who allege that their rights under the ICRA have been denied by their tribes, substantially undermines the goal of the ICRA

---

[53] [32] A tribe's right to define its own membership for tribal purposes has long been recognized as central to its existence as an independent political community. *See Roff v. Burney*, 168 U.S. 218 (1897); *Cherokee Intermarriage Cases*, 203 U.S. 76 (1906). Given the often vast gulf between tribal traditions and those with which federal courts are more intimately familiar, the judiciary should not rush to create causes of action that would intrude on these delicate matters.

and in particular frustrates Title I's purpose [to protect Indians from arbitrary actions by their governments].

Many tribal constitutions adopted pursuant to 25 U.S.C. § 476, though not that of the Santa Clara Pueblo, include provisions requiring that tribal ordinances not be given effect until the Department of Interior gives its approval. See I American Indian Policy Review Commission, *supra*, at 187–188; 1961 Hearings (Pt. I), *supra*, at 95. In these instances, persons aggrieved by tribal laws may, in addition to pursuing tribal remedies, be able to seek relief from the Department of Interior.

NOTES

1. **The Impact of *Santa Clara Pueblo***: *Santa Clara Pueblo* brought a temporary halt to federal courts' ability to review tribal governmental decisions. Because of the *Martinez* decision two formidable legal barriers faced any litigant attempting to get federal review of tribal decisions: tribal sovereign immunity and the need to establish a federal cause of action. Since *Martinez* held that the tribal sovereign immunity defense did not extend to tribal officials, including the tribal Governor, where only injunctive or declaratory relief was sought, the first barrier was not as significant as the second. *But see Linneen v. Gila River Indian Community*, 276 F.3d 489 (9th Cir. 2002); *United States v. Oregon*, 657 F.2d 1009, 1013 n.8 (9th Cir. 1981) (both suggesting, perhaps inconsistently with *Martinez*, that federal doctrines of tribal sovereign immunity bar suits against tribal officials). If the ICRA does not create any claim in federal court, what forum is available to redress violations of civil rights? Must a tribe provide a tribal court system to adjudicate such disputes? If the tribe has a tribal court must the jurisdiction of the tribal court necessarily include claims under the ICRA? If the ICRA creates no *federal* right of action may a tribe decline to imply a tribal right of action to enforce the ICRA? While some tribes have constitutional provisions that provide a clear separation of powers between the judiciary and the legislative branch, others have no clear delineation of separation of powers. Few expressly provide for judicial review of tribal council actions in their tribal codes. Can a tribal court enforce the ICRA in civil contexts in tribes lacking separation of powers or any express provisions for judicial review? Can adversely affected persons take their ICRA claims to tribal council? Does the *Martinez* Court deem that an adequate remedy?

Shortly after *Santa Clara Pueblo* was decided, Alvin Ziontz wrote an illuminating article suggesting that the development of judicial review and the enforcement of Bill of Rights limitations did not occur overnight in the federal system and reminding readers that the civil rights enforcement regime currently operating in federal courts was a relatively recent phenomenon that took almost 200 years to develop. He noted that tribes were developing far more rapidly, but responding to the demands of the ICRA might take time. Nevertheless, he commented: "If tribal governments fail, however, to deal responsibly with ICRA problems, *Martinez* will only have resulted in a reprieve, and there will be calls for Congress to amend the Indian Civil Rights Act so as to empower federal courts to review tribal action." Alvin J. Ziontz, *After* Martinez: *Indian Civil Rights Under Tribal Government*, 12 U.C. Davis L. Rev. 1, 26 (1979) (footnote omitted). In light of the cases in Sec. C, this chapter, his views may have been prophetic.

Could *Martinez* be read as a federal judicial effort to read statutes altering the tribal-federal balance narrowly in order to temper the rigors of the broad constitutional plenary power doctrine it has recognized in Indian affairs? The Supreme Court conventionally has done the same thing in construing statutes that affect the federalism balance between states and the federal government. *E.g.*, *United States v. Bass*, 404 U.S. 336 (1971).

2. The 1986 Amendments to the ICRA and the Tribal Law and Order Act of 2010: The version of the ICRA referred to in *Martinez* prevented tribes from imposing more than six months in jail or $500 in fines, or both. In 1986 Congress increased the length of imprisonment to one year and the fine to $5,000. The Anti-Drug Abuse Act of 1986, Pub. L. No. 99-570, § 4217, 100 Stat. 3207, 3207–146 (1986). Further augmenting tribal court sentencing authority, the Tribal Law and Order Act of 2010, Pub. L. 111-211, 124 Stat. 2258, § 234, amends section 1302 of the Indian Civil Rights Act to allow tribal courts to impose sentences as long as three years and fines as great as $15,000 for any one offense, up to a total limit of nine years' imprisonment. This enhanced sentencing authority may only be exercised, however, if the tribe provides effective assistance of counsel to indigent defendants at government expense, makes tribal criminal laws publicly available, maintains a record of the proceedings, and appoints judges who "have sufficient legal training" and are licensed to practice law in "any jurisdiction in the United States." Are these federal requirements reasonable in light of the fact that imprisonment is a feature of the non-Indian legal system, rather than a traditional tribal penalty? Or is the Congress making excessive demands that tribal criminal justice conform to non-Indian norms in order to achieve community safety? Are there mechanisms, such as waivers by defendants of their procedural rights, that can facilitate alternate forms of tribal justice, such as peacemaking or wellness courts? Note that the Indian Law and Order Commission, discussed in Ch. 1, Sec. B.2.I and Ch. 4, Sec. A.3, recommended that Congress legislate a tribal option to exercise exclusive Indian country criminal jurisdiction, regardless of the identity of the defendant, and with no limits on sentencing authority. The Commission also recommended, however, that Congress establish a specialized federal appellate court to hear appeals from tribal convictions, limited to procedural claims of violations of rights protected by the U.S. Bill of Rights. Indian Law and Order Commission, A Roadmap For Making Native America Safer: Report to Congress and the President of the United States 23–27 (November 2013).

The Ninth Circuit Court of Appeals has ruled that section 1302(7) of the Indian Civil Rights Act "unambiguously permits tribal courts to impose up to a one-year term of imprisonment for each discrete criminal violation" in a single transaction. *Miranda v. Anchondo*, 684 F.3d 844 (9th Cir. 2011) (sentence was decided prior to passage of the Tribal Law and Order Act). However, a federal district court in Arizona has held that the Tribal Law and Order Act requirements may apply when a tribal court sentences a defendant to consecutive one-year sentences. *See Johnson v. Tracy*, 2012 U.S. Dist. Lexis 140837 (D. Ariz. Sept. 28, 2012) (crime was committed before TLOA came into effect but conviction occurred after, so procedural protections of the legislation should have been afforded). For a thoughtful analysis of these issues, see Seth J. Fortin, *The Two-Tiered Program of the Tribal Law and*

Order Act, 61 UCLA L. REV. DISC. 88 (2013). For further discussion of tribal sentencing authority, see Ch. 4, sec. C.3.

3. **The Search for *Martinez* Exceptions:** In Kevin Gover & Robert Laurence, *Avoiding* Santa Clara Pueblo v. Martinez: *The Litigation in Federal Court of Civil Actions Under the Indian Civil Rights Act*, 8 HAMLINE L. REV. 497 (1985), the authors document the search for ways around the *Martinez* ruling. In one noted case, *Dry Creek Lodge, Inc. v. Arapahoe & Shoshone Tribes*, 623 F.2d 682 (10th Cir. 1980), the Tenth Circuit all but ignored *Martinez*, holding it inapplicable because the tribal court had determined in a case brought by the plaintiff that it had no jurisdiction in the case without the consent of the Tribal Council, which was not forthcoming. Claiming that the *Martinez* limitations applied only where an available remedy existed in tribal courts, the Tenth Circuit affirmed a monetary judgment levied directly against the Tribe for blocking the access road to the plaintiffs' commercial lodge within the reservation thereby forcing the closure of the lodge. As the Tenth Circuit put it "There must exist a remedy for parties in the position of plaintiffs to have the dispute resolved in an orderly manner. To hold that they have access to no court is to hold that they have constitutional rights but have no remedy." In *Dry Creek Lodge*, a dissenting judge chastised the majority of the panel for ignoring the *Martinez* sovereign immunity holding. Had the Arapahoe and Shoshone Tribes provided a tribal court forum to Dry Creek Lodge, Inc., in which it could litigate its ICRA claims, would the case have been decided in the same manner? A later decision in the Tenth Circuit limited *Dry Creek Lodge* to its facts. *White v. Pueblo of San Juan*, 728 F.2d 1307, 1312 (10th Cir. 1984) (*Dry Creek Lodge* distinguished because plaintiff in *White* had not sought a remedy in any tribal forum, unlike the plaintiff in *Dry Creek Lodge*). Was *Martinez* premised on the availability of an alternative tribal remedy? *Dry Creek Lodge* has been expressly rejected by the Ninth Circuit, *R.J. Williams v. Ft. Belknap Hous. Auth.*, 719 F.2d 979, 981 (9th Cir. 1983) (*Dry Creek* analysis foreclosed by *Martinez*), and further limited by the Tenth Circuit. *See, e.g., Ramey Constr. Co. v. Apache Tribe*, 673 F.2d 315, 319 n.4 (10th Cir. 1982) (*Dry Creek Lodge* based on "particularly egregious allegations of personal restraint and deprivation of personal rights").

In what turned out to be a prophetic observation, Gover and Laurence also noted in 1985 that a number of cases had sought to bypass the *Martinez* limitations on federal court review by arguing that the tribal court or tribal council lacked jurisdiction over the matter. Thus, the claim brought into federal court was not an ICRA claim, but rather, a claim that under federal law the tribe lacked legislative or judicial authority. The authors criticized this trend, suggesting:

> The irony, of course, is the effect of the *Oliphant* spin-off theory [permitting non-Indian litigants to attack tribal court jurisdiction in federal courts] on *Martinez*. That case, wary of Anglo-American intrusions into tribal business, falls to a much more intrusive interference. The federal court, unable to slap the hand of the process server — must handcuff the tribal judge and prevent him from exercising even the fairest jurisdiction.

Kevin Gover & Robert Laurence, *supra*, 8 HAMLINE L. REV. at 522. As it turns out, the authors' worst fears were realized several months later when the court decided *National Farmers Union Ins. Cos. v. Crow Tribe*, 471 U.S. 845 (1985), recognizing a federal common law right of action for claims of lack of jurisdiction in tribal courts over which federal district courts could exercise jurisdiction under 28 U.S.C. § 1331, albeit only after the plaintiffs exhausted any available tribal remedies. The nature of the *National Farmers Union* case reflects how such jurisdictional attacks sought to bypass *Martinez*. At core, the insurance company plaintiff in *National Farmers Union* sought to collaterally attack a default judgment based on failure of notice issued in tribal court against its insured. Given that the due process avenue was closed to it by *Martinez*, it argued that the tribal court lacked subject matter jurisdiction altogether over its non-Indian insured. *National Farmers Union* sets the stage for federal court review and federal judicial curtailment of tribal court civil jurisdiction. Since *Martinez* refused to imply a federal right of action from a statute actually creating rights, how could the Court in *National Farmers Union* imply a federal right of action to attack tribal jurisdiction where no federal statute existed at all on the subject?

4. The Membership Rule in *Martinez*: Control over tribal membership or citizenship has long been recognized as an essential power of the tribe. Should a federally imposed norm of gender equality be given greater weight in *Martinez*? What, if anything, is the basis for the assumption by Congress that it has power to control the tribal government or to affect the decisions of tribal courts? Professor Clinton has pointed out that the supremacy clause expressly subordinates state, not tribal, law to federal supremacy and questioned the existence of any doctrine of national supremacy on such questions. Robert N. Clinton, *There Is No Federal Supremacy Clause for Indian Tribes*, 34 Ariz. St. L.J. 113 (2002). Does the plenary power doctrine provide an adequate substitute for the supremacy clause in this regard? Since Professor Clinton questions and attacks the theoretical roots of the plenary power doctrine, he thinks not.

Professor Judith Resnik notes that federal courts and Congress often impose federal norms on Indian tribes. Nevertheless, she suggests, "One explanation of *Santa Clara Pueblo* is, in general, that Indian tribes' treatment of their members is not of central concern to federal law, and, in particular, that membership rules that subordinate women do not threaten federal norms (either because federal law tolerates women holding lesser status than men or because federal law has labeled the issue one of 'private' ordering and non-normative)." Judith Resnik, *Dependent Sovereigns: Indian Tribes, States, and the Federal Courts*, 56 U. Chi. L. Rev. 671, 755 (1989); *see also* Catharine MacKinnon, Feminism Unmodified: Discourses on Life and Law 63–69 (1987) (critique of *Martinez* as denying women's cultural participation). Should one assume that the gendered membership rule of the Santa Clara Pueblo necessarily subordinates women or necessarily reflect a Eurocentric conception of gender roles? If the Pueblo has been a matriarchy and had a matrilineal membership rule would we make the same assumption? Donna Goldsmith has warned American feminists against imposing their own assumptions about gender hierarchy on Indian societies or Indian women: "One of the dangers we face as feminists is believing that we are capable of constructing a universal set of truths that will benefit all women." Donna Goldsmith, *Individual v. Collective Rights: The Indian Child Welfare Act*, 13 Harv. Women's L.J. 1 (1990); *see also* Angela P. Harris, *Race and Essentialism in Feminist Legal Theory*, 42 Stan. L. Rev. 581, 588–93 (1990). For more information about the cultural context and the stories behind the case, *see* Gloria Valencia-Weber, *Three Stories in One: The Story of* Santa Clara Pueblo v. Martinez *in* INDIAN LAW STORIES (Carole Goldberg, Kevin K. Washburn & Philip P. Frickey, eds., 2011).

If a case like *Martinez* comes into tribal court, how should the tribal court interpret the equal protection clause of the ICRA? Does *Martinez* hold that the tribe is at liberty to ignore it, as some seem to think? Assuming, as *Martinez* suggests, that the limitations on tribal governing powers set forth in the ICRA can be constitutionally justified, must a tribal court interpret the equal protection clause of the ICRA as applied in a tribal context to a tribal membership rule in precisely the same fashion a federal or state court would interpret the equal protection clause of the Fourteenth Amendment as applied to the states? Does the difference in tribal context or, perhaps, the gendered nature of tribal origin stories and culture count for anything? Even if it need not reach the same result given the differences in context, culture, and governmental interests, must it apply the same tests? Does it make any difference that the major case including gender equality within the heightened scrutiny of the equal protection clause, *Frontiero v. Richardson*, 411 U.S. 677 (1973), was not decided until five years after the ICRA was enacted? Is the adoption of constitutional-like rights in the ICRA static (*i.e.*, including only extent rights at the time the Act was adopted) or dynamic (*i.e.*, including both existing and after-decided rights)? For an analysis of how one tribal court dealt with these questions under a tribal constitutional Bill of Rights worded identically to the ICRA, see *Winnebago Tribe v. Bigfire*, 25 Ind. L. Rep. 6229 (Winn. Sup. Ct. 1998), presented in Sec. D.2, this chapter. Had the defendants in *Bigfire* made an ICRA claim (which they did not), would the Winnebago Supreme Court have had the same liberty to depart from federal constitutional interpretations of gender equality?

In 2003, the University of Kansas School of Law's Tribal Law and Government Center sponsored a reconsideration of the case of *Martinez v. Santa Clara Pueblo* before the hypothetical Supreme Court of the American Indian Nations. Briefs for the petitioner and respondents, as well as the Court's decision, can be found at 14 KAN. J.L. & PUB. POL'Y 67, 79 & 91 (2004). The Supreme Court of the American Indian Nations agreed with the United States Supreme Court that the federal courts lack jurisdiction to review tribal government actions. The Indian Nations Court did not rest its decision on interpretation of the Indian Civil Rights Act, however. Rather, echoing points made in Porter's article, discussed above, the Indian Nations Court rested on the fact that Santa Clara Pueblo had never consented to suit. According to the court, "The foremost factor for consideration in this instance is the self-determination of the Santa Clara Pueblo. Any federal review of tribal decisions is an unlawful intrusion on the sovereignty of indigenous nations." That same journal issue also features "Testimony of a Santa Clara Woman," by Rina Swentzell, a woman who was raised at the Pueblo and went on to receive a Ph.D. from the University of New Mexico and marry a non-Santa Claran. Rina Swentzell, *Testimony of a Santa Clara Woman*, 14 KAN. J.L. & PUB. POL'Y 97 (2004). Dr. Swentzell observes that the Santa Clara social order "was not traditionally either/or, not matriarchal or patriarchal. It was both." Although she finds the exclusion of her children from tribal membership under Santa Clara law painful, she also prefers that decision-making about tribal membership stay within the community, which has been considering an amendment to base membership on criteria other than gender. She notes that in the dichotomous non-Indian world, "We are even tempted to think that American law can bring equality by written mandates, making us forget that we are capable of remembering a system in which focus on relationships might lead us to different solutions." Does Dr. Swentzell's testimony affect your assessment of the outcome in *Martinez*? *See also* Gloria Valencia-Weber, Santa Clara Pueblo v. Martinez: *Twenty-Five Years of Disparate Cultural Visions, An Essay Introducing the Case for Re-Argument Before the American Indian Nations Supreme Court*, 14 KAN. J.L. & PUB. POL'Y 49 (2004); Bethany R. Berger, *Indian Policy and the Imagined Indian Woman*, 14 KAN. J.L. & PUB. POL'Y 104 (2004).

2. Individual Rights in Tribal Courts

As Professor Frank Pommersheim has noted, typical IRA constitutions "omitted at least two hallmark provisions from the 'model' United States Constitution, namely the protections of the Bill of Rights and the doctrine of separation of powers."[54] According to Professor Pommersheim, it is no coincidence that "these very omissions are the ones that tribes are most criticized for, when in fact the blame lies elsewhere." Frank Pommersheim, *A Path Near the Clearing: An Essay on Constitutional Adjudication in Tribal Courts*, 27 GONZ. L. REV. 393, 396 (1991–92). Because tribal governments today possess far more centralized power and economic leverage with individuals than they did in the past, tribal members can be among the most vociferous critics. At the same time, non-Indians express concern that they will not receive fair treatment in tribal court, although a recent study of one year's reported tribal court decisions concluded that "non-Indian parties were treated fairly. . . . [T]he tribe does not always win against the individual, and the tribal member does not always defeat the non-Indian." Nell Jessup Newton, *Tribal Court Praxis: One Year in the Life of Twenty Indian Tribal Courts*, 22 AM. INDIAN L. REV. 285, 352 (1998).

Indian nations are increasingly aware of the need to make their constitutional governments more legitimate with their own people as well as with outsiders. One solution has been to develop tribal bills of rights that function in the same way as the federal Bill of Rights — to articulate fundamental values about the proper operation of government in relation to individuals. The growth in tribal provisions for independent judiciaries with powers of judicial review, combined with limited waivers of sovereign immunity in tribal court for purposes of injunctive and declaratory actions, has made enforcement of such rights increasingly available under tribal law. *See* Sec F, this chapter. Some tribal enumerations of rights track language in the United States constitution, or even incorporate wholesale the Indian Civil Rights Act of 1968. *See, e.g.*, Hoopa Valley Constitution, Art. VIII. Because tribal conceptions of the individual in relation to the collective do not always resemble non-Indian understandings, however, these tribal bills of rights

---

[54] A 1934 document by Felix S. Cohen, entitled "Basic Memorandum on Drafting of Tribal Constitutions," suggests that these provisions were not encouraged because of New Deal members' dissatisfaction with the substantive due process agenda of the United States Supreme Court, which was using the Bill of Rights to invalidate New Deal legislation. *See* ON THE DRAFTING OF TRIBAL CONSTITUTIONS BY FELIX S. COHEN (D. Wilkins, ed., 2007).

sometimes choose to protect a different or additional set of rights than their federal counterpart. Alternatively, the phrases used in tribal bills of rights may look the same as their federal equivalents, but tribal courts may interpret those phrases to fit tribal notions of fairness and individualism.

While Western liberalism posits the individual as the atomistic primary unit, independent of social role and context, Native cultures generally hold that the individual has moral worth stemming from equality of status and interdependence of individuals within the cosmic order. The logic of liberalism leads to the institutionalization of guarantees to protect the individual from the state. In contrast, the logic of Native cultures spawns efforts to restore community harmony and to insure a place of dignity for each individual within the social order. *See* Angela R. Riley, *(Tribal) Sovereignty and Illiberalism*, 95 CAL. L. REV. 799 (2007); Bruce G. Miller, *The Individual, the Collective, and Tribal Code*, 21:1 AM. IND. CULTURE & RESEARCH J. 107 (1997). Rather than expressing an adversarial relationship between the individual and the community, tribal constitutions, particularly as interpreted by tribal courts, often emphasize individual responsibilities, equal access to common resources, and balance among potentially competing kinship groups.

Thus, for example, Art. VII of the Muckleshoot Constitution protects civil liberties and rights of the accused, but also guarantees that "All members of the tribe shall be accorded equal opportunities to participate in the economic resources and activities of the reservation." Art. VII. And the concept of due process has been elaborated by the Navajo Nation Supreme Court in light of Navajo common law, the Court stating:

> Although due process of law is expressly guaranteed by section 3 of the Navajo Nation Bill of Rights, this Court has noted that "[t]he concept of due process was not brought to the Navajo Nation by the Indian Civil Rights Act . . . [nor] the Navajo Bill of Rights." Instead, due process is "fundamental fairness in a Navajo cultural context," and "strict standards of fairness and equity . . . are inherent in the Navajo common law." Due process is found by synthesizing the principles of Navajo custom and government, and it is applied "with fairness and respect."

> This Court has held that Navajo due process ensures notice and an opportunity to be heard for all parties to a dispute; entitles parties to representation; protects the right to seek political office; prevents the enforcement of ambiguous statutes affecting personal and property rights; must be provided when the government takes private property without the owner's consent; and applies to juvenile proceedings to the same extent as to adult proceedings.

In re Estate of Begay #2, 19 Ind. L. Rep. 6130, 6131 (Navajo 1992). The following case illustrates another tribe's approach to fundamental guarantees.

Winnebago Tribe of Nebraska v. Bigfire, 25 Ind. L. Rep. 6229 (Winn. Sup. Ct. 1998):[55] In three separate cases, males under the age of 18 were prosecuted under § 3-419(C) of the Winnebago Tribal Code, which states that "Any person who subjects another person to sexual contact and . . . (C) Any person who subjects an unemancipated minor to sexual penetration is guilty of sexual assault in the second degree." The females involved, who were several years younger than the males, were not prosecuted. The defendants appealed their convictions, arguing that they had been subject to selective prosecution on the basis of gender, in violation of the equal protection guarantee of Article IV, § 3(h) of the Winnebago Constitution. That provision declares that "The Winnebago Tribe of Nebraska in exercising its powers of self-government shall not: . . . (h) deny to any person within its jurisdiction the equal protection of the laws." On appeal, defendants did not invoke rights under the Indian Civil Rights Act, having failed to raise them at trial.

The Winnebago Supreme Court first determined that despite the similarities between Article IV § 3(h) and language in the Indian Civil Rights Act and the Fourteenth Amendment to the United States Constitution, it was not bound to apply state or federal law to the case. The court stated:

> Just as a state court may interpret provisions of an identically worded state constitution to mean something different and more protective than a similar federal constitutional guarantee, so a tribal court is free to interpret the tribal constitution independently of the meaning afforded similar language in federal law. This independence is not only a logical result of the sovereignty of the tribe as a separate political community within the United States, but also a necessary option to protect the separate and different cultural heritage of the tribe and to adapt the meaning of legal concepts derived from Anglo-American roots to the unique cultural context of communal tribal life. It is only with such sensitive adaptation of such legal concepts to the precise tribal community served by tribal law that such legal concepts will take on true meaning and provide real and meaningful legal protection.

The Winnebago Tribal Code instructed Winnebago courts to look first to the constitution, laws, and customs of the Tribe, and to turn to federal or state law only when tribal law failed to address an issue. Here, tribal law clearly dealt with the issue posed by the defendants.

Having determined that tribal law should be applied, the court next considered the relative weight to give to the tribal constitution versus tribal custom and usage. Although the Winnebago Tribal Code gave priority to written law, the court noted that "The harder problem, of course, is when will the adoption of a new written tribal positive law . . . be found to displace prior tribal customs and usages." According to the court,

> Like most tribes, the Winnebago Tribe of Nebraska agreed to removal from their ancestral homelands and to the acceptance of new reservation lands precisely to preserve their separate cultural and political identity as a

---

[55] Robert N. Clinton, one of the authors of this casebook, sat as Chief Justice on the panel in the *Bigfire* matter.

people. Therefore, while it is true that the people of the Winnebago Tribe of Nebraska can directly through constitutional amendment or indirectly by tribal ordinance alter their tribal traditions and customs, they should not be found to have done so unless they do so explicitly or unless the new positive law creates such an irreconcilable conflict with tribal traditions and customary law that the two cannot conceivably be harmonized and coexist. Otherwise all tribal written law . . . should be interpreted against the backdrop of and in harmony with evolving tribal custom and tradition. . . . Insofar as the Winnebago Tribal Constitution is unclear or vague as to meaning or interpretation of any of its provisions, this Court can and will look to tribal law, customs, and usages to provide background for and illuminate the meaning of such constitutional provisions.

Under these circumstances, the court refused to "parrot" equal protection standards found in the U.S. Constitution or the Indian Civil Rights Act, and chose to "fashion a standard for determining equal protection issues that may be analogous to federal or state standards but which also draws upon the rich cultural, social, and political heritage of the Winnebago Tribe."

The standard the court applied to the problem at hand differed from the federal equal protection standard for gender discrimination in two ways. First, the court indicated that it "take[s] gender discrimination quite seriously," and therefore applied "strict scrutiny" rather than the federal intermediate scrutiny standard. Thus, only a "compelling governmental interest, not merely an important governmental interest, must be found and the discrimination must be essential to furthering that interest." Second, the court determined that "a compelling justification for a gender or other differentiation can be found in the rich culture, history and traditions of the Winnebago Tribe," and "[o]nly invidious and irrational discriminations and disparities in governmental treatment unsupported by tribal law, customs, and usages therefore will be struck down under the equal protection provisions of the Winnebago Constitution."

Finally arriving at the merits of the defendants' gender-based prosecution claim, the court assessed the compelling government interests offered by the Tribe: preventing unwanted underage sexual activity and pregnancy, which have "devastating economic, cultural, and social impacts on young Winnebago women," and differences in the way that Winnebago tradition and culture treat men and women with respect to procreation. Like many tribal communities, the worldview of the Ho-Chunk people who comprise the Winnebago Tribe is gendered, a phenomena that occurs in many tribes because of gender roles assigned in tribal origin stories and because of gender-based assignment of clan membership or other significant affiliations within the tribal community through either matrilineal or patrilineal lines. Defendants argued that these gender-based concerns enshrined "archaic stereotypes" and "remnant[s] of patriarchy" into Winnebago law. Drawing upon trial court testimony from the Cultural Preservation Officer and Tribal Historian of the Tribe, respected anthropological sources, and personal knowledge of the teachings of tribal elders, the court characterized the Ho-Chunk thinking on gender relations as follows:

Gender differences constitute a natural part of life. Indeed, the Earth, the Grandmother who gives life, is female. Thus, gender role differentiation and gender differences in legal or customary treatment related to those roles are natural and expected. In Ho-Chunk culture, therefore, gender differences or disparities in treatment do not signal hierarchy, lack of respect or invidious discrimination, but, rather, are a respected and natural part of life. They are, indeed, part of the way that the Winnebago worldview brings meaning to life.

To support this view, the court quoted a tribal teaching found in one of the anthropological works:

My son, never abuse your wife. The women are sacred. If you abuse your wife and make her life miserable, you will die early. Our grandmother, the earth, is a woman, and in mistreating your wife you will be mistreating her. Most assuredly will you be abusing our grandmother if you act thus. And as it is she that is taking care of us you will really be killing yourself by such behavior.

Paul Radin, The Winnebago Tribe 122 (1990 [1923]).

The court viewed itself as combining both Western and Winnebago perspectives on equal treatment, with the Western approach rejecting gender differences that are "unjustified," and the Winnebago approach supplying the culture-based justification. Accordingly, the court found,

. . . [I]n applying the strict scrutiny standard . . . it must recognize that traditional differentiations, commonly accepted and practiced by the Tribe without pejorative or discriminatory implications, such as gender distinctions related to sexual conduct, must be sustained as involving the compelling tribal governmental interest of preserving tribal traditions and culture. What is tribally appropriate under Ho-Chunk tradition and customary law certainly was not rendered illegal and unconstitutional by the Tribe's own constitution!

In the context of these cases, it certainly was appropriate within a tribal legal system to apply tribal laws on second degree sexual abuse only to older males who had committed the crime and to make them more accountable. This Court's research into and understanding of Ho-Chunk tradition and customary law suggests that within the Winnebago culture, the male clearly is assigned the obligation of protecting the women. The areas of sexual misconduct and domestic abuse were specifically singled out as areas in which the Winnebago tradition and customary law assigned roles and responsibilities based on gender. Thus, even if a discriminatory effect and motivation could be shown clearly by the defendants in these cases (which the Court doubts given the limited universe of cases and the prosecutor's explanation of his prosecutorial policy [based on age difference]), the Tribe has a compelling governmental interest based on tribal traditions and usages for such gender differentiation in the area of sexual misconduct.

The court thus rejected defendants' equal protection claim, and upheld the prosecutions in every case but one, where the appeal was dismissed because of a double jeopardy problem.

NOTES

1. **Positive vs. Common or Customary Law:** Principles of Anglo-American law generally privilege positive law, certainly constitutional law, over common law. Why might a tribal court be less inclined to show such deference, as in the *Bigfire* opinion?

2. **Tribal vs. Federal Standards of Gender Equality:** *Bigfire* purports to apply a more demanding test to gender classifications than the federal standard. Is the standard really more demanding as the Court applies it? What would happen if the Court had applied a *less* demanding test? If tribal courts deploying tribal bills of rights afford fewer rights to criminal defendants than those guaranteed by the Indian Civil Rights Act, defendants may proceed to federal courts and petition for the writ of habeas corpus, at least if they have properly exhausted tribal remedies. *See* Sec. C.5. Does the availability of a separate set of federal rights render tribal law opinions, such as the one in *Bigfire*, pointless? *See* Robert N. Clinton, *There Is No Federal Supremacy Clause for Indian Tribes*, 34 Ariz. St. L.J. 113 (2002). Keep in mind that in *Bigfire*, the defendants had failed to exhaust their tribal remedies. But even if the exhaustion requirement had been satisfied, might a federal court pay heed to the tribal court's interpretation of equal protection? When phrases such as "equal protection" appear both in the United States Constitution and the Indian Civil Rights Act, are federal courts obliged to give them the same interpretation? In a portion of the *Bigfire* opinion not reproduced above, the Court went out of its way to suggest that federal constitutional law would reach the same result. Why might it have done so?

3. Tribal Power to Define Membership

While Indian tribes frequently employ the term members to refer to those who are full participating citizens of their tribal community, tribal membership is synonymous with and denotes tribal citizenship, *i.e.*, the right of full political and economic participation in the tribal political community. The right of an Indian tribe to determine its own membership was recognized by the United States Supreme Court in *Roff v. Burney*, 168 U.S. 218, 222 (1896), where the Court noted:

> The citizenship which the Chickasaw legislature could confer it could withdraw. The only restriction on the power of the Chickasaw Nation to legislate in respect to its internal affairs is that such legislation shall not conflict with the constitution or laws of the United States, and we know of no provision of such constitution or laws which would be set at naught by the action of a political community like this in withdrawing privileges of membership in the community once conferred.

In *Santa Clara Pueblo v. Martinez*, 436 U.S. 49, 54 (1978), the Supreme Court quoted the district court opinion for the proposition that "membership rules were 'no more or less than a mechanism of social . . . self-definition,' and as such were basic to the tribe's survival as a cultural and economic entity. The power of a tribe to define and control its membership, therefore, is critical to its definition of identity." Elsewhere in the opinion, the Court indicated that "[a] tribe's right to define its own membership for tribal purposes has long been recognized as central to its existence as an independent polity community." As noted in Chapter 2, most federal definitions of Indian defer to tribal definitions of membership by simply defining an Indian, more or less, as a member of a tribe recognized by the federal government.

Traditionally, tribal membership identification was often undertaken through kinship identity. In fact, Vine Deloria, the great scholar of Indian policy, has defined an Indian tribe as "a group of people living pretty much in the same place who know who their relatives are." Quoted in F. M. BORDEWICH, KILLING THE WHITE MAN'S INDIAN: REINVENTING NATIVE AMERICANS AT THE END OF THE TWENTIETH CENTURY 68 (1996). Thus, under the traditional law of many tribal communities, one who married into the tribe, even though not ancestrally descended from that tribe, might acquire tribal membership through kinship. *See, e.g., United States v. Rogers*, 45 U.S. 567 (1846) (discussing, and rejecting for federal law purposes, the Cherokee practice of granting nonmembers, including whites, who married tribal members full citizenship rights in the Cherokee Nation); *Nofire v. United States*, 164 U.S. 657 (1897) (same with opposite federal result). In addition to marrying into a tribe, many tribes recognized adoption as a traditional mechanism of establishing the kinship ties necessary to become part of the community. *See* John Rockwell Snowden et al., *American Indian Sovereignty and Naturalization: It's a Race-Thing*, 80 NEB. L. REV. 171 (2001).

While it remains true that the Native nations have the primary authority and responsibility to define who constitutes a citizen of their tribal community, Indian identity and tribal citizenship are far more complicated today and those complications create significant legal problems. No longer is tribal membership reckoned simply through kinship. Instead, legal membership rules have complicated the governance of many tribal communities. That complication was created by multiple factors. First, beginning with the late nineteenth century, the federal government's need to enumerate the tribal citizenry for allotment purposes required the Bureau of Indian Affairs to commence maintaining tribal enrollment lists, often based on blood quantum, *i.e.*, tribal ancestry. *See United States ex rel. West v. Hitchcock*, 205 U.S. 80 (1907) (agreement between tribe and federal government authorized Secretary to determine tribal membership for purposes of receiving allotments); *Stephens v. Cherokee Nation*, 174 U.S. 445 (1899) (membership for purposes of sharing in tribal funds). While such blood quantum or descent requirements sometimes conflicted with more traditional ways of reckoning kinship, they nevertheless gradually supplanted the more traditional, and less racial, ways of measuring tribal identity. Therefore Indian tribes gradually began to measure tribal membership or citizenship based on some type of blood quantum or tribal descent rule. Either a blood quantum or tribal descent rule became nearly universal in Indian country as a means of determining tribal citizenship. In one of the first cases to marshal an equal protection attack on such blood quantum definitions of tribal membership, when ratified by the federal government, the court wrote "it seems obvious that whenever Congress deals with Indians and defines what constitutes Indians or members of Indian tribes, it must necessarily do so by reference to Indian blood." *Simmons v. Eagle Seelatsee*, 244 F. Supp. 808, 814 (E.D. Wash. 1965), *aff'd*, 384 U.S. 209 (1966); *see also* Memo. Sol. I.D., October 1, 1941 (upholding provisions limiting tribal membership to persons of tribal blood). Since some tribes traditionally had clan divisions that for each tribe were reckoned either through patriarchal or matriarchal lines, tribes sometimes added additional membership rules that required not only the requisite blood-quantum or tribal descent, but also required that the tribal blood quantum or ancestry come through, for example, the father's line in a tribe with a traditional means of determining clan identification for both men and women through the father's line. For a recounting of the early history of blood quantum requirements in federal Indian law, see Paul Spruhan, *A Legal History of Blood Quantum in Federal Indian Law to 1935*, 51 S.D. L. Rev. 1 (2006).

Second, when Indian Reorganization Act constitutions were drafted in the 1930s, most of the tribal IRA constitutions enshrined tribal membership rules within the fabric of the tribal constitution, often in the form of minimum blood quantum requirements. The Bureau of Indian Affairs actively promoted inclusion of such criteria, through a circular stating that the IRA's definition of "Indian" — as persons of "one-half or more Indian blood" — should influence the design of membership provisions in tribal constitutions. According to the circular, Bureau employees should "urge and insist that any constitutional provision conferring automatic tribal membership upon children hereafter born, should limit such membership to persons who reasonably can be expected to participate in tribal relations and affairs." Circular No. 3123, United States Dept. of Interior (Nov. 18, 1935). Examples of appropriate provisions included requirements that both parents be tribal members, that the parents reside within the reservation, or that the children have a minimum blood quantum. Once these criteria were introduced into tribal constitutions, efforts to alter tribal citizenship requirements often raised serious tribal constitutional questions and frequently became the most critical battleground in any effort to amend or otherwise reform tribal constitutions. *See* Carole Goldberg, *Members Only? Designing Citizenship Requirements for Indian Nations*, 50 Kan. L. Rev. 437 (2002).

Third, the post-World War II mobility of the Native population frequently meant that large numbers of Indians considered members under a system reckoned by blood quantum or tribal descent, rather than residence, no longer lived on the reservation. Yet, as tribal citizens, they could vote in tribal elections and fully participate in tribal governance, even though they seldom were subject to laws it passed. Indeed, on many reservations the majority of eligible tribal voters live *off* the reservation and can control the governance of the remaining tribal members who live on the reservation lands and are therefore subject to tribal governance.

Fourth, as Indian gaming and other economic enterprises undertaken by tribes during the 1990s brought wealth to a few fortunate tribes, membership lists determined both who could share in the wealth of the tribe and how widely that wealth had to be spread, thereby affecting the size of *per capita* distribution payments from tribal revenues. Contests over the economic fruits of tribal investments have produced a number of significant membership disputes in recent years. Mark Neath, *American Indian Gaming Enterprises and Tribal Member-*

ship: Race, Exclusivity and a Perilous Future, 2 U. CHI. L. SCH. ROUNDTABLE 689 (1995). For all these reasons, tribal membership rules and their enforcement have increasingly become legal and political battlegrounds both inside and outside of Indian country.

POODRY v. TONAWANDA BAND OF SENECA INDIANS
United States Court of Appeals, Second Circuit
85 F.3d 874 (1996)

JUDGE JOSE A. CABRANES delivered the opinion for the Second Circuit:

I

The Tonawanda Band of Seneca Indians is a federally recognized Indian tribe occupying a 7,500-acre reservation near Akron, New York. Along with Seneca Indians now occupying the Cattaraugus and Allegany reservations in upstate New York, the Band was formerly recognized as the Seneca Nation, one of six nations known collectively as the Haudenosaunee or the Iroquois Confederacy. Unlike the Indians currently recognized as the Seneca Nation — i.e., the Seneca Indians of the Cattaraugus and Allegany Reservations — the Tonawanda Band retains the traditional governing institution of the Confederacy: the tribal Council of Chiefs ("the Council"), which carries out the views of the tribe on matters of internal governance. The petitioners claim, and the respondents do not appear to dispute, that this traditional form of Seneca government is based on consensus. The Tonawanda Band consists of eight "clans": the Snipe, the Heron, the Hawk, the Deer, the Wolf, the Beaver, the Bear, and the Turtle. Each clan appoints a clan mother, who in turn appoints an individual to serve as Chief. The clan mother retains the power to remove a Chief and, in consultation with members of the clan, provides recommendations to the Chief on matters of tribal government. The clan mothers cannot disregard the views of the clan, nor can the Chiefs disregard the recommendations of the clan mothers.

. . . .

In November and December 1991, a dispute arose on the Tonawanda Reservation concerning alleged misconduct by certain members of the Tonawanda Council of Chiefs. The petitioners, Peter L. Poodry, David C. Peters, Susan LaFromboise, John A. Redeye, and Stonehorse Lone Goeman, and others, apparently accused members of the Council, particularly its Chairman, respondent Bernard Parker, of misusing tribal funds, suspending tribal elections, excluding members of the Council of Chiefs from the tribe's business affairs, and burning tribal records. Allegedly in consultation with other members of the tribe, the petitioners formed an Interim General Council of the Tonawanda Band.

Petitioners Poodry, Peters, and LaFromboise claim that on January 24, 1992, they were accosted at their homes by groups of fifteen to twenty-five persons bearing the following notice:

It is with a great deal of sorrow that we inform you that you are now banished from the territories of the Tonawanda Band of the Seneca Nation. You are to leave now and never return.

According to the customs and usage of the Tonawanda Band of the Seneca Nation and the HAUDENOSAUNEE, no warnings are required before banishment for acts of murder, rape, or treason.

Your actions to overthrow, or otherwise bring about the removal of, the traditional government at the Tonawanda Band of Seneca Nation, and further by becoming a member of the Interim General Council, are considered treason. Therefore, banishment is required.

According to the customs and usage of the Tonawanda Band of Seneca Nation and the HAUDENOSAUNEE, your name is removed from the Tribal rolls, your Indian name is taken away, and your lands will become the responsibility of the Council of Chiefs. You are now stripped of your Indian citizenship and permanently lose any and all rights afforded our members.

YOU MUST LEAVE IMMEDIATELY AND WE WILL WALK WITH YOU TO THE OUTER BORDERS OF OUR TERRITORY.

The individuals bearing the notices attempted (without success) to take petitioners Poodry, Peters, and LaFromboise into custody and eject them from the reservation. Petitioners John A. Redeye and Stonehorse Lone Goeman received identical notices by mail. . . .

The five targeted individuals filed petitions for writs of habeas corpus in the United States District Court for the Western District of New York on November 10, 1992, claiming that they had been denied several rights guaranteed under Title I of the Indian Civil Rights Act of 1968[.]

. . . .

II

We face here a question of federal Indian law not yet addressed by any federal court: whether an Indian stripped of tribal membership and "banished" from a reservation has recourse in a federal forum to test the legality of the tribe's actions. More specifically, the issue is whether the habeas corpus provision of the Indian Civil Rights Act of 1968, 25 U.S.C. § 1303, allows a federal court to review punitive measures imposed by a tribe upon its members, when those measures involve "banishment" rather than imprisonment. . . .

[The Court first held that the tribal action was "criminal," rather than "civil" in nature and thus fit for habeas review. It concluded that]. . . . Santa Clara Pueblo simply does not compel the conclusion that all membership determinations are "civil in nature" and therefore insulated from federal habeas review. While ordinarily the inquiry into whether a sanction is "criminal" or "civil" is neither simple nor mechanical, we have no doubt about its resolution here. The documents that the members of the Council of Chiefs served upon the petitioners and circulated to various government agencies indicate that the respondents themselves view the petitioners' conduct as "criminal": the petitioners are claimed to have engaged in "unlawful activities," including "actions to overthrow, or otherwise bring about the removal of, the traditional government" of the Tonawanda Band. For these actions, the petitioners were "convicted of TREASON." Moreover, "banishment" has clearly and historically been punitive in nature. Examining a statute imposing forfeiture of citizenship upon a natural-born citizen who evaded military service, the Supreme Court found reference to history "peculiarly appropriate":

> [F]orfeiture of citizenship and the related devices of banishment and exile have throughout history been used as punishment. . . . Banishment was a weapon in the English legal arsenal for centuries, but it was always adjudged a harsh punishment even by men who were accustomed to brutality in the administration of criminal justice.

Kennedy v. Mendoza-Martinez, 372 U.S. 144, 170 n. 23 (1963) (citations and internal quotation marks omitted).

. . . .

The determination that we deal here with a criminal sanction does not end our inquiry. We must ascertain whether the petitioners are being "detained" within the meaning of § 1303. . . . The district court [concluded] that the banishment orders failed to give rise to a sufficient restraint on liberty to satisfy the traditional test for the availability of habeas relief.

. . . .

Section 1303 of the ICRA provides that "[t]he privilege of the writ of habeas corpus shall be available to any person, in a court of the United States, to test the legality of his detention by order of an Indian tribe." In contrast, 28 U.S.C. § 2241(c)(3), along with § 2254(a), serves as a basis for a federal court to exercise jurisdiction over one held "in custody" by a state "in violation of the Constitution or laws or treaties of the United States." Similarly, 28 U.S.C. § 2255 permits a district court to entertain a motion by "a prisoner in custody under sentence" of a federal court; § 2241(c)(1), which authorizes relief from federal restraint mainly in non-criminal settings, also uses the phrase "in custody."

The question is whether we should look to the interpretation of the "custody" requirement of these cognate federal statutes to inform our interpretation of the term "detention" in § 1303. The petitioners seize upon the difference in language to urge that Congress's use of the term "detention" in the ICRA was deliberate, and was intended to empower district courts to entertain a petition for habeas relief in a wider range of circumstances than the analogous provisions for relief from state and federal custody permit.

. . . .

We are not persuaded. . . . Congress appears to use the terms "detention" and "custody" interchangeably in the habeas context. We are therefore reluctant to attach great weight to Congress's use of the word "detention" in § 1303.

. . . .

The conclusion that § 1303 is no broader than analogous statutory provisions for collateral relief does not foreclose the possibility of habeas relief in this case. It is well established that actual physical custody is not a jurisdictional prerequisite for federal habeas review. *See, e.g., Jones v. Cunningham,* 371 U.S. 236, 243 (1963). The respondents acknowledge as much, but claim that habeas review requires "restraints far more closely related to actual imprisonment than the disabilities allegedly suffered by the appellants in this case." The district court agreed, finding that, "[i]n the absence of the imminent possibility of incarceration or at least some other form of on-going supervision by the Tonawanda Band" or "any tribal official," *Poodry v. Tonawanda Band of Seneca Indians,* No. 92-CV-738A, at 11 (W.D.N.Y. Apr. 13, 1995), the petitioners had "failed to establish that [they are] 'in custody' within the meaning of the habeas corpus statute," *id.* at 10.

We disagree. We begin with three decades of case law rejecting the notion that a writ of habeas corpus, as applied to one subject to a judgment of conviction by a state court, is a formalistic remedy whose availability is strictly limited to persons in actual physical custody. In the 1963 case of *Jones v. Cunningham,* the Supreme Court concluded that the conditions routinely placed on parolees — and the possibility of re-arrest if parole officers believe a violation of those conditions has occurred — constitute restraints on liberty significant enough to render parole a species of "custody" for habeas purposes:

> History, usage, and precedent can leave no doubt that, besides physical imprisonment, there are other restraints on a man's liberty, restraints not shared by the public generally, which have been thought sufficient in the English-speaking world to support the issuance of habeas corpus.
>
> . . . .
>
> . . . Of course, [the] writ always could and still can reach behind prison walls and iron bars. But it can do more. It is not now and never has been a static, narrow, formalistic remedy; its scope has grown to achieve its grand purpose — the protection of individuals against erosion of their right to be free from wrongful restraints upon their liberty.

371 U.S. 236, 240, 243 (1963) (emphasis supplied).

In a series of cases following *Jones,* the Court explored the contours of habeas review for individuals facing restraints on their liberty outside of conventional notions of physical custody or for whom the grant of a writ of habeas corpus would not achieve a release from custody. The Court held that a person released on his own recognizance pending sentencing after a state court conviction is "in custody" for habeas jurisdictional purposes.

As *Jones* and its progeny make clear, while the requirement of physical custody historically served to restrict access to habeas relief to those most in need of judicial attention, physical custody is no longer an adequate proxy for identifying all circumstances in which federal adjudication is necessary to guard against governmental abuse in the imposition of "severe restraints on individual liberty." . . . The custody requirement is simply designed to limit the availability of habeas review "to cases of special urgency, leaving more conventional remedies for cases in which the restraints on liberty are neither severe nor immediate." Thus, the inquiry into whether a petitioner has satisfied the jurisdictional prerequisites for habeas review requires a court to judge the "severity" of an actual or potential restraint on liberty. The most important example of this inquiry is a line of cases holding that a petition for a writ of habeas corpus cannot be used to challenge a conviction that resulted only in a cash fine or a short-lived suspension of privileges[.]

The petitioners have surely identified severe restraints on their liberty. . . . The respondents contend that the district court is without subject matter jurisdiction because the revocation of the petitioners' tribal membership is, as a legal matter, not a significant restraint on liberty. They do not appear to contest certain relevant jurisdictional facts: that the banishment notices were served upon three of the petitioners by groups of fifteen to twenty-five people demanding the petitioners' removal; that there have since been other attempts to remove the petitioners from the reservation; that certain petitioners have been threatened or assaulted by individuals purporting to act on the respondents' behalf; and that the petitioners have been denied electrical service. The district court acknowledged the alleged "interfere[nce] with [the petitioners'] peaceful life on the Tonawanda Reservation" and the attempts at forcible removal. Nonetheless, the court found no "on-going supervision by the Tonawanda Band" or "any tribal official," nor any requirement that the petitioners receive "prior approval to do things that an unconvicted person would be free to do."

"Restraint" does not require "on-going supervision" or "prior approval." As long as the banishment orders stand, the petitioners may be removed from the Tonawanda Reservation at any time. That they have not been removed thus far does not render them "free" or "unrestrained." While "supervision" (or harassment) by tribal officials or others acting on their behalf may be sporadic, that only makes it all the more pernicious. Unlike an individual on parole, on probation, or serving a suspended sentence — all "restraints" found to satisfy the requirement of custody — the petitioners have no ability to predict if, when, or how their sentences will be executed. The petitioners may currently be able to "come and go" as they please, cf. *Hensley [v. Municipal Court]*, 411 U.S. [345,] 351 [(1973)], but the banishment orders make clear that at some point they may be compelled to "go," and no longer welcome to "come." That is a severe restraint to which the members of the Tonawanda Band are not generally subject. . . . To determine the severity of the sanction, we need only look to the orders of banishment themselves, which suggest that banishment is imposed (without notice) only for the most severe of crimes: murder, rape, and treason. Had the petitioners been charged with lesser offenses and been subjected to the lesser punishment of imprisonment, there is no question that a federal court would have the power to inquire into the legality of the tribe's action. The respondents would have us turn the ordinary custody inquiry on its head: the question is not whether a punishment less severe than imprisonment — e.g., a fine, probation, or a temporary suspension of privileges — satisfies the custody requirement, but whether a more severe punishment does. We believe that Congress could not have intended to permit a tribe to circumvent the ICRA's habeas provision by permanently banishing, rather than imprisoning, members "convicted" of the offense of treason.

The severity of banishment as a restraint on liberty is well demonstrated by the Supreme Court's treatment of (1) "denaturalization" proceedings, initiated where an individual has obtained a certificate of U.S. naturalization illegally or through willful misrepresentation; and (2) statutes imposing a penalty of "denationalization" — forfeiture of American citizenship — on a natural-born U.S. citizen. Although a denaturalization proceeding is thought to be "civil" or "administrative" in nature, the Supreme Court has long recognized that a deprivation of citizenship is "an extraordinarily severe penalty" with consequences that "may be more grave than consequences that flow from conviction for crimes." *Klapprott v. United States*, 335 U.S. 601, 611–12 (1949).[56] . . .

To suggest that banishment is a fate "universally decried by civilized people" is not, of course, to say that this was always so. The practice of banishment has existed throughout the history of traditional societies, and in our Anglo-American tradition as well. Although Blackstone described exile as "punishment [ ] . . . unknown to the common law," 1 William Blackstone, Commentaries, it was not unknown to Parliament. Early in American history, the punishment of banishment was imposed upon British loyalists, and was even celebrated as a matter of sound policy in dictum by a Justice of the Supreme Court. *See Cooper v. Telfair*, 4 U.S. (4 Dall.) 14 (1800) ("The right to confiscate and banish, in the case of an offending citizen, must belong to every government.") (Cushing, J.).

The fact that permanent banishment has in the past been imposed as a punitive sanction, in our culture and in others, does not mean that under the laws of the United States it is a sanction not involving a severe restraint on liberty. Where, as here, petitioners seek to test the legality of orders of permanent banishment, a federal district court has subject matter jurisdiction to entertain applications for writs of habeas corpus.

In reaching this conclusion, we recall that this is a case of first impression, and that, if not considered in due course by the Supreme Court, the holding of the case may have significance in the future. This is especially true at a time when some Indian tribal communities have achieved unusual opportunities for wealth, thereby unavoidably creating incentives for dominant elites to "banish" irksome dissidents for "treason." Be that as it may, whatever doubts we might entertain about our construction of this legislation specially crafted for the benefit of Indian tribes is assuaged by the knowledge that, if we are wrong, Congress will have ample opportunity to correct our mistake.

. . . .

---

[56] [22] Concurring in *Klapprott*, Justice Wiley T. Rutledge wrote:

To take away a man's citizenship deprives him of a right no less precious than life or liberty, indeed of one which today comprehends those rights and almost all others. To lay upon the citizen the punishment of exile for committing murder, or even treason, is a penalty thus far unknown to our law and at most but doubtfully within Congress' power. Yet by the device or label of a civil suit, carried forward with none of the safeguards of criminal procedure provided by the Bill of Rights, this most comprehensive and basic right of all, so it has been held, can be taken away and in its wake may follow the most cruel penalty of banishment.

III

Finally, we address briefly a tension inevitable in any case involving questions of rights and questions of culture: whether the principles that guide our inquiry into the "criminal" or "civil" nature of the tribal action in this case or the severity of the restraint imposed must be "culturally defined" by the tribe, or whether we can approach these questions guided by general American legal norms or certain universal principles. Here, the respondents adopt a stance of cultural relativism, claiming that while "treason" may be a crime under the law of the United States, it is a civil matter under tribal law; and that while "banishment" may be thought to be a harsh punishment under the law of the United States — indeed, Chief Justice Warren described it as a "fate universally decried by civilized people," — it is necessary to and consistent with the culture and tradition of the Tonawanda Band.

We are unpersuaded. . . . [S]tatements submitted to the district court on behalf of the petitioners in this case counsel against accepting the respondents' attempt to avoid jurisdiction on grounds of tradition and culture at face value. If true, those statements would support a finding that "banishment" has not occurred within the Tonawanda Band within living memory, and that, to the extent that "banishment" is appropriate at all, it was not here imposed in the manner that tribal traditions actually prescribe. Were the mere invocation of cultural difference and tradition to preclude jurisdiction — even in the face of sworn statements suggesting the possibility that the "tradition" is not as claimed — our recognition of cultural relativism could only create a refuge for repression.

But we need not resolve the debate on whether basic rights can or should be culturally defined to resolve this case. We deal here not with a foreign state, but with admittedly distinct communities that have had a unique relationship with our federal government for centuries — a relationship that exists within the framework of American institutions and, in the last analysis, under American law. We need not condone policies pursued in the early years of our nation to conclude that federal influence — such as the role of the Bureau of Indian Affairs in recognizing a ruling council of the Tonawanda Band — is intertwined with tribal power. In this respect, the wide dissemination of material proclaiming to federal and state officials the petitioners' "convict [ion]" and "banishment" — indeed, seeking aid in removing the petitioners from the Tonawanda Reservation — speaks for itself. The respondents wish to use their connection with federal authorities as a sword, while employing notions of cultural relativism as a shield from federal court jurisdiction. We need not question the power of Indian nations to govern, to establish membership criteria, to exclude outsiders, or to regulate the use of their land and resources in order to acknowledge and vindicate a federal responsibility for those American citizens subject to tribal authority when that authority imposes criminal sanctions in denial of rights guaranteed by the laws of the United States. In sum, there is simply no room in our constitutional order for the definition of basic rights on the basis of cultural affiliations, even with respect to those communities whose distinctive "sovereignty" our country has long recognized and sustained.

NOTES ON TRIBAL MEMBERSHIP/CITIZENSHIP
AND BANISHMENT

1. Tribal Membership and Governance of the Reservation: Simple reliance on blood quantum or descent to determine tribal membership increasingly is creating major problems for the governance of tribes. When all members remained on the reservation, ascertaining membership solely by blood quantum or descent posed few problems since most adult tribal members eligible to vote in tribal elections also lived on the reservation and were subject to tribal governance. With increased post-World War II mobility of Indian populations and far less than half of the nation's Native population living in Indian country today, many Native nations find that the majority of their voting members live outside of, and often far removed from, the reservation. For the largest tribe in the country, the Cherokee Nation of Oklahoma, a majority of the members live outside the Nation's occupancy area, its former reservation. Yet, providing them full membership rights, including voting privileges, as the Cherokee Nation does, could result in a tribal government increasingly divorced from and not fully politically accountable to the reservation population that it serves. Since tribal membership is also often the passport to important tribal and federal benefits and a source of individual income for those tribes fortunate enough to have wealth sufficient to make *per capita* distributions to members, significant disincentives and political pressures operate to prevent the tribe from addressing such political imbalances of power.

Such questions have become an increasing source of internal friction within Native nations. While many have not addressed this problem, a few have. First, some tribes have responded by imposing residency requirements, often of six months or a year, for eligibility to vote in tribal elections or for holding elective tribal political office, or both. The Cheyenne River Sioux Tribe has a six month residency requirement for voting and the Leech Lake Chippewa impose a year residency for holding elective office. Such solutions leave all tribal members eligible for tribal or federal services or benefits or *per capita* distributions but limit political participation to those directly governed by the tribal government. Second, other tribes, either overtly or covertly, discourage tribal enrollment of children born to parents living *off* the reservation. Amendment III of Colville Constitution, for example, draws a distinction for enrollment purposes between children born to Colville parents living on the reservation and those living off the reservation. Children possessing the requisite degree of Indian blood born to a Colville tribal member living on the reservation may be enrolled at any time. For children possessing the requisite degree of tribal blood born to a Colville parent living off the reservation, however, Amendment III (1)(c) provides that "[t]o indicate a willingness to maintain tribal affiliation, the parent or guardian, shall within six months after the birth of the child submit a written application to have the child enrolled." If the application is not submitted within the six month window the child cannot be enrolled. Other tribes informally accomplish the same result by refusing to mail tribal membership application forms or requiring the application to be made within a limited period after birth and in person. Third, some tribes have adopted a residence requirement, either as a precondition for tribal enrollment or as a condition of the continued maintenance of tribal membership. *E.g.*, Constitution and Bylaws of the Sac and Fox Tribe of the Mississippi in Iowa, Article II (loss of tribal membership if adult resides off the reservation for longer than 10 years without returning). Would adopting a residency requirement for voting and holding office cure most of these problems? Are the main goals of such limitations assuring political accountability to those residing on the reservation or are other property-related issues at stake? Can a tribe legally distinguish among its citizens/members on the basis of their residency in the exercise of their political rights? When confronted with this question a quarter of a century ago, the Eighth Circuit held in *Daly v. United States*, 483 F.2d 700 (8th Cir. 1973), that the Crow Creek Sioux could limit eligibility for service on the Tribal Council to those of one-half or more Indian blood even though their membership blood quantum was lower. The Eighth Circuit stated "the tribe has a sufficient cultural interest in setting a higher blood quantum requirement to hold office than for mere membership in the tribe if it so desires." Would a residency requirement for voting raise a more difficult or easier question? What about a higher blood quantum for voting? In a constitution revision proposal developed by the Cherokee Constitution Convention Commission, voting for the Tribal Council is by residence district, with non-resident Cherokees voting for two at-large Council members. For a discussion of tribal considerations in designing citizenship provisions, as well as design options for such provisions, see Carole Goldberg, *Members Only? Designing Citizenship Requirements for Indian Nations*, 50 KAN. L. REV. 437, 458–71 (2002).

2. **Limitations on Tribal Power to Control Membership:** As noted above, during the late nineteenth and early twentieth centuries the federal government sought to control enrollment lists for purposes of determining eligibility for allotments and funds due from the federal government. Another departure from the usual rule that tribes have unrestricted right to determine their own membership occurred after the Civil War. Many of the so-called Five Tribes, initially from the southeast and, ultimately, removed to the Indian Territory, now part of Oklahoma, had been slave holding, having acquired the institution of slavery from their white neighbors in southern states. *See generally* ANNIE HELOISE ABEL, THE SLAVEHOLDING INDIANS (1915). Portions of some of those tribes allied and fought with the Confederacy during the Civil War. As a result, by treaty the federal government forced these tribes to absorb their slaves and gave the former slaves a right to share in tribal property. *E.g.*, Treaty with the Seminole Nation, Mar. 21, 1866, art. 2, 14 Stat. 756. When these tribes were authorized to reorganize under the Oklahoma Indian Welfare Act of 1936, however, surprisingly little was said of these prior provisions, perhaps reflecting the changes in the racial climate of the nation. This history continues to have modern legal repercussions for many of the Five Tribes. *E.g.*, *Seminole Nation v. Norton*, 223 F. Supp. 2d 122 (D.D.C. 2002) (upholding the Secretary of the Interior's decision to refuse to recognize a Seminole Tribal Council elected under tribal rules that unlawfully sought to remove two freedmen's bands from tribal membership). In *Allen v. Cherokee Nation Tribal Council*, No. JAT-04-09 (Cherokee Nation Jud. App. Trib., Mar. 7, 2006), the highest court for the Cherokee Nation of Oklahoma, which had a similar post-Civil War treaty and no requirement of Indian blood in the membership requirements of its 1975 Constitution, decided in a split 2-1 decision that the descendants of the Cherokee Freedman were entitled to enrollment in the Cherokee Nation. The court, however, did indicate that the Nation could amend its Constitution to require that all tribal members possess Cherokee blood, but noted "if the Cherokee people wish to limit

tribal citizenship, and such limitation would terminate the pre-existing citizenship of even one Cherokee citizen, then it must be done in the open. It cannot be accomplished through silence." The *Allen* decision touched off a racially charged political debate in the Cherokee Nation as to whether Cherokee citizenship should be limited to those of Indian blood with Principal Chief Chad Smith strongly urging such a change.

On March 3, 2007, Freedmen descendants were denied citizenship in the Cherokee Nation in a special election for an amendment to the Cherokee Nation constitution. Shortly after the vote, Principal Chief Chad Smith defended the results against charges of racism: "Of the 270,000 Cherokee citizens, there are many who are racially black, racially white, racially Hispanic and racially Asian. However, each one shares a common bond of having a Cherokee ancestor on the base roll of 1906." He called the vote "an affirmation of identity" and said that "the Cherokee Nation is an Indian tribe made up of Indians, just like other Indian tribes all over the country." "Smith: Cherokees Vote for Indian Blood," Indian Country Today, March 9, 2007.

Supporters of Cherokee citizenship for Freedmen descendants have been challenging the constitutional amendment vote in several different venues. They have brought an action for injunctive relief in the Cherokee courts, alleging violation of the Thirteenth Amendment and the 1866 Treaty. *Raymond Nash v. CN Registrar*, papers available at www.cherokeecourts.org. In May, 2007, Cherokee District Court Judge John T. Cripps approved a temporary injunction restoring citizenship to the Freedmen until the litigation is completed. This Cherokee litigation runs concurrently with a federal lawsuit filed before the 2007 constitutional amendment vote. In that federal suit, the Freedmen have sought to overturn earlier Cherokee actions denying them the vote. In *Vann v. Kempthorne*, 467 F. Supp. 2d 56 (D.D.C. 2006), a federal trial judge rejected the Cherokee Nation's effort to dismiss the suit on sovereign immunity grounds, stating that the Thirteenth Amendment's ban on slavery and the 1866 Treaty abrogated tribal sovereign immunity. On July 29, 2008, the D.C. Circuit reversed the district court's decision as it applied to the Cherokee Nation, but affirmed as to the claim for injunctive relief against tribal officials, relying on the reasoning of *Ex parte Young*, 209 U.S. 123 (1908) (authorizing injunctive actions against state officials notwithstanding state sovereign immunity under the Eleventh Amendment).

The Cherokee Freedmen have also mounted a political campaign against the 2007 Cherokee constitutional amendment that denied them citizenship. In June 2007, members of the Congressional Black Caucus and others introduced a bill into the House of Representatives to sever all government relations with the Cherokee Nation until the Freedmen's citizenship was restored. H.R. 2824, 110th Cong., 1st Sess. (2007). To date, this bill has not passed either house of Congress. In September 2007, the House passed a version of the Native American Housing Assistance and Self-Determination Reauthorization Act of 2007 which included a provision denying funds to the Cherokee Nation until citizenship was reinstated. The Senate version of the bill, passed in May, 2008, did not include that language. *See* H.R. 2786, 110th Cong., 1st Sess. (2007); S. 2062, 110th Cong., 1st Sess. (2007).

Principal Chief Chad Smith of the Cherokee Nation has argued that the 1866 Treaty was thoroughly abrogated by the United States, and the Cherokee should no longer be bound by it. Furthermore, he has contended that the language of that treaty, guaranteeing Cherokee citizenship to those former slaves "who have been liberated by voluntary act of their former owners or by law, as well as all free colored persons who were in the country at the commencement of the rebellion, and are now residents therein, or who may return within six months, and their descendants," limits the benefit of the treaty protections to a smaller group than all descendants of former Cherokee slaves. Are these arguments convincing?

3. **Banishment and Exclusion of Members:** Excluding a tribal member from her homeland has a profoundly serious impact on access to political participation, services, employment opportunities, and family members. When that exclusion is accompanied by a termination of tribal membership or citizenship, the impact can be even more devastating, extending to one's personal identity. In *Roff v. Burney*, 168 U.S. 218, 222 (1897), the Supreme Court sustained the authority of a tribal legislature to "cancel the rights of citizenship" granted to certain individuals and to direct the removal of those individuals "beyond the limits of the nation," reasoning as follows:

> The only restriction on the power of the [Tribe] to legislate in respect to its internal affairs is that such legislation shall not conflict with the Constitution or laws of the United States, and we know of no provision of such Constitution or laws which would be set at naught by the action of a political community like this in withdrawing privileges of membership in the community once conferred.

Seventy-one years later, Congress passed the Indian Civil Rights Act. Should an excluded tribal member be permitted to challenge tribal action under the Indian Civil Rights Act via a petition for a writ of habeas corpus filed in federal court?

The Indian Civil Rights Act (ICRA) provides that "[t]he privilege of the writ of habeas corpus shall be available to any person, in a court of the United States, to test the legality of his detention by order of an Indian tribe." Indian Civil Rights Act of 1968, 25 U.S.C. § 1303 (2011). As the ICRA does not define the term, courts have had to define the contours of what constitutes a "detention" under the statute. To that end, the Ninth Circuit has held that the "detention" requirement in the ICRA is analogous to the "in custody" requirement applied to habeas cases in the non-tribal context. *Jeffredo v. Macarro*, 599 F.3d 913, 918 (9th Cir. 2009). In *Moore v. Nelson*, the Ninth Circuit stated that "[t]here is no reason to conclude that the requirement of 'detention' set forth in the Indian Civil Rights Act . . . is any more lenient than the requirement of 'custody' set forth in the other habeas statutes." *Moore v. Nelson*, 270 F.3d 789, 791 (9th Cir. 2001). While there has been no extensive analysis of whether the collateral consequences doctrine strictly applies to tribal actions that have expired but still severely restrain individual liberty, federal courts appear to require that the detention in question remains ongoing in some manner in order to sustain a habeas petition under the ICRA.

Consider the effect of the *Poodry* decision on a tribe's ability to determine its own membership and disciplinary practices. Were the canons of construction for federal statutes properly applied in construing the word "detention" in the Indian Civil

Rights Act? Is federal court the place to be determining contested questions of tribal legal tradition as a first step in deciding whether a proceeding is punitive in nature or consistent with the culture of the tribe? Is it proper for the court to emphasize "our constitutional order" and the petitioners' rights as "American citizens" when the deprivation in question concerns the basic elements — the constitutional order — of a tribal society? How could a federal court hope to supervise an order decreeing the treatment of individuals as members within a very different tribal society? Under various colonial models of tribal-federal relations, it is permissible for federal standards to supercede tribal laws, even those pertaining to citizenship. Under a self-determination model, what role is there for the federal government's concerns about banishment of tribal citizens? Should it suffice to inquire whether a tribe's actions reach the level of an international human rights violation? Is the effect of *Poodry* to displace traditional decision-making mechanisms with non-Indian adversarial courts? *See* Robert B. Porter, *Strengthening Tribal Sovereignty Through Peacemaking: How the Anglo-American Legal Tradition Destroys Indigenous Societies*, 28 COLUM. HUM. RTS. L. REV. 235 (1997).

   4. Disenrollment Decisions and Appeal: Banishment orders sometimes accompany increasingly common disenrollment decisions. In those tribes that permit disenrollment, such decisions frequently are left finally to the tribal council, sometimes on recommendation of a membership committee or official. This fact relegates disenrollment to tribal political processes, which sometimes pay scant attention to the actual membership rules in tribal constitutions or ordinances. Instead, disenrollment decisions sometimes are fueled by political considerations, family factionalism, desires to rid the community of dissidents (as in the *Poodry* case), or economic concerns, such as enlarging *per capita* distributions by reducing the number of members sharing in such distributions. Frequently, tribal law limits or precludes tribal judicial review of such disenrollment decisions. *See, e.g., Terry-Carpenter v. Las Vegas Paiute Tribal Council*, No. CA-01-01 (Las Vegas Paiute Ct. App. 2002) (Las Vegas Paiute Tribal Code limited review in membership cases including disenrollment to procedure error, leaving final substantive decisions to the Tribal Council). What role should the BIA, federal or state courts play if former tribal members claimed their legal rights have been violated by disenrollment?

   In *Alto v. Black*, 738 F.3d 1111 (9th Cir. 2013), the San Pasqual Band of Mission Indians disenrolled some of their members because they were descended from an adopted person, and allegedly did not possess the blood quantum required for membership. The Band's Constitution gives final authority over enrollment decisions to the Secretary of the Interior, and the BIA issued a decision upholding the Band's disenrollment order. The disenrolled individuals sued the BIA in federal court, requesting a preliminary injunction against the agency's decision, which the district court granted. The Band, acting as an intervener, requested that the Ninth Circuit dissolve the injunction based on lack of federal jurisdiction. The Court refused, holding that because the Band's governing documents gave review authority to the BIA, the lower court had jurisdiction to review the BIA's actions under the Administrative Procedure Act. *But see Cahto Tribe of Laytonville Rancheria*, 715 F.3d 1225 (9th Cir. 2013) (holding that when tribe filed suit under APA, seeking to set aside decision of BIA directing tribe to re-enroll disenrolled members, and tribe's governing documents did not authorize BIA review of disenrolled members' appeal, BIA could not review tribe's disenrollment decision).

Should it make any difference whether disenrolled members' claims are predicated on the substantive and procedural membership requirements of tribal law or they claim equal protection or due process deprivations under the Indian Civil Rights Act of 1968 (ICRA)? Recall that the leading ICRA case, *Santa Clara Pueblo v. Martinez*, 436 U.S. 49 (1978), discussed in Sec. D.1, this chapter, was itself a challenge to a tribal membership requirement and held that the federal courts had no jurisdiction to hear such ICRA claims. In cases where Congress has authorized state courts to entertain cases arising in Indian country involving Indians, such as those reservations governed by Public Law 280, can the state courts hear such cases? In *Lamere v. Superior Court of the County of Riverside*, 131 Cal. App. 4th 1059 (2005), a California state court held that Public Law 280 "does not provide jurisdiction over disputes involving a *tribe*" and further indicated that tribal sovereign immunity barred state court review of tribal membership. In *Lamere*, the plaintiffs based their claims on both tribal law and the Indian Civil Rights Act of 1968. The California courts were fully aware that Temecula Band of Luiseno Mission Indians of the Pechanga Reservation had not established a tribal court and that their decision left the final resolution of the legal questions raised by the plaintiffs regarding their disenrollment to the same political process responsible for the disenrollment decisions. Should disenrolled tribal members have access to some independent non-political process to adjudicate their legal claims? If so, what is the most desirable forum? Does the failure of a tribe to provide such an independent non-political forum justify intervention by federal or state courts or by the Bureau of Indian Affairs?

In *Quair v. Sisco*, 2007 U.S. Dist. LEXIS 36858 (E.D. Cal. May 18, 2007), Judge Levi considered whether a federal court could entertain a habeas corpus action challenging the decision of a tribe's General Council to disenroll and banish two members. The Santa Rosa Tachi Yokut Tribe had determined that the two individuals had been working against tribal interests, cooperating with an attorney who had threatened to destroy the Tribe's essential economic relations with outside sources of financing. Challenging this action, the two individuals asserted that they were denied due process under the Indian Civil Rights Act, because the General Council did not follow the procedures of an adversarial court system. Applying *Martinez*, Judge Levi found that the habeas corpus provision of the Indian Civil Rights Act would be available to challenge the Tribe's decision to banish, but not to disenroll. Subsequently, the case settled. The individuals involved agreed to drop their suit in exchange for another opportunity to address the General Council directly. Following their appearance, the General Council agreed to reinstate them as members. By that time, the two had been excluded from the Tribe for several years. For an insightful analysis of the issues surrounding banishment of tribal members, and recommendations for treatment of such issues by tribes under principles of "good governance," see Angela R. Riley, *Good (Native) Governance*, 107 COLUM. L. REV. 1049 (2007).

E. INTERJURISDICTIONAL RESPECT AND COOPERATION

1. Extradition, Full Faith and Credit, and Comity

Sovereignty — that is, a group's political autonomy — does not exist in a vacuum. If other governments are unwilling to recognize it, sovereignty is most difficult to sustain.

Not only is interjurisdictional respect essential to sustaining sovereignty, respect and cooperation among governments are necessary to accommodate the limited jurisdictional reach of all governments, federal and state as well as tribal. Nations enter into extradition treaties and agreements, for example. The United States Constitution also recognizes this necessity for states to cooperate with one another. Article IV, sections 1 and 3 impose binding federal legal obligations on states of the Union to provide full faith and credit to the judicial acts and laws of sister states and to afford extradition of fugitives from justice to other states.

This subsection focuses on laws and legal doctrines addressing interjurisdictional respect and cooperation affecting tribal governments. We begin with some history.

During the period of treaty federalism, Indian tribes and the United States negotiated provisions dealing with intergovernmental cooperation. Many Indian treaties contain provisions facilitating the treatment of fugitives from justice and those who allegedly committed crimes against citizens of the other party. Recall from Chapter 1 that the Fort Pitt Treaty with the Delaware Nation actually contemplated the establishment of cooperative joint criminal prosecution for such cases. Later treaties commonly included extradition provisions. The provisions in Article I of the Fort Laramie Treaty with the Sioux Nation and Others, April 29, 1868, 15 Stat. 635, are illustrative:

> If bad men among the Indians shall commit a wrong or depredation upon the person or property of any one, white, black, or Indian, subject to the authority of the United States, and at peace therewith, the Indians herein named solemnly agree that they will, upon proof made to their agent and notice by him, deliver up the wrong-doer to the United States, to be tried and punished according to its laws; and in case they wilfully refuse so to do, the person injured shall be re-imbursed for his loss from the annuities or other moneys due or to become due to them under this or other treaties made with the United States. And the President, on advising with the Commissioner of Indian Affairs, shall prescribe such rules and regulations for ascertaining damages under the provisions of this article as in his judgment may be proper. But no one sustaining loss while violating the provisions of this treaty or the laws of the United States shall be re-imbursed therefor.

Such provisions, of course, recognized the complete territorial sovereignty of the tribe over its territory and sought its cooperation in returning fugitives. When confronted with this provision in *Ex parte Crow Dog*, 109 U.S. 556 (1883), the United States Supreme Court properly understood the provision as an extradition agreement that recognized the Sioux Nation's sovereignty, rather than as a relinquishment of that sovereignty. Modern cases occasionally rely on these treaty extradition provisions to limit state authority to seize fugitives in Indian country. *E.g., Arizona ex rel. Merrill v. Turtle*, 413 F.2d 683 (9th Cir. 1969) (Arizona has no authority to extradite a Cheyenne Indian living on the Navajo Reservation to face criminal charges in Oklahoma since such extradition authority rests with the Navajo Nation). Complying with such extradition agreements, many tribes today have included extradition provisions in their tribal codes. *E.g.*, Cheyenne River Sioux Tribal Rules of Criminal Procedure, Rule 33. Since these treaties were signed with the United States, the federal government at one time certainly assumed it did not have authority simply to enter Indian country and seize accused Indians or others charged with federal or state crimes. What, if anything, has changed to give the federal government such authority today?

Today, most legal debate regarding intergovernmental cooperation involving Indian tribal courts centers on the civil, rather than criminal, area, although continuing interjurisdictional problems crop up that require cooperation between sovereign governments to facilitate tribal, federal, or state criminal prosecutions. *E.g., Tracy v. Superior Court of Maricopa County*, 810 P.2d 1030 (Ariz. 1991) (Arizona upholds employing Uniform Act to Secure the Attendance of Witnesses to enforce subpoenas originally issued by the Navajo Nation in connection with a criminal case).

Since few banks have branches in Indian country, most liquid assets and perhaps the bulk of other property that can be attached for purposes of enforcement of a tribal court judgment usually are found *off* reservation. The ability of tribal courts to effectively resolve civil disputes therefore frequently will turn on whether other forums, such as state or federal courts, will recognize and enforce their judgments. Two very different models for such enforcement exist: (1) full faith and credit (generally used in enforcement of judgments between states) and (2) comity (generally used in the enforcement of judgments of foreign nations). While both the full faith and credit model and the comity model for recognition of the sovereign acts of another jurisdiction, including its judicial judgments, contemplate normal recognition of such actions, the level of legal force and judicial discretion available in each differs significantly. Full faith and credit generally is sought, depending on context, to be a matter of *federal* legal obligation imposed either constitutionally or by statute. Judicial discretion is therefore significantly reduced in the full faith and credit model, and enforcing courts may decline to enforce judgments otherwise subject to full faith and credit only if they determine both that the judgment was rendered by a court that lacked personal or subject matter jurisdiction and that such questions had not been finally or could not be resolved in the prior proceedings. By contrast, comity is usually thought to be a matter of local, rather than federal, law and constitutes a matter of judicial discretion. Generally, under comity rules, a foreign judgment would be expected to be enforced by an enforcing court if the enforcing court finds that the issuing court had personal and subject matter jurisdiction, complied with fundamental norms of fairness or due process in issuing the judgment, the judgment was not secured by bribery or fraud, and the judgment did not contravene the public policy of the enforcing jurisdiction. Notice under the comity model, unlike the full faith and credit model, *all* of these questions are finally determined by the enforcing court, even if previously addressed by the issuing forum. Given the differences, which model better serves the tribal objectives of securing full enforcement of their judgments? Must tribes be willing to enforce the judgments of other jurisdictions if they expect their judgments to be enforced?

EBERHARD v. EBERHARD
Cheyenne River Sioux Court of Appeals
24 Ind. L. Rep. 6059 (1997)[57]

PER CURIAM

[This case addresses the proper application of the Parental Kidnapping Prevention Act (PKPA), 28 U.S.C. § 1738A, to a tribal court custody proceeding in the context of a later-filed divorce proceeding pending in a California state court.]

Facts

[Appellant Shawn Travis Eberhard and the minor child are both enrolled members of the Cheyenne River Sioux Tribe (Tribe) and legal residents of the Cheyenne River Sioux Reservation (Reservation). . . . In 1995, the Appellant met the Appellee, Angela M. Coontz Eberhard, [and both litigants were] stationed at the same military base in California . . . The parties were married and had a daughter. Shortly after their marriage, Appellant was reassigned and reported to a new duty station at the United States military base in Okinawa, Japan.

After hearing claims of marital misconduct and child neglect by Appellee, Appellant instituted this divorce proceeding in the Cheyenne River Sioux Tribal Trial Court on February 16, 1996. On the same day, Appellant filed a petition for temporary custody pending divorce with the Cheyenne River Sioux Tribal Children's Court and an emergency, temporary order granting such custody was entered the same day.

Appellee refused to turn over the minor child in accordance with the Children's Court order. Thereafter, she fled to her parents' home in Snohomish, Washington, with the child. On February 26, 1996, the Appellee was again served with the Divorce Complaint and Custody Order by the Sheriff for Snohomish Country, Washington, and honored the temporary custody order by turning over the minor child to the Appellant . . . The minor child remains in the care and custody of her paternal grandmother pending Appellant's return from duty in Okinawa.

On March 20, 1996, over a month after the filing of proceedings in the courts of the Tribe, Appellee initiated a divorce action in the Superior Court of California for San Bernardino County seeking essentially the same relief sought by the Appellant in this proceeding. On April 22, 1996, the California court concluded that it had jurisdiction over all the issues as to the divorce of the parties and the custody of the minor child and ordered the return of the minor child to California and to the custody of the mother.

---

[57] [Robert N. Clinton, one of the authors of this casebook, sat as a member of the panel that decided the *Eberhard* matter.— Eds.].

On April 29, 1996, Appellee finally specially appeared before the Cheyenne River Sioux Tribal Trial Court to contest jurisdiction and to enforce the California order. On May 6, 1996, the CRST Superior Court entered an order sustaining the jurisdiction of the CRST courts over all issues, but ordering release of the child from temporary protection and custody upon the order of the California court. That order was specifically premised on a finding that the Parental Kidnapping Prevention Act (PKPA), 28 U.S.C. § 1738A, applied to this case and that California was the "home state" of the minor child within the meaning of the PKPA. Both parties appealed this ruling, the Appellant contesting the release of the minor child from custody under the CRST court orders and the Appellee contesting the jurisdiction of the CRST courts over all issues in the proceeding.

On May 28, 1996, the California court conducted a further hearing, at which the Appellant was not present, regarding both the divorce and custody issues. It again ordered the minor child returned to California. The California court appointed counsel for the Appellant under the provisions of the Soldiers and Sailor's Relief Act, 509 U.S.C. § 520 . . . .

Jurisdiction

The Tribal Trial Court was obviously correct that the CRST court system has jurisdiction over both the divorce and custody issues in this case. . . . [I]t is clear that the minor child is a legal resident of the Reservation since, as noted above, her father was at the time he entered military service, and still is, a legal resident of the Reservation and a member of the Tribe . . . . Therefore, except insofar as the exercise of such jurisdiction may be precluded by the federal Parental Kidnapping Prevention Act, 28 U.S.C. § 1738A, the Cheyenne River Sioux Tribal Trial Court correctly ruled under tribal law that tribal courts clearly had jurisdiction over the parties and jurisdiction over the subject matter of both the divorce and custody proceedings. Its decision in this respect therefore must be affirmed.

Application and Effect of the Parental Kidnapping Prevention Act

This court must decide therefore whether the PKPA applies to tribal courts and their orders and, if so, what the effect of that federal statute is on the obligation of the tribal courts in this case to defer to and recognize the orders of the California court. For the reasons indicated below, the Court finds that the PKPA does apply to tribal courts and their orders, but holds that it does not require in this case that the tribal courts defer to or recognize the California court orders or to cease their exercise of jurisdiction over the custody issues, since under California law the California court was patently without jurisdiction to interfere with an earlier tribal filed custody proceeding and was required to cease its exercise of jurisdiction, which it failed to do.

The federal Parental Kidnapping Prevention Act, 28 U.S.C. § 1738A, was enacted by Congress in 1980 . . . to reduce interjurisdictional conflict over judicial proceedings between parents which involve child custody. Reduced to its basics, the PKPA requires covered jurisdictions to enforce and provide full faith and credit, generally without modification, to any child custody decree made in conformity with the PKPA if the court that issued the order had jurisdiction and satisfied certain other requirements of the Act. While statutory directives of the PKPA are worded to apply to any "State," the term "State," as used in this legislation, is a defined term that includes "a State of the United States, the District of Columbia, the Commonwealth of Puerto Rico, or a territory or possession of the United States." 28 U.S.C. § 1738A(b)(8). The preliminary question for this Court, therefore, is whether Indian tribes and their reservations are within the phrase "State" or "a territory or possession of the United States," as used in the statutory definition of State found in the PKPA. While the Court finds this issue to pose a very close and troubling question, on balance it concludes both that Congress meant to include Indians tribes and their reservations within the statutory phrases "State" and "a territory or possession of the United States" and that coverage of Indian tribes by the PKPA best furthers both the purposes of that legislation and the sovereign interests of the tribes.

[T]he PKPA was originally proposed as part of a larger piece of legislation, H.R. 2977, that became stalled in the Senate after Conference Committee. H.R. 2977 was reported out of the Conference Committee as the Domestic Violence Prevention and Services Act. It then consisted of four sections. The first section was titled, Title I — Domestic Violence Prevention. This section provided for participation at the state and local level in an effort to prevent domestic violence and to provide shelter for victims funded by federal grants. Indian tribes were included in this program by express language found in Section 102(a)(3)(b)(1) and (3)

Section 113 of the proposed bill set forth definitions for this Title. Subsection (3) stated: "The term 'Indian tribe' means any Indian tribe, band, nation, or other organized group or community, including any Alaska Native village or group or regional or village corporation as defined in or established pursuant to the Alaska Native Claims Settlement Act (85 Stat. 688), which is recognized as eligible for the special programs and services provided by the United States to Indians because of their status as Indians."

The third section of the Act was titled, Title III — Parental Kidnapping Prevention Act. Section 303(a) of this Title added a new provision immediately after 28 U.S.C. § 1738, which is the current section 1738A — "Full faith and credit given to child custody determinations." Subsection (b) stated, "As used in this section, the term — (8) State means a State of the United States, the District of Columbia, the Commonwealth of Puerto Rico, or a territory or possession of the United States."

As the conference report shows, the House and Senate conferees on the Act considered and negotiated over precisely which Indian groups would be included in Title I relating to domestic violence. The Senate-passed version of H.R. 2977 included Indian tribes, bands, and groups including urban Indian organizations, as grantees under Title I; while the House-passed version made no provision at all for Indians. The House conferees agreed to the inclusion of Indian tribes, bands, and groups as grantees but refused to agree to the inclusion of urban Indian organizations.

[Through the legislative process,] the PKPA [eventually] became detached from the Domestic Violence Prevention legislation to which it was originally appended, [was passed as part of a different bill, and signed into law as P.L. 96-611. This law did not expressly mention Indian Tribes.]

[B]oth the Appellant and the Tribe now contend that the intent of Congress with respect to the inclusion of tribes in the PKPA is to be found in the Conference Report on H.R. 2977 since tribes were expressly included and defined in Title I of H.R. 2977, but were never included in Title III (the original version of the PKPA) and were not included in other provisions of H.R. 8406, which became P.L. 96-611 and enacted the PKPA into law. The Tribe, in particular, argues that because of the sovereign status of an Indian tribe, any curtailment of its sovereignty by Congress must be expressed with a clear Congressional intent . . . .

While there is considerable force to these arguments and this Court would normally agree with the Tribe that any Congressional curtailment of tribal sovereignty requires a clear and express showing of Congressional intent, the Court is convinced that Congress intended the PKPA to apply to tribal courts as a means of integrating them, and other courts, into the cooperative federalism framework of the national union. Furthermore, this Court believes that this conclusion does not diminish tribal sovereignty, as suggested by the Tribe, but, rather, protects tribal sovereignty and the right of self-government of the Lakota people in many instances. Consequently . . . this Court finds that the PKPA applies to tribal proceedings involving child custody and also applies to tribally issued child custody orders . . . .

Congress and the courts have long addressed the question of full faith and credit in an effort to integrate first the states and, later the tribes, territories, and possessions, into an national union with reciprocal full faith and credit recognition of judgments and laws. In 1790 Congress passed the Full Faith and Credit Act, now found at 28 U.S.C. § 1738, which required "courts *within* the United States and its Territories and Possessions" to recognize and enforce the records and judicial proceedings "of any court of such State, Territory or Possession . . . ." As early as 1856, the United States Supreme Court held in *United States ex. rel. Mackey v. Coxe*, 59 U.S. (18 How.) 100 (1855), that the courts of the Cherokee Nation were included in the term territories. . . .

While Indian tribes and their governments do not owe their political authority to federal or state delegation, but, rather, derive their power from inherent aboriginal sovereignty, *United States v. Wheeler*, 435 U.S. 313 (1978); *Talton v. Mayes*, 163 U.S. 376 (1896); *Ex parte Crow Dog*, 109 U.S. 556 (1883); *Worcester v. Georgia*, 31 U.S. (6 Pet.) 515, 556 (1832), from the outset the United States Supreme Court has recognized that Indian lands, while under the separate sovereign authority of the affected tribe, are nevertheless included within the exterior boundaries of the United States and of any state or territory in which they are located. *Worcester v. Georgia*, 31 U.S. (6 Pet.) at 560. Consequently . . . the Supreme Court of the United States has generally recognized . . . that full faith and credit statutes applicable to courts of the states, territories, or possessions apply to Indian tribes . . . . Furthermore, to the extent that Congress has directly addressed the question of the applicability of full faith and credit concepts to tribal courts, it has consistently directly applied full faith and credit legislation to tribal courts and their decisions. *E.g.* 25 U.S.C. § 1911(d) (Indian Child Welfare Act of 1978); 25 U.S.C. § 1725(g) (Maine Indian Claims Settlement Act); 28 U.S.C. § 1738B (Full Faith and Credit for

Child Support Orders Act); 18 U.S.C. § 2265 (Violence Against Women Act); 25 U.S.C. § 2207 (Indian Land Consolidation Act).[58]

With this background, it is apparent to this Court that when Congress enacted the Parental Kidnapping Prevention Act, it legislated against a well-established interpretive backdrop under which the courts had interpreted designations like state, territory, or possession found in federal full faith and credit recognition statutes to adopt geographic, rather than political, meanings. Such terms were meant to include the courts of Indian tribes, as in *Mackey.* Consequently, it is quite understandable why Congress would specifically refer to Indian tribes in Title I of HR 2977, but make no reference to them in Title III, which later became the PKPA. Title I dealt with domestic violence, a relatively new subject for the federal government to address and one which lacked the well-developed interpretive regime evident in the area of full faith and credit. Consequently, Congress supplied careful definitions of its terms that expressly included Indian tribes and certain Indian organizations to make them eligible for grant projects. By contrast, Title III, which later became the PKPA, dealt with full faith and credit and incorporated references to states, territories, and possessions, which, since 1856, had been interpreted to include Indian tribes in this area of legislation. In this context, Congress was not required to explicitly refer to Indian tribes since the judicial interpretive backdrop against which it legislated, including the *Mackey* case, clearly reflected that tribes were included within the states, territories, or possessions of the United States . . . .

[T]he Tribe argues that the PKPA should not be interpreted to apply to tribal courts or their orders since such an interpretation would curtail tribal sovereignty and, therefore, under traditional maxims of federal law requires an express showing of Congressional intent. While the Court agrees with the Tribe that the federal canons of statutory construction require any curtailment of Indian immunities to be made expressly, *e.g. Bryan v. Itasca County*, 426 U.S. 373, 379 (1976); *Menominee Tribe v. United States*, 391 U.S. 404 (1968), the Court does not find this case to be one to which this canon of construction can be properly applied. The PKPA is not intended to and does not diminish the sovereignty of the courts to which it applies. Rather, it protects their jurisdiction by assuring that other sovereigns will not "second guess" child custody orders granted full faith and credit under the Act.

---

[58] [38] This Court is aware, as argued by the Tribe, that perhaps a majority of the state courts that have considered the question, and a number of the commentators have rejected the application of federal full faith and credit concepts to tribal courts and their judgments where not expressly commanded by federal statute. . . . Most of the state cases that reject general application of federal full faith and credit concepts to tribal courts and their orders merely cite to the constitutional full faith and credit clause and note that it is inapplicable since tribes are not states. *Desjarlait v. Desjarlait*, 379 N.W.2d 139 (Minn. Ct. App. 1985); *Mexican v. Circle Bear*, 370 N.W.2d 737 (S.D. 1985); *Wippert v. Black Feet Tribe*, 654 P.2d 512 (Mont. 1982); *Malaterre v. Malaterre*, 293 N.W.2d 139 (N.D. 1980); *Red Fox v. Red Fox*, 542 P.2d 918 (Or. Ct. App. 1975); *Lynch's Estate*, 377 P.2d 199 (Ariz. 1962). Relying on *Hilton v. Guyot*, 159 U.S. 113 (1895), and the doctrine of international comity announced in that case, these courts generally adopt a more discretionary comity approach to the recognition and enforcement of tribal judgments. This approach has the twin disadvantages of being both relatively discretionary and a matter of state law, therefore unreviewable from a state court decision to the United States Supreme Court. Some states have adopted state statutes or court rules to implement, structure, and codify the exercise of their comity relationships with tribal courts, often labeling such rules as full faith and credit rules. . . .

The conclusion that the PKPA applies to the courts of this Tribe and its orders only starts the analysis, it does not end it. The trial court in this matter found that California was the "home State" within the meaning of the PKPA, 28 U.S.C. § 1738A(b)(4) . . . . The language of the PKPA, however, suggests that this assumption is not completely accurate on the facts of this case. Indeed, for reasons set forth below, this Court finds it need not reach the question of whether the lower court correctly determined that California was the "home State" of the minor child as that term is used in the PKPA — an issue that is not completely free from doubt.

Under the commands of 28 U.S.C. § 1738A(a), a "State" court must enforce according to its terms any child custody determination "made consistently with the provisions of this section by the court of another State." According to 28 U.S.C. § 1738A(c) . . . , to require enforcement of an order determining child custody, the PKPA demands that there be *both* a showing that the court which issued the order had jurisdiction *and* that there be some contact of that "State" with the child of the type set forth in section 1738A(c)(2), one of which is that the state is the "home State." Additionally, the limitation on the exercise of "State" court jurisdiction set forth in section 1738(g)[59] is limited to those situations in which another "State" court is exercising jurisdiction "consistently with the provisions of this section" and, consequently, requires the same determination.

In this case, the lower court was only required to enforce the later filed child custody order of the California court issued in a subsequently filed divorce action and to cease the exercise of tribal court jurisdiction over the custody proceeding if (1) the California court had jurisdiction and (2) California constituted the "home State." A determination that California is the "home State" is, under the PKPA, an analytically separate determination from the question of whether the California court had jurisdiction . . . Unlike certain other full faith and credit contexts, the PKPA appears to expressly require an *independent* determination of that jurisdiction by the enforcing court by making a finding of the existence of jurisdiction an express precondition to the enforceability of the order in the court of another "State." This court therefore finds that it must make an independent determination of the jurisdiction of the California court before it can determine whether the tribal courts are bound under the PKPA to enforce the California child custody determination . . .

California, like most states, but not the Cheyenne River Sioux Tribe, has adopted the Uniform Child Custody Jurisdiction Act (UCCJA). California Family Code §§ 3400 *et seq.* Under the express provisions of California Family Code § 3406(a), the California courts are divested of jurisdiction over a child custody proceeding if another earlier proceeding involving child custody had been commenced and the court was "exercising jurisdiction substantially in conformity with this part."

Consequently, since the tribal court child custody determination was the first

---

[59] [39] 28 U.S.C. § 1738A(g) provides:

> A court of a State shall not exercise jurisdiction in any proceeding for a custody determination commenced during the pendency of a proceeding in a court of another State where such court of that other State is exercising jurisdiction consistently with the provisions of this section to make a custody determination.

filed action, the tribal court had jurisdiction over the subject matter and over the person, and will exercise jurisdiction in conformity with the PKPA, and therefore in substantial conformity to the UCCJA, it is clear that the California court lacked jurisdiction over the child custody proceeding under California law. It is also clear under the PKPA, the California court is required to cease its exercise of jurisdiction and defer to the jurisdiction and orders of courts of the Cheyenne River Sioux Tribe in this matter . . .

[The Cheyenne River Sioux Tribal Court of Appeals therefore concluded that since the California court lacked jurisdiction under the California version of the UCCJA, the Cheyenne River tribal courts had a legal obligation under the PKPA to enforce the California custody order, and therefore reversed.]

Separate Concurring opinion of CHIEF JUSTICE POMMERSHEIM

I concur with the judgment in this case and the erudite opinion of the Court, but write separately (and briefly) to emphasize . . . [that] . . . the inclusion of "tribes" within the meaning of "State" in the PKPA in no way demeans tribal sovereignty but rather takes it to another and quite appropriate level. This is the level where tribal courts are treated with the same dignity and respect accorded state and federal courts within the national system of law and jurisprudence. Indeed, such a doctrinal regime bespeaks a true sovereign equality under enduring principles of law.

WILSON v. MARCHINGTON
United States Court of Appeals, Ninth Circuit
127 F.3d 805 (1997)

THOMAS, CIRCUIT JUDGE.

This appeal presents the question of whether, and under what circumstances, a tribal court tort judgment is entitled to recognition in the United States Courts. We conclude that the principles of comity, not full faith and credit, govern whether a district court should recognize and enforce a tribal court judgment. In this instance, because the tribal court lacked jurisdiction, its judgment is not entitled to recognition in the United States courts.

I

The traffic accident which precipitated this action involved Mary Jane Wilson, who is an enrolled member of the Blackfeet Indian Tribe, and Thomas Marchington, who is not. On July 17, 1989, Marchington was driving on U.S. Highway 2 within the boundaries of the Blackfeet Indian Reservation in Montana on assignment for his employer Inland Empire Shows, an Idaho carnival company. Wilson, driving ahead of Marchington on the two-lane road, signaled a left turn. Marchington, in ignorance or in disregard of Wilson's intent, attempted to pass her on the left, careening into her car as she exited Highway 2.

Wilson sued Marchington and Inland Empire in the Blackfeet Tribal Court. The tribal jury found in favor of Wilson and awarded her $246,100. The Blackfeet Court of Appeals reversed for a hearing on whether punitive damages had been improperly awarded, but the Blackfeet Supreme Court reversed the Blackfeet Court of Appeals and reinstated the original judgment in favor of Wilson.

Claiming her judgment was entitled to full faith and credit or comity, Wilson brought suit in the United States District Court for the District of Montana to register the tribal court judgment in the federal court system. The district court granted summary judgment in favor of Wilson.

II

No legal judgment has any effect, of its own force, beyond the limits of the sovereignty from which its authority is derived. Because states and Indian tribes coexist as sovereign governments, they have no direct power to enforce their judgments in each other's jurisdictions. By contrast, the United States Constitution and implementing legislation require full faith and credit be given to judgments of sister states, territories, and possessions of the United States. U.S. Const. art. IV, § 1, cl. 1; 28 U.S.C. § 1738. The extent to which the United States, or any state, honors the judicial decrees of foreign nations is a matter of choice, governed by "the comity of nations." *Hilton v. Guyot*, 159 U.S. 113, 163 (1895).

Determining comity to be a proper basis for recognizing a tribal court judgment is not a remarkable notion; indeed, both parties agree that it is appropriate. However, Wilson asserts comity only as an alternative analysis, contending that a tribal judgment must be recognized by the United States under 28 U.S.C. § 1738, the implementing legislation of the United States Constitution's Full Faith and Credit Clause.

The Constitution's Full Faith and Credit Clause provides:

> Full Faith and Credit shall be given in each State to the public Acts, Records, and judicial Proceedings of every other State. And the Congress may by general Laws prescribe the Manner in which such Acts, Records and Proceedings shall be proved, and the Effect thereof.

U.S. Const. art. IV, § 1.

By its terms, the Full Faith and Credit Clause applies only to the states. Nothing in debates of the Constitutional Convention concerning the clause indicates the framers thought the clause would apply to Indian tribes. The Constitution is silent about recognition of tribal judgments, though it specifically addresses other tribal concerns. See U.S. Const. art. I, § 2, cl. 3 (excluding non-taxed Indians from the calculation of representative apportionment); art. I, § 8, cl. 3 (providing Congress the power to regulate commerce with the Indian tribes); amend. XIV, § 2 (excluding non-taxed Indians from the calculation of representative apportionment). Thus, the Constitution itself does not afford full faith and credit to Indian tribal judgments.

Initial legislation implementing the full faith and credit clause was passed in 1790. The statute was modified in 1804 to include the extension of full faith and credit to United States territories and possessions. Subsequent technical amendments were made and the current full faith and credit statute reads in relevant part:

> Such Acts, records, and judicial proceedings or copies thereof, so authenticated, shall have the same full faith and credit in every court within the United States and its Territories and Possessions as they have by law or usage in the courts of such State, Territory or Possession from which they are taken.

28 U.S.C. § 1738.

Because Indian nations are not referenced in the statute, the question is whether tribes are "territories or possessions" of the United States under the statute. The United States Supreme Court has not ruled on the precise issue and its pronouncements on collateral matters are inconclusive. For example, in *United States ex rel. Mackey v. Coxe*, 59 U.S. (18 How.) 100, 103–04 (1855), the Court held the Cherokee nation was a territory as that term was used in a federal letters of administration statute. By contrast, in *New York ex rel. Kopel v. Bingham*, 211 U.S. 468, 474–75 (1909), the Court cited with approval *Ex Parte Morgan*, 20 F. 298, 305 (W.D. Ark. 1883) in which the district court held that the Cherokee nation was not a "territory" under the federal extradition statute. State courts have reached varied results, citing either *Mackey* or *Morgan* as authority, depending on the outcome.[60]

In our view, the decisive factor in determining Congress's intent was the enactment of subsequent statutes which expressly extended full faith and credit to certain tribal proceedings: the Indian Land Consolidation Act, 25 U.S.C. §§ 2201–2211 (1983) (extending full faith and credit for certain actions involving trust, restricted or controlled lands), the Maine Indian Claims Settlement Act, 25 U.S.C. § 1725(g) (1980) (requiring the Passamaquoddy Tribe, the Penobscot Nation and the State of Maine to "give full faith and credit to the judicial proceedings of each other"), and the Indian Child Welfare Act of 1978, 25 U.S.C. § 1911 (d) (extending full faith and credit to tribal custody proceedings in the courts of the U.S. "every territory or possession" of the U.S., and every tribe). . . .

A later legislative act can be regarded as a legislative interpretation of an earlier act and "is therefore entitled to great weight in resolving any ambiguities and doubts." If full faith and credit had already been extended to Indian tribes, enactment of the Indian Land Consolidation Act, the Maine Indian Claims Settlement Act, and the Indian Child Welfare Act would not have been necessary. Further, the separate listing of territories, possessions and Indian tribes in the Indian Child Welfare Act provides an indication that Congress did not view these terms as synonymous. Thus, we conclude that Congress did not extend full faith and credit to the tribes under 28 U.S.C. § 1738.

Further, if Congress had specifically intended to include Indian tribes under the umbrella of 28 U.S.C. § 1738, it could have easily done so either by specifically referencing them in the 1804 amendments, or by further amending the statute once ambiguous judicial constructions appeared. It chose not to, but rather elected to

---

[60] [2] *Compare Jim v. CIT Fin. Servs.*, 87 N.M. 362, 533 P.2d 751 (1975) (citing *Mackey* and holding that tribes are entitled to full faith and credit) and *In re Buehl*, 87 Wash.2d 649, 555 P.2d 1334 (1976) (citing *CIT* and concluding that tribes are entitled to full faith and credit) with *Brown v. Babbitt Ford, Inc.*, 117 Ariz. 192, 571 P.2d 689 (1977) (citing *Morgan* and holding that an Indian reservation is not a territory for purposes of full faith and credit).

create a special exception in cases of Indian child custody determinations and land trusts.

Given this history, it would be imprudent of us to now construe the phrase "territories and possessions" in the 1804 statute to assume the meaning of the language Congress used in the Indian Child Welfare Act ("every territory or possession of the United States, *and every Indian tribe*") (emphasis added) and Indian Land Consolidation Act.

Certainly, there are policy reasons which could support an extension of full faith and credit to Indian tribes. Those decisions, however, are within the province of Congress or the states,[61] not this Court. Full faith and credit is not extended to tribal judgments by the Constitution or Congressional act, and we decline to extend it judicially.

III

In absence of a Congressional extension of full faith and credit, the recognition and enforcement of tribal judgments in federal court must inevitably rest on the principles of comity. Comity "is neither a matter of absolute obligation, on the one hand, nor of mere courtesy and good will, upon the other." *Hilton v. Guyot*, 159 U.S. 113, 163–64, 16 S. Ct. 139, 143–44 (1895). As a general policy, "[c]omity should be withheld only when its acceptance would be contrary or prejudicial to the interest of the nation called upon to give it effect." *Somportex Ltd. v. Philadelphia Chewing Gum Corp.*, 453 F.2d 435, 440 (3d Cir. 1971). At its core, comity involves a balancing of interests. "[I]t is the recognition which one nation allows within its territory to the legislative, executive, or judicial acts of another nation, having due regard both to international duty and convenience, and to the rights of its own citizens, or of other persons who are under the protection of its laws." *Hilton*, 159 U.S. at 164. Although the status of Indian tribes as "dependent domestic nations" presents some unique circumstances, comity still affords the best general analytical framework for recognizing tribal judgments.

As we recognized in *Her Majesty the Queen v. Gilbertson*, 597 F.2d 1161, 1163 n.4 (9th Cir. 1979), *Hilton* provides the guiding principles of comity.[62] More recently, the Restatement (Third) of Foreign Relations Law of the United States (1986)

---

[61] [3] *See, e.g.*, Okla. Stat. tit. 12, § 728 (permitting the Supreme Court of the State of Oklahoma to extend full faith and credit to tribal court judgments); Wis. Stat. § 806.245 (granting full faith and credit to judgments of Wisconsin Indian tribal courts); Wyo. Stat. Ann. § 5-1-111 (granting full faith and credit to judicial decisions of the Eastern Shoshone and Northern Arapaho Tribes of the Wind River Reservation). Montana has judicially refused to extend full faith and credit to tribal orders, judgments, and decrees. *In re Day*, 272 Mont. 170, 900 P.2d 296, 301 (1995).

[62] [4] [W]here there has been opportunity for a full and fair trial abroad before a court of competent jurisdiction, conducting the trial upon regular proceedings, after due citation or voluntary appearance of the defendant, and under a system of jurisprudence likely to secure an impartial administration of justice between the citizens of its own country and those of other countries, and there is nothing to show either prejudice in the court, or in the system of laws under which it was sitting, or fraud in procuring the judgment, or any other special reason why the comity of this nation should not allow it full effect, the merits of the case should not, in an action brought in this country upon the judgment, be tried afresh, as on a new trial or an appeal, upon the mere assertion of the party that the judgment was erroneous in law or in fact. *Hilton*, 159 U.S. at 202–03, 16 S. Ct. at 158.

[hereinafter Restatement (Third)] suggested two mandatory and six discretionary grounds for non-recognition of foreign judgments.[63] While Hilton and the Restatement (Third) provide sound guidance for assessing legal judgments of other nations, special considerations arising out of existing Indian law merit some modification in the application of comity to tribal judgments. In synthesizing the traditional elements of comity with the special requirements of Indian law, we conclude that, as a general principle, federal courts should recognize and enforce tribal judgments. However, federal courts must neither recognize nor enforce tribal judgments if:

(1)   the tribal court did not have both personal and subject matter jurisdiction; or

(2)   the defendant was not afforded due process of law.

In addition, a federal court may, in its discretion, decline to recognize and enforce a tribal judgment on equitable grounds, including the following circumstances:

(1)   the judgment was obtained by fraud;

(2)   the judgment conflicts with another final judgment that is entitled to recognition;

(3)   the judgment is inconsistent with the parties' contractual choice of forum; or

(4)   recognition of the judgment, or the cause of action upon which it is based, is against the public policy of the United States or the forum state in which recognition of the judgment is sought.

The lack of personal jurisdiction mandates rejection of a foreign judgment under the Restatement (Third) and that requirement must logically extend to tribal judgments. Although the Restatement (Third) lists subject matter jurisdiction as a discretionary inquiry, the existence of subject matter jurisdiction is a threshold inquiry in virtually every federal examination of a tribal judgment. *E.g., Strate v. A-1 Contractors*, 520 U.S. 438, 449 (1997); *Montana v. United States*, 450 U.S. 544, 565–66 (1981). Additionally, the existence of subject matter jurisdiction is mandatory under the Uniform Foreign Money-Judgments Recognition Act which has been

---

[63]   [5] The Restatement (Third) § 482 provides:

(1)   A court in the United States may not recognize a judgment of the court of a foreign state if:

    (a)   the judgment was rendered under a judicial system that does not provide impartial tribunals or procedures compatible with due process of law; or

    (b)   the court that rendered the judgment did not have jurisdiction over the defendant in accordance with the law of the rendering state and with the rules set forth in § 421.

(2)   A court in the United States need not recognize a judgment of the court of a foreign state if:

    (a)   the court that rendered the judgment did not have jurisdiction of the subject matter of the action;

    (b)   the defendant did not receive notice of the proceedings in sufficient time to enable him to defend;

    (c)   the judgment was obtained by fraud;

    (d)   the cause of action on which the judgment was based, or the judgment itself, is repugnant to the public policy of the United States or of the State where recognition is sought;

    (e)   the judgment conflicts with another final judgment that is entitled to recognition; or

    (f)   the proceeding in the foreign country was contrary to an agreement between the parties to submit the controversy on which the judgment is based to another forum.

adopted by twenty-five states, including Montana. Louise E. Teitz, Transnational Litigation 253 & n. 5 (1996); Mont. Code Ann. § 25-9-601 et seq. Accordingly, the existence of both personal and subject matter jurisdiction is a necessary predicate for federal court recognition and enforcement of a tribal judgment.

A federal court must also reject a tribal judgment if the defendant was not afforded due process of law. "It has long been the law of the United State that a foreign judgment cannot be enforced if it was obtained in a manner that did not accord with the basics of due process." *Bank Melli Iran v. Pahlavi*, 58 F.3d 1406, 1410 (9th Cir.), *cert. denied*, 516 U.S. 989 (1995). The guarantees of due process are vital to our system of democracy. We demand that foreign nations afford United States citizens due process of law before recognizing foreign judgments; we must ask no less of Native American tribes.

Due process, as that term is employed in comity, encompasses most of the *Hilton* factors, namely that there has been opportunity for a full and fair trial before an impartial tribunal that conducts the trial upon regular proceedings after proper service or voluntary appearance of the defendant, and that there is no showing of prejudice in the tribal court or in the system of governing laws. Further, as the Restatement (Third) noted, evidence "that the judiciary was dominated by the political branches of government or by an opposing litigant, or that a party was unable to obtain counsel, to secure documents or attendance of witnesses, or to have access to appeal or review, would support a conclusion that the legal system was one whose judgments are not entitled to recognition." Restatement (Third) § 482 comment b.

Comity does not require that a tribe utilize judicial procedures identical to those used in the United States Courts. "Foreign-law notions are not per se disharmonious with due process by reason of their divergence from the common-law notions of procedure." *Panama Processes, S.A. v. Cities Serv. Co.*, 796 P.2d 276, 286 n. 36 (Okla. 1990). Indeed, *Hilton* rejected challenges to a judgment based on lack of adequate cross-examination and unsworn testimony. 159 U.S. at 205. Federal courts must also be careful to respect tribal jurisprudence along with the special customs and practical limitations of tribal court systems. Extending comity to tribal judgments is not an invitation for the federal courts to exercise unnecessary judicial paternalism in derogation of tribal self-governance. However, the tribal court proceedings must afford the defendant the basic tenets of due process or the judgment will not be recognized by the United States.

Marchington urges us to require reciprocal recognition of judgments as an additional mandatory prerequisite. In *Hilton*, the Supreme Court determined that a judgment from a foreign country would not be enforced by the United States courts if the foreign country would not enforce a similar American judgment in its courts. However, the reciprocity requirement has fallen into disfavor. In *Banco Nacional de Cuba v. Sabbatino*, 376 U.S. 398 (1964), the Supreme Court stated, "[a]lthough *Hilton v. Guyot* . . . contains some broad language about the relationship of reciprocity to comity, the case in fact imposed a requirement of reciprocity only in regard to conclusiveness of judgments, and even then only in limited circumstances." According to the Restatement (Second) of Conflict of Laws (1988) [hereinafter Restatement (Second)], "[e]xcept when otherwise required by local statute, the great majority of State and federal courts have extended recognition to judgments of foreign nations without regard to any question of reciprocity." § 98 cmt. f. The Restatement (Second) addresses the *Hilton* problem by noting that the decision involved "one isolated situation," and suggesting that *Hilton* be limited to its facts. Id. Additionally, Judge Learned Hand has observed that the Supreme Court "certainly did not mean to hold that an American court was to recognize no obligations or duties arising elsewhere until it appeared that the sovereign of the locus reciprocally recognized similar obligations existing here. That doctrine I am happy to say is not a part of American jurisprudence." *Direction der Disconto-Gesellschaft v. United States Steel Corp.*, 300 F. 741, 747 (S.D.N.Y. 1924), *aff'd*, 267 U.S. 22 (1925).

Although courts have expressed disaffection for the reciprocity requirement, they have not entirely disavowed it. . . . However, we also noted that reciprocity "certainly remains a factor which may be considered in deciding whether to recognize a foreign country's judgment for taxes."

The general rationale underlying rejection of the reciprocity requirement is that it is a matter of diplomacy, best negotiated by the executive and legislative branches. There are, of course, substantive differences between foreign relations with other nations and domestic relations with Native American tribes. Further, a policy of requiring reciprocity with foreign nations has practical limits which would not affect a domestic analysis. If a litigant sought recognition of a Djibouti judgment in Montana, for example, it is unlikely that Djibouti would have had the prior opportunity to consider recognition of a Montana judgment.

Despite these dissimilarities, the theory that the imposition of a reciprocity requirement is not a matter for courts to decide independently is generally sound. The question of whether a reciprocity requirement ought to be imposed on an Indian tribe before its judgments may be recognized is essentially a public policy question best left to the executive and legislative branches. The fact that some states have chosen to impose such a condition by statute reinforces this conclusion,[64] as does the judicial response of looking to applicable statutes to decide reciprocity issues. . . .

Neither the State of Montana nor, more relevantly, Congress has spoken on this question and we do not believe that *Hilton* or any controlling case law concerning recognition of foreign judgments requires a district court to reject a tribal judgment for lack of reciprocity. Thus, we decline Marchington's suggestion to adopt reciprocity as a judicially-created mandatory requirement.[65]

---

[64] [6] *See, e.g.*, S.D. Codified Laws § 1-1-25(2)(b) (permitting South Dakota courts to recognize a tribal judgment if the courts of that tribe recognize the orders and judgments of the South Dakota courts); Okla. Stat. tit. 12, § 728(B) (allowing the Supreme Court of Oklahoma to recognize tribal court judgments where the tribal courts agree to grant reciprocity of judgments); Wis. Stat. § 806.245(1)(e) (granting full faith and credit to judgments of Wisconsin Indian tribal court judgments if, inter alia, the tribe grants full faith and credit to the judgments of Wisconsin courts); Wyo. Stat. Ann. § 5-1-111(a)(iv) (granting full faith and credit to the Eastern Shoshone and Northern Arapaho Tribes if, inter alia, the tribal court certifies that it grants full faith and credit to the orders and judgments of Wyoming).

[65] [7] Whether a district court may, in the exercise of its discretion, reject a judgment for lack of reciprocity is a question we leave for another day. Although best left to our sister branches of

Lack of tribal jurisdiction and absence of due process, then, are the only mandatory reasons for a district court to reject a tribal judgment. The court may, in the exercise of its discretion, choose not to honor a tribal judgment for one of the other enumerated reasons. This approach satisfies two competing concerns: it provides tribes with a mechanism by which the judgments of their courts may be recognized by the United States while assuring defendants of due process of law and other safeguards inherent in our judicial system.

[The Ninth Circuit went on to hold that the judgment of the Blackfeet Tribal Court was not entitled to recognition and enforcement under the principles of comity since the Tribal Court lacked subject matter jurisdiction over the case. The court relied on *Strate v. A-1 Contractors*, 520 U.S. 438 (1997) (holding that a tribal court lacked jurisdiction over an automobile accident involving two nonmembers occurring on a state highway right-of-way traversing the reservation), discussed in the next chapter. In arriving at its holding, the court rejected the claim that since a tribal member was the plaintiff in the *Wilson* litigation, the case was distinguishable from *Strate*.]

NOTES ON FULL FAITH AND CREDIT AND COMITY

1. **Full Faith and Credit or Comity Models for Interjurisdictional Cooperation:** As the juxtaposition of *Eberhard* and *Wilson* demonstrates there are two different models of civil interjurisdictional cooperation commonly employed to recognize the judicial acts of other sovereigns. Outside of Indian country, American courts employ full faith and credit to recognize and enforce the judgments of federal or state courts, and comity to recognize and enforce judgments issued by the courts of foreign nations. Which of these two approaches best reflects the status and relationship of Indian tribes? Can that question be answered in isolation or must one determine the appropriate model of tribal-federal relations to answer the question? Consider whether adopting self-determination paradigms or treaty federalism or more colonialist views of the nature of the relationship should alter which model is selected. Before deciding which is the best model to govern the relationship of tribal courts to the remainder of the nation, consider two other matters discussed in the following notes: (1) the practical operational differences between full faith and credit models and the comity paradigm and (2) congressional and judicial pronouncements on the subject.

Traditionally, full faith and credit obligations are matters of federal law. Thus, the refusal of a federal or state court to enforce a judgment subject to a full faith and credit obligation constitutes a question that can be reviewed ultimately by the United States Supreme Court. By contrast, comity constitutes a discretionary accommodation of the forum to other sovereign governments and, therefore, when in state courts, is governed by state law. That approach affords no appeal to the United States Supreme Court from a decision to decline to grant comity to a foreign judgment. More importantly, in addition to the fact that comity permits a forum to

---

government, there may be an appropriate case in which the record demonstrates significant public policy factors which might be sufficient for the district court to consider reciprocity under the "public policy" discretionary exception. Thus, we decline to endorse or preclude its discretionary consideration in a proper case.

decline to enforce a judgment it deems inconsistent with the forum's public policy, full faith and credit and comity models also differ fundamentally on the question of who gets to decide important questions of jurisdiction or compliance with due process or other fundamental fairness considerations. Under the full faith and credit model, unless the party did not appear in the initial proceeding, as in *Eberhard* where the father did not appear in the California proceeding, the *issuing* jurisdiction gets to *finally* decide whether it had jurisdiction. The enforcing court is bound by any jurisdictional determination that was made or could have been made on such jurisdictional questions. In *Eberhard*, the tribal court was free to redetermine the jurisdictional question both because the PKPA appeared to depart somewhat from the classic full faith and credit model by placing jurisdiction at issue in the *enforcing* court and because the father had not appeared in the California proceeding. Additionally, in the full faith and credit model, other procedural questions of due process compliance and fairness must be presented to and resolved exclusively by the *issuing* court, not the *enforcing* court. Would this model help tribal courts seeking recognition of their judgments in other forums, as in *Wilson*? Which model would be more helpful to tribes if state judgments are brought into tribal courts for enforcement, as in *Eberhard*? Can different models be used for each purpose or must the system settle on a single model? Which one has greater long-term importance to Indian nations?

In the comity model employed to enforce foreign judgments, the courts of the *enforcing* sovereign have wide discretion to determine whether the issuing court had jurisdiction, whether the process under which the foreign court judgment was secured complied with fundamental notions of fairness or procedural due process, whether the judgment was secured by bribery or fraud, and whether the judgment or its theory violates the public policy of the enforcing forum. The ability of enforcing courts under the comity model to redetermine or second-guess the issuing court on issues of jurisdiction has wide implications for colonial oversight of tribal courts by other nontribal forums to which tribal judgments are taken, as *Wilson v. Marchington* demonstrates.

In *Bird v. Glacier Elec. Coop., Inc.*, 255 F.3d 1136 (9th Cir. 2001), the Ninth Circuit made good on some of the dicta in *Wilson v. Marchington*, declining to recognize and enforce a judgment of the Blackfeet Tribal Court because it claimed that appeals to racial bias contained in the closing statement of counsel for one of the parties in the tribal court offended fundamental fairness and violated the due process clause of the Indian Civil Rights Act of 1968, 25 U.S.C. § 1302. In his closing argument to the jury in the tribal court, the plaintiffs' counsel included mention of General Custer, analogies to "killing" and "massacre" of Indians, contrasts between "white man's magic" and the "lowly" Indians, references to the cavalry riding into town to kill an Indian business, and comment about the lands of the Indian people being taken by the "conquering people." Can the result of the *Bird* case be reconciled with the holding of *Santa Clara Pueblo v. Martinez*, 436 U.S. 49 (1978), refusing to imply a federal cause of action to enforce the Indian Civil Rights Act? *See* Sec. D.1, this chapter. More importantly, since the remark was made by plaintiffs' counsel, *without objection by the defendant*, how can it be said that *the tribal court* denied fundamental fairness or due process? If made in closing argument in a state civil case, would such statements constitute a civil rights violation actionable under 42 U.S.C. § 1983? If not, why is the tribal court being held to a higher standard as a precondition of the recognition of its judgments? A critical review of both the *Wilson* and *Bird* decisions can be found in Robert N. Clinton, *Comity and Colonialism: The Federal Courts' Frustration of Tribal-Federal Cooperation*, 36 ARIZ. ST. L. J. 1 (2004).

Not all tribal courts have followed the *Eberhard* decision. *E.g., In re Guardianship of Chewiwi*, 1 Navajo Rptr. 120 (1970); *Ameach v. Reed*, 98-CV-332 (Cherokee 2000) (PKPA inapplicable to tribes). With respect to *Eberhard* specifically, it should be noted that the Indian Child Welfare Act, 25 U.S.C. § 1911(d) already adopts a full faith and credit model of enforcement for child custody orders arising from any Indian child placement proceeding governed by the Act, which does not include a custody order ancillary to divorce. Likewise, the Federal Full Faith and Credit for Child Support Orders Act, 28 U.S.C. § 1738B, imposes the full faith and credit model for child support orders. Notice that the *Eberhard* decision rested in part on the point that no rational Congressional policy could be discerned that would suggest a comity model be employed for child custody orders emanating from divorce actions while a full faith and credit model is expressly adopted by Congress for other Indian child custody proceedings or orders of support. Have any of the critics of the *Eberhard* decision or any of the cases rejecting *Eberhard* supplied an answer to this point?

2. Congressional and Judicial Responses to Interjurisdictional Civil Cooperation: Congress has adopted at least nine federal full faith and credit statutes that could affect Indian tribes. In seven of those nine, it expressly included Indian tribes within the definition of the full faith and credit obligation. *See* 28 U.S.C. 1738B (Federal Full Faith and Credit for Child Support Orders Act); 18 U.S.C. § 2265 (Federal Violence Against Women Act); 25 U.S.C. § 1911(d) (Indian Child Welfare Act); 25 U.S.C. 2207 (Indian Land Consolidation Act); 25 U.S.C. § 3106 (National Indian Forest Resources Management Act); 25 U.S.C.§ 3713 (American Indian Agricultural Resources Management Act); 25 U.S.C. § 1725(g) (Maine Indian Claims Settlement Act).

Only the Parental Kidnapping Act, 28 U.S.C. § 1738A, involved in *Eberhard*, and the federal Full Faith and Credit Act, 28 U.S.C. § 1738, involved in *Wilson*, lack express references to Indian tribes in their coverage. The *Eberhard* and *Wilson* courts split on the significance of those omissions. The *Eberhard* court indicted that it could not find any rational Congressional policy that would require full faith and credit for custody orders not ancillary to divorce, as required by 28 U.S.C. § 1911(d), and for child support orders, as required by 28 U.S.C. § 1738(B), but to withhold such recognition for child custody orders ancillary to divorce, the primary issue covered by the PKPA, 28 U.S.C. § 1738A. Does *Wilson* try to answer these concerns? By contrast, the *Wilson* court indicated that the existence of express obligations to enforce tribal orders in 28 U.S.C. § 1738B, 25 U.S.C. § 2265, and 28 U.S.C. § 1911(d) indicated that Congress meant to exclude a full faith and credit obligation where it had not expressly included such obligations. Does *Eberhard* adequately respond to this concern?

The most recent United States Supreme pronouncement in the areas involved a brief approving citation to *Mackey* in *Martinez*, in which the Court said:

Judgments of tribal courts, as to matters properly within their jurisdiction, have been regarded in some circumstances as entitled to full faith and credit in other courts. *See, e.g., United States ex rel. Mackey v. Coxe*, 15 L. Ed. 299, 18 How. 100 (1856); *Standley v. Roberts*, 59 F. 836, 845 (CA8 1894), appeal dismissed, 17 S. Ct. 999, 41 L. Ed. 1177 (1896).

Santa Clara Pueblo v. Martinez, 436 U.S. 49, 65–66 n.21 (1978). Notwithstanding this Supreme Court endorsement of the full faith and credit approach, some federal courts and, perhaps, a majority of state courts that have considered the question have opted for comity, rather than full faith and credit models, except, of course, where federal statutes compel a contrary result. *E.g., John v. Baker*, 982 P.2d 738 (Alaska 1999); *Mexican v. Circle Bear*, 370 N.W.2d 737 (S.D. 1985) (adopting comity approaches). *But see Sheppard v. Sheppard*, 655 P.2d 895 (Idaho 1982); *Jim v. CIT Financial Services*, 533 P.2d 751 (N.M. 1975); *In re Adoption of Buehl*, 555 P.2d 1334 (Wash. 1976) (adopting full faith and credit approaches). Why would a state court likely prefer a comity over a full faith and credit approach?

In 1996, Congress enacted another statute specifically referencing tribes, although this one denies rather than affirms the obligation to give full faith and credit. The Defense of Marriage Act (DOMA), 28 U.S.C. § 1738C, provides:

> No State, territory, or possession of the United States, or Indian tribe, shall be required to give effect to any public act, record, or judicial proceeding of any other State, territory, possession, or tribe respecting a relationship between persons of the same sex that is treated as a marriage under the laws of such other State, territory, possession, or tribe, or a right or claim arising from such relationship.

Some have argued that DOMA is inconsistent with the constitutional obligation of Article IV, § 1 requiring states to grant full faith and credit to the "public Acts, Records, and judicial Proceedings of every other State." *Compare, e.g.*, Andrew Koppelman, *Same-Sex Marriage, Choice of Law, and Public Policy*, 76 Tex. L. Rev. 921, 974 (1998) (finding constitutionality doubtful), *with* Jeffrey L. Rensberger, *Same-Sex Marriages and the Defense of Marriage Act: A Deviant View of an Experiment in Full Faith and Credit*, 32 Creighton L. Rev. 409 (1998) (arguing in favor of constitutionality). Is this argument available to Indian tribes? Given the language of DOMA, do Indian Tribes require this argument? Under DOMA, do they retain the sovereign authority to recognize, or decline to recognize, same sex marriages performed by other tribes or states? Does the inclusion of Indian tribes in DOMA deprive them of any sovereign authority? In particular, is it an infringement on tribal sovereignty if a state refuses to recognize a tribal same-sex marriage? To date, same-sex marriage has not been embraced as formal law in Indian country. The Navajo Nation Tribal Council recently enacted a ban on same-sex marriage, and then overrode a veto of the law by the Nation's President. On August 2, 2005, the highest court of the Cherokee Nation dismissed, for lack of standing, a suit seeking to enjoin implementation of the only marriage license that that Nation had issued to a same-sex couple. Shortly after the couple wed, the Cherokee Nation Tribal Council unanimously approved a resolution defining marriage as between a man and a woman. *See generally* Matthew L.M. Fletcher,

Same-Sex Marriage, Indian Tribes, and the Constitution, 61 U. MIAMI L. REV. 53 (2006).

3. **State Full Faith and Credit/Comity Statutes and Rules:** As footnote 6 of *Wilson v. Marchington* highlights, a number of states have adopted statutes or court rules extending full faith and credit, or sometimes comity, to tribal court judgments, irrespective of what federal law requires. *E.g.,* Arizona Rules of Procedure for the Recognition of Tribal Court Civil Judgments. If 28 U.S.C. § 1738 already requires such full faith and credit, can state rules or statutes vary the requirements of section 1738? The Wisconsin provision, Wis. Stat. § 806.245, is illustrative. It provides that "The judicial records, orders and judgments of an Indian tribal court in Wisconsin and acts of an Indian tribal legislative body shall have the same full faith and credit in the courts of this state as do the acts, records, orders and judgments of any other governmental entity," subject to certain conditions. The tribal entity must be organized under the IRA; its tribal documents must be authenticated in accordance with state law; the tribal court must be a court of record; the tribal court judgment must be a "valid judgment;" and the tribe in question must grant reciprocal full faith and credit to state judgments and legislative acts. When such a state rule or statute adopts the language "full faith and credit" to describe the recognition obligation, has it eliminated the independent discretion of the enforcing forum which normally would operate under a comity regime to redetermine jurisdiction and due process compliance?

In *Teague v. Bad River Band of Lake Superior Tribe of Chippewa Indians,* 612 N.W.2d 709 (Wis. 2000), the plaintiff brought suit in Wisconsin state courts seeking to compel arbitration under his employment contract after he ceased employment with the tribe as the general manager of the Bad River Casino. While the state case was pending, and after the state judge had denied the Tribe's motion to dismiss, the Tribe filed suit in tribal court seeking a declaration of the invalidity of the employment agreement. The former employee accepted service in the tribal action through his counsel but failed to appear in the tribal court proceeding. The Tribe unsuccessfully sought to have the state court stay its proceeding in favor of exhaustion of tribal remedies. Ultimately, the tribal court entered a default judgment against the former employee and found the employment contract invalid. When the Tribe sought to use the final tribal judgment in the state proceeding, the question of whether the state court was bound to provide full faith and credit to the tribal judgment under section 806.245 ultimately was appealed to the Wisconsin Supreme Court. That court held that the Tribe, as an independent sovereign, was under no obligation to refrain from exercising its jurisdiction merely because the same matter was simultaneously pending in state court. It therefore rejected the former employee's argument that winning the race to the courthouse divested the tribal court of jurisdiction and obviated any obligation to enforce its judgment under section 806.245. Nevertheless, the court wrote:

> Unlike the Uniform Foreign Judgments Act, Wis. Stat. § 806.245 by its terms clearly contemplates a discretionary judicial inquiry into the juris-dictional and procedural validity of tribal court judgments before full faith and credit will be afforded. Several commentators have indicated that the Wisconsin tribal full faith and credit statute is more accurately character-ized as a codification of principles of comity rather than the statutory

equivalent of constitutional full faith and credit. See Darby L. Hoggatt, *The Wyoming Tribal Full Faith and Credit Act: Enforcing Tribal Judgments and Protecting Tribal Sovereignty*, 30 LAND & WATER L. REV. 531, 552–56 (1995); *Recognition of Tribal Court Orders in Wisconsin: An Overview of State and Federal Law*, State Bar of Wisconsin, Indian Law News, Vol. 7, No. 1 (Spring 1999).

612 N.W.2d 716–717. Ultimately, however, the Wisconsin Supreme Court declined to enforce the tribal court judgment under section 806.245. Instead, it suggested:

> This, ultimately, is not a question of full faith and credit under the statute but of judicial allocation of jurisdiction pursuant to principles of comity. Unfortunately, the law currently provides no protocols for state or tribal courts to follow in this situation. Similar problems exist between the courts of different states, and in this context, states have in some areas of the law developed procedures to follow in cases of jurisdictional conflict, where two sovereigns have jurisdiction over the same matter. See, e.g., Uniform Child Custody Jurisdiction Act, Wis. Stat. ch. 822; Wis. Stat. § 767.025(1). The development of similar protocols between state and tribal courts in Wisconsin is a matter of high priority and should be pursued.

Id. at 404–05. Did the Wisconsin Supreme Court successfully distinguish section 806.245 from the case it had before it? If you were a tribal judge would you deem it appropriate in this context to cooperate in developing the jurisdictional protocol suggested by the Wisconsin Supreme Court? In a later proceeding in the *Teague* litigation, the lower court rejected any recognition of the tribal judgment, quashed the tribal judgment, and awarded judgment in *Teague*'s favor. The Wisconsin Supreme Court reversed. A majority of the Court claimed that the Wisconsin full faith and credit statute, Wis. Stat. § 806.245, did not address the situation of parallel judicial proceedings in concurrent jurisdictions evident in the case. They therefore concluded that comity, rather than the state full faith and credit statute, should govern resolution of the matter.

Nevertheless, finding the *Hilton* standards satisfied, they held that the tribal judgment was entitled to recognition and the lower court erred in quashing the tribal judgment. One member of the majority, however, would have applied the state full faith and credit statute to the dispute. He suggested that all elements of Wis. Stat. § 806.245 had been satisfied, based on the tribal court record and the record made in the state court, and therefore indicated that the lower courts were required by Wis. Stat. § 806.245 to accord full faith and credit to the default judgment rendered by the tribal court. The two dissenters joined the other justices in the majority in rejecting application of Wis. Stat. § 806.245 to the case, claiming that it had no place in case of current jurisdiction and competing judgments. *Teague v. Bad River Band of Lake Superior Tribe of Chippewa Indians*, 665 N.W.2d 899 (Wis. 2003). Is that a correct analysis of a state statute intended to accord full faith and credit? Do such questions of full faith and credit or comity only arise where concurrent jurisdiction exists? Why was the Wisconsin Supreme Court so resistant to application of its own *state* statute compelling full faith and credit to a tribal judgment, a clearly non-constitutional question?

4. Enforcement of Foreign Legislative Acts in Judicial Proceedings: The doctrine of full faith and credit also applies to recognition and application of foreign laws. Sometimes, it therefore will influence the question of choice of law. In *Jim v. CIT Financial Servs. Corp.*, 533 P.2d 751 (N.M. 1975), New Mexico gave full faith and credit to a Navajo tribal law. In contrast, Arizona in *Brown v. Babbitt Ford, Inc.*, 571 P.2d 689 (Ariz. Ct. App. 1977) held that the doctrine of comity governed the question whether the same Navajo ordinance at issue in *Jim* was entitled to enforcement. Does full faith and credit have more compulsive force in choice of law questions or in recognition of foreign judgments? *See Allstate Ins. Co. v. Hague*, 449 U.S. 302 (1981). *See generally* Comment, *Conflicts Between State and Tribal Law: The Application of Full Faith and Credit Legislation to Indian Tribes*, 1981 ARIZ. ST. L.J. 801.

5. Habitual Offenders with Prior Tribal Court Convictions in Federal Court: In *U.S. v. Bryant*, 769 F.3d 671 (9th Cir. 2014), the Ninth Circuit held that the Sixth Amendment precluded uncounseled tribal court convictions from counting as predicate offenses under a federal habitual offender domestic violence statute. This decision put the Ninth Circuit in conflict with the Eighth and Tenth Circuits, which held that use of an uncounseled tribal court conviction could not violate the Sixth Amendment if the Sixth Amendment did not apply in tribal court. *See United States v. Cavanaugh*, 643 F.3d 592 (8th Cir. 2011); *United States v. Shavanaux*, 647 F.3d 993 (10th Cir. 2011). Should federal courts refuse to recognize tribal court decisions that do not provide defendants with the same protections that federal law requires? Why might some tribal courts refrain from providing counsel to indigent defendants?

2. Intergovernmental Agreements

Jurisdiction in Indian country is complex, and the possibilities for interjurisdictional conflict legion. While federal Indian law privileges Congress as the ultimate arbiter of jurisdictional arrangements, federal statutes do not provide comprehensive resolutions to the complicated situations arising in Indian country. Furthermore, even where federal statutes exist, such as Public Law 280, thorny interpretive questions remain. And the complex doctrines, sometimes differentiating jurisdiction based on land and tribal membership status, often deny both Indian nations and states the possibility of effective regulation if they act on their own.

Intergovernmental agreements, especially agreements between Indian nations and state or local governments, can reduce such conflicts and debilitating uncertainties. Through these agreements, Indian nations and states may agree to disagree about jurisdiction issues, and then cooperate through such means as sharing tax revenues or other resources, cross-deputizing officers, recognizing one another's judgments, or jointly producing land use plans. Such agreements may affect jurisdiction, especially taxation, law enforcement, judicial matters — such as protocols for concurrent jurisdiction and enforcement of judgments — and regulation of matters such as child welfare, the environment, gaming, and land use. States and tribes might also make agreements regarding rights to land, water, and other natural resources, often but not always in settlement of litigation over such matters. Some of these agreements also address jurisdictional matters. Scholars have argued that intergovernmental agreements reintroduce the "consent principle" into relations between Indian nations and other governments. Rebecca Tsosie, *Negotiating Economic Survival: The Consent Principle and Tribal-State Gaming Compacts Under the Indian Gaming Regulatory Act*, 29 Ariz. St. L.J. 25 (1997).

In its 2013 report to Congress and the President, the Indian Law and Order Commission (ILOC), discussed in Ch. 1, Sec. B.2.I and Ch. 4, Sec. A.3, notes that, in the realm of criminal jurisdiction, in particular, "the recognition of Tribal government and jurisdictional powers through agreements with local jurisdictions will develop partnerships, allow the sharing of knowledge and resources, and result in better chances to coordinate police enforcement, thereby strengthening public safety for Tribal reservations and nearby communities." Indian Law and Order Commission, A Roadmap For Making Native America Safer: Report to Congress and the President of the United States 105 (November 2013). As the ILOC report illustrates, jurisdictional complexities in the realm of criminal justice have had devastating consequences in Indian country, leaving already vulnerable communities with limited access to justice and resources. Some states and tribes have turned to intergovernmental agreements and cooperation as a means to improve services for both tribal and non-tribal communities. In Public Law 280 states, these types of agreements may not only help to facilitate communication and resource sharing, but also to ensure tribal members receive culturally specific treatment and education. *Id.* at 172. *See, e.g.*, Oregon Youth Authority, 2012 Government-to-Government Report on Tribal Relations: Supporting the Rights and Needs of Oregon's Tribal Youth, available at http:// www.oregon.gov/oya/ reports/SB770Report_2012.pdf. *See also* Hannah Bobee et al., *Criminal Jurisdiction in Indian Country: The Solution of Cross Deputization* 18–19 (Indigenous Law and Policy Center Working Paper 2008) available at www.law.msu.edu/ indigenous/papers/2008-01.pdf.

Under what circumstances are such agreements likely to arise and succeed for both sides? What legal requirements, if any, restrict the authority of Indian nations and states to make such agreements? How may such agreements be enforced? These are the questions addressed in the following section.

a. Why Enter into Intergovernmental Agreements?

At their best, cooperative agreements between Indian nations and state or local governments can limit costly and uncertain litigation, arrive at mutually respectful adjustments of competing sovereign interests, share expertise, provide a stable environment for mutually beneficial economic development, fill in regulatory gaps, and assign responsibility for regulation or public services to the agency best positioned to serve the affected community. Both Indian nations and state governments are coming to appreciate these benefits. But what underlying conditions, understandings, and more formal arrangements enable such agreements to come into being? What are the potential pitfalls of making such agreements, particularly for the oftentimes politically weaker partner, the Indian nations?

NATIONAL CONGRESS OF AMERICAN INDIANS & NATIONAL CONFERENCE OF STATE LEGISLATURES, GOVERNMENT TO GOVERNMENT: MODELS OF COOPERATION BETWEEN STATES AND TRIBES
3–5, 32–33 (2002)

Smart for States, Smart for Tribes

State-tribal relationships can be mutually beneficial, helping neighboring governments generally to do their jobs more effectively and also yielding many specific benefits. Effective state-tribal relationships, for example, help states serve their tribal citizens. All tribal members also are citizens of the state in which they reside, and all tribal lands lie within state legislative districts. As such, tribal members are eligible for state services and programs, just as any other state citizens. The difficulty for states in serving these particular citizens, however, often lies in cultural differences or the remoteness of populations. . . .

Building state-tribal relationships can create an opportunity for tribal governments to contract for the administration of some state programs on Indian lands. While relieving the state of its obligation to provide services to a particular group of people that frequently may be "hard-to-serve" because they reside on-reservation in a remote, rural area, tribally administered programs also can benefit both the state and tribe by meeting the specific needs of tribal citizens and using their particular cultural philosophies in the design of their programs, whether for managing natural resources, sustaining a healthy environment, or providing assistance to tribal members in a culturally appropriate manner and environment. Additionally, exercising tribal self-determination by interacting with state governments on the basis of tribal governmental status can serve to reinforce tribal sovereignty, rather than to diminish it, as some tribal leaders fear.

Positive tribal-state relations also can reduce legal problems. Both tribes and states have erred in first seeking a conclusive legal opinion about who has jurisdiction over a particular matter. Given the unclear state of federal Indian law, this formula can produce a significant amount of time-consuming, expensive litigation that may produce unpredictable and undesirable results for all parties. . . .

As the Alaska Commission on Rural Governance and Empowerment noted, "Collaborative arrangements among municipal, tribal, regional, state and federal governments, institutions and agencies provide the means for strengthened local self-governance. Increased participation in decision making, more efficient service provision, and more effective management of environmental, land, and fish and game resources are results of cooperative efforts."

Economic development often can be enhanced by effective tribal-state partnerships. Economic development helps infuse resources into the tribal economy, allowing for greater development of human capital, providing jobs on reservations, and assisting tribes to become self-sufficient. State governments also benefit from tribal economic development, both directly (taxation and gaming compact payments) and indirectly (increased tribal revenue and spending, purchase of goods and services from surrounding, off-reservation businesses). Studies consistently show that tribal economic growth contributes significantly to surrounding communities. . . .

The Devolution Factor

The transfer of federal resources and responsibilities to state, local or tribal governments — often through block grants or other funding mechanisms — is commonly referred to as devolution. . . . In recent years, a variety of governmental functions have been devolved from the federal government to states and, to differing degrees, to tribal governments. . . .

The devolution of federal authorities and resources to state, tribal and local governments has increased the opportunity for and the benefits of enhanced state-tribal relations. More than ever, states and tribes find themselves with parallel or overlapping responsibilities and many incentives for cooperation. According to Stephen Cornell, the director of the Udall Center for Studies in Public Policy at the University of Arizona, and Jonathan Taylor of the Udall Center and the Harvard Project on Indian Economic Development:

> [T]ribes and states are in relationships that are much more complex and uncertain than ever before. . . . The evidence is compelling that where tribes have taken advantage of the federal self-determination policy to gain control of their own resources and of economic and other activity within their borders, and have backed up that control with good governance, they have invigorated their economies and produced positive economic spillovers to states.

Devolution is bringing policymaking to the local level. . . . For state, tribal and local policymaking to be successful, however, neighboring governments will want to consider collaborating and, at least, coordinating the making of policy and administration of programs. . . .

Of all the state-tribal relationships, institutions and agreements in various states, one particular mechanism does not appear to be inherently better than another. Instead, general principles and functions have been shown to lead to better working relationships. . . . The principles that provide the basis for these functions are cooperation, understanding, communication, process, and institutionalization.

   . . . .

The establishment of guiding principles for a government-to-government relationship between state executive branches and tribes has been a significant development in recent years in state-tribal relations. . . .

NOTES ON TRIBAL-STATE
INTERGOVERNMENTAL AGREEMENTS

1. **Analyzing Gains and Losses to Tribes and States or Local Governments from the Agreements:** For an example of a tribal-state policing agreement, see Interlocal Agreement for Deputization and Mutual Law Enforcement Assistance Between the Little Traverse Bay Bands of Odawa Indians and the County of Emmet, Michigan, available at http://www.ncai.org/ncai/resource/agreements/ Little%20Traverse%20Bay%20Bands%20-%20County%20of%20Emmet.pdf 2003). An example of a tribal-state tax agreement is Cigarette Tax Contract Between the Squaxin Island Tribe and the State of Washington, available at http://www. squaxinisland.org/wp/wp-content/uploads/2010/04/cigarette_compact.pdf (2004). Carefully review both of these agreements online. What do the preambles of these agreements suggest to you about what may have prompted each of these governments to make the agreements? Are there differences between them in terms of the underlying purpose? Are any jurisdictional disputes avoided through these agreements? To answer this question, it is necessary to review the material in this chapter and Chapter 4 on criminal jurisdiction and taxing authority in Indian country. If the agreements do avoid jurisdictional disputes, how is it possible for them to do so, given that each agreement acknowledges that it is not altering preexisting jurisdictional arrangements? The major device for doing so in the deputization agreement is granting state law enforcement authority to tribal police. In the case of the tax agreement, the state agrees to substitute tribal for state taxes, without denying its own taxing authority. What sovereign authority, if any, do the tribes forego in these two agreements? To answer this question, you must examine each agreement closely to determine the implications for tribal sovereign immunity, exclusive tribal jurisdiction, and tribal control of entry into tribal territory. Is it a measure of sovereignty for tribes to trade off some elements of sovereignty in exchange for what the tribes deem valuable benefits from the state? Do the gains to the two tribes from these particular agreements seem substantial? To understand what those gains are, consider the services provided to the two tribes, the financial benefits, if any, and the benefits from foregoing litigation over disputed jurisdiction.

2. **Paying for Authority?** Native nations sometimes find that the price of an agreement with a state or local government recognizing tribal authority is that the tribe must expend its funds for services that the state is already obligated to provide, such as law enforcement or education. For example, under a deputization agreement, tribal officers may be able to cite non-Indian traffic violators on the reservation into state court. Think about which government is spending the resources for law enforcement and which government is receiving the traffic fines under such an arrangement. Should lawyers representing tribes encourage their clients to make such agreements? What is the alternative?

3. **Unintended Consequences for Tribal Sovereignty?** In 1965, the Nez Perce Tribe and the State of Idaho entered into an agreement extending state jurisdiction over minor crimes committed by Indians, crimes that would have otherwise been within the Tribe's exclusive jurisdiction. This agreement was made under the auspices of Public Law 280, as Idaho had previously assumed jurisdiction under that Act conditioned on tribal consent. *See* Sec. A.1, this chapter. More than 20 years

later, a county sheriff, acting pursuant to the agreement, arrested a tribal member on the reservation for disturbing the peace. After the charge was dismissed on grounds that the defendant's behavior had occurred in a private home rather than in public, the defendant attempted to bring tort actions and a federal civil rights claim against the sheriff and the county in tribal court. A tribal jury found for the plaintiff, and the sheriff and county brought suit in federal court challenging the tribal court's jurisdiction, invoking *Montana* and *Strate*, presented and discussed in Ch. 3, Sec. C.3. The federal court concluded:

> Under the Agreement, county law enforcement officers . . . have an express right to come onto the reservation and exercise jurisdiction over Indians. . . . The logical consequence of this arrangement is that the officers should not be subject to tribal court civil jurisdiction for conduct arising directly out of their criminal law enforcement activities. . . .
>
> . . . [T]he Nez Perce Tribe ceded its "gatekeeping right," by consenting to and receiving the benefits of state law enforcement protection. The tribe gave up its landowner's right to exclude state officials engaged in law enforcement activities on the reservation. This is a significant alienation of tribal sovereignty and control. . . .
>
> . . . Having divested itself of sovereignty over the very activities that gave rise to the civil claim, nothing in this case can be seen as threatening self-government or the political integrity, economic security or health and welfare of the tribe.

County of Lewis v. Allen, 163 F.3d 509 (9th Cir. 1998). The court also refused to treat the agreement as evidence of a "consensual relationship" between the tribe and the state warranting tribal jurisdiction under *Montana*.

If tribal court is not available to address the consequences of tribal-state agreements, will Indian nations be less likely to enter into such agreements? How might attorneys for the Nez Perce have drafted the agreement so as to prevent the result in this case?

Another potential hidden danger for tribal sovereignty emerges in litigation related to a child welfare agreement made between the Shoshone and Arapaho Tribes and the State of Wyoming. The agreement was designed to ensure that reservation children received social services at a level at least commensurate with services provided by the state to children outside the reservation. The Tribes established a social services agency to supply these services, and the state furnished the agency with necessary funds. Among other provisions, the agreement incorporated state law, provided for state training, and allowed the state to inspect and review the tribal social services agency's case records. The agreement specifically provided that the tribal social services agency was not acting as a representative of the state, and that the Tribes did not waive their sovereign immunity.

Thereafter the tribal social services agency and its officers were sued in federal court by a mother who had been charged with abuse and neglect in tribal court. The tribal member sued under the federal civil rights statutes, including 42 U.S.C. § 1983, claiming that the agreement constituted a waiver of tribal sovereign immunity and rendered the tribal officials actors "under color of state law." To buttress these assertions, the complaint emphasized that the tribal agency had adopted the administrative rules and regulations of a state agency and had agreed to use state forms. Although the Tenth Circuit rejected these arguments, *E.F.W. v. St. Stephen's Mission Indian High School*, 264 F.3d 1297 (10th Cir. 2001), the court's decision relies heavily on specific provisions in the agreement. Should a tribe's choice to adopt state law be interpreted as an exercise or as a forfeiture of sovereignty? Should Indian nations be advised to avoid incorporating state law, even if that is necessary to seal an intergovernmental agreement?

4. Sources on Intergovernmental Agreements: Intergovernmental agreements, both in general and in particular realms of governance, have attracted widespread scholarly interest. In addition to the NCAI and NCSL document excerpted above, general treatments can be found in JEFFREY S. ASHLEY & SECODY J. HUBBARD, NEGOTIATED SOVEREIGNTY: WORKING TO IMPROVE TRIBAL-STATE RELATIONS (2004); David Getches, *Negotiated Sovereignty: Intergovernmental Agreements with American Indian Tribes as Models for Expanding Self-Government*, 1 REVIEW OF CONSTITUTIONAL STUDIES 120 (1993); Joel H. Mack & Gwynn Goodson Timms, *Cooperative Agreements: Government-to-Government Relations to Foster Reservation Business Development*, 20 PEPP. L. REV. 1295 (1993); Frank Pommersheim, *Tribal-State Dispute Resolution: Hope for the Future?*, 36 S.D. L. REV. 239 (1991); Gover, Stetson & Williams, P.C., *Tribal-State Dispute Resolution: Recent Attempts*, 36 S.D. L. REV. 277 (1991); Note, *Intergovernmental Compacts in Native American Law: Models for Expanded Usage*, 112 HARV. L. REV. 922 (1999). An appendix to the publication of the NCAI and NCSL excerpted above includes detailed descriptions of several different types of tribal-state agreements.

b. Authority to Enter into Tribal-State Agreements

Before Native nations and states form intergovernmental agreements, each should be authorized under its own law to do so. Several tribes have enacted enabling legislation for tribal-state agreements, including the Navajo Nation (Navajo Tribal Code tit. 2, § 824, empowering the Council's Intergovernmental Relations Committee to recommend approval of agreements); Cheyenne River Sioux Tribal Code tit. 9, § 2 (allowing cooperative law enforcement agreements); and Blackfeet Constitution (Blackfeet Const. art. VI(1)(a), authorizing the Tribal Council to negotiate with federal, state, and local governments on behalf of the Tribe). Legislation also exists in many states that authorizes and allocates power to make agreements with Indian nations. Many of these statutes provide general authority to local governments and state agencies to form agreements with tribes on a wide range of topics, subject to approval by a designated state official or committee. *See, e.g.,* Mont. Code Ann. § 18-11-101 et seq.; Neb. Rev. Stat. § 13-1502 et seq. Others are limited to particular areas of public services, regulation, or law enforcement. *See, e.g.,* Cal. Pub. Res. Code Ann. § 44201 et seq. (solid waste management); Minn. Stat. § 626.90 et seq. (law enforcement); N.M. Stat. Ann. § 9-11-12.1 (tax administration). Where tribal or state legislation does not clearly specify which officer or branch of government has the power to make such agreements, litigation has predictably ensued. *See, e.g., Kansas v. Finney*, 836 P.2d 1169 (Kan. 1992) (invalidating state gaming compact entered into by governor on the ground that such agreements are legislative in nature, requiring prior legislative authorization or subsequent ratification); *State ex rel. Clark v. Johnson*, 904 P.2d 11 (N.M. 1995) (finding that New Mexico's Joint Powers Agreement Act, N.M. Stat. Ann. § 11-1-2(A),which authorized public agencies to enter into agreements with tribes, required legislative approval of agreements to which the state is a party).

Even if tribal-state agreements are properly authorized under tribal and state law, further questions arise about the necessity for federal approval. Both before and after the enactment of Public Law 280 in 1953 (*see* Sec. A, this chapter), some Indian nations made agreements or resolutions designed to transfer or share their civil and criminal jurisdiction with states. In *Kennerly v. District Court of Montana*, 400 U.S. 423 (1971), the Court held that, notwithstanding a 1967 Blackfeet Tribal Council resolution suggesting that state courts could exercise jurisdiction concurrent with tribal courts over suits involving tribal members, Montana state courts lacked jurisdiction over a debt action commenced against two resident members of the Blackfeet Indian Tribe where the cause of action arose on the Blackfeet Reservation. The *per curiam* opinion for the Court noted that before the 1968 amendments Public Law 280 "conditioned the assumption of state jurisdiction on 'affirmative legislative action' by the State; the Act made no provision whatsoever for tribal consent, either as a necessary or sufficient condition to the assumption of state jurisdiction." The Court further rejected the argument that the 1968 tribal consent amendments might retroactively validate the assumption of state authority, since under the amendment the tribal consent "must be manifested by majority vote of the enrolled Indians within the affected area of Indian country." The Court therefore concluded that "[l]egislative action by the Tribal Council does not comport with the explicit requirements of the Act." *Id.* at 429.

Does *Kennerly* mean that Public Law 280 ousted tribes and states of their preexisting authority to make such agreements, except in the manner provided in the statute? Or would pre-1953 agreements be invalid as well, because of a general requirement of federal approval for *all* tribal-state arrangements altering jurisdictional limits? The leading treatise in Indian law, NELL JESSUP NEWTON ET AL., COHEN'S HANDBOOK OF FEDERAL INDIAN LAW (2012 ed.), declares (at page 590), "Because of federal supremacy over Indian affairs, tribes and states may not make agreements altering the scope of their jurisdiction without congressional consent." *But see Bad Horse v. Bad Horse*, 517 P.2d 893 (Mont. 1974) (upholding state jurisdiction under pre-1953 tribal resolutions). Should agreements where tribes deputize one another's officers or jointly provide services be subject to any such approval requirement, given that neither government purports to grant additional jurisdiction to the other? Is there some general rule of federal preemption that precludes Indian nations and states from entering into government-to-government relations altogether?

Congress has actually enacted several laws empowering states and tribes to alter preexisting jurisdictional limits. Public Law 280 is often included in this group, because before the 1968 amendments states could condition their assumption of jurisdiction on tribal agreement, and after 1968 states may assume jurisdiction under the Act only if there is Indian consent manifest in a vote of the tribal members. *See County of Lewis v. Allen*, 163 F.3d 509 (9th Cir. 1998) (describing a 1965 agreement by the Nez Perce Tribe consenting to Idaho's exercise of concurrent jurisdiction over minor crimes). Is it proper to characterize such jurisdiction-shifting measures as "agreements," given that Public Law 280 grants the states complete control over returning or retroceding such jurisdiction to the federal government? *See* Sec. A.1, this chapter. Or should Indian nations bargain for terms binding states to retrocede jurisdiction under specified conditions?

Other federal statutes that authorize jurisdictional shifts by agreement are the Indian Child Welfare Act (ICWA) (*see* Sec. D, this chapter) and the Indian Gaming Regulatory Act (IGRA) (*see* Sec. E, this chapter). Under ICWA, 25 U.S.C. § 1919(a), "States and Indian tribes are authorized to enter into agreements with each other respecting care and custody of Indian children and jurisdiction over child custody proceedings, including agreements which may provide for orderly transfer of jurisdiction on a case-by-case basis and agreements which provide for concurrent jurisdiction. . . . " Federal approval of such agreements is not required. The compacting provisions in IGRA are discussed in Rebecca Tsosie, *Negotiating Economic Survival: The Consent Principle and Tribal-State Gaming Compacts Under the Indian Gaming Regulatory Act*, 29 Ariz. St. L.J. 25 (1997), and include authority to address jurisdictional allocations directly related to the gaming operation. *See* Sec. E.1, this chapter.

c. Enforcement Issues

Suppose a party to a tribal-state agreement believes that the other has breached the agreement. What enforcement arrangements are legally possible? What are the potential practical or symbolic drawbacks to such arrangements? Review the deputization and tax agreements presented above to determine what enforcement arrangements are included. Are there provisions requiring conferral or mediation before any legal action is taken? Is sovereign immunity waived on either side? Note that waiving tribal sovereign immunity may produce the unintended consequence of federal civil rights actions. *See E.F.W. v. St. Stephen's Mission Indian High School*, 264 F.3d 1297 (10th Cir. 2001) (discussed above).

Assuming sovereign immunity is waived in a tribal-state agreement, questions remain about which forum — federal, tribal, or state — has jurisdiction to entertain an enforcement action. An arbitration clause can sidestep that dilemma. In the absence of such a clause, however, the problem of subject matter jurisdiction nags. Just because one party to an intergovernmental agreement is an Indian nation doesn't mean that an enforcement action "arises under" federal law for purposes of federal subject matter jurisdiction. *See* Mack & Timms, *Cooperative Agreements*, *supra*, at 1333–34.

What do the general rules of state and tribal adjudicative jurisdiction suggest about the possibility of bringing such enforcement actions in either state or tribal court? Interestingly, in his brief presented to the Supreme Court in *Nevada v. Hicks*, 533 U.S. 353 (2001) (*see* Ch. 3, Sec. A.3.a), Hicks argued that if state officials were granted a blanket immunity from tribal jurisdiction, "the developing framework of tribal-state cooperation could easily be crippled." Elaborating on this point, Hicks contended:

> States and their officials may no longer see the need to negotiate cooperative agreements with the tribes if they are immunized for all actions

in Indian country. Tribes would also be less likely to enter into negotiations or uphold current obligations if the reality were that the state party or its agents could in fact be completely immune from any review and monitoring power by tribes and their courts.

Is this prediction well-founded? What kinds of provisions in tribal-state agreements would facilitate use of state court or tribal court, depending on the agreement of the parties? Should Indian nations agree to enforcement in state court? Note that even in a Public Law 280 state, where states have been granted jurisdiction over civil lawsuits, courts have found that the statute does not extend to Indian nations as opposed to individual Indians. *See* NELL JESSUP NEWTON ET AL., COHEN'S HANDBOOK OF FEDERAL INDIAN LAW, *supra*, § 6.04[3][b][v].

F.   TRIBAL SOVEREIGN IMMUNITY

All sovereigns possess inherent common law sovereign immunity from suit as an attribute of that sovereignty. *See Kawananakoa v. Polyblank*, 205 U.S. 349 (1907) (Holmes, J.) (supplying a rationale for the sovereign immunity doctrine). Indeed, the very first reported decision of the United States Supreme Court, *Chisholm v. Georgia*, 2 U.S. (2 Dall.) 419 (1793) concerned precisely this question, holding that references to states in Article III, section 2 of the United States Constitution waived sovereign immunity of the states from suit by citizens of another state, a result overturned by adoption of the Eleventh Amendment. Even without a formal waiver many sovereigns employed private legislation or formal petition directly to the crown as alternative means of providing redress instead of litigation. Today, most sovereigns, such as the federal or state governments, have waived much of that immunity through federal or state tort claims acts and other provisions that authorize litigation against the government for breach of contracts, torts, or other related claims. Since tribes are sovereign, the same governmental immunity from suit without their consent possessed by federal and state sovereigns is also shared by tribes. Suits against Indian tribes, however, remain a highly contentious issue. For a thorough treatment of the subject, see Andrea M. Seielstad, *The Recognition and Evolution of Tribal Sovereign Immunity Under Federal Law: Legal Historical, and Normative Reflections on a Fundamental Aspect of American Indian Sovereignty*, 37 TULSA L. REV. 661 (2002).

1.   In Federal and State Courts

OKLAHOMA TAX COMMISSION v. CITIZEN BAND POTAWATOMI INDIAN TRIBE OF OKLAHOMA
United States Supreme Court
498 U.S. 505 (1991)

CHIEF JUSTICE REHNQUIST delivered the opinion of the Court.

The issue presented in this case is whether a State that has not asserted jurisdiction over Indian lands under Public Law 280 may validly tax sales of goods to tribesmen and nontribal members occurring on land held in trust for a federally recognized Indian tribe. We conclude that, under the doctrine of tribal sovereign immunity, the State may not tax such sales to Indians, but remains free to collect taxes on sales to nontribal members.

Respondent, the Citizen Band Potawatomi Indian Tribe of Oklahoma (Potawatomis or Tribe), owns and operates a convenience store in Oklahoma on land held in trust for it by the federal government. For many years, the Potawatomis have sold cigarettes at the convenience store without collecting Oklahoma's state cigarette tax on these sales. In 1987, petitioner, the Oklahoma Tax Commission (Oklahoma or Commission), served the Potawatomis with an assessment letter, demanding that they pay $2.7 million for taxes on cigarette sales occurring between 1982 and 1986. The Potawatomis filed suit to enjoin the assessment in the United States District Court for the Western District of Oklahoma.

Oklahoma counterclaimed, asking the District Court to enforce its $2.7 million claim against the Tribe and to enjoin the Potawatomis from selling cigarettes in the future without collecting and remitting state taxes on those sales. The Potawatomis moved to dismiss the counterclaim on the ground that the Tribe had not waived its sovereign immunity, and therefore could not be sued by the State. The District Court denied the Potawatomis' motion to dismiss and proceeded to trial. On the merits, the District Court concluded that the Commission lacked the authority to tax the on-reservation cigarette sales to tribal members or to tax the Tribe directly. It held, therefore, that the Tribe was immune from Oklahoma's suit to collect past unpaid taxes directly from the Tribe. Nonetheless, the District Court held that Oklahoma could require the Tribe to collect taxes prospectively for on-reservation sales to nontribal members. Accordingly, the court ordered the Tribe to collect taxes on sales to nontribal members, and to comply with all statutory recordkeeping requirements.

The Tribe appealed the District Court's denial of its motion to dismiss, and the court's order requiring it to collect and remit taxes on sales to nontribal members. The United States Court of Appeals for the Tenth Circuit reversed. That court held that the District Court erred in entertaining Oklahoma's counterclaims because the Potawatomis enjoy absolute sovereign immunity from suit, and had not waived that immunity by filing an action for injunctive relief. The Court of Appeals further held that Oklahoma lacked the authority to impose a tax on any sales that occur on the reservation, regardless of whether they are to tribesmen or nontribal members. It concluded that "because the convenience store is located on land over which the Potawatomis retain sovereign powers, Oklahoma has no authority to tax the store's transactions unless Oklahoma has received an independent jurisdictional grant of authority from Congress." Finding no independent jurisdictional grant of authority to tax the Potawatomis, the Court of Appeals ordered the District Court to grant the Potawatomis' request for an injunction.

We granted certiorari to resolve an apparent conflict with this Court's precedents and to clarify the law of sovereign immunity with respect to the collection of sales taxes on Indian lands. We now affirm in part and reverse in part.

I

Indian tribes are "domestic dependent nations," which exercise inherent sovereign authority over their members and territories. *Cherokee Nation v. Georgia*, 5 Pet. 1, 17 (1831). Suits against Indian tribes are thus barred by sovereign immunity absent a clear waiver by the tribe or congressional abrogation. *Santa Clara Pueblo v. Martinez*, 436 U.S. 49, 58 (1978). Petitioner acknowledges that Indian tribes generally enjoy sovereign immunity, but argues that the Potawatomis waived their sovereign immunity by seeking an injunction against the Commission's proposed tax assessment. It argues that, to the extent that the Commission's counterclaims were "compulsory" under Federal Rule of Civil Procedure 13(a), the District Court did not need any independent jurisdictional basis to hear those claims.

We rejected an identical contention over a half-century ago in *United States v. United States Fidelity & Guaranty Co.*, 309 U.S. 506, 511–512 (1940). In that case, a surety bondholder claimed that a federal court had jurisdiction to hear its state law counterclaim against an Indian tribe because the tribe's initial action to enforce the bond constituted a waiver of sovereign immunity. We held that a tribe does not waive its sovereign immunity from actions that could not otherwise be brought against it merely because those actions were pleaded in a counterclaim to an action filed by the tribe. "Possessing . . . immunity from direct suit, we are of the opinion [the Indian nations] possess a similar immunity from cross-suits." Petitioner does not argue that it received congressional authorization to adjudicate a counterclaim against the Tribe, and the case is therefore controlled by *Fidelity & Guaranty*. We uphold the Court of Appeals' determination that the Tribe did not waive its sovereign immunity merely by filing an action for declaratory relief.

Oklahoma offers an alternative, and more far-reaching, basis for reversing the Court of Appeals' dismissal of its counterclaims. It urges this Court to construe more narrowly, or abandon entirely, the doctrine of tribal sovereign immunity. Oklahoma contends that the tribal sovereign immunity doctrine impermissibly burdens the administration of state tax laws. At the very least, petitioner proposes that the Court modify *Fidelity & Guaranty*, because tribal business activities such as cigarette sales are now so detached from traditional tribal interests that the tribal sovereignty doctrine no longer makes sense in this context. The sovereignty doctrine, it maintains, should be limited to the tribal courts and the internal affairs of tribal government, because no purpose is served by insulating tribal business ventures from the authority of the States to administer their laws.

A doctrine of Indian tribal sovereign immunity was originally enunciated by this Court, and has been reaffirmed in a number of cases. *Turner v. United States*, 248 U.S. 354, 358 (1919); *Santa Clara Pueblo v. Martinez*, supra, at 58. Congress has always been at liberty to dispense with such tribal immunity or to limit it. Although Congress has occasionally authorized limited classes of suits against Indian tribes, it has never authorized suits to enforce tax assessments. Instead, Congress has consistently reiterated its approval of the immunity doctrine. See, e.g., Indian Financing Act of 1974, 88 Stat. 77, 25 U.S.C. 1451 et seq., and the Indian Self-Determination and Education Assistance Act, 88 Stat. 2203, 25 U.S.C. 450 et seq. These Acts reflect Congress's desire to promote the "goal of Indian self-government, including its 'overriding goal' of encouraging tribal self-sufficiency and economic development." *California v. Cabazon Band of Mission Indians*, 480 U.S. 202, 216 (1987). Under these circumstances, we are not disposed to modify the long-established principle of tribal sovereign immunity.

Finally, Oklahoma asserts that, even if sovereign immunity applies to direct actions against tribes arising from activities on the reservation, that immunity should not apply to the facts of this case. The State contends that the Potawatomis' cigarette sales do not, in fact, occur on a "reservation." Relying upon our decision in *Mescalero Apache Tribe v. Jones*, 411 U.S. 145 (1973), Oklahoma argues that the tribal convenience store should be held subject to State tax laws because it does not operate on a formally designated "reservation," but on land held in trust for the Potawatomis. Neither *Mescalero* nor any other precedent of this Court has ever drawn the distinction between tribal trust land and reservations that Oklahoma urges. In *United States v. John*, 437 U.S. 634 (1978), we stated that the test for determining whether land is Indian country does not turn upon whether that land is denominated "trust land" or "reservation." Rather, we ask whether the area has been "validly set apart for the use of the Indians as such, under the superintendence of the Government." *Id.*, at 648–649; *see also United States v. McGowan*, 302 U.S. 535, 539 (1938).

II

. . . .

Although the doctrine of tribal sovereign immunity applies to the Potawatomis, that doctrine does not excuse a tribe from all obligations to assist in the collection of validly imposed state sales taxes. *Washington v. Confederated Tribes of Colville Reservation*, 447 U.S. 134 (1980). Oklahoma argues that, the Potawatomis' tribal immunity notwithstanding, it has the authority to tax sales of cigarettes to nontribal members at the Tribe's convenience store. We agree. In *Moe v. Confederated Salish and Kootenai Tribes*, 425 U.S. 463 (1976), this Court held that Indian retailers on an Indian reservation may be required to collect all state taxes applicable to sales to non-Indians. We determined that requiring the tribal seller to collect these taxes was a minimal burden justified by the State's interest in assuring the payment of these concededly lawful taxes. "Without the simple expedient of having the retailer collect the sales tax from non-Indian purchasers, it is clear that wholesale violations of the law by the latter class will go virtually unchecked." Only four years later, we reiterated this view, ruling that tribal sellers are obliged to collect and remit state taxes on sales to nontribal members at Indian smoke-shops on reservation lands. *Colville*. . . .

In view of our conclusion with respect to sovereign immunity of the Tribe from suit by the State, Oklahoma complains that, in effect, decisions such as *Moe* and *Colville* give them a right without any remedy. There is no doubt that sovereign immunity bars the State from pursuing the most efficient remedy, but we are not persuaded that it lacks any adequate alternatives. We have never held that individual agents or officers of a tribe are not liable for damages in actions brought by the State. *See Ex parte Young*, 209 U.S. 123 (1908). And under today's decision, States may of course collect the sales tax from cigarette wholesalers, either by seizing unstamped cigarettes off the reservation, or by assessing wholesalers who supplied unstamped cigarettes to the tribal stores. States may also enter into agreements with the tribes to adopt a mutually satisfactory regime for the collection of this sort of tax. See 48 Stat. 987, as amended, 25 U.S.C. 476. And if Oklahoma and other States similarly situated find that none of these alternatives produce the revenues to which they are entitled, they may of course seek appropriate legislation from Congress.

Affirmed in part and reversed in part.

JUSTICE STEVENS, concurring.

The doctrine of sovereign immunity is founded upon an anachronistic fiction. See *Nevada v. Hall*, 440 U.S. 410, 414–416 (1979). In my opinion all Governments — federal, state, and tribal — should generally be accountable for their illegal conduct. The rule that an Indian tribe is immune from an action for damages absent its consent is, however, an established part of our law. *See United States v. United States Fidelity & Guaranty Co.*, 309 U.S. 506, 512–513 (1940). Nevertheless, I am not sure that the rule of tribal sovereign immunity extends to cases arising from a tribe's conduct of commercial activity outside its own territory, cf. 28 U.S.C. 1605(a) ("A foreign state shall not be immune from the jurisdiction of courts of the United States or of the States in any case . . . (2) in which the action is based upon a commercial activity carried on in the United States by a foreign state. . . . "), or that it applies to claims for prospective equitable relief against a tribe, cf. *Edelman v. Jordan*, 415 U.S. 651, 664–665 (1974) (Eleventh amendment bars suits against States for retroactive monetary relief, but not for prospective injunctive relief).

KIOWA TRIBE OF OKLAHOMA v. MANUFACTURING TECHNOLOGIES, INC.
United States Supreme Court
523 U.S. 751 (1998)

JUSTICE KENNEDY delivered the opinion of the Court.

In this commercial suit against an Indian Tribe, the Oklahoma Court of Civil Appeals rejected the Tribe's claim of sovereign immunity.

I

Petitioner Kiowa Tribe is an Indian Tribe recognized by the federal government. The Tribe owns land in Oklahoma, and, in addition, the United States holds land in that State in trust for the Tribe. Though the record is vague about some key details, the facts appear to be as follows: In 1990, a tribal entity called the Kiowa Industrial Development Commission agreed to buy from respondent Manufacturing Technologies, Inc., certain stock issued by Clinton-Sherman Aviation, Inc. On April 3, 1990, the then-chairman of the Tribe's business committee signed a promissory note in the name of the Tribe. By its note, the Tribe agreed to pay Manufacturing Technologies $285,000 plus interest. The face of the note recites it was signed at Carnegie, Oklahoma, where the Tribe has a complex on land held in trust for the

Tribe. According to respondent, however, the Tribe executed and delivered the note to Manufacturing Technologies in Oklahoma City, beyond the Tribe's lands, and the note obligated the Tribe to make its payments in Oklahoma City. The note does not specify a governing law. In a paragraph entitled "Waivers and Governing Law," it does provide: "Nothing in this Note subjects or limits the sovereign rights of the Kiowa Tribe of Oklahoma." App. 14.

The Tribe defaulted; respondent sued on the note in state court; and the Tribe moved to dismiss for lack of jurisdiction, relying in part on its sovereign immunity from suit. The trial court denied the motion and entered judgment for respondent. The Oklahoma Court of Civil Appeals affirmed, holding Indian tribes are subject to suit in state court for breaches of contract involving off-reservation commercial conduct. The Oklahoma Supreme Court declined to review the judgment, and we granted certiorari.

II

As a matter of federal law, an Indian tribe is subject to suit only where Congress has authorized the suit or the tribe has waived its immunity. See *Three Affiliated Tribes of Fort Berthold Reservation v. Wold Engineering*, 476 U.S. 877, 890 (1986); *Santa Clara Pueblo v. Martinez*, 436 U.S. 49, 59 (1978); *United States Fidelity & Guaranty Co. (USF&G)*, 309 U.S. 506, 512 (1940). To date, our cases have sustained tribal immunity from suit without drawing a distinction based on where the tribal activities occurred. In one case, a state court had asserted jurisdiction over tribal fishing "both on and off its reservation." *Puyallup Tribe, Inc. v. Department of Game of Wash.*, 433 U.S. 165, 167 (1977). We held the Tribe's claim of immunity was "well founded," though we did not discuss the relevance of where the fishing had taken place. *Id.*, at 168, 172. Nor have we yet drawn a distinction between governmental and commercial activities of a tribe. See, *e.g., ibid.* (recognizing tribal immunity for fishing, which may well be a commercial activity); *Oklahoma Tax Comm'n v. Citizen Band Potawatomi Indian Tribe of Okla.*, 498 U.S 505 (1991) (recognizing tribal immunity from suit over taxation of cigarette sales). . . . Though respondent asks us to confine immunity from suit to transactions on reservations and to governmental activities, our precedents have not drawn these distinctions.

Our cases allowing States to apply their substantive laws to tribal activities are not to the contrary. We have recognized that a State may have authority to tax or regulate tribal activities occurring within the State but outside Indian country. See *Mescalero Apache Tribe v. Jones*, 411 U.S. 145, 148–149; see also *Organized Village of Kake v. Egan*, 369 U.S. 60, 75 (1962). To say substantive state laws apply to off-reservation conduct, however, is not to say that a tribe no longer enjoys immunity from suit. In *Potawatomi*, for example, we reaffirmed that while Oklahoma may tax cigarette sales by a Tribe's store to nonmembers, the Tribe enjoys immunity from a suit to collect unpaid state taxes. 498 U.S., at 510. There is a difference between the right to demand compliance with state laws and the means available to enforce them. See *id.*, at 514.

The Oklahoma Court of Civil Appeals nonetheless believed federal law did not mandate tribal immunity, resting its holding on the decision in *Hoover v. Kiowa*

Tribe of Oklahoma, 909 P.2d 59 (Okla. 1995), cert. denied, 517 U.S. 1188 (1996). In *Hoover*, the Oklahoma Supreme Court held that tribal immunity for off-reservation commercial activity, like the decision not to exercise jurisdiction over a sister State, is solely a matter of comity. 909 P.2d, at 62 (citing *Nevada v. Hall*, 440 U.S. 410, 426 (1979)). According to *Hoover*, because the State holds itself open to breach of contract suits, it may allow its citizens to sue other sovereigns acting within the State. We have often noted, however, that the immunity possessed by Indian tribes is not coextensive with that of the States. See, *e.g.*, *Blatchford v. Native Village of Noatak*, 501 U.S. 775 (1991). In *Blatchford*, we distinguished state sovereign immunity from tribal sovereign immunity, as tribes were not at the Constitutional Convention. They were thus not parties to the "mutuality of . . . concession" that "makes the States' surrender of immunity from suit by sister States plausible." *Id.*, at 782; accord, *Idaho v. Coeur d'Alene Tribe of Idaho*, 521 U.S. 261, 268–269 (1997). So tribal immunity is a matter of federal law and is not subject to diminution by the States. *Three Affiliated Tribes*, *supra*, at 891; *Washington v. Confederated Tribes of Colville Reservation*, 447 U.S. 134, 154 (1980).

Though the doctrine of tribal immunity is settled law and controls this case, we note that it developed almost by accident. The doctrine is said by some of our own opinions to rest on the Court's opinion in *Turner v. United States*, 248 U.S. 354 (1919). See, *e.g.*, *Potawatomi*, *supra*, at 510. Though *Turner* is indeed cited as authority for the immunity, examination shows it simply does not stand for that proposition. The case arose on lands within the Creek Nation's "public domain" and subject to "the powers of [the] sovereign people." 248 U.S., at 355. The Creek Nation gave each individual Creek grazing rights to a portion of the Creek Nation's public lands, and 100 Creeks in turn leased their grazing rights to Turner, a non-Indian. He built a long fence around the land, but a mob of Creek Indians tore the fence down. Congress then passed a law allowing Turner to sue the Creek Nation in the Court of Claims. The Court of Claims dismissed Turner's suit, and the Court, in an opinion by Justice Brandeis, affirmed. The Court stated: "The fundamental obstacle to recovery is not the immunity of a sovereign to suit, but the lack of a substantive right to recover the damages resulting from failure of a government or its officers to keep the peace." *Id.*, at 358. "No such liability existed by the general law." *Id.*, at 357.

The quoted language is the heart of *Turner*. It is, at best, an assumption of immunity for the sake of argument, not a reasoned statement of doctrine. One cannot even say the Court or Congress assumed the congressional enactment was needed to overcome tribal immunity. There was a very different reason why Congress had to pass the Act: "The tribal government had been dissolved. Without authorization from Congress, the Nation could not then have been sued in any court; at least without its consent." *Id.*, at 358. The fact of tribal dissolution, not its sovereign status, was the predicate for the legislation authorizing suit. *Turner*, then, is but a slender reed for supporting the principle of tribal sovereign immunity.

Turner's passing reference to immunity, however, did become an explicit holding that tribes had immunity from suit. We so held in *USF&G*, saying: "These Indian Nations are exempt from suit without Congressional authorization." 309 U.S., at 512 (citing *Turner, supra*, at 358). As sovereigns or quasi sovereigns, the Indian Nations enjoyed immunity "from judicial attack" absent consent to be sued. 309 U.S., at

513–514. Later cases, albeit with little analysis, reiterated the doctrine. *E.g.*, *Puyallup*, 433 U.S., at 167, 172–173; *Santa Clara Pueblo*, 436 U.S., at 58; *Three Affiliated Tribes*, 476 U.S., at 890–891; *Blatchford, supra*, at 782; *Coeur d'Alene, supra*, at 268.

The doctrine of tribal immunity came under attack a few years ago in *Potawatomi, supra.* The petitioner there asked us to abandon or at least narrow the doctrine because tribal businesses had become far removed from tribal self-governance and internal affairs. We retained the doctrine, however, on the theory that Congress had failed to abrogate it in order to promote economic development and tribal self-sufficiency. *Id.*, at 510. The rationale, it must be said, can be challenged as inapposite to modern, wide-ranging tribal enterprises extending well beyond traditional tribal customs and activities. Justice Stevens, in a separate opinion, criticized tribal immunity as "founded upon an anachronistic fiction" and suggested it might not extend to off-reservation commercial activity. *Id.*, at 514–515 (concurring opinion).

There are reasons to doubt the wisdom of perpetuating the doctrine. At one time, the doctrine of tribal immunity from suit might have been thought necessary to protect nascent tribal governments from encroachments by States. In our interdependent and mobile society, however, tribal immunity extends beyond what is needed to safeguard tribal self-governance. This is evident when tribes take part in the Nation's commerce. Tribal enterprises now include ski resorts, gambling, and sales of cigarettes to non-Indians. See *Mescalero Apache Tribe v. Jones*, 411 U.S. 145 (1973); *Potawatomi, supra*; *Seminole Tribe of Fla. v. Florida*, 517 U.S. 44 (1996). In this economic context, immunity can harm those who are unaware that they are dealing with a tribe, who do not know of tribal immunity, or who have no choice in the matter, as in the case of tort victims.

These considerations might suggest a need to abrogate tribal immunity, at least as an overarching rule. Respondent does not ask us to repudiate the principle outright, but suggests instead that we confine it to reservations or to noncommercial activities. We decline to draw this distinction in this case, as we defer to the role Congress may wish to exercise in this important judgment.

Congress has acted against the background of our decisions. It has restricted tribal immunity from suit in limited circumstances. See, *e.g.*, 25 U.S.C. § 450(f)(c)(3) (mandatory liability insurance); § 2710(d)(7)(A)(ii) (gaming activities). And in other statutes it has declared an intention not to alter it. See, *e.g.*, § 450n (nothing in financial-assistance program is to be construed as "affecting, modifying, diminishing, or otherwise impairing the sovereign immunity from suit enjoyed by an Indian tribe"); see also *Potawatomi*, 498 U.S., at 510 (discussing Indian Financing Act of 1974, 88 Stat. 77, 25 U.S.C. § 1451 *et seq.*).

In considering Congress's role in reforming tribal immunity, we find instructive the problems of sovereign immunity for foreign countries. As with tribal immunity, foreign sovereign immunity began as a judicial doctrine. Chief Justice Marshall held that United States courts had no jurisdiction over an armed ship of a foreign state, even while in an American port. *The Schooner Exchange v. McFaddon*, 7 Cranch 116 (1812). While the holding was narrow, "that opinion came to be regarded as extending virtually absolute immunity to foreign sovereigns." *Verlinden B.V. v.*

Central Bank of Nigeria, 461 U.S. 480, 486 (1983). In 1952, the State Department issued what came to be known as the Tate Letter, announcing the policy of denying immunity for the commercial acts of a foreign nation. See *id.*, at 486–487. Difficulties in implementing the principle led Congress in 1976 to enact the Foreign Sovereign Immunities Act, resulting in more predictable and precise rules. See *id.*, at 488–489 (discussing the Foreign Sovereign Immunities Act of 1976, 28 U.S.C. §§ 1604, 1605, 1607).

Like foreign sovereign immunity, tribal immunity is a matter of federal law. *Verlinden, supra*, at 86 Although the Court has taken the lead in drawing the bounds of tribal immunity, Congress, subject to constitutional limitations, can alter its limits through explicit legislation. See, *e.g., Santa Clara Pueblo, supra*, at 58.

In both fields, Congress is in a position to weigh and accommodate the competing policy concerns and reliance interests. The capacity of the Legislative Branch to address the issue by comprehensive legislation counsels some caution by us in this area. Congress "has occasionally authorized limited classes of suits against Indian tribes" and "has always been at liberty to dispense with such tribal immunity or to limit it." *Potawatomi, supra*, at 510. It has not yet done so.

In light of these concerns, we decline to revisit our case law and choose to defer to Congress. Tribes enjoy immunity from suits on contracts, whether those contracts involve governmental or commercial activities and whether they were made on or off a reservation. Congress has not abrogated this immunity, nor has petitioner waived it, so the immunity governs this case. The contrary decision of the Oklahoma Court of Civil Appeals is *Reversed.*

JUSTICE STEVENS, with whom JUSTICE THOMAS and JUSTICE GINSBURG join, dissenting.

"Absent express federal law to the contrary, Indians going beyond reservation boundaries have generally been held subject to nondiscriminatory state law otherwise applicable to all citizens of the State." *Mescalero Apache Tribe v. Jones*, 411 U.S. 145, 148–149, 93 S. Ct. 1267, 1270, 36 L. Ed. 2d 114 (1973). There is no federal statute or treaty that provides petitioner, the Kiowa Tribe of Oklahoma, any immunity from the application of Oklahoma law to its off-reservation commercial activities. Nor, in my opinion, should this Court extend the judge-made doctrine of sovereign immunity to pre-empt the authority of the state courts to decide for themselves whether to accord such immunity to Indian tribes as a matter of comity.

I

. . . [I]n litigation that consumed more than a decade and included three decisions by this Court, we rejected a Tribe's claim that the doctrine of sovereign immunity precluded the State of Washington from regulating fishing activities on the Puyallup Reservation. *Puyallup Tribe, Inc. v. Department of Game of Wash.*, 433 U.S. 165, 175–176, 97 S. Ct. 2616, 2622–2623, 53 L. Ed. 2d 667 (1977). It is true that as an incident to that important holding, we vacated the portions of the state-court decree that were directed against the Tribe itself. *Id.*, at 172–173, 97 S. Ct., at 2621–2622. That action, however, had little practical effect because we upheld the portions of the decree granting relief against the entire class of Indians that was represented by the Tribe. Although Justice Blackmun, one of the "strongest supporters of Indian rights on the Court,"[66] wrote separately to express his "doubts . . . about the continuing vitality in this day of the doctrine of tribal immunity as it was enunciated in *United States v. United States Fidelity & Guaranty Co.*," *id.*, at 178, 97 S. Ct., at 2624, our opinion did not purport to extend or to explain the doctrine. Moreover, as the Tribe's predominant argument was that "the state courts of Washington are without jurisdiction to regulate fishing activities on its reservation," *id.*, at 167, 97 S. Ct., at 2618–2619, we had no occasion to consider the validity of an injunction relating solely to off-reservation fishing.

In several cases since *Puyallup*, we have broadly referred to the tribes' immunity from suit, but "with little analysis," *ante*, at 1704, and only considering controversies arising on reservation territory. In *Santa Clara Pueblo v. Martinez*, 436 U.S. 49, 98 S. Ct. 1670, 56 L. Ed. 2d 106 (1978), a Tribe member and her daughter who both lived on the Santa Clara Pueblo reservation sued in federal court to challenge the validity of a tribal membership law. We agreed with the Tribe that the court lacked jurisdiction to decide this "intratribal controvers[y] affecting matters of tribal self-government and sovereignty." *Id.*, at 53, 98 S. Ct., at 1674. Our decision in *Three Affiliated Tribes of Fort Berthold Reservation v. Wold Engineering*, 476 U.S. 877, 106 S. Ct. 2305, 90 L. Ed. 2d 881 (1986), held that North Dakota could not require a Tribe's blanket waiver of sovereign immunity as a condition for permitting the Tribe to sue private parties in state court. That condition was "unduly intrusive on the Tribe's common law sovereign immunity, and thus on its ability to govern itself according to its own laws," because it required "that the Tribe open itself up to the coercive jurisdiction of state courts for *all* matters occurring on the reservation." *Id.*, at 891, 106 S. Ct., at 2313.[67] Most recently, we held that a federal court lacked authority to entertain Oklahoma's claims for unpaid taxes on cigarette sales made on tribal trust land, which is treated the same as reservation territory. *Oklahoma Tax Comm'n v. Citizen Band Potawatomi Tribe of Okla.*, 498 U.S. 505, 509–511, 111 S. Ct. 905, 909–910, 112 L. Ed. 2d 1112 (1991).[68]

In sum, we have treated the doctrine of sovereign immunity from judicial jurisdiction as settled law, but in none of our cases have we applied the doctrine to purely off-reservation conduct. Despite the broad language used in prior cases, it is quite wrong for the Court to suggest that it is merely following precedent, for we have simply never considered whether a tribe is immune from a suit that has no meaningful nexus to the tribe's land or its sovereign functions. Moreover, none of our opinions has attempted to set forth any reasoned explanation for a distinction

---

[66] [3] Dussias, *Heeding the Demands of Justice: Justice Blackmun's Indian Law Opinions*, 71 N D. L. Rev. 41, 43 (1995).

[67] [4] The particular counter-claims asserted by the private party, which we assumed would be barred by sovereign immunity, concerned the construction of a water-supply system on the Tribe's reservation. *Three Affiliated Tribes*, 476 U.S. at 881.

[68] [5] The Court cites *Blatchford v. Native Village of Noatak*, 501 U.S. 775, 115 L. Ed. 2d 686, 111 S. Ct. 2578 (1991), and *Idaho v. Coeur d' Alene Tribe of Idaho*, 521 U.S. 261, 138 L. Ed. 2d 438, 117 S. Ct. 2028 (1997), as having "reiterated the doctrine" of tribal sovereign immunity. *Ante*, at 5. Each of those cases upheld a State's sovereign immunity under the Eleventh Amendment from being sued in federal court by an Indian tribe. The passing references to tribes' immunity from suit did not discuss the scope of that immunity and were, of course, dicta.

between the States' power to regulate the off-reservation conduct of Indian tribes and the States' power to adjudicate disputes arising out of such off-reservation conduct. Accordingly, while I agree with the Court that it is now too late to repudiate the doctrine entirely, for the following reasons I would not extend the doctrine beyond its present contours.

II

Three compelling reasons favor the exercise of judicial restraint.

First, the law-making power that the Court has assumed belongs in the first instance to Congress. The fact that Congress may nullify or modify the Court's grant of virtually unlimited tribal immunity does not justify the Court's performance of a legislative function. . . .

Second, the rule is strikingly anomalous. Why should an Indian tribe enjoy broader immunity than the States, the federal government, and foreign nations? As a matter of national policy, the United States has waived its immunity from tort liability and from liability arising out of its commercial activities. See 28 U.S.C. §§ 1346(b), 2674 (Federal Tort Claims Act); §§ 1346(a)(2), 1491 (Tucker Act). Congress has also decided in the Foreign Sovereign Immunities Act of 1976 that foreign states may be sued in the federal and state courts for claims based upon commercial activities carried on in the United States, or such activities elsewhere that have a "direct effect in the United States." § 1605(a)(2). And a State may be sued in the courts of another State. *Nevada v. Hall*, 440 U.S. 410, 99 S. Ct. 1182, 59 L. Ed. 2d 416 (1979). The fact that the States surrendered aspects of their sovereignty when they joined the Union does not even arguably present a legitimate basis for concluding that the Indian tribes retained — or, indeed, ever had — any sovereign immunity for off-reservation commercial conduct.

Third, the rule is unjust. This is especially so with respect to tort victims who have no opportunity to negotiate for a waiver of sovereign immunity; yet nothing in the Court's reasoning limits the rule to lawsuits arising out of voluntary contractual relationships. Governments, like individuals, should pay their debts and should be held accountable for their unlawful, injurious conduct.

I respectfully dissent.

MICHIGAN v. BAY MILLS INDIAN COMMUNITY
United States Supreme Court
134 S. Ct. 2024 (2014)

JUSTICE KAGAN delivered the opinion of the Court.

The question in this case is whether tribal sovereign immunity bars Michigan's suit against the Bay Mills Indian Community for opening a casino outside Indian lands. We hold that immunity protects Bay Mills from this legal action. . . .

I

The Indian Gaming Regulatory Act (IGRA or Act), 102 Stat. 2467, 25 U.S.C. § 2701 *et seq.*, creates a framework for regulating gaming activity on Indian lands.[69] See § 2702(3) (describing the statute's purpose as establishing "regulatory authority . . . [and] standards for gaming on Indian lands"). The Act divides gaming into three classes. Class III gaming, the most closely regulated and the kind involved here, includes casino games, slot machines, and horse racing. See § 2703(8). A tribe may conduct such gaming on Indian lands only pursuant to, and in compliance with, a compact it has negotiated with the surrounding State. See § 2710(d)(1)(C). A compact typically prescribes rules for operating gaming, allocates law enforcement authority between the tribe and State, and provides remedies for breach of the agreement's terms. See §§ 2710(d)(3)(C)(ii), (v). Notable here, IGRA itself authorizes a State to bring suit against a tribe for certain conduct violating a compact: Specifically, § 2710(d)(7) (A)(ii) allows a State to sue in federal court to "enjoin a class III gaming activity located on Indian lands and conducted in violation of any Tribal-State compact . . . that is in effect."

Pursuant to the Act, Michigan and Bay Mills . . . entered into a compact in 1993. . . . The compact empowers Bay Mills to conduct class III gaming on "Indian lands"; conversely, it prohibits the Tribe from doing so outside that territory. . . . The compact also contains a dispute resolution mechanism, which sends to arbitration any contractual differences the parties cannot settle on their own. . . . A provision within that arbitration section states that "[n]othing in this Compact shall be deemed a waiver" of either the Tribe's or the State's sovereign immunity. . . . Since entering into the compact, Bay Mills has operated class III gaming, as authorized, on its reservation in Michigan's Upper Peninsula.

In 2010, Bay Mills opened another class III gaming facility in Vanderbilt, a small village in Michigan's Lower Peninsula about 125 miles from the Tribe's reservation. Bay Mills had bought the Vanderbilt property with accrued interest from a federal appropriation, which Congress had made to compensate the Tribe for nineteenth-century takings of its ancestral lands. See Michigan Indian Land Claims Settlement Act, 111 Stat. 2652. Congress had directed that a portion of the appropriated funds go into a "Land Trust" whose earnings the Tribe was to use to improve or purchase property. According to the legislation, any land so acquired "shall be held as Indian lands are held." § 107(a)(3), *id.*, at 2658. Citing that provision, Bay Mills contended that the Vanderbilt property was "Indian land" under IGRA and the compact; and the Tribe thus claimed authority to operate a casino there.

Michigan disagreed: The State sued Bay Mills in federal court to enjoin operation of the new casino, alleging that the facility violated IGRA and the compact because it was located outside Indian lands. . . .

---

[69] [1] The Act defines "Indian lands" as "(A) all lands within the limits of any Indian reservation; and (B) any lands title to which is either held in trust by the United States for the benefit of any Indian tribe or individual[,] or held by any Indian tribe or individual subject to restriction by the United States against alienation and over which an Indian tribe exercises governmental power." § 2703(4).

II

Indian tribes are "domestic dependent nations" that exercise "inherent sovereign authority." *Oklahoma Tax Comm'n v. Citizen Band Potawatomi Tribe of Okla.*, 498 U.S. 505, 509 (1991) (Potawatomi) (quoting *Cherokee Nation v. Georgia*, 5 Pet. 1 (1831)). As dependents, the tribes are subject to plenary control by Congress. . . . And yet they remain "separate sovereigns pre-existing the Constitution." *Santa Clara Pueblo v. Martinez*, 436 U.S. 49, 56 (1978). Thus, unless and "until Congress acts, the tribes retain" their historic sovereign authority. *United States v. Wheeler*, 435 U.S. 313, 323 (1978).

Among the core aspects of sovereignty that tribes possess — subject, again, to congressional action — is the "common-law immunity from suit traditionally enjoyed by sovereign powers." *Santa Clara Pueblo*, 436 U.S., at 58. That immunity, we have explained, is "a necessary corollary to Indian sovereignty and self-governance." *Three Affiliated Tribes of Fort Berthold Reservation v. Wold Engineering, P. C.*, 476 U.S. 877, 890 (1986); cf. The Federalist No. 81, p. 511 (B. Wright ed. 1961) (A. Hamilton) (It is "inherent in the nature of sovereignty not to be amenable" to suit without consent) . . .

In doing so, we have held that tribal immunity applies no less to suits brought by States (including in their own courts) than to those by individuals. First in *Puyallup Tribe, Inc. v. Department of Game of Wash.*, 433 U.S. 165, 167–168, 172–173 (1977), and then again in *Potawatomi*, 498 U.S., at 509–510, 111 S. Ct. 905, we barred a State seeking to enforce its laws from filing suit against a tribe, rejecting arguments grounded in the State's own sovereignty. In each case, we said a State must resort to other remedies, even if they would be less "efficient." *Id.*, at 514; see *Kiowa*, 523 U.S., at 755 ("There is a difference between the right to demand compliance with state laws and the means available to enforce them"). That is because, as we have often stated (and contrary to the dissent's novel pronouncement, see *post* (opinion of THOMAS, J.) (hereinafter the dissent)), tribal immunity "is a matter of federal law and is not subject to diminution by the States." 523 U.S., at 756. . . . Or as we elsewhere explained: While each State at the Constitutional Convention surrendered its immunity from suit by sister States, "it would be absurd to suggest that the tribes" — at a conference "to which they were not even parties" — similarly ceded their immunity against state-initiated suits. *Blatchford v. Native Village of Noatak*, 501 U.S. 775, 782.

Equally important here, we declined in *Kiowa* to make any exception for suits arising from a tribe's commercial activities, even when they take place off Indian lands. [W]e opted to "defer" to Congress about whether to abrogate tribal immunity for off-reservation commercial conduct. *Id.*, at 758, 760.

Our decisions establish as well that such a congressional decision must be clear. The baseline position, we have often held, is tribal immunity; and "[t]o abrogate [such] immunity, Congress must 'unequivocally' express that purpose." *C & L Enterprises, Inc. v. Citizen Band Potawatomi Tribe of Okla.*, 532 U.S. 411, 418 (2001) (quoting *Santa Clara Pueblo*, 436 U.S., at 58. That rule of construction reflects an enduring principle of Indian law: Although Congress has plenary authority over tribes, courts will not lightly assume that Congress in fact intends to undermine Indian self-government. See, *e.g.*, *id.*, at 58–60 . . . .

The upshot is this: Unless Congress has authorized Michigan's suit, our precedents demand that it be dismissed.[70] And so Michigan, naturally enough, makes two arguments: first, that IGRA indeed abrogates the Tribe's immunity from the State's suit; and second, that if it does not, we should revisit — and reverse — our decision in *Kiowa*, so that tribal immunity no longer applies to claims arising from commercial activity outside Indian lands. We consider — and reject — each contention in turn.

III

IGRA partially abrogates tribal sovereign immunity in § 2710(d)(7)(A)(ii) — but this case, viewed most naturally, falls outside that term's ambit. The provision, as noted above, authorizes a State to sue a tribe to "enjoin a class III gaming activity located on Indian lands and conducted in violation of any Tribal-State compact." See *supra*, at 2028; *Kiowa*, 523 U.S., at 758 (citing the provision as an example of legislation "restrict[ing] tribal immunity from suit in limited circumstances"). A key phrase in that abrogation is "on Indian lands" — three words reflecting IGRA's overall scope (and repeated some two dozen times in the statute). A State's suit to enjoin gaming activity *on* Indian lands (assuming other requirements are met, see n. 6, *infra*) falls within § 2710(d)(7)(A)(ii); a similar suit to stop gaming activity *off* Indian lands does not. And that creates a fundamental problem for Michigan. After all, the very premise of this suit — the reason Michigan thinks Bay Mills is acting unlawfully — is that the Vanderbilt casino is *outside* Indian lands. . . . By dint of that theory, a suit to enjoin gaming in Vanderbilt is correspondingly outside § 2710(d)(7)(A)(ii)'s abrogation of immunity.

Michigan first attempts to fit this suit within § 2710(d)(7)(A)(ii) by relocating the "class III gaming activity" to which it is objecting. True enough, Michigan states, the Vanderbilt casino lies outside Indian lands. But Bay Mills "authorized, licensed, and operated" that casino from within its own reservation. . . . According to the State, that necessary administrative action — no less than, say, dealing craps — is "class III gaming activity," and because it occurred on Indian land, this suit to enjoin it can go forward.

But that argument comes up snake eyes, because numerous provisions of IGRA show that "class III gaming activity" means just what it sounds like — the stuff involved in playing class III games. . . .

Stymied under § 2710(d)(7)(A)(ii), Michigan next urges us to adopt a "holistic method" of interpreting IGRA that would allow a State to sue a tribe for illegal gaming off, no less than on, Indian lands. . . . Michigan asks here that we consider "IGRA's text and structure as a whole." . . . But . . . Michigan fails to identify any specific textual or structural features of the statute to support its proposed result. Rather, Michigan highlights a (purported) anomaly of the statute as written: that it enables a State to sue a tribe for illegal gaming inside, but not outside, Indian country. . . . Michigan argues [that] [w]hatever words Congress may have used in IGRA, it could not have intended that senseless outcome. . . .

---

[70] [4] Michigan does not argue here that Bay Mills waived its immunity from suit. Recall that the compact expressly preserves both the Tribe's and the State's sovereign immunity. . . .

But this Court does not revise legislation, as Michigan proposes, just because the text as written creates an apparent anomaly as to some subject it does not address. . . .

And the resulting world, when considered functionally, is not nearly so "enigma[tic]" as Michigan suggests. . . . True enough, a State lacks the ability to sue a tribe for illegal gaming when that activity occurs off the reservation. But a State, on its own lands, has many other powers over tribal gaming that it does not possess (absent consent) in Indian territory. Unless federal law provides differently, "Indians going beyond reservation boundaries" are subject to any generally applicable state law. See *Wagnon v. Prairie Band Potawatomi Nation*, 546 U.S. 95, 113 (2005) (quoting *Mescalero Apache Tribe v. Jones*, 411 U.S. 145, 148 (1973)). So, for example, Michigan could, in the first instance, deny a license to Bay Mills for an off-reservation casino. See Mich. Comp. Laws Ann. §§ 432.206–432.206a. And if Bay Mills went ahead anyway, Michigan could bring suit against tribal officials or employees (rather than the Tribe itself) seeking an injunction for, say, gambling without a license. See § 432.220; see also § 600.3801(1)(a) (designating illegal gambling facilities as public nuisances). . . .

Finally, if a State really wants to sue a tribe for gaming outside Indian lands, the State need only bargain for a waiver of immunity. . . . States have more than enough leverage to obtain such terms because a tribe cannot conduct class III gaming on its lands without a compact, see § 2710(d)(1)(C), and cannot sue to enforce a State's duty to negotiate a compact in good faith, see *Seminole Tribe*, 517 U.S., at 47 (holding a State immune from such suits). So as Michigan forthrightly acknowledges, "a party dealing with a tribe in contract negotiations has the power to protect itself by refusing to deal absent the tribe's waiver of sovereign immunity from suit." . . .

Because IGRA's plain terms do not abrogate Bay Mills's immunity from this suit, Michigan (and the dissent) must make a more dramatic argument: that this Court should "revisit *Kiowa*'s holding" and rule that tribes "have no immunity for illegal commercial activity outside their sovereign territory." . . . Michigan argues that tribes increasingly participate in off-reservation gaming and other commercial activity, and operate in that capacity less as governments than as private businesses. . . . Further, Michigan contends, tribes have broader immunity from suits arising from such conduct than other sovereigns — most notably, because Congress enacted legislation limiting foreign nations' immunity for commercial activity in the United States. See 28 U.S.C. § 1605(a)(2). It is time, Michigan concludes, to "level[ ] the playing field." . . .

But this Court does not overturn its precedents lightly. *Stare decisis*, we have stated, "is the preferred course because it promotes the evenhanded, predictable, and consistent development of legal principles, fosters reliance on judicial decisions, and contributes to the actual and perceived integrity of the judicial process." *Payne v. Tennessee*, 501 U.S. 808, 827 (1991) . . . .

And that is more than usually so in the circumstances here. First, *Kiowa* itself was no one-off: Rather, in rejecting the identical argument Michigan makes, our decision reaffirmed a long line of precedents, concluding that "the doctrine of tribal immunity" — without any exceptions for commercial or off-reservation conduct —

"is settled law and controls this case." 523 U.S., at 756; see *id.*, at 754–755. Second, we have relied on *Kiowa* subsequently: In another case involving a tribe's off-reservation commercial conduct, we began our analysis with *Kiowa*'s holding that tribal immunity applies to such activity (and then found that the Tribe had waived its protection). See *C & L Enterprises*, 532 U.S., at 418. Third, tribes across the country, as well as entities and individuals doing business with them, have for many years relied on *Kiowa* (along with its forebears and progeny), negotiating their contracts and structuring their transactions against a backdrop of tribal immunity. As in other cases involving contract and property rights, concerns of *stare decisis* are thus "at their acme." *State Oil Co. v. Khan*, 522 U.S. 3, 20 (1997). And fourth . . . , Congress exercises primary authority in this area and "remains free to alter what we have done" — another factor that gives "special force" to *stare decisis. Patterson v. McLean Credit Union*, 491 U.S. 164, 172–173 (1989). To overcome all these reasons for this Court to stand pat, Michigan would need an ace up its sleeve.[71] . . . But instead, all the State musters are retreads of assertions we have rejected before. . . .

We ruled [the way we did in *Kiowa*] for a single, simple reason: because it is fundamentally Congress's job, not ours, to determine whether or how to limit tribal immunity. . . .

All that we said in *Kiowa* applies today, with yet one more thing: Congress has now reflected on *Kiowa* and made an initial (though of course not irrevocable) decision to retain that form of tribal immunity. Following *Kiowa*, Congress considered several bills to substantially modify tribal immunity in the commercial context. Two in particular — drafted by the chair of the Senate Appropriations Subcommittee on the Interior — expressly referred to *Kiowa* and broadly abrogated tribal immunity for most torts and breaches of contract. See S. 2299, 105th Cong., 2d Sess. (1998); S. 2302, 105th Cong., 2d Sess. (1998). But instead of adopting those reversals of *Kiowa*, Congress chose to enact a far more modest alternative requiring tribes either to disclose or to waive their immunity in contracts needing the Secretary of the Interior's approval. See Indian Tribal Economic Development and Contract Encouragement Act of 2000, § 2, 114 Stat. 46 (codified at 25 U.S.C. § 81(d)(2)); see also F. Cohen, Handbook of Federal Indian Law § 7.05[1][b], p. 643 (2012). . . .

Reversing *Kiowa* in these circumstances would scale the heights of presumption: Beyond upending "long-established principle[s] of tribal sovereign immunity," that action would replace Congress's considered judgment with our contrary opinion. *Potawatomi*, 498 U.S., at 510 . . . .

---

[71] [8] Adhering to *stare decisis* is particularly appropriate here given that the State, as we have shown, has many alternative remedies: It has no need to sue the Tribe to right the wrong it alleges. . . . We need not consider whether the situation would be different if no alternative remedies were available. We have never, for example, specifically addressed (nor, so far as we are aware, has Congress) whether immunity should apply in the ordinary way if a tort victim, or other plaintiff who has not chosen to deal with a tribe, has no alternative way to obtain relief for off-reservation commercial conduct. The argument that such cases would present a "special justification" for abandoning precedent is not before us. *Arizona v. Rumsey*, 467 U.S. 203, 212 (1984).

V

. . . Accordingly, Michigan may not sue Bay Mills to enjoin the Vanderbilt casino, but must instead use available alternative means to accomplish that object.

We affirm the Sixth Circuit's judgment and remand the case for further proceedings consistent with this opinion.

It is so ordered.

JUSTICE SOTOMAYOR, concurring.

. . . The doctrine of tribal immunity has been a part of American jurisprudence for well over a century. . . . I write separately to further detail why both history and comity counsel against limiting Tribes' sovereign immunity in the manner the principal dissent advances.

[T]he principal dissent analogizes tribal sovereign immunity to foreign sovereign immunity. Foreign sovereigns (unlike States) are generally not immune from suits arising from their commercial activities. . . . This analogy, however, lacks force. Indian Tribes have never historically been classified as "foreign" governments in federal courts even when they asked to be.

[In] *Cherokee Nation v. Georgia*, 8 L.Ed. 25, 5 Pet. 1 (1831), . . . this Court concluded that it lacked jurisdiction because Tribes were not "foreign state[s]." *Id.*, at 20. . . . Tribes were more akin to "domestic dependent nations," the Court explained, than to foreign nations. *Id.*, at 17. We have repeatedly relied on that characterization in subsequent cases. . . . Two centuries of jurisprudence therefore weigh against treating Tribes like foreign visitors in American courts.

II

The principal dissent contends that whenever one sovereign is sued in the courts of another, the question whether to confer sovereign immunity is not a matter of right but rather one of "comity." . . . But in my view, the premise leads to a different conclusion than the one offered by the dissent. Principles of comity strongly counsel in favor of continued recognition of tribal sovereign immunity, including for off-reservation commercial conduct.

Comity — "that is, 'a proper respect for [a sovereign's] functions,'" *Sprint Communications, Inc. v. Jacobs*, 571 U.S. —, —, 134 S. Ct. 584, 591 (2013) — fosters "respectful, harmonious relations" between governments, *Wood v. Milyard*, 566 U.S. —, —, 132 S. Ct. 1826, 1832–1833 (2012). For two reasons, these goals are best served by recognizing sovereign immunity for Indian Tribes, including immunity for off-reservation conduct, except where Congress has expressly abrogated it. First, a legal rule that permitted States to sue Tribes, absent their consent, for commercial conduct would be anomalous in light of the existing prohibitions against Tribes' suing States in like circumstances. Such disparate treatment of these two classes of domestic sovereigns would hardly signal the federal government's respect for tribal sovereignty. Second, Tribes face a number of barriers to raising revenue in traditional ways. If Tribes are ever to become more self-sufficient, and fund a more substantial portion of their own governmental functions, commercial enterprises will likely be a central means of achieving that goal. . . .

Both history and proper respect for tribal sovereignty — or comity — counsel against creating a special "commercial activity" exception to tribal sovereign immunity. For these reasons, and for the important reasons of *stare decisis* and deference to Congress outlined in the majority opinion, I concur.

JUSTICE SCALIA, dissenting.

In *Kiowa* . . . , this Court expanded the judge-invented doctrine of tribal immunity to cover off-reservation commercial activities. *Id.,* at 760. I concurred in that decision. For the reasons given today in Justice THOMAS's dissenting opinion, which I join, I am now convinced that *Kiowa* was wrongly decided. . . .

JUSTICE THOMAS, with whom JUSTICE SCALIA, JUSTICE GINSBURG, and JUSTICE ALITO join, dissenting.

In *Kiowa* . . . , this Court extended the judge-made doctrine of tribal sovereign immunity to bar suits arising out of an Indian tribe's commercial activities conducted outside its territory. That was error. Such an expansion of tribal immunity is unsupported by any rationale for that doctrine, inconsistent with the limits on tribal sovereignty, and an affront to state sovereignty.

That decision, wrong to begin with, has only worsened with the passage of time. In the 16 years since *Kiowa*, tribal commerce has proliferated and the inequities engendered by unwarranted tribal immunity have multiplied. . . .

I

A

There is no substantive basis for *Kiowa*'s extension of tribal immunity to off-reservation commercial acts. . . .

1

. . . [It] is unobjectionable when a tribe raises immunity as a defense in its own courts. . . . [But] to the extent an Indian tribe may claim immunity in federal or state court, it is because federal or state law provides it, not merely because the tribe is sovereign. Outside of tribal courts, the majority's inherent-immunity argument is hardly persuasive.

2

Immunity for independent foreign nations in federal courts is grounded in international "comity," *Verlinden B. v. Central Bank of Nigeria*, 461 U.S. 480, 486 (1983). . . . But whatever its relevance to tribal immunity, comity is an ill-fitting justification for extending immunity to tribes' off-reservation commercial activities.

Even with respect to fully sovereign foreign nations, comity has long been discarded as a sufficient reason to grant immunity for commercial acts. In 1976, Congress provided that foreign states are not immune from suits based on their "commercial activity" in the United States or abroad. Foreign Sovereign Immunities Act, 28 U.S.C. § 1605(a)(2) . . . .

There is a further reason that comity cannot support tribal immunity for off-reservation commercial activities. At bottom, comity is about one sovereign respecting the dignity of another. See *Nevada v. Hall*, 440 U.S. 410, 416 (1979). But permitting immunity for a tribe's off-reservation acts represents a substantial affront to a different set of sovereigns — the States, whose sovereignty is guaranteed by the Constitution, see *New York v. United States*, 505 U.S. 144, 188 (1992) . . . . When an Indian tribe engages in commercial activity outside its own territory, it necessarily acts within the territory of a sovereign State. . . .

3

This Court has previously suggested that recognizing tribal immunity furthers a perceived congressional goal of promoting tribal self-sufficiency and self-governance. . . . Whatever the force of this assertion as a general matter, it is easy to reject as a basis for extending tribal immunity to off-reservation commercial activities. . . . Nor is immunity for off-reservation commercial acts necessary to protect tribal self-governance. . . . And no party has suggested that immunity from the isolated suits that may arise out of extraterritorial commercial dealings is somehow fundamental to protecting tribal government or regulating a tribe's internal affairs. . . .

B

This [Court's] asserted "deference" to Congress was a fiction and remains an enigma . . . because the *Kiowa* Court did not actually leave to Congress the decision whether to extend tribal immunity. Tribal immunity is a common-law doctrine adopted and shaped by this Court. . . .

II

. . . I turn now to *stare decisis*. Contrary to the majority's claim, that policy does not require us to preserve this Court's mistake in *Kiowa*. The Court's failure to justify *Kiowa*'s rule and the decision's untoward consequences outweigh the majority's arguments for perpetuating the error.

A

. . . In the 16 years since *Kiowa*, the commercial activities of tribes have increased dramatically. This is especially evident within the tribal gambling industry. Combined tribal gaming revenues in 28 States have more than tripled — from $8.5 billion in 1998 to $27.9 billion in 2012. . . . But tribal businesses extend well beyond gambling and far past reservation borders. In addition to ventures that take advantage of on-reservation resources (like tourism, recreation, mining, forestry, and agriculture), tribes engage in "domestic and international business ventures" including manufacturing, retail, banking, construction, energy, telecommunications, and more. Graham, An Interdisciplinary Approach to American Indian Economic Development, 80 N.D. L. Rev. 597, 600–604 (2004). Tribal enterprises run the gamut: they sell cigarettes and prescription drugs online; engage in foreign financing; and operate greeting cards companies, national banks, cement plants, ski resorts, and hotels. *Ibid.* . . . These manifold commercial enterprises look the same as any other — except immunity renders the tribes largely litigation-proof.

As the commercial activity of tribes has proliferated, the conflict and inequities brought on by blanket tribal immunity have also increased. Tribal immunity significantly limits, and often extinguishes, the States' ability to protect their citizens and enforce the law against tribal businesses. . . .

In sum, any number of Indian tribes across the country have emerged as substantial and successful competitors in interstate and international commerce, both within and beyond Indian lands. As long as tribal immunity remains out of sync with this reality, it will continue to invite problems, including *de facto* deregulation of highly regulated activities; unfairness to tort victims; and increasingly fractious relations with States and individuals alike. The growing harms wrought by *Kiowa*'s unjustifiable rule fully justify overruling it.

B

In support of its adherence to *stare decisis*, the majority asserts that "Congress has now reflected on *Kiowa*" and has decided to "retain" the decision. . . . On its face, however, this is a curious assertion. To this day, Congress has never granted tribal sovereign immunity in *any* shape or form — much less immunity that extends as far as *Kiowa* went. What the majority really means, I gather, is that the Court must stay its hand because Congress has implicitly approved of *Kiowa*'s rule by *not* overturning it.

This argument from legislative inaction is unavailing. . . .

C

. . . In *Kiowa*, this Court adopted a rule without a reason: a sweeping immunity from suit untethered from commercial realities and the usual justifications for immunity, premised on the misguided notion that only Congress can place sensible limits on a doctrine we created. The decision was mistaken then, and the Court's decision to reaffirm it in the face of the unfairness and conflict it has engendered is doubly so. I respectfully dissent.

JUSTICE GINSBURG, dissenting.

I join Justice THOMAS' dissenting opinion with one reservation. *Kiowa* . . . held for the first time that tribal sovereign immunity extends to suits arising out of an Indian tribe's off-reservation commercial activity. For the reasons stated in the dissenting opinion I joined in *Kiowa, id.,* at 760–766 (opinion of Stevens, J.), and cogently recapitulated today by Justice THOMAS, this Court's declaration of an immunity thus absolute was and remains exorbitant. But I also believe that the Court has carried beyond the pale the immunity possessed by States of the United States. . . . Neither brand of immoderate, judicially confirmed immunity, I anticipate, will have staying power.

NOTES ON TRIBAL SOVEREIGN IMMUNITY IN FEDERAL AND STATE COURTS

1. **Rationales for Federal Protection of Tribal Sovereign Immunity:** Some of the earliest cases, such as *United States Fidelity and Guaranty*, cited in *Citizen Band* and *Kiowa*, seemed to suggest that federally protected sovereign immunity of Tribes derived from the federal trust obligation to protect tribal property and the tribal treasury, thereby suggesting that tribal sovereign immunity was derivative from federal sovereign immunity. This theory would surely explain Justice Kennedy's assumption in *Kiowa* that Congress has the power to waive tribal sovereign immunity for suits in federal and state courts, a power which Congress has not exercised. It now seems clear, however, that tribal sovereign immunity is not derivative from federal sovereign immunity, but, rather, derived from the inherent sovereignty of the Indian tribes. This understanding of tribal sovereign immunity is evident in the majority opinion in *Bay Mills* as well as in earlier circuit court decisions. For example, in *Bottomly v. Passamaquoddy Tribe*, 599 F.2d 1061 (1st Cir. 1979), the First Circuit held that the Passamaquoddy Tribe, which was then *not* federally recognized and which did not then have any property held in trust by the federal government, nevertheless had sovereign immunity when sued in a federal diversity action by its former attorney for unpaid legal fees. The First Circuit noted, "Congress has taken no action to deprive the Passamaquoddy Indians of their inherent immunity from suit. Surely its inattention would not suffice."

How can the *Kiowa* Court's assertion that "[the doctrine of tribal immunity] developed almost by accident" be reconciled with the understanding that, as *Bay Mills* acknowledges, sovereign immunity is derived from inherent tribal sovereignty? Is the statement a historically accurate assessment of the development of the Supreme Court's doctrine regarding tribal sovereign immunity? For an extensive analysis of this issue, *see* William Wood, *It Wasn't an Accident: The Tribal Sovereign Immunity Story*, 62 AM. U. L. REV. 1587, 1590 (2013) (arguing that the Court "ignored some of the foundational tribal sovereign immunity cases [in *Kiowa*], including cases cited in its own precedent, which . . . make clear that the doctrine did not develop by accident").

Since the cases now clearly concede that the source of the tribal sovereign immunity doctrine in federal common law is the inherent sovereignty of the Indian tribes, what, if any justifications, exist for the Court's assumption in *Bay Mills* that Congress has power to waive or eliminate that sovereign immunity by legislation? Waiver of tribal sovereign immunity is discussed later in this section.

2. **Suits Against Tribal Officials:** In *Santa Clara Pueblo v. Martinez*, 436 U.S. 49, 56 (1978), after holding that the Pueblo was immune from suit under the doctrine of tribal sovereign immunity, the Supreme court held that the Governor of the Santa Clara Pueblo did not have tribal sovereign immunity. Justice Marshall

wrote, "As an officer of the Pueblo, petitioner Lucario Padilla is not protected by the tribe's immunity from suit. . . . cf. *Ex parte Young*, 209 U.S. 123 (1908)." In so holding, the Court appeared to adopt for tribal sovereign immunity, precisely the same distinction that the doctrine of *Ex parte Young*, 209 U.S. 123 (1908) applies to the states. That case generally holds that seeking relief directly from a state official does not implicate state sovereign immunity concerns. Indeed, in its opinion in *Citizen Band* the Court cited *Ex parte Young* approvingly as a vehicle by which the state could enforce its cigarette taxes, and *Bay Mills* reiterates that tribal officials may be subject to suits for injunctive relief. To what extent can claimants circumvent the federal doctrine of tribal sovereign immunity by suing tribal officials?

A decision in the Ninth Circuit tried to extend tribal sovereign immunity to tribal officials. In *Linneen v. Gila River Indian Community*, 276 F.3d 489 (9th Cir. 2002), the court held that the Tribe's sovereign immunity extended to the Tribe's Governor and a tribal ranger in a suit brought for money damages after the tribal ranger allegedly detained and threatened the non-Indian plaintiffs while they were walking their dogs on the Gila River Reservation. The Ninth Circuit wrote, " 'Indian tribes have long been recognized as possessing the common-law immunity from suit traditionally enjoyed by sovereign powers.' *Santa Clara Pueblo v. Martinez*, 436 U.S. 49 (1978). 'This immunity extends to tribal officials when acting in their official capacity and within the scope of their authority.' *United States v. Oregon*, 657 F.2d 1009, 1013 n.8 (9th Cir. 1981)." *Id.* at 492; *see also Davis v. Littell*, 398 F.2d 83, 84–85 (9th Cir. 1968). Is this statement consistent with the ruling in *Santa Clara Pueblo* that the Governor could not assert the Pueblo's sovereign immunity?

In *Maxwell v. County of San Diego*, 708 F.3d 1075 (9th Cir. 2013), family members of a shooting victim filed suit against the officials who responded to the crime, including paramedics in an ambulance from the Viejas Band of Kumeyaay Indians, arguing that the victim's death was caused by their unreasonable delay in transporting her to an emergency facility for appropriate medical treatment. The Ninth Circuit held that tribal sovereign immunity did not bar a tort lawsuit against tribal paramedics in their individual capacities because any monetary damages judgment would be assessed directly against the individuals and not the tribal treasury. The court announced that, under these circumstances, the Viejas Band of Kumeyaay Indians was not the "real party in interest," and even if an indemnification agreement existed between the Tribe and the paramedics, this would not confer tribal immunity on the individual employees of the tribe. After this decision, is it proper to say that tribal employees acting in their official capacity share in the tribe's immunity? Is the decision consistent with *Linneen*?

In the arguably analogous field of state sovereign immunity, protected by the Eleventh Amendment, the courts have limited the ability to circumvent the doctrine by suing state officials. In *Edelman v. Jordan*, 415 U.S. 651 (1974), the Court held that the Eleventh Amendment bars an ostensibly equitable suit brought against state officials seeking compensatory damages or "equitable restitution" payable out of the state treasury, while claims for prospective injunctive relief were not precluded despite the need for state financing to comply with the order. Seeking injunctive relief, however, does not provide an automatic exemption from Eleventh Amendment sovereign immunity. In *Idaho v. Coeur d'Alene Tribe*, 521 U.S. 261

(1997), the Court held that Eleventh Amendment sovereign immunity barred an Indian tribe from suing state officials in federal court in order to contest title to a lakebed, the ownership of which was disputed between the Tribe and the State of Idaho. Since the property was actually adversely claimed by the state, rather than the state officials, suit against the state officials was tantamount to a suit against the state since it sought to adjudicate the validity of state title to the lakebed. The action was therefore functionally the equivalent of a suit to quiet title brought against the state. *See also In re Ayers*, 123 U.S. 443 (1887) (sovereign immunity bars suit against state officers to perform contractual obligations of the state). Should these same limitations apply to suits against tribal officials in federal or state courts? Should they apply if the tribal official is sued in tribal court?

Bay Mills may have finally extinguished the hopes of tribal adversaries that the Supreme Court would overrule *Kiowa* and diminish or eliminate tribal sovereign immunity. In a footnote, however, Justice Kagan leaves open some future possibility of limiting the doctrine: "We have never, for example, specifically addressed (nor, so far as we are aware, has Congress) whether immunity should apply in the ordinary way if a tort victim, or other plaintiff who has not chosen to deal with a tribe, has no alternative way to obtain relief for off-reservation commercial conduct. The argument that such cases would present a 'special justification' for abandoning precedent is not before us." Should the cases addressing immunity of tribal officials dampen tribal concerns raised by this language? To the extent those cases expose tribal officials (and through indemnification agreements, tribes) to potential liability, are they cause for even greater concern?

3. **Scope of Federal Protection of Tribal Sovereign Immunity:** Generally, the federal common law doctrines protecting tribal sovereign immunity extend to tribes, their governing bodies, including tribal councils, and their executive branch agencies. *Garcia v. Akwesasne Housing Authority*, 268 F.3d 76 (2d Cir. 2001) (tribal housing authority); *Burlington Northern R. Co. v. Blackfeet Tribe of Blackfeet Indian Reservation*, 924 F.2d 899 (9th Cir. 1991); *Dillon v. Yankton Sioux Tribe Housing Auth.*, 144 F.3d 581, 583 (8th Cir. 1998) (tribal housing authority); *Hagen v. Sisseton-Wahpeton Community College*, 205 F.3d 1040 (8th Cir. 2000) (separately chartered and incorporated tribal college); *Tamiami Partners, Ltd. v. Miccosukee Tribe*, 63 F.3d 1030 (11th Cir. 1995) (tribal council and tribal gaming agency).

The courts generally hold that a tribe cannot assert its tribal sovereign immunity against suits or demands from the United States or United States agencies. *E.g., United States v. Red Lake Band of Chippewa Indians*, 827 F.2d 380, 382 (8th Cir. 1987) ("It is an inherent application of superior power exercised by the United States over Indian tribes that a tribe may not interpose its sovereign immunity against the United States"). Thus, in *E.E.O.C. v. Karuk Tribe Housing Authority*, 260 F.3d 1071 (9th Cir. 2001), the court held that the Tribe enjoyed no sovereign immunity that would immunize it from an administrative subpoena issued in connection with an investigation of the federal Equal Employment Opportunity Commission into alleged age discrimination in employment in the tribal housing authority. The Ninth Circuit indicated, "We know of no principle of law (and the Tribe does not cite any) that differentiates a federal agency such as the EEOC from 'the United States itself' for the purpose of sovereign immunity analysis." *Id.* at 1075.

In *Agua Caliente Band of Cahuilla Indians v. Superior Court*, 148 P.3d 1126 (Cal. 2006), a sharply divided California Supreme Court concluded that the California Fair Political Practices Commission (FPPC) could sue the Agua Caliente Band in state court for alleged violations of state campaign contribution and lobbying disclosure laws. The court acknowledged that the United States Supreme Court's sovereign immunity doctrine protects the tribe from state court suit without its consent regardless whether the tribal activities in question take place on or off the reservation. Nonetheless, it found that tribal sovereign suit immunity is a creature of federal common law, and therefore the reservation of rights to the states in the Tenth Amendment as well as the "guarantee to every State . . . [of] a Republican Form of Government" in Article IV, § 4, as constitutional requirements, trump tribal immunity from suit. The decision grants the Tenth Amendment a wide role in supporting state authority over Indian matters, and goes beyond established United States Supreme Court doctrine treating claims under the Guaranty Clause as political questions. Does the state court's approach properly account for the constitutional provision in the Indian commerce clause granting Congress control over Indian affairs, exclusive of the states? If the state is unable to bring suit in state court to enforce its campaign control laws against tribal participants in the state electoral process, is the integrity of that process seriously endangered, considering the potential for some gaming tribes to make substantial contributions to candidates and ballot measures? Can't the state insist that the recipients of campaign contributions make the disclosures? The Agua Caliente Band had made an offer to the state to establish an agreement that would yield voluntary disclosures by the tribe, but the state refused. Nonetheless, the California high court insisted that practical exigencies demanded that state power overcome tribal sovereign immunity. As the majority opinion observed,

> Tribal members, as citizens of the United States, are allowed to participate in state elections. Allowing the Tribe immunity from suit in this context would allow tribal members to participate in elections and make campaign contributions (using the tribal organization) unfettered by regulations designed to ensure the system's integrity. Allowing tribal members to participate in our state electoral process while leaving the state powerless to effectively guard against political corruption puts the state in an untenable and indefensible position without recourse.

Was this opinion exaggerating how "powerless" the state would be, under the "unique facts" of that case, given that the Tribe had offered to report its contributions on a voluntary basis? For a recent federal Court of Appeals case reaffirming the vitality of tribal sovereign immunity, see *Allen v. Gold Country Casino*, 464 F.3d 1044 (9th Cir. 2006).

4. Tribal Immunity from Process: Recent cases have raised the question whether tribal sovereign immunity bars either state or federal authorities from enforcing process on Indian tribes in connection with civil and criminal investigations. The issue becomes especially charged when a federal or state agency is attempting to serve a search warrant or subpoena in connection with the investigation of a tribal member. In *Bishop Paiute Tribe v. County of Inyo*, 291 F.3d 549 (9th Cir. 2002), *vacated on other grounds sub nom. Inyo County v. Paiute-Shoshone Indians of the Bishop Cmty. of the Bishop Colony*, 538 U.S. 701 (2003), the Ninth

Circuit held that the State of California could not execute a search warrant on a tribal facility to obtain personnel information about a tribal member who was under investigation for state welfare fraud. The tribe had a personnel policy prohibiting disclosure of the information in question without employee consent, but had offered to accept copies of the suspects' state welfare applications as evidence of that consent. After the District Attorney rejected the tribe's proposal, state police, purporting to act under the authority of a search warrant, used bolt cutters to break into the tribal records, seizing payroll documents that contained confidential information from not only the three employees who were the subject of the investigation, but also 78 others. Relying on an earlier Ninth Circuit decision that had invalidated a federal subpoena for tribal records sought in the course of a criminal investigation, the *Inyo County* court concluded that the county's search violated the tribe's sovereign immunity. Although the United States Supreme Court later vacated that decision on jurisdictional grounds, declining to address the merits, at least one court has followed the Ninth Circuit's lead. *See Catskill Development v. Park Place Entertainment Corp.*, 206 F.R.D. 78 (S.D.N.Y. 2002) (disallowing third party subpoenas against tribal officials in a contracts dispute). Prior to the Ninth Circuit's decision in *County of Inyo*, several other federal courts had taken an opposing view, choosing to enforce subpoenas directed at tribes, at least where they were sought by the United States in a criminal proceeding. *See, e.g., United States v. Velarde*, 40 F. Supp. 2d 1314 (D.N.M. 1999). A review of the case law and a recommended legal framework for resolving conflicts between tribal sovereignty, on the one hand, and state and federal law enforcement needs on the other, see Jon W. Monson, *Tribal Immunity from Process: Limiting the Government's Power to Enforce Search Warrants and Subpoenas on American Indian Land*, 56 RUTGERS L. REV. 271 (2003).

C & L ENTERPRISES, INC. v. CITIZEN BAND POTAWATOMI INDIAN TRIBE OF OKLAHOMA
United States Supreme Court
532 U.S. 411 (2001)

JUSTICE GINSBURG delivered the opinion of the Court.

In *Kiowa Tribe of Okla. v. Manufacturing Technologies, Inc.*, 523 U.S. 751 (1998), this Court held that an Indian tribe is not subject to suit in a state court — even for breach of contract involving off-reservation commercial conduct — unless "Congress has authorized the suit or the tribe has waived its immunity." *Id.*, at 754 This case concerns the impact of an arbitration agreement on a tribe's plea of suit immunity. The document on which the case centers is a standard form construction contract signed by the parties to govern the installation of a foam roof on a building, the First Oklahoma Bank, in Shawnee, Oklahoma. The building and land are owned by an Indian Tribe, the Citizen Potawatomi Nation (Tribe). The building is commercial, and the land is off-reservation, nontrust property. The form contract, which was proposed by the Tribe and accepted by the contractor, C & L Enterprises, Inc. contains an arbitration clause.

The question presented is whether the Tribe waived its immunity from suit in state court when it expressly agreed to arbitrate disputes with C & L relating to the contract, to the governance of Oklahoma law, and to the enforcement of arbitral awards "in any court having jurisdiction thereof."

I

Respondent Citizen Potawatomi Nation is a federally recognized Indian Tribe. In 1993, it entered into a contract with petitioner C & L for the installation of a roof on a Shawnee, Oklahoma, building owned by the Tribe. The building, which housed the First Oklahoma Bank, is not on the Tribe's reservation or on land held by the federal government in trust for the Tribe. The contract at issue is a standard form agreement copyrighted by the American Institute of Architects. The Tribe proposed the contract; details not set out in the form were inserted by the Tribe and its architect. Two provisions of the contract are key to this case. First, the contract contains an arbitration clause:

> All claims or disputes between the Contractor [C & L] and the Owner [the Tribe] arising out of or relating to the Contract, or the breach thereof, shall be decided by arbitration in accordance with the Construction [I]ndustry Arbitration Rules of the American Arbitration Association currently in effect unless the parties mutually agree otherwise. . . . The award rendered by the arbitrator or arbitrators shall be final, and judgment may be entered upon it in accordance with applicable law in any court having jurisdiction thereof.

App. to Pet. for Cert. 46.

The American Arbitration Association Rules to which the clause refers provide: "Parties to these rules shall be deemed to have consented that judgment upon the arbitration award may be entered in any federal or state court having jurisdiction thereof." American Arbitration Association, Construction Industry Dispute Resolution Procedures, R-48(c) (Sept. 1, 2000).

Second, the contract includes a choice-of-law clause that reads: "The contract shall be governed by the law of the place where the Project is located." Oklahoma has adopted a Uniform Arbitration Act, which instructs that "[t]he making of an agreement . . . providing for arbitration in this state confers jurisdiction on the court to enforce the agreement under this act and to enter judgment on an award thereunder." Okla. Stat., Tit. 15, § 802.B (1993). The Act defines "court" as "any court of competent jurisdiction of this state." *Ibid.*

After execution of the contract but before C & L commenced performance, the Tribe decided to change the roofing material from foam (the material specified in the contract) to rubber guard. The Tribe solicited new bids and retained another company to install the roof. C & L, claiming that the Tribe had dishonored the contract, submitted an arbitration demand. The Tribe asserted sovereign immunity and declined to participate in the arbitration proceeding. It notified the arbitrator, however, that it had several substantive defenses to C & L's claim. On consideration of C & L's evidence, the arbitrator rendered an award in favor of C & L for $25,400 in damages (close to 30% of the contract price), plus attorney's fees and costs.

Several weeks later, C & L filed suit to enforce the arbitration award in the District Court of Oklahoma County, a state court of general, first instance, jurisdiction. The Tribe appeared specially for the limited purpose of moving to dismiss the action on the ground that the Tribe was immune from suit. The District Court denied the motion and entered a judgment confirming the award.

The Oklahoma Court of Civil Appeals affirmed, holding that the Tribe lacked immunity because the contract giving rise to the suit was "between an Indian tribe and a non-Indian" and was "executed outside of Indian Country." App. to Pet. for Cert. 14 (citation omitted). The Oklahoma Supreme Court denied review, and the Tribe petitioned for certiorari in this Court.

While the Tribe's petition was pending here, the Court decided *Kiowa*, holding: "Tribes enjoy immunity from suits on contracts, whether those contracts involve governmental or commercial activities and whether they were made on or off a reservation." 523 U.S., at 760. *Kiowa* reconfirmed: "[A]n Indian tribe is subject to suit only where Congress has authorized the suit or the tribe has waived its immunity." *Id.*, at 754. Thereafter, we granted the Tribe's petition in this case, vacated the judgment of the Court of Civil Appeals, and remanded for reconsideration in light of *Kiowa*. 524 U.S. 901 (1998).

On remand, the Court of Civil Appeals changed course. It held that, under *Kiowa*, the Tribe here was immune from suit on its contract with C & L, despite the contract's off-reservation subject matter. The court then addressed whether the Tribe had waived its immunity. "The agreement of [the] Tribe to arbitration, and the contract language regarding enforcement in courts having jurisdiction," the court observed, "seem to indicate a willingness on [the] Tribe's part to expose itself to suit on the contract." But, the court quickly added, "the leap from that willingness to a waiver of immunity is one based on implication, not an unequivocal expression." Concluding that the Tribe had not waived its suit immunity with the requisite clarity, the appeals court instructed the trial court to dismiss the case. The Oklahoma Supreme Court denied C & L's petition for review.

Conflicting with the Oklahoma Court of Civil Appeals' current decision, several state and federal courts have held that an arbitration clause, kin to the one now before us, expressly waives tribal immunity from a suit arising out of the contract. See *Sokaogon Gaming Enterprise Corp. v. Tushie-Montgomery Associates, Inc.*, 86 F.3d 656, 661 (7th Cir. 1996) (clause requiring arbitration of contractual disputes and authorizing entry of judgment upon arbitral award "in any court having jurisdiction thereof" expressly waived Tribe's immunity); *Native Village of Eyak v. GC Contractors*, 658 P.2d 756 (Alaska 1983) (same); *Val/Del, Inc. v. Superior Court*, 145 Ariz. 558 (Ct. App. 1985) (same). But cf. *Pan American Co. v. Sycuan Band of Mission Indians*, 884 F.2d 416 (9th Cir. 1989) (clause requiring arbitration of contractual disputes did not expressly waive Tribe's immunity). We granted certiorari to resolve this conflict and now reverse.

II

Kiowa, in which we reaffirmed the doctrine of tribal immunity, involved an off-reservation, commercial agreement (a stock purchase) by a federally recognized

Tribe. The Tribe signed a promissory note agreeing to pay the seller $285,000 plus interest. The note recited: "Nothing in this Note subjects or limits the sovereign rights of the *Kiowa Tribe of Oklahoma*." 523 U.S., at 753–754, 118 S. Ct. 1700. The Tribe defaulted, the seller sued on the note in state court, and the Tribe asserted sovereign immunity. We upheld the plea. Tribal immunity, we ruled in *Kiowa*, extends to suits on off-reservation commercial contracts. *Id.*, at 754–760. The Kiowa Tribe was immune from suit for defaulting on the promissory note, we held, because "Congress ha[d] not abrogated [the Tribe's] immunity, nor ha[d] petitioner waived it." *Id.*, at 760. Like *Kiowa*, this case arises out of the breach of a commercial, off-reservation contract by a federally recognized Indian Tribe. The petitioning contractor, C & L, does not contend that Congress has abrogated tribal immunity in this setting. The question presented is whether the Tribe has waived its immunity.

To abrogate tribal immunity, Congress must "unequivocally" express that purpose. *Santa Clara Pueblo v. Martinez*, 436 U.S. 49 (1978) (citing *United States v. Testan*, 424 U.S. 392, 399 (1976)). Similarly, to relinquish its immunity, a tribe's waiver must be "clear." *Oklahoma Tax Comm'n v. Citizen Band Potawatomi Tribe of Okla.*, 498 U.S. 505, 509 (1991). We are satisfied that the Tribe in this case has waived, with the requisite clarity, immunity from the suit C & L brought to enforce its arbitration award.

The construction contract's provision for arbitration and related prescriptions lead us to this conclusion. The arbitration clause requires resolution of all contract-related disputes between C & L and the Tribe by binding arbitration; ensuing arbitral awards may be reduced to judgment "in accordance with applicable law in any court having jurisdiction thereof." For governance of arbitral proceedings, the arbitration clause specifies American Arbitration Association Rules for the construction industry, *ibid.*, and under those Rules, "the arbitration award may be entered in any federal or state court having jurisdiction thereof," American Arbitration Association, Construction Industry Dispute Resolution Procedures, R-48(c) (Sept. 1, 2000).

The contract's choice-of-law clause makes it plain enough that a "court having jurisdiction" to enforce the award in question is the Oklahoma state court in which C & L filed suit. By selecting Oklahoma law ("the law of the place where the Project is located") to govern the contract, App. to Pet. for Cert. 56, the parties have effectively consented to confirmation of the award "in accordance with" the Oklahoma Uniform Arbitration Act, *id.*, at 46 ("judgment may be entered upon [the arbitration award] in accordance with applicable law"); Okla. Stat., Tit. 15, § 802.A (1993) ("This act shall apply to . . . a provision in a written contract to submit to arbitration any controversy thereafter arising between the parties.").[72]

The Uniform Act in force in Oklahoma prescribes that, when "an agreement . . . provid[es] for arbitration in this state," *i.e.*, in Oklahoma, jurisdiction to enforce the

---

[72] [1] The United States, as *amicus* supporting the Tribe, urges us to remain within the "four corners of the contract" and refrain from reliance on "secondary sources." Brief for United States as *Amicus Curiae* 19, and n. 7. The American Arbitration Association Rules and the Uniform Arbitration Act, however, are not secondary interpretive aides that supplement our reading of the contract; they are prescriptions incorporated by the express terms of the agreement itself.

agreement vests in "any court of competent jurisdiction of this state." § 802.B. On any sensible reading of the Act, the District Court of Oklahoma County, a local court of general jurisdiction, fits that statutory description.[73]

In sum, the Tribe agreed, by express contract, to adhere to certain dispute resolution procedures. In fact, the Tribe itself tendered the contract calling for those procedures. The regime to which the Tribe subscribed includes entry of judgment upon an arbitration award in accordance with the Oklahoma Uniform Arbitration Act. That Act concerns arbitration in Oklahoma and correspondingly designates as enforcement forums "court[s] of competent jurisdiction of [Oklahoma]." *Ibid.* C & L selected for its enforcement suit just such a forum. In a case involving an arbitration clause essentially indistinguishable from the one to which the Tribe and C & L agreed, the Seventh Circuit stated:

> There is nothing ambiguous about th[e] language [of the arbitration clause]. The tribe agrees to submit disputes arising under the contract to arbitration, to be bound by the arbitration award, and to have its submission and the award enforced in a court of law.
>
> . . . .
>
> . . . "The [tribal immunity] waiver . . . is implicit rather than explicit only if a waiver of sovereign immunity, to be deemed explicit, must use the words 'sovereign immunity.' " No case has ever held that.

Sokaogon, 86 F.3d, at 659–660.

That cogent observation holds as well for the case we confront.[74]

The Tribe strenuously urges, however, that an arbitration clause simply "is not a waiver of immunity from suit." Brief for Respondent 13. The phrase in the clause providing for enforcement of arbitration awards "in any court having jurisdiction thereof," the Tribe maintains, "begs the question of what court has jurisdiction." *Id.*, at 22. As counsel for the Tribe clarified at oral argument, the Tribe's answer is "no court," on earth or even on the moon. Tr. of Oral Arg. 32–33. No court — federal, state, or even tribal — has jurisdiction over C & L's suit, the Tribe insists, because it has not expressly waived its sovereign immunity in any judicial forum. *Ibid.*; cf. *Sokaogon*, 86 F.3d, at 660 (facing a similar argument, Seventh Circuit gleaned that

---

[73] [2] The United States argues that the Oklahoma Uniform Arbitration Act is inapplicable in this case because it does not reach all arbitrations properly held in Oklahoma, but only those in which the agreement explicitly "provide[s] for arbitration in [Oklahoma]." Tr. of Oral Arg. 47–48 (referring to § 802.B). No Oklahoma authority is cited for this constricted reading of an Act that expressly "appl[ies] to . . . a provision in a written contract to submit to arbitration any controversy thereafter arising between the parties." § 802.A. We decline to attribute to the Oklahoma lawmakers and interpreters a construction that so severely shrinks the Act's domain.

[74] [3] Instructive here is the law governing waivers of immunity by foreign sovereigns. Cf. *Kiowa Tribe of Okla. v. Manufacturing Technologies, Inc.*, 523 U.S. 751, 759 (1998) ("In considering Congress' role in reforming tribal immunity, we find instructive the problems of sovereign immunity for foreign countries."). "Under the law of the United States . . . an agreement to arbitrate is a waiver of immunity from jurisdiction in . . . an action to enforce an arbitral award rendered pursuant to the agreement. . . . " Restatement (Third) of the Foreign Relations Law of the United States § 456(2)(b)(ii) (1987).

counsel meant only a statement to this effect will do: "The tribe will not assert the defense of sovereign immunity if sued for breach of contract.").[75]

Instead of waiving suit immunity in any court, the Tribe argues, the arbitration clause waives simply and only the parties' rights to a court trial of contractual disputes; under the clause, the Tribe recognizes, the parties must instead arbitrate. Brief for Respondent 21 ("An arbitration clause is what it is: a clause submitting contractual disputes to arbitration."). The clause no doubt memorializes the Tribe's commitment to adhere to the contract's dispute resolution regime. That regime has a real world objective; it is not designed for regulation of a game lacking practical consequences. And to the real world end, the contract specifically authorizes judicial enforcement of the resolution arrived at through arbitration. See *Eyak*, 658 P.2d, at 760 ("[W]e believe it is clear that any dispute arising from a contract cannot be resolved by arbitration, as specified in the contract, if one of the parties intends to assert the defense of sovereign immunity. . . . The arbitration clause . . . would be meaningless if it did not constitute a waiver of whatever immunity [the Tribe] possessed."); *Val/Del*, 145 Ariz., at 565 (because the Tribe has "agree[d] that any dispute would be arbitrated and the result entered as a judgment in a court of competent jurisdiction, we find that there was an express waiver of the tribe's sovereign immunity"); cf. *Rosebud Sioux Tribe v. Val-U Constr. Co.*, 50 F.3d 560, 562 (8th Cir. 1995) (agreement to arbitrate contractual disputes did not contain provision for court enforcement; court nonetheless observed that "disputes could not be resolved by arbitration if one party intended to assert sovereign immunity as a defense").[76]

The Tribe also asserts that a form contract, designed principally for private parties who have no immunity to waive, cannot establish a clear waiver of tribal suit immunity. Brief for Respondent 20; Tr. of Oral Arg. 27–28. In appropriate cases, we apply "the common-law rule of contract interpretation that a court should construe ambiguous language against the interest of the party that drafted it." *Mastrobuono v. Shearson Lehman Hutton, Inc.*, 514 U.S. 52, 62 (1995) (construing form contract containing arbitration clause). That rule, however, is inapposite here. The contract, as we have explained, is not ambiguous. Nor did the Tribe find itself holding the short end of an adhesion contract stick: The Tribe proposed and prepared the contract; C & L foisted no form on a quiescent Tribe. Cf. *United States v. Bankers Ins. Co.*, 245 F.3d 315, 319–320 (4th Cir. 2001) (where federal agency prepared

---

[75] [4] Relying on our state sovereign immunity jurisprudence, the United States maintains that "courts must be especially reluctant to construe ambiguous expressions as consent by a Tribe to be sued in state court." Brief for United States as *Amicus Curiae* 23; see also *id.*, at 25 (arguing that a State's generalized consent to suit, without an express selection of the forum in which suit may proceed, "should be construed narrowly as the State's consent to be sued in its *own* courts of competent jurisdiction, and not its consent to be subjected to suits in *another* sovereign's courts") (citing, *e.g.*, *Kennecott Copper Corp. v. State Tax Comm'n*, 327 U.S. 573 (1946) (State statute authorizing suits against State in "any court of competent jurisdiction" did not waive State's immunity from suit in federal court)). But in this case, as we explained *supra*, the Tribe has plainly consented to suit in Oklahoma state court. We therefore have no occasion to decide whether parallel principles govern state and tribal waivers of immunity.

[76] [5] The Tribe's apparent concession — that the arbitration clause embodies the parties' agreement to resolve disputes through arbitration — is not altogether consistent with the Tribe's refusal to participate in the arbitration proceedings.

agreement, including its arbitration provision, sovereign immunity does not shield the agency from engaging in the arbitration process).[77]

. . . .

For the reasons stated, we conclude that under the agreement the Tribe proposed and signed, the Tribe clearly consented to arbitration and to the enforcement of arbitral awards in Oklahoma state court; the Tribe thereby waived its sovereign immunity from C & L's suit. The judgment of the Oklahoma Court of Civil Appeals is therefore reversed, and the case is remanded for further proceedings not inconsistent with this opinion.

It is so ordered.

NOTES ON WAIVER OF TRIBAL SOVEREIGN IMMUNITY

1. **Scope of the *C & L Enterprises* Holding:** In light of the language of the contractual waiver in *C & L Enterprises*, would the result have been any different if the case had involved litigation to compel arbitration, rather than an effort to enforce the award? Does the contractual clause expressly contemplate litigation to enforce the obligation to arbitrate? Must it? Might the result in *C & L Enterprises* have been different had the contractual agreement to arbitrate omitted the last sentence? Does *C & L Enterprises* overturn a line of lower court cases holding that an agreement to arbitrate standing alone does not constitute a waiver of sovereign immunity? *E.g., Pan American Co. v. Sycuan Band of Mission Indians*, 884 F.2d 416 (9th Cir. 1989); *cf. Val-U Constr. Co. v. Rosebud Sioux Tribe*, 146 F.3d 573 (8th Cir. 1998).

The Supreme Court of Montana revisited the question of waivers of sovereign immunity in *Bradley v. Crow Tribe of Indians*, 67 P.3d 306 (Mont. 2003). The case arose after the indictment and conviction of the former Chairperson of the Crow Tribe for embezzlement. Based on the financial improprieties of the prior administration, the new government of the Crow Tribe required all prior contracts to be ratified anew by the Tribal Council prior to payment. Bradley, a tribal member, allegedly had a seven year contract under the prior administration to provide consulting services and act as program director of a power plant project for the Tribe. When his contract was not ratified by the new administration and he was not paid, he filed suit for breach of contract in the Montana state courts. The Tribe objected to personal and subject matter jurisdiction on the grounds of sovereign immunity. While there is no doubt the prior tribal administration authorized the project and the contract, discovery could not produce an executed copy of the contract signed by the prior chairperson. Nevertheless, she filed a signed affidavit indicating that she believes she had signed the contract and the contract was partially performed by Bradley. The copies that existed contained the following clause:

---

[77] [6] The Tribe alternatively urges affirmance on the grounds that the contract is void under 25 U.S.C. § 81 and that the members of the Tribe who executed the contract lacked the authority to do so on the Tribe's behalf. These issues were not aired in the Oklahoma courts and are not within the scope of the questions on which we granted review. We therefore decline to address them.

11. MONTANA LAW AND VENUE

The parties agree that any action at law, suit in equity, or judicial proceeding for the enforcement of this **AGREEMENT** or any provision thereof shall be instituted only in the courts of the **STATE OF MONTANA**, and it is mutually agreed that this **AGREEMENT** shall be governed by the laws of the **STATE OF MONTANA**, both as to interpretation and performance.

(Emphasis in original.)

While the trial court dismissed the action based on tribal sovereign immunity, the Montana Supreme Court, over the dissents of three justices, reversed. They found that under their state Statute of Frauds, partial performance overcame the lack of a signed contract the terms of which were otherwise not in dispute. Furthermore, and more to the present point, they found the foregoing language to constitute a waiver of sovereign immunity. Was that holding correct? Does the quoted language differ in any material respect from the contractual language found to be a waiver in *C & L Enterprises*? What are the similarities? Should the differences or similarities be controlling? Why?

2.   **Who Can Waive Tribal Sovereign Immunity:** In *Santa Clara Pueblo v. Martinez*, 436 U.S. 49, 58 (1978), the Court held:

Indian tribes have long been recognized as possessing the common-law immunity from suit traditionally enjoyed by sovereign powers. This aspect of tribal sovereignty, like all others, is subject to the superior and plenary control of Congress. But "without congressional authorization," the "Indian Nations are exempt from suit." [quoting] *United States v. United States Fidelity & Guaranty Co.*, [309 U.S. 506, 512 (1940).]

It is settled that a waiver of sovereign immunity "cannot be implied but must be unequivocally expressed." [quoting] *United States v. Testan*, [424 U.S. 392, 399 (1976).]

In *Seminole Tribe v. Florida*, 517 U.S. 44 (1996), the Court held that Congress has no power under the Indian commerce clause to waive *state* sovereign immunity guaranteed by the Eleventh Amendment. Why should Congress have any power to waive tribal sovereign immunity? Other cases recognize the tribe also has power to waive tribal sovereign immunity protected by federal common law. For example, in *Puyallup Tribe v. Department of Game*, 433 U.S. 165, 173 (1977), the Court held the Tribe immune from suit because it could find no indication that "either the Tribe or Congress has waived its claim of immunity." Why should an Indian tribe be able to waive tribal sovereign immunity protected in federal and state court by federal common law?

3.   **Waiver of Tribal Sovereign Immunity by Congress:** *Santa Clara Pueblo v. Martinez, supra*, sustained the Pueblo's claim of sovereign immunity, finding that the Indian Civil Rights Act of 1968, 25 U.S.C. §§ 1301–03, contained no waiver of that immunity. As the quoted language from *Martinez* set forth above suggests, any congressional waiver of tribal sovereign immunity must be "unequivocally expressed." An illustration of the enforcement of that requirement is found in the

judicial reaction to the amendments to Public Law 93-638, the Indian Self-Determination Act, 25 U.S.C. §§ 450–450n. That Act permits tribes to enter into contracts with the federal government, often called "638 contracts," to operate federally-funded service programs for tribal members. Public Law 93-638 was amended in 1988 to require the Secretary of the Interior to obtain insurance for tribes carrying out 638 contracts and to further require the insurance carrier to explicitly waive any right to invoke sovereign immunity in defending suits that arise under those contracts. 25 U.S.C. § 450f(c). The Ninth Circuit construed these changes in *Evans v. McKay*, 869 F.2d 1341 (9th Cir. 1989) and held that the provision only precluded the insurer from raising tribal sovereign immunity; it did not constitute a general waiver of the tribe's immunity. The Ninth Circuit relied significantly on 25 U.S.C. § 450n, which provides "[n]othing in this Act shall be construed as (a) affecting, modifying, diminishing, or otherwise impairing the sovereign immunity upon suit enjoyed by an Indian tribe." *See also* Ch. 5, Sec. A.2 (discussing whether Public Law 280 constitutes a waiver of tribal sovereign immunity).

While Congress generally has not acted to waive tribal sovereign immunity, leaving such decisions primarily to the tribes, there are some rare instances in which congressional waivers have been found. For example, in *Hopi Tribe v. Navajo Tribe*, 46 F.3d 908 (9th Cir. 1995), the Ninth Circuit held that section 18(e) of the Navajo-Hopi Settlement Act of 1974, 25 U.S.C. § 640d-17(e), waived Navajo Nation tribal sovereign immunity from prejudgment interest on rentals involved in the Navajo-Hopi land dispute. The Eighth Circuit arrived at a similar conclusion in *Blue Legs v. BIA*, 867 F.2d 1094 (8th Cir. 1989), when it held that the Resource Conservation and Recovery Act (RCRA), 42 U.S.C. § 6901 et seq., waived tribal sovereign immunity for claims filed in federal court under the Act. RCRA contained express authorization for civil actions to be brought in federal district court against any person who violated its terms. The Act expressly included Indian tribes within the definition of municipalities. The term person in the Act, in turn, was specifically defined to include municipalities. While the language of the Act addressed jurisdiction, rather than sovereign immunity, the Court nevertheless found the language referencing Indian tribes sufficiently specific in contemplating suit against them that it waived sovereign immunity. Is this result consistent with the Supreme Court's later decision in *C & L Enterprises*? Is it consistent with the requirement that any waiver be unequivocally expressed?

4. **Waiver of Sovereign Immunity by Tribe:** Indian tribes, as sovereign governments, generally have authority to waive their own tribal sovereign immunity. *E.g., Native Village of Eyak v. GC Contractors*, 658 P.2d 756 (Alaska 1983) (Native village had inherent sovereignty to waive its own sovereign immunity by contract). Notwithstanding the ability of a tribe to unilaterally waive its sovereign immunity, federal law places some limits on the manner in which it can be exercised, particularly by contract. For example, as amended in the year 2000 by Pub. Law 106-179, section 2, 25 U.S.C. § 81, now requires the approval of the Secretary of the Interior or a designee for a contract "that encumbers Indian lands for a period of 7 or more years." The amendment worked a major limitation on this long-standing requirement of federal approval of tribal contracts since the prior provision required approval of any contract with a tribe or individual Indian "calling for the

payment or delivery of any money or thing of value . . . in consideration of services for said Indians relative to their lands" or related to moneys due from or held by the United States. Under the amended version of 25 U.S.C. § 81(d)(2), the Secretary is not permitted to approve the contract if the contract fails to include a provision that either affords remedies for breach of the contract, references a provision of tribal law disclosing the tribe's right to assert sovereign immunity, or expressly waives that immunity. The requirement that federally approved contracts include an express waiver of tribal sovereign immunity to secure secretarial approval would have worked a very substantial change in the law, had not the amendments also substantially narrowed the class of contracts requiring secretarial approval. *See* Sec. F.1, this chapter.

Contracts that fail to secure required section 81 approval are null and void and, consequently, any waiver of sovereign immunity contained in such a contract is also invalid. *E.g., A.K. Management Co. v. San Manuel Band of Mission Indians*, 789 F.2d 785, 789 (9th Cir. 1986); *Calvello v. Yankton Sioux Tribe*, 899 F. Supp. 431 (D.S.D. 1995). Furthermore, management for class II gaming establishments must under the express provisions of 25 U.S.C. § 2711 secure approval from the Chair of the National Indian Gaming Commission. The Commission has taken the position that this provision applies both to contacts that formally call for a contracting party to engage in management activities and to other agreements structured as consulting or other arrangements that result in *de facto* management of the gaming operation by a non-tribal contracting party. Where such contracts fail to secure the required federal approval, they are null and void and any waiver of sovereign immunity contained therein is therefore invalid. *See generally Tamiami Partners, Ltd. v. Miccosukee Tribe of Indians of Florida*, 63 F.3d 1030, 1036–37 (11th Cir. 1995).

Congress also recently amended 25 U.S.C. § 415, the federal statute governing surface leasing of tribal lands, to add a new subsection (f) authorizing, but not mandating, any lease entered into under the provision to "contain a provision for the binding arbitration of disputes arising out of such lease or contract" and further providing that such leases or contracts shall be considered within the meaning of commerce as employed in the Federal Arbitration Act, 9 U.S.C. § 1 authorizing the enforcement of arbitration agreements. Since the Federal Arbitration Act requires the existence of an independent ground of federal jurisdiction separate from that Act, the amendment further provided that any refusal to submit to arbitration or abide by the award would create a claim "deemed to be a civil action arising under the Constitution, laws or treaties of the United States" within the meaning of the general federal question jurisdiction statute, 28 U.S.C. § 1331. Does this federal statute waive tribal sovereign immunity or merely authorize the tribe to do so in any affected lease or contract? Why would a tribe desire to waive sovereign immunity to a forum other than its own? The federal and state governments rarely waive their own sovereign immunity to forums other than their own. Why, if at all, should tribes? Are statutes like new provisions of section 415(f) or tribal contractual waivers of sovereign immunity to forums other than tribal court required by business necessity?

Where the practical effect of a judgment does not reach tribal assets, courts sometimes have taken a looser view of tribal sovereign immunity. In *Namekagon*

Dev. Co. v. Bois Forte Reservation Hous. Auth., 517 F.2d 508 (8th Cir. 1975), the court found that a developer could sue a tribal housing authority for breach of contract in order to collect its judgments out of federal program funds received by the Tribe designed to pay the contractual obligations of the developer, but could not execute its judgment against tribal funds. By contrast, in *Atkinson v. Haldane*, 569 P.2d 151 (Alaska 1977), the court held that existence of tribal insurance from which a judgment could be paid did not prevent the tribe from asserting tribal sovereign immunity since the insurance was designed to protect the tribe from a judicial determination hostile to the tribe's sovereign immunity. When a tribe sues in federal or state courts, it has not waived its sovereign immunity with respect to counter-claims or cross-claims. *See, e.g., Citizen Band Potawatomi Indian Tribe v. Oklahoma Tax Commission*, 498 U.S. 505 (1991).

Indian tribes with corporate charters issued under section 17 of the Indian Reorganization Act, 25 U.S.C. § 477, often have clauses in their corporate charter that grant various powers to the tribal corporation, including the power to "sue or be sued." *E.g.*, Corporate Charter of the Minnesota Chippewa Tribe, November 13, 1937, Article 5(i); *cf.* Corporate Charter of the Winnebago Tribe, amended September 22, 1995, Article 5(h) (authorizing the tribal corporation "[t]o sue and consent to be sued in courts of competent jurisdiction within the United States"). While such clauses are common in charters of commercial corporations and are generally understood only to grant the corporation the *capacity* to sue or be sued, some courts have held that such "sue or be sued" clauses waive tribal sovereign immunity for tribes conducting operations through their section 17 corporation. *E.g., Padilla v. Pueblo of Acoma*, 754 P.2d 845, 848 (N.M. 1988); *Parker Drilling Co. v. Metlakatla Indian Comm.*, 451 F. Supp. 1127 (D. Alaska 1978). Courts that find waivers of sovereign immunity in such "sue or be sued" provisions in section 17 charters limit their effect to assets devoted to the tribal corporation and such waivers generally do not affect the sovereign immunity of the tribal government operating under section 16 of the IRA, 25 U.S.C. § 476. *E.g., Ramey Constr. Co. v. Apache Tribe*, 673 F.2d 315, 320 (10th Cir. 1982).

5. Counterclaims and Waivers of Tribal Sovereign Immunity: In *Oklahoma Tax Comm'n v. Citizen Band of Potawatomi Tribe*, 498 U.S. 505 (1991), the United States Supreme Court clearly held that the mere filing of legal action by a tribe does not waive its sovereign immunity and open it up to legal claims that would otherwise be barred. *See also Oneida Indian Nation of New York v. New York*, 194 F. Supp. 2d 104, 136 (N.D.N.Y. 2002). *See also Contour Spa at the Hard Rock Inc. v. Seminole Tribe of Florida*, 692 F.3d 1200 (11th Cir. 2012) (holding that tribe's removal of action to federal court did not constitute a waiver of sovereign immunity).

Nevertheless, that does not mean that filing a legal action may not have some consequences. Usually, counterclaims in the nature of recoupment or offset or which request declaratory relief no broader than the tribal claim are permitted. In *Cayuga Indian Nation of New York v. Village of Union Springs*, 293 F. Supp. 2d 183 (N.D.N.Y. 2003), the district court invoked this principle. The suit arose when the Cayuga Nation, a previously landless federally recognized tribe, purchased property in the Village of Union Springs and commenced renovation. The Village insisted that the Tribe comply with local building and zoning laws and the Tribes resisted, filing suit in federal district court to enjoin enforcement of those laws. The Village counterclaimed, seeking only a declaratory judgment that it could enforce those laws against the Tribe's property. When the Tribe moved to dismiss the counterclaim based on tribal sovereign immunity, the district court denied the dismissal based on the foregoing principle. It concluded that "claims in recoupment are not limited to claims for monetary damages, and a claim for declaratory relief may, in fact, be deemed a claim for recoupment as long as it arises out of the same subject as the original cause of action and is based on issues asserted in the complaint." Since the Village's request for declaratory judgment was not broader than the relief requested by the Tribe, the district court refused to dismiss the counterclaim. Notice that the Village would have been able to file the counterclaim against the Tribe on its own. Thus, the fact that the Tribe sued first opened it up to adjudication of the Village's declaratory relief request since that issue was subsumed in the questions presented to the court by the Tribe's complaint.

6.   Participation in Arbitration as a Waiver of Sovereign Immunity by the Tribe: In *Oglala Sioux Tribe v. C & W Enterprises, Inc.*, 542 F.3d 224 (8th Cir. 2008), the Eighth Circuit decided that participation in arbitration can trigger a tribal waiver of sovereign immunity. C & W Enterprises, Inc., a Native American-owned business, entered into four separate contracts with the Oglala Sioux Tribe. Each contract obligated C & W to perform road construction on the Pine Ridge Indian Reservation. The first three contracts contained explicit clauses waiving the Tribe's sovereign immunity and providing a claims resolution process. However, the fourth contract contained different language and a different dispute resolution plan which allowed the Oglala Sioux Tribal Court to resolve all disputes arising under this contract with tribal substantive laws regarding contracts.

Disputes arose concerning C & W's performance and payment and the parties attempted to resolve their disputes through non-binding mediation by the Oglala Sioux Tribal Executive Committee. In 2006, C & W filed a claim with the American Arbitration Association ("AAA") concerning all four contracts, seeking $6 million. The Tribe agreed to arbitrate and, although not required to do so, agreed to include the fourth contract in the arbitration. The Tribe moved to dismiss certain claims on grounds of sovereign immunity, but not involving the fourth contract. The Tribe fully participated in five months of arbitration. At a later date, the Tribe moved the arbitrator to dismiss the fourth claim from arbitration, claiming sovereign immunity. The arbitrator denied the motion, finding the Tribe's active participation in arbitrating the fourth contract waived its immunity. Eventually, the arbitrator entered a final award of $1,250,552.58 in favor of C & W. C & W then filed an action in South Dakota state court to confirm the award, pursuant to South Dakota's Uniform Arbitration Act. Default judgment was entered against the Tribe. After various court actions in the state and tribal courts, the Tribe filed an action in federal court to stop the enforcement proceeding in state court. The United States District Court for the District of South Dakota vacated two executions of judgment for C & W entered by the state court and enjoined the state court from confirming the arbitration award against tribe.

In reviewing the matter on appeal, the Eighth Circuit held that the Tribe waived its sovereign immunity on all four contracts. The court also considered whether the waiver extended to South Dakota state court enforcement. It concluded that it did, finding that "[t]he parties opted to use arbitration, and in doing so, opted for the AAA's Rules." When it agreed to arbitrate disputes and incorporated the AAA's claim resolution procedures into the contracts, and when it participated in the South Dakota arbitration, the Tribe acquiesced in the arbitrator's decision, placing jurisdiction over the award in South Dakota's courts.

2. Scope of Sovereign Immunity in Tribal Courts

Tribes and tribal officials also enjoy sovereign immunity when sued in tribal courts. Many tribes have enacted provisions in tribal ordinances waiving sovereign immunity for specific causes of action and/or for particular types of relief. Some scholars have argued that at least limited waivers of tribal sovereign immunity are an essential component of good governance. *See* Angela R. Riley, *Good (Native) Governance*, 107 COLUM. L. REV. 1049 (2007). For a valuable discussion of tribal sovereign immunity in tribal court and issues of waiver, see Patrice Kunesh, *Tribal Self-Determination in the Age of Scarcity*, 54 S.D. L. REV. 398 (2009).

CHARBONNEAU v. ST. PAUL INSURANCE COMPANY
Turtle Mountain Tribal Court of Appeals
TMAC-08-019 (July 20, 2009)

PER CURIAM:

This appeal stems from an order by the lower court on October 1, 2008 dismissing the Estate's wrongful death suit against St. Paul. The Estate's Personal Representative is Earl Charbonneau, an enrolled member of the Turtle Mountain Band of Chippewa Indians. The deceased, Lonnie Charbonneau, was an enrolled member of the Turtle Mountain Band of Chippewa Indians before his death.

The Estate alleges on or about November 8, 2003 Lonnie Charbonneau was a passenger in a motor vehicle driven by his brother, Greg Charbonneau, that hit a light pole on Sky Dancer Casino premises. The Estate's lawsuit alleged that the motor vehicle accident was proximately caused by the negligence of the Casino because employees allegedly continued providing shots of alcohol and other alcoholic beverages to Greg Charbonneau even though he was obviously intoxicated. The Estate argues that the Casino servers should have known that the alcohol would impair Greg's ability to drive and could likely result in the physical harm or death of others.

St. Paul Insurance Co. provides liability insurance for Sky Dancer Casino. The Estate argues that, under clearly-established precedents of this Court, St. Paul steps into the shoes of Sky Dancer Casino and therefore may directly be sued for negligent acts of Sky Dancer Casino.

The Estate filed this instant lawsuit against Sky Dancer Casino in 2004. Sky Dancer moved to dismiss the suit based upon sovereign immunity grounds. Before the motion was granted, the Estate moved to amend the summons and complaint to include St. Paul. On March 16, 2006, the Tribal Court granted the Estate's motion to amend the complaint to add St. Paul as a defendant while dismissing Sky Dancer Casino from the suit.

. . . .

St. Paul brought a motion for Summary Judgment seeking dismissal of the direct action. The Tribal Court granted summary judgment in St. Paul's favor on October 1, 2008, dismissing the Estate's Complaint with prejudice, stating "the [Estate] cannot make a direct claim against St. Paul because there is no statute, law, or ordinance mandating liability coverage for the [Estate's] claims against Sky Dancer Casino. . . . "

DISCUSSION

I. Waiver of Sovereign Immunity Analysis

In determining whether a tribe or tribal entity has waived its sovereign immunity we must complete a three step analysis:

First, we must look to see if the tribe or tribal entity (the Sky Dancer Casino in this current case) has sovereign immunity to waive. *Champagne v. Sky Dancer Hotel & Casino*, TMAC 07-006 p. 3–4. Second, if it has been determined that there is sovereign immunity to waive, we must determine whether it was expressly (not impliedly) waived. *Thomas v. Sky Dancer Hotel & Casino*, TMAC p. 4 and *Champagne*, p. 3–4. Third, and lastly since the Casino is no longer a party to this case this Court must determine if a direct action may lie against the insurance carrier for the immune party . . .

. . . .

Generally, a tribe "is subject to suit only where Congress has authorized the suit or the tribe has waived its immunity." *Champagne* p. 7 citing *Kiowa Tribe of Okla v. Mfg. Technologies, Inc.*, 523 U.S. 751, 754 (1998). If a tribe elects to waive its sovereign immunity, that waiver must be *express, not implied. Champagne* p. 7 citing *Satiacum v. Sterud*, No. 82-1157 (Puy. Tr. Ct. 1982); see also *Allen*, 464 F.3d at 1047 (9th Cir. 2006). As such, there is a strong presumption against waiver of tribal sovereign immunity . . . .

[The court then engaged in an analysis as to whether any component of federal law, including the Indian Gaming Regulatory Act or the gaming compact between the State of North Dakota and the Turtle Mountain Band of Chippewa Indians, waived sovereign immunity of the tribe.]

The Gaming Compact is a document created through negotiations between the Tribe and the State. Both the State and Tribe must agree to the terms of the compact by signing it . . . .

Looking at Paragraph 18.1B of the Gaming Compact, the court finds it perfectly clear that the Tribe expressly waived its sovereign immunity for personal injury arising out of its gaming activities up to its liability insurance coverage limits.

Paragraph 18.1B of the Gaming Compact reads:

Sovereign immunity must be asserted by the Tribe itself and may not be asserted by insurers or agents. The tribe waives sovereign immunity for personal injury arising out of its gaming activities, but only to the extent of its liability insurance coverage limits.

This is wording the tribe agreed to when it decided to sign and enter into the Gaming Compact. Thus, the tribe has expressly waived its sovereign immunity for personal injury arising out of its gaming activities up to its liability insurance coverage limits.

Chapter 4

FEDERAL AND STATE AUTHORITY IN INDIAN COUNTRY

During the treaty period, the Native nations negotiated for and secured treaty guarantees of their exclusive jurisdiction and sovereignty over their dwindling domains. While implicit in all the treaties, these guarantees were perhaps made most explicit in the removal treaties involving the southeastern tribes since those tribes were the first to feel the illegal encroachment of state authority over their lands and people, a practice condemned as illegal by Chief Justice Marshall in *Worcester v. Georgia*, 31 U.S. (6 Pet.) 515 (1832), set forth and discussed in Chapter 1. Thus, the Choctaws sought and secured a treaty promise from the United States that it would

> secure to the said Choctaw Nation of Red People the jurisdiction and government of *all the persons and property* that may be within their limits west, so that no Territory or State shall ever have a right to pass laws for the government of the Choctaw Nation of Red People and their descendants; and that no part of the land granted them shall ever be embraced in any Territory or State. . . .

Treaty of Dancing Rabbit Creek with the Choctaw Nation, Feb. 21, 1831, Art. 4, 7 Stat. 333 (emphasis added). Similarly, the Cherokee Nation insisted as a precondition of removal that they be assured that

> in no future time without their consent, [would they] be included within the territorial limits or jurisdiction of any State or Territory. But [the United States] shall secure to the Cherokee nation the right by their national councils to make and carry into effect all such laws as they may deem necessary for the government and protection *of the persons and property within their own country belonging to their people or such persons as have connected themselves with them*: provided always that they shall not be inconsistent with the constitution of the United States and such acts of Congress as have been or may be passed regulating trade and intercourse with the Indians. . . .

Treaty of New Echota with the Cherokee Nation, Dec. 29, 1835, Art. 5, 7 Stat. 478. Similarly, when the Fort Laramie Treaty of 1868 was negotiated with Sioux and other tribes, the Lakota, among others, were assured that the Great Sioux Reservation would be set apart for the "absolute and undisturbed use and occupation of the Indians herein named." Treaty of Fort Laramie with Sioux Nation and other tribes, April 29, 1868, Art. 2, 15 Stat. 635. All of these provisions and, many more like them, suggest that the jurisdictional model that emerged from the period of treaty federalism was clear and simple — tribes had complete territorial jurisdiction over all persons and property located within their territory, just as states had such territorial jurisdiction outside of Indian country. Under this model, states and the federal government had almost no authority to enforce any laws in Indian country and the primary governance over both Indians and non-Indians (other than federal officials and employees performing diplomatic or military duties) was left to the tribes.

Had the United States fully honored these treaty promises, the pattern of sovereignty and jurisdiction in Indian country would have been quite clear — it would have rested almost completely with the tribes. Thus this chapter of the book would have been short on that narrative of history. Like many promises made to the Indian tribes to induce them to part with their lands, however, the treaty promises to the tribes of complete tribal political control over their remaining lands have not been fully honored. Beginning in the late nineteenth century, the United States government began to unilaterally assert increased political hegemony in Indian country. Much more recently, in the last quarter of the twentieth century, a trend began that has greatly eroded the clear holding of *Worcester* and sustained increasing state authority over, at least non-Indians, in Indian country. In short, to the extent that the Indian tribes sought clear reservation boundaries to definitively demarcate their jurisdiction, the reservation boundaries have become more permeable as barriers against the exercise of, first, federal and, later, state authority.

This chapter is devoted to exploring these doctrinal developments, the difficulties they pose for the tribes, and the legal foundations, if any, upon which they rest. As you consider the materials in this chapter keep in mind three sets of questions.

First, if current legal doctrines and recent developments regarding federal and state authority in Indian country are not consistent with the treaty federalism model of tribal-federal relations, what model do they most closely resemble and how appropriate is that model for dealing with Native nations in a post-colonial world? Do the federal and state cases you read in this chapter demonstrate any appreciation for these larger questions of intergovernmental history and sovereign paradigms? Should they?

Second, what are the sources of judicial decision-making in these cases? For states, the model of state-federal relations frequently emerges from debates over interpretation of the United States Constitution. For tribes, do the courts craft a model of tribal-federal relations based on any model supplied by the United States Constitution? Is any such model provided in that document? If so, what is it and has it been followed? If not, why not? If the Constitution does not supply an answer to many of these questions, has Congress addressed many of them by statute? Could it? Do most of the court opinions in this chapter rest on statutory grounds? If not, what, if any, is the source of the federal judiciary's authority to unilaterally impose a model of tribal-federal relations? From which sources does it derive its conception of the appropriate model and how legitimate are those sources both factually and legally?

Third, as the Treaty of Dancing Rabbit Creek with the Choctaw Nation demonstrates, the treaty federalism model required tribal consent for any inroad on the Tribe's complete territorial jurisdiction over "*all the persons and property* that may be within their limits." To what extent has that consent been given? If a tribe takes a jurisdictional challenge to a federal court, has it consented to abide by the outcome of the litigation, including any resultant diminution of its sovereignty? Does it consent if a member does so? In what form should such consent be manifested? Should tribal consent be required today for inroads on tribal sovereignty or is this nicety merely an outdated relic of the first 300 years of Native/Anglo-American diplomacy? Do international models of self-determination have anything to say on this subject?

A. THE FEDERAL GOVERNMENT'S PLENARY POWER OVER INDIANS AND INDIAN COUNTRY

1. Sources and Scope of the Power

The material in Ch. 1, Secs. C and D traced United States law regarding the sources, scope, and limitations on federal power over Indian affairs, at least until the first decades of the twentieth century. You saw that the earliest understanding of the federal-tribal relationship, reflected in the Treaty of 1778 with the Delaware, was that Indian tribes and their members were not subject to federal governmental authority while within their own territory except through their own agreement. Indeed, as the readings at the beginning of this book point out, several treaties contain provisions by which the affected tribes agree to curtail their authority and abide by federal law, particularly the early Trade and Intercourse Acts, or to extradite fugitives. The earliest federal Indian legislation, namely the Trade and Intercourse Acts, are consistent with this understanding, as they purport to regulate or protect only those who deal with Indian nations, not to assert unilateral power over the nations themselves or their peoples. *See* Robert N. Clinton, *There Is No Supremacy Clause for Indian Tribes*, 34 Ariz. St. L. J. 113 (2002). These limitations on federal power were so well-understood in those early decades that in diplomatic correspondence with Great Britain that preceded the War of 1812, the United States formally took the position that "the Indians residing within the United States are so far independent that they live under their own customs, *and not under the laws of the United States.*"

As Supreme Court decisions from the late nineteenth and early twentieth centuries forecast, however, modern federal Indian law no longer recognizes that limitation, and the tribal-federal relationship therefore has been markedly changed since the baseline understanding emerged through treaty negotiations between the tribes and the federal government. Since the scope of federal powers over Indian affairs set forth in the United States Constitution was drafted while the original understanding of the tribal-federal relationship prevailed, perhaps the most interesting question is what authority the federal courts have to alter that relationship. Did adoption of the Indian commerce clause in Article I, section 8, clause 3 of the United States Constitution constitutionalize the original tribal-federal relationship, or did it grant the federal government a broader plenary power over Indians, Indian tribes, and Indian lands, as the federal judiciary now claims? Should this question only be answered in historical terms or should courts take a more dynamic approach, considering subsequent changes in the nature of

Indian land holdings (such as allotment) and imposed colonial changes in the tribal-federal relationship?

Although the Supreme Court's 1886 decision in *United States v. Kagama*, presented in Ch. 1, Sec. D.2, suggested otherwise for federal Indian law, modern-day constitutional theory normally requires some grounding in the constitutional text for any assertion of congressional power. So long as federal power was based upon tribal consent through treaty-making, a constitutional source for the exercise of that power was readily available. Basic American constitutional law recognizes that a treaty "may endow Congress with a source of legislative authority independent of the powers enumerated in Article I (although, of course, still limited by the Constitution's explicit constraint on federal action)." 1 LAURENCE H. TRIBE, AMERICAN CONSTITUTIONAL LAW 645–46 (3d ed. 2000); *see generally, Missouri v. Holland*, 252 U.S. 416 (1920). But if Congress wanted to step beyond treaties as a mode of regulating Indian affairs, some alternate source of authority would be required.

The Constitution contains three explicit references to Indians, in the two apportionment clauses and in the commerce clause. Article 1, section 2, clause 3 and section 2 of the Fourteenth Amendment exclude "Indians not taxed" for purposes of calculating the representation apportioned to each state in the House of Representatives. While some erroneously believe that these clauses create a general tax exemption, that was not their intent. Rather, the reference to "Indians not taxed" was a shorthand way of describing Indians who continued their tribal relations. Indians are subject to some federal taxation today; thus, these clauses have not had any legal or practical effect for some time (*see* Sec. A.4.a, this chapter). The more significant reference to Indians is contained in the Indian commerce clause. U.S. Const., Art. I, § 8, cl. 3. This clause provides, "The Congress shall have Power . . . To regulate Commerce . . . with the Indian Tribes." As Professor Clinton's article points out, the roots of the Indian commerce clause derive from the perceived inadequacies of national power set forth in the Indian affairs clause of Article IX of the Articles of Confederation, which granted Congress "the sole and exclusive right and power of . . . regulating the trade and managing all affairs with the Indians, not members of any of the States, provided that the legislative right of any State within its own limits be not infringed or violated." Article IX and its two provisos attempted to strike a balance between federal and state power by giving the federal government power over relations with tribes, with states retaining control over assimilated Indians living within their borders. The article's language and purpose created chronic questions over which Indians could be considered "members" of the states and thus subject to the legitimate scope of the legislative rights of the states. The 1787 report of a special committee of the Continental Congress concluded that the drafters of Article IX had intended that the Continental Congress exercise exclusive power in dealing with tribal Indians. Nevertheless, state claims to sole power to regulate "their" Indians caused an Indian war on the very eve of the Constitutional Convention. *See* 33 J. CONT. CONG. 458–59; *see also* Robert N. Clinton, *Book Review*, 47 U. CHI. L. REV. 846, 856 n.50 (1980).

In commenting on the Indian commerce clause in number 42 of the *Federalist Papers*, James Madison criticized article IX as "obscure and contradictory." He added:

> [W]hat description of Indians are to be deemed members of a state is not yet settled, and has been a question of frequent perplexity and contention in the federal councils. And how the trade with Indians, though not members of a State, yet residing within its legislative jurisdiction can be regulated by an external authority, without so far intruding on the internal rights of legislation, is absolutely incomprehensible.

Id. Do the text and history of Article IX shed any light on the role, if any, the framers envisioned for Indian tribes to play in the American constitutional system? What scope should be given the term "commerce" in the clause? Should it be construed to include, as did the Indian affairs clause of the Articles, "regulating the trade and managing all affairs with the Indians" or should it be limited to regulation of the economic intercourse with the Indian tribes? Assuming that the broad sweep of the Indian affairs clause of the Articles of Confederation supplies a meaning for the term "commerce . . . with the Indian tribes," does the grant of power to regulate trade and manage affairs *with* the Indians include the power to regulate the affairs *of* the Indian tribes? How did Justice Marshall answer this question in *Worcester v. Georgia*, 31 U.S. (6 Pet.) 515 (1832), set forth and discussed in Ch. 1, Sec. C.2?

The historical account of tribal-federal relations in Ch. 1, Sec. B.2.c, explains how the conclusion of the War of 1812 led the United States to reach further in controlling tribal lands and peoples. From the earliest time of North American colonization by British, French, Dutch, and Spanish governments, the tribes had achieved political leverage by playing one off against the other. The combination of the Louisiana Purchase in 1803, which eliminated the French as a potential ally for Indian tribes, and the War of 1812, which permanently ended the possibility of British intrusion into United States interests, ended the geopolitical conditions that had governed Indian relations since contact. With the departure of the British as a danger to the fledgling American nation, Indian nations could no longer realistically threaten a foreign alliance. Thereafter, Indian tribes would continue, often alone, to resist, forcibly or otherwise, American colonial expansion and forced relocation, resulting in some armed confrontations, such as Geronimo's resistance with the Chiricahua Apaches and the Battle of Greasy Grass (Little Big Horn) in which the Lakota decimated General George Armstrong Custer and his Seventh Cavalry.

This change in the geopolitical reality in North America, occasioned by the British defeat in the War of 1812, subtly altered the negotiating posture of the federal government. While Indian consent was still sought and required, increasingly the federal government thought it could dictate terms in treaty negotiations, rather than bargain with the tribes as equals as it had done in the Fort Pitt Treaty. Thus in the Indian Removal Act of 1830, the federal government established the removal policy but expressly provided that it could not be implemented without tribal consent. Consequently, Indian treaties remained the major device for adjusting the tribal-federal relationship until 1871, when Congress statutorily forbade the making of future treaties. *See* 25 U.S.C. § 71. *See generally* NELL JESSUP NEWTON ET AL., COHEN'S HANDBOOK OF FEDERAL INDIAN LAW § 1.03 (2012 ed.) (providing examples of treaty provisions). By the late nineteenth century the perceived necessity of tribal consent had waned, and it totally disappeared in the early twentieth century. Should these changing geopolitical realities on the North American continent alter the scope of federal authority granted to the United States government in a constitution ratified in 1789? The late nineteenth and early twentieth century cases you read in Ch. 1, Sec. D.2 display the Supreme Court's initial struggles with this question, struggles that suggest the difficulty of justifying its results under a traditional legal analysis. As you review the more contemporary materials below, ask whether the Court still considers the justification of federal power over internal tribal affairs a troubling matter. If not, are there any intervening legal developments, such as the expansion of federal power over interstate commerce since the 1930s, which may support the Court's current position? Given what you have read about the origins of the Indian commerce clause, do you think it should be interpreted in lockstep with the interstate commerce clause?

UNITED STATES v. JOHN
United States Supreme Court
437 U.S. 634 (1978)

MR. JUSTICE BLACKMUN delivered the opinion of the Court.

I

In October 1975, in the Southern District of Mississippi, Smith John was indicted by a federal grand jury for assault with intent to kill Artis Jenkins, in violation of 18 U.S.C. §§ 1153 and 113(a). He was tried before a jury and, on December 15, was convicted of the lesser included offense of simple assault. On appeal, the United States Court of Appeals for the Fifth Circuit, considering the issue on its own motion, ruled that the District Court was without jurisdiction over the case because the lands designated as a reservation for the Choctaw Indians residing in Mississippi, and on which the offense took place, were not "Indian country," and that, therefore, § 1153 did not provide a basis for federal prosecution. The United States sought review, and we granted its petition for certiorari.

II

There is no dispute that Smith John is a Choctaw Indian, and it is presumed by all that he is a descendant of the Choctaws who for hundreds of years made their homes in what is now central Mississippi. . . .

At the time of the Revolutionary War, these Indians occupied large areas of what is now the State of Mississippi. In the years just after the formation of our country, they entered into a treaty of friendship with the United States. Treaty at Hopewell, 7 Stat. 21 (1786). But the United States became anxious to secure the lands the Indians occupied in order to allow for westward expansion. The Choctaws, in an attempt to avoid what proved to be their fate, entered into a series of treaties gradually relinquishing their claims to these lands.

Despite these concessions, when Mississippi became a State on December 10, 1817, the Choctaws still retained claims, recognized by the federal government, to more than three-quarters of the land within the State's boundaries. The popular pressure to make these lands available to non-Indian settlement, and the responsibility for these Indians felt by some in the Government, combined to shape a federal policy aimed at persuading the Choctaws to give up their lands in Mississippi completely and to remove to new lands in what for many years was known as the Indian Territory, now a part of Oklahoma and Arkansas. The first attempt to effectuate this policy, the Treaty at Doak's Stand, 7 Stat. 210 (1820), resulted in an exchange of more than 5 million acres. Because, however, of complications arising when it was discovered that much of the land promised the Indians already had been settled, most Choctaws remained in Mississippi. A delegation of Choctaws went to Washington, D. C., to untangle the situation and to negotiate yet another treaty. See 7 Stat. 234 (1825). Still, few Choctaws moved.

Only after the election of Andrew Jackson to the Presidency in 1828 did the federal efforts to persuade the Choctaws to leave Mississippi meet with some success. Even before Jackson himself had acted on behalf of the federal government, however, the State of Mississippi, grown impatient with federal policies, had taken steps to assert jurisdiction over the lands occupied by the Choctaws. In early 1829, legislation was enacted purporting to extend legal process into the Choctaw territory. 1824–1838 Miss.Gen.Laws 195 (Act of Feb. 4, 1829). In his first annual address to Congress on December 8, 1829, President Jackson made known his position on the Indian question and his support of immediate removal. S. Doc. No. 1, 21st Cong., 1st Sess., 15–16 (1829). Further encouraged, the Mississippi Legislature passed an Act purporting to abolish the Choctaw government and to impose a fine upon anyone assuming the role of chief. The Act also declared that the rights of white persons living within the State were to be enjoyed by the Indians, and that the laws of the State were to be in effect throughout the territory they occupied. 1824–1838 Miss.Gen.Laws 207 (Act of Jan. 19, 1830).

In Washington, Congress debated whether the States had power to assert such jurisdiction and whether such assertions were wise. But the only message heard by the Choctaws in Mississippi was that the federal government no longer would stand between the States and the Indians. Appreciating these realities, the Choctaws again agreed to deal with the federal government. On September 27, 1830, the Treaty at Dancing Rabbit Creek, 7 Stat. 333, was signed. It provided that the Choctaws would cede to the United States all lands still occupied by them east of the Mississippi, more than 10 million acres. They were to remove to lands west of the river, where they would remain perpetually free of federal or state control, by the fall of 1833. The Government would help plan and pay for this move. Each Choctaw "head of a family being desirous to remain and become a citizen of the States," *id.*, at 335, however, was to be permitted to do so by signifying his intention within six months to the federal agent assigned to the area. Lands were to be reserved, at least 640 acres per household, to be held by the Indians in fee simple if they would remain upon the lands for five years. *Ibid.* Other lands were reserved to the various chiefs and to others already residing on improved lands. *Id.*, at 335–336. Those who remained, however, were not to "lose the privilege of a Choctaw citizen," *id.*, at 335, although they were to receive no share of the annuity provided for those who chose to remove.

The relations between the federal government and the Choctaws remaining in Mississippi did not end with the formal ratification of the Treaty at Dancing Rabbit Creek by the United States Senate in February 1831. 7 Cong. Deb. 347 (1831). The account of the federal attempts to satisfy the obligations of the United States both to those who remained, and to those who removed, is one best left to historians. It is enough to say here that the failure of these attempts, characterized by incompetence, if not corruption, proved an embarrassment and an intractable problem for the federal government for at least a century. It remained federal policy, however, to try to induce these Indians to leave Mississippi.

During the 1890's, the federal government became acutely aware of the fact that not all the Choctaws had left Mississippi. At that time federal policy toward the Indians favored the allotment at tribal holdings, including the Choctaw holdings in the Indian Territory, in order to make way for Oklahoma's statehood. The inclusion of the Choctaws then residing in Mississippi in the distribution of these holdings proved among the largest obstacles encountered during the allotment effort. But even during this era, when federal policy again supported the removal of the Mississippi Choctaws to join their brethren in the West, there was no doubt that there remained persons in Mississippi who were properly regarded both by the Congress and by the Executive Branch as Indians.

It was not until 1916 that this federal recognition of the presence of Indians in Mississippi was manifested by other than attempts to secure their removal. The appropriations for the Bureau of Indian Affairs in that year included an item (for $1,000) to enable the Secretary of the Interior "to investigate the condition of the Indians living in Mississippi" and to report to Congress "as to their need for additional land and school facilities." 39 Stat. 138. See H.R. Doc. No. 1464, 64th Cong., 2d Sess. (1916). In March 1917, hearings were held in Union, Miss., by the House Committee on Investigation of the Indian Service, again exploring the desirability of providing federal services for these Indians. The efforts resulted in an inclusion in the general appropriation for the Bureau of Indian Affairs in 1918. This appropriation, passed only after debate in the House, 56 Cong. Rec. 1136–1140 (1918), included funds for the establishment of an agency with a physician, for the maintenance of schools, and for the purchase of land and farm equipment. Lands purchased through these appropriations were to be sold on contract to individuals in keeping with the general pattern of providing lands eventually to be held in fee by individual Indians, rather than held collectively.

In the 1930's, the federal Indian policy had shifted back toward the preservation of Indian communities generally. This shift led to the enactment of the Indian Reorganization Act of 1934, 48 Stat. 984, and the discontinuance of the allotment program. The Choctaws in Mississippi were among the many groups who, before the legislation was enacted, voted to support its passage. . . .

By this time, it had become obvious that the original method of land purchase authorized by the 1918 appropriations — by contract to a particular Indian purchaser — not only was inconsistent with the new federal policy of encouraging the preservation of Indian communities with commonly held lands, but also was not providing the Mississippi Choctaws with the benefits intended. . . . In 1939, Congress passed an Act providing essentially that title to all the lands previously purchased for the Mississippi Choctaws would be "in the United States in trust for such Choctaw Indians of one-half or more Indian blood, resident in Mississippi, as shall be designated by the Secretary of the Interior." Ch. 235, 53 Stat. 851. In December 1944, the Assistant Secretary of the Department of the Interior officially proclaimed all the lands then purchased in aid of the Choctaws in Mississippi, totaling at that time more than 15,000 acres, to be a reservation. 9 Fed. Reg. 14907.

In April 1945, again as anticipated by the Indian Reorganization Act, the Mississippi Band of Choctaw Indians adopted a constitution and bylaws; these were duly approved by the appropriate federal authorities in May 1945.

With this historical sketch as background, we turn to the jurisdictional issues presented by Smith John's case.

III

. . . .

The Mississippi lands in question here were declared by Congress to be held in trust by the federal government for the benefit of the Mississippi Choctaw Indians who were at that time under federal supervision. There is no apparent reason why these lands, which had been purchased in previous years for the aid of those Indians, did not become a "reservation," at least for the purposes of federal criminal jurisdiction at that particular time. But if there were any doubt about the matter in 1939 when, as hereinabove described, Congress declared that title to lands previously purchased for the Mississippi Choctaws would be held in trust, the situation was completely clarified by the proclamation in 1944 of a reservation and the subsequent approval of the constitution and bylaws adopted by the Mississippi Band.

The Court of Appeals and the Mississippi Supreme Court held, and the State now argues, that the 1944 proclamation had no effect because the Indian Reorganization Act of 1934 was not intended to apply to the Mississippi Choctaws. Assuming for the moment that authority for the proclamation can be found only in the 1934 Act, we find this argument unpersuasive. The 1934 Act defined "Indians" not only as "all persons of Indian descent who are members of any recognized [in 1934] tribe now under Federal jurisdiction," and their descendants who then were residing on any Indian reservation, but also as "all other persons of one-half or more Indian blood." There is no doubt that persons of this description lived in Mississippi, and were recognized as such by Congress and by the Department of the Interior, at the time the Act was passed. The references to the Mississippi Choctaws in the legislative history of the Act, confirm our view that the Mississippi Choctaws were not to be excepted from the general operation of the 1934 Act.

IV

Mississippi appears to concede, that if § 1153 provides a basis for the prosecution of Smith John for the offense charged, the State has no similar jurisdiction. This concession, based on the assumption that § 1153 ordinarily is pre-emptive of state jurisdiction when it applies, seems to us to be correct.

The State argues, however, that the federal government has no power to produce this result. It suggests that since 1830 the Choctaws residing in Mississippi have become fully assimilated into the political and social life of the State, and that the federal government long ago abandoned its supervisory authority over these Indians. Because of this abandonment, and the long lapse in the federal recognition of a tribal organization in Mississippi, the power given Congress "[t]o regulate Commerce . . . with the Indian Tribes," Const. Art. I, § 8, cl. 3, cannot provide a basis for federal jurisdiction. To recognize the Choctaws in Mississippi as Indians over whom special federal power may be exercised would be anomalous and arbitrary.

We assume for purposes of argument, as does the United States, that there have been times when Mississippi's jurisdiction over the Choctaws and their lands went unchallenged. But, particularly in view of the elaborate history, recounted above, of relations between the Mississippi Choctaws and the United States, we do not agree that Congress and the Executive Branch have less power to deal with the affairs of the Mississippi Choctaws than with the affairs of other Indian groups. Neither the fact that the Choctaws in Mississippi are merely a remnant of a larger group of Indians, long ago removed from Mississippi, nor the fact that federal supervision over them has not been continuous, destroys the federal power to deal with them. *United States v. Wright*, 53 F.2d 300 [4th Cir. 1931].

The State also argues that the federal government may not deal specially with the Indians within the State's boundaries because to do so would be inconsistent with the Treaty at Dancing Rabbit Creek. This argument may seem to be a cruel joke to those familiar with the history of the execution of that treaty, and of the treaties that renegotiated claims arising from it. And even if that treaty were the only source regarding the status of these Indians in federal law, we see nothing in it inconsistent with the continued federal supervision of them under the Commerce Clause. It is true that this treaty anticipated that each of those electing to remain in Mississippi would become "a citizen of the States," but the extension of citizenship status to Indians does not, in itself, end the powers given Congress to deal with them.

V

We therefore hold that § 1153 provides a proper basis for federal prosecution of the offense involved here, and that Mississippi has no power similarly to prosecute Smith John for that same offense. Reversed.

NOTES

1. **Congressional Power to Recognize Tribes:** The *John* case sustains the power of Congress to acknowledge new tribes within states, notwithstanding treaty or other limitations to the contrary. Congress, therefore, obviously has the power to recognize tribes and, occasionally, has directly done so, *e.g.*, 25 U.S.C. § 711a (Siletz Indians); 25 U.S.C. § 1751 et seq. (Mashantucket Pequot), although most of the

recognition work is undertaken through the BIA's Office of Federal Acknowledgment, formerly the Branch of Acknowledgment and Research, pursuant to 25 C.F.R. Pt. 83. *See* Ch. 2, Sec. A.1.c. Are there any limitations on what group could be dealt with as an Indian tribe within the meaning of the Constitution? In *Baker v. Carr*, 369 U.S. 186, 215–17 (1962), the Supreme Court noted that the Court had long deferred to the political departments in determining whether Indians are recognized as a tribe because this issue "reflects familiar attributes of political questions." Nevertheless, citing *United States v. Sandoval*, presented and discussed in Ch. 1, Sec. D.2, the Court added: "Able to discern what is 'distinctly Indian,' the courts will strike down any heedless extension of that label. They will not stand impotent before an obvious instance of a manifestly unauthorized exercise of power."

In the last decade of the nineteenth century, the United States government supported the overthrow of the Hawaiian monarchy, the forced cession of Native Hawaiian lands, and the annexation of the islands. No treaties or reservations were ever provided for the Native Hawaiians as a political entity, though over the following decades Congress passed a variety of laws allocating lands and certain benefits for Native Hawaiian people. In the 2002 Native Hawaiian Education Act, 20 U.S.C. § 7511 et seq., Congress acknowledged that the United States "has established a trust relationship" with Native Hawaiians, and declared: "[T]he political status of Native Hawaiians is comparable to that of American Indians and Alaska Natives." 20 U.S.C. § 7512(12)(B), (D). The Act authorized special educational programs for Native Hawaiians, and created a Native Hawaiian Education Council to enable Native Hawaiians to participate in planning and managing those programs. More recently, bills have been introduced in Congress to recognize Native Hawaiians as an Indian tribe and facilitate their political organization. *See, e.g.*, S. 1011, Native Hawaiian Government Reorganization Act, 111th Cong. (2009). Does the movement to recognize Native Hawaiians as an Indian tribe or provide services to them pose any major constitutional problems? Can such legislation be grounded on the Indian commerce clause? Is the term "Indian tribes" as employed in Article I synonymous with all indigenous peoples? If not, what basis, if any, is there for recognizing Native Alaskans or Pueblo Indians as subject to the federal Indian affairs power when neither of these communities lived within the geographic confines of the United States when the Indian commerce clause was drafted? Does the Native Hawaiian problem really pose a distinctly different situation? How? For further discussion of the federal Indian law treatment of Native Hawaiians, see Ch. 5, Sec. B.2.

2. Indian Commerce Clause as a Source for Federal Power over Indian Affairs: Please review *United States v. Lara* in Ch. 3, Sec. C.2. Justice Breyer states in *Lara* that the Court has "traditionally" identified the sources of federal power over Indian affairs as the Indian commerce clause and the treaty clause. Is that statement an accurate depiction of the development of the doctrine of plenary power? Looking back at the late nineteenth and early twentieth century cases delineating federal power over Indian affairs, *United States v. Kagama*, *United States v. Sandoval*, and *Lone Wolf v. Hitchcock*, all presented in Ch. 1, Sec. D.2, are they grounded on the Indian commerce clause or some general notion of trusteeship? For a historically-based rejection of the idea that the Indian commerce clause (or any other constitutional source) can support the notion of any broad federal power in Indian affairs, see Robert N. Clinton, *There Is No Federal Supremacy Clause for Indian Tribes*, 34 ARIZ. ST. L.J. 113 (2002); FRANK POMMERSHEIM, BROKEN LANDSCAPE: INDIANS, INDIAN TRIBES, AND THE CONSTITUTION (2009). For general debate over the legitimacy of the plenary power doctrine, see Robert A. Williams, Jr., *The Algebra of Federal Indian Law: The Hard Trail of Decolonizing and Americanizing the White Man's Indian Jurisprudence*, 1986 WIS. L. REV. 219; Robert Laurence, *Learning to Live with the Plenary Power of Congress over the Indian Nations: An Essay in Reaction to Professor Williams' Algebra*, 30 ARIZ. L. REV. 413 (1988); Robert A. Williams, Jr., *Learning Not to Live with Eurocentric Myopia: A Reply to Professor Laurence's Learning to Live with the Plenary Power of Congress over the Indian Nations*, 30 ARIZ. L. REV. 439 (1988). If the Court now rejects the trusteeship as a source of congressional power in Indian affairs, and the Indian commerce clause cannot sustain any broad authority in Indian affairs, should not the federal judiciary rethink the plenary power doctrine in the field of Indian affairs?

While overtly abandoning the trusteeship roots of the federal plenary power doctrine, the modern Supreme Court to date has shown no signs of reevaluating the scope of federal Indian affairs powers. *United States v. Lara* shows how broad a path the Court has cleared for Congress, encompassing the power to "terminate . . . the existence of individual tribes" as well as to remove obstacles to the exercise of their inherent powers. Earlier, in *Santa Clara Pueblo v. Martinez*, 436 U.S. 49, 57 (1978), presented in Ch. 3, Sec. D.1, the Court, in upholding congressional power to enact the Indian Civil Rights Act of 1968 wrote:

> Congress has plenary authority to limit, modify or eliminate the powers of local self-government which the tribes otherwise possess. *Ibid. See, e.g., United States v. Kagama, supra,* 118 U.S., at 379–381, 383–384; *Cherokee Nation v. Hitchcock,* 187 U.S. 294, 305–307 (1902). Title I of the ICRA, 25 U.S.C. §§ 1301–1303, represents an exercise of that authority. In 25 U.S.C. § 1302, Congress acted to modify the effect of *Talton* and its progeny by imposing certain restrictions upon tribal governments similar, but not identical, to those contained in the Bill of Rights and the Fourteenth Amendment.

In the arena of federal-state relations, the United States Supreme Court recently has been quite active in limiting the scope of the power of Congress in order to protect state sovereignty on the ostensible ground that the states and their people never consented to or delegated broad, plenary commerce powers to the federal government. *E.g., United States v. Morrison,* 529 U.S. 598 (2000); *Alden v. Maine,* 527 U.S. 706 (1999); *Printz v. United States,* 521 U.S. 898 (1997); *United States v. Lopez,* 514 U.S. 549 (1995). At core, these cases are quite inconsistent with the idea that Congress has broad authority to curtail or eliminate the sovereign power of states as *Lara* and *Martinez* suggest it can do for tribes. Why should such differences exist? Given the nature of the treaty relationship, would not an even-handed application to Indian tribes of the same legal principles the Court applies to states suggest a total lack of federal authority over the tribes and their members without their consent reflected in a treaty or treaty-substitute? Why has the Supreme Court not applied the same principles even-handedly between protecting state sovereignty through the New Federalism cases and protecting tribal sovereignty from the excesses of the exercise of congressional power? Professor Judith Resnik has asserted that "For better and worse, but time and again, jurists doing Federal Indian Law keep trying to assimilate the interaction between federal power and tribes to American constitutional precepts that, somewhere and somehow, boundaries exist on the powers claimed by government." Judith Resnik, *Tribes, Wars, and the Federal Courts: Applying the Myths and the Methods of* Marbury v. Madison *to Tribal Courts' Criminal Jurisdiction*, 36 ARIZ. ST. L. J. 77, 89 (2004). Does *Lara* suggest a Court much concerned with defining such boundaries? What of the Court's efforts to explain how the particular exercise of congressional power in the *Duro*-fix was not unusual and was limited in nature? Do those efforts suggest any real restraints on a Congress prepared to curtail or eliminate tribal governmental powers? Given the contemporary realities of tribal economic development and political participation, should Indian nations be more concerned about threats to their sovereignty from congressional power or from an activist Supreme Court?

In a sweeping challenge to conventional thinking in the field of Indian law, Professor Robert Odawi Porter has asserted that practitioners, scholars, and tribal officials should stop assuming the applicability of American law to Indian nations. *See* Robert Odawi Porter, *The Inapplicability of American Law to the Indian Nations*, 89 IOWA L. REV. 1595 (2004). Porter's central point is that unless tribes have consented to American law through treaty or otherwise, nothing but "colonial fiat" sustains federal power. While acknowledging that the doctrine of federal "plenary power" holds up from an American perspective, he points out that it has no standing from the viewpoint of tribal law. He therefore urges tribal courts and practitioners to respond to conflicts between federal law and tribal law by analyzing the issues from both perspectives, in effect offering alternate rulings. Is Porter giving up too much in conceding the legitimacy of federal plenary power from the vantage of U.S. law? Is his proposed response to conflicts between tribal and federal law one that can be implemented as a practical matter?

DELAWARE TRIBAL BUSINESS COMMITTEE v. WEEKS
United States Supreme Court
430 U.S. 73 (1977)

MR. JUSTICE BRENNAN delivered the opinion of the Court.

[The Delaware Indians had become geographically and politically divided into four present-day groups, called the Cherokee, Absentee, Munsee, and Kansas Delawares. The Cherokee and Absentee Delawares were both federally recognized Indian tribes. The Kansas Delawares had elected to take individual parcels of land in Kansas in 1866; their descendants are not members of a federally recognized tribe. At issue was the distribution of an Indian Claims Commission judgment awarded to the modern day descendants of members of the historic Delaware Nation. The congressional distribution scheme awarded 90% of the judgment to be distributed per capita solely to the Cherokee and Absentee Delawares, with the rest to go into the tribal treasuries of the two tribes. As a result, the Kansas Delawares received nothing. Weeks brought an action on behalf of all the Kansas Delawares alleging that the exclusion of the Kansas Delawares denied them equal protection of the laws.]

II

Appellants differ on the issue of whether this suit presents a nonjusticiable political question because of Congress's pervasive authority, rooted in the Constitution, to control tribal property. Stated in other words, they differ on the issue of whether congressional exercise of control over tribal property is final and not subject to judicial scrutiny, since the power over distribution of tribal property has "been committed by the Constitution" to the Congress, *Baker v. Carr*, 369 U.S. 186, 211 (1962), and since "[the] nonjusticiability of a political question is primarily a function of the separation of powers." Appellants Cherokee and Absentee Delawares, citing [*Lone Wolf v. Hitchcock*], argue that Congress's distribution plan reflects a congressional determination not subject to scrutiny by the Judicial Branch, and that the District Court therefore erred in reaching the merits of this action. Appellant Secretary of the Interior, on the other hand, submits that the plenary power of Congress in matters of Indian affairs "does not mean that all federal legislation concerning Indians is . . . immune from judicial scrutiny or that claims, such as those presented by [appellees], are not justiciable." [Brief for Appellants.] We agree with the Secretary of the Interior.

The statement in *Lone Wolf* that the power of Congress "has always been deemed a political one, not subject to be controlled by the judicial department of the government," however pertinent to the question then before the Court of congressional power to abrogate treaties, has not deterred this Court, particularly in this day, from scrutinizing Indian legislation to determine whether it violates the equal protection component of the fifth amendment. *See, e.g.,* [*Morton v. Mancari*]. "The power of Congress over Indian affairs may be of a plenary nature; but it is not absolute." *United States v. Alcea Band of Tillamooks*, 329 U.S. 40 (1946) (plurality opinion).

The question is therefore what judicial review of Pub. L. 92-456 is appropriate in light of the broad congressional power to prescribe the distribution of property of the Indian tribes. The general rule emerging from our decisions ordinarily requires the judiciary to defer to congressional determination of what is the best or most efficient use for which tribal funds should be employed. *Sizemore v. Brady*, 235 U.S. 441, 449 (1914). Thus, Congress may choose to differentiate among groups of Indians in the same tribe in making a distribution, *Simmons v. Seelatsee*, 384 U.S. 209 (1966), or on the other hand to expand a class of tribal beneficiaries entitled to share in royalties from tribal lands, *United States v. Jim*, [409 U.S. 80 (1972)], or to devote to tribal use mineral rights under allotments that otherwise would have gone to individual allottees, Northern *Cheyenne Tribe v. Hollowbreast*, 425 U.S. 649 (1976). The standard of review most recently expressed is that the legislative judgment should not be disturbed "as long as the special treatment can be tied rationally to the fulfillment of Congress's unique obligation toward the Indians. . . . " [*Morton v. Mancari*, set forth and discussed in Ch. 2, Sec. B.1.]

IV

We are persuaded on the record before us that Congress's omission of [Kansas Delawares] was "tied rationally to the fulfillment of Congress's unique obligation toward the Indians."

First, the Kansas Delawares are not a recognized tribal entity, but are simply individual Indians with no vested rights in any tribal property. Public Law 92-456 distributes tribal rather than individually owned property, for the funds were appropriated to pay an award redressing the breach of a treaty with a tribal entity, the Delaware Nation. [The tribal entity brought the claim before the Indian Claims Commission, and the judgment was designed to compensate the tribe.] As tribal property, the appropriated funds were subject to the exercise by Congress of its traditional broad authority over the management and distribution of lands and property held by recognized tribes, an authority "drawn both explicitly and implicitly from the Constitution itself." *Morton v. Mancari, supra,* at 551–52.

[The Kansas Delawares' ancestors] severed their relations with the tribe when they elected under [a] treaty to become United States citizens entitled to participate in tribal assets only to the extent of their "just proportion . . . of the cash value of the credits of said tribe . . . *then held in trust by the United States.*" (Emphasis supplied.) We cannot say that the decision of Congress to exclude [them] and to distribute the appropriated funds only to members of or persons closely affiliated with the Cherokee and Absentee Delaware Tribes, was not "tied rationally to the fulfillment of Congress's unique obligation toward the Indians."

[The] conclusion that the exclusion of the Kansas Delawares from distribution under Pub. L. 92-456 does not offend the Due Process Clause of the fifth amendment of course does not preclude Congress from revising the distribution scheme to include the Kansas Delawares. The distribution authorized by Pub. L. 92-456 has not yet occurred, and Congress has the power to revise its original allocation. *United States v. Jim,* 409 U.S., at 82–83.

Reversed.

NOTES ON THE BILL OF RIGHTS AND PLENARY POWER

1. **Plenary Power and the Political Question Doctrine:** As you saw in Ch. 1, Sec. D.2, plenary power over Indian affairs arose in the late nineteenth and early twentieth century in cases like *Lone Wolf* and *Sandoval* in part because of a refusal by the Supreme Court to permit the federal judiciary to question the legality of congressional actions under the guise of the political question doctrine. *Weeks* represents the culmination of a lengthy, slow legal development in which the Court appeared to repudiate the notion that the political question doctrine barred consideration of the merits of a tribal claim attacking the constitutionality of an exercise of congressional power. That development probably began when the Supreme Court in *Choate v. Trapp,* 224 U.S. 665 (1912), refused to find an implied repeal of federal tax immunity statutes involving Choctaw and Chickasaw allotments because to abrogate the tax immunity granted to individual Indians would potentially constitute a taking. As the Court put it, "there was no intimation that the

power of wardship conferred authority on Congress to lessen any of the rights of property which had been vested in the individual Indian by prior laws or contracts. Such rights are protected from repeal by the provisions of the 5th Amendment." Nevertheless, as recently as 1980 in the appeal of the Sioux Nation's claim for damages for the taking of the Black Hills, the federal government argued that under *Lone Wolf* Congress had broad power to take tribal property which could only be minimally reviewed by the courts. Brief for the United States at 57–59 & n.49, *United States v. Sioux Nation*, 448 U.S. 371 (1980). In rejecting that argument the Court distinguished *Lone Wolf* by saying: "[T]he [*Lone Wolf*] Court's conclusive presumption of congressional good faith was based in large measure on the idea that relations between this Nation and the Indian tribes are a political matter, not amenable to judicial review. That view, of course, has long since been discredited in taking cases, and was expressly laid to rest in [*Weeks*]." *Morton v. Mancari*, *United States v. Antelope*, and *Rice v. Cayetano*, set forth and discussed in Ch. 2, Sec. B, also suggest that the federal courts are prepared to review Fifth, Fourteenth, and Fifteenth Amendment claims of racial discrimination in federal and state Indian affairs statutes.

Notice that *Choate v. Trapp*, *Sioux Nation*, *Weeks*, *Morton*, *Antelope*, and many cases like them, involve the application of external constraints on federal power imposed by Bill of Rights limitations, often the Fifth Amendment due process or takings clauses, rather than reconsidering the inherent scope of the grant of power itself.

2.   **Plenary Power and the Bill of Rights:** The preceding discussion indicates that the modern change in the method of analyzing the scope of federal power over Indian affairs involves a judicial willingness to enforce federal external constraints, many of them derived from the Bill of Rights, on the exercise of the so-called plenary power doctrine in Indian affairs. Since that change occurred, the Supreme Court on at least three occasions has declared unconstitutional an act of Congress affecting Indian country. *Babbitt v. Youpee*, 519 U.S. 234 (1997); *Hodel v. Irving*, 481 U.S. 704 (1987) (holding that the General Allotment Act of 1887 created a vested right to devise or bequeath Indian allotments, therefore invalidating a congressional effort to repair the problem of fractionated allotments); *Seminole Tribe of Florida v. Florida*, 517 U.S. 44 (1996) (provisions of the Indian Gaming Regulatory Act, designed to protect tribes from state overreaching in compact negotiations, violate the Eleventh Amendment); *see also Muskrat v. United States*, 219 U.S. 346 (1911) (federal statutory authorization for certain suits contesting Cherokee allotment system are unconstitutional for violating the case or controversy limitations of Article III in their grant of jurisdiction for federal courts). *Babbitt* and *Hodel* are discussed in Ch. 6, Sec. A.6; *Seminole Tribe* is discussed in Ch. 5, Sec. D.1.

In addition to the Fifth Amendment due process and taking clauses, another constitutional right frequently invoked to limit federal (and state) actions affecting Indians is the First Amendment, particularly the free exercise of religion clause. After some initial successes in lower federal and state courts, *e.g., People v. Woody*, 394 P.2d 813, 817–818 (Cal. 1964), Indian tribes and their members recently have been notably unsuccessful invoking the First and Fourteenth Amendments to protect their ceremonial and religious practices in cases heard in the United States Supreme Court. *See* Ch. 6, Sec. B.1. Professor Goldberg has noted the double standard evident in Supreme Court decisions that have upheld Congress's power to destroy tribal rights, but have invalidated, on individual rights grounds, Congress's later attempts to repair those same harms. *See* Carole Goldberg, *Individual Rights and Tribal Revitalization*, 35 Ariz. St. L.J. 889 (2003) (comparing decisions upholding allotment with decisions invalidating Congress's efforts to restore tribal land bases).

3. ***Weeks* and Judicial Deference:** Unlike *Lone Wolf v. Hitchcock*, in *Weeks*, the Court reached the merits of the Fifth Amendment equal protection attack made by the plaintiffs against the federal statute. Was its analysis of the merits of the equal protection claim any less deferential to federal congressional power in Indian affairs than the Court's decision in *Lone Wolf*, which refused to reach the merits of a different Fifth Amendment claim? The Court noted that the ancestors of the Kansas Delawares had severed their relations with the Tribe when, under an 1866 treaty, they elected to become United States citizens entitled only to participate in tribal assets by taking allotments constituting their pro-rata proportion of assets then held in trust by the United States. The Supreme Court therefore found the statute's exclusion of the Kansas Delawares from participation in the claims award to be "tied rationally to the fulfillment of Congress's unique obligation toward the Indians" and dismissed their due process challenge. Justice Stevens' dissent pointed out that the legislative record indicated Congress's omission of the Kansas Delawares from those entitled to participate in the claims distribution was nothing more than a legislative oversight. He thus would have invalidated the law as violating "the due process of lawmaking." *Weeks*, 430 U.S. at 97–98 (Stevens, J., dissenting).

2. Non-Constitutional Limitations on Legislative Plenary Power: Canons of Construction, Treaty Abrogation, and Political Accountability

UNITED STATES v. DION
United States Supreme Court
476 U.S. 734 (1986)

Justice Marshall delivered the opinion of the Court.

Respondent Dwight Dion, Sr., a member of the Yankton Sioux Tribe, was convicted of shooting four bald eagles on the Yankton Sioux reservation in South Dakota in violation of the Endangered Species Act, 87 Stat. 884, as amended, 16 U.S.C. § 1531 et seq. (1982 ed. and Supp. II). The District Court dismissed before trial a charge of shooting a golden eagle in violation of the Bald Eagle Protection Act, 54 Stat. 250, 16 U.S.C. § 668 et seq. (Eagle Protection Act). Dion was also convicted of selling carcasses and parts of eagles and other birds in violation of the Eagle Protection Act and the Migratory Bird Treaty Act, 40 Stat. 755, as amended, 16 U.S.C. § 703 et seq. The Court of Appeals for the Eighth Circuit affirmed all of Dion's convictions except those for shooting bald eagles in violation of the Endangered Species Act. As to those, it stated that Dion could be convicted only upon a jury determination that the birds were killed for commercial purposes. It also affirmed the District Court's dismissal of the charge of shooting a golden eagle in violation of the Eagle Protection Act. We granted certiorari, and we now reverse the judgment of the Court of Appeals insofar as it reversed Dion's convictions under the Endangered Species Act and affirmed the dismissal of the charge against him under the Eagle Protection Act.

I

The Eagle Protection Act by its terms prohibits the hunting of the bald or golden eagle anywhere within the United States, except pursuant to a permit issued by the Secretary of the Interior. The Endangered Species Act imposes an equally stringent ban on the hunting of the bald eagle. The Court of Appeals for the Eighth Circuit, however, sitting en banc, held that members of the Yankton Sioux Tribe have a treaty right to hunt bald and golden eagles within the Yankton reservation for noncommercial purposes. It further held that the Eagle Protection Act and Endangered Species Act did not abrogate this treaty right. It therefore directed that Dion's convictions for shooting bald eagles be vacated, since neither the District Court nor the jury made any explicit finding whether the killings were for commercial or noncommercial purposes[1]. [In the Treaty with the Yancton Sioux, Apr. 19, 1858, 11 Stat. 743,] the Yankton ceded to the United States all but 400,000 acres of the land then held by the tribe. The treaty bound the Yanktons to remove to, and settle on, their reserve land within one year. The United States in turn agreed to guarantee the Yanktons quiet and undisturbed possession of their reserved land, and to pay to the Yanktons, or expend for their benefit, various moneys in the years to come. The area thus reserved for the tribe was a legally constituted Indian reservation. The treaty did not place any restriction on the Yanktons' hunting rights on their reserved land.

All parties to this litigation agree that the treaty rights reserved by the Yankton included the exclusive right to hunt and fish on their land. As a general rule, Indians enjoy exclusive treaty rights to hunt and fish on lands reserved to them, unless the rights were clearly relinquished by treaty or have been modified by Congress. F. Cohen, Handbook of Federal Indian Law 449 (1982 ed.) (hereinafter Cohen). These rights need not be expressly mentioned in the treaty. *See Menominee Tribe v.*

---

[1] [3] On remand from the *en banc* court, an Eighth Circuit panel rejected a religious freedom claim raised by Dion. Dion does not pursue that claim here, and accordingly we do not consider it. A statement made by the panel in rejecting that claim, though, casts some doubt on whether the issue of whether Dion had a treaty right to kill eagles for noncommercial purposes is squarely before us. The panel stated: "The record reveals that Dion, Sr. was killing eagles and other protected birds for commercial gain. . . . " 762 F.2d 674, 680 (1980). Notwithstanding its statement that Dion's killings were for commercial gain, apparently inconsistent with the *en banc* court's refusal to pass on that issue, it issued a judgment vacating Dion's convictions for shooting bald eagles "pursuant to the opinion of this Court *en banc.*" *Id.*, at 694.

We find that this case properly presents the issue whether killing eagles for noncommercial purposes is outside the scope of the Eagle Protection Act and the Endangered Species Act. The Eighth Circuit panel did not disturb the *en banc* court's holding that Dion cannot be convicted absent a jury determination of whether the killings were for a commercial purpose, and vacated his convictions for shooting bald eagles because the jury made no such finding. The Solicitor General argues that Dion's convictions should have been affirmed whether the killings were for commercial or noncommercial purposes. The correctness of the holding below that killing for noncommercial purposes is not punishable, therefore, is squarely before us.

United States, 391 U.S. 404 (1968). Those treaty rights, however, little avail Dion if, as the Solicitor General argues, they were subsequently abrogated by Congress. We find that they were.

II

It is long settled that "the provisions of an act of Congress, passed in the exercise of its constitutional authority, . . . if clear and explicit, must be upheld by courts, even in contravention of express stipulations in an earlier treaty" with a foreign power. *Fong Yue Ting v. United States*, 149 U.S. 698, 720 (1893). This Court applied that rule to congressional abrogation of Indian treaties in [*Lone Wolf v. Hitchcock*]. Congress, the Court concluded, has the power "to abrogate the provisions of an Indian treaty, though presumably such power will be exercised only when circumstances arise which will not only justify the government in disregarding the stipulation of the treaty, but may demand, in the interest of the country and the Indians themselves, that it should do so."

We have required that Congress's intention to abrogate Indian treaty rights be clear and plain. "Absent explicit statutory language, we have been extremely reluctant to find congressional abrogation of treaty rights. . . . " *Washington v. Fishing Vessel Ass'n*, 443 U.S. 658, 690 (1979). We do not construe statutes as abrogating treaty rights in "a backhanded way," *Menominee Tribe v. United States*, 391 U.S. 404, 412 (1968); in the absence of explicit statement, " 'the intention to abrogate or modify a treaty is not to be lightly imputed to the Congress.' " *Id.*, at 413. Indian treaty rights are too fundamental to be easily cast aside.

We have enunciated, however, different standards over the years for determining how such a clear and plain intent must be demonstrated. In some cases, we have required that Congress make "express declaration" of its intent to abrogate treaty rights. See *Leavenworth, Lawrence & Galveston R. Co. v. United States*, 92 U.S. 733, 741–742 (1876); see also Wilkinson & Volkman [63 CAL. L. REV. at] 627–630, 645–659. In other cases, we have looked to the statute's " 'legislative history' " and " 'surrounding circumstances' " as well as to " 'the face of the Act.' " *Rosebud Sioux Tribe v. Kneip*, 430 U.S. 584 587 (1977), quoting *Mattz v. Arnett*, 412 U.S. 481, 505 (1973). Explicit statement by Congress is preferable for the purpose of ensuring legislative accountability for the abrogation of treaty rights. We have not rigidly interpreted that preference, however, as a per se rule; where the evidence of congressional intent to abrogate is sufficiently compelling, "the weight of authority indicates that such an intent can also be found by the reviewing court from clear and reliable evidence in the legislative history of a statute." Cohen [at] 223. What is essential is clear evidence that Congress actually considered the conflict between its intended action on the one hand and Indian treaty rights on the other, and chose to resolve that conflict by abrogating the treaty.

A

The Eagle Protection Act renders it a federal crime to "take, possess, sell, purchase, barter, offer to sell, purchase or barter, transport, export or import, at any time or in any manner any bald eagle commonly known as the American eagle or any golden eagle, alive or dead, or any part, nest, or egg thereof." 16 U.S.C. § 668(a). The prohibition is "sweepingly framed"; the enumeration of forbidden acts is "exhaustive and careful." *Andrus v. Allard*, 444 U.S. 51, 56 (1979). The Act, however, authorizes the Secretary of the Interior to permit the taking, possession, and transportation of eagles "for the religious purposes of Indian Tribes," and for certain other narrow purposes, upon a determination that such taking, possession or transportation is compatible with the preservation of the bald eagle or the golden eagle.

Congressional intent to abrogate Indian treaty rights to hunt bald and golden eagles is certainly strongly suggested on the face of the Eagle Protection Act. The provision allowing taking of eagles under permit for the religious purposes of Indian tribes is difficult to explain except as a reflection of an understanding that the statute otherwise bans the taking of eagles by Indians, a recognition that such a prohibition would cause hardship for the Indians, and a decision that [the] problem should be resolved not by exempting Indians from the coverage of the statute, but by authorizing the Secretary to issue permits to Indians where appropriate.

The legislative history of the statute supports that view. The Eagle Protection Act was originally passed in 1940, and did not contain any explicit reference to Indians. Its prohibitions related only to bald eagles; it cast no shadow on hunting of the more plentiful golden eagle. In 1962, however, Congress considered amendments to the Eagle Protection Act extending its ban to the golden eagle as well. As originally drafted by the staff of the Subcommittee on Fisheries and Wildlife Conservation of the House Committee on Merchant Marine and Fisheries, the amendments simply would have added the words "or any golden eagle" at two places in the Act where prohibitions relating to the bald eagle were described.

Before the start of hearings on the bill, however, the Subcommittee received a letter from Assistant Secretary of the Interior Frank Briggs on behalf of the Interior Department. The Interior Department supported the proposed bill. It noted, however, the following concern [quoting from Assistant Secretary Briggs' letter regarding the golden eagle's importance]:

> "[I]n enabling many Indian tribes, particularly those in the Southwest, to continue ancient customs and ceremonies that are of deep religious or emotional significance to them," [and concluding: "In the circumstances, it is evident that the Indians are deeply interested in the preservation of both the golden and the bald eagle. If enacted, the bill should therefore permit the Secretary of the Interior, by regulation, to allow the use of eagles for religious purposes by Indian tribes."].

The House Committee reported out the bill. In setting out the need for the legislation, it explained in part:

> Certain feathers of the golden eagle are important in religious ceremonies of some Indian tribes and a large number of the birds are killed to obtain these feathers, as well as to provide souvenirs for tourists in the Indian country. In addition, they are actively hunted by bounty hunters in Texas and some other States. As a result of these activities if steps are not taken

as contemplated in this legislation, there is grave danger that the golden eagle will completely disappear. H.R. Rep. No. 1450, 87th Cong., 2d Sess., 2 (1962).

The Committee also reprinted Assistant Secretary Briggs' letter in its Report, and adopted an exception for Indian religious use drafted by the Interior Department. The bill as reported out of the House Committee thus made three major changes in the law, along with other more technical ones. It extended the law's ban to golden eagles. It provided that the Secretary may exempt, by permit, takings of bald or golden eagles "for the religious purposes of Indian tribes." And it added a final proviso: "Provided, That bald eagles may not be taken for any purpose unless, prior to such taking, a permit to do so is procured from the Secretary of the Interior." The bill, as amended, passed the House and was reported to the Senate Committee on Commerce.

At the Senate hearings, representatives of the Interior Department reiterated their position that, because "the golden eagle is an important part of the ceremonies and religion of many Indian tribes," the Secretary should be authorized to allow the use of eagles for religious purposes by Indian tribes. The Senate Committee agreed, and passed the House bill with an additional amendment allowing the Secretary to authorize permits for the taking of golden eagles that were preying on livestock. That Committee again reprinted Assistant Secretary Briggs' letter, S. Rep. No. 1986, 87th Cong., 2d Sess., 5–7 (1962), and summarized the bill as follows: "The resolution as hereby reported would bring the golden eagle under the 1940 act, allow their taking under permit for the religious use of the various Indian tribes (their feathers are an important part of Indian religious rituals) and upon request of a Governor of any State, be taken for the protection of livestock and game." The bill passed the Senate, and was concurred in by the House, with little further discussion.

It seems plain to us, upon reading the legislative history as a whole, that Congress in 1962 believed that it was abrogating the rights of Indians to take eagles. Indeed, the House Report cited the demand for eagle feathers for Indian religious ceremonies as one of the threats to the continued survival of the golden eagle that necessitated passage of the bill. Congress expressly chose to set in place a regime in which the Secretary of the Interior had control over Indian hunting, rather than one in which Indian on-reservation hunting was unrestricted. Congress thus considered the special cultural and religious interests of Indians, balanced those needs against the conservation purposes of the statute, and provided a specific, narrow exception that delineated the extent to which Indians would be permitted to hunt the bald and golden eagle.

Respondent argues that the 1962 Congress did not in fact view the Eagle Protection Act as restricting Indian on-reservation hunting. He points to an internal Interior Department memorandum circulated in 1962 stating with little analysis, that the Eagle Protection Act did not apply within Indian reservations. Memorandum from Assistant Solicitor Vaughn, Branch of Fish and Wildlife, Office of the Solicitor to the Director, Bureau of Sport Fisheries and Wildlife, April 26, 1962. We have no reason to believe that Congress was aware of the contents of the Vaughn memorandum. More importantly, however, we find respondent's contention that the

1962 Congress did not understand the Act to ban all Indian hunting of eagles simply irreconcilable with the statute on its face.

Respondent argues, and the Eighth Circuit agreed, that the provision of the statute granting permit authority is not necessarily inconsistent with an intention that Indians would have unrestricted ability to hunt eagles while on reservations. Respondent construes that provision to allow the Secretary to issue permits to non-Indians to hunt eagles "for Indian religious purposes," and supports this interpretation by pointing out testimony during the hearings to the effect that large-scale eagle bounty hunters sometimes sold eagle feathers to Indian tribes. We do not find respondent's argument credible. Congress could have felt such a provision necessary only if it believed that Indians, if left free to hunt eagles on reservations, would nonetheless be unable to satisfy their own needs and would be forced to call on non-Indians to hunt on their behalf. Yet there is nothing in the legislative history that even remotely supports that patronizing and strained view. Indeed, the Interior Department immediately after the passage of the 1962 amendments adopted regulations authorizing permits only to "individual Indians who are authentic, bona fide practitioners of such religion." 28 Fed. Reg. 976 (1963).[2]

Congress's 1962 action, we conclude, reflected an unmistakable and explicit legislative policy choice that Indian hunting of the bald or golden eagle, except pursuant to permit, is inconsistent with the need to preserve those species. We therefore read the statute as having abrogated that treaty right.

B

Dion also asserts a treaty right to take bald eagles as a defense to his Endangered Species Act prosecution. He argues that evidence that Congress intended to abrogate treaty rights when it passed the Endangered Species Act is considerably more slim than that relating to the Eagle Protection Act. The Endangered Species Act and its legislative history, he points out, are to a great extent silent regarding Indian hunting rights. In this case, however, we need not resolve the question of whether the Congress in the Endangered Species Act abrogated Indian treaty rights. We conclude that Dion's asserted treaty defense is barred in any event.

Dion asserts that he is immune from Endangered Species Act prosecution because he possesses a treaty right to hunt and kill bald eagles. We have held, however, that Congress in passing and amending the Eagle Protection Act divested Dion of his treaty right to hunt bald eagles. He therefore has no treaty right to hunt bald eagles that he can assert as a defense to an Endangered Species Act charge.

We do not hold that when Congress passed and amended the Eagle Protection Act, it stripped away Indian treaty protection for conduct not expressly prohibited

---

[2] [8] Respondent's argument that Congress in amending the Eagle Protection meant to benefit nontreaty tribes is also flawed. Indian reservations created by statute, agreement, or executive order normally carry with them the same implicit hunting rights as those created by treaty. *See* Cohen [at] 224; *Antoine v. Washington*, 420 U.S. 194 (1975).

by that statute. But the Eagle Protection Act and the Endangered Species Act, in relevant part, prohibit exactly the same conduct, and for the same reasons. Dion here asserts a treaty right to engage in precisely the conduct that Congress, overriding Indian treaty rights, made criminal in the Eagle Protection Act. Dion's treaty shield for that conduct, we hold, was removed by that statute, and Congress's failure to discuss that shield in the context of the Endangered Species Act did not revive that Treaty right.

It would not promote sensible law to hold that while Dion possesses no rights derived from the 1858 treaty that bar his prosecution under the Eagle Protection Act for killing bald eagles, he nonetheless possesses a right to hunt bald eagles, derived from that same treaty, that bars his Endangered Species Act prosecution for the same conduct. Even if Congress did not address Indian treaty rights in the Endangered Species Act sufficiently expressly to effect a valid abrogation, therefore, respondent can assert no treaty defense to a prosecution under the Act for a taking already explicitly prohibited under the Eagle Protection Act.

III

We hold that the Court of Appeals erred in recognizing Dion's treaty defense to his Eagle Protection Act and Endangered Species Act prosecutions. For the reasons stated in n. 3, *supra*, we do not pass on the claim raised by *amici* that the Eagle Protection Act, if read to abrogate Indian treaty rights, invades religious freedom. Cf. *United States v. Abeyta*, 632 F. Supp. 1301 (NM 1986). Nor do we address respondent's argument, raised for the first time in this Court, that the Statutes under which he was convicted do not authorize separate convictions for taking and for selling the same birds.

[*Reversed and remanded.*]

NOTES ON TREATY ABROGATION

1. **Tests Used to Determine Whether a Later Statute Abrogates a Treaty:** *Lone Wolf v. Hitchcock*, presented in Ch. 1, Sec. D.2, answered in the affirmative the question whether Congress by subsequent statute had the *constitutional* power to abrogate or modify Indian rights found in a prior Indian treaty. Therefore, like treaties with foreign nations, Indian treaties can be abrogated by enactment of a later inconsistent federal statute. In such cases, the courts treat treaties and statutes as being of equal weight and generally apply a last-in-time rule in cases of patent conflict. *Cherokee Tobacco*, 78 U.S. (11 Wall.) 616, 621 (1871) (Indian treaties accorded no higher sanctity than treaties with foreign nations). The courts have consistently treated the relevant judicial inquiry as a search for clearly expressed congressional intent to abrogate the treaty. *See, e.g., Rosebud Sioux Tribe v. Kneip*, 430 U.S. 584, 586 (1977). Despite the *Lone Wolf* holding that Congress has power to unilaterally abrogate Indian treaty rights, many treaties executed over 100 years ago are still in effect and serve as important sources of rights. *See, e.g., Richard v. United States*, 677 F.3d 1141 (Fed. Cir. 2012) (discussed in Ch. 2, Sec. C) (Sioux treaty promising reimbursement for wrongs committed by "bad men among the whites" still in effect; therefore U.S. could be sued for damages for death of two

tribal members caused by a non-Indian drunk driver on the reservation). The obvious inconsistency between the existence of the *Lone Wolf* principle and the continued vitality of most Indian treaties suggests that important legal mediating principles are at work protecting Indian nations from the full implications of the federal constitutional power recognized in *Lone Wolf*. The *Dion* case illustrates the application of such a mediating principle.

To understand the *Dion* principle, it is important to recognize that the mere fact that Congress possesses a constitutional power to unilaterally abrogate or modify Indian treaty rights by subsequent federal statute does not mean that it must exercise or has exercised that power in any particular case. Notice that in *Dion* the question was not, as it was in *Lone Wolf*, whether Congress had constitutional power to abrogate Yankton Sioux hunting rights, including the right to take eagles, guaranteed by the 1858 treaty. Rather, the question posed for decision was whether Congress by amending the Eagle Protection Act in 1962 had in fact exercised that power. Another way to see that question is to understand that Congress has *power* to abrogate or modify Indian treaty rights by creating a clear conflict between a later federal statute and the prior treaty right, but some principle of law is required to construe federal statutes to determine when congressional action creates such a "clear conflict" with prior Indian treaty rights as to constitute a congressional abrogation or modification of those rights. As argued in one of the seminal articles on the question, cases have long required some type of clear showing of congressional intent to abrogate Indian treaties. Charles F. Wilkinson & John M. Volkman, *Judicial Review of Indian Treaty Abrogation*, 63 CAL. L. REV. 601 (1975). The most recent incarnation of this test, the one suggested in *Dion*, requires a fairly clear showing of congressional intent to abrogate treaty rights. Specifically, *Dion* holds that "[w]hat is essential is clear evidence that Congress actually considered the conflict between its intended action on the one hand and Indian treaty rights on the other, and chose to resolve that conflict by abrogating the treaty." Do the facts of the *Dion* case really satisfy its stated test? Would the test have been satisfied if Congress had never broadened the Act through the 1962 amendments or sought to protect Indian religious rights to take eagles? Does your answer to that question suggest a certain perversity of the holding in *Dion*?

When rigorously enforced by federal courts, the *Dion* principle can constitute a potent limitation on the exercise of federal power. During the 1970s and 1980s courts generally only found termination or abrogation of Indian treaty rights on a rather clear congressional record. In *United States v. Winnebago Tribe*, 542 F.2d 1002 (8th Cir. 1976), for example, the Eighth Circuit held that general congressional approval for the Oxbow Lakes, Snyder-Winnebago Complex did not authorize the Army Corps of Engineers to condemn lands guaranteed to the Winnebago Tribe of Nebraska by an 1865 treaty. The only reference to the tribal lands associated with the project in the legislative record was a 1943 letter from the Chief of Engineers to the Chairman of the House Committee on Flood Control in connection with the Flood Control Act of 1944 and some brief references in the hearings. The Eighth Circuit noted that no reference to tribal lands appeared in the committee reports or the statutory language relevant to the project. The court therefore held "[t]hese references to the Oxbow Lakes, Snyder-Winnebago Complex made during the appropriation hearings do not indicate the clear intent of the Congress to abrogate the Treaty. The United States, through the Army Corps of Engineers, was without authority to take the Tribal lands at issue by eminent domain." *Contra Seneca Nation of Indians v. United States*, 338 F.2d 55, 56 (2d Cir. 1964) (*Seneca II*); *Seneca Nation of Indians v. Brucker*, 262 F.2d 27 (D.C. Cir. 1958) (*Seneca I*) (contrary holdings regarding condemnation of Seneca lands for Kinzua Damn and related projects where legislative record referenced the need for Indian lands). *See generally* ALVIN M. JOSEPHY, JR., NOW THAT THE BUFFALO'S GONE: A STUDY OF TODAY'S AMERICAN INDIANS 127 (1982) (history of the land and the dam construction). Notice the extraordinary rigor with which the Eighth Circuit in the *Winnebago Tribe* case applied the principles reflected in *Dion*. Does the Supreme Court in *Dion* employ the same level of rigor?

The *Dion* principle limiting treaty abrogation presupposes the existence of a treaty right; and any such claims of right must be resolved within the framework of the federal Indian law canons of treaty construction. *See* Ch. 2, Sec. C. Thus, courts applying *Dion* must first determine, applying the canons, whether the treaty right is broad enough to create a conflict with the later-enacted federal statute. Should a tribe's treaty right to exclude nonmembers bar application of federal occupational and safety laws, because federal inspectors must enter the reservation in order to enforce the law? *See Solis v. Matheson*, 563 F.3d 425 (9th Cir. 2009). Should tribal members' right to hunt on the reservation bar application of federal laws prohibiting ex-felons from carrying firearms? *See United States v. Fox*, 573 F.3d 1050 (10th Cir. 2009). In both of these cases, the treaty right was insufficient to defeat application of the federal statute. Should the strength of the federal policy involved influence the resolution of such disputes?

2.   The Endangered Species Act After *Dion*: Because of its holding that the amended Eagle Protection Act abrogated Yankton Sioux treaty rights to take eagles, when the Court considered the Endangered Species Act (ESA) charge based on the taking of an eagle, it concluded that no conflict existed between any currently valid Indian treaty right and the Endangered Species Act. If the second count had been based on the taking of a listed endangered species other than an eagle, would the Court have been required to apply its *Dion* test to the Endangered Species Act?

In *United States v. Billie*, 667 F. Supp. 1485 (S.D. Fla. 1987), the federal district court reached the issue whether the Endangered Species Act abrogated Indian treaty rights. The case involved the tribal chairman of the Florida Seminole Nation who was charged with violating the Endangered Species Act by taking a Florida panther. Testimony indicated that only 20 to 50 Florida panthers remained in the wild although disputes existed as to how differentiated the Florida panther was from other species of the cat.

In addressing whether Chairman Billie had a treaty right to take the panther that prevented the application of the Endangered Species Act, the district court applied the *Dion* test. Thus, it found there must be "clear evidence that Congress actually considered the conflict between its intended action on the one hand and Indian treaty rights on the other, and chose to resolve that conflict by abrogating" the Indian rights.

From its review of the legislative record, the district court found the requisite *Dion* test satisfied. Noting that the express language of the statute contemplated a comprehensive legislative scheme that appeared to apply to all persons, the district court indicated that Congress meant the Act to apply to Indians. The Act contained very few exceptions. The only stated exception in the Act relevant to Indian peoples involved a narrow exemption for hunting for subsistence purposes for Alaskan Natives. Since Alaskan Native peoples had no treaties with the federal government, this exception, unlike the one involved in *Dion*, could not involve treaty rights, a point on which the court did not dwell.

The district court also reviewed the legislative history, specifically relying on Senate and House hearings on two bills that had *not* passed the year before the ESA was enacted. Both of these proposed bills contained broader exemptions for Indians hunting for religious purposes. In a hearing on one of the bills, officials from the Department of the Interior testified in favor of affording Indians a carefully regulated exemption permitting Native peoples to take endangered specifies for cultural and survival purposes. Another bill contained a provision expressly extinguishing Indian treaty rights. Testimony from the Department of the Interior on that legislation suggested that Indians should not be able to exercise their treaty guaranteed hunting or fishing rights to extinguish imperiled species. Finally, the same official advised Congress that it must make a clear statement if it intended to abrogate Indian hunting rights.

While these two bills did not pass, the ESA bill that eventually did pass came out of the same committees and contained no exemptions whatsoever for Indian treaty hunting and fishing, but only the narrow exemption for Native Alaskan subsistence activities. Based on this record, the district court ruled "that Congress would have also circumscribed non-Alaskan Indians' rights had it intended to preserve them." As a result, the court concluded: "Congress must have known that the limited Alaskan exemption would be interpreted to show congressional intent not to exempt other Indians." Is this result consistent with the standard articulated in *Dion*? Cf. *United States v. Bresette*, 761 F. Supp. 658, 664 (D. Minn. 1991) (reading *Billie* as a case resting on the broad coverage of the ESA, and not "stand[ing] for the proposition that the inclusion of Alaskan natives' concerns in a statute is evidence that Congress has considered Indian treaty rights. . . . ") Since Congress was advised that treaty abrogation required an express statement, might the lack of such a statement reflect a contrary resolution? *See generally* Carl H. Johnson, *Balancing Species Protection with Tribal Sovereignty: What Does the Tribal Rights-Endangered Species Order Accomplish?*, 83 MINN. L. REV. 523 (1998) (discussing 1997 order signed by Secretaries of Commerce and Interior that attempts to clarify the responsibilities of each department when actions are taken under the ESA involving tribal trust land, and provides that tribes should not bear a "disproportionate burden" for the conservation of listed species).

3. **Constitutional Limitations on Treaty Abrogation — Ceremonial Species Gathering and the Free Exercise Clause:** Recall that in footnote 3 of *Dion*, the Supreme Court declined to address the question whether the free exercise clause of the First Amendment protected the ceremonial and religious taking of a protected species. In *Billie*, the district court expressly rejected the defendant's free exercise claim on the grounds that the defendant failed to prove that the use of panther parts

by medicine men was essential to the practice of the Seminoles' traditional religion.

In contrast, a federal district judge in New Mexico ruled a few months before *Dion* that the free exercise clause protects the religious taking of a protected species, the golden eagle, even where the accused failed to apply for a permit available to effect a religious accommodation. *United States v. Abeyta*, 632 F. Supp. 1301 (D.N.M. 1986). Abeyta, a member of the Isleta Pueblo, had been charged with shooting the eagle for use in religious ceremonies of his secret religious society, the Katsina Society. The district court held that even if the defendant did not have a treaty right to hunt eagles, the federal government could not constitutionally punish him for the ceremonial act of taking an eagle since such punishment violated his free exercise rights. After determining that the use of eagle feathers, "particularly from the tail and wings, is indispensable to the ceremonies of the Katsina Society and other pueblo ritual" (*Id.* at 1303), the court held that the government's interest in protecting the golden eagle was not compelling, since the testimony reflected that the golden eagle was no longer endangered. Even if protecting the golden eagle were regarded as a compelling governmental interest, the district court held the Eagle Protection Act's provisions forbidding the taking of eagles and requiring Indians to obtain eagle parts and feathers through the Secretary of the Interior did not constitute the least restrictive means of achieving the government's objective of conserving the species.

Could the court reach the same result after *Employment Division, Dept. of Human Res., Or. v. Smith*, 494 U.S. 872 (1990), set forth and discussed in Ch. 6, Sec. B.1, which held that Indians do not have a free exercise clause right of exemption from criminal controlled substances laws for the ceremonial use of peyote as members of the Native American Church? Part of the analysis of that case suggested that religiously motivated conduct was not exempted from laws of general application, particularly criminal laws, by the free exercise clause. How would *Smith* impact the *Abeyta* ruling? Today, Indians and non-Indians challenging limits on possession of eagle feathers invoke instead the Religious Freedom Restoration Act (RFRA), 42 U.S.C. § 2000bb et seq., which Congress enacted in the wake of *Smith*. *See* Ch. 6, Sec. B.1.

4.   Constitutional Limitations on Treaty Abrogation — The Just Compensation Clause: The rights guaranteed Indians by treaty and statute were often secured in exchange for large cessions of land by the tribes. Additionally, many other treaty or statutory rights that Congress might wish to abrogate involve vested property rights protected under the Fifth Amendment from taking without just compensation. The *Dion* clear statement rule therefore helps insulate the United States from unintended monetary liability. In *Menominee Tribe v. United States*, 391 U.S. 404, 413 (1968), the United States Supreme Court made precisely this point:

> We find it difficult to believe that Congress, *without explicit statement*, would subject the United States to a claim for compensation by destroying property rights conferred by treaty, particularly when Congress was purporting by the Termination Act to settle the Government's financial obligations toward the Indians (emphasis added).

Would the holding of *Dion* that the United States abrogated completely Indian treaty hunting rights to take eagles give the defendant or the Yankton Sioux Tribe any claim in the United States Court of Federal Claims for a taking? If so, how could a court measure the value of the property right? Would any Indian or Indian tribe think to bring such a claim?

3.   Criminal Jurisdiction as an Illustration of the Exercise of Federal Power over Indian Affairs

a.   Introduction

Unlike most issues of civil regulatory, taxing, and adjudicative jurisdiction, criminal jurisdiction in Indian country is substantially governed by a limited number of federal statutes. This statutory regime supplements federal criminal jurisdiction over crimes of nationwide application, such as drug and mail fraud offenses, which federal courts generally uphold with equal force in Indian country in the absence of a more specific conflict with guaranteed treaty or other Indian rights.

For reservations on which the primary jurisdiction pattern has not been altered by Public Law 280 or like statutes authorizing state jurisdiction, the main federal Indian country criminal jurisdiction provisions are the definition of Indian country found at 18 U.S.C. § 1151, discussed in Ch. 2, Sec. A.3, the Indian Country Crimes Act (sometimes also known as the General Crimes Act), 18 U.S.C. § 1152, and the Major Crimes Act, 18 U.S.C. § 1153. Additionally, 18 U.S.C. § 3242 specifies the procedure governing prosecutions under the Major Crimes Act. Students should carefully review the statutory language contained in these provisions. For reservations affected by Public Law 280, the primary governing provision is 18 U.S.C. § 1162. Public Law 280 is presented and discussed in greater detail in Ch. 5, Sec. A. Other reservation or state specific provisions exist elsewhere in federal law. *E.g.*, 18 U.S.C. § 3243 (all reservations in Kansas); 25 U.S.C. § 232 (all reservations in New York). Since many of the federal Indian country criminal jurisdiction statutes seem to overlap or, at times, appear inconsistent, they are not easily understood unless set in a historical context.

As evidenced in *Ex parte Crow Dog*, 109 U.S. 556 (1883), set forth and discussed in Ch. 1, Sec. D.1, there was a long-standing federal policy implementing Indian treaties that contemplated primary tribal jurisdiction over offenses committed on the reservation. *See, e.g.*, Treaty with the Cherokees, July 19, 1866, art. XIII, 14 Stat. 803 ("the judicial tribunals of the [Cherokee] nation shall be allowed to retain exclusive jurisdiction in all civil and criminal cases arising within their country in which members of the nation, by nativity or adoption, shall be the only parties, or where the cause of action shall arise in the Cherokee nation"); Treaty with the Creeks and Seminoles, Aug. 7, 1856, art. IV, 11 Stat. 700 (treaty guarantee assuring that tribal lands would never become part of or subject to the jurisdiction of any state or federal territory). Thus, the primary model of tribal jurisdiction that emerged from the treaty federalism model of the early nineteenth century was relatively complete tribal criminal jurisdiction over the reservation, which then contained primarily tribal residents. The only major exception to that model was the authorization for the federal government to try non-Indians who committed crimes against the person or property of Indians in Indian country or to try Indians, when not already punished by the laws of their tribe, for crimes committed against American citizens. While these provisions evolved over time, they are traceable to an 1817 federal statute and are now codified in 18 U.S.C. § 1152. The historic exclusion of Indians who had already been punished by the laws of their tribe reflects that federal policy relied primarily on tribal jurisdiction in Indian country and would only intervene where tribal cooperation was not forthcoming. Compare these provisions to the federal government's assertion of extraterritorial jurisdiction today to protect American citizens or federal employees from crimes committed abroad. *See e.g.*, 18 U.S.C. § 7(7); 21 U.S.C. § 846; 46 U.S.C. app. § 1903(h).

The pattern underwent significant change in the late nineteenth century after the *Crow Dog* decision reaffirmed this long-standing federal policy. *See generally* SIDNEY L. HARRING, CROW DOG'S CASE: AMERICAN INDIAN SOVEREIGNTY, TRIBAL LAW, AND UNITED STATES LAW IN THE NINETEENTH CENTURY (1994). *Crow Dog* provoked the first major congressional deviation from the traditional reliance on tribal jurisdiction over offenses committed in Indian country. In 1885, in direct response to *Crow Dog*, Congress enacted the Major Crimes Act now codified in amended form at 18 U.S.C. § 1153. This Act, the constitutionality of which was upheld in *United States v. Kagama*, discussed in Ch. 1, Sec. D.2, extended federal criminal jurisdiction for the first time to cover seven enumerated crimes committed by Indians in Indian country against the person or property of "another Indian or other person." In reviewing the materials that follow consider the extent to which this federal incursion on tribal self-government has expanded. Is the model of tribal-federal relations reflected in the Major Crimes Act consistent with the treaty federalism model? If not, what model of the tribal-federal relationship explains the continued existence of the jurisdictional patterns established by the Major Crimes Act?

Public Law 280 and other statewide or reservation-specific federal statutes authorizing state jurisdiction in Indian country came much later than the Indian Country Crimes Act and the Major Crimes Act. They are products of the post-World War II federal termination policy, aimed at preparing Indians for termination by incorporating them into state legal systems. Congress also wanted to reduce federal expenditures for Indian country law enforcement and criminal justice, and therefore eliminated federal criminal jurisdiction under sections 1152 and 1153 for the states named in Public Law 280.

As you will see, the federal criminal jurisdiction regime created by all of these statutes is a "jurisdictional maze." Robert N. Clinton, *Criminal Jurisdiction over Indian Lands: A Journey Through a Jurisdictional Maze*, 18 ARIZ. L. REV. 503 (1976). The scheme was not designed at one point in time to implement a single, coherent vision of the tribal-federal relationship. Rather, individual elements were piled upon one another at various points in time, when different conceptions of the tribal-federal relationship prevailed. This section focuses on the kinds of offenses and defendants these statutes reach within Indian country, as well as the statutes' possible preemption of state and tribal criminal authority. For a thorough treatment of criminal jurisdiction in Indian country, see NELL JESSUP NEWTON ET AL., COHEN'S HANDBOOK OF FEDERAL INDIAN LAW Ch. 9 (2012 ed.).

Responding to widespread tribal complaints about federal law enforcement and criminal justice in Indian country, as well as unacceptably high crime rates — particularly crimes of domestic violence and sexual assault — Congress passed in 2010 the Tribal Law and Order Act (TLOA), Pub. L. 111-211, 124 Stat. 2258. President Obama signed TLOA in an emotion-filled ceremony that included testimony by a Rosebud Sioux tribal member who had been the victim of a violent sexual assault that was never prosecuted in federal court. The Act altered federal criminal jurisdiction for Indian country in limited ways (discussed below in this section), and established a commission to conduct a "comprehensive study of law enforcement and criminal justice in tribal communities," including criminal jurisdiction. The Commission was bi-partisan and multi-branch, with appointees by the President and both parties in the House and the Senate. In November 2013, the Indian Law and Order Commission issued its report, recommending an overhaul of Indian country criminal jurisdiction to enable greater tribal control, including a tribe-by-tribe option to exit federal and/or state Indian country criminal jurisdiction. *See* Indian Law and Order Commission, A Roadmap for Making Native America Safer 1–30 (2013), available at http://www.aisc.ucla.edu/iloc/report/files/Chapter_1_Jurisdiction.pdf. The report provides helpful charts mapping the complexity of Indian country criminal jurisdiction (p. 7), and goes on to indict the system for its lack of effectiveness in providing safety and justice to tribal communities. Summarizing its views on jurisdiction, the Commission wrote:

> . . . [C]riminal jurisdiction in Indian country is an indefensible maze of complex, conflicting, and illogical commands, layered in over decades via congressional policies and court decisions, and without the consent of Tribal nations. Ultimately, the imposition of non-Indian criminal justice institutions in Indian country extracts a terrible price: delayed prosecutions, too few prosecutions, and other prosecution inefficiencies; trials in distant courthouses; justice systems and players unfamiliar with or hostile to Indians and tribes; and the exploitation of system failures by criminals, more criminal activity, and further endangerment of everyone living in and near Tribal communities. When Congress and the Administration ask why is the crime rate so high in Indian country, they need look no further than the archaic system in place, in which Federal and State authority displaces Tribal authority at the expense of local Tribal control and accountability. When Tribal law enforcement and courts are supported — rather than discouraged — from taking primary responsibility over the dispensation of local justice, they are often better, stronger, faster, and more effective in providing justice in Indian country than their non-Native counterparts located elsewhere. After listening to and hearing from Tribal communities, the Commission strongly believes that for public safety to be achieved in Indian country, Tribal justice systems must be allowed to flourish, Tribal authority should be restored to Tribal governments when they request it, and the Federal government in particular needs to take a back seat in Indian country, enforcing only those crimes that it would enforce in any case, on or off reservation. The Federal trust responsibility to Tribes turns on the consent of Tribes, not the imposition of Federal will. The Commission also believes that what is not warranted is a top-down, prescriptive Federal solution to the problem.

The Commission also recommended that tribes opting out of federal criminal jurisdiction (and federally authorized state jurisdiction) should be congressionally empowered to assert criminal jurisdiction over all offenders within their territory, and should have all their convictions directly reviewed by a specialized federal appellate court, whose jurisdiction would be limited to examining criminal procedure violations under the Bill of Rights. Note that the Commission's recommendations apply to Indian country criminal jurisdiction only, so federal criminal laws of general applicability (*see* Ch. 2, Sec. C) would remain enforceable even after a tribe opted out of federal or state Indian country jurisdiction.

The Commission's recommendations will be more understandable after you have mastered the existing regime of criminal jurisdiction in Indian country. To avoid getting lost in the maze, keep your eye on the central question of the type of tribal-federal relationship federal Indian country criminal laws do and should reflect. Did the Indian Law and Order Commission strike the right balance between respect for tribal sovereignty and protection of the rights of individual criminal defendants? How could appointees from the political right and left come to an agreement on the Commission's recommendations, which would so thoroughly upend the existing jurisdictional scheme?

b.   Federal Criminal Jurisdiction Statutes

Section 1152, the Indian Country Crimes Act, stems from criminal jurisdiction provisions in the early Nonintercourse Acts, which implemented treaty language reserving tribal sovereignty and jurisdiction over intratribal matters. As Professor Clinton points out,

> The actual statutory crimes covered by section 1152 are relatively easy to describe. The first paragraph extends to Indian country the body of criminal law applied "within the sole and exclusive jurisdiction of the United States, except the District of Columbia"; that is, the body of federally defined crimes which Congress has established for other federal enclaves, such as national parks and military installations, as well as for admiralty and maritime law. Insofar as these crimes are promulgated, and their punishment prescribed by federal statute, the coverage of section 1152 is ascertainable from the United States Code.

Robert N. Clinton, *Criminal Jurisdiction over Indian Lands*, *supra*, 18 ARIZ. L. REV. at 523. Because Congress has not promulgated the kind of comprehensive criminal code found under state law, many less serious offenses, such as traffic and game violations, are not defined as crimes under federal law. In addition to applying federally-defined crimes to Indian country, however, section 1152 incorporates state-defined offenses "in force at the time of such act or omission" through the Assimilative Crimes Act, 18 U.S.C. § 13. The Supreme Court assumed as much, without analysis, in *Williams v. United States*, 327 U.S. 711 (1946), and lower federal courts and the United States Department of Justice have adopted that view. Nonetheless, there is reason to question an interpretation of sections 1152 and 13 that allows state offenses to become federal crimes within Indian country. *See* NELL JESSUP NEWTON ET AL., COHEN'S HANDBOOK OF FEDERAL INDIAN LAW § 9.02[1][c] (2012 ed.). The Assimilative Crimes Act was designed to fill gaps in law enforcement that arise on federal lands because of the absence of state criminal jurisdiction. Is there a similar gap that needs to be filled in Indian country, where tribal law enforcement is available? Furthermore, introduction of state law and expansion of federal criminal law enforcement through the Assimilative Crimes Act are major incursions into tribal self-government. States are granted certain criminal legislative powers over Indian reservations located within their boundaries which they would otherwise not have. In the absence of any explicit statement in either statute authorizing such consequences, should courts conclude that by incorporating "general criminal laws" in section 1152, the Congress intended to include state law through the Assimilative Crimes Act?

In *United States v. Marcyes*, 557 F.2d 1361, 1365 n.1 (9th Cir. 1977), the court considered and rejected arguments against the application of the Assimilative Crimes Act in Indian country. The court said:

> Amicus argues that *Williams v. United States*, 327 U.S. 711 (1946) did not decide the question of whether the A.C.A. [Assimilative Crimes Act] is applicable to Indian country. We disagree. In *Williams* the petitioner, a married white man, was convicted of having had sexual intercourse, within an Indian reservation, with an unmarried Indian girl who was over the age of 16 but under 18 years of age. This act was made punishable under the laws of the State of Arizona and was incorporated as a federal crime under the provisions of 18 U.S.C. § 468 (the predecessor to 18 U.S.C. § 13). The Supreme Court's initial statement was "[t]his case turns upon the applicability of the Assimilative Crimes Act. . . . " Since it was undisputed that the act took place within an Indian reservation, the threshold question necessarily decided was whether the A.C.A. even applied to Indian country. Amicus' argument that the court merely assumed its applicability without deciding the question is belied by the court's own words. The court stated:
>
> > It is not disputed that this Indian reservation is "reserved or acquired for the use of the United States, and under the exclusive or concurrent jurisdiction thereof," or that it is "Indian country" within the meaning of Rev. Stat. § 2145. [the predecessor to 18 U.S.C. § 1152]. This means that many sections of the Federal Criminal Code *apply to the reservation, including not only the Assimilative Crimes Act. . . .* 327 U.S. at 713, 66 S. Ct. at 779 (emphasis added).
>
> We would also note that the *Williams* court's ultimate decision, that the A.C.A. did not apply to the particular crime charged because the precise acts were made penal by Federal law and therefore the State's laws could not be incorporated, would never have been reached had the court felt that the A.C.A. did not apply to any crime committed upon Indian lands. Our own review of the language of 18 U.S.C. § 13 and 18 U.S.C. § 1152 convinces us that the district court was correct in holding that the A.C.A., by its own terms and through § 1152, is applicable to Indian country.

Marcyes affirmed the federal convictions of several Indians under the Assimilative Crimes Act for selling fireworks on the Puyallup Reservation in East Tacoma, Washington, in violation of the laws of the State of Washington. As you will see below, the court arguably should have found section 1152 inapplicable because the alleged offense was a victimless crime committed by an Indian. The court did, however, limit application of the Assimilative Crimes Act to Indian country by holding that the Act does not incorporate state regulatory crimes and make them applicable to Indian country. Rather, the Act only incorporates conduct which the state absolutely forbids to its citizens, such as the sale of fireworks, not conduct which it permits, but extensively regulates. The distinction between prohibitory criminal laws and regulatory statutes to which criminal sanctions are appended, drawn in *Marcyes*, is consistent with the same distinction drawn by the courts in Public Law 280 cases involving the application in state courts of state law to Indians for offenses committed on their reservations.

Notwithstanding these limitations on incorporation of state law through the Assimilative Crimes Act, should Congress clarify that the Assimilative Crimes Act does not apply to Indian country? Consider this view:

> It has been a continuous tenet of Federal-Indian policy to leave tribes free to govern themselves under their own code of laws within the Indian country. The wholesale adoption of State laws onto reservations by way of the Assimilative Crimes Act runs completely counter to that long standing Federal policy. It is the tribe, not the State or the Federal Government, which should determine whether Indian stick games may be played within the reservation, whether bingo games will be sanctioned, whether fire-crackers may be sold within the reservation. It may well be that Congress would want to control certain activities of a more substantial nature, but this should be done by specific legislation and only after a showing that the tribes themselves have failed to pass regulatory laws.

AMERICAN INDIAN POLICY REVIEW COMMISSION, FINAL REPORT 198 (1977). According to the Indian Law and Order Commission, discussed above, which is the more serious problem with federal Indian country jurisdiction: overreaching by federal statutes or underenforcement by federal prosecutors?

The first paragraph of section 1152 seems to provide a broad and complete grant of federal criminal jurisdiction within Indian country. Yet several exceptions, some statutory and some judge-made, have substantially reduced the coverage of that act. The most important statutory exception excludes "offenses committed by one Indian against the person or property of another Indian." These intra-Indian crimes are withdrawn from the grant of criminal jurisdiction in section 1152 because of federal treaty commitments and policies affording tribes a measure of self-government. For a discussion of who counts as an Indian for purposes of this statute, see Ch. 2, Sec. A.2.

The statute does not mention victimless crimes committed by Indians, leaving courts to determine whether the Indian-against-Indian exception encompasses such offenses. Any solution to this problem must grapple with the difficulty attendant on determining whether a crime is truly victimless. Should the general public, which may include Indians and non-Indians, be treated as the victims of reckless driving, given that they may all be endangered? If the criminal act involves consensual behavior, should third parties affected by the act (*e.g.*, spouses in an adultery prosecution) be considered victims? In *United States v. Quiver*, 241 U.S. 602 (1916), and *Ex parte Mayfield*, 141 U.S. 107 (1891), the Supreme Court refused to find victims where the offense of adultery was consensual, and applied the section 1152 exception for intra-Indian offenses. The *Quiver* Court offered the following rationale in the form of a rhetorical question: "[Are not the words of the exception] intended to be in accord with the policy reflected by the legislation of Congress and its administration for many years, that the relations of the Indians among themselves — the conduct of one toward another — is to be controlled by the customs and laws of the tribe, save when Congress expressly or clearly directs otherwise?"

Notwithstanding the opinion in *Quiver*, several lower courts have applied section 1152 to apparently victimless crimes, emphasizing public impact of the offenses and a lack of tribal tradition of punishing the conduct in question. *See, e.g., United States v. Thunder Hawk*, 127 F.3d 705 (8th Cir. 1997). Consider the impact that such holdings can have in light of the incorporation of state law, including many lesser offenses, as federal law through the Assimilative Crimes Act. Victimless or consensual crime statutes enacted by the states generally involve legislation of morals in one sense or another. To allow the states, through the Act, to make moral judgments for the tribes, undermines the purpose for continuing reservation policy — permitting the Indian tribes to maintain their own separate, evolving, cultural traditions and government. As Cohen's Handbook points out, "Charging tribal members with violations of state-defined victimless crimes such as traffic or public decency laws would give 'assimilative' an unintended double meaning." NELL JESSUP NEWTON ET AL., COHEN'S HANDBOOK OF FEDERAL INDIAN LAW 744 (2012 ed.). Do the Indian law canons of construction have any role to play in addressing the question of the application of section 1152 to victimless crimes committed by Indians?

Another statutory exception to section 1152 involves crimes committed by Indians, whether against Indians or non-Indians, that have been "punished by the local law of the tribe." This double jeopardy protection underscores the primary role of tribal justice systems within the scheme envisioned under section 1152. If the offense is covered by the Major Crimes Act, 18 U.S.C. § 1153, the exception does not apply, and protection against multiple prosecution is unavailable. *See United States v. Wheeler*, 435 U.S. 313 (1978).

The third and final statutory exception to federal criminal jurisdiction under section 1152 extends to "any case where by treaty stipulations, the exclusive jurisdiction over such offenses is or may be secured to the Indian tribes respectively." After considering the scope of section 1152 and the potentially relevant treaty provisions, Professor Clinton was able to find several such provisions that arguably have not been abrogated. Robert N. Clinton, *Criminal Jurisdiction over Indian Lands, supra*, 18 ARIZ. L. REV. at 530–32.

In addition to section 1152's statutory exceptions, an important judge-crafted exception exists for crimes committed by one non-Indian against another. Professor Clinton points out:

> . . . This exception is not based on any language contained in section 1152 but rather is a judicially created exception. Its roots are found in a trilogy

of Supreme Court decisions spanning 65 years: *United States v. Bratney,*[3] *Draper v. United States,*[4] and *New York ex rel. Ray v. Martin.*[5]

In each case, the Supreme Court found that proper jurisdiction for a crime committed on Indian lands between non-Indians was in the state courts rather than the federal forum which the language of section 1152 seemingly provided. The Court paid scant attention to the language of section 1152, relying instead on the inherent jurisdiction exercised by the states over Indian lands within their borders as a consequence of their admission to the Union without an express disclaimer of jurisdiction. Although the logic of this argument would apply equally well to interracial or even intra-Indian crimes committed on Indian lands, the Supreme Court has applied the *McBratney* analysis only to crimes committed on Indian lands between non-Indians. Indeed, dicta in later cases suggests that the rationale in *McBratney* and *Draper* has little to do with state sovereignty. Rather, the cases suggest that the non-ward status of the accused and the victim divests the federal government of any interest in prosecution despite the occurrence of the crime in Indian country.[6]

The combined impact of the *McBratney* trilogy and the express intra-Indian crime exclusion indicates that section 1152 jurisdiction is limited to interracial crimes, crimes in which an Indian is involved either as the

---

[3] [97] 104 U.S. 621 (1881). . . .

[4] [98] 164 U.S. 240 (1896). . . .

[5] [99] 326 U.S. 496 (1946). . . .

[6] [102] *United States v. Ramsey*, 271 U.S. 467, 469 (1926); *Donnelly v. United States*, 228 U.S. 243, 271–72 (1913). In *Ramsey*, two white men were charged with murdering a fullblood Osage Indian upon a reservation. Discussing the issue of federal court jurisdiction, the Court stated:

> The authority of the United States under § 2145 to punish crimes occurring within the State of Oklahoma, not committed by or against Indians, was ended by the grant of statehood. [citing *McBratney* and *Draper*] But authority in respect of crimes committed by or against Indians continued after the admission of the state as it was before . . . in virtue of the long-settled rule that such Indians are wards of the nation in respect of whom there is devolved upon the Federal Government "the duty of protection, and with it the power." . . . The guardianship of the United States over the Osage Indians has not been abandoned; they are still the wards of the nation . . . and it rests with Congress alone to determine when that relationship shall cease.

271 U.S. at 469. In *Donnelly*, the defendant, a white man, was charged for a crime committed within the Hoopa Valley Reservation. Utilizing the logic of *McBratney*, he argued that when California was admitted to the Union, it received authority to punish crimes committed within its borders, even on land set aside for Indian reservations. Rejecting this argument, the Court stated:

> Upon full consideration we are satisfied that offenses committed by or against Indians are not within the principle of the *McBratney* and *Draper* Cases. This was in effect held, as to crimes committed *by* the Indians, in the *Kagama* Case, . . . where the constitutionality of the second branch of § 9 of the act of March 3, 1885, . . . was sustained upon the ground that the Indian tribes are the wards of the nation. This same reason applies — perhaps *a fortiori* — with respect to crimes committed by white men against the persons or property of the Indian tribes while occupying reservations set apart for the very purpose of segregating them from the whites and others not of Indian blood.

Id. at 271–72 (citations omitted).

defendant or the accused. One problem not confronted in the cases is how section 1152 is to be construed with reference to a crime involving multiple defendants or multiple victims.

Id. at 524–27.

Whatever the analytical and other deficiencies in the *McBratney* doctrine, it appears to be well-settled law. When the United States Department of Justice attacked the interpretation of section 1152 offered in the *McBratney* trilogy of cases and invited its overruling to avoid the otherwise racial nature of the jurisdictional classification drawn by the law, the United States Supreme Court tersely reaffirmed the doctrine, stating: "Not all crimes committed within Indian country are subject to federal or tribal jurisdiction, however. Under *United States v. McBratney*, 104 U.S. 621 (1882), a non-Indian charged with committing crimes against other non-Indians in Indian country is subject to prosecution under state law." *United States v. Antelope*, 430 U.S. 641, 642 n.2 (1977).

What if a non-Indian commits a victimless crime within Indian country? Should the tribal community be treated as the true victim, making the *McBratney* exception inapplicable? Or would consistent application of *Quiver*, the case discussed above involving a victimless crime committed by an Indian, suggest that the jurisdiction should be exclusively vested in the state courts under the *McBratney* trilogy? As a practical consideration, which set of prosecutors, federal or state, would you expect to give higher priority to prosecuting victimless crimes such as driving under the influence? For a rather formalistic analysis of the issue, see *United States v. Langford*, 641 F.3d 1195 (10th Cir. 2011) (addressing the crime of being a spectator at a cockfight, which could become a federal offense by virtue of the Assimilative Crimes Act).

The Federal Major Crimes Act, now codified as amended at 18 U.S.C. § 1153, was first enacted in 1885, in response to the Supreme Court's holding in *Ex Parte Crow Dog* (presented in Ch. 1, Sec. D.1) that federal criminal jurisdiction under section 1152 did not extend to a homicide committed by one Indian against another. Its application is limited to fourteen enumerated crimes when committed within Indian country by an Indian against "another Indian or other person;" thus, unlike the jurisdiction conferred in section 1152, the race or political affiliation of the victim is irrelevant. Since the Assimilative Crimes Act applies only to Indians in Indian country through section 1152, it does not insert itself into prosecutions brought solely through the Major Crimes Act.

The operation of section 1153 is affected by a related federal statute, 18 U.S.C. § 3242, which specifies that persons tried under section 1153 are to be tried "in the same courts, and in the same manner, as are all other persons committing any of the above crimes within the exclusive jurisdiction of the United States." Since federal defendants are ordinarily entitled to an instruction on a lesser included offense if a rational jury could find that the evidence supports conviction of the lesser crime and not the greater one, defendants prosecuted under section 1153 have claimed they are entitled to such instructions, even though the crimes enumerated in section 1153 are the only ones a federal district court has jurisdiction to entertain under the statute. In *Keeble v. United States*, 412 U.S. 205 (1973), an Indian who was charged with assault resulting in serious bodily injury, one of the crimes enumerated in section 1153, requested a jury instruction on simple assault, a lesser-included offense. The trial judge denied the request, resting on the fact that simple assault was not one of the offenses enumerated in section 1153. Reversing, the Supreme Court, in an opinion by Justice Brennan, emphasized the language of section 3242, which requires Indian offenses heard under section 1153 to be tried in the same manner as other offenses within the exclusive jurisdiction of the United States. According to the Court, that language required the section 1153 defendant to be treated the same as a non-Indian tried under section 1152 for the same crime. Since the section 1152 defendant would be entitled to a lesser-included offense instruction, Keeble was entitled to receive one as well.

Although *Keeble* did not explicitly determine that the federal court giving such a lesser included offense instruction could convict and sentence for the lesser crime, several circuit courts have upheld the practice. *Keeble* also left open the question whether prosecutors as well as defendants should be able to request the lesser-included offense instruction, whether federal courts should be allowed to accept guilty pleas to lesser included offenses, and whether state as well as federally-defined crimes may be included within the lesser included offense instruction. *See* NELL JESSUP NEWTON ET AL., COHEN'S HANDBOOK OF FEDERAL INDIAN LAW § 9.02[2][g] (2012 ed.). How does allowing such instructions, convictions, and plea bargains affect the scope of federal criminal jurisdiction over intra-Indian offenses within Indian country? Recall that such offenses are excluded from federal criminal jurisdiction under section 1152, and are therefore exclusively tribal unless covered by the Major Crimes Act. Should tribal rather than state law therefore be used to define the lesser-included offenses that are not defined under federal law?

The federal criminal jurisdiction regime established by sections 1152 and 1153 excludes concurrent state jurisdiction. *See* NELL JESSUP NEWTON ET AL., COHEN'S HANDBOOK OF FEDERAL INDIAN LAW § 9.03 (2012 ed.). By congressional statute, however, nearly one-quarter of the reservation Indian population in the lower 48 states — representing 51% of all such tribes — and all Alaska Natives are affected by statutes that specifically authorize state jurisdiction. Most of these statutes also eliminate the application of sections 1152 and 1153 to the affected Indian country, although a number of ambiguities remain. The drive to supplant federal with state criminal jurisdiction arose during the period of federal termination policy immediately following World War II, but has also found a home in congressional acts of the 1970s and later directed at tribal land settlement and restoration, where state opposition was assuaged with tribal agreements to accept state criminal and civil jurisdiction. *See, e.g.*, 25 U.S.C. § 1775d (Mohegan Nation Land Claims Settlement Act).

The most sweeping of the congressional acts authorizing state criminal jurisdiction, Public Law 280, required six states — Alaska, California, Minnesota, Nebraska, Oregon, and Wisconsin — to assume broad criminal (as well as civil) jurisdiction over most of the reservations located within their boundaries. Codified at 18 U.S.C. § 1162, this criminal jurisdiction provision also states that within the affected reservations in these "mandatory" states, "[t]he provisions of sections 1152 and 1153 of this chapter *shall not be applicable* . . . as areas over which the several States have exclusive jurisdiction." (Emphasis supplied.) In 1970, this provision was amended to clarify that "states shall have exclusive jurisdiction" with respect to the offenses covered by those two federal Indian country statutes in the reservations included in the mandatory states.

Public Law 280 not only compelled six states to assume jurisdiction, it also permitted the assumption of Indian jurisdiction by any other states that desired to do so. In 25 U.S.C. § 1321, Public Law 280 gave congressional consent to the assumption by the states of criminal and civil jurisdiction "by affirmative legislative action," and furthermore gave congressional consent to the amendment of state constitutions which contained disclaimers of jurisdiction over Indian lands, presumably a necessary predicate to the assumption of jurisdiction. As originally enacted, Public Law 280 required no tribal consent for a state's discretionary assumption of jurisdiction. A number of states assumed such jurisdiction despite contrary desires on the part of resident Indian tribes, although only three such states — Florida, Idaho, and Washington — currently exercise such authority in criminal matters, either fully or over certain subject areas. *See* NELL JESSUP NEWTON ET AL., COHEN'S HANDBOOK OF FEDERAL INDIAN LAW § 6.04[3][a] (2012 ed.).

Public Law 280 was amended by the Indian Civil Rights Act of 1968 to prospectively require tribal consent, and to allow retrocession (or return) of jurisdiction undertaken by either mandatory or discretionary states pursuant to Public Law 280. 25 U.S.C. §§ 1323, 1326. Since that time, no tribe has formally consented to the extension of state criminal jurisdiction over its lands, and seven states — Minnesota, Montana, Nebraska, Nevada, Oregon, Washington, and Wisconsin — have retroceded some or all of the criminal jurisdiction they assumed under Public Law 280. *See* DUANE CHAMPAGNE AND CAROLE GOLDBERG, CAPTURED JUSTICE: NATIVE NATIONS AND PUBLIC LAW 280 14–18 (2011) (listing tribes subject to Public Law 280, by state). A few states, such as Washington, have acted to facilitate the retrocession process for tribes desiring to exit state jurisdiction. *See* Robert T. Anderson, *Negotiating Jurisdiction: Retroceding State Authority over Indian Country Granted by Public Law 280*, 87 WASH. L. REV. 915 (2012).

Because Public Law 280 tribes often complain that states are unresponsive to the safety and justice needs on reservations, the Tribal Law and Order Act of 2010 amended Public Law 280, 18 U.S.C. § 1162 and 25 U.S.C. § 1321(a), to allow affected tribes to request federal criminal jurisdiction under sections 1152 and 1153 *concurrent with* state jurisdiction. Federal jurisdiction can be reestablished only "after consultation and consent by the Attorney General." At least one tribe (White Earth, in Minnesota) has successfully reinstated federal jurisdiction, and several other Public Law 280 tribes have made requests. Is layering another government with criminal jurisdiction in Indian country, especially the federal government, a sound response to the types of concerns voiced by the Indian Law and Order Commission, *supra*? As noted above, the Indian Law and Order Commission has recommended that tribes be authorized to opt out of state criminal jurisdiction under Public Law 280, either in whole or in part.

Augmenting the Indian Country Crimes Act, the Major Crimes Act, and the various congressional acts authorizing state criminal jurisdiction in Indian country are a collection of subject-specific federal criminal laws targeting Indian country. They include a federal law penalizing unauthorized hunting, trapping, or fishing on Indian land (18 U.S.C. § 1165, discussed in Ch. 7, Sec. A.1), several laws prohibiting the introduction and sale of liquor in Indian country (*e.g.*, 18 U.S.C. § 1154, discussed in Ch. 5, Sec. E), and a prohibition on gambling in Indian country unless authorized pursuant to federal law (18 U.S.C. § 1166, discussed in Ch. 5, Sec. D). When laws such as Public Law 280 specify that federal criminal jurisdiction under sections 1152 and 1153 will no longer exist, these other federal criminal statutes, by implication, remain in force. To the extent these laws are exclusive of state jurisdiction over the same subject, they remain exclusively federal under Public Law 280. *See, e.g., Sycuan Band of Mission Indians v. Roache*, 38 F.3d 402, 407 (9th Cir. 1994), *amended* 54 F.3d 535 (1995) (addressing the gambling prohibition in 18 U.S.C. § 1166). The persistence of such federal criminal jurisdiction in Public Law 280 states has important implications for the conduct of tribal law enforcement on reservations in those states. *See* Sec. A.3.d, this chapter.

NOTE ON JUVENILE OFFENDERS AND FEDERAL JURISDICTION

The handling of juvenile offenders under the basic jurisdictional scheme established for Indian country by sections 1152 and 1153 rarely has surfaced in decided federal cases. In *United States v. Male Juvenile (Pierre Y.)*, 280 F.3d 1008 (9th Cir. 2002), however, the Ninth Circuit Court of Appeals confronted the interplay of the federal Indian country jurisdictional statutes and the Federal Juvenile Delinquency Act, 18 U.S.C. § 5031 et seq. Under 18 U.S.C. § 5032, federal jurisdiction exists outside of Indian country only if the juvenile has committed a "violation of a law of the United States" *and* if the Attorney General certifies either (1) the juvenile court or other appropriate court of a State does not have or refuses to exercise jurisdiction; or (2) the State does not have available programs or services adequate to the needs of the juvenile; or (3) the offense charged involves certain described crimes of violence.

The juvenile in *Male Juvenile (Pierre Y.)* was an Indian adjudicated delinquent for committing two burglaries on the Fort Peck Indian Reservation, where the state has no criminal jurisdiction over Indians. Since proper certification of the case under section 5032 constituted a jurisdictional requirement, the Ninth Circuit was immediately confronted with the inconsistency between a certification requirement focused on the "State" and the lack of jurisdiction of the state over the offense. The court looked closely at the word "State" employed in the statute and found that it was defined to include "territories." Nevertheless, it rejected the notion that Congress meant to include Indian tribes within the meaning of the word "State," based on the legislative history of the statute. Consequently, the Ninth Circuit held that the Attorney General was not required to consult with the affected tribal government before making any certification under section 2032.

This ruling, of course, left states within the Ninth Circuit with primary jurisdiction over their juveniles but left Indian tribal governments to the mercy of the Attorney General of the United States and without formal input. Can this disparity be justified on statutory language alone? What model of tribal-federal relationship does this decision suggest? Worse still, while the juvenile was charged with residential burglary, burglary while an enumerated offense under the Major Crimes Act, 18 U.S.C. § 1153, is not defined by federal law. The lower federal court relied on the Montana state definition of burglary to supply the omission, as required by section 1153. The juvenile argued that the offense therefore was not a "violation of a law of the United States" as required by section 5032. The Ninth Circuit rejected that argument, suggesting that the enumeration of the crime in the Major Crimes Act, the jurisdictional statute, made it a federal crime, irrespective of the fact that state law was employed to define the elements of and penalty for the offense. Thus, the Ninth Circuit sustained federal jurisdiction. Despite the fact that the Major Crimes Act expressly required any offender convicted of a state defined crime to be sentenced in accordance with the penalties afforded by state law, the court, in a decision having ramifications for adults as well as juveniles, held that the Federal Sentencing Reform Act of 1990 displaced the prior provisions of the Major Crimes Act and that the juvenile was properly sentenced under those provisions. The Ninth Circuit relied on its prior decision involving burglary committed by an adult Indian, which had reached the same result on the sentencing question. *United States v. Bear*, 932 F.2d 1279, 1281 (9th Cir. 1990).

Should 18 U.S.C. § 5032 be amended to include tribes with states, so that most federal juvenile proceedings for Indian country offenses would be barred where tribal jurisdiction exists? The 2013 report of the Indian Law and Order Commission, discussed earlier in this chapter, devoted an entire chapter to juvenile justice, focusing on the special difficulties experienced by Native children and the inadequacies of the federal justice system for juveniles. Native youth, the report explained, suffers from intergenerational trauma due to tribes' history of dispossession, coerced assimilation, and federal boarding schools that forcibly separated children from their parents. Their exposure to violence is highest among all groups in the U.S., and they are 2.5 times more likely to commit suicide than other youth. The federal justice system is ill-equipped to deal with Native youth, who typically comprise half of the docket of juvenile cases in that system each year. According to the Indian Law and Order Commission:

> The Federal court system has no juvenile division — no specialized juvenile court judges, no juvenile probation system — and the Bureau of Prisons (BOP), a DOJ component, has no juvenile detention, diversion, or rehabilitation facilities. Federal judges and magistrates, for whom juvenile cases represent 2 percent or less of their caseload, hear juvenile cases along with all others. Native youth processed at the Federal level, along with their families and Tribes, face significant challenges, such as great physical distance between reservations and Federal facilities and institutions, and cultural differences with federal personnel involved in Federal prosecution. If juveniles are detained through the Federal system, it is through contract with State and local facilities, which may be several States away from the juvenile's reservation.

> Within Federal juvenile detention facilities for misdemeanor violations operated in Indian country by the Office of Justice Services (OJS), a component of the Bureau of Indian Affairs (BIA), secondary educational services are either lacking or entirely non-existent. Officials of the Federal Bureau of Indian Education, which is statutorily responsible for providing secondary educational services and programs within OJS juvenile deten-

tion centers, confirmed for the Commission that Congress has not appropriated any Federal funds for this purpose in recent years. This means that Native children behind bars are not receiving any classroom teaching or other educational instruction or services at all.

INDIAN LAW AND ORDER COMMISSION, A ROADMAP FOR MAKING NATIVE AMERICA SAFER 155 (2013). The Commission also recommended that tribes be authorized to remove themselves from federal Indian country juvenile jurisdiction under sections 1152 and 1153 entirely or in part. Why might a tribe choose *not* to exit federal juvenile jurisdiction entirely? Might some tribes be concerned that they lack the resources to deal with the most serious offenders? Recall that under the Commission's recommendations, federal criminal laws of general applicability would continue to apply within Indian country, even after a tribe withdrew from federal jurisdiction under sections 1152 and 1153.

c.   Implications of Federal Criminal Jurisdiction Statutes for Tribal Jurisdiction

As you will recall from *Talton v. Mayes* and *United States v. Wheeler*, presented and discussed in Ch. 3, Sec. B.1, and *United States v. Lara*, presented and discussed in Ch. 3, Sec. C.2, Indian nations exercise inherent criminal jurisdiction over Indians that need not be conferred by the United States. While the United States claims the power to divest tribes of such jurisdiction, the Indian law canons of construction suggest that courts will find such divestment only if Congress clearly indicates its intent to produce that result. Only one of the federal statutes addressing criminal jurisdiction is explicit about the existence of concurrent tribal jurisdiction. Since the Indian Country Crimes Act, 18 U.S.C. § 1152, expressly excludes from federal jurisdiction crimes by Indians against non-Indians where the Indian was already punished by the laws of the tribe, that statute must not have preempted tribal jurisdiction over the same offenses. Thus, tribes clearly have concurrent jurisdiction over Indian Country Crimes Act offenses. The language of the Major Crimes Act, 18 U.S.C. § 1153, is notably less clear about its effect on tribal jurisdiction. Yet the legislative history of the Major Crimes Act strongly suggests that it was not intended to be preemptive of tribal authority. While there are critical remarks about the tribal custom of the blood feud in the legislative debates and a statement by the sponsor of the Act that "the law of the tribe, . . . is just no law at all," 16 CONG. REC. 934 (1885), the Act should be read in light of the fact that Congress had rejected a similar bill in 1874 because it conflicted with the exercise of tribal jurisdiction:

> The Indians, while their tribal relations subsist, generally maintain law, customs, and usages of their own for the punishment of offenses. They have no knowledge of the laws of the United States, and the attempt to enforce their own ordinances might bring them in direct conflict with existing statutes and subject them to prosecution for their violations.

S. REP. No. 367, 43d Cong., 1st Sess. (1874), *quoted in* FELIX S. COHEN, HANDBOOK OF FEDERAL INDIAN LAW 147 n.222 (1942). The original bill proposed in 1885 had provided that Indians committing any of the enumerated offenses "shall be tried therefor in the same courts and in the same manner *and not otherwise*" (emphasis added). The bill was amended to strike the italicized phrase, the sponsor of the amendment explaining:

> The effect of this modification will be to give the courts of the United States concurrent jurisdiction with the Indian courts in the Indian country. But if these words be not struck out, all jurisdiction of these offenses will be taken from the existing tribunals of the Indian country. I think it sufficient that the courts of the United States should have concurrent jurisdiction in these cases.

16 CONG. REC. 934 (1885). The amended portion of this part of the Major Crimes Act is now found at 18 U.S.C. § 3242, a provision which therefore originally was enacted with the predecessor of 18 U.S.C. § 1153.

In *Talton v. Mayes*, 163 U.S. 376 (1896), set forth and discussed in Ch. 3, Sec. B.1, the Supreme Court sustained the murder conviction of an Indian imposed by the courts of the Cherokee Nation, which, as a result of a long evolution, were patterned after Anglo-American models and employed a written criminal code. *See generally* RENNARD STRICKLAND, FIRE AND SPIRITS: CHEROKEE LAW FROM CLANS TO COURT (1975). The fact that the United States Supreme Court did not question the Cherokee courts' authority to hear a murder case, even after passage of the Major Crimes Act, probably reflects the fact that by treaties and statute, the Cherokee were guaranteed the right to enact laws necessary for their public welfare. *See, e.g.*, Treaty with the Cherokees, July 19, 1866, art. XIII, 14 Stat. 803, discussed above. In the 1890 act establishing the Territory of Oklahoma, Congress provided "That the judicial tribunals of the Indian nations shall retain exclusive jurisdiction in all civil and criminal cases arising in the country in which members of the Nation by nativity or by adoption shall be the only parties. . . . "

Where such treaty-based or statutory recognition of tribal authority over major crimes is lacking, the Supreme Court has more recently suggested in dicta that the Major Crimes Act preempts tribal court jurisdiction over serious crimes committed by tribal members. In *Oliphant v. Suquamish Indian Tribe*, 435 U.S. 191, 203 n.14 (1978), then Justice Rehnquist commented:

> The Major Crimes Act provides that Indians committing any of the enumerated offenses "shall be subject to the same laws and penalties as all other persons committing any of the above offenses, *within the exclusive jurisdiction of the United States*." (Emphasis added.) While the question has never been directly addressed by this Court, Courts of Appeals have read this language to exclude tribal jurisdiction over the Indian offender. *See, e.g., Sam v. United States*, 385 F.2d 213, 214 (CA10 1967); *Felicia v. United States*, 495 F.2d 353, 354 (CA8 1974). We have no reason to decide today whether jurisdiction under the Major Crimes Act is exclusive. . . .

> . . . The issue of exclusive jurisdiction over major crimes was mooted for all practical purposes by the passage of the Indian Civil Rights Act of 1968 which limits the punishment that can be imposed by Indian tribal courts to a term of 6 months or a fine of $500 [since increased to 1 year and $5,000].

Similarly, in *United States v. Antelope*, 430 U.S. 641, 642 n.2 (1977), the Court without any further analysis or support wrote "[e]xcept for the offenses enumerated in the Major Crimes Act, all crimes committed by enrolled Indians against other Indians within Indian country are subject to the jurisdiction of tribal courts. 18 U.S.C. § 1152."

Was the Major Crimes Act intended to preempt tribal jurisdiction? Remember that the Indian Country Crimes Act, 18 U.S.C. § 1152, clearly does not do so. Yet, *both* provisions start out by referring to crimes within the "exclusive jurisdiction of the United States" (section 1153) or "the sole and exclusive jurisdiction of the United States" (section 1152). Justice Rehnquist suggested (but did not decide) in a footnote in *Oliphant* that the use of this phrase "exclusive jurisdiction of the United States" in the Major Crimes Act meant that Congress intended to preempt tribal court criminal jurisdiction over serious felonies covered by the Act. In light of the use of a similar phrase in section 1152, could that result really have been the intended meaning? The Ninth Circuit was required to confront the preemptive effect of section 1153 on tribal criminal jurisdiction in the following case, and looked beyond the earlier dicta.

Wetsit v. Stafne, 44 F.3d 823 (9th Cir. 1995): Wetsit, a member of the Fort Peck Tribes, was accused of killing her common law husband, another tribal member, on the Fort Peck Reservation. After she was acquitted of voluntary manslaughter for the killing by a federal court jury in a Major Crimes Act prosecution, the tribe initiated a manslaughter prosecution. She was convicted in tribal court, sentenced to a year incarceration, fined $2,500, and ordered to participate in mental health treatment and a domestic abuse program. Thereafter, she sought federal habeas corpus contesting the Tribe's jurisdiction over the offense. Specifically, she argued that the federal courts had exclusive jurisdiction over Major Crimes Act offenses and that tribal jurisdiction was therefore preempted by federal law. The Ninth Circuit rejected her argument, holding that tribal criminal jurisdiction over felonies covered by 18 U.S.C. § 1153 is concurrent.

Insofar as Wetsit rested her argument on the exclusivity of federal jurisdiction under 18 U.S.C. § 1153, the Ninth Circuit rejected the premise of her complaint. It wrote:

> That the tribes retain jurisdiction over crimes within the Major Crimes Act is the conclusion already reached by distinguished authorities on the subject. It has been noted for example that "the great majority of tribes have for many years exercised jurisdiction over the crime of theft, which duplicates larceny, a crime rather surprisingly included in the original Major Crimes Act." William C. Canby, Jr., AMERICAN INDIAN LAW IN A NUTSHELL 135 (2d ed. 1988). Such a practice was, indeed, necessary because federal prosecution of the crime of theft on reservations was "virtually nonexistent." *Id.* at 106. Without the exercise of this jurisdiction by a tribe many crimes on a reservation would still go unpunished. D. Getches, ed., *National American Indian Court Judges Association, Indian Courts in the Future* 33–35 (1978), quoted in DAVID H. GETCHES AND CHARLES F. WILKINSON, FEDERAL INDIAN LAW: CASES AND MATERIALS 403 (2nd ed. 1986). Logic also points in the same direction because federal jurisdiction under the Major Crimes Act permits conviction of the lesser offenses included within the crime specified, and to hold that the tribal jurisdiction is thereby

preempted would preempt a large part of a tribe's criminal jurisdiction. See F. COHEN, HANDBOOK OF FEDERAL INDIAN LAW 339–41 (1982 ed.).

Jurisdiction over Wetsit's offense existed in the tribal court of the Fort Peck Tribes despite her acquittal under the Major Crimes Act. As Brandeis long ago observed, "responsibility is the great developer." See ALPHEUS THOMAS MASON, BRANDEIS, A FREE MAN'S LIFE (1946) 642; cf. 281. Retention of this jurisdiction by the tribes can only increase their responsibility for efficient and fair justice.

For reasons more fully explained in the *Wheeler* case (*see* Ch. 3, Sec. B.1), the Ninth Circuit also rejected Wetsit's claim that tribal prosecution constituted double jeopardy.

NOTES ON CONCURRENT TRIBAL JURISDICTION OVER "MAJOR" CRIMES AND DOUBLE JEOPARDY

1. **Tribal Criminal Jurisdiction Revisited:** Recall that *Oliphant v. Suquamish Indian Tribe*, 435 U.S. 191 (1978), set forth and discussed in Ch. 3, Sec. C.1, held that Indian tribes have no inherent criminal jurisdiction over non-Indians based on a somewhat tortured analysis of the history of tribal jurisdiction. The Court found a tacit assumption that the historical lack of such jurisdiction rendered its exercise inconsistent with a tribe's dependent status. Jettisoning the historical methodology employed in *Oliphant*, the Court in *Duro v. Reina*, 495 U.S. 676 (1990), also set forth and discussed in Ch. 3, Sec. C.1, nevertheless expanded the *Oliphant* holding to limit tribal criminal jurisdiction over nonmember Indians. While the holding of *Oliphant* remains substantially unchanged, Congress purported to overturn prospectively the result of *Duro* in the 1990 amendments to the Indian Civil Rights Act, 25 U.S.C. § 1301, thereby leaving tribes with criminal jurisdiction over all Indians, but not non-Indians. This statute was upheld as against a double jeopardy challenge in *United States v. Lara*. Questions remain about the validity of the statute as against equal protection and due process challenges. *See* Note 2 in Ch. 3, Sec. C.1. Finally, in 2013, Congress enacted amendments to the Violence Against Women Act that authorize tribes, under certain conditions, to exercise criminal jurisdiction over non-Indians who commit specified crimes of domestic violence, dating violence, or violation of domestic violence restraining orders against Indian victims. As discussed in Ch. 3, Sec. C.1, the defendant must have sufficient ties to the prosecuting tribal community, and the prosecuting tribe must include non-Indians in the jury pool and afford the defendant the rights provided under the Tribal Law and Order Act (see Note 2, *infra*) and all those constitutional rights "whose protection is necessary under the Constitution of the United States in order for Congress to recognize and affirm the inherent power of the participating tribe to exercise special domestic violence criminal jurisdiction over the defendant." Pub. L. 113-4, Title IX.

2. **Tribal Efforts to Prosecute Major Crimes:** The Indian Civil Rights Act of 1968 (ICRA) expressly limited punishment options, but not the crimes, available to tribal courts. The initial limitation enacted in 1968 as part of 25 U.S.C. § 1302(7) limited tribal criminal punishments to a term of not more than 6 months or a fine of not more than $500 for any one offense. In 1986, Congress amended 25 U.S.C.

§ 1302(7) to permit tribal courts to impose sentences of up to one year and fines up to $5,000 for any one offense. Tribes in fact have always exercised some concurrent jurisdiction over lesser Major Crimes Act offenses. For example, many tribes regularly prosecuted theft even though larceny was a Major Crimes Act offense until 1984, when Congress substituted felony theft for larceny in the Major Crimes Act. The increase in the permissible penalties occasioned by the 1986 amendments to the Indian Civil Rights Act encouraged tribes to take concurrent jurisdiction over more Major Crimes Act offenses. *See, e.g.*, Makah Criminal Code § 5.1.04 (criminal homicide provision), available at http://www.narf.org/nill/Codes/makahcode/makahlawt5.htm. Furthermore, in 1987, Assistant Secretary for Indian Affairs Ross Swimmer issued a decision stating that henceforth the BIA would approve tribal law and order codes including crimes covered by the Major Crimes Act, based on a legal analysis and "the inadequacy of prosecutions of major crimes in the federal courts." Letter from Ross Swimmer, Assistant Secretary-Indian Affairs to Peter J. Sfarrazza (on behalf of the Washoe Tribe), April 8, 1987. The problem of federal prosecutorial declination has continued. For example, from 2005–2009, U.S. Attorneys declined to prosecute 52% of reservation violent crimes, including 67% of crimes of sexual violence.

As tribal legal systems continued to grow in the 1990s, and some tribes acquired the capacity to detain offenders for longer periods, tribal prosecutors began to pursue lengthier sentences for more serious offenses, by charging multiple crimes and "stacking" consecutive one-year sentences. *See Miranda v. Anchondo*, 684 F.3d 844 (9th Cir. 2011) (§ 1302(7) allows "stacking" for each discrete criminal violation). The Tribal Law and Order Act of 2010 further enlarged tribal sentencing authority by amending § 1302(7) to allow tribes to impose sentences of up to three years imprisonment and $15,000 per offense, subject to a cap of nine years imprisonment for combined offenses, where:

- the defendant has already been convicted of the same offense or the offense is one where the penalty is greater than one year under United States or any state law;

- the tribe guarantees defendants the right to effective assistance of counsel as specified under federal law;

- the tribe provides defense counsel at government expense to indigent defendants, and that defense counsel is licensed to practice law in any jurisdiction that applies appropriate professional licensing standards and "effectively ensures the competence and professional responsibility of its licensed attorneys;"

- the tribal judge who imposes the sentence has "sufficient legal training" and is licensed to practice in any jurisdiction in the United States;

- the tribe publicizes its criminal laws and rules, including rules on the recusal of judges;

- the tribe maintains an audio or written recording of the proceedings.

The courts have not yet determined whether these procedural requirements only apply for the expanded sentencing authority under the TLOA, or if they also apply to stacked sentences that, combined, last longer than one year. In *Miranda v.*

Achondo, involving a defendant who had been sentenced before TLOA, the court suggested that the requirements might apply to stacked sentences as well. *Id.* at 849, n.4.

A separate provision of TLOA establishes a pilot project that would allow tribal courts to sentence their longer-term defendants to federal Bureau of Prison facilities, rather than BIA or tribal jails. Tribes are obviously not required to opt for enhanced sentencing authority, and may prefer (for reasons of cost and/or policy) to continue functioning under the one year/$5,000 limit per offense. For example, some tribes, such as the Navajo Nation, have deliberately chosen to emphasize traditional peacemaking over incarceration, even for some serious offenses. *See* Chief Justice Robert Yazzie, *Healing as Justice: The Navajo Response to Crime in* JUSTICE AS HEALING: INDIGENOUS WAYS 121 (Wanda D. McCaslin, ed., 2005). It is unclear how the newest ICRA amendments will affect current disputes regarding stacking of one-year sentences, and how many tribal bar associations will satisfy the require- ments for enhanced sentencing authority.

A 2012 report by the Government Accountability Office found that no tribes had opted for the enhanced sentencing authority allowed under the Tribal Law and Order Act, and that funding limitations were the main reason. See U.S. Gov't Accountability Office, GAO-12-658R, *Tribal Law and Order Act: None of the Surveyed Tribes Reported Exercising the New Sentencing Authority, and the Department of Justice Could Clarify Tribal Eligibility for Certain Grant Funds* (2012), available at http://www.gao.gov/products/GAO-12-658R. Since that time, a few tribes, including the Cherokee Nation (Oklahoma) and the Tulalip Tribes (Washington) have amended their codes to meet the requirements for imposing the longer sentences authorized by TLOA. To facilitate greater tribal control over criminal justice, including the capacity to impose longer sentences, the Indian Law and Order Commission recommended fundamental alteration of the system of federal funding for tribal justice systems, currently split between the Departments of Justice and Interior. *See* INDIAN LAW AND ORDER COMMISSION, A ROADMAP FOR MAKING NATIVE AMERICA SAFER 65–96 (2013), available at http://www.aisc.ucla.edu/ iloc/report/files/Chapter_3_STJ.pdf. For example, the Commission recommended consolidation of funding in the Department of Justice, greater emphasis on base funding (as compared with grant funding), and funding for tribal courts at a level of parity with state courts. For further discussion of the relative roles of Justice and Interior in contemporary Indian affairs, see Sec. 6, this chapter.

Do the conditions attached to the enhanced sentencing provisions of TLOA force tribes to conform to a non-Indian, adversarial system of justice, thereby undermin- ing any gains to tribal sovereignty from greater tribal capacity to manage more serious criminal offenses? Once a tribal justice system is proceeding against a defendant on an adversarial basis, do international human rights norms suggest the need to provide rights as specified in TLOA? *See* STEFAN TRECHSEL & SARAH SUMMERS, HUMAN RIGHTS IN CRIMINAL PROCEEDINGS (2006). Over the past several decades, tribes have found ways to operate dual court systems, partly to satisfy the different preferences of their community members. For example, an adversarial tribal criminal justice system may co-exist with a more traditional peacemaking or wellness court, with defendants given the option to waive their rights to an adversarial proceeding and consent to the alternative. *See, e.g.*, Mississippi Band of

Choctaw Code, Title XXIV, Choctaw Peacemaker Code, Choctaw Itti-kana-ikbi Code, § 24-1-8, available at http://www.choctaw.org/government/tribal_code/Title%2024%20-%20Choctaw%20Peacemaker%20Code.pdf (allowing transfer of criminal cases to Itti-kana-ikbi (Peacemaking) Court upon consent of the parties). Does the possibility of waiver by individual defendants diminish or obviate any threats to tribal sovereignty from the demands of TLOA?

Apart from enhanced sentencing for tribes, TLOA attempted to address the problem of inadequate federal prosecution of Indian country offenses in two ways: by requiring federal prosecutors to supply reports on the cases where they decline prosecution (§ 212), and by authorizing U.S. Attorneys to appoint tribal prosecutors as special federal prosecutors for Indian country offenses (§ 213). Because declination has always been viewed as a matter of prosecutorial discretion, not subject to reporting or judicial review, the new requirement was designed to make the federal system more transparent and accountable to tribal communities. The use of tribal prosecutors in federal court was also designed to empower tribes to establish priorities for federal criminal proceedings. Are these changes to the federal system an adequate substitute for expanded tribal jurisdiction over criminal activity in Indian country?

  3. Double Jeopardy, Double Punishment and Tribal Criminal Jurisdiction: This would be a good time to review *United States v. Wheeler*, presented and discussed in Ch. 3, Sec. B.1. While *Wheeler* plainly holds that the double jeopardy guarantee affords no constitutional protection against multiple trials and punishments in federal and tribal courts, 18 U.S.C. § 1152 does except from its coverage "any Indian committing any offense in the Indian country who has been punished by the local law of the tribe." This statutory clause provides limited protection for Indians, but not non-Indians, from multiple punishment by both tribal and federal courts. *United States v. La Plant*, 156 F. Supp. 660 (D. Mont. 1957). The Major Crimes Act, 18 U.S.C. § 1153, contains no similar exception. As *Wheeler* notes, the existence of dual sovereignty and concurrent criminal jurisdiction between federal and state governments poses absolutely no issue of double jeopardy since under the holdings of *Abbate* and *Bartkus*, both cited and discussed in *Wheeler*, each government is regarded as a separate sovereign and the constitutional guarantee against double jeopardy is only thought to protect against multiple punishment or multiple trials for the same crime by the same sovereignty.

Notwithstanding the *Wheeler* decision on double jeopardy at least two vexing double jeopardy problems remain. First, as noted in footnote 26 of the *Wheeler* opinion, Courts of Indian Offenses still exist for more than a dozen tribes, many of which are in Oklahoma. Unlike tribal courts, Courts of Indian Offenses are established and governed by *federal* regulations found in 25 C.F.R. Part 11. These courts are the descendants of the Courts of Indian Offenses sustained in *United States v. Clapox*, discussed in Ch. 1, Sec. D.2. Under 25 C.F.R. § 11.201(a) "[e]ach magistrate shall be appointed by the Assistant Secretary-Indian Affairs or his or her designee *subject to confirmation by a majority vote of the tribal governing body of the tribe occupying the Indian country over which the court has jurisdiction.*" (Emphasis added.) Magistrates of the Courts of Indian Offenses are technically federal employees and are paid from federal, rather than tribal, sources. Nevertheless, under 25 C.F.R. § 11.202, the governing body of the affected tribe can file a written recommendation to the Assistant Secretary that any magistrate be removed, although it cannot remove him or her directly. Furthermore, CFR Courts exist on Indian reservations today at the sufferance of tribes since under 25 C.F.R. 11.100(c) any affected tribe can displace its CFR Court by adopting a law and order code and assuming primary judicial responsibility. Should CFR Courts be seen as tribal or federal courts for purposes of *Wheeler*?

More significantly, recall that the so-called *Duro* fix legislation amended 25 U.S.C. § 1301(2) to overturn the holding of *Duro* that tribes lacked inherent tribal criminal jurisdiction over nonmember Indians. Congress did not phrase the legislation as a delegation of authority, but, rather, merely purported to confirm the very tribal jurisdiction the *Duro* Court held did not exist. Nonetheless, the lower federal courts wrestled with whether the statute delegated or confirmed jurisdiction and whether the fact that the source of the authority was a federal statute might mean that a prior tribal criminal prosecution of a nonmember Indian might bar subsequent federal prosecution for the same crime under double jeopardy. In *United States v. Lara*, 541 U.S. 193 (2004), the United States Supreme Court construed the statute as a confirmation of inherent tribal authority, rather than a delegation. Furthermore, the Court found the statute, as so construed, to be a constitutional exercise of Congress's power over Indian affairs. In light of those determinations, the Court concluded that the federal prosecution following a tribal conviction was permissible under the double jeopardy clause. Should this holding come as any surprise, given that a state's criminal jurisdiction under Public Law 280 has presented no double jeopardy problems when the federal government later prosecutes the same individual for the same underlying conduct? For a fuller discussion of *Lara*, see Ch. 3, Sec. C.2.

WALKER v. RUSHING
United States Court of Appeals, Eighth Circuit
898 F.2d 672 (1990)

LAY, CHIEF JUDGE.

On August 24, 1987, Ann Walker, a member of the Omaha Tribe of Nebraska, was driving on a public road within the boundaries of the Omaha Indian Reservation when she struck and killed two persons, also members of the Omaha Tribe. The tribe brought two counts of criminal homicide against Walker in the Omaha Tribal Court pursuant to Title III, Section 3-4-8 of the Omaha Tribal Code.[7] After the tribal court denied her motion to dismiss for lack of subject matter jurisdiction, Walker applied to federal district court for a writ of habeas corpus pursuant to 25 U.S.C. § 1303 (1982). The district court granted the writ, ruling that Walker's charged offense lay within the exclusive jurisdiction of the federal courts under the Major Crimes Act, 18 U.S.C. § 1153 (1982). The tribe appeals; we reverse and vacate the grant of the writ.

---

[7] [1] Section 3-4-8 provides: "(1) A person is guilty of criminal homicide if he purposely, knowingly, recklessly or negligently causes the death of another human being."

Statutory Background

Congress enacted the Major Crimes Act in 1885. In *Ex parte Crow Dog*, 109 U.S. 556, 572, (1883), the Supreme Court held that in the absence of explicit congressional authorization a federal court lacked jurisdiction to try an Indian for a crime committed against another Indian within Indian country. Congress responded by extending certain provisions of federal enclave law, including the offense of manslaughter, to conduct by Indians against other Indians within Indian country. 18 U.S.C. § 1153; *see also Keeble v. United States*, 412 U.S. 205, 209–10, 93 S. Ct. 1993, 36 L. Ed. 2d 844 (1973). In passing the Major Crimes Act, Congress intended that no Indians would go unpunished for committing what Congress considered to be the most serious crimes. *Id.*

In 1953, Congress altered this jurisdictional grant. *See* Act of Aug. 15, 1953, ch. 505, 67 Stat. 588, *codified in part at* 18 U.S.C. § 1162 (Public Law 280). Public Law 280 gave certain states the right to exercise criminal jurisdiction over specified Indian country within their respective borders "to the same extent that such State or Territory has jurisdiction over offenses committed elsewhere within the State or Territory * * *." 18 U.S.C. § 1162(a).[8] Public Law 280 specifically granted the State of Nebraska the right to exercise criminal jurisdiction over all Indian country within its borders. *Id.* Congress expressly repealed the Major Crimes Act insofar as it applied to those areas covered by 18 U.S.C. § 1162(a). 18 U.S.C. § 1162(c).

In 1968, Congress once again altered the jurisdictional scheme by authorizing the United States to "accept retrocession by any State of all or any measure of criminal or civil jurisdiction, or both, acquired by such State pursuant to [Public Law 280]." Act of April 11, 1968, Title IV, § 403, 82 Stat. 79, codified at 25 U.S.C. § 1323(a). The United States Secretary of Interior was designated by the President to accept such retrocession on behalf of the United States. Exec. Order No. 11,435, 33 Fed. Reg. 17,339 (1968). Pursuant to 25 U.S.C. § 1323(a), the Nebraska legislature passed a resolution offering to retrocede to the United States all criminal jurisdiction over offenses committed by Indians in Indian country located in Thurston County, Nebraska (which included both the Omaha and Winnebago Indian Reservations). Res. 37, 80th Neb. Leg. (1969), *quoted in full in Omaha Tribe v. Village of Walthill*, 334 F. Supp. 823, 827 n. 6 (D. Neb. 1971), *aff'd per curiam*, 460 F.2d 1327 (8th Cir. 1972), *cert. denied*, 409 U.S. 1107, 93 S. Ct. 898, 34 L. Ed. 2d 687 (1973). However, Nebraska's offer contained an exception: "That the retrocession of jurisdiction * * * shall not apply to any offenses involving the operation of motor vehicles on public roads or highways." *Id.* The Secretary of Interior accepted this offer of retrocession as to the Omaha Tribe, and the retrocession was upheld as valid by this court. *Omaha Tribe*, 460 F.2d at 1328.[9]

---

[8] [3] It has long been held that the states are severely limited in exercising jurisdiction over Indians within Indian country absent authorization by Congress. *E.g., McClanahan v. Arizona State Tax Comm'n*, 411 U.S. 164, 168–69, (1973); *Worcester v. Georgia*, 31 U.S. (6 Pet.) 515, 557 (1832); F. Cohen, Cohen's handbook of Federal Indian Law 349–52 (1982).

[9] [5] In *Omaha Tribe* the United States District Court for the District of Nebraska held that 25 U.S.C. § 1323(a) authorized the United States to accept any part of the jurisdiction offered to it by Nebraska. Therefore, the court upheld the power of the Secretary of Interior to accept the Nebraska legislature's offer to retrocede jurisdiction over the Omaha Tribe and to reject the legislature's offer to retrocede

Discussion

An Indian tribe's power to punish members who commit crimes within Indian country is a fundamental attribute of the tribe's sovereignty. *United States v. Wheeler*, 435 U.S. 313, 326–27, (1978); *Talton v. Mayes*, 163 U.S. 376, 379–80 (1896). Unlike certain other aspects of tribal sovereignty, this power was not "implicitly lost by virtue of [the tribe's] dependent status." This power may be limited only by a treaty or federal statute. Walker argues, and the district court held, that the Major Crimes Act imposes such a limit by divesting the tribal court of jurisdiction over offenses that are equivalent to the enumerated "Major Crimes."[10]

We need not decide this issue, however. In holding that the Major Crimes Act places a limitation on tribal jurisdiction, the district court reasoned that the federal jurisdiction authorized by the Major Crimes Act extends to Walker's conduct. The tribe, and the United States as amicus curiae, urge that this premise is erroneous because Walker's conduct involved a motor vehicle on a Nebraska public road and is therefore a matter that was never retroceded back to the federal government pursuant to 25 U.S.C. § 1323(a). We agree.

Because Nebraska withheld motor vehicle matters from its offer of retrocession, the federal government's acceptance of retrocession did not reestablish Major Crimes Act jurisdiction over such matters. Walker stipulated that the offense with which she is charged involves the "operation of a motor vehicle on public roads or highways" within the meaning of the exception contained in Resolution 37. We agree with the United States that Nebraska's retention of jurisdiction over "*any offenses involving the operation of motor vehicles * * *,*" cannot be read as limiting the exception to minor traffic offenses. Moreover, even if we were to find that the exception applies merely to offenses that specifically include operation of a motor vehicle as an element, this would not affect our conclusion because Nebraska has specifically enacted a statute penalizing "motor vehicle homicide." Neb. Rev. Stat. app. § 28–306 (1985). Therefore, even if the Major Crimes Act could be construed as imposing a limitation on tribal jurisdiction, the limitation cannot affect this case. The Major Crimes Act simply does not apply here.

Although Walker's brief cites only the Major Crimes Act as an obstacle to tribal jurisdiction, we agree with the district court's conclusion that Public Law 280 did not itself divest Indian tribes of their sovereign power to punish their own members for violations of tribal law. Nothing in the wording of Public Law 280 or its legislative history precludes concurrent tribal authority. F. Cohen, *Cohen's Handbook of Federal Indian Law* 344. As both the Supreme Court and this court have made clear, limitations on an Indian tribe's power to punish its own members must be clearly set forth by Congress. *Quiver*, 241 U.S. at 606; *Greywater v. Joshua*, 846 F.2d 486, 489 (8th Cir. 1988); *see also White Mountain Apache Tribe v. Bracker*, 448 U.S. 136, 143–44, 100 S. Ct. 2578, 65 L. Ed. 2d 665 (1980) (ambiguities in federal law are generously construed in favor of tribal sovereignty). We find no such clear

jurisdiction over the Winnebago Tribe. *Omaha Tribe*, 334 F. Supp. at 835. We upheld the district court's ruling in a per curiam opinion. 460 F.2d at 1328.

[10] [6] The Supreme Court has expressly acknowledged this issue on three occasions, but has not yet resolved it. *See United States v. John*, 437 U.S. 634, 651 n. 21 (1978); *Wheeler*, 435 U.S. at 325 n. 22; *Oliphant v. Suquamish Indian Tribe*, 435 U.S. 191, 203 n. 14 (1978).

expression of congressional intent in Public Law 280.

Conclusion

No applicable federal law ousts the Omaha Tribal Court of jurisdiction in this case. We therefore find no basis for the district court's issuance of the writ of habeas corpus to prohibit the tribe's prosecution of Walker. The order of the district court is reversed and the writ is vacated.

NOTES ON CONCURRENT TRIBAL CRIMINAL JURISDICTION UNDER PUBLIC LAW 280 AND LIKE STATUTES

1. **Concurrent Tribal Criminal Jurisdiction and Public Law 280:** Neither Public Law 280 nor many other federal statutes transferring the criminal jurisdiction for crimes in Indian country to the states expressly address their preemptive effect on tribal jurisdiction. Since most of these statutes, like the Kansas and Iowa statutes, were enacted precisely because the tribes were not then formally exercising such jurisdiction through any tribal courts, the question simply was not a salient one when the statutes were enacted. Furthermore, since the federal government long refused to fund tribal courts in Public Law 280 jurisdictions or other reservations affected by similar statutes on the theory (not always realized in practice) that law enforcement was already adequately served through state jurisdiction, tribal courts were quite late in developing in these areas. Thus, the question of concurrent tribal jurisdiction rarely arose under Public Law 280 or similar statutes. As affected tribes westernized their governments and acquired more resources from gaming and otherwise with which to fund tribal courts, such questions have emerged with far greater frequency. Often tribes have chosen to undertake such expenditures because they are dissatisfied with the poor level of protection provided by local and state authorities and the discriminatory conduct that sometimes has accompanied state and local policing of Indian reservations. *See generally* Duane Champagne & Carole Goldberg, Captured Justice: Native Nations and Public Law 280 (2011).

The *Walker* case clearly holds that nothing in Public Law 280 preempts the exercise of concurrent tribal criminal jurisdiction on Public Law 280 reservations. Note that the major point of Public Law 280 was to divest the federal government of fiscal responsibility for such policing, not to curtail the long-recognized inherent sovereignty of the tribes over such matters. Unlike the intent behind Public Law 280, the Kansas and Iowa statutes delegating criminal jurisdiction to the states were partially motivated by the lack of any western-style tribal court exercising criminal jurisdiction over such matters. These statutes, therefore, were meant to fill a void in law enforcement. Could those affected tribes decide to exercise criminal jurisdiction today by creating tribal courts with concurrent criminal jurisdiction? For example, the Meskwaki Tribe in Iowa established a western-style Tribal Court in 2004. Could it do so without express congressional repeal of the 1948 federal statute that delegated criminal jurisdiction to the State of Iowa over the reservation?

2. Double Jeopardy Issues: The double jeopardy clauses of the United States Constitution and the Indian Civil Rights Act (25 U.S.C. § 1302(3)) permit multiple prosecutions so long as the prosecutions are carried out by separate sovereigns. The United States Supreme Court has held that Indian nations are separate from the federal government for this purpose, and the same reasoning applies to the states. *See United States v. Lara*, Ch. 3, Sec. C.2; *United States v. Wheeler*, Ch. 3, Sec. B.1. Thus, multiple prosecutions by states and tribes for the same offense should not raise federal double jeopardy issues. Nevertheless, about half of all states have enacted laws that either limit or extinguish their power to prosecute a defendant after another sovereign has already done so. While most of these laws fail to mention Indian nations as among those sovereigns whose prior exercise of criminal jurisdiction will bar the state's own prosecution, some state courts have interpreted language such as "territories" and "any jurisdiction within the United States" to include tribes. *See, e.g., Hill v. Eppolito*, 5 A.D.3d 854 (N.Y. App. Div. 2004); *Booth v. Alaska*, 903 P.2d 1079 (Alaska Ct. App. 1995); *People v. Morgan*, 785 P.2d 1294 (Colo. 1990). *But see Washington v. Moses*, 37 P.3d 1216 (Wash. 2002) (refusing to include tribes within the scope of the double jeopardy statute's reference to prosecution by any "other state or country"). Should tribes in Public Law 280 and similar jurisdictions use their concurrent criminal jurisdiction to try to foreclose prosecution of Indian country offenders under state law, especially state law that may be unpopular, such as California's "three strikes" provisions? Remember the sentencing limitations on tribal courts, discussed above. For a thoughtful analysis of double jeopardy issues where states exercise Indian country criminal jurisdiction, see Ross Naughton, *State Statutes Limiting the Dual Sovereignty Doctrine: Tools for Tribes to Reclaim Criminal Jurisdiction Stripped by Public Law 280?*, 55 UCLA L. Rev. 489 (2007).

d. Criminal Jurisdiction, Policing, and Extradition

When courts determine criminal jurisdiction in Indian country, they are establishing the subject matter jurisdiction of the respective courts to adjudicate the crimes in question. Policing authority may sometimes be broader. For example, even though most tribes do not in fact exercise jurisdiction over the serious felonies covered by the Major Crimes Act, tribal police frequently are the first responders to such crimes, particularly on remote reservations. Not infrequently, tribal police officers undertake the initial investigation and, sometimes, make the arrest, ultimately turning any suspect over to federal authorities for prosecution. *E.g., United States v. Boyles*, 57 F.3d 535, 538 n.3 (7th Cir. 1995) (Menominee tribal police officers undertook initial investigation in sexual assault and kidnapping case and turned information over to FBI for further investigation and prosecution). Thus, policing powers may be somewhat greater than the criminal jurisdiction of the sovereign may suggest.

Questions of the scope of police authority often arise when an act that takes place outside Indian country causes state police to follow the suspect or seek to investigate on a reservation where the police cannot invoke state criminal jurisdiction. In such situations, the general test for state authority in Indian country, discussed in section B of this chapter, generally applies — namely whether the state's action infringes on the inherent sovereign power of the tribe to make its own laws and be governed by them.

The most limited action by the police is stopping a suspect to determine whether jurisdiction exists. As you know by now, the Indian or non-Indian status of the suspect can make all the difference. In *United States v. Patch*, 114 F.3d 131 (9th Cir. 1997), for example, the Ninth Circuit upheld the authority of a state police officer to pursue a member of the Colorado River Indian Tribe (CRIT) both on the state highway within the CRIT Reservation and after he exited the vehicle and entered his own front porch on the Reservation, even though it conceded the state had no criminal jurisdiction on the Reservation. While the accused refused to stop because he knew the state officer had no jurisdiction on the Reservation, the Ninth Circuit upheld the stop. It noted that a state highway running through a reservation is subject to overlapping jurisdiction, with state and municipal police authorized to stop and arrest non-Indians. It then held:

> As a practical matter, without a stop and inquiry, it is impossible for an Arizona officer to tell who is operating an offending vehicle. In this case, [the state officer] did not know who was driving the pickup truck. The question therefore is whether [he] had the authority to stop offending vehicles to determine whether he had authority to arrest.

Id. at 133–134. While the county police officer pursued the tribal member to his front porch, the court upheld this action on the grounds that the porch, while private property, was in public view and the pursuit therefore was lawful under the doctrine of hot pursuit. The Ninth Circuit also noted that on many reservations in Arizona, and elsewhere, this problem is resolved through cross-deputization agreements, but that none existed between CRIT and La Paz County, Arizona. In a similar case, the New Mexico Supreme Court followed *Patch* and observed: "Cross-commission agreements are consistent with this State's venerable tradition of cooperation and comity between state and tribal governments, and we encourage San Juan County to enter into such an agreement with the Navajo Nation in order to protect the citizens of this State, who reside both on and off the reservation, from the danger of DWI, a problem which transcends borders." *State v. Harrison*, 238 P.3d 869 (N.M. 2010). What would be the advantage to a state, city, or county that would encourage it to enter into a cross-deputization agreement? What advantages would accrue to the tribe from such an agreement? Are there any disadvantages? Can a cross-deputization agreement alter the basic criminal jurisdiction of the respective parties without congressional approval? For an example of a deputization and mutual law enforcement agreement entered into by the Little Traverse Bay Bands of Odawa Indians and Emmet County, Michigan, and discussion of cooperative law enforcement agreements more generally, see Ch. 3, Sec. E.5. For discussion of policing arrangements on reservations subject to state jurisdiction under Public Law 280 and similar statutes, see Ch. 5, Sec. A.

In the absence of criminal jurisdiction or a cross-deputization agreement, may police go beyond stopping a suspect and turning her over to the proper authorities? What about effecting an arrest or conducting an investigation? Recall that many of the early Indian treaties contained extradition provisions that required tribes to deliver up Indian fugitives for criminal trial by the United States. *E.g.*, Treaty of

Fort Laramie, with the Sioux Nation and Others, Art. 1, 15 Stat. 635; Treaty of Fort Sumner with the Navajo, Art. 1, 15 Stat. 667. What does the routine existence of such extradition provisions suggest about the historic assumptions under the treaty federalism model regarding the scope of federal or state arrest powers in Indian country, even for crimes over which the federal government had jurisdiction? Whatever the historic assumptions, today, the FBI and other federal law enforcement agencies simply assume that they have arrest powers in Indian country and regularly make such arrests without resort to tribal extradition or even seeking cooperation from tribal police. Indeed, the FBI routinely removes accused individuals from tribal custody for federal criminal trial while their cases are pending in tribal courts, thereby interfering with the tribal criminal justice systems. What is the basis for such a claim of federal arrest authority in Indian country? Can federal authorities secure it without tribal consent? Can they exercise it without express federal statutory authorization specifically referencing Indian country?

Problems of policing authority to arrest and investigate are even greater where state or county authorities are involved and the state has not been authorized to exercise criminal jurisdiction under Public Law 280 or a similar statute. In *State v. Harrison*, *supra*, the state police officer followed a suspected drunk driver onto the reservation, administered a field sobriety test (which the suspect failed), and then attempted, unsuccessfully, to secure assistance from the tribal police. Because the Indian suspect could not reach a friend or family member to drive him home, he walked back to his house. Afterward, the county officer secured an arrest warrant, following procedures specified in the Navajo Nation's code. Could the officer have made the arrest on the spot? Until recently it was universally recognized that state and municipal police officers had no authority to arrest Indians, or at least tribal members, in Indian country unless Congress had authorized state criminal jurisdiction through Public Law 280 or a similar statute. A more vexing question has been whether state or local police lacking jurisdiction under such a federal statute have authority to make such arrests following hot pursuit for an off-reservation crime. *Compare State v. Smith*, 268 P.3d 644 (Or. Ct. App. 2011) (permitting arrest after pursuit under state law that permits tribal police to do the same off the reservation), *with State v. Spotted Horse*, 462 N.W.2d 463 (S.D. 1990) (disallowing arrest after pursuit). *See generally* Judith V. Royster & Rory SnowArrow Fausett, *Fresh Pursuit Onto Native American Reservations: State Rights "To Pursue Savage Hostile Indian Marauders Across the Border,"* 59 UNIV. COLO. L. REV. 191 (1988). On those non-Public Law 280 reservations taking the view against such authority, states seeking to arrest Indians found on the reservation for crimes they were accused of committing off the reservation had to seek their extradition through tribal authorities. *E.g., State of Ariz. ex rel. Merrill v. Turtle*, 413 F.2d 683 (9th Cir. 1969). For example, in *Patch*, discussed above, while the Ninth Circuit held that a state officer had lawful authority to stop Patch to ascertain whether he was a tribal member, it clearly recognized that having ascertained his tribal membership the officer was without lawful authority to arrest him on the reservation. In *Harrison*, the county officer resorted to Navajo procedures to effect the arrest, but only after administering a field sobriety test. Did the administration of that test exceed police authority? Should your answer to that question vary depending on whether the Navajo Nation has its own laws regulating the administration of such tests?

How should *Nevada v. Hicks*, 533 U.S. 353 (2001), discussed in Ch. 3, Sec. C, affect the analysis of police arresting and investigative authority in the absence of criminal jurisdiction? While the case was technically about the jurisdiction of a tribal court to entertain a tribal tort and federal Civil Rights Act claim against state conservation officers, the majority opinion, written by Justice Scalia, went considerably beyond the issues posed by the case and suggested that state police officers had the power to execute search warrants on Indian lands and to arrest Indians on the reservation for crimes committed off the reservation over which the state otherwise had subject matter jurisdiction. Ironically, even the facts of the *Hicks* case indicated that state authorities fully understood that they had no such lawful authority on Indian lands, since the state search warrant issued in the case expressly provided that the warrant had no force on the Fallon Reservation and any search thereunder was "subject to obtaining approval from the Fallon Tribal Court in and for the Fallon Paiute-Shoshone Tribes." Notwithstanding the fact that the Nevada court claimed no authority to execute search or arrest warrants in Indian country, Justice Scalia claimed they had it, writing:

> Nothing in the federal statutory scheme prescribes, or even remotely suggests, that state officers cannot enter a reservation (including Indian-fee land) to investigate or prosecute violations of state law occurring off the reservation. To the contrary, 25 U.S.C. § 2806 affirms that "the provisions of this chapter alter neither . . . the law enforcement, investigative, or judicial authority of any . . . State, or political subdivision or agency thereof. . . . "

Id. at 366. Justice O'Connor, in a separate concurring opinion, called this portion of the majority opinion "unmoored from our precedents" and a "sweeping opinion, [that] without cause, undermines the authority of tribes to 'make their own laws and be ruled by them.'" Indeed, seven members of the unanimous Court in separate concurring opinions purported to resolve the case without addressing the question of state jurisdiction unilaterally raised by Justice Scalia. Does that fact suggest that Justice Scalia's dicta, while contained in a designated majority opinion, did not in fact have the support of a majority of the Court?

In *Hicks*, the Fallon Tribe had no treaty. Would the exercise of state search or arrest jurisdiction on the reservation of a tribe that had such a treaty be consistent with the existence of extradition provisions in the treaty? Does not the existence of the extradition provisions assume that states and the federal government generally have no arrest and detention authority over Indians in Indian country, irrespective of the existence of any treaty, without the cooperation of the tribe? Should the existence or non-existence of such a treaty provision make any difference to the scope of the state's arrest power over Indians in Indian country? Ironically, Justice Scalia's opinion in *Hicks* totally ignores the existence of the extradition provisions in the treaties. What model of tribal-federal relations does Justice Scalia's *Hicks* opinion posit?

The force and scope of Justice Scalia's statements in *Hicks* were tested in *State v. Cummings*, 679 N.W.2d 484 (S.D. 2004). Under a pre-*Hicks* South Dakota precedent, *State v. Spotted Horse*, 462 N.W.2d 463 (S.D. 1990), state police lacked authority to arrest an Indian followed into Indian country in hot pursuit for commission of an off-reservation offense. Following *Hicks*, the State of South Dakota argued that such an arrest was valid under that case's holding. The South Dakota Supreme Court declined to overrule its earlier decision, stating that its review of *Hicks* "reveals that its holding does not apply in this case and that the language the State relies upon in support of its argument, quoted above, is insufficient to allow such an incursion on tribal sovereignty, especially without specific direction from the United States Congress or a clear holding by a majority of the Supreme Court." The South Dakota Supreme Court emphasized that *Hicks* was narrowly focused on tribal, not state, jurisdiction, and that here "the State is attempting to extend its jurisdiction into the boundaries of the Tribe's Reservation without consent of the Tribe or a tribal-state compact allowing such jurisdiction" (citing *Williams v. Lee*). Furthermore, the quoted language from Justice Scalia merely acknowledges that federal law doesn't prohibit state law enforcement officers from entering reservations to make arrests for off-reservation offenses, it doesn't show that federal law actually authorizes such action. According to the court, "[O]ur State never effectively asserted jurisdiction over the reservations in South Dakota [under Public Law 280]." As the court noted:

> Nothing in current federal enactments has overruled the general proposition that the State has no jurisdiction to act on the reservations in South Dakota. It is difficult to maintain the proposition that the State, after having failed to effectively assert jurisdiction when given the opportunity by Congress, now suddenly gains that jurisdiction through no action of the State or the Tribe.

679 N.W.2d at 488.

Finally, the court emphasized the fact that Justice Scalia's statements in *Hicks* only attracted two other Justices. In conclusion, the court stated:

> [T]he question in *Hicks* was whether the tribal court had jurisdiction over state officers acting in their individual or official capacity on tribal land. *Hicks* should be construed to address that question only, and in fact, several federal courts have done so. *See, e.g., McDonald v. Means*, 309 F.3d 530 (9th Cir. 2002); *Macarthur v. San Juan County*, 309 F.3d 1216 (10th Cir. 2002); *United States v. Archambault*, 174 F. Supp. 2d 1009 (D.S.D. 2001); *Fidelity and Guaranty Insurance Co. v. Bradley*, 212 F. Supp.2d 163 (W.D.N.C. 2002). The question whether a state officer in fresh pursuit for a crime committed off the reservation has jurisdiction to enter the reservation without tribal permission or a warrant was not squarely before the Court. We decline to usurp the power of the United States Congress to make laws with respect to Native American rights and sovereignty and the authority of the Supreme Court to interpret those laws by relying on dicta from a factually and legally distinguishable case.

Id. at 489. In other states, *Hicks* has been credited with more robust impact on state arresting and investigation powers. In *State v. Clark*, 308 P.3d 590 (Wash. 2013), for example, the Washington Supreme Court affirmed the power of county police to execute a state search warrant on Colville reservation land over which the state had no criminal jurisdiction, for a crime committed elsewhere that the state *did* have authority to prosecute. Colville tribal law included provisions regarding search warrants, and requiring cooperation among state, federal, and tribal police. Nonetheless, relying on *Hicks*, the court upheld the search. Dismissing arguments that statements in *Hicks* about state authority to execute criminal process were dictum, the *Clark* court stated: "Because the *Hicks* Court relied on its discussion of tribal sovereignty and federal preemption to reach its holding, this portion of *Hicks* is binding law." *Clark* also rejected arguments that a majority of Justices had not signed onto this portion of the *Hicks* opinion: "Six members of the Court signed the majority opinion in full; none of these justices withheld their signatures from part II, the portion discussing the execution of the search warrants." The search warrant in *Clark* was arguably a more intrusive act of policing than the hot pursuit arrest in *Cummings*. Review the Supreme Court's opinion in *Hicks*. Which state's highest court, South Dakota's or Washington's, properly interpreted the scope of *Hicks*?

e. Problems

One of the best ways to master the complex federal statutory pattern governing criminal jurisdiction over Indian lands is to establish an analytical framework and then work through a number of hypothetical problems.

Of course, Indian tribes generally have criminal jurisdiction over their reservation unless divested of that authority by federal statute or to the extent that the federal courts find it inconsistent with their dependent status, as in *Oliphant*. As *Lara* reminds us, however, Congress can augment their criminal authority by statute, as well.

One of the first questions that must be answered for any criminal jurisdictional problem is whether Congress has altered the basic jurisdictional scheme for the reservation or land area in question through Public Law 280 or some other specific statutory delegation of criminal jurisdiction to the state. If such a statute exists, care must be taken to carefully examine its scope and effect on concurrent federal or tribal jurisdiction, as *Walker v. Rushing* and the cases construing Public Law 280 illustrate.

In areas of Indian country not governed by Public Law 280 or some other specific statutory transfer of criminal jurisdiction to the states, the jurisdictional pattern will be governed by the crime charged, the locus of the crime, and the status of the parties. *See* Tim Vollman, *Criminal Jurisdiction in Indian Country: Tribal Sovereignty and Defendants' Rights in Conflict*, 22 Kan. L. Rev. 387 (1974). In analyzing any jurisdictional question, it is worthwhile to approach the inquiry in an orderly fashion. The first question that should be asked is whether the crime in question is a federal crime of nationwide application, such as assault on a federal officer in the performance of duties, or, rather, constitutes an *enclave* crime, such as murder, rape, or theft, that normally would be prosecuted by state authorities but is handled by federal or tribal authorities in Indian country. If the crime is a federal crime of nationwide application, federal jurisdiction exists irrespective of the locus of the crime or the status of the parties *unless the prosecution for the crime would interfere with Indian treaty or other rights*. If any conflicting Indian rights exist, a careful statutory analysis must be made as to whether Congress clearly and specifically intended to abrogate preexisting Indian rights when it enacted the federal criminal statute in question.

If the crime in question, however, constitutes an *enclave* crime a more complicated analysis is required. In the case of an enclave crime, the second logical question to ask is whether the locus of the crime is in Indian country. The legal concept of Indian country is explored at some length in Ch. 2, Sec. A.3. For enclave crimes occurring outside of Indian country the state generally will have jurisdiction irrespective of the status of the parties unless state prosecution of Indians for the crime will interfere with treaty or other guarantees of off-reservation rights. For enclave or other crimes occurring in Indian country, however, the state will *not* have jurisdiction unless *both* the accused and the victim were non-Indians, or the non-Indian stands accused of a victimless crime. State jurisdiction over enclave crimes in Indian country involving only non-Indians is sanctioned by the controversial *McBratney* decision discussed in Professor Clinton's article in Sec. A.1.b, this chapter. For enclave crimes occurring in Indian country, careful inquiry must be made regarding the status of the parties. The status of the parties will determine not only the existence of state jurisdiction in a *McBratney* situation, but also which of the two federal jurisdictional statutes applies, a question with considerable significance.

The problem of who constitutes an Indian for purposes of the criminal jurisdiction statutes involves considerable uncertainty. For a detailed examination of this question, turn to Ch. 2, Sec. A.2. In the context of tribal jurisdiction the Supreme Court has held that tribes may not exercise criminal jurisdiction over nonmember Indians, *Duro v. Reina*, 495 U.S. 676 (1990), set forth and discussed in Ch. 3, Sec. C.1, a decision which Congress overturned by virtue of the 1990 amendments to the Indian Civil Rights Act, 25 U.S.C. § 1301, and the Supreme Court upheld in *United States v. Lara*, presented and discussed in Ch. 3, Sec. C.2.

In *United States v. Kagama*, 118 U.S. 375 (1886), the Court justified federal jurisdiction over the Indian crimes covered by the Major Crimes Act in part on the basis of the potential prejudice of local juries against Indians. Justice Miller stated, "[b]ecause of local ill feeling, the people of the States where they are found are often their deadliest enemies." Is prejudice or hostility toward Indians accused of crime, especially those who reside on reservations, likely to be any less just because they are not enrolled members of any tribe? Notwithstanding potential prejudice, Indians of *terminated* tribes apparently are considered non-Indians for purposes of sections 1152 and 1153. *Compare United States v. Heath*, 509 F.2d 16, 19 (9th Cir. 1974) ("While anthropologically a Klamath Indian even after the Termination Act obviously remains an Indian, his unique status *vis-à-vis* the federal government no longer exists."), *with St. Cloud v. United States*, 702 F. Supp. 1456 (D.S.D. 1988) (Indian from terminated tribe constitutes an Indian under 18 U.S.C. § 1153 for purposes of crime committed on the reservation of a non-terminated tribe).

If the crime in question is interracial, *i.e.*, committed by a non-Indian against the person or property of an Indian, or committed by an Indian against the person or property of a non-Indian, the crime is governed by the Indian Country Crimes Act, 18 U.S.C. § 1152. In that case, prosecution would be proper under federal law for any federally defined enclave crime contained in the United States Code, and prosecution would also be possible under the Assimilative Crimes Act, 18 U.S.C. § 13, and the Indian Country Crimes Act in *federal* court for any state prohibitory crime not otherwise covered by a federally defined offense. If the accused is an

Indian, however, she may not be prosecuted in federal court under the Indian Country Crimes Act if already punished for the same offense under the laws of the tribe. If the enclave crime in question is intra-Indian, rather than interracial, federal prosecution is possible only under the Major Crimes Act, 18 U.S.C. § 1153. That Act covers fourteen enumerated felonies. If the crime constitutes one of the enumerated crimes, federal jurisdiction exists. If not, the jurisdiction lies exclusively with the tribe. Note that, for intra-Indian crimes, adoption of state law under the Assimilative Crimes Act is not possible. In order to preserve exclusive tribal jurisdiction over lesser intra-Indian crimes, section 1153(b) expressly limits adoption of state law to offenses listed in section 1153(a) which are not defined and punished by federal law. The Assimilative Crimes Act only applies in Indian country through the Indian Country Crimes Act, 18 U.S.C. § 1152, and therefore only applies to the interracial crimes to which that section applies.

In order to apply these principles consider the following problems. In evaluating these problems also consider whether the result is consistent with the underlying reasons for a separate federal Indian policy. Also consider what model of tribal-federal relationship the answers to these problems suggest. For purposes of these problems, assume all Indians mentioned are enrolled tribal members.

Problem No. 1. Albert Rodgers, an enrolled member of the Cherokee Nation, and John Smith, a non-Indian, are suspected of the murder of Harvey Doe, a non-Indian, on a restricted Indian trust allotment within the former boundaries of the now extinguished reservation of the Cherokee Nation in eastern Oklahoma. Which courts have jurisdiction to try Rodgers or Smith for murder? Can they be tried together? Explain.

Problem No. 2. Joan Bear, an enrolled member of the Tohono O'Odham Nation, and John Doe, a non-Indian, are suspected of the murder of Ms. Bear's Indian husband, Jim Bear, on the Tohono O'Odham Reservation in southern Arizona. Which courts have jurisdiction to try Bear and Doe for murder? Explain.

Problem No. 3. Harvey MacDonald, an enrolled member of the Navajo Nation, and Harold Carr, a non-Indian, are alleged to have conspired to pass a bad check to the Indian owner and operator of a store at Window Rock, Arizona, on the Navajo Reservation. No provision in Title 18 of the United States Criminal Code defines or punishes the forgery of a private check on an Indian reservation or other federal enclave. Which courts have authority to try MacDonald or Carr for forgery? Explain. Would the result in this problem be changed if the owner and operator of the store to whom the check was negotiated was a non-Indian? Explain.

Problem No. 4. Lenore White, a Chippewa Indian, is alleged to have embezzled funds from the non-Indian-owned corporation for which she worked as a bookkeeper on the Red Lake Reservation in Minnesota. While 18 U.S.C. § 1163 prohibits embezzlement from tribal governments or other tribal enterprises, no provision of the United States Code defines and punishes private embezzlements occurring in Indian country or other federal enclaves. In which courts could White be tried for embezzlement? Explain. Might the result in Problem No. 4 be altered if the corporation for which White worked was wholly owned by an Indian or the Red Lake Chippewa Tribe? Explain. How, if at all, might the result be different if the crime has occurred on the Mille Lacs Chippewa Reservation in Minnesota instead of the Red Lake Reservation?

Problem No. 5. Harvey Roberts, a member of the Sac and Fox Tribe of Oklahoma, allegedly killed a non-Indian while driving a motor vehicle under the influence of alcohol on the Salt River Pima Maricopa Indian Community in Arizona. In which courts could Roberts be tried for manslaughter? In which courts could he be *convicted* of driving while under the influence of alcohol? What determines the answer to the last question? Would your answers to any of these questions be different if the victim were a member of the Salt River Pima Maricopa Indian Community?

4. Federal Civil Jurisdiction

As you have just seen, federal statutes allocate criminal jurisdiction in Indian country among tribes, the federal government, and the states. But Congress has not set out a comparably complete system for Indian country civil jurisdiction. Even on reservations affected by federal statutes authorizing state jurisdiction in Indian country (*see* Ch. 5, Sec. A), the provision for civil jurisdiction is not comprehensive. Regarding taxation and regulation, Congress has occasionally intervened to assign jurisdiction among federal, tribal, and state authorities. Examples include federal laws allowing state taxation of allotments (*see* Sec. B.4.b, this chapter) and federal laws dividing jurisdiction over gaming and liquor among the three sets of governments (*see* Ch. 5, Secs. D, E). Regarding judicial jurisdiction, Congress has intervened to assign jurisdiction to tribes in many child welfare proceedings involving Indian children (*see* Ch. 5, Sec. C).

Such allocations are exceptional, however. Absent any clearly applicable congressional pronouncement, basic principles of tribal, federal, and state authority, presented in Chapters 3 and 4, must be applied to determine the existence of civil jurisdiction within Indian country. In addition, some special doctrines are necessary to address problems of overlapping or conflicting assertions of jurisdiction. This section focuses on the reach of federal civil jurisdiction in Indian country, including taxing, regulatory, and adjudicative jurisdiction, with special attention to the way Indian law shapes the application of general federal statutes.

a. Federal Jurisdiction to Tax and Regulate

SQUIRE v. CAPOEMAN
United States Supreme Court
351 U.S. 1 (1956)

MR. CHIEF JUSTICE WARREN delivered the opinion of the Court.

The question presented is whether the proceeds of the sale by the United States Government of standing timber on allotted lands on the Quinaielt Indian Reservation may be made subject to capital-gains tax, consistently with applicable treaty and statutory provisions and the Government's role as respondents' trustee and guardian.

When white men first came to the Olympic Peninsula, in what is now the State of Washington, they found the Quinaielt Tribe of Indians and their neighboring allied tribes occupying a tract of country lying between the Coast Range and the Pacific Ocean. This vast tract, with the exception of a small portion reserved for their exclusive use, was ceded by the Quinaielts and their neighbors to the United States in exchange for protection and tutelage by the treaty of July 1, 1855, and January 25, 1856, 12 Stat. 971. According to this treaty, the Quinaielts were to have exclusive use of their reservation "and no white man shall be permitted to reside thereon without permission of the tribe. . . . " Article II. Years later, Congress passed the General Allotment Act of 1887. Thereunder, Indians were to be allotted lands on their reservations not to exceed 160 acres of grazing land or 80 acres of agricultural land, and 25 years after allotment the allottees were to receive the lands discharged of the trust under which the United States had theretofore held them, and to obtain a patent "in fee, discharged of said trust and free of all charge or incumbrance whatsoever," though the President might extend the period.[11]

Respondents, husband and wife, were born on the reservation, and are described by the Government as full-blood, noncompetent Quinaielt Indians. They have lived on the reservation all their lives with the exception of the time served by respondent husband in the Armed Forces of the United States during World War II.

Pursuant to the treaty and under the General Allotment Act of 1887, respondent husband was allotted from the treaty-guaranteed reservation 93.25 acres and received a trust patent therefor dated October 1, 1907.[12] During the tax year here in question, the fee title to this land was still held by the United States in trust for him, and was not subject to alienation or encumbrance by him, except with the consent of the United States Government, which consent had never been given. The land was forest land, covered by coniferous trees from one hundred years to several hundred years old. It was not adaptable to agricultural purposes, and was of little value after the timber was cut.

In the year 1943, the Bureau of Indian Affairs of the United States Department of the Interior entered into a contract of sale for the standing timber on respondent's allotted land for the total price of $ 15,080.80. The Government received the sum of $ 8,418.28 on behalf of respondent in that year.[13]

---

[11] [4] The trust period here involved has regularly been extended by Executive Order.

[12] [6] In pertinent part, the patent provides:

"Now know ye, That the United States of America, in consideration of the premises, has allotted, and by these presents does allot, unto the said Horton Capoeman, the land above described, and hereby declares that it does and will hold the land thus allotted (subject to all statutory provisions and restrictions) for the period of twenty-five years, in trust for the sole use and benefit of the said Indian, and that at the expiration of said period the United States will convey the same by patent to said Indian, in fee, discharged of said trust and free of all charge or incumbrance whatsoever, . . ."

[13] [7] This sale seems to have followed a pattern generally adopted by the Government in selling timber from Indian allotments. Huge areas of forest are put up for competitive bids by lumber companies. These tracts include the tribal forest lands and individual allotments, with the consent of

Upon demand of petitioner, Collector of Internal Revenue for the District of Washington, respondents filed a joint income tax return on October 10, 1947, for the tax year 1943, reporting long-term capital gain from the sale of the timber in that year. Simultaneously, they paid the taxes shown due. Thereafter, they filed a timely claim for refund of the taxes paid and contended that the proceeds from the sale of timber from the allotted land were not subject to federal income taxation because such taxation would be in violation of the provisions of the Quinaielt Treaty, the trust patent, and the General Allotment Act. The claim for refund was denied, and this action was instituted. The District Court found that the tax had been unlawfully collected and ordered the refund. The Court of Appeals, agreeing with the District Court but recognizing a conflict between this case and the decision of the Tenth Circuit in the case of *Jones v. Taunah*, 186 F.2d 445, affirmed. Because of the apparent conflict, we granted certiorari.

The Government urges us to view this case as an ordinary tax case without regard to the treaty, relevant statutes, congressional policy concerning Indians, or the guardian-ward relationship between the United States and these particular Indians. It argues:

> As citizens of the United States they are taxable under the broad provisions of Sections 11 and 22 (a) of the Internal Revenue Code of 1939, which imposes a tax on the net income of every individual, derived from any source whatever. There is no exemption from tax in the Quinaielt Treaty, the General Allotment Act, the taxing statute, or in any other legislation dealing with taxpayers' affairs. . . .

> Even if it be assumed that the United States would be prohibited from imposing a direct tax on the allotted land held in trust for the taxpayers, there would, nevertheless, be no prohibition against a federal tax on the income derived from the land, since a tax on such income is not the same as a tax on the source of the income, the land.

We agree with the Government that Indians are citizens and that in ordinary affairs of life, not governed by treaties or remedial legislation, they are subject to the payment of income taxes as are other citizens. We also agree that, to be valid, exemptions to tax laws should be clearly expressed. But we cannot agree that taxability of respondents in these circumstances is unaffected by the treaty, the trust patent or the Allotment Act.

The courts below held that imposition of the tax here in question is inconsistent with the Government's promise to transfer the fee "free of all charge or incum-

---

tribal councils and individual allottees. The successful bidder is required to make an immediate advance payment of a large proportion of the estimated value of the lumber in the tract. Since as much as 640 million board feet have been sold at one time, this requirement makes it economically infeasible for any but the largest companies to submit bids. The uncertainties of such large scale operations, which are to be carried on over twenty-five- or thirty-year periods, coupled with local quality and accessibility variables, has resulted in substantially lower than prevailing market bids. In some instances, the return to other sellers of comparable timber was two or three times that received by the Indians. See Transcript of November 28, 1955, Joint Hearing of Subcommittee on Legislative Oversight Function of the Senate Committee on Interior and Insular Affairs and of Subcommittee on Public Works and Resources of the House Committee on Government Operations, 2151–2217, and *passim*.

brance whatsoever." Although this statutory provision is not expressly couched in terms of nontaxability, this Court has said that

> Doubtful expressions are to be resolved in favor of the weak and defense-less people who are the wards of the nation, dependent upon its protection and good faith. Hence, in the words of Chief Justice Marshall, "The language used in treaties with the Indians should never be construed to their prejudice. If words be made use of, which are susceptible of a more extended meaning than their plain import, as connected with the tenor of the treaty, they should be considered as used only in the latter sense." *Worcester v. The State of Georgia*, 6 Pet. 515, 582. *Carpenter v. Shaw*, 280 U.S. 363, 367.

Thus, the general words "charge or incumbrance" might well be sufficient to include taxation. But Congress, in an amendment to the General Allotment Act, gave additional force to respondents' position. Section 6 of that Act was amended to include a provision:

> That the Secretary of the Interior may, in his discretion, and he is authorized, whenever he shall be satisfied that any Indian allottee is competent and capable of managing his or her affairs at any time to cause to be issued to such allottee a patent in fee simple, and thereafter all restrictions as to sale, incumbrance, or taxation of said land shall be removed and said land shall not be liable to the satisfaction of any debt contracted prior to the issuing of such patent. . . . [14]

The Government argues that this amendment was directed solely at permitting state and local taxation after a transfer in fee, but there is no indication in the legislative history of the amendment that it was to be so limited. The fact that this amendment antedated the federal income tax by 10 years also seems irrelevant. The literal language of the proviso evinces a congressional intent to subject an Indian allotment to all taxes only after a patent in fee is issued to the allottee. This, in turn, implies that, until such time as the patent is issued, the allotment shall be free from all taxes, both those in being and those which might in the future be enacted.

The first opinion of an Attorney General touching on this question seemed to construe the language of the amendment to Section 6 as exempting from the income tax income derived from restricted allotments.[15] And even without such a clear statutory basis for exemption, a later Attorney General advised that he was

> [u]nable, by implication, to impute to Congress under the broad language of our Internal Revenue Acts an intent to impose a tax for the benefit of the Federal Government on income derived from the restricted property of these wards of the nation; property the management and control of which rests largely in the hands of officers of the Government charged by law with the responsibility and duty of protecting the interests and welfare of these

---

[14] [9] 25 U.S.C. § 349.

[15] [12] 34 Op. Atty. Gen. 275, 281 (1924). And see *id.*, 302 (1924).

dependent people. In other words, it is not lightly to be assumed that Congress intended to tax the ward for the benefit of the guardian.[16]

Two of these opinions were published as Treasury Decisions. On the basis of these opinions and decisions, and a series of district and circuit court decisions, it was said by Felix S. Cohen, an acknowledged expert in Indian law, that "It is clear that the exemption accorded tribal and restricted Indian lands extends to the income derived directly therefrom."[17] These relatively contemporaneous official and unofficial writings are entitled to consideration. The Government makes much of a subsequent Attorney General's opinion, which expressly overruled an earlier opinion, on the authority of *Superintendent of Five Civilized Tribes v. Commissioner*, 295 U.S. 418.

That case is distinguishable from the case at hand. It involved what the Court characterized as "income derived from investment of surplus income from land,"[18] or income on income, which Cohen termed "reinvestment income." The purpose of the allotment system was to protect the Indians' interest and "to prepare the Indians to take their place as independent, qualified members of the modern body politic." *Board of Commissioners v. Seber*, 318 U.S. 705, 715. To this end, it is necessary to preserve the trust and income derived directly therefrom, but it is not necessary to exempt reinvestment income from tax burdens. It is noteworthy that the *Superintendent* case did not involve an attempt to tax the land "surplus."

The wisdom of the congressional exemption from tax embodied in Section 6 of the General Allotment Act is manifested by the facts of the instant case. Respondent's timber constitutes the major value of his allotted land. The Government determines the conditions under which the cutting is made. Once logged off, the land is of little value. The land no longer serves the purpose for which it was by treaty set aside to his ancestors, and for which it was allotted to him. It can no longer be adequate to his needs and serve the purpose of bringing him finally to a state of competency and independence. Unless the proceeds of the timber sale are preserved for respondent, he cannot go forward when declared competent with the necessary chance of economic survival in competition with others. This chance is guaranteed by the tax exemption afforded by the General Allotment Act, and the solemn undertaking in the patent. It is unreasonable to infer that, in enacting the income tax law, Congress intended to limit or undermine the Government's undertaking. To tax respondent under these circumstances would, in the words of the court below, be "at the least, a sorry breach of faith with these Indians."[19]

The judgment of the Court of Appeals is *Affirmed*.

---

[16] [13] *Id.*, 439, 445 (1925). This ruling was followed in 35 Op. Atty. Gen. 1 (1925). And cf. *id.*, 107 (1926).

[17] [15] Cohen, Handbook of Federal Indian Law, 265. He distinguished cases permitting the imposition of income taxes upon income derived from unrestricted lands, and upon reinvestment income. *Id.*, at 265–266. Mr. Cohen was Chairman of the Department of Interior Board of Appeals, and Assistant Solicitor of the Department. The Handbook has a foreword by Harold L. Ickes, then Secretary of the Interior, and was printed by the United States Government Printing Office.

[18] [18] 295 U.S. at 421.

[19] [22] 220 F.2d [349] at 350.

LAZORE v. COMMISSIONER OF INTERNAL REVENUE
United States Court of Appeals, Third Circuit
11 F.3d 1180 (1993)

ROTH, CIRCUIT JUDGE:

This appeal arises from the United States Tax Court's determination that appellants, Glenny and Carol Lazore, were not exempt from paying federal income taxes and that they were subject to both late filing and negligence penalties on the basis of their unexcused two-week delay in filing their return. . . .

I.

Appellants Glenny and Carol Lazore are residents of the St. Regis Mohawk Indian Reservation, located within the State of New York. The Mohawk Nation, along with the Oneida, the Seneca, the Onondaga, the Cayuga and the Tuscarora Nations, is part of the Six Nations Confederacy. The Six Nations are also known as the Iroquois or Haudenosaunee ("the People of the Long House"). We shall refer to them as the Haudenosaunee. The Haudenosaunee Nation exists within the territorial limits of the United States, but in many ways functions as a separate government. It has its own governing bodies, known as the Grand Council and the Council of Chiefs, and issues passports which are recognized by the United States and other nations. The Haudenosaunee may travel freely between the United States and Canada on identification cards issued by the Haudenosaunee Nation. Both Mr. and Ms. Lazore consider themselves to be citizens of the Mohawk Nation and not citizens of the United States.

Appellants are husband and wife; they filed their joint 1986 federal income tax return on May 1, 1987. During 1986, Mr. Lazore worked for the Reynolds Metals Company in New York State as a plant mechanic and received compensation in the amount of $30,332.31. Ms. Lazore worked for the Mohawk Indian Housing Corporation as its executive director and received compensation in the amount of $18,427.20. Appellants reported these amounts as income on their tax return along with $31.03 of interest income. However, they reported no taxable income and no tax. They attached an affidavit to their return in which they declared that they were exempt from tax based on the 1794 Treaty of Canandaigua, the Jay Treaty, the Treaty of Ghent, and the U.S. Constitution.

. . . .

III.

. . . The notion that Congress has the power to unilaterally abrogate provisions of treaties with Indians is firmly established. See *Rosebud Sioux Tribe v. Kneip*, 430 U.S. 584, 587–88 (1977); *Lone Wolf v. Hitchcock*, 187 U.S. 553 (1903). Consistent with this power, Congress has repeatedly asserted its legislative jurisdiction over Indians without regard to whether any treaty provisions concerned the subject of the law. Beginning with the Seven Major Crimes Act of 1885, for example, and continuing through 1988, Congress has removed major criminal jurisdiction from all

Indian tribes. Similarly, the Indian Civil Rights Act of 1968, specifies the maximum penalties which tribal courts may impose upon convicted defendants, and sets out a list of rights — including six-person juries and review of tribal court detention orders by federal District Courts through issuance of writs of habeas corpus — that must be provided to participants in tribal criminal proceedings. Congress has also legislated frequently with respect to the right of all Indians within the United States to alienate reservation lands by lease or transfer.

Related to the power to abrogate treaty provisions is the Supreme Court's holding that "a general statute applying to all persons includes Indians and their property interests." *Federal Power Comm'n v. Tuscarora Indian Nation*, 362 U.S. 99, 116 (1960). Thus, for example, Congress has successfully asserted the power to draft Indians.

In the area of taxation, Congress has passed neither a statute specifically abrogating the provisions of Indian treaties nor a statute of general application that has the effect of abrogating Indian treaties. To be sure, § 1 of the Internal Revenue Code is a general statute which subjects the income of every individual to taxation. Furthermore, this tax extends to "all income from whatever source derived." I.R.C. § 61(a). However, provisions of the income tax law are to be applied "with due regard to any treaty obligation of the United States which applies to such taxpayer." I.R.C. § 894(a)(1). Thus, "in ordinary affairs of life, not governed by treaties or remedial legislation, [Indians] are subject to the payment of income taxes as are other citizens." *Squire v. Capoeman*, 351 U.S. 1, 6 (1956) (emphasis added).

Despite the fact that the United States stopped dealing with Indians by treaty long before the establishment of the income tax, the Supreme Court has held that a treaty-based tax exemption must be supported by the text of a treaty. In *Superintendent of Five Civilized Tribes v. Commissioner*, 295 U.S. 418 (1935), the Court, faced with a claim that an Indian's investment income was exempt from taxation, stated that "[t]he general terms of the taxing act include the income under consideration, and if exemption exists it must derive plainly from agreements with the Creeks or some Act of Congress dealing with their affairs." *Id.* at 420. Similarly, in *Choteau v. Burnet*, 283 U.S. 691 (1931), the Court concluded that "[n]o provision in any of the treaties referred to . . . has any bearing upon the question of the liability of an individual Indian to pay tax upon income derived by him from his own property." *Id.* at 694. We interpret the Court's statement that an exemption must "derive plainly" from a treaty, together with its conclusion in Choteau that treaties cannot support an exemption without a "provision" concerning "the liability of an individual to pay tax upon income," to stand for the proposition that an exemption must be rooted in the text of a treaty. Furthermore, because all Indian treaties were entered into long before the passage of the income tax, the fact that the parties to a treaty did not negotiate with the federal income tax in mind is immaterial. As such, silence as to matters of taxation will never be sufficient to establish an exemption.

At first glance, these doctrines appear to conflict to such an extent as to nullify one another. Since there was no income tax contemplated when these treaties were drafted, it is virtually inconceivable that any treaty would contain an exemption to the tax. Thus, short of a provision creating an exemption from all taxation, there would appear to be no way for a treaty to contain language that could support an exemption from the income tax. The Court has avoided this result by crafting a special set of rules to be used in interpreting treaties between the United States and Indian nations. In general, "doubts concerning the meaning of a treaty with an Indian tribe should be resolved in favor of the tribe." *Oregon Dept. of Fish & Wildlife v. Klamath Indian Tribe*, 473 U.S. 753 (1985).

The language used in treaties with the Indians should never be construed to their prejudice. If words be made use of, which are susceptible of a more extended meaning than their plain import, as connected with the tenor of the treaty, they should be considered as used only in the latter sense. . . . How the words of the treaty were understood by this unlettered people, rather than their critical meaning, should form the rule of construction. *Worcester v. Georgia*, 31 U.S. (6 Pet.) 515, 582 (1832). Furthermore, the words of such treaties must be construed, not according to their technical meaning, but "in the sense in which they would naturally be understood by the Indians." *Jones v. Meehan*, 175 U.S. 1, 11 (1899).

. . . The effect of these rules of interpretation is to make it possible for language that could not have been concerned with the income tax to nevertheless create an exemption from it. An example is the language at issue in *Hoptowit v. Commissioner of Internal Revenue*, 709 F.2d 564 (9th Cir. 1983). In *Hoptowit* the taxpayer argued that the Treaty with the Yakimas of 1855, 12 Stat. 951, which provided that a certain tract of land was set apart "for the exclusive use and benefit of said confederated tribes and bands of Indians," expressed a tax exemption as clearly as was possible before the income tax existed. 709 F.2d at 566. The Ninth Circuit, though it held that the treaty did not create a blanket exemption from the income tax, allowed that the language might create an exemption from taxation on income derived directly from the land. *Id.*

Consistent with this reasoning, we accept the approach adopted by the Eighth Circuit. In *Holt v. Commissioner*, 364 F.2d 38, 40 (8th Cir. 1966), that court concluded that the principle that Indian treaties should be liberally construed to favor the Indians "comes into play only if such . . . treaty contains language which can reasonably be construed to confer income exemptions." This formulation gives appropriate weight to the notion that a treaty-based tax exemption must have a textual basis and accounts for the interpretive rules applicable to Indian treaties. We specifically reject the Ninth Circuit's requirement that a treaty contain a "definitely expressed exemption," *Confederated Tribes of Warm Springs Reservation v. Kurtz*, 691 F.2d 878, 882 (9th Cir. 1982), because we believe that it insufficiently accounts for these rules of liberal construction.

IV.

We must now consider whether any of the treaties on which the Lazores rely contain a textual basis for an exemption from the federal income tax. The Lazores bottom their claim of exemption primarily on provisions of the Treaty of Canandaigua, 7 Stat. 44 (1794), supported by the Treaty of Amity, Commerce, and Navigation, known as the Jay Treaty, 8 Stat. 116 (1794), and the Treaty of Ghent, 8 Stat. 218 (1815). The relevant sections of the Treaty of Canandaigua provide as follows:

ARTICLE II.

The United States acknowledge the lands reserved to the Oneida, Onondaga, and Cayuga Nations in their respective treaties . . . to be their property; and the United States will never claim the same, nor disturb them or either of the Six Nations, nor their Indian friends residing thereon and united with them, in the free use and enjoyment thereof. . . .

ARTICLE III.

. . . Now, the United States acknowledge all the land within the aforementioned boundaries, to be the property of the Seneka nation: and the United States will never claim the same, nor disturb the Seneka nation, nor any of the Six Nations, or of their Indian friends residing thereon and united with them, in the free use and enjoyment thereof. . . .

ARTICLE IV.

The United States having thus described and acknowledged what lands belong to the Oneidas, Onondagas, Cayugas and Senekas, and engaged never to claim the same, not to disturb them, or any of the Six Nations, or their Indian friends residing thereon and united with them in free use and enjoyment thereof: Now, the Six Nations, and each of them, hereby engage that they will never claim any other lands within the boundaries of the United States; nor ever disturb the people of the United States in the free use and enjoyment thereof.

In particular, the Lazores point to the treaty's statement that the United States and its citizens will not "disturb . . . any of the Six Nations, or their Indian friends residing thereon and united with them, in the free use and enjoyment" of their lands.

At trial the Lazores presented a substantial amount of uncontradicted historical evidence concerning the Haudenosaunee understanding of the treaty's meaning. Witnesses stated that the Haudenosaunee know, through their oral tradition, that the treaty recognizes them as a separate nation over which the United States has no power, of taxation or otherwise. Kevin Deer, an Iroquois faithkeeper, and Jake Swamp, a Mohawk Chief, testified that the Haudenosaunee understanding of the treaty is embodied in the Two Row Wampum, a belt consisting of two parallel rows of dark colored beads on a background of lighter colored beads. The two rows signify the two peoples — Indian and European — coexisting peacefully, neither imposing their laws or religion on the other. The Two Row Wampum initially reflected the principles of the agreement between the Haudenosaunee and the Dutch in 1645 to remain separate peoples. These principles became known to the Haudenosaunee as the "chain of friendship," and, in the view of the Haudenosaunee, were the basis for treaties with France, Great Britain, and the United States, including the Treaty of Canandaigua.

. . . .

While we are sympathetic to the Lazores' claim that the Treaty of Canandaigua recognized the Haudenosaunee as a separate nation, we are unable to accept it as sufficient to create an exemption from the federal income tax. As we have concluded above, we are constrained from finding an exemption in the absence of some textual support. Nor do we find that the treaty's statement that the United States will not disturb the Haudenosaunee in "the free use and enjoyment" of their lands to be capable of being reasonably construed as supporting an exemption from the income tax. Both the Eighth and Ninth Circuits have rejected claims of exemption based on similar treaty provisions. In *Jourdain v. Commissioner of Internal Revenue*, 617 F.2d 507, 508–09 (8th Cir. 1980), the court rejected the taxpayer's claim that federal taxation of his income violated the prohibition on "molestation from the United States" in the Treaty with the Tribes of Indians of Greenville, 7 Stat. 49 (1795). In *Dillon v. United States*, 792 F.2d 849 (9th Cir. 1986), the taxpayers argued that they were exempt from the income tax by virtue of a treaty provision that exempted the land assigned to them from taxation until the formation of a state constitution and another provision that placed geographic limits on the scope of the Indians' trading activities. *Id.* at 852–53. The court, despite "substantial historical evidence offered by the taxpayers," concluded that neither provision amounted to an exemption. *Id.* at 853. . . .

The language relied on by the Lazores might be sufficient to support an exemption from a tax on income derived directly from the land. In order to hold that the Treaty of Canandaigua exempted the Haudenosaunee from the federal income tax, however, we would need to find language capable of being construed more broadly. We cannot find any such language.

. . . .

For the foregoing reasons, the decision of the Tax Court holding that the Lazores are not exempted from the federal income tax based on the Treaty of Canandaigua will be affirmed. . . .

NOTES ON FEDERAL TAXATION OF TRIBES AND TRIBAL MEMBERS

1. **"Indians Not Taxed"**: In a section not printed above, the *Lazore* court adopts the dominant scholarly view of the "Indians not taxed" clauses in Article I and Amendment XIV of the Constitution, which is that they describe the class of Indians still maintaining their tribal relations and historically subject only to tribal law, but do not grant such Indians any tax exemption. *See* NELL JESSUP NEWTON ET AL., COHEN'S HANDBOOK OF FEDERAL INDIAN LAW § 8.01[2] (2012 ed.). Evidently many Iroquois understand the impact of that constitutional phrase differently. Because traditionalists rejected United States citizenship and claim sole allegiance to the Haudenosaunee Confederacy, they continue to see themselves as outside the regulatory or taxing power of the federal government. For an account of Iroquois opposition to United States citizenship, see Robert Porter, *The Demise of the Ongwehoweh and the Rise of the Native Americans: Redressing the Genocidal Act of Forcing American Citizenship upon Indigenous Peoples*, 15 HARV. BLACK LETTER L.J. 107, 126–28 (1999).

At the time the "Indians not taxed" clauses were included in the Constitution, there was no federal income tax. The category "Indians not taxed" encompassed those who were not counted for purposes of assessing a direct per capita tax. After ratification of the Sixteenth Amendment in 1913, the federal government began to impose an income tax. For somewhat obscure reasons, Indian nations have been treated as exempt from this tax. The Internal Revenue Service "has taken the position that the income tax statutes do not purport to tax the political entity embodied in the concept of an Indian tribe and no attempt has ever been made to tax the tribe with respect to tribal income." Gen. Couns. Mem. 38,853 (May 17, 1982). The exemption applies to tribal income earned inside or outside Indian country, as well as to income generated by a tribally-owned business entity. Rev. Rul. 94-16, 1994-1 C.B. 19. Somewhat inconsistently, the IRS insists that federal employment taxes, especially FICA and FUTA, do apply to tribes. *See generally* Scott Taylor, *An Introduction and Overview of Taxation and Indian Gaming*, 29 Ariz. St. L.J. 251, 252–55 (1997). For a comprehensive assessment of the question whether Congress should tax tribes, both from a tax policy and an Indian policy perspective, see Mark J. Cowan, *Leaving Money on the Table(s): An Examination of Federal Income Tax Policy Toward Indian Tribes*, 6 Fla. Tax Rev. 345 (2004). Cowan concludes that taxing tribes "would put tribes and states on different footings from a tax standpoint," raising concerns of horizontal equity. It would also frustrate federal Indian policies favoring tribal sovereignty and economic development, and contradict the general trend of federal legislation favoring treatment of tribes as states for purposes of tax, environmental, and other laws.

2. Canons of Construction and Treaty Provisions as Limits on Federal Taxation: The federal courts' broad conception of federal "plenary power" over Indian affairs would seem to allow a free flow of federal power to tax tribal members. Furthermore, general interpretive canons for federal tax laws require that tax exemptions be clearly expressed. What happens when these principles confront tax exemption claims by individual Indians, especially claims resting on federal statutes or treaties, coupled with the federal trust responsibility and associated Indian law canons of construction, discussed in Ch. 2, Sec. C? The outcome of this struggle is not entirely clear. The Supreme Court in *Squire* acknowledges that even in Indian tax cases, tax exemptions must be "clearly expressed." But as the opinion demonstrates, no specifically-worded reference to exemption is required, and the language need "not [be] expressly couched in terms of nontaxability." In *Squire* itself, the Court uses ordinary Indian law canons of construction to determine whether language arguably offering a statutory exemption is "clearly [enough] expressed."

Treaty-based claims of tax exemption precipitate the same clash of canons. As the *Lazore* opinion indicates, the Eighth and Ninth Circuits have called the fight differently. Although the Eighth Circuit insisted that a treaty-based exemption "must be rooted in the text of a treaty" and the Third Circuit denied the Lazores' claim on that basis, the *Lazore* court also acknowledged that "language that could not have been concerned with the income tax [may] nevertheless create an exemption from it," and "the principle that Indian treaties should be liberally construed to favor the Indians [may come into] play" if the treaty "contains language which can reasonably be construed to confer income exemptions." The

Lazore court contrasts this approach to that of the Ninth Circuit, which insists upon a "definitely expressed exemption."

In practice, how do these two different approaches produce different results? Does the Ninth Circuit's insistence on "express exemptive language" confuse exemptions conferred by the Internal Revenue Code or other statutes with those based on treaties? Does it give too little regard to the doctrine that Indian treaties must be liberally construed to favor the Indians? Does it unrealistically demand that treaties have anticipated forms of taxation that did not yet even exist?

Consider the following statement by a leading scholar of Indian taxation:

> The treaties negotiated with Indians until the end of the treaty-making period did not contain any reference to federal taxation. Such references were not necessary because during this period Congress did not attempt to tax activity within Indian Country and the tribes probably believed that Congress would never tax member activity taking place within Indian Country. Treaties ought to be read as having implicit in them a promise that the federal government would not tax member activity within Indian Country. Accordingly, treaties provide a basis for asserting that members are exempt from federal taxation for their on-reservation activity. Congress, by its plenary power, can abrogate treaties. But general federal legislation does not abrogate a treaty unless it is clear that Congress intended this result. Because the federal statute imposing the federal income tax does not mention Indians, no federal income tax statute abrogates the treaties.

Scott Taylor, *An Introduction and Overview of Taxation and Indian Gaming*, 29 ARIZ. ST. L.J. 251, 263 (1997). What, if anything, is wrong with this view?

b. Federal Civil Adjudicative Jurisdiction

Federal courts are courts of limited subject matter jurisdiction, the outer contours of which are specified in Article III, section 1, clause 1 of the United States Constitution. Because Congress need not confer the full extent of federal subject matter jurisdiction on the federal courts, federal statutes determine the actual scope of their jurisdiction. The most important implementing jurisdictional provisions for Indian country are 28 U.S.C. §§ 1331 (federal question jurisdiction), 1332 (diversity jurisdiction), 1362 (jurisdiction over suits brought by tribes and raising federal questions), and 1505 (jurisdiction over claims brought by tribes against the United States). The following cases address their reach and significance in an Indian country context. Ask yourself how well they engage the Indian law canons of construction set forth in Ch. 2, Sec. C, and the model(s) of the tribal-federal relationship they articulate or assume.

County of Oneida v. Oneida Indian Nation, 414 U.S. 661 (1974): The Oneida Indian Nation filed suit in federal district court against certain named counties, claiming that an alleged conveyance made by the Tribe in a 1795 agreement with the State of New York and without federal approval violated the federal statutory restraint on alienation of land found in the Trade and Intercourse Act of 1793, a section sometimes called the Nonintercourse Act and now codified as amended at 25

U.S.C. § 177. That law provided that no person or entity could purchase Indian land without the approval of the federal government and further provided that any agreements made without federal approval were void. Claiming that the alleged conveyance on which the counties' title claim rested was void, the Tribe sought damages representing the fair rental value for a 2-year period from the defendants for that part of the land they occupied. The district court dismissed the case for want of federal jurisdiction and the Second Circuit affirmed. The Second Circuit found that the Oneida's complaint "shatters on the rock of the 'well-pleaded complaint' rule for determining federal question jurisdiction." 464 F.2d 916, 918 (2d Cir. 1972). While that court conceded that the "decision would ultimately turn on whether the deed of 1795 complied with what is now 25 U.S.C. § 177 and what the consequences would be if it did not," *id.*, at 919, it found that this fact alone did not establish federal question jurisdiction because the federal issue was not one of the necessary elements required to be plead in the complaint, which the court saw as one that basically sought relief based on the right to possession of real property. The Court of Appeals relied on *Taylor v. Anderson*, 234 U.S. 74 (1914), which held that an ejectment claim, although stating a federally-created right to property title, did not state a claim within the federal question jurisdiction since the right to relief was created by state law.

In an opinion by Justice Powell, the United States Supreme Court unanimously reversed the dismissal of the complaint, finding federal question jurisdiction under 28 U.S.C. § 1331. Central to that decision was its conclusion that federal common law must create an implied cause of action to protect Indian tribal title otherwise guaranteed by federal treaty and by the provisions of 25 U.S.C. § 177. The Court noted:

> It very early became accepted doctrine in this Court that although fee title to the lands occupied by Indians when the colonists arrived became vested in the sovereign — first the discovering European nation and later the original States and the United States — a right of occupancy in the Indian tribes was nevertheless recognized. That right, sometimes called Indian title and good against all but the sovereign, could be terminated only by sovereign act. Once the United States was organized and the Constitution adopted, these tribal rights to Indian lands became the exclusive province of the federal law. Indian title, recognized to be only a right of occupancy, was extinguishable only by the United States. The Federal Government took early steps to deal with the Indians through treaty, the principal purpose often being to recognize and guarantee the rights of Indians to specified areas of land. This the United States did with respect to the various New York Indian tribes, including the Oneidas. The United States also asserted the primacy of federal law in the first Nonintercourse Act passed in 1790, 1 Stat. 137, 138, which provided that "no sale of lands made by any Indians . . . within the United States, shall be valid to any person . . . or to any state . . . unless the same shall be made and duly executed at some public treaty, held under the authority of the United States." This has remained the policy of the United States to this day. See 25 U.S.C. § 177.

In *United States v. Santa Fe Pacific R. Co.*, 314 U.S. 339, 345 (1941), a unanimous Court succinctly summarized the essence of past cases in relevant respects:

> "Unquestionably it has been the policy of the Federal Government from the beginning to respect the Indian right of occupancy, which could only be interfered with or determined by the United States." *Cramer v. United States*, 261 U.S. 219, 227. This policy was first recognized in *Johnson v. M'Intosh*, 8 Wheat. 543, and has been repeatedly reaffirmed. *Worcester v. Georgia*, 6 Pet. 515; *Mitchel v. United States*, 9 Pet. 711; *Chouteau v. Molony*, 16 How. 203; *Holden v. Joy*, 17 Wall. 211; *Buttz v. Northern Pacific Railroad*[, 119 U.S. 55]; *United States v. Shoshone Tribe*, 304 U.S. 111. As stated in *Mitchel v. United States*, Indian "right of occupancy is considered as sacred as the fee simple of the whites."

The *Santa Fe* case also reaffirmed prior decisions to the effect that a tribal right of occupancy, to be protected, need not be "based upon a treaty, statute, or other formal government action." Tribal rights were nevertheless entitled to the protection of federal law, and with respect to Indian title based on aboriginal possession, the "power of Congress . . . is supreme."

As indicated in *Santa Fe*, the fundamental propositions which it restated were firmly rooted in earlier cases. In *Johnson v. M'Intosh*, 21 U.S. 543 (1823), the Court refused to recognize land titles originating in grants by Indians to private parties in 1773 and 1775; those grants were contrary to the accepted principle that Indian title could be extinguished only by or with the consent of the general government. The land in question, when ceded to the United States by the State of Virginia, was "occupied by numerous and warlike tribes of Indians; but the exclusive right of the United States to extinguish their title, and to grant the soil, has never, we believe, been doubted." The possessory and treaty rights of Indian tribes to their lands have been the recurring theme of many other cases.

The rudimentary propositions that Indian title is a matter of federal law and can be extinguished only with federal consent apply in all of the States, including the original 13. It is true that the United States never held fee title to the Indian lands in the original States as it did to almost all the rest of the continental United States and that fee title to Indian lands in these States, or the pre-emptive right to purchase from the Indians, was in the State, *Fletcher v. Peck*, 10 U.S. 87 (1810). But this reality did not alter the doctrine that federal law, treaties, and statutes protected Indian occupancy and that its termination was exclusively the province of federal law.

For example, in *Worcester v. Georgia*, 6 Pet. 515 (1832), the State of Georgia sought to prosecute a white man for residing in Indian country contrary to the laws of the State. This Court held the prosecution a nullity, the Chief Justice referring to the treaties with the Cherokees and to the

> universal conviction that the Indian nations possessed a full right to the lands they occupied, until that right should be extinguished by the

United States, with their consent: that their territory was separated from that of any state within whose chartered limits they might reside, by a boundary line, established by treaties: that, within their boundary, they possessed rights with which no state could interfere: and that the whole power of regulating the intercourse with them, was vested in the United States. *Id.* at 560.

Thus, the Court concluded that Indian title had long been protected by federal law. On that basis, the Court reasoned:

In the present case, however, the assertion of a federal controversy does not rest solely on the claim of a right to possession derived from a federal grant of title whose scope will be governed by state law. Rather, it rests on the not insubstantial claim that federal law now protects, and has continuously protected from the time of the formation of the United States, possessory right to tribal lands, wholly apart from the application of state law principles which normally and separately protect a valid right of possession.

For the same reasons, we think the complaint before us satisfies the additional requirement formulated in some cases that the complaint reveal a "dispute or controversy respecting the validity, construction or effect of such a law, upon the determination of which the result depends." Here, the Oneidas assert a present right to possession based in part on their aboriginal right of occupancy which was not terminable except by act of the United States. Their claim is also asserted to arise from treaties guaranteeing their possessory right until terminated by the United States, and "it is to these treaties [that] we must look to ascertain the nature of these [Indian] rights, and the extent of them." *The New York Indians*, 5 Wall., at 768. Finally, the complaint asserts a claim under the Nonintercourse Acts which put in statutory form what was or came to be the accepted rule — that the extinguishment of Indian title required the consent of the United States. To us, it is sufficiently clear that the controversy stated in the complaint arises under the federal law within the meaning of the jurisdictional statutes and our decided cases.

NATIONAL FARMERS UNION
INSURANCE COS. v. CROW TRIBE
United States Supreme Court
471 U.S. 845 (1985)

Justice Stevens delivered the opinion of the Court.

[The parents of an Indian student injured by a motorcycle in the parking lot of a state school on the Crow Indian reservation filed suit in tribal court against the state school district seeking $153,000 in compensatory damages — $3,000 for medical expenses and $150,000 for pain and suffering. The Complaint and summons were duly served by Dexter Falls Down on the Chairman of the School Board, Wesley Falls Down, and the school board chairman failed to notify either the School

Board or National Farmers Union Insurance, the school district's insurer. The first time the insurance company learned of the suit was after a default judgment had already been entered in the tribal court on October 29, 1982 and while the plaintiffs sought to enforce the judgment by seizing property of the school. National and the school district then filed suit in the federal district court seeking to enjoin enforcement of the default judgment, ultimately claiming that the tribal court lacked subject matter jurisdiction over the case. On November 3, 1982, the district court granted the insurance company and the school district a temporary restraining order in response to National's allegations that an application for a writ of execution was pending in tribal court. Finding the court had federal question jurisdiction, the district court later granted a permanent injunction on the ground that the tribal court lacked subject matter jurisdiction over the dispute.

A divided panel of the Ninth Circuit Court of Appeals reversed (736 F.2d 1320 (1984)), holding there was no ground for the district court to exercise jurisdiction over the matter. The majority concluded that the district court's exercise of jurisdiction could not be supported on any constitutional, statutory, or common-law ground. One judge concurred in the result, believing that the petitioners had a duty to exhaust their tribal court remedies before invoking the jurisdiction of a federal court, and therefore concurred in the judgment directing that the complaint be dismissed. The Supreme Court ultimately found a compromise between these two positions.]

I

Section 1331 of the Judicial Code provides that a federal district court "shall have original jurisdiction of all civil actions arising under the Constitution, laws, or treaties of the United States." It is well settled that [f]ederal common law as articulated in rules that are fashioned by court decisions are "laws" as that term is used in § 1331. [Nevertheless it was] necessary [for petitioners] to assert a claim "arising under" federal law. [The right petitioners assert] — a right to be protected against an unlawful exercise of Tribal Court judicial power — has its source in federal law because federal law defines the outer boundaries of an Indian tribe's power over non-Indians.

As we have often noted, Indian tribes occupy a unique status under our law. At one time they exercised virtually unlimited power over their own members as well as those who were permitted to join their communities. Today, however, the power of the federal government over the Indian tribes is plenary. Federal law, implemented by statute, by treaty, by administrative regulations, and by judicial decisions, provides significant protection for the individual, territorial, and political rights of the Indian tribes. The tribes also retain some of the inherent powers of the self-governing political communities that were formed long before Europeans first settled in North America.

This Court has frequently been required to decide questions concerning the extent to which Indian tribes have retained the power to regulate the affairs of non-Indians. [T]he governing rule of decision has been provided by federal law. [W]hether an Indian tribe retains the power to compel a non-Indian property owner to submit to the civil jurisdiction of a tribal court is [a question] that must be answered by reference to federal law and is a "federal question" under § 1331. [Since] petitioners contend that federal law has divested the Tribe of this aspect of sovereignty, it is federal law on which they rely as a basis for the asserted right of freedom from Tribal Court interference. They have, therefore, filed an action "arising under" federal law within the meaning of § 1331. The District Court correctly concluded that a federal court may determine under § 1331 whether a tribal court has exceeded the lawful limits of its jurisdiction.

II

Respondents contend that, even though the District Court's jurisdiction was properly invoked under § 1331, the Court of Appeals was correct in ordering that the complaint be dismissed because the petitioners failed to exhaust their remedies in the tribal judicial system. They further assert that the underlying tort action "has turned into a procedural and jurisdictional nightmare" because petitioners did not pursue their readily available Tribal Court remedies. Petitioners, in response, relying in part on *Oliphant v. Suquamish Indian Tribe*, 435 U.S. 191 (1978), assert that resort to exhaustion as a matter of comity "is manifestly inappropriate."

In *Oliphant* we held that the Suquamish Indian Tribal Court did not have criminal jurisdiction to try and to punish non-Indians for offenses committed on the reservation. That holding adopted the reasoning of early opinions of two United States Attorneys General, and concluded that federal legislation conferring jurisdiction on the federal courts to try non-Indians for offenses committed in Indian Country had implicitly pre-empted tribal jurisdiction. We wrote:

> "While Congress never expressly forbade Indian tribes to impose criminal penalties on non-Indians, we now make express our implicit conclusion of nearly a century ago that Congress consistently believed this to be the necessary result of its repeated legislative actions."

If we were to apply the *Oliphant* rule here, it is plain that any exhaustion requirement would be completely foreclosed because federal courts would always be the only forums for civil actions against non-Indians. For several reasons, however, the reasoning of *Oliphant* does not apply to this case. First, although Congress's decision to extend the criminal jurisdiction of the federal courts to offenses committed by non-Indians against Indians within Indian Country supported the holding in *Oliphant*, there is no comparable legislation granting the federal courts jurisdiction over civil disputes between Indians and non-Indians that arise on an Indian reservation. Moreover, the opinion of one Attorney General on which we relied in *Oliphant*, specifically noted the difference between civil and criminal jurisdiction. Speaking of civil jurisdiction, Attorney General Cushing wrote:

> "But there is no provision of treaty, and no statute, which takes away from the Choctaws jurisdiction of a case like this, a question of property strictly internal to the Choctaw nation; nor is there any written law which confers jurisdiction of such a case in any court of the United States.

> "The conclusion seems to me irresistible, not that such questions are justiciable nowhere, but that they remain subject to the local jurisdiction of

the Choctaws.

> "Now, it is admitted on all hands . . . that Congress has 'paramount right' to legislate in regard to this question, in all its relations. *It has legislated, in so far as it saw fit, by taking jurisdiction in criminal matters, and omitting to take jurisdiction in civil matters. . . . By all possible rules of construction the inference is clear that jurisdiction is left to the Choctaws themselves of civil controversies arising strictly within the Choctaw Nation."*

7 Op. Atty. Gen. 175, 179–181 (1855) (emphasis added).

Thus, we conclude that the answer to the question whether a tribal court has the power to exercise civil subject-matter jurisdiction over non-Indians in a case of this kind is not automatically foreclosed, as an extension of *Oliphant* would require. Rather, the existence and extent of a tribal court's jurisdiction will require a careful examination of tribal sovereignty, the extent to which that sovereignty has been altered, divested, or diminished, as well as a detailed study of relevant statutes, Executive Branch policy as embodied in treaties and elsewhere, and administrative or judicial decisions.

We believe that examination should be conducted in the first instance in the Tribal Court itself. Our cases have often recognized that Congress is committed to a policy of supporting tribal self-government and self-determination. That policy favors a rule that will provide the forum whose jurisdiction is being challenged the first opportunity to evaluate the factual and legal bases for the challenge.[20] Moreover the orderly administration of justice in the federal court will be served by allowing a full record to be developed in the Tribal Court before either the merits or any question concerning appropriate relief is addressed.[21] The risks of the kind of "procedural nightmare" that has allegedly developed in this case will be minimized if the federal court stays its hand until after the Tribal Court has had a full opportunity to determine its own jurisdiction and to rectify any errors it may have made. Exhaustion of tribal court remedies, moreover, will encourage tribal courts to explain to the parties the precise basis for accepting jurisdiction, and will also provide other courts with the benefit of their expertise in such matters in the event of further judicial review.

III

Our conclusions that § 1331 encompasses the federal question whether a tribal court has exceeded the lawful limits of its jurisdiction, and that exhaustion is

---

[20] [21] We do not suggest that exhaustion would be required where an assertion of tribal jurisdiction "is motivated by a desire to harass or is conducted in bad faith," *cf. Juidice v. Vail*, 430 U.S. 327, 338 (1977), or where the action is patently violative of express jurisdictional prohibitions, or where exhaustion would be futile because of the lack of an adequate opportunity to challenge the court's jurisdiction.

[21] [22] Four days after receiving notice of the default judgment, petitioners requested that the District Court enter an injunction. Crow Tribal Court Rule of Civil Procedure 17(d) provides that a party in a default [action] may move to set aside the default judgment at any time within 30 days. Petitioners did not utilize this legal remedy. It is a fundamental principle of long standing that a request for an injunction will not be granted as long as an adequate remedy at law is available.

required before such a claim may be entertained by a federal court, require that we reverse the judgment of the Court of Appeals. Until petitioners have exhausted the remedies available to them in the Tribal Court system, . . . it would be premature for a federal court to consider any relief. Whether the federal action should be dismissed, or merely held in abeyance pending the development of further Tribal Court proceedings, is a question that should be addressed in the first instance by the District Court.

[*Reversed and remanded.*]

Iowa Mutual Insurance Co. v. LaPlante, 480 U.S. 9 (1987): While *National Farmers Union* recognized that section 1331 could be invoked to bring a federal common law claim based on *Oliphant* alleging that a tribal court lacked jurisdiction to adjudicate certain claims arising in Indian country involving non-Indians, it also closed off quick and easy access to the federal courts by imposing an exhaustion of tribal remedies requirement for most cases. Some non-Indians residing in a state different from that in which the reservation was located (often businesses incorporated in other states), began to invoke diversity jurisdiction, 28 U.S.C. § 1332, to secure federal jurisdiction and avoid tribal forums. In *Iowa Mutual*, the Supreme Court faced the question whether diversity jurisdiction could be invoked in that manner. The case arose when LaPlante, a member of the Blackfeet Tribe, was injured while driving a cattle truck for the Wellman Ranch Company, a Montana corporation with its principal place of business on the Blackfeet Indian Reservation. It was owned by members of the Wellman family, who are also Blackfeet Indians residing on the Reservation. LaPlante filed a personal injury suit against the Wellmans and the Ranch in tribal court, and the defendants questioned jurisdiction. After the tribal court first dismissed the complaint for failure to sufficiently allege facts establishing jurisdiction, LaPlante amended and the tribal court sustained its jurisdiction. Since the tribal court did not permit interlocutory appeals, the Wellmans' insurance carrier, Iowa Mutual, instead filed suit in federal district court naming both LaPlante, the Wellmans, and the Wellman Ranch Company as defendants, seeking a declaratory judgment that it had no obligation to defend and indemnify the Wellmans in the tribal court litigation. As an out-of-state corporation, Iowa Mutual predicated its invocation of federal court jurisdiction on diversity of citizenship. The district court dismissed the suit for lack of federal jurisdiction and the Ninth Circuit affirmed the dismissal. The Supreme Court applied the *National Farmers Union* exhaustion rule to the exercise of diversity jurisdiction, but nevertheless held that dismissal for want of jurisdiction, as opposed to failure to exhaust, was improper and therefore reversed and remanded.

Justice Marshall's opinion for the Court noted:

> We have repeatedly recognized the Federal Government's longstanding policy of encouraging tribal self-government. *See, e.g., Three Affiliated Tribes v. Wold Engineering*, 476 U.S. 877, 890 (1986); *Merrion v. Jicarilla Apache Tribe*, 455 U.S. 130, 138, n. 5 (1982); *White Mountain Apache Tribe v. Bracker*, 448 U.S. 136, 143–144, and n. 10 (1980); *Williams v. Lee*, 358 U.S. 217, 220–221 (1959).[22] This policy reflects the fact that Indian tribes retain

---

[22] [5] Numerous federal statutes designed to promote tribal government embody this policy. *See, e.g.,*

"attributes of sovereignty over both their members and their territory," *United States v. Mazurie*, 419 U.S. 544, 557 (1975), to the extent that sovereignty has not been withdrawn by federal statute or treaty. The federal policy favoring tribal self-government operates even in areas where state control has not been affirmatively pre-empted by federal statute. "[Absent] governing Acts of Congress, the question has always been whether the state action infringed on the right of reservation Indians to make their own laws and be ruled by them." *Williams v. Lee, supra*, at 220.

Tribal courts play a vital role in tribal self-government, cf. *United States v. Wheeler*, 435 U.S. 313, 332 (1978), and the Federal Government has consistently encouraged their development.[23] Although the criminal jurisdiction of the tribal courts is subject to substantial federal limitation, see *Oliphant v. Suquamish Indian Tribe*, 435 U.S. 191 (1978), their civil jurisdiction is not similarly restricted. See *National Farmers Union, supra*, at 854–855, and nn. 16 and 17. If state-court jurisdiction over Indians or activities on Indian lands would interfere with tribal sovereignty and self-government, the state courts are generally divested of jurisdiction as a matter of federal law. *See Fisher v. District Court*, 424 U.S. 382 (1976); *Williams v. Lee, supra*.

The Court therefore saw a great potential for the exercise of federal jurisdiction under diversity to interfere with the federally protected functioning of tribal courts.

To accommodate these two interests, the Court, while recognizing that federal diversity jurisdiction existed, indicated that abstention in favor of exhaustion of tribal remedies should be required for federal diversity jurisdiction as well as federal question jurisdiction. Thus, Justice Marshall wrote:

A federal court's exercise of jurisdiction over matters relating to reservation affairs can also impair the authority of tribal courts, as we recognized in *National Farmers Union*.[24] [In *National Farmers Union* promotion] of tribal self-government and self-determination required that the Tribal Court have "the first opportunity to evaluate the factual and legal bases for the challenge" to its jurisdiction. We remanded th[at] case to the District Court to determine whether the federal action should be dismissed or stayed pending exhaustion of the remedies available in the tribal court system.[25]

---

25 U.S.C. §§ 450, 450a (Indian Self-Determination and Education Assistance Act); 25 U.S.C. §§ 476–479 (Indian Reorganization Act); 25 U.S.C. §§ 1301–1341 (Indian Civil Rights Act).

[23] [6] For example, Title II of the Indian Civil Rights Act provides "for the establishing of educational classes for the training of judges of courts of Indian offenses." 25 U.S.C. § 1311(4).

[24] [7] *See also Santa Clara Pueblo v. Martinez*, 436 U.S. 49, 60 (1978) (providing a federal forum for claims arising under the Indian Civil Rights Act interferes with tribal autonomy and self-government).

[25] [8] As the Court's directions on remand in *National Farmers Union* indicate, the exhaustion rule enunciated in *National Farmers Union* did not deprive the federal courts of subject-matter jurisdiction. Exhaustion is required as a matter of comity, not as a jurisdictional prerequisite. In this respect, the rule is analogous to principles of abstention articulated in *Colorado River Water Conservation Dist. v. United States*, 424 U.S. 800 (1976): even where there is concurrent jurisdiction in both the state and federal courts, deference to state proceedings renders it appropriate for the federal courts to decline jurisdiction

Although petitioner alleges that federal jurisdiction in this case is based on diversity of citizenship, rather than the existence of a federal question, the exhaustion rule announced in *National Farmers Union* applies here as well. Regardless of the basis for jurisdiction, the federal policy supporting tribal self-government directs a federal court to stay its hand in order to give the tribal court a "full opportunity to determine its own jurisdiction." *Ibid.* In diversity cases, as well as federal-question cases, unconditional access to the federal forum would place it in direct competition with the tribal courts, thereby impairing the latter's authority over reservation affairs. See *Santa Clara Pueblo v. Martinez*, 436 U.S. 49, 59 (1978). Adjudication of such matters by any nontribal court also infringes upon tribal lawmaking authority, because tribal courts are best qualified to interpret and apply tribal law.

As *National Farmers Union* indicates, proper respect for tribal legal institutions requires that they be given a "full opportunity" to consider the issues before them and "to rectify any errors." The federal policy of promoting tribal self-government encompasses the development of the entire tribal court system, including appellate courts. At a minimum, exhaustion of tribal remedies means that tribal appellate courts must have the opportunity to review the determinations of the lower tribal courts. In this case, the Tribal Court has made an initial determination that it has jurisdiction over the insurance dispute, but Iowa Mutual has not yet obtained appellate review, as provided by the Tribal Code, ch. 1, § 5. Until appellate review is complete, the Blackfeet Tribal Courts have not had a full opportunity to evaluate the claim and federal courts should not intervene.

The Court also rejected the most common reason claimed for the existence of diversity jurisdiction — avoiding local bias — as a justification for avoiding exhaustion. The Court wrote:

Petitioner also contends that the policies underlying the grant of diversity jurisdiction — protection against local bias and incompetence — justify the exercise of federal jurisdiction in this case. We have rejected similar attacks on tribal court jurisdiction in the past. See, *e.g.*, *Santa Clara Pueblo v. Martinez*, 436 U.S., at 65, and n. 21. The alleged incompetence of tribal courts is not among the exceptions to the exhaustion requirement established in *National Farmers Union*, 471 U.S., at 856, n. 21, n12, and would be contrary to the congressional policy promoting the development of tribal courts. Moreover, the Indian Civil Rights Act, 25 U.S.C. § 1302, provides non-Indians with various protections against unfair treatment in the tribal courts.

Since the Court held that the exhaustion limitation constituted an abstention rule vindicating the comity interests between tribal and federal courts, rather than a jurisdictional limitation, it found dismissal for lack of jurisdiction improper and reversed.

---

in certain circumstances. In *Colorado River*, as here, strong federal policy concerns favored resolution in the nonfederal forum.

The Court recognized that its rule would mean that the matter might return to federal court after a final tribal judgment. Expanding on the significance of the *National Farmers Union* exhaustion rule, the Court noted:

> Although petitioner must exhaust available tribal remedies before instituting suit in federal court, the Blackfeet Tribal Courts' determination of tribal jurisdiction is ultimately subject to review. If the Tribal Appeals Court upholds the lower court's determination that the tribal courts have jurisdiction, petitioner may challenge that ruling in the District Court. Unless a federal court determines that the Tribal Court lacked jurisdiction, however, proper deference to the tribal court system precludes relitigation of issues raised by the LaPlantes' bad-faith claim and resolved in the Tribal Courts.

Thus, the Court seemed to suggest that in a case predicated on diversity jurisdiction, the only matter left for the federal district court to decide after exhaustion of tribal remedies is the federal question involving the existence of tribal jurisdiction. If the federal court sustains the existence of that jurisdiction, it must defer to the tribal adjudication.

Justice Stevens, the author of the *National Farmers Union* opinion wrote a separate opinion concurring in part and dissenting in part. Comparing the effect of diversity jurisdiction on state court authority with the impact of *Iowa Mutual*'s holding on the relationship with tribal courts, Justice Stevens expressed his disagreement with the majority approach as follows:

> Until today, we have never suggested that an Indian tribe's judicial system is entitled to a greater degree of deference than the judicial system of a sovereign State. Today's opinion, however, requires the federal court to avoid adjudicating the merits of a controversy also pending in Tribal Court although it could reach those merits if the case instead were pending in state court. Thus, although I of course agree with the Court's conclusion that the Federal District Court had subject-matter jurisdiction over the case, I respectfully dissent from its exhaustion holding.

Can one easily explain this anomaly for federal diversity jurisdiction that *Iowa Mutual* creates?

NOTES ON FEDERAL CIVIL JURISDICTION INVOLVING INDIAN COUNTRY

1. **Indians, Indian Country, and Federal Jurisdiction:** Despite the special tribal-federal relationship, as *Oneida*, *National Farmers Union*, and *Iowa Mutual* indicate, the mere fact that a case involves Indians or arises in Indian country does not create federal jurisdiction, and such jurisdiction cannot be created by consent through choice of forum clauses. *E.g.*, *Iowa Management & Consultants, Inc. v. Sac & Fox Tribe of Mississippi in Iowa*, 207 F.3d 488 (8th Cir. 2000) (federal district court lacked subject matter jurisdiction over enforcement of a contractual arbitration agreement arising from alleged breach of casino consulting/management contract). Rather, as the Supreme Court held as early as *Cherokee Nation v.*

Georgia, 30 U.S. (5 Pet.) 1 (1831), a party seeking to invoke federal jurisdiction must demonstrate through allegations in the complaint that the case falls within both the federal statutes conferring jurisdiction and the boundaries of federal court jurisdiction specified in Article III, section 2, clause 1 of the United States Constitution. Generally, to do so, the party must invoke federal question jurisdiction under 28 U.S.C. §§ 1331, 1343 (claim arises under federal civil rights statutes), or 1362. Some parties claim federal jurisdiction under diversity jurisdiction, 28 U.S.C. § 1332, which is now subject to the *Iowa Mutual* exhaustion rule. Furthermore, some cases, such as tribal claims brought against the United States, come into federal court because the United States is a party. 28 U.S.C. § 1505.

2. **Federal Question Jurisdiction and Indian Law:** By far the most common provisions invoked to establish federal question jurisdiction for cases arising in Indian country are 28 U.S.C. §§ 1362 and 1331. Indian tribes frequently invoke section 1362 to establish federal jurisdiction over claims brought against state or federal officials seeking to enforce tribal sovereignty by limiting state or federal efforts to regulate or tax transactions arising on the reservation. *E.g., Arizona v. San Carlos Apache Tribe*, 463 U.S. 545, 559 n.10 (1983); *Moe v. Confederated Salish and Kootenai Tribes*, 425 U.S. 463, 472–73 (1976) (discussing the legislative history and purpose of section 1362); *Citizen Potawatomi Nation v. Norton*, 248 F.3d 993 (10th Cir. 2001). *But see Canadian St. Regis Band of Mohawk Indians v. New York*, 146 F. Supp. 2d 170 (N.D.N.Y. 2001) (because of the requirement in section 1362 that the tribe be federally recognized, a recognized Canadian Indian band cannot invoke section 1362 as a basis for federal question jurisdiction to litigate the legal validity of an 1824 treaty with the State of New York raising similar claims to those posed in *Oneida*). Congress passed 28 U.S.C. § 1362 in 1966 in order to give Indian tribes access to federal courts on federal issues without regard to the $10,000 amount-in-controversy requirement then included in 28 U.S.C. § 1331. The legislative history suggests that Congress contemplated section 1362 would be used particularly in situations in which the United States suffered from a conflict of interest or was otherwise unable or unwilling to bring suit as trustee for the Indians. *See* S. Rep. No. 1507, 89th Cong., 2d Sess. 2–3 (1966); H. Rep. No. 2040, 89th Cong., 2d Sess. 2, 4 (1966). Recall also that *Cherokee Nation v. Georgia*, 30 U.S. (5 Pet.) 1 (1831), set forth and discussed in Ch. 1, Sec. C.2, had suggested that at the time the Constitution was framed no one anticipated Indian tribes coming to federal courts for redress of their grievances, thereby raising some questions about the standing of tribes to sue on their own without the United States government suing on their behalf. Section 1362 therefore actually had far greater impact than Congress imagined by freeing Indian tribes from any perceived necessity of having the federal government sue on their behalf. Consequently, it permitted tribes to bring long dormant claims the federal government refused to pursue such as the land claims at issue in *Oneida*, and unleashed a flood of similar litigation, particularly on the east coast. *See* Ch. 6, Sec. A.5 for further discussion of these land claims.

Both *Oneida* and *National Farmers Union* highlight the fact that for a case to arise under federal law for purposes of either 28 U.S.C. § 1331 or 28 U.S.C. § 1362, federal law must not only be involved in the disposition, it must create the cause of action, *i.e.*, the claim or the right to relief. Notice that in both cases, the Court creates an implied common law right of action to supply the requirements of the well-pleaded complaint rule. By contrast, in *Santa Clara Pueblo v. Martinez*, 436 U.S. 49, 60 (1978), set forth and discussed in Ch. 3, Sec. D.1, the Court refused to imply a federal cause of action to enforce the provisions of the Indian Civil Rights Act of 1968, 25 U.S.C. §§ 1301–03, since asserting federal jurisdiction in that case was thought inconsistent with the delicate balance between federal intervention and tribal sovereignty Congress drew in enacting that statute. Thus, not all federal statutes affecting Indians necessarily can be enforced in federal courts. For further discussion of this issue in connection with tribal claims against state officers for violation of federal common law rules governing the scope of state jurisdiction in Indian country, see Note 7, *infra*.

3.   **Diversity Jurisdiction:** Since federal law now treats Indians as citizens of the states in which they reside (although the analytic justification for this result remains obscure), *Iowa Mutual* highlights the fact that diversity jurisdiction might be possible under 28 U.S.C. § 1332 for reservation related causes of action. The broad exhaustion of tribal remedies holding of *Iowa Mutual* would seem to relegate the initial decisions in such cases to tribal court. At least one commentator has noted that "*LaPlante*'s sweeping conclusion of nonjurisdictional nonreviewability grants potentially enormous authority to tribal courts acting within their jurisdiction in civil cases." Dennis W. Arrow, *Contemporary Tensions in Constitutional Indian Law*, 12 OKLA. CITY U. L. REV. 469, 491 (1987).

If, however, after exhaustion of tribal remedies a court finds that the tribal court lacked jurisdiction or if for other reasons determines that exhaustion is unnecessary, the reach of federal diversity jurisdiction becomes quite important. Certainly, for individual Indians, the normal domicile rule will establish their state citizenship. The harder problem not raised in *Iowa Mutual* is whether tribally or federally chartered Indian corporations have state citizenship and whether agencies of the tribal government have state citizenship for purposes of section 1332. Notice that in *Iowa Mutual*, the Wellman Ranch Company was incorporated under state law. Under the express language of section 1332(c)(1), the Wellman Ranch Company therefore was "deemed to be a citizen of any State in which it has been incorporated *and* of the State where it has its principal place of business," in that case both of which were Montana. That result occurred notwithstanding the fact that it was wholly owned by tribal members who resided on and did business on the reservation. What if the Wellmans had chosen the Fort Peck Indian Tribe, rather than the State of Montana, as the government to which they looked to incorporate their ranch? Would the Ranch still have state citizenship for diversity purposes? Does the fact that the statute is phrased in the conjunctive mean that a corporation should not be ascribed state citizenship based on its principal place of business unless it also is incorporated by a state? The cases, have tended to ignore the precise language of the statute and ascribed to a tribally chartered corporation the citizenship of its principal place of business in order to create diversity jurisdiction. *E.g., Wells Fargo Bank, N.A. v. Lake of the Torches Econ. Dev. Corp.*, 658 F.3d 684 (7th Cir. 2011); *Cook v. AVI Casino Enters., Inc.*, 548 F.3d 718, 722–724 (9th Cir. 2008). Can tribes avoid state citizenship for diversity jurisdiction purposes by declining to incorporate their organizations or entities altogether, and setting them up as agencies of the government? At least four federal circuits have concluded that

Indian tribes, tribal authorities, and tribal agencies do not have any state citizenship for purposes of section 1332. *American Vantage Companies, Inc. v. Table Mountain Rancheria*, 292 F.3d 1091 (9th Cir. 2002); *Ninigret Dev. Corp. v. Narragansett Indian Wetuomuck Hous. Auth.*, 207 F.3d 21, 27 (1st Cir. 2000); *Romanella v. Hayward*, 114 F.3d 15, 16 (2d Cir. 1997) (per curiam); *Gaines v. Ski Apache*, 8 F.3d 726, 729 (10th Cir. 1993). How should a federal court for diversity jurisdiction purposes treat a federally-chartered tribal corporation incorporated under section 17 of the Indian Reorganization Act? Must these questions be considered in establishing the form of business organization for any tribal enterprise, such as a casino, or does the holding of *Iowa Mutual* totally resolve such concerns?

The Ninth Circuit applied the *Iowa Mutual* exhaustion rule to prevent an Indian *plaintiff* from invoking diversity jurisdiction to sue a non-Indian defendant for breach of contract for a claim arising on the reservation. *Wellman v. Chevron U.S.A., Inc.*, 815 F.2d 577 (9th Cir. 1987). Was this approach a proper application of the *Iowa Mutual* rule? Was the requirement of exhaustion of tribal remedies a personal right or one which affected the sovereignty of the tribe and therefore could not be waived by a tribal member?

4. The Exhaustion Rule: As footnote 8 in *Iowa Mutual* indicates, the requirement of exhaustion of tribal remedies imposed on federal question jurisdiction by *National Farmers Union* and on diversity jurisdiction by *Iowa Mutual*, is not a jurisdictional limitation, but rather a rule of comity-based abstention. Furthermore, as footnote 21 in *National Farmers Union* indicates, exhaustion of tribal remedies is not invariably required. In *Strate v. A-1 Contractors*, 520 U.S. 438 (1997), set forth and discussed in Ch. 3, Sec. C.1, the Court specifically indicated that it would no longer require exhaustion of tribal remedies after it held that an auto accident claim between two non-Indians arising on a highway right-of-way running through the reservation was not within the Tribe's jurisdiction.

The nature and extent of the requirement of exhaustion of tribal remedies has been heavily litigated in lower federal courts in a wide variety of circumstances. *E.g., Sharber v. Spirit Mountain Gaming Inc.*, 343 F.3d 974 (9th Cir. 2003) (stay of federal action for purposes of exhaustion of tribal remedies required on question of tribal jurisdiction to hear actions based on the federal Family and Medical Leave Act); *Garcia v. Akwesasne Housing Authority*, 268 F.3d 76 (2d Cir. 2001) (exhaustion of tribal remedies not required where no tribal action pending and existence of tribal avenue of relief uncertain); *Krempel v. Prairie Island Indian Community*, 125 F.3d 621 (8th Cir. 1997) (no requirement of exhaustion of tribal remedies where no tribal court exists); *United States v. Tsosie*, 92 F.3d 1037 (10th Cir. 1996) (exhaustion of tribal remedies required in a suit brought by the United States on behalf of a Navajo allottee raising trespass and ejectment claims against another Navajo allegedly illegally occupying the property); *see generally* Timothy W. Joranko, *Exhaustion of Tribal Remedies in the Lower Courts After* National Farmers Union *and* Iowa Mutual: *Toward a Consistent Treatment of Tribal Courts by the Federal Judicial System*, 78 MINN. L. REV. 259 (1993); Laurie Reynolds, *Adjudication in Indian Country: The Confusing Parameter of State, Federal, and Tribal Jurisdiction*, 38 WM. & MARY L. REV. 539 (1997); Laurie Reynolds, *Exhaustion of Tribal Remedies: Extolling Tribal Sovereignty While Expanding Federal Jurisdiction*, 73 N.C. L. REV. 1089 (1995). One of the leading commentators on tribal courts has suggested that the exhaustion of tribal remedies requirement announced in *National Farmers Union* and *Iowa Mutual* "further spurred the development of tribal courts as the locus — at least in the first instance — for important civil litigation arising on the reservation." Frank Pommersheim, *Tribal Courts and the Federal Judiciary: Opportunities and Challenges for a Constitutional Democracy*, 58 MONT. L. REV. 313, 323 (1997).

Despite Professor Pommersheim's optimistic predictions for tribal courts, the exhaustion of tribal remedies requirement of *National Farmers Union* and *Iowa Mutual* has proved to be a two-edged sword for Indian tribes. Predictably, after these decisions were announced a brief lull in federal litigation occurred while parties exhausted their tribal remedies. After the parties exhausted their tribal remedies, notice, however, that both cases contemplate the cases will return to federal courts since each sustains the district court's jurisdiction and treats the exhaustion requirement as one of comity abstention rather than jurisdictional limitation. Significantly, none of the cases considered the fact that after exhaustion of tribal remedies the parties might have a final tribal judgment that perhaps might be entitled to full faith and credit under 28 U.S.C. § 1738 or at least comity. *See* Ch. 3, Sec. E.1. Neither concept was mentioned in either opinion and the Court simply assumed, without considering the question, that the federal courts might be free to completely relitigate the question of jurisdiction after it has been fully and fairly litigated in the tribal forum. *Contrast, Baldwin v. Iowa State Traveling Men's Ass'n*, 283 U.S. 522 (1931) (issuing court's determination on jurisdiction precluded redetermination of the question on collateral attack).

Predictably, such cases did return to federal courts in large numbers after exhaustion and set the stage for the development of the modern judicial plenary power cases introduced in Ch. 3, Sec. A. Once those cases returned to federal courts, the courts worked out a doctrinal regime to review the tribal determination of its own jurisdiction, as contemplated by *National Farmers Union* and *Iowa Mutual* without considering the full faith and credit or comity implications of such review. In *FMC v. Shoshone-Bannock Tribes*, 905 F.2d 1311 (9th Cir. 1990), the Ninth Circuit Court of Appeals reversed the district court's determination that a tribe did not have jurisdiction to enforce in tribal court a Tribal Employment Rights Ordinance against a non-Indian owned company operating a phosphorus plant on the reservation. In reaching its conclusion the Ninth Circuit sought to establish the appropriate deference under *National Farmers* which the district court should have applied. Without ever considering full faith and credit or comity, it concluded that a clearly erroneous standard must be applied to a tribal court's finding of fact on the jurisdictional issue, but that it could review *de novo*. Reaching the merits, the Ninth Circuit reversed the district court's determination of lack of tribal jurisdiction, agreeing with the tribal court that under *Montana v. United States*, which provided the appropriate rule, the tribe retained its power to regulate employment practices because the company had entered into a consensual relationship with the tribe. The Ninth Circuit also rejected as prematurely brought Indian Civil Rights Act (ICRA) claims which had not been raised in the tribal court and relegated the company back to the tribal court to afford an opportunity to challenge the ordinance under ICRA. If the tribal court rejects the ICRA claims raised by the company, can the district court review those claims after exhaustion? *See AT&T Corp. v. Coeur*

D'Alene Tribe, 295 F.3d 899, 904 (9th Cir. 2002) (federal courts may not readjudicate tribal court determinations of federal law "absent a finding that the tribal court lacked jurisdiction or that its judgment be denied comity for some other valid reason").

Later Ninth Circuit decisions have affirmed that in conducting de novo review of tribal court decisions regarding their own jurisdiction, federal courts owe some deference: " . . . [B]ecause tribal courts are competent law-applying bodies, the tribal court's determination of its own jurisdiction is entitled to 'some deference.' " *Water Wheel Camp Rec. Area, Inc. v. Larance*, 642 F.3d 802, 808 (9th Cir. 2011) (agreeing with tribal court in supporting tribal jurisdiction). How does "some deference" operate, especially if the federal court's legal analysis points it toward a different conclusion on questions such as "consent" under *Montana*? Is "some deference" analogous to a canon of construction? For a critique of the practice of federal de novo review, see Robert N. Clinton, *Comity and Colonialism: The Federal Courts' Frustration of Tribal-Federal Cooperation*, 36 ARIZ. ST. L.J. 1 (2004). Are the results of *National Farmers Union* and *Iowa Mutual* actually the federal colonial domination of tribal courts by the federal judiciary?

A perfect example of the problem involves a case on which Professor Pommersheim sat as a member of the Rosebud Sioux Supreme Court, the dispute over Crazy Horse Malt Liquor. Seth Big Crow was appointed executor of the estate of Crazy Horse (Tasunke Witko) by the Rosebud Tribal Court. In that capacity, he sued the brewers and distributors of Crazy Horse Malt Liquor in Rosebud Tribal Court on a variety of tribal and federal claims including invasion of the right of publicity, violation of Lakota law regarding the ownership of names, trademark violation under the federal Lanham Act, and violation of the Indian Arts and Crafts Act. The complaint sought both an injunction against the use of the name of Crazy Horse and various traditional Lakota compensatory remedies. The Rosebud trial court dismissed the complaint for lack of jurisdiction, noting that the defendants were not located or otherwise doing business on the reservation, and while the defendants through other retailers sold various other products they manufactured, on the reservation, they had refrained from selling Crazy Horse Malt Liquor anywhere in South Dakota, including the Rosebud Sioux Reservation. The Rosebud Sioux Supreme Court, sitting en banc, reversed the dismissal and remanded the case to the tribal court. *Estate of Tasunke Witko v. G. Heilman Brewing Co. (In re Tasunke Witko)*, Civ. No. 93-204, slip op. at 2 (Rosebud Sioux Sup. Ct. 1996). It reasoned that the label on the beer, by referring to the Black Hills and Crazy Horse, had specifically targeted traditional Lakota territory and that the continuing pattern of selling other nonalcoholic products through retailers in South Dakota and on the Reservation had created sufficient contacts with the Rosebud Sioux Tribe that the Tribe had both personal and subject matter jurisdiction. The Rosebud Sioux Supreme Court first held the tests of *Montana v. United States*, 450 U.S. 544 (1981), set forth and discussed in Ch. 3, Sec. C.1, inapplicable to the case, reasoning that a tribal court's civil jurisdiction, like that of a state court was not limited to cases arising in its territory, so long as sufficient contacts could be established to sustain the exercise of personal jurisdiction. Ultimately, however, the Rosebud Sioux Supreme Court ruled in the alternative that if *Montana* were applicable to the case, the defendants' conduct satisfied both of the *Montana* exceptions. First, the court stated the defendants' failure to enter into a consensual relationship with the Estate for the use of the name and reputation of Crazy Horse satisfies the first exception. Second, the court further found that the defendants' conduct satisfies the second exception, because the Tribe's health and welfare depend upon the Tribe's ability to provide a forum for resolution of the defendants' allegedly harmful conduct. *See generally* Joseph William Singer, *Publicity Rights and the Conflict of Laws: Tribal Court Jurisdiction in the Crazy Horse Case*, 41 S.D. L. REV. 1, 36 (1996).

Rather than completing the tribal process, including ultimate trial of the matter, the defendants filed suit in federal district court to enjoin the prosecution of the matter on the ground that the tribal court had no jurisdiction. The federal district court remanded the case to the tribal court for further proceedings on the questions of personal and subject matter jurisdiction and the brewer and distributor appealed. In *Hornell Brewing Co. v. Rosebud Sioux Tribal Court*, 133 F.3d 1087 (8th Cir. 1998), the Eighth Circuit vacated the district court judgment and directed the injunction be granted, finding that the tribal court had no subject matter jurisdiction. Giving absolutely no deference to the reasoning or findings of law of the Rosebud Sioux Supreme Court, the Eighth Circuit wrote:

> It is a fundamental fact in the present case that the Breweries do not manufacture, sell, or distribute Crazy Horse Malt Liquor on the Reservation. The tribal court asserts that the Breweries do engage in the sale of other beverages, including some alcoholic beverages, on the Reservation. We find, as did the district court, that this argument is irrelevant. This is not the activity for which complaint is made. The only grounds upon which the Rosebud Sioux Supreme Court asserted subject matter jurisdiction was that the Breweries' conduct affects the health and welfare of the Tribe in that the Tribe should be able to provide a forum for resolution of harm suffered by its members on the Reservation. The district court rejected this reasoning and stated:
>
> > If providing a forum for its members would be a sufficient reason to confer subject matter jurisdiction upon the tribal courts when a tribal member is a party to a lawsuit, it follows that the tribal courts would always have civil subject matter jurisdiction over non-Indians. There would have been no reason for the discussion in *Montana* regarding the broad general rule of no civil jurisdiction over non-Indians and the two narrow exceptions to that general rule. Therefore, this Court does not agree that the second *Montana* exception provides tribal civil subject matter jurisdiction over the brewing companies in this case, under the present record.
>
> We agree with this conclusion.

133 F.3d at 1093.

The inconsistency between the exhaustion of tribal remedies requirement of *National Farmers Union* and concepts of full faith and credit surfaced in the Ninth Circuit in *Wilson v. Marchington*, 127 F.3d 805 (9th Cir. 1997), in which a party sought full faith and credit for a tribal judgment which the judgment debtor tried to collaterally attack defensively in the enforcement proceedings based on lack of tribal jurisdiction. In order to facilitate the collateral review of the tribal court jurisdiction contemplated by *National Farmers Union*, the Ninth Circuit rejected the application of the Full Faith and Credit Act, 28 U.S.C. § 1738, to tribal judgments and instead adopted a flexible comity approach to recognition. Since comity, unlike full faith and credit, permits the enforcing court to redetermine jurisdiction, even if already litigated in the issuing forum, the Ninth Circuit independently reviewed the tribal court's jurisdiction over a suit brought by a tribal member against a non-Indian for an automobile accident arising on a state highway right-of-way within the reservation and, affording no deference to the legal conclusions of the tribal court, concluded that the tribal court lacked jurisdiction under the authority of *Strate v. A-1 Contractors*, 520 U.S. 438 (1997).

In another article, written shortly after *National Farmers Union* and *Iowa Mutual*, Professor Pommersheim wrote:

> Before *Santa Clara Pueblo, National Farmers Union*, and *Iowa Mutual*, it was relatively easy to circumvent tribal courts. The notions of a direct federal cause of action under the Indian Civil Rights Act, federal question jurisdiction, and diversity jurisdiction permitted a significant bulk of civil causes of action arising on the reservation to be brought directly in federal courts, without any concern for the tribal forum. As a result, there was little federal concern for what occurred in tribal courts. There was also scant interest in the question of federal review and in the overall relationship of tribal courts to the federal system. But when direct access to federal courts was sharply curtailed, there was a concomitant growth of tribal court litigation and a renewed litigant and federal interest in prescribing the boundaries of tribal authority.

Frank Pommersheim, *The Crucible of Sovereignty: Analyzing Issues of Tribal Jurisdiction*, 31 ARIZ. L. REV. 329, 360–61 (1989) (footnotes omitted).

With the benefit of hindsight, has the exhaustion of tribal remedies requirement proved as helpful to tribal courts as it sounded, or have *National Farmers Union* and *Iowa Mutual* merely invented out of the whole cloth commonly known as federal common law a review procedure *not authorized by federal statute* by which federal courts review the jurisdictional determinations of tribal courts? By what authority did they gain that power?

5.   State Sovereign Immunity: One problem frequently encountered by Indian tribes filing suit against states, state agencies, or sometimes state officials involves the state sovereign immunity the Supreme Court has found protected by the Eleventh Amendment. Interestingly, one of the earliest contexts in which the United States Supreme Court applied the Eleventh Amendment was the case of *Cherokee Nation v. Georgia*, 30 U.S. (5 Pet.) 1 (1831), set forth and discussed in Ch. 1, Sec. C.2. In that case, Georgia claimed sovereign immunity and refused to respond to the process issued from the Supreme Court, declining to appear to defend its position. Chief Justice Marshall's single-sentence response to the claim of state sovereign immunity clearly demonstrated that the Court then thought the Eleventh Amendment should be read literally, rather than protecting some broader concept of state immunity. On its face, the amendment protects states against suit only from citizens of other states and citizens of "any foreign state." Marshall wrote, "The party defendant [the State of Georgia] may then unquestionably be sued in this court."

The later decisions of the Supreme Court, however, have ascribed a far broader meaning to the Eleventh Amendment, reading it to protect state sovereign immunity generally, irrespective of who files the suit. In *Blatchford v. Native Village of Noatak*, 501 U.S. 775 (1991), for example, a Native village sued a state official in federal court seeking payment of funds from him of money allegedly due and unpaid under a state revenue sharing program. The official thought the scheme unconstitutional since he viewed Native governments as "racially exclusive groups" or "racially exclusive organizations," the membership in which derived exclusively from the racial ancestry of their members. The defendant interposed an Eleventh Amendment sovereign immunity defense, and the issue worked its way to the United States Supreme Court. Since 28 U.S.C. § 1362 was intended to permit federally recognized Indian tribes to sue where the United States previously could or would have done so and since the United States was not barred under the Eleventh Amendment from suing a state, *United States v. Texas*, 143 U.S. 621 (1892), the Native Village argued that 28 U.S.C. § 1362 should be read to waive state sovereign immunity in cases filed by an Indian tribe under that section. The Village's position was that Congress had essentially delegated the federal function of suit to the tribes. The Court rejected the notion, finding:

> [Even] assuming that delegation of exemption from state sovereign immunity is theoretically possible, there is no reason to believe that Congress ever contemplated such a strange notion. Even if our decision in *Moe* could be regarded as in any way related to sovereign immunity, it could nevertheless not be regarded as in any way related to congressional "delegation." The opinion does not mention that word, and contains not the slightest suggestion of such an analysis. To say that "§ 1362 . . . suggests that in certain respects tribes suing under this section were to be accorded treatment similar to that of the United States had it sued on their behalf," 425 U.S. at 474, does not remotely imply delegation-only equivalence of treatment. The delegation theory is entirely a creature of respondents' own invention.

501 U.S. at 785–86. The Court by a 7-2 vote therefore rejected the notion that section 1362 waived state sovereign immunity and held the suit barred by the Eleventh Amendment.

While *Native Village of Noatak* seemingly assumed that Congress could waive state sovereign immunity in suits by Indian tribes but had not done so, five years later the Court in a narrowly divided 5-4 decision held that Congress generally had no power to do so under the Indian commerce clause. In *Seminole Tribe of Florida v. Florida*, 517 U.S. 44 (1996), set forth and discussed in Ch. 5, Sec. D.1, the Court held unconstitutional a provision of the Indian Gaming Regulatory Act found in 28 U.S.C. § 2710(d)(7), which expressly authorized an Indian tribe to file suit in federal district court against a state to enforce the obligation of the state contained in that Act to bargain in good faith toward a compact that would permit Class III gaming to occur on Indian lands. In so doing, the Court also overturned a relatively recent holding that Congress had power to abrogate state sovereign immunity pursuant to the interstate commerce clause.

In *Seminole Tribe of Florida*, the Tribe had also sued the Governor of the state to enforce the IGRA statutory obligations. Normally under the doctrine of *Ex parte Young*, 209 U.S. 123 (1908), state officials can be sued without violating Eleventh Amendment sovereign immunity since suits against state officials charging illegal conduct are not generally viewed as suits against the state unless they seek funds from the state treasury, seek to enforce contractual obligations of the state, or seek to adjudicate title to property claimed by the state. In *Seminole Tribe of Florida*, however, the Court refused to permit the suit to proceed against the Governor since Congress in section 2710(d)(7) had prescribed an exclusive remedy that involved an unconstitutional suit against the state itself. The Court held that where Congress had spoken, the Tribe could not substitute the Governor for the suit against the state specified by Congress. Thus, the Court refused to invoke *Ex parte Young* to save the remedial scheme that Congress had sought to create, claiming that substituting the Governor for the state violated the statutory language.

Where tribes have property disputes with states, as they frequently will with respect to adjoining lands or lakebeds and streambeds, tribes may have trouble invoking *Ex parte Young* to permit suit against a state officer in federal court to adjudicate the title dispute. In *Idaho v. Coeur d'Alene Tribe*, 521 U.S. 261 (1997), the Court held that the Tribe could not invoke the *Ex parte Young* doctrine to sue state officials to contest title to the submerged lands and bed of Lake Coeur d'Alene through a quiet title action, but insofar as the Tribe only sought declaratory and injunctive relief against state officials to prevent continuing violations of federal law, the suit could proceed. The Tribe's title to the submerged lands and bed of the Lake was adjudicated in an action brought by the United States on behalf of the Tribe against the State of Idaho. *Idaho v. United States*, 533 U.S. 262 (2001). Note also that while the Native Village of Noatak named a state official as party defendant in its suit, the Supreme Court still held the action barred by Eleventh Amendment sovereign immunity because the complaint required the payment of funds from the state treasury, rather than seeking individual damages from the defendant. Do these cases suggest that where tribes have property, public fund payment, or contractual disputes with a state that only the United States and not the tribe itself can effectively secure relief in federal courts? What model of tribal-federal relations does this line of cases further?

6. Suits Against the United States: For large portions of the nation's history most of the Indian cases litigated involved claims brought against the United States either under special jurisdictional statutes, see *United States v. Sioux Nation of Indians*, 448 U.S. 371, 384 (1980) (Black Hills taking case brought under special statute), the former jurisdiction of the Indian Claims Commission, or the Indian Tucker Act, 28 U.S.C. § 1505. Since many, but not all, of the Indian Tucker Act claims involve breach of trust, the contours of jurisdiction under the Indian Tucker Act are considered in connection with the *Mitchell* cases, set forth and discussed in Sec. A.5, this chapter.

As a product of amendments to the Indian Self-Determination and Education Assistance Act of 1975 (commonly known as Public Law 93-638), another very important source of jurisdiction will involve the Federal Tort Claims Act, 28 U.S.C. §§ 1346(b), 2671 et seq. Section 314 of Public Law 93-638, as amended, provides:

> [w]ith respect to claims resulting from the performance of functions . . . under a contract, grant agreement, or cooperative agreement authorized by the Indian Self-determination and Education Assistance Act . . . an Indian tribe, tribal organization or Indian contractor is deemed hereafter to be part of the Bureau of Indian Affairs in the Department of the Interior . . . while carrying out any such contract or agreement and its employees are deemed employees of the Bureau . . . while acting within the scope of their employment in carrying out the contract agreement: Provided, That after September 30, 1990, any civil action or proceeding involving such claims brought hereafter against any tribe, tribal organization, Indian contractor or tribal employee covered by this provision shall be deemed to be an action against the United States and will be defended by the Attorney General and be afforded the full protection and coverage of the Federal Tort Claims Act. . . .

Pub. L. No. 101-512, Title III, § 314, 104 Stat. 1959, codified at 25 U.S.C. § 450f. In essence, this provision makes tribal contractors and tribal employees federal employees and treats tort actions for personal or property damage as suits against the United States governed by the provisions of the Federal Torts Claims Act. This provision has raised important questions as to which tribal contractors and employees are deemed federal employees for which the United States is liable to defend under the jurisdiction created by the Federal Tort Claims Act. *E.g., FGS Constructors v. Carlow*, 64 F.3d 1230 (8th Cir. 1995) (negligence of tribally contracted engineering firm on federally-funded dam project within Pine Ridge Indian Reservation not within 25 U.S.C. § 450f); *Locke v. United States*, 215 F. Supp. 2d 1033 (D.S.D. 2002) (alleged assault with an air pistol by a tribal police officer on dispatch officer while on break in the police duty room within jurisdiction, but case dismissed on other grounds). Under 25 U.S.C. § 2674, in Federal Tort Claims cases the United States is held "liable, respecting the provisions of this title relating to tort claims, in the same manner and to the same extent as a private individual under like circumstances." Outside of Indian country, this statutory standard generally requires application of state tort law. On reservations where the state has no regulatory or civil adjudicative jurisdiction over matters involving Indians in Indian country should the governing law to which the federal courts look in such cases be tribal law? Some courts, following their practice in non-Indian related cases, adopt state law as the governing principle even though the state law would not otherwise be applicable in a like private suit. *E.g., Locke v. United States*, 215 F. Supp. 2d 1033 (D.S.D. 2002). This approach creates the strange anomaly that the standard of care governing the duties of a *tribal* employee in a suit governed by section 450f is controlled by state law, rather than the law of the tribal government that employs the alleged wrongdoer. Can this result be justified by anything in the language of either section 450f or the Federal Tort Claims Act? The same issue arises when suits are brought against *federal* employees for actions undertaken on tribal land. *Compare Lafromboise v. Leavitt*, 439 F.3d 792 (8th Cir. 2006) (in suit by a tribal member against a non-Indian doctor practicing with the Indian Health Service, state rather than tribal malpractice law applies, because otherwise the federal government would be susceptible to the application of 550 different bodies of tribal law) *with Cheromiah v. United States*, 55 F. Supp. 2d 1295 (D.N.M. 1999) (applying tribal law in a similar suit and relying on plain language of the statute and respect for the political authority of the tribe in the place where the malpractice occurred).

7.   Tribal Suits Against State Officers: In *Inyo County v. Paiute-Shoshone Indians of the Bishop Community of the Bishop Colony*, 538 U.S. 701 (2003), the Tribe sued for damages when county law enforcement officers broke into the tribal casino and seized confidential tribal personnel documents under a search warrant in connection with a state welfare fraud investigation. The complaint invoked, *inter alia*, 42 U.S.C. § 1983, which authorizes suits against state officers for violations of federally protected rights. The Tribe claimed it was denied its rights under the Fourth and Fourteenth Amendments because its sovereign immunity protected it from state process. After the federal District Court granted defendants' motion to dismiss, the Ninth Circuit ruled that even though Public Law 280 allowed the county to enforce state criminal law on the reservation, including welfare fraud against the tribal employee, Public Law 280 did not apply to the Tribe, and any interference with tribal self-government would have to bear a heavy burden of justification based on compelling state law enforcement concerns. No such concerns were manifest. On further appeal to the United States Supreme Court, the Court held that an Indian tribe does not qualify as a person under 42 U.S.C. § 1983 and therefore the suit could not proceed under that statutory authority. Without ruling on the Tribe's immunity claims, Justice Ginsburg's opinion for the Court described 42 U.S.C. § 1983 as "designed to secure private rights against government encroachment . . . not to advance a sovereign's prerogative to withhold evidence relevant to a criminal investigation." The Court sent the case back to the Ninth Circuit to determine whether the case could proceed as a claim "arising under federal law" for purposes of 28 U.S.C. § 1331 or some other federal jurisdictional statute.

Does it make sense to bar Indian nations from access to 42 U.S.C. § 1983 for claims that state officers violated their federal rights? Do tribes even have the kinds of rights that § 1983 — essentially a civil rights statute — was designed to protect? Do states? What about tribes in their capacity as property owners? If a county or city conducted zoning proceedings involving off-reservation tribal land, and failed to comply with due process requirements, would the tribe be able to bring suit after *Bishop Paiute*? Cf. *Jicarilla Apache Nation v. Rio Arriba County*, 440 F.3d 1202 (10th Cir. 2006) (without discussion or reference to *Bishop Paiute*, court entertains and dismisses Tribe's § 1983 suit against county officials for discriminatory assessment of a property tax).

The Tribe also argued that it could bring its claims for injunctive and declaratory relief against the state officers under the general federal common law of jurisdiction in Indian country, and therefore could invoke federal jurisdiction under 28 U.S.C. § 1331. Is that a good argument? If such claims are not allowable, how would you explain the Supreme Court's decisions in cases such as *California v. Cabazon Band of Mission Indians* (suit by tribes against state seeking declaratory judgment that county had no authority to enforce state bingo laws inside reservations, and an injunction against their enforcement), and *New Mexico v. Mescalero Apache Tribe* (suit by tribe to enjoin state from enforcing its hunting and fishing laws against nonmembers on the reservation), both presented in Sec. B.4.b, this chapter? Note that the most important practical consequence of being denied a claim under 42 U.S.C. § 1983 is that prevailing tribes are unable to recover attorneys fees otherwise available under 42 U.S.C. § 1988.

5. Federal Executive Power and the Executive Trust Responsibility

a. The Bureau of Indian Affairs and the Administration of Federal Indian Programs

Since 1789 the federal government has exclusively managed relations with the Indian tribes. Initially, responsibility for that effort was lodged in the Department of War, a department that today is known as the Department of Defense. The Office of Indian Affairs was created in 1824 to centralize all the activities of the Department of War dealing with Indian affairs. In 1849, those responsibilities were transferred to the Department of the Interior at its inception and remains there today. Until the 1950's, the Bureau of Indian Affairs (BIA), as it is known today, remained the central federal home for all federal programs dealing with Indians. Since that time, some federal Indian functions have been separated and reorganized into other agencies. As part of the massive federal bureaucratic reorganization during the Eisenhower administration, the Indian Health Service (IHS) was separated from BIA and moved to the federal department now known as Health and Human Services. Later, the Departments of Commerce, Education, Justice, and Housing and Urban Development each developed separate programmatic initiatives aimed at Indian country. Even within the Department of the Interior, internal reorganization and new statutes have vested portions of the BIA's prior authority in new parts of the Department. The Indian Gaming Regulatory Act of 1988 created the National Indian Gaming Commission within the Department of the Interior and vested it with certain regulatory oversight and management contract approval authority, portions of which were formerly exercised within the BIA. *See* Ch. 5, Sec. E. The American Indian Trust Fund Management Reform Act of 1994, 25 U.S.C. § 4001 et seq. established the Office of the Special Trustee for American Indians to oversee the management of Indian trust assets. Most recently, responding to pending trust litigation, the Secretary of the Interior has created an Office of Historical Trust Accounting to attempt to reconcile and report on old trust accounts.

Since 1977, an Assistant Secretary of the Interior for Indian Affairs has headed the BIA and supervised other Indian related divisions of the Department of the Interior. Previously, the BIA was led by a Commissioner of Indian Affairs who reported, usually through an assistant secretary, to the Secretary of the Interior. A broad account and analysis of the BIA's responsibilities can be found in Robert McCarthy, *The Bureau of Indian Affairs and the Federal Trust Obligation to American Indians*, 19 BYU J. Pub. L. 1 (2004).

The fact that Indian affairs began in the War Department and that the federal bureaucracy supporting Indian affairs predates the emergence of the modern administrative state and the various rules of federal administrative law reflected in the Administrative Procedure Act has created a very unique administrative relationship between the BIA and Congress. While most federal programs are created by explicit federal authorizing statutes spelling out criteria and eligibility, the BIA traditionally was the moving force and initiator of many of the programs it ran. This relationship probably was the result of the fact that the day-to-day formulation of Indian policy was frequently left to the Indian Service during the first 150 years of national Indian policy. The BIA therefore came to be a policy organ unto itself. Congress only mapped out in the broadest possible terms the purposes and objectives of national Indian policy; the Service was left to create programs and initiate action to implement those and other policy objectives. A good historical example of this phenomenon was the creation of the Courts of Indian Offenses or the Indian boarding schools that the BIA imposed on many Indian reservations without explicit statutory authorization. Recall from Chapter 1 that when Indians challenged the legality of the Courts of Indian Offenses for lack of an authorizing statute they were unsuccessful in *United States v. Clapox.*

After repeatedly being asked to approve appropriations from programs that it never created or approved by statute, Congress in 1921 finally enacted the Snyder Act now codified at 25 U.S.C. § 13. This legislation, while directly creating no programs itself, authorizes the BIA to expend appropriated funds "for the benefit, care, and assistance of the Indians throughout the United States" for a long laundry list of purposes. This statute therefore ratified a historical structure in which federal programs benefiting Indians were primarily created by the executive branch rather than through legislative enactment.

This structure poses major problems when federal program or policy initiatives in the field of Indian affairs are challenged for lack of statutory authorization. Consider the next case and ask whether like principles of administrative law would be applied today to any agency other than the BIA.

United States v. Eberhardt, 789 F.2d 1354 (9th Cir. 1986): Members of the Yurok Tribe and the Hoopa Valley Tribe had rights to on-reservation fishing created by the statutes creating the Hoopa Valley Reservation. While the Hoopa Valley members had an organized non-IRA government, at the time no federally-recognized government existed for the Yuroks and other non-Hoopa Valley Indians of the Reservation. In view of this lack of regulatory authority and the endangerment of the fishery, the United States Department of the Interior issued emergency regulations prohibiting commercial fishing by Indians on that part of the Klamath River flowing through the Reservation. Several Yuroks were prosecuted in federal court on charges of unlawful sale of anadromous fish taken within the Reservation in violation of these emergency regulations. They defended against the criminal charges by contesting the legality of the regulations, claiming they interfered with federally-protected rights to fish established by the statutes creating the Hoopa Valley Reservation.

The defendants argued that no statute authorized the emergency regulations and the curtailment of their fishing rights violated federal law. The Court of Appeals rejected the argument. It noted that "[t]he validity of the moratorium depends on whether Congress has given Interior express or implied statutory authority to regulate Indian fishing." As is often true of regulations issued by the Bureau of

Indian Affairs, no express statutory authorization was apparent for the type of commercial fishing moratorium it applied through regulation to the Hoopa Valley Reservation. Nevertheless, the Ninth Circuit found an implied source of authority in the broad contours of 25 U.S.C. §§ 2, 9:

> Interior's authority for issuing the Hoopa Valley Reservation fishing regulations arises from the statutory delegation of powers contained in 25 U.S.C. §§ 2, 9 (1982).

> These provisions generally authorize the Executive to manage Indian affairs but do not expressly authorize Indian fishing regulation. However, ever since these statutes were enacted in the 1830's, they have served as the source of Interior's plenary administrative authority in discharging the federal government's trust obligations to Indians. We conclude that these statutory provisions give Interior sufficient authority to promulgate the Indian fishing regulations at issue here and consequently, we reject appellees' argument that the regulations are invalid in the absence of specific legislation giving Interior authority to regulate Indian fishing.

> . . . .

> We hold that the general trust statutes in Title 25 do furnish Interior with broad authority to supervise and manage Indian affairs and property commensurate with the trust obligations of the United States.

NOTES ON STATUTORY AUTHORITY FOR ADMINISTRATIVE ACTION

1. **Broad Delegations of Power:** Consider the language of the statutory delegations of power to the President and Commissioner of Indian Affairs (now the Assistant Secretary of Interior for Indian Affairs), now contained in 25 U.S.C. §§ 2 and 9. Would such statutes in other contexts be given the expansive interpretation employed in *Eberhardt*? Are these statutes any more than the usual statutes found for any agency that create the agency and describe its general area of responsibility and create rulemaking authority to implement the grants of power contained in authorizing statutes? In other contexts are such provisions considered grants of policymaking authority? Is the expansive commitment of the "management of all Indian affairs" to the BIA subject to any limitations? Is it subject to the grant of power to Congress to regulate commerce with the Indian tribes or to individual rights guarantees of the Constitution?

The *Eberhardt* approach to interpreting 25 U.S.C. §§ 2 and 9 is, of course, not new. These statutes are successors to the precise statutes relied upon in the *Clapox* case, discussed in Ch. 1, Sec. D.2, to uphold the Courts of Indian Offenses. Similarly, more than a century ago in *Rainbow v. Young*, 161 F. 835 (8th Cir. 1908), the Eighth Circuit employed the predecessors of sections 2 and 9 to uphold an order issued by a local BIA agency superintendent barring bill collectors from the Winnebago Reservation on the day lease payments were to be made to tribal members. In all these cases, the courts uphold policy initiatives that originated in the BIA with no greater congressional authorization or guidance than that afforded by sections 2 and 9. Nonetheless, a careful analysis of some cases frequently relied upon for the view that the Secretary's authority is nearly limitless reveals the courts frequently rested in part on more specific statutes relating to federal control over Indian trade or Indian trust property. *See, e.g., United States ex rel. West v. Hitchcock*, 205 U.S. 80 (1907) (agreement with Tribe that Secretary of the Interior had power to determine membership of Tribe for purposes of receiving allotments from ceded land).

2.   Administrative Review in the Context of Broad Delegations of Authority: Since most federal administrative review includes consideration of whether the actions of an administrative agency were authorized by the statute establishing the agency or program, the lack of such clear authorizing statutes for much of what the BIA does poses serious problems for review under the federal Administrative Procedure Act. Tribes often invoke the Administrative Procedure Act (APA), 5 U.S.C. §§ 701–706, to contest BIA action adverse to their economic or political interests. *See, e.g., Navajo Tribe v. United States Dep't of Interior*, 667 F. Supp. 747 (D.N.M. 1987) (failure to follow department's own procedures violated APA); *Joint Tribal Council of Passamaquoddy Tribe v. Morton*, 388 F. Supp. 649 (D. Me.), *aff'd*, 528 F.2d 370 (1st Cir. 1975) (federal government's refusal to initiate litigation on behalf of a tribe reviewable under the APA where the refusal was predicated upon an error of law).

A classic case reflecting the problems caused by lack of authorizing statutes is *Morton v. Ruiz*, 415 U.S. 199 (1974). In *Ruiz*, Indians living near a reservation attacked the limitations developed by BIA for its general assistance program which required the applicants to live on the reservation. While a reviewing court normally might have looked to an authorizing statute to determine whether the agency qualification criteria were in conformity with the law, in *Ruiz* the only authorizing statute was the Snyder Act, 25 U.S.C. § 13, which authorized the BIA to expend funds for the benefit of Indians "throughout the United States." Instead of relying on this broad authorizing statute, the Supreme Court was forced to look to the purposes for which the BIA represented it would spend the funds requested when it sought appropriations from Congress. Finding that the BIA had represented that it would serve Indians living on or near the reservation, the Supreme Court invoked the requirements of the APA to hold that a regulation limiting availability for the general assistance program to Indians living on a reservation was invalid. A further part of its analysis was that the regulation had not been published in the Federal Register or in the Code of Federal Regulations. Although the decision sparked a harsh comment from the leading expert on administrative law, *see* Kenneth C. Davis, *Administrative Law Surprises in the* Ruiz *Case*, 75 COLUM. L. REV. 823 (1975), the requirement that regulations affecting Indian peoples must be published has become part of the administrative law of Indian law.

Likewise, in *Tooahnippah v. Hickel*, 397 U.S. 598 (1970), the Supreme Court held that the decision of the Regional Solicitor disapproving an Indian decedent's will was subject to judicial review under the APA. While 25 U.S.C. § 373 which granted the Secretary or his designee the authority to approve or disapprove Indian wills where trust property was involved contained no standards whatsoever for the exercise of that power, the Supreme Court held that in exercising the secretarial power, the Secretary had no power to deny approval to a will that reflected a rational testamentary scheme based on an administrative concept of equity.

In its most recent foray into this problem, *Lincoln v. Vigil*, 508 U.S. 182 (1993), the Supreme Court's ruling suggested that the lack of a clearly delineated authorizing statute operated to curtail the level of administrative review that could be provided by a court. In the *Vigil* case the beneficiaries of an IHS program benefiting handicapped Indian children in the southwest sued the Director of IHS to prevent the cancellation of the program. Since the contested program, like most IHS and BIA programs was not directly created by statute, but merely involved the administrative agency's decision on how to use lump sum appropriations, the Court held that the decision on how to use the appropriated funds, including the decision to cancel the program, was "committed to the agency's discretion" and therefore under the provisions of the APA not subject to review. Furthermore, for similar reasons the cancellation was not subject to the normal notice and comment period that might otherwise accompany major programmatic changes. Given the lack of clear statutory delineation for much of what the BIA and IHS undertake, does the *Vigil* decision portend the possibility of broad virtually unreviewable discretion in those agencies? Given the lack of statutory delineation of their responsibilities would that outcome be wise? Do any other doctrines operate to rein in executive excess? Consider the role of the trust relationship in accomplishing that result in the materials that follow.

b.   The Trust Relationship

The idea of a trust relationship by Euro-American powers over the indigenous occupants of the Americas can be traced to the earliest colonial discussions in Europe over the rationalizations for invading and controlling the Americas. As noted in Chapter 1, after first contact with the Americas one idea that emerged in Spain was the paternalistic notion that "in [the Indians'] own interests the sovereigns of Spain might undertake the administration of their country, providing them with prefects and governors for their towns, and might even give them new lords, so long as this was clearly for their benefit." FRANCISCO VITORIA, DE INDIS ET DE IURE BELLI RELECTIONES (E. Nys ed., J. Bate trans., 1917). Early British colonial authorities also employed such notions, going so far as to appoint formal trustees for the Mohicans in the colony of Connecticut.

In federal Indian law, the notion of trusteeship has had a long and constantly evolving role. In *Cherokee Nation v. Georgia*, 30 U.S. (5 Pet.) 1 (1831), Chief Justice Marshall described the Indian nations as "domestic dependent nations" and described the tribal-federal relationship as one that "resembles that of a ward to his guardian." In the context of the case, Chief Justice Marshall employed the trusteeship to describe tribal status and explain that Indian nations were not foreign nations within the meaning of Article III of the United States Constitution, but, rather, domestic dependent nations. The focus of the guardianship referenced in *Cherokee Nation* appeared to be the obligations of protection which the United States assumed in the Treaties of Hopewell and Holston with the Cherokee Nation, obligations on which the political branches of the federal government were reneging at the time of the decision. This status, as *Cherokee Nation* conceived it, constituted a protective shield for the tribes against the excesses of hostile outsiders. For Chief Justice Marshall, however, these trust obligations clearly were *not* judicially enforceable by the tribes. As he put it, like other foreign governments, "[t]heir appeal was to the tomahawk, or to the government." Thus, as he put it:

> If it be true that the Cherokee nation have rights, this is not the tribunal in which those rights are to be asserted. If it be true that wrongs have been inflicted, and that still greater are to be apprehended, this is not the tribunal which can redress the past or prevent the future.

The earliest forms of the federal trusteeship therefore neither involved a source of federal power nor a source of judicially enforceable rights. Rather, it involved a description of legal status.

In the late nineteenth century, as federal colonial authority expanded over Indian peoples, the trusteeship was invoked as a nontextual source of federal power *over* Indian peoples. Recall from the *Kagama*, *Lone Wolf*, and *Sandoval* cases that the United States Supreme Court purported to justify the so-called plenary power doctrine in Indian affairs primarily on the basis of unilaterally claimed trust obligations to protect, educate, and elevate the Indians. Fueled by racially charged late nineteenth century notions of social Darwinism, these cases, while repeatedly citing *Cherokee Nation*, did not employ the trusteeship to protect the tribes in the manner *Cherokee Nation* contemplated. Rather, in the late nineteenth century, the trusteeship became a sword the federal government could employ as a source of power to attack tribal governance. The reliance on the political question doctrine in *Lone Wolf* illustrated the fact that, as in *Cherokee Nation*, the Court did not conceive its refashioned trust power to be judicially enforceable or judicially limitable.

Professor Milner Ball characterized the origins of this more paternalistic trust doctrine as follows:

> The likely origin of the trust doctrine is not Marshall's notion of wardship but the later ethnocentrism that also produced the notions of superiority and unrestrained power. For example, in the 1877 case of *Beecher v. Wetherby* the Court announced its presumption that, in dealings with tribes, "the United States would be governed by such considerations of justice as would control a Christian people in their treatment of an ignorant and dependent race." The "semi-barbarous condition" of Indians was expected some day to "give place to the higher civilization of our race."
>
> This uninspiring heritage gave rise to the trust doctrine.

Milner S. Ball, *Constitution, Courts, Indian Tribes*, 1987 A.B.F. RES. J. 1, 63.

Again, in the middle of the twentieth century Indian trusteeship assumed yet another role, that of providing judicially enforceable rights. That development probably evolved slowly as Congress first by special statute and then through the Indian Claims Commission Act permitted Indian tribes for the first time to bring long-standing historical grievances to American courts or administrative tribunals to secure redress. Before the Indian Claims Commission Act was enacted in 1946, Indian tribes could not sue in the Court of Claims without first obtaining a special jurisdictional act from Congress. A number of decisions based on these special jurisdictional statutes began to award damages for breach of trust in the 1940s. *See, e.g., Menominee Tribe v. United States*, 101 Ct. Cl. 10 (1944) (special act instructed court to apply same standards applicable to a private trustee in determining whether United States liable for mismanaging resources); *Seminole Nation v. United States*, 316 U.S. 286 (1942) (government's disbursement of treaty annuity payments at the request of the Tribe to the tribal treasurer and creditors of the Tribe when the government had reason to know that tribal officials were misappropriating tribal funds breached the government's fiduciary obligations to the Indians). In addition, tribes sometimes successfully claimed mismanagement of trust assets in suits before the Indian Claims Commission under provisions permitting adjudication of claims based on statutes and treaties or the so-called "fair and honorable dealing" jurisdiction established by that Act. The Indian Claims Commission served from 1946 to 1978 as a specialized administrative tribunal with jurisdiction to remedy old Indian claims arising before 1946 once and for all. Since the Indian Claims Commission was an administrative tribunal, its breach of trust decisions had little value as precedent in courts of general jurisdiction.

As in the *Menominee Tribe* case, *supra*, early breach of trust claims cases frequently drew analogies to the obligations of private fiduciaries. For example, in *Cheyenne-Arapaho Tribes v. United States*, 512 F.2d 1390 (Ct. Cl. 1975), the Court of Claims held that the United States had breached its trust obligations by failing to invest tribal trust funds at the highest rate of return authorized by law. After setting forth the various investment opportunities for tribal trust funds available under various federal statutes including 25 U.S.C. § 162a and noting that different rates of return might be had by investing trust funds in various investment opportunities afforded by law, the court looked to private trust analogies and described the trusteeship obligations of the federal government as follows:

> The fiduciary duty which the United States undertook with respect to these funds includes the "obligation to maximize the trust income by prudent investment," and the trustee has the burden of proof to justify less than a maximum return. *See Blankenship v. Boyle*, 329 F. Supp. 1089, 1096 (D.D.C. 1971). *See also* Restatement of Trusts 2d § 181 (1959). A corollary duty is the responsibility to keep informed so that when a previously proper investment becomes improper, perhaps because of the opportunity for better (and equally safe) investment elsewhere, funds can be reinvested. While the trustee has a reasonable time in which to make the initial investment or to reinvest, he becomes liable for a breach of trust if that reasonable time is exceeded. Restatement of Trusts 2d §§ 231 and comm. *b*, 181 and comm. *c* (1959).

512 F.2d at 1394. Since federal law did not afford the United States the luxury of investing in securities, including the equity markets, the court was not suggesting that the federal government had to secure the same rate of return as a private trustee. Rather, the federal government was only required to maximize trust income within the available investment alternatives authorized by law. *See also Manchester Band of Pomo Indians v. United States*, 363 F. Supp. 1238 (N.D. Cal. 1973) (federal government liable for failure to maximize return on tribal funds held in trust by the federal government). To what extent do the later cases that follow analogize the duties of the federal government to those of a private trustee? Are the two situations totally analogous? Does the analogy make more sense as applied to

the federal management of real property and other natural resources as compared with other federal actions on behalf of Native nations?

UNITED STATES v. MITCHELL
United States Supreme Court
463 U.S. 206 (1983)

Justice Marshall delivered the opinion of the Court.

The principal question in this case is whether the United States is accountable in money damages for alleged breaches of trust in connection with its management of forest resources on allotted lands of the Quinault Indian Reservation.

I

A

In the 1850's, the United States undertook a policy of removing Indian tribes from large areas of the Pacific Northwest in order to facilitate the settlement of non-Indians. [In the Treaty of Olympia] the Indians ceded to the United States a vast tract of land on the Olympic Peninsula in the State of Washington, and the United States agreed to set aside a reservation for the Indians.

[S]ince the coastal tribes drew their subsistence almost entirely from the water, [it was recommended they] be collected on a reservation suitable for their fishing needs. Acting on this suggestion, President Grant issued an Executive Order on November 4, 1873, designating about 200,000 acres along the Washington coast as an Indian reservation. The vast bulk of this land consisted of rain forest covered with huge, coniferous trees.

In 1905 the federal government began to allot the Quinault Reservation in trust to individual Indians under the [General Allotment Act and] the Quinault Allotment Act of Mar. 4, 1911, ch. 246, 36 Stat. 1345. [T]he entire Reservation had been divided into 2,340 trust allotments, most of which were 80 acres of heavily timbered land [by 1935]. About a third of the Reservation has since gone out of trust, but the bulk of the land has remained in trust status.

The forest resources on the allotted lands have long been managed by the Department of the Interior, which exercises "comprehensive" control over the harvesting of Indian timber. The Secretary of the Interior has broad statutory authority over the sale of timber on reservations. See 25 U.S.C. §§ 406, 407. Sales of timber "shall be based upon a consideration of the needs and best interests of the Indian owner and his heirs," § 406(a), and the proceeds from such sales are to be used for the benefit of the Indians or transferred to the Indian owner, §§ 406(a), 407. Congress has directed the Secretary to adhere to principles of sustained-yield forestry on all Indian forest lands under his supervision. 25 U.S.C. § 466. Under these statutes, the Secretary has promulgated detailed regulations governing the management of Indian timber. 25 CFR pt. 163 (1983). The Secretary is authorized to deduct an administrative fee for his services from the timber revenues paid to

Indian allottees. 25 U.S.C. §§ 406(a), 413.

B

The respondents are 1,465 individuals owning interests in allotments on the Quinault Reservation, an unincorporated association of Quinault Reservation allottees, and the Quinault Tribe, which now holds some portions of the allotted lands. In 1971 respondents [sued in the Court of Claims seeking damages for] mismanagement of timberlands on the Quinault Reservation. More specifically, respondents claimed that the Government (1) failed to obtain a fair market value for timber sold; (2) failed to manage timber on a sustained-yield basis; (3) failed to obtain any payment at all for some merchantable timber; (4) failed to develop a proper system of roads and easements for timber operations and exacted improper charges from allottees for maintenance of roads; (5) failed to pay any interest on certain funds from timber sales held by the Government and paid insufficient interest on other funds; and (6) exacted excessive administrative fees from allottees. Respondents assert that the alleged misconduct constitutes a breach of the fiduciary duty owed them by the United States as trustee under various statutes.

[When the United States moved to dismiss for lack of jurisdiction over these breach of trust claims, the Court of Claims] denied the motion, holding that the General Allotment Act created a fiduciary duty on the United States' part to manage the timber resources properly and thereby provided the necessary authority for recovery of damages against the United States. In *United States v. Mitchell*, 445 U.S. 535 (1980), this Court reversed the ruling of the Court of Claims, stating that the General Allotment Act "created only a limited trust relationship between the United States and the allottee that does not impose any duty upon the Government to manage timber resources." We concluded that "[a]ny right of the respondents to recover money damages for Government mismanagement of timber resources must be found in some source other than [the General Allotment] Act." Since the Court of Claims had not considered respondents' assertion that other statutes render the United States answerable in money damages for the alleged mismanagement in this case, we remanded the case for consideration of these alternative grounds for liability.

On remand, the Court of Claims once again held the United States subject to suit for money damages on most of respondents' claims. [664 F.2d 265 (1981).] The court ruled that [other statutes] imposed fiduciary duties upon the United States in its management of forested allotted lands. The court concluded that the statutes and regulations implicitly required compensation for damages sustained as a result of the Government's breach of its duties. Thus, the court held that respondents could proceed on their claims.

Because the decision of the Court of Claims raises issues of substantial importance concerning the liability of the United States,[26] we granted the Government's petition for certiorari [and] affirm.

---

[26] [7] The Government has informed us that the damages claimed in this suit alone may amount to $100 million. Pet. for Cert. 24.

II

Respondents have invoked the jurisdiction of the Court of Claims under the Tucker Act, 28 U.S.C. § 1491, and its counterpart for claims brought by Indian tribes, 28 U.S.C. § 1505, known as the Indian Tucker Act. The Tucker Act states in pertinent part:

> The Court of Claims shall have jurisdiction to render judgment upon any claim against the United States founded either upon the Constitution, or any Act of Congress, or any regulation of any executive department or implied contract with the United States, or for liquidated or unliquidated damages in cases not sounding in tort.

It is axiomatic that the United States may not be sued without its consent and that the existence of consent is a prerequisite for jurisdiction. [W]e conclude that by giving the Court of Claims jurisdiction over specified types of claims against the United States, the Tucker Act constitutes a waiver of sovereign immunity with respect to those claims. [The Court reviewed the history of the Tucker Act, concluding that its purpose was to permit persons the right to sue the government. The Court also concluded that the Indian Tucker Act, enacted as part of the Indian Claims Commission Act of 1946 conferred jurisdiction on the Court of Claims to hear tribal claims "of a character which would be cognizable in the Court of Claims if the claimant were not an Indian tribe," had "a similar history."] For decades this Court consistently interpreted the Tucker Act as having provided the consent of the United States to be sued *eo nomine* for the classes of claims described in the Act. These decisions confirm the unambiguous thrust of the history of the Act.

In *United States v. Testan*, 424 U.S. 392, 398, 400 (1976), and in *United States v. Mitchell*, 445 U.S., at 538, this Court employed language suggesting that the Tucker Act does not effect a waiver of sovereign immunity. Such language was not necessary to the decision in either case. Without in any way questioning the result in either case, we conclude that this isolated language should be disregarded. If a claim falls within the terms of the Tucker Act, the United States has presumptively consented to suit.

B

It nonetheless remains true that the Tucker Act " 'does not create any substantive right enforceable against the United States for money damages.' " [*United States v. Testan.*] A substantive right must be found in some other source of law, such as "the Constitution, or any Act of Congress, or any regulation of an executive department." 28 U.S.C. § 1491. [The claim must be for money damages against the United States and the claimant must prove that the law relied upon "can fairly be interpreted as mandating compensation by the Federal Government for the damage sustained." *Eastport S.S. Corp. v. United States*, 372 F.2d 1002, 1009 (Ct. Cl. 1967).] In [*Mitchell I*] this Court concluded that the General Allotment Act [providing that the government hold the land "in trust" for the allottees] creates only a limited trust relationship [preventing] improvident alienation of the allotted lands and assur[ing] their immunity from state taxation.

[In conclusion] a court need not find a separate waiver of sovereign immunity in the substantive provision, [although] in determining the general scope of the Tucker Act, this Court has not lightly inferred the United States' consent to suit.

In this case, however, there is simply no question that the Tucker Act provides the United States' consent to suit for claims founded upon statutes or regulations that create substantive rights to money damages. If a claim falls within this category, the existence of a waiver of sovereign immunity is clear. The question in this case is thus analytically distinct: whether the statutes or regulations at issue can be interpreted as requiring compensation.

III

Respondents have based their money claims against the United States on various Acts of Congress and executive department regulations. We begin by describing these sources of substantive law. We then examine whether they can fairly be interpreted as mandating compensation for damages sustained as a result of a breach of the duties they impose.

A

The Secretary of the Interior's pervasive role in the sales of timber from Indian lands began with the Act of June 25, 1910 [as amended 25 U.S.C. §§ 406, 407.] The 1910 Act empowered the Secretary to sell timber on unallotted lands and apply the proceeds of the sales for the benefit of the Indians, § 7, and authorized the Secretary to consent to sales by allottees, with the proceeds to be paid to the allottees or disposed of for their benefit, § 8. Congress thus sought to provide for harvesting timber "in such a manner as to conserve the interests of the people on the reservations, namely, the Indians." From the outset, the Interior Department recognized its obligation to supervise the cutting of Indian timber. In 1911, the Department's Office of Indian Affairs promulgated detailed regulations [addressing] virtually every aspect of forest management, including the size of sales, contract procedures, advertisements and methods of billing, deposits and bonding requirements, administrative fee deductions, procedures for sales by minors, allowable heights of stumps, tree marking and scaling rules, base and top diameters of trees for cutting, and the percentage of trees to be left as a seed source. The regulations applied to allotted as well as tribal lands, and the Secretary's approval of timber sales on allotted lands was explicitly conditioned upon compliance with the regulations.

Over time, deficiencies in the Interior Department's performance of its responsibilities became apparent. [Thus] Congress expressly directed that the Interior Department manage Indian forest resources "on the principle of sustained-yield management." [25 U.S.C. § 466.]

Regulations promulgated under the Act [were] designed to assure that the Indians receive " 'the benefit of whatever profit [the forest] is capable of yielding.' " *White Mountain Apache Tribe v. Bracker*, 448 U.S., at 149 (quoting 25 C.F.R § 41.3(a)(3) (1979)).

In 1964 [amendments directed the Secretary to] consider "the needs and best interests of the Indian owner and his heirs." 25 U.S.C. § 406(a). In performing this duty, the Secretary was specifically required to take into account: ["the need for maintaining the productive capacity of the land for the benefit of the owner and his heirs," the "highest and best use of the land," and "the present and future financial needs of the owner and his heirs"].

[In sum, the] Department of the Interior — through the Bureau of Indian Affairs — "exercises literally daily supervision over the harvesting and management of tribal timber." [*White Mountain Apache Tribe v. Bracker.*] Virtually every stage of the process is under federal control.

B

In [*Mitchell I* the Court held that the General Allotment Act] could not be read "as establishing that the United States has a fiduciary responsibility for management of allotted forest lands." In contrast to the bare trust created by the General Allotment Act, the statutes and regulations now before us clearly give the federal government full responsibility to manage Indian resources and land for the benefit of the Indians. They thereby establish a fiduciary relationship and define the contours of the United States' fiduciary responsibilities.

The language of these statutory and regulatory provisions directly supports the existence of a fiduciary relationship. For example, § 8 of the 1910 Act, as amended, expressly mandates that sales of timber from Indian trust lands be based upon the Secretary's consideration of "the needs and best interests of the Indian owner and his heirs" and that proceeds from such sales be paid to owners "or disposed of for their benefit." 25 U.S.C. § 406(a). Similarly, even in its earliest regulations, the Government recognized its duties in "managing the Indian forests so as to obtain the greatest revenue for the Indians consistent with a proper protection and improvement of the forests." U.S. Office of Indian Affairs, Regulations and Instructions for Officers in Charge of Forests on Indian Reservations 4 (1911). Thus, the Government has "expressed a firm desire that the Tribe should retain the benefits derived from the harvesting and sale of reservation timber." [*White Mountain Apache Tribe v. Bracker.*]

Moreover, a fiduciary relationship necessarily arises when the Government assumes such elaborate control over forests and property belonging to Indians. All of the necessary elements of a common-law trust are present: a trustee (the United States), a beneficiary (the Indian allottees), and a trust corpus (Indian timber, lands, and funds).[27] "[W]here the Federal Government takes on or has control or supervision over tribal monies or properties, the fiduciary relationship normally exists with respect to such monies or properties (unless Congress has provided otherwise) even though nothing is said expressly in the authorizing or underlying statute (or other fundamental document) about a trust fund, or a trust or fiduciary connection." [*Navajo Tribe v. United States*, 624 F.2d 981, 987 (Ct. Cl. 1980).]

Our construction of these statutes and regulations is reinforced by the undisputed existence of a general trust relationship between the United States and the

---

[27] [30] *See* RESTATEMENT (SECOND) OF TRUSTS § 2, Comment h, p. 10 (1959).

Indian people. This Court has previously emphasized "the distinctive obligation of trust incumbent upon the Government in its dealings with these dependent and sometimes exploited people." *Seminole Nation v. United States*, 316 U.S. 286, 296 (1942).

Because the statutes and regulations at issue in this case clearly establish fiduciary obligations of the Government in the management and operation of Indian lands and resources, they can fairly be interpreted as mandating compensation by the federal government for damages sustained. Given the existence of a trust relationship, it naturally follows that the Government should be liable in damages for the breach of its fiduciary duties. It is well established that a trustee is accountable in damages for breaches of trust. See Restatement (Second) of Trusts §§ 205–212 (1959); G. Bogert, Law of Trusts and Trustees § 862 (2d ed. 1965); 3 A. Scott, Law of Trusts § 205 (3d ed. 1967). This Court and several other federal courts have consistently recognized that the existence of a trust relationship between the United States and an Indian or Indian tribe includes as a fundamental incident the right of an injured beneficiary to sue the trustee for damages resulting from a breach of the trust.

The recognition of a damages remedy also furthers the purposes of the statutes and regulations [to] generate proceeds for the Indians. It would be anomalous to conclude that these enactments create a right to the value of certain resources when the Secretary lives up to his duties, but no right to the value of the resources if the Secretary's duties are not performed. "Absent a retrospective damages remedy, there would be little to deter federal officials from violating their trust duties, at least until the allottees managed to obtain a judicial decree against future breaches of trust." [Justice White's dissent from *Mitchell I*.]

The Government contends that violations of duties imposed by the various statutes may be cured by actions for declaratory, injunctive, or mandamus relief against the Secretary. [P]rospective equitable remedies are totally inadequate. [T]he Indian allottees are in no position to monitor federal management of their lands on a consistent basis. Many are poorly educated, most are absentee owners, and many do not even know the exact physical location of their allotments. Indeed, it was the very recognition of the inability of the Indians to oversee their interests that led to federal management in the first place. A trusteeship would mean little if the beneficiaries were required to supervise the day-to-day management of their estate by their trustee or else be precluded from recovery for mismanagement.

In addition, by the time Government mismanagement becomes apparent, the damage to Indian resources may be so severe that a prospective remedy may be next to worthless. For example, if timber on an allotment has been destroyed through Government mismanagement, it will take many years for nature to restore the timber.

[T]he statutes and regulations at issue here can fairly be interpreted as mandating compensation by the federal government for violations of its fiduciary responsibilities in the management of Indian property. The Court of Claims therefore has jurisdiction over respondents' claims for alleged breaches of trusts.

[*Affirmed.*]

JUSTICE POWELL, with whom JUSTICE REHNQUIST and JUSTICE O'CONNOR join, dissenting.

Today [the Court] has effectively reversed the presumption that absent "affirmative statutory authority," the United States has not consented to be sued for damages. It has substituted a contrary presumption, applicable to the conduct of the United States in Indian affairs, that the United States has consented to be sued for statutory violations and other departures from the rules that govern private fiduciaries. I dissent from the Court's departure from long-settled principles.

I

The Court does not — and clearly cannot — contend that any of the statutes standing alone reflects the necessary legislative authorization of a damages remedy. None of the statutes contains any "provision . . . that expressly makes the United States liable" for [mismanagement] or grants a right of action "with specificity." [*Testan.*] Indeed, nothing in the timber-sales statutes addresses in any respect the institution of damages actions against the United States. Nor is there any indication in the legislative history [indicating congressional intent to consent to damages actions for mismanagement].

The Court for the most part rests its decision on the implausible proposition that statutes that do not in terms create a right to payment of money nonetheless may support a damages action against the United States.

The Court defends its departure from our precedents on the ground that the statutes and regulations upon which respondents rely need not be "construed in the manner appropriate to waivers of sovereign immunity." The Court in effect is overruling *Mitchell I sub silentio.*

II

[The Court's] conclusion rests on two dubious assumptions. First, the Court decides that the statutes create or recognize fiduciary duties. It then reasons that because a private express trust normally imports a right to recover damages for breach, and because injunctive relief is perceived to be inadequate, Congress necessarily must have authorized recovery of damages for failure to perform the statutory duties properly. The relevancy of the first conclusion is questionable, and the other departs from our precedents, chiefly *Testan* and *Mitchell I.*

The Court simply asserts that the statutes here "clearly establish fiduciary obligations." [According to Judge Nichols in the Court of Claims]: "The federal power over Indian lands is so different in nature and origin from that of a private trustee . . . that caution is taught in using the mere label of a trust plus a reading of *Scott on Trusts* to impose liability on claims where assent is not unequivocally expressed." [664 F.2d 265,] at 283.[28]

---

[28] [8] "There are a number of widely varying relationships which more or less closely resemble trusts, but which are not trusts, although the term 'trust' is sometimes used loosely to cover such relationships. It is important to differentiate trusts from these other relationships, since many of the rules applicable

The trusteeships to which the Court has referred in the past have manifested more the view that pervasive control over Indian life is such a high attribute of federal sovereignty that States cannot infringe upon that control. The Court today turns this shield into a sword.

[I]t is clear that "[n]othing on the face" of any of the statutes at issue, or in their legislative histories, "fairly [can] be interpreted as mandating compensation" for the conduct alleged by respondents. [T]he Court concludes that the mere existence of a trust of some kind necessarily establishes that Congress has consented to a recovery of damages. In effect we are told to accept on faith the existence of a damages cause of action: "Given the existence of a trust relationship, it naturally follows that the Government should be liable in damages for the breach of its fiduciary duties." [T]he Court is influenced by its view that an injunctive remedy is inadequate to redress the violations alleged. [It is the nature] of sovereign immunity that unconsented claims for money damages are barred. The fact that damages cannot be recovered without the sovereign's consent hardly supports the conclusion that consent has been given. Yet this, in substance, is the Court's reasoning. If it is saying that a remedy is necessary to redress every injury sustained, the doctrine of sovereign immunity will have been drained of all meaning. Moreover, "many of the federal statutes . . . that expressly provide money damages as a remedy against the United States in carefully limited circumstances would be rendered superfluous." [*Testan.*]

NOTES ON TRUST MISMANAGEMENT CLAIMS

1. **Who Does the Trust Doctrine Limit?** Notice that at the core of the efforts by the Kiowa to prevent allotment of their reservation in *Lone Wolf* was a kind of mismanagement claim, a claim that the federal government's allotment policy breached obligations under the Medicine Lodge Treaty to protect their traditional way of life. In *Lone Wolf*, it was Congress that had made the decision to act contrary to the desires of at least some of the tribal leadership. In light of *Lone Wolf* could the trust doctrine impose judicially enforceable limitations on the actions of Congress? If the trust doctrine operated to limit congressional action would it

---

to trusts are not applicable to them." Restatement (Second) of Trusts § 4, Introductory Note, p. 15 (1959). For example, the Court often has described the fiduciary relationship between the United States and Indians as one between a guardian and a ward. But "[a] guardianship is not a trust." Restatement (Second) of Trusts § 7. There is no explanation, however, why the Court chooses one analogy and not another. The choice appears to be influenced by the fact that "[t]he duties of a trustee are more intensive than the duties of some other fiduciaries." *Id.*, § 2, Comment b.

[T]wo persons and a parcel of real property, without more, do not create a trust. Rather, "[a] trust . . . arises as a result of a manifestation of an intention to create it." Restatement (Second) of Trusts § 2. This is the element that is missing in this case, and the Court does not, and cannot, find that Congress has manifested its intent to make the statutory duties upon which respondents rely trust duties.

Indeed, given the language of the statute at issue in *Mitchell I*, the case for finding that Congress intended to impose fiduciary obligations on the United States was much stronger there than it is here. [In Justice White's dissent in *Mitchell I*, he cited *Scott on Trusts*, which] specifically discusses the General Allotment Act as an example of the United States acting as a trustee. Furthermore, a trustee can "reserv[e] powers with respect to the administration of the trust." Restatement (Second) of Trusts § 37. Unless the United States agrees to be held liable in damage, even the existence of a trust does not necessarily establish that the Government has surrendered its immunity from damages.

effectively have constitutional force? Recall the discussion of *Delaware Tribal Business v. Weeks*, and the possibility that the due process clause may require that congressional acts be "tied rationally" to the fulfillment of Congress's "unique obligations" to the Indians. *See* Sec. A.1, this chapter. Suggesting that the trust doctrine has not been found to *legally* limit acts of Congress does not mean that the trust relationship has not been used as a powerful *political* tool in arguing for or against federal legislative action affecting Indian tribes. Congressional hearings, reports, and debates are replete with references to the Indian trust obligation as a political factor in passing or defeating legislation. *E.g.*, 25 U.S.C. § 1901(2) (trust obligation "for the protection and preservation of Indian tribes and their resources" employed by Congress to justify the Indian Child Welfare Act of 1978). One should not confuse, however, the political arguments based on the federal trust relationship with the notion that the trust can legally limit the plenary power that the federal cases unilaterally claim for Congress in Indian affairs. The political and legal uses of the Indian trust doctrine are simply not the same.

If the Indian trust doctrine cannot directly limit the exercise of federal congressional power in Indian affairs, can it operate to limit executive authority? Certainly, where the BIA or other executive agencies are merely carrying out express congressional directives, it is hard to find any separate limitations imposed by the trust. Where, however, they are acting without express congressional directive in creating or structuring programs or other actions, the Indian trust doctrine has far greater force. Notice that the claims involved in *Mitchell I* and *Mitchell II* contest BIA actions allegedly constituting mismanagement taken without any clear congressional directive. The idea that the actions of the executive branch not directly mandated by Congress might be limited by the Indian trust doctrine probably began with two early Supreme Court decisions employing the Indian trust doctrine to protect tribal ownership of land. The Court first moved in this direction in *Lane v. Pueblo of Santa Rosa*, 249 U.S. 110 (1919). In *Lane*, the Court enjoined the Secretary of the Interior from disposing of tribal lands under the general public land laws. Focusing on the trust aspect of the power described in *Lone Wolf*, the Court found that the executive had an obligation to regulate Indian lands for the benefit and protection of Indians. As the Court put it, this power and obligation "certainly . . . would not justify . . . treating the lands of the Indians as public lands of the United States, and disposing of the same under the Public Land Laws." According to the *Lane* Court such actions "would not be an exercise of the guardianship, but an act of confiscation." Four years later in *Cramer v. United States*, 261 U.S. 219 (1923), the Court expanded the effect of its *Pueblo of Santa Rosa* decision (although it never cited that decision) by invalidating a federal patent improvidently issued 19 years previously for lands thought to be in the public domain but in fact held by individual Indians who had actually enclosed and were farming part of it, albeit without the benefit of any ratified treaty, statute, or executive order confirming their aboriginal title. These two cases probably mark the beginnings of enforcement of the Indian trust obligations against federal executive officials and those who benefited from their mismanagement.

Notice, however, that in neither *Pueblo of Santa Rosa* nor *Cramer* were the parties asking for compensatory damage relief, as was commonly requested in many later Indian trust cases. The idea that the Indian trust doctrine could be enforced through compensatory damage relief had to await a waiver of sovereign immunity that might permit the federal government to be sued for such relief. Most thought that waiver came in the form of the Indian Claims Commission Act, 25 U.S.C. § 70 et seq. That statute not only set up an administrative tribunal to hear old claims arising prior to 1946, section 24 of that Act also enacted the provisions of the so-called Indian Tucker Act, 28 U.S.C. § 1505, the interpretation of which was at issue in both *Mitchell I* and *Mitchell II*.

   2.   The Background — *Mitchell I*: *Mitchell I* and *Mitchell II* involve two different appeals to the United States Supreme Court from decisions of the Court of Claims in the case brought by the Quinault Nation and some of its tribal members claiming mismanagement of their timber resources and the proceeds from sale. In *Mitchell I*, the Court of Claims had denied the federal government's motion to dismiss on grounds of sovereign immunity on the basis of the Indian Tucker Act, 25 U.S.C. § 1505 and it ruled that the General Allotment Act of 1887 provided the Indian allottees a right of action against the federal government. The United States took an interlocutory appeal of that order to the Supreme Court in *United States v. Mitchell*, 445 U.S. 535 (1980) (*Mitchell I*). A divided Court in *Mitchell I* appeared to suggest two points, both of which represented changes from prior law developed by the lower courts. First, language in the *Mitchell I* opinion suggested that 25 U.S.C. § 1505 itself did not constitute a waiver of sovereign immunity. Justice Marshall wrote:

> The Tucker Act is "only a jurisdictional statute; it does not create any substantive right enforceable against the United States for money damages." *United States v. Testan*, 424 U.S. 392, 398 (1976). The Act merely "confers jurisdiction upon [the Court of Claims] whenever the substantive right exists." The individual claimants, therefore, must look beyond the jurisdictional statute for a waiver of sovereign immunity with respect to their claims.

445 U.S. at 538. Three dissenting members of the Court, including Justice Brennan, thought that 28 U.S.C. § 1505 itself constituted a waiver of sovereign immunity and tribes needed to look no further to find such a waiver. Do their views prevail in *Mitchell II*?

   Second, despite the fact that the express language of section 5 of the General Allotment Act required the United States to "hold the land . . . in trust for the sole use and benefit of the" allottee, the Court held that section 5 did not create the kind of statutorily-based trust claim upon which they could rest a cause of action. The Supreme Court argued that section 5 must be read in conjunction with the overall purpose of the General Allotment Act that was designed to facilitate Indian economic independence and encourage economic assimilation into American society. The trust period was designed to restrain alienation and insulate the Indian allottees from state property taxation. After reviewing the legislative history of the General Allotment Act, the Court therefore concluded that:

> [The General Allotment] Act created only a limited trust relationship between the United States and the allottee that does not impose any duty upon the Government to manage timber resources. The Act does not unambiguously provide that the United States has undertaken full fidu-

ciary responsibilities as to the management of allotted lands.

Id. at 542. Thus, despite the fact that section 5 expressly created a trust relationship, the Court held that the limited nature of the trust established did not cover the mismanagement claim brought by the Quinault Tribe and its members since they were alleging active mismanagement and nothing in the General Allotment Act, including section 5, contemplated active federal management of allotted or tribal lands. The Court remanded the case back to the Court of Claims to consider whether the remaining claims created a statutory cause of action that might form the basis for liability against the United States. Its decision, of course, set up the appeal in *Mitchell II*.

   3.   **The Impact of *Mitchell I & II* on Trust Mismanagement Cases:** In Indian breach of trust cases like *Cheyenne-Arapaho* decided before the decisions in *Mitchell I* and *II*, the federal courts rarely sought any statutory basis for the trust claim asserted by any Indian tribe or its members. Rather, as in *Cheyenne-Arapaho*, federal statutes might sometimes establish the operational parameters of federal trust management, but the existence of the trust relationship and the cause of action from its breach were rarely sought in existing federal statutes or regulations. *Mitchell I* and *II* both obviously place extraordinary emphasis on finding a statutory or regulatory basis for the claim of trust mismanagement against the United States. Was this changed emphasis on a federal positive law, as opposed to common law, basis for an Indian breach of trust claim based on any substantive need to demonstrate the existence of a trust obligation in positive federal law or was it the result of the fact that the plaintiffs in the case sought *damage* relief under the Indian Tucker Act, 28 U.S.C. § 1505? Does the requirement of a statutory or regulatory basis for the assumption of trust obligations prevent federal courts from enforcing the Indian trust doctrine against executive officials where only equitable or declaratory relief is sought and the basis of jurisdiction is not the Indian Tucker Act? The Supreme Court has not definitively addressed these questions.

   The impact of the decisions in *Mitchell I* and *II* on the manner in which Indian trust mismanagement cases are handled can be seen by comparing two cases brought by the Navajo Nation in the Court of Claims arising before and after the *Mitchell* decisions. Both involved the same basic type of claim, an assertion that during World War II the United States breached its trust responsibility to the Navajo Nation by exploiting Navajo natural resources to further the war effort in a manner that did not bring maximum economic return to the Navajo Nation and which further involved major conflicts of interest and self-dealing on the part of the United States government. In *Navajo Tribe v. United States*, 364 F.2d 320 (Ct. Cl. 1966), the Court of Claims held the federal government liable for damages for its self-dealing in helium exploitation on the Navajo Nation during World War II. The federal government had approved and overseen oil and gas leases with a private corporation on lands in the Navajo Reservation. Oil and gas exploration pursuant to the leases did not discover the desired resource but indicated the presence of helium-bearing gas. When the corporation decided to relinquish the lease since it had no need for helium, the Bureau of Mines sought to develop the helium deposits for the war effort during World War II. It took an assignment of the lease without notifying the Navajo Nation either of the existence of the helium resource or of the lessee's desire to surrender the lease. The Court of Claims held that the failure to inform the tribe of the lessee's desire to surrender the lease constituted the usurpation by the trustee of a valuable tribal business opportunity, and held the federal government liable for self-dealing in its role as trustee. The court analogized the government's action to "that of a fiduciary who learns of an opportunity, prevents the beneficiary from getting it, and seizes it for himself. The *Navajo Tribe* helium case was decided before the *Mitchell* cases and consequently placed almost no emphasis on finding a statutory basis for the trust management or a statutory basis for establishing the obligation of the federal government not to engage in self-dealing in its management of Indian resources. Rather, as the quote suggests, the mere fact of trust management of Indian assets was thought to impose on the federal government the normal fiduciary obligations of a private trustee.

By contrast, in *Navajo Tribe v. United States*, 9 Cl. Ct. 227 (1985), the United States Claims Court analyzed a similar case very differently after the *Mitchell* decisions. The case arose out of the events surrounding the then top secret Manhattan Project to develop the atomic bomb during World War II. The Navajo Nation claimed the federal government engaged in mismanagement based on its failure to collect rental payments on uranium mining leases and its failure to require filling of uranium mines to minimize harm to tribal members from exposure to the residual uranium tailings that are a byproduct of uranium mining. The Nation also claimed the government had breached its duty of loyalty and engaged in self-dealing when it failed to charge a secret federal agency created as part of the Manhattan Project for exploring Navajo land for uranium needed to develop the atomic bomb. The court dismissed the tailings claim as time-barred, but did hold the government accountable for failing to collect rents and royalties from third persons. More importantly, in evaluating the self-dealing claim, the same type of claim involved in the helium *Navajo Tribe* case, the court noted that no statutes or regulations spoke to the issue of permits or permission from landowners and, in fact, the government sought no permission. While the court conceded that such an action if undertaken by a private trustee would constitute self-dealing and therefore would render the trustee liable for a breach of the duty of loyalty, it nevertheless held that the federal government could not be held liable. In part the court relied on the *Mitchell* decisions but it also relied on *Nevada v. United States*, 463 U.S. 110 (1983), set forth and discussed below, which suggested that the United States could not be held to the normal standards otherwise applied to a private fiduciary when its fiduciary obligation to the Indians conflicts with a competing public policy dictated by Congress. Insofar as the self-dealing claim was concerned the uranium exploration caused no actual harm to the land, because there had been no drilling or other harmful activity antecedent to the actual mining. Once the uranium was found, the Tribe did in fact benefit from the mineral royalties under the lease. While the last point might distinguish the helium *Navajo Tribe* case from the uranium *Navajo Tribe* case, the intervening *Mitchell* decisions and *Nevada v. United States* certainly resulted in very marked differences in the actual mode of analysis in the two cases. Those differences reflect the manner in which these Supreme Court decisions have moved mismanagement cases away from simple private fiduciary analogies.

United States v. White Mountain Apache Tribe, 537 U.S. 465 (2003): In 1870

Congress created a military post known as Fort Apache on 7,500 acres of land within what later would become the White Mountain Apache Reservation. In 1960, Congress passed a statute which declared the Fort to be "held by the United States in trust for the White Mountain Apache Tribe, subject to the right of the Secretary of the Interior to use any part of the land and improvements for administrative or school purposes for as long as they are needed for that purpose." Pub. L. No. 86-392, 74 Stat. 8 (1960). As a result of this statute, the federal government held in trust and had responsibility for approximately 35 buildings on the site, including a school that supported very few students and the continued viability of which was under active review. The federal government allegedly had the exclusive responsibility for these buildings and some fell into such bad disrepair that they were unsafe. Consequently, the Department of the Interior condemned and demolished some of them. After allegedly making numerous requests to the Secretary of the Interior to repair and restore the buildings on the site, the Tribe developed a master plan for the restoration of the site, which estimated the cost at $14 million. The Tribe commenced a breach of trust claim against the United States seeking payment of that sum for failure to maintain the site. The federal government responded that it had maintained some of the buildings but admitted that others had been permitted to fall into disrepair. Nevertheless, it claimed that under the *Mitchell* decisions the Tribe had no statutory basis for asserting a claim against the United States.

While both parties agreed that the 1960 Act created a trust, they disagreed whether the trust created was of a type pursuant to which the federal government could be found liable under the Indian Tucker Act, 28 U.S.C. § 1505. The Federal Circuit reviewed its subsequent cases and held the 1960 Act was sufficient to maintain the Tribe's cause of action against the United States. In a 5-4 decision the United States Supreme Court affirmed. Justice Souter's opinion for the narrow majority emphasized that *Mitchell II* had held that the Indian Tucker Act constituted a waiver of federal sovereign immunity but did not create an independent right of action:

> As we said in *Mitchell II*, a statute creates a right capable of grounding a claim within the waiver of sovereign immunity if, but only if, it "can fairly be interpreted as mandating compensation by the Federal Government for the damage sustained."

> This "fair interpretation" rule demands a showing demonstrably lower than the standard for the initial waiver of sovereign immunity. "Because the Tucker Act supplies a waiver of immunity for claims of this nature, the separate statutes and regulations need not provide a second waiver of sovereign immunity, nor need they be construed in the manner appropriate to waivers of sovereign immunity." *Mitchell II*. It is enough, then, that a statute creating a Tucker Act right be reasonably amenable to the reading that it mandates a right of recovery in damages. While the premise to a Tucker Act claim will not be "lightly inferred," a fair inference will do.

In the context of the *White Mountain Apache* case, a majority of the Court found this standard satisfied. Justice Souter wrote:

> The 1960 Act goes beyond a bare trust and permits a fair inference that the Government is subject to duties as a trustee and liable in damages for

breach. The statutory language, of course, expressly defines a fiduciary relationship in the provision that Fort Apache be "held by the United States in trust for the White Mountain Apache Tribe." 74 Stat. 8. Unlike the Allotment Act, however, the statute proceeds to invest the United States with discretionary authority to make direct use of portions of the trust corpus. The trust property is "subject to the right of the Secretary of the Interior to use any part of the land and improvements for administrative or school purposes for as long as they are needed for the purpose," and it is undisputed that the Government has to this day availed itself of its option. As to the property subject to the Government's actual use, then, the United States has not merely exercised daily supervision but has enjoyed daily occupation, and so has obtained control at least as plenary as its authority over the timber in *Mitchell II*. While it is true that the 1960 Act does not, like the statutes cited in that case, expressly subject the Government to duties of management and conservation, the fact that the property occupied by the United States is expressly subject to a trust supports a fair inference that an obligation to preserve the property improvements was incumbent on the United States as trustee. This is so because elementary trust law, after all, confirms the commonsense assumption that a fiduciary actually administering trust property may not allow it to fall into ruin on his watch.

Writing for the four dissenting members of the Court, Justice Thomas emphasized that the basic test, first announced in *United States v. Testan*, 424 U.S. 392, 400 (1976), for determining if Congress has conferred a substantive right enforceable against the Government in a suit for money damages is whether an Act "can fairly be *interpreted* as mandating compensation by the Federal Government for the damage sustained." The dissenting opinion insisted that the 1960 Act could not fairly be interpreted to support any requirement mandating compensation by the United States for any damage sustained.

United States v. Navajo Nation, 537 U.S. 488 (2003): In 1964 the Navajo Nation entered into a lease agreement with the Sentry Royalty Company (the predecessor in interest to the present Peabody Coal Company). The lease covered mining of coal deposits on Navajo lands. As negotiated, the agreement provided for payment of a royalty not to exceed 37.5 cents per ton. It further authorized the Secretary of the Interior to readjust the royalty rate to a "reasonable" level on the twentieth anniversary of the lease.

As the twentieth year of the lease approached it was clear that the old lease royalty rate was quite low due to interim changes in the market price for coal. As a result of interim increases in that market price the rate of 37.5 cents per ton constituted only about 2% of the gross proceeds. Such a rate was well below the then-prevailing royalty rates. Negotiations proceeded directly between the Navajo and Peabody. No agreement was reached, and the Navajo asked the Department of the Interior to resolve the issue and to set the royalty at a fair market rate.

Based on technical advice secured from the Bureau of Mines, the BIA Area Real Property Management Officer issued an Initial Decision to increase the royalty rate to 20% of gross proceeds. The BIA's Navajo Area Director adopted this decision and so notified Peabody.

Given the large increase in royalty payments such a change envisioned, Peabody appealed to the Deputy Assistant Secretary for Indian Affairs pursuant to 25 C.F.R. §§ 211.2, 211.3. He affirmed the decision. His decision, however, was later withdrawn at the instruction of the Secretary of the Interior. The Secretary of the Interior wrote, "I suggest that you inform the involved parties that a decision on this appeal is not imminent and urge them to continue with efforts to resolve this matter in a mutually agreeable fashion." 46 Fed. Cl. 217, 237 (2000). The Deputy Assistant Secretary complied with this instruction.

When the case was ultimately litigated, it became apparent that Peabody Coal had numerous contacts during the appeals period with Interior officials including the Secretary. The Navajo were not informed that a decision on Peabody's appeal initially had been made in their favor. Facing severe economic pressures, the Navajo eventually agreed to an adjusted royalty rate of 12.5% of the gross proceeds without any knowledge that the appeals process in the Department of the Interior initially had approved the 20% royalty rate.

Once the Navajo Nation fully discovered these facts, it sued the United States for breach of trust. The United States Court for the Federal Circuit found that the government's actions "violated the most fundamental fiduciary duties of care, loyalty and candor," 46 Fed. Cl. at 227 and held the federal government liable. On appeal to the Federal Circuit, that court affirmed and described these facts by suggesting that "[i]t can not be reasonably disputed that the Secretary's actions were in Peabody's interest and contrary to the Navajo's interest." When the case reached the United States Supreme Court, the Court reversed by a 6-3 vote.

Justice Ginsburg, who joined in the *White Mountain Apache* decision, wrote the *Navajo Nation* decision. The majority opinion stated the relevant standard as follows:

> To state a claim cognizable under the Indian Tucker Act, *Mitchell I* and *Mitchell II* thus instruct, a Tribe must identify a substantive source of law that establishes specific fiduciary or other duties, and allege that the Government has failed faithfully to perform those duties. If that threshold is passed, the court must then determine whether the relevant source of substantive law "can fairly be interpreted as mandating compensation for damages sustained as a result of a breach of the duties [the governing law] imposes." Although "the undisputed existence of a general trust relationship between the United States and the Indian people" can "reinforce" the conclusion that the relevant statute or regulation imposes fiduciary duties, that relationship alone is insufficient to support jurisdiction under the Indian Tucker Act. Instead, the analysis must train on specific rights-creating or duty-imposing statutory or regulatory prescriptions. Those prescriptions need not, however, expressly provide for money damages; the availability of such damages may be inferred.

Applying these standard, the majority opinion focused attention on the nature of the federal obligations assumed in the Indian Mineral Leasing Act of 1938 (IMLA), 25 U.S.C. §§ 396a et seq., and the regulations issued pursuant to that statute. Finding that the only statutory obligation imposed on the federal government was the approval by the Secretary of the Interior of mineral leases ostensibly negotiated by the tribes, the Court concluded that the legislation failed to meet the prescribed standard:

> The Tribe's principal contention is that the IMLA's statutory and regulatory scheme, viewed in its entirety, attaches fiduciary duties to each Government function under that scheme, and that the Secretary acted in contravention of those duties by approving the 12 1/2 percent royalty contained in the amended Lease. We read the IMLA differently. As we see it, the statute and regulations at issue do not provide the requisite "substantive law" that "mandates compensation by the Federal Government."
>
> The IMLA and its implementing regulations impose no obligations resembling the detailed fiduciary responsibilities that *Mitchell II* found adequate to support a claim for money damages. The IMLA simply requires Secretarial approval before coal mining leases negotiated between Tribes and third parties become effective, 25 U.S.C. § 396a, and authorizes the Secretary generally to promulgate regulations governing mining operations, § 396d. Yet the dissent concludes that the IMLA imposes "one or more specific statutory obligations, as in *Mitchell II*, at the level of fiduciary duty whose breach is compensable in damages." The endeavor to align this case with *Mitchell II* rather than *Mitchell I*, however valiant, falls short of the mark. Unlike the "elaborate" provisions before the Court in *Mitchell II*, the IMLA and its regulations do not "give the Federal Government full responsibility to manage Indian resources . . . for the benefit of the Indians." The Secretary is neither assigned a comprehensive managerial role nor, at the time relevant here, expressly invested with responsibility to secure "the needs and best interests of the Indian owner and his heirs." (quoting 25 U.S.C. § 406(a) [a statute involved in *Mitchell II*]).

In a footnote, the majority noted, however, that its ruling was limited to the application of the IMLA to coal leases. The opinion noted:

> We rule only on the Government's role in the coal leasing process under the IMLA. [B]oth the IMLA and its implementing regulations address oil and gas leases in considerably more detail than coal leases. Whether the Secretary has fiduciary or other obligations, enforceable in an action for money damages, with respect to oil and gas leases is not before us.

The Court of Appeals and the Navajo Nation had relied heavily on the Secretary's alleged violation of 25 U.S.C. § 399. The majority rejected the claim, however, finding that "[§ 399] is not part of the IMLA and does not govern [the Navajo lease in question]. Enacted almost 20 years before the IMLA, section 399 authorizes *the Secretary* to lease certain unallotted Indian lands for mining purposes on terms she sets, and does not provide for input from the Tribes concerned." Since the IMLA governed the Navajo lease in question, the Court also rejected the Tribe's reliance on provisions from the Indian Mineral Development Act of 1982, 25 U.S.C. § 2101 et seq. Thus, the majority concluded that:

[N]either the IMLA nor any of its regulations establishes anything more than a bare minimum royalty. Hence, there is no textual basis for concluding that the Secretary's approval function includes a duty, enforceable in an action for money damages, to ensure a higher rate of return for the Tribe concerned. Similarly, no pertinent statutory or regulatory provision requires the Secretary, on pain of damages, to conduct an independent "economic analysis" of the reasonableness of the royalty to which a Tribe and third party have agreed.

Three members of the Court, led by Justice Souter, dissented in *Navajo Nation*. They differed from the majority in that they found "the Secretary's obligation to approve mineral leases under 25 U.S.C. § 396a as raising a substantial fiduciary obligation to the Navajo Nation (Tribe), which has pleaded and shown enough to survive the Government's motion for summary judgment."

In 2009, the Supreme Court revisited the Navajo Nation breach of trust case, with Justice Scalia delivering the opinion for a unanimous Court. *United States v. Navajo Nation*, 556 U.S. 287 (2009). On remand from *United States v. Navajo Nation*, 537 U.S. 488 (2003), the Tribe had argued that even if its suit could not be maintained on the basis of the Indian Mineral Leasing Act (IMLA), the Indian Mineral Development Act (IMDA), or 25 U.S.C. § 399, a "network" of other treaties, statutes, and regulations provided a basis for the claims. The Government maintained that the Court's 2003 opinion foreclosed the arguments, but the U.S. Court of Appeals for the Federal Circuit disagreed and remanded the case for consideration. The Court of Federal Claims again dismissed the Tribe's claim. The Federal Circuit again reversed, relying on three statutory provisions to allow the Tribe's claim to proceed: two sections of the Navajo-Hopi Rehabilitation Act of 1950 and one section of the Surface Mining Control and Reclamation Act of 1977. The Federal Circuit held that the Government had violated the specific duties created by those statutes, as well as "common law trust duties of care, candor, and loyalty" that arise from the comprehensive control over tribal coal that is exercised by the Government. 501 F.3d 1327, 1346 (2007).

The Supreme Court once again granted the Government's petition for a writ of certiorari. The Court specifically noted the 2003 opinion did not analyze any statutes beyond the IMLA, the IMDA, and § 399. Thus, the Court acknowledged it was "conceivable, albeit unlikely, that some other relevant statute, though invoked by the Tribe at the outset of the litigation, might have gone unmentioned by the Federal Circuit and unanalyzed by this Court." The Court first looked at 25 U.S.C. § 635(a) in the Navajo-Hopi Rehabilitation Act of 1950, which permits Indians to lease reservation lands if the Secretary approves of the deal. The Court noted that the provision was only relevant if Lease 8580 was issued under this authority, recognizing that in its earlier review the Court had presumed that the lease had been issued pursuant to the IMLA. The Tribe argued that the lease was approved under this authority and the Government contended that Section 635(a) permits leasing only for "public, religious, educational, recreational, or business purposes," and that mining was not covered by those terms. The Court found that because the lease in this case fell outside of § 635(a)§ s "domain," the Tribe could not invoke it as a source of money-mandating rights or duties. Next, the Court looked at 25 U.S.C. § 638, another provision in the Navajo-Hopi Rehabilitation Act. The Navajo

Nation argued that the Secretary violated the provision by "failing promptly to abide by its wishes to affirm the Area Director's order increasing the royalty rate under Lease 8580 to a full 20% of gross proceeds." The Court disagreed. Finally, the Court looked at the Surface Mining Control and Reclamation Act of 1977 (SMCRA), 30 U.S.C. § 1201 *et seq.*, the comprehensive statute that regulates all surface coal mining operations. The Navajo Nation argued that the provision of the Act involving coal mining on Indian lands, and specifically § 1300, subsection (e) required the Secretary to enforce whatever terms the Indians request with respect to coal leases. However, the Court noted that subsections (c) and (d) of the Act refer exclusively to environmental protection standards, and since Lease 8580 was issued in 1964, 13 years before the date of enactment of the SMCRA, the provision was categorically inapplicable. Thus, the Court found that SMCRA was irrelevant. The Court also analyzed whether the Government's "comprehensive control" over coal on Indian land gave rise to fiduciary duties based on common-law trust principles. However, the Court found that "the Federal Government's liability cannot be premised on control alone." Accordingly, the Supreme Court held that none of the sources of law cited by the Federal Circuit and relied upon by the Tribe provided any more sound a basis for its breach-of-trust lawsuit against the federal government than those previously analyzed. The Court concluded by stating, "[t]his case is at an end."

Justice Souter, with whom Justice Stevens joined, concurred and stated "I am not through regretting that my position in *United States v. Navajo Nation*, 537 U.S. 488, 514–521 (2003) (dissenting opinion) did not carry the day. But it did not, and I agree that the precedent of that case calls for the result reached here."

NOTE ON RECENT MISMANAGEMENT CLAIMS

The timber management regulations require active oversight of on-going timber operations. By contrast the mineral leasing statutes and regulations at issue in *Navajo Nation* do not involve active federal oversight of the on-going mineral extraction process. Rather, under the Mineral Leasing Act the federal government's role primarily involves oversight and approval of the lease process itself. Does this fact distinguish *Mitchell II* from *Navajo Nation*? Does it make any difference that the claim at issue in *Navajo Nation* involved the actual lease renegotiation process, rather than the mineral extraction itself?

Both the *White Mountain Apache* case and the *Navajo Nation* case arrived at the United States Supreme Court when a very high visibility breach of trust case for historical mismanagement of individual (not tribal) Indian trust accounts (often known as Individual Indian Money (IIM) accounts) was pending in the United States District Court for the District of Columbia. *Cobell v. Norton*, No. 96-1285. This action resulted from efforts by Congress to turn the management of Indian trust assets over to a special trustee in the American Indian Trust Fund Management Reform Act of 1994, Public Law 103-412. This legislation established the Office of the Special Trustee for American Indians to oversee the management of such Indian trust assets. As part of the handover the trustee reasonably insisted on an audit of accounts, the preliminary studies for which promptly revealed that the records maintained by the BIA were either missing, inaccurate, or insufficient to audit the historic flow of funds through these accounts. As a result, the plaintiffs in *Cobell v. Norton* filed the class-action lawsuit on June 10, 1996, to force the federal government to account for amounts alleged to include billions of dollars belonging to approximately 500,000 American Indians and their heirs, which had been held in trust since the late nineteenth century. Discovery orders filed in the case against the federal government were repeatedly frustrated either by the government's refusal or inability to supply the requested documentation for the accounts. Discovery and courtroom testimony revealed a pattern of poor record keeping, ineptitude, and mismanagement by federal officials in connection with these IIM accounts. Reviewing these facts, then presiding District Judge, Royce Lamberth, described the federal conduct as "fiscal and governmental irresponsibility in its purest form." These events led to multiple contempt citations against the Secretary of the Interior, the Assistant Secretary of Indian Affairs, and others in both the Clinton and second Bush administrations, although citations directed at Bush's Secretary of the Interior were overturned by the D.C. Circuit based on an absence of evidence that the Secretary knew that reports filed with the court were false and fraudulent. *Cobell v. Norton*, 334 F.3d 1128 (D.C. Cir. 2003).

Judge Lamberth bifurcated trial in the case. In Phase One, focused on reform of the system, Judge Lamberth ruled in 1999 that the Secretaries of Interior and Treasury had breached their trust obligations to the Indians. The court retained judicial oversight of the system for a minimum of five years, to ensure that the federal management system was overhauled. He further ordered the Secretary of the Interior to provide an historical accounting of all trust funds, an accounting which to date the Secretary has been unable or unwilling to provide. In 2001, an interlocutory appeal by the government, arguing that the judge had overreached his authority, was unanimously rejected by the United States Court of Appeals for the District of Columbia in an opinion set forth below. A website containing all of the orders and many other documents filed in the case can be found at www. indiantrust.com/documents.

To help oversee compliance with his orders, Judge Lamberth appointed both a special master to oversee the preservation and production of trust documents, and a federal monitor to provide the judge with assessments of the truthfulness of Interior's representations to the Court regarding execution of trust reform. The D.C. Circuit overturned the monitor's appointment because it believed his charge entailed excessive intrusion into Department of the Interior's internal business. *Cobell v. Norton*, 334 F.3d 1128, 1140–43 (D.C. Cir. 2003). And on April 6, 2004, Judge Lamberth accepted the resignation of Special Master Alan L. Balaran "with profound regret." Special Master Balaran's letter of resignation noted that for the past several months the Department of the Interior had been making motions to disqualify him from the case, and that the agency was doing so because he had been uncovering numerous instances of wrongful appraisal and record-keeping practices. According to Balaran, "[M]y recent findings implicated the agency's systematic failure to properly monitor the activities of energy companies leasing minerals on individual Indian lands. The consequences of these findings could cost the very companies with which senior Interior officials maintain close ties, millions of dollars."

In light of this description of *Cobell* and the Court of Appeals decision set forth below, what impact, if any, might the *White Mountain Apache Tribe* and *Navajo*

Nation decisions have had on the *Cobell* litigation? Does it make any difference that the basis for jurisdiction in *Cobell* was 28 U.S.C. § 1331, *not* 28 U.S.C. § 1505, as it was in *Mitchell I* and *II, White Mountain Apache,* and *Navajo Nation*?

Cobell v. Norton, 240 F.3d 1081 (D.C. Cir. 2001) (Cobell VI): *Cobell* is a class action suit brought on behalf of the beneficiaries of Individual Indian Money ("IIM") trust accounts against Interior Secretary Gale A. Norton and other federal officials who serve, in their official capacities, as trustee-delegates on behalf of the federal government in managing the IIM accounts. The complaint alleged breach of fiduciary duties and sought a declaratory judgment delineating appellants' trust obligations to IIM trust beneficiaries and injunctive relief to ensure that such trust obligations are carried out. No compensatory damages were sought.

After a lengthy trial on the merits, the district court concluded that the federal government and its officers had breached their trust obligations and remanded the matter back to the Interior and Treasury Departments ordering them to discharge their fiduciary responsibilities. The district court retained jurisdiction and ordered the defendants to file quarterly reports detailing their compliance with their trust obligations. The initial finding of breach of trust obligations was certified to the Court of Appeals for interlocutory appeal.

After detailing the history of the trust doctrine and of the allotment policy that led to creation of IIM accounts, the Court of Appeals described the federal role with respect to these accounts as follows:

> Because the United States holds IIM lands in trust for individual Indian beneficiaries, it assumes the fiduciary obligations of a trustee. " '[W]here the Federal Government takes on or has control or supervision over tribal monies or properties, the fiduciary relationship normally exists with respect to such monies or properties (unless Congress has provided otherwise) even though nothing is said expressly in the authorizing or underlying statute (or other fundamental document) about a trust fund, or a trust or fiduciary connection.' " *United States v. Mitchell ("Mitchell II"),* 463 U.S. 206, 225 (1983) (quoting *Navajo Tribe of Indians v. United States,* 624 F.2d 981, 224 Ct. Cl. 171, 183 (1980)). As a result of allotment, individual Indians became beneficiaries of the trust lands, but lost the right to sell, lease, or burden the property without the federal government's approval. The federal government also probates estates related to Indian trust lands and receives and distributes income from the lease of allotted lands. Income generated from the trust lands is to be paid to the individual beneficiaries.

> Under current law, the Secretary of the Interior and the Secretary of the Treasury are the designated trustee-delegates for the IIM trust. Each Secretary, or his designates, has specific fiduciary responsibilities that must be fulfilled lest the United States breach its fiduciary obligations. Several governmental agencies have specific trust obligations. These include, among others, BIA, Office of Trust Funds Management ("OTFM"), and Office of the Special Trustee ("OST"). (Their responsibilities are exten-sively detailed in the decision below. See Cobell V, 91 F. Supp. 2d at 9–12.)

BIA is responsible for trust land management, including the approval of leases and land transfers, and income collection. As noted above, BIA is also required to contract with qualifying tribes for the management of IIM accounts. OTFM, with the assistance of the Treasury Department, deposits IIM land revenues, maintains the individual IIM accounts, and ensures that money is distributed to IIM account holders or special deposit accounts where money cannot be distributed to the individual account holder. OST, created in 1994 by the Indian Trust Fund Management Reform Act, oversees IIM trust reform efforts. 25 U.S.C. §§ 4042–43.

While the Interior Department is responsible for executing most of the federal government's trust duties, the Treasury Department has substantial trust responsibilities as well. In particular, Treasury holds and invests IIM funds at the Interior Department's direction and provides accounting and financial management services. The Treasury Department maintains only a single "IIM account" for all IIM funds, rather than individuated accounts for each individual IIM beneficiary, leaving the maintenance of individualized accounting records to OTFM. OTFM relies upon the Treasury Department's accounting records to reconcile its own IIM records. Of note, when OTFM issues a check to an IIM trust beneficiary, the amount is deducted from the relevant fund, even though the money remains in the Treasury's general account. Thus, the IIM beneficiary loses any interest that would be accrued between issuance and cashing of the check. The district court found that while "this time lapse may be short in the private sector, it can be much longer in the IIM trust context because OTFM often has incorrect addresses for the recipients."

The federal government does not know the precise number of IIM trust accounts that it is to administer and protect. At present, the Interior Department's system contains over 300,000 accounts covering an estimated 11 million acres,[29] but the Department is unsure whether this is the proper number of accounts. Plaintiffs claim that the actual number of accounts is far higher, exceeding 500,000 trust accounts. Not only does the Interior Department not know the proper number of accounts, it does not know the proper balances for each IIM account, nor does Interior have sufficient records to determine the value of IIM accounts. As the district court found, "[a]lthough the United States freely gives out 'balances' to plaintiffs, it admits that currently these balances cannot be supported by adequate transactional documentation." Current account reconciliation procedures are insufficient to ensure that existing account records, reported account balances, or payments to IIM beneficiaries are accurate. As the Interior Secretary testified at trial, the Department is presently unable to render an accounting for a majority of the IIM trust beneficiaries. As a result, the government regularly issues payments to trust beneficiaries "in erroneous amounts — from unreconciled accounts — some of which are known to have incorrect balances." Thus, the district court concluded, and the government does not deny, that "[i]t is entirely possible that tens of thousands of IIM

---

[29] [1] Note that these figures are in addition to land and accounts held in trust for tribes.

trust beneficiaries should be receiving different amounts of money — their own money — than they do today. Perhaps not. But no one can say. . . . "

240 F.3d at 1088–1089. The Court of Appeals also noted the importance of the Indian Trust Fund Management Act of 1994 in crystallizing both the dispute and the description of the federal government's fiduciary duties:

> In 1994, Congress enacted the Indian Trust Fund Management Reform Act ("1994 Act"), Pub. L. No. 103-412 (1994). This law recognized the federal government's preexisting trust responsibilities.[30] It further identified some of the Interior Secretary's duties to ensure "proper discharge of the trust responsibilities of the United States." 25 U.S.C. § 162a(d). These "include (but are not limited to) the following":
>
> - "Providing adequate systems for accounting for and reporting trust fund balances";
> - "Providing adequate controls over receipts and disbursements";
> - "Providing periodic, timely reconciliations to assure the accuracy of accounts";
> - "Preparing and supplying . . . periodic statements of . . . account performance" and balances to account holders; and
> - "Establishing consistent, written policies and procedures for trust fund management and accounting."
>
> There is no dispute that the federal government owes IIM beneficiaries — the plaintiffs/appellees — these duties. The district court so found and the Interior Department conceded as much at trial. While arguing that plaintiffs' claims should be evaluated on the basis of what is contained in the Act alone, the Interior Department did not dispute that these duties "must be interpreted in light of the common law of trusts and the United States' Indian policy." Most significantly, the Interior Department stipulated that many of the duties owed under the 1994 Act were not being fulfilled. In other words, the federal government readily acknowledges that it is in breach of at least some of the fiduciary duties owed to IIM beneficiaries.

Id. at 1090.

While the federal government defended in part based on federal sovereign immunity, the Court of Appeals rejected that defense. It noted that the claim was partially based on section 702 of the Administrative Procedure Act, 5 U.S.C. § 702, and that section had been interpreted to include a waiver of federal sovereign immunity. The Court of Appeals noted "[t]hat plaintiffs rely upon common law trust principles in pursuit of their claim is immaterial, as here they seek specific relief other than money damages, and federal courts have jurisdiction to hear such claims under the APA."

In the most critical portion of its lengthy opinion, the Court of Appeals described the federal government's general trust obligations toward the IIM accounts and the

---

[30] [2] That the law recognized, rather than created, the government's IIM trust duties is clear from the Act's text and structure. Indeed, Title I of the Act is titled "Recognition of Trust Responsibility."

duties imposed by the Indian Trust Fund Management Reform Act of 1994 as follows:

A. The Trust Relationship

There is no doubt that the federal government has a longstanding fiduciary obligation to IIM trust beneficiaries. "[T]he law is 'well established that the Government in its dealings with Indian tribal property acts in a fiduciary capacity.' " *Lincoln v. Vigil*, 508 U.S. 182, 194 (1993) (quoting *United States v. Cherokee Nation of Oklahoma*, 480 U.S. 700, 707 (1987)). In the leading case on Indian trust responsibilities, *United States v. Mitchell ("Mitchell II")*, the Supreme Court was clear:

> A fiduciary relationship necessarily arises when the Government assumes such elaborate control over forests and property belonging to Indians. All of the necessary elements of a common-law trust are present: a trustee (the United States), a beneficiary (the Indian allottees), and a trust corpus (Indian timber, lands, and funds).

463 U.S. 206, 225 (1983) (citing Restatement (Second) of Trusts § 2, cmt. h (1959)).

This rule operates as a presumption. *See Loudner v. United States*, 108 F.3d 896, 900 (8th Cir. 1997) (" '[T]here is a presumption that absent explicit language to the contrary, all funds held by the United States for Indian tribes are held in trust.' " (quoting *Rogers v. United States*, 697 F.2d 886, 890 (9th Cir. 1983))). Therefore, courts correctly recognize a trust relationship even where it is not explicitly laid out by statute. Specifically, " 'where the Federal Government takes on or has control or supervision over tribal monies or properties, the fiduciary relationship normally exists with respect to such monies or properties (unless Congress has provided otherwise) even though nothing is said expressly in the authorizing or underlying statute (or other fundamental document) about a trust fund, or a trust or fiduciary connection.' " *Mitchell II*, 463 U.S. at 225 (quoting *Navajo Tribe of Indians v. United States*, 624 F.2d 981, 224 Ct. Cl. 171, 183 (1980)).

It is no doubt true that "the government's fiduciary responsibilities necessarily depend on the substantive laws creating those obligations." *Shoshone-Bannock Tribes v. Reno*, 56 F.3d 1476, 1482 (D.C. Cir. 1995); *see also Mitchell II*, 463 U.S. at 224 (the relevant statutes and regulations "define the contours of the United States' fiduciary responsibilities."). This does not mean that the failure to specify the precise nature of the fiduciary obligation or to enumerate the trustee's duties absolves the government of its responsibilities. It is well understood that "[t]he extent of [a trustee's] duties and powers is determined by the trust instrument and the rules of law which are applicable." Restatement (Second) of Trusts § 201, at 442 (1959). It is the nature of any instrument that establishes a trust relationship that many of the duties and powers are implied therein. They arise from the nature of the relationship established.

While the government's obligations are rooted in and outlined by the relevant statutes and treaties, they are largely defined in traditional equitable terms. "Where Congress uses terms that have accumulated settled meaning under either equity or the common law, a court must infer, unless the statute otherwise dictates, that Congress means to incorporate the established meaning of these terms." *NLRB v. Amax Coal Co.*, 453 U.S. 322, 329 (1981). Courts "must infer that Congress intended to impose on trustees traditional fiduciary duties unless Congress has unequivocally expressed an intent to the contrary." Much as the Supreme Court has regularly turned to the Restatement and other authorities to construe trust responsibilities, it is appropriate for the district court to consult similar sources.

Despite the imposition of fiduciary duties, federal officials retain a substantial amount of discretion to order their priorities. In *Lincoln v. Vigil*, for example, the Supreme Court held that the government's fiduciary relationship with Indians "could not limit" an agency's discretion "to reorder its priorities" as among beneficiaries. 508 U.S. 182, 195 (1993). In *Lincoln*, the Court rejected a challenge to the Indian Health Service's decision to discontinue a health program for handicapped Indian children in one region of the country in order to devote greater resources to a national program. Nonetheless, the Secretary "cannot escape his role as trustee by donning the mantle of administrator" to claim that courts must defer to his expertise and delegated authority. *Jicarilla Apache Tribe v. Supron Energy Corp.*, 728 F.2d 1555, 1567 (10th Cir. 1984) (Seymour, J., concurring in part and dissenting in part), adopted as majority opinion as modified en banc, 782 F.2d 855 (10th Cir. 1986).

The Secretary has an "overriding duty . . . to deal fairly with Indians." *Morton v. Ruiz*, 415 U.S. 199, 236 (1974). This duty necessarily constrains the Secretary's discretion. When faced with several policy choices, an administrator is generally allowed to select any reasonable option. Yet this is not the case when acting as a fiduciary for Indian beneficiaries as "stricter standards apply to federal agencies when administering Indian programs." Summarizing federal case law on fiduciary obligations owed to Indian tribes, the Tenth Circuit concluded that where "the Secretary is obligated to act as a fiduciary . . . his actions must not merely meet the minimal requirements of administrative law, but must also pass scrutiny under the more stringent standards demanded of a fiduciary." The federal government has "charged itself with moral obligations of the highest responsibility and trust" in its relationships with Indians, and its conduct "should therefore be judged by the most exacting fiduciary standards." *Seminole Nation v. United States*, 316 U.S. 286, 297 (1942); cf. *Muscogee (Creek) Nation v. Hodel*, 851 F.2d 1439, 1445 n. 8 (D.C. Cir. 1988) (giving "careful consideration to Interior's interpretation" of the Oklahoma Indian Welfare Act, but not deferring to it).

B. The 1994 Act

The crux of appellants' argument is that there was no material breach of their fiduciary obligations as defined by the 1994 Act. Specifically, appellants contend that the district court found obligations beyond those enumerated in the Act, when Congress had intended that OST would determine the proper content and timing of policies and procedures to discharge appellants' fiduciary obligations. Therefore, insofar as this process has yet to be completed, appellants contend that there is no basis for the district court to find that appellants unlawfully withheld or unreasonably delayed discharge of their obligations.

The fundamental problem with appellants' claims is the premise that their duties are solely defined by the 1994 Act. The Indian Trust Fund Management Reform Act reaffirmed and clarified preexisting duties; it did not create them. It further sought to remedy the government's longstanding failure to discharge its trust obligations; it did not define and limit the extent of appellants' obligations. While appellants are right to quibble with some of the district court's specific findings, the premise upon which much of their appeal rests is unsustainable.

The trust nature of the federal government's IIM responsibilities was recognized long before passage of the 1994 Act. See Felix S. Cohen, HANDBOOK OF FEDERAL INDIAN LAW, 630–31 (1982 ed.). As early as 1831, the Supreme Court recognized that the relationship between Indians and the federal government was like "that of a ward to his guardian." *Cherokee Nation v. Georgia*, 30 U.S. (5 Pet.) 1, 17 (1831) (Marshall, C.J.). . . . The fiduciary nature of the government's duty was made explicit in *Seminole Nation v. United States*, 316 U.S. 286 (1942). In *Seminole Nation* the Court applied the "most exacting fiduciary standards" of the common law in assessing the government's discharge of its duties. And in *Mitchell II*, the Court reiterated the existence of a "general trust relationship" which imposes "distinctive obligation[s]" in addition to those established by statute.

Enactment of the Indian Trust Fund Management Reform Act in 1994 did not alter the nature or scope of the fiduciary duties owed by the government to IIM trust beneficiaries. Rather, by its very terms the 1994 Act identified a portion of the government's specific obligations and created additional means to ensure that the obligations would be carried out. Indeed, the 1994 Act explicitly reaffirmed the Interior Secretary's obligation to fulfill the "trust responsibilities of the United States." 25 U.S.C. § 1629(d). From this express language, "we must infer that Congress intended to impose on trustees traditional fiduciary duties unless Congress has unequivocally expressed an intent to the contrary." *NLRB v. Amax Coal Co.*, 453 U.S. 322, 330 (1981). Section 101 of the 1994 Act states that the Interior Secretary's "proper discharge of the trust responsibilities shall include (but are not limited to)" eight enumerated actions, 25 U.S.C. § 1629(d) (emphasis added). In other words, the government has other trust responsibilities not enumerated in the 1994 Act. . . .

Section 101 of the 1994 Act does not create "trust responsibilities of the United States." . . . This view of the federal government's fiduciary duties is supported by *Mitchell II* which held that "a fiduciary relationship necessarily arises when the government assumes such elaborate control over . . . property belonging to Indians" — in particular where, as here, "[a]ll of the necessary elements of a common-law trust are present." The general "contours" of the government's obligations may be defined by statute, but the interstices must be filled in through reference to general trust law. While *Mitchell II* involved a claim for damages, nothing in that decision or other Indian cases would imply that appellants are not entitled to declaratory or injunctive relief. Such remedies are the traditional ones for violations of trust duties.

Having concluded that general trust principles and the 1994 legislation imposed judicially enforceable trust obligations on the defendants in the management of the IIM accounts and that the defendants had breached those legal obligations, the Court of Appeals concluded that the 1994 legislation entitled the plaintiffs to an historic accounting of all funds deposited with the United States in IIM accounts. In so ruling, it rejected the argument offered by the federal defendants that the legislation only required a prospective, not historic, accounting of IIM funds. The Court noted:

Contrary to [defendants'] claims, Section 102 of the 1994 Act makes clear that the Interior Secretary owes IIM trust beneficiaries an accounting for "*all funds* held in trust by the United States for the benefit of an Indian tribe or an individual Indian which are deposited or invested pursuant to the Act of June 24, 1938." 25 U.S.C. § 4011(a) (emphasis added). "All funds" means all funds, irrespective of when they were deposited (or at least so long as they were deposited after the Act of June 24, 1938). Therefore, the 1994 Act reaffirms the government's preexisting fiduciary duty to perform a complete historical accounting of trust fund assets.

Accordingly, the Court of Appeals affirmed the lower court ruling that the federal defendants had breached their trust responsibilities and that the plaintiff class was entitled to an accurate historic accounting of their IIM accounts. Because the numerous decisions in this case make it difficult to keep track of different opinions, this decision is normally referenced as *Cobell VI*.

NOTE ON FURTHER DEVELOPMENTS IN THE *COBELL* LITIGATION

Following the D.C. Circuit's affirmance and a trial on the second part of the bifurcated lawsuit, Judge Lamberth issued a detailed injunctive order specifying the type of historical accounting the defendants must provide. This order differed from the plan proposed by the United States in significant ways. Among other things, it required coverage of accounts of deceased beneficiaries, included accounting for transactions before 1938, and precluded the use of statistical sampling as a method for verifying the accuracy of transactions for individual accounts. According to the United States, it would cost between $6 and $14 billion to carry out the type of accounting ordered by Judge Lamberth; the government's alternative, in contrast, would cost an estimated $335 million. The United States appealed, and the D.C. Circuit, struggling to establish a "balance between exactitude and cost," decided that Judge Lamberth had failed to grant sufficient deference to Interior's plan for random sampling of accounts valued at less than $5,000. The D.C. Circuit was influenced by the fact that the taxpayers, not the plaintiffs, would bear the cost of the accounting, something that distinguished this claim from an ordinary beneficiary's breach of trust claim, and by the fact that the estimated cost of auditing claims worth less than $5,000 would exceed that amount. *Cobell v. Norton*, 428 F.3d 1070 (D.C. Cir. 2005). The appeals court was careful to point out, however, that once the accounting project is completed plaintiffs could make "challenges to the correctness of specific account balances."

If the random sampling establishes overall accuracy in the accounting for revenues and investments of the covered accounts, is a class member with one of those smaller accounts ever going to be able to demonstrate that he or she was shortchanged? Should that matter? Interestingly, the plaintiffs in the case had questioned Judge Lamberth's order as well, largely because they believed that the government's destruction or loss of paper and electronic records had rendered an effective accounting impossible.

As of May 2006, the litigation was a decade old and the docket sheet contained over 3,000 entries. In the course of granting a motion to require the Department of the Interior to send notices to the entire 500,000-member plaintiff class of the continuing inability or refusal of the United States to discharge its fiduciary duties, Judge Lamberth offered a harsh assessment of the federal government's conduct in the case. Among his more quotable passages are the following:

> [W]hen one strips away the convoluted statutes, the technical legal complexities, the elaborate collateral proceedings, and the layers upon layers of interrelated orders and opinions from this Court and the Court of Appeals, what remains is the raw, shocking, humiliating truth at the bottom: After all these years, our government still treats Native American Indians as if they were somehow less than deserving of the respect that should be afforded to everyone in a society where all people are supposed to be equal. . . .

> For those harboring hope that the stories of murder, dispossession, forced marches, assimilationist policy programs, and other incidents of cultural genocide against the Indians are merely the echoes of a horrible, bigoted government-past that has been sanitized by the good deeds of more recent history, this case serves as an appalling reminder of the evils that result when large numbers of the politically powerless are placed at the mercy of institutions engendered and controlled by a politically powerful few. It reminds us that even today our great democratic enterprise remains unfinished. And it reminds us, finally, that the terrible power of government, and the frailty of the restraints on the exercise of that power, are never fully revealed until government turns against the people. . . .

> Despite Interior's near wholesale abdication of its trust duties, the vast majority of the Indian beneficiaries remain unaware that anything is out of

order. . . .

The entire record in this case tells the dreary story of Interior's degenerate tenure as Trustee-Delegate for the Indian trust — a story shot through with bureaucratic blunders, flubs, goofs and foul-ups, and peppered with scandals, deception, dirty tricks and outright villainy — the end of which is nowhere in sight. Despite the breadth and clarity of this record, Interior continues to litigate and relitigate, in excruciating fashion, every minor, technical legal issue. *See Cobell v. Norton*, 357 F. Supp. 2d 298, 306–07 (D.D.C. 2005). This is yet another factor forestalling the final resolution of the issues in this case and delaying the relief the Indians so desperately need. See id. It is against this background of mismanagement, falsification, spite, and obstinate litigiousness that this Court is to evaluate the general reliability of the information Interior distributes to IIM account holders. . . .

CONCLUSION

While it is undeniable that Interior has failed as a Trustee-Delegate, it is nevertheless difficult to conjure plausible hypotheses to explain Interior's default. Perhaps Interior's past and present leaders have been evil people, deriving their pleasure from inflicting harm on society's most vulnerable. Interior may be consistently populated with apathetic people who just cannot muster the necessary energy or emotion to avoid complicity in the Department's grossly negligent administration of the Indian trust. Or maybe Interior's officials are cowardly people who dodge their responsibilities out of a childish fear of the magnitude of effort involved in reforming a degenerate system. Perhaps Interior as an institution is so badly broken that even the most well-intentioned initiatives are polluted and warped by the processes of implementation.

The government as a whole may be inherently incapable of serving as an adequate fiduciary because of some structural flaw. Perhaps the Indians were doomed the moment the first European set foot on American soil. Who can say? It may be that the opacity of the cause renders the Indian trust problem insoluble. On numerous occasions over the last nine years, the Court has wanted to simply wash its hands of Interior and its iniquities once and for all. The plaintiffs have invited the Court to declare that Interior has repudiated the Indian trust, appoint a receiver to liquidate the trust assets, and finally relieve the Indians of the heavy yoke of government stewardship. The Court may eventually do all these things — but not yet. Giving up on rehabilitating Interior would signal more than the downfall of a single administrative agency. It would constitute an announcement that negligence and incompetence in government are beyond judicial remedy, that bureaucratic recalcitrance has outpaced and rendered obsolete our vaunted system of checks and balances, and that people are simply at the mercy of governmental whim with no chance for salvation. The Court clings to a slim and quickly receding hope that future progress may vitiate the need for such a grim declaration.

This hope is sustained in part by the fact that the Indians who brought this case found it in themselves to stand up, draw a line in the sand, and tell the government: Enough is enough — this far and no further. Perhaps they regret having done so now, nine years later, beset on all sides by the costs of protracted litigation and the possibility that their efforts may ultimately prove futile; but still they continue. The notice requirement established by the Court today represents a significant victory for the plaintiffs. For the first time in the history of this case, the majority of Indian beneficiaries will be aware of the lawsuit, the plaintiffs' efforts, and the danger involved in placing any further confidence in the Department of the Interior. Perhaps more importantly, the Indians will be advised that they may contact class counsel for guidance on their trust-related concerns. This likely will bring to light a wealth of new evidence concerning Interior's mismanagement of the trust; it will also open an avenue to relief for individuals throughout Indian country whose suffering might otherwise be buried forever in a bureaucratic tomb.

Real justice for these Indians may still lie in the distant future; it may never come at all. This reality makes a statement about our society and our form of government that we should be unwilling to let stand. But perhaps the best that can be hoped for is that people never forget what the plaintiffs have done here, and that other marginalized people will learn about this case and follow the Indians' example.

Cobell v. Norton, 229 F.R.D. 5 (D.D.C. 2005).

Based on this language, among other passages, the United States asked the D.C. Circuit to remove Judge Lamberth from the case, arguing that he was biased against the United States because he had "viciously and baselessly denounced" the Interior Department as "villainous racists." Does this kind of assessment of United States history reflect bias any more or any differently than the opinion in *Johnson v. M'Intosh*, which you read in Ch. 1, Sec. C.1?

Relying on the language quoted above and on numerous reversals of Judge Lamberth's rulings in procedural matters, the D.C. Circuit ordered Judge Lamberth removed from the case. *Cobell v. Kempthorne*, 455 F.3d 317 (D.C. Cir. 2006). While acknowledging that the government bore "a heavy burden" if it were to prevail on such a motion based on the judge's "strong words" rather than specific acts of favoritism toward one side, the appeals court found that Judge Lamberth's language was sufficiently extreme and that it displayed a " 'clear inability to render fair judgment' " (citing *Liteky v. United States*, 510 U.S. 540, 551 (1994)). According to the D.C. Circuit panel, much of that language, though "harsh — even incendiary" was "nothing more than the views of an experienced judge who, having presided over this exceptionally contentious case for almost a decade, has become 'exceedingly ill disposed towards [a] defendant' that has flagrantly and repeatedly breached its fiduciary obligations. *Liteky*, 510 U.S. at 550." Where the D.C. Circuit drew the line, however, was at the point where Judge Lamberth accused the Department of the Interior of "racism."

Senators John McCain and Byron Dorgan of the Senate Indian Affairs Committee introduced legislation in 2005 that called for the Treasury and Interior

Departments to figure out how much money flowed through the individual accounts since 1980, and use that as a basis for a guesstimate of what the overall settlement amount should be. Estimates of the money owed to the class members range from $500 million to $27.5 billion, the government's lower number based on efforts to account for possible errors in collections, deposits, and payments, and the plaintiffs' higher number based on a presumption that Indians still are owed a fifth of the $100–$170 billion in royalties they should have received (mostly in accrued interest). Perhaps signifying broad exhaustion with the process, voices on both sides of the dispute were urging Congress to come up with an "arbitrary" number to settle this historical wrong, rather than waiting for a costly and probably unilluminating accounting procedure. Assuming that Congress could identify such a figure, how would such an amount be distributed among the class members?

A new judge, James Robertson, was assigned the *Cobell* case. Judge Robertson held a trial in June of 2008, and in *Cobell v. Kempthorne*, 532 F. Supp. 2d 37 (D.D.C. 2008) (*Cobell* XX), he concluded that the Department of the Interior continued to breach its duty to account for trust funds. The court further held that accounting for the funds was impossible "as a conclusion of law" because the government could not "achieve an accounting that passes muster as a trust accounting" given inadequate present and (likely) future funding from Congress. In *Cobell v Kempthorne*, 569 F. Supp. 2d 223 (D.D.C. 2008) (*Cobell XXI*), Judge Robertson granted equitable restitution to the plaintiff class based on the unproven shortfall of the trust's actual value as compared with its statistically likely value. The court awarded $455,600,000 to the plaintiff class in what it called a restitutionary award. Lawyers for the plaintiffs had been arguing that they were entitled to $47 billion.

The D.C. Circuit proceeded to vacate *Cobell XX* and *Cobell XII* and remand for further proceedings.

COBELL v. SALAZAR
United States Court of Appeals, District of Columbia Circuit
573 F.3d 808 (2009)

SENTELLE, CHIEF JUDGE:

Plaintiffs and defendants cross appeal from two orders of the district court. The first, "*Cobell XX*," held that the Department of the Interior continued to breach its duty to account for trust funds . . . [and] . . . further held that accounting for the funds was impossible "as a conclusion of law" because the government could not "achieve an accounting that passes muster as a trust accounting" given inadequate present and (likely) future funding from Congress. The second order of the district court, "*Cobell XXI*," granted equitable restitution to the plaintiff class based on the unproven shortfall of the trust's actual value as compared with its statistically likely value. The district court stressed that breaching the duty to account did not generate the government's financial liability. Rather, the government's "failure properly to allocate and pay trust funds to beneficiaries" gave rise to "restitution or disgorgement of the very money that ha[d] been withheld." Accordingly, the court awarded $455,600,000 to the plaintiff class in what it called a restitutionary award.

. . . .

Bowing to our directive in *Cobell v. Kempthorne*, 455 F.3d 301 (D.C. Cir. 2006) (*Cobell XVII*) — that because "both the APA and the common law of trusts apply in this case[,] the specific question to be addressed determines which body of law becomes most prominent," *id.* at 303–04 — the district court sought to determine "which body of law [wa]s more prominent with respect to specific aspects of Interior's 2007 accounting plan," *Cobell XX*, 532 F.Supp.2d [37], 89 [D.D.C. 2008]. Most importantly, the district court divided the issues into those relating to the methodology and to the scope of the accounting. *Id.* The district court correctly held that Interior's methodology was "owed the greatest deference," *id.* at 89, because it "ar[ose] out of an administrative balancing of cost, time, and accuracy," *id.* at 91. In contrast, the court observed that the scope "is the result . . . of a legal interpretation of the 1994 Act and other statutes governing the IIM trust." *Id.* at 89. It further noted that scope is not "only a temporal matter. It also relates to the elements that are present within and missing from the statements of account Interior proposes to issue. . . ." *Id.* at 90. That said, the court went on to conclude that Interior's choices on scope, particularly as to the latter aspects, "were not dictated by administrative cost-benefit analyses to which judicial deference is owed. . . ." *Id.* In that conclusion, the district court went too far.

We recognize, as did the district court, that the courts face two mandates of deference in construing the relevant statutes at issue in this case. First, there is the familiar Chevron deference upon which the district court relied in reviewing Interior's methodology. However, as the court observed, Chevron deference can be " 'trumped by the requirement that statutes are to be construed liberally in favor of the Indians, with ambiguous provisions interpreted to their benefit.' " *Id.* at 89. Nonetheless, Chevron deference does not disappear from the process of reviewing an agency's interpretation of those statutes it is trusted to administer for the benefit of the Indians, although that deference applies with muted effect. Granted, the Indians' benefit remains paramount. But where Congress has entrusted to the agency the duty of applying, and therefore interpreting, a statutory duty owed to the Indians, we cannot ignore the responsibility of the agency for careful stewardship of limited government resources. Applying even a muted Chevron deference leads us to a different conclusion than that reached by the district court.

. . . In *Cobell XVII* we opined that "neither congressional language nor common law trust principles (once translated to this context) establish a definite balance between exactitude and cost." While we understand that it may not have been clear to the *Cobell XX* court that this balance applied beyond the accounting methodology, we now hold that the scope of the accounting must also be balanced in equity.

Therefore, the district court was not completely correct when it said that "the proper scope of the accounting obligation . . . is the result . . . of a legal interpretation of the 1994 Act and other statutes governing the IIM trust." *Cobell XX*, 532 F. Supp. 2d at 89. The district court was correct to the extent that the scope of the accounting is derived from statutory law. But when Congress affords courts equitable jurisdiction — as it has done in this case — it draws on a tradition of flexibility, not rigidity, in equity. The unique nature of this trust has been emphasized by the district court. . . . The unique nature of this trust requires the district court to exercise equitable powers in resolving the paradox between classical accounting and limited government resources. . . . Therefore, the district court was incorrect insofar as it assumed that the scope of the accounting obligation could not be adjusted in equity.

The plaintiffs are entitled to an accounting under the statute. 25 U.S.C. § 4011(a). The district court sitting in equity must do everything it can to ensure that Interior provides them an equitable accounting. The district court's holding of impossibility contradicts the requirement of an equitable accounting — one that makes most efficient use of limited government resources. Given the realities of congressional appropriations, it would be inequitable for Interior to throw up its hands and stop the accounting. This is what the district court declared Interior should do in *Cobell XX*, leading to the money judgment of *Cobell XXI*. That judgment was substantial, but without an accounting, it is impossible to know who is owed what. The best any trust beneficiary could hope for would be a government check in an arbitrary amount. Even if this did justice for the class, it would be inaccurate and unfair to an unknown number of individual trust beneficiaries. There will be uncertainty in any accounting for this trust. Interior's job is to minimize that uncertainty with a finite budget. Equity requires the courts to assure that Interior provides the best accounting it can.

The proper scope of the accounting ultimately remains a question for the district court, but we will provide as much guidance as we can on appropriate methodology, and principles to guide the analysis of unforeseen circumstances. The overarching aim of the district court should be for Interior to provide the trust beneficiaries the best accounting possible, in a reasonable time, with the money that Congress is willing to appropriate

In *Cobell XVII*, we made clear that an equitable accounting may include the use of statistical sampling when verifying transactions. A primary reason for this decision was that, "for the subset of transactions valued at less than $500, Interior estimated that the average cost of accounting, per transaction, would exceed the average value of the transactions." Because of this, Interior proposed to study only "about 0.3% of the roughly 25 million transactions under $500." We now instruct the district court to extend this reasoning to the rest of the accounting. [Vacated and remanded].

NOTE ON SETTLEMENT OF THE *COBELL* LITIGATION

On December 8, 2009, the plaintiffs in the *Cobell* lawsuit and the federal government announced that the parties had entered into a settlement agreement. Under the terms of the settlement, which required and received congressional approval, the federal government agreed to:

- establish a $1.4 billion fund to settle historic trust mismanagement and accounting claims;

- create a $2 billion fund that the Department of the Interior will use to buy back fractionated Indian lands to ensure the problems raised by *Cobell* do not occur again;

- in order to provide an incentive for account holders to sell their interests in fractionated lands, direct up to 5% of the value of fractionated land into a college scholarship fund of up to $60 million for American Indian students.

See Claims Resolution Act of 2010, Pub. L. No. 111-291, § 101, 124 Stat. 3064 (2010). On the same day, Secretary of the Interior Ken Salazar announced he had signed a Secretarial Order establishing a 5-member Secretarial Commission on Indian Trust Administration and Reform to examine ongoing trust account improvement efforts and the management of Individual Indian Money accounts.

In June 2011, the D.C. District Court held a fairness hearing during which the court heard arguments from the attorneys on behalf of the parties regarding the terms of the proposed settlement. One month later Judge Thomas F. Hogan issued an order granting final approval for the settlement and directing the clerk to enter final judgment in accordance with the order. Among other things, the court expressly found that "the requirements for settlement under Rule 23(e) are satisfied, and that the terms of the settlement are 'fair, reasonable and adequate' from the perspective of absent class members." The court also concluded that adequate due process had been afforded to class members, and that they had been adequately represented in the proceedings. Individuals who are entitled to participate in the settlement as a class member were encouraged (via a nationwide advertising campaign) to submit claim forms to opt in the settlement. On May 22, 2012, the D.C. Circuit Court of Appeals affirmed the *Cobell* class action settlement agreement against a challenge filed by a class member asserting that the settlement was unfair because it rested on an impermissible "intra-class conflict" and violated principles of due process, as well as Federal Rule of Civil Procedure 23. *See Cobell v. Salazar*, 679 F.3d 909 (D.C. Cir. 2012).

The *Cobell* litigation directed unprecedented attention to the weaknesses of federal trust administration, and was directly responsible for creation of the Secretarial Commission on Indian Trust Administration and Reform. That commission released its final report in December 2013, available at http://www.doi. gov/cobell/commission/upload/Report-of-the-Commission-on-Indian-Trust-Administration-and-Reform_FINAL_Approved-12-10-2013.pdf. Its recommendations for transformation of federal trust administration are sweeping, ranging from a broad redefinition of the fiduciary standard to details of management of individual Indian trust accounts. To overcome the Supreme Court's narrow construction of the federal trust responsibility in damages cases such as those discussed earlier in this section, the Commission urges Congress to enact legislation that would provide: "The trustee is a fiduciary in which the law demands an unusually high standard of ethical or moral conduct with reference to the beneficiary. The trustee owes a duty to act solely in the interest of the beneficiary, and must not consider their own personal advantage." *Id.* at 24–25. Can you see how such language could alter the outcomes in the damages cases such as *White Mountain Apache* and *Navajo Nation*? For management of Department of Interior (DOI) trust funds, the Commission recommends that the department create a fully independent and centralized Indian Trust Administration Commission, with structural, reporting, and funding autonomy from DOI. Why does the Commission want this new trust administration entity to be both "independent" and under the umbrella of DOI? If these functions were removed from the DOI, as some Interior officials have advocated in light of the *Cobell* litigation, what would happen to Indian hiring preference obligations under the Indian Reorganization Act, 25 U.S.C. § 472, and contracting requirements for federal Indian programs under the Indian Self-Determination Act, 25 U.S.C. § 450a? Still other Commission recommendations tackle the problems that arise because "[t]he United States both litigates cases as trustee for Indian tribes and also defends lawsuits brought by Indian tribes against the federal government and various agencies." *Id.* at 25.

c.   Conflicts of Interest Between Government Departments and the Prospect of Equitable Relief

A common problem in the federal trust administration of Indian natural resources is the conflict of interest between the government's need to further national policy objectives and its trust obligations to the Indians. In the seminal article on the subject, Reid Peyton Chambers, *Judicial Enforcement of the Federal Trust Responsibility to Indians*, 27 Stan. L. Rev. 1213, 1213–48 (1975), the author notes that the federal government has a built-in conflict of interest that it somehow must manage. These problems often are exacerbated when agencies with conflicting interests, such as the Bureau of Mines or the Bureau of Reclamation, co-exist in the Department of the Interior with the BIA and other federal agencies charged with trust administration of Indian assets. Should the role of the Secretary of the Interior or of the Solicitor's Office in the Department of the Interior be to manage, mediate, or decide such conflicts or to assure that each side gets maximum representation and permit the courts to resolve the conflicts that emerge? Furthermore, as then Professor Chambers pointed out, if such conflicts of interest must be resolved by the federal courts, they cannot effectively enforce the Indian trust doctrine or understand how to manage such conflicts of interest unless there is some clear delineation of the purposes of the Indian trust relationship with the federal government. As he put it:

> The underlying purposes of the trust responsibility thus are probably determinative of the proper extent of judicial review. If it is a short-term "guardianship" designed to last until the wards become competent — *i.e.*, acclimated to the ways of the dominant culture and/or assimilated into it — then specific performance of trust obligations seems less important and property can be more readily transmuted into money. Even if the trust relationship were seen as permanent, its purposes could be limited to providing financial support for Indians and to ensuring that their lands and resources were not sold for an unconscionable consideration; in this event, judicial remedies limited to money damages for breach of trust would again seem adequate. A more expansive reading of the trust relationship, however, would suggest that the preservation of the trust corpus in a particular form — land and natural resources instead of money — is itself a critical value. If, as the Cherokee cases suggest, a chief objective of the trust responsibility is to protect tribal status as self-governing entities, executive extinguishment of the tribal land base diminishes the territory over which tribal authority is exercised and thereby imperils fulfillment of the guarantee of tribal political and cultural autonomy. If this is the correct interpretation of the trust responsibility, equitable relief in appropriate cases seems essential. Such relief is particularly vital to accommodate the

conflicts between Indian trustee responsibilities and competing government projects that affect countless federal agencies.

Id. at 1235–36. Decades later, the problem persists, as the following case illustrates.

UNITED STATES v. JICARILLA APACHE NATION
United States Supreme Court
131 S. Ct. 2313 (2011)

JUSTICE ALITO delivered the opinion of the Court.

The attorney-client privilege ranks among the oldest and most established evidentiary privileges known to our law. The common law, however, has recognized an exception to the privilege when a trustee obtains legal advice related to the exercise of fiduciary duties. In such cases, courts have held, the trustee cannot withhold attorney-client communications from the beneficiary of the trust.

In this case, we consider whether the fiduciary exception applies to the general trust relationship between the United States and the Indian tribes. We hold that it does not. Although the Government's responsibilities with respect to the management of funds belonging to Indian tribes bear some resemblance to those of a private trustee, this analogy cannot be taken too far. The trust obligations of the United States to the Indian tribes are established and governed by statute rather than the common law, and in fulfilling its statutory duties, the Government acts not as a private trustee but pursuant to its sovereign interest in the execution of federal law. The reasons for the fiduciary exception — that the trustee has no independent interest in trust administration, and that the trustee is subject to a general common-law duty of disclosure — do not apply in this context.

I

The Jicarilla Apache Nation (Tribe) occupies a 900,000-acre reservation in northern New Mexico that was established by Executive Order in 1887. The land contains timber, gravel, and oil and gas reserves, which are developed pursuant to statutes administered by the Department of the Interior. Proceeds derived from these natural resources are held by the United States in trust for the Tribe pursuant to the American Indian Trust Fund Management Reform Act of 1994, 108 Stat. 4239, and other statutes.

In 2002, the Tribe commenced a breach-of-trust action against the United States in the Court of Federal Claims (CFC). The Tribe sued under the Tucker Act, 28 U.S.C. § 1491 (2006 ed. and Supp. III), and the Indian Tucker Act, § 1505, which vest the CFC with jurisdiction over claims against the Government that are founded on the Constitution, laws, treaties, or contracts of the United States. The complaint seeks monetary damages for the Government's alleged mismanagement of funds held in trust for the Tribe. The Tribe argues that the Government violated various laws, including 25 U.S.C. §§ 161a and 162a, that govern the management of funds held in trust for Indian tribes. See 88 Fed.Cl. 1, 3 (2009).

From December 2002 to June 2008, the Government and the Tribe participated in alternative dispute resolution in order to resolve the claim. During that time, the Government turned over thousands of documents but withheld 226 potentially relevant documents as protected by the attorney-client privilege, the attorney work-product doctrine, or the deliberative-process privilege.

In 2008, at the request of the Tribe, the case was restored to the active litigation docket. The CFC divided the case into phases for trial and set a discovery schedule. The first phase, relevant here, concerns the Government's management of the Tribe's trust accounts from 1972 to 1992. The Tribe alleges that during this period the Government failed to invest its trust funds properly. Among other things, the Tribe claims the Government failed to maximize returns on its trust funds, invested too heavily in short-term maturities, and failed to pool its trust funds with other tribal trusts. During discovery, the Tribe moved to compel the Government to produce the 226 withheld documents. In response, the Government agreed to withdraw its claims of deliberative-process privilege and, accordingly, to produce 71 of the documents. But the Government continued to assert the attorney-client privilege and attorney work-product doctrine with respect to the remaining 155 documents. The CFC reviewed those documents *in camera* and classified them into five categories: (1) requests for legal advice relating to trust administration sent by personnel at the Department of the Interior to the Office of the Solicitor, which directs legal affairs for the Department, (2) legal advice sent from the Solicitor's Office to personnel at the Interior and Treasury Departments, (3) documents generated under contracts between Interior and an accounting firm, (4) Interior documents concerning litigation with other tribes, and (5) miscellaneous documents not falling into the other categories.

The CFC granted the Tribe's motion to compel in part. The CFC held that communications relating to the management of trust funds fall within a "fiduciary exception" to the attorney-client privilege. Under that exception, which courts have applied in the context of common-law trusts, a trustee who obtains legal advice related to the execution of fiduciary obligations is precluded from asserting the attorney-client privilege against beneficiaries of the trust. The CFC concluded that the trust relationship between the United States and the Indian tribes is sufficiently analogous to a common-law trust relationship that the exception should apply. Accordingly, the CFC held, the United States may not shield from the Tribe communications with attorneys relating to trust matters. . . .

The Government sought to prevent disclosure of the documents by petitioning the Court of Appeals for the Federal Circuit for a writ of mandamus directing the CFC to vacate its production order. The Court of Appeals denied the petition because, in its view, the CFC correctly applied the fiduciary exception. The court held that "the United States cannot deny an Indian tribe's request to discover communications between the United States and its attorneys based on the attorney-client privilege when those communications concern management of an Indian trust and the United States has not claimed that the government or its attorneys considered a specific competing interest in those communications." *In re United States*, 590 F.3d 1305, 1313 (C.A. Fed. 2009). In qualifying its holding, the court recognized that sometimes the Government may have other statutory obligations that clash with its fiduciary duties to the Indian tribes. But because the Government had not alleged that the legal advice in this case related to such conflicting interests, the court reserved judgment on how the fiduciary exception might apply in that situation. The court rejected the Government's argument that, because its duties to the Indian tribes were governed by statute rather than the common law, it had no general duty of disclosure that would override the attorney-client privilege. The court also disagreed with the Government's contention that a case-by-case approach made the attorney-client privilege too unpredictable and would impair the Government's ability to obtain confidential legal advice.

We granted certiorari, 562 U.S. —, 131 S. Ct. 856, 178 L. Ed. 2d 622 (2011), and now reverse and remand for further proceedings. . . .

II

The Federal Rules of Evidence provide that evidentiary privileges "shall be governed by the principles of the common law . . . in the light of reason and experience." Fed. Rule Evid. 501. The attorney-client privilege "is the oldest of the privileges for confidential communications known to the common law." *Upjohn Co. v. United States,* 449 U.S. 383, 389 (1981) (citing 8 J. Wigmore, Evidence § 2290 (J. McNaughton rev. 1961)). Its aim is "to encourage full and frank communication between attorneys and their clients and thereby promote broader public interests in the observance of law and administration of justice." 449 U.S., at 389; *Hunt v. Blackburn,* 128 U.S. 464, 470 (1888).

The objectives of the attorney-client privilege apply to governmental clients. . . . Unless applicable law provides other-wise, the Government may invoke the attorney-client privilege in civil litigation to protect confidential communications between Government officials and Government attorneys. *Id.,* at 574 ("[G]overnmental agencies and employees enjoy the same privilege as nongovernmental counterparts"). The Tribe argues, however, that the common law also recognizes a fiduciary exception to the attorney-client privilege and that, by virtue of the trust relationship between the Government and the Tribe, documents that would otherwise be privileged must be disclosed. As preliminary matters, we consider the bounds of the fiduciary exception and the nature of the trust relationship between the United States and the Indian tribes.

A

English courts first developed the fiduciary exception as a principle of trust law in the nineteenth century. The rule was that when a trustee obtained legal advice to guide the administration of the trust, and not for the trustee's own defense in litigation, the beneficiaries were entitled to the production of documents related to that advice. *Wynne v. Humberston,* 27 Beav. 421, 423–424, 54 Eng. Rep. 165, 166 (1858); *Talbot v. Marshfield* 2 Dr. & Sm. 549, 550–551, 62 Eng. Rep. 728, 729 (1865). The courts reasoned that the normal attorney-client privilege did not apply in this situation because the legal advice was sought for the beneficiaries' benefit and was obtained at the beneficiaries' expense by using trust funds to pay the attorney's fees. *Ibid.; Wynne, supra,* at 423–424, 54 Eng. Rep., at 166.

The fiduciary exception quickly became an established feature of English common law, see, *e.g.*, *In re Mason*, 22 Ch. D. 609 (1883), but it did not appear in this country until the following century. . . .

The leading American case on the fiduciary exception is *Riggs Nat. Bank of Washington, D.C. v. Zimmer*, 355 A.2d 709 (Del. Ch. 1976). In that case, the beneficiaries of a trust estate sought to compel the trustees to reimburse the estate for alleged breaches of trust. The beneficiaries moved to compel the trustees to produce a legal memorandum related to the administration of the trust that the trustees withheld on the basis of attorney-client privilege. The Delaware Chancery Court, observing that "American case law is practically nonexistent on the duty of a trustee in this context," looked to the English cases. *Id.*, at 712. Applying the common-law fiduciary exception, the court held that the memorandum was discoverable. It identified two reasons for applying the exception.

First, the court explained, the trustees had obtained the legal advice as "mere representative[s]" of the beneficiaries because the trustees had a fiduciary obligation to act in the beneficiaries' interest when administering the trust. *Ibid.* For that reason, the beneficiaries were the "real clients" of the attorney who had advised the trustee on trust-related matters, and therefore the attorney-client privilege properly belonged to the beneficiaries rather than the trustees. *Id.*, at 711–712. The court based its "real client" determination on several factors: (1) when the advice was sought, no adversarial proceedings between the trustees and beneficiaries had been pending, and therefore there was no reason for the trustees to seek legal advice in a personal rather than a fiduciary capacity; (2) the court saw no indication that the memorandum was intended for any purpose other than to benefit the trust; and (3) the law firm had been paid out of trust assets. . . . The court distinguished between "legal advice procured at the trustee's *own* expense and for his *own* protection," which would remain privileged, "and the situation where the trust itself is assessed for obtaining opinions of counsel where interests of the beneficiaries are presently at stake." *Ibid.* In the latter case, the fiduciary exception applied, and the trustees could not withhold those attorney-client communications from the beneficiaries.

Second, the court concluded that the trustees' fiduciary duty to furnish trust-related information to the beneficiaries outweighed their interest in the attorney-client privilege. "The policy of preserving the full disclosure necessary in the trustee-beneficiary relationship," the court explained, "is here ultimately more important than the protection of the trustees' confidence in the attorney for the trust." *Id.*, at 714. Because more information helped the beneficiaries to police the trustees' management of the trust, disclosure was, in the court's judgment, "a weightier public policy than the preservation of confidential attorney-client communications." *Ibid.*

The Federal Courts of Appeals apply the fiduciary exception based on the same two criteria. See, *e.g.*, *In re Long Island Lighting Co.*, 129 F.3d 268, 272 (C.A.2 1997). . . . Not until the decision below had a federal appellate court held the exception to apply to the United States as trustee for the Indian tribes.

B

In order to apply the fiduciary exception in this case, the Court of Appeals analogized the Government to a private trustee. 590 F.3d, at 1313. We have applied that analogy in limited contexts, see, *e.g., United States v. Mitchell*, 463 U.S. 206, 226 (1983) *(Mitchell II)*, but that does not mean the Government resembles a private trustee in every respect. On the contrary, this Court has previously noted that the relationship between the United States and the Indian tribes is distinctive, "different from that existing between individuals whether dealing at arm's length, *as trustees and beneficiaries*, or otherwise." *Klamath and Moadoc Tribes v. United States*, 296 U.S. 244, 254 (1935) (emphasis added). "The *general* relationship between the United States and the Indian tribes is not comparable to a private trust relationship." *Cherokee Nation of Okla. v. United States*, 21 Cl. Ct. 565, 573 (1990) (emphasis added).

The Government, of course, is not a private trustee. Though the relevant statutes denominate the relationship between the Government and the Indians a "trust," see, *e.g.*, 25 U.S.C. § 162a, that trust is defined and governed by statutes rather than the common law. See *United States v. Navajo Nation*, 537 U.S. 488, 506 (2003) *(Navajo I)* ("[T]he analysis must train on specific rights-creating or duty-imposing statutory or regulatory prescriptions.") As we have recognized in prior cases, Congress may style its relations with the Indians a "trust" without assuming all the fiduciary duties of a private trustee, creating a trust relationship that is "limited" or "bare" compared to a trust relationship between private parties at common law. *United States v. Mitchell*, 445 U.S. 535, 542, (1980) *(Mitchell I); Mitchell II, supra*, at 224.[31]

The difference between a private common-law trust and the statutory Indian trust follows from the unique position of the Government as sovereign. The distinction between "public rights" against the Government and "private rights" between private parties is well established. The Government consents to be liable to private parties "and may yield this consent upon such terms and under such restrictions as it may think just." *Murray's Lessee v. Hoboken Land & Improvement Co.*, 15 L. Ed. 372, 18 How. 272, 283 (1856). This creates an important distinction "between cases of private right and those which arise between the Government and persons subject to its authority in connection with the performance of the constitutional functions of the executive or legislative departments." *Crowell v. Benson*, 285 U.S. 22, 50 (1932).

Throughout the history of the Indian trust relationship, we have recognized that the organization and management of the trust is a sovereign function subject to the plenary authority of Congress. See *Merrion v. Jicarilla Apache Tribe*, 455 U.S. 130, 169, n. 18, 102 (1982) ("The United States retains plenary authority to divest the

---

[31] [4] "There are a number of widely varying relationships which more or less closely resemble trusts, but which are not trusts, although the term 'trust' is sometimes used loosely to cover such relationships. It is important to differentiate trusts from these other relationships, since many of the rules applicable to trusts are not applicable to them." Restatement (Second) of Trusts § 4, Introductory Note, p. 15 (1957) (hereinafter Restatement 2d); *see also Begay v. United States*, 16 Cl. Ct. 107, 127, n. 17 (1987) ("[T]he provisions relating to private trustees and fiduciaries, while useful as analogies, cannot be regarded as finally dispositive in a government-Indian trustee-fiduciary relationship").

tribes of any attributes of sovereignty"); *United States v. Wheeler,* 435 U.S. 313, 319 (1978) ("Congress has plenary authority to legislate for the Indian tribes in all matters, including their form of government"); *Winton v. Amos,* 255 U.S. 373, 391(1921) ("Congress has plenary authority over the Indians and all their tribal relations, and full power to legislate concerning their tribal property"); *Lone Wolf v. Hitchcock,* 187 U.S. 553, 565 (1903) ("Plenary authority over the tribal relations of the Indians has been exercised by Congress from the beginning, and the power has always been deemed a political one, not subject to be controlled by the judicial department of the government"); *Cherokee Nation v. Hitchcock,* 187 U.S. 294, 308 (1902) ("The power existing in Congress to administer upon and guard the tribal property, and the power being political and administrative in its nature, the manner of its exercise is a question within the province of the legislative branch to determine, and is not one for the courts"); see also *United States v. Candelaria,* 271 U.S. 432, 439 (1926); *Tiger v. Western Investment Co.,* 221 U.S. 286, 315 (1911).

Because the Indian trust relationship represents an exercise of that authority, we have explained that the Government "has a real and direct interest" in the guardianship it exercises over the Indian tribes; "the interest is one which is vested in it as a sovereign." *United States v. Minnesota,* 270 U.S. 181, 194 (1926). This is especially so because the Government has often structured the trust relationship to pursue its own policy goals. Thus, while trust administration "relat[es] to the welfare of the Indians, the maintenance of the limitations which Congress has prescribed as a part of its plan of distribution is distinctly an interest of the United States." *Heckman v. United States,* 224 U.S. 413, 437 (1912); see also *Candelaria, supra,* at 443–444.

In *Heckman,* the Government brought suit to cancel certain conveyances of allotted lands by members of an Indian tribe because the conveyances violated restrictions on alienation imposed by Congress. This Court explained that the Government brought suit as the representative of the very Indian grantors whose conveyances it sought to cancel, and those Indians were thereby bound by the judgment. 224 U.S., at 445–446. But while it was formally acting as a trustee, the Government was in fact asserting its own sovereign interest in the disposition of Indian lands, and the Indians were precluded from intervening in the litigation to advance a position contrary to that of the Government. *Id.,* at 445. Such a result was possible because the Government assumed a fiduciary role over the Indians not as a common-law trustee but as the governing authority enforcing statutory law.

We do not question "the undisputed existence of a general trust relationship between the United States and the Indian people." *Mitchell II,* 463 U.S., at 225. The Government, following "a humane and self imposed policy . . . has charged itself with moral obligations of the highest responsibility and trust," *Seminole Nation v. United States,* 316 U.S. 286, 296–297 (1942), obligations "to the fulfillment of which the national honor has been committed," *Heckman, supra,* at 437. Congress has expressed this policy in a series of statutes that have defined and redefined the trust relationship between the United States and the Indian tribes. In some cases, Congress established only a limited trust relationship to serve a narrow purpose. See *Mitchell I,* 445 U.S., at 544 (Congress intended the United States to hold land " 'in trust' " under the General Allotment Act "simply because it wished to prevent alienation of the land and to ensure that allottees would be immune from state taxation"); *Navajo I,* 537 U.S., at 507–508 (Indian Mineral Leasing Act imposes no "detailed fiduciary responsibilities" nor is the Government "expressly invested with responsibility to secure 'the needs and best interests of the Indian owner' ").

In other cases, we have found that particular "statutes and regulations . . . clearly establish fiduciary obligations of the Government" in some areas. *Mitchell II, supra,* at 226,; see also *United States v. White Mountain Apache Tribe,* 537 U.S. 465, 475 (2003). Once federal law imposes such duties, the common law "could play a role." *United States v. Navajo Nation,* 556 U.S. 287, 301 (2009) *(Navajo II).* We have looked to common-law principles to inform our interpretation of statutes and to determine the scope of liability that Congress has imposed. See *White Mountain Apache Tribe, supra,* at 475–476. But the applicable statutes and regulations "establish [the] fiduciary relationship and define the contours of the United States' fiduciary responsibilities." *Mitchell II, supra,* at 224. When "the Tribe cannot identify a specific, applicable, trust-creating statute or regulation that the Government violated, . . . neither the Government's 'control' over [Indian assets] nor common-law trust principles matter." *Navajo II, supra,* at 302.[32] The Government assumes Indian trust responsibilities only to the extent that it expressly accepts those responsibilities by statute.[33]

Over the years, we have described the federal relationship with the Indian tribes using various formulations. The Indian tribes have been called "domestic dependent nations," *Cherokee Nation v. Georgia,* 5 Pet. 1, 17 (1831), under the "tutelage" of the United States, *Heckman, supra,* at 444, and subject to "the exercise of the Government's guardianship over . . . their affairs," *United States v. Sandoval,* 231 U.S. 28, 48 (1913). These concepts do not necessarily correspond to a common-law trust relationship. See, *e.g.,* Restatement 2d, § 7 ("A guardianship is not a trust"). That is because Congress has chosen to structure the Indian trust relationship in different ways. We will apply common-law trust principles where Congress has indicated it is appropriate to do so. For that reason, the Tribe must point to a right conferred by statute or regulation in order to obtain otherwise privileged information from the Government against its wishes.

III

In this case, the Tribe's claim arises from 25 U.S.C. §§ 161–162a and the American Indian Trust Fund Management Reform Act of 1994, § 4001 *et seq.* These provisions define "the trust responsibilities of the United States" with respect to tribal funds. § 162a(d). The Court of Appeals concluded that the trust relationship between the United States and the Indian tribes, outlined in these and other statutes, is "sufficiently similar to a private trust to justify applying the fiduciary exception." 590 F.3d, at 1313. We disagree.

As we have discussed, the Government exercises its carefully delimited trust

---

[32] [5] Thus, the dissent's reliance on the Government's "managerial control" (opinion of SOTOMAYOR, J.) is misplaced.

[33] [6] Cf. Restatement 2d, § 25, Comment *a* ("[A]lthough the settlor has called the transaction a trust[,] no trust is created unless he manifests an intention to impose duties which are enforceable in the courts").

responsibilities in a sovereign capacity to implement national policy respecting the Indian tribes. The two features justifying the fiduciary exception — the beneficiary's status as the "real client" and the trustee's common-law duty to disclose information about the trust — are notably absent in the trust relationship Congress has established between the United States and the Tribe.

A

The Court of Appeals applied the fiduciary exception based on its determination that the Tribe rather than the Government was the "real client" with respect to the Government attorneys' advice. *Ibid.* In cases applying the fiduciary exception, courts identify the "real client" based on whether the advice was bought by the trust corpus, whether the trustee had reason to seek advice in a personal rather than a fiduciary capacity, and whether the advice could have been intended for any purpose other than to benefit the trust. *Riggs,* 355 A.2d, at 711–712. Applying these factors, we conclude that the United States does not obtain legal advice as a "mere representative" of the Tribe; nor is the Tribe the "real client" for whom that advice is intended. See *ibid.*

Here, the Government attorneys are paid out of congressional appropriations at no cost to the Tribe. . . .

The payment structure confirms our view that the Government seeks legal advice in its sovereign capacity rather than as a conventional fiduciary of the Tribe. Undoubtedly, Congress intends the Indian tribes to benefit from the Government's management of tribal trusts. That intention represents "a humane and self imposed policy" based on felt "moral obligations." *Seminole Nation,* 316 U.S., at 296–297. This statutory purpose does not imply a full common-law trust, however. . . . We have said that "the United States continue[s] as trustee to have an active interest" in the disposition of Indian assets because the terms of the trust relationship embody policy goals of the United States. *McKay v. Kalyton,* 204 U.S. 458, 469 (1907).

In some prior cases, we have found that the Government had established the trust relationship in order to impose its own policy on Indian lands. See *Mitchell I,* 445 U.S., at 544 (Congress "intended that the United States 'hold the land . . . in trust' . . . because it wished to prevent alienation of the land"). In other cases, the Government has invoked its trust relationship to prevent state interference with its policy toward the Indian tribes. See *Minnesota v. United States,* 305 U.S. 382, 386 (1939); *Candelaria,* 271 U.S., at 442–444; *United States v. Kagama,* 118 U.S. 375, 382–384 (1886). And the exercise of federal authority thereby established has often been "left under the acts of Congress to the discretion of the Executive Department." *Heckman, supra,* at 446. In this way, Congress has designed the trust relationship to serve the interests of the United States as well as to benefit the Indian tribes. See *United States v. Rickert,* 188 U.S. 432, 443 (1903) (trust relationship " 'authorizes the adoption on the part of the United States of such policy as their own public interests may dictate' " (quoting *Choctaw Nation v.*

United States, 119 U.S. 1, 28 (1886))).[34]

We cannot agree with the Tribe and its *amici* that "[t]he government and its officials who obtained the advice have no stake in [the] substance of the advice, beyond their trustee role," Brief for Respondent 9, or that "the United States' interests in trust administration were identical to the interests of the tribal trust fund beneficiaries," Brief for National Congress of American Indians et al. as *Amici Curiae* 5. The United States has a sovereign interest in the administration of Indian trusts distinct from the private interests of those who may benefit from its administration. . . . For that reason, when the Government seeks legal advice related to the administration of tribal trusts, it establishes an attorney-client relationship related to its sovereign interest in the execution of federal law. In other words, the Government seeks legal advice in a "personal" rather than a fiduciary capacity. See *Riggs*, 355 A.2d, at 711.

Moreover, the Government has too many competing legal concerns to allow a case-by-case inquiry into the purpose of each communication. When "multiple interests" are involved in a trust relationship, the equivalence between the interests of the beneficiary and the trustee breaks down. *Id.*, at 714. That principle applies with particular force to the Government. Because of the multiple interests it must represent, "the Government cannot follow the fastidious standards of a private fiduciary, who would breach his duties to his single beneficiary solely by representing potentially conflicting interests without the beneficiary's consent." *Nevada v. United States*, 463 U.S. 110, 128 (1983).

As the Court of Appeals acknowledged, the Government may be obliged "to balance competing interests" when it administers a tribal trust. 590 F.3d, at 1315. The Government may need to comply with other statutory duties, such as the environmental and conservation obligations that the Court of Appeals discussed. See *id.*, at 1314–1315. The Government may also face conflicting obligations to different tribes or individual Indians. . . . The Government may seek the advice of counsel for guidance in balancing these competing interests. Indeed, the point of consulting counsel may be to determine whether conflicting interests are at stake.

---

[34] [8] Congress has structured the trust relationship to reflect its considered judgment about how the Indians ought to be governed. For example, the Indian General Allotment Act of 1887, 24 Stat. 388, was "a comprehensive congressional attempt to change the role of Indians in American society." F. Cohen, Handbook of Federal Indian Law § 1.04, p. 77 (2005) (hereinafter Cohen). Congress aimed to promote the assimilation of Indians by dividing Indian lands into individually owned allotments. The federal policy aimed "to substitute a new individual way of life for the older Indian communal way." *Id.*, at 79. The Indian Reorganization Act of 1934, 48 Stat. 984, marked a shift away "from assimilation policies and toward more tolerance and respect for traditional aspects of Indian culture." Cohen § 1.05, at 84. The Act prohibited further allotment and restored tribal ownership. *Id.*, at 86. The Indian Self-Determination and Education Assistance Act of 1975, 88 Stat. 2203, and the Tribal Self-Governance Act of 1994, 108 Stat. 4270, enabled tribes to run health, education, economic development, and social programs for themselves. Cohen § 1.07, at 103. This strengthened self-government supported Congress's decision to authorize tribes to withdraw trust funds from Federal Government control and place the funds under tribal control. American Indian Trust Fund Management Reform Act of 1994, 108 Stat. 4239, 4242–4244; *see* 25 U.S.C. §§ 4021–4029 (2006 ed. and Supp. III). The control over the Indian tribes that has been exercised by the United States pursuant to the trust relationship — forcing the division of tribal lands, restraining alienation — does not correspond to the fiduciary duties of a common-law trustee. Rather, the trust relationship has been altered and administered as an instrument of federal policy.

The Court of Appeals sought to accommodate the Government's multiple obligations by suggesting that the Government may invoke the attorney-client privilege if it identifies "a specific competing interest" that was considered in the particular communications it seeks to withhold. 590 F.3d, at 1313. But the conflicting interests the Government must consider are too pervasive for such a case-by-case approach to be workable.

We have said that for the attorney-client privilege to be effective, it must be predictable. See *Jaffee v. Redmond,* 518 U.S. 1, 18, (1996); *Upjohn,* 449 U.S., at 393. If the Government were required to identify the specific interests it considered in each communication, its ability to receive confidential legal advice would be substantially compromised. The Government will not always be able to predict what considerations qualify as a "specific competing interest," especially in advance of receiving counsel's advice. Forcing the Government to monitor all the considerations contained in each communication with counsel would render its attorney-client privilege "little better than no privilege at all." *Ibid.*

B

The Court of Appeals also decided the fiduciary exception properly applied to the Government because "the fiduciary has a duty to disclose all information related to trust management to the beneficiary." 590 F.3d, at 1312. In general, the common-law trustee of an irrevocable trust must produce trust-related information to the beneficiary on a reasonable basis, though this duty is sometimes limited and may be modified by the settlor. Restatement (Third) of Trusts § 82 (2005) (hereinafter Restatement 3d); Bogert §§ 962, 965.[35] The fiduciary exception applies where this duty of disclosure overrides the attorney-client privilege. *United States v. Mett,* 178 F.3d 1058, 1063 (C.A.9 1999) ("[T]he fiduciary exception can be understood as an instance of the attorney-client privilege giving way in the face of a competing legal principle.")

The United States, however, does not have the same common-law disclosure obligations as a private trustee. As we have previously said, common-law principles are relevant only when applied to a "specific, applicable, trust-creating statute or regulation." *Navajo II,* 556 U.S., at 302. The relevant statute in this case is 25 U.S.C. § 162a(d), which delineates "trust responsibilities of the United States" that the Secretary of the Interior must discharge. The enumerated responsibilities include

---

[35] [9] We assume for the sake of argument that an Indian trust is properly analogized to an irrevocable trust rather than to a revocable trust. A revocable trust imposes no duty of the trustee to disclose information to the beneficiary. "[W]hile a trust is revocable, only the person who may revoke it is entitled to receive information about it from the trustee." Bogert § 962, at 25, § 964; Restatement 3d, § 74, Comment e, at 31 ("[T]he trustee of a revocable trust is not to provide reports or accountings or other information concerning the terms or administration of the trust to other beneficiaries without authorization either by the settlor or in the terms of the trust or a statute"). In many respects, Indian trusts resemble revocable trusts at common law because Congress has acted as the settlor in establishing the trust and retains the right to alter the terms of the trust by statute, even in derogation of tribal property interests. *See Winton v. Amos,* 255 U.S. 373, 391 (1921) ("It is thoroughly established that Congress has plenary authority over the Indians . . . and full power to legislate concerning their tribal property"); Cohen § 5.02 [4], at 401–403. The Government has not advanced the argument that the relationship here is similar to a revocable trust, and the point need not be addressed to resolve this case.

a provision identifying the Secretary's obligation to provide specific information to tribal account holders: The Secretary must "suppl[y] account holders with periodic statements of their account performance" and must make "available on a daily basis" the "balances of their account." § 162a(d)(5). The Secretary has complied with these requirements by adopting regulations that instruct the Office of Trust Fund Management to provide each tribe with a quarterly statement of performance, 25 CFR § 115.801 (2010), that identifies "the source, type, and status of the trust funds deposited and held in a trust account; the beginning balance; the gains and losses; receipts and disbursements; and the ending account balance of the quarterly statement period," § 115.803. Tribes may request more frequent statements or further "information about account transactions and balances." § 115.802.

The common law of trusts does not override the specific trust-creating statute and regulations that apply here. Those provisions define the Government's disclosure obligation to the Tribe. The Tribe emphasizes, Brief for Respondent 34, that the statute identifies the list of trust responsibilities as nonexhaustive. See § 162a(d) (trust responsibilities "are not limited to" those enumerated). . . . Whatever Congress intended, we cannot read the clause to include a general common-law duty to disclose all information related to the administration of Indian trusts. When Congress provides specific statutory obligations, we will not read a "catchall" provision to impose general obligations that would include those specifically enumerated. *Massachusetts Mut. Life Ins. Co. v. Russell*, 473 U.S. 134, 141–142 (1985).

. . . Reading the statute to incorporate the full duties of a private, common-law fiduciary would vitiate Congress's specification of narrowly defined disclosure obligations.[36]

By law and regulation, moreover, the documents at issue in this case are classed "the property of the United States," while other records are "the property of the tribe." 25 CFR § 115.1000 (2010); see also §§ 15.502, 162.111, 166.1000. Just as the source of the funds used to pay for legal advice is highly relevant in identifying the "real client" for purposes of the fiduciary exception, we consider ownership of the resulting records to be a significant factor in deciding who "ought to have access to the document." See *Riggs*, 355 A.2d, at 712. In this case, that privilege belongs to the United States.[37]

---

[36] [10] Our reading of 25 U.S.C. § 162a(d) receives additional support from another statute in which Congress expressed its understanding that the Government retains evidentiary privileges allowing it to withhold information related to trust property from Indian tribes. The Indian Claims Limitation Act of 1982, 96 Stat. 1976, addressed Indian claims that the claimants desired to have litigated by the United States. If the Secretary of the Interior decided to reject a claim for litigation, he was required to furnish a report to the affected Indian claimants and, upon their request, to provide "any nonprivileged research materials or evidence gathered by the United States in the documentation of such claim." Id., at 1978. That Congress authorized the withholding of information on grounds of privilege makes us doubt that Congress understood the Government's trust obligations to override so basic a privilege as that between attorney and client.

[37] [11] The dissent tells us that applying the fiduciary exception is even more important against the Government than against a private trustee because of a "history of governmental mismanagement." *Post*, at 2342. While it is not necessary to our decision, we note that the Indian tribes are not required to keep their funds in federal trust. *See* 25 U.S.C. § 4022 (authorizing tribes to withdraw funds held in trust by

. . . .

Courts and commentators have long recognized that "[n]ot every aspect of private trust law can properly govern the unique relationship of tribes and the federal government." Cohen § 5.02[2], at 434–435. The fiduciary exception to the attorney-client privilege ranks among those aspects inapplicable to the Government's administration of Indian trusts. The Court of Appeals denied the Government's petition for a writ of mandamus based on its erroneous view to the contrary. We leave it for that court to determine whether the standards for granting the writ are met in light of our opinion.[38] We therefore reverse the judgment of the Court of Appeals and remand the case for further proceedings consistent with this opinion.

It is so ordered.

Justice Kagan took no part in the consideration or decision of this case.

Justice Ginsburg, with whom Justice Breyer joins, concurring in the judgment.

I agree with the Court that the Government is not an ordinary trustee. Unlike a private trustee, the Government has its own "distinc[t] interest" in the faithful carrying out of the laws governing the conduct of tribal affairs. *Heckman v. United States*, 224 U.S. 413, 437 (1912). This unique "national interest" obligates Government attorneys, in rendering advice, to make their own "independent evaluation of the law and facts" in an effort "to arrive at a single position of the United States," App. to Pet. for Cert. 124a (Letter from Attorney General Griffin B. Bell to Secretary of the Interior Cecil D. Andrus (May 31, 1979)). "For that reason," as the Court explains, "the Government seeks legal advice in a 'personal' rather than a fiduciary capacity." The attorney-client privilege thus protects the Government's communications with its attorneys from disclosure.

Going beyond attorney-client communications, the Court holds that the Government "assumes Indian trust responsibilities only to the extent it expressly accepts those responsibilities by statute." The Court therefore concludes that the trust relationship described by 25 U.S.C. § 162a does not include the usual "common-law disclosure obligations." Because it is unnecessary to decide what information *other than* attorney-client communications the Government may withhold from the beneficiaries of tribal trusts, I concur only in the Court's judgment.

Justice Sotomayor, dissenting.

Federal Indian policy, as established by a network of federal statutes, requires the United States to act strictly in a fiduciary capacity when managing Indian trust fund accounts. The interests of the federal government as trustee and the Jicarilla Apache Nation (Nation) as beneficiary are thus entirely aligned in the context of

---

the United States); 25 CFR pt. 1200(B). If the Tribe wishes to have its funds managed by a "conventional fiduciary," *post*, at 2336, it may seek to do so.

[38] [12] If the Court of Appeals declines to issue the writ, we assume that the CFC on remand will follow our holding here regarding the applicability of the fiduciary exception in the present context.

Indian trust fund management. Where, as here, the governing statutory scheme establishes a conventional fiduciary relationship, the Government's duties include fiduciary obligations derived from common-law trust principles. Because the common-law rationales for the fiduciary exception fully support its application in this context, I would hold that the Government may not rely on the attorney-client privilege to withhold from the Nation communications between the Government and its attorneys relating to trust fund management.

The Court's decision to the contrary rests on false factual and legal premises and deprives the Nation and other Indian tribes of highly relevant evidence in scores of pending cases seeking relief for the Government's alleged mismanagement of their trust funds. But perhaps more troubling is the majority's disregard of our settled precedent that looks to common-law trust principles to define the scope of the Government's fiduciary obligations to Indian tribes. Indeed, aspects of the majority's opinion suggest that common-law principles have little or no relevance in the Indian trust context, a position this Court rejected long ago. Although today's holding pertains only to a narrow evidentiary issue, I fear the upshot of the majority's opinion may well be a further dilution of the Government's fiduciary obligations that will have broader negative repercussions for the relationship between the United States and Indian tribes.

I

A

Federal Rule of Evidence 501 provides in relevant part that "the privilege of a . . . government . . . shall be governed by the principles of the common law as they may be interpreted by the courts of the United States in the light of reason and experience." Rule 501 "was adopted precisely because Congress wished to leave privilege questions to the courts rather than attempt to codify them." *United States v. Weber Aircraft Corp.*, 465 U.S. 792, 804, n. 25 (1984).

As the majority notes, the purpose of the attorney-client privilege "is to encourage full and frank communication between attorneys and their clients and thereby promote broader public interests in the observance of law and administration of justice." *Upjohn Co. v. United States*, 449 U.S. 383, 389 (1981). But the majority neglects to explain that the privilege is a limited exception to the usual rules of evidence requiring full disclosure of relevant information. . . . Because it "has the effect of withholding relevant information from the factfinder," courts construe the privilege narrowly. *Fisher v. United States*, 425 U.S. 391, 403 (1976). It applies "only where necessary to achieve its purpose," *ibid.*; "[w]here this purpose ends, so too does the protection of the privilege," *Wachtel v. Health Net, Inc.*, 482 F.3d 225, 231 (C.A.3 2007).

. . . The majority correctly identifies the two rationales courts have articulated for applying the fiduciary exception, *ante*, at 2322, but its description of those rationales omits a number of important points. With regard to the first rationale, courts have characterized the trust beneficiary as the "real client" of legal advice relating to trust administration because such advice, provided to a trustee to assist in his management of the trust, is ultimately for the benefit of the trust beneficiary, rather than for the trustee in his personal capacity. . . . If the advice was rendered for the benefit of the beneficiary and not for the trustee in any personal capacity, the "real client" of the advice is the beneficiary.

As to the second rationale for the fiduciary exception — rooted in the trustee's fiduciary duty to disclose all information related to trust management — the majority glosses over the fact that this duty of disclosure is designed "to enable the beneficiary to prevent or redress a breach of trust and otherwise to enforce his or her rights under the trust." Third Restatement § 82, Comment *a(2)*, at 184. . . . The majority fails to appreciate the important oversight and accountability interests that underlie this rationale for the fiduciary exception, or explain why they operate with any less force in the Indian trust context.

B

The question in this case is whether the fiduciary exception applies in the Indian trust context such that the Government may not rely on the attorney-client privilege to withhold from the Nation communications between the Government and its attorneys relating to the administration of the Nation's trust fund accounts. Answering that question requires a proper understanding of the nature of the Government's trust relationship with Indian tribes, particularly with regard to its management of Indian trust funds.

Since 1831, this Court has recognized the existence of a general trust relationship between the United States and Indian tribes. See *Cherokee Nation v. Georgia*, 5 Pet. 1, 17 (1831) (Marshall, C.J.). Our decisions over the past century have repeatedly reaffirmed this "distinctive obligation of trust incumbent upon the Government" in its dealings with Indians. *Seminole Nation v. United States*, 316 U.S. 286, 296 (1942); see *United States v. Mitchell*, 463 U.S. 206, 225–226 (1983) *(Mitchell II)* (collecting cases and noting "the undisputed existence of a general trust relationship between the United States and the Indian people"). Congress, too, has recognized the general trust relationship between the United States and Indian tribes. Indeed, "[n]early every piece of modern legislation dealing with Indian tribes contains a statement reaffirming the trust relationship between tribes and the federal government." F. Cohen, Handbook of Federal Indian Law § 5.04[4][a], pp. 420–421 (2005 ed.) (hereinafter Cohen).[39]

Against this backdrop, Congress has enacted federal statutes that "define the contours of the United States' fiduciary responsibilities" with regard to its management of Indian tribal property and other trust assets. *Mitchell II*, 463 U.S., at 224. The Nation's claims as relevant in this case concern the Government's

---

[39] [2] See, *e.g.*, 25 U.S.C. § 458cc(a) (directing Secretary of the Interior to enter into funding agreements with Indian tribes "in a manner consistent with the Federal Government's laws and trust relationship to and responsibility for the Indian people"); § 3701 (finding that the Government "has a trust responsibility to protect, conserve, utilize, and manage Indian agricultural lands consistent with its fiduciary obligation and its unique relationship with Indian tribes"); 20 U.S.C. § 7401 ("It is the policy of the United States to fulfill the Federal Government's unique and continuing trust relationship with and responsibility to the Indian people for the education of Indian children").

alleged mismanagement of its tribal trust fund accounts. See *ante*, at 2319.

The system of trusteeship and federal management of Indian funds originated with congressional enactments in the nineteenth century directing the Government to hold and manage Indian tribal funds in trust. See, *e.g.*, Act of June 9, 1837, 5 Stat. 135; see also Misplaced Trust: The Bureau of Indian Affairs' Mismanagement of the Indian Trust Fund, H.R. Rep. No. 102-449, p. 6 (1992) (hereinafter Misplaced Trust). Through these and later congressional enactments, the United States has come to manage almost $3 billion in tribal funds and collects close to $380 million per year on behalf of tribes. Cohen § 5.03[3][b], at 407.[40]

Today, numerous statutes outline the federal government's obligations as trustee in managing Indian trust funds. In particular, the Secretary of the Treasury, at the request of the Secretary of the Interior, must invest "[a]ll funds held in trust by the United States . . . to the credit of Indian tribes" in certain securities "suitable to the needs of the fund involved." 25 U.S.C. § 161a(a). The Secretary of the Interior may deposit in the Treasury and pay mandatory interest on Indian trust funds when "the best interests of the Indians will be promoted by such deposits, in lieu of investments." § 161. Similarly, the Secretary of the Interior may invest tribal trust funds in certain public debt instruments "if he deems it advisable and for the best interest of the Indians." § 162a(a). And Congress has set forth a nonexhaustive list of the Secretary of the Interior's "trust responsibilities" with respect to Indian trust funds, which include a series of accounting, auditing, management, and disclosure obligations. § 162a(d). These and other statutory provisions[41] give the United States "full responsibility to manage Indian [trust fund accounts] for the benefit of the Indians." *Mitchell II*, 463 U.S., at 224.

"[A] fiduciary relationship necessarily arises when the Government assumes such elaborate control over [trust assets] belonging to Indians." *Id.*, at 225. Under the statutory regime described above, the Government has extensive managerial control over Indian trust funds, exercises considerable discretion with respect to their investment, and has assumed significant responsibilities to account to the tribal beneficiaries. As a result, "[a]ll of the necessary elements of a common-law trust are present: a trustee (the United States), a beneficiary (the Indian [Tribe]), and a trust corpus (Indian . . . funds)." *Ibid.* Unlike in other contexts where the statutory scheme creates only a "bare trust" entailing only limited responsibilities, *United States v. Navajo Nation*, 537 U.S. 488, 505 (2003) *(Navajo I)* (internal quotation marks omitted), the statutory regime governing the United States's obligations with regard to Indian trust funds "bears the hallmarks of a conventional fiduciary relationship," *United States v. Navajo Nation*, 556 U.S. 287, 301 (2009)

---

[40] [3] Trust fund accounts are "comprised mainly of money received through the sale or lease of trust lands and include timber stumpage, oil and gas royalties, and agriculture fees," as well as "judgment funds awarded to tribes." H.R. Rep. No. 103-778, p. 9 (1994). The Nation's claims involve proceeds derived from the Government's management of the Nation's timber, gravel, and other resources and leases of reservation lands. The Government has held these funds in trust for the Nation since the late 1880's. *See* App. to Pet. for Cert. 98a–100a, 105a.

[41] [4] *See, e.g.*, 25 U.S.C. § 4011(a) (requiring Secretary of the Interior to account "for the daily and annual balance of all funds held in trust by the United States for the benefit of an Indian tribe"); § 4041(1) (creating the Office of Special Trustee for American Indians "to provide for more effective management of, and accountability for the proper discharge of, the Secretary's trust responsibilities to Indian tribes").

(*Navajo II*) (internal quotation marks omitted); see *Lincoln v. Vigil*, 508 U.S. 182, 194 (1993) ("[T]he law is 'well established that the Government in its dealings with Indian tribal property acts in a fiduciary capacity' ") (quoting *United States v. Cherokee Nation of Okla.*, 480 U.S. 700, 707 (1987)). . . .

II

In light of Federal Rule of Evidence 501 and the Government's role as a conventional fiduciary in managing Indian trust fund accounts, I would hold as a matter of federal common law that the fiduciary exception is applicable in the Indian trust context, and thus the Government may not rely on the attorney-client privilege to withhold communications related to trust management. As explained below, the twin rationales for the fiduciary exception fully support its application in this context. The majority's conclusion to the contrary rests on flawed factual and legal premises.

A

When the Government seeks legal advice from a government attorney on matters relating to the management of the Nation's trust funds, the "real client" of that advice for purposes of the fiduciary exception is the Nation, not the Government. The majority's rejection of that conclusion is premised on its erroneous view that the Government, in managing the Nation's trust funds, "has its own independent interest in the implementation of federal Indian policy" that diverges from the interest of the Nation as beneficiary.

The majority correctly notes that, as a general matter, the Government has sovereign interests in managing Indian trusts that distinguish it from a private trustee. See, *e.g., United States v. Minnesota*, 270 U.S. 181, 194 (1926). . . .

In the specific context of Indian trust fund management, however, federal Indian policy entirely aligns the interests of the Government as trustee and the Indian tribe as beneficiary. As explained above, Congress has enacted an extensive network of statutes regulating the Government's management of Indian trust fund accounts. That statutory framework establishes a "conventional fiduciary relationship" in the context of Indian trust fund administration. *Navajo Nation II*, 556 U.S., at 301 (internal quotation marks omitted).

As a conventional fiduciary, the Government's management of Indian trust funds must "be judged by the most exacting fiduciary standards." *Seminole Nation.* Among the most fundamental fiduciary obligations of a trustee is "to administer the trust solely in the interest of the beneficiaries." 2A A. Scott & W. Fratcher, Law of Trusts § 170, p. 311 (4th ed. 1987) . . . .

Because federal Indian policy requires the Government to act strictly as a conventional fiduciary in managing the Nation's trust funds, the Government acts in a "representative" rather than "persona[l]" capacity when managing the Nation's trust funds. *Riggs*, 355 A.2d, at 713. By law, the Government cannot pursue any "independent" interest, distinct from its responsibilities as a fiduciary. . . . In other words, any uniquely sovereign interest the Government may have in other contexts of its trust relationship with Indian tribes does not exist in the specific context of Indian trust fund administration. It naturally follows, then, that when the Government seeks legal advice from government attorneys relating to the management of the Nation's trust funds, the "real client" of the advice for purposes of the fiduciary exception is the Nation, not the Government.

This conclusion holds true even though government attorneys are "paid out of congressional appropriations at no cost to the [Nation]." *Ante*, at 2326. As noted above, although the source of funding for legal advice may be relevant, the ultimate inquiry is for whose benefit the legal advice was rendered. See *supra*, at 2319–2320. And, for all the emphasis the majority places on the funding source here, see *ante*, at 2322, 2326, the majority never suggests that the fiduciary exception would apply if Congress amended federal law to permit Indian tribes to pay government attorneys out of their own trust funds.[42]

The majority also suggests that, even if the interests of the United States and Indian tribes may be equivalent in some contexts, that "equivalence" "breaks down" when there are "multiple interests" involved in a trust relationship. *Ante*, at 2327–2328. . . .

Preliminarily, while the Government in certain circumstances may have sovereign obligations that conflict with its duties as a fiduciary for Indian tribes, see, *e.g.*, *Nevada v. United States*, 463 U.S. 110 (1983),[43] the existence of competing interests is not unique to the Government as trustee. Indeed, the issue of competing interests arises frequently in the private trust context. . . . In such circumstances, "a trustee — and ultimately a court — may need to provide some response that offers a compromise between the confidentiality or privacy concerns of some and the interest-protection needs of others." *Id.*, § 82, Comment *f*, at 188. . . .

The majority's categorical rejection of the fiduciary exception in the Indian trust context sweeps far broader than necessary

The majority's categorical approach fails to appreciate that privilege determina-

---

[42] [6] The majority also states that ownership of the requested documents is "a significant factor" in deciding whether the fiduciary exception applies, *ante*, at 2330, but the only case it cites as support deals with the source of payment for the legal advice, not the ownership of the documents. *See ibid.* (citing *Riggs Nat'l Bank of Washington, D.C. v. Zimmer*, 355 A.2d 709, 712 (Del. Ch. 1976)).

[43] [7] In *Nevada*, the Government represented certain tribes in litigation involving water rights even though it was also required by statute to represent the water rights of a reclamation project. *See* 463 U.S., at 128, 103 S. Ct. 2906 (noting that Congress delegated to the Secretary of the Interior "both the responsibility for the supervision of the Indian tribes and the commencement of reclamation projects in areas adjacent to reservation lands"). Because of this dual litigating responsibility, we noted that "it is simply unrealistic to suggest that the Government may not perform its obligation to represent Indian tribes in litigation when Congress has obliged it to represent other interests as well." *Ibid.* We thus observed in the context of that case that "the Government cannot follow the fastidious standards of a private fiduciary, who would breach his duties to his single beneficiary solely by representing potentially conflicting interests without the beneficiary's consent." *Ibid.* We expressly distinguished the context "where only a relationship between the Government and the tribe is involved." *Id.*, at 142, 103 S. Ct. 2906. In that context, we acknowledged that "the law respecting obligations between a trustee and a beneficiary in private litigation will in many, if not all, respects adequately describe the duty of the United States." *Ibid.*

tions are by their very nature made on a case-by-case — indeed, document-by-document — basis. . . .

Rather than fashioning a blanket rule against application of the fiduciary exception in the Indian trust context, I would, consistent with Rule 501 and principles of judicial restraint, decide the question solely on the facts before us. See *Upjohn*, 449 U.S., at 386 (noting that "we sit to decide concrete cases and not abstract propositions of law" and "declin[ing] to lay down a broad rule or series of rules to govern all conceivable future questions in this area"). On those facts, the fiduciary exception applies to the communications in this case.

B

Like the "real client" rationale, the second rationale for the fiduciary exception, rooted in a trustee's fiduciary duty to disclose all matters relevant to trust administration to the beneficiary, fully supports disclosure of the communications in this case. . . . Because the statutory scheme requires the Government to act as a conventional fiduciary in managing the Nation's trust funds, the Government's fiduciary duty to keep the Nation informed of matters relating to trust administration includes the concomitant duty to disclose attorney-client communications relating to trust fund management. See Third Restatement § 82, Comment *f,* at 187–188; Restatement of the Law (Third) Governing Lawyers § 84, pp. 627–628 (1998).

Notably, the majority does not suggest that the Nation needs less information than a private beneficiary to exercise effective oversight over the Government as trustee. Instead, the majority contends that the Nation is entitled to less disclosure because the Government's disclosure obligations are more limited than a private trustee. In particular, the majority states that the Government "assumes Indian trust responsibilities only to the extent it expressly accepts those responsibilities by statute," and thus the Nation "must point to a right conferred by statute or regulation in order to obtain otherwise privileged information from the Government against its wishes." The majority cites a single statutory provision and its implementing regulations as "defin[ing] the Government's disclosure obligation to the [Nation]." Because those "narrowly defined disclosure obligations" do not provide Indian tribes with a specific statutory right to disclosure of attorney-client communications relating to trust administration, *ante,* at 2330, the majority concludes that the Government has no duty to disclose those communications to the Nation.

The majority's conclusion employs a fundamentally flawed legal premise. We have never held that all of the Government's trust responsibilities to Indians must be set forth expressly in a specific statute or regulation. To the contrary, where, as here, the statutory framework establishes that the relationship between the Government and an Indian tribe "bears the hallmarks of a conventional fiduciary relationship," *Navajo II,* 556 U.S., at 287, (internal quotation marks omitted), we have consistently looked to general trust principles to flesh out the Government's fiduciary obligations.

For example, in *United States v. White Mountain Apache Tribe,* 537 U.S. 465

(2003), we construed a statute that vested the Government with discretionary authority to "use" trust property for certain purposes as imposing a concomitant duty to preserve improvements that had previously been made to the land. *Id.,* at 475 (quoting 74 Stat. 8). Even though the statute did not "expressly subject the Government to duties of management and conservation," we construed the Government's obligations under the statute by reference to "elementary trust law," which "confirm[ed] the commonsense assumption that a fiduciary actually administering trust property may not allow it to fall into ruin on his watch." 537 U.S., at 475 .Similarly, in *Seminole Nation,* we relied on general trust principles to conclude that the Government had a fiduciary duty to prevent misappropriation of tribal trust funds by corrupt members of a tribe, even though no specific statutory or treaty provision expressly imposed such a duty. See 316 U.S., at 296.[44]

Accordingly, although the "general 'contours' of the government's obligations" are defined by statute, the "interstices must be filled in through reference to general trust law." *Cobell,* 240 F.3d, at 1101 (quoting *Mitchell II,* 463 U.S., at 224). . . .

Contrary to the majority's view, the Government's disclosure obligations are not limited solely to the "narrowly defined disclosure obligations" set forth in § 162a(d)(5) and its implementing regulations, *ante,* at 2329–2330; rather, given that the statutory regime requires the Government to act as a conventional fiduciary in managing Indian trust funds, the Government's disclosure obligations include those of a fiduciary under common-law trust principles. . . .

This conclusion, moreover, is supported by the plain text of the very statute cited by the majority. Section 162a(d), which was enacted as part of the American Indian Trust Fund Management Reform Act of 1994 (1994 Act), 108 Stat. 4239, sets forth eight "trust responsibilities of the United States." But that provision also specifically states that the Secretary of the Interior's "proper discharge of the trust responsibilities of the United States shall include *(but are not limited to)* " those specified duties. 25 U.S.C. § 162a(d) (emphasis added). By expressly including the italicized language, Congress recognized that the Government has pre-existing trust responsibilities that arise out of the broader statutory scheme governing the management of Indian trust funds.[45] Indeed, Title I of the 1994 Act is entitled

---

[44] [8] To be sure, in decisions involving the jurisdiction of the Court of Federal Claims under the Tucker Act, we have explained that the jurisdictional analysis "must train on specific rights-creating or duty-imposing statutory or regulatory prescriptions." *Navajo I,* 537 U.S., at 506. But even assuming *arguendo* that those jurisdictional decisions have relevance here, they do not stand for the proposition that the Government's fiduciary duties are defined exclusively by express statutory provisions. Indeed, those decisions relied specifically on general trust principles to determine whether the relevant statutory scheme permitted a damages remedy, a prerequisite for jurisdiction under the Tucker Act. See, *e.g., Mitchell II,* 463 U.S., at 226 (noting that common-law trust sources establish that "a trustee is accountable in damages for breaches of trust" and that, "[g]iven the existence of a trust relationship, it naturally follows that the Government should be liable in damages for the breach of its fiduciary duties"); *see also Navajo II,* 556 U.S., at 301, (affirming that general "trust principles . . . could play a role in inferring that the trust obligation is enforceable by damages" (internal quotation marks and brackets omitted)).

[45] [9] The majority invokes the canon against superfluity and argues that the "catchall" phrase (by which it means the "shall include (but are not limited to)" language) cannot be read to "include a general common-law duty to disclose all information related to the administration of Indian trusts" because doing

"*Recognition* of Trust Responsibility," 108 Stat. 4240 (emphasis added), and courts have similarly observed that the Act "recognized and reaffirmed . . . that the government has longstanding and substantial trust obligations to Indians." *Cobell*, 240 F.3d, at 1098; see also H.R. Rep. No. 103-778, p. 9 (1994) ("The responsibility for management of Indian Trust Funds by the [Government] has been determined through a series of court decisions, treaties, and statutes"). That conclusion accords with common sense, as not even the Government argues that it had no disclosure obligations with respect to Indian trust funds prior to the enactment of the 1994 Act.[46]

The majority requires the Nation to "point to a right conferred by statute" to the attorney-client communications at issue, *ante*, at 2325, and finding none, denies the Nation access to those communications. The upshot of that decision, I fear, may very well be to reinvigorate the position of the dissenting Justices in *White Mountain Apache* and *Mitchell II*, who rejected the use of common-law principles to inform the scope of the Government's fiduciary obligations to Indian tribes. See *White Mountain Apache*, 537 U.S., at 486–487 (THOMAS, J., dissenting); *Mitchell II*, 463 U.S., at 234–235 (Powell, J., dissenting). That approach was wrong when *Mitchell II* was decided nearly 30 years ago, and it is wrong today. Under our governing precedents, common-law trust principles play an important role in defining the Government's fiduciary duties where, as here, the statutory scheme establishes a conventional fiduciary relationship. Applying those principles in this context, I would hold that the fiduciary exception is fully applicable to the communications in this case. . . .

III

We have described the federal government's fiduciary duties toward Indian tribes as consisting of "moral obligations of the highest responsibility and trust," to be fulfilled through conduct "judged by the most exacting fiduciary standards." *Seminole Nation*, 316 U.S., at 297; see also *Mitchell II*, 463 U.S., at 225–226

---

so would "impose general obligations that would include those specifically enumerated." *Ante*, at 2330. But the flaw in the majority's argument is that it misperceives the function of the relevant language. Rather than serving as a "catchall" provision that affirmatively "incorporate[s]" common-law trust duties into § 162a(d), that language simply makes clear that § 162a(d) does not set forth an exhaustive list of the Government's trust responsibilities in managing Indian trust funds; nothing in that language itself imports any substantive obligations into the statute.

[46] [10] The majority also contends that its reading of § 162a(d) is supported by a provision in the Indian Claims Limitation Act of 1982 (ICLA), 96 Stat. 1976, which provided that if the Secretary of the Interior rejected a claim for litigation by an Indian claimant, he was required to provide upon request "any nonprivileged research materials or evidence gathered by the United States in the documentation of such claim." § 5(b), *id.*, at 1978. According to the majority, this provision reflected Congress's understanding that "the Government retains evidentiary privileges allowing it to withhold information related to trust property from Indian tribes." *Ante*, at n. 11. But this provision cannot bear the weight the majority places on it. Even putting aside the undisputed fact that the ICLA is inapplicable to the claims in this case, the majority's reliance on the ICLA provision fails to recognize that documents subject to the fiduciary exception are, under the "real client" rationale, *per se* nonprivileged. See, *e.g.*, *Mett*, 178 F.3d, at 1063. Accordingly, if anything, the ICLA's requirement that the Government disclose "nonprivileged" materials to Indian claimants supports the conclusion that Congress intended communications related to trust fund management to be disclosed to Indian tribes.

(collecting cases). The sad and well-documented truth, however, is that the Government has failed to live up to its fiduciary obligations in managing Indian trust fund accounts. See, *e.g., Cobell*, 240 F.3d, at 1089 ("The General Accounting Office, Interior Department Inspector General, and Office of Management and Budget, among others, have all condemned the mismanagement of [Indian] trust accounts over the past twenty years"); Misplaced Trust 8 ("[T]he [Government's] indifferent supervision and control of the Indian trust funds has consistently resulted in a failure to exercise its responsibility and [to meet] any reasonable expectations of the tribal and individual accountholders, Congress, and taxpayers"); *id.*, at 56 ("[H]ad this type of mismanagement taken place in any other trust arrangements such as Social Security, there would be war").

As Congress has recognized, "[t]he Indian trust fund is more than balance sheets and accounting procedures. These moneys are crucial to the daily operations of native American tribes and a source of income to tens of thousands of native Americans." *Id.*, at 5. Given the history of governmental mismanagement of Indian trust funds, application of the fiduciary exception is, if anything, even more important in this context than in the private trustee context. The majority's refusal to apply the fiduciary exception in this case deprives the Nation — as well as the Indian tribes in the more than 90 cases currently pending in the federal courts involving claims of tribal trust mismanagement, App. to Pet. for Cert. 126a–138a — of highly relevant information going directly to the merits of whether the Government properly fulfilled its fiduciary duties. Its holding only further exacerbates the concerns expressed by many about the lack of adequate oversight and accountability that has marked the Government's handling of Indian trust fund accounts for decades.

But perhaps even more troubling than the majority's refusal to apply the fiduciary exception in this case is its disregard of our established precedents that affirm the central role that common-law trust principles play in defining the Government's fiduciary obligations to Indian tribes. By rejecting the Nation's claim on the ground that it fails to identify a specific statutory right to the communications at issue, the majority effectively embraces an approach espoused by prior dissents that rejects the role of common-law principles altogether in the Indian trust context. Its decision to do so in a case involving only a narrow evidentiary issue is wholly unnecessary and, worse yet, risks further diluting the Government's fiduciary obligations in a manner that Congress clearly did not intend and that would inflict serious harm on the already-frayed relationship between the United States and Indian tribes. Because there is no warrant in precedent or reason for reaching that result, I respectfully dissent.

NEVADA v. UNITED STATES
United States Supreme Court
463 U.S. 110 (1983)

Justice Rehnquist delivered the opinion of the Court.

In 1913 the United States sued to adjudicate water rights to the Truckee River for the benefit of the Pyramid Lake Indian Reservation and the planned Newlands

Reclamation Project. Thirty-one years later, in 1944, the United States District Court for the District of Nevada entered a final decree in the case pursuant to a settlement agreement. In 1973 the United States filed the present action in the same court on behalf of the Pyramid Lake Indian Reservation seeking additional water rights to the Truckee River. The issue thus presented is whether the Government may partially undo the 1944 decree, or whether principles of res judicata prevent it, and the intervenor Pyramid Lake Paiute Tribe, from litigating this claim on the merits.

I

Nevada has, on the average, less precipitation than any other State in the Union. [T]he Truckee River, one of the three principal rivers flowing through west central Nevada, [flows] into Pyramid Lake, which has no outlet.

[I]n early 1844, Pyramid Lake was some 50 miles long and 12 miles wide. Since that time the surface area of the lake has been reduced by about 20,000 acres. [Created by President Grant in 1874, the] Reservation includes Pyramid Lake, and land surrounding it, the lower reaches of the Truckee River, and the bottom land alongside the lower Truckee.

[The Reclamation Act of 1902, 32 Stat. 388,] directed the Secretary of the Interior to withdraw from public entry arid lands in specified Western States, reclaim the lands through irrigation projects, and then to restore the lands to entry pursuant to the homestead laws and certain conditions imposed by the Act itself. Accordingly, the Secretary withdrew from the public domain approximately 200,000 acres in western Nevada, which ultimately became the Newlands Reclamation Project.

[The Newlands Project diverted water] from the Truckee River to the Carson River by constructing the Derby Diversion Dam on the Truckee River, and constructing the Truckee Canal through which the diverted waters would be transported to the Carson River. [The] Lahontan Dam [and] Lahontan Reservoir [were created for storage]. The combined waters of the Truckee and Carson Rivers impounded in Lahontan Reservoir are distributed for irrigation and related uses on downstream lands by means of lateral canals within the Newlands Reclamation Project.

Before the works contemplated by the Project went into operation, a number of private landowners had established rights to water in the Truckee River under Nevada law. The Government also asserted on behalf of the Indians of the Pyramid Lake Indian Reservation a reserved right under the so-called "implied-reservation-of-water" doctrine set forth in *Winters v. United States*, 207 U.S. 564 (1908). [In 1913 the] United States [instituted] what became known as the *Orr Ditch* litigation. The Government, for the benefit of both the Project and the Pyramid Lake Reservation, asserted a claim to 10,000 cubic feet of water per second for the Project and a claim to 500 cubic feet per second for the Reservation. The complaint named as defendants all water users on the Truckee River in Nevada. The Government expressly sought a final decree quieting title to the rights of all parties.

[A] Special Master issued a report and proposed decree in July 1924 [awarding] the Reservation an 1859 priority date in the Truckee River for 58.7 second-feet and 12,412 acre-feet annually of water to irrigate 3,130 acres of Reservation lands. The Project was awarded a 1902 priority date for 1,500 cubic feet per second to irrigate, to the extent the amount would allow,[47] 32,800 acres of land within the Newlands Reclamation Project. In February 1926 the District Court entered a temporary restraining order declaring the water rights as proposed by the Special Master. "One of the primary purposes" for entering a temporary order was to allow for an experimental period during which modifications of the declared rights could be made if necessary. Not until almost 10 years later, in the midst of a prolonged drought, was interest stimulated in concluding the *Orr Ditch* litigation. Settlement negotiations were commenced in 1934 by the principal organizational defendants in the case, [and] the representatives of the Project and the Reservation. The United States still acted on behalf of the Reservation's interests, but the Project was now under the management of the Truckee-Carson Irrigation District (TCID). The defendants and TCID proposed an agreement along the lines of the temporary restraining order. The United States objected, demanding an increase in the Reservation's water rights to allow for the irrigation of an additional 2,745 acres of Reservation land. After some resistance, the Government's demand was accepted and a settlement agreement was signed on July 1, 1935. The District Court entered a final decree adopting the agreement on September 8, 1944. No appeal was taken. Thus, 31 years after its inception the *Orr Ditch* litigation came to a close.

[In] 1973, the Government instituted [this action] seeking additional rights to the Truckee River for the Pyramid Lake Indian Reservation; the Pyramid Lake Paiute Tribe was permitted to intervene in support of the United States. The Government named as defendants all persons presently claiming water rights to the Truckee River and its tributaries in Nevada. The defendants include the defendants in the *Orr Ditch* litigation and their successors, approximately 3,800 individual farmers that own land in the Newlands Reclamation Project, and TCID. The District Court certified the Project farmers as a class and directed TCID to represent their interests.

[The Government argues] that *Orr Ditch* determined only the Reservation's right to "water for irrigation," not the claim now being asserted for "sufficient waters of the Truckee River . . . [for] the maintenance and preservation of Pyramid Lake, [and for] the maintenance of the lower reaches of the Truckee River as a natural spawning ground for fish." The complaint further averred that in establishing the Reservation the United States had intended that the Pyramid Lake fishery be maintained. Since the additional water now being claimed is allegedly necessary for that purpose, the Government alleged that the Executive Order creating the Reservation must have impliedly reserved a right to this water.[48]

---

[47] [3] Notwithstanding the Project's 1902 priority, it was awarded far less water than the Government had claimed. [According to the Court of Appeals:] "there has never been irrigated more than about 65,000 acres of land in the Project."

[48] [7] Between 1920 and 1940 the surface area of Pyramid Lake was reduced by about 20,000 acres. The decline [prevented the fish] from reaching their spawning grounds in the Truckee River, resulting in the near extinction of [the] species. [Efforts to restore the fish include fish] hatcheries operated by both the State of Nevada and the United States [and] the Marble Bluff Dam and Fishway [which] enabl[e] the fish to [reach] their spawning grounds in the Truckee. Both the District Court and Court of

The defendants below asserted res judicata as an affirmative defense. [T]he District Court sustained the defense and dismissed the complaint in its entirety. [T]he District Court first determined that all of the parties in this action were parties, or in privity with parties, in the *Orr Ditch* case. [According to the court, the Government intended] "to assert as large a water right as possible for the Indian reservation" [in the *Orr Ditch* litigation]. [The District Court explained]:

> The plaintiff and the Tribe may not litigate several different types of water use claims, all arising under the *Winters* doctrine and all derived from the same water source in a piece-meal fashion. There was but one cause of action in equity to quiet title in plaintiff and the Tribe based upon the *Winters* reserved right theory.

[T]he Court of Appeals found that the *Orr Ditch* decree did not conclude the dispute between the Tribe and the owners of Newlands Project lands. The court said that litigants are not to be bound by a prior judgment unless they were adversaries under the earlier pleadings or unless the specific issue in dispute was actually litigated in the earlier case and the court found that neither exception applied here.

The Court of Appeals conceded that "[a] strict adversity requirement does not necessarily fit the realities of water adjudications." Nevertheless, the court found that since neither the Tribe nor the Project landowners were parties in *Orr Ditch* but instead were both represented by the United States, and since their interests may have conflicted in that proceeding, the court would not find that the Government had intended to bind these nonparties inter se absent a specific statement of adversity in the pleadings. We granted certiorari in the cases challenging the Court of Appeals's decision, and we now affirm in part and reverse in part.

II

The Government [argues]: "The court of appeals has simply permitted a reallocation of the water decreed in *Orr Ditch* to a single party — the United States — from reclamation uses to a Reservation use with an earlier priority. The doctrine of res judicata does not bar a single party from reallocating its water in this fashion. . . . " We are bound to say that the Government's position, if accepted, would do away with half a century of decided case law relating to the Reclamation Act of 1902 and water rights in the public domain of the West.

[The Court then summarized the history of the Reclamation Act, quoting extensively from *Ickes v. Fox*, 300 U.S. 82 (1937), holding that projects built under the Reclamation Act did not vest water rights in the government. According to *Ickes*:]

> "Appropriation was made not for the use of the government, but, under the Reclamation Act, for the use of the land owners; and by the terms of the law and of the contract already referred to, the water-rights became the property of the land owners, wholly distinct from the property right of the

---

Appeals observed that "these restoration efforts 'appear to justify optimism for eventual success.' "

government in the irrigation works. [I]t long has been established law that the right to the use of water can be acquired only by prior appropriation for a beneficial use; and that such right when thus obtained is a property right, which, when acquired for irrigation, becomes, by state law and here by express provision of the Reclamation Act as well, part and parcel of the land upon which it is applied."

The law of Nevada, in common with most other Western States, requires for the perfection of a water right for agricultural purposes that the water must be beneficially used by actual application on the land. Such a right is appurtenant to the land on which it is used.

In the light of these cases, we conclude that the Government is completely mistaken if it believes that the water rights confirmed to it by the *Orr Ditch* decree in 1944 for use in irrigating lands within the Newlands Reclamation Project were like so many bushels of wheat, to be bartered, sold, or shifted about as the Government might see fit. Once these lands were acquired by settlers in the Project, the Government's "ownership" of the water rights was at most nominal; the beneficial interest in the rights confirmed to the Government resided in the owners of the land within the Project to which these water rights became appurtenant upon the application of Project water to the land. [T]he law of the relevant State and the contracts entered into by the landowners and the United States make this point very clear.

The Government's brief is replete with references to its fiduciary obligation to the Pyramid Lake Paiute Tribe of Indians, as it properly should be. But the Government seems wholly to ignore in the same brief the obligations that necessarily devolve upon it from having mere title to water rights for the Newlands Project, when the beneficial ownership of these water rights resides elsewhere.

Both the briefs of the parties and the opinion of the Court of Appeals focus their analysis of res judicata on provisions relating to the relationship between private trustees and fiduciaries, especially those governing a breach of duty by the fiduciary to the beneficiary. While these undoubtedly provide useful analogies in cases such as these, they cannot be regarded as finally dispositive of the issues. This Court has long recognized "the distinctive obligation of trust incumbent upon the Government" in its dealings with Indian tribes, see, e.g., *Seminole Nation v. United States*, 316 U.S. 286, 296 (1942). These concerns have been traditionally focused on the Bureau of Indian Affairs within the Department of the Interior. *Poafpybitty v. Skelly Oil Co.*, 390 U.S. 365, 374 (1968). See 25 U.S.C. § 1.

But Congress in its wisdom, when it enacted the Reclamation Act of 1902, required the Secretary of the Interior to assume substantial obligations with respect to the reclamation of arid lands in the western part of the United States. Additionally, in § 26 of the Act of Apr. 21, 1904, 33 Stat. 225, Congress provided for the inclusion of irrigable lands of the Pyramid Lake Indian Reservation within the Newlands Project, and further authorized the Secretary, after allotting five acres of such land to each Indian belonging to the Reservation, to reclaim and dispose of the remainder of the irrigable Reservation land to settlers under the Reclamation Act.

Today, particularly from our vantage point nearly half a century after the enactment the Indian Reorganization Act, it may well appear that Congress was requiring the Secretary of the Interior to carry water on at least two shoulders when it delegated to him both the responsibility for the supervision of the Indian tribes and the commencement of reclamation projects in areas adjacent to reservation lands. But Congress chose to do this, and it is simply unrealistic to suggest that the Government may not perform its obligation to represent Indian tribes in litigation when Congress has obliged it to represent other interests as well. In this regard, the Government cannot follow the fastidious standards of a private fiduciary, who would breach his duties to his single beneficiary solely by representing potentially conflicting interests without the beneficiary's consent. The Government does not "compromise" its obligation to one interest that Congress obliges it to represent by the mere fact that it simultaneously performs another task for another interest that Congress has obligated it by statute to do.

With these observations in mind, we turn to the principles of res judicata that we think are involved in this case.

III

[The doctrine of res judicata] "is essential to the maintenance of social order; for, the aid of judicial tribunals would not be invoked for the vindication of rights of person and property, if . . . conclusiveness did not attend the judgments of such tribunals." *Southern Pacific R. Co. v. United States*, 168 U.S. 1, 49 (1897).[49]

[W]hen a final judgment has been entered on the merits of a case, "[i]t is a finality as to the claim or demand in controversy, concluding parties and those in privity with them, not only as to every matter which was offered and received to sustain or defeat the claim or demand, but as to any other admissible matter which might have been offered for that purpose." *Cromwell v. County of Sac*, 94 U.S. 351, 352 (1877). The final "judgment puts an end to the cause of action, which cannot again be brought into litigation between the parties upon any ground whatever." *Commissioner v. Sunnen*, 333 U.S. 591, 597 (1948). *See Chicot County Drainage District v. Baxter State Bank*, 308 U.S. 371, 375, 378 (1940).

To determine the applicability of res judicata to the facts before us, we must decide first if the "cause of action" which the Government now seeks to assert is the "same cause of action" that was asserted in *Orr Ditch*; we must then decide whether the parties in the instant proceeding are identical to or in privity with the parties in *Orr Ditch*. We address these questions in turn.

---

[49] [10] The policies advanced by the doctrine of res judicata perhaps are at their zenith in cases concerning real property, land and water. [Q]uiet title actions for the adjudication of water rights, such as the *Orr Ditch* suit, [are] distinctively equipped to serve these policies because "[they enable] the court of equity to acquire jurisdiction of all the rights involved and also of all the owners of those rights, and thus settle and permanently adjudicate in a single proceeding all the rights, or claims to rights, of all the claimants to the water taken from a common source of supply." 3 C. Kinney, Law of Irrigation and Water Rights § 1535, p. 2764 (2d ed. 1912).

A

Definitions of what constitutes the "same cause of action" have not remained static over time. Compare Restatement of Judgments § 61 (1942) with Restatement (Second) of Judgments § 24 (1982). We find it unnecessary in these cases to parse any minute differences which these differing tests might produce, because whatever standard may be applied the only conclusion allowed by the record in the *Orr Ditch* case is that the Government was given an opportunity to litigate the Reservation's entire water rights to the Truckee, and that the Government intended to take advantage of that opportunity.

[The Court compared the *Orr Ditch* decree and the complaint in the present case, concluding that both "show[ed] the Government's intention to assert in *Orr Ditch* the Reservation's full water rights."]

B

[W]e must next determine which of the parties before us are bound by the earlier decree. As stated earlier, the general rule is that a prior judgment will bar the "parties" to the earlier lawsuit, "and those in privity with them," from relitigating the cause of action. *Cromwell v. County of Sac*, 94 U.S., at 352.

There is no doubt but that the United States was a party to the *Orr Ditch* proceeding, acting as a representative for the Reservation's interests and the interests of the Newlands Project, and cannot relitigate the Reservation's "implied-reservation-of-water" rights with those who can use the *Orr Ditch* decree as a defense. We also hold that the Tribe, whose interests were represented in *Orr Ditch* by the United States, can be bound by the *Orr Ditch* decree.[50] This Court left little room for an argument to the contrary in *Heckman v. United States*, 224 U.S. 413 (1912), where it plainly said that "it could not, consistently with any principle, be tolerated that, after the United States on behalf of its wards had invoked the jurisdiction of its courts . . . these wards should themselves be permitted to relitigate the question." See also Restatement (Second) of Judgments § 41(1)(d) (1982). We reaffirm that principle now.[51]

---

[50] [14] We, of course, do not pass judgment on the quality of representation that the Tribe received. In 1951 the Tribe sued the Government before the Indian Claims Commission for damages, basing its claim of liability on the Tribe's receipt of less water for the fishery than it was entitled to. *Northern Paiute Tribe v. United States*, 30 Ind. Cl. Comm'n 210 (1973). In a settlement the Tribe was given $8 million in return for its waiver of further liability on the part of the United States.

[51] [15] This Court held in *Hansberry v. Lee*, 311 U.S. 32, 44 (1940), that persons vicariously represented in a class action could not be bound by a judgment in the case where the representative parties had interests that impermissibly conflicted with those of persons represented. See also RESTATEMENT (SECOND) OF JUDGMENTS § 42(1)(d) (1982). The Tribe seeks to take advantage of this ruling, arguing that the Government's primary interest in *Orr Ditch* was to obtain water rights for the Newlands Reclamation Project and that by definition any water rights given to the Tribe would conflict with that interest. We reject this contention.

We have already said that the Government stands in a different position than a private fiduciary where Congress has decreed that the Government must represent more than one interest. When the Government performs such duties it does not by that reason alone compromise its obligation to any of the interests involved.

We then turn to the issue of which defendants in the present litigation can use the *Orr Ditch* decree against the Government and the Tribe. There is no dispute but that the *Orr Ditch* defendants were parties to the earlier decree and that they and

---

[Once the Justice Department decided to get involved in the *Orr Ditch* suit a] Special Assistant United States Attorney assigned to the matter was apparently the first to recognize that the Government should in the same suit seek to establish the water rights to the Pyramid Lake Indian Reservation. [He] advanced the view that "[t]hese Indian reservation water rights are important and should be established to the fullest extent because they are senior and superior to most if not all the other rights on the river."

[At the same time the Commissioner of Indian Affairs was notified] that an assertion of the Reservation's rights should be included in *Orr Ditch*. The claim was advanced accordingly and thereafter the Bureau of Indian Affairs was kept aware of the *Orr Ditch* proceedings; during the settlement negotiations the BIA directly participated. The BIA is the agency of the Federal Government "charged with fulfilling the trust obligations of the United States" to Indians, *Poafpybitty v. Skelly Oil Co.*, 390 U.S. 365, 374 (1968), and there is nothing in the record of this case to indicate that any official outside of the BIA attempted to influence the BIA's decisions in a manner inconsistent with these obligations. The record suggests that the BIA alone may have made the decision not to press claims for a fishery water right, for reasons which hindsight may render questionable, but which did not involve other interests represented by the Government. For instance, in a 1926 letter to a federal official on the Pyramid Lake Reservation, the Commissioner of Indian Affairs explained:

> "We feel that the Indians would be wise to assume that Truckee River water will be used practically as far as it can be for irrigation, and that the thing for the Indians to do is, if possible, instead of trying to stop such development to direct it so that it will inure to their benefit.

> . . . "[I]f their ultimate welfare depends in part on their being able to hold their own in a civilized world . . . they should look forward to a different means of livelihood, in part at least, from their ancestral one, of fishing and hunting. They should expect not only to farm their allotments but also to do other sorts of work and have other ways of making a living."

Furthermore, the District Court found that during the pendency of the *Orr Ditch* proceedings "a serious and reasonable doubt existed as to whether any *Winters* reserved water right could be claimed at all for an executive order Indian reservation."

In pressing for a different conclusion, the Tribe relies primarily on a finding by the District Court that it was the intention of the Government in *Orr Ditch* "to assert as large a water right as possible for the Indian reservation, and to do everything possible to protect the fish for the benefit of the Indians and the white population insofar as it was 'consistent with the larger interests involved in the propositions having to do with the reclamation of thousands of acres of arid and now useless land for the benefit of the country as a whole.' " The Tribe's focus on this ambiguous finding, however, has not blinded us to the District Court's specific finding on the alleged conflict.

> "[T]here was a foreseeable conflict of purposes created by the Congress within the Interior Department and as between the Bureau of Reclamation on the one hand in asserting large water rights for its reclamation projects and the Bureau of Indian Affairs on the other in the performance of its obligations to protect the rights and interests of the Indians on the Pyramid Lake Paiute Indian Reservation. [T]his conflict of purposes was apparent prior to and during the *Orr Ditch* proceedings and was resolved within the executive department of government by top-level executive officers acting within the scope of their Congressionally-delegated duties and authority and were political and policy decisions of those officials charged with that responsibility, which decisions resulted in the extinguishment of the alleged fishery purposes water right. . . . The government lawyers in *Orr Ditch*, both departmental, agency and bureaus, as well as those charged with the responsibility for the actual conduct of the litigation, are not chargeable with an impermissible conflict of purpose or interest in carrying out the decisions and directions of their superiors in the executive department of government. . . ."

The District Court's finding reflects the nature of a democratic government that is charged with more than one responsibility; it does not describe conduct that would deprive the United States of the authority to conduct litigation on behalf of diverse interests.

their successors can rely on the decree. The Court of Appeals so held, and we affirm.

The Court of Appeals reached a different conclusion concerning TCID and the Project farmers that it now represents. The Court of Appeals conceded that the Project's interests, like the Reservation's interests, were presented in *Orr Ditch* by the United States and thus that TCID, like the Tribe, stands with respect to that litigation in privity with the United States. The court further stated, however, that "[a]s a general matter, a judgment does not conclude parties who were not adversaries under the pleadings," and that in "representative litigation we should be especially careful not to infer adversity between interests represented by a single litigant." Since the pleadings in *Orr Ditch* did not specifically allege adversity between the claims asserted on behalf of the Newlands Project and those asserted on behalf of the Reservation, the Court of Appeals ruled that the decree did not conclude the dispute between them.

[A]s the Court of Appeals noted:

> "A strict adversity requirement does not necessarily fit the realities of water adjudications. All parties' water rights are interdependent. Stability in water rights therefore requires that all parties be bound in all combinations. Further, in many water adjudications there is no actual controversy between the parties; the proceedings may serve primarily an administrative purpose." 649 F.2d, at 1309.

We agree with these observations of the Court of Appeals. That court felt, however, that these factors did not control these cases because the "Tribe and the Project were neither parties nor co-parties, however. They were non-parties who were represented simultaneously by the same government attorneys." We disagree with the Court of Appeals as to the consequence of this fact.

It has been held that the successors in interest of parties who are not adversaries in a stream adjudication nevertheless are bound by a decree establishing priority of rights in the stream. [The] rule seems to be generally applied in stream adjudications in the Western States, where these actions play a critical role in determining the allocation of scarce water rights, and where each water rights claim by its "very nature raise[s] issues inter se as to all such parties for the determination of one claim necessarily affects the amount available for the other claims." *Marlett v. Prosser*, [179 P. 141, 142 (1919)].

In these cases, as we have noted, the Government as a single entity brought the action seeking a determination both of the Tribe's reserved rights and of the water rights necessary for the irrigation of land within the Newlands Project. But it separately pleaded the interests of both the Project and the Reservation. During the settlement negotiations the interests of the Project, and presumably of the landowners to whom the water rights actually accrued, were represented by the newly formed TCID and the interests of the Reservation were represented by the Bureau of Indian Affairs. The settlement agreement was signed by the Government and by TCID. It would seem that at this stage of the litigation the interests of the Tribe and TCID were sufficiently adverse for the latter to oppose the Bureau's claim for additional water rights for the Reservation during the settlement negotiations.

The Court of Appeals held, however, that "in representative litigation we should be especially careful not to infer adversity between interests represented by a single litigant," 649 F.2d, at 1309, analogizing the Government's position to that of a trustee under the traditional law of trusts. But as we have indicated previously, we do not believe that this analogy from the world of private law may be bodily transposed to the present situation.

The Court of Appeals went on to conclude: "By representing the Tribe and the Project against the *Orr Ditch* defendants, the government compromised its duty of undivided loyalty to the Tribe. See Restatement (Second) of Trusts, *supra*, § 170 & Comments p, q, r." *Id.*, at 1310. This section of the Restatement (Second) of Trusts (1959) is entitled "Duty of Loyalty," and states that: "(1) the trustee is under a duty to the beneficiary to administer the trust solely in the interest of the beneficiary." Comments p, q, and r deal respectively with "[c]ompetition with the beneficiary," "[a]ction in the interest of a third person," and "[d]uty of trustee under separate trusts."

As we previously intimated, we think the Court of Appeals's reasoning here runs aground because the Government is simply not in the position of a private litigant or a private party under traditional rules of common law or statute. [I]n the very area of the law with which we deal in these cases, this Court said in *Heckman v. United States*, 224 U.S., at 444–445:

> "There can be no more complete representation than that on the part of the United States in acting on behalf of these dependents — whom Congress, with respect to the restricted lands, has not yet released from tutelage. Its effacacy [sic] does not depend on the Indian's acquiescence. It does not rest upon convention, nor is it circumscribed by rules which govern private relations. It is a representation which traces its source to the plenary control of Congress in legislating for the protection of the Indians under its care, and it recognizes no limitations that are inconsistent with the discharge of the national duty."

These cases, we believe, point the way to the correct resolution of the instant cases. The United States undoubtedly owes a strong fiduciary duty to its Indian wards. See [*Seminole Nation*]; *Shoshone Tribe v. United States*, 299 U.S. 476, 497–498 (1937). It may be that where only a relationship between the Government and the tribe is involved, the law respecting obligations between a trustee and a beneficiary in private litigation will in many, if not all, respects adequately describe the duty of the United States. But where Congress has imposed upon the United States, in addition to its duty to represent Indian tribes, a duty to obtain water rights for reclamation projects, and has even authorized the inclusion of reservation lands within a project, the analogy of a faithless private fiduciary cannot be controlling for purposes of evaluating the authority of the United States to represent different interests.

At least by 1926, when TCID came into being, and very likely long before, when conveyances of the public domain to settlers within the Reclamation Project necessarily carried with them the beneficial right to appropriate water reserved to the Government for this purpose, third parties entered into the picture. The legal relationships were no longer simply those between the United States and the Paiute

Tribe, but also those between the United States, TCID, and the several thousand settlers within the Project who put the Project water to beneficial use. We find it unnecessary to decide whether there would be adversity of interests between the Tribe, on the one hand, and the settlers and TCID, on the other, if the issue were to be governed by private law respecting trusts. We hold that under the circumstances described above, the interests of the Tribe and the Project landowners were sufficiently adverse so that both are now bound by the final decree entered in the *Orr Ditch* suit.

[I]n the final analysis we agree with the Court of Appeals that [the defendants who appropriated water afterwards] can use the *Orr Ditch* decree against the plaintiffs below. [E]xceptions to the res judicata mutuality [of estoppel] requirement have been found necessary, and we believe that such an exception is required in these cases. [E]ven though quiet title actions are in personam actions, water adjudications are more in the nature of in rem proceedings. Nonparties such as the subsequent appropriators in these cases have relied just as much on the *Orr Ditch* decree in participating in the development of western Nevada as have the parties of that case. We agree with the Court of Appeals that under "these circumstances it would be manifestly unjust not to permit subsequent appropriators" to hold the Reservation to the claims it made in *Orr Ditch*; "[a]ny other conclusion would make it impossible ever finally to quantify a reserved water right." 649 F.2d, at 1309.[52]

IV

In conclusion we affirm the Court of Appeals's finding that the cause of action asserted below and the cause of action asserted in *Orr Ditch* are one and the same. We also affirm the Court of Appeals's finding that the *Orr Ditch* decree concluded the controversy on this cause of action between, on the one hand, the *Orr Ditch* defendants, their successors in interest, and subsequent appropriators of the Truckee River, and, on the other hand, the United States and the Tribe. We reverse the Court of Appeals, however, with respect to its finding concerning TCID, and the Project farmers it represents, and hold instead that the *Orr Ditch* decree also ended the dispute raised between these parties and the plaintiffs below.

[*Affirmed in part, reversed in part.*]

---

[52] [16] The Tribe makes the argument that even if res judicata would otherwise apply, it cannot be used in these cases because to do so would deny the Tribe procedural due process. The Tribe argues that in *Orr Ditch* they were given neither the notice required by *Mullane v. Central Hanover Bank & Trust Co.*, 339 U.S. 306 (1950), nor the full and fair opportunity to be heard required by *Hansberry v. Lee*, 311 U.S. 32 (1940), and *Logan v. Zimmerman Brush Co.*, 455 U.S. 422 (1982). *Mullane*, which involved a final accounting between a trustee and beneficiaries, is of course inapposite. *Hansberry* was based upon an impermissible conflict in a class action between the representatives of the class and certain class members; we have already said that such a conflict did not exist in these cases and that in any event this litigation is governed by different rules than those that apply in private representative litigation. *Logan* did not involve a fiduciary relationship, and like *Mullane*, was a suit where the complaining party would be left without recourse. In these cases, the Tribe, through the Government as their representative, was given adequate notice and a full and fair opportunity to be heard. If in carrying out their role as representative, the Government violated its obligations to the Tribe, then the Tribe's remedy is against the Government, not against third parties. As we have noted earlier, the Tribe has already taken advantage of that remedy.

JUSTICE BRENNAN, concurring.

The mere existence of a formal "conflict of interest" does not deprive the United States of authority to represent Indians in litigation, and therefore to bind them as well. If, however, the United States actually causes harm through a breach of its trust obligations the Indians should have a remedy against it. I join the Court's opinion on the understanding that it reaffirms that the Pyramid Lake Paiute Tribe has a remedy against the United States for the breach of duty that the United States has admitted. [See note 16.]

In the final analysis, our decision today is that thousands of small farmers in northwestern Nevada can rely on specific promises made to their forebears two and three generations ago, and solemnized in a judicial decree, despite strong claims on the part of the Pyramid Lake Paiutes. Here, as elsewhere in the West, [water] is insufficient to satisfy all claims. In the face of such fundamental natural limitations, the rule of law cannot avert large measures of loss, destruction, and profound disappointment, no matter how scrupulously evenhanded are the law's doctrines and administration. Yet the law can and should fix responsibility for loss and destruction that should have been avoided, and it can and should require that those whose rights are appropriated for the benefit of others receive appropriate compensation.[53]

NOTES ON INJUNCTIVE ENFORCEMENT OF THE TRUST

1. **The Recurring Proposal for an Independent Trust Counsel:** In 1973, President Nixon recommended that Congress establish an Indian Trust Counsel Authority independent of both the Department of the Interior and the Department of Justice. The trust counsel would have had the authority to bring suit against federal agencies as well as states and private parties in the name of the United States as trustee. In explaining the rationale for creating an independent counsel, the President stated:

> The United States Government acts as a legal trustee for the land and water rights of American Indians. These rights are often of critical economic importance to the Indian people; frequently they are also the subject of extensive legal dispute. In many of these legal confrontations, the Federal government is faced with an inherent conflict of interest. The Secretary of the Interior and the Attorney General must at the same time advance *both* the *national* interest in the use of land and water rights *and* the *private* interests of Indians in land which the government holds as trustee.

---

[53] [*] [O]ne of the purposes for establishment of the Pyramid Lake Reservation was "to provide the Indians with access to Pyramid Lake . . . in order that they might obtain their sustenance, at least in part, from these historic fisheries." As a consequence, the Tribe retains a *Winters* right, at least in theory, to water to maintain the fishery, a right which today's ruling does not question. To some extent it may be possible to satisfy the Tribe's claims consistent with the *Orr Ditch* decree — for instance, through judicious management of the Derby Dam and Lahontan Reservoir, improvement of the quality of the Newlands Project irrigation works, application of heretofore unappropriated floodwaters, or invocation of the decree's provisions for restricting diversions in excess of those allowed by the decree.

Every trustee has a legal obligation to advance the interests of the beneficiaries of the trust without reservation and with the highest degree of diligence and skill. Under present conditions, it is often difficult for the Department of the Interior and the Department of Justice to fulfill this obligation. No self-respecting law firm would ever allow itself to represent two opposing clients in one dispute; yet the Federal government has frequently found itself in precisely that position. There is considerable evidence that the Indians are the losers when such situations arise. More than that, the credibility of the Federal government is damaged whenever it appears that such a conflict of interest exists.

Message from the President of the United States Transmitting Recommendations for Indian Policy, H.R. Doc. 363, 91st Cong., 2d Sess. (1970). Although President Nixon's suggestion was well-received in Indian country, it was not immediately implemented. The 1977 American Indian Policy Review Commission Report took up the cause, recommending establishment of an Office of Indian Rights Protection, which would take responsibility for litigating Indian matters. AMERICAN INDIAN POLICY REVIEW COMMISSION, FINAL REPORT at 137–38 (1977). More recently, in 2013, the report of the Commission on Indian Trust Administration and Reform, discussed above, stated, somewhat cautiously, that "[t]he independent counsel concept has been around for a long time and deserves further consideration by the federal government. The Commission recommends that the Secretary evaluate the options in this area." COMMISSION ON INDIAN TRUST ADMINISTRATION AND REFORM, FINAL REPORT at 26 (2013). The Commission also recommended more conscientious and effective consultation with tribes before federal agencies before decisions are made affecting tribal interests: "Federal officials must establish clear protocols for disclosing and minimizing conflicts of interest, which should be implemented after full consultation with Indian nations. This must go beyond conflicts that meet minimal legal standards applicable to non-fiduciary relationships and extend to appearances of conflicts of interest that affect tribal and individual Indian interests in any transactions or actions related to trust assets, or the government-to-government relationship." *Id.* at 31.

2. Concern for Potential Conflicts in Refusing to Order the Government to Represent Tribes: Another arena in which conflicts of interest often affect federal decisions relating to Indian nations and their members involves the decision to initiate litigation to protect Indian resources or rights. Since 1893, federal law has provided that: "In all States and Territories where there are reservations or allotted Indians the [United States Attorney] shall represent them in all suits of law and in equity." 25 U.S.C. § 175. Despite the apparent mandatory language of the codified version of this statute, courts have relied on potential conflicts of interest and language of discretion in the session laws from which the codified statute derived to hold Congress did not intend to create a judicially enforceable obligation to represent tribes attempting to preserve property rights. *See, e.g., Black Spotted Horse v. Else*, 767 F.2d 516 (8th Cir. 1985) (no duty to represent federal prisoner in suit against prison); *Rincon Band of Mission Indians v. Escondido Mut. Water Co.*, 459 F.2d 1082, 1085 (9th Cir. 1972) (contrary decision would force the United States to take an opposite position than one taken in another pending case to which it was a party); *Siniscal v. United States*, 208 F.2d 406, 410 (9th Cir. 1953) (government would be on opposite sides of same case, creating a conflict of interest).

3. Enforcing the Trust After *Nevada*: Does *Nevada* undercut the cases permitting application to the federal executive department of equitable fiduciary standards that would be applied to a private fiduciary? *E.g.*, *Pyramid Lake Paiute Tribe v. Morton*, 354 F. Supp. 252 (D.D.C. 1972) (requiring the Secretary of the Interior to apply fiduciary principles and discharge his trust obligations to the Indians, rather than making a "judgment call," in the allocation of federal water along to Truckee-Carson flowage). Consider how the *Cobell* court or the Court of Claims in both *Navajo Nation* and the uranium *Navajo Tribe* case handled this question. Does *Nevada* stand for the proposition that there can be no breach of duty claim where the federal government represents both an Indian tribe and an agency like the Bureau of Reclamation that has an inconsistent interest? In *White Mountain Apache Tribe v. Hodel*, 784 F.2d 921 (9th Cir. 1986), the Tribe sought a declaratory judgment that the United States was not able to represent both the Tribe and the Bureau of Land Management adequately in a water rights adjudication in state court. Relying on *Nevada*, the Ninth Circuit held that representing both clients did not per se constitute an actionable conflict of interest. It nevertheless suggested that should a tribe offer evidence of actual malfeasance in the federal government's representation of the tribe, the tribe could press a claim for breach of trust. The Ninth Circuit further recognized that the Tribe could attempt to intervene in the state court water proceeding to protect its interests and further could appeal any adverse decision caused by the government's misrepresentation.

Examples of federal conflicts in water rights litigation and settlement are provided in Ann Juliano, *Conflicted Justice: The Department of Justice's Conflict of Interest in Representing Native American Tribes*, 37 Ga. L. Rev. 1307, 1362–64 (2003). *See also* Ch. 7, Sec. B. For thorough analyses of the trust responsibility doctrine, see Mary Christina Wood, *Indian Land and the Promise of Native Sovereignty: The Trust Doctrine Revisited*, 1994 Utah L. Rev. 1471; Mary Christina Wood, *Protecting the Attributes of Native Sovereignty: A New Trust Paradigm for Federal Actions Affecting Tribal Lands and Resources*, 1995 Utah L. Rev. 109; Mary C. Wood, *The Federal Trust Responsibility: Protecting Tribal Lands and Resources Through Claims of Injunctive Relief Against Federal Agencies*, 39 Tulsa L. Rev. 355 (2003).

For the Pyramid Lake Paiute Indians, Congress finally took a step toward restoring their fishery, passing the Truckee-Carson Pyramid Lake Water Rights Settlement Act of 1990 (PL101-618, section. 206(f)), which mandated studies of federal water rights repurchase and rehabilitation of the lower Truckee River for the benefit of the Tribe's fishery. The long saga of the Pyramid Lake Paiute litigation and negotiations is recounted in Ann Carey Juliano, *A Step Backward in the Government's Representation of Tribes: The Story of* Nevada v. United States *in* Indian Law Stories (Carole Goldberg, Kevin K. Washburn, and Philip P. Frickey, eds., 2011).

4. The Limits of the Trust Relationship: Both the trust doctrine and the so-called "fair and honorable dealings" jurisdiction established by section 5 of the Indian Claims Commission Act of 1946 might initially be thought to encompass broad political and social wrongs, in addition to economic claims. *See* Ch. 6, Sec.

A.5.a. Efforts to push the judicial enforceability of the Indian trust doctrine into such unfamiliar territory for courts have met with little notable success. When the Menominee Tribe sued the United States in the Court of Claims for breach of trust resulting from passage of the Menominee Termination Act and its costs to the Tribe, the Court held that sovereign immunity barred the claim, because it was not based on the Constitution or on a breach of a statute. *Menominee Tribe v. United States*, 607 F.2d 1335 (Ct. Cl. 1979). In *Fort Sill Apache Tribe v. United States*, 477 F.2d 1360, 1366 (Ct. Cl. 1973), the Court of Claims held that the federal government could not be held legally accountable in damages for wrongfully imprisoning the entire Chiracahua Apache Tribe for 27 years. Absent specific language in a statute, the court stated, the trust relationship could not be extended to "intangible factors of tribal well-being, cultural advancement, and maintenance of tribal form and structure."

Fort Sill Apache was based on the fair and honorable dealings jurisdiction of the Indian Claims Commission, 60 Stat. 1049, 1050, § (2)(5), which encompassed "claims based upon fair and honorable dealings that are not recognized by any existing rule of law or equity." Despite the fact that considerable legislative history of the 1946 Act suggested a congressional intent to permit Indian tribes to bring every sort of past grievance to the Commission, even those raising only moral rather than legal issues, the Commission narrowly interpreted the clause to require a breach of an affirmative duty to act created by statute, treaty, or other agreement. In *Gila River Pima-Maricopa Indian Community v. United States*, 427 F.2d 1194 (Ct. Cl. 1970), the Tribe sought damages for failure to provide education or medical services for the Tribe, alleging that the duty to provide for the Tribe arose when the government "undertook to, and did, subjugate the petitioner under wardship to a stagnation of self-expression . . . [and] bridled petitioner into cultural impotency." The court denied the relief because of the absence of any specific statutory duty to act. Notice that this grudging approach to interpreting the fair and honorable dealings provisions presaged the like approach later taken in the *Mitchell* decisions to narrow the reach of the Indian Tucker Act, 28 U.S.C. § 1505. Does it not stand to reason if the broader fair and honorable dealings jurisdiction of the Indian Claims Commission Act did not encompass such moral claims unsupported by a statutory duty, the narrower jurisdiction of section 1505, enacted at the same time, similarly might not have the legal reach that its moral force suggests?

Professor Nancy Lurie has criticized the grudging and narrow interpretations of the Indian Claims Commission Act offered in cases like *Fort Sill*. She suggested the Commission

> put a very fine point on the language of the act and moved the preparation of cases in the direction of simple, quantifiable issues. . . . The *Fort Sill* case not only eliminated the need for the commission to wrestle with compensating for cruel and unusual punishment and other intangibles implied in the exceedingly broad grounds for suit in the act, but also eliminated grievances with which many tribes were directly familiar, knowing exactly how they had been cheated, and for which they sought justice.

Nancy O. Lurie, *Epilogue, in* IRREDEEMABLE AMERICA: THE INDIAN'S ESTATE AND LAND CLAIMS 363, 372 (I. Sutton ed., 1985); *see also* Note, *Rethinking the Trust Doctrine in Federal Indian Law*, 98 HARV. L. REV. 422, 436 (1984).

6.   Federal Power in the Era of Self-Determination

Tribal governments exercise similar responsibilities to state governments, overseeing programs for health, education, housing, law enforcement, and social services for tribal members. However, the trust relationship with the federal government means that many of these services will be undertaken in partnership with the federal government, often through self-determination contracts ("638" contracts). *See* Ch. 1, Sec. B. The Bureau of Indian Affairs historically provided services to tribal governments and their members, and the 638 process is perhaps most apparent in relation to BIA programs that are assumed by tribal governments. However, in the modern era, other agencies have also entered the picture. So, for example, the Indian Health Service, located with the Department of Health and Human Services, administers health services to tribal members. The Secretary of Health and Human Services oversees this process. This model of inter-agency collaboration to effectuate the trust responsibility is intended to streamline the functions and increase efficiency. However, it also creates challenges for tribal governments who must contract with the agencies to provide services and may experience the consequences of deficiencies in funding.

In *Salazar v. Ramah Navajo Chapter*, 132 S. Ct. 2181 (2012), the question presented to the Justices was whether the federal government must pay the full amount of contract support costs incurred by tribes in performing their contracts, even when Congress has not appropriated sufficient funds to cover the aggregate amount due to each contractor. Note the different ways that Justice Sotomayor, for the majority, and Chief Justice Roberts, for the dissent, construe the relevant language in the Indian Self-Determination and Education Assistance Act.

SALAZAR v. RAMAH NAVAJO CHAPTER
United States Supreme Court
132 S. Ct. 2181 (2012)

JUSTICE SOTOMAYOR delivered the opinion of the Court.

The Indian Self-Determination and Education Assistance Act (ISDA), 25 U.S.C. § 450 et seq., directs the Secretary of the Interior to enter into contracts with willing tribes, pursuant to which those tribes will provide services such as education and law enforcement that otherwise would have been provided by the federal government. ISDA mandates that the Secretary shall pay the full amount of "contract support costs" incurred by tribes in performing their contracts. At issue in this case is whether the Government must pay those costs when Congress appropriates sufficient funds to pay in full any individual contractor's contract support costs, but not enough funds to cover the aggregate amount due every contractor. Consistent with longstanding principles of Government contracting law, we hold that the Government must pay each tribe's contract support costs in full.

I

A

Congress enacted ISDA in 1975 in order to achieve "maximum Indian participation in the direction of educational as well as other Federal services to Indian communities so as to render such services more responsive to the needs and desires of those communities." 25 U.S.C. § 450a(a). To that end, the Act directs the Secretary of the Interior, "upon the request of any Indian tribe . . . to enter into a self-determination contract . . . to plan, conduct, and administer" health, education, economic, and social programs that the Secretary otherwise would have administered. § 450f(a)(1).

As originally enacted, ISDA required the Government to provide contracting tribes with an amount of funds equivalent to those that the Secretary "would have otherwise provided for his direct operation of the programs." § 106(h), 88 Stat. 2211. It soon became apparent that this secretarial amount failed to account for the full costs to tribes of providing services. Because of "concern with Government's past failure adequately to reimburse tribes' indirect administrative costs," *Cherokee Nation of Okla. v. Leavitt*, 543 U.S. 631, 639, 125 S. Ct. 1172, 161 L. Ed. 2d 66 (2005), Congress amended ISDA to require the Secretary to contract to pay the "full amount" of "contract support costs" related to each self-determination contract, § 450j–1(a)(2), (g).[54] The Act also provides, however, that "[n]otwithstanding any other provision in [ISDA], the provision of funds under [ISDA] is subject to the availability of appropriations." § 450j–1(b).

Congress included a model contract in ISDA and directed that each tribal self-determination contract "shall . . . contain, or incorporate [it] by reference." § 450l (a)(1). . . .

During each relevant FY, Congress appropriated sufficient funds to pay in full any individual tribal contractor's contract support costs. Congress did not, however, appropriate sufficient funds to cover the contract support costs due all tribal contractors collectively. Between FY 1994 and 2001, appropriations covered only between 77% and 92% of tribes' aggregate contract support costs. The extent of the shortfall was not revealed until each fiscal year was well underway, at which point a tribe's performance of its contractual obligations was largely complete. See 644 F.3d 1054, 1061 (C.A.10 2011). Lacking funds to pay each contractor in full, the Secretary paid tribes' contract support costs on a uniform, pro rata basis. Tribes responded to these shortfalls by reducing ISDA services to tribal members, diverting tribal resources from non-ISDA programs, and forgoing opportunities to contract in furtherance of Congress's self-determination objective. GAO, V. Rezen-

---

[54] [1] As defined by ISDA, contract support costs "shall consist of an amount for the reasonable costs for activities which must be carried on by a tribal organization as a contractor to ensure compliance with the terms of the contract and prudent management, but which . . . (A) normally are not carried on by the respective Secretary in his direct operation of the program; or (B) are provided by the Secretary in support of the contracted program from resources other than those under contract." § 450j–1(a)(2). Such costs include overhead administrative costs, as well as expenses such as federally mandated audits and liability insurance. See *Cherokee Nation of Okla.*, 543 U.S., at 635, 125 S. Ct. 1172.

des, Indian Self-Determination Act: Shortfalls in Indian Contract Support Costs Need to Be Addressed 3–4 (GAO/RCED-99-150, 2009).

Respondent Tribes sued for breach of contract pursuant to the Contract Disputes Act, 41 U.S.C. §§ 601–613, alleging that the Government failed to pay the full amount of contract support costs due from FY 1994 through 2001, as required by ISDA and their contracts. The United States District Court for the District of New Mexico granted summary judgment for the Government. A divided panel of the United States Court of Appeals for the Tenth Circuit reversed. The court reasoned that Congress made sufficient appropriations "legally available" to fund any individual tribal contractor's contract support costs, and that the Government's contractual commitment was therefore binding. 644 F.3d, at 1063–1065. In such cases, the Court of Appeals held that the Government is liable to each contractor for the full contract amount. Judge Hartz dissented, contending that Congress intended to set a maximum limit on the Government's liability for contract support costs. We granted certiorari to resolve a split among the Courts of Appeals, 565 U.S. —, 132 S. Ct. 995, 181 L. Ed. 2d 725 (2012), and now affirm.

II

A

In evaluating the Government's obligation to pay tribes for contract support costs, we do not write on a clean slate. Only seven years ago, in *Cherokee Nation*, we also considered the Government's promise to pay contract support costs in ISDA self-determination contracts that made the Government's obligation "subject to the availability of appropriations." 543 U.S., at 634–637, 125 S. Ct. 1172. For each FY at issue, Congress had appropriated to the Indian Health Service (IHS) a lump sum between $1.277 and $1.419 billion, "far more than the [contract support cost] amounts" due under the Tribes' individual contracts. *Id.*, at 637; see *id.*, at 636 (Cherokee Nation and Shoshone-Paiute Tribes filed claims seeking $3.4 and $3.5 million, respectively). The Government contended, however, that Congress had appropriated inadequate funds to enable the IHS to pay the Tribes' contract support costs in full, while meeting all of the agency's competing fiscal priorities.

As we explained, that did not excuse the Government's responsibility to pay the Tribes. We stressed that the Government's obligation to pay contract support costs should be treated as an ordinary contract promise, noting that ISDA "uses the word 'contract' 426 times to describe the nature of the Government's promise." *Id.*, at 639. As even the Government conceded, "in the case of ordinary contracts . . . 'if the amount of an unrestricted appropriation is sufficient to fund the contract, the contractor is entitled to payment even if the agency has allocated the funds to another purpose or assumes other obligations that exhaust the funds.' " *Id.*, at 641. It followed, therefore, that absent "something special about the promises at issue," the Government was obligated to pay the Tribes' contract support costs in full. *Id.*, at 638.

We held that the mere fact that ISDA self-determination contracts are made "subject to the availability of appropriations" did not warrant a special rule. *Id.*, at

643 (internal quotation marks omitted). That commonplace provision, we explained, is ordinarily satisfied so long as Congress appropriates adequate legally unrestricted funds to pay the contracts at issue. See *ibid.* Because Congress made sufficient funds legally available to the agency to pay the Tribes' contracts, it did not matter that the BIA had allocated some of those funds to serve other purposes, such that the remainder was insufficient to pay the Tribes in full. Rather, we agreed with the Tribes that "as long as Congress has appropriated sufficient legally unrestricted funds to pay the contracts at issue," the Government's promise to pay was binding. *Id.*, at 637–638.

Our conclusion in *Cherokee Nation* followed directly from well-established principles of Government contracting law. When a Government contractor is one of several persons to be paid out of a larger appropriation sufficient in itself to pay the contractor, it has long been the rule that the Government is responsible to the contractor for the full amount due under the contract, even if the agency exhausts the appropriation in service of other permissible ends. See *Ferris v. United States*, 27 Ct. Cl. 542, 546 (1892); *Dougherty v. United States*, 18 Ct. Cl. 496, 503 (1883); see also 2 GAO, Principles of Federal Appropriations Law, p. 6–17 (2d ed. 1992) (hereinafter GAO Redbook). That is so "even if an agency's total lump-sum appropriation is insufficient to pay all the contracts the agency has made." *Cherokee Nation*, 543 U.S., at 637. In such cases, "[t]he United States are as much bound by their contracts as are individuals." *Lynch v. United States*, 292 U.S. 571, 580 (1934) (internal quotation marks omitted). Although the agency itself cannot disburse funds beyond those appropriated to it, the Government's "valid obligations will remain enforceable in the courts." GAO Redbook, p. 6–17.

. . . .

B

The principles underlying *Cherokee Nation* and *Ferris* dictate the result in this case. Once "Congress has appropriated sufficient legally unrestricted funds to pay the contracts at issue, the Government normally cannot back out of a promise to pay on grounds of 'insufficient appropriations,' even if the contract uses language such as 'subject to the availability of appropriations,' and even if an agency's total lump-sum appropriation is insufficient to pay all the contracts the agency has made." *Cherokee Nation*, 543 U.S., at 637; see also *id.*, at 638 ("[T]he Government denies none of this").

That condition is satisfied here. . . .

. . . .

IV

As the Government points out, the state of affairs resulting in this case is the product of two congressional decisions that the BIA has found difficult to reconcile. On the one hand, Congress obligated the Secretary to accept every qualifying ISDA contract, which includes a promise of "full" funding for all contract support costs. On the other, Congress appropriated insufficient funds to pay in full each tribal contractor. The Government's frustration is understandable, but the dilemma's resolution is the responsibility of Congress.

Congress is not short of options. For instance, it could reduce the Government's financial obligation by amending ISDA to remove the statutory mandate compelling the BIA to enter into self-determination contracts, or by giving the BIA flexibility to pay less than the full amount of contract support costs. It could also pass a moratorium on the formation of new self-determination contracts, as it has done before. See § 328, 112 Stat. 2681–291 to 292. Or Congress could elect to make line-item appropriations, allocating funds to cover tribes' contract support costs on a contractor-by-contractor basis. On the other hand, Congress could appropriate sufficient funds to the BIA to meet the tribes' total contract support cost needs. Indeed, there is some evidence that Congress may do just that. See H.R.Rep. No. 112–151, p. 42 (2011) ("The Committee believes that the Bureau should pay all contract support costs for which it has contractually agreed and directs the Bureau to include the full cost of the contract support obligations in its fiscal year 2013 budget submission").

The desirability of these options is not for us to say. We make clear only that Congress has ample means at hand to resolve the situation underlying the Tribes' suit. Any one of the options above could also promote transparency about the Government's fiscal obligations with respect to ISDA's directive that contract support costs be paid in full. For the period in question, however, it is the Government — not the Tribes — that must bear the consequences of Congress's decision to mandate that the Government enter into binding contracts for which its appropriation was sufficient to pay any individual tribal contractor, but "insufficient to pay all the contracts the agency has made." *Cherokee Nation*, 543 U.S., at 637.

The judgment of the Court of Appeals is affirmed.

It is so ordered.

CHIEF JUSTICE ROBERTS, with whom JUSTICE GINSBURG, JUSTICE BREYER, and JUSTICE ALITO join, dissenting.

Today the Court concludes that the federal government must pay the full amount of contract support costs incurred by the respondent Tribes, regardless of whether there are any appropriated funds left for that purpose. This, despite the facts that payment of such costs is "subject to the availability of appropriations," a condition expressly set forth in both the statute and the contracts providing for such payment, 25 U.S.C. §§ 450j-1(b), 450l (c) (Model Agreement § 1(b)(4)); that payment of the costs for all tribes is "not to exceed" a set amount, e.g., 108 Stat. 2511, an amount that would be exceeded here; and that the Secretary "is not required to reduce funding for programs, projects, or activities serving a tribe to make funds available to another tribe," § 450j-1(b). Because the Court's conclusion cannot be squared with these unambiguous restrictions on the payment of contract support costs, I respectfully dissent.

. . . .

This is hardly a typical government contracts case. Many government contracts contain a "subject to the availability of appropriations" clause, and many appropriations statutes contain "not to exceed" language. But this case involves not only those provisions but a third, relieving the Secretary of any obligation to make funds "available" to one contractor by reducing payments to others. Such provisions will not always appear together, but when they do, we must give them effect. Doing so here, I would hold that the Tribes are not entitled to payment of their contract support costs in full, and I would reverse the contrary judgment of the Court of Appeals for the Tenth Circuit.

NOTE ON FEDERAL PROGRAMS AND ADMINISTRATIVE AUTHORITY OF FEDERAL AGENCIES FOR TRIBAL SERVICES

The federal obligation to provide services to American Indian and Alaska Native people arises from treaties, statutes, and the trust relationship. The trust relationship, by itself, exists as a moral obligation. However, when specific guarantees are extended by treaty or statute, there may be a legally cognizable claim if an agency fails to honor the obligation. In such cases, federal administrative law may guide the ways in which claims can be made to require an agency to adhere to its legal obligations.

The Indian Self-Determination and Education Assistance Act (PL 93-638) is the law that effectuated the most dramatic change in the implementation of federal services. The Act allows tribes to enter into self-determination contracts with the federal government to take control of federal programs and schools for Indians. *See generally* NELL JESSUP NEWTON ET AL., COHEN'S HANDBOOK OF FEDERAL INDIAN LAW § 22.02 (2012 ed.). The Tribal Self-Governance Act extended this model to allow tribal governments to negotiate a single annual funding agreement or "self-governance compact" for the administration of all programs that the tribe is administering in cooperation with the Department of Interior. Tribal governments have similar authorities with respect to services provided by the Indian Health Service, although the contracts and compacts in that area must be negotiated with the Department of Health and Human Services.

In all applicable substantive areas, tribal governments negotiate the terms of self-governance with the lead federal agency. The negotiations cover funding and allocation of responsibility. In addition, tort claims against tribes and tribal organizations may be considered claimed against the United States, for purposes of the Federal Tort Claims Act. *See* Sec. A.4, this chapter. In addition, tribal members are entitled to receive state services on an equal basis to any other citizen, so there may be a need to coordinate some services between tribal, state, and federal agencies. Thus, the provision of services to tribal governments and tribal members is dependent upon a complex interaction of governance authorities, in many cases requiring intergovernmental agreements. *See* Ch. 3, Sec. E. As you read through the examples below, notice that the federal trust responsibility may be shared by more than one federal agency, requiring inter-agency coordination to fully effectuate the federal responsibility.

HEALTH CARE

The historic policy of the United States to assume responsibility for the healthcare of tribal members originated in the need of the BIA to prevent disease epidemics but grew into a novel system designed to serve tribal members in their basic healthcare needs. *See generally* Emery A. Johnson, M.D. & Everett R, Rhodes, M.D., *The History and Organization of Indian Health Services and Systems in* AMERICAN INDIAN HEALTH: INNOVATIONS IN HEALTH CARE, PROMOTION, AND POLICY 74–100 (Everett R. Rhoades, ed., 2000). The BIA operated healthcare programs with the assistance of the U.S. Public Health Service, resulting in a cumbersome partnership between the two entities. In 1954, the responsibility for tribal healthcare was formally transferred to the U.S. Public Health Service in an effort to improve coordination of healthcare and access to services. In 1968, the Indian Health Service was created as the formal entity to provide health services to tribal members. The IHS is a separate agency within the Department of Health and Human Services responsible for providing federal health services to American Indian and Alaska Natives, including behavioral health programs. The IHS also has the primary responsibility over water, sanitation, and waste disposal services within Indian Country.

American Indian and Alaska Native people are entitled to receive state health care services on the same basis as all other state citizens. However, because of the federal responsibility to provide healthcare to tribal members, states were unclear on whether they had an obligation to provide services to Indians covered by the IHS system. Today, federal law explicitly declares that the IHS is the payor of last resort, which forecloses state laws attempting to deny care to Indians eligible for IHS services under alternative resource rules. 25 U.S.C. § 1623(b). The Indian Healthcare Improvement Act was permanently reauthorized in 2010 as part of the Patient Protection and Affordable Care Act (P.L. 111-148), explicitly acknowledging the federal government's duty to provide healthcare to American Indian and Alaska Native people.

EDUCATION

The historic policy of the United States to provide education to American Indian and Alaska Native people was rooted in the policy of assimilation, first through the use of federally-operated boarding schools and then, in the mid-twentieth century, espousing cooperation with state educational programs. *See generally* 2014 Native Youth Report, Executive Office of the President, December 2014 at pp. 7–12. However, in 2001, Congress enacted the Native American Education Improvement Act to formalize the obligation to provide educational services to American Indian and Alaska Native peoples, consistent with the responsibility to ensure that Native peoples enjoy equal educational opportunity.

Today, BIA educational programs are operated by the Bureau of Indian Education, which was created in 2006 as an independent office within the BIA that is responsible for BIE-funded elementary and secondary schools, tribally controlled colleges, higher education grants, and Johnson O'Malley contracts. All BIE-funded schools receive funds through the Indian School Equalization Program (ISEP), which uses a funding formula to determine the respective needs of the schools. BIE schools also receive funds from the U.S. Department of Education. The Indian Education Act establishes the authority of the Department of Education to address the specific educational and cultural needs of American Indian and Alaska Native students, and provide funding for these programs. The Native Hawaiian Education Act of 1988 addresses the unique educational needs of Native Hawaiian students and provides discretionary grants to encourage development of culturally-relevant educational programs for these students.

The Tribally Controlled College or University Assistance Act of 1998 formalizes the role of the BIA in supporting higher education, and is an outgrowth of the 1978 Tribally Controlled Community College Act. Tribal colleges are important institutions for furthering trial self-determination, and Congressional policy supports the development of tribally-controlled colleges and the provision of operational support.

Despite these important advances in federal policy, American Indian and Alaska Native youth continue to experience significant disparities in educational attainment when compared to other groups within U.S. society. 2014 Native Youth Report at 13–26. They are also disproportionately represented in the school discipline system. *Id.* at 15. As a result of these disparities, the 2014 Native Youth Report concludes that American Indians and Alaska Natives continue to experience limited opportunity in higher education and the employment market. The authors of the report highlight the need for increased participation by tribal governments, as well as improved coordination between the agencies that are responsible for providing educational services.

LAW ENFORCEMENT

Today, law enforcement on reservation lands is a shared responsibility of the tribal government, the Bureau of Indian Affairs, and the Department of Justice, consistent with the shared jurisdictional authorities of the federal and tribal governments. In P.L. 280 states, tribal governments must formally coordinate jurisdiction with the state government. However, even in other states, tribal governments and state governments often find it helpful to enter agreements to enhance the provision of services and deal with intra-jurisdictional issues.

The Indian Law Enforcement Reform Act of 1990 created the Office of Justice Services within the BIA to carry out the BIA's law enforcement responsibilities in Indian Country. *See* NELL JESSUP NEWTON ET AL., COHEN'S HANDBOOK OF FEDERAL INDIAN LAW § 22.07 (2012 ed.). Tribal governments may contract to administer these programs under the authority of the Indian Self-Determination Act. These authorities are enhanced by the provisions of the Tribal Law and Order Act of 2010.

The Department of Justice oversees the investigation and prosecution of serious crimes under federal jurisdiction. In addition, the DOJ funds discretionary grant programs and assists tribal governments in developing capacity to exercise enhanced law enforcement authorities under the TLOA and the Violence Against Women Act. The TLOA also institutionalized the Office of Tribal Justice within the Department of Justice. The OTJ is the point of contact for tribal governments with DOJ and also serves as the primary adviser to the Attorney General.

In November 2013, the Indian Law and Order Commission released its comprehensive report, A Roadmap for Making Native American Safer, to the President and Congress of the United States. The Commission's findings constitute the most comprehensive assessment ever undertaken on the state of the criminal justice system that serves American Indian and Alaska Native Communities, documenting the "unacceptably high rates of violent crime that have plagued Indian Country for decades." The Report includes a lengthy set of recommendations for improving the criminal justice system in Indian Country. *See* INDIAN LAW AND ORDER COMMISSION, A ROADMAP FOR MAKING NATIVE AMERICA SAFER 82–92 (November 2013). The Commission "views tribal governments as having the lead role in strengthening Tribal justice" systems, but notes that tribal governments require increased financial support and a "more rational Federal administrative structure" in order to accomplish their goals. The Report notes that the Department of Justice funding for tribal governments has been disproportionately directed toward short-term "competitive grants for specific activities," rather than long-term structural improvements. In addition, the Report notes that the Federal administrative structure suffers from "overlapping functions" among federal agencies because both DOI and DOJ provide funding for law enforcement, criminal investigation, prosecution, Tribal courts and detention," leading to program duplication, confusion, decreased accountability, and wasteful outcomes. The Commission outlined alternatives that might be pursued to enhance effective tribal-federal law enforcement programs in Indian Country. For further discussion of the Commission's Report, see Sec. A.3.a, this chapter.

HOUSING

The federal role in providing housing services to American Indian and Alaska Native peoples traces back to the treaties made during the Removal Era, which pledged federal assistance in securing homes for Indians in the Indian territory which would replace the ones that they were forced to leave. *See* NELL JESSUP NEWTON ET AL., COHEN'S HANDBOOK OF FEDERAL INDIAN LAW § 22.05 (2012 ed.). In addition, as federal policy shifted during the latter part of the nineteenth century to favor allotment of land in severalty to tribal members, the notion of housing became tied to the norm of private property.

For many years, housing appropriations were sporadic and tied to specific programs, such as the revolving loan fund authorized by the Indian Reorganization Act. In 1961, a report on Indian housing revealed striking deficiencies in the housing available to tribal members, promoting a change in the law that allowing Indian Housing Authorities to participate in the programs authorized by the Public Housing Administration. However, a 2003 Report by the U.S. Commission on Civil Rights declared that housing in Indian country was still so far below the national standards that it "raised civil rights concerns." COHEN'S HANDBOOK at 1429 and note 18 (citing U.S. Comm'n on Civil Rights, A Quiet Crisis: Federal Funding and Unmet Needs in Indian Country).

Until 1998, most HUD programs for tribal members were created under the authority of the Housing Act of 1937. However, in 1996, Congress enacted the Native American Housing Assistance and Self-Determination Act which affirmed the federal trust responsibility to provide housing assistance to Indian people and enabled tribal governments to tailor housing programs to the needs of the community. 25 U.S.C.§ 4101 et seq. NAHASDA consolidated funding for nine of the fourteen former HUD housing programs and enabled flexible grants to be made to tribal governments to develop building plans consistent with community needs. Thus, HUD oversees a significant portion of the federal responsibility to provide housing assistance to tribal governments and their members. The BIA continues to provide funds for housing improvement, which assists tribal members with their immediate need for repairs and improvements. In addition, the BIA oversees title records on trust lands and Indian allotments, which necessitates coordination between the two agencies.

B.   STATE AUTHORITY IN INDIAN COUNTRY

1.   Tribal Expectations

Cherokee Council, 1830
in FROM THE HEART: VOICES OF THE AMERICAN INDIAN
155 (L. Miller ed., 1995)

Of late years . . . much solicitude was occasioned among our people by the claims of Georgia. This solicitude arose from an apprehension that by extreme importunity, threats, and other undue influence, a treaty would be made, which should cede the territory, and thus compel the inhabitants to remove. But it never occurred to us for a moment, that without any new treaty, without any assent of our rules and people, without even a pretended compact, and against our vehement and unanimous protestations, we should be delivered over to the discretion of those, who had declared by a legislative act, that they wanted the Cherokee lands and would have them.

George W. Harkins (Choctaw), *Farewell Letter to the American People, 1832*
in GREAT DOCUMENTS IN AMERICAN INDIAN HISTORY
152 (W. Moquin & C. Van Doren eds., 1973)

We were hedged in by two evils, and we chose that which we thought least. Yet we could not recognize the right that the State of Mississippi had assumed to legislate for us. Although the legislature of the state were qualified to make laws for their own citizens, that did not qualify them to become law makers to a people who were so dissimilar in manners and customs as the Choctaws are to the Mississippians. . . . Amid the gloom and horrors of the present separation, we are cheered with a hope that ere long we shall reach our destined home, and that nothing short of the basest acts of treachery will be able to wrest it from us, and that we may live free . . .

Treaty with the Creek and Seminole Tribes
Aug. 7, 1856, 11 Stat. 699

ARTICLE 4. The United States do hereby, solemnly agree and bind themselves, that no State or Territory shall ever pass laws for the government of the Creek or Seminole tribes of Indians, and that no portion of either of the tracts of country defined in the first and second articles of this agreement shall ever be embraced or included within, or annexed to, any Territory or State, nor shall either, or any part of either, ever be erected into a Territory without the full and free consent of the legislative authority of the tribe owning the same.

NOTE ON TRIBAL EXPECTATIONS REGARDING STATE AUTHORITY

When lands were reserved or set aside by treaty with the United States for the occupation of Indian nations, tribal communities assumed that states would have no authority within those lands. Typically, the treaties provided for federal control over traders, and federal jurisdiction over non-Indian offenders or unauthorized intruders. *See* Articles VIII, X, and XII, Treaty of Dancing Rabbit Creek with the Choctaw, Feb. 21, 1831, 7 Stat. 333. No realm of state authority was acknowledged or provided in the treaties. As Article IV of the Treaty with the Creek and Seminole demonstrates, state authority was sometimes expressly denied.

But even where such strong denials were absent from the treaty language, the very fact of treating with Indians reflected a conception of Native nations as distinct groups separate from the states. And the regime of demarcating Indian reservations carried with it the idea of jurisdictional as well as physical separation of Indians from surrounding state populations. For example, in his account of the 1863 treaty negotiations between the Nez Perce and Governor Stevens, Chief Joseph recites, "He said there were a great many white people in the country, and many more would come; that he wanted the land marked out so that the Indians and white men could be separated. If they were to live in peace it was necessary, he said, that the Indians should have a country set apart for them. . . . " *The Fate of the Nez Perces Tribe 1879, in* GREAT DOCUMENTS IN AMERICAN INDIAN HISTORY 239 (W. Moquin & C. Van Doren eds., 1973). The treaty itself refers to the reserved lands of the Nez Perce as being for the "sole use and occupation" and the "exclusive use and benefit" of the Tribe. "White men" are allowed onto the reservation only with the permission of the Tribe and the federal agent. And the state is expressly precluded from taxing or allowing transfer of lands absent permission of Congress. Arts. II & III, Treaty with the Nez Perce Indians, June 9, 1863, 14 Stat. 647. At one point Congress even considered admission of the Indian Territory (now Oklahoma) as a separate Indian state governed by a confederation of tribes. Annie Heloise Abel, *Proposals for an Indian State 1778–1878,* ANNUAL REPORT OF THE AMERICAN HISTORICAL ASSOCIATION 89, 94–102 (1907). What model of tribal-federal relations would that arrangement have exemplified? What would have been the implications for tribal sovereignty and cultures?

Early visions of complete separation did not match the later reality. Pressures for non-Indian settlement and control within Indian country had prompted the removal of the Cherokee, Choctaw, and other southeastern Indian nations early in the nineteenth century. Within 20 years of signing the Nez Perce treaty, western tribes were experiencing the same population pressures and demands for state control over tribal territories. Beginning in the 1880's, reservation allotment and sale of "surplus" reservation lands brought large numbers of non-Indian landowners onto reservation lands. In 1907, Oklahoma statehood breached agreements with the southeastern tribes that had been removed to the Indian Territory. By the time of the 1990 census, nearly 50% of those living on reservations and trust lands identified themselves as non-Indian. States have viewed the end of complete separation as the occasion for asserting their authority within reservation boundaries, and conflicts over these assertions continue to churn.

Why would the exclusion of state power have been so important to Indian nations? Is the exercise of state sovereignty over tribal lands and peoples necessarily inconsistent with the continued existence of tribal Indian societies as separate political entities? If so, cannot the same thing be said of the coexistence of federal authority and tribal power in Indian country? Is there something about the differences between the operation of federal and state authority in Indian country that makes the exercise of the latter less compatible with the continued existence of separate Indian tribal societies, cultures, and governments? Any likely difference in the set of non-Indian interests that tribes must contend with? *See* THOMAS BIOLSI, DEADLIEST ENEMIES: LAW AND THE MAKING OF RACE RELATIONS ON AND OFF ROSEBUD RESERVATION (2001). Which model(s) of the tribal-federal relationship leave room for the exercise of state power within Indian country? As in the Treaty of 1863 with the Nez Perce, Congress claims authority to empower states within tribal territories. Which model(s) support congressional exercise of that authority, and to what ends?

2. Early Approaches to Inherent State Power in Indian Country

Reread *Worcester v. Georgia*, set forth in Ch. 1, Sec. C.2. In that case, the Court held that Georgia could not criminally prosecute and convict several white missionaries to the Cherokees, including Samuel A. Worcester, for violating an 1830 law enacted by the Georgia legislature that required any person residing within the Cherokee Nation to have a license or permit from the Georgia governor and to take an oath of loyalty. Georgia law also purported to annex the Cherokee Nation to the state, extend state law over the Cherokees, and disqualify Indians from testifying in state court. The Court held that the state laws violated the Indian commerce clause, the federal treaties with the Cherokee protecting their lands and political autonomy, and the Trade and Intercourse Acts, and therefore were preempted by federal law.

NOTES

1. Jurisdiction of Colonies and States Under British Rule and the Articles of Confederation: During the colonial period, England and the colonies struggled continuously over management of Indian affairs. England was concerned to avoid costly warfare and conflict with the tribes that might sap its treasury and endanger its position vis-à-vis other European contenders for North America. Accordingly, English law upheld central control over Indian relations, and generally followed international law in recognizing tribes as politically and legally autonomous within their unceded territory. Measures such as the English Proclamation of 1763 were enacted to separate tribes from colonists, thereby reducing white encroachments on Indian lands.

The colonists preferred their own control over Indian affairs in order to facilitate land acquisitions. Viewing tribes as obstacles to land development rather than as autonomous peoples, colonial law offered no remedies when tribes complained of fraudulent land acquisitions or trespass. Colonies engaged in diplomatic relations only with the most powerful tribes, such as the Six Nations of the Haudenosaunee. Yet by the mid-eighteenth century, even colonists began to understand that mistreatment of tribes might engender threats to collective safety.

The problems of defining tribal status and centralizing management of Indian affairs received no satisfactory solution under the Articles of Confederation. Despite early treaties between the Continental Congress and Indian nations guaranteeing tribal autonomy, states persisted in conducting diplomatic and land transactions, and in seeking to govern tribal territories. At one point, New York officials actually disrupted treaty negotiations between national representatives and the Haudenosaunee, claiming that the state possessed the exclusive right to treat with those Indians. Article IX of the Articles of Confederation offered no decisive statement favoring federal control. Instead, it granted the Continental Congress "the sole and exclusive [authority of] regulating the trade and managing all affairs with Indians not members of any of the states; provided, that the legislative right of any state within its own limits be not infringed or violated." Were Indians living in tribal communities on reserved lands within state boundaries "members" of those states? Or did that language refer only to Indians who had severed their tribal ties and gone to live among the non-Indians? Did the "legislative right of any state" encompass the former or only the latter?

2. **Analytical Underpinnings of *Worcester*:** Note that Chief Justice Marshall stated three separate grounds, each of which is sufficient by itself to preempt state authority. First, the Court held that the State of Georgia wholly lacked any inherent sovereignty over Indians or Indian country because the framers of the Constitution had exclusively vested the Indian affairs power in the federal government. This approach suggests that whatever state jurisdiction exists in Indian country must be based on federal statutory delegation of authority under the Indian commerce clause. Second, the Court held that treaties recognizing the Cherokee Nation's political autonomy and setting land aside for the Cherokee reservation preempted state authority. This second approach suggests a broad preemptive force for treaties (and later statutes and executive orders) that recognize tribal autonomy; this broad preemption analysis is known as "Indian country preemption." Third, the Court held that specific federal statutes, in this case the Trade and Intercourse Acts, preempted the Georgia laws. Under this last form of preemption, specific statutes, regulations, or treaties are read broadly in light of federal policy toward Indians to preempt state regulation.

Of the three potential methods of analyzing questions of state interference first employed in *Worcester*, the negative implications of the Indian commerce clause, Indian country preemption, and statutory preemption, which is most fully supported by the history of the Indian commerce clause? Professor Clinton has provided some history of the Indian commerce clause which strongly suggests that the framers intended "negative implications" for state power as well as a grant of federal power.

> [James] Madison was . . . the primary proponent and architect of the Indian Commerce Clause and the meaning he sought to convey is clear. He desired explicitly to prevent state encroachments on the exclusive commitment of power to the federal government to regulate affairs with the Indian tribes. Both the Convention and Madison also intended to protect the separate and sovereign status of the Indian tribes. It was the claim by various states that the Indian tribes were not separate and sovereign, but rather were "members" of the states wherein they resided, that had produced the rift in Indian affairs during the confederation period. It was this claim Madison explicitly set out to demolish. Further evidence that the Convention was united in its effort to constitutionally protect the separate and sovereign status of the Indian tribes is found in (1) the exclusion of "Indians not taxed" from the apportionment formula for representation and direct taxation from the states; (2) the phrasing of the Indian affairs clause by the Committee of Detail which declared that Indian tribes within the states were "not subject to the laws thereof;" and (3) the inclusion by the Committee of Eleven of the Indian tribes among the other sovereigns, foreign and domestic, in the Commerce Clause.

> While the meaning of the Indian Commerce Clause and the intent of the framers seems reasonably clear, it is remarkable that the clause provoked so little debate or overt attention at the Constitutional Convention. While it might be argued that this lack of attention occurred because Indian affairs simply was not a serious constitutional problem deserving of protracted attention, the history of the period refutes this argument. The constitutional rifts between the states and the national government over Indian affairs during the confederation period were well known. They had brought the nation to the brink of a general Indian war or, at least, serious frontier clashes in Georgia, Virginia and Northern Carolina, on the very eve of the Convention. The Continental Congress was simultaneously engaged in efforts to avert the threat of Indian warfare and on August 3, 1787 the Committee on Southern Indian Affairs issued its report forcefully asserting exclusive federal authority over Indian affairs and condemning state initiatives for the deterioration in relations with the Indian tribes. . . .

> Rather, the Convention's lack of discussion or division over the Indian affairs clause may be better attributed to the role the Convention was playing vis-à-vis the Indian affairs power. In this field, the Convention was not shaping a new frame of governance out of whole cloth. Rather, in the arena of Indian affairs, the Convention was tinkering with the prior decision of the Articles to commit to the national government "the sole and exclusive right and power . . . regulating the trade and managing all affairs

with the Indians. . . . " The framers were curing rather than creating. Indeed, as suggested above, there already existed in the Continental Congress a dominant view that the national government had the sole and exclusive right to regulate affairs with all sovereign Indian tribes, wherever located, and this view was well presented in the report of the Committee on Southern Indian Affairs to the Continental Congress just two weeks before steps were taken in the Convention to include the Indian Commerce Clause in the Constitution. All the framers did at the Convention was ratify this dominant view, an action that required and consumed little debate. . . .

The debates over the ratification of the Constitution, both in the state conventions and in the popular press, also failed to focus extensively on the Indian Commerce Clause. These discussions, however, were not entirely unenlightening. Rather, they reinforced the view that the Constitutional Convention, in adopting the Indian Commerce Clause, sought to constitutionally protect from state encroachment the exclusive power of the national government over Indian affairs and to constitutionally protect the legal status of the Indian tribes as separate and sovereign peoples. . . .

The debates in the popular press . . . contained some brief reference to the Indian affairs. Robert Yates, writing in the New York Journal on June 3, 1788 under the pen name Sydney, compared the proposed Constitution to the constitution of the State of New York in order to show in what respects "the powers of the state government will be either totally or partially absorbed. . . . " After noting that under the New York constitution all purchases or contracts for the sale of lands from the Indians within the limits of the state must be made under the authority and with the consent of the state legislature, Yates argued that the "whole history of this spurious constitution for the government of the United States, from its origin to the present day, and the measures taken by Congress respecting the Indian affairs in this state, are a series of violations of these paragraphs, and of . . . the confederation. Yates then entered into a long historical discourse to show that management of Indian affairs, and particularly affairs with the Five Nations, properly belonged to the states. He concluded:

> It is therefore evident that this state, by adopting the new government, will enervate their legislative rights, and totally surrender into the hands of Congress the management and regulation of the Indian trade to an improper government, and the traders to be fleeced by iniquitous impositions, operating at one and the same time as a monopoly and a poll tax.

Thus, Yates, an opponent of the Constitution, understood full well that the Indian Commerce Clause removed the last vestige of state claims to authority over Indian tribes within their boundaries and vested the full, complete and exclusive power over managing all affairs with the Indian tribes in the federal government. . . .

While problems of defense against the Indians and Indian affairs are briefly adverted to elsewhere in The Federalist, by far the single most important comment on the Indian Commerce Clause offered by proponents of the Constitution during the ratification debates was advanced by James Madison, the father of the clause, in Federalist Number 42, dated January 22, 1788.

[B]oth Madison and Yates agreed that the Indian Commerce Clause was intended to ratify the exclusive commitment of the management of Indian affairs and trade to the federal government to the exclusion of the states. They disagreed only as to the desirability of that decision. . . .

Ratification of the Constitution, with its attendant Indian Commerce Clause, therefore, was intended to resolve constitutionally three legal issues, the origins of which lay deep in the colonial experience. First, the intent of the framers to grant the national government full and complete power to manage all affairs and trade with the Indian tribes was evident in the debates in the Convention and expressly conceded by both proponents and opponents of the Constitution. The critical need for centralized management of Indian affairs had become too evident to ignore, whatever the countervailing commercial and property interests of the states. Second, perhaps the most critical part of this centralization of power in the national government was the concomitant curtailment of any claims to state authority through the elimination of the provisos contained in the Articles of Confederation which had so hampered the power of the Congress under the Articles. Finally, the framers' determination to protect the sovereignty of the Indian tribes as peoples separate from the states was evident in their enumeration among the states and foreign nations in the Commerce Clause and in the apportionment formula which excluded Indians not taxed. The Convention thus wholly abandoned any notion that tribal Indians were members of the state in which they resided, a point made by both Madison and Yates. Since Indian sovereignty and national power were also asserted during the Articles, perhaps the most important marginal contribution of the Indian Commerce Clause was to limit state authority. In short, the framers not only intended a dormant Indian Commerce Clause, it was the central focal point of their drafting efforts with respect to the Indian affairs powers.

Robert N. Clinton, *The Dormant Indian Commerce Clause*, 27 CONN. L. REV. 1055, 1155–1164 (1995).

3. State Jurisdiction When No Indian Interests Are Involved: Nineteenth-century legal developments did not, however, completely bear out the broadest possible readings of *Worcester*. Where no Indian interest whatsoever was involved, some late nineteenth and early twentieth century cases suggested the existence of some limited state sovereignty in Indian country. In *United States v. McBratney*, 104 U.S. 621 (1882), and *Draper v. United States*, 164 U.S. 240 (1896), discussed in Sec. A.3.b, this chapter, the Supreme Court held that state courts, rather than federal or tribal courts, had the jurisdiction to try non-Indians who committed crimes against the person or property of other non-Indians in Indian country. On the other hand, where any Indian interest existed, the early cases consistently held that state jurisdiction was lacking. In *The New York Indians*, 72 U.S. (5 Wall.) 761

(1867), and *The Kansas Indians*, 72 U.S. (5 Wall.) 737 (1867), the Court held that Indians were immune from state taxation, even if their land was allotted or they were scheduled for removal. And in *Harkness v. Hyde*, 98 U.S. 476 (1879), and *Langford v. Monteith*, 102 U.S. 145 (1880), the Court held that the civil process of state and territorial courts did not reach into Indian country even with respect to non-Indian defendants, at least where the cause of action arose on an Indian reservation. Dicta in *Langford* purported to limit the holding in *Harkness*, however, only to those reservations for which there was an explicit treaty or statutory disclaimer of state or territorial jurisdiction.

4. State Jurisdictional Disclaimers and the Equal Footing Doctrine: The dicta in *Langford, supra*, draw attention to a very confusing and now repudiated line of cases involving state disclaimers of jurisdiction. As the removal policy was winding down, the pace at which states were being settled, formed, and admitted to the Union began to outstrip the speed with which the federal government could remove tribes from the states prior to statehood. Thus, beginning with the admission of Wisconsin and Kansas, Congress began to insist that *some* states disclaim authority and jurisdiction over lingering vestiges of Indian country by including such disclaimers in the enabling or statehood legislation or by requiring the affected states to include such irrevocable disclaimers in their state constitutions. For example, Article XXI, § 2 of the New Mexico Constitution contains a specific disclaimer

> to all lands lying within said boundaries owned or held by any Indian or Indian tribes, the right or title to which shall have been acquired through the United States, [and that] until the title of such Indian or Indian tribes shall have been extinguished the same shall be and remain subject to the disposition and under the absolute jurisdiction and control of the Congress of the United States.

See also Art. 4, Alaska Statehood Act, 72 Stat. 339 (1958); Montana, 25 Stat. 676, 677 (1889); Utah, 28 Stat. 107, 108 (1894); New Mexico, 36 Stat. 557, 558–77 (1910); Wyoming Const., 1890, Art. 21, § 26; Idaho Const., 1890, Art. 21, § 19.

The state disclaimers soon took on an historical significance beyond their initial intent. Seemingly ignoring the lessons of *Worcester*, the Supreme Court in a few instances suggested that negative implications could be drawn from the lack of such a disclaimer. For example, the *McBratney* decision was based in part on the lack of such a disclaimer in the Colorado Constitution. Similarly, in *Ward v. Race Horse*, 163 U.S. 504 (1896), the Court held that treaty rights of the Shoshone-Bannock to hunt and fish on unoccupied lands of the federal government were displaced or abrogated in Wyoming when the state entered the union on an equal footing with other states and without such a disclaimer, because such rights were incompatible with state sovereignty. Contrary to the negative implications of the Indian commerce clause and basic canons of construction in federal Indian law (*see* Ch. 2, Sec. C), this doctrine meant that states had some residual sovereignty over Indian affairs unless Congress chose to place them in an unequal position through a disclaimer. Indeed, adherence to this doctrine would mean that Congress could not recognize a tribe, create a new reservation, or otherwise create Indian country after statehood in a state that did not have a constitutional disclaimer involving the tribe in question.

The fundamental flaws in these "equal footing" cases challenged courts to find ingenious ways of distinguishing them. Thus the *McBratney* case has come to be thought about as a case involving criminal jurisdiction over a crime by a non-Indian against the person or property of another non-Indian in Indian country, an approach which limits the case to its facts and ignores its rationale. Rather than focusing on the state disclaimer, courts have emphasized the absence of a federal Indian affairs interest warranting application of federal criminal laws, an interesting point given that reservation-based crimes threaten the entire surrounding population. The "equal footing" holding in *Ward* was all but overruled in *Minnesota v. Mille Lacs Band of Chippewa Indians*, 526 U.S. 172, 203–04 (1999), presented in Ch. 2, Sec. C, where the Court said:

> . . . [The "equal footing" doctrine] prevents the Federal Government from impairing fundamental attributes of state sovereignty when it admits new States into the Union. According to the *Race Horse* Court, because the Treaty rights conflicted irreconcilably with state regulation of natural resources — "an essential attribute of its governmental existence," — the Treaty rights were held an invalid impairment of Wyoming's sovereignty. Thus, those rights could not survive Wyoming's admission to the Union on "equal footing" with the original States.

> But *Race Horse* rested on a false premise. As this Court's subsequent cases have made clear, an Indian tribe's treaty rights to hunt, fish, and gather on state land are not irreconcilable with a State's sovereignty over the natural resources in the State. Rather, Indian treaty rights can coexist with state management of natural resources. Although States have important interests in regulating wildlife and natural resources within their borders, this authority is shared with the Federal Government when the Federal Government exercises one of its enumerated constitutional powers, such as treaty making. U.S. Const., Art. VI, cl. 2. . . . Thus, because treaty rights are reconcilable with state sovereignty over natural resources, statehood by itself is insufficient to extinguish Indian treaty rights to hunt, fish, and gather on land within state boundaries.

5. **Toward the Modern Era:** Beyond its somewhat confused decisions involving disclaimers and the equal footing doctrine, the Supreme Court did not return in a substantial manner to the problem of inherent state authority over Indians in Indian country until 1959. In the interim, allotment and termination policies had focused attention on unsuccessful legislative solutions to these jurisdictional questions. Thus, as recently as 1945, Justice Black could proclaim, "The policy of leaving Indians free from state jurisdiction and control is deeply rooted in the Nation's history." *Rice v. Olson*, 324 U.S. 786, 789 (1945). In 1981, Professor Clinton summarized the long-standing federal rule still prevailing as late as 1959 as follows: "[I]n the absence of clear and specific congressional authorization state law had no force in Indian country except in those cases where no Indian was involved and no Indian interest affected." Robert N. Clinton, *State Power over Indian Reservations: A Critical Comment on Burger Court Doctrine*, 26 S.D. L. REV. 434, 438 (1981). Is

such a rule consistent with the self-determination model of tribal-federal relations, or even a treaty federalism model? Would these models admit a congressional role in allowing state jurisdiction?

3. Congressionally Authorized State Power in Indian Country

During the period of treaty-making, the federal government allowed states little or no role within Indian country. At most, as in the Treaty with the Nez Perce, *supra*, a treaty might forbid state power (in that instance, taxing power over tribal lands) *unless* Congress specifically permits it. However, treaty references to congressional authorization of state power suggested that Congress could properly exercise its treaty-making and commerce powers by lifting limits on state authority arising from the negative implications of the Indian commerce clause. In other words, these provisions suggest that the Indian commerce clause simultaneously denied state power and allowed Congress to approve state power over Indian affairs.

Congress's initial forays into authorizing state jurisdiction in Indian country involved taxation of allotments, and extended beyond tribes such as the Nez Perce that had treaties alluding to such impositions. *See, e.g.*, 25 U.S.C. § 349 (providing that upon issuance of a fee patent to an allottee under the General Allotment Act of 1887, "all restrictions as to . . . taxation of said land shall be removed"). Allotment attacked the conceptual foundation of legal doctrines barring state authority, by weakening collective tribal structures and pushing individual Indians toward assimilation. In this colonial domination model of tribal-federal relations, Congress treated state taxing jurisdiction over allotted lands as a stepping-stone toward complete integration of tribal members, preparing them for broader responsibilities and gradually weaning them from federal protection. In fact, the financial burden of state taxes, coupled with Indians' lack of preparation for economic development of their allotments, often forced them into tax sales or leasing decisions. JANET A. McDONNELL, THE DISPOSSESSION OF THE AMERICAN INDIAN 1887–1934, 100–101, 106–07 (1991).

The Supreme Court upheld state taxing jurisdiction exercised under congressional auspices, never doubting that Congress could allow states such inroads into tribal self-rule. *See Goudy v. Meath*, 203 U.S. 146 (1906). Coming at the height of the Supreme Court's "plenary power" holdings, these cases depict federal laws authorizing state jurisdiction as just another tool effectuating federal Indian policy. But a federal law authorizing state jurisdiction pursuant to a treaty provision such as the one with the Nez Perce is quite different from one allowing state taxation in the far more common cases where treaties are silent on that subject or actually promise freedom from application of state law. Tribes protested the state taxation provisions, rightly perceiving the threats to their land bases and the well-being of their members. *See* BLUE CLARK, LONE WOLF V. HITCHCOCK: TREATY RIGHTS AND INDIAN LAW AT THE END OF THE NINETEENTH CENTURY (1994).

Some federal allotment laws also suggested that Indian allottees, not merely their allotted property, would be subject to state law. In the Burke Act of 1906, Congress provided that upon expiration of the trust period of an allotment and issuance of a patent in fee, "each and every allottee shall have the benefit of and be subject to the laws, both civil and criminal, of the State or Territory in which they may reside. . . . " 25 U.S.C. § 349. Such provisions made sense, however, only if federal allotment policies ultimately attained their intended goal, which was the extinguishment of tribal sovereignty. If instead Indian nations persisted as governments within defined territories, conflicts and confusion would erupt between states and tribes as jurisdiction varied with land status. In fact, pursuit of allotment's assimilationist goal came to a halt when Congress adopted the Indian Reorganization Act of 1934 (IRA). The IRA ended further allotment, extended indefinitely the trust period of existing allotments, and established a framework for the restoration of tribal integrity. Taking account of the IRA, the Supreme Court subsequently held that language of the Burke Act subjecting allottees to state jurisdiction applied only to the allottees themselves, not to their Indian grantees, devisees, or heirs. *Moe v. Confederated Salish & Kootenai Tribes*, 425 U.S. 463, 478–79 (1976).

In the 1940s and 1950s, Congress again turned to state jurisdiction as an instrument of pro-assimilationist federal Indian policy. First with respect to individual reservations and states, and later on a more comprehensive basis in Public Law 280, passed in 1953, Congress empowered states to exercise some criminal and civil jurisdiction over Indians within Indian country. *See* Ch. 5, Sec. A. In some instances, the states were directed to exercise such jurisdiction, but only after federal consultation with the states to assure that they were willing to take over federal functions such as law enforcement. Before Public Law 280 was amended in 1968, Congress rarely sought or secured tribal consent to such state jurisdiction.

Exercises of federal power to authorize state jurisdiction are often described as "delegations," with Congress delegating its otherwise preemptive authority over Indian affairs to the states. Courts have assumed or concluded, with only limited analysis, that Congress's power over Indian affairs extends to such delegations, even in the face of conflicting treaty provisions. *Anderson v. Britton*, 318 P.2d 291 (Or. 1957); *Anderson v. Gladden*, 293 F.2d 463 (9th Cir. 1961); *Robinson v. Sigler*, 187 N.W.2d 756 (Neb. 1971); *Robinson v. Wolff*, 349 F. Supp. 514 (D. Neb. 1972); *Idaho v. Fanning*, 759 P.2d 937 (Ida. Ct. App. 1988); *Oyler v. Allenbrand*, 23 F.3d 292 (10th Cir. 1994) (Kansas Act); *United States v. Burns*, 725 F. Supp. 116 (N.D.N.Y. 1989) (N.Y. Act). The United States Supreme Court has construed statutes delegating jurisdiction to states without closely examining Congress's power to enact such laws. *See California v. Cabazon Band of Mission Indians*, 480 U.S. 202 (1987); *Washington v. Confederated Bands & Tribes of the Yakima Indian Nation*, 439 U.S. 463 (1979); *Bryan v. Itasca County*, 426 U.S. 373 (1976).

What does it mean to describe state power as "delegated" from the federal government? Early lower court decisions examined federal statutes that introduced obligatory state criminal jurisdiction in place of federal jurisdiction under Indian country criminal statutes. They upheld state jurisdiction on the theory that states possess inherent jurisdiction over Indians in Indian country, authority which is suppressed while federal jurisdiction exists but which becomes liberated when federal jurisdiction is withdrawn. *See, e.g., Anderson v. Gladden*, 293 F.2d 463, 468 (9th Cir. 1961). On this view, Congress was not conferring jurisdiction on the state, but merely abandoning its preemptive role in the field by eliminating the application of its Indian country criminal laws. Does this theory properly reflect the Supreme Court's analysis of state jurisdiction issues in the absence of congressional action? If Congress failed to assert federal jurisdiction over reservation Indians (as it does in most civil matters), would state jurisdiction exist under this theory even without congressional action? Recall *Worcester*'s pronouncement that "The Cherokee Nation . . . is a distinct community, occupying its own territory, . . . in which the laws of Georgia can have no force."

An alternative approach would be to recognize that states forfeited their inherent authority over reservation Indians by virtue of joining the constitutional order, but that Congress may act affirmatively to lift the jurisdictional ban. This alternative approach suggests that a congressional delegation statute has in some sense "conferred" jurisdiction on the states. Under this approach, when Congress does approve state jurisdiction, does the state become an arm of the federal government, subject to all the Bill of Rights provisions applicable only to federal acts, such as the Seventh Amendment? Or is it still possible that Congress has only lifted a ban, albeit a constitutional ban, and the resulting state jurisdiction is an exercise of state rather than federal power? Should this analysis differ from the analysis of federal statutes that authorize tribal jurisdiction that otherwise would be deemed outside "inherent" tribal authority? *See* Ch. 3, Sec. C.2.

If Congress must act to establish state jurisdiction over reservation Indians, then its acts must be tested against constitutional or other limits on the exercise of congressional power. As one Idaho appellate court has noted, federal statutes "delegating" jurisdiction to states should be examined in light of Supreme Court decisions placing limits on the exercise of federal "plenary" power. *Idaho v. Fanning, supra.* More specifically, such statutes should be reviewed to determine whether they are "tied rationally to the fulfillment of Congress's unique obligation toward the Indians." *Morton v. Mancari*, 417 U.S. 535 (1974). *See* Ch. 2, Sec. B.1; Sec. A.1, this chapter. The rationale for Public Law 280 and similar federal statutes focused on the need to address "lawlessness" in Indian Country and the value of state jurisdiction as a means of achieving assimilation through the application of non-Indian norms. *See* Carole E. Goldberg, *Public Law 280 and the Problem of Lawlessness in California Indian Country*, 44 UCLA L. REV. 1405 (1997). Should state jurisdiction that is imposed on such bases be deemed a lawful pursuit of Congress's obligation to treat with tribes as governments? Is there any other "unique obligation" to the Indians that a law such as Public Law 280 might be advancing? For purposes of this inquiry, should it matter that some of the objectives of Public Law 280, such as reducing "lawlessness," could be advanced by federal support for tribal institutions rather than authorizing state jurisdiction?

Apart from constitutional objections, federal statutes delegating jurisdiction to states have been challenged because they violate federal treaty promises to shield Indian nations from state authority. For example, Article X of the Treaty with the Shawnee of 1831 provides that "the United States guarantees that [the lands granted to the Shawnees] shall never be within the bounds of any State or territory, nor subject to the laws thereof. . . . " Other treaty provisions, such as Article IX of the Treaty with the Klamath and Modoc of 1870, contain agreements by the Indians to submit to federal law, implicitly excluding the application of state law. In the absence of tribal consent, federal laws delegating jurisdiction to states over these tribes therefore constitute treaty abrogations. Does that make them invalid? *See* Ch. 1, Sec. D.2; Sec. A.1, this chapter. What principles of construction should be applied when a federal statute authorizing state jurisdiction conflicts with treaty promises?

In *Washington v. Confederated Bands and Tribes of the Yakima Nation*, 439 U.S. 463 (1979), the Supreme Court entertained a wholesale challenge to Public Law 280 on the ground that it authorized future state assumptions of jurisdiction without regard to the particular tribes affected or their specific treaty guarantees. In rejecting this challenge, the Court assumed Congress's power to abrogate, and confined its inquiry to whether Congress had expressed the requisite intent to set aside treaty guarantees given that it had not designated all the tribes that would be subjected to future assumptions of state jurisdiction. After nodding to the canons of construction, the Court characterized the Tribe's argument as "tendentious." According to the Court,

> The treaty right asserted by the Tribe is jurisdictional. So also is the entire subject matter of Pub. L. 280. To accept the Tribe's position would be to hold that Congress could not pass a jurisdictional law of general applicability to Indian country unless in so doing it itemized all potentially conflicting treaty rights that it wished to affect. This we decline to do. The intent to abrogate inconsistent treaty rights is clear enough from the express terms of Pub. L. 280.

Does the Court's analysis merely underscore Congress's disregard for Indian nations' reasonable expectations and lack of consent to be governed by state law when it enacted Public Law 280? In contrast, a court construing the federal statute that delegated jurisdiction to New York refused to apply it to internal tribal disputes out of concern for treaty guarantees to the Seneca. *Bowen v. Doyle*, 880 F. Supp. 99 (W.D.N.Y. 1995). Reflecting concerns for community safety as well as respect for local tribal authority, the Indian Law and Order Commission, discussed in Sec. A.3, above, recommended that Congress allow tribes to opt out of state criminal jurisdiction, in whole or in part. For further discussion of this recommendation, see Ch. 5, Sec. A.

If Congress specifies a comprehensive method for states to acquire jurisdiction over Indians within Indian country, can a state later assert jurisdiction if it *hasn't* followed the prescribed method? What if the tribe involved has voted in favor of state jurisdiction or entered into a cooperative agreement? Apart from the six mandatory jurisdiction states named in the statute, Public Law 280 set out a precise scheme for all others wishing to assume jurisdiction. *See* Ch. 5, Sec. A. Thus, as the modern era for state jurisdiction opened, courts had to factor this open invitation into their decisions. In effect, the federal government had said to the states: if you want to become the instruments of our colonial domination, you must follow our procedures.

4. The Modern Era

To understand the scope of state authority in Indian country, it is helpful to make several analytical distinctions. First is the distinction between inherent and federally authorized jurisdiction, developed above. Second is the distinction between criminal and civil jurisdiction. Questions of state criminal jurisdiction are relatively easier to resolve than questions of state civil jurisdiction because most state criminal jurisdiction in Indian country is preempted by a reasonably clear set of federal statutes specifically addressed to jurisdiction over non-Indians as well as Indians, discussed in Sec. A.3, this chapter. Absent federal authorization through Public Law 280 or some similar statute, state criminal jurisdiction within Indian country has been limited to crimes involving only non-Indians, in keeping with the decision in *McBratney, supra.*

In contrast, there is no set of preemptive federal statutes that asserts federal power over the range of civil jurisdiction matters, both adjudicative and regulatory, that arise in Indian country. Throughout the nineteenth century and first half of the twentieth century, the BIA flexed this federal power administratively, under general congressional authorization to manage Indian affairs. For the past forty years, Congress has generally conceded such matters to tribal authority. The main congressional intervention in the area of civil jurisdiction has been through Public Law 280, which directed some states to open their courts to civil actions against Indians and enabled all others to do so. But the language of Public Law 280 does not address the full range of civil jurisdiction, especially not civil regulatory jurisdiction or civil adjudicative jurisdiction over non-Indians. *See* Ch. 5, Sec. A. Where Public Law 280 does not apply or have preemptive effect, questions of civil jurisdiction have been primarily resolved by analyzing the inherent reach of state authority and the preemptive implications of statutes and treaties that may not deal expressly with jurisdiction.

A third set of distinctions involves subcategories of questions subsumed within the general category of civil jurisdiction. For example, analytically there is a discernible distinction between the legislative authority of the state, *e.g.*, the power to regulate or tax, in Indian country and the civil adjudicative jurisdiction of the state courts to resolve private disputes. Basic principles of conflicts of law suggest that adjudicative power, especially the power of courts exercising inherent or "general" jurisdiction, may extend to matters to which the forum state could not apply its laws. *See Home Ins. v. Dick*, 281 U.S. 397 (1930) (denying application of forum state law to a controversy over property within the court's jurisdiction because of lack of sufficient state contacts with the parties and the occurrence). Underlying this principle is the view that adjudicative jurisdiction merely creates a process for private dispute resolution, without threatening the sovereignty of other political entities in the way extension of regulatory or taxing power would do. From a tribal perspective, does state taxing or regulatory power have a greater impact on self-rule than state adjudication of a dispute arising within tribal territory? Professor Robert Porter claims that non-adversarial tribal processes of dispute resolution are integral to the harmonious functioning of tribal communities. Offering the example of the Iroquois, he shows how channeling intra-tribal disputes into adversarial non-Indian courts has made it much more difficult to sustain traditional tribal organization. Robert B. Porter, *Strengthening Tribal Sovereignty Through Peacemaking: How the Anglo-American Legal Tradition Destroys Indigenous Societies*, 28 COLUM. HUM. RTS. L. REV. 235 (1997). With this observation in mind, should the same rules or principles apply to the resolution of a question of the reach of a state's taxing authority in Indian country that would be applied to determine the scope of state court subject matter jurisdiction, whether the parties are Indian or non-Indian? Even within the issue of the scope of civil adjudicative jurisdiction of state courts in Indian country, there are separate sub-issues, such as the distinction between subject matter and personal jurisdiction, discussed below.

If the jurisdictional patterns largely excluding state law from operating in Indian country are to be altered, which body has been charged by the Constitution with the power to so affect tribal sovereignty, Congress or the Court? How has the Supreme Court justified its development of legal doctrine in this area? Is its implicit model of the tribal-federal relationship the same as the one that Congress seems to be using?

a.   State Adjudicative Jurisdiction

WILLIAMS v. LEE
United States Supreme Court
358 U.S. 217 (1959)

MR. JUSTICE BLACK delivered the opinion of the Court.

Respondent, who is not an Indian, operates a general store in Arizona on the Navajo Indian Reservation under a license required by federal statute.[55] He brought this action in the Superior Court of Arizona against petitioners, a Navajo Indian and his wife who live on the Reservation, to collect for goods sold them there on credit. Over petitioners' motion to dismiss on the ground that jurisdiction lay in the tribal court rather than in the state court, judgment was entered in favor of respondent. The Supreme Court of Arizona affirmed, holding that since no Act of Congress expressly forbids their doing so Arizona courts are free to exercise jurisdiction over civil suits by non-Indians against Indians though the action arises on an Indian reservation. Because this was a doubtful determination of the important question of state power over Indian affairs, [certiorari was granted].

Despite bitter criticism and the defiance of Georgia which refused to obey this Court's mandate in *Worcester* the broad principles of that decision came to be accepted as law. Over the years this Court has modified these principles in cases where essential tribal relations were not involved and where the rights of Indians would not be jeopardized, but the basic policy of *Worcester* has remained. Thus,

---

[55] [1] 31 Stat. 1066, as amended, 32 Stat. 1009, 25 U.S.C. § 262, provides:

> Any person desiring to trade with the Indians on any Indian reservation shall, upon establishing the fact, to the satisfaction of the Commissioner of Indian Affairs, that he is a proper person to engage in such trade, be permitted to do so under such rules and regulations as the Commissioner of Indian Affairs may prescribe for the protection of said Indians.

suits by Indians against outsiders in state courts have been sanctioned. [*E.g.,*] *Felix v. Patrick*, 145 U.S. 317, 332. And state courts have been allowed to try non-Indians who committed crimes against each other on a reservation. *E.g., New York ex rel. Ray v. Martin*, 326 U.S. 496. But if the crime was by or against an Indian, tribal jurisdiction or that expressly conferred on other courts by Congress has remained exclusive. *Donnelly v. United States*, 228 U.S. 243, 269–272; *Williams v. United States*, 327 U.S. 711. Essentially, absent governing Acts of Congress, the question has always been whether the state action infringed on the right of reservation Indians to make their own laws and be ruled by them. *Cf. Utah & Northern Railway v. Fisher*, 116 U.S. 28.

Congress has also acted consistently upon the assumption that the States have no power to regulate the affairs of Indians on a reservation. To assure adequate government of the Indian tribes it enacted comprehensive statutes in 1834 regulating trade with Indians and organizing a Department of Indian Affairs. 4 Stat. 729, 735. Not satisfied solely with centralized government of Indians, it encouraged tribal governments and courts to become stronger and more highly organized. *E.g.,* [the IRA.] Congress has followed a policy calculated eventually to make all Indians full-fledged participants in American society. This policy contemplates criminal and civil jurisdiction over Indians by any State ready to assume the burdens that go with it as soon as the educational and economic status of the Indians permits the change without disadvantage to them. *See* H.R. Rep. No. 848, 83d Cong., 1st Sess. 3, 6, 7 (1953). Significantly, when Congress has wished the States to exercise this power it has expressly granted them the jurisdiction which *Worcester v. Georgia* had denied.[56]

No departure from the policies which have been applied to other Indians is apparent in the relationship between the United States and the Navajos. On June 1, 1868, a treaty was signed between General William T. Sherman, for the United States, and numerous chiefs and headmen of the "Navajo nation or tribe of Indians."[57] At the time this document was signed the Navajos were an exiled people, forced by the United States to live crowded together on a small piece of land on the Pecos River in eastern New Mexico, some 300 miles east of the area they had occupied before the coming of the white man. In return for their promises to keep peace, this treaty "set apart" for "their permanent home" a portion of what had been their native country, and provided that no one, except United States Government personnel, was to enter the reserved area. Implicit in these treaty terms, as it was in the treaties with the Cherokees involved in *Worcester v. Georgia*, was the understanding that the internal affairs of the Indians remained exclusively within the jurisdiction of whatever tribal government existed. Since then, Congress

---

[56] [6] *See, e.g.*, 62 Stat. 1224, 64 Stat. 845, 25 U.S.C. §§ 232, 233 (1952) (granting broad civil and criminal jurisdiction to New York); 18 U.S.C. § 1162, 28 U.S.C. § 1360 (granting broad civil and criminal jurisdiction to California, Minnesota, Nebraska, Oregon, and Wisconsin). The series of statutes granting extensive jurisdiction over Oklahoma Indians to state courts are discussed in Cohen, [Handbook of Federal Indian Law] at 985–1051.

[57] [7] 15 Stat. 667. In 16 Stat. 566 (1871), Congress declared that no Indian tribe or nation within the United States should thereafter be recognized as an independent power with whom the United States could execute a treaty but provided that this should not impair the obligations of any treaty previously ratified. Thus the 1868 treaty with the Navajos survived this Act.

and the Bureau of Indian Affairs have assisted in strengthening the Navajo tribal government and its courts. See the Navajo-Hopi Rehabilitation Act of 1950, § 6, 64 Stat. 46, 25 U.S.C. § 636. The Tribe itself has in recent years greatly improved its legal system through increased expenditures and better-trained personnel. Today the Navajo Courts of Indian Offenses exercise broad criminal and civil jurisdiction which covers suits by outsiders against Indian defendants. No Federal Act has given state courts jurisdiction over such controversies.[58] In a general statute Congress did express its willingness to have any State assume jurisdiction over reservation Indians if the State Legislature or the people vote affirmatively to accept such responsibility. To date, Arizona has not accepted jurisdiction, possibly because the people of the State anticipate that the burdens accompanying such power might be considerable.

There can be no doubt that to allow the exercise of state jurisdiction here would undermine the authority of the tribal courts over Reservation affairs and hence would infringe on the right of the Indians to govern themselves. It is immaterial that respondent is not an Indian. He was on the Reservation and the transaction with an Indian took place there. The cases in this Court have consistently guarded the authority of Indian governments over their reservations. Congress recognized this authority in the Navajos in the Treaty of 1868, and has done so ever since. If this power is to be taken away from them, it is for Congress to do it. [*Lone Wolf v. Hitchcock.*]

Reversed.

NOTES

1. ***Williams* and State Courts of General Jurisdiction:** *Williams v. Lee* is an extraordinary decision from the perspective of conflicts of law. Normally state courts, as courts of general subject matter jurisdiction, may hear cases arising anywhere and under any set of laws, so long as they can secure personal jurisdiction over the defendant. The persistence of transient personal jurisdiction means, for example, that a state court could hear a case between two Italian citizens over a dispute that arose in Italy so long as the plaintiff preferred an American forum and the defendant was served while visiting the state for business or pleasure. If the defendant in *Williams* had been served while traveling in Arizona outside the Navajo reservation, could the Arizona court have heard the case against him? What makes Indian country different for purposes of state court jurisdiction? For an overview of the events and historical context leading up to the *Williams* dispute, *see* Bethany R. Berger, *Sheep, Sovereignty, and the Supreme Court: The Story of* Williams v. Lee *in* INDIAN LAW STORIES (Carole Goldberg, Kevin K. Washburn, and Philip P. Frickey, eds., 2011).

---

[58] [9] In the 1949 Navajo-Hopi Rehabilitation Bill, S. 1407, 81st Cong., 1st Sess., setting up a 10-year program of capital and other improvements on the Reservation, Congress provided for concurrent state, federal and tribal jurisdiction. President Truman vetoed the bill because he felt that subjecting the Navajo and Hopi to state jurisdiction was undesirable in view of their illiteracy, poverty and primitive social concepts. He was also impressed by the fact that the Indians vigorously opposed the bill. 95 Cong. Rec. 14784–14785. After the objectionable features of the bill were deleted it was passed again and became law. 64 Stat. 44, 25 U.S.C. §§ 631–640.

2. The Rationale of *Williams*: Does Justice Black's opinion in *Williams v. Lee* draw a sharp line between those occasions when the state can and when it cannot assume jurisdiction? The principle derived is one which could cause extraordinary debate: When does state jurisdiction "undermine the authority of the tribal courts over Reservation affairs and [therefore] infringe on the right of the Indians to govern themselves?" Upon what legal theory did the exclusion of state authority in *Williams* rest? Was state power limited merely because of the existence of tribal sovereignty? Would the result in the case have been the same had the Navajo not been a tribe recognized by the federal government in treaty and statute as possessing tribal self-governing authority? Was federal law, then, preemptive of state jurisdiction? If so, was the preemptive federal law (1) the Indian commerce clause, (2) the treaties or statutes recognizing tribal self-government, (3) Public Law 280, or (4) some combination of the foregoing? What practical difference does it make as to which source of federal law is seen as preemptive?

3. The Infringement Test: A Sword for State Power or a Shield for the Tribes? Some state courts initially regarded the negative implications of the *Williams v. Lee* infringement test as an invitation to extend state jurisdiction to many situations in Indian country that they did not think involved tribal self-government. *McClanahan v. State Tax Comm'n*, presented in Sec. 4.B.2 below, illustrates this state strategy, as Arizona argued that a state personal income tax on reservation-based tribal members was no infringement because it was directed at individual tribal members, not the Navajo Nation itself or tribal property. In rejecting that argument, the Supreme Court seemed to grasp that any exercise of state governing power could complicate or even impede tribal efforts to establish government policy. Note that the Navajo Nation did not impose its own personal income tax on tribal members, yet the Supreme Court still found the state tax invalid. Should a tribe's decision not to exercise subject matter jurisdiction over a particular type of dispute justify state jurisdiction? What if the tribe believes the matters should be resolved without court intervention altogether, through spiritual leaders or community elders? By contrast, some federal courts regarded the infringement test as an important shield of tribal sovereignty against the intrusions of state authority. *Arizona ex rel. Merrill v. Turtle*, 413 F.2d 683 (9th Cir. 1969) (finding no state extradition authority over Indian accused discovered on Navajo Reservation and wanted for a crime in another state). If Public Law 280 has the preemptive effect described in *Williams* and *McClanahan*, is there any need to struggle with the infringement test in such cases?

4. Infringement Test and Nonmembers: Of what significance to the decision in *Williams* is the fact that a non-Indian is involved in the adjudication? Most obviously, the non-Indian plaintiff is required to have his rights adjudicated in a tribal court, a form of tribal jurisdiction over non-Indians. *See* Ch. 3, Sec. C.1. Would the result and rationale have been the same if a Navajo, or for that matter a Cheyenne, had been the plaintiff in the case?

Notice, however, that the non-Indian is a *plaintiff* in the *Williams* action, not the defendant. Had the non-Indian trader been sued by a Navajo consumer for breach of warranty in the Arizona state courts, would the result be the same? Consider Justice Black's statement that "suits by Indians against outsiders in state courts have been sanctioned." Can that statement be reconciled with the general rationale in *Williams* and the infringement test in particular? *See, e.g., Paiz v. Hughes*, 417 P.2d 51 (N.M. 1966) ("Permitting the [Indian] plaintiffs in these cases to prosecute their claims [against non-Indian defendants] for personal injuries and alleged wrongful death, in the New Mexico courts, will not affect the rights of the Jicarilla-Apache Indians to make their own laws and be ruled by them, will not affect their tribal relations, and will not affect the rights of the Federal Government.").

Can the result in *Paiz v. Hughes* be reconciled with tribal sovereignty? Should an individual tribal member be permitted to waive the authority of the tribe over the subject matter of the suit? Is tribal self-government an individual or a group right? Is this dilemma easier to resolve if a state court hearing such a case applies tribal law based on the fact that the claim arose within Indian country? Should a state court be *obliged* to apply tribal law in such a case, as a matter of federal Indian law? The Supreme Court has assumed, without much discussion, that state courts are available to hear reservation-based civil claims brought by one nonmember against another, even when there are substantial tribal contacts with the lawsuit. *See Strate v. A-1 Contractors*, 520 U.S. 438, 459 (1997), presented in Ch. 3, Sec. C.1. Should the state court apply, or be obliged to apply, tribal law under those circumstances as well? *Cf.* 28 U.S.C. § 1360(c) (requiring state courts hearing civil suits pursuant to Public Law 280 to apply any "tribal ordinance or custom heretofore or hereafter adopted . . . if not inconsistent with any applicable civil law of the State. . . . ").

The question of tribal power to sue a non-Indian in state court was presented in *Three Affiliated Tribes of the Fort Berthold Reservation v. Wold Eng'g, P.C.*, 467 U.S. 138 (1984) (*Three Tribes I*), which involved a suit by a tribe against a non-Indian for breach of contract and negligence in conjunction with work on a tribal water project. The Three Affiliated Tribes were suing in state court because the tribal court lacked jurisdiction, and out of concern that even if the Tribes authorized such jurisdiction, any tribal court judgment might not be enforced in North Dakota. North Dakota had permitted such suits in its courts before Public Law 280, but subsequently adopted a statute prohibiting jurisdiction over claims arising in Indian country unless the Indian party consented to full state jurisdiction. In practice, that meant that the Tribes could not sue the non-Indian unless there was a waiver of tribal sovereign immunity. North Dakota argued that it was merely disclaiming jurisdiction that federal law barred under the *Williams* infringement test. The Supreme Court held,

> [W]e fail to see how the exercise of state-court jurisdiction in this case would interfere with the right of tribal Indians to govern themselves under their own laws. . . . This Court . . . repeatedly has approved the exercise of jurisdiction by state courts over claims by Indians against non-Indians, even when those claims arose in Indian country. See *McClanahan v. Arizona State Tax Comm'n*, 411 U.S., at 173 (dictum); *Poafpybitty v. Skelly Oil Co.*, 390 U.S. 365 (1968); *Williams v. Lee*, 358 U.S., at 219 (dictum); *United States v. Candelaria*, 271 U.S. 432, 444 (1926); *Felix v. Patrick*, 145 U.S. 317, 332 (1892); *Fellows v. Blacksmith*, 19 How. 366 (1857). The interests implicated in such cases are very different from those present in *Williams v. Lee*, where a non-Indian sued an Indian in state court for debts incurred in Indian country, or in *Fisher v. District Court*, where this Court

held that a tribal court had exclusive jurisdiction over an adoption proceeding in which all parties were tribal Indians residing on a reservation. As a general matter, tribal self-government is not impeded when a State allows an Indian to enter its courts on equal terms with other persons to seek relief against a non-Indian concerning a claim arising in Indian country. *The exercise of state jurisdiction is particularly compatible with tribal autonomy when, as here, the suit is brought by the tribe itself and the tribal court lacked jurisdiction over the claim at the time the suit was instituted.*

467 U.S. at 148–149 (emphasis added). Is the Court suggesting that infringement should be found if an individual Indian litigant sues a non-Indian and a tribal forum is available? Should Public Law 280's preemptive effect extend to suits brought by Indians against non-Indians?

   5.   The Preemptive Effect of Public Law 280: The Supreme Court has insisted on strict compliance with Public Law 280 when states attempt to exercise adjudicative jurisdiction over Indians, regardless of possible arguments that there is no "infringement" of tribal sovereignty. When Montana tried to rely on a Blackfeet tribal resolution rather than compliance with Public Law 280 to hear suits against tribal members, the United States Supreme Court balked. *Kennerly v. District Court of Montana*, 400 U.S. 423 (1971). The Court made it sound simple: "Here it is conceded that Montana took no affirmative legislative action with respect to the Blackfeet Reservation [as required by Public Law 280]. The unilateral action of the Tribal Council was insufficient to vest Montana with jurisdiction over Indian country. . . . "

   Under the broadest possible reading, Public Law 280 could operate to outlaw all state jurisdiction in Indian country outside its framework, including jurisdiction over non-Indians and regulatory jurisdiction. However, following *Kennerly*, the Court has not always given an expansive reading to the preemptive effect of Public Law 280. For example, cases such as *Washington v. Confederated Tribes of the Colville Reservation*, and *Montana v. United States* (discussed in Sec. B.4, this chapter, and Ch. 3, Sec. C.1), without significant reference to Public Law 280, suggested that states had considerable inherent authority over non-Indians in Indian country and had limited, indirect authority to require Indians to conform to state laws as a means of facilitating enforcement of legitimate state taxation or regulation of non-Indians in Indian country. Precisely why Public Law 280 was not preemptive in such situations is difficult to imagine, unless the Court was strictly confining the preemptive scope of the legislation to statutory provisions that conferred jurisdiction in criminal cases "over offenses committed by or against Indians [within] Indian country," 18 U.S.C. § 1162, and "over civil causes of action between Indians or to which Indians are parties which arise [within] Indian country," 28 U.S.C. § 1360. In *Three Tribes I, supra*, the Court declined to find that Public Law 280 preempted a suit in state court by a tribe against a non-Indian arising in Indian country, stating:

   This Court previously has recognized that Pub. L. 280 was intended to facilitate rather than to impede the transfer of jurisdictional authority to the States. *Washington v. Yakima Indian Nation*, 439 U.S., at 490; see also

Bryan v. Itasca County, 426 U.S., at 383–390. Nothing in the language or legislative history of Pub. L. 280 indicates that it was meant to divest States of pre-existing and otherwise lawfully assumed jurisdiction. Section 6 of the federal statute authorized a State whose enabling Act and constitution contained jurisdictional disclaimers "to remove any legal impediment to the *assumption* of civil and criminal jurisdiction" (emphasis added). Similarly, § 7 gave congressional consent to the assumption of jurisdiction by any other State "not having jurisdiction." By their terms, therefore, both § 6 and § 7 were designed to eliminate obstacles to the assumption of jurisdiction rather than to require pre-existing jurisdiction to be disclaimed.

467 U.S. at 150.

Yet in a second round of the same case, the Court gave a wider reading to the preemptive scope of Public Law 280. At this point in the litigation the question was whether Public Law 280 prevented the state from disclaiming exercise of its authority over Indian country lawsuits absent an Indian plaintiff's full consent to jurisdiction, including a waiver of tribal sovereign immunity. The Court treated North Dakota's disclaimer of jurisdiction over Indian country lawsuits as equivalent to "retrocession" under Public Law 280, a statutory process provided by Congress in 1968 that allowed states which had assumed Public law 280 jurisdiction to give it up. Since North Dakota had not complied with the federal procedures for carrying out retrocession, its disclaimer was preempted. *Three Affiliated Tribes of the Fort Berthold Reservation v. Wold Engineering (Three Tribes II)*, 476 U.S. 877, 885–87 (1986). Importantly, the specific language of Public Law 280 does not refer to suits brought by Indians against *non-Indians*. Furthermore, while Public Law 280 did establish a mechanism for states to return or "retrocede" jurisdiction to the federal government, by its terms this mechanism applied only to jurisdiction acquired under the Act. In the *Three Tribes* litigation, the state was disclaiming jurisdiction that it had previously assumed outside the framework of Public Law 280. Nonetheless, the Court found preemption.

   6.   Implications of *Strate v. A-1 Contractors* for State Jurisdiction: Some of the United States Supreme Court's recent decisions limiting tribal jurisdiction (*see* Ch. 3, Sec. C.1) have been read by states as an invitation to broaden state jurisdiction over the same matters. Indeed, if *Williams v. Lee*'s infringement test rests on protection of tribal powers, won't litigants want to use cases like *Strate v. A-1 Contractors*, 520 U.S. 438 (1997), which curtail those tribal powers, to argue that state jurisdiction causes no infringement? Recall that in *Strate*, the Court denied a tribal court's jurisdiction to hear a tort action between two non-Indians that arose on a state right-of-way within the reservation, land that qualified as Indian country under 18 U.S.C. § 1151(a). What if that suit had been against a tribal member, making it analogous to *Williams v. Lee*? Would *Strate* alter the *Williams* outcome of exclusive tribal jurisdiction solely because the accident occurred on a state right-of-way?

   Presented with just such a scenario in *Winer v. Penny Enterprises, Inc.*, 674 N.W.2d 9 (N.D. 2004), the Supreme Court of North Dakota answered "no." According to that court, *Strate*'s analysis was limited to questions of tribal governance over nonmembers, and thus does not govern questions of state jurisdiction. Describing *Williams v. Lee* as still the "seminal" authority on state civil jurisdiction in Indian country, and citing for this proposition the AMERICAN INDIAN LAW DESKBOOK published by the Conference of Western Attorneys General, the Court went on to note that "The interests implicated when a non-Indian is sued are 'very different from those present' when a non-Indian sues an Indian in state court over an incident occurring in Indian country" (citing *Three Affiliated Tribes v. Wold Engineering, P.C.*, 476 U.S. 877 (1986)). The Court concluded, "If *Strate* signals a drastic departure from the state court jurisdictional principles in *Williams v. Lee* and its progeny, it is well hidden in the *Strate* decision. *Strate* is distinguishable from the situation in this case, and until the United States Supreme Court declares otherwise, we conclude *Strate* does not govern our analysis."

7. Personal or Subject Matter Jurisdiction? Is the result in *Williams v. Lee* predicated upon a lack of subject matter jurisdiction over the controversy, upon the lack of jurisdiction over the person of the defendant in the state court, or some other principle? If the sale of the goods in *Williams* had occurred outside of the Navajo Reservation in Flagstaff, Arizona, for example, would the courts of the State of Arizona lack subject matter jurisdiction over the controversy? If the state courts have subject matter jurisdiction over the case, does that mean that state officials may enter the Reservation and lawfully serve process on an Indian defendant domiciled there? In two nineteenth-century cases, *Harkness v. Hyde*, 98 U.S. 476 (1879), and *Langford v. Monteith*, 102 U.S. 145 (1880), the Supreme Court seemed to suggest that Indian reservations were jurisdictional enclaves outside of the reach of process issuing from the courts of the state or federal territory in which they were located. The breadth of that holding is clouded, however, since the *Langford* opinion contained dicta suggesting the now discredited approach that this special jurisdictional enclave status was dependent upon the existence of explicit treaty or statutory language applicable to the particular reservation that expressly disclaimed such state or territorial jurisdiction. Unfortunately, the Supreme Court has not returned to the issue to clarify it. Does the Court's decision in *Nevada v. Hicks*, presented in Ch. 3, Sec. C.1, bear in any way on this question? Does *Hicks* undermine *Harkness* and *Langford*? In default of a definitive Supreme Court decision, the courts are split on the question of exercise of jurisdiction over the person of an individual located in Indian country. *Compare Francisco v. State*, 556 P.2d 1 (Ariz. 1976) ("based on the reasoning in *McClanahan* [and *Williams v. Lee*] that the Executive Order [setting aside the Papago Reservation] would preclude the extension of state law to Indians on the reservation, including the laws which effectuate the authority in the Sheriff to serve process"), *with State Sec., Inc. v. Anderson*, 506 P.2d 786 (N.M. 1973) ("State jurisdiction does not eliminate Indian jurisdiction, it exists concurrently with it. There is no interference with Indian self-government."). Should it make any difference whether the person upon whom state process is served in Indian country is a member of the tribe or, for that matter, even an Indian? *See State v. Zaman*, 984 P.2d 528 (Ariz. 1999) (sheriff may serve process on a non-Indian residing on reservation in a paternity action over which state court has jurisdiction). Does it make any difference whether process is served by a state official, by a private process server, or by mail? Given the expansion of concepts of jurisdiction beyond territorial boundaries under *International Shoe Co. v. Washington*, 326 U.S. 310 (1945), cannot states that are frequently confronted with this problem, like Arizona or New Mexico, eliminate whatever legal impediment exists by enacting long-arm type statutes authorizing service by mail on persons domiciled on Indian reservations? For an excellent article setting forth proposals to use long-arm statutes to solve problems of jurisdiction over persons and property in Indian country, see William C. Canby, Jr., *Civil Jurisdiction and the Indian Reservation*, 1973 UTAH L. REV. 206. If states may secure jurisdiction over persons located in Indian country by simply enacting a long-arm statute, why should they not be authorized to secure process more directly by sending a state sheriff onto the reservation to serve process personally on the defendant? Does *Hicks* affect Judge Canby's analysis in any way?

JOE v. MARCUM
United States Court of Appeals, Tenth Circuit
621 F.2d 358 (1980)

McWILLIAMS, CIRCUIT JUDGE.

Garnishment proceedings to enforce a $247.35 default judgment trigger the present proceeding, which involves, among other things, the United States Constitution, the Navajo Treaty of 1868, the New Mexico Enabling Act, the Civil Rights Act of 1968, and Navajo Tribal Statutes. The facts are simple, though the legal issues are not.

Tom S. Joe is a Navajo Indian who resides on the Navajo Indian Reservation at Shiprock, New Mexico. Joe borrowed money from USLife Credit Corporation, a New Mexico corporation. This transaction occurred in Farmington, New Mexico, which is outside the Navajo Indian Reservation. Joe apparently defaulted in repayment of the loan, and USLife brought a breach of contract action against him in the Magistrate Court of the Honorable Roy Marcum at Farmington, New Mexico. Service of process was made. Joe did not respond to the summons and complaint, and a default judgment was entered against him in the amount of $247.35. The validity of this default judgment is not in issue.

Utah International, Inc., is a Delaware corporation qualified to do business in New Mexico. Utah International operates a strip mine, known as the Navajo Mine, located on the Navajo Indian Reservation near Fruitland, New Mexico. Utah International maintains its offices on the Navajo Reservation. Joe is employed by Utah International and works at the Navajo Mine.

In an effort to enforce its judgment against Joe, USLife caused a writ of garnishment to issue out of Judge Marcum's court. Utah International was the named defendant in the garnishment proceeding. The garnishee summons was served on Utah International at its offices on the Navajo Reservation. Under New Mexico law, up to 25% of Joe's weekly salary was subject to garnishment under the writ issued by Judge Marcum.

It was in this general setting that Joe sought relief in the United States District Court for the District of New Mexico. Specifically, Joe brought suit against Marcum, USLife Credit Corporation, and Utah International, Inc. Joe asked for declaratory judgment and injunctive relief, alleging that Judge Marcum had no jurisdiction to garnish, or otherwise attach, wages due him and then in the possession of Utah International. It was further alleged that the garnishment of wages due Joe from Utah International for the use of USLife constituted a deprivation of property without due process of law, and, having been done under the color of state law, was contrary to 42 U.S.C. § 1983.

The case was presented to the United States District Court on an agreed statement of facts. Based on the pleadings, and the stipulated facts, Joe moved for summary judgment. The district court granted the motion, and entered judgment in favor of Joe. More specifically, the defendants were permanently enjoined from enforcing the writ of garnishment issued by Judge Marcum, and served on Utah International, attaching wages earned by Joe from his employment on the Navajo Reservation with Utah International. Both Judge Marcum and USLife now appeal.

[T]he basis for the district court's action is contained in paragraph 7 of its findings and conclusions. That paragraph reads as follows:

> 7. The Magistrate Court lacked jurisdiction to issue the writ of garnishment herein because of federal pre-emption of the field: Applicable federal treaties and statutes reserve to the Navajos the right to make and be governed by their own laws, and the State of New Mexico cannot empower its courts to encroach upon the right.

[W]e conclude that the action of the federal district court was correct. In thus holding, we recognize that there is authority to the contrary, and that an argument can be made that Joe should not be allowed to use the Navajo Reservation as a sanctuary to insulate himself from state court garnishment proceedings arising from an off-reservation transaction with a non-Indian lending agency. In our view, however, this argument does not withstand close analysis, as it overlooks the central and dominant factor here involved, namely, that to allow the present garnishment proceeding to stand would impinge upon tribal sovereignty.

25 U.S.C. § 1322, a part of the Civil Rights Act of 1968, provides a method whereby a state may assume jurisdiction of civil causes of action between Indians, or to which Indians are parties, which arise in areas of Indian country, with the consent of the tribe. In the instant case New Mexico has not sought to assume such jurisdiction. However, according to the appellants, any failure by New Mexico to thus assume jurisdiction is not dispositive of the controversy. It is argued that the local New Mexico state court nonetheless had jurisdiction to run the present garnishment, and that such did not in any wise impinge on tribal sovereignty. It is with this line of argument that we are not in accord.

The basic tenet of the Navajo Treaty of 1868 is that the Navajo Tribe is a sovereign entity and that, upon the reservation, the tribe possesses the right of self-government. This fundamental tenet, which is reinforced by applicable federal statutes, is the basis for our conclusion that state jurisdiction of the sort sought to be exercised here has been pre-empted. In thus holding, we recognize that the doctrine of tribal sovereignty is not an absolute, but we do believe this doctrine controls the present fact situation.

We are advised that the Navajo Tribe has its own scheme of self-government, which includes a judicial branch consisting of six district courts, a Court of Appeals, and a Supreme Judicial Council. The Navajo Tribal Code permits enforcement of judgments obtained in tribal courts by execution upon specific property owned by the judgment debtor. However, the Navajo Tribal Code does not permit the garnishment of wages. The fact that the Tribal Code provides methods of post-judgment enforcement, but not garnishment, is in our view significant.

Garnishment is a statutory remedy, which does not exist at common law. Whether wages should be subject to garnishment is a matter upon which there is no unanimity of thought. Some states, New Mexico included, permit garnishment of wages. Other states do not. Similarly, a sovereign entity such as the Navajo Tribe need not provide garnishment, if it so chooses. As indicated, such is the Navajo policy, as the tribal code does not provide for garnishment, although it does provide other means of enforcing judgments. Under such circumstances, to permit a state court of New Mexico to run a garnishment against Utah International, on the reservation, and attach wages earned by Joe for on-reservation labor, would thwart the Navajo policy not to allow garnishment. Such impinges upon tribal sovereignty, and runs counter to the letter and the spirit of the Navajo Treaty of 1868, the New Mexico Enabling Act, and other applicable federal statutes.

We believe our disposition of this appeal to be in line with the pronouncements of the Supreme Court in such benchmark cases as *McClanahan v. Arizona Tax Commissioners*, 411 U.S. 164 (1973), *Kennerly v. District Court*, 400 U.S. 423 (1971), and *Williams v. Lee*, 358 U.S. 217 (1959). In *Williams*, a non-Indian operated a general store on the Navajo Indian Reservation in Arizona. He brought an action in an Arizona state court against a Navajo Indian to collect for goods sold on credit. The transaction sued on occurred on the reservation. The defendant moved to dismiss on the ground that jurisdiction lay in the tribal court rather than the state court. The motion was denied, and judgment entered against the Navajo defendant. On appeal, the Arizona State Court affirmed. On certiorari, the United States Supreme Court reversed. In reversing, the Supreme Court commented as follows:

> There can be no doubt that to allow the exercise of state jurisdiction here would undermine the authority of the tribal courts over Reservation affairs and hence would infringe on the right of the Indians to govern themselves. It is immaterial that respondent is not an Indian. He was on the Reservation and the transaction with an Indian took place there. Cf. *Connelly v. United States, supra, Williams v. United States, supra.* The cases in this Court have consistently guarded the authority of Indian governments over their reservations. Congress recognized this authority in the Navajos in the Treaty of 1868, and has done so ever since. If this power is to be taken away from them, it is for Congress to do it. *Lone Wolf v. Hitchcock*, 187 U.S. 553, 564–566.

In *Kennerly*, suit was commenced in a Montana state court by a non-Indian against members of the Blackfeet Tribe for a debt arising out of a transaction occurring on the reservation. A motion to dismiss on the ground that the state court lacked jurisdiction because the defendants were members of the Blackfeet Tribe and because the transactions sued on took place on the Indian reservation, was denied. The Montana Supreme Court affirmed. On certiorari, the Supreme Court reversed. In reversing, the Supreme Court held that the State of Montana, not having complied with either the provisions of § 7 of the Act of August 15, 1953, 67 Stat. 590, or Title IV of the Civil Rights Act, did not have jurisdiction over the case.

In the instant case, also, there has been no compliance with applicable federal statutes regarding state assumption of civil jurisdiction over transactions occurring on an Indian reservation.

In *McClanahan*, the Supreme Court held that the State of Arizona had no jurisdiction to impose a tax on the income of Navajo Indians residing on the Navajo Reservation where the income is wholly derived from reservation sources, citing in support thereof the relevant treaty with the Navajos and the implementing federal statutes.

The appellants' continuing argument in this Court is that the garnishment proceeding is merely ancillary to the default judgment entered against Joe in the New Mexico state court, and that since there is no challenge to the validity of the default judgment against Joe, it necessarily follows that the New Mexico state court has jurisdiction to pursue the garnishment proceedings through to conclusion. We do not agree with this reasoning, though such does find support in *Little Horn State Bank v. Stops*, 170 Mont. 510, 555 P.2d 211 (1976), *cert. denied*, 431 U.S. 924 (1977). Garnishment proceedings are indeed ancillary proceedings in the sense that they are in aid of a judgment previously obtained. However, such are independent proceedings in the sense that they are against the judgment debtor's employer, to attach wages held by the employer and due the judgment debtor. The subject matter of the present garnishment proceedings is money held by Utah International and due Joe. Utah International was served on the reservation. The garnishment res is located on the reservation and represents wages due for services rendered by Joe to Utah International on the reservation. Under such circumstances, to uphold the present garnishment would thwart the Navajo policy which does not permit garnishment of wages.

Annis v. Dewey County Bank, 335 F. Supp. 133 (D.S.D. 1971) is quite similar to the instant case. There, Chief Judge Nichol enjoined state officials from enforcing a state judgment by attaching property located on the Cheyenne River Sioux Indian Reservation in South Dakota. In the instant case, the federal district court enjoined the defendants from enforcing a state judgment by garnishing wages which were earned, and in a real sense are "located," on the Navajo Reservation.

Judgment affirmed.

NOTE ON ENFORCEMENT OF JUDGMENTS IN INDIAN COUNTRY

Notice that in *Joe v. Marcum* the loan transaction occurred off the reservation and no one doubted the jurisdiction of the state court to adjudicate the breach of contract claim that resulted in the judgment. Just because a state court has jurisdiction over an off-reservation cause of action, does that afford the state court power to levy execution on Indian owned property located on the reservation or garnish Indian wages earned on the reservation to satisfy a valid judgment? *Joe v. Marcum* and *Annis v. Dewey County Bank*, cited therein, state the prevailing view that separate jurisdiction must exist for garnishment or seizure proceedings, and if property is located on the reservation, tribal courts generally must be employed to enforce the state judgment. In such cases, the available remedies to enforce the judgment generally will be governed by the law of the tribe, rather than state law.

Some courts have taken a contrary position. In *Little Horn State Bank v. Stops*, 555 P.2d 211 (Mont. 1976), the court reached the opposite result, explaining, "It had been a long standing doctrine that any court having jurisdiction to render a judgment also has the power to enforce that judgment through any order or writ necessary to carry its judgment into effect." Is that statement accurate?

TEAGUE v. BAD RIVER BAND OF LAKE SUPERIOR TRIBE OF CHIPPEWA INDIANS
Wisconsin Supreme Court
665 N.W.2d 899 (2003)

SHIRLEY S. ABRAHAMSON, CHIEF JUSTICE (concurring) [but delivering the opinion for the court]

This is a case in which both a state court and a tribal court have exercised jurisdiction over the same dispute between Teague and the Bad River Band about termination of Teague's employment [as casino general manager] with the tribe. Teague first commenced an action in the circuit court for Ashland County [for breach of contract]. A second action was begun by the Bad River Band in tribal court one year later [seeking a declaration that the employment contract was invalid because it was not properly approved]. Both courts had personal and subject matter jurisdiction. Though each court knew about the lawsuit pending in the other court, neither court communicated with the other. Either court could have followed the judicial doctrine of abstention and deferred to the other court but neither did.

The tribal court reached judgment first and the Bad River Tribe sought a stay of the proceedings in the circuit court. The circuit court refused to stay its proceedings or enforce the tribal court judgment. Instead, the circuit court also proceeded to judgment.

The two courts reached opposite results. Each party now wants this court to give effect to the judgment in its favor. The Bad River Band wants us to enforce the tribal court's judgment in its favor. Teague wants us to enforce the circuit court's judgment in his favor. Tensions abound when jurisdiction is concurrent.[59]

This is the second time we have been asked to resolve the dispute between Teague and the Bad River Band by deciding what effect should be given to each judgment. The first opinion proposed that principles of comity must guide both the circuit court and tribal court when they are faced with the dilemma of concurrent jurisdiction. . . .

In our first decision, *Teague II*, the court froze the action when both the circuit and tribal courts were exercising jurisdiction and before either court had reached

---

[59] [25] For a discussion of these tensions, see Judith Resnik, Multiple Sovereignties: Indian Tribes, States, and the Federal Government, 79 Judicature 118 (Nov./Dec. 1995).

a judgment.[60] At that moment, this court refused to apply the "prior action pending rule" from *Syver v. Hahn*, 6 Wis. 2d 154, 94 N.W.2d 161 (1959), otherwise referred to as the race-to-the-courthouse rule. That is, we refused to hold that the first court in which the action was filed (here, the circuit court) should be the prevailing court by virtue of this timing alone. When both courts were exercising concurrent jurisdiction, this court also refused to hold that the first court to reach judgment (here, the tribal court) should prevail.

In *Teague II* this court concluded, as I read the opinion, that when a state court and a tribal court exercise concurrent jurisdiction over the parties and subject matter and each court knows of the other's proceedings, Wis. Stat. § 806.245 [Wisconsin's law requiring that full faith and credit be given to tribal court orders if certain conditions are met] is not yet applicable. Rather, each court should stop its proceedings, consult with the other, and as a matter of comity decide which court should proceed. Consequently, in *Teague II* we sent the case back for the two courts to get together and decide retrospectively as a matter of comity which court's proceedings should have gone forward. [Following *Teague II*, the circuit courts in the 10th Judicial Administrative District and the Chippewa tribal courts successfully drafted and agreed to protocols for managing concurrent jurisdiction. Tribal/State Protocol for the Judicial Allocation of Jurisdiction Between the Four Chippewa Tribes of Northern Wisconsin and the Tenth Judicial District of Wisconsin, often referred to as the Teague Protocol. This Protocol was only in draft form at the time the circuit court was required to address the tribal court judgment.]

Unfortunately each court refused to give way and the case is back in this court.

[In what is called the "lead opinion" in this case, but which functions as a concurring opinion, Justice Crooks interprets state law, Wisconsin Stat. § 806.245, to require that the state court give "full faith and credit" to the first-delivered tribal court judgment if the specified statutory conditions are met. The opinion for the Court first explains why the case should not be resolved on the basis of that statute.]

First, the statute says nothing about what a state court should do when an action is instituted in both a tribal court and state court and the tribal court reaches judgment while the case is still pending in the state court. [In particular, the statute does not direct] the state court to halt its proceedings and apply full faith and credit to the tribal court judgment.

Second, [invoking full faith and credit would eliminate] any incentive for tribal courts and state courts to cooperate with each other in cases of concurrent jurisdiction. [If we adopt the position that the first judgment must be respected by the other court system, then] if either court disagrees with the decision reached under the protocol, or no protocol exists, each court can unilaterally take precedence by proceeding to judgment faster than the other court. [Such a first-to-judgment principle] undercuts the *Teague II* decision and renders it a nullity.

Third, [applying] Wis. Stat. § 806.245 [in the present situation] leads to a

---

[60] [26] *Teague v. Bad River Band of Lake Superior Tribe of Chippewa Indians*, 2000 WI 79, 236 Wis. 2d 384, 612 N.W.2d 709 (*Teague II*).

potentially absurd result. That is, should a state court and a tribal court reach valid judgments at the same time, or both proceed to judgment unaware of the other's proceedings, the state court must give effect to the tribal court judgment and the tribal court must give effect to the state court judgment.[61] Each courts' judgment has no effect in its own jurisdiction but is entitled to full faith and credit in the other court's jurisdiction.[62] This result cannot be right.

The issue here is which court properly proceeded to reach a judgment in this case despite its awareness that proceedings on the exact same dispute were taking place in the other court. Consequently, our focus must return to that point in the proceedings, pre-judgment, when both courts became aware of the other's concurrent exercise of jurisdiction.

I conclude, consistent with *Teague II*, that Wis. Stat. § 806.245 does not apply at that moment in time. Rather, general principles of comity, including principles of abstention, must be used to resolve the jurisdictional dispute presented to us. . . .

Comity is based on respect for the proceedings of another system of government and a spirit of cooperation. Comity endorses the principle of mutual respect between legal systems, recognizing the sovereignty and sovereign interests of each governmental system and the unique features of each legal system. It is a doctrine that recognizes, accepts, and respects differences in process. . . . Comity is discretionary, highly fact specific, and reviewable on appeal for erroneous exercise of discretion.

In the context of state-tribal relations, principles of comity must be applied with an understanding that the federal government is, and the state courts should be, fostering tribal self-government and tribal self-determination. Through principles of comity, federal and state governments can develop an increased understanding of tribal sovereignty, encourage deference to and support for tribal courts, and advance cooperation, communication, respect and understanding in interacting with tribal courts.[63] "Central to tribal sovereignty is the capacity for self-government through tribal justice mechanisms. . . . Tribal justice systems are 'essential to the maintenance of the culture and identity of Indian tribes.'"[64]

Against this backdrop, courts and scholars have developed a number of factors to help state and tribal courts determine, in the spirit of cooperation, not competition, which of two courts should proceed to judgment and which court should abstain and

---

[61] [32] Wisconsin Stat. § 806.245 provides that for a tribal court judgment to be given full faith and credit in state court, the tribal court must give full faith and credit to state court judgments.

[62] [33] Wisconsin Stat. § 806.245(1)(e) provides that full faith and credit will be accorded to the laws and judgments of a tribal legal system only if the tribal legal system accords full faith and credit to the laws and judgments of the state.

[63] [36] The cooperative protocol adopted by the 10th Judicial District and tribes is an important advance in this jurisdictional dilemma. *See also* Stanley G. Feldman & David L. Withey, Resolving State-Tribal Jurisdictional Dilemmas, 79 Judicature 154 (Nov./Dec. 1995).

[64] [37] Janet Reno, A Federal Commitment to Tribal Justice Systems, 79 Judicature 113, 113–14 (Nov./Dec. 1995) (quoting Indian Tribal Justice Act, 25 U.S.C. § 3601); *see also* Douglas B.L. Endreson, The Challenges Facing Tribal Courts Today, 79 Judicature 142 (Nov./Dec. 1995); Raymond L. Niblock & William C. Plouffe, Federal Courts, Tribal Courts, and Comity: Developing Tribal Judiciaries and Forum Selection, 19 U. Ark. Little Rock L. Rev. 219, 227 (1997).

cede its jurisdiction. Though the weight to be given each factor will vary from case to case, the factors to be considered include the following:[65]

1. Where the action was first filed and the extent to which the case has proceeded in the first court.

2. The parties' and courts' expenditures of time and resources in each court and the extent to which the parties have complied with any applicable provisions of either court's scheduling orders.

3. The relative burdens on the parties, including cost, access to and admissibility of evidence and matters of process, practice, and procedure, including whether the action will be decided most expeditiously in tribal or state court.

4. Whether the nature of the action implicates tribal sovereignty, including but not limited to the following:

   a. The subject matter of the litigation.

   b. The identities and potential immunities of the parties.

5. Whether the issues in the case require application and interpretation of a tribe's law or state law.

6. Whether the case involves traditional or cultural matters of the tribe.

7. Whether the location of material events giving rise to the litigation is on tribal or state land.

8. The relative institutional or administrative interests of each court.

9. The tribal membership status of the parties.

10. The parties' choice by contract, if any, of a forum in the event of dispute.

11. The parties' choice by contract, if any, of the law to be applied in the event of a dispute.

12. Whether each court has jurisdiction over the dispute and the parties and has determined its own jurisdiction.

13. Whether either jurisdiction has entered a final judgment that conflicts with another judgment that is entitled to recognition.

In this case, principles of comity have been discussed but never properly applied. The circuit court attempted to apply principles of comity when the Bad River Band sought a stay of the state court proceedings in January 1997. The state court denied the Band's motion for a stay based on its belief that the case could not be resolved in its entirety by the tribal court, and on the grounds that the action was in state court first and was subject to Wisconsin state contract law.

Moreover, on remand from *Teague II*, the circuit court and tribal court attempted to cooperate and select between their competing judgments through principles of comity. Unable to do so, the circuit court again exercised its discretion

---

[65] [38] I have compiled these factors from a number of sources discussing comity, allocation of jurisdiction, and enforcement of judgments. See, e.g., Niblock & Plouffe, supra note 37 at 237–39; Tribal/State Protocol for the Judicial Allocation of Jurisdiction Between the Four Chippewa Tribes of Northern Wisconsin and the Tenth Judicial District of Wisconsin (2001).

in its March 27, 2001, order, concluding that "comity does not require that jurisdiction in this particular case be allocated to the tribal court."

The circuit court's March 27, 2001, order concluding that maintaining jurisdiction in state court is appropriate identified and discussed several of the above factors. The circuit court noted that the action was first filed in state court, that state court proceedings were relatively advanced by the time a jurisdictional allocation conference should have originally been held, that the law to be applied was predominately Wisconsin law, and that the parties' contractual choice of forum was state court. While it appears that the contract had actually selected a choice of law (state arbitration law), not a choice of forum, the plaintiff selected the state court forum when he brought his action in the circuit court for Ashland County. The plaintiff's decision about where to bring the action is properly entitled to great weight.

I agree that these are appropriate factors for consideration and that, as identified by the state court, they favor state court jurisdiction in the present case. The state court's order, however, identified and discussed only those factors that weighed in favor of state court jurisdiction. The state court never considered those factors that weigh in favor of tribal court jurisdiction, and the circuit court's failure to identify and balance those factors supporting tribal jurisdiction in the present case against the factors favoring state court jurisdiction was an erroneous exercise of discretion.

In the present case, balanced against the factors identified by the circuit court, are the following factors that favor the circuit court ceding jurisdiction to the tribal court:

(a)   The nature of the action implicates tribal sovereignty. The subject matter of the litigation is the power of the tribe to enter into a contract, as well as the potential immunity of the tribe.

(b)   The case also requires interpretation of tribal law.

(c)   The material events relating to the litigation occurred on tribal land.

(d)   The tribal court has an institutional interest in determining the validity of contracts between Indians and non-Indians, especially those involving contracts in which the tribe is a party and which relate to tribal business; here the contract was between the tribe and a non-Indian relating to gaming run by the tribe.

Clearly, the decision in this case is difficult. There are factors that favor each court's exercise of jurisdiction. Yet in the end, I must conclude that the principles of comity favor the circuit court ceding jurisdiction to the tribal court in the present case.

The principles of comity applicable to state court-tribal court relations are built upon the goal of fostering tribal self-government through recognition of tribal justice mechanisms. Consequently, the significance of the plaintiff's choice of a forum and the application and interpretation of state law are outweighed by the fact that the litigation involves tribal sovereignty and the interpretation of tribal law, and that the material events occurred on tribal land. Moreover, the fact that the circuit court had conducted significant proceedings before the tribal court even began to hear the case is outweighed by the tribal court's institutional interest in determining the validity of contracts made with the tribe.

Because the circuit court should not have proceeded to judgment, we now have only the tribal court judgment, and the issue is whether this judgment should be given effect under Wis. Stat. § 806.245. The lead opinion concludes that the tribal court judgment is entitled to full faith and credit under § 806.245 by formalistically applying the enumerated factors under § 806.245(1) [the pre-conditions for full faith and credit under the statute, including whether the tribe is organized under the IRA, the proceedings complied with the Indian Civil Rights Act, and the tribal court certifies that it will give full faith and credit to state court judgments].

I am concerned, however, with this approach. Although titled and incorporating the phrase "full faith and credit," and recognizing the sovereignty of tribes, the statute seems to be a blend of elements of constitutional full faith and credit, statutory full faith and credit, and comity.

Indeed the statute has been described as being more akin to international comity standards than to federal constitutional or state statutory full faith and credit standards for state court judgments.[66] As this court noted in *Teague II*, "Several commentators have indicated that the Wisconsin tribal full faith and credit statute is more accurately characterized as a codification of principles of comity rather than the statutory equivalent of constitutional full faith and credit."[67] Persuasive authority characterizes Wis. Stat. § 806.245 as a comity statute that gives greater

---

[66] [39] *See* David S. Clark, State Court Recognition of Tribal Court Judgments: Securing the Blessings of Civilization, 23 Okla. City U. L. Rev. 353 (1998):

> Wisconsin and Wyoming enacted what they call full faith and credit statutes to recognize the judgments of their own state tribes, but in actuality these statutes function according to a comity standard. These states require that the tribes maintain an impartial court system according to an idiosyncratic list of four elements and that the tribal court in the case at hand correctly apply its own procedural law (which can be examined sua sponte by the court in Wisconsin).

Id. at 368–369 (citations omitted); Stacy L. Leeds, Cross-Jurisdictional Recognition and Enforcement of Judgments: A Tribal Court Perspective, 76 N.D. L. Rev. 311 (2000):

> Although many states dignify their policy with a "full faith and credit" title, most are more akin to international comity standards.

> . . . .

> Wisconsin's legislature also inappropriately labeled its tribal court recognition statute "full faith and credit," when the statute more accurately embodies principles of comity. The Wisconsin statute mirrors the Wyoming statute. . . .

Id. at 341, 344; Carol Tebben, Trifederalism in the Aftermath of *Teague*: The Interaction of State and Tribal Courts in Wisconsin, 26 Am. Indian L. Rev. 177 (2001–02):

> Wisconsin's tribal full faith and credit statute encourages state court judges to honor decisions made in tribal courts, but allows state judges to evaluate tribal courts . . . and to grant full faith and credit on a discretionary basis. In this sense, the statute is not written in the words of a full faith and credit requirement.

Id. at 184 (citations omitted).

[67] [40] *See Teague II*, 236 Wis. 2d 384, P28 (citing Darby L. Hoggatt, The Wyoming Tribal Full Faith and Credit Act: Enforcing Tribal Judgments and Protecting Tribal Sovereignty, 30 Land & Water L. Rev. 531, 552–56 (1995); Recognition of Tribal Orders in Wisconsin: An Overview of State and Federal Law, Indian Law News (State Bar of Wisconsin, Spring 1999)).

flexibility to both state and tribal courts in giving effect to the other's judgments than does the constitutional doctrine of full faith and credit.[68]

Nevertheless, Wis. Stat. § 806.245 may not be a pure comity statute. The statute lists specific criteria under which a tribal court judgment would not be given "full faith and credit." The criteria are broad, including the requirement that the tribal court proceedings comply with the Indian Civil Rights Act, which requires the guarantees of equal protection and due process.[69] It is not entirely clear, however, whether these statutory grounds are exclusive and thus limit a state court's discretion in applying the discretionary doctrine of comity.

Despite these problems with the interpretation of the statute, I conclude that the principles of full faith and credit and comity stated explicitly in or embedded in Wis. Stat. § 806.245 require us to enforce the tribal court judgment in the present case. For the reasons set forth above, I would REVERSE the order denying the motion to reopen the judgment of the Circuit Court for Ashland County and REMAND the cause for dismissal of the complaint, along with the garnishment action brought on behalf of Teague.

WILCOX, J., dissenting.

I believe that principles of comity constitute the proper approach in this case, and I believe the circuit court's discretionary decision based on those principles should be upheld. . . . Unlike the majority . . . I conclude that the outcome resulting from application of [principles of comity] favors enforcement of the circuit court's judgment. . . .

Here, the action in state court was filed first and proceeded for over a year before the Bad River Band even brought suit in tribal court. Motions were ruled upon and extensive discovery had taken place in the circuit court action long before the action in tribal court began. In fact, in ruling to deny the motion to reopen, the circuit court noted that it had ruled upon the waiver of sovereign immunity issue before the tribal court proceedings began. At the conference, the judges and parties discussed the issue of the validity of the contracts. Following the discussion, [the circuit court judge] decided the contract predominantly dealt with state contract law and also found that the choice of forum clause in the contracts favored state jurisdiction. . . .

The finding of state court jurisdiction is in no way a statement regarding the ability of tribal courts to address cases such as this. Judge Gallagher [of the circuit court] openly conceded that jurisdiction was concurrent. Rather the question is which judgment to enforce when both courts went ahead, cognizant of the other's proceedings. I believe that Judge Gallagher could appropriately find that, under the specific circumstances presented, the extent of the state court proceedings and the nature of action itself outweighed the factors favoring tribal court jurisdiction.

---

[68] [41] *See* William C. Canby, Jr., American Indian Law 173 (2d ed. 1988); Felix S. Cohen, Handbook of Federal Indian Law 385 (1982); Fred L. Ragsdale, Jr., Problems in the Application of Full Faith and Credit for Indian Tribes, 7 N.M. L. Rev. 133 (1977).

[69] [42] *See* 25 U.S.C. § 1302(8).

While members of this court may reach a different conclusion, our review is whether there is basis for the circuit court's decision. Because I believe such a basis exists, I respectfully dissent.

PROSSER, J., dissenting.

This case presents a wide array of delicate legal issues. The issue on which the case turns is the applicability and interpretation of Wis. Stat. § 806.245. . . .

The Bad River Band seeks a "full faith and credit" equivalent to the full faith and credit between two states. It is in effect asking this court to hold that the Wisconsin legislature intended to accord judgments of the Bad River Tribal Court on any subject the same status as judgments of courts in, say, Michigan and Minnesota. The reasonableness of this proposition may be judged by looking at the evidence presented to the legislature by the Advisory Committee on Tribal Courts.

The Advisory Committee conducted a survey of Wisconsin tribal courts in 1988. Four of the state's tribes and bands indicated that they did not have a tribal court. . . .

Today, Wisconsin tribal courts are more mature and sophisticated than they once were. Even so, given the structure of some tribes and bands, there are lingering concerns about judicial independence. In truth, there is little evidence that the Wisconsin legislature understood in 1991 [when it enacted § 806.245 in its present form] the possible ramifications of § 806.245 for this state's courts and sovereignty.

This court needs to consider questions that it has never faced before. For instance, are there any circumstances in which a Wisconsin circuit court may refuse to give full faith and credit to a tribal court judgment if all the conditions in § 806.245 are met and there is no competing circuit court action or judgment? The majority opinion does not answer this question, while the lead opinion appears to say "no."

Suppose, for example, a tribal member suffers injury and damages on account of the negligence of a Wisconsin local government employee acting in an official capacity on tribal land. May the tribal member sue the local government employee in tribal court? If the answer is yes, suppose the tribal court refuses to apply the limitations on liability in Wis. Stat. § 893.80. Would the circuit court be bound by § 806.245 to give full faith and credit to the tribal court judgment?

The circuit court might look to § 806.245(4)(a) to determine whether the tribal court had jurisdiction of the subject matter and over the person named in the judgment. Even under constitutional full faith and credit, the court of one state may examine whether the other state had jurisdiction to decide the case. *See Underwriters Nat'l Assurance v. North Carolina Life & Accident & Health Ins. Guar. Ass'n*, 455 U.S. 691, 704–05 (1982). Our hypothetical assumes, however, that all the conditions in the statute have been satisfied, including jurisdiction. It should be noted, parenthetically, that each tribe or band determines the jurisdiction of its own court, so long as that jurisdiction conforms to any limitations imposed by federal law.

The bottom line is this: If a Wisconsin court were to extend full faith and credit to the judgment of the tribal court in this hypothetical circumstance, it would treat one of our citizens differently from the way it would treat the rest of our citizens, and it would disregard the conditions the legislature has set on tort suits against our own local governments. In my view, the text of § 806.245 does not provide the answer to how a Wisconsin court should proceed.

Wisconsin has been given concurrent jurisdiction over civil causes of action to which Indians are parties that arise in the areas of Indian Country in Wisconsin. *See* Public Law 280, as codified at 28 U.S.C. § 1360(a). In my view, § 806.245 does not require Wisconsin courts to yield this jurisdiction and extend full faith and credit to a tribal court judgment in every circumstance. Our legislature would not expect or intend that Wisconsin courts subordinate Wisconsin laws and policies or undercut Wisconsin courts if a tribal court judgment intruded too deeply into an area of fundamental concern. *See* Ruth B. Ginsburg, *Judgments in Search of Full Faith and Credit: The Last-In-Time Rule for Conflicting Judgments*, 82 HARV. L. REV. 798, 832 (1969). . . .

The statute provides that "judgments of an Indian tribal court in Wisconsin . . . shall have the same full faith and credit in the courts of this state as . . . the judgments of any other governmental entity." What does the phrase "judgments of any other governmental entity" mean? We have already established that "judgments of any other governmental entity" does not mean the judgments of another state, for § 806.245 does not require a circuit court to treat judgments of a Wisconsin tribal court the same as judgments of another state. Quebec, Canada, and Chiapas, Mexico, are governmental entities, but Wisconsin courts are not required to give full faith and credit to the judgments of these foreign governmental entities. The Navajo Tribe and the San Carlos Apache Tribe are governmental entities, but § 806.245 does not require that circuit courts accord full faith and credit to the judgments of these out-of-state tribes.[70] A Wisconsin municipal court is a governmental entity, but the judgments of a municipal court are often subject to a de novo trial. See Wis. Stat. § 800.14(4). Clearly, the phrase "judgments of any other governmental entity" needs construction.

In my view, until the legislature clarifies its intent, judgments of a Wisconsin tribal court should be treated the same as judgments of a Wisconsin circuit court. Under this theory, the Ashland County Circuit Court's invocation of *Syver v. Hahn*, 6 Wis. 2d 154, 94 N.W.2d 161 (1959), which embodies the "prior action pending rule," makes perfect sense and should have been affirmed, leaving only legal issues about the merits of the circuit court's judgment.

In *Teague II*, we held otherwise [because the state and tribal courts belong to different sovereigns, and "it would be incorrect, given the tribe's sovereign status, to apply a state court common law rule to find an erroneous assumption of jurisdiction by the tribal court," and because applying that rule "would distort the purposes of Public Law 280. Public Law 280 was not designed to deprive tribal courts of jurisdiction where they properly have it."]

---

[70] [49] By contrast, Wis. Stat. § 806.245(1) appears to state that the acts of any Indian tribal legislative body shall have the same full faith and credit in the courts of this state as do the acts of any other governmental entity.

In retrospect, this analysis misses the point. The fact that a Wisconsin Indian tribe is "an independent sovereign" does not dictate the applicable law. The intent of the Wisconsin legislature dictates the applicable law. The legislature intended to treat the judgments of a Wisconsin tribal court the "same" as the judgments of a Wisconsin circuit court, not superior to a Wisconsin circuit court. Section 806.245 should not be construed to deprive Wisconsin courts of jurisdiction that has been expressly given to them by Congress.

NOTES

1.　**Teague Protocol:** This case gave rise to a process of cooperation between the state and tribal courts for resolving jurisdictional disputes. Soon after the decision was issued, an agreement was reach between the state and tribal courts in the north-central area of Wisconsin regarding the allocation of jurisdiction among state and tribal courts where they adopted verbatim the comity principles outlines in the *Teague* decision. Under the Teague Protocol, Wisconsin state courts now have the ability to transfer civil cases of concurrent jurisdiction to tribal courts when deemed appropriate through the application of the enumerated standards. See http://www. tribal-institute.org/2004/handouts/Closing-Tribal%20Perspective%20-%20David% 20Raasch-State%20Tribal%20Courts%20Work%20to%20Build%20-%20Handouts. pdf.

2.　**State Civil Adjudicative Jurisdiction in Public Law 280 States:** *Teague* illustrates the civil jurisdictional problems that can emerge in Public Law 280 jurisdictions. Public Law 280, which is discussed more fully in Ch. 5, Sec. A, clearly vests the states in which covered reservations are located with civil subject matter and personal jurisdiction over suits involving Indians in Indian country. Thus, it removes the normal federal preemption of state jurisdiction that *Williams v. Lee* and its progeny create in a non-Public Law 280 reservation. State courts therefore have greater civil adjudicative jurisdiction over Public Law 280 reservations, although in states that opted into the statutory scheme the precise limits of that jurisdiction may depend on the state statute enacted to assume such jurisdiction. Nevertheless, Public Law 280 did not terminate the preexisting tribal civil jurisdiction over matters arising on the reservation.

Until recently, the existence of concurrent state and tribal jurisdiction on Public Law 280 reservations raised few problems since the BIA historically refused to underwrite the operating costs for tribal courts and police on Public Law 280 reservations. Without such federal financial support, most Public Law 280 reservations lacked tribal courts of general jurisdiction. Recent economic development trends, including the emergence of tribal gaming in Indian country, have facilitated the emergence of tribal courts on Public Law 280 reservations, such as the tribal court for the Bad River Band of Lake Superior Chippewa involved in *Teague*. Furthermore, since the 1990s, the United States Department of Justice has been funding initiatives for tribal court development and enhancement that have reached tribes in Public Law 280 states. *See* DUANE CHAMPAGNE & CAROLE GOLDBERG, CAPTURED JUSTICE: NATIVE NATIONS AND PUBLIC LAW 280 (2011).

The existence of concurrent tribal and state civil jurisdiction over claims arising on the reservation can cause serious questions about jurisdictional priority of the type advanced in *Teague*. Had the tribal court action been filed first, would the state's *Syver* "pending action" rule have prevented the state court from entertaining the action? Should it? Does the exhaustion of tribal remedies rule of *National Farmers Union*, discussed in Sec. A.4.b, this chapter, apply to a state court, particularly where the state court has jurisdiction pursuant to Public Law 280? *See* Ch. 5, Sec. A.3.

In *Teague*, the Wisconsin Supreme Court holds that the question is not one of full faith and credit under the Wisconsin full faith and credit statute, but, rather, one of jurisdictional priority to be resolved ideally through mutual accession to an intergovernmental protocol, and if not, through principles of comity. The protocol, which was only in draft form at the time the state trial judge had to decide whether to proceed in *Teague*, established a method for dealing with the type of tribal-state deadlock that eventually occurred in that case: appointment of a third judge from a standing pool of tribal and state court judges, through a complex process of striking names and random selection. Given that the protocol was unavailable in *Teague*, which of the four opinions in the case produced the strongest analysis? Was the lead opinion, which opted to treat the Wisconsin statute as mandating enforcement of the tribal judgment, providing the best reading of the statute? What should the Wisconsin Supreme Court have made of the fact that the statute establishes various conditions on the enforcement of tribal court judgments? If the legislature took the trouble to identify a limited set of conditions, should the Court then interpret the statute as allowing it to create a flexible range of additional requirements before a tribal court judgment will be respected, such as the absence of a first-filed state court proceeding? What should be the significance of the fact that the legislature gave the statute a "Full Faith and Credit" label? Did that label simplify the Wisconsin Supreme Court's task or make it more confusing? Finally, how justified are dissenting Justice Prosser's concerns about the hypothetical case of a tribal court failing to observe state law limits on the liability of a state officer? Could such a suit even proceed in tribal court after *Nevada v. Hicks*, discussed in Ch. 3, Sec. C.1? Why should Justice Prosser be any more concerned about a tribal court declining to apply state law in a case within its jurisdiction than another state doing the same? Full faith and credit or comity for tribal court judgments is considered in greater detail in Ch. 3, Sec. E.1.

Was Justice Abrahamson's opinion in *Teague* correct in weighing the governmental interest of the Tribe with respect to its contracts as greater than the state court's interest in efficient disposition of litigation? What model of tribal-federal relations propels the particular application of comity by the Wisconsin Supreme Court in *Teague*? Are the intergovernmental relations issues presented in this case any different from problems that would arise if an American court and a Canadian court both had personal jurisdiction over the parties to a dispute that was within their subject matter jurisdiction? How do foreign countries normally address problems of simultaneous and competing litigation involving the same dispute? *See* ANDREAS F. LOWENFELD, INTERNATIONAL LITIGATION AND ARBITRATION 273–80 (2d ed. 2002) (suggesting that anti-suit injunctions should be disfavored, and that in an international legal system based largely on comity, there may be situations where a forum is not the first to receive a filing related to a particular dispute, but nonetheless may consider itself the more appropriate forum and may wish to go ahead with the litigation anyway). Could Congress enact legislation that would prescribe the sequence and relationship of concurrent tribal and state lawsuits? Would that be preferable to the kind of protocol that was established between tribal and state courts in Wisconsin?

b.   State Taxing and Regulatory Jurisdiction

McCLANAHAN v. ARIZONA STATE TAX COMMISSION
United States Supreme Court
411 U.S. 164 (1973)

MR. JUSTICE MARSHALL delivered the opinion of the Court.

This case requires us once again to reconcile the plenary power of the States over residents within their borders with the semi-autonomous status of Indians living on tribal reservations. In this instance, the problem arises in the context of Arizona's efforts to impose its personal income tax on a reservation Indian whose entire income derives from reservation sources. Although we have repeatedly addressed the question of state taxation of reservation Indians, the problems posed by a state income tax are apparently of first impression in this Court. The Arizona courts have held that such state taxation is permissible. 14 Ariz. App. 452, 484 P. 2d 221 (1971). We noted probable jurisdiction, 406 U.S. 916 (1972), and now reverse. We hold that by imposing the tax in question on this appellant, the State has interfered with matters which the relevant treaty and statutes leave to the exclusive province of the federal government and the Indians themselves. The tax is therefore unlawful as applied to reservation Indians with income derived wholly from reservation sources.

I

Appellant is an enrolled member of the Navajo tribe who lives on that portion of the Navajo Reservation located within the State of Arizona. Her complaint alleges that all her income earned during 1967 was derived from within the Navajo Reservation. Pursuant to Ariz. Rev. Stat. Ann. § 43-188 (f) (Supp. 1972–1973), $16.20 was withheld from her wages for that year to cover her state income tax liability. At the conclusion of the tax year, appellant filed a protest against the collection of any taxes on her income and a claim for a refund of the entire amount withheld from her wages. When no action was taken on her claim, she instituted this action in Arizona Superior Court on behalf of herself and those similarly situated, demanding a return of the money withheld and a declaration that the state tax was unlawful as applied to reservation Indians.

The trial court dismissed the action for failure to state a claim, and the Arizona Court of Appeals affirmed. Citing this Court's decision in *Williams v. Lee*, 358 U.S. 217 (1959), the Court of Appeals held that the test "is not whether the Arizona state income tax infringes on plaintiff's rights as an individual Navajo Indian, but whether such a tax infringes on the rights of the Navajo tribe of Indians to be self-governing." 14 Ariz. App., at 454, 484 P. 2d, at 223. The court thus distinguished cases dealing with state taxes on Indian real property on the ground that these taxes, unlike the personal income tax, infringed tribal autonomy.

The court then pointed to cases holding that state employees could be required to pay federal income taxes and that the State had a concomitant right to tax federal employees. See Helvering v. Gerhardt, 304 U.S. 405 (1938); Graves v. New York ex rel. O'Keefe, 306 U.S. 466 (1939). Reasoning by analogy from these cases, the court argued that Arizona's income tax on individual Navajo Indians did not "[cause] an impairment of the right of the Navajo tribe to be self governing." 14 Ariz. App., at 455, 484 P. 2d, at 224.

Nor did the court find anything in the Arizona Enabling Act, 36 Stat. 557, to prevent the State from taxing reservation Indians. . . . The Arizona Supreme Court denied a petition for review of this decision, and the case came here on appeal. See 28 U. S. C. § 1257 (2).

II

It may be helpful to begin our discussion of the law applicable to this complex area with a brief statement of what this case does not involve. We are not here dealing with Indians who have left or never inhabited reservations set aside for their exclusive use or who do not possess the usual accoutrements of tribal self-government [citing, *e.g.*, *Organized Village of Kake v. Egan*, 369 U.S. 60 (1962)]. Nor are we concerned with exertions of state sovereignty over non-Indians who undertake activity on Indian reservations [citing, *e.g.*, *United States v. McBratney*, discussed in Sec. A.3, this chapter]. Nor, finally, is this a case where the State seeks to reach activity undertaken by reservation Indians on nonreservation lands [citing *Mescalero Apache Tribe v. Jones*, discussed in Sec. B, this chapter]. Rather, this case involves the narrow question whether the State may tax a reservation Indian for income earned exclusively on the reservation.

The principles governing the resolution of this question are not new. On the contrary, "the policy of leaving Indians free from state jurisdiction and control is deeply rooted in the Nation's history." *Rice v. Olson*, 324 U.S. 786, 789 (1945). This policy was first articulated by this Court 141 years ago when Mr. Chief Justice Marshall held that Indian nations were "distinct political communities, having territorial boundaries, within which their authority is exclusive, and having a right to all the lands within those boundaries, which is not only acknowledged, but guarantied by the United States." *Worcester v. Georgia*, 6 Pet. 515, 557 (1832). It followed from this concept of Indian reservations as separate, although dependent nations, that state law could have no role to play within the reservation boundaries. "The Cherokee nation . . . is a distinct community, occupying its own territory, with boundaries accurately described, in which the laws of Georgia can have no force, and which the citizens of Georgia have no right to enter, but with the assent of the Cherokees themselves, or in conformity with treaties, and with the acts of Congress. The whole intercourse between the United States and this nation, is, by our Constitution and laws, vested in the government of the United States." *Id.*, at 561. *See also United States v. Kagama*, 118 U.S. 375 (1886); Ex parte *Crow Dog*, 109 U.S. 556 (1883).

Although *Worcester* on its facts dealt with a State's efforts to extend its criminal jurisdiction to reservation lands, the rationale of the case plainly extended to state taxation within the reservation as well. Thus, in *The Kansas Indians*, 5 Wall. 737 (1867), the Court unambiguously rejected state efforts to impose a land tax on reservation Indians. "If the tribal organization of the Shawnees is preserved intact, and recognized by the political department of the government as existing, then they are a 'people distinct from others,' capable of making treaties, separated from the jurisdiction of Kansas, and to be governed exclusively by the government of the Union. If under the control of Congress, from necessity there can be no divided authority." *Id.*, at 755. *See also The New York Indians*, 5 Wall. 761 (1867).

It is true, as the State asserts, that some of the later Indian tax cases turn, not on the Indian sovereignty doctrine, but on whether or not the State can be said to have imposed a forbidden tax on a federal instrumentality. *See, e.g., Leahy v. State Treasurer of Oklahoma*, 297 U.S. 420 (1936); *United States v. Rickert*, 188 U.S. 432 (1903). To the extent that the tax exemption rests on federal immunity from state taxation, it may well be inapplicable in a case such as this involving an individual income tax. But it would vastly oversimplify the problem to say that nothing remains of the notion that reservation Indians are a separate people to whom state jurisdiction, and therefore state tax legislation, may not extend. . . . As a leading text on Indian problems summarizes the relevant law: "State laws generally are not applicable to tribal Indians on an Indian reservation except where Congress has expressly provided that State laws shall apply. It follows that Indians and Indian property on an Indian reservation are not subject to State taxation except by virtue of express authority conferred upon the State by act of Congress." U.S. DEPT. OF THE INTERIOR, FEDERAL INDIAN LAW 845 (1958) (hereafter FEDERAL INDIAN LAW).

This is not to say that the Indian sovereignty doctrine, with its concomitant jurisdictional limit on the reach of state law, has remained static during the 141 years since *Worcester* was decided. Not surprisingly, the doctrine has undergone considerable evolution in response to changed circumstances. As noted above, the doctrine has not been rigidly applied in cases where Indians have left the reservation and become assimilated into the general community. See, e.g., *Oklahoma Tax Comm'n v. United States*, 319 U.S. 598 (1943). Similarly, notions of Indian sovereignty have been adjusted to take account of the State's legitimate interests in regulating the affairs of non-Indians. *See, e. g., New York* ex rel. *Ray v. Martin*, 326 U.S. 496 (1946); *Draper v. United States*, 164 U.S. 240 (1896); *Utah & Northern R. Co. v. Fisher*, 116 U.S. 28 (1885). This line of cases was summarized in this Court's landmark decision in *Williams v. Lee*, 358 U.S. 217 (1959): [quoting legal standard as "whether the state action infringed on the right of reservation Indians to make their own laws and be ruled by them."].

Finally, the trend has been away from the idea of inherent Indian sovereignty as a bar to state jurisdiction and toward reliance on federal pre-emption.[71] *See Mescalero Apache Tribe v. Jones, ante*, p. 145. The modern cases thus tend to avoid

---

[71] The source of federal authority over Indian matters has been the subject of some confusion, but it is now generally recognized that the power derives from federal responsibility for regulating commerce with Indian tribes and for treaty making. See U.S. Const. Art. I, § 8, cl. 3; Art. II, § 2, cl. 2. *See also Williams v. Lee*, 358 U.S. 217, 219 n. 4 (1959); *Perrin v. United States*, 232 U.S. 478, 482 (1914); FEDERAL INDIAN LAW 3.

reliance on platonic notions of Indian sovereignty and to look instead to the applicable treaties and statutes which define the limits of state power. *Compare, e.g., United States v. Kagama*, 118 U.S. 375 (1886), *with Kennerly v. District Court*, 400 U.S. 423 (1971). [72]

The Indian sovereignty doctrine is relevant, then, not because it provides a definitive resolution of the issues in this suit, but because it provides a backdrop against which the applicable treaties and federal statutes must be read. It must always be remembered that the various Indian tribes were once independent and sovereign nations, and that their claim to sovereignty long predates that of our own Government. Indians today are American citizens. They have the right to vote, to use state courts, and they receive some state services. But it is nonetheless still true, as it was in the last century, that "the relation of the Indian tribes living within the borders of the United States . . . [is] an anomalous one and of a complex character. . . . They were, and always have been, regarded as having a semi-independent position when they preserved their tribal relations; not as States, not as nations, not as possessed of the full attributes of sovereignty, but as a separate people, with the power of regulating their internal and social relations, and thus far not brought under the laws of the Union or of the State within whose limits they resided." *United States v. Kagama*, 118 U.S., at 381–382.

III

When the relevant treaty and statutes are read with this tradition of sovereignty in mind, we think it clear that Arizona has exceeded its lawful authority by attempting to tax appellant. The beginning of our analysis must be with the treaty which the United States Government entered with the Navajo Nation in 1868. The agreement provided, in relevant part, that a prescribed reservation would be set aside "for the use and occupation of the Navajo tribe of Indians" and that "no persons except those herein so authorized to do, and except such officers, soldiers, agents, and employees of the government, or of the Indians, as may be authorized to enter upon Indian reservations in discharge of duties imposed by law, or the orders of the President, shall ever be permitted to pass over, settle upon, or reside in, the territory described in this article." 15 Stat. 668.

The treaty nowhere explicitly states that the Navajos were to be free from state law or exempt from state taxes. But the document is not to be read as an ordinary contract agreed upon by parties dealing at arm's length with equal bargaining positions. We have had occasion in the past to describe the circumstances under which the agreement was reached. "At the time this document was signed the Navajos were an exiled people, forced by the United States to live crowded together on a small piece of land on the Pecos River in eastern New Mexico, some 300 miles east of the area they had occupied before the coming of the white man. In return for their promises to keep peace, this treaty 'set apart' for 'their permanent home' a

---

[72] The extent of federal pre-emption and residual Indian sovereignty in the total absence of federal treaty obligations or legislation is therefore now something of a moot question. *Cf. Organized Village of Kake v. Egan*, 369 U.S. 60, 62 (1962); FEDERAL INDIAN LAW 846. The question is generally of little more than theoretical importance, however, since in almost all cases federal treaties and statutes define the boundaries of federal and state jurisdiction.

portion of what had been their native country." *Williams v. Lee*, 358 U.S., at 221.

It is circumstances such as these that have led this Court in interpreting Indian treaties, to adopt the general rule that "doubtful expressions are to be resolved in favor of the weak and defenseless people who are the wards of the nation, dependent upon its protection and good faith." *Carpenter v. Shaw*, 280 U.S. 363, 367 (1930). When this canon of construction is taken together with the tradition of Indian independence described above, it cannot be doubted that the reservation of certain lands for the exclusive use and occupancy of the Navajos and the exclusion of non-Navajos from the prescribed area was meant to establish the lands as within the exclusive sovereignty of the Navajos under general federal supervision. It is thus unsurprising that this Court has interpreted the Navajo treaty to preclude extension of state law — including state tax law — to Indians on the Navajo Reservation. *See Warren Trading Post Co. v. Arizona Tax Comm'n*, 380 U.S. 685, 687, 690 (1965); *Williams v. Lee, supra*, at 221–222.

Moreover, since the signing of the Navajo treaty, Congress has consistently acted upon the assumption that the States lacked jurisdiction over Navajos living on the reservation [citing Arizona Enabling Act, 36 Stat. 569, 570, prohibiting state jurisdiction over Indian country but allowing state taxation of land "outside of an Indian reservation owned or held by any Indian"]. It is true, of course, that exemptions from tax laws should, as a general rule, be clearly expressed. But we have in the past construed language far more ambiguous than this as providing a tax exemption for Indians. *See, e. g., Squire v. Capoeman*, 351 U.S. 1, 6 (1956) [presented in Sec. A.4, this chapter], and we see no reason to give this language an especially crabbed or restrictive meaning.

Indeed, Congress's intent to maintain the tax-exempt status of reservation Indians is especially clear in light of the Buck Act, 4 U. S. C. § 105 et seq., which provides comprehensive federal guidance for state taxation of those living within federal areas. Section 106 (a) of Title 4 U. S. C. grants to the States general authority to impose an income tax on residents of federal areas, but § 109 expressly provides that "nothing in sections 105 and 106 of this title shall be deemed to authorize the levy or collection of any tax on or from any Indian not otherwise taxed." To be sure, the language of the statute itself does not make clear whether the reference to "any Indian not otherwise taxed" was intended to apply to reservation Indians earning their income on the reservation. But the legislative history makes plain that this proviso was meant to except reservation Indians from coverage of the Buck Act, *see* S. Rep. No. 1625, 76th Cong., 3d Sess., 2, 4 (1940); 84 Cong. Rec. 10685, and this Court has so interpreted it. *See Warren Trading Post Co. v. Arizona Tax Comm'n*, 380 U.S., at 691 n. 18. While the Buck Act itself cannot be read as an affirmative grant of tax-exempt status to reservation Indians, it should be obvious that Congress would not have jealously protected the immunity of reservation Indians from state income taxes had it thought that the States had residual power to impose such taxes in any event. Similarly, narrower statutes authorizing States to assert tax jurisdiction over reservations in special situations are explicable only if Congress assumed that the States lacked the power to impose the taxes without special authorization.

Finally, it should be noted that Congress has now provided a method whereby

States may assume jurisdiction over reservation Indians. Title 25 U. S. C. § 1322 (a) grants the consent of the United States to States wishing to assume criminal and civil jurisdiction over reservation Indians, and 25 U. S. C. § 1324 confers upon the States the right to disregard enabling acts which limit their authority over such Indians. But the Act expressly provides that the State must act "with the consent of the tribe occupying the particular Indian country," 25 U. S. C. § 1322 (a), 17 and must "appropriately [amend its] constitution or statutes." 25 U. S. C. § 1324. Once again, the Act cannot be read as expressly conferring tax immunity upon Indians. But we cannot believe that Congress would have required the consent of the Indians affected and the amendment of those state constitutions which prohibit the assumption of jurisdiction if the States were free to accomplish the same goal unilaterally by simple legislative enactment. *See Kennerly v. District Court*, 400 U.S. 423 (1971).

Arizona, of course, has neither amended its constitution to permit taxation of the Navajos nor secured the consent of the Indians affected. Indeed, a startling aspect of this case is that appellee apparently concedes that, in the absence of compliance with 25 U. S. C. § 1322 (a), the Arizona courts can exercise neither civil nor criminal jurisdiction over reservation Indians. *See* Brief for Appellee 24–26. 19. But the appellee nowhere explains how, without such jurisdiction, the State's tax may either be imposed or collected. Unless the State is willing to defend the position that it may constitutionally administer its tax system altogether without judicial intervention, *cf. Ward v. Board of County Comm'rs*, 253 U.S. 17 (1920), the admitted absence of either civil or criminal jurisdiction would seem to dispose of the case.

IV

When Arizona's contentions are measured against these statutory imperatives, they are simply untenable. The State relies primarily upon language in *Williams v. Lee* stating that the test for determining the validity of state action is "whether [it] infringed on the right of reservation Indians to make their own laws and be ruled by them." 358 U.S., at 220. Since Arizona has attempted to tax individual Indians and not the tribe or reservation as such, it argues that it has not infringed on Indian rights of self-government.

In fact, we are far from convinced that when a State imposes taxes upon reservation members without their consent, its action can be reconciled with tribal self-determination. But even if the State's premise were accepted, we reject the suggestion that the *Williams* test was meant to apply in this situation. It must be remembered that cases applying the *Williams* test have dealt principally with situations involving non-Indians. *See also Organized Village of Kake v. Egan*, 369 U.S., at 75–76. In these situations, both the tribe and the State could fairly claim an interest in asserting their respective jurisdictions. The *Williams* test was designed to resolve this conflict by providing that the State could protect its interest up to the point where tribal self-government would be affected.

The problem posed by this case is completely different. Since appellant is an Indian and since her income is derived wholly from reservation sources, her activity is totally within the sphere which the relevant treaty and statutes leave for the federal government and for the Indians themselves. Appellee cites us to no cases holding that this legislation may be ignored simply because tribal self-government has not been infringed. On the contrary, this Court expressly rejected such a position only two years ago. In *Kennerly v. District Court*, 400 U.S. 423 (1971), the Blackfoot Indian Tribe had voted to make state jurisdiction concurrent within the reservation. Although the State had not complied with the procedural prerequisites for the assumption of jurisdiction, it argued that it was nonetheless entitled to extend its laws to the reservation since such action was obviously consistent with the wishes of the Tribe and, therefore, with tribal self-government. But we held that the Williams rule was inapplicable and that "the unilateral action of the Tribal Council was insufficient to vest Montana with jurisdiction." *Id.*, at 427. If Montana may not assume jurisdiction over the Blackfeet by simple legislation even when the Tribe itself agrees to be bound by state law, it surely follows that Arizona may not assume such jurisdiction in the absence of tribal agreement. . . .

Finally, we cannot accept the notion that it is irrelevant "whether the . . . state income tax infringes on [appellant's] rights as an individual Navajo Indian," as the State Court of Appeals maintained. 14 Ariz. App., at 454, 484 P. 2d, at 223. To be sure, when Congress has legislated on Indian matters, it has, most often, dealt with the tribes as collective entities. But those entities are, after all, composed of individual Indians, and the legislation confers individual rights. This Court has therefore held that "the question has always been whether the state action infringed on the right of reservation *Indians* to make their own laws and be ruled by them." *Williams v. Lee, supra*, at 220 (emphasis added). In this case, appellant's rights as a reservation Indian were violated when the state collected a tax from her which it had no jurisdiction to impose. Accordingly, the judgment of the court below must be

Reversed.

WASHINGTON v. CONFEDERATED TRIBES OF THE COLVILLE RESERVATION
United States Supreme Court
447 U.S. 134 (1980)

MR. JUSTICE WHITE delivered the opinion of the Court.

In recent Terms we have more than once addressed the intricate problem of state taxation of matters involving Indian tribes and their members. *Moe v. Salish & Kootenai Tribes*, 425 U.S. 463 (1976); *McClanahan v. Arizona State Tax Comm'n*, 411 U.S. 164 (1973); *Mescalero Apache Tribe v. Jones*, 411 U.S. 145 (1973). We return to that vexing area in the present cases. Although a variety of questions are presented, perhaps the most significant is whether an Indian tribe ousts a State from any power to tax on-reservation purchases by nonmembers of the tribe by imposing its own tax on the transaction or by otherwise earning revenues from the tribal business. A three-judge District Court held for the Tribes. We affirm in part and reverse in part.

I

[The Confederated Tribes of Colville, Makah and Lummi and the United States on behalf of the Yakima tribe, filed separate cases that were consolidated,] contend[ing] that the State's cigarette and tobacco products taxes[73] could not lawfully be applied to sales by on-reservation tobacco outlets. They sought declaratory judgments to that effect, as well as injunctions barring the State from taking any measures to enforce the challenged taxes. In particular, the plaintiffs sought to enjoin the State from seizing as contraband untaxed cigarettes destined for delivery to their reservations. In the *Colville* case, the Tribes also challenged the State's assumption of civil and criminal jurisdiction over their reservations and, by amended pleadings, attacked the application of the State's vehicle excise taxes to Indian-owned vehicles. The *Yakima* case did not present these latter issues, but it did make a broad attack on the application of the State's general retail sales tax to on-reservation transactions.

[Both cases were tried] on Mar. 28, 1977, and the three-judge court entered its consolidated decision on Feb. 22, 1978. The court concluded (1) that it had jurisdiction as a three-judge court to consider the issues presented; (2) that the state cigarette tax could not be applied to on-reservation transactions because it was pre-empted by the tribal taxing ordinances and constituted an impermissible interference with tribal self-government; (3) that the state retail sales tax could not be applied to tribal cigarette sales, but could be applied to sales of other goods to non-Indians; (4) that the State could not impose certain recordkeeping requirements in connection with various tax-exempt sales; (5) that the State could not impose its vehicle excise taxes upon vehicles owned by the Tribes and their members, and (6) that the State's assumption of civil and criminal jurisdiction over the Makah and Lummi Tribes was unconstitutional. The court enjoined enforcement of the statutes it had struck down, and the State moved unsuccessfully for a new trial [and this appeal followed].

We begin by sketching the relevant factual background, which is not seriously in dispute. Thereafter, we explore the jurisdictional questions previously postponed and then turn to the merits.

II

The State of Washington levies a cigarette excise tax of $1.60 per carton, on the "sale, use, consumption, handling, possession or distribution" of cigarettes within the State. Wash. Rev. Code § 82.24.020 (1976). The tax is enforced with tax stamps; and dealers are required to sell only cigarettes to which such stamps have been affixed. § 82.24.030. Indian tribes are permitted to possess unstamped cigarettes for purposes of resale to members of the tribe, but are required by regulation to collect the tax with respect to sales to nonmembers. § 82.24.260; Wash. Admin. Code § 458-20-192 (1977). The District Court found, on the basis of its examination of

---

[73] [2] The state tobacco products tax, which is imposed on cigars and pipe tobacco pursuant to Wash. Rev. Code § 82.26 (1976), is not before us. The District Court concluded that that tax fell upon the Indian sellers and not upon the non-Indian purchasers. The State did not appeal from this holding, and all parties agree that in consequence the tobacco products tax may not be imposed on sales by tribal dealers.

state authorities, that the legal incidence of the tax is on the purchaser in transactions between an Indian seller and a non-Indian buyer.

The State has sought to enforce its cigarette tax by seizing as contraband unstamped cigarettes bound for various tribal reservations. It claims that it is entitled to make such seizures whenever the cigarettes are destined to be sold to non-Indians without affixation of stamps or collection of the tax.

Washington also imposes a sales tax on sales of personal property, including cigarettes. Wash. Rev. Code § 82.08.020 (1976). This tax, which was 5% during the relevant period, is collected from the purchaser by the retailer. § 82.08.050. It does not apply to on-reservation sales to reservation Indians. Wash. Admin. Code § 458-20-192 (1977).

The state motor vehicle excise tax is imposed on "the privilege of using in the state any motor vehicle." Wash. Rev. Code § 82.44.020 (1976). The tax is assessed annually, and during the relevant period the amount was two percent of the fair market value of the vehicle in question. In addition, the State imposes an annual tax in the amount of one percent of fair market value on the privilege of using campers and trailers in the State. § 82.50.400.

Each of the Tribes involved in this litigation is recognized by the United States as a sovereign Indian tribe. Each is governed by a business or tribal council approved by the Secretary of the Interior. . . .

The Colville, Lummi, and Makah Tribes have nearly identical cigarette sales and taxing schemes. Each Tribe has enacted ordinances pursuant to which it has authorized one or more on-reservation tobacco outlets. These ordinances have been approved by the Secretary of the Interior; and the dealer at each tobacco outlet is a federally licensed Indian trader. All three Tribes use federally restricted tribal funds to purchase cigarettes from out-of-state dealers. The Tribes distribute the cigarettes to the tobacco outlets and collect from the operators of those outlets both the wholesale distribution price and a tax of 40 to 50 cents per carton. The cigarettes remain the property of the Tribe until sale. The taxing ordinances specify that the tax is to be passed on to the ultimate consumer of the cigarettes. From 1972 through 1976, the Colville Tribe realized approximately $266,000 from its cigarette tax; the Lummi Tribe realized $54,000 and the Makah Tribe realized $13,000.

While the Colville, Lummi, and Makah Tribes function as retailers, retaining possession of the cigarettes until their sale to consumers, the Yakima Tribe acts as a wholesaler. It purchases cigarettes from out-of-state dealers and then sells them to its licensed retailers. The Tribe receives a markup over the wholesale price from those retailers as well as a tax of 22.5 cents per carton. There is no requirement that this tax be added to the selling price. In 1975, the Yakima Tribe derived $278,000 from its cigarette business.

Indian tobacco dealers make a large majority of their sales to non-Indians — residents of nearby communities who journey to the reservation especially to take advantage of the claimed tribal exemption from the state cigarette and sales taxes. The purchaser saves more than a dollar on each carton, and that makes the trip worthwhile. All parties agree that if the State were able to tax sales by Indian smoke shops and eliminate that one-dollar saving the stream of non-Indian bargain hunters would dry up. In short, the Indian retailer's business is to a substantial degree dependent upon his tax-exempt status, and if he loses that status his sales will fall off sharply.

III

We first address our jurisdiction to hear the State's appeal. Two attacks are made upon that jurisdiction, one grounded in the intricacies of the now-repealed statute governing three-judge district courts and the other having to do with the timing of the State's appeal.

[The provisions of section 2281 do not require] a three-judge court where a constitutional challenge to a state statute is grounded only in the Supremacy Clause. [Furthermore] § 2281 is not brought into play by constitutional claims that are "insubstantial."

[The plaintiffs had claimed that the] state taxes were unconstitutional under the Indian Commerce Clause as well as the Supremacy Clause. [There is] language in footnote 17 [of] *Moe v. Salish & Kootenai Tribes*, 425 U.S. 463, 481, n.17 (1976) [suggesting] that the insubstantiality of Commerce Clause claims such as those before us flows from *Mescalero Apache Tribe v. Jones*, 411 U.S. 145 (1973), and *McClanahan v. Arizona State Tax Comm'n*, — both of which were decided before the present suits were filed.[74] [T]he United States reads too much into [the language of these decisions]. Neither *Mescalero* nor *McClanahan* "inescapably render[s] the [Tribes' Commerce Clause] claims frivolous" because neither holds that that clause is wholly without force in situations like the present. And even footnote 17 merely rejects the stark and rather unhelpful notion that the Commerce Clause provides an "*automatic* exemptio[n] 'as a matter of constitutional law' " in such cases. (Emphasis added.) It does not take that clause entirely out of play in the field of state regulation of Indian affairs. . . .

---

[74] [22] Footnote 17 in its entirety reads as follows:

It is thus clear that the basis for the invalidity of these taxing measures, which we have found to be inconsistent with existing federal statutes, is the Supremacy Clause, and not any automatic exemptions 'as a matter of constitutional law' either under the Commerce Clause or the intergovernmental-immunity doctrine as laid down originally in *M'Culloch v. Maryland*, 4 Wheat. 316 (1819). If so, then the basis for convening a three-judge court in this type of case has effectively disappeared, for this Court has expressly held that attacks on state statutes raising only Supremacy Clause invalidity do not fall within the scope of 28 U.S.C. § 2281. *Swift & Co. v. Wickham*, 382 U.S. 111 (1965). Here, however, the District Court properly convened a § 2281 court, because at the outset the Tribe's attack asserted unconstitutionality of these statutes under the Commerce Clause, a not insubstantial claim since *Mescalero* and *McClanahan* had not yet been decided. See *Goosby v. Osser*, 409 U.S. 512 (1973). 425 U.S., at 481.

IV

A

In [*Moe*] we considered a state taxing scheme remarkably similar to the cigarette and sales taxes at issue in the present cases. Montana there sought to impose a cigarette tax on sales by smoke shops operated by tribal members and located on leased trust lands within the reservation, and sought to require the smoke shop operators to collect the tax. We upheld the tax, insofar as sales to non-Indians were concerned, because its legal incidence fell on the non-Indian purchaser. Hence, "the competitive advantage which the Indian seller doing business on tribal land enjoys over all other cigarette retailers, within and without the reservation, is dependent on the extent to which the non-Indian purchaser is willing to flout *his* legal obligation to pay the tax." (Emphasis in original.) We upheld the collection requirement, as applied to purchases by non-Indians, on the ground that it was a "minimal burden" designed to aid the State in collecting an otherwise valid tax.

Moe establishes several principles relevant to the present cases. The State may sometimes impose a nondiscriminatory tax on non-Indian customers of Indian retailers doing business on the reservation. Such a tax may be valid even if it seriously disadvantages or eliminates the Indian retailer's business with non-Indians.[75] And the State may impose at least "minimal" burdens on the Indian retailer to aid in enforcing and collecting the tax. There is no automatic bar, therefore, to Washington's extending its tax and collection and recordkeeping requirements onto the reservation in the present cases.

Although it narrows the issues in the present cases, *Moe* does not definitively resolve several important questions. First, unlike in *Moe*, each of the Tribes imposes its own tax on cigarette sales, and obtains further revenues by participating in the cigarette enterprise at the wholesale or retail level. Second, Washington requires the Indian retailer to keep detailed records of exempt and nonexempt sales in addition to simply precollecting the tax. *Moe* expressed no opinion regarding the "complicated problems" of enforcement that distinctions between exempt and nonexempt purchasers might entail. Third, *Moe* left unresolved the question of whether a State can tax purchases by on-reservation Indians not members of the governing tribe, as Washington seeks to do in the present cases. Finally, unlike in *Moe*[,] Washington has seized and threatens to continue seizing, shipments of unstamped cigarettes en route to the reservations from wholesalers outside the State. We address each of these questions.[76]

---

[75] [27] The United States reads *Moe* too parsimoniously in asserting its inapplicability to cases, such as the present ones, in which the economic impact on tribal retailers is particularly severe. *Moe* makes clear that the Tribes have no vested right to a certain volume of sales to non-Indians, or indeed to any such sales at all.

[76] [28] The incidence of the Colville, Lummi, and Makah taxes falls on the cigarette purchaser, since the tribal ordinances specify that the tax is to be passed on to the ultimate consumer. The Yakima ordinance, in contrast, does not require that the tax be added to the selling price, and the incidence of the Yakima tax therefore does not fall on the purchaser. The State's challenge is directed only at the Colville, Lummi, and Makah taxes.

B

[*Oliphant* posed no barrier to the tribal taxation of non-Indians. Because they have exercised this power to tax, the tribes further] contend that their involvement in the operation and taxation of cigarette marketing on the reservation ousts the State from any power to exact its sales and cigarette taxes from nonmembers purchasing cigarettes at tribal smoke shops. The primary argument is economic. It is asserted that smoke shop cigarette sales generate substantial revenues for the Tribes which they expend for essential governmental services, including programs to combat severe poverty and underdevelopment at the reservations. Most cigarette purchasers are outsiders attracted on to the reservations by the bargain prices the smoke shops charge by virtue of their claimed exemption from state taxation. If the State is permitted to impose its taxes, the Tribes will no longer enjoy any competitive advantage vis-à-vis businesses in surrounding areas. Indeed, because the Tribes themselves impose a tax on the transaction, if the state tax is also collected the price charged will necessarily be higher and the Tribes will be placed at a competitive *disadvantage* as compared to businesses elsewhere. Tribal smoke shops will lose a large percentage of their cigarette sales and the Tribes will forfeit substantial revenues. Because of this economic impact, it is argued, the state taxes are (1) pre-empted by federal statutes regulating Indian affairs; (2) inconsistent with the principle of tribal self-government; and (3) invalid under "negative implications" of the Indian Commerce Clause.

It is painfully apparent that the value marketed by the smoke shops to persons coming from outside is not generated on the reservations by activities in which the Tribes have a significant interest. Cf. *Moe v. Salish & Kootenai Tribes; McClanahan v. Arizona State Tax Comm'n.* What the smoke shops offer these customers, and what is not available elsewhere, is solely an exemption from state taxation. The Tribes assert the power to create such exemptions by imposing their own taxes or otherwise earning revenues by participating in the reservation enterprises. If this assertion were accepted, the Tribes could impose a nominal tax and open chains of discount stores at reservation borders, selling goods of all descriptions at deep discounts and drawing customers from surrounding areas. We do not believe that principles of federal Indian law, whether stated in terms of pre-emption, tribal self-government, or otherwise, authorize Indian tribes thus to market an exemption from state taxation to persons who would normally do their business elsewhere.

The federal statutes cited to us, even when given the broadest reading to which they are fairly susceptible, cannot be said to pre-empt Washington's sales and cigarette taxes. The [IRA], the Indian Financing Act of 1974, and the Indian Self-Determination and Education Assistance Act of 1975, evidence to varying degrees a congressional concern with fostering tribal self-government and economic development, but none goes so far as to grant tribal enterprises selling goods to nonmembers an artificial competitive advantage over all other businesses in a State. The Indian traders statutes, 25 U.S.C. §§ 261 et seq., incorporate a congressional desire comprehensively to regulate businesses selling goods to reservation Indians for cash or exchange, see *Warren Trading Post v. Arizona Tax Comm'n*, 380 U.S. 685 (1965), but no similar intent is evident with respect to sales by Indians to nonmembers of the Tribe. [A]lthough the Tribes themselves could perhaps pre-empt state taxation through the exercise of properly delegated federal power to do so, cf. *Fisher v. District Court*, 424 U.S. 382, 390 (1976) (per curiam); [*United States v. Mazurie*,] we do not infer from the mere fact of federal approval of the Indian taxing ordinances, or from the fact that the Tribes exercise congressionally sanctioned powers of self-government, that Congress has delegated the far-reaching authority to pre-empt valid state sales and cigarette taxes otherwise collectible from nonmembers of the Tribe.

Washington does not infringe the right of reservation Indians to "make their own laws and be ruled by them," [*Williams v. Lee*], merely because the result of imposing its taxes will be to deprive the Tribes of revenues which they currently are receiving. The principle of tribal self-government, grounded in notions of inherent sovereignty and in congressional policies, seeks an accommodation between the interests of the Tribes and the federal government, on the one hand, and those of the State, on the other. [*McClanahan*.] While the Tribes do have an interest in raising revenues for essential governmental programs, that interest is strongest when the revenues are derived from value generated on the reservation by activities involving the Tribes and when the taxpayer is the recipient of tribal services. The State also has a legitimate governmental interest in raising revenues, and that interest is likewise strongest when the tax is directed at off-reservation value and when the taxpayer is the recipient of state services. As we have already noted, Washington's taxes are reasonably designed to prevent the Tribes from marketing their tax exemption to nonmembers who do not receive significant tribal services and who would otherwise purchase their cigarettes outside the reservations.

It can no longer be seriously argued that the Indian Commerce Clause, of its own force, automatically bars all state taxation of matters significantly touching the political and economic interests of the Tribes. See *Moe v. Salish & Kootenai Tribes*, n.17. That clause may have a more limited role to play in preventing undue discrimination against, or burdens on, Indian commerce. But Washington's taxes are applied in a nondiscriminatory manner to all transactions within the State. And although the result of these taxes will be to lessen or eliminate tribal commerce with nonmembers, that market existed in the first place only because of a claimed exemption from these very taxes. The taxes under consideration do not burden commerce that would exist on the reservations without respect to the tax exemption.

We cannot fault the State for not giving credit on the amount of tribal taxes paid. It is argued that if a credit is not given, the tribal retailers will actually be placed at a competitive disadvantage, as compared to retailers elsewhere, due to the overlapping impact of tribal and state taxation. While this argument is not without force, we find that the Tribes have failed to demonstrate that business at the smoke shops would be significantly reduced by a state tax without a credit as compared to a state tax with a credit. With a credit, prices at the smoke shops would presumably be roughly the same as those off the reservation, assuming that the Indian enterprises are operated at an efficiency similar to that of businesses elsewhere; without a credit, prices at smoke shops would exceed those off the reservation by the amount of the tribal taxes, about 40 to 50 cents per carton for the Lummi, Makah, and Colville Tribes, and 22.5 cents per carton for the Yakima Tribe. It is evident that even if credit were given, the bulk of the smoke shops' present business would still be eliminated, since nonresidents of the reservation could purchase cigarettes at the same price and with greater convenience nearer their homes and would have no incentive to travel to the smoke shops for bargain purchases as they do [at present].

A second asserted ground for the invalidity of the state taxes is that they somehow conflict with the Tribes' cigarette ordinances and thereby are subject to pre-emption or contravene the principle of tribal self-government. This argument need not detain us. There is no direct conflict between the state and tribal schemes, since each government is free to impose its taxes without ousting the other. Although taxes can be used for distributive or regulatory purposes, as well as for raising revenue, we see no nonrevenue purposes to the tribal taxes at issue in these cases, and, as already noted, we perceive no intent on the part of Congress to authorize the Tribes to pre-empt otherwise valid state taxes. Other provisions of the tribal ordinances do comprehensively regulate the marketing of cigarettes by the tribal enterprises; but the State does not interfere with the Tribes' power to regulate tribal enterprises when it simply imposes its tax on sales to nonmembers. Hence, we perceive no conflict between state and tribal law warranting invalidation of the State's taxes.

C

We recognized in *Moe* that if a State's tax is valid, the State may impose at least minimal burdens on Indian businesses to aid in collecting and enforcing that tax. The simple collection burden imposed by Washington's cigarette tax on tribal smoke shops is legally indistinguishable from the collection burden upheld in *Moe*, and we therefore hold that the State may validly require the tribal smoke shops to affix tax stamps purchased from the State to individual packages of cigarettes prior to the time of sale to nonmembers of the Tribe.

The state sales tax scheme requires smoke shop operators to keep detailed records of both taxable and nontaxable transactions. The operator must record the number and dollar volume of taxable sales to nonmembers of the Tribe. With respect to nontaxable sales, the operator must record and retain for state inspection the names of all Indian purchasers, their tribal affiliations, the Indian reservations within which sales are made, and the dollar amount and dates of sales. In addition, unless the Indian purchaser is personally known to the operator he must present a tribal identification card. . . .

Contrary to the District Court, we find the State's recordkeeping requirements valid *in toto*. The Tribes, and not the State as the District Court supposed, bear the burden of showing that the recordkeeping requirements which they are challenging are invalid. The District Court made the factual finding, which we accept, that there was no evidence of record on this question. Applying the correct burden of proof to the District Court's finding, we hold that the Tribes have failed to demonstrate that the State's recordkeeping requirements for exempt sales are not reasonably necessary as a means of preventing fraudulent transactions.

D

The State asserts the power to apply its sales and cigarette taxes to Indians resident on the reservation but not enrolled in the [Tribe imposing the taxes]. Federal statutes, even given the broadest reading to which they are reasonably susceptible, cannot be said to pre-empt Washington's power to impose its taxes on Indians not members of the Tribe. We do not so read the Major Crimes Act, which at most provides for federal-court jurisdiction over crimes committed by Indians on another Tribe's reservation. Similarly, the mere fact that nonmembers resident on the reservation come within the definition of "Indian" for purposes of the [IRA] does not demonstrate a congressional intent to exempt such Indians from state taxation.

Nor would the imposition of Washington's tax on these purchasers contravene the principle of tribal self-government, for the simple reason that nonmembers are not constituents of the governing Tribe. For most practical purposes those Indians stand on the same footing as non-Indians resident of the reservation. There is no evidence that nonmembers have a say in tribal affairs or significantly share in tribal disbursements. We find, therefore, that the State's interest in taxing these purchasers outweighs any tribal interest that may exist in preventing the State from imposing its taxes.

E

Finally, the State contends that it has the power to seize unstamped cigarettes as contraband if the Tribes do not cooperate in collecting the State's taxes. . . .

We find that Washington's interest in enforcing its valid taxes is sufficient to justify these seizures. Although the cigarettes in transit are as yet exempt from state taxation, they are not immune from seizure when the Tribes, as here, have refused to fulfill collection and remittance obligations which the State has validly imposed. It is significant that these seizures take place outside the reservation, in locations where state power over Indian affairs is considerably more expansive than it is within reservation boundaries. Cf. *Mescalero Apache Tribe v. Jones*, 411 U.S. 145 (1973). By seizing cigarettes en route to the reservation, the State polices against wholesale evasion of its own valid taxes without unnecessarily intruding on core tribal interests.

[T]he judgments of the District Court are *Reversed in part and affirmed in part*.

MR. JUSTICE BRENNAN, with whom MR. JUSTICE MARSHALL joins, concurring in part and dissenting in part.

[T]he State of Washington's cigarette taxing scheme should be invalidated both because it undermines the Tribes' sovereign authority to regulate and tax the distribution of cigarettes on trust lands and because it conflicts with tribal activities and functions that have been expressly approved by the federal government. . . .

The Court draws support for its result from the suggestion that a decision invalidating these taxes would give the Tribes carte blanche to establish vast tax exempt shopping centers dealing in every imaginable good. I think these fears are substantially overdrawn. *Moe* made clear that Indians do not have an absolute entitlement to achieve some particular sales volume by passing their tax-exempt status to non-Indian customers, and I do not question that conclusion today. I would simply hold that the State may not impose a tax that forces the Tribes to choose between federally sanctioned goals and places their goods at an actual competitive disadvantage. Nothing in such a holding would emasculate state taxing authority or bring the specter of enormous tribal tax havens closer to reality. On the contrary, I am confident that the State could devise a taxing scheme without the flaws which mar the present one. . . .

MR. JUSTICE STEWART, concurring in part and dissenting in part.

[W]hen a State and an Indian Tribe tax in a functionally identical manner the same on-reservation sales to nontribal members, it is my view that congressional policy conjoined with the Indian Commerce Clause requires the State to credit against its own tax the amount of the Tribe's tax. This solution fully effectuates the State's goal of assuring that its citizens who are not tribal members do not cash in on the exemption from state taxation that the Tribe and its members enjoy. On the other hand, it permits the Tribe to share with the State in the tax revenues from cigarette sales, without at the same time placing the Tribe's federally encouraged enterprises at a competitive disadvantage compared to similarly situated off-reservation businesses. . . .

MR. JUSTICE REHNQUIST, concurring and dissenting.

Since early in the last century, this Court has been struggling to develop a coherent doctrine by which to measure with some predictability the scope of Indian immunity from state taxation. In recent years, it appeared such a doctrine was well on its way to being established. I write separately to underscore what I think the contours of that doctrine are because I am convinced that a well-defined body of principles is essential in order to end the need for case-by-case litigation which has plagued this area of the law for a number of years. That doctrine, I had thought, was at bottom a preemption analysis based on the principle that Indian immunities are dependent upon congressional intent, at least absent discriminatory state action prohibited by the Indian Commerce Clause. I see no need for this Court to balance the state and tribal interests in enacting particular forms of taxation in order to determine their validity. Absent discrimination, the question is only one of congressional intent. Either Congress intended to pre-empt the state taxing authority or it did not. Balancing of interests is not the appropriate gauge for determining validity since it is that very balancing which we have reserved to Congress. I concur in the Court's conclusion, however, that the cigarette tax is valid because Congress has not pre-empted state authority to impose the tax. . . .

NOTES

1. **The Indian Commerce Clause, Preemption, and "Inherent" State Authority:** *Colville* indicates that under the proper circumstances (found to exist in that case), states may exercise taxing and regulatory power within Indian country

over transactions between Indians and non-Indians, even without express congressional permission to do so. In adopting this approach, has the Court lost sight of *Worcester*, with its holding that Indian country is outside state authority by virtue of, among other things, the negative implications of the Indian commerce clause? In *Worcester*, Chief Justice Marshall said that the state statute purporting to exercise authority over Worcester and other non-Indian missionaries in the Cherokee Nation was unconstitutional, in part because it "interfere[d] forcibly with the relations established between the United States and the Cherokee nation, the regulation of which, according to the settled principles of our constitution, are *committed exclusively* to the government of the Union." In contrast, Justice White's opinion in *Colville* restricts the force of the Indian commerce clause to situations where there is "undue discrimination against, or burdens on, Indian commerce." Even if one accepts this limited role for the Indian commerce clause, did the Court arrive at the correct conclusion? While it is reasonably easy to see why the Washington taxes in *Colville* or the Montana taxes in *Moe* were not discriminatory, could it not be said that they impose undue "burdens" on Indian commerce? How can this statement in *Colville* be reconciled with the comment in *Williams v. Lee* that "essentially, absent governing Acts of Congress, the question has always been whether the state action infringed on the right of reservation Indians to make their own laws and be ruled by them?" Did *McClanahan*'s admonition that courts should "avoid reliance on platonic notions of Indian sovereignty and . . . look instead to the applicable treaties and statutes which define the limits of state power" effectively modify *Williams v. Lee*'s infringement test? What did the Court mean in *McClanahan* when it described "[t]he Indian sovereignty doctrine" as "relevant, then, not because it provides a definitive resolution of the issues in this suit, but because it provides a backdrop against which the applicable treaties and federal statutes must be read?"

Should the involvement of non-Indians as customers in *Colville* trigger a different judicial approach from *Worcester*, *Williams*, and *McClanahan*? Recall that in *Worcester*, the state was prevented from exercising jurisdiction over a *non-Indian* minister who had entered Cherokee territory to work with the Indians. Furthermore, later nineteenth century cases upholding limited state authority over non-Indians within Indian country confined those results to situations where the Court found the complete absence of any "Indian interest." *See* Sec. B.1, this chapter. Can an Indian interest be denied in *Colville*, where the Tribes were involved in the businesses and seeking to tax the same transactions as the state?

The idea that states could tax transactions between Indians and non-Indians first surfaced in the Supreme Court decision in *Moe v. Salish & Kootenai Tribes*, 425 U.S. 463 (1976), discussed in *Colville*. *Moe* did not cite *Worcester* or even examine the negative implications of the Indian commerce clause. It did, however, cite to the case of *Thomas v. Gay*, 169 U.S. 264 (1898), where the Court had rejected an Indian commerce clause challenge to a state personal property tax on non-Indian cattle grazing on lands leased by non-Indians from tribes. But in *Thomas*, the Court had been careful to deny the existence of any Indian interest. Even though the state tax might have some indirect impact on the value of the land for leasing, the Court found that a tax put upon the cattle of the lessees is too remote and indirect to be deemed a tax upon the lands or privileges of the [Indians or their tribes]. . . . The taxes in question here were not imposed on the business of grazing, or on the rents received by the Indians, but on the cattle as property of the lessees, and, as we have heretofore said that as such a tax is too remote and indirect to be deemed a tax or burden on interstate commerce, so is it too remote and indirect to be regarded as an interference with the legislative power of Congress.

Id. at 273–74. Even assuming that *Thomas* is correct in analogizing the Indian commerce clause to the interstate commerce clause, does the result in *Moe* follow from the holding and reasoning in *Thomas*?

After discarding the Indian commerce clause as a restraint, *Moe* and *Colville* analyze the state cigarette tax solely from the perspective of preemption by federal treaty or statute, and find them to create no bar. But is it reasonable to interpret a treaty setting aside lands for the sole use and benefit of a tribe as permitting the intrusion of state law where tribal interests are involved and tribal taxing authority might be impaired? In *Worcester* Chief Justice Marshall relied in part on the preemptive effect of the federal promises of tribal sovereignty and self-government that he inferred from the terms of the Treaty of Hopewell. The argument seemed to be that the federal policy of recognizing an Indian tribe and protecting its homeland and legal autonomy wholly preempted state power in Indian country, even over *non-Indian* missionaries such as Worcester. Is *Williams* consistent with that approach? Are *Moe* and *Colville* consistent with this theme from *Worcester*? *Moe* assumed without discussion that states had inherent authority to tax *non-Indians* in Indian country and *Colville* expands that assumption even to resident nonmember Indians. From what source does the state derive this authority? In light of *Worcester* and *Williams*, should not the same doctrinal test control the issue of state power over either tribal members or nonmembers in Indian country? As you consider these questions, keep in mind the canon of construction requiring interpretation of treaties as the Indians would have understood them, with ambiguities resolved in their favor. *See* Ch. 2, Sec. C.

Colville treats federal *statutory* preemption as a prime means of determining whether state tax laws can be applied to dealings between tribes and nonmembers. The Court's Indian country preemption analysis can be best understood when juxtaposed against federal statutory preemption analysis used in non-Indian law contexts. *See generally* LAURENCE H. TRIBE, AMERICAN CONSTITUTIONAL LAW 1172–1204 (3d ed. 2000). This non-Indian preemption law, derived from the supremacy clause of Article IV of the Constitution, has two branches. According to the first branch, an exercise of state power that directly conflicts with a federal statute or that could pose a serious threat of conflicting enforcement efforts is preempted by federal law.

Can this branch of preemption analysis explain *Colville*, given that the case does not inquire whether state law conflicts with any clear federal statutory or treaty provision? At the time of *Colville*, no federal laws addressed state taxation of tribal retail sales. It is precisely the absence of a requirement of a clear and express preemptive federal statutory provision that provoked Justice Rehnquist to insist in his *Colville* concurrence that "Indian immunities [should be] dependent upon congressional intent. . . . Either Congress intended to pre-empt the state taxing authority or it did not." In light of the history of the Indian commerce clause and the historic lack of state authority in Indian country, should the courts require the existence of a clear and specific federal law that preempts state authority merely because such clear statutory conflict is frequently required to find preemption in other fields?

A second branch of non-Indian preemption law provides that federal preemption of state law can occur where the federal regulation is either so pervasive or involves a field of such dominant national concern that the federal statutory action has "occupied the field" to the exclusion of even consistent state laws. *E.g., Ray v. Atlantic Richfield Co.*, 435 U.S. 151 (1978); *Rice v. Santa Fe Elev. Corp.*, 331 U.S. 218 (1947). Sometimes the federal statutory objective may not be fully attainable in the face of concurrent state legislation, no matter how congenial that state law may be to the federal policies involved. For example, the federal statute may reflect a legislative compromise that would be disturbed by state regulation of the same subject. In the *Rice* case Justice Douglas stated, "The question in each case is what the purpose of Congress was. . . . It is often a perplexing question whether Congress has precluded a state action or by the choice of selective regulatory measures has left the police power of the States undisturbed except as the state and federal regulations collide." Does this branch of non-Indian preemption law adequately explain the analytic approach or result in *Colville*? Is there a pervasive regulatory statute in that case? *McClanahan* treats the *implied* protections of tribal sovereignty derived from treaty or statute as a federal occupation of the geographic "field" of Indian country. But even adopting that approach, difficult problems remain. If federal regulations, or at least protections of the legal autonomy of Indian country, are either so pervasive or so infused with a dominant national interest, how can one explain the inherent state power over non-Indians and over Indians who are not tribal members that is recognized in *Colville*? Of course, it may be necessary in each case to determine the outer boundaries of the realm of tribal self-government that Congress has protected. However, is there any justification for drawing this boundary line in a fashion that results in federal preemption of matters involving tribal members in Indian country but excludes from the preemptive effect of federal law in Indian country state taxation of non-Indians or even Indians who are not tribal members? Can this result be reconciled with *Worcester* or *Williams v. Lee*?

2. Preemption Where States Seek to Tax Tribes or Individual Indians: In contrast to the first branch of non-Indian preemption law, in cases where the incidence of a tax is on a tribe or its members, the Court, following *McClanahan*, has said it has adopted a "categorical approach," which would deny all state taxing authority regardless whether Congress has clearly banned such taxation. *See, e.g., Oklahoma Tax Commission v. Chickasaw Nation*, 515 U.S. 450 (1995). Consistent with *Worcester*, the *implied* federal protection of tribal self-government derived from federal treaties and statutes recognizing the Indian reservation and protecting its autonomy establishes the preemption in such cases. *Cf., e.g., Jones v. Rath Packing Co.*, 430 U.S. 519 (1977); *City of Burbank v. Lockheed Air Term., Inc.*, 411 U.S. 624 (1973). Is that strict "categorical approach" the same method of analysis the Court deploys in *Colville*, where a tax falls on nonmembers? Was such a "categorical approach" followed in *City of Sherrill v. Oneida Indian Nation*, 544 U.S. 197 (2005), upholding a state property tax imposed on Oneida tribal land held in fee within its reservation? In *City of Sherrill*, presented in Ch. 6, Sec. A.5.b., the Court allowed imposition of the state tax without questioning the reservation status of the land, which the Nation had reacquired in fee nearly 200 years after its loss in a transaction with the State of New York that violated the Nonintercourse Act. A tribal lawsuit to enjoin the tax was dismissed on grounds of laches, even though the suit was brought very shortly after the Nation reacquired the land and the state began assessing the tax. Is there any way to justify such a result without overturning fundamental principles of federal Indian law, which the Court did not purport to do? As you will see in Note 6, *infra*, the Court has always required some clear indication from a federal statute before allowing state taxation of tribal lands, including fee lands. In *City of Sherrill*, the Court attempted to distinguish those cases as ones where the Indians had "continuously occupied" the tax-exempt lands. Should it matter for purposes of a claim of exemption from state taxation that the tribe had only recently reacquired its on-reservation land, many years after an illegal transfer?

3. **Applying *Colville*'s Preemption Approach:** In cases like *Colville*, where states seek to tax non-Indians on reservations, if state law is not categorically permitted absent clear conflict with federal law (Rehnquist's preferred approach in *Colville*) and not categorically invalidated because of tribal government and reservation status (Chief Justice Marshall's approach in *Worcester*), how does *Colville* determine whether states may tax tribal transactions with nonmembers? Rather than insisting on a single, critical federal regulatory statute that can sweep away incompatible state law, the Court seems willing to find preemption when a pattern of discrete federal laws and regulations evidences federal support for or supervision of Indian activities. For example, the Department of the Interior may have approved tribal ordinances establishing the business enterprise the state seeks to tax or regulate, or the federal government may be helping to fund the tribal activity or the tribal activity may be advancing fulfillment of the federal trust responsibility. Why wasn't the manifestation of federal interest sufficient in *Colville*? Does it make sense, in an era when federal policy favors tribal self-determination and assumption of federal service responsibilities by tribes, to make preemption turn on the pervasiveness and strength of federal involvement in tribal activities? Doesn't such a doctrine put pressure on Congress to maintain unnecessary regulatory regimes?

In addition to accepting a more diffuse expression of congressional purpose, the Indian law preemption doctrine in cases involving nonmember suppliers or customers has expressly considered state as well as federal and tribal interests. This three-way balancing gives weight to state interests in deriving tax revenue from nonmembers who benefit from state services, and denies weight to tribal interests in taxation where the tribe is not providing any services to the non-Indian. According to this approach, what would the Tribes in *Colville* have had to do to establish preemption? What if they had located the smoke shops in strip malls that had small restaurants and restrooms, as well as a playground for children? What if the smokeshops were located in a tribal campground, designed to attract smokers?

What if the Tribes provided their own packaging and brand name for the cigarettes? This balancing process has made it extremely difficult to predict whether states possess taxing and regulatory authority over nonmembers within Indian country, and a stampede of litigation has been the predictable consequence. To avoid the considerable costs of such litigation, tribes and states sometimes enter into cooperative agreements where they agree to disagree about jurisdiction and go about the business of tax revenue sharing and cooperative allocation of regulatory responsibilities. *See* Note 7 following *Cotton Petroleum Corp. v. New Mexico, infra*; Ch. 5, Sec. G.

For a general review of the preemption doctrine in the field of Indian affairs, see NELL JESSUP NEWTON ET AL., COHEN'S HANDBOOK OF FEDERAL INDIAN LAW §§ 6.01–6.03 (2012 ed.); Robert N. Clinton, *The Dormant Indian Commerce Clause*, 27 CONN. L. REV. 1055 (1995); Rebecca Tsosie, *Separate Sovereigns, Civil Rights, and the Sacred Text: The Legacy of Justice Thurgood Marshall's Indian Law Jurisprudence*, 26 ARIZ. ST. L.J. 494, 504 (1994); Philip P. Frickey, *Congressional Intent, Practical Reasoning, and the Dynamic Nature of Federal Indian Law*, 78 CAL. L. REV. 1137 (1990).

4. **"Incidental" State Power:** The decisions in *Moe* and *Colville* seem to suggest that state authority to tax cigarette sales to non-Indians and nonmember Indians derives primarily from the fact that the legal incidence of the tax, that is the formal transaction upon which the tax falls, is the purchase by the non-Indian. In *California State Bd. of Equalization v. Chemehuevi Tribe*, 474 U.S. 9 (1985), a tribal smoke shop sought to distinguish *Moe* and *Colville* on the ground that the structure of the California cigarette tax imposed the legal incidence of the tax on the Indian retailer of the cigarettes without any requirement that the tax be passed through to the ultimate consumer. In a brief *per curiam* opinion, the Court rejected the argument, stating:

> None of our cases has suggested that an express statement that the tax is to be passed on to the ultimate purchaser is necessary before a State may require a tribe to collect cigarette taxes from non-Indian purchasers and remit the amounts of such tax to the State. Nor do our cases suggest that the only test for whether the legal incidence of such a tax falls on purchasers is whether the taxing statute contains an express "pass on and collect" provision.

474 U.S. at 11–12. The Court ultimately rejected the premise of the Tribe's argument and concluded that the legal incidence of the California cigarette tax actually fell on the consumer. Does *Chemehuevi* suggest that permitting state taxation or regulation of transactions involving non-Indians or nonmembers in Indian country only starts a slippery analytical slope that inevitably leads to some state taxation or regulation of *Indians* in Indian country in contravention of *Worcester*, not to mention the intent of the framers of the Indian commerce clause? In *Moe*, the Court sustained a state requirement that forced Indian retailers to *precollect* the tax and keep records, and in *Colville* the Court broadened the record-keeping obligations and sustained cigarette stamp requirements as a precollection device. *See also Department of Taxation & Finance of N.Y. v. Milhelm Attea & Bros.*, 512 U.S. 61 (1994) (upholding New York cigarette tax regulations

which imposed burdensome recordkeeping requirements and cigarette sale quotas on non-Indian wholesalers who had been licensed under the federal Indian Trader statutes). Ostensibly, the Court sustained all of these devices as *means* toward the end of collecting the tax on sales to non-Indians and nonmembers. Are not these regulations, however, a substantial expansion of state power over Indians in Indian country, albeit through a doctrinal "back door"?

In *California v. Cabazon Band of Mission Indians*, 480 U.S. 202 (1987), presented and discussed below, the Supreme Court hinted that even without congressional permission, states may be able to exercise jurisdiction over Indian nations or their members within Indian country "in exceptional circumstances." Despite these statements, it is nearly impossible to find a Supreme Court holding that supports state jurisdiction of this type. For example, in *Cabazon* itself, the Court denied the application of state law banning high stakes bingo to a tribal gaming enterprise, despite the existence of off-reservation impacts on non-Indian customers. The only case that has been described as offering such an "exceptional circumstance" involved application of state fishing laws to on-reservation tribal members when those laws were reasonable and necessary for conservation of the species and for protection of fishing rights shared by Indians and non-Indians. *Puyallup Tribe, Inc. v. Washington Game Dep't*, 433 U.S. 165, 176–77 (1977). The existence of a shared fishing right makes this case *sui generis*. Why isn't such "incidental" state jurisdiction over tribes preempted by the limitations in Public Law 280?

5. State Taxing Authority over Nonmember Indians: The decision in *Colville* to exclude Indians who were not members of the affected tribes from the preemptive effect of federal law and thereby to authorize state taxation of their purchases in Indian country was certainly novel. *Cf. Arizona ex rel. Merrill v. Turtle*, 413 F.2d 683 (9th Cir. 1969) (State of Arizona lacked authority to extradite to Oklahoma a Cheyenne Indian who resided on the Navajo reservation with his Navajo wife since the exercise of such power would infringe on tribal government and interfere with the Navajo extradition procedures). One can reasonably question the support for and origins of such differential treatment of Indians. *See* Ch. 3, Sec. C. Note that the exclusion of nonmembers from the federal preemption analysis seemingly applies to all Indians who are not members of the governing tribe. Thus, even Indians who are members of a recognized Indian tribe must pay the state taxes if they are not members of the tribe governing the reservation where the sale took place. Is this result a logical outgrowth of *Morton v. Mancari*, which sustained the Indian employment preference for BIA hiring and advancement on the ground that it was a rational political preference related to self-government rather than a racial classification? *See* Ch. 2, Sec. B.1. Under the BIA employment preference, a member of the Navajo Nation would still receive employment preference over a non-Indian for a BIA position involving work with the Red Lake Chippewa in Minnesota.

Under the rule of *Colville*, however, this same Navajo would *not* be immune from state taxation for on-reservation transactions if he married a Santa Clara woman and lived for the rest of his life on the Santa Clara Pueblo. Moreover, the children of this union, if ineligible for enrollment as Santa Clarans, would also have to pay state taxes even if they spoke Tewa and otherwise fully participated in the cultural and social life of the Pueblo, like the Martinez children in *Santa Clara Pueblo v. Martinez*. *See* Ch. 3, Sec. C.5. Is there any sufficient justification for subjecting them to state taxation while exempting Julia Martinez? On the other hand, a member of the Santa Clara Pueblo who lived in Phoenix, Arizona, for example, but returned periodically to the reservation, seemingly would be exempt from state taxation for on-reservation transactions despite nonresidency. Note also that the Court's holding in *Colville* was not merely addressed to Indians who are temporarily and casually on a reservation other than their own. It is specifically addressed to "Indians who are *resident* on the reservation but not enrolled in the governing Tribe" (emphasis supplied). Did the Court fully appreciate the complexities of the tribal community in its ruling? Should the holding in *Colville* survive Congress's 1991 amendments to the Indian Civil Rights Act, which were designed to overturn *Duro*'s analogous decision regarding tribal criminal jurisdiction over nonmember Indians? *See* Ch. 3, Sec. C.1. Should those amendments be read solely as an affirmation of the similar status of member and nonmember Indians for purposes of inherent *tribal* jurisdiction? Or should they be read more broadly to mean that Congress intended for nonmember Indians to have the same status as member Indians for all purposes, including *state* jurisdiction? Hasn't the Court said that its task in developing federal common law is to work within the framework of Congress's expressed policies and objectives? *See, e.g., Oliphant v. Suquamish Indian Tribe*, Ch. 3, Sec. C.1.

Consider the facts of *Mike v. Franchise Tax Bd.*, 182 Cal. App. 4th 817 (2010), in which a member of the Twenty-Nine Palms Band of Mission Indians, a Cahuilla tribe, challenged imposition of state taxes on income she earned while living and working on the nearby reservation of the Agua Caliente Band of Cahuilla Indians, located in Palm Springs, California. To contest the tax, Mike invoked *McClanahan* and the *Duro*-fix legislation. She also pointed out that her own Tribe had long had close relations with the Agua Caliente, and her own reservation was too small for her to live and work there. In upholding the state tax, the Court of Appeal found no inconsistency with *McClanahan*, emphasizing language from *McClanahan* that cautioned it was not "dealing with Indians who have left . . . reservations set aside for their exclusive use. . . . ." *McClanahan*, 411 U.S. at 167. Couldn't this language be read to exclude exemption from state taxes for tribal members who live outside Indian country altogether, rather than on a reservation other than their own? The *Mike* court also rejected arguments resting on the *Duro*-fix legislation, claiming that if Congress had wanted to extend the common treatment of member and nonmember Indians outside the realm of tribal criminal jurisdiction, it could have done so. Does the California Court of Appeal's insistence on a clear expression of congressional intent to exclude state taxation consistent with the analytical framework established in *McClanahan* and even in *Oliphant*? Did that court ignore the Indian law canons of construction in refusing to give force to the *Duro*-fix legislation, or was Mike trying to push those canons too far? Should Mike have filed this suit in federal rather than state court?

6. State Taxation with Federal Authorization: Any analysis of state taxing authority within Indian country should begin with an inquiry into any possible congressional grant of such authority. Such an affirmative congressional grant to the state would represent an exercise of federal "plenary power" to remove obstacles to state jurisdiction grounded in tribal sovereignty and federal law. Congress has granted six states criminal and civil jurisdiction under Public Law 280, and allowed other states to opt into this regime under specified conditions. *See* Ch. 5, Sec. A. But in *Bryan v. Itasca County*, 426 U.S. 373 (1976), the Court interpreted Public Law 280 to exclude federal authorization for state taxing or regulatory power. *Bryan* reasoned that the statute was ambiguous on this important matter affecting tribal sovereignty, and that canons of construction dictated that such ambiguities be resolved in favor of the tribe. History and context also supported this result, as it was clear from the legislative record that Congress had mostly been concerned about lack of criminal and civil justice forums for reservation problems. Congress was not attempting through Public Law 280 to terminate the affected tribes or to deny their governmental status. Yet, if Public Law 280 were read to give states taxing and regulatory power on reservations, tribes would be diminished to the status of municipalities or less. Both in *Bryan*, and later in *California v. Cabazon Band of Mission Indians*, presented and discussed below, the Court sought to draw a line between criminal law enforcement and civil court jurisdiction, on the one hand, and more elaborate forms of government intervention in the form of taxation and regulation, on the other. Difficulties in drawing this line, known in shorthand as the prohibitory/regulatory distinction, are discussed in Ch. 5, Sec. A. Outside of Public Law 280, the Court has been more disposed to find federal authorization of state taxation.

In *County of Yakima v. Confederated Tribes & Bands of the Yakima Indian Nation*, 502 U.S. 251 (1992), the Court interpreted the General Allotment Act of 1887, 25 U.S.C. § 331 et seq., as authorizing state taxation of Indian trust allotments that had passed out of trust and into fee ownership. Writing for the Court, Justice Scalia refused to treat the final phrase of this provision as a dead letter in light of subsequent congressional acts. In particular, Congress's repudiation of allotment in the Indian Reorganization Act of 1934, its inclusion of reservation-based fee patent land in the definition of Indian country in 1948, and its enactment in 1953 of Public Law 280 (with arguably preemptive procedures) failed to convince the Court that Congress had abandoned its authorization to the states.

In *Cass County v. Leech Lake Band of Chippewa Indians*, 524 U.S. 103 (1998), the Court had to decide whether the allotment act for the Chippewa tribes in Minnesota, known as the Nelson Act, gave the local county authority to tax parcels within the reservation that had been sold to nonmembers and then repurchased by the Tribe. Some of the parcels had initially found their way into non-Indian ownership through the allotment process, which was carried out under the terms of the General Allotment Act. Others had been sold at auction as timber lands or opened for homesteading as agricultural lands. By 1977, when the Tribe's repurchasing program began, less than 5% of the reservation was owned by the Tribe or its members. Writing for the Court, Justice Thomas reiterated the longstanding doctrinal principle that state taxation will not be deemed permitted by Congress unless Congress has "made its intention . . . unmistakably clear." 524 U.S. at 111 (quoting *County of Yakima*). Thomas then proceeded to infer this intention from the fact that land was made freely alienable, even as he conceded that Congress could choose to make the land alienable without intending that it be taxed. As to lands that had been patented under the General Allotment Act, the Court also relied on the same language in that Act that proved dispositive in *County of Yakima, supra.* However, no comparable statutory language supported state taxation of the timber or agricultural lands; and the Eighth Circuit had ruled against state taxation of those lands for that reason. Justice Thomas untied himself from this dilemma by effectively switching the presumption regarding state taxing authority when reservation land has been rendered freely alienable. According to Thomas, "once Congress has demonstrated . . . a clear intent to subject the land to taxation by making it alienable, Congress must make an unmistakably clear statement in order to render it non-taxable."

What happened to the canons of construction in *Cass County*? What happened to the Tribe's effort to undo what has been called "the legacy of allotment"? Judith V. Royster, *The Legacy of Allotment*, 27 ARIZ. ST. L.J. 1 (1995). What underlying model of the tribal-federal relationship would impel the Court to privilege policies derived from the earlier allotment era over policies from the later reorganization and self-determination eras, even when Congress has not made its intention "unmistakably clear"?

WHITE MOUNTAIN APACHE TRIBE v. BRACKER
United States Supreme Court
448 U.S. 136 (1980)

MR. JUSTICE MARSHALL delivered the Opinion of the Court.

[Pursuant to a contract with an organization of petitioner White Mountain Apache Tribe, petitioner Pinetop Logging Co. (Pinetop), a non-Indian enterprise authorized to do business in Arizona, felled tribal timber on the Fort Apache Reservation and transported it to the tribal organization's sawmill. Pinetop's activities were performed solely on the reservation. Respondents, state agencies and members thereof, sought to impose on Pinetop Arizona's motor carrier license tax, which is assessed on the basis of the carrier's gross receipts, and its use fuel tax, which is assessed on the basis of diesel fuel used to propel a motor vehicle on any highway within the State. Pinetop paid the taxes under protest and then brought suit in state court, asserting that under federal law the taxes could not lawfully be imposed on logging activities conducted exclusively within the reservation or on hauling activities on Bureau of Indian Affairs (BIA) and tribal roads. The trial court awarded summary judgment to respondents, and the Arizona Court of Appeals affirmed in pertinent part rejecting petitioners' preemption claim.]

II

Congress has broad power to regulate tribal affairs under the Indian Commerce Clause, Art. 1, § 8, cl. 3. This congressional authority and the "semi-independent position" of Indian tribes have given rise to two independent but related barriers to the assertion of state regulatory authority over tribal reservations and members. First, the exercise of such authority may be pre-empted by federal law. *See, e.g., Warren Trading Post Co. v. Arizona Tax Comm'n*, 380 U.S. 685 (1965); [*McClanahan*]. Second, it may unlawfully infringe "on the right of reservation Indians to make their own laws and be ruled by them." [*Williams v. Lee.*] See also *Washington v. Yakima Indian Nation*, 439 U.S. 463, 470 (1979); *Fisher v. District Court*, 424 U.S. 382 (1976) *(per curiam)*; *Kennerly v. District Court of Montana*, 400 U.S. 423 (1971). The two barriers are independent because either, standing alone, can be a sufficient basis for holding state law inapplicable to activity undertaken on the reservation or by tribal members. They are related, however, in two important ways. The right of tribal self-government is ultimately dependent on and subject to the broad power of Congress. Even so, traditional notions of Indian self-government are so deeply engrained in our jurisprudence that they have provided an important "backdrop," [*McClanahan*] against which vague or ambiguous federal enactments must always be measured.

The unique historical origins of tribal sovereignty make it generally unhelpful to apply to federal enactments regulating Indian tribes those standards of pre-emption that have emerged in other areas of the law. Tribal reservations are not States, and the differences in the form and nature of their sovereignty make it treacherous to import to one notions of pre-emption that are properly applied to the other. The tradition of Indian sovereignty over the reservation and tribal members must inform the determination whether the exercise of state authority has been pre-empted by operation of federal law. *Moe v. Salish & Kootenai Tribes*, [425 U.S. at] 475. As we have repeatedly recognized, this tradition is reflected and encouraged in a number of congressional enactments demonstrating a firm federal policy of promoting tribal self-sufficiency and economic development. Ambiguities in federal law have been construed generously in order to comport with these traditional notions of sovereignty and with the federal policy of encouraging tribal independence. See [*McClanahan*]. We have thus rejected the proposition that in order to find a particular state law to have been preempted by operation of federal law, an express congressional statement to that effect is required.[77] *Warren Trading Post Co. v. Arizona State Tax Comm'n, supra*. At the same time any applicable regulatory interest of the State must be given weight, [*McClanahan*] and "automatic exemptions 'as a matter of constitutional law' " are unusual. *Moe v. Salish & Kootenai Tribes, supra*, 425 U.S., at 481, n.17.

When on-reservation conduct involving only Indians is at issue, state law is generally inapplicable, for the State's regulatory interest is likely to be minimal and the federal interest in encouraging tribal self-government is at its strongest. More difficult questions arise where, as here, a State asserts authority over the conduct of non-Indians engaging in activity on the reservation. In such cases we have examined the language of the relevant federal treaties and statutes in terms of both the broad policies that underlie them and the notions of sovereignty that have developed from historical traditions of tribal independence. This inquiry is not dependent on mechanical or absolute conceptions of State or tribal sovereignty, but has called for a particularized inquiry into the nature of the State, Federal, and tribal interests at stake, an inquiry designed to determine whether, in the specific context, the exercise of state authority would violate federal law. Compare *Warren*

---

[77] [11] In the case of "Indians going beyond reservation boundaries," however, "a nondiscriminatory state law" is generally applicable in the absence of "express federal law to the contrary." *Mescalero Apache Tribe v. Jones, supra* at 148–149.

Trading Post Co. v. Arizona State Tax Comm'n, supra, and *Williams v. Lee, supra,* with *Moe v. Salish & Kootenai Tribes, supra,* and *Thomas v. Gay,* 169 U.S. 264 (1898). Cf. [*McClanahan*]; *Mescalero Apache Tribe v. Jones, supra,* 411 U.S., at 148.

III

With these principles in mind, we turn to the respondents' claim that they may, consistent with federal law, impose the contested motor vehicle license and use fuel taxes on the logging and hauling operations of petitioner Pinetop. At the outset we observe that the federal government's regulation of the harvesting of Indian timber is comprehensive. That regulation takes the form of Acts of Congress, detailed regulations promulgated by the Secretary of the Interior, and day-to-day supervision by the Bureau of Indian Affairs. Under 25 U.S.C. §§ 405–407, the Secretary of the Interior is granted broad authority over the sale of timber on the reservation. Timber on Indian land may be sold only with the consent of the Secretary, and the proceeds from any such sales, less administrative expenses incurred by the federal government, are to be used for the benefit of the Indians or transferred to the Indian owner. Sales of timber must "be based upon a consideration of the needs and best interests of the Indian owner and his heirs." 25 U.S.C. § 406. The statute specifies the factors which the Secretary must consider in making that determination. In order to assure the continued productivity of timber-producing land on tribal reservations, timber on unallotted lands "may be sold in accordance with the principles of sustained yield." 25 U.S.C. § 407. The Secretary is granted power to determine the disposition of the proceeds from timber sales. He is authorized to promulgate regulations for the operation and management of Indian forestry units. 25 U.S.C. § 466.

Acting pursuant to this authority, the Secretary has promulgated a detailed set of regulations to govern the harvesting and sale of tribal timber. Among the stated objectives of the regulations is the "development of Indian forests by the Indian people for the purpose of promoting self-sustaining communities, to the end that the Indians may receive from their own property not only the stumpage value, but also the benefit of whatever profit it is capable of yielding and whatever labor the Indians are qualified to perform." 25 C.F.R. § 141.3(a)(3). [Part 141 of 25 C.F.R. is now 25 C.F.R. Part 163.] The regulations cover a wide variety of matters: for example, they restrict clear-cutting, § 141.5; establish comprehensive guidelines for the sale of timber, § 141.7; regulate the advertising of timber sales, §§ 141.8–141.9; specify the manner in which bids may be accepted and rejected, § 141.11; describe the circumstances in which contracts may be entered into, §§ 141.12–141.13; require the approval of all contracts by the Secretary, § 141.13; call for timber cutting permits to be approved by the Secretary, § 141.19; specify fire protective measures, § 141.21; and provide a board of administrative appeals, § 141.23. Tribes are expressly authorized to establish commercial enterprises for the harvesting and logging of tribal timber. § 141.6.

Under these regulations, the Bureau of Indian Affairs exercises literally daily supervision over the harvesting and management of tribal timber. In the present case, contracts between FATCO and Pinetop must be approved by the Bureau; indeed, the record shows that some of those contracts were drafted by employees of the federal government. Bureau employees regulate the cutting, hauling, and marking of timber by FATCO and Pinetop. The Bureau decides such matters as how much timber will be cut, which trees will be felled, which roads are to be used, which hauling equipment Pinetop should employ, the speeds at which logging equipment may travel, and the width, length, height, and weight of loads.

The Secretary has also promulgated detailed regulations governing the roads developed by the Bureau of Indian Affairs. 25 C.F.R. Part 162 [now 25 C.F.R. Part 170]. Bureau roads are open to "[f]ree public use." § 162.8. Their administration and maintenance are funded by the federal government, with contributions from the Indian tribes. §§ 162.6–162.6a. On the Fort Apache Reservation the Forestry Department of the Bureau has required FATCO and its contractors, including Pinetop, to repair and maintain existing Bureau and tribal roads and in some cases to construct new logging roads. Substantial sums have been spent for these purposes. In its federally approved contract with FATCO, Pinetop has agreed to construct new roads and to repair existing ones. A high percentage of Pinetop's receipts are expended for those purposes, and it has maintained separate personnel and equipment to carry out a variety of tasks relating to road maintenance.

In these circumstances we agree with petitioners that the federal regulatory scheme is so pervasive as to preclude the additional burdens sought to be imposed in this case. Respondents seek to apply their motor vehicle license and use fuel taxes on Pinetop for operations that are conducted solely on Bureau and tribal roads within the reservation.[78] There is no room for these taxes in the comprehensive federal regulatory scheme. In a variety of ways, the assessment of state taxes would obstruct federal policies. And equally important, respondents have been unable to identify any regulatory function or service performed by the State that would justify the assessment of taxes for activities on Bureau and tribal roads within the reservation.

At the most general level, the taxes would threaten the overriding federal objective of guaranteeing Indians that they will "receive . . . the benefit of whatever profit [the forest] is capable of yielding. . . . " 25 C.F.R. § 141.3(a)(3). Underlying the federal regulatory program rests a policy of assuring that the profits derived from timber sales will inure to the benefit of the Tribe, subject only to administrative expenses incurred by the federal government. That objective is part of the general federal policy of encouraging tribes "to revitalize their self-government" and to assume control over their "business and economic affairs." *Mescalero Apache Tribe v. Jones, supra*, 411 U.S., at 151. The imposition of the taxes at issue would undermine that policy in a context in which the federal government has undertaken to regulate the most minute details of timber production and expressed a firm

---

[78] [14] In oral argument counsel for respondents appeared to concede that the asserted state taxes could not lawfully be applied to tribal roads and was unwilling to defend the contrary conclusion of the court below, which made no distinction between Bureau and tribal roads under state and federal law. Tr. of Oral Arg., at 34–37. Contrary to respondents' position throughout the litigation and in their brief in this Court, counsel limited his argument to a contention that the taxes could be asserted on the roads of the Bureau of Indian Affairs. *Ibid.* For purposes of federal pre-emption, however, we see no basis, and respondents point to none, for distinguishing between roads maintained by the Tribe and roads maintained by the Bureau of Indian Affairs.

desire that the Tribes should retain the benefits derived from the harvesting and sale of reservation timber.

In addition, the taxes would undermine the Secretary's ability to make the wide range of determinations committed to his authority concerning the setting of fees and rates with respect to the harvesting and sale of tribal timber. The Secretary reviews and approves the terms of the Tribe's agreements with its contractors, sets fees for services rendered to the tribe by the federal government, and determines stumpage rates for timber to be paid to the Tribe. Most notably in reviewing or writing the terms of the contracts between FATCO and its contractors, federal agents must predict the amount and determine the proper allocation of all business expenses, including fuel costs. The assessment of state taxes would throw additional factors into the federal calculus, reducing tribal revenues and diminishing the profitability of the enterprise for potential contractors.

Finally, the imposition of state taxes would adversely affect the Tribe's ability to comply with the sustained-yield management policies imposed by federal law. Substantial expenditures are paid out by the federal government, the Tribe, and its contractors in order to undertake a wide variety of measures to ensure the continued productivity of the forest. These measures include reforestation, fire control, wildlife promotion, road improvement, safety inspections, and general policing of the forest. The expenditures are largely paid for out of tribal revenues, which are in turn derived almost exclusively from the sale of timber. The imposition of state taxes on FATCO's contractors would effectively diminish the amount of those revenues and thus leave the Tribe and its contractors with reduced sums with which to pay out federally required expenses.

As noted above, this is not a case in which the State seeks to assess taxes in return for governmental functions it performs for those on whom the taxes fall. Nor have respondents been able to identify a legitimate regulatory interest served by the taxes they seek to impose. They refer to a general desire to raise revenue, but we are unable to discern a responsibility or service that justifies the assertion of taxes imposed for on-reservation operations conducted solely on tribal and Bureau of Indian Affairs roads. Pinetop's business in Arizona is conducted solely on the Fort Apache Reservation. Though at least the use fuel tax purports to "compensat[e] the state for the use of its highways," Ariz. Rev. Stat. Ann. § 28-1552, no such compensatory purpose is present here. The roads at issue have been built, maintained, and policed exclusively by the federal government, the Tribe, and its contractors. We do not believe that respondents' generalized interest in raising revenue is in this context sufficient to permit its proposed intrusion into the federal regulatory scheme with respect to the harvesting and sale of tribal timber.

Respondents' argument is reduced to a claim that they may assess taxes on non-Indians engaged in commerce on the reservation whenever there is no express congressional statement to the contrary. That is simply not the law. In a number of cases we have held that state authority over non-Indians acting on tribal reservations is pre-empted even though Congress has offered no explicit statement on the subject. See *Warren Trading Post, supra; Williams v. Lee, supra; Kennerly v. District Court of Montana, supra.* The Court has repeatedly emphasized that there is a significant geographical component to tribal sovereignty, a component which remains highly relevant to the pre-emption inquiry; though the reservation boundary is not absolute, it remains an important factor to weigh in determining whether state authority has exceeded the permissible limits. " 'The cases in this Court have consistently guarded the authority of Indian governments over their reservations.' " *United States v. Mazurie, supra,* 419 U.S., at 558, quoting *Williams v. Lee,* 358 U.S. 217, 223 (1959). Moreover, it is undisputed that the economic burden of the asserted taxes will ultimately fall on the Tribe.[79] Where, as here, the federal government has undertaken comprehensive regulation of the harvesting and sale of tribal timber, where a number of the policies underlying the federal regulatory scheme are threatened by the taxes respondents seek to impose, and where respondents are unable to justify the taxes except in terms of a generalized interest in raising revenue, we believe that the proposed exercise of state authority is impermissible.[80]

Both the reasoning and result in this case follow naturally from our unanimous decision in *Warren Trading Post Co. v. Arizona Tax Comm'n, supra.* . . . The present case, we conclude, is in all relevant respects indistinguishable from *Warren Trading Post.*

[*Reversed.*]

MR. JUSTICE STEVENS, with whom MR. JUSTICE STEWART and MR. JUSTICE REHNQUIST join, dissenting.

[Given the posture of this case] I think the most appropriate disposition would be to vacate the judgment of the Arizona Court of Appeals and remand for further consideration in light of the concessions made on behalf of the State in this Court. As the Court and Mr. Justice Powell point out, it is difficult to see why those concessions are not an acknowledgement that the State has no authority to tax the use of roads in which it has no interest. . . .

Even assuming, however, that the state courts would uphold the imposition of taxes based on the use of BIA roads, despite their similarities with private and tribal roads, I would not find those taxes to be pre-empted by federal law. In *Warren Trading Post v. Arizona Tax Commission,* 380 U.S. 685, the Court held that state taxation of a non-Indian doing business with a tribe on the reservation was pre-empted because the taxes threatened to "disturb and disarrange" a pervasive

---

[79] [15] Of course, the fact that the economic burden of the tax falls on the Tribe does not by itself mean that the tax is pre-empted, as *Moe v. Salish & Kootenai Tribes,* 425 U.S. 463 (1976), makes clear. Our decision today is based on the pre-emptive effect of the comprehensive federal regulatory scheme, which, like that in *Warren Trading Post Co. v. Arizona Tax Comm'n, supra,* leaves no room for the additional burdens sought to be imposed by state law.

[80] [16] Respondents also contend that the taxes are authorized by the Buck Act, 4 U.S.C. § 105 *et seq.,* and the Hayden-Cartwright Act, 4 U.S.C. § 104. In *Warren Trading Post Co. v. Arizona State Tax Comm'n, supra,* [380 U.S. at] 691, n.18 (1965), we squarely held that the Buck Act did not apply to Indian reservations, and respondents present no sufficient reason for us to depart from that holding. We agree with petitioners that the Hayden-Cartwright Act, which authorizes state taxes "on United States military or other reservations," was not designed to overcome the otherwise pre-emptive effect of federal regulation of tribal timber. We need not reach the more general question whether the Hayden-Cartwright Act applies to Indian reservations at all.

scheme of federal regulation and because there was no governmental interest on the State's part in imposing such a burden. See [*Central Machinery Co.*] (Stewart, J., dissenting). In this case we may assume *arguendo* that the second factor relied upon in *Warren Trading Post* is present. As a result, Pinetop may well have a right to be free from taxation as a matter of due process or equal protection.[81] But I cannot agree that it has a right to be free from taxation because of its business relationship with the petitioner tribe.

As the Court points out, the federal government has imposed a detailed scheme of regulation on the tribal logging business. Thus, among other things, the BIA approves and sometimes drafts contracts between the tribe and non-Indian logging companies such as Pinetop and requires the tribe and its contractors to follow its dictates as to where to cut, haul and mark timber, and as to which roads to construct and repair.

[T]he Court's prediction of massive interference with federal forest-management programs seems overdrawn, to say the least. The logging operations involved in this case produced a profit of $1,508,713 for the Indian tribal enterprise in 1973. As noted above, the maximum annual taxes Pinetop would be required to pay would be $5,000–$6,000 or less than 1% of the total annual profits. Given the State's concession in this Court that the use of certain roads should not have been taxed as a matter of state law, the actual taxes Pinetop would be required to pay would probably be considerably less. It is difficult to believe that these relatively trivial taxes could impose an economic burden that would threaten to "obstruct federal policies."

Under these circumstances I find the Court's reliance on the indirect financial burden imposed on the Indian tribe by state taxation of its contractors disturbing. As a general rule, a tax is not invalid simply because a nonexempt taxpayer may be expected to pass all or part of the cost of the tax through to a person who is exempt from tax. . . .

MR. JUSTICE POWELL, dissenting and concurring.

I write separately because I would distinguish [*Central Machinery Co.*] [and] *White Mountain Apache Tribe v. Bracker*. [I concur with the Court] that a non-Indian contractor continuously engaged in logging upon a reservation is subject to such pervasive federal regulation as to bring into play the pre-emption doctrine of *Warren Trading Post Co. v. Arizona Tax Comm'n*, 380 U.S. 685 (1965). But *Warren Trading Post* simply does not apply to routine state taxation of a non-Indian corporation that makes a single sale to reservation Indians. I therefore join the Court's opinion in *White Mountain Apache Tribe*, but I dissent from its decision in *Central Machinery*.

---

[81] [7] The Due Process Clause may prohibit a State from imposing a tax on the use of completely private roads if the tax is designed to reimburse it for use of state-owned roads. Or it may be that once the State has decided to exempt private roads from its taxing system, it is also required, as a matter of equal protection, to exempt other types of roads that are identical to private roads in all relevant respects.

I

Central Machinery

Warren Trading Post held that Arizona could not levy its transaction privilege tax against a company regularly engaged in retail trading with the Indians upon a reservation. The company operated under a federal license, and it was subject to the federal regulatory scheme authorized by 25 U.S.C. §§ 261–264. "These apparently all-inclusive regulations," the Court concluded, "show that Congress has taken the business of Indian trading on reservations so fully in hand that no room remains for state laws imposing additional burdens upon traders." 380 U.S., at 690.

The Court today is too much persuaded by the superficial similarity between *Warren Trading Post* and *Central Machinery*. The Court mistakenly concludes that a company having no license to trade with the Indians and no place of business within a reservation is engaged in "the business of Indian trading on reservations. . . . " *Ibid*. Although "any person" desiring to sell goods to Indians inside a reservation must secure federal approval, see 25 U.S.C. §§ 262, 264, the federal regulations — and the facts of this case — show that a person who makes a single approved sale need not become a fully regulated Indian trader. Even itinerant peddlers who engage in a pattern of selling within a reservation are merely "considered as traders" for purposes of the licensing requirement. 25 C.F.R. § 251.9(b). "The business of a licensed trader," in fact, "must be managed by the bonded principal, who must habitually reside upon the reservation. . . . " 25 C.F.R. § 251.14.[82] Since *Warren Trading Post* involved a resident trader subject to the complete range of federal regulation, the Court had no occasion to consider whether federal regulation also pre-empts state taxation of a seller who enters a reservation to make a single transaction.

Our most recent cases undermine the notion that 25 U.S.C. §§ 261–264 occupy the field so as to pre-empt all state regulation affecting licensed Indian traders. The unanimous Court in *Moe v. Salish and Kootenai Tribes*, 425 U.S. 463, 481–483 (1976), concluded that a State could require tribal retailers to prepay a tax validly imposed on non-Indian customers. Rejecting an argument based on *Warren Trading Post*, the Court concluded that federal laws "passed to protect and guard [the Indians] only affect the operation, within the [reservation], of such state laws as conflict with the federal enactments." 425 U.S., at 483 quoting *United States v. McGowan*, 302 U.S. 535, 539 (1938). In [*Colville,*] the Court holds that a State can require licensed traders to keep detailed tax records of their sales to both Indians and non-Indians.

Finally, unlike taxes imposed upon an Indian trader engaged in a continuous course of dealing within the reservation, the tax assessed against *Central Machinery* does not "to a substantial extent frustrate the evident congressional purpose of ensuring that no burden shall be imposed upon Indian traders for trading with

---

82 [1] The regulation dealing with itinerant peddlers was promulgated after the decision in *Warren Trading Post*. See 30 Fed. Reg. 8267 (1965). Thus, the regulations before the Court in *Warren Trading Post* required all licensed Indian traders to conduct their businesses under the management of a habitual resident upon the reservation. 25 C.F.R. § 251.14 (1958).

Indians except as authorized by Acts of Congress or by valid regulations promulgated under those Acts." . . .

II

White Mountain Apache Tribe

White Mountain Apache Tribe presents a different situation. Petitioner Pinetop Logging Co. operates solely and continuously upon an Indian reservation under its contract with a tribal enterprise. Pinetop's daily operations are controlled by a comprehensive federal regulatory scheme designed to assure the Indian tribes the greatest possible return from their timber. Federal officials direct Pinetop's hauling operations down to such details as choice of equipment, selection of routes, speeds of travel, and dimensions of the loads. Pinetop does all of the hauling at issue in this case over roads constructed, maintained, and regulated by the White Mountain Apache Tribe and the Bureau of Indian Affairs. The Bureau requires the Tribe and its contractors to repair existing roads and to construct new roads necessary for sustained logging. Pinetop exhausts a large percentage of its gross income in performing these contractual obligations.

Since the federal government, the Tribe, and its contractors are solely responsible for the roads that Pinetop uses, I "cannot believe that Congress intended to leave to the State the privilege of levying" road use taxes upon Pinetop's operations. See *Warren Trading Post, supra*, at 691. The State has no interest in raising revenues from the use of Indian roads that cost it nothing and over which it exercises no control. See [*Colville*]. The addition of these taxes to the road construction and repair expenses that Pinetop already bears also would interfere with the federal scheme for maintaining roads essential to successful Indian timbering. See 380 U.S., at 691. The Tribe or its contractors would pay twice for use of the same roads. This double exaction could force federal officials to reallocate work from non-Indian contractors to the tribal enterprise itself or to make costly concessions to the contractors. I therefore join the Court in concluding that this case "is in all relevant respects indistinguishable from *Warren Trading Post*."

COTTON PETROLEUM CORP. v. NEW MEXICO
United States Supreme Court
490 U.S. 163 (1989)

JUSTICE STEVENS delivered the opinion of the Court.

This case is a sequel to *Merrion v. Jicarilla Apache Tribe*, 455 U.S. 130 (1982),[83] in which we held that the Jicarilla Apache Tribe (Tribe) has the power to impose a severance tax on the production of oil and gas by non-Indian lessees of wells located on the Tribe's reservation. We must now decide whether the State of New Mexico can continue to impose its severance taxes on the same production of oil and gas.

---

[83] [*Merrion* is set forth and discussed in Ch. 3, Sec. A.3.a.— Eds.].

I

All 742,135 acres of the Jicarilla Apache Reservation are located in northwestern New Mexico [on a reservation created by executive order].

The Tribe, which consists of approximately 2500 enrolled members, is organized under the [IRA]. The Indian Mineral Leasing Act of 1938 grants the Tribe authority, subject to the approval of the Secretary of the Interior (Secretary), to execute mineral leases. 52 Stat. 347, 25 U.S.C. § 396a et seq. Since at least as early as 1953, the Tribe has been leasing reservation lands to non-members for the production of oil and gas. [Such mineral leases currently] encompass a substantial portion of the reservation and constitute the primary source of the Tribe's general operating revenues. In 1969, the Secretary approved an amendment to the Tribe's Constitution authorizing it to enact ordinances, subject to his approval, imposing taxes on non-members doing business in the reservation. The Tribe enacted such an ordinance in 1976, imposing a severance tax on "any oil and natural gas severed, saved and removed from Tribal lands." Oil and Gas Severance Tax, Ordinance No. 77-0-02, Jicarilla Apache Tribal Code, Tit. II, ch. 1 (1978) (Equity) (hereinafter J.A.T.C.). [The Secretary of the Interior approved the ordinance in 1976] and in 1982 this Court upheld the Tribe's power to impose a severance tax on pre-existing as well as future leases. See *Merrion*. Subsequently, the Tribe enacted a privilege tax, which the Secretary also approved. See Oil and Gas Privilege Tax, Ordinance No. 85-0-434 (1985), J.A.T.C. Tit. II, ch. 2.[84]

In 1976, Cotton Petroleum Corporation (Cotton), a non-Indian company in the business of extracting and marketing oil and gas, acquired five leases covering approximately 15,000 acres of the reservation. There were then 15 operating wells on the leased acreage and Cotton has since drilled another 50 wells. The leases were issued by the Tribe and the United States under the authority of the Indian Mineral Leasing Act of 1938. Pursuant to the terms of the leases, Cotton pays the Tribe a rent of $125 per acre, plus a royalty of 12 1/2 percent of the value of its production. In addition, Cotton pays the Tribe's oil and gas severance and privilege taxes, which amount to approximately six percent of the value of its production. Thus, Cotton's aggregate payment to the Tribe includes an acreage rent in excess of one million dollars, plus royalties and taxes amounting to about 18 1/2 percent of its production.

Prior to 1982, Cotton paid, without objection, five different oil and gas production taxes to the State of New Mexico. The state taxes amount to about eight percent of the value of Cotton's production. The same eight percent is collected from producers throughout the State. Thus, on wells outside the reservation, the total tax burden is only eight percent, while Cotton's reservation wells are taxed at a total rate of 14 percent (eight percent by the State and six percent by the Tribe). No state tax is imposed on the royalties received by the Tribe.

At the end of our opinion in *Merrion*, 455 U.S., at 158–159, n.26, we added a

---

[84] [2] Effective January 1, 1988, the Tribe added a third tax, which is based on the value of possessory interests — including leasehold interests — held by taxpayers on the reservation. [Since] Cotton does not seek refund of state taxes paid after the possessory interest tax took effect, and because this tax was not enacted until after the New Mexico Court of Appeals issued its decision, we leave it to the side for purposes of our decision.

footnote rejecting the taxpayer's argument that the tribal tax was invalid as a "multiple tax burden on interstate commerce" because imposed on the same activity already taxed by the State. One of the reasons the argument failed was that the taxpayer had made no attempt to show that the Tribe was "seek[ing] to seize more tax revenues than would be fairly related to the services provided by the Tribe." *Ibid.* After making that point, the footnote suggested that the state tax might be invalid under the Commerce Clause if in excess of what "the *State's* contact with the activity would justify."[85] *Ibid.* (emphasis in original).

In 1982, Cotton paid its state taxes under protest and then brought an action in state court challenging the taxes under the Indian Commerce, Interstate Commerce, Due Process and Supremacy Clauses of the Federal Constitution. Relying on the *Merrion* footnote, Cotton contended that state taxes imposed on reservation activity are only valid if related to actual expenditures by the State in relation to the activity being taxed. In support of this theory, Cotton presented evidence at trial tending to prove that the amount of tax it paid to the State far exceeded the value of services that the State provided to it and that the taxes paid by all non-member oil producers far exceeded the value of services provided to the reservation as a whole.[86] Cotton did not, however, attempt to prove that the state taxes imposed any burden on the Tribe.

After trial, the Tribe sought, and was granted, leave to file a brief *amicus curiae*.

[T]he New Mexico district court issued a decision upholding the state taxes. [It]

---

[85] [5] The entire footnote reads as follows:

"Petitioners contend that because New Mexico may tax the same mining activity at full value, the Indian tax imposes a multiple tax burden on interstate commerce in violation of the Commerce Clause. The multiple taxation issue arises where two or more taxing jurisdictions point to some contact with an enterprise to support a tax on the entire value of its multi-state activities, which is more than the contact would justify. *E.g., Standard Oil Co. v. Peck*, 342 U.S. 382, 384–385 (1952). This Court has required an apportionment of the tax based on the portion of the activity properly viewed as occurring within each relevant State. *See, e.g., Exxon Corp. v. Wisconsin Dep't of Revenue*, 447 U.S. 207, 219 (1980); *Washington Revenue Dep't v. Association of Washington Stevedoring Cos.*, 435 U.S. 734, 746, and n.16 (1978).

"This rule has no bearing here, however, for there can be no claim that the Tribe seeks to tax any more of petitioners' mining activity than the portion occurring within tribal jurisdiction. Indeed, petitioners do not even argue that the Tribe is seeking to seize more tax revenues than would be fairly related to the services provided by the Tribe. . . . In the absence of such an assertion, and when the activity taxed by the Tribe occurs entirely on tribal lands, the multiple taxation issue would arise only if a *State* attempted to levy a tax on the same activity, which is more than the *State's* contact with the activity would justify. In such a circumstance, any challenge asserting that tribal and state taxes create a multiple burden on interstate commerce should be directed at the state tax, which, in the absence of congressional ratification, might be invalidated under the Commerce Clause. These cases, of course, do not involve a challenge to state taxation, and we intimate no opinion on the possibility of such a challenge."

455 U.S., at 158–159, n.26 (emphasis in the original).

[86] [6] Cotton's evidence tended to prove that for the tax years 1981-1985 it paid New Mexico $2,298,953, while only receiving the equivalent of $89,384 in services to its operations in return. Cotton's evidence further suggested that over the same period the State received total tax revenues of $47,483,306 from the on-reservation, non-member oil and gas producers, while only providing $10,704,748 in services to the reservation as a whole.

found that "New Mexico provides substantial services to both the Jicarilla Tribe and Cotton"[87] and concluded that the State had a valid interest in imposing taxes on non-Indians on the reservation. After squarely rejecting Cotton's theory of the case, the court stated that "[t]he theory of public finance does not require expenditures equal to revenues." . . .

The New Mexico Court of Appeals affirmed. [Participating as *amicus curiae*, the Tribe] urged a different approach to the case. Unlike Cotton, the Tribe argued that the state taxes could not withstand traditional pre-emption analysis. The Tribe conceded that state laws, to the extent they do not interfere with tribal self-government, may control the conduct of non-Indians on the reservation. It maintained, however, that the taxes at issue interfered with its ability to raise taxes and thus with its right to self-government. The Court of Appeals rejected this argument because the record contained no evidence of any adverse impact on the Tribe and, indeed, indicated that the Tribe could impose even higher taxes than it had without adverse effect.[88]

The New Mexico Supreme Court granted, but then quashed, a writ of certiorari. We then noted probable jurisdiction and invited the parties to brief and argue the following additional question:

> "Does the Commerce Clause require that an Indian Tribe be treated as a State for purposes of determining whether a state tax on nontribal activities conducted on an Indian Reservation must be apportioned to account for taxes imposed on those same activities by the Indian Tribe?"

We now affirm the judgment of the New Mexico Court of Appeals.

II

This Court's approach to the question whether a State may tax on-reservation oil production by non-Indian lessees has varied over the course of the past century. At one time, such a tax was held invalid unless expressly authorized by Congress; more recently, such taxes have been upheld unless expressly or impliedly prohibited by Congress. The changed approach to these taxes is one aspect of the evolution of the doctrine of intergovernmental tax immunity that we recently discussed in detail in *South Carolina v. Baker*, 485 U.S. [505] (1988).

---

[87] [7] The district court found that New Mexico spends approximately three million dollars per year in providing on-reservation services to Cotton and the Tribe. [The court also] found that New Mexico does not discriminate against the Tribe or its members in providing state services; indeed, the State spends as much or more per capita on members of the Tribe than on non-members. The court further found that New Mexico provides services on the reservation not provided by either the Tribal or federal governments, and provides additional services off the reservation that benefit the reservation and members of the Tribe. Finally, the court found that the State regulates the spacing and mechanical integrity of wells located both on and off the reservation.

[88] [9] The Court of Appeals noted that Cotton, and not the Tribe, paid the taxes at issue; that "[t]he record contains no evidence of an impact [on] tribal sovereignty"; that Cotton drilled twelve new wells while subject to both the state and tribal taxes and "shows no signs of disrupting production because of the tax burden"; and that at trial "[t]he Tribe's own consultant indicated that the Tribe could charge an even higher tax despite the state taxes imposed on Cotton." 106 N.M., at 522, 745 P.2d, at 1175.

During the first third of this century, this Court frequently invalidated state taxes that arguably imposed an indirect economic burden on the federal government or its instrumentalities by application of the "intergovernmental immunity" doctrine. [I]n 1922, the Court applied the intergovernmental immunity doctrine to invalidate a state tax on income derived by a non-Indian lessee from the sale of his interest in oil produced on Indian land. See *Gillespie v. Oklahoma*, 257 U.S. 501 (1922). Consistently with the view of intergovernmental immunity that then prevailed, the Court stated that "a tax upon such profits is a direct hamper upon the effort of the United States to make the best terms that it can for its wards." *Id.*, at 506 (citing *Weston v. Charleston*, 2 Pet. 449, 468 (1829)). The same reasoning was used to invalidate a variety of other state taxes imposed on non-Indian lessees at that time.[89]

Shortly after reaching its zenith in the *Gillespie* decision, the doctrine of intergovernmental tax immunity started a long path in decline and has now been "thoroughly repudiated" by modern case law. [I]n *Helvering v. Mountain Producers Corp.*, 303 U.S. 376, 386–387 (1938), the Court squarely overruled *Gillespie*. Thus, after *Mountain Producers Corp.* was decided, oil and gas lessees operating on Indian reservations were subject to nondiscriminatory state taxation as long as Congress did not act affirmatively to pre-empt the state taxes. See also *Oklahoma Tax Comm'n v. Texas Co.*, 336 U.S. 342 (1949).

In sum, it is well-settled that, absent express congressional authorization, a State cannot tax the United States directly. See *McCulloch v. Maryland*, 4 Wheat. 316 (1819). It is also clear that the tax immunity of the United States is shared by the Indian tribes for whose benefit the United States holds reservation lands in trust. See *Montana v. Blackfeet Tribe of Indians*, 471 U.S. 759, 764 (1985). Under current doctrine, however, a State can impose a nondiscriminatory tax on private parties with whom the United States or an Indian tribe does business, even though the financial burden of the tax may fall on the United States or tribe. [While] a lessee's oil production on Indian lands is therefore not "automatically exempt from state taxation," Congress does, of course, retain the power to grant such immunity. *Mescalero Apache Tribe v. Jones*, 411 U.S. 145, 150 (1973). Whether such immunity shall be granted is a question that "is essentially legislative in character." *Texas Co., supra*, at 365–366.

The question for us to decide is whether Congress has acted to grant the Tribe such immunity, either expressly or by plain implication. In addition, we must consider Cotton's argument that the "multiple burden" imposed by the state and tribal taxes is unconstitutional.

III

[W]e have applied a flexible pre-emption analysis sensitive to the particular facts and legislation involved. Each case "requires a particularized examination of the relevant state, federal, and tribal interests." *Ramah Navajo School Bd., Inc. v.*

---

[89] [10] The Court [has] held that non-Indian mineral lessees were exempt from state occupation and privilege taxes, exempt from state taxes on the value of their leasehold, exempt from state gross production taxes, and exempt from state ad valorem taxes in some circumstances.

Bureau of Revenue of New Mexico, 458 U.S. 832, 838 (1982). Moreover, in examining the pre-emptive force of the relevant federal legislation, we are cognizant of both the broad policies that underlie the legislation and the history of tribal independence in the field at issue. It bears emphasis that although congressional silence no longer entails a broad-based immunity from taxation for private parties doing business with Indian tribes, federal pre-emption is not limited to cases in which Congress has expressly — as compared to impliedly — pre-empted the state activity. Finally, we note that although state interests must be given weight and courts should be careful not to make legislative decisions in the absence of congressional action, ambiguities in federal law are, as a rule, resolved in favor of tribal independence.

Against this background, Cotton argues that the New Mexico taxes are pre-empted by the "federal laws and policies which protect tribal self-government and strengthen impoverished reservation economies." Most significantly, Cotton contends that the Indian Mineral Leasing Act of 1938, 52 Stat. 347, 25 U.S.C. § 396a et seq. (1938 Act), exhibits a strong federal interest in guaranteeing Indian tribes the maximum return on their oil and gas leases. Moreover, Cotton maintains that the Federal and Tribal Governments, acting pursuant to the 1938 Act, its accompanying regulations, and the Jicarilla Apache Tribal Code, exercise comprehensive regulatory control over Cotton's on-reservation activity. Cotton describes New Mexico's responsibilities, in contrast, as "significantly limited." Thus, weighing the respective state, federal and tribal interests, Cotton concludes that the New Mexico taxes unduly interfere with the federal interest in promoting tribal economic self-sufficiency and are not justified by an adequate state interest. We disagree.

The 1938 Act neither expressly permits state taxation nor expressly precludes it, but rather simply provides that "unallotted lands within any Indian reservation or lands owned by any tribe . . . may, with the approval of the Secretary of the Interior, be leased for mining purposes, by authority of the tribal council . . . . for terms not to exceed ten years and as long thereafter as minerals are produced in paying quantities." 25 U.S.C. § 396a. The Senate and House Reports that accompanied the Act, moreover — even when considered in their broadest possible terms — shed little light on congressional intent concerning state taxation of oil and gas produced on leased lands. See S. Rep. No. 985, 75th Cong., 1st Sess. (1937); H.R. Rep. No. 1872, 75th Cong., 3d Sess. (1938). Both Reports reflect that the proposed legislation was suggested by the Secretary and considered by the appropriate committees, which recommended that it pass without amendment. Beyond this procedural summary, the Reports simply rely on the Secretary's letter of transmittal to describe the purpose of the Act. That letter provides that the legislation was intended, in light of the disarray of federal law in the area, "to obtain uniformity so far as practicable of the law relating to the leasing of tribal lands for mining purposes," and, in particular, was designed to "bring all mineral leasing matters in harmony with the Indian Reorganization Act" of 1934. *Id.*, at 1, 3; S. Rep. No. 985, *supra*, at 2, 3. In addition, the letter contains the following passage:

> *It is not believed that the present law is adequate to give the Indians the greatest return from their property.* As stated, present law provides for locating and taking mineral leases in the same manner as mining locations are made on the public lands of the United States; but there are

disadvantages in following this procedure on Indian lands that are not present in applying for a claim on the public domain. For instance, on the public domain the discoverer of a mineral deposit gets extralateral rights and can follow the ore beyond the side lines indefinitely, while on the Indian lands under the act of June 30, 1919, he is limited to the confines of the survey markers not to exceed 600 feet by 1,500 feet in any one claim. The draft of the bill herewith would permit the obtaining of sufficient acreage to remove the necessity for extralateral rights with all of its attending controversies. *Id.*, at 2; H.R. Rep. No. 1872, *supra*, at 2 (emphasis supplied).

Relying on the first sentence in this paragraph, Cotton argues that the 1938 Act embodies a broad congressional policy of maximizing revenues for Indian tribes. [T]he proposition that, in authorizing mineral leases, Congress sought to provide Indian tribes with a profitable source of revenue [certainly is not remarkable]. It is however quite remarkable, indeed unfathomable in our view, to suggest that Congress intended to remove all state imposed obstacles to profitability by attaching to the Senate and House Reports a letter from the Secretary that happened to include the phrase "the greatest return from their property." Read in the broadest terms possible, the relevant paragraph suggests that Congress sought to remove "disadvantages in [leasing mineral rights] on Indian lands that are not present in applying for a claim on the public domain." S. Rep. No. 985, *supra*, at 2; H.R. Rep. No. 1872, *supra*, at 2. By 1938, however, it was established that oil and gas lessees of public lands were subject to state taxation. See *Mid-Northern Oil Co. v. Walker*, 268 U.S. 45 (1925). It is thus apparent that Congress was not concerned with state taxation, but with matters such as the unavailability of extralateral mineral rights on Indian land. . . .

We thus agree that a purpose of the 1938 Act is to provide Indian tribes with badly needed revenue, but find no evidence for the further supposition that Congress intended to remove all barriers to profit maximization. The Secretary's letter of transmittal, even when read permissively for broad policy goals and even when read to resolve ambiguities in favor of tribal independence, supports no more.

Our review of the legislation that preceded the 1938 Act provides no additional support for Cotton's expansive view of the Act's purpose. This history is relevant in that it supplies both the legislative background against which Congress enacted the 1938 Act and the relevant "backdrop" of tribal independence. Congress first authorized mineral leasing on Indian lands in 1891. See Act of Feb. 28, 1891, § 3, 26 Stat. 795, 25 U.S.C. § 397 (1891 Act). That legislation, which empowered tribes to enter into grazing and mining leases, only applied to lands "occupied by Indians who have bought and paid for the same," and was thus interpreted to be inapplicable to Executive Order reservations. Mineral leasing on reservations created by Executive Order — like the Jicarilla Apache reservation — was not authorized until almost four decades later. After years of debate concerning whether Indians had any right to share in royalties derived from oil and gas leases in Executive Order reservations,[90] Congress finally enacted legislation in 1927 that authorized such

[90] [12] This history is recounted in L. Kelly, The Navajo Indians and Federal Indian Policy 48–103 (1968) (hereinafter Kelly). Of particular significance, in 1922, the Secretary took the position that Executive Order reservations "are without question lands 'owned by the United States,'" and thus

leases. See Indian Oil Act of 1927, 44 Stat. (part 2) 1347, 25 U.S.C. § 398a (1927 Act).

While both the 1891 and 1927 Acts were in effect, *Gillespie* was the prevailing law and, under its expansive view of inter-governmental tax immunity, States were powerless to impose severance taxes on oil produced on Indian reservations unless Congress expressly waived that immunity. Just two years after *Gillespie* was decided, Congress took such express action and authorized state taxation of oil and gas production in Treaty reservations. See Indian Oil Leasing Act of 1924, 43 Stat. 244, current version at 25 U.S.C. § 398. See also *British-American Oil Producing Co. v. Board of Equalization, supra* (applying 1924 Act to uphold state tax imposed on the production of oil and gas in the Blackfeet Indian Reservation). More significantly for purposes of this case, when Congress first authorized oil and gas leasing on Executive Order reservations in the 1927 Act, it expressly waived immunity from state taxation of oil and gas lessees operating in those reservations. See Indian Oil Act of 1927, 44 Stat. (part 2) 1347, 25 U.S.C. § 398c. Thus, at least as to Executive Order reservations, state taxation of non-member oil and gas lessees was the norm from the very start. There is, accordingly, simply no history of tribal independence from state taxation of these lessees to form a "backdrop" against which the 1938 Act must be read.

We are also unconvinced that the contrast between the 1927 Act's express waiver of immunity and the 1938 Act's silence on the subject suggests that Congress intended to repeal the waiver in the 1938 Act and thus to diametrically change course by implicitly barring state taxation. The general repealer clause contained in the 1938 Act provides that "[a]ll Act[s] or parts of Act[s] inconsistent herewith are hereby repealed." 52 Stat. 348. Although one might infer from this clause that all preceding, nonconflicting legislation in the area, like the 1927 Act's waiver provision, is implicitly incorporated, we need not go so far to simply conclude that the 1938 Act's omission demonstrates no congressional purpose to close the door to state taxation. Moreover, the contrast between the 1927 and 1938 Acts is easily explained by the contemporaneous history of the doctrine of intergovernmental tax immunity. In 1927, *Gillespie* prevailed, and States were only permitted to tax lessees of Indian lands if Congress expressly so provided. By the time the 1938 Act was enacted, however, *Gillespie* had been overruled and replaced by the modern rule permitting

---

subject to leasing under the Mineral Lands Leasing Act of 1920, 41 Stat. 450, 30 U.S.C. § 189. Harrison, 49 L.D. 139, 144. As such, the Executive Order tribes had no right to share in royalties derived from oil and gas leases. Two years later, then-Attorney General Stone rendered an opinion concluding that the Mineral Lands Leasing Act did not apply to Executive Order reservations. 34 Op. Atty. Gen. 171, 181. This decision made clear that new federal legislation would be required to open Executive Order reservations to oil and gas leasing. For the next few years, a number of legislative solutions were proposed and considered. For example, in 1926, Representative Carl Hayden introduced legislation that would have provided for Executive Order reservation leasing in accordance with the Indian Oil Leasing Act of 1924, 43 Stat. 244, but which, in lieu of permitting a state production tax, would have given to the relevant State 37 ½% of the royalties, rent, and bonuses received by the tribe. This payment was to be used for building and maintaining roads on the reservation or to support public schools attended by Indian children. A bill introduced in the Senate would have attached no qualification to how the State might spend its 37 1/2% share. Finally, Congress settled on the terms of the Indian Oil Act of 1927, which authorized oil and gas leasing in Executive Order reservations and allowed States to tax "any lessee upon lands within Executive order Indian reservations in the same manner as such taxes are otherwise levied and collected." 44 Stat. (part 2) 1347, 25 U.S.C. § 398c.

such taxes absent congressional disapproval.[91] Thus, Congress's approaches to both the 1927 and 1938 Acts were fully consistent with an intent to permit state taxation of non-member lessees.[92]

Cotton nonetheless maintains that our decisions in [*Bracker*] and *Ramah Navajo School Bd., Inc. v. Bureau of Revenue of New Mexico*, 458 U.S. 832 (1982), compel the conclusion that the New Mexico taxes are pre-empted by federal law. In pressing this argument, Cotton ignores the admonition included in both of those decisions that the relevant pre-emption test is a flexible one sensitive to the particular state, federal, and tribal interests involved.

The factual findings of the New Mexico district court clearly distinguish this case from both *Bracker* and *Ramah Navajo School Bd.* After conducting a trial, that court found that "New Mexico provides substantial services to both the Jicarilla Tribe and Cotton," costing the State approximately three million dollars per year. Indeed, Cotton concedes that from 1981 through 1985 New Mexico provided its operations with services costing $89,384, but argues that the cost of these services is disproportionate to the $2,298,953 in taxes the State collected from Cotton. Neither *Bracker*, nor *Ramah Navajo School Bd.*, however, imposes such a proportionality requirement on the States.[93] Rather, both cases involved complete

---

[91]   [13] Although *Gillespie* was not explicitly overruled until 1938 in *Helvering v. Mountain Producers Corp.*, 303 U.S. 376, the holding in that case was plainly foreshadowed by the development of the law in this area during the preceding decade. The fact that the text of the 1938 Act had been drafted before our decision in *Mountain Producers* was actually handed down does not, therefore, have the significance that the dissent ascribes to it.

[92]   [14] Our decision in *Montana v. Blackfeet Tribe of Indians*, 471 U.S. 759 (1985), is not to the contrary. In that case we considered the distinct question of whether the 1938 Act, through incorporation of the 1927 Act, expressly authorized direct taxation of Indian royalties. In concluding that it did not, we made clear that our holding turned on the rule that Indian tribes, like the Federal Government itself, are exempt from direct state taxation and that this exemption is "lifted only when Congress has made its intention to do so unmistakably clear." *Id.*, at 765. We stressed that the 1938 Act (contains no explicit consent to state taxation," and that the reverse implication of the general repealer clause that the 1927 waiver might be incorporated "does not satisfy the requirement that Congress clearly consent to state taxation." *Id.*, at 766–767. Our conclusion that the 1938 Act does not expressly authorize direct taxation of Indian tribes does not entail the further step that the Act impliedly prohibits taxation of non-members doing business on a reservation.

Nor can a congressional intent to pre-empt state taxation be found in the Indian Reorganization Act of 1934, 48 Stat. 964, 25 U.S.C. § 461 et seq., the Indian Financing Act of 1974, 38 Stat. 77, 25 U.S.C. § 1451 et seq., or the Indian Self-Determination Act of 1975, 88 Stat. 2208, 25 U.S.C. § 450 et seq. Although these statutes "evidence to varying degrees a congressional concern with fostering tribal self-government and economic development," *Washington v. Confederated Tribes of Colville Indian Reservation*, 447 U.S. 134, 155 (1980), they no more express a congressional intent to pre-empt state taxation of oil and gas lessees than does the 1938 Act. More instructive is the Crude Oil Windfall Profit Tax Act of 1980, 94 Stat. 229, 26 U.S.C. § 4985 et seq. In imposing the Windfall Profits Tax, Congress expressly exempted certain Indian producers, see 26 U.S.C. § 4994(d), but decided not to exempt "oil received by non-Indian lessees of tribal interests." See S. Rep. No. 96-394, p. 61 (1979). See also H.R. Conf. Rep. No. 96-817, p. 108 (1980). If Congress was of the view that taxing non-Indian lessees would interfere with the goal of promoting tribal economic self-sufficiency, it seems unlikely that it would have imposed this additional tax on those lessees.

[93]   [15] Nor are we inclined to do so today. Not only would such a proportionality requirement create nightmarish administrative burdens, but it would also be antithetical to the traditional notion that taxation is not premised on a strict quid pro quo relationship between the taxpayer and the tax collector.

abdication or noninvolvement of the State in the on-reservation activity. The present case is also unlike *Bracker*, and *Ramah Navajo School Bd.*, in that the district court found that "[n]o economic burden falls on the tribe by virtue of the state taxes," and that the Tribe could, in fact, increase its taxes without adversely affecting on-reservation oil and gas development. Finally, the district court found that the State regulates the spacing and mechanical integrity of wells located on the reservation. Thus, although the federal and tribal regulations in this case are extensive,[94] they are not exclusive, as were the regulations in *Bracker* and *Ramah Navajo School Bd.*

We thus conclude that federal law, even when given the most generous construction, does not pre-empt New Mexico's oil and gas severance taxes. This is not a case in which the State has had nothing to do with the on-reservation activity, save tax it. Nor is this a case in which an unusually large state tax has imposed a substantial burden on the Tribe.[95] It is, of course, reasonable to infer that the New Mexico taxes have at least a marginal effect on the demand for on-reservation leases, the value to the Tribe of those leases, and the ability of the Tribe to increase its tax rate. Any impairment to the federal policy favoring the exploitation of on-reservation oil and gas resources by Indian tribes that might be caused by these effects, however, is simply too indirect and too insubstantial to support Cotton's claim of pre-emption. To find pre-emption of state taxation in such indirect burdens on this broad congressional purpose, absent some special factor such as those present in *Bracker* and *Ramah Navajo School Bd.*, would be to return to the pre-1937 doctrine of intergovernmental tax immunity.[96] Any adverse effect on the

---

See *Carmichael v. Southern Coal & Coke Co.*, 301 U.S. 495, 521–523 (1987).

[94] [16] The federal regulations provide, inter alia, that tribal leases may only be offered for sale pursuant to specified standards governing notice and bidding, 25 CFR § 211.3(a) (1988), that the Secretary reserves "the right to reject all bids when in his judgment the interests of the Indians will be best served by so doing," § 211.3(b), that corporate bidders must submit detailed information concerning their officers, directors, shareholders, and finances, § 211.5, that no single lease for oil and gas may exceed 2,560 acres, § 211.9, and that a primary lease may not exceed ten years, § 211.10. The regulations also address the manner of payment and amount of rents and royalties, §§ 211.12, 211.13(a), and provide for Interior Department inspection of lessees' premises and records, § 211.18. Other federal regulations address the spacing, drilling, and plugging of wells, and impose reporting requirements concerning production and environmental protection. See 43 CFR §§ 3160.0-1-3186.4 (1987).

The Tribe imposes further regulations, including a requirement that anyone seeking to conduct oil and gas operations in the reservation must obtain a permit from the Tribal Oil and Gas Administration, J.A.T.C., Tit. 18, ch. 1, § 3, must post a bond, § 4(B), must open covered premises for inspection, § 5(C)(2), and must comply with the Tribe's environmental protection ordinance, § 6(A)(3).

[95] [17] We therefore have no occasion to reexamine our summary affirmance of the Court of Appeals for the Ninth Circuit's conclusion that Montana's unique severance and gross proceeds taxes may not be imposed on coal mined on Crow tribal property. See *Montana v. Crow Tribe of Indians*, 484 U.S. 997 (1988), summarily aff'g 819 F.2d 895 (1987). In that case, as the Ninth Circuit noted, the state taxes had a negative effect on the marketability of coal produced in *Montana*. See id., at 900. Moreover, as the Solicitor General stated in urging that we affirm the judgment of the Court of Appeals, the Montana taxes at issue were "extraordinarily high." Motion to Affirm for United States, O.T. 1987, No. 87-343, p. 12. According to the Crow Tribe's expert, the combined effective rate of the Montana taxes was 32.9%, "more than twice that of any other state's coal taxes." 819 F.2d, at 899, n.2. See also JUSTICE BLACKMUN's discussion of the "enormous revenues" generated by the Montana severance tax in *Commonwealth Edison Co. v. Montana*, 453 U.S. 609, 641–642 (1981) (BLACKMUN, J., dissenting).

[96] [18] It is important to keep in mind that the primary burden of the state taxation falls on the

Tribe's finances caused by the taxation of a private party contracting with the Tribe would be ground to strike the state tax. Absent more explicit guidance from Congress, we decline to return to this long-discarded and thoroughly repudiated doctrine.

IV

Cotton also argues that New Mexico's severance taxes — "insofar as they are imposed without allocation or apportionment on top of Jicarilla Apache tribal taxes" — impose "an unlawful multiple tax burden on interstate commerce." In support of this argument, Cotton relies on three facts: (1) that the State and the Tribe tax the same activity; (2) that the total tax burden on Cotton is higher than the burden on its off-reservation competitors who pay no tribal tax; and (3) that the state taxes generate revenues that far exceed the value of the services it provides on the reservation.

As we pointed out in the *Merrion* footnote, see n.5, *supra*, a multiple taxation issue may arise when more than one State attempts to tax the same activity. If a unitary business derives income from several States, each State may only tax the portion of that income that is attributable to activity within its borders. See, e.g., *Exxon Corp. v. Wisconsin Department of Revenue*, 447 U.S. 207 (1980). Thus, in such a case, an apportionment formula is necessary in order to identify the scope of the taxpayer's business that is within the taxing jurisdiction of each State. In this case, however, all of Cotton's leases are located entirely within the borders of the State of New Mexico and also within the borders of the Jicarilla Apache reservation. Indeed, they are also within the borders of the United States. There are, therefore, three different governmental entities, each of which has taxing jurisdiction over all of the non-Indian wells. Cf. [*Colville*] (Indian tribe did not oust State of power to impose cigarette tax on on-reservation sales to non-Indian customers by imposing its own tax on transaction). The federal sovereign has the undoubted power to prohibit taxation of the Tribe's lessees by the Tribe, by the State, or by both, but since it has not exercised that power, concurrent taxing jurisdiction over all of Cotton's on-reservation leases exists. . . .

It is, of course, true that the total taxes paid by Cotton are higher than those paid by off-reservation producers. But neither the State nor the Tribe imposes a discriminatory tax. The burdensome consequence is entirely attributable to the fact that the leases are located in an area where two governmental entities share jurisdiction. As we noted in *Merrion*, the tribal tax does "not treat minerals transported away from the reservation differently than it treats minerals that might be sold on the reservation." 455 U.S., at 157–158. Similarly, the New Mexico taxes are administered in an even-handed manner and are imposed at a uniform rate throughout the State — both on and off the reservation.

Cotton's most persuasive argument is based on the evidence that tax payments by reservation lessees far exceed the value of services provided by the State to the

---

non-Indian taxpayers. Amicus curiae briefs supporting the position of Cotton Petroleum Corp. in this case have been filed by [twelve oil companies]. Apparently all of those oil companies correctly interpreted the import of the 1988 Act until a seed of doubt was [sown] by our footnote in *Merrion*.

lessees, or more generally, to the reservation as a whole. There are, however, two sufficient reasons for rejecting this argument. First, the relevant services provided by the State include those that are available to the lessees and the members of the Tribe off the reservation as well as on it. The intangible value of citizenship in an organized society is not easily measured in dollars and cents; moreover, the district court found that the actual per capita state expenditures for Jicarilla members are equal to or greater than the per capita expenditures for non-Indian citizens. Second, there is no constitutional requirement that the benefits received from a taxing authority by an ordinary commercial taxpayer — or by those living in the community where the taxpayer is located — must equal the amount of its tax obligations.

[I]n effect, [Cotton] asks us to divest New Mexico of its normal latitude because its taxes have "some connection" to commerce with the Tribe. The connection, however, is by no means close enough. There is simply no evidence in the record that the tax has had an adverse effect on the Tribe's ability to attract oil and gas lessees. It is, of course, reasonable to infer that the existence of the state tax imposes some limit on the profitability of Indian oil and gas leases — just as it no doubt imposes a limit on the profitability of off-reservation leasing arrangements — but that is precisely the same indirect burden that we rejected as a basis for granting non-Indian contractors an immunity from the state taxation in *Helvering v. Mountain Producers Corp.*, 303 U.S. 376 (1938), *Oklahoma Tax Comm'n v. United States*, 319 U.S. 598 (1943), *Oklahoma Tax Comm'n v. Texas Co.*, 336 U.S. 342 (1949), [*Moe*,] and [*Colville*].

V

In our order noting probable jurisdiction we invited the parties to address the question whether the Tribe should be treated as a State for the purpose of determining whether New Mexico's taxes must be apportioned. All of the Indian tribes that have filed amicus curiae briefs addressing this question — including the Jicarilla Apache Tribe — have uniformly taken the position that Indian tribes are not States within the meaning of the Commerce Clause. This position is supported by the text of the Clause itself. Article I, § 8, cl. 3, provides the "Congress shall have the power . . . To regulate Commerce with foreign Nations, and among the several States, and with the Indian Tribes." Thus, the Commerce Clause draws a clear distinction between "States" and "Indian Tribes." As Chief Justice Marshall observed in [*Cherokee Nation*]: "The objects to which the power of regulating commerce might be directed, are divided into three distinct classes — foreign nations, the several states, and Indian Tribes. When forming this article, the convention considered them as entirely distinct." In fact, the language of the Clause no more admits of treating Indian tribes as States than of treating foreign nations as States.

It is also well-established that the Interstate Commerce and Indian Commerce Clauses have very different applications. In particular, while the Interstate Commerce Clause is concerned with maintaining free trade among the States even in the absence of implementing federal legislation, see *McLeod v. J.E. Dilworth Co.*, 322 U.S. 327, 330 (1944); *Pike v. Bruce Church, Inc.*, 397 U.S. 137 (1970), the central function of the Indian Commerce Clause is to provide Congress with plenary power to legislate in the field of Indian affairs, see *Morton v. Mancari*, 417 U.S. 535, 551–552 (1974); F. Cohen, Handbook of Federal Indian Law 207–208, and nn.2, 3 and 9–11 (1982). The extensive case law that has developed under the Interstate Commerce Clause, moreover, is premised on a structural understanding of the unique role of the States in our constitutional system that is not readily imported to cases involving the Indian Commerce Clause. Most notably, as our discussion of Cotton's "multiple taxation" argument demonstrates, the fact that States and tribes have concurrent jurisdiction over the same territory makes it inappropriate to apply Commerce Clause doctrine developed in the context of commerce "among" States with mutually exclusive territorial jurisdiction to trade "with" Indian tribes.

Accordingly, we have no occasion to modify our comment on this question in the *Bracker* case:

> Tribal reservations are not States, and the differences in the form and nature of their sovereignty make it treacherous to import to one notions of pre-emption that are properly applied to the other. 448 U.S., at 143.

[*Affirmed.*]

JUSTICE BLACKMUN, with whom JUSTICE BRENNAN and JUSTICE MARSHALL join, dissenting.

Although the Jicarilla Apache Tribe is not a party to the appeal, this case centrally concerns "the boundaries between state regulatory authority and [the Tribe's] self-government." [*Bracker*]. The basic principles that define those boundaries are well established. The Court today, while faithfully reciting these principles, is less faithful in their application.

Pre-emption is essentially a matter of congressional intent. In this case, our goal should be to determine whether the State's taxation of Cotton Petroleum's reservation oil production is consistent with federal Indian policy as expressed in relevant statutes and regulations. First and foremost, we must look to the statutory scheme Congress has established to govern the activity the State seeks to tax in order to see whether the statute itself expresses Congress's views on the question of state taxation. As the discussion in Part I below reveals, the statute most relevant to this case makes clear that Congress intended to foreclose the kind of tax New Mexico has imposed. Second, we must consider other indications of whether federal policy permits the tax in question. Part II below demonstrates that, under established principles, state taxation is pre-empted by federal and tribal interests in this case. Because the record is more than adequate to demonstrate the pre-emptive force of federal and tribal interests, I dissent.[97]

---

[97] [1] The Court today addresses, in addition to pre-emption, the question whether the Interstate Commerce Clause applies to problems of multiple state and Indian taxation. I agree with the majority's conclusion in Part V of its opinion that an Indian tribe is not to be equated with a State for purposes of the Interstate Commerce Clause. It would seem to follow that the Clause has no application to this case. I thus see no purpose in the majority's detailed application of Interstate Commerce Clause analysis in Part IV of its opinion.

I

The most relevant statute is the Indian Mineral Leasing Act of 1938, pursuant to which the Jicarilla Apache entered into mineral leases with appellant Cotton Petroleum. The 1938 Act is silent on the question of state taxation. But, as interpreted by this Court in *Montana v. Blackfeet Tribe*, the silence of the 1938 Act is eloquent and argues forcefully against the result reached by the majority. . . .

The argument that the 1938 congressional silence regarding lessee taxation is consistent with an intent to permit such taxation cannot, for two reasons, withstand close scrutiny. First, even if the majority is correct in seeking the meaning of Congress's silence in changes in this Court's intergovernmental tax immunity jurisprudence, the facts defeat the majority's theory. Second, and fundamentally, the majority's court-centered approach fails to give due weight to a far more significant intervening event: the major change in federal Indian policy embodied in the Indian Reorganization Act of 1934.

The case which overruled Justice Holmes's opinion for the Court in *Gillespie* was *Helvering v. Mountain Producers Corp.*, 303 U.S. 376 (1938). *Mountain Producers* was decided on March 7, 1938. The majority, indeed, is correct that the 1938 Act was enacted on May 11, 1938, after that case was decided. But a review of the history of the 1938 Act reveals that it had assumed final form well before this Court's March 7, 1938, decision in *Mountain Producers*. The majority's chronology thus is somewhat misleading, at least if the realities of the legislative process are to have any relevance to the analysis of legislative intent.

[A]lthough the majority is technically correct that the 1938 Act did not become law until after the announcement of this Court's decision in *Mountain Producers*, the legislation was formulated, considered by the House and Senate committees, referred out of the committees without amendment, and passed by the Senate, all before *Mountain Producers* on March 7, 1938, changed the law of intergovernmental tax immunity. Up until that point, the clear meaning of the statute, as our decision in *Montana* makes clear, is that the State lacked power to impose the tax at issue in this case. There is no evidence that the change in the law wrought by *Mountain Producers* was brought to the attention of the House. It defies historical sense to make *Mountain Producers* the centerpiece of the interpretation of a statute which reached final form before *Mountain Producers* was decided.

. . . .

In sum, we are given to choose between two possible interpretations of the silence of the 1938 Act. One, adopted by the majority, focuses on the change in this Court's intergovernmental immunity doctrine which took place at the very end of the process leading to the 1938 Act. The other focuses on a fundamental change in congressional Indian policy which took place shortly before the process began, and was expressly noted as its motivating force. The latter interpretation is clearly the more compelling. I must conclude that, contrary to the majority's view, the silence of the 1938 Act is not consistent with a congressional intent that non-Indian lessees of Indian mineral lands shall be subject to state taxation for their on-reservation activities.[98] This conclusion does not constitute, as the majority says, a "return to [the] long-discarded and thoroughly repudiated doctrine" of constitutional inter-governmental tax immunity. Rather, it reflects a fuller understanding of the policies underlying federal Indian law in the mid to late-1930s and continuing, in relevant part, into the present time.

II

Even if we did not have such direct evidence of Congress's intent to preclude state taxation of non-Indian oil production on Indian lands, that conclusion would be amply supported by a routine application of the traditional tools of Indian pre-emption analysis. . . .

Federal regulation of leasing of Indian oil lands "is both comprehensive and pervasive." *Ramah*, 458 U.S., at 839. Provisions of the 1938 Act regulate all stages of the process of oil and gas leasing and production on Indian reservations. The auction or bidding process through which leases are acquired is supervised by the Department of the Interior. 25 U.S.C. § 396b. Successful lessees must furnish a bond to secure compliance with lease terms, § 396c, and each lessee's operations are in all respects subject to federal rules and regulations, § 396d. Longstanding regulations promulgated pursuant to the 1938 Act govern the minute details of the bidding process, 25 CFR § 211.3 (1988), and give the Secretary of the Interior the power to reject bids that are not in the best interest of the Indian lessor, § 211.9, [and that govern] the term of each lease, §§ 211.13 and 211.16. Turning to the regulation of the lessee's operations, federal law controls when operations may start, § 211.20, and federal supervisory personnel are empowered to ensure the conservation of resources and prevention of waste, §§ 211.19–211.21. Additional restrictions are placed on lessees by the Federal Oil and Gas Royalty Management Act of 1982, 96 Stat. 2447, 30 U.S.C. §§ 1701 et seq., which further safeguards tribal interests by imposing additional inspection, collection, auditing security, and conservation requirements on lessees.

In addition, the Jicarilla Apache, as expressly authorized by their Constitution, have enacted regulations of their own to supplement federal guidelines, and have created a tribal Oil and Gas Administration to exercise tribal authority in this area.[99] See Jicarilla Apache Tribal Code, Tit. 18, ch. 1, §§ 1–7 (1987) and their Revised Constitution, Art. XI, § 1(a)(3). Indeed, just as we earlier found of the Mescalero Apache: "The . . . Tribe has engaged in a concerted and sustained undertaking to develop and manage the reservation's . . . resources specifically for the benefit of its members." *New Mexico v. Mescalero Apache Tribe*, 462 U.S. 324, 341 (1983).

---

[98] [7] Even if the silence of the 1938 Act simply were held to be ambiguous, our precedents consistently have required that ambiguities in statutes affecting tribal interests be resolved in favor of Indian independence. *Ramah Navajo School Board, Inc. v. Bureau of Revenue*, 458 U.S. 832, 838 (1982); *White Mountain Apache Tribe v. Bracker*, 448 U.S. 136, 143–144 (1980). That canon of interpretation would require rejecting the conclusion the majority reaches here.

[99] [8] Tribal regulation is expressly contemplated by regulations promulgated under the 1938 Act, which specify that certain statutory and regulatory provisions "may be superseded by the provisions" of tribal law enacted pursuant to the IRA. 25 CFR § 211.29 (1988).

. . . .

Finally, the majority sorely underestimates the degree to which state taxation of oil and gas production adversely affects the interests of the Jicarilla Apache. Assuming that the Tribe continues to tax oil and gas production at present levels, on-reservation taxes will remain 75% higher (14% as opposed to 8% of gross value) than off-reservation taxes within the State. The state trial court was not disturbed by this fact: it found that Cotton Petroleum had plans to dig new wells, and took that to be proof positive that the taxes imposed by the State did not deter drilling. But the court failed to recognize that Cotton Petroleum's new wells were infield (or "infill") wells, drilled between existing producing wells to increase the efficiency of drainage on lands already leased. An infill well is essentially a no-risk proposition, in that there is little doubt that the well will be productive. Therefore, Cotton Petroleum's willingness to drill infill wells does not reflect its willingness to develop new lands. Federal and tribal interests legitimately include long-term planning for development of lease revenues on new lands, where there is greater economic risk, and a greater probability that difference in tax rates will have an adverse effect on a producer's willingness to drill new wells and on the competitiveness of Jicarilla leases. "[B]oth the rate at which mining companies acquire Indian land leases and the rate at which they develop them are dependent on the future balance between the deterrents to and the advantages of Indian land leasing. Where the balance will be struck cannot be predicted, for there are simply too many variables involved." Federal Trade Commission, Staff Report on Mineral Leasing on Indian Lands 48 (1975) (FTC Report). Dual state and tribal taxation inevitably affects that balance.

In weighing the effect of state taxation on tribal interests, logic dictates that it is necessary not only to consider the size of the tax, but also the importance of the taxed activity to the tribal economy. See *California v. Cabazon Band of Mission Indians*, 480 U.S. 202, 218 (1987) (noting, in invalidating state regulation of tribal bingo operations, that bingo games constituted the sole source of tribal income). In this case, too, it is undisputed that oil and gas production is the Jicarilla Apache economy — a common pattern in reservations with substantial oil and gas reserves.

Furthermore, where, as here, the Tribe has made the decision to tax oil and gas producers, the long-term impact of state taxation on the Tribe's freedom of action in the sphere of taxation must also be considered. Tribal taxation has been widely perceived as necessary to protect Indian interests. The fact that the Jicarilla Apache have seen fit to impose their own taxes renders the threat to tribal interests which is always inherent in state taxation all the more apparent.[100] The market can bear only so much taxation, and it is inevitable that a point will be reached at which the State's taxes will impose a ceiling on tribal tax revenues. That the Jicarilla Apache have not yet raised their taxes to a level at which the combined effect of tribal and state taxation has been proved to diminish tribal revenues cannot be dispositive.

---

[100] [14] Although this Court ruled in [*Colville*] that the mere fact of Indian taxation does not oust a State's power to tax, this Court clearly relied in *Colville* on the fact that value generated by the activity there at issue (smokeshops) was not developed on the reservation by activities in which the Tribe has an interest. We observed in *Colville* that the Tribe was basically importing goods and marketing its tax immunity. That is not so here. Indeed, our decision in *Colville* expressly left open the possibility that "the Tribe themselves could perhaps pre-empt state taxation through the exercise of properly delegated federal power to do so."

Our decisions have never required a case-specific showing that state taxation in fact has deterred tribal activity; the potential for conflict is sufficient.

The majority observes that this is not "a case in which an unusually large state tax has imposed a substantial burden on the Tribe," and deems the tribal interest "indirect and . . . insubstantial." But the majority does not explain why interferences with federal policy of only the dramatic magnitude of the tax at issue in *Montana v. Crow Tribe of Indians*, 484 U.S. 997 (1988), meet the pre-emption threshold. In *Warren Trading Post Co. v. Arizona Tax Comm'n*, 380 U.S. 685, 691 (1965), the Court rejected a 2% tax on the gross proceeds of a non-Indian trader on an Indian reservation because it put "financial burdens on [the trader] or the Indians . . . in addition to those Congress or the tribes have prescribed, and could thereby disturb and disarrange the statutory plan Congress set up in order to protect Indians." Indeed, the dissenters in *White Mountain Apache* characterized the less-than-1% tax struck down in that case as "relatively trivial" and "unlikely to have a serious adverse impact on the tribal business," 448 U.S., at 159 (dissenting opinion of STEVENS, J.). That the tax burden was held sufficient to support a finding of pre-emption in *White Mountain Apache* and *Warren Trading Post* undermines the majority's position here. . . .

I respectfully dissent.

NOTES ON STATE TAXING JURISDICTION

1. Applying Federal Indian Law Preemption Doctrines: Since *Colville* indicates that states have some inherent authority over non-Indians in Indian country, preemption doctrines are particularly critical where, as in the two preceding cases, non-Indians are involved in business dealings with Indians either as suppliers or as customers. While the framers of the Constitution probably intended the Indian commerce clause to deprive states of any claims to authority over such transactions, the modern case law has not sustained that role for dormant Indian commerce clause claims. Rather, as suggested in *Colville*, the modern role of dormant Indian commerce clause doctrine is to prevent states from discriminating against or placing undue burdens upon such Indian commerce. By default, the primary role of structuring state power in this area therefore has fallen to statutory preemption doctrines of the type exemplified in the preceding cases.

While the courts use the term preemption as if it referred to a single doctrine, actually a broad range of approaches recently has been lumped together under this general rubric. For example, see *Central Machinery Co. v. Arizona State Tax Commission*, 448 U.S. 160 (1980) (federal Indian trader statutes pre-empted state tax on the sale of farm machinery to an Indian tribe when the sale took place on an Indian reservation and was made by a corporation that did not reside on the reservation and was not licensed to trade with Indians). In that case, one critical regulatory statute, the Federal Licensed Trader Act, Act of July 22, 1790, ch. 33, 1 Stat. 137, codified as amended at 25 U.S.C. § 261, preempted state authority to tax the transactions of even off-reservation non-Indian vendors subject to the regulatory regime of the Act, even if they had failed to comply with the Act by securing the required licenses. By contrast, in *White Mountain Apache v. Bracker*, the complex pattern of factors suggesting federal administrative support for or supervision of various Indian activities preempted the application of state law.

The preemption principles of *Bracker* were reaffirmed in *Ramah Navajo School Bd., Inc. v. Bureau of Revenue*, 458 U.S. 832 (1982). In *Ramah* the Supreme Court held that New Mexico's attempt to impose a gross receipts tax on a non-Indian construction company involved in the construction of a school for Indian children on the Navajo Reservation was preempted by federal law. The Navajo tribal organization had contracted with the BIA for the construction of the new school, and the Tribe then subcontracted, subject to BIA approval, with the non-Indian construction company that did business both on and off the reservation. The Court relied on several congressional statutes that authorized the BIA to provide for Indian education, both on and off the reservation, including the Snyder Act, 25 U.S.C. § 13, the Johnson-O'Malley Act, 25 U.S.C. § 452 et seq., the Navajo-Hopi Rehabilitation Act, 25 U.S.C. § 631 et seq., and the Indian Self-Determination and Education Assistance Act, 25 U.S.C. § 450 et seq. The Court noted that federal education policies had recently shifted toward encouraging Indian-controlled educational institutions on the reservation, reflected in the Indian Self-Determination and Education Assistance Act of 1975. Pursuant to these statutes, the Secretary of the Interior had promulgated regulations now found in 25 C.F.R. pt. 274, for "school construction for previously private schools now controlled and operated by tribes." *Id.* at 840–41 *quoting* 25 C.F.R. § 274.1 (1981). The Court held that the burden of the state tax, "although nominally falling on the non-Indian contractor, necessarily impedes the clearly expressed federal interest in promoting the 'quality and quantity' of educational opportunities for Indians for depleting the funds available for the construction of Indian schools." *Id.* at 842.

In his dissent in *Ramah*, Justice Rehnquist objected that the majority was more concerned with the extent of economic burden on the Tribe than with the preemptive effect of federal regulations. He claimed that the regulatory scheme relied upon in *Ramah* to demonstrate comprehensive and pervasive federal regulation of the subject matter amounted to little more than a grant application process, detailing procedures by which tribes may apply for federal funds in order to carry out school construction.

Is it clear that the asserted state tax in *Ramah* would obstruct the federal policy, particularly if the cost of construction is assumed to include various applicable taxes? Although the economic burden of the state-imposed gross receipts tax was held to fall on the Tribe in *Ramah*, the Tribe was paying for the construction of the school through congressional appropriations earmarked for that purpose. In *United States v. New Mexico*, 455 U.S. 720 (1982), decided the same term as *Ramah*, the Court held in a non-Indian context that New Mexico could impose its gross receipts, sales, and compensating use taxes on private contractors that conduct business with the federal government and that "immunity may not be conferred simply because the tax has an effect on the United States, or even because the federal government shoulders the entire economic burden of the levy." Are these principles of inter-governmental tax immunity relevant to the Indian preemption analysis? Does *Ramah* suggest that where a tribe is acting to effect congressionally expressed policies, any state tax whose economic burden ultimately falls on the tribe, irrespective of the legal incidence of the tax, will be preempted?

2. The Preemption Doctrine in *Cotton Petroleum*: Professor Frickey has labeled *Cotton Petroleum* "the Rehnquist Court's prime offender of the Marshall legacy. [T]his case expressed the general proposition, completely contrary to *Worcester*, that an Indian reservation is within the territorial jurisdiction of three sovereigns: the state, the tribe, and the federal government." Philip P. Frickey, *Marshalling Past and Present: Colonialism, Constitutionalism, and Interpretation in Federal Indian Law*, 107 Harv. L. Rev. 381, 433–34 (1993). Professor Frickey provides both an extended critique of *Cotton* and his own reimagining of an analysis of the case in keeping with Justice Marshall's legacy.

Might *Cotton Petroleum* stand for the proposition that state taxation, and maybe regulation, of non-Indian enterprises leasing Indian land and resources can be sustained unless it has a *direct* effect on the tribe? If so, has the Court adopted the same direct/indirect effects tests for the Indian preemption doctrine that it rejected in favor of a more pragmatic test a half-century ago in the Court's dormant commerce clause cases? *Compare Buck v. Kuykendall*, 267 U.S. 307 (1925) (direct/indirect effects test), *with Southern Pac. Co. v. Arizona*, 325 U.S. 761 (1945) (rejection of direct/indirect effects test in favor of practical assessment of "the nature and extent of the burden" of the state regulation and a balancing of state interests against freedom of interstate commerce). In 1988 the Supreme Court summarily affirmed a Ninth Circuit decision holding two Montana taxes with an effective rate of 32.9% of the value of coal mined by non-Indian producers on tribal land preempted. *Montana v. Crow Tribe*, 484 U.S. 997 (1988), *aff'g, Crow Tribe v. Montana*, 819 F.2d 895 (9th Cir. 1987). How can *Cotton Petroleum* and *Montana v. Crow Tribe* be reconciled? Does either the majority or the dissent in *Cotton Petroleum* provide any insights into this question?

Recall that the Indian commerce clause originally was adopted to prevent state frustration of federal efforts to protect Indian lands and resources. In light of that history, how can one justify the Court's willingness to permit multiple taxation and burdens on the development of Indian resources which make such development *more* expensive in Indian country within the state than outside of Indian country? Why does not such a tax pattern constitute a discriminatory pattern of taxation? Is not the tax apportionment doctrine of the interstate commerce clause precisely designed to prevent such discrimination against commerce? Should *Cotton Petroleum* be treated as the oddball case where double taxation was found to have absolutely no impact on tribal capacity to generate tax revenue from the same source?

Cotton Petroleum considers federal preemption in the context of the Indian Mineral Leasing Act of 1938; but the Tenth Circuit reached the same conclusion where a non-Indian's mineral lease was made under the Indian Mineral Development Act of 1982. That later Act gives tribes more flexibility in establishing lease terms, in order to promote economic development; but it also does not mention taxation. *See Ute Mt. Ute Tribe v. Rodriguez*, 660 F.3d 1177 (10th Cir. 2011). What if the non-Indian lessee has a surface lease of land taken into trust under the Indian Reorganization Act, 25 U.S.C. § 465, rather than a mineral lease, and the state wants to tax buildings or the value of the rental? In 2012, the Department of Interior promulgated regulations on leasing tribal trust lands that purport to preempt state and local taxes levied on improvements on these lands. *See* 25 CFR

162.017. Should it matter that section 465 does not expressly bar state taxation? In considering this question, review *Mescalero Apache Tribe v. Jones*, 411 U.S. 145 (1973), presented and discussed in Sec. B, this chapter.

4. Impact of the Dormant Indian Commerce Clause and *Seminole Tribe of Florida v. Florida*: In *Cotton Petroleum*, Justice Stevens contrasts the interstate and Indian commerce clauses. The interstate commerce clause, he asserts, both empowers Congress and operates in "dormant" fashion to invalidate state laws that could impede free trade. In contrast, "the central function of the Indian Commerce Clause is to provide Congress with plenary power to legislate in the field of Indian affairs." By implication, the Indian commerce clause has no comparable "dormant" impact on state law. Does Justice Stevens's position accord with the framers' intent and constitutional history? In an extensive article detailing the history of the Indian commerce clause, Professor Clinton contends that the Indian commerce clause was intended by the framers to limit state authority. Robert N. Clinton, *The Dormant Indian Commerce Clause*, 27 CONN. L. REV. 1055 (1995). Professor Clinton argues that, as Chief Justice Marshall noted in *Worcester*, the Indian commerce clause, unlike the interstate and foreign commerce clauses, had an antecedent in Article IX of the Articles of Confederation. The Indian affairs clause of Article IX had been plagued, like the earlier colonial management of Indian affairs, by competing and conflicting claims of residual state sovereignty and power in Indian affairs. These claims repeatedly frustrated the initiatives of the central government in the field of Indian affairs during the confederation period. Professor Clinton argues that while Justice Stevens correctly notes that the Indian commerce clause affirmatively granted Indian affairs powers to Congress, its primary marginal contribution to the American constitutional framework over the Articles was to eliminate provisos found in Article IX that formed the basis of the states' claims to residual power in Indian affairs. The Supreme Court revisited the issue of the impact of the Indian commerce clause on state power in *Seminole Tribe of Florida v. Florida*, 517 U.S. 44 (1996), asking "whether the Indian Commerce Clause, like the Interstate Commerce Clause, is a grant of authority to the federal Government at the expense of the States?" The Court responded, "the answer to that question is obvious. If anything, the Indian Commerce Clause accomplishes a greater transfer of power from the States to the federal government than does the Interstate Commerce Clause. This is clear enough from the fact that the States still exercise some authority over interstate trade but have been divested of virtually all authority over Indian commerce and Indian tribes." Elsewhere in the opinion, the Court indicated that the Indian commerce clause gave the power to deal with Indian tribes and Indian affairs exclusively to the federal government. *Seminole Tribe* is set forth in Ch. 5, Sec. D.1. Does *Seminole* signal a rejection of Justice Stevens's *Cotton Petroleum* treatment of the effects of the Indian commerce clause on state power?

5. Lower Courts Struggle with State Jurisdiction to Tax Nonmembers: In *Hoopa Valley Tribe v. Nevins*, 881 F.2d 657 (9th Cir. 1989), the Ninth Circuit distinguished *Cotton Petroleum* and held that federal law preempted assessment of a state timber yield tax. The Hoopa Valley Indian Reservation consists of over 80,000 acres of commercial timber land. Remoteness of the reservation limits tribal employment opportunities and therefore the Tribe relied primarily on timber-related revenues for its economic well-being. In an effort to promote timber management, conservation and production, the State of California adopted a timber yield tax. Cal. Rev. & Tax Code §§ 38101–38908. The tax is assessed judging the value of the timber when it is harvested and is imposed on the first non-exempt entity procuring ownership of the timber. The Hoopa Valley Tribe filed suit challenging application of the tax to private companies purchasing Tribal timber. The district court held "that the exercise of state authority in assessing the timber yield tax against companies which purchase Tribal timber . . . is preempted by the pervasive federal regulation of Indian timber and is thus in violation of federal law." *Hoopa Valley Tribe v. Nevins*, 590 F. Supp. 198, 203 (N.D. Cal. 1984). Affirming the district court's determination, the Ninth Circuit carefully distinguished the factual situation from *Cotton Petroleum*. The court noted that, in *Cotton Petroleum*, New Mexico "regulated the oil and gas activities affected by the tax" and that the "New Mexico tax primarily burdened non-Indian taxpayers." *Hoopa*, 881 F.2d at 660. In contrast, the Ninth Circuit noted that "California plays no role in the Hoopa Valley Tribe's timber activities" and "the burden of the tax concededly falls on the tribe." *Id.* (making reference to the district court opinion). Although the state provided a variety of services to residents of the reservation, because those services were not related to timber activities, the court was unpersuaded by the state's argument that the tax serves any legitimate state interests of raising revenues for services provided. *Id.* at 660–61.

Subsequent Ninth Circuit decisions have split on state taxing jurisdiction in situations where Indian nations enlisted non-Indian companies in economic development projects on their reservations. *Compare Gila River Indian Community v. Waddell (Gila I)*, 967 F.2d 1404 (9th Cir. 1992) (rejecting state tax on ticket revenues of non-Indian operator of performing arts theater, where theater was developed by the Tribe with BIA assistance and approval and leased to the non-Indian, with improvements belonging to the Tribe, the Tribe receiving a percentage of gross receipts from each performance, and the Tribe levying its own sales tax on theater tickets and concessions), *and Cabazon Band of Mission Indians v. Wilson*, 37 F.3d 430 (1994) (rejecting state tax on non-Indian racing associations that Tribe contracted with to broadcast signals to Tribe's off-track betting facilities, where gaming was regulated by federal law, facility was built and operated by the Tribe, and gaming was the main source of tribal revenue), *with Salt River Pima-Maricopa Indian Community v. Arizona*, 50 F.3d 734 (9th Cir. 1995) (allowing state sales and rental taxes on transactions at shopping mall operated by non-Indian developer who leased land from the Tribe on behalf of allottees, with buildings to revert to allottees, and the Tribe imposing its own sales tax and providing the majority of services to the mall), *and Gila River Indian Community v. Waddell (Gila II)*, 91 F.3d 1232 (9th Cir. 1996) (allowing state tax on entertainment events at tribally-constructed facility leased to non-Indian, Tribe provided most services to the facility, few tribal members worked at the facility, and Tribe had the right to shut down scheduled events in cases of threats to public safety), *and Yavapai-Prescott Indian Tribe v. Scott*, 117 F.3d 1107 (9th Cir. 1997) (allowing state business transaction privilege tax on room rentals, food, and beverage sales by non-Indian hotel operator, where hotel was built by Tribe partly with funds from HUD and tribal loans, Tribe received rent from operator based on gross revenue, Tribe subleased part of hotel for its gaming operation, Tribe did not have an active role in the business of the hotel, tribal members were not employed at the hotel, and most services were provided by the state but paid for by the Tribe). Do these cases form a coherent pattern? How much and what kind of involvement must a tribe have in non-Indian economic activities on its reservation before state taxation can be precluded? How much time must non-Indian customers spend in connection with tribal retail or entertainment establishments before it is safe to say that the tribe is not merely "marketing a tax exemption"? Is the Ninth Circuit properly taking into account factors such as the extent of tribal employment and the tribe's sharing in profits? For example, shouldn't a tribe be able to choose taxation rather than a share of profits as its source of revenue without triggering state taxation? Should it matter whether the state is providing services roughly comparable in value to the amount of tax revenue it seeks to extract? For an analysis of these cases, see Richard R. Ansson, Jr., *State Taxation of Non-Indians Who Do Business with Indian Tribes: Why Several Recent Ninth Circuit Holdings Reemphasize the Need for Indian Tribes to Enter into Taxation Compacts with Their Respective States*, 78 OR. L. REV. 501 (1999).

Test your understanding by considering the following facts: The Mashantucket Pequot Tribe in Connecticut operates a large-scale gaming enterprise, compensating the local town of Ledyard for law enforcement services and compacting with the state to pay over 25% of proceeds from slot machines. Following standard practices in the gaming industry, it leases gaming machines from a non-Indian company, and agrees to bear the burden of any taxes imposed on the machines. The local town, which maintains roads to and from the reservation and provides education to the on-reservation children, wants to impose a personal property tax on the non-Indian owner of the leased machines. Is that local government tax preempted, either by direct conflict with a federal statute or otherwise? How would you go about analyzing the problem? *See Mashantucket Pequot Tribe v. Town of Ledyard*, 722 F.3d 457 (2d Cir. 2013), and consider whether the District Court or the Court of Appeals did a better job.

6. **Tribal Resistance to State Taxation:** The tribal ordinances involved in *Colville* and in *Milhelm Attea* made the tribes the retailers of the cigarettes, and the tribes retained ownership of the cigarettes until they were sold. In light of this feature of the tribal schemes, how can states enforce the record keeping requirements that the Court has sustained? Recall that Indian tribes generally have sovereign immunity. In *McClanahan*, *supra*, the Supreme Court invalidated the state income tax on reservation-based Indians earning their income on the reservation, partly because the state could not enforce its purported tax. Justice Marshall wrote, "[The state] nowhere explains how, without such jurisdiction, the State's tax may either be imposed or collected." Is the states' power to seize unstamped cigarettes that are destined for a tribe outside the reservation, a power sustained in *Colville*, a sufficient enforcement mechanism? Do states have any other enforcement powers available to them? See the discussion above, in *Milhelm Attea*, of *Oklahoma Tax Commission v. Citizen Band Potawatomi Indian Tribe of Oklahoma*, 498 U.S. 505, 514 (1991) (suggesting additional remedies, including an appeal to Congress), as well as the discussion of upstream taxation of distributors in Sec. B.5, this chapter. Tribal taxation expert Scott Taylor has stated in a congressional hearing, "My own experience with tribes shows that they are inclined to comply with state withholding and payment requirements when the taxes are

legally imposed and reasonably applied." Testimony of Scott A. Taylor, Committee on Resources, U.S House of Representatives, 106th Cong., October 12, 1999.

Some tribes have resisted making tax payments to states for on-reservation transactions with nonmembers, believing that the tribal-federal relationship does not allow state interference with tribal economic development initiatives. In New York, Haudenosaunee tribes and the state nearly succeeded in establishing a cooperative agreement that would have substituted tribal cigarette taxes for state taxes on sales to nonmembers. *See* Joseph J. Heath, *Review of the History of the April 1997 Trade and Commerce Agreement Among the Traditional Haudenosaunee Councils of Chiefs and New York State and the Impact Thereof on Haudenosaunee Sovereignty*, 46 BUFF. L. REV. 1011 (1998). After negotiations broke down, the Governor tried blocking delivery and seizing untaxed cigarettes, but the enforcement attempts resulted in demonstrations, confrontations with state police, tire-burnings, and threats of violence by Indian groups. Eventually, the state Department of Revenue made a judgment to refrain from attempting to collect the taxes, and non-Indian retailers sued to reinstate the enforcement efforts. The state's decision was sustained by the New York courts in *New York Ass'n of Convenience Stores v. Urbach*, 694 N.Y.S.2d 885 (1999).

In Montana, the Confederated Salish and Kootenai Tribes refused to collect a state lodging tax on hotel rooms rented by nonmembers at the Tribes' lakeside KwaTaqNuk resort. The Tribes' position has been that as a sovereign Indian nation, it should not be required to collect taxes for the state without first negotiating an agreement. When the Montana Revenue Department filed suit in state court to force the resort to collect the tax, the trial judge dismissed the action based on lack of state jurisdiction and tribal sovereign immunity. What do these actions say about Indian nations' views of the proper tribal-federal relationship, as it affects the extent of state power? How should the terms of that relationship be established? Can states circumvent tribal resistance by going upstream in the commercial chain to tax off-reservation non-Indian distributors?

7. **Tribal-State Tax Compacts:** As of 1998, more than 200 Tribes in eighteen states had resolved taxation disputes by forming intergovernmental agreements. Testimony of W. Ron Allen, President National Congress of American Indians, Committee on Resources, U.S. House of Representatives, June 24, 1998. More have been adopted in the ensuing years. These agreements spare costly litigation, and may include terms addressing tax compliance problems, revenue sharing, reimbursement for tribal or state services, and off-reservation business's concerns with reservations as low-tax competitors. For example, Nevada and Louisiana have actually agreed that tribes may keep all revenues from on-reservation sales to nonmembers, so long as the tribes impose taxes at the same rate as the state. Likewise, the Navajo Nation recently established its own motor vehicle fuel excise tax, expected to raise approximately $10 million per year for building and maintaining tribal roads. Because its reservation includes land in three states, each with its own fuel excise tax system, the Navajo Nation attempted to form agreements. Arizona entered into an intergovernmental agreement that eliminated multiple taxation and provided for revenue sharing based on a statistical study. New Mexico and Utah, in contrast, amended their fuel taxes to allow stations owned by the Nation or its members to deduct tribal fuel taxes from the respective state

taxes, thereby eliminating most multiple taxation. *See, e.g.*, Utah Sess. Law Chapter 232, effective March 19, 2001. An example of a tax agreement, this one between the Squaxin Island Tribe and the State of Washington, is referenced in Ch. 3, Sec. E.2 along with discussion of the advantages and disadvantages of such jurisdiction agreements.

Has the Supreme Court doctrine on tribal and state taxing jurisdiction put Indian nations in a strong position as they enter into negotiations for such agreements? The following cases extend the analysis of state taxation to state regulation within Indian country, revealing many of the same doctrinal challenges and practical initiatives.

NEW MEXICO v. MESCALERO APACHE TRIBE
United States Supreme Court
462 U.S. 324 (1983)

JUSTICE MARSHALL delivered the opinion of the Court.

We are called upon to decide in this case whether a State may restrict an Indian Tribe's regulation of hunting and fishing on its reservation. With extensive federal assistance and supervision, the Mescalero Apache Tribe has established a comprehensive scheme for managing the reservation's fish and wildlife resources. Federally approved tribal ordinances regulate in detail the conditions under which both members of the Tribe and nonmembers may hunt and fish. New Mexico seeks to apply its own laws to hunting and fishing by nonmembers on the reservation. We hold that this application of New Mexico's hunting and fishing laws is pre-empted by the operation of federal law.

I

The Mescalero Apache Tribe (Tribe) resides on a reservation located within Otero County in south central New Mexico. The reservation, which represents only a small portion of the aboriginal Mescalero domain, was created by a succession of Executive Orders promulgated in the 1870's and 1880's. The present reservation comprises more than 460,000 acres, of which the Tribe owns all but 193.85 acres. Approximately 2,000 members of the Tribe reside on the reservation, along with 179 non-Indians, including resident federal employees of the [BIA] and the [IHS].

The Tribe is organized under the [IRA. Its Constitution] requires the Tribal Council

> [t]o protect and preserve the property, wildlife and natural resources of the tribe, and to regulate the conduct of trade and the use and disposition of tribal property upon the reservation, providing that any ordinance directly affecting non-members of the tribe shall be subject to review by the Secretary of Interior. App. 53a.

The Constitution further provides that the Council shall

adopt and approve plans of operation to govern the conduct of any business or industry that will further the economic well-being of the members of the tribe, and to undertake activity of any nature whatsoever, not inconsistent with Federal law or with this constitution, designed for the social or economic improvement of the Mescalero Apache people, . . . subject to review by the Secretary of the Interior. *Ibid.*

Anticipating a decline in the sale of lumber which has been the largest income-producing activity within the reservation, the Tribe has recently committed substantial time and resources to the development of other sources of income. The Tribe has constructed a resort complex financed principally by federal funds,[101] and has undertaken a substantial development of the reservation's hunting and fishing resources. These efforts provide employment opportunities for members of the Tribe, and the sale of hunting and fishing licenses and related services generates income which is used to maintain the tribal government and provide services to Tribe members.[102]

Development of the reservation's fish and wildlife resources has involved a sustained, cooperative effort by the Tribe and the federal government. Indeed, the reservation's fishing resources are wholly attributable to these recent efforts. Using federal funds, the Tribe has established eight artificial lakes which, together with the reservation's streams, are stocked by the Bureau of Sport Fisheries and Wildlife of the United States Fish and Wildlife Service, Department of the Interior, which operates a federal hatchery located on the reservation. None of the waters are stocked by the State.[103] The United States has also contributed substantially to the creation of the reservation's game resources. Prior to 1966 there were only 13 elk in the vicinity of the reservation. In 1966 and 1967 the National Park Service donated a herd of 162 elk which was released on the reservation. Through its management and range development the Tribe has dramatically increased the elk population, which by 1977 numbered approximately 1,200. New Mexico has not contributed significantly to the development of the elk herd or the other game on the reservation, which includes antelope, bear, and deer.

The Tribe and the federal government jointly conduct a comprehensive fish and management program. Pursuant to its Constitution and to an agreement with the Bureau of Sport Fisheries and Wildlife,[104] the Tribal Council adopts hunting and

---

[101] [3] Financing for the complex, the Inn of the Mountain Gods, came principally from the Economic Development Administration (EDA), an agency of the United States Department of Commerce, and other federal sources. In addition, the Tribe obtained a $6 million loan from the Bank of New Mexico, 90% of which was guaranteed by the Secretary of the Interior under the Indian Financing Act of 1974, 25 U.S.C. § 1451 et seq. (1976 ed. and Supp. V), and 10% of which was guaranteed by trial funds. Certain additional facilities at the Inn were completely funded by the EDA as public works projects, and other facilities received 50% funding from the EDA. . . .

[102] [4] Income from the sale of hunting and fishing licenses, "package hunts" which combine hunting and fishing with use of the facilities at the Inn, and campground and picnicking permits totaled $269,140 in 1976 and $271,520 in 1977. The vast majority of the nonmember hunters and fishermen on the reservation are not residents of the State of New Mexico.

[103] [5] The State has not stocked any waters on the reservation since 1976.

[104] [8] That agreement, which provides for the stocking of the reservation's artificial lakes by the Bureau, obligates the Tribe to "designate those waters of the Reservation which shall be open to public

fishing ordinances each year. The tribal ordinances, which establish bag limits and seasons and provide for licensing of hunting and fishing, are subject to approval by the Secretary under the Tribal Constitution and have been so approved. The Tribal Council adopts the game ordinances on the basis of recommendations submitted by a Bureau of Indian Affairs' range conservationist who is assisted by full-time conservation officers employed by the Tribe. The recommendations are made in light of the conservation needs of the reservation, which are determined on the basis of annual game counts and surveys. Through the Bureau of Sport Fisheries and Wildlife, the Secretary also determines the stocking of the reservation's waters based upon periodic surveys of the reservation.

Numerous conflicts exist between state and tribal hunting regulations. For instance, tribal seasons and bag limits for both hunting and fishing often do not coincide with those imposed by the State. The Tribe permits a hunter to kill both a buck and a doe; the State permits only buck to be killed. Unlike the State, the Tribe permits a person to purchase an elk license in two consecutive years. Moreover, since 1977, the Tribe's ordinances have specified that state hunting and fishing licenses are not required for Indians or non-Indians who hunt or fish on the reservation.[105] The New Mexico Department of Game and Fish has enforced the State's regulations by arresting non-Indian hunters for illegal possession of game killed on the reservation in accordance with tribal ordinances but not in accordance with state hunting regulations.

In 1977 the Tribe filed suit against the State and the Director of its Game and Fish Department in the United States District Court for the District of New Mexico, seeking to prevent the State from regulating on-reservation hunting or fishing by members or nonmembers. On August 2, 1978, the District Court ruled in favor of the Tribe and granted declaratory and injunctive relief against the enforcement of the State's hunting and fishing laws against any person for hunting and fishing activities conducted on the reservation. The United States Court of Appeals for the Tenth Circuit affirmed. Following New Mexico's petition for a writ of certiorari, this Court vacated the Tenth Circuit's judgment, and remanded the case for reconsideration in light of *Montana v. United States*, 450 U.S. 544 (1981). On remand, the Court of Appeals adhered to its earlier decision. We granted *certiorari* [and] now affirm.

II

New Mexico concedes that on the reservation the Tribe exercises exclusive jurisdiction over hunting and fishing by members of the Tribe and may also regulate the hunting and fishing by nonmembers. New Mexico contends, however, that it may exercise concurrent jurisdiction over nonmembers and that therefore its regulations governing hunting and fishing throughout the State should also apply to hunting and fishing by nonmembers on the reservation. Although New Mexico does not claim that it can require the Tribe to permit nonmembers to hunt and fish on the

---

fishing" and to "establish regulations for the conservation of the fishery resources." App. 71a.

[105] [10] Prior to 1977 the Tribe consented to the application to the reservation of the State's hunting and fishing regulations.

reservation, it claims that, once the Tribe chooses to permit hunting and fishing by nonmembers, such hunting and fishing is subject to any state-imposed conditions. Under this view the State would be free to impose conditions more restrictive than the Tribe's own regulations, including an outright prohibition. The question in this case is whether the State may so restrict the Tribe's exercise of its authority.

Our decision in *Montana v. United States, supra*, does not resolve this question. Unlike this case, *Montana* concerned lands located within the reservation but not owned by the Tribe or its members. We held that the Crow Tribe could not as a general matter regulate hunting and fishing on those lands.[106] But as to "land belonging to the Tribe or held by the United States in trust for the Tribe," we "readily agree[d]" that a Tribe may "prohibit nonmembers from hunting or fishing . . . [or] condition their entry by charging a fee or establish bag and creel limits." *Id.*, at 557. We had no occasion to decide whether a Tribe may only exercise this authority in a manner permitted by a State.

On numerous occasions this Court has considered the question whether a State may assert authority over a reservation. The decision in [*Worcester v. Georgia*] reflected the view that Indian tribes were wholly distinct nations within whose boundaries "the laws of [a State] can have no force." We long ago departed from the "conceptual clarity of Mr. Chief Justice Marshall's view in *Worcester*," *Mescalero Apache Tribe v. Jones*, 411 U.S. 145, 148 (1973), and have acknowledged certain limitations on tribal sovereignty. For instance, we have held that Indian tribes have been implicitly divested of their sovereignty in certain respects by virtue of their dependent status, that under certain circumstances a State may validly assert authority over the activities of nonmembers on a reservation, and that in exceptional circumstances a State may assert jurisdiction over the on-reservation activities of tribal members.

Nevertheless, in demarcating the respective spheres of state and tribal authority over Indian reservations, we have continued to stress that Indian tribes are unique aggregations possessing " 'attributes of sovereignty over both their members and their territory,' " [*Bracker*] quoting *United States v. Mazurie*, 419 U.S. 544, 557 (1975). Because of their sovereign status, tribes and their reservation lands are insulated in some respects by a "historic immunity from state and local control," *Mescalero Apache Tribe v. Jones, supra*, at 152, and tribes retain any aspect of their historical sovereignty not "inconsistent with the overriding interests of the National Government." [*Colville*]

The sovereignty retained by tribes includes "the power of regulating their internal and social relations," [*United States v. Kagama*]. A tribe's power to prescribe the conduct of tribal members has never been doubted, and our cases

---

[106] [12] Even so, the Court acknowledged that "Indian tribes retain inherent sovereign power to exercise some forms of civil jurisdiction over non-Indians on their reservations, even on non-Indian fee lands." 450 U.S., at 565. The Court stressed that in *Montana* the pleadings "did not allege that non-Indian hunting and fishing on [non-Indian] reservation lands [had] impaired [the Tribe's reserved hunting and fishing privileges]," *id.*, at 558, n. 6, or "that non-Indian hunting and fishing on fee lands imperil the subsistence or welfare of the Tribe," *id.*, at 566, and that the existing record failed to suggested "that such non-Indian hunting and fishing . . . threaten the Tribe's political or economic security." *Ibid.*

establish that " 'absent governing Acts of Congress,' " a State may not act in a manner that " 'infringed on the right of reservation Indians to make their own laws and be ruled by them.' " [*McClanahan*, quoting *Williams v. Lee*].

A tribe's power to exclude nonmembers entirely or to condition their presence on the reservation is equally well established. See, *e.g.*, *Montana v. United States*, 450 U.S. 544 (1981); *Merrion v. Jicarilla Apache Tribe*, 455 U.S. 130 (1982). Whether a State may also assert its authority over the on-reservation activities of nonmembers raises "[m]ore difficult questions," *Bracker, supra*, at 144. While under some circumstances a State may exercise concurrent jurisdiction over non-Indians acting on tribal reservations, see, *e.g.*, [*Colville*;] *Moe v. Salish & Kootenai Tribes*, 425 U.S. 463 (1976), such authority may be asserted only if not pre-empted by the operation of federal law. [*E.g.*, *Ramah Navajo School Bd., Inc. v. Bureau of Revenue of New Mexico*, 458 U.S. 832 (1982).]

In *Bracker* we reviewed our prior decisions concerning tribal and state authority over Indian reservations and extracted certain principles governing the determination whether federal law pre-empts the assertion of state authority over nonmembers on a reservation. We stated that that determination does not depend "on mechanical or absolute conceptions of state or tribal sovereignty, but call[s] for a particularized inquiry into the nature of the state, federal, and tribal interests at stake." 448 U.S., at 145.

We also emphasized the special sense in which the doctrine of pre-emption is applied in this context. Although a State will certainly be without jurisdiction if its authority is pre-empted under familiar principles of pre-emption, we cautioned that our prior cases did not limit pre-emption of state laws affecting Indian tribes to only those circumstances. "The unique historical origins of tribal sovereignty" and the federal commitment to tribal self-sufficiency and self-determination make it "treacherous to import . . . notions of pre-emption that are properly applied to . . . other [contexts]." *Bracker, supra*, at 143. By resting pre-emption analysis principally on a consideration of the nature of the competing interests at stake, our cases have rejected a narrow focus on congressional intent to pre-empt state law as the sole touchstone. They have also rejected the proposition that pre-emption requires " 'an express congressional statement to that effect.' " *Bracker, supra*, at 144. State jurisdiction is pre-empted by the operation of federal law if it interferes or is incompatible with federal and tribal interests reflected in federal law, unless the state interests at stake are sufficient to justify the assertion of state authority. *Bracker, supra*, at 145. See also *Ramah Navajo School Bd., supra*, at 845, quoting *Hines v. Davidowitz*, 312 U.S. 52, 67 (1941).[107]

Certain broad considerations guide our assessment of the federal and tribal interests. The traditional notions of Indian sovereignty provide a crucial "backdrop," *Bracker, supra*, at 143, citing *McClanahan, supra*, at 172, against which any assertion of state authority must be assessed. Moreover, both the tribes and the federal government are firmly committed to the goal of promoting tribal self-

---

[107] [16] The exercise of state authority may also be barred by an independent barrier — inherent tribal sovereignty — if it "unlawfully infringe[s] on 'the right of reservation Indians to make their own laws and be ruled by them.' " *White Mountain Apache Tribe v. Bracker*, 448 U.S. 136, 142 (1980), quoting *Williams v. Lee*, 358 U.S. 217, 220 (1959).

government, a goal embodied in numerous federal statutes.[108] We have stressed that Congress's objective of furthering tribal self-government encompasses far more than encouraging tribal management of disputes between members, but includes Congress's overriding goal of encouraging "tribal self-sufficiency and economic development." *Bracker*, 448 U.S., at 143 (footnote omitted). In part as a necessary implication of this broad federal commitment, we have held that tribes have the power to manage the use of their territory and resources by both members and nonmembers,[109] to undertake and regulate economic activity within the reservation, *Merrion*, 455 U.S., at 137, and to defray the cost of governmental services by levying taxes. *Ibid.* Thus, when a tribe undertakes an enterprise under the authority of federal law, an assertion of state authority must be viewed against any interference with the successful accomplishment of the federal purpose. See generally [*Bracker*;] *Ramah Navajo School Bd.*, 458 U.S., at 845, quoting *Hines v. Davidowitz, supra*, at 67 (state authority precluded when it " 'stands as an obstacle to the accomplishment of the full purposes and objectives of Congress' ").

Our prior decisions also guide our assessment of the state interest asserted to justify state jurisdiction over a reservation. The exercise of state authority which imposes additional burdens on a tribal enterprise must ordinarily be justified by functions or services performed by the State in connection with the on-reservation activity. *Ramah Navajo School Bd., supra*, at 843, and n.7; [*Bracker*; *Central Machinery*] (Powell, J., dissenting). Thus a State seeking to impose a tax on a transaction between a tribe and nonmembers must point to more than its general interest in raising revenues. See, e.g., [*Warren Trading Post*; *Bracker*; *Ramah Navajo School Bd.*]. See also [*Colville*], 447 U.S., at 157 (governmental interest in raising revenues is . . . strongest when the tax is directed at off-reservation value and when the taxpayer is the recipient of state services); *Moe*, 425 U.S., at 481–483 (State may require tribal shops to collect state cigarette tax from nonmember purchasers). A State's regulatory interest will be particularly substantial if the State can point to off-reservation effects that necessitate state intervention. Cf. *Puyallup Tribe v. Washington Game Dept.*, 433 U.S. 165 (1977).

---

[108] [17] For example, the Indian Financing Act of 1974, 25 U.S.C. § 1451 et seq. (1976 ed. and Supp. V), states: "It is hereby declared to be the policy of Congress . . . to help develop and utilize Indian resources, both physical and human, to a point where the Indians will fully exercise responsibility for the utilization and management of their own resources and where they will enjoy a standard of living from their own productive efforts comparable to that enjoyed by non-Indians in neighboring communities." § 1451. Similar policies underlie the Indian Self-Determination and Education Assistance Act of 1975, 25 U.S.C. § 450 et seq., as well as the Indian Reorganization Act of 1934, 25 U.S.C. § 461 et seq. (1976 ed. and Supp. V), pursuant to which the Mescalero Apache Tribe adopted its Constitution. The "intent and purpose of the Reorganization Act was 'to rehabilitate the Indian's economic life and to give him a chance to develop the initiative destroyed by a century of oppression and paternalism.' " *Mescalero Apache Tribe v. Jones*, 411 U.S. 145, 152 (1973), quoting H.R. Rep. No. 1804, 73d Cong., 2d Sess., 6 (1934). The Indian Civil Rights Act of 1968, 25 U.S.C. § 1301 et seq., likewise reflects Congress's intent "to promote the well-established federal 'policy of furthering Indian self-government.' " *Santa Clara Pueblo v. Martinez*, 436 U.S. 49, 62 (1978), quoting *Morton v. Mancari*, 417 U.S. 535, 551 (1974).

[109] [18] Our cases have recognized that tribal sovereignty contains a "significant geographical component." *Bracker, supra*, at 151. Thus the off-reservation activities of Indians are generally subject to the prescriptions of a "nondiscriminatory state law" in the absence of "express federal law to the contrary." *Mescalero Apache Tribe v. Jones, supra*, at 148–149.

III

With these principles in mind, we turn to New Mexico's claim that it may superimpose its own hunting and fishing regulations on the Mescalero Apache Tribe's regulatory scheme.

A

It is beyond doubt that the Mescalero Apache Tribe lawfully exercises substantial control over the lands and resources of its reservation, including its wildlife. As noted [above], and as conceded by New Mexico,[110] the sovereignty retained by the Tribe under the Treaty of 1852 includes its right to regulate the use of its resources by members as well as nonmembers. In *Montana v. United States*, we specifically recognized that tribes in general retain this authority.

Moreover, this aspect of tribal sovereignty has been expressly confirmed by numerous federal statutes.[111] Pub. L. 280 specifically confirms the power of tribes to regulate on-reservation hunting and fishing. 67 Stat. 588, 18 U.S.C. § 1162(b); see also 25 U.S.C. § 1321(b). This authority is afforded the protection of the federal criminal law by 18 U.S.C. § 1165, which makes it a violation of federal law to enter Indian land to hunt, trap, or fish without the consent of the tribe. See *Montana v. United States*, 450 U.S., at 562.[112] The 1981 Amendments to the Lacey Act, 16 U.S.C. § 3371 et seq. (1976 ed., Supp. V), further accord tribal hunting and fishing regulations the force of federal law by making it a federal offense "to import, export, transport, sell, receive, acquire, or purchase any fish or wildlife . . . taken or possessed in violation of any . . . Indian tribal law." § 3372(a)(1).

B

Several considerations strongly support the Court of Appeals's conclusion that the Tribe's authority to regulate hunting and fishing pre-empts state jurisdiction. It is important to emphasize that concurrent jurisdiction would effectively nullify the Tribe's authority to control hunting and fishing on the reservation. Concurrent jurisdiction would empower New Mexico wholly to supplant tribal regulations. The State would be able to dictate the terms on which nonmembers are permitted to

---

[110] [19] New Mexico concedes that the Tribe originally relied on wildlife for subsistence, that tribal members freely took fish and game in ancestral territory, and that the Treaty of July 1, 1852, 10 Stat. 979, between the Tribe and the United States confirmed the Tribe's rights regarding hunting and fishing on the small portion of the aboriginal Mescalero domain that was eventually set apart as the Tribe's reservation. See also *United States v. Winans*, 198 U.S. 371, 381 (1905) (recognizing that hunting and fishing "were not much less necessary to the existence of the Indians than the atmosphere they breathed").

[111] [20] The Tribe's authority was also confirmed more generally by the Indian Reorganization Act of 1934, 25 U.S.C. § 476, which reaffirms "all powers vested in any Indian tribe or tribal council by existing law."

[112] [21] The provision of Pub. L. 280 granting States criminal jurisdiction over Indian reservations under certain conditions provides that States are not thereby authorized to deprive any Indian or any Indian tribe, band, or community of any right, privilege, or immunity afforded under Federal treaty, agreement, or statute with respect to hunting, trapping, or fishing *or the control, licensing or regulation thereof.* 18 U.S.C. § 1162(b) (emphasis added). The same language is contained in 25 U.S.C. § 1321(b).

utilize the reservation's resources. The Tribe would thus exercise its authority over the reservation only at the sufferance of the State. The tribal authority to regulate hunting and fishing by nonmembers, which has been repeatedly confirmed by federal treaties and laws and which we explicitly recognized in [*Montana*], would have a rather hollow ring if tribal authority amounted to no more than this.

Furthermore, the exercise of concurrent state jurisdiction in this case would completely "disturb and disarrange," *Warren Trading Post Co. v. Arizona Tax Comm'n, supra,* at 691, the comprehensive scheme of federal and tribal management established pursuant to federal law. As described [in *Warren*], federal law requires the Secretary to review each of the Tribe's hunting and fishing ordinances. Those ordinances are based on the recommendations made by a federal range conservationist employed by the Bureau of Indian Affairs. Moreover, the Bureau of Sport Fisheries and Wildlife stocks the reservation's waters based on its own determinations concerning the availability of fish, biological requirements, and the fishing pressure created by on-reservation fishing.[113]

Concurrent state jurisdiction would supplant this regulatory scheme with an inconsistent dual system: members would be governed by tribal ordinances, while nonmembers would be regulated by general state hunting and fishing laws. This could severely hinder the ability of the Tribe to conduct a sound management program. Tribal ordinances reflect the specific needs of the reservation by establishing the optimal level of hunting and fishing that should occur, not simply a maximum level that should not be exceeded. State laws in contrast are based on considerations not necessarily relevant to, and possibly hostile to, the needs of the reservation. For instance, the ordinance permitting a hunter to kill a buck and a doe was designed to curb excessive growth of the deer population on the reservation. Enforcement of the state regulation permitting only buck to be killed would frustrate that objective. Similarly, by determining the tribal hunting seasons, bag limits, and permit availability, the Tribe regulates the duration and intensity of hunting. These determinations take into account numerous factors, including the game capacity of the terrain, the range utilization of the game animals, and the availability of tribal personnel to monitor the hunts. Permitting the State to enforce different restrictions simply because they have been determined to be appropriate for the State as a whole imposed on the Tribe the possibly insurmountable task of ensuring that the patchwork application of state and tribal regulations remains consistent with sound management of the reservation's resources.

Federal law commits to the Secretary and the Tribal Council the responsibility to manage the reservation's resources. It is most unlikely that Congress would have authorized, and the Secretary would have established, financed, and participated in tribal management if it were true that New Mexico was free to nullify the entire arrangement.[114] Requiring tribal ordinances to yield whenever state law is more

---

[113] [23] In addition, as noted earlier, the Federal Government played a substantial role in the development of the Tribe's resources.

[114] [24] The Secretary assumed precisely the opposite is true — that state jurisdiction is pre-empted — when he approved a tribal ordinance which provided that nonmembers hunting and fishing on the reservation need not obtain state licenses. That assumption is also embodied in an agreement between the Tribe and the Department of the Interior's Bureau of Sport Fisheries and Wildlife, [that] openly

restrictive would seriously "undermine the Secretary's [and the Tribe's] ability to make the wide range of determinations committed to [their] authority." *Bracker*, 448 U.S., at 149.

The assertion of concurrent jurisdiction by New Mexico not only would threaten to disrupt the federal and tribal regulatory scheme, but would also threaten Congress's overriding objective of encouraging tribal self-government and economic development. The Tribe has engaged in a concerted and sustained undertaking to develop and manage the reservation's wildlife and land resources specifically for the benefit of its members. The project generates funds for essential tribal services and provides employment for members who reside on the reservation. This case is thus far removed from those situations, such as on-reservation sales outlets which market to nonmembers goods not manufactured by the tribe or its members, in which the tribal contribution to an enterprise is de minimis. See [*Colville*].[115]

The tribal enterprise in this case clearly involves "value generated on the reservation by activities involving the Trib[e]." *Id.*, at 156–157. The disruptive effect that would result from the assertion of concurrent jurisdiction by New Mexico would plainly " 'stan[d] as an obstacle to the accomplishment of the full purposes and objectives of Congress,' " *Ramah Navajo School Bd.*, 458 U.S., at 845, quoting *Hines v. Davidowitz*, 312 U.S., at 67.

C

The State has failed to "identify the regulatory function or service . . . that would justify" the assertion of concurrent regulatory authority. *Bracker, supra*, at 148. The hunting and fishing permitted by the Tribe occur entirely on the reservation. The fish and wildlife resources are either native to the reservation or were created by the joint efforts of the Tribe and the federal government. New Mexico does not contribute in any significant respect to the maintenance of these resources, and can point to no other "governmental functions it provides," *Ramah Navajo School Bd., supra*, at 843, in connection with hunting and fishing on the reservation by nonmembers that would justify the assertion of its authority.

The State also cannot point to any off-reservation effects that warrant state intervention. Some species of game never leave tribal lands, and the State points to no specific interest concerning those that occasionally do. Unlike *Puyallup Tribe v. Washington Game Dept.*, this is not a case in which a treaty expressly subjects a tribe's hunting and fishing rights to the common rights of nonmembers and in which a State's interest in conserving a scarce, common supply justifies state intervention. 433 U.S., at 174, 175–177. The State concedes that the Tribe's management has "not had an adverse impact on fish and wildlife outside the Reservation." App. to Brief in Opposition 35a. . . .

---

acknowledges that tribal regulations need not agree with state laws. The agreement provides that "*[i]nsofar as possible* said regulations shall be in agreement with State regulations." App. 71a. (Emphasis added.)

[115] [26] In [*Colville*] the Court held that the sales of tribal smokeshops which sold cigarettes to nonmembers were subject to the state sales and cigarette taxes. The Court relied on the fact that the tribal smokeshops were not marketing "value generated on the reservation," but instead were seeking merely to market a "tax exemption to nonmembers who do not receive significant tribal services."

IV

In this case the governing body of an Indian Tribe, working closely with the federal government and under the authority of federal law, has exercised its lawful authority to develop and manage the reservation's resources for the benefit of its members. The exercise of concurrent jurisdiction by the State would effectively nullify the Tribe's unquestioned authority to regulate the use of its resources by members and nonmembers, interfere with the comprehensive tribal regulatory scheme, and threaten Congress's firm commitment to the encouragement of tribal self-sufficiency and economic development. Given the strong interests favoring exclusive tribal jurisdiction and the absence of state interests which justify the assertion of concurrent authority, we conclude that the application of the State's hunting and fishing laws to the reservation is pre-empted.

[*Affirmed*].

CALIFORNIA v. CABAZON BAND OF MISSION INDIANS
United States Supreme Court
480 U.S. 202 (1987)

JUSTICE WHITE delivered the opinion of the Court.

The Cabazon and Morongo Bands of Mission Indians, federally recognized Indian tribes, occupy reservations in Riverside County, California. Each Band, pursuant to an ordinance approved by the Secretary of the Interior, conducts bingo games on its reservation. The Cabazon Band has also opened a card club at which draw poker and other card games are played. The games are open to the public and are played predominantly by non-Indians coming onto the reservations. The games are a major source of employment for tribal members, and the profits are the Tribes' sole source of income. The State of California seeks to apply to the two Tribes Cal. Penal Code Ann. § 326.5 (West Supp. 1987). That statute does not entirely prohibit the playing of bingo but permits it when the games are operated and staffed by members of designated charitable organizations who may not be paid for their services. Profits must be kept in special accounts and used only for charitable purposes; prizes may not exceed $250 per game. Asserting that the bingo games on the two reservations violated each of these restrictions, California insisted that the Tribes comply with state law.[116] Riverside County also sought to apply its local Ordinance No. 558 regulating bingo, as well as its Ordinance No. 331, prohibiting the playing of draw poker and the other card games.

---

[116] [3] The Tribes admit that their games violate the provision governing staffing and the provision setting a limit on jackpots. They dispute the State's assertion that they do not maintain separate funds for the bingo operations. At oral argument, counsel for the State asserted, contrary to the position taken in the merits brief and contrary to the stipulated facts in this case, App. 65, p. 24, 82–83, p. 15, that the Tribes are among the charitable organizations authorized to sponsor bingo games under the statute. It is therefore unclear whether the State intends to put the tribal bingo enterprises out of business or only to impose on them the staffing, jackpot limit, and separate fund requirements. The tribal bingo enterprises are apparently consistent with other provisions of the statute: minors are not allowed to participate, the games are conducted in buildings owned by the Tribes on tribal property, the games are open to the public, and persons must be physically present to participate.

The Tribes sued the county in Federal District Court seeking a declaratory judgment that the county had no authority to apply its ordinances inside the reservations and an injunction against their enforcement. The State intervened, the facts were stipulated and the District Court granted the Tribes' motion for summary judgment, holding that neither the State nor the county had any authority to enforce its gambling laws within the reservations. The Court of Appeals for the Ninth Circuit affirmed [and this appeal followed].

I

The Court has consistently recognized that Indian tribes retain "attributes of sovereignty over both their members and their territory," *United States v. Mazurie*, 419 U.S. 544 (1975), and that "tribal sovereignty is dependent on, and subordinate to, only the Federal Government, not the States," *Washington v. Confederated Tribes of the Colville Indian Reservation*, 447 U.S. 134, 154 (1980). It is clear, however, that state laws may be applied to tribal Indians on their reservations if Congress has expressly so provided. Here, the State insists that Congress has twice given its express consent: first in Pub. L. 280 in 1953, 67 Stat. 588, as amended, 18 U.S.C. § 1162, 28 U.S.C. § 1360 (1982 ed. and Supp. III), and second in the Organized Crime Control Act in 1970, 84 Stat. 937, 18 U.S.C. § 1955. We disagree in both respects.

In Pub. L. 280, Congress expressly granted six States, including California, jurisdiction over specified areas of Indian country within the States and provided for the assumption of jurisdiction by other States. In § 2, California was granted broad criminal jurisdiction over offenses committed by or against Indians within all Indian country within the State. Section 4's grant of civil jurisdiction was more limited. In *Bryan v. Itasca County*, 426 U.S. 373 (1976), [presented in Ch. 5, Sec. D.1.b.] we interpreted § 4 to grant states jurisdiction over private civil litigation involving reservation Indians in state court, but not to grant general civil regulatory authority. We held, therefore, that Minnesota could not apply its personal property tax within the reservation. [Consequently,] when a State seeks to enforce a law within an Indian reservation under the authority of Pub. L. 280, it must be determined whether the law is criminal in nature, and thus fully applicable to the reservation under § 2, or civil in nature, and applicable only as it may be relevant to private civil litigation in state court. The Minnesota personal property tax at issue in *Bryan* was unquestionably civil in nature. The California bingo statute is not so easily categorized. California law permits bingo games to be conducted only by charitable and other specified organizations, and then only by their members who may not receive any wage or profit for doing so; prizes are limited and receipts are to be segregated and used only for charitable purposes. Violation of any of these provisions is a misdemeanor. California insists that these are criminal laws which Pub. L. 280 permits it to enforce on the reservations.

Following its earlier decision in *Barona Group of the Capitan Grande Band of Mission Indians, San Diego County, Cal. v. Duffy*, 694 F.2d 1185 (9th Cir. 1982), which also involved the applicability of § 326.5 of the California Penal Code to Indian reservations, the Court of Appeals rejected this submission. 783 F.2d [900], at 901–903. In *Barona*, applying what it thought to be the civil/criminal dichotomy drawn in *Bryan v. Itasca County*, the Court of Appeals drew a distinction between state "criminal/prohibitory laws" and state "civil/regulatory" laws: if the intent of a state law is generally to prohibit certain conduct, it falls within Pub. L. 280's grant of criminal jurisdiction, but if the state law generally permits the conduct at issue, subject to regulation, it must be classified as civil/regulatory and Pub. L. 280 does not authorize its enforcement on an Indian reservation. The shorthand test is whether the conduct at issue violates the State's public policy. Inquiring into the nature of § 326.5, the Court of Appeals held that it was regulatory rather than prohibitory. This was the analysis employed, with similar results, by the Court of Appeals for the Fifth Circuit in *Seminole Tribe of Florida v. Butterworth*, 658 F.2d 310 (1981), which the Ninth Circuit found persuasive.

We are persuaded that the prohibitory/regulatory distinction is consistent with *Bryan's* construction of Pub. L. 280. It is not a bright-line rule, however; and as the Ninth Circuit itself observed, an argument of some weight may be made that the bingo statute is prohibitory rather than regulatory. But in the present case, the court reexamined the state law and reaffirmed its holding in *Barona*, and we are reluctant to disagree with that court's view of the nature and intent of the state law at issue here.

There is surely a fair basis for its conclusion. California does not prohibit all forms of gambling. California itself operates a state lottery, and daily encourages its citizens to participate in this state-run gambling. California also permits parimutuel horse-race betting. Although certain enumerated gambling games are prohibited under Cal. Penal Code Ann. § 330 (West Supp. 1987), games not enumerated, including the card games played in the Cabazon card club, are permissible. The Tribes assert that more than 400 card rooms similar to the Cabazon card club flourish in California, and the State does not dispute this fact. Also, as the Court of Appeals noted, bingo is legally sponsored by many different organizations and is widely played in California. There is no effort to forbid the playing of bingo by any member of the public over the age of 18. Indeed, the permitted bingo games must be open to the general public. Nor is there any limit on the number of games which eligible organizations may operate, the receipts which they may obtain from the games, the number of games which a participant may play, or the amount of money which a participant may spend, either per game or in total. In light of the fact that California permits a substantial amount of gambling activity, including bingo, and actually promotes gambling through its state lottery, we must conclude that California regulates rather than prohibits gambling in general and bingo in particular.[117]

California argues, however, that high stakes, *unregulated* bingo, the conduct which attracts organized crime, is a misdemeanor in California and may be prohibited on Indian reservations. But that an otherwise regulatory law is enforceable by criminal as well as civil means does not necessarily convert it into a criminal law within the meaning of Pub. L. 280. Otherwise, the distinction between § 2 and § 4 of that law could easily be avoided and total assimilation permitted. This

---

[117] [10] Nothing in this opinion suggests that cockfighting, tattoo parlors, nude dancing, and prostitution are permissible on Indian reservations within California. [S]tate laws governing an activity must be examined in detail before they can be characterized as regulatory or prohibitory. . . .

view, adopted here and by the Fifth Circuit in the *Butterworth* case, we find persuasive. Accordingly, we conclude that Pub. L. 280 does not authorize California to enforce Cal. Penal Code Ann. § 326.5 (West Supp. 1987) within the Cabazon and Morongo Reservations.

California and Riverside County also argue that the Organized Crime Control Act (OCCA) authorizes the application of their gambling laws to the tribal bingo enterprises. The OCCA makes certain violations of state and local gambling laws violations of federal law. The Court of Appeals rejected appellants' argument, relying on its earlier decisions in *United States v. Farris*, 624 F.2d 890 (9th Cir. 1980), and *Barona Group of the Capitan Grande Band of Mission Indians, San Diego County, Cal. v. Duffy*, 694 F.2d 1185 (9th Cir. 1982). The court explained that whether a tribal activity is "a violation of the law of a state" within the meaning of OCCA depends on whether it violates the "public policy" of the State, the same test for application of state law under Pub. L. 280, and similarly concluded that bingo is not contrary to the public policy of California.[118]

The Court of Appeals for the Sixth Circuit has rejected this view. *United States v. Dakota*, 796 F.2d 186 (1986).[119] Since the OCCA standard is simply whether the gambling business is being operated in "violation of the law of a State," there is no basis for the regulatory/prohibitory distinction that it agreed is suitable in construing and applying Pub. L. 280. And because enforcement of OCCA is an exercise of federal rather than state authority, there is no danger of state encroachment on Indian tribal sovereignty. This latter observation exposes the flaw in appellants' reliance on OCCA. That enactment is indeed a federal law that, among other things, defines certain federal crimes over which the district courts have exclusive jurisdiction. There is nothing in OCCA indicating that the States are to have any part in enforcing federal crimes or are authorized to make arrests on Indian reservations that in the absence of OCCA they could not effect. We are not informed of any federal efforts to employ OCCA to prosecute the playing of bingo on Indian reservations, although there are more than 100 such enterprises currently in operation, many of which have been in existence for several years, for the most part with the encouragement of the federal government.[120] Whether or not, then, the Sixth Circuit is right and the Ninth Circuit wrong about the coverage

---

[118] [13] In *Farris*, in contrast, the court had concluded that a gambling business, featuring blackjack, poker, and dice, operated by tribal members on the Puyallup Reservation violated the public policy of Washington; the United States, therefore, could enforce OCCA against the Indians.

[119] [14] In *Dakota*, the United States sought a declaratory judgment that a gambling business, also featuring the playing of blackjack, poker, and dice, operated by two members of the Keweenaw Bay Indian Community on land controlled by the community, and under a license issued by the community, violated OCCA. The Court of Appeals held that the gambling business violated Michigan law and OCCA.

[120] [16] See S. Rep. No. 99-493, p. 2 (1986). Federal law enforcement officers have the capability to respond to violations of OCCA on Indian reservations, as is apparent from *Farris* and *Dakota*. This is not a situation where the unavailability of a federal officer at a particular moment would likely result in nonenforcement. OCCA is directed at large scale gambling enterprises. If state officers discover a gambling business unknown to federal authorities while performing their duties authorized by Pub. L. 280, there should be ample time for them to inform federal authorities, who would then determine whether investigation or other enforcement action was appropriate. A federal police officer is assigned by the Department of the Interior to patrol the Indian reservations in southern California. App. to Brief for Appellees 1d-7d.

of OCCA, a matter that we do not decide, there is no warrant for California to make arrests on reservations and thus, through OCCA, enforce its gambling laws against Indian tribes.

II

Because the state and county laws at issue here are imposed directly on the Tribes that operate the games, and are not expressly permitted by Congress, the Tribes argue that the judgment below should be affirmed without more. They rely on the statement in *McClanahan v. Arizona State Tax Comm'n*, 411 U.S. 164, 170–171 (1973), that " '(s)tate laws generally are not applicable to tribal Indians on an Indian reservation except where Congress has expressly provided that State laws shall apply' " (quoting U.S. Dept. of the Interior, Federal Indian Law 845 (1958)). Our cases, however, have not established an inflexible per se rule precluding state jurisdiction over tribes and tribal members in the absence of express congressional consent. "(U)nder certain circumstances a State may validly assert authority over the activities of nonmembers on a reservation, and . . . in exceptional circumstances a State may assert jurisdiction over the on-reservation activities of tribal members." *New Mexico v. Mescalero Apache Tribe*, 462 U.S. 324, 331–332 (1983) (footnotes omitted). Both *Moe v. Confederated Salish and Kootenai Tribes*, 425 U.S. 463 (1976), and *Washington v. Confederated Tribes of the Colville Indian Reservation*, 447 U.S. 134 (1980), are illustrative. In those decisions we held that, in the absence of express congressional permission, a State could require tribal smoke shops on Indian reservations to collect state sales tax from their non-Indian customers. Both cases involved nonmembers entering and purchasing tobacco products on the reservations involved. The State's interest in assuring the collection of sales taxes from non-Indians enjoying the off-reservation services of the State was sufficient to warrant the minimal burden imposed on the tribal smoke shop operators.

This case also involves a state burden on tribal Indians in the context of their dealings with non-Indians since the question is whether the State may prevent the Tribes from making available high stakes bingo games to non-Indians coming from outside the reservations. Decision in this case turns on whether state authority is pre-empted by the operation of federal law; and "[s]tate jurisdiction is pre-empted . . . if it interferes or is incompatible with federal and tribal interests reflected in federal law, unless the state interests at stake are sufficient to justify the assertion of state authority." *Mescalero*, 462 U.S., at 333, 334. The inquiry is to proceed in light of traditional notions of Indian sovereignty and the congressional goal of Indian self-government, including its "overriding goal" of encouraging tribal self-sufficiency and economic development.

These are important federal interests. They were reaffirmed by the President's 1983 Statement on Indian Policy. More specifically, the Department of the Interior, which has the primary responsibility for carrying out the federal government's trust obligations to Indian tribes, has sought to implement these policies by promoting tribal bingo enterprises. Under the Indian Financing Act of 1974, 25 U.S.C. § 1451 et seq. (1982 ed. and Supp. III), the Secretary of the Interior has made grants and has guaranteed loans for the purpose of constructing bingo facilities. See S. Rep.

No. 99-493, p. 5 (1986); *Mashantucket Pequot Tribe v. McGuigan*, 626 F. Supp. 245, 246 (Conn. 1986). The Department of Housing and Urban Development and the Department of Health and Human Services have also provided financial assistance to develop tribal gaming enterprises. See S. Rep. No. 99-493, *supra*, at 5. Here, the Secretary of the Interior has approved tribal ordinances establishing and regulating the gaming activities involved. See H.R. Rep. No. 99-488, p. 10 (1986). The Secretary has also exercised his authority to review tribal bingo management contracts under 25 U.S.C. § 81, and has issued detailed guidelines governing that review. App. to Motion to Dismiss Appeal or Affirm Judgment, 63a-70a.

These policies and actions, which demonstrate the Government's approval and active promotion of tribal bingo enterprises, are of particular relevance in this case. The Cabazon and Morongo Reservations contain no natural resources which can be exploited. The tribal games at present provide the sole source of revenues for the operation of the tribal governments and the provision of tribal services. They are also the major sources of employment on the reservations. Self-determination and economic development are not within reach if the Tribes cannot raise revenues and provide employment for their members. The Tribes' interests obviously parallel the federal interests. California seeks to diminish the weight of these seemingly important tribal interests by asserting that the Tribes are merely marketing an exemption from state gambling laws. In *Washington v. Confederated Tribes of the Colville Indian Reservation*, 447 U.S., at 155, we held that the State could tax cigarettes sold by tribal smoke shops to non-Indians, even though it would eliminate their competitive advantage and substantially reduce revenues used to provide tribal services, because the Tribes had no right "to market an exemption from state taxation to persons who would normally do their business elsewhere." We stated that "(i)t is painfully apparent that the value marketed by the smoke shops to persons coming from outside is not generated on the reservations by activities in which the Tribes have a significant interest." *Ibid.* Here, however, the Tribes are not merely importing a product onto the reservations for immediate resale to non-Indians. They have built modern facilities which provide recreational opportunities and ancillary services to their patrons, who do not simply drive onto the reservations, make purchases and depart, but spend extended periods of time there enjoying the services the Tribes provide. The Tribes have strong incentive to provide comfortable, clean and attractive facilities and well-run games in order to increase attendance at the games.[121] The tribal bingo enterprises are similar to the resort complex, featuring hunting and fishing, that the Mescalero Apache Tribe operates on its reservation through the "concerted and sustained" management of reservation land and wildlife resources. *New Mexico v. Mescalero Apache Tribe*, 462

---

[121] [23] An agent of the California Bureau of Investigation visited the Cabazon bingo parlor as part of an investigation of tribal bingo enterprises. The agent described the clientele as follows:

> In attendance for the Monday evening bingo session were about 300 players. . . . On row 5, on the front left side were a middle-aged latin couple, who were later joined by two young latin males. These men had to have the game explained to them. The middle table was shared with a senior citizen couple. The aisle table had 2 elderly women, 1 in a wheelchair, and a middle-aged woman. . . . A goodly portion of the crowd were retired age to senior citizens. App. 176.

We are unwilling to assume that these patrons would be indifferent to the services offered by the Tribes.

U.S., at 341. The Mescalero project generates funds for essential tribal services and provides employment for tribal members. We there rejected the notion that the tribe is merely marketing an exemption from state hunting and fishing regulations and concluded that New Mexico could not regulate on-reservation fishing and hunting by non-Indians. *Ibid.* Similarly, the Cabazon and Morongo Bands are generating value on the reservations through activities in which they have a substantial interest. . . .

The sole interest asserted by the State to justify the imposition of its bingo laws on the Tribes is in preventing the infiltration of the tribal games by organized crime. To the extent that the State seeks to prevent any and all bingo games from being played on tribal lands while permitting regulated, off-reservation games, this asserted interest is irrelevant and the state and county laws are pre-empted. See n.3, *supra.* Even to the extent that the State and county seek to regulate short of prohibition, the laws are pre-empted. The State insists that the high stakes offered at tribal games are attractive to organized crime, whereas the controlled games authorized under California law are not. This is surely a legitimate concern, but we are unconvinced that it is sufficient to escape the pre-emptive force of federal and tribal interests apparent in this case. California does not allege any present criminal involvement in the Cabazon and Morongo enterprises [and] the prevailing federal policy continues to support these tribal enterprises, including those of the Tribes involved in this case.

We conclude that the State's interest in preventing the infiltration of the tribal bingo enterprises by organized crime does not justify state regulation of the tribal bingo enterprises in light of the compelling federal and tribal interests supporting them. State regulation would impermissibly infringe on tribal government, and this conclusion applies equally to the county's attempted regulation of the Cabazon card club. We therefore affirm the judgment of the Court of Appeals and remand the case for further proceedings consistent with this opinion.

It is so ordered.

JUSTICE STEVENS, with whom JUSTICE O'CONNOR and JUSTICE SCALIA join, dissenting.

Unless and until Congress exempts Indian-managed gambling from state law and subjects it to federal supervision, I believe that a State may enforce its laws prohibiting high-stakes gambling on Indian reservations within its borders. Congress has not pre-empted California's prohibition against high-stakes bingo games and the Secretary of the Interior plainly has no authority to do so. While gambling provides needed employment and income for Indian tribes, these benefits do not, in my opinion, justify tribal operation of currently unlawful commercial activities. Accepting the majority's reasoning would require exemptions for cock fighting, tattoo parlors, nude dancing, houses of prostitution, and other illegal but profitable enterprises. As the law now stands, I believe tribal entrepreneurs, like others who might derive profits from catering to non-Indian customers, must obey applicable state laws.

In my opinion the plain language of Pub. L. 280 authorizes California to enforce its prohibition against commercial gambling on Indian reservations.

NOTES ON STATE JURISDICTION TO REGULATE

1. **Federal Authorization of State Regulation:** In *Cabazon*, the Court first inquired whether any federal statutes authorized the state regulation. Federal authorization of this type would have represented an exercise of federal "plenary power" to remove obstacles to state jurisdiction grounded in tribal sovereignty and federal law. Congress had granted California criminal and civil jurisdiction under Public Law 280. But in *Bryan v. Itasca County*, 426 U.S. 373 (1976), presented and discussed in Ch. 5, Sec. A, the Court had interpreted Public Law 280 to exclude federal authorization for state regulatory power. After a careful analysis, the *Cabazon* court concluded that California allowed so many different types of gambling that it would be improper to characterize high-stakes bingo as "prohibited" and against the state's public policy. Even the fact that the bingo regulations were enforced by misdemeanor sanctions did not lead the Court onto the "prohibitory" side of the line.

Having rejected Public Law 280 as a source of state jurisdiction, the *Cabazon* court turned to the Organized Crime Control Act of 1970, 18 U.S.C. § 1955. While this federal statute makes certain violations of state gambling laws violations of federal law, the Court had no difficulty dismissing it as a source of state jurisdiction over the Cabazons' gaming. By its terms, the Act restricts enforcement power to federal prosecutors and federal courts.

In contrast, in *New Mexico v. Mescalero Apache Tribe*, there were no arguable federal laws authorizing New Mexico to regulate hunting and fishing within Indian country. New Mexico had not opted into Public Law 280, and there were no federal laws addressing state jurisdiction over hunting and fishing in Indian country. Should New Mexico's failure to opt into Public Law 280 have worked to invalidate the state law in that case on preemption grounds? If that were an effective means of establishing preemption in matters involving non-Indians, would the state tax in *Colville* have survived?

Another case refusing to find federal authorization for state regulation, this one involving Indian-owned fee land, is *Gobin v. Snohomish County*, 304 F.3d 909 (9th Cir. 2002). There the Ninth Circuit rejected Washington's attempt to zone fee land owned by Tulalip tribal members within their reservation. The Tribe had enacted its own zoning law, under which tribal members had received approval to build a residential development. Yet the county threatened civil and criminal action if the landowners did not also receive a county permit. The County tried to analogize its zoning authority to state taxing power over allotments that are no longer in trust.

Recall that in *Cass County v. Leech Lake Band of Chippewa Indians*, 524 U.S. 103 (1998), and *County of Yakima v. Confederated Tribes & Bands of the Yakima Indian Nation*, 502 U.S. 251 (1992), discussed above, the Court had interpreted the federal allotment acts as authorizing state taxation once the trust was lifted. Distinguishing these earlier cases involving taxation of allotted land in fee status and applying rigorously the Indian law canons of construction, the Ninth Circuit found in *Gobin* that Congress did not authorize state land use regulation when it made Indian fee lands freely alienable and encumberable. It also found no "exceptional circumstances" that would justify state jurisdiction over tribal members, rejecting County concerns about protecting endangered species, regulating county-maintained sewers and road, and assuring the health and safety of county citizens. Launching its analysis, the court declared that "The policy of leaving Indians free from State jurisdiction is deeply rooted in our Nation's history." Is there any other federal law that might have preempted the state's assertion of jurisdiction, even if "exceptional circumstances" had been found?

2.   **Application of Preemption Doctrines:** While *Mescalero* clearly involved an issue of regulation of non-Indian conduct, suggesting application of the *Colville/ Bracker* interest-balancing analysis, *Cabazon* involved the state's effort to regulate a tribally-owned and operated bingo hall. Under the line of taxation cases, if the State of California had attempted to tax the tribal bingo operation, wouldn't the tax have been barred under the "categorical approach" articulated in *Oklahoma Tax Commission v. Chickasaw Nation*, 515 U.S. 450 (1995), discussed above? In other words, should the Court have even bothered to examine state or federal interests in *Cabazon* once it acknowledged that an Indian interest existed by virtue of the Tribe owning and operating the bingo hall? Should the fact that nearly all of the bingo players were off-reservation non-Indians alter the required analysis? Is the Court eschewing formalism in favor of an approach that emphasizes factual context and practical consequences? Does it do that consistently in the tax cases? *Cf. Wagnon v. Prairie Band Potawatomi Nation*, discussed in Sec. B.5, this chapter. Keep in mind that *Cabazon* preceded (in fact prompted) enactment of the Indian Gaming Regulatory Act of 1988, 25 U.S.C. §§ 2701–2721, which allowed for limited state authority over tribal gaming. *See* Ch. 5, Sec. D.

3.   **Perverse Consequences of Applying the Court's Preemption Doctrine:** In *Mescalero*, as well as in *Cabazon*, the Court requires some evidence of active federal involvement in tribal projects before state regulatory authority is displaced and tribal jurisdiction may become exclusive. That federal involvement may take the form of funding, supporting, or regulating the tribe's undertaking. At a time when policy of the federal executive and legislative branches has turned to tribal-self-determination (*see* Ch. 1, Sec. B.2.i-j), including tribal contracts to provide federal services and overall budget compacting with tribes, why should the prerequisite for tribal autonomy be federal micromanagement? Consider that Professors Joseph Kalt and Stephen Cornell, experts in tribal economic development, have concluded that Indian nations experience far greater economic success when they make economic decisions for themselves. *See* Stephen Cornell & Joseph P. Kalt, *Reloading the Dice: Improving the Chances for Economic Development on American Indian Reservations, in* WHAT CAN TRIBES DO? STRATEGIES AND INSTITUTIONS IN AMERICAN INDIAN ECONOMIC DEVELOPMENT (S. Cornell & J. Kalt eds., 1992).

4.   **State Regulation of Nonmembers on Nonmember Fee Land Within Reservation Boundaries:** Most cases posing questions of state jurisdiction over nonmembers within Indian country, such as *Mescalero* and *Cabazon*, presuppose the existence of at least concurrent, if not exclusive, tribal authority. In analyzing whether state jurisdiction exists, courts thus have considered whether state jurisdiction would interfere with the tribe's assertion of its own powers. But what if there were no tribal jurisdiction with which the state's power could conflict? Wouldn't the argument for state jurisdiction be stronger, at least absent federal preemption in the non-Indian law sense? Where nonmembers are engaged in activity on reservation fee land owned by nonmembers, the Supreme Court has

been developing a doctrine that denies tribal jurisdiction under some circumstances, often resulting in the substitution of state jurisdiction for tribal authority. This line of authority stems from the Court's 1981 decision in *Montana v. United States*, 450 U.S. 544 (1981), presented and discussed in Ch. 3, Sec. C.1, which created a presumption against tribal jurisdiction over nonmembers on nonmember-owned fee land. This presumption can be overcome only if the non-Indian object of regulation has entered into a consensual relationship with the tribe or a tribal member, or is engaged in activity seriously endangering the health, safety, economic security, or political integrity of the tribe. The Court has also chosen to apply the *Montana* presumption and exceptions to at least one case arising on trust land. *See Nevada v. Hicks*, 533 U.S. 353, 357–60 (2001).

As the discussion in Chapter 3 notes, this line of authority has been severely criticized by tribes and by scholars because it dismisses all but the most urgent Indian interests in such regulatory matters, and ignores the preemptive effect of the Indian commerce clause and federal statutes and treaties establishing or recognizing lands as tribal homelands. So long as the *Montana* doctrine is not repudiated by the Court or overturned by Congress, however, that doctrine holds potential for expanding state jurisdiction.

5. State Jurisdiction over Indians and Indian Property Outside Indian Country

Mescalero Apache Tribe v. Jones, 411 U.S. 145 (1973): The Mescalero Apache Tribe operated a ski resort adjacent to their reservation on lands leased from the National Forest Service. With the exception of some of the cross-country ski trails, no part of the ski resort facility was located within the exterior boundary of the Mescalero Apache Reservation. The land was leased, instead of sold, to the Tribe because "it would have been meaningless for the United States, which already had title to the forest, to convey title to itself for the use of the Tribe." The State of New Mexico asserted a right to impose both a gross receipts tax on the proceeds of the resort and a use sales tax on certain items purchased out of state for the ski lift, claiming that the operations were off-reservation.

The Court, in an opinion by Justice White, upheld the gross receipts tax but struck down the application of the use tax. Justice White's opinion began by noting that no automatic tax immunity applied merely because an Indian tribe was involved:

> At the outset, we reject — as did the state court — the broad assertion that the Federal Government has exclusive jurisdiction over the Tribe for all purposes and that the State is therefore prohibited from enforcing its revenue laws against any tribal enterprise "[w]hether the enterprise is located on or off tribal land." Generalizations on this subject have become particularly treacherous. The conceptual clarity of Mr. Chief Justice Marshall's view in [*Worcester v. Georgia*] has given way to more individualized treatment of particular treaties and specific federal statutes, including statehood enabling legislation, as they, taken together, affect the respective rights of States, Indians, and the Federal Government. [I]n the special area of state taxation, absent cession of jurisdiction or other federal

statutes permitting it, there has been no satisfactory authority for taxing Indian reservation lands or Indian income from activities carried on within the boundaries of the reservation, and [*McClanahan*] lays to rest any doubt in this respect by holding that such taxation is not permissible absent congressional consent.

But tribal activities conducted outside the reservation present different considerations. "State authority over Indians is yet more extensive over activities . . . not on any reservation." *Organized Village of Kake*, [369 U.S. 60] at 75. Absent express federal law to the contrary, Indians going beyond reservation boundaries have generally been held subject to nondiscriminatory state law otherwise applicable to all citizens of the State. [*E.g.*], *Puyallup Tribe v. Department of Game*, 391 U.S. 392, 398 (1968); *Tulee v. Washington*, 315 U.S. 681, 683 (1942); *Ward v. Race Horse*, 163 U.S. 504 (1896). That principle is as relevant to a State's tax laws as it is to state criminal laws, and applies as much to tribal ski resorts as it does to fishing enterprises.

The three dissenters, led by Justice Douglas, found Justice White's first paragraph above to be inconsistent with the exclusive grant to the federal government of authority for regulating commerce with Indian tribes under Article I, section 8, clause 3 of the United States Constitution, and, therefore, with the *Worcester* decision. Justice White's opinion, nevertheless, paid no heed to the Indian commerce clause and, instead, assumed that states had power to regulate and tax Indian activities in a nondiscriminatory manner outside the reservation except where preempted by federal treaty or statute. The Court found neither the disclaimer of jurisdiction in the New Mexico Constitution, which focuses on Indian lands, nor the Indian Reorganization Act of 1934 preemptive of state power to impose its gross business receipts tax on the off-reservation tribal ski resort. The Court also rejected the claim that the tax immunity set forth as part of the Indian Reorganization Act in 25 U.S.C.§ 465 preempted the state gross receipts tax. Focusing on the off-reservation site of the ski resort, the Court noted "absent clear statutory guidance, courts ordinarily will not imply tax exemptions and will not exempt off-reservation income from tax simply because the land from which it is derived, or its other source, is itself exempt from tax." From the plain language of section 465, the Court concluded that the "statute exempts land and rights in land, not income derived from its use." Reviewing the history of the Indian Reorganization Act, the Court concluded that the Act was "designed to encourage tribal enterprises 'to enter the white world on a footing of equal competition.' 78 Cong. Rec. 11732. In this context, we will not imply an expansive immunity from ordinary income taxes that businesses throughout the State are subject to."

The out-of-state goods purchased for use in the ski resort, however, posed a far different problem. According to a stipulation of the parties those items of personal property had been incorporated into the ski lift and had been permanently attached to the realty. Those items therefore fell within the express tax immunity for lands set forth in 25 U.S.C. § 465 because "use of permanent improvements upon land is so intimately connected with use of the land itself that an explicit provision relieving the latter of state tax burdens must be construed to encompass an exemption for the former. . . . " The State of New Mexico therefore could not apply its use tax to such items despite the fact they were located off-reservation as a result of the express federal statutory tax immunity.

NOTES

1. Off- vs. On-Reservation Activity: As a statement of general principle, *Mescalero Apache* is correct in suggesting that, historically, Indians have usually been subject to state authority for various conduct, including crimes, occurring off the reservation. Ever since the Trade and Intercourse Acts many (but not all) preemptive federal statutes have applied only to Indian country or other federally designated territory, leaving to state authorities the management of affairs elsewhere. For example, the Indian Gaming Regulatory Act of 1988 (IGRA), discussed in Ch. 5, Sec. D, restricts tribal gaming to federally defined "Indian lands," and authorizes states to sue tribes only for breach of tribal-state compacts directed at tribal gaming on such lands. When Michigan sued to enjoin the Bay Mills Indian Community for conducting gaming activities outside "Indian lands," the Supreme Court found that tribal sovereign immunity barred the action because the suit was not governed by IGRA. At the same time, the Court pointed out that Michigan still had means to regulate or close down the gaming *because* it was off-reservation and outside any federally-defined Indian territory. For example, Michigan could deny a gaming license to the casino and then bring civil or criminal actions against individuals working or gambling at the facility, regardless whether they are tribal members. *See Michigan v. Bay Mills Indian Community*, 134 S. Ct. 2024 (2014), presented and discussed in Ch. 3, Sec. F.1.

A few federal Indian law statutes do address activities outside Indian country. *See, e.g.,* Passamaquoddy *Tribe v. Morton*, 528 F.2d 370 (1st Cir. 1975) (federal statutory restraints on alienation of Indian land apply to all tribal land within the United States irrespective of lack of federal recognition of the tribe); Indian Child Welfare Act, 25 U.S.C. § 1901 et seq. (creating procedural rules and placement preferences for off-reservation Indian children).

The difference in federal Indian law within and outside Indian country makes it imperative to characterize accurately the location of activities and property. *See* Ch. 2, Sec. A (addressing the definition of "Indian country"). Was the Court correct in treating the Sierra Blanca Ski Enterprises in *Mescalero Apache* as an off-reservation enterprise, when it was located on land adjacent to the tribal reservation leased to it by the United States Forest Service in order (according to footnote 11) to avoid the meaningless gesture of having "the United States, which already had title to the forest, . . . convey title to itself for the use of the Tribe?" Had the land in fact been conveyed rather than leased would it not have become part of the tribal estate and thereby part of the reservation? The answer to that question is more complex than first appears. While not noted in the *Mescalero Apache* opinion, section 7 of the Indian Reorganization Act, 25 U.S.C. § 467, authorizes

> [t]he Secretary of the Interior . . . to proclaim new Indian reservations on lands acquired pursuant to any authority conferred [by the Indian Reorganization Act], or to add such lands to existing reservations. *Provided,* That lands added to existing reservations shall be designated for the

exclusive use of Indians entitled by enrollment or by tribal membership to residence at such reservations.

Apparently, no such proclamation had been issued over the leased lands involved in *Mescalero Apache*, in part because the Secretary has been extremely reluctant to invoke the authority conferred by section 7 and has issued such proclamations only rarely. In light of the proviso in section 7 could a proclamation have been issued adding the leased lands to the Mescalero Apache's Reservation? Does the lack of a proclamation under section 7 of the IRA help explain why the Court treated the Sierra Blanca Ski Enterprises as an off-reservation business? As discussed in Ch. 2, Sec. A.3.b.i, failure to issue a section 7 proclamation has not prevented the Supreme Court from treating land acquired under section 5 of the Indian Reorganization Act, 25 U.S.C. § 465, as part of the tribal reservation and therefore as Indian country. Sometimes the Court has even referred to trust land for which there is no proclamation as an "informal reservation." *Oklahoma Tax Commission v. Sac and Fox Nation*, 508 U.S. 114, 128 (1993). By this criterion, why didn't the Mescalero ski resort qualify?

2. *Kake v. Egan* and Federal Authority to Preempt State Jurisdiction over Off-Reservation Matters: In *Organized Village of Kake v. Egan*, 369 U.S. 60 (1962), the Supreme Court held that the State of Alaska's authority to apply its anti-fish-trap conservation laws to members of two Native villages was not preempted by federal law or policy even though the federal government had authorized use of the traps. The Secretary of the Interior had relied on the White Act, a conservation statute, and the general provisions of the Snyder Act as providing authority for the regulation permitting the traps. The Court held that the statutory authority was not sufficiently specific to preempt the contrary state law. Unfortunately, Justice Frankfurter's opinion contained some very broad language regarding the reach of state law both on and off Indian reservations. First, the language in the opinion intimated that the presumption is in favor of state jurisdiction absent specific preemptive statutes even for activity occurring on Indian reservations. But *Kake* was a case involving state jurisdiction where there was no reservation at all. The existence of a reservation is critical in determining the scope of state jurisdiction. *Metlakatla Indian Community v. Egan*, 369 U.S. 45 (1962), decided the same day as *Kake*, held that the federal government, rather than the State of Alaska, had jurisdiction over the use of traps in the Metlakatla Indian Community, a federally recognized reservation created by statute. The extent to which *Kake* has added to judicial confusion is a tribute to the power of a scholarly opinion, even where that scholarship is faulty.

Second, the *Kake* Court asserted that states have full authority to regulate all Indian activity off of reservations, even activity exercising aboriginal rights:

> [S]tate regulation of off-reservation fishing certainly does not impinge on treaty-protected reservation self-government, the factor found decisive in *Williams v. Lee*. Nor have appellants any fishing rights derived from federal laws. This Court has never held that States lack power to regulate the exercise of aboriginal Indian rights, such as claimed here, or of those based on occupancy. Because of the migratory habits of salmon, fish traps at Kake and Angoon are not merely local matters.

Is such a broad statement consistent with the history and purposes of the Indian commerce clause? If the relationship between tribes and states is solely a matter of federal law, should not federal law control the extent to which states may affect aboriginal rights? Were many of the tribes affected by the Indian commerce clause federally recognized by treaty at the time that the Constitution was drafted in 1787? Is *Kake* limited to the peculiar problems of the aboriginal rights of Alaskan Natives prior to enactment of the Alaska Native Claims Settlement Act of 1971 (discussed in Ch. 5, Sec. B.1)? If so, why were those claims treated differently? Does *Kake* have any application to tribes in the east coast that are not federally recognized but trace their title to land from aboriginal sources or from colonial grants and treaties?

Although it is true that Indians are generally subject to state authority for transactions occurring off reservations, federal authority under the Indian commerce clause does reach off reservation so that the actual exercises of that power in statute or treaty may nevertheless have preemptive effects on state authority. The narrow holding in *Kake* is merely that the statutory authority was not sufficiently precise to preempt state authority. Consider, for example, the treatment of the taxability of the materials used in the ski lift in *Mescalero Apache*. Does the statutory preemption doctrine operate with the same strength and in the same manner for off-reservation activities as for on-reservation matters? What differences, if any, exist in these two contexts?

For other examples of off-reservation preemption of state authority, consider the materials on child welfare proceedings involving off-reservation tribal children in Ch. 5, Sec. C, and off-reservation hunting and fishing rights in Ch. 7, Sec. A.2.

3. Identifying Whether the Incidence of a State Tax Is On or Off the Reservation: In *Wagnon v. Prairie Band Potawatomi Nation*, 546 U.S. 95 (2005), the Supreme Court determined that a state tax on wholesale distributors of motor fuel to tribally-owned, reservation-based retailers was imposed on distributors outside the reservation, and hence was not subject to the balancing of governmental interests prescribed for on-reservation state taxes through *White Mountain Apache v. Bracker*, discussed above. In doing so, it rejected an argument by the Nation that the tax arose out of the distributor's on-reservation transaction with the Tribe and was therefore subject to the *Bracker* balancing test. The Nation had argued that various exemptions granted under state law, including for fuel that distributors sold to other states or to the United States or held as inventory, demonstrated that the tax was on the resale or use of the fuel, not on its receipt by the distributor. Furthermore, the Nation had contended that exemptions for other sovereigns but not for Indian nations indicated an unlawful discrimination against Indian commerce. The Court rejected this contention as well, concluding that Kansas provides roads services to the Nation that it does not provide to those other sovereigns. Did the Court apply an overly formalistic analysis, ignoring the practical impact on the Nation? Compare the Court's approach in *California State Bd. of Equalization v. Chemehuevi Tribe*, 474 U.S. 9 (1985), discussed in Note 4 following *Colville*, where despite the fact that a state cigarette tax appeared on its face to be on the tribal retailer rather than on non-Indian consumers, the Court determined that the burden was actually borne by the consumer. Can a good argument be made that the *Bracker* balancing test should apply even if the transaction is deemed wholly off-reservation, at least where a tribe is attempting to impose its own tax on the retail sale? Would expanding such an amorphous legal standard outside Indian country be desirable as a matter of policy? Writing for herself and Justice Kennedy, Justice Ginsburg dissented, agreeing with the Nation that the taxable event was the sale of the fuel to the tribal retailer. Applying the *Bracker* test, she would have struck that balance in favor of the Nation because the Nation was not marketing a tax exemption, but was instead collecting a tax to meet important transportation needs not addressed by the State. One benefit she saw of applying the *Bracker* test was that it encouraged states and tribes to resolve tax disputes through the use of state-tribal tax agreements. The impact of *Wagnon* is likely to be limited to motor fuel and tobacco taxes because these are generally the only taxes where the point of collection is shifted up the distribution chain. And some states already have agreements with tribes regarding such taxes. For further discussion of such tribal-state tax agreements, see Note 7 following the *Cotton Petroleum* opinion, above and Ch. 3, Sec. E.2.

Test your understanding by considering the following facts: A member of the Seneca Nation of Indians in New York operates an Internet cigarette sales business from the Seneca Reservation. Residents of Idaho have purchased millions of cigarettes through the business's website, which ships the cigarettes to the buyers' Idaho homes. Idaho insists that the tribal seller comply with a state law that implements the sweeping national settlement between states and major cigarette manufacturers over the health costs of smoking. This state law would impose sizeable tax burdens on the tribal seller. Should the state's power be analyzed under the law applicable to on-reservation or off-reservation transactions? What difference would that make? *See State v. Maybee*, 224 P.3d 1109 (Idaho 2010).

4. Transactions Occurring Both On- and Off-Reservation: What if a state wants to tax or regulate a nonmember's conduct that takes place partly within and partly outside Indian country? Activities are likely to have connections both within and outside Indian country where reservations are very small or in Oklahoma, where reservations were abolished and Indian country consists of many dispersed trust allotments and small parcels of tribal trust land. Does *Colville, supra*, hold that where a state purports to tax Indians for conduct occurring both on- and off-reservation that it must always prorate the tax to the extent of the off-reservation conduct? Is that approach equally applicable to the problem of regulation? How, if at all, would such an approach be applied to the issues of jurisdiction over a series of transactions (*e.g.*, the negotiation of the sale of securities), some of which occurred off-reservation?

Recent cases from the Ninth and Tenth Circuits indicate that states must recognize and respect sovereign tribal activities that take place partially within and partially outside Indian country, if strong tribal interests are at stake and the state interests in refusing to do so are so weak as to suggest discrimination against tribal governments. The Tenth Circuit emphasized a preemption analysis that balanced tribal, federal, and state interests. The Ninth Circuit focused more heavily on the question of discrimination against tribal entities.

The Ninth Circuit case involves the Cabazon Band of Mission Indians in California, which encountered resistance from the Riverside County Sheriff's Department when the Band's police officers drove vehicles with light bars while conducting patrols and responding to calls on the Band's two noncontiguous reservation parcels. The Sheriff's Department insisted that the tribal police could not use the light bars on state roads and highways connecting the two parcels because state law did not allow them. Indeed, state law permitted a wide range of other emergency vehicles, including police cars from other states, to have the light bars. Concerned that the absence of light bars on tribal vehicles would impair public safety, Cabazon sued in federal court to enjoin enforcement of the state prohibition. The County argued that it had authority to regulate the tribal vehicles because the driving occurred on state roads outside of Indian country. In *Cabazon Band of Mission Indians v. Smith*, 388 F.3d 691 (9th Cir. 2004), the Ninth Circuit held that application of the state law was discriminatory against tribal emergency vehicles, and thus preempted by federal law. The only justification the County could offer for denying the tribal emergency vehicles access to state roads was that their presence might slow down traffic; and the court couldn't see how that explanation could provide a legitimate basis for singling out tribal governments for adverse treatment.

The Tenth Circuit case, *Prairie Band Potawatomi Nation v. Wagnon*, 402 F.3d 1015 (10th Cir. 2005), *vacated and remanded on other grounds sub nom. Wagnon v. Prairie Band Potawatomi Nation*, 546 U.S. 95 (2005), determined that the State of Kansas could not enforce its motor vehicle registration laws against owners of vehicles housed in Indian country and registered under tribal law, even when those vehicles were driven outside Indian country. Applying the balancing test of *White Mountain Apache Tribe v. Bracker* (presented in Sec. B.4.b., this chapter), the court found that the tribal and federal interests in tribal economic development and sovereignty outweighed the state's negligible marginal interest in public safety. Reinforcing the court's conclusion was the fact that the State of Kansas routinely recognized the registration and titling laws of other states and neighboring foreign countries.

The following United States Supreme Court case poses this problem of activity with links both on and off the reservation, by bringing us full circle to the type of treaty provision that opened this section.

OKLAHOMA TAX COMMISSION v. CHICKASAW NATION
United States Supreme Court
515 U.S. 450 (1995)

Justice Ginsburg delivered the opinion of the Court.

This case concerns the taxing authority of the State of Oklahoma over the Chickasaw Nation and its members. We take up two questions: (1) May Oklahoma impose its motor fuels excise tax upon fuel sold by Chickasaw Nation retail stores on tribal trust land; (2) May Oklahoma impose its income tax upon members of the Chickasaw Nation who are employed by the Tribe but who reside in the State outside Indian country.

. . . .

The Chickasaw Nation, a federally recognized Indian Tribe, commenced this civil action in the United States District Court for the Eastern District of Oklahoma, to stop the State of Oklahoma from enforcing several state taxes against the Tribe and its members. Pertinent here, the District Court, ruling on cross-motions for summary judgment, held for the State on the motor fuels tax imposition and largely for the Tribe on the income tax issue. The Court of Appeals for the Tenth Circuit ruled for the Tribe and its members on both issues: It held that the State may not apply the motor fuels tax to fuel sold by the Tribe's retail stores, and, further, that the State may not tax the wages of members of the Chickasaw Nation who work for the Tribe, even if they reside outside Indian country. 31 F.3d 964 (1994).

. . . .

The initial and frequently dispositive question in Indian tax cases, therefore, is who bears the legal incidence of a tax. If the legal incidence of an excise tax rests on a tribe or on tribal members for sales made inside Indian country, the tax cannot be enforced absent clear congressional authorization. See, e.g., *Moe*, 425 U.S. at 475–481 (Montana's cigarette sales tax imposed on retail consumers could not be applied to on-reservation "smoke shop" sales to tribal members). But if the legal incidence of the tax rests on non-Indians, no categorical bar prevents enforcement of the tax; if the balance of federal, state, and tribal interests favors the State, and federal law is not to the contrary, the State may impose its levy, see *Washington v. Confederated Tribes of Colville Reservation*, 447 U.S. 134, 154–157 (1980), and may place on a tribe or tribal members "minimal burdens" in collecting the toll, *Department of Taxation and Finance of N.Y. v. Milhelm Attea & Bros.*, 512 U.S. 61, 73 (1994). Thus, the inquiry proper here is whether the legal incidence of Oklahoma's fuels tax rests on the Tribe (as retailer), or on some other transactors — here, the wholesalers who sell to the Tribe or the consumers who buy from the Tribe.

Judicial focus on legal incidence in lieu of a more venturesome approach accords due deference to the lead role of Congress in evaluating state taxation as it bears on Indian tribes and tribal members. See Yakima, 502 U.S. at 267. The State complains, however, that the legal incidence of a tax " 'has no relationship to economic realities.' " Brief for Petitioner 30 (quoting *Complete Auto Transit, Inc. v. Brady*, 430 U.S. 274, 279 (1977)). But our focus on a tax's legal incidence accommodates the reality that tax administration requires predictability. The factors that would enter into an inquiry of the kind the State urges are daunting. If we were to make "economic reality" our guide, we might be obliged to consider, for example, how completely retailers can pass along tax increases without sacrificing sales volume — a complicated matter dependent on the characteristics of the market for the relevant product. Cf. *Yakima*, 502 U.S. at 267–268 (categorical approach safeguards against risk of litigation that could "engulf the States' annual assessment and taxation process, with the validity of each levy dependent upon a multiplicity of factors that vary from year to year, and from parcel to parcel").

By contrast, a "legal incidence" test, as 11 States with large Indian populations have informed us, "provide[s] a reasonably bright-line standard which, from a tax administration perspective, responds to the need for substantial certainty as to the permissible scope of state taxation authority." Brief for South Dakota et al. as Amici Curiae 2. And if a State is unable to enforce a tax because the legal incidence of the impost is on Indians or Indian tribes, the State generally is free to amend its law to shift the tax's legal incidence. So, in this case, the State recognizes and the Tribe agrees that Oklahoma could accomplish what it here seeks "by declaring the tax to fall on the consumer and directing the Tribe to collect and remit the levy." Pet. for Cert. 17; see Brief for Respondent 10–13.

The State also argues that, even if legal incidence is key, the Tenth Circuit erred in holding that the fuels tax's legal incidence rests on the retailer (here, the Tribe). We consider the Court of Appeals's ruling on this point altogether reasonable, and therefore uphold it. See, e.g., *Haring v. Prosise*, 462 U.S. 306, 314, n. 8 (1983) (noting "our practice to accept a reasonable construction of state law by the court of appeals").

The Oklahoma legislation does not expressly identify who bears the tax's legal incidence — distributors, retailers, or consumers; nor does it contain a "pass through" provision, requiring distributors and retailers to pass on the tax's cost to consumers. Cf. *Moe*, 425 U.S. at 482 (statute at issue provided that Montana cigarette tax " 'shall be conclusively presumed to be [a] direct [tax] on the retail consumer precollected for the purpose of convenience and facility only' ").

In the absence of such dispositive language, the question is one of "fair interpretation of the taxing statute as written and applied." *California Bd. of Equalization v. Chemehuevi Tribe*, 471 U.S. 9, 11 (1985) (per curiam). Oklahoma's law requires fuel distributors to "remit" the amount of tax due to the Tax Commission; crucially, the statute describes this remittal by the distributor as "on behalf of a licensed retailer." Okla. Stat., Tit. 68, § 505(C) (1991). The inference that the tax obligation is legally the retailer's, not the distributor's, is supported by the prescriptions that sales between distributors are exempt from taxation, § 507, but sales from a distributor to a retailer are subject to taxation, § 505(E). Further, if the distributor remits taxes it subsequently is unable to collect from the retailer, the distributor may deduct the uncollected amount from its future payments to the Tax Commission. § 505(C). The distributor, then, "is no more than a transmittal agent for the taxes imposed on the retailer." 31 F.3d at 971. And for their services as "agent of the state for [tax] collection," distributors retain a small portion of the taxes they collect. § 506(a).

The fuels tax law contains no comparable indication that retailers are simply collection agents for taxes ultimately imposed on consumers. No provision sets off the retailer's liability when consumers fail to make payments due; neither are retailers compensated for their tax collection efforts. And the tax imposed when a distributor sells fuel to a retailer applies whether or not the fuel is ever purchased by a consumer. See, e.g., § 502 ("There is hereby levied an excise tax . . . upon the sale of each and every gallon of gasoline sold, or stored and distributed, or withdrawn from storage. . . . "). Finally, Oklahoma's law imposes no liability of any kind on a consumer for purchasing, possessing, or using untaxed fuel; in contrast, the legislation makes it unlawful for distributors or retailers "to sell or offer for sale in this state, motor fuel or diesel fuel while delinquent in the payment of any excise tax due the state." § 505(C).

As the Court of Appeals fairly and reasonably concluded: "[T]he import of the language and the structure of the fuel tax statutes is that the distributor collects the tax from the retail purchaser of the fuel"; the "motor fuel taxes are legally imposed on the retailer rather than on the distributor or the consumer." 31 F.3d at 971–972.

Regarding Oklahoma's income tax, the Court of Appeals declared that the State may not tax the wages of members of the Chickasaw Nation who work for the Tribe, including members who reside in Oklahoma outside Indian country.

The holding on tribal members who live in the State outside Indian country runs up against a well-established principle of interstate and international taxation — namely, that a jurisdiction, such as Oklahoma, may tax all the income of its residents, even income earned outside the taxing jurisdiction: "That the receipt of income by a resident of the territory of a taxing sovereignty is a taxable event is universally recognized. Domicil itself affords a basis for such taxation. Enjoyment of the privileges of residence in the state and the attendant right to invoke the protection of its laws are inseparable from responsibility for sharing the costs of government. . . . These are rights and privileges which attach to domicil within the state. . . . Neither the privilege nor the burden is affected by the character of the source from which the income is derived." *New York ex rel. Cohn v. Graves*, 300 U.S. 308, 312–313 (1937).

This "general principl[e] . . . ha[s] international acceptance." American Law Institute, Federal Income Tax Project: International Aspects of United States Income Taxation 4, 6 (1987. . . . It has been applied both to the States, . . . , and to the federal government. . . .

Concerning salaries of United States resident "diplomats and employees of international organizations," . . . the dissent speaks of "treaties" as the wellsprings of "an exception" to otherwise governing tax law. That is not quite right. It is dominantly United States internal law that sets the ground rules for exemptions accorded employees of foreign governments and international organizations. In return for exemption of foreign government employees from United States federal taxation, § 893 of the Internal Revenue Code requires that the employer government grant equivalent exemption to United States Government employees performing similar services abroad. 26 U.S.C. § 893(a)(3). . . .

The Tribe seeks to block the State from exercising its ordinary prerogative to tax the income of every resident; in particular, the Tribe seeks to shelter from state taxation the income of tribal members who live in Oklahoma outside Indian country but work for the Tribe on tribal lands. For the exception the Tribe would carve out of the State's taxing authority, the Tribe gains no support from the rule that Indians and Indian tribes are generally immune from state taxation, *McClanahan v. Arizona Tax Comm'n*, 411 U.S. 164 (1973), as this principle does not operate outside Indian country. *Oklahoma Tax Comm'n v. Sac and Fox Nation*, 508 U.S. 114, 123–126 (1993).

Notably, the Tribe has not asserted here, or before the Court of Appeals, that the State's tax infringes on tribal self-governance. . . . Instead, the Tribe relies on the argument that Oklahoma's levy impairs rights granted or reserved by federal law. See *Mescalero Apache Tribe v. Jones*, 411 U.S. at 148–149 ("[E]xpress federal law to the contrary" overrides the general rule that "Indians going beyond reservation boundaries have generally been held subject to nondiscriminatory state law otherwise applicable to all citizens of the State.").

The Tribe invokes the Treaty of Dancing Rabbit Creek, Sept. 27, 1830, Art. IV, 7 Stat. 333–334, which provides in pertinent part:

> The Government and people of the United States are hereby obliged to secure to the said [Chickasaw] Nation of Red People the jurisdiction and government of all the persons and property that may be within their limits west, so that no Territory or State shall ever have a right to pass laws for the government of the [Chickasaw] Nation of Red People and their descendants . . . but the U.S. shall forever secure said [Chickasaw] Nation from, and against, all [such] laws. . . .

According to the Tribe, the State's income tax, when imposed on tribal members employed by the Tribe, is a law "for the government of the [Chickasaw] Nation of Red People and their descendants," and it is immaterial that these "descendants" live outside Indian country.

. . . By its terms, the Treaty applies only to persons and property "within [the Nation's] limits." We comprehend this Treaty language to provide for the Tribe's sovereignty within Indian country. We do not read the Treaty as conferring supersovereign authority to interfere with another jurisdiction's sovereign right to tax income, from all sources, of those who choose to live within that jurisdiction's limits.

The Tribe and the United States further urge us to read the Treaty in accord with the repudiated view that an income tax imposed on government employees should be treated as a tax on the government. See *Dobbins v. Commissioners of Erie Cty.*, 41 U.S. (16 Pet.) 435 (1842). But see *Graves v. New York ex rel. O'Keefe*, 306 U.S. 466, 480 (1939) ("The theory, which once won a qualified approval, that a tax on income is legally or economically a tax on its source, is no longer tenable. . . . "). Under this view, a tax on tribal members employed by the Tribe would be seen as an impermissible tax on the Tribe itself.

We doubt the signatories meant to incorporate this now-defunct view into the Treaty. They likely gave no thought to a State's authority to tax the income of tribal members living in the State's domain, because they did not expect any members to be there. On the contrary, the purpose of the Treaty was to put distance between the Tribe and the States. Under the Treaty, the Tribe moved across the Mississippi River, from its traditional lands within Mississippi and Alabama, to unsettled lands not then within a State. See D. HALE & A. GIBSON, THE CHICKASAW 46–59 (1991).

. . . .

For the reasons stated, we affirm the judgment of the Court of Appeals as to the motor fuels tax, reverse that judgment as to the income tax, and remand the case for proceedings consistent with this opinion.

It is so ordered.

JUSTICE BREYER, with whom JUSTICE STEVENS, JUSTICE O'CONNOR, and JUSTICE SOUTER join, concurring in part and dissenting in part.

I dissent from the portion of the Court's decision that permits Oklahoma to tax the wages that (1) the Tribe pays (2) to members of the Tribe (3) who work for the Tribe (4) within Indian country, but (5) who live outside Indian country, and, apparently, commute to work. The issue is whether such a tax falls within the scope of a promise this Nation made to the Chickasaw Nation in 1837 — a promise that no "State shall ever have a right to pass laws for the government of the [Chickasaw] Nation of Red People and their descendants . . . but the U.S. shall forever secure said [Chickasaw] Nation from, and against, all laws" except those the Tribe made itself (and certain others not relevant here). Treaty of Dancing Rabbit Creek, 7 Stat. 333 (1830) (See the Appendix to the Opinion of the Court); Treaty of Jan. 17, 1837, 11 Stat. 573. In my view, this language covers the tax.

For one thing, history suggests that the signatories to the Treaty intended the language to provide a broad guarantee that state law would not apply to the Chickasaws if they moved west of the Mississippi River — which they did. The promise's broad reach was meant initially to induce the Choctaws to make such a move in 1830, and it was extended, in 1837, to the Chickasaws for the same reason, all with the hope that other tribes would follow. . . .

For another thing, the language of this promise, read broadly and in light of its purpose, fits the tax at issue. The United States promised to secure the "[Chickasaw] Nation from, and against, all laws" for the government of the Nation, except those the Nation made itself or that Congress made. Treaty of Dancing Rabbit Creek, supra (emphasis added). The law in question does not fall within one of the explicit exceptions to this promise. Nor need the Court read the Treaty as creating an additional implied exception where, as here, the law in question likely affects significantly and directly the way in which the Tribe conducts its affairs in areas subject to tribal jurisdiction — how much, for example, it will likely have to pay workers on its land and what kinds of tribal expenditures it consequently will be able to afford. The impact of the tax upon tribal wages, tribal members, and tribal land makes it possible, indeed reasonable, to consider Oklahoma's tax (insofar as it applies to these tribal wages) as amounting to a law "for the government of" the Tribe. Indeed, in 1837, when the United States made its promise to the Chickasaws, the law considered a tax like the present one to be a tax on its source — i.e., the Tribe itself. . . . The Treaty's basic objective, namely, practical protection for the Tribe, suggests that this unchanging empirical impact, rather than shifting legal tax theory, is the critical consideration.

The majority sets forth several strong arguments against the Treaty's application. But, ultimately, I do not find them convincing. It is true, as the majority points out, that well-established principles of tax law permit States to tax those who reside within their boundaries. It is equally true that the Chickasaws whom Oklahoma seeks to tax live in the State at large, although they work in Indian country. But, these truths simply pose the question in this case: Does the Treaty provide an exception to well-established principles of tax law, roughly the same way as do, say, treaties governing diplomats and employees of international organizations? . . . The statement of basic tax principles, by themselves, cannot provide the answer.

The majority is also concerned about a "line-drawing" problem. If the Treaty invalidates the law before us, what about an Oklahoma tax, for example, on residents who work for, but are not members of, the Tribe? I acknowledge the problem of line drawing, but that problem exists irrespective of where the line is drawn here. And, because this tax (1) has a strong connection to tribal government (i.e., it falls on tribal members, who work for the Tribe, in Indian country), (2) does not regulate conduct outside Indian country, and (3) does not (as the Solicitor General points out) represent an effort to recover a proportionate share of, say, the cost of providing state services to residents, I am convinced that it falls on the side of the line that the Treaty's language and purpose seek to prohibit. To decide that the Treaty prohibits the law here is not to decide whether or not it would prohibit a law with a weaker link to tribal government or a stronger impact outside Indian country.

. . . Thus, in my view, whether we construe the Treaty's language liberally or literally, Oklahoma's tax falls within its scope. For these reasons, I believe the Treaty bars the tax. And, although I join the remainder of the Court's opinion, I respectfully dissent on this point.

NOTE

Oklahoma Tax Commission v. Chickasaw Nation seems to treat as noncontroversial the idea that federal law can create federally protected tribal interests outside Indian country. Justices Ginsburg and Breyer merely differ about whether any such federal law exists. Are there any limits on Congress's power to create such interests? Recall Judge Kozinski's skeptical queries in *Babbitt v. Williams*, discussed in Ch. 2, Sec. B, about whether Congress could afford Indians a blanket preference for federal civil service positions or for defense contracts. How seriously should one take Justice Ginsburg's concern that if the Treaty of Dancing Rabbit Creek were interpreted to allow a state tax exemption for tribal member-employees living off reservation, it would necessarily have to exempt all tribal employees, including nonmembers, as well? In his dissent, Justice Breyer claims that the line-drawing dilemma is unavoidable, and that a reasonable interpretation of the Treaty language could limit it to member-employees. Can you articulate and justify such an interpretation of the Treaty? Because the Chickasaw Nation had not previously raised the argument that the state tax infringed upon its powers of self-governance, the Supreme Court refused to consider that argument for the first time. Had the point been properly presented, should it have prevailed?

Chapter 5

JURISDICTION UNDER SPECIAL STATUTES

As the preceding two chapters have demonstrated, tribal, federal, and state courts have developed jurisdictional principles for Indian country as default rules in the absence of direction from Congress or some other appropriate legislative body. Within relevant constitutional limits, legislatures can supercede these principles. For instance, legislatures may decline to exercise the full range of their governments' powers as acknowledged by the judiciary. In this way, Congress has declined to exercise federal criminal jurisdiction over "minor" crimes committed by one Indian against another, despite the judge-made doctrine of federal "plenary power" (*see* Ch. 4, Sec. A). Similarly, even though court decisions have affirmed tribal civil jurisdiction over non-Indians, some Indian nations' constitutions have declined to assert such authority, or have made their assertions of jurisdiction contingent upon approval of the Secretary of the Interior. For example, Articles VI(j) and (h) of the Constitution of the Tule River Tribe include as powers of the Tribal Council,

> To promulgate ordinances for the purpose of safeguarding the peace and safety of residents of the reservation, and to establish courts for the adjudication of claims or disputes arising *among the members of the tribe*, and for the trial and penalizing *of members of the tribe* charged with the commission of offenses set forth in such ordinances.

> To create and maintain a tribal fund by accepting grants or donations from any person, State, or the United States, . . . or by levying taxes and license fees, *subject to review by the Secretary of the Interior*, upon persons doing business within the reservation (emphasis added).

Section 1(c) of the Bylaws of that Tribe states the tribal court "shall have jurisdiction over *all Indians* upon the reservation and over such disputes or lawsuits as shall occur between Indians on the reservation or *between Indians and non-Indians where such cases are brought before it by stipulation of the parties*" (emphasis added).

These latter acts of self-restraint were likely influenced by officials of the Bureau of Indian Affairs, which had approval power over tribal constitutions established through the Indian Reorganization Act. In recent years, many Indian nations have removed such limitations (*see* Ch. 3, Sec. A.1).

Illustrations of legislative control over jurisdiction arise when Congress uses its broad authority over Indian affairs to allow the exercise of tribal or state jurisdiction that courts have denied, or to forbid the exercise of such jurisdiction that courts might otherwise allow. Congress has sometimes effected these allocations over particular reservations, or the reservations in a particular state. *See, e.g.,* Act of June 30, 1948, ch. 759, 62 Stat. 1161 (criminal jurisdiction to Iowa over the Sac and Fox Reservation); 25 U.S.C. §§ 232, 233 (criminal and civil jurisdiction to New York over all reservations in the state).

This chapter examines both geographic-specific jurisdictional regimes affecting particular tribes or groups of tribes, as well as subject matter-specific legislation affecting jurisdiction over particular subject areas for all tribes. The more geographic-specific legislation includes Public Law 280, enacted in 1953 and significantly amended in 1968, which authorized certain states to assume more significant criminal and civil authority in Indian country. It also includes the special regimes established for indigenous peoples of Alaska and Hawaii, laws that relate to property as well as jurisdiction. The subject matter-specific legislation presented in this chapter includes statutory schemes for child welfare, tribal gaming, liquor control on reservations, and environmental protection. We will look at the following:

- the Indian Child Welfare Act of 1978, in which Congress supported the tribal role and diminished the state role in adjudications affecting the custody and adoption of Indian children outside the context of divorce;

- the Indian Gaming Regulatory Act of 1988, in which Congress authorized states to ban casino-type gaming on reservations under very limited circumstances, although only the federal government can prosecute violators. This Act also required states to make compacts with Indian nations regarding forms of gaming allowed for any purpose under state law, and gave tribes control over high-stakes bingo;

- federal laws governing sale and use of liquor in Indian country, which have approved both tribal and state authority to restrict such activity, and have made the federal government the primary enforcement agency;

- federal laws determining jurisdiction over water quality, air quality, and other environmental concerns within Indian country, including federal certification of tribes to enforce environmental standards at least as strict as federal law.

Federal jurisdictional allocation statutes implicitly or explicitly posit models of tribal-federal relations. These models also underpin court decisions seeking to interpret the meaning of the texts and the drafters' intent. The very fact that Congress takes unilateral control of jurisdictional arrangements suggests a colonial domination model. However, federal statutes allocating jurisdiction vary in the extent to which they incorporate or reflect Indian nations' preferences and consent. Particularly in the 1940s and 1950s, when the goal of assimilating Indian people dominated federal policy, Congress conferred jurisdiction upon states over Indian protests and against tribal wishes. More recently, Congress has often insisted on some measure of Indian consent before jurisdictional arrangements go into effect, or the statutes have embodied the results of prior negotiations among federal, tribal, and state representatives. *See, e.g.*, Mohegan Nation Land Claims Settlement Act, 25 U.S.C. § 1775d (prior negotiations limited state jurisdiction to criminal matters, and affirmed concurrent tribal jurisdiction). Where federal statutes allocating jurisdiction incorporate or require Indian consent, they may approximate more closely an international self-determination model or a federalism model. As you examine the individual sections of this chapter, focusing on Public Law 280, Alaska, and Hawaii, the Indian Child Welfare Act, the Indian Gaming Regulatory

Act, the Indian country liquor laws, and the environmental laws affecting Indian country, consider how these statutes and the administrative and court decisions construing their terms model Native nations' relationships to the federal government and its constituent units, the states.

A.   PUBLIC LAW 280 AND RELATED STATUTES

1.   Text and History

Public Law 280 drastically expanded state criminal and civil jurisdiction within Indian country without tribal consent. You will find the text of Public Law 280, including the 1968 amendments that prospectively condition state jurisdiction on Indian consent, in 18 U.S.C. § 1162, 25 U.S.C. §§ 1321–1326, and 28 U.S.C. § 1360. Since 1968, Congress has passed numerous other statutes that impose state jurisdiction on individual reservations as if the tribe involved had given its consent under Public Law 280. These statutes are generally the product of negotiations related to land claims, tribal recognition claims, and/or restoration of previously terminated tribes. One example you should examine is the Connecticut Indian Land Claims Settlement Act of 1983, 25 U.S.C. § 1755. Public Law 280 was further amended by section 221 of the Tribal Law and Order Act of 2010, but only to allow tribes under state jurisdiction to request restoration of federal jurisdiction *over and above* state jurisdiction, which would remain unaffected. *See* Sec. A.3, this chapter.

The federal government never polled Indian nations to determine whether they welcomed state jurisdiction under the original version of Public Law 280. Indeed, the law was passed even though many tribes registered their opposition. According to a representative of the Yakima Indian Nation who testified against the predecessor version of Public Law 280 in the early 1950s:

> The Yakima Indians . . . feel that in the State Courts they will not be treated as well as they are in the Federal courts, because they believe that many of the citizens of the State are still prejudiced against the Indians. . . .

> They are now under the Federal laws and have their own tribal laws, customs, and regulations. This system is working well and the Yakima Tribe believes that it should be continued and not changed at this time.

Although a few large and well-organized tribes were exempted from the law's application at their request, tribes throughout the United States were left at the mercy of state legislatures that might opt to assume jurisdiction. Thus, for example, Public Law 280 authorized Washington to take jurisdiction over the Yakimas without their consent. The state subsequently asserted partial jurisdiction over some subject areas throughout the reservation and complete jurisdiction over non-trust lands within reservation boundaries. It was not until 2012, when Washington State enacted a process for retroceding (or returning) state jurisdiction back to the tribes and federal government, that the Yakama Nation was able to reclaim control over those subject areas previously under state jurisdiction. *See* Robert T. Anderson, *Negotiating Jurisdiction: Retroceding State Authority over*

Indian Country Granted by Public Law 280, 87 WASH. L. REV. 915 (2012). The process finally reached conclusion for the Yakama in January 2014.

Carole E. Goldberg, *Public Law 280: The Limits of State Jurisdiction over Reservation Indians*
22 UCLA LAW REVIEW 535, 537–47, 549–52, 558–59 (1975)

Passed in 1953, PL-280[1] was an attempt at compromise between wholly abandoning the Indians to the states and maintaining them as federally protected wards, subject only to federal or tribal jurisdiction. The statute originally transferred to five willing states and offered all others, civil and criminal jurisdiction over reservation Indians regardless of the Indians' preference for continued autonomy. PL-280 did not, however, terminate the trust status of reservation lands.

From the outset, PL-280 left both the Indians and the states dissatisfied, the Indians because they did not want state jurisdiction thrust upon them against their will, the states because they resented the remaining federal protection which seemed to deprive them of the ability to finance their newly acquired powers. Predictably, disagreement between the Indians and the states erupted over the scope of jurisdiction offered by PL-280 and the means by which transfers of jurisdiction were to be effected. Among the matters in dispute were whether states assuming jurisdiction under PL-280 acquired the power to tax and zone on Indian reservations, and whether states asserting PL-280 jurisdiction had satisfied the procedural prerequisites for doing so.

Recent social, economic, and political developments have made the Indians and states especially anxious that their respective interpretations of PL-280 prevail. The expansion of metropolitan areas near Indian reservations has increased the states' interest in regulating and exploiting residential and recreational development on trust land. States have been notably desirous of acquiring pollution and subdivision control. The discovery of substantial energy resources on reservations, and consequent industrial development, have spurred similar state interest in regulating and taxing those activities. At the same time, tribal governments have been receiving encouragement from the federal government to develop tribal enterprises and strengthen their administrative apparatus, increasing their interest in freedom from state power. Finally, growing demands on the part of Indians that they receive their share of state services and their share of representation in state legislatures have produced concomitant demands on the part of the states that Indians submit to state jurisdiction.

The jurisdictional stakes are considerably higher today than they were when PL-280 was enacted; at the same time federal Indian policy is more devoted to fulfilling federal responsibility for Indians and building effective tribal governments. Broadly speaking, the model for federal Indian policy seems to be changing from one favoring state power with minimum protection for Indian interests to one favoring tribal autonomy with minimum protection for state interests. Nevertheless, since PL-280 is the most direct evidence of congressional intent with respect

---

[1] [10] Act of Aug. 15, 1953, ch. 505, 67 Stat. 588–90 (now codified as amended in scattered sections of 18, 28 U.S.C.).

to state jurisdiction, the debate over the scope of state power on Indian reservations must contend with policy choices Congress made when PL-280 was enacted. Amendments to the Act adopted in 1968 did, however, bring PL-280 more in conformity with current policy by rendering all *future* assertions of state jurisdiction under the Act subject to the affected Indians' consent, and authorizing states to return jurisdiction to the federal government. But controversies persist over jurisdiction claimed by the states prior to [the 1968 amendments].

II.

Legislative Background

PL-280 differed from earlier relinquishments of federal Indian jurisdiction in that it authorized every state to assume jurisdiction at any time in the future. Previous transfers had been limited to some or all the reservations in a single state,[2] and had followed consultation with the individual state and affected tribes by the Bureau of Indian Affairs (hereinafter referred to as B.I.A.). Although PL-280 itself had begun as an attempt to confer jurisdiction on California only, by the time it was reported out of the Senate, the prevailing view was that "any legislation in [the] area should be on a general basis, making provision for all affected States to come within its terms. . . . " The Senate Report of the bill in committee suggests why Congress was concerned with effectuating a general transfer of jurisdiction after years of an ad hoc policy which had involved careful evaluation in each case from the point of view of both Indians and the states. The Report indicates the foremost concern of Congress at the time of enacting of PL-280 was lawlessness on the reservations and the accompanying threat to Anglos living nearby. In 1953, responsibility for law enforcement on the reservations was irrationally fractionated. If a non-Indian committed a crime against another non-Indian or a crime without an apparent victim, such as gambling or drunk driving, only state authorities could prosecute him under state law. But if either the offender or victim was Indian, the federal government had exclusive jurisdiction to prosecute, applying state law in federal court under the Assimilative Crimes Act. Finally, if offender and victim were both Indians, the federal government had exclusive jurisdiction if the offense was one of the "Ten Major Crimes;" otherwise, tribal courts had exclusive jurisdiction. Since federal law enforcement was typically neither well-financed nor vigorous, and tribal courts often lacked the resources and skills to be effective, the result, described by House Indian Affairs Subcommittee member Wesley D'Ewart, of Montana, was "[t]he complete breakdown of law and order on many of the Indian reservations. . . . " Throughout the hearings of PL-280 and its predecessor bills in the previous Congress, Representative D'Ewart repeatedly voiced "[t]he desire of all law abiding citizens living on or near Indian reservations for law and order." The

---

[2] [20] Act of June 8, 1940, ch. 276, 54 Stat. 249 (criminal jurisdiction to Kansas); Act of May 31, 1946, ch. 279, 60 Stat. 229 (criminal jurisdiction to North Dakota over the Devils Lake Reservation); Act of June 30, 1948, ch. 759, 62 Stat. 1161 (criminal jurisdiction to Iowa over the Sac and Fox Reservations); Act of July 2, 1948, ch. 809, 62 Stat. 1224 (criminal jurisdiction to New York) (codified at 25 U.S.C. § 232 (1970)); Act of Oct. 5, 1949, ch. 604, 63 Stat. 705 (civil and criminal jurisdiction to California over Agua Caliente Reservation); Act of Sept. 13, 1950, ch. 947, 64 Stat. 845 (civil jurisdiction to New York).

primary law enforcement thrust of PL-280 is further evidenced by the fact that several predecessor bills offered the states criminal jurisdiction only, and PL-280 itself exempted several reservations completely from state jurisdiction solely because they had legal systems and organizations "functioning in a reasonably satisfactory manner."

Of course, conferring jurisdiction on the states was not the only available solution to the very real law enforcement problem. [Conferring state] criminal jurisdiction was preferred to other alternatives however, because it was the cheapest solution; Congress was interested in saving money as well as bringing law and order to the reservations.

There is much less evidence of the congressional rationale for conferring civil jurisdiction on the states, and much less factual support for that decision. State civil jurisdiction over reservation Indians was believed to have been somewhat more extensive than state criminal jurisdiction, though typically, state courts were powerless to resolve claims against reservation Indians arising on the reservation. Since federal law governed many important civil relations involving Indians, the B.I.A., charged with administering these laws, played a considerable governing role on the reservations. In this context, the Senate Report on PL-280 declared that the Indians "have reached a stage of acculturation and development that makes desirable extension of State civil jurisdiction. . . . " The implication of this and similar statements was that Indians were just as socially advanced as other state citizens, and should therefore be released from second-class citizenship as well as the paternalistic supervision of the B.I.A.

Considering the absence of any significant investigation of the Indians' stage of social development prior to the broad delegation of jurisdiction to every state by PL-280, it seems unlikely that Congress knew or cared about the Indians' readiness for state jurisdiction. Furthermore, it is difficult to reconcile this theme of advanced acculturation with the prevailing notion that state criminal jurisdiction was necessary because the Indians were disorderly and incapable of self-government. Most likely, civil jurisdiction was an afterthought in a measure aimed primarily at bringing law and order to the reservations, added because it comported with the pro-assimilationist drift of federal policy, and because it was convenient and cheap.

The choice Congress made in PL-280 did not wholly satisfy either the tribes or the states. The source of the Indians' displeasure was the absence of a provision for tribal consent prior to state assumption of jurisdiction. The states, on the other hand, were unhappy about the absence of a provision either granting federal subsidies to states that accepted jurisdiction or removing reservation lands from tax-exempt trust status. These aspects of the law have generated efforts directed at Congress, the state legislatures, and the courts to mold or remold PL-280 to suit [the preferences of the Indians or the states].

III.

Objections to PL-280

A. Controversy Over Indian Consent

Indian antagonism to PL-280 has stemmed almost entirely from its initial unilateral imposition of state law. Congress omitted a tribal consent requirement from PL-280 for the same reasons it abandoned its policy of conferring jurisdiction state by state after consultation with the affected tribes. In both instances, concern about bringing law and order to the reservations at reduced federal expense dictated immediate transfers of jurisdiction to the states. Thus, when Congressperson D'Ewart inserted a tribal consent provision in one of the predecessor bills to PL-280 in order to obtain the support of the tribes in his state, B.I.A. Commissioner Dillon S. Meyer stated:

> [I]t might be possible to pass a referendum in some of the reservations against action by the State, where they have a completely inadequate law and order code and completely inadequate court system and completely inadequate policing system, and we would recommend if we found that situation that they be included anyhow.

Indian opposition to the absence of a tribal consent provision in PL-280 was initially based on the principle of tribal sovereignty. The departure from past practice of consulting with the Indians prior to transferring jurisdiction was considered a deliberate slight.

Another reason for opposition was the fear that state jurisdiction would in practice operate to the disadvantage of the Indians. The Indians in many instances preferred federal to state jurisdiction because the B.I.A., for all its faults, at least perceived the Indians as its special responsibility and concern. Many Indians feared that their people would be discriminated against in state courts and given longer sentences simply because they were Indians; that state law enforcement officials would ignore crimes when Indians were the victims but act vigorously when a white was harmed; and that many of their elders were not sufficiently fluent in the language and customs of white America to enable them to cope with state jurisdiction. They disliked the ousting of their functioning tribal courts and law-making bodies and feared that the state institutions taking their place would be neither sufficiently sensitive to Indian traditions nor adequately staffed and financed. The latter fear was especially warranted in view of PL-280's failure to provide a tax base or subsidies to the states to support their newly acquired law enforcement obligations.

Between 1953 and 1968, a wide variety of influential persons and organizations urged Congress to add an Indian consent provision to PL-280. Some states, however, did not wait for Congress to act. Instead, they undertook by themselves to accommodate the Indians' desire to determine when and how state jurisdiction should be assumed. Since the 1968 amendments (adding Indian consent provisions) to PL-280 did not affect prior assertions of jurisdiction under the Act, the nature and validity of these efforts retain importance.

The five, later six, states that were granted PL-280 jurisdiction immediately and irrevocably (mandatory states) lacked the flexibility to condition their jurisdiction on Indian consent. By virtue of language in PL-280 any jurisdiction other than state jurisdiction on the reservations was henceforth invalid, except as provided in the Act. While Congress had consulted with these states prior to passage of PL-280 in order to ascertain their desire for such jurisdiction, and had exempted certain reservations in these states at the Indians' request, it had not authorized the mandatory states to create further exemptions in response to Indian wishes. In contrast, the states merely authorized to assume jurisdiction at their discretion (optional states) could take the Indians' wishes into account before asserting their power, and many did so, either formally or informally. For some states, this recognition of Indian sovereignty was spontaneous; in others, it was formed by the bitter experience of states such as Wyoming,[3] South Dakota,[4] Washington,[5] and New Mexico, in which the Indians had waged vigorous and successful battles against bills and constitutional amendments imposing state jurisdiction unilaterally. Although Arizona[6] and Iowa[7] simply asserted jurisdiction without seeking concurrence of the affected Indians, and Idaho and Washington ignored Indian preferences as to some subject matters,[8] Florida first solicited the consent of the Seminole tribe, Nevada consulted with every tribe in the state prior to assuming jurisdiction, and Idaho,[9] Montana,[10] North Dakota,[11] South Dakota,[12] and Washington[13] established some form of Indian consent procedure despite the absence of a requirement in PL-280.

---

[3] [56] In a state referendum in 1964, Wyoming rejected an attempt to amend its constitution to empower the legislature to accept PL-280 jurisdiction. The sponsor of the measure had not bothered to consult with the Indians prior to introducing [the bill].

[4] [57] In 1964, after the South Dakota legislature had enacted a measure unilaterally extending state jurisdiction to the reservations, the Indians instituted a referendum, bombarded the voters of the state with publicity and literature opposing the measure, and secured the law's defeat. Dep't of Indian Affairs, State of Montana, Tribal Governments and Law and Order 19–20 (1968) [hereinafter cited as Tribal Governments].

[5] [58] Washington's first attempt to accept PL-280 jurisdiction met with strong Indian opposition and was defeated. Thereafter, in 1957, a bill was passed with the support of the Indians which permitted Washington to assume jurisdiction only after a tribe had requested that it do so. See Civil Rights Report, *supra* note 50, at 145. The Indians were partially defeated on the tribal consent issue in 1963, however, when jurisdiction was extended unilaterally to some subject matters. Wash. Rev. Code §§ 37.12.010–.060 (Supp. 1971).

[6] [60] Ariz. Rev. Stat. Ann. §§ 36-1801, 36-1856 (Supp. 1973) (water pollution control).

[7] [61] Iowa Code Ann. §§ 1.12–.15 (Supp. 1974). Iowa extended its civil jurisdiction over the Sac and Fox Reservations, which were already subject to state criminal jurisdiction.

[8] [62] Idaho Code § 67-5101 (1973); Wash. Rev. Code §§ 37.12.010–.060 (Supp. 1971).

[9] [65] Idaho Code § 67-5102 (1973).

[10] [66] Mont. Rev. Code Ann. §§ 83-802, 83-806 (1966). For a discussion of the considerations that influenced Montana's decision to include a tribal consent provision, refer to Dep't of Indian Affairs, State of Montana, A Study of Problems Arising from the Transfer of Law & Order Jurisdiction on Indian Reservations to the State of Montana 11 (1961).

[11] [67] N.D. Cent. Code § 27-19-02 (1974).

[12] [68] S.D. Compiled Laws Ann. § 1-1-13 (1967). The law provides for state jurisdiction unless within three months the tribe rejects it in a referendum held at [the expense of the tribe].

[13] [69] Wash. Rev. Code § 37.12.021 (Supp. 1971).

[In the Indian Civil Rights Act of 1968], Congress eliminated the need for self-imposed limits on state jurisdiction in the future by establishing a tribal consent provision in PL-280 itself. Congress provided in the Civil Rights Act of 1968 that henceforth no state could acquire PL-280 jurisdiction over the objections of the affected Indians. Furthermore, in an action which most legislators believed did no more than make explicit existing law, the 1968 Act declared that state jurisdiction could be acquired one tribe at a time, so long as a majority of the adult enrolled members of the tribe expressed their consent in a special election. Finally, in a more controversial action, it allowed acceptance of jurisdiction over some subject matters, but not others.[14]

This change in PL-280 is significant evidence of a shift in federal Indian policy from the pro-assimilationist orientation of the 1950s to a greater concern for strengthening tribal institutions and encouraging economic development on reservations. Interestingly, the opposition to tribal consent was not couched in law and order language this time. Rather, the opponents stressed the need for state control of economic development on the reservations, a need which has precipitated much conflict over PL-280 in recent years, especially in the Southwest. Later actions by Congress indicate a willingness to permit enclaves of tribal sovereignty within a state, so long as the federal government maintained control over tribal decisions that might seriously endanger state interests.

The significance of the addition of a tribal consent provision to PL-280 lies not only in its recognition of the principle of Indian self-determination, but also in its new conception of the role of state jurisdiction on reservations. The tribal consent provision transformed PL-280 from a law that justified state jurisdiction on law enforcement, budgetary, and assimilationist grounds to one that justified state jurisdiction as a means of providing services to Indian communities. Among the strongest arguments in favor of the 1968 Act's amendment was that the institution of state jurisdiction under PL-280, far from improving reservation law and order and elevating Indians from second-class citizenship, had subjected them to discriminatory treatment in the courts, as well as discrimination in the provision of state services. Once tribal consent became a prerequisite to state jurisdiction, and jurisdiction could be acquired one subject matter at a time, the way was opened for tribes and states to negotiate for the extension of state jurisdiction in those situations where it was to their mutual advantage.

The beneficial impact of the 1968 amendments to PL-280 should not be overemphasized, however. The Indian consent provision was not made retroactive, and thus earlier assumptions of state jurisdiction over Indian objections were not affected. Moreover, it did not enable Indians who had consented to state jurisdiction under a state-initiated consent provision to reconsider their decisions.

---

[14] [81] 25 U.S.C. § 1321(a) (1970) provides that states may assume criminal jurisdiction "over any or all . . . offenses"; 25 U.S.C. § 1322(a) (1970) provides that states may assume civil jurisdiction over "any or all . . . civil causes of action arising within . . . Indian country. . . . "

B. Controversy Over Financing State Jurisdiction

The absence of an Indian consent provision in PL-280 reflected insensitivity to the interests of the Indians; the absence of federal subsidies to PL-280 states demonstrated similar insensitivity to the dilemma of states handed jurisdiction but simultaneously denied the means to finance it. This financial dilemma derives from a basic inconsistency in federal policy. On the one hand, Congress wished to satisfy state demands for improved law and order on the reservation; on the other hand, Congress was itself unwilling to pay for such improvements or to enable the states to do so by lifting the tax-exempt status of Indian trust lands.[15]

The failure to resolve this inconsistency had disastrous consequences for states acquiring PL-280 jurisdiction. Local governments acquiring jurisdiction were required to hire more police, more judges, more prison guards, more probation and parole officers, and more juvenile aid officers, and to build new police stations, courthouses, and jails. It could have been predicted that a state which undertook law enforcement on the reservation as vigorously as elsewhere in the state would incur higher expenses than the federal government, even allowing for the greater expense of operating a federal as opposed to a municipal court. The new resources available to the states under PL-280 such as fines and court costs were clearly inadequate; estimates based on federal experience indicated such funds would cover only about 10 percent of all newly-acquired law enforcement expenses. The mandatory PL-280 states were hardest hit; they could not avoid the economic consequences of federal withdrawal from the reservations by refusing jurisdiction under the Act.

Financial hardship for the states translated into inadequate law enforcement for the reservations. The most notable failure among the mandatory states was Nebraska, where the Omaha and Winnebago reservations were left without any law enforcement at all once federal officers withdrew [from providing such services].

C. Retrocession

Had PL-280 originally contained a provision permitting the states and the tribes to demand the return or "retrocession" of state PL-280 jurisdiction to the federal

---

[15] [87] This inconsistency was exposed during the hearings on PL-280 when Congressperson Young of Nevada confronted counsel for the B.I.A., Harry Sellery, with the questionable value of offering the states jurisdiction but denying them the power to tax Indian property as the means of financing it. Counsel responded that if federal financial assistance were made available to fill the gap,

> there [would] be some tendency . . . for the Indian to be thought of and perhaps to think of himself because of the financial assistance which comes from the Federal Government as still somewhat a member of a race or group which is set apart from other citizens of the State. And it is desired to give him and the other citizens of the State the feeling of a conviction that he is in the same status and has access to the same services, including the courts, as other citizens of the State who are not Indians.

Hearings Transcript I, *supra* note 22, at 8. When counsel was reminded that differentiation between Indians and non-Indians would be *increased* by the failure to provide federal financial aid, since the Indians would enjoy a unique exemption from state property taxes, he replied curtly: "The Department [of the Interior] has recommended, nevertheless, that no financial assistance be afforded to the States." *Id.* at 9.

government, much of the dissatisfaction with the Act would have been avoided, though federal dissatisfaction might have been greater. Retrocession would have allowed both states and tribes to experiment with state jurisdiction, the states to determine whether it was too costly, and the tribes to determine whether it fairly met their needs. In addition, retrocession would have permitted jurisdictional arrangements to reflect changed circumstances. If a tribe subject to PL-280 jurisdiction developed new economic resources, or a new generation of tribal members wished to establish strong tribal governing institutions, the state could be required to relinquish jurisdiction.

Notwithstanding these potential benefits from retrocession, the device received little attention during the debates over PL-280 and its predecessor bills, and no recognition in the statute itself. The failure to include a means by which states could effect retrocession is perhaps attributable to a congressional wish to rid the federal government forever of its costly supervisory responsibilities on the reservations. The omission of a provision allowing tribes to demand retrocession is undoubtedly explained by the same pro-assimilationist impulses responsible for the absence of an Indian consent provision.

Eventually, however, Congress extended the advantages of retrocession to the states, although not to the tribes. By 1968, the states' financial difficulties with PL-280 had become so apparent that relief was provided in the form of a section of the 1968 Civil Rights Act enabling any state which had previously assumed jurisdiction under PL-280 to offer the return of all or any measure of its jurisdiction to the federal government by sending a resolution to the Secretary of the Interior. The Secretary could accept or reject the retrocession in his discretion.[16] Under this provision, tribes could not participate in the retrocession decision, although they might attempt to do so informally through appeals directly to the Secretary of the Interior.

The absence of a tribal veto over state-initiated retrocession was undesirable from the tribe's point of view because the states could decide to retrocede only part of their PL-280 jurisdiction, and might use that power to relieve themselves of the most costly forms of jurisdiction while retaining those most offensive to the Indians. Perhaps Congress believed that the Secretary's veto power over a state's proposed retrocession would make a tribal veto unnecessary in those situations where a state's partial retrocession seriously disadvantaged the Indians, or where the Indians actually preferred to retain complete state jurisdiction.

A more glaring omission was the failure to create any mechanism by which Indians could initiate and *force* retrocession on an unwilling state that had acquired jurisdiction. It is difficult to justify this omission on assimilationist grounds or on the ground of the inadequacy of tribal law enforcement facilities because other

---

[16] [112] 25 U.S.C. § 1323 (1970). Why this opportunity was not extended to states acquiring jurisdiction *after* 1968 is somewhat unclear, since both optional and mandatory states were authorized to return jurisdiction accepted before 1968. A possible ground for distinction is that the 1968 Act, by expressly authorizing partial assumptions of jurisdiction, rendered retrocession less financially imperative for the states. In addition, Congress may have felt that states should not be as free to retrocede jurisdiction acquired after Indian consent which the 1968 Act's amendments of PL-280 required before jurisdiction could be acquired.

language in the 1968 Act required tribal consent before any initial extension of state jurisdiction, regardless of the quality of law enforcement machinery on the reservation. Perhaps objections to allowing tribal-initiated retrocession derived from concern that the tribes would seek to retrocede less than all of the jurisdiction the state had initially assumed, under circumstances where the state was unwilling to exercise only the remainder. Or perhaps Congress felt that reservations that had already been subjected to PL-280 jurisdiction were so weakened as to be incapable of resuming self-government.

2. Acquiring and Exercising State Jurisdiction Under Public Law 280

BRYAN v. ITASCA COUNTY
United States Supreme Court
426 U.S. 373 (1976)

Mr. Justice Brennan delivered the opinion of the Court.

This case presents the question reserved in [*McClanahan*]: whether the grant of civil jurisdiction to the States conferred by § 4 of [Public Law 280] 28 U.S.C. § 1360, is a congressional grant of power to the States to tax reservation Indians except insofar as taxation is expressly excluded by the terms of the statute.

Petitioner Russell Bryan, an enrolled member of the Minnesota Chippewa Tribe, resides in a mobile home on land held in trust by the United States for the Chippewa Tribe on the Leech Lake Reservation in Minnesota. In June 1972, petitioner received notices from the auditor of respondent Itasca County, Minn., that he had been assessed personal property tax liability on the mobile home totaling $147.95. Thereafter, in September 1972, petitioner brought this suit in the Minnesota District Court seeking a declaratory judgment that the State and county were without authority to levy such a tax on personal property of a reservation Indian on the reservation and that imposition of such a tax was contrary to federal law. The Minnesota District Court [upheld the tax, the] Minnesota Supreme Court affirmed, [w]e granted certiorari, and now reverse.

I

[This Court's decisions in] *McClanahan* and *Moe* preclude any authority in respondent county to levy a personal property tax upon petitioner's mobile home in the absence of congressional consent. Our task therefore is to determine whether § 4 of Pub. L. 280, 28 U.S.C. § 1360, constitutes such consent. [Section 1360] does not in terms provide that the tax laws of a State are among "civil laws . . . of general application to private persons or private property." The Minnesota Supreme Court concluded, however, that they were, finding in § 4(b) of the statute a negative implication of inclusion in § 4(a) of a general power to tax. . . . The Minnesota Supreme Court reasoned that "unless paragraph (a) is interpreted as a general grant of the power to tax, then the exceptions contained in paragraph (b) are limitations on a nonexistent power." 303 Minn. [395], at 402, 228 N.W.2d [249], at

253. Therefore, the state court held: "Public Law 280 is a clear grant of the power to tax." *Id.* at 406, 228 N.W.2d at 256. We disagree. That conclusion is foreclosed by the legislative history of Pub. L. 280 and the application of canons of construction applicable to congressional statutes claimed to terminate Indian immunities.

II

The primary concern of Congress in enacting Pub. L. 280 that emerges from its sparse legislative history was with the problem of lawlessness on certain Indian reservations, and the absence of adequate tribal institutions for law enforcement. See Goldberg, *Public Law 280: The Limits of State Jurisdiction over Reservation Indians*, 22 UCLA L. Rev. 535, 541–542 (1975). The House Report states:

> These States lack jurisdiction to prosecute Indians for most offenses committed on Indian reservations or other Indian country, with limited exceptions. . . .

> As a practical matter, the enforcement of law and order among the Indians in the Indian country has been left largely to the Indian groups themselves. In many States, tribes are not adequately organized to perform that function; consequently, there has been created a hiatus in law-enforcement authority that could best be remedied by conferring criminal jurisdiction on States indicating an ability and willingness to accept such responsibility. H.R. Rep. No. 848, 83d Cong., 1st Sess., 5–6 (1953).

Thus, provision for state criminal jurisdiction over offenses committed by or against Indians on the reservations was the central focus of Pub. L. 280 and is embodied in § 2 of the Act, 18 U.S.C. § 1162.

In marked contrast in the legislative history is the virtual absence of expression of congressional policy or intent respecting § 4's grant of civil jurisdiction to the States. Of special significance for our purposes, however, is the total absence of mention or discussion regarding a congressional intent to confer upon the States an authority to tax Indians or Indian property on reservations. Neither the Committee Reports nor the floor discussion in either House mentions such authority. This omission has significance in the application of the canons of construction applicable to statutes affecting Indian immunities, as some mention would normally be expected if such a sweeping change in the status of tribal government and reservation Indians had been contemplated [by the Congress].

Piecing together as best we can the sparse legislative history of § 4, subsection (a) seems to have been primarily intended to redress the lack of adequate Indian forums for resolving private legal disputes between reservation Indians, and between Indians and other private citizens, by permitting the courts of the States to decide such disputes; this is definitely the import of the statutory wording conferring upon a State "jurisdiction over civil causes of action between Indians or to which Indians are parties which arise in . . . Indian country . . . to the same extent that such State . . . has jurisdiction over other civil causes of action." With this as the primary focus of § 4(a), the wording that follows in § 4(a) — "and those civil laws of such State . . . that are of general application to private persons or private property shall have the same force and effect within such Indian country as they have elsewhere within the State" — authorizes application by the state courts of their rules of decision to decide such disputes.[17] Cf. 28 U.S.C. § 1652. This construction finds support in the consistent and uncontradicted references in the legislative history to "permitting" *"State courts to adjudicate* civil controversies" arising on Indian reservations, H.R. Rep. No. 848, pp. 5, 6 (emphasis added), and the absence of anything remotely resembling an intention to confer general state civil regulatory control over Indian reservations. In short, the consistent and exclusive use of the terms "civil causes of action," "aris[ing] on," "civil laws . . . of general application to private persons or private property," and "adjudicat[ion]," in both the Act and its legislative history virtually compels our conclusion that the primary intent of § 4 was to grant jurisdiction over private civil litigation involving reservation Indians in state court.

[This] construction is also more consistent with Title IV of the Civil Rights Act of 1968, 82 Stat. 78, 25 U.S.C. §§ 1321–1326. Title IV repeals § 7 of Pub. L. 280 and requires tribal consent as a condition to further state assumptions of the jurisdiction provided in 18 U.S.C. § 1162 and 28 U.S.C. § 1360. Section 402 of Title IV, 25 U.S.C. § 1322, tracks the language of § 4 of Pub. L. 280. Section 406 of Title IV, 25 U.S.C. § 1326, which provides for Indian consent, refers to "State jurisdiction acquired pursuant to this subchapter with respect to criminal offenses or civil causes of action. . . . " It is true, of course, that the primary interpretation of § 4 must have reference to the legislative history of the Congress that enacted it rather than to the history of Acts of a later Congress. Nevertheless, Title IV of the 1968 Act is intimately related to § 4, as it provides the method for further state assumptions of the jurisdiction conferred by § 4, and we previously have construed the effect of legislation affecting reservation Indians in light of "intervening" legislative enactments. *Moe v. Salish & Kootenai Tribes*, 425 U.S. [463], at 472–475. It would be difficult to suppose that Congress in 1968 intended the meaning of § 4 to vary depending upon the time and method by which particular States acquired jurisdiction. And certainly the legislative history of Title IV makes it difficult to construe § 4 jurisdiction acquired pursuant to Title IV as extending general state civil regulatory authority, including taxing power, to govern Indian reservations. Senator Ervin, who offered and principally sponsored Title IV, see *Kennerly v. District Court of Montana, supra*, at 429 n.5, referred to § 1360 civil jurisdiction as follows:

> Certain representatives of municipalities have charged that the repeal of [§ 7 of] Public Law 280 would hamper air and water pollution controls and provide a haven for undesirable, unrestricted business establishments within tribal land borders. Not only does this assertion show the lack of faith that certain cities have in the ability and desire of Indian tribes to better themselves and their environment, but, *most importantly, it is*

[17] Cf. Israel & Smithson, [*Indian Taxation, Tribal Sovereignty and Economic Development,* 49 N.D.L. Rev. 267, 296 (1973).]

"A fair reading of these two clauses suggests that Congress never intended 'civil laws' to mean the entire array of state noncriminal laws, but rather that Congress intended 'civil laws' to mean those laws which have to do with private rights and status. Therefore, 'civil laws . . . of general application to private persons or private property' would include the laws of contract, tort, marriage, divorce, insanity, descent, etc., but would not include laws declaring or implementing the states' sovereign powers, such as the power to tax, grant franchises, etc. These are not within the fair meaning of 'private' laws."

irrelevant, since Public Law 280 relates primarily to the application of state civil and criminal law in court proceedings, and has no bearing on programs set up by the States to assist economic and environmental development in Indian territory. (Emphasis added.) Hearing before the Subcommittee on Indian Affairs of the House Committee on Interior and Insular Affairs, No. 90-23, 90th Cong., 2d Sess., 136 (1968).

III

Other considerations also support our construction. Today's congressional policy toward reservation Indians may less clearly than in 1953 favor their assimilation, but Pub. L. 280 was plainly not meant to effect total assimilation. Public L. 280 was only one of many types of assimilationist legislation under active consideration in 1953. H.R. Rep. No. 848, pp. 3–5; *Santa Rosa Band of Indians v. Kings County*, 532 F.2d 655, 662 (CA9 1975). And nothing in its legislative history remotely suggests that Congress meant the Act's extension of civil jurisdiction to the States should result in the undermining or destruction of such tribal governments as did exist and a conversion of the affected tribes into little more than " 'private, voluntary organizations,' " *United States v. Mazurie*, 419 U.S. 544, 557 (1975) — a possible result if tribal governments and reservation Indians were subordinated to the full panoply of civil regulatory powers, including taxation, of state and local governments. The Act itself refutes such an inference: there is notably absent any conferral of state jurisdiction over the tribes themselves, and § 4(c), 28 U.S.C. § 1360(c), providing for the "full force and effect" of any tribal ordinances or customs "heretofore or hereafter adopted by an Indian tribe . . . if not inconsistent with any applicable civil law of the State," contemplates the continuing vitality of tribal government.

Moreover, the same Congress that enacted Pub. L. 280 also enacted several termination Acts — legislation which is cogent proof that Congress knew well how to express its intent directly when that intent was to subject reservation Indians to the full sweep of state laws and state taxation. These termination enactments provide expressly for subjecting distributed property "and any income derived therefrom by the individual, corporation, or other legal entity . . . to the same taxes, State and Federal, as in the case of non-Indians," 25 U.S.C. §§ 564j, 749, 898, and provide that "all statutes of the United States which affect Indians because of their status as Indians shall no longer be applicable to the members of the tribe, and the laws of the several States shall apply to the tribe and its members in the same manner as they apply to other citizens or persons within their jurisdiction." 25 U.S.C. §§ 564q, 757, 899; cf. 25 U.S.C. § 726. These contemporaneous termination Acts are *in pari materia* with Pub. L. 280. *Menominee Tribe v. United States*, 391 U.S. [404], at 411. Reading this express language respecting state taxation and application of the full range of state laws to tribal members of these contemporaneous termination Acts, the negative inference is that Congress did not mean in § 4(a) to subject reservation Indians to state taxation. Thus, rather than inferring a negative implication of a grant of general taxing power in § 4(a) from the exclusion of certain taxation in § 4(b), we conclude that construing Pub. L. 280 *in pari materia* with these Acts shows that if Congress in enacting Pub. L. 280 had intended to confer upon the States general civil regulatory powers, including taxation, over reservation Indians, it would have expressly said so.

IV

Additionally, we note that § 4(b), excluding "taxation of any real or personal property . . . belonging to any Indian or any Indian tribe . . . that is held in trust by the United States or is subject to a restriction against alienation imposed by the United States," is not obviously the narrow exclusion of state taxation that the Minnesota Supreme Court read it to be. On its face the statute is not clear whether the exclusion is applicable only to taxes levied directly on the trust property specifically, or whether it also excludes taxation on activities taking place in conjunction with such property and income deriving from its use. And even if read narrowly to apply only to taxation levied against trust property directly, § 4(b) certainly does not expressly authorize all other state taxation of reservation Indians.

Moreover, the express prohibition of any "alienation, encumbrance, or taxation" of any trust property can be read as prohibiting state courts, acquiring jurisdiction over civil controversies involving reservation Indians pursuant to § 4, from applying state laws or enforcing judgments in ways that would effectively result in the "alienation, encumbrance, or taxation" of trust property. Indeed, any other reading of this provision of § 4(b) is difficult to square with the identical prohibition contained in § 2(b) of the Act, which applies the same restrictions upon States exercising criminal jurisdiction over reservation Indians. It would simply make no sense to infer from the identical language of § 2(b) a general power in § 2(a) to tax Indians in all other respects since § 2(a) deals only with criminal jurisdiction.

Indeed, § 4(b) in its entirety may be read as simply a reaffirmation of the existing reservation Indian-federal government relationship in all respects save the conferral of state-court jurisdiction to adjudicate private civil causes of action involving Indians. . . .

Finally, in construing this "admittedly ambiguous" statute, *Board of Comm'rs v. Seber*, 318 U.S. [705], at 713, we must be guided by that "eminently sound and vital canon," *Northern Cheyenne Tribe v. Hollowbreast*, 425 U.S. 649, 655 n.7 (1976), that "statutes passed for the benefit of dependent Indian tribes . . . are to be liberally construed, doubtful expressions being resolved in favor of the Indians." *Alaska Pacific Fisheries v. United States*, 248 U.S. 78, 89 (1918). See *Choate v. Trapp*, 224 U.S. 665, 675 (1912); *Antoine v. Washington*, 420 U.S. 194, 199–200 (1975). This principle of statutory construction has particular force in the face of claims that ambiguous statutes abolish by implication Indian tax immunities. *McClanahan v. Arizona State Tax Comm'n*, 411 U.S., at 174; *Squire v. Capoeman*, 351 U.S. 1, 6–7 (1956); *Carpenter v. Shaw*, 280 U.S. 363, 366–367 (1930). "This is so because . . . Indians stand in a special relation to the federal government from which the states are excluded unless the Congress has manifested a clear purpose to terminate [a tax] immunity and allow states to treat Indians as part of the general community." *Oklahoma Tax Comm'n v. United States*, 319 U.S. 598, 613–614 (1943) (Murphy, J., dissenting). What we recently said of a claim that Congress had terminated an Indian reservation by means of an ambiguous statute is equally applicable here to the respondent's claim that § 4(a) of Pub. L. 280 is a clear grant of power to tax, and hence a termination of traditional Indian immunity from state taxation:

> Congress was fully aware of the means by which termination could be effected. But clear termination language was not employed in the . . . Act. This being so, we are not inclined to infer an intent to terminate. . . . A congressional determination to terminate must be expressed on the face of the Act or be clear from the surrounding circumstances and legislative history. *Mattz v. Arnett*, 412 U.S. 481, 504–505 (1973).

[*Reversed.*]

NOTES

1. **Applying *Bryan* in *Cabazon*:** The Supreme Court famously applied the criminal/prohibitory versus civil/regulatory distinction from *Bryan* in *California v. Cabazon Band of Mission Indians*, 480 U.S. 202 (1987) to invalidate application of California's laws against high-stakes bingo to tribal games. Reread that opinion, which is presented and analyzed in Ch. 4, Sec. B.4.b. Insofar as *Cabazon* gave rise to the Indian Gaming Regulatory Act of 1988, 25 U.S.C. § 2701 et seq., which in turn triggered large-scale tribal gaming, one could say that *Bryan* spawned today's tribal gaming industry. For a detailed account of the litigation strategy behind *Bryan* as well as the key role the case played in bringing about the tribal gaming phenomenon, see Kevin K. Washburn, *How a $147 County Tax Notice Helped Bring Tribes More than $200 Billion in Indian Gaming Revenue: The Story of* Bryan v. Itasca County, *in* INDIAN LAW STORIES (Carole Goldberg, Kevin K. Washburn, and Philip P. Frickey, eds., 2011).

2. **Tribes Affected by Public Law 280:** The six "mandatory" states mentioned in Public Law 280 in 1953 encompass 359 of the over 550 federally recognized tribes and Native villages. Today, aggregating the tribes in those states with those affected by assumptions of jurisdiction between 1953 and 1968, 70% of all federally recognized tribes and Native villages have been subjected to state jurisdiction under Public Law 280. Twenty-three percent of the tribal population in the lower 48 states and all Alaskan Natives are affected by Public Law 280 and like statutes authorizing state jurisdiction, although the Court's decision in *Alaska v. Native Village of Venetie*, 522 U.S. 520 (1998), reducing Indian country in Alaska, has made Public Law 280 less relevant there. The only remaining Indian country in Alaska consists of the Metlakatla Reservation on the Annette Islands and parcels of Native allotments and townsites, estimated at 4 to 6 million acres. *See* Ch. 2, Sec. A.3.b; Sec. B.1, this chapter; Natalie Landreth & Erin Dougherty, *The Use of the Alaskan Native Claims Settlement Act to Justify Disparate Treatment of Alaska's Tribes*, 36 AM. INDIAN L. REV. 321 (2012). Public Law 280 applies only within Indian country. Today, only a handful of states exercise full or partial jurisdiction as a result of having opted into Public Law 280 before 1968 — Florida, Idaho (limited subjects), Montana (felony jurisdiction only on one reservation), and Washington (complex scheme with different arrangements on different reservations). A few other states attempted to opt into Public Law 280, but had their efforts invalidated, or they subsequently retroceded (returned) their jurisdiction to the United States. For a complete listing of tribes affected by Public Law 280, including optional as well as mandatory states, retroceded tribes, and excluded tribes, see DUANE CHAMPAGNE &

CAROLE GOLDBERG, CAPTURED JUSTICE: NATIVE NATIONS AND PUBLIC LAW 280, 14–18 (2011).

3. **Models of Tribal-Federal Relations:** As a nonconsensual imposition of state jurisdiction, Public Law 280 fits the colonial domination model of tribal-federal relations. If Congress was correct in 1953 about the lack of effective law enforcement and access to civil dispute resolution within Indian country, what were the alternatives to establishing state jurisdiction? Which alternative(s) might reflect an international self-determination model of tribal-federal relations? Which might reflect a federalism model? Which would be most consistent with the federal trust responsibility to Indian nations?

4. **Federal Power to Authorize State Jurisdiction:** The exercise of federal power to authorize state jurisdiction is usually described as a delegation, with Congress delegating its otherwise preemptive authority over Indian nations to the states. Courts have assumed or concluded, with only limited analysis, that Congress's power over Indian affairs extends to such delegations, even in the face of conflicting treaty provisions. For an in-depth examination of this question, see Ch. 4, Sec. B.3.

5. **Express Exceptions in Public Law 280:** Public Law 280 specifically prohibits application of state law that would alienate, encumber, regulate, or probate Indian or tribal trust or restricted property. 28 U.S.C. § 1360(b). It likewise prevents state jurisdiction over hunting and fishing rights protected by "treaty, agreement, or statute." 18 U.S.C. § 1162(b). Before *Bryan*, the courts gave a broad reading to these restrictions on state authority. Thus, for example, the Ninth Circuit in *Santa Rosa Band of Indians v. Kings County*, 532 F.2d 655 (9th Cir. 1975) stated in a case challenging state and local authority to zone trust lands:

> Relying on the canon of construction applied in favor of Indians, the Court has ruled in different contexts that the word "encumbrance" [in 28 U.S.C. § 1360(b)] is to be broadly construed and is not limited to a burden which hinders alienation of the fee . . . , rather focusing on the effect the challenged state action would have on the value, use and enjoyment of the land. Following the Court's lead, and resolving, as we must, doubts in favor of the Indians, we think that the word as used here may reasonably be interpreted to deny the state the power to apply zoning regulations to trust property.

532 F.2d at 667. Likewise, courts broadly construed the protection for hunting and fishing rights to include rights created by executive orders and Interior Department regulations. *Quechan Tribe v. Rowe*, 350 F. Supp. 106 (S.D. Cal. 1972), *aff'd and remanded*, 531 F.2d 408 (9th Cir. 1976); *Metlakatla Indian Comm. v. Egan*, 369 U.S. 45, 56–57 (1962).

Did *Bryan* and *Cabazon* diminish the significance of these decisions? While courts have had little difficulty characterizing local zoning laws or rent control laws as "regulatory" within the meaning of the Supreme Court's decisions, they have struggled to find the proper characterization of state hunting and fishing laws. *Compare Quechan Indian Tribe v. McMullen*, 984 F.2d 304, 307 (9th Cir. 1993) (characterizing hunting and fishing as a "regulatory scheme" because "a person who wants to hunt or fish merely has to pay a fee and obtain a license"), *with Jones v. State*, 936 P.2d 1263, 1266–67 (Alaska Ct. App. 1997) (calling the state's hunting and fishing laws "prohibitory" because unlicensed acts are outlawed altogether).

Today, because of *Bryan* and *Cabazon*, most interpretive issues surrounding the exception clause of Public Law 280 have been situated in private disputes. When interests in trust property are acknowledged to be the basis for the lawsuit, the proviso clearly operates to bar state jurisdiction. Thus, for example, state jurisdiction under Public Law 280 does not encompass unlawful detainer actions (*i.e.*, evictions), quiet title or ejectment actions, and suits to establish the existence of a state easement where reservation or trust allotments are involved. *See, e.g., All Mission Indian Housing Authority v. Silvas*, 680 F. Supp. 330 (C.D. Ca. 1987). What if the purpose of a private lawsuit is to test whether property is in fact Indian trust or restricted property? For example, in *Boisclair v. Superior Court*, 801 P.2d 305 (Cal. 1990), the California Supreme Court had to decide whether there was state jurisdiction over a declaratory judgment action to affirm a private or public easement for a road across tribal trust land. The plaintiff argued and the tribe denied that the road had lost its trust status. How should courts analyze such cases?

In state court domestic relations lawsuits under Public Law 280, special care is needed to avoid direct or indirect effects on trust property in violation of section 1360(b). Of course, a state court order in a marital dissolution case may not divide trust property belonging to one or both of the spouses. *See Wellman v. Wellman*, 852 P.2d 559, 562–63 (Mont. 1993). More difficult issues arise, however, when the state court seeks to take the value of trust property into account in ordering a property distribution, spousal support, or child support. *See Sheppard v. Sheppard*, 655 P.2d 895 (Idaho 1982). When a divorcing spouse's sole income is from trust property, does section 1360(b) of Public Law 280 allow a state court to base support obligations on that stream? *See In re Marriage of Purnel*, 52 Cal. App. 4th 527 (1997).

6. **Applying *Bryan*'s and *Cabazon*'s Regulatory/Prohibitory Distinction:** When *Cabazon* invoked the criminal prohibitory/civil regulatory distinction, the Court acknowledged that it was not creating a "bright-line rule," and noted that the state laws governing a particular realm of activity would have to be "examined in detail before they can be characterized as regulatory or prohibitory." Nonetheless, the Court expressed some confidence that courts could effectively manage this line-drawing process, pointing to lower federal courts' apparent success in applying a similar distinction under the Assimilative Crimes Act. *See* Ch. 4, Sec. A.3. Subsequent case law, issued largely by state courts, has demonstrated that the Court's confidence was misplaced. For example, some courts have found that state laws restricting sale and use of fireworks are regulatory for purposes of Public Law 280, and others have declared them prohibitory. *Compare Wisconsin v. Cutler*, 527 N.W.2d 400 (Wis. Ct. App. 1994), *with Quechan Indian Tribe v. McMullen*, 984 F.2d 304 (9th Cir. 1993). Courts have also reached conflicting results in deciding whether state laws that address traffic infractions such as speeding, and state laws that penalize driving with a revoked, restricted, or suspended driver's license or without proof of insurance should be treated as regulatory or prohibitory.

In *State v. Stone*, 572 N.W.2d 725 (Minn. 1997), for example, the Minnesota Supreme Court considered whether the state could enforce citations directed at Indians driving on the reservation for no motor vehicle insurance and no proof of insurance, driving with an expired registration, driving without a license, driving with an expired license, speeding, no seat belt, and failure to have a child in a child restraint seat. Quite sensibly, the court realized that it could not resolve the question by asking whether the conduct involved was generally allowed but regulated vs. altogether prohibited, because the answer would depend on which "conduct" was the focus of the analysis. If the relevant conduct was driving, it was surely allowed but regulated. But if the relevant conduct was each form of unlawful driving, then it was absolutely prohibited. To overcome this formalist dilemma, the court offered a pragmatic approach:

> The first step is to determine the focus of the *Cabazon* analysis. The broad conduct will be the focus of the test unless the narrow conduct presents substantially different or heightened public policy concerns. If this is the case, the narrow conduct must be analyzed apart from the broad conduct. After identifying the focus of the *Cabazon* test, the second step is to apply it. If the conduct is generally permitted, subject to exceptions, then the law controlling the conduct is civil/regulatory. If the conduct is generally prohibited, the law is criminal/prohibitory. In making this distinction in close cases, we are aided by *Cabazon*'s "shorthand public policy test," which provides that conduct is criminal if it violates the state's public policy.

> While this shorthand test is helpful, we note that all laws implicate some public policy. Therefore, in light of the purpose of Public Law 280 to combat lawlessness, we interpret "public policy," as used in the *Cabazon* test, to mean public criminal policy. Public criminal policy goes beyond merely promoting the public welfare. It seeks to protect society from serious breaches in the social fabric which threaten grave harm to persons or property. We find the following factors to be useful in determining whether an activity violates the state's public policy in a nature serious enough to be considered "criminal": (1) the extent to which the activity directly threatens physical harm to persons or property or invades the rights of others; (2) the extent to which the law allows for exceptions and exemptions; (3) the blameworthiness of the actor; (4) the nature and severity of the potential penalties for a violation of the law. This list is not meant to be exhaustive, and no single factor is dispositive.

572 N.W.2d at 730.

Applying this approach, the court found that none of the citations in question raised heightened or substantially different public policy concerns as compared to the policy underlying the general scheme of traffic and driving laws — to protect the safety of persons and property on the roadways. The court suggested, however, that other traffic-related laws, such as prohibitions on driving while intoxicated or reckless driving, might be viewed as criminal/prohibitory because their violation creates a greater risk of direct injury to persons and property on the roadways, indicating a heightened public policy concern.

In contrast to the Minnesota approach, in *State v. George*, 905 P.2d 626 (Idaho 1995), the Idaho Supreme Court upheld state citations for failure to stop at a posted stop sign, failure to provide proof of insurance, and speeding, after a tribal member was stopped while driving on the reservation. The driver had insisted that the officer lacked authority, and eventually received citations for obstructing and delaying an officer and resisting arrest as well. Unlike the Minnesota court, the Idaho court focused on whether state law treated traffic violations as criminal in nature, stressing that although such laws were defined as infractions under the state traffic code (which labeled them "civil public offense[s], not constituting a crime"), the state courts had treated them as criminal for purposes of the right to jury trial and double jeopardy protections. Why are courts having so much difficulty applying the regulatory/prohibitory distinction?

The source of these troubles may be some conflicting signals from *Cabazon* itself. First, the Court uses both narrow and broad language to define the distinction between state regulatory and prohibitory laws. The narrower, or more specific, definition provides that "if the state law generally permits the conduct at issue, subject to regulation, it must be classified as civil/regulatory. . . . " The Court then offers a relatively broad definition, stating "[t]he shorthand test is whether the conduct at issue violates the State's public policy. . . . " Because these tests often dictate contrary results, state and lower federal courts applying the regulatory/prohibitory distinction have been able to select the formulation that best supports their desired outcome. Courts that characterize state laws as regulatory usually stress that the conduct in question is a subset of a larger, permissible category of conduct. For example, speeding is a subset of driving, or shooting a deer out of season is a subset of hunting. If the subset of outlawed conduct is small relative to the entire class of activity, then courts are likely to find the state law regulatory. In contrast, courts that find state laws to be prohibitory usually focus on the fact that state "public policy" opposes the specific conduct in question, often losing sight of the fact that "the violation of any statute would in some sense go against the public policy of the state." As one commentator has written,

> Public policy . . . is often used as an excuse for courts that do not want tribes to have exclusive authority, because protecting life and property (public policy) is, to some extent, the purpose of all statutes, whether they be pollution controls, driving regulations, or traditional criminal offenses. Unfortunately, public policy analysis is often used to disguise a court's decision to base a case's outcome on the criminal or regulatory importance of the law to the state and not on the actual criminal or regulatory nature of the specific regulation.

Arthur Foerster, *Divisiveness and Delusion: Public Law 280 and the Evasive Criminal/Regulatory Distinction*, 46 UCLA L. Rev. 1333, 1358 (1999).

How does the Minnesota Supreme Court attempt to avoid a tautological "public policy" analysis in *State v. Stone*? What convinces the Idaho Supreme Court that the traffic laws in *State v. George* are criminal/prohibitory rather than regulatory? Which case, *State v. Stone* or *State v. George*, is more faithful to the reasoning and values of *Bryan* and *Cabazon*? Are the different results attributable to differences between the state laws rather than to differences in the interpretation and application of Supreme Court precedents?

The *Stone* case did not put an end to conflict and confusion in Minnesota over the regulatory/prohibitory distinction. In *State v. Losh*, 755 N.W.2d 736 (Minn. 2008), a divided Minnesota Supreme Court decided that the state law penalizing driving with a revoked license was criminal/prohibitory rather than civil/regulatory for purposes of Public Law 280, at least where the basis for license revocation was "driving while impaired." The same court had previously held that driving with a revoked license was civil/regulatory where the basis for revocation was failure to maintain insurance. Majority and dissent clashed over whether the underlying offense that led to revocation should matter when interpreting the reach of Public Law 280. In particular, they could not agree on whether "heightened public policy concerns" should arise because of the offense that led to revocation, given that the later unlicensed driving might not, itself, create any heightened dangers to the public. According to the dissent, consideration of the underlying offense threatens to create uncertainty and to overextend state jurisdiction: "any offense leading to revocation or cancellation may, depending on the views of the individual judges sitting on this court, seem to raise heightened public safety concerns." Does this exceedingly difficult line-drawing problem suggest the need to amend or repeal Public Law 280? What kind of amendment would help?

7. **Civil Regulatory Laws Versus Private Civil Actions:** A related but separate line-drawing problem presented by Public Law 280 has been the distinction between state judicial proceedings that are regulatory in nature and those that constitute private civil actions. Under *Bryan* and *Cabazon*, only the latter fall within Public Law 280's grant of civil authority. As with the regulatory/prohibitory distinction, courts have struggled with this regulatory/private civil action dichotomy. The dividing line is inevitably obscure, because adjudication of civil controversies normally entails the application of a body of legal rules that regulate private conduct. Furthermore, some state regulation reflects public refinement or incorporation of private actions, such as nuisance. If a state court could apply, for example, common law nuisance doctrine, does it make sense to bar the use of environmental protection statutes?

Some of the most confounding cases have been those initiated by state or local government entities and implicating state services: civil commitment proceedings brought by mental health agencies; petitions by social services agencies to terminate parental rights; and suits by counties on behalf of children against their noncustodial parent to establish paternity, collect reimbursement for state welfare payments, and obtain future support. Courts have had to assess whether the civil suit is handmaiden to an essentially regulatory proceeding, or whether it is more akin to a private lawsuit.

For example, in suits by local governments to obtain reimbursement for welfare payments, courts in different Public Law 280 states have arrived at opposite conclusions regarding the proper characterization of these matters as regulatory or civil actions, and hence the existence of state jurisdiction. Courts that have found the proceedings to be regulatory have stressed the "public, regulatory character" of the agency acting to recoup the welfare payments and obtain support orders; the extent of state interest in and control over the proceeding; and the resemblance between the collection scheme and taxation because of assessment of collection charges. *E.g., State Department of Human Services v. Whitebreast*, 409 N.W.2d 460, 463–64 (Iowa 1987). Courts resolving this issue in favor of state jurisdiction have pointed out that "the test should be one of substance rather than form," meaning that the presence of a government party should not automatically transform the action into a regulatory matter if the suit is essentially a suit on behalf of a private party. *E.g., County of Inyo v. Jeff*, 227 Cal. App. 3d 487, 494–95 (1991); *Becker County Welfare Department v. Bellcourt*, 453 N.W.2d 543 (Minn. Ct. App. 1990). These same courts have dismissed as irrelevant the existence of additional administrative methods for collecting child support, and analogize collection charges to ordinary court costs for private parties. Finally, the courts that have allowed such suits in state court under Public Law 280 have noted the absence of tribal courts with jurisdiction over child support cases, a consideration that should have no bearing on the delegation issue. Is it surprising that states shouldering the burden of federal obligations to provide services to reservation Indians are disposed to assert jurisdiction over associated matters so long as no tribal court or other appropriate tribal forum exists? What is the explanation for the absence of formal tribal dispute resolution mechanisms under these circumstances?

In a similar vein, the Wisconsin Supreme Court has considered the absence of a tribal forum in deciding to assume Public Law 280 jurisdiction over state civil actions for commitment of sexually violent persons. *State v. Burgess*, 665 N.W.2d 124 (Wis. 2003). In finding that the proceeding was a civil adjudication rather than an exercise of regulatory power, the court focused on a law review article that the *Bryan* court referenced, in which the authors claimed that Public Law 280's civil jurisdiction provision directed application of state laws having to do with "private rights and status," and therefore includes areas such as " 'contract, tort, marriage, divorce, insanity, descent, etc., but would not include laws . . . such as the power to tax, grant franchises, etc.' " *Bryan*, 426 U.S. at 384 n.10 (quoting Israel & Smithson, *Indian Taxation, Tribal Sovereignty and Economic Development*, 49 N.D. L. Rev. 267, 296 (1973)). The Wisconsin Court concluded that the adjudication of an individual as a sexually violent person is a status determination, "which is more similar to adjudications like those involving insanity, rather than regulations such as the power to tax. Furthermore, the tribal court in this case declined to accept jurisdiction because the Lac du Flambeau Tribe had not yet passed an ordinance regarding the commitment of sexually violent persons."

Following the Wisconsin Supreme Court's decision, Burgess petitioned for federal habeas corpus, raising the same argument that the involuntary commitment proceeding for sexually violent persons was regulatory, and therefore outside the state's civil jurisdiction under Public Law 280. While the Seventh Circuit found Burgess's position "certainly reasonable" as an interpretation of *Bryan*, it concluded that the opposing view — that state-initiated proceedings to determine personal status qualified as adjudicative rather than regulatory — also had some reasonable support. *Burgess v. Watters*, 467 F.3d 676 (7th Cir. 2006). Under current law, habeas corpus relief is available only when the underlying conviction was based on an "unreasonable application of, clearly established Federal law." 28 U.S.C. § 2254. Habeas corpus was therefore denied. Minnesota's Supreme Court has followed the path of *Burgess*, finding that state involuntary commitment proceedings for sexually dangerous offenders are authorized by Public Law 280 as "civil proceedings" to adjudicate the status of individuals. *In re Civil Commitment of Johnson*, 800 N.W.2d 134 (Minn. 2011).

There is no neat, precise way to separate regulatory matters from private civil suits for purposes of Public Law 280. Under these circumstances, what role, if any, should the canons of construction play? Taking the canons into account, the Wisconsin Attorney General has determined that suits brought by state agencies to terminate parental rights are regulatory. 70 Op. Wisc. Att'y Gen. 237 (1981). In contrast, the Ninth Circuit has held that these proceedings are civil actions adjusting children's status, despite the heavy involvement of agency officials in regulating parental conduct. *Doe v. Mann*, 415 F.3d 1038 (9th Cir. 2005). The opinion construes Public Law 280 in light of the Indian Child Welfare Act, which Congress passed 25 years *after* Public Law 280, and exhibits a cavalier attitude toward the Indian law canons of construction. Most remarkably, it uses a questionable reading of the Indian Child Welfare Act, a statute that was designed to curtail state power over such proceedings, to justify a broad reading of state power under Public Law 280. *See* Sec. C, this chapter.

8. **Recent Extension of Public Law 280 Through the Adam Walsh Act:** Despite language in the 1968 Indian Civil Rights Act stating that future extensions of Public Law 280 jurisdiction should occur only with tribal consent, Congress broadened the scope of state jurisdiction in 2006 with passage of the Adam Walsh Child Protection and Safety Act, 42 U.S.C. § 16901. The Act requires states to establish and maintain sex offender registries, imposing substantial burdens on individuals convicted of a broad range of offenses. Sex offenders covered by the Act must maintain their registration in all of the jurisdictions where they reside, work, and attend school. Tribes other than those covered by mandatory Public Law 280 jurisdiction may elect whether to maintain registries of their own, or to delegate that authority to their respective states. But mandatory Public Law 280 tribes are denied that choice, and must accept state jurisdiction over registration of sex offenders living, working, or attending school within their territory. Is sex offender registration a civil regulatory matter, and therefore outside the states' ordinary Public Law 280 jurisdiction? Is the Adam Walsh Act thus an expansion of state jurisdiction for the mandatory tribes? For a ruling that a state sex offender registration law is criminal/prohibitory rather than civil regulatory, see *State v. Jones*, 729 N.W.2d 1 (Minn. 2007). In enacting the Public Law 280 provision of the Adam Walsh Act, was Congress disregarding the spirit of the 1968 amendments to Public Law 280, or was it taking a practical step in light of the reduced law enforcement capability of some Public Law 280 tribes? See Sec. A.4, this chapter.

3. Concurrent Tribal and State Jurisdiction Under Public Law 280

Reread *Walker v. Rushing*, set forth in Ch. 4, Sec. A.3.c and *Teague v. Bad River Band of Lake Superior Tribe of Chippewa Indians*, set forth in Ch. 4, Sec. B.4.a. Both cases involve situations where tribal and state jurisdiction overlap under Public Law 280. In *Walker v. Rushing*, the concurrent jurisdiction in criminal, and in *Teague* the concurrent jurisdiction is civil.

NOTES

1. **Tribal Courts and Law Enforcement in Public Law 280 States:** *Walker v. Rushing* and *Teague* reflect a wide consensus among federal, state, and tribal courts, as well as several state attorneys general, the Solicitor for the Department of Interior, and scholars, that Indian nations retain concurrent jurisdiction in Public Law 280 states. *See, e.g.,* 70 Op. Att'y Gen. Wisc. 237, 243 (1981) (child welfare matters); Op. Att'y Gen. Neb. No. 48 (1985); Opinion of Solicitor of the Department of the Interior M36907, Nov. 14, 1978; Carole Goldberg-Ambrose & Timothy Carr Seward, *Tribal Courts in California: Hope for the Future, in* Carole Goldberg-Ambrose, Planting Tail Feathers: Public Law 280 and Tribal Survival (1997); Vanessa J. Jimenez & Soo C. Song, *Concurrent Tribal and State Jurisdiction Under Public Law 280*, 47 Am. U. L. Rev. 1627 (1998).

This landslide of authority in support of concurrent tribal jurisdiction is relatively recent, however. Previously, many Public Law 280 states, especially California, vigorously resisted the claim that Indian nations retained their inherent jurisdiction under the statute. Moreover, the federal government used Public Law 280 as an excuse for declining to distribute federal funds for development of tribal courts and law enforcement to Indian nations in those states. The position of the Department of the Interior was that state law enforcement and court systems could manage reservation needs. Consequently, in the 1970s and 1980s, when many Indian nations in non-Public Law 280 states were using these funds to build court systems that could repel state incursions and cultivate their own legal traditions and values, tribes in Public Law 280 states were unable to participate. As a consequence, Public Law 280 tribes lagged behind in the development of tribal police, judicial, and detention institutions. Meanwhile, tribes continued to complain that they were not receiving adequate or fair law enforcement and criminal justice from state and local authorities. *See* Duane Champagne & Carole Goldberg, A Second Century of Dishonor: Federal Inequities and California Tribes (1996), *available at* http://www.aisc.ucla.edu/ca/Tribes.htm; Duane Champagne & Carole Goldberg, Captured Justice: Native Nations and Public Law 280 at 67–111 (2011).

If Public Law 280 did not eliminate tribal jurisdiction, does the federal government's past policy with respect to tribal courts in Public Law 280 states comport with the federal trust responsibility? If not, what legal remedy, if any, is available to Indian nations in states such as California? The Los Coyotes Band of Cahuilla and Cupeño Indians in California requested that the Bureau of Indian Affairs enter a contract for its Law Enforcement Services Program under the Indian Self-Determination Act of 1975 (ISDA), commonly known as a 638 contract. According to evidence later presented by the Tribe, its 40,000-acre reservation is secluded and hilly, and has been the site of murders, theft, serious drug offenses, and other violent and non-violent crimes. The sole full-time tribal officer who patrols the reservation "is often asked to pay for training and equipment out of his own pocket. Moreover, the inability of the County Sheriff's office to pay overtime limits its officers' ability to respond and investigate crimes on the reservation. Tribal members report that they often wait up to two hours for a sheriff's officer to respond to a call." *Los Coyotes Band of Cahuilla & Cupeño Indians v. Jewell*, 729 F.3d 1025, 1032 (9th Cir. 2013). The BIA refused to contract with the Tribe, stating that the "amount of money that the BIA's Office of Justice Services spends in

California for law enforcement services is zero . . . . The principal reason for this is that, as you know, California is a [Public Law] 280 state, and so the cost of law enforcement on Indian reservations is borne by the State, not the BIA." (Letter from BIA to the Tribe, quoted in *Los Coyotes* at 1034.) In its *Los Coyotes* opinion, the Ninth Circuit upheld the BIA's decision, finding that the ISDA does not require a 638 contract where the BIA has decided not to provide any funds for a law enforcement program of its own. The Indian Law and Order Commission, discussed in Ch. 4, Sec. A.3.a, has condemned the BIA's position, recommending parity of federal funding for all tribal courts and law enforcement systems, regardless of Public Law 280 status. *See* INDIAN LAW AND ORDER COMMISSION, A ROADMAP FOR MAKING NATIVE AMERICA SAFER 71 (November 2013).

What recourse does Los Coyotes have at this point? The Ninth Circuit pointed out that section 221 of the Tribal Law and Order Act of 2010, amending 18 U.S.C. § 1161 and 25 U.S.C. § 1321, authorized Public Law 280 tribes to request reinstatement of federal Indian country criminal jurisdiction under 18 U.S.C. §§ 1152 and 1153. The Attorney General is allowed to accept or deny the request. Where such a request is granted, state jurisdiction remains, so there is three-way concurrent criminal jurisdiction — tribal, state, and federal. Although this provision does not achieve retrocession of state criminal jurisdiction under Public Law 280, it does open the possibility of greater tribal deputization under special BIA commissions to conduct federal law enforcement activities. It also may make it easier for tribes to argue in favor of retrocession in the future, at least if the federal government is already assuming significant law enforcement and criminal justice responsibility. Finally, it may provide a partial remedy where tribes have difficulty securing adequate law enforcement and prosecutorial services from state and local governments. The Tribal Law and Order Act also makes it clear that state duties to provide such services to Indian country under Public Law 280 are not diminished. The Department of Justice has issued a final rule establishing procedures for Indian tribes in Public Law 280 states to request that the U.S. accept concurrent criminal jurisdiction within the tribe's Indian country, and providing that the Attorney General's office may decide whether to consent to such a request. 28 C.F.R. Part 50, published at 76 Fed. Reg. 76037. At least one Public Law 280 tribe, White Earth in Minnesota, has succeeded in adding federal Indian country criminal jurisdiction. Given the difficulties that non-Public Law 280 tribes have experienced with federal prosecutors declining to pursue criminal matters in Indian country (see Ch. 4, Sec. A.3), how much confidence should a tribe like Los Coyotes have in a federal solution to their community safety issues?

Without waiting for a change in BIA policy or the questionable benefits of concurrent federal jurisdiction, many Public Law 280 tribes have realized that tribal courts are an essential element of their sovereignty. Using funds from economic development enterprises such as gaming, from federal self-governance programs, and from recent United States Department of Justice technical assistance programs, they have begun to establish their own law enforcement and court systems. Today, a growing number of the more than 100 federally recognized Indian nations in California operate tribal courts, among them the Hoopa Valley Tribe, the Karuk Tribe, the San Manuel Band of Mission Indians, and the dozen tribes participating in the Intertribal Court of Southern California. Tribal courts can be found in other parts of Indian country affected by Public Law 280 as well, including the Stockbridge-Munsee and Ho-Chunk reservations in Wisconsin and the Shakopee Sioux in Minnesota.

While the exercise of concurrent tribal jurisdiction can partially overcome deficiencies in state criminal justice, it often does not go far enough. First, tribal governments lack criminal jurisdiction over most non-Indian offenders. Second, because of the sentencing limits in the Indian Civil Rights Act, tribes often cannot take sufficient effective action against serious offenders. Third, as explained above, some tribes cannot secure adequate funding to carry out comprehensive criminal jurisdiction. Thus, some tribes have entered into cooperative agreements with counties whereby tribal police receive authority to make arrests under state law. Prosecution is then carried out by state authorities. For example, one Public Law 280 state, Minnesota, enacted a law encouraging such agreements where a tribe's officers meet state certification requirements and the tribe agrees to waive its sovereign immunity with respect to claims arising from actions of their officers. Minn. Stat. § 626.93(2). The statute is careful to emphasize that it does not alter or expand either state or tribal criminal jurisdiction. In a case where a tribal police officer arrested a tribal member for violating state law, the Supreme Court of Minnesota upheld the statute, rejecting claims that it contravened Public Law 280. *State v. Manypenny*, 662 N.W.2d 183 (Minn. 2003). How would you argue that Public Law 280 preempts these agreements and their authorizing statute? Does such an argument depend for its success on an interpretation of Public Law 280 as vesting exclusive jurisdiction in the designated states? Some states, such as Oregon, have gone even further, enacting statutes that confer state "peace officer" status on appropriately trained tribal police, without the need to establish a cross-deputization agreement with the state. See Oregon Rev. Stat. § 801.395. Under what conditions could such arrangements meet tribal needs for safety, fairness, and cultural compatibility of justice? Is there something inherently wrong with a tribe paying for law enforcement when the state has an obligation under Public Law 280 to provide it?

2.   **Tribal-State Court Relations Under Conditions of Concurrent Jurisdiction:** The recent consensus about concurrent tribal and state jurisdiction under Public Law 280 has left both sets of courts and law enforcement officers with the task of developing principles of coexistence and comity. Intergovernmental agreements can be very helpful in anticipating and resolving potential areas of conflict, both for civil and criminal matters. What kinds of provisions would you want to include in such an agreement if you were representing an Indian nation affected by Public Law 280? A state or local government? The material that follows addresses the legal doctrines that will apply in civil matters in the absence of intergovernmental agreements. The interplay of concurrent tribal and state criminal jurisdiction in Public Law 280 states, including double jeopardy issues, is addressed in the Notes following *Walker v. Rushing* in Ch. 4, Sec. A.3.c.

In civil cases, concurrent tribal and state jurisdiction under Public Law 280 leads to the possibility of each disputant racing to litigate to judgment in the forum of choice. One incentive for such behavior is that state and tribal courts with concurrent jurisdiction might choose to apply different bodies of law to the same dispute. State courts are directed to apply tribal law, but only if that law does not conflict with the law of the state. 25 U.S.C. § 1360(c). And nothing in Public Law 280 requires tribal courts to apply state law. If each sovereign is under some obligation to respect the judgments of the other (*see* Ch. 3, Sec. E), then the first forum to reach a judgment will determine the outcome, regardless of the duration or extent of completion of the parallel proceeding. If the sovereigns do not view themselves as under any compulsion to respect one another's judgments, then the litigants may be subjected to conflicting and mutually inconsistent orders.

The *Teague* case is illustrative. Recall that the *Teague* court expressed its preference for a process whereby the courts of states and Indian nations would establish protocols to govern situations of overlapping jurisdiction, much as federal and state judges have done for matters within their concurrent jurisdiction. Another route to avoiding conflicts would be to borrow a legal doctrine developed for situations of concurrent tribal and federal jurisdiction, the requirement of exhaustion of tribal remedies. *See* Ch. 4, Sec. A.4.b.

In *Drumm v. Brown*, 716 A.2d 50 (Conn. 1998), state police officers formerly assigned to a tribal casino and a casino security officer sued the tribe and several tribal officials, alleging infliction of emotional distress, defamation, and interference with contractual relations, among other claims. According to the complaint, defendants had attempted to interfere with plaintiffs' investigation of certain casino break-ins. Defendants argued that the plaintiffs should be required to exhaust their tribal remedies before bringing their state court action under the state's version of Public Law 280. After the state trial court agreed with defendants that tribal exhaustion was required and dismissed the suit, plaintiffs filed their same action in tribal court. The Connecticut Supreme Court concluded that exhaustion was required, "superseding the general obligation upon our courts to exercise their jurisdiction," but only if a tribal lawsuit is pending at the time the state action is filed. Since two defendants had filed such an action, exhaustion would be mandatory "absent satisfaction of one of a narrow set of exceptions. . . . " The court concluded further that those exceptions were inapplicable "when both the tribal and state court proceedings have been initiated by the same party or parties."

The federal exhaustion doctrine is designed to avoid interference with Indian nations' self-government and to afford federal courts the benefits of tribal consideration of matters within the tribes' realm of special expertise. As the *Drumm* court points out, this doctrine may well embody a federal common law of deference to tribal courts that binds state along with federal courts. Even if the doctrine is not binding on state courts as a matter of federal common law, however, the same considerations of comity and efficiency that animate the federal exhaustion doctrine counsel in favor of state courts establishing an identical rule of deference.

A growing number of state courts have embraced such an exhaustion doctrine, requiring plaintiffs to bring their claims to tribal court even though the state may possess concurrent jurisdiction under Public Law 280. Most of the state cases adopting the exhaustion doctrine, like *Drumm*, have involved suits against tribal entities or officers, with attendant issues of sovereign immunity and privilege. *See, e.g., Cohen v. Little Six, Inc.*, 543 N.W.2d 376, 381 n.3 (Minn. Ct. App. 1996), *aff'd*, 561 N.W.2d 889 (Minn. 1997). Exhaustion in the name of respect for tribal self-government is particularly appropriate in such cases. Should the exhaustion doctrine be applied to private lawsuits as well? A few state courts have answered "no." *McCrea v. Denison*, 885 P.2d 856 (Wash. Ct. App. 1994); *Nenana Fuel Co. Inc. v. Native Village of Venetie*, 834 P.2d 1229 (Alaska 1992). Is there good reason to distinguish purely private suits from suits involving tribal officials?

Through amendment to Public Law 280, Congress could legislate a priority for tribal courts where concurrent state/tribal jurisdiction exists. For example, it could require removal or transfer of suits against tribes or tribal officers from state to tribal court. A model for such legislation can be found in the Indian Child Welfare Act, and is discussed in Sec. C.4, this chapter. Would such an amendment be advisable?

4. Practical Effects and the Future of Public Law 280

In 1974, Wendell Chino, then President of the National Congress of American Indians, had this to say about Public Law 280:

> Public Law 280 . . . as far as the American Indians are concerned it is a despicable law. Public Law 280 if it is not amended, will destroy Indian self-government and result in further loss of Indian lands. On those reservations where states have assumed jurisdiction under the provisions of Public Law 280, lawlessness and crimes have substantially increased and have become known as a no man's land because the state and federal officials will not assume the responsibility of Public Law 280.

Despite this complaint and others, in the 50 years following passage of Public Law 280, the federal government made no serious effort to assess the availability and effectiveness of state jurisdiction under Public Law 280. Finally, the National Institute of Justice, the research arm of the U.S. Department of Justice, funded a major study of policing and the criminal process as they operate on Public Law 280 reservations. The results of this study have been published as DUANE CHAMPAGNE & CAROLE GOLDBERG, CAPTURED JUSTICE: NATIVE NATIONS AND PUBLIC LAW 280 (2011). Champagne and Goldberg gathered qualitative and quantitative data from seventeen reservation sites, including those subject to Public Law 280, those not subject to Public Law 280, and some that operated under both regimes because they straddled state lines. The results show that reservation residents in Public Law 280 jurisdictions rate the availability and quality of law enforcement and criminal justice lower than reservation residents in non-Public Law 280 jurisdiction. The results also support the view that "when tribal governments and federal and county-state governments are more cooperative or share decision-making authority, criminal justice is more effectively administered." *Id.* at 199. Furthermore, the study revealed widespread support for retrocession among reservation residents in Public Law 280 jurisdictions, at least if federal support were available for development and expansion of tribal policing and criminal justice agencies. Among those tribes that had effected retrocession, satisfaction levels were high. For further reading on the effects of Public Law 280 on income level and rates of crime in Indian Country, *see also* Valentina Dimtrova-Grajzl, Peter Grajzl & A. Joseph Guse, *Jurisdiction, Crime, and Development: The Impact of Public Law 280 in Indian Country*, 48 LAW AND SOC'Y REV. 127 (2014).

NOTE ON THE FUTURE OF PUBLIC LAW 280

Professor Robert B. Porter, former Attorney General of the Seneca Nation of Indians, in an article entitled *A Proposal to the Hanodaganyas to Decolonize Federal Indian Control Law*, 31 U. Mich. J.L. Reform 899, 955–56 (1998), has urged total repeal of Public Law 280 and other federal laws that imposed state jurisdiction on reservations without tribal consent. He writes,

> [T]ribal justice systems would be strengthened, and others might be encouraged to do the same, if state criminal justice systems did not have concurrent criminal jurisdiction. Similarly, tribal courts would be strengthened by eliminating state civil adjudicatory jurisdiction and not having to compete with the state courts over matters involving reservation Indians or arising within Indian country. I have seen firsthand how concurrent state court jurisdiction can undermine the tribal courts and can assure you that access to the state courts undermines tribal sovereignty. . . .

As alternative to repeal, Congress could amend Public Law 280 to allow Indian nations to initiate retrocession. A provision of this sort was included in the Indian Child Welfare Act of 1978, allowing Indian nations to petition for reassumption of exclusive jurisdiction over certain child custody matters. *See* 25 U.S.C. § 1918; Sec. C, this chapter. The report of the Indian Law and Order Commission, discussed in Ch. 4, Sec. A, recommends that Congress amend Public Law 280 and similar laws to allow tribes to remove themselves from state jurisdiction. *See* Indian Law and Order Commission, A Roadmap for Making Native America Safer 23–27 (November 2013).

If you were asked to advise an Indian nation in a Public Law 280 state about its policy agenda, which alternative would you recommend? What are the advantages and disadvantages for Indian nations of repeal versus amendment to make it more like the Indian Child Welfare Act?

B. UNIQUE TRIBAL-FEDERAL RELATIONSHIPS

1. Alaska

The term "Alaska Natives" encompasses three distinct groups of Native peoples, historically understood as "Indian, Eskimo, and Aleut." *See generally*, David S. Case and David A. Voluck, Alaska Natives and American Laws (2nd ed. 2002). The term "Eskimo" encompasses the Inuit, Inupiat, and Yupik peoples. The term "Indian" encompasses the Tlingit, Haida, and Athabascan peoples. Although these groups are ethnically distinct, federal law has long treated all as "Indians" for purposes of federal Indian policy. *See, e.g.*, 53 Interior Decisions 593 (1932). Today, these various Native peoples are organized into a complex array of communities and political organizations, due to the unique legal structure established by the Alaska Native Claims Settlement Act of 1971 (ANCSA), codified at 43 U.S.C. § 1601 et seq., as well as the unique history that characterizes Alaska.

Russia was the first non-Indigenous nation to colonize the territory that makes up Alaska today, but that nation only established two permanent settlements, at

Kodiak and Sitka. The United States purchased Russia's interests in Alaska from Russia in an 1867 Treaty. The United States did not make treaties with Alaska Natives, although it did establish certain reservations by executive order. However, Alaska Natives held aboriginal use and occupancy rights similar to those of other Native groups. *See Tee-Hit-Ton Indians v. United States*, 348 U.S. 272 (1955), presented and discussed in Ch. 6 Sec. A.1. The 1958 Act that admitted Alaska to statehood set the stage for legislative action regarding Native land claims. On the one hand, the Act provided that "all right and title . . . to any lands or other property (including fishing rights), the right or title to which may be held by any Indians, Eskimos, or Aleuts . . . or is held by the United States in trust for said natives . . . shall be and remain under the absolute jurisdiction and control of the United States until disposed of under its authority, except to such extent as the Congress has prescribed or may hereafter prescribe." This language was incorporated into the Alaska State Constitution. Section 6(b) of the Act, however, granted the State of Alaska the right to select 102.5 million acres of land from the "vacant, unappropriated and unreserved" public lands within the boundaries of the state. Native groups protested the state's attempt to claim public lands that were rich in natural resources, including oil and gas, but still subject to unextinguished aboriginal title interests. In 1969, Secretary of Interior Stewart Udall imposed a freeze upon the processing of these applications, pending settlement of Native lands claims. The incentive to settle the Native land claims increased when oil companies holding leases in Prudhoe Bay sought a right of way to serve the proposed Trans-Alaska Pipeline. Several of the affected Native villages objected, leading a federal court to enjoin construction of the pipeline until the Native land claims could be settled. This led to the enactment of ANCSA.

a.   The Alaska Native Claims Settlement Act of 1971 (ANCSA)

ANCSA disclaimed a trust model of protection for Native peoples and resources, in favor of a market-based system of corporate land ownership. The federal act expressly abolished all but one of the existing reservations in Alaska (the Metlakatla Indian Community Annette Island Reserve) and implemented the settlement "without establishing any "permanent racially defined institutions, rights, privileges, or obligations, without creating a reservation system or lengthy wardship or trusteeship, and without adding to the categories of property and institutions enjoying special tax privileges." 43 U.S.C. § 1601(b). This new business-oriented model of tribal autonomy was intended to free Alaska Natives from the bureaucratic control of the federal government. In fact, however, it also stripped these Native communities of many federal protections for tribal sovereignty and land.

True to its intended purpose, ANCSA extinguished all aboriginal title rights in over 360 million acres of land within Alaska. 43 U.S.C. § 1603(1). Because many Native Alaskans practice traditional subsistence-based lifeways, the failure to protect their aboriginal hunting and fishing resources caused tremendous hardships for affected communities. In 1980, Congress enacted the Alaska National Interest Lands Conservation Act (ANILCA) to remedy the problems. In keeping with the racially "neutral" theme of ANCSA, ANILCA grants a statutory preference for "rural Alaska residents" to engage in subsistence uses on public lands, although it was clearly directed toward the protection of Native peoples engaged in subsistence lifeways. The statute expressly acknowledges that "the continuation of the opportunity for subsistence uses by rural residents of Alaska . . . is essential to Native physical, economic, traditional, and cultural existence." 16 U.S.C. § 3111(1). *See* NELL JESSUP NEWTON ET AL., COHEN'S HANDBOOK OF FEDERAL INDIAN LAW 345 (2012 ed.).

In exchange for giving up their aboriginal title claims, ANCSA awarded Alaska Natives fee title to over 40 million acres of land, federal payments of $462.5 million over an eleven-year period, and a royalty of 2% to a ceiling of $500 million on mineral development in Alaska. To manage these resources, ANCSA created thirteen "regional" corporations and more than 200 village corporations, which are incorporated under state law. The villages were eligible to receive fee patents to land in the vicinity of their villages. The regional corporations retain ownership of other lands as well as the legal interest in the subsurface estate of the village lands. They also participate in a scheme of revenue-sharing. Membership in the regional corporations and village corporations depends upon a complex set of rules and initially was intended to minimize the shares of "afterborn" generations, who could only take by inheritance. This provision was ultimately changed by a statutory amendment, as the plan was to open ownership to non-Natives after 20 years. In 1988, Congress passed the "1991 amendments," which allowed the corporations to retain decisionary control over these issues and amend their articles and by-laws accordingly. To date, no corporation has elected to make its stock alienable. In addition, the statutory amendments indefinitely extended the property tax exemptions for lands conveyed to Natives and Native corporations, unless the land is developed or leased. The amendments also prevented the seizure of undeveloped Native corporation lands by creditors, adverse possession, or bankruptcy or other involuntary proceedings.

Although Congress may have intended ANCSA to assimilate the traditional Native governments to a corporate structure, Alaska Natives have steadfastly held to their traditional governance systems. Nothing in ANCSA required the dissolution of tribal governments and the tribal governments continued to exist alongside the new corporations. Tribal governments maintain their inherent sovereign powers of self-government. The regional and village corporations, however, are chartered under state law to perform proprietary, rather than governmental, functions. Today, there are more than 200 federally recognized Alaska Native tribes. About 150 of these maintain traditional governments. The rest have organized under the IRA and maintain tribal councils according to that model. In 1993, the Department of the Interior clarified in its revised list of federally-recognized tribes that "the villages and regional tribes listed . . . are distinctly Native communities and have the same status as tribes in the contiguous 48 states." 58 Fed. Reg. 54,364, 54,365; *see also* 58 Fed. Reg. 54,368.

NOTES ON THE ALASKA NATIVE CLAIMS SETTLEMENT ACT

1. **ANCSA as a Treaty Substitute:** ANCSA has been described as a "treaty substitute." CHARLES F. WILKINSON, AMERICAN INDIANS, TIME, AND THE LAW 8 (1987). Implicit in this characterization is a portrayal of ANCSA as the result of negotiations between Alaska Natives and the United States. In what respects does ANCSA resemble a treaty? What kind of prior review or approval process would have to take place within the affected Native villages or representative organizations before the Act could fairly be called "bilateral"? ANCSA's process was criticized by some Native leaders as reflecting the United States's historic tendency to negotiate with certain individuals or groups that would be receptive to U.S. interests, rather than truly engaging all of the official tribal organizations. *See* THOMAS R. BERGER, VILLAGE JOURNEY: THE REPORT OF THE ALASKA NATIVE REVIEW COMMISSION 118–19 (1985). Referring back to the discussion in Chapter 1, what models of the tribal-federal relationship are reflected by ANCSA?

2. **ANCSA as a Model for Federal Indian Policy?** ANCSA squarely poses the question whether the "survival" of Native nations depends upon maintenance of separate Native governing institutions and landbases. ANCSA's corporate model of landholding and governance has posed significant challenges for the persistence of tribal sovereignty, including the taxation issue posed in the *Venetie* case, presented in Ch. 2, Sec. A.3.b.ii. Some commentators have queried whether ANCSA's focus on economic self-sufficiency, development of natural resources, and capitalist institutions was an exercise in "self-determination" or "termination." *See, e.g.*, Comment, *The Alaska Native Claims Settlement Act: An Illusion in the Quest for Self-Determination*, 66 OR. L. REV. 185, 211–14 (1987); Arthur Lazarus Jr. & W. Richard West Jr., *The Alaska Native Claims Settlement Act: A Flawed Victory*, 40 LAW & CONTEMP. PROBS. 132 (1976). How well did ANCSA integrate the existing cultural norms and political structures of Alaska Native communities with the federal government's goals and purposes? Is ANCSA a template for future domestic policy with respect to Native nations? Does its regime comport with evolving international standards of indigenous peoples' rights?

3. **Alaska Native Subsistence Rights and Alaska National Interest Lands Conservation Act:** ANILCA gives a statutory preference to "rural Alaska residents" who engage in subsistence uses on public lands. While it was clearly directed toward the protection of Native peoples, the statute utilizes "race-neutral" language. Congress initially anticipated that the state would regulate all lands within its jurisdiction and would also assume regulatory jurisdiction over subsistence uses on federal lands, in accordance with ANILCA's requirements. Thus, ANILCA authorized the state to assume active regulatory authority so long as state law provided for the same definition, preference, and priorities established in the federal Act. 16 U.S.C. § 3115(d). ANILCA also allowed claimants to bring a suit in federal court to enforce the subsistence priority if the state or federal government violated ANILCA's statutory provisions. 16 U.S.C. § 3117. The State of Alaska assumed management responsibility in 1982, when it was certified to have the requisite definition, preference, and participation required under ANILCA. *See Bobby v. Alaska*, 718 F. Supp. 764, 788 (D. Alaska 1989). However, subsequent

litigation in the state Supreme Court highlighted tensions between the federal law and the state constitution. Ultimately, the Alaska Supreme Court ruled in *McDowell v. Alaska*, 785 P.2d 1 (Alaska 1989), that the equal access provisions of the state constitution barred the state legislature from creating a "rural" priority for subsistence uses.

Following this opinion, and in the wake of a series of federal cases finding the State of Alaska in violation of ANILCA, the federal government assumed management of all subsistence uses on public lands within the State of Alaska. *See* 55 Fed. Reg. 23,522 (June 8, 1990). The current conflicts over federal management largely concern the geographic scope of "public lands." COHEN'S HANDBOOK OF FEDERAL INDIAN LAW, *supra*, 350–51. The federal government has asserted authority over all "federally owned uplands and waters subject to a federal reserved water right." *Id.* The regulations, however, do not define "public lands" to include Native allotments, or waters within or adjacent to those allotments. 64 Fed. Reg. 1279 (Jan. 8, 1999). Moreover, the United States Supreme Court has held that the outer continental shelf is not within Alaska's boundary, as defined by ANILCA, and therefore, the Secretary had no duty to evaluate the impacts of oil and gas leasing on the outer continental shelf on Native subsistence uses. *See Amoco Production Co. v. Village of Gambell*, 480 U.S. 531 (1987). Further constraining Native rights, the Ninth Circuit, sitting en banc, recently found that several Alaska Native villages had failed to meet their burden of proving by a preponderance of the evidence that they had an aboriginal right to engage in subsistence fishing within the outer continental shelf. *Native Village of Eyak v. Blank*, 688 F.3d 619 (9th Cir. 2012). The court perceived their aboriginal use of the area as "intermittent" and "opportunistic," and therefore found that the Native villages could not prove that they exercised exclusive control of the area they claimed.

More favorably for Alaska Natives, in *John v. U.S.*, the Ninth Circuit has upheld the 1999 Final Rules against both a challenge from the State of Alaska seeking to limit the application of the federal reserved water rights doctrine, and a challenge from tribes and inter-tribal groups. The tribal litigants asserted that the Secretaries should have categorically designated the waters appurtenant to all Alaska Native allotments as "public lands" subject to ANILCA's rural subsistence priority. Without deciding whether Alaska Native allotments can give rise to federal reserved water rights, the court held that:

> the Secretaries reasonably decided to resolve this difficult issue on a case by case basis. We uphold the 1999 Rules, and affirm the district court's conclusion that it was "lawful and reasonable" for the Secretaries to delegate authority to the Federal Subsistence Board to decide which Native allotments falling outside of federal reservations, if any, give rise to federal reserved water rights which justify imposing ANILCA's rural subsistence priority on appurtenant waters. Ultimately, the court refused to expand or limit the doctrine, and stated that "reserved water rights for Alaska Native Settlement allotments are best determined on a case-by-case basis."

John v. United States, 720 F.3d 1214, 1244 (9th Cir. 2013). The court thus deferred to the Secretaries' approach to identify federal reserved water rights for Alaska

Native settlement allotments, though it encouraged them to undertake the "process in a reasonably efficient manner." *Id.* Thus, the federal government will continue to have control over Native subsistence uses in much of rural Alaska, at least until such time as Alaska may choose to amend its constitution to include a Native preference.

4. Change in Land into Trust Policy in Alaska: After Congress passed ANCSA in 1971, the Native Village of Venetie asked the federal government to return its former reservation land, converted into fee land by ANCSA, to trust status. In a 1978 legal opinion to the Assistant Secretary of Indian Affairs about the request, a DOI official wrote that ANCSA evidenced Congress's intent to "permanently remove all Native lands in Alaska from trust status." *Quoted in* Land Acquisitions in the State of Alaska, 79 Fed. Reg. 24648, 24649 (2014). Following this memo, DOI promulgated regulations that prohibited land into trust in Alaska, except for the Metlakatla Indian Community. *See* 25 C.F.R. § 151.1. In the following decades, DOI continued to follow this policy, refusing to take land into trust on behalf of Alaska Natives. Alaska Natives have challenged the Alaska exclusion, both in court and before the Department of the Interior. They were initially successful in a federal trial court, which held that ANCSA did not prohibit land into trust, and the regulation violated the Indian Reorganization Act. *See Akiachak Native Community v. Salazar*, 935 F. Supp. 2d 197 (D.D.C. Cir. 2013), *modified, Akiachak Native Community v. Jewell*, 995 F. Supp. 2d 1 (D.D.C. Cir. 2013) (limiting the holding of earlier opinion regarding its description of IRA provisions). Soon thereafter, in late 2013, two different federal commissions, the Indian Law and Order Commission (discussed in Ch. 4, Sec. A.3) and the Secretarial Commission on Indian Trust Administration and Reform (discussed in Ch. 4, Sec. A.5), recommended that the Secretary of the Interior remove the Alaska exclusion for land into trust. In April 2014, the Bureau of Indian Affairs proposed removal of the exception, and, following a period of comment, the rule was finalized in December 2014. 79 Fed. Reg. 76888 (2014). Why would a commission on Indian country criminal justice have been concerned about land into trust policy in Alaska? What result would you expect if the State of Alaska challenges the new regulation as a violation of ANCSA?

b. Indian Country and Tribal Government Jurisdiction

The territorial jurisdiction of Alaska Native villages was substantially limited by the United States Supreme Court's holding in *Alaska v. Native Village of Venetie*, 522 U.S. 520 (1998), presented in Ch. 2, Sec. A.3.b.ii, that former reservation lands reacquired by a village corporation in fee could not constitute "Indian country" for purposes of the tribe's ability to tax a nonmember company doing business on these lands. The Court found that ANCSA had expressly revoked the Venetie reservation, as it had most reservations within Alaska, and had also expressed a congressional intent "to avoid a lengthy wardship or trusteeship." According to the Court, these lands could not constitute "dependent Indian communities" for purposes of the statutory definition of Indian country because they were neither "validly set apart for the use of Indians" nor "under the superintendence" of the federal government. The fact that state-chartered corporations held the lands in fee was pivotal to this conclusion, as was the fact that the federal government effectively disclaimed any "superintendence" by revoking the existing reservations and advocating a policy of self-determination, rather than "dependency." Although this holding arguably is limited to the case of former reservation lands now held in fee by a Native village, it has cast a great deal of ambiguity on the nature and extent of tribal territorial jurisdiction in Alaska.

Tribal authority over members, however, may exist outside of Indian country. In *John v. Baker*, 982 P.2d 738 (Alaska 1999), the Alaska Supreme Court considered whether a Native village could adjudicate a custody issue between unmarried tribal members residing outside of Indian country. The Court was careful to note that tribal jurisdiction over child custody disputes between village members is not exclusive, rather it is concurrent with the State of Alaska's jurisdiction. The court found that "federal law suggests that the only bar to state jurisdiction over Indians and Indian affairs is the presence of Indian country. Outside Indian country, all disputes arising within the State of Alaska, whether tribal or not, are within the state's general jurisdiction." Nor is there any principle that would give "tribal courts, priority or presumptive authority, in disputes involving tribal members." Having said that, the court noted several reasons why Alaska Natives would seek to "resolve internal disputes in their own forums," where they would not encounter "barriers of culture, geography, and language" within a "foreign and inaccessible" state court system. According to the court, this creates an opportunity for "Native villages and the state to cooperate in the child custody arena by sharing resources." The court found that "the tribe only has subject matter jurisdiction over the internal disputes of tribal members" and thus, has authority to make custody determinations only "of children who are members or eligible for membership." Importantly, the Alaska Supreme Court found that because "Alaska Native tribes have inherent sovereignty to adjudicate internal tribal disputes, the tribes must be able to apply their tribal law to those disputes. Thus, tribal sovereignty over issues like family relations includes the right to enforce tribal law in resolving disputes." Finally the court found that the "comity doctrine provides the proper framework for deciding when state courts should recognize tribal court decisions." The court held that "as a general rule, our courts should respect tribal court decisions under the comity doctrine." The Alaska Supreme Court has extended its acknowledgment of concurrent tribal jurisdiction to child welfare matters. *See Simmonds v. Parks*, 329 P.3d 995 (Alaska 2014); Sec. C, this Chapter. *See also Healy Lake Village v. Mt. McKinley Bank*, 322 P.3d 866 (Alaska 2014) (denying state court jurisdiction over tribal election dispute and describing election matters as part of tribe's "retained inherent sovereignty").

NOTE

1. **The "Alaska Exceptions," Tribal Jurisdiction, and Public Safety After ANCSA and *Venetie*:** Following ANCSA and *Venetie*, federal lawmakers have often exempted Alaska from laws, programs, and regulations that apply to all other tribes in the United States, leaving Alaska Native communities either without federal funding, programming, and protections, or excluded from the removal of federal limitations on tribal jurisdiction.

As noted above, the district court in *Akiachak Native Community v. Salazar* held that land-into-trust regulations exempting Alaska tribes violated the Indian Reorganization Act. The relevant provision of the IRA states:

Any regulation or administrative decision or determination of a department . . . that classifies, enhances, or diminishes the privileges and immunities available to a federally recognized Indian tribe relative to the privileges and immunities available to other federally recognized tribes by virtue of their status as Indian tribes shall have no force and effect.

25 U.S.C. § 476(g). Should courts consider other "Alaska exceptions" a violation of this provision? Why or why not? Alaska tribes (except the Metlakatla Indian Community) were originally excluded from the special jurisdiction provision in the 2013 reauthorization of the Violence Against Women Act. The 2013 VAWA permitted all other tribes in the United States to once again exercise criminal jurisdiction over non-Indian perpetrators of statutorily specified acts of domestic violence, sexual assault, and restraining order violations. 25 U.S.C § 1304. However, in December 2014, following strenuous protest by Native and women's groups, Congress amended VAWA to repeal the Alaska exception. Alaska Safe Families and Villages Act of 2014, Pub. L. No. 113- 275 (2014).

The Attorney General of Alaska has contended that the state has exclusive criminal jurisdiction over all tribal lands in the state through Public Law 280, asserting that, after *Venetie* and ANCSA, there is no "Indian country" on which tribes may exercise jurisdiction. Can the state have it both ways — denying there is Indian country, and asserting jurisdiction under Public Law 280, which applies only *within* Indian country? Moreover, as the report of the Indian Law and Order Commission (discussed in Ch. 4, Sec. A.3) points out, *Venetie* only addressed the status of former reservation fee land. It did not address whether Alaska Native allotments or Alaska Native townsites, estimated at 4–6 million acres, constitute Indian Country. INDIAN LAW AND ORDER COMMISSION, A ROADMAP FOR MAKING NATIVE AMERICA SAFER: REPORT TO CONGRESS AND THE PRESIDENT OF THE UNITED STATES 45 (2013) (ILOC Report). *See also* Natalie Landreth & Erin Dougherty, *The Use of the Alaskan Native Claims Settlement Act to Justify Disparate Treatment of Alaska's Tribes*, 36 AM. INDIAN L. REV. 321 (2012). For more information about Public Law 280, see Sec. A, this chapter.

The Indian Law and Order Commission devoted an entire chapter of its report to Alaska. The Commission found that due to the small, rural, and remote character of many tribal communities, a uniquely centralized state government, large geographical distances, and a lack of collaboration and culturally appropriate services, state law enforcement's services to these communities are limited, at best. Native Alaskan communities are often unable to adequately address the public safety of their own citizens, due to the hurdles created by federal and state policy. Largely because of these realities, Native Alaskans experience extraordinarily high rates of violence, incarceration, and suicide, with few resources to address these problems. What solutions might help these issues? What steps can tribal, state, and federal governments take? How might tribal assumption of jurisdiction over Native Alaskan communities and their lands change the current situation? After extensive onsite research, the Indian Law and Order Commission compiled suggested solutions. For its recommendations and further reading on the state of justice for Native Alaskans, *see* ILOC Report, Chapter 2.

2. Hawai'i

While Native Hawaiians are ethnically classified as "Polynesians," rather than "Indians," federal law increasingly models the body of law governing its relationship with Native Hawaiians after federal Indian law. Politically and historically, however, the experience of Native Hawaiians is quite disparate from that of the American Indian nations. Prior to European contact in 1778, the eight main Hawaiian Islands were divided into separate kingdoms. NELL JESSUP NEWTON ET AL., COHEN'S HANDBOOK OF FEDERAL INDIAN LAW 358 (2012 ed.). The islands were divided into self-sufficient landholding units, known as "ahupua'a," also under a hierarchical structure of leadership. Traditional norms governed the relationship of the chiefs to the people living under their rule, and ensured a fair distribution of use rights in the land and resources. The indigenous economy underwent a radical transformation after European contact emphasized the strategic position of the Hawaiian islands in international trade routes. In response to foreign pressure, the Native Hawaiian people unified their autonomous island governments under the leadership of a monarch, King Kamehameha I. The Kingdom of Hawai'i signed treaties of peace and commerce with many European and Asian countries, as well as the United States. U.S. Secretary of State, Daniel Webster, even acknowledged that the Doctrine of Discovery, which had been applied to American Indian nations, should not be applied to the Hawaiian Kingdom. Thus, unlike any other indigenous group currently within the United States, the United States and many other nations explicitly acknowledged Hawai'i as a foreign nation.

Non-Native Hawaiians pressured the Hawaiian monarchy to conform its political organization and property system to European norms. In the middle of the nineteenth century, the non-Native advisors to the Hawaiian monarchs persuaded them to adopt a process (called the Mahele or division) that would separate the traditionally intertwined rights of the government, king, chiefs and people in the land, and would also eventually open land to non-Native ownership. COHEN'S HANDBOOK OF FEDERAL INDIAN LAW, *supra*, 359. As a result of the Mahele, the king received a million acres as Crown lands, the government received 1.5 million acres, and 251 subchiefs and "konohiki" (land agents) held approximately 1.5 million acres of land. All awards were made subject to the rights of Native tenants, and ultimately the Native tenants received small plots totaling approximately 1% of the total lands in Hawaii. In 1850, the Kingdom enacted a law permitting any resident, regardless of citizenship, to own and convey land. After the Mahele, the King and Chiefs held approximately 65% of the land. The monarchy conveyed some of this land to non-Natives, who were working to establish a plantation economy staffed by foreign labor. By 1897, non-Natives owned 67% of the land in Hawaii, while Native Hawaiians owned a mere 24%. COHEN'S HANDBOOK OF FEDERAL INDIAN LAW, *supra*, 360 (*citing* ANDREW LIND, AN ISLAND COMMUNITY: ECOLOGICAL SUCCESSION IN HAWAII 57 (1938)).

In 1893, a group of American imperialists, motivated by economic interests and backed by a contingent of U.S. Marines, coerced the surrender of Queen Lili'uokalani and imprisoned her in Iolani palace, proclaiming the creation of a new "Republic of Hawaii." The Queen made a formal protest to the United States, and President Grover Cleveland ordered an investigation. The President condemned the overthrow of Queen Lili'uokalani as a breach of American foreign policy, morality, and international law, and called for the restoration of the monarchy. Cleveland's successor, President William McKinley disregarded the findings of the report and pushed for annexation of the "Republic of Hawaii." The so-called "Republic" had formed a provisional government that expropriated Crown lands without compensation and placed political control in the hands of a small group of non-Native property owners.

Native Hawaiians turned out in force to block annexation, protesting the actions of the Republic and filing anti-annexation petitions with Congress. These efforts were successful in that proponents of annexation were unable to obtain the 2/3 vote necessary for treaty ratification in the Senate. Undeterred, the proponents ultimately were successful in achieving annexation through a joint resolution of Congress, passed in 1898. The Joint Resolution ceded "all public, Government, or Crown lands" including some 1.8 million acres of land to the United States, but directed that the proceeds from the lands be used "solely for the benefit of the inhabitants of the Hawaiian Islands for educational and other public purposes." J. Res. 55, 30 Stat. 750 (1898). The Joint Resolution and the subsequent Organic Act for the territory of Hawai'i preserved Hawaiian land laws, but also allowed the United States to withdraw public lands for its own uses. Organic Act of 1900, sec. 73, 31 Stat. 154. The Organic Act also established a territorial legislature, which set up a government for the Territory of Hawaii. Under this structure, Native Hawaiians were recognized as citizens of the United States and of the Territory of Hawaii, another departure from the policies applied to American Indian nations, who at this time were held not to be citizens of the United States. *See, e.g., Elk v. Wilkins*, 112 U.S. 94 (1884), discussed in Ch. 1, Sec. D.2. For more information about this history, *see* Eric K. Yamamoto and Catherine Corpus Betts, *Disfiguring Civil Rights to Deny Indigenous Hawaiian Self-Determination: The Story of* Rice v. Cayetano *in* RACE LAW STORIES (Rachel F. Moran and Devon W. Carbado, eds., 2008). *See also* Melody Kapilialoha MacKenzie, *Ke Ala Loa — The Long Road: Native Hawaiian Sovereignty and the State of Hawai'i*, 47 TULSA L. REV. 621 (2011–2012) (providing historical overview and discussing law and cultural sovereignty in the Native Hawaiian context

In the fall of 2011, Governor Neil Abercrombie signed into law a measure recognizing the Native Hawaiian people as the "only indigenous, aboriginal, maoli people of Hawaii" and provided a process that would "implement the recognition of the Native Hawaiian people" as a political unit entitled to exercise self-governance and protect their rights to land and resources, programmatic entitlements, and cultural heritage." Act 195 accords the Governor the power to appoint a five-member Native Hawaiian Roll Commission that will build the foundation for self-determination, and expressly refers to the United States's endorsement of the United Nations Declaration on the Rights of Indigenous Peoples, as well as the many federal laws that already protect the distinctive rights and interests of Native Hawaiian people. The text of Act 195 is available as S.B. No. 1520, 26th Legislature, 2011, State of Hawaii. How might this Act advance the efforts of Native Hawaiians to secure recognition through federal legislation, discussed below?

a. The Hawaiian Homes Commission Act of 1921

The Native Hawaiian culture, like many indigenous cultures, is strongly connected to the traditional land base. The massive confiscation of Hawaiian lands (including Crown lands and Government lands) caused tremendous cultural and economic harm to the Hawaiian people. In addition, many of the Native Hawaiians who held individual or family land rights were disenfranchised by the registration system established to validate land claims, which was operative for a very short period of time. *See Pai 'Ohana v. United States*, 875 F. Supp. 680 (D. Haw. 1995). In 1921, Congress passed the Hawaiian Homes Commission Act (HHCA), which allows Native homesteads on specific lands. 42 Stat. 108, ch. 42. The HHCA placed approximately 200,000 acres under the jurisdiction of the Hawaiian Homes Commission, which was a branch of the Territorial government, in order to "rehabilitate" persons of at least 50% Native Hawaiian blood and foster an agricultural and pastoral lifestyle. This program still operates today. Qualified applicants may receive an initial lease of 99 years, with a maximum extension of another 100 years. The lessee pays nominal rent. Most leases are for residential lots. COHEN'S HANDBOOK OF FEDERAL INDIAN LAW, *supra*, 371. Homesteads are initially obtained through application, but may be transferred to other parties upon approval of the Commission or through inheritance.

The entire Hawaiian Homes Commission program was transferred to the State of Hawai'i upon admission in 1959, and the Admissions Act specified that the HHCA, as amended, would be adopted as part of the Hawai'i State Constitution. Pub. L. No. 86-3, sec. 4, 73 Stat. 4, 5 (1959). With this transfer, the state assumed administrative responsibility over the HHCA lands, and in return agreed to accept a trust responsibility with respect to the administration of the HHCA. The United States retained residual authority, giving the Secretary of Interior the right to approve any land exchanges involving Hawaiian Home lands, and giving Congress the right to alter, amend or repeal the provisions of the HHCA, including the qualifications or benefits available to lessees. The United States also reserved the right to sue the State of Hawai'i for breach of trust concerning mismanagement of the lands or use of the proceeds for any other than the stated purposes. Pub. L. No. 86-3, sec. 5(f), 73 Stat. 4 (1959). To date, the federal government has never brought suit to challenge a state action related to Hawaiian home lands. *See Han v. U.S. Dept. of Justice*, 45 F.3d 333 (9th Cir. 1995) (holding that federal officials have no fiduciary duty to bring suit against the state for an alleged breach of trust).

Since the 1921 enactment of the HHCA, both federal and state officials have engaged in misuse of Hawaiian home-lands, including illegal land exchanges and use of the lands for other public uses. In 1995, the Hawaiian State Legislature attempted to remediate the state's past misuse of the Hawaiian home-lands with corrective legislation that authorized a settlement to be paid into a trust fund, as well as a transfer of 16,518 acres of public lands to the Department. Act 14, Haw. Special Sess. Laws. In 1995, Congress passed analogous legislation at the federal level. The Hawaiian Home Lands Recovery Act requires the Secretary of Interior to determine the value of lands originally designated as Hawaiian home lands under the HHCA, which were wrongfully acquired by the federal government, as well as the value of lost use of the lands. The statute then authorizes the Secretary to convey federal lands in Hawai'i of equivalent value to the Department, in exchange for the land wrongfully acquired by the federal government. Pub. L. 104-42, Title II (1995).

The administration of the HHCA has been problematic. COHEN'S HANDBOOK OF FEDERAL INDIAN LAW, *supra*, 374. Currently, there are over 19,600 Native Hawaiians on the waiting list for a homesite. Some have been on the waiting list for over 30 years. Less than 25% of the Department's lands are actually in use by approved lessees. Most controversies concerning Hawaiian Home Lands have been litigated in state courts. The Hawai'i state courts have acknowledged that the state has a trust responsibility to Native Hawaiian beneficiaries and have held that the administration of the trust is governed by the same exacting fiduciary standards that would govern a trustee of a private trust. *See, e.g., Ahuna v. Department of Hawaiian Home Lands*, 640 P.2d 1161 (Haw. 1982). Most cases have held that general state laws enacted in the exercise of the state's public health, safety, and welfare powers, such as criminal laws and environmental regulations, are applicable on Hawaiian Home Lands. *See Kepo'o v. Watson*, 952 P.2d 379 (Haw. 1998); *State v. Jim*, 907 P.2d 754 (Haw. 1995).

b.   The Hawai'i State Constitution and the 1982 Amendments

The act that admitted Hawai'i to the United States gave the federal government the authority to retain certain lands that had been set aside for federal use including military installations. The remaining public lands in Hawaii, as well as any proceeds from that land, were transferred to the state to be held in trust for five permissible purposes, one of which was the "betterment of conditions" of those persons with 50% or more Native Hawaiian ancestry.

In 1978, Hawai'i amended its State Constitution to clarify that the lands transferred to the state in the Admission Act, except the lands under the authority of the Hawaiian Homes Commission, are held in trust for Native Hawaiians and the general public. Haw. Const., art. XII, sec. 4. The amendments to the Constitution also established an Office of Hawaiian Affairs (OHA), which is governed by a board of trustees, and charged with administering the 20% pro rata share of the trust lands designated for Native Hawaiians. The OHA was also empowered to provide benefits to "Hawaiians," who were defined as anyone descended from the peoples who lived on the islands prior to 1778. As initially structured, the Board of Trustees was envisioned to be composed of Hawaiians, and only Hawaiians were to have the right to vote for the OHA trustees. However, in *Rice v. Cayetano*, 528 U.S. 495 (2000), presented and discussed in Ch. 2, Sec. B.3, the United States Supreme Court invalidated this scheme, holding that restricting voting rights to persons of Hawaiian descent was "race-based" voting and violated the Fifteenth Amendment of the federal Constitution.[18] The Court did not address the equal protection

---

[18] In a subsequent case, the Ninth Circuit found similar violations of the Fifteenth Amendment and the Voting Rights Act with respect to a Hawai'i state law that required OHA trustee candidates to be of Hawaiian ancestry. *See Arakaki v. Hawaii*, 314 F.3d 1091 (9th Cir. 2002). In the wake of *Rice v. Cayetano*, litigants have filed challenges to the constitutionality of OHA and the Hawaiian Home Lands program on Fourteenth Amendment equal protection grounds. Most of these cases have been dismissed for lack of standing. *See, e.g., Carroll v. Nakatani*, 188 F. Supp. 2d 1219 (D. Haw. 2001). In, *Arakaki v. Lingle*, 423

dimensions of the issue, reserving for another day the questions whether Congress has determined that Native Hawaiians have a "political status" similar to that of Indian tribes, and, if this is the case, whether it could delegate to the state the authority to preserve that status. The Court merely held that Congress could not authorize the state to create a voting scheme that limited voters for state office to those of a particular race.

c. Ceded Lands Controversy

At the time of annexation, the Republic of Hawai'i ceded approximately 1.8 million acres of former Government and Crown lands to the United States. When Hawai'i was admitted to statehood in 1959, the United States transferred about 1.4 million acres of the ceded lands to the state, including the 200,000 acres reserved for homesteading purposes under the Hawaiian Homes Commission Act. The federal government retained about 375,000 acres of the ceded lands for its military installations and national parks. The Admission Act specified that the lands and revenue from the ceded lands were to be used for five specified public purposes, including for the "betterment of the conditions of native Hawaiians." The 1978 amendments to the Hawaiian Constitution specified that the revenues from this pro-rata share of the state-controlled ceded lands, except the Hawaiian home lands, should go to the Office of Hawaiian Affairs. There are approximately 1.2 million acres of ceded lands under state control, and a great deal of litigation has ensued regarding OHA's share of the ceded lands revenue, other state commitments for the revenue, the process to be used to determine the amounts payable to OHA, and the different rules that apply to income derived from the state's proprietary functions and income derived from its sovereign functions. These cases are discussed in detail in NELL JESSUP NEWTON ET AL., COHEN'S HANDBOOK OF FEDERAL INDIAN LAW, *supra*, 366–370.

The Hawai'i Supreme Court reversed a lower court ruling to hold that the State of Hawai'i should be enjoined from selling or transferring 1.2 million acres of "ceded lands," currently owned by the state, until a political settlement is reached with Native Hawaiian people about the status of that land. *Office of Hawaiian Affairs v. Housing and Community Development Corp. of Hawaii*, 177 P.3d 884 (Haw. 2008). In reaching this decision, the Hawai'i Supreme Court found that "the Apology Resolution [adopted by Congress in 1993] and related state legislation give rise to a fiduciary duty by the State, as trustee, to preserve the corpus of the public lands trust, specifically, the ceded lands, until such time as the unrelinquished claims of the native Hawaiians have been resolved." The United States Supreme Court reversed.

F.3d 954 (9th Cir. 2005), the Ninth Circuit upheld the dismissal of all claims against the HHC and most claims against OHA on standing grounds, and remanded a claim challenging the expenditure of state tax funds for OHA's programs to the district court for a determination on the merits. The United States Supreme Court vacated the Ninth Circuit's opinion and remanded the case to that court for further consideration in light of a recent standing decision outside the Indian law field. Lingle v. Arakaki, 547 U.S. 1189 (2006).

HAWAII v. OFFICE OF HAWAIIAN AFFAIRS
United States Supreme Court
556 U.S. 163 (2009)

JUSTICE ALITO delivered the opinion of the Court.

I

A

In 1893, "[a] so-called Committee of Safety, a group of professionals and businessmen with the active assistance of John Stevens, the United States Minister to Hawaii, acting with the United States Armed Forces, replaced the [Hawaiian] monarchy with a provisional government." *Rice v. Cayetano*, 528 U.S. 495, 504–505 (2000). "That government sought annexation by the United States," which the United States granted, see Joint Resolution to Provide for Annexing the Hawaiian Islands to the United States, No. 55, 30 Stat. 750 (hereinafter Newlands Resolution). Pursuant to the Newlands Resolution, the Republic of Hawaii "cede[d] absolutely and without reserve to the United States of America all rights of sovereignty of whatsoever kind" and further "cede[d] and transfer[red] to the United States the absolute fee and ownership of all public, Government, or Crown lands, public buildings or edifices, ports, harbors, military equipment, and all other public property of every kind and description belonging to the Government of the Hawaiian Islands, together with every right and appurtenance thereunto appertaining" (hereinafter ceded lands).[19] The Newlands Resolution further provided that all "property and rights" in the ceded lands "are vested in the United States of America."

Two years later, Congress established a government for the Territory of Hawaii. See Act of Apr. 30, 1900, ch. 339, 31 Stat. 141 (hereinafter Organic Act). The Organic Act reiterated the Newlands Resolution and made clear that the new Territory consisted of the land that the United States acquired in "absolute fee" under that resolution. See § 2, ibid. The Organic Act further provided:

> [T]he portion of the public domain heretofore known as Crown land is hereby declared to have been, on [the effective date of the Newlands Resolution], and prior thereto, the property of the Hawaiian government, and to be free and clear from any trust of or concerning the same, and from all claim of any nature whatsoever, upon the rents, issues, and profits thereof. It shall be subject to alienation and other uses as may be provided by law." § 99, id., at 161; see also § 91, id., at 159.

In 1959, Congress admitted Hawaii to the Union. See Pub. L. 86-3, 73 Stat. 4 (hereinafter Admission Act). Under the Admission Act, with exceptions not relevant here, "the United States grant[ed] to the State of Hawaii, effective upon its

---

[19] [1] "Crown lands" were lands formerly held by the Hawaiian monarchy. "Public" and "Government" lands were other lands held by the Hawaiian government.

admission into the Union, the United States' title to all the public lands and other public property within the boundaries of the State of Hawaii, title to which is held by the United States immediately prior to its admission into the Union." § 5(b). These lands, "together with the proceeds from the sale or other disposition of [these] lands and the income therefrom, shall be held by [the] State as a public trust" to promote various public purposes, including supporting public education, bettering conditions of Native Hawaiians, developing home ownership, making public improvements, and providing lands for public use. § 5(f). Hawaii state law also authorizes the State to use or sell the ceded lands, provided that the proceeds are held in trust for the benefit of the citizens of Hawaii. See, e.g., Haw. Rev. Stat. §§ 171-45, 171-18 (1993).

In 1993, Congress enacted a joint resolution "to acknowledge the historic significance of the illegal overthrow of the Kingdom of Hawaii, to express its deep regret to the Native Hawaiian people, and to support the reconciliation efforts of the State of Hawaii and the United Church of Christ with Native Hawaiians." Joint Resolution to Acknowledge the 100th Anniversary of the January 17, 1893 Overthrow of the Kingdom of Hawaii, Pub. L. 103-150, 107 Stat. 1510, 1513 (hereinafter Apology Resolution). In a series of the preambular "whereas" clauses, Congress made various observations about Hawaii's history. For example, the Apology Resolution states that "the indigenous Hawaiian people never directly relinquished their claims . . . over their national lands to the United States" and that "the health and well-being of the Native Hawaiian people is intrinsically tied to their deep feelings and attachment to the land." In the same vein, the resolution's only substantive section — entitled "Acknowledgement and Apology" — states that Congress:

> (1) . . . acknowledges the historical significance of this event which resulted in the suppression of the inherent sovereignty of the Native Hawaiian people;

> (2) recognizes and commends efforts of reconciliation initiated by the State of Hawaii and the United Church of Christ with Native Hawaiians;

> (3) apologizes to Native Hawaiians on behalf of the people of the United States for the overthrow of the Kingdom of Hawaii on January 17, 1893 with the participation of agents and citizens of the United States, and the deprivation of the rights of Native Hawaiians to self-determination;

> (4) expresses its commitment to acknowledge the ramifications of the overthrow of the Kingdom of Hawaii, in order to provide a proper foundation for reconciliation between the United States and the Native Hawaiian people; and

> (5) urges the President of the United States to also acknowledge the ramifications of the overthrow of the Kingdom of Hawaii and to support reconciliation efforts between the United States and the Native Hawaiian people. Id., at 1513.

Finally, § 3 of the Apology Resolution states that "Nothing in this Joint Resolution is intended to serve as a settlement of any claims against the United States." *Id.*, at 1514.

B

This suit involves a tract of former crown land on Maui, now known as the "Leiali'i parcel," that was ceded in "absolute fee" to the United States at annexation and has been held by the State since 1959 as part of the trust established by § 5(f) of the Admission Act. The Housing Finance and Development Corporation (HFDC) — Hawaii's affordable housing agency — received approval to remove the Leiali'i parcel from the § 5(f) trust and redevelop it. In order to transfer the Leiali'i parcel out of the public trust, HFDC was required to compensate respondent Office of Hawaiian Affairs (OHA), which was established to receive and manage funds from the use or sale of the ceded lands for the benefit of native Hawaiians. Haw. Const., Art. XII, §§ 4–6.

In this case, however, OHA demanded more than monetary compensation. Relying on the Apology Resolution, respondent OHA demanded that HFDC include a disclaimer preserving any native Hawaiian claims to ownership of lands transferred from the public trust for redevelopment. HFDC declined to include the requested disclaimer because "to do so would place a cloud on title, rendering title insurance unavailable."

Again relying on the Apology Resolution, respondents then sued the State, its Governor, HFDC (since renamed), and its officials [to enjoin sale of the property on grounds of breach of trust to the Native Hawaiian people].

III

Turning to the merits, we must decide whether the Apology Resolution "strips Hawaii of its sovereign authority to sell, exchange, or transfer" the lands that the United States held in "absolute fee" (30 Stat. 750) and "grant[ed] to the State of Hawaii, effective upon its admission into the Union" (73 Stat. 5). We conclude that the Apology Resolution has no such effect.

A

"We begin, as always, with the text of the statute." *Permanent Mission of India to United Nations v. City of New York*, 551 U.S. 193, 197 (2007). The Apology Resolution contains two substantive provisions. See 107 Stat. 1513–1514. Neither justifies the judgment below.

The resolution's first substantive provision uses six verbs, all of which are conciliatory or precatory. Specifically, Congress "acknowledge[d] the historical significance" of the Hawaiian monarchy's overthrow, "recognize[d] and commend[ed] efforts of reconciliation" with native Hawaiians, "apologize[d] to [n]ative Hawaiians" for the monarchy's overthrow, "expresse[d] [Congress's] commitment to acknowledge the ramifications of the overthrow," and "urge[d] the President of the United States to also acknowledge the ramifications of the overthrow. . . . " § 1. Such terms are not the kind that Congress uses to create substantive rights — especially those that are enforceable against the cosovereign States. See, e.g.,

Pennhurst State School and Hospital v. Halderman, 451 U.S. 1, 17–18 (1981).[20]

The Apology Resolution's second and final substantive provision is a disclaimer, which provides: "Nothing in this Joint Resolution is intended to serve as a settlement of any claims against the United States." § 3. By its terms, § 3 speaks only to those who may or may not have "claims against the United States." The court below, however, held that the only way to save § 3 from superfluity is to construe it as a congressional recognition — and preservation — of claims against Hawaii and as "the foundation (or starting point) for reconciliation" between the State and native Hawaiians. 117 Hawai'i, at 192, 177 P.3d, at 902.

"We must have regard to all the words used by Congress, and as far as possible give effect to them," *Louisville & Nashville R. Co. v. Mottley*, 219 U.S. 467, 475 (1911), but that maxim is not a judicial license to turn an irrelevant statutory provision into a relevant one. And we know of no justification for turning an express disclaimer of claims against one sovereign into an affirmative recognition of claims against another. Cf. *Pacific Bell Telephone Co. v. linkLine Communications, Inc.*, 555 U.S. 438, 457, 129 S. Ct. 1109, 1123 (2009) ("Two wrong claims do not make one that is right"). The Supreme Court of Hawaii erred in reading § 3 as recognizing claims inconsistent with the title held in "absolute fee" by the United States (30 Stat. 750) and conveyed to the State of Hawaii at statehood. See supra, at 1440–1441.

B

Rather than focusing on the operative words of the law, the court below directed its attention to the 37 "whereas" clauses that preface the Apology Resolution. See 107 Stat. 1510–1513. "Based on a plain reading of" the "whereas" clauses, the Supreme Court of Hawaii held that "Congress has clearly recognized that the native Hawaiian people have unrelinquished claims over the ceded lands." 117 Hawai'i, at 191, 177 P.3d, at 901. That conclusion is wrong for at least three reasons.

First, "whereas" clauses like those in the Apology Resolution cannot bear the weight that the lower court placed on them. As we recently explained in a different context, "where the text of a clause itself indicates that it does not have operative effect, such as 'whereas' clauses in federal legislation . . . , a court has no license to make it do what it was not designed to do." *District of Columbia v. Heller*, 554 U.S. 570, 578, n. 3, (2008). See also *Yazoo & Mississippi Valley R. Co. v. Thomas*, 132 U.S. 174, 188 (1889) ("[A]s the preamble is no part of the act, and cannot enlarge or confer powers, nor control the words of the act, unless they are doubtful or ambiguous, the necessity of resorting to it to assist in ascertaining the true intent and meaning of the legislature is in itself fatal to the claim set up").

---

[20] [3] The Apology Resolution's operative provisions thus stand in sharp contrast with those of other "apologies," which Congress intended to have substantive effect. *See, e.g.*, Civil Liberties Act of 1988, 102 Stat. 903, 50 U.S.C.App. § 1989 (2000 ed.) (acknowledging and apologizing "for the evacuation, relocation and internment" of Japanese citizens during World War II and providing $20,000 in restitution to each eligible individual); Radiation Exposure Compensation Act, 104 Stat. 920, notes following 42 U.S.C. § 2210 (2000 ed. and Supp. V) ("apologiz[ing] on behalf of the Nation . . . for the hardships" endured by those exposed to radiation from above-ground nuclear testing facilities and providing $100,000 in compensation to each eligible individual).

Second, even if the "whereas" clauses had some legal effect, they did not "chang[e] the legal landscape and restructur[e] the rights and obligations of the State." 117 Hawai'i, at 190, 177 P.3d, at 900. As we have emphasized, "repeals by implication are not favored and will not be presumed unless the intention of the legislature to repeal [is] clear and manifest." *National Assn. of Home Builders v. Defenders of Wildlife*, 551 U.S. 644, 662 (2007) (internal quotation marks omitted). The Apology Resolution reveals no indication — much less a "clear and manifest" one — that Congress intended to amend or repeal the State's rights and obligations under Admission Act (or any other federal law); nor does the Apology Resolution reveal any evidence that Congress intended sub silentio to "cloud" the title that the United States held in "absolute fee" and transferred to the State in 1959. On that score, we find it telling that even respondent OHA has now abandoned its argument, made below, that "Congress . . . enacted the Apology Resolution and thus . . . change[d]" the Admission.

Third, the Apology Resolution would raise grave constitutional concerns if it purported to "cloud" Hawaii's title to its sovereign lands more than three decades after the State's admission to the Union. We have emphasized that "Congress cannot, after statehood, reserve or convey submerged *Idaho v. United States* lands that have already been bestowed upon a State." 533 U.S. 262, 280, n. 9 (2001) (internal quotation marks and alteration omitted); . . . . And that proposition applies a fortiori where virtually all of the State's public lands — not just its submerged ones — are at stake. In light of those concerns, we must not read the Apology Resolution's nonsubstantive "whereas" clauses to create a retroactive "cloud" on the title that Congress granted to the State of Hawaii in 1959. See, e.g., *Clark v. Martinez*, 543 U.S. 371, 381–382 (2005) (the canon of constitutional avoidance "is a tool for choosing between competing plausible interpretations of a statutory text, resting on the reasonable presumption that Congress did not intend the alternative which raises serious constitutional doubts").

When a state supreme court incorrectly bases a decision on federal law, the court's decision improperly prevents the citizens of the State from addressing the issue in question through the processes provided by the State's constitution. Here, the State Supreme Court incorrectly held that Congress, by adopting the Apology Resolution, took away from the citizens of Hawaii the authority to resolve an issue that is of great importance to the people of the State. Respondents defend that decision by arguing that they have both state-law property rights in the land in question and "broader moral and political claims for compensation for the wrongs of the past." Brief for Respondents 18. But we have no authority to decide questions of Hawaiian law or to provide redress for past wrongs except as provided for by federal law. The judgment of the Supreme Court of Hawaii is reversed, and the case is remanded for further proceedings not inconsistent with this opinion.

It is so ordered.

In 2012, the Hawaiian legislature passed a bill conveying land worth approximately 200 million dollars to the Office of Hawaiian Affairs to settle OHA's claims to ceded lands proceeds. In exchange for the land, the legislation "extinguishe[d], discharge[d] and bar[red] all claims, suits, and actions relating to OHA's portion of income and proceeds from the public trust lands" for the period of time between 1978 and 2012. S.B. 2783, 2012 Leg., Reg. Sess. (Haw. 2012). In addition to the settlement, the state will continue making contributions to the OHA.

d. Native Hawaiian Political Status and Legal Rights

Since the 1893 overthrow of Queen Lili'uokalani and President Grover Cleveland's direction to reinstate the Hawaiian monarchy, the United States has not formally recognized the sovereignty of the Native Hawaiian people. The United States has offered special programs to assist individual Native Hawaiians, such as the Hawaiian Home Lands program, and has selectively included Native Hawaiians as a group in laws directed toward the protection of Native American rights, such as the Native American Languages Act (25 U.S.C. §§ 2901–2912), the Native American Graves Protection and Repatriation Act (25 U.S.C. §§ 3001–3013), the American Indian Religious Freedom Act (42 U.S.C. § 1996), and the Drug Abuse Prevention, Treatment, and Rehabilitation Act (21 U.S.C. § 1177(d)). There are indications that the federal government has established a trust relationship with the Native Hawaiian people, and yet the federal government hasn't designated Native Hawaiian people as a federally recognized group. For these reasons, there is an active debate among contemporary Native Hawaiians and federal and state policymakers about the legal status of Native Hawaiians. Significantly, the federal courts have largely refrained from entering these political debates. For example, in *Kahawaiolaa v. Norton*, 386 F.3d 1271 (9th Cir. 2004), Native Hawaiians brought an action against the Secretary of the Interior contesting both the refusal to provide to Native Hawaiians some of the programs available to Indian tribes and also their exclusion from the federal administrative tribal recognition process. After surveying the history of the legal treatment of Native Hawaiians and contrasting it with American Indians, the district court dismissed the action as raising a nonjusticiable political question, and the Ninth Circuit affirmed.

The future of Native Hawaiian rights will likely depend upon congressional actions. In 1993, Congress enacted a joint resolution that acknowledged the 100th anniversary of the overthrow of the Kingdom of Hawaii. Pub. L. No. 103-150, 107 Stat. 1510 (1993). In the joint resolution, Congress apologized for the United States's participation in the overthrow and called for a reconciliation process to commence. This movement toward "reconciliation" received heightened attention after the Supreme Court issued its decision in *Rice v. Cayetano*, describing OHA's voting scheme as a race-based restriction of voting rights in violation of the Fifteenth Amendment. *See* Ch. 2, Sec. B.3. This decision cast significant doubt on the nature of "Native Hawaiian" identity as a "political" classification, at least for purposes of state laws and benefits. Non-Native claimants drew on the opinion's language describing Hawai'i as a "multicultural society" of United States citizens from different backgrounds and ethnicities and began to attack state and private programs directed toward Native Hawaiian beneficiaries as "racially discriminatory," largely on equal protection and civil rights grounds. Some of these claims have failed for lack of standing. *See Carroll v. Nakatani*, 342 F.3d 934 (9th Cir. 2003); *Arakaki v. Lingle, supra*. Others, however, have at least partially succeeded in eroding special programs for Native Hawaiians.

For example, in *Doe v. Kamehameha Schools*, 416 F.3d 1025 (9th Cir. 2005), a divided panel of the Ninth Circuit (later overturned en banc) used the 1866 Civil Rights Act, 42 U.S.C. § 1981, to invalidate the admissions policies favoring Native Hawaiians of the Kamehameha Schools administered under a trust established by Princess Bernice Pauahi Bishop, for the express purpose of educating Native Hawaiians. Under those policies, all qualified applicants of Native Hawaiian descent are admitted before any non-Native Hawaiians will be considered. The Kamehameha Schools are private and do not take state or federal funds. The Ninth Circuit panel, however, rejected the district court's ruling that this was a valid race-conscious remedial plan seeking to preserve the Native Hawaiian indigenous culture and identity against a history of discrimination and lost sovereignty. *See Doe v. Kamehameha Schools/Bernice Pauahi Bishop Estate*, 295 F. Supp. 2d 1141 (D. Haw. 2003). The Ninth Circuit held instead that the admissions policy should be measured against the same type of standard that would apply in a Title VII civil rights action. This holding was overturned by an en banc panel of the Ninth Circuit, which affirmed the district court's ruling and held that a private, non-profit school that receives no federal funds does not violate section 1981 by preferring Native Hawaiians in its admission policy. 470 F.3d 827 (9th Cir. 2006). For background and an assortment of Amicus Curiae briefs submitted during the case, *see* Susan K. Serrano, Eric K. Yamamoto, Melody Kapilialoha MacKenzie & David M. Forman, *Restorative Justice for Hawai'i's First People: Selected Amicus Curiae Briefs in* Doe v. Kamehameha Schools, 14 ASIAN AM. L.J. 205 (2007).

In response to these cases, some Native Hawaiians and policymakers have increased efforts to pass federal legislation promoting development of a "Native Hawaiian governing entity" that would be eligible for recognition by the United States government. In 2000, legislation to establish a process for federal recognition of a Native Hawaiian governing entity was introduced in Congress. "A Bill to Express the Policy of the United States Regarding the United States' Relationship with Native Hawaiians," S. 2899 and H.R. 4904, 106th Cong. (2000). Several other bills relating to this topic have been introduced over the years and have received varying degrees of congressional attention. However, none has passed. While these bills have enjoyed support from many Native Hawaiians and policymakers, other citizens and politicians have argued that such a bill would constitute an impermissible "racial preference." Some opponents have even argued that Congress lacks the authority to create a political relationship with Native Hawaiians under the "Indian Commerce Clause." For a scholarly article that makes this argument, see Stuart M. Benjamin, *Equal Protection and the Special Relationship: The Case of Native Hawaiians*, 106 YALE L.J. 537 (1996). In 2014, the Department of the Interior gave notice that it was considering adopting an administrative rule that would "facilitate the reestablishment of a government-to-government relationship with the Native Hawaiian community, to more effectively implement the special political and trust relationship that Congress has established between that community and the United States." *Procedures for Reestablishing a Government-to-Government Relationship with the Native Hawaiian Community*, 79 Fed. Reg. 35296 (2014)

Some of the opposition to federal recognition of a "Native Hawaiian governing entity" has come from Native Hawaiians themselves. There is a strong Independence movement in Hawai'i that recognizes the distinctive status of the Kingdom of

Hawaii, which enjoyed international status as a "foreign nation" and received diplomatic recognition from the United States on this basis. The proponents of Independence point out that the annexation of Hawai'i as a "state of the Union" violated both domestic and international law, and was thus invalid. They maintain that Hawai'i is under illegal military occupation by the United States and that international law demands "decolonization" of Hawai'i and the restoration of the sovereign Hawaiian nation. They fear that "consent" to incorporation into the United States as a "domestic dependent nation" will destroy their claim for independence.

One Hawaiian sovereignty leader, Poka Laenui, has described the movement's goals as follows:

> Today, there is a growing vision of Hawai'i becoming an independent nation, rejoining the ranks of other nations of the world. Within this vision, the question of citizenship and residence would be settled not by racial extraction but by one's relationship to Hawai'i — measured by some standard of acculturation, vows of loyalty to Hawaii, ancestry from Hawaiian citizens prior to the American invasion of 1893, and other similar means. The native Hawaiians' position in this nation is still being considered. Some possibilities are
>
> 1. a weighted voting system for public officials, within an electoral process such that the native vote would not be less than 50 percent of the total votes cast;
>
> 2. a bicameral legislature in which the members of one body would be selected exclusively by native Hawaiian voters;
>
> 3. the creation of a council of customs, protocol, and 'aina (land) within which certain matters would be controlled by native Hawaiians; and
>
> 4. Special provisions for land rights, access and gathering rights, and other rights recognized by developing international organizations such as the International Labour Office and the United Nations.

See Poka Laenui, *The Rediscovery of Hawaiian Sovereignty*, 17 AM. IND. CULTURE & RES. J. 79, 96 (1993).

NOTES ON NATIVE HAWAIIAN SOVEREIGNTY

1. **Modeling the Native Hawaiian-Federal Relationship:** Which models of tribal-federal relationships can be discerned in the alternatives identified by Poka Laenui? Do these alternatives reflect emerging international human rights law norms applicable to "indigenous peoples"? *See* S. James Anaya, *The Native Hawaiian People and International Human Rights Law: Toward a Remedy for Past and Continuing Wrongs*, 28 GA. L. REV. 309 (1994).

2. **Nationhood vs. Indigenous Rights:** Notice how different the claims are of Native Hawaiians for independent "nationhood" (*i.e.*, the decolonization argument based on the internationally recognized political status of the Kingdom of Hawaii) from the claims of Native Hawaiians as "indigenous peoples" for recognition of their

unique cultural rights and separate political status under domestic United States law. Is the situation of Native Hawaiians more analogous to that of Tibet, which continues to argue for independence from China using arguments of separate nation status and "self-determination?" Culturally, Native Hawaiians share many similarities with the Maori peoples of New Zealand and other Polynesian groups throughout the South Pacific. If Native Hawaiians are recognized as being similar to "Indian tribes" for purposes of United States domestic law, will this status be sufficient to protect their unique cultural and political identity?

3. **Recognition of Hawaiian Customary Law:** Importantly, a number of Hawaiian rights that date back from the Kingdom of Hawai'i are currently preserved through the adherence to "customary law" that has long been embodied in Hawaiian state court jurisprudence. Traditional Hawaiian usage is admissible in state court, and also controls inconsistent common law. *See* Haw. Rev. Stat. § 1-1. Customs may be proven through oral testimony from witnesses familiar with them. *See In re Kamakana*, 574 P.2d 1346 (Haw. 1978). Native Hawaiian traditional law is applied in a variety of areas, including family law and property law. Customary uses of property for purposes of ceremonies, subsistence, and gathering or access rights, have been recognized under Hawai'i State law. In November 1978, state voters amended the Hawai'i constitution to include a provision specifically protecting traditional and customary rights of ahupua'a tenants. Haw. Const. art. XII, sec. 7. *See, e.g., Kalipi v. Haw. Trust Co.*, 656 P.2d 745 (Haw. 1982) (customary right to gather may be exercised by Native tenant residing within ahupua'a on undeveloped land); *Pele Defense Fund v. Paty*, 837 P.2d 1247 (Haw. 1992) (Native Hawaiian rights may extend beyond boundaries of ahupua'a in which Native Hawaiian resides if they are consistent with the exercise of subsistence, cultural, and religious practices according to ancient custom and usage). The rights provided by the constitution can be used as a defense in criminal trespass cases. *See, e.g., State of Hawai'i v. Hanapi*, 970 P.2d 485 (Haw. 1998) (establishing three-part test to determine if a defendant's conduct is constitutionally protected). *See also State v. Pratt*, 277 P.3d 300 (Haw. 2012) (balancing state's interest in regulating land use with defendant's interest in exercising customary practices) The Hawai'i Supreme Court has also relied on the constitutional provision in holding that the state may impose appropriate regulations to protect Native Hawaiian customary rights in conjunction with permits issued for the development of land. *See Public Access Shoreline Hawai'i v. Haw. County Planning Comm'n*, 903 P.2d 1246 (Haw. 1995); *see also Ka Pa'Akai O Ka'Aina v. Land Use Comm'n*, 7 P.3d 1068 (Haw. 2000).

C. INDIAN CHILD WELFARE ACT

1. Introduction

Jurisdictional conflicts between Indian nations and states over the guardianship, foster care placement, and adoption of Indian children have stemmed from fundamentally different conceptions of the place and needs of Indian children in relation to their communities. States intervene in child welfare matters out of concern for children's wellbeing within nuclear families; and the job of state child welfare proceedings is to police, ameliorate, sever, or recreate strong bonds between children and parents in cases of parental abuse, neglect, or voluntary relinquishment. In the case of Indian children, the history of forced assimilation, cultural misunderstanding, and reservation poverty has led state courts to emphasize severing parental bonds in order to place the children with non-Indian families. Studies presented to the United States Senate in 1974 revealed that approximately one-third of Indian children had been removed from their families and placed in non-Indian foster care, institutions, or adoptive homes.

Because Indian nations hold different views about intimate relationships and responsibility for their children, they often dispute both the authority and the objectives of state intervention. Not only have state interventions diminished Indian nations' population bases and wellspring of new leadership, they have disrupted the most fundamental and intimate aspects of Native cultures. As networks of kinship groups, clans, and similar social units, Native nations are inspired by creation stories and other narratives to experience links and obligations to children among a broader set of community institutions. Thus from a Native perspective, the diagnosis and appropriate response to family problems may differ considerably from comparable assessments by non-Indian institutions. Consider the following statements from tribal court opinions:

> [T]he Navajo view of the relationship of children to parents is not one of a simple parent and child relationship, but an entire pattern of expectation and desirable action surrounding children. . . . The Navajo common law principle is one of the expectation that children are to be taken care of and that obligation is not simply one of the child's parents. The Navajos have very strong family ties and clan ties. . . . [Navajo adoption law is concerned] with the obligation in family members, usually aunts or grandparents or a family member, who are best suited to assist the child to support and assist children in need by taking care of them for such periods of time as are necessary under the circumstances, or permanently, in the case of a permanent tragedy affecting the parents. (*In Re: J.J.S.*, 4 Navajo Rep. 192, 194–95 (1983)).

> Under traditional Indian law of Southeast Alaska there is no question as to jurisdiction and responsibility for children of female clan members. Traditional law holds children of female members of a clan are children of the clan regardless of where or under what circumstances they may be found. Clan membership does not wash off, nor can such membership be removed by any force, or any distance, or over time. Even in death clan membership continues, and in rebirth is it renewed. (Finding of Traditional Law by the Sitka Community Association Court of Elders in *Hepler v. Perkins*, 13 Ind. L. Rep. 6011, 6016 (Sitka C. Ass'n Tr. Ct., Apr. 7, 1986).)

Thus for Indian nations, the well-being of children is to be found in situating and caring for them within the larger social networks of the communities into which they were born. Non-Indian courts, scholars, and social services personnel have often interpreted the Native view as sacrificing children's welfare for the sake of collective interests such as tribal survival and cultural continuity. One legal scholar, commenting on the possibility that Indian children would be left in foster care with a Native family rather than being adopted into a non-Indian home, wrote,

Clearly, preference for the interests of the tribe is at the expense of the child's emotional development. If best interests means a placement most conducive to healthy psychological growth, this result is contrary to it. . . . [T]he child pays the price for the tribe's welfare.

Margaret Howard, *Transracial Adoption: Analysis of the Best Interests Standard*, 59 NOTRE DAME L. REV. 503, 544 (1984). Is there any way to reconcile Native and non-Indian views about children's needs and the appropriate goals of intervention? For different attempts at doing so, see Barbara Atwood, *Flashpoints under the Indian Child Welfare Act: Toward a New Understanding of State Court Resistance*, 51 EMORY L.J. 587 (2002); Lorie Graham, *"The Past Never Vanishes": A Contextual Critique of the Existing Indian Family Doctrine*, 23 AM. INDIAN L. REV. 1 (1998).

Inevitably, conflicting understandings of child welfare have translated into jurisdictional struggles between state and tribal courts. For purposes of United States law, jurisdictional questions associated with guardianship, foster care placement, and adoption of Indian children turn on considerations such as physical location of the child, prior court intervention, and the tribal status of the child and her biological parents. Increases in the mobility and intermarriage of tribal members have emboldened state courts to assert more authority over Indian children. Where a Native family has had connections both on and off the reservation, some family members are tribal members and others are not, or an Indian parent has left the reservation to place a child for adoption, state courts have often claimed jurisdiction to pursue their view of child welfare. At the same time, the growing numbers of tribal courts, social services agencies, and foster care networks have made Indian nations more forceful in advancing their own jurisdictional claims in pursuit of tribal conceptions of children's needs.

Before passage of the Indian Child Welfare Act, 25 U.S.C. § 1901 et seq., in 1978, it was clear that tribal courts possessed exclusive jurisdiction over child placement proceedings involving tribal children when both parents and child lived on the reservation and the state had not been allocated jurisdiction under Public Law 280 or some similar law. *Fisher v. District Court*, 424 U.S. 382 (1976). If all of these conditions were not met, however, tribal and state courts often competed for control over the same cases. In the case of a tribally-enrolled child living outside Indian country, for example, the tribe would assert jurisdiction based on the child's status as an enrolled member, and the state would assert jurisdiction based on the child's residence. The case that follows lays out some of this history and indicates how the Indian Child Welfare Act (ICWA) resolves some of these conflicts. Before reading the case, review the statute carefully and note the different methods it employs to advance Indian nations concerns for their children. One way Congress addressed the tensions between states and tribes was by establishing substantive criteria and procedural requirements for Indian child welfare cases that would be heard in state courts. *See, e.g.*, 25 U.S.C. § 1915 (placement preferences for Indian families); 25 U.S.C. § 1912(f) (setting burden of proof as "beyond a reasonable doubt" before parental rights of Indian parents could be terminated). In addition to prescribing the process and criteria for Indian child welfare cases heard in state court, ICWA also responded to the tension between state and tribal courts by reallocating jurisdiction between them based on the status of the child and the child's residence or domicile. The jurisdictional innovations in ICWA consist of an affirmation of exclusive tribal jurisdiction for some cases; a provision for transfer of some other cases from state to tribal court; and an authorization for tribally-initiated reassumption of jurisdiction previously exercised by states under Public Law 280. Under ICWA, as you will see, much turns on the finding that an Indian child is domiciled on or off the reservation. What law of domicile should be applied in such situations — tribal, federal or state? The statute does not directly resolve this question, shifting the burden to the courts.

For an overview and critical assessment of ICWA, see MATTHEW L. M. FLETCHER, WENONA T. SINGEL & KATHRYN E. FORT, FACING THE FUTURE: THE INDIAN CHILD WELFARE ACT AT 30 (2009).

2. Jurisdiction and "Domicile" Under ICWA

MISSISSIPPI BAND OF CHOCTAW INDIANS v. HOLYFIELD
United States Supreme Court
490 U.S. 30 (1989)

JUSTICE BRENNAN delivered the opinion of the Court.

This appeal requires us to construe the provisions of the Indian Child Welfare Act that establish exclusive tribal jurisdiction over child custody proceedings involving Indian children domiciled on the tribe's reservation.

I

A

The Indian Child Welfare Act of 1978 (ICWA), 92 Stat. 3069, 25 U.S.C. §§ 1901–1963, was the product of rising concern in the mid-1970s over the consequences to Indian children, Indian families, and Indian tribes of abusive child welfare practices that resulted in the separation of large numbers of Indian children from their families and tribes through adoption or foster care placement, usually in non-Indian homes. Senate oversight hearings in 1974 yielded numerous examples, statistical data, and expert testimony documenting what one witness called "the wholesale removal of Indian children from their homes, . . . the most tragic aspect of Indian life today." Indian Child Welfare Program, Hearings before the Subcommittee on Indian Affairs of the Senate Committee on Interior and Insular Affairs, 93d Cong., 2d Sess., 3 (hereinafter 1974 Hearings) (statement of William Byler). Studies undertaken by the Association on American Indian Affairs in 1969 and 1974, and presented in the Senate hearings, showed that 25 to 35 percent of all Indian children had been separated from their families and placed in adoptive families, foster care, or institutions. *Id.*, at 15; see also H. R. Rep. No. 95-1386, p. 9 (1978) (hereinafter House Report). Adoptive placements counted significantly in this total: in the State of Minnesota, for example, one in eight Indian children under the age of 18 was in an adoptive home, and during the year 1971–1972 nearly one in every four infants under one year of age was placed for adoption. The adoption rate of

Indian children was eight times that of non-Indian children. Approximately 90% of the Indian placements were in non-Indian homes. 1974 Hearings, at 75–83. A number of witnesses also testified to the serious adjustment problems encountered by such children during adolescence,[21] as well as the impact of the adoptions on Indian parents and the tribes themselves. See generally 1974 Hearings.

Further hearings, covering much the same ground, were held during 1977 and 1978 on the bill that became the ICWA.[22] While much of the testimony again focused on the harm to Indian parents and their children who were involuntarily separated by decisions of local welfare authorities, there was also considerable emphasis on the impact on the tribes themselves of the massive removal of their children. For example, Mr. Calvin Isaac, Tribal Chief of the Mississippi Band of Choctaw Indians and representative of the National Tribal Chairmen's Association, testified as follows:

> Culturally, the chances of Indian survival are significantly reduced if our children, the only real means for the transmission of the tribal heritage, are to be raised in non-Indian homes and denied exposure to the ways of their People. Furthermore, these practices seriously undercut the tribes' ability to continue as self-governing communities. Probably in no area is it more important that tribal sovereignty be respected than in an area as socially and culturally determinative as family relationships. 1978 Hearings, at 193. See also *id.*, at 62.[23]

[21] [1] For example, Dr. Joseph Westermeyer, a University of Minnesota social psychiatrist, testified about his research with Indian adolescents who experience difficulty coping in white society, despite the fact that they had been raised in a purely white environment:

> [T]hey were raised with a white cultural and social identity. They are raised in a white home. They attended predominantly white schools, and in almost all cases, attended a church that was predominantly white, and really came to understand very little about Indian culture, Indian behavior, and had virtually no viable Indian identity. They can recall such things as seeing cowboys and Indians on TV and feeling that Indians were a historical figure but were not a viable contemporary social group.

> Then during adolescence, they found that society was not to grant them the white identity that they had. They began to find this out in a number of ways. For example, a universal experience was that when they began to date white children, the parents of the white youngsters were against this, and there were pressures among white children from the parents not to date these Indian children. . . .

> The other experience was derogatory name calling in relation to their racial identity. . . .

> [T]hey were finding that society was putting on them an identity which they didn't possess and taking from them an identity that they did possess.

1974 Hearings, at 46.

[22] [2] Hearing on S. 1214 before the Senate Select Committee on Indian Affairs, 95th Cong., 1st Sess. (1977) (hereinafter 1977 Hearings); Hearings on S. 1214 before the Subcommittee on Indian Affairs and Public Lands of the House Committee on Interior and Insular Affairs, 95th Cong., 2d Sess. (1978) (hereinafter 1978 Hearings).

[23] [3] These sentiments were shared by the ICWA's principal sponsor in the House, Rep. Morris Udall, see 124 Cong. Rec. 38102 (1978) ("Indian tribes and Indian people are being drained of their children and, as a result, their future as a tribe and a people is being placed in jeopardy"), and its minority sponsor, Rep. Robert Lagomarsino, see *ibid.* ("This bill is directed at conditions which . . . threaten . . . the future of American Indian tribes. . . . ").

Chief Isaac also summarized succinctly what numerous witnesses saw as the principal reason for the high rates of removal of Indian children:

> One of the most serious failings of the present system is that Indian children are removed from the custody of their natural parents by nontribal government authorities who have no basis for intelligently evaluating the cultural and social premises underlying Indian home life and childrearing. Many of the individuals who decide the fate of our children are at best ignorant of our cultural values, and at worst contemptful of the Indian way and convinced that removal, usually to a non-Indian household or institution, can only benefit an Indian child. *Id.*, at 191–192.[24]

The congressional findings that were incorporated into the ICWA reflect these sentiments. The Congress found:

> (3) that there is no resource that is more vital to the continued existence and integrity of Indian tribes than their children . . . ;
>
> (4) that an alarmingly high percentage of Indian families are broken up by the removal, often unwarranted, of their children from them by nontribal public and private agencies and that an alarmingly high percentage of such children are placed in non-Indian foster and adoptive homes and institutions; and
>
> (5) that the States, exercising their recognized jurisdiction over Indian child custody proceedings through administrative and judicial bodies, have often failed to recognize the essential tribal relations of Indian people and the cultural and social standards prevailing in Indian communities and families. 25 U.S.C. § 1901.

At the heart of the ICWA are its provisions concerning jurisdiction over Indian child custody proceedings. Section 1911 lays out a dual jurisdictional scheme. Section 1911(a) establishes exclusive jurisdiction in the tribal courts for proceedings concerning an Indian child "who resides or is domiciled within the reservation of such tribe," as well as for wards of tribal courts regardless of domicile. Section 1911(b), on the other hand, creates concurrent but presumptively tribal jurisdiction in the case of children not domiciled on the reservation: on petition of either parent or the tribe, state-court proceedings for foster care placement or termination of parental rights are to be transferred to the tribal court, except in cases of "good

---

[24] [4] One of the particular points of concern was the failure of non-Indian child welfare workers to understand the role of the extended family in Indian society. The House Report on the ICWA noted: "An Indian child may have scores of, perhaps more than a hundred, relatives who are counted as close, responsible members of the family. Many social workers, untutored in the ways of Indian family life or assuming them to be socially irresponsible, consider leaving the child with persons outside the nuclear family as neglect and thus as grounds for terminating parental rights." House Report, at 10. At the conclusion of the 1974 Senate hearings, Senator Abourezk noted the role that such extended families played in the care of children: "We've had testimony here that in Indian communities throughout the Nation there is no such thing as an abandoned child because when a child does have a need for parents for one reason or another, a relative or a friend will take that child in. It's the extended family concept." 1974 Hearing 473. See also *Wisconsin Potowatomies of Hannahville Indian Community v. Houston*, 393 F. Supp. 719 (W.D. Mich. 1973) (discussing custom of extended family and tribe assuming responsibility for care of orphaned children).

cause," objection by either parent, or declination of jurisdiction by the tribal court.

Various other provisions of ICWA Title I set procedural and substantive standards for those child custody proceedings that do take place in state court. The procedural safeguards include requirements concerning notice and appointment of counsel; parental and tribal rights of intervention and petition for invalidation of illegal proceedings; procedures governing voluntary consent to termination of parental rights; and a full faith and credit obligation in respect to tribal court decisions. See §§ 1901–1914. The most important substantive requirement imposed on state courts is that of § 1915(a), which, absent "good cause" to the contrary, mandates that adoptive placements be made preferentially with (1) members of the child's extended family, (2) other members of the same tribe, or (3) other Indian families.

The ICWA thus, in the words of the House Report accompanying it, "seeks to protect the rights of the Indian child as an Indian and the rights of the Indian community and tribe in retaining its children in its society." House Report, at 23. It does so by establishing "a Federal policy that, where possible, an Indian child should remain in the Indian community," *ibid.*, and by making sure that Indian child welfare determinations are not based on "a white, middle-class standard which, in many cases, forecloses placement with [an] Indian family." *Id.*, at 24.[25]

Beyond its jurisdictional and other provisions concerning child custody proceedings, the ICWA also created, in its Title II, a program of grants to Indian tribes and organizations to aid in the establishment of child welfare programs. See 25 U.S.C. §§ 1981–1984.

B

This case involves the status of twin babies, known for our purposes as B. B. and G. B., who were born out of wedlock on December 29, 1985. Their mother, J. B., and father, W. J., were both enrolled members of appellant Mississippi Band of Choctaw Indians (Tribe), and were residents and domiciliaries of the Choctaw Reservation in Neshoba County, Mississippi. J. B. gave birth to the twins in Gulfport, Harrison County, Mississippi, some 200 miles from the reservation. On January 10, 1986, J. B. executed a consent-to-adoption form before the Chancery Court of Harrison County. Record 8–10.[26] W. J. signed a similar form.[27] On January 16, appellees

---

[25] [6] The quoted passages are from the House Report's discussion of § 1915, in which the ICWA attempts to accomplish these aims, in regard to nondomiciliaries of the reservation, through the establishment of standards for state-court proceedings. In regard to reservation domiciliaries, these goals are pursued through the establishment of exclusive tribal jurisdiction under § 1911(a).

[26] [7] Section 1913(a) of the ICWA requires that any voluntary consent to termination of parental rights be executed in writing and recorded before a judge of a "court of competent jurisdiction," who must certify that the terms and consequences of the consent were fully explained and understood. Section 1913(a) also provides that any consent given prior to birth or within 10 days thereafter is invalid. In this case the mother's consent was given 12 days after the birth. See also n.26, *infra*.

[27] [8] W. J.'s consent to adoption was signed before a notary public in Neshoba County on January 11, 1986. Record 11–12. Only on June 3, 1986, however — well after the decree of adoption had been entered and after the Tribe had filed suit to vacate the decree — did the chancellor of the Chancery Court certify that W. J. had appeared before him in Harrison County to execute the consent to adoption. *Id.*, at 12-A.

Orrey and Vivian Holyfield filed a petition for adoption in the same court, *id.*, at 1–5, and the chancellor issued a Final Decree of Adoption on January 28. *Id.*, at 13–14.[28] Despite the court's apparent awareness of the ICWA,[29] the adoption decree contained no reference to it, nor to the infants' Indian background.

Two months later the Tribe moved in the Chancery Court to vacate the adoption decree on the ground that under the ICWA exclusive jurisdiction was vested in the tribal court. *Id.*, at 15–18.[30] On July 14, 1986, the court overruled the motion, holding that the Tribe "never obtained exclusive jurisdiction over the children involved herein. . . . " The court's one-page opinion relied on two facts in reaching that conclusion. The court noted first that the twins' mother "went to some efforts to see that they were born outside the confines of the Choctaw Indian Reservation" and that the parents had promptly arranged for the adoption by the Holyfields. Second, the court stated: "At no time from the birth of these children to the present date have either of them resided on or physically been on the Choctaw Indian Reservation." *Id.*, at 78.

The Supreme Court of Mississippi affirmed. 511 So. 2d 918 (1987). It rejected the Tribe's arguments that the state court lacked jurisdiction and that it, in any event, had not applied the standards laid out in the ICWA. The court recognized that the jurisdictional question turned on whether the twins were domiciled on the Choctaw Reservation. It answered that question as follows:

> At no point in time can it be said the twins resided on or were domiciled within the territory set aside for the reservation. Appellant's argument that living within the womb of their mother qualifies the children's residency on the reservation may be lauded for its creativity; however, apparently it is unsupported by any law within this state, and will not be addressed at this time due to the far-reaching legal ramifications that would occur were we to follow such a complicated tangential course. *Id.*, at 921.

The court distinguished Mississippi cases that appeared to establish the principle that "the domicile of minor children follows that of the parents," *ibid.*; see *Boyle v. Griffin*, 84 Miss. 41, 36 So. 141 (1904); *Stubbs v. Stubbs*, 211 So. 2d 821 (Miss. 1968); see also *In re Guardianship of Watson*, 317 So. 2d 30 (Miss. 1975). It noted that "the Indian twins . . . were voluntarily surrendered and legally abandoned by the

---

[28] [10] Mississippi adoption law provides for a 6-month waiting period between interlocutory and final decrees of adoption, but grants the chancellor discretionary authority to waive that requirement and immediately enter a final decree of adoption. See Miss. Code Ann. § 93-17-13 (1972). The chancellor did so here, Record 14, with the result that the final decree of adoption was entered less than one month after the babies' birth.

[29] [11] The chancellor's certificates that the parents had appeared before him to consent to the adoption recited that "the Consent and Waiver was given in full compliance with Section 103(a) of Public Law 95-608" (i.e., 25 U.S.C. § 1913(a)). Record 10, 12-A.

[30] [12] The ICWA specifically confers standing on the Indian child's tribe to participate in child custody adjudications. Section 1914 authorizes the tribe (as well as the child and its parents) to petition a court to invalidate any foster care placement or termination of parental rights under state law "upon a showing that such action violated any provision of sections 1911, 1912, and 1913" of the ICWA. See also § 1911(c) (Indian child's tribe may intervene at any point in state-court proceedings for foster care placement or termination of parental rights). "Termination of parental rights" is defined in § 1908(1)(ii) as "any action resulting in the termination of the parent-child relationship."

natural parents to the adoptive parents, and it is undisputed that the parents went to some efforts to prevent the children from being placed on the reservation as the mother arranged for their birth and adoption in Gulfport Memorial Hospital, Harrison County, Mississippi." 511 So. 2d, at 921. Therefore, the court said, the twins' domicile was in Harrison County and the state court properly exercised jurisdiction over the adoption proceedings. Indeed, the court appears to have concluded that, for this reason, none of the provisions of the ICWA was applicable. *Ibid.* ("these proceedings . . . actually escape applicable federal law on Indian Child Welfare"). In any case, it rejected the Tribe's contention that the requirements of the ICWA applicable in state courts had not been followed: "[T]he judge did conform and strictly adhere to the minimum federal standards governing adoption of Indian children with respect to parental consent, notice, service of process, etc." *Ibid.*[31]

Because of the centrality of the exclusive tribal jurisdiction provision to the overall scheme of the ICWA, as well as the conflict between this decision of the Mississippi Supreme Court and those of several other state courts,[32] we granted plenary review [and now reverse].

II

Tribal jurisdiction over Indian child custody proceedings is not a novelty of the ICWA. Indeed, some of the ICWA's jurisdictional provisions have a strong basis in pre-ICWA case law in the federal and state courts. *See, e.g., Fisher v. District Court*, 424 U.S. 382 (1976) (per curiam) (tribal court had exclusive jurisdiction over adoption proceeding where all parties were tribal members and reservation residents); *Wisconsin Potowatomies of Hannahville Indian Community v. Houston*, 393 F. Supp. 719 (WD Mich. 1973) (tribal court had exclusive jurisdiction over custody of Indian children found to have been domiciled on reservation); *Wakefield v. Little Light*, 276 Md. 333, 347 A.2d 228 (1975) (same); *In re Adoption of Buehl*, 87 Wash. 2d 649, 555 P.2d 1334 (1976) (state court lacked jurisdiction over custody of Indian children placed in off-reservation foster care by tribal court order); see also *In re Lelah-puc-ka-chee*, 98 F. 429 (ND Iowa 1899) (state court lacked jurisdiction to appoint guardian for Indian child living on reservation). In enacting the ICWA Congress confirmed that, in child custody proceedings involving Indian children

---

[31] [13] The lower court may well have fulfilled the applicable ICWA procedural requirements. But see n.8, *supra*, and n.26, *infra*. It clearly did not, however, comply with or even take cognizance of the substantive mandate of § 1915(a): "In any adoptive placement of an Indian child under State law, a preference shall be given, in the absence of good cause to the contrary, to a placement with (1) a member of the child's extended family; (2) other members of the Indian child's tribe; or (3) other Indian families" (emphasis added). Section 1915(e), moreover, requires the court to maintain records "evidencing the efforts to comply with the order of preference specified in this section." Notwithstanding the Tribe's argument below that § 1915 had been violated, see Brief for Appellant 20–22 and Appellant's Brief in Support of Petition for Rehearing 11–12 in No. 57,659 (Miss. Sup. Ct.), the Mississippi Supreme Court made no reference to it, merely stating in conclusory fashion that the "minimum federal standards" had been met. 511 So. 2d 918, 921 (1987).

[32] [14] See, e.g., *In re Adoption of Halloway*, 732 P.2d 962 (Utah 1986); *In re Adoption of Baby Child*, 102 N.M. 735, 700 P.2d 198 (App. 1985); *In re Appeal in Pima County Juvenile Action No. S-903*, 130 Ariz. 202, 635 P.2d 187 (App. 1981), *cert. denied sub nom. Catholic Social Services of Tucson v. P. C.*, 455 U.S. 1007 (1982).

domiciled on the reservation, tribal jurisdiction was exclusive as to the States.

The state-court proceeding at issue here was a "child custody proceeding." That term is defined to include any "'adoptive placement' which shall mean the permanent placement of an Indian child for adoption, including any action resulting in a final decree of adoption." 25 U.S.C. § 1903(1)(iv). Moreover, the twins were "Indian children." See 25 U.S.C. § 1903(4). The sole issue in this case is, as the Supreme Court of Mississippi recognized, whether the twins were "domiciled" on the reservation.[33]

Section 1911(a) does not apply "where such jurisdiction is otherwise vested in the State by existing Federal law." This proviso would appear to refer to Pub. L. 280, 67 Stat. 588, as amended, which allows States under certain conditions to assume civil and criminal jurisdiction on the reservations. ICWA § 1918 permits a tribe in that situation to reassume jurisdiction over child custody proceedings upon petition to the Secretary of the Interior. The State of Mississippi has never asserted jurisdiction over the Choctaw Reservation under Public Law 280. See F. COHEN, HANDBOOK OF FEDERAL INDIAN LAW 362–363, and nn.122–125 (1982); cf. *United States v. John*, 437 U.S. 634 (1978).

A

The meaning of "domicile" in the ICWA is, of course, a matter of Congress's intent. The ICWA itself does not define it. The initial question we must confront is whether there is any reason to believe that Congress intended the ICWA definition of "domicile" to be a matter of state law. While the meaning of a federal statute is necessarily a federal question in the sense that its construction remains subject to this Court's supervision, [nevertheless] Congress sometimes intends that a statutory term be given content by the application of state law. [We start] with the general assumption that "in the absence of a plain indication to the contrary, . . . Congress when it enacts a statute is not making the application of the federal act dependent on state law." [One important] reason for this rule of construction is that federal statutes are generally intended to have uniform nationwide application. [Thus], the cases in which we have found that Congress intended a state-law definition of a statutory term have often been those where uniformity clearly was not intended. [Another] reason for the presumption against the application of state law is the danger that "the federal program would be impaired if state law were to control." [Thus], "we look to the purpose of the statute to ascertain what is intended." . . .

First, and most fundamentally, the purpose of the ICWA gives no reason to believe that Congress intended to rely on state law for the definition of a critical term; quite the contrary. It is clear from the very text of the ICWA, not to mention its legislative history and the hearings that led to its enactment, that Congress was concerned with the rights of Indian families and Indian communities vis-à-vis state

---

[33] [16] "Reservation" is defined quite broadly for purposes of the ICWA. See 25 U.S.C. § 1903(10). There is no dispute that the Choctaw Reservation falls within the definition.

authorities.[34] More specifically, its purpose was, in part, to make clear that in certain situations the state courts did not have jurisdiction over child custody proceedings. Indeed, the congressional findings that are a part of the statute demonstrate that Congress perceived the States and their courts as partly responsible for the problem it intended to correct. See 25 U.S.C. § 1901(5) (state "judicial bodies . . . have often failed to recognize the essential tribal relations of Indian people and the cultural and social standards prevailing in Indian communities and families").[35] Under these circumstances it is most improbable that Congress would have intended to leave the scope of the statute's key jurisdictional provision subject to definition by state courts as a matter of state law.

Second, Congress could hardly have intended the lack of nationwide uniformity that would result from state-law definitions of domicile. An example will illustrate. In a case quite similar to this one, the New Mexico state courts found exclusive jurisdiction in the tribal court pursuant to § 1911(a), because the illegitimate child took the reservation domicile of its mother at birth — notwithstanding that the child was placed in the custody of adoptive parents two days after its off-reservation birth and the mother executed a consent to adoption ten days later. *In re Adoption of Baby Child*, 102 N.M. 735, 737–738, 700 P.2d 198, 200–201 (App. 1985).[36] Had that mother traveled to Mississippi to give birth, rather than to Albuquerque, a different result would have obtained if state-law definitions of domicile applied. The same, presumably, would be true if the child had been transported to Mississippi for adoption after her off-reservation birth in New Mexico. While the child's custody proceeding would have been subject to exclusive tribal jurisdiction in her home State, her mother, prospective adoptive parents, or an adoption intermediary could have obtained an adoption decree in state court merely by transporting her across state lines.[37] Even if we could conceive of a federal statute under which the rules of

---

34 [17] This conclusion is inescapable from a reading of the entire statute, the main effect of which is to curtail state authority. See especially §§ 1901, 1911, 1912, 1913, 1914, 1915, 1916, 1918.

35 [18] See also 124 Cong. Rec. 38103 (1978) (letter from Rep. Morris K. Udall to Assistant Attorney General Patricia M. Wald) ("state courts and agencies and their procedures share a large part of the responsibility" for crisis threatening "the future and integrity of Indian tribes and Indian families"); House Report, at 19 ("contributing to this problem has been the failure of State officials, agencies, and procedures to take into account the special problems and circumstances of Indian families and the legitimate interest of the Indian tribe in preserving and protecting the Indian family as the wellspring of its own future"). See also *In re Adoption of Halloway*, 732 P.2d, at 969 (Utah state court "quite frankly might be expected to be more receptive than a tribal court to [Indian child's] placement with non-Indian adoptive parents. Yet this receptivity of the non-Indian forum to non-Indian placement of an Indian child is precisely one of the evils at which the ICWA was aimed").

36 [19] Some details of the *Baby Child* case are taken from the briefs in *Pino v. District Court*, O.T. 1984, No. 84-248. That appeal was dismissed under this Court's Rule 58, 472 U.S. 1001 (1985), following the appellant's successful collateral attack, in the case cited in the text, on the judgment from which appeal had been taken.

37 [20] Nor is it inconceivable that a State might apply its law of domicile in such a manner as to render inapplicable § 1911(a) even to a child who had lived several years on the reservation but was removed from it for the purpose of adoption. Even in the less extreme case, a state-law definition of domicile would likely spur the development of an adoption brokerage business. Indian children, whose parents consented (with or without financial inducement) to give them up, could be transported for adoption to States like Mississippi where the law of domicile permitted the proceedings to take place in state court.

domicile (and thus of jurisdiction) applied differently to different Indian children, a statute under which different rules apply from time to time to the same child, simply as a result of her transport from one State to another, cannot be what Congress had in mind.

We therefore think it beyond dispute that Congress intended a uniform federal law of domicile for the ICWA.[38]

B

It remains to give content to the term "domicile" in the circumstances of the present case. The holding of the Supreme Court of Mississippi that the twin babies were not domiciled on the Choctaw Reservation appears to have rested on two findings of fact by the trial court: (1) that they had never been physically present there, and (2) that they were "voluntarily surrendered" by their parents. 511 So. 2d, at 921; see Record 78. The question before us, therefore, is whether under the ICWA definition of "domicile" such facts suffice to render the twins nondomiciliaries of the reservation.

We have often stated that in the absence of a statutory definition we "start with the assumption that the legislative purpose is expressed by the ordinary meaning of the words used." [Therefore, we] look both to the generally accepted meaning of the term "domicile" and to the purpose of the statute.

That we are dealing with a uniform federal rather than a state definition does not, of course, prevent us from drawing on general state-law principles to determine "the ordinary meaning of the words used." Well-settled state law can inform our understanding of what Congress had in mind when it employed a term it did not define. Accordingly, we find it helpful to borrow established common-law principles of domicile to the extent that they are not inconsistent with the objectives of the congressional scheme.

"Domicile" is, of course, a concept widely used in both federal and state courts for jurisdiction and conflict-of-laws purposes, and its meaning is generally uncontroverted. See generally RESTATEMENT §§ 11–23; R. LEFLAR, L. McDOUGAL & R. FELIX, AMERICAN CONFLICTS LAW 17–38 (4th ed. 1986); R. WEINTRAUB, COMMENTARY ON THE CONFLICT OF LAWS 12–24 (2d ed. 1980). "Domicile" is not necessarily synonymous with residence. "[O]ne can reside in one place but be domiciled in another. [D]omicile is established [for adults] by physical presence in a place in connection with a certain state of mind concerning one's intent to remain there." *Texas v. Florida*, 306 U.S. 398, 424 (1939). One acquires a "domicile of origin" at birth, and that domicile continues until a new one (a "domicile of choice") is acquired. "[Because] most minors are legally incapable of forming the requisite intent to establish a domicile, their domicile is determined by that of their parents." *Yarborough v. Yarborough*, 290 U.S. 202, 211 (1933). In the case of an illegitimate

---

[38] [22] We note also the likelihood that, had Congress intended a state-law definition of domicile, it would have said so. Where Congress did intend that ICWA terms be defined by reference to other than federal law, it stated this explicitly. See § 1903(2) ("extended family member" defined by reference to tribal law or custom); § 1903(6) ("Indian custodian" defined by reference to tribal law or custom and to state law).

child, that has traditionally meant the domicile of its mother. [Based on] these principles, it is entirely logical that "[o]n occasion, a child's domicile of origin will be in a place where the child has never been." RESTATEMENT § 14, Comment b.

It is undisputed in this case that the domicile of the mother (as well as the father) has been, at all relevant times, on the Choctaw Reservation. [Therefore], it is clear that at their birth the twin babies were also domiciled on the reservation, even though they themselves had never been there. The statement of the Supreme Court of Mississippi that "[a]t no point in time can it be said the twins . . . were domiciled within the territory set aside for the reservation," 511 So. 2d, at 921, may be a correct statement of that State's law of domicile, but it is inconsistent with generally accepted doctrine in this country and cannot be what Congress had in mind when it used the term in the ICWA.

Nor can the result be any different simply because the twins were "voluntarily surrendered" by their mother. Tribal jurisdiction under § 1911(a) was not meant to be defeated by the actions of individual members of the tribe, for Congress was concerned not solely about the interests of Indian children and families, but also about the impact on the tribes themselves of the large numbers of Indian children adopted by non-Indians. See 25 U.S.C. §§ 1901(3) ("there is no resource that is more vital to the continued existence and integrity of Indian tribes than their children"), 1902 ("promote the stability and security of Indian tribes"). The numerous prerogatives accorded the tribes through the ICWA's substantive provisions, e.g., §§ 1911(a) (exclusive jurisdiction over reservation domiciliaries), 1911(b) (presumptive jurisdiction over nondomiciliaries), 1911(c) (right of intervention), 1912(a) (notice), 1914 (right to petition for invalidation of state-court action), 1915(c) (right to alter presumptive placement priorities applicable to state-court actions), 1915(e) (right to obtain records), 1919 (authority to conclude agreements with States), must, accordingly, be seen as a means of protecting not only the interest of individual Indian children and families, but also of the tribes themselves.

In addition, it is clear that Congress's concern over the placement of Indian children in non-Indian homes was based in part on evidence of the detrimental impact on the children themselves of such placements outside their culture.[39] Congress determined to subject such placements to the ICWA's jurisdictional and

---

[39] [24] In large part the concerns that emerged during the congressional hearings on the ICWA were based on studies showing recurring developmental problems encountered during adolescence by Indian children raised in a white environment. See n.1, supra. See also 1977 Hearings, at 114 (statement of American Academy of Child Psychiatry); S. Rep. No. 95-597, p. 43 (1977) (hereinafter Senate Report). More generally, placements in non-Indian homes were seen as "depriving the child of his or her tribal and cultural heritage." Id., at 45; see also 124 Cong. Rec. 38102–38103 (1978) (remarks of Rep. Lagomarsino). The Senate Report on the ICWA incorporates the testimony in this sense of Louis La Rose, chairman of the Winnebago Tribe, before the American Indian Policy Review Commission:

> I think the cruelest trick that the white man has ever done to Indian children is to take them into adoption courts, erase all of their records and send them off to some nebulous family that has a value system that is A-1 in the State of Nebraska and that child reaches 16 or 17, he is a little brown child residing in a white community and he goes back to the reservation and he has absolutely no idea who his relatives are, and they effectively make him a non-person and I think . . . they destroy him. Senate Report, at 43.

Thus, the conclusion seems justified that, as one state court has put it, "[t]he Act is based on the fundamental assumption that it is in the Indian child's best interest that its relationship to the tribe be

other provisions, even in cases where the parents consented to an adoption, because of concerns going beyond the wishes of individual parents. As the 1977 Final Report of the congressionally established American Indian Policy Review Commission stated, in summarizing these two concerns, "[r]emoval of Indian children from their cultural setting seriously impacts a long-term tribal survival and has damaging social and psychological impact on many individual Indian children." Senate Report, at 52.[40]

These congressional objectives make clear that a rule of domicile that would permit individual Indian parents to defeat the ICWA's jurisdictional scheme is inconsistent with what Congress intended.[41] *See In re Adoption of Child of Indian Heritage*, 111 N.J. 155, 168–171, 543 A.2d 925, 931–933 (1988). The appellees in this case argue strenuously that the twins' mother went to great lengths to give birth off the reservation so that her children could be adopted by the Holyfields. But that was precisely part of Congress's concern. Permitting individual members of the tribe to avoid tribal exclusive jurisdiction by the simple expedient of giving birth off the reservation would, to a large extent, nullify the purpose the ICWA was intended to accomplish.[42] The Supreme Court of Utah expressed this well in its scholarly and sensitive opinion in what has become a leading case on the ICWA:

---

protected." *In re Appeal in Pima County Juvenile Action No. S-903*, 130 Ariz., at 204, 635 P.2d, at 189.

[40] [25] While the statute itself makes clear that Congress intended the ICWA to reach voluntary as well as involuntary removal of Indian children, the same conclusion can also be drawn from the ICWA's legislative history. For example, the House Report contains the following expression of Congress's concern with both aspects of the problem:

> One of the effects of our national paternalism has been to so alienate some Indian [parents] from their society that they abandon their children at hospitals or to welfare departments rather than entrust them to the care of relatives in the extended family. Another expression of it is the involuntary, arbitrary, and unwarranted separation of families. House Report, at 12.

[41] [26] The Bureau of Indian Affairs pointed out, in issuing nonbinding ICWA guidelines for the state courts, that the terms "residence" and "domicile" "are well defined under existing state law. There is no indication that these state law definitions tend to undermine in any way the purposes of the Act." 44 Fed. Reg. 67584, 67585 (1979). The clear implication is that state law that did tend to undermine the ICWA's purpose could not be taken to express Congress's intent. There is some authority for the proposition that abandonment can effectuate a change in the child's domicile, *In re Adoption of Halloway*, 732 P.2d, at 967, although this may not be the majority rule. *See* RESTATEMENT § 22, Comment *e* (abandoned child generally retains the domicile of the last-abandoning parent). In any case, as will be seen below, the Supreme Court of Utah declined in the *Halloway* case to apply Utah abandonment law to defeat the purpose of the ICWA. Similarly, the conclusory statement of the Supreme Court of Mississippi that the twin babies had been "legally abandoned," 511 So. 2d, at 921, cannot be determinative of ICWA jurisdiction. There is also another reason for reaching this conclusion. The predicate for the state court's abandonment finding was the parents' consent to termination of their parental rights, recorded before a judge of the state Chancery Court. ICWA § 1913(a) requires, however, that such a consent be recorded before "a judge of a court of competent jurisdiction." See n.7, *supra*. In the case of reservation- domiciled children, that could be only the tribal court. The children therefore could not be made nondomiciliaries of the reservation through any such state-court consent.

[42] [27] It appears, in fact, that all Choctaw women give birth off the reservation because of the lack of appropriate obstetric facilities there. See Juris. Statement 4, n.2. In most cases, of course, the mother and child return to the reservation after the birth, and this would presumably be sufficient to make the child a reservation domiciliary even under the Mississippi court's theory. Application of the Mississippi domicile rule would, however, permit state authorities to avoid the tribal court's exclusive § 1911(a) jurisdiction by removing a newborn from an allegedly unfit mother while in the hospital, and seeking to terminate her parental rights in state court.

To the extent that [state] abandonment law operates to permit [the child's] mother to change [the child's] domicile as part of a scheme to facilitate his adoption by non-Indians while she remains a domiciliary of the reservation, it conflicts with and undermines the operative scheme established by subsections [1911(a)] and [1913(a)] to deal with children of domiciliaries of the reservation and weakens considerably the tribe's ability to assert its interest in its children. The protection of this tribal interest is at the core of the ICWA, which recognizes that the tribe has an interest in the child which is distinct from but on a parity with the interest of the parents. This relationship between Indian tribes and Indian children domiciled on the reservation finds no parallel in other ethnic cultures found in the United States. It is a relationship that many non-Indians find difficult to understand and that non-Indian courts are slow to recognize. It is precisely in recognition of this relationship, however, that the ICWA designates the tribal court as the exclusive forum for the determination of custody and adoption matters for reservation-domiciled Indian children, and the preferred forum for nondomiciliary Indian children. [State] abandonment law cannot be used to frustrate the federal legislative judgment expressed in the ICWA that the interests of the tribe in custodial decisions made with respect to Indian children are as entitled to respect as the interests of the parents. *In re Adoption of Halloway*, 732 P.2d 962, 969–970 (1986).

We agree with the Supreme Court of Utah that the law of domicile Congress used in the ICWA cannot be one that permits individual reservation-domiciled tribal members to defeat the tribe's exclusive jurisdiction by the simple expedient of giving birth and placing the child for adoption off the reservation. Since, for purposes of the ICWA, the twin babies in this case were domiciled on the reservation when adoption proceedings were begun, the Choctaw tribal court possessed exclusive jurisdiction pursuant to 25 U.S.C. § 1911(a). The Chancery Court of Harrison County was, accordingly, without jurisdiction to enter a decree of adoption; under ICWA § 1914 its decree of January 28, 1986, must be vacated.

III

We are not unaware that over three years have passed since the twin babies were born and placed in the Holyfield home, and that a court deciding their fate today is not writing on a blank slate in the same way it would have in January 1986. Three years' development of family ties cannot be undone, and a separation at this point would doubtless cause considerable pain.

Whatever feelings we might have as to where the twins should live, however, it is not for us to decide that question. We have been asked to decide the legal question of who should make the custody determination concerning these children — not what the outcome of that determination should be. The law places that decision in the hands of the Choctaw tribal court. Had the mandate of the ICWA been followed in 1986, of course, much potential anguish might have been avoided, and in any case the law cannot be applied so as automatically to "reward those who obtain custody, whether lawfully or otherwise, and maintain it during any ensuing (and protracted) litigation." *Halloway, supra,* at 972. It is not ours to say whether the trauma that might result from removing these children from their adoptive family should outweigh the interest of the Tribe — and perhaps the children themselves — in having them raised as part of the Choctaw community.[43] Rather, "we must defer to the experience, wisdom, and compassion of the [Choctaw] tribal courts to fashion an appropriate remedy." *Ibid.*

The judgment of the Supreme Court of Mississippi is reversed and the case remanded for further proceedings not inconsistent with this opinion. It is so ordered.

JUSTICE STEVENS, with whom THE CHIEF JUSTICE and JUSTICE KENNEDY join, dissenting.

The parents of these twin babies unquestionably expressed their intention to have the state court exercise jurisdiction over them. J. B. gave birth to the twins at a hospital 200 miles from the reservation, even though a closer hospital was available. Both parents gave their written advance consent to the adoption and, when the adoption was later challenged by the Tribe, they reaffirmed their desire that the Holyfields adopt the two children. . . .

. . . I agree with the Court that Congress intended a uniform federal law of domicile for the Indian Child Welfare Act of 1978 (ICWA), 92 Stat. 3069, 25 U.S.C. §§ 1901–1963, and that domicile should be defined with reference to the objectives of the congressional scheme. [However], I cannot [accept] the cramped definition the Court gives that term. To preclude parents domiciled on a reservation from deliberately invoking the adoption procedures of state court, the Court gives "domicile" a meaning that Congress could not have intended and distorts the delicate balance between individual rights and group rights recognized by the ICWA. . . .

While the Act's substantive and procedural provisions effect a major change in state child custody proceedings, its jurisdictional provision is designed primarily to preserve tribal sovereignty over the domestic relations of tribe members and to confirm a developing line of cases which held that the tribe's exclusive jurisdiction could not be defeated by the temporary presence of an Indian child off the reservationWhile the Act's substantive and procedural provisions effect a major change in state child custody proceedings, its jurisdictional provision is designed primarily to preserve tribal sovereignty over the domestic relations of tribe members and to confirm a developing line of cases which held that the tribe's exclusive jurisdiction could not be defeated by the temporary presence of an Indian child off the reservation. . . .

Although parents of Indian children are shielded from the exercise of state jurisdiction when they are temporarily off the reservation, the Act also reflects a recognition that allowing the tribe to defeat the parents' deliberate choice of jurisdiction would be conducive neither to the best interests of the child nor to the stability and security of Indian tribes and families. Section 1911(b), providing for

---

[43] [28] We were assured at oral argument that the Choctaw court has the authority under the tribal code to permit adoption by the present adoptive family, should it see fit to do so. Tr. of Oral Arg. 17.

the exercise of concurrent jurisdiction by state and tribal courts when the Indian child is not domiciled on the reservation, gives the Indian parents a veto to prevent the transfer of a state court action to tribal court.[44]

. . . As Mr. Calvin Isaac, Tribal Chief of the Mississippi Band of Choctaw Indians stated in testimony to the House Subcommittee on Indian Affairs and Public Lands with respect to a different provision: "The ultimate responsibility for child welfare rests with the parents and we would not support legislation which interfered with that basic relationship." Hearings on S. 1214 before the Subcommittee on Indian Affairs and Public Lands of the House Committee on Interior and Insular Affairs, 95th Cong., 2d Sess., 62 (1978).[45]

If J. B. and W. J. had established a domicile off the reservation, the state courts would have been required to give effect to their choice of jurisdiction; there should not be a different result when the parents have not changed their own domicile, but have expressed an unequivocal intent to establish a domicile for their children off the reservation. . . .

When an Indian child is temporarily off the reservation, but has not been abandoned to a person off the reservation, the tribe has an interest in exclusive jurisdiction. The ICWA expresses the intent that exclusive tribal jurisdiction is not so frail that it should be defeated as soon as the Indian child steps off the reservation. Similarly, when the child is abandoned by one parent to a person off the reservation, the tribe and the other parent domiciled on the reservation may still have an interest in the exercise of exclusive jurisdiction. That interest is protected by the rule that a child abandoned by one parent takes on the domicile of the other. But when an Indian child is deliberately abandoned by both parents to a person off the reservation, no purpose of the ICWA is served by closing the state courthouse door to them. The interests of the parents, the Indian child, and the tribe in preventing the unwarranted removal of Indian children from their families and from

---

[44] [8] The explanation of this subsection in the House Committee Report reads as follows:

> Subsection (b) directs a State court having jurisdiction over an Indian child custody proceeding to transfer such proceeding, absent good cause to the contrary, to the appropriate tribal court upon the petition of the parents or the Indian tribe. Either parent is given the right to veto such transfer. The subsection is intended to permit a State court to apply a modified doctrine of forum non conveniens, in appropriate cases, to insure that the rights of the child as an Indian, the Indian parents or custodian, and the tribe are fully protected. *Id.*, at 21.

In commenting on the provision, the Department of Justice suggested that the section should be clarified to make it perfectly clear that a state court need not surrender jurisdiction of a child custody proceeding if the Indian parent objected. The Department of Justice letter stated:

> Section 101(b) should be amended to prohibit clearly the transfer of a child placement proceeding to a tribal court when any parent or child over the age of 12 objects to the transfer. *Id.*, at 32.

[45] [9] Chief Isaac elsewhere expressed a similar concern for the rights of parents with reference to another provision. *See* Hearing, *supra* n.1, at 158 (Statement of Calvin Isaac on behalf of National Tribal Chairmen's Association) ("We believe the tribe should receive notice in all such cases but where the child is neither a resident nor domiciliary of the reservation intervention should require the consent of the natural parents or the blood relative in whose custody the child has been left by the natural parents. It seems there is a great potential in the provisions of section 101(c) for infringing parental wishes and rights").

the reservation are protected by the Act's substantive and procedural provisions. In addition, if both parents have intentionally invoked the jurisdiction of the state court in an action involving a non-Indian, no interest in tribal self-governance is implicated. See *McClanahan v. Arizona State Tax Comm'n*, 411 U.S. 164, 173 (1973); *Williams v. Lee*, 358 U.S. 217, 219–220 (1959); *Felix v. Patrick*, 145 U.S. 317, 332 (1892).

The interpretation of domicile adopted by the Court requires the custodian of an Indian child who is off the reservation to haul the child to a potentially distant tribal court unfamiliar with the child's present living conditions and best interests. Moreover, it renders any custody decision made by a state court forever suspect, susceptible to challenge at any time as void for having been entered in the absence of jurisdiction.[46] Finally, it forces parents of Indian children who desire to invoke state court jurisdiction to establish a domicile off the reservation. Only if the custodial parent has the wealth and ability to establish a domicile off the reservation will the parent be able use the processes of state court. I fail to see how such a requirement serves the paramount congressional purpose of "promot[ing] the stability and security of Indian tribes and families." 25 U.S.C. § 1902.

The Court concludes its opinion with the observation that whatever anguish is suffered by the Indian children, their natural parents, and their adoptive parents because of its decision today is a result of their failure to initially follow the provisions of the ICWA. Ante, at 18. By holding that parents who are domiciled on the reservation cannot voluntarily avail themselves of the adoption procedures of state court and that all such proceedings will be void for lack of jurisdiction, however, the Court establishes a rule of law that is virtually certain to ensure that similar anguish will be suffered by other families in the future. Because that result is not mandated by the language of the ICWA and is contrary to its purposes, I respectfully dissent.

NOTES

1. **The Ultimate Disposition in *Holyfield*:** After the Supreme Court's decision, the Mississippi Choctaw Tribal Court appointed a guardian ad litem for the twins, demanded proof of paternity from the father, and conducted a home investigation of

---

[46] [12] The facts of *In re Adoption of Halloway*, 732 P.2d 962 (Utah 1986), which the Court cites approvingly, *ante*, at 21–22, vividly illustrate the problem. In that case, the mother, a member of an Indian Tribe in New Mexico, voluntarily abandoned an Indian child to the custody of the child's maternal aunt off the Reservation with the knowledge that the child would be placed for adoption in Utah. The mother learned of the adoption two weeks after the child left the Reservation and did not object and, two months later, she executed a consent to adoption. Nevertheless, some two years after the petition for adoption was filed, the Indian Tribe intervened in the proceeding and set aside the adoption. The Tribe argued successfully that regardless of whether the Indian parent consented to it, the adoption was void because she resided on the Reservation and thus the tribal court had exclusive jurisdiction. Although the decision in *Halloway*, and the Court's approving reference to it, may be colored somewhat by the fact that the mother in that case withdrew her consent (a fact which would entitle her to relief even if there were only concurrent jurisdiction, see 25 U.S.C. § 1913(c)), the rule set forth by the majority contains no such limitation. As the Tribe acknowledged at oral argument, any adoption of an Indian child effected through a state court will be susceptible of challenge by the Indian tribe no matter how old the child and how long it has lived with its adoptive parents.

Ms. Holyfield. On February 9, 1990, the Tribal Court granted adoption of the children to Ms. Holyfield, after deciding it was in the children's best interest that they remain with her. Coyle, *After the Gavel Comes Down*, Nat'l L.J., Feb. 25, 1991, at 1. Does this disposition call into question the Tribe's decision to fight this case all the way to the United States Supreme Court? Does the disposition suggest a response to critics of ICWA who worry that "the best interests" of affected children will be ignored? After canvassing tribal court decisions in ICWA cases, Professor Carole Goldberg concluded,

> Reading state court decisions, one's strong impression is that state judges perceive tribal justice as ignoring children's well-being in favor of some reflexive support for Indian parents (if parents' interests are threatened by a state welfare department) or the tribe (if an Indian parent wants to place an Indian child for adoption with a non-Indian family). These state courts do not open themselves to understand or respect the alternative vision of child welfare that governs much tribal decision-making. Neither do they appreciate the concern for individual Indian children that pervades tribal codes and court decisions. . . . Closer attention by state judges to this tribal law would reveal that tribal justice embraces a less individualistic conception of child welfare than is found in state courts, but without eclipsing the concern for individual needs that so preoccupies those state court judges.

Carole Goldberg-Ambrose, *Heeding the "Voice" of Tribal Law in Indian Child Welfare Proceedings*, 7 Law & Anthropology 1, 3–4 (1994).

2. **Ascertaining Domicile:** As *Holyfield* demonstrates, domicile is critical to the Indian Child Welfare Act since it represents the primary dividing line between exclusive tribal jurisdiction and potential concurrent state authority. In *Holyfield*, the Court relied heavily on the definition of domicile developed in the highly publicized case of *Matter of Adoption of Halloway*, 732 P.2d 962 (Utah 1986). *Halloway* involved an Indian child who lived on a reservation for almost three years — six months spent with his natural mother and the remainder with his grandmother. A maternal aunt removed the child from the reservation with his mother's consent. The record indicated that the natural mother believed that the child would be placed in temporary foster care, although she had discussed adoption as an option with the aunt prior to the removal. Two weeks later the mother learned of the proposed adoption of the child by a non-Indian family. After another two months the natural mother executed a consent for adoption in a Utah district court. The adoptive family immediately filed a petition for adoption and upon the court's order notified the Navajo Nation of the adoption proceeding five months later. Two years after the petition was filed, the Navajo Nation intervened in the adoption proceeding. The aunt testified that she did not want the child placed in an Indian home and removed him from the reservation for that purpose. The trial court decided that the child's domicile was in Utah and not on the reservation. In addition, the court held that the time the child spent with the adoptive parents satisfied the good cause requirement of § 1911(b) to preclude transfer of jurisdiction over a child domiciled off reservation from state court to the tribal court. The Utah Supreme Court reversed, finding that if state law were applicable, the trial court correctly determined that the domicile had changed. Jeremiah's mother had abandoned him,

and under Utah law the domicile of an illegitimate child is that of the mother even when the child and mother are separated, unless the mother abandons the child. In the case of abandonment the child assumes the domicile of the person who is acting parent at the time of abandonment. Nevertheless, the Court ruled that federal, rather than state, definitions of domicile controlled since federal law preempts state law in cases of conflict. The Utah Supreme Court stated:

> There certainly is nothing in the ICWA or its legislative history to suggest that state law controls if, in application, its subtleties bring it into conflict with the ICWA in ways that Congress apparently did not foresee. Under general supremacy principles, state law cannot be permitted to operate "as an obstacle to the accomplishment and execution of the full purposes and objectives of Congress."

Id. at 967 (quoting *Hines v. Davidowitz*, 312 U.S. 52, 67–68 (1941)). Had the passage of time been allowed to dictate a contrary result, would states have been given an incentive to delay their decisions in ICWA cases, in order to alter conditions "on the ground"?

In *Father v. Mother*, No. 3 Mash. 204 (Mashantucket Pequot Tribal Ct. 1999), the Mashantucket Pequot Tribal Court found subject matter jurisdiction over a child custody proceeding involving a child who lived with her father on the reservation, where the parents were not married and the mother lived elsewhere. The court agreed with the decision of the Cheyenne River Sioux Tribal Court of Appeals in *Eberhard v. Eberhard*, 24 IND. L. REP. 6059, 6061 (Cheyenne River Sioux Tribal Ct. App. 1997), which had rejected "the historically gendered and sexist rules of the western common law" referenced in *Holyfield* in favor of a gender-neutral rule which looks to the legal residence or domicile of the parent who is a tribal member. According to the Mashantucket Pequot court, the *Holyfield* domicile rule failed to protect the Tribe's sovereign interest in asserting jurisdiction over all children enrolled by virtue of their parentage, and was especially inapt where the child is not an infant, and may move to be with her father for a variety of reasons. The court preferred "to look at each parent-child relationship on a case by case basis in a gender neutral fashion." The court also declined to establish a minimum duration of residency requirement, finding that all tribal members, including tribal children who may never have set foot on the reservation, have "special ties . . . to their ancestral homelands and reservations, and to the tribal history, culture and extended family relations that are alive there." The court pointed to the law of the Penobscot Nation, which states: "By virtue of longstanding customs and tradition of the Penobscot Nation, its lands are viewed, and so defined, as the domicile for enrolled members." Penobscot Nation Land and Residency Laws, Subchapter VI, Residency, § 1. If state courts hearing ICWA cases were obliged to apply tribal law of domicile, Penobscot law would produce exclusive tribal jurisdiction over proceedings involving every enrolled child. Should Indian nations be able to dictate domicile in ICWA matters?

3. Special Jurisdiction Issues for Public Law 280 Tribes: ICWA mandates exclusive tribal jurisdiction over child welfare proceedings involving Indian children residing or domiciled on the reservation or who have been made wards of the tribal court, except in circumstances where states exercise authority under Public Law

280 or some similar act. 25 U.S.C. § 1911(a). It also enables Indian nations in Public Law 280 states and others to petition to reassume exclusive jurisdiction. 25 U.S.C. § 1918. Soon after enactment of ICWA, the Attorney General of Wisconsin, a mandatory Public Law 280 state, opined that Public Law 280 does not confer state jurisdiction over involuntary proceedings, because they are "regulatory" in nature. 70 Op. Wisc. Att'y Gen. 237, *3 (1981). *See* Sec. A.2, this chapter. Under that view, the Wisconsin tribes have exclusive jurisdiction over involuntary foster care placements and termination of parental rights even without filing a petition for reassumption of exclusive jurisdiction under ICWA. Only in voluntary proceedings (such as voluntary adoptions) would a Wisconsin tribe need to initiate the reassumption process in order to acquire exclusive authority. In the absence of such a petition, the tribe's jurisdiction would still be concurrent with the state's over those voluntary matters. *Native Village of Venetie I.R.A. Council v. Alaska*, 944 F.2d 548, 562 (9th Cir. 1991), *rev'd on other grounds sub nom. Alaska v. Native Village of Venetie*, 522 U.S. 520 (1998). Another mandatory Public Law 280 state, Minnesota, has by statute relinquished its jurisdiction over child placement proceedings involving Indian children who reside on the reservation or are under a custody order issued by a tribal court. Minn. Stat. § 260.771(1).

When an Indian parent in California, a mandatory Public Law 280 state, challenged the state's authority over an involuntary child welfare proceeding involving an on-reservation Indian child, the state secured a ruling from the Ninth Circuit affirming concurrent state jurisdiction. *Doe v. Mann*, 415 F.3d 1038 (9th Cir. 2005). The court found the state's involuntary child welfare proceedings to be fundamentally determinations of the children's status, and thus concluded that the proceedings are civil adjudicative rather than regulatory for purposes of Public Law 280. The court conceded that "California's child dependency statute may not fit neatly into any of the Public Law 280 jurisdictional boxes [meaning criminal prohibitory, regulatory, or civil adjudicative]," but stated that "construing ICWA as a whole and considering child dependency proceedings in the context of both ICWA and Public Law 280, we conclude that the California statute does not fall within Public Law 280's criminal jurisdiction, but that it does fall within Public Law 280's civil adjudicatory jurisdiction." Influential in the court's reasoning was its perception that § 1911 of ICWA, together with its reassumption provision in § 1918, reflected Congress's understanding as of 1978 that Public Law 280 states had concurrent jurisdiction over all Indian child welfare matters.

Does *Doe v. Mann* adequately consider all the interventions into family life (*e.g.*, home visits by social workers, drug testing, mandatory parent education classes) associated with involuntary child welfare proceedings? Would a parent involved in such a proceeding view it as "regulatory" in the Public Law 280 sense? Is it a sufficient response to this point that the court is merely adjudicating the child's status, with these additional measures being imposed on the parents as a condition of keeping their child? If involuntary child welfare proceedings don't "fit neatly into any of the Public Law 280 boxes," shouldn't the court have invoked the Indian law canons and ruled against state jurisdiction? Focusing on the court's use of ICWA, was it at all appropriate to invoke a statute enacted 25 years afterwards to interpret Congress's underlying intent in Public Law 280? Assuming that such use is permissible, was it correct for the court to infer from the presence of ICWA's reassumption provision that the 1978 Congress understood tribes in Public Law 280 states to lack exclusive jurisdiction? If that were Congress's understanding, why didn't it come right out and say so, rather than couching § 1911(a) in conditional terms? In any event, is it appropriate to draw inferences from ICWA's reassumption provision? Would finding exclusive tribal jurisdiction over the involuntary proceedings make the reassumption provision pointless? The Wisconsin Attorney General, in his opinion, concluded otherwise. More broadly, in view of the overall purposes of ICWA and the Indian law canons of construction, does it make sense to interpret the statute as effectively expanding state jurisdiction?

In applying the civil regulatory/adjudicative distinction in child welfare cases, what weight should courts give to the fact that many tribes in California and other Public Law 280 states do not have formal tribal court systems, and may rely on their tribal councils to resolve child custody matters? Should it matter that ICWA defines a "tribal court" to include not only courts "established and operated under the code or custom of an Indian tribe," but also "any other administrative body of a tribe which is vested with authority over child custody proceedings"? Should it matter that under ICWA, tribes with exclusive jurisdiction are authorized to make agreements with states for concurrent jurisdiction? 25 U.S.C. § 1919.

4. Applicability of ICWA in Tribal Courts: Although a few tribal courts have found otherwise, the dominant view is that ICWA's procedural and substantive provisions do not control Indian child custody proceedings in tribal courts. Thus, for example, the Chitimacha Indian Tribal Court of Appeals declined to apply ICWA's standard of proof of "beyond a reasonable doubt" to an involuntary proceeding, stating:

> We are quite satisfied . . . that the intent of the I.C.W.A., having been enacted to protect Indian families from non-tribal tribunals and agencies, that the burden of proof provided for in Section 1912(f), was to apply to proceedings in non-tribal courts; and that tribal courts, dealing with their own families and children, were free to adopt and impose their own rules and standards for use within their own membership; and that consequently, the standard of clear and convincing evidence provided by the CCCJ [Chitimacha Comprehensive Codes of Justice] is the applicable standard to be employed in the instant case.

In re J.D.M., 2000.NACH.0000001 (Chitimach Indian Tribal Ct. App. 2000); *see also C.B. v. Little Flower Freedom Center*, No. CV-16-16-90 (Northern Plains Intertribal Ct. App. 1991). Accordingly, when the Mississippi Choctaw Tribal Court received the case on remand in *Holyfield*, it was not bound by the placement preferences of section 1915(a). Rather, the determination was governed by tribal law. Other than the coverage definitions and jurisdictional provisions found in sections 1903 and 1911, most of the procedural and substantive provisions of the Act apply only to child custody proceedings heard in a state court under state law. Does the added flexibility available to tribal courts suggest a reason for supporting tribal jurisdiction in such cases?

3. "Indian Child" Under ICWA

None of the special jurisdictional, procedural, and substantive rules of ICWA applies unless the child involved qualifies as an "Indian child." In 25 U.S.C. § 1903(4), ICWA defines an Indian child as "any unmarried person who is under age eighteen and is either (a) a member of an Indian tribe or (b) eligible for membership in an Indian tribe and is the biological child of a member of an Indian tribe." Some state courts, reluctant to cede their traditional authority over child welfare matters in accordance with ICWA, have tried to narrow this definition beyond what the statute prescribes. Creating what has come to be known as the "existing Indian family" doctrine, these state courts have declined to apply ICWA to children who fit the statutory definition of an "Indian child" because, in the courts' view, the children have never been sufficiently affiliated with an Indian parent or tribe. Most recently, however, the trend in both state courts and state legislatures has been to reject any judge-made restrictions on the application of ICWA.

IN RE A.J.S.
Kansas Supreme Court
204 P.3d 543 (2009)

JUSTICE BEIER delivered the opinion of the Court.

This dispute between the unmarried natural mother and natural father of A.J.S. requires us to revisit our state's adherence to the existing Indian family doctrine. The doctrine was first articulated in *In re Adoption of Baby Boy L.*, 231 Kan. 199, 643 P.2d 168 (1982), and since then has been invoked in Kansas and elsewhere to except certain custody proceedings involving children with Indian ancestry from the provisions of the Indian Child Welfare Act (ICWA), 25 U.S.C. § 1901et seq. (2000).

Father is an enrolled member of the Cherokee Nation. Mother consented to adoption of their child, A.J.S., by members of her family and sought to terminate Father's parental rights. The district judge rejected Father's effort to transfer this matter to tribal court and rejected the tribe's attempt to intervene, basing his decision on *Baby Boy L.* This is an interlocutory appeal from those rulings.

Mother had been dating Father approximately 1 month before she became pregnant with A.J.S. The day after the baby was born, Mother filed a petition to terminate Father's parental rights. She also signed a consent to the adoption of A.J.S. by members of her family. A temporary order placing A.J.S. in the custody of the intended adoptive parents was entered, and A.J.S. has resided with the intended adoptive parents since that order.

Father filed an Indian Heritage Affidavit, acknowledging that he was the father of A.J.S. and that he was an enrolled member of the Cherokee Nation. He invoked the placement preferences of the ICWA; requested that the tribal court assume jurisdiction; and requested that A.J.S. be placed with him, pending further proceedings. In his answer to Mother's petition, filed the same day, he denied allegations that he was unfit; suggested that Mother also was of Indian heritage;

and requested the be dismissed, stayed, or transferred to the tribal court pursuant to ICWA.

Mother objected to the transfer request, denied any Indian heritage, and sought placement for adoption with her own family. She also sought a declaration that ICWA was inapplicable under the existing Indian family doctrine of *Baby Boy L.*, 231 Kan. 199, 643 P.2d 168.

The Cherokee Nation filed a motion to intervene, arguing that ICWA applied.

At the ensuing evidentiary hearing in district court, Mother testified that she was not a member of any tribe, that she had never lived on a reservation, and that she knew nothing of tribal customs. She also testified that Father never mentioned his ties to the Cherokee Nation and that she had never known he was a member of the tribe. According to Mother, Father never had contact with or provided any support for A.J.S. She also testified that she would revoke her consent to the adoption and raise A.J.S. by herself to prevent A.J.S. being raised by Father or the tribe. The evidence before the district judge also included printouts of information from Father's MySpace web page in which he had listed his heritage as white/Caucasian.

The parties stipulated that A.J.S. qualified as an Indian child under ICWA's definition. Nevertheless, the district judge ruled that ICWA was not applicable to this termination and adoption because A.J.S. had never been part of any Indian family relationship. Under these circumstances, the district judge also denied the Cherokee Nation's motion to intervene and declined to modify the temporary custody order. Trial was set to determine whether Father's parental rights should be severed, and permission was granted for this appeal.

These proceedings were initiated under provisions of the Kansas Adoption and Relinquishment Act, K.S.A. 59-2111 et seq., governing relinquishment and adoption and the associated termination of the rights of natural parents. See K.S.A. 59-2136. As Father and the tribe point out, however, federal law preempts nonconforming or conflicting state law. By its terms, ICWA applies to any child custody proceeding, including a termination of parental rights proceeding and a foster care or adoptive placement proceeding, involving an Indian child. 25 U.S.C. § 1903(1)(i), (ii) (2000).

There is no dispute that A.J.S. is an Indian child within the meaning of ICWA, see 25 U.S.C. § 1903(4), or that this is a state court child custody proceeding, see 25 U.S.C. § 1903(1)(ii), (iv). Generally, when such a child is not domiciled or residing on a reservation and the child's father objects to severance of his rights and the child's adoption, the tribe is permitted to intervene in the proceeding. 25 U.S.C. § 1911(c); see, e.g., *Mississippi Band of Choctaw Indians v. Holyfield*, 490 U.S. 30, 36 (1989). Moreover, ICWA's procedural and substantive provisions govern the case to avoid a risk of invalidation of its result. See, e.g., 25 U.S.C. § 1912 (2000) (notice); 25 U.S.C. § 1914 (2000) (invalidation); 25 U.S.C. § 1915 (2000) (placement preferences).

The parties appreciate that, to this point, Kansas has departed from the ICWA norm through the existing Indian family doctrine, adopted unanimously by this court in *Baby Boy L.*, 231 Kan. 199, 643 P.2d 168. Since *Baby Boy L.* was decided in 1982, 4 years after enactment of ICWA, the doctrine has been consistently applied in Kansas. Thus the parties' principal arguments focus on the logic and wisdom of the doctrine and the similarity or lack of similarity between the facts of this case and those before this court in *Baby Boy L.*

Baby Boy L. was born to an unmarried, non-Indian woman, who gave consent for adoption by non-Indian appellees. The district judge granted temporary custody to the appellees, who later filed a petition for termination of the parental rights of Baby Boy L.'s natural father, C.P. C.P., who was incarcerated, contested the petition and sought denial of the adoption. The district court judge bifurcated the proceedings, dealing first with the termination action and then the adoption. The parties presented their evidence, and, before ruling, the judge learned that C.P. was an enrolled member of the Kiowa Tribe. The tribe was then notified. It sought intervention, invoked ICWA, requested that the proceeding be transferred to tribal court, and demanded Baby Boy L. be placed with C.P.'s parents and/or the tribe.

The district judge ruled that ICWA did not apply and he denied the tribe's motion to intervene. The judge reasoned that ICWA was designed to prevent the unilateral break-up of Indian families. Baby Boy L. had never been, and, in the judge's view, absent his mother's consent, would never be part of an Indian family. The district judge terminated C.P.'s parental rights and granted the adoption. [The father and Tribe appealed.]

On appeal, this court focused on the language, history, and purpose of ICWA in order to determine whether Congress intended it to be applicable on these facts. The court concluded "that the ICWA, by its own terms, does not apply to these proceedings." *Baby Boy L.*, 231 Kan. at 207. Justice Richard W. Holmes wrote for the court:

> A careful study of the legislative history behind the Act and the Act itself discloses that the overriding concern of Congress and the proponents of the Act was the maintenance of the family and tribal relationships existing in Indian homes and to set minimum standards for the removal of Indian children from their existing Indian environment. It was not to dictate that an illegitimate infant who has never been a member of an Indian home or culture, and probably never would be, should be removed from its primary cultural heritage and placed in an Indian environment over the express objections of its non-Indian mother. Section 1902 of the Act makes it clear that it is the declared policy of Congress that the Act is to adopt minimum federal standards 'for the removal of Indian children from their [Indian] families.' Numerous provisions of the Act support our conclusion that it was never the intent of Congress that the Act would apply to a factual situation such as is before the court. *Baby Boy L.*, 231 Kan. at 205–06.

The court noted that its position was not without criticism, from appellants as well as commentators, but suggested that, even if it had concluded ICWA applied, there would be no reversible error in Baby Boy L.'s situation because his mother's consent to adoption was contingent on the appellees' identity. She had made it clear that

> if this adoption was denied for any reason, or if an attempt was made to place the child for adoption under the terms of the Act, she would revoke her consent and again take custody of her child, and never consent to his

placement with his father or with the father's extended Indian family, the Kiowa Tribe, the grandparents or anyone else. *Baby Boy L.*, 231 Kan. at 208.

This meant, the court said, that Baby Boy L. would be placed with a non-Indian family under either ICWA or Kansas law. *Baby Boy L.*, 231 Kan. at 209.

The validity of the existing Indian family doctrine has been called into repeated question by a variety of courts and commentators over the course of the 27 years since *Baby Boy L.* was decided. See, e.g., *In re Baby Boy C. Jeffrey A.*, 27 A.D.3d 34, 46–47, 805 N.Y.S.2d 313 (2005); Atwood, *Flashpoints Under the Indian Child Welfare Act: Toward a New Understanding of State Court Resistance*, 51 Emory L.J. 587, 624–34 (2002); Prim, *The Indian Child Welfare Act and the Existing Indian Family Exception: Rerouting the Trail of Tears?*, 24 Law & Psychol. Rev. 115, 118–19 (2000).

Although the United States Supreme Court has not addressed the issue before us and has consistently denied review of cases dealing with the constitutionality of ICWA, its 1989 decision in *Mississippi Band of Choctaw Indians v. Holyfield*, underscored the central importance of the relationship between an Indian child and his or her tribe, independent of any parental relationship. *Holyfield*, 490 U.S. at 50. . . . Although focused on whether "domicile" should be defined by state law or by ICWA for purposes of determining jurisdiction, rather than on the existing Indian family doctrine, it is significant that the Court relied extensively on testimony from Congressional hearings leading to the passage of ICWA and on ICWA's explicit statement of Congress's purpose. [The court then quotes extensively from the *Holyfield* opinion.]

The Court's result and rationale in *Holyfield* recognized that ICWA grew in part out of concern for preservation of tribal interests in Indian children and that those interests could not necessarily be defeated by the desires of parents or concerns over placement permanency.

The majority of our sister states who have considered the existing Indian family doctrine have rejected it. See *In the Matter of the Adoption of T.N.F.*, 781 P.2d 973 (Alaska 1989); *Michael J., Jr. v. Michael J., Sr.*, 198 Ariz. 154, 7 P.3d 960 (Ariz. App. 2000); *In re N.B.*, 199 P.3d 16, 2007 WL 2493906 (Colo. App. 2007) (unpublished opinion); *In re Baby Boy Doe*, 123 Idaho 464, 849 P.2d 925 (1993); *In re Adoption of S.S.*, 252 Ill. App. 3d 33, 42–43, 622 N.E.2d 832, 190 Ill. Dec. 802 (1993), *rev'd on other grounds* 167 Ill.2d 250, 657 N.E.2d 935, 212 Ill. Dec. 590 (1995); *In re Elliott*, 218 Mich. App. 196, 203, 554 N.W.2d 32 (1996); *In the Matter of the Adoption of Riffle*, 277 Mont. 388, 922 P.2d 510 (1996); *Matter of Adoption of a Child of Indian Heritage*, 111 N.J. 155, 543 A.2d 925 (1988); see also Kunesh, *Borders Beyond Borders — Protecting Essential Tribal Relations Off Reservation Under the Indian Child Welfare Act*, 42 New Eng. L. Rev. 15, 59 n.226, 227 (2007); *In re Baby Boy C.*, 27 A.D.3d 34, 805 N.Y.S.2d 313 (2005); *In re A.B.*, 2003 ND 98, 663 N.W.2d 625 (N.D. 2003); *Quinn v. Walters*, 117 Ore. App. 579, 583–84, 845 P.2d 206 (1993), *rev'd on other grounds* 320 Or. 233, 881 P.2d 795 (1994); *State in Interest of D.A.C.*, 933 P.2d 993 (Utah App. 1997).

Other states, having once adopted the doctrine, have now abandoned it. See *In the Matter of Baby Boy L.*, 2004 OK 93, 103 P.3d 1099 (Okla. 2004) (holding the existing Indian family exception to application of Indian Child Welfare Act no longer viable, overruling prior state cases). Such changes of heart can be traced to changes in state law. See Wash. Rev. Code § 26.10.034(1) (2004); Wash. Rev. Code § 26.33.040(1) (2004); *Adoption of Crews*, 118 Wash. 2d 561, 825 P.2d 305 (1992); *In re R.E.K.F.*, 698 N.W.2d 147, 151 (Iowa 2005); Okla. Stat. tit. 10, § 40.3 (2001). In South Dakota, the court merely recognized that the existing Indian family doctrine was inconsistent with ICWA's motivating impulse and the United States Supreme Court's decision in *Holyfield*. *See Matter of Adoption of Baade*, 462 N.W.2d 485, 489–90 (S.D. 1990).

California's courts are split on the viability of the existing Indian family doctrine. Compare *In re Vincent M.*, 150 Cal. App. 4th 1247, 1265, 59 Cal. Rptr. 3d 321 (2007) (rejecting existing Indian family doctrine based on California statutory amendment); *In re Bridget R.*, 41 Cal. App. 4th 1483, 49 Cal. Rptr. 2d 507 (1996) (upholding validity of doctrine on constitutional ground); *Crystal R. v. Superior Court*, 59 Cal. App. 4th 703, 69 Cal. Rptr. 2d 414 (1997) (accepting, applying doctrine).

The doctrine has been employed by a few of our sister states on facts such as those before us; rationales have included perceived congressional intent and avoidance of constitutional infirmities in ICWA's placement preferences. See *In the Matter of Adoption of T.R.M.*, 525 N.E.2d 298, 303 (Ind. 1988); *Rye v. Weasel*, 934 S.W.2d 257, 43 12 Ky. L. Summary 23 (Ky. 1996); *Hampton v. J.A.L.*, 658 So. 2d 331 (La. App. 1995); *C.E.H. v. L.M.W.*, 837 S.W.2d 947, 952 (Mo. App. 1992); *In Interest of S.A.M.*, 703 S.W.2d 603 (Mo. App. 1986); see also *S.A. v. E.J.P.*, 571 So. 2d 1187 (Ala. Civ. App. 1990). Alabama has specifically limited application of the doctrine to facts similar to those here and in *Ex parte C.L.J.*, 946 So. 2d 880 (Ala. Civ. App. 2006) (doctrine applies only if child illegitimate, never member of Indian family or culture, non-Indian mother relinquishing child voluntarily).

We also note that there have been numerous amendments to and attempts to amend ICWA since its original enactment. On occasion, unsuccessful efforts have addressed the existing Indian family doctrine, but these efforts have been conflicting, directed at overruling it and endorsing it. Compare S. 1976, 100th Cong. (1987), and H.R. 3275, 104th Cong. (1996).

From this point in ICWA interpretation and the development of common law, we are persuaded that abandonment of the existing Indian family doctrine is the wisest future course. Although we do not lightly overrule precedent, neither are we inextricably bound by it. See *Crist v. Hunan Palace, Inc.*, 277 Kan. 706, 715, 89 P.3d 573 (2004). *Baby Boy L.* is ready to be retired.

First, the existing family doctrine appears to be at odds with the clear language of ICWA, which makes no exception for children such as A.J.S. See 25 U.S.C. § 1903(4); Jaffke, *The "Existing Indian Family" Exception to the Indian Child Welfare Act: The States' Attempt to Slaughter Tribal Interests in Indian Children*, 66 La. L. Rev. 733, 745–51 (2006).

Further, as recognized by the *Holyfield* decision, 490 U.S. at 36–37, tribal interests in preservation of their most precious resource, their children, drove passage of ICWA; and its expressly declared policy is

> to protect the best interests of Indian children and to promote the stability
> and security of Indian tribes and families by the establishment of minimum
> Federal standards for the removal of Indian children from their families
> and the placement of such children in foster or adoptive homes which will
> reflect the unique values of Indian culture, and by providing for assistance
> to Indian tribes in the operation of child and family service programs. 25
> U.S.C. § 1902.

As counsel for the Cherokee Nation emphasized at oral argument before us, a
child removed now from the tribe cannot later be a voice for the tribe.

We also detect illogic in the *Baby Boy L.* opinion's secondary justification for its
result, also invoked by the district judge here, that the non-Indian mother's refusal
to consent to adoption of her infant by anyone other than the proposed non-Indian
adoptive parents inevitably means a non-Indian upbringing for the child. In *Baby
Boy L.*, as here, the mother's testimony was evidence of her intention only. That
intention extends only as far as the mother's unilateral control. If ICWA applies, a
father's fitness to parent and the child's placement will not be governed solely by the
mother's expressed desires. The father and the tribe also will be heard, and ICWA's
preferences will apply in the absence of "good cause to the contrary." 25 U.S.C.
§ 1915(a). Although the result reached may be the same as that dictated by the
existing Indian family doctrine, it may not be. See *Baby Boy C.*, 27 A.D.3d at 52–53;
In re Alicia S., 65 Cal. App. 4th 79, 88–89, 76 Cal. Rptr. 2d 121 (1998). A.J.S.'s
unmarried mother's status as a non-Indian or another factor or set of factors may
militate in favor of or against a certain ICWA preference or constitute "good cause"
to ignore all of the preferences. We cannot know and neither could the members of
this court who decided *Baby Boy L.* Simply put, an Indian family may yet be
recognized or created if ICWA is not avoided through the existing Indian family
doctrine.

We are also influenced by our sister states' and commentators' widespread and
well-reasoned criticism of the doctrine. For example, in *Baby Boy C.*, 27 A.D.3d 34,
805 N.Y.S.2d 313, in which an unmarried Indian mother and non-Indian father
attempted to relinquish their parental rights to facilitate their infant's adoption by
non-Indian parents, the court convincingly detailed inconsistencies between the
existing Indian family doctrine and the plain language of ICWA, as well as the
doctrine's deviation from ICWA's core purpose of "preserving and protecting the
interests of Indian tribes in their children." 27 A.D.3d at 47. The court said:

> Because Congress has clearly delineated the nature of the relationship
> between an Indian child and tribe necessary to trigger application of the
> Act, judicial insertion of an additional criterion for applicability is plainly
> beyond the intent of Congress and must be rejected. . . .

> Another problem with the [doctrine] is that its acceptance would under-
> mine the significant tribal interests recognized by the Supreme Court in
> *Holyfield*. The Supreme Court made it clear in *Holyfield* that Indian tribes
> have an interest in applying ICWA that is distinct from that of the child's
> parents, and that such parents may not unilaterally defeat its application

by deliberately avoiding any contact with the tribe or reservation (490 U.S. at 51–52). In many respects, that is what occurred in this case. By divorcing herself from tribal life and by putting her child up for adoption away from the reservation immediately after birth, [the mother] singlehandedly destroyed the notion of an "existing Indian family." If the [doctrine] were applied in this instance, [the mother] would have succeeded in nullifying ICWA's purpose at the expense of the interests of the Tribe. However, as *Holyfield* recognized, Congress intended otherwise by specifically mandating that tribal interests be considered ['protection of this tribal interest is at the core of the ICWA, which recognizes that the tribe has an interest in the child which is distinct from but on a parity with the interest of the parents']; see also *Matter of Baby Boy Doe*, 123 Idaho [464, 470–71, 849 P.2d 925, 931–32 (1993)]; *In re A.B.*, 2003 ND 98, 663 N.W.2d [625, 636 (N.D. 2003)].

Nor can we agree . . . that 'relinquishing control over a child born to parents uninvolved in Indian life costs the tribe nothing.' [Citation omitted.] Where, as here, [the mother] has rejected Indian life and culture and then, voluntarily relinquished her newborn Indian child to be adopted by a non-Indian couple, the detriment to the Tribe is quite significant — the loss of two generations of Indian children instead of just one.

The [doctrine] also conflicts with the Congressional policy underlying ICWA that certain child custody determinations be made in accordance with Indian cultural or community standards (see *Holyfield*, 490 U.S. at 34–35 [one of the most serious failings of the present system is that Indian children are removed from natural parents by nontribal governmental authorities who have no basis for intelligently evaluating the cultural and social premises underlying Indian home life and child rearing]; 25 U.S.C. § 1915(d) [applicable standards 'shall be the prevailing social and cultural standards of the Indian community'].

The [doctrine] is clearly at odds with this policy because it requires state subjective factual determination as to the 'Indianness' of a particular Indian child or parent, a determination that state courts 'are ill-equipped to make' (In re Alicia S., 65 Cal. App. 4th at 90, 76 Cal. Rptr. 2d at 128). Since ICWA was passed, in part, to curtail state authorities from making child custody determinations based on misconceptions of Indian family life, the [doctrine], which necessitates such an inquiry, clearly frustrates this purpose (*Holyfield*[, 490 U.S. at 34–35]; *Quinn*, [*v. Walters*, 117 Ore. App. 579, 584 n.2, 845 P.2d 206 (1993)]; [*State in Interest of D.A.C.*, 933 P.2d 993, 999 (Utah App. 1997)]." *Baby Boy C.*, 27 A.D.3d at 48–49.

See also Jaffke, 66 La. L. Rev. at 745–58; Atwood, 51 Emory L.J. at 625–42; Prim, 24 Law & Pyschol. Rev. at 118–24; Graham, *"The Past Never Vanishes": A Contextual Critique of the Existing Indian Family Doctrine*, 23 Am. Indian. L. Rev. 1, 34–43 (1998); Cross, *The Existing Indian Family Exception: Is it Appropriate to Use a Judicially Created Exception to Render the Indian Child Welfare Act of 1978 Inapplicable?* 26 Cap. U. L. Rev. 847, 864–90 (1998); Parnell, *The Existing Indian Family Exception: Denying Tribal Rights Protected by the*

Indian Child Welfare Act, 34 San Diego L. Rev. 381, 397–401, 408–28 (1997); Davis, *The Existing Indian Family Exception to the Indian Child Welfare Act*, 69 N.D. L. Rev. 465, 475–96 (1993); Lehmann, *The Indian Child Welfare Act of 1978: Does it Apply to the Adoption of an Illegitimate Child?* 38 Cath. U. L. Rev. 511, 533–37 (1989).

Given all of the foregoing, we hereby overrule *Baby Boy L.*, 231 Kan. 199, 643 P.2d 168, and abandon its existing Indian family doctrine. Indian heritage and the treatment of it has a unique history in United States law. A.J.S. has both Indian and non-Indian heritage, and courts are right to resist essentializing any ethnic or racial group. However, ICWA's overall design, including its "good cause" threshold in 25 U.S.C. § 1915, ensures that all interests — those of both natural parents, the tribe, the child, and the prospective adoptive parents — are appropriately considered and safeguarded. ICWA applies to this state court child custody proceeding involving A.J.S., and the Cherokee Nation must be permitted to intervene. The contrary rulings of the district judge are reversed, and the case remanded for further proceedings consistent with this opinion.

Reversed and *remanded.*

NOTES

1. **Significance of *In re A.J.S.*:** The Kansas Supreme Court was the first state high court to articulate the "existing Indian family" exception to ICWA's definition of "Indian child." Numerous state courts followed suit, as the *A.J.S.* opinion points out. So repudiation of the exception by the Kansas court marks a significant turning point. Scholarly criticism of the doctrine seems to have had a major impact on the courts' analysis. There are still state courts applying the "existing Indian family" exception, however.

2. **State Judicial Resistance and the Constitutionality of ICWA:** The "existing Indian family" doctrine, overruled in *In re A.J.S.*, has been applied in some states to involuntary child welfare proceedings to terminate parental rights, as well as to voluntary adoptions. For example, in *In re Santos Y.*, 92 Cal. App. 4th 1274 (2001), one California Court of Appeal overturned the decision to place an Indian child with a member of his extended family on the Grand Portage Chippewa Reservation, in accordance with ICWA's placement preferences, following termination of parental rights. The child had been living with a non-Indian foster family for 18 months since birth, and the court found that he had never been part of an "existing Indian family." Although California had enacted legislation forbidding application of the "existing Indian family" exception, California Welfare and Institutions Code § 360.6, the Court of Appeal found that provision unconstitutional under the due process clause, the equal protection clause, and the Tenth Amendment. As a matter of due process, the court stated, it violates the child's liberty interest in continuing an existing family relationship to separate him from his foster parents solely because of his Indian ancestry. According to the court, only a compelling government interest could overcome this deprivation, and the court found no such interest, observing:

> The Minor's sole connection with the Tribe is a one-quarter "Minnesota Chippewa Tribe" genetic contribution from an enrolled bloodline, and enrollment based on that genetic contribution. While placing the Minor for adoption on the Reservation would, in the most attenuated sense, promote the stability and security of the Tribe by providing one more individual to carry on Minnesota Chippewa cultural traditions, we find the "repatriation" to the Reservation of a child of assimilated parents, solely because of the child's one-quarter Minnesota Chippewa Tribe genetic heritage, to be a constitutionally impermissible application of the statue.

The court also rejected application of the more relaxed equal protection standard of review in *Morton v. Mancari* (presented in Ch. 2, Sec. B.1), and found the "existing Indian family" doctrine constitutionally compelled on equal protection and Tenth Amendment grounds for essentially the same reason.

Santos Y. was not the first occasion for a court to consider the constitutionality of ICWA. Soon after Congress passed ICWA, the South Dakota Supreme Court sustained its constitutionality as applied to Indian children who had spent some time living in a group foster home outside their reservation. Both of the parents were tribal members domiciled on the Lower Brule Sioux reservation, and the tribal court was asserting exclusive jurisdiction under the Act. The court rejected challenges based on the Tenth Amendment, equal protection, and due process, relying on *Williams v. Lee*, 358 U.S. 217 (1959), to establish that state jurisdiction would infringe upon tribal self-government, and *Fisher v. District Court*, 424 U.S. 382 (1976), to explain that the jurisdictional treatment was based on a political rather than a racial classification. *Matter of Guardianship of D.L.L. & C.L.L.*, 291 N.W.2d 278 (S.D. 1980). According to the South Dakota court, "The locus of the act of a member is not conclusive. Rather, the test is a broader one, hinging on whether the matter demands exercise of the tribe's responsibility of self-government. . . . There can be no greater threat to essential tribal relations and to the tribal power of self-government than to interfere in questions of custody of tribal members." *See also Armell v. Prairie Band of Potawatomi Indians*, 550 N.E.2d 1060 (Ill. App. Ct. 1990) (rejecting an equal protection challenge to ICWA).

The constitutional questions raised in these cases and in *Santos Y.* were debated with even greater vigor by Congress in connection with the passage of ICWA. In letters to the congressional committee, Assistant Attorney General (later Judge) Patricia M. Wald raised questions regarding the constitutionality of the bill. First, the Department of Justice questioned whether the broad definition of "Indian child" contained in the proposed legislation might constitute invidious racial discrimination in violation of the Fifth Amendment. Second, the Department of Justice questioned whether such pervasive federal legislation in an area of traditional state concern, such as child welfare and custody, might violate the Tenth Amendment. Finally, the Department of Justice challenged the constitutionality of authorizing Indian tribes to exercise jurisdiction over children domiciled off the reservation and over nonmember children domiciled on or off reservation, stating:

> An eligible Indian who has chosen, for whatever reasons, not to enroll in a tribe would be in a position to argue that depriving him of access to the State courts on matters related to family life would be invidious. Such an

Indian presumably has, under the first amendment, the same right of association as do all citizens, and indeed would appear to be in no different situation from a non-Indian living on reservation who . . . would have access to State courts. The only difference between them would, in fact, be the racial characteristics of the former.

H. Rep. No. 95-1386, 95th Cong., 2d Sess. 37 (1978). In another letter, the Department stated:

[W]e are not convinced that Congress' power to control the incidents of such litigation involving nonreservation Indian children and parents pursuant to the Indian commerce clause is sufficient to override the significant State interest in regulating the procedure to be followed by its courts in exercising State jurisdiction over what is a traditionally state matter. It seems to us that the Federal interest in the off-reservation context is so attenuated that the 10th Amendment and general principles of federalism preclude the wholesale invasion of State power contemplated by section 102 (25 U.S.C. § 1912).

Id. at 40.

In response to these concerns, some changes were made in the proposed legislation. To what extent does the text of ICWA resolve these questions? The congressional reports responded to some of these concerns by noting that the committees disagreed with the constitutional assessments offered by the Department of Justice. Thus, the House report offered an extensive brief to support the constitutionality of ICWA, the major outlines of which are evident in the preamble to the statute.

First, responding to the concern that the definition of Indian child might constitute invidious racial discrimination because it included persons who are not enrolled tribal members, the report noted that the definition of "Indians" contained in section 19 of the IRA also was not limited to tribal members and, yet, was approved in *Morton v. Mancari* (set forth and discussed in Ch. 2, Sec. B.). The report noted that a number of cases decided in the wake of federal efforts to wind up the affairs of the Oklahoma tribes at the turn of the century had sustained the power of Congress to disregard tribal membership rolls and make its own judgments about entitlements to per capita distribution. *See, e.g., Stephens v. Cherokee Nation*, 174 U.S. 445 (1899); *Sizemore v. Brady*, 235 U.S. 441 (1914); *see also* FELIX S. COHEN, HANDBOOK OF FEDERAL INDIAN LAW 45 n.10 (1942). Thus, the report stated,

[T]he constitutional and plenary power of Congress over Indians and Indian tribes and affairs cannot be made to hinge upon the cranking into operation of a mechanical [enrollment] process established under tribal law, particularly with respect to Indian children who, because of their minority, cannot make a reasoned decision about their tribal and Indian identity.

In *Santos Y.*, the Court of Appeal insisted that unless Santos Y.'s mother has had ongoing and significant cultural, political, or social connections with her tribe, any special treatment of Santos Y. under ICWA must be attributed solely to his "genetic association" with the tribe, an impermissible racial classification. The court thus declined to apply *Morton v. Mancari*. Professor Carole Goldberg describes the court's approach as "an erroneous act of racialization." According to Professor Goldberg,

> . . . The court characterizes Santos Y. as a "multi-ethnic child who has had a minimal relationship with his assimilated parents. . . . " At another point, the court finds ICWA unconstitutional as applied to any individual "who is in all respects, except in genetic heritage, indistinguishable from other residents of th[e] state. . . . " Yet Santos Y. was indeed distinguishable from children ineligible for tribal membership. He was entitled to special tribal and federal benefits relating to health and education. At an appropriate age, he could vote in tribal elections or hold tribal office. He enjoyed treaty-based hunting, fishing, and gathering rights as a tribal member, as well as rights to assignment of tribal lands. Most important, however, he had access to the vast resources of his tribal culture, including kinship and clan relations prescribed by Chippewa or Anishnabe creation stories. These duties are ascribed to one by birth and transcend individual rejection, even death. It may be true that Santos Y.'s own mother had not participated in her tribal community. But the adoption offered by his mother's extended family member, who worked as the Tribe's director of education, opened the prospect of cultural integration for Santos Y.

Carole Goldberg, *Descent into Race*, 49 UCLA L. REV. 1373, 1383–84 (2002).

In making the equal protection analysis turn on the extent of the family's tribal associations, the Court of Appeal in *Santos Y.* followed the path of *Babbitt v. Williams*, discussed in Ch. 2, Sec. B.3, which stated that rational basis review under *Morton v. Mancari* would apply only "to legislation involving uniquely Indian concerns." According to another California Court of Appeal decision, *In re Bridget R.*, 41 Cal. App. 4th 1483, 1515 (1996), that would mean assessing whether the parents

> privately observed tribal customs and, among other things, whether despite their distance from the reservation, they participated in tribal community affairs, voted in tribal elections, or otherwise took an interest in tribal politics, contributed to tribal or Indian charities, subscribed to tribal newsletters or other periodicals of special interest to Indians, participated in Indian religious, social, cultural or politics events which are held in their own locality, or maintained social contacts with other members of the Tribe.

Does it make sense to have state courts serving as arbiters of Indian identity, for the purpose of determining applicable standards of review in equal protection cases or for any other purpose? Do the criteria in *Bridget R.* (for example, subscription to tribal newsletters) reflect non-Indian notions of cultural affiliation, or forms of cultural affiliation accepted by the tribal groups themselves?

Insofar as the Tenth Amendment was concerned, the House report on ICWA took the position that so long as the statute constituted an appropriate exercise of the plenary power of Congress over Indian affairs, the supremacy clause of Article VI, clause 2 of the Constitution required inconsistent state policies to yield. Relying on *Wakefield v. Little Light*, 347 A.2d 228 (Md. 1975), and *Wisconsin Band of*

Potowatomies of Hannahville Indian Community v. Houston, 393 F. Supp. 719 (W.D. Mich. 1973), the report noted that "a tribe's children are vital to its integrity and future. Since the United States has the responsibility to protect the integrity of the tribes, we can say with the *Kagama* court, ' . . . there arises the duty of protection, and with it the power.' " H. Rep. No. 95-1386, 95th Cong., 2d Sess. 15 (1978). The legislative history of ICWA further indicated that Indian children were being placed in foster care or adopted at alarming rates, often because social workers did not understand Indian extended family child-rearing practices or because poverty was equated with neglect. *See* Hearings on S. 1214 Before the Senate Select Comm. on Indian Affairs, 95th Cong., 1st Sess., 538–40 (1977).

Despite Congress's finding that ICWA was necessary to preserve the very existence of Indian nations by preventing the cultural removal of their children, *In re Santos Y.* finds a violation of the Tenth Amendment because ICWA has no adequate "nexus" to Congress's Indian commerce clause power when the parents lack sufficient social, political, or cultural ties to their tribe. Was the House report on ICWA relying exclusively on Congress's Indian commerce clause power when it invoked the *Kagama* decision, discussed in Ch. 1, Sec. D.2? Consider the implications of the United States Supreme Court's decision in *United States v. John,* 437 U.S. 634 (1978), presented and discussed in Ch. 4, Sec. A.1. In *John,* the United States wanted to prosecute an Indian under the Major Crimes Act and to preclude state prosecution for the same offense. The Indian had committed the crime on the Mississippi Choctaw reservation, which had not been under continuous federal supervision since the attempted removal of the Choctaw in the nineteenth century, but which was now held in trust for the federally recognized tribe. The State of Mississippi argued that the Mississippi Choctaw had become "fully assimilated into the political and social life of the State," and therefore the Indian commerce clause could not supply a basis for federal jurisdiction. In rejecting this argument, the Supreme Court stated, "we do not agree that Congress and the Executive Branch have less power to deal with the affairs of the Mississippi Choctaws than with the affairs of other [non-assimilated] Indian groups." The required nexus to the Indian commerce clause was supplied by the "elaborate history . . . of relations between the [Indian tribes] and the United States . . . [including the fact that in] the early 1950s . . . federal Indian policy . . . emphasized assimilation. . . . " The *Santos Y.* court did not discuss *United States v. John.*

The *Santos Y.* court invoked the "existing Indian family" doctrine and the Tenth Amendment even in the face of state legislation directing it to apply ICWA. Why might a state court be asserting "state interests" under these circumstances? The court also declares that state Indian child welfare legislation is preempted because it involves tribes, but then finds ICWA unconstitutional as applied to the facts before it because no tribal interest is sufficiently implicated. Are these two positions consistent? Is the implication of the court's Tenth Amendment analysis that states may never legislate with respect to tribes? Minnesota, for example, has adopted a state counterpart to ICWA. Minnesota Indian Family Preservation Act, Minn. Stat. §§ 260.751–260.835.

Finally, the House report on ICWA did not anticipate the due process challenge accepted in *Santos Y.,* probably because there has never been a United States Supreme Court decision indicating that such a challenge could succeed. As one careful commentator has pointed out, the *Santos Y.* court,

> by constitutionalizing the children's interest in remaining in their adoptive/
> foster homes, interpreted federal constitutional principles to go beyond
> existing Supreme Court precedent. . . . Moreover, even if children were
> recognized as possessing a constitutional liberty interest in preserving
> family-like relationships, it is not at all clear that the ICWA is therefore
> unconstitutional under circumstances such as those presented in *Santos*.
> Instead, the presence of a child's constitutional liberty interest would seem
> to require a careful adjudication at the placement stage where the court
> would take into account the child's interest in remaining with his de facto
> family.

Barbara Atwood, *Flashpoints Under the Indian Child Welfare Act: Toward a New Understanding of State Court Resistance*, 51 EMORY L.J. 587, 639–41 (2002). In other words, does *Santos Y.* erroneously treat the child's asserted liberty interest as absolute? Is it possible that *Santos Y.* also failed to acknowledge other competing liberty interests, including those of the Indian child to be associated with her tribe, and the tribe's interest in its stability and security, both acknowledged in ICWA itself? Would these interests supply the "compelling government purpose" required when an individual is deprived of liberty under the due process clause? What about the long string of Supreme Court decisions, such as *Morton v. Mancari* itself, declaring that Congress is entitled to considerable deference when it exercises its power under the Indian commerce clause? For an extended analysis of these questions, see Christine Metteer, *The Existing Indian Family Exception: An Impediment to the Trust Responsibility to Preserve Tribal Existence and Culture as Manifested in the Indian Child Welfare Act*, 30 LOY. L.A. L. REV. 647, 672–81 (1997). Professor Rachel Moran has interpreted the "existing Indian family" cases denying application of ICWA as the tacit creation of a right of children who have been defined as "white" to remain with a white family. RACHEL F. MORAN, INTERRACIAL INTIMACY: THE REGULATION OF RACE AND ROMANCE 134–52 (2001). Now that some tribes are developing lucrative forms of economic development such as tribal gaming, with the potential for significant per capita distributions and tribal support for their citizens' education, health, and welfare, should state courts be paying greater heed to Indian children's "right to be Indian"? For one state court's analysis and rejection of the position that ICWA is unconstitutional in the absence of the existing Indian family exception, see *Baby Boy C. v. Tohono O'odham Nation*, 27 A.D.3d 34 (N.Y. App. Div. 2005).

Given growing state court disapproval of the "existing Indian family" exception, is it likely that other courts will follow the lead of *In re Santos Y.*? The United States Supreme Court's 2013 decision in *Adoptive Couple v. Baby Girl*, presented in Sec. D.4, below, could revitalize constitutional challenges to ICWA. Justice Alito's majority opinion does not directly address the constitutional issues posed by ICWA or the "existing Indian family" doctrine. Instead, it interprets the language in ICWA providing protections to Indian parents, and decides that biological fathers who have never had physical or legal custody of their children are excluded. Nonetheless, Justice Thomas's concurring opinion attacks the constitutionality of ICWA, both as outside Congress's powers and as a violation of due process/equal protection, concluding that the statute would be invalid unless interpreted to exclude such fathers.

3.   **State Legislative Attempts to Achieve ICWA Compliance:** As the Kansas Supreme Court notes in *In re A.J.S.*, several states have recently passed laws aimed at improving state court compliance with ICWA. For example, the Iowa Indian Child Welfare Act, Iowa Code chapter 232B, enacted during the 2003 legislative session, specifies that state policy requires full cooperation with Indian tribes and tribal citizens to ensure the intent and provisions of ICWA are enforced. The law also requires notice to the tribe and family at every stage of a child welfare proceeding to help parties understand and participate in the legal process. A portion of this statute was held unconstitutional on equal protection grounds in *In the Interest of A.W. and S.W.*, 741 N.W.2d 793 (Iowa 2007), discussed in Ch. 2, Sec. B.3. The Iowa high court found that the state law erred in extending protection to children of Indian ancestry who did not qualify as "Indian children" under ICWA. During its 2002 legislative session, the Colorado legislature passed HB 1064, which, among other things, established an Indian Child Welfare Act Team comprised of officials from around the state to monitor ICWA compliance. *See also* Kathryn E. Fort, *Waves of Education: Tribal-State Court Cooperation and the Indian Child Welfare Act*, 47 TULSA L. REV. 530 (2012), (discussing the history of cooperation between tribal and state representatives in developing state ICWA laws in Michigan.)

4.   When Does ICWA Protect an Indian Parent?

Even when a child unquestionably qualifies as an "Indian child," some state courts have resisted application of ICWA by refusing the claims of Indian biological fathers when non-Indians attempt an adoption. In the case that follows, the state trial court refused such claims, only to be reversed on appeal within the state's own system. The United States Supreme Court sided with the trial court, finding that ICWA did not protect the rights of a biological father because he never had custody of the child and the adoption thus did not interfere with parental custody, or cause the "breakup of an Indian family," and no other eligible Indian relative had attempted to adopt the child. As you read the opinion, consider the implications of the case for the definition of who is an "Indian" (note the Court's view that the child is "classified as Indian because she is 1.2% (3/256) Cherokee") and the scope of federal power to regulate the domestic affairs of individual Indians living outside of Indian country (see Justice Thomas's concurring opinion). Does the decision have consequences beyond Indian law, challenging the rights of unwed biological fathers to establish a relationship with their children (see Justice Sotomayor's dissent)? Also, where are the Indian law canons of construction to be found in this dispute over the interpretation of a federal Indian law statute?

ADOPTIVE COUPLE v. BABY GIRL
United States Supreme Court
133 S. Ct. 2552 (2013)

JUSTICE ALITO delivered the opinion of the Court.

This case is about a little girl (Baby Girl) who is classified as an Indian because she is 1.2% (3/256) Cherokee. Because Baby Girl is classified in this way, the South Carolina Supreme Court held that certain provisions of the federal Indian Child Welfare Act of 1978 required her to be taken, at the age of 27 months, from the only parents she had ever known and handed over to her biological father, who had attempted to relinquish his parental rights and who had no prior contact with the child. The provisions of the federal statute at issue here do not demand this result.

Contrary to the State Supreme Court's ruling, we hold that 25 U. S. C. § 1912(f) — which bars involuntary termination of a parent's rights in the absence of a heightened showing that serious harm to the Indian child is likely to result from the parent's "continued custody" of the child — does not apply when, as here, the relevant parent never had custody of the child. We further hold that § 1912(d) — which conditions involuntary termination of parental rights with respect to an Indian child on a showing that remedial efforts have been made to prevent the "breakup of the Indian family" — is inapplicable when, as here, the parent abandoned the Indian child before birth and never had custody of the child. Finally, we clarify that § 1915(a), which provides placement preferences for the adoption of Indian children, does not bar a non-Indian family like Adoptive Couple from adopting an Indian child when no other eligible candidates have sought to adopt the child. We accordingly reverse the South Carolina Supreme Court's judgment and remand for further proceedings.

I

"The Indian Child Welfare Act of 1978 (ICWA), 92 Stat. 3069, 25 U. S. C. §§ 1901–1963, was the product of rising concern in the mid-1970's over the consequences to Indian children, Indian families, and Indian tribes of abusive child welfare practices that resulted in the separation of large numbers of Indian children from their families and tribes through adoption or foster care placement, usually in non-Indian homes." *Mississippi Band of Choctaw Indians v. Holyfield*, 490 U.S. 30, 32 (1989). Congress found that "an alarmingly high percentage of Indian families [were being] broken up by the removal, often unwarranted, of their children from them by nontribal public and private agencies." § 1901(4). This "wholesale removal of Indian children from their homes" prompted Congress to enact the ICWA, which establishes federal standards that govern state-court child custody proceedings involving Indian children. *Id.*, at 32, 36 (internal quotation marks omitted); see also § 1902 (declaring that the ICWA establishes "minimum Federal standards for the removal of Indian children from their families").[47]

---

[47] [1] It is undisputed that Baby Girl is an "Indian child" as defined by the ICWA because she is an unmarried minor who "is eligible for membership in an Indian tribe and is the biological child of a

Three provisions of the ICWA are especially relevant to this case. *First*, "[a]ny party seeking" an involuntary termination of parental rights to an Indian child under state law must demonstrate that "active efforts have been made to provide remedial services and rehabilitative programs designed to prevent the breakup of the Indian family and that these efforts have proved unsuccessful." § 1912(d). *Second*, a state court may not involuntarily terminate parental rights to an Indian child "in the absence of a determination, supported by evidence beyond a reasonable doubt, including testimony of qualified expert witnesses, that the continued custody of the child by the parent or Indian custodian is likely to result in serious emotional or physical damage to the child." § 1912(f). *Third*, with respect to adoptive placements for an Indian child under state law, "a preference shall be given, in the absence of good cause to the contrary, to a placement with (1) a member of the child's extended family; (2) other members of the Indian child's tribe; or (3) other Indian families." § 1915(a).

II

In this case, Birth Mother (who is predominantly Hispanic) and Biological Father (who is a member of the Cherokee Nation) became engaged in December 2008. One month later, Birth Mother informed Biological Father, who lived about four hours away, that she was pregnant. After learning of the pregnancy, Biological Father asked Birth Mother to move up the date of the wedding. He also refused to provide any financial support until after the two had married. The couple's relationship deteriorated, and Birth Mother broke off the engagement in May 2009. In June, Birth Mother sent Biological Father a text message asking if he would rather pay child support or relinquish his parental rights. Biological Father responded via text message that he relinquished his rights.

Birth Mother then decided to put Baby Girl up for adoption. Because Birth Mother believed that Biological Father had Cherokee Indian heritage, her attorney contacted the Cherokee Nation to determine whether Biological Father was formally enrolled. The inquiry letter misspelled Biological Father's first name and incorrectly stated his birthday, and the Cherokee Nation responded that, based on the information provided, it could not verify Biological Father's membership in the tribal records.

Working through a private adoption agency, Birth Mother selected Adoptive Couple, non-Indians living in South Carolina, to adopt Baby Girl. Adoptive Couple supported Birth Mother both emotionally and financially throughout her pregnancy. Adoptive Couple was present at Baby Girl's birth in Oklahoma on September 15, 2009, and Adoptive Father even cut the umbilical cord. The next morning, Birth Mother signed forms relinquishing her parental rights and consenting to the adoption. Adoptive Couple initiated adoption proceedings in South Carolina a few days later, and returned there with Baby Girl. After returning to South Carolina, Adoptive Couple allowed Birth Mother to visit and communicate with Baby Girl.

---

member of an Indian tribe," § 1903(4)(b). It is also undisputed that the present case concerns a "child custody proceeding," which the ICWA defines to include proceedings that involve "termination of parental rights" and "adoptive placement," § 1903(1).

It is undisputed that, for the duration of the pregnancy and the first four months after Baby Girl's birth, Biological Father provided no financial assistance to Birth Mother or Baby Girl, even though he had the ability to do so. Indeed, Biological Father "made no meaningful attempts to assume his responsibility of parenthood" during this period. App. to Pet. for Cert. 122a (Sealed; internal quotation marks omitted).

Approximately four months after Baby Girl's birth, Adoptive Couple served Biological Father with notice of the pending adoption. (This was the first notification that they had provided to Biological Father regarding the adoption proceeding.) Biological Father signed papers stating that he accepted service and that he was "not contesting the adoption." But Biological Father later testified that, at the time he signed the papers, he thought that he was relinquishing his rights to Birth Mother, not to Adoptive Couple.

Biological Father contacted a lawyer the day after signing the papers, and subsequently requested a stay of the adoption proceedings. In the adoption proceedings, Biological Father sought custody and stated that he did not consent to Baby Girl's adoption. Moreover, Biological Father took a paternity test, which verified that he was Baby Girl's biological father. A trial took place in the South Carolina Family Court in September 2011, by which time Baby Girl was two years old. The Family Court concluded that Adoptive Couple had not carried the heightened burden under § 1912(f) of proving that Baby Girl would suffer serious emotional or physical damage if Biological Father had custody. The Family Court therefore denied Adoptive Couple's petition for adoption and awarded custody to Biological Father. On December 31, 2011, at the age of 27 months, Baby Girl was handed over to Biological Father, whom she had never met.

The South Carolina Supreme Court affirmed the Family Court's denial of the adoption and the award of custody to Biological Father. The State Supreme Court first determined that the ICWA applied because the case involved a child custody proceeding relating to an Indian child. It also concluded that Biological Father fell within the ICWA's definition of a "parent." The court then held that two separate provisions of the ICWA barred the termination of Biological Father's parental rights. *First*, the court held that Adoptive Couple had not shown that "active efforts ha[d] been made to provide remedial services and rehabilitative programs designed to prevent the breakup of the Indian family." § 1912(d). *Second*, the court concluded that Adoptive Couple had not shown that Biological Father's "custody of Baby Girl would result in serious emotional or physical harm to her beyond a reasonable doubt." § 1912(f). Finally, the court stated that, even if it had decided to terminate Biological Father's parental rights, § 1915(a)'s adoption-placement preferences would have applied.

III

It is undisputed that, had Baby Girl not been 3/256 Cherokee, Biological Father would have had no right to object to her adoption under South Carolina law. See Tr. of Oral Arg. 49; 398 S. C., at 644, n. 19, 731 S. E. 2d, at 560, n. 19 ("Under state law, [Biological] Father's consent to the adoption would not have been required"). The South Carolina Supreme Court held, however, that Biological Father is a "parent" under the ICWA and that two statutory provisions — namely, § 1912(f) and § 1912(d) — bar the termination of his parental rights. In this Court, Adoptive Couple contends that Biological Father is not a "parent" and that § 1912(f) and § 1912(d) are inapplicable. We need not — and therefore do not — decide whether Biological Father is a "parent." See § 1903(9) (defining "parent"). Rather, assuming for the sake of argument that he is a "parent," we hold that neither § 1912(f) nor § 1912(d) bars the termination of his parental rights.

A

Section 1912(f) addresses the involuntary termination of parental rights with respect to an Indian child. Specifically, § 1912(f) provides that "[n]o termination of parental rights may be ordered in such proceeding in the absence of a determination, supported by evidence beyond a reasonable doubt, . . . that the *continued custody* of the child by the parent or Indian custodian is likely to result in serious emotional or physical damage to the child." (Emphasis added.) The South Carolina Supreme Court held that Adoptive Couple failed to satisfy § 1912(f) because they did not make a heightened showing that Biological Father's "*prospective* legal and physical custody" would likely result in serious damage to the child (emphasis added). That holding was error.

Section 1912(f) conditions the involuntary termination of parental rights on a showing regarding the merits of "*continued* custody of the child by the parent." (Emphasis added.) The adjective "continued" plainly refers to a pre-existing state. As JUSTICE SOTOMAYOR concedes (dissenting opinion) (hereinafter the dissent), "continued" means "[c]arried on or kept up without cessation" or "[e]xtended in space without interruption or breach of conne[ct]ion." Compact Edition of the Oxford English Dictionary 909 (1981 reprint of 1971 ed.) (Compact OED); see also American Heritage Dictionary 288 (1981) (defining "continue" in the following manner: "1. To go on with a particular action or in a particular condition; persist. . . . 3. To remain in the same state, capacity, or place"); Webster's Third New International Dictionary 493 (1961) (Webster's) (defining "continued" as "stretching out in time or space esp. without interruption"); *Aguilar v. FDIC*, 63 F. 3d 1059, 1062 (CA11 1995) (*per curiam*) (suggesting that the phrase "continue an action" means "go on with . . . an action" that is "preexisting"). The term "continued" also can mean "resumed after interruption." Webster's 493; see American Heritage Dictionary 288. The phrase "continued custody" therefore refers to custody that a parent already has (or at least had at some point in the past). As a result, § 1912(f) does not apply in cases where the Indian parent *never* had custody of the Indian child.

Biological Father's contrary reading of § 1912(f) is nonsensical. Pointing to the provision's requirement that "[n]o termination of parental rights may be ordered . . . in the absence of a determination" relating to "the continued custody of the child by the parent," Biological Father contends that if a determination relating to "continued custody" is inapposite in cases where there is no "custody," the statutory text *prohibits* termination. But it would be absurd to think that Congress enacted a provision that *permits* termination of a custodial parent's rights, while simultaneously *prohibiting* termination of a noncustodial parent's rights. If the statute draws any distinction between custodial and noncustodial parents, that distinction surely does not provide greater protection for noncustodial parents.[48]

Our reading of § 1912(f) comports with the statutory text demonstrating that the primary mischief the ICWA was designed to counteract was the unwarranted *removal* of Indian children from Indian families due to the cultural insensitivity and biases of social workers and state courts. The statutory text expressly highlights the primary problem that the statute was intended to solve: "an alarmingly high percentage of Indian families [were being] broken up by the *removal*, often unwarranted, of their children from them by nontribal public and private agencies." § 1901(4) (emphasis added); see also § 1902 (explaining that the ICWA establishes "minimum Federal standards for the *removal* of Indian children from their families" (emphasis added)); *Holyfield*, 490 U.S., at 32–34. And if the legislative history of the ICWA is thought to be relevant, it further underscores that the Act was primarily intended to stem the unwarranted removal of Indian children from intact Indian families. See, *e.g.*, H. R. Rep. No. 95-1386, p. 8 (1978) (explaining that, as relevant here, "[t]he purpose of [the ICWA] is to protect the best interests of Indian children and to promote the stability and security of Indian tribes and families by establishing minimum Federal standards for the *removal* of Indian children from their families and the placement of such children in foster or adoptive homes" (emphasis added)); *id.*, at 9 (decrying the "wholesale separation of Indian children" from their Indian families); *id.*, at 22 (discussing "the removal" of Indian children from their parents pursuant to §§ 1912(e) and (f)). In sum, when, as here, the adoption of an Indian child is voluntarily and lawfully initiated by a non-Indian parent with sole custodial rights, the ICWA's primary goal of preventing the unwarranted removal of Indian children and the dissolution of Indian families is not implicated.

The dissent fails to dispute that nonbinding guidelines issued by the Bureau of Indian Affairs (BIA) shortly after the ICWA's enactment demonstrate that the BIA envisioned that § 1912(f)'s standard would apply only to termination of a *custodial* parent's rights. Specifically, the BIA stated that, under § 1912(f), "[a] child may not be *removed* simply because there is someone else willing to raise the child who is likely to do a better job"; instead, "[i]t must be shown that . . . it is dangerous for the child to *remain* with his or her *present* custodians." Guidelines for State Courts; Indian Child Custody Proceedings, 44 Fed. Reg. 67593 (1979) (emphasis added) (hereinafter Guidelines). Indeed, the Guidelines recognized that § 1912(f) applies only when there is pre-existing custody to evaluate. See *ibid.* ("[T]he issue on which qualified expert testimony is required is the question of whether or not serious damage to the child is likely to occur if the child is not removed").

Under our reading of § 1912(f), Biological Father should not have been able to invoke § 1912(f) in this case, because he had never had legal or physical custody of Baby Girl as of the time of the adoption proceedings. As an initial matter, it is undisputed that Biological Father never had *physical* custody of Baby Girl. And as

---

[48] [6] The dissent criticizes us for allegedly concluding that a biological father qualifies for "substantive" statutory protections "only when [he] has physical or state-recognized legal custody." But the dissent undercuts its own point when it states that "numerous" ICWA provisions not at issue here afford "meaningful" protections to biological fathers regardless of whether they ever had custody.

a matter of both South Carolina and Oklahoma law, Biological Father never had *legal* custody either. See S. C. Code Ann. § 63-17-20(B) (2010) ("Unless the court orders otherwise, the custody of an illegitimate child is solely in the natural mother unless the mother has relinquished her rights to the child"); Okla. Stat., Tit. 10, § 7800 (West Cum. Supp. 2013) ("Except as otherwise provided by law, the mother of a child born out of wedlock has custody of the child until determined otherwise by a court of competent jurisdiction").**49**

In sum, the South Carolina Supreme Court erred in finding that § 1912(f) barred termination of Biological Father's parental rights.

B

Section 1912(d) provides that "[a]ny party" seeking to terminate parental rights to an Indian child under state law "shall satisfy the court that active efforts have been made to provide remedial services and rehabilitative programs designed *to prevent the breakup of the Indian family* and that these efforts have proved unsuccessful." (Emphasis added.) The South Carolina Supreme Court found that Biological Father's parental rights could not be terminated because Adoptive Couple had not demonstrated that Biological Father had been provided remedial services in accordance with § 1912(d). We disagree.

Consistent with the statutory text, we hold that § 1912(d) applies only in cases where an Indian family's "breakup" would be precipitated by the termination of the parent's rights. The term "breakup" refers in this context to "[t]he discontinuance of a relationship," American Heritage Dictionary 235 (3d ed. 1992), or "an ending as an effective entity," Webster's 273 (defining "breakup" as "a disruption or dissolution into component parts: an ending as an effective entity"). See also Compact OED 1076 (defining "break-up" as, *inter alia*, a "disruption, separation into parts, disintegration"). But when an Indian parent abandons an Indian child prior to birth and that child has never been in the Indian parent's legal or physical custody, there is no "relationship" that would be "discontinu[ed]"— and no "effective entity" that would be "end[ed]" — by the termination of the Indian parent's rights. In such a situation, the "breakup of the Indian family" has long since occurred, and § 1912(d) is inapplicable.

Our interpretation of § 1912(d) is, like our interpretation of § 1912(f), consistent with the explicit congressional purpose of providing certain "standards for the *removal* of Indian children from their families." § 1902 (emphasis added); see also, *e.g.,* § 1901(4); *Holyfield*, 490 U.S., at 32–34. In addition, the BIA's Guidelines confirm that remedial services under § 1912(d) are intended "to alleviate the need to *remove* the Indian child from his or her parents or Indian custodians," not to

---

49 [7] In an effort to rebut our supposed conclusion that "Congress *could not* possibly have intended" to require legal termination of Biological Father's rights with respect to Baby Girl, the dissent asserts that a minority of States afford (or used to afford) protection to similarly situated biological fathers (emphasis added). This is entirely beside the point, because we merely conclude that, based on the statute's text and structure, Congress *did not* extend the heightened protections of § 1912(d) and § 1912(f) to all biological fathers. The fact that state laws may provide certain protections to biological fathers who have abandoned their children and who have never had custody of their children in no way undermines our analysis of these two federal statutory provisions.

facilitate a *transfer* of the child *to* an Indian parent. See 44 Fed. Reg., at 67592 (emphasis added).

Our interpretation of § 1912(d) is also confirmed by the provision's placement next to § 1912(e) and § 1912(f), both of which condition the outcome of proceedings on the merits of an Indian child's "continued custody" with his parent. That these three provisions appear adjacent to each other strongly suggests that the phrase "breakup of the Indian family" should be read in harmony with the "continued custody" requirement. See *United Sav. Assn. of Tex. v. Timbers of Inwood Forest Associates, Ltd.*, 484 U.S. 365, 371 (1988) (explaining that statutory construction "is a holistic endeavor" and that "[a] provision that may seem ambiguous in isolation is often clarified by the remainder of the statutory scheme"). None of these three provisions *creates* parental rights for unwed fathers where no such rights would otherwise exist. Instead, Indian parents who are already part of an "Indian family" are provided with access to "remedial services and rehabilitative programs" under § 1912(d) so that their "custody" might be "continued" in a way that avoids foster-care placement under § 1912(e) or termination of parental rights under § 1912(f). In other words, the provision of "remedial services and rehabilitative programs" under § 1912(d) supports the "continued custody" that is protected by § 1912(e) and § 1912(f).[50]

Section 1912(d) is a sensible requirement when applied to state social workers who might otherwise be too quick to remove Indian children from their Indian families. It would, however, be unusual to apply § 1912(d) in the context of an Indian parent who abandoned a child prior to birth and who never had custody of the child. The decision below illustrates this point. The South Carolina Supreme Court held that § 1912(d) mandated measures such as "attempting to stimulate [Biological] Father's desire to be a parent." But if prospective adoptive parents were required to engage in the bizarre undertaking of "stimulat[ing]" a biological father's "desire to be a parent," it would surely dissuade some of them from seeking to adopt Indian children.[51] And this would, in turn, unnecessarily place vulnerable Indian children at a unique disadvantage in finding a permanent and loving home, even in cases where neither an Indian parent nor the relevant tribe objects to the adoption.[52]

In sum, the South Carolina Supreme Court erred in finding that § 1912(d) barred

---

[50] [8] The dissent claims that our reasoning "necessarily extends to *all* Indian parents who have never had custody of their children," even if those parents have visitation rights. As an initial matter, the dissent's concern about the effect of our decision on individuals with visitation rights will be implicated, at most, in a relatively small class of cases. For example, our interpretation of § 1912(d) would implicate the dissent's concern only in the case of a parent who abandoned his or her child prior to birth and *never* had physical or legal custody, but *did* have some sort of visitation rights. Moreover, in cases where this concern is implicated, such parents might receive "comparable" protections under state law. And in any event, it is the *dissent's* interpretation that would have far-reaching consequences: Under the dissent's reading, *any* biological parent — even a sperm donor — would enjoy the heightened protections of § 1912(d) and § 1912(f), even if he abandoned the mother and the child immediately after conception.

[51] [9] Biological Father and the Solicitor General argue that a tribe or state agency could provide the requisite remedial services under § 1912(d). But what if they don't? And if they don't, would the adoptive parents have to undertake the task?

[52] [10] The dissent repeatedly mischaracterizes our opinion. As our detailed discussion of the terms of the ICWA makes clear, our decision is not based on a "[p]olicy disagreement with Congress's judgment."

termination of Biological Father's parental rights.

IV

In the decision below, the South Carolina Supreme Court suggested that if it had terminated Biological Father's rights, then § 1915(a)'s preferences for the adoptive placement of an Indian child would have been applicable. 398 S. C., at 655–657, 731 S. E. 2d, at 566–567. In so doing, however, the court failed to recognize a critical limitation on the scope of § 1915(a).

Section 1915(a) provides that "[i]n any adoptive placement of an Indian child under State law, a preference shall be given, in the absence of good cause to the contrary, to a placement with (1) a member of the child's extended family; (2) other members of the Indian child's tribe; or (3) other Indian families." Contrary to the South Carolina Supreme Court's suggestion, § 1915(a)'s preferences are inapplicable in cases where no alternative party has formally sought to adopt the child. This is because there simply is no "preference" to apply if no alternative party that is eligible to be preferred under § 1915(a) has come forward.

In this case, Adoptive Couple was the only party that sought to adopt Baby Girl in the Family Court or the South Carolina Supreme Court. Biological Father is not covered by § 1915(a) because he did not seek to *adopt* Baby Girl; instead, he argued that his parental rights should not be terminated in the first place.[53] Moreover, Baby Girl's paternal grandparents never sought custody of Baby Girl. Nor did other members of the Cherokee Nation or "other Indian families" seek to adopt Baby Girl, even though the Cherokee Nation had notice of — and intervened in — the adoption proceedings.[54]

. . . .

The Indian Child Welfare Act was enacted to help preserve the cultural identity and heritage of Indian tribes, but under the State Supreme Court's reading, the Act would put certain vulnerable children at a great disadvantage solely because an ancestor — even a remote one — was an Indian. As the State Supreme Court read §§ 1912(d) and (f), a biological Indian father could abandon his child *in utero* and refuse any support for the birth mother — perhaps contributing to the mother's

---

[53] [11] Section 1915(c) also provides that, in the case of an adoptive placement under § 1915(a), "if the Indian child's tribe shall establish a different order of preference by resolution, the agency or court effecting the placement shall follow such order so long as the placement is the least restrictive setting appropriate to the particular needs of the child, as provided in [§ 1915(b)]." Although we need not decide the issue here, it may be the case that an Indian child's tribe could alter §1915's preferences in a way that includes a biological father whose rights were terminated, but who has now reformed. See § 1915(c). If a tribe were to take such an approach, however, the court would still have the power to determine whether "good cause" exists to disregard the tribe's order of preference. See §§ 1915(a), (c); *In re Adoption of T. R. M.*, 525 N. E. 2d 298, 313 (Ind. 1988).

[54] [12] To be sure, an employee of the Cherokee Nation testified that the Cherokee Nation certifies families to be adoptive parents and that there are approximately 100 such families "that are ready to take children that want to be adopted." However, this testimony was only a general statement regarding the Cherokee Nation's practices; it did not demonstrate that a specific Indian family was willing to adopt Baby Girl, let alone that such a family formally sought such adoption in the South Carolina courts. See Reply Brief for Petitioners 13–14; see also Brief for Respondent Cherokee Nation 21–22.

decision to put the child up for adoption — and then could play his ICWA trump card at the eleventh hour to override the mother's decision and the child's best interests. If this were possible, many prospective adoptive parents would surely pause before adopting any child who might possibly qualify as an Indian under the ICWA. Such an interpretation would raise equal protection concerns, but the plain text of §§ 1912(f) and (d) makes clear that neither provision applies in the present context. Nor do § 1915(a)'s rebuttable adoption preferences apply when no alternative party has formally sought to adopt the child. We therefore reverse the judgment of the South Carolina Supreme Court and remand the case for further proceedings not inconsistent with this opinion.

It is so ordered.

JUSTICE THOMAS, concurring.

I join the Court's opinion in full but write separately to explain why constitutional avoidance compels this out-come. Each party in this case has put forward a plausible interpretation of the relevant sections of the Indian Child Welfare Act (ICWA). However, the interpretations offered by respondent Birth Father and the United States raise significant constitutional problems as applied to this case. Because the Court's decision avoids those problems, I concur in its interpretation.

I

The threshold question, then, is whether the Constitution grants Congress power to override state custody law whenever an Indian is involved.

II

The ICWA asserts that the Indian Commerce Clause, Art. I, § 8, cl. 3, and "other constitutional authority" provides Congress with "plenary power over Indian affairs." § 1901(1). The reference to "other constitutional authority" is not illuminating, and I am aware of no other enumerated power that could even arguably support Congress's intrusion into this area of traditional state authority (citations omitted). The assertion of plenary authority must, therefore, stand or fall on Congress's power under the Indian Commerce Clause. Although this Court has said that the "central function of the Indian Commerce Clause is to provide Congress with plenary power to legislate in the field of Indian affairs," *Cotton Petroleum Corp. v. New Mexico*, 490 U.S. 163, 192 (1989), neither the text nor the original understanding of the Clause supports Congress's claim to such "plenary" power.

A

The Indian Commerce Clause gives Congress authority "[t]o regulate *Commerce* . . . with the Indian tribes." Art. I, § 8, cl. 3 (emphasis added). "At the time the original Constitution was ratified, 'commerce' consisted of selling, buying, and bartering, as well as transporting for these purposes." *United States v. Lopez*, 514 U.S. 549, 585 (1995) (THOMAS, J., concurring).

The Indian Commerce Clause contains an additional textual limitation relevant to this case: Congress is given the power to regulate Commerce "with the Indian *tribes*." The Clause does not give Congress the power to regulate commerce with all Indian *persons* any more than the Foreign Commerce Clause gives Congress the power to regulate commerce with all foreign nationals traveling within the United States. A straightforward reading of the text, thus, confirms that Congress may only regulate commercial interactions — "commerce" — taking place with established Indian communities — "tribes." That power is far from "plenary."

B

Congress's assertion of "plenary power" over Indian affairs is also inconsistent with the history of the Indian Commerce Clause. At the time of the founding, the Clause was understood to reserve to the States general police powers with respect to Indians who were citizens of the several States. The Clause instead conferred on Congress the much narrower power to regulate trade with Indian tribes — that is, Indians who had not been incorporated into the body politic of any State.

III

In light of the original understanding of the Indian Commerce Clause, the constitutional problems that would be created by application of the ICWA here are evident. First, the statute deals with "child custody proceedings," § 1903(1), not "commerce." It was enacted in response to concerns that "an alarmingly high percentage of Indian families [were] broken up by the removal, often unwarranted, of their children from them by nontribal public and private agencies." § 1901(4). The perceived problem was that many Indian children were "placed in non-Indian foster and adoptive homes and institutions." *Ibid.* This problem, however, had nothing to do with commerce.

Second, the portions of the ICWA at issue here do not regulate Indian tribes as tribes. Sections 1912(d) and (f), and § 1915(a) apply to all child custody proceedings involving an Indian child, regardless of whether an Indian tribe is involved. This case thus does not directly implicate Congress's power to "legislate in respect to Indian *tribes*." *United States v. Lara*, 541 U.S. 193, 200 (2004) (emphasis added). Baby Girl was never domiciled on an Indian Reservation, and the Cherokee Nation had no jurisdiction over her. Cf. *Mississippi Band of Choctaw Indians v. Holyfield*, 490 U.S. 30, 53–54 (1989) (holding that the Indian Tribe had exclusive jurisdiction over child custody proceedings, even though the children were born off the reservation, because the children were "domiciled" on the reservation for purposes of the ICWA). Although Birth Father is a registered member of The Cherokee Nation, he did not live on a reservation either. He was, thus, subject to the laws of the State in which he resided (Oklahoma) and of the State where his daughter resided during the custody proceedings (South Carolina). Nothing in the Indian Commerce Clause permits Congress to enact special laws applicable to Birth Father merely because of his status as an Indian.[55]

---

[55] [3] Petitioners and the guardian ad litem contend that applying the ICWA to child custody

Because adoption proceedings like this one involve neither "commerce" nor "Indian tribes," there is simply no constitutional basis for Congress's assertion of authority over such proceedings. Also, the notion that Congress can direct state courts to apply different rules of evidence and procedure merely because a person of Indian descent is involved raises absurd possibilities. Such plenary power would allow Congress to dictate specific rules of criminal procedure for state-court prosecutions against Indian defendants. Likewise, it would allow Congress to substitute federal law for state law when contract disputes involve Indians. But the Constitution does not grant Congress power to override state law whenever that law happens to be applied to Indians. Accordingly, application of the ICWA to these child custody proceedings would be unconstitutional.

Because the Court's plausible interpretation of the relevant sections of the ICWA avoids these constitutional problems, I concur.

JUSTICE BREYER, concurring.

I join the Court's opinion with three observations. First, the statute does not directly explain how to treat an absentee Indian father who had next-to-no involvement with his child in the first few months of her life. That category of fathers may include some who would prove highly unsuitable parents, some who would be suitable, and a range of others in between. Most of those who fall within that category seem to fall outside the scope of the language of 25 U. S. C. §§ 1912(d) and (f). Thus, while I agree that the better reading of the statute is, as the majority concludes, to exclude most of those fathers, I also understand the risk that, from a policy perspective, the Court's interpretation could prove to exclude too many [citing dissent of JUSTICE SOTOMAYOR].

Second, we should decide here no more than is necessary. Thus, this case does not involve a father with visitation rights or a father who has paid "all of his child support obligations." Neither does it involve special circumstances such as a father who was deceived about the existence of the child or a father who was prevented from supporting his child. The Court need not, and in my view does not, now decide whether or how § 1912(d) and (f) apply where those circumstances are present.

Third, other statutory provisions not now before us may nonetheless prove relevant in cases of this kind. Section 1915(a) grants an adoptive "preference" to "(1) a member of the child's extended family; (2) other members of the Indian child's tribe; or (3) other Indian families . . . in the absence of good cause to the contrary." Further, § 1915(c) allows the "Indian child's tribe" to "establish a different order of preference by resolution." Could these provisions allow an absentee father to re-enter the special statutory order of preference with support from the tribe, and subject to a court's consideration of "good cause?" I raise, but do not here try to answer, the question.

---

proceedings on the basis of race implicates equal protection concerns. See Brief for Petitioners 45 (arguing that the statute would be unconstitutional "if unwed fathers with no preexisting substantive parental rights receive a statutory preference based solely on the Indian child's race"); Brief for Respondent Guardian Ad Litem 48–49 (same). I need not address this argument because I am satisfied that Congress lacks authority to regulate the child custody proceedings in this case.

JUSTICE SCALIA, dissenting.

I join JUSTICE SOTOMAYOR's dissent except as to one detail. I reject the conclusion that the Court draws from the words "continued custody" in 25 U. S. C § 1912(f) not because "literalness may strangle meaning," but because there is no reason that "continued" must refer to custody in the past rather than custody in the future. I read the provision as requiring the court to satisfy itself (beyond a reasonable doubt) not merely that initial or temporary custody is not "likely to result in serious emotional or physical damage to the child," but that continued custody is not likely to do so. See Webster's New International Dictionary 577 (2d ed. 1950) (defining "continued" as "[p]rotracted in time or space, esp. without interruption; constant"). For the reasons set forth in JUSTICE SOTOMAYOR's dissent, that connotation is much more in accord with the rest of the statute.

While I am at it, I will add one thought. The Court's opinion, it seems to me, needlessly demeans the rights of parenthood. It has been the constant practice of the common law to respect the entitlement of those who bring a child into the world to raise that child. We do not inquire whether leaving a child with his parents is "in the best interest of the child." It sometimes is not; he would be better off raised by someone else. But parents have their rights, no less than children do. This father wants to raise his daughter, and the statute amply protects his right to do so. There is no reason in law or policy to dilute that protection.

JUSTICE SOTOMAYOR, with whom JUSTICE GINSBURG and JUSTICE KAGAN join, and with whom JUSTICE SCALIA joins in part, dissenting.

A casual reader of the Court's opinion could be forgiven for thinking this an easy case, one in which the text of the applicable statute clearly points the way to the only sensible result. In truth, however, the path from the text of the Indian Child Welfare Act of 1978 (ICWA) to the result the Court reaches is anything but clear, and its result anything but right . . . Unlike the majority, I cannot adopt a reading of ICWA that is contrary to both its text and its stated purpose. I respectfully dissent.

I

When it excludes noncustodial biological fathers from the Act's substantive protections, [the Majority's] textually backward reading misapprehends ICWA's structure and scope. Moreover, notwithstanding the majority's focus on the perceived parental shortcomings of Birth Father, its reasoning necessarily extends to *all* Indian parents who have never had custody of their children, no matter how fully those parents have embraced the financial and emotional responsibilities of parenting. The majority thereby transforms a statute that was intended to provide uniform federal standards for child custody proceedings involving Indian children and their biological parents into an illogical piecemeal scheme.

A

Better to start at the beginning and consider the operation of the statute as a whole. ICWA commences with express findings. Congress recognized that "there is no resource that is more vital to the continued existence and integrity of Indian tribes than their children," 25 U. S. C. § 1901(3), and it found that this resource was threatened. State authorities insufficiently sensitive to "the essential tribal relations of Indian people and the cultural and social standards prevailing in Indian communities and families" were breaking up Indian families and moving Indian children to non-Indian homes and institutions. See §§ 1901(4)–(5). As § 1901(4) makes clear, and as this Court recognized in *Mississippi Band of Choctaw Indians v. Holyfield*, 490 U.S. 30, 33 (1989), adoptive placements of Indian children with non-Indian families contributed significantly to the overall problem. See § 1901(4) (finding that "an alarmingly high percentage of [Indian] children are placed in non-Indian . . . adoptive homes").

Consistent with these findings, Congress declared its purpose "to protect the best interests of Indian children and to promote the stability and security of Indian tribes and families by the establishment of minimum Federal standards" applicable to child custody proceedings involving Indian children. §1902.

First, ICWA defines the term "parent" broadly to mean "any biological parent . . . of an Indian child or any Indian person who has lawfully adopted an Indian child." §1903(9). It is undisputed that Baby Girl is an "Indian child" within the meaning of the statute, see §1903(4); *ante*, at 2, n. 1, and Birth Father consequently qualifies as a "parent" under the Act.

Second, the Act's comprehensive definition of "child custody proceeding" includes not only "adoptive placement[s]," "preadoptive placement[s]," and "foster care placement[s]," but also "termination of parental rights" proceedings. § 1903(1). This last category encompasses "*any* action resulting in the termination of the *parent child relationship*," § 1903(1)(ii) (emphasis added). So far, then, it is clear that Birth Father has a federally recognized status as Baby Girl's "parent" and that his "parent-child relationship" with her is subject to the protections of the Act.

These protections are numerous . . . [Among them,] any voluntary consent Birth Father gave to Baby Girl's adoption would have been invalid unless written and executed before a judge and would have been revocable up to the time a final decree of adoption was entered.[56] See §§ 1913(a), (c). And § 1912, the center of the dispute here, sets forth procedural and substantive standards applicable in "involuntary proceeding[s] in a State court," including foster care placements of Indian children and termination of parental rights proceedings. § 1912(a).

Section 1912(a) requires that any party seeking "termination of parental rights t[o] an Indian child" provide notice to both the child's "parent or Indian custodian" and the child's tribe "of the pending proceedings and of their right of intervention." Section 1912(b) mandates that counsel be provided for an indigent "parent or Indian custodian" in any "termination proceeding." Section 1912(c) also gives all "part[ies]" to a termination proceeding — which, thanks to §§ 1912(a) and (b), will always include a biological father if he desires to be present — the right to inspect all

---

[56] [1] For this reason, the South Carolina Supreme Court held that Birth Father did not give valid consent to Baby Girl's adoption when, four months after her birth, he signed papers stating that he accepted service and was not contesting the adoption. See 398 S. C. 625, 645–646, 731 S. E. 2d 550, 561 (2012). Petitioners do not challenge this aspect of the South Carolina court's holding.

material "reports or other documents filed with the court." By providing notice, counsel, and access to relevant documents, the statute ensures a biological father's meaningful participation in an adoption proceeding where the termination of his parental rights is at issue . . . These protections are consonant with the principle, recognized in our cases, that the biological bond between parent and child is meaningful . . .

The majority does not and cannot reasonably dispute that ICWA grants biological fathers, as "parent[s]," the right to be present at a termination of parental rights proceeding and to have their views and claims heard there.[57] . . . Having assumed a uniform federal definition of "parent" that confers certain procedural rights, the majority then illogically concludes that ICWA's *substantive* protections are available only to a subset of "parent[s]": those who have previously had physical or state-recognized legal custody of his or her child. The statute does not support this departure. The majority would hold that the use of the phrase "breakup of the Indian family" in this subsection means that it does not apply where a birth father has not previously had custody of his child . . . .

The majority, reaching the contrary conclusion, asserts baldly that "when an Indian parent abandons an Indian child prior to birth and that child has never been in the Indian parent's legal or physical custody, there is no 'relationship' that would be 'discontinu[ed]' . . . by the termination of the Indian parent's rights." Says who? Certainly not the statute. Section 1903 recognizes Birth Father as Baby Girl's "parent," and, in conjunction with ICWA's other provisions, it further establishes that their "parent-child relationship" is protected under federal law . . .

In light of the structure of § 1912, which indicates that subsection (f) is applicable to the same actions to which subsections (a) through (d) are applicable; the use of the phrase "such proceeding[s]" at the start of subsection (f) to reinforce this structural inference; and finally, the provision's explicit statement that it applies to "termination of parental rights" proceedings, the necessary conclusion is that the word "custody" does not strictly denote a state-recognized custodial relationship. If one refers back to the Act's definitional section, this conclusion is not surprising. Section 1903(1) includes "any action resulting in the termination of the parent-child relationship" within the meaning of "child custody proceeding," thereby belying any congressional intent to give the term "custody" a narrow and exclusive definition throughout the statute.

In keeping with § 1903(1) and the structure and language of § 1912 overall, the phrase "continued custody" is most sensibly read to refer generally to the continuation of the parent-child relationship that an ICWA "parent" has with his or her child . . . . The majority chooses instead to focus on phrases not statutorily defined that it then uses to exclude Birth Father from the benefits of his parental status. When one must disregard a statute's use of terms that have been explicitly defined by Congress, that should be a signal that one is distorting, rather than faithfully reading, the law in question.

---

[57] [2] Petitioners concede that, assuming Birth Father is a "parent" under ICWA, the notice and counsel provisions of 25 U. S. C. §§ 1912(a) and (b) apply to him.

B

The majority also does not acknowledge the full implications of its assumption that there are some ICWA "parent[s]" to whom §§ 1912(d) and (f) do not apply. Its discussion focuses on Birth Father's particular actions, but nothing in the majority's reasoning limits its manufactured class of semiprotected ICWA parents to biological fathers who failed to support their child's mother during pregnancy. Its logic would apply equally to noncustodial fathers who have actively participated in their child's upbringing.

Consider an Indian father who, though he has never had custody of his biological child, visits her and pays all of his child support obligations.[58] Suppose that, due to deficiencies in the care the child received from her custodial parent, the State placed the child with a foster family and proposed her ultimate adoption by them. Clearly, the father's parental rights would have to be terminated before the adoption could go forward.[59] On the majority's view, notwithstanding the fact that this father would be a "parent" under ICWA, he would not receive the benefit of either § 1912(d) or § 1912(f). Presumably the court considering the adoption petition would have to apply some standard to determine whether termination of his parental rights was appropriate. But from whence would that standard come?

---

[58] [8] The majority attempts to minimize the consequences of its holding by asserting that the parent-child relationships of noncustodial fathers with visitation rights will be at stake in an ICWA proceeding in only "a relatively small class of cases." *Ante*, at n. 8. But it offers no support for this assertion, beyond speculating that there will not be many fathers affected by its interpretation of § 1912(d) because it is qualified by an "abandon[ment]" limitation. *Ibid.* Tellingly, the majority has nothing to say about § 1912(f), despite the fact that its interpretation of that provision is not limited in a similar way. In any event, this example by no means exhausts the class of semiprotected ICWA parents that the majority's opinion creates. It also includes, for example, biological fathers who have not yet established a relationship with their child because the child's mother never informed them of the pregnancy, see, *e.g.*, *In re Termination of Parental Rights of Biological Parents of Baby Boy W.*, 1999 OK 74, 988 P. 2d 1270, told them falsely that the pregnancy ended in miscarriage or termination, see, *e.g.*, *A Child's Hope, LLC v. Doe*, 178 N. C. App. 96, 630 S. E. 2d 673 (2006), or otherwise obstructed the father's involvement in the child's life, see, *e.g.*, *In re Baby Girl W.*, 728 S. W. 2d 545 (Mo. App. 1987) (birth mother moved and did not inform father of her whereabouts); *In re Petition of Doe*, 159 Ill. 2d 347, 638 N. E. 2d 181 (1994) (father paid pregnancy expenses until birth mother cut off contact with him and told him that their child had died shortly after birth).And it includes biological fathers who did not contribute to pregnancy expenses because they were unable to do so, whether because the father lacked sufficient means, the expenses were covered by a third party, or the birth mother did not pass on the relevant bills. See, *e.g.*, *In re Adoption of B. V.*, 2001 UT App 290, ¶¶ 24–31, 33 P.3d 1083, 1087–1088.

The majority expresses the concern that my reading of the statute would produce "far-reaching consequences," because "even a sperm donor" would be entitled to ICWA's protections. *Ante*, at n. 8. If there are any examples of women who go to the trouble and expense of artificial insemination and then carry the child to term, only to put the child up for adoption or be found so unfit as mothers that state authorities attempt an involuntary adoptive placement — thereby necessitating termination of the parental rights of the sperm donor father — the majority does not cite them. As between a possibly overinclusive interpretation of the statute that covers this unlikely class of cases, and the majority's underinclusive interpretation that has the very real consequence of denying ICWA's protections to all noncustodial biological fathers, it is surely the majority's reading that is contrary to ICWA's design.

[59] [9] With a few exceptions not relevant here, before a final decree of adoption may be entered, one of two things must happen: "the biological parents must either voluntarily relinquish their parental rights or have their rights involuntarily terminated." 2A. Haralambie, Handling Child Custody, Abuse and Adoption Cases § 14.1, pp. 764–765 (3d ed. 2009) (footnote omitted).

. . . .

II

The majority's textually strained and illogical reading of the statute might be explicable, if not justified, if there were reason to believe that it avoided anomalous results or furthered a clear congressional policy. But neither of these conditions is present here.

A

There is nothing "bizarre" about placing on the party seeking to terminate a father's parental rights the burden of showing that the step is necessary as well as justified. "For . . . natural parents, . . . the consequence of an erroneous termination [of parental rights] is the unnecessary destruction of their natural family." *Santosky*, 455 U.S., at 766. In any event, the question is a nonissue in this case given the family court's finding that Birth Father is "a fit and proper person to have custody of his child" who "has demonstrated [his] ability to parent effectively" and who possesses "unwavering love for this child." Petitioners cannot show that rehabilitative efforts have "proved unsuccessful," 25 U. S. C. § 1912(d), because Birth Father is not in need of rehabilitation.[60]

B

On a more general level, the majority intimates that ICWA grants Birth Father an undeserved windfall: in the majority's words, an "ICWA trump card" he can "play . . . at the eleventh hour to override the mother's decision and the child's best interests." The implicit argument is that Congress could not possibly have intended to recognize a parent-child relationship between Birth Father and Baby Girl that would have to be legally terminated (either by valid consent or involuntary termination) before the adoption could proceed.

But this supposed anomaly is illusory.

Without doubt, laws protecting biological fathers' parental rights can lead — even outside the context of ICWA — to outcomes that are painful and distressing for both would — be adoptive families, who lose a much wanted child, and children who must make a difficult transition (citations omitted). On the other hand, these rules recognize that biological fathers have a valid interest in a relationship with their child. And children have a reciprocal interest in knowing their biological parents.

---

[60] [11] The majority's concerns about what might happen if no state or tribal authority stepped in to provide remedial services are therefore irrelevant here. *Ante*, at n. 9. But as a general matter, if a parent has rights that are an obstacle to an adoption, the state- and federal-law safeguards of those rights must be honored, irrespective of prospective adoptive parents' understandable and valid desire to see the adoption finalized. "We must remember that the purpose of an adoption is to provide a home for a child, not a child for a home." *In re Petition of Doe*, 159 Ill. 2d, at 368, 638 N. E. 2d, at 190 (Heiple, J,. supplemental opinion supporting denial of rehearing).

ICWA, on a straightforward reading of the statute, is consistent with the law of those States that protected, and protect, birth fathers' rights more vigorously. This reading can hardly be said to generate an anomaly. ICWA, as all acknowledge, was "the product of rising concern . . . [about] abusive child welfare practices that resulted in the separation of large numbers of Indian children from their families." *Holyfield*, 490 U.S., at 32. It stands to reason that the Act would not render the legal status of an Indian father's relationship with his biological child fragile, but would instead grant it a degree of protection commensurate with the more robust state-law standards.[61]

C

The majority also protests that a contrary result to the one it reaches would interfere with the adoption of Indian children. This claim is the most perplexing of all. A central purpose of ICWA is to "promote the stability and security of Indian . . . families," 25 U. S. C. § 1902, in part by countering the trend of placing "an alarmingly high percentage of [Indian] children . . . in non-Indian foster and adoptive homes and institutions." § 1901(4). The Act accomplishes this goal by, first, protecting the familial bonds of Indian parents and children, see *supra*, at 4–12; and, second, establishing placement preferences should an adoption take place, see § 1915(a). ICWA does not interfere with the adoption of Indian children except to the extent that it attempts to avert the necessity of adoptive placement and makes adoptions of Indian children by non-Indian families less likely . . .

The majority may consider this scheme unwise. But no principle of construction licenses a court to interpret a statute with a view to averting the very consequences Congress expressly stated it was trying to bring about. Instead, it is the "judicial duty to give faithful meaning to the language Congress adopted in the light of the evident legislative purpose in enacting the law in question." *Graham County Soil and Water Conservation Dist. v. United States ex rel. Wilson*, 559 U.S. 280, 298 (2010) (quoting *United States v. Bornstein*, 423 U.S. 303, 310 (1976)).

The majority further claims that its reading is consistent with the "primary" purpose of the Act, which in the majority's view was to prevent the dissolution of "intact" Indian families. We may not, however, give effect only to congressional goals we designate "primary" while casting aside others classed as "secondary"; we must apply the entire statute Congress has written . . . Congress also recognized that "there is no resource that is more vital to the continued existence and integrity of Indian tribes than their children," § 1901(3). As we observed in *Holyfield*, ICWA protects not only Indian parents' interests but also those of Indian tribes. See 490 U.S., at 34, 52. A tribe's interest in its next generation of citizens is adversely

---

[61] [14] It bears emphasizing that the ICWA standard for termination of parental rights of which Birth Father claims the benefit is more protective than, but not out of step with, the clear and convincing standard generally applied in state courts when termination of parental rights is sought. Birth Father does not claim that he is entitled to custody of Baby Girl unless petitioners can satisfy the demanding standard of § 1912(f). The question of custody would be analyzed independently, as it was by the South Carolina Supreme Court. Of course, it will often be the case that custody is subsequently granted to a child's fit parent, consistent with the presumption that a natural parent will act in the best interests of his child.

affected by the placement of Indian children in homes with no connection to the tribe, whether or not those children were initially in the custody of an Indian parent.[62]

Moreover, the majority's focus on "intact" families begs the question of what Congress set out to accomplish with ICWA. In an ideal world, perhaps all parents would be perfect. They would live up to their parental responsibilities by providing the fullest possible financial and emotional support to their children. They would never suffer mental health problems, lose their jobs, struggle with substance dependency, or encounter any of the other multitudinous personal crises that can make it difficult to meet these responsibilities. In an ideal world, parents would never become estranged and leave their children caught in the middle. But we do not live in such a world. Even happy families do not always fit the custodial-parent mold for which the majority would reserve [ICWA]'s substantive protections; unhappy families all too often do not. They are families nonetheless. Congress understood as much. ICWA's definitions of "parent" and "termination of parental rights" provided in § 1903 sweep broadly. They should be honored.

D

The majority does not rely on the theory pressed by petitioners and the guardian ad litem that the canon of constitutional avoidance compels the conclusion that ICWA is inapplicable here. It states instead that it finds the statute clear.[63] But the majority nevertheless offers the suggestion that a contrary result would create an equal protection problem.

It is difficult to make sense of this suggestion in light of our precedents, which squarely hold that classifications based on Indian tribal membership are not impermissible racial classifications. See *United States v. Antelope*, 430 U.S. 641, 645–647 (1977); *Morton v. Mancari*, 417 U.S. 535, 553–554 (1974). The majority's repeated, analytically unnecessary references to the fact that Baby Girl is 3/256 Cherokee by ancestry do nothing to elucidate its intimation that the statute may violate the Equal Protection Clause as applied here. See *ante* (stating that ICWA "would put certain vulnerable children at a great disadvantage solely because an ancestor — *even a remote one* — was an Indian" (emphasis added)). . . .

The majority's treatment of this issue, in the end, does no more than create a lingering mood of disapprobation of the criteria for membership adopted by the Cherokee Nation that, in turn, make Baby Girl an "Indian child" under the statute.

---

[62] [15] Birth Father is a registered member of the Cherokee Nation, a fact of which Birth Mother was aware at the time of her pregnancy and of which she informed her attorney. See 398 S. C. 625, 632–633, 731 S. E. 2d 550, 554 (2012).

[63] [16] JUSTICE THOMAS concurs in the majority's interpretation because, although he finds the statute susceptible of more than one plausible reading, he believes that the majority's reading avoids "significant constitutional problems" concerning whether ICWA exceeds Congress's authority under the Indian Commerce Clause. No party advanced this argument, and it is inconsistent with this Court's precedents holding that Congress has "broad general powers to legislate in respect to Indian tribes, powers that we have consistently described as plenary and exclusive," founded not only on the Indian Commerce Clause but also the Treaty Clause. *United States v. Lara*, 541 U.S. 193, 200–201 (2004) (internal quotation marks omitted).

Its hints at lurking constitutional problems are, by its own account, irrelevant to its statutory analysis, and accordingly need not detain us any longer.

III

Because I would affirm the South Carolina Supreme Court on the ground that § 1912 bars the termination of Birth Father's parental rights, I would not reach the question of the applicability of the adoptive placement preferences of § 1915. I note, however, that the majority does not and cannot foreclose the possibility that on remand, Baby Girl's paternal grandparents or other members of the Cherokee Nation may formally petition for adoption of Baby Girl. If these parties do so, and if on remand Birth Father's parental rights are terminated so that an adoption becomes possible, they will then be entitled to consideration under the order of preference established in § 1915 . . . It would indeed be an odd result for this Court, in the name of the child's best interests, to purport to exclude from the proceedings possible custodians for Baby Girl, such as her paternal grandparents, who may have well-established relationships with her.

The majority opinion turns § 1912 upside down, reading it from bottom to top in order to reach a conclusion that is manifestly contrary to Congress's express purpose in enacting ICWA: preserving the familial bonds between Indian parents and their children and, more broadly, Indian tribes' relationships with the future citizens who are "vital to [their] continued existence and integrity." § 1901(3).

. . . .

The majority casts Birth Father as responsible for the painful circumstances in this case, suggesting that he intervened "at the eleventh hour to override the mother's decision and the child's best interests." I have no wish to minimize the trauma of removing a 27-month-old child from her adoptive family. It bears remembering, however, that Birth Father took action to assert his parental rights when Baby Girl was four months old, as soon as he learned of the impending adoption. As the South Carolina Supreme Court recognized, "[h]ad the mandate of . . . ICWA been followed [in 2010], . . . much potential anguish might have been avoided[;] and in any case the law cannot be applied so as automatically to 'reward those who obtain custody, whether lawfully or otherwise, and maintain it during any ensuing (and protracted) litigation.'" 398 S. C., at 652, 731 S. E. 2d, at 564 (quoting *Holyfield*, 490 U.S., at 53–54).

The majority's hollow literalism distorts the statute and ignores Congress's purpose in order to rectify a perceived wrong that, while heartbreaking at the time, was a correct application of federal law and that in any case cannot be undone. Baby Girl has now resided with her father for eighteen months. However difficult it must have been for her to leave Adoptive Couple's home when she was just over two years old, it will be equally devastating now if, at the age of 3½, she is again removed from her home and sent to live halfway across the country. Such a fate is not foreordained, of course. But it can be said with certainty that the anguish this case has caused will only be compounded by today's decision.

I believe that the South Carolina Supreme Court's judgment was correct, and I would affirm it. I respectfully dissent.

NOTES

1. Subsequent Proceedings Regarding Placement of Baby Girl Veronica: Following the Supreme Court's decision in *Adoptive Couple v. Baby Girl*, the case was remanded to the South Carolina Supreme Court for further proceedings. However, the South Carolina Supreme Court summarily ordered Baby Girl Veronica's immediate transfer to the non-Indian pre-adoptive couple without conducting a "best interest of the child" hearing. Veronica's biological father, stepmother, and paternal grandparents filed petitions to adopt Veronica, but were rebuffed. When the Cherokee Nation then joined these family members in seeking relief from the order to transfer, their pleas were rejected by South Carolina and the U.S. Supreme Court.

Veronica's biological father did not immediately comply with the order to relinquish his daughter, so an arrest warrant was issued and he was charged with "custodial interference" under South Carolina law. At the same time, litigation on Veronica's behalf was filed in tribal, state, and federal court. A Cherokee Nation tribal court ordered that Veronica could remain with her biological father's family members while he was undergoing National Guard training, and an Oklahoma state trial court entered a stay of extradition on the father's South Carolina charge. Ultimately, however, the Oklahoma Supreme Court found it lacked jurisdiction over the matter and dissolved the stay. Veronica's biological father then reluctantly turned her over to the non-Indian South Carolina couple. Press coverage of the case was extensive, and often tilted against Veronica's biological father. The Supreme Court had failed to mention that he was on active duty in the military during all of the time Veronica's biological mother pursued the adoption by the non-Indian couple, and the press largely portrayed him as a father who had abandoned his child and her mother. Would the fact that he had been on active duty abroad affect your view of his conduct and obligations throughout the proceedings?

2. Reach of the *Adoptive Couple* Decision: In what ways are Justice Breyer's concurring opinion and Justice Sotomayor's dissenting opinion in *Adoptive Couple* overlapping? Does Breyer's concurrence leave open some issues regarding the applicability of ICWA to an "Indian parent"?

3. Seeds of Constitutional Doubt?: Compare Justice Thomas's concurring opinion in *Adoptive Couple* with his concurrence in *U.S. v. Lara*, 541 U.S. 193 (2004), presented in Ch. 3, Sec. C.2. What are the common threads running through his constitutional arguments in both cases? Which concerns him more — whether ICWA is authorized under the Indian commerce clause, or whether ICWA violates constitutional due process/equal protection? Should the majority opinion fuel worries that ICWA is unconstitutional or that *Morton v. Mancari* may be overruled? Consider the closing passage of Justice Alito's opinion:

> The Indian Child Welfare Act was enacted to help preserve the cultural identity and heritage of Indian tribes, but under the State Supreme Court's reading, the Act would put certain vulnerable children at a great disadvantage solely because an ancestor — even a remote one — was an Indian. As the State Supreme Court read §§ 1912(d) and (f), a biological Indian father could abandon his child *in utero* and refuse any support for the birth mother — perhaps contributing to the mother's decision to put the child up

for adoption — and then could play his ICWA trump card at the eleventh hour to override the mother's decision and the child's best interests. If this were possible, many prospective adoptive parents would surely pause before adopting any child who might possibly qualify as an Indian under the ICWA. Such an interpretation would raise equal protection concerns, but the plain text of §§ 1912(f) and (d) makes clear that neither provision applies in the present context. Nor do § 1915(a)'s rebuttable adoption preferences apply when no alternative party has formally sought to adopt the child.

Does this passage fairly portray the state Supreme Court's decision below or Justice Sotomayor's dissent? How serious are the equal protection concerns it raises?

5. "Good Cause" and Transfer of ICWA Cases from State to Tribal Court

The novel transfer provision in ICWA has transformed cases involving Indian children that otherwise would have been within exclusive or concurrent state court jurisdiction into cases where tribal court is presumptively the proper forum. For child welfare proceedings involving an "Indian child" not domiciled on the reservation or a ward of the tribal court, ICWA makes tribal court jurisdiction "presumptive," requiring transfer of state court cases so long as both parents and the tribe agree, and "in the absence of good cause to the contrary." 25 U.S.C. § 1911(b). For Public Law 280 tribes, where state jurisdiction over child welfare matters extends to Indian children who *are* domiciled on the reservation, the transfer provision applies to on-reservation cases as well.

What qualifies as "good cause to the contrary" that would justify a state court refusing to transfer an Indian child welfare case to tribal court? The language of ICWA offers no definition. For help in interpreting this phrase, the best resource is a set of guidelines, promulgated by the Bureau of Indian Affairs, which are advisory only.

Bureau of Indian Affairs Guidelines for State Court Indian Child Custody Proceedings
44 Fed. Reg. 67584 (1979)

C.3. Determination of Good Cause to the Contrary

a. Good cause not to transfer the proceeding exists if the Indian child's tribe does not have a tribal court as defined by the Act to which the case can be transferred.

b. Good cause not to transfer this proceeding may exist if any of the following circumstances exists:

i. The proceeding was at an advanced stage when the petition to transfer was received and the petitioner did not file the petition promptly after receiving notice of the hearing.

ii. The Indian child is over twelve years of age and objects to the transfer.

iii. The evidence necessary to decide the case could not be adequately presented in the tribal court without undue hardship to the parties or the witnesses.

iv. The parents of a child over five years of age are not available and the child has had little or no contact with the child's tribe or members of the child's tribe.

c. Socio-economic conditions and the perceived adequacy of tribal or Bureau of Indian Affairs social services or judicial systems may not be considered in a determination that good cause exists.

d. The burden of establishing good cause to the contrary shall be on the party opposing the transfer.

Commentary: C.3. Commentary

It is recommended that in most cases state court judges not be called upon to determine whether or not a child's contacts with a reservation are so limited that a case should not be transferred. This may be a valid consideration since the shock of changing cultures may, in some cases, be harmful to the child. This determination, however, can be made by the parent, who has a veto — over transfer to tribal court.

This reasoning does not apply, however, where there is no parent available to make that decision. The guidelines recommend that state courts be authorized to make such determinations only in those cases where there is no parent available to make it.

State court authority to make such decisions is limited to those cases where the child is over five years of age. Most children younger than five years can be expected to adjust more readily to a change in cultural environment.

The fifth criterion [ii in the Guidelines] has been retained. It is true that teenagers may make some unwise decisions, but it is also true that their judgment has developed to the extent that their views ought to be taken into account in making decisions about their lives.

The existence of a tribal court is made an absolute requirement for transfer of a case. Clearly, the absence of a tribal court is good cause not to ask the tribe to try the case.

Consideration of whether or not the case can be properly tried in tribal court without hardship to the parties or witnesses was included on the strength of the section-by-section analysis in the House Report on the Act, which stated with respect to the § 1911(b), "The subsection is intended to permit a State court to apply a modified doctrine of *forum non conveniens*, in appropriate cases, to insure that the rights of the child as an Indian, the Indian parents or custodian, and the tribe are fully protected." Where a child is in fact living in a dangerous situation, he or she should not be forced to remain there simply because the witnesses cannot afford to travel long distances to court.

Application of this criterion will tend to limit transfers to cases involving Indian children who do not live very far from the reservation. This problem may be alleviated in some instances by having the court come to the witnesses. The Department is aware of one case under that Act where transfer was conditioned on having the tribal court meet in the city where the family lived. Some cities have substantial populations of members of tribes from distant reservations. In such situations some tribes may wish to appoint members who live in those cities as tribal judges.

The timeliness of the petition for transfer . . . is listed as a factor to be considered. Inclusion of this criterion is designed to encourage the prompt exercise of the right to petition for transfer in order to avoid unnecessary delays. Long periods of uncertainty concerning the future are generally regarded as harmful to the well-being of children. For that reason, it is especially important to avoid unnecessary delays in child custody proceedings.

Almost all commenters favored retention of the paragraph stating that reservation socio-economic conditions and the perceived adequacy of tribal institutions are not to be taken into account in making good cause determinations. Come commenters did suggest, however, that a case not be transferred if it is clear that a particular disposition of the case that could only be made by the state court held especially great promise of benefiting the child.

Such considerations are important but they have not been listed because the Department believes such judgments are best made by tribal courts. Parties who believe that state court adjudication would be better for such reasons can present their reasons to the tribal court and urge it to decline jurisdiction. The Department is aware of one case under the Act where this approach is being used and believes it is more in keeping with the confidence Congress has expressed in tribal courts.

Since Congress has established a policy of preferring tribal control over custody decisions affecting tribal members, the burden of proving that an exception to that policy ought to be made in a particular case rests on the party urging that an exception be made. The rule is reflected in subsection (d).

NOTES ON TRANSFER OF CASES FROM STATE TO TRIBAL COURT

1. **Considering "Best Interest" of the Child:** When they apply the ICWA transfer provision, some state courts have chosen to add another factor to the consideration of "good cause": whether they think the transferee tribal court will make placement decisions or take other actions that the state court views as contrary to the best interest of the child, such as parenting abilities and stability of homes of individuals seeking custody and emotional and physical needs of the child, particularly where the children are living (sometimes in violation of ICWA) in non-Indian foster homes. *See, e.g., In re M.E.M.*, 635 P.2d 1313, 1314 (Mont. 1981); *In re Robert T.*, 200 Cal. App. 3d 657 (1988). Other state courts have resisted this temptation. *See, e.g., In re Zylena R. v. Elise M.*, 825 N.W.2d 173 (Neb. 2012); *In re A.B.*, 663 N.W.2d 625, 632 (N.D. 2003).

A case that illuminates the issues surrounding use of "best interests of the child" is *Yavapai-Apache Tribe v. Mejia*, 906 S.W.2d 152 (Tex. App. 1995), where a state trial court had taken "best interests" into account, and the Texas appeals court found that consideration to be improper under ICWA's notion of "good cause." While noting that section 1902 of ICWA states that the policy of the Act is "to protect the best interest of Indian children," the court explained that the phrase "best interests of Indian children" in the context of the ICWA is different from the general Anglo-American "best interest of the child" standard used in cases involving non-Indian children. Citing to *Holyfield*, the Texas appeals court stated that "Under the ICWA, what is best for an Indian child is to maintain ties with the Indian tribe, culture, and family." Joining states such as Colorado, Illinois, Minnesota, Missouri, and New Mexico that had rejected use of "best interest" to decide whether to transfer cases to tribal court, the Texas court offered two distinct reasons for its holding:

> First, the use of the best interest standard when determining whether good cause exists defeats the very purpose for which the ICWA was enacted, for it allows Anglo cultural biases into the picture. Second, the best interest test is relevant to issues of placement, not jurisdiction.
>
> As the historical context of the Act shows, it was specifically directed at preventing the infiltration of Anglo standards, standards which created the outrageous situation of child welfare agencies and state courts removing Indian children from the stability of their tribes and families. The ICWA precludes the imposition of Anglo standards by creating a broad presumption of jurisdiction in the tribes. Thus, the jurisdictions provisions in section 1911(a) and (b) are at the very heart of the ICWA. We decline to embrace a test that would, in our judgment, eviscerate the spirit of the Act.
>
> Secondly, we reject the best interest standard because it is relevant to issues of placement, not jurisdiction. The only issue in cases involving motions to transfer is the determination of the proper tribunal to resolve the custody issue. Thus, the question of whether a parent or guardian is abusive, neglectful, or otherwise unfit is irrelevant at this point. For a court to use this standard when deciding a purely jurisdictional matter, alters the focus of the case, and the issue becomes not what judicial entity should decide custody, but the standard by which the decision itself is made. The utilization of the best interest standard and fact findings made on that basis reflects the Anglo-American legal system's distrust of Indian legal competence by its assuming that an Indian determination would be detrimental to the child. Jeanne Louise Carriere, *Representing the Native American: Culture, Jurisdiction, and the Indian Child Welfare Act*, 79 Iowa L. Rev. 585, 628 (1994). The underlying assumption is that relying on an Indian determination of best interest would not truly result in what is best for the Indian child. *Id.* We view this as an arrogant idea that defeats the sovereignty of Indian tribes in custody matters; the very idea for which the ICWA was enacted.

906 S.W.2d at 170.

The court also found support for its rejection of the "best interest" standard in the Supreme Court's *Holyfield* decision, particularly its statement that "Whatever feeling we might have as to where the twins should live . . ., it is not for us to decide that question. We have been asked to decide the legal question of *who* should make the custody determination concerning these children — not what the outcome of that determination should be. The law places that decision in the hands of the Choctaw tribal court." 490 U.S. at 53 (emphasis in the original).

The Texas trial court in the *Yavapai-Apache v. Prescott* case had also based its finding of "good cause" not to transfer on two other factors: the lack of contact between the children and the Tribe and the difficulty of presenting the case to the tribal court without undue hardship to the parties and witnesses. The Texas appeals court decided that the trial judge had abused discretion in taking the lack of contact into account, given that all but one of the children were under the age of 5 and all had at least one parent available, making BIA Guideline (iv), quoted above, inapplicable. The court noted that an earlier version of the Guidelines, which had allowed for consideration of this factor without regard to age and parental availability, had been criticized and limited, because it ignored the legitimate interest that tribes retained in the welfare of members who did not have previous significant contact with the tribe or reservation, and because it "invited the state courts to make the kind of cultural decisions that the Act contemplated should be made by Indian tribes."

Ultimately, however, the Texas appeals court affirmed the trial court's decision not to transfer based on "undue hardship" to parties and witnesses if the case were sent to tribal court, a consideration approved in BIA Guideline (iii), quoted above. This Guideline has been called a "modified forum non conveniens" doctrine, enabling state courts to take into account such factors as the convenience of parties and witnesses, as well as the location of the evidence. One of these relevant factors is whether the proceeding is at an "advanced stage" at the time the motion to transfer is made. In a situation where a dependent child has been placed in foster care, and later a petition is filed to terminate parental rights, should a motion to transfer that is made at the time of the termination petition be considered at "an advanced stage" because of all the time spent on the earlier foster care placement? Might a tribe be more interested in intervening to make a transfer motion when severance of parental rights is at stake? *See In re Zylena R. v. Elise M., supra; Puyallup Tribe of Indians v. State (In re M.S.)*, 237 P.3d 161 (Okla. 2010). In the *Yavapai-Apache* case, the Tribal Court had offered to address forum non conveniens concerns by holding its proceedings in Houston; but the Texas trial court refused to take this possibility into account, relying on state court decisions stating that a court could not take official actions outside its territorial boundaries. For a critique of state courts' use of the "best interests" standard, see B.J. Jones, *The Indian Child Welfare Act: In Search of a Federal Forum to Vindicate the Rights of Indian Tribes and Children Against the Vagaries of State Courts*, 73 N.D. L. Rev. 395, 422–29 (1997).

2. **Enforcing ICWA's Transfer Provision:** What if some state court persists in factoring the "best interest of the child," as the state court understands it, into transfer decisions, and an Indian parent or tribe wants to challenge the state court's refusal to transfer? Does ICWA afford a role for federal courts in achieving

nationwide uniformity and advancing the intent of the statute? In his article cited in Note 1, above, B.J. Jones, Director of the Northern Plains Tribal Judicial Training Institute, has pointed out that most federal courts have answered this question in the negative, despite ICWA's implicit "distrust of the competency and institutional capability of state courts to handle proceedings involving Indian children," and "Congress's discerning focus on state courts as participants in the devastation of Indian families and culture. . . . " Jones offers an analysis of the proper federal role in policing state court compliance with ICWA, an analysis that applies not only to state court decisions regarding transfer, but also to their determinations regarding exclusive tribal court jurisdiction, the "existing Indian family" doctrine, and tribal motions to intervene. Section 1914 of ICWA appears to offer Indian or tribal litigants some help from the federal judiciary, as it provides:

> Any Indian child who is the subject of any action for foster care placement or termination of parental rights under state law, any parent or Indian custodian from whose custody such child was removed, and the Indian child's tribe may petition any court of competent jurisdiction to invalidate such action upon a showing that such action violated any provision of sections 1911, 1912, and 1913

Since the transfer provision of ICWA is found in section 1911(b), section 1914 seems on its face to offer a mechanism for challenging state court decisions rejecting such transfer. However, as Jones explains, "To date, no federal court has invalidated an arguably erroneous state court decision because the majority of federal courts have emasculated their authority to do so under the principles of full faith and credit." Invoking doctrines of abstention and preclusion, federal courts have refused to overturn individual state court decisions. Jones urges that federal courts interpret section 1914 as an exception to the application of the federal full faith and credit statute, 28 U.S.C. § 1738, rather than as a grant of jurisdiction to the federal courts.

In *Doe v. Mann*, discussed in Sec. C.2, this chapter, the Ninth Circuit sidestepped the full faith and credit issues because the state did not raise them, and allowed an Indian parent to bring a federal court action challenging the state's exercise of jurisdiction over an involuntary child welfare proceeding involving an on-reservation child. While this case does not involve a denial of transfer to a tribal court, and does not address the hurdles presented by 28 U.S.C. § 1738, it does suggest a more robust role for section 1914 of ICWA. In particular, the court swept aside objections to federal jurisdiction under that provision based on what is known as the *Rooker-Feldman* doctrine, which bars federal courts from exercising subject-matter jurisdiction over a proceeding in "which a party losing in state court" seeks "what in substance would be appellate review of the state judgment in a United States district court, based on the losing party's claim that the state judgment itself violates the loser's federal rights." *Johnson v. De Grandy*, 512 U.S. 997, 1005–06 (1994). The court found that section 1914 was a grant of federal authority that "counteracts" the *Rooker-Feldman* doctrine, invoking congressional intent and the Indian law canons.

3. Funding Issues Associated with Transfer from State to Tribal Court: Tribes as well as parents can prevent transfer of ICWA cases from state to tribal court. In the past, one reason why some tribes have not welcomed transfer is because tribal courts were unable to access federal funds for foster care placements. Under Title IV-E of the Social Security Act, these funds were only disbursed to states, and the states were under no obligation to allocate funds to the tribes. In practice, many state child welfare agencies were unwilling to make agreements to pass funding through to the tribes. In 2008, however, Congress passed legislation authorizing direct federal funding of tribal IV-E foster care programs, and requiring states to negotiate Title IV-E agreements with tribes "in good faith." Fostering Connections to Success and Increasing Adoptions Act of 2008, Public Law 110-351. Since October 2009, tribes have been able to apply to operate their own Title IV-E programs.

6. ICWA and the Adoption and Safe Families Act

The Adoption and Safe Families Act of 1997 (ASFA), P.L. 105-89, amending 42 U.S.C. § 620 et seq. and 42 U.S.C. § 670 et seq., attached new federal requirements to funding that states and tribes receive for child welfare programs, foster care, and adoption assistance. Its fundamental objective is to minimize the duration of foster care placements in circumstances where reunification is highly unlikely, and to facilitate permanent adoption. *See* DAVID SIMMONS & JACK TROPE, P.L. 105-89 ADOPTION AND SAFE FAMILIES ACT OF 1997: ISSUES FOR TRIBES AND STATES SERVING INDIAN CHILDREN 6–7 (National Resource Center for Organizational Improvement, Edmund S. Muskie School of Public Service, University of Southern Maine 1999), *available at* http://www.nicwa.org/policy/law/adoption_safe/asfa-issues.pdf.

Among other things, ASFA encourages states to place the health and safety of children ahead of family unification efforts where the parent has a pattern of abusive behavior with the child in question, criminal behavior with another child of the parent, or the parental rights of the parent to a sibling of the child in question have previously been terminated involuntarily. 42 U.S.C. § 671(a)(15). It provides incentive payments to increase the number of foster children placed for adoption, 42 U.S.C. § 673b, and expedites permanent placement for children through a variety of procedural requirements. *See, e.g.,* 42 U.S.C. § 675(5)(C) (requiring a permanency hearing within 12 months after the initial foster care placement).

Because ASFA and ICWA deal with related matters, one might ask whether ASFA modifies ICWA. Imagine, for example, off-reservation Indian parents who have behaved abusively toward their children. The state child welfare agency places the children temporarily in foster care, and moves to terminate parental rights. The parents, in turn, request remedial help and reunification services. Under ICWA, such services are required to prevent breakup of the Indian family. 25 U.S.C. § 1912(d). Under ASFA, those services may be bypassed. Should a state court follow the ICWA requirement even when ASFA would allow otherwise? If the legislative history of ASFA reveals no congressional intent to alter ICWA, how should the courts resolve this question? Consider what weight, if any, should be given to the fact that ASFA deals with all children in the foster care or adoption system, while ICWA is a more specific statute dealing with Indian children involved in child custody proceedings. *Cf. Morton v. Mancari*, 417 U.S. 535 (1974) (presented and discussed in Ch. 2, Sec. B.1). Also consider the import of the fact that state and tribal courts affected by ASFA can normally comply with both statutes, because

ASFA provides state courts with greater rather than less flexibility in deciding whether to terminate parental rights, and because ASFA's procedural requirements can be followed without violating ICWA. Thus, for example, a state is permitted to cut off reunification efforts under specified circumstances, but is not required to do so. 42 U.S.C. § 471(15). The state courts in Alaska and South Dakota have responded to these questions differently. Alaska carved out an exception to the ICWA reunification requirements for "aggravated circumstances." *J. S. v. State*, 50 P.3d 388, 389–90 (Alaska 2002). South Dakota chose instead to follow ICWA. *Ex rel. J.S.B., Jr., Minor Child*, 691 N.W.2d 611, 617 (S.D. 2005). *See* C. Eric Davis, *In Defense of the Indian Child Welfare Act in Aggravated Circumstances*, 13 MICH. J. RACE & L. 433 (2008).

D.   INDIAN GAMING REGULATORY ACT

1.   The Jurisdictional Regime for Tribal Gaming

The United States Supreme Court's 1976 opinion in *Bryan v. Itasca County*, presented in Sec. A.2, this chapter, sets forth a distinction between civil/regulatory and criminal/prohibitory laws for purposes of determining the application of state law under Public Law 280, a distinction that set the stage for development of a thriving and lucrative tribal gaming industry precisely at the time when federal support for Indian tribal programs was shrinking. Following that decision, many lower federal courts took this distinction to be the proper standard for interpreting not only Public Law 280 but also the Organized Crime Control Act of 1970, 18 U.S.C. § 1955, which makes it a federal crime to violate state gaming laws. Beginning with the Fifth Circuit's decision in *Seminole Tribe v. Butterworth*, 658 F.2d 310 (5th Cir. 1981), several lower courts found that state laws prohibiting high stakes bingo and limiting bingo games to religious, charitable, and civic groups were "civil/regulatory," and hence outside state authority in Indian country. The *Butterworth* court distinguished *United States v. Marcyes*, 557 F.2d 1361 (9th Cir. 1977) (Washington fireworks laws apply to Indians in Indian country under the Assimilative and Indian Country Crimes Acts, 18 U.S.C. §§ 13, 1152), on the ground that the bingo games, unlike fireworks, were regulated rather than banned by the state. The court also expressly rejected an argument based on *Colville* (*see* Ch. 4, Sec. B.4.b) that a distinction had to be drawn between Indian and non-Indian players. It said, "In the present case the only regulation is directed at the Indian operators of the bingo hall, not its non-Indian bingo players." *See also Barona Group of Capitan Grande Band of Mission Indians v. Duffy*, 694 F.2d 1185 (9th Cir. 1982) (same result).

In 1987, the United States Supreme Court decided *California v. Cabazon Band of Mission Indians*, 480 U.S. 202 (1987), set forth and discussed in Ch. 4, Sec. B.4.b, which confirmed the *Butterworth* holding as to Public Law 280 but declined to resolve the Organized Crime Control Act issue. Review the *Cabazon* decision, and see how it jeopardized all potential assertions of state authority over tribal gaming, at least where the state already allows many types of games, and even sponsors a state lottery. Ever since *Butterworth* and similar cases, Congress had been considering legislation to limit and control tribal gaming, at the behest of state officials. *Cabazon* lent new urgency to these efforts, and simultaneously offered the tribes a strengthened hand in the negotiations. Tribal gaming was generating considerable controversy, mostly from state lotteries and non-Indian gaming interests fearing competition, as well as from law enforcement agencies expressing (unproven) fears of infiltration by organized crime.

Congress responded with the Indian Gaming Regulatory Act of 1988, 25 U.S.C. § 2701 et seq., which is discussed in the readings that follow. Review the statute carefully online, and consider how it alters the preexisting jurisdictional regime. Given the decision in *Cabazon*, as well as federal anti-gaming laws such as the Organized Crime Control Act and the Johnson Act, 15 U.S.C. §§ 1171–78, is it clear that tribes could have mounted slot machines and other forms of casino gaming in the absence of the Act? While the statute attempted to clarify the conditions under which tribal gaming could and could not go forward, it also gave rise to tough legal and political conflicts, explored below. For an in-depth history of Indian gaming and IGRA, *see* Robert N. Clinton, *Enactment of the Indian Gaming Regulatory Act of 1988: The Return of the Buffalo to Indian Country or Another Federalism Usurpation of Tribal Sovereignty?*, 42 Ariz. St. L.J. 17 (2011).

Kevin K. Washburn, *Recurring Problems in Indian Gaming*
1 Wyo. L. Rev. 427, 428–30, 435–36, 440–41 (2001)

II. The Indian Gaming Regulatory Act

Following the *Cabazon* decision, Indian tribes increased development of Indian gaming establishments. Meanwhile, states went to Congress, seeking a legislative limitation to the tribal power recognized in the *Cabazon* decision. Congress responded by enacting the Indian Gaming Regulatory Act of 1988 (IGRA). In IGRA, Congress provided that tribes have the unilateral authority to conduct bingo and similar games such as "pull-tabs" games (which are defined as "Class II" games in the Act) on Indian lands, if such games are not prohibited in the state in which the tribe is situated.

In contrast to Class II gaming, Congress realized that states were likely to have more serious and more legitimate public policy concerns related to more expansive casino-type gaming which is defined as "Class III" gaming in IGRA. Accordingly, Congress stopped short of giving tribes the unilateral power to conduct full casino-style Class III gaming. Congress limited Class III gaming to those states that already allow some measure of Class III gaming and gave states a voice in tribal decisions to conduct such gaming.

As for Class III gaming, Congress adopted the criminal-prohibitory versus civil-regulatory distinction set forth in the *Cabazon* decision. IGRA allows tribes to offer Class III gaming if a state permits Class III gaming for any purpose by any person, organization or entity. In other words, if a state allows a limited class of organizations such as charitable groups to offer low stakes gambling on a limited number of occasions each year, a tribe may offer such gambling activities. The theory is that state public policy toward such activity is merely regulatory rather than prohibitory. On the other hand, IGRA forbids a tribe from conducting Class

III gaming if the state has adopted a "no-Class III-gaming-and-no-exceptions" approach.

A. *State Tribal Compacts for Class III Casino-style Gaming*

Congress imposed one other major requirement for Class III gaming. IGRA provides that tribes may engage in Class III casino-style gaming only if they first negotiate "compacts" with states. Through the compacting process, Congress empowered states to negotiate with tribes to address seven areas of legitimate state concerns related to public safety and regulation of gaming. Each of the seven subjects are directly related to the operation of gaming establishments.

Alex Tallchief Skibine, *The Indian Gaming Regulatory Act at 25: Successes, Shortcomings, and Dilemmas*
60 FED. LAW. 35, 37–38, 40 (2013)
(First published in the April 2013 issue of *The Federal Lawyer*)

II: ASSESSING THE SUCCESS OF IGRA 25 YEARS LATER

What Went Right or Wrong for the Tribes

If the purposes as stated in the bill were indeed the true purposes, there is no question that IGRA has been a success. IGRA had two main purposes. The first one was to establish a statutory framework that would allow gaming to generate tribal revenues as a "means of promoting tribal economic development, self-sufficiency, and strong tribal governments." 25 U.S.C. § 2702(1). The second purpose was to shield tribal gaming from "organized crime and other corrupting influences." 25 U.S.C. § 2702(2). I think it is fair to say that in the last twenty-five years, tribal gaming has not been infiltrated by organized crime and has been largely free of corrupting influences. Furthermore, Indian gaming has been a financial success for many Indian tribes. Since 2007, Indian gaming has generated approximately $26 billion a year in net revenues. Along with such revenues, Indian gaming has also generated close to 700,000 jobs. In a recent article, Profs. Steven Light and Kathryn Rand detail how gaming revenues have been used by Indian tribes to first, boost services provided by tribal governments, second, build up governmental administrative capabilities and institutions, and, finally, to provide opportunities for tribes to diversify their economies so as not to be solely relying on gaming for tribal governmental revenues.[64] I would also add to their conclusions this: greater independence from the federal government and less reliance on federal governmental programs.

The major setback has obviously been the Supreme Court decision in *Seminole Tribe v. Florida* [517 U.S. 44 (1996), presented later in this section], which held that Congress could not authorize the tribes to sue states in federal court because it could not abrogate the states' eleventh amendment sovereign immunity from suit

---

[64] [10] Steven Andrew Light & Kathryn R.L. Rand, *The Hand That's Been Dealt: The Indian Gaming Regulatory Act at 20*, 57 DRAKE L. REV. 413 (2009)

using its Commerce Clause power. This has resulted in some legal uncertainty as to what remedies are available to tribes in cases where states fail to negotiate a compact in good faith and that uncertainty has given the states the upper hand in re-negotiating tribal state compacts. As a result, the states have been receiving increasing amounts of revenue from the tribes using the controversial revenue sharing agreements.[65] One also has to mention the fact that gaining has not been a success for all tribes. As noted by Ezekiel Fletcher, 22 gaming facilities account for 42% of all tribal gaming revenues while there were 210 tribal casinos which accounted for less than 2% of all tribal gaming revenues.

What Went Right or Wrong for the States

If the intent of the states during the negotiations that led to IGRA was to somehow stop or derail Indian gaming, then IGRA has been a failure from that point of view. If, however, their intent was the promotion of economic development within the states through Indian gaming, the Act has been a success. One study reported that 75% of all jobs generated by Indian gaming are held by non-Indians. In addition, these controversial revenue sharing agreements have generated a substantial amount of revenues to the states. Professors Light and Rand reported that in 2007 alone, "tribes made over $1 billion in revenue-sharing payments to states and another $155 million in payments to local governments." Although tribes may rightly feel that these revenue sharing agreements give out too much cash to the states, the silver lining here is that such arrangements have ensured that both tribes and states have a vested interest in the success of Indian gaming.

III: MAJOR ISSUES IN NEED OF CLARIFICATION

IGRA has never been substantially amended in its twenty-five-year history . . . Yet, there are some serious unresolved issues concerning the interpretation of IGRA . . . The most important unresolved issue is the validity of the secretarial regulations for issuance of Class III gaming procedures when a state claims sovereign immunity after being sued for failing to negotiate in good faith. After *Seminole Tribe*, IGRA's abrogation of the states' sovereign immunity is no longer constitutional. The Secretary of the Interior has taken the position that if a state invoked sovereign immunity in such situations, the tribes can directly petition the Secretary of the Interior to issue Class III gaming procedures. Under IGRA, the Secretary can issue such gaming procedures but only after a court ruled that a state has not negotiated in good faith and has rejected the court-appointed mediator's proposal. The few lower courts that have reached this issue have disagreed. While the U.S. Court of Appeals for the Fifth Circuit in *Texas v. United States* [497 F.3d 491 (5th Cir. 2007)], held that the Secretary had no power to issue gaming procedures in such cases, the U.S. Court of Appeals for the Ninth Circuit and the U.S. Court of Appeals for the Eleventh Circuit indicated that they would probably

---

[65] [11] For a recent article on problems generated by the Supreme Court opinion, see Ezekiel J.N. Fletcher, *Negotiating Meaningful Concessions from Statutes in Gaming Compacts to Further Tribal Economic Development: Satisfying the Economic Benefits Test*, 54 S.D. L. REV. 419 (2009)

uphold the regulations.[66]

Another area that has been very controversial, has generated much litigation, and could use some clarification, has been the process of placing off-reservation fee land into trust for the purpose of gaming.[67] Unfortunately much of this litigation has involved tribes against other tribes.

Another still unresolved issue is the meaning of "good-faith negotiation" when it comes to tribal state negotiation over the scope of gaming and the validity of revenue sharing agreements. This issue concerns what type of Class III games a state has to negotiate with a tribe. Under IGRA "Class III gaming shall be lawful on Indian lands only if such activities are . . . located in a State that permits such gaming for any purpose by any person." There are currently two judicial views on the meaning of this sentence: [a] broad view adopted by the U.S. Court of Appeals for the Second Circuit in *Mashantucket Pequot Tribe v. Connecticut*[, 913 F.2d 1024 (2d Cir. 1990)], is under which any state allowing one type of Class III gaming activity has to negotiate over all Class III gaming activities, and a narrow view (a.k.a. as the game-specific approach) adopted by the U.S. Court of Appeals for the Eighth and Ninth Circuits, where a state should only have to negotiate over the types of Class III gaming that are specifically authorized under state law.[68]

The other good-faith issue involves the validity of the revenue sharing agreements that some states have been insisting on as a condition of agreeing to a tribal state Class III compact. Although these revenue sharing agreements sound like a form of state taxation, something that is prohibited under IGRA, courts have held that they will not be considered taxation as long as they are directly related to the operation of gaming activities and are not "imposed" on the tribes because the tribes have acquired in return some meaningful concessions from the states. Two Ninth Circuit decisions, *In re Gaming Related Cases*, 312 F.3d 1094 (9th Cir. 2003) and *Rincon Band v. Schwarzenegger*, 602 F.3d 1019 (9th Cir. 2010) epitomize the difference between what is legal and what is not when it comes to revenue sharing agreements. The agreements were held valid in the first case but not valid in the second.

Another issue that has generated a substantial amount of litigation and could use some legislative clarification has been the difference between Class II and Class III gaming when it comes to distinguishing between various electronic bingo machines. Some have argued that technological innovations in this area have rendered distinctions between some of these machines meaningless, at least from a policy point of view.[69] The key issue here is distinguishing between electronic or

---

[66] [14] See United States v. Spokane Tribe of Indians, 139 F.3d 1297, 1302 (9th Cir. 1998) and Seminole Tribe v. Florida, 11 F.3d 1016, 1029 (11th Cir. 1994). See also Santee Sioux v. Norton, No. 8:05CV147, [2006 U.S. Dist. Lexis 70790] (D. Neb. Sept. 26, 2006).

[67] [15] For a recent critical analysis of the fee to trust process under IGRA, see Brian L. Lewis, *A Day Late and a Dollar Short: Section 2719 of the Indian Gaming Regulatory Act, the Interpretation of Its Exception, and the Part 292 Regulations*, 12 T.M. Cooley J. Prac. & Clinical L. 147 (2010). *See also* Eric M. Jensen, *Indian Gaming on Newly Acquired Lands*, 47 Washburn L. Rev. 675 (2008).

[68] [16] See *Rumsey Indian Rancheria v. Wilson*, 64 F.3d 1250 (1994) and *Cheyenne River Sioux Tribe v. South Dakota*, 3 F.3d 273 (1993).

[69] [17] See Antonia Cowan, *You Can't Get There From Here: IGRA Needs Reinvention Into a*

electromechanical facsimiles of any game of chance or slot machines which is considered Class III, and bingo that has been enhanced by electronic, computer, or other techno-logical aids which is allowed under Class II. This issue has gained much importance for tribes after the Seminole Tribe decision since compact negotiations with the states [for class III gaming have] been rendered much more difficult as a result of the legal uncertainties created by the decision. As long as an electronically aided bingo machine can be classified as Class II, it does not need to be approved by a state pursuant to a tribal state compact.

A somewhat related issue that could use some clarification is whether the Johnson Act prohibition on gaming devices, which has been lifted when gaming is conducted pursuant to a tribal state compact, has also been lifted when a gaming device is considered a Class II machine . . . .[70]

CONCLUSION

Whenever there is a perception that an unregulated problem exists in Indian country, the knee jerk reaction of some always seems to be the same: have the tribes completely regulated by the states, or federally prohibit the tribal activity outright as in the Johnson Act . . . IGRA came up with an innovative compromise: a quasi-independent commission, a majority of whose members had to be tribal members, and a tribal state compact mechanism that gave tribes a meaningful opportunity to negotiate, at least before the Supreme Court upset the apple cart in *Seminole Tribe*. It was not a perfect solution, and it remains controversial but it ended up working much better than the alternative the anti-tribal gaming interests were pushing which was to have tribal gaming under state jurisdiction. . . .

RUMSEY INDIAN RANCHERIA OF WINTUN INDIANS v. WILSON
United States Court of Appeals, Ninth Circuit
64 F.3d 1250 (1994), *as amended,*
1996 U.S. App. LEXIS 27929 (9th Cir. Oct. 29, 1996)

O'SCANNLAIN, CIRCUIT JUDGE:

We decide whether certain gaming activities are permitted under California law and thus subject to tribal-state negotiation under the Indian Gaming Regulatory Act.

Relevant Statute for Mature Industry, 17 VILL. SPORTS & ENT. L.J. 309 (2010)

[70] [There is currently a split in the circuits on this issue. The U.S. Court of Appeals for the District of Columbia (D.C.) Circuit in Diamond Game v. Reno, 23 and the Tenth Circuit in Seneca-Cayuga Tribe v. NIGC,24 ruled that the Johnson Act does not apply to Class II gaming while the Eighth Circuit in United States v. Santee Sioux," took the position that the Johnson Act's prohibition did apply to Class II machines. The NIGC has sided with the D.C. and Tenth Circuit's position. Its views are set out at 67 Fed. Reg. 41,166 (2002).— *Eds.*]

I

Numerous federally recognized Indian tribes currently engage in various gaming activities on tribal lands in California. . . . Desiring to engage in additional activities (the "Proposed Gaming Activities"), several tribes asked the State of California (the "State") to negotiate a compact permitting the operation of certain stand-alone electronic gaming devices[71] and live banking and percentage card games.[72] The State refused to negotiate with the tribes, asserting that the Proposed Gaming Activities were illegal under California law. The State and seven tribes subsequently entered into a stipulation to seek judicial determination of whether the State was obligated to negotiate with the tribes. . . .

II

A tribe seeking to operate Class III gaming activities [under IGRA] on tribal lands generally may do so only under a compact [with the state.] . . . If a state refuses to negotiate in good faith, the tribe can bring a civil suit, whereupon a federal district court may order the state and tribe to conclude a compact within 60 days. *Id.* at § 2710(d)(7)(A)–(B). . . . In the instant case, the State opted not to negotiate over the Proposed Gaming Activities. The State asserts two reasons why it need not negotiate with the Tribes. The first reason is that the Act itself does not require negotiation. The second reason is that the Act violates the tenth amendment. Because the first reason persuades us, we do not reach the second.

The State contends that IGRA does not obligate it to negotiate with the Tribes over the Proposed Gaming Activities. IGRA provides that "Class III gaming activities shall be lawful on Indian lands *only if* such activities are . . . located in a State that *permits such gaming* for any purpose by any person, organization, or entity. . . . " 25 U.S.C. § 2710 (d)(1)(B) (emphasis added). Consequently, where a state does not "permit" gaming activities sought by a tribe, the tribe has no right to engage in these activities, and the state thus has no duty to negotiate with respect to them.

The parties disagree as to whether California "permits" the Proposed Gaming Activities. The State's argument is straightforward: the Proposed Gaming Activities are illegal. California law prohibits the operation of a banked or percentage card game as a misdemeanor offense. Cal. Penal Code § 330 (Deering 1993). In addition, according to the State, the stand-alone electronic gaming machines sought by the Tribes are electronic "slot machines." California law prohibits the operation of slot machines as a misdemeanor offense, Cal. Penal Code §§ 330a, 330b, and a California appellate court has indicated that electronic machines of the sort requested by the Tribes fall within the scope of this prohibition. *Score Family Fun Center, Inc. v.*

---

[71] [1] Included among these electronic games are electronic pull tab machines, video poker devices, video bingo devices, video lotto devices, and video keno devices. The parties agree that California allows these games to be played in nonelectronic formats.

[72] [2] A card game is "banked" if a gaming operator participates in the game with the players and acts as a house bank, paying all winners and retaining all other players' losses. . . . A card game is a "percentage" game if the gaming operator has no interest in the outcome of a game but takes a percentage of all amounts wagered or won. *Id.*

County of San Diego, 225 Cal. App. 3d 1217, 275 Cal. Rptr. 358 (1990).

The Tribes offer a broader reading of IGRA, claiming that a state "permits" a specific gaming activity if it "regulates" the activity *in general* rather than prohibiting it entirely as a matter of public policy. Under this approach, a specific illegal gaming activity is "regulated," rather than "prohibited," if the state allows the operation of similar gaming activities. The Tribes observe that video lottery terminals, parimutuel horse racing, and nonbanked, nonpercentage card gaming are legal in California. Because the Tribes view these activities as functionally similar to the Proposed Gaming Activities, they conclude that California regulates, and thus permits, these activities.

The Tribes cite to the Supreme Court's pre-IGRA decision, in support of their view. In *Cabazon* . . . the Court observed that, "when a State seeks to enforce a law within an Indian reservation under the authority of Public Law 280, it must be determined whether the law is criminal in nature, and thus fully applicable to the reservation . . . , or civil in nature." 480 U.S. at 208. [In *Cabazon*], the Court held that the fact that "an otherwise regulatory law is enforceable by criminal as well as civil means does not necessarily convert it into a criminal law within the meaning of Pub. L. 280." *Id.* at 211. Instead, it explained that there was:

> a distinction between state "criminal/prohibitory" laws and state "civil/regulatory" laws: if the intent of a state law is generally to prohibit certain conduct, it falls within Pub. L. 280's grant of criminal jurisdiction, but if the state law generally permits the conduct at issue, subject to regulation, it must be classified as civil/regulatory and Pub. L. 280 does not authorize its enforcement on an Indian reservation. *The shorthand test is whether the conduct at issue violates the State's public policy.*

Id. at 209 (emphasis added). Applying this test to bingo gaming in California, the Court found that California law permitted a large variety of gaming activities, including bingo. It concluded that the state "regulates rather than prohibits gambling in general and bingo in particular," *id.* at 211, and held that the Indian tribes thus were entitled to engage in their gaming activities.

Congress enacted IGRA in response to *Cabazon*. The Tribes assert that IGRA codified *Cabazon*'s "criminal/regulatory" test . . . We reject this reading of IGRA. In interpreting IGRA, we [turn to the plain meaning of the statute . . . A]lthough statutes benefiting Native Americans generally are construed liberally in their favor, we will not rely on this factor to contradict the plain language of a statute. *Cf. Seldovia Native Ass'n v. Lujan*, 904 F.2d 1335, 1342 (9th Cir. 1987).

Section 2710(d)(1)(b) is unambiguous. In *United States v. Launder*, 743 F.2d 686 (9th Cir. 1984), we adopted a dictionary definition of the term "permit" as meaning " 'to suffer, allow, consent, let; to give leave or license; to acquiesce, by failure to prevent, or to expressly assent or agree to the doing of an act.' " *Id.* at 689 (quoting from *Black's Law Dictionary*). Clearly, California does not allow banked or percentage card gaming. The fact that California allows games that share some characteristics with banked and percentage card gaming . . . is not evidence that the State permits the Proposed Gaming Activities. Nor is it significant that the state lottery, if not technically a slot machine, is functionally similar to one . . . .

IGRA does not require a state to negotiate over one form of Class III gaming activity simply because it has legalized another, albeit similar form of gaming . . . In other words, a state need only allow Indian tribes to operate games that others can operate, but need not give tribes what others cannot have.[73]

III

Because we find the plain meaning of the word "permit" to be unambiguous, we need not look to IGRA's legislative history. However, a brief examination helps to clarify [that] the word has different meanings with respect to Class II and Class III gaming.

. . . The only relevant passages occur in the Senate Report [accompanying IGRA in the] discussion of *Class II* gaming . . . Relying upon the maxim that identical language in a statute should be interpreted to have the same meaning, the Tribes infer that the Senate Report establishes the applicability of the *Cabazon* test to Class III gaming. However, that inference is incorrect. "Identical words appearing more than once in the same act, and even in the same section, may be construed differently if it appears they were used in different places with different intent." *Vanscoter v. Sullivan*, 920 F.2d 1441, 1448 (9th Cir. 1990). Such is the case for Class III gaming. The Senate Report repeatedly links the *Cabazon* test to Class II gaming while remaining silent as to Class III gaming — a fact that itself suggests that Class II and III provisions should be treated differently. . . .

IV

With the possible exception of slot machines in the form of video lottery terminals, California has no obligation to negotiate with the Tribes on the Proposed Gaming Activities, and the trial court judgment is reversed to that extent. . . . We remand to the district court to consider the limited question of whether California permits the operation of slot machines in the form of the state lottery or otherwise.

Affirmed in part, *Reversed* in part, and *Remanded*.

---

[73] [5] Our decision in *Sycuan Band of Mission Indians v. Roache*, 54 F.3d 535, slip op. 4879 (9th Cir. Apr. 1995) is not to the contrary. In *Sycuan Band*, this court held that California lacked jurisdiction to enforce its laws against certain Class III gaming activities on tribal lands because IGRA vests exclusive jurisdiction with the federal government. Slip op. at 4889 (citing 18 U.S.C. § 1166(d)). In the course of its analysis, the court also suggested that, even if the gaming devices at issue were Class II gaming, California would lack authority to enforce its law on tribal lands. The court relied on the statement in *Cabazon* that California "regulates rather than prohibits gambling in general and bingo in particular." Slip op. at 4889 (quoting *Cabazon*, 480 U.S. at 211). The court interpreted this statement expansively to mean that California's gambling laws regarding Class II-type gaming fall on the civil/regulatory side of *Cabazon*'s test; thus, California lacked jurisdiction to enforce these laws on tribal lands.

As an initial matter, the *Sycuan Band* court's analysis of *Cabazon Band* in the context of Class II gaming is dicta; the court expressly held that the gaming at issue was Class III gaming. Slip op. at 4892–98. Moreover, in its discussion of *Cabazon Band*, the *Sycuan Band* court expressed no opinion on its relevance for Class III-type gaming, slip op. at 4888, the type of gaming at issue here. For the reasons expressed above, we have determined that the analysis of whether a type of gaming is permitted by a state under IGRA differs depending on the class of gaming involved.

CANBY, CIRCUIT JUDGE, dissenting, and joined by PREGERSON, REINHARDT, and HAWKINS, CIRCUIT JUDGES, dissenting from the denial of rehearing en banc:

Rumsey holds that California, which permits several varieties of Class III gambling, has no duty under IGRA to negotiate with the tribes over the tribes' ability to conduct any game that is illegal under California law. This ruling effectively frustrates IGRA's entire plan governing Class III Indian gaming. The primary purpose of IGRA, as set forth in the Act, is "to provide a statutory basis for the operation of gaming by Indian tribes as a means of promoting tribal . . . The whole idea was to foster [tribal-state] compacts. That goal is defeated if the details of the state's regulatory schemes, allowing some games and prohibiting others, apply if the state does nothing. Thus the Second Circuit, in arriving at a conclusion precisely opposite to that of *Rumsey*, stated:

> Under the State's approach, . . . even where a state does not prohibit class III gaming as a matter of criminal law and public policy, an Indian tribe could nonetheless conduct such gaming only in accord with, and by acceptance of, the entire state corpus of laws and regulations governing such gaming. The compact process that Congress established as the centerpiece of the IGRA's regulation of class III gaming would thus become a dead letter; there would be nothing to negotiate, and no meaningful compact would be possible.

Mashantucket Pequot Tribe v. Connecticut, 913 F.2d 1024, 1030–31 (2d Cir. 1990).[74]

. . . If a state has a genuine prohibitory public policy against all Class III gaming, as some states do, it can rest on that policy and not entertain the possibility of Indian Class III gaming within its borders . . . IGRA imposes on the states [that have no such wholesale public policy] a duty to negotiate [gaming] compacts in good faith. That duty is enforceable in federal court . . . 25 U.S.C. § 2710(d)(7). But under *Rumsey*, this whole process is nipped in the bud if the tribe seeks to operate games that state law, criminal *or* regulatory, happens to prohibit. The state has no duty to begin negotiations, even though under IGRA a compact may permit the tribe to operate games that state law otherwise prohibits. 18 U.S.C. § 1166(c)(2). The State thus has no incentive to negotiate, and there is no system to require negotiation. IGRA is rendered toothless.

Such a nullifying interpretation . . . is not [required by the statute.] *Rumsey* defeats the congressional plan for Class III gaming by a manifestly flawed interpretation of the statutory language . . . [T]he state must negotiate with a tribe if the state "permits such gaming." The *Rumsey* opinion regards the key question as being whether the word "permits" is ambiguous; it holds that the word is not ambiguous, so the State need not bargain. But the proper question is not what Congress meant by "permits," but what Congress meant by "such gaming." Did it mean the particular game or games in issue, or did it mean the entire category of Class III gaming? The structure of IGRA makes clear that Congress was dealing categorically, and that a state's duty to bargain is not to be determined game-by-

---

[74] [1] We recognize that *Rumsey*'s approach is supported by the Eighth Circuit, *Cheyenne River Sioux Tribe v. South Dakota*, 3 F.3d 273 (8th Cir. 1993), but for the reasons stated we believe that the Second Circuit has much the better overview of IGRA.

game. The time to argue over particular games is during the negotiation process.

The only natural reading of section 2710(d)(1)(B) is that, when Congress says "Class III gaming activities shall be lawful . . . if located in a State that permits such gaming," then "such gaming" refers back to the category of "Class III gaming," which is the next prior use of the word "gaming." *Rumsey* interprets the statutory language as if it said: "A Class III game shall be lawful . . . if located in a State that permits that game." But that is not what Congress said, and it is not a natural reading of the statutory language. The plain language cuts directly against *Rumsey* . . . .

. . . We have held that the state cannot allow or disallow Class II Indian gaming game-by-game. *Sycuan Band of Mission Indians v. Miller*, 54 F.3d 535 (9th Cir. 1995) (amended opinion). Our decision in *Sycuan Band* followed the reasoning of the Supreme Court in *California v. Cabazon Band of Mission Indians*, 480 U.S. 202 (1987), the seminal Indian gaming case that ultimately led to the passage of IGRA. In deciding for purposes of Public Law 280 whether California's prohibition of high-stakes bingo could be enforced against the Band, the Supreme Court noted that "the shorthand test is whether the conduct at issue violates the State's public policy." After reviewing California's treatment of gambling, the Court stated:

> In light of the fact that California permits a substantial amount of gambling activity, including bingo, and actually promotes gambling through its state lottery, we must conclude that California regulates rather than prohibits *gambling in general* and bingo in particular.

Id. at 211 (emphasis added). Thus, *Cabazon Band* ascertained California's public policy at a level of generality far above that of the individual game in issue, and concluded that the Band could conduct high-stakes bingo even though California made that activity a misdemeanor. We applied a similarly broad and categorical approach to Class II gaming in *Sycuan Band*.

The *Rumsey* opinion refuses to apply the reasoning of *Cabazon Band* and *Sycuan Band*, and instead holds that a class-wide, categorical approach is precluded by the "unambiguous" plain words of section 2710(d)(1)(B), even though identical words in section 2710(b)(1)(A) require a contrary result for Class II gaming. The majority in *Rumsey* justifies its interpretation by referring to the Senate Committee Report on IGRA . . . . *See* Sen. Rep. No. 100-446, 1988 U.S.C.C.A.N. 3071, 3076. But we should not read a congressional negative into a committee report's failure to mention *Cabazon Band* in regard to Class III gaming. *Cabazon Band* dealt with games that IGRA placed in Class II, and that is explanation enough why the discussion of *Cabazon Band* in the Committee's report arose only in connection with Class II gaming. The fact remains that Congress wrote provisions of essentially identical wording and structure to govern both Class II and Class III gaming. We should give them both the same categorical meaning.

Rumsey has thus misconstrued IGRA's Class III gaming provisions, and has done so in a manner that defeats Congress's intention and causes great economic harm to numerous tribes. With all respect to the *Rumsey* panel, we dissent from the denial of rehearing en banc.

FERGUSON and NORRIS, SENIOR CIRCUIT JUDGES:

We agree with the views expressed by JUDGE CANBY.

SEMINOLE TRIBE OF FLORIDA v. FLORIDA
United States Supreme Court
517 U.S. 44 (1996)

CHIEF JUSTICE REHNQUIST delivered the opinion of the Court.

[Under the Indian Gaming Regulatory Act of 1988, if a state refuses or fails to negotiate in good faith for a class III gaming compact, the affected tribe may sue the state in federal court to secure first an order to negotiate in good faith and, if that fails, the appointment of a mediator. If appointed, the mediator conducts a bottom-line arbitration of the competing positions and selects one which ultimately is referred to the Secretary of the Interior for approval if not accepted by the parties. A number of states attempted to thwart the process by resisting negotiations and claiming that the provisions that authorize suit against the state violate the eleventh amendment to the Constitution. In *Seminole Tribe* the Eleventh Circuit accepted that argument but ruled that if a state declines to participate in the federal litigation and asserts eleventh amendment sovereign immunity, the Act authorized the Secretary to promulgate regulations under which such gaming could take place. *Seminole Tribe v. Florida*, 11 F.3d 1016 (11th Cir. 1994). The Supreme Court affirmed the eleventh amendment ruling, albeit not on the analysis offered by the Eleventh Circuit. It further declined to address the question of secretarial power to unilaterally approve class III gaming in such circumstances. Critical excerpts from the lengthy *Seminole Tribe* opinions are set forth below.]

The Indian Gaming Regulatory Act provides that an Indian tribe may conduct certain gaming activities only in conformance with a valid compact between the tribe and the State in which the gaming activities are located. 25 U.S.C. § 2710(d)(1)(C). The Act, passed by Congress under the Indian Commerce Clause, U.S. Const., Art. I, section 8, cl. 3, imposes upon the States a duty to negotiate in good faith with an Indian tribe toward formation of a compact, 25 U.S.C. § 2710(d)(3)(A), and authorizes a tribe to bring suit in federal court against a State in order to compel performance of that duty, § 2710(d)(7). We hold that notwithstanding Congress's clear intent to abrogate the States' sovereign immunity, the Indian Commerce Clause does not grant Congress that power, and therefore § 2710(d)(7) cannot grant jurisdiction over a State that does not consent to be sued. We further hold that the doctrine of *Ex parte Young*, 209 U.S. 123 (1908), may not be used to enforce § 2710(d)(3) against a state official. . . .

[O]ur inquiry into whether Congress has the power to abrogate unilaterally the States' immunity from suit is narrowly focused on one question: Was the Act in question passed pursuant to a constitutional provision granting Congress the power to abrogate? *See, e.g., Fitzpatrick v. Bitzer*, 427 U.S. 445, 452–456 (1976). Previously in conducting that inquiry, we have found authority to abrogate under only two provisions of the Constitution. In *Fitzpatrick*, we recognized that the fourteenth amendment, by expanding federal power at the expense of state autonomy, had fundamentally altered the balance of state and federal power struck by the Constitution. *Id.* at 455.

In only one other case has congressional abrogation of the States' eleventh amendment immunity been upheld. In *Pennsylvania v. Union Gas Co.*, 491 U.S. 1 (1989), a plurality of the Court found that the Interstate Commerce Clause, Art. I, § 8, cl. 3, granted Congress the power to abrogate state sovereign immunity, stating that the power to regulate interstate commerce would be "incomplete without the authority to render States liable in damages." *Union Gas*, 491 U.S., at 19–20. . . .

Both parties make their arguments from the plurality decision in *Union Gas*, and we, too, begin there. We think it clear that Justice Brennan's opinion finds Congress's power to abrogate under the Interstate Commerce Clause from the States' cession of their sovereignty when they gave Congress plenary power to regulate interstate commerce. See *Union Gas*, 491 U.S. at 17 ("The important point . . . is that the provision both expands federal power and contracts state power"). Respondents' focus elsewhere is misplaced. While the plurality decision states that Congress's power under the Interstate Commerce Clause would be incomplete without the power to abrogate, that statement is made solely in order to emphasize the broad scope of Congress's authority over interstate commerce. *Id.* at 19–20. Moreover, respondents' rationale would mean that where Congress has less authority, and the States have more, Congress's means for exercising that power must be greater. We read the plurality opinion to provide just the opposite. Indeed, it was in those circumstances where Congress exercised complete authority that Justice Brennan thought the power to abrogate most necessary. *Id.* at 20 ("Since the States may not legislate at all in [the aforementioned] situations, a conclusion that Congress may not create a cause of action for money damages against the States would mean that no one could do so. And in many situations, it is only money damages that will carry out Congress' legitimate objectives under the Commerce Clause").

Following the rationale of the *Union Gas* plurality, our inquiry is limited to determining whether the Indian Commerce Clause, like the Interstate Commerce Clause, is a grant of authority to the federal government at the expense of the States. The answer to that question is obvious. If anything, the Indian Commerce Clause accomplishes a greater transfer of power from the States to the federal government than does the Interstate Commerce Clause. This is clear enough from the facts that the States still exercise some authority over interstate trade but have been divested of virtually all authority over Indian commerce and Indian tribes. Under the rationale of *Union Gas*, if the States' partial cession of authority over a particular area includes cession of the immunity from suit, then their virtually total cession of authority over a different area must also include cession of the immunity from suit. *See, Union Gas*, supra, at 42 (Scalia, J., dissenting) ("[I]f the Article I commerce power enables abrogation of state sovereign immunity, so do all the other Article I powers"); *see, Ponca Tribe of Oklahoma v. Oklahoma*, 37 F.3d 1422, 1428 (C.A. 10 1994) (Indian Commerce Clause grants power to abrogate; *Cheyenne River Sioux Tribe v. South Dakota*, 3 F.3d 273, 281 (C.A. 8 1993) (same); *cf. Chavez v. Arte Publico Press*, 59 F.3d 539, 546–547 (C.A. 5 1995) (After *Union Gas*, Copyright Clause, U.S. Const., Art. I, § 8, cl. 8, must grant Congress power to abrogate). We agree with the petitioner that the plurality opinion in *Union Gas* allows no principled distinction in favor of the States to be drawn between the Indian Commerce Clause and the Interstate Commerce Clause. . . .

In overruling *Union Gas* today, we reconfirm that the background principle of state sovereign immunity embodied in the eleventh amendment is not so ephemeral as to dissipate when the subject of the suit is an area, like the regulation of Indian commerce, that is under the exclusive control of the federal government. Even when the Constitution vests in Congress complete law-making authority over a particular area, the eleventh amendment prevents congressional authorization of suits by private parties against unconsenting States. The eleventh amendment restricts the judicial power under Article III, and Article I cannot be used to circumvent the constitutional limitations placed upon federal jurisdiction. Petitioner's suit against the State of Florida must be dismissed for a lack of jurisdiction.

[*Affirmed.*]

[Justice Stevens dissented, asserting that the majority had made a "sharp break with the past" in denying Congress's power to create a private federal cause of action against a State for violation of a federal right, and that it was "illogical" for the Court to carve out a limited exception to this rule for statutes enacted pursuant to the Enforcement Clause of the fourteenth amendment. He pointed out that the decision would have broad ramifications outside the realm of Indian law, affecting antitrust and environmental matters, among others. Justice Stevens found no basis in the text or interpretations of Article III or the eleventh amendment to support such a denial of congressional power, especially when suit is brought by a citizen of the state that is sued. He read prior decisions involving state sovereign immunity as creating no more than a common law presumption of such immunity, something that Congress had not overcome through the enactment of general subject matter jurisdiction statutes such as 28 U.S.C. § 1331 (federal question) and § 1332 (diversity). With IGRA, however, Congress had plainly manifest an intent to overcome that immunity. At the conclusion of his dissent, Justice Stevens noted:]

Fortunately, and somewhat fortuitously, a jurisdictional problem that is unmentioned by the Court may deprive its opinion of precedential significance. The Indian Gaming Regulatory Act establishes a unique set of procedures for resolving the dispute between the Tribe and the State. If each adversary adamantly adheres to its understanding of the law, if the District Court determines that the State's inflexibility constitutes a failure to negotiate in good faith, and if the State thereafter continues to insist that it is acting within its rights, the maximum sanction that the Court can impose is an order that refers the controversy to a member of the Executive Branch of the Government for resolution. 25 U.S.C. § 2710(d)(7)(B). As the Court of Appeals interpreted the Act, this final disposition is available even though the action against the State and its Governor may not be maintained. 11 F.3d 1016, 1029 (CA11 1994). (The Court does not tell us whether it agrees or disagrees with that disposition.) In my judgment, it is extremely doubtful that the obviously dispensable involvement of the judiciary in the intermediate stages of a procedure that begins and ends in the Executive Branch is a proper exercise of judicial power. See Gordon v. United States, 117 U.S. App. 697, 702–703 (1864) (opinion of Taney, C. J.); United States v. Ferreira, 54 U.S. 40, 14 L. Ed. 42, 13 How 40, 48 (1852). It may well follow that the misguided opinion of today's majority has nothing more than an advisory character.

[Justices Souter, Ginsburg, and Breyer filed a separate dissent, a lengthy and heavily researched opinion that examined the original understanding of state sovereign immunity, the eleventh amendment, and the power of legislatures to amend the common law. The dissenting Justices wrote that "In ignoring the reasons for this pervasive understanding at the time of the ratification, and in holding that a nontextual common-law rule limits a clear grant of congressional power under Article I, the Court follows a course that has brought it to grief before in our history, and promises to do so again." They also challenged the Court's decision to disallow suit against the Governor of the state, thereby displacing *Ex parte Young*, 209 U.S. 123 (1908).]

Pueblo of Santa Ana v. Kelly, 104 F.3d 1546 (10th Cir. 1997): The Governor of New Mexico signed separate gaming compacts with thirteen Indian nations, and the Secretary of the Interior approved these compacts under the terms of IGRA and published notice in the Federal Register. Subsequently, the state's supreme court found that the Governor lacked authority to bind the state absent legislative confirmation. The tribes argued that secretarial approval overcame any deficiencies of the compacts under state law. The Tenth Circuit disagreed, holding that IGRA contains two distinct compact-related requirements before Class III gaming may be exempt from the application of federal and state criminal prohibitions: the compact must have been "entered into" by the tribe and the state, 25 U.S.C. § 2710(d)(1)(C), and the compact must be "in effect" pursuant to secretarial approval and notice, 25 U.S.C. § 2710(d)(3)(B). *See also* 25 U.S.C. § 2710(d)(6). IGRA does not specify the meaning of "entered into" or "in effect." The first of these requirements, according to the court, was governed by state law, and the court chose to accept the state supreme court's interpretation of that law. Furthermore, the court found that the Secretary of the Interior was not obliged to inquire into such matters during the 45-day period in which the Secretary must sign compacts under IGRA.

The tribes had argued that allowing state law challenges to disrupt federally approved compacts would undermine the primary purpose of IGRA, which was to promote tribal self-sufficiency and to minimize state involvement in the regulation of economic development within Indian country. They raised concerns that state law challenges would undermine the finality of compacts and inhibit investment. According to the Tenth Circuit, however,

> While preservation of tribal sovereignty was clearly of great concern to Congress, respect for state interests relating to class III gaming was also of great concern. We are hesitant to conclude that Congress intended to permit a state to be bound by a compact regulating class III gaming which it never validly entered. . . .

> A compact is a form of contract. As with any contract, parties entering into one must assure themselves that each contracting party is authorized to enter into the contract.

The court also expressed concern over imposing affirmative regulatory obligations upon states that they had never properly assumed.

Is the court properly characterizing a tribal-state gaming compact as just another contract? Isn't the fact of federal involvement in approving the compacts a sign that these agreements bear a special federal interest? Professor Tsosie has pointed out that unlike most tribal-state agreements, which rely on "voluntary compliance and mutual forbearance," IGRA compacts grant states power otherwise withheld from them by the Constitution and exclusively within federal concern. Rebecca Tsosie, *Negotiating Economic Survival: The Consent Principle and Tibal States Compacts Under the Indian Gaming Regulatory Act*, 29 ARIZ ST. L.J., 25, 58–59 (1997). While the former might be appropriate for contract analysis, the latter, she suggests, calls for application of federal law.

The Tenth Circuit's treatment of tribal-state gaming compacts contrasts with the legal regime for interstate compacts. In the case of interstate compacts, which as a matter of federal law must be adopted by state legislatures and ratified by Congress, the congressional ratification transforms the compact into federal law, and disputes about the validity of the compact into federal issues. Professor Tsosie contends, "Federal sovereignty has always served an important function in mediating the struggles between states and tribes for regulatory power in Indian Country, and, conceivably, the requirement of federal approval of gaming compacts serves a similar role in guarding federal supremacy. . . . " *Id.* at 61. She notes that interstate compacts, like IGRA compacts, trigger affirmative duties, and the Supreme Court has never been troubled by applying federal law in situations where states commit themselves to such duties, inducing reliance by other states, and then later attack an interstate compact as invalid under state law. Does the fact that federal law specifies state legislative approval before making an interstate compact suggest that the federal interest is greater in interstate compact situations than in IGRA compacts, or that the chances for claims of invalidity under state law are smaller?

NOTES

1. IGRA and Jurisdiction in Indian Country: How, if at all, does IGRA alter the allocation of jurisdiction within Indian country? In the ongoing competition between Indian nations and states for control, IGRA offers something for both sides.

First, confirming the result in *Cabazon*, it affords Indian nations regulatory power over Class II gaming (including high-stakes bingo, pull-tabs and lotto, in electronic or any other form). 25 U.S.C. § 2710(b). This feature of IGRA has become increasingly important to tribes and threatening to states, as inventive manufacturers using advanced chip technology have found ways to make these games function much the same as highly popular casino-style slot machines. *See* Note 6, *infra*.

Second, it makes violation of applicable state gaming laws a federal offense, and gives the federal courts exclusive authority to enforce state gaming prohibitions that may still be effective after IGRA, thereby displacing any state criminal/

prohibitory jurisdiction that states may have retained under Public Law 280 following *Cabazon*. 18 U.S.C. § 1166(d). *See Sycuan Band of Mission Indians v. Roache*, 54 F.3d 535 (9th Cir. 1995) (discussed in both the majority and dissenting opinions in *Rumsey*, and holding that only the federal government can enforce state gaming prohibitions made applicable under IGRA). This provision was important in the struggle between California tribes and state authorities, as it placed the United States Attorney in the key role of determining whether and when action should be taken against tribes that were engaging in Class III gaming without a compact while arguing to the courts, ultimately without success, that the state was compelled to negotiate with them over slot machines.

Third, and most important, it requires Indian nations to make compacts with states in order to carry out potentially lucrative Class III gaming, and allows states that ban Class III gaming to decline to negotiate such compacts. As the opinions in *Rumsey* reveal, how much power this provision confers on the states depends on how one interprets IGRA. As the *Rumsey* majority and the Eighth Circuit would have it, states should have the power to veto any type of Class III gaming that is absolutely prohibited under state law. Judge Canby in his *Rumsey* dissent, agreeing with the Second Circuit, interprets IGRA to require compact negotiations over all forms of Class III gaming whenever the state permits any games falling into that category. Which interpretation of 25 U.S.C. § 2710(d)(1)(B) makes more sense of the text itself? Which is more consistent with the legislative history, especially Congress's desire to enshrine the distinction presented in *Cabazon*? Which is more faithful to the Indian law canons of construction? What understandings of the tribal-federal relationship undergird the two opinions in *Rumsey*?

After two tribally-led initiatives resulted in a California state constitutional amendment authorizing slot machines and house-banked black jack on reservations with Class III compacts under specified terms (*see* Note 3, *infra*), off-reservation horse-racing and card room owners brought another challenge under IGRA, this time arguing that a Class III compact was not permissible under the act unless the state authorized the types of games in question *off* the reservation as well as on. The challengers rested their claim on the "permits such gaming" language of 25 U.S.C. § 2710(d)(1)(B), pointing to earlier federal court decisions that had said it would be "patent bootstrapping" to find that a tribal-state compact for Class III gaming satisfied both the "permits such gaming" requirement and also the compacting requirement. In *Artichoke Joe's Cal. Grand Casino v. Norton*, 353 F.3d 712 (9th Cir. 2003), the Ninth Circuit rejected this argument, observing that California's constitutional amendment separately legalized the designated forms of gaming and authorized the Governor to enter into compacts. It also swept aside the contention that California had no authority to "permit" gaming on Indian lands because of *Cabazon*, making it impossible for any reservation-specific state measure to satisfy IGRA's requirement. If one reads IGRA as restoring some of the state's regulatory authority lost under *Cabazon*, then there would be some room for the state to "permit" on-reservation Class III gaming. Applying the Indian law canons of construction, the court chose that interpretation. The challengers also contended that IGRA's requirement, also found in section 2710(d)(1)(B), that a state permit class III gaming by "any person, organization, or entity" did not include Indian tribes. Their position was that if no other Class III gaming is permitted in a state, then federal law must bar Indians from conducting such gaming. The tribes, in contrast, argued that since the statute did not specify whether tribes were included, a state should be free to give tribes a monopoly, even though, under *Rumsey*, states could not be forced to negotiate a compact at all for games absolutely prohibited to non-Indians. Again, finding ambiguities and applying the Indian law canons, the Ninth Circuit ruled for the tribes.

Fourth, IGRA provides that in the Class III gaming compacts themselves, Indian nations and states may negotiate and reach agreements about a variety of matters, including allocation of civil and criminal jurisdiction that is "directly related to, and necessary for, the licensing and regulation" of gaming activity, and "any other subjects that are directly related to the operation of gaming activities." 25 U.S.C. § 2710(d)(3)(C). These agreements could conceivably alter preexisting jurisdictional allocations. Under this provision, could states and Indian nations agree to tribal criminal jurisdiction over non-Indians who pass bad checks to the casino? Could an Indian nation in a non-Public Law 280 state introduce state criminal jurisdiction over tribal members who get into altercations with patrons on casino grounds or application of state laws regarding types of wagers? Under tribal compacts with the State of New Mexico, any crime committed by a nonmember of the tribe "against the Gaming Enterprise or any employee thereof or that occurs on the premises of the Tribal Gaming Facility" is within the state's criminal jurisdiction. Recently, a nonmember who embezzled more than $1.2 million from the Sandia Pueblo was sentenced in state court to 50 years in prison. Scott Sandlin, *Casino Embezzler Receives 50 Years*, ALBUQUERQUE J., Oct. 29, 2009, at 1. Is that a good result under IGRA? Should tribes welcome such prosecutions?

A related issue reached the New Mexico Supreme Court in *Jane Doe v. Santa Clara Pueblo*, 154 P.3d 644 (N.M. 2007), involving civil rather than criminal jurisdiction. Santa Clara Pueblo and New Mexico had included a provision in their compact relating to tort claims by casino patrons: "[A]ny such claim may be brought in state district court, including claims arising on tribal land, unless it is finally determined by a state or federal court that IGRA does not permit the shifting of jurisdiction over visitors' personal injury suits to state court." Do the provisions of 25 U.S.C. § 2710(d)(3)(C) regarding civil and criminal jurisdiction, quoted in the preceding paragraph, encompass patron lawsuits? If not, does the catch-all language of IGRA, also quoted in that paragraph, provide sufficient support? How should these two provisions be read together, especially in light of the Indian law canons of construction? The case of *Kennerly v. District Court*, 400 U.S. 423 (1971), discussed in Sec. A, this chapter, holds that states and tribes may not make agreements to extend state jurisdiction on reservations unless Congress has given its consent. Does the compact provision above even demonstrate tribal consent to state jurisdiction? If so, would the language of IGRA count as adequate evidence of congressional consent? Over a dissent from Justice Minzner, the New Mexico Supreme Court upheld state jurisdiction. *See also Pueblo of Santa Ana v. Nash*, 972 F. Supp. 2d 1254 (D.N.M. 2013) (holding that IGRA did not authorize state courts to take jurisdiction over a personal injury claim that arose from negligent service of alcohol within tribal land).

Some states, such as California, have interpreted section 2710(d)(3)(C) as license to negotiate over application of a broad range of state regulatory legislation, ranging from labor laws to coastal zone management laws. Tribes anticipated this problem during legislative debates over IGRA, and some opposed enactment of the law for that reason. To allay such concerns, Senator Inouye, Chair of the Committee on Indian Affairs pronounced on the floor of the Senate,

> There is no intent on the part of Congress that the compacting methodology be used in such areas such as taxation, water rights, environmental regulation, and land use. On the contrary, the tribal power to regulate such activities . . . remains fully intact. The exigencies caused by the rapid growth of gaming in Indian country and the threat of corruption and infiltration by criminal elements in class III gaming warranted the utilization of existing State regulatory capabilities in this one narrow area. No precedent is meant to be set as to other areas.

134 Cong. Rec. 12651, Sept. 15, 1988. Speaking during the House debates, Rep. Coehlo added, "Nor is it the intent of Congress that States use negotiations on gaming compacts as a means to pressure Indian tribes to cede rights in any other area." Given the language of section 2710(d)(3)(C), should a state be able to insist that application of state labor or environmental laws be a subject of gaming compact negotiations?

In *In re Gaming Related Cases*, 331 F.3d 1094 (9th Cir. 2003), the Ninth Circuit considered whether California could properly inject the issue of labor relations into gaming compact negotiations. The Coyote Valley Tribe, which had initiated the lawsuit, argued that labor relations "are too far afield from tribal gaming to be an appropriate topic. . . . " The state's position was that "because thousands of its citizens are employed at tribal casinos, it is proper for the State to insist on some minimal level of protection for those workers as a precondition to entering a Tribal-State compact." In ruling for the state, the Ninth Circuit panel first refused to find labor relations categorically outside the scope of permissible topics. Without engaging the legislative history quoted above, the panel found that labor relations is "directly related to the operation of gaming activities," and thus permissible under IGRA, because "without the 'operation of gaming activities,' the jobs this provision covers would not exist; nor, conversely, could Indian gaming activities operate without someone performing these jobs." The Tribe argued that the state's insistence on a specific Tribal Labor Relations Ordinance demonstrated bad faith. But the panel rejected this argument as well, finding that the ordinance "provides only modest organizing rights to tribal gaming employees and contains several provisions protective of tribal sovereignty." Further, an organization of tribes, including Coyote Valley, had met with union representatives and participated in the shaping of the TLRO, all the compacting tribes in California had adopted it, and the state had granted concessions in exchange for it.

In the same case, the Ninth Circuit also upheld the state's bargaining stance that compacting tribes must contribute funds to a Revenue Sharing Trust Fund for nongaming tribes, as well as a Special Distribution Fund to affected local governments. Again, the panel emphasized connections between these funds and the tribal gaming enterprises, the accession of other tribes to these terms, and the concessions provided by the state. Revenue-sharing provisions in IGRA gaming compacts are discussed further in Note 3, below.

The former chair of the National Indian Gaming Association, Leonard Prescott, has said that NIGA views IGRA as an incursion on the tribal right of self-government. On behalf of NIGA he has said, "IGRA did not confer any rights on Indian tribes to engage in, or regulate, gaming. We already had those rights. IGRA took away some of our rights to serve the economic interests of the non-Indian gaming industry." Implementation and Enforcement of the Indian Gaming Regulatory Act, P.L. 100-497, Before the House Committee on Interior and Insular Affairs, 102d Cong. 2d Sess. (1992). Is that a proper characterization of IGRA? For a thoughtful account of IGRA as a legal and political compromise, see STEVEN ANDREW LIGHT & KATHRYN R.L. RAND, INDIAN GAMING AND TRIBAL SOVEREIGNTY: THE CASINO COMPROMISE (2005).

2. *Seminole* and the Resolution of Tribal-State Conflicts over Gaming Compacts: After *Seminole*, what options do Indian nations have if states resist negotiating gaming compacts, or refuse to negotiate in good faith? Can they sue in state courts, where the Eleventh Amendment does not on its face apply? Can the United States, which is not mentioned in the Eleventh Amendment, sue states on behalf of the tribes to enforce IGRA's requirements? Would it be a violation of the federal trust responsibility if the federal government declined to bring such an action? *See Chemehuevi Indian Tribe v. Wilson*, 987 F. Supp. 804 (N.D. Cal. 1997). The Ninth Circuit has strongly suggested that in the absence of a state's waiver of Eleventh Amendment immunity, the compact requirements of IGRA may have to fall under the weight of *Seminole*. *United States v. Spokane Tribe of Indians*, 139 F.3d 1297 (9th Cir. 1998). The court found clear indications that Congress would not have instituted the compact requirements absent the provision for judicial enforcement struck down in *Seminole*. The State of California has waived its Eleventh Amendment immunity in suits by Indian nations to compel good faith negotiations under IGRA.

The *Seminole* Court mentioned but declined to rule on another alternative means of resolving tribal-state conflicts over compact negotiations — notifying the Secretary of the Interior, who may address the problem by regulation. *Seminole Tribe of Florida v. Florida*, 11 F.3d 1016, 1029 (11th Cir. 1994). Although it took considerable time, the Interior Department has adopted regulations allowing the Secretary to prescribe gaming procedures if a state's assertion of sovereign immunity results in the dismissal of a tribal claim. These regulations can be found at 25 C.F.R. Part 291. What if the state waives Eleventh Amendment sovereign immunity but successfully challenges the constitutionality of the IGRA procedures on some other grounds? In such circumstances, do the provisions of 25 C.F.R. Part 291 apply? If the state waives sovereign immunity but the IGRA-prescribed judicial procedures fail to generate an agreed upon compact, do the provisions of 25 C.F.R. Part 291 apply? Perhaps as a result of Part 291, several states have already waived sovereign immunity in post-*Seminole* IGRA litigation and permitted the litigation to go forward. *See, e.g., Northern Arapaho Tribe v. Wyoming*, 389 F.3d 1308 (10th Cir. 2004).

Taking a position at odds with the Eleventh and Ninth Circuits, a split panel of the Fifth Circuit, with one judge dissenting and the other concurring only in the judgment, has found the Part 291 regulations violate IGRA because they contain no requirement of bad faith. Compare *Texas v. United States*, 497 F.3d 491 (5th Cir.

2007) with *Seminole Tribe of Fla. v. Florida*, 11 F.3d 1016, 1029 (11th Cir. 1994) and *United States v. Spokane Tribe*, 139 F.3d 1297, 1301–1302 (9th Cir. 1998). The impact of the *Texas* case is limited by the absence of a majority opinion. But which of the federal circuits offers a better reading of IGRA, given that the statute imposed a limitation on pre-existing tribal gaming authority as recognized in *Cabazon*? Given your reading of IGRA, are the Part 291 regulations a reasonable response to the statutory dilemma presented by the Supreme Court's decision in *Seminole*?

The discussion in this Note focuses on tribal remedies against states refusing to bargain or to enter into compacts. What if the compact is made, and the state wants to sue the tribe for breach? IGRA provides for a waiver of tribal immunity and authorization for injunctive actions with respect to any "class III gaming activity . . . conducted in violation of any Tribal-State compact entered into [in accordance with IGRA] . . . that is in effect." 25 U.S.C. § 2710(d)(7)(A)(ii). Should a tribe's failure to make payments under a compact's revenue-sharing provisions trigger the operation of this provision? Or should suit be allowed against the tribe only when the actual operations of the tribal casino are being conducted in violation of the compact's terms? In *Wisconsin v. Ho-Chunk Nation*, 512 F.3d 921 (7th Cir. 2008), Wisconsin sued the Ho-Chunk Nation to compel arbitration in a dispute over tribal payments to the state under its revenue-sharing agreement. The Seventh Circuit said that the language of IGRA allowed suits against tribes for compact violations, but only for terms addressing the seven items listed in 25 U.S.C. § 2710(d)(3)(C)(i)–(vii). The Ninth and Eleventh Circuits have adopted even more restrictive readings of the IGRA language waiving tribal sovereign immunity and authorizing suits. See *Florida v. Seminole Tribe of Florida*, 181 F.3d 1237, 1242 (11th Cir. 1999); *Cabazon Band of Mission Indians v. Wilson*, 124 F.3d 1050, 1059–1060 (9th Cir. 1997).

3. **Revenue-Sharing Agreements in Tribal-State Compacts:** Though revenue sharing agreements between tribe and states were rare in the past, they have become quite frequent since the Court's decision in *Seminole Tribe*. With limited legal recourse to demand fair bargaining practices in compact negotiations, tribes must often agree to share large percentages of their profits before states approve Class III compact agreements. According to scholars Kathryn Rand, Steven Light, and Alan Meister, revenue sharing agreements "take a number of forms, including percentage payments, fixed compact payments, impact/mitigation fees and taxes, contributions to community funds, and redistribution to non-gaming tribes." Kathryn Rand, Steven Light & Alan Meister, *Spreading the Wealth: Indian Gaming and Revenue Sharing Agreements*, N.D. L. REV. 657, 667 (2004). Many have criticized the fairness of these agreements. *See* Gavin Clarkson & Jim Sebenius, *Leveraging Tribal Sovereignty for Economic Opportunity: A Strategic Negotiations Perspective*, 76 MO. L. REV. 1045, 1109 (2011).

IGRA specifically prohibits states from taxing tribal gaming. 25 U.S.C. § 2710(d)(4). Furthermore IGRA specifies and limits the proper uses of gaming revenues. 25 U.S.C. § 2710(b)(2)(B)(i)–(v). Nonetheless, several states, including Connecticut, California, Michigan, New Mexico, and Wisconsin, have succeeded in securing significant contributions from tribes. The Department of Interior has been willing to approve such compact provisions if the state provides exclusivity in exchange, on the theory that the power to make such an economic deal is part of the tribes' sovereignty that IGRA did not withdraw. However, this "exclusivity" — which limits or restrains other gaming interests — is often tenuous or meaningless in practice. As scholar Eric Lent states, "In practice, tribes are not paying for a valuable asset (the right to exclusive gaming), but instead are paying for the right to conduct gaming in the first place. Significantly, only when tribes have an established right to gaming would exclusivity be of any value; without a preexisting gaming right, exclusivity. . . is practically worthless." *See* Eric S. Lent, *Are States Beating the House?: The Validity of Tribal-State Revenue Sharing Under the Indian Gaming Regulatory Act*, 91 GEO L.J. 451, 470 (2003). Does the DOI's rationale hold up in light of the other ways in which IGRA compromises tribal economic sovereignty and the overriding purposes of IGRA?

4. **Revenue Sharing Agreements in California:** In California, gaming tribes that negotiated compacts in 1999 pay a percentage of their compact revenues into the "Indian Gaming Revenue Sharing Trust Fund." Money from the RSTF is distributed to non-gaming tribes in the state. California gaming tribes under the 1999 compacts also pay into the state's "Special Distribution Fund," which is redistributed for costs associated with gaming to affected local governments. Compacts negotiated under Governor Schwarzenegger, beginning in 2004, changed this arrangement to a system in which tribes deposited money directly into the state's general fund, in exchange for the ability to use more slot machines. Around this time, the Rincon Band of Luiseño Mission Indians sought to renegotiate its compact, hoping to expand its casino operations. The State offered the tribe the ability to add 900 additional slot machines, but asked Rincon to pay 10–15% of its profits to the state. As consideration, the State promised that Rincon would not have to compete with non-Tribal casinos — something already provided by the California Constitution. In *Rincon Band of Luiseno Mission Indians v. Schwarzenegger*, 602 F.3d 1019 (9th Cir. 2010), the Ninth Circuit held that California negotiated in bad faith and characterized the state's demand that the Rincon Band agree to pay a portion of its net profits into the state treasury as an impermissible tax under IGRA. Further, the Court held that the state could not use a promise of illusory exclusivity as consideration for revenue sharing. Recall that California has agreed to a limited waiver of sovereign immunity in IGRA good faith suits, meaning that the tribes can sue the state, despite the holding in *Seminole*.

5. **Referenda and Initiative — Avoiding the IGRA Litigation Process:** Another response that some tribes have successfully invoked to resolve problems created by *Seminole Tribe* and recalcitrant state officials involves by-passing or displacing the negotiations processes by taking their proposed compacts directly to a vote of the state electorate through state initiative or referendum procedures. For example, in the 2002 election, the State of Arizona approved Proposition 202 sponsored by a consortium of 17 Arizona tribes that mandated the governor to sign compacts in a format specified by the referendum. *See* Az. Rev. Stat. § 5-601.2. Earlier, the Salt River Pima-Maricopa Indian Community had successfully deployed the Arizona initiative process to secure a gaming compact through a vote of the people over objections from the governor. *See Salt River Pima-Maricopa Indian Community v. Hull*, 945 P.2d 818 (Ariz. 1997).

California tribes were particularly successful in invoking that state's initiative processes to overcome gubernatorial resistance to Indian gaming and highly intrusive proposals made by the state and accepted by one tribe. They first employed the California initiative process to pass Proposition 5 authorizing more acceptable class III gaming compacts. As Professors Carole Goldberg and Duane Champagne explain in *Ramona Redeemed? The Rise of Tribal Political Power in California*, 17 WICAZO SA REV. 43, 47–56 (2001), "In *International Union (HERE) v. Davis*, [981 P.2d 990 (Cal. 1999),] the opposition [to Indian gaming in California] argued that Proposition 5, a law by initiative, violated the 1984 state constitutional amendment prohibiting Nevada and New Jersey style gaming in California as well as inconsistent with IGRA. In a vote of 6-1, the California Supreme Court ruled that Proposition 5 was unlawful under the state constitution, and declined to reach the IGRA issue." The California tribes consequently successfully submitted a constitutional amendment labeled Proposition 1A to the California electorate as authorized by the California Constitution, which overcame the impediments created by the California Supreme Court decision and created a new detailed form of compact agreement. Professors Goldberg and Champagne describe the aftermath of the passage of Proposition 1A as follows:

> Passage of Proposition 1A created terms for agreements between the Indian tribes of California and the State of California. The proposition allowed casino-style gaming on reservations, but the state enforced several compromises on tribal governments. Apart from the provisions relating to labor, licensing, and customer suits, tribes were restricted to 2000 slot machines per tribe and a limit of two casinos per tribe. Banking and percentage card games such as blackjack were allowed, tribes were to share 1.1 million per year with nongaming tribes, a joint state-tribal oversight agency was created with two representatives from each gaming tribe, tribal funding was provided for compulsive gaming treatment, and the tribes were required to adopt ordinances for environmental protection, worker safety, building codes, and were required to waive limited sovereign immunity for injuries to patrons . . .

> The passage of Proposition 1A was derived from considerable public support, but also strong support from within the Davis administration and California legislature. . . . Not only did the Governor and state legislature place Proposition 1A on the March 2000 ballot, but several prominent state office holders also began to sponsor and support bills and issues that tribal leaders and Indian communities wanted and needed. . . .

> After passage of Proposition 1A, many Nevada and New Jersey investors became more interested in California Indian gaming tribes. Previously, gaming investors feared that California Indian gaming might be ultimately ruled illegal, and therefore curtailed investments in California Indian gaming. However, after the election many gaming investors quickly starting negotiating investment plans with California Indian tribes, and several tribes announced plans for significant expansions in larger casinos, new hotels, and recreation centers.

17 WICAZO SA REV. at 54–56.

6. Restrictions on the Location of Tribal Gaming Under IGRA: Under IGRA, gaming may only be conducted on "Indian lands," 25 U.S.C. § 2710, which are defined to include lands within reservations and other lands held in trust by the United States for tribes or individual Indians. 25 U.S.C. § 2703(4). To contain the potential spread of tribal gaming, IGRA provides that "gaming regulated by this Act shall not be conducted on lands acquired by the Secretary in trust for the benefit of an Indian tribe after [the date of enactment of this Act, October 17th, 1988]. . . . " 25 U.S.C. § 2719(a). Limited exceptions exist for lands within or contiguous to an existing reservation, lands acquired by virtue of land claims settlement, lands provided for newly recognized or restored tribes, and other lands approved both by the Secretary of the Interior and the governor of the state in question. In 2013, a district court in New York held that the restriction against gaming on lands acquired after 1988 only applied to lands held in trust, and did not restrict gaming on tribal lands held in fee. *Citizens Against Casino Gambling in Erie County v. Stevens* 945 F. Supp. 2d 391 (D.N.Y. 2013).

IGRA's restrictions on gaming locations have created a financial incentive for tribes to pursue the federal recognition and restoration processes, as well as to file land claims litigation. For example, the Mohegan Nation in Connecticut settled its land claims litigation by negotiating a compact with the state to open a casino. In response, gaming opponents have begun to attack the federal recognition process, demanding a freeze on all recognition decisions until the procedures are reformed. *See* Light & Rand, Indian Gaming and Tribal Sovereignty, *supra*, at 59–65. *See also* Ch. 2, Sec. A.1, for further discussion of the federal recognition process. For already recognized tribes, IGRA's provision for gubernatorial and Interior Secretary approval of off-reservation gaming has led some tribes and investors to court well-located but economically depressed non-Indian communities eager for the infusion of gaming-related jobs and dollars. This practice has alarmed non-Indian gaming opponents as well as some already established gaming tribes.

To address many of these questions, the Bureau of Indian Affairs has published implementing regulations. See 25 C.F.R. 292 (Interior; Final Rule, 2008). For example, for a parcel of land to qualify under the "initial reservation" exception to § 2719(b)(1)(B)(ii), the tribe must have present and historical connections to the land, and the Department of the Interior must proclaim the land a new reservation under the Indian Reorganization Act. Also, with the United States Supreme Court's decision in *Carcieri v. Salazar*, presented in Ch. 6, Sec. 6 and discussed in Ch. 2, Sec. A.2, it will be more difficult for tribes that were not federally recognized in 1934 to secure initial reservations in the first place. Additionally, the new Interior regulations clarify that a tribe submitting a gaming ordinance to the National Indian Gaming Commission for approval must also supply Indian lands information. Before that regulation was instituted, a tribe could secure approval of a gaming ordinance without indicating the specific site where the gaming would be conducting, or demonstrating that the chosen site was allowable under IGRA. *See N. County Cmty. Alliance, Inc. v. Salazar*, 573 F.3d 738 (9th Cir. 2009).

7. The Constitutionality of IGRA: Apart from the Eleventh Amendment challenge that succeeded in *Seminole*, the main vehicle for constitutional attack on IGRA has been the equal protection requirement built into the Fifth Amendment due process clause. For example, in *Artichoke Joe's Cal. Grand Casino v. Norton*,

353 F.3d 712 (9th Cir. 2003), discussed in Note 1, *supra*, non-Indian businesses contended that IGRA violates equal protection insofar as it enables tribes to conduct gaming enterprises that are forbidden elsewhere within the state. They also challenged California's Proposition 1A under the equal protection clause of the Fourteenth Amendment insofar as it implemented that regime. Plaintiffs argued that strict scrutiny review should be applied to IGRA and Proposition 1A rather than the more deferential standard established in *Morton v. Mancari*. *See* Ch. 2, Sec. B.1. Alternatively, they argued that the law does not survive even under *Morton v. Mancari*'s more lenient criterion. The Ninth Circuit panel held that *Morton v. Mancari* is still good law, and that IGRA and Proposition 1A both pass muster under its standard of review. Analyzing IGRA, it distinguished *Williams v. Babbitt*, discussed in Ch. 2, Sec. B.3, which had raised constitutional questions about a federal law that could be interpreted to give a preference to individual Alaska Natives in the reindeer industry, finding:

> IGRA falls squarely within the rule of *Mancari*. *Williams* continued to recognize that a statute relating to tribal self-government, to tribal status, or to Indian lands is subject to rational-basis review. IGRA is just such a statute, notwithstanding the dictum in *Williams* that doubted whether Congress could give "Indians a complete monopoly on the casino industry." As our lengthy discussion of the statute has made clear, IGRA does not give "Indians" a monopoly; it neither relates to "Indians" (as distinct from federally recognized tribes) nor, itself, creates a monopoly.

353 F.3d at 735. The panel then had little difficulty concluding that IGRA met the *Mancari* rational basis standard because it is "rationally related to Congress' stated purposes of encouraging tribal autonomy and economic development."

Turning to California's Proposition 1A, which made tribal exclusivity or monopoly an important feature of the gaming compacts it authorized, the panel likewise found that *Mancari*'s rational basis test applies because "in ratifying Proposition 1A, the people of California were legislating with reference to the authority that Congress had granted to the State of California in IGRA." *See Washington v. Confederated Bands & Tribes of Yakima Indian Nation*, discussed in Ch. 2, Sec. B.1. While the state's grant of a monopoly made the issue more difficult, the court noted that "States have wide latitude in establishing classifications to balance interests and remedy perceived problems," including the grant of a monopoly itself when there exists "an appropriate connection to the state's police power." California could cite to two legitimate interests supporting the exclusivity provisions in Proposition 1A — the regulation of "vice" activity "by permitting certain forms of gambling only on the lands of sovereign tribal entities that enter into government-to-government compacts with the State," and the promotion of "cooperative relationships between the tribes and the State by fostering tribal sovereignty and self-sufficiency."

Plaintiffs had argued that upholding Proposition 1A would lead to state-granted tribal monopolies in other areas, such as automobile dealerships. Does the holding in *Artichoke Joe's* mean that states constitutionally can grant tribes exclusive rights to conduct enterprises other than casino gambling? For an interesting discussion of issues surrounding exclusivity of tribal gaming under state law, see Kevin K.

Washburn, *Cross-Border Issues in Gaming: Federal Law, State Policy, and Indian Gaming*, 4 NEV. L.J. 285 (2003). A vast literature has developed on IGRA and the policy issues associated with tribal gaming. Among the most useful compilations of articles are: *Indian Gaming Symposium*, Vol. 29, No. 1, ARIZ. ST. L.J. (1997); INDIAN GAMING: WHO WINS? (A. Mullis & D. Kamper eds., 2000). An insightful book on the subject is STEVEN ANDREW LIGHT & KATHRYN R.L. RAND, INDIAN GAMING AND TRIBAL SOVEREIGNTY: THE CASINO COMPROMISE (2005). The Harvard Project on American Indian Economic Development has published an analysis of the 1990 and 2000 censuses for Indians residing on reservations, which demonstrates that improvements across socio-economic measures were significantly greater for Indians on reservations with gaming than for those on non-gaming reservations. Rates of improvement were generally higher for reservation Indians than for the United States population as a whole. *See* THE HARVARD PROJECT ON AMERICAN INDIAN ECONOMIC DEVELOPMENT, THE STATE OF THE NATIVE NATIONS: CONDITIONS UNDER U.S. POLICIES OF SELF-DETERMINATION 150–153 (2008).

In *KG Urban Enterprises, LLC v. Patrick*, a non-tribal applicant for a gaming license argued that a Massachusetts gaming law granted an unconstitutional race-based preference to Indian tribes. Without reaching that question, the First Circuit stated:

> [I]t is quite doubtful that *Mancari's* language can be extended to apply to preferential state classifications based on tribal status. *Mancari* itself relied on several sources of federal authority to reach its holding, including the portion of the Commerce Clause relating to Indian tribes, the treaty power, and the special trust relationship between Indian tribes and the federal government. The states have no such equivalent authority, which is ceded by the Constitution to the federal government. [Citations omitted].

693 F.3d 1 (1st Cir. 2012). Is that statement consistent with what you learned in Ch. 2, Sec. B about the application of *Mancari* to state classifications?

8. **Class II or Class III Gaming?** The dividing line between Class II and Class III gaming marks an important legal boundary under IGRA between primary tribal regulation and adoption of state regulatory law as federal law. As a result, this dividing line has become critical for tribes located in states unwilling to approve the gaming compacts necessary to conduct Class III gaming, or involved in compacts that restrict the number of gaming machines to a number below what the market will bear. Tribes in such states sometimes have tried to enhance their tribal gaming revenue by moving beyond face to face bingo through the use of electronic machines that simulate or assist in the playing of bingo, pull tabs or like games. Many such games have produced litigation attempting to ascertain whether the electronic game constitutes permissible Class II gaming.

IGRA specifically excludes from the definition of Class II gaming "electronic or electromechanical facsimiles of any game of chance or slot machines of any kind." 25 U.S.C. § 2703(7)(B)(ii). On the other hand, "bingo (*whether or not electronic, computer or other technologic aids are used in connection therewith*)" is specifically included within the definition of Class II gaming. 25 U.S.C. § 2703(7)(A) (emphasis added). Navigating the distinction between a technological aid and an electromechanical facsimile has produced considerable litigation. For example, in *Seneca-*

Cayuga Tribe of Oklahoma v. National Indian Gaming Commission, 327 F.3d 1019 (10th Cir. 2003), the court held that the Magical Irish Instant Bingo Dispenser machine constituted a Class II aid to the playing of pull-tabs. In this case, the machine consisted of "[t]hree physically separate components . . . — the dispenser, the base, and the verifier." Human intervention was required to integrate use and integrate the three components. Relying on the National Indian Gaming Commission's recently promulgated regulation set forth at 25 C.F.R. § 502.7, the Tenth Circuit held that any machine or device that assists a player or the playing of the game, that does not constitute a self-contained "electronic or electromechanical facsimile" and is operated in accordance with applicable regulations of the Federal Communications Commission constitutes a Class II technological aid. Critical to the result was the need for human intervention in the playing of the game. The court also held that any Class II technological aid did not constitute a prohibited gambling machine under the Johnson Act. 15 U.S.C. § 1575. *See also United States v. 162 MegaMania Gambling Devices*, 231 F.3d 713, 717 (10th Cir. 2000) (MegaMania machines constituted Class II technological aids in playing bingo); *Sycuan Band of Mission Indians v. Roache*, 54 F.3d 535, 541–42 (9th Cir. 1994) (a self-contained machine containing a computer linked to a video monitor and a printer constituted a Class III electronic facsimile of pull-tabs); *Cabazon Band Mission Indians v. NIGC*, 14 F.3d 633 (D.C. Cir. 1994) (pull-tabs game was a "computerized version" of pull-tabs and therefore a Class III facsimile). The National Indian Gaming Commission, which has regulatory control over Class II gaming, has so far declined to give a restrictive definition to the term. For a detailed discussion of this controversy, see Heidi McNeil Staudenmeier & Andrew D. Lynch, *The Class II Gaming Debate: The Johnson Act v. The Indian Gaming Regulatory Act*, 8 GAMING L. REV. 227 (2004).

9. **Private Challenges to Indian Gaming:** While many conflicts surrounding the ability of tribes to conduct gaming are between states and tribes, a number of private anti-gaming organizations have filed suit to block tribal gaming enterprises, often basing their challenges on location of proposed gaming sites, validity of land-into-trust-decisions, and compliance with environmental standards. *See, e.g., Citizens Against Casino Gambling in Erie County v. Stevens*, 945 F. Supp. 2d 391 (D.N.Y. 2013) (challenging gaming site); *Citizens Exposing Truth About Casinos v. Kempthorne*, 492 F.3d 460 (D.C. Cir. 2007) (challenging federal decision to take land into trust); *Stand Up for California! v. U.S. Dept. of the Interior*, 919 F. Supp. 2d 51 (D.D.C. 2013) (challenging environmental review process as well as federal authority to take land into trust). In *Match-E-Be-Nash-She-Wish Band of Pottawatomi Indians v. Patchak*, 132 S. Ct. 2199 (2012), presented in Ch. 6, Sec. A, a private citizen who lived near a proposed gaming site challenged the Secretary of Interior's decision to take the land into trust. The Court held that the United States had waived its sovereign immunity and that the citizen had standing to sue because he lived near the site and had economic, environmental, and aesthetic interests in how the proposed gaming operation might impact his property.

2. Business Disputes Related to Gaming

Before the 1988 passage of IGRA, in the early days of Indian gaming, many tribes entered into gaming management contracts with outside firms, some of which provided venture capital, but also took large portions of the profits and left tribes with sizable debts. For accounts of such situations, see *United States ex rel. Citizen Band of the Potawatomi Indian Tribe v. Enterprise Mgt. Consultants*, 883 F.2d 886 (10th Cir. 1989); *United States ex rel. Shakopee Mdewakanton Sioux Community v. Pan American Management Co.*, 616 F. Supp. 1200 (D. Minn. 1985), *appeal dismissed*, 789 F.2d 632 (8th Cir. 1986). In those days, many tribes successfully invoked the Secretarial approval requirement of 25 U.S.C. § 81, discussed in Ch. 3, Sec. D, to void such disadvantageous agreements. At that time, section 81 required certain documentation and federal approval of contracts between tribal and non-tribal parties "relative to [Indian] lands." Resting on a premise of Indian incompetence, the statute included a draconian *qui tam* provision allowing suit against a nonconforming non-tribal party to void the agreement and restore any previous payments under the agreement to the tribe. The law swept broadly, and in the pre-IGRA era courts found that section 81 included gaming management contracts, even though the Secretary of the Interior had not made a practice of reviewing such agreements before 1984. *See, e.g., Barona Group of Capitan Grande Band of Mission Indians v. American Management & Amusement, Inc.*, 840 F.2d 1394 (9th Cir. 1987). Unlike tribal sovereign immunity, the requirements of section 81 could not be waived. For a discussion of the 2000 amendments to 25 U.S.C. § 81, which decreased its scope, clarified the criteria for Secretarial approval, and protected non-tribal parties by insisting that tribes expressly indicate whether they are waiving sovereign immunity, see Ch. 3, Sec. D.

For contracts relating to the management of tribal gaming, the Indian Gaming Regulatory Act adopted a separate set of rules and requirements, independent of section 81. IGRA's regime for gaming management contracts delegates to the National Indian Gaming Commission (NIGC) the approval power over such contracts previously exercised by the Secretary of the Interior under section 81. Reflecting the broad authority delegated to the presidentially appointed Chair of the NIGC, 25 U.S.C. §§ 2711 and 2712 provide minimum standards for such contracts and require review by the Chair and the Commission of all existing contracts. This review includes certain terms of the agreement, background investigations of management personnel, and environmental impact. The NIGC has promulgated regulations to implement this authority at 25 C.F.R. §§ 531–539. For a detailed account of how NIGC goes about reviewing gaming management contracts, see Kevin K. Washburn, *The Mechanics of Indian Gaming Management Contract Approval*, 8 GAMING L. REV. 333 (2004).

Although IGRA sets some presumptive guidelines for the duration and management compensation provisions in gaming management contracts, IGRA does not require the NIGC to review gaming management contracts to ensure that tribes obtain the maximum advantage from their gaming projects. At the same time, the NIGC Chair is supposed to disapprove a management contract if a theoretical trustee for the tribe, "exercising the skill and diligence to which a trustee is commonly held, would not approve the contract." Should this provision be read to give the NIGC Chair discretionary power to second-guess business decisions by the tribe? Dean Washburn has pointed out that the exercise of such power "would not be consistent with current federal policies of treating tribes a self-governing sovereigns," and he notes (as of 2004), that this power in the NIGC has not resulted in disapproval of contracts. *Id.* at 337.

Because failure to secure the necessary federal approval renders the contracts null and void, including any waivers of sovereign immunity, it is essential to know which contracts are subject to this new set of requirements. Determining which courts have jurisdiction to decide such questions — tribal, federal, or state — has also presented some difficult challenges, as the following case demonstrates.

Bruce H. Lien Company v. Three Affiliated Tribes, 93 F.3d 1412 (8th Cir. 1996): The parties to this dispute came together for the purpose of constructing and operating a tribal casino. They entered into a management contract under IGRA, whereby Lien was to assist in the financing, construction, and management of the Tribes' casino in exchange for a share of the profits. The agreement further provided that all disputes would be subject to binding arbitration, that the arbitration process would be deemed sufficient to exhaust the parties' tribal court remedies, and that the tribe would waive its sovereign immunity for purposes of this dispute resolution procedure. The agreement also specified that, pending arbitration of a dispute arising out of the agreement, either party could seek injunctive relief in federal court. The local BIA Area Director, who had interim authority under IGRA to approve gaming management contracts until the National Indian Gaming Commission (NIGC) was functioning, gave his approval in 1993, and construction and operation of the casino ensued shortly thereafter.

After the gaming enterprise was up and running, there was a change in tribal leadership, and those newly elected raised questions about the prior Chairman's authority to bind the Tribes to the agreement. Although the casino appeared to be operating to the financial benefit of both sides, Lien began to claim amounts in excess of those expressly provided in the contract, and the Tribal Gaming Commission dramatically increased licensing fees charged to Lien.

Lien eventually filed a demand for binding arbitration pursuant to the management agreement, seeking resolution of the construction costs and license fees issues. Not long after the arbitrators were selected in accordance with the agreement, the NIGC notified the parties that it would be conducting its mandatory review of the contract and requested all documentation be submitted within 60 days. *See* 25 C.F.R. Part 533.1 et. seq. The Tribes unsuccessfully sought a postponement of the arbitration, and then filed an action in tribal court for a declaration that the management contract signed by the former Chairman was null and void under tribal law due to lack of proper authority and failure to garner approval by the Tribal Business Council. The Tribes also requested and received an injunction against the arbitration proceeding until the question of the contract's validity was established in tribal court or the NIGC completed its review. In turn, Lien sued in federal court to enforce the arbitration agreement, to enjoin tribal interference with that proceeding, and to compel arbitration.

Although the federal district court concluded that the NIGC had primary jurisdiction to determine the contract's validity, the Eighth Circuit panel disagreed. The court summarized:

> . . . Our interpretation of IGRA and the regulations promulgated thereunder lead to the conclusion that disposition regarding the legal validity of the management contract is beyond the authority of the NIGC. It further appears obvious that resolution of any or all collateral issues would be pointless until a decision regarding the validity of the contract is achieved. That being the case, the issue becomes where the decision regarding the contract's validity is to be made. In the end we are convinced that the question must first be promptly addressed in the Tribal Court, subject to appropriate review by the District Court [relying on *National Farmers Union Insurance Cos. v. Crow Tribe*, 471 U.S. 845 (1985) and *Iowa Mut. Ins. Co. v. LaPlante*, 480 U.S. 9 (1987), discussed in Ch. 4, Sec. A.4.b].

The court noted that IGRA and its regulations prescribe six essential terms to be included before a management contract may be approved. 25 U.S.C. § 2711(b)(1–6); 25 C.F.R. §§ 531.1, 531.2, and 533. Also, "IGRA and the rules and regulations of the NIGC require that all management contracts approved prior to the organization of the NIGC be reviewed and approved by that agency's Chairman." 25 U.S.C. § 2512. But that review, the court pointed out, focuses solely on compliance with IGRA and its regulations. "Has all of the proper documentation been submitted? Does the document contain provisions addressing the required essential topics? Do the backgrounds of 'interested parties' check out?" The legal validity of the document does not fit within the scope of such a review. In fact, the NIGC review did not generate any pronouncement on the validity of the contract. While the Commission found some serious deficiencies in the agreement and threatened to shut down the casino, these deficiencies involved the absence of a tribal gaming license and the lack of background checks on certain employees, not the contract's invalidity.

In deferring to the tribal court for a determination of the validity of the agreement, the Eighth Circuit panel rejected arguments that the arbitration agreement and IGRA ousted the tribal court of jurisdiction. As the court pointed out,

> Questions regarding whether IGRA or the NIGC divest the Tribal Court of authority to rule on the issues regarding the contract's validity, whether IGRA is applicable to the Tribal Court action, and whether the validity of the management contract can be affected by an interpretation of Tribal law, are issues relating to the Tribal Court's jurisdiction which should be dealt with first by the Tribal Court itself.

NOTES ON TRIBAL GAMING DISPUTES

1.   Politics and Business: Note that the *Bruce H. Lien* lawsuit emerged in the wake of a transfer of power within tribal government. According to Professors Stephen Cornell and Joseph Kalt, who have conducted extensive research on the conditions for economic development success in Indian country, "natural, human, and financial resources aren't the key to economic development." Rather, what matters most is whether tribes adopt a "nation building" approach to development, which emphasizes effective self-governance, including provision of stable institutions and policies, fair and effective dispute resolution, separation of politics from business management, a competent bureaucracy, and "match" between the tribe's culture and the system of governance. This approach is necessary, they argue, to attract human and financial capital investment. Stephen Cornell & Joseph Kalt, *Sovereignty and Nation-Building: The Development Challenge in Indian Country Today*, 22(3) AM. INDIAN CULTURE & RES. J. 187 (1998). Does the factual pattern in *Bruce H. Lien* suggest a failure of tribal political stability, or the triumph of culturally appropriate institutions?

2.   Jurisdiction over Gaming Contract Disputes: The *Bruce H. Lien* court defers to the Tribes' initial jurisdiction under established federal law. What if a tribe has no tribal court? Is the possibility of such litigation reason to create a tribal court? Assuming a state court cannot take jurisdiction over a gaming contract dispute, even under Public Law 280 (*see* Sec. A.2, this chapter, pointing out that Public Law 280 does not confer jurisdiction over tribes), the federal court has rejected jurisdiction, and the tribe has no tribal court, should there be any forum that can hear such a claim? Should the federal court claim jurisdiction under a theory of "complete federal preemption?" *See American Vantage Companies v. Table Mountain Rancheria*, 102 Cal. App. 4th 954 (2002). The prevalence of arbitration provisions and sovereign immunity waivers in gaming contracts has obviously not prevented uncertainty and confusion. In *Bruce H. Lien*, Judge Bogue wrote for the Eighth Circuit,

> . . . Two courts have this dispute on active status; the NIGC continues its review and continues in its attempt to bring the contract and gaming operation into compliance with IGRA; arbitrators, once chosen, presumably await notification that their activity is to resume. The vessel which is the orderly administration of justice is leaking all over and making a big mess.

93 F.3d at 1419. What legal changes, if any, could avert the kind of litigation nightmare this case presents?

A more recent Eighth Circuit case that follows *Bruce H. Lien*, and cites decisions from other circuits doing the same, is *Gaming World International, Ltd. v. White Earth Band of Chippewa Indians*, 317 F.3d 840 (8th Cir. 2003). The Sixth Circuit distinguished *Bruce H. Lien* and refused to restrain enforcement of an arbitration clause in *Match-E-Be-Nash-She-Wish Band of Pottawatomi Indians v. Kean-Argovitz Resorts*, 383 F.3d 512 (6th Cir. 2004). The difference, according to the court, was that *Bruce H. Lien* involved a challenge to the validity of the contract by virtue of lack of signing authority on the part of the tribal official who signed it, while the *Match-E-Be-Nash-She-Wish* case involved a challenge to the "substance" of the agreement, namely whether it was properly approved by the Chair of the National Indian Gaming Commission. Are you persuaded by this distinction, given the nature of the Tribes' challenge to the contract in *Bruce H. Lien*?

3.   Rights of Action Under IGRA: The jurisdictional complexity of *Bruce H. Lien* is matched, if not exceeded, in *Tamiami Partners v. Miccosukee Tribe of Indians*, 63 F.3d 1030 (5th Cir. 1995). In that case, the management company,

Tamiami, alleged that the Tribe and its individual officers had wrongfully terminated the contract based on the denial of tribal gaming licenses to its key employees. As in *Bruce H. Lien*, arbitrators, the tribal court, and a federal court all got into the act. The Indian Gaming Regulatory Act, 25 U.S.C. § 2710(b)(2)(F), requires tribes to conduct background investigations on such employees as well as to maintain a system of licensing as conditions to NIGC approval of the tribal gaming operation. That part of IGRA does not, however, authorize private rights of action for violation of its terms. Tamiami alleged that the Tribe had abused its licensing authority and that the individual officials had carried out the Tribe's plan to wrest control of the operation from Tamiami, all in violation of IGRA. Given that IGRA does provide private rights of action for *other* kinds of claims, such as challenges to NIGC decisions regarding approval of tribal ordinances and management contracts, should Tamiami be permitted to pursue its claims in federal court? Note that the Tenth Circuit has affirmed that IGRA creates no private rights of action for casino employees claiming wrongful dismissal. *Hartman v. Kickapoo Tribe Gaming Commission*, 319 F.3d 1230 (10th Cir. 2003).

4. **Tortious Interference with Gaming-Related Contracts:** The broad reach of IGRA's contract approval requirement can be seen in *Catskill Dev, L.L.C. v. Park Place Entm't Corp.*, 547 F.3d 115 (2d Cir. 2008). Two non-Indian companies were vying with one another for the opportunity to develop a gaming facility with the Mohawk Indian Tribe. When one tried to sue the other for tortious interference with its contractual relations, the Second Circuit would not allow the litigation to proceed, pointing out that the plaintiff's alleged contract with the Tribe was void because it had not been approved by the National Indian Gaming Commission. The approval requirement applied even though the Tribe had not yet secured the necessary trust lands for the gaming facility.

E. FEDERAL INDIAN LIQUOR CONTROL STATUTES

Eight sections of the federal criminal code establish federal jurisdiction over illegal possession, sale, or manufacture of liquor in Indian country. *See* 18 U.S.C. §§ 1154, 1156, 1161, 3055, 3113, 3488, 3618–3619. In addition, 25 U.S.C. § 251 announces a prohibition enforced by civil penalties. These provisions apply to Indian as well as non-Indian defendants. *Hallowell v. United States*, 221 U.S. 317 (1911) (Indians); *United States v. Mazurie*, 419 U.S. 544 (1975) (non-Indians).

Federal regulation of liquor traffic with Indians dates back to the earliest years of the nation, and continued British colonial practice. Tribes themselves have sometimes sought these restrictions; notably, the first federal law on the subject responded to an appeal from an Indian leader to President Jefferson in 1802. Act of Mar. 30, 1802, ch. 13, § 21, 2 Stat. 139, 146. Prohibitions carrying monetary penalties were included in the Trade and Intercourse Act of 1834, and imprisonment became possible in 1862. Act of Feb. 13, 1862, ch. 24, 12 Stat. 338, 339. At one point the laws applied outside as well as within Indian country, prohibiting selling liquor to any Indian deemed under "federal superintendence." Although this provision is still in the criminal code, it is confined to Indian country by § 1161. Furthermore, under that same statute, liquor transactions are not subject to federal prohibitions "provided such act or transaction is in conformity both with the laws of the State in which such act or transaction occurs and with an ordinance duly adopted by the tribe having jurisdiction." For purposes of federal liquor control laws, "Indian country" has a special meaning, which excludes "fee-patented lands in non-Indian communities or rights-of-way through Indian reservations" absent federal statute or treaty specifying otherwise. 18 U.S.C. § 1154(c). *See* Ch. 2, Sec. A.3.

In *United States v. Mazurie*, 419 U.S. 544 (1975), set forth and discussed in Ch. 3, Sec. A.2, the United States Supreme Court approved tribal jurisdiction to regulate liquor sales by non-Indians on reservation fee land, citing 18 U.S.C. §§ 1154 and 1161. Not long thereafter, the Court had occasion to consider the scope of state authority over liquor transactions within Indian country. While the same federal statutes involved in *Mazurie* required compliance with state as well as tribal law, it was unclear whether this regime contemplated application of state licensing requirements. These licensing requirements represented a far greater intrusion of state regulation into Indian country transactions.

Rice v. Rehner, 463 U.S. 713 (1983): The provisions of 18 U.S.C. § 1161 created local option with respect to liquor sales in Indian country by exempting from the federal liquor control laws any "act or transaction [that] is in conformity both with the laws of the State in which such act or transaction occurs and with an ordinance duly adopted by the tribe having jurisdiction over such area of Indian country." *United States v. Mazurie*, 419 U.S. 544, 557 (1975), held that the Act legally could require non-Indians selling liquor on fee lands within an Indian reservation to secure a tribal license and comply with tribal laws. In *Rice*, the issue was whether a member of the governing tribe named "Rehner [who] is a federally licensed Indian trader[75] [and] who operates a general store on the Pala Reservation in San Diego, California" was required to secure a state license to sell liquor on the Reservation. While this issue would appear to involve a clear question of statutory interpretation, Justice O'Connor's opinion for the Court, holding that California could require a tribal member and a federally licensed Indian trader to secure a state liquor license to sell liquor on the Reservation, announced and relied upon far broader principles. Noting that judicial conceptions of tribal sovereignty have not been static over time, Justice O'Connor wrote:

> The role of tribal sovereignty in pre-emption analysis varies in accordance with the particular "notions of sovereignty that have developed from historical traditions of tribal independence." These traditions themselves reflect the "accommodation between the interests of the Tribes and the Federal Government, on the one hand, and those of the State, on the other." However, it must be remembered that "tribal sovereignty is dependent on, and subordinate to, only the Federal Government, not the States." "The sovereignty that the Indian tribes retain is of a unique and limited character. It exists only at the sufferance of Congress and *is subject to*

---

[75] [2] There is some confusion among the parties and amici as to whether the court below held that the tribes had exclusive jurisdiction over the licensing and distribution of liquor on reservations irrespective of the identity of the vendor. Although we acknowledge that the decision below is somewhat ambiguous in this respect, we construe the opinion as applying only to vendors, like Rehner, who are members of the governing tribe.

complete defeasance." United States v. Wheeler, 435 U.S. 313, 323 (1978) (emphasis added).

Thus, the Court surveyed the history of federal liquor regulation to "determine the nature of the 'backdrop' of tribal sovereignty that will inform our pre-emption analysis." Justice O'Connor rejected the argument that tribal control of Indian liquor sales in Indian country constituted an essential element of the Tribe's sovereignty since:

> tradition simply has not recognized a sovereign immunity or inherent authority in favor of liquor regulation by Indians. The colonists regulated Indian liquor trading before this Nation was formed, and Congress exercised its authority over these transactions as early as 1802. Congress imposed complete prohibition by 1832, and these prohibitions are still in effect subject to suspension conditioned on compliance with state law and tribal ordinances.

Thus, focusing on federal, rather than tribal, law, the Court found no historic tradition of tribal regulation of liquor sales. Rather, it believed such matters historically were regulated by federal and state legislation. Justice O'Connor further argued that such a regulatory scheme was justified by the effects of liquor sales:

> This historical tradition of concurrent state and federal jurisdiction over the use and distribution of alcoholic beverages in Indian country is justified by the relevant state interests involved. Rehner's distribution of liquor has a significant impact beyond the limits of the Pala Reservation. The State has an unquestionable interest in the liquor traffic that occurs within its borders, and this interest is independent of the authority conferred on the States by the Twenty-first Amendment. *Crowley v. Christensen*, 137 U.S. 86, 91 (1890). Liquor sold by Rehner to other Pala tribal members or to non-members can easily find its way out of the reservation and into the hands of those whom, for whatever reason, the State does not wish to possess alcoholic beverages, or to possess them through a distribution network over which the State has no control. This particular "spillover" effect is qualitatively different from any "spillover" effects of income taxes or taxes on cigarettes. "A State's regulatory interest will be particularly substantial if the State can point to off-reservation effects that necessitate State intervention." *New Mexico v. Mescalero Apache Tribe*, 462 U.S. 324, 336 (1983).

The Court therefore found that:

> The court below erred in thinking that there was some single notion of tribal sovereignty that served to direct any preemption analysis involving Indians. Because we find that there is no tradition of sovereign immunity that favors the Indians in this respect, and because we must consider that the activity in which Rehner seeks to engage potentially has a substantial impact beyond the reservation, we may accord little if any weight to any asserted interest in tribal sovereignty in this case.

Having thereby undermined Rehner's tribal sovereignty argument, Justice O'Connor turned to interpreting section 1161. She wrote:

> We must next determine whether the State authority to license the sale of liquor is pre-empted by federal law. [Below, the court] held that § 1161 pre-empted state regulation of licensing and distribution, and that the reference to state law in § 1161 was not sufficiently explicit to permit application of the state licensing law.
>
> We disagree with both aspects of the court's analysis. As we explained [above], the tribes have long ago been divested of any inherent self-government over liquor regulation by both the explicit command of Congress and "as a necessary implication of their dependent status." [Furthermore, Congress] has also historically permitted concurrent state regulation through the imposition of criminal penalties on those who supply Indians with liquor, or who introduce liquor into Indian country. Therefore, this is not a case in which we apply a presumption of a lack of state authority.
>
> The presumption of preemption derives from the rule against construing legislation to repeal by implication some aspect of tribal self-government. See *Bryan v. Itasca County*, 426 U.S. 373, 391–392 (1976); *Morton v. Mancari*, 417 U.S. 535, 549–551 (1974). Because there is no aspect of exclusive tribal self-government that requires the deference reflected in our requirement that Congress expressly provide for the application of state law, we have only to determine whether application of the state licensing laws would "impair a right granted or reserved by federal law." [By enacting section 1161] Congress authorized, rather than pre-empted, state regulation over Indian liquor transactions.
>
> [A review of the legislative history indicates] that Congress viewed § 1161 as abolishing federal prohibition, and as legalizing Indian liquor transactions as long as those transactions conformed both with tribal ordinance and state law. It is also clear that Congress contemplated that its absolute but not exclusive power to regulate Indian liquor transactions would be delegated to the tribes themselves, and to the States, which historically shared concurrent jurisdiction with the federal government in this area. Early administrative practice and our prior decision in *United States v. Mazurie*, confirm this understanding of § 1161.
>
> [The Ninth Circuit and Rehner both] believed that § 1161 was merely an exemption from *federal* criminal liability, and affirmatively empowered neither Indian tribes nor the State to regulate liquor transactions. [*Mazurie*] rejected this argument with respect to Indian tribes, and there is no reason to accept it with respect to the State. In *Mazurie* we held that in enacting § 1161 Congress intended to *delegate* to the tribes a portion of its authority over liquor transactions on reservations. Since we found this delegation on the basis of the statutory language requiring that liquor transactions conform "*both* with the laws of the State . . . and with an ordinance duly adopted" by the governing tribe (emphasis added), we

would ignore the plain language of the statute if we failed to find this same delegation in favor of the States.[76]

The thrust of Rehner's argument, and the primary focus of the court below, is that state authority in this area is preempted because such authority requires an express statement by Congress in the light of the canon of construction that we quoted in *McClanahan*: " 'State laws generally are not applicable to tribal Indians on an Indian reservation except where Congress has expressly provided that State laws shall apply.' " 411 U.S., at 170–171 (quoting Indian Law, at 845). As we have established above, because of the lack of a tradition of self-government in the area of liquor regulation, it is not necessary that Congress indicate expressly that the State has jurisdiction to regulate the licensing and distribution of alcohol.[77]

. . . Even if this canon of construction were applicable to this case, our result would be the same. The canon is quoted from the 1958 edition of the Federal Indian Law, published by the Dept. of the Interior. See Indian Law, at 845. In that same volume, the Solicitor of the Interior assumed that § 1161 would result in state prosecutions for failing to have a state license. Whatever Congress had to do to provide "expressly" for the application of state law, the Solicitor obviously believed that Congress had done it in § 1161. Indeed, even in *McClanahan*, we suggested that § 1161 satisfied the canon of construction requiring that Congress expressly provide for application of state law. In discussing statutes that did satisfy the canon, we cited § 1161 and stated that "state liquor laws may be applicable within reservations." More important, we have consistently refused to apply such a canon of construction when application would be tantamount to a formalistic disregard of congressional intent.

[In conclusion,] § 1161 was intended to remove federal discrimination that resulted from the imposition of liquor prohibition on Native Americans. Congress was well aware that the Indians never enjoyed a tradition of tribal self-government insofar as liquor transactions were concerned. Congress was also aware that the States exercised concurrent authority insofar as prohibiting liquor transactions with Indians was concerned. By

---

[76] [14] Indeed, given the history of concurrent state jurisdiction and the tradition of complete prohibition imposed on the Indians, the delegation to the States is more readily apparent than the delegation to the tribes.

[77] [15] This canon is based, in part, on the notion that we normally resolve any doubt in a pre-emption analysis in favor of the Indians because of their status as "wards of the nation." McClanahan v. Arizona State Tax Commission, 411 U.S. 164, 174 (1973) (quoting Carpenter v. Shaw, 280 U.S. 363, 367 (1930)). Even if this canon properly informed a pre-emption analysis that involved a historic tradition of federal and state regulation, its application in the context of liquor licensing and distribution would be problematic. Liquor trade has been regulated among the Indians largely due to early attempts by the tribes themselves to seek assistance in controlling Indian access to liquor. See Talk delivered by Little Turtle to President Thomas Jefferson on January 4, 1802, reprinted in IV American State Papers, Indian Affairs, Vol. I, Class II, at 655 (1802). In many respects, the concerns about liquor expressed by the tribes were responsible for the development of the dependent status of the tribes. When the substance to be regulated is that primarily responsible for "dependent" status, it makes no sense to say that the historical position of Indians as federal "wards" militates in favor of giving exclusive control over licensing and distribution to the tribes.

enacting § 1161, Congress intended to delegate a portion of its authority to the tribes as well as to the States, so as to fill the void that would be created by the absence of the discriminatory federal prohibition. Congress did not intend to make tribal members "super citizens" who could trade in a traditionally regulated substance free from all but self-imposed regulations. Rather, we believe that in enacting § 1161, Congress intended to recognize that Native Americans are not "weak and defenseless," and are capable of making personal decisions about alcohol consumption without special assistance from the Federal Government. Application of the state licensing scheme does not "impair a right granted or reserved by federal law." On the contrary, such application of state law is "specifically authorized by . . . Congress . . . and [does] not interfere with federal policies concerning the reservations." *Warren Trading Post Co. v. Arizona Tax Commission*, 380 U.S. 685, 687, n.3 (1965).

Justice O'Connor also noted that enforcing the state license requirement was facilitated by the fact that California was a Public Law 280 state. Would the *Rice* issue be decided differently in a non-Public Law 280 jurisdiction?

Justice Blackmun, joined by Justices Brennan and Marshall, dissented, relying on *Central Machinery* and *Warren Trading* Post and focusing on the fact that Rehner was a federally licensed trader. Justice Blackmun also wrote in dissent:

The Court gives far too much weight to the fact that Indian tribes historically have not exercised regulatory authority over sales of liquor. In prior pre-emption cases, the Court's focus properly and consistently has been on the reach and comprehensiveness of applicable federal law, colored by the recognition that "traditional notions of Indian self-government are so deeply engrained in our jurisprudence that they have provided an important 'backdrop' . . . against which vague or ambiguous federal enactments must always be measured." [*Bracker*] quoting [*McClanahan*]. The Court's analysis has never turned on whether the particular area being regulated is one traditionally within the tribe's control.

. . . .

[In conclusion, the] Court obviously argues to a result that it strongly feels is desirable and good. But that, however strong the feelings may be, is activism in which this Court should not indulge. I therefore dissent.

NOTES ON FEDERAL INDIAN LIQUOR CONTROL LAWS

1. **Implications of *Rice v. Rehner*:** States eagerly read *Rice v. Rehner* to mean that tribes would henceforth lack jurisdiction over any subject matters not "traditionally" subject to their control. Furthermore, they interpreted it to mean that states could regulate any activity within Indian country so long as the activity produced significant spillover effects outside reservation boundaries. Thus, for example, when property owners near the Campo Reservation in California sought to curtail solid waste disposal on tribal trust lands, the legislation their representatives introduced found its justification in *Rice v. Rehner. See* DAN MCGOVERN, THE CAMPO LAND FILL WAR 125–27 (1995).

Was it ever necessary to take *Rice v. Rehner* that far? Despite the dissent's protestations to the contrary, was it so difficult to find that Congress had authorized state regulation as well as the application of state standards for liquor sales under 18 U.S.C. § 1161? In fact, largely because of the Court's subsequent decision in *Cabazon*, rejecting state jurisdiction over tribal high-stakes bingo, *Rice v. Rehner* has been confined to liquor regulation, and the case has not served as the template for expanded state jurisdiction. While gaming was common in Indian tribes, extensive tribal regulation of Indian gaming operations serving both non-Indian and Indian clients was historically unknown. Furthermore, just like the liquor regulations involved in *Rice*, the gaming operations were said to have externalities off the reservation. Nevertheless, in *Cabazon*, the Court did not rely on the analysis in *Rice* and, instead, suggested that the state gaming laws were preempted by federal law.

A further problem with the *Rice* analysis is the manner in which it locks Indian tribes into *historical* conceptions of their sovereignty and precludes Indian polities from evolving to meet the new demands of modern tribal societies. Indian tribes, like all societies and governments, are continually evolving as they cope with new and changing internal and external demands. *Cf.* FELIX S. COHEN, HANDBOOK OF FEDERAL INDIAN LAW 288 (1942 ed.) (cautioning against a menagerie theory of Indian property rights that denied Indians ownership because they merely roamed over their property). Near extinction of the buffalo herds, loss of vital hunting or fishing areas, and other changes forced Indian tribes to adapt their cultural practices to new circumstances. Does Justice O'Connor's opinion in *Rice v. Rehner* fall prey to a menagerie theory of Indian law that treats Indian reservations as historic human zoos? Does this approach risk curtailing tribal sovereignty in ways that preordain tribal failures for want of authority in coping with new and changing tribal problems?

Rice v. Rehner continues to spawn controversy. A serious question is whether 18 U.S.C. § 1161, as interpreted in *Rice v. Rehner*, waives tribal sovereign immunity in state courts and allows application of state dram shop laws. (State dram shop laws establish liability for those who provide alcoholic drinks to individuals who subsequently cause injury while under the influence of alcohol.) For two sharply contrasting views of section 1161 and *Rice v. Rehner*, see *Bittle v. Bahe*, 192 P.3d 810 810 (Okla. 2008) (state court has jurisdiction over claim under dram shop law and tribe has no tribal sovereign immunity) and *Foxworthy v. Puyallup Tribe of Indians Association*, 169 P.3d 53 (Wa. Ct. App. 2007) (state court lacks jurisdiction and Congress has not abrogated tribal sovereign immunity). Recently the Eleventh Circuit Court of Appeals held that section 1161 and *Rice v. Rehner* did not abrogate tribal sovereign immunity, reiterating that "congressional abrogation of tribal sovereign immunity must be express and unequivocal." *Furry v. Miccosukee Tribe of Indians*, 685 F.3d 1224, 1234 n.7 (11th Cir. 2012).

2. Tribal Regulation of Liquor Transactions by Non-Indians: The tribal jurisdiction upheld in *Mazurie* has given rise to conflict between Indian nations and the non-Indians living within their reservation boundaries. In 2000, the Yakama Indian Nation voted to ban the possession, distribution, or sale of alcohol on its reservation, with the ban to take effect six months later. The Yakamas saw the ban as a necessary step to curb a major alcoholism problem, and tribal prohibition already applied on tribal lands, the tribal casino and convenience store, and at powwows and Yakama ceremonies. As one tribal council member pointed out, the rate of children born with fetal alcohol syndrome is about 500% higher on the Yakama reservation than in the surrounding community, and 78% of motor vehicle deaths on the reservation in recent years have been alcohol-related compared with 39% statewide and 48% nationwide. Linda Ashton, *State Suit Challenges Tribe's Beer Ban*, Seattle Times (Oct. 8, 2000).

The 1.2 million-acre Yakama reservation is predominantly non-Indian: of the 38,000 residents, 29,000 are non-Indians. State officials believed that the state controlled liquor sales in Washington, and took up the cause of 47 non-Indian businesses that were engaged in alcohol sales, mostly in the cities of Toppenish and Wapato. A suit by the state to enjoin enforcement by the Yakamas was dismissed on sovereign immunity grounds, leaving the ban to take effect. The Yakama Nation chose to focus on sales, not on use of alcohol in residents' homes. Rather than attempt to enforce the law directly, the Nation gathered evidence for the U.S. Attorney, to be used in prosecutions under 18 U.S.C. §§ 1154 and 1156. However, in March 2001, the U.S. Attorney found that bars in the cities of Toppenish and Wapato would likely be exempt from the ban on alcohol because those cities are probably not Indian country within the meaning of 18 U.S.C. § 1154(c), which excludes reservation fee lands in "non-Indian communities." This opinion still left eight businesses outside of those cities that the Yakama leaders wanted to shut down because they were some of the worst establishments. The Yakama Nation has continued its fight against alcoholism, deciding in June 2001 to ban advertisements for alcoholic beverages on its land.

If the Yakamas had wanted to prosecute, civilly penalize, or enjoin the non-Indian liquor sales outlets throughout their reservation, could they have done so under tribal law? *See* Ch. 3, Sec. A.3.a. The answer to that question may turn on whether the special definition of Indian country excluding fee land in non-Indian communities applies only to federal criminal jurisdiction, or also to tribal authority. For an answer supporting tribal injunctive power, see *City of Timber Lake v. Cheyenne River Sioux Tribe*, 10 F.3d 554 (8th Cir. 1993). Under what conception of the tribal-federal relationship would it make sense to preclude the Yakamas from regulating an activity that they viewed as threatening the health and well-being of their children and adults, indeed their very survival?

F.   FEDERAL ENVIRONMENTAL LAWS

1.   Introduction: Tribal Perspectives on Economic Development and the Environment

John Echohawk, *We Are Sovereign Peoples*
in Lois Crozier-Hogle & Darryl Babe Wilson, Surviving in Two Worlds: Contemporary Native American Voices 67–68 (1997)

[T]ribes are governments. . . . Not all tribes are going to take a totally anti-development stance in regard to their lands. Some tribes are going to choose for social and economic reasons to do some development that certain environmentalists are not going to like.

This puts some environmentalists in a difficult spot. They may be against any development, yet they see a tribe finally getting control of their own lands and making a decision the environmentalists don't necessarily support. It's the tribes' right to do that.

Tribes, just like states, are bound by the federal environmental laws in meeting the minimum standards required by law. This is a sovereign power they have now — to regulate their own environment, to increase those standards if they choose to do that. To me, that's only right.

I think what you will see is that tribal governments will be a different kind of government than most environmentalists are used to. Tribes, because of who they are, are going to have a different perspective. They understand that they don't really control the land they have, or the earth in general. They have a relationship, they are a part of that land. They're the same as the creatures who live on that land. Tribes have been living on the land since time immemorial. As a tribe, they're looking to the future in a way that sees their future generations always living on that land. It's home to them. They are not going to pollute and destroy their home, the place that belongs to their future generations.

––––––––––

Until the advent of federal self-determination policy in the mid-1970s and the increased organization of resource-rich tribes, the Bureau of Indian Affairs dominated and directed economic development decisions for most of Indian country. These decisions followed a predictable pattern with grim environmental consequences. If the reservation contained valued natural resources — coal, lumber, uranium, oil — then they were leased out at below-market rates to non-Indians, with no requirements for mitigation of environmental consequences or restoration of ecosystems. The disastrous results for Indian country are captured in the following testimony by Asa Bazhonoodah, an elderly Navajo woman living near the Peabody Coal Company's open pit coal mine atop Black Mesa, a sacred place to Navajo and Hopi people:

> The particles of coal dust that contaminate the water kill our animals. I know this for a fact because many of the sheep belonging to my children were killed. I have some cows and they started dying off. And now it has become too frequent, almost every day. . . .
>
> . . . .
>
> Air is one of the Holy Elements, it is important in prayer. Wooded areas are being cut down. Now the air is becoming bad; not working. The herbs that are taken from Mother Earth and given to a woman during childbirth no longer grow in the cut area. The land looks burned.
>
> The Earth is our mother. The white man is ruining our mother. I don't know the white man's ways, but to us the Mesa, the air, the water, are Holy Elements. We pray to these Holy Elements in order for our people to flourish and perpetuate the well-being of each generation.

. . . .

This pollution is what I'm especially against. When I first realized I had eyes, I saw that it was clear. Now it is getting hazy and gray outside. The coal mine is causing it. Because of the bad air, animals are not well, they don't feel well. They know what is happening and are dying. . . .

The reason why is that the things that we ask blessings for are being tampered with. . . . The plants no longer grow because the elements have been tampered with. . . .

Quoted in PETER NABOKOV, NATIVE AMERICAN TESTIMONY: A CHRONICLE OF INDIAN WHITE-RELATIONS FROM PROPHECY TO THE PRESENT, 1492–2000, 398–400 (1999). For other accounts of the environmental damage done to reservation lands through resource extraction, see Winona LaDuke, *Indigenous Environmental Perspectives: A North American Primer, in* STEVE LOBO & SUSAN TALBOT, NATIVE AMERICAN VOICES: A READER 316–32 (1998); DONALD GRINDE & BRUCE JOHANSEN, ECOCIDE OF NATIVE AMERICA: ENVIRONMENTAL DESTRUCTION OF INDIAN LANDS AND PEOPLE (1995).

Managing trade-offs between economic development and environmental quality is a central governmental function, as is negotiating with other governments over environmental spillover effects. Before the 1970s, tribal governments lacked the ability to fulfill these functions, largely because of lack of information and BIA interference. Not surprisingly, Indian nations today seek control over development decisions with environmental consequences, sometimes to encourage development and sometimes to limit its adverse effects within their territories. Depending on its location and topography, its economic condition, its cultural practices, and its social norms, a given tribal community may prefer to use its sovereignty to attract industry with more flexible environmental controls than apply off-reservation. Alternatively, it may prefer to invoke its power to protect its territory from environmental impacts generated both within and outside. The latter set of choices is not necessarily anti-development. Whether a reservation ecosystem can "afford" economic development — whether through ecotourism or power generation — will depend at least partly on how much surrounding non-Indian populations are polluting the shared water, air, and land.

The opposite face of tribal effort to promote or resist development through environmental regulation has been state activity to seize such control. Indian nations and states have competed over environmental authority on two fronts: tribes accusing states of approving off-reservation development projects in order to concentrate adverse impacts on reservation environments, and states complaining that tribes approve on-reservation development projects that endanger off-reservation communities. States have also sought to assert their environmental authority over nonmember-owned fee lands within reservations, imperiling comprehensive environmental control by *any* government within tribal territories.

Federal environmental laws resolve many of these conflicts through statutory schemes and implementing regulations that, with some exceptions, set minimum federal standards, enable states and tribes to implement those standards and introduce more stringent requirements within their respective territories, and afford mediation when competing governments clash. As you read the materials in this section, consider the model of tribal-federal relations undergirding federal environmental laws. In what ways do these laws seek to incorporate Indian nations into the federal Union? Are they a sound model for federal Indian law more generally? Why might greater federal respect for tribal sovereignty find its way into environmental legislation in particular? Do popular and romanticized images of Indians as "the first environmentalists" figure into this policy? Are Indian nations more successful when they seek to use their environmental authority to repel development than when they seek to accommodate it? Is there a principled basis for treating the two types of tribal environmental authority differently?

This section explores these questions by first presenting federal law and policy regarding allocation of authority over reservation environments. Next, it considers cases where tribes and states contend over tribal economic development initiatives. Finally, it examines cases where tribes act to protect their territories against non-Indian development, whether the projects are on reservations or outside their boundaries.

2. The Basic Framework of Federal Environmental Law and Policy

A comprehensive review of federal environmental legislation and implementing regulations is impossible within the confines of a book on Indian law. This section will focus on four major pieces of legislation: the National Environmental Policy Act (NEPA) (environmental review), the Clean Water Act (CWA) (water quality), the Clean Air Act (CAA) (air quality), and the Resource Conservation and Recovery Act (RCRA) (solid and hazardous waste disposal). The first is procedural, requiring certain assessments before projects requiring federal action may go forward. The latter three are substantive as well as procedural, establishing federal environmental standards as well as allocating responsibility among governments for implementation of those standards. For useful summaries and analyses of these statutes for purposes of Indian law, see JUDITH V. ROYSTER & MICHAEL C. BLUMM, NATIVE AMERICAN NATURAL RESOURCES LAW 227–299 (2d ed. 2007).

The CWA and CAA, though not RCRA, now equate tribes with states for purposes of program implementation. If a state or tribe does not secure approval from the federal Environmental Protection Agency (EPA) to assume "primacy" over implementation within its territory, the federal government carries out administration and enforcement of the minimum national standards. Most but not all federal environmental standards apply to tribal activities as well as pollution by private individuals or businesses, effectively waiving tribal sovereign immunity. See, e.g., Blue Legs v. United States Bureau of Indian Affairs, 867 F.2d 1094 (8th Cir. 1989) (RCRA interpreted as a waiver of the tribes' sovereign immunity). The Clean Air Act contains no such waiver.

a. EPA's Indian Policy

When a tribe wants to draw in outside businesses for purposes of economic development, such as energy production, resource extraction, waste disposal, or a business park, which government's standards apply? What environmental review requirements, if any, apply? The following EPA policy, first adopted in 1984 and reaffirmed in 2001, offers the view of the agency responsible for administering federal environmental statutes and entitled to deference in its interpretation of federal statutory requirements under general principles of administrative law. *Chevron, U.S.A. Inc. v. Natural Resources Defense Council*, 467 U.S. 837 (1984).

EPA Policy for the Administration of Environmental Programs on Indian Reservations
available at http://www.epa.gov/tribalportal/pdf/indian-policy-84.pdf (1984)

Introduction:

The President [Reagan] published a Federal Indian Policy on January 24, 1983, supporting the primary role of Tribal Governments in matters affecting American Indian reservations. That policy stressed two related themes: (1) that the federal government will pursue the principle of Indian "self-government" and (2) that it will work directly with Tribal Governments on a "government-to-government" basis. . . .

Policy:

1. The Agency stands ready to work directly with Indian Tribal Governments on a one-to-one basis (the "government-to-government" relationship), rather than as subdivisions of other governments.

EPA recognizes Tribal Governments as sovereign entities with primary authority and responsibility for the reservation populace. Accordingly, EPA will work directly with Tribal Governments as the independent authority for reservation affairs, and not as political subdivisions of States or other governmental units.

2. The Agency will recognize tribal governments as the primary parties for setting standards, making environmental policy decisions and managing programs for reservations, consistent with Agency standards and regulations.

In keeping with the principle of Indian self-government, the Agency will view Tribal Governments as the appropriate non-federal parties for making decisions and carrying out program responsibilities affecting Indian reservations, their environments, and the health and welfare of the reservation populace. Just as EPA's deliberations and activities have traditionally involved the interests and/or participation of State Governments, EPA will look directly to Tribal Governments to play this lead role for matters affecting reservation environments.

3. The Agency will take affirmative steps to encourage and assist tribes in assuming regulatory and program management responsibilities for reservation lands.

The Agency will assist interested Tribal Governments in developing programs and in preparing to assume regulatory and program management responsibilities for reservation lands. Within the constraints of EPA's authority and resources, this aid will include providing grants and other assistance to Tribes, similar to what we provide State Governments. The Agency will encourage Tribes to assume delegable responsibilities, (i.e. responsibilities which the Agency has traditionally delegated to State Governments for non-reservation lands) under terms similar to those governing delegations to States.

Until Tribal Governments are willing and able to assume full responsibility for delegable programs, the Agency will retain responsibility for managing programs for reservations (unless the State has an expressed grant of jurisdiction from Congress sufficient to support delegation to the State Government). Where EPA retains such responsibility, the Agency will encourage the Tribe to participate in policy-making and to assume appropriate lesser or partial roles in the management of reservation programs.

4. The Agency will take appropriate steps to remove existing legal and procedural impediments to working directly and effectively with tribal governments on reservation programs. . . .

5. The Agency, in keeping with the federal trust responsibility, will assure that tribal concerns and interests are considered whenever EPA's actions and/or decisions may affect reservation environments. . . .

6. The Agency will encourage cooperation between tribal, state and local governments to resolve environmental problems of mutual concern.

. . . [This principle] recognizes that in the field of environmental regulation, problems are often shared and the principle of comity between equals and neighbors often serves the best interests of both.

. . . .

8. The Agency will strive to assure compliance with environmental statutes and regulations on Indian reservations.

In those cases where facilities owned or managed by Tribal Governments are not in compliance with federal environmental statutes, EPA will work cooperatively with Tribal leadership to develop means to achieve compliance, providing technical support and consultation as necessary to enable Tribal facilities to comply. Because of the distinct status of Indian Tribes and the complex legal issues involved, direct EPA action through the judicial or administrative process will be considered where the Agency determines, in its judgment, that: (1) a significant threat to human health or the environment exists, (2) such action would reasonably be expected to achieve effective results in a timely manner, and (3) the federal government cannot utilize other alternatives to correct the problem in a timely fashion.

In those cases where reservation facilities are clearly owned or managed by private parties and there is no substantial Tribal interest or control involved, the Agency will endeavor to act in cooperation with the affected Tribal Government, but will otherwise respond to noncompliance by private parties on Indian reservations as the Agency would to noncompliance by the private sector elsewhere in the country. . . . When the Tribe has a substantial proprietary interest in, or control over, the privately owned or managed facility, EPA will respond as described in the first paragraph above. . . .

b.   Implications for Application of State Environmental Laws

Washington Department of Ecology v. EPA, 752 F.2d 1465 (9th Cir. 1985):
Subchapter C of the Resource Conservation and Recovery Act (RCRA), 42 U.S.C.
§ 6901 et seq., creates a comprehensive federal program of hazardous waste
management administered by the Environmental Protection Agency (EPA). RCRA
also authorizes the states to develop and implement their own hazardous waste
management programs "in lieu of" the federal program. The State of Washington
applied to the EPA for primacy to apply its hazardous waste program throughout
the state, including to all persons on "Indian lands," a term which EPA treated as
synonymous with "Indian country." EPA denied the application as it affected the
"Indian lands," concluding that the state had not adequately demonstrated that it
had jurisdiction over such lands, either inherently or through a delegation via
RCRA. Washington asked the Ninth Circuit to overturn that ruling, arguing that
RCRA applies to all persons, including Indians and tribes, and that the statute
specifically authorizes states to impose requirements "more stringent than those
imposed by [federal] regulations." 42 U.S.C. § 6929. Because RCRA does not
expressly preserve similar tribal powers, Washington argued that the state must
have authority over tribal territory, shared with the federal government.

In an opinion written by Judge William Canby, an Indian law scholar before and
since joining the bench, the Ninth Circuit rejected this position, upholding EPA's
decision, at least with respect to Indians on Indian lands. It declined to address the
legality of a state program limited in application to non-Indians on such lands.

Acknowledging, along with the state and tribal amici, that industrial development on reservations "create[s] a potentially significant hazardous waste problem,"
the court found that RCRA does not expressly grant states authority over Indian
tribes or lands. The only reference to Indians in the statute is in 42 U.S.C.
§ 6903(13), which defines "municipality" to include "an Indian tribe or authorized
tribal organization." While this provision authorizes enforcement of RCRA against
tribes (since "municipalities" are "persons" under the Act) it does not empower
states to regulate "Indian lands." Not a single mention of "Indian lands" appears in
the legislative history, suggesting that Congress did not advert to the question.

The court then explained that in the absence of statutory direction, it was
required to defer to any reasonable interpretation rendered by the responsible
administrative agency. *Chevron, U.S.A. Inc. v. Natural Resources Defense Council*,
467 U.S. 837 (1984). According to the court, "The agency's interpretation is
especially weighty where statutory construction involves 'reconciling conflicting
policies, and a full understanding of the force of the statutory policy in the given
situation (depends) upon more than ordinary knowledge respecting the matters
subjected to agency regulations.' " [*Chevron*, 467 U.S. at 844–45, *quoting United
States v. Shimer*, 367 U.S. 374, 382 (1961).] The court reasoned:

> . . . Implementation of hazardous waste management programs on Indian
> lands raises questions of Indian policy as well as environmental policy. It is
> appropriate for us to defer to EPA's expertise and experience in reconciling

these policies, gained through administration of similar environmental statutes on Indian lands.

Our conclusion that the EPA construction is a reasonable one is buttressed by well-settled principles of federal Indian law. States are generally precluded from exercising jurisdiction over Indians in Indian country unless Congress has clearly expressed an intention to permit it. This rule derives in part from respect for the plenary authority of Congress in the area of Indian affairs [citing *Merrion* and *White Mountain Apache Tribe*, presented in Ch. 3, Sec. A.1 and Ch. 4, Sec. B.4.b, respectively]. Accompanying the broad congressional power is the concomitant federal trust responsibility toward the Indian tribes. That responsibility arose largely from the federal role as a guarantor of Indian rights against state encroachment [citing *Kagama*, presented in Ch. 1, Sec. D.2]. We must presume that Congress intended to exercise its power in a manner consistent with the federal trust obligation.

The Washington tribes that appeared as amici in this case fear that their reservations will become "dumping grounds" for off-reservation hazardous wastes if the state is permitted to control the hazardous waste program on the reservations. Whether or not that fear is well-founded, the United States in its role as primary guarantor of Indian interests legitimately may decide that such tribal concerns can best be addressed by maintaining federal control over Indian lands. EPA's interpretation of RCRA permits this option.

Respect for the long tradition of tribal sovereignty and self-government also underlies the rule that state jurisdiction over Indians in Indian country will not be easily implied. Vague or ambiguous federal statutes must be measured against the "backdrop" of tribal sovereignty, especially when the statute affects an area in which the tribes historically have exercised their sovereign authority or contemporary federal policy encourages tribal self-government.

In this case, of course, the state is being required to yield to an exercise of jurisdiction by the federal government, not by a tribe. The sovereign role of the tribes, however, does not disappear when the federal government takes responsibility for the management of a federal program on tribal lands. The federal government has a policy of encouraging tribal self-government in environmental matters. That policy has been reflected in several environmental statutes [such as the Clean Air Act] that give Indian tribes a measure of control over policymaking or program administration or both.

The court refused to treat RCRA's lack of language expressly delegating authority to tribes — a contrast with some other federal environmental statutes — as proof that Congress meant for states to have power within Indian country. According to the court, "This contention, if accepted, would reverse the fundamental principle that the established jurisdictional relationships between Indian tribes and the states remain intact unless Congress clearly expresses its desire to change them." EPA's decision was also consistent with a broader federal policy of "tribal self-regulation in environmental matters," manifest in federal decisions to amend several other environmental statutes to "expressly permit tribal participation."

The court further noted that before they were so amended, several other environmental statutes were interpreted by EPA to allow delegation of authority over Indian country only to tribes, not to states, and these determinations had been upheld in the courts. *See Nance v. EPA*, 645 F.2d 701 (9th Cir. 1981) (upholding EPA's delegation of authority to tribes under the Clean Air Act, despite the absence of an express delegation at that time). The court emphasized that as in *Nance*, "the tribal interest in managing the reservation environment and the federal policy of encouraging tribes to assume or at least share in management responsibility are controlling." In conclusion, the court reasoned:

> . . . We cannot say that RCRA clearly evinces a Congressional purpose to revise federal Indian policy or to diminish the independence of Indian tribes. Section 3006 of RCRA is far less explicit than the Clean Air Act provision at issue in *Nance*, which gave the states primary responsibility for the "entire geographic region" within the state. RCRA merely authorizes state hazardous waste programs "in lieu of" the federal program. Since EPA could exclude state authority from Indian lands in *Nance*, it can certainly do so here.

> EPA, having retained regulatory authority over Indian lands in Washington under the interpretation of RCRA that we approve today, can promote the ability of the tribes to govern themselves by allowing them to participate in hazardous waste management. To do so, it need not delegate its full authority to the tribes. We therefore need not decide, and do not decide, the extent to which program authority under Section 3006 of RCRA is delegable to Indian governments. It is enough that EPA remains free to carry out its policy of encouraging tribal self-government by consulting with the tribes over matters of hazardous waste management policy, such as the siting of waste disposal facilities. Other avenues of accommodating tribal sovereignty will doubtless become clear in the concrete administration of the federal program. The "backdrop" of tribal sovereignty, in light of federal policies encouraging Indian self-government, consequently supports EPA's interpretation of RCRA.

> We therefore conclude that EPA correctly interpreted RCRA in rejecting Washington's application to regulate all hazardous waste-related activities on Indian lands. We recognize the vital interest of the State of Washington in effective hazardous waste management throughout the state, including on Indian lands. The absence of state enforcement power over reservation Indians, however, does not leave a vacuum in which hazardous wastes go unregulated. EPA remains responsible for ensuring that the federal standards are met on the reservations. Those standards are designed to protect human health and the environment. See 42 U.S.C. § 6924. The state and its citizens will not be without protection.

The decision of the EPA Regional Administrator is AFFIRMED.

NOTES

1. **Federal Preemption of State Authority Under Environmental Statutes:** Since the adoption of its Indian Policy in 1984, EPA has worked for the passage of amendments to federal environmental laws clarifying that Indian nations may assume "primacy" over Indian country, as well as inclusion of such language in any new environmental laws. The most common label for these provisions is "treatment as a state" or "treatment in the manner of a state" (often abbreviated TAS). As indicated above, both the Clean Water Act and the Clean Air Act, but not RCRA, contain such provisions. Indeed, RCRA is now the only major piece of federal environmental legislation lacking such a provision. For discussion of the various federal environmental statutes and their provisions regarding tribal regulatory authority, *see* NELL JESSUP NEWTON ET AL., COHEN'S HANDBOOK OF FEDERAL INDIAN LAW § 10.2 (2012 ed.). Where statutory language of this type exists, combined with EPA's 1984 Indian Policy, the possibility of state jurisdiction within Indian country is largely foreclosed. Hence most controversy has centered on RCRA. Should the exclusion of RCRA from this trend influence courts' interpretation of the scope of state jurisdiction?

2. **Continuing State Claims to Environmental Authority Within Indian Country:** Following the Ninth Circuit's decision in *Washington Department of Ecology v. EPA*, Washington petitioned EPA for authority over non-Indian hazardous waste activities within Indian country, including fee as well as trust lands. EPA denied the application, finding that the state lacked any independent source of regulatory power over all such lands. 51 Fed. Reg. 3782, 3783 (1986).

In *Yankton Sioux Tribe v. Southern Missouri Waste Management Dist.*, 890 F. Supp. 878, 890–91 (D.S.D. 1995), *aff'd*, 99 F.3d 1439 (8th Cir. 1996), *rev'd on other grounds*, 522 U.S. 329 (1998), the Tribe sued to stop state approval of a non-Indian landfill project on fee lands arguably within their reservation. EPA was taking the position that neither tribes (because of *Montana v. United States*, Ch. 3, Sec. A.3.a) nor states (because of lack of delegation under RCRA or any inherent authority) possessed jurisdiction that would support their departure from federal landfill construction standards in accordance with RCRA. The United States District Court Judge agreed with EPA that federal regulations would apply. Eventually, however, the United States Supreme Court found that the lands were not within the reservation boundaries because that part of the reservation had been disestablished. As a consequence, state authority to approve landfills was the same as elsewhere within the state. Assuming that the fee land had been within Indian country, was EPA correct to reject state authority over the nonmember-owned fee land? Could federal policy preferences for unitary regulation of Indian country, expressed in RCRA and EPA's 1984 Indian Policy, support EPA's refusal to single out the nonmember fee lands? *See* Judith V. Royster & Rory S. Fausett, *Control of the Reservation Environment: Tribal Primacy, Federal Delegation, and the Limits of State Intrusion*, 64 WASH. L. REV. 581 (1989).

What if a Public Law 280 state wants to apply its tougher solid or hazardous waste regulations to Indian country? Would the state's authority under Public Law 280 support such efforts? *Bryan v. Itasca County*, presented in Sec. A.2, this chapter, should squelch any hopes of such state regulatory jurisdiction. But in 1990, the California legislature passed a bill asserting state authority over waste disposal on trust as well as fee lands, ignoring opinions from the EPA, the Department of the Interior, and the state's own legislative analyst that neither inherent state authority nor Public Law 280 could sustain such legislation. The bill was inspired by a conflict that had erupted over plans by the Campo Band of Mission Indians to develop a commercial solid waste landfill on remote and otherwise unproductive tribal lands. Neighbors opposed the project, claiming that it would threaten local groundwater supplies. Jana Walker & Kevin Gover, *Commercial Solid and Hazardous Waste Disposal Projects on Indian Lands*, NAT. RESOURCES J., 6 Feb. 1992, at 58. After the Governor vetoed the bill, new legislation was enacted that authorizes the California Environmental Protection Agency to form agreements with tribes concerning waste disposal facilities on reservations. Cal. Health & Safety Code §§ 25198.1–.9 and Cal. Pub. Res. Code §§ 44201–44210. A tribe wishing to enter into such an agreement receives benefits of state testing and expertise in exchange for instituting tribal standards for the construction and operation of the facility that are the "functional equivalent" of state licensing requirements. Joel H. Mack & Gwynn Goodson Timms, *Cooperative Agreements: Government-to-Government Relations to Foster Reservation Business Development*, 20 PEPP. L. REV. 1295, 1325–26 (1993).

3. Federal Laws Regulating Tribal Activities

As noted above, most federal anti-pollution statutes, such as the Clean Water Act and the Resource Conservation and Recovery Act (RCRA) apply to tribes when they are the polluters. In addition to these laws affecting specific environmental media, tribes must contend with two federal environmental laws that may limit tribal economic and subsistence activity within reservations and anywhere Indians enjoy hunting or fishing rights. One of these laws, the National Environmental Policy Act (1969), imposes no substantive limits on development, but demands extensive review and analysis of the environmental impacts of such activity. The other, the Endangered Species Act (1973) shuts down both economic and subsistence activity that may harm animals or plants listed as endangered. The sections that follow focus on the interplay of these two laws with issues of tribal sovereignty.

a. Environmental Review Requirements

DAVIS v. MORTON
United States Court of Appeals, Tenth Circuit
469 F.2d 593 (1972)

HILL, CIRCUIT JUDGE.

This is an appeal from the United States District Court for the District of New Mexico for dismissing appellants' action against the United States government. Appellants allege the government failed to follow the provisions of the National Environmental Policy Act (NEPA), 42 U.S.C. § 4321 et seq., and of 25 U.S.C. § 415 before approving a ninety-nine-year lease on the Tesuque Indian Reservation in Santa Fe County, New Mexico.

The facts are simple and uncontroverted. On April 17, 1970, a ninety-nine-year lease of restricted Indian lands was executed by the Pueblo of Tesuque (Pueblo), as lessor, and Sangre de Cristo Development Company, Inc. (Sangre), a New Mexico corporation, as lessee. The agreement granted Sangre a lease on a 1300-acre tract of land called "Tract 1" and granted lease options on four other tracts, thereby subjecting approximately 5400 acres to the lease. The purpose of the lease is to develop the property for residential, recreational and commercial purposes. Ultimately a small city is planned with a population of approximately 15,000 inhabitants.

On May 24, 1970, appellee Walter O. Olson, Area Supervisor for the New Mexico District of the Bureau of Indian Affairs of the Department of the Interior, approved the lease agreement pursuant to 25 U.S.C. § 415. . . . Appellants charged that appellees were without authority to grant the lease since no environmental impact study was conducted prior to approval of the lease as required by NEPA, 42 U.S.C. § 4332 (2)(C).[78]

. . . .

[Does the Secretary's authority to ratify or reject leases relating to Indian lands under section 415 constitute major federal action and therefore trigger the requirement of an environmental impact study under NEPA?]

Appellees' primary thesis is that although the contractual relationship between Sangre and the Pueblo is a lease, it is not a federal lease and therefore does not constitute major federal action. The United States did not initiate the lease, was not a party, possessed no interest in either the lease or the development, did not participate financially or benefit from the lease in any way. Before federal action will constitute major federal action under the mandates of NEPA, the government must initiate, participate in or benefit from the project.

We feel the government's interpretation of NEPA is too constrained for our court to adopt. Title 42 U.S.C. § 4331 (b) states:

> [I]t is the continuing responsibility of the Federal Government to use all practicable means, consistent with other essential considerations of national policy, to . . . (2) assure for all Americans safe, healthful, productive, and esthetically and culturally pleasing surroundings; (3) attain the widest range of beneficial uses of the environment without degradation, risk to health or safety, or other undesirable and unintended consequences; (4) preserve important historic, cultural, and natural aspects of our national heritage, and maintain, wherever possible, an environment which supports diversity and variety of individual choice. . . .

---

[78] [18] The Congress authorizes and directs that, to the fullest extent possible: . . . (2) all agencies of the Federal Government shall — . . . (C) include in every recommendation or report on proposals for legislation and other major Federal actions significantly affecting the quality of the human environment, a detailed statement by the responsible official on — (i) the environmental impact of the proposed action, (ii) any adverse environmental effects which cannot be avoided should the proposal be implemented, (iii) alternatives to the proposed action, (iv) the relationship between local short-term uses of man's environment and the maintenance and enhancement of long-term productivity, and (v) any irreversible and irretrievable commitments of resources which would be involved in the proposed action should it be implemented. . . .

[Taking into account both the language of the Act and its legislative history], there is little doubt that Congress intended all agencies under their authority to follow the substantive and procedural mandates of NEPA.

The problem boils down to whether granting leases on Indian lands constitutes major federal action as required in NEPA § 102(2) (C). Upon review of the lease and relevant case law, we feel the lower court erred in holding the lease did not constitute major federal action. The lease refers to the United States government countless times. All notices and approvals must be made by the Pueblo and the United States. The Secretary is required to give written approval before encumbrances can be made on the leased land. The lease protects the United States government against damage or injury to people or property on the leased premises. Certainly the fact the United States government might be held liable for injury or damages incurred on the Indian land unless the lease provides otherwise makes the government more than an impartial, disinterested party to the contract between Pueblo and Sangre.

[W]here a federal license or permit is involved, or where Congress possesses and has utilized its plenary power of regulation under the interstate commerce clause or other constitutional authority, federal approval constitutes major federal action. [Appellees, however,] argue the government is operating in a different capacity when dealing with Indian lands. It is the appellees' contention that Indian lands, such as those of the Pueblo, are held in trust by the government for the Indians. Therefore, the appellees should approve the lease if it is advantageous to the beneficiaries of the trust.

Appellees also charge that Congress did not intend to enmesh the discretionary execution of these fiduciary duties in the procedural and bureaucratic web that NEPA § 102(2) (C) imposes. To impose this burden on private Indian land places the Indians at an economic and competitive disadvantage, and subjects their property to judicial challenge by non-Indian competitors laboring under no such environmental restriction.

It is interesting to note that appellees proffer no case law to support their arguments. The fact Indian lands are held in trust does not take it out of NEPA's jurisdiction. Cf. *Federal Power Comm'n v. Tuscarora*, 362 U.S. 99, 116 (1960). All public lands of the United States are held by it in trust for the people of the United States. *Utah Power & Light v. United States*, 243 U.S. 389, 409 (1916). To accept appellees' contention would preclude all federal lands from NEPA jurisdiction, something clearly not intended by Congress in passing the Act.

Appellees' second contention that Congress did not intend to enmesh the discretionary execution of these fiduciary duties in the procedural and bureaucratic web imposed by NEPA § 102(2) (C) also falls on deaf ears. In *Calvert Cliffs' Coord. Comm. v. United States A. E. Comm'n, supra*, the court answered this problem by stating that "Section 102 duties are not inherently flexible. . . . Considerations of administrative difficulty, delay or economic cost will not suffice to strip the section of its fundamental importance." (449 F.2d p. 1115).

We conclude approving leases on federal lands constitutes major federal action and thus must be approved according to NEPA mandates. As our court had occasion to consider once before, this Act was intended to include all federal agencies, including the Bureau of Indian Affairs. See *National Helium Corporation v. Morton*, 455 F.2d 650 (10th Cir. 1971).

The lower court felt NEPA did not apply to Indian lands or otherwise the amendment to 25 U.S.C. § 415 would not have addressed the problem of environmental concerns. We do not draw that conclusion. NEPA is a very broad statute covering both substantive and procedural problems relating to the environment. The amendment to 25 U.S.C. § 415 deals primarily with the addition of Indian tribes to the group having long-term lease authority. Only briefly is the environmental problem discussed. The amendment only requires the Secretary to satisfy himself on the environmental issue; nowhere are any specific procedural guidelines set out as in NEPA. In *Calvert Cliffs' Coord. Comm. v. United States A. E. Comm'n, supra*, a similar problem arose. The court correctly determined that unless the obligations of another statute are clearly mutually exclusive with the mandates of NEPA, the specific requirements of NEPA will remain in force. The reasoning is applicable in the instant case. The general statement in § 415 in no way implies leases on Indian lands were not covered by NEPA. The amendment merely reaffirms congressional intent that environmental considerations are to play a factor in any Bureau of Indian Affairs decisions.

For the reasons stated above, we feel the lower court erred in dismissing appellants' request for a temporary and permanent injunction enjoining appellees from approving or acting on any submissions or approvals under the lease until the environmental impact of the project is studied and evaluated.

The judgment appealed from is reversed, and the case is remanded to the trial court with directions to grant the relief prayed for.

NOTES ON FEDERAL ENVIRONMENTAL REVIEW REQUIREMENTS

1.   **Aftermath of *Davis v. Morton*:** For more than four years after the Tenth Circuit's decision, the Bureau of Indian Affairs and several other federal agencies worked with the developer to prepare an environmental impact statement. During that period, the Pueblo acquired new leadership and tribal support for the lease declined. In 1977, at the request of the Pueblo, the Department of the Interior rescinded its approval of the lease, citing environmental concerns as well as the Pueblo's opposition. Soon thereafter, the developer went into bankruptcy. The Tenth Circuit ultimately rejected Sangre de Cristo's challenges to the lease rescission. *Sangre de Cristo Development Company, Inc. v. United States of America*, 932 F.2d 891 (10th Cir. 1991).

The Jicarilla Apache were less successful than the Pueblo of Tesuque in using a NEPA violation to void an unfavorable lease. In *Jicarilla Apache Tribe v. Andrus*, 687 F.2d 1324 (10th Cir. 1982), the court invoked the doctrine of laches to deny such a claim, even though the Tribe demonstrated that its delay in challenging the lease was attributable to inadequate advice from the Bureau of Indian Affairs.

2.   **Federal or Tribal Action?** A discordant note as to the federal government's trusteeship responsibility is introduced by NEPA according to *Davis*. The trustee is obliged to consider the impact of a tribal decision on the environment of lands of nontribal people. *Cf.* 25 U.S.C. § 415(e). When and how do we require such consideration of externalities when development on private lands is involved? Does *Davis* place special duties of environmental solicitude on Indian lands?

In *Oliver v. Udall*, 306 F.2d 819 (D.C. Cir. 1962), the court held that the secretarial approval of a tribal ordinance did not constitute a sufficient federal action to render the decision subject to First Amendment challenge. Rather, according to the court, "the Secretary's approval of tribal action in 1959 was entirely in keeping with that abstinence from federal intervention in the internal affairs of an Indian tribe which the law clearly requires. The Secretary had simply recognized the valid governing authority of the Tribal Council." In approving a tribal lease does the Secretary do any more than "[recognize] the valid governing authority of the Tribal Council"? Can the *Davis* result be reconciled with *Oliver*? Can the difference in results be reconciled based solely on the externalities involved in a lease approval decision?

The National Environmental Policy Act is seemingly silent on its applicability to Indian country. In the face of such congressional silence, should the statute be read to apply to the leasing or development of Indian lands? *See* Ch. 2, Sec. C and Ch. 4, Sec. A.2 regarding the general treatment under federal Indian law of federal laws of general applicability. Should it make any difference whether the development is being undertaken by the Indians or by non-Indian lessees? Should the approach to such issues be affected by whether the reservation's ownership of the land is based on treaty-guaranteed title or executive order? Note that minimum national standards established under federal environmental laws such as the Clean Air Act and Clean Water Act apply to Indian country. Since the 1980s this arrangement could be justified by the provisions in most of these statutes for treatment of tribes in the manner of states. But the minimum national standards were applied to Indian country even during the earlier period when those statutes were silent as to tribal lands. Does this pattern of interpretation support the decision in *Davis v. Morton*? Or can one distinguish NEPA from these other statutes?

3.   Secretarial Approval and Environmental Impact Statements — Environmental and Tribal Protections or Tools for Frustrating Indian Economic Development? The *Davis* case demonstrates how environmental protection statutes can be used to attempt to delay or frustrate tribal or federal development plans for Indian land. In the *Davis* case the decisions under attack were made by the tribal council. In light of the strong federal policy of protecting Indian self-government and avoiding federal court intrusions on tribal decisions, as reflected in *Santa Clara Pueblo v. Martinez* (presented in Ch. 3, Sec. C.5), is such a use of federal environmental statutes appropriate? Can it be justified by the overriding federal concern for protecting environmental values? Does your view of the appropriateness of the application of federal environmental laws to Indian lands change when the tribal government invokes such laws, as in *Nance v. Environmental Protection Agency, supra*, to protect its members from the development goals of non-Indians and, sometimes, other agencies of the federal government? Even when the tribal government seeks to invoke such federal environmental legislation, there may be

some long-term costs to tribal sovereignty. For example, the reclassification of the Northern Cheyenne Reservation as a Class I air quality area, secured by the Northern Cheyenne governing body in the 1970s, prevents future tribal governments, as well as non-Indian lessees, from significantly developing the Northern Cheyenne Reservation. The redesignation thus delimits future uses of reservation land that may be supported by transient majorities of the Northern Cheyenne tribe. While federal environmental statutes, in this instance, no doubt added stability to the land management process, was such redesignation an appropriate intrusion of the federal government on the vagaries of local tribal control?

One consequence of the secretarial approval and NEPA impact statement requirements set forth in *Davis* is that third parties sometimes can challenge, and therefore sometimes delay implementation of, federal action approving tribal development plans. In *Ringsred v. City of Duluth*, 828 F.2d 1305 (8th Cir. 1987), disaffected members of the Duluth community filed suit to prevent construction of a parking ramp in downtown Duluth as part of a larger bingo project proposed jointly by the Fond du Lac Band of Lake Superior Chippewa and the City of Duluth with the approval of the Secretary of the Interior. While the court doubted that an outsider to the deal had any standing to challenge secretarial approval under the provisions of 25 U.S.C. § 81, the Eighth Circuit entertained and rejected the outside challenger's NEPA challenge.

Adopting the same kind of strategy, the State of Utah was able to intervene in the Nuclear Regulatory Commission's EIS (environmental impact statement) and licensing proceedings in connection with a lease of land by the Skull Valley Band of Goshute Indians for temporary storage of high-level nuclear waste. When Utah went further and demanded intervenor status for the lease approval process underway before the BIA, the Tenth Circuit found the claim unripe because the EIS had not yet been completed. *State of Utah v. United States Department of the Interior*, 210 F.3d 1193 (10th Cir. 2000).

Are federal environmental review requirements under NEPA protecting Indian nations or defeating their legitimate economic development objectives? Does your answer depend in part on your assessment of the history of federal involvement in reshaping tribal governments, and the extent to which contemporary governments of Indian nations reflect the legitimate aspirations of their communities? If traditional communities on some reservations feel excluded from decision-making within tribal governments, is the proper solution more extensive federal environmental review or is it internal tribal government reform efforts? In the case of the Rosebud Sioux, community members and environmental activists filed suit to cancel a BIA-approved lease for the establishment of a multi-site hog production facility. Their claim was that the BIA had acted improperly in issuing a Finding of No Significant Impact (FONSI), and thereby obviating the need for a full environmental assessment under NEPA. In response to the lawsuit, the BIA voided the lease. Not long thereafter, the Tribe held general elections that changed the composition of the Tribal Council. The new tribal government no longer favored the hog production project, and defended the BIA's action when the lessee sued to uphold the lease. *See Rosebud Sioux Tribe v. McDivitt*, 286 F.3d 1031 (8th Cir. 2002). Should one generalize from this one case?

A valuable source of context for understanding the Tribe's initial decision to develop economically through a hog farm, and the wellsprings of later resistance to that plan, is Winona LaDuke, *The Hogs of Rosebud*, *in* 7 MULTINAT'L MONITOR 34 (July 1, 2003). For a discussion of the implications of the *McDivitt* case for future economic development on tribal lands, see Dani Daugherty, *In Hogs We Trust — A Million Pigs in a Parlor: The Bureaucracy of the Bureau of Indian Affairs' Conflicting Trust Rules*, 7 GREAT PLAINS NAT. RESOURCES J. 267 (2002). By 2003, the firm that had contracted to develop the hog farm had already invested approximately $20 million in the venture, and the Tribe was attempting to shut down the first phase of the project, which had already located 48,000 hogs on the reservation. The firm sued the Tribe and the Department of the Interior for failing to live up to the contract. The Tribe argued in response that the firm must first exhaust tribal remedies, and that its waiver of sovereign immunity in the contract is no longer valid since the Secretary of the Interior refused to approve it. In May 2005, the parties arrived at a settlement that allowed a very small number of existing facilities to remain but barred further expansion.

4. NEPA and the Taking of Land into Trust: Tribal economic development sometimes requires acquisition of additional land, with such land taken into trust for the tribe by the United States. If such development does not entail a federal lease, *Davis v. Morton* will not demand NEPA review. Does NEPA apply to decisions by the Department of the Interior to take land into trust for purposes of the tribe's own economic development? In *State of Nevada v. United States*, 221 F. Supp. 2d 1241 (D. Nev. 2002), a federal court refused to find NEPA applicable to a trust acquisition for the Fallon Paiute-Shoshone Tribe that was congressionally mandated. The Tribe was intending to use the land to develop a gas station. The court explained that NEPA applies only to discretionary acts. *See also Sac & Fox Nation v. Norton*, 240 F.3d 1250 (10th Cir. 2001). Current federal regulations specify that NEPA review applies to discretionary decisions by the Department of the Interior to take land into trust, even within reservation boundaries. 25 C.F.R. § 151.10 (h). Should such assessments take account of planned tribal economic development? How far along should those plans have to be in order to figure into NEPA review? What are the tribe's incentives under these circumstances?

5. Environmental Review Requirements for Mineral Development and Gaming: The Indian Mineral Development Act of 1982, 25 U.S.C. § 2101 et seq., allows Indian nations to form joint ventures and other types of minerals agreements more favorable than leases. Unlike 25 U.S.C. § 415(a), which requires the Secretary of the Interior to assess very broadly "the effect on the environment of the uses to which the leased land will be subject," the Mineral Development Act asks the Secretary of the Interior to consider only environmental impacts on the tribe. 25 U.S.C. § 2103(b). However, the Mineral Development Act also contemplates that NEPA will often apply to secretarial approval of such agreements. 25 U.S.C. § 2103(a)(2).

A form of tribal economic development that has inspired real or pretextual environmental complaints is gaming. Particularly when gaming facilities are constructed in sparsely settled rural areas, off-reservation neighbors fear uncontrolled traffic congestion, waste, and sewage. If there is no lease associated with a gaming facility, will NEPA apply?

Under the statutory scheme established by the Indian Gaming Regulatory Act of 1988 (IGRA), 25 U.S.C. § 2701 et seq. (*see* Sec. E, this chapter), a federal agency, the National Indian Gaming Commission, is heavily involved in tribal gaming projects. This involvement, in turn, may trigger federal environmental review requirements. In addition, IGRA requires that tribal governments adopt ordinances governing gaming activities covered by the Act, and these ordinances must include, among other things, provisions ensuring that "the construction and maintenance of the gaming operation, and the operation of that gaming is conducted in a manner that adequately protects the environment and the public health and safety." 25 U.S.C. § 2710(b)(2)(E). Ordinances are not valid unless approved by the National Indian Gaming Commission. To implement its approval power, the Commission has issued regulations that require gaming tribes to adopt standards designed to ensure that those operations are constructed, operated, and maintained in a manner that adequately protects the environment, and to enforce compliance with those standards through monitoring conducted by qualified personnel. 67 Fed. Reg. 46109–46112 (July 12, 2002).

Will this requirement likely satisfy the complaining off-reservation neighbors? Recall that the most lucrative forms of tribal gaming, labeled "Class III" under IGRA, may only be conducted pursuant to a tribal-state compact. *See* Sec. E, this chapter. May states properly insist that application of their environmental controls or environmental review requirements be one of the subjects of compact negotiations? During the legislative debates over IGRA, Senator Daniel Inouye, Chair of the Committee on Indian Affairs, pronounced that "There is no intent on the part of Congress that the compacting methodology be used in such areas such as taxation, water rights, environmental regulation, and land use. On the contrary, the tribal power to regulate such activities . . . remains fully intact." 134 Cong. Rec. 12651, Sept. 15, 1988. In the standard gaming compact that more than 60 California Indian nations have made with the State of California, they agreed only to make good faith efforts to incorporate the policies of federal and state laws regarding environmental review of off-reservation impacts, "consistent with the Tribe's governmental interests." Tribal-State Gaming Compact, § 10.8.1 (1999), available at http://www.cgcc.ca.gov/documents/enabling/tsc.pdf.

The tribes also agreed to submit environmental impact reports to state and local governments, to afford off-reservation residents an opportunity to voice their environmental concerns, to consult with local officials regarding mitigation in advance of construction, and to carry out mitigation during construction. *Id.* at §§ 10.8.2 & 10.8.3. In more recent compact amendments, a few California tribes have agreed, in addition, to conduct negotiations and enter into enforceable agreements with counties for mitigation of significant effects on the off-reservation environment. Binding arbitration is specified if the two sides can't agree. *See, e.g.*, Amendment to Tribal-State Compact between the State of California and the Rumsey Band of Wintun Indians, § 10.8.8 (2004), available at http://www.cgcc.ca. gov/documents/compacts/amended_compacts/rumseyamend082004.pdf.

b.   The Endangered Species Act in Indian Country

For millennia, Native peoples have conserved and managed plant and animal life, and have held certain animals and plants sacred. Not surprisingly, in numerous treaties, Indians insisted that their rights to hunt, fish, and gather be protected, often designating ceded, off-reservation lands as places where these rights would extend. *See* Ch. 7, Sec. A. But as tribes have become enmeshed in non-Indian economies and ecosystems that diminish wildlife, questions have arisen about the proper application of federal species conservation measures, such as the Endangered Species Act (ESA), to activities on tribal lands and to tribal off-reservation resources. That Act places severe restrictions on development, hunting, and other activities in areas identified as critical habitats for species formally listed as endangered. Recall *United States v. Dion*, 476 U.S. 734 (1986), presented in Ch. 4, Sec. A.2, where the Supreme Court held the Bald Eagle Protection Act applicable to a tribal member who had killed an eagle on his own reservation, and declined to also consider whether the Endangered Species Act applied to the hunt. How should the Endangered Species Act's drastic provisions be applied in the face of tribal treaty rights, religious ceremonial needs, and sovereign need to balance development decisions with environmental concerns? Implications of the ESA for Indian religious practices are discussed in Ch. 6, Sec. B.1. The relationship between ESA and Indian hunting and fishing rights is considered in Ch. 7, Sec. A.2. This section focuses on ESA's habitat protections, and their consequences for tribal development activities.

The United States Fish and Wildlife Service, within the Department of Commerce, is charged with designating critical habitats for purposes of the Endangered Species Act. Since the 1990s, it has had a policy of declining to designate tribal lands as critical habitats where the tribe has developed its own protection plan, taking the position that the benefits of allowing tribes to pursue their own management plans outweigh any benefits from additional federal designation. The Secretarial Order that follows is an internal guidance memorandum for the agencies, much like EPA's Indian Policy and the Indian Child Welfare Act guidelines presented in Sec. D.4, this chapter.

SECRETARIAL ORDER #3206
available at http://www.fws.gov/nativeamerican/pdf/
tek-secretarial-order-3206.pdf (1997)

Subject: American Indian Tribal Rights, Federal-Tribal Trust Responsibilities, and the Endangered Species Act

Jointly Issued by the Secretaries of the Interior and Commerce

Sec. 1. Purpose and Authority. This Order is issued by the Secretary of the Interior and the Secretary of Commerce (Secretaries) pursuant to the Endangered Species Act of 1973, 16 U.S.C. 1531, as amended (the Act), the federal-tribal trust relationship, and other federal law. . . . Accordingly, the Departments will carry out their responsibilities under the Act in a manner that harmonizes the Federal trust responsibility to tribes, tribal sovereignty, and statutory missions of the Departments, and that strives to ensure that Indian tribes do not bear a disproportionate burden for the conservation of listed species, so as to avoid or minimize the potential for conflict and confrontation. . . .

Sec. 3. Definitions. For the purposes of this Order, except as otherwise expressly provided, the following terms shall apply:

. . . (C) The term "tribal rights" means those rights legally accruing to a tribe or tribes by virtue of inherent sovereign authority, unextinguished aboriginal title, treaty, statute, judicial decisions, executive order or agreement, and which give rise to legally enforceable remedies.

Sec. 4. Background. The unique and distinctive political relationship between the United States and Indian tribes is defined by treaties, statutes, executive orders, judicial decisions, and agreements, and differentiates tribes from other entities that deal with, or are affected by, the federal government. This relationship has given rise to a special federal trust responsibility, involving the legal responsibilities and obligations of the United States toward Indian tribes and the application of fiduciary standards of due care with respect to Indian lands, tribal trust resources, and the exercise of tribal rights.

The Departments recognize the importance of tribal self-governance and the protocols of a government-to-government relationship with Indian tribes. Long-standing Congressional and Administrative policies promote tribal self-government, self-sufficiency, and self-determination, recognizing and endorsing the fundamental rights of tribes to set their own priorities and make decisions affecting their resources and distinctive ways of life. The Departments recognize and respect, and shall consider, the value that tribal traditional knowledge provides to tribal and federal land management decision-making and tribal resource management activities. The Departments recognize that Indian tribes are governmental sovereigns; inherent in this sovereign authority is the power to make and enforce laws, administer justice, manage and control Indian lands, exercise tribal rights and protect tribal trust resources. The Departments shall be sensitive to the fact that Indian cultures, religions, and spirituality often involve ceremonial and medicinal uses of plants, animals, and specific geographic places.

Because of the unique government-to-government relationship between Indian tribes and the United States, the Departments and affected Indian tribes need to establish and maintain effective working relationships and mutual partnerships to promote the conservation of sensitive species (including candidate, proposed and listed species) and the health of ecosystems upon which they depend. Such relationships should focus on cooperative assistance, consultation, the sharing of information, and the creation of government-to-government partnerships to promote healthy ecosystems. . . .

Sec. 5. Responsibilities. To achieve the objectives of this Order, the heads of all agencies, bureaus and offices within the Department of the Interior, and the Administrator of the National Oceanic and Atmospheric Administration (NOAA) within the Department of Commerce, shall be responsible for ensuring that the following directives are followed:

Principle 1. THE DEPARTMENTS SHALL WORK DIRECTLY WITH INDIAN TRIBES ON A GOVERNMENT-TO-GOVERNMENT BASIS TO PROMOTE HEALTHY ECOSYSTEMS.

The Departments shall recognize the unique and distinctive political and constitutionally based relationship that exists between the United States and each Indian tribe, and shall view tribal governments as sovereign entities with authority and responsibility for the health and welfare of ecosystems on Indian lands. The Departments recognize that Indian tribes are governmental sovereigns with inherent powers to make and enforce laws, administer justice, and manage and control their natural resources. Accordingly, the Departments shall seek to establish effective government-to-government working relationships with tribes to achieve the common goal of promoting and protecting the health of these ecosystems. Whenever the agencies, bureaus, and offices of the Departments are aware that their actions planned under the Act may impact tribal trust resources, the exercise of tribal rights, or Indian lands, they shall consult with, and seek the participation of, the affected Indian tribes to the maximum extent practicable. This shall include providing affected tribes adequate opportunities to participate in data collection, consensus seeking, and associated processes. To facilitate the government-to-government relationship, the Departments may coordinate their discussions with a representative from an intertribal organization, if so designated by the affected tribe(s). . . .

Principle 2. THE DEPARTMENTS SHALL RECOGNIZE THAT INDIAN LANDS ARE NOT SUBJECT TO THE SAME CONTROLS AS FEDERAL PUBLIC LANDS.

. . . Indian lands are not federal public lands or part of the public domain, but are rather retained by tribes or set aside for tribal use pursuant to treaties, statutes, court orders, executive orders, judicial decisions, or agreements. Accordingly, Indian tribes manage Indian lands in accordance with tribal goals and objectives, within the framework of applicable laws.

Principle 3. THE DEPARTMENTS SHALL ASSIST INDIAN TRIBES IN DEVELOPING AND EXPANDING TRIBAL PROGRAMS SO THAT HEALTHY ECOSYSTEMS ARE PROMOTED AND CONSERVATION RESTRICTIONS ARE UNNECESSARY.

(A) . . . The Departments shall offer and provide such scientific and technical assistance and information as may be available for the development of tribal conservation and management plans to promote the maintenance, restoration, enhancement and health of the ecosystems upon which sensitive species (including candidate, proposed, and listed species) depend, including the cooperative identification of appropriate management measures to address concerns for such species and their habitats.

(B) The Departments shall recognize that Indian tribes are appropriate governmental entities to manage their lands and tribal trust resources. The Departments acknowledge that Indian tribes value, and exercise responsibilities for, management of Indian lands and tribal trust resources. In keeping with the federal policy of promoting tribal self-government, the Departments shall respect the exercise of tribal sovereignty over the management of Indian lands, and tribal trust resources. Accordingly, the Departments shall give deference to tribal conservation and management plans for tribal trust resources that: (a) govern activities on Indian lands, including, for the purposes of this section, tribally-owned fee lands, and (b) address the conservation needs of listed species. The Departments shall conduct government-to-government consultations to discuss the extent to which tribal resource management plans for tribal trust resources outside Indian lands can be incorporated into actions to address the conservation needs of listed species.

(C) The Departments, as trustees, shall support tribal measures that preclude the need for conservation restrictions.

At the earliest indication that the need for federal conservation restrictions is being considered for any species, the Departments, acting in their trustee capacities, shall promptly notify all potentially affected tribes, and provide such technical, financial, or other assistance as may be appropriate, thereby assisting Indian tribes in identifying and implementing tribal conservation and other measures necessary to protect such species.

In the event that the Departments determine that conservation restrictions are necessary in order to protect listed species, the Departments, in keeping with the trust responsibility and government-to-government relationships, shall consult with affected tribes and provide written notice to them of the intended restriction as far in advance as practicable. If the proposed conservation restriction is directed at a tribal activity that could raise the potential issue of direct (directed) take under the Act, then meaningful government-to-government consultation shall occur, in order to strive to harmonize the federal trust responsibility to tribes, tribal sovereignty and the statutory missions of the Departments. In cases involving an activity that could raise the potential issue of an incidental take under the Act, such notice shall include an analysis and determination that all of the following conservation standards have been met: (i) the restriction is reasonable and necessary for conservation of the species at issue; (ii) the conservation purpose of the restriction cannot be achieved by reasonable regulation of non-Indian activities; (iii) the measure is the least restrictive alternative available to achieve the required conservation purpose; (iv) the restriction does not discriminate against Indian activities, either as stated or applied; and, (v) voluntary tribal measures are not adequate to achieve the necessary conservation purpose.

Principle 4. THE DEPARTMENTS SHALL BE SENSITIVE TO INDIAN CULTURE, RELIGION AND SPIRITUALITY.

The Departments shall take into consideration the impacts of their actions and policies under the Act on Indian use of listed species for cultural and religious purposes. The Departments shall avoid or minimize, to the extent practicable, adverse effects upon the noncommercial use of listed sacred plants and animals in medicinal treatments and in the expression of cultural and religious beliefs by Indian tribes. When appropriate, the Departments may issue guidelines to accommodate Indian access to, and traditional uses of, listed species, and to address unique circumstances that may exist when administering the Act.

Principle 5. THE DEPARTMENTS SHALL MAKE AVAILABLE TO INDIAN

TRIBES INFORMATION RELATED TO TRIBAL TRUST RESOURCES AND INDIAN LANDS, AND, TO FACILITATE THE MUTUAL EXCHANGE OF INFORMATION, SHALL STRIVE TO PROTECT SENSITIVE TRIBAL INFORMATION FROM DISCLOSURE.

Sec. 6. Federal-Tribal Intergovernmental Agreements. The Departments shall, when appropriate and at the request of an Indian tribe, pursue intergovernmental agreements to formalize arrangements involving sensitive species (including candidate, proposed, and listed species) such as, but not limited to, land and resource management, multi-jurisdictional partnerships, cooperative law enforcement, and guidelines to accommodate Indian access to, and traditional uses of, natural products. Such agreements shall strive to establish partnerships that harmonize the Departments' missions under the Act with the Indian tribe's own ecosystem management objectives.

NOTES ON TRIBES AND THE ENDANGERED SPECIES ACT

1. **Tribal Leadership in Species Protection and Recovery:** Even before this Secretarial Order was issued, the Fish and Wildlife Service had entered into an agreement with the Nez Perce Tribe of Idaho that put the Tribe in the position of primary manager of the statewide protection and recovery effort for the endangered gray wolf. While the non-Indian population held extremely negative views of the wolves, in Nez Perce culture, the wolf is considered a brother, and many Nez Perce narratives include the wolf as a spiritual guide. *See* Marren Sanders, *Ecosystem Co-Management Agreements: A Study of Nation Building or a Lesson on Erosion of Tribal Sovereignty?* 15 BUFF. ENVT'L. L.J. 97, 155 (2007). When the State of Idaho refused an invitation from the Fish and Wildlife Service to direct the recovery effort, the Tribe built its capacity and made an agreement with Fish and Wildlife, in 1995, to assume responsibility. Ten years later, Idaho altered its position, and made an agreement with the Nez Perce to "work in concert as sovereign governments to maintain self sustaining wolf populations and to avoid the potential of wolves returning to federal protection." Among other things, the Tribe and Idaho establish "fair shares" for harvests of gray wolves for sport and subsistence.

2. **Judicial Response to Secretarial Order #3206:** In *Center for Biological Diversity v. Norton*, 240 F. Supp. 2d 1090 (D. Ariz. 2003), involving a conflict over designation of critical habitat for the Mexican spotted owl, the district court rejected the policy of tribal management plans incorporated in Secretarial Order #3206 as a clear violation of the statute, and found additional problems in the fact that the agency had not even produced one of the tribal management plans in question for public comment. Given that most of the danger to plant and animal species has come from non-Indian development that is already entrenched, and given that tribes are relatively late to the pursuit of economic development, is the Endangered Species Act disproportionately curtailing tribal economic prospects? How similar is this concern to the concern expressed by some developing countries that tough international environmental standards are under consideration only after the West has already gained the benefits of economic development at the expense of the environment? Should it matter whether a tribe is interested in conducting ceremonial activities that involve use of endangered species as opposed

to economic activity that might threaten some of the species? For defense of the policy embodied in Secretarial Order #3206, see Charles Wilkinson, *The Role of Bilateralism in Fulfilling the Federal-Tribal Relationship: The Tribal Rights-Endangered Species Secretarial Order*, 72 WASH. L. REV. 1063 (1997); Sandi B. Zellmer, *Indian Lands as Critical Habitat for Indian Nations and Endangered Species: Tribal Survival and Sovereignty Come First*, 43 S.D. L. REV. 381 (1998).

4. Federal Protection for Tribal Environments and Economic Activities from Non-Indian Economic Development

WISCONSIN v. ENVIRONMENTAL PROTECTION AGENCY
United States Court of Appeals, Seventh Circuit
266 F.3d 741 (2001)

WOOD, CIRCUIT JUDGE

Although the general model of sovereignty suggests that different sovereign states normally occupy different geographic territories, *see, e.g.*, Restatement (3d) of the Foreign Relations Law of the United States, § 201 (1986), the existence of federations and confederations shows that overlapping sovereignty is also a common feature of modern political organization. In this case, we confront one of the more complex kinds of overlapping sovereignty that exists in the United States today: that between the States and Indian tribes. . . . A[n] . . . aspect of [that] relationship is before us here: namely, whether the Environmental Protection Agency (EPA), acting through authority delegated to it by statute, was empowered to treat a particular tribe as a "state" for purposes of certain water quality rules. Like the district court, we conclude that the EPA acted properly in doing so, and we thus affirm the district court's judgment rejecting the challenge Wisconsin has brought to the EPA's action.

A. The Clean Water Act

The Clean Water Act (the Act) prohibits the discharge of pollutants into navigable waters unless the discharge is sanctioned by a permit or statute. See 33 U.S.C. § 1311(a). Permits are issued by the EPA or by state agencies subject to EPA review. Id. at § 1342. The Act also gives states the authority to establish water quality standards for waters within their boundaries (*id.* at § 1313), to certify compliance with those standards (*id.* at § 1341), and to issue and enforce discharge permits (*id.* at §§ 1342, 1319), all under the watchful eye of the EPA. Like other states, Wisconsin has enacted its own federally approved comprehensive water pollution regulatory system. . . .

In 1987, Congress amended the Act to authorize the EPA to treat Indian tribes as states under § 518 of the Act. Once a tribe has treatment-as-state (TAS) status, the statute permits it to establish water quality standards for bodies of water within its reservation and to require permits for any action that may create a discharge into those waters. 33 U.S.C. § 1377(e). In 1991, after full notice-and-comment rule-making, the EPA issued a final rule implementing this provision and setting forth the requirements Indian tribes would have to meet in order to be granted TAS status:

(1)   the tribe must be federally recognized;

(2)   the tribe must have a governing body carrying out substantial governmental duties and powers;

(3)   the functions to be exercised by the tribe must pertain to the management and protection of water resources which are held by the tribe, held by the United States in trust for the tribe, or otherwise within the borders of the reservation; and

(4)   the tribe must be capable of carrying out the functions of the Act.

40 C.F.R. 131.8(a); see also 33 U.S.C. §§ 1377(e)(1)–(3).

Relying heavily on the Supreme Court's decision in *Montana v. United States*, 450 U.S. 544 (1981), the EPA concluded that this was neither a plenary delegation of inherent authority to tribes to regulate all reservation waters, nor was it a standard that precluded tribal regulation of any non-member or any off-reservation activity. See 56 Fed. Reg. at 64877. Instead, the agency chose a case-by-case approach under which a tribe attempting to satisfy element (3) of the regulation would have to show that it possesses inherent authority over the waters in light of evolving case law. See 56 Fed. Reg. at 64878. There was no question that tribes could regulate the activities of tribal members, undertaken on the reservation, in order to protect the quality of reservation waters. In addition, the EPA concluded that "a tribe may regulate the activities of non-Indians on fee lands within its reservations when those activities threaten or have a direct effect on the political integrity, the economic security, or the health or welfare of the tribe." *Id.*

The EPA acknowledged that this will usually be an easy showing, based on "generalized findings" that water quality is related to human health and welfare. See *id.* Although the EPA stated that it would make a case-specific determination with regard to the scope of each tribe's authority, once a tribe has shown that impairment of the waters on the reservation would have a serious and substantial effect on the health and welfare of the tribe, the EPA presumes that there has been an adequate showing of inherent authority. *Id.* at 64879.

B. The Mole Lake Band and its Application For TAS Status

The waters at issue in this case are lakes and streams adjacent to or surrounded by the reservation of the Sokaogon Chippewa Community, also known as the Mole Lake Band of Lake Superior Chippewa Indians (the Band), located in northeastern Wisconsin. The Mole Lake reservation is unusual in two respects. First, the Band is heavily reliant on the availability of the water resources within the reservation for food, fresh water, medicines, and raw materials. In particular, Rice Lake, the largest body of water on the reservation, is a prime source of wild rice, which serves as a significant dietary and economic resource for the Band. Second, all of the 1,850 acres within the reservation are held in trust by the United States for the tribe. None of the land within the reservation is controlled or owned in fee by non-members of the tribe.

In August 1994, the Band applied for TAS status under the Act. Wisconsin opposed the application, arguing that it was sovereign over all of the navigable waters in the state, including those on the reservation, and that its sovereignty precluded any tribal regulation. Nevertheless, after elaborate administrative proceedings, on September 29, 1995, the EPA approved the Band's application, finding that the tribe had satisfied all of the requirements of 40 C.F.R. § 131.8, including the necessary demonstration of its inherent authority over all water resources on the reservation. In keeping with its earlier positions, the EPA noted that the inherent authority question did not turn on who had title to the land underneath the waters.

This grant of TAS status alarmed the State of Wisconsin, which saw it as both an affront to the state's sovereignty and, more pragmatically, as an action with the potential to throw a wrench into the state's planned construction of a huge zinc-copper sulfide mine on the Wolf River, upstream from Rice Lake. Concerned about its loss of authority over certain territory within its outer boundaries and worried that the tribal water standards might limit the activities of the mine by prohibiting some or all of the discharge from the mine, Wisconsin filed this action in district court on January 25, 1996, reiterating its challenge to the EPA's grant of TAS status to the Band. (The United States and the EPA waived immunity under 5 U.S.C. § 702.) The state's case raises a fundamental challenge to the TAS grant; the relief it seeks is outright revocation of the grant, rather than mere accommodation for any particular project. We are therefore satisfied that the issue is ripe now and need not await the Band's promulgation of specific water quality standards. If Wisconsin is right, it is entitled to have the EPA's creation of a state-like entity within its borders voided — an action that lies within the power of the court. . . .

In April 1999, the district court upheld the TAS grant, finding that the EPA's determination that a tribe could regulate all water within the reservation, regardless of ownership, was a reasonable interpretation of the relevant statutes and regulations. Wisconsin now appeals.

II

. . . We should uphold the agency's determination as long as it considered relevant data under the correct legal standards and offered a satisfactory explanation for its actions. Moreover, the EPA here has interpreted the statute by promulgating formal regulations, using plenary notice-and-comment procedures, and then implementing its rule with respect to the Band through a formal process in which the state was entitled to be heard. Its regulations and subsequent decision are therefore entitled to deference. . . .

Wisconsin is challenging the EPA's findings only with respect to the third requirement for TAS status — the demonstration of the tribe's inherent authority to regulate water quality within the borders of the reservation. . . .

. . . Wisconsin argues that the tribe does not have authority over the water resources on the reservation because the state has ownership of the underlying lake beds. We will assume for the purposes of this appeal that, pursuant to the Equal

Footing Doctrine, the state does indeed have title to the lake beds within the reservation.

This court has indeed held that, in some situations, state ownership of lake beds may restrict a tribe's authority to regulate the waters running over those beds. In *Wisconsin v. Baker*, 698 F.2d 1323, 1335 (7th Cir. 1983), we found that, because the State of Wisconsin held title to the underlying lake beds in a reservation, the Chippewa Band was precluded from restricting hunting and fishing in the reservation waters.

But contrary to Wisconsin's assertions, *Baker* does not dispose of this case. Most importantly, *Baker* did not involve a particular statute under which Congress specified that tribes would be entitled to be treated as states under particular circumstances, and both Congress and the responsible agency outlined the regulatory authority tribes were to exercise. . . .

We find pertinent instead a number of legal principles all of which support the EPA's determination that a state's title to a lake bed does not in itself exempt the waters from all outside regulation. First, "the power of Congress to regulate commerce among the states involves the control of the navigable waters of the United States." *Coyle v. Smith*, 221 U.S. 559, 573 (1911). This power has not been eroded in any way by the Equal Footing Doctrine cases, which "involved only the shores of and lands beneath navigable waters. [The doctrine] cannot be accepted as limiting the broad powers of the United States to regulate navigable waters under the Commerce Clause." *Arizona v. California*, 373 U.S. 546, 597–98 (1963). . . .

The breadth of federal authority over Indian affairs is equally well-established: "The Constitution vests the Federal Government with exclusive authority over relations with Indian tribes." *Montana v. Blackfeet Tribe*, 471 U.S. 759, 764 (1985); *United States v. Wheeler*, 435 U.S. 313, 319 (1978) ("Congress has plenary authority to legislate for the Indian tribes in all matters."); U.S. Const., Art. I, § 8, cl. 3. In fact, in the absence of tribal TAS status, the EPA and not the State of Wisconsin might well be the proper authority to administer Clean Water Act programs for the reservation, because state laws may usually be applied to Indians on their reservations only if Congress so expressly provides. *See California v. Cabazon Band of Mission Indians*, 480 U.S. 202, 207 (1987).

Because the state does not contend that its ownership of the beds would preclude the federal government from regulating the waters within the reservation, it cannot now complain about the federal government allowing tribes to do so. It was reasonable for the EPA to determine that ownership of the waterbeds did not preclude federally approved regulation of the quality of the water, and we uphold that determination. . . .

Finally, Wisconsin argues that the Band did not make the required showing of authority over those activities potentially affected by its imposition of water quality standards. Because the EPA has determined that, unlike the Clean Air Act, the Clean Water Act is not an express delegation of power to tribes, see 56 Fed. Reg. at 64880, the EPA requires tribes to show that they already possessed inherent authority over the activities undoubtedly affected by the water regulations. EPA regulations allow a tribe to establish this authority by showing that impairment of the reservation's waters would affect "the political integrity, the economic security, or the health or welfare of the tribe." 56 Fed. Reg. at 64877.

This regulatory language tracks the Supreme Court's decision in *Montana v. United States, supra,* in which the Court recognized the general rule that "the inherent sovereign powers of an Indian tribe do not extend to the activities of nonmembers of the tribe," 450 U.S. at 565, but went on to hold that "[a] tribe may also retain inherent power to exercise civil authority over the conduct of non-Indians on fee lands within its reservation when that conduct threatens or has some direct effect on the political integrity, the economic security, or the health or welfare of the tribe." *Id.* at 566. The regulations also track the more recent Supreme Court language in *Strate v. A-1 Contractors,* 520 U.S. 438 (1997), by noting that authority is usually proper because "water quality management serves the purpose of protecting public health and safety, which is a core governmental function, whose exercise is critical to self-government." 56 Fed. Reg. at 64879. . . .

Once a tribe is given TAS status, it has the power to require upstream off-reservation dischargers, conducting activities that may be economically valuable to the state (*e.g.,* zinc and copper mining), to make sure that their activities do not result in contamination of the downstream on-reservation waters (assuming for the sake of argument that the reservation standards are more stringent than those the state is imposing on the upstream entity). *See Albuquerque v. Browner,* 97 F.3d 415 (10th Cir. 1996). Such compliance may impose higher compliance costs on the upstream company, or in the extreme case it might have the effect of prohibiting the discharge or the activities altogether. This is a classic extraterritorial effect, which Wisconsin argues is impermissible and takes this case beyond the scope of *Montana,* which concerned only tribal authority over non-member activities on reservation fee lands.

But this is not the only situation where upstream and downstream users may have different standards and some accommodation is necessary. Wisconsin's argument could be made equally if the downstream regulator were Illinois, yet in that case the need for the two states to coordinate their standards, or for the upstream company to comply with the more stringent rules, would be clear. In fact, Congress anticipated this very problem in the statute, and it had the following to say about it:

> The Administrator shall, in promulgating such regulations [for TAS status], consult affected States sharing common water bodies and provide a mechanism for the resolution of any unreasonable consequences that may arise as a result of differing water quality standards that may be set by States and Indian tribes located on common bodies of water. Such mechanism shall provide for explicit consideration of relevant factors including, but not limited to, the effects of differing water quality permit requirements on upstream and downstream dischargers, economic impacts, and present and historical uses and quality of the waters subject to such standards. Such mechanism should provide for the avoidance of such unreasonable consequences in a manner consistent with the objective of this chapter.

33 U.S.C. § 1377(e).

The EPA has developed the mechanism called for by the statute, which allows it to mediate conflicting interests when a tribe's standards differ from those of a state. See also 33 U.S.C. § 1341(a). In addition, once a tribe is given TAS status, the Act gives it the same right as that given to states to object to permits issued for upstream off-reservation activities. See 56 Fed. Reg. at 64887. In deciding whether to issue a permit for discharge within a state that may violate the water quality standards of a downstream tribe, the EPA may ask the parties to engage in mediation or arbitration, in which the decision-maker and the EPA administrator, who has the final authority over the issuance of the permit, will consider such factors as "the effects of differing water quality permit requirements on upstream and downstream dischargers, economic impacts, and present and historical uses and quality of the waters subject to such standards." 33 U.S.C. § 1377(e). The EPA may then ask the tribe to issue a temporary variance from its standards for the particular discharge or may ask the state to provide additional water pollution controls. See 54 Fed. Reg. at 39099–101; 56 Fed. Reg. at 64885–89; 40 C.F.R. §§ 121.11 through 121.16. This mechanism, rather than a futile effort to avoid extraterritorial effects, is the way both Congress and the agency sought to accommodate the inevitable differences that would arise.

We say "inevitable" because activities located outside the regulating entity (here the reservation), and the resulting discharges to which those activities can lead, can and often will have "serious and substantial" effects on the health and welfare of the downstream state or reservation. There is no case that expressly rejects an application of *Montana* to off-reservation activities that have significant effects within the reservation, and it would be exceedingly hard to say that the EPA's interpretation is contrary to law in the face of the express recognition of this issue and the choice of a solution in the statute itself. It was reasonable for the EPA to determine that, since the Supreme Court has held that a tribe has inherent authority over activities having a serious effect on the health of the tribe, this authority is not defeated even if it exerts some regulatory force on off-reservation activities.

Finally, we think Wisconsin exaggerates the power of the tribe to veto upstream discharge activities. The tribe cannot impose any water quality standards or take any action that goes beyond the federal statute or the EPA's power. To the contrary, the EPA supervises all standards and permits. Far from allowing a tribe to veto a state permit, granting TAS status to tribes simply allows the tribes some say regarding those standards and permits. It is quite possible that, in particular cases, perhaps through the vehicle of the statutory mediation mechanism, the EPA may require the tribe's more stringent standards to give way to upstream discharge and development. Whether the tribe or the state ultimately "wins" in the dispute, it is the EPA, not the tribe or the state, that has the ultimate authority to decide whether or not to issue a permit.

Because the Band has demonstrated that its water resources are essential to its survival, it was reasonable for the EPA, in line with the purposes of the Clean Water Act and the principles of *Montana*, to allow the tribe to regulate water quality on the reservation, even though that power entails some authority over off-reservation activities. Since a state has the power to require upstream states to comply with its water quality standards, to interpret the statutes to deny that power to tribes because of some kind of formal view of authority or sovereignty would treat tribes as second-class citizens. Nothing in § 1377(e) indicates that Congress authorized any such hierarchy. Particularly in light of the deference we owe to the EPA's decisions here, we see nothing that would justify our setting aside the agency's action.

III

We conclude that the EPA's grant of TAS status to the Band is not arbitrary, unreasonable, or contrary to law and we therefore AFFIRM the district court's judgment. We note once again in closing that the EPA's decision in each case seeking TAS status is fact-specific. In this case, both parties conceded that the waters within the Band's reservation are very important to the Band's economic and physical existence. Additionally, the reservation here is unusual in that there are no parcels of fee land within the reservation owned by non-members of the tribe. We have no occasion to say whether, on a different set of facts, the EPA might extend the notion of a tribe's "inherent authority" to affect off-reservation activities so far as to go beyond the standards of the statute or the regulations. If it ever arises, that will be another case, for another day.

NOTES ON TRIBAL ENVIRONMENTAL CONTROLS AFFECTING OFF-RESERVATION DEVELOPMENT

1. **Purposes of Environmental Controls:** The Mole Lake community wanted clean water for two distinct but interrelated purposes: to carry out traditional subsistence and ceremonial activities, and to maintain an important form of economic development — harvesting and selling wild rice. A similar convergence of goals of cultural maintenance and economic development can occur when a tribe's primary source of revenue is tourism or agriculture. *See, e.g., City of Albuquerque v. Browner*, 97 F.3d 415 (10th Cir. 1996) (Pueblo of Isleta's strict water quality standards, designed to protect agriculture and ceremonies, may limit City of Albuquerque's power to discharge pollution into Rio Grande River). Does it matter for purposes of legal analysis why a Native nation has established environmental standards beyond federal minimum requirements? Should it matter? What if a tribe is attempting to control upstream users in order to engage in polluting activities of its own?

2. **Comparing the Clean Water Act with the Clean Air Act:** As reflected in *Wisconsin v. EPA*, the EPA interprets the Clean Water Act as not delegating federal jurisdiction to tribes. Rather, EPA views the "treatment as a state" language of the Act as allowing the agency to delegate authority to tribes that can demonstrate their governing power over their territory. Furthermore, EPA has made it relatively easy for Indian nations to make such showings with respect to nonmember-owned fee lands by treating water quality as essential to the health and welfare of the tribe.

In contrast, EPA understands the 1990 "treatment as a state" amendment to the Clean Air Act, 42 U.S.C. § 7601(d)(2)(B), as a direct delegation of federal power to tribes, and the D.C. Circuit has upheld this interpretation in *Arizona Public Service*

Co. v. Environmental Protection Agency, 211 F.3d 1280 (D.C. Cir. 2000). The most important operational difference between these two interpretations is that tribes seeking TAS status under the Clean Air Act do not need to justify their jurisdiction over nonmember-owned fee lands. Thus tribes are free to set air quality standards higher than federal minima and to fashion Tribal Implementation Plans under the Act, regardless of the pattern of land ownership within their communities.

EPA has rested its different treatment of the Clean Water and Clean Air Acts on differences in language and legislative history. Language in the Clean Air Act, which does not appear in the Clean Water Act, strongly suggests that Congress viewed all parts of a reservation as "within the area of the tribal government's jurisdiction." Legislative history, especially different versions of the Clean Air Act amendments introduced into the Congress, supported this implication. In the absence of such evidence for delegation in the Clean Water Act, EPA concluded that the legislative history of the Clean Water Act was "ambiguous and inconclusive." *Amendments to the Water Quality Standards Regulation That Pertain to Standards on Indian Reservations,* 56 Fed. Reg. 64,876, 64,880 (1991) (codified at 40 C.F.R. pt. 131). However, at least one federal court has been willing to travel further on a limb, commenting in dicta that "statutory language [in the Clean Water Act] seems to indicate plainly that Congress did intend to delegate . . . authority to tribes." *State of Montana v. EPA,* 941 F. Supp. 945, 951 (D. Mont. 1996). Given the ease with which tribes are able to satisfy the EPA's criteria for delegation under the Clean Water Act, does the difference in interpretation have significant practical or legal consequences?

3. Other Methods for Protecting Tribal Environmental Quality from Non-Indian Development: In addition to regulations and enforcement under the auspices of federal environmental laws, Native nations may seek to protect their environments from outside polluters through citizen suits in federal court under those federal laws, or through what are known as toxic tort actions. These other options are described at length in Allan Kanner, Ryan Casey & Barrett Ristroph, *New Opportunities for Native American Tribes to Pursue Environmental and Natural Resource Claims,* 14 Duke Envnmt'l L. & Pol'y F. 155 (2003).

Chapter 6

TRIBAL RIGHTS TO LAND AND CULTURAL RESOURCES

> God created this Indian country and it was like He spread out a big blanket. He put the Indians on it. They were created here in this country, truly and honestly, and that was the time this river started to run. Then God created fish in this river and put deer in these mountains and made laws through which has come the increase of fish and game. Then the Creator gave us Indians life; we awakened and as soon as we saw the game and the fish we knew they were made for us. . . . I was not brought from a foreign country and did not come here. I was put here by the Creator.

Chief Meninock, Yakama Nation, *Testimony of Chief Meninock (Yakama) During a 1915 Trial for Violating a Washington State Code on Salmon Fishing, in* GREAT DOCUMENTS IN AMERICAN INDIAN HISTORY 297–98 (W. Moquin & C. Van Doren eds., 1973).

> The head chief told us that there was not a family in that whole Nation that had not a home of its own. There was not a pauper in that Nation, and the Nation did not owe a dollar. It built its own capitol . . . and it built its schools and its hospitals. Yet the defect of the system was apparent. They had got as far as they can go, because they own their land in common . . . and under that there is no enterprise to make your home any better than that of your neighbors. There is no selfishness, which is at the bottom of civilization. Till this people will consent to give up their lands, and divide them among their citizens so that each can own the land he cultivates, they will not make much more progress.

Sen. Henry M. Dawes, following a visit to the Cherokee Nation, 1885, *quoted in* Kenneth H. Bobroff, *Retelling Allotment: Indian Property Rights and the Myth of Common Ownership*, 54 VAND. L. REV. 1559, 1564 (2001).

Chief Meninock's words describe a world in which the Native people, the land, and its resources interact under a Divine plan created for a particular place on earth. The people who are "indigenous" to the land — placed there by the Creator — exist under the same set of laws that governs all other living things, which results in order, balance, and abundance. This cultural understanding of land is fundamentally important to comprehending the conflicts over land, sovereignty, and resources that characterize much of federal Indian law.

While Native nations differ from one another in their social and cultural organization, there is a striking similarity among their traditional attitudes toward the land and environment. Indigenous peoples' land ethics developed in accordance with these values. As Professor Tsosie has pointed out,

[I]ndigenous environmental belief systems share a number of features revolving around a cyclical and comprehensive understanding of the environment. . . . Under indigenous systems of environmental ethics, humans are part of nature and the secular is part of spiritual life: "Aboriginal land ethics reflect this sense of unity by emphasizing balance and sustainability." [These land ethics share] several important aspects: a perception of the earth as an animate being; a belief that humans are in a kinship system with other living things; a perception of the land as essential to the identity of the people; and a concept of reciprocity and balance that extends to relationships among humans, including future generations, and between humans and the natural world.

For Indian peoples, who traditionally interpreted their relationship with the land and with future generations as holistic, cyclical, and permanent, sustainability was the natural result, if not the conscious goal, of deeply rooted environmental ethics and traditional land-based economies. Many contemporary indigenous peoples thus advocate a Native concept of sustainability that "means ensuring the survival of the people, the land and the resources for seven generations."

Rebecca Tsosie, *Tribal Environmental Policy in an Era of Self-Determination: The Role of Ethics, Economics, and Traditional Ecological Knowledge*, 21 VT. L. REV. 225, 286–87 (1996).

However, as Senator Dawes's statement reflects, European peoples arrived in North America with a normatively different set of land ethics, which characterized the land as a material resource to be exploited for economic and political gain. This different land ethic, as well as the property law regime which supported it, precluded the European settlers from comprehending the systems of property law that prevailed within Native nations.

Native peoples have continually battled the common Western misperception that they lacked "property" rights, when, in reality they hold concepts that are normatively distinct from the analogous European constructs of these concepts. For example, like Senator Dawes, outsiders routinely described the Indians' property systems as communal, when in fact the systems were far more complex. In a comprehensive analysis of tribal property regimes, Professor Kenneth Bobroff notes that within the broad understanding of land as a sacred gift, Native nations as a group manifest nearly every element of Anglo-American private property except the right to alienate land to those outside the nation. Kenneth H. Bobroff, *Retelling Allotment: Indian Property Rights and the Myth of Common Ownership*, 54 VAND. L. REV. 1559, 1590 (2001). For example, the potlatch, a ceremonial giving away of material goods, served to resolve disputes over ownership of fishing sites, with the party who gave away or destroyed the most goods becoming entitled to the spot. Rights to use specific tracts, to exclude others, to allow access, to inherit, and to transfer can be found in tribal property systems. Interests comparable to leases, easements, life estates, licenses, and condominiums are also present. *See also* Stacy L. Leeds, *The Burning of Blackacre: A Step Toward Reclaiming Tribal Property Law*, 10 KAN. J.L. & PUB. POL'Y 491 (2001) (discussing the Cherokee conception of property rights). When Native peoples told the Europeans and later Americans that land is not a commodity to be bought and sold, the outsiders leapt to the conclusion that Indians had no systems of private property at all. Tragically and ironically, such systems of property were denounced by outsiders as proof of the wastefulness of the tribes who practiced them.

For land-hungry settlers, this view of Indians' relationship to the land afforded a convenient rationalization for colonization and appropriation. To an Anglo-American legal system that venerated private property, forcibly displacing existing property holders was problematic. But if the claims of the indigenous peoples could be cast as something short of true property rights, the dilemma would disappear. As this chapter will demonstrate, the accommodation has not always been easy. Federal Indian law developed as a means of asserting federal control over the definition and administration of Native property, justifying dispossession and instituting concepts largely modeled after Western European rather than Native notions of property. Nonetheless, the nagging sense that peoples were wrongfully displaced continues, however erratically, to find its way into federal legislation and legal decisions.

This chapter is devoted to an understanding of how federal Indian law has defined the property rights of Native peoples and how Native people have responded. It focuses on land and cultural resources, saving hunting, fishing, gathering, and water rights for Chapter 7. To understand the tribal-federal relationship with respect to property, it is useful to consider Laura Underkuffler-Freund's definition of "property right":

> Property rights are, by nature, social rights; they embody how we, as a society, have chosen to reward the claims of some people to finite and critical goods, and to deny the claims to the same goods by others. Try as we might to separate this right from choice, conflict, and vexing social questions, it cannot be done.

Laura S. Underkuffler-Freund, *Property: A Special Right*, 71 NOTRE DAME L. REV. 1033, 1046 (1996). Under this definition, the institution of property orders the relationships among people in a society with respect to finite resources. This appears to be a rational way to order such relationships among the individuals who collectively comprise a unitary society. In such a society, individuals may rationally order their claims according to prevailing social ideals, such as equal access, distributive justice, and fairness. However, this understanding is highly problematic when applied to the rights of distinctive *peoples*, who preexisted the formation of the society and who were involuntarily annexed (as sovereign groups) into that society through acts of colonialism. This question of intercultural justice is at the heart of this relationship, and the way we conceptualize the institution of property can continue to strip Native peoples of their lands and other resources, and consequently their autonomy. *See* Rebecca Tsosie, *Land, Culture, and Community: Reflections on Native Sovereignty and Property in America*, 34 IND. L. REV. 1291, 1300–01 (2001). For an account of the Supreme Court's jurisprudence surrounding Indian lands and property rights, *see* Angela R. Riley, *The History of Native American Lands and the Supreme Court*, 38 J. SUP. CT. HIST. 369 (2013). We turn now to that discussion.

A. TRIBAL PROPERTY INTERESTS

1. Aboriginal Title

Review *Johnson v. M'Intosh*, 21 U.S. (8 Wheat.) 543 (1823), presented in Ch. 1, Sec. C.1. In that case, two non-Indians claimed title to the same land, one tracing his claim to a direct conveyance from the Illinois and Piankashaw Indians, the other basing his claim on a patent from the United States, which had procured the land through a subsequent treaty with those nations. Chief Justice Marshall held that under the Doctrine of Discovery, the United States, as successor to England, had acquired the preemptive right to acquire tribal land by purchase or conquest. Thus, the title granted by a tribe to a private individual could not prevail over a patent from the United States. In the course of that decision, the Court stated that "the principle which has been supposed to be recognised by all European governments, from the first settlement of America," is that "[t]he absolute ultimate title has been considered as acquired by discovery, subject only to the Indian title of occupancy, which title the discoverers possessed the exclusive right of acquiring." The Court analogized this "Indian title of occupancy" to a lease, and declared it just as effectual to preclude ejectment. The Indians had their own view, exemplified by the Creek Council's statement in 1824 that although they knew that "we now hold our land by right of occupancy only," they still considered themselves "the original proprietors of the soil as an inheritance left to us by our forefathers." Little Prince et al. to unidentified federal officials, 11 December 1824, document TCC181, *Southeastern Native American Documents, 1730–1842, available at* http://dlg.galileo.usg.edu/CollectionsA-Z/zlna_information.html?Welcome.

UNITED STATES EX REL. HUALPAI INDIANS v. SANTA FE PACIFIC RAILROAD CO.
United States Supreme Court
314 U.S. 339 (1941)

Mr. Justice Douglas delivered the opinion of the Court.

This is a suit brought by the United States, in its own right and as guardian of the Indians of the Walapai (Hualpai) Tribe in Arizona (28 U.S.C. § 41(1), § 24 Judicial Code) to enjoin respondent from interfering with the possession and occupancy by the Indians of certain land in northwestern Arizona. Respondent claims full title to the lands in question under the grant to its predecessor, the Atlantic and Pacific Railroad Co., provided for in the Act of July 27, 1866, 14 Stat. 292. The bill sought to establish that respondent's rights under the grant of 1866 are subject to the Indians' right of occupancy both inside and outside their present reservation which was established by the Executive Order of President Arthur, January 4, 1883. The bill consists of two causes of action — the first relating to lands inside, and the second, to lands outside, that reservation. The bill prayed, *inter alia*, that title be quieted and that respondent "account for all rents, issues and profits derived from the leasing, renting or use of the lands subject to said right of occupancy" by the Indians. Respondent moved to dismiss on the ground that the facts alleged were "insufficient to constitute a valid cause of action in equity." The

District Court granted that motion [and the] Court of Appeals affirmed. We granted the petition for certiorari because of the importance of the problems raised in the administration of the Indian laws and the land grants.

Sec. 2 of the Act of July 27, 1866, the Act under which respondent's title to the lands in question derived, provided: "The United States shall extinguish, as rapidly as may be consistent with public policy and the welfare of the Indians, and only by their voluntary cession, the Indian title to all lands falling under the operation of this act and acquired in the donation to the road named in the act."

Basic to the present causes of action is the theory that the lands in question were the ancestral home of the Walapais, that such occupancy constituted "Indian title" within the meaning of § 2 of the 1866 Act, which the United States agreed to extinguish, and that in absence of such extinguishment the grant to the railroad "conveyed the fee subject to this right of occupancy." *Buttz v. Northern Pacific Railroad*, 119 U.S. 55, 66. The Circuit Court of Appeals concluded that the United States had never recognized such possessory rights of Indians within the Mexican Cession[1] and that in absence of such recognition the Walapais had no such right good against grantees of the United States.

Occupancy necessary to establish aboriginal possession is a question of fact to be determined as any other question of fact. If it were established as a fact that the lands in question were, or were included in, the ancestral home of the Walapais in the sense that they constituted definable territory occupied exclusively by the Walapais (as distinguished from lands wandered over by many tribes), then the Walapais had "Indian title" which, unless extinguished, survived the railroad grant of 1866.

"Unquestionably it has been the policy of the Federal Government from the beginning to respect the Indian right of occupancy, which could only be interfered with or determined by the United States." *Cramer v. United States*, 261 U.S. 219, 227. This policy was first recognized in [*Johnson v. M'Intosh*] and has been repeatedly reaffirmed. [*E.g., Worcester v. Georgia.*] As stated in *Mitchel v. United States*, [9 Pet. 711,] 746, the Indian "right of occupancy is considered as sacred as the fee simple of the whites." Whatever may have been the rights of the Walapais under Spanish law, the *Cramer* case assumed that lands within the Mexican Cession were not excepted from the policy to respect Indian right of occupancy. Though the *Cramer* case involved the problem of individual Indian occupancy, this Court stated that such occupancy was not to be treated differently from "the original nomadic tribal occupancy." (p. 227.) Perhaps the assumption that aboriginal possession would be respected in the Mexican Cession was, like the generalizations in *Johnson v. M'Intosh*, *supra*, not necessary for the narrow holding of the case. But such generalizations have been so often and so long repeated as respects land under the prior sovereignty of the various European nations, including Spain, that, like other rules governing titles to property they should now be considered no longer open. Furthermore, treaties negotiated with Indian tribes, wholly or partially within the Mexican Cession, for delimitation of their occupancy rights or for the settlement and adjustment of their boundaries, constitute clear recognition that no different

---

[1] [2] See Treaty of Guadalupe Hidalgo, 9 Stat. 922.

policy as respects aboriginal possession obtained in this area than in other areas. Certainly it would take plain and unambiguous action to deprive the Walapais of the benefits of that policy. For it was founded on the desire to maintain just and peaceable relations with Indians. The reasons for its application to other tribes are no less apparent in case of the Walapais, a savage tribe which in early days caused the military no end of trouble.

Nor is it true, as respondent urges, that a tribal claim to any particular lands must be based upon a treaty, statute, or other formal government action. As stated in the *Cramer* case, "The fact that such right of occupancy finds no recognition in any statute or other formal governmental action is not conclusive." 261 U.S. at 229.

Extinguishment of Indian title based on aboriginal possession is of course a different matter. The power of Congress in that regard is supreme. The manner, method and time of such extinguishment raise political, not justiciable, issues. As stated by Chief Justice Marshall in *Johnson v. M'Intosh, supra*, p. 586, "the exclusive right of the United States to extinguish" Indian title has never been doubted. And whether it be done by treaty, by the sword, by purchase, by the exercise of complete dominion adverse to the right of occupancy, or otherwise, its justness is not open to inquiry in the courts. If the right of occupancy of the Walapais was not extinguished prior to the date of definite location of the railroad in 1872, then the respondent's predecessor took the fee subject to the encumbrance of Indian title. For on that date the title of respondent's predecessor attached as of July 27, 1866.

Certainly, prior to 1865 any right of occupancy of the Walapais to the lands in question was not extinguished; nor was the policy of respecting such Indian title changed. The Indian Trade and Intercourse Act of June 30, 1834, 4 Stat. 729, was extended over "the Indian tribes in the Territories of New Mexico and Utah" by § 7 of the Act of February 27, 1851, 9 Stat. 574, 587. The 1834 Act, which derived from the Act of July 22, 1790, 1 Stat. 137, made it an offense to drive stock to range or feed "on any land belonging to any Indian or Indian tribe, without the consent of such tribe" (§ 9); gave the superintendent of Indian affairs authority "to remove from the Indian country all persons found therein contrary to law" (§ 10); made it unlawful to settle on (any lands belonging, secured, or granted by treaty with the United States to any Indian tribe" (§ 11); and made invalid any conveyance of lands (from any Indian nation or tribe of Indians." (§ 12).

[In] the Act of March 3, 1865, 13 Stat. 541, 559, which provided:

> All that part of the public domain in the Territory of Arizona, lying west of a direct line from Half-Way Bend to Corner Rock on the Colorado River, containing about seventy-five thousand acres of land, shall be set apart for an Indian reservation for the Indians of said river and its tributaries.

It is plain that the Indians referred to included the Walapais. The suggestion for removing various Indian tribes in this area to a reservation apparently originated with a former Indian agent, Superintendent Poston, who was a Territorial Representative in Congress in 1865. His explanation on the floor of the House of the bill, which resulted in the creation of the 1865 reservation, indicates that he had called a council of the confederated tribes of the Colorado, including the Walapais, and had told them that "they should abandon" their lands and confine themselves to the place on the Colorado river which was later proposed for a reservation. He entered into no agreement with them nor did he propose a treaty. He merely stated that if elected to Congress he would try to get Congress to provide for them. As stated by the Commissioner of Indian Affairs in 1864, "Assuming that the Indians have a right of some kind to the soil, Mr. Poston's arrangement proposes a compromise with [them]."

We search the public records in vain for any clear and plain indication that Congress in creating the Colorado River reservation was doing more than making an offer to the Indians, including the Walapais, which it was hoped would be accepted as a compromise of a troublesome question. We find no indication that Congress by creating that reservation intended to extinguish all of the rights which the Walapais had in their ancestral home. That Congress could have effected such an extinguishment is not doubted. But an extinguishment cannot be lightly implied in view of the avowed solicitude of the Federal Government for the welfare of its Indian wards. As stated in *Choate v. Trapp*, 224 U.S. 665, 675, the rule of construction recognized without exception for over a century has been that "doubtful expressions, instead of being resolved in favor of the United States, are to be resolved in favor of a weak and defenseless people, who are wards of the nation, and dependent wholly upon its protection and good faith." Nor was there any plain intent or agreement on the part of the Walapais to abandon their ancestral lands if Congress would create a reservation. Furthermore, the Walapais did not accept the offer which Congress had tendered. In 1874 they were, however, forcibly removed to the Colorado River reservation on order from the Indian Department. But they left it in a body the next year. And it was decided "to allow them to remain in their old range during good behavior." They did thereafter remain in their old country and engaged in no hostilities against the whites. No further attempt was made to force them onto the Colorado River reservation, even though Congress had made various appropriations to defray the costs of locating the Arizona Indians in permanent abodes, including the Colorado River reservation. On these facts we conclude that the creation of the Colorado River reservation was, so far as the Walapais were concerned, nothing more than an abortive attempt to solve a perplexing problem. Their forcible removal in 1874 was not pursuant to any mandate of Congress. It was a high-handed endeavor to wrest from these Indians lands which Congress had never declared forfeited.[2] No forfeiture can be predicated on an unauthorized attempt to effect a forcible settlement on the reservation,

---

[2] [13] *See Walapai Papers*, [S. Doc. No. 273, 74th Cong., 2d Sess.,] p. 108. General Schofield reported on May 24, 1875, to the Adjutant General as follows:

"The Hualpai Indians have been our firm friends for many years, and our active allies whenever their services have been required against the hostile Apaches. In return for their fidelity they have been treated with great injustice and cruelty. They were forced to leave their homes in the mountains and go upon a reservation in the Colorado desert, where they have suffered from the extreme heat, to which they were unaccustomed, from disease, and from hunger."

"The injustice and bad faith shown by the government toward the Hualpais and the Indians which Gen'l. Crook had collected upon the Verde reservation are calculated to undo as far as possible the good work which Gen'l. Crook and his troops had accomplished with so much wisdom and gallantry. It is useless to attempt to disguise the fact that such treatment of the

unless we are to be insensitive to the high standards for fair dealing in light of which laws dealing with Indian rights have long been read. Certainly, a forced abandonment of their ancestral home was not a "voluntary cession" within the meaning of § 2 of the Act of July 27, 1866.

The situation was, however, quite different in 1881. Between 1875 and that date there were rather continuous suggestions for settling the Walapais on some reservation. In 1881 the matter came to a head. A majority of the tribe, "in council assembled," asked an officer of the United States Army in that region "to aid them and represent to the proper authorities" the following proposal:

> They say that in the country, over which they used to roam so free, the white men have appropriated all the water; that large numbers of cattle have been introduced and have rapidly increased during the past year or two; that in many places the water is fenced in and locked up; and they are driven from all waters. They say that the Railroad is now coming, which will require more water, and will bring more men who will take up all the small springs remaining. They urge that the following reservation be set aside for them while there is still time; that the land can never be of any great use to the Whites; that there are no mineral deposits upon it, as it has been thoroughly prospected; that there is little or no arable land; that the water is in such small quantities, and the country is so rocky and void of grass, that it would not be available for stock raising. I am credibly informed, and from my observations believe, the above facts to be true. I, therefore, earnestly recommend that the hereafter described Reservation be, at as early a date as practicable, set aside for them.

Pursuant to that recommendation, the military reservation was constituted on July 8, 1881, subject to the approval of the President. The Executive Order creating the Walapai Indian Reservation was signed by President Arthur on January 4, 1883. There was an indication that the Indians were satisfied with the proposed reservation. A few of them thereafter lived on the reservation; many of them did not. While suggestions recurred for the creation of a new and different reservation, this one was not abandoned. For a long time it remained unsurveyed. Cattlemen used it for grazing, and for some years the Walapais received little benefit from it. But in view of all of the circumstances, we conclude that its creation at the request of the Walapais and its acceptance by them amounted to a relinquishment of any tribal claims to lands which they might have had outside that reservation and that relinquishment was tantamount to an extinguishment by "voluntary cession" within the meaning of § 2 of the Act of July 27, 1866. The lands were fast being populated. The Walapais saw their old domain being preempted. They wanted a reservation while there was still time to get one. That solution had long seemed desirable in view of recurring tensions between the settlers and the Walapais. [Given] this historical setting, it cannot now be fairly implied that tribal rights of the Walapais in lands outside the reservation were preserved. [Consequently,] acquiescence in that arrangement must be deemed to have been a relinquishment of tribal rights in lands outside the reservation and notoriously claimed by others.

Indians is in violation of the just and humane policy prescribed by the President and a disgrace to any civilized country."

On January 23, 1941, the date of the filing of this petition for certiorari, respondent quitclaimed to the United States [the lands it claimed under the 1866 Act] within the Walapai Indian Reservation. Since the decree below must stand as to the second cause of action and since by virtue of the quitclaim deeds the United States has received all the lands to which the first cause of action relates, the decree will not be reversed. It is apparent, however, that it must be modified so as to permit the accounting as respects lands in the first cause of action. It does not appear whether those lands were included in the ancestral home of the Walapais in the sense that they were in whole or in part occupied exclusively by them or whether they were lands wandered over by many tribes. As we have said, occupancy necessary to establish aboriginal possession is a question of fact. The United States is entitled to an accounting as respects any or all of the lands in the first cause of action which the Walapais did in fact occupy exclusively from time immemorial.[3] Such an accounting is not precluded by the Act of February 20, 1925, 43 Stat. 954, which authorized the Secretary of the Interior "to accept reconveyances to the Government of privately owned and State school lands and relinquishments of any valid filings, under the homestead laws, or of other valid claims within the Walapai Indian Reservation." The implication is that there may be some land within the reservation that is not subject to Indian occupancy. But that Act certainly cannot be taken as an extinguishment of any and all Indian title that did exist or as a repeal by implication of § 2 of the Act of July 27, 1866, requiring such extinguishment by "voluntary cession." It was passed so that lands "retained for Indian purposes may be consolidated and held in a solid area so far as may be possible." Such statements by the Secretary of the Interior as that "title to the odd-numbered sections" was in the respondent do not estop the United States from maintaining this suit. For they could not deprive the Indians of their rights any more than could the unauthorized leases in *Cramer v. United States, supra*.

Hence, an accounting as respects such lands in the reservation which can be proved to have been occupied by the Walapais from time immemorial can be had. To the extent that the decree below precludes such proof and accounting, it will be modified. And as so modified, it is

Affirmed.

NOTES ON ABORIGINAL TITLE

1. **Justifications for Taking Indian Land:** Professor Robert Williams, Jr. has produced a sustained study of the Doctrine of Discovery, revealing its roots in medieval European legal discourse that denied the humanity of "normatively divergent" peoples, including the Irish and Arabs. ROBERT A. WILLIAMS, JR., THE AMERICAN INDIAN IN WESTERN LEGAL THOUGHT: THE DISCOURSES OF CONQUEST (1990). *See also*, ROBERT A. WILLIAMS, JR., SAVAGE ANXIETIES: THE INVENTION OF WESTERN CIVILIZATION (2012). For example, 10 years after *Johnson v. M'Intosh*, United States

---

[3] [24] In case of any lands in the reservation which were not part of the ancestral home of the Walapais and which had passed to the railroad under the 1866 Act, the railroad's title would antedate the creation of the reservation in 1883 and hence not be subject to the incumbrance of Indian title.

Supreme Court Justice Joseph Story, a contemporary of Chief Justice Marshall, wrote:

> [A]s between themselves, [European nations] treated the dominion and title of territory as resulting from the priority of discovery. . . . The title of the Indians was not treated as a right of property and dominion, but as a mere right of occupancy. As infidels, heathens, and savages, they were not allowed to possess the prerogatives belonging to absolute, sovereign, and independent nations. The territory over which they wandered, and which they used for this temporary and fugitive purposes, was, in respect to Christians, deemed as if it were inhabited only by brute animals.

JOSEPH STORY, COMMENTARIES § 152 (1833).

As a factual claim about Indian land use, Story's statement, echoing similar language in *Johnson v. M'Intosh*, is patently incorrect. Many Native nations throughout the eastern United States, the Midwest, and parts of the Southwest engaged in agriculture. As an assertion about the legal implications of Indian possession and use, the Story excerpt is inconsistent with the English common law of its day and earlier American legal practice as well. In an examination of the common law roots of the doctrine of aboriginal title, Professor Kent McNeil, has shown that English common law presumed that a person in factual occupation had possession and, absent proof to the contrary (*e.g.*, an act of expropriation or proof of wrongful possession), valid title as well. KENT MCNEIL, COMMON LAW ABORIGINAL TITLE 298 (1989). Indeed, throughout the eighteenth century American law treated Indians as the owners of their lands in fee simple, with the government holding no more than a preemptive or exclusive right of purchase. As Washington's Secretary of War, Henry Knox explained, Indians "possess the right of the soil." McNeil contends that *Johnson v. M'Intosh* "ignored common law principles and constructed a vague theory of Indian title on the basis of doubtful premises drawn to some extent from his own perceptions of international law. In effect, what Marshall did was invent a body of law which was virtually without precedent." *Id.* at 301.

In a study of how the Indians lost their land, Professor Stuart Banner suggests instead that during the period from the ratification of the United States Constitution to *Johnson v. M'Intosh*, American conceptions of Indian property underwent a transformation, fed by the stereotype of Indians as hunters rather than farmers, as well as by a growing market in preemption rights (that is rights to buy land once Indian claims were extinguished by treaty). By the end of this period, the generally accepted view that Indians owned their lands in fee simple until they were purchased by the government gave way to the view that Indians had only a right of occupancy, with fee title in the original thirteen states or the federal government. *See* STUART BANNER, HOW THE INDIANS LOST THEIR LAND (2005). Alternately, scholar Michael Blumm contends that the holding of *Johnson v. M'Intosh* has been misinterpreted and should be understood as affirming Indian tribes' fee simple absolute title in their lands. Michael C. Blumm, *Why Aboriginal Title Is a Fee Simple Absolute*, 15 LEWIS & CLARK L. REV. 975 (2011).

Scholarship suggests that the government's right of preemption and the later doctrine of aboriginal title also served an economic function for the European and American governments engaged in land transactions with the tribes. Indeed, it seems fair to say that the doctrine helped the United States to carry out land purchases rather than outright seizures as a means of acquiring land. As discussed in Ch. 1, Sec. C, *Johnson v. M'Intosh* afforded the United States monopsonist power in negotiating with Native nations over land transfers. Because tribes could deal only with the United States, and not with competing individual land speculators, prices remained artificially low. *See* Eric Kades, *The Dark Side Of Efficiency: Johnson v. M'Intosh and the Expropriation of American Indian Lands*, 148 U. Pa. L. Rev. 1065 (2000).

For further discussion of the justifications offered for taking Indian lands, see Francis Jennings, The Invasion of America (1975); Bernard W. Sheehan, *Indian-White Relations in Early America, A Review Essay*, Third Series, 26 (1969); Wilcomb E. Washburn, *The Moral and Legal Justifications for Dispossessing the Indians, in* Seventeenth Century America 15–32 (J. Smith ed., 1959); Robert J. Miller, *American Indians, the Doctrine of Discovery, and Manifest Destiny*, 11 Wyo. L. Rev. 329 (2011). Professor Williams has suggested that an alternative, indigenous vision of law to govern the property and other relations between the West and non-Western peoples can be found in the Haudenosaunee's Gus-Wen-Tah, or Two Row Wampum. The origins and practical implications of this vision are presented in Robert A. Williams, Jr., Linking Arms Together: American Indian Treaty Visions of Law and Peace 1600–1800 (1997).

2. Incidents of the Tribal Right of Occupancy: *Johnson v. M'Intosh* invalidated a particular grant of land by a tribe, but not because the Tribe lacked the legal right to alienate its lands to non-Indians. The Court expressly acknowledged that the internal law of the tribe could authorize such transfers. Furthermore, the Court decided soon thereafter that grants by tribes to non-Indians would be valid if ratified by the United States. *Mitchel v. United States*, 34 U.S. (9 Pet.) 711, 758–59 (1835). While the right of occupancy and its limitation on alienation provided the United States with an advantageous negotiating position, as discussed above, it also could be viewed as a mechanism for preserving the separateness and integrity of Indian territory for purposes of tribal self-government. Furthermore, it established a tribal federal relationship regarding land status that precluded state intervention. Should Native nations therefore have welcomed the decision? *See* Howard R. Berman, *The Concept of Aboriginal Rights in the Early Legal History of the United States*, 27 Buff. L. Rev. 637, 644 (1978) ("the reasoning of the case created a theory of conquest that stands as a centerpiece for the judicial diminution of native rights"). Would a victory for the idea of free alienability of Indian lands have benefited Native nations given the economic, political, and demographic pressures of the early eighteenth century? Would reliance on tribal law to regulate transfers of tribal lands have been a possible third alternative?

Other Supreme Court opinions from the Marshall era declare the Indian right of occupancy to be "sacred as the fee simple of the Whites." *See, e.g., Mitchel v. United States*, 34 U.S. (9 Pet.) 711, 746 (1835) (quoting *Cherokee Nation v. Georgia*, 30 U.S. (5 Pet.) 1, 48 (1831) (Baldwin, J., concurring)). As a consequence, aboriginal title has been deemed a full beneficial interest, including full use and enjoyment of the surface and mineral estate, timber resources, and other things growing on the land. *See, e.g., United States v. Northern Paiute Nation*, 393 F.2d 786 (Ct. Cl. 1968). The extension of aboriginal rights to hunting and fishing is discussed in *Village of*

Gambell v. Hodel, 869 F.2d 1273 (9th Cir. 1989) (Alaska Native Claims Settlement Act did not extinguish aboriginal rights to hunt and fish in the Outer Continental Shelf). For further treatment of resource rights, see Ch. 7.

As *United States ex rel. Hualpai Indians v. Santa Fe Pacific Railroad Co.* illustrates, the tribal right of occupancy also includes the power to bring legal action against trespassers. Tribes holding aboriginal title are entitled to an accounting for third parties' trespasses on unextinguished land, even if they no longer inhabit the land. The tribes' rights are enforceable against private parties and also against the states, even though the original thirteen states hold fee title to all lands acquired as successors to the Crown. From their inception, the Trade and Intercourse Acts were designed to provide federal protection for tribal possessory rights against unauthorized entry or injury by third persons, including possessory rights derived from aboriginal title. *See Joint Tribal Council of Passamaquoddy Tribe v. Morton*, 528 F.2d 370 (1st Cir. 1975), discussed in Sec. A.4.a, this chapter. For example, the Acts prohibited trespasses involving persons settling on Indian lands, driving livestock upon Indian lands, and hunting or trapping game on Indian lands. Ch. 151, 4 Stat. 729 (repealed in part), now codified in various parts of 18 and 25 U.S.C. As Chief Justice Vincent wrote in *United States v. Alcea Band of Tillamooks*, 329 U.S. 40, 46 (1946), "As against any but the sovereign, original Indian title was accorded the protection of complete ownership; but it was vulnerable to affirmative action by the sovereign, which possessed exclusive power to extinguish the right of occupancy at will."

Courts continue to recognize that aboriginal title rights persist until clearly extinguished by the United States. *See, e.g., Alabama-Coushatta Tribe v. United States*, 2000 U.S. Claims Lexis 287 (Ct. Fed. Cl. 2000) (ruling that tribe established aboriginal title to approximately 5.5 million acres of land in east Texas by 1830, and that subsequent land grants and settlement did not extinguish the Tribe's aboriginal title). Courts may deny aboriginal title claims based on a failure to show historical use and occupancy of the land at the exclusion of other tribes. *See Native Village of Eyak v. Blank*, 688 F.3d 619 (9th Cir. 2012) (holding Native Alaskan Villages did not possess aboriginal title to portions of the outer continental shelf because they failed to establish that they exercised exclusive control over them.) For other detailed treatments of the evolution of the concept of aboriginal title, see Felix S. Cohen, *Original Indian Title*, 32 MINN. L. REV 28 (1947) (aboriginal title in the United States); KENT MCNEIL, COMMON LAW ABORIGINAL TITLE (1989) (aboriginal title in Canada).

3. Extinguishment and Compensability: *Johnson v. M'Intosh* recognizes the right of the United States to extinguish aboriginal title by purchase or conquest. Aboriginal or Indian title may also be lost through abandonment. *See, e.g., Wichita Indian Tribe v. United States*, 696 F.2d 1378 (Fed. Cir. 1983). The standard for finding abandonment is high, however, and is not satisfied merely by establishing that the Indians failed to resist illegal non-Indian encroachment or moved temporarily in response to raids from other tribes.

The Third Circuit Court of Appeals held that the Delaware Nation's aboriginal rights to a portion of their historic territories had been validly extinguished in 1737, even though the purchase was made by a private individual, William Penn, and under fraudulent circumstances involving a forged document and overt misrepresentations to tribal leaders. *Delaware Nation v. Commonwealth of Pennsylvania*, 446 F.3d 410 (3d Cir. 2006). The court acknowledged that there was uncertainty about whether William Penn possessed the sovereign authority to extinguish Native title, but held that because the Delaware had not raised that issue in the district court proceeding, it could not be raised on appeal. The court refused to accept the Delaware's contention that a fraudulent purchase should have no valid legal effect, finding that "the manner, method, and time of the sovereign's extinguishment of aboriginal title raise political, not justiciable issues."

Likewise, the Vermont Supreme Court rejected an argument by members of the Missisquoi Tribe, a subpart of the Western Abenaki Tribe, that they could not be charged with fishing without a license under 10 V.S.A. 4251(a), 4266 because they held "aboriginal title" to the land. *State of Vermont v. Elliott*, 616 A.2d 210 (Vt. 1992). The court recognized the *Johnson v. McIntosh* rule, that "aboriginal title" continues until those lands have been abandoned or the sovereign extinguishes the right. The court also noted, however, that "[e]xtinguishment may be accomplished 'by treaty, by the sword, by purchase, by the exercise of complete dominion adverse to the right of occupancy, or otherwise'" and, once extinguishment occurs, it is "irrevocable." The court examined voluminous documentation regarding the settlement of the area and the eventual statehood of Vermont in 1791. Based on the "cumulative effect of many historical events," the court concluded that the aboriginal title of the Missisquoi Tribe had been extinguished.

There has been considerable criticism of the *Vermont v. Elliot* case. Consider whether the Vermont Supreme Court or the trial court correctly applied the principles regarding extinguishment of aboriginal title from the *Santa Fe* case? Is there any precedent for "extinguishment by the weight of history"? As with other aboriginal title claims, is it possible the court was concerned about the expectations of other Vermont citizens who had purchased the lands in good faith? Professor Joseph Singer offers a critical view:

> Even if one concludes that it would be unjust or unlawful to dispossess current non-Indian residents in Vermont it is a logical error to conclude that the original inhabitants must, therefore, have been lawfully deprived of their property rights. One wrong does not make another wrong right. Two just claims may exist and conflict with each other; it may be unjust to dispossess current residents and also have been unjust to dispossess the Abenakis.

> This "either/or" reasoning misunderstands the character of property rights. It presumes that the relevant question is "who is the owner?" and that, once that owner is identified, others have no legally cognizable claims. Ruling that the Abenakis had never been lawfully divested of their title would not automatically entitle them to oust the current residents of Vermont or even to collect rent from them. Given the conflicting property rights in question, it would have been a matter for further discussion how to resolve the conflicting property rights.

> The Vermont Supreme Court failed to recognize that the most likely and most appropriate resolution to the case would have been a negotiated and

ultimately legislative one. If the court had recognized that the Abenakis had never been lawfully deprived of their title to the tribes' lands in the "State of Vermont, the United States could have negotiated with the tribe to settle the matter by providing some land and compensation, as it did in the case of the Passamaquoddy and Penobscot nations in Maine and the natives in Alaska. In other words, the United States could have negotiated a treaty with the Missisquoi Abenaki Nation. This way of resolving the conflict would have recognized property rights and sovereignty on both sides.

Joseph William Singer, *Well-Settled?: The Increasing Weight of History in American Indian Land Claims*, 28 GA. L. REV. 481, 530–31 (1994); *see also* John P. Lowndes, *When History Outweighs Law: Extinguishment of Abenaki Aboriginal Title*, 42 BUFF. L. REV. 77 (1994).

What happens if the United States merely grants a patent for lands subject to the Indians' right of occupancy, as in the *Santa Fe* case? As the United States sought to encourage the spread of railroads across the continent, the lands astride the rights of way that it sought to grant the railroads were often Indian lands. The government would typically couple the prospective cession to the railroad with the promise to extinguish the Indian title and to establish treaty commissions, thus preserving at least the appearance of legality. Note that the Court says that extinguishment may take place through "the exercise of complete dominion adverse to the right of occupancy." Does *Johnson v. M'Intosh* mention or endorse such a method for extinguishing the Indians' right of occupancy? One must look to the early allotment era to find cases that articulate the concept of extinguishment by federal grant. The case which *Santa Fe* relies on for this proposition, *Buttz v. Northern Pacific Railroad*, 119 U.S. 55 (1886), states that the manner and timing of extinguishment of Indian title are nonjusticiable matters. *Buttz* did not, however, reject the principle that conveyances of the fee by the United States are subject to the Indians' right of occupancy until that right is properly extinguished. Indeed, in that case the Indians' right was extinguished by treaty.

Assuming, nonetheless, that *Santa Fe* is correct in allowing extinguishment by congressional grant alone, does a conveyance extinguish the Indians' right of occupancy if Congress fails to provide express recognition of continued tribal rights as part of the grant? What role do the Indian law canons of construction play in the Court's answer to this question in the *Santa Fe* case? Recent efforts by tribes to claim interference with tribal ownership rights by railroads operating rights of way through reservation lands have been successful. *See, e.g., United States v. Southern Pac. Transp. Co.*, 543 F.2d 676 (9th Cir. 1976) (successful trespass claim against railroad; congressional grant to railroad of right of way not sufficient to grant land within boundaries of reservation); *Burlington N. R.R. v. Ft. Peck Tribal Exec. Bd.*, 701 F. Supp. 1493 (D. Mont. 1988) (tribal property tax based on tribal ownership upheld; congressional grant to railroad of right of way did not extinguish tribal interest in land).

Supreme Court decisions from the Marshall era through *Santa Fe* refer to the Indians' right of occupancy as a "legal right" to the land and "sacred as the fee simple of the Whites." These statements suggest the existence of a property interest in the constitutional sense. However, these cases involved claims among non-Indians or by Indians against individuals or states. They were not suits by Native nations against the United States. At last, in the twentieth century, the United States Supreme Court received a case by a tribe seeking compensation from the United States for an alleged taking.

TEE-HIT-TON INDIANS v. UNITED STATES
United States Supreme Court
348 U.S. 272 (1955)

MR. JUSTICE REED delivered the opinion of the Court.

This case rests upon a claim under the Fifth Amendment by petitioner, an identifiable group of American Indians of between 60 and 70 individuals residing in Alaska, for compensation for a taking by the United States of certain timber from Alaskan lands allegedly belonging to the group.[4] The area claimed is said to contain over 350,000 acres of land and 150 square miles of water. The Tee-Hit-Tons, a clan of the Tlingit Tribe, brought this suit in the Court of Claims under 28 U.S.C. § 1505. The compensation claimed does not arise from any statutory direction to pay. Payment, if it can be compelled, must be based upon a constitutional right of the Indians to recover. This is not a case that is connected with any phase of the policy of the Congress, continued throughout our history, to extinguish Indian title through negotiation rather than by force, and to grant payments from the public purse to needy descendants of exploited Indians. The legislation in support of that policy has received consistent interpretation from this Court in sympathy with its compassionate purpose.

[The Court of Claims found] that petitioner was an identifiable group of American Indians residing in Alaska; that its interest in the lands prior to purchase of Alaska by the United States in 1867 was "original Indian title" or "Indian right of occupancy." It was further held that if such original Indian title survived the Treaty of 1867, 15 Stat. 539, Arts. III and VI, by which Russia conveyed Alaska to the United States, such title was not sufficient basis to maintain this suit as there had been no recognition by Congress of any legal rights in petitioner to the land in question. The court said that no rights inured to plaintiff by virtue of legislation by Congress.

[The] petitioner claims a compensable interest [in land] located near and within the exterior lines of the Tongass National Forest. By Joint Resolution of August 8, 1947, 61 Stat. 920, the Secretary of Agriculture was authorized to contract for the sale of national forest timber located within this National Forest "notwithstanding any claim of possessory rights." The Resolution defines "possessory rights"[5] and provides for all receipts from the sale of timber to be maintained in a special account

---

[4] [1] A partial taking is compensable (citations omitted).

[5] [7] *Id.*, 1: "That 'possessory rights' as used in this resolution shall mean all rights, if any should exist, which are based upon aboriginal occupancy or title, or upon section 8 of the Act of May 17, 1884 (23 Stat. 24), section 14 of the Act of March 3, 1891 (26 Stat. 1095), or section 27 of the Act of June 6, 1900 (31 Stat. 321), whether claimed by native tribes, native villages, native individuals, or other persons, and which have not been confirmed by patent or court decision or included within any reservation."

in the Treasury until the timber and land rights are finally determined. Section 3(b) of the Resolution provides:

> Nothing in this resolution shall be construed as recognizing or denying the validity of any claims of possessory rights to lands or timber within the exterior boundaries of the Tongass National Forest.

The Secretary of Agriculture, on August 20, 1951, pursuant to this authority contracted for sale to a private company of all merchantable timber in the area claimed by petitioner. This is the sale of timber which petitioner alleges constitutes a compensable taking by the United States of a portion of its proprietary interest in the land.

The problem presented is the nature of the petitioner's interest in the land, if any. Petitioner claims a "full proprietary ownership" of the land; or, in the alternative, at least a "recognized" right to unrestricted possession, occupation and use. Either ownership or recognized possession, petitioner asserts, is compensable. If it has a fee simple interest in the entire tract, it has an interest in the timber and its sale is a partial taking of its right to "possess, use and dispose of it." *United States v. General Motors Corp.*, 323 U.S. 373, 378. It is petitioner's contention that its tribal predecessors have continually claimed, occupied and used the land from time immemorial; that when Russia took Alaska, the Tlingits had a well-developed social order which included a concept of property ownership; that Russia while it possessed Alaska in no manner interfered with their claim to the land; that Congress has by subsequent acts confirmed and recognized petitioner's right to occupy the land permanently and therefore the sale of the timber off such lands constitutes a taking pro tanto of its asserted rights in the area.

The Government denies that petitioner has any compensable interest. It asserts that the Tee-Hit-Tons's property interest, if any, is merely that of the right to the use of the land at the Government's will; that Congress has never recognized any legal interest of petitioner in the land and therefore without such recognition no compensation is due the petitioner for any taking by the United States.

I. Recognition.— The question of recognition may be disposed of shortly. Where the Congress by treaty or other agreement has declared that thereafter Indians were to hold the lands permanently, compensation must be paid for subsequent taking. The petitioner contends that Congress has sufficiently "recognized" its possessory rights in the land in question so as to make its interest compensable. Petitioner points specifically to two statutes to sustain this contention. The first is § 8 of the Organic Act for Alaska of May 17, 1884, 23 Stat. 24. The second is § 27 of the Act of June 6, 1900, which was to provide for a civil government for Alaska, 31 Stat. 321, 330. The Court of Appeals in the *Miller* case, *supra*, felt that these Acts constituted recognition of Indian ownership. 159 F.2d 997, 1002–1003.

We have carefully examined these statutes and the pertinent legislative history and find nothing to indicate any intention by Congress to grant to the Indians any permanent rights in the lands of Alaska occupied by them by permission of Congress. Rather, it clearly appears that what was intended was merely to retain the status quo until further congressional or judicial action was taken. There is no particular form for congressional recognition of Indian right of permanent occupancy. It may be established in a variety of ways but there must be the definite intention by congressional action or authority to accord legal rights, not merely permissive occupation. *Hynes v. Grimes Packing Co.*, 337 U.S. 86, 101.

This policy of Congress toward the Alaskan Indian lands was maintained and reflected by its expression in the Joint Resolution of 1947 under which the timber contracts were made.

II. Indian Title.— (a) The nature of aboriginal Indian interest in land and the various rights as between the Indians and the United States dependent on such interest are far from novel as concerns our Indian inhabitants. It is well settled that in all the States of the Union the tribes who inhabited the lands of the States held claim to such lands after the coming of the white man, under what is sometimes termed original Indian title or permission from the whites to occupy. That description means mere possession not specifically recognized as ownership by Congress. After conquest they were permitted to occupy portions of territory over which they had previously exercised "sovereignty," as we use that term. This is not a property right but amounts to a right of occupancy which the sovereign grants and protects against intrusion by third parties but which right of occupancy may be terminated and such lands fully disposed of by the sovereign itself without any legally enforceable obligation to compensate the Indians.

This position of the Indian has long been rationalized by the legal theory that discovery and conquest gave the conquerors sovereignty over and ownership of the lands thus obtained. 1 Wheaton's International Law, c. V. The great case of *Johnson v. M'Intosh*, 8 Wheat. 543, denied the power of an Indian tribe to pass their right of occupancy to another. It confirmed the practice of two hundred years of American history "that discovery gave an exclusive right to extinguish the Indian title of occupancy, either by purchase or by conquest." 8 Wheat. at page 587.

[In another case,] *Beecher v. Wetherby*, 95 U.S. 517, a tract of land which Indians were then expressly permitted by the United States to occupy was granted to Wisconsin. In a controversy over timber, this Court held the Wisconsin title good.

> "The grantee, it is true, would take only the naked fee, and could not disturb the occupancy of the Indians: that occupancy could only be interfered with or determined by the United States. It is to be presumed that in this matter the United States would be governed by such considerations of justice as would control a Christian people in their treatment of an ignorant and dependent race. Be that as it may, the propriety or justice of their action towards the Indians with respect to their lands is a question of governmental policy, and is not a matter open to discussion in a controversy between third parties, neither of whom derives title from the Indians. The right of the United States to dispose of the fee of lands occupied by them has always been recognized by this court from the foundation of the government." [*Id.* at] 525.

In 1941 a unanimous Court wrote, concerning Indian title, the following:

> "Extinguishment of Indian title based on aboriginal possession is of course a different matter. The power of Congress in that regard is supreme. The

manner, method and time of such extinguishment raise political, not justiciable, issues." *United States v. Santa Fe Pacific R. Co.*, 314 U.S. 339, 347.

No case in this Court has ever held that taking of Indian title or use by Congress required compensation. The American people have compassion for the descendants of those Indians who were deprived of their homes and hunting grounds by the drive of civilization. They seek to have the Indians share the benefits of our society as citizens of this Nation. Generous provision has been willingly made to allow tribes to recover for wrongs, as a matter of grace, not because of legal liability.

(b) There is one opinion in a case decided by this Court that contains language indicating that unrecognized Indian title might be compensable under the Constitution when taken by the United States. *United States v. Tillamooks*, 329 U.S. 40.

Recovery was allowed under a jurisdictional Act of 1935, 49 Stat. 801, that permitted payments to a few specific Indian tribes for "legal and equitable claims arising under or growing out of the original Indian title" to land, because of some unratified treaties negotiated with them and other tribes. The other tribes had already been compensated. Five years later this Court unanimously held that none of the former opinions in Vol. 329 of the United States Reports expressed the view that recovery was grounded on a taking under the fifth amendment. *United States v. Tillamooks*, 341 U.S. 48. Interest, payable on recovery for a taking under the Fifth Amendment, was denied.

Before the second *Tillamook* case, a decision was made on Alaskan Tlingit lands held by original Indian title. *Miller v. United States*, 159 F.2d 997. That opinion holds such a title compensable under the Fifth Amendment on reasoning drawn from the language of this Court's first *Tillamook* case. After the *Miller* decision, this Court had occasion to consider the holding of that case on Indian title in *Hynes v. Grimes Packing Co.*, 337 U.S. 86, 106, note 28. We there commented as to the first *Tillamook* case: "That opinion does not hold the Indian right of occupancy compensable without specific legislative direction to make payment." We further declared "we cannot express agreement with that [compensability of Indian title by the *Miller* case] conclusion."

[T]his Court in the second *Tillamook* case, 341 U.S. 48, held that the first case was not "grounded on a taking under the Fifth Amendment." Therefore no interest was due. This latter *Tillamook* decision by a unanimous Court supported the Court of Claims in its view of the law in this present case. We think it must be concluded that the recovery in the *Tillamook* case was based upon statutory direction to pay for the aboriginal title in the special jurisdictional act to equalize the Tillamooks with the neighboring tribes, rather than upon a holding that there had been a compensable taking under the Fifth Amendment.[6] This leaves unimpaired the rule

---

[6] [18] In *Carino v. Insular Government of Philippine Islands*, 212 U.S. 449, this Court did uphold as valid a claim of land ownership in which tribal custom and tribal recognition of ownership played a part. Petitioner was an Igorot who asserted the right to register ownership of certain land although he had no document of title from the Spanish Government and no recognition of ownership had been extended by Spain or by the United States. The United States Government had taken possession of the land for a public use and disputed the fact that petitioner had any legally recognizable title.

derived from *Johnson v. McIntosh* that the taking by the United States of unrecognized Indian title is not compensable under the Fifth Amendment.

This is true, not because an Indian or an Indian tribe has no standing to sue or because the United States has not consented to be sued for the taking of original Indian title, but because Indian occupation of land without government recognition of ownership creates no rights against taking or extinction by the United States protected by the Fifth Amendment or any other principle of law.

(c) What has been heretofore set out deals largely with the Indians of the Plains and east of the Mississippi. The Tee-Hit-Tons urge, however, that their stage of civilization and their concept of ownership of property takes them out of the rule applicable to the Indians of the States. They assert that Russia never took their lands in the sense that European nations seized the rest of America. The Court of Claims, however, saw no distinction between their use of the land and that of the Indians of the Eastern United States. That court had no evidence that the Russian handling of the Indian land problem differed from ours. The natives were left the use of the great part of their vast hunting and fishing territory but what Russia wanted for its use and that of its licensees, it took. The court's conclusion on this issue was based on strong evidence.

In considering the character of the Tee-Hit-Tons's use of the land, the Court of Claims had before it the testimony of a single witness who was offered by plaintiff. He stated that he was the chief of the Tee-Hit-Ton tribe. He qualified as an expert on the Tlingits, a group composed of numerous interconnected tribes including the Tee-Hit-Tons. His testimony showed that the Tee-Hit-Tons had become greatly reduced in numbers. Membership descends only through the female line. At the present time there are only a few women of childbearing age and a total membership of some 65

The witness pointed out that their claim of ownership was based on possession and use. The use that was made of the controverted area was for the location in winter of villages in sheltered spots and in summer along fishing streams and/or bays. The ownership was not individual but tribal. As the witness stated, "Any member of the tribe may use any portion of the land that he wishes, and as long as he uses it that is his for his own enjoyment, and is not to be trespassed upon by anybody else, but the minute he stops using it then any other member of the tribe can come in and use that area."

The basis of the Court's decision, however, distinguishes it from applicability to the Tee-Hit-Ton claim. The Court relied chiefly upon the purpose of our acquisition of the Philippines as disclosed by the Organic Act of July 1, 1902, which was to administer property and rights (for the benefit of the inhabitants thereof." 32 Stat. 695. This purpose in acquisition and its effect on land held by the natives was distinguished from the settlement of the white race in the United States where (the dominant purpose of the whites in America was to occupy the land." 212 U.S., at 458. The Court further found that the Spanish law and exercise of Spanish sovereignty over the islands tended to support rather than defeat a prescriptive right. Since this was no communal claim to a vast uncultivated area, it was natural to apply the law of prescription rather than a rule of sovereign ownership or dominium. Cariqo's claim was to a 370-acre farm which his grandfather had fenced some fifty years before and was used by three generations as a pasture for livestock and some cultivation of vegetables and grain. The case bears closer analogy to the ordinary prescriptive rights situation rather than to a recognition by this Court of any aboriginal use and possession amounting to fee simple ownership.

When the Russians first came to the Tlingit territory, the most important of the chiefs moved the people to what is now the location of the town of Wrangell. Each tribe took a portion of Wrangell harbor and the chief gave permission to the Russians to build a house on the shore.

The witness learned the alleged boundaries of the Tee-Hit-Ton area from hunting and fishing with his uncle after his return from Carlisle Indian School about 1904. From the knowledge so obtained, he outlined in red on the map, which petitioner filed as an exhibit, the territory claimed by the Tee-Hit-Tons. Use by other tribal members is sketchily asserted. This is the same 350,000 acres claimed by the petition. On it he marked six places to show the Indians' use of the land: (1) his great uncle was buried here, (2) a town, (3) his uncle's house, (4) a town, (5) his mother's house, (6) smokehouse. He also pointed out the uses of this tract for fishing salmon and for hunting beaver, deer and mink.

The testimony further shows that while membership in the tribe and therefore ownership in the common property descended only through the female line, the various tribes of the Tlingits allowed one another to use their lands. Before power boats, the Indians would put their shelters for hunting and fishing away from villages. With the power boats, they used them as living quarters.

In addition to this verbal testimony, exhibits were introduced by both sides as to the land use. These exhibits are secondary authorities but they bear out the general proposition that land claims among the Tlingits, and likewise of their smaller group, the Tee-Hit-Tons, was wholly tribal. It was more a claim of sovereignty than of ownership. The articles presented to the Court of Claims by those who have studied and written of the tribal groups agree with the above testimony. There were scattered shelters and villages moved from place to place as game or fish became scarce. There was recognition of tribal rights to hunt and fish on certain general areas, with claims to that effect carved on totem poles. From all that was presented, the Court of Claims concluded, and we agree, that the Tee-Hit-Tons were in a hunting and fishing stage of civilization, with shelters fitted to their environment, and claims to rights to use identified territory for these activities as well as the gathering of wild products of the earth. We think this evidence introduced by both sides confirms the Court of Claims' conclusion that the petitioner's use of its lands was like the use of the nomadic tribes of the States Indians.[7]

------

[7] [20] It is significant that even with the Pueblo Indians of the Mexican Land Sessions, despite their centuries-old sedentary agricultural and pastoral life, the United States found it proper to confirm to them a title in their lands. The area in which the Pueblos are located came under our sovereignty by the Treaty of Guadalupe Hidalgo, 9 Stat. 922, and the Gadsden Purchase Treaty of December 30, 1853, 10 Stat. 1031. The treaty of Guadalupe Hidalgo contained a guarantee by the United States to respect the property rights of Mexicans located within the territory acquired. Art. VIII, Stat. 929. This provision was incorporated by reference into the Gadsden Treaty. Art. V, 10 Stat. 1035. The latter treaty also contained a provision that no grants of land within the ceded territory made after a certain date would be recognized or any grants "made previously [would] be respected or be considered as obligatory which have not been located and duly recorded in the archives of Mexico." Art. VI, 10 Stat. 1035. This provision was held to bar recognition of fee ownership in the Pueblo of Santa Rosa which claimed such by immemorial use and possession as well as by prescription against Spain and Mexico because they could produce no paper title to the lands. *Pueblo of Santa Rosa v. Fall*, 12 F.2d 332, 335, reversed on other grounds, 273 U.S. 315. Disputes as to the Indian titles in the Pueblos and their position as wards required congressional action for settlement. *See* Brayer, Pueblo Indian Land Grants of the "Rio Abajo," New

The line of cases adjudicating Indian rights on American soil leads to the conclusion that Indian occupancy, not specifically recognized as ownership by action authorized by Congress, may be extinguished by the Government without compensation.[8] Every American schoolboy knows that the savage tribes of this continent were deprived of their ancestral ranges by force and that, even when the Indians ceded millions of acres by treaty in return for blankets, food and trinkets, it was not a sale but the conquerors' will that deprived them of their land.

[Given] the history of Indian relations in this Nation, no other course would meet the problem of the growth of the United States except to make congressional contributions for Indian lands rather than to subject the Government to an obligation to pay the value when taken with interest to the date of payment. Our conclusion does not uphold harshness as against tenderness toward the Indians, but it leaves with Congress, where it belongs, the policy of Indian gratuities for the termination of Indian occupancy of Government-owned land rather than making compensation for its value a rigid constitutional principle.

Affirmed.

MR. JUSTICE DOUGLAS, with whom THE CHIEF JUSTICE and MR. JUSTICE FRANKFURTER concur, dissenting.

The first Organic Act for Alaska became a law on May 17, 1884, 23 Stat. 24. It contained a provision in § 8 which reads as follows:

> the Indians or other persons in said district shall not be disturbed in the possession of any lands actually in their use or occupation or now claimed

---

Mexico; Cohen, Handbook of Federal Indian Law, c. 20. These problems were put in the way of solution only by congressional recognition of the Pueblos' title to their land and the decisions of this Court as to their racial character as Indians, subject to necessary federal tutelage. 10 Stat. 308, Creation of Office of Surveyor-General of New Mexico to report area of bona fide holdings; Report of Secretary of the Interior, covering that of the Surveyor-General of New Mexico, S. Exec. Doc. No. 5, 34th Cong., 3d Sess. 174, 411; Confirmation of titles for approved Pueblo Land Claims, 11 Stat. 374; S. Doc. No. 1117, 37th Cong., 2d Sess. 581–582, Report of Secretary of Interior showing New Mexico Pueblos with confirmed titles. Representative Sandidge, who reported the first Pueblo Confirmation Act to the House of Representatives, stated that the Pueblo claims, "although they are valid, are not held to be so by this Government, nor by any of its courts, until the claim shall have been acted on specifically. I will say, furthermore, that the whole land system of the Territory of New Mexico is held in abeyance until these private land claims shall have been acted on by Congress." Cong. Globe, 35th Cong., 1st Sess. 2090 (1858). The position as Indians of the inhabitants of the Pueblos was considered in *United States v. Joseph*, 94 U.S. 614, and *United States v. Sandoval*, 231 U.S. 28. . . . Thus it is seen that congressional action was deemed necessary to validate the ownership of the Pueblos whose claim was certainly founded upon stronger legal and historical basis than the Tlingits.

   [8] [21] The Departments of Interior, Agriculture and Justice agree with this conclusion. *See* Committee Print No. 12, Supplemental Reports dated January 11, 1954, on H.R. 1921, 83d Cong., 2d Sess. Department of Interior: "That the Indian right of occupancy is not a property right in the accepted legal sense was clearly indicated when *United States v. Alcea Band of Tillamooks*, 341 U.S. 48 (1951), was reargued. The Supreme Court stated, in a per curiam decision, that the taking of lands to which Indians had a right of occupancy was not a taking within the meaning of the fifth amendment entitling the dispossessed to just compensation. "Since possessory rights based solely upon aboriginal occupancy or use are thus of an unusual nature, subject to the whim of the sovereign owner of the land who can give good title to third parties by extinguishing such rights, they cannot be regarded as clouds upon title in the ordinary sense of the word. . . ."

by them but the terms under which such persons may acquire title to such lands is reserved for future legislation by Congress: And provided further, That parties who have located mines or mineral privileges therein under the laws of the United States applicable to the public domain, or who have occupied and improved or exercised acts of ownership over such claims, shall not be disturbed therein, but shall be allowed to perfect their title to such claims by payment as aforesaid.

[The conclusion] seems clear that Congress in the 1884 Act recognized the claims of these Indians to their Alaskan lands. What those lands were was not known. Where they were located, what were their metes and bounds, were also unknown. Senator Plumb thought they probably were small and restricted. But all agreed that the Indians were to keep them, wherever they lay. It must be remembered that the Congress was legislating about a Territory concerning which little was known. No report was available showing the nature and extent of any claims to the land. No Indian was present to point out his tribe's domain. Therefore, Congress did the humane thing of saving to the Indians all rights claimed; it let them keep what they had prior to the new Act. The future course of action was made clear-conflicting claims would be reconciled and the Indian lands would be put into reservations.

That purpose is wholly at war with the one now attributed to the Congress of reserving for some future day the question whether the Indians were to have any rights to the land.

There remains the question what kind of "title" the right of use and occupancy embraces. Some Indian rights concern fishing alone. *See Tulee v. Washington*, 315 U.S. 681. Others may include only hunting or grazing or other limited uses. Whether the rights recognized in 1884 embraced rights to timber, litigated here, has not been determined by the finders of fact. The case should be remanded for those findings. It is sufficient now only to determine that under the jurisdictional Act the Court of Claims is empowered to entertain the complaint by reason of the recognition afforded the Indian rights by the Act of 1884.

Nell Jessup Newton, *At the Whim of the Sovereign: Aboriginal Title Reconsidered*
31 HASTINGS L.J. 1215, 1241–53 (1980)

In holding in *Tee-Hit-Ton* that aboriginal title was not a compensable property interest under the fifth amendment, Justice Reed relied heavily on the doctrine of discovery cases, and in particular on *Johnson v. M'Intosh*. Unfortunately, the portion of the *Tee-Hit-Ton* opinion discussing these cases is poorly structured. The Court first quoted several lengthy passages from *Johnson*, followed with several assertions of fact regarding the case in controversy, and finished by purporting to state the obvious conclusion. Despite the Court's poor drafting, one can nevertheless discern a semblance of logic in the opinion. Initially, the Court noted that conquest was a legitimate means of extinguishing aboriginal title. Recognizing this, the Court went on to suggest that the government and its predecessors, as a matter of historical fact, had conquered the Indians, either through actual warfare or by forcing treaties on the Indians. Consequently, all aboriginal title had been extinguished before *Tee-Hit-Ton*, with the exception of the title Congress had chosen to grant back to the Indians.

The Court in *Tee-Hit-Ton* relied on *Johnson* to provide the cornerstone for converting the doctrine of discovery to this doctrine of conquest. Two passages from *Johnson* regarding extinguishment of Indian title by conquest were cited, including the statement that "[c]onquest gives a title which the Courts of the conqueror cannot deny, whatever the private and speculative opinions of individuals may be respecting the original justice of the claim which has been successfully asserted." The Court's reliance on these passages from *Johnson* was misplaced for several reasons. The only war relevant to the decision in *Johnson* was the war between France and England to settle England's claim to the land east of the Mississippi, including the land in controversy in the case. This war in no way affected the Indian tribes' interest in their land, as the opinion pointed out. Hence, the language was merely dicta.

The dicta in *Johnson* regarding extinguishment of Indian title by conquest does not support Justice Reed's conclusion that all Indian land had been conquered. Authorities differ on whether Justice Marshall actually recognized conquest as a valid method of extinguishment of Indian title under American law. Regardless of how the passages in *Johnson* are interpreted, however, it is evident that *Johnson* did not establish that all Indian title had been extinguished by conquest, for *Johnson* itself, as well as its progeny, recognized that purchase was the primary method of extinguishment of Indian title. Had discovery itself extinguished Indian title to land, most of the decisions in those cases would have been unnecessary.

In addition, Justice Reed's use of the term "conquest" is itself questionable. Both at the time of *Johnson* and today, conquest has been a narrow concept with clearly defined effects on the conquered people. For example, conquest generally requires some sort of physical possession by force of arms. Thus, the conclusion that all Indian land has been conquered was as illogical as it was unprecedented. Even if Justice Reed meant only that the congressional resolution at issue in *Tee-Hit-Ton* was the functional equivalent of a declaration of war followed by conquest, such a conclusion was not warranted by either the language of the resolution or the rules of international law regarding conquest. Finally, even if the federal government's actions in the forty-eight contiguous states could have been interpreted as examples of the "conqueror's will," the Alaska natives had never fought a skirmish with either Russia or the United States, but instead welcomed newcomers to Alaska with open arms. To say that the Alaska natives were subjugated by conquest stretches the imagination too far. The only sovereign act that can be said to have conquered the Alaska native was the *Tee-Hit-Ton* opinion itself.

Extinguishment as a Political Question

In constructing the rule of *Tee-Hit-Ton*, Justice Reed asserted that the decision of Congress to recognize aboriginal title was not subject to judicial review. This conclusion logically followed from two unexpressed premises: first, that political questions, such as the decision to declare war, are not justiciable; and second, that extinguishment of Indian title is a purely political question. In support of the latter premise, the court placed critical reliance on language from two cases, *Beecher v.*

Wetherby[9] and *United States ex rel. Hualpai Indians v. Santa Fe Pacific Railroad*[10] (*Walapai Tribe*).

Beecher involved a dispute over tribal land the United States granted to Wisconsin in 1848, before the tribe's aboriginal title had been extinguished. The United States Government subsequently attempted to cede the land back to the tribe, despite its prior grant of the land to Wisconsin. Both the plaintiff and defendant claimed title to lumber taken from the land, the plaintiff's claim based on a United States patent issued in 1872 and the defendant's claim based on the State's issuance of patents in 1865 and 1870. In holding only the grant by Wisconsin valid, the Court stated that "the propriety or justice of . . . [the government's] action towards the Indians with respect to their lands is a question of governmental policy, and is not a matter open to discussion in a controversy between third parties, neither of whom derives title from the Indians."

The Court's position in *Beecher* was sound. Because many land titles can be traced to a period of Indian occupancy, judicial time and individual resources would be wasted if third parties were permitted to contest the sovereign's decision to extinguish the tribal right of occupancy. Additionally, there seems little justification in allowing a third party to contest the sovereign's decision with respect to a tribe if the tribe itself is an uninterested party. *Tee-Hit-Ton* was not a controversy between third parties, but a direct controversy between a native Alaska tribe and the government. Hence, what proved to be a compelling justification in *Beecher* was wholly lacking under the facts of *Tee-Hit-Ton*. Indeed, contest between a tribe and the government regarding the consequences of congressional extinguishment or the government's liability seems to be precisely the sort of matter subject to judicial review. . . .

NOTES

1. **The Debate over Compensability Before *Tee-Hit-Ton*:** In *United States v. Alcea Band of Tillamooks*, 329 U.S. 40 (1946), Chief Justice Vinson, in an opinion joined by three other justices (including Justice Frankfurter), held that a special jurisdictional act authorized recovery for the extinguishment of aboriginal title. Regarding compensation, the plurality stated: "[T]aking original Indian title without compensation and without consent does not satisfy the 'high standards for fair dealing' required of the United States in controlling Indian affairs. The Indians have more than a merely moral claim for compensation." *Id.* at 47. The plurality also declined the government's invitation to distinguish between recognized and aboriginal title, noting:

> . . . [S]ome cases speak of the unlimited power of Congress to deal with those Indian lands which are held by what petitioner would call "recognized" title, yet it cannot be doubted that, given the consent of the United States to be sued, recovery may be had for an involuntary, uncompensated taking of "recognized title." We think the same rule applicable to a taking

---

[9] [183] 95 U.S. 517 (1877).

[10] [184] 314 U.S. 339 (1941).

of original Indian title. "Whether this tract . . . was properly called a reservation . . . or unceded Indian country, . . . is a matter of little moment. . . . [T]he Indians' right of occupancy has always been held to be sacred; something not be taken from him except by his consent, and then upon such consideration as should be agreed upon."

Justice Reed, joined by two other justices, dissented, stating:

This distinction between rights from recognized occupancy and from Indian title springs from the theory under which the European nations took possession of the lands of the American aborigines. This theory was that discovery by the Christian nations gave them sovereignty over and title to the lands discovered. *Johnson v. M'Intosh*, 8 Wheat. 543, 572–86; 1 Story, Commentaries on the Constitution (5th Ed.) (152). While Indians were permitted to occupy these lands under their Indian title, the conquering nations asserted the right to extinguish that Indian title without legal responsibility to compensate the Indian for his loss. It is not for the courts of the conqueror to question the propriety or validity of such an assertion of power. Indians who continued to occupy their aboriginal homes, without definite recognition of their right to do so are like paleface squatters on public lands without compensable rights if they are evicted.

Id. at 51–52, 58.

Justice Black merely concurred in the result in *Tillamooks I*, resting his brief opinion solely on the statute. In *United States v. Alcea Band of Tillamooks (Tillamooks II)*, 341 U.S. 48 (1951), the Court explained the result in the first case as derived from the jurisdictional statute, not from the fifth amendment. Consequently, the Tribe was not entitled to interest, which would have been recoverable if there had been a constitutional taking.

2. **Speculation Regarding the *Tee-Hit-Ton* Court's Motivation:** Scholars have offered numerous theories as to the motivation for the Court's decision in *Tee-Hit-Ton*. In her piece, *At the Whim of the Sovereign: Aboriginal Title Reconsidered*, 31 HASTINGS L.J. 1215, 1241–53 (1980), Dean Nell Newton posits realism, fiscal considerations, and ethnocentricism as possible rationales, finding all of them grossly inaccurate and insufficient as a basis for the decision. For additional treatment of the *Tee-Hit-Ton* case, see, Joseph William Singer, *Erasing Indian Country: The Story of* Tee-Hit-Ton Indians v. United States *in* INDIAN LAW STORIES (Carole Goldberg, Kevin K. Washburn & Philip P. Frickey, eds., 2011); Angela R. Riley, *The History of Native American Lands and the Supreme Court*, 38 J. SUP. CT. HIST. 369 (2013).

3. **The Role of Conquest:** Was it prior conquest, as Justice Reed's comments might suggest or, rather, the 1947 Joint Resolution that represented the "conquest" that extinguished the Tee-Hit-Ton's original title? What difference does it make? If Justice Reed's comments are given their full scope, could aboriginal title enforceable against third parties exist anywhere in the United States today? Furthermore, if Justice Reed's comments are taken seriously, how does one explain the compensability of "recognized" Indian title, acknowledged as protected even in *Tee-Hit-Ton*?

4. Retroactive Extinguishment: Recall that Indians claiming lands by aboriginal possession have an enforceable right of occupancy against third parties under which damages or an accounting for trespass may be awarded. Are the accrued damage claims protected by the Fifth Amendment takings clause even if the underlying aboriginal title is not? In other words, can Congress not only extinguish aboriginal title at will but also retroactively extinguish accrued Indian rights against third parties based on violations of the Indian right of occupancy? In *United States v. Atlantic Richfield Co.*, 612 F.2d 1132, 1135–38 (9th Cir. 1980), the Ninth Circuit held that the provisions of the Alaska Native Claims Settlement Act (ANCSA) extinguishing retroactively both aboriginal title and claims based on aboriginal title included claims against third parties for trespass and did not violate the due process clause. This settlement act was not a true agreement, but rather imposed on the Alaska Natives after some period of consultation. The Inupiat Community subsequently sued in the Court of Claims for compensation, arguing that the statutory extinguishment of claims based on aboriginal title was a taking of vested property rights. The Court of Claims held that if aboriginal title itself was not a compensable property interest, claims based on aboriginal title could not be protected either. *Inupiat Community of the Arctic Slope v. United States*, 680 F.2d 122 (Ct. Cl. 1982). For more extensive discussion of the terms of ANCSA as they affect property as well as sovereignty of Alaska Native villages, see Ch. 5, Sec. B.

2. Recognized Title

UNITED STATES v. SHOSHONE TRIBE OF INDIANS
United States Supreme Court
304 U.S. 111 (1938)

Mr. Justice Butler delivered the opinion of the Court.

. . . .

The sole question for decision is whether, as the United States contends, the Court of Claims erred in holding that the right of the tribe included the timber and mineral resources within the reservation.

The findings show: The United States, by the treaty of July 2, 1863, set apart for the Shoshone Tribe a reservation of 44,672,000 acres located in Colorado, Utah, Idaho and Wyoming. By the treaty of July 3, 1868, the tribe ceded that reservation to the United States. And by it the United States agreed that the "district of country" 3,054,182 acres definitely described "shall be and the same is set apart for the absolute and undisturbed use and occupation of the Shoshone Indians . . . , and the United States now solemnly agrees that no persons," with exceptions not important here, "shall ever be permitted to pass over, settle upon, or reside in" that territory. The Indians agreed that they would make the reservation their permanent home. The treaty provided that any individual member of the tribe having specified qualifications, might select a tract within the reservation which should then cease to be held in common, and be occupied and held in the exclusive possession of the person selecting it, and of his family, while he or they continued to cultivate it. It declared: " . . . Congress shall provide for protecting the rights of the Indian settlers . . . and may fix the character of the title held by each. The United States may pass such laws on the subject of alienation and descent of property as between Indians, and on all subjects connected with the government of the Indians on said reservation, and the internal police thereof, as may be thought proper."

The treaty emphasized the importance of education; the United States agreed to provide a schoolhouse and teacher for every thirty children, and the tribe promised to send the children to school. The United States also agreed to provide instruction by a farmer for members cultivating the soil, clothing for members of the tribe, and a physician, carpenter, miller, engineer and blacksmith. It stipulated that no treaty for the cession of any portion of the reservation held in common should be valid as against the Indians, unless signed by at least a majority of all interested male adults; and that no cession by the tribe should be construed to deprive any member of his right to any tract of land selected by him.

When the treaty of 1868 was made, the tribe consisted of full blood blanket Indians, unable to read, write, or speak English. Upon consummation of the treaty, the tribe went, and has since remained, upon the reservation. It was known to contain valuable mineral deposits — gold, oil, coal and gypsum. It included more than 400,000 acres of timber, extensive well-grassed bench lands and fertile river valleys conveniently irrigable. It was well protected by mountain ranges and a divide, and was the choicest and best-watered portion of Wyoming.

. . . .

The substance of the Government's point is that in fixing the value of the tribe's right, the lower court included as belonging to the tribe substantial elements of value, ascribable to mineral and timber resources, which in fact belonged to the United States.

It contends that the Shoshones's right to use and occupy the lands of the reservation did not include the ownership of the timber and minerals and that the opinion of the court below departs from the general principles of law regarding Indian land tenure and the uniform policy of the Government in dealing with Indian tribes. It asks for reversal with "directions to determine the value of the Indians' right of use and occupancy but to exclude therefrom 'the net value of the lands' and 'the net value of any timber or minerals.' "

. . . .

In this case we have held, 299 U.S. 476, 484, that the tribe had the right of occupancy with all its beneficial incidents; that, the right of occupancy being the primary one and as sacred as the fee, division by the United States of the Shoshones's right with the Arapahoes was an appropriation of the land pro tanto; that although the United States always had legal title to the land and power to control and manage the affairs of the Indians, it did not have power to give to others or to appropriate to its own use any part of the land without rendering, or assuming the obligation to pay, just compensation to the tribe, for that would be, not the exercise of guardianship or management, but confiscation.

It was not then necessary to consider, but we are now called upon to decide, whether, by the treaty, the tribe acquired beneficial ownership of the minerals and timber on the reservation. The phrase "absolute and undisturbed use and occupation" is to be read, with other parts of the document, having regard to the purpose of the arrangement made, the relation between the parties, and the settled policy of the United States fairly to deal with Indian tribes. In treaties made with them the United States seeks no advantage for itself; friendly and dependent Indians are likely to accept without discriminating scrutiny the terms proposed. They are not to be interpreted narrowly, as sometimes may be writings expressed in words of art employed by conveyancers, but are to be construed in the sense in which naturally the Indians would understand them. *Worcester v. Georgia*, 6 Pet. 515, 582. *Jones v. Meehan*, 175 U.S. 1, 11. *Starr v. Long Jim*, 227 U.S. 613, 622–623.

The principal purpose of the treaty was that the Shoshones should have, and permanently dwell in, the defined district of country. To that end the United States granted and assured to the tribe peaceable and unqualified possession of the land in perpetuity. Minerals and standing timber are constituent elements of the land itself. *United States v. Cook*, 19 Wall. 591. *British-American Oil Co. v. Board*, 299 U.S. 159, 164–165. For all practical purposes, the tribe owned the land. Grants of land subject to the Indian title by the United States, which had only the naked fee, would transfer no beneficial interest. *Leavenworth, L. & G. R. Co. v. United States*, 92 U.S. 733, 742–743. *Beecher v. Wetherby*, 95 U.S. 517, 525. The right of perpetual and exclusive occupancy of the land is not less valuable than full title in fee. *See Holden v. Joy*, 17 Wall. 211, 244. *Western Union Tel. Co. v. Pennsylvania R. Co.*, 195 U.S. 540, 557.

The treaty, though made with knowledge that there were mineral deposits and standing timber in the reservation, contains nothing to suggest that the United States intended to retain for itself any beneficial interest in them. The words of the grant, coupled with the Government's agreement to exclude strangers, negative the idea that the United States retained beneficial ownership. The grant of right to members of the tribe severally to select and hold tracts on which to establish homes for themselves and families, and the restraint upon cession of land held in common or individually, suggest beneficial ownership in the tribe. As transactions between a guardian and his wards are to be construed favorably to the latter, doubts, if there were any, as to ownership of lands, minerals or timber would be resolved in favor of the tribe. . . .

Although the United States retained the fee, and the tribe's right of occupancy was incapable of alienation or of being held otherwise than in common, that right is as sacred and as securely safeguarded as is fee simple absolute title. *Cherokee Nation v. Georgia*, 5 Pet. 1, 48. *Worcester v. Georgia, supra*, 580. Subject to the conditions imposed by the treaty, the Shoshone Tribe had the right that has always been understood to belong to Indians, undisturbed possessors of the soil from time immemorial. Provisions in aid of teaching children and of adult education in farming, and to secure for the tribe medical and mechanical service, to safeguard tribal and individual titles, when taken with other parts of the treaty, plainly evidence purpose on the part of the United States to help to create an independent permanent farming community upon the reservation.

United States v. Cook, supra, gives no support to the contention that in ascertaining just compensation for the Indian right taken, the value of mineral and timber resources in the reservation should be excluded. That case did not involve adjudication of the scope of Indian title to land, minerals or standing timber, but only the right of the United States to replevin logs cut and sold by a few unauthorized members of the tribe. We held that, as against the purchaser from the wrongdoers, the United States was entitled to possession. It was not there decided that the tribe's right of occupancy in perpetuity did not include ownership of the land or mineral deposits or standing timber upon the reservation, or that the tribe's right was the mere equivalent of, or like, the title of a life tenant.

The lower court did not err in holding that the right of the Shoshone Tribe included the timber and minerals within the reservation.

Affirmed.

Mr. Justice Stone and Mr. Justice Cardozo took no part in the consideration or decision of this case.

Mr. Justice Reed dissents.

UNITED STATES v. SIOUX NATION
United States Supreme Court
448 U.S. 371 (1980)

Mr. Justice Blackmun delivered the opinion of the Court.

This case concerns the Black Hills of South Dakota, the Great Sioux Reservation, and a colorful, and in many respects tragic, chapter in the history of the Nation's West. Although the litigation comes down to a claim of interest since 1877 on an award of over $17 million, it is necessary, in order to understand the controversy, to review at some length the chronology of the case and its factual setting.

I

For over a century now the Sioux Nation has claimed that the United States unlawfully abrogated the Fort Laramie Treaty of April 29, 1868, 15 Stat. 635, in Art. II of which the United States pledged that the Great Sioux Reservation, including the Black Hills, would be "set apart for the absolute and undisturbed use and occupation of the Indians herein named." *Id.*, at 636. The Fort Laramie Treaty was concluded at the culmination of the Powder River War of 1866–1867, a series of military engagements in which the Sioux tribes, led by their great chief, Red Cloud, fought to protect the integrity of earlier-recognized treaty lands from the incursion of white settlers.

The Fort Laramie Treaty included several agreements central to the issues presented in this case. First, it established the Great Sioux Reservation, a tract of land bounded on the east by the Missouri River, on the south by the northern border of the State of Nebraska, on the north by the forty-sixth parallel of north latitude, and on the west by the one hundred and fourth meridian of west longitude, in addition to certain reservations already existing east of the Missouri. The United States "solemnly agree[d]" that no unauthorized persons "shall ever be permitted to pass over, settle upon, or reside in [this] territory."

Second, the United States permitted members of the Sioux tribes to select lands within the reservation for cultivation. In order to assist the Sioux in becoming civilized farmers, the Government promised to provide them with the necessary services and materials, and with subsistence rations for four years.

Third, in exchange for the benefits conferred by the treaty, the Sioux agreed to relinquish their rights under the Treaty of September 17, 1851, to occupy territories outside the reservation, while reserving their "right to hunt on any lands north of North Platte, and on the Republican Fork of the Smoky Hill river, so long as the buffalo may range thereon in such numbers as to justify the chase." The Indians also expressly agreed to withdraw all opposition to the building of railroads that did not pass over their reservation lands, not to engage in attacks on settlers, and to withdraw their opposition to the military posts and roads that had been established south of the North Platte River.

Fourth, Art. XII of the treaty provided:

> "No treaty for the cession of any portion or part of the reservation herein described which may be held in common shall be of any validity or force as against the said Indians, unless executed and signed by at least three fourths of all the adult male Indians, occupying or interested in the same."

The years following the treaty brought relative peace to the Dakotas, an era of tranquility that was disturbed, however, by renewed speculation that the Black Hills, which were included in the Great Sioux Reservation, contained vast quantities of gold and silver. In 1874 the Army planned and undertook an exploratory expedition into the Hills, both for the purpose of establishing a military outpost from which to control those Sioux who had not accepted the terms of the Fort Laramie Treaty, and for the purpose of investigating "the country about which dreamy stories have been told." D. Jackson, Custer's Gold 14 (1966) (quoting the 1874 annual report of Lieutenant General Philip H. Sheridan, as Commander of the Military Division of the Missouri, to the Secretary of War). Lieutenant Colonel George Armstrong Custer led the expedition of close to 1,000 soldiers and teamsters, and a substantial number of military and civilian aides. Custer's journey began at Fort Abraham Lincoln on the Missouri River on July 2, 1874. By the end of that month they had reached the Black Hills, and by mid-August had confirmed the presence of gold fields in that region. The discovery of gold was widely reported in newspapers across the country. Custer's florid descriptions of the mineral and timber resources of the Black Hills, and the land's suitability for grazing and cultivation, also received wide circulation, and had the effect of creating an intense popular demand for the "opening" of the Hills for settlement. The only obstacle to "progress" was the Fort Laramie Treaty that reserved occupancy of the Hills to the Sioux.

Having promised the Sioux that the Black Hills were reserved to them, the United States Army was placed in the position of having to threaten military force, and occasionally to use it, to prevent prospectors and settlers from trespassing on lands reserved to the Indians. For example, in September 1874, General Sheridan sent instructions to Brigadier General Alfred H. Terry, Commander of the Department of Dakota, at Saint Paul, directing him to use force to prevent companies of prospectors from trespassing on the Sioux reservation. At the same time, Sheridan let it be known that he would "give a cordial support to the settlement of the Black Hills," should Congress decide to "open up the country for settlement, by extinguishing the treaty rights of the Indians." App. 62–63. Sheridan's instructions were published in local newspapers. *See id.*, at 63.

Eventually, however, the Executive Branch of the Government decided to abandon the Nation's treaty obligation to preserve the integrity of the Sioux territory. In a letter dated November 9, 1875, to Terry, Sheridan reported that he had met with President Grant, the Secretary of the Interior, and the Secretary of War, and that the President had decided that the military should make no further resistance to the occupation of the Black Hills by miners, "it being his belief that such resistance only increased their desire and complicated the troubles." *Id.*, at 59. These orders were to be enforced "quietly," *ibid.*, and the President's decision was to remain "confidential." *Id.*, at 59–60 (letter from Sheridan to Sherman).

With the Army's withdrawal from its role as enforcer of the Fort Laramie Treaty, the influx of settlers into the Black Hills increased. The Government concluded that the only practical course was to secure to the citizens of the United States the right to mine the Black Hills for gold. Toward that end, the Secretary of the Interior, in the spring of 1875, appointed a commission to negotiate with the Sioux. The commission was headed by William B. Allison. The tribal leaders of the Sioux were aware of the mineral value of the Black Hills and refused to sell the land for a price less than $70 million. The commission offered the Indians an annual rental of $400,000, or payment of $6 million for absolute relinquishment of the Black Hills. The negotiations broke down.

In the winter of 1875–1876, many of the Sioux were hunting in the unceded territory north of the North Platte River, reserved to them for that purpose in the Fort Laramie Treaty. On December 6, 1875, for reasons that are not entirely clear, the Commissioner of Indian Affairs sent instructions to the Indian agents on the reservation to notify those hunters that if they did not return to the reservation agencies by January 31, 1876, they would be treated as "hostiles." Given the severity of the winter, compliance with these instructions was impossible. On February 1, the Secretary of the Interior nonetheless relinquished jurisdiction over all hostile Sioux, including those Indians exercising their treaty-protected hunting rights, to the War Department. The Army's campaign against the "hostiles" led to Sitting Bull's notable victory over Custer's forces at the battle of the Little Big Horn on June 25. That victory, of course, was short-lived, and those Indians who surrendered to the Army were returned to the reservation, and deprived of their weapons and horses, leaving them completely dependent for survival on rations provided them by the Government.

In the meantime, Congress was becoming increasingly dissatisfied with the failure of the Sioux living on the reservation to become self-sufficient. The Sioux' entitlement to subsistence rations under the terms of the Fort Laramie Treaty had expired in 1872. Nonetheless, in each of the two following years, over $1 million was appropriated for feeding the Sioux. In August 1876, Congress enacted an appropriations bill providing that "hereafter there shall be no appropriation made for the subsistence" of the Sioux, unless they first relinquished their rights to the hunting grounds outside the reservation, ceded the Black Hills to the United States, and reached some accommodation with the Government that would be calculated to enable them to become self-supporting. Act of August 15, 1876, 19 Stat. 176, 192. Toward this end, Congress requested the President to appoint another commission to negotiate with the Sioux for the cession of the Black Hills.

This commission, headed by George Manypenny, arrived in the Sioux country in early September and commenced meetings with the head men of the various tribes. The members of the commission impressed upon the Indians that the United States no longer had any obligation to provide them with subsistence rations. The commissioners brought with them the text of a treaty that had been prepared in advance. The principal provisions of this treaty were that the Sioux would relinquish their rights to the Black Hills and other lands west of the one hundred and third meridian, and their rights to hunt in the unceded territories to the north, in exchange for subsistence rations for as long as they would be needed to ensure the Sioux' survival. In setting out to obtain the tribes' agreement to this treaty, the commission ignored the stipulation of the Fort Laramie Treaty that any cession of the lands contained within the Great Sioux Reservation would have to be joined in by three-fourths of the adult males. Instead, the treaty was presented just to Sioux chiefs and their leading men. It was signed by only 10% of the adult male Sioux population.[11]

Congress resolved the impasse by enacting the 1876 "agreement" into law as the Act of Feb. 28, 1877 (1877 Act), 19 Stat. 254. The Act had the effect of abrogating the earlier Fort Laramie Treaty, and of implementing the terms of the Manypenny Commission's "agreement" with the Sioux leaders.[12]

---

[11] [13] The commission's negotiations with the chiefs and head men is described by [D.] Robinson, [A History of the Dakota or Sioux Indians] at 439–42 [where he] states: "As will be readily understood, the making of a treaty was a forced put, so far as the Indians were concerned. Defeated, disarmed, dismounted, they were at the mercy of a superior power and there was no alternative but to accept the conditions imposed upon them. This they did with as good grace as possible under all of the conditions existing. . . ."

[12] [14] The 1877 Act "ratified and confirmed" the agreement reached by the Manypenny Commission with the Sioux tribes. 19 Stat. 254. It altered the boundaries of the Great Sioux Reservation by adding some 900,000 acres of land to the north, while carving out virtually all that portion of the reservation between the one hundred and third and one hundred and fourth meridians, including the Black Hills, an area of well over 7 million acres. The Indians also relinquished their rights to hunt in the unceded lands recognized by the Fort Laramie Treaty, and agreed that three wagon roads could be cut through their reservation. *Id.*, at 255. In exchange, the Government reaffirmed its obligation to provide all annuities called for by the Fort Laramie Treaty, and "to provide all necessary aid to assist the said Indians in the work of civilization; to furnish to them schools and instruction in mechanical and agricultural arts, as provided for by the treaty of 1868." *Id.*, at 256. In addition, every individual was to receive fixed quantities of beef or bacon and flour, and other foodstuffs, in the discretion of the Commissioner of Indian Affairs, which "shall be continued until the Indians are able to support themselves." *Ibid.* The provision of rations was to be conditioned, however, on the attendance at school by Indian children, and on the labor of those who resided on lands suitable for farming. The Government also promised to assist the Sioux in finding markets for their crops and in obtaining employment in the performance of Government work on the reservation. *Ibid.* Later congressional actions having the effect of further reducing the domain of the

The passage of the 1877 Act legitimized the settlers' invasion of the Black Hills, but throughout the years it has been regarded by the Sioux as a breach of this Nation's solemn obligation to reserve the Hills in perpetuity for occupation by the Indians. . . .

II

[Pursuant to a special statute enacted by Congress to permit the Sioux to relitigate their claim to compensation for the taking of the Black Hills free from a res judicata defense based on prior unsuccessful litigation of the same issue,] a majority of the Court of Claims, sitting en banc, in an opinion by Chief Judge Friedman, affirmed the Commission's holding that the 1877 Act effected a taking of the Black Hills and of rights-of-way across the reservation.[13] In doing so, the court applied the test it had earlier articulated in *Fort Berthold*, 390 F.2d [686], at 691, asking whether Congress had made (a good faith effort to give the Indians the full value of the land," in order to decide whether the 1877 Act had effected a taking or whether it had been a noncompensable act of congressional guardianship over tribal property. The court characterized the Act as a taking, an exercise of Congress's power of eminent domain over Indian property. It distinguished broad statements seemingly leading to a contrary result in *Lone Wolf v. Hitchcock*, 187 U.S. 553 (1903) inapplicable to a case involving a claim for just compensation.

The court thus held that the Sioux were entitled to an award of interest, at the annual rate of 5%, on the principal sum of $17.1 million, dating from 1877.

We granted the Government's petition for a writ of certiorari, in order to review the important constitutional questions presented by this case, questions not only of long-standing concern to the Sioux, but also of significant economic import to the Government. . . .

IV

A

In reaching its conclusion that the 1877 Act effected a taking of the Black Hills for which just compensation was due the Sioux under the fifth amendment, the Court of Claims relied upon the "good faith effort" test developed in its earlier decision in *Three Tribes of Fort Berthold Reservation v. United States*, 390 F.2d 686 (1968). The *Fort Berthold* test had been designed to reconcile two lines of cases decided by this Court that seemingly were in conflict. The first line, exemplified by *Lone Wolf v. Hitchcock*, 187 U.S. 553 (1903), recognizes "that Congress possesse[s] a paramount power over the property of the Indians, by reason of its exercise of

---

Great Sioux Reservation are described in *Rosebud Sioux Tribe v. Kneip*, 430 U.S. 584, 589 (1977).

[13] [19] While affirming the Indian Claims Commission's determination that the acquisition of the Black Hills and the rights-of-way across the reservation constituted takings, the court reversed the Commission's determination that the mining of gold from the Black Hills by prospectors prior to 1877 also constituted a taking. The value of the gold, therefore, could not be considered as part of the principal on which interest would be paid to the Sioux.

guardianship over their interests, and that such authority might be implied, even though opposed to the strict letter of a treaty with the Indians." *Id.*, at 565. The second line, exemplified by the more recent decision in *Shoshone Tribe v. United States*, 299 U.S. 476 (1937), concedes Congress's paramount power over Indian property, but holds, nonetheless, that "[t]he power does not extend so far as to enable the Government 'to give the tribal lands to others, or to appropriate them to its own purposes, without rendering, or assuming an obligation to render, just compensation.'" *Id.*, at 497 (quoting *United States v. Creek Nation*, 295 U.S. 103, 110 (1935)). In *Shoshone Tribe*, Mr. Justice Cardozo, in speaking for the Court, expressed the distinction between the conflicting principles in a characteristically pithy phrase: "Spoliation is not management." 299 U.S., at 498.

The *Fort Berthold* test distinguishes between cases in which one or the other principle is applicable:

> "It is obvious that Congress cannot simultaneously (1) act as trustee for the benefit of the Indians, exercising its plenary powers over the Indians and their property, as it thinks is in their best interests, and (2) exercise its sovereign power of eminent domain, taking the Indians' property within the meaning of the Fifth Amendment to the Constitution. In any given situation in which Congress has acted with regard to Indian people, it must have acted either in one capacity or the other. Congress can own two hats, but it cannot wear them both at the same time.

> "Some guideline must be established so that a court can identify in which capacity Congress is acting. The following guideline would best give recognition to the basic distinction between the two types of congressional action: Where Congress makes a good faith effort to give the Indians the full value of the land and thus merely transmutes the property from land to money, there is no taking. This is a mere substitution of assets or change of form and is a traditional function of a trustee." 390 F.2d, at 691.

Applying the *Fort Berthold* test to the facts of this case, the Court of Claims concluded that, in passing the 1877 Act, Congress had not made a good-faith effort to give the Sioux the full value of the Black Hills. The principal issue presented by this case is whether the legal standard applied by the Court of Claims was erroneous.[14]

---

[14] [26] It should be recognized at the outset that the inquiry presented by this case is different from that confronted in the more typical of our recent "taking" decisions. *E.g., Kaiser Aetna v. United States*, 444 U.S. 164 (1979); *Penn Central Transp. Co. v. New York*, 438 U.S. 104 (1978). In those cases the Court has sought to "determin[e] when 'justice and fairness' require that economic injuries caused by public action be compensated by the Government, rather than remain disproportionately concentrated on a few persons." *Penn Central*, 438 U.S., at 124. Here, there is no doubt that the Black Hills were "taken" from the Sioux in a way that wholly deprived them of their property rights to that land. The question presented is whether Congress was acting under circumstances in which that "taking" implied an obligation to pay just compensation, or whether it was acting pursuant to its unique powers to manage and control tribal property as the guardian of Indian welfare, in which event the Just Compensation Clause would not apply.

B

The Government contends that the Court of Claims erred insofar as its holding that the 1877 Act effected a taking of the Black Hills was based on Congress's failure to indicate affirmatively that the consideration given the Sioux was of equivalent value to the property rights ceded to the Government. It argues that "the true rule is that Congress must be assumed to be acting within its plenary power to manage tribal assets if it reasonably can be concluded that the legislation was intended to promote the welfare of the tribe." Brief for United States 52. The Government derives support for this rule principally from this Court's decision in *Lone Wolf v. Hitchcock*.

In the penultimate paragraph of the opinion, however, the Court in *Lone Wolf* went on to make some observations seemingly directed to the question whether the Act at issue might constitute a taking of Indian property without just compensation. The Court there stated:

> "The act of June 6, 1900, which is complained of in the bill, was enacted at a time when the tribal relations between the confederated tribes of Kiowas, Comanches, and Apaches still existed, and that statute and the statutes supplementary thereto dealt with the disposition of tribal property and purported to give an adequate consideration for the surplus lands not allotted among the Indians or reserved for their benefit. Indeed, the controversy which this case presents is concluded by the decision in *Cherokee Nation v. Hitchcock*, 187 U.S. 294, decided at this term, where it was held that full administrative power was possessed by Congress over Indian tribal property. In effect, the action of Congress now complained of was but an exercise of such power, a mere change in the form of investment of Indian tribal property, the property of those who, as we have held, were in substantial effect the wards of the government. *We must presume that Congress acted in perfect good faith in the dealings with the Indians of which complaint is made, and that the legislative branch of the government exercised its best judgment in the premises.* In any event, as Congress possessed full power in the matter, the judiciary cannot question or inquire into the motives which prompted the enactment of this legislation. If injury was occasioned, which we do not wish to be understood as implying, by the use made by Congress of its power, relief must be sought by an appeal to that body for redress and not to the courts. The legislation in question was constitutional." *Ibid.* (Emphasis supplied.)

The Government relies on the italicized sentence in the quotation above to support its view "that Congress must be assumed to be acting within its plenary power to manage tribal assets if it reasonably can be concluded that the legislation was intended to promote the welfare of the tribe." Several adjoining passages in the paragraph, however, lead us to doubt whether the *Lone Wolf* Court meant to state a general rule applicable to cases such as the one before us.

First, *Lone Wolf* presented a situation in which Congress "purported to give an adequate consideration" for the treaty lands taken from the Indians. In fact, the act at issue set aside for the Indians a sum certain of $2 million for surplus reservation lands surrendered to the United States. 31 Stat. 678; see 187 U.S., at 555. In contrast, the background of the 1877 Act "reveals a situation where Congress did not 'purport' to provide 'adequate consideration,' nor was there any meaningful negotiation or arm's-length bargaining, nor did Congress consider it was paying a fair price." 601 F.2d [1157], at 1176 (concurring opinion).

Second, given the provisions of the act at issue in *Lone Wolf*, the Court reasonably was able to conclude that "the action of Congress now complained of was but . . . a mere change in the form of investment of Indian tribal property." Under the Act of June 6, 1900, each head of a family was to be allotted a tract of land within the reservation of not less than 320 acres, an additional 480,000 acres of grazing land were set aside for the use of the tribes in common, and $2 million was paid to the Indians for the remaining surplus. 31 Stat. 677–678. In contrast, the historical background to the opening of the Black Hills for settlement, and the terms of the 1877 Act itself, *see* Part I, *supra*, would not lead one to conclude that the Act effected "a mere change in the form of investment of Indian tribal property."

Third, it seems significant that the views of the Court in *Lone Wolf* were based, in part, on a holding that "Congress possessed full power in the matter." Earlier in the opinion the Court stated: "Plenary authority over the tribal relations of the Indians has been exercised by Congress from the beginning, and the power has always been deemed a political one, not subject to be controlled by the judicial department of the government." 187 U.S., at 565. Thus, it seems that the Court's conclusive presumption of congressional good faith was based in large measure on the idea that relations between this Nation and the Indian tribes are a political matter, not amenable to judicial review. That view, of course, has long since been discredited in taking cases, and was expressly laid to rest in *Delaware Tribal Business Comm. v. Weeks*, [430 U.S. 73, 84 (1977).]

Fourth, and following up on the political question holding, the *Lone Wolf* opinion suggests that where the exercise of congressional power results in injury to Indian rights, (relief must be sought by an appeal to that body for redress and not to the courts." Unlike *Lone Wolf*, this case is one in which the Sioux have sought redress from Congress, and the Legislative Branch has responded by referring the matter to the courts for resolution. Where Congress waives the Government's sovereign immunity, and expressly directs the courts to resolve a taking claim on the merits, there would appear to be far less reason to apply *Lone Wolf*'s principles of deference.

The foregoing considerations support our conclusion that the passage from *Lone Wolf* here relied upon by the Government has limited relevance to this case. More significantly, *Lone Wolf*'s presumption of congressional good faith has little to commend it as an enduring principle for deciding questions of the kind presented here. In every case where a taking of treaty-protected property is alleged,[15] a reviewing court must recognize that tribal lands are subject to Congress's power to

---

[15] [29] Of course, it has long been held that the taking by the United States of "unrecognized" or "aboriginal" Indian title is not compensable under the Fifth Amendment. *Tee-Hit-Ton Indians v. United States*, 348 U.S. 272, 285 (1955). The principles we set forth today are applicable only to instances in which "Congress by treaty or other agreement has declared that thereafter Indians were to hold the lands permanently." *Id.*, at 277. In such instances, "compensation must be paid for subsequent taking." *Id.*, at 277–278.

control and manage the tribe's affairs. But the court must also be cognizant that "this power to control and manage [is] not absolute. While extending to all appropriate measures for protecting and advancing the tribe, it [is] subject to limitations inhering in . . . a guardianship and to pertinent constitutional restrictions." *United States v. Creek Nation*, 295 U.S. 103 (1935).

As the Court of Claims recognized in its decision below, the question whether a particular measure was appropriate for protecting and advancing the tribe's interests, and therefore not subject to the constitutional command of the Just Compensation Clause, is factual in nature. The answer must be based on a consideration of all the evidence presented. We do not mean to imply that a reviewing court is to second-guess, from the perspective of hindsight, a legislative judgment that a particular measure would serve the best interests of the tribe. We do mean to require courts, in considering whether a particular congressional action was taken in pursuance of Congress's power to manage and control tribal lands for the Indians' welfare, to engage in a thoroughgoing and impartial examination of the historical record. A presumption of congressional good faith cannot serve to advance such an inquiry.

C

We turn to the question whether the Court of Claims' inquiry in this case was guided by an appropriate legal standard. We conclude that it was. In fact, we approve that court's formulation of the inquiry as setting a standard that ought to be emulated by courts faced with resolving future cases presenting the question at issue here:

> "In determining whether Congress has made a good faith effort to give the Indians the full value of their lands when the government acquired [them], we therefore look to the objective facts as revealed by Acts of Congress, congressional committee reports, statements submitted to Congress by government officials, reports of special commissions appointed by Congress to treat with the Indians, and similar evidence relating to the acquisition. . . .

> "The 'good faith effort' and 'transmutation of property' concepts referred to in *Fort Berthold* are opposite sides of the same coin. They reflect the traditional rule that a trustee may change the form of trust assets as long as he fairly (or in good faith) attempts to provide his ward with property of equivalent value. If he does that, he cannot be faulted if hindsight should demonstrate a lack of precise equivalence. On the other hand, if a trustee (or the government in its dealings with the Indians) does not attempt to give the ward the fair equivalent of what he acquires from him, the trustee to that extent has taken rather than transmuted the property of the ward. In other words, an essential element of the inquiry under the *Fort Berthold* guideline is determining the adequacy of the consideration the government gave for the Indian lands it acquired. That inquiry cannot be avoided by the

government's simple assertion that it acted in good faith in its dealings with the Indians."[16]

D

We next examine the factual findings made by the Court of Claims, which led it to the conclusion that the 1877 Act effected a taking. First, the Court found that "[t]he only item of 'consideration' that possibly could be viewed as showing an attempt by Congress to give the Sioux the 'full value' of the land the government took from them was the requirement to furnish them with rations until they became self-sufficient." This finding is fully supported by the record, and the Government does not seriously contend otherwise.[17]

Second, the court found, after engaging in an exhaustive review of the historical record, that neither the Manypenny Commission, nor the congressional committees that approved the 1877 Act, nor the individual legislators who spoke on its behalf on the floor of Congress, ever indicated a belief that the Government's obligation to provide the Sioux with rations constituted a fair equivalent for the value of the Black Hills and the additional property rights the Indians were forced to surrender. This finding is unchallenged by the Government.

A third finding lending some weight to the Court's legal conclusion was that the conditions placed by the Government on the Sioux' entitlement to rations "further show that the government's undertaking to furnish rations to the Indians until they could support themselves did not reflect a congressional decision that the value of the rations was the equivalent of the land the Indians were giving up, but instead was an attempt to coerce the Sioux into capitulating to congressional demands."

[T]he Court of Claims [also] rejected the Government's contention that the fact that it subsequently had spent at least $43 million on rations for the Sioux (over the course of three quarters of a century) established that the 1877 Act was an act of

---

[16] [30] An examination of this standard reveals that, contrary to the Government's assertion, the Court of Claims in this case did not base its finding of a taking solely on Congress's failure in 1877 to state affirmatively that the "assets" given the Sioux in exchange for the Black Hills were equivalent in value to the land surrendered. Rather, the court left open the possibility that, in an appropriate case, a mere assertion of congressional good faith in setting the terms of a forced surrender of treaty-protected lands could be overcome by objective indicia to the contrary. And, in like fashion, there may be instances in which the consideration provided the Indians for surrendered treaty lands was so patently adequate and fair that Congress's failure to state the obvious would not result in the finding of a compensable taking. To the extent that the Court of Claims' standard, in this respect, departed from the original formulation of the *Fort Berthold* test, such a departure was warranted. The Court of Claims's present formulation of the test, which takes into account the adequacy of the consideration given, does little more than reaffirm the ancient principle that the determination of the measure of just compensation for a taking of private property (is a judicial, and not a legislative, question." *Monongahela Navigation Co. v. United States*, 148 U.S. 312, 327 (1893).

[17] [31] The 1877 Act [*supra* n.14] purported to provide the Sioux with "all necessary aid to assist the said Indians in the work of civilization," and "to furnish to them schools and instruction in mechanical and agricultural arts, as provided for by the treaty of 1868." 19 Stat. 256.

The Court of Claims correctly concluded that the first item "was so vague that it cannot be considered as constituting a meaningful or significant element of payment by the United States." As for the second, it "gave the Sioux nothing to which they were not already entitled [under the 1868 treaty]."

guardianship taken in the Sioux' best interest. The court concluded: "The critical inquiry is what Congress did — and how it viewed the obligation it was assuming — at the time it acquired the land, and not how much it ultimately cost the United States to fulfill the obligation." It found no basis for believing that Congress, in 1877, anticipated that it would take the Sioux such a lengthy period of time to become self-sufficient, or that the fulfillment of the Government's obligation to feed the Sioux would entail the large expenditures ultimately made on their behalf. We find no basis on which to question the legal standard applied by the Court of Claims, or the findings it reached, concerning Congress's decision to provide the Sioux with rations.

E

The aforementioned findings fully support the Court of Claims' conclusion that the 1877 Act appropriated the Black Hills "in circumstances which involved an implied undertaking by [the United States] to make just compensation to the tribe." *United States v. Creek Nation*, 295 U.S., at 111. We make only two additional observations about this case. First, dating at least from the decision in *Cherokee Nation v. Southern Kansas Railway Co.*, 135 U.S. 641, 657 (1890), this Court has recognized that Indian lands, to which a tribe holds recognized title, "are held subject to the authority of the general government to take them for such objects as are germane to the execution of the powers granted to it; provided only, that they are not taken without just compensation being made to the owner." In the same decision the Court emphasized that the owner of such lands "is entitled to reasonable, certain and adequate provision for obtaining compensation before his occupancy is disturbed." *Id.*, at 659. The Court of Claims gave effect to this principle when it held that the Government's uncertain and indefinite obligation to provide the Sioux with rations until they became self-sufficient did not constitute adequate consideration for the Black Hills.

Second, it seems readily apparent to us that the obligation to provide rations to the Sioux was undertaken in order to ensure them a means of surviving their transition from the nomadic life of the hunt to the agrarian lifestyle Congress had chosen for them. Those who have studied the Government's reservation policy during this period of our Nation's history agree. It is important to recognize that the 1877 Act, in addition to removing the Black Hills from the Great Sioux Reservation, also ceded the Sioux' hunting rights in a vast tract of land extending beyond the boundaries of that reservation. Under such circumstances, it is reasonable to conclude that Congress's undertaking of an obligation to provide rations for the Sioux was a *quid pro quo* for depriving them of their chosen way of life, and was not intended to compensate them for the taking of the Black Hills.

V

In sum, we conclude that the legal analysis and factual findings of the Court of Claims fully support its conclusion that the terms of the 1877 Act did not effect "a mere change in the form of investment of Indian tribal property." *Lone Wolf v. Hitchcock*, 187 U.S., at 568. Rather, the 1877 Act effected a taking of tribal property, property which had been set aside for the exclusive occupation of the Sioux by the

Fort Laramie Treaty of 1868. That taking implied an obligation on the part of the Government to make just compensation to the Sioux Nation, and that obligation, including an award of interest, must now, at last, be paid.

[*Affirmed.*]

Mr. Justice Rehnquist, dissenting.

III

Even if I could countenance the Court's decision to reach the merits of this case, I also think it has erred in rejecting the 1942 Court's interpretation of the facts. That Court rendered a very persuasive account of the congressional enactment. As the dissenting judges in the Court of Claims opinion under review pointedly stated, "The majority's view that the rations were not consideration for the Black Hills is untenable. What else was the money for?"

I think the Court today rejects that conclusion largely on the basis of a view of the settlement of the American West which is not universally shared. There was undoubtedly greed, cupidity, and other less-than-admirable tactics employed by the government during the Black Hills episode in the settlement of the West, but the Indians did not lack their share of villainy either. It seems to me quite unfair to judge by the light of "revisionist" historians or the mores of another era actions that were taken under pressure of time more than a century ago.

Different historians, not writing for the purpose of having their conclusions or observations inserted in the reports of congressional committees, have taken different positions than those expressed in some of the materials referred to in the Court's opinion. This is not unnatural, since history, no more than law, is an exact (or for that matter an inexact) science. . . .

That there was tragedy, deception, barbarity, and virtually every other vice known to man in the 300-year history of the expansion of the original 13 colonies into a Nation which now embraces more than three million square miles and 50 States cannot be denied. But in a Court opinion, as a historical and not a legal matter, both settler and Indian are entitled to the benefit of the Biblical adjuration: "Judge not, that ye be not judged."

NOTES ON RECOGNIZED TITLE

1. **Origins of the Term:** As *United States v. Shoshone Tribe* demonstrates, the Court has not always distinguished between recognized and aboriginal title, often using the term "Indian title" to describe Indian land. When the Court did use the term "recognized," it was generally to identify treaty-based claims for purposes of special jurisdictional statutes, or to identify the boundaries of previously ceded land for purposes of an unconscionable consideration claim before the Indian Claims Commission. *See, e.g., Northwestern Bands of Shoshone Indians v. United States,* 324 U.S. 335 (1945) (claim under special jurisdictional act for taking 15 million acres did not arise from the Treaty of Box Elder); *Quapaw Tribe v. United States,* 1 Ind. Cl. Comm'n 474, 491 (1951), *aff'd,* 120 F. Supp. 283 (Ct. Cl. 1954) (boundary

"recognized" by prior treaty, therefore tribe did not need to prove aboriginal title). "Recognized title" took on special meaning when the Supreme Court used the term in *Tee-Hit-Ton* to differentiate between compensable and noncompensable takings under the Fifth Amendment. Should the term "recognition" in these earlier cases be read as having the same meaning as the term "recognition" in *Tee-Hit-Ton*?

2. **Treaty Language Recognizing Title:** *Tee-Hit-Ton* states that recognition requires congressional action. Treaties or statutes setting aside land as a permanent home for the Indians will generally vest the tribe with recognized Indian title. As *Shoshone* notes, the question is ultimately one of congressional intent, requiring a careful analysis of the language and history of the treaty or statute. Will Congressional ratification of such a treaty invariably supply the predicate for recognition?

In *United States v. Kiowa, Comanche & Apache Tribes*, 479 F.2d 1369 (Ct. Cl. 1973), the Court of Claims denied the tribes' claim that the following language recognized title:

> Article II. The United States hereby agree that the district of country embraced within the following limits, or such portion of the same as may hereafter from time to time be designated by the President of the United States for that purpose . . . shall be and is hereby set apart for the absolute use and occupation of the tribes who are parties to the treaty. . . .

Treaty of October 18, 1865, 14 Stat. 717, 718. The Court of Claims found that because the treaty gave the President discretion to alter the boundaries of the reservation, the language setting apart the land "for the absolute use and occupation of the tribes" could not create a compensable interest. The court distinguished *United States v. Klamath & Moadoc Tribes*, 304 U.S. 119 (1938), a pre-*Tee-Hit-Ton* case, in which compensation was awarded despite the fact that the treaty specified that the grant was qualified by "until otherwise directed by the President," because the treaty in the earlier case "was seen as overturned by subsequent action." What accounts for such differences in the construction of the operative effects of a treaty or statute? What role, if any, should the canons of statutory and treaty construction, discussed in Ch. 2, Sec. C., play in the resolution of recognition questions? Should post-treaty official actions influence the determination of recognition through a treaty?

3. **Other Acts Recognizing Title:** Indian tribes have also acquired land by purchase, as in the case of the Choctaw of Mississippi, or by grant from a prior sovereign, as in the case of the Pueblos, whose title was recognized under Spanish law. Statutes can also serve to recognize title, supplying the necessary congressional action. Some statutes directly confirm title, while others establish a land claims process permitting Indian claims to be made along with other claims deriving from a prior sovereign. *See* Act of Dec. 15, 1970, Pub. L. No. 91-550, 84 Stat. 1437 (returning Blue Lake to Taos Pueblo); *Tee-Hit-Ton, supra,* n.20 (describing a general process for confirmation of Pueblo titles). Is any particular congressional language required to produce "recognized title"? For example, the act returning Blue Lake to Taos Pueblo, *supra,* states "The lands held in trust pursuant to this section shall be part of the Pueblo de Taos Reservation, and shall be administered

under the laws and regulations applicable to other trust lands." Does that language suffice?

4. **Incidents of Recognized Title:** The issue of the scope and extent of recognized title raised in the *Shoshone* case had been clouded by the Supreme Court's prior decision in *United States v. Cook*, 86 U.S. (19 Wall.) 591 (1874). *Cook* involved a replevin action brought by the United States against the vendees of standing timber that was cut on the Oneida Reservation in Wisconsin by individual Indians without authority from the Department of the Interior. The Supreme Court, analogizing the status of the Indian title to "a tenant for life" with the United States holding the fee (*i.e.*, the remainder interest), applied the doctrine of waste. Thus, the Court held that the cutting of standing timber, which was part of the realty, for commercial sale, rather than for Indian use "of improving the land, or the better adapting it to convenient occupation," was illegal since it infringed on the federal government's interest in the land. Peculiarities of the Oneida's land rights upon moving from New York to Wisconsin may best explain the decision in *Cook*, as there was specific treaty language suggesting that the Oneidas's land was held under a right of occupancy only, and giving the United States special rights to the timber. How does the *Shoshone* Court distinguish *Cook*?

Whatever doubts *Cook* may have cast on tribal mineral and timber interests in recognized tribal lands has now been laid to rest by the *Shoshone* decision and by a series of statutes authorizing commercial exploitation of such resources for the benefit of Indians. *See* Felix S. Cohen, *Original Indian Title*, 32 MINN. L. REV. 28, 54–55 (1947). Why was the tribe denied the value of the gold taken by the miners in *Sioux Nation*? *Cf. Black Hills Institute of Geological Research v. South Dakota School of Mines and Technology*, 12 F.3d 737 (8th Cir. 1993), Sec. A.6, this chapter.

5. **Tribal Property and the *Sioux Nation* Rule:** Is a taking of recognized title treated differently than any other taking of property? Should it be? If the Black Hills had been non-Indian property, any physical invasion would establish a compensable taking. *See, e.g., Loretto v. Teleprompter Manhattan CATV Corp.*, 458 U.S. 419 (1982). Given that recognized title is a protectable property interest after *Tee-Hit-Ton*, and given that the Court found the Sioux's treaty-based recognized title to have been taken "in a way that wholly deprived [the Sioux] of their property rights to that land" (*see* n.26), was there anything more to discuss? Does the Court give any credence to the notion, derived from *Lone Wolf v. Hitchcock* (presented in Ch. 1, Sec. D.2), that Indian property questions are political questions? If not, does *Lone Wolf* carry any other weight in *Sioux Nation*? The Court seems to reinterpret *Lone Wolf* as a case alleging mismanagement, the federal guardian having transmuted the tribal property into money. Thus it establishes a legal test requiring a distinction between the government's role when it acts as a guardian changing the form of tribal property as in *Lone Wolf*, and when it acts as a sovereign exercising its power of eminent domain. How exactly does the Court formulate the legal test for this crucial determination? Is the test easy to apply? Should negligent, but good faith actions by the government, such as a gross undervaluation, spare it from liability for a taking? Why should such considerations determine whether there has been a taking? Professor (now Dean) Newton has argued that the appropriate test ought to be whether the tribe consented to the taking, instead of a test requiring a determination of whether the government has "fairly (or in good faith) attempt[ed]

to provide his ward with property of equivalent value." Nell Jessup Newton, *The Judicial Role in Fifth Amendment Takings of Indian Land: An Analysis of the Sioux Nation Rule*, 61 Or. L. Rev. 245 (1982). For a collection of the critical appraisals of the Court's takings analysis, see John P. LaVelle, *Rescuing Paha Sapa: Achieving Environmental Justice by Restoring the Great Grasslands and Returning the Sacred Black Hills to the Great Sioux Nation*, 5 Great Plains Nat. Resources J. 40, 63 n.74 (2001).

Unlike most claims against the government, including breach of trust claims under the Indian Claims Commission Act and others, claims for just compensation under the takings clause accrue prejudgment interest. Because the Sioux Nation claim was so old, the amount of the award was $122 million, despite the federal government's success in depressing Indian land prices through its monopoly of buyer's rights. Does the fact that a successful constitutional claim would result in the payment of large amounts of interest while a breach of trust claim would not require payment of any interest affect the Court's adoption of the *Sioux Nation* test rather than the simpler test for takings in non-Indian cases? *See* Howard M. Friedman, *Interest on Indian Claims: Judicial Protection of the Fisc*, 5 Val. U. L. Rev. 26 (1970).

Despite the large amount of the *Sioux Nation* award, and the extreme poverty of the Sioux people, a majority of the Sioux tribes have refused to accept the money, insisting that they are entitled to reclaim their ancestral lands in accordance with their treaty rights. William Means, executive director of the International Indian Treaty Council and citizen of the Oglala Lakota Nation, offered this assessment of the *Sioux Nation* decision in 1986 testimony before the Senate Select Committee on Indian Affairs:

> First of all, the courts [in *Sioux Nation*] identified the thief of the Black Hills in 1877 as the U.S. Congress. The second thing the court did was allow the thief to keep what he had stolen. The third thing the court did was allow the thief to determine the value of the land. The fourth thing they did was allow the thief to impose or attempt to impose that monetary judgment upon our people in exchange for the land.

The opposition to payment in lieu of land includes not only the claims adjudicated in the *Sioux Nation* case, but also treaty-based claims resolved in a separate docket before the Court of Claims. In 1987, the Oglala Sioux Tribe and Rosebud Sioux Tribe sought relief from the entry of judgment based on a settlement of the treaty-based claims, contending that the attorneys who appeared on behalf of the plaintiffs had agreed to this entry without notice to the plaintiffs or their approval. Though with a blistering dissent by Judge Newman, the motion was denied, and the U.S. Court of Appeals for the Federal Circuit affirmed. *Oglala Sioux Tribe and Rosebud Sioux Tribe v. Untied States*, 862 F.2d 275 (Fed. Cir. 1988). For a discussion of ethical considerations faced by tribal attorneys, see Kristen A. Carpenter, *Lawyering for Groups: The Case of American Indian Tribal Attorneys*, 81 Fordham L. Rev. 3–8 (with E. Wald) (2013).

As of 2009, the total award for Sioux Nation cases had reached an estimated $900,000,000. A class action filed in April 2009 by some individual Sioux is seeking a court order to compel the Secretary of the Interior to distribute the judgment funds. Would the Sioux tribes be indispensable parties to such a suit? If so, could they be joined without their consent?

Bills to restore 1.3 million acres of federal land in the Black Hills to the Sioux have been introduced into the Congress, but have failed to pass. *See, e.g.,* "The Sioux Nation Black Hills Act," S. 1453, 99th Cong., 1st Sess. (1985). Professor John LaVelle has made a powerful case for environmentalists to join in support of the legislation. John P. LaVelle, *Rescuing Paha Sapa: Achieving Environmental Justice by Restoring the Great Grasslands and Returning the Sacred Black Hills to the Great Sioux Nation,* 5 GREAT PLAINS NAT. RESOURCES J. 40 (2001). For a chronology of events before and after the Supreme Court's decision in the *Sioux Nation* case, see MARIO GONZALEZ & ELIZABETH COOK-LYNN, THE POLITICS OF HALLOWED GROUND: WOUNDED KNEE AND THE STRUGGLE FOR INDIAN SOVEREIGNTY 331–57 (1999). An account of the litigation written by the son of one of the attorneys is EDWARD LAZARUS, BLACK HILLS/WHITE JUSTICE THE SIOUX NATION VERSUS THE UNITED STATES, 1775 TO THE PRESENT (1999).

6. **Damages Claims for Violations of Treaty Rights:** In *United States ex rel. Hualpai Indians v. Santa Fe Pac. R.R. Co.,* discussed in Sec. A.1, this chapter, the Supreme Court upheld the right of the United States, in its own right and on behalf of the tribe, to enjoin third parties from interfering with aboriginal property rights. The Court's opinion indicated that the tribe's property rights deserved no less protection because of the absence of a treaty, implying that protection would have been assured if the tribe's property rights were recognized by treaty. Several United States courts of appeal have extended this incident of aboriginal title, and by implication of treaty title, to claims for damages. *See United States v. Pend Oreille Pub. Util. Dist. No. 1,* 28 F.3d 1544, 1548–51 (9th Cir. 1994) (allowing the Kalispel Indian Tribe to seek damages from a county utility district for the flooding of aboriginal lands that had been set aside by executive order); *Mescalero Apache Tribe v. Burgett Floral Co.,* 503 F.2d 336, 337–38 (10th Cir. 1974) (allowing damages to a tribe for a private company's unlawful tree-cutting). In fact, the Supreme Court's decision in *County of Oneida v. Oneida Indian Nation,* 470 U.S. 226 (1985), presented in Ch. 4, Sec. A.4.b, allowed a suit under federal common law against a non-signatory third party for unlawful use and occupation of lands in violation of aboriginal rights reserved by treaty.

It is quite surprising, then, that the Ninth Circuit, en banc, decided that the Skokomish Tribe could not bring an action against the City of Tacoma and Tacoma Public Utility for massive damage caused to tribal land and other treaty-protected property rights by a hydroelectric project. *Skokomish Indian Tribe v. United States,* 410 F.3d 506 (9th Cir. 2005) (also discussed at Ch. 7, Sec. A.1). Allegedly the project caused flooding of tribal lands, failure of septic tanks, contamination of water wells, blockage of fish migration, and silting of shellfish beaches, among other harms. Yet the en banc majority determined that an action to redress this harm could be brought against third parties only if the treaty specifically envisioned or authorized such a suit. The majority in *Skokomish* attempted to distinguish the Oneida case on the basis that the Oneida claim involved aboriginal title. Does that move work? In any event, if there is an appropriate difference in treatment between aboriginal and treaty rights, should aboriginal rights receive more or less protection? In addition, is it appropriate to distinguish the *Santa Fe* case on the basis that the claim there involved injunctive relief rather than damages? The court also disallowed tribal claims against the City and utility under 42 U.S.C. § 1983, relying on *Inyo County v. Paiute-Shoshone Indians of the Bishop Cmty. of the Bishop Colony*, 538 U.S. 701 (2003), discussed in Ch. 4, Sec. A.4.b. It sent claims against the United States to the Court of Federal Claims, as they sounded under the Indian Tucker Act, 28 U.S.C. § 1505, rather than the Federal Tort Claims Act. Writing for a group of dissenting judges, Judge Berzon accused the majority of "reinvent[ing] established doctrine," and "largely ignor[ing] two centuries of understandings concerning the federal protection of Indian aboriginal and treaty-based rights — in particular, the understanding that Indian treaties in large part simply preserve some pre-existing aboriginal rights in exchange for cession of a portion of Indian land." Is that an overstatement?

3. Executive Order Reservations

After Congress abandoned treaty-making in 1871, 25 U.S.C. § 71, the federal government nevertheless continued the process of land cessions and the allocation and protection of Indian tribal reserves. This process was sometimes accomplished by agreements with the Indian tribes that were ratified by statutory enactment, thereby generally recognizing the Indian title so protected. *See, e.g.*, Act of Feb. 28, 1877, ch. 72, 19 Stat. 254 (Sioux Nation, Northern Arapaho, and Cheyenne Indians). In addition, presidents also set aside over twenty-three million acres from the public domain by executive orders for the use and occupancy of the Indians until 1918-1919, when Congress declared an end to the practice. 25 U.S.C. § 211 (codification of 1918 Act prohibiting the creation of new reservations in New Mexico and Arizona "except by Act of Congress"); 43 U.S.C. § 150 (codification of 1919 Act stating: "No public lands of the United States shall be withdrawn by Executive Order, proclamation, or otherwise, for or as an Indian reservation except by act of Congress."). *See also* 25 U.S.C. § 398d (prohibiting changes in boundaries of executive order Indian reservations "except by Act of Congress").

Article IV, section 3, clause 2 of the Constitution provides "The Congress shall have Power to dispose of and make all needful Rules and Regulations respecting the Territory and other Property belonging to the United States." This provision raises a host of complex, interrelated, constitutionally based questions regarding executive order lands not affirmatively authorized or recognized by Congress. Included among the questions are:

(1) whether the President has the power to set aside portions of the public domain for the Indians without congressional authorization;

(2) whether the title acquired under a mere executive order is recognized or unrecognized; and

(3) whether the President, without participation by the Congress, may terminate and extinguish Indian land rights created by executive order.

SIOUX TRIBE v. UNITED STATES
United States Supreme Court
316 U.S. 317 (1942)

MR. JUSTICE BYRNES delivered the opinion of the Court.

This is an action to recover compensation for some 5 million acres of land allegedly taken from the petitioner tribe in 1879 and 1884. The suit was initiated under the Act of June 3, 1920, 41 Stat. 738, permitting petitioner to submit to the Court of Claims any claims arising from the asserted failure of the United States to pay money or property due, without regard to lapse of time or statutes of limitation. The Court of Claims denied recovery, 94 Ct. Cls. 150, and we brought the case here on certiorari.

The facts as found by the Court of Claims are as follows:

In 1868 the United States and the Sioux Tribe entered into the Fort Laramie Treaty (15 Stat. 635). By Article II of this treaty, a certain described territory, known as the Great Sioux Reservation and located in what is now South Dakota and Nebraska, was "set apart for the absolute and undisturbed use and occupation" of the Tribe. The United States promised that no persons, other than government officers and agents discharging their official duties, would be permitted "to pass over, settle upon, or reside in the territory described in this article, or in such territory as may be added to this reservation for the use of said Indians." For their part, the Indians relinquished "all claims or right in and to any portion of the United States or Territories, except such as is embraced within the limits aforesaid." No question arises in this case with respect to the lands specifically included within the Reservation by this treaty.

The eastern boundary of the Great Sioux Reservation, as constituted by the Ft. Laramie Treaty, was the low water mark on the east bank of the Missouri River. The large tract bordering upon and extending eastward from the east bank of the river remained a part of the public domain open to settlement and afforded easy access to the Reservation. As a result, great numbers of white men "infested" the region for the purpose of engaging in the liquor traffic. Anxiety over this development led the Commissioner of Indian Affairs, on January 8, 1875, to suggest to the Secretary of the Interior that he request the President to issue an executive order withdrawing from sale and setting apart for Indian purposes a certain large tract of the land along the eastern bank of the Missouri River. In the Commissioner's letter to the Secretary of the Interior, and in the latter's letter of January 9th to the President, the reason advanced for the proposed executive order was that it was "deemed necessary for the suppression of the liquor traffic with the Indians upon the Missouri River." On January 11, 1875, the President signed the suggested order.

[Three other small tracts of land were similarly later withdrawn from the public domain to suppress the liquor traffic.]

About two and a half years after the last of these four executive orders withdrawing lands from sale and setting them apart for the use of the Sioux, the Commissioner of Indian Affairs submitted to the Secretary of the Interior a report upon a suggestion that the orders be modified so as to permit the return of the lands to the public domain. The report, dated June 6, 1879, reviewed the problems arising from the liquor trade during the years following the Fort Laramie treaty, recalled that the purpose of the four executive orders of 1875 and 1876 had been to eliminate this traffic, observed that they had "to a great extent accomplished the object desired, viz: the prevention of the sale of whiskey to the Indians," and concluded that any change in the boundaries established by the executive orders would "give renewed life to this unlawful traffic, and be detrimental to the best interests of the Indians."

Three weeks later, however, upon reconsideration, the Commissioner informed the Secretary that, in his opinion, the lands included in the executive orders of 1875 and 1876 might be "restored to the public domain, and the interests of the Indians still be protected." [Consequently,] he recommended that the lands withdrawn from sale by the President in 1875 and 1876 be returned to the public domain, with the exception of three small tracts directly opposite the Cheyenne, Grand River, and Standing Rock agencies. On August 9, 1879, an executive order to this effect was promulgated and the land, with the exceptions indicated, was "restored to the public domain." Five years later, the Commissioner informed the Secretary that the Grand River Agency had ceased to exist and that the agents at Cheyenne and Standing Rock considered it no longer necessary to withhold the tracts opposite their agencies from the public domain "for the purpose for which they have thus far been retained." Consequently, an executive order was prepared and signed by the President on March 20, 1884, restoring these three small pieces of land to the public domain, "the same being no longer needed for the purpose for which they were withdrawn from sale and settlement."

One additional event remains to be noted. In the Indian Appropriation Act for 1877, approved August 15, 1876 (19 Stat. 176, 192), Congress provided: . . .

> [H]ereafter there shall be no appropriation made for the subsistence of said Indians [i.e., the Sioux], unless they shall first agree to relinquish all right and claim to any country outside the boundaries of the permanent reservation established by the treaty of eighteen hundred and sixty-eight [the Fort Laramie treaty] for said Indians; and also so much of their said permanent reservation as lies west of the one hundred and third meridian of longitude [the western boundary set by the Fort Laramie treaty had been the 104th meridian], and shall also grant right of way over said reservation to the country thus ceded for wagon or other roads, from convenient and accessible points on the Missouri River. . . .

On September 26, 1876 — a date subsequent to the first three of the four executive orders setting apart additional lands for the use of the Sioux, but about two months prior to the last of those orders — the Sioux Tribe signed an agreement conforming to the conditions imposed by Congress in the Indian Appropriation Act and promised to "relinquish and cede to the United States all the territory lying outside the said reservation, as herein modified and described. . . ."

Petitioner's position is that the executive orders of 1875 and 1876 were effective to convey to the Tribe the same kind of interest in the lands affected as it had acquired in the lands covered by the Fort Laramie Treaty, that the executive orders of 1879 and 1884 restoring the lands to the public domain deprived petitioner of this interest, and that it is entitled to be compensated for the fair value of the lands as of 1879 and 1884.

[Art. IV, § 3] of the Constitution confers upon Congress exclusively "the power to dispose of and make all needful rules and regulations respecting the territory or other property belonging to the United States." Nevertheless, "from an early period in the history of the government it has been the practice of the President to order, from time to time, as the exigencies of the public service required, parcels of land belonging to the United States to be reserved from sale and set apart for public uses." *Grisar v. McDowell*, 6 Wall. 363, 381. As long ago as 1830, Congress revealed its awareness of this practice and acquiesced in it. By 1855 the President had begun to withdraw public lands from sale by executive order for the specific purpose of establishing Indian reservations. From that date until 1919, hundreds of reservations for Indian occupancy and for other purposes were created by executive order. Department of the Interior, *Executive Orders Relating to Indian Reservations, passim; United States v. Midwest Oil Co.*, 236 U.S. 459, 469–470. Although the validity of these orders was occasionally questioned, doubts were quieted in *United States v. Midwest Oil Co., supra*. In that case, it was squarely held that, even in the absence of express statutory authorization, it lay within the power of the President to withdraw lands from the public domain. *Cf. Mason v. United States*, 260 U.S. 545.

The Government therefore does not deny that the executive orders of 1875 and 1876 involved here were effective to withdraw the lands in question from the public domain. It contends, however, that this is not the issue presented by this case. It urges that, instead, we are called upon to determine whether the President had the power to bestow upon the Sioux Tribe an interest in these lands of such a character as to require compensation when the interest was extinguished by the executive orders of 1879 and 1884. Concededly, where lands have been reserved for the use and occupation of an Indian Tribe by the terms of a treaty or statute, the tribe must be compensated if the lands are subsequently taken from them. *Shoshone Tribe v. United States*, 299 U.S. 476; *United States v. Shoshone Tribe*, 304 U.S. 111; *United States v. Klamath Indians*, 304 U.S. 119. Since the Constitution places the authority to dispose of public lands exclusively in Congress, the executive's power to convey any interest in these lands must be traced to Congressional delegation of its authority. The basis of decision in *United States v. Midwest Oil Co.* was that, so far as the power to withdraw public lands from sale is concerned, such a delegation could be spelled out from long continued Congressional acquiescence in the executive practice. The answer to whether a similar delegation occurred with respect to the power to convey a compensable interest in these lands to the Indians must be found in the available evidence of what consequences were thought by the executive and Congress to flow from the establishment of executive order reservations.

It is significant that the executive department consistently indicated its understanding that the rights and interests which the Indians enjoyed in executive order reservations were different from and less than their rights and interests in treaty or statute reservations. The annual reports of the Commissioner of Indian Affairs during the years when reservations were frequently being established by executive order contain statements that the Indians had "no assurance for their occupation of these lands beyond the pleasure of the Executive," that they "are mere tenants at will, and possess no permanent rights to the lands upon which they are temporarily permitted to remain," and that those occupying land in executive order reservations "do not hold it by the same tenure with which Indians in other parts of the Indian Territory possess their reserves."

Although there are abundant signs that Congress was aware of the practice of establishing Indian reservations by executive order, there is little to indicate what it understood to be the kind of interest that the Indians obtained in these lands. However, in its report in 1892 upon a bill to restore to the public domain a portion of the Colville executive order reservation, the Senate Committee on Indian Affairs expressed the opinion that under the executive order "the Indians were given a license to occupy the lands described in it so long as it was the pleasure of the Government they should do so, and no right, title, or claim to such lands has vested in the Indians by virtue of this occupancy."

[T]he most striking proof of the belief shared by Congress and the Executive that the Indians were not entitled to compensation upon the abolition of an executive order reservation is the very absence of compensatory payments in such situations. It was a common practice, during the period in which reservations were created by executive order, for the President simply to terminate the existence of a reservation by canceling or revoking the order establishing it. That is to say, the procedure followed in the case before us was typical. No compensation was made, and neither the Government nor the Indians suggested that it was due. It is true that on several of the many occasions when Congress itself abolished executive order reservations, it provided for a measure of compensation to the Indians. In the Act of July 1, 1892, restoring to the public domain a large portion of the Colville reservation, and in the Act of February 20, 1893, restoring a portion of the White Mountain Apache Indian Reservation, Congress directed that the proceeds from the sale of the lands be used for the benefit of the Indians. But both acts contained an explicit proviso: "That nothing herein contained shall be construed as recognizing title or ownership of said Indians to any part of said . . . Reservation, whether that hereby restored to the public domain or that still reserved by the Government for their use and occupancy." Consequently, the granting of compensation must be regarded as an act of grace rather than a recognition of an obligation.

We conclude therefore that there was no express constitutional or statutory authorization for the conveyance of a compensable interest to petitioner by the four executive orders of 1875 and 1876, and that no implied Congressional delegation of the power to do so can be spelled out from the evidence of Congressional and executive understanding. The orders were effective to withdraw from sale the lands affected and to grant the use of the lands to the petitioner. But the interest which the Indians received was subject to termination at the will of either the executive or Congress and without obligation to the United States. The executive orders of 1879 and 1884 were simply an exercise of this power of termination, and the payment of compensation was not required.

Affirmed.

NOTES

1. **The Nature of Executive Order Title:** Does *Sioux Tribe* hold that all lands held solely under executive order are unrecognized for purposes of the Fifth Amendment and may be extinguished at the will of the Chief Executive, or is its holding limited by the narrow and peculiar reasons for which the executive order lands were set aside in the case? In *Confederated Bands of Ute Indians v. United States*, 330 U.S. 169 (1947), the Court, relying on *Sioux Tribe*, held that lands set apart for the Utes by executive order in 1875 in an effort to resolve a boundary dispute created by an erroneous survey of the line established in an 1868 treaty were not recognized Indian property. Thus, such lands could be withdrawn without compensation by a subsequent 1882 executive order restoring the lands to the public domain in the aftermath of the so-called "Meeker massacre" perpetrated by the Utes. The Court stressed, "There is not one word in [any] Act showing a congressional purpose to convey the Executive Order lands, or any other lands, to the Indians." Might the result in *Sioux Tribe* or *Confederated Bands of Ute Indians* be different if the executive orders creating the reservations had remained in force for longer periods of time?

What if evidence showed that Congress had appropriated funds to improve the reservation for the benefit of the Indians or had repeatedly supplied educational benefits to Indians on the reservation? What should be the consequences of the many federal statutes, such as those regulating mineral and timber extraction, that treat tribes as rightful occupants or even owners of executive order land? Recall that subsequent treatment by the executive and the general public, as well as by Congress, has figured into determinations of congressional intent in other types of cases, including those involving the boundaries of a reservation and establishment of recognized title. *See, e.g., Solem v. Bartlett*, 465 U.S. 463 (1984) (set forth and discussed in Ch. 2, Sec. A.3.b); *United States v. Klamath & Moadoc Tribes*, 304 U.S. 119 (1938). Should decades of Congress treating Indians inhabiting executive order reservations the same as those inhabiting treaty or statutory reservations have the effect of turning executive order reservations into compensable property interests for purposes of the Fifth Amendment, either by demonstrating sufficient congressional intent to protect existing reservations or by creating a reliance interest in the tribes that has risen to the status of a property interest? *Cf.* Joseph William Singer, *The Reliance Interest in Property*, 40 STAN. L. REV. 611 (1988).

2. **General Recognition of All Executive Order Reservations:** By one estimate over two million acres of executive order land remained unrecognized by explicit statutory provision as of 1953. Note, *Tribal Property Interests in Executive-Order Reservations: A Compensable Indian Right*, 69 YALE L.J. 627, 629 n.14 (1960). Could there be a general federal law recognizing all of this land? In *Sioux Tribe*, the Tribe argued that Congress had demonstrated an intent to give executive order lands recognized Indian title status in the General Allotment Act of 1887, ch. 119, § 1, 24 Stat. 389, codified as amended at 25 U.S.C. § 331, by expressly authorizing the allotment in severalty to tribal members of land located on reservations "created for [Indian] use, either by treaty stipulation or by virtue of an Act of Congress or Executive order." The Court rejected this contention, stating:

> We think that the inclusion of executive order reservations meant no more than that Congress was willing that the lands within them should be allotted to individual Indians according to the procedure outlined. It did not amount to a recognition of tribal ownership of the lands prior to allotment. Since the lands involved in the case before us were never allotted — indeed, the executive orders of 1879 and 1884 terminated the reservation even before the Allotment Act was passed, — we think the Act has no bearing upon the issue presented.

316 U.S. at 330. What should be the result regarding recognized title if the question arises as to an allotted reservation?

A 1927 Act of Congress, enacted in response to litigation raising the question whether Indians claiming title to executive order lands were entitled to the royalties from mineral, oil, and gas development of such lands, expressly authorized such mineral development and leasing for the benefit of the Indians. Act of Mar. 3, 1927, ch. 299, 44 Stat. 1347, §§ 1–3, codified at 25 U.S.C. §§ 398a–398e. At least one commentator has viewed this Act as an intentional blanket recognition of unrecognized executive order lands by Congress. Note, *Tribal Property Interests in Executive Order Reservations: A Compensable Indian Right*, 69 YALE L.J. 627, 631–39 (1960). *But see Sekaquaptewa v. MacDonald*, 448 F. Supp. 1183, 1192–93 (D. Ariz. 1978), *aff'd in part and rev'd in part*, 619 F.2d 801 (9th Cir. 1980) (explicitly rejecting the argument, but holding that the Navajo Boundary Act of 1934, ch. 521, 48 Stat. 960, recognized nine million acres of executive order land).

Finally, in 1994, Congress amended the Indian Reorganization Act by adding sections that prohibit any new or existing regulations of the United States from classifying, enhancing, or diminishing "the privileges and immunities" of any federally recognized tribe relative to any other federally recognized tribe. Act of May 31, 1994, Pub. L. No. 103-263, § 5(b), 108 Stat. 707, 709, amending 25 U.S.C. § 476. Could this provision be used to preclude different treatment of tribal executive order land?

3. Recognition of Specific Executive Order Reservations: Some executive order reservations were created under the authority of a treaty or statute. *See, e.g.*, Act of Apr. 8, 1864, § 2, 13 Stat. 39, 40, providing "[T]here shall be set apart by the President, and at his discretion, not exceeding four tracts of land, within the limits of [California], to be retained by the United States for the purpose of Indian reservations, which shall be of suitable extent for the accommodation of the Indians of said state. . . ." In 1876, President Grant issued an executive order formally setting apart land in Northern California which has become part of the Hoopa Valley Reservation, declaring that the land "be and hereby is, withdrawn from public sale and set apart for Indian purposes, as one of the Indian reservations authorized to be set apart, in California, by act of Congress approved April 8, 1864." 1 CHARLES J. KAPPLER, INDIAN AFFAIRS: LAWS & TREATIES 815 (1904). Could the Indians of that reservation argue that their land had been recognized? The Hoopa were afforded clear Congressional affirmation of their title in the Hoopa-Yurok Settlement Act, 25 U.S.C. § 1300i-1(b). Other tribes have received similar recognition for their executive order reservations. *See, e.g., Three Affiliated Tribes of the Ft. Berthold Reservation v. United States*, 390 F.2d 686 (Ct. Cl. 1968).

4. Incidents of Unrecognized Executive Order Title: The Supreme Court has not generally distinguished between types of title when questions arise regarding the property rights that attach to reservation status. In *United States v. Dion*, presented in Ch. 4, Sec. A.2, the Court rejected a statutory interpretation argument that rested on the distinction between treaty and nontreaty hunting rights, stating: "Indian reservations created by statute, agreement, or executive order normally carry with them the same implicit hunting rights as those created by treaty." *United States v. Dion*, 476 U.S. 734, 745 n.8 (1986); *see also Winters v. United States*, 207 U.S. 564, 577 (1908) (water rights attach to executive order reservation). For more information on the *Winters* case, *see* Judith V. Royster, *Water, Legal Rights, and the Actual Consequences: The Story of* Winters v. United States *in* INDIAN LAW STORIES (Carole Goldberg, Kevin K. Washburn & Philip P. Frickey, eds., 2011). Indian hunting, fishing, and water rights are presented in Ch. 7.

5. The Navajo-Hopi Dispute over Executive Order Land: In 1882, President Chester Arthur set aside a reservation that enclosed 2.5 million acres, or 3,900 square miles, surrounding the three mesas on which all but two of the present-day twelve Hopi villages are located. This reservation encompassed the entire Hopi population, and was established in order to evict several Anglos who were helping the Hopis resist federal attempts to send their children to boarding schools. As there were an estimated 300–600 Navajos living among the Hopis, the reservation provided that it should be for the Hopi "and such other Indians as the Secretary of the Interior may see fit to settle thereon." Executive Order of President Chester Arthur, December 16, 1882, reprinted in *Healing v. Jones*, 210 F. Supp. 125, 129 n.1 (D. Ariz. 1962). The balance of later settlement in that area strongly favored the much larger Navajo Nation.

In 1958, at the request of Hopi tribal leaders, Congress enacted a law authorizing suit to be brought settling title to the land. A court decision, *Healing v. Jones*, 174 F. Supp. 211 (D. Ariz. 1959), *aff'd*, 373 U.S. 758 (1963) (per curiam), found that this jurisdictional act confirmed title in both tribes, a ruling that only intensified the dispute. In 1966, Commissioner of Indian Affairs Robert Bennett, with authorization from Congress, ordered a "freeze" on development in 1.5 million acres, making it impossible for residents to build or make repairs or improvements to their homes, and preventing construction of roads, sewers, or any other public infrastructure. Despite this hardship, by 1974 10,000 Navajos inhabited the Hopi land. Congress enacted the Navajo and Hopi Relocation Act, Pub. L. No. 93-531, 88 Stat. 1712, codified as amended at 25 U.S.C. §§ 640d–640d-28, providing for a judicial partition of the disputed Joint Use Area and setting up a commission charged with devising a plan to relocate members of each tribe to their tribe's portion of the area. The Commission's work was to have been done by July 6, 1986, but many delays occurred, creating enormous difficulties for Navajos left in the disputed area, and sparking a concerted resistance movement, with international support.

The partition itself was a highly unusual remedy, especially in light of the wrenching displacement of so many Navajos. Was it justified by concerns that the more numerous Navajo, who mainly herded livestock, would deprive the more sedentary, agrarian Hopis of reasonable access to the jointly held area? Given the history of federal Indian policy, which economic interest — livestock or farming — would you expect the United States to favor? As Attorney Hollis Whitson has noted, there is another way of understanding the Navajo-Hopi dispute, which "focuses more on the common ground between the two peoples and the problems created by decades of federal intrusion into tribal affairs." Hollis A. Whitson, *A Policy Review of the Federal Government's Relocation of Navajo Indians Under P.L. 93-531 and P.L. 96-305*, 27 Ariz. L. Rev. 371, 373–74 (1985). For a history of the dispute containing interviews with Hopi and Navajo traditionals, see Anita Parlow, Cry Sacred Ground: Big Mountain, USA (1988).

A claim by 47 traditional Navajos that the relocation violated both First Amendment free exercise rights and international law was rejected in *Manybeads v. United States*, 730 F. Supp. 1515 (D. Ariz. 1989). By that time, at least 12,000 Navajos had been forced to leave land that their families had occupied for generations, but some 3,000 Navajos remained on the Hopi Partitioned Lands (HPL). *See*, Eric T. Cheyfitz, *Theory and Practice: The Case of the Navajo-Hopi Land Dispute*, 10 Am. U. J. Gender Soc. Pol'y & L. 619, 629 (2002). In 2006, the Navajo and Hopi settled their remaining issues, allowing religious access and use by members of each tribe on the land of the other, and lifting the construction ban imposed by the 1966 Bennett Freeze. In May 2009, President Obama signed federal legislation that repealed authorization for the Freeze, an action which seems to have brought some closure to the dispute.

4.   Placing Indian Land in Trust

Trust title arises when the United States holds title to Indian lands for the benefit of either an Indian tribe or specific Indian allottees. Decisions covered elsewhere in this book indicate the importance of placing Indian land in federal trust for various legal purposes. For example, *Alaska v. Native Village of Venetie Tribal Government*, 522 U.S. 520 (1998), set forth and discussed in Ch. 2, Sec. A.3.b.ii, indicates that federal supervision of tribal lands through trust title or otherwise (as illustrated by the Pueblos or the Five Tribes in Oklahoma) may be required to establish that tribal lands constitute Indian country. *See also Buzzard v. Oklahoma Tax Comm'n*, 992 F.2d 1073 (10th Cir. 1993). Similarly, in *County of Yakima v. Confederated Tribes and Bands of Yakima Indian Nation*, 502 U.S. 251 (1992), and *Cass County, Minn. v. Leech Lake Band of Chippewa Indians*, 524 U.S. 103 (1998), the Court held that when an Indian tribe repurchased former tribal lands and held them in fee simple within its reservation, the lands nevertheless were not tax exempt when not placed in trust since Congress had manifested an intent through various allotment statutes to permit taxation of freely alienable land. These cases indicate the importance of placing lands a tribe desires to safeguard in trust title. Indeed, many tribes experiencing economic development success through gaming or otherwise are trying to reconstruct the ancestral territories from which they were dispossessed by purchasing land in fee and asking the Department of the Interior to take the land into trust. Which model of tribal-federal relations do these decisions reflect when they require trust land status before tribal authority and immunities attach? Why does federal Indian law insist on tribal trust title to secure the full implementation of tribal rights?

This emphasis on tribal trust title, of course, focuses attention on the mechanisms through which Indian tribes and tribal members place lands in federal trust. The process has become highly contentious, because state and local governments resist the loss of their property tax base and their loss of jurisdiction once the land becomes Indian country. How can and should tribes allay these concerns? Should they offer payments to local governments in lieu of taxes, as the Oneida Indian Nation of New York, a successful gaming tribe, has done? Should they underscore the amount of services and special funding opportunities that accompany Indian country status? For some non-Indian communities, these economic arguments carry little weight compared with their fears of loss of control to a Native government. For example, an organization called Upstate Citizens for Equality, operating in New York, indicates on its website: "The fundamental issue is sovereignty. UCE adamantly opposes the establishment of an independent, sovereign Cayuga Indian nation within New York State." *See* http://www.upstate-citizens.org/sovereignty.htm. Is there any tribal response, short of litigation, that can answer such concerns?

The only general federal statutes expressly authorizing the federal government to take Indian lands into trust title are found in sections 5 and 7 of the Indian Reorganization Act of 1934 (IRA), 25 U.S.C. §§ 465, 467. Section 5 of the IRA, 25 U.S.C. § 465, authorizes the Secretary of the Interior to acquire any interest in lands, water rights, or surface rights for Indians "within or without reservation" through "purchase, relinquishment, gift, exchange or assignment." That section specifically indicates that acquisition must be "for the purpose of providing land for Indians." When the Secretary acquires land under section 5, "[t]itle to any lands or rights acquired . . . shall be taken in the name of the United States in trust for the Indian tribe or individual Indian for which the land is acquired, and such lands or rights shall be exempt from State and local taxation." Section 7 of the IRA, 25 U.S.C. § 467, authorizes the Secretary to proclaim such newly acquired lands as either a new Indian reservation or as an addition to an existing reservation, but requires that the land added to existing reservations "shall be designated for the exclusive use of Indians entitled by enrollment or by tribal membership to residence at such reservations."

While administrative practice of the Bureau of Indian Affairs has frequently invoked the power granted in section 5 to take land in trust, it has far less frequently issued proclamations under section 7, apparently believing that taking the land into trust was sufficient to establish its Indian country status. In *Mescalero Apache Tribe v. Jones*, 411 U.S. 145 (1973), the Supreme Court considered the state tax status of a tribal ski enterprise operated on lands leased to the tribe by the United States from national forest lands adjacent to the reservation. The lands had been acquired under section 5 and had been leased rather than conveyed by actually transferring title in trust for the tribe because "it would have been meaningless for the United States, which already had title to the forest, to convey title to itself for the use of the Tribe." Although no mention of this fact is made in the opinion, apparently no proclamation was ever issued under section 7 of the 1934 Act to cover the land so acquired. The Court treated the ski enterprise as a tribal activity conducted outside of the reservation, thereby upholding a nondiscriminatory state gross receipts tax on the tribal revenues from the enterprise. Noting that section 5 of the 1934 Act, however, expressly exempted real estate acquired under its provision from state and local taxation, the Court did hold that the state could not impose a use tax on certain fixtures purchased by the enterprise — a reminder that federal Indian statutes sometimes operate outside of Indian country. *Cf. Santa Rosa Band of Indians v. Kings County*, 532 F.2d 655 (9th Cir. 1975) (land acquired under section 5 exempt from local building and zoning ordinances).

Originally, 25 U.S.C. § 478, provided that section 465 applied only to tribes that voted to adopt the Indian Reorganization Act of 1934. Other tribally-specific authorizations to take land into trust are found in settlement legislation and other federal statutes, such as the Maine Indian Claims Settlement Act of 1980, 25 U.S.C. §§ 1724(d). Notwithstanding the lack of any general express statutory authority for taking land in trust for non-IRA tribes, however, the Bureau of Indian Affairs historically drew no distinction between IRA and non-IRA tribes with respect to its authority to take land into trust for their benefit, so long as the tribal government was federally recognized at the time of the trust decision. Ultimately, section 203 of the Indian Land Consolidation Act of 1983, Pub.L. 97-459, Title II, § 203, Jan. 12, 1983, 96 Stat. 2517, codified at 25. U.S.C. § 2202, resolved this problem by making section 465 applicable to "all tribes," while simultaneously providing that it did supersede "any other provision of Federal law which authorizes, prohibits, or restricts the acquisition of land for Indians with respect to any specific tribe, reservation, or state(s)." *See* Note 7 in Section A.5, this chapter. Thus, except where otherwise prohibited by federal law, section 465 now authorizes the Secretary to take land in trust for both IRA and non-IRA tribes. For an historical in-depth discussion of land-into-trust policy and process, tribal-state relations regarding the issue, and analysis of Supreme Court doctrine, *see* Frank Pommersheim, *Land Into Trust: An Inquiry Into Law, Policy, and History*, 49 IDAHO L. REV. 519 (2012–2013).

In *South Dakota v. U.S. Dept. of the Interior*, 69 F.3d 878 (8th Cir. 1995), *judgment vacated by, Department of the Interior v. South Dakota*, 519 U.S. 919 (1996), the Eighth Circuit declared section 5 of the Indian Reorganization Act unconstitutional for lack of standards. While the plaintiffs in the case felt aggrieved that the lack of notice or meaningful participation in the administrative process deprived them of any effective opportunity to prevent the removal of land taken in trust from the tax roles, the Eighth Circuit objected to the statutory authority pursuant to which the land was taken into trust. It noted:

> There are no perceptible "boundaries," no "intelligible principles," within the four corners of the statutory language that constrain this delegated authority — except that the acquisition must be "for Indians." It delegates unrestricted power to acquire land from private citizens for the private use and benefit of Indian tribes or individual Indians.

69 F.3d at 882. Consequently, in an extraordinarily rare invocation of the non-delegation doctrine (which, at least in theory, prevents congressional delegation of authority to executive agencies without adequate standards), the Eighth Circuit declared section 5 unconstitutional pursuant to that doctrine. Responding to this decision, the Secretary of the Interior promulgated new regulations that provided greater notice and opportunity for state and local governments to be heard in connection with applications to take land into trust for Indian tribes and individuals. Department of the Interior, Land Acquisitions (Nongaming), 61 Fed. Reg. 18083 (1996), codified at 25 C.F.R. § 151.12. Responding to this regulation, the United

States Supreme Court voted, over three dissents, to vacate the judgments below and remand the case to the Secretary of the Interior for reconsideration in light of the new regulations. While this decision vacated the *South Dakota* decision and eliminated its effect as precedent, did it resolve the non-delegation issue? Does section 5 contain adequate standards to satisfy the non-delegation doctrine?

Following the Court's remand, the Department of the Interior initiated a new review of the request to take the Lower Brule Sioux land in South Dakota into trust. After the Department approved the request, the state of South Dakota and affected local governments renewed their federal court challenge to section 5 of the IRA, arguing again that that the land- into-trust provisions constitute an unconstitutional delegation of power to the Executive Branch. The Eighth Circuit eventually concluded that the delegation in section 5 provides sufficient guidance to withstand a challenge based upon nondelegation doctrine grounds. *South Dakota v. United States DOI*, 423 F.3d 790 (8th Cir. 2005). In the court's view, "the purposes evident in the whole of the IRA and its legislative history sufficiently narrow the delegation and guide the Secretary's discretion in deciding when to take land into trust." Those purposes involve stemming the loss of Indian lands and revitalizing reservations as sites of tribal self-government.

Other federal circuits have upheld Interior's land-into-trust regulations in the face of nondelegation challenges. *See Michigan Gambling Opposition v. Kempthorne*, 525 F.3d 23 (D.C. Cir. 2008); *United States v. Roberts*, 185 F.3d 1125, 1136–37 (10th Cir. 1999). After experiencing the defeat of their nondelegation challenges, state and local governments initiated a different line of attack on Interior's land-into-trust decisions.

As explained in Ch. 2, Sec. A.3 and Ch. 5, Sec. B.1.a, the Alaska Native Claims Settlement Act of 1971 (ANCSA) resulted in much of the territory of Alaska Native tribes being held in fee by Native corporations or in the Native villages themselves. The Secretary of the Interior interpreted ANCSA as barring the federal government from taking such fee lands into trust. Recently, in *Akiachak Native Community v. Salazar*, 935 F. Supp. 2d 195 (D.D.C. 2013), the district court for the District of Columbia struck down the regulatory prohibition on taking land in trust in Alaska. The Bureau of Indian Affairs has now repealed the prohibition, relying in part on the recommendations of two separate federal commissions. For discussion of this development, see Ch. 5, Sec. B.1.a (Note 4).

CARCIERI v. SALAZAR
United States Supreme Court
555 U.S. 379 (2009)

Justice Thomas delivered the opinion of the Court.

The Indian Reorganization Act (IRA or Act) authorizes the Secretary of the Interior, a respondent in this case, to acquire land and hold it in trust "for the purpose of providing land for Indians." Ch. 576, § 5, 48 Stat. 985, 25 U.S.C. § 465. The IRA defines the term "Indian" to "include all persons of Indian descent who are members of any recognized Indian tribe now under Federal jurisdiction." § 479. The

Secretary notified petitioners — the State of Rhode Island, its Governor, and the town of Charlestown, Rhode Island — that he intended to accept in trust a parcel of land for use by the Narragansett Indian Tribe in accordance with his claimed authority under the statute. In proceedings before the Interior Board of Indian Appeals (IBIA), the District Court, and the Court of Appeals for the First Circuit, petitioners unsuccessfully challenged the Secretary's authority to take the parcel into trust.

In reviewing the determination of the Court of Appeals, we are asked to interpret the statutory phrase "now under Federal jurisdiction" in § 479. Petitioners contend that the term "now" refers to the time of the statute's enactment, and permits the Secretary to take land into trust for members of recognized tribes that were "under Federal jurisdiction" in 1934. The respondents argue that the word "now" is an ambiguous term that can reasonably be construed to authorize the Secretary to take land into trust for members of tribes that are "under Federal jurisdiction" at the time that the land is accepted into trust.

We agree with petitioners and hold that, for purposes of § 479, the phrase "now under Federal jurisdiction" refers to a tribe that was under federal jurisdiction at the time of the statute's enactment. As a result, § 479 limits the Secretary's authority to taking land into trust for the purpose of providing land to members of a tribe that was under federal jurisdiction when the IRA was enacted in June 1934. Because the record in this case establishes that the Narragansett Tribe was not under federal jurisdiction when the IRA was enacted, the Secretary does not have the authority to take the parcel at issue into trust. We reverse the judgment of the Court of Appeals.

I

At the time of colonial settlement, the Narragansett Indian Tribe was the indigenous occupant of much of what is now the State of Rhode Island. See Final Determination of Federal Acknowledgement of Narragansett Indian Tribe of Rhode Island, 48 Fed.Reg. 6177 (1983) (hereinafter Final Determination). Initial relations between colonial settlers, the Narragansett Tribe, and the other Indian tribes in the region were peaceful, but relations deteriorated in the late 17th century. The hostilities peaked in 1675 and 1676 during the two-year armed conflict known as King Philip's War. Hundreds of colonists and thousands of Indians died. See E. Schultz & M. Tougias, King Philip's War 5 (1999). The Narragansett Tribe, having been decimated, was placed under formal guardianship by the Colony of Rhode Island in 1709. 48 Fed.Reg. 6177.

Not quite two centuries later, in 1880, the State of Rhode Island convinced the Narragansett Tribe to relinquish its tribal authority as part of an effort to assimilate tribal members into the local population. See *Narragansett Indian Tribe v. National Indian Gaming Comm'n*, 158 F.3d 1335, 1336 (C.A.D.C.1998). The Tribe also agreed to sell all but two acres of its remaining reservation land for $5,000. Almost immediately, the Tribe regretted its decisions and embarked on a campaign to regain its land and tribal status. In the early 20th century, members of the Tribe sought economic support and other assistance from the federal government. But, in correspondence spanning a ten-year period from 1927 to 1937, federal officials declined their request, noting that the Tribe was, and always had been, under the jurisdiction of the New England States, rather than the federal government.

Having failed to gain recognition or assistance from the United States or from the State of Rhode Island, the Tribe filed suit in the 1970's to recover its ancestral land, claiming that the State had misappropriated its territory in violation of the Indian Non-Intercourse Act, 25 U.S.C. § 177. The claims were resolved in 1978 by enactment of the Rhode Island Indian Claims Settlement Act, 92 Stat. 813, 25 U.S.C. § 1701 et seq. Under the agreement codified by the Settlement Act, the Tribe received title to 1,800 acres of land in Charlestown, Rhode Island, in exchange for relinquishing its past and future claims to land based on aboriginal title. The Tribe also agreed that the 1,800 acres of land received under the Settlement Act "shall be subject to the civil and criminal laws and jurisdiction of the State of Rhode Island." § 1708(a); see also § 1712(a).

The Narragansett Tribe's ongoing efforts to gain recognition from the United States Government finally succeeded in 1983. 48 Fed.Reg. 6177. In granting formal recognition, the Bureau of Indian Affairs (BIA) determined that "the Narragansett community and its predecessors have existed autonomously since first contact, despite undergoing many modifications." *Id.*, at 6178. The BIA referred to the Tribe's "documented history dating from 1614" and noted that "all of the current membership are believed to be able to trace to at least one ancestor on the membership lists of the Narragansett community prepared after the 1880 Rhode Island 'detribalization' act." After obtaining federal recognition, the Tribe began urging the Secretary to accept a deed of trust to the 1,800 acres conveyed to it under the Rhode Island Indian Claims Settlement Act. 25 CFR § 83.2 (2008) (providing that federal recognition is needed before an Indian tribe may seek "the protection, services, and benefits of the Federal government"). The Secretary acceded to the Tribe's request in 1988.

In 1991, the Tribe's housing authority purchased an additional 31 acres of land in the town of Charlestown adjacent to the Tribe's 1,800 acres of settlement lands. Soon thereafter, a dispute arose about whether the Tribe's planned construction of housing on that parcel had to comply with local regulations. *Narragansett Indian Tribe v. Narragansett Elec. Co.*, 89 F.3d 908, 911–912 (C.A.1 1996). The Tribe's primary argument for noncompliance — that its ownership of the parcel made it a "dependent Indian community" and thus "Indian country" under 18 U.S.C. § 1151 — ultimately failed. [*See* Ch. 2, Sec. A.3.b.ii.] But, while the litigation was pending, the Tribe sought an alternative solution to free itself from compliance with local regulations: It asked the Secretary to accept the 31-acre parcel into trust for the Tribe pursuant to 25 U.S.C. § 465. By letter dated March 6, 1998, the Secretary notified petitioners of his acceptance of the Tribe's land into trust. Petitioners appealed the Secretary's decision to the IBIA, which upheld the Secretary's decision.

Petitioners sought review of the IBIA decision pursuant to the Administrative Procedure Act, 5 U.S.C. § 702. The District Court granted summary judgment in favor of the Secretary and other Department of Interior officials. As relevant here, the District Court determined that the plain language of 25 U.S.C. § 479 defines

"Indian" to include members of all tribes in existence in 1934, but does not require a tribe to have been federally recognized on that date. *Carcieri v. Norton*, 290 F.Supp.2d 167, 179–181 (D.R.I.2003). According to the District Court, because it is currently "federally-recognized" and "existed at the time of the enactment of the IRA," the Narragansett Tribe "qualifies as an 'Indian tribe' within the meaning of § 479." *Id.*, at 181. As a result, "the secretary possesses authority under § 465 to accept lands into trust for the benefit of the Narragansetts."

The Court of Appeals for the First Circuit affirmed, first in a panel decision, *Carcieri v. Norton*, 423 F.3d 45 (2005), and then sitting en banc, 497 F.3d 15 (C.A.1 2007). Although the Court of Appeals acknowledged that "[o]ne might have an initial instinct to read the word 'now' [in § 479] . . . to mean the date of [the] enactment of the statute, June 18, 1934," the court concluded that there was "ambiguity as to whether to view the term . . . as operating at the moment Congress enacted it or at the moment the Secretary invokes it." The Court of Appeals noted that Congress has used the word "now" in other statutes to refer to the time of the statute's application, not its enactment. The Court of Appeals also found that the particular statutory context of § 479 did not clarify the meaning of "now." On one hand, the Court of Appeals noted that another provision within the IRA, 25 U.S.C. § 472, uses the term "now or hereafter," which supports petitioners' argument that "now," by itself, does not refer to future events. But on the other hand, § 479 contains the particular application date of "June 1, 1934," suggesting that if Congress had wanted to refer to the date of enactment, it could have done so more specifically. The Court of Appeals further reasoned that both interpretations of "now" are supported by reasonable policy explanations, and it found that the legislative history failed to "clearly resolve the issue."

Having found the statute ambiguous, the Court of Appeals applied the principles set forth in *Chevron U.S.A. Inc. v. Natural Resources Defense Council, Inc.*, 467 U.S. 837, 843 (1984), and deferred to the Secretary's construction of the provision. The court rejected petitioners' arguments that the Secretary's interpretation was an impermissible construction of the statute. It also held that petitioners had failed to demonstrate that the Secretary's interpretation was inconsistent with earlier practices of the Department of Interior. Furthermore, the court determined that even if the interpretation were a departure from the Department's prior practices, the decision should be affirmed based on the Secretary's "reasoned explanation for his interpretation."

We granted certiorari, 552 U.S. 1229, 128 S. Ct. 1443, 170 L. Ed. 2d 274 (2008), and now reverse.

II

This case requires us to apply settled principles of statutory construction under which we must first determine whether the statutory text is plain and unambiguous. *United States v. Gonzales*, 520 U.S. 1, 4 (1997). If it is, we must apply the statute according to its terms. See, e.g., *Dodd v. United States*, 545 U.S. 353, 359 (2005).

The Secretary may accept land into trust only for "the purpose of providing land for Indians." 25 U.S.C. § 465. "Indian" is defined by statute as follows:

The term 'Indian' as used in this Act shall include all persons of Indian descent who are members of *any recognized Indian tribe now under Federal jurisdiction*, and all persons who are descendants of such members who were, on June 1, 1934, residing within the present boundaries of any Indian reservation, and shall further include all other persons of one-half or more Indian blood. . . . The term 'tribe' wherever used in this Act shall be construed to refer to any Indian tribe, organized band, pueblo, or the Indians residing on one reservation. . . . § 479 (emphasis added).

The parties are in agreement, as are we, that the Secretary's authority to take the parcel in question into trust depends on whether the Narragansetts are members of a "recognized Indian Tribe now under Federal jurisdiction." That question, in turn, requires us to decide whether the word "now under Federal jurisdiction" refers to 1998, when the Secretary accepted the 31-acre parcel into trust, or 1934, when Congress enacted the IRA.

We begin with the ordinary meaning of the word "now," as understood when the IRA was enacted. *Director, Office of Workers' Compensation Programs v. Greenwich Collieries*, 512 U.S. 267, 272 (1994); *Moskal v. United States*, 498 U.S. 103, 108–109 (1990). At that time, the primary definition of "now" was "[a]t the present time; at this moment; at the time of speaking." Webster's New International Dictionary 1671 (2d ed.1934); see also Black's Law Dictionary 1262 (3d ed.1933) (defining "now" to mean "[a]t this time, or at the present moment" and noting that "'[n]ow' as used in a statute *ordinarily* refers to the date of its taking effect . . . " (emphasis added)). This definition is consistent with interpretations given to the word "now" by this Court, both before and after passage of the IRA, with respect to its use in other statutes. See, e.g., *Franklin v. United States*, 216 U.S. 559, 568–569 (1910) (interpreting a federal criminal statute to have "adopted such punishment as the laws of the State in which such place is situated now provide for the like offense"); *Montana v. Kennedy*, 366 U.S. 308, 310–311 (1961) (interpreting a statute granting citizenship status to foreign-born "children of persons who now are, or have been citizens of the United States").

It also aligns with the natural reading of the word within the context of the IRA. For example, in the original version of 25 U.S.C. § 465, which provided the same authority to the Secretary to accept land into trust for "the purpose of providing land for Indians," Congress explicitly referred to current events, stating "[t]hat no part of such funds shall be used to acquire additional land outside of the exterior boundaries of [the] Navajo Indian Reservation . . . in the event that the proposed Navajo boundary extension measures *now* pending in Congress . . . become law." IRA, § 5, 48 Stat. 985 (emphasis added). In addition, elsewhere in the IRA, Congress expressly drew into the statute contemporaneous and future events by using the phrase "now or hereafter." See 25 U.S.C. § 468 (referring to "the geographic boundaries of any Indian reservation now existing or established hereafter"); § 472 (referring to "Indians who may be appointed . . . to the various positions maintained, now or hereafter, by the Indian Office"). Congress's use of the word "now" in this provision, without the accompanying phrase "or hereafter," thus provides further textual support for the conclusion that the term refers solely to events contemporaneous with the Act's enactment. See *Barnhart v. Sigmon Coal Co.*, 534 U.S. 438, 452 (2002) ("[W]hen Congress includes particular language in one section of a statute but omits it in another section of the same Act, it is generally presumed that Congress acts intentionally and purposely in the disparate inclusion or exclusion").

Furthermore, the Secretary's current interpretation is at odds with the Executive Branch's construction of this provision at the time of enactment. In correspondence with those who would assist him in implementing the IRA, the Commissioner of Indian Affairs, John Collier, explained that:

> Section 19 of the Indian Reorganization Act of June 18, 1934 (48 Stat. L., 988), provides, in effect, that the term 'Indian' as used therein shall include — (1) all persons of Indian descent who are members of any recognized tribe *that was under Federal jurisdiction at the date of the Act.* . . . Letter from John Collier, Commissioner, to Superintendents (Mar. 7, 1936), Lodging of Respondents (emphasis added).[18]

Thus, although we do not defer to Commissioner Collier's interpretation of this unambiguous statute, we agree with his conclusion that the word "now" in § 479 limits the definition of "Indian," and therefore limits the exercise of the Secretary's trust authority under § 465 to those members of tribes that were under federal jurisdiction at the time the IRA was enacted.

The Secretary makes two other arguments in support of his contention that the term "now" as used in § 479 is ambiguous. We reject them both. First, the Secretary argues that although the "use of 'now' can refer to the time of enactment" in the abstract, "it can also refer to the time of the statute's application." But the susceptibility of the word "now" to alternative meanings "does not render the word . . . whenever it is used, ambiguous," particularly where "all but one of the meanings is ordinarily eliminated by context." *Deal v. United States*, 508 U.S. 129, 131–132 (1993). Here, the statutory context makes clear that "now" does not mean "now or hereafter" or "at the time of application." Had Congress intended to legislate such a definition, it could have done so explicitly, as it did in §§ 468 and 472, or it could have omitted the word "now" altogether. Instead, Congress limited the statute by the word "now" and "we are obliged to give effect, if possible, to every word Congress used." *Reiter v. Sonotone Corp.*, 442 U.S. 330, 339 (1979).

Second, the Secretary argues that § 479 left a gap for the agency to fill by using the phrase "shall include" in its introductory clause. The Secretary, in turn, claims to have permissibly filled that gap by defining "'Tribe'" and "'Individual Indian'" without reference to the date of the statute's enactment. But, as explained above, Congress left no gap in 25 U.S.C. § 479 for the agency to fill. Rather, it explicitly and

---

[18] [5] In addition to serving as Commissioner of Indian Affairs, John Collier was "a principal author of the [IRA]." *United States v. Mitchell*, 463 U.S. 206, 221, n. 21 (1983). And, as both parties note, he appears to have been responsible for the insertion of the words "now under Federal jurisdiction" into what is now 25 U.S.C. § 479. *See* Hearings on S. 2755 et al.: A Bill to Grant Indians Living Under Federal Tutelage the Freedom to Organize for Purposes of Local Self-Government and Economic Enterprise, before the Senate Committee on Indian Affairs, 73d Cong., 2d Sess., pt. 2, p. 266 (1934). Also, the record contains a 1937 letter from Commissioner Collier in which, even after the passage of the IRA, he stated that the Federal Government still lacked any jurisdiction over the Narragansett Tribe. App. 23a–24a. Commissioner Collier's responsibilities related to implementing the IRA make him an unusually persuasive source as to the meaning of the relevant statutory language and the Tribe's status under it.

comprehensively defined the term by including only three discrete definitions: "[1] members of any recognized Indian tribe now under Federal jurisdiction, and [2] all persons who are descendants of such members who were, on June 1, 1934, residing within the present boundaries of any Indian reservation, and . . . [3] all other persons of one-half or more Indian blood." In other statutory provisions, Congress chose to expand the Secretary's authority to particular Indian tribes not necessarily encompassed within the definitions of "Indian" set forth in § 479.[19] Had it understood the word "include" in § 479 to encompass tribes other than those satisfying one of the three § 479 definitions, Congress would have not needed to enact these additional statutory references to specific Tribes.

The Secretary and his amici also go beyond the statutory text to argue that Congress had no policy justification for limiting the Secretary's trust authority to those tribes under federal jurisdiction in 1934, because the IRA was intended to strengthen Indian communities as a whole, regardless of their status in 1934. Petitioners counter that the main purpose of § 465 was to reverse the loss of lands that Indians sustained under the General Allotment Act, see *Atkinson Trading Co. v. Shirley*, 532 U.S. 645, 650, n. 1 (2001), so the statute was limited to tribes under federal jurisdiction at that time because they were the tribes who lost their lands. We need not consider these competing policy views, because Congress's use of the word "now" in § 479 speaks for itself and "courts must presume that a legislature says in a statute what it means and means in a statute what it says there." *Connecticut Nat. Bank v. Germain*, 503 U.S. 249, 253–254 (1992).

III

The Secretary and his supporting amici also offer two alternative arguments that rely on statutory provisions other than the definition of "Indian" in § 479 to support the Secretary's decision to take this parcel into trust for the Narragansett Tribe. We reject both arguments.

First, the Secretary and several amici argue that the definition of "Indian" in § 479 is rendered irrelevant by the broader definition of "tribe" in § 479 and by the fact that the statute authorizes the Secretary to take title to lands "in the name of the United States in trust for the *Indian tribe* or individual Indian for which the land is acquired." § 465 (emphasis added). But the definition of "tribe" in § 479 itself refers to "any *Indian* tribe" (emphasis added), and therefore is limited by the temporal restrictions that apply to § 479's definition of "Indian." See § 479 ("The term 'tribe' wherever used in this Act shall be construed to refer to any *Indian* tribe, organized band, pueblo, or the Indians residing on one reservation" (emphasis added)). And, although § 465 authorizes the United States to take land in trust for an Indian tribe, § 465 limits the Secretary's exercise of that authority "for the purpose of providing land for Indians." There simply is no legitimate way to

---

[19] [6] *See, e.g.*, 25 U.S.C. § 473a ("Sections . . . 465 . . . and 479 of this title shall after May 1, 1936, apply to the Territory of Alaska"); § 1041e(a) ("The [Shawnee] Tribe shall be eligible to have land acquired in trust for its benefit pursuant to section 465 of this title . . . "); § 1300b-14(a) ("[Sections 465 and 479 of this title are] hereby made applicable to the [Texas] Band [of Kickapoo Indians] . . . "); § 1300g-2(a) ("[Sections 465 and 479] shall apply to the members of the [Ysleta Del Ser Pueblo] tribe, the tribe, and the reservation").

circumvent the definition of "Indian" in delineating the Secretary's authority under §§ 465 and 479.[20]

Second, amicus National Congress of American Indians (NCAI) argues that 25 U.S.C. § 2202, which was enacted as part of the Indian Land Consolidation Act (ILCA), Title II, 96 Stat. 2517, overcomes the limitations set forth in § 479 and, in turn, authorizes the Secretary's action. Section 2202 provides:

> The provisions of section 465 of this title shall apply to all tribes notwithstanding the provisions of section 478 of this title: *Provided*, That nothing in this section is intended to supersede any other provision of Federal law which authorizes, prohibits, or restricts the acquisition of land for Indians with respect to any specific tribe, reservation, or state(s). (Alteration in original.)

NCAI argues that the "ILCA independently grants authority under Section 465 for the Secretary to execute the challenged trust acquisition." We do not agree.

The plain language of § 2202 does not expand the power set forth in § 465, which requires that the Secretary take land into trust only "for the purpose of providing land for Indians." Nor does § 2202 alter the definition of "Indian" in § 479, which is limited to members of tribes that were under federal jurisdiction in 1934.[21] Rather, § 2202 by its terms simply ensures that tribes may benefit from § 465 even if they opted out of the IRA pursuant to § 478, which allowed tribal members to reject the application of the IRA to their tribe. § 478 ("This Act shall not apply to any reservation wherein a majority of the adult Indians . . . shall vote against its application"). As a result, there is no conflict between § 2202 and the limitation on the Secretary's authority to take lands contained in § 465. Rather, § 2202 provides additional protections to those who satisfied the definition of "Indian" in § 479 at the time of the statute's enactment, but opted out of the IRA shortly thereafter.

NCAI's reading of § 2202 also would nullify the plain meaning of the definition of "Indian" set forth in § 479 and incorporated into § 465. Consistent with our obligation to give effect to every provision of the statute, we will not assume that Congress repealed the plain and unambiguous restrictions on the Secretary's exercise of trust authority in §§ 465 and 479 when it enacted § 2202. "We have repeatedly stated . . . that absent 'a clearly expressed congressional intention,' . . . [a]n implied repeal will only be found where provisions in two statutes are in 'irreconcilable conflict,' or where the latter Act covers the whole subject of the

---

[20] [8] For this reason, we disagree with the argument made by Justice Stevens that the term "Indians" in § 465 has a different meaning than the definition of "Indian" provided in § 479, and that the term's meaning in § 465 is controlled by later-enacted regulations governing the Secretary's recognition of tribes like the Narragansetts. When Congress has enacted a definition with "detailed and unyielding provisions," as it has in § 479, this Court must give effect to that definition even when "'it could be argued that the line should have been drawn at a different point.'" *INS v. Hector*, 479 U.S. 85, 88–89 (1986) (per curium).

[21] [9] NCAI notes that the ILCA's definition of "tribe" "means any Indian tribe, band, group, pueblo, or community for which, or for the members of which, the United States holds lands in trust." § 2201. But § 2201 is, by its express terms, applicable only to Chapter 24 of Title 25 of the United States Code. The IRA is codified in Chapter 14 of Title 25. See § 465. Section 2201, therefore, does not itself alter the authority granted to the Secretary by § 465.

earlier one and 'is clearly intended as a substitute.'" *Branch v. Smith*, 538 U.S. 254, 273 (2003) (plurality opinion) (quoting Morton v. Mancari, 417 U.S. 535, 551 (1974)).

IV

We hold that the term "now under Federal jurisdiction" in § 479 unambiguously refers to those tribes that were under the federal jurisdiction of the United States when the IRA was enacted in 1934. None of the parties or amici, including the Narragansett Tribe itself, has argued that the Tribe was under federal jurisdiction in 1934. And the evidence in the record is to the contrary. 48 Fed.Reg. 6177. Moreover, the petition for writ of certiorari filed in this case specifically represented that "[i]n 1934, the Narragansett Indian Tribe . . . was neither federally recognized nor under the jurisdiction of the federal government." Pet. for Cert. 6. The respondents' brief in opposition declined to contest this assertion. See Brief in Opposition 2–7. Under our rules, that alone is reason to accept this as fact for purposes of our decision in this case. See this Court's Rule 15.2. We therefore reverse the judgment of the Court of Appeals.

It is so ordered.

JUSTICE BREYER, concurring.

I join the Court's opinion with three qualifications. First, I cannot say that the statute's language by itself is determinative. Linguistically speaking, the word "now" in the phrase "now under Federal jurisdiction," 25 U.S.C. § 479, may refer to a tribe's jurisdictional status as of 1934. But one could also read it to refer to the time the Secretary of the Interior exercises his authority to take land "for Indians." § 465. *Compare Montana v. Kennedy*, 366 U.S. 308, 311–312 (1961) ("now" refers to time of statutory enactment), *with Difford v. Secretary of HHS*, 910 F.2d 1316, 1320 (C.A.6 1990) ("now" refers to time of exercise of delegated authority); In re Lusk's Estate, 336 Pa. 465, 467–468, 9 A.2d 363, 365 (1939) (property "now" owned refers to property owned when a will becomes operative). I also concede that the Court owes the Interior Department the kind of interpretive respect that reflects an agency's greater knowledge of the circumstances in which a statute was enacted, *cf. Skidmore v. Swift & Co.*, 323 U.S. 134 (1944). Yet because the Department then favored the Court's present interpretation, that respect cannot help the Department here. . . .

Second, I am persuaded that "now" means "in 1934" not only for the reasons the Court gives but also because an examination of the provision's legislative history convinces me that Congress so intended. . . .

Third, an interpretation that reads "now" as meaning "in 1934" may prove somewhat less restrictive than it at first appears. That is because a tribe may have been "under Federal jurisdiction" in 1934 even though the Federal Government did not believe so at the time. We know, for example, that following the Indian Reorganization Act's enactment, the Department compiled a list of 258 tribes covered by the Act; and we also know that it wrongly left certain tribes off the list. See Brief for Law Professors Specializing in Federal Indian Law as *Amicus Curiae* 22–24; Quinn, Federal Acknowledgment of American Indian Tribes: The Historical

Development of a Legal Concept, 34 Am. J. Legal Hist. 331, 356–359 (1990). The Department later recognized some of those tribes on grounds that showed that it should have recognized them in 1934 even though it did not. And the Department has sometimes considered that circumstance sufficient to show that a tribe was "under Federal jurisdiction" in 1934 — even though the Department did not know it at the time.

The statute, after all, imposes no time limit upon recognition. See § 479 ("The term 'Indian' . . . shall include all persons of Indian descent who are members of *any recognized* Indian tribe now under Federal jurisdiction . . . " (emphasis added)). And administrative practice suggests that the Department has accepted this possibility. The Department, for example, did not recognize the Stillaguamish Tribe until 1976, but its reasons for recognition in 1976 included the fact that the Tribe had maintained treaty rights against the United States since 1855. Consequently, the Department concluded that land could be taken into trust for the Tribe. See Memorandum from Associate Solicitor, Indian Affairs to Assistant Secretary, Indian Affairs, Request for Reconsideration of Decision Not to Take Land in Trust for the Stillaguamish Tribe (Oct. 1, 1980). Similarly, in 1934 the Department thought that the Grand Traverse Band of Ottawa and Chippewa Indians had long since been dissolved. Grand Traverse Band of Ottawa & Chippewa Indians v. Office of U.S. Attorney for Western Dist. of Mich., 369 F.3d 960, 961, and n. 2 (C.A.6 2004). But later the Department recognized the Tribe, considering it to have existed continuously since 1675. 45 Fed.Reg. 19321 (1980). Further, the Department in the 1930's thought that an anthropological study showed that the Mole Lake Tribe no longer existed. But the Department later decided that the study was wrong, and it then recognized the Tribe. See Memorandum from the Solicitor to the Commissioner of Indian Affairs 2758, 2762–2763 (Feb. 8, 1937) (recognizing the Mole Lake Indians as a separate tribe).

In my view, this possibility — that later recognition reflects earlier "Federal jurisdiction" — explains some of the instances of early Department administrative practice to which JUSTICE STEVENS refers. I would explain the other instances to which JUSTICE STEVENS refers as involving the taking of land "for" a tribe with members who fall under that portion of the statute that defines "Indians" to include "persons of one-half or more Indian blood," § 479. See 1 Dept. of Interior, Opinions of the Solicitor Relating to Indian Affairs, 1917–1974, pp. 706–707 (Shoshone Indians), 724–725 (St. Croix Chippewas), 747–748 (Nahma and Beaver Indians) (1979).

Neither the Narragansett Tribe nor the Secretary has argued that the Tribe was under federal jurisdiction in 1934. Nor have they claimed that any member of the Narragansett Tribe satisfies the "one-half or more Indian blood" requirement. And I have found nothing in the briefs that suggests the Narragansett Tribe could prevail on either theory. Each of the administrative decisions just discussed involved post-1934 recognition on grounds that implied a 1934 relationship between the tribe and Federal Government that could be described as jurisdictional, for example, a treaty with the United States (in effect in 1934), a (pre-1934) congressional appropriation, or enrollment (as of 1934) with the Indian Office. I can find no similar indication of 1934 federal jurisdiction here. Instead, both the State and Federal Government considered the Narragansett Tribe as under state, but not under federal, jurisdiction in 1934. And until the 1970's there was "little Federal contact with the Narragansetts as a group." Memorandum from Deputy Assistant Secretary-Indian Affairs (Operations) to Assistant Secretary-Indian Affairs, Recommendation and Summary of Evidence for Proposed Finding for Federal Acknowledgment of Narragansett Indian Tribe of Rhode Island Pursuant to 25 CFR 83, p. 8 (July 29, 1982). Because I see no realistic possibility that the Narragansett Tribe could prevail on the basis of a theory alternative to the theories argued here, I would not remand this case.

With the qualifications here expressed, I join the Court's opinion and its judgment.

JUSTICE SOUTER, with whom JUSTICE GINSBURG joins, concurring in part and dissenting in part.

Save as to one point, I agree with JUSTICE BREYER's concurring opinion, which in turn concurs with the opinion of the Court, subject to the three qualifications JUSTICE BREYER explains. I have, however, a further reservation that puts me in the dissenting column.

The disposition of the case turns on the construction of the language from 25 U.S.C. § 479, "any recognized Indian tribe now under Federal jurisdiction." Nothing in the majority opinion forecloses the possibility that the two concepts, recognition and jurisdiction, may be given separate content. As JUSTICE BREYER makes clear in his concurrence, the statute imposes no time limit upon recognition, and in the past, the Department of the Interior has stated that the fact that the United States Government was ignorant of a tribe in 1934 does not preclude that tribe from having been under federal jurisdiction at that time. See Memorandum from Associate Solicitor, Indian Affairs, to Assistant Secretary, Indian Affairs, Request for Reconsideration of Decision Not to Take Land in Trust for the Stillaguamish Tribe (Oct. 1, 1980). And giving each phrase its own meaning would be consistent with established principles of statutory interpretation.

During oral argument, however, respondents explained that the Secretary's more recent interpretation of this statutory language had "understood recognition and under Federal jurisdiction at least with respect to tribes to be one and the same." Given the Secretary's position, it is not surprising that neither he nor the Tribe raised a claim that the Tribe was under federal jurisdiction in 1934: they simply failed to address an issue that no party understood to be present. The error was shared equally all around, and there is no equitable demand that one side be penalized when both sides nodded.

I can agree with JUSTICE BREYER that the current record raises no particular reason to expect that the Tribe might be shown to have been under federal jurisdiction in 1934, but I would not stop there. The very notion of jurisdiction as a distinct statutory condition was ignored in this litigation, and I know of no body of precedent or history of practice giving content to the condition sufficient for gauging the Tribe's chances of satisfying it. So I see no reason to deny the Secretary and the Narragansett Tribe an opportunity to advocate a construction of the "jurisdiction" phrase that might favor their position here.

I would therefore reverse and remand with opportunity for respondents to pursue a "jurisdiction" claim and respectfully dissent from the Court's straight reversal.

JUSTICE STEVENS, dissenting.

Congress has used the term "Indian" in the Indian Reorganization Act of 1934 to describe those individuals who are entitled to special protections and benefits under federal Indian law. The Act specifies that benefits shall be available to individuals who qualify as Indian either as a result of blood quantum or as descendants of members of "any recognized Indian tribe now under Federal jurisdiction." 25 U.S.C. § 479. In contesting the Secretary of the Interior's acquisition of trust land for the Narragansett Tribe of Rhode Island, the parties have focused on the meaning of "now" in the Act's definition of "Indian." Yet to my mind, whether "now" means 1934 (as the Court holds) or the present time (as respondents would have it) sheds no light on the question whether the Secretary's actions on behalf of the Narragansett were permitted under the statute. The plain text of the Act clearly authorizes the Secretary to take land into trust for Indian tribes as well as individual Indians, and it places no temporal limitation on the definition of "Indian tribe."[22] Because the Narragansett Tribe is an Indian tribe within the meaning of the Act, I would affirm the judgment of the Court of Appeals. . . .

II

The Secretary's trust authority is located in 25 U.S.C. § 465. That provision grants the Secretary power to take "in trust for [an] Indian tribe or individual Indian" "any interest in lands . . . for the purpose of providing land for Indians." The Act's language could not be clearer: To effectuate the Act's broad mandate to revitalize tribal development and cultural self-determination, the Secretary can take land into trust for a tribe or he can take land into trust for an individual Indian. . . .

Having separate definitions for "Indian" and "tribe" is essential for the administration of IRA benefits. The statute reflects Congress's intent to extend certain benefits to individual Indians, e.g., 25 U.S.C. § 471 (offering loans to Indian students for tuition at vocational and trade schools); § 472 (granting hiring preferences to Indians seeking federal employment related to Indian affairs), while directing other benefits to tribes, e.g., § 476 (allowing tribes to adopt constitutions and bylaws); § 470 (giving loans to Indian-chartered corporations).

Section 465, by giving the Secretary discretion to steer benefits to tribes and individuals alike, is therefore unique. But establishing this broad benefit scheme was undoubtedly intentional: The original draft of the IRA presented to Congress directed the Secretary to take land into trust only for entities such as tribes. Compare H.R. 7902, 73d Cong., 2d Sess., 30 (1934) ("Title to any land acquired pursuant to the provisions of this section shall be taken in the name of the United

---

[22] [1] . . . Notably the word "now," which is used to define one of the categories of Indians, does not appear in the definition of "tribe."

States in trust for the Indian tribe or community for whom the land is acquired" (emphasis added)), with 25 U.S.C. § 465 ("Title to any lands or rights acquired pursuant to this Act . . . shall be taken in the name of the United States in trust for the Indian tribe or individual Indian for which the land is acquired" (emphasis added)).

The Secretary has long exercised his § 465 trust authority in accordance with this design. In the years immediately following the adoption of the IRA, the Solicitor of the Department of the Interior repeatedly advised that the Secretary could take land into trust for federally recognized tribes and for individual Indians who qualified for federal benefits by lineage or blood quantum.

For example, in 1937, when evaluating whether the Secretary could purchase approximately 2,100 acres of land for the Mole Lake Chippewa Indians of Wisconsin, the Solicitor instructed that the purchase could not be "completed until it is determined whether the beneficiary of the trust title should be designated as a band or whether the title should be taken for the individual Indians in the vicinity of Mole Lake who are of one half or more Indian blood." Memorandum from the Solicitor to the Commissioner of Indian Affairs 2758 (Feb. 8, 1937). Because the Mole Lake Chippewa was not yet recognized by the Federal Government as an Indian tribe, the Solicitor determined that the Secretary had two options: "Either the Department should provide recognition of this group, or title to the purchased land should be taken on behalf of the individuals who are of one half or more Indian blood."

The tribal trust and individual trust options were similarly outlined in other post-1934 opinion letters, including those dealing with the Shoshone Indians of Nevada, the St. Croix Chippewa Indians of Wisconsin, and the Nahma and Beaver Island Indians of Michigan. See 1 Dept. of Interior, Opinions of the Solicitor Relating to Indian Affairs, 1917–1974, pp. 706–707, 724–725, 747–748 (1979). Unless and until a tribe was formally recognized by the Federal Government and therefore eligible for trust land, the Secretary would take land into trust for individual Indians who met the blood quantum threshold.

Modern administrative practice has followed this well-trodden path. [Several illustrations follow, demonstrating that the Department of the Interior has acquired land in trust for tribes following administrative recognition through the OFA (formerly BAR) process described in Ch. 2, Sec. A.1.b].

This brief history of § 465 places the case before us into proper context. Federal recognition, regardless of when it is conferred, is the necessary condition that triggers a tribe's eligibility to receive trust land. No party has disputed that the Narragansett Tribe was properly recognized as an Indian tribe in 1983. See 48 Fed.Reg. 6177. Indeed, given that the Tribe has a documented history that stretches back to 1614 and has met the rigorous criteria for administrative recognition, Recommendation for Acknowledgment 1, 7–18, it would be difficult to sustain an objection to the Tribe's status. With this in mind, and in light of the Secretary's longstanding authority under the plain text of the IRA to acquire tribal trust land, it is perfectly clear that the Secretary's land acquisition for the Narragansett was entirely proper.

III

Despite the clear text of the IRA and historical pedigree of the Secretary's actions on behalf of the Narragansett, the majority holds that one word ("now") nestled in one clause in one of § 479's several definitions demonstrates that the Secretary acted outside his statutory authority in this case. . . .

Petitioners' argument works only if one reads "Indians" (in the phrase in § 465 "providing land for Indians") to refer to individuals, not an Indian tribe. To petitioners, this reading is obvious; the alternative, they insist, would be "nonsensical." This they argue despite the clear evidence of Congress' intent to provide the Secretary with the option of acquiring either tribal trusts or individual trusts in service of "providing land for Indians." And they ignore unambiguous evidence that Congress used "Indian tribe" and "Indians" interchangeably in other parts of the IRA. See § 475 (discussing "any claim or suit of any Indian tribe against the United States" in the first sentence and "any claim of such *Indians* against the United States" in the last sentence (emphasis added)).

In any event, this much must be admitted: Without the benefit of context, a reasonable person could conclude that "Indians" refers to multiple individuals who each qualify as "Indian" under the IRA. An equally reasonable person could also conclude that "Indians" is meant to refer to a collective, namely, an Indian tribe. Because "[t]he meaning — or ambiguity — of certain words or phrases may only become evident when placed in context," *FDA v. Brown & Williamson Tobacco Corp.*, 529 U.S. 120, 132 (2000), the proper course of action is to widen the interpretive lens and look to the rest of the statute for clarity. Doing so would lead to § 465's last sentence, which specifies that the Secretary is to hold land in trust "for the Indian tribe or individual Indian for which the land is acquired." Put simply, in § 465 Congress used the term "Indians" to refer both to tribes and individuals.

The majority bypasses a straightforward explanation on its way to a circular one. Requiring that a tribe be an "Indian tribe" does not demand immediate reference to the definition of "Indian"; instead, it simply reflects the requirement that the tribe in question be formally recognized as an Indian tribe. . . .

The majority's retort, that because "tribe" refers to "Indian," the definition of "Indian" must control which groups can be considered a "tribe," is entirely circular. Yes, the word "tribe" is defined in part by reference to "Indian tribe." But the word "Indian" is also defined in part by reference to "Indian tribe." Relying on one definition to provide content to the other is thus "completely circular and explains nothing." *Nationwide Mut. Ins. Co. v. Darden*, 503 U.S. 318, 323 (1992). . . .

IV

The Court today adopts a cramped reading of a statute Congress intended to be "sweeping" in scope. *Morton v. Mancari*, 417 U.S. 535, 542 (1974). In so doing, the Court ignores the "principle deeply rooted in [our] Indian jurisprudence" that " 'statutes are to be construed liberally in favor of the Indians.' " *County of Yakima v. Confederated Tribes and Bands of Yakima Nation*, 502 U.S. 251, 269 (1992)); see also Cohen § 2.02[1], p. 119 ("The basic Indian law canons of construction require that treaties, agreements, statutes, and executive orders be liberally construed in favor of the Indians").

Given that the IRA plainly authorizes the Secretary to take land into trust for an Indian tribe, and in light of the Narragansett's status as such, the Court's decision can be best understood as protecting one sovereign (the State) from encroachment from another (the Tribe). Yet in matters of Indian law, the political branches have been entrusted to mark the proper boundaries between tribal and state jurisdiction. See U.S. Const., Art. I, § 8, cl. 3; *Cotton Petroleum Corp. v. New Mexico*, 490 U.S. 163, 192 (1989); *Worcester v. Georgia*, 6 Pet. 515, 559 (1832). With the IRA, Congress drew the boundary in a manner that favors the Narragansett. I respectfully dissent.

NOTES ON LAND-INTO-TRUST AND *CARCIERI*

1. **Questions Remaining After *Carcieri*, and a Possible "*Carcieri* Fix":** Neither the Narragansett Tribe nor the United States argued that the Tribe had been "under Federal jurisdiction" in 1934, within the meaning of 25 U.S.C. § 479. Thus, the Supreme Court's decision left open the possibility that a tribe could satisfy that requirement even though it was not expressly or formally recognized as a tribe by the United States at that time. *See* the concurring opinion of Justice Breyer and the partially concurring, partially dissenting opinion of Justices Souter and Ginsburg. Could one argue that any tribe presently recognized by the United States was necessarily "under federal jurisdiction" as of 1934? Recall the requirements for administrative recognition as a tribe through the Office of Federal Acknowledgment within the Department of the Interior. *See* Ch. 2, Sec. A.1.c. If an Indian group has sufficient continuity of political and social organization to satisfy those administrative criteria, would that trigger federal jurisdiction over Indian affairs dating back to 1934 and much further? See Testimony of the National Congress of American Indians on the Supreme Court Decision in *Carcieri v. Salazar*, Executive Branch Authority to Acquire Trust Land for Indians, United States Senate Committee on Indian Affairs, May 21, 2009, available at http://indian.senate.gov/public/_files/Allentestimony.pdf. If Congress doesn't amend the IRA to adopt NCAI's view of "under Federal jurisdiction," are tribes vulnerable to costly and protracted litigation challenges by non-Indian citizen groups and state or local governments that oppose taking land into trust? Could longstanding BIA actions taking land into trust be reversed? NCAI's Testimony urges Congress to amend the IRA. How would you draft such an amendment to eliminate uncertainty and maximize tribes' access to the land-into-trust process? NCAI offered its own proposal in the testimony cited above.

Congress continues to debate the merits of a legislative "fix" to correct the problems caused by the Supreme Court's opinion in the *Carcieri* case. See S.2188, 113th Cong. (2013) (entitled "A bill to amend the Act of June 18th, 1934, to reaffirm the authority of the Secretary of the Interior to take land into trust for Indian tribes"; reported to Committee, June 2014).

2. **Procedures for Placing Lands into Trust:** The federal government acquires land in trust for Indians under the procedures set forth in 25 C.F.R. Part 151. The regulations apply to Indian trust acquisitions for both tribes and individual Indians, and cover acquisitions both on and off the reservation. *See generally* Mary

Jane Sheppard, *Taking Indian Land into Trust*, 44 S.D. L. Rev. 681 (1999) (describing in greater detail the process under 25 C.F.R. Part 151). These regulations have been highly controversial, but have survived attempts at revision from both the Clinton and Bush II administrations.

The regulations provide that land not held in trust or restricted status for an Indian tribe or tribal members may be acquired in trust status only "when such acquisition is authorized by an act of Congress." 25 C.F.R. § 151.3. Application of this provision has been complicated by the *Carcieri* decision. Assuming statutory authorization exists, the purposes and standards for such acquisitions are spelled out in 25 C.F.R. § 151.3 and may include a determination that "the acquisition of the land is necessary to facilitate tribal self-determination, economic development, or Indian housing."

The regulations draw a distinction between the taking of land into trust within or contiguous to an existing Indian reservation and off-reservation acquisitions. When potential trust lands are located within or adjacent to an existing Indian reservation, 25 C.F.R. § 151.10 requires formal notification to state and local governments that exercise regulatory jurisdiction over the land. Once the application is complete, the Secretary considers a number of facts including compliance with the National Environmental Policy Act and its implementing procedures, the "impact on the States and its political subdivisions resulting from the removal of the land from the tax rolls," and "jurisdictional problems and potential conflicts of land which may arise." Under this requirement, a tribe seeking to place land in trust must either secure a finding of no significant impact (FONSI) on the environment, or conduct an exhaustive and expensive environmental impact study.

For lands located outside of and noncontiguous with an existing Indian reservation (off-reservation acquisitions), 25 C.F.R. § 151.11 provides additional requirements. Most important, "as the distance between the tribe's reservation and the land to be acquired increases, the Secretary [gives] greater scrutiny to the tribe's justification of anticipated benefits from the acquisition." Applicant tribes must also submit a business plan for any such lands acquired for business purposes.

3.   Special Limitations on the Use of Newly-Acquired Lands for Gaming Purposes: Section 20 of the Indian Gaming Regulatory Act of 1988 (IGRA), codified at 25 U.S.C. § 2719, contains express prohibitions on the use of newly acquired lands for gaming purposes, with some exceptions. The section provides that "gaming regulated by this chapter shall not be conducted on lands acquired by the Secretary in trust for the benefit of an Indian tribe" after October 17, 1988 (the date IGRA was enacted). In addition to a number of tribally-specific and Oklahoma-specific exceptions found in section 2719(b)(2), the statute provides narrow exceptions to the prohibition for lands on or contiguous to a tribe's existing reservation, lands that are part of a settlement of a land claim, or lands provided for a newly recognized tribe or returned to a tribe restored to federal recognition. Finally, the statute makes an exception when the Secretary of the Interior, after consultation with tribal, state, and local officials determines that "a gaming establishment on the newly acquired lands would be in the best interest of the Indians tribe and its members, and would not be detrimental to the surrounding community," and the Governor of the state in which the land is located agrees with the Secretary's determination. Few tribes have been able to muster the combination of federal, state, and local political support necessary to invoke the third exception. Tribes attempting to take advantage of this exception may also battle other tribes in whose ancestral territory the new gaming facility would be located. Notably, the Forest County Potawatomi Tribe in northeastern Wisconsin successfully obtained a trust-status determination under this exception on a parcel of land for gaming in the city of Milwaukee, hundreds of miles from its reservation.

The Department of the Interior issued implementing regulations for the exceptions listed in section 2719. These regulations, are discussed in Note 6 on the Indian Gaming Regulatory Act in Ch. 5, Sec. D.1. How easy do you think it should be for newly recognized or restored tribes to obtain trust land for gaming purposes beyond their reservation borders or outside their ancestral territories? Recall that one of the purposes of IGRA is to promote economic development for tribal nations. How might geographical limitations on tribal gaming affect the success of potential gaming ventures? Note that the California gaming compacts entered in 1999 created a fund for distribution to tribes located in more remote places that cannot sustain lucrative gaming facilities. Tribal-State Gaming Compact between the State of California and the [Named] Tribe, Sec. 4.3.2.1 (1999), *available at* http://www.cgcc.ca.gov/documents/enabling/tsc.pdf.

The latest round of litigation over the Secretary's power to take land into trust emerged when a non-Indian landowner challenged the Secretary of Interior's decision to take land into trust for the Match-E-Be-Nash-She-Wish Band of Pottawatomi Indians for purposes of a tribal casino. The Department of the Interior (DOI) formally recognized the Band in 1999, and the DOI followed the requisite statutory procedures to take the land into trust for gaming purposes. However, an individual landowner in the vicinity brought a challenge asserting that his interests had been impaired by the decision.

MATCH-E-BE-NASH-SHE-WISH BAND OF POTTAWATOMI INDIANS v. PATCHAK
United States Supreme Court
132 S. Ct. 2199 (2012)

JUSTICE KAGAN delivered the opinion of the Court.

A provision of the Indian Reorganization Act (IRA), 25 U.S.C. § 465, authorizes the Secretary of the Interior (Secretary) to acquire property "for the purpose of providing land for Indians." Ch. 576, § 5, 48 Stat. 985. The Secretary here acquired land in trust for an Indian tribe seeking to open a casino. Respondent David Patchak lives near that land and challenges the Secretary's decision in a suit brought under the Administrative Procedure Act (APA), 5 U.S.C. § 701 et seq. Patchak claims that the Secretary lacked authority under § 465 to take title to the land, and alleges economic, environmental, and aesthetic harms from the casino's operation.

We consider two questions arising from Patchak's action. The first is whether the United States has sovereign immunity from the suit by virtue of the Quiet Title Act

(QTA), 86 Stat. 1176. We think it does not. The second is whether Patchak has prudential standing to challenge the Secretary's acquisition. We think he does. We therefore hold that Patchak's suit may proceed.

I

The Match-E-Be-Nash-She-Wish Band of Pottawatomi Indians (Band) is an Indian tribe residing in rural Michigan. Although the Band has a long history, the Department of the Interior (DOI) formally recognized it only in 1999. See 63 Fed.Reg. 56936 (1998). Two years later, the Band petitioned the Secretary to exercise her authority under § 465 by taking into trust a tract of land in Wayland Township, Michigan, known as the Bradley Property. The Band's application explained that the Band would use the property "for gaming purposes," with the goal of generating the "revenue necessary to promote tribal economic development, self-sufficiency and a strong tribal government capable of providing its members with sorely needed social and educational programs." App. 52, 41.

In 2005, after a lengthy administrative review, the Secretary announced her decision to acquire the Bradley Property in trust for the Band. See 70 Fed.Reg. 25596. In accordance with applicable regulations, the Secretary committed to wait 30 days before taking action, so that interested parties could seek judicial review. See *ibid.*; 25 CFR § 151.12(b) (2011). Within that window, an organization called Michigan Gambling Opposition (or MichGO) filed suit alleging that the Secretary's decision violated environmental and gaming statutes. The Secretary held off taking title to the property while that litigation proceeded. Within the next few years, a District Court and the D.C. Circuit rejected MichGO's claims. See *Michigan Gambling Opposition v. Kempthorne*, 525 F.3d 23, 27–28 (C.A.D.C. 2008); *Michigan Gambling Opposition v. Norton*, 477 F.Supp.2d 1 (D.D.C. 2007).

Shortly after the D.C. Circuit ruled against MichGO (but still before the Secretary took title), Patchak filed this suit under the APA advancing a different legal theory. He asserted that § 465 did not authorize the Secretary to acquire property for the Band because it was not a federally recognized tribe when the IRA was enacted in 1934. See App. 37. To establish his standing to bring suit, Patchak contended that he lived "in close proximity to" the Bradley Property and that a casino there would "destroy the lifestyle he has enjoyed" by causing "increased traffic," "increased crime," "decreased property values," "an irreversible change in the rural character of the area," and "other aesthetic, socioeconomic, and environmental problems." *Id.*, at 30–31. Notably, Patchak did not assert any claim of his own to the Bradley Property. He requested only a declaration that the decision to acquire the land violated the IRA and an injunction to stop the Secretary from accepting title. See *id.*, at 38–39. The Band intervened in the suit to defend the Secretary's decision.

In January 2009, about five months after Patchak filed suit, this Court denied certiorari in MichGO's case, 555 U.S. 1137 (201), and the Secretary took the Bradley Property into trust. That action mooted Patchak's request for an injunction to prevent the acquisition, and all parties agree that the suit now effectively seeks to divest the federal government of title to the land. See Brief for Match-E-Be-Nash-She-Wish Band of Pottawatomi Indians 17 (hereinafter Tribal Petitioner); Brief for

Federal Petitioners 11; Brief for Respondent 24–25. The month after the Government took title, this Court held in *Carcieri v. Salazar*, 555 U.S. 379 (2009), that § 465 authorizes the Secretary to take land into trust only for tribes that were "under federal jurisdiction" in 1934.

The District Court dismissed the suit without considering the merits (including the relevance of *Carcieri*), ruling that Patchak lacked prudential standing to challenge the Secretary's acquisition of the Bradley Property. The court reasoned that the injuries Patchak alleged fell outside § 465's "zone of interests." 646 F.Supp.2d 72, 76 (D.D.C. 2009). The D.C. Circuit reversed that determination. See 632 F.3d 702, 704–707 (2011). The court also rejected the Secretary's and the Band's alternative argument that by virtue of the QTA, sovereign immunity barred the suit. See *id.*, at 707–712. The latter ruling conflicted with decisions of three Circuits holding that the United States has immunity from suits like Patchak's. See *Neighbors for Rational Development, Inc. v. Norton*, 379 F.3d 956, 961–962 (C.A.10 2004); *Metropolitan Water Dist. of Southern Cal. v. United States*, 830 F.2d 139, 143–144 (C.A.9 1987) (per curiam); *Florida Dept. of Bus. Regulation v. Department of Interior*, 768 F.2d 1248, 1253–1255 (C.A.11 1985). We granted certiorari and we now affirm.

II

We begin by considering whether the United States's sovereign immunity bars Patchak's suit under the APA. That requires us first to look to the APA itself and then, for reasons we will describe, to the QTA. We conclude that the United States has waived its sovereign immunity from Patchak's action.

The APA generally waives the federal government's immunity from a suit "seeking relief other than money damages and stating a claim that an agency or an officer or employee thereof acted or failed to act in an official capacity or under color of legal authority." 5 U.S.C. § 702. That waiver would appear to cover Patchak's suit, which objects to official action of the Secretary and seeks only non-monetary relief. But the APA's waiver of immunity comes with an important carve-out: The waiver does not apply "if any other statute that grants consent to suit expressly or impliedly forbids the relief which is sought" by the plaintiff. Ibid. That provision prevents plaintiffs from exploiting the APA's waiver to evade limitations on suit contained in other statutes. The question thus becomes whether another statute bars Patchak's demand for relief.

The Government and Band contend that the QTA does so. The QTA authorizes (and so waives the Government's sovereign immunity from) a particular type of action, known as a quiet title suit: a suit by a plaintiff asserting a "right, title, or interest" in real property that conflicts with a "right, title, or interest" the United States claims. 28 U.S.C. § 2409a(d). The statute, however, contains an exception: The QTA's authorization of suit "does not apply to trust or restricted Indian lands." § 2409a(a). According to the Government and Band, that limitation on quiet title suits satisfies the APA's carve-out and so forbids Patchak's suit. In the Band's words, the QTA exception retains "the United States' full immunity from suits seeking to challenge its title to or impair its legal interest in Indian trust lands." Brief for Tribal Petitioner 18.

Two hypothetical examples might help to frame consideration of this argument. First, suppose Patchak had sued under the APA claiming that he owned the Bradley Property and that the Secretary therefore could not take it into trust. The QTA would bar that suit, for reasons just suggested. True, it fits within the APA's general waiver, but the QTA specifically authorizes quiet title actions (which this hypothetical suit is) except when they involve Indian lands (which this hypothetical suit does). In such a circumstance, a plaintiff cannot use the APA to end-run the QTA's limitations. "[W]hen Congress has dealt in particularity with a claim and [has] intended a specified remedy"— including its exceptions — to be exclusive, that is the end of the matter; the APA does not undo the judgment. *Block v. North Dakota ex rel. Board of Univ. and School Lands*, 461 U.S. 273, 286, n. 22 (1983) (quoting H.R.Rep. No. 94-1656, p. 13 (1976), 1976 U.S.C.C.A.N. 6121, 6133).

But now suppose that Patchak had sued under the APA, claiming only that use of the Bradley Property was causing environmental harm, and raising no objection at all to the Secretary's title. The QTA could not bar that suit because even though involving Indian lands, it asserts a grievance altogether different from the kind the statute concerns. Justice SCALIA, in a former life as Assistant Attorney General, made this precise point in a letter to Congress about the APA's waiver of immunity (which we hasten to add, given the author, we use not as legislative history, but only for its persuasive force). When a statute "is not addressed to the type of grievance which the plaintiff seeks to assert," then the statute cannot prevent an APA suit. *Id.*, at 28 (May 10, 1976, letter of Assistant Atty. Gen. A. Scalia).

We think that principle controls Patchak's case: The QTA's "Indian lands" clause does not render the Government immune because the QTA addresses a kind of grievance different from the one Patchak advances. As we will explain, the QTA — whose full name, recall, is the Quiet Title Act — concerns (no great surprise) quiet title actions. And Patchak's suit is not a quiet title action, because although it contests the Secretary's title, it does not claim any competing interest in the Bradley Property. That fact makes the QTA's "Indian lands" limitation simply inapposite to this litigation. . . .

Patchak does not contend that he owns the Bradley Property, nor does he seek any relief corresponding to such a claim. He wants a court to strip the United States of title to the land, but not on the ground that it is his and not so that he can possess it. Patchak's lawsuit therefore lacks a defining feature of a QTA action. He is not trying to disguise a QTA suit as an APA action to circumvent the QTA's "Indian lands" exception. Rather, he is not bringing a QTA suit at all. He asserts merely that the Secretary's decision to take land into trust violates a federal statute — a garden-variety APA claim. See 5 U.S.C. § 706(2)(A), (C) ("The reviewing court shall . . . hold unlawful and set aside agency action . . . not in accordance with law [or] in excess of statutory jurisdiction [or] authority"). Because that is true — because in then–Assistant Attorney General Scalia's words, the QTA is "not addressed to the type of grievance which [Patchak] seeks to assert," H.R. Rep. 94-1656, at 28, 1976 U.S.C.C.A.N. 6121 at 6147 — the QTA's limitation of remedies has no bearing. The APA's general waiver of sovereign immunity instead applies.

The Band and Government, along with the dissent, object to this conclusion on three basic grounds. First, they contend that the QTA speaks more broadly than we have indicated, waiving immunity from suits "to adjudicate a disputed title to real property in which the United States claims an interest." 28 U.S.C. § 2409a(a). That language, the argument goes, encompasses all actions contesting the Government's legal interest in land, regardless whether the plaintiff claims ownership himself. See Brief for Federal Petitioners 19–20; Reply Brief for Tribal Petitioner 4–6; *post*, at 2215–2216 (SOTOMAYOR, J., dissenting). The QTA (not the APA) thus becomes the relevant statute after all — as to both its waiver and its "corresponding" reservation of immunity from suits involving Indian lands. Reply Brief for Tribal Petitioner 6.

But the Band and Government can reach that result only by neglecting key words in the relevant provision. That sentence, more fully quoted, reads: "The United States may be named as a party defendant in *a civil action under this section* to adjudicate a disputed title to real property in which the United States claims an interest." § 2409a(a) (emphasis added). And as we have already noted, "this section" — § 2409a — includes a host of indications that the "civil action" at issue is an ordinary quiet title suit: Just recall the section's title ("Real property quiet title actions"), and its pleading requirements (the plaintiff "shall set forth with particularity the nature of the right, title, or interest which [he] claims"), and its permission to the Government to remedy an infraction by paying "just compensation." Read with reference to all these provisions (as well as to the QTA's contemporaneously enacted jurisdictional and venue sections), the waiver clause rebuts, rather than supports, the Band's and the Government's argument: That clause speaks not to any suit in which a plaintiff challenges the Government's title, but only to an action in which the plaintiff also claims an interest in the property.

The Band and Government next invoke cases holding that "when a statute provides a detailed mechanism for judicial consideration of particular issues at the behest of particular persons," the statute may "impliedly preclude [ ]" judicial review "of those issues at the behest of other persons." *Block v. Community Nutrition Institute*, 467 U.S. 340, 349 (1984); see *United States v. Fausto*, 484 U.S. 439, 455 (1988). Here, the Band and Government contend, the QTA's specific authorization of adverse claimants' suits creates a negative implication: *non*-adverse claimants like Patchak cannot challenge Government ownership of land under any other statute. See Reply Brief for Tribal Petitioner 7–10; Reply Brief for Federal Petitioners 7–9; see also post, at 2213–2214. The QTA, says the Band, thus "preempts [Patchak's] more general remedies." Brief for Tribal Petitioner 23 (internal quotation marks omitted).

But we think that argument faulty, and the cited cases inapposite, for the reason already given: Patchak is bringing a different claim, seeking different relief, from the kind the QTA addresses. . . .

Last, the Band and Government argue that we should treat Patchak's suit as we would an adverse claimant's because they equally implicate the "Indian lands" exception's policies. According to the Government, allowing challenges to the Secretary's trust acquisitions would "pose significant barriers to tribes['] . . . ability to promote investment and economic development on the lands." Brief for Federal Petitioners 24. That harm is the same whether or not a plaintiff claims to own the land himself. Indeed, the Band argues that the sole difference in this suit cuts in its direction, because non-adverse claimants like Patchak have "the most remote injuries and indirect interests in the land." Brief for Tribal Petitioner 13; see Reply Brief for Federal Petitioners 11–12; see also *post*, at 2212, 2215, 2216.

That argument is not without force, but it must be addressed to Congress. In the QTA, Congress made a judgment about how far to allow quiet title suits — to a point, but no further. (The "no further" includes not only the "Indian lands" exception, but one for security interests and water rights, as well as a statute of limitations, a bar on jury trials, jurisdictional and venue constraints, and the just compensation option discussed earlier.) Perhaps Congress would — perhaps Congress should — make the identical judgment for the full range of lawsuits pertaining to the Government's ownership of land. But that is not our call. The Band assumes that plaintiffs like Patchak have a lesser interest than those bringing quiet title actions, and so should be precluded *a fortiori*. But all we can say is that Patchak has a different interest. Whether it is lesser, as the Band argues, because not based on property rights; whether it is greater because implicating public interests; or whether it is in the end exactly the same — that is for Congress to tell us, not for us to tell Congress. As the matter stands, Congress has not assimilated to quiet title actions all other suits challenging the Government's ownership of property. And so when a plaintiff like Patchak brings a suit like this one, it falls within the APA's general waiver of sovereign immunity.

III

We finally consider the Band's and the Government's alternative argument that Patchak cannot bring this action because he lacks prudential standing. This Court has long held that a person suing under the APA must satisfy not only Article III's standing requirements, but an additional test: The interest he asserts must be "arguably within the zone of interests to be protected or regulated by the statute" that he says was violated. . . .

The prudential standing test Patchak must meet "is not meant to be especially demanding." . . . We apply the test in keeping with Congress's "evident intent" when enacting the APA "to make agency action presumptively reviewable." *Ibid.* We do not require any "indication of congressional purpose to benefit the would-be plaintiff." *Id.*, at 399–400. And we have always conspicuously included the word "arguably" in the test to indicate that the benefit of any doubt goes to the plaintiff. The test forecloses suit only when a plaintiff's "interests are so marginally related to or inconsistent with the purposes implicit in the statute that it cannot reasonably be assumed that Congress intended to permit the suit." *Id.*, at 399.

Patchak's suit satisfies that standard, because § 465 has far more to do with land use than the Government and Band acknowledge. . . .

The Department's regulations make this statutory concern with land use crystal clear. Those regulations permit the Secretary to acquire land in trust under § 465 if the "land is necessary to facilitate tribal self-determination, economic development, or Indian housing." 25 CFR § 151.3(a)(3). And they require the Secretary to consider, in evaluating any acquisition, both "[t]he purposes for which the land will be used" and the "potential conflicts of land use which may arise." §§ 151.10(c), 151.10(f); see § 151.11(a). For "off-reservation acquisitions" made "for business purposes" — like the Bradley Property — the regulations further provide that the tribe must "provide a plan which specifies the anticipated economic benefits associated with the proposed use." § 151.11(c). DOI's regulations thus show that the statute's implementation centrally depends on the projected use of a given property. . . .

And so neighbors to the use (like Patchak) are reasonable — indeed, predictable — challengers of the Secretary's decisions: Their interests, whether economic, environmental, or aesthetic, come within § 465's regulatory ambit.

. . . .

The QTA's reservation of sovereign immunity does not bar Patchak's suit. Neither does the doctrine of prudential standing. We therefore affirm the judgment of the D.C. Circuit, and remand the case for further proceedings consistent with this opinion.

It is so ordered.

JUSTICE SOTOMAYOR, dissenting.

In enacting the Quiet Title Act (QTA), Congress waived the Government's sovereign immunity in cases seeking "to adjudicate a disputed title to real property in which the United States claims an interest." 28 U.S.C. § 2409a(a). In so doing, Congress was careful to retain the Government's sovereign immunity with respect to particular claimants, particular categories of land, and particular remedies. Congress and the Executive Branch considered these "carefully crafted provisions" essential to the immunity waiver and "necessary for the protection of the national public interest." *Block v. North Dakota ex rel. Board of Univ. and School Lands*, 461 U.S. 273, 284–285 (1983).

The Court's opinion sanctions an end-run around these vital limitations on the Government's waiver of sovereign immunity. After today, any person may sue under the Administrative Procedure Act (APA) to divest the federal government of title to and possession of land held in trust for Indian tribes — relief expressly forbidden by the QTA — so long as the complaint does not assert a personal interest in the land. That outcome cannot be squared with the APA's express admonition that it confers no "authority to grant relief if any other statute that grants consent to suit expressly or impliedly forbids the relief which is sought." 5 U.S.C. § 702. The Court's holding not only creates perverse incentives for private litigants, but also exposes the Government's ownership of land to costly and prolonged challenges. Because I believe those results to be inconsistent with the QTA and the APA, I respectfully dissent.

I

A

Congress enacted the QTA to provide a comprehensive solution to the problem of real-property disputes between private parties and the United States. The QTA strikes a careful balance between private parties' desire to adjudicate such disputes, and the Government's desire to impose " 'appropriate safeguards' " on any waiver of sovereign immunity to ensure " 'the protection of the public interest.' " *Block*, 461 U.S., at 282–283; see also S.Rep. No. 92-575, p. 6 (1971).

Section 2409a(a) provides expansively that "[t]he United States may be named as a party defendant in a civil action under this section to adjudicate a disputed title to real property in which the United States claims an interest." That language mirrors the title proposed by the Executive Branch for the legislation that Congress largely adopted: "A Bill To permit suits to adjudicate disputed titles to lands in which the United States claims an interest." *Id.*, at 7.

The remainder of the Act, however, imposes important conditions upon the Government's waiver of sovereign immunity. First, the right to sue "does not apply to trust or restricted Indian lands." § 2409a(a). The Indian lands exception reflects the view that "a waiver of immunity in this area would not be consistent with specific commitments [the Government] ha[s] made to the Indians through treaties and other agreements." *Block*, 461 U.S., at 283 (internal quotation marks omitted). By exempting Indian lands, Congress ensured that the Government's "solemn obligations" to tribes would not be "abridg[ed] . . . without the consent of the Indians." S.Rep. No. 92–575, at 4.

Second, the Act preserves the United States's power to retain possession or control of any disputed property, even if a court determines that the Government's property claim is invalid. To that end, § 2409a(b) "allow[s] the United States the option of paying money damages instead of surrendering the property if it lost a case on the merits." *Block*, 461 U.S., at 283. . . .

Finally, the Act limits the class of individuals permitted to sue the Government to those claiming a "right, title, or interest" in disputed property. § 2409a(d). . . .

Congress considered these conditions indispensable to its immunity waiver. "[W]hen Congress attaches conditions to legislation waiving the sovereign immunity of the United States, those conditions must be strictly observed, and exceptions thereto are not to be lightly implied." *Block*, 461 U.S., at 287 . . .

For that reason, we held that Congress did not intend to create a "new supplemental remedy" when it enacted the APA's general waiver of sovereign immunity. *Block*, 461 U.S., at 286, n. 22,. "It would require the suspension of disbelief," we reasoned, "to ascribe to Congress the design to allow its careful and thorough remedial scheme to be circumvented by artful pleading." *Id.*, at 285, 103 S. Ct. 1811 (quoting *Brown v. GSA*, 425 U.S. 820, 833 (1976)). If a plaintiff could oust the Government of title to land by means of an APA action, "all of the carefully crafted provisions of the QTA deemed necessary for the protection of the national public interest could be averted," and the "Indian lands exception to the QTA would be rendered nugatory." *Block*, 461 U.S., at 284–285. . . .

It is undisputed that Patchak does not meet the conditions to sue under the QTA. He seeks to challenge the Government's title to Indian trust land (strike one); he seeks to force the Government to relinquish possession and title outright, leaving it no alternative to pay compensation (strike two); and he does not claim any personal right, title, or interest in the property (strike three). Thus, by its express terms, the

QTA forbids the relief Patchak seeks. . . .

B

The majority nonetheless permits Patchak to circumvent the QTA's limitations by filing an action under the APA. It primarily argues that the careful limitations Congress imposed upon the QTA's waiver of sovereign immunity are "simply inapposite" to actions in which the plaintiff advances a different "grievance" to that underlying a QTA suit, *i.e.*, cases in which a plaintiff seeks to "strip the United States of title to the land . . . not on the ground that it is his," but rather because "the Secretary's decision to take land into trust violates a federal statute." *Ante*, at 2206, 2207. This analysis is unmoored from the text of the APA. . . .

The relief Patchak admittedly seeks — to oust the Government of title to Indian trust land — is identical to that forbidden by the QTA. . . .

The majority attempts to bolster its reading by emphasizing an unexpected source within § 2409a: the clause specifying that the United States may be sued " 'in *a civil action under this section.*' " *Ante*, at 11. . . .

Regardless of how one reads the clause, however, it does not alter the APA's clear command that suits seeking relief forbidden by other statutes are not authorized by the APA. And the QTA forbids the relief sought here: injunctive relief forcing the Government to relinquish title to Indian lands.

Even if the majority were correct that the QTA itself reached only as far as ordinary quiet title actions, that would establish only that the QTA does not expressly forbid the relief Patchak seeks. The APA, however, does not waive the Government's sovereign immunity where any other statute "expressly or *impliedly* forbids the relief which is sought." 5 U.S.C. § 702 (emphasis added). The text and history of the QTA, as well as this Court's precedent, make clear that the United States intended to retain its sovereign immunity from suits to dispossess the Government of Indian trust land. Patchak's suit to oust the Government of such land is therefore, at minimum, impliedly forbidden.

II

Three consequences illustrate the difficulties today's holding will present for courts and the Government. First, it will render the QTA's limitations easily circumvented. Although those with property claims will remain formally prohibited from bringing APA suits because of *Block*, savvy plaintiffs and their lawyers can recruit a family member or neighbor to bring suit asserting only an "aesthetic" interest in the land but seeking an identical practical objective — to divest the Government of title and possession. § 2409a(a), (b). Nothing will prevent them from obtaining relief that the QTA was designed to foreclose.

Second, the majority's holding will frustrate the Government's ability to resolve challenges to its fee-to-trust decisions expeditiously. When a plaintiff like Patchak asserts an "aesthetic" or "environmental" concern with a planned use of Indian trust land, he may bring a distinct suit under statutes like the National Environmental Policy Act of 1969 and the Indian Gaming Regulatory Act. Those challenges generally may be brought within the APA's ordinary six-year statute of limitations. Suits to contest the Government's decision to take title to land in trust for Indian tribes, however, have been governed by a different rule. Until today, parties seeking to challenge such decisions had only a thirty-day window to seek judicial review. 25 CFR § 151.12 (2011); 61 Fed.Reg. 18,082–18,083 (1996). That deadline promoted finality and security — necessary preconditions for the investment and "economic development" that are central goals of the Indian Reorganization Act. *Ante*, at 2210. Today's result will promote the opposite, retarding tribes' ability to develop land until the APA's six-year statute of limitations has lapsed.

Finally, the majority's rule creates substantial uncertainty regarding who exactly is barred from bringing APA claims. The majority leaves unclear, for instance, whether its rule bars from suit only those who "claim any competing interest" in the disputed land in their complaint, *ante*, at 2206, or those who could claim a competing interest, but plead only that the Government's title claim violates a federal statute. If the former, the majority's holding would allow Patchak's challenge to go forward even if he had some personal interest in the Bradley Property, so long as his complaint did not assert it. That result is difficult to square with *Block* and *Mottaz*. If the latter, matters are even more peculiar. Because a shrewd plaintiff will avoid referencing her own property claim in her complaint, the Government may assert sovereign immunity only if its detective efforts uncover the plaintiff's unstated property claim. Not only does that impose a substantial burden on the Government, but it creates perverse incentives for private litigants. What if a plaintiff has a weak claim, or a claim that she does not know about? Did Congress really intend for the availability of APA relief to turn on whether a plaintiff does a better job of overlooking or suppressing her own property interest than the Government does of sleuthing it out?

As these observations illustrate, the majority's rule will impose a substantial burden on the Government and leave an array of uncertainties. Moreover, it will open to suit lands that Congress and the Executive Branch thought the "national public interest" demanded should remain immune from challenge. Congress did not intend either result.

. . . .

For the foregoing reasons, I would hold that the QTA bars the relief Patchak seeks. I respectfully dissent.

NOTES

1. **Regulatory "*Patchak* Patches," Challenges, and Remaining Questions:** Justice Sotomayor lists three consequences of the *Patchak* decision in her dissent. Are there other potential consequences that tribes might face following the decision? For more information on the potential impacts of the case, as well as the story behind it, *see* J. Matthew Martin, *The Supreme Court Erects a Fence Around Indian Gaming*, 39 OKLA. CITY. U. L. REV. 45 (2014). The Court's decision in *Patchak* focuses on gaming, but this decision impacts other tribal economic development projects as well. How have public perceptions and court decisions about tribal

gaming affected the ability of tribes to take land into trust for both gaming and non-gaming purposes?

The Department of Interior implemented new regulations, seeking to limit potential lawsuits against tribes in the wake of *Patchak*. The new rule ends the 30-day waiting period for the Secretary of the Interior to take land into trust for tribes planning to use the land for gaming. While opponents may still file suit opposing such land-into-trust decisions, closing the waiting period means that they will do so only after the Department has already taken the land into trust. Further, the rule includes a 30-day appeal period for non-gaming land-into-trust decisions. If opponents do not appeal within this period, they lose their right to do so. 25 C.F.R. § 151 (2014). Do the Department of Interior's new rules effectively address the potential difficulties the *Patchak* litigation might cause for tribes seeking to place their land into trust? Why might the rules differentiate between land taken into trust for gaming versus land taken into trust for non-gaming purposes?

In September of 2014, Congress passed a bill reaffirming the trust status of the land at issue in *Patchak* on behalf of the Match-E-Be-Nash-She-Wish Band of Pottawatomi. The law also mandated that federal courts should "promptly dismiss" any action, including those pending relating to the parcel of land. *Gun Lake Trust Land Reaffirmation Act*, Pub. L. No. 113-179, 128 Stat. 1913 (2014). However, the act did not address any of the broader implications of the *Patchak* litigation. What action might Congress take to address tribal concerns about the litigation's impact on tribes' ability to take land into trust?

2. Prudential Standing and State Challenges to Land-Into-Trust Claims: In *South Dakota v. United States Department of Interior*, 665 F.3d 986 (8th Cir. 2012), South Dakota challenged the Department of Interior's decision to take land into trust on behalf of the Sisseton-Wahpeton Oyate of the Lake Traverse Reservation, noting economic consequences due to lost tax revenue. The state based its claim in the Fifth Amendment's due process clause, but did not seek to enforce a right arising from the statutes authorizing the Secretary to take land into trust on behalf of tribes. The court held that the state, while meeting the minimum requirements for standing, did not satisfy the prudential standing requirement because it was not a person within the meaning of the due process clause. *Id.* at 990.

5. Land Claims

a. The Indian Claims Commission

Even if the *Tee-Hit-Ton* case, presented in Section A.1, this chapter, is correct in stating that Congress is not constitutionally compelled to compensate tribes for the extinguishment of aboriginal title, Congress has consistently done so. Typically, Congress has paid compensation far in excess of the blankets, food, and trinkets suggested by Justice Reed in the *Tee-Hit-Ton* opinion. However, Congress has not compensated tribes for the full fair market value of their lost land, or provided interest from the time of loss.

The early nineteenth century cession treaties generally extinguished aboriginal title in exchange for recognition of diminished holdings as a reservation or, during the removal period, for new lands guaranteed to the tribes and for substantial annuities. *See, e.g.*, Treaty with the Ponca, Mar. 12, 1858, 12 Stat. 997 (land ceded in exchange for inter alia a recognized reservation; annual annuities of $12,000 for five years, $10,000 thereafter for 10 years, and $8,000 for the succeeding fifteen years; expenditures of $20,000 for removal and housing; $5,000 for education; the establishment of saw and grist mills and mechanics shops; the expenditure of up to $7,500 for assisting the Poncas in pursuing agricultural and mechanical pursuits; and $20,000 to adjust and settle the Poncas's outstanding debts). To address instances in which tribes were deprived of their aboriginal homelands without compensation or with less than fair compensation (for example, the Sioux Nation's loss of the Black Hills), Congress passed special jurisdictional acts authorizing Indian tribes to pursue claims in the Court of Claims.

The history of aboriginal title and land loss in California affords an instructive example. Soon after California was admitted to the Union in 1850, federal representatives negotiated eighteen treaties with 139 tribes throughout the state, setting aside approximately 7.5 million acres for their reservations. Concerned that this land might contain valuable gold deposits, the California congressional delegation prevented ratification of the treaties, and had them placed in secret files. Contemporaneous with these treaty negotiations, Congress passed the Land Claims Act of 1851, Act of March 3, 1851, 9 Stat. 631, which provided that all lands in California, the claim to which was invalid or not presented within two years of the date of the Act, would pass into the public domain. Unsurprisingly, Congress didn't notify the indigenous peoples of California that they needed to present claims to their lands, and they failed to meet the 1853 deadline. Even if they had known of the Land Claims Act, it was not clear that it applied to aboriginal lands. See William Wood, *The Trajectory of Indian Country in California: Rancherías, Villages, Pueblos, Missions, Ranchos, Reservations, Colonies, and Rancherias*, 44 Tulsa L. Rev. 317, 343–44 n.140 (2008). Nonetheless, federal officials treated tribal lands as if they had been forfeited under the Act. *See* Bruce S. Flushman & Joe Barbieri, *Aboriginal Title: The Special Case of California*, 17 Pac. L.J. 391 (1986) (arguing that the Indians' failure to present these claims extinguished their aboriginal title). Seventy-five years later, after the treaties were "discovered" in the secret files, Congress passed the California Indian Jurisdictional Act, 45 Stat. 602, authorizing "the Indians of California," to bring suit in the Court of Claims for the loss of their lands, although the statute limited compensation to no more than $1.25 per acre and provided an offset for the costs of BIA administration in California. For a thorough and learned study of the history of Indian lands in California, see William Wood, *The Trajectory of Indian Country in California, supra.*

As a general matter, since individual claims statutes waived the federal government's sovereign immunity, they were construed narrowly. For example, in *Northwestern Bands of Shoshone Indians v. United States*, 324 U.S. 335 (1945), the Court, in an opinion by Justice Reed, held that a special jurisdictional act authorizing suits for claims "arising under or growing out of the treaty [of Box Elder]" did not authorize a claim based on aboriginal title when the Court's construction of the treaty indicated that it had not recognized the Indians' title to the affected land.

After dealing with Indian claims through 142 ad hoc jurisdictional statutes for nearly a century, in 1946 Congress enacted the Indian Claims Commission Act, Pub. L. No. 79-726, 60 Stat. 1049 (codified at 28 U.S.C. § 1505, 25 U.S.C. § 70 et seq., and omitted from 25 U.S.C. on termination of the Commission, September 30, 1978). The act created a special Commission to hear Indian claims accruing before August 13, 1946, and defined the Commission's jurisdiction as follows:

> The Commission shall hear and determine the following claims against the United States on behalf of any Indian tribe, band, or other identifiable group of American Indians residing within the territorial limits of the United States or Alaska: (1) claims in law or equity arising under the Constitution, laws, treaties of the United States, and Executive orders of the President; (2) all other claims in law or equity, including those sounding in tort, with respect to which the claimant would have been entitled to sue in a court of the United States if the United States was subject to suit; (3) claims which would result if the treaties, contracts, and agreements between the claimant and the United States were revised on the ground of fraud, duress, unconscionable consideration, mutual or unilateral mistake, whether of law or fact, or any other ground cognizable by a court of equity; (4) claims arising from the taking by the United States, whether as the result of a treaty of cession or otherwise, of lands owned or occupied by the claimant without the payment for such lands of compensation agreed to by the claimant; and (5) claims based upon fair and honorable dealings that are not recognized by any existing rule of law or equity.

All claims had to be filed within five years of the enactment of the Act. Additionally, the statute provided that the claims were to be heard notwithstanding any defense of statute of limitations or laches and that the Commission could deduct offsets and counterclaims from its award, including expenditures for goods, rations, or provisions that the United States had given to tribes if it found that "the nature of the claims and the entire course of dealings and accounts between the United States and the claimant in good conscience warrant[ed] such actions. . . ." The Commission was given a limited ten-year life, which was extended periodically because the Commission was unable to complete the task of adjudicating the 375 claims filed with it in the time available. A survey of the Commission's work, including an index of its decisions, can be found In UNITED STATES INDIAN CLAIMS COMMISSION, FINAL REPORT (1978). The Commission expired on September 31, 1978, and transferred the remaining 102 dockets to the Court of Claims (now the United States Court of Federal Claims). *See also* HARVEY D. ROSENTHAL, THEIR DAY IN COURT: A HISTORY OF THE INDIAN CLAIMS COMMISSION (1990); IRREDEEMABLE AMERICA: THE INDIANS' ESTATE AND LAND CLAIMS (I. Sutton ed., 1985); Russel L. Barsh, *Indian Land Claims Policy in the United States*, 58 N.D. L. REV. 7 (1982); John T. Vance, *The Congressional Mandate and the Indian Claims Commission*, 45 N.D. L. REV. 325 (1969).

The Indian Claims Commission could only award monetary relief, not the return of land. Indeed, judgments and settlements in Indian Claims Commission litigation resulted in the formal extinguishment of aboriginal title claim to lands for which compensation was paid. Attorneys who prosecuted claims before the Commission were compensated on a contingent fee basis, which led them to favor taking the cases to judgment or settlement. Thus, tribes that wished to forego payments and maintain ties to their ancestral lands sometimes found themselves at odds with their attorneys. For an example of this phenomenon, *see United States v. Sioux Nation*, presented in Section A.2, this chapter. In that case, the claim brought to the Indian Claims Commission had involved loss of land guaranteed in a treaty. In the case that follows, the claim before the Commission involves land held in aboriginal title.

UNITED STATES v. DANN
United States Supreme Court
470 U.S. 39 (1985)

JUSTICE BRENNAN delivered the opinion of the Court.

The question presented in this case is whether the appropriation of funds into a Treasury account pursuant to 31 U.S.C. § 724a (1976 ed., Supp. V) constitutes "payment" under § 22(a) of the Indian Claims Commission Act, 60 Stat. 1055, 25 U.S.C. § 70u(a) (1976 ed.).

I

This case is an episode in a longstanding conflict between the United States and the Shoshone Tribe over title to lands in the western United States. In 1951 certain members of the Shoshone Tribe sought compensation for the loss of aboriginal title to lands located in California, Colorado, Idaho, Nevada, Utah, and Wyoming. Eleven years later, the Indian Claims Commission entered an interlocutory order holding that the aboriginal title of the Western Shoshone had been extinguished in the latter part of the nineteenth century, *Shoshone Tribe v. United States*, 11 Ind. Cl. Comm'n 387, 416 (1962), and later awarded the Western Shoshone in excess of $26 million in compensation. *Western Shoshone Identifiable Group v. United States*, 40 Ind. Cl. Comm'n 318 (1977). The Court of Claims affirmed this award. *Temoak Band of Western Shoshone Indians v. United States*, 593 F.2d 994 (Ct. Cl. 1979). On December 6, 1979, the Clerk of the Court of Claims certified the Commission's award to the General Accounting Office. Pursuant to 31 U.S.C. § 724a (1976 ed., Supp. V), this certification automatically appropriated the amount of the award and deposited it for the Tribe in an interest-bearing trust account in the Treasury of the United States.

Under 25 U.S.C. § 1402(a) and § 1403(a), the Secretary of the Interior is required, after consulting with the Tribe, to submit to Congress within a specified period of time a plan for the distribution of the fund. In this case, the Secretary has yet to submit a plan of distribution of the $26 million owing to the refusal of the Western Shoshone to cooperate in devising the plan. The fund apparently has now grown to $43 million.

In 1974, the United States brought an action in trespass against two sisters, Mary and Carrie Dann, members of an autonomous band of the Western Shoshone, alleging that the Danns, in grazing livestock without a permit from the United States, were acting in violation of regulations issued by the Secretary of the Interior under the authority of the Taylor Grazing Act, 43 U.S.C. § 315b. The 5,120 acres at issue in the suit are located in the northeast corner of Nevada. In response to the United States's suit, the Danns claimed that the land has been in the possession of their family from time immemorial and that their aboriginal title to the land precluded the Government from requiring grazing permits. The United States District Court for the District of Nevada rejected the Danns' argument and ruled that aboriginal title had been extinguished by the collateral-estoppel effect of the Indian Claims Commission's judgment in 1962. The Court of Appeals for the Ninth Circuit reversed and remanded, however, on the ground that "[w]hatever may have been the implicit assumptions of both the United States and the Shoshone Tribes during the litigation . . . , the extinguishment question was not necessarily in issue, it was not actually litigated, and it has not been decided."

On remand, the District Court held that aboriginal title was extinguished when the final award of the Indian Claims Commission was certified for payment on December 6, 1979. On appeal, the Government defended the judgment of the District Court on the ground that the "full discharge" language of § 22(a) of the Indian Claims Commission Act, see n.2, *supra*, precluded the Danns from raising the defense of aboriginal title. Although Congress had not yet approved a plan for the distribution of the funds to the Western Shoshone, the United States maintained that the requirement of "payment" under § 22(a) was satisfied by the congressional appropriation of the $26 million award into the Treasury account. The Danns argued that until Congress approved a plan for the distribution of the money to the Tribe, "payment" was not satisfied.

The Court of Appeals held that "payment" had not occurred within the meaning of § 22(a) and reversed the District Court. The court reasoned that until a plan of distribution was adopted by the Congress, there remained "significant legal blocks in the way of delivery to the payee," and thus the "ordinary meaning" of payment was not satisfied. We granted certiorari to resolve the question of whether the certification of the award and appropriation under § 724a constitutes payment under § 22(a). We reverse.

II

The legislative purposes of the Indian Claims Commission Act and the principles of payment under the common law of trust as they have been applied to the context of relations between Native American communities and the United States require that we hold that "payment" occurs under § 22(a) when funds are placed by the United States into an account in the Treasury of the United States for the Tribe pursuant to 31 U.S.C. § 724a (1976 ed., Supp. V).

A

The Indian Claims Commission Act had two purposes. The "chief purpose of the [Act was] to dispose of the Indian claims problem with finality." H.R. Rep. No. 1466, 79th Cong., 1st Sess., 10 (1945). This purpose was effected by the language of § 22(a): "When the report of the Commission determining any claimant to be entitled to recover has been filed with Congress, such report shall have the effect of a final judgment of the Court of Claims. . . . " Section 22(a) also states that the "payment of any claim . . . shall be a full discharge of the United States of all claims and demands touching any of the matters involved in the controversy." To hold, as the court below has, that payment does not occur until a final plan of distribution has been approved by Congress would frustrate the purpose of finality by postponing the preclusive effects of § 22(a) while subjecting the United States to continued liability for claims and demands that "touch" the matter previously litigated and resolved by the Indian Claims Commission.

The second purpose of the Indian Claims Commission Act was to transfer from Congress to the Indian Claims Commission the responsibility for determining the merits of Native American claims. [Congressman Jackson, chairman of the House Committee on Indian Affairs noted during the floor debate] that the House was acting in response to a study by the Brookings Institution that had concluded that "there ought to be a prompt and final settlement of all claims between the Government and its Indian citizens, and that the best way to accomplish this purpose is to set up temporarily an Indian Claims Commission which will sift all these claims, subject to appropriate judicial review, and bring them to a conclusion once and for all." 92 Cong. Rec. 5312 (1946).

[L]anguage that Attorney General Clark asserted would give the decisions of the Indian Claims Commission the effect of a final judgment binding upon Congress [was deleted in the Senate version]. The Conference adopted the House version "in order to make perfectly clear the intention of both houses that the determinations of the Commission should, unless reversed [by the Court of Claims], have the same finality as judgments of the Court of Claims." H.R. Conf. Rep. No. 2693, 79th Cong., 2d Sess., 8 (1946). As enacted, the Indian Claims Commission Act explicitly incorporated this standard of finality in § 22(a).

The court below justified its decision on the ground that in making "payment" turn on the submission and approval of a final plan of distribution, Congress would have one last opportunity to review the merits of claims litigated before the Indian Claims Commission. This justification for delay obviously conflicts with the purpose of relieving Congress of the burden of having to resolve these claims.

B

[T]he Court of Appeals' interpretation is in conflict with the accepted legal uses of the word "payment" (uses we assume Congress intended to adopt when it enacted § 22(a). To accept the argument of the Court of Appeals would give the word "payment" a meaning that differs markedly from its common-law meaning, which has long been applied by this Court to the relations between Native American tribes and the United States.

The common law recognizes that payment may be satisfied despite the absence of actual possession of the funds by the creditor. Funds transferred from a debtor to an agent or trustee of the creditor constitute payment, and it is of no consequence that the creditor refuses to accept the funds from the agent or the agent misappropriates the funds. The rationale for this is that fiduciary obligations and the rules of agency so bind the trustee or agent to the creditor (i.e., the beneficiary or principal) as to confer effective control of the funds upon the creditor.

The Court has applied these principles to relations between Native American communities and the United States. In *Seminole Nation v. United States*, 316 U.S. 286 (1942), the United States was obligated by treaty to pay annual annuities to members of the Seminole Nation. Instead, the Government transferred the money to the Seminole General Council. Members of the Tribe argued that because the Seminole General Council had misappropriated the money, the Government had not satisfied its obligation to pay the individual members of the Tribe. In disposing of the case, the Court relied upon the rule that "a third party who pays money to a fiduciary for the benefit of the beneficiary, with knowledge that the fiduciary intends to misappropriate the money or otherwise be false to his trust, is a participant in the breach of trust and liable therefor to the beneficiary." *Id.*, at 296. The Court's holding was based on its recognition of the traditional rule that a debtor's payment to a fiduciary of the creditor satisfies the debt.

[T]he general rule in *Seminole Nation* is authority for our holding that the United States has made "payment" under § 22(a). The final award of the Indian Claims Commission placed the Government in a dual role with respect to the Tribe: the Government was at once a judgment debtor, owing $26 million to the Tribe, and a trustee for the Tribe responsible for ensuring that the money was put to productive use and ultimately distributed in a manner consistent with the best interests of the Tribe. In short, the Indian Claims Commission ordered the Government qua judgment debtor to pay $26 million to the Government qua trustee for the Tribe as the beneficiary. Once the money was deposited into the trust account, payment was effected.

[*Reversed and remanded.*]

NOTES ON THE *DANN* CASE AND THE INDIAN CLAIMS COMMISSION

1. Scope of Indian Claims Commission Jurisdiction: Although the list of claims recognized in the Indian Claims Commission did not distinguish between aboriginal and recognized title, the United States argued that the Act extended only to claims involving recognized title lands. For example, the United States contended that the term "treaties" in clause (3) included only those treaties relating to land held by Indians under fee simple or recognized title, and that the reference to "dealings" in clause (5) was intended to exclude dealings relative to aboriginal title. In *Otoe & Missouria Tribe of Indians v. United States*, 131 F. Supp. 265 (Ct. Cl. 1955), the Court of Claims reviewed the legislative history of the Indian Claims Commission Act and held that the Commission had jurisdiction under subdivisions (2) and (5) to award compensation for the extinguishments of aboriginal Indian title. Noting that under *Tee-Hit-Ton* such claims did not represent compensable takings under the Fifth Amendment, the Court relied on language in the *Tee-Hit-Ton* opinion recognizing that Congress could "allow tribes to recover for wrongs, as a matter of grace, not because of legal liability." The court also acknowledged that its holding conflicted with the general, but not absolute, rule that jurisdictional grants in claims involving the United States were not usually construed to create a cause of action where none existed independently of the jurisdictional statute. But it relied on the statute's plain language as well as its history. Note that such awards do not include accrued interest. In contrast, claims based on loss of recognized title would accrue such interest. *See United States v. Sioux Nation*, presented in Sec. A.2, this chapter.

Under 28 U.S.C. § 1505 the Court of Claims is authorized to exercise jurisdiction over claims accruing after August 13, 1946 on behalf of tribes arising under the Constitution, laws, or treaties of the United States, or Executive orders, of "which otherwise would be cognizable in the Court of Claims if the claimant were not an Indian tribe, band, or group." Under this section, are claims for the extinguishment of aboriginal title compensable if they accrue after that date? *Cf. Tee-Hit-Ton v. United States, supra.*

2. **Money vs. Land:** Soon after it began its work, the Indian Claims Commission ruled that its jurisdiction was confined to money damages awards. *Osage Nation v. United States*, 1 Ind. Cl. Comm'n 54 (1948), *rev'd on other grounds*, 97 F. Supp. 381 (Ct. Cl. 1951). Other cases before *Dann* had held that the Indian Claims Commission's jurisdiction was exclusive, thereby precluding suits by tribes to block distribution of ICC judgments and to secure alternative remedies. *See, e.g., Oglala Sioux Tribe v. United States*, 650 F.2d 140 (8th Cir. 1981) (Indian treaty claims); *Six Nations Confederacy v. Andrus*, 610 F.2d 996, 998 (D.C. Cir. 1979) (suit to prevent distribution of ICC award). In *Navajo Tribe v. New Mexico*, 809 F.2d 1455 (10th Cir. 1987), the Tenth Circuit went even further, holding that the Tribe was relegated to the Indian Claims Commission remedy for a claim that Executive Order land had been restored to the public domain by President Teddy Roosevelt in violation of a federal statute requiring that the land be allotted to Navajos before being restored. Even though the Tribe requested a declaration that it still possessed equitable title, and no claim had been filed or paid in the Indian Claims Commission, the Tenth Circuit found the Indian Claims Commission remedy both exclusive and time-barred. Citing language in *Dann* that the purpose of the Claims Commission was to settle all Indian land claims, the court found that the restriction of ICC remedies to money damages was designed to prevent tribes from dispossessing third parties currently in possession. *Cf. City of Sherrill v. Oneida Indian Nation*, presented in Sec. A.5.b, this chapter (finding a Nonintercourse Act claim barred under the doctrine of laches, partly for the same reason).

Congress has occasionally acted to restore land to a tribe. The return of Blue Lake to the Taos Pueblo is a well-known illustration, but other tribes have had some modest success. *See* Russel Barsh, *Indian Land Claims Policy in the United States*, 58 N.D. L. Rev. 7, 73 & n.358 (collecting statutes); John F. Martin, *From Judgment to Restoration: The Havasupai Land Claims Case, in* Irredeemable America: The Indians' Estate and Land Claims 71 (I. Sutton ed., 1985) (return of 185,000 acres to reservation and grant of exclusive use for traditional purposes of 95,300 acres of National Forest). Land has also been restored in connection with tribal recognition or restoration legislation. *See, e.g.,* Timbisha Shoshone Homeland Act, Act of Nov. 1, 2000, P.L. 106-423, 114 Stat. 1875. For an account of the long struggle by the Tule River Indian Tribe of California to retrieve the most valuable portion of their reservation, lost to them through a fraudulent federal survey, see Gelya Frank & Carole Goldberg, Defying the Odds: The Tule River Tribe's Struggle for Sovereignty in Three Centuries (2010).

3. History of the Western Shoshone Title Litigation: The *Dann* case holds that the Indian Claims Commission (ICC) proceeding extinguished the Dann Band's land, even though the Dann Band was not a party and the Dann sisters had never ceased to occupy their land. One commentator explains how this could come about:

> [O]nce the representative of an identifiable group is recognized, this claimant group is the exclusive representative of all tribal descendants, even though not all of the competing interests are represented. This situation arises where Indians still occupy aboriginal land, and are therefore unlikely to file a claim with the ICC for lands to which they apparently still hold title. Members who were displaced by the government from a portion of the tribal land, however, had a monetary incentive to include the entire ancestral parcel in their claim. Furthermore, Indians still living on aboriginal land may not have had notice that a separate descendant group claimed the extinguishment of aboriginal title. Then, when the Indians occupying aboriginal land attempted to intervene in the ICC proceedings, they were usually denied the right because the proceedings were at an advanced stage.

Caroline Orlando, *Aboriginal Title Claims in the Indian Claims Commission*: United States v. Dann *and Its Due Process Implications*, 13 B.C. ENVTL. AFF. L. REV. 241, 261 (1986). But how can this procedure be reconciled with due process? *See Hansberry v. Lee*, 311 U.S. 32 (1940) (due process violated when a class action judgment is given binding effect and the class members were not notified about the litigation or given an opportunity to opt out). If the Court is correct in stating that a major purpose of the Indian Claims Commission was to provide a forum for the full and final litigation of Indian land claims, why wasn't the Claims Commission obliged to afford interested autonomous groups like the Dann Band an opportunity to intervene? Does the Court in Dann address the due process issues? Orlando, *supra*, offers a highly critical analysis of the decision.

United States v. Dann represents just one installment in a long saga of struggle by various bands of Western Shoshone to secure a judicial ruling that their right to their ancestral lands has never been extinguished by the United States. The decentralized nature of Western Shoshone social and political organization, functioning as a loose confederation of autonomous bands held together by cultural and clan connections has been a complicating factor. The claim for taking aboriginal title filed by the Temoak Bands of Western Shoshone was designated by the Indian Claims Commission as on behalf of an entity called "the Western Shoshone Identifiable Group." This group was chosen at meetings called by the Temoak Band's attorneys, and existed for purposes of the litigation only. It did not correspond to any pre-existing Western Shoshone political entity. The ICC found that "gradual encroachment by whites, settlers and others, and the acquisition, disposition or taking of their lands by the United States for its own use and benefit" had extinguished Western Shoshone land claims. In the absence of a single, identifiable date for the taking, the Western Shoshone Identifiable Group entered into a stipulation with the United States setting a formal taking date in the nineteenth century, enabling the case to proceed to the valuation phase. Eventually the ICC awarded the Group a judgment of $26 million. *Western Shoshone*

Identifiable Group v. United States, 29 Ind. Cl. Comm'n 5, 7 (1972) (decision and description of stipulation).

As the litigation proceeded, Western Shoshone people became increasingly concerned about its potential impact on those who continued to live on approximately 3 million acres of land held under unextinguished aboriginal title. The plaintiffs believed that their stipulation regarding the date of taking affected only land that Western Shoshone people no longer held. In the early 1970's, a group of Western Shoshone petitioned to intervene in the Indian Claims Commission proceeding and obtain a stay of the judgment pending presentation of an amended compensation claim to excise land presently occupied by Western Shoshone people. The Court of Claims characterized the attempted intervention as an intra-tribal disagreement over the proper litigation strategy and rejected the intervention as untimely. *Western Shoshone Legal Defense & Educ. Ass'n v. United States*, 531 F.2d 495 (Ct. Cl. 1976).

Mary and Carrie Dann, active participants in the effort to escape the effects of the judgment, were cited for trespass in 1974 by the U.S. government. In 1975 and 1976, the Temoak Band dismissed their attorney and adopted a position similar to that of the Danns, claiming that the Band's previous attorney had not presented them with the choice whether to include all of the ancestral lands in the claim or only the unoccupied portion. In a letter to the Secretary of the Interior, the Band's Chairman protested that the lawyers

> "no longer report to us but to a 'claims committee' which was elected by just a few Indians and has no rules or any way for the people to control them. These lawyers not only have refused to protect the title to the land we still have but have fought our people who have tried to do it themselves through the Western Shoshone Legal Defense and Education Association."

Respondents' Appendix at R2–R3, *United States v. Dann*, 470 U.S. 39 (1985). Accordingly, they attempted to stay the proceedings in the ICC and before the Court of Claims so they could address this issue. However, the ICC denied the stay and entered a final judgment, and on appeal the Court of Claims affirmed the ICC's ruling on the basis that it was too late for the Temoak Band to change their litigation strategy. 40 Ind. Cl. Comm'n 305 (1977), *aff'd*, *Temoak Band v. United States*, 593 F.2d 994 (Ct. Cl. 1979).

Meanwhile, the Danns were fighting their trespass case, arguing that their aboriginal title had never been extinguished. Following the decision by the United States Supreme Court, the matter was once again remanded to the District Court to resolve a question left open by the high court — whether the Dann sisters could claim individual aboriginal rights. The Supreme Court recognized individual aboriginal title rights in the case of *Cramer v. United States*, 261 U.S. 219 (1923), which protected rights of occupancy on public lands that were not aboriginal in the usual sense of long or indefinite duration. In that case, the Court relied heavily on assimilationist federal policy in place at the time the individual Indians first occupied public lands, policy that encouraged Indians to abandon their nomadic existence in favor of settlement in one place. Ultimately, the Ninth Circuit distinguished *Cramer*, finding that federal policy had shifted after 1934 in favor of withdrawal of federal lands from entry, and recognizing individual aboriginal title only on lands that had been occupied continuously since before that date. The court also extended the principle of *Cramer* to use rights, affirming the District Court's decision that the Dann sisters had acquired grazing rights during the period before the Taylor Grazing Act established an exclusive mechanism for securing such rights. *United States v. Dann*, 873 F.2d 1189 (9th Cir. 1989).

In 1991, the Bureau of Land Management (BLM) was granted an injunction against trespass by the Dann's livestock. However, the BLM was only partially successful in enforcing the injunction. The sisters became a symbol of indigenous resistance, and an international cause celebre, with supporters from around the world who sent letters of protest to the agency. In a trespass case brought by a neighboring rancher, a BLM officer testified, "When officials tried to load animals into trucks, Carrie Dann placed her own body into the loading chute. And when the Dann sisters' brother, Clifford Dann, threatened to immolate himself with gasoline, the BLM backed off. Clifford Dann tossed gasoline on Federal officers, and ultimately went to prison for this assault." *Alves v. United States*, 133 F.3d 1454, 1455 (Fed. Cir. 1998).

In 1993, the Dann sisters, represented by the Indian Law Resource Center, filed a complaint with the Inter-American Commission on Human Rights, alleging violations of the American Declaration of the Rights and Duties of Man as well as other international human rights norms and principles. In September of 2002, the Commission ruled in favor of the Danns, concluding that the Danns "did not play a full or effective role in retaining, authorizing, or instructing the Western Shoshone claimants in the ICC process," and that the finding of extinguishment was "not based upon a judicial evaluation of pertinent evidence, but rather was based upon apparently arbitrary stipulations as between the U.S. government and the Temoak Band regarding the extent and timing of the loss of indigenous title to the entirety of the Western Shoshone ancestral lands." In September 2002, heavily armed federal agents, joined by helicopters, rounded up 232 head of the Danns' cattle, which were later sold at auction. On February 6, 2003, the BLM began rounding up approximately 800 horses belonging to the sisters. *U.S. Agents Seize Horses of 2 Defiant Indian Sisters*, NEW YORK TIMES (Feb. 7, 2003), at A16.

In 2003, the Western Shoshone filed suit to invalidate the ICC ruling, claiming that the judgment of the ICC was void under Rule of the Court of Federal Claims (RCFC) 60(b)(4) because the ICC denied them due process in reaching its judgment. Alternatively, the Western Shoshone claimed entitlement to pre-judgment interest on the ICC's award. Further, they asked for royalties on minerals mined and extracted under the Treaty of Ruby Valley; an accounting of the proceeds from the United States' use of the land; and damages for breach of fiduciary duties related to land mismanagement and noncompliance with the Treaty of Ruby Valley. In an unpublished 2008 opinion, the Federal Circuit Court of Appeals upheld the U.S. government's motion to dismiss for lack of subject matter jurisdiction and for failure to state a claim, finding that the suit was untimely because it was filed 24 years after the Court of Claims affirmed the ICC judgment. *Western Shoshone National Council v. United States* (No. 2007-5020), 279 Fed.App. 980 (Fed. Cir. 2008).

The most recent development in the longstanding battle of the Western Shoshone people for protection of their ancestral lands and resources came in the form of a special decision from the United Nations Committee for the Elimination of Racial Discrimination (CERD). *Early Warning and Urgent Action Procedure Decision 1(68): United States of America*, 68th Session, Geneva, 20 February–10 March 2006. CERD noted that the planned development was proceeding, despite the opposition of the Western Shoshone, in a manner that might "cumulatively lead to irreparable harm to these communities." Because of this, CERD decided to "adopt the present decision under its early warning and urgent action procedure." CERD's decision expresses concern about the United States's failure to take action to address the Committee's earlier findings (based on the Inter-American Commission of Human Rights ruling in *Mary and Carrie Dann versus United States*, case 11.140, 27 December 2002). In particular, CERD expresses concern about the United States's position that the Western Shoshone peoples' legal rights to ancestral lands have been "extinguished," given the fact that the Western Shoshone people continue to use and occupy their lands and natural resources in their "traditional land tenure patterns." CERD emphasizes that the United States's position, founded on the finality of the Indian Claims Commission judgment, did not comply with contemporary international human rights norms regarding indigenous property interests because the ICC process was procedurally flawed.

According to CERD, the failure of the United States to respect the Western Shoshone peoples' rights on their traditional land breached the Convention's obligation "to guarantee the right of everyone to equality before the law in the enjoyment of civil, political, economic, social and cultural rights, without discrimination based on race, colour or national or ethnic origin." CERD listed several actions that breached this obligation, including legislative efforts to privatize Western Shoshone ancestral lands for energy development, destruction of sacred sites and denial of access to the Shoshone to such lands, the resumption of nuclear testing on Western Shoshone ancestral lands, and the intimidation and harassment of Western Shoshone people by federal officials through imposition of grazing fees, trespass notices, and livestock impoundment. CERD further noted that the Western Shoshone people have been denied access to the courts based on "domestic technicalities" and that the United States was undertaking the destructive activities without consultation and despite the protests of the Western Shoshone people. CERD recommended that the United States freeze any plan to privatize the lands and desist from all of the above activities pending a full dialogue with representatives of the Western Shoshone people and the negotiation of a final settlement that is acceptable to the Western Shoshone and complies with their rights under the Convention. In a 2007 response, the United States contended:

> Because they have been unsuccessful in pursuing their objections, the dissenting Western Shoshone descendants now seek to bring before the CERD Committee what is essentially an internal dispute among the Western Shoshone, despite ample recourse before U.S. courts, including the U.S. Supreme Court, and despite the fact that their position is at odds with the decisions of the representatives of the Western Shoshone made at the time the case was litigated, and that their position does not now

represent the views of all Western Shoshone descendants, most of whom wish to receive the compensation as awarded by the ICC.

For more discussion of the historical and legal background and development of the Danns' struggle to assert their title, *see* Rebecca Tsosie, *Property Power, and American "Justice": The Story of* United States v. Dann in INDIAN LAW STORIES (Carole Goldberg, Kevin K. Washburn & Philip P. Frickey, eds., 2011).

4.   **Attorney-Client Relationships in Claims Cases:** The *Dann* case is not the only one in which lawyers and clients clashed over the claims to make and remedies to pursue in Indian Claims Commission proceedings. Time and again tribes had to decide whether to restrict their takings claims to instances where a prior extinguishment was unquestionable, thereby preserving their lands, or to press for more sweeping takings in order to maximize immediate cash recovery. Unfortunately, the latter option was always in the interest of the attorneys, who stood to recover 10% on the amount of the award actually paid by the defendant, but no portion of the value of the land retained by the tribe. *See, e.g., Pueblo of Santo Domingo v. United States*, 647 F.2d 1087 (Ct. Cl. 1981) (refusing to set aside a stipulation filed with the ICC that tribal lands had in fact been taken, where the stipulation shifted the claimants' theory of the case from trespass to a taking). For criticisms of the role of claims attorneys, see VINE DELORIA, JR., BEHIND THE TRAIL OF BROKEN TREATIES 23–41 (1974); Monroe E. Price, *Lawyers on the Reservation: Some Implications for the Legal Profession*, 1969 ARIZ. ST. L.J. 161, 187–90.

5.   **Evaluating the ICCA as Federal Indian Policy:** Assessments of the Indian Claims Commission process have not been kind, focusing on the long and costly proceedings, the failure to create an investigative division to collect testimony, the reconstruction of tribal territory much more narrowly than the tribes and their experts, the inadequacy of awards, the frequency of per capita distributions rather than tribal investment, and the limitation on remedies to cash rather than return of homelands. Wilcomb Washburn has criticized the Lands Division of the Justice Department, which represented the United States in the proceedings, for "stubbornly fighting and appealing even the weakest case," "[losing] sight of the humane and benevolent purpose of the . . . Act," and acting "as though it must fight, obstruct, extend, delay, and frustrate any effort on the Indians' part, or inclination on the government's part, to settle claims with generosity and good will." WILCOMB E. WASHBURN, RED MAN'S LAND/WHITE MAN'S LAW: A STUDY OF THE PAST AND PRESENT STATUS OF THE AMERICAN INDIAN 116 (1971). Anthropologist Nancy Oestreich Lurie, who testified as an expert witness before the Commission, has written:

> [W]ith only a few exceptions, the benefits to the tribes were negligible. Money was appropriated, distributed, spent, and forgotten and did little if any thing to overcome the sense of Indian grievance. It is easy to attribute the failure of the Act to do much good to the familiar complaint that Indians are profligate and too "factional" to get together on plans to use their money wisely. The failure really must be attributed to the interpretation and implementation of the Act.

Nancy O. Lurie, *Epilogue, in* IRREMDEEMABLE AMERICA: THE INDIANS' ESTATE AND LAND CLAIMS 363 (I. Sutton ed., 1985). Rather than a genuine attempt at reparations and apology, the Indian Claims Commission came to look like a closing of accounts by the United States, designed to open the way for a termination policy that swiftly followed. *See* Ch. 1, Sec. B.2.h. As the Court of Claims acknowledged in *Pawnee Tribe v. United States*, 109 F. Supp. 860, 869 (Ct. Cl. 1953), "It was anticipated that with the settlement of these claims, many Indians would abandon their connection with the tribes and their dependence upon the United States." Professor Sheleff describes the work of the Commission as carried out "in an atmosphere devoid of the jurisprudence of regret," because "it was not set up for the purpose of achieving a rapprochement between the indigenous population and the descendants of the settlers, but merely to seek a more efficient — and possibly less costly — way of achieving closure to the accumulated consequences of past policies." LEON SHELEFF, THE FUTURE OF TRADITION: CUSTOMARY LAW, COMMON LAW, AND LEGAL PLURALISM 423–24 (1999). A policy more concerned with "a deep moral accounting," reconciliation, better future relations, and an overall sense of justice, he suggests, would have included land as well as money. *See also* HARVEY ROSENTHAL, THEIR DAY IN COURT: A HISTORY OF THE INDIAN CLAIMS COMMISSION 245 (1990). What does the United Nations Declaration on the Rights of Indigenous Peoples, discussed in Ch. 1, Sec. E.1 say about the proper remedy for dispossession of Native lands? Article 28 is especially instructive.

b. Claims Under the Nonintercourse Act

As noted in Ch. 4, Sec. A.4.b, before 1966, when Congress authorized federal question jurisdiction in suits brought by Indian tribes, it was unclear whether tribes had standing to sue to protect their property rights, without the United States government suing on their behalf. Moreover, tribes had considerable difficulty securing adequate legal representation in the days before federally funded legal services and public interest law firms made lawyers available free of charge. But beginning in the late 1960s, these zealous new attorneys worked with Native nations to identify a store of substantial legal claims — many of them property claims that should have been brought on the tribes' behalf long ago by their trustee, the United States. In conducting this litigation, the attorneys' most effective tool was a statute dating back to the 1790s, the Nonintercourse Act, now codified at 25 U.S.C. § 177.

COUNTY OF ONEIDA v. ONEIDA INDIAN NATION
United States Supreme Court
470 U.S. 226 (1985)

JUSTICE POWELL delivered the opinion of the Court.[23]

These cases present the question whether three Tribes of the Oneida Indians may bring a suit for damages for the occupation and use of tribal land allegedly conveyed unlawfully in 1795.

---

[23] [*] THE CHIEF JUSTICE, JUSTICE WHITE, and JUSTICE REHNQUIST join only Part V of this opinion.

I

The Oneida Indian Nation of New York, the Oneida Indian Nation of Wisconsin, and the Oneida of the Thames Band Council (the Oneidas) instituted this suit in 1970 against the Counties of Oneida and Madison, New York. The Oneidas alleged that their ancestors conveyed 100,000 acres to the State of New York under a 1795 agreement that violated the Trade and Intercourse Act of 1793 (Nonintercourse Act), 1 Stat. 329, and thus that the transaction was void. The Oneidas' complaint sought damages representing the fair rental value of that part of the land presently owned and occupied by the Counties of Oneida and Madison, for the period January 1, 1968, through December 31, 1969.

The United States District Court for the Northern District of New York initially dismissed the action on the ground that the complaint failed to state a claim arising under the laws of the United States. The United States Court of Appeals for the Second Circuit affirmed. We then granted certiorari and reversed. *Oneida Indian Nation v. County of Oneida*, 414 U.S. 661 (1974) (*Oneida I*). We held unanimously that, at least for jurisdictional purposes, the Oneidas stated a claim for possession under federal law. The case was remanded for trial.

On remand, the District Court trifurcated trial of the issues. In the first phase, the court found the counties liable to the Oneidas for wrongful possession of their lands. In the second phase, it awarded the Oneidas damages in the amount of $16,694, plus interest, representing the fair rental value of the land in question for the two-year period specified in the complaint. Finally, the District Court held that the State of New York, a third-party defendant brought into the case by the counties, must indemnify the counties for the damages owed to the Oneidas. The Court of Appeals affirmed the trial court's rulings with respect to liability and indemnification. It remanded, however, for further proceedings on the amount of damages. The counties and the State petitioned for review of these rulings. Recognizing the importance of the Court of Appeals' decision not only for the Oneidas, but potentially for many eastern Indian land claims, we granted certiorari, to determine whether an Indian tribe may have a live cause of action for a violation of its possessory rights that occurred 175 years ago. We hold that the Court of Appeals correctly so ruled.

II

The respondents in these cases are the direct descendants of members of the Oneida Indian Nation, one of the six nations of the Iroquois, the most powerful Indian Tribe in the Northeast at the time of the American Revolution. From time immemorial to shortly after the Revolution, the Oneidas inhabited what is now central New York State. Their aboriginal land was approximately six million acres, extending from the Pennsylvania border to the St. Lawrence River, from the shores of Lake Ontario to the western foothills of the Adirondack Mountains.

Although most of the Iroquois sided with the British, the Oneidas actively supported the colonists in the Revolution. This assistance prevented the Iroquois from asserting a united effort against the colonists, and thus the Oneidas' support was of considerable aid. After the War, the United States recognized the importance of the Oneidas' role, and in the Treaty of Fort Stanwix, 7 Stat. 15 (Oct. 22, 1784), the National Government promised that the Oneidas would be secure (in the possession of the lands on which they are settled." Within a short period of time, the United States twice reaffirmed this promise, in the Treaties of Fort Harmar, 7 Stat. 33 (Jan. 9, 1789), and of Canandaigua, 7 Stat. 44 (Nov. 11, 1794).[24]

During this period, the State of New York came under increasingly heavy pressure to open the Oneidas' land for settlement. Consequently, in 1788, the State entered into a "treaty" with the Indians, in which it purchased the vast majority of the Oneidas' land. The Oneidas retained a reservation of about 300,000 acres, an area that, the parties stipulated below, included the land involved in this suit.

In 1790, at the urging of President Washington and Secretary of War Knox, Congress passed the first Indian Trade and Intercourse Act, ch. 33, 1 Stat. 137. The Act prohibited the conveyance of Indian land except where such conveyances were entered pursuant to the treaty power of the United States. In 1793, Congress passed a stronger, more detailed version of the Act, providing that "no purchase or grant of lands, or of any title or claim thereto, from any Indians or nation or tribe of Indians, within the bounds of the United States, shall be of any validity in law or equity, unless the same be made by a treaty or convention entered into pursuant to the constitution . . . [and] in the presence, and with the approbation of the commissioner or commissioners of the United States" appointed to supervise such transactions. 1 Stat. 330, § 8. Unlike the 1790 version, the new statute included criminal penalties for violation of its terms.

Despite Congress's clear policy that no person or entity should purchase Indian land without the acquiescence of the federal government, in 1795 the State of New York began negotiations to buy the remainder of the Oneidas' land. When this fact came to the attention of Secretary of War Pickering, he warned Governor Clinton, and later Governor Jay, that New York was required by the Nonintercourse Act to request the appointment of federal commissioners to supervise any land transaction with the Oneidas. The State ignored these warnings, and in the summer of 1795 entered into an agreement with the Oneidas whereby they conveyed virtually all of their remaining land to the State for annual cash payments. It is this transaction that is the basis of the Oneidas' complaint in this case.

The District Court found that the 1795 conveyance did not comply with the requirements of the Nonintercourse Act. In particular, the court stated that "[t]he only finding permitted by the record . . . is that no United States Commissioner or other official of the federal government was present at the . . . transaction." The petitioners did not dispute this finding on appeal. Rather, they argued that the Oneidas did not have a federal common-law cause of action for this violation. Even if such an action once existed, they contended that the Nonintercourse Act

---

[24] [1] The Treaty of Fort Harmar stated that the Oneidas and the Tuscaroras were "again secured and confirmed in the possession of their respective lands." 7 Stat. 34. The Treaty of Canandaigua of 1794 provided: "The United States acknowledge the lands reserved to the Oneida, Onondaga and Cayuga Nations, in their respective treaties with the state of New-York, and called their reservations, to be their property; and the United States will never claim the same, nor disturb them . . . in the free use and enjoyment thereof: but the said reservations shall remain theirs, until they choose to sell the same to the people of the United States, who have the right to purchase." 7 Stat. 45.

pre-empted it, and that the Oneidas could not maintain a private cause of action for violations of the Act. Additionally, they maintained that any such cause of action was time-barred or nonjusticiable, that any cause of action under the 1793 Act had abated, and that the United States had ratified the conveyance. The Court of Appeals, with one judge dissenting, rejected these arguments. Petitioners renew these claims here; we also reject them and affirm the court's finding of liability.

III

At the outset, we are faced with petitioner counties' contention that the Oneidas have no right of action for the violation of the 1793 Act. Both the District Court and the Court of Appeals rejected this claim, finding that the Oneidas had the right to sue on two theories: first, a common-law right of action for unlawful possession; and second, an implied statutory cause of action under the Nonintercourse Act of 1793. We need not reach the latter question as we think the Indians' common-law right to sue is firmly established.

A

Federal Common Law

By the time of the Revolutionary War, several well-defined principles had been established governing the nature of a tribe's interest in its property and how those interests could be conveyed. It was accepted that Indian nations held "aboriginal title" to lands they had inhabited from time immemorial. *See* Cohen, *Original Indian Title*, 32 Minn. L. Rev. 28 (1947). The "doctrine of discovery" provided, however, that discovering nations held fee title to these lands, subject to the Indians' right of occupancy and use. As a consequence, no one could purchase Indian land or otherwise terminate aboriginal title without the consent of the sovereign. *See* Clinton & Hotopp, *Judicial Enforcement of the Federal Restraints on Alienation of Indian Land: The Origins of the Eastern Land Claims*, 31 Me. L. Rev. 17, 19–49 (1979).

With the adoption of the Constitution, Indian relations became the exclusive province of federal law. From the first Indian claims presented, this Court recognized the aboriginal rights of the Indians to their lands. The Court spoke of the "unquestioned right" of the Indians to the exclusive possession of their lands, [*Cherokee Nation,*] and stated that the Indians' right of occupancy is "as sacred as the fee simple of the whites." *Mitchel v. United States*, 9 Pet. 711, 746 (1835). This principle has been reaffirmed consistently. Thus, as we concluded in *Oneida I*, the "possessory right claimed [by the Oneidas] is a *federal* right to the lands at issue in this case." 414 U.S., at 671 (emphasis in original).

Numerous decisions of this Court prior to *Oneida I* recognized at least implicitly that Indians have a federal common-law right to sue to enforce their aboriginal land rights. [For example,] the Court held that Indians have a common-law right of action for an accounting of "all rents, issues and profits" against trespassers on their land. [*United States v. Santa Fe Pacific R. Co.*] [The] opinion in *Oneida I* implicitly assumed that the Oneidas could bring a common-law action to vindicate their aboriginal rights. [W]e noted that the Indians' right of occupancy need not be based on treaty, statute, or other formal Government action. We stated that "absent federal statutory guidance, the governing rule of decision would be fashioned by the federal court in the mode of the common law." *Id.* at 674.

In keeping with these well-established principles, we hold that the Oneidas can maintain this action for violation of their possessory rights based on federal common law.

B

Pre-emption

[Congressional action after the 1793 statute was enacted] and later versions of the Nonintercourse Act demonstrate that the Acts did not pre-empt common-law remedies. In 1822 Congress amended the 1802 version of the Act to provide that "in all trials about the right of property, in which Indians shall be party on one side and white persons on the other, the burden of proof shall rest upon the white person, in every case in which the Indian shall make out a presumption of title in himself from the fact of previous possession and ownership." § 4, 3 Stat. 683; see 25 U.S.C. § 194. Thus, Congress apparently contemplated suits by Indians asserting their property rights.

[I]n *Wilson v. Omaha Indian Tribe*, 442 U.S. 653 (1979), [this] Court construed the 1822 amendment to apply to suits brought by Indian tribes as well as individual Indians. Citing the very sections of the Act that petitioners contend pre-empt a common-law action by the Indians, the Court interpreted the amendment to be part of the overall "design" of the Nonintercourse Acts "to protect the rights of Indians to their properties." *Id.*, at 664.

We recognized in *Oneida I* that the Nonintercourse Acts simply "put in statutory form what was or came to be the accepted rule — that the extinguishment of Indian title required the consent of the United States." Nothing in the statutory formulation of this rule suggests that the Indians' right to pursue common-law remedies was thereby pre-empted. Accordingly, we hold that the Oneidas' right of action under federal common law was not pre-empted by the passage of the Nonintercourse Acts.

IV

Having determined that the Oneidas have a cause of action under federal common law, we address the question whether there are defenses available to the counties. We conclude that none has merit.

A

Statute of Limitations

There is no federal statute of limitations governing federal common-law actions by Indians to enforce property rights. In the absence of a controlling federal limitations period, the general rule is that a state limitations period for an analogous cause of action is borrowed and applied to the federal claim, provided that the application of the state statute would not be inconsistent with underlying federal policies.[25] We think the borrowing of a state limitations period in these cases would be inconsistent with federal policy. Indeed, on a number of occasions Congress has made this clear with respect to Indian land claims.

In adopting the statute that gave jurisdiction over civil actions involving Indians to the New York courts, Congress included this proviso: "[N]othing herein contained shall be construed as conferring jurisdiction on the courts of the State of New York or making applicable the laws of the State of New York in civil actions involving Indian lands or claims with respect thereto which relate to transactions or events transpiring prior to September 13, 1952." 25 U.S.C. § 233. This proviso was added specifically to ensure that the New York statute of limitations would not apply to pre-1952 land claims. In *Oneida I*, we relied on the legislative history of 25 U.S.C. § 233 in concluding that Indian land claims were exclusively a matter of federal law. This history also reflects congressional policy against the application of state statutes of limitations in the context of Indian land claims

Congress recently reaffirmed this policy in addressing the question of the appropriate statute of limitations for certain claims brought by the United States on behalf of Indians. Originally enacted in 1966, this statute provided a special limitations period of six years and ninety days for contract and tort suits for damages brought by the United States on behalf of Indians. 28 U.S.C. §§ 2415(a), (b). The statute stipulated that claims that accrued prior to its date of enactment, July 18, 1966, were deemed to have accrued on that date. § 2415(g). Section 2415(c) excluded from the limitations period all actions "to establish the title to, or right of possession of, real or personal property."

In 1972 and again in 1977, 1980, and 1982, as the statute of limitations was about to expire for pre-1966 claims, Congress extended the time within which the United States could bring suits on behalf of the Indians. The legislative history of the 1972, 1977, and 1980 amendments demonstrates that Congress did not intend § 2415 to apply to suits brought by the Indians themselves, and that it assumed that the Indians' right to sue was not otherwise subject to any statute of limitations. Both proponents and opponents of the amendments shared these views.

With the enactment of the 1982 amendments, Congress for the first time imposed a statute of limitations on certain tort and contract claims for damages brought by

---

[25] [13] Under the Supremacy Clause, state-law time bars, e.g., adverse possession and laches, do not apply of their own force to Indian land title claims. *See Ewert v. Bluejacket*, 259 U.S. 129, 137–138 (1922); *United States v. Ahtanum Irrigation District*, 236 F. 2d 321, 334 (CA9 1956), *cert. denied*, 352 U.S. 988 (1957).

individual Indians and Indian tribes. These amendments, enacted as the Indian Claims Limitation Act of 1982, Pub. L. 97-394, 96 Stat. 1976, note following 28 U.S.C. § 2415, established a system for the final resolution of pre-1966 claims cognizable under §§ 2415(a) and (b). The Act directed the Secretary of the Interior to compile and publish in the Federal Register a list of all Indian claims to which the statute of limitations provided in 28 U.S.C. § 2415 applied. The Act also directed that the Secretary notify those Indians who may have an interest in any such claims. The Indians were then given an opportunity to submit additional claims; these were to be compiled and published on a second list. Actions for claims subject to the limitations periods of § 2415 that appeared on neither list were barred unless commenced within 60 days of the publication of the second list. If at any time the Secretary decides not to pursue a claim on one of the lists, "*any* right of action shall be barred unless the complaint is filed within one year after the date of publication [of the notice of the Secretary's decision] in the Federal Register." Pub. L. 97-394, 96 Stat. 1978, § 5(c) (emphasis added). Thus, § 5(c) implicitly imposed a one-year statute of limitations within which the Indians must bring contract and tort claims that are covered by §§ 2415(a) and (b) and not listed by the Secretary. So long as a listed claim is neither acted upon nor formally rejected by the Secretary, it remains live.[26]

The legislative history of the successive amendments to § 2415 is replete with evidence of Congress's concern that the United States had failed to live up to its responsibilities as trustee for the Indians, and that the Department of the Interior had not acted with appropriate dispatch in meeting the deadlines provided by § 2415. *E.g.*, Authorizing Indian Tribes to Bring Certain Actions on Behalf of their Members with Respect to Certain Legal Claims, and for Other Purposes, H.R. Rep. No. 97-954, p. 5 (1982). By providing a one-year limitations period for claims that the Secretary decides not to pursue, Congress intended to give the Indians one last opportunity to file suits covered by §§ 2415(a) and (b) on their own behalf. Thus, we think the statutory framework adopted in 1982 presumes the existence of an Indian right of action not otherwise subject to any statute of limitations. It would be a violation of Congress's will were we to hold that a state statute of limitations period should be borrowed in these circumstances.

---

[26] [15] The two lists were published in the Federal Register on March 31, 1983, and November 7, 1983, respectively. 48 Fed. Reg. 13698, 51204. The Oneidas' claims are on the first list compiled by the Secretary. *Id.*, at 13920. These claims would not be barred, however, even if they were not listed. The Oneidas commenced this suit in 1970 when no statute of limitations applied to claims brought by the Indians themselves. Additionally, if claims like the Oneidas', *i.e.*, damages actions that involve litigating the continued vitality of aboriginal title, are construed to be suits "to establish the title to, or right of possession of, real or personal property," they would be exempt from the statute of limitations of the Indian Claims Limitations Act of 1982. The Government agrees with this view. Brief for United States as *Amicus Curiae* 24–25.

B

Laches

The dissent argues that we should apply the equitable doctrine of laches to hold that the Oneidas' claim is barred. Although it is far from clear that this defense is available in suits such as this one,[27] we do not reach this issue today. While petitioners argued at trial that the Oneidas were guilty of laches, the District Court ruled against them and they did not reassert this defense on appeal. As a result, the Court of Appeals did not rule on this claim, and we likewise decline to do so. [In Section IV-C, the Court held that language of formal repeal in the 1796 version of the Nonintercourse Act did not abate the cause of action.]

D

Ratification

We are similarly unpersuaded by petitioners' contention that the United States has ratified the unlawful 1795 conveyances. Petitioners base this argument on federally approved treaties in 1798 and 1802 in which the Oneidas ceded additional land to the State of New York.

[C]anons of construction applicable in Indian law are rooted in the unique trust relationship between the United States and the Indians. Thus, it is well established that treaties should be construed liberally in favor of the Indians. [This] Court has applied similar canons of construction in nontreaty matters. Most importantly, the Court has held that congressional intent to extinguish Indian title must be "plain and unambiguous," *United States v. Santa Fe Pacific R. Co.* at 346, and will not be "lightly implied," *id.* at 354. Relying on the strong policy of the United States "from the beginning to respect the Indian right of occupancy," *id.*, at 345 (citing *Cramer v. United States*, 261 U.S. 219, 227 (1923)), the Court concluded that it "[c]ertainly" would require "plain and unambiguous action to deprive the [Indians] of the benefits of that policy," *id.* at 346.

In view of these principles, the treaties relied upon by petitioners are not

---

[27] [16] We note, as Justice STEVENS properly recognizes, that application of the equitable defense of laches in an action at law would be novel indeed. Moreover, the logic of the Court's holding in *Ewert v. Bluejacket*, 259 U.S. 129 (1922), seems applicable here: "the equitable doctrine of laches, developed and designed to protect good-faith transactions against those who have slept on their rights, with knowledge and ample opportunity to assert them, cannot properly have application to give vitality to a void deed and to bar the rights of Indian wards in lands subject to statutory restrictions." *Id.*, at 138. Additionally, this Court has indicated that extinguishment of Indian title requires a sovereign act. *See, e.g., Oneida I*, 414 U.S. 661, 670 (1974); *United States v. Candelaria*, 271 U.S. 432, 439 (1926), quoting *United States v. Sandoval*, 231 U.S. 28, 45–47 (1913). In these circumstances, it is questionable whether laches properly could be applied. Furthermore, the statutory restraint on alienation of Indian tribal land adopted by the Nonintercourse Act of 1793 is still the law. *See* 25 U.S.C. § 177. This fact not only distinguishes the cases relied upon by the dissent, but also suggests that, as with the borrowing of state statutes of limitations, the application of laches would appear to be inconsistent with established federal policy. Although the issue of laches is not before us, we add these observations in response to the dissent.

sufficient to show that the United States ratified New York's unlawful purchase of the Oneidas' land. The language cited by petitioners, a reference in the 1798 treaty to "the last purchase" and one in the 1802 treaty to "land heretofore ceded," far from demonstrates a plain and unambiguous intent to extinguish Indian title. There is no indication that either the Senate or the President intended by these references to ratify the 1795 conveyance.

E

Nonjusticiability

The claim also is made that the issue presented by the Oneidas' action is a nonjusticiable political question. The counties contend first that Art. 1, § 8, cl. 3, of the Constitution explicitly commits responsibility for Indian affairs to Congress. Moreover, they argue that Congress has given exclusive civil remedial authority to the Executive for cases such as this one, citing the Nonintercourse Acts and the 1794 Treaty of Canandaigua. Thus, they say this case falls within the political question doctrine because of "a textually demonstrable constitutional commitment of the issue to a coordinate political department." *Baker v. Carr*, 369 U.S. 186, 217 (1962). Additionally, the counties argue that the question is nonjusticiable because there is "an unusual need for unquestioning adherence to a political decision already made." *Ibid.* None of these claims is meritorious.

This Court has held specifically that Congress's plenary power in Indian affairs under Art. 1, § 8, cl. 3, does not mean that litigation involving such matters necessarily entails nonjusticiable political questions. [*E.g.*, *Sioux Nation.*] If Congress's constitutional authority over Indian affairs does not render the Oneidas' claim nonjusticiable, *a fortiori*, Congress's delegation of authority to the President does not do so either.

We are also unpersuaded that petitioners have shown "an unusual need for unquestioning adherence to a political decision already made." *Baker v. Carr, supra,* at 217. The basis for their argument is the fact that in 1968, the Commissioner of Indian Affairs declined to bring an action on behalf of the Oneidas with respect to the claims asserted in these cases. The counties cite no cases in which analogous decisions provided the basis for nonjusticiability. Our cases suggest that such "unusual need" arises most of the time, if not always, in the area of foreign affairs. Nor do the counties offer convincing reasons for thinking that there is a need for "unquestioning adherence" to the Commissioner's decision. Indeed, the fact that the Secretary of the Interior has listed the Oneidas' claims under the § 2415 procedure suggests that the Commissioner's 1968 decision was not a decision on the merits of the Oneidas' claims. *See* n.15, *supra.*

VI

The decisions of this Court emphasize " 'Congress' unique obligation toward the Indians." *Morton v. Mancari*, 417 U.S. 535, 555 (1974). The Government, in an *amicus curiae* brief, urged the Court to affirm the Court of Appeals. The Government recognized, as we do, the potential consequences of affirmance. It was observed, however, that "Congress has enacted legislation to extinguish Indian title and claims related thereto in other eastern States, . . . and it could be expected to do the same in New York should the occasion arise." See Rhode Island Indian Claims Settlement Act, 25 U.S.C. § 1701 *et seq.*; Maine Indian Claims Settlement Act, 25 U.S.C. § 1721 *et seq.* We agree that this litigation makes abundantly clear the necessity for congressional action.

One would have thought that claims dating back for more than a century and a half would have been barred long ago. As our opinion indicates, however, neither petitioners nor we have found any applicable statute of limitations or other relevant legal basis for holding that the Oneidas' claims are barred or otherwise have been satisfied. The judgment of the Court of Appeals is affirmed with respect to the finding of liability under federal common law,[28] and reversed with respect to the exercise of ancillary jurisdiction over the counties' cross-claim for indemnification. The cases are remanded to the Court of Appeals for further proceedings consistent with our decision.

Affirmed in part, reversed in part, and remanded.

JUSTICE STEVENS, with whom THE CHIEF JUSTICE, JUSTICE WHITE, and JUSTICE REHNQUIST join, dissenting in No. 83-1065.[29]

In 1790, the President of the United States notified Cornplanter, the Chief of the Senecas, that federal law would securely protect Seneca lands from acquisition by any State or person:

> "If . . . you have any just cause of complaint against [a purchaser] and can make satisfactory proof thereof, the federal courts will be open to you for redress, as to all other persons." 4 American State Papers, Indian Affairs, Vol, 1, p. 142 (1832).

The elders of the Oneida Indian Nation received comparable notice of their capacity to maintain the federal claim that is at issue in this litigation. They made no attempt to assert the claim, and their successors in interest waited 175 years before bringing suit to avoid a 1795 conveyance that the Tribe freely made, for a valuable consideration. The absence of any evidence of deception, concealment, or interference with the Tribe's right to assert a claim, together with the societal interests that always underlie statutes of repose — particularly when title to real property is at stake — convince me that this claim is barred by the extraordinary passage of time. It is worthy of emphasis that this claim arose when George Washington was the President of the United States.

The Court refuses to apply any time bar to this claim, believing that to do so

---

[28] [27] The question whether equitable considerations should limit the relief available to the present day Oneida Indians was not addressed by the Court of Appeals or presented to this Court by petitioners. Accordingly, we express no opinion as to whether other considerations may be relevant to the final disposition of this case should Congress not exercise its authority to resolve these far-reaching Indian claims.

[29] [*] JUSTICE STEVENS concurred in the judgment that the federal court lacked ancillary jurisdiction over the counties' cross claims against the state.

would be inconsistent with federal Indian policy. This Court, however, has always applied the equitable doctrine of laches when Indians or others have sought, in equity, to set aside conveyances made under a statutory or common-law incapacity to convey. Although this action is brought at law, in ejectment, there are sound reasons for recognizing that it is barred by similar principles.

In reaching a contrary conclusion, the Court relies on the legislative histories of a series of recent enactments. In my view, however, the Oneida were barred from avoiding their 1795 conveyance long before 1952, when Congress enacted the first statute that the Court relies on today. Neither that statute, nor any subsequent federal legislation, revived the Oneida's dormant claim.

CITY OF SHERRILL, N.Y. v. ONEIDA INDIAN NATION OF NEW YORK
United States Supreme Court
544 U.S. 197 (2005)

JUSTICE GINSBURG delivered the opinion of the Court.

This case concerns properties in the city of Sherrill, New York, purchased by the Oneida Indian Nation of New York (OIN or Tribe) in 1997 and 1998. The separate parcels of land in question, once contained within the Oneidas' 300,000-acre reservation, were last possessed by the Oneidas as a tribal entity in 1805. For two centuries, governance of the area in which the properties are located has been provided by the State of New York and its county and municipal units. In *County of Oneida v. Oneida Indian Nation of N.Y.*, 470 U.S. 226 (1985) (*Oneida II*), this Court held that the Oneidas stated a triable claim for damages against the County of Oneida for wrongful possession of lands they conveyed to New York State in 1795 in violation of federal law. In the instant action, OIN resists the payment of property taxes to Sherrill on the ground that OIN's acquisition of fee title to discrete parcels of historic reservation land revived the Oneidas' ancient sovereignty piecemeal over each parcel. Consequently, the Tribe maintains, regulatory authority over OIN's newly purchased properties no longer resides in Sherrill.

Our 1985 decision recognized that the Oneidas could maintain a federal common-law claim for damages for ancient wrongdoing in which both national and state governments were complicit. Today, we decline to project redress for the Tribe into the present and future, thereby disrupting the governance of central New York's counties and towns. Generations have passed during which non-Indians have owned and developed the area that once composed the Tribe's historic reservation. And at least since the middle years of the nineteenth century, most of the Oneidas have resided elsewhere. Given the longstanding, distinctly non-Indian character of the area and its inhabitants, the regulatory authority constantly exercised by New York State and its counties and towns, and the Oneidas' long delay in seeking judicial relief against parties other than the United States, we hold that the Tribe cannot unilaterally revive its ancient sovereignty, in whole or in part, over the parcels at issue. The Oneidas long ago relinquished the reins of government and cannot regain them through open-market purchases from current titleholders.

I

A

OIN is a federally recognized Indian Tribe and a direct descendant of the Oneida Indian Nation (Oneida Nation), "one of the six nations of the Iroquois, the most powerful Indian Tribe in the Northeast at the time of the American Revolution." *Id.*, at 230. At the birth of the United States, the Oneida Nation's aboriginal homeland comprised some six million acres in what is now central New York.

In the years after the Revolutionary War, "the State of New York came under increasingly heavy pressure to open the Oneidas' land for settlement." *Oneida II*, 470 U.S., at 231. Reflective of that pressure, in 1788, New York State and the Oneida Nation entered into the Treaty of Fort Schuyler. For payments in money and kind, the Oneidas ceded to New York "all their lands." App. to Pet. for Cert. A136. Of the vast area conveyed, "[t]he Oneidas retained a reservation of about 300,000 acres," *Oneida II*, 470 U.S., at 231, 105 S. Ct. 1245, "for their own use and cultivation," App. to Pet. for Cert. A137 (internal quotation marks omitted).[30] OIN does not here contest the legitimacy of the Fort Schuyler conveyance or the boundaries of the reserved area.

The federal government initially pursued a policy protective of the New York Indians, undertaking to secure the Tribes' rights to reserved lands. See *Oneida II*, 470 U.S., at 231–232; *Oneida I*, 414 U.S., at 667; F. Cohen, Handbook of Federal Indian Law 418–419 (1942 ed.); F. Cohen, Handbook of Federal Indian Law 73–74 (1982 ed.) (hereinafter Handbook). In 1790, Congress passed the first Indian Trade and Intercourse Act, commonly known as the Nonintercourse Act. Act of July 22, 1790, ch. 33, 1 Stat. 137. Periodically renewed, see *Oneida I*, 414 U.S., at 667–668, and n. 4, and remaining substantially in force today, see Rev. Stat. § 2116, 25 U.S.C. § 177, the Act bars sales of tribal land without the acquiescence of the federal government.[31]

---

[30] [1] Under the "doctrine of discovery," *County of Oneida v. Oneida Indian Nation of N.Y.*, 470 U.S. 226, 234 (1985) (*Oneida II*), "fee title to the lands occupied by Indians when the colonists arrived became vested in the sovereign — first the discovering European nation and later the original States and the United States," *Oneida Indian Nation of N.Y. v. County of Oneida*, 414 U.S. 661, 667 (1974) (*Oneida I*). In the original 13 States, "fee title to Indian lands," or "the pre-emptive right to purchase from the Indians, was in the State." *Id.*, at 670; see *Oneida Indian Nation of N.Y. v. New York*, 860 F.2d 1145, 1159–1167 (C.A. 2 1988). Both before and after the adoption of the Constitution, New York State acquired vast tracts of land from Indian tribes through treaties it independently negotiated, without National Government participation. See Gunther, Governmental Power and New York Indian Lands — A Reassessment of a Persistent Problem of Federal — State Relations, 8 Buffalo L. Rev. 1, 4–6 (1959) (hereinafter Gunther).

[31] [2] By its terms, the 1790 Nonintercourse Act governed Indian lands within the boundaries of the original 13 States. The Act provided "[t]hat no sale of lands made by any Indians, or any nation or tribe of Indians within the United States, shall be valid to any person or persons, *or to any state, whether having the right of pre-emption to such lands or not*, unless the same shall be made and duly executed at some public treaty, held under the authority of the United States." Act of July 22, 1790, ch. 33, § 4, 1 Stat. 138 (emphasis added). Our prior decisions state in this regard that, "[w]ith the adoption of the Constitution, Indian relations became the exclusive province of federal law." *Oneida II*, 470 U.S., at 234 (citing *Oneida I*, 414 U.S., at 670). See generally Clinton & Hotopp, Judicial Enforcement of the Federal Restraints on Alienation of Indian Land: The Origins of the Eastern Land Claims, 31 Me. L. Rev. 17,

In 1794, in further pursuit of its protective policy, the United States entered into the Treaty of Canandaigua with the Six (Iroquois) Nations. Act of Nov. 11, 1794, 7 Stat. 44. That treaty both "acknowledge[d]" the Oneida Reservation as established by the Treaty of Fort Schuyler and guaranteed the Oneidas' "free use and enjoyment" of the reserved territory. *Id.*, at 45, Art. II. The Oneidas in turn agreed they would "never claim any other lands within the boundaries of the United States." *Id.*, at 45, Art. IV.

New York State nonetheless continued to purchase reservation land from the Oneidas. The Washington administration objected to New York's 1795 negotiations to buy 100,000 acres of the Oneidas' Reservation without federal supervision. *Oneida II*, 470 U.S., at 229, 232. Later administrations, however, "[made not] even a pretense of interfer[ing] with [the] State's attempts to negotiate treaties [with the Oneidas] for land cessions." *Oneida Nation of N.Y. v. United States*, 43 Ind. Cl. Comm'n 373, 385 (1978); see also *id.*, at 390; Campisi, The Oneida Treaty Period, 1783–1838, in The Oneida Indian Experience: Two Perspectives 48, 59 (J. Campisi & L. Hauptman eds., 1988) (hereinafter Campisi). See generally Gunther 6 ("New York acquired much land from Indians through treaties — perhaps as many as 200 — not participated in, though apparently known and not objected to, by the national government." (footnote omitted)).

The federal government's policy soon veered away from protection of New York and other east coast reservations. In lieu of the commitment made in the Treaty of Canandaigua, the United States pursued a policy designed to open reservation lands to white settlers and to remove tribes westward. D. Getches, C. Wilkinson & R. Williams, Cases and Materials on Federal Indian Law 94 (4th ed. 1998) (After the Louisiana Purchase in 1803, federal policymakers "began to debate the tactics of inducing [eastern Indians] to exchange their remaining ancestral lands for a permanent territory in the West."). As recounted by the Indian Claims Commission in 1978, early nineteenth-century federal Indian agents in New York State did not simply fail to check New York's land purchases, they "took an active role . . . in encouraging the removal of the Oneidas . . . to the west." *Oneida Nation of N.Y.*, 43 Ind. Cl. Comm'n, at 390; see *id.*, at 391 (noting that some federal agents were "deeply involved" in "plans . . . to bring about removal of the [Oneidas]" and in the State's acquisition of Oneida land). Beginning in 1817, the federal government accelerated its efforts to remove Indian tribes from their east coast homelands. Handbook 78–79, and n. 142.

Pressured by the removal policy to leave their ancestral lands in New York, some 150 Oneidas, by 1825, had moved to Wisconsin. Horsman, The Wisconsin Oneidas in the Preallotment Years, in The Oneida Indian Experience, *supra*, at 65, 67. In 1838, the Oneidas and the United States entered into the Treaty of Buffalo Creek, which envisioned removal of all remaining New York Indians, including the Oneidas, to Kansas. Act of Jan. 15, 1838, 7 Stat. 550. By this time, the Oneidas had sold all but 5,000 acres of their original reservation. 337 F.3d 139, 149 (C.A. 2 2003). Six hundred of their members resided in Wisconsin, while 620 remained in New York State. 7 Stat. 556 (Sched. A).

23–38 (1979) (discussing Indian relations under the Articles of Confederation and the Constitution).

In Article 13 of the Buffalo Creek Treaty, the Oneidas agreed to remove to the Kansas lands the United States had set aside for them "as soon as they c[ould] make satisfactory arrangements" for New York State's "purchase of their lands at Oneida." *Id.*, at 554. As a condition of the treaty's ratification, the Senate directed that a federal commissioner "fully and fairly explai[n]" the terms to each signatory tribe and band. *New York Indians v. United States*, 170 U.S. 1, 21–22 (1898). Commissioner Ransom H. Gillet, who had originally negotiated the treaty terms with the Oneidas, met with them again and assured them they would not be forced to move but could remain on "their lands *where they reside*," *i.e.*, they could "if they ch[ose] to do so remain *where they are* forever." App. 146 (emphases added).

The Oneidas who stayed on in New York after the proclamation of the Buffalo Creek Treaty continued to diminish in number and, during the 1840's, sold most of their remaining lands to the State. *New York Indians v. United States*, 40 Ct. Cl. 448, 458, 469–471 (1905). A few hundred Oneidas moved to Canada in 1842, *id.*, at 458, and "by the mid-1840s, only about 200 Oneidas remained in New York State," Introduction to Part I, The Oneida Indian Journey: From New York to Wisconsin, 1784–1860, pp. 9, 13 (L. Hauptman & L. McLester eds., 1999). By 1843, the New York Oneidas retained less than 1,000 acres in the State. Campisi 61. That acreage dwindled to 350 in 1890; ultimately, by 1920, only 32 acres continued to be held by the Oneidas. *Ibid.*

The United States eventually abandoned its efforts to remove the New York Indians to Kansas. In 1860, the Federal Government restored the Kansas lands to the public domain, and sold them thereafter. *New York Indians*, 170 U.S., at 24, 28–29, 31, 18 S. Ct. 531.

B

Early litigation concerning the Oneidas' land claims trained on monetary recompense from the United States for past deprivations. In 1893, the United States agreed to be sued for disposing of the Kansas lands to settlers, and the Oneidas in New York shared in the resulting award of damages. See *New York Indians*, 170 U.S. 1; *New York Indians*, 40 Ct. Cl. 448 (identifying the Tribes qualified to share in the distribution of the sum recovered).

Seeking further compensation from the United States a half century later, the New York and Wisconsin Oneidas initiated proceedings before the Indian Claims Commission in 1951. *Oneida Indian Nation of N.Y. v. County of Oneida*, 622 F.2d 624, 626 (C.A. 2 1980). They sought redress for lands New York had acquired through 25 treaties of cession concluded between 1795 and 1846. The Oneidas alleged, and the Claims Commission agreed, that under the Nonintercourse Act of 1790 and successor statutes, the federal government had a fiduciary duty to assure that the Oneidas received from New York "conscionable consideration" for the lands in question. *Oneida Nation of N.Y. v. United States*, 26 Ind. Cl. Comm'n 138, 145 (1971). The Court of Claims affirmed the Commission's core determination, but held that the United States's duty extended only to land transactions of which the Government had knowledge. *United States v. Oneida Nation of N.Y.*, 477 F.2d 939, 944, 201 Ct. Cl. 546, 554 (1973). Accordingly, the Court of Claims directed the Commission to determine whether the Government actually or constructively knew of the land transactions at issue. *Id.*, at 555, 477 F.2d, at 945.

On remand, the Commission found that the Federal Government had actual or constructive knowledge of all of the treaties and would be liable if the Oneidas had not received conscionable consideration. *Oneida Nation of N.Y.*, 43 Ind. Cl. Comm'n, at 375, 406–407. The Commission anticipated further proceedings to determine the Federal Government's ultimate liability, but the Oneidas had by then decided to pursue a different course. On the Oneidas' request, the Court of Claims dismissed the proceedings. See *Oneida Nation of N.Y. v. United States*, 231 Ct. Cl. 990, 991 (1982) (*per curiam*).

In lieu of concentrating on recovery from the United States, the Oneidas pursued suits against local governments. In 1970, the Oneidas of New York and Wisconsin, asserting federal-question jurisdiction under 28 U.S.C. § 1331 or § 1362, instituted a "test case" against the New York Counties of Oneida and Madison. They alleged that the cession of 100,000 acres to New York State in 1795, see *supra*, at 1484, violated the Nonintercourse Act and thus did not terminate the Oneidas' right to possession under the applicable federal treaties and statutes. In this initial endeavor to gain compensation from governmental units other than the United States, the Oneidas confined their demand for relief. They sought only damages measured by the fair rental value, for the years 1968 and 1969, of 872 acres of their ancestral land owned and occupied by the two counties. The District Court, affirmed by the Court of Appeals, dismissed the Oneidas' complaint for failure to state a claim arising under federal law. We reversed that determination, holding that federal jurisdiction was properly invoked. *Oneida I*, 414 U.S., at 675.

In the next round, the Oneidas prevailed in the lower courts. On review in *Oneida II*, we rejected various defenses the counties presented that might have barred the action for damages, 470 U.S., at 240–250, and held that the Oneidas could maintain their claim to be compensated "for violation of their possessory rights based on federal common law," *id.*, at 236. [*County of Oneida v. Oneida Indian Nation*, presented above.] While upholding the judgment of the Court of Appeals regarding the counties' liability under federal common law, we noted that "[t]he question whether equitable considerations should limit the relief available to the present day Oneida Indians was not addressed by the Court of Appeals or presented to this Court." *Id.*, at 253, n. 27. Accordingly, "we express[ed] no opinion as to whether other considerations m[ight] be relevant to the final disposition of this case." *Ibid.* On remand, the District Court entered a final judgment which fixed the amount of damages payable by the counties. Allowing setoffs for the counties' good-faith improvements to the land, the court ordered recoveries of $15,994 from Oneida County and $18,970 from Madison County, plus prejudgment interest. *Oneida Indian Nation of N.Y. v. County of Oneida*, 217 F. Supp. 2d 292, 310 (N.D.N.Y. 2002).

In 2000, litigation resumed in an action held in abeyance during the pendency of the test case. In that revitalized action, the Oneidas sought damages from Oneida and Madison Counties for a period spanning over 200 years. The amended complaint alleged that, through a series of agreements concluded during the years 1795 to 1846, approximately 250,000 acres of the Oneidas' ancestral land had been unlawfully conveyed to New York. *Oneida Indian Nation of N.Y. v. County of*

Oneida, 199 F.R.D. 61, 66–68 (N.D.N.Y. 2000).

The Oneidas further sought to enlarge the action by demanding recovery of land they had not occupied since the 1795–1846 conveyances. They attempted to join as defendants, *inter alia*, approximately 20,000 private landowners, and to obtain declaratory relief that would allow the Oneidas to eject these landowners. *Id.*, at 67–68. The District Court refused permission to join the landowners so late in the day, resting in part on the Oneidas' bad faith and undue delay. *Id.*, at 79–85. Further, the court found the proposed amendment "futile." *Id.*, at 94. In this regard, the court emphasized the "sharp distinction between the *existence* of a federal common law right to Indian homelands," a right this Court recognized in *Oneida II*, "and how to *vindicate* that right." 199 F.R.D., at 90. That distinction "must be drawn," the court stated, *ibid.*, for in the two centuries since the alleged wrong, "development of every type imaginable has been ongoing," *id.*, at 92. Referring to the "practical concerns" that blocked restoration of Indians to their former lands, the court found it high time "to transcend the theoretical." *Ibid.* Cases of this genre, the court observed, "cr[ied] out for a pragmatic approach." *Ibid.* The District Court therefore excluded the imposition of any liability against private landowners. *Id.*, at 93–95.

This brings us to the present case, which concerns parcels of land in the city of Sherrill, located in Oneida County, New York. According to the 2000 census, over 99% of the population in the area is non-Indian: American Indians represent less than 1% of the city of Sherrill's population and less than 0.5% of Oneida County's population. OIN owns approximately 17,000 acres of land scattered throughout the Counties of Oneida and Madison, representing less than 1.5% of the counties' total area. OIN's predecessor, the Oneida Nation, had transferred the parcels at issue to one of its members in 1805, who sold the land to a non-Indian in 1807. The properties thereafter remained in non-Indian hands until OIN's acquisitions in 1997 and 1998 in open-market transactions. OIN now operates commercial enterprises on these parcels: a gasoline station, a convenience store, and a textile facility.

Because the parcels lie within the boundaries of the reservation originally occupied by the Oneidas, OIN maintained that the properties are exempt from taxation, and accordingly refused to pay the assessed property taxes. The city of Sherrill initiated eviction proceedings in state court, and OIN sued Sherrill in federal court. In contrast to *Oneida I* and *II*, which involved demands for monetary compensation, OIN sought equitable relief prohibiting, currently and in the future, the imposition of property taxes. OIN also sued Madison County, seeking a declaration that the Tribe's properties in Madison are tax exempt. The litigation involved a welter of claims and counterclaims. Relevant here, the District Court concluded that parcels of land owned by the Tribe in Sherrill and Madison are not taxable. See 145 F. Supp. 2d 226, 254–259 (N.D.N.Y. 2001).

A divided panel of the Second Circuit affirmed. 337 F.3d 139. . . .

We granted the city of Sherrill's petition for a writ of certiorari, and now reverse the judgment of the Court of Appeals.

II

OIN and the United States argue that because the Court in *Oneida II* recognized the Oneidas' aboriginal title to their ancient reservation land and because the Tribe has now acquired the specific parcels involved in this suit in the open market, it has unified fee and aboriginal title and may now assert sovereign dominion over the parcels. When the Oneidas came before this Court 20 years ago in *Oneida II*, they sought money damages only. 470 U.S., at 229, 105 S. Ct. 1245; see also *id.*, at 244, n. 16 (recognizing that the suit was an "action at law"). The Court reserved for another day the question whether "equitable considerations" should limit the relief available to the present-day Oneidas. *Id.*, at 253, n. 27.

"The substantive questions whether the plaintiff has any right or the defendant any duty, and if so what it is, are very different questions from the remedial questions whether this remedy or that is preferred, and what the measure of the remedy is." D. Dobbs, Law of Remedies § 1.2, p. 3 (1973); see also *Navajo Tribe of Indians v. New Mexico*, 809 F.2d 1455, 1467 (C.A. 10 1987) ("The distinction between a claim or substantive right and a remedy is fundamental."). "[S]tandards of federal Indian law and federal equity practice" led the District Court, in the litigation revived after *Oneida II*, see *supra*, at 1487–1488, to reject OIN's plea for ejectment of 20,000 private landowners. *Oneida Indian Nation of N.Y.*, 199 F.R.D., at 90 (internal quotation marks omitted); *ibid.* ("[T]here is a sharp distinction between the *existence* of a federal common law right to Indian homelands and how to *vindicate* that right. . . ."). In this action, OIN seeks declaratory and injunctive relief recognizing its present and future sovereign immunity from local taxation on parcels of land the Tribe purchased in the open market, properties that had been subject to state and local taxation for generations.[32] We now reject the unification theory of OIN and the United States and hold that "standards of federal Indian law and federal equity practice" preclude the Tribe from rekindling embers of sovereignty that long ago grew cold.[33]

The appropriateness of the relief OIN here seeks must be evaluated in light of the long history of state sovereign control over the territory. From the early 1800's into the 1970's, the United States largely accepted, or was indifferent to, New York's governance of the land in question and the validity *vel non* of the Oneidas' sales to the State. See generally Gunther 23–25 (attributing much of the confusion and conflict in the history of New York Indian affairs to "Federal inattention and ambivalence"). In fact, the United States's policy and practice through much of the early nineteenth century was designed to dislodge east coast lands from Indian possession. See *supra*, at 1485–1486. Moreover, the properties here involved have greatly increased in value since the Oneidas sold them 200 years ago. Notably, it

---

[32] [7] The dissent suggests that, compatibly with today's decision, the Tribe may assert tax immunity defensively in the eviction proceeding initiated by Sherrill. Post, at 1496. We disagree. The equitable cast of the relief sought remains the same whether asserted affirmatively or defensively.

[33] [8] We resolve this case on considerations not discretely identified in the parties' briefs. But the question of equitable considerations limiting the relief available to OIN, which we reserved in Oneida II, is inextricably linked to, and is thus "fairly included" within, the questions presented. See this Court's Rule 14.1(a) ("The statement of any question presented is deemed to comprise every subsidiary question fairly included therein."); . . .

was not until lately that the Oneidas sought to regain ancient sovereignty over land converted from wilderness to become part of cities like Sherrill. See *supra*, at 1487–1489; *Oneida II*, 470 U.S., at 264–265 (STEVENS, J., dissenting in part).

This Court has observed in the different, but related, context of the diminishment of an Indian reservation that "[t]he longstanding assumption of jurisdiction by the State over an area that is over 90% non-Indian, both in population and in land use," may create "justifiable expectations." *Rosebud Sioux Tribe v. Kneip*, 430 U.S. 584, 604–605 (1977); accord *Hagen v. Utah*, 510 U.S. 399, 421 (1994) ("jurisdictional history" and "the current population situation . . . demonstrat[e] a practical acknowledgment" of reservation diminishment; "a contrary conclusion would seriously disrupt the justifiable expectations of the people living in the area" (some internal quotation marks omitted)).[34] Similar justifiable expectations, grounded in two centuries of New York's exercise of regulatory jurisdiction, until recently uncontested by OIN, merit heavy weight here.[35]

The wrongs of which OIN complains in this action occurred during the early years of the Republic. For the past two centuries, New York and its county and municipal units have continuously governed the territory. The Oneidas did not seek to regain possession of their aboriginal lands by court decree until the 1970's. And not until the 1990's did OIN acquire the properties in question and assert its unification theory to ground its demand for exemption of the parcels from local taxation. 337 F.3d, at 144.[36] This long lapse of time, during which the Oneidas did not seek to revive their sovereign control through equitable relief in court, and the attendant dramatic changes in the character of the properties, preclude OIN from gaining the disruptive remedy it now seeks.

The principle that the passage of time can preclude relief has deep roots in our law, and this Court has recognized this prescription in various guises. It is well established that laches, a doctrine focused on one side's inaction and the other's legitimate reliance, may bar long-dormant claims for equitable relief. See, *e.g.*, *Badger v. Badger*, 2 Wall. 87, 94 (1865) ("[C]ourts of equity act upon their own inherent doctrine of discouraging, for the peace of society, antiquated demands, refuse to interfere where there has been gross laches in prosecuting the claim, or

---

[34] [9] The Court has recognized that "only Congress can divest a reservation of its land and diminish its boundaries." *Solem v. Bartlett*, 465 U.S. 463, 470 (1984); see also 18 U.S.C. § 1151 (defining Indian country); *South Dakota v. Yankton Sioux Tribe*, 522 U.S. 329, 343 (1998) ("[O]nly Congress can alter the terms of an Indian treaty by diminishing a reservation."). The Court need not decide today whether, contrary to the Second Circuit's determination, the 1838 Treaty of Buffalo Creek disestablished the Oneidas' Reservation, as Sherrill argues. The relief OIN seeks — recognition of present and future sovereign authority to remove the land from local taxation — is unavailable because of the long lapse of time, during which New York's governance remained undisturbed, and the present-day and future disruption such relief would engender.

[35] [10] Citing *Montana v. Blackfeet Tribe*, 471 U.S. 759 (1985), *The Kansas Indians*, 5 Wall. 737 (1867), and *The New York Indians*, 5 Wall. 761 (1867), the dissent notes that only Congress may revoke the tax-exempt status of Indian reservation land. Post, at 1495–1496, and n. 3. Those cases, however, concerned land the Indians had continuously occupied. . . .

[36] [11] The fact that OIN brought this action promptly after acquiring the properties does not overcome the Oneidas' failure to reclaim ancient prerogatives earlier or lessen the problems associated with upsetting New York's long-exercised sovereignty over the area. OIN's claim concerns grave, but ancient, wrongs, and the relief available must be commensurate with that historical reality.

long acquiescence in the assertion of adverse rights." (internal quotation marks omitted)); . . .

This Court applied the doctrine of laches in *Felix v. Patrick*, 145 U.S. 317 (1892), to bar the heirs of an Indian from establishing a constructive trust over land their Indian ancestor had conveyed in violation of a statutory restriction. In the nearly three decades between the conveyance and the lawsuit, "[a] large part of the tract ha[d] been platted and recorded as an addition to the city of Omaha, and . . . sold to purchasers." *Id.*, at 326. "[A]s the case stands at present," the Court observed, "justice requires only what the law . . . would demand — the repayment of the value of the [illegally conveyed] scrip." *Id.*, at 334. The Court also recognized the disproportion between the value of the scrip issued to the Indian ($150) and the value of the property the heirs sought to acquire (over $1 million). *Id.*, at 333. The sort of changes to the value and character of the land noted by the *Felix* Court are present in even greater magnitude in this suit. Cf. *Galliher v. Cadwell*, 145 U.S. 368, 373 (1892) ("[L]aches is not . . . a mere matter of time; but principally a question of the inequity of permitting the claim to be enforced — an inequity founded upon some change in the condition or relations of the property or the parties.").

As between States, long acquiescence may have controlling effect on the exercise of dominion and sovereignty over territory. *Ohio v. Kentucky*, 410 U.S. 641, 651 (1973) ("The rule, long-settled and never doubted by this court, is that long acquiescence by one state in the possession of territory by another and in the exercise of sovereignty and dominion over it is conclusive of the latter's title and rightful authority." (quoting *Michigan v. Wisconsin*, 270 U.S. 295, 308 (1926))); . . . The acquiescence doctrine does not depend on the original validity of a boundary line; rather, it attaches legal consequences to acquiescence in the observance of the boundary. *California v. Nevada*, 447 U.S. 125, 131 (1980) (No relationship need exist "between the *origins* of a boundary and the legal *consequences* of acquiescence in that boundary. . . . Longstanding acquiescence by California and Nevada can give [the boundary lines] the force of law whether or not federal authorities had the power to draw them.")

This Court's original-jurisdiction state-sovereignty cases do not dictate a result here, but they provide a helpful point of reference: When a party belatedly asserts a right to present and future sovereign control over territory,[37] longstanding observances and settled expectations are prime considerations. There is no dispute that it has been two centuries since the Oneidas last exercised regulatory control over the properties here or held them free from local taxation. Parcel-by-parcel revival of their sovereign status, given the extraordinary passage of time, would dishonor "the historic wisdom in the value of repose." *Oneida II*, 470 U.S., at 262 (Stevens, J., dissenting in part).

Finally, this Court has recognized the impracticability of returning to Indian control land that generations earlier passed into numerous private hands. See *Yankton Sioux Tribe v. United States*, 272 U.S. 351, 357 (1926) ("It is impossible

---

[37] [12] It bears repetition that for generations, the Oneidas dominantly complained, not against New York or its local units, but about "[mis]treatment at the hands of the United States Government." Oneida II, 470 U.S., at 269 (Stevens, J., dissenting in part); . . .

. . . to rescind the cession and restore the Indians to their former rights because the lands have been opened to settlement and large portions of them are now in the possession of innumerable innocent purchasers. . . ."); *Felix*, 145 U.S. [317], at 334, 12 S. Ct. 862 (observing, in declining to award equitable relief, "[t]hat which was wild land thirty years ago is now intersected by streets, subdivided into blocks and lots, and largely occupied by persons who have bought upon the strength of Patrick's title, and have erected buildings of a permanent character"). The District Court, in the litigation dormant during the pendency of *Oneida II*, rightly found these pragmatic concerns about restoring Indian sovereign control over land "magnified exponentially here, where development of every type imaginable has been ongoing for more than two centuries." *Oneida Indian Nation of N.Y.*, 199 F.R.D., at 92.

In this case, the Court of Appeals concluded that the "impossibility" doctrine had no application because OIN acquired the land in the open market and does not seek to uproot current property owners. 337 F.3d, at 157. But the unilateral reestablishment of present and future Indian sovereign control, even over land purchased at the market price, would have disruptive practical consequences similar to those that led this Court in *Yankton Sioux* to initiate the impossibility doctrine. The city of Sherrill and Oneida County are today overwhelmingly populated by non-Indians. A checkerboard of alternating state and tribal jurisdiction in New York State — created unilaterally at OIN's behest — would "seriously burde[n] the administration of state and local governments" and would adversely affect landowners neighboring the tribal patches. *Hagen*, 510 U.S., at 421 (quoting *Solem v. Bartlett*, 465 U.S. 463, 471–472, n. 12 (1984)). If OIN may unilaterally reassert sovereign control and remove these parcels from the local tax rolls, little would prevent the Tribe from initiating a new generation of litigation to free the parcels from local zoning or other regulatory controls that protect all landowners in the area. See *Felix*, 145 U.S., at 335 ("decree prayed for in this case, if granted, would offer a distinct encouragement to . . . similar claims"); cf. *Brendale v. Confederated Tribes and Bands of Yakima Nation*, 492 U.S. 408, 433–437 (1989) (opinion of STEVENS, J.) (discussing tribal land-use controls); *post*, at 1497, n. 6 (STEVENS, J., dissenting) (noting that "the balance of interests" supports continued state zoning jurisdiction).[38]

Recognizing these practical concerns, Congress has provided a mechanism for the acquisition of lands for tribal communities that takes account of the interests of others with stakes in the area's governance and well being. Title 25 U.S.C. § 465 authorizes the Secretary of the Interior to acquire land in trust for Indians and provides that the land "shall be exempt from State and local taxation." See *Cass County v. Leech Lake Band of Chippewa Indians*, 524 U.S. 103, 114–115 (1998). The

---

[38] [13] Other tribal entities have already sought to free historic reservation lands purchased in the open market from local regulatory controls. See *Seneca-Cayuga Tribe of Okla. v. Town of Aurelius, New York*, No. 5:03-CV-00690 (NPM), [2004 U.S. Dist. LEXIS 17481,] 2004 WL 1945359, *1–3 (N.D.N.Y. Sept. 1, 2004) (tribe seeks declaratory and injunctive relief to avoid application of municipal zoning and land use laws to 229 acres); *Cayuga Indian Nation of N.Y. v. Village of Union Springs*, 317 F. Supp. 2d 128, 131–134, 147–148 (N.D.N.Y. 2004) (granting declaratory and injunctive relief to tribe, to block application of zoning regulations to property — "located within 300 yards" of a school — under renovation by the tribe for use as a gaming facility).

regulations implementing § 465 are sensitive to the complex interjurisdictional concerns that arise when a tribe seeks to regain sovereign control over territory. Before approving an acquisition, the Secretary must consider, among other things, the tribe's need for additional land; "[t]he purposes for which the land will be used"; "the impact on the State and its political subdivisions resulting from the removal of the land from the tax rolls"; and "[j]urisdictional problems and potential conflicts of land use which may arise." 25 CFR § 151.10 (2004). Section 465 provides the proper avenue for OIN to reestablish sovereign authority over territory last held by the Oneidas 200 years ago.

In sum, the question of damages for the Tribe's ancient dispossession is not at issue in this case, and we therefore do not disturb our holding in *Oneida II.* However, the distance from 1805 to the present day, the Oneidas' long delay in seeking equitable relief against New York or its local units, and developments in the city of Sherrill spanning several generations, evoke the doctrines of laches, acquiescence, and impossibility, and render inequitable the piecemeal shift in governance this suit seeks unilaterally to initiate.[39]

For the reasons stated, the judgment of the Court of Appeals for the Second Circuit is reversed, and the case is remanded for further proceedings consistent with this opinion.

It is so ordered.

JUSTICE STEVENS, dissenting.

This case involves an Indian tribe's claim to tax immunity on its own property located within its reservation. It does not implicate the tribe's immunity from other forms of state jurisdiction, nor does it concern the tribe's regulatory authority over property owned by non-Indians within the reservation.

For the purposes of its decision the Court assumes that the District Court and the Court of Appeals correctly resolved the major issues of fact and law that the parties debated in those courts and that the City of Sherrill (City) presented to us in its petition for certiorari. Thus, we accept those courts' conclusions that the Oneida Indian Nation of New York (Tribe) is a federally recognized Indian Tribe; that it is the successor-in-interest to the original Oneida Nation; that in 1788 the Treaty of Fort Schuyler created a 300,000 acre reservation for the Oneida; that in 1794 the Treaty of Canandaigua established that tract as a federally protected reservation; and that the reservation was not disestablished or diminished by the Treaty of Buffalo Creek in 1838. It is undisputed that the City seeks to collect

---

[39] [14] Justice STEVENS, after vigorously urging the application of laches to block further proceedings in *Oneida II*, 470 U.S., at 255, now faults the Court for rejecting the claim presented here. The majority indicated in *Oneida II* that application of a nonstatutory time limitation in an action for damages would be "novel." 470 U.S., at 244, n. 16; *cf. id.*, at 261–262 (STEVENS, J., dissenting in part) (acknowledging "the application of a traditional equitable defense in an action at law is something of a novelty"). No similar novelty exists when the specific relief OIN now seeks would project redress for the Tribe into the present and future. The claim to a sovereign's prerogative asserted by OIN, we hold, does "not survive eternally," *id.*, at 272 (STEVENS, J., dissenting in part); rather, it is a claim "best left in repose." *Id.*, at 273 (same).

property taxes on parcels of land that are owned by the Tribe and located within the historic boundaries of its reservation.

Since the outset of this litigation it has been common ground that if the Tribe's properties are "Indian Country," the City has no jurisdiction to tax them without express congressional consent. For the reasons set forth at length in the opinions of the District Court and the Court of Appeals, it is abundantly clear that all of the land owned by the Tribe within the boundaries of its reservation qualifies as Indian country. Without questioning the accuracy of that conclusion, the Court today nevertheless decides that the fact that most of the reservation has been occupied and governed by non-Indians for a long period of time precludes the Tribe "from rekindling embers of sovereignty that long ago grew cold." This is a novel holding, and in my judgment even more unwise than the Court's holding in *County of Oneida v. Oneida Indian Nation of N.Y.*, 470 U.S. 226 (1985), that the Tribe may recover damages for the alleged illegal conveyance of its lands that occurred in 1795. In that case, I argued that the "remedy for the ancient wrong established at trial should be provided by Congress, not by judges seeking to rewrite history at this late date," *id.*, at 270 (opinion dissenting in part). In the present case, the Tribe is not attempting to collect damages or eject landowners as a remedy for a wrong that occurred centuries ago; rather, it is invoking an ancient immunity against a city's present-day attempts to tax its reservation lands.

Without the benefit of relevant briefing from the parties, the Court has ventured into legal territory that belongs to Congress. Its decision today is at war with at least two bedrock principles of Indian law. First, only Congress has the power to diminish or disestablish a tribe's reservation [citing *South Dakota v. Yankton Sioux Tribe*, discussed in Ch. 2, Sec. A.3.b.iv, and *Solem v. Bartlett*, presented in the same section]. Second, as a core incident of tribal sovereignty, a tribe enjoys immunity from state and local taxation of its reservation lands, until that immunity is explicitly revoked by Congress [citing *Montana v. Blackfeet Tribe*, 471 U.S. 759, 764–765 (1985) and *Cass County v. Leech Lake Band of Chippewa Indians*, discussed in Ch. 4, Sec. B.4.b]. Far from revoking this immunity, Congress has specifically reconfirmed it with respect to the reservation lands of the New York Indians.[40] Ignoring these principles, the Court has done what only Congress may do — it has effectively proclaimed a diminishment of the Tribe's reservation and an abrogation of its elemental right to tax immunity. Under our precedents, whether it is wise policy to honor the Tribe's tax immunity is a question for Congress, not this Court, to decide.

---

[40] [4] In providing New York state courts with jurisdiction over civil actions between Indians, Congress emphasized that the statute was not to be "construed as subjecting the lands within any Indian reservation in the State of New York to taxation for State or local purposes." 25 U.S.C. § 233. *See Oneida Indian Nation of N.Y. v. County of Oneida*, 414 U.S. 661, 680–681, n. 15 (1974) (" 'The text and history of the new legislation are replete with indications that congressional consent is necessary to validate the exercise of state power over tribal Indians and, most significantly, that New York cannot unilaterally deprive Indians of their tribal lands or authorize such deprivations. The civil jurisdiction law, to make assurance doubly sure, contains a proviso that explicitly exempts reservations from state and local taxation. . . . Moreover, both federal and state officials agreed that the bills would retain ultimate federal power over the Indians and that federal guardianship, particularly with respect to property rights, would continue' " (quoting Gunther, *Governmental Power and New York Indian Lands — A Reassessment of a Persistent Problem of Federal — State Relations*, 8 BUFFALO L. REV. 1, 16 (1958))).

As a justification for its lawmaking decision, the Court relies heavily on the fact that the Tribe is seeking *equitable* relief in the form of an injunction. The distinction between law and equity is unpersuasive because the outcome of the case turns on a narrow legal issue that could just as easily, if not most naturally, be raised by a tribe as a *defense* against a state collection proceeding. In fact, that scenario actually occurred in this case: The City brought an eviction proceeding against the Tribe based on its refusal to pay property taxes; that proceeding was removed to federal court and consolidated with the present action; the District Court granted summary judgment for the Tribe; and the Court of Appeals affirmed on the basis of tribal tax immunity. Either this defensive use of tax immunity should still be available to the Tribe on remand, but see *ante*, at 1489, n. 7, or the Court's reliance on the distinctions between law and equity and between substantive rights and remedies, see *ante*, at 1489, is indefensible.[41]

In any event, as a matter of equity I believe that the "principle that the passage of time can preclude relief," *ante*, should be applied sensibly and with an even hand. It seems perverse to hold that the reliance interests of non-Indian New Yorkers that are predicated on almost two centuries of inaction by the Tribe do not foreclose the Tribe's enforcement of judicially created damages remedies for ancient wrongs, but do somehow mandate a forfeiture of a tribal immunity that has been consistently and uniformly protected throughout our history. In this case, the Tribe reacquired reservation land in a peaceful and lawful manner that fully respected the interests of innocent landowners — it purchased the land on the open market. To now deny the Tribe its right to tax immunity — at once the most fundamental of tribal rights and the least disruptive to other sovereigns — is not only inequitable, but also irreconcilable with the principle that only Congress may abrogate or extinguish tribal sovereignty. I would not decide this case on the basis of speculation about what may happen in future litigation over other regulatory issues.[42] For the answer to the question whether the City may require the Tribe to pay taxes on its own property within its own reservation is pellucidly clear. Under settled law, it may not.

---

[41] [5] *See* 337 F.3d 139, 167 (C.A. 2 2003). Additionally, to the extent that we are dealing with genuine equitable defenses, these defenses are subject to waiver. Here, the City sought to add the defense of laches to its answer; the District Court refused on the ground of futility, 145 F. Supp. 2d, at 259; the Court of Appeals upheld this determination, 337 F.3d, at 168–169; and the City failed to preserve this point in its petition for certiorari or brief on the merits. The City similarly failed to preserve its impossibility defense in its submissions to this Court, and there is no indication that the City ever raised an acquiescence defense in the proceedings below.

[42] [6] It is not necessary to engage in any speculation to recognize that the majority's fear of opening a Pandora's box of tribal powers is greatly exaggerated. Given the State's strong interest in zoning its land without exception for a small number of Indian-held properties arranged in checkerboard fashion, the balance of interests obviously supports the retention of state jurisdiction in this sphere. See *California v. Cabazon Band of Mission Indians*, 480 U.S. 202, 215 (1987) (" '[I]n exceptional circumstances a State may assert jurisdiction over the on-reservation activities of tribal members' "). Nor, as the Tribe acknowledges, Brief for Respondents 19, n. 4, could it credibly assert the right to tax or exercise other regulatory authority over reservation land owned by non-Indians. See *Atkinson Trading Co. v. Shirley*, 532 U.S. 645 (2001); *Strate v. A-1 Contractors*, 520 U.S. 438, 456 (1997) (denying tribal jurisdiction in part because the Tribe could not "assert a landowner's right to occupy and exclude" over the land in question); see also *Brendale v. Confederated Tribes and Bands of Yakima Nation*, 492 U.S. 408, 444–445 (1989) (opinion of STEVENS, J.) ("Because the Tribe no longer has the power to exclude nonmembers from a large portion of this area, it also lacks the power to define the essential character of the territory [through zoning]").

Accordingly, I respectfully dissent.

NOTES ON THE ONEIDA LITIGATION AND THE NONINTERCOURSE ACT

1. ***Sherrill's* Impact:** In footnote 11 of *City of Sherrill*, Justice Ginsberg writes that the "OIN's claim concerns grave, but ancient wrongs . . . ." The opinion focuses on the Oneidas' delay in reclaiming their land, which had been transferred nearly 200 years earlier in violation of the federal Nonintercourse Act. However, as Justice Stevens points out in his dissent, the parties had not briefed the issue of laches, making resolution of the case on those grounds beyond the scope of the Court. *Id.* at 1495. Nevertheless, the Court's decision has had far-reaching effects.

After *Sherrill*, the Nation agreed to a settlement with the City. *Oneida Indian Nation v. Madison County*, 665 F.3d 408 (2d Cir. 2011) (noting settlement). While OIN obtained an agreement with the City, Madison and Oneida counties pursued foreclosure actions against the Nation for its refusal to pay county taxes. Additionally, the Court's holding in *Sherrill* made the Nation vulnerable to litigation over its casino's compliance with IGRA. In response to this uncertainty, the Nation requested that the Department of Interior take the land into trust. The DOI approved the petition in part and the two counties challenged the DOI's positive land status determination. *See Town of Verona v. Cuomo*, 2013 U.S. Dist. LEXIS 155283 (N.D.N.Y. Oct. 30, 2013) (addressing other legal issues, but outlining the history of the Nation's legal battles over its land). After the Second Circuit held that the Nation's sovereign immunity barred the counties' foreclosure proceedings, the Supreme Court granted their writ of certiorari. In response, the Oneida Indian Nation waived its sovereign immunity, and the Court remanded the case. *Oneida Indian Nation v. Madison County, id.* at 414.

Ultimately, following these protracted legal battles, the counties, the state, and OIN entered into a settlement agreement in 2013. The Nation agreed to pay the state a one-time sum of 11 million dollars, and 25% of its "net-win"[43] earnings from the casino. The state in turn allocated yearly payments to the counties, and the one-time 11 million dollars to Madison County. These payments provided "full satisfaction of all existing tax liens that [the counties] claims as against the Nation and in full satisfaction of tax revenues that the Counties [would not receive in the future] under the agreement or because of the trust status of the Nation land." While the agreement dictated that specific areas of the Nation's land were non-taxable, it also stated that in the future, the Nation would not seek additional property tax "exemptions" on its reacquired lands beyond the areas designated in the agreement. The counties agreed not to pursue legal claims against the Nation in the future over land or taxation issues, and the Nation agreed to cap its trust land acquisitions to 25,000 acres. Settlement Agreement by The Oneida Nation, The State of New York, The County of Madison & The County of Oneida, O.I.N.-N.Y.-

---

[43] According to the settlement, "net-win" means "the amount wagered on gaming devices less the payout from [the devices], but before expenses, to be calculated on a quarterly basis. . ." and less "free play" amounts. Settlement Agreement by The Oneida Nation, The State of New York, The County of Madison & The County of Oneida, O.I.N.-N.Y.-Cnty of Madison-Cnty of Oneida, May 16th, 2013.

Cnty of Madison-Cnty of Oneida, May 16th, 2013.

2. **Types of Tribal Property Rights Protected by the Nonintercourse Act:**
The land in question in the Oneida litigation was guaranteed to the Tribe through
a treaty. The Nonintercourse Act also protects land held in aboriginal title, and
some tribal land held in fee simple. *See United States v. Candelaria*, 271 U.S. 432,
440–44 (1926) (protecting land held by a Pueblo that possessed fee simple title
during Spanish rule). Non-federally recognized tribes may also be protected under
the Act. *See Joint Tribal Council of the Passamaquoddy Tribe v. Morton*, 528 F.2d
370 (1st Cir. 1975) (United States has a trust responsibility under the Nonintercourse Act to a non-federally recognized tribe that had no treaty with the United
States, but had maintained continuous relationships with the State of Maine).

If a tribe acquires an office building in downtown Los Angeles or a hotel in
Washington, D.C. for investment purposes, would it be prohibited from mortgaging
or selling the property without the permission of the United States under the
Nonintercourse Act? Some recent Supreme Court decisions suggest that a purchase
of this type would not trigger application of the Nonintercourse Act, though the
legal result is not certain. *See, e.g., County of Yakima v. Confederated Tribes &
Bands of the Yakima Indian Nation*, 502 U.S. 251, 263 (1992) (discussing the
alienability of tribal land in connection with the issue of taxation). For more
extended consideration of this issue, see NELL JESSUP NEWTON ET AL., COHEN'S
HANDBOOK OF FEDERAL INDIAN LAW 1034–1036 (2012 ed.). Given that some of the
tribal land acquisitions in fee are for investment purposes only, how might you
structure the legal entities making the purchases in order to avoid uncertainties
originating in the Nonintercourse Act?

3. **Settlement of Many Nonintercourse Act Claims:** Beginning in the 1970s,
a host of highly publicized cases involving east coast Indian tribes invoked this
federal restraint on alienation. Although the state and local government defendants
injected a variety of defenses, the high stakes and legal uncertainty led, in the early
years, to numerous Congressional settlement acts. For example, the Maine Indian
Claims Settlement Act of 1980, codified at 25 U.S.C. §§ 1721–1735, settled claims on
behalf of the Passamaquoddy, Penobscot, and Maliseet Indians to large portions of
the State of Maine. It established two trust funds, one for payment of income to the
Passamaquoddy and Penobscot, and the other for land acquisition for all three
tribes. Existing and future land holdings of the Tribes were to be put in trust by the
federal government. Unlike the original terms of the Alaska Native Claims
Settlement Act (discussed in Ch. 5, Sec. B), the Maine Indian Claims Settlement Act
adopts a modified sovereignty approach rather than a corporate model. The state is
authorized to exercise civil and criminal jurisdiction, in the manner of Public Law
280 (*see* Ch. 5, Sec. A). 25 U.S.C. § 1725. Suits against the Tribes in federal and state
courts are allowed. Under implementing legislation adopted by the State of Maine,
tribal sovereign immunity is protected in state court when the Tribe is acting in its
governmental capacity, and tribal exclusive jurisdiction over a limited range of civil
and criminal matters is recognized. Me. Rev. Stat. Ann. tit. 30, §§ 6206(2), 6209-a,
6209-b. Maine also provides for cooperation between tribal and state law enforcement officers. *Id.* at § 6210. Other sections of the Settlement Act address issues of
taxation (25 U.S.C. § 6208(2)) and tribal hunting and fishing rights (25 U.S.C.
§ 6207). In *Passamaquoddy Tribe v. Maine*, 75 F.3d 784 (1st Cir. 1996), the court

held that the Settlement Act precluded the Tribes from pursuing a tribal-state gaming compact under the Indian Gaming Regulatory Act of 1988 (*see* Ch. 5, Sec. D). The court relied on the following language of the Act:

> The provisions of any federal law enacted after October 10, 1980 [the effective date of the Settlement Act], for the benefit of Indians, Indian nations, or tribes or bands of Indians, which would affect or preempt the application of the laws of the State of Maine, . . . shall not apply within the State of Maine, unless such provision of such subsequently enacted Federal law is specifically made applicable within the State of Maine.

25 U.S.C. § 1735(b). Do the terms of the Settlement Act suggest that the Tribes' claims were seen to be strong and credible? Imposition of state jurisdiction is a common feature of many settlement acts of this period. *See* NELL JESSUP NEWTON ET AL., COHEN'S HANDBOOK OF FEDERAL INDIAN LAW 582–583 (2012 ed.). For a complete history of the Maine litigation, see PAUL BRODEUR, RESTITUTION (1985). Examples of other land claims settlements can be found at 25 U.S.C. §§ 1751–1760 (Mashantucket Pequot Tribe) and 25 U.S.C. §§ 1701–1706 (Narragansett Tribe).

4. Defenses to Nonintercourse Act Litigation: Although Congress settled many Nonintercourse Act claims through settlement acts, some tribes did not agree to settle their claims. One impediment to settlement was fragmentation of some tribes caused by dispossession and removal from their ancestral territory. As noted in the *County of Oneida v. Oneida Indian Nation* opinion, there were three Oneida plaintiffs, including those Oneidas who had moved to Wisconsin as part of the federal removal effort of the early nineteenth century, and those who had remained in New York. The various Oneida groups would all have to agree if any settlement were to occur. Other tribes refused to settle because they did not want to accede to settlement terms such as state jurisdiction.

Even before the Supreme Court's 2005 decision in the *City of Sherrill* case, litigation posed substantial risks for tribes bringing Nonintercourse Act claims. For tribes that lacked federal recognition, the biggest obstacle was the requirement that the claimant demonstrate that it has functioned as an Indian tribe continuously since the time of the challenged land transaction (*e.g.*, *Mashpee Tribe v. New Seabury Corp.*, 592 F.2d 575 (1st Cir. 1979), discussed in Ch. 2, Sec. A.1.c). For recognized tribes, the *County of Oneida* decision appeared to clear away certain important defenses, such as state statutes of limitation, but the defendants kept injecting other objections to recovery. For example, they argued, to no avail, that Nonintercourse Act claims were barred by prior Indian Claims Commission litigation. *See, e.g.*, Cayuga *Indian Nation v. Cuomo*, 667 F. Supp. 938 (N.D.N.Y. 1987).

After reading the opinion in *County of Oneida*, would you have anticipated that laches would be an effective defense to a Nonintercourse Act claim for damages or ejectment? Recall that the *County of Oneida* opinion points out that laches is an equitable doctrine, not generally considered relevant to a legal claim for damages or ejectment. For an extended argument that *City of Sherrill* broke from precedent in its use of laches, see Kathryn E. Fort, *The New Laches: Creating Title Where None Existed*, 16 GEO. MASON L. REV. 357 (2009). *See also* Kathryn E. Fort, *Disruption and Impossibility: The New Laches and the Unfortunate Resolution of the*

Iroquois Land Claims in Federal Courts, 11 Wyo. L. Rev. 375 (2011).

In *Sherrill*, the Court asserts that the OIN's exercise of jurisdiction over the ancestral territory that it bought in fee would disrupt "settled expectations" of state and local governments and non-Indians, including the ability to obtain tax revenues from the properties. Should such rationales be used to foreclose Indian land and jurisdiction claims? *See also* Matthew L.M. Fletcher, Kathryn E. Fort & Dr. Nicholas J. Reo, *Tribal Disruption and Indian Claims*, 112 Mich. L. Rev. First Impressions 65 (2013) (discussing the theory of "tribal disruption" post-*Sherrill*) and Wenona T. Singel & Matthew L.M. Fletcher, *Power, Authority, and Tribal Property*, 41 Tulsa L. Rev. 21, 48–49 (2005). Do other areas of federal Indian law rely on rationales similar to the idea of "settled expectations" used in *Sherrill*? Consider and compare the doctrine of "diminishment" presented in Ch. 2, Sec. A.3.b.

5. Judicial vs. Congressional Control over Indian Policy and Implications for Further Litigation: As Justice Stevens notes in his dissent in *Sherrill*, the majority does not question that the Oneida land in question is located within the Nation's reservation, and therefore within Indian country. Yet under longstanding principles of Indian law, Indian nations are not subject to state taxing power within Indian country, unless Congress has affirmatively authorized the state to tax. *See* Ch. 4, Sec. B.4.b (especially Note 2 following *Washington v. Confederated Tribes of the Colville Reservation*). Does Justice Ginsburg address this point in her opinion? Why shouldn't it be up to Congress to determine whether the City of Sherrill should be able to tax Oneida-owned land?

Justice Ginsburg's majority opinion appears to draw a distinction between legal remedies for tribal land claims, such as damages (permitted under the Court's 1985 decision, *County of Oneida*, presented above) and equitable remedies for such claims, such as injunctions (not permitted). Does the Court's preference for compensatory legal remedies flow out of the traditional preference for legal over equitable remedies or out of non-Indian demands for retaining Indian resources once taken, legally or otherwise? Does the Court address the adequacy of the legal remedy in the *City of Sherrill* analysis, as it traditionally did in courts of equity?

While Justice Ginsburg prefers legal remedies for tribal land claims, she relies on equitable doctrines, such as laches and impossibility, as the basis for denying injunctive relief to the OIN. As any student of the common law writs will recall, ejectment (or eviction) from land is a legal rather than an equitable remedy, notwithstanding its resemblance to forward-looking equitable remedies such as injunctions. Does *City of Sherrill* foreclose tribal efforts to reclaim possession of lands transferred in violation of 25 U.S.C. § 177 through writs of ejectment? In a post-*Sherrill* decision, *Cayuga Indian Nation of N.Y. v. Pataki*, 413 F.3d 266 (2d Cir. 2005), a divided panel of the Second Circuit interpreted *Sherrill* as precluding any "disruptive" claim (see Note 5, above), regardless of the equitable or legal nature of the relief sought. The court then applied equitable defenses to both the Cayugas' ejectment claim, and the damages claim that had yielded a $247,000,000 judgment in federal district court. Indeed, the panel majority did so even though it conceded that the Cayugas were not to blame for the delay in bringing their claim, and despite the fact that the United States, which is not normally subject to a defense of laches, had joined the litigation as a plaintiff. Review the Supreme

Court's 1985 *County of Oneida* decision, and consider whether the Second Circuit's opinion in *Cayuga* properly applies it.

6. Allotted Lands

NORTHERN CHEYENNE TRIBE v. HOLLOWBREAST
United States Supreme Court
425 U.S. 649 (1976)

Mr. Justice Brennan delivered the opinion of the Court.

The question to be decided is whether the Northern Cheyenne Allotment Act, Act of June 3, 1926, 44 Stat. 690, gave the allottees of surface lands vested rights in the mineral deposits underlying those lands. The District Court for the District of Montana held that the Act did not grant the allottees vested rights in the mineral deposits. 349 F. Supp. 1302 (1972). The Court of Appeals for the Ninth Circuit reversed. 505 F. 2d 268 (1974). We agree with the District Court and reverse.

I

The 1926 Act statutorily established the Northern Cheyenne Reservation pursuant to the federal policy expressed in the General Allotment Act of 1887, 24 Stat. 388, and provided for the allotment of tracts of land to individual tribal members. Section 1 of the Act declared the lands constituting the reservation "to be the property of [the Northern Cheyenne] Indians, subject to such control and management of said property as the Congress of the United States may direct." Section 2 set up a procedure for allotment of agricultural and grazing lands. Section 3, 44 Stat. 691, upon which the question for decision in this case turns, reads as follows:

> "That the timber, coal or other minerals, including oil, gas, and other natural deposits, on said reservation are hereby reserved for the benefit of the tribe and may be leased with the consent of the Indian council under such rules and regulations as the Secretary of the Interior may prescribe: Provided, That at the expiration of fifty years from the date of the approval of this Act the coal or other minerals, including oil, gas, and other natural deposits, of said allotments shall become the property of the respective allottees or their heirs: Provided further, That the unallotted lands of said tribe of Indians shall be held in common, subject to the control and management thereof as Congress may deem expedient for the benefit of said Indians."

On its face, § 3 provides that title to the mineral deposits would pass to the allottees, or their heirs,[44] fifty years after approval of the Act, or in 1976. But the

---

[44] [2] In 1961 Congress amended the Act to add the allottees' devisees as beneficiaries. Act of Sept. 22, 1961, Pub. L. 87-287, 75 Stat. 586. At the same time Congress amended § 3 to permit the Tribe to lease mineral rights beyond 1976 and provided that any interest that might be taken by the allottees would be "subject to any outstanding leases." Congress also prohibited the allottees from conveying their future

phrasing might also be read to imply a reserved power in Congress to terminate the allottees' interest before that date. Thus, the critical question is whether Congress could, as it purports to have done in 1968, terminate the grant without rendering the United States constitutionally liable to pay the allottees just compensation.

A supervening event of particular significance was the considerable increase in value of coal reserves under the allotted lands that occurred in the 1960's due to increasing energy demand and the concomitant need for new sources of energy.[45] Until this occurred, the reservation of the deposits until 1976 for the benefit of the Tribe had not significantly benefited it, because mining of most of the coal was not economically feasible. There was also substantial concern that, because one-third of the allottees did not live on the reservation, if control of strip mining passed in 1976 to the individual allottees, serious adverse consequences might be suffered by the Indians living on the reservation. In addition, Congress believed that injustice might result if the benefits to be realized by individual Indians depended upon whether coal was found under particular allotted lands. S. Rep. No. 1145, 90th Cong., 2d Sess., 2 (1968); H.R. Rep. No. 1292, 90th Cong., 2d Sess., 2 (1968). These considerations led Congress in 1968 to terminate the grant to allottees and to reserve the mineral rights "in perpetuity for the benefit of the Tribe." Act of July 24, 1968, Pub. L. 90-424, 82 Stat. 424. The termination was, however, expressly conditioned upon a prior judicial determination that the allottees had not been granted vested rights to the mineral deposits by the 1926 Act. Congress so conditioned the termination to avoid the possibility of a successful claim for damages against the United States by the allottees under the Just Compensation Clause of the fifth amendment. The 1968 amendment authorized the Tribe to commence an action against the allottees in the District Court for Montana "to determine whether under [the 1926 Act] the allottees, their heirs or devisees, have received a vested property right in the minerals which is protected by the fifth amendment," and provided that the reservation of the minerals in perpetuity for the benefit of the Tribe "shall cease to have any force or effect" if the court determines that "the allottees, their heirs or devisees, have a vested interest in the minerals which is protected by the fifth amendment."

The Tribe sued 10 allottees, individually and as representatives of the class of allottees, heirs, and devisees, and sought a declaratory judgment that the class had no vested rights and that the Tribe owned the coal and other minerals in perpetuity. We shall refer to the class as "allottees."

II

Both the Tribe and the allottees argue that the plain meaning of § 3 of the 1926 Act, providing that the mineral deposits "shall become the property of the respective allottees" fifty years after the effective date of the Act, compels a declaratory judgment in their favor. The Tribe argues that this provision can only

---

interest and voided any conveyances entered into prior to 1961. Previously § 3 had been amended to grant the allottees the timber on the allotted lands. Act of July 24, 1947, c. 314, 61 Stat. 418.

[45] [3] Petitioner informs us that its "conservative" estimate of the value of the coal reserves is $2 billion, based on a recent offer for coal under the Crow Reservation, which adjoins the Northern Cheyenne Reservation.

be read to grant an expectancy, while the allottees maintain that it unequivocally grants a vested future interest. Both interpretations are consistent with the wording of the Act, and we therefore must determine the intent of Congress by looking to the legislative history against the background of principles governing congressional power to alter allotment plans.

The District Court agreed with the Tribe, reading "unallotted lands" in § 3 as including the mineral deposits, since the Act expressly severed the mineral deposits from the surface of the allotted lands and subjected unallotted lands "to the control and management thereof as Congress may deem expedient for the benefit of said Indians." 349 F. Supp., at 1309–1310. The Court of Appeals rejected the District Court's interpretation of "unallotted lands" as including the severed mineral deposits, rendering them subject to congressional control and management; rather, it read § 3 to be an "unconditional, noncontingent grant of [the mineral] deposits to the allottees," and noted the absence of any "clear expression of Congress's retained power." 505 F. 2d, at 271–272

The Court of Appeals erred in its basic approach to construction of the 1926 Act. Its view was that Congress must be regarded as having relinquished its control over Indian lands in the absence of an express statement of its intent to retain the power.[46] Just the opposite is true. The Court has consistently recognized the wide-ranging congressional power to alter allotment plans until those plans are executed. *E.g., Chase v. United States*, 256 U.S. 1, 7 (1921); *United States v. Rowell*, 243 U.S. 464, 468 (1917); *Sizemore v. Brady*, 235 U.S. 441, 449–450 (1914); *Gritts v. Fisher*, 224 U.S. 640, 648 (1912); *Stephens v. Cherokee Nation*, 174 U.S. 445, 484 (1899). This principle has specifically been applied to uphold congressional imposition on allottees of restraints against alienation of their interests or expansion of the class of beneficiaries under an allotment Act. *E.g., United States v. Jim*, 409 U.S. 80 (1972); *Brader v. James*, 246 U.S. 88 (1918). The extensiveness of this congressional authority, as well as "Congress' unique obligation toward the Indians," *Morton v. Mancari*, 417 U.S. 535, 555 (1974), underlies the judicially fashioned canon of construction that these statutes are to be read to reserve Congress's powers in the absence of a clear expression by Congress to the contrary. *Chippewa Indians v. United States*, 307 U.S. 1, 5 (1939).

Read in this light, the statutory history of the Northern Cheyenne Reservation allotment supports the District Court's reading of the Act. Although prior to 1925 allotment acts had been enacted for nearly all Indian reservations, none yet applied to the Northern Cheyenne Reservation. The Tribe in 1925 petitioned Senator Walsh of Montana to have the reservation allotted. The petition read in pertinent part:

> "We, the undersigned members of the Northern Cheyenne Indian Tribe, of the State of Montana, do hereby humbly beseech you to do all in your power to have a Bill introduced and passed in Congress, to have an allotment of not less than 320 acres of tillable farm land made to each and every member of the Northern Cheyenne Indians.

---

[46] [7] The court also relied on the canon that "statutes passed for the benefit of the Indians are to be liberally construed and all doubts are to be resolved in their favor." 505 F. 2d, at 272. But this eminently sound and vital canon has no application here; the contesting parties are an Indian tribe and a class of individuals consisting primarily of tribal members.

"To reserve all mineral, timber, and coal lands for the benefit of the Northern Cheyenne Indian Tribe, said tribe to have absolute control of same."

Thus, the Tribe from the outset sought allotment provisions that would retain, for the benefit of the entire Tribe, the rights to the coal and other minerals underlying the reservation.

Shortly thereafter Hubert Work, Secretary of the Interior, sent Representative Leavitt of Montana, Chairman of the House Committee on Indian Affairs, a proposed draft of an allotment bill for the Northern Cheyenne Reservation. An accompanying letter reiterated the Tribe's desire to give individual Indians agricultural and grazing lands. Secretary Work also suggested that a survey of the land be made and further proposed that "[i]n the event any of the land listed for allotting is found to contain coal or other minerals, it is contemplated to reserve all such minerals for the tribe and to allot the surface only." H.R. Rep. No. 383, 69th Cong., 1st Sess., 2 (1926).

The proposed bill (H.R. 9558) introduced in the House two days later by Representative Leavitt followed this suggestion. Section 2 of this bill provided for a geological survey and required that

"if any of the land shall be found to contain coal or other minerals, only the surface thereof may be allotted, and all minerals on said lands are hereby reserved for the benefit of the tribe."

This language is clear evidence of an intent to sever the surface estate from the interest in the minerals, at least wherever minerals are found to exist. But nothing appears in the legislative history explaining the object of the proviso:

"Provided, That at the expiration of fifty years from the date of the approval of this Act, the coal or other mineral deposits of said allotments shall become the property of the respective allottees or their heirs or assigns."

We are persuaded for several reasons that it was not intended to grant the allottees a vested future interest in the mineral deposits and thereby relinquish congressional "control and management thereof as Congress may deem expedient for the benefit of said Indians."

The proposed bill plainly reveals a purpose to sever the mineral rights from the surface estate; "only the surface . . . may be allotted" under the bill. In fact, the limited object of the bill, as stated in its title, was "to provide for allotting in severalty agricultural lands" within the reservation. This limited object carries out Secretary Work's suggestion, and honors the Tribe's request, to limit the allotment to the surface lands to enable the Tribe to enjoy the full benefit of the mineral rights. Nothing in the legislative history shows any congressional purpose not to follow the Secretary's proposal; every indication is to the contrary. Only the surface lands were to be subject to allotment. The House Committee's amendments to the bill make this purpose even clearer; the Committee retained the language that limited the allotment to surface lands but omitted the language imposing this limitation only in the event that minerals were found on the land. H.R. Rep. No. 383, supra, at 1. The House passed the bill as amended by the Committee. 67 Cong. Rec. 6522 (1926).

The Senate Committee reported out the House bill with several amendments, two of which have significance in support of our conclusion. S. Rep. No. 638, 69th Cong., 1st Sess. (1926). A new opening section, eventually § 1 of the Act, see supra, at 651, confirmed the Tribe's title to the reservation lands and expressly retained Congress's authority to manage those lands. The Committee also rewrote § 2 of the House bill and substituted the following as § 3 of its bill:

> "That the timber, coal or other minerals, including oil, gas, and other natural deposits on said reservation, are hereby reserved for the benefit of the tribe: Provided, That at the expiration of fifty years from the date of the approval of this act the coal or other minerals, including oil, gas, and other natural deposits of said allotments shall become the property of the respective allottees or their heirs: Provided further, That the unallotted lands of said tribe of Indians shall be held in common, subject to the control and management thereof as Congress may deem expedient for the benefit of said Indians."

The changes from the House bill indicate no difference in purpose. The coal and other mineral rights were still "reserved for the benefit of the tribe," with no suggestion from the Senate Committee that it attached any more import to the fifty-year provision than had the House. Most significantly, and a critical fact supporting the District Court's construction of § 3, the Committee added an express reservation of congressional authority over "unallotted lands." Since the House bill clearly allotted only the surface lands, we are compelled to conclude that when both Houses adopted the bill as amended by the Senate, "unallotted lands" in § 3 included the mineral deposits.[47]

The conclusion we reach is also supported by the wording of the allotment trust patents. The patents "reserved for the benefit of the Northern Cheyenne Indians, all the coal or other minerals, including oil, gas, and all natural deposits in said land," without any reference to the allottees' future interest. Thus, the agency charged with executing the Act construed it as not granting the allottees any vested rights. . . .

Reversed.

MR. JUSTICE BLACKMUN, concurring.

For me, and obviously for the Congress, this case is much closer and the legislative history much less clear than the Court's opinion makes them out to be.

---

[47] [11] A reasonable explanation for the provision that the mineral rights would become the property of the allottees after 50 years is that it may have been thought to further the policy of assimilation underlying the allotment policy, see n. 1, supra; the provision is consistent with a desire to give the mineral rights to the allottees after they became assimilated. On the other hand, the vesting of an irrevocable future interest in 1926 would not be wholly consistent with that policy, particularly since the policy as reflected in allotment statutes was already losing its appeal by 1926, and Congress might more logically be expected to have been reluctant to surrender its power to modify the Act.

There are factors that distinctly favor the respondents. For one example, in other comparable statutes, there are specific reservations (*e.g.*, "unless otherwise provided by Congress") of the kind of congressional power that the Court finds implicit here. Our National Legislature obviously knew how expressly to reserve the power and yet did not employ the "magic words" here. On balance, however, the strength of the case rests with the petitioner. It is of some importance, I feel, that the minerals could have been leased and depleted during the fifty-year period. This possibility surely diminishes the reliance interest of any allottee and his successors. I therefore join the Court's opinion and its judgment.

Black Hills Institute of Geological Research v. South Dakota School of Mines and Technology, 12 F.3d 737 (8th Cir. 1993): A valuable Tyrannosaurus rex fossil named Sue was found by a Black Hills geologist on a trust allotment. During the excavation of the fossil, Black Hills purported to purchase the right to excavate from the allottee for $5,000. After Black Hills removed the fossil, the United States seized it (placing it in the South Dakota School of Mines and Technology) on the ground that the removal violated federal criminal statutes relating to federal lands. Black Hills then sued to quiet title.

The United States had acquired the allotment in question pursuant to the Indian Reorganization Act of 1934 (25 U.S.C. § 465), and had issued the trust patent to Williams, the allottee, under a provision of the General Allotment Act of 1887 (25 U.S.C. § 348). Under the Indian Reorganization Act, alienation of trust allotments is prohibited without the prior approval of the Secretary of the Interior. Any attempt to sell an interest in a trust allotment in violation of legal requirements is void. Williams never applied for nor received approval from the Secretary for the transaction with Black Hills regarding the right to excavate Sue. The Court observed:

> All parties agree that the fossil is now personal property because it has been severed from the land. In *Starr v. Campbell*, 208 U.S. 527, 534 (1908), however, the Supreme Court held that timber from Indian trust land that the beneficial owner sold was subject to the trust patent's restraint on alienation even though the timber became personal property after the purchaser severed it from the land.[48]

Thus, the question before the court was whether Sue was personal property or land *before* Black Hills excavated it. Only if the fossil was land within the meaning of the relevant federal statutes at the time of excavation would the transaction with

---

[48] [4] The Supreme Court has held that a beneficial owner of Indian trust land could sell timber from his land without violating the restraint on alienation because "the cutting was incidental to the preparation of [the] land for agricultural uses." Felix S. Cohen, Handbook of Federal Indian Law, at 539 n.94 (1982 ed.) (citing *United States v. Paine Lumber*, 206 U.S. 467, 473–74, 27 S. Ct. 697, 51 L. Ed. 1139 (1907)). The Court distinguished *Paine*, however, in *Starr*. In *Starr*, the Court found the timber subject to the restraint on alienation because the timber constituted 15/16 of the value of the land and the land was "timber land" unsuitable for farming. 208 U.S. at 534. Holding otherwise, the Court reasoned, would reduce the restraint on alienation to "small consequence." Id. Thus, *Paine* does not apply here because Sue was a valuable part of the land and nothing in the record suggests that she was excavated to clear the land for farming or other similar purposes.

Williams be void. While appreciating that the question was one of federal law, the court sought guidance from state law in the absence of a federal definition. Under South Dakota law, real property consists of land, things affixed to the land, things incidental or appurtenant to the land, and items immovable by law. From this starting point, the court concluded:

> We hold that the fossil was "land" within the meaning of § 464 and § 483. Sue Hendrickson found the fossil embedded in the land. Under South Dakota law, the fossil was an "ingredient" comprising part of the "solid material of the earth." It was a component part of Williams' land, just like the soil, the rocks, and whatever other naturally-occurring materials make up the earth of the ranch. Black Hills makes several arguments to the contrary, none of which we find persuasive. That the fossil once was a dinosaur which walked on the surface of the earth and that part of the fossil was protruding from the ground when Hendrickson discovered it are irrelevant. The salient point is that the fossil had for millions of years been an "ingredient" of the earth that the United States holds in trust for Williams. The case very well might be different had someone found the fossil elsewhere and buried it in Williams' land or somehow inadvertently left it there. Here, however, a Tyrannosaurus rex died some 65 million years ago on what is now Indian trust land and its fossilized remains gradually became incorporated into that land. Although it is movable, personal property now, at the time Hendrickson discovered the fossil it was part of Williams' land and thus is subject to § 464 and § 483. As in *Starr*, 208 U.S. at 534, where an Indian sold timber constituting 15/16 of the value of the land, we would render the statutory restraint on alienation here essentially meaningless if Williams could transfer the right to excavate a priceless fossil derived from otherwise nondescript land without the Secretary's permission. Because he did not seek the Secretary's approval, we hold that Williams' attempted sale to Black Hills is void and that the United States holds Sue in trust for Williams pursuant to the trust patent.

The court next addressed Black Hills's contention that the government's trust duties over Williams's land did not include protection of fossils. Black Hills relied on *United States v. Mitchell*, presented and discussed in Ch. 4, Sec. A.5.b. The court rejected this argument, noting that the fiduciary duties of the government to beneficial owners of allotted lands are a separate matter from the ability of beneficial owners to alienate trust lands. Moreover, alienation of a fossil that is part of the land is a central concern of the General Allotment Act, whose purpose was to prevent alienation of trust land.

Black Hills next argued that holding Williams's sale invalid was bad policy because Williams was competent to sell the fossil and restrictions on alienation defeat Congress's policies favoring self-determination. The court responded:

> These points are matters of policy for Congress to consider, not federal courts. The current statutory scheme reflects Congress's desire to protect beneficial owners of Indian trust land like Williams regarding disposition of interests in such land. *See* 25 U.S.C. §§ 348, 464, 483; *see also Tooahnippah v. Hickel*, 397 U.S. 598, 609, 90 S. Ct. 1316, 25 L. Ed. 2d 600 (1970)

(explaining that the GAA's legislative history "reflects the concern of the Government to protect Indians from improvident acts or exploitation by others"). Congress may very well determine that the historic practice of shielding beneficial owners from their own improvident decisions, unscrupulous offerors, and whatever other evils the enacting Congresses contemplated decades ago is no longer wise. Until it does, however, we are bound to apply the statutes and regulations forbidding such owners from alienating trust land without the Secretary's approval.

In conclusion, the court noted that "although it is unfortunate that Black Hills spent a great deal of time and resources adding value to a fossil it does not own," it should have been on notice of the federal government's interest in Sue because the fossil was embedded in land located within the boundaries of the Cheyenne River Sioux Indian Reservation. Accordingly, the court ruled in favor of the United States as trustee for Williams, the allottee. For a discussion of tribal understandings of fossils, see, Allison M. Dussias, *Science, Sovereignty, and the Sacred Text: Paleontological Resources and Native American Rights*, 55 MD. L. REV. 84, 158 (1996) (drawing together examples of ways in which Native cultures, and especially Sioux culture, have extended the sacred nature of land to stones and fossils).

NOTES ON ALLOTTED LANDS

1. **Ongoing Consequences of Allotment:** The history of the allotment policy has been treated elsewhere in this book. *See* Ch. 1, Sec. B.2.f. Although that policy has been repudiated, the problems of Indian land tenure caused by allotment remain. Allotment issues are complex and form a separate and specialized body of jurisprudence important to the field of Indian law beyond the scope of this book and its focus on the tribe. What follows is, thus, a brief summary of some of the ways the allotment policy continues to affect Indian tribes today. *See generally* NELL JESSUP NEWTON ET AL., COHEN'S HANDBOOK OF FEDERAL INDIAN LAW § 16.03 (2012 ed.); Judith Royster, *The Legacy of Allotment*, 27 ARIZ. ST. L.J. 1 (1995).

The most important effect of the policy was the great loss of Indian land. During the allotment era the Indian land base shrank by nearly two-thirds, from 138 million acres held in trust for Indian tribes in 1887 to 48 million acres in 1934, when the Indian Reorganization Act withdrew the authority to allot Indian lands in severalty. 25 U.S.C. § 461. The legal processes by which land was transferred from Indian to non-Indian hands varied. First, the allotment policy and the implementing agreements specifically envisioned the ceding and subsequent sale to non-Indian settlers of "surplus" land, not needed for limited-acreage allotments to tribal members. Second, upon the expiration of the 25-year restrictions against alienation, or the shortening of that period by the proper issuance of a certificate of competency to an allottee, sale of the land by the individual Indian holder was authorized. Significant land sales, including evidence of land frauds, occurred through the second method.

The Indian Reorganization Act of 1934 ended this second method of land loss. For tribes that approved the IRA, the law indefinitely extended the trust periods for allotted lands as to which the twenty-five-year period had not expired. 25 U.S.C. § 462. Executive Orders extended other unexpired trust periods. 25 C.F.R. appendix. Nevertheless, Congress did not completely end the practice of issuing patents in fee. In 1948, Congress authorized the Secretary of the Interior to remove the restraints on allotted land, issue patents in fee, and approve conveyances upon application of the Indian owners. 25 U.S.C. § 483. *See Sampson v. Andrus*, 483 F. Supp. 240 (D.S.D. 1980) (section 483 permits Secretary to partition land upon request by one of two owners); *see also* 25 U.S.C. §§ 404, 405.

A third method of land loss continues today. Some land has been removed from restricted trust status by its descent and distribution to non-Indian legatees or heirs. The individualization of Indian land title brought about by the allotment policy required some procedures for the descent and distribution of Indian property upon the death of the allottee. Thus, 25 U.S.C. § 348 authorized the issuance of the patent to the allottee's "heirs" according to the laws of the state or territory where such land is located, and the Secretary of the Interior was further authorized under 25 U.S.C. § 373 to approve Indian wills for the descent and distribution of property of the allottee. To enforce these provisions, the Department of the Interior has become a land records office for individual claims to allotted land. Furthermore, the United States has set up an administrative probate system, independent of the probate systems of the states, for the administration of the estates of Indians holding restricted trust property. *See, e.g., Tooahnippah v. Hickel*, 397 U.S. 598 (1970) (Secretary of the Interior does not have unlimited discretion under 25 U.S.C. § 373 "to revoke or rewrite a will that reflects a rational testamentary scheme"). Provisions for the administrative probate of the estates of allottees holding restricted trust lands are found at 25 U.S.C. §§ 371–380.

The land tenure of allotted Indian lands differs from tribal land tenure in a number of other ways that can result in present-day land loss. For example, the holders of allotted lands may execute a mortgage or deed of trust to such lands and such lands are thereafter subject to foreclosure or sale under the mortgage or deed of trust in the manner provided by state law, 25 U.S.C. § 483a. The mortgagee may have to foreclose in tribal court, however. *See Northwest South Dakota Prod. Credit Ass'n v. Smith*, 784 F.2d 323 (8th Cir. 1986). In addition, 25 U.S.C. § 357 authorizes states to condemn allotted lands for any public purpose, but requires the state to pay compensation to the allottee. Such a condemnation action, however, must be prosecuted in federal court and the United States is an indispensable party to any such proceeding. *Minnesota v. United States*, 305 U.S. 382 (1939). Moreover, the state may not simply seize the land even if inverse condemnation is permissible under state law, but must invoke formal condemnation procedures. *United States v. Clarke*, 445 U.S. 253 (1980).

In sum, loss of allotted land continues today, although not nearly on the same scale as during the allotment era. Over the past 20 years, allottees have begun to make claims for the return of allotted land lost through defective or invalid transfers of allotted Indian land. For background and description of these claims, see Edward Michael Peterson Jr., *That So-Called Warranty Deed: Clouded Land Titles on the White Earth Indian Reservation in Minnesota*, 59 N.D. L. REV. 159 (1983) (over 900 individual claims involving 90,000 acres); LeAnn Larson LaFave, *South Dakota's Forced Fee Indian Land Claims: Will Landowners Be Liable for Government's Wrongdoing?*, 30 S.D. L. REV. 59 (1984) (estimate of 9,500 forced fee claims affecting 1.5 to 2 million acres in western U.S.). Claims against the United States, however, are governed by the applicable federal statute of limitations. *See*

United States v. Mottaz, 476 U.S. 834 (1986) (twelve-year statute of limitations of Quiet Title Act, the exclusive means to challenge U.S. title, bars the claim). Concluding that the federal statute of limitations bars the forced fee claims, courts have also dismissed suits against states, counties, and individual parties, ruling that the U.S. was an indispensable party. *See, e.g., Nichols v. Rysavy*, 809 F.2d 1317 (8th Cir. 1987); *Manypenny v. United States*, 125 F.R.D. 497 (D. Minn. 1989). In 1985, Congress enacted the White Earth Reservation Land Settlement Act to extinguish the forced fee claims on the White Earth Reservation and provide for a mechanism to obtain compensation in the amount of fair market value plus 5% interest. The law was upheld in *Littlewolf v. Lujan*, 877 F.2d 1058 (D.C. Cir. 1989) (even if law a taking, it provides a reasonable mechanism to obtain just compensation). Responses to the serious problem of fractionated allotments are addressed below.

In addition to individualizing Indian land tenure, the allotment policy also had other long-term effects on Indian reservations. Allotment opened Indian reservation enclaves to non-Indian settlement. Thus, it impaired the possibility of a purely geographically based concept of tribal sovereignty by interspersing non-Indian and Indian ownership, often in a checkerboard pattern. This result has given rise to many of the jurisdictional issues already discussed above in Chapters 3 and 4. For further discussion of the allotment policy and its history, see JANET A. McDONNELL, THE DISPOSSESSION OF THE AMERICAN INDIAN (1991); KIRKE KICKINGBIRD & KAREN DUCHENEAUX, ONE HUNDRED MILLION ACRES (1972); D. S. Otis, *History of the Allotment Policy*, in Readjustment of Indian Affairs, Hearings on H.R. 7902 Before the Committee on Indian Affairs, 73d Cong., 2d Sess., pt. 9, at 428 et seq. (1934).

2. **Confiscation of Allotments:** Do allottees have recognized title in the *Tee-Hit-Ton* sense? Does the answer to that question turn on whether the land from which allotments originally were carved was held by the tribe under recognized title? Does it turn on specific language in the allotment statute, agreement, or patent? In *Choate v. Trapp*, 224 U.S. 665 (1912), the Court held that allottees had a vested property right in the tax immunity that Congress had established for their lands, and that any statutory abrogation of that immunity would trigger a right to just compensation. The Court stressed the fact that allottees had consented to give up their claims to tribal property in exchange for their allotments, and used the Indian law canons to interpret the statutes as creating private property rights "vested in the individual Indian by prior laws and contracts." In *Hollowbreast*, the allotment statute of 1926 was held not to vest property rights in the allottees to subsurface minerals despite what seemed like a straightforward grant in the statute. What happened to the Indian law canons of construction in that case? Was it significant that the coal reserves on the affected lands were conservatively estimated at that time to have a value of more than two billion dollars? Was the Court taking into account the change in policy regarding allotment reflected in the Indian Reorganization Act of 1934?

3. **Individual vs. Tribal Interests in Allotments:** Both *Hollowbreast* and *Black Hills* involve allotments, on the Northern Cheyenne and Cheyenne River Sioux Reservations respectively. In the former case, the Court holds that the allotment act did not vest the allottees with subsurface mineral rights despite relatively straightforward language stating that "at the expiration of 50 years . . . the coal or other minerals . . . of said allotments shall become the property of the

respected allottees or their heirs. . . ." In the latter case, the Eighth Circuit does not consider that the fossils might belong to the Tribe rather than to the individual allottee. What is the difference? The answer may be found in a 1954 statute that confirmed to certain Cheyenne River allottees all timber, mineral, water, and other rights that had been conveyed to the Tribe under a land consolidation program established by the Department of the Interior following the Indian Reorganization Act of 1934. *See* Patrick K. Duffy & Lois A. Lofgren, *Jurassic Farce: A Critical Analysis of the Government's Seizure of "Sue [TM]," a Sixty-Five-Million-Year-Old Tyrannosaurus Rex Fossil*, 39 S.D. L. REV. 478, 509–10 (1994) (written by attorneys for the geologist party).

4. Difficulties in Determining Jurisdiction and Land Status of Allotment and Former Allotment Lands Outside the Reservation: While federal and tribal courts have exclusive jurisdiction over allotted lands, determinations about land status and corresponding jurisdictional questions regarding formerly allotted lands outside of reservation borders are often complicated. The patchwork nature of allotment lands; unique and varied agreements and legislation applied to different tribes, transfer of land parcels through the generations, as well as the previously discussed issues resulting from fractionated inheritance, and individualization of allotment land all contribute to potential confusion over which land remains allotted land and is therefore under tribal jurisdiction. Due to these issues, such lands are arguably more vulnerable to jurisdictional challenges by states than lands within the interior bounds of an established reservation, because their status as Indian lands may not be immediately apparent.

In *Magnan v. Trammell*, 719 F.3d 1159 (10th Cir. 2013), the Tenth Circuit granted a habeas petition of an inmate on death row in Oklahoma after determining that his crime had occurred in Indian country, not on state land. The parcel of land in question had been allotted to a member of the Seminole Nation in the early nineteenth century. The court held that even though a 1947 statute authorized the removal of federal restrictions on the inherited allotment land, the Secretary of the Interior had never approved their removal, as was required by statute.

In *Oklahoma Dep't of Environmental Quality v. EPA*, 740 F.3d 185 (D.C. Cir. 2014), the court held that under the Clean Air Act, the State of Oklahoma had regulatory jurisdiction over allotment land outside the boundaries of Indian reservations until either the Environmental Protection Agency or a tribe demonstrated that the tribe held jurisdiction over the land, due to the Act's statutory distinction between reservation and allotment land. Recall that in Oklahoma, the General Allotment Act did not apply — a conglomeration of agreements and legislation extended varied allotment policies to the 38 tribes as a precondition for statehood. Congress later terminated and diminished many reservations in the state, leaving some tribal lands outside reservation boundaries. This history makes Oklahoma tribes vulnerable to impositions of jurisdictional authority by the state government. Despite the fact that the majority of the land in the state is Indian country — as the cases above demonstrate, whether or not individual parcels of land are subject to tribal or state jurisdiction may be determined in a piecemeal fashion.

HODEL v. IRVING
United States Supreme Court
481 U.S. 704 (1987)

JUSTICE O'CONNOR delivered the opinion of the Court.

The question presented is whether the original version of the "escheat" provision of the Indian Land Consolidation Act of 1983, Pub. L. 97-459, Tit. II, 96 Stat. 2519, effected a "taking" of appellees' decedents' property without just compensation.

I

Towards the end of the nineteenth century, Congress enacted a series of land Acts which divided the communal reservations of Indian tribes into individual allotments for Indians and unallotted lands for non-Indian settlement. This legislation seems to have been in part animated by a desire to force Indians to abandon their nomadic ways in order to "speed the Indians' assimilation into American society," *Solem v. Bartlett*, 465 U.S. 463, 466 (1984), and in part a result of pressure to free new lands for further white settlement. Two years after the enactment of the General Allotment Act of 1887, ch. 119, 24 Stat. 388, Congress adopted a specific statute authorizing the division of the Great Reservation of the Sioux Nation into separate reservations and the allotment of specific tracts of reservation land to individual Indians, conditioned on the consent of three-fourths of the adult male Sioux. Act of Mar. 2, 1889, ch. 405, 25 Stat. 888. Under the Act, each male Sioux head of household took 320 acres of land and most other individuals 160 acres. In order to protect the allottees from the improvident disposition of their lands to white settlers, the Sioux allotment statute provided that the allotted lands were to be held in trust by the United States. Until 1910 the lands of deceased allottees passed to their heirs "according to the laws of the State or Territory" where the land was located, and after 1910, allottees were permitted to dispose of their interests by will in accordance with regulations promulgated by the Secretary of the Interior. 25 U.S.C. § 373. Those regulations generally served to protect Indian ownership of the allotted lands.

The policy of allotment of Indian lands quickly proved disastrous for the Indians. Cash generated by land sales to whites was quickly dissipated and the Indians, rather than farming the land themselves, evolved into petty landlords, leasing their allotted lands to white ranchers and farmers and living off the meager rentals. The failure of the allotment program became even clearer as successive generations came to hold the allotted lands. 40-, 80-, and 160-acre parcels became splintered into multiple undivided interests in land, with some parcels having hundreds and many parcels having dozens of owners. Because the land was held in trust and often could not be alienated or partitioned the fractionation problem grew and grew over time.

A 1928 report commissioned by the Congress found the situation administratively unworkable and economically wasteful. LEWIS MERIAM, INSTITUTE FOR GOVERNMENT RESEARCH, THE PROBLEM OF INDIAN ADMINISTRATION 40–41. Good, potentially productive, land was allowed to lie fallow, amidst great poverty, because of the difficulties of managing property held in this manner. In discussing the Indian

Reorganization Act of 1934, Representative Howard said:

> It is in the case of the inherited allotments, however, that the administrative costs become incredible . . . . On allotted reservations, numerous cases exist where the shares of each individual heir from lease money may be 1 cent a month. Or one heir may own minute fractional shares in 30 or 40 different allotments. The cost of leasing, bookkeeping, and distributing the proceeds in many cases far exceeds the total income. The Indians and the Indian Service personnel are thus trapped in a meaningless system of minute partition in which all thought of the possible use of land to satisfy human needs is lost in a mathematical haze of bookkeeping. 78 Cong. Rec. 11728 (1934) (remarks of Rep. Howard).

In 1934, in response to arguments such as these, the Congress acknowledged the failure of its policy and ended further allotment of Indian lands [by enacting the Indian Reorganization Act].

But the end of future allotment by itself could not prevent the further compounding of the existing problem caused by the passage of time. Ownership continued to fragment as succeeding generations came to hold the property, since, in the order of things, each property owner was apt to have more than one heir. In 1960, both the House and the Senate undertook comprehensive studies of the problem. These studies indicated that one-half of the approximately 12 million acres of allotted trust lands were held in fractionated ownership, with over three million acres held by more than six heirs to a parcel. Further hearings were held in 1966, but not until the Indian Land Consolidation Act of 1983 did the Congress take action to ameliorate the problem of fractionated ownership of Indian lands.

Section 207 of the Indian Land Consolidation Act — the escheat provision at issue in this case — provided:

> No undivided fractional interest in any tract of trust or restricted land within a tribe's reservation or otherwise subjected to a tribe's jurisdiction shall descendent [sic] by intestacy or devise but shall escheat to that tribe if such interest represents 2 per centum or less of the total acreage in such tract and has earned to its owner less than $100 in the preceding year before it is due to escheat.

Congress made no provision for the payment of compensation to the owners of the interests covered by § 207. The statute was signed into law on January 12, 1983 and became effective immediately.

The three appellees — Mary Irving, Patrick Pumpkin Seed, and Eileen Bisonette — are enrolled members of the Oglala Sioux Tribe. They are, or represent, heirs or devisees of members of the Tribe who died in March, April, and June 1983. Eileen Bisonette's decedent, Mary Poor Bear-Little Hoop Cross, purported to will all her property, including property subject to § 207, to her five minor children in whose name Bisonette claims the property. Chester Irving, Charles Leroy Pumpkin Seed, and Edgar Pumpkin Seed all died intestate. At the time of their deaths, the four decedents owned 41 fractional interests subject to the provisions of § 207. The Irving estate lost two interests whose value together was approximately $100; the Bureau of Indian Affairs placed total values of approximately $2,700 on the 26 escheatable interests in the Cross estate and $1,816 on the 13 escheatable interests in the Pumpkin Seed estates. But for § 207, this property would have passed, in the ordinary course, to appellees or those they represent.

Appellees filed suit in the United States District Court for the District of South Dakota, claiming that § 207 resulted in a taking of property without just compensation in violation of the fifth amendment. The District Court concluded that the statute was constitutional. It held that appellees had no vested interest in the property of the decedents prior to their deaths and that Congress had plenary authority to abolish the power of testamentary disposition of Indian property and to alter the rules of intestate succession.

The Court of Appeals for the Eighth Circuit reversed. Although it agreed that the appellees had no vested rights in the decedents' property, it concluded that their decedents had a right, derived from the original Sioux Allotment Statute, to control disposition of their property at death. The Court of Appeals held that the appellees had standing to invoke that right and that the taking of that right without compensation to decedents' estates violated the fifth amendment.

III

The Congress, acting pursuant to its broad authority to regulate the descent and devise of Indian trust lands, *Jeferson v. Fink*, 247 U.S. 288, 294 (1918), enacted § 207 as a means of ameliorating, over time, the problem of extreme fractionation of certain Indian lands. By forbidding the passing on at death of small, undivided interests in Indian lands, Congress hoped that future generations of Indians would be able to make more productive use of the Indians' ancestral lands. We agree with the Government that encouraging the consolidation of Indian lands is a public purpose of high order. The fractionation problem on Indian reservations is extraordinary and may call for dramatic action to encourage consolidation. The Sisseton-Wahpeton Sioux Tribe, appearing as amicus curiae in support of the United States, is a quintessential victim of fractionation. Forty-acre tracts on the Sisseton-Wahpeton Lake Traverse reservation, leasing for about $1,000 annually, are commonly subdivided into hundreds of undivided interests, many of which generate only pennies a year in rent. The average tract has 196 owners and the average owner undivided interests in fourteen tracts. The administrative headache this represents can be fathomed by examining Tract 1305, [a 43-acre tract valued at $8,000, which] has 439 owners, one-third of whom receive less than $.05 in annual rent and two-thirds of whom receive less than $1. The largest interest holder receives $82.85 annually. The common denominator used to compute fractional interests in the property is 3,394,923,840,000.

The smallest heir receives $.01 every 177 years. If the tract were sold (assuming the 439 owners could agree) for its estimated $8,000 value, he would be entitled to $.000418. The administrative costs of handling this tract are estimated by the Bureau of Indian Affairs at $17,560 annually. This Court has held that the Government has considerable latitude in regulating property rights in ways that may adversely affect the owners. *See Keystone Bituminous Coal Assn. v. DeBenedictis*, 480 U.S. [470] (1987); *Penn Central Transportation Co. v. New York City*, 438 U.S. 104, 125–127 (1978); *Goldblatt v. Hempstead*, 369 U.S. 590, 592–593 (1962). The framework for examining the question of whether a regulation of property amounts to a taking requiring just compensation is firmly established and has been regularly and recently reaffirmed. As the Chief Justice has written:

> "[T]his Court has generally 'been unable to develop any "set formula" for determining when "justice and fairness" require that economic injuries caused by public action be compensated by the government, rather than remain disproportionately concentrated on a few persons.' *Penn Central Transportation Co. v. New York City*, 438 U.S.], at 124. Rather, it has examined the 'taking' question by engaging in essentially ad hoc, factual inquiries that have identified several factors — such as the economic impact of the regulation, its interference with reasonable investment backed expectations, and the character of the governmental action — that have particular significance. *Ibid." Kaiser Aetna v. United States*, [444 U.S. 164,] at 175 [1979].

There is no question that the relative economic impact of § 207 upon the owners of these property rights can be substantial. Section 207 provides for the escheat of small undivided property interests that are unproductive during the year preceding the owner's death. Even if we accept the Government's assertion that the income generated by such parcels may be properly thought of as de minimis, their value may not be. While the Irving estate lost two interests whose value together was only approximately $100, the Bureau of Indian Affairs placed total values of approximately $2,700 and $1,816 on the escheatable interests in the Cross and Pumpkin Seed estates. These are not trivial sums. There are suggestions in the legislative history regarding the 1984 amendments to § 207 that the failure to "look back" more than one year at the income generated by the property had caused the escheat of potentially valuable timber and mineral interests. Of course, the whole of appellees' decedents' property interests were not taken by § 207. Appellees' decedents retained full beneficial use of the property during their lifetimes as well as the right to convey it inter vivos. There is no question, however, that the right to pass on valuable property to one's heirs is itself a valuable right. Depending on the age of the owner, much or most of the value of the parcel may inhere in this "remainder" interest.

The extent to which any of the appellees' decedents had "investment-backed expectations" in passing on the property is dubious. Though it is conceivable that some of these interests were purchased with the expectation that the owners might pass on the remainder to their heirs at death, the property has been held in trust for the Indians for 100 years and is overwhelmingly acquired by gift, descent, or devise. Because of the highly fractionated ownership, the property is generally held for lease rather than improved and used by the owners. None of the appellees here can point to any specific investment-backed expectations beyond the fact that their ancestors agreed to accept allotment only after ceding to the United States large parts of the original Great Sioux Reservation.

Also weighing weakly in favor of the statute is the fact that there is something of an "average reciprocity of advantage," *Pennsylvania Coal Co. v. Mahon*, 260 U.S. 393, 415 (1922), to the extent that owners of escheatable interests maintain a nexus to the Tribe. Consolidation of Indian lands in the Tribe benefits the members of the

Tribe. All members do not own escheatable interests, nor do all owners belong to the Tribe. Nevertheless, there is substantial overlap between the two groups. The owners of escheatable interests often benefit from the escheat of others' fractional interests. Moreover, the whole benefit gained is greater than the sum of the burdens imposed since consolidated lands are more productive than fractionated lands.

If we were to stop our analysis at this point, we might well find § 207 constitutional. But the character of the Government regulation here is extraordinary. In *Kaiser Aetna v. United States*, 444 U.S., at 176, we emphasized that the regulation destroyed "one of the most essential sticks in the bundle of rights that are commonly characterized as property — the right to exclude others." Similarly, the regulation here amounts to virtually the abrogation of the right to pass on a certain type of property — the small undivided interest — to one's heirs. In one form or another, the right to pass on property — to one's family in particular — has been part of the Anglo-American legal system since feudal times. The fact that it may be possible for the owners of these interests to effectively control disposition upon death through complex inter vivos transactions such as revocable trusts, is simply not an adequate substitute for the rights taken, given the nature of the property. Even the United States concedes that total abrogation of the right to pass property is unprecedented and likely unconstitutional. Moreover, this statute effectively abolishes both descent and devise of these property interests even when the passing of the property to the heir might result in consolidation of property — as for instance when the heir already owns another undivided interest in the property. Compare 25 U.S.C. § 2206(b) (1982 ed., Supp. III). Since the escheatable interests are not, as the United States argues, necessarily de minimis, nor, as it also argues, does the availability of inter vivos transfer obviate the need for descent and devise, a total abrogation of these rights cannot be upheld. *But cf. Andrus v. Allard*, 444 U.S. 51 (1979) (upholding abrogation of the right to sell endangered eagles' parts as necessary to environmental protection regulatory scheme).

In holding that complete abolition of both the descent and devise of a particular class of property may be a taking, we reaffirm the continuing vitality of the long line of cases recognizing the States's, and where appropriate, the United States's, broad authority to adjust the rules governing the descent and devise of property without implicating the guarantees of the Just Compensation Clause. The difference in this case is the fact that both descent and devise are completely abolished; indeed they are abolished even in circumstances when the governmental purpose sought to be advanced, consolidation of ownership of Indian lands, does not conflict with the further descent of the property.

There is little doubt that the extreme fractionation of Indian lands is a serious public problem. It may well be appropriate for the United States to ameliorate fractionation by means of regulating the descent and devise of Indian lands. Surely it is permissible for the United States to prevent the owners of such interests from further subdividing them among future heirs on pain of escheat. It may be appropriate to minimize further compounding of the problem by abolishing the descent of such interests by rules of intestacy, thereby forcing the owners to formally designate an heir to prevent escheat to the Tribe. What is certainly not appropriate is to take the extraordinary step of abolishing both descent and devise of these property interests even when the passing of the property to the heir might result in consolidation of property. Accordingly, we find that this regulation, in the words of Justice Holmes, "goes too far." *Pennsylvania Coal Co. v. Mahon*, 260 U.S., at 415.

Affirmed.

JUSTICE BRENNAN, with whom JUSTICE MARSHALL and JUSTICE BLACKMUN join, concurring.

I find nothing in today's opinion that would limit *Andrus v. Allard*, 444 U.S. 51 (1979) to its facts. Indeed, largely for reasons discussed by the Court of Appeals, I am of the view that the unique negotiations giving rise to the property rights and expectations at issue here make this case the unusual one. Accordingly, I join the opinion of the Court.

JUSTICE SCALIA, with whom THE CHIEF JUSTICE and JUSTICE POWELL join, concurring.

I join the opinion of the Court. I write separately to note that in my view the present statute, insofar as concerns the balance between rights taken and rights left untouched, is indistinguishable from the statute that was at issue in *Andrus v. Allard*, 444 U.S. 51 (1979). Because that comparison is determinative of whether there has been a taking, in finding a taking today our decision effectively limits *Allard* to its facts.

JUSTICE STEVENS, with whom JUSTICE WHITE joins, concurring in the judgment.

The Government has a legitimate interest in eliminating Indians' fractional holdings of real property. Legislating in pursuit of this interest, the Government might constitutionally have consolidated the fractional land interests affected by § 207 of the Indian Land Consolidation Act of 1983, in three ways: It might have purchased them; it might have condemned them for a public purpose and paid just compensation to their owners; or it might have left them untouched while conditioning their descent by intestacy or devise upon their consolidation by voluntary conveyances within a reasonable period of time. . . .

Since Congress plainly did not authorize either purchase or condemnation and the payment of just compensation, the statute is valid only if Congress, in § 207, authorized the third alternative. In my opinion, therefore, the principal question in this case is whether § 207 represents a lawful exercise of the sovereign's prerogative to condition the retention of fee simple or other ownership interests upon the performance of a modest statutory duty within a reasonable period of time.

III

[T]he Secretary contends that § 207 falls within the permissible boundaries of legislation that may operate to limit or extinguish property rights. The Secretary places great emphasis on the minimal value of the property interests affected by § 207, the legitimacy of the governmental purpose in consolidating such interests, and the fact that the tribe, rather than the United States, is the beneficiary of the so-called "escheat." These points, considered in turn and as a whole, provide absolutely no basis for reversing the judgment of the Court of Appeals.

The value of a property interest does not provide a yardstick for measuring "the scope of the dual constitutional guarantees that there be no taking of property without just compensation, and no deprivation of property without the due process of law." *Texaco, Inc. v. Short*, 454 U.S. 516, 540–541 (1982) (BRENNAN, J., dissenting). The sovereign has no license to take private property without paying for it and without providing its owner with any opportunity to avoid or mitigate the consequences of the deprivation simply because the property is relatively inexpensive. *Loretto v. Teleprompter Manhattan CATV Corp.*, 458 U.S. 419, 436–437 and 438, n.16 (1982). The Fifth Amendment draws no distinction between grand larceny and petty larceny.

The legitimacy of the governmental purposes served by § 207 demonstrates that the statute is not arbitrary, *see Delaware Tribal Business Committee v. Weeks*, 430 U.S. 73 (1977), and that the alleged "taking" is for a valid "public use" within the meaning of the fifth amendment. Those facts, however, do not excuse or mitigate whatever obligation to pay just compensation arises when an otherwise constitutional enactment effects a taking of property. Nor does it lessen the importance of giving a property owner fair notice of a major change in the rules governing the disposition of his property.

The fact that § 207 provides for an "escheat" to the tribe rather than to the United States does not change the unwarned impact of the statute on an individual Indian who wants to leave his property to his children. The statute takes the disposition of decedent's fractional land interests out of the control of the decedent's will or the laws of intestate succession; whether the United States or the Tribe retains the property, the landowner's loss is the same. The designation of the Tribe as beneficiary is an essential feature, however, in two respects. Since the Tribe is the beneficiary, its own interests conflict with its duty to bring the workings of the statute to the attention of the property owner. In addition, the designation of the Tribe as beneficiary highlights the inappropriateness of the majority's takings analysis. The use of the term "escheat" in § 207 differs in a substantial way from the more familiar uses of that term. At common law the property of a person who died intestate and without lawful heirs would escheat to the sovereign; thus the doctrine provided a mechanism for determining ownership of what otherwise would have remained abandoned property. In contrast, under § 207 the statutory escheat supersedes the rights of claimants who would otherwise inherit the property; it allocates property between two contending parties.

Section 207 differs from more conventional escheats in another important way. It contains no provisions assuring that the property owner was given a fair opportunity to make suitable arrangements to avoid the operation of the statute. Legislation authorizing the escheat of unclaimed property, such as real estate, bank accounts, and other earmarked funds, typically provides as a condition precedent to the escheat an appropriate lapse of time and the provision of adequate notice to make sure that the property may fairly be treated as abandoned. Similarly, interpleader proceedings in District Court provide procedural safeguards, including an opportunity to appear, for those whose rights will be affected by the judgment.

See 28 U.S.C. § 1335; Federal Rule of Civil Procedure 22. The statute before us, in contrast, contained no such mechanism, apparently relying on the possibility that appellees' decedents would simply learn about the statute's consequences one way or another.

While § 207 therefore does not qualify as an escheat of the kind recognized at common law, it might be regarded as a statute imposing a duty on the owner of highly fractionated interests in allotted lands to consolidate his interests with those of other owners of similar interests. The method of enforcing such a duty is to treat its nonperformance during the owner's lifetime as an abandonment of the fractional interests. This release of dominion over the property might justify its escheat to the use of the sovereign.

[A] statute providing for the lapse, escheat, or abandonment of private property cannot impose conditions on continued ownership that are unreasonable, either because they cost too much or because the statute does not allow property owners a reasonable opportunity to perform them and thereby to avoid the loss of their property. . . .

The Due Process Clause of the fifth amendment thus applies to § 207's determination of which acts and omissions may validly constitute an abandonment, just as the Takings Clause applies to whether the statutory escheat of property must be accompanied by the payment of just compensation. It follows, I believe, that § 207 deprived decedents of due process of law by failing to provide an adequate "grace period" in which they could arrange for the consolidation of fractional interests in order to avoid abandonment. Because the statutory presumption of abandonment is invalid under the precise facts of this case, I do not reach the ground relied upon by the Court of Appeals — that the resulting escheat of abandoned property would effect a taking of private property for public use without just compensation.

[C]itizens "are presumptively charged with knowledge of the law," [but] that presumption may not apply when "the statute does not allow a sufficient 'grace period' to provide the persons affected by a change in the law with an adequate opportunity to become familiar with their obligations under it." [*Atkins v. Parker*, 472 U.S. 115, 130 (1985) (citing *Texaco, Inc.*, 454 U.S., at 532).] Unlike the food stamp recipients in *Parker*, who received a grace period of over 90 days and individual notice of the substance of the new law, [*Id.*] at 130–131, the Indians affected by § 207 did not receive a reasonable grace period. Nothing in the record suggests that appellees' decedents received an adequate opportunity to put their affairs in order.

The conclusion that Congress has failed to provide appellees' decedents with a reasonable opportunity for compliance implies no rejection of Congress's plenary authority over the affairs and the property of Indians. The Constitution vests Congress with plenary power "to deal with the special problems of Indians." [*Morton v. Mancari*, 417 U.S. 535, 551 (1974).] As the Secretary acknowledges, however, the Government's plenary power over the property of Indians "is subject to constitutional limitations." The Due Process Clause of the fifth amendment required Congress to afford reasonable notice and opportunity for compliance to Indians that § 207 would prevent fractional interests in land from descending by intestate or testate succession. In omitting any opportunity at all for owners of fractional interests to order their affairs in light of § 207, Congress has failed to afford the affected Indians the due process of law required by the fifth amendment.

Accordingly, I concur in the judgment.

———————

Babbitt v. Youpee, 519 U.S. 234 (1997): This case takes up the question of the constitutionality of the 1984 amendments to the Indian Land Consolidation Act (ILCA), a question left unresolved in *Hodel v. Irving*. While *Irving* was still pending in the Eighth Circuit, Congress amended 25 U.S.C. § 207 in three ways. First, under the amended version, fractionated allotments return to the tribe if they fail to earn $100 in any one of the five years following the decedent's death (as opposed to one year before the decedent's death); and if the interest failed to earn $100 in any of the five years preceding the decedent's death a rebuttable presumption arises that it was incapable of earning that much in any one of the five years following the decedent's death. Second, devise of the designated fractionated interests is permitted to anyone else holding such an interest in the same parcel (as opposed to a total ban on devise). Third, tribes are allowed for the first time to override the provisions of section 207 by adopting their own probate codes governing the disposition of fractionated interests, subject to approval by the Secretary of the Interior.

Heirs of the holder of a fractional allotment that fell under the terms of amended section 207 sued the Secretary of the Interior for a taking of their property. The Ninth Circuit found a Fifth Amendment taking. In an opinion by JUSTICE GINSBURG, the Supreme Court agreed that the amendments were insufficient to cure the constitutional difficulties identified in *Hodel v. Irving*. The Court stated:

> [Although amended § 207 permits a five-year window rather than a one-year window to assess the income-generating capacity of the interest, it] still trains on income generated from the land, not on the value of the parcel. The Court observed in *Irving* that "even if . . . the income generated by such parcels may be properly thought of as de minimis," the value of the land may not fit that description. 481 U.S. at 714. The parcels at issue in *Irving* were valued by the Bureau of Indian Affairs at $2,700 and $1,816, amounts we found "not trivial." *Ibid.* The value of the disputed parcels in this case is not of a different order; as the Ninth Circuit reported, the value of decedent Youpee's fractional interests was $1,239. 67 F.3d [194] at 199. In short, the economic impact of amended § 207 might still be palpable.

> Even if the economic impact of amended § 207 is not significantly less than the impact of the original provision, the United States correctly comprehends that *Irving* rested primarily on the "extraordinary" character of the governmental regulation [in virtually abrogating the right to devise property]. . . . As the United States construes *Irving*, Congress cured the fatal infirmity in § 207 when it revised the section to allow transmission of fractional interests to successors who already own an interest in the allotment.

Congress' creation of an ever-so-slight class of individuals equipped to receive fractional interests by devise does not suffice, under a fair reading of *Irving*, to rehabilitate the measure. Amended § 207 severely restricts the right of an individual to direct the descent of his property. Allowing a decedent to leave an interest only to a current owner in the same parcel shrinks drastically the universe of possible successors. And, as the Ninth Circuit observed, the "very limited group [of permissible devisees] is unlikely to contain any lineal descendants." 67 F.3d at 199–200. Moreover, amended § 207 continues to restrict devise "even in circumstances when the governmental purpose sought to be advanced, consolidation of ownership of Indian lands, does not conflict with the further descent of the property." *Irving*, 481 U.S. [704] at 718. William Youpee's will, the United States acknowledges, bequeathed each fractional interest to one heir. Giving effect to Youpee's directive, therefore, would not further fractionate Indian land holdings.

The United States also contends that amended § 207 satisfies the Constitution's demand because it does not diminish the owner's right to use or enjoy property during his life-time, and does not affect the right to transfer property at death through non-probate means. These arguments did not persuade us in *Irving* and they are no more persuasive today.

The third alteration made in amended § 207 also fails to bring the provision outside the reach of this Court's holding in *Irving*. Amended § 207 permits tribes to establish their own codes to govern the disposition of fractional interests; if approved by the Secretary of the Interior, these codes would govern in lieu of amended § 207. See 25 U.S.C. § 2206(c). The United States does not rely on this new provision to defend the statute. Nor does it appear that the United States could do so at this time: Tribal codes governing disposition of escheatable interests have apparently not been developed.

For the reasons stated, the judgment of the Court of Appeals for the Ninth Circuit is

Affirmed.

Justice Stevens dissented, reiterating his view that so long as property owners are on notice that they must consolidate interests or dispose of their allotment during their lifetime or risk escheat, Congress can force them to take such action or lose their property.

NOTES ON FRACTIONATED ALLOTMENTS

1. **Assessing *Irving* and *Youpee*:** It seems that although the requirement of compensation to tribes did not restrain the initial allotment process, the requirement of compensation to allottees must burden and inhibit the process of restoring tribal land bases to productive use and to collective pursuits such as tribal enterprises. What is the difference? Recall that under the doctrine of *Lone Wolf v. Hitchcock*, 187 U.S. 553 (1903), presented in Ch. 1, Sec. D.2, the Supreme Court would not even decide whether the forced allotment of tribal lands constituted a "taking" from the tribe in violation of the Fifth Amendment, calling the matter a

"political question" and presuming that the United States had acted in good faith as a trustee. Could you make the case that the forced distribution of tribal lands to individual tribal citizens constitutes a taking of the tribe's property? *See* Joseph William Singer, Lone Wolf, *or How to Take Property by Calling It a "Mere Change in the Form of Investment,"* 38 TULSA L. REV. 37 (2003). Recall also that in *Sioux Nation*, presented in Sec. A.2, this chapter, the Court relaxed the *Lone Wolf* rule sufficiently to allow for judicial review of tribal takings claims, but determined that it must still establish whether the United States has in fact acted in good faith as a trustee before it could find a taking of tribal property. Given the Court's reluctance to act when taking of tribal lands is at stake, why is the Court being so scrupulous about compensating the individual property owners now that Congress wants to repair the harm perpetrated by allotment? Is it a good sign that Indian takings doctrine is becoming normalized — that is, more like takings doctrine in a non-Indian setting? Or is it a bad sign that the Court is constitutionalizing the relationship between a Native nation and its citizens, privileging individual property rights of the allottee over the common interests of the tribe? *See* Rebecca Tsosie, *American Indians and the Politics of Recognition: Soifer on Law, Pluralism, and Group Identity*, 22 LAW & SOCIAL INQUIRY 359, 371 (1997) ("The Court overlooked both the importance of communal land ownership to the tribes and the fact that the owner of a land interest measured in the thousandths is unlikely to be able to make beneficial use of the property. The notion of private property interests, exalted under Anglo-American law, prevailed.").

With one notable exception, Katheleen R. Guzman, *Give or Take an Acre: Property Norms and the Indian Land Consolidation Act*, 85 IOWA L. REV. 595 (2000), property law scholars have not been kind in their evaluation of *Irving* and *Youpee*. The most common critique is that the Court has abandoned a more flexible analysis of the circumstances giving rise to a taking, and created a new and unjustified category of property right — an absolute right to devise even the most economically pointless interest. For critical assessments, see Frank I. Michelman, *Takings, 1987*, 88 COLUM. L. REV. 1600, 1621–25 (1988); Ronald Chester, *Essay: Is the Right to Devise Property Constitutionally Protected? — The Strange Case of* Hodel v. Irving, 24 SW. U. L. REV. 1195, 1197 (1995). In the most sustained analysis of the Indian Land Consolidation Act, Professor Guzman defends the Court's decisions, pointing out the economic and social significance to allottees even of highly fractionated allotments, and noting that several tribes joined in the assault on forced escheat of those interests. She concludes that decisions about escheat should be made within Native nations rather than by Congress, especially since Congress has its own concerns about reducing the cost of administering the proliferating tiny interests. As she puts it, the decisions "preserve . . . a tribe's ability to define its own history and future, rather than forcing it to accept Congress's proffer." Do you agree? Consider the following response by Professor Carole Goldberg:

> Achieving tribal consensus on heavily allotted reservations will require convincing the allottees that it is in their interest as tribal members. The very process of allotment, however, was designed to inculcate in the recipients an ethos that focuses more on their individual interests than on their community connections. If that process was even partly effective,

there will be sources of internal tribal resistance to land consolidation through forced escheat, even of tiny, economically unproductive parcels. The irony is that the source of that resistance will be the very wrongful (and probably unconstitutional) policy of allotment that Congress is attempting to remedy. Indian nations might be able to alleviate some internal concerns about forced escheat through creative land assignment codes and by tempering the onset of the escheat with life estates; but gaining political consensus may still be difficult. At least a federal statute compelling escheat spares tribes such political challenges.

Carole E. Goldberg, *Individual Rights and Tribal Revitalization*, 35 ARIZ. ST. L.J. 889, 933–34 (2003).

2. 2000 and 2004 Amendments to ILCA: In an attempt to address the fractionated heirship problem without running afoul of *Hodel v. Irving* and *Babbitt v. Youpee*, Congress amended ILCA once again in 2000, changing the offending escheat provisions. P.L. 106-462, 114 Stat. 1991 (2000). The scheme was quite complex, and led some allottees to complain that its provisions regarding disposition to non-Indian children actually encouraged removal of allotments from trust status. The 2004 amendments, titled the American Indian Probate Reform Act of 2004, P.L. 108-374 (codified at 25 U.S.C. § 2201 et seq.), address this objection and reorganize ILCA. Key provisions of ILCA as amended in 2004 include, among others: authorization for tribes to purchase "highly fractionated" trust land and interests in allotments that were devised to persons not entitled to take the interest in trust; establishment of a uniform tribal probate code governing both intestate and testamentary dispositions; authorization for tribes to enact probate codes, subject to approval by the Secretary of the Interior, and assistance and funding for estate planning and code development; authorization for certain "eligible purchasers," including tribes, to purchase interests in trust lands at probate from willing sellers, or from unwilling sellers of interests less than 5%; appropriation of significant funds for acquisition by the Secretary of the Interior of trust interests, which may then be sold to Indians already owning interests in the same parcel; and a reduction in the percentage of consents required from owners of interests for leasing of allotments.

The 2004 amendments also encourage tribes to enact their own probate codes, because such codes, once approved by the Secretary of the Interior, supercede ILCA's uniform probate code when the BIA probates individual trust lands. Assuming it passed review with the Secretary of the Interior, would a tribal probate code that prohibited devise of interests in trust allotments to non-Indian lineal descendants violate the Indian Civil Rights Act? Would the Secretary violate the Fifth Amendment in approving such a code? For a proposal regarding a distinct Cherokee property system that would reduce or prevent fractionation problems in that Nation's territory, see Stacy L. Leeds, *The Burning of Blackacre: A Step Toward Reclaiming Tribal Property Law*, 10 KAN. J.L. & PUB. POL'Y 491 (2001). Could a tribal probate code provide for escheat to the tribe that would be unconstitutional if the federal government carried it out? *See* Katheleen R. Guzman, *Give or Take an Acre: Property Norms and the Indian Land Consolidation Act*, 85 IOWA L. REV. 595, 659–61 & n.269 (2000) (suggesting that such a tribal law should be valid).

Apart from their constitutionality, will the 2004 amendments to ILCA effectively reduce fractionation? Does the answer depend on how well informed allottees are about making wills? The Indian Land Working Group, formed in 1991, is an organization of tribes, individual Indians, and interested groups working to reverse the history of fractionation, land loss, and loss of trust status. Education of allottees in the probate process and estate management is an important part of the mission, as well as sponsorship of land acquisition programs. *See* Jack Welliver, *CP 87 and CP 100: Allotment and Fractionation Within the Citizen Potawatomi Nation*, 2 TRIBAL L.J. 2 (2002) (description of the Indian Land Working Group's work). Another non-profit group with a similar mission is the Indian Land Tenure Foundation. According to a 2001 statement of the Indian Land Working Group:

> The future of Indian land tenure depends upon action by tribes and Indian landowners. Indian people's survival depends on land ownership. Tribal societies are tied to their lands through history, culture, religion, and economies. The land is the heart of the people. It must be made whole again for tribal cultures to emerge strong.

3. Fractionated Allotments and Settlement of the *Cobell* litigation: The settlement of the *Cobell* litigation, presented in Ch. 4 sec. A.5.b addressed Indian trust mismanagement claims resulting from the federal government's failure to adequately compensate owners of fractionated interests in Indian land. It allocated 3.4 billion dollars to compensation for fractionated interests, scholarship funds, and a federal program to repurchase fractionated lands and return them to tribal ownership. Claims Resolution Act of 2010, Pub. L. No. 111-291, §101, 124 Stat. 3064 (2010). Review the description of the settlement in Ch. 4. Does the settlement, along with the 2004 amendments to the ILCA, adequately address the problems caused by fractionation of Indian land under allotment policies?

B. CULTURAL RESOURCES

Anglo-American law has traditionally segregated the cultural or religious aspects of land use from the property aspects of land use, as demonstrated by the Sioux Nation's litigation to reclaim the Black Hills, presented in Sec. A.2, this chapter. Furthermore, as Anglo-American law developed a concept of "cultural resources" for purposes of historical preservation or protection of archaeological resources, it has recognized only material resources that have significant historical or archaeological value. *See, e.g.,* National Historic Preservation Act (NHPA), 16 U.S.C. § 470 et seq.; Archaeological Resources Protection Act (ARPA), 16 U.S.C. §§ 470aa–mm. In comparison, Native peoples often define cultural resources more expansively, to include tribal symbols, stories, ceremonies, sacred sites, ceremonial objects, objects of cultural patrimony, and even their own genetic resources. *See* Kristen A. Carpenter, Sonia K. Katyal & Angela R. Riley, *In Defense of Property*, 118 YALE L. J. 1022 (2009). This section focuses on this broader understanding of cultural property, including both tangible and intangible resources. In recent years, Native peoples in the United States have increasingly been able to inform the development of cultural resources laws at the tribal, national, and international levels through incorporation of indigenous and human rights concepts. *See,* Kristen A. Carpenter

& Angela R. Riley, *Indigenous Peoples and the Jurisgenerative Moment in Human Rights*, 102 CAL. L. REV. 173 (2014).

1. Sacred Sites and Religious Freedom

As the preceding materials demonstrate, Native peoples hold deep attachments to their land. Part of that attachment involves ceremonial and spiritual connections to specific sacred sites on the landscape, some of which are still owned by Indian tribes or tribal members and many others of which have passed out of Indian ownership, but often remain under federal or state control. To what extent do the freedom of religion clauses of the First Amendment and their incorporation into and application to the states through the Fourteenth Amendment protect Indian religious freedom and its association with such sacred sites?

In *Wisconsin v. Yoder*, 406 U.S. 205 (1972), the Court dealt with the right of an Amish community, acting on its religiously derived beliefs, to resist generally applicable state compulsory education laws. In somewhat grudging fashion, the Court recognized the right of the Amish community to some zone of immunity in order to fulfill their special beliefs.

> Aided by a history of three centuries as an identifiable religious sect and a long history as a successful and self-sufficient segment of American society, the Amish in this case have convincingly demonstrated the sincerity of their religious beliefs, the interrelationship of belief with their mode of life, the vital role which belief and daily conduct play in the continued survival of Old Order Amish communities and their religious organization, and the hazards presented by the state's enforcement of a statute generally valid as to others. Beyond this, they have carried the even more difficult burden of demonstrating the adequacy of their alternative mode of continuing informal vocational education in terms of precisely those over-all interests that the state advances in support of its program of compulsory high school education. In light of this convincing showing, one which probably few other religious groups or sects could make, and weighing the minimal difference between what the state would require and what the Amish already accept, it was incumbent on the state to show with more particularity how its admittedly strong interest in compulsory education would be adversely affected by granting an exemption to the Amish.

Id. at 235–236. Later Supreme Court cases, many involving Indian religious beliefs, were far less supportive than *Yoder* of special First Amendment legal protections for religious exercise and sacred sites. In an effort to safeguard traditional Indian religious activity, Congress passed the American Indian Religious Freedom Act of 1978, Pub. L. No. 95-341, 92 Stat. 469, codified at 42 U.S.C. § 1996. As originally enacted, this legislation provided in relevant part:

> It shall be the policy of the United States to protect and preserve for American Indians their inherent right of freedom to believe, express, and exercise the traditional religions of the American Indian, Eskimo, Aleut, and Native Hawaiians, including but not limited to access to sites, use and

possession of sacred objects, and the freedom to worship through ceremonial and traditional rites.

The Act also required the President to survey the various federal departments and agencies to evaluate in consultation with Indian religious leaders what changes, if any, were needed in their policies and procedures and to report to Congress within a year. Senate Select Committee on Indian Affairs, Hearings Before Senate Select Committee on Indian Affairs on S.J. Res. 102 (American Indian Religious Freedom), 95th Cong., 2d Sess. (1978); Federal Agencies Task Force, U.S. Department of Interior, American Indian Religious Freedom Act Report, P.L. 95-341 (1979). *See generally* Robert S. Michaelsen, *Is the Miner's Canary Silent? Implications of the Supreme Court's Denial of American Indian Religious Freedom*, 6 J.L. & RELIGION 97 (1988).

However, efforts to invoke the Act to limit federal policies adversely affecting Indian access to religious sites were largely unsuccessful. *E.g., Badoni v. Higginson*, 638 F.2d 172 (10th Cir. 1980)(unsuccessful challenge under Act to federal operation of Rainbow Bridge National Monument); *Sequoyah v. Tennessee Valley Auth.*, 620 F.2d 1159 (6th Cir. 1980) (unsuccessful effort to halt flooding of Indian burial site through federal construction of Tellico Dam); *Wilson v. Block*, 708 F.2d 735 (D.C. Cir. 1983) (unsuccessful effort to halt expansion of ski facilities of the Arizona Snow Bowl in the San Francisco Peaks, an area that is sacred to members of both the Hopi and Navajo Tribes); *Crow v. Gullet*, 541 F. Supp. 785 (D.S.D. 1982), *aff'd*, 706 F.2d 856 (8th Cir. 1983) (unsuccessful challenge to restrictions on Indian access to and public desecration of ceremonial sites located in Bear Butte State Park in the Black Hills). This does not mean, of course, that tribes are limited in enacting their own protection for religious practices and sacred sites. State law, too, may have a role to play. For a concrete and practical guide to tribal action in this area, see DARBY C. STAPP & MICHAEL S. BURNEY, TRIBAL CULTURAL RESOURCE MANAGEMENT: THE FULL CIRCLE OF STEWARDSHIP (2002).

Conflicts over securing Indian religious freedom have been exacerbated by the delicate doctrinal interplay between the free exercise and establishment clauses of the First Amendment. *See Bowen v. Roy*, 476 U.S. 693 (1986) (federal government could constitutionally require a state to employ a social security number to identify a child in connection with food stamp and AFDC welfare programs, despite claims of the father, an Indian of Abenaki descent, that control over one's life was essential to spiritual purity). Subsequent to *Bowen*, tribes in Northern California relied on the First Amendment's free exercise clause to object to the building of a road through a sacred site. This case followed.

LYNG v. NORTHWEST INDIAN CEMETERY PROTECTIVE ASSOCIATION
United States Supreme Court
485 U.S. 439 (1988)

JUSTICE O'CONNOR delivered the opinion of the Court.

This case requires us to consider whether the first amendment's Free Exercise Clause forbids the Government from permitting timber harvesting in, or constructing a road through, a portion of a National Forest that has traditionally been used for religious purposes by members of three American Indian tribes in northwestern California. We conclude that it does not.

As part of a project to create a paved 75-mile road linking two California towns, Gasquet and Orleans, the United States Forest Service has upgraded 49 miles of previously unpaved roads on federal land. In order to complete this project (the G-O road), the Forest Service must build a 6-mile paved segment through the Chimney Rock section of the Six Rivers National Forest. That section of the forest is situated between two other portions of the road that are already complete.

In 1977, the Forest Service issued a draft environmental impact statement that discussed proposals for upgrading an existing unpaved road that runs through the Chimney Rock area. In response to comments on the draft statement, the Forest Service commissioned a study of American Indian cultural and religious sites in the area. The Hoopa Valley Indian reservation adjoins the Six Rivers National Forest, and the Chimney Rock area has historically been used for religious purposes by Yurok, Karok, and Tolowa Indians. The commissioned study, which was completed in 1979, found that the entire area "is significant as an integral and indispensible (sic) part of Indian religious conceptualization and practice." [Certain] sites are used for certain rituals, and "successful use of the (area) is dependent upon and facilitated by certain qualities of the physical environment, the most important of which are privacy, silence, and an undisturbed natural setting." [The commissioned] study concluded that constructing a road along any of the available routes "would cause serious and irreparable damage to the sacred areas which are an integral and necessary part of the belief systems and lifeway of Northwest California Indian peoples." Accordingly, the report recommended that the G-O road not be completed.

In 1982, the Forest Service decided not to adopt this recommendation, and it prepared a final environmental impact statement for construction of the road. The Regional Forester selected a route that avoided archeological sites and was removed as far as possible from the sites used by contemporary Indians for specific spiritual activities. Alternative routes that would have avoided the Chimney Rock area altogether were rejected because they would have required the acquisition of private land, had serious soil stability problems, and would in any event have traversed areas having ritualistic value to American Indians. [Simultaneously], the Forest Service adopted a management plan allowing for the harvesting of significant amounts of timber in this area of the forest. The management plan provided for one-half mile protective zones around all the religious sites identified in the report that had been commissioned in connection with the G-O road.

After exhausting their administrative remedies, respondents — an Indian organization, individual Indians, nature organizations and individual members of those organizations, and the State of California — challenged both the road-building and timber-harvesting decisions in the United States District Court for the Northern District of California. Respondents claimed that the Forest Service's decisions violated the Free Exercise Clause, the Federal Water Pollution Control Act (FWPCA), 86 Stat. 896, as amended, 33 U.S.C. section 1251 et seq., the National Environment Policy Act of 1969 (NEPA), 83 Stat. 852, 42 U.S.C. section 4321 et seq., several other federal statutes, and governmental trust responsibilities to Indians living on the Hoopa Valley Reservation.

After a trial, the District Court issued a permanent injunction forbidding the Government from constructing the Chimney Rock section of the G-O road or putting the timber-harvesting management plan into effect. *See Northwest Indian Cemetery Protective Assn. v. Peterson*, 565 F. Supp. 586 (ND Cal. 1983). The court found that both actions would violate the Free Exercise Clause because they "would seriously damage the salient visual, aural, and environmental qualities of the high country." Id., at 594–595. The court also found that both proposed actions would violate the FWPCA, and that the environmental impact statements for construction of the road were deficient under the National Environmental Policy Act. Finally, the court concluded that both projects would breach the Government's trust responsibilities to protect water and fishing rights reserved to the Hoopa Valley Indians.

[T]he Ninth Circuit affirmed in part. *Northwest Indian Cemetery Protective Assn. v. Peterson*, 795 F.2d 688 (1986). The panel unanimously rejected the District Court's conclusion that the Government's proposed actions would breach its trust responsibilities to Indians on the Hoopa Valley Reservation [and affirmed the District Court's constitutional ruling by a divided decision].

II

We begin by noting that the courts below did not articulate the bases of their decisions with perfect clarity. A fundamental and long-standing principle of judicial restraint requires that courts avoid reaching constitutional questions in advance of the necessity of deciding them. *See[, e.g.,] Three Affiliated Tribes of Ft. Berthold Reservation v. Wold Engineering, P. C.*, 467 U.S. 138, 157–158 (1984). This principle required the courts below to determine, before addressing the constitutional issue, whether a decision on that question could have entitled respondents to relief beyond that to which they were entitled on their statutory claims. If no additional relief would have been warranted, a constitutional decision would have been unnecessary and therefore inappropriate.

Neither the District Court nor the Court of Appeals explained or expressly articulated the necessity for their constitutional holdings. Were we persuaded that those holdings were unnecessary, we could simply vacate the relevant portions of the judgment below without discussing the merits of the constitutional issue. The structure and wording of the District Court's injunctive order, however, suggests that the statutory holdings would not have supported all the relief granted.

[Since] it appears reasonably likely that the first amendment issue was necessary to the decisions below, we believe that it would be inadvisable to vacate and remand without addressing that issue on the merits. This conclusion is strengthened by considerations of judicial economy [and convenience].

III

A

The Free Exercise Clause of the First Amendment provides that "Congress shall make no law . . . prohibiting the free exercise [of religion]." U.S. Const., Amdt. 1. It is undisputed that the Indian respondents' beliefs are sincere and that the Government's proposed actions will have severe adverse effects on the practice of their religion. Respondents contend that the burden on their religious practices is heavy enough to violate the Free Exercise Clause unless the Government can demonstrate a compelling need to complete the G-O road or to engage in timber harvesting in the Chimney Rock area. We disagree.

In *Bowen v. Roy*, 476 U.S. 693 (1986), we considered a challenge to a federal statute that required the States to use Social Security numbers in administering certain welfare programs. Two applicants for benefits under these programs contended that their religious beliefs prevented them from acceding to the use of a Social Security number for their two-year-old daughter because the use of a numerical identifier would "'rob the spirit' of (their) daughter and prevent her from attaining greater spiritual power." Similarly, in this case, it is said that disruption of the natural environment caused by the G-O road will diminish the sacredness of the area in question and create distractions that will interfere with "training and ongoing religious experience of individuals using (sites within) the area for personal medicine and growth . . . and as integrated parts of a system of religious belief and practice which correlates ascending degrees of personal power with a geographic hierarchy of power." ("Scarred hills and mountains, and disturbed rocks destroy the purity of the sacred areas, and (Indian) consultants repeatedly stressed the need of a training doctor to be undistracted by such disturbance"). The Court rejected this kind of challenge in *Roy*.

The Free Exercise Clause simply cannot be understood to require the Government to conduct its own internal affairs in ways that comport with the religious beliefs of particular citizens. Just as the government may not insist that (the Roys) engage in any set form of religious observance, so (they) may not demand that the Government join in their chosen religious practices by refraining from using a number to identify their daughter. . . .

. . . The Free Exercise Clause affords an individual protection from certain forms of governmental compulsion; it does not afford an individual a right to dictate the conduct of the Government's internal procedures. 476 U.S., at 699–700.

The building of a road or the harvesting of timber on publicly owned land cannot meaningfully be distinguished from the use of a Social Security number in *Roy*. In both cases, the challenged government action would interfere significantly with private persons' ability to pursue spiritual fulfillment according to their own religious beliefs. In neither case, however, would the affected individuals be coerced by the Government's action into violating their religious beliefs; nor would either governmental action penalize religious activity by denying any person an equal share of the rights, benefits, and privileges enjoyed by other citizens.

We are asked to distinguish this case from *Roy* on the ground that the infringement on religious liberty here is "significantly greater," or on the ground that the government practice in *Roy* was "purely mechanical" whereas this case involves "a case-by-case substantive determination as to how a particular unit of land will be managed." [W]e are [also] told that this case can be distinguished from *Roy* because "the government action is not at some physically removed location where it places no restriction on what a practitioner may do." [The State argues] that the Social Security number in *Roy* "could be characterized as interfering with Roy's religious tenets from a subjective point of view, where the government's conduct of 'its own internal affairs' was known to him only secondhand and did not interfere with his ability to practice his religion." [Here], however, it is said that the proposed road will "physically destro(y) the environmental conditions and the privacy without which the (religious) practices cannot be conducted."

[The plaintiffs'] efforts to distinguish *Roy* are unavailing. This Court cannot determine the truth of the underlying beliefs that led to the religious objections here or in *Roy*, [and therefore] cannot weigh the adverse effects on the Roys and compare them with the adverse effects on respondents. Without the ability to make such comparisons, we cannot say that the one form of incidental interference with an individual's spiritual activities should be subjected to a different constitutional analysis than the other. Respondents insist, nonetheless, that the courts below properly relied on a factual inquiry into the degree to which the Indians' spiritual practices would become ineffectual if the G-O road were built. They rely on several cases in which this Court has sustained free exercise challenges to government programs that interfered with individuals' ability to practice their religion. *See Wisconsin v. Yoder*, 406 U.S. 205 (1972) (compulsory school-attendance law). . . .

Even apart from the inconsistency between *Roy* and respondents' reading of these cases, their interpretation will not withstand analysis. It is true that this Court has repeatedly held that indirect coercion or penalties on the free exercise of religion, not just outright prohibitions, are subject to scrutiny under the First Amendment. [This point] does not and cannot imply that incidental effects of government programs, which may make it more difficult to practice certain religions but which have no tendency to coerce individuals into acting contrary to their religious beliefs, require government to bring forward a compelling justification for its otherwise lawful actions. The crucial word in the constitutional text is "prohibit": "For the Free Exercise Clause is written in terms of what the government cannot do to the individual, not in terms of what the individual can exact from the government." . . .

Whatever may be the exact line between unconstitutional prohibitions on the free exercise of religion and the legitimate conduct by government of its own affairs, the location of the line cannot depend on measuring the effects of a governmental action on a religious objector's spiritual development. The Government does not dispute, and we have no reason to doubt, that the logging and road-building projects at issue in this case could have devastating effects on traditional Indian religious practices.

Those practices are intimately and inextricably bound up with the unique features of the Chimney Rock area, which is known to the Indians as the "high country." Individual practitioners use this area for personal spiritual development; some of their activities are believed to be critically important in advancing the welfare of the tribe, and indeed, of mankind itself. The Indians use this area, as they have used it for a very long time, to conduct a wide variety of specific rituals that aim to accomplish their religious goals. According to their beliefs, the rituals would not be efficacious if conducted at other sites than the ones traditionally used, and too much disturbance of the area's natural state would clearly render any meaningful continuation of traditional practices impossible. [We] assume that the threat to the efficacy of at least some religious practices is extremely grave.

Even if we assume that we should accept the Ninth Circuit's prediction, according to which the G-O road will "virtually destroy the Indians' ability to practice their religion" 795 F.2d, at 693 (opinion below), the Constitution simply does not provide a principle that could justify upholding respondents' legal claims. However much we might wish that it were otherwise, government simply could not operate if it were required to satisfy every citizen's religious needs and desires. A broad range of government activities — from social welfare programs to foreign aid to conservation projects — will always be considered essential to the spiritual well-being of some citizens, often on the basis of sincerely held religious beliefs. Others will find the very same activities deeply offensive, and perhaps incompatible with their own search for spiritual fulfillment and with the tenets of their religion. The First Amendment must apply to all citizens alike, and it can give to none of them a veto over public programs that do not prohibit the free exercise of religion. The Constitution does not, and courts cannot, offer to reconcile the various competing demands on government, many of them rooted in sincere religious belief, that inevitably arise in so diverse a society as ours. That task, to the extent that it is feasible, is for the legislatures and other institutions. Cf. The Federalist No. 10 (suggesting that the effects of religious factionalism are best restrained through competition among a multiplicity of religious sects).

One need not look far beyond the present case to see why the analysis in *Roy* [advances] a sound reading of the Constitution. Respondents attempt to stress the limits of the religious servitude that they are now seeking to impose on the Chimney Rock area of the Six Rivers National Forest. While defending an injunction against logging operations and the construction of a road, they apparently do not at present object to the area's being used by recreational visitors, other Indians, or forest rangers. Nothing in the principle for which they contend, however, would distinguish this case from another lawsuit in which they (or similarly situated religious objectors) might seek to exclude all human activity but their own from sacred areas of the public lands. The Indian respondents insist that "(p)rivacy during the power quests is required for the practitioners to maintain the purity needed for a successful journey." [Likewise]: "The practices conducted in the high country entail intense meditation and require the practitioner to achieve a profound awareness of the natural environment. Prayer seats are oriented so there is an unobstructed view, and the practitioner must be surrounded by undisturbed naturalness." No disrespect for these practices is implied when one notes that such beliefs could easily require de facto beneficial ownership of some rather spacious tracts of public property. Even without anticipating future cases, the diminution of the Government's property rights, and the concomitant subsidy of the Indian religion, would in this case be far from trivial: the District Court's order permanently forbade commercial timber harvesting, or the construction of a two-lane road, anywhere within an area covering a full 27 sections (i.e. more than 17,000 acres) of public land.

The Constitution does not permit government to discriminate against religions that treat particular physical sites as sacred, and a law forbidding the Indian respondents from visiting the Chimney Rock area would raise a different set of constitutional questions. Whatever rights the Indians may have to the use of the area, however, those rights do not divest the Government of its right to use what is, after all, its land. Cf. *Bowen v. Roy*, 476 U.S., at 724–727 (O'CONNOR, J., concurring in part and dissenting in part) (distinguishing between the Government's use of information in its possession and the Government's requiring an individual to provide such information).

B

Nothing in our opinion should be read to encourage governmental insensitivity to the religious needs of any citizen. The Government's rights to the use of its own land, for example, need not and should not discourage it from accommodating religious practices like those engaged in by the Indian respondents. [T]he Government has taken numerous steps in this very case to minimize the impact that construction of the G-O road will have on the Indians' religious [practices].

Except for abandoning its project entirely, and thereby leaving the two existing segments of road to dead-end in the middle of a National Forest, it is difficult to see how the Government could have been more solicitous. Such solicitude accords with "the policy of the United States to protect and preserve for American Indians their inherent right of freedom to believe, express, and exercise the traditional religions of the American Indian . . . including but not limited to access to sites, use and possession of sacred objects, and the freedom to worship through ceremonials and traditional rites." American Indian Religious Freedom Act (AIRFA), Pub. L. 95-341, 92 Stat. 469, 42 U.S.C. section 1996.

Respondents, however, suggest that AIRFA goes further and in effect enacts their interpretation of the first amendment into statutory law. Although this contention was rejected by the District Court, they seek to defend the judgment below by arguing that AIRFA authorizes the injunction against completion of the G-O road. This argument is without merit. After reciting several legislative findings, AIRFA "resolves" upon the policy quoted above. A second section of the statute, 92 Stat. 470, required an evaluation of federal policies and procedures, in consultation with native religious leaders, of changes necessary to protect and preserve the rights and practices in question. The required report dealing with this evaluation was completed and released in 1979. Nowhere in the law is there so much as a hint of any intent to create a cause of action or any judicially enforceable individual rights.

What is obvious from the face of the statute is confirmed by numerous indications in the legislative history. The sponsor of the bill that became AIRFA, Representative Udall, called it "a sense of Congress joint resolution," aimed at ensuring that "the basic right of the Indian people to exercise their traditional religious practices is not infringed without a clear decision on the part of the Congress or the administrators that such religious practices must yield to some higher consideration." 124 Cong. Rec. 21444 (1978). Representative Udall emphasized that the bill would not "confer special religious rights on Indians," would "not change any existing State or Federal law," and in fact "has no teeth in it." *Id.*, at 21444–21445.

C

The dissent proposes an approach to the first amendment that is fundamentally inconsistent with the principles on which our decision rests. Notwithstanding the sympathy that we all must feel for the plight of the Indian respondents, it is plain that the approach taken by the dissent cannot withstand analysis. On the contrary, the path towards which it points us is incompatible with the text of the Constitution, with the precedents of this Court, and with a responsible sense of our own institutional role.

The dissent begins by asserting that the "constitutional guarantee we interpret today . . . is directed against any form of government action that frustrates or inhibits religious practice." . . . The Constitution, however, says no such thing. Rather, it states: "Congress shall make no law . . . prohibiting the free exercise (of religion)." U.S. Const., Amdt. 1 (emphasis added).

[So that] the District Court's injunction may be reconsidered in light of this holding, and in light of any other relevant events that may have intervened since the injunction issued, the case is remanded for further proceedings consistent with this opinion.

It is so ordered.

JUSTICE BRENNAN, with whom JUSTICE MARSHALL and JUSTICE BLACKMUN join, dissenting.

"[T]he Free Exercise Clause," the Court explains today, "is written in terms of what the government cannot do to the individual, not in terms of what the individual can exact from the government." [Claiming] fidelity to the unremarkable constitutional principle, the Court nevertheless concludes that even where the Government uses federal land in a manner that threatens the very existence of a Native American religion, the Government is simply not "doing" anything to the practitioners of that faith. Instead, the Court believes that Native Americans who request that the Government refrain from destroying their religion effectively seek to exact from the Government de facto beneficial ownership of federal property. These two astonishing conclusions follow naturally from the Court's determination that federal land-use decisions that render the practice of a given religion impossible do not burden that religion in a manner cognizable under the Free Exercise Clause, because such decisions neither coerce conduct inconsistent with religious belief nor penalize religious activity. The constitutional guarantee we interpret today, however, draws no such fine distinctions between types of restraints on religious exercise, but rather is directed against any form of governmental action that frustrates or inhibits religious practice. Because the Court today refuses even to acknowledge the constitutional injury respondents will suffer, and because this refusal essentially leaves Native Americans with absolutely no constitutional protection against perhaps the gravest threat to their religious practices, I dissent.

I

For at least 200 years and probably much longer, the Yurok, Karok, and Tolowa Indians have held sacred an approximately 25 square-mile area of land situated in what is today the Blue Creek Unit of Six Rivers National Forest in northwestern California. As the Government readily concedes, regular visits to this area, known to respondent Indians as the "high country," have played and continue to play a "critical" role in the religious practices and rituals of these tribes. [Such] beliefs, only briefly described in the Court's opinion, are crucial to a proper understanding of respondents' claims.

As the Forest Service's commissioned study, the Theodoratus Report, explains, for Native Americans religion is not a discrete sphere of activity separate from all others, and any attempt to isolate the religious aspects of Indian life "is in reality an exercise which forces Indian concepts into non-Indian categories." [To] most Native Americans, "(t)he area of worship cannot be delineated from social, political, cultural and other aspects of Indian lifestyle." American Indian Religious Freedom, Hearings on S. J. Res. 102 Before the Select Comm. on Indian Affairs, U.S. Sen. 95th Cong., 2d Sess. at 86 (Statement of Barney Old Coyote, Crow Tribe). A pervasive feature of this lifestyle is the individual's relationship with the natural world; this relationship, which can accurately though somewhat incompletely be characterized as one of stewardship, forms the core of what might be called, for want of a better nomenclature, the Indian religious experience. While traditional western religions view creation as the work of a deity "who institutes natural laws which then govern the operation of physical nature," tribal religions regard creation as an ongoing process in which they are morally and religiously obligated to participate. [The] Native Americans fulfill this duty through ceremonies and rituals designed to preserve and stabilize the earth and to protect humankind from disease and other catastrophes. Failure to conduct these ceremonies in the manner and place specified, adherents believe, will result in great harm to the earth and to the people whose welfare depends upon it.

In marked contrast to traditional western religions, the belief systems of Native Americans do not rely on doctrines, creeds, or dogmas. Established or universal truths — the mainstay of western religions — play no part in Indian faith. Ceremonies are communal efforts undertaken for specific purposes in accordance with instructions handed down from generation to generation. Commentaries on or interpretations of the rituals themselves are deemed absolute violations of the ceremonies, whose value lies not in their ability to explain the natural world or to enlighten individual believers but in their efficacy as protectors and enhancers of tribal existence. Where dogma lies at the heart of western religions, Native American faith is inextricably bound to the use of land. The site-specific nature of Indian religious practice derives from the Native American perception that land is itself a sacred, living being. See Dean B. Suagee, *American Indian Religious*

Freedom and Cultural Resources Management: Protecting Mother Earth's Caretakers, 10 AMER. IND. L. REV. 1, 10 (1982). Rituals are performed in prescribed locations not merely as a matter of traditional orthodoxy, but because land, like all other living things, is unique, and specific sites possess different spiritual properties and significance. Within this belief system, therefore, land is not fungible; indeed, at the time of the Spanish colonization of the American southwest, "all . . . Indians held in some form a belief in a sacred and indissoluble bond between themselves and the land in which their settlements were located." EDWARD H. SPICER, CYCLES OF CONQUEST: THE IMPACT OF SPAIN, MEXICO, AND THE UNITED STATES ON THE INDIANS OF THE UNITED STATES 576 (1962).

For respondent Indians, the most sacred of lands is the high country where, they believe, pre-human spirits moved with the coming of humans to the earth. Because these spirits are seen as the source of religious power, or "medicine," many of the tribes' rituals and practices require frequent journeys to the [high country].

Recognizing that the high country is "indispensable" to the religious lives of the approximately 5,000 tribe members who reside in that area, [the Court of Appeals] concluded "that the proposed government operations would virtually destroy the Indians' ability to practice their religion." [Like the district court], the Court of Appeals found the Government's interests in building the road and permitting limited timber harvesting — interests which of course were considerably undermined by passage of the California Wilderness Act — did not justify the destruction of respondents' religion.

II

The Court does not for a moment suggest that the interests served by the G-O road are in any way compelling, or that they outweigh the destructive effect construction of the road will have on respondents' religious practices. Instead, the Court embraces the Government's contention that its prerogative as landowner should always take precedence over a claim that a particular use of federal property infringes religious practices. Attempting to justify this rule, the Court argues that the first amendment bars only outright prohibitions, indirect coercion, and penalties on the free exercise of religion. All other "incidental effects of government programs," it concludes, even those "which may make it more difficult to practice certain religions but which have no tendency to coerce individuals into acting contrary to their religious beliefs," simply do not give rise to constitutional concerns. [Ever since] our recognition nearly half a century ago that restraints on religious conduct implicate the concerns of the Free Exercise Clause, [this Court has] never suggested that the protections of the guarantee are limited to so narrow a range of governmental burdens. . . .

A

[I cannot] accept the Court's premise that the form of the Government's restraint on religious practice, rather than its effect, controls our constitutional analysis. [T]he proposed logging and construction activities will virtually destroy respondents' religion, and will therefore necessarily force them into abandoning those practices [completely].

B

Federal land-use decisions, [in contrast to the demand for social security numbers involved in *Roy*], are likely to have substantial external effects that government decisions concerning office furniture and information storage obviously will not, and they are correspondingly subject to public scrutiny and public challenge in a host of ways that office equipment purchases are not. Indeed, in the American Indian Religious Freedom Act (AIRFA), 42 U.S.C. section 1996, Congress expressly recognized the adverse impact land-use decisions and other governmental actions frequently have on the site-specific religious practices of Native Americans, and the Act accordingly directs agencies to consult with Native American religious leaders before taking actions that might impair those practices. Although I agree that the Act does not create any judicially enforceable rights, [the] absence of any private right of action in no way undermines the statute's significance as an express congressional determination that federal land management decisions are not "internal" governmental "procedures," but are instead governmental actions that can and indeed are likely to burden Native American religious practices. That such decisions should be subject to constitutional challenge, and potential constitutional limitations, should hardly come as a surprise.

C

[Before] today's decision, several courts of appeals had attempted to fashion a test that accommodates the competing "demands" placed on federal property by the two cultures. Recognizing that the Government normally enjoys plenary authority over federal lands, the courts of appeals required Native Americans to demonstrate that any land-use decisions they challenged involved lands that were "central" or "indispensable" to their religious practices. *See, e.g.,* [*Wilson v. Block*, 708 F.2d 735 (DC Cir.), *cert. denied*, 464 U.S. 956 (1983)]. Although this requirement limits the potential number of free exercise claims that might be brought to federal land management decisions, and thus forestalls the possibility that the Government will find itself ensnared in a host of lilliputian lawsuits, it has been criticized as inherently ethnocentric, for it incorrectly assumes that Native American belief systems ascribe religious significance to land in a traditionally western hierarchical manner. *See* Robert S. Michaelsen, *American Indian Religious Freedom Litigation: Promise and Perils*, 3 J. Law & Rel. 47 (1985); Stephen L. Pepper, *Conundrum of the Free Exercise Clause — Some Reflections on Recent Cases*, 9 N. Ky. L. Rev. 265, 283–284 (1982). It is frequently the case in constitutional litigation, however, that courts are called upon to balance interests that are not readily translated into rough equivalents. At their most absolute, the competing claims that both the Government and Native Americans assert in federal land are fundamentally incompatible, and unless they are tempered by compromise, mutual accommodation will remain impossible.

I believe it appropriate, therefore, to require some showing of "centrality" before the Government can be required either to come forward with a compelling justification for its proposed use of federal land or to forego that use altogether. "Centrality," however, should not be equated with the survival or extinction of the religion itself. [W]hile Native Americans need not demonstrate, as respondents did here, that the Government's land-use decision will assuredly eradicate their faith, I do not think it is enough to allege simply that the land in question is held sacred. Rather, adherents challenging a proposed use of federal land should be required to show that the decision poses a substantial and realistic threat of frustrating their religious practices. Once such a showing is made, the burden should shift to the Government to come forward with a compelling state interest sufficient to justify the infringement of those practices.

III

[It is hard] to imagine conduct more insensitive to religious needs than the Government's determination to build a marginally useful road in the face of uncontradicted evidence that the road will render the practice of respondents' religion impossible. Nor do I believe that respondents will derive any solace from the knowledge that although the practice of their religion will become "more difficult" as a result of the Government's actions, they remain free to maintain their religious beliefs. Given today's ruling, that freedom amounts to nothing more than the right to believe that their religion will be destroyed. The safeguarding of such a hollow freedom not only makes a mockery of the "policy of the United States to protect and preserve for American Indians their inherent right of freedom to believe, express, and exercise the(ir) traditional religions," [the decision] fails utterly to accord with the dictates of the first amendment.

I dissent.

NOTE ON *LYNG*Events Following *Lyng*: Notwithstanding the Tribes' loss in *Lyng*, the G-O road at issue was actually stopped, albeit not before timber clearing of portions of the right of way had done significant damage to the environment of the sacred High Country. Specifically, in alliance with various environmental groups, the Tribes secured legislation that added the Six Rivers National Forest, which included the High Country, to the national wilderness system through Public Law 101-612, 104 Stat. 3209. National wilderness designation prevented the completion of the G-O road. This case study indicates that often political strategies not rooted exclusively in Indian law or constitutional protections can be deployed to protect Indian rights. For a creative approach to problems of Native access to sacred sites on public lands, employing property law concepts, *see* Kristen Carpenter, *A Property Rights Approach to Sacred Sites Cases: Asserting a Place for Indians as Nonowners*, 52 UCLA L. REV. 1061 (2005). For background and cultural context of the Lyng case, see also Amy Bowers & Kristen Carpenter, *Challenging the Narrative of Conquest: The Story of* Lyng v. Northwest Indian Cemetery Protective Association *in* INDIAN LAW STORIES (Carole Goldberg, Kevin K. Washburn & Philip P. Frickey eds., 2011).

EMPLOYMENT DIVISION, DEPARTMENT OF HUMAN RESOURCES OF OREGON v. SMITH
United States Supreme Court
494 U.S. 872 (1990)

JUSTICE SCALIA delivered the opinion of the Court.

This case requires us to decide whether the Free Exercise Clause of the first amendment permits the State of Oregon to include religiously inspired peyote use within the reach of its general criminal prohibition on use of that drug, and thus permits the State to deny unemployment benefits to persons dismissed from their jobs because of such religiously inspired use.

I

Oregon law prohibits the knowing or intentional possession of a "controlled substance" unless the substance has been prescribed by a medical practitioner. Ore. Rev. Stat. § 475.992(4) (1987). The law defines "controlled substance" as a drug classified in Schedules I through V of the Federal Controlled Substances Act, 21 U.S.C. §§ 811–812 (1982 ed. and Supp. V), as modified by the State Board of Pharmacy. Ore. Rev. Stat. § 475.005(6) (1987). Persons who violate this provision by possessing a controlled substance listed on Schedule I are "guilty of a Class B felony." § 475.992(4)(a). As compiled by the State Board of Pharmacy under its statutory authority, see Ore. Rev. Stat. § 475.035 (1987), Schedule I contains the drug peyote, a hallucinogen derived from the plant Lophophorawilliamsii Lemaire. Ore. Admin. Rule 855-80-021(3)(s) (1988).

Respondents Alfred Smith and Galen Black were fired from their jobs with a private drug rehabilitation organization because they ingested peyote for sacramental purposes at a ceremony of the Native American Church, of which both are members. When respondents applied to petitioner Employment Division for unemployment compensation, they were determined to be ineligible for benefits because they had been discharged for work-related "misconduct." The Oregon Court of Appeals reversed that determination, holding that the denial of benefits violated respondents' free exercise rights under the first amendment.

On appeal to the Oregon Supreme Court, petitioner argued that the denial of benefits was permissible because respondents' consumption of peyote was a crime under Oregon law. The Oregon Supreme Court reasoned, however, that the criminality of respondents' peyote use was irrelevant to resolution of their constitutional claim — since the purpose of the "misconduct" provision under which respondents had been disqualified was not to enforce the State's criminal laws but to preserve the financial integrity of the compensation fund, and since that purpose was inadequate to justify the burden that disqualification imposed on respondents' religious practice. Citing our decisions in *Sherbert v. Verner*, 374 U.S. 398 (1963), and *Thomas v. Review Board, Indiana Employment Security Div.*, 450 U.S. 707 (1981), the court concluded that respondents were entitled to payment of unemployment benefits. We granted certiorari.

Before this Court in 1987, petitioner continued to maintain that the illegality of respondents' peyote consumption was relevant to their constitutional claim. We agreed, concluding that "if a State has prohibited through its criminal laws certain kinds of religiously motivated conduct without violating the First Amendment, it certainly follows that it may impose the lesser burden of denying unemployment compensation benefits to persons who engage in that conduct." *Employment Div., Dept. of Human Resources of Oregon v. Smith*, 485 U.S. 660, 670 (1988) (*Smith I*). We vacated the judgment of the Oregon Supreme Court and remanded for further proceedings [to determine the legality of religious use under Oregon law].

On remand, the Oregon Supreme Court held that respondents' religiously inspired use of peyote fell within the prohibition of the Oregon statute, which "makes no exception for the sacramental use" of the drug. It then considered whether that prohibition was valid under the Free Exercise Clause, and concluded that it was not. The court therefore reaffirmed its previous ruling that the State could not deny unemployment benefits to respondents for having engaged in that practice.

We again granted certiorari.

II

Respondents' claim for relief rests on our decisions in *Sherbert v. Verner, Thomas v. Review Board, Indiana Employment Security Div.*, and *Hobbie v. Unemployment Appeals Comm'n of Florida*, 480 U.S. 136 (1987), in which we held that a State could not condition the availability of unemployment insurance on an individual's willingness to forgo conduct required by his religion. As we observed in *Smith I*, however, the conduct at issue in those cases was not prohibited by law. We held that distinction to be critical, for "if Oregon does prohibit the religious use of peyote, and if that prohibition is consistent with the Federal Constitution, there is no federal right to engage in that conduct in Oregon," and "the State is free to withhold unemployment compensation from respondents for engaging in work-related misconduct, despite its religious motivation." Now that the Oregon Supreme Court has confirmed that Oregon does prohibit the religious use of peyote, we proceed to consider whether that prohibition is permissible under the Free Exercise Clause.

A

The Free Exercise Clause of the first amendment, which has been made applicable to the States by incorporation into the fourteenth amendment, *see Cantwell v. Connecticut*, 310 U.S. 296, 303 (1940), provides that "Congress shall make no law respecting an establishment of religion, or prohibiting the free exercise thereof. . . . " U.S. Const. Am. I (emphasis added). The free exercise of religion means, first and foremost, the right to believe and profess whatever religious doctrine one desires. Thus, the first amendment obviously excludes all "governmental regulation of religious beliefs as such." The government may not compel affirmation of religious belief, *see Torcaso v. Watkins*, 367 U.S. 488 (1961), punish the expression of religious doctrines it believes to be false, *United States v. Ballard*, 322 U.S. 78, 86–88 (1944), impose special disabilities on the basis of religious views or religious status, [*e.g.*, *McDaniel v. Paty*, 435 U.S. 618 (1978)], or lend its power to one or the other side in controversies over religious authority or dogma, [*e.g.*, *Presbyterian Church v. Hull Church*, 393 U.S. 440, 445–452 (1969)].

But the "exercise of religion" often involves not only belief and profession but the performance of (or abstention from) physical acts: assembling with others for a worship service, participating in sacramental use of bread and wine, proselytizing, abstaining from certain foods or certain modes of transportation. It would be true, we think (though no case of ours has involved the point), that a state would be "prohibiting the free exercise [of religion]" if it sought to ban such acts or abstentions only when they are engaged in for religious reasons, or only because of the religious belief that they display. It would doubtless be unconstitutional, for example, to ban the casting of "statues that are to be used for worship purposes," or to prohibit bowing down before a golden calf.

Respondents in the present case, however, seek to carry the meaning of "prohibiting the free exercise [of religion]" one large step further. They contend that their religious motivation for using peyote places them beyond the reach of a criminal law that is not specifically directed at their religious practice, and that is concededly constitutional as applied to those who use the drug for other reasons. They assert, in other words, that "prohibiting the free exercise [of religion]" includes requiring any individual to observe a generally applicable law that requires (or forbids) the performance of an act that his religious belief forbids (or requires). As a textual matter, we do not think the words must be given that meaning. It is no more necessary to regard the collection of a general tax, for example, as "prohibiting the free exercise [of religion]" by those citizens who believe support of organized government to be sinful, than it is to regard the same tax as "abridging the freedom . . . of the press" of those publishing companies that must pay the tax as a condition of staying in business. It is a permissible reading of the text, in the one case as in the other, to say that if prohibiting the exercise of religion (or burdening the activity of printing) is not the object of the tax but merely the incidental effect of a generally applicable and otherwise valid provision, the First Amendment has not been offended. *Compare Citizen Publishing Co. v. United States*, 394 U.S. 131, 139 (1969) (upholding application of antitrust laws to press), *with Grosjean v. American Press Co.*, 297 U.S. 233, 250–251 (1936) (striking down license tax applied only to newspapers with weekly circulation above a specified level); *see generally Minneapolis Star & Tribune Co. v. Minnesota Commissioner of Revenue*, 460 U.S. 575, 581 (1983).

Our decisions reveal that the latter reading is the correct one. We have never held that an individual's religious beliefs excuse him from compliance with an otherwise valid law prohibiting conduct that the State is free to regulate. On the contrary, the record of more than a century of our free exercise jurisprudence contradicts that proposition. As described succinctly by Justice Frankfurter in *Minersville School Dist. Bd. of Educ. v. Gobitis*, 310 U.S. 586, 594–595 (1940): "Conscientious scruples have not, in the course of the long struggle for religious toleration, relieved the individual from obedience to a general law not aimed at the promotion or restriction of religious beliefs. The mere possession of religious convictions which contradict the relevant concerns of a political society does not relieve the citizen from the discharge of political responsibilities (footnote omitted)." We first had occasion to assert that principle in *Reynolds v. United States*, 98 U.S. 145 (1879), where we rejected the claim that criminal laws against polygamy could not be constitutionally applied to those whose religion commanded the practice. "Laws," we said, "are made for the government of actions, and while they cannot interfere with mere religious belief and opinions, they may with practices. . . . Can man excuse his practices to the contrary because of his religious belief? To permit this would be to make the professed doctrines of religious belief superior to the law of the land, and in effect to permit every citizen to become a law unto himself."

Subsequent decisions have consistently held that the right of free exercise does not relieve an individual of the obligation to comply with a "valid and neutral law of general applicability on the ground that the law proscribes (or prescribes) conduct that his religion prescribes (or proscribes)." *United States v. Lee*, 455 U.S. 252, 263, n. 3 (1982) (STEVENS, J., concurring in judgment); *see Minersville School Dist. Bd. of Educ. v. Gobitis, supra*, at 595 (collecting cases). In *Prince v. Massachusetts*, 321 U.S. 158 (1944), we held that a mother could be prosecuted under the child labor laws for using her children to dispense literature in the streets, her religious motivation notwithstanding. We found no constitutional infirmity in "excluding [these children] from doing there what no other children may do." In *Braunfield v. Brown*, 366 U.S. 599 (1961) (plurality opinion), we upheld Sunday-closing laws against the claim that they burdened the religious practices of persons whose religions compelled them to refrain from work on other days. In *Gillette v. United States*, 401 U.S. 437, 461 (1971), we sustained the military selective service system against the claim that it violated free exercise by conscripting persons who opposed a particular war on religious grounds.

Our most recent decision involving a neutral, generally applicable regulatory law that compelled activity forbidden by an individual's religion was *United States v. Lee*, 455 U.S. at 258–261. There, an Amish employer, on behalf of himself and his employees, sought exemption from collection and payment of Social Security taxes on the ground that the Amish faith prohibited participation in governmental support programs. We rejected the claim that an exemption was constitutionally required. There would be no way, we observed, to distinguish the Amish believer's objection to Social Security taxes from the religious objections that others might have to the collection or use of other taxes. "If, for example, a religious adherent believes war is a sin, and if a certain percentage of the federal budget can be identified as devoted to war-related activities, such individuals would have a similarly valid claim to be exempted from paying that percentage of the income tax. The tax system could not function if denominations were allowed to challenge the tax system because tax payments were spent in a manner that violates their religious belief."

The only decisions in which we have held that the first amendment bars application of a neutral, generally applicable law to religiously motivated action have involved not the Free Exercise Clause alone, but the Free Exercise Clause in conjunction with other constitutional protections, such as freedom of speech and of the press, *see Cantwell v. Connecticut*, 310 U.S. at 304–307 (invalidating a licensing system for religious and charitable solicitations under which the administrator had discretion to deny a license to any cause he deemed nonreligious); *Murdock v. Pennsylvania*, 319 U.S. 105 (1943) (invalidating a flat tax on solicitation as applied to the dissemination of religious ideas); *Follett v. McCormick*, 321 U.S. 573 (1944) (same), or the right of parents, acknowledged in *Pierce v. Society of Sisters*, 268 U.S. 510 (1925), to direct the education of their children, *see Wisconsin v. Yoder*, 406 U.S. 205 (1972) (invalidating compulsory school-attendance laws as applied to Amish parents who refused on religious grounds to send their children to school). Some of our cases prohibiting compelled expression, decided exclusively upon free speech grounds, have also involved freedom of religion, cf. *Wooley v. Maynard*, 430 U.S. 705 (1977) (invalidating compelled display of a license plate slogan that offended individual religious beliefs); *West Virginia Board of Education v. Barnette*, 319 U.S. 624 (1943) (invalidating compulsory flag salute statute challenged by religious objectors). And it is easy to envision a case in which a challenge on freedom of association grounds would likewise be reinforced by Free Exercise Clause concerns.

The present case does not present such a hybrid situation, but a free exercise claim unconnected with any communicative activity or parental right. Respondents urge us to hold, quite simply, that when otherwise prohibitable conduct is accompanied by religious convictions, not only the convictions but the conduct itself must be free from governmental regulation. We have never held that, and decline to do so now. There being no contention that Oregon's drug law represents an attempt to regulate religious beliefs, the communication of religious beliefs, or the raising of one's children in those beliefs, the rule to which we have adhered ever since *Reynolds* plainly controls. "Our cases do not at their farthest reach support the proposition that a stance of conscientious opposition relieves an objector from any colliding duty fixed by a democratic government."

B

Respondents argue that even though exemption from generally applicable criminal laws need not automatically be extended to religiously motivated actors, at least the claim for a religious exemption must be evaluated under the balancing test set forth in *Sherbert v. Verner*, 374 U.S. 398 (1963). Under the *Sherbert* test, governmental actions that substantially burden a religious practice must be justified by a compelling governmental interest. [While we have applied this test three times to unemployment compensation cases, we] have never invalidated any governmental action on the basis of the *Sherbert* test except the denial of unemployment compensation. Although we have sometimes purported to apply the *Sherbert* test in contexts other than that, we have always found the test satisfied, *see United States v. Lee*, 455 U.S. 252 (1982); *Gillette v. United States*, 401 U.S. 437 (1971). In recent years we have abstained from applying the *Sherbert test* (outside the unemployment compensation field) at all. In *Bowen v. Roy*, 476 U.S. 693 (1986), we declined to apply *Sherbert* analysis to a federal statutory scheme that required benefit applicants and recipients to provide their Social Security numbers. The plaintiffs in that case asserted that it would violate their religious beliefs to obtain and provide a Social Security number for their daughter. We held the statute's application to the plaintiffs valid regardless of whether it was necessary to effectuate a compelling interest. In *Lyng v. Northwest Indian Cemetery Protective Assn.*, 485 U.S. 439 (1988), we declined to apply *Sherbert* analysis to the Government's logging and road construction activities on lands used for religious purposes by several Native American Tribes, even though it was undisputed that the activities "could have devastating effects on traditional Indian religious practices."

Even if we were inclined to breathe into *Sherbert* some life beyond the unemployment compensation field, we would not apply it to require exemptions from a generally applicable criminal law. The *Sherbert* test, it must be recalled, was developed in a context that lent itself to individualized governmental assessment of the reasons for the relevant conduct. As a plurality of the Court noted in *Roy*, a distinctive feature of unemployment compensation programs is that their eligibility criteria invite consideration of the particular circumstances behind an applicant's unemployment: "The statutory conditions [in *Sherbert* and *Thomas*] provided that a person was not eligible for unemployment compensation benefits if, 'without good cause,' he had quit work or refused available work. The 'good cause' standard created a mechanism for individualized exemptions." As the plurality pointed out in *Roy*, our decisions in the unemployment cases stand for the proposition that where the State has in place a system of individual exemptions, it may not refuse to extend that system to cases of "religious hardship" without compelling reason.

Whether or not the decisions are that limited, they at least have nothing to do with an across-the-board criminal prohibition on a particular form of conduct. Although, as noted earlier, we have sometimes used the *Sherbert* test to analyze free exercise challenges to such laws, we have never applied the test to invalidate one. We conclude today that the sounder approach, and the approach in accord with the vast majority of our precedents, is to hold the test inapplicable to such challenges. The government's ability to enforce generally applicable prohibitions of socially harmful conduct, like its ability to carry out other aspects of public policy, "cannot depend on measuring the effects of a governmental action on a religious objector's spiritual development." *Lyng, supra*, at 451. To make an individual's obligation to obey such a law contingent upon the law's coincidence with his religious beliefs, except where the State's interest is "compelling" — permitting him, by virtue of his beliefs, "to become a law unto himself," *Reynolds v. United States*, 98 U.S., at 167 — contradicts both constitutional tradition and common sense.

The "compelling government interest" requirement seems benign, because it is familiar from other fields. But using it as the standard that must be met before the government may accord different treatment on the basis of race, or before the government may regulate the content of speech, is not remotely comparable to using it for the purpose asserted here. What it produces in those other fields — equality of treatment, and an unrestricted flow of contending speech — are constitutional norms; what it would produce here — a private right to ignore generally applicable laws — is a constitutional anomaly.

Nor is it possible to limit the impact of respondents' proposal by requiring a "compelling state interest" only when the conduct prohibited is "central" to the individual's religion. *Cf. Lyng v. Northwest Indian Cemetery Protective Assn.*, (BRENNAN, J., dissenting). It is no more appropriate for judges to determine the "centrality" of religious beliefs before applying a "compelling interest" test in the free exercise field, than it would be for them to determine the "importance" of ideas before applying the "compelling interest" test in the free speech field. What principle of law or logic can be brought to bear to contradict a believer's assertion that a particular act is "central" to his personal faith? Judging the centrality of different religious practices is akin to the unacceptable "business of evaluating the relative merits of differing religious claims." *United States v. Lee*, 455 U.S., at 263 n. 2 (STEVENS, J., concurring). As we reaffirmed only last Term, "[i]t is not within the judicial ken to question the centrality of particular beliefs or practices to a faith, or the validity of particular litigants' interpretation of those creeds." *Hernandez v. Commissioner*, [109 S. Ct. 2136, 2149]. Repeatedly and in many different contexts, we have warned that courts must not presume to determine the place of a particular belief in a religion or the plausibility of a religious claim.

Nor is this difficulty avoided by Justice BLACKMUN's assertion that "although courts should refrain from delving into questions of whether, as a matter of religious doctrine, a particular practice is 'central' to the religion, I do not think this means that the courts must turn a blind eye to the severe impact of a State's restrictions on the adherents of a minority religion." (BLACKMUN, J. dissenting). As Justice BLACKMUN's opinion proceeds to make clear, inquiry into "severe impact" is no different from inquiry into centrality. He has merely substituted for the question "How important is X to the religious adherent?" the question "How great will be the harm to the religious adherent if X is taken away?" There is no material difference.

If the "compelling interest" test is to be applied at all, then, it must be applied across the board, to all actions thought to be religiously commanded. Moreover, if "compelling interest" really means what it says (and watering it down here would subvert its rigor in the other fields where it is applied), many laws will not meet the test. Any society adopting such a system would be courting anarchy, but that danger increases in direct proportion to the society's diversity of religious beliefs, and its determination to coerce or suppress none of them. Precisely because "we are a cosmopolitan nation made up of people of almost every conceivable religious preference," and precisely because we value and protect that religious divergence, we cannot afford the luxury of deeming presumptively invalid, as applied to the religious objector, every regulation of conduct that does not protect an interest of the highest order. The rule respondents favor would open the prospect of constitutionally required religious exemptions from civic obligations of almost every conceivable kind — ranging from compulsory military service, to the payment of taxes, to health and safety regulation such as manslaughter and child neglect laws, compulsory vaccination laws, drug laws, and traffic laws; to social welfare legislation such as minimum wage laws, child labor laws, animal cruelty laws, environmental protection laws, and laws providing for equality of opportunity for the races. The first amendment's protection of religious liberty does not require this.

Values that are protected against government interference through enshrinement in the Bill of Rights are not thereby banished from the political process. Just as a society that believes in the negative protection accorded to the press by the first amendment is likely to enact laws that affirmatively foster the dissemination of the printed word, so also a society that believes in the negative protection accorded to religious belief can be expected to be solicitous of that value in its legislation as well. It is therefore not surprising that a number of States have made an exception to their drug laws for sacramental peyote use. *See, e.g.*, Ariz. Rev. Stat. Ann. § 13-3402(b)(1)–(3) (1989); Colo. Rev. Stat. § 12-22-317(3) (1985); N. M. Stat. Ann. § 30-31-6(D) (Supp. 1989). But to say that a nondiscriminatory religious-practice exemption is permitted, or even that it is desirable, is not to say that it is constitutionally required, and that the appropriate occasions for its creation can be discerned by the courts. It may fairly be said that leaving accommodation to the political process will place at a relative disadvantage those religious practices that are not widely engaged in; but that unavoidable consequence of democratic government must be preferred to a system in which each conscience is a law unto itself or in which judges weigh the social importance of all laws against the centrality of all religious beliefs.

. . . .

Because respondents' ingestion of peyote was prohibited under Oregon law, and because that prohibition is constitutional, Oregon may, consistent with the Free Exercise Clause, deny respondents unemployment compensation when their dismissal results from use of the drug. The decision of the Oregon Supreme Court is accordingly reversed.

It is so ordered.

JUSTICE O'CONNOR, with whom JUSTICE BRENNAN, JUSTICE MARSHALL, and JUSTICE BLACKMUN join as to Parts I and II, concurring in the judgment.

Although I agree with the result the Court reaches in this case, I cannot join its opinion. In my view, today's holding dramatically departs from well-settled first amendment jurisprudence, appears unnecessary to resolve the question presented, and is incompatible with our Nation's fundamental commitment to individual religious liberty.

B

Respondents . . . do not contend that their conduct is automatically immune from all governmental regulation simply because it is motivated by their sincere religious beliefs. . . . Rather, respondents invoke our traditional compelling interest test to argue that the Free Exercise Clause requires the State to grant them a limited exemption from its general criminal prohibition against the possession of peyote. The Court today, however, denies them even the opportunity to make that argument, concluding that "the sounder approach, and the approach in accord with the vast majority of our precedents, is to hold the [compelling interest] test inapplicable to" challenges to general criminal prohibitions.

In my view, however, the essence of a free exercise claim is relief from a burden imposed by government on religious practices or beliefs, whether the burden is imposed directly through laws that prohibit or compel specific religious practices, or indirectly through laws that, in effect, make abandonment of one's own religion or conformity to the religious beliefs of others the price of an equal place in the civil community.

Indeed, we have never distinguished between cases in which a State conditions receipt of a benefit on conduct prohibited by religious beliefs and cases in which a State affirmatively prohibits such conduct. The *Sherbert* compelling interest test applies in both kinds of cases. [Hence] I would reaffirm that principle today: a neutral criminal law prohibiting conduct that a State may legitimately regulate is, if anything, more burdensome than a neutral civil statute placing legitimate conditions on the award of a state benefit.

The compelling interest test reflects the first amendment's mandate of preserving religious liberty to the fullest extent possible in a pluralistic society. For the Court to deem this command a "luxury," is to denigrate "[t]he very purpose of a Bill of Rights."

III

The Court's holding today not only misreads settled first amendment precedent; it appears to be unnecessary to this case. I would reach the same result applying our established free exercise jurisprudence.

A

There is no dispute that Oregon's criminal prohibition of peyote places a severe burden on the ability of respondents to freely exercise their religion. Peyote is a sacrament of the Native American Church, and is regarded as vital to respondents' ability to practice their religion. [In addition, there] is also no dispute that Oregon has a significant interest in enforcing laws that control the possession and use of controlled substances by its citizens.

B

Thus, the critical question in this case is whether exempting respondents from the State's general criminal prohibition "will unduly interfere with fulfillment of the governmental interest." Although the question is close, I would conclude that uniform application of Oregon's criminal prohibition is "essential to accomplish" *Lee, supra,* at 257, its overriding interest in preventing the physical harm caused by the use of a Schedule I controlled substance. Oregon's criminal prohibition represents that State's judgment that the possession and use of controlled substances, even by only one person, is inherently harmful and dangerous. Because the health effects caused by the use of controlled substances exist regardless of the motivation of the user, the use of such substances, even for religious purposes, violates the very purpose of the laws that prohibit them. . . .

For these reasons, I believe that granting a selective exemption in this case would seriously impair Oregon's compelling interest in prohibiting possession of peyote by its citizens. Under such circumstances, the Free Exercise Clause does not require the State to accommodate respondents' religiously motivated conduct. . . .

I would therefore adhere to our established free exercise jurisprudence and hold that the State in this case has a compelling interest in regulating peyote use by its citizens and that accommodating respondents' religiously motivated conduct "will unduly interfere with fulfillment of the governmental interest." *Lee,* 455 U.S., at 259. Accordingly, I concur in the judgment of the Court.

JUSTICE BLACKMUN, with whom JUSTICE BRENNAN and JUSTICE MARSHALL join, dissenting.

This Court over the years painstakingly has developed a consistent and exacting standard to test the constitutionality of a state statute that burdens the free exercise of religion. Such a statute may stand only if the law in general, and the State's refusal to allow a religious exemption in particular, are justified by a compelling interest that cannot be served by less restrictive means.

Until today, I thought this was a settled and inviolate principle of this Court's first amendment jurisprudence. The majority, however, perfunctorily dismisses it as a "constitutional anomaly." As carefully detailed in Justice O'CONNOR's concurring opinion, the majority is able to arrive at this view only by mischaracterizing this Court's precedents. . . .

This distorted view of our precedents leads the majority to conclude that strict scrutiny of a state law burdening the free exercise of religion is a "luxury" that a well-ordered society cannot afford, and that the repression of minority religions is an "unavoidable consequence of democratic government." I do not believe the Founders thought their dearly bought freedom from religious persecution a "luxury," but an essential element of liberty — and they could not have thought religious intolerance "unavoidable," for they drafted the Religion Clauses precisely in order to avoid that intolerance.

For these reasons, I agree with Justice O'Connor's analysis of the applicable free exercise doctrine, and I join Parts I and II of her opinion. As she points out, "the critical question in this case is whether exempting respondents from the State's general criminal prohibition 'will unduly interfere with fulfillment of the governmental interest.'" I do disagree, however, with her specific answer to that question.

I

In weighing respondents' clear interest in the free exercise of their religion against Oregon's asserted interest in enforcing its drug laws, it is important to articulate in precise terms the state interest involved. It is not the State's broad interest in fighting the critical "war on drugs" that must be weighed against respondents' claim, but the State's narrow interest in refusing to make an exception for the religious, ceremonial use of peyote. Failure to reduce the competing interests to the same plane of generality tends to distort the weighing process in the State's favor. *See* J. Morris Clark, *Guidelines for the Free Exercise Clause*, 83 HARV. L. REV. 327, 330–331 (1969) ("The purpose of almost any law can be traced back to one or another of the fundamental concerns of government: public health and safety, public peace and order, defense, revenue. To measure an individual interest directly against one of these rarified values inevitably makes the individual interest appear the less significant"); Roscoe Pound, *A Survey of Social Interests*, 57 HARV. L. REV. 1, 2 (1943) ("When it comes to weighing or valuing claims or demands with respect to other claims or demands, we must be careful to compare them on the same plane . . . [or else] we may decide the question in advance in our very way of putting it").

It is surprising, to say the least, that this Court which so often prides itself about principles of judicial restraint and reduction of federal control over matters of state law would stretch its jurisdiction to the limit in order to reach, in this abstract setting, the constitutionality of Oregon's criminal prohibition of peyote use.

The State's interest in enforcing its prohibition, in order to be sufficiently compelling to outweigh a free exercise claim, cannot be merely abstract or symbolic. The State cannot plausibly assert that unbending application of a criminal prohibition is essential to fulfill any compelling interest, if it does not, in fact, attempt to enforce that prohibition. In this case, the State actually has not evinced any concrete interest in enforcing its drug laws against religious users of peyote. Oregon has never sought to prosecute respondents, and does not claim that it has made significant enforcement efforts against other religious users of peyote. The State's asserted interest thus amounts only to the symbolic preservation of an unenforced prohibition. But a government interest in "symbolism, even symbolism for so worthy a cause as the abolition of unlawful drugs," cannot suffice to abrogate the constitutional rights of individuals.

Similarly, this Court's prior decisions have not allowed a government to rely on mere speculation about potential harms, but have demanded evidentiary support for a refusal to allow a religious exception. In this case, the State's justification for refusing to recognize an exception to its criminal laws for religious peyote use is entirely speculative.

The State proclaims an interest in protecting the health and safety of its citizens from the dangers of unlawful drugs. It offers, however, no evidence that the religious use of peyote has ever harmed anyone. The factual findings of other courts cast doubt on the State's assumption that religious use of peyote is harmful. *See State v. Whittingham*, 19 Ariz. App. 27, 30, 504 P.2d 950, 953 (1973) ("the State failed to prove that the quantities of peyote used in the sacraments of the Native American Church are sufficiently harmful to the health and welfare of the participants so as to permit a legitimate intrusion under the State's police power"); *People v. Woody*, 61 Cal. 2d 716, 722–723, 394 P.2d 813, 818 (1964) ("as the Attorney General . . . admits, the opinion of scientists and other experts is 'that peyote . . . works no permanent deleterious injury to the Indian'").

The fact that peyote is classified as a Schedule I controlled substance does not, by itself, show that any and all uses of peyote, in any circumstance, are inherently harmful and dangerous. The Federal Government, which created the classifications of unlawful drugs from which Oregon's drug laws are derived, apparently does not find peyote so dangerous as to preclude an exemption for religious use. Moreover, other Schedule I drugs have lawful uses.

[Furthermore], 23 States, including many that have significant Native American populations, have statutory or judicially crafted exemptions in their drug laws for religious use of peyote. *See Smith v. Employment Division*, 307 Ore. 68, 73, n. 2, 763 P.2d 146, 148, n. 2 (1988). Although this does not prove that Oregon must have such an exception too, it is significant that these States, and the Federal Government, all find their (presumably compelling) interests in controlling the use of dangerous drugs compatible with an exemption for religious use of peyote.

The carefully circumscribed ritual context in which respondents used peyote is far removed from the irresponsible and unrestricted recreational use of unlawful drugs.[49] The Native American Church's internal restrictions on, and supervision of, its members' use of peyote substantially obviate the State's health and safety concerns.

Moreover, just as in *Yoder*, the values and interests of those seeking a religious exemption in this case are congruent, to a great degree, with those the State seeks to promote through its drug laws. Not only does the Church's doctrine forbid nonreligious use of peyote; it also generally advocates self-reliance, familial responsibility, and abstinence from alcohol. There is considerable evidence that the spiritual and social support provided by the Church has been effective in combatting the tragic effects of alcoholism on the Native American population. Two noted experts on peyotism, Dr. Omer C. Stewart and Dr. Robert Bergman, testified by affidavit to this effect on behalf of respondent Smith before the Employment Appeal Board. Far from promoting the lawless and irresponsible use of drugs, Native American Church members' spiritual code exemplifies values that Oregon's drug laws are presumably intended to foster.

The State also seeks to support its refusal to make an exception for religious use of peyote by invoking its interest in abolishing drug trafficking. There is, however, practically no illegal traffic in peyote.

[Lastly,] the State argues that granting an exception for religious peyote use would erode its interest in the uniform, fair, and certain enforcement of its drug laws. The State fears that, if it grants an exemption for religious peyote use, a flood of other claims to religious exemptions will follow. It would then be placed in a dilemma, it says, between allowing a patchwork of exemptions that would hinder its law enforcement efforts, and risking a violation of the Establishment Clause by arbitrarily limiting its religious exemptions. This argument, however, could be made in almost any free exercise case. *See* Ira C. Lupu, *Where Rights Begin: The Problem of Burdens on the Free Exercise of Religion*, 102 HARV. L. REV. 933, 947 (1989) ("Behind every free exercise claim is a spectral march; grant this one, a voice whispers to each judge, and you will be confronted with an endless chain of exemption demands from religious deviants of every stripe"). This Court, however, consistently has rejected similar arguments in past free exercise cases, and it should do so here as well.

The State's apprehension of a flood of other religious claims is purely speculative. Almost half the States, and the Federal Government, have maintained an exemption for religious peyote use for many years, and apparently have not found themselves overwhelmed by claims to other religious exemptions. Allowing an exemption for religious peyote use would not necessarily oblige the State to grant a similar exemption to other religious groups. The unusual circumstances that make the religious use of peyote compatible with the State's interests in health and safety and in preventing drug trafficking would not apply to other religious claims. Some religions, for example, might not restrict drug use to a limited ceremonial context,

---

[49] [6] During Prohibition, the federal government exempted such use of wine from its general ban on possession and use of alcohol. See National Prohibition Act, Title II, § 3, 41 Stat. 308. However compelling the Government's then general interest in prohibiting the use of alcohol may have been, it could not plausibly have asserted an interest sufficiently compelling to outweigh Catholics' right to take communion.

as does the Native American Church. Some religious claims involve drugs such as marijuana and heroin, in which there is significant illegal traffic, with its attendant greed and violence, so that it would be difficult to grant a religious exemption without seriously compromising law enforcement efforts. That the State might grant an exemption for religious peyote use, but deny other religious claims arising in different circumstances, would not violate the Establishment Clause. Though the State must treat all religions equally, and not favor one over another, this obligation is fulfilled by the uniform application of the "compelling interest" test to all free exercise claims, not by reaching uniform results as to all claims. A showing that religious peyote use does not unduly interfere with the State's interests is "one that probably few other religious groups or sects could make," this does not mean that an exemption limited to peyote use is tantamount to an establishment of religion.

III

Finally, although I agree with Justice O'CONNOR that courts should refrain from delving into questions of whether, as a matter of religious doctrine, a particular practice is "central" to the religion, I do not think this means that the courts must turn a blind eye to the severe impact of a State's restrictions on the adherents of a minority religion. Cf. Yoder, 406 U.S., at 219 (since "education is inseparable from and a part of the basic tenets of their religion . . . [just as] baptism, the confessional, or a sabbath may be for others," enforcement of State's compulsory education law would "gravely endanger if not destroy the free exercise of respondents' religious beliefs").

Respondents believe, and their sincerity has never been at issue, that the peyote plant embodies their deity, and eating it is an act of worship and communion. Without peyote, they could not enact the essential ritual of their religion.

If Oregon can constitutionally prosecute them for this act of worship, they, like the Amish, may be "forced to migrate to some other and more tolerant region." This potentially devastating impact must be viewed in light of the federal policy — reached in reaction to many years of religious persecution and intolerance — of protecting the religious freedom of Native Americans. See American Indian Religious Freedom Act, 92 Stat. 469, 42 U.S.C. § 1996 ("it shall be the policy of the United States to protect and preserve for American Indians their inherent right of freedom to believe, express, and exercise the traditional religions . . . , including but not limited to access to sites, use and possession of sacred objects, and the freedom to worship through ceremonials and traditional rites"). Congress recognized that certain substances, such as peyote, "have religious significance because they are sacred, they have power, they heal, they are necessary to the exercise of the rites of the religion, they are necessary to the cultural integrity of the tribe, and, therefore, religious survival." H.R. Rep. No. 95-1308, p. 2 (1978).

Indeed, Oregon's attitude toward respondents' religious peyote use harkens back to the repressive federal policies pursued a century ago:

"In the government's view, traditional practices were not only morally degrading, but unhealthy. 'Indians are fond of gatherings of every description,' a 1913 public health study complained, advocating the restriction of dances and 'sings' to stem contagious diseases. In 1921, the Commissioner of Indian Affairs Charles Burke reminded his staff to punish any Indian engaged in 'any dance which involves . . . the reckless giving away of property . . . frequent or prolonged periods of celebration . . . in fact, any disorderly or plainly excessive performance that promotes superstitious cruelty, licentiousness, idleness, danger to health, and shiftless indifference to family welfare.' Two years later, he [forbade] Indians under the age of 50 from participating in any dances of any kind, and directed federal employees 'to educate public opinion' against them." *Id.*, at 370–371 (footnotes omitted).

The American Indian Religious Freedom Act, in itself, may not create rights enforceable against government action restricting religious freedom, but this Court must scrupulously apply its free exercise analysis to the religious claims of Native Americans, however unorthodox they may be. Otherwise, both the first amendment and the stated policy of Congress will offer to Native Americans merely an unfulfilled and hollow promise.

IV

For these reasons, I conclude that Oregon's interest in enforcing its drug laws against religious use of peyote is not sufficiently compelling to outweigh respondents' right to the free exercise of their religion. Since the State could not constitutionally enforce its criminal prohibition against respondents, the interests underlying the State's drug laws cannot justify its denial of unemployment benefits. Absent such justification, the State's regulatory interest in denying benefits for religiously motivated "misconduct," is indistinguishable from the state interests this Court has rejected in *Frazee, Hobbie, Thomas,* and *Sherbert.* The State of Oregon cannot, consistently with the Free Exercise Clause, deny respondents unemployment benefits.

I dissent.

NOTES

1. **Peyote, the Native American Church, and the First Amendment:** The decision in *Smith* was preceded by many cases from state and federal courts upholding the right of Native individuals who belonged to the Native American Church to practice the ceremonial use of peyote. *See, e.g., Native American Church of New York v. United States,* 468 F. Supp. 1247 (S.D.N.Y. 1979), *aff'd,* 633 F.2d 205 (2d Cir. 1980); *In re Grady,* 394 P.2d 728 (Cal. 1964); *State v. Whittingham,* 504 P.2d 950 (Ariz. Ct. App. 1964). One of the earliest and most influential cases was the California Supreme Court's 1964 decision in *People v. Woody,* 394 P.2d 813 (Cal. 1964). In that case, the court reversed the convictions of several Navajo Indians who had been charged with violating state controlled substances laws for the ceremonial use of peyote in a NAC meeting held in a remote California desert area. The court found that the practice was protected by the First Amendment free exercise clause, and that the state's asserted interest in remediating the "primitive condition" of Indians was not sufficient to outweigh the defendants' free exercise right. The court

distinguished the *Reynolds* polygamy case, finding that polygamy was not "essential" to the practice of Mormonism, while peyote is essential to the practice of the NAC religion, and that polygamy jeopardized the institution of marriage, while the ceremonial use of peyote does not jeopardize any democratic institution of the state.

In addition, at the time *Smith* was decided, existing federal regulations and a large number of state statutes explicitly exempted ceremonial use of peyote in bona fide religious ceremonies of the Native American Church from the controlled substance restrictions. See, e.g., 21 C.F.R. sec. 1307/31 (1989) (exempting "the nondrug use of peyote in bona fide religious ceremonies of the Native American Church" from the listing of peyote as a controlled substance, and exempting "members of the Native American Church so using peyote" from registration"). *See generally Olsen v. Drug Enforcement Admin.*, 878 F.2d 1458, 1463–64 (D.C. Cir. 1989). *See also* Ariz. Rev. Stat. Ann. § 13-3402(b)(1)–(3); Colo. Rev. Stat. § 12-22-317(3); N. M. Stat. Ann. § 30-31-6(D). These religious exemptions were generally limited to Indians who are members of the Native American Church, and were not extended to other groups and individuals asserting that they, too, should have a right to use peyote. *See, e.g., Peyote Way Church of God v. Thornburg*, 922 F.2d 1210 (5th Cir. 1991) (upholding Texas state law exempting the ceremonial use of peyote by NAC members, which tracked the federal language, against an equal protection challenge by an individual asserting that other religions should be entitled to the exemption, too).

Following *Smith*, Congress enacted the American Indian Religious Freedom Act Amendments of 1994, Pub. L. 103-344, 108 Stat. 3125, codified at 42 U.S.C. § 1996, which provide that:

> Nothwithstanding any other provision of law, the use, possession, or transportation of peyote by an Indian for bona fide traditional ceremonial purposes in connection with the practice of a traditional Indian religion is lawful, and shall not be prohibited by the United States or any State. No Indian shall be penalized or discriminated against on the basis of such use, possession, or transportation, including, but not limited to, denial of otherwise applicable benefits under public assistance programs.

The Act defines "Indian" as a member of an Indian tribe, but does not specify that this must be a federally recognized tribe. It also recognizes limited rights of federal agencies to impose reasonable regulations for cultivating, harvesting, and distributing peyote in conformity with the Act, and for reasonable regulations on the use of peyote in certain military, transportation, or other sensitive employments.

2. Federal Efforts to Protect Indian Sacred Sites: While Congress repeatedly considered legislation during the 1990s to overturn *Lyng* and protect Indian sacred sites, no such legislation was immediately enacted. *See generally* Jack F. Trope, *Protecting Native American Religious Freedom: The Legal, Historical, and Constitutional Basis for the Proposed Native American Free Exercise of Religion Act*, 20 N.Y.U. Rev. L. & Soc. Change 373 (1993). In the absence of Congressional action, President Clinton issued an Executive Order on May 24, 1996, dealing with protection of sacred sites located on federally managed lands. Executive Order, Indian Sacred Sites, 61 FR 26771 (May 24, 1996). While this Executive Order expressly provides in section 4 that it is "intended only to improve the internal management of the executive branch and is not intended to, nor does it, create any right, benefit, or trust responsibility, substantive or procedural, enforceable at law or in equity against the United States, it agencies, officers, or any person," section 1 of the Order does mandate that in managing Federal lands:

> each executive branch agency with statutory or administrative responsibility for the management of Federal lands shall, to the extent practicable, permitted by law, and not clearly inconsistent with essential agency functions, (1) accommodate access to and ceremonial use of Indian sacred sites by Indian religious practitioners and (2) avoid adversely affecting the physical integrity of such sacred sites.

Section 1 also mandates executive agencies to "maintain the confidentiality of sacred sites" where appropriate. Section 2 of the Sacred Sites Executive Order mandates agencies affected by the Order to establish procedures for implementing the mandate of the Order. Does the President have the same powers to protect Indian sacred sites that Congress could exercise? *See generally* Shawna Lee, Note, *Government Managed Shrines: Protection of Native American Sacred Site Worship*, 35 VAL. U. L. REV. 265, 294–296 (2000).

3. **The Religious Freedom Restoration Act:** Responding to *Bowen, Lyng* and *Smith*, Congress passed the Religious Freedom Restoration Act (RFRA), Pub. L. 103-141, 107 Stat. 1488, codified in significant part at 28 U.S.C. § 1988 and 42 U.S.C. §§ 2000bb–2000bb-4. This statute purported to overturn both the result and analysis of *Smith* by creating a new federal statutory cause of action for infringement of religious exercise rights. Under the RFRA standard, courts must employ the compelling governmental interest test, including a new least restrictive alternative component of the test. Initially, RFRA was used, sometimes successfully, to see protection for Native American religious rights, particularly in the prison context. *E.g., Werner v. McCotter*, 49 F.3d 1476, 1480 (10th Cir. 1995); *Hinkle v. Ariz. Dept. of Corrections*, 1995 U.S. App. LEXIS 4186 (9th Cir. Feb. 21, 1995); *Belgard v. Hawaii*, 883 F. Supp. 510, 512–17 (D. Haw. 1995); *Francis v. Keane*, 888 F. Supp. 568 (S.D.N.Y. 1995). *But see Hamilton v. Schriro*, 74 F.3d 1545 (8th Cir. 1996) (rejecting Indian prisoner long-hair and sweat lodge claims on both free exercise and RFRA grounds. For a discussion of the developments in federal law regarding American Indian religious freedom, as well as contemporary challenges, *see* Kristen A. Carpenter, *Limiting Principles and Empowering Practices in American Indian Religious Freedoms*, 45 CONN. L. REV. 387 (2012)

In *City of Boerne v. Flores*, 521 U.S. 507 (1997), the Supreme Court held, however, that Congress lacked power under section 5 of the Fourteenth Amendment to enact RFRA as a remedial statute restricting state and local governmental action impinging on religiously motivated conduct. The Court reasoned that the statute's prohibitions were too broad and lacked congruence and proportionality to the level of constitutional violations. The Court also suggested that by not giving full force and effect to Smith, RFRA effectively violated the separation of powers. Nevertheless, the Supreme Court subsequently held in *Gonzales v. O Centro Espirita Beneficente Uniao do Vegetal*, 546 U.S. 418, 433 (2006) that RFRA is still in full force and effect as against the federal government.

4. The Religious Land Use and Institutionalized Persons Act (RLUIPA): In 2000, Congress enacted RLUIPA, which provides, "No government shall impose a substantial burden on the religious exercise of a person residing in or confined to an institution" without "a compelling governmental interest" carried out with the "least restrictive means." 42 U.S.C. § 2000cc-1. *See also Cutter v. Wilkinson,* 544 U.S. 709 (2005) (upholding the constitutionality of the RLUIPA.) Even under a strict scrutiny standard, Native prisoners face particular hurdles in vindicating their religious freedom rights, because courts have often held that prison officials possess strong interests in prisoner safety and security. S*ee Fowler v. Crawford,* 534 F.3d 931 (8th Cir. 2008) (prohibiting an inmate's access to a sweatlodge was the least restrictive means to further a compelling government interest of prison safety and security); *Knight v. Thompson,* 723 F.3d 1275 (11th Cir. 2013) (corrections policy prohibiting male Native American inmates from wearing long hair furthered a compelling state interest in security, discipline, hygiene, and safety, and the policy was the least restrictive means of achieving this goal).

In addition to policies regarding hair-cutting and sweatlodges, in recent years, departments of corrections in several states have issued bans and prohibitions on items often associated with Native American religious practices, such as tobacco, kinnikinnick, and beads, among other materials. *See* HUY, JOINT SUBMISSION TO THE U.N. HUMAN RIGHTS COMMITTEE CONCERNING RELIGIOUS FREEDOMS OF INDIGENOUS PERSONS DEPRIVED OF THEIR LIBERTY IN THE UNITED STATES OF AMERICA 9 (2013) (submitted jointly by Huy, the National Native American Bar Association, the Indigenous Peoples Law and Policy Program, the National Congress of American Indians, and the Native American Rights Fund, among other groups and organizations).

Even when the government does not initially provide a compelling interest for its actions in RLUIPA cases, courts often remand the case with the caveat that prison officials provide additional evidence regarding the allegedly "compelling state interest." *See Yellowbear v. Lampert,* 741 F.3d 48 (10th Cir. 2014) (dismissing a summary judgment claim against Northern Arapaho prisoner who wanted to use the prison's sweatlodge, but was denied access because he was not in the general population of the prison); *Haight v. Thompson,* 763 F.3d 554 (6th Cir. 2014) (whether death-row inmates had a right to access prison sweatlodge and whether inmates had a right to consume traditional foods before a faith-based powwow were triable issues of fact). Note also that every circuit to consider the issue has held that the RLUIPA does not permit money damages against state prison officials in their official capacity. *Haight v. Thompson, supra,.* at 570.

5. Assessing the Impact of Indian Religious Freedom Legislation: The impact of recent legislation regarding Indian religious freedoms and the protection of sacred sites is a subject of continuing controversy in the federal courts. Thus, the central issue of whether RFRA is more protective of Native interests than the Supreme Court's pre-*Smith* case law under the First Amendment free exercise clause is still open. The U.S. Supreme Court denied the Navajo Nation's petition for a writ of certiorari in *Navajo Nation v. U.S. Forest Service,* 535 F.3d 1058 (9th Cir. 2008), an en banc opinion of the Ninth Circuit which upheld the U.S. Forest Service's approval of a permit allowing the Snowbowl ski resort on the San Francisco Peaks to make certain modifications to its facility, including the manufacture of artificial snow from treated sewage effluent. In an opinion authored by Judge Bea, a majority of the panel held that the government-approved use of artificial snow made from recycled sewage effluent did not violate RFRA or any other federal law and affirmed the district court's denial of relief to plaintiffs on all grounds. The court held that in order to establish a prima facie RFRA claim, a plaintiff must prove that (1) the activities the plaintiff claims are burdened by the government action constitute an "exercise of religion," and (2) the government action "substantially burdens" the exercise of religion. If the plaintiff proves both elements, the burden shifts to "the government to prove that the challenged government action is in furtherance of a 'compelling government interest' and is implemented by 'the least restrictive means.'"

The en banc majority found that the plaintiffs had proven that the religious activities in question constitute an "exercise of religion." However, the court found that plaintiffs had not proven that the use of recycled wastewater on the Snowbowl would impose a "substantial burden" on the exercise of plaintiffs' religion. Consequently, there was no need to engage the analysis of whether the government had a compelling interest in approving the use of recycled wastewater on the sacred mountain or whether its action constituted the least restrictive means of achieving such a purpose. In reaching this holding, the court found that, in enacting RFRA, Congress had intended to incorporate the pre-*Smith* case law on what constitutes a "substantial burden," including the *Sherbert* and *Yoder* decisions. The court found that this case law supported its conclusion that:

> Under RFRA, a "substantial burden" is imposed only when individuals are forced to choose between following the tenets of their religion and receiving a government benefit (*Sherbert*) or coerced to act contrary to their religious beliefs by the threat of civil or criminal sanctions (*Yoder*). Any burden imposed on the exercise of religion short of that described by *Sherbert* or *Yoder* is not a "substantial burden" within the meaning of RFRA, and does not require the application of the compelling interest test set forth in those two cases.

Using this analysis, the court found that the harm to plaintiffs in this case was merely offense to their "subjective, emotional religious experience." Because there was no "physical effect" on plaintiffs' religious experience, neither factor in the substantial burden test was met. The court found that a claim of "damaged spiritual feelings" is not actionable under RFRA. The court cited *Lyng v. Northwest Indian Cemetery Protective Association* as the closest precedent on point because in that case, the Supreme Court concluded that the Native plaintiffs' "belief" that the government's construction of a road through a sacred site on government land would "destroy" their ability to practice their religion did not constitute a "substantial burden" on the religion, when tribal members remained free to access the area and perform ceremonial activities. The Ninth Circuit en banc majority found that RFRA incorporated all of the Supreme Court's prior free exercise analysis, including *Lyng*.

The policy underpinning the Ninth Circuit's decision is reflected in its finding that the government could not function if it was forced to respond to the preferences of all citizens about what is offensive to their religious beliefs. "Were it otherwise, any action the federal government were to take, including action on its own land, would be subject to the personalized oversight of millions of citizens." The court maintained that "[W]e are a cosmopolitan nation made up of people of almost every conceivable religious preference," and that the government meets its obligation to respect that pluralism by protecting the right of citizens to "believe" as they choose, but it does not have the obligation to conform its conduct to those beliefs. The majority further found that the plaintiffs' NEPA claim that the Forest Service had not adequately evaluated the risks posed by human ingestion of artificial snow had not been properly raised in the district court and was therefore waived on appeal.

Judge William Fletcher authored a strong dissent, joined by Judge Pregerson and Judge Fisher, concluding that "the proposed expansion of the Arizona Snowbowl, which would entail spraying up to 1.5 million gallons per day of treated sewage effluent on the holiest of the San Francisco Peaks, violates RFRA" because the expansion "would impose a 'substantial burden' on the Indians' 'exercise of religion' and is not justified by a 'compelling government interest.' " In a carefully documented and reasoned opinion, the dissent found that the majority had misstated the law under RFRA and had misunderstood the very nature of the religions under consideration.

The dissent observed that RFRA had been amended by the Religious Land Use and Institutionalized Persons Act of 2000 (RLUIPA), which replaced the original "First Amendment definition of 'exercise of religion' with a broader statutory definition." This statutory mandate requires the government to consider the effects of its actions on "any exercise of religion, whether or not compelled by, or central to, a system of religious belief." Thus, the government had an obligation to consider the effects of its action on the land-based religions of American Indian peoples, which are necessarily different from the religions of any other group. Moreover, the dissent found that in several other ways, "RFRA provides greater protection for religious practices than did the Supreme Court's pre-*Smith* cases." For example, "RFRA 'goes beyond the constitutional language that forbids the 'prohibiting' of the free exercise of religion and uses the broader verb 'burden.'" RFRA also "imposes in every case a least restrictive means requirement" that was not used in the pre-*Smith* jurisprudence. And finally, RFRA "applies *Sherbert* and *Yoder*'s compelling interest test 'in all cases' where the exercise of religion is substantially burdened." In particular, the dissent found that that the majority had misstated the law under RFRA by developing such a restrictive definition of "substantial burden," by ignoring the impact of RLUIPA and cases interpreting RLUIPA, and by suggesting that it is an "open question whether RFRA applies to the federal government's use of its own land."

The dissent also found that the Forest Service had failed to satisfy its obligation under NEPA to evaluate the possible risks posed by human ingestion of artificial snow. The dissent noted that the NEPA violation could be cured, but the RFRA violation could not be cured: "Because of the majority's decision today, there will be a permanent expansion of the Arizona Snowbowl," with a daily release of sewage effluent on the mountain that would forever desecrate the mountain and impair the Indians' exercise of their religion. The dissent read the majority's opinion as "effectively read[ing] American Indians out of RFRA," and criticized the majority for treating the mountain as a "public park" that "belongs to everyone," conveniently ignoring the historical fact that the mountains were taken "from the Indians by force" and using that fact as a "justification for spraying treated sewage effluent on the holiest of the Indians' holy mountains." The dissent also noted the sweeping effect of the majority's analysis on Native peoples: "RFRA was passed to protect the exercise of all religions, including the religions of American Indians. If Indians' land-based exercise of religion is not protected by RFRA in this case, I cannot imagine a case in which it will be."

The Ninth Circuit has rejected the plaintiffs' most recent attempt to stop the snowmaking on the ground that the plan posed unacceptable environmental risks that were inadequately evaluated under NEPA, characterizing plaintiffs' claim as a "gross abuse of the judicial process." *Save the Peaks Coalition v. U.S. Forest Service*, 669 F.3d 1025, 1028 (9th Cir. 2012).

6.   **Other Avenues for Indian Religious Freedom Protection:** One additional statute that may provide at least procedural protection for Native Americans is the National Historic Preservation Act, 16 U.S.C. § 470 et seq. The NHPA requires federal agencies to assess the impacts of development activities on significant historic resources, including any structure, area, or district listed or eligible for listing on the National Register of Historic Places. See 16 U.S.C. § 470f. It applies to agency decisions affecting private development *(e.g.,* water discharge permits issued by the Army Corps of Engineers) as well as development on public lands. The NHPA's "section 106" process imposes consultation requirements and other proce-dural protections which allow agencies to adequately consider the impacts of the proposed development. The NHPA covers "Traditional Cultural Properties," which are sites that are associated with the cultural practices and beliefs of a living community and are important in maintaining the community's continuing cultural identity. *See* Patricia L. Parker & Thomas E. King, *National Park Service, National Register Bulletin No. 38: Guidelines for Evaluating and Documenting Traditional Cultural Properties*, U.S. Dept. of Interior, National Park Service National Register. Thus, the NHPA may provide a means to protect places that are considered sacred to an Indian nation or several Indian nations but are no longer within tribal ownership. *See generally* Rebecca Tsosie, *The Conflict Between the "Public Trust" and the "Indian Trust" Doctrines: Federal Public Land Policy and Native Nations*, 39 Tulsa L. Rev. 271 (2003); Dean Suagee, *The Cultural Heritage of American Indian Tribes and the Preservation of Biological Diversity*, 31 Ariz. St. L.J. 483 (1999). NHPA's section 106 process is discussed further in Sec. B.3.a, this chapter.

At the international level, the United Nations Declaration on the Rights of Indigenous Peoples, discussed in Ch. 1, Sec. E, recognizes that "indigenous peoples have the right to maintain and strengthen their distinctive spiritual relationship with their traditionally owned or otherwise occupied and used lands, territories, waters and coastal seas and other resources and to uphold their responsibilities to future generations in this regard." The United States officially offered its support of the Declaration in 2010. Is there any way the Navajo, Hopi, and Apache can employ this provision to prevent expansion of the Snowbowl ski resort? Assuming those tribes could persuade the Obama administration to do so, is it too late for the U.S. Forest Service to retract its permit? For a thoughtful analysis of the issues posed by the *Navajo Nation* case within a property law framework, see Kristen A.

Carpenter, Sonia K. Katyal & Angela R. Riley, *In Defense of Property*, 118 YALE
LAW JOURNAL 1022 (2009). For a helpful synthesis of the constitutional principles,
statutory requirements, and federal policies that affect Native American sacred
sites in public land management decisions, *see* Sandi Zellmer, *Sustaining Geogra-
phies of Hope: Cultural Resources on Public Lands*, 73 U. COLO. L. REV. 413 (2002).

Finally, there is still the opportunity for the voluntary accommodation of Indian
religious freedom claims. While *Smith* holds that the First Amendment does not
require religiously-based exemptions to state laws of general application, it does not
hold that federal or state governments cannot voluntarily decide to accommodate
Indian religious practices, including ceremonial practices at federal or state owned
Indian sacred sites. Justice Scalia's majority opinion in *Smith* specifically noted that
"a nondiscriminatory religious-practice exemption is permitted."

However, to the extent that federal officials do comply with AIRFA and seek to
accommodate Indian religious practices at sacred sites, they may find themselves
vulnerable to an establishment clause challenge. This occurred in *Bear Lodge
Multiple Use Association v. Babbitt*, 175 F.3d 814 (10th Cir. 1999). In that case, the
National Park Service issued a Final Climbing Management Plan for the Devil's
Tower National Monument that sought to reconcile Native peoples' religious use of
the monument with its recreational use by rock climbers by instituting a voluntary
closure to rock climbing during the month of June. This site is sacred to several of
the Plains tribes, including the Kiowa, Crow, Lakota, Northern Cheyenne and
Arapaho, and the month of June is particularly significant for the religious and
cultural practices of the various tribes. A group of recreational climbers challenged
the policy, claiming that it constituted an "establishment of religion" in violation of
the First Amendment. The district court upheld the voluntary climbing ban on the
ground that the establishment clause does not prevent the federal government from
accommodating the free exercise of religion at a sacred site on federally-owned
lands so long as the accommodation does not deprive others of their use of the area.
Bear Lodge Multiple Use Association v. Babbitt, 2 F. Supp. 2d 1448 (D. Wyo. 1988).
The Tenth Circuit ultimately ruled that the plaintiffs lacked standing to contest the
Management Plan since they could not establish any injury from the voluntary
accommodation of Indian religious ceremonies at the site and therefore, the court
did not reach the establishment clause issue. Would the result have been different
if the Climbing Management Plan had instituted a mandatory ban on climbing?
Does it affect the establishment clause analysis that the various tribes have
different religions and that the site has significant cultural and historical value to
these groups? *Cf. Access Fund v. U.S. Dept. of Agriculture* 499 F.3d 1036 (9th Cir.
2007) (upholding Forest Service ban on climbing at Cave Rock site in Nevada, which
was sacred to the Washoe Tribe, on the basis that the ban was intended to preserve
the historic and cultural value of the site and not to advance or endorse a particular
religion).

**7. Other Native American Cultural Practices That Implicate Religious
Freedom:** There are many contexts beyond sacred sites and the ceremonial use of
peyote that raise issues for Native Americans under the First Amendment free
exercise clause and RFRA. For example, many Native peoples engage in particular
hunting and fishing practices for cultural and religious reasons. Should the state or
the federal government have the right to restrict these practices to effectuate

general laws intended to conserve the species? In *United States v. Dion* (set forth and discussed in Ch. 4, Sec. A.2), the Supreme Court upheld the conviction of a tribal member for hunting eagles on the reservation in violation of the Eagle Protection Act in a case which did not feature the free exercise claim. Other courts have adjudicated the religious claims raised by taking eagles for ceremonial purposes in violation of the statutory permit requirements. *See, e.g., United States v. Abeyta*, 632 F. Supp. 1301 (D.N.M. 1986) (upholding the right of a Pueblo Indian to take eagles for religious purposes under the First Amendment free exercise clause); *cf. United States v. Friday*, 525 F.3d 938 (10th Cir. 2008) (upholding the indictment of a tribal member for hunting eagles on the reservation without the requisite federal permit against a RFRA challenge on the grounds that the Bald and Golden Eagle Protection Act and its regulations are the least restrictive means of pursuing the government's compelling interest in preserving the bald eagle). *See Frank v. Alaska*, 604 P.2d 1068 (Alaska 1979) (upholding the right of Athabascan Indians to kill and possess a moose out of season when fresh moose meat was found to be an integral part of a potlatch ceremony honoring the passing of a tribal member). Other cases involve cultural practices that may come into conflict with institutional regulations, such as those applied to prisoners (see above) or students. *See New Rider v. Board of Educ.*, 480 F.2d 693 (10th Cir. 1973) (characterizing long hair as an expression of cultural pride rather than a religious observance). *See also A.A. v. Needville Independent School District*, 611 F.3d 248 (5th Cir. 2010) (holding Native American child's religious freedoms were violated under the Texas Religious Freedom Restoration Act when he had a sincere religious belief in wearing his hair uncut). As you read the materials in the next section of this casebook, consider whether the distinction between "culture" and "religion" accurately reflects these issues as they arise in a Native American context.

2. Cultural Property

As scholars have observed, "fluid conceptions of property underlie indigenous peoples' group claims to those items most closely and intimately tied to peoplehood and group identity: indigenous cultural property." Kristen A. Carpenter, Sonia K. Katyal, and Angela R. Riley, *In Defense of Property*, 118 YALE L.J. 1022, 1088 (2009). In this sense, the categories of "property" represented under Anglo-American law-real property, material cultural heritage and intellectual property-are not easily aligned with the multiple understandings that accompany indigenous claims to their cultural heritage. This section of the casebook presents concepts of "tangible" and "intangible" cultural property and discusses the statutes and doctrines that have been used to address these claims, as well as noting the deficiencies of existing law in protecting indigenous peoples' interests. The deficiencies arise from normative differences between Anglo-American and indigenous concepts about the appropriate relationship of these forms of "property" to their holders. *See generally* Christopher S. Byrne, *Communal Property Rights in Cultural Objects*, 8 J. ENVTL. L. & LITIG. 109, 116 (1993). For example, indigenous cultural property is generally considered to be under the "ownership" (or "stewardship") of the group in perpetuity and is most often inalienable by individual tribal members. In comparison, the norm of Anglo-American law is the free transferability and alienability of all forms of property.

Furthermore, indigenous cultural property is often imbued with characteristics that represent group values about healing, sharing, historical memory, and reciprocity. Maintenance of the property is therefore considered essential to the group's cultural survival through successive generations. In comparison, the utilitarian values undergirding Anglo-American property law focus on the economic value of the resource to the individual and restraints on alienation are strictly construed as a matter of public policy.

a. Tangible Cultural Property

Material forms of Native American cultural property have been the subject of avid interest by non-Indian art collectors, who tend to see objects like medicine bundles, masks, shields, and prayer sticks as objects of "ethnic art," which can be bought, sold and collected like any form of art. Because of the commercial demand for "Native American antiquities," many art collectors have appropriated cultural objects or attempted to coerce tribal members into alienating tribal cultural property, leading tribes to take action to prevent the transfer of certain objects or gain return of objects that were already transferred into museum collections. Prior to the enactment of NAGPRA, there were limited remedies available to prevent the unauthorized transfer of objects from the tribe, and tribes were often unsuccessful in replevin actions seeking the return of objects plundered from Indian nations during earlier eras. The Chilkat Indian Village's struggle to protect its cultural heritage, detailed in the two cases below, provides a good example of the difficulties faced by Native Americans prior to the enactment of NAGPRA.

The most important federal legislative response to the appropriation of tangible tribal cultural property has been NAGPRA, which defines two categories of protected cultural property (in addition to the sections on Native American human remains and funerary objects, which are separately addressed below) and imposes criminal sanctions on anyone who sells or otherwise profits from any Native American "sacred object" or "object of cultural patrimony." The statute also requires federal agencies and federally-funded museums to prepare summaries of any sacred objects or objects of cultural patrimony that are within their collections, transmit those summaries to potentially affected tribes or Native Hawaiian organizations, and repatriate the objects to culturally affiliated groups upon their request. 25 U.S.C. §§ 3004–3005. "Sacred objects" are defined as "specific ceremonial objects which are needed by traditional Native American religious leaders for the practice of traditional Native American religion by their present day adherents." 25 U.S.C. § 3001 (3)(C). The determination of "sacredness" is to be made by Native American religious leaders themselves, and may vary according to the traditions of the particular community. "Objects of cultural patrimony" are objects that have "ongoing historical, traditional, or cultural importance central to the Native American group or culture itself, rather than property owned by an individual Native American, and which, therefore, cannot be alienated, appropriated, or conveyed by any individual, regardless of whether or not the individual is a member of the Indian tribe." 25 U.S.C. § 3001 (3)(D). Such objects must have been considered inalienable by the Native American group at the time the object was separated from the group. As you read *United States v. Corrow*, which follows the *Chilkat* cases, consider whether one or both categories of cultural property are represented by the facts of the case, and why the United States might have decided to prosecute the case as it did.

Chilkat Indian Village v. Johnson, 870 F.2d 1469 (9th Cir. 1989): Four wooden carved posts and a wooden partition known as a rain screen, traditionally held by the Alaska Native Village of Chilkat, have been called "the finest example of Native art, either Tlingit, or Tsimshian, in Alaska." George T. Emmons, The *Whale House of Chilkat, in* Raven's Bones 81 (1982). A Chilkat member claimed that she had inherited these artifacts under the Tlingit system of descent and distribution. When the Village prevented her from removing them, she was unable to sue in federal court because of the Village's sovereign immunity. *Johnson v. Chilkat Indian Village*, 457 F. Supp. 384 (D. Alaska 1978). Some years later, the artifacts were removed from the Village and sold to an art dealer named Johnson. State officers seized and held them. Meanwhile, the Village sued Johnson and sixteen others in federal court, alleging that defendants had violated both village and federal law by removing the artifacts from their lands. In 1976, the Village had adopted an ordinance prohibiting removal of "artifacts, clan crests, or other traditional Indian art work owned or held by members of the Chilkat Indian Village [or kept within the Village's property] without first requesting and obtaining permission to do so from the Chilkat Indian Village Council."

The Village's complaint made out claims for conversion of tribal property, violation of the tribal ordinance, and violation of a federal criminal statute, 18 U.S.C. § 1163, which penalizes theft or conversion of tribally-owned property. The United States District Court dismissed the claim for lack of jurisdiction, finding that the Village had not stated a claim arising under federal law.

The Ninth Circuit agreed with the trial court that the criminal statute did not give rise to a private claim on behalf of the Village. It also agreed that the claim for conversion was not a federal claim, because the property in question was neither trust property nor property held pursuant to federal statute or common law. Thus the Court distinguished the Chilkat claim from the property claim found to arise under federal law in *Oneida Indian Nation v. County of Oneida*, 414 U.S. 661 (1974) (finding that a suit to aboriginal title arises under federal law because the possessory right itself is a creation of federal common law).

The Ninth Circuit parted company with the District Court, however, over the Village's claim that it was entitled to enforce its ordinance against Johnson and the other defendants. Because the defendants were non-Indian, the Village's claim lay "on the boundaries of tribal jurisdiction." Judge Canby noted:

> [T]he state of the law is such that the heart of the controversy over the claim will be the Village's power, under federal law, to enact its ordinance and apply it to non-Indians. Indeed, the meaning of the ordinance is barely open to dispute, but the Village's power under the federal statute or common law to enact and apply it is open to immense dispute. The State of Alaska placed in issue in district court questions whether the Village was a federally-recognized tribe, whether it ever had or ever could qualify as one, and whether it had any legislative jurisdiction in general or over the artifacts and defendants in particular. Alaska also stated that it was prepared to dispute the Village's contention that its fee lands were Indian

country; Alaska further asserted that, even if they were, the Village thereby acquired or retained no legislative powers. These issues are not before us now, but they are federal questions and they lie at the heart of the Village's claim to enforce its ordinance.

Defendants argued that these federal issues were entirely defensive, and therefore could not count for purposes of establishing a claim that arises under federal law. While viewing the question as a close one, Judge Canby explained, "It would be too technical . . . to focus only on the ultimate ordinance, which is not federal, and to ignore the necessity for the Village to prove its disputed federal power to enact and apply it to those outside of its community. We conclude, therefore, that the Village's claim against Johnson and his corporation arise under federal law." Following this reasoning, the Ninth Circuit held that the Village's claims against its own members did not arise under federal law, because they posed issues of tribal, not federal law.

The Ninth Circuit remanded the case with some hints to the District Court to apply the tribal court exhaustion requirement of *National Farmers Union*, presented in Ch. 4, Sec. A.4.b. The District Court found that the Village was indeed a federally recognized tribe with inherent governmental powers, that the fee land from which the artifacts were taken was a "dependent Indian community" (and hence Indian country) subject to the jurisdiction of the Village,[50] and that exhaustion was therefore appropriate.

CHILKAT INDIAN VILLAGE, IRA v. JOHNSON
Chilkat Trial Court
20 Indian L. Rep. 6127 (1993)

BOWEN, TRIBAL COURT JUDGE

[On January 8, 1990, the Village filed two claims against Johnson and others (both Village members and nonmembers) responsible for removing the house posts and rain screen. One claim was for conversion of tribal trust property, the other for violation of the tribal ordinance. The Village sought declaratory and injunctive relief, as well as money damages. Defendants' answer denied the allegations and counterclaimed against the Village. At trial, testimony included the following, as described by the Tribal Court in its opinion.]

Mr. Hotch [President of the Chilkat Indian Village Council] . . . is a member of the Eagle (or Wolf) moiety, Eagle Clan, and Bear and Killer Whale houses. He is the caretaker, *i.e.,* "*hitsati*" of the Killer Whale House. . . . Mr. Hotch emphasized that a *hitsati* has the duty under tribal law to care for the property of the house *and* clan, and has no right to sell or otherwise dispose of clan property.

Mr. Hotch's testimony addressed several aspects of Tlingit social structure, . . . All Tlingits are either of the Raven or Eagle (also called Wolf) moiety, which exists primarily for marital purposes. Under Tlingit custom law one must marry only a member of the opposite moiety. . . .

[50] This decision preceded the Supreme Court's ruling in the *Venetie* case, presented in Ch. 2, Sec. A.3.b.ii, that such lands are not "dependent Indian communities."

Although identification by Tlingits as members of a particular village is very significant for many purposes, the clan is the primary and most important affiliation. . . . Finally, within each clan there are different house groups. . . . "Houses" in this context refer to physical structures, which traditionally housed nuclear families.

Regarding the four house posts (sometimes called poles or totems) and rain screen here at issue, Joe Hotch testified that they were "clan trust property," with great spiritual significance to the Ganexteidi Clan, which has primary custodial rights over them. Mr. Hotch and other witnesses explained that the tribe on the whole also has an interest in the artifacts because they have tremendous significance not just for Ravens, but for all Eagles in Klukwan as well.

Joe Hotch described in eloquent terms the healing quality which the artifacts assume. For example, when a member of an opposite clan (of the Eagle moiety) died, and a potlatch was held as a part of the progression of Tlingit funeral arrangements, members of the grieving clan would be brought before the rain screen and told that it constituted medicine which would relieve the loss of their clan member.

Mr. Hotch also provided detailed testimony regarding how certain property is confirmed as being clan trust property, which includes presenting it in a ceremony in which members of the opposite "tribe" (*i.e.*, in this case members of clans of the Eagle moiety) are invited, which completes the confirmation of the clan trust status of property such as the Whale House artifacts, which, according to Mr. Hotch, were subject to this process. Joe Hotch recalled attending many ceremonies at the Whale House in which the artifacts played a central role.

[Mr. Hotch further testified about numerous instances when in which art dealers, and Johnson in particular, had attempted to acquire the artifacts by offering large sums of money to individual clan members and had also paid others to seize and carry away the artifacts, only to be thwarted by Village members. The 1976 Village ordinance was a response to these monetary and physical assaults against the artifacts, and was posted conspicuously in the Village.]

Rosita Worl [a social anthropologist who is Tlingit with roots in Klukwan] testified that the Whale House artifacts are crest objects which are owned by the Ganexteidi Clan on the whole. They were commissioned in the traditional way and brought out in a potlatch, in which members of the opposite side (Eagles) played a central role. Under Tlingit law, such objects cannot be sold, unless for some reason (such as restitution for a crime) the entire clan decides to do so. The participants in a clan decision such as this would include all adult males, and high-ranking women. The witness testified that the traditional penalty for an individual selling artifacts in violation of tribal law was death.

Mr. Katzeek [a Tlingit born in Klukwan, known for his expertise in tribal law] was asked . . . to explain the historical significance of the Whale House artifacts, and then whether there is a spiritual significance to the artifacts. His answers were as follows:

> The primary significance is knowing who you are . . . with us, these
> particular artifacts tell a story. . . . When you're selling an artifact . . .

you're not only getting rid of a piece of wood . . . you're getting rid of the music, the song, the dance, and the good, the bad, and the ugly.

CONCLUSIONS

I. The Whale House Rain Screen and House Posts as Artifacts, Clan Crests, and Indian Art Within the Meaning of the Ordinance

The artifacts consist of four elaborately carved wooden posts (made of spruce and over nine feet high) and a wooden partition (made of thin cedar boards) called a rain screen. . . . The record indicates that if the artifacts were sold on the open market they would likely reap a price of several million dollars.

The artifacts were created around 1830. A prominent leader in Klukwan, Xetsuwu, resolved to build a new house (Whale House) in order to unify certain existing house groups of the Ganexteidi Clan. He commissioned the house posts from a famous carver who resided in the Stikine River area, near what is currently referred to as Old Wrangell, Alaska. The name of that artist remained unknown until 1987, when a written account was discovered, which identified his name as Kadjisdu.axtc. The artist, who made detailed sketches while being told about the clan's stories during the canoe trip to Klukwan, is said to have resided in Klukwan for one year while carving the posts. By some accounts he was paid 10 slaves, 50 dressed moose skins, and several blankets.

The four posts represented the four groups that were brought together to form the new Whale House. The posts and rain screen tell stories of the clan; not just of the Whale House. The artifacts and the Whale House itself were created and dedicated in the traditional manner. The Ganexteidi hired Eagles to construct the original house. The Eagles were then repaid in a traditional "payback party," and the property was brought out in a potlatch and dedicated as clan property.

[X]etsuwu's vision to unify the Ganexteidi under a new house with these clan crests was successfully implemented. The clan, as well as the Chilkat Indians generally, became a strong and powerful people. They maintained control of valuable trade routes to interior Alaska, and became quite prosperous.

The historical resistance by members of the clan to a series of efforts by outsiders to purchase these great works is testimony in itself of the clan crest nature of the artifacts, which are held in trust by the clan.

Around 1899, Yeilgooxu (whose English name was George Shotridge), *hitsati* of the Whale House, organized the construction of a new Whale House because the original one was in disrepair. Although a mudslide destroyed it before completion, the artifacts were rescued. Yeilgooxu refused the offers of his friend George Emmons to acquire the artifacts. Following the death of Yeilgooxu, Yeilxaak, who was *hitsati* of the Raven House, was chosen to be *hitsati* of the Whale House, in part because of his close ties with the Whale House.

Louis Shotridge, the son of Yeilgooxu, caused a furor in the tribal community when he attempted to purchase the Whale House artifacts for the University of Pennsylvania's University Museum. In 1922 he arranged a meeting of Ganexteidi leaders, and offered $3,500 for the artifacts. Although that was a tremendous amount of money at that time and place, the clan turned him down.

As a function of the matrilineal nature of Tlingit social structure, Louis Shotridge, like his mother, was a member of the Kaagwantan Clan of the Wolf moiety — the opposite side of his father's clan (Ganexteidi) and moiety (Raven) affiliations. His disingenuous claims to the property under Western inheritance law were rejected by the village. Shotridge became obsessed with acquiring the artifacts, continued his efforts during the 1920s and 1930s, but was never successful. [Shotridge soon thereafter suffered an agonizing and mysterious death.]

Obsession with acquiring the Whale House artifacts did not end with Louis Shotridge. Defendant art dealer Michael Johnson has also been obsessed with the artifacts' acquisition, and his actions in this respect have caused tremendous conflicts and ill will at Klukwan. While the Tlingit defendants cooperated with him to remove the artifacts in 1984, the evidence brought out at trial leads this court to conclude that they seem to regret their 1984 actions in concert with Michael Johnson. Their spokesman Bill Thomas expressed such regret, and all of the Tlingit defendants now want the artifacts returned to Klukwan, and want nothing more to do with Michael Johnson and his attempts to sell the artifacts.

This court concludes that, inexorably, the Whale House property at issue constitutes "artifacts, clan crests, or other Indian art works" within the meaning of the tribe's 1976 Ordinance prohibiting removal of such property without first obtaining the consent of the council at Klukwan.

II. Power of the Village to Enact the Ordinance and Enforce It Against the Defendants

[The court found that Chilkat has retained, inherent power to adopt the Ordinance in question, and that jurisdiction over the non-Indian defendant Johnson is warranted under the test established in *Montana v. United States*, because Johnson "entered into contractual relations with the Tlingit defendants regarding the removal and sale of the Whale House artifacts." In addition, the court pointed to the powerful importance of the artifacts to the Village community as satisfying the requirement in *Montana* that tribal jurisdiction over nonmembers be necessary to protect the political integrity, health, and welfare of the tribe. As the court noted, "All members of the village continue to rely on the artifacts for essential ceremonial purposes. The artifacts embody the clan's history." Finally, the court agreed with the United States District Court that Chilkat's fee land was a "dependent Indian community" and therefore Indian country for tribal jurisdiction purposes. Several years later, the United States Supreme Court reached a contrary conclusion in the *Venetie* case, presented in Ch. 2, Sec. A.3.b.ii.]

RELIEF AND ORDER

. . . This court is convinced that as a matter of tribal law the artifacts must be returned to Klukwan. Placing them in the Whale House will return the parties to the status that existed before the illegal 1984 removal. . . . This court also recognizes that there may be a lack of adequate custodial capacity of the Whale

House, and possibly the Ganexteidi Clan as a whole in Klukwan. After all, the clan, through its leaders, requested that the village (which enacted the 1976 Ordinance) bring this action enforcing the ordinance, and seek the return of the artifacts to the village on its behalf. Accordingly, this court hereby makes it clear that plaintiff Chilkat Indian Village, in consultation with the Ganexteidi Clan, has ultimate authority to enforce its ordinance, effect the return of the artifacts to Klukwan, and otherwise exercise all necessary custodial responsibility in overseeing the care and future custodial arrangements of the Whale House artifacts.

[With respect to the Village's claims for damages,] this court finds that the evidence presented at trial compels a fundamental distinction between the Tlingit defendants and Michael Johnson and his corporation — even though no legal rationale was established for the 1984 actions of any of the defendants. Although the Tlingit defendants were undoubtedly motivated in part by greed, they also believed — mistakenly as it turns out — that as members of the Whale House they had a right to assume custody of the artifacts. The bad faith conduct of their uncle Clarence Hotch and Michael Johnson contributed to their incorrect assumption — as of 1984 — that they had the right to take the actions resulting in violation of the tribe's ordinance. They appeared at trial, attempted in good faith to justify their actions, but also expressed responsibility for their actions. The Tlingit defendants, in their own way, expressed regret, and all of them now want the artifacts returned to the village.

Michael Johnson, on the other hand, remains relentless in his efforts to acquire the artifacts, which he intends to sell to the highest bidder. He is unremorseful, and has become vindictive. . . ." [The court ordered Michael Johnson to pay the costs of returning the artifacts to Whale House and to pay the Village's costs and fees.]

UNITED STATES v. CORROW
United States Court of Appeals, Tenth Circuit
119 F.3d 796 (1997)

PORFILIIO, CIRCUIT JUDGE

This appeal raises issues of first impression in this Circuit under the Native American Graves Protection and Repatriation Act, 25 U.S.C. §§ 3001–3013 (NAGPRA). . . . Richard Nelson Corrow challenges the constitutionality of 25 U.S.C. § 3001(3)(D) of NAGPRA which defines "cultural patrimony," the basis for his conviction of trafficking in protected Native American cultural items in violation of 18 U.S.C. § 1170(b). [H]e contends the definition is unconstitutionally vague, an argument the district court rejected in denying his motion to dismiss that count of the indictment and to reverse his conviction. *United States v. Corrow*, 941 F. Supp. 1553, 1562 (D.N.M. 1996). . . . We affirm.

I. Background

[Richard Corrow, the owner of Artifacts Display Stands in Scottsdale, Arizona, and an aficionado of Navajo culture and religion, purchased twenty-two Yei B'Chei from the widow of Ray Winni, a hataali, a Navajo religious singer. Traditionally, the

Yei B'Chei would pass from family or clan to those who had studied the ceremonies. This is how Mr. Winnie acquired his Yei B'Chei. Mr. Corrow paid $10,000 to the family for the Yei B'Chei, as well as five headdresses and other artifacts. Mrs. Winnie spoke no English, but agreed to the sale, indicating so by placing her thumbprint on the document of sale after a relative read it to her in Navajo.

Subsequently, a National Park Service ranger operating undercover offered to buy the Yei B'Chei for $70,000. The F.B.I. agents arrested Mr. Corrow with the twenty-two Yei B'Chei at the Albuquerque airport, and he was charged with trafficking in Native American cultural items in violation of 18 U.S.C. § 1170, 25 U.S.C. §§ 3001(3)(D), 3002(c), and 18 U.S.C. § 2; . . . .]

The court rejected Mr. Corrow's pretrial motion to dismiss Count one [trafficking in Native American cultural items] based on its purported unconstitutional vagueness, and the trial proceeded comprised predominantly of the testimony of expert witnesses clashing over whether the Yei B'Chei constitute "cultural patrimony" protected by NAGPRA. Having concluded they do, the jury convicted Mr. Corrow of illegal trafficking in cultural items, Count one. . . .

In this renewed challenge, Mr. Corrow asserts the court erred in failing to dismiss Count one on the ground the NAGPRA definition of cultural patrimony is unconstitutionally vague, trapping the unwary in its multitude of meanings and creating easy prey for the untrammeled discretion of law enforcement.[51] Were NAGPRA's definitional bounds nevertheless discernible, Mr. Corrow then urges the evidence was insufficient to support his conviction on either count.

II. NAGPRA

Congress enacted NAGPRA in 1990 to achieve two principle objectives: to protect Native American human remains, funerary objects, sacred objects and objects of cultural patrimony presently on Federal or tribal lands; and to repatriate Native American human remains, associated funerary objects, sacred objects, and objects of cultural patrimony currently held or controlled by Federal agencies and museums. H.R. Rep. No. 101-877, 101st Cong., 2d Sess. 1990, reprinted in 1990 U.S.C.C.A.N. 4367, 4368. The legislation and subsequent regulations, 43 C.F.R. §§ 10.1–10.17, provide a methodology for identifying objects; determining the rights of lineal descendants, Indian tribes and Native Hawaiian organizations; and retrieving and repatriating that property to Native American owners. NAGPRA's reach in protecting against further desecration of burial sites and restoring countless ancestral remains and cultural and sacred items to their tribal homes warrants its aspirational characterization as "human rights legislation." Jack F. Trope & Walter R. Echo-Hawk, *The Native American Graves Protection and Repatriation Act: Background and Legislative History*, 24 ARIZ. ST. L.J. 35, 37 (1992). Indeed, a Panel of National Dialogue on Museum-Native American Relations, which was convened to address the divergent interests of the museum and

---

[51] [2] Mr. Corrow does not specifically address 25 U.S.C. § 3002(c) which prohibits the intentional removal of Native American cultural items unless done with (1) a permit; (2) after consultation with or consent of the Indian tribe; and (3) proof of tribal consultation or consent. Our disposition of § 3001(3)(D) subsumes without directly addressing the issue.

Native American communities, reported to Congress that "respect for Native human rights is the paramount principle that should govern resolution of the issue when a claim is made." 1990 U.S.C.C.A.N. 4369–70.

Nonetheless to give teeth to this statutory mission, 18 U.S.C. § 1170 penalizes trafficking in Native American human remains and cultural items and creates a felony offense for a second or subsequent violation. Subsection 1170(b), the basis for prosecution here, states:

> Whoever knowingly sells, purchases, uses for profit, or transports for sale or profit any Native American cultural items obtained in violation of the Native American Grave Protection and Repatriation Act shall be fined in accordance with this title, imprisoned not more than one year, or both, and in the case of a second or subsequent violation, be fined in accordance with this title, imprisoned not more than 5 years, or both.

One must look to NAGPRA, 25 U.S.C. § 3001, for the definition of "cultural item." Section 3001(3) states:

> "cultural items" means human remains and—

> (D) "cultural patrimony" which shall mean an object having ongoing historical, traditional, or cultural importance central to the Native American group or culture itself, rather than property owned by an individual Native American, and which, therefore, cannot be alienated, appropriated, or conveyed by any individual regardless of whether or not the individual is a member of the Indian tribe or Native Hawaiian organization and such object shall have been considered inalienable by such Native American group at the time the object was separated from such group.[52]

Thus, to be judged "cultural patrimony"[53] the object must have (1) ongoing historical, cultural or traditional importance; and (2) be considered inalienable by the tribe by virtue of the object's centrality in tribal culture. That is, the cultural item's essential function within the life and history of the tribe engenders its inalienability such that the property cannot constitute the personal property of an individual tribal member. "The key aspect of this definition is whether the property was of such central importance to the tribe or group that it was owned communally." Francis P. McManamon & Larry V. Nordby, *Implementing the Native American Graves Protection and Repatriation Act*, 24 Ariz. St. L.J. 217, 233–34 (1992). The regulations mirror this definition and incorporate the Senate Report for its version of the bill which did not pass, S. Rep. No. 473, 101st Cong., 2d Sess. 1 (1990). 43 C.F.R. § 10.2(d)(4).

---

[52] [3] There are three other components of "cultural items" included in § 3001(3): (A) "associated funerary objects"; (B) "unassociated funerary objects" and (C) "sacred objects." The government alleged the Yei B'Chei are "cultural patrimony" and has not argued they constitute "sacred objects," defined as "specific ceremonial objects which are needed by traditional Native American religious leaders for the practice of traditional Native American religions by their present day adherents." 16 U.S.C. § 3001(3)(C).

[53] [4] Webster's Third New International Dictionary defines "patrimony" as "anything derived one's father or ancestors: HERITAGE; an inheritance from the past; an estate or property held by ancient right."

In this prosecution, then, the definition of cultural patrimony divided into its three component parts required the government prove Mr. Corrow trafficked in an object that (1) was not owned by an individual Native American; (2) that could not be alienated, appropriated, or conveyed by an individual; and (3) had an ongoing historical, traditional, or cultural importance central to the Native American group. [Mr. Corrow challenges the statute on the grounds that it violates the due process clause of the fourteenth amendment for failure to give notice of prohibited conduct.]

In support, Mr. Corrow arrays the conflicting expert testimony, characterized by the amicus curiae[54] as a conflict between orthodox and moderate Navajo religious views. For the government, Alfred Yazzie, an ordained hataali and Navajo Nation Historic Preservation representative, testified the Yei B'Chei must remain within the four sacred mountains of the Navajo for they represented the "heartbeat" of the Navajo people.[55] Also for the government, Harry Walters, a Navajo anthropologist, stated there is "no such thing as ownership of medicine bundles and that these are viewed as living entities." He equated ownership with use, knowing the rituals, but acknowledged often cultural items are sold because of economic pressures. For Mr. Corrow, Jackson Gillis, a medicine man from Monument Valley, testified that if no claim is made by a clan relative or other singer, the jish pass to the widow who must care for them. If the widow feels uncomfortable keeping the jish, Mr. Gillis stated she has the right to sell them. Harrison Begay, another of Mr. Corrow's expert witnesses, agreed, explaining that because the masks themselves are "alive," a widow, uneasy about their remaining unused, may sell them. Billy Yellow, another hataali testifying for Mr. Corrow, reiterated the traditional disposition of a hataali's Yei B'Chei to a spouse, the children, and grandchildren, although he stated nobody really owns the jish because they are living gods.

Given these conflicting views on the alienability of the Yei B'Chei, Mr. Corrow asks how an individual, even one educated in Navajo culture, indeed, one accepting the responsibility of inquiring further about the status of the item as the district court deduced from its reading of NAGPRA, can "ascertain ownership when the group itself cannot agree on that point"? The shadow cast by this question, he insists, sufficiently clouds the meaning of "cultural patrimony" to render it unconstitutional. . . .

[The Court undertook an analysis of the void-for-vagueness doctrine and determined that Mr. Corrow's complaint failed to meet the burden to demonstrate a lack of constitutionality of the statute.]

Mr. Corrow cannot meet that burden. First, deciding whether the statute gave

---

[54] [7] The Antique Tribal Art Dealers Association, a trade organization promoting authenticity and ethical dealing in the sale of Native American artifacts, filed an amicus brief contending the government in this case "exploited a controversy between orthodox and moderate Navajo religious perspectives."

[55] [8] He stated, "This is my heartbeat, this is my life, this is my teaching. This causes me to behave right. It allows me to teach my children to behave. So it's a God-given gift to the Navajos and it has everything to do with the welfare and the health and wisdom." He explained the hataali is responsible for caring for the jish, restoring them in the event of exposure to the wrong people or places: "when they do come back we would have to use what we call a diagnosis to see what can be done and how we can treat them and bring them back to the respect that they should have." He explained the Navajo tradition of compensating a person who gives his Yei B'Chei to another chanter.

him fair notice, the district court found, after reviewing all of the expert testimony, Mr. Corrow is knowledgeable about Navajo traditions and culture and "would have been aware that various tribal members viewed ownership of property differently." 941 F. Supp. at 1560. The court cited the testimony of Ms. Charlotte Frisbie, author of Navajo Medicine Bundles or Jish: Acquisition, Transmission and Disposition in the Past and Present (1987). Ms. Frisbie related several calls from Mr. Corrow inquiring about the prices of certain Navajo artifacts. Although she stated he did not specifically ask her about these Yei B'Chei, she expressed her objection to dealers and commercial handlers selling Native American cultural objects in the open market. Ms. Frisbie also reminded him both of the Navajo Nation's implementing procedures to return cultural items and of the enactment of NAGPRA. *Id.* Most damning, Ms. Bia, Mrs. Winnie's granddaughter, recounted Mr. Corrow's representation that he wanted to buy the Yei B'Chei to pass on to another young chanter in Utah. Reasonably, a jury could infer from that representation that Mr. Corrow appreciated some dimension of the Yei B'Chei's inherent inalienability in Navajo culture. Although Mrs. Winnie stated she believed the Yei B'Chei belonged to her, she testified, "there was another man that knew the ways and he had asked of [the Yei B'Chei] but I was the one that was stalling and ended up selling it." Although this man trained with her husband, he had not offered her any money. This is not a case of an unsuspecting tourist happening upon Mrs. Winnie's hogan and innocently purchasing the set of Yei B'Chei. Nor is it even close to . . . *Kolender* where the unwary had no means or ability to discern their conduct violated the acts in question.

Surely, this evidence establishes Mr. Corrow had some notice the Yei B'Chei he purchased were powerfully connected to Navajo religion and culture. While it may be true that even the experts in that culture differed in their views on alienability, no expert testified it was acceptable to sell Yei B'Chei to non-Navajos who planned to resell them for a profit, the very conduct § 1170(b) penalizes. All experts testified the Yei B'Chei resided within the Four Corners of the Navajo people and acknowledged the ritual cleansing and restoration required were the Yei B'Chei to be defiled in any way. Thus, while the parameters of the designation "cultural patrimony" might be unclear in some of its applications and at its edges, there is no doubt, in this case as applied to Mr. Corrow, the Yei B'Chei were cultural items which could not be purchased for a quick $40,000 turn of profit. Indeed, the Court observed in *Hoffman Estates*, 455 U.S. at 494 n.6, that "ambiguous meanings cause citizens to 'steer far wider of the unlawful zone' . . . than if the boundaries of the forbidden areas were clearly marked." *Baggett v. Bullitt*, 377 U.S. 360, 372 (1964) (quoting *Speiser v. Randall*, 357 U.S. 513, 526 (1958)) (internal quotation marks omitted).

Consequently, even if the term cultural patrimony "might reflect some uncertainty as applied to extreme situations, the conduct for which [defendant] was prosecuted and convicted falls squarely within the core of the [Act]." *United States v. Amer*, 110 F.3d 873, 878 (2d Cir. 1997) (challenge to International Parental Kidnapping Crime Act attacking such terms as "lawful exercise of parental rights" as unconstitutionally vague failed where defendant's retention of three children in Egypt when at least two of the children were born in New York and other child had stayed in New York for eight years was clearly proscribed by IPKCA). Consequently, we believe Mr. Corrow had fair notice — if not of the precise words of NAGPRA — of their meaning that Native American objects "having ongoing historical, traditional, or cultural importance central to the Native American group . . . rather than property owned by an individual Native American" could not be bought and sold absent criminal consequences. Moreover, contrary to Mr. Corrow's assertion, § 3001(3)(D) is not infirm because it fails to list examples of cultural items. "In short, due process does not require that citizens be provided actual notice of all criminal rules and their meanings. The Constitution is satisfied if the necessary information is reasonably obtainable by the public." *United States v. Vasarajs*, 908 F.2d 443, 449 (9th Cir. 1990) (citations to La Fave & Scot omitted) (statute barring reentry onto military base was not unconstitutionally vague because it failed to inform individuals of the precise boundaries of the base).

While not dispositive, we would add § 1170(b) includes scienter as an element of the offense ("Whoever knowingly sells, purchases, uses for profit. . . . "). "A statutory requirement that an act must be willful or purposeful may not render certain, for all purposes, a statutory definition of the crime which is in some respects uncertain. But it does relieve the statute of the objection that it punishes without warning an offense of which the accused was unaware." *Screws v. United States*, 325 U.S. 91, 101–02 (1945) (Douglas, J., concurring). Here, the government was required to prove Mr. Corrow knowingly used the Yei B'Chei for profit assuring his understanding of the prohibited zone of conduct. "[A] scienter requirement may mitigate a criminal law's vagueness by ensuring that it punishes only those who are aware their conduct is unlawful." *Gaudreau*, 860 F.2d at 360 .. . . .

We conclude, therefore, as applied to Mr. Corrow, § 1170(b) provides sufficient guidance to law enforcement to dispel the fear of subjective enforcement.[56] We affirm the district court's denial of Mr. Corrow's motion to dismiss Count one.

Having failed in his constitutional challenge, Mr. Corrow urges we examine the same evidence which defeated the legal claim to support his contention the government failed to prove Mrs. Winnie was not the rightful owner of the Yei B'Chei. The evidence we detailed *infra* — the expert and family members' testimony as well as that of Forest Service agents — viewed in the government's favor satisfies us that a rational jury could find beyond a reasonable doubt the Yei B'Chei are cultural patrimony which Mr. Corrow could not resell for profit. We

---

[56] [12] We would note there have been similar challenges to federal statutes protecting items deemed antiquities under the Antiquities Act of 1906, 16 U.S.C. § 431–433 (1988), and the Archeological Resources Protection Act (ARPA), 16 U.S.C. §§ 470aa–470mm. Although the Ninth Circuit invalidated the Antiquities Act, sustaining a challenge to its penalizing appropriating "objects of antiquity situated on lands owned and controlled by the Government of the United States," as applied to taking three or four year old face masks from a cave, *United States v. Diaz*, 499 F.2d 113 (9th Cir. 1974), we upheld the same act in *United States v. Smyer*, 596 F.2d 939 (10th Cir. 1979), where defendants excavated a prehistoric Mimbres ruin at an archeological site, removing objects of antiquity. We held in light of defendants' conduct, the Antiquities Act was not unconstitutionally vague. Later, the Ninth Circuit upheld the Antiquities' Act's successor, ARPA, in *United States v. Austin*, 902 F.2d 743 (9th Cir. 1990). Defendant there unsuccessfully argued the terms, "weapons" and "tools" were unconstitutionally vague, the court's having found regarding defendant "there can be no doubt nor lack of fair notice that the scrapers and arrow points for which he was convicted are indeed weapons and tools." *Id.* at 745. These predecessors were instructive to the district court's analysis.

therefore affirm the district court's denial of the motion for judgment of acquittal on Count one.

We therefore *affirm* the judgment of the district court.

NOTES ON TANGIBLE CULTURAL PROPERTY

1. The Struggle for Protection of Native Cultural Property: Late in the nineteenth century, the New York State Museum obtained 26 belts of "wampum" — colored clam and conch shells used by the Onondaga Tribe of the Iroquois or Haudenosaunee Nation for trade and for recording their most significant community events. When the Museum refused to return the belts, the Onondaga went to court, and lost. *Onondaga Nation v. Thacher*, 61 N.Y.S. 1027 (Sup. Ct. Onondaga County 1899). Public outcry against the decision was so strong, however, that New York passed a law providing for repatriation of five of the belts so long as the Iroquois would preserve them at the level of the Museum's standards.

More recently, the Zuni Pueblo has battled with art collectors and museums in order to secure the return of ceremonial war gods, which are central to ceremonies associated with the bow priest society. After the ceremonies, the war gods are placed on mountain peaks located on sacred lands, where their religious function continues. Through sales by tribal members as well as thefts, the war gods have turned up on the art market. Early efforts by the Zuni to retrieve the gods met with resistance at first. One museum made a statement that "To our knowledge no legal precedent exists of a museum donating an object to any religious group on the basis that the object is of religious significance and should be presumed to have been stolen by virtue of having been communal religious property. . . . [T]o set such a precedent can cause immensely complex problems for museums. . . ." LEONARD DUBOFF, THE DESKBOOK OF ART LAW IV-41–43 (Supp. 1984), quoted in Christopher S. Byrne, *Communal Property Rights in Cultural Objects*, 8 J. ENVTL. L. & LITIG. 109, 125 (1993). Through persistent pressure, however, the Zuni were able to establish an expectation that these items would be returned. Can an individual American sell the original of the Declaration of Independence? Why should the Iroquois or Zuni cases be treated any differently? Given the direction of Supreme Court decisions regarding tribal jurisdiction over non-Indians, discussed in Chapters 3 and 4, will it be as easy for tribes in the future to assert the kind of authority that Chilkat Village did? Can a tribe prevent a nonmember from excavating artifacts found on fee land within the boundaries of a "checkerboard" reservation? Does the new federal offense under NAGPRA take care of that problem?

In recent years, in a series of high-profile auctions, French auction houses have put up for sale over a hundred Hopi katsinam. The katsinam are visages used in sacred, religious ceremonies within the community. Those at issue in the auctions were acquired by an anonymous collector, and are believed to have been removed from Hopi territory in late 1800's and early 1900's by a combination of theft, duress, and sale. When the Hopi learned of the pending auctions, they attempted to intervene legally in the United States and in France, but their claims were rejected. The United States State Department indicated it had no legal grounds upon which to stop the auction. In two cases, a private collector and the Annenberg Foundation, respectively, purchased the katsinam at auction and returned them to the Hopi.

What options for recourse do Native American tribes have in cases where their cultural property rights are violated outside of the United States? Diane Hume-tewa, a federal judge appointed by President Obama, held meetings with French officials about the auctions. *See* Dominique Godreche, *Lawyer Has Hope That Auctions of Sacred Items Will Someday Stop*, Dec. 22, 2014, *available at indiancountrytodaymedianetwork.com/2014/12/22/lawyer-has-hope-auctions-sacred-items-will-someday-stop-158421*. Should the United States have any obligation to engage with France on behalf of the Hopi as part of its trust responsibility? What kind of actions should it take?

2. **Cultural Property as Cultural Patrimony Under NAGPRA:** The Whale House artifacts at issue in the *Chilkat* case were taken before the enactment of NAGPRA. If the incident had occurred post-NAGPRA, would the four posts and rain screen have qualified as "cultural patrimony" for purposes of the criminal provisions of the Act? Would Johnson's actions have violated the Act? Note that under section 3001(3)(D), the object must have "ongoing historical, traditional, or cultural importance central to the Native American group or culture," not be "property owned by an individual Native American," and be "considered inalienable by such Native American group at the time the object was separated from such group." Are these requirements separate and independent? In other words, could a tribe view the artifact as inalienable, but a court find that the artifact is insufficiently "central" to the culture to warrant characterization of it as cultural patrimony, or that it "belongs" to an individual tribal member? Does tribal law or custom have the final say on whether an object qualifies as cultural patrimony? While highly publicized cases such as the Onondaga wampum belts and the Zuni war gods, as well as the Chilkat artifacts, present clear cases, what about those objects that are less emblematic of a particular tribe in the eyes of the outside world? How does the *Corrow* case respond to the claim that the statute is unconstitutionally vague with respect to such matters?

Apart from the taking of cultural property, NAGPRA addresses the return or repatriation of cultural patrimony items that have entered the art market. Publicly funded museums have obligations to repatriate objects to tribes with which they are culturally affiliated. Reclaiming Native artifacts from private parties is far more difficult. The tribe must be able to make a prima facie showing that the party in possession of the artifact does not have a valid right of possession (*i.e.*, consent from the individual or group that has authority to alienate), and then the burden shifts to the opposing party to rebut that case. Jack F. Trope & Walter R. Echo-Hawk, *The Native American Graves Protection and Repatriation Act: Background and Legislative History*, 24 ARIZ. ST. L. J. 35 (1992). As one commentator has complained, however, NAGPRA does not "provide criteria by which to determine whether the object belongs to the community or an individual member." It simply begs the question. What is needed, says the author, is a modification of existing tenets of property law to recognize communal cultural property. Christopher S. Byrne, *Communal Property Rights in Cultural Objects*, 8 J. ENVTL. L. & LITIG. 109, 130–31 (1993). Why isn't the inherent power of the tribe to define property law within its territory, as implemented in the *Chilkat* case, sufficient to do this job?

3. **Sacred Objects:** In *Corrow*, the government alleged the Yei B'Chei were "cultural patrimony" within the meaning of NAGPRA, not "sacred objects," which

NAGPRA defines as "specific ceremonial objects which are needed by traditional Native American religious leaders for the practice of traditional Native American religions by their present day adherents." 16 U.S.C. § 3001(3)(C). The legislative history demonstrates that this definition is to include objects necessary to renew traditional religious ceremonies as well as items used in current ceremonies. Furthermore, the definition reveals deference to the judgment of Native American religious leaders themselves in judging the continuing sacredness of the objects. Why do you think the United States steered clear of this provision? Is it any more vulnerable to a void-for-vagueness attack? Would the artifacts in *Chilkat* have qualified as sacred objects within the meaning of NAGPRA?

b. Intangible Cultural Property

The intangible aspects of Native culture include songs, stories, symbols, ceremonies, and traditional knowledge. Recently, there has been an effort to define indigenous genetic resources as part of protected cultural property. While NAGPRA protects certain tangible forms of Native American cultural property, it does not extend to intangible components of culture. This is also true of the harm suffered by Native people. NAGPRA is set up according to the idea that Native peoples suffer a cognizable harm if they are denied rightful ownership of their cultural objects and ancestral remains. This is similar to the harm of conversion under Anglo-American law. In comparison, as illustrated by the *Na Iwi* case, there is no category within Anglo-American law to recognize "spiritual harm" or other "intangible" cultural harms, such as the injury suffered by the misappropriation of tribal songs and ceremonies. Consider the following excerpt from an article by Professor Angela Riley on the need for more expansive protections for indigenous cultural property:

> The eclectic hip-hop/funk super duo OutKast brought down the house at the 2004 Grammy Awards when they introduced their performance of "Hey Ya!" with an ethereal, Indian-sounding melody. This serene, mystical introduction was immediately juxtaposed with a thumping bass and the descent of spaceship — like tipis as OutKast's Big Boi and Andre 3000 (a.k.a. Dre) appeared on stage amidst a scantily clad dance troupe. Flanked by the University of Southern California marching band (wearing hats adorned with feathers), OutKast belted out the hit single. The duo racked up a total of three Grammy's that night, including one for the coveted Album of the Year. The raucous Grammy audience stayed on its feet for the duration of the performance and grew more excited as OutKast's back-up dancers-most of whom appeared to be African-American women-bopped around the stage wearing buckskin bikinis, long braids and feathers in their hair. The dancers' choreography included a sequence wherein they hit their open mouths with flat palms, imitating a traditional Plains-tribe war cry
> . . . .
>
> Soon thereafter . . . [there was] an outcry . . . from Native communities . . . Complaints ranged from a feeling of violation over the use of Indian symbols reserved for ceremonial purposes, like feathers and war paint, to anger over the perpetuation of Tomahawk-and-tipi stereotypes." The greatest shock came when *Indian Country Today* revealed that the melody

piped in to introduce "Hey Ya!" was the sacred Navajo (Dine) "Beauty Way" song. According to the Navajo, the song is "meant to restore peace and harmony," and it is improper to use the song for entertainment purposes.

Angela R. Riley, *"Straight-Stealing": Towards an Indigenous System of Cultural Property Protection*, 80 WASH. L. REV. 69, 70–71 (2005). What, if any, legal harm was suffered by the Navajo Nation in this case? Could there be harm to all Native Americans by virtue of the stereotyping and caricatures presented in the OutKast dance performance? As Professor Riley goes on to explain, the unauthorized downloading of "Hey Ya!" would constitute a violation of U.S. copyright law and thus be considered "legal harm." The appropriation of the Navajo "Beauty Way" song, however, is not protected by copyright law and there is no other law protecting "against OutKast's appropriation of Native culture, Native symbols, Native dance, or Native music." *Id.* at 72.

In fact, Native claimants are often unable to protect the intangible aspect of their cultures within the existing legal framework. Anglo-American intellectual property law provides several mechanisms to protect a person's commercial interest in generating new ideas and technology, without allowing the type of monopoly on knowledge that is considered harmful to society. The economic underpinnings of Anglo-American property law dominate the approach of American courts to these issues. Other nations, such as France, have broader jurisprudential structures for intellectual property law, which rest in part upon a moral rights theory. Indigenous peoples have generally been required to litigate their claims according to the available legal frameworks established by the domestic law of the nation-state which encompasses them. In the United States, the available legal structures are generally not protective of the interests that indigenous peoples seek to protect. For a general discussion of intellectual property rights and Native interests, see Richard Guest, *Intellectual Property Rights and Native American Tribes*, 20 AM. IND. L. REV. 111 (1995).

At the center of most indigenous claims is the concept of "cultural appropriation." Lenore Keeshig-Tobias, a First Nations scholar and activist in Canada, has defined cultural appropriation as a "taking, from a culture that is not one's own, intellectual property, cultural expressions and artifacts, history and ways of knowledge." Marchand, *Dancing to the Pork Barrel Polka*, TORONTO STAR, Aug. 5, 1992, at B6. Cultural appropriation can relate to the tangible or intangible aspects of culture, and it is of vital importance to Native peoples because Native culture is essential to the survival of Native nations as distinctive cultural and political groups.

Rebecca Tsosie, *Reclaiming Native Stories: An Essay on Cultural Appropriation and Cultural Rights*
34 ARIZ. ST. L.J. 299, 311–12 (2002)

Cultural appropriation from Native peoples takes many forms in contemporary society. "New Age" people seek to learn Native American traditional spirituality, sometimes turning this into a business. Movies such as *Dances with Wolves* and books focusing on real or imagined Native Americans or Native American traditions become huge hits. Artists frequently appropriate tribal symbolism for use in their paintings, jewelry and pottery. Non-Indian corporations promote products like the

Hornell Brewing Company's "Crazy Horse" beer and the Jeep "Cherokee," and some use Native Americans as team mascots. Pharmaceutical companies seek to learn about traditional medicines and use the knowledge to market products based on traditional healing practices. In short, "Indian" culture is a commodity in modern America. It is sold, exploited, probed, catalogued and controlled by outsiders in many different markets, both economic and intellectual. Some individual Native Americans participate, to some degree, in the commodification of Native culture. For example, Professor Huhndorf points to specific Native individuals who sell "spiritual services" to non-Native New Age adherents. Other Native people, particularly those who urge tribal control over tribal cultures, wonder where this will all stop. Will Native cultures continue to be perceived as the "common property" of the United States, or even the world?

NOTES

1.   **Cultural Appropriation and Cultural Harm:** Professor Tsosie's article identifies four distinct categories of claims that relate to the central objection of cultural appropriation. First, the acts of outsiders who remove an Indian nation's cultural objects, such as sacred objects or objects of cultural patrimony. Second, the actions of outsiders who take a Native group's sacred symbols (*e.g.*, the Hopi Kachina), designs, or artforms and appropriate them for commercial use. Third, the acts of non-Indians who appropriate tribal rituals or songs for "New Age" religions. And finally, the portrayal of Indian people and tribal cultures in movies, literature, and art by non-Indians. Professor Tsosie asserts that these and similar actions result in a variety of separate harms to Native people, which would require different forms of redress, depending upon the circumstances. Current law may recognize certain forms of economic harm caused by cultural appropriation; however, existing law does not account for the "cultural harm" caused to Native people by such actions. As you read the notes below, consider how concepts of "cultural harm" are litigated under domestic law. How can tribal communities protect themselves from the harms caused by cultural appropriation?

2.   **Copyright and Patent Law:** Copyrights stem from federal law, and to some extent, state common law, and are designed to protect original creations that are "fixed" in a tangible medium, such as literature, music, or art. Under federal law, the protection arises when the author fixes the expression in a permanent medium and lasts for the life of the author plus an additional amount of time, depending on the nature of the work. *See generally* 17 U.S.C. §§ 101–914. Significantly, the copyright protects only the original expression of the idea and not the idea itself. The author's copyright gives her the exclusive right to make copies of the work, and to control derivative works. When the copyright expires, the work enters the "public domain" and may be used by others without restriction

Patents offer limited protection for new and useful inventions and discoveries. The federal government uses its patent power to provide incentives for the development of new technology. *See generally* 35 U.S.C. §§ 1–376. Unlike copyrights, no property right exists until the government approves the patent. To prove eligibility, the potential patentee must demonstrate that she has developed a new, useful and nonobvious process or technology. Once granted, the patent lasts for seventeen years. It cannot be renewed. After the patent expires, the technology enters the "public domain," which means that the patentee loses the exclusive rights to the patent and anyone else may make, use, or sell the invention.

There are several conceptual problems with according copyright or patent protection to protect Native peoples' concerns over the misuse of intangible aspects of culture such as songs, ceremonies, symbols, or knowledge of plant resources. First, both copyrights and patents protect "new" knowledge (novel inventions or "original" expression), not knowledge that already exists. Much of what tribes seek to protect would be considered "traditional" knowledge, of long-standing importance to the group. In addition, some of that traditional knowledge is now considered to be in the "public domain" as a result of anthropologists publishing their data and research. Second, copyrights and patents establish limited, rather than perpetual, protection of the invention or creation. Anglo-American property law seeks to encourage productive behavior by granted limited monopolies. Perpetual monopolies are viewed as detrimental to beneficial competition. Indigenous peoples, on the other hand, often believe that these intangible aspects of culture are solely to be retained by the indigenous cultures themselves, and should not be shared with others. Finally, copyrights and patents confer property rights on individuals (or corporations which are legal entities acting as individuals), rather than groups. The point of recognizing a property right is to enable the individual to exclude other members of society from unauthorized use of the property. With respect to indigenous interests, it is unclear who within the group would have the authority to control or limit the use of the knowledge. Should these rights reside with the traditional spiritual leaders? The political leaders? Each tribal member? Would it depend upon the nature of the resource? For a thorough discussion of these and related issues, see INTELLECTUAL PROPERTY RIGHTS FOR INDIGENOUS PEOPLES, A SOURCEBOOK (T. Greaves ed., 1994); MICHAEL F. BROWN, WHO OWNS NATIVE CULTURE? (2003). For an interesting account of how Australian courts have attempted to deal with protection of Native cultural property, and a possible application to indigenous North America, see Amina Para Matlon, *Safeguarding Native American Sacred Art by Partnering Tribal Law and Equity: An Exploratory Case Study Applying the Bulun Bulun Equity to Navajo Sandpainting*, 27 COLUM. J.L. & ARTS 211 (2004).

3. **Trademark Law:** Trademark law originated under English common law as a device to identify in the marketplace the craftsmen responsible for producing goods for sale. Under state law, trademarks were intended to prevent one person from "passing off" his goods as those of another. Federal trademark law provides a structure to enforce the state-derived common law of trademark. The Lanham Act recognizes various categories of "marks" (*e.g.*, trademark, servicemark, certification mark, collective mark), provides protection against unfair competition, and prevents deceptive marketing of goods and services that cause injury to other competitors. *See generally* 15 U.S.C. §§ 1051–1127. Trademark law focuses on preventing injury to the market, including producers and consumers. Trademark law requires the mark to be "distinctive," *e.g.*, it must indicate the origin of the goods and identify the producer of the goods, so as to avoid confusion, deception or mistake as to either.

Two sections of the Lanham Act are potentially applicable to protect against unauthorized commercial use of Native American beliefs, cultures, and traditions.

Under section 2(a) of the Lanham Act, trademark registration may be denied if the mark "consists of or comprises immoral, deceptive or scandalous matter; or matter which may falsely suggest a connection with persons, living or dead, institutions, beliefs, or national symbols, or bring them into contempt or disrepute." This section formed the basis for a claim by several Native Americans that the "Washington Redskins" mark should be cancelled because the term "Redskin" is a pejorative, derogatory, degrading and offensive designation for a Native American person. The mark was ultimately cancelled as a result of this action. *See Harjo v. Pro-Football, Inc.*, 50 U.S.P.Q.2d 1705 (Trademark Tr. & App. Bd. 1999). However, the result is less than satisfactory for many Native people. By canceling the mark, the football team no longer has the "exclusive" right to use the term "Redskins." However, there is no requirement that the football team cease using the name altogether. On October 30, 1998, President Clinton signed Public Law 105-330. Title III of this law requires the United States Patent and Trademark Office (USPTO) to study how official insignia of Native American tribes may better be protected under trademark law. Under the law, the Commissioner must complete the study and submit a report to the Judiciary Committees of the House and Senate addressing a variety of issues, including the impact of any changes on the international legal obligations of the United States, the definition of "official insignia" of a federally or state recognized Native American tribe, and the administrative feasibility, including the cost, of changing current law or policy in light of any recommendations. Implementing one of the recommendations of the report, the USPTO announced in August 2001 that it was establishing a database to record the official tribal insignia. This database assists the agency in reviewing trademark applications. Inclusion of official insignia in this database allows attorneys searching a mark that is confusingly similar to an official insignia to find and consider the official insignia before making a determination of registrability. The USPTO uses recorded official insignia as evidence of what a federally or state recognized tribe considers to be its official insignia.

In a June 25, 2008 memorandum opinion in the United States District Court for the District of Columbia, Judge Colleen Kollar-Kotelly ruled that the youngest of the seven Native American plaintiffs waited too long after turning 18 to file the lawsuit attempting to revoke the Redskins trademarks and therefore the lawsuit was barred by laches. *See Pro-Football, Inc. v. Harjo*, (Civ. Action No. 99-1385) (D.D.C. 2008). The court granted Pro-Football's motion for summary judgment on the laches issue, but underscored its earlier ruling that the "opinion should not be read as . . . making any statement of the appropriateness of Native American imagery for team names."

In 2012, five Native Americans brought a cancellation proceeding to the Trademark Trial and Appeal Board (TTAB), again challenging the name in the case of *Pro-Football Inc. v. Blackhorse*. As in the *Harjo* case, the plaintiffs argued that the six trademarks were disparaging of Native Americans at the time the trademarks were registered, and thus not entitled to trademark protection. The five plaintiffs turned eighteen between the years of 2000–2005. Cancellation Proceeding No. 92/046, 185 (Trademark Tr. & App. Bd. Aug. 11, 2006), available at http://apps.washingtonpost.com/g/page/local/Redskins-trademark-order/1105/.

The TTAB issued its ruling in June 2014. The TTAB applied a two-part test for finding disparagement: (1) what is the meaning of the matter in question as it appears in the marks and as those marks are used in connection with the goods and services identified in the trademark registration; and (2) is the meaning of the marks one that may disparage a substantial composite of the relevant population (i.e., Native Americans)? *Id.* at 15. The TTAB found the term "when used in connection with [the Washington team] retains the meaning Native American." *Id.* at 20. In addressing the second prong, the Court emphasized that pro football's "alleged honorable intent and manner of use of the term" were not relevant in determining whether the term was disparaging during the time period, because the Native American meaning of the term still existed. *Id.* at 23. The Board looked to expert testimony, dictionary definitions, and reference books to find that at least 30% of Native Americans during the relevant period — a substantial composite — found the term that was used in connection with pro football to be disparaging. *Id.* at 24, 71.

In terms of the laches defense, the Board first highlighted a new statute, the America Invests Act of 2011, which changed the venue for appeals from the District Court of Columbia to the Eastern District of Virginia. *Id.* at 74. The Board held "that laches does not apply to a disparagement claim where the disparagement pertains to a group of which the individual plaintiff or plaintiffs simply comprise one or more members." The Board further held that the laches defense does not apply to instances where broader public policy concern is at play. *Id.* at 74–75. The Board found that there was a broader public interest here because the "marks may have disparaged a substantial composite of Native Americans at the time." *Id.* at 76.

However, even if the laches defense does apply, the Board found that pro football has not met its burden of proof in demonstrating that the plaintiffs caused unreasonable and inexcusable delay and that pro football has been prejudiced as a result. The case has been appealed. *Pro-Football Inc. v. Blackhorse*, 2014 U.S. Dist. LEXIS 166889 (E.D. Va. Nov. 25, 2014).

In the case of *In re Shinnecock Smoke Shop*, 571 F.3d 1171 (Fed. Cir. 2009), a member of the Shinnecock Indian Nation who is also the sole proprietor of the Shinnecock Smokeshop filed two trademark applications with the U.S. Patent and Trademark office seeking to register the marks of "Shinnecock Brand Full Flavor" and "Shinnecock Brand Lights" for cigarettes. The PTO refused to register the marks because they falsely suggested a connection to the Shinnecock Tribe, a non-sponsoring entity. This decision was affirmed by Trademark Trial and Appeal Board, and also upheld in the Federal Circuit's opinion which observes that 15 U.S.C. § 1052(a) protects against marks that "falsely suggest a connection with persons, living or dead, institutions, beliefs, or national systems" and holds that the Shinnecock Indian Nation is an "institution" for purposes of section 1052(a) and is protected by that section.

The related issue of how to stop the use of tribal names and images as "mascots" continues to perplex Native claimants. *See generally* Jeff Dolley, *The Four R's: Use of Indian Mascots in Educational Facilities*, 32 J. L. & Educ. 21 (2003). In a move that provoked some controversy, the NCAA announced in August 2005 that it was banning the use of Native mascots by member teams in postseason tournaments, unless the team sought and was granted permission by the relevant tribe.

Section 43(a) of the Lanham Act regulates unfair trade practices, independent of any trademark rights. This statutory provision creates a federal "common law" of unfair competition. The statute is limited to activities subject to the interstate commerce clause, and a cause of action is triggered by such an activity that includes: (1) a false statement of fact concerning defendant's products or services; (2) that deceives consumers or creates a likelihood of deception; and (3) is material to the consumer's decision to purchase; and (4) causes injury or the likelihood of injury to the plaintiff. To the extent that the use of a tribal name or symbol suggests an association with the tribe, which is "false or misleading," the product or activity could potentially be regulated under this section. For an assessment of the harm that may come to tribes and individual Native people from the unauthorized use of Indian symbols and names to sell products or as mascots for sports teams, including reinforcement of negative stereotypes, perpetuation of offensive and inaccurate messages about Indians, and treatment of Indians as less than fully human, see Gavin Clarkson, *Racial Imagery and Native Americans: A First Look at the Empirical Evidence Behind the Indian Mascot Controversy*, 11 Cardozo J. Int'l & Comp. L. 393 (2003).

4. **The Indian Arts and Crafts Act:** The Indian Arts and Crafts Act (IACA) is a federal statute largely based on the same policies that underlie the trademark statute, but specifically directed toward protecting Indian tribes. *See* 25 U.S.C. § 305 et seq. Some states have enacted similar statutes, designed to prohibit the sale of any products falsely represented to be authentic Indian arts and crafts. *See*, e.g., Ariz. Rev. Stat. §§ 44-1231–1233. The first version of the federal IACA was enacted in 1935 and provided criminal penalties for selling goods with misrepresentations that they were Indian-produced. The penalties were minimal (a maximum fine of $500 and/or 6 months in prison), and the standard for proof of illegal conduct necessitated a showing of "willfulness" and "intent." As of 1990, there were still no convictions under the Act. After holding hearings on the problem of counterfeit "Indian art," Congress enacted the Indian Arts and Crafts Act of 1990. Under the 1990 Act, criminal and civil actions are possible. The Attorney General may bring a civil or criminal action against the defendant; and tribal governments, tribal artisans and tribal arts organizations also have the power to bring a civil action. The IACA specifies that it is unlawful to "offer or display for sale or to sell any good, with or without a Government trademark, in a manner that falsely suggests that it is Indian produced, an Indian product, or the product of a particular Indian tribe." Is this language sufficient to regulate products that are "Indian-inspired" (*e.g.*, "Navajo-style rugs") if there is no indication that the product is intended to or would mislead a consumer into thinking that the item is an "Indian product"?

5. **Commercial Speech:** One of the most significant obstacles to broad and pervasive regulation of non-Indian conduct that seeks to appropriate tribal names, symbols, designs and other expression, is the First Amendment of the United States Constitution, which protects "freedom of speech" and includes "commercial speech" as a protected category of speech. Perhaps the best-known example of this concerns the Hornell Brewing Company's attempt to market Crazy Horse Malt Beer. In that case, also discussed in Ch. 4, Sec. A.4.b, the liquor company appropriated the name of a revered Lakota leader for an alcoholic beverage which was marketed with images of Sioux Warriors, the U.S. Cavalry, and the Black Hills

as a "romantic and colorful episode in the history of the American West." The harms to the Lakota people were profound. Crazy Horse, by name and by reputation, exemplifies the cultural and political resistance of the Lakota people during the nineteenth century, and this leader was legendary for his firm opposition to alcohol and for his refusal to surrender to the United States. Moreover, within Lakota tradition, as for many Native peoples, names carry a special significance and essence. Even without the defamatory connection to a non-Indian alcoholic beverage, it would have been inappropriate to use the name of this great leader without the family's permission.

After holding hearings on the potential for increased alcohol use by Native youth if a product carried the name of a Lakota leader, Congress attempted to alleviate the harm to the Lakota people by passing a statute prohibiting the use of the name "Crazy Horse" on any "distilled spirit, wine or malt beverage product." Hornell Brewing Company then brought a First Amendment claim challenging the constitutionality of the statute. The court agreed with the liquor company that the statute was unconstitutional, finding that use of Crazy Horse's name was "commercial speech" and that the statute was not closely-tailored toward meeting the government's stated interest in preventing the enhanced appeal of alcohol use among Native Americans. *Hornell Brewing Co. v. Brady*, 819 F. Supp. 1227 (E.D.N.Y. 1993). Eventually, a descendant of Crazy Horse filed a lawsuit in the Rosebud Sioux Tribal Court, on behalf of the estate of Crazy Horse, to enjoin the use of the name by the Hornell Brewing Company. The case contained claims for defamation, violation of the Estate's right of publicity, and negligent and intentional infliction of emotional distress, and sought injunctive and declaratory relief as well as damages. No. Civ. 93-204, 23 I.L.R. 6104 (Rbd. Sx. Sup. Ct. 1996). Ultimately the case failed for procedural reasons when a federal court of appeals held that the Rosebud Sioux Tribal Court lacked jurisdiction to adjudicate the conduct of a non-Indian Brewing Company that was not doing business on the reservation. *Hornell Brewing Co. v. Rosebud Sioux Tribal Court*, 133 F.3d 1087 (8th Cir. 1998). For further discussion of this litigation, see Nell Jessup Newton, *Memory and Misrepresentation: Representing Crazy Horse in Tribal Court*, in BORROWED POWER: ESSAYS ON CULTURAL APPROPRIATION (B. Ziff & P. Rao eds., 1997); Jessica R. Herrera, *Not Even His Name: Is the Denigration of Crazy Horse Custer's Final Revenge?*, 29 HARV. C.R.-C.L. L. REV. 175 (1994).

6. The Role of Tribal Law: Importantly, the substantive rights that were asserted in the tribal court spoke to the unique harms that the descendants of Crazy Horse had suffered and were framed under tribal law. For example, the defamation claim would likely have failed under state law because of the Anglo-American view that the dead cannot be harmed. However, the "defamation of spirit" claim under tribal customary law responded to the Lakota belief that the spirits of the dead have feelings and volition, and can sustain harm. Similarly, the "right of publicity" claim under tribal customary law cited the importance of names within Lakota tradition, including the "naming ceremony" that ought to attach to an authorized use of a Lakota individual's name. How can these harms to Native people be adjudicated without access to a tribal forum? In *"Straight Stealing,"* Professor Angela Riley provides a compelling account of the potential role of tribal law in articulating a legal framework capable of securing protection for intangible cultural property. 80

WASH. L. REV. at 92–117. Professor Riley acknowledges the jurisdictional limitations on enforcement of tribal law, but claims that even though a tribe like the Navajo Nation might "be unable to assert jurisdiction" over a non-Indian performer like OutKast, "'living sovereignty' requires that the Navajo Nation enact laws to address these harms and demonstrate a commitment to enforce them." *Id.* at 119.

7. **Genetic Prospecting:** Indigenous peoples across the globe have been vocal opponents of the "bioprospecting" activities of pharmaceutical companies and the efforts of other multinational companies to patent seed stocks, alleging that these activities threaten indigenous peoples' existence, which is closely tied to the appropriate use of plant resources. There are several international conventions that inform these issues, which are generally associated with the protection of biodiversity and international trade equities. *See, e.g.*, Agreement on Trade Related Aspects of Intellectual Property Rights, Including Trade in Counterfeit Goods (TRIPS), Apr. 15, 1994, art. 27, 33 I.L.M. 81; U.N. Convention on Biological Diversity (in particular, Art. 8(j) of the Convention discusses the role of indigenous peoples and local communities). However, aside from the relevant provisions of the Declaration on the Rights of Indigenous Peoples (see, for example, Art. 24, which recognizes that "Indigenous peoples have the right to their traditional medicines and to maintain their health practices, including the conservation of their vital medicinal plants, animals and minerals."), there has been no concerted effort to develop a separate convention that would protect indigenous peoples from exploitation as the international community continues its process of globalization. For further discussion of issues of biodiversity as they relate to indigenous peoples, *see* INTELLECTUAL PROPERTY RIGHTS FOR INDIGENOUS PEOPLES, *supra*; Dean Suagee, *The Cultural Heritage of American Indian Tribes and the Preservation of Biological Diversity*, 31 ARIZ. ST. L.J. 483 (1999).

Many indigenous groups have also protested the efforts of biomedical researchers to conduct genetic testing on indigenous populations and collect the data for use in other research activities, such as archaeological research on the origin of human populations. These issues were raised in an Arizona Case that recently settled out of court in satisfaction of the Havasupais' claims against a team of researchers from Arizona State University. *See Havasupai Tribe v. Arizona State University* (CV 2004-0146, AZ Superior Ct. Coconino County) (Havasupai Tribe's claim against University researchers who conducted diabetes study with tribal consent and then used genetic materials for other studies and purposes that were not authorized by the Tribe or its members); *Tilousi v. AZ State University* (CV 2004-0115, AZ Superior Ct., Coconino County) (related claim filed by individual tribal members who participated in the study without knowledge that samples would be used for unauthorized purposes). The Havasupai case illustrates many of the complex legal issues that may arise in the future given the rapid development of genomics research. *See generally* Rebecca Tsosie, *Cultural Challenges to Biotechnology: Native American Genetic Resources and the Concept of Cultural Harm*, 35 J. L. MED. & ETHICS 396 (2007).

3.   Protections for Native American Human Remains

NAGPRA has played an important role in shifting the historical treatment of Native American human remains, which differs dramatically from the legal protections accorded to Anglo-American cemeteries and the remains of other deceased individuals under Anglo-American common law. All states have in place statutes that preclude desecration of cemeteries, and most such statutes provide for significant penalties for "grave robbery." Similarly, state common law generally recognized the right in the decedent's next of kin to dictate the disposition of remains, where this was otherwise not prescribed in a will or other written document. It would be considered unthinkable for a third party to excavate state cemeteries and place the remains or funerary objects into commerce. However, until the passage of NAGPRA, courts routinely denied legal rights to Native peoples to protect their burial grounds from desecration under a variety of theories. Moreover, until the passage of NAGPRA, it was not illegal to collect Native American skeletal remains and funerary objects and sell these to interested consumers.

NAGPRA must be understood within its appropriate context. According to Walter Echo-Hawk and Jack Trope, the Native American Graves Protection and Repatriation Act is at its core "human rights legislation," designed to remedy the historical inequality in treatment accorded to Caucasian and Native American human remains. Jack F. Trope & Walter R. Echo-Hawk, *The Native American Graves Protection and Repatriation Act: Background and Legislative History*, 24 ARIZ. ST. L. J. 35 (1992). Pawnee Historian James Riding In has documented that gruesome history in an article which delineates the interaction of federal policies, such as the 1868 Surgeon General's order to collect Native crania for study in Washington, D.C., with the efforts of nineteenth century scientists and archaeologists to study the remains of Native people and document them as "specimens" of a different race. *See* James Riding In, *Without Ethics and Morality: A Historical Overview of Imperial Archaeology and American Indians*, 24 ARIZ. ST. L.J. 11 (1992). The 1868 Surgeon General's Order directed Army personnel to procure Indian crania and other body parts for the Army Medical Museum. Trope & Echo-Hawk, *supra*, at 40. Over the next decades, over 4,000 Native American heads were taken from battlefields, hospitals, and even burial grounds. The result of the 1868 Order and similar practices was the removal of thousands of sets of Native American human remains from cemeteries and from battlefields across the country. The remains were, in many cases, disarticulated and sent to distant locations, to be housed in the collections of federal agencies and museums such as the Smithsonian.

In the 1980s, national attention began to focus on the legacy of this disparate history as a result of several events. In 1986, a group of Northern Cheyenne leaders discovered that about 18,500 sets of Native American human remains were being warehoused in the Smithsonian Museum. This discovery served as a catalyst for a national effort by Indian tribes and organizations to further assess the state of federal collections and obtain legislation to repatriate these human remains, as well as cultural artifacts, to Indian tribes and descendants. Trope & Echo-Hawk, *supra*, at 54–55. In an unrelated event, over 500 graves of Native Americans were plundered at a site in northern Kentucky known as "Slack Farm" in 1987. *See* Gene A. Marsh, *Walking the Spirit Trail: Repatriation and Protection of Native American Remains and Sacred Cultural Items*, 24 ARIZ. ST. L.J. 79, 81 (1992). This incident pointed out the fact that Native American burials often did not merit legal protection under state cemetery laws, and also that the prevailing national attitude still supported the idea that the bones of Native ancestors were "relics" which could be plundered, looted, and sold in commercial markets.

With respect to Native American human remains and funerary objects, NAGPRA contains two sets of provisions. One set covers human remains and funerary objects which are in the possession of federal agencies and federally funded museums as of the effective date of the statute (Nov. 16, 1990). NAGPRA requires each institution to prepare an inventory of its collection of Native American human remains and associated funerary objects, distribute this to any potentially affected tribe or Native Hawaiian organization, and repatriate the remains and funerary objects to culturally affiliated groups or lineal descendants upon their request. 25 U.S.C. sec. 3003. If the Native American human remains or funerary objects are discovered on federal or tribal lands *after* the effective date of the statute, then another section of the statute applies, which establishes a process to secure the site and protect the remains pending appropriate notice and consultation with affected tribes. 25 U.S.C. sec. 3002. In such cases, the statutory procedures are designed to determine which group has the appropriate relationship to establish "ownership" of the remains and funerary objects, and this process culminates with a transfer to that group.

Although there can be overlap (for example, because remains that are exhumed should be "transferred" to the custody of the "owner" and this is also a form of "repatriation"), the following materials track the basic approach of NAGPRA, which differentiates the process which protects the intentional or inadvertent excavation of Native American human remains from ancestral burial sites (exhumation), from the process applicable to Native American human remains that are in museum or agency collections, which is intended to identify the appropriate claimant for a "repatriation." The cases and notes below present both "pre-NAGPRA" and "post-NAGPRA" approaches to determine the rights that Native people have to control their ancestral remains. As you read the cases, try to determine what principles the court is using to arrive at its legal conclusions about these rights.

a. Exhumation of Human Remains

CHARRIER v. BELL
Louisiana Court of Appeal
496 So. 2d 601 (1986)

PONDER, J.

Plaintiff appealed the trial court's judgment denying both his claim as owner of Indian artifacts and his request for compensation for his excavation work in uncovering those artifacts under the theory of unjust enrichment. We affirm.

Plaintiff is a former Corrections Officer at the Louisiana State Penitentiary in Angola, Louisiana, who describes himself as an "amateur archeologist." After researching colonial maps, records and texts, he concluded that Trudeau Plantation,[57] near Angola, was the possible site of an ancient village of the Tunica Indians. He alleges that in 1967 he obtained the permission of Mr. Frank Hoshman, Sr., who he believed was the owner of Trudeau Plantation, to survey the property with a metal detector for possible burial locations. After locating and excavating approximately 30 to 40 burial plots, lying in a circular pattern, plaintiff notified Mr. Hoshman that he had located the Tunica village. Although the evidence is contradictory, plaintiff contends that it was at that time that Mr. Hoshman first advised that he was the caretaker, not the owner, of the property.

Plaintiff continued to excavate the area for the next three years until he had located and excavated approximately 150 burial sites, containing beads, European ceramics, stoneware, glass bottles; iron kettles, vessels and skillets; knives, muskets, gunflints, balls and shots; crucifixes, rings and bracelets; and native pottery. The excavated artifacts are estimated to weigh two to two and one-half tons.

In search of a buyer for the collection, plaintiff talked to Dr. Robert S. Neitzel of Louisiana State University, who, in turn, informed Dr. Jeffrey D. Brain of Harvard University. Dr. Brain, who was involved in a survey of archeology along the lower Mississippi River, viewed the artifacts and began discussions of their sale to the Peabody Museum of Harvard University. The discussions resulted in the lease of the artifacts to the Museum, where they were inventoried, catalogued and displayed.

Plaintiff initially informed Dr. Neitzel and Dr. Brain that he had found the artifacts in a cave in Mississippi, so as to conceal their source; later he did disclose the actual site of the find to Dr. Brain, who had expressed his concern over the title of the artifacts. Dr. Brain then obtained permission from the landowners to do further site testing and confirmed that it was the true source of the artifacts.

Confronted with the inability to sell the collection because he could not prove ownership, plaintiff filed suit against the six nonresident landowners of Trudeau Plantation, requesting declaratory relief confirming that he was the owner of the artifacts. Alternatively, plaintiff requested that he be awarded compensation under the theory of unjust enrichment for his time and expenses.

The State of Louisiana intervened in the proceeding on numerous grounds, including its duty to protect its citizens in the absence of the lawful heirs of the artifacts. In 1978, the State purchased Trudeau Plantation and the artifacts from the six landowners and agreed to defend, indemnify and hold the prior owners harmless from any and all actions.

In 1981 the Tunica and Biloxi Indians were recognized as an American Indian Tribe by the Bureau of Indian Affairs of the Department of the Interior . . . .

---

[57] [1] Trudeau Plantation consists of approximately 150 acres located on a bluff in the southeast quadrant of the meeting of the Mississippi River and Tunica Bayou. Angola is on the other side of the bayou.

The trial judge held that the Tunica-Biloxi Tribe is the lawful owner of the artifacts, finding that plaintiff was not entitled to the artifacts under La. C.C. art. 3423 as it read prior to amendment by Act No. 187 of 1982, which required discovery "by chance." The judge also found that plaintiff had no claim to the artifacts on the basis of abandonment under La. C.C. art. 3421, as it read prior to the amendment by Act No. 187 of 1982, because the legal concept of abandonment does not extend to burial goods.

The trial court also denied relief under the theory of unjust enrichment, finding that any impoverishment claimed by plaintiff was a result of his attempts "for his own gain" and that his presence and actions on the property of a third party placed him in a "precarious position, if not in legal bad faith."

The issues before this court are the adequacy of proof that the Tunica-Biloxi Indians are descendants of the inhabitants of Trudeau, the ownership of the artifacts, and the applicability of the theory of unjust enrichment.

Plaintiff first argues that the evidence that the members of the Tunica-Biloxi Indians of Louisiana, Inc., are legal descendants of the inhabitants of Trudeau Plantation was insufficient to entitle them to the artifacts. He asserts that federal recognition of the tribe "merely proves that the Tribe is the best representative of the Tunica Indians for purposes of receiving federal benefits," and points to evidence of intermixing by the Tunica tribe with other tribes.

The fact that members of other tribes are intermixed with the Tunicas does not negate or diminish the Tunicas' relationship to the historical tribe. Despite the fact that the Tunicas have not produced a perfect "chain of title" back to those buried at Trudeau Plantation, the tribe is an accumulation of the descendants of former Tunica Indians and has adequately satisfied the proof of descent.

Plaintiff next argues that the Indians abandoned the artifacts when they moved from Trudeau Plantation, and the artifacts became *res nullius* until found and reduced to possession by plaintiff who then became the owner.

Plaintiff contends that he has obtained ownership of the property through occupancy, which is a "mode of acquiring property by which a thing which belongs to nobody, becomes the property of the person who took possession of it, with the intention of acquiring a right of ownership upon it." La. C.C. art. 3412, prior to amendment by Act No. 187 of 1982.

One of the five methods of acquiring property by occupancy is "By finding (that is, by discovering precious stones on the sea shore, or things abandoned, or a treasure.)" La. C.C. art. 3414, prior to amendment by Act No. 187 of 1982. Plaintiff contends that the artifacts were abandoned by the Tunicas and that by finding them he became the owner.

Both sides presented extensive expert testimony on the history of the Tunica Indians, the French, English and Spanish occupation of the surrounding territory and the presence or absence of duress causing the Tunicas to abandon the Trudeau site.

However, the fact that the descendants or fellow tribesmen of the deceased Tunica Indians resolved, for some customary, religious or spiritual belief, to bury certain items along with the bodies of the deceased, does not result in a conclusion that the goods were abandoned. While the relinquishment of immediate possession may have been proved, an objective viewing of the circumstances and intent of the relinquishment does not result in a finding of abandonment. Objects may be buried with a decedent for any number of reasons. The relinquishment of possession normally serves some spiritual, moral, or religious purpose of the descendant/owner, but is not intended as a means of relinquishing ownership to a stranger. Plaintiff's argument carried to its logical conclusion would render a grave subject to despoliation either immediately after interment or definitely after removal of the descendants of the deceased from the neighborhood of the cemetery.

Although plaintiff has referred to the artifacts as *res nullius*, under French law, the source of Louisiana's occupancy law, that term refers specifically to such things as wild game and fish, which are originally without an owner. The term *res derelictae* refers to "things voluntarily abandoned by their owner with the intention to have them go to the first person taking possession." P. Esmein, *Aubry & Rau Droit Civil Francais*, Vol. II, 168, p. 46 (7th ed. 1966). Some examples of *res derelictae* given by *Aubry and Rau* include things left on public ways, in the cities or to be removed by garbage collectors.

The artifacts fall into the category of *res derelictae*, if subject to abandonment. The intent to abandon *res derelictae* must include the intent to let the first person who comes along acquire them. Obviously, such is not the case with burial goods.

French sources have generally held that human remains and burial goods located in cemeteries or burial grounds are not "treasure" under article 716 of the French Civil Code and thereby not subject to occupancy upon discovery. The reasoning has been that any contrary decision would lead to and promote commercial speculation and despoilment of burial grounds. . .

The same reasoning that the French have used to treat burial goods applies in determining if such items can be abandoned. The intent in interring objects with the deceased is that they will remain there perpetually, and not that they are available for someone to recover and possess as owner.

For these reasons, we do not uphold the transfer of ownership to some unrelated third party who uncovers burial goods. The trial court concluded that La. C.C. art. 3421, as it read prior to passage of Act No. 187 of 1982, was not intended to require that objects buried with the dead were abandoned or that objects could be acquired by obtaining possession over the objections of the descendants. We agree with this conclusion. . . .

Plaintiff next argues that he is entitled to recover a sum of money to compensate his services and expenses on the basis of an *actio de in rem verso* [unjust enrichment]. We first question whether there has been an enrichment. While the nonresident landowners were "enriched" by the sale of the property to the state, the ultimate owners of the artifacts presented substantial evidence that the excavation caused substantial upset over the ruin of "ancestral burial grounds," rather than any enrichment.

Even if the Indians have been enriched, plaintiff has failed to prove that he has sustained [impoverishment]. The *actio de in rem verso* [is] derived from the similar

French action [and] is influenced greatly by French Civil Code articles from which our own are copied. The impoverishment element in French law is met only when the factual circumstances show that it was not a result of the plaintiff's own fault or negligence or was not undertaken at his own risk. Obviously the intent is to avoid awarding one who has helped another through his own negligence or fault or through action taken at his own risk. Plaintiff was acting possibly out of his own negligence, but more probably knowingly and at his own risk [because he knew he was on the property without the owner's consent]. Under these circumstances, plaintiff has not proven the type of impoverishment necessary for a claim of unjust enrichment.

Additionally, plaintiff has failed to show that any enrichment was unjustified, entitling him to an action to recover from the enriched party. [Under Louisiana law] descendants have a right to enjoin the disinterment of their deceased relatives, as well as to receive damages for the desecration involved. Such a right would be subverted if descendants were obliged to reimburse for the expenses of the excavation. [Thus, there] is a legal justification for any enrichment received by the Tribe and plaintiff is not entitled to invoke the equitable theory.

[*Affirmed.*]

NOTES

1. **Archaeological Sites on Public Lands:** Can tribes prevent the destruction of archaeological sites on public land? The Archaeological Resources Protection Act of 1979, 16 U.S.C. § 470 et seq., is designed to protect "archaeological resources" on federal and Indian lands from individual and commercial interests, and to foster the professional gathering of information for future benefit. ARPA requires the issuance of permits to excavate archaeological resources on public or tribal lands. ARPA also criminalizes the illegal excavation of remains or cultural objects on federal or tribal lands, trafficking in illegal cultural property, or the sale, purchase or transport of archaeological resources in interstate or foreign commerce assuming that the item was removed from state or privately-owned lands in violation of state or local law. "Archaeological resources" are defined as "any material remains of past human life or activities which are at least 100 years of age." The definition includes human remains and burial sites, as well as cultural objects, such as pottery, basketry and weapons. Once excavated or removed, archaeological resources are deemed to be the property of the United States if taken from public lands. 16 U.S.C. § 470cc(b)(3). Native interests are represented in both the text of the statute and its enforcement. For example, the statute requires the public land manager to notify an Indian tribe when granting a permit on public land might harm "any religious or cultural site." 16 U.S.C. § 470cc(c). The law also mandates compliance with AIRFA and requires consultation with Indian tribes in formulating regulations. To the extent that Native American remains or cultural objects are excavated on public land, the disposition of such remains or objects must be in accordance with NAGPRA.

2. **Sites on Private Land:** As *Charrier v. Bell* illustrates, ownership of artifacts excavated from private lands by or under the supervision of the landowner presents unique problems. What was the court's rationale for finding that the Tribe owned

the artifacts? If the private landowners had not sold their land to the state and the state had not subordinated its interest to the Tribe, would the result be the same? Do owners of property always acquire all items buried in the soil? Could an argument be made that the Tribe in ceding land to the United States never intended to cede burial sites contained in the ceded land? Can it be argued that the United States took the land with an obligation to protect burial sites?

Tribal-state agreements regarding repatriation and protection can be a very effective method to protect tribal artifacts and human remains. Beginning with Iowa in 1974, many states have enacted or are considering such measures. Wolinsky, *Unburying Indian Bones: Science vs. Spirituality*, 9 AM. C. PHYSICIANS OBS. 1 (1989). For example, California has enacted a provision preventing anyone from possessing "artifacts or human remains" taken from a "Native American grave or cairn" after January 1, 1984. Cal. Pub. Resources Code § 5097.99. The law also gives the California Native American Heritage Commission, five of whose members must be "elder, traditional people, or spiritual leaders of California Native American tribes nominated by Native American organizations, tribes, or groups within the state," *id.* § 5097.92, authority to mediate disputes and enforce the law.

In *People v. Van Horn*, 218 Cal. App. 3d 1378 (1990), the state court upheld the statute in a case affirming an injunction against a California archaeologist who refused to return two metates (millstones) found in a site he excavated on private land while making a survey for the city of Vista, which was considering acquisition of the land. The defendant argued that the law was void for vagueness, violated the due process and equal protection clauses of the Fourteenth Amendment, and violated the establishment clause of the First Amendment. The court rejected defendant's arguments, examining the legislature's purposes in enacting the statute: (1) to provide protection to Native American human burials and skeletal remains from vandalism and inadvertent destruction; and (2) to provide a regular means by which Native American descendants can make known their concerns regarding the need for sensitive treatment and disposition of Native American burials. The legislature anticipated that the Commission would mediate disputes between landowners and Native Americans and assist them in reaching agreements that would serve these goals.

Where excavations or other disturbance of private lands involves expenditure of federal funds or issuance of a federal permit, the National Historic Preservation Act (NHPA), 16 U.S.C. §§ 470–470x-6, provides some avenues for Native advocates to seek protection of human remains as well as cultural items. *See also* discussion in the Notes at Sec. B.1, this chapter. For example, if a private development entails discharge into waters covered by the Clean Water Act, the Army Corps of Engineers will have to issue a permit before the development can go forward. In such a case, state environmental reviews will be supplemented by what is commonly known as the "section 106 process." Administered in accordance with regulations promulgated by the Advisory Council on Historic Preservation, this review process applies to any "traditional cultural property," defined in National Park Service Bulletin 38 as a property that is eligible for inclusion in the National Register of Historic Places "because of its association with cultural practices or beliefs of a living community that (a) are rooted in that community's history, and (b) are important in maintaining the continuing cultural identity of the community." Oral tradition is treated as important in evaluating the historic significance of such sites. The review process itself requires the federal agency to take into account the effect of proposed activity on the site and to consult with tribes and Native Hawaiian organizations that might attach religious or cultural significance to it. The final step in the process is "resolution of adverse effects," where an agreement is typically made on how to avoid, minimize, or mitigate any identified adverse effects. 36 C.F.R. § 800.6. *See Muckleshoot Indian Tribe v. U.S. Forest Service*, 177 F.3d 800 (9th Cir. 1999) (discussing whether documenting a site before destroying it constitutes "mitigation"). Outside tribal lands, however, tribes and Native Hawaiian organizations that have been included as consulting parties are not required signatories to such an agreement, although they may be invited to participate.

The Advisory Council on Historic Preservation may enter the process at this final stage at the request of tribes and Native Hawaiian organizations. A very valuable resource by a longtime expert in the field is THOMAS F. KING, CULTURAL RESOURCE LAWS & PRACTICE: AN INTRODUCTORY GUIDE (2d ed. 2004).

As a practical matter, how helpful is NHPA to Native nations seeking to protect burial sites and other culturally important sites on private lands? Will the section 106 process, which provides only procedural guarantees, do anything to protect the sites from disturbance, as opposed to merely sanctioning removal and reburial? Nonfederally recognized tribes have had the greatest difficulty making effective use of NHPA, often because private developers are able to exploit decentralized tribal organization and internal political rifts to find the most receptive tribal representatives.

A case in point is the recent controversy over the discovery of a Tongva cemetery during the excavation of a drainage waterway for a large-scale development known as Playa Vista near the Pacific Ocean in Los Angeles. During the section 106 process, certain tribal representatives of the nonfederally recognized Tongva had agreed to a protocol for handling and reburial of human remains, on the expectation that only a few individual burials might be disturbed. The developers eventually excavated more than 200 sets of remains complete with ceremonial shell beads and other burial artifacts, dating from centuries ago until the post-contact period. Under California law, such cemeteries (defined as six or more human bodies buried at one place) are protected from disinterment, but only if they were created after 1872. *Wana the Bear v. Community Construction, Inc.*, 128 Cal. App. 3d 536 (1982). The developer has agreed to reinter the remains elsewhere on the property, and to establish a cultural center for the Tongva, but many tribal representatives insist the bones should be returned to their original burial site and the drainage corridor relocated. The City of Los Angeles has approved the environmental impact report, and it appears that the project will be going forward in accordance with the developer's plans. For an account of this controversy, see Nick Madigan, *Developer Unearths Burial Ground and Stirs Up Anger Among Indians*, N.Y. TIMES, June 2, 2004, at A-13. Commentaries by anthropologists who have worked closely with Native communities on cultural resource issues include Nabokov, *City Is Losing a Part of Its Soul in Playa Vista*, L.A. TIMES, June 7, 2004, at B-9; C. King & Gibson, *Skeletons in Playa Vista's Closet*, L.A. TIMES, June 20, 2004, at M-3.

Would any changes in the law, state or federal, have made a difference in this situation? What changes, if any, should be made?

3. **The Role of Tribal Law:** To what extent can or should state courts defer to tribal courts and legislatures in the articulation of the appropriate standards to govern treatment of deceased Native people? In *Mexican v. Circle Bear*, 370 N.W.2d 737 (S.D. 1985), *see* Ch. 3, Sec. C.3, a state court recognized a tribal court judgment regarding the disposition of a dead body of a tribal member who died off the reservation, even though tribal law regarding control over the burial differed from state law. The case is responsive to the ethic of respect, which Native people argue should govern the treatment of their ancestral remains. The Eastern Band of Cherokee Indians is among the tribes that have issued specific protection for all ancestral human remains in their tribal code. The Code specifies that "the graves of Cherokee people and their ancestors are sacred and shall not be disturbed or excavated." The Code applies to trust lands and to non-trust lands, and provides for immediate reburial of remains that are excavated, along with associated funerary objects. Remains that are disinterred at any location within "aboriginal Cherokee lands" should be "buried at the original site where possible." If remains are disinterred outside Cherokee trust lands, they may be reburied at the Cherokee Memorial Cemetery in Vanore, Tennessee. The Code goes beyond NAGPRA in requiring repatriation of Cherokee remains in the possession of any museums, universities, or federal agencies or other institutions or persons. The Code also specifies that "the remains of Cherokee people" or Cherokee ancestors "should not be subjected to destructive skeletal analysis."

4. **The Implications of International Human Rights Law:** Indigenous peoples' claims for protection of ancestral human remains are also present within the sphere of international human rights law. In *Francis Hopu v. France*, the Human Rights Committee established under Article 28 of the International Covenant on Civil and Political Rights considered a claim by two Native Polynesians against France for protection of an ancestral burial site in Tahiti, which was due to be excavated and developed as a luxury hotel complex. Communication No. 549/1993: France.29/12/97. CCPR/C60/D/549/1993/Rev. 1. (Jurisprudence). The site was a pre-European burial ground of the Polynesian people and was treated as a sacred site. In addition, the adjacent lagoon was used for fishing and subsistence purposes by the Native people. The claim was litigated under several provisions of the International Covenant on Civil and Political Rights, including Article 27, which applies to the cultural rights of ethnic groups, and Articles 17 and 23, which protect rights to family and privacy.

In this case, although France had signed onto the Covenant, it had reserved itself from Article 27 on Cultural Rights. Therefore, a majority of the Committee held that Article 27 was not binding on France. The question, therefore, was whether the Native claimants could assert that their right to protect their ancient ancestors triggered rights to family and privacy. A majority of the Committee held that construction of the hotel complex on ancestral burial grounds would interfere with the claimants' rights to family and privacy. The Committee found that these rights must be interpreted within the Native framework for establishing kinship, and thus the failure to establish a "direct kinship link" in European terms could not be used against the claimants "where the burial grounds in question pre-date the arrival of the European settlers and are recognized as including the forbears of present Polynesian inhabitants of Tahiti." Does this opinion have any bearing on the current controversy over the disposition of the Ancient One known as "Kennewick Man"? Should it? On a related point, the NAGPRA Review Committee continues to struggle with how to draft regulations governing the disposition of so-called "culturally unidentifiable" Native American human remains. These are remains that museums and scientists believe cannot be "culturally affiliated" to any contemporary Native group. Many Native people, on the other hand, argue that all Native ancestors are "culturally affiliated" to contemporary Native people and that it is inappropriate to apply Western kinship standards or scientific notions of "genetic descendency" to this inquiry. What would the Human Rights Committee advise on this point?

b.   "Repatriation" and "Ownership" of Human Remains Under NAGPRA

Native peoples' interest in protecting their ancestral remains and cultural objects, as well as the land containing cultural sites, has sometimes clashed with the interests of archaeologists. Many Native peoples believe that it is disrespectful and potentially dangerous to treat ancestral remains as scientific subjects or museum displays. Although some Native people might consent to limited scientific inquiry for a specific and legitimate objective (e.g., cultural affiliation), most groups are opposed to scientific study of human remains for the sake of general intellectual inquiry and many are vehemently opposed to destructive (e.g., DNA) analysis of ancestral remains. Most Native groups believe that Native American human remains and cultural objects belong with the descendant groups, and are to be treated with the utmost respect, given the pervasive belief that such remains and objects contain an active agency or essence that can affect living people.

Native people object to the fact that their ancestors, unlike those of Caucasian people, are considered "archaeological resources," to be studied and displayed. They are frequently reluctant to divulge any information on burial sites known to them either on or off reservations. Archaeologists, however, often argue that Native American remains are a "resource" for scientific study, and some equate the reburial of remains as akin to burning a library. Many archaeologists insist that bones, particularly ancient skeletal remains, are a valuable source of knowledge about the origins of human populations and disease epidemiology. Even where they may not have developed the techniques necessary to draw out such information, they believe that the advancement of science will lead to such understanding. They often seek disclosure of burial sites on the theory that this is necessary to prevent looting by "amateur" pothunters, which is equally destructive to the quest for knowledge that they are committed to. For a comprehensive summary of these disparate views, see NATIVE AMERICANS AND ARCHAEOLOGISTS: STEPPING STONES TO COMMON GROUND (N. Swidler et al. ed., 1997).

Some of the most contentious disputes between Native Americans and archaeologists have centered around the discovery of "ancient remains." The *Bonnichsen* case, below, presents one of the most controversial. Under ARPA, the federal Archaeological Resources Protection Act, 16 U.S.C. § 470aa et seq., the plaintiff archaeologists applied to the Army Corps of Engineers for a permit to engage in scientific testing of the "Kennewick Man" remains, categorized as an "archaeological resource" under that Act. The five tribes that claimed an aboriginal connection to the site where the remains were found claimed rights under NAGPRA, which entitled them to custody of the remains if they could demonstrate "cultural affiliation" by a preponderance of the evidence. This litigation ensued.

BONNICHSEN v. UNITED STATES
United States Court of Appeals, Ninth Circuit
367 F.3d 864 (2004)

GOULD, CIRCUIT JUDGE.

This is a case about the ancient human remains of a man who hunted and lived, or at least journeyed, in the Columbia Plateau an estimated 8,340 to 9,200 years ago, a time predating all recorded history from any place in the world, a time before the oldest cities of our world had been founded, a time so ancient that the pristine and untouched land and the primitive cultures that may have lived on it are not deeply understood by even the most well-informed men and women of our age. Seeking the opportunity of study, a group of scientists as Plaintiffs[58] in this case brought an action against, *inter alia*, the United States Department of the Interior, challenging various Indian tribes'[59] claim to one of the most important American anthropological and archaeological discoveries of the late twentieth century, and challenging the Interior Department's decision honoring the tribes' claim. The discovery that launched this contest was that of a human skeleton, estimated by carbon dating to be 8,340 to 9,200 years old, known popularly and commonly as "Kennewick Man," but known as "the Ancient One" to some American Indians who now inhabit regions in Washington, Idaho, and Oregon, roughly proximate to the site on the Columbia River at Kennewick, Washington, where the bones were found. From the perspective of the scientists-Plaintiffs, this skeleton is an irreplaceable source of information about early New World populations that warrants careful scientific inquiry to advance knowledge of distant times. Yet, from the perspective of the intervenor-Indian tribes the skeleton is that of an ancestor who, according to the tribes' religious and social traditions, should be buried immediately without further testing.

Plaintiffs filed this lawsuit seeking to stop the transfer of the skeleton by the government to the tribes for burial, and the district court held in favor of the scientists-Plaintiffs. The Secretary of the Interior and the intervenor-Indian tribes

---

[58] [1] Plaintiffs are experts in their respective fields. Plaintiff Bonnichsen is Director of the Center for the Study of the First Americans at Oregon State University. Plaintiff Brace is Curator of Biological Anthropology at the University of Michigan Museum of Anthropology. Plaintiffs Gill, Haynes, Jantz, and Steele are anthropology professors. Plaintiff Owsley is division head for physical anthropology at the Smithsonian Institution's National Museum of Natural History. Plaintiff Stanford is Director of the Smithsonian's Paleo Indian Program.

[59] [2] The Tribal Claimants — present in this appeal as intervenors — are the Confederated Tribes & Bands of the Yakama Indian Nation, the Nez Perce Tribe of Idaho, the Confederated Tribes of the Umatilla Indian Reservation, and the Confederated Tribes of the Colville Reservation.

appeal. We have jurisdiction under 28 U.S.C. § 1291 and affirm the judgment of the district court barring the transfer of the skeleton for immediate burial and instead permitting scientific study of the skeleton.

I

In July 1996, teenagers going to a boat race discovered a human skull and bones near the shore of the Columbia River just outside Kennewick, Washington. The remains were found on federal property under the management of the United States Army Corps of Engineers ("Corps") and, at the request of the county coroner, were removed for analysis by an anthropologist, Dr. James Chatters, pursuant to an Archaeological Resources Protection Act of 1979 ("ARPA"), 16 U.S.C. §§ 470aa–470mm, permit. Because of physical features such as the shape of the skull and facial bones, anthropologists at first thought the remains were those of an early European settler. But the anthropologists then found a stone projectile point embedded in the skeleton's upper hip bone. The object's design, when viewed with x-rays and CT scans of the hip, resembled a style that was common before the documented arrival of Europeans in the region. Further study of the remains revealed characteristics unlike those of a European settler, yet also inconsistent with any American Indian remains previously documented in the region. A minute quantity of metacarpal bone was radiocarbon dated. The laboratory estimated the age of the bones to be between 8,340 and 9,200 years old.[60]

The skeleton attracted attention because some of its physical features, such as the shape of the face and skull, differed from those of modern American Indians. Many scientists believed the discovery might shed light on the origins of humanity in the Americas. On August 31, 1996, Dr. Douglas Owsley, Division Head for Physical Anthropology at the Smithsonian Institution in Washington, D.C., made arrangements for Dr. Chatters to bring this important find to the Smithsonian's National Museum of Natural History for further study.

Indian tribes from the area of the Columbia River opposed scientific study of the remains on religious and social grounds.[61]

Four Indian groups (the "Tribal Claimants") demanded that the remains be turned over to them for immediate burial. The Tribal Claimants based their demand

---

[60] [6] Human skeletons this old are rare in the Western Hemisphere, and most found have consisted of only fragmented remains. The record indicates that less than twelve securely dated human crania older than 8,000 years have been found in the United States. By contrast, about 90% of this skeleton was recovered in good condition.

[61] [8] For example, the Tribal Claimants urged that "when a body goes into the ground, it is meant to stay there until the end of time. When remains are disturbed and remain above the ground, their spirits are at unrest. . . . To put these spirits at ease, the remains must be returned to the ground as soon as possible." *Bonnichsen III*, 217 F. Supp. 2d [1116] at 1121 (quoting Joint Tribal Amici Memorandum (1997) at 4–5). We note that the Ethnic Minority Council of America, in its amicus brief, urges that: "Potential descendants [of Kennewick Man] may not be members of the Joint Tribal Claimants or believe in the expressed 'Indian' religious interpretations made by the political leaders of the tribes." Further, as suggested by amicus Ohio Archaeological Council, in the absence of a conclusive determination of cultural affiliation, the Tribal Claimants cannot establish that permitting Plaintiffs-scientists to study the Kennewick Man's remains offends their religious views or customs.

on the Native American Graves Protection and Repatriation Act ("NAGPRA"), 25 U.S.C. § 3001 et seq. The Corps agreed with the Tribal Claimants and, citing NAGPRA, seized the remains on September 10, 1996, shortly before they could be transported to the Smithsonian. The Corps also ordered an immediate halt to DNA testing, which was being done using the remainder of the bone sample that had been submitted earlier for radiocarbon dating. After investigation, the Corps decided to give the remains to the Tribal Claimants for burial. As required by NAGPRA, the Corps published a "Notice of Intent to Repatriate Human Remains" in a local newspaper on September 17, 1996, and September 24, 1996.

The scientists and others, including the Smithsonian Institution, objected to the Corps' decision, arguing that the remains were a rare discovery of national and international significance. In late September and early October 1996, several scientists asked Major General Ernest J. Herrell, Commander of the Corps' North Pacific Division, to allow qualified scientists to study the remains.

The scientists did not convince the Corps to permit them to study the remains, and commenced this litigation on October 16, 1996, in the United States District Court for the District of Oregon. . . . [After denying motions by both plaintiff and defendant for disposition in their favor, and finding that the Army Corps had failed to resolve difficult legal questions and had assumed facts that proved to be erroneous, the District Court judge remanded the case to the Army Corps for further proceedings.]

On March 24, 1998, the Corps and the Secretary of the Interior entered into an agreement that effectively assigned to the Secretary responsibility to decide whether the remains were "Native American" under NAGPRA, and to determine their proper disposition. The Department of the Interior then assumed the role of lead agency on this case.

Almost two years after this matter was remanded, the Secretary's experts began to examine the remains in detail. The experts could not determine, from non-destructive examination of the skeleton alone, when Kennewick Man lived. Further study of the sediment was recommended, but the Corps' decision to bury the discovery site in April 1998 prevented completion of those studies.[62]

The experts concluded that Kennewick Man's remains were unlike those of any known present-day population, American Indian or otherwise.

The Secretary's experts cautioned, however, that an apparent lack of physical resemblance between the Kennewick Man's remains and present-day American Indians did not completely rule out the possibility that the remains might be

---

[62] [10] The Corps buried the discovery site of the remains under approximately two million pounds of rubble and dirt, topped with 3700 willow, dogwood, and cottonwood plants. The lengthy administrative record that Defendants filed with the district court documents only a portion of the process by which the decision to bury the site was made. Nevertheless, that record suggested to the district court that the Corps' primary objective in covering the site was to prevent additional remains or artifacts from being discovered, not to "preserve" the site's archaeological value or to remedy a severe erosion control problem as Defendants represented. Burial of the discovery site hindered efforts to verify the age of Kennewick Man's remains, and effectively ended efforts to determine whether other artifacts are present at the site which might shed light on the relationship between the remains and contemporary American Indians.

biologically ancestral to modern American Indians. Moreover, although Kennewick Man's morphological traits did not closely resemble those of modern American Indian populations, the Secretary's experts noted that Kennewick Man's physical attributes are generally consistent with the very small number of human remains from this period that have been found in North America.

Relying solely on the age of the remains and the fact that the remains were found within the United States, on January 13, 2000, the Secretary pronounced Kennewick Man's remains "Native American" within NAGPRA's meaning. And on September 25, 2000, the Secretary determined that a preponderance of the evidence supported the conclusion that the Kennewick remains were culturally affiliated with present-day Indian tribes. For this reason, the Secretary announced his final decision to award Kennewick Man's remains to a coalition of the Tribal Claimants. The Corps and the Secretary also denied Plaintiffs' request to study the remains.

Plaintiffs filed an amended complaint in the district court challenging the Secretary's decisions. The district court again ruled in Plaintiffs' favor. As pertinent to this appeal, the district court vacated the Secretary's decisions as contrary to the Administrative Procedure Act, 5 U.S.C. § 706(2)(A) ("APA"), on the ground that the Secretary improperly concluded that NAGPRA applies. The district court also held that, because NAGPRA did not apply, Plaintiffs should have the opportunity to study Kennewick Man's remains under ARPA. Defendants and the Tribal Claimants appealed, and we stayed the district court's order granting Plaintiffs-scientists' study of the remains pending our decision herein.

II

[The court found both that it had jurisdiction over the case and that the plaintiffs had standing to bring the suit, based upon the fact that the plaintiffs would benefit if the court found that ARPA rather than NAGPRA applies, and because NAGPRA broadly authorizes "any person" alleging a violation of that statute, regardless of whether he or she satisfies the prudential "zone of interests" test for standing and regardless whether he or she alleges underenforcement or overenforcement of the Act. . . .]

III

Our review of the Secretary's decision to transfer Kennewick Man to the Tribal Claimants is governed by the APA, which instructs courts to "hold unlawful and set aside agency action, findings, and conclusions found to be . . . arbitrary, capricious, an abuse of discretion, or otherwise not in accordance with law." 5 U.S.C. § 706(2)(A).

NAGPRA vests "ownership or control" of newly discovered Native American human remains in the decedent's lineal descendants or, if lineal descendants cannot be ascertained, in a tribe "affiliated" with the remains. 25 U.S.C. § 3002(a). NAGPRA mandates a two-part analysis. The first inquiry is whether human remains are Native American within the statute's meaning. If the remains are not Native American, then NAGPRA does not apply. However, if the remains are Native

American, then NAGPRA applies, triggering the second inquiry of determining which persons or tribes are most closely affiliated with the remains.

The parties dispute whether the remains of Kennewick Man constitute Native American remains within NAGPRA's meaning. NAGPRA defines human remains as "Native American" if the remains are "of, or relating to, a tribe, people, or culture that is indigenous to the United States." 25 U.S.C. § 3001(9). The text of the relevant statutory clause is written in the present tense ("of, or relating to, a tribe, people, or culture that is indigenous"). Thus the statute unambiguously requires that human remains bear some relationship to a presently existing tribe, people, or culture to be considered Native American . . . .

In the context of NAGPRA, we conclude that Congress's use of the present tense is significant. The present tense "in general represents present time." R. Pence and D. Emery, A Grammar of Present-Day English 262 (2d ed. 1963). Congress, by using the phrase "is indigenous" in the present tense, referred to *presently existing* tribes, peoples, or cultures. We must presume that Congress gave the phrase "is indigenous" its ordinary or natural meaning. We conclude that Congress was referring to presently existing Indian tribes when it referred to "a tribe, people, or culture *that is* indigenous to the United States." 25 U.S.C. § 3001(9) (emphasis added).

NAGPRA also protects graves of persons not shown to be of current tribes in that it protects disjunctively remains "of, or relating to" current indigenous tribes. Thus, NAGPRA extends to all remains that relate to a tribe, people, or culture that is indigenous to the United States, see 25 U.S.C. § 3001(9) (defining human remains as Native American if they are "of, or relating to, a tribe, people, or culture that is indigenous to the United States") (emphasis added).

Our conclusion that NAGPRA's language requires that human remains, to be considered Native American, bear some relationship to a presently existing tribe, people, or culture accords with NAGPRA's purposes . . . .

Congress's purposes would not be served by requiring the transfer to modern American Indians of human remains that bear no relationship to them. Yet, that would be the result under the Secretary's construction of the statute, which would give Native American status to any remains found within the United States regardless of age and regardless of lack of connection to existing indigenous tribes.[63] The exhumation, study, and display of ancient human remains that are unrelated to modern American Indians was not a target of Congress's aim, nor was it precluded by NAGPRA.

---

[63] [17] At oral argument, the government urged that its interpretation of remains as Native American when found within the United States would apply even to remains as old as 100,000 or 150,000 years, close to the dawn of homo sapiens. Indeed, the government at oral argument even said that if remains of a mythical first man and woman, an "Adam and Eve," were found in the United States, those remains would be "Native American" under the government's interpretation of NAGPRA. Thus the government's unrestricted interpretation based solely on geography, calling any ancient remains found in the United States "Native American" if they pre-date the arrival of Europeans has no principle of limitation beyond geography. This does not appear to us to be what Congress had in mind. Nor does the legislative history support NAGPRA coverage of bones of such great antiquity.

NAGPRA was also intended to protect the dignity of the human body after death by ensuring that Native American graves and remains be treated with respect. *See* S. Rep. No. 101-473, at 6 (1990). . . . Congress's purpose is served by requiring the return to modern-day American Indians of human remains that bear some significant relationship to them.

[The Ninth Circuit panel rejected the Secretary's argument that the district court's interpretation "improperly collapses" NAGPRA's first inquiry (asking whether human remains are Native American) into NAGPRA's second inquiry (asking which American Indians or Indian tribe bears the closest relationship to Native American remains). According to the panel, "[t]he second inquiry requires a more specific finding that remains are most closely affiliated . . . to a specific Indian tribe," not simply that they are Native American. Plaintiffs could not satisfy the second inquiry because "the record shows no relationship of Kennewick Man to the Tribal Claimants." The panel also refused to give *Chevron* deference to the Secretary's interpretation of NAGPRA, finding that the Secretary's interpretation was contrary to "unambiguous" language in the statute. *Chevron U.S.A. v. Natural Res. Def. Council*, 467 U.S. 837 (1984). The statute's "unambiguous" language also led the panel to refuse to apply the Indian law canons of construction. *See* Ch. 2, Sec. C.]

    . . . .

The Secretary's interpretation would mean that the finding of any remains in the United States in and of itself would automatically render these remains "Native American." This interpretation would leave no meaning for the "relating to" clause, unless we were to interpret the clause to cover remains found outside the United States. But we cannot conclude that Congress intended an absurd result, for Congress could not be considered to have jurisdiction over disposition of human remains found in some other country. By reading NAGPRA's definition of "Native American" literally, meaning is given to each of its terms. Some remains may be covered because they are remains of a tribe, people, or culture that is indigenous, while other remains may be covered because they are "related to" a currently existing indigenous tribe, people, or culture. . . .

Congress enacted NAGPRA to give American Indians control over the remains of their genetic and cultural forbearers, not over the remains of people bearing no special and significant genetic or cultural relationship to some presently existing indigenous tribe, people, or culture.

The age of Kennewick Man's remains, given the limited studies to date, makes it almost impossible to establish any relationship between the remains and presently existing American Indians. At least no significant relationship has yet been shown. We cannot give credence to an interpretation of NAGPRA advanced by the government and the Tribal Claimants that would apply its provisions to remains that have at most a tenuous, unknown, and unproven connection, asserted solely because of the geographical location of the find.

IV

Finally, we address the Secretary's determination that Kennewick Man's remains are Native American, as defined by NAGPRA. We must set aside the Secretary's decision if it was "arbitrary" or "capricious" because the decision was based on inadequate factual support. *See* 5 U.S.C. § 706(2)(A). Here, after reviewing the record, we conclude that the record does not contain substantial evidence that Kennewick Man's remains are Native American within NAGPRA's meaning.[64]

The administrative record contains no evidence — let alone substantial evidence — that Kennewick Man's remains are connected by some special or significant genetic or cultural relationship to any presently existing indigenous tribe, people, or culture. An examination of the record demonstrates the absence of evidence that Kennewick Man and modern tribes share significant genetic or cultural features.[65]

The Secretary's only evidence, perhaps, of a possible cultural relationship between Kennewick Man and modern-day American Indians comes in the form of oral histories. One of the Secretary's experts, Dr. Daniel Boxberger, concluded that modern day Plateau tribes' oral histories — some of which can be interpreted to refer to ancient floods, volcanic eruptions, and the like — are "highly suggestive of long-term establishment of the present-day tribes." Stated another way, Dr. Boxberger noted that oral traditions showed no necessary tale of a superseding migration with newer peoples displacing older ones. But evidence in the record demonstrates that oral histories change relatively quickly, that oral histories may be based on later observation of geological features and deduction (rather than on the first teller's witnessing ancient events), and that these oral histories might be from a culture or group other than the one to which Kennewick Man belonged. The oral traditions relied upon by the Secretary's expert, Dr. Boxberger, entail some published accounts of Native American folk narratives from the Columbia Plateau region, and statements from individual tribal members. But we conclude that these accounts are just not specific enough or reliable enough or relevant enough to show a significant relationship of the Tribal Claimants with Kennewick Man. Because oral accounts have been inevitably changed in context of transmission, because the traditions include myths that cannot be considered as if factual histories, because the value of such accounts is limited by concerns of authenticity, reliability, and accuracy, and because the record as a whole does not show where historical fact ends and mythic tale begins, we do not think that the oral traditions of interest to Dr. Boxberger were adequate to show the required significant relationship of the Kennewick Man's remains to the Tribal Claimants.[66] As the district court observed,

---

[64] [20] In so holding, we necessarily determine that no reasonable person could conclude on this record that Kennewick Man is "Native American" under NAGPRA.

[65] [21] As pointed out by amici Texas Historical Commission, under the framework proposed by the government and the Tribal Claimants, as soon as any remains are determined to be pre-Columbian, any study or testing of such remains would have to stop. This blanket prohibition could result in improper disposition of remains to parties wholly unrelated to the remains.

[66] [23] We find of considerable help the explanations of the uses and limits on oral narratives as explained and documented with scholarly authority by *amicus curiae* Dr. Andrei Simic, Professor of Anthropology at the University of Southern California, in Los Angeles since 1971 who has specialized in study of the role of folklore and oral tradition in developing cultural identity of ethnic groups, and Dr.

8340 to 9200 years between the life of Kennewick Man and the present is too long a time to bridge merely with evidence of oral traditions.

Considered as a whole, the administrative record might permit the Secretary to conclude reasonably that the Tribal Claimants' ancestors have lived in the region for a very long time.

However, because Kennewick Man's remains are so old and the information about his era is so limited, the record does not permit the Secretary to conclude reasonably that Kennewick Man shares special and significant genetic or cultural features with presently existing indigenous tribes, people, or cultures. We thus hold that Kennewick Man's remains are not Native American human remains within the meaning of NAGPRA and that NAGPRA does not apply to them. Studies of the Kennewick Man's remains by Plaintiffs-scientists may proceed pursuant to ARPA.[67]

We remand to the district court for further proceedings consistent with this opinion.

Affirmed.

NOTES

1. **The Problem of Ancient Remains:** NAGPRA defines "cultural affiliation" as the existence of "a relationship of shared group identity which can be reasonably traced historically or prehistorically between a present day Indian tribe or Native Hawaiian organization and an identifiable earlier group." 25 U.S.C. § 3001(2). Why is the Ninth Circuit unwilling to allow them the opportunity to make such a showing, given that the tribes have the burden of proof on this matter?

Consider whether the Ninth Circuit panel adequately responds to the contention that its interpretation of "Native American" renders the "cultural affiliation" provisions of NAGPRA pointless. Was the court's chosen interpretation of this phrase so obviously required by the language and purpose of NAGPRA that the panel was justified in ignoring the administrative interpretation of that phrase, an interpretation normally entitled to deference under federal law? For example, does the specific language used to define "sacred objects," referring to "present day adherents," support the panel's interpretation of "Native American," or could it be used to show that Congress knows how to insist on a present-day connection, and didn't do so with respect to the term "Native American"? For a critical appraisal of the court's decision, see Allison M. Dussias, *Kennewick Man, Kinship, and the "Dying Race": The Ninth Circuit's Assimilationist Assault on the Native American Graves Protection and Repatriation Act*, 84 NEB. L. REV. 55 (2005).

NAGPRA expressly provides that acceptable evidence of cultural affiliation

---

Harry Glynn Custred, Jr., Professor of Anthropology at California State University in Hayward since 1971, who teaches anthropology, linguistics, and folklore and who has written on the subject of oral traditions.

[67] [24] As pointed out by amici Texas Historical Commission, Plaintiffs-scientists plan to engage in the following general types of testing: (1) morphometric cranial and post-cranial measurements comparing the Kennewick Man's remains with other populations; (2) dental characteristic studies; (3) DNA studies; and (4) diet analysis.

includes linguistic patterns, folklore, and oral tradition. One reading of the statute is that the inclusion of such evidence reflects Congress's intent to respect the systems of knowledge found within Native American communities. Reading the footnotes and text of *Bonnichsen*, how much respect do Native sources of knowledge receive, compared to non-Native anthropologists' sources? Interestingly, to assess the weight to give to oral tradition, the panel turns to two non- Native folklorists, one of whom specializes in peoples of the Balkans. For a different perspective on the proper uses of oral tradition, *see* John Borrows, *Listening for a Change: The Courts and Oral Tradition*, 39 OSGOODE HALL L. J. 1 (2001).

The Ninth Circuit's opinion did not spell the end to controversy over testing of the Ancient One. After the intervening Tribes chose not to appeal the decision to the United States Supreme Court, the anthropologists complained that the Army Corps of Engineers objected to too many aspects of their study plan, and threatened to sue again. Under ARPA, the Corps is entitled to place reasonable terms and conditions on the study, and the Tribes are hoping to have some voice in how the bones are studied, in order to minimize "desecration." *See* Tomas Alex Tizon, *Skeleton Case's New Bone of Contention*, L.A. TIMES, Aug. 2, 2004, at A-12. Indian advocates have also focused their attention on urging Congress to amend NAGPRA's definitions to eliminate the conflation of "Native American" with determinations of "cultural affiliation," and to shift NAGPRA implementation from the National Park Service to a different federal agency. The heart of these various bills and riders is the addition of "or was" to the definition of "Native American," so the term would mean of, or relating to, a tribe, people, or culture that "is or was" indigenous to any geographic area that is now located within U.S. boundaries. *See* Testimony of Susan Shown Harjo, Walter Echohawk, Paul Bender et al. before the Senate Indian Affairs Committee, July 14, 2004.

At the 2004 hearings, the Department of Interior indicated to Congress that it agreed with the court's decision in *Bonnichsen*, and the Department's representative stated:

> We believe that NAGPRA should protect the sensibilities of currently existing tribes, cultures, and people while balancing the need to learn about past cultures and customs. In the situation where remains are not significantly related to any existing tribe, people, or culture they should be available for appropriate scientific analysis. The proposed legislation would shift away from this balance.

One of the leading proponents of NAGPRA, Morning Star Institute President Susan Shown Harjo, has characterized Interior's position as

> bowing to the "Kennewick" decision as the law of the land, even though none of the other judicial circuits have misread repatriation law in the same way. This paves the way for regulations that the scientists want to protect their "studies" on the myriad dead Indians they view as their property.

Suzan Shown Harjo, *How Many Dead Indians Will Satisfy Feds and Scientists?*, INDIAN COUNTRY TODAY, Aug. 4, 2005. For further discussion of this case and the context within which it arose, see DAVID H. THOMAS, SKULL WARS: KENNEWICK MAN AND THE BATTLE FOR NATIVE AMERICAN IDENTITY (2000); Rebecca Tsosie, *Privileging*

Claims to the Past: Ancient Human Remains and Contemporary Cultural Values,
31 ARIZ. ST. L.J. 583 (1999). Both of these works were published before the Ninth
Circuit's decision in *Bonnichsen.*

In a broader sense, is there any reason to distinguish between "ancient" Native
American remains and those of more modern origin for purposes of Native claims
to ancestral human remains? Many tribes do not possess a concept of "prehistory"
within their languages or traditions. Why should this concept be used to confine
their claims to those that post-date historic European contact? Are the evidentiary
standards under NAGPRA responsive to Native concerns as to how to prove
"cultural affiliation"? What would happen to NAGPRA if it is amended to require
proof of "genetic descendency" in order to claim cultural affiliation?

   2. Legal Treatment of Native Claims for Cultural Harm: The Ninth Circuit's
opinion in *Bonnichsen* allows scientific testing of the Ancient One to proceed on the
basis that he is not "Native American" for purposes of NAGPRA, in part by limiting
NAGPRA's definition of "Native American" to "presently existing" tribes, peoples or
cultures. Because of this ruling, there is no legal mechanism to prevent the harm
that the Native claimants believed would result from scientific testing of the
skeleton.

   This type of injury, which might be designated as "cultural harm," has similarly
failed to receive recognition in cases where the remains are "Native American," so
long as the agency is acting within the scope of the law. For example, in *Na Iwi O
Na Kupuna O Mokapu v. Dalton,* 894 F. Supp. 1397 (D. Haw. 1995), the
Department of Defense had contracted with the Bishop Museum to prepare an
inventory of human remains disinterred from the Mokapu Peninsula during
construction of a military installation. At the time, this was the "largest single group
of Native Hawaiian remains housed at the Bishop Museum." Due to the nature of
the excavation and the way the remains were stored for many years, the remains
were in substantial disarray and numerous experts were retained to assemble the
parts into identifiable individual skeletal remains. The ensuing scientific analysis
and documentation was extensive and resulted in a final inventory, which consisted
of the narrative report and appendices containing the documentation. The issue was
whether this inventory could be released to interested members of the public. The
Native Hawaiian claimant, Hui Malama, brought suit against the Department of
Defense to prevent release of the document, claiming that the release of detailed
information as to the identity and characteristics of the ancestors would cause grave
harm, both to the ancestors and to their contemporary descendants. Hui Malama's
lawsuit named the ancestral remains (Iwi) as parties in interest, as well as the
organization, which was acting on their behalf as a "guardian." Hui Malama claimed
that public disclosure should be barred under specific exemptions within the federal
Freedom of Information Act. The court ruled against the plaintiffs on all counts.
The court first held that the ancestors ("Na Iwi") had no independent standing to
bring a claim, as there was no case indicating that "human remains have legal
standing" and no indication that Congress intended such a result. Although some
"inanimate entities" (*e.g.,* ships and corporations) have been deemed to have legal
standing because this "furthers societal interests and benefits individual persons,"
the court saw no comparable benefits to granting standing to human remains. And,
while the court found that Hui Malama had standing to bring the claim on the

ancestors' behalf, it concluded that FOIA mandates the disclosure of all information controlled by the federal government, and declined to find that any FOIA exemptions applied to exclude the Inventory from this requirement.

3. Implementing Regulations Regarding Culturally Unaffiliated Remains: On March 15, 2010, the final rule on "Disposition of Culturally Unidentifiable Human Remains" was published as 43 C.F.R. 10.11. This new regulation implements section 8(c)(5) of NAGPRA and "applies to human remains previously determined to be Native American under section 10.9, but for which no lineal descendant or culturally affiliated Indian tribe or Native Hawaiian organization has been identified." The rule requires agencies, educational institutions, or museums to transfer these human remains to appropriate Native American parties when those institutions do not have a "right of possession" to the deceased persons, and prescribes a process for this to occur. The transfer of these remains is mandatory upon the conclusion of the requisite process. The transfer of "associated funerary objects" is recommended where "State or Federal law does not preclude" this, but remains discretionary under the rule

According to the rule, the process begins with a mandatory consultation process between the institutions and specified Native American officials and religious leaders. That consultation ideally would result in a mutually agreeable disposition. Section 10.11(c) requires the entity to offer to transfer control of human remains to Indian tribes and Native Hawaiian organizations, according to a specified order of priority that largely relates to the geographic connections of the remains to historical patterns of tribal land ownership and aboriginal occupancy. If none of the parties agrees to accept control, the institution may transfer control to "an Indian group that is not federally-recognized" or may "reinter the remains according to State or other law" provided that this is recommended by the Secretary of the Interior and there is no objection from the Indian tribes or Native Hawaiian organizations who were entitled to receive the remains.

The rule is of great significance given the fact that there are approximately 118,000 sets of Native American human remains and thousands of associated funerary objects still in the custody of agencies, museums, and educational institutions. Not surprisingly, many archeologists have objected to the rule, which would apply to ancient human remains, such as those at issue in the *Bonnichsen* case, asserting that valuable data will be lost and that these remains cannot be culturally affiliated to any contemporary tribe. Native Nations and their advocates, however, assert that this is a human rights issue and that all deceased Native American persons are entitled to a decent burial and should not be treated as "research specimens."

Under this new regulation, archaeologists and museums opposed to repatriation can no longer prevent the return of remains by demonstrating the absence of "cultural affiliation," at least where the claiming tribe can show that the remains were removed from its aboriginal lands. In cases involving very old remains, some archaeologists have responded by shifting their argument against repatriation from lack of "cultural affiliation" to lack of proof that the remains are "American Indian" within the meaning of NAGPRA. *See* Duane Champagne, *A New Attack on Repatriation*, INDIAN COUNTRY TODAY, Apr. 9, 2012, *available at* http://

indiancountrytodaymedianetwork.com/2012/04/09/new-attack-repatriation-107181; *see also* Rebecca Tsosie, *NAGPRA and the Problem of Culturally Unidentifiable Remains: The Argument for a Human Rights Framework*, 44 ARIZ. ST. L. J. 809 (2012).

In *White v. University of California* 765 F.3d 1010 (9th Cir. 2014), archeologists unearthed human remains beneath the Chancellor's residence at the University of California-San Diego. The place where the remains were found was the ancestral territory of the Kumeyaay Nation. The Nation's member tribes made a repatriation request under NAGPRA, but professors in the University of California system opposed their request, because they wished to study the remains. In 2009, the University's assessment of the remains to determine their affiliation concluded that the remains were culturally unaffiliated with any tribe. However, in 2010, the Department of Interior promulgated the regulations discussed above, which meant that the remains would have to be repatriated if they were determined to be Native American. The University issued a decision that they were. In response, scientist professors filed suit against the University's determination. The Ninth Circuit held that the scientists had standing to assert their claims, based on their interest in studying the remains. However, it concluded that NAGPRA did not abrogate tribal sovereign immunity, and because the Tribes and their Repatriation Committee were indispensible parties with sovereign immunity, the scientist's claims were properly dismissed.

4. **Conflicts Between Native Peoples and Archaeologists:** Native peoples' interest in protecting their ancestral remains and cultural objects, as well as the land containing cultural sites, has sometimes clashed with the interests of archaeologists. Many Native peoples believe that it is disrespectful and potentially dangerous to treat ancestral remains as scientific subjects or museum displays. Although some Native people might consent to limited scientific inquiry for a specific and legitimate objective (*e.g.*, cultural affiliation), most groups are opposed to scientific study of human remains for the sake of general intellectual inquiry and many are vehemently opposed to destructive (*e.g.*, DNA) analysis of ancestral remains. Most Native groups believe that Native American human remains and cultural objects belong with the descendant groups, and are to be treated with the utmost respect, given the pervasive belief that such remains and objects contain an active agency or essence that can affect living people.

Native people object to the fact that their ancestors, unlike those of Caucasian people, are considered to be "archaeological resources," to be studied and displayed. They are frequently reluctant to divulge any information on burial sites known to them either on or off reservations. Archaeologists, however, often argue that Native American remains are a "resource" for scientific study, and some equate the reburial of remains as akin to burning a library. Many archaeologists insist that bones, particularly ancient skeletal remains, are a valuable source of knowledge about the origins of human populations and disease epidemiology. Even where they may not have developed the techniques necessary to draw out such information, they believe that the advancement of science will lead to such understanding. They often seek disclosure of burial sites on the theory that this is necessary to prevent looting by "amateur" pothunters, which is equally destructive to the quest for knowledge that they are committed to. For a comprehensive summary of these disparate views, see NATIVE AMERICANS AND ARCHAEOLOGISTS: STEPPING STONES TO COMMON GROUND (N. Swidler et al. ed., 1997).

Chapter 7

THE OPERATION OF THE RESERVED RIGHTS DOCTRINE: HUNTING, FISHING, AND WATER RIGHTS

When Native nations reserved, or the federal government set aside, lands for Indian reservations, these actions did far more than allocate the beneficial use of real estate. The demarcation of Indian country created jurisdictional lines that protected Indian peoples and, to a more limited extent, Indian culture from outside influences. As Chief Justice Marshall noted in *Johnson v. M'Intosh*, 21 U.S. (8 Wheat.) 543 (1823), traditional Indian cultures often were built in part on a hunter-gatherer tradition in which Indian people derived some of their subsistence and some of their commercial trade goods from the wildlife of the forests, from the fisheries of the rivers and lakes, and from other natural food resources, such as wild rice, that might be available in the tribe's traditional resource area. Federal Indian law long has recognized the importance of such food-gathering activities to traditional Indian cultures by treating land used seasonally as hunting, fishing, or food-gathering grounds as protected by aboriginal title. *See, e.g., Confederated Tribes of the Warm Springs Reservation v. United States*, 177 Ct. Cl. 184, 194 (1966); *Spokane Tribe of Indians v. United States*, 163 Ct. Cl. 58 (1963); *State v. Coffee*, 556 P.2d 1185, 1188 (Idaho 1976) ("[A]boriginal title was more than just a right to remain camped on the land. It was a right to continue, at least temporarily, a way of life. To the extent that hunting or fishing was an integral part of the Indian's way of life prior to the coming of the white man, it became a part of the way of life allowed to continue after establishment of the sovereign. Thus, hunting and fishing rights are part and parcel with aboriginal title."). Indeed, this tradition stretches back to a seventeenth century royal commission that criticized colonial expropriation of Indian hunting areas. Robert N. Clinton, *The Proclamation of 1763: Colonial Prelude to Two Centuries of Federal-State Conflict over the Management of Indian Affairs*, 69 B.U. L. REV. 329, 333 (1989).

Despite the stereotype painted in Chief Justice Marshall's opinions, Indian tribes were not merely hunter-gatherer societies. Most tribes at one point in their history engaged in significant agricultural pursuits. Indeed, the hunter-gatherer stereotype of Indian culture is rapidly dispelled when one recalls that it was the Indians who taught the European colonists how to grow many agricultural products that are now staples in North American and world cultures, including tobacco, squash, sweet potatoes, and corn. In order to engage in such agricultural pursuits, the Indian tribes relied heavily on water resources. Reliance on water was a comparatively small problem for the agricultural pursuits of the Creek and Cherokee towns in the water-rich southeastern United States. The Pueblos of the arid Southwest, however, also developed highly sophisticated flood plain or dry farming methods, and the

Anasazi and other ancestors relied on complex irrigation systems to further their agricultural pursuits. Even the hunter-gatherer societies of the arid West, such as the Shoshones, or the buffalo hunters of the Plains, like the Sioux, relied heavily on water resources for subsistence and for processing their gathered food supplies.

If Indian peoples and societies were to be protected in the Indian reservations guaranteed to tribal communities, access to food resources and to water was essential. This chapter is devoted to analyzing the body of legal doctrine that has emerged surrounding the protection of Indian food-gathering activities and water rights. The chapter also explores another major theme in the history of Indian law — the competition between Indian and non-Indian for access to and control over scarce resources. When food and water resources were plentiful, the competition posed few legal problems because the two competing claimants could fully satisfy their needs without affecting one another or endangering the survival of the resources. The resources appeared unlimited. Beginning with the massive disloca- tion of Native economies engendered by the Euro-American induced disappearance of the buffalo herds, the late nineteenth and twentieth centuries brought serious shortages of wildlife, fisheries, and other natural food supplies, caused by environ- mental destruction and over-intensive harvesting of the resources. The twentieth century also brought a scarcity of water resources created by urban development, irrigation projects, mining, and power projects in the arid West.

In times of shortage, law often steps in to sort out the competing demands for scarce resources and to try to prevent violent self-help remedies. In the field of Indian law, such decisions, like many others affecting Indian peoples, are compli- cated by the competition for jurisdiction and control between the federal govern- ment, the states, and the tribes. Indeed, resolution of the jurisdictional questions in some cases determines the allocation of the resource. As will be seen in the Pacific Northwest fishing dispute, discussed at the end of Sec. A, this chapter, the long-term exercise of jurisdiction over Indian fishing by the states of Washington and Oregon resulted in allocating virtually all of the harvest of fisheries in the region to non-Indian commercial fishers despite treaty rights guaranteeing certain substantive fishing rights to the affected Indians. Recent intervention by the federal courts has produced a major reallocation of the resource in favor of the Indians.

This chapter pulls together themes of jurisdiction and property previously reviewed and indicates how they interact in the resolution of concrete disputes. It presents two case studies of a much broader and long-term theme in the history of the tribal-federal relationship — the role of federal law in resolving competing claims to resources held by Indians but needed or wanted for non-Indian economic development. Since the first colonists made the North American continent their home by displacing a resident Indian population, these competing claims have pervaded the history of contact between Indians and non-Indians. In the federal courts, attempts to relieve this tension stretch back at least to the two early nineteenth-century decisions by the Supreme Court in the Cherokee cases. Carefully appraise modern judicial resolutions to determine whether, or why, they provide any greater permanency than previous efforts.

This chapter also provides important insights into the manner in which treaties, statutes, or executive orders creating Indian land should be construed. Many of the food-gathering and water rights covered in this chapter are the product of the so-called reserved rights doctrine. As briefly summarized in *United States v. Winans*, 198 U.S. 371, 381 (1905), this rule of construction provides that a "treaty was not a grant of rights to the Indians, but a grant of rights from them — a reservation of those not granted." In reviewing these materials consider what effect the historical perspective enshrined in this rule of construction has on Indian rights.

Finally, this chapter presents some of the modern-day negotiated arrangements between tribes and competing government or private claimants to animals, plants, and water resources. Increasingly, Native nations have been finding that such agreements offer greater flexibility in structuring access to resources. This flexibility enables tribes to advance their needs for economic resources to facilitate their actual enjoyment of theoretical rights. Negotiated agreements also protect against the risk of adverse litigation outcomes.

A.   HUNTING, FISHING, AND FOOD-GATHERING RIGHTS

Aleck Paul (Chippewa), *Our Stock of Food & Clothes*
in NATIVE AMERICAN TESTIMONY: A CHRONICLE OF
INDIAN-WHITE RELATIONS FROM PROPHECY TO THE PRESENT
85–87 (Peter Nabokov ed., 1991)

In the early times the Indians owned this land where they lived bounded by the lakes, and rivers, and hills, or determined by a certain number of days' journey in this direction or that. These tracts formed the hunting grounds owned and used by the different families. Wherever they went the Indians took care of the game animals, especially the beaver, just as the Government takes care of the land today.

So these families of hunters would never think of damaging the abundance or the source of supply of the game, because this had come to them from their father and grandfather and those behind them. . . .

The Indian families use to hunt in a certain section for beaver. They would only kill the small beaver and leave the old ones to keep on breeding. Then when they got too old they too would be killed, just as a farmer kills his pigs, preserving the stock for his supply of young. The beaver is the Indian's pork, the moose his beef, the partridge his chicken. And there was the caribou or red deer, that was his sheep. All these formed the stock on his family hunting ground, which would be parceled out among the sons when the owner died.

He says to his sons, "You take this part. Take care of this tract. See that it always produces enough." That was what my grandfather told us. His land was divided among two sons, my father and Pisha'bo (Tea Water), my uncle. We were to own this land so no other Indians could hunt on it. Other Indians could travel through it and go there, but could not go there to kill the beaver. Each family had its own district where they belonged and owned the game. That was each one's stock, for food and clothes.

If another Indian hunted on our territory we, the owners, could shoot him. This division of the land started in the beginning of time, and always remained unchanged. I remember about twenty years ago some Nipissing Indians came north to hunt on my father's land. He told them not to hunt beaver. "This is our land," he told them; "you can fish but must not touch the fur, as that is all we have to live on." Sometimes an owner would give permission for strangers to hunt for a certain time or on a certain tract. This was often done for friends or when neighbors had had a poor season. Later the favor might be returned.

When the white people came they commenced killing all the game. They left nothing on purpose to breed and keep up the supply, because the white man don't care about the animals. They are after the money. After the white man kills all the game in one place he can take the train and go three hundred miles or more to another and do the same there.

You can write this down for me. If an Indian went to the old country, England, and sold hunting licenses to the old country people for them to hunt on their own land, the white people would not stand for that. The Government sells our big game, our moose, for $50.00 license and we don't get any of it. The Government sells our fish and our islands or gets the money, but we don't get any share.

What we Indians want is for the Government to stop the white people killing our game, as they do it only for sport and not for support. We Indians do not need to be watched about protecting the game; we must protect the game or starve. We can take care of the game just as well as the game warden and better, because we are going to live here all the time.

1. On-Reservation Rights

MENOMINEE TRIBE v. UNITED STATES
United States Supreme Court
391 U.S. 404 (1968)

MR. JUSTICE DOUGLAS delivered the opinion of the Court.

The Menominee Tribe of Indians was granted a reservation in Wisconsin by the Treaty of Wolf River in 1854, 10 Stat. 1064. By this treaty the Menominees retroceded certain lands they had acquired under an earlier treaty and the United States confirmed to them the Wolf River Reservation "for a home, to be held as Indian lands are held." Nothing was said in the 1854 treaty about hunting and fishing rights. Yet we agree with the Court of Claims that the language "to be held as Indian lands are held" includes the right to fish and to hunt. The record shows that the lands covered by the Wolf River Treaty of 1854 were selected precisely because they had an abundance of game. See *Menominee Tribe v. United States*, 95 Ct. Cl. 232, 240–241 (1941). The essence of the Treaty of Wolf River was that the Indians were authorized to maintain on the new lands ceded to them as a reservation their way of life which included hunting and fishing.

What the precise nature and extent of those hunting and fishing rights were we need not at this time determine. For the issue tendered by the present decision of the Court of Claims, 179 Ct. Cl. 496, 388 F.2d 998, is whether those rights, whatever their precise extent, have been extinguished.

That issue arose because, beginning in 1962, Wisconsin took the position that the Menominees were subject to her hunting and fishing regulations. Wisconsin prosecuted three Menominees for violating those regulations and the Wisconsin Supreme Court held that the state regulations were valid, as the hunting and fishing rights of the Menominees had been abrogated by Congress in the Menominee Indian Termination Act of 1954. 68 Stat. 250, as amended, 25 U.S.C. §§ 891–902.

Thereupon the tribe brought suit in the Court of Claims against the United States to recover just compensation for the loss of those hunting and fishing rights. The Court of Claims by a divided vote held that the tribe possessed hunting and fishing rights under the Wolf River Treaty; but it held, contrary to the Wisconsin Supreme Court, that those rights were not abrogated by the Termination Act of 1954. We granted the petition for a writ of certiorari in order to resolve that conflict between the two courts. On oral argument both petitioner and respondent urged that the judgment of the Court of Claims be affirmed. The State of Wisconsin appeared as *amicus curiae* and argued that the judgment be reversed.

In 1953 Congress by concurrent resolution instructed the Secretary of the Interior to recommend legislation for the withdrawal of federal supervision over certain American Indian tribes, including the Menominees. Several bills were offered, one for the Menominee Tribe that expressly preserved hunting and fishing rights. But the one that became the Termination Act of 1954, *viz.*, H.R. 2828, did not mention hunting and fishing rights. Moreover, counsel for the Menominees spoke against the bill, arguing that its silence would by implication abolish those hunting and fishing rights. It is therefore argued that they were abolished by the Termination Act.

The purpose of the 1954 Act was by its terms "to provide for orderly termination of Federal supervision over the property and members" of the tribe. Under its provisions, the tribe was to formulate a plan for future control of tribal property and service functions theretofore conducted by the United States. On or before April 30, 1961, the Secretary was to transfer to a tribal corporation or to a trustee chosen by him all property real and personal held in trust for the tribe by the United States.

The Menominees submitted a plan, looking toward the creation of a county in Wisconsin out of the former reservation and the creation by the Indians of a Wisconsin corporation to hold other property of the tribe and its members. The Secretary of the Interior approved the plan with modifications; the Menominee Enterprises, Inc., was incorporated;[1] and numerous ancillary laws were passed by Wisconsin integrating the former reservation into its county system of government.

---

[1] [10] Wisconsin questions whether Menominee Enterprises, Inc., to which all tribal assets were conveyed pursuant to the termination plan (26 Fed. Reg. 3726), should be viewed as the successor entity to the tribe and the present holder of the hunting and fishing rights, and, if so, to what extent the corporation or the tribal members thereof can withhold or parcel out these rights. The Menominees, on the other hand, claim the rights are held by Menominee Indian Tribe of Wisconsin, Inc., a tribal body organized in 1962. . . . The corporation adopted a resolution defining those persons entitled to exercise the hunting and fishing rights. . . . We believe it inappropriate, however, to resolve the question of who the beneficiaries of the hunting and fishing rights may be; and we expressly reserve decision on it. Neither it nor the nature of those rights nor the extent, if any, to which Wisconsin may regulate them has been fully briefed and argued by the parties either in the Court of Claims or in this Court, and the posture of the present litigation does not require their resolution.

The Termination Act provided that after the transfer by the Secretary of title to the property of the tribe, all federal supervision was to end and "the laws of the several States shall apply to the tribe and its members in the same manner as they apply to other citizens or persons within their jurisdiction."

It is therefore argued with force that the Termination Act of 1954, which became fully effective in 1961, submitted the hunting and fishing rights of the Indians to state regulation and control. We reach, however, the opposite conclusion. The same Congress that passed the Termination Act also passed Public Law 280, 67 Stat. 588, as amended, 18 U.S.C. § 1162. The latter came out of the same committees of the Senate and the House as did the Termination Act; and it was amended[2] in a way that is critical here only two months after the Termination Act became law. As amended, Public Law 280 granted designated States, including Wisconsin, jurisdiction "over offenses committed by or against Indians in the areas of Indian country" named in the Act, which in the case of Wisconsin was described as "All Indian country within the State." But Public Law 280 went on to say that "Nothing in this section . . . shall deprive any Indian or any Indian tribe, band, or community of any right, privilege, or immunity afforded under Federal treaty, agreement, or statute *with respect to hunting, trapping, or fishing* or the control, licensing, or regulation thereof." (Emphasis added.) That provision on its face contains no limitation; it protects any hunting, trapping, or fishing right granted by a federal treaty. Public Law 280, as amended, became the law in 1954, nearly seven years *before* the Termination Act became fully effective in 1961. In 1954, when Public Law 280 became effective, the Menominee Reservation was still "Indian country" within the meaning of Public Law 280.

Public Law 280 must therefore be considered *in pari materia* with the Termination Act. The two Acts read together mean to us that, although federal supervision of the tribe was to cease and all tribal property was to be transferred to new hands, the hunting and fishing rights granted or preserved by the Wolf River Treaty of 1854 survived the Termination Act of 1954. . . .

We decline to construe the Termination Act as a backhanded way of abrogating the hunting and fishing rights of these Indians. While the power to abrogate those rights exists (see [*Lone Wolf v. Hitchcock*]) "the intention to abrogate or modify a treaty is not to be lightly imputed to the Congress." *Pigeon River Co. v. Cox Co.*, 291 U.S. 138, 160.

Our conclusion is buttressed by the remarks of the legislator chiefly responsible for guiding the Termination Act to enactment, Senator Watkins, who stated upon

---

[2] [11] As originally enacted Public Law 280 exempted the Menominees from its provisions. The House Reports on Pub. L. 280 (H.R. 1063, 83d Cong., 1st Sess.) and on Pub. L. 661 (H.R. 9821, 83d Cong., 2d Sess.) indicate that the Menominees had specifically asked for exemption from the provisions of the bill that eventually became Pub. L. 280, on the ground that their tribal law and order program was functioning satisfactorily. Subsequently, the tribe reconsidered its position and sponsored H.R. 9821, amending Pub. L. 280 to extend its provisions to the Menominee Reservation. The Department of the Interior recommended favorable action on the proposed amendment, and the amendment was enacted into law on August 24, 1954 (68 Stat. 795), two months after the passage of the Menominee Termination Act.

the occasion of the signing of the bill that it "in no way violates any treaty obligation with this tribe."

We find it difficult to believe that Congress, without explicit statement, would subject the United States to a claim for compensation by destroying property rights conferred by treaty, particularly when Congress was purporting by the Termination Act to settle the Government's financial obligations toward the Indians.[3]

[*Affirmed.*]

Mr. Justice Marshall took no part in the consideration or decision of this case.

Mr. Justice Stewart, with whom Mr. Justice Black joins, dissenting.

[The Menominee termination] statute is plain on its face: after termination the Menominees are fully subject to state laws just as other citizens are, and no exception is made for hunting and fishing laws. Nor does the legislative history contain any indication that Congress intended to say anything other than what the unqualified words of the statute express. In fact two bills which would have explicitly preserved hunting and fishing rights were rejected in favor of the bill ultimately adopted — a bill which was opposed by counsel for the Menominees because it failed to preserve their treaty rights.

The Court today holds that the Termination Act does not mean what it says. The Court's reason for reaching this remarkable result is that it finds "in pari materia" another statute which, I submit, has nothing whatever to do with this case.

[The Menominee Termination Act] by its very terms provides:

[A]ll statutes of the United States which affect Indians because of their status as Indians shall no longer be applicable to the members of the tribe. . . . 25 U.S.C. § 899.

Public Law 280 is such a statute. It has no application to the Menominees now that their reservation is gone.

The 1854 Treaty granted the Menominees special hunting and fishing rights. The 1954 Termination Act, by subjecting the Menominees without exception to state law, took away those rights. The Menominees are entitled to compensation.

I would reverse the judgment of the Court of Claims.

---

[3] [15] Compare the hearings on the Klamath Termination bill, which took place shortly before the Menominee bills were reached, in which Senator Watkins expressed the view that perhaps the Government should "buy out" the Indians' hunting and fishing rights rather than preserve them after termination. See Joint Hearings, Subcommittees of the Committees on Interior and Insular Affairs, 83d Cong., 2d Sess., Pt. 4, on S. 2745 and H.R. 7320, pp. 254–255

NOTES ON ON-RESERVATION
HUNTING AND FISHING RIGHTS

1. **The Property Basis of On-Reservation Food-Gathering Rights:** Indian tribes generally enjoy full hunting, fishing, and food-gathering rights on their own reservation. Thus, the courts uniformly hold that except where absolutely essential to the conservation of a species, state conservation and licensing laws have no application to tribal members hunting, fishing, or gathering food on their own reservation. *See, e.g., Mattz v. Arnett*, 412 U.S. 481 (1973); *Cheyenne-Arapaho Tribes v. Oklahoma*, 618 F.2d 665 (10th Cir. 1980); *Moore v. United States*, 157 F.2d 760 (9th Cir. 1946). The only major exception is *Sac & Fox v. Licklider*, 576 F.2d 145 (8th Cir. 1978), where the Sac and Fox Tribe (now the Meskwaki Nation) had ceded its land in Iowa in connection with removal to Kansas in the 19th century, and then returned to purchased land in Iowa, which the Governor of the state held in trust for them. When the United States later accepted the land into trust from the Governor, it agreed that the state would retain civil and criminal jurisdiction over the reservation. Congress later confirmed the state's civil and criminal jurisdiction through a special statute (criminal) and Public Law 280 (which Iowa used to opt into civil jurisdiction). Even though hunting and fishing are property rights normally associated with the trust status of land, the Eighth Circuit seemed to view Iowa's historic insistence on jurisdiction as justification for subjecting the Tribe to state season and take limits. Doctrinally, the court treated the on-reservation food-gathering rights as a property right voluntarily ceded by the Sac and Fox in their 1842 removal treaty and not regained by their subsequent purchase of land within Iowa.

While the case law almost uniformly recognizes on-reservation Indian hunting and fishing rights, the cases are not as explicit in defining the origins, nature, and scope of such rights. In general, Indian hunting, fishing, and food-gathering rights often derive from aboriginal title, treaties, and agreements, statutes, and executive orders promulgated after the 1871 prohibition of further treaties with Indian tribes. The theoretical basis of the Indian on-reservation hunting and fishing rights nevertheless is somewhat mixed. Indian food-gathering rights are frequently preserved in treaties. Some treaties expressly provide for exclusive hunting and fishing rights. *See, e.g.*, Treaty with the Klamaths, Moadocs, and Yahooshin Band of Snakes, Oct. 14, 1864, art. 1, 16 Stat. 707, 708. Nevertheless, a treaty is "not a grant of rights to the Indians, but a grant of rights from them — a reservation of those not granted." *United States v. Winans*, 198 U.S. 371, 381 (1905). Therefore, express provision for food-gathering rights in the treaty is not necessary to establish their existence. For example, the *Menominee Tribe* case found the creation of hunting and fishing rights in the Treaty of Wolf River despite the fact that the treaty never explicitly mentions such rights. Rather, the rights were created by merely recognizing that the tribal land would be "held as Indian lands are held." Thus, *Menominee Tribe* suggests that hunting, fishing, and food-gathering rights are property rights that derive from the very nature and purpose of tribal land tenure. As the Minnesota Supreme Court once put it, "Certainly, it would be incongruous to construe the treaty as denying the Indians their very means of existence while purporting to grant them a home." *Minnesota v. Clark*, 282 N.W.2d 902, 909 (Minn. 1979).

Because of communication and translation difficulties between Indians and non-Indians during most treaty negotiations, courts follow a general rule that language in treaties must be construed in favor of the Indians. *See, e.g., Washington v. Washington State Com. Passenger Fishing Vessel Ass'n*, 443 U.S. 658 (1979). After 1871, Congress prohibited further treaties with Indian tribes. Consequently, agreements with the tribes were entered into under statute, executive order, or agreement later approved by statute. Courts have generally applied the same rules of liberal construction to such laws as are applied to treaties. *See, e.g., Antoine v. Washington*, 420 U.S. 194 (1975).

In *Menominee Tribe*, the Supreme Court treated hunting and fishing rights as property rights protected under the Treaty of Wolf River and not extinguished by the Menominee Termination Act. For example, referring to the tribal hunting and fishing rights guaranteed in the Treaty of Wolf River, the *Menominee Tribe* opinion noted: "We find it difficult to believe that Congress, without explicit statement, would subject the United States to a claim for compensation by destroying *property rights* conferred by treaty, particularly when Congress was purporting by the Termination Act to settle the Government's financial obligations toward the Indians." *Menominee Tribe* also suggested that Indian hunting and fishing rights are compensable property rights protected under the takings clause of the Fifth Amendment. With respect to this compensation issue, the origin of the hunting and fishing rights is significant. If the rights are based solely on aboriginal title, Indians generally would not be entitled to compensation based on the harsh rule of *Tee-Hit-Ton Indians v. United States*, 348 U.S. 272 (1955), presented in Ch. 6, Sec. A.1. If, on the other hand, such rights are based on a treaty or statute their abrogation gives rise to a claim for compensation. *See, e.g., Confederated Tribes v. United States*, 43 Indian Cl. Comm'n 505 (1978); *Shoshone Tribe v. United States*, 299 U.S. 476 (1937).

2.   **The Jurisdictional Basis of On-Reservation Food-Gathering Rights:** An additional legal theory often may support on-reservation hunting and fishing rights — preemption of state regulatory and law enforcement authority. As discussed in Chapters 4 and 5, generally state regulatory laws, such as conservation laws, do not apply to tribal members in Indian country, and state governments often lack law enforcement authority in Indian country. Thus, absent some federal statutory authority for the enforcement of state conservation laws in Indian country, application of the usual rules of preemption applicable to Indians in Indian country would preclude enforcement of state conservation and licensing laws against tribal members for on-reservation activity. For example, the Eastern Band of Cherokee Tribe was found to be exempt from state hunting and fishing laws on its reservation in North Carolina despite the fact that, like the Sac and Fox (Meskwaki) community in Iowa, discussed in Note 1 above, its current reservation was created by the process of federal recognition of a tribal community that remained in its aboriginal homeland on purchased land in violation of a removal treaty. *See Eastern Band of Cherokee Indians v. North Carolina Wildlife Resources Comm'n*, 588 F.2d 75 (4th Cir. 1978).

Would a tribe like the Sac and Fox (Meskwaki) in Iowa, that had been subjected to state civil and criminal jurisdiction by congressional act, lose its rights to hunt and fish free of state control? Recall that *Bryan v. Itasca County*, 426 U.S. 373

(1976), discussed in Ch. 5, Sec. A.2, holds that Public Law 280, the main federal law authorizing state jurisdiction, gives states civil adjudicative jurisdiction but not taxing or regulatory authority. Furthermore, Public Law 280 expressly denies states civil and criminal authority over hunting and fishing rights. 25 U.S.C. § 1322(b); 18 U.S.C. § 1162(b). The Attorney General of California, a mandatory Public Law 280 state, has determined that since there were no ratified treaties in that state there is no operative limit on state jurisdiction in California. *See* 41 Op. Cal. Att'y Gen. 17 (Op. No. 227, 1963); 42 Op. Cal. Att'y Gen. 147 (Op. No. 90, 1963). *But see Donahue v. California Justice Ct.*, 15 Cal. App. 3d 557 (1971). By contrast, the Wisconsin Attorney General, operating in another mandatory Public Law 280 state, has taken a position more protective of Indian hunting rights. 56 Op. Wis. Att'y Gen. 11 (1967) (reversing a prior ruling). Aren't many, if not most, state hunting and fishing, laws excluded from state jurisdiction anyway under Public Law 280 because they are "civil/regulatory," rather than "criminal/prohibitory"? What should happen if a Public Law 280 state tries to prosecute an Indian for possession of a gun on the reservation without a state permit, when the tribal member is carrying the gun in order to hunt for deer that he might encounter on his way to or from work? Should it matter whether the hunting was legal during that season under tribal law? *See Minnesota v. Folstrom*, 331 N.W.2d 231 (Minn. 1983) (upholding state authority).

It is important to see that jurisdictional protections supplement rather than displace tribal property rights to hunt and fish. If Indian on-reservation fishing rights were *merely* the incidental product of the jurisdictional arrangements for Indian country, why would they involve compensable property rights protected under the takings clause, as indicated in the *Menominee Tribe* case? For further review of the case law on Indian hunting and fishing rights, see Robert J. Miller, *Indian Hunting and Fishing Rights*, 21 ENVT'L. L. 1291 (1991); Laurie Reynolds, *Indian Hunting and Fishing Rights: The Role of Tribal Sovereignty and Preemption*, 62 N.C. L. REV. 743 (1984); Charles F. Wilkinson, *To Feel the Summer in the Spring: The Treaty Fishing Rights of the Wisconsin Chippewa*, 1991 WIS. L. REV. 375.

3.   On-Reservation Food-Gathering Rights and Reservation Diminishment: The rather uniform recognition of Indian on-reservation food-gathering rights obviously places an important premium on determining whether the food-gathering activity occurred on-reservation or in Indian country. Thus, many on-reservation hunting and fishing rights cases turn on questions of title to land or its status as a reservation. *Compare Mattz v. Arnett*, 412 U.S. 481 (1973), *with Organized Village of Kake v. Egan*, 369 U.S. 60 (1962). In particular, many hunting and fishing cases ultimately turn on the question of reservation diminishment or termination discussed at greater length in Ch. 2, Sec. A.3.b.iv. *E.g., Lower Brule Sioux Tribe v. South Dakota*, 711 F.2d 809 (8th Cir. 1983); *White Earth Band of Chippewa Indians v. Alexander*, 683 F.2d 1129 (8th Cir. 1982). Thus, one unforeseen consequence of a finding of reservation diminishment under the doctrines discussed previously may be that tribal members may no longer have rights to fish, hunt, or gather food in the diminished portions of the reservation free of state conservation laws, including license requirements and season and bag limits.

The comparison of two Minnesota cases involving the food-gathering rights of various bands of Chippewa Indians decided by the same judge illustrates the importance of reservation status. In *Leech Lake Band of Chippewa Indians v. Herbst*, 334 F. Supp. 1001 (D. Minn. 1971), the Leech Lake Band sought the right to hunt, fish, and gather wild rice unhindered by state regulation on lands owned by county, state, and federal governments within the Leech Lake reservation boundaries. Although the Band had ceded this land to the federal government under the Nelson Act of 1889 and a contemporaneous written agreement pursuant to the Act, Judge Devitt held that Congress had not intended reservation disestablishment with respect to the ceded lands. Following *Menominee*, Judge Devitt found no express congressional intent to abrogate the Band's food-gathering rights on the ceded land; thus, state game laws were not applicable. In *United States v. Minnesota*, 466 F. Supp. 1382 (D. Minn. 1979), *aff'd sub nom. Red Lake Band of Chippewa Indians v. Minnesota*, 614 F.2d 1161 (8th Cir. 1980), the Red Lake Band sought declaratory judgment that its members retained food-gathering rights free from state regulation on lands ceded to the federal government under virtually identical circumstances as found in *Herbst*. In this case, however, Judge Devitt asserted that hunting and fishing rights were mere incidents of Indian title, extinguished once such title was extinguished. Therefore, with respect to the ceded lands, *Menominee Tribe* did not control and the Red Lake Band's rights were subject to state regulation. *Compare Minnesota v. Clark*, 282 N.W.2d 902 (Minn. 1979) (despite land cessions by the White Earth Band of Chippewa under the Nelson Act, their reservation was not disestablished; following *Menominee*, food-gathering rights were not abrogated), *with Minnesota v. Keezer*, 292 N.W.2d 714 (Minn. 1980) (relinquishment of title to Neds Lake area of Minnesota by the Sioux eliminated any residual Chippewa hunting and fishing rights held pursuant to a treaty between the tribes).

As a general rule, the prior cession of Indian land by treaty, agreement, or statute extinguishes the preexisting on-reservation hunting and fishing rights unless some express language in the treaty or act ceding the land preserves the pre-existing rights as, now, off-reservation rights. In *Oregon Dep't of Fish & Wildlife v. Klamath Indian Tribe*, 473 U.S. 753 (1985), for example, the Court ruled that a 1901 agreement clarifying and diminishing the boundaries of the Klamath Reservation did not preserve the right to fish on ceded lands within the former boundaries of the reservation even though such land areas were covered by a 1864 treaty that had guaranteed "the exclusive right of taking fish in the streams and lakes" included in said reservation, and the 1901 agreement and its legislative history were absolutely silent on the question of abrogation of the preexisting fishing rights. Justice Stevens's opinion for the majority carefully canvassed the purposes and legislative history of the 1864 treaty and the 1901 agreement and concluded:

> [E]ven though "legal ambiguities are resolved to the benefit of the Indians," [the] courts cannot ignore plain language that, viewed in historical context and given a "fair appraisal," [very] clearly runs counter to the tribes' later claims. Careful examination of the entire record in this case leaves us with the firm conviction that the exclusive right to hunt, fish, and gather roots, berries, and seeds on lands reserved to the Klamath Tribe by the 1864

Treaty was not intended to survive as a right to be free of state regulation in the ceded lands that were outside the reservation after the 1901 agreement.

Id. at 774. For an example of a treaty that expressly protects food-gathering rights on ceded lands, see *Minnesota v. Mille Lacs Band of Chippewa Indians*, 526 U.S. 172 (1999), presented in Ch. 2, Sec. C and Sec. A.2, this chapter.

4. Aboriginal Food-Gathering Rights: As previously noted, federal law recognizes and protects the aboriginal right to hunt and fish by treating lands to which the Indian tribes customarily resorted for food-gathering as subject to aboriginal title. Courts have generally required a showing of actual use and occupancy of the lands over an extended period of time to determine the existence of aboriginal title. *See Confederated Tribes v. United States*, 177 Ct. Cl. 184 (1966). Aboriginal title to the lands, however, is not necessary to the existence of aboriginal hunting and fishing rights. *See United States ex rel. Hualpai Indians v. Santa Fe Pac. R.R.*, 314 U.S. 339 (1941), presented and discussed in Ch. 6, Sec. A.1. Generally aboriginal hunting and fishing rights remain in the Indians unless granted to the United States by treaty, abandoned, or extinguished by statute. For example, many such rights were extinguished when payments were made through the Indian Claims Commission Act. *See* Ch. 6, Sec. A.5.a. Without such extinguishment, the aboriginal rights may be exercised to the same extent as other non-reservation rights are under treaties, statutes, agreements, or executive orders. *But cf. Organized Village of Kake v. Egan*, 369 U.S. 60 (1963) ("This Court has never held that States lack power to regulate the exercise of aboriginal Indian [fishing] rights, such as claimed here, or of those based on occupancy.").

State v. Elliott, 616 A.2d 210 (Vt. 1992), set forth and discussed at greater length in Ch. 6, Sec. A.1, began as a prosecution of 36 Western Abenaki of the Missisquoi Tribe, a non-federally recognized tribe, for fishing without a license in a "fish-in" demonstration. When the case reached the Vermont Supreme Court, it turned into a dispute over land ownership. Since the Abenakis relied on claims of aboriginal rights to hunt and fish in their original territory, the Court went to great pains to attempt to establish that their aboriginal ownership of the area had been extinguished, although it could give no clear account of precisely what action constituted the extinguishment. Ultimately, it concluded that the historical course of events, particularly land grants made by the independent Vermont prior to accepting statehood extinguished their title to their aboriginal lands and with it any attendant aboriginal rights to hunt and fish on that land.

The Alaska Native Claims Settlement Act (*see* Ch. 5, Sec. B.1) did not extinguish the Natives' aboriginal claims to the outer continental shelf (the territory seaward of three miles off the coast), where they traditionally hunted and fished. Do Alaska Native villages that have hunted and fished on the outer continental shelf for thousands of years have aboriginal hunting and fishing rights in that territory? When the federal government placed strict limits and imposed permitting requirements for fishing off the Alaska coast, several Native villages sued to enjoin interference with their aboriginal rights. Should they prevail? The United States has asserted a paramount interest in the outer continental shelf based on national security concerns, denying states any claim to such territory; and the United States

Supreme Court has affirmed that the federal government's "paramountcy" precludes state property claims. *See United States v. Texas*, 339 U.S. 707 (1950). Tribes have argued that because the federal government must approve the transfer of aboriginal title, and can even extinguish that title, aboriginal title is not incompatible with federal paramountcy interests. Although this argument has straightforward appeal, a Ninth Circuit panel rejected it in *Native Village of Eyak v. Trawler Diane Marie, Inc.*, 154 F.3d 1090, 1091 (9th Cir. 1998). The Ninth Circuit en banc has reopened the question, directing a federal court faced with an aboriginal title claim to the outer continental shelf to ascertain whether the tribe in question could actually make legitimate claims to aboriginal title. *See Native Village of Eyak v. Evans*, 375 F.3d 1218 (9th Cir. 2004). For the argument that the aboriginal hunting and fishing rights should prevail, see David J. Bloch, *Colonizing the Last Frontier*, 29 AM. INDIAN L. REV. 1 (2005).

5. **Food-Gathering Rights and Habitat Protection:** What is the property protected when courts protect Indian food-gathering rights? Is it the wild game that lives on or periodically migrates over Indian land? Does the right include the habitat for the wildlife resource? *See United States v. Washington*, 759 F.2d 1353 (9th Cir. 1985) (en banc) (reversing district court's declaration that tribes were entitled to a fish habitat free from environmental despoliation because the terms of the declaration were too imprecise to enforce). In further litigation over the content of the Washington tribes' treaty-based fishing rights, a federal district court judge has enjoined the state of Washington from maintaining culverts rather than bridges where roadways cross rivers and streams. *United States v. Washington*, 20 F. Supp. 3d 828 (W.D. Wash. 2007). The tribes maintained that these culverts blocked the passage of fish up and down the streams, diminishing the supply of fish available to them. Federal District Court Judge Martinez read the Ninth Circuit's 1985 opinion as resting on the general nature of the claim for habitat protection made at that time (described by the Ninth Circuit as an "environmental servitude"). Judge Martinez pointed to language in that opinion acknowledging the tribal right to protection of the fish supply or catch, and insisting only that any attempt to enforce that right invoke concrete facts and a particular dispute. For general discussion of the issues posed in this case, see Ruth Langridge, *The Rights to Habitat Protection*, 29 PUB. LAND & RESOURCES L. REV. 42 (2008); O. Yale Lewis, *Treaty Fishing Rights: A Habitat Right as Part of the Trinity of Rights Implied by the Fishing Clause of the Stevens Treaties*, 27 AM. INDIAN L. REV. 281 (2003).

6. **Limitations on On-Reservation Food-Gathering Rights:** While on-reservation hunting and fishing rights historically involved exemption of Indians exercising such rights from all state, but not tribal or federal, conservation regulations, some cases suggest that state regulation of such rights is permissible where necessary to the conservation of fish and game. *See Puyallup Tribe v. Department of Game*, 433 U.S. 165, 173–77 (1977), *infra*; *United States v. Oregon*, 657 F.2d 1009, 1016 (9th Cir. 1981); *see also Puyallup Tribe v. Department of Game*, 391 U.S. 392, 402 n.14 (1968) (origin of the "necessary for the conservation of fish" standard in an off-reservation case), *infra*. On reservations not covered by Public Law 280 or some other federal law authorizing state jurisdiction in Indian country, it is unclear how, if at all, the state conservation officials could enforce such conservation measures against Indians exercising their on-reservation hunting and

fishing rights. Even on Public Law 280 reservations, state jurisdiction probably does not extend to regulation of hunting and fishing. *See* Note 2, above.

7. Nonmember Food-Gathering in Indian Country: While tribal members generally enjoy on-reservation hunting and fishing rights, the situation with respect to non-Indians is substantially less clear, as the Supreme Court briefly noted in *Oliphant v. Suquamish Indian Tribe*, 435 U.S. 191 (1978), presented in Ch. 3, Sec. A.3.a. In 1960, Congress enacted a statute now codified at 18 U.S.C. § 1165 to supplement or complement tribal enforcement of conservation and game licensing rules by providing for federal prosecution of those who illegally take game or fish on Indian lands. Under section 1165 the term "lands" includes waterways. *See United States v. Pollman*, 364 F. Supp. 995 (D. Mont. 1973). Section 1165 does not apply to tribal members who hunt or fish in Indian country in violation of tribal ordinances even where the tribe lacks any enforcement mechanism for its prohibition. *United States v. Jackson*, 600 F.2d 1283 (9th Cir. 1979). The act therefore applies principally to nonmembers. *United States v. Sanford*, 547 F.2d 1085 (9th Cir. 1976). Should that include nonmember Indians? One federal trial court opinion, issued before the Supreme Court's decision in *Duro v. Reina*, 495 U.S. 676 (1990), presented in Ch. 3, Sec. A.3.a, held that because a nonmember Indian was subject to tribal criminal jurisdiction, section 1165 would not apply. *United States v. Greyfox*, 727 F. Supp. 576 (D. Ore. 1989). Recall that *Duro v. Reina* denied inherent tribal criminal jurisdiction over nonmember Indians, but Congress subsequently affirmed such jurisdiction over *all* Indians in 25 U.S.C. § 1301(2). Does the rationale for excluding tribal members from section 1165 now also extend to nonmember Indians?

Section 1165 undoubtedly authorizes Indian tribes to adopt laws and ordinances regulating hunting and fishing by nonmembers, including non-Indians, on trust and tribal land within Indian country. Criminal enforcement of such ordinances, at least for non-Indians, is, however, left to the federal courts. *See generally* NELL JESSUP NEWTON ET AL., COHEN'S HANDBOOK OF FEDERAL INDIAN LAW § 18.06 (2005 ed.). A further important question involves whether section 1165 and tribal ordinances preempt state conservation authority in Indian country. In *New Mexico v. Mescalero Apache Tribe*, 462 U.S. 324 (1983), set forth and discussed in Ch. 4, Sec. B.4.b, the Court held that the Mescalero Apache Tribe had the exclusive right to license nonmembers for hunting occurring on its reservation, which was unallotted, where its officials managed the elk herd in question and it worked jointly with the federal government to renew the resource. State jurisdiction was barred based on a balance of relative federal, tribal, and state interests.

Tribal regulatory rights over nonmember hunting and fishing, just like tribal hunting rights, can be lost if Indian title to the land in question is lost and the tribe cannot establish that its control of nonmember hunting and fishing is essential to its economic sufficiency. For example, in *South Dakota v. Bourland*, 508 U.S. 679 (1993), a divided Court held that the Cheyenne River Sioux Tribe had no power to license and regulate nonmember hunting and fishing on portions of its reservation that had been condemned pursuant to the Flood Control Act of 1944, ch. 665, 58 Stat. 887 and the Cheyenne River Act of Sept. 3, 1954, 68 Stat. 1191, to construct the Oahe Dam and Reservoir Project. Relying heavily on the Court's prior decisions in *Montana v. United States*, 450 U.S. 544 (1981), and *Brendale v. Confederated Tribes and Bands of Yakima Indian Nation*, 492 U.S. 408 (1989), the Court held that the loss of Indian ownership created by federal condemnation created a strong presumption that the Cheyenne River Sioux Tribe lost the power to control entry and therefore its prior authority to license and regulate nonmember hunting on the affected lands even though they remained part of the reservation. Justice Blackmun, in dissent, protested:

> The United States did not take this land with the purpose of destroying tribal government or even with the purpose of limiting tribal authority. It simply wished to build a dam. The Tribe's authority to regulate hunting and fishing on the taken area is consistent with the uses to which Congress has put the land, and, in my view, that authority must be understood to continue until Congress clearly decides to end it.

508 U.S. at 698.

Sometimes states actually seek to prohibit hunting or fishing by nonmembers within Indian country. In *State v. Shook*, 67 P.3d 863 (Mont. 2002), a nonmember was prosecuted for violating a regulation promulgated by Montana's Fish, Wildlife, and Parks Commission, prohibiting non-tribal members from hunting big game on all reservations in the state. The offense occurred on fee land within the reservation. Should that regulation be able to survive an equal protection challenge? *See* Ch. 2, Sec. B.

8. **Rights of Access and Indian Hunting and Fishing Rights:** It has long been recognized that Indian hunting and fishing rights often include rights of access, in the nature of easements, to protect treaty-guaranteed access to customary fishing or hunting sites. *United States v. Winans*, 198 U.S. 371 (1905). By contrast, in *Blake v. Arnett*, 663 F.2d 906 (9th Cir. 1981), the court held that the patents secured by non-Indian owners of reservation land conveyed to them after trust restrictions on Indian allotments expired were not encumbered by any easement of access to the Klamath River to permit members of the Yurok Tribe to exercise customary fishing rights. Even though the court recognized that some of the land in *Winans* had never been part of any Indian reservation and the land involved in the *Blake* case was within the Hoopa Valley Reservation, the court nevertheless distinguished *Winans*:

> Under *Winans*, patents did not cut off the fishing and hunting rights there involved, which were expressly reserved by treaty. Here whether we look at the Executive Order of 1885 that created the old Klamath River Reservation or to the Executive Order of 1891, which created the Hoopa Valley Reservation Extension, we find no such express reservation or creation of fishing or hunting rights. This may be because all of the reservation, when created, was riparian to the Klamath River, thus affording complete access for fishing by the reservation Indians to the lower twenty miles of the river. It probably did not occur to anyone to mention fishing rights. Similarly, the tribe occupied the reservation and could of course hunt upon it, so long as no action by the United States prevented it.

We conclude that Congress intended that the allotments and patents, granted under the Act of 1887, would grant an unencumbered title to the

Indian allottees and their successors in interest, which would not be subject to any interest in the land that might be implied from the mere creation of the reservation.

Id. at 911.

9. Federal Abrogation of and Authority over Indian Hunting and Fishing Rights: In *United States v. Dion*, 474 U.S. 900 (1985), set forth and discussed in Ch. 4, Sec. A.2, the Court held that the Eagle Protection Act abrogated Indian treaty-guaranteed hunting rights to take bald and golden eagles in Indian country except as permitted by the Act under a permit system for religious uses. *Dion* indicates that Congress has the constitutional authority to unilaterally abrogate Indian food-gathering rights and may do so through a clear and specific legislative statement. The *Menominee Tribe* case, however, suggests that congressional abrogation of Indian hunting and fishing rights can render the United States liable to a Fifth Amendment claim for just compensation, since such food-gathering rights generally constitute a vested property right protected by the takings clause.

Instead of abrogation, can the federal government regulate or tax the exercise of Indian hunting and fishing rights? If Indian hunting and fishing rights guarantee an unlimited opportunity to gather food for subsistence, religious, commercial, and other purposes, subject only to those externally imposed regulations that are absolutely necessary to the conservation of the species, would not federal regulation or taxation of the exercise of such rights constitute a partial abrogation of the right, thereby subjecting the United States to liability for just compensation under the Fifth Amendment? On the other hand, if Indian food-gathering rights are not so expansive, precisely what is the scope and nature of the right?

Building on the conception of plenary federal authority in the area of Indian affairs, the cases suggest considerable federal authority to regulate and therefore to partially limit guaranteed Indian hunting and fishing rights. In *Northern Arapahoe Tribe v. Hodel*, 808 F.2d 741 (10th Cir. 1987), the court sustained the authority of the Secretary of the Interior to issue interim game regulations for the Wind River Reservation to preserve the reservation game resources after the Shoshone Tribe and the Northern Arapahoe Tribe could not agree on a game code and after the Shoshone Tribe requested the Secretary to act to protect game resources. The court said:

> Congress has delegated to the Secretary broad authority to manage Indian affairs, see 25 U.S.C. § 2, and to promulgate regulations relating to Indians affairs, see *id.* at § 9. Sections 2 and 9, however, do not vest the Secretary with general regulatory authority. See *Organized Village of Kake v. Egan*, 369 U.S. 60, 63 (1962). Section 2 delegates the general management of Indian affairs and relations to the Secretary of the Interior and Commissioner of Indian Affairs. The language of section 9 vests authority "for carrying into effect the various provisions of any act relating to Indian affairs," 25 U.S.C. § 9. Given the language of the statute and the fact that hunting on the reservation has historically been a matter of tribal self-regulation, we are reluctant to hold that sections 2 and 9 by themselves could support the regulations. [H]owever, we conclude that sections 2 and 9 together with the Treaty [of July 3, 1868, 15 Stat. 673], construed in

accordance with the special relationship between the United States and Indian tribes, provide the necessary authority for the Secretary to enact these regulations.

Id. at 749. In particular, in justifying the interim federal game regulations the court stressed the Shoshone's request for regulation and the clear risk of endangerment or extinction to the large game resources of the reservation caused by the severity of winter snowstorms that had driven big game resources down to lower elevations where they were easy prey.

Likewise, in *United States v. Eberhardt*, set forth and discussed in Ch. 4, Sec. A.5.a, the court also relied on 25 U.S.C. §§ 2 and 9 to reverse a district court opinion invalidating federal fishing regulations prohibiting tribal members on the Hoopa Valley Reservation from engaging in commercial fishing for anadromous fish. Believing that the Department of the Interior had no lawful authority to unilaterally abrogate or modify Indian fishing rights where not essential to conservation, the district court had invalidated the regulations. The court of appeals reversed. Its opinion noted that "[o]nly Congress can modify or abrogate Indian tribal rights; it will be held to have done so only when its intention to do so has been made absolutely clear." Nevertheless, the appellate court concluded that the regulations were promulgated pursuant to the Department's rulemaking authority and there-fore could be set aside under the relevant provision of the Administrative Procedure Act, 5 U.S.C. § 706(2)(A), only if they were arbitrary, capricious, an abuse of discretion, or otherwise not in accordance with the law. Finding that modification of Indian fishing rights was not alone a sufficient ground to invalidate the federal regulations, the court remanded to the district court to determine whether the regulations were arbitrary or capricious.

The Lacey Act, 16 U.S.C. § 3372, makes it a federal criminal offense in Indian country "to import, export, transport, sell, receive, acquire, or purchase any fish or wildlife or plant taken or possessed in violation of any law, treaty, or regulation of the United States or in violation of any Indian tribal law." In *United States v. Sohappy*, 770 F.2d 816 (9th Cir. 1985), the court affirmed the convictions of David Sohappy and others for transporting, selling, or acquiring fish in violation of the Lacey Act. The court rejected the defendants' contention that the Lacey Act did not apply to Indian defendants who transported fish in violation of tribal law, arguing that the Act manifested Congress' general desire to protect wildlife for the general welfare. The court noted that "[g]iven Congress' goal of preserving wildlife, it is only reasonable to assume that Congress intended the Lacey Act to encompass everyone, including Indians." *See also, United States v. March*, 111 Fed. Appx. 888 (9th Cir. 2004) (sustaining Lacey Act conviction for violation of a tribal law that prohibited presentation of false information to obtain hunting permits or tags).

After repeated conflicts between the United States Internal Revenue Service and Native Americans exercising their hunting and fishing rights over the taxation of the proceeds of commercial food gathering, Congress passed subtitle E of the Technical and Miscellaneous Revenue Act of 1988, Pub. L. 100-647, 102 Stat. 3640–42, to resolve such questions. Basically, this legislation amends the United States Internal Revenue Code to clearly indicate that no income, business, social security, or like taxes are due from any tribal members or qualified Indian entity exercising "fishing rights secured as of March 17, 1988, by treaty between such tribe and the United States or by an Executive order or an act of Congress." The Act also indicates that distributions with respect to equity interests in qualified Indian entities are subject to similar rules so long as the distribution derives from income attributable to Indian fishing rights-related activity. The legislation also amends 25 U.S.C. § 71 to preempt state and local taxation of such activities to the same extent that they are immune from federal taxation.

Issues presented by the application of the Endangered Species Act to tribal treaty rights are considered in Sec. A.2, this chapter. For discussion of the Endangered Species Act as applied to reservation habitats, see Ch. 5, Sec. G.3.b.

10. Suing for Harm or Damage to Food-Gathering Rights: In *Skokomish Indian Tribe v. United States*, 410 F.3d 506 (9th Cir. 2005), discussed in Ch. 6, Sec. A.2, an en banc panel of the Ninth Circuit precluded the Skokomish from bringing an action for damages to their treaty-protected fishing and shellfish gathering rights. In a departure from prior circuit court and Supreme Court cases, the court held that because the treaty did not itself authorize a claim for damages, none should be derived or implied from the treaty terms and general intent. Furthermore, it refused to permit a claim under 42 U.S.C. § 1983 for redress of tribal property rights to fish and gather shellfish, because those rights are "communal, rather than individual rights," even when the claim is brought by an individual Indian. Is that conclusion consistent with the notion, advanced in the *Menominee Tribe* case, that tribes may sue for just compensation when their federally protected hunting and fishing rights are extinguished? For a case granting relief where individual Indians claimed a taking of their interest in tribal hunting and fishing rights, see *Kimball v. Callahan*, 493 F.2d 564 (9th Cir. 1974).

2. Off-Reservation Food-Gathering Rights

As a general rule, Indian conduct outside of Indian reservations is subject to nondiscriminatory state law otherwise applicable to all citizens of the state. *See Mescalero Apache Tribe v. Jones*, 411 U.S. 145 (1973). Subject to constitutional and federal statutory restraints, protection of wildlife and regulation of hunting and fishing are within the police power of the states. *See Baldwin v. Fish & Game Comm'n*, 436 U.S. 371 (1978). Thus, the Supreme Court has never held that the states lack power to regulate the exercise of off-reservation hunting and fishing rights based on aboriginal title or occupancy. *Organized Village of Kake v. Egan*, 369 U.S. 60 (1962).

Establishing off-reservation hunting and fishing rights based on aboriginal title can be quite difficult. Indians sometimes have argued for the existence of off-reservation rights based on aboriginal claims or on substantially less than explicit treaty language. Where made, such claims have generally failed. *See, e.g., Minnesota v. Keezer*, 292 N.W.2d 714 (Minn. 1980). In *State v. Quigley*, 324 P.2d 827 (Wash. 1958), for example, the Washington Supreme Court held that once aboriginal rights to land are extinguished and the land passes into private ownership, aboriginal hunting rights are also extinguished. Thus, even though an Indian purchased land within his aboriginal hunting region, his right to hunt was subject to state regulation. In *State v. Coffee*, 556 P.2d 1185 (Idaho 1976), the Idaho

Supreme Court held that the Kootenai Indians did retain their aboriginal right to hunt on open and unclaimed lands despite congressional extinguishment of the Tribe's right to the land. Nevertheless, the court held that the Tribe did not retain aboriginal hunting rights on privately owned land and that state regulations would be applicable on such land. Tribes have sometimes claimed that outright cessions of land made in prior treaties did not include a cession of hunting and fishing rights because such rights were not explicitly mentioned. These claims have also been unsuccessful. *See, e.g., Red Lake Band of Chippewa Indians v. Minnesota*, 614 F.2d 1161 (8th Cir. 1980).

In *Oregon Dep't of Fish & Wildlife v. Klamath Indian Tribe*, 473 U.S. 753 (1985), the United States Supreme Court held that despite the fact that the Klamath Tribe had an 1864 Treaty that guaranteed the Tribe "the exclusive right of taking fish in the streams and lakes, included in said reservation," such rights were not preserved as to ceded lands formerly within the reservation after a 1901 Agreement that, among other things, ceded certain lands to resolve a boundary dispute based on claimed erroneous survey. Tribal members therefore had no right to be free of state regulation of their fishing activities on lands formerly within the reservation that had been ceded by the 1901 Agreement. Justice Stevens' opinion for the Court noted:

> The Court of Appeals' holding was predicated on its understanding that the hunting and fishing rights reserved to the Tribe by the 1864 Treaty were not appurtenant to the land within the reservation boundaries. We agree with the Court of Appeals that Indians may enjoy special hunting and fishing rights that are independent of any ownership of land, and that, as demonstrated in 25 U.S.C. § 564m(b), the 1954 Termination Act for the Klamath Tribe, such rights may survive the termination of an Indian reservation. Moreover, the Court of Appeals was entirely correct in its view that doubts concerning the meaning of a treaty with an Indian tribe should be resolved in favor of the tribe. *See Washington v. Washington Commercial Passenger Fishing Vessel Assn.*, 443 U.S. 658, 675–676 (1979); *Carpenter v. Shaw*, 280 U.S. 363, 36 7 (1930). Nevertheless, we cannot agree with the court's interpretation of the 1901 Cession Agreement or with its reading of the 1864 Treaty.

> . . . .

> Before the 1864 Treaty was executed, the Tribe claimed aboriginal title to about 22 million acres of land. The Treaty language that ceded that entire tract — except for the 1.9 million acres set apart for the Klamath Reservation — stated only that the Tribe ceded "all their right, title, and claim" to the described area. Yet that general conveyance unquestionably carried with it whatever special hunting and fishing rights the Indians had previously possessed in over 20 million acres outside the reservation. Presumptively, the similar language used in the 1901 Cession Agreement should have the same effect.

> More importantly, the language of the 1864 Treaty plainly describes rights intended to be exercised *within the limits of the reservation.*

. . . .

> [The] 1901 Agreement thus was both a divestiture of the Tribe's ownership of the ceded lands and a diminution of the boundaries of the reservation within which the Tribe exercised its sovereignty. In the absence of any language reserving any specific rights in the ceded lands, the normal construction of the words used in the 1901 Agreement unquestionably would encompass any special right to use the ceded lands for hunting and fishing.

Id. at 766, 768 (emphasis supplied).

More recently, in *Menominee Tribe v. Thompson*, 161 F.3d 449 (7th Cir. 1998), the Menominee Tribe, in addition to certain treaty claims, asserted a right to fish in Lake Winnebago, Lake Michigan, and the Wisconsin River based on aboriginal rights never having been affirmatively extinguished by treaty. The Seventh Circuit disagreed, ruling:

> "Extinguishment of Indian title based on aboriginal possession . . . [can] be done by treaty, by the sword, by purchase, by the exercise of complete dominion adverse to the right of occupancy, or otherwise, [and] its justness is not open to inquiry in the courts." *United States v. Santa Fe Pacific R.R. Co.*, 314 U.S. 339, 347 (1941). Abrogation of aboriginal title occurs "without any legal responsibility in the sovereign [United States] to compensate the Indian for his loss." *Northwestern Bands of Shoshone Indians*, 324 U.S. at [335] 339; *see also Lac Courte Oreilles*, 700 F.2d at [341] 351 (citing *Tee-Hit-Ton Indians v. United States*, 348 U.S. 272, 288–89 (1955)). *Furthermore, the creation and acceptance of an Indian reservation by treaty constitutes a relinquishment of aboriginal rights to lands outside the reservation. Santa Fe Pacific R.R.*, 314 U.S. at 357–58, *Lac Courte Oreilles*, 700 F.2d at 352. *The Tribe signed the 1854 Treaty which created the Wolf River reservation and extinguished any aboriginal rights the Menominee possessed, including aboriginal rights in land or water not specifically mentioned in any treaty.* It is irrelevant whether members of the Tribe continued to use these off-reservation resources. Because the Menominee can prove no set of facts under which they would be entitled to exercise aboriginal rights, this claim was properly dismissed as well.

Id. at 462 (emphasis supplied).

Off-reservation food-gathering rights therefore are created primarily by language guaranteeing off-reservation food-gathering activities or in some instances by the persistence of prior guarantees of on-reservation rights after the reservation in question was diminished or otherwise reduced in size by cession. The rule requiring express guarantees of such rights, of course, is the opposite of the liberal construction given to treaties to create on-reservation hunting and food-gathering rights. *See Menominee Tribe v. United States*, 391 U.S. 404 (1968), presented in Sec. A.1, this chapter. The approach nevertheless is consistent with the more grudging construction given to statutes affecting Indian off-reservation activities. *See Mescalero Apache Tribe v. Jones*, 411 U.S. 145 (1973) (presented in Ch. 4, Sec. B.5). The *Mescalero Apache Tribe* case did recognize that specific federal treaty or statutory provisions may preempt state jurisdiction outside of Indian country.

While not universal, a number of treaties in the Pacific Northwest, New York, and the Great Lakes areas contain such explicit guarantees of off-reservation hunting or fishing rights. *See, e.g.*, Treaty with the Confederated Tribes and Bands of Indians Residing in Middle Oregon, June 25, 1855, 12 Stat. 963; Treaty with the Quinaielt and Quillehute, Jan. 22, 1856, and July 1, 1855, 12 Stat. 971. Typical of Pacific Northwest provisions is the following:

> The right of taking fish, at all usual and accustomed grounds and stations, is further secured to said Indians in common with all citizens of the Territory, and of erecting temporary houses for the purpose of curing, together with the privilege of hunting, gathering roots and berries, and pasturing their horses on open and unclaimed lands: *Provided, however,* That they shall not take shellfish from any beds staked or cultivated by citizens. . . .

Treaty with Nisqually, Payallup and Other Tribes, Dec. 26, 1855, art. 3, 10 Stat. 1133 (commonly known as the Treaty of Medicine Creek). The 1836 Treaty with the Ottawa and Chippewa provided: "The Indians stipulate for the right of hunting on the lands ceded, with the other usual privileges of occupancy, until the land is required for settlement." Treaty with the Ottawa and Chippewa, Mar. 28, 1836, art. 13, 7 Stat. 491.

The extent of federal preemption of state regulation by an Indian treaty turns on the intent of the parties as reflected in the language of the treaty and the circumstances under which the treaty was negotiated. *See, e.g., Washington v. Washington State Com. Passenger Fishing Vessel Ass'n*, 443 U.S. 658 (1979), *infra*. Treaty or statutory provisions purporting to reserve such off-reservation rights are subject to the rules requiring liberal construction of Indian treaties in a manner that executes the Indian understanding of the agreement, as the cases in this section will indicate. Even where off-reservation rights are recognized, significant questions remain regarding the meaning, scope, and extent of such rights and the power of the states, tribes, and the federal government to regulate the exercise of such off-reservation rights.

UNITED STATES v. WINANS
United States Supreme Court
198 U.S. 371 (1905)

Mr. Justice McKenna delivered the opinion of the Court.

This suit was brought to enjoin the respondents from obstructing certain Indians of the Yakima Nation in the State of Washington from exercising fishing rights and privileges on the Columbia River in that State, claimed under the provisions of the treaty between the United States and the Indians, made in 1859.

There is no substantial dispute of facts, or none that is important to our inquiry. The treaty is as follows:

. . . .

> The exclusive right of taking fish in all the streams where running through or bordering said reservation, is further secured to said confederated tribes and bands of Indians, as also the right of taking fish at all usual and accustomed places, in common with citizens of the Territory, and of erecting temporary buildings for curing them; together with the privilege of hunting, gathering roots and berries, and pasturing their horses and cattle upon open and unclaimed land. . . .

The respondents or their predecessors in title claim under patents of the United States the lands bordering on the Columbia River and under grants from the State of Washington to the shore land which, it is alleged, fronts on the patented land. They also introduced in evidence licenses from the State to maintain devices for taking fish, called fish wheels.

At the time the treaty was made the fishing places were part of the Indian country, subject to the occupancy of the Indians, with all the rights such occupancy gave. The object of the treaty was to limit the occupancy to certain lands and to define rights outside of them.

The pivot of the controversy is the construction of the second paragraph. Respondents contend that the words "the right of taking fish at all usual and accustomed places *in common* with the citizens of the Territory" confer only such rights as a white man would have under the conditions of ownership of the lands bordering on the river, and under the laws of the State, and, such being the rights conferred, the respondents further contend that they have the power to exclude the Indians from the river by reason of such ownership.

[W]e have said we will construe a treaty with the Indians as "that unlettered people" understood it, and "as justice and reason demand in all cases where power is exerted by the strong over those to whom they owe care and protection," and counterpoise the inequality "by the superior justice which looks only to the substance of the right without regard to technical rules." How the treaty in question was understood may be gathered from the circumstances.

The right to resort to the fishing places in controversy was a part of larger rights possessed by the Indians, upon the exercise of which there was not a shadow of impediment, and which were not much less necessary to the existence of the Indians than the atmosphere they breathed. New conditions came into existence, to which those rights had to be accommodated. Only a limitation of them, however, was necessary and intended, not a taking away. In other words, the treaty was not a grant of rights to the Indians, but a grant of rights from them — a reservation of those not granted. And the form of the instrument and its language was adapted to that purpose. Reservations were not of particular parcels of land, and could not be expressed in deeds as dealings between private individuals. The reservations were in large areas of territory and the negotiations were with the tribe. They reserved rights, however, to every individual Indian, as though named therein. They imposed a servitude upon every piece of land as though described therein. There was an exclusive right of fishing reserved within certain boundaries. There was a right outside of those boundaries reserved "in common with citizens of the Territory." As a mere right, it was not exclusive in the Indians. Citizens might share it, but the Indians were secured in its enjoyment by a special provision of means for its exercise. They were given "the right of taking fish at all usual and accustomed places," and the right "of erecting temporary buildings for curing them." The contingency of the future ownership of the lands, therefore, was foreseen and provided for — in other words, the Indians were given a right in the land — the right of crossing it to the river — the right to occupy it to the extent and for the purpose mentioned. No other conclusion would give effect to the treaty. And the right was intended to be continuing against the United States and its grantees as well as against the State and its grantees.

The respondents urge an argument based upon the different capacities of white men and Indians to devise and make use of instrumentalities to enjoy the common right. Counsel say: "The fishing right was in common, and aside from the right of the State to license fish wheels the wheel fishing is one of the civilized man's methods, as legitimate as the substitution of the modern combined harvester for the ancient sickle and flail." But the result does not follow that the Indians may be absolutely excluded. It needs no argument to show that the superiority of a combined harvester over the ancient sickle neither increased nor decreased rights to the use of land held in common. In the actual taking of fish white men may not be confined to a spear or crude net, but it does not follow that they may construct and use a device which gives them exclusive possession of the fishing places, as it is admitted a fish wheel does. Besides, the fish wheel is not relied on alone. Its monopoly is made complete by a license from the State. The argument based on the inferiority of the Indians is peculiar. If the Indians had not been inferior in capacity and power, what the treaty would have been, or that there would have been any treaty, would be hard to guess.

The construction of the treaty disposes of certain subsidiary contentions of respondents. The Land Department could grant no exemptions from its provisions. It makes no difference, therefore, that the patents issued by the Department are absolute in form. They are subject to the treaty as to the other laws of the land.

It is further contended that the rights conferred upon the Indians are subordinate to the powers acquired by the State upon its admission into the Union. In other words, it is contended that the State acquired, by its admission into the Union "upon an equal footing with the original States," the power to grant rights in or to dispose of the shore lands upon navigable streams, and such power is subject only to the paramount authority of Congress with regard to public navigation and commerce. The United States, therefore, it is contended, could neither grant nor retain rights in the shore or to the lands under water.

The elements of this contention and the answer to it are expressed in *Shively v. Bowlby*, 152 U.S. 1. It is unnecessary, and it would be difficult, to add anything to the reasoning of that case. The power and rights of the States in and over shore lands were carefully defined, but the power of the United States, while it held the country as a Territory, to create rights which would be binding on the States was also announced, opposing the dicta scattered through the cases, which seemed to assert a contrary view.

[E]xtinguishment of the Indian title, opening the land for settlement and preparing the way for future States, were appropriate to the objects for which the United States held the Territory. And surely it was within the competency of the

Nation to secure to the Indians such a remnant of the great rights they possessed as "taking fish at all usual and accustomed places." Nor does it restrain the State unreasonably, if at all, in the regulation of the right. It only fixes in the land such easements as enables the right to be exercised.

The license from the State, which respondents plead to maintain a fishing wheel, gives no power to them to exclude the Indians, nor was it intended to give such power. It was the permission of the State to use a particular device. What rights the Indians had were not determined or limited. This was a matter for judicial determination regarding the rights of the Indians and rights of the respondents. And that there may be an adjustment and accommodation of them the Solicitor General concedes and points out the way. We think, however, that such adjustment and accommodation are more within the province of the Circuit Court in the first instance than of this court.

[*Reversed and remanded.*]

Mr. Justice White dissents.

NOTES ON *WINANS* AND ITS AFTERMATH

1. **History of Interpretation of Off-Reservation Hunting and Fishing Rights Treaty Guarantees:** The decision in *Winans* represented the beginning of the evolution in the construction of the meaning and scope of off-reservation hunting and fishing rights. Prior to *Winans*, a divided Court had held in *Ward v. Race Horse*, 163 U.S. 504 (1896), that the right reserved to the Bannock Indians in an 1868 treaty "to hunt on unoccupied lands of the United States, so long as game may be found thereon" did not survive the admission of Wyoming to statehood. The Court majority argued that

> [t]o suppose that the words of the treaty intended to give to the Indian the right to enter into already established States and seek out every portion of unoccupied government land and there exercise the right of hunting, in violation of the municipal law, would be to presume that the treaty was so drawn as to frustrate the very object it had in view.

Id. at 509. The Court noted that the treaty right was "temporary and precarious" because it was wholly dependent on retention of title to unoccupied lands by the federal government. The Court further argued that a contrary construction would frustrate the unquestioned power of a state to control and regulate the taking of game. Thus, the Court found that the 1868 treaty, if construed as the Indians argued, violated the so-called "equal footing" doctrine because Wyoming was admitted to the Union on an equal footing with all other states and was therefore entitled to regulate the taking of game throughout the state.

Winans clearly rejected the view that the equal footing doctrine limits the exercise of treaty-guaranteed off-reservation hunting and fishing rights. However, *Winans* left a legacy of confusion as to the nature and scope of such rights. Fundamentally, *Winans* involved the question of access to a usual and accustomed fishing station with which the defendants had interfered by the operation of their fish wheel. Thus, the most limited holding of *Winans* treats the off-reservation rights as merely a guarantee of access to fishing sites in the nature of an easement or encumbrance on the title of subsequent title holders. Such a construction guarantees the Indians neither specific rights in the fishery resource nor freedom from state regulation. Two aspects of *Winans* suggest, however, that the Court had in mind a broader construction of the off-reservation treaty rights. First, the Court noted that the fish wheel interfered with the movement of the fish upstream and therefore depleted the available resource. Second, the defendants' fish wheel was state licensed. Thus, the Court's ruling suggested that the Indians' treaty-guaranteed off-reservation fishing rights imposed some limits on the usually unquestioned power of the state to control and regulate the taking of game. The subsequent cases on off-reservation food gathering are best understood as representing an evolutionary effort to work out these ambiguities in *Winans*. As is often true in the long-term development of a path of cases, these cases include some false starts and dead ends.

The early cases after *Winans* seemed to stress in particular the access aspects of *Winans*. Either as a product of their facts or their holdings, the early cases treated off-reservation fishing rights primarily as a guarantee of access to traditional fisheries sites even when held in private hands — the "easement" view of the right. For example, in *Seufert Bros. v. United States*, 249 U.S. 194 (1919), the Court affirmed an injunction against a private company and its employees restraining them from interfering with the treaty-guaranteed fishing rights of the Yakima. The suit was brought by the United States to enforce the Indians' rights to establish fish wheels on sites adversely claimed by the defendant corporation. The Court construed the Yakima treaty rights as the Indians understood them, "that they had the right to resort to these fishing grounds and make use of them in common with other citizens of the United States. . . ." 249 U.S. at 198–99. Responding to the defendants' suggestion that the Indians in exercising their off-reservation rights were limited to the methods employed in primitive times, the district court had said, "I see no reason why Indians may not be permitted to advance in the arts and sciences as well as any other people, and, if they can catch their supply of food fish by a more scientific and expeditious method, there exists no good reason why they may not be permitted to do so." *United States ex rel. Williams v. Seufert Bros.*, 233 Fed. Rep. 579, 584 (D. Or. 1916).

In *New York ex rel. Kennedy v. Becker*, 241 U.S. 556 (1916), the Supreme Court indicated that the easement construction of off-reservation hunting rights might subsume their entire scope. This case involved the state prosecution of Seneca Indians for violation of state conservation laws when exercising rights reserved under a federally approved indenture to exercise "the privilege of fishing and hunting on the said tract of land hereby intended to be conveyed [by the federal indenture to private claimants]." According to the Court:

> It has frequently been said that treaties with the Indians should be construed in the sense in which the Indians understood them. But it is idle to suppose that there was any actual anticipation at the time the treaty was made of the conditions now existing to which the legislation in question was addressed. Adopted when game was plentiful — when the cultivation contemplated by the whites was not expected to interfere with its abun-

dance — it can hardly be supposed that the thought of the Indians was concerned with the necessary exercise of inherent power under modern conditions for the preservation of wild life. But the existence of the sovereignty of the State was well understood, and this conception involved all that was necessarily implied in that sovereignty, whether fully appreciated or not. We do not think that it is a proper construction of the reservation in the conveyance to regard it as an attempt either to reserve sovereign prerogative or so to divide the inherent power of preservation as to make its competent exercise impossible.

Id. at 563.

In 1942, the Court began to limit the sweeping dicta in *Kennedy* suggesting that Indian hunting and fishing rights were wholly subject to state control. In *Tulee v. Washington*, 315 U.S. 681 (1942), the Court held that the state of Washington could not impose a licensing fee for the exercise of the Yakimas' off-reservation treaty fishing rights. The Court said:

[W]e are of the opinion that the state is without power to charge the Yakimas a fee for fishing. A stated purpose of the licensing act was to provide for "the support of the state government and its existing public institutions." Laws of Washington (1937) 529, 534. The license fees prescribed are regulatory as well as revenue producing. But it is clear that their regulatory purpose could be accomplished otherwise, that the imposition of license fees is not indispensable to the effectiveness of a state conservation program. Even though this method may be both convenient and, in its general impact, fair, it acts upon the Indians as a charge for exercising the very right their ancestors intended to reserve. We believe that such exaction of fees as a prerequisite to the enjoyment of fishing in the "usual and accustomed places" cannot be reconciled with a fair construction of the treaty. We therefore hold the state statute invalid as applied in this case.

Id. at 685. *Tulee* clearly indicated, as *Winans* had previously suggested, that off-reservation treaty rights preempted the force of state conservation laws to some extent. It remained for later cases to work out the scope and contours of that preemption.

2. The *Puyallup* Cases and the Start of the Modern Litigation: In *Puyallup Tribe v. Department of Game*, 391 U.S. 392 (1968) (*Puyallup I*), the Court was faced with suits by the state of Washington to secure a declaratory judgment that the Puyallup Tribe was subject to state conservation measures in the exercise of their off-reservation fishing rights and to enjoin the Nisqually Indians from using set nets and drift nets in violation of state law. The Court assumed that the off-reservation fishing rights of the affected tribes historically and presently had "commercial aspects" and said that Indian right "may, of course, not be qualified by the State, even though all Indians born in the United States are now citizens of the United States." Nevertheless, the Court held that "the manner of fishing, the size of the take, the restriction of commercial fishing, and the like may be regulated by the state in the interest of conservation, provided that the regulation meets appropriate standards and does not discriminate against the Indians." The Court described its appropriate standards by saying, "the power of the State was to be measured by whether it was "necessary for the conservation of fish." The Court remanded the case to the trial court for determination of the measures reasonable and necessary for conservation with the admonition that "the conservation issue must also cover the issue of equal protection implicit in the phrase 'in common with.' "

The late Professor Ralph Johnson (who was probably the first to regularly teach Indian law in an American law school) was severely critical of the *Puyallup I* decision, stating:

> Because agreements with the Indians are treaties, the Indians are not subject to state regulation unless the treaty so provides or unless Congress so legislates. The treaties with the Indians do not provide for state regulation and Congress has never authorized such regulation. Therefore, the Supreme Court should clearly hold that the states have no power to regulate Indian off-reservation fishing unless and until Congress expressly delegates the power to do so. . . .
>
> [T]he vagueness of the case law standards portends a continuing series of clashes between the Indians and the states, each seeking to carve out the broadest possible claim in this legal thicket. But the creation of adequate standards will not be an easy task.

Ralph Johnson, *The States Versus Indian Off-Reservation Fishing: A United States Supreme Court Error*, 47 WASH. L. REV. 207, 208–09 (1972).

Professor Johnson's prediction regarding the difficulty of working out the scope of state jurisdiction through adjudication proved correct, as *Puyallup I* engendered a flood of litigation in the Pacific Northwest during the next decade. In *Department of Game v. Puyallup Tribe*, 414 U.S. 44 (1973) (*Puyallup II*), the same litigation returned to the Court, this time to resolve the question whether the state conservation authorities could prohibit all Indian net fishing for steelhead trout in order to conserve the steelhead fish runs. The state authorities argued that after the allotment of steelhead caught by sport fishers, the remainder was necessary for spawning in order to replenish the run. The Court struck down the state regulations because they discriminated against Indian treaty fishers. "There is discrimination here because all Indian net fishing is banned and only hook-and-line fishing entirely preempted by non-Indians is allowed." The Court, however, cautioned:

> The aim is to accommodate the rights of Indians under the Treaty and the rights of other people.
>
> We do not imply that these fishing rights persist down to the very last steelhead in the river. Rights can be controlled by the need to conserve a species; and the time may come when the life of a steelhead is so precarious in a particular stream that all fishing should be banned until the species regains assurance of survival. The police power of the State is adequate to prevent the steelhead from following the fate of the passenger pigeon; and the Treaty does not give the Indians a federal right to pursue the last living steelhead until it enters their nets.

Id. at 49. Justice White noted in a brief concurring opinion, joined by Chief Justice Burger and Justice Stewart, that the state of Washington through its hatchery program was responsible for a substantial proportion of the steelhead run in question. He then commented, ". . . the Treaty does not obligate the State of Washington to subsidize the Indian fishery with planted fish paid for by sports fishermen."

The *Puyallup* litigation again returned to the Court in *Puyallup Tribe v. Department of Game*, 433 U.S. 165 (1977) (*Puyallup III*). *Puyallup III* involved the review of the state regulations governing Puyallup treaty fishing rights promulgated after the remand in *Puyallup II*. Before the state courts considered these regulations on remand, a crucial change in the facts of the case occurred. In *United States v. Washington*, 496 F.2d 620 (9th Cir. 1974), the Ninth Circuit Court of Appeals held that the Puyallup Reservation had not been extinguished. Under this ruling, the reservation boundaries thus included almost all of the area where the fishing in *Puyallup I* and *Puyallup II* had taken place. From the commencement of the Puyallup litigation in 1963, the state of Washington had conceded that it had no right to regulate fishing on the reservation. Nevertheless, the Washington Supreme Court both recognized the Ninth Circuit's decision and held that the state could regulate Indian fishing *off* and *on* the reservation. Thus, before the Supreme Court in *Puyallup III*, the Tribe shifted its defense to one based on on-reservation rights.

The Tribe claimed both sovereign immunity from suit and that its reservation still existed and included large sections of the city of Tacoma. On the sovereign immunity issue, the Court sustained the Tribe's claim and therefore vacated that portion of the lower court order requiring the Tribe to report the catch of its members each week. However, the Court treated the designation of the Tribe as a surrogate for designating the various members of the Tribe and permitted the case to proceed without any reference to potential indispensable party issues. The Court rejected the significance of the Tribe's belated on-reservation fishing rights claim, noting that of the original 18,000-acre reservation, the Tribe retains only 22 acres, none of which abutted the Puyallup River. Nevertheless, the Court stopped short of finding that the Puyallup Reservation had been disestablished. Rather, the Court's opinion noted:

> The resource being regulated is indigenous to the Puyallup River. Virtually all adult steelhead in the river have returned after being spawned or planted by respondent upstream from the boundaries of the original Puyallup Reservation, which encompass the lowest seven miles of the river. Though it would be decidedly unwise, if Puyallup treaty fishermen were allowed untrammeled on-reservation fishing rights, they could interdict completely the migratory fish run and "pursue the last living [Puyallup River] steelhead until it enters their nets." . . . In practical effect, therefore, the petitioner is reasserting the right to exclusive control of the steelhead run that was unequivocally rejected in both *Puyallup I* and *Puyallup II*. At this stage of this protracted litigation, we are unwilling to re-examine those unanimous decisions or to render their holdings virtually meaningless. We therefore reject petitioner's claim to an exclusive right to take steelhead while passing through the reservation.

433 U.S. at 176–177. Finally, the Court reviewed the state standards and found that they met appropriate conservation standards in that "the court determined the number of steelhead in the river and how many could be taken without diminishing the number in future years; the court then allocated 45% of the annual natural steelhead run available for taking to the treaty fishermen's net fishery." The Court withheld comment on the lower court's exclusion of hatchery fish from the calculation as not available to the Indians since this issue was not presented in the petition for certiorari.

Puyallup III indicates that questions of conservation and state regulation not infrequently mask the true underlying dispute: allocation of the resource between Indians and non-Indians. Thus, in *United States v. Washington*, 384 F. Supp. 312 (W.D. Wash. 1974) (Boldt, J.), *aff'd*, 520 F.2d 676 (9th Cir. 1975), the courts construed guarantees of off-reservation fishery rights to require that "[t]reaty Indians thus are to have the opportunity to take up to 50 percent of the available harvest at their traditional grounds." This ruling spawned a major political and legal dispute in the Pacific Northwest. *See, e.g., Puget Sound Gillnetters Ass'n v. United States District Court*, 573 F.2d 1123 (9th Cir. 1978); *Washington State Com. Passenger Fishing Vessel Ass'n v. Tollefson*, 571 P.2d 1373 (Wash. 1977), *vacated*, 434 U.S. 586 (1979); *Purse Seine Vessel Owners Ass'n v. Moos*, 567 P.2d 205 (Wash. 1977). The political and legal conflict engendered by those cases ultimately led the Supreme Court to intervene.

WASHINGTON v. WASHINGTON STATE COMMERCIAL PASSENGER FISHING VESSEL ASSOCIATION
United States Supreme Court
443 U.S. 658 (1979)

MR. JUSTICE STEVENS delivered the opinion of the Court.

To extinguish the last group of conflicting claims to lands lying west of the Cascade Mountains and north of the Columbia River in what is now the State of Washington, the United States entered into a series of treaties with Indian tribes in 1854 and 1855.[4] The Indians relinquished their interest in most of the territory in exchange for monetary payments. In addition, certain relatively small parcels of land were reserved for their exclusive use, and they were afforded other guarantees, including protection of their "right of taking fish at usual and accustomed grounds and stations . . . in common with all citizens of the Territory."

The principal question presented by this litigation concerns the character of that treaty right to take fish. Various other issues are presented, but their disposition

---

[4] [2] Treaty of Medicine Creek (10 Stat. 1132), the Treaty of Point Elliott (12 Stat. 927), the Treaty of Point No Point (12 Stat. 933), the Treaty of Neah Bay (12 Stat. 939), the Treaty with the Yakimas (12 Stat. 951), and the Treaty of Olympia (12 Stat. 971). The parties to the treaties and to this litigation include these Indian Tribes: Hoh; Lower Elwha Band of Clallam Indians; Lummi; Makah; Muckleshoot; Nisqually; Nooksack Tribe; Port Gamble Band of Clallam Indians; Puyallup; Quileute; Quinault; Sauk-Suiattle; Skokomish; Sqaxin Island; Stillaguamish; Suquamish; Swinomish; Tulalip; Upper Skagit; The Yakima Nation.

depends on the answer to the principal question. Before answering any of these questions, or even stating the issues with more precision, we shall briefly describe the anadromous fisheries of the Pacific Northwest, the treaty negotiations, and the principal components of the litigation complex that led us to grant these three related petitions for certiorari.

I

Anadromous fish hatch in fresh water, migrate to the ocean where they are reared and reach mature size, and eventually complete their life cycle by returning to the fresh-water place of their origin to spawn. Different species have different life cycles, some spending several years and travelling great distances in the ocean before returning to spawn and some even returning to spawn on more than one occasion before dying. The regular habits of these fish make their "runs" predictable; this predictability in turn makes it possible for both fishermen and regulators to forecast and to control the number of fish that will be caught or "harvested." Indeed, as the terminology associated with it suggests, the management of anadromous fisheries is in many ways more akin to the cultivation of "crops" — with its relatively high degree of predictability and productive stability, subject mainly to sudden changes in climatic patterns — than is the management of most other commercial and sports fisheries.

Regulation of the anadromous fisheries of the Northwest is nonetheless complicated by the different habits of the various species of salmon and trout involved, by the variety of methods of taking the fish, and by the fact that a run of fish may pass through a series of different jurisdictions. Another complexity arises from the fact that the State of Washington has attempted to reserve one species, steelhead trout, for sport fishing and therefore conferred regulatory jurisdiction over that species upon its Department of Game, whereas the various species of salmon are primarily harvested by commercial fishermen and are managed by the State's Department of Fisheries. Moreover, adequate regulation must not only take into account the potentially conflicting interests of sport and commercial fishermen, as well as those of Indian and nontreaty fishermen, but also must recognize that the fish runs may be harmed by harvesting either too many or too few of the fish returning to spawn.

The anadromous fish constitute a natural resource of great economic value to the State of Washington. Millions of salmon, with an average weight of from four or five to about 20 pounds, depending on the species, are harvested each year. Over 6,600 nontreaty fishermen and about 800 Indians make their livelihood by commercial fishing; moreover, some 280,000 individuals are licensed to engage in sport fishing in the State.

II

One hundred and twenty-five years ago when the relevant treaties were signed, anadromous fish were even more important to most of the population of western Washington than they are today. At that time, about three-fourths of the approximately 10,000 inhabitants of the area were Indians. Although in some respects the cultures of the different tribes varied — some bands of Indians, for example, had little or no tribal organization[5] while others, such as the Makah and the Yakima, were highly organized — all of them shared a vital and unifying dependence on anadromous fish.

Religious rites were intended to insure the continual return of the salmon and the trout; the seasonal and geographic variations in the runs of the different species determined the movements of the largely nomadic tribes. Fish constituted a major part of the Indian diet, was used for commercial purposes, and indeed was traded in substantial volume.[6] The Indians developed food preservation techniques that enabled them to store fish throughout the year and to transport it over great distances. They used a wide variety of methods to catch fish, including the precursors of all modern netting techniques. Their usual and accustomed fishing places were numerous and were scattered throughout the area, and included marine as well as fresh water areas.

All of the treaties were negotiated by Isaac Stevens, the first Governor and first Superintendent of Indian Affairs of the Washington territory, and a small group of advisors. Contemporaneous documents make it clear that these people recognized the vital importance of the fisheries to the Indians and wanted to protect them from the risk that non-Indian settlers might seek to monopolize their fisheries. There is no evidence of the precise understanding the Indians had of any of the specific English terms and phrases in the treaty. It is perfectly clear, however, that the Indians were vitally interested in protecting their right to take fish at usual and accustomed places, whether on or off the reservations, and that they were invited by the white negotiators to rely and in fact did rely heavily on the good faith of the United States to protect that right.

Referring to the negotiations with the Yakima Nation, by far the largest of the Indian tribes, the District Court found:

> At the treaty council the United States negotiators promised, and the Indians understood, that the Yakimas would forever be able to continue the same off-reservation food gathering and fishing practices as to time, place, method, species and extent as they had or were exercising. The Yakimas

---

[5] [5] Indeed, the record shows that the territorial officials who negotiated the treaties on behalf of the United States took the initiative in aggregating certain loose bands into designated tribes and even appointed many of the chiefs who signed the treaties.

[6] [7] "At the time of the treaties, trade was carried on among the Indian groups throughout a wide geographic area. Fish was a basic element of the trade. There is some evidence that the volume of this intra-tribal trade was substantial, but it is not possible to compare it with the volume of present day commercial trading in salmon. Such trading was, however, important to the Indians at the time of the treaties. In addition to potlatching, which is a system of exchange between communities in a social context often typified by competitive gifting, there was a considerable amount of outright sale and trade beyond the local community and sometimes over great distances. In the decade immediately preceding the treaties, Indian fighting increased in order to accommodate increased demand for local non-Indian consumption and for export, as well as to provide money for purchase of introduced commodities and to obtain substitute non-Indian goods for native products which were no longer available because of the non-Indian movement into the area. Those involved in negotiating the treaties recognized the contribution that Indian fishermen made to the territorial economy because Indians caught most of the non-Indians' fish for them, plus clams and oysters." 384 F. Supp., at 351 (citations to record omitted). See also *id.*, at 364 (Makah Tribe "maintained from time immemorial a thriving economy based on commerce" in "marine resources").

relied on these promises and they formed a material and basic part of the treaty and of the Indians' understanding of the meaning of the treaty. *Id.*, at 381 (record citations omitted).

See also *Id.*, at 363 (similar finding regarding negotiations with the Makah tribe).

The Indians understood that non-Indians would also have the right to fish at their off-reservation fishing sites. But this was not understood as a significant limitation on their right to take fish. Because of the great abundance of fish and the limited population of the area, it simply was not contemplated that either party would interfere with the other's fishing rights. The parties accordingly did not see the need and did not intend to regulate the taking of fish by either Indians or non-Indians, nor was future regulation foreseen.

Indeed, for several decades after the treaties were signed, Indians continued to harvest most of the fish taken from the waters of Washington, and they moved freely about the territory and later the State in search of that resource. The size of the fishery source continued to obviate the need during the period to regulate the taking of fish by either Indians or non-Indians. Not until major economic developments in canning and processing occurred in the last few years of the 19th century did a significant non-Indian fishery develop. It was as a consequence of these developments, rather than of the treaty, that non-Indians began to dominate the fisheries and eventually to exclude most Indians from participating in it — a trend that was encouraged by the onset of often-discriminatory state regulation in the early decades of the 20th century.

In sum, it is fair to conclude that when the treaties were negotiated, neither party realized or intended that their agreement would determine whether, and if so how, a resource that had always been thought inexhaustible would be allocated between the native Indians and the incoming settlers when it later became scarce.

III

Unfortunately, that resource has now become scarce, and the meaning of the Indians' treaty right to take fish has accordingly become critical. The United States Court of Appeals for the Ninth Circuit and the Supreme Court of the State of Washington have issued conflicting decisions on its meaning. In addition, their holdings raise important ancillary questions that will appear from a brief review of this extensive litigation. . . .

The District Court agreed with the parties who advocated an allocation to the Indians, and it essentially agreed with the United States as to what that allocation should be. It held that the Indians were then entitled to a 45% to 50% share of the harvestable fish that will at some point pass through recognized tribal fishing grounds in the case area.[7]

---

[7] [16] The Solicitor General estimates that over half of the anadromous fish in the case area do not pass through such grounds and are exempt from the order. Brief for the United States, at 72–73. This estimate is consistent with the State's figures on the number of salmon caught in 1977, see JA 635–639, which indicate that the Indians caught only about 18% of the fish taken in the case area that year. Of course, the Indians claim that they were prevented from catching as many fish that year as they were

The share was to be calculated on a river-by-river, run-by-run basis, subject to certain adjustments. Fish caught by Indians for ceremonial and subsistence purposes as well as fish caught within a reservation were excluded from the calculation of the tribes' share. In addition, in order to compensate for fish caught outside of the case area, *i.e.*, beyond the State's jurisdiction, the court made an "equitable adjustment" to increase the allocation to the Indians. The court left it to the individual tribes involved to agree among themselves on how best to divide the Indian share of runs that pass through the usual and accustomed grounds of more than one tribe, and it postponed until a later date the proper accounting for hatchery-bred fish. [T]he Court of Appeals for the Ninth Circuit affirmed, and we denied certiorari.

The injunction entered by the District Court required the Department of Fisheries ("Fisheries") to adopt regulations protecting the Indians' treaty rights. After the new regulations were promulgated, however, they were immediately challenged by private citizens in suits commenced in the Washington state courts. The State Supreme Court, in two cases that are herein consolidated form in No. 77-983, ultimately held that Fisheries could not comply with the federal injunction. *Puget Sound Gillnetters Ass'n v. Moos*, 88 Wn. 2d 677, 565 P.2d 1151; *Fishing Vessel Ass'n v. Tollefson*, 89 Wn. 2d 276, 571 P.2d 1373.

As a matter of federal law, the state court first accepted the Game Department's and rejected the District Court's interpretation of the treaty and held that it did not give the Indians a right to a share of the fish runs, and second concluded that recognizing special rights for the Indians would violate the Equal Protection Clause of the Fourteenth Amendment. The opinions might also be read to hold, as a matter of state law, that Fisheries had no authority to issue the regulations because they had a purpose other than conservation of the resource. In this Court, however, the Attorney General of the State disclaims the adequacy and independence of the state law ground and argues that the state-law authority of Fisheries is dependent on the answers to the two federal-law questions discussed above. We defer to that interpretation, subject, of course, to later clarification by the State Supreme Court. Because we are also satisfied that the constitutional holding is without merit,[8] our review of the state court's judgment will be limited to the treaty issue.

When Fisheries was ordered by the state courts to abandon its attempt to promulgate and enforce regulations in compliance with the federal court's decree — and when the Game Department simply refused to comply — the District Court

---

entitled to under the District Court's order because of interference by non-Indian fishermen. But even if the 18% figure were increased by the amount of fish the Indians claim they should have caught, the Indians' take would only amount to about 20% of the total number of fish taken in the case area.

[8] [20] The Washington Supreme Court held that the treaties would violate equal protection principles if they provided fishing rights to Indians that were not also available to non-Indians. The simplest answer to this argument is that this Court has already held that these treaties confer enforceable special benefits on signatory Indian tribes, *e.g.*, *Tulee v. Washington*, 315 U.S. 681; *United States v. Winans*, 198 U.S. 371, and has repeatedly held that the peculiar semisovereign and constitutionally recognized status of Indians justifies special treatment on their behalf when rationally related to the Government's "unique obligation toward the Indians." *Morton v. Mancari*, 417 U.S. 535, 555. See *United States v. Antelope*, 430 U.S. 641; *Antoine v. Washington*, 420 U.S. 194. See also *Fishing Vessel Assn. v. Tollefson*, 89 Wash. 2d 276, 287–288, 571 P. 2d 1373, 1379–1380 (1977) (Utter, J., dissenting).

entered a series of orders enabling it, with the aid of the United States Attorney for the Western District of Washington and various federal law enforcement agencies, directly to supervise those aspects of the State's fisheries necessary to the preservation of treaty fishing rights. The District Court's power to take such direct action and, in doing so, to enjoin persons who were not parties to the proceeding was affirmed by the United States Court of Appeals for the Ninth Circuit. That court, in a separate opinion, also held that regulations of the International Pacific Salmon Fisheries Commission posed no impediment to the District Court's interpretation of the treaty language and to its enforcement of that interpretation. Subsequently, the District Court entered an Enforcement Order regarding the salmon fisheries for the 1978 and subsequent seasons, which, prior to our issuance of a writ of certiorari to review the case, was pending on appeal in the Court of Appeals.

Because of the widespread defiance of the District Court's orders, this litigation has assumed unusual significance. We granted certiorari in the state and federal cases to interpret this important treaty provision and thereby to resolve the conflict between the state and federal courts regarding what, if any, right the Indians have to a share of the fish, to address the implications of international regulation of the fisheries in the area, and to remove any doubts about the federal court's power to enforce its orders.

IV

The treaties secure a "right of taking fish." The pertinent articles provide:

> The right of taking fish at usual and accustomed grounds and stations is further secured to said Indians in common with all citizens of the Territory, and of erecting temporary houses for the purpose of curing, together with the privilege of hunting and gathering roots and berries on open and unclaimed lands. *Provided, however,* That they shall not take shell-fish from any beds staked or cultivated by citizens.

At the time the treaties were executed there was a great abundance of fish and a relative scarcity of people. No one had any doubt about the Indians' capacity to take as many fish as they might need. Their right to take fish could therefore be adequately protected by guaranteeing them access to usual and accustomed fishing sites which could be — and which for decades after the treaties were signed were — comfortably shared with the incoming settlers.

Because the sparse contemporaneous written materials refer primarily to assuring access to fishing sites "in common with citizens of the Territory," the State of Washington and the commercial fishing associations, having all adopted the Game Department's original position, argue that it was merely access that the negotiators guaranteed. . . .

A treaty, including one between the United States and an Indian tribe, is essentially a contract between two sovereign nations. *E.g.,* [*Lone Wolf v. Hitchcock*]. When the signatory nations have not been at war and neither is the vanquished, it is reasonable to assume that they negotiated as equals at arms length. There is no reason to doubt that this assumption applies to the treaty at issue here.

Accordingly, it is the intention of the parties, and not solely that of the superior side, that must control any attempt to interpret the treaties. When Indians are involved, this Court has long given special meaning to this rule. It has held that the United States, as the party with the presumptively superior negotiating skills and superior knowledge of the language in which the treaty is recorded, has a responsibility to avoid taking advantage of the other side. "[T]he treaty must therefore be construed, not according to the technical meaning of its words to learned lawyers, but in the sense in which they would naturally be understood by the Indians." *Jones v. Meehan*, 175 U.S. 1, 10. This rule, in fact, has thrice been explicitly relied on by the Court in broadly interpreting these very treaties in the Indians' favor.

Governor Stevens and his associates were well aware of the "sense" in which the Indians were likely to view assurances regarding their fishing rights. During the negotiations, the vital importance of the fish to the Indians was repeatedly emphasized by both sides, and the Governor's promises that the treaties would protect that source of food and commerce were crucial in obtaining the Indians' assent. It is absolutely clear, as Governor Stevens himself said, that neither he nor the Indians intended that the latter "should be excluded from their ancient fisheries," and it is accordingly inconceivable that either party deliberately agreed to authorize future settlers to crowd the Indians out of any meaningful use of their accustomed places to fish. That each individual Indian would share an "equal opportunity" with thousands of newly arrived individual settlers is totally foreign to the spirit of the negotiations. Such a "right," along with the $207,500 paid the Indians, would hardly have been sufficient to compensate them for the millions of acres they ceded to the Territory.

[W]e think greater importance should be given to the Indians' likely understanding of the other words in the treaty and especially the reference to the "right of *taking* fish" — a right that had no special meaning at common law but that must have had obvious significance to the tribes relinquishing a portion of their pre-existing rights to the United States in return for this promise. This language is particularly meaningful in context of anadromous fisheries — which were not the focus of the common law — because of the relative predictability of the "harvest." In this context, it makes sense to say that a party has a right to "take" — rather than merely the "opportunity" to try to catch — some of the large quantities of fish that will almost certainly be available at a given place at a given time. This interpretation is confirmed by additional language in the treaty. The fishing clause speaks of "securing" certain fishing rights, a term the Court has previously interpreted as synonymous with "reserving" rights previously exercised. Because the Indians had always exercised the right to meet their subsistence and commercial needs by taking fish from treaty area waters, they would be unlikely to perceive a "reservation" of that right as merely the chance, shared with millions of other citizens, occasionally to dip their nets into the territorial waters. Moreover, the phrasing of the clause quite clearly avoids placing each individual Indian on an equal footing with each individual citizen of the State. The referent of the "said Indians" who are to share the right of taking fish with "all citizens of the Territory" is not the individual Indians but the various signatory "tribes and bands of Indians" listed in the opening article of each treaty. Because it was the tribes that were given a right in common with non-Indian citizens, it is especially likely that a class right to a share of fish, rather than a personal right to attempt to land fish, was intended.

In our view, the purpose and language of the treaties are unambiguous; they secure the Indians' right to take a share of each run of fish that passes through tribal fishing areas. But our prior decisions provide an even more persuasive reason why this interpretation is not open to question. For notwithstanding the bitterness that this litigation has engendered, the principal issue involved is virtually a "matter decided" by our previous holdings.

The Court has interpreted the fishing clause in these treaties on six prior occasions. In all of these cases the Court placed a relatively broad gloss on the Indians' fishing rights and — more or less explicitly — rejected the State's "equal opportunity" approach; in the earliest and the three most recent cases, moreover, we adopted essentially the interpretation that the United States is reiterating here.

[The Court discusses its opinions in *Winans, Seufert Bros., Tulee*, and the three *Puyallup* cases.]

Not only all six of our cases interpreting the relevant treaty language but all federal courts that have interpreted the treaties in recent times have reached the foregoing conclusions, see *Sohappy v. Smith*, 302 F. Supp. 899, 908, 911 (Ore. 1969) (citing cases), as did the Washington Supreme Court itself prior to the present litigation. *State v. Satiacum*, 50 Wn. 2d 513, 523–524, 414 P.2d 400 (1957). A like interpretation, moreover, has been followed by the Court with respect to hunting rights explicitly secured by treaty to Indians "in common with all other persons," *Antoine v. Washington*, 420 U.S. 94, 205–206, and to water rights that were merely implicitly secured to the Indians by treaties reserving land — treaties that the Court enforced by ordering an apportionment to the Indians of enough water to meet their subsistence and cultivation needs. *Arizona v. California*, 373 U.S. 546, 598-601, following *United States v. Powers*, 305 U.S. 527, 528–533; *Winters v. United States*, 207 U.S. 564, 576.

The purport of our cases is clear. Nontreaty fishermen may not rely on property law concepts, devices such as the fish wheel, license fees, or general regulations to deprive the Indians of a fair share of the relevant runs of anadromous fish in the case area. Nor may treaty fishermen rely on their exclusive right of access to the reservations to destroy the rights of other "citizens of the territory." Both sides have a right, secured by treaty, to take a fair share of the available fish. That, we think, is what the parties to the treaty intended when they secured to the Indians the right of taking fish in common with other citizens.

V

We also agree with the Government that an equitable measure of the common right should initially divide the harvestable portion of each run that passes through a "usual and accustomed" place into approximately equal treaty and non-treaty shares, and should then reduce the treaty share if tribal needs may be satisfied by a lesser amount. Although this method of dividing the resource, unlike the right to *some* division, is not mandated by our prior cases, it is consistent with the 45%-55% division arrived at by the Washington state courts, and affirmed by this Court, in

Puyallup III with respect to the steelhead run on the Puyallup River. The trial court in the *Puyallup* litigation reached those figures essentially by starting with a 50% allocation based on the Indians' reliance on the fish for their livelihoods and then adjusting slightly downward due to other relevant factors. The District Court took a similar tack in this case, *i.e.*, by starting with a 50-50 division and adjusting slightly downward on the Indians' side when it became clear that they did not need a full 50%.

The division arrived at by the District Court is also consistent with our earlier decisions concerning Indian treaty rights to scarce natural resources. In those cases, after determining that at the time of the treaties the resource involved was necessary to the Indians' welfare, the Court typically ordered a trial judge or special master, in his discretion, to devise some apportionment that assured that the Indians' reasonable livelihood needs would be met. This is precisely what the District Court did here, except that it realized that some ceiling should be placed on the Indians' apportionment to prevent their needs from exhausting the entire resource and thereby frustrating the treaty right of "all other citizens of the Territory."

Thus, it first concluded that at the time the treaties were signed, the Indians, who comprised three-fourths of the territorial population, depended heavily on anadromous fish as a source of food, commerce, and cultural cohesion. Indeed, it found that the non-Indian population depended on Indians to catch the fish that the former consumed. Only then did it determine that the Indian's present-day subsistence and commercial needs should be met, subject, of course, to the 50% ceiling.

It bears repeating, however, that the 50% figure imposes a maximum but not a minimum allocation. As in *Arizona v. California* and its predecessor cases, the central principle here must be that Indian treaty rights to a natural resource that once was thoroughly and exclusively exploited by the Indians secures so much as, but not more than, is necessary to provide the Indians with a livelihood — that is to say, a moderate living. Accordingly, while the maximum possible allocation to the Indians is fixed at 50%,[9] the minimum is not; the latter will, upon proper submissions to the District Court, be modified in response to changing circumstances. If, for example, a tribe should dwindle to just a few members, or if it should find other sources of support that lead it to abandon its fisheries, a 45% or 50% allocation of an entire run that passes through its customary fishing grounds would be manifestly inappropriate because the livelihood of the tribe under those circumstances could not reasonably require an allotment of large number of fish.

Although the District Court's exercise of its discretion, as slightly modified by

---

[9] [27] Because the 50% figure is only a ceiling, it is not correct to characterize our holding "as guaranteeing the Indians a specified percentage" of the fish. See POWELL, J., dissenting. The logic of the 50% ceiling is manifest. For an equal division . . . especially between parties who presumptively treated with each other as equals — is suggested, if not necessarily dictated, by the word "common" as it appears in the treaties. Since the days of Solomon, such as division has been accepted as a fair apportionment of a common asset, and Anglo-American common law has presumed that division when, as here, no other percentage is suggested by the language of the agreement or the surrounding circumstances. E.g., 2 American Law of Property § 6.5, at 19 (A. Casner ed., 1952); E. Hopkins, Handbook on the Law of Real Property § 209, at 336 (1896).

the Court of Appeals, is in most respects unobjectionable, we are not satisfied that all of the adjustments it made to its division are consistent with the preceding analysis.

The District Court determined that the fish taken by the Indians on their reservations should not be counted against their share. It based this determination on the fact that Indians have the exclusive right under the treaties to fish on their reservations. But this fact seems to us to have no greater significance than the fact that some nontreaty fishermen may have exclusive access to fishing sites that are not "usual and accustomed" places. Shares in the fish runs should not be affected by the place where the fish are taken. Cf. *Puyallup III*, 433 U.S., at 173–177.[10] We therefore disagree with the District Court's exclusion of the Indians' on-reservation catch from their portion of the runs.[11]

This same rationale, however, validates the Court-of-Appeals-modified equitable adjustment for fish caught outside the jurisdiction of the State by nontreaty fishermen from the State of Washington. So long as they take fish from identifiable runs that are destined for traditional tribal fishing grounds, such persons may not rely on the location of their take to justify excluding it from their share. . . .

On the other hand, as long as there are enough fish to satisfy the Indians' ceremonial and subsistence needs, we see no justification for the District Court's exclusion from the treaty share of fish caught for these purposes. We need not now decide whether priority for such uses would be required in a period of short supply in order to carry out the purposes of the treaty. See 384 F. Supp., at 343. For present purposes, we merely hold that the total catch — rather than the commercial catch — is the measure of each party's right.

Accordingly, any fish (1) taken in Washington waters or in United States waters off the coast of Washington and (2) taken from runs of fish that pass through the Indians' usual and accustomed fishing grounds and (3) taken by either members of the Indian tribes that are parties to this litigation, on the one hand, or by non-Indian citizens of Washington, on the other hand, shall count against that party's respective share of the fish.

VI

Regardless of the Indians' other fishing rights under the treaties, the State argues that an agreement between Canada and the United States pre-empts their

---

[10] [28] This Court's decision in *Puyallup III*, which approved state regulation of on-reservation fishing in the interest of conservation, was issued after the District Court excluded the Indians' on-reservation take and the Court of Appeals affirmed. See 520 F.2d, at 690. There is substantial doubt in my mind that those courts would have decided the question as they did had *Puyallup III* been on the books.

[11] [29] A like reasoning requires the fish taken by treaty fisherman off of the reservations and at locations other than "usual and accustomed" sites, to be counted as part of the Indians share. Of course, the District Court, in its discretion, may determine that so few fish fit into this, or any other, category (e.g., "take-home" fish caught by non-treaty commercial fishermen for personal use) that accounting for them individually is unnecessary, and that an estimated figure may be relied on in making the annual computation. Indeed, if the amount is truly de minimis, no accounting at all may be required.

rights with respect to the sockeye and pink salmon runs on the Fraser River.

In 1930 the United States and Canada agreed that the catch of Fraser River salmon should be equally divided between Canadian and American fishermen. Convention of May 26, 1930, 50 Stat. 1355, as amended by 8 U.S.T. 1058. To implement this agreement, the two governments established the International Pacific Salmon Fisheries Commission (IPSFC). Each year that Commission proposes regulations to govern the time, manner, and number of the catch by the fishermen of the two countries; those regulations become effective upon approval of both countries. . . .

First, we agree with the Court of Appeals that the Convention itself does not implicitly extinguish the Indians' treaty rights. Absent explicit statutory language, we have been extremely reluctant to find congressional abrogation of treaty rights, e.g., *Menominee Tribe v. United States*, 391 U.S. 404, and there is no reason to do so here. Indeed, the Canadian Government has long exempted Canadian Indians from regulations promulgated under the Convention and afforded them special fishing rights. . . .

VII

In addition to their challenges to the District Court's basic construction of the treaties, and to the scope of its allocation of fish to treaty fishermen, the State and the commercial fishing associations have advanced two objections to various remedial orders entered by the District Court. It is claimed that the District Court has ordered a state agency to take action that it has no authority to take as a matter of state law and that its own assumption of the authority to manage the fisheries in the State after the state agencies refused or were unable to do so was unlawful.

These objections are difficult to evaluate in view of the representations to this Court by the Attorney General of the State that definitive resolution of the basic federal question of construction of the treaties will both remove any state-law impediment to enforcement of the State's obligations under the treaties, and enable the State and its Fisheries to carry out those obligations. Once the state agencies comply, of course, there would be no issue relating to federal authority to order them to do so nor any need for the District Court to continue its own direct supervision of enforcement efforts.

The representations of the Attorney General are not binding on the courts and legislature of the State, although we assume they are authoritative within its executive branch. Moreover, the State continues to argue that the District Court exceeded its authority when it assumed control of the fisheries in the State, and the commercial fishing groups continue to argue that the District Court may not order the state agencies to comply with its orders when they have no state-law authority to do so. Accordingly, although adherence to the Attorney General's representations by the executive, legislative, and judicial officials in the State would moot these two issues, a brief discussion should foreclose the possibility that they will not be respected. State-law prohibition against compliance with the District Court's decree cannot survive the command of the Supremacy Clause of the United States Constitution. *Cooper v. Aaron*, 358 U.S. 1; *Abelman v. Booth*, 62 U.S. 506. It is also clear that Game and Fisheries, as parties to this litigation, may be ordered to prepare a set of rules that will implement the Court's interpretation of the rights of the parties even if state law withholds from them the power to do so. E.g., *North Carolina Board of Education v. Swann*, 402 U.S. 43; *Griffin v. County School Board*, 377 U.S. 218; *Tacoma v. Taxpayers of Tacoma*, 357 U.S. 320. Once again the answer to a question raised by this litigation is largely dictated by our *Puyallup* trilogy. There, this Court mandated that state officers make precisely the same type of allocation of fish as the District Court ordered in this case. See *Puyallup III*, 433 U.S., at 177.

Whether Game and Fisheries may be ordered actually to promulgate regulations having effect as a matter of state law may well be doubtful. But the District Court may prescind that problem by assuming direct supervision of the fisheries if state recalcitrance or state-law barriers should be continued. It is therefore absurd to argue as do the fishing associations, both that the state agencies may not be ordered to implement the decree and also that the District Court may not itself issue detailed remedial orders as a substitute for state supervision. The federal court unquestionably has the power to enter the various orders that state official and private parties have chosen to ignore, and even to displace local enforcement of those orders if necessary to remedy the violations of federal law found by the court. [E.g.], *Milliken v. Bradley*, 433 U.S. 267, 280–281, 290; *Swann v. Charlotte-Mecklenburg Board of Education*, 402 U.S. 1, 14. Even if those orders may have been erroneous in some respects, all parties have an unequivocal obligation to obey them while they remain in effect.

In short, we trust that the spirit of cooperation motivating the Attorney General's representation will be confirmed by the conduct of state officials. But if it is not, the District Court has the power to undertake the necessary remedial steps and to enlist the aid of the appropriate federal-law enforcement agents in carrying out those steps. Moreover, the comments by the Court of Appeals strongly imply that it is prepared to uphold the use of stern measures to require respect for federal court orders.[12]

The judgments of the Court of Appeals for the Ninth Circuit, the District Court for the Western District of Washington, and the Supreme Court of the State of Washington are vacated and the respective causes are remanded to those courts for further proceedings not inconsistent with this opinion, except that the judgment in *United States v. Washington*, 573 F.2d 1118 (the International Fisheries case) is affirmed.

[Dissenting opinion of MR. JUSTICE POWELL, joined by JUSTICES STEWART and REHNQUIST has been omitted.]

---

[12] [36] "The state's extraordinary machinations in resisting the [1974] decree have forced the district court to take over a large share of the management of the state's fishery in order to enforce its decrees. Except for some desegregation cases [citations omitted], the district court has faced the most concerted official and private efforts to frustrate a decree of a federal court witnessed in this century. The challenged orders in this appeal must be reviewed by this court in the context of events forced by litigants who offered the court no reasonable choice."

NOTES ON OFF-RESERVATION FOOD GATHERING RIGHTS

1. Further Developments in the Pacific Northwest Fishing Litigation: The continuing sensitivity of the issues in the *Washington Fishing* case is revealed by an unusual modification by the Court of its opinion in the above case. Upon consideration of a motion by the state of Washington, footnote 16 of *Washington v. Washington State Com. Passenger Fishing Vessel Ass'n* was modified as follows:

> A factual dispute exists on the question of what percentage of the fish in the case area actually passes through Indian fishing areas and is therefore subject to the District Court's allocations. In the absence of any relevant findings by the courts below, we are unable to express any view on the matter.

444 U.S. 816 (1979). Was the modification necessary?

The Pacific Northwest litigation moved into a second phase, which involved Indian efforts to assert their off-reservation treaty rights to protect the fishery resource. In *United States v. Washington*, 506 F. Supp. 187 (W.D. Wash. 1980), the court held that hatchery fish should not be excluded from the Indian treaty allocation because "the State lacks an ownership interest in released hatchery fish. . . ." The court also held "that implicitly incorporated in the treaties' fishery clause is the right to have the fishery habitat protected from man-made despoliation." The Ninth Circuit, while affirming this decision as to the hatchery fish, reversed on the issue of protection from man-made pollution since the case was not ripe on that issue. *United States v. Washington*, 759 F.2d 1353 (9th Cir. 1985). Other cases now pending in Washington courts have reopened the pollution question. *E.g.*, *United States v. Washington*, Subproceeding No. 01-01 (Culverts), No. C70-9213.

The orders in the Pacific Northwest cases were subject to the continued monitoring and adjustment of the federal courts. Recently, the Pacific Northwest tribes have found themselves in competition with one another for the fisheries resource, and the Skokomish Tribe actually asked the *United States v. Washington* court to make an equitable apportionment of the shared tribal fishery. United States District Court Judge Martinez and the Ninth Circuit both rebuffed the effort. The Ninth Circuit likened the suit to one among states for equitable apportionment of anadromous fish, and noted that because such claims are brought against sovereign governments, courts will intervene only if the claimant can show that "the threatened invasion of rights is of serious magnitude and established by clear and convincing evidence." Applying that same test to a claim against a tribe, the court found no evidence of such a calamitous threat. Ultimately, the court observed, private dispute resolution among the tribes was preferable to a judicial resolution, "because of their greater familiarity with and sensitivity to the details of the problem and any cultural factors that may bear on the solution, if there is one." *United States v. Washington*, 573 F.3d 701 (9th Cir. 2009). Should the tribes have brought this dispute to a federal court in the first place? What other alternatives were there?

Meanwhile, Washington commercial fishing interests have continued to challenge both state and federal regulations allocating fisheries to tribal fishing, often with declining success. *E.g., Midwater Trawlers Co-operative v. Department of Commerce*, 282 F.3d 710 (9th Cir. 2002) (rejecting challenge by commercial fishing interests and State of Oregon to order increasing and allocating portion of commercial fishery to Indian tribes based on standing and other grounds). The boundaries of usual and accustomed stations have also been a continuing source of dispute. *E.g., Midwater Trawlers Co-operative v. Department of Commerce*, 282 F.3d 710 (9th Cir. 2002); *United States v. Lummi Tribe*, 235 F.3d 443 (9th Cir. 2000). In the Skokomish equitable apportionment case discussed above, the court displayed impatience with its continuing jurisdiction:

> We are puzzled, but need not reach the question, about why the equitable decree in this case remains in force at all. . . . The goal of "provid[ing] a volume of fish sufficient to the fair needs of the tribes" seems . . . to have been achieved. . . . The original injunction, entered 35 years ago, was intended to resolve the treaty right fishing disputes once and for all. Yet this case has become a Jarndyce and Jarndyce [the suit at the center of Charles Dickens' Bleak House], with judges dying out of it and whole Indian tribes being born into it. . . . Judges in the Western District of Washington have now been regulating fishing in the Puget Sound for 35 years, with the aid of a Fishery Advisory Board that the court created. [The] Constitution does not establish the district courts as permanent administrative agencies. Now that treaty enforcement is no longer at issue, it is hard to see why the court still displaces state and federal fish management agencies.
>
> We need not in this case decide whether the 1974 decree should now be released, modified, or dissolved, because no party has asked us to. Such a motion, if made, would be directed to the discretion of the district court, as would sua sponte consideration.

573 F.3d at 709–710. Given the ongoing tension between state and tribal interests, is there reason for the federal courts to retain jurisdiction in *United States v. Washington*?

2. **Off-Reservation Hunting Rights and the Makah Whaling Dispute:** While most of the cases in this section involve the exercise of off-reservation fishing rights, treaties and agreements also reserved off-reservation hunting and food-gathering rights to certain tribes. For example, in *Antoine v. Washington*, 420 U.S. 194 (1975), the Supreme Court held that Washington conservation laws were preempted in application to an Indian hunting on the north half of the former Colville Indian Reservation when the statute ceding the land provided "the right to hunt and fish in common with all other persons on lands not allotted to said Indians shall not be taken away or in anywise abridged." The Court disposed of the conservation issue by briefly noting: "The State of Washington has not argued, let alone established, that applying the ban on out-of-season hunting of deer by the Indians on the land in question is in any way necessary or even useful for the conservation of deer."

Questions of abrogation and federal regulatory authority over off-reservation hunting rights surfaced again in litigation over the right of the Makah Tribe, under the 1855 Treaty of Neah Bay, "of taking fish and of whaling or sealing at usual and accustomed grounds and stations. . . ." *See* 12 Stat. 939, 940 (1855). In exchange for this right, the Tribe gave up most of its land on the Olympic Peninsula. Indeed, the

Treaty of Neah Bay is the only treaty between the United States and an Indian nation that specifically protects the right to hunt whales, which suggests the centrality of whaling in the culture of the Makah. For a variety of reasons, including depletion of the gray whale due to excessive hunting by non-Indians, the Makah ceased conducting whaling expeditions in the 1920s. In the 1990s, as part of a cultural revitalization movement and coinciding with removal of the gray whale from the Endangered Species List, the Makah sought to resume whaling. By that time, federal and international law had introduced strict regulation of such activity, and the Makah required a permit pursuant to United States implementation of the International Convention for the Regulation of Whaling. 62 Stat. 1716, 161 U.N.T.S. 72 (Dec. 2, 1946). This Convention created a quota system to accommodate Native whaling for subsistence purposes.

When the United States proceeded on behalf of the Makah with the International Whaling Commission and announced a quota for Makah whaling based on a Makah whaling management plan, animal rights activists filed suit alleging that the United States had failed to conduct an environmental impact review under NEPA and had failed to comply with the Marine Mammal Protection Act (MMPA), 16 U.S.C. § 1361 et. seq., which prohibits the taking of marine mammals absent a permit or waiver. The federal agencies had found insufficient environmental impact on the whales to warrant a formal NEPA review (known as a FONSI, or Finding of No Significant Impact), and claimed that the international and domestic treaty rights of the Makah rendered the MMPA permit requirement inapplicable.

In *Anderson v. Evans*, 371 F.3d 475 (9th Cir. 2004), the Ninth Circuit took up this issue for the second time, finding that full NEPA review was required and that the Tribe must obtain a permit under the MMPA. The court found that the plaintiffs had raised "substantial questions" about whether the project would have a significant effect on the environment, focusing specifically on the impact of the Makah whaling plan on the whale population in the Tribe's local area (as opposed to the total species), and the potential precedential impact of United States support for the International Whaling Commission, which had chosen for the first time to defer to domestic law determinations regarding which groups met the Convention's subsistence exception.

With regard to the MMPA, the court refused to apply the statutory exemption for hunting that has been "expressly provided for by an international treaty, convention, or agreement to which the United States is a party and which was entered into before [1972] or by any statute implementing any such treaty, convention, or agreement." 16 U.S.C. § 1372(a)(2). In the court's view, the International Whaling Commission's 1997 allowance for United States aboriginal uses, which had formed the basis for the Makah's quota, was too vague and could not relate back to the 1946 date of the International Convention for the Regulation of Whaling. The court then held the permitting requirement of the MMPA applicable to the Tribe, despite the existence of treaty rights, because such application is "necessary to achieve [the statute's] conservation purpose." Here the court cited to cases, such as *Antoine v. Washington*, *supra*, approving, at least in principle, state regulation of Indian treaty rights where the regulation is a "reasonable and necessary conservation measure," as well as to *United States v. Eberhardt* (*see* Sec. A.1, this chapter; Ch. 4, Sec. A.5.a). While acknowledging that the major United

States Supreme Court decision on abrogation of treaty hunting and fishing rights, *United States v. Dion* (Ch. 4, Sec. A.2), did not incorporate a "conservation necessity" principle, the court insisted that it could employ that principle to determine whether a general federal statute may be applied despite some impact on treaty rights, regardless whether that impact constitutes an abrogation.

The court's view of "conservation necessity" extended considerably beyond species preservation, and incorporated the MMPA's goals of ensuring that marine mammals maintain an "optimum sustainable population" and remain "significant functioning elements in the ecosystem." According to the court, if tribal whaling were allowed without navigation of the MMPA's permitting process, there would be no guarantee that future whaling would not "jeopardize" the gray whale population, because international limits may not apply, other Pacific Northwest tribes might claim the right to whale under their general treaty hunting rights, and the Tribe could decide to employ different technologies and kill more whales under future management plans. In the court's words, "The intent of Congress cannot be hostage to the goodwill or good judgment or good sense of the particular leaders empowered by the Tribe at present; it must be assumed that Congress intended to effectuate policies for the United States and its residents, including the Makah Tribe, that transcend the decisions of any subordinate group."

The court also reasoned that application of the MMPA under the conservation principle "goes hand in hand with the principles embedded in the Treaty of Neah Bay itself," which gave the Tribe rights, but "in common with" other citizens of the United States. Under the court's reading of the Northwest fishing rights cases construing similar treaty language, "in common with" means that the Makah are entitled only to their "fair share" of whales, and that "the Makah cannot, consistent with the plain terms of the treaty, hunt whales without regard to processes in place and designed to advance conservation values. . . ." The court claimed to be deciding only that the MMPA's permitting process and "conservation principles" applied, not whether "treaty rights must be considered and given weight [by the agency] in implementing the MMPA," whether the Tribe "may have sufficient justification to gain a permit or waiver," or whether treaty rights are abrogated by the MMPA. If, as the court concludes, the MMPA allows taking of marine mammals "only when it will not diminish the sustainability and optimum level of the resource for all citizens," and given the sorts of considerations (such as whalewatching, scientific study, and other nonconsumptive uses) that the court includes in determining what is optimum, do you expect the Makah will agree that the court has not sanctioned an abrogation of their treaty rights?

As noted in Zachary Tomlinson, *Abrogation or Regulation? How* Anderson v. Evans *Discards the Makah's Treaty Whaling Right in the Name of Conservation Necessity*, 78 WASH. L. REV. 1101 (2003), other lower courts have interpreted the scope of a state's conservation necessity power quite narrowly, all requiring proof of substantial species peril. Furthermore, the Supreme Court, in cases such as *Dion* and *Mille Lacs* (Ch. 4, Sec. A.2 and Ch. 2, Sec. C, respectively), has not used the conservation necessity principle in resolving treaty abrogation issues, but instead has required a clear indication that Congress considered and determined to override treaty rights. Can *Anderson*'s analysis be reconciled with *Dion*? If Makah whaling were really to get to the point that it jeopardized the gray whales, couldn't

Congress then exercise its acknowledged power to abrogate the Tribe's treaty right? Is the *Anderson* court usurping Congress's authority in this area?

In 1999, before the *Anderson* plaintiffs were able to secure an injunction, the Makah actually carried out one whale hunt. According to an open letter that the President of the Makah Whaling Commission sent to the SEATTLE TIMES:

> Whaling has been part of our tradition for over 2,000 years. Although we had to stop in the 1920s because of the scarcity of gray whales, their abundance now makes it possible to resume our ancient practice of whale hunting. Many of our Tribal members feel that our health problems result from the loss of our traditional sea food and sea mammal diet. We would like to restore the meat of the whale to that diet. We also believe that the problems which are troubling our young people stem from lack of discipline and pride and we hope that the restoration of whaling will help to restore that discipline and pride. But we also want to fulfill the legacy of our forefathers and restore a part of our culture which was taken from us.

SEATTLE TIMES, Aug. 23, 1998. While the *Anderson* litigation has certainly delayed further Makah whaling, it may not prevent it altogether, depending on the outcome of environmental review and permitting processes and any further litigation.

In September, 2007, several Makah tribal members, impatient with the slow pace of federal review and approvals, embarked on a whale hunt without waiting for tribal permission. While out to sea, the tribal members killed a gray whale. The Tribe prosecuted them for hunting without a tribal license, though difficulties empanelling a tribal jury led the tribal prosecutor to drop his request for a sentence of one year in jail, and limit the sentence to community service. A federal prosecution followed, which resulted in jail sentences for two of the five tribal defendants, and two years' probation for the other three. Linda V. Mapes, "2 Makahs to Serve Time for Illegally Killing Whale," SEATTLE TIMES, July 1, 2008. In May, 2008, the National Oceanic and Atmospheric Administration released a draft environmental impact report for public comment. As of early 2010, the federal environmental review process still has not been completed.

3. Pacific Northwest Shellfish Gathering Rights: In addition to providing for off-reservation fishing rights, some the Pacific Northwest treaties, particularly for more coastal tribes, included or referenced an off-reservation right to harvest shellfish, with the exception of "beds staked or cultivated by private citizens." Since most of the commercial salmon runs declined almost to the point of collapse during or, shortly after, the *Washington Passenger Fishing Vessel Association* case, many of the tribes sought other ways to economically sustain their fishing traditions, and shellfish harvesting emerged as a larger issue. The issue was exacerbated by the fact that shellfish harvesting required access to shellfish beds on the coast or Puget Sound, many of which were adjacent to privately-owned luxury residences. Just as the commercial salmon industry fought the exercise of Indian off-reservation fishing rights, private property owners blocked and otherwise fought Indians exercising off-reservation shellfish gathering rights.

In *United States v. Washington*, 157 F.2d 630 (9th Cir. 1998), sixteen western Washington tribes sought to establish their basic shellfishing rights. The Ninth

Circuit reaffirmed the principles of *Washington Passenger Fishing Vessel Association* in application to shellfish gathering. It ruled that the treaty exclusion of "beds staked or cultivated by private citizens" only applied to artificial shellfish beds created by private citizens, generally as part of a shellfish farming operation, and that the lower court had erred in excluding human enhanced natural shellfish beds from the exercise of the off-reservation right. Nevertheless, the Ninth Circuit ruled that the tribal share of the shellfish beds was limited to 50% of the available take that might have been taken from the beds had not their capacity been enhanced. It also ruled that the state of Washington was not a private citizen for purposes of the treaties and, therefore, the Indians could exercise their rights on beds created or cultivated by the State. It also ruled that while the right to conduct shellfish gathering included the right of access to the beds across private property, the district court did not abuse its discretion in either limiting access through private property only to those situations where no other feasible public access was available and in imposing reasonable time, place, and manner restrictions on such access.

4.   The Great Lakes Off-Reservation Hunting and Fishing Rights: Concurrent with the Pacific Northwest litigation, a similar series of cases arose in state and federal courts in the Great Lakes region, commencing in Michigan. At issue in the Michigan cases was the application of state gill-net fishing regulations to Indians fishing under an 1836 treaty with the Chippewa and Ottawa tribes that guaranteed "the right of hunting the lands ceded, with the other usual privileges of occupancy, until the land is required for settlement." In *People v. Le Blanc*, 248 N.W.2d 199 (Mich. 1976), the Michigan Supreme Court held that this language reserved off-reservation fishing rights for the tribes, but these rights were not exclusive and Indian fishers would be subject to state gill-net regulations under the rule in *Puyallup I*. Three years later, after extensive hearings on the historical circumstances surrounding the treaty negotiations, a federal district court rejected the *LeBlanc* construction of the treaty. Because the 1836 treaty did not contain the phrase "in common with," a crucial term of the Puyallup treaties, the District Court held that the state of Michigan had no power to regulate off-reservation fishing by Ottawa and Chippewa Indians in the Great Lakes region.

Before this ruling reached the Sixth Circuit Court of Appeals, the Department of the Interior issued regulations governing the exercise of off-reservation fishing rights. 25 C.F.R. pt. 256 (1980). On appeal, the Sixth Circuit remanded the case to determine whether these regulations preempted the force of state conservation laws over Indian treaty fishers. *United States v. Michigan*, 623 F.2d 448 (6th Cir. 1980). Before the district court could consider the case on remand, the Reagan Administration entered office and its new Secretary of the Interior announced his decision not to renew the federal regulations at issue. Despite eight years of the government's urgings to the contrary, the Secretary opined that *LeBlanc* accurately stated the law applicable to treaty fishing. In response to the state's emergency motion to set aside the remand and put in place state regulations to replace the lapsed federal regulations, the Sixth Circuit held that, indeed, *LeBlanc* did accurately state the rule of the case. *United States v. Michigan*, 653 F.2d 277 (6th Cir. 1981).

The Court of Appeals established several criteria for evaluating the state fishing regulations. The court cautioned that, under *LeBlanc*, "any such state regulations restricting Indian fishing rights under the 1836 treaty, including gill-net fishing, (a) must be a necessary conservation measure, (b) must be the least restrictive alternative method available for preserving fisheries in the Great Lakes from irreparable harm, and (c) must not discriminatorily harm Indian fishing or favor other classes of fishermen." *Id.* at 279. Moreover, the Sixth Circuit held that "[o]nly upon a finding of necessity, irreparable harm and the absence of effective Indian tribal self-regulation should the District Court sanction and permit state regulation of gill net fishing." *Id.*

When the case finally reached the District Court on remand, the court held that the federal preemption issue was moot. Nevertheless, the court retained jurisdiction to determine whether any future attempts by the state to impose regulations on treaty fishers would meet the *LeBlanc* requirements. *United States v. Michigan*, 520 F. Supp. 207 (W.D. Mich. 1981). The exercise of Indian off-reservation fishing rights in Michigan subsequently has been governed by a series of regulatory consent orders issued by the court after agreement of the parties. The first consent decree was entered in 1985 and operated to the satisfaction of neither the tribes nor the state of Michigan. A new decree was renegotiated pursuant to a long and complex mediation process and signed in a special ceremony atop a bluff on the Bay Mills Indian Community on August 7, 2000. Among other things, the 2000 consent decree works with the Chippewa Ottawa Resource Authority (CORA) formed in 2001 to serve as an inter-tribal regulatory body for the exercise of tribal off-reservation rights.

After the Michigan treaties became an issue for courts within the Sixth Circuit, treaties containing off-reservation rights involving the Chippewa and other tribes became volatile legal and political issues in Wisconsin. In an 1837 treaty with the Chippewa, Article V provided:

> The privilege of hunting, fishing and gathering the wild rice, upon the lands, the rivers and the lakes included in the territory ceded, is guarantied to the Indians during the pleasure of the President of the United States.

Treaty of St. Peters with the Chippewa Nation, July 29, 1837, 5 Stat. 158. Later treaties in 1842 and 1854, while ceding more tribal land, were silent on the preservation of this right or other off-reservation rights, although in 1850 the President purported to issue an Executive Order as part of a never implemented removal scheme to terminate the off-reservation rights. In long, volatile, and protracted litigation in Wisconsin, the courts in the Seventh Circuit established the continued vitality of the Wisconsin Chippewa's off-reservation fishing and food gathering rights under the 1837 treaty. The courts generally held that the land cessions in subsequent treaties that did not explicitly extinguish the off-reservation rights contained in the 1837 treaty did not implicitly have that effect. *E.g., Lac Courte Oreilles Band of Lake Superior Chippewa Indians v. Wisconsin*, 700 F.2d 341 (7th Cir. 1983); *Lac Courte Oreilles Band of Lake Superior Chippewa Indians v. Wisconsin*, 707 F. Supp. 1034 (W.D. Wis. 1989). For an excellent summary of the history and legal theories of the Wisconsin cases, see Charles F. Wilkinson, *To Feel the Summer in the Spring: The Treaty Fishing Rights of the Wisconsin Chippewa*, 1991 WIS. L. REV. 375.

More recently, the Menominee Tribe, relying on an 1831 treaty, unsuccessfully sought to assert off-reservation rights in Wisconsin. *Menominee Indian Tribe v. Thompson*, 161 F.3d 449 (7th Cir 1998). Specifically, the Treaty provided:

> The Menomonee [sic] tribe of Indians shall be at liberty to hunt and fish on the lands they have now ceded to the United States, on the east side of Fox river [sic] and Green bay [sic], with the same privileges they at present enjoy, until it be surveyed and offered for sale by the President; they conducting themselves peaceably and orderly.

1831 Treaty Art. Sixth at 1. Subsequently, the Menominee signed three other treaties with the United States, including one in 1848 that purported to cede all of its land in Wisconsin as prelude to a removal. That treaty, while signed and ratified, was never fully implemented as the Tribe entered into the Treaty of Wolf River of May 12, 1854 establishing its present reservation. When the Tribe filed its complaint, it attached these supportive documents and the district court granted a motion to dismiss, finding, among other things, that the 1831 Treaty rights were expressly limited by extinguishing events, which had occurred when the Tribe ceded all of its lands in Wisconsin and agreed to removal in the 1848 Treaty, notwithstanding the fact that the removal was never fully implemented. The Seventh Circuit affirmed the dismissal. It distinguished *Lac Courte Oreilles*, noting that:

> [In *Lac Courte Oreilles*] we interpreted the treaty to mean that the President would be pleased as long as the Indians lived peacefully with the settlers, and that the Indians thus had the right to use the land for as long as they remained peaceful. Our holding in *Lac Courte Oreilles* is not relevant to the question presented here. In *Lac Courte Oreilles*, the determinative issue was how to interpret the phrase "the pleasure of the President." In this case we are not set the task of analyzing the meaning of "until the President of the United States shall deem it expedient." Instead, the question is whether the terms of the treaty inextricably joined the Tribe's usufructuary rights to the Tribe's title to the land, and thus whether those usufructuary rights were extinguished when the Tribe ceded its title to the land.

161 F.3d at 460. Thus, the Seventh Circuit held that the outright cession by the Menominee Tribe of all land title in Wisconsin contained in the 1848 removal treaty extinguished the Tribe's off-reservation rights, even though the removal was later suspended by the Treaty of Wolf River of 1854.

After the resolution of most of the Wisconsin Chippewa cases, the focus of the Great Lakes litigation shifted to Minnesota, where the 1837 Chippewa Treaty was also applicable to numerous tribes. Despite initial seemingly successful efforts to settle the matter, sport fishing and tourism interests sabotaged the settlements in the state legislature and forced the state of Minnesota (within the Eighth federal circuit) to defend a claim that had already been sustained by courts in the Sixth and Seventh Circuits.

Predictably, the lower courts ruled in favor of the continued vitality of the tribal off-reservation hunting and fishing rights. *Mille Lacs Band of Chippewa Indians v. Minnesota*, 952 F. Supp. 1362 (D. Minn.), *aff'd*, 124 F.3d 904 (8th Cir. 1997). Despite the fact that the various courts in the Sixth, Seventh, and Eighth Circuit and the state of Michigan were in unanimous agreement regarding the survival of the Chippewa off-reservation fishing rights, particularly those contained in the 1837 Treaty, the United States Supreme Court, in a highly unusual decision in the face of such unanimity, granted certiorari to review the Eighth Circuit decision in *Mille Lacs*. In *Minnesota v. Mille Lacs Band of Chippewa Indians*, 526 U.S. 172 (1999), set forth and discussed in Ch. 2, Sec. C, the Supreme Court ruled 5-4 that the off-reservation fishing rights guaranteed in the 1837 Treaty survived despite later cessions in treaties in 1842 and 1854 that did not mention the prior off-reservation rights and despite the fact that President Taylor purported to issue a Presidential Order in 1850 as part of a removal effort that expressly sought to terminate the off-reservation rights. Relying heavily on the Indian law canons of treaty construction, the majority opinion, written by Justice O'Connor, followed the conventional rule that a subsequent land cession by a tribe which fails to reference earlier treaty guarantees of off-reservation rights does not extinguish those off-reservation rights where no intent to do so is demonstrated clearly and specifically from the text or history of subsequent treaties. More importantly, in light of the express provisions in section 3 of the Removal Act of 1830, § 3, 4 Stat. 411, requiring tribal consent for removal, the Court held that the removal Order of 1850 was invalid since it conflicted with an act of Congress. The Court further held that the provisions in that Order purporting to extinguish the guarantees of off-reservation fishing rights guaranteed by the 1837 Treaty were also invalid since they constituted an integral part of the removal Order and therefore were inseparable from the otherwise illegal Order, a point vigorously disputed by the dissent. In addition to sustaining the continued vitality of the off-reservation rights guaranteed by the 1837 Treaty, the Court also discussed and dismissed the continued significance of the so-called equal footing doctrine to the assertion of off-reservation hunting, fishing, and food gathering rights, as discussed in the next note.

While the *Mille Lacs* case reaffirmed Chippewa off-reservation fishing rights, at least one court has subsequently held that those rights are limited. In *United States v. Gotchnik*, 222 F.3d 506 (8th Cir. 2000), the Eighth Circuit affirmed the convictions of members of the Bois Forte Band of Chippewa Indians for using motorboats and motor vehicles to hunt and fish in the Boundary Waters Canoe Area in violation of the regulations under the federal Boundary Waters Canoe Area Wilderness Act, which closed the area to motorboats and motor vehicles. The Court held that the Act did not abrogate Chippewa off-reservation fishing rights in the area. It also conceded that tribal members could employ evolving fishing and hunting technologies in the exercise of their rights. It concluded, however, that these rights did not similarly authorize the use of modern means of transportation to reach the most desirable hunting and fishing locations in areas otherwise closed to such transportation traffic. It therefore distinguished hunting and fishing from preparatory travel. Is that a justifiable distinction?

Both the *Mille Lacs* and *Menominee* cases turned on the effect of subsequent removal efforts on off-reservation fishing and food gathering rights contained in prior treaties. *Menominee* was decided by the Seventh Circuit before the Supreme Court decision in *Mille Lacs* was handed down. Can these two cases be reconciled or does the subsequent decision in *Mille Lacs* cast doubt on the vitality of the

Menominee holding? Does it make any difference that the Menominee signed the ratified, but unimplemented, 1848 removal Treaty, while the 1850 removal Order in *Mille Lacs* constituted a Presidential initiative?

5. **The Equal Footing Doctrine and Off-Reservation Hunting, Fishing, and Food Gathering Rights:** In *Ward v. Race Horse*, 163 U.S. 504 (1896), the United States Supreme Court ruled that the treaty-guaranteed right of a tribe "to hunt on the unoccupied lands of the United States, so long as game may be found thereon, and so long as peace subsists among the whites and Indians on the borders of the hunting districts" terminated when Wyoming was admitted to statehood in 1890. Part of the rationale of the case involved the long-accepted doctrine that all states are admitted to the Union on an equal footing, *i.e.*, with the same attributes of sovereignty, as the original thirteen states. *Ward v. Race Horse* claimed that permitting the continued exercise of the off-reservation hunting rights on open lands of the state free from state regulation embarrassed and impaired that federally-guaranteed equal sovereignty. Most had assumed that the foundations of the *Ward v. Race Horse* equal footing doctrine claim had been laid to rest when the Court's decision eight years later in *United State v. Winans*, 198 U.S. 371, 382–384 (1905), set forth above, undermined its analytical foundations. Nevertheless, in *Crow Tribe of Indians v. Repsis*, 73 F.3d 982 (10th Cir. 1995), the Tenth Circuit resurrected the doctrine from near desuetude to hold that the Crow Tribe had lost certain off-reservation hunting rights contained in the 1868 Fort Laramie Treaty when Wyoming became a state. As *Mille Lacs* demonstrates, however, this rejuvenation of the equal footing doctrine in Indian off-reservation hunting and fishing cases proved to be short lived. Justice O'Connor's opinion points out:

> *Race Horse* rested on a false premise, namely that an Indian tribe's treaty rights to hunt, fish, and gather on state land are not irreconcilable with a State's sovereignty over the natural resources in the State. The state's rights to protect wildlife are not absolute, and must coexist with federal power to make treaties with the Indians. Moreover, the Indians' treaty-based rights are not absolute either, but are subject to state authority to impose reasonable and necessary nondiscriminatory regulations on Indian hunting, fishing, and gathering rights in the interest of conservation. Thus, because treaty rights are reconcilable with state sovereignty over natural resources, statehood by itself is insufficient to extinguish Indian treaty rights to hunt, fish, and gather on land within state boundaries. Justice O'Connor noted in conclusion that "there is nothing inherent in the nature of reserved treaty rights to suggest that they can be extinguished by implication at statehood. Treaty rights are not impliedly terminated upon statehood.

526 U.S. at 204–207.

6. **Federal Power and Off-Reservation Rights:** Could the President issue an Executive Order today terminating the Chippewa off-reservation fishing and food gathering rights guaranteed under the 1837 Treaty? If he did so, would the various Chippewa tribes have a viable takings claims against the United States that they could bring in the United States Court of Federal Claims under the Indian Tucker Act, 28 U.S.C. § 1505? Could the President issue such an extinguishment order with

respect to the off-reservation hunting, fishing, and food gathering rights of the Pacific Northwest tribes guaranteed in the Stevens treaties? Would federal extinguishment of those rights, however accomplished, constitute an actionable taking?

B. COMPETITION FOR CONTROL OF WATER

Indian water rights are to the late twentieth and early twenty-first centuries what Indian land rights were to the nineteenth century. In the Mountain Basin and the Southwest, water is in exceedingly short supply and the competition for it is intense. It is water ownership, not land ownership, that primarily dictates development. Yet, the extent of Indian title to most water in this area is indefinite. Many of the same utilitarian arguments made with respect to land in the nineteenth century have been applied to water in the last several decades. The question often becomes not who owns the water but how can it best be used: for the reservations and their relatively few inhabitants or for the industrial metropolises of the Southwest?

Water rights are as critical for Indian well-being and development now as land rights were in the late nineteenth century. As with land, Congress has assumed enormous powers in the definition of Indian rights to water. And the pressures and techniques to encourage Indian consent to the modification of Indian water rights are strikingly reminiscent of the acquisitive practices of the non-Indian community during the nineteenth century. Faced with costly and uncertain litigation outcomes, as well as tremendous needs for investment capital to make water rights actually useable, Native nations increasingly have turned to negotiated settlements as the way to make their water rights into building blocks for real nation-building.

In order to understand the nature of Indian water rights, a basic knowledge of western water is in order as background. Unlike water-rich eastern riparian states, in the western states the doctrine of "prior appropriation" controls. The prior appropriation doctrine holds that actual beneficial use of the water is the basis of the property right. The owner is entitled to take a specific quantity of water, deriving from his beneficial use, and such water user's priority to that amount of water dates from the time it was first applied to such beneficial uses. This scheme creates a temporal and quantitative ladder of priorities among competing water users. Just as important is the rule governing what happens in time of shortage. During shortages, the senior appropriator's right is satisfied *in full* before the junior appropriator obtains any of his share. The theory of Indian water rights is inconsistent with both these elements of western water law. As reflected in the *Winters* case, set forth below, the Indian right to the water does not depend on present use or priority but, rather, on future need. The seniority of the right usually is not measured by the date of first beneficial use of the right. Rather, Indian rights date from reservation creation.

Water rights are important to understand because of their relationship to the underlying philosophy of development of the land to which they apply. The western law of prior appropriation rests on basic and fundamental assumptions about the value of using, presently, a scarce and important resource. It is a harsh, pragmatic, pioneer doctrine that places a premium on development and has little regard for conservation. The assumptions underlying the Indian reserved rights doctrine, as will be seen, are far different. The seeming conflict between the two — an ideological and economic conflict — is reflected in FRANK TRELEASE, FEDERAL-STATE RELATIONS IN WATER LAW (1971), and in the important water law study for which the Trelease report was a foundation, UNITED STATES NATIONAL WATER COMMISSION, WATER POLICIES FOR THE FUTURE, FINAL REPORT TO THE PRESIDENT AND TO THE CONGRESS OF THE UNITED STATES (1972). *See also* Harold A. Ranquist, *The* Winters *Doctrine and How It Grew: Federal Reservation of Rights to the Use of Water*, 1975 B.Y.U. L. REV. 639.

1.   Source, Quantity, and Use of Indian Water Rights

WINTERS v. UNITED STATES
United States Supreme Court
207 U.S. 564 (1908)

[After the United States obtained cessions of land from the Gros Ventre and Assiniboine Tribes, patents were issued to individuals who wished to establish farms upstream on the Milk River. Some years after those farmers had established diversion and irrigation works, the United States determined to build irrigation works for the Indian reservation to enable farming to take place there. The contest arose because the water available was insufficient to meet the needs both of the upstream farmers and the Indian reservation. Under western water law, the prior appropriation by the farmers of Milk River water for irrigation purposes should prevail, but it did not due to the nature of Indian water rights established in this opinion.]

MR. JUSTICE MCKENNA delivered the opinion of the Court.

[This] case, as we view it, turns on the agreement of May, 1888, resulting in the creation of Fort Belknap Reservation. In the construction of this agreement there are certain elements to be considered that are prominent and significant. The reservation was a part of a very much larger tract which the Indians had the right to occupy and use and which was adequate for the habits and wants of a nomadic and uncivilized people. It was the policy of the Government, it was the desire of the Indians, to change those habits and to become a pastoral and civilized people. If they should become such the original tract was too extensive, but a smaller tract would be inadequate without a change of conditions. The lands were arid and, without irrigation, were practically valueless. And yet, it is contended, the means of irrigation were deliberately given up by the Indians and deliberately accepted by the Government. The lands ceded were, it is true, also arid; and some argument may be urged, and is urged, that with their cession there was the cession of the waters, without which they would be valueless, and "civilized communities could not be established thereon." And this, it is further contended, the Indians knew, and yet made no reservation of the waters. We realize that there is a conflict of implications, but that which makes for the retention of the waters is of greater force than that which makes for their cession. The Indians had command of the lands and the waters — command of all their beneficial use, whether kept for hunting, "and grazing roving herds of stock," or turned to agriculture and the arts of civilization.

Did they give up all this? Did they reduce the area of their occupation and give up the waters which made it valuable or adequate? And, even regarding the allegation of the answer as true, that there are springs and streams on the reservation flowing about 2,900 inches of water, the inquiries are pertinent. If it were possible to believe affirmative answers, we might also believe that the Indians were awed by the power of the Government or deceived by its negotiators. Neither view is possible. The Government is asserting the rights of the Indians. But extremes need not be taken into account. By a rule of interpretation of agreements and treaties with the Indians, ambiguities occurring will be resolved from the standpoint of the Indians. And the rule should certainly be applied to determine between two inferences, one of which would support the purpose of the agreement and the other impair or defeat it. On account of their relations to the Government, it cannot be supposed that the Indians were alert to exclude by formal words every inference which might militate against or defeat the declared purpose of themselves and the Government, even if it could be supposed that they had the intelligence to foresee the "double sense" which might some time be urged against them.

Another contention of appellants is that if it be conceded that there was a reservation of the waters of Milk River by the agreement of 1888, yet the reservation was repealed by the admission of Montana into the Union, February 22, 1889, c. 180, 25 Stat. 676, "upon an equal footing with the original States." The language of counsel is that "any reservation in the agreement with the Indians, expressed or implied, whereby the waters of Milk River were not to be subject of appropriation by the citizens and inhabitants of said State, was repealed by the act of admission." But to establish the repeal counsel rely substantially upon the same argument that they advance against the intention of the agreement to reserve the waters. The power of the Government to reserve the waters and exempt them from appropriation under the state laws is not denied, and could not be. *The United States v. The Rio Grande Ditch & Irrigation Co.*, 174 U.S. 690, 702; *United States v. Winans*, 198 U.S. 371. That the Government did reserve them we have decided, and for a use which would be necessarily continued through years. This was done May 1, 1888, and it would be extreme to believe that within a year Congress destroyed the reservation and took from the Indians the consideration of their grant, leaving them a barren waste — took from them the means of continuing their old habits, yet did not leave them the power to change to new ones.

Appellants' argument upon the incidental repeal of the agreement by the admission of Montana into the Union and the power over the waters of Milk River which the State thereby acquired to dispose of them under its laws, is elaborate and able, but our construction of the agreement and its effect make it unnecessary to answer the argument in detail. For the same reason we have not discussed the doctrine of riparian rights urged by the Government.

[*Affirmed.*]

ARIZONA v. CALIFORNIA
United States Supreme Court
373 U.S. 546 (1963)

MR. JUSTICE BLACK delivered the opinion of the Court.

[T]he United States has asserted claims to waters in the main [Colorado] river and in some of the tributaries for use on Indian Reservations, National Forests, Recreational and Wildlife Areas and other government lands and works. While the Master passed upon some of these claims, he declined to reach others, particularly those relating to tributaries. We approve his decision as to which claims required adjudication, and likewise we approve the decree he recommended for the government claims he did decide. We shall discuss only the claims of the United States on behalf of the Indian Reservations.

The Government, on behalf of five Indian Reservations in Arizona, California, and Nevada, asserted rights to water in the mainstream of the Colorado River.[13] The Colorado River Reservation, located partly in Arizona and partly in California, is the largest. It was originally created by an Act of Congress in 1865, but its area was later increased by Executive Order. Other reservations were created by Executive Orders and amendments to them, ranging in dates from 1870 to 1907. The Master found both as a matter of fact and law that when the United States created these reservations or added to them, it reserved not only land but also the use of enough water from the Colorado to irrigate the irrigable portions of the reserved lands. The aggregate quantity of water which the Master held was reserved for all the reservations is about 1,000,000 acre-feet, to be used on around 135,000 irrigable acres of land. Here, as before the Master, Arizona argues that the United States had no power to make a reservation of navigable waters after Arizona became a State; that navigable waters could not be reserved by Executive Orders; that the United States did not intend to reserve water for the Indian Reservations; that the amount of water reserved should be measured by the reasonably foreseeable needs of the Indians living on the reservation rather than by the number of irrigable acres; and, finally, that the judicial doctrine of equitable apportionment should be used to divide the water between the Indians and the other people in the State of Arizona.

The last argument is easily answered. The doctrine of equitable apportionment is a method of resolving water disputes between States. It was created by this Court in the exercise of its original jurisdiction over controversies in which States are parties. An Indian Reservation is not a State. And while Congress has sometimes left Indian Reservations considerable power to manage their own affairs, we are not convinced by Arizona's argument that each reservation is so much like a State that its rights to water should be determined by the doctrine of equitable apportionment. Moreover, even were we to treat an Indian Reservation like a State, equitable apportionment would still not control since, under our view, the Indian claims here are governed by the statutes and Executive Orders creating the reservations.

---

[13] [97] The Reservations were Chemehuevi, Cocopah, Yuma, Colorado River and Fort Mohave.

Arizona's contention that the Federal Government had no power, after Arizona became a State, to reserve waters for the use and benefit of federally reserved lands rests largely upon statements in *Pollard's Lessee v. Hagan*, 3 How. 212 (1845), and *Shively v. Bowlby*, 152 U.S. 1 (1894). Those cases and others that followed them gave rise to the doctrine that lands underlying navigable waters within territory acquired by the Government are held in trust for future States and that title to such lands is automatically vested in the States upon admission to the Union. But those cases involved only the shores of and lands beneath navigable waters. They do not determine the problem before us and cannot be accepted as limiting the broad powers of the United States to regulate navigable waters under the Commerce Clause and to regulate government lands under Art. IV, § 3, of the Constitution. We have no doubt about the power of the United States under these clauses . . . to reserve water rights for its reservations and its property.

Arizona also argues that, in any event, water rights cannot be reserved by Executive Order. Some of the reservations of Indian lands here involved were made almost 100 years ago, and all of them were made over 45 years ago. In our view, these reservations, like those created directly by Congress, were not limited to land, but included waters as well. Congress and the Executive have ever since recognized these as Indian Reservations. Numerous appropriations, including appropriations for irrigation projects, have been made by Congress. They have been uniformly and universally treated as reservations by map makers, surveyors, and the public. We can give but short shrift at this late date to the argument that the reservations either of land or water are invalid because they were originally set apart by the Executive.[14]

Arizona also challenges the Master's holding as to the Indian Reservations on two other grounds; first, that there is a lack of evidence showing that the United States in establishing the reservations intended to reserve water for them; second, that even if water was meant to be reserved the Master has awarded too much water. We reject both of these contentions. Most of the land in these reservations is and always has been arid. If the water necessary to sustain life is to be had, it must come from the Colorado River or its tributaries. It can be said without overstatement that when the Indians were put on these reservations they were not considered to be located in the most desirable area of the Nation. It is impossible to believe that when Congress created the great Colorado River Indian Reservation and when the Executive Department of this Nation created the other reservations they were unaware that most of the lands were of the desert kind — hot, scorching sands — and that water from the river would be essential to the life of the Indian people and to the animals they hunted and the crops they raised. In the debate leading to approval of the first congressional appropriation for irrigation of the Colorado River Indian Reservation, the delegate from the Territory of Arizona made this statement:

> Irrigating canals are essential to the prosperity of these Indians. Without water there can be no production, no life; and all they ask of you is to give them a few agricultural implements to enable them to dig an irrigating

---

[14] [102] See *United States v. Midwest Oil Co.*, 236 U.S. 459, 469–475 (1915); *Winters v. United States*, 207 U.S. 564 (1908).

canal by which their lands may be watered and their fields irrigated, so that they may enjoy the means of existence. You must provide these Indians with the means of subsistence or they will take by robbery from those who have. During the last year I have seen a number of these Indians starved to death for want of food. Cong. Globe, 38th Cong., 2d Sess. 1321 (1865).

[In *Winters*, the Court] concluded that the Government, when it created that Indian Reservation, intended to deal fairly with the Indians by reserving for them the waters without which their lands would have been useless. *Winters* has been followed by this Court as recently as 1939 in *United States v. Powers*, 305 U.S. 527. We follow it now and agree that the United States did reserve the water rights for the Indians effective as of the time the Indian Reservations were created. This means, as the Master held, that these water rights, having vested before the Act became effective on June 25, 1929, are "present perfected rights" and as such are entitled to priority under the Act.

We also agree with the Master's conclusion as to the quantity of water intended to be reserved. He found that the water was intended to satisfy the future as well as the present needs of the Indian Reservations and ruled that enough water was reserved to irrigate all the practicably irrigable acreage on the reservations. Arizona, on the other hand, contends that the quantity of water reserved should be measured by the Indians' "reasonably foreseeable needs," which, in fact, means by the number of Indians. How many Indians there will be and what their future needs will be can only be guessed. We have concluded, as did the Master, that the only feasible and fair way by which reserved water for the reservations can be measured is irrigable acreage. The various acreages of irrigable land which the Master found to be on the different reservations we find to be reasonable. . . .

NOTES ON *WINTERS* RIGHTS

1. **Meaning of the Reserved Rights Doctrine:** The reserved rights doctrine has been interpreted in distinct ways with important differences in implication. As enunciated in the *Winters* case, the doctrine stands for the proposition that, on making a treaty with the United States, the Indians *themselves* reserved for their own use sufficient water to make their reservations productive. Thus, "when the Indians made the treaty granting rights to the United States, they reserved the right to use the waters of Milk River, at least to an extent reasonably necessary to irrigate their lands. The right so reserved continues to exist against the United States and its grantees, as well as against the state and its grantees." *Winters v. United States*, 143 F. 740, 749 (9th Cir. 1906).

The second interpretation of the reserved rights doctrine holds that when the United States created the various Indian reservations, the United States reserved the necessary water from the adjacent rivers and streams for those reservations. Thus, in *Arizona v. California*, "[t]he Master found both as a matter of fact and law that when the United States created these reservations or added to them, it reserved not only land but also the use of enough water from the Colorado to irrigate the irrigable portions of the reserved lands." The Supreme Court went on to hold that "[w]e have no doubt about the power of the United States to reserve water rights for its reservations and its property." Under this theory, the reservations for Indian use are much like federal reservations for other uses, such as national forests or parks. The *Winters* construction of the reserved rights doctrine gives greater recognition to tribal sovereignty and may suggest entitlement to a greater quantum of water. Under this interpretation, the reserved water rights may be seen as recognized property rights vested in the Indians, which may be defended against all comers, including the United States; therefore, the taking of such property is compensable. In *Arizona v. California (Arizona I)*, 373 U.S. at 595–601, the Supreme Court seemed to adopt a public domain theory with respect to such land. When the federal government removes land from the public domain for federal uses — including Indian reservations — it has the power also to reserve sufficient water from the public domain for use on these lands. *See also Report of the Special Master* in *Arizona v. California*, 259 (1960): "In the *Winters* case the United States exercised its power to reserve water by treaty; but the power itself stems from the United States' property rights in the water, not from the treaty power." While the original *Winters* construction of the reserved rights doctrine is more compatible with vested Indian property rights in the reserved water, the second interpretation is more easily reconcilable with the protection of Indian water rights on reservations that were created not by treaty but by act of Congress or executive order.

Regardless of which construction is placed upon the reserved rights doctrine, however, it is clear that Indians on reservations — no matter how the reservation was created — have the right to use sufficient water from included and adjacent streams and rivers and groundwater to make those reservations productive, that the Indian water right is superior to all subsequently created state water rights, and that it is when created unquantified, albeit not unquantifiable. Reserved rights attach to reservations whether or not the instruments creating them mention water rights. Water rights were not mentioned in the treaty involved in the *Winters* case nor in the act of Congress and executive orders creating the Indian reservations involved in *Arizona v. California*. In both cases, the Supreme Court held that an implied reservation of water rights was made at the time the Indian reservations were created.

The right to control and have access to available water has been one of absolute necessity for Indians living on arid reservations. Without reserving existing water rights, these reservations would be useless. This point was recognized by the courts as early as 1905 when the Supreme Court held that certain rights necessary to the development of the reservation, such as fishing, hunting, and water, were reserved by the Indians rather than granted to the United States. *United States v. Winans*, set forth and discussed in the preceding section. For a history of the *Winters* decision that emphasizes the period in which the decision was made, see JOHN SHURTS, INDIAN RESERVED WATER RIGHTS: THE *WINTERS* DOCTRINE AND ITS SOCIAL AND LEGAL CONTEXT, 1880–1930 (2000).

2. Scope of Indian Water Rights: Both *Winters* and *Arizona v. California* (*Arizona I*) suggest that the scope of Indian water rights may be summarized as follows:

> a. State-created water rights in existence before the date the reservation was created are superior to the reserved right; those state-created water rights arising thereafter are subordinate.

b. The reserved right, unlike state-created appropriative rights, does not depend upon diversion from the stream and application to beneficial use. The reserved right arises when the reservation is established even though the water right is not exercised for decades thereafter. In this respect the right is like a riparian right. In time of shortage, however, it is unlike a riparian right, for it does not share the available supply pro rata but rather takes its place on the priority schedule and receives water ahead of all rights of later date.

c. The federal reserved right need not be created or exercised in accordance with state law. Not only does creation of the reserved right not depend on diversion of water and application of it to beneficial use, but the right does not depend upon a filing with the state water agency or upon recording of the claim and it is not subject to state laws on forfeiture and abandonment.

d. The quantity of water to be enjoyed under a reserved right is measured by the quantity necessary to fulfill the purposes of the reservation, both at the present time and in the future.

Arizona v. California quantified this amount for the Indian reservations as the amount of water necessary to irrigate all the irrigable land on each reservation. This quantity represents for those reservations the amount of water they are entitled to for all time unless, of course, the reservations are enlarged by additional withdrawals. For the five Indian reservations and two wildlife refuges involved in that case, reserved water rights aggregated just under one million acre-feet in diversions. *Arizona v. California (Arizona II)*, 376 U.S. 340 (1964); *see also Arizona v. California (Arizona III)*, 439 U.S. 419 (1979). *See generally* Charles Meyers, *The Colorado River*, 19 STAN. L. REV. 1, 65–66 (1966). Subject to changes to technology, practicably irrigable acreage (often known in the litigation as the PIA standard) constitutes a relatively determinative and predictable standard facilitating settlement since the size and amount of irrigable acreage of a reservation are readily ascertained and not subject to sizable variation. For that reason, it has been an attractive formula for the judiciary. What if a reservation was formed for other purposes, however, such as to preserve timber habitat or to preserve a tribal fishery? Should the standard change?

3. Indian Water Rights Based on Theories Other than the Reserved Rights Doctrine: The reasoning of *Winters* assumes a bargained arrangement where water was reserved for the prospering of the reserved lands. Is the *Winters* reasoning applicable in the context, say, of New Mexico Pueblos where the land now held has been held from time immemorial and there has been no cession, treaty, or executive agreement establishing the Pueblo? In *New Mexico v. Aamodt*, 537 F.2d 1102 (10th Cir. 1976), the court held that when Congress confirmed the Pueblos' title to their land in 1858, no reservation of either land or water was created for the Indians. Therefore, the later recognition of reserved water rights under *Winters* may not be applicable to the Pueblos. This point was made more recently in *State ex rel. Martinez v. Kerr-McGee Corp.*, 898 P.2d 1256, 1265 (N.M. Ct. App. 1995). Since *Winters* reasoning may not be directly applicable, should Pueblo lands be bound by state rules governing appropriation of water? The *New Mexico v. Aamodt* court said no, stating that the federal government had not relinquished jurisdiction and control over the Pueblos as trustee and guardian when it relinquished the fee title. *See* Note, *Water Law: Pueblo Indians' Water Rights*, 54 DEN. L.J. 302 (1977). The court indicated that the Pueblos' claim to water was derived from their aboriginal rights, which are established by continuous and exclusive use of property over a long period of time and which were recognized by the United States under the Treaty of Guadalupe Hidalgo to the extent recognized by the prior Spanish and Mexican sovereigns. *See* James L. Merrill, *Aboriginal Water Rights*, 20 NAT. RESOURCES J. 45 (1980). For a thorough discussion of Pueblo water rights, see NELL JESSUP NEWTON ET AL., COHEN'S HANDBOOK OF FEDERAL INDIAN LAW § 4.07[2][c] (2005 ed.). Are Pueblo aboriginal water rights any less "paper" rights than the Navajo reserved rights? Also, will there be any less temptation to agree to extinguishment of potentially substantial, but possibly historically unverifiable, aboriginal rights for immediate monetary compensation or promises of economic assistance?

Besides the reserved right to a particular quantity of water, is there a right to a particular quality of water embedded in the *Winters* doctrine? Off-reservation activities — whether agricultural, industrial, or silvicultural — can potentially affect the water quality on reservation, and thus may impact Indian farm and fishery efforts. Assuming the existence of a reserved right, can it be satisfied by the delivery of nonpotable or overly saline water? Consider, for example, both the high salinity of the Colorado River by the time it approaches the Mexican border, and the presence of a portion of the Cocopah Indian Reservation on its bank in the southwestern corner of Arizona. *See* ALAN P. KLEINMAN & BRUCE N. BROWN, COLORADO RIVER SALINITY: IMPACTS ON AGRICULTURAL, MUNICIPAL, AND INDUSTRIAL USERS, WATER AND POWER RESOURCES SERVICES (Dec. 1981).

IN RE GENERAL ADJUDICATION OF ALL RIGHTS TO USE WATER IN GILA RIVER SYSTEM AND SOURCE
Arizona Supreme Court
35 P.3d 68 (2001)

[As part of the on-going general stream adjudication to rights in water of the Gila River system, which affects perhaps two-thirds of the state, the Arizona Supreme Court heard an interlocutory appeal of a number of issues pending in the matter. Among the issues posed to the court was the applicability of the PIA standard to all of the tribes affected by the litigation. While some of the tribes in valley areas were large tribes with sizable irrigable acreage that had a long history as irrigation farmers, others held upland, mountainous, forested reservations with little irrigable acreage. Application of the PIA standard therefore had varying impacts on the affected tribes. The Arizona Supreme Court found that in adjudicating the tribes' rights under the *Winters* reserved water rights doctrine the state trial court was not bound by the PIA standard of *Arizona v. California*.]

CHIEF JUSTICE ZLAKET

Indian reservations . . . are different. In its role as trustee of such lands, the government must act for the Indians' benefit. *See United States v. Mitchell*, 463 U.S.

206, 225–26 (1983). This fiduciary relationship is referred to as "one of the primary cornerstones of Indian law." Felix S. Cohen, Handbook of Federal Indian Law 221 (1982). Thus, treaties, statutes, and executive orders are construed liberally in the Indians' favor. *County of Yakima v. Confederated Tribes & Bands of the Yakima Indian Nation*, 502 U.S. 251, 269 (1992) (citations omitted). Such an approach is equally applicable to the federal government's actions with regard to water for Indian reservations. "The purposes of Indian reserved rights . . . are given broader interpretation in order to further the federal goal of Indian self sufficiency."

The parties dispute the purposes of the several Indian reservations involved in this case. The United States and the tribal litigants argue that federal case law has preemptively determined that every Indian reservation was established as a permanent tribal homeland. The state litigants disagree, contending instead that the trial court must analyze each tribe's treaty or enabling documentation to determine that reservation's individual purpose. We need not decide whether federal case law has preemptively determined the issue. We agree with the Supreme Court that the essential purpose of Indian reservations is to provide Native American people with a "permanent home and abiding place," *Winters*, 207 U.S. at 565, that is, a "livable" environment. *Arizona I*, 373 U.S. at 599.

While courts may choose to examine historical documents in determining the purpose and reason for creating a federal reservation on non-Indian lands, the utility of such an exercise with respect to Indian reservations is highly questionable.[15] This is so for a variety of reasons.

First, as pointed out by the state litigants, many Indian reservations were pieced together over time. For example, the boundaries of the Gila River Indian Community changed ten times from its creation in 1859 until 1915, resulting in overall growth from 64,000 to 371,422 acres. But some of the changes along the way actually decreased the size of the reservation or limited the scope of previous additions. If these alterations had different purposes, as the state litigants suggest, it might be argued that water reserved to a specific parcel could not be utilized elsewhere on the same reservation, or that water once available could no longer be accessed. Such an arbitrary patchwork of water rights would be unworkable and inconsistent with the concept of a permanent, unified homeland.

A second problem lies in the fact that congressional intent to reserve water for tribal land is not express, but implied. As Franks points out, "because the intent is merely imputed — that is, its historical reality is irrelevant for purposes of establishing reserved rights — it seems strained to impute an historical definition to that imputed intent for the purpose of quantifying an extremely valuable right to a scarce resource."

Courts construe Indian treaties according to the way in which the Indians

---

[15] [2] One commentator, in fact, suggests that "the effort to inform the quantification of federal [Indian] reserved rights with historical considerations is futile and should be abandoned." Martha C. Franks, *The Uses of the Practicably Irrigable Acreage Standard in the Quantification of Reserved Water Rights*, 31 Nat. Resources J. 549, 563 (1991). While we generally agree with this observation, we believe that tribal history may play an important role in quantifying the amount of water necessary to fulfill an Indian reservation's purpose as a permanent homeland.

themselves would have understood them. *Minnesota v. Mille Lacs Band of Chippewa Indians*, 526 U.S. 172, 196 (1999) (citations omitted). But the historical search for a reservation's purpose tends to focus only on the motives of Congress — tribal intent is easily and often left out of the equation. It is doubtful that any tribe would have agreed to surrender its freedom and be confined on a reservation without some assurance that sufficient water would be provided for its well-being.

The most recognizable difficulty with the historical approach is that many documents do not accurately represent the true reasons for which Indian reservations were created. It is well known that in the nineteenth century, the federal government made conflicting promises. On one hand, it offered white settlers free land, an abundance of resources, and safety if they would travel to and inhabit the West. The government also assured Indians that they would be able to live on their lands in peace. The promises to the tribes were not kept. As recognized in 1863 by the Superintendent of Indian Affairs, M. Steck, the invasion of white settlement caused the Apache Indian people to be

> divested . . . of all their peculiar and former means of subsistence, in contending with a race who, under the circumstances, can feel no sympathy with them, [such that] the Indian must soon be swept from the face of the earth. If every red man were a Spartan, they would find it impossible to withstand this overpowering influx of immigration. Humanity and religion, therefore, demand of us that we interpose a barrier for their safety. . . .

S. Rep. 102-133, at 2 (1991). Even after this humanitarian "barrier" was imposed, however, General William T. Sherman made clear that "if [the Indians] wander outside they at once become objects of suspicion, liable to be attacked by the troops as hostile." In a November 9, 1871 letter to the Secretary of War, Sherman closed by stating that General Crook, head of the Army in Arizona, "may feel assured that whatever measures of severity he may adopt to reduce these Apaches to a peaceful and subordinate condition will be approved by the War Department and the President."

Despite what may be set forth in official documents, the fact is that Indians were forced onto reservations so that white settlement of the West could occur unimpeded. See Walter Rusinek, Note, *A Preview of Coming Attractions?* Wyoming v. United States *and the Reserved Rights Doctrine*, 17 Ecology L.Q. 355, 406 (1990) ("Cynical motives aside, the goals of the reservation system were to move Indian tribes out of the path of white settlement, provide them a homeland, and 'civilize' individual tribal members, often by attempting to transform them into yeoman farmers."). As recognized by former Arizona Congressman Morris K. Udall, the federal government "can be kindly described as having been less than diligent in its efforts to secure sufficient water supplies for the [Indian] community to develop its arable lands and achieve meaningful economic self-sufficiency and self-determination." 134 Cong. Rec. E562-02 (Mar. 8, 1988) (statement of Rep. Udall).

The trial court here failed to recognize any particular purpose for these Indian reservations, only finding that the PIA standard should be applied when quantifying tribes' water rights. It is apparent that the judge was leery of being "drawn into a potential racial controversy" based on historical documentation. But it seems clear to us that each of the Indian reservations in question was created as a "permanent home and abiding place" for the Indian people, as explained in *Winters*. This conclusion comports with the belief that "[t]he general purpose, to provide a home for the Indians, is a broad one and must be liberally construed." *Colville Confederated Tribes v. Walton*, 647 F.2d 42, 47 (9th Cir. 1981). Such a construction is necessary for tribes to achieve the twin goals of Indian self-determination and economic self-sufficiency. See Yavapai-Prescott Indian Tribe Water Rights Settlement Act of 1994, Pub. L. 103-434, § 102(a)(1), 108 Stat. 4526, 4526; Fort McDowell Indian Community Water Rights Settlement Act of 1990, Pub. L. 101-628, § 402(a)(1), 104 Stat. 4469, 4480; *Greely*, 712 P.2d at 768.

Limiting an Indian reservation's purpose to agriculture, as the PIA standard implicitly does,

> assumes that the Indian peoples will not enjoy the same style of evolution as other people, nor are they to have the benefits of modern civilization. I would understand that the homeland concept assumes that the homeland will not be a static place frozen in an instant of time but that the homeland will evolve and will be used in different ways as the Indian society develops.

In re General Adjudication of All Rights to Use Water in the Big Horn River System, 753 P.2d 76, 119 (Wyo.1988) (Thomas, J., dissenting) [*Big Horn I*]; *see also Walton*, 647 F.2d at 47 (stating that courts consider Indians' "need to maintain themselves under changed circumstances" when determining a reservation's purpose).[16]

. . . .

D. Quantifying Winters Rights

The *Winters* doctrine retains the concept of "minimal need" by reserving "only that amount of water necessary to fulfill the purpose of the reservation, no more." The method utilized in arriving at such an amount, however, must satisfy both present and future needs of the reservation as a livable homeland.

E. The PIA Standard

The trial court in this matter held that each Indian reservation was entitled to "the amount of water necessary to irrigate all of the practicably irrigable acreage

---

[16] [4] Even where reservations were created so that tribes could engage in agricultural pursuits, Congress only envisioned this as "a first step in the 'civilizing'." *In re the General Adjudication of all Rights to Use Water in the Big Horn River System*, 835 P.2d 273, 278–79 (Wyo.1992) [*Big Horn II*] (following the test). Nevertheless, we believe the significant differences between Indian and non-Indian reservations preclude application of the test to the former. As Judge Canby has noted, "[w]hile the purpose for which the federal government reserves other types of lands may be strictly construed, the purposes of Indian reservations are necessarily entitled to broader interpretation if the goal of Indian self-sufficiency is to be attained." W. Canby, American Indian Law 245–46 (1981) (citation omitted); see also Yavapai-Prescott Indian Tribe Water Rights Settlement Act of 1994, Pub. L. 103-434, § 102(a)(1), 108 Stat. 4526 (declaring United States' policy "to promote Indian self-determination and economic self-sufficiency"). Parenthetically, even if the New Mexico test were to apply, tribes would be entitled to the full measure of their reserved rights because water use necessary to the establishment of a permanent homeland is a primary, not secondary, purpose.

(P.I.A.) on that reservation." The PIA standard was developed by Special Master Rifkind in *Arizona I*, 373 U.S. 546 (1963). That case dealt with the water rights of similarly-situated tribes in Arizona, California, and Nevada. Without much amplification, the Supreme Court declared:

> We also agree with the Master's conclusion as to the quantity of water intended to be reserved. He found that the water was intended to satisfy the future as well as the present needs of the Indian Reservations and ruled that enough water was reserved to irrigate all the practicably irrigable acreage on the reservations.

Id. at 600. Other courts have since adopted the PIA standard in quantifying reserved water rights for Indian tribes. *See Walton*, 647 F.2d at 47–48 (applying PIA "to provide a homeland for the Indians to maintain their agrarian society"); *Greely*, 712 P.2d at 764 (utilizing PIA to fulfill a reservation's agricultural purpose).

PIA constitutes "those acres susceptible to sustained irrigation at reasonable costs." This implies a two-step process. First, it must be shown that crops can be grown on the land, considering arability and the engineering practicality of irrigation. Second, the economic feasibility of irrigation must be demonstrated. *See generally Arizona v. California*, 460 U.S. 605 (1983) [*Arizona II*] (adopting the Special Master's PIA analysis requiring this methodology); Andrew C. Mergen & Sylvia F. Liu, *A Misplaced Sensitivity: The Draft Opinions in* Wyoming v. United States, 68 U. COLO. L. REV. 683, 696 (1997) (acknowledging that, since *Arizona II*, the economic feasibility requirement in PIA analysis has "become the norm"). This is accomplished by subjecting proposed irrigation projects to a cost-benefit analysis, "comparing the likely costs of the project to the likely financial returns. If the latter outweighs the former, the project can be found economically feasible, and the underlying land 'practicably irrigable'. . . . "

The United States and tribal litigants argue that federal case law has preemptively established PIA as the standard by which to quantify reserved water rights on Indian reservations. We disagree. As observed by Special Master Tuttle in his *Arizona II* report, "the Court did not necessarily adopt this standard as the universal measure of Indian reserved water rights. . . ." Indeed, nothing in *Arizona I* or *II* suggests otherwise.

On its face, PIA appears to be an objective method of determining water rights. But while there may be some "value of the certainty inherent in the practicably irrigable acreage standard," its flaws become apparent on closer examination.

The first objection to an across-the-board application of PIA lies in its potential for inequitable treatment of tribes based solely on geographical location. Arizona's topography is such that some tribes inhabit flat alluvial plains while others dwell in steep, mountainous areas. This diversity creates a dilemma that PIA cannot solve. As stated by two commentators:

> There can be little doubt that the PIA standard works to the advantage of tribes inhabiting alluvial plains or other relatively flat lands adjacent to stream courses. In contrast, tribes inhabiting mountainous or other agriculturally marginal terrains are at a severe disadvantage when it comes to demonstrating that their lands are practicably irrigable.

Mergen & Liu, supra, at 695. Tribes who fail to show either the engineering or economic feasibility of proposed irrigation projects run the risk of not receiving any reserved water under PIA. *See, e.g., State ex rel. Martinez v. Lewis*, 116 N.M. 194, 861 P.2d 235, 246–51 (Ct. App. 1993) (denying water rights to the Mescalero Apache Tribe, situated in a mountainous region of southern New Mexico, for failure to prove irrigation projects were economically feasible). This inequity is unacceptable and inconsistent with the idea of a permanent homeland.

Another concern with PIA is that it forces tribes to pretend to be farmers in an era when "large agricultural projects . . . are risky, marginal enterprises. This is demonstrated by the fact that no federal project planned in accordance with the Principles and Guidelines [adopted by the Water Resources Council of the Federal Government] has been able to show a positive benefit/cost ratio in the last decade [1981 to 1991]." A permanent homeland requires water for multiple uses, which may or may not include agriculture. The PIA standard, however, forces "tribes to prove economic feasibility for a kind of enterprise that, judging from the evidence of both federal and private willingness to invest money, is simply no longer economically feasible in the West."

Limiting the applicable inquiry to a PIA analysis not only creates a temptation for tribes to concoct inflated, unrealistic irrigation projects, but deters consideration of actual water needs based on realistic economic choices. We again agree with the analysis of Justice Richard V. Thomas in *Big Horn I:*

> I would be appalled . . . if the Congress . . . began expending money to develop water projects for irrigating these Wyoming lands when far more fertile lands in the midwestern states now are being removed from production due to poor market conditions. I am convinced that . . . those lands which were included as practicably irrigable acreage, based upon the assumption of the construction of a future irrigation project, should not be included for the purpose of quantification of the Indian peoples' water rights. They may be irrigable academically, but not as a matter of practicality. . . .

753 P.2d at 119 (Thomas, J., dissenting).

The PIA standard also potentially frustrates the requirement that federally reserved water rights be tailored to minimal need. Rather than focusing on what is necessary to fulfill a reservation's overall design, PIA awards what may be an overabundance of water by including every irrigable acre of land in the equation.

For the foregoing reasons, we decline to approve the use of PIA as the exclusive quantification measure for determining water rights on Indian lands.

F. Proper Factors for Consideration

Recognizing that the most likely reason for PIA's endurance is that "no satisfactory substitute has emerged," Dan A. Tarlock, *One River, Three Sovereigns: Indian and Interstate Water Rights*, 22 LAND & WATER L. REV. 631, 659 (1987), we now enter essentially uncharted territory. In *Gila III*, this court stated that determining the amount of water necessary to accomplish a reservation's purpose is a "fact-intensive inquir[y] that must be made on a reservation-by-reservation basis." 195 Ariz. [411] at 420, 989 P.2d [739] at 748. We still adhere to the belief that this is the only way federally reserved rights can be tailored to meet each reservation's minimal need.

When *Big Horn I* went before the Supreme Court, one of the present state litigants, in an amicus brief, argued that there should be a "balancing of a myriad of factors" in quantifying reserved water rights. Rusinek, supra, at 397 (quoting Brief of Amicus Curiae Salt River Project Agric. Improvement & Power Dist. at 19, *Wyoming v. United States*, 492 U.S. 406 (1989)). During oral argument in the present case, counsel for the Apache tribes made a similar argument. Considering the objective that tribal reservations be allocated water necessary to achieve their purpose as permanent homelands, such a multi-faceted approach appears best-suited to produce a proper outcome.

Tribes have already used this methodology in settling water rights claims with the federal government. One feature of such settlements has been the development of master land use plans specifying the quantity of water necessary for different purposes on the reservation. See, e.g., S. Rep. 101-479 (1990) (Fort McDowell Indian Community utilized a land use plan in conjunction with its water rights settlement based on agricultural production, commercial development, industrial use, residential use, recreational use, and wilderness).

While we commend the creation of master land use plans as an effective means of demonstrating water requirements, tribes may choose to present evidence to the trial court in a different manner. The important thing is that the lower court should have before it actual and proposed uses, accompanied by the parties' recommendations regarding feasibility and the amount of water necessary to accomplish the homeland purpose. In viewing this evidence, the lower court should consider the following factors, which are not intended to be exclusive.

A tribe's history will likely be significant. Deference should be given to practices requiring water use that are embedded in Native American traditions. Some rituals may date back hundreds of years, and tribes should be granted water rights necessary to continue such practices into the future. An Indian reservation could not be a true homeland otherwise.

In addition to history, the court should consider tribal culture when quantifying federally reserved rights. Preservation of culture benefits both Indians and non-Indians; for this reason, Congress has recognized the "unique values of Indian culture" in our society. 25 U.S.C. § 1902 (1994) (recognizing the importance of culture when placing Indian children in foster care); see also 20 U.S.C. § 7801 (1994) (finding that education should "build on Indian culture"). Water uses that have particular cultural significance should be respected, where possible. The length of time a practice has been engaged in, its nature (e.g., religious or otherwise), and its importance in a tribe's daily affairs may all be relevant.

The court should also consider the tribal land's geography, topography, and natural resources, including groundwater availability. As mentioned earlier, one of the biggest problems with PIA is that it does not allow for flexibility in this regard. It has also been observed that "irrigation is one of the most inefficient and ecologically damaging ways to use water. . . . [I]ncreasing the use of water for irrigation runs counter to a historic trend in western water use — the transition from agricultural to less consumptive and higher-valued municipal and industrial uses." This does not mean that tribes are prohibited from including agriculture/irrigation as part of their development plans. However, future irrigation projects are subject to a PIA-type analysis: irrigation must be both practically and economically feasible. Tribes should be free to develop their reservations based on the surroundings they inhabit. We anticipate that any development plan will carefully consider natural resources (including potential water uses), so that the water actually granted will be put to its best use on the reservation.

In conjunction with natural resources, the court should look to a tribe's economic base in determining its water rights. Tribal development plans or other evidence should address, and the court should consider, "the optimal manner of creating jobs and income for the tribes [and] the most efficient use of the water. . . ." Economic development and its attendant water use must be tied, in some manner, to a tribe's current economic station. Physical infrastructure, human resources, including the present and potential employment base, technology, raw materials, financial resources, and capital are all relevant in viewing a reservation's economic infrastructure.

Past water use on a reservation should also be considered when quantifying a tribe's rights. The historic use of water may indicate how a tribe has valued it. Logically, tribal prioritization of past water use will affect its future development. For example, a tribe that has never used water to irrigate is less likely to successfully and economically develop irrigation projects in the future. This does not mean that Indians may not use their water allocations for new purposes on a reservation. However, any proposed projects should be scrutinized to insure that they are practical and economical. Such projects should also be examined to determine that they are, in fact, appropriate to a particular homeland.

While it should never be the only factor, a tribe's present and projected future population may be considered in determining water rights. We recognize that the Supreme Court has rejected any quantification standard based solely on the "number of Indians." *Arizona II.* However, if a federally reserved water right is to be tailored to a reservation's "minimal need," as we believe it must, then population necessarily must be part of the equation. To act without regard to population would ignore the fact that water will always be used, most importantly, for human needs. Therefore, the number of humans is a necessary element in quantifying water rights. Such consideration is not at odds with the need to satisfy tribes' "future as well as . . . present needs." *Arizona I.* Population forecasts are common in today's society and are recognized and relied upon by the legal system. It is therefore proper to use population evidence in conjunction with other factors in quantifying a tribe's *Winters* rights.

The state litigants argue that courts should act with sensitivity toward existing state water users when quantifying tribal water rights. They claim that this is necessary because when a water source is fully appropriated, there will be a gallon-for-gallon decrease in state users' water rights due to the tribes' federally reserved rights. When an Indian reservation is created, the government impliedly reserves water to carry out its purpose as a permanent homeland. *See Winters*, 207 U.S. at 566–67, 577. The court's function is to determine the amount of water necessary to effectuate this purpose, tailored to the reservation's minimal need. We believe that such a minimalist approach demonstrates appropriate sensitivity and consideration of existing users' water rights, and at the same time provides a realistic basis for measuring tribal entitlements.

Again, the foregoing list of factors is not exclusive. The lower court must be given the latitude to consider other information it deems relevant to determining tribal water rights. We require only that proposed uses be reasonably feasible. As with PIA, this entails a two-part analysis. First, development projects need to be achievable from a practical standpoint — they must not be pie-in-the-sky ideas that will likely never reach fruition. Second, projects must be economically sound. When water, a scarce resource, is put to efficient uses on the reservation, tribal economies and members are the beneficiaries.

[*Vacated and remanded.*]

NOTES ON *WINTERS* RIGHTS QUANTIFICATION

1. **Quantification Formulae:** Debate has raged with particular energy over the formula for quantification of Indian reserved water rights. The Court in *Arizona v. California* adopted the practicably irrigable acreage [PIA] standard under which the quantum of the reserved right can be fixed for reservations created primarily for agricultural uses by reference to the number of irrigable acres located on a reservation. Thus, in its supplemental decree to *Arizona v. California* (*Arizona III*), 439 U.S. 419 (1979), the Supreme Court stated that while usage of adjudicated water rights by the lower Colorado tribes was not restricted to agricultural application, the quantity of water needed to supply consumptive use required for irrigation constituted the measure for determining the quantity of adjudicated rights. This formula has the virtue of providing a relatively fixed and stable allocation to the Indians, thereby enabling other water users to plan for their own withdrawals. But it may not be the optimal formula if the reservation sees as its future a use other than agriculture that requires a greater supply of water, or if the tribe envisioned a supply adequate to maintain the level of groundwater sources of springs on the reservation or the level of a lake. *See Cappaert v. United States*, 426 U.S. 128 (1976) (holding that federal reserved rights include groundwater). *Contra In re General Adjudication of All Rights to Use Water in the Big Horn River Sys.*, 753 P.2d 76 (Wyo. 1988), *aff'd on equally divided vote*, 492 U.S. 406 (1989) (rejecting application of *Winters* doctrine to groundwater for lack of precedent, while recognizing that "[t]he logic which supports a reservation of surface water to fulfill the purpose of the reservation also supports reservation of groundwater"). For competing views on the quantum of Indian reserved rights, compare William H. Veeder, *Indian Prior and Paramount Rights to the Use of Water*, 16 ROCKY MT. MIN. L. INST. 631 (1971) with Paul Bloom, *Indian "Paramount" Rights to Water Use*, 16 ROCKY MT. MIN. L. INST. 669 (1971).

Recall that in *Washington v. Washington State Passenger Fishing Vessel Ass'n*, Justice Stevens' opinion for the Court relied on analogies to *Winters* and *Arizona v. California* in analyzing the appropriate accommodation of Indian and non-Indian allocation of the fisheries resources involved in that case. Thus, he described *Arizona v. California* as having authorized the Court or a special master "to devise some apportionment that assured that the Indians' reasonable needs would be met." He continued the analogy, stating:

> As in *Arizona v. California* and its predecessor cases, the central principle here must be that Indian treaty rights to a natural resource that once was thoroughly and exclusively exploited by the Indians secures so much as, but not more than, is necessary to provide the Indians with a livelihood — that is to say, a moderate living.

443 U.S. at 686. Does Justice Stevens' focus on the income and livelihood derived from a natural resource comport with the prior thrust of the Court's decisions in *Winters* and *Arizona v. California* or does it herald a new departure and a potentially novel approach to allocating or quantifying Indian water rights and other resources? In *Arizona v. California*, were the present population of the reservation, the standard of living of tribal members, or the level of their income significant factors in the quantification calculations?

In the cases following *Winters*, courts struggled with the problem of reconciling the changing Indian need for water with the non-Indian need for a definite allocation to permit development of the off-reservation lands sharing the same watershed with the Indians. Thus, in *Conrad Inv. Co. v. United States*, 161 F. 829 (9th Cir. 1908), decided shortly after the Supreme Court decision in *Winters*, the court stated:

> It is further objected that the decree of the Circuit Court provides that, whenever the needs and requirements of the [Indian] complainant for the use of the waters of Birch Creek for irrigating and other useful purposes upon the reservation exceed the amount of water reserved by the decree for that purpose, the complainant may apply to the court for a modification of the decree. This is entirely in accord with complainant's rights as adjudged by the decree. Having determined that the Indians on the reservation have a paramount right to the waters of Birch Creek, it follows that the permission given to the defendant to have the excess over the amount of water specified in the decree should be subject to modification, should the conditions on the reservation at any time require such modification.

Id. at 835.

In 1939 the Ninth Circuit reversed itself. In *United States v. Walker River Irrig. Dist.*, 104 F.2d 334 (9th Cir. 1939), the court permanently fixed that reservation's entitlement by making a determination of the population of the tribe over a period of seventy years, the number of acres cultivated, the quantity of water in the area, and the needs for domestic, stock-watering, and power-generating purposes.

In *United States v. Ahtanum Irrig. Dist.*, 236 F.2d 321 (9th Cir. 1956), the court rejected any notion that the amount of water reserved to an Indian reservation was to be measured by the Indians' needs at the time the reservation was created:

> It is plain from our decision in the *Conrad Inv. Co.* case . . . that the paramount right of the Indians to the waters of Ahtanum Creek was not

limited to use of the Indians at any given date but this right extended to the ultimate needs of the Indians as those needs and requirements should grow to keep pace with the development of Indian agriculture upon the reservation.

Id. at 327; *see also United States v. Ahtanum Irrig. Dist.*, 330 F.2d 897 (9th Cir. 1964). And, of course, *Arizona v. California* adopted as the most practical test the amount of water necessary to irrigate reservation land susceptible of irrigation.

In *United States v. New Mexico*, 438 U.S. 696 (1978), Justice Rehnquist, writing for the majority, stated that:

> [w]hile many of the contours of what has come to be called the "implied-reservation-of-water doctrine" remains unspecified, the Court has repeatedly emphasized that Congress reserved "only that amount of water necessary to fulfill the purpose of the reservation, no more." *Cappaert*, 426 U.S., at 141. See *Arizona v. California*, 373 U.S., at 600, 601; *District Court for Eagle County*, 401 U.S. [520], at 523. Each time this Court has applied the "implied-reservation-of-water doctrine," it has carefully examined both the asserted water right and the specific purposes for which the land was reserved, and concluded that without the water the purposes of the reservation would be entirely defeated.

Id. at 700. The Court addressed itself specifically to the extent of federal reserved water rights in national forests. It held that the federal reserved rights doctrine was limited to the original purposes for creation of such national forest lands, namely continuous timber supply and watershed conservation. Any expansion in the purposes for which national forests were managed subsequent to the Forest Service Organic Act of 1897, which established the national forest system, had no effect and could not be used to maintain minimum instream flows in the forests to meet the newer needs such as the preservation of fish and wildlife and the protection of recreational and aesthetic values. The Court noted that such an expansion could cut deeply into the water used by state and private appropriators in a fully appropriated river. The relevance of the New Mexico decision to Indian reserved water rights lies in the idea of the specific purposes for which the land was reserved. Though the decision is limited in its application to non-Indian federal reservations, one may query whether the Court might some day consider whether recreational or aesthetic purposes were implied in a treaty's provisions dealing with tribal reserved water rights. In *United States v. Finch*, 548 F.2d 822 (9th Cir. 1976), *rev'd on other grounds*, 433 U.S. 676 (1977), the Ninth Circuit broadly interpreted the original purpose of an Indian reservation to include fishery management even though agriculture was the sole purpose mentioned at the reservation's creation in 1868.

2. Water for Instream Flowage to Preserve Fisheries: One issue that has particularly plagued the quantification of Indian water rights is the frequent Indian demand to maintain minimum stream flows and lake levels to support tribal fisheries. *E.g., Pyramid Lake Paiute Tribe v. Morton*, 354 F. Supp. 252 (D.D.C. 1973), *rev'd*, 499 F.2d 1095 (D.C. Cir. 1974) (effort to maintain lake level of Pyramid Lake to preserve natural fishery spawning areas). In light of *Winters* and *New Mexico*, the recent cases raising such questions generally have focused attention on whether fishing and fishery preservation were within the original purposes for which the reservation was created. For example, in *Joint Bd. of Control of the Flathead, Mission & Jocko Irrig. Dists. v. United States*, 832 F.2d 1127 (9th Cir. 1987), the court was asked to adjudicate a dispute between the Confederated Salish and Kootenai Tribes and the local federal irrigation projects over the manner in which the Department of the Interior allocated its water. The court noted that at the time of the Treaty of Hell Gate of 1859, which established the Flathead Reservation, the Tribes were heavily dependent on fishing and the treaty protected their prior aboriginal fishing rights. Thus, the court rejected the district court's conclusion that the Indians must share water rights needed to exercise their prior fishing rights with junior appropriators, such as the irrigation district. *See also United States v. Adair*, 723 F.2d 1394 (9th Cir. 1983); *Colville Confederated Tribes v. Walton*, 752 F.2d 397 (9th Cir. 1985).

In *United States v. Adair*, 187 F. Supp. 2d 1273 (D. Ore. 2002), the United States District Court for Oregon recognized that the water rights of the Klamath Indian Tribe specifically included a right to water necessary to support the resources the Tribe hunted, fished, and trapped *and* the food resources that it gathered pursuant to express treaty guarantees of food gathering rights. Thus, providing insufficient water to the habitat necessary to support the natural resource basis for tribal hunting, fishing, trapping, and food gathering would constitute a denial of the Tribe's reserved water rights guaranteed under their treaty. On appeal, however, the Ninth Circuit found the issue unripe for resolution, because further factual development of the Klamath Basin Adjudication was needed to determine what standard the Oregon Water Resources Department would apply to quantify the tribes' rights. *United States v. Braren*, 338 F.3d 971, 974 (9th Cir. 2003). That meant the Klamath would have to wait many years for completion of the Klamath Basin Adjudication, a process that began in the 1970s and is unlikely to end any time soon. As Blumm, Becker, and Smith observed in 2006:

> Over a quarter-century after the court in *Adair I* recognized the Klamath Tribes' reserved instream flow rights, the Klamath tribes continue to await the outcome of the state comprehensive adjudication process in order to obtain river water to which their treaty entitles them. Although the litigation that the tribes undertook to obtain recognition of their reserved water rights was a critical first step on the road to obtaining "wet rights" to instream flows, it is quite evident that that was only the first step in a process which has yet to come to full fruition. And partly because the tribes' water rights claims have languished in the state administrative process, Klamath River salmon runs reached critically low levels, requiring the closure of the off-shore salmon harvesting along the Oregon and northern California coasts in 2006. Litigation and negotiations continue over the relicensing or removal of four dams licensed to PacifiCorp, currently blocking treaty-reserved fish from passing up the Klamath River into Oregon. The scope of the Klamath Tribes' reserved water rights might be resolved as part of a settlement focusing on fish survival and dam removal, making the state administrative water rights adjudication moot.

Michael C. Blumm, David H. Becker & Joshua D. Smith, *The Mirage of Indian Reserved Water Rights and Western Streamflow Restoration in the McCarran Amendment Era: A Promise Unfulfilled*, 36 ENVTL. L. 1157, 1169–1170 (2006).

The Washington Supreme Court rejected the Yakama claims for instream flowage to protect the Yakama's treaty-guaranteed fishing rights in *In the Matter of the Determination of the Rights to the Use of the Surface Waters of the Yakama River Drainage Basin*, 121 Wash. 2d 257, 850 P.2d 1306 (1993) (en banc). While recognizing the basic guarantee of water necessary to protect treaty-guaranteed fishing rights, the court held that the 1968 settlement by the Yakama Nation of a claim filed against the United States in the Indian Claims Commission for loss and impairment of the treaty fishing rights precluded their assertion of any water claim to support those rights found to have been impaired or lost in litigation with the United States. The Washington high court apparently was unaware that the Indian Claims Commission had jurisdiction to award damages only, and could not take or diminish treaty rights. *See State ex rel. Martinez v. Kerr-McGee Corp.*, 898 P.2d 1256, 1260 (N.M. Ct. App. 1995) (refusing to follow the Washington decision). But despite that litigation loss, the Yakamas have enjoyed some success in maintaining instream flows. A subsequent Washington Supreme Court decision acknowledged a limited habitat right to some flow to maintain the tribal fishery; in 1994, Congress passed the Yakima River Basin Water Enhancement Project Act, Pub. L. No. 103-434, tit. XII, 108 Stat. 4526, 4550, one goal of which was to provide increased instream flows to protect salmon and steelhead runs; the Tribe has worked cooperatively with the Bureau of Reclamation in setting the level of instream flows that implement the Project; and through negotiations with non-Indian irrigation districts, the Tribe has secured agreements that reduce demand on the river in exchange for assistance with water conservation. *See* Blumm, Becker & Smith, *supra*, at 1180–83.

In *Wyoming v. Owl Creek Irrig. Dist. (In re General Adjudication of All Rights to Use Water in the Big Horn River Sys.)*, 750 P.2d 681, 753 P.2d 76 (Wyo. 1988), *aff'd by equally divided vote*, 492 U.S. 406 (1989), the court held that the Shoshone and Arapahoe Tribes of the Wind River Reservation had no right to preserve minimum stream flow for fisheries. The court noted that the 1868 Treaty with the Shoshones and Bannacks which established the reservation sought to encourage only agriculture, while only mentioning other activities such as hunting, lumbering, and milling. The court held that even though the Tribes' evidence established that historically they were partially dependent on fish for their diet, they had not established sufficient evidence to be entitled to *any* water for fishery maintenance. The court distinguished other cases permitting such fisheries in stream flow rights on the ground that the tribes in question were "heavily, if not totally, dependent on fish for their livelihood." Even though the special master had concluded that at least some water should be awarded on a showing that the Tribes historically were partially dependent on fish, the Wyoming Supreme Court affirmed the district court's deletion of the award. In the wake of this loss, the Tribes have been focusing on Clean Water Act litigation, to improve the quality of the water that they do have. *See* Blumm, Becker & Smith, *supra*, at 1176.

Finally, in the case of *Pyramid Lake*, discussed *supra* and in Ch. 4, Sec. A.5.c, the Tribe has been able to restore some instream flows to the Truckee River, thereby supplying water for its fishery in Pyramid Lake, despite its devastating loss in the United States Supreme Court. Recall that in *Nevada v. United States*, 463 U.S. 110, 116–19 (1983), the Court denied the Tribe an opportunity to assert water rights for that fishery, finding the claim foreclosed by a prior judgment, obtained by the United States, that had limited the Tribe's water rights to agricultural use. Nonetheless, the Tribe has used legislative lobbying as well as threats of lawsuits under the Clean Water Act and the Endangered Species Act to produce more water for instream flow. In 1998, the Nevada State Engineer, acting on the basis of authority conferred by the federal court decree regarding water rights in the Truckee River, granted applications from the Tribe to transfer water rights available for irrigation to instream use for protection of fisheries. In support of this action, the State Engineer concluded that the fishery was one of the "primary uses" for which the Pyramid Lake Reservation was created. The United States District Court for Nevada upheld the Engineer's action in *United States v. Orr Water Ditch Co.*, 309 F. Supp. 2d 1245 (D. Nev. 2004), rejecting arguments by the water districts that the rights emanating from the decree were not federally reserved rights, that they had been abandoned for lack of perfection, and that the transfer would impair existing rights.

What do these brief case studies suggest about the relative efficacy of litigation, legislation, administrative action, and negotiated agreements in enhancing instream flows? Are the most successful tribes always the ones with the most favorable litigation outcomes? Does a litigation loss necessarily signal the end of all opportunity to achieve greater instream flows? Is it fair to say that litigation success is necessary but not sufficient to produce enhanced instream flows? Relying on the Pyramid Lake experience, Blumm, Becker & Smith observe that "dexterous use of judicial recognition of their reserved rights can enable tribes to bargain to transform those federal rights into state-recognized rights capable of implementation by established state water regimes." Blumm, Becker & Smith, *supra* at 1203.

3. **Water for Modern Industrial, Commercial, Domestic, or Mining Purposes:** As economies on Indian reservations have evolved away from agrarian activities and diversified, questions have emerged as to whether reserved Indian water rights include water for activities such as mining, industrial, commercial, municipal, and domestic consumption. Recent cases have relied heavily on the theory of the *New Mexico* case, which seems to limit the *measure* of federal, but not necessarily Indian, reserved rights to the purposes for which the federal reservation *originally* was created. One might distinguish Indian reserved water rights on the basis that, unlike the National Forest lands involved in *New Mexico*, discussed in Note 1 above, and most other federal reservations, Indian reservations were reserved for human habitation by Indian tribes which, like all other civilizations, evolve over time. While some have suggested that *New Mexico* does not directly apply to Indian reserved rights, *State ex rel. Greely v. Confederated Salish & Kootenai Tribes of the Flathead Reservation*, 712 P.2d 754, 766–67 (Mont. 1985); Felix S. Cohen, Handbook of Federal Indian Law 1217–18 (2012 ed.), many of the cases have looked to the *New Mexico* case for guidance on these questions. *E.g.*, *United States v. Adair, supra*, at 1408. For example, in *Wyoming v. Owl Creek Irrig. Dist., supra*, the court rejected any water allocation for mineral and industrial uses. Even though the court conceded that the parties were fully aware of the valuable minerals that lay beneath the reservation when the treaty was signed that created the reservation, the court found that there was no evidence that parties to the treaty originally created the Wind River Reservation for mineral or industrial purposes.

Similarly, the court rejected any allocation of water for wildlife management or aesthetic uses since neither use fell within the original purposes for which the reservation was created. By contrast, the court noted that no separate allocation for municipal, domestic, livestock, and commercial uses was necessary since such allocations properly were included within the agricultural reserved water award. For the court, the practicably irrigable acreage standard established in *Arizona v. California* (*Arizona I*), 373 U.S. at 601, specifically included the water necessary for agriculture and related purposes. Taken together, these cases indicate that the *Arizona v. California* practicably irrigable acreage standard for quantification represents an expansive concept which includes municipal, domestic, livestock, and commercial uses on Indian reservations intended primarily for agriculture. The cases also suggest that where a tribe proves that other uses, such as hunting and fishing, were originally intended when the reservation was established, the court may award water allocations beyond the practicably irrigable acreage standard.

Which standard better accommodates modern water usage needs of reservations, the PIA standard or the totality of circumstances test of *Gila River*? Which provides greater predictability in the case of claims settlements during protracted water litigation? Which is therefore preferable? Were all tribes in the *Gila River* litigation helped by the standards it advanced or only some? Which ones? In general, which is more advantageous to Indian tribes, rigorous adherence to the PIA standard of *Arizona v. California* or the more flexible approach of *Gila River*? Does it make any difference that many of the cases where the standard is applied will be heard in state court, as was true in the *Gila River* litigation, for reasons explained in *San Carlos Apache*, the next major case in this section?

Standards such as the practicably irrigable acreage standard generally do not control Indian *use* of their reserved water rights but, rather, merely quantify the *amount* of water to which Indians are entitled under the *Winters* doctrine. Thus, water allocated on this standard can be diverted for mining, industrial, or other purposes never originally contemplated in the treaty. The point of any such standard is that it limits the quantity of water to which the tribes have title under the *Winters* doctrine. By quantifying Indian reserved rights under such standards, the courts prevent the usually prior Indian reserved rights from expanding with technology and use and thereby posing a serious threat to the utility of the rights held by junior appropriators under state law.

The seeming conflict between non-Indian needs and Indian rights was the subject of scrutiny by the National Water Commission, a governmental entity created in 1968. Its 1973 Final Report states that "the future utilization of Indian rights on fully appropriated streams will divest prior uses initiated under state law . . . and will impose economic hardship, amounting to disaster in some cases, on users with large investments made over long periods of time." FINAL REPORT OF THE NATIONAL WATER COMMISSION 477 (1973). The solution proposed is that at any time construction of a reservation water resource project impairs a pre-existing non-Indian right "valid under state law" and initiated prior to 1963, the United States should pay the non-Indian just compensation. The report realizes that such a law would make even more unlikely federal financing of water rights projects on Indian reservations since the cost would now include compensation to non-Indian users. The basis for the Commission's proposed recommendation is that non-Indian users could not have reasonably known, prior to 1963 (the date of the *Arizona v. California* decision), the extent of Indian rights. But what kind of a right did the non-Indians have? What were their reasonable expectations of the length of time they could use the water? Recall that the tribes probably did not have the funds for irrigation works and it could reasonably have appeared to the settlers that massive irrigation on the reservation was at least several decades away. Should the fact that the United States has not adequately financed reservation water projects be a basis for legitimating non-Indian use? Should the non-Indian users have been on notice as a consequence of *Winters* that their own use was in constant jeopardy? Ironically, these non-Indian users often had been federally financed. The Commission's recommendation for compensation to non-Indian water rights holders has never been enacted into law.

In the face of the uncertainties of existing water law and the substantial capital investment necessary to realize the economic benefit of reserved water rights, tribes may find themselves modifying their rights through other means of quantification in order to gain a measure of economic security. In the case of the Navajo Tribe (now the Navajo Nation), for example, there were two occasions when it found it desirable to bargain its unquantified reserved rights under *Winters* for other gains. In 1962, Congress confirmed a tribal determination providing for federal financing of the massive Navajo Indian Irrigation Project on the eastern portion of the reservation in exchange for surrender of the Navajo priority to waters needed for the San Juan-Chama Diversion project to divert headwaters of the San Juan System into the Rio Grande River System that serves Albuquerque. In 1968, the Tribe resolved to forebear from using Colorado River water on the western portion of the reservation in exchange for some monetary consideration and the promise of beneficial economic development, actions that made possible the construction of the Navajo Generating Station and the availability of the water needed by the Salt River Project to operate it.

There is some question whether the information to which the Tribe had access was sufficient to allow for an informed decision to compromise and whether the disparity in economic strength between the Tribe and the non-Navajo interests that it negotiated with, such as the federal Bureau of Reclamation, Upper Colorado River Commission, Salt River Project, and New Mexico Interstate Stream Commission, resulted in an inequitable settlement. *See* Monroe E. Price & Gary Weatherford, *Indian Water Rights in Theory and Practice: Navajo Experience in the Colorado River Basin*, 40 LAW & CONTEMP. PROBS. 97 (1976); *see also* Charles DuMars & Helen Ingram, *Congressional Quantification of Indian Reserved Water Rights: A Definitive Solution or a Mirage?*, 20 NAT. RESOURCES J. 17 (1980) (raising questions concerning the competing values involved when the Navajos exchanged certain reserved rights upon receipt of federal projects).

Should changed technology be taken into account in defining the scope of the reserved right? When the Navajo Reservation was created, most Colorado River water was inaccessible because its flow was so far below ground level. Enormous investment and the construction of Navajo Dam now make the water more readily available. Upstream and downstream uses (including the development of cities) may have been premised on a view of the Indian right based on the productivity of water diversion techniques at the time the reservation was created. Now, as a consequence of advances, there is a shift in water availability. Assuming that the Indian reserved right encompasses exploitation made possible by the development of superior technology, who should bear the increased cost of water for competing users? Should it be the taxpayers as a whole or the users themselves? Often, the only means of financing the expensive diversion works that increase the Indians' share of water is through congressional appropriations. But a member of Congress might be loath to vote an appropriation that will lead to the permanent diversion of scarce water from powerful urban and rural constituents to Indian users.

4. **Modification or Abrogation of Indian Water Rights and the Takings Clause:** What are the Fifth Amendment consequences of modifying Indian water rights? Do they have the status of aboriginal Indian title, and therefore, the fragile quality assigned by the Supreme Court in *Tee-Hit-Ton*, set forth and discussed in Ch. 6, Sec. A.1, where land held under such title was deemed not covered by the takings clause of the Fifth Amendment? Professor Meyers has argued that all water rights may not be compensable, though no definitive answer has yet been provided. Charles Meyers, *The Colorado River*, 10 STAN. L. REV. 1, 47 (1966). *But see United States v. 5,677.94 Acres of Land*, 162 F. Supp. 108 (D. Mont. 1958). Under Professor Meyers' theory that the United States may assert its superior easement of navigation to condemn water rights, is it possible that some uses or diversions are not compensable but that others are? *See California v. United States*, 438 U.S. 645 (1978); *Dugan v. Rank*, 372 U.S. 609 (1963); *International Paper Co. v. United States*, 282 U.S. 399 (1931) (all suggesting the compensability of water rights under the Fifth Amendment). In *United States v. Shoshone Tribe*, 304 U.S. 111 (1938), the Court held that the Tribe's beneficial interest in the land of its reservation included the timber and minerals, so just compensation was due upon federal appropriation of the resources. Attention must be paid to the jurisdiction statute that establishes the grounds for recovery. The treaty with the Shoshone contained nothing to suggest that the United States intended to retain beneficial interest. Where a reservation is created by treaty or statute, the reserved water rights would seem to be as compensable as timber or minerals. The result might differ if the reservation was created by executive order and never afterward recognized by statute. *See Sioux Tribe v. United States*, 316 U.S. 317 (1942), presented in Ch. 6, Sec. A.3. The existing case law, including *Winters* and *Arizona v. California*, suggests that unlike aboriginal title, however, Indian water rights, once defined, are usually vested property rights and specifically enforceable.

NELL JESSUP NEWTON ET AL., COHEN'S HANDBOOK OF FEDERAL INDIAN LAW § 19.03[4] (2005 ed.), notes that "State water laws do not govern the use of water by Indians and Indian tribes on Indian lands with respect to any of the purposes of a reservation," citing *Bryan v. Itasca County*, 426 U.S. 373 (1976), presented in Ch. 5, Sec. A.2, among other cases for this proposition. *See also id.* at § 19.04[2]. In Justice Brennan's opinion for the majority in *Bryan*, he quotes prior cases to the effect that " 'Congress has . . . acted consistently upon the assumption that the States have no power to regulate the affairs of Indians on a reservation,' *Williams v. Lee*, 358 U.S. 217, 220 (1959), and therefore 'State laws generally are not applicable to tribal Indians on an Indian reservation except where Congress has expressly provided that State laws shall apply.' *McClanahan v. Arizona State Tax Comm'n*, 411 U.S. 164, 170, 171 (1973) (quoting . . . FEDERAL INDIAN LAW 845

(1958))." It is at least conceivable that Congress could change the rules of the game and allow for state regulation of on-reservation water use by Indians. If Congress did so, would such legislation effectuate a compensable taking of Indian water rights? *See Menominee Tribe v. United States*, 391 U.S. 404 (1968).

5. Unsettling Quantified Tribal Water Allocations: In *Arizona v. California* (*Arizona IV*), 460 U.S. 605 (1983), certain tribes, noting that a prior water decree was subject to "appropriate adjustment," sought to reopen a 1979 final water decree adjudicating rights in the lower Colorado River. Over three dissents, the Court, noting that "[c]ertainty of rights is particularly important with respect to water rights in the Western United States," declined based on the doctrines of law of the case and *res judicata* to reopen the 1979 decree in order to recalculate the Indians practicably irrigable acreage (the water quantification test applied to Indian *Winters* rights in this case) to take account of lands omitted in error and developments in irrigation technology. Justice White's opinion for the Court observed:

> Recalculating the amount of practicably irrigable acreage runs directly counter to the strong interest in finality in this case. A major purpose of this litigation, from its inception to the present day, has been to provide the necessary assurance to States of the Southwest and to various private interests, of the amount of water they can anticipate to receive from the Colorado River system. "In the arid parts of the West . . . claims to water for use on federal reservations vie with other public and private claims for the limited quantities to be found in the rivers and streams." *United States v. New Mexico*, 438 U.S. 696 (1978). If there is no surplus of water in the Colorado River, an increase in federal reserved water rights will require a "gallon-for-gallon reduction in the amount of water available for water-needy state and private appropriators."

Id. at 620–621.

Later, the same term, the Court considered and rejected the efforts of the Pyramid Lake Paiute to reopen an earlier 1944 decree in which the tribal water rights had been quantified. The Tribe recognized that the amount of water allocated under the decree was inadequate to sustain the lake level of Pyramid Lake and, consequently, the natural spawning of its valuable fishery. Consequently, the Tribe sought to reopen the decree, claiming that their interests, which had been represented by the United States in the prior litigation, had been inadequately represented because the United States, which was also seeking water in the same litigation for upstream federal irrigation projections, had a conflict of interest. In *Nevada v. United States*, 463 U.S. 110 (1983), set forth and discussed in Ch. 4, Sec. A.5.c, the Court rejected the Tribe's claim. It emphasized the importance of finality particularly in water law litigation in the West where investment backed development decisions relied upon prior water decrees. The Court further emphasized that, unlike a private trustee, the United States had two statutorily mandated, albeit conflicting, obligations, neither of which it could divest itself from pursuing. Consequently, the Court deemed it unfair to subject the United States to the rigorous fiduciary responsibilities applied to a private trustee. Nevertheless, in a footnote, the Court carefully scrutinized the manner in which the United States handled the Pyramid Lake Tribe's water claims, noting approvingly that the United States essentially filed what would later come to be called a split brief, separately seeking water for the Pyramid Lake Paiute Tribe and the upstream federal irrigation project in different sections of the brief, thereby leaving the decisions regarding the division of water between the conflicting federal claimants to the court. Thus, the Court declined to reopen the 1944 water decree.

If water adjudications like those involved in *Nevada* and *Arizona* finally quantify and adjudicate Indian water rights irrespective of error, later technological developments, or conflicts of interest in representation, careful attention should be paid to the procedure by which adjudication and quantification of Indian water rights occurs. The next case, *Arizona v. San Carlos Apache Tribe*, and *Colorado River Water Conservation District*, discussed in the next opinion, address this question. Do they provide sufficient protections for Indian *Winters* rights?

6.   Leasing Indian Water Rights: May a tribe or restricted allottee lease or sell water rights for off-reservation uses? Aboriginal title to land, it was said, was a right of use only and could not be alienated. Is the same true of Indian water rights? Do they exist for the present and potential use of the Indian owners only? Or can the rights be conveyed to others, even if Indian lands are not sold? On the Colorado River Indian Reservation, there is an active program of leasing tribal agricultural lands, almost wholly to non-Indians, for the purpose of taking advantage of the reservation's Colorado River allocation. It is generally assumed that the rights are alienable.

Both statutory and case law have provided answers with regard to certain types of alienation, but interstices in the law remain. In *Skeem v. United States*, 273 F. 93 (9th Cir. 1921), the court held that the lease of allotments to non-Indians did not affect the tribal water rights if the Indians chose not to maintain residency. The use of reserved water rights by lessees, by virtue of continued Indian ownership of the allotments, still bore a relationship to the tribe. However, here both Indian land and water were leased together. What benefits and disadvantages might be foreseen if reserved water rights were leased for use off-reservation by non-Indians? What would be the economic and cultural implications of turning these *Winter* rights into clearly saleable commodities?

The National Water Commission, mentioned in a previous Note, recommended that the governing body of an Indian tribe should have the right to lease water appurtenant to a reservation at fair market value, and proposed that the United States should have the obligation to buy such water when offered. FINAL REPORT, *supra*, at 480. The virtue to the tribe of leasing reserved rights arises from the possibility to realize income immediately and steadily. An example may be helpful: Suppose a Pueblo along the Rio Grande has an unperfected reserved right to 15,000 acre-feet of water. At the present time, it has only a modest irrigation program, and there is not the prospect of substantially more irrigation in the near future. The tribe would benefit by being able to lease the 15,000 acre-feet to the United States. Reservations with a need for reliable income might favor an approach that would so reward them.

Some hazard to the tribe lies in the implications of severing the water right from the reservation. The economic use of unexploited assets may make sense but the effect on the future of the reservation may be substantial. Under the National Water Commission's set of proposals, it is clear that non-Indian users can begin to make investments based on the reliability of the supply of water. Vested economic interests will be established based on the Indian water. Where water rights are leased, it would be natural to ask whether the Indians could recapture the right for their own benefit at the expiration of the lease. The answer must be that there will be difficulties in effective recapturing, unless alternative supplies of water are developed during the lease period by the non-Indian users. This conclusion is based on two reasons. First, effective implementation and exploitation of reserved rights usually requires congressional appropriations for the massive investments necessary on the reservation. Funds needed for irrigation works, reservoirs, pumping facilities, and the like are unlikely to be provided by Congressmen with other constituents who will be adversely affected if the Indians can, themselves, exploit through sale or lease the water to which they are entitled. And the moral pressure to provide substantial funds for such irrigation works will be eased by the fact that the tribe is already exploiting its water through the mechanism of a lease. A likely result of adopting the Water Commission's proposals is that the congressional appropriations for water-based economic development on Indian reservations would be adversely affected. Second, consistent with nineteenth-century judicial decisions, the United States Congress may have the power unilaterally to convert water resources permanently into cash, that is to open up the Indian water rights for non-Indian settlement. Under existing doctrine the trust responsibility is not legally violated because, as courts have put it, the trust *res* is merely converted from one form (water) to another (cash). As long as fair market value is obtained, the United States is not liable as a fiduciary.

In light of the discussion of quantification above, leasing reserved rights, therefore, may be seen as appealing on two grounds: It provides an income source for the reservation and it provides more security to non-Indian water users in the West. However, it is troublesome for another much more complicated reason. Quantification and leasing are at war with the fundamental reasoning of the *Winters* decision and with the idea of development and growth by the Indian community on the reservation. Yet, in some instances, the sort of "progress" envisioned by *Winters* may be impossible or unwanted, and the substitution of income for a large portion of water rights may be welcome. For assessments of the legality, benefits, and detriments of Indian water rights leasing, see David H. Getches, *Management and Marketing of Indian Water: From Conflict to Pragmatism*, 58 U. COLO. L. REV. 515 (1988); Karen M. Schapiro, *An Argument for the Marketability of Indian Reserved Water Rights: Tapping the Untapped Reservoir*, 23 IDAHO L. REV. 277 (1987); Lee Herold Storey, *Comment, Leasing Indian Water Off the Reservation: A Use Consistent with the Reservation's Purpose*, 76 CAL. L. REV. 179 (1988).

The express provisions of 25 U.S.C. § 177 limit the conveyance of "lands, or of any title or claim thereto, from any Indian nation or tribe of Indians" without federal approval and specify that any nonconforming grant is null and void. To what extent are Indian water rights governed by this federal restraint against alienation? In *United States v. Ahtanum Irrig. Dist.*, 236 F.2d 321 (9th Cir. 1956), the court was confronted with the validity of a 1908 agreement which the Chief Engineer of the Indian Irrigation Service entered into with a large number of white users of water from Ahtanum Creek that bargained away valuable Indian water rights by quantifying the Indians' claim to twenty-five percent of the natural flow of the creek. The agreement was never specifically approved by Congress. The opinion of the Ninth Circuit made repeated references to section 177 and seemed to assume that the alienation of water rights required congressional approval. The court, however, sustained the 1908 agreement on the basis that Congress had explicitly authorized the Secretary of the Interior to "have the management of all Indian affairs, and of all matters arising out of Indian relations," 25 U.S.C. § 2, and that in conferring these powers upon the Secretary of the Interior Congress must have had it in mind that a part of the Secretary's task of supervisor and of management of Indian affairs would necessarily deal with certain relations between Indians on the one hand and their white neighbors on the other.

In *United States v. Truckee-Carson Irrig. Dist.*, 5 Ind. L. Rep. F-13 (D. Nev. No. R. 1987-JBA, filed Dec. 12, 1977), *rev'd on other grounds*, 649 F.2d 1286 (9th Cir. 1981), *rev'd*, 463 U.S. 110 (1983), the court confronted a similar question involving the power of the judiciary to adjudicate and alienate Indian water rights without congressional approval. Responding to the claim that under section 177 ownership of Indian water rights could only be altered by congressional legislation rather than adjudication, the district court held that a water law decree was not a "conveyance" within the meaning of section 177. The court also found federal approval by the fact that the United States appeared in the prior adjudication and therefore consented to the consequences of the litigation. Finally, considering whether water rights constituted "lands, or . . . any title or claim thereto" within the meaning of section 177, the district court said:

> Dealing with the second requirement, "of lands," the Tribe cites *North Side Canal Co. v. Twin Falls Canal Co.*, 12 F.2d 311 (D. of Idaho), in which the court stated:

> "Land," in a statute of this general nature must necessarily be given a broad and comprehensive meaning. "Land," in such sense, includes water upon the land, and water claimed to be appropriated for use in the development, by irrigation, of the land.

> The Tribe also cites *Holmes v. United States*, 53 F.2d 960 (9th Cir. 1931), in which the court stated:

> The primary meaning of the word "land" at common law is "any ground, soil or earth whatsoever; as arable, meadows, pastures, woods, waters, marshes, furzes and heath." 2 Blackstone, Com. 18.

> However, it could also be argued that since section 177 was derived from the Act of June 30, 1834, long before the concept of the *Winters* doctrine was recognized, that Congress was concerned with the typical situation wherein the backward, unschooled Indians were being taken advantage of by the white men in trading or selling their lands for inadequate prices. The concept that the Indians also were reserved sufficient water to go along with their lands was not conceived of until *Winters v. United States*, which was decided in 1908.

Ind. L. Rep. at F-16.

Should tribes have any greater right to lease or otherwise alienate their water than they have to alienate their land? For affirmative answers, albeit answers based on different theories, see Steven J. Shupe, *Indian Tribes in the Water Marketing Arena*, 15 AM. INDIAN L. REV. 185, 197 (1990); Richard B. Collins, *The Future Course of the* Winters *Doctrine*, 56 COLO. L. REV. 481, 489 (1985). For discussion of a separate problem with leasing of Indian water rights across state lines, see Chris Seldin, *Interstate Marketing of Indian Water Rights: The Impact of the Commerce Clause*, 87 CAL. L. REV. 1545 (1999).

2. Adjudicating and Regulating Indian Water Rights

ARIZONA v. SAN CARLOS APACHE TRIBE
United States Supreme Court
463 U.S. 545 (1983)

JUSTICE BRENNAN delivered the opinion of the Court.

These consolidated cases form a sequel to our decision in *Colorado River Water Conservation District v. United States*, 424 U.S. 800 (1976). That case held that (1) the McCarran Amendment, 66 Stat. 560, 43 U.S.C. § 666, which waived the sovereign immunity of the United States as to comprehensive state water rights adjudications,[17] provides state courts with jurisdiction to adjudicate Indian water rights held in trust by the United States, and (2), in light of the clear federal policies underlying the McCarran Amendment, a water rights suit brought by the United States in federal court was properly dismissed in favor of a concurrent comprehensive adjudication reaching the same issues in Colorado state court. The questions in these cases are parallel: (1) What is the effect of the McCarran Amendment in those States which, unlike Colorado, were admitted to the Union subject to federal legislation that reserved "absolute jurisdiction and control" over Indian lands in the Congress of the United States? (2) If the courts of such States do have jurisdiction to adjudicate Indian water rights, should concurrent federal suits brought by Indian tribes, rather than by the United States, and raising only Indian claims, also be subject to dismissal under the doctrine of *Colorado River*?

---

[17] [1] The McCarran Amendment provides in relevant part:

"(a) Consent is hereby given to join the United States as a defendant in any suit (1) for the adjudication of rights to the use of water of a river system or other source, or (2) for the administration of such rights, where it appears that the United States is the owner of or is in the process of acquiring water rights by appropriation under State law, by purchase, by exchange, or otherwise, and the United States is a necessary party to such suit. The United States, when a party to any such suit, shall (1) be deemed to have waived any right to plead that the State laws are inapplicable or that the United States is not amenable thereto by reason of its sovereignty, and (2) shall be subject to the judgments, orders and decrees of the court having jurisdiction, and may obtain review thereof, in the same manner and to the same extent as a private individual under like circumstances. . . ."

I

Colorado River arose out of a suit brought by the Federal Government in the United States District Court for the District of Colorado seeking a declaration of its rights, and the rights of a number of Indian Tribes, to waters in certain rivers and their tributaries located in one of the drainage basins of the State of Colorado. In the suit, the Government asserted reserved rights, governed by federal law, as well as rights based on state law. Shortly after the federal suit was commenced, the United States was joined, pursuant to the McCarran Amendment, as a party in the ongoing state-court comprehensive water adjudication being conducted for the same drainage basin. The Federal District Court, on motion of certain of the defendants and intervenors, dismissed the federal suit, stating that the doctrine of abstention required deference to the state proceedings. The Court of Appeals reversed the District Court, and we in turn reversed the Court of Appeals.

We began our analysis in *Colorado River* by conceding that the District Court had jurisdiction over the federal suit under 28 U.S.C. § 1345, the general provision conferring district court jurisdiction over most civil actions brought by the Federal Government. We then examined whether the federal suit was nevertheless properly dismissed in view of the concurrent state-court proceedings. This part of the analysis began by considering "whether the McCarran Amendment provided consent to determine federal reserved rights held on behalf of Indians in state court," since "given the claims for Indian water rights in [the federal suit], dismissal clearly would have been inappropriate if the state court had no jurisdiction to decide those claims." We concluded:

> "Not only the Amendment's language, but also its underlying policy, dictates a construction including Indian rights in its provisions. [*United States v. District Court for Eagle County*, 401 U.S. 520 (1971),] rejected the conclusion that federal reserved rights in general were not reached by the Amendment for the reason that the Amendment '[deals] with an all-inclusive statute concerning "the adjudication of rights to the use of water of a river system.'" This consideration applies as well to federal water rights reserved for Indian reservations."

In sum, considering the important federal interest in allowing all water rights on a river system to be adjudicated in a single comprehensive state proceeding, and "bearing in mind the ubiquitous nature of Indian water rights in the Southwest," it was clear to us "that a construction of the Amendment excluding those rights from its coverage would enervate the Amendment's objective."

We buttressed this conclusion with an examination of the legislative history of the McCarran Amendment. We also noted:

> "Mere subjection of Indian rights to legal challenge in state court . . . would no more imperil those rights than would a suit brought by the Government in district court for their declaration. . . . The Government has not abdicated any responsibility fully to defend Indian rights in state court, and Indian interests may be satisfactorily protected under regimes of state law. The Amendment in no way abridges any substantive claim on behalf of Indians under the doctrine of reserved rights. Moreover, as Eagle

County said, 'questions [arising from the collision of private rights and reserved rights of the United States], including the volume and scope of particular reserved rights, are federal questions which, if preserved, can be reviewed [by the Supreme Court] after final judgment by the Colorado court'."

We then considered the dismissal itself. We found that the dismissal could not be supported under the doctrine of abstention in any of its forms, but that it was justified as an application of traditional principles of " '[w]ise judicial administration giving regard to conservation of judicial resources and comprehensive disposition of litigation.' " [A]lthough the federal courts had a "virtually unflagging obligation . . . to exercise the jurisdiction given them," there were certain very limited circumstances outside the abstention context in which dismissal was warranted in deference to a concurrent state-court suit. [W]e noted the comprehensive nature of the state proceedings and the considerable expertise and technical resources available in those proceedings.

We concluded:

"[A] number of factors clearly counsel against concurrent federal proceedings. The most important of these is the McCarran Amendment itself. The clear federal policy evinced by that legislation is the avoidance of piecemeal adjudication of water rights in a river system. This policy is akin to that underlying the rule requiring that jurisdiction be yielded to the court first acquiring control of property, for the concern in such instances is with avoiding the generation of additional litigation through permitting inconsistent dispositions of property. This concern is heightened with respect to water rights, the relationships among which are highly interdependent. Indeed, we have recognized that actions seeking the allocation of water essentially involve the disposition of property and are best conducted in unified proceedings. The consent to jurisdiction given by the McCarran Amendment bespeaks a policy that recognizes the availability of comprehensive state systems for adjudication of water rights as the means for achieving these goals." *Id.*, at 819 (citations omitted).

For these reasons, and others,[18] we affirmed the judgment of the District Court dismissing the federal complaint.

II

The two petitions considered here arise out of three separate consolidated appeals that were decided within three days of each other by the same panel of the Court of Appeals for the Ninth Circuit. In each of the underlying cases, either the United States as trustee or certain Indian Tribes [including the Northern Cheyenne Tribe in Montana, the San Carlos Apache and Navajo Tribes in Arizona] on their

---

[18] [3] The other factors were the apparent absence at the time of dismissal of any proceedings in the District Court other than the filing of the complaint, the extensive involvement of state water rights in the suit, the 300-mile distance between the Federal District Court in Denver and the state tribunal, and the Government's apparent willingness to participate in other comprehensive water proceedings in the state courts.

own behalf, or both, asserted the right to have certain Indian water rights in Arizona or Montana adjudicated in federal court.

[The Enabling Acts under which both Montana and Arizona were admitted to statehood and the state constitutions contain disclaimers of jurisdiction over Indian property phrased in a substantially identical fashion. For example, in response to the requirements of the Montana Enabling Act, the Montana Constitution provided that the people of Montana

> agree and declare that they forever disclaim all right and title to . . . all lands . . . owned or held by any Indian or Indian tribes; and that until title thereto shall have been extinguished by the United States, the same shall be and remain subject to the disposition of the United States, and said Indian lands shall remain under the absolute jurisdiction and control of the Congress of the United States.

Enabling Act of Feb. 22, 1889, § 4, 25 Stat. 677 (North Dakota, South Dakota, Montana, and Washington); Mont. Const., Ordinance No. 1 (1895). In the Ninth Circuit, the tribes successfully claimed that these constitutional disclaimers disabled Arizona and Montana state courts from adjudicating Indian water claims, thereby seeking to distinguish *Colorado River*.]

We granted certiorari, 459 U.S. 821 (1982), in order to resolve a conflict among the Circuits regarding the role of federal and state courts in adjudicating Indian water rights.[19]

We now reverse.

III

A

At the outset of our analysis, a number of propositions are clear. First, the federal courts had jurisdiction here to hear the suits brought both by the United States and the Indian Tribes. Second, it is also clear in these cases, as it was in *Colorado River*, that a dismissal or stay of the federal suits would have been improper if there was no jurisdiction in the concurrent state actions to adjudicate the claims at issue in the federal suits. Third, the parties here agree that the Court of Appeals erred in believing that, in the absence of state jurisdiction otherwise, Pub. L. 280 would have authorized the States to assume jurisdiction over the adjudication of Indian water rights. To the contrary, Pub. L. 280 specifically withheld from state courts jurisdiction to adjudicate ownership or right to possession "of any real or personal property, *including water rights*, belonging to any Indian or any Indian tribe, band, or community that is held in trust by the United States or is subject to a restriction against alienation imposed by the United

---

[19] [9] In *Jicarilla Apache Tribe v. United States*, 601 F.2d 1116 (1979), the Court of Appeals for the Tenth Circuit held that the Enabling Act under which New Mexico was admitted to the Union (whose language is essentially the same as the Enabling Acts at issue in these cases) did not bar state jurisdiction over Indian water rights, and upheld the District Court's dismissal of a general water adjudication brought in federal court by the Jicarilla Apache Tribe.

States." 28 U.S.C. § 1360(b) (emphasis added). Thus, the presence or absence of jurisdiction must rise or fall without reference to whether the States have assumed jurisdiction under Pub. L. 280.

Finally, it should be obvious that, to the extent that a claimed bar to state jurisdiction in these cases is premised on the respective State Constitutions, that is a question of state law over which the state courts have binding authority. Because, in each of these cases, the state courts have taken jurisdiction over the Indian water rights at issue here, we must assume, until informed otherwise, that — at least insofar as state law is concerned — such jurisdiction exists. We must therefore look, for our purposes, to the federal Enabling Acts and other federal legislation, in order to determine whether there is a federal bar to the assertion of state jurisdiction in these cases.

B

That we were not required in *Colorado River* to interpret the McCarran Amendment in light of any statehood Enabling Act was largely a matter of fortuity, for Colorado is one of the few Western States that were not admitted to the Union pursuant to an Enabling Act containing substantially the same language as is found in the Arizona and Montana Enabling Acts. Indeed, a substantial majority of Indian land — including most of the largest Indian reservations — lies in States subject to such Enabling Acts. Moreover, the reason that Colorado was not subject to such an Enabling Act, and Arizona and Montana were, has more to do with historical timing than with deliberate congressional selection. Colorado was admitted to the Union in 1876. In 1882, this Court held in *United States v. McBratney*, 104 U.S. 621, that the federal courts in Colorado had no criminal jurisdiction in a murder committed by one non-Indian against another on an Indian reservation, pointing out that the case did not concern "the punishment of crimes committed by or against Indians, the protection of the Indians in their improvements, or the regulation by Congress of the alienation and descent of property and the government and internal policy of the Indians." We also suggested, however, that the result might have been different if Congress had expressly reserved all criminal jurisdiction on Indian reservations when Colorado was admitted to the Union, pointing to a similar disclaimer contained in the legislation by which Kansas was admitted to statehood in 1861. Probably in response to the *McBratney* decision, Congress resumed the practice of including reservations in Enabling Acts, and did so in the case of virtually every State admitted after 1882.

Despite *McBratney* and *The Kansas Indians*[, 5 Wall. 737 (1867)], the presence or absence of specific jurisdictional disclaimers has rarely been dispositive in our consideration of state jurisdiction over Indian affairs or activities on Indian lands. In *Draper v. United States*, 164 U.S. 240 (1896), for example, this Court held that, despite the jurisdictional reservation in the Montana Enabling Act, a federal court still did not have jurisdiction over a crime committed on an Indian reservation by one non-Indian against another. We stated:

> "As equality of statehood is the rule, the words relied on here to create an exception cannot be construed as doing so, if, by any reasonable meaning, they can be otherwise treated. The mere reservation of jurisdiction and

control by the United States of 'Indian lands' does not of necessity signify a retention of jurisdiction in the United States to punish all offenses committed on such lands by others than Indians or against Indians."

Similarly, in *Organized Village of Kake v. Egan*, 369 U.S. 60 (1962), we held that a reservation in the Alaska Enabling Act did not deprive the State of the right to regulate Indian fishing licensed by the Department of the Interior, finding that the state regulation neither interfered with Indian self-government nor impaired any right granted or reserved by federal law. Conversely, *Worcester v. Georgia*, 6 Pet. 515 (1832), perhaps the most expansive declaration of Indian independence from state regulation ever uttered by this Court, pertained to one of the original 13 States, unbound by any Enabling Act whatsoever. See also, e.g., *The New York Indians*, 5 Wall. 761, 769–770 (1867) (reaching same conclusion as *The Kansas Indians, supra*, but without benefit of disclaimer). And our many recent decisions recognizing crucial limits on the power of the States to regulate Indian affairs have rarely either invoked reservations of jurisdiction contained in statehood Enabling Acts by anything more than a passing mention or distinguished between disclaimer States and nondisclaimer States.

In light of this history, the parties in these cases have engaged in a vigorous debate as to the exact meaning and significance of the Arizona and Montana Enabling Acts. We need not resolve that debate, however, nor need we resort to the more general doctrines that have developed to chart the limits of state authority over Indians, because we are convinced that, whatever limitation the Enabling Acts or federal policy may have originally placed on state-court jurisdiction over Indian water rights, those limitations were removed by the McCarran Amendment. Congress clearly would have had the right to distinguish between disclaimer and nondisclaimer States in passing the McCarran Amendment. But the Amendment was designed to deal with a general problem arising out of the limitations that federal sovereign immunity placed on the ability of the States to adjudicate water rights, and nowhere in its text or legislative history do we find any indication that Congress intended the efficacy of the remedy to differ from one State to another. Moreover, we stated in *Colorado River* that "bearing in mind the ubiquitous nature of Indian water rights in the Southwest, it is clear that a construction of the Amendment excluding those rights from its coverage would enervate the Amendment's objective." The "ubiquitous nature of Indian water rights" is most apparent in the very States to which Congress attached jurisdictional reservations. To declare now that our holding in *Colorado River* applies only to that minority of Indian water claims located in States without jurisdictional reservations would constitute a curious and unwarranted retreat from the rationale behind our previous holding, and would work the very mischief that our decision in *Colorado River* sought to avoid. We need not rely on the possibly overbroad statement in *Draper v. United States* that "equality of statehood is the rule," in order to conclude that, in this context at least, "equality of statehood" is sensible, necessary, and, most important, consistent with the will of Congress.

IV

The second crucial issue in these cases is whether our analysis in *Colorado River* applies with full force to federal suits brought by Indian tribes, rather than by the United States, and seeking adjudication only of Indian water rights.[20] "This question is not directly answered by *Colorado River*, because we specifically reserved in that case "[w]hether similar considerations would permit dismissal of a water suit brought by a private party in federal district court." On reflection, however, we must agree with Justice STEVENS, who, in dissenting from our decision, wrote:

> "[T]he Federal Government surely has no lesser right of access to the federal forum than does a private [party], such as an Indian asserting his own claim. If this be so, today's holding will necessarily restrict the access to federal court of private plaintiffs asserting water rights claims in Colorado."

The United States and the various Indian respondents raise a series of arguments why dismissal or stay of the federal suit is not appropriate when it is brought by an Indian tribe and only seeks to adjudicate Indian rights. (1) Indian rights have traditionally been left free of interference from the States. (2) State courts may be inhospitable to Indian rights. (3) The McCarran Amendment, although it waived United States sovereign immunity in state comprehensive water adjudications, did not waive Indian sovereign immunity. It is therefore unfair to force Indian claimants to choose between waiving their sovereign immunity by intervening in the state proceedings and relying on the United States to represent their interests in state court, particularly in light of the frequent conflict of interest between Indian claims and other federal interests and the right of the Indians under 28 U.S.C. § 1362 to bring suit on their own behalf in federal court.[21] (4) Indian

---

[20] [16] As is apparent from our discussion of the facts, [some of suits here involved cases] brought by the United States. In light of our express holding in *Colorado River*, what we say here with regard to the suits brought by the Indians must apply a fortiori to the suits brought by the United States. In addition, some of the cases before us sought adjudication of all the rights to a particular water system, rather than merely Indian or other federal water rights, and it is argued that these suits avoid the "piecemeal adjudication of water rights" which we found in Colorado River to be inconsistent with federal policy. [Since] one of the best arguments in favor of retaining federal jurisdiction in Indian water cases is that Indian water rights can be adjudicated separately and then incorporated into the results of the comprehensive state proceedings, [the correct] analysis of the more ambitious federal suits at issue here must also follow a fortiori from our discussion in text. A comprehensive federal adjudication going on at the same time as a comprehensive state adjudication might not literally be "piecemeal." It is, however, duplicative, wasteful, inconsistent with the McCarran Amendment's policy of "recogniz[ing] the availability of comprehensive state systems for adjudication of water rights as the means for [conducting unified water rights proceedings]," 424 U.S., at 819, likely to "generat[e] . . . additional litigation "as a result of inconsistent dispositions of property," *ibid.*, and permeated with state-law issues entirely tangential to any conceivable federal interest. . . .

[21] [17] This argument, of course, suffers from the flaw that, although the McCarran Amendment did not waive the sovereign immunity of Indians as parties to state comprehensive water adjudications, it did (as we made quite clear in *Colorado River*) waive sovereign immunity with regard to the Indian rights at issue in those proceedings. Moreover, contrary to the submissions by certain of the parties, any judgment against the United States, as trustee for the Indians, would ordinarily be binding on the Indians. In addition, there is no indication in these cases that the state courts would deny the Indian parties leave to intervene to protect their interests. Thus, although the Indians have the right to refuse

water rights claims are generally based on federal rather than state law. (5) Because Indian water claims are based on the doctrine of "reserved rights," and take priority over most water rights created by state law, they need not as a practical matter be adjudicated inter sese with other water rights, and could simply be incorporated into the comprehensive state decree at the conclusion of the state proceedings.

Each of these arguments has a good deal of force. We note, though, that very similar arguments were raised and rejected in *United States v. District Court for Eagle County*, 401 U.S. 520 (1971), and *Colorado River*. More important, all of these arguments founder on one crucial fact: If the state proceedings have jurisdiction over the Indian water rights at issue here, as appears to be the case, then concurrent federal proceedings are likely to be duplicative and wasteful, generating "additional litigation through permitting inconsistent dispositions of property." Moreover, since a judgment by either court would ordinarily be *res judicata* in the other, the existence of such concurrent proceedings creates the serious potential for spawning an unseemly and destructive race to see which forum can resolve the same issues first — a race contrary to the entire spirit of the McCarran Amendment and prejudicial, to say the least, to the possibility of reasoned decisionmaking by either forum. The United States and many of the Indian Tribes recognize these concerns, but in responding to them they cast aside the sort of sound argument generally apparent in the rest of their submissions and rely instead on vague statements of faith and hope. The United States, for example, states that adjudicating Indian water rights in federal court, despite the existence of a comprehensive state proceeding, would not

> "entail any duplication or potential for inconsistent judgments. The federal court will quantify the Indian rights only if it is asked to do so before the State court has embarked on the task. And, of course, once the United States district court has indicated its determination to perform that limited role, *we assume* the State tribunal will turn its attention to the typically more complex business of adjudicating all other claims on the stream. *In the usual case*, the federal court will have completed its function earlier and its quantification of Indian water rights will simply be incorporated in the comprehensive State court decree." Brief for United States 30 (emphasis added).

Similarly, the Navajo Nation states:

> "There is no reasonably foreseeable danger that [the] federal action [brought by the Navajo] will duplicate or delay state proceedings or waste judicial resources. While the Navajo claim proceeds in federal court, the state court *can* move forward to assess, quantify, and rank the 58,000 state claims. The Navajo federal action will be concluded long before the state court has finished its task." Brief for Respondent Navajo Nation in No. 81-2147, p. 22 (emphasis added; footnote omitted).

The problem with these scenarios, however, is that they assume a cooperative

---

to intervene even if they believe that the United States is not adequately representing their interests, the practical value of that right in this context is dubious at best.

attitude on the part of state courts, state legislatures, and state parties which is neither legally required nor realistically always to be expected. The state courts need not "turn their attention" to other matters if they are prompted by state parties to adjudicate the Indian claims first. Moreover, considering the specialized resources and experience of the state courts, it is not at all obvious that the federal actions "will be concluded long before" the state courts have issued at least preliminary judgments on the question of Indian water rights.

The McCarran Amendment, as interpreted in *Colorado River*, allows and encourages state courts to undertake the task of quantifying Indian water rights in the course of comprehensive water adjudications. Although adjudication of those rights in federal court instead might in the abstract be practical, and even wise, it will be neither practical nor wise as long as it creates the possibility of duplicative litigation, tension and controversy between the federal and state forums, hurried and pressured decisionmaking, and confusion over the disposition of property rights.

Colorado River, of course, does not require that a federal water suit must always be dismissed or stayed in deference to a concurrent and adequate comprehensive state adjudication. Certainly, the federal courts need not defer to the state proceedings if the state courts expressly agree to stay their own consideration of the issues raised in the federal action pending disposition of that action. Moreover, it may be in a particular case that, at the time a motion to dismiss is filed, the federal suit at issue is well enough along that its dismissal would itself constitute a waste of judicial resources and an invitation to duplicative effort. [W]e do not deny that, in a case in which the arguments for and against deference to the state adjudication were otherwise closely matched, the fact that a federal suit was brought by Indians on their own behalf and sought only to adjudicate Indian rights should be figured into the balance. But the most important consideration in *Colorado River*, and the most important consideration in any federal water suit concurrent to a comprehensive state proceeding, must be the "policy underlying the McCarran Amendment." [D]espite the strong arguments raised by the respondents, we cannot conclude that water rights suits brought by Indians and seeking adjudication only of Indian rights should be excepted from the application of that policy or from the general principles set out in *Colorado River*. In the cases before us, assuming that the state adjudications are adequate to quantify the rights at issue in the federal suits, and taking into account the McCarran Amendment policies we have just discussed, the expertise and administrative machinery available to the state courts, the infancy of the federal suits, the general judicial bias against piecemeal litigation, and the convenience to the parties, we must conclude that the District Courts were correct in deferring to the state proceedings.[22]

---

[22] [21] We leave open for determination on remand as appropriate whether the proper course in such cases is a stay of the federal suit or dismissal without prejudice. *See Moses H. Cone Hospital*, 460 U.S. [1], at 28 (reserving issue). In either event, resort to the federal forum should remain available if warranted by a significant change of circumstances, such as, for example, a decision by a state court that it does not have jurisdiction over some or all of these claims after all.

V

Nothing we say today should be understood to represent even the slightest retreat from the general proposition we expressed so recently in *New Mexico v. Mescalero Apache Tribe*, 462 U.S., at 332: "Because of their sovereign status, [Indian] tribes and their reservation lands are insulated in some respects by a 'historic immunity from state and local control,' and tribes retain any aspect of their historical sovereignty not 'inconsistent with the overriding interests of the National Government.'" Nor should we be understood to retreat from the general proposition, expressed in *Colorado River*, that federal courts have a "virtually unflagging obligation . . . to exercise the jurisdiction given them." But water rights adjudication is a virtually unique type of proceeding, and the McCarran Amendment is a virtually unique federal statute, and we cannot in this context be guided by general propositions.

We also emphasize, as we did in *Colorado River*, that our decision in no way changes the substantive law by which Indian rights in state water adjudications must be judged. State courts, as much as federal courts, have a solemn obligation to follow federal law. Moreover, any state-court decision alleged to abridge Indian water rights protected by federal law can expect to receive, if brought for review before this Court, a particularized and exacting scrutiny commensurate with the powerful federal interest in safeguarding those rights from state encroachment.

The judgment of the Court of Appeals in each of these cases is reversed, and the cases are remanded for further proceedings consistent with this opinion.

So ordered.

JUSTICE MARSHALL, dissenting.

In *Colorado River Water Conservation District v. United States*, 424 U.S. 800 (1976), this Court recognized a narrow rule of abstention governing controversies involving federal water rights. We stated that in light of "the virtually unflagging obligation of the federal courts to exercise the jurisdiction given them," "[o]nly the clearest of justifications," will warrant abstention in favor of a concurrent state proceeding. Substantially for the reasons set forth in Justice STEVENS' dissenting opinion, I believe that abstention is not appropriate in these cases. Unlike the federal suit in *Colorado River*, the suits here are brought by Indian Tribes on their own behalf. These cases thus implicate the strong congressional policy, embodied in 28 U.S.C. § 1362, of affording Indian tribes a federal forum. . . .

JUSTICE STEVENS, with whom JUSTICE BLACKMUN joins, dissenting.

"Nothing in the McCarran Amendment or in its legislative history can be read as limiting the jurisdiction of the federal courts." *Colorado River Water Conservation District v. United States*, 424 U.S. 800, 821, n.2 (1976) (Stewart, J., dissenting). That Amendment is a waiver, not a command. It permits the United States to be joined as a defendant in state water rights adjudications; it does not purport to diminish the United States' right to litigate in a federal forum and it is totally silent on the subject of Indian tribes' rights to litigate anywhere. Yet today the majority somehow concludes that it commands the federal courts to defer to state-court water rights proceedings, even when Indian water rights are involved. Although it is customary for the Court to begin its analysis of questions of statutory construction by examining the text of the relevant statute, one may search in vain for any textual support for the Court's holding today.

. . . .

One important aspect of the special relationship [between the federal government and Indian tribes] is 28 U.S.C. § 1362, which embodies a federal promise that Indian tribes will be able to invoke the jurisdiction of federal courts to resolve matters in controversy arising under federal law. Congress thereby assured Indians a neutral federal forum — a guarantee whose importance should not be underestimated.[23] The Senate Report noted:

> "There is great hesitancy on the part of tribes to use State courts. This reluctance is founded partially on the traditional fear that tribes have had of the States in which their reservations are situated. Additionally, the Federal courts have more expertise in deciding questions involving treaties with the Federal Government, as well as interpreting the relevant body of Federal law that has developed over the years." S. Rep. No. 1507, 89th Cong., 2d Sess., 2 (1966).

Section 1362 also assured the tribes that they need not rely on the Federal Government to protect their interests, an important safeguard in light of the undeniable potential for conflicts of interest between Indian claims and other Federal Government claims.

Despite the silence of the McCarran Amendment regarding Indian tribal claims, and the clear promise of a federal forum embodied in § 1362, the Court holds that considerations of "wise judicial administration" require that Indian claims, governed by federal law, must be relegated to the state courts. It is clear to me that the words "wise judicial administration" have been wrenched completely from their ordinary meaning. One of the Arizona proceedings, in which process has been served on approximately 58,000 known water claimants, illustrates the practical consequences of giving the state courts the initial responsibility for the adjudication of Indian water rights claims. Because this Court may not exercise appellate jurisdiction in state-court litigation until after a final judgment has been entered by

---

[23] [8] The majority recognizes that there is "a good deal of force" to the assertion that "[s]tate courts may be inhospitable to Indian rights." Federal officials responsible for Indian affairs have consistently recognized the appropriateness of deciding Indian claims in federal, not state, courts. See, e.g., H.R. Rep. No. 2040, 89th Cong., 2d Sess., 2 (1966) (describing position of Interior Department); National Water Comm'n, Water Policies for the Future, Final Report to the President and to the Congress of the United States 478–479 (1973). American Indian Policy Review Commission, Task Force Four, Report on Federal, State, and Tribal Jurisdiction 176 (Comm. Print 1976); American Indian Policy Review Commission, Final Report 333–334 (Comm. Print 1977).

Although the Court correctly observes that state courts, "as much as federal courts, have a solemn obligation to follow federal law," state judges, unlike federal judges, tend to be elected and hence to be more conscious of the prevailing views of the majority. Water rights adjudications, which will have a crucial impact on future economic development in the West, are likely to stimulate great public interest and concern.

the highest court of the State, no federal tribunal will be able to review any federal question in the case until the entire litigation has been concluded. The Court promises that "any state-court decision alleged to abridge Indian water rights protected by federal law can expect to receive, if brought for review before this Court, a particularized and exacting scrutiny commensurate with the powerful federal interest in safeguarding those rights from state encroachment." If a state court errs in interpreting the *Winters* doctrine or an Indian treaty, and this Court ultimately finds it necessary to correct that error, the entire comprehensive state-court water rights decree may require massive readjustment. If, however, the quantification of Indian rights were to be adjudicated in a separate federal proceeding — which presumably would be concluded long before the mammoth, conglomerate state adjudication comes to an end — the state judgment would rest on a solid foundation that this Court should never need to examine.

The Court acknowledges the logical force of these propositions, but sets them aside because the exercise of concurrent federal-court jurisdiction would create "the possibility of duplicative litigation, tension and controversy between the federal and state forums, hurried and pressured decisionmaking, and confusion over the disposition of property rights."

NOTES ON STATE ADJUDICATION OF INDIAN WATER RIGHTS

1. **Problematic Features of State Adjudication:** When state courts adjudicate Indian water rights under the McCarran Amendment and *Colorado River Water Conservation District* and *San Carlos Apache*, whose law governs issues regarding the priority, quantity, and use of Indian water rights? What problems, if any, does this system of adjudication pose? Where states use administrative, rather than judicial, processes to resolve water rights claims, at least one court surprisingly held that *Colorado River Water Conservation District* and *San Carlos Apache* still apply to relegate the United States and the tribes to state administrative tribunals, even where the adjudication sought an alteration of a prior *federal* court water decree. *United States v. Walker River Irrig. Dist.*, 15 Ind. L. Rep. 3083 (D. Nev. No. C-125-ECR, decided May 17, 1988).

The Court stated in *Colorado River Water Conserv. Dist.*, 424 U.S. 800, 812–13 (1976), and in *United States v. District Court for Eagle County*, 401 U.S. 520, 525–26 (1971), that it stands ready to correct abuses in reserved water rights cases that are adjudicated in state courts or administrative processes by exercising its certiorari jurisdiction. Whether such vigilance is actually being exercised is another matter entirely. According to Nell Jessup Newton et al., Cohen's Handbook of Federal Indian Law 1210 (2005 ed.), "The efficacy of this solution may be doubted, however, particularly when the quantification of reserved water rights is predicated on complex factual determinations." This leading treatise also collects a number of cases where the federal courts declined to intervene where tribes offered evidence of state judges' conflicts of interest or improper ex parte contacts with the state water agency. *Id.* at 1210–1211, n. 313; *see also Wilson v. Omaha Indian Tribe*, 442 U.S. 653, 673–74 (1979). State court adjudication of *Winters* rights, without a significant possibility of Supreme Court review, presents non-Indian private appropriators and both local and state governments in water-scarce areas with the opportunity to have judges who may be more responsive to local political pressures adjudicate such claims. *See* extract of letter from Anthony Rogers to Senator Edward M. Kennedy (June 23, 1976), reproduced in Michael C. Nelson, *The* Winters *Doctrine: Seventy Years of Application of "Reserved" Water Rights to Indian Reservations*, ARID LANDS RESOURCE INFORMATION PAPER No. 9, n. 158 (University of Arizona 1977). For another negative assessment of state adjudication of Indian water rights, specifically tribal claims for instream flow, see Michael C. Blumm, David H. Becker & Joshua D. Smith, *The Mirage of Indian Reserved Water Rights and Western Streamflow Restoration in the McCarran Amendment Era: A Promise Unfulfilled*, 36 ENVTL. L. 1157, 1169–1170 (2006).

The assumption that state tribunals will provide less neutral adjudication obviously is not shared by the Court. On what premises can such an assumption be justified? Does it make any difference that state judges are elected or appointed, often with far less judicial independence that federal judges are assured under Article III, section 1 of the United States Constitution? Should the fact that state administrative agencies often have little job security affect the adequacy of the forum? On the other hand, the worst fears of tribal water advocates have not always been realized in state court. For example, in *In re General Adjudication of All Rights to Water in the Gila River Sys. & Source*, 15 Indian L. Rep. 5099 (Ariz. Super. Ct., Maricopa County, Nos. W-1, W-2, W-3, and W-4, decided Sept. 9, 1988), the state court accepted most of the Indian positions. It held that Indian *Winters* rights applied to both surface and groundwater sources and rejected the efforts by adverse claimants to exclude their groundwater wells from the stream adjudication.

While state courts may have jurisdiction to adjudicate and quantify Indian water rights, the special jurisdictional status of Indian country and the sovereign immunity of Indian tribes continue to pose significant barriers for states and others seeking information on water usage or seeking to monitor and enforce water law decrees. *See, e.g., Joint Bd. of Control of the Flathead, Mission & Jocko Irrig. Dists. v. Bureau of Indian Affairs*, 16 Indian L. Rep. 3001 (D. Mont. No. CV 87-217-BLG-JFB, decided Sept. 9, 1988) (information on water resources on the Flathead Indian Reservation exempt from disclosure under Freedom of Information Act).

2.   Authority to Regulate Water Use in Indian Country: In the case of *In re General Adjudication of All Rights to Use Water in Big Horn River System*, 835 P.2d 273 (Wyo. 1992) (*Big Horn III*), the Wyoming Supreme Court held that water allocated to the Wind River Reservation under the PIA standard could not be used for purposes other than irrigation, such as to preserve instream flowage for fishery preservation, without complying with state law. The Court wrote:

> The Tribes further contend that an unbroken chain of decisions exists in the United States determining that the Tribes' water rights are governed by federal law. The Tribes, however, fail to direct us to any of these decisions. The Tribes' additional reasoning that historical federal and tribal regulation of Indian water use is strong evidence that state control is federally preempted is not persuasive. We are persuaded by *United States v. New Mexico*, 438 U.S. 696 (1978), wherein the United States Supreme Court held that water is impliedly reserved only to the extent necessary to meet

the primary purpose(s) for which a reservation is made and that, where water is valuable for a secondary purpose, the inference arises that Congress intended for water to be acquired in the same manner as is employed by any other private or public appropriator. In *United States v. Adair*, 723 F.2d 1394 (9th Cir. 1983), *cert. denied*, 467 U.S. 1252 (1984), the United States attempted to convert Indian reserved water rights to forest and wildlife programs. The Ninth Circuit Court of Appeals rejected the attempt and stated:

> The purpose of a federal reservation of land defines the scope and nature of impliedly reserved water rights. Because the reserved rights doctrine is an exception to Congress's explicit deference to state water law in other areas, the Supreme Court has emphasized the importance of the limitation of such rights to only so much water as is essential to accomplish the purpose for which the land was reserved. We conclude that it would be inconsistent with the principles expressed in *United States v. New Mexico* to hold that the Government may "tack" a currently claimed *Winters* right to a prior one by asserting that it has merely changed the purpose of its previously reserved water right.

835 P.2d at 278–279.

The effect of the *Big Horn III* decision was to bring the Tribes within the Wyoming water regulatory regime and to require state permission to alter the use of water the Tribes owned under their *Winters* rights. In the absence of the McCarran Amendment would the state water engineer normally have jurisdiction to regulate the Tribes' use of their *Winters* rights water? Was there anything in the McCarran Amendment that authorized state regulation of tribal water use? Do the *Gila River* and *Big Horn III* cases demonstrate any problems with having state courts adjudicate tribal water rights as part of general stream adjudications? Could the tribes of the Wind River Reservation or their members now go to federal court seeking an injunction against the Wyoming Water Engineer preventing them from using their water for purposes other than irrigation? Would that suit be barred by *Colorado River Conservation District* or *San Carlos Apache?* Would the suit be barred by full faith and credit under 28 U.S.C. § 1738? Does it make any difference that the McCarran Amendment, which permitted the tribal claims to be litigated in *Big Horn III*, involved a waiver of federal sovereign immunity and that statutes waiving sovereign immunity generally are narrowly construed?

In Robert Pelcyger, *Indian Water Rights: Some Emerging Frontiers*, 21 ROCKY MT. MIN. L. INST. 743 (1976), the author argued that:

> The tribe may have jurisdiction to regulate non-Indians' water uses even though some of the non-Indians' substantive rights may be governed by state law. A non-Indian's right to obtain water for land located within a reservation may be governed by substantive considerations found in state law, such as whether a surplus is found to exist, but the decision on whether or not those substantive considerations are met, that is whether there is, in fact, a surplus, may properly reside with the tribe to the exclusion of the state.

Id. at 769–70 (footnote omitted). Pelcyger wrote before the Supreme Court decision in *Montana v. United States*, 450 U.S. 544 (1981) (tribes have no regulatory authority over nonmember activity on non-Indian owned land unless they satisfy the "*Montana* exceptions"), set forth and discussed in Ch. 3, Sec. A.3.a, and other court decisions limiting tribal jurisdiction. Considering these cases as well as the *Colorado River* and *San Carlos* decisions, how much vitality is left of Pelcyger's argument? Does the *Brendale* decision rejecting tribal authority to zone non-Indian land on "open" portions of a reservation, discussed in Ch. A.6, undermine the Pelcyger argument? Might your analysis of these problems depend in part on the legal source and theory of non-Indian water rights in Indian country? In that connection, consider the materials that follow on rights derived from Indian allotments. Even prior to *Brendale*, the Ninth Circuit had rejected the Yakima Nation Water Code as invalid insofar as it purported to control use by non-Indians of excess waters on or passing through the Yakima Indian Reservation. *Holly v. Confederated Tribes & Bands of the Yakima Indian Nation*, 655 F. Supp. 557 (E.D. Wash. 1986), *aff'd sub nom. Holly v. Totus*, 812 F.2d 714 (9th Cir. 1987); *see also United States v. Anderson*, 736 F.2d 1358 (9th Cir. 1984) (tribes cannot use criminal or quasi-criminal sanctions to regulate non-Indian use of excess water within their reservations).

In *Confederated Salish & Kootenai Tribes v. Clinch*, 297 Mont. 448, 997 P.2d 244 (Mont. Sup. Ct. 1999), the Montana Supreme Court took the unusual procedural step of exercising its original jurisdiction to enjoin the Montana Department of Natural Resources and Conservation and its Director from issuing water use permits to non-Indians on the Flathead Reservation until such time as the tribal rights had been quantified. Since the Montana Water User Act limited permits to water that was "legally available," Mont. Code Ann. § 85-2-311, the court construed the language to "mean there is water available which, among other things, has not been federally reserved for Indian tribes." Thus, the court held that on the Flathead Reservation, water was not legally available within the meaning of the Act until the reserved rights of the tribes had been quantified. Despite the evident clarity of the Montana Supreme Court's ruling in *Clinch*, the State Department of Natural Resources and Conservation proceeded to grant a permit for reservation ground-water to a non-Indian applicant. The state Supreme Court responded sharply to this action, stopping just short of holding the agency's director in contempt, and remanding that issue to the trial court. *See Confederated Salish and Kootenai Tribes of the Flathead Reservation v. Stults*, 59 P.3d 1093 (Mont. 2002). The Court held that tribes are not required to defend their water rights in the context of individual permit applications, and reaffirmed that the only basis upon which the McCarren Amendment allows adjudication of Indian water rights in state court is through a comprehensive stream adjudication.

When the case returned to the Montana Supreme Court after remand, the state's Department of Natural Resources and Conservation seemed to be given more leeway to process applications for *changes* of water uses by non-Indians on the Flathead Reservation, even though the Tribe's water rights have not yet been quantified. *Confederated Salish and Kootenai Tribes v. Clinch*, 336 Mont. 302, 158 P.2d 377 (2007). The court remanded the case again, however, so that the trial judge could determine whether the state even has sovereign authority to process applications, given the United States Supreme Court's line of cases dealing with state regulatory and taxing jurisdiction over non-Indians on reservations. *See* Ch. 4, Sec. B.4.b. In the court's view, the important issue arising from this line of cases is whether the proposed changes in water use would adversely affect the tribes' reserved water rights, and thereby have some direct impact on their political integrity, economic security, health, or welfare. Once again, the court remanded for factual findings. In framing the issue this way, wasn't the Montana high court conflating the legal test for state jurisdiction with the legal test for tribal jurisdiction over non-Indian fee land, the line of cases beginning with *United States v. Montana*, presented in Ch. 3, Sec. C.1? How do those two legal analyses differ, and how might that difference affect the issue of state regulatory jurisdiction in the Montana litigation? Crucial to the court's decision was an assumption that the unquantified nature of the Tribes' rights shouldn't matter when only a change of use is at stake. Dissenting Justice James C. Nelson challenged that assumption, pointing out:

> While an applicant might not divert any more water after a proposed change than he or she has diverted historically, the change in use still could increase or decrease the flow in a protected stretch of a stream, raise or lower a water table, artesian pressure, or water level in a protected area, or impede aboriginal practices. For instance, the change could adversely affect the use of water rights reserved by the Tribes for aboriginal hunting and fishing, which may require that a particular quantity of water is located (or not located) at a particular location. Indeed, the [Department] conceded this point in the District Court.

What might be the burden, both legal and practical, of the latest *Clinch* decision on the Confederated Salish and Kootenai Tribes? Should the Tribes have to bear that burden so long as the Tribes' water rights haven't been quantified?

3.   Water Rights of Allottees and Their Successors

Difficult questions surround Indian allottees' water rights. A pair of articles by knowledgeable experts in the field frames the issues, though the authors do not always reach the same conclusions. *See* Richard B. Collins, *Indian Allotment Water Rights*, 20 LAND & WATER L. REV. 421 (1985); David Getches, *Water Rights on Indian Allotments*, 26 S.D. L. REV. 405, 416 (1981); *see also* NELL JESSUP NEWTON ET AL., COHEN'S HANDBOOK OF FEDERAL INDIAN LAW § 19.03[8] (2005 ed.). In the absence of clear congressional guidance, courts have had to develop the governing rules. Court decisions, primarily *United States v. Powers*, 305 U.S. 527 (1930), have established that Indian-held allotments took some portion of the *Winters* water rights held by the tribe prior to allotment and that their successors in interest, whether Indian or non-Indian, acquired some right to water. The precise nature and extent of those rights, however, remains the subject of considerable dispute. The quantification of such Indian rights, their impact on the tribal allocation, and their transferability to non-Indians when the land was alienated or passed out of trust have remained substantially less clear despite the importance of these questions to the economic development of such lands. For Indian owners of allotments, the rule seems to be that they hold a percentage of the prior tribal reserved water rights in a water system that is equal to the percentage that their practically irrigable acreage bears to the irrigable acreage contained in the reservation itself. The problem for their successors in interest is considerably more complex, as the articles mentioned above indicate.

In *Colville Confederated Tribes v. Walton*, 647 F.2d 42 (9th Cir. 1981), the court held that a ratable share of the reserved tribal water rights of the Colville Tribes passed to allottees and that these rights could be and were conveyed to their non-Indian successors in interest subject to loss if not put to use "with reasonable diligence." The published 1981 opinion followed a withdrawn 1980 opinion in which the court had held that a non-Indian purchaser of Indian allotted land acquired no reserved water rights. In a footnote to the withdrawn 1980 *Walton* opinion, the court had stated that this reading of *Powers* was erroneous, since the Supreme Court in *Powers* "expressly reserved the issue of transferability" by not considering the extent or precise nature of water rights of non-Indian successors to Indian allottees. The Ninth Circuit in the published 1981 *Walton* opinion, however, found in *Powers* a recognition that some sort of water right was appurtenant to and passed with an allotment when purchased by non-Indians. In a later opinion, *Colville Confederated Tribes v. Walton*, 752 F.2d 397 (9th Cir. 1985), the court reviewed the water allocation awarded by the district court and reduced the award to the non-Indian owner since the court erred in permitting the perfection of reserved water rights by the reasonable diligence of *subsequent* non-Indian successors beyond the immediate successor in interest. The opinion noted:

> A careful reading [of the Court's earlier *Walton* opinion] leaves no doubt that the immediate grantee of the original allottee must exercise due diligence to perfect his or her inchoate right to the allottee's ratable share of reserved waters. This interpretation is supported by our reference to *Walton II* in subsequent cases. *See, e.g., United States v. Anderson*, 736 F.2d 1358, 1362 (9th Cir. 1984) ("use it or lose it"); *United States v. Adair*, 723 F.2d 1394, 1417 (9th Cir. 1983), *cert. denied*, 104 S. Ct. 3536 (1984). Once perfected, the water right must be "maintained by continued use [or] it is lost." *Walton II*, 647 F.2d at 51.

> The district court on remand was to "calculate the respective rights of the parties." *Id.* at 53. Calculating Walton's share required an investigation into the diligence with which the *immediate* grantee from the Indian allottees appropriated water, and the extent to which successor grantees, up to and including Walton, continued to use the water thus appropriated. Otherwise, any remote purchaser could appropriate enough water to irrigate all irrigable acreage with a priority date as of the creation of the Reservation. The reasonable diligence requirement of *Walton II* would be meaningless.

752 F.2d at 402.

In an earlier case, *United States ex rel. Ray v. Hibner*, 27 F.2d 909 (D. Idaho 1928), the United States sought an adjudication of the rights of Indians of the Fort Hall Reservation and their successors in interest to the waters of Toponce Creek. The Fort Bridger Treaty of 1869, which established the reservation, also granted twenty-two allotments to Indians occupying and cultivating land that was within the reservation. In addition, the treaty stated that the water of streams within the allotments that was necessary for irrigation in land in actual cultivation was reserved for the Indian allottees. The court held that non-Indian successors to these allottees were entitled to reserved water rights "for the actual acreage that was under irrigation at the time title passed from the Indians, and such increased acreage as [the non-Indians] might with reasonable diligence place under irrigation, which would give . . . , under the doctrine of relation, the same priority as owned by the Indians." Since there was no forfeiture of water rights by failure to cultivate the allotments during a period of Indian ownership, the priority date was not that time at which the Indian allottee began to put the water to beneficial use, but rather the time of the creation of the reservation. Thus, the non-Indian successor's priority date would relate back to the date of the creation of the reservation and not just to the actual date of appropriation. While such a successor was not governed by the state law of prior appropriation with respect to priority date, the court did find that policy recognized in the development of arid lands such as those dealt with in the case required that the successor continue to put the water to beneficial use in order to preserve the rights to it. Also, the Court stated that "granting to the Indian lands the (reserved) right to . . . water . . . will not prohibit the next appropriator on the stream from using the water, when it is not diverted and used from the stream by the Indians and applied by them to a beneficial use. . . . "

In his article, referenced above, Professor David Getches argued that while the Supreme Court in *Powers* did recognize an Indian allottee's right to that part of the tribal water necessary for farming the allotment, there was "nothing in the General Allotment Act to suggest that Congress was dividing up and conveying tribal water rights in severalty as it did tribal lands." If that was indeed the case, then the reserved water rights would continue to be owned by the tribe both after creation of allotments and conveyance of the fee patents to Indian allottees. Thus, no reserved rights would pass to non-Indian purchasers of allotments. Getches contended that because the goal of the Allotment Act was to integrate Indian allottees into mainstream society, ending their status as government wards and their dependence on the tribe, it followed that they would no longer receive the benefit of preferential treatment under the reserved water rights doctrine once the federal trust period had expired. The end of the trust period would free the allottee from restrictions on encumbrancing or disposing of the property, but it would also expose the property to taxes and local and state regulation. The state laws relative to the perfection and maintenance of water rights would be among those regulations applying to the allotments.

Clearly differing with his colleague Professor Collins, who thought that allottees should be able to transfer such rights conditioned on their perfection by the transferee within a reasonable time, Getches argued that a pro rata reserved right for allottees would place them at an advantage over non-Indian homesteaders governed by the appropriative rights doctrine and over Indian allottees whose land was still in trust. Getches noted that a pro rata reserved right for allottees and their successors would even call into question the extent of the tribe's rights when water use for irrigation was subject to abatement due to scarcity. In the latter case, because the allottees would have reserved rights allowing for full pro rata shares, during droughts the tribal water requirements would be in conflict with allotment requirements without benefit of a hierarchy of dominant and subordinate water rights. Whereas non-Indian appropriators whose perfection of a water right was prior to the creation of a reservation would be senior to the right of the tribe, and non-Indian appropriators whose perfection was subsequent to the creation would be junior, tribal and allottee rights would be equal and thus difficult to adjudicate. Getches cautioned that reserved rights could extend to potentially thousands of individuals, advising that the trust ownership of the tribal reserved water rights remain with the government even after the fee patents to land are conveyed to allottees. Getches argued that allottees should be allowed to transfer rights only if they had been perfected by use during the trust period and had been maintained in accordance with state law after expiration of the trust.

Do the holdings in *Hibner* and the 1981 published *Walton* opinion, particularly the "due or reasonable diligence" element for the establishment of water rights for non-Indian purchasers of allotments, create too great an incentive for non-Indian purchasers to seek out Indian allotments rather than other lands, thereby reducing tribal water allocations and individual allottees' incentives to develop their water rights during the period of Indian ownership? Can you see why this might be so?

In *Wyoming v. Owl Creek Irrig. Dist.* (*In re General Adjudication of All Rights to Use Water in the Big Horn River Sys.*), 750 P.2d 681, 753 P.2d 76 (Wyo. 1988), *aff'd by equally divided vote sub nom. United States v. Wyoming*, 492 U.S. 406 (1989) (*Big Horn I*), the court held that Indian allottees who held fee lands shared in the tribal reserved rights with a priority as of the date of the creation of the Wind River Reservation, and it remanded the case to calculate the water rights of non-Indian grantees of the allottees "with an 1868 priority date for the PIA [practicably irrigable acreage] they can show were irrigated by their Indian predecessors or put under irrigation within a reasonable time thereafter." 753 P.2d at 113–14. What constitutes a "reasonable time"? Some of the former allotments drawing upon the Big Horn River had not come under irrigation for ten to thirty years. In *In re General Adjudication of All Rights to Use Water in the Big Horn River System*, 48 P.3d 1040 (Wyo. 2002), the Wyoming Supreme Court found that such delays were consistent with a reasonable time standard, so long as the delays were attributable to diligent but time-consuming pursuit of development of a federal irrigation project, and state law was followed to protect rights while the development was pending. The court acknowledged that state law favored efforts to achieve federally funded irrigation projects. Should federal or state law govern whether the reasonable time standard has been met for maintaining *Walton* rights?

4. Water Rights Settlements as Alternatives to Litigation

The costs, time, and potential for bias experienced by tribes in state general stream adjudications, coupled with the tribal need for funds to turn "paper" water rights into useable flow, have led many tribes to negotiate settlements of their water rights claims. According to NELL JESSUP NEWTON ET AL., COHEN'S HANDBOOK OF FEDERAL INDIAN LAW § 19.05[2] (2005 ed.) and its 2009 Cumulative Update, Congress has enacted 21 settlement acts into law between 1978 and 2008. Typically these settlements quantify the tribe's right and provide federal funds for tribal water development. They may also address issues such as the relationship of ground and surface water, water marketing, permissible tribal uses, and ways of increasing the total amount of water available for all users (*e.g.*, by lining irrigation canals). Are there any major disadvantages for tribes in negotiating rather than litigating over their water rights? Have Supreme Court decisions addressing the extent of Indian water rights and the procedures for adjudicating them given tribes a strong hand in such negotiations? How might the need for large-scale investment to make water rights meaningful affect tribes' choice between negotiating and litigating? The following article addresses these questions, and offers a specific illustration, the 2004 Snake River Water Settlement.

Robert T. Anderson, *Indian Water Rights: Litigation and Settlements*
42 Tulsa L. Rev. 23 (2006)

B. Ambiguity in the Law and its Application

Ten years ago Professor Judith Royster wrote an article about Indian reserved water rights titled, *A Primer on Indian Water Rights: More Questions than Answers*. Courts in the intervening years have published dozens of opinions dealing with Indian reserved water rights, but it is safe to say that there are still more questions than answers. The United States Supreme Court has not decided a substantive Indian water rights case since the 1989 affirmance by a four-to-four vote of the Wyoming Supreme Court's ruling on the application of the practicably irrigable acreage doctrine. There was no opinion for the Court although draft majority and dissent opinions were circulated within the Court and have become public. The draft majority opinion would have cautioned courts to be "sensitive" to non-Indian water use when determining the amount reserved for an Indian tribe. How would the current Supreme Court answer the question presented? No one knows, but the tension in the draft opinions invites speculation.

[The author identifies numerous areas of "significant debate," including whether the purposes of a reservation of water for Indian use should be construed broadly or narrowly; whether reserved rights extend to groundwater; the water rights of individual allotment holders and non-Indians who have acquired land that was allotted.]

These vague standards encourage resolution through settlement legislation as demonstrated by the following example.

III. THE SNAKE RIVER SETTLEMENT EXAMPLE

Congress passed the Snake River Water Rights Act of 2004 [Pub. L. No. 108-447, § 8(g), 118 Stat. 2809] "to achieve a fair, equitable, and final settlement of all claims of the Nez Perce Tribe, its members, and allottees and the United States on behalf of the Tribe, its members, and allottees to the water of the Snake River Basin within Idaho." The settlement was achieved despite a trial court ruling that rejected all claims by the Tribe and the United States for instream flows to support the Tribe's right to fish at all "usual and accustomed stations." While the court's reasoning had many serious flaws and an appeal was taken, the parties to the adjudication were already heavily invested in negotiations to resolve not just tribal water rights disputes but also to deal with Endangered Species Act matters, which gravely concerned non-Indian water users in Idaho. The settlement involved three major components, with the first two serving as the incentive for the State of Idaho and private water users to support a favorable settlement of tribal claims. First was the desire for security for Upper Snake River water users pursuant to a thirty-year negotiated flow augmentation plan. Second was agreement on the fairly specific plan for an agreement under § 6 of the Endangered Species Act for habitat protection and restoration in the Salmon and Clearwater Basins. Having satisfied those desires, private water users and the State supported a tribal settlement with the following primary components.

The Settlement Act and "mediator's term sheet" provide:

1. water for a variety of tribal uses on the reservation;

2. recognition of allotment water rights and a due process requirement for tribal regulation of such rights;

3. for the transfer of on-reservation land valued at $7 million (estimated to be approximately 11,000 acres) from the federal Bureau of Land Management to the tribe;

4. a right to access and use of approximately six hundred springs and fountains on federal lands in off-reservation areas;

5. tribal control of 200,000 acre-feet of water from Dworshak reservoir;

6. authorization of nearly $90 million for tribal water- and habitat-related improvements; and

7. instream flow minimums at over two hundred "locations selected by the Tribe as a matter of biological and cultural priority."

There is an additional $38 million allocated for a Salmon and Clearwater River Basins Habitat Fund.

The settlement agreement provides an excellent outcome for all parties involved. It accomplishes far more in terms of benefits for the Tribe that would have been possible in litigation because it returns land to the Tribe and provides funds to improve water and sanitation systems. It also funds habitat restoration projects throughout the basin. Moreover, one reason the settlement seems so favorable is because it provided an escape from a state court system hostile to federal and Indian water rights. The stakes for Indian tribes are too high for the United States to participate solely in a reactive mode and seek settlement as a way out of desperate situations. The National Water Commission in 1973 documented the federal government's miserable performance with respect to the protection of Indian water rights. The commission made some concrete recommendations for improvement, prompted in part by the fact that the federal government had promoted and subsidized non-Indian water development at the expense of vested tribal rights. Yet the settlement process in place during the first Bush Administration is governed — in theory at least — by guidelines that were developed without consultation with the affected tribes. This is despite the fact that the guidelines themselves declare that "Indian water rights are vested property rights for which the United States has a trust responsibility, with the United States holding legal title to such water in trust for the benefit of the Indians."

A major concern in the settlement process is the amount of the federal monetary contribution to resolve the dispute. The Senate Report to the Snake River Settlement Act demonstrates Congress's awareness of the need for federal funds to settle litigation and remedy past injustices:

> A significant additional shortcoming from the tribal perspective is that although a decree in a general stream adjudication might recognize an Indian tribe's rights to substantial quantities of water with an early priority date, this may do little, if anything, to deliver real (or "wet") water to dry Indian lands.

The shortcomings of the general stream adjudication process as a device for water rights dispute resolution have led to an increasing number of agreed-to water rights settlements on streams in the western States — where the parties, including Indian tribes, negotiate and compromise among themselves as to quantity, priority dates and other issues, and where the Federal government contributes money to the settlement in order to achieve various goals that could not otherwise be achieved within the confines of a general stream adjudication, such as monetary and other compensation to the Indian tribe, including construction of water delivery systems that bring "wet" water to the Indian lands as well as other tangible benefits to the tribe or its members.

The federal contribution to settle the Nez Perce claims would be in the neighborhood of $130 million, with $90 million to the Tribe for water- and fishery-related projects.

How did the federal government determine that the amount of money in the bill was justified? The Criteria and Procedures for the Participation of the Federal Government in Negotiations for the Settlement of Indian Water Rights Claims provide that:

> Federal contributions to a settlement should not exceed the sum of the following two elements: a. First, calculable legal exposure — litigation cost and judgment obligations if the case is lost; Federal and non-Federal exposure should be calculated on a present value basis taking into account the size of the claim, value of the water, timing of the award, [and] likelihood of loss. b. Second, additional costs related to Federal trust or programmatic responsibilities (assuming the U.S. obligation as trustee can be compared to existing precedence.) — Federal contributions relating to programmatic responsibilities should be justified as to why such contributions cannot be funded through the normal budget process.

How this language is converted into the government's position in any given settlement context is not really known, but many suspect that it is more a matter of whether the Administration has the political will to advance a settlement with a large federal contribution than some sort of a principled economic calculation. And of course, the Administration's political will is dependent on factors such as the influence and power of the affected state's congressional delegation and whether other sectors of the water use community are in strong support of the settlement and stand to obtain significant benefits from the settlement. The powerful coalition of Idaho water users, the Nez Perce Tribe, and other industry groups provided a strong foundation for enactment of the legislation, but even so the manner in which it became law was serendipitous. Nowhere in the course of these events is it revealed how the Administration determined that the federal contribution to the settlement passed muster under the criteria and procedures noted above. It is commonly understood that the federal position on the funding issue is driven by the Office of Management and Budget and that the figures associated with federal calculable legal exposure are subject to a wide range of estimates. Frequently, it appropriately includes the federal government's legal exposure based on its past failures to protect Indian water rights. In addition, "federal contributions relating to programmatic responsibilities" are frequently rolled into a settlement because, as in the Nez Perce settlement, it is politically expedient to do so.

The current Secretary of the Interior, Dirk Kempthorne [as of 2006], was the governor of Idaho when the Snake River Settlement Act became law. His lead negotiator for water rights matters in Idaho, Counselor Michael Bogert, [was] the lead policy official in the Secretary's office. Recent remarks from Bogert mention the financial contribution limitations of the Criteria and Procedures, but the Snake River experience may cause there to be more flexibility and creativity employed in forthcoming settlements. Bogert stated:

> We will also be considering a more holistic problem-solving approach to those issues, and some settlements could include discussion of strategic approaches to the endangered species act and the clean water act.

> We will also consider non-monetary elements such as land transfers, habitat management and facility operations. These were key ingredients to the success of the Nez Perce agreement.

This apparent endorsement of non-monetary contributions to facilitate settlement of water rights disputes is a welcome development. Likewise, the recognition of federal expenditures as appropriate to further habitat improvements and facilitate resolution of at least portions of Endangered Species Act controversies is a step forward. The federal contribution should point the way for future settlements. The fact is that the Snake River Settlement also funded a tribal domestic water system, funded a tribal fisheries and water program, and turned over federal land, a total of $102 million in value to the Nez Perce Tribe. It would be fascinating to see how the federal government's "calculable legal exposure" led to arrival at this figure (plus $26 million for the State of Idaho) under the Criteria and Procedures.

It is time to call it like it is and simply drop the pretext of a pseudo-economic analysis of the value of certain claims and simply acknowledge that Indian water settlements happen when all parties — including Congress and the Administration — see fit to get behind a particular proposal. This would not give carte blanche to those seeking gold-plated settlements, but it would remove an artificial barrier to Indian water settlements and place the focus on the merits of disputes. The creative Snake River approach demonstrates how two different federal administrations were able to support a settlement that provides substantial benefits to the Nez Perce Tribe, protects the interests of state water right holders, and promotes salmon habitat protection. Future administrations should hold its creativity forth as a model for other settlements.

NOTE ON INDIAN WATER SETTLEMENTS

Blumm, Becker, and Smith offer a more cautious analysis of the Snake River settlement:

> As part of the settlement, the state — the only entity allowed to hold instream flow rights under Idaho water law — promised to establish instream flow rights at nearly 200 locations, selected by the tribe, in the Salmon and Clearwater basins and also protect 600 springs on federal lands ceded by the tribe. These instream flow rights will be subordinated to water rights existing at the date of the settlement and also to future domestic, commercial, industrial and municipal water rights, but they will not be subordinated to future agricultural water use, except as to a small, varying percentage of use based on land ownership in each subbasin. The state may change the use of these instream flow rights only after consultation with the tribe. Despite the consultation requirement, the state retains ultimate authority to change uses. The state must also identify other flow-limited streams, take measures to augment instream flows, and undertake other habitat improvement projects, although these commitments are quite vague.
>
> The Nez Perce decision to settle its reserved water right claims has yielded a promise of enhanced instream flows outside its reservation through the instream flow rights contained in the SRBA [Snake River Basin Adjudication] Agreement and through the congressional funding provided in the SRBA Agreement to the tribe and state in separate accounts. The tribe is likely to prioritize use of these funds based on biological and cultural importance, and the state is likely to prioritize these funds based on ESA exposure. It remains to be seen whether the 2005 SRBA settlement will enable the tribe to successfully transform its treaty fishing and water rights into sustainable and meaningful instream flows that can help restore its damaged fishing culture.

Michael C. Blumm, David H. Becker & Joshua D. Smith, *The Mirage of Indian Reserved Water Rights and Western Streamflow Restoration in the McCarran Amendment Era: A Promise Unfulfilled*, 36 ENVTL. L. 1157, 1200–1201 (2006). Their central focus is the instream flow component of the settlement. Considering the negative decision the trial court dealt to the Nez Perce, are they expecting too much from the settlement?

The rapid resort to water settlements as a means for both establishing and ensuring wet water rights as well as settling long and complicated water adjudications, has led to legislation approving several tribes' water rights in one Act. In 2010 Congress supported and enacted the Claims Resolution Act of 2010, Pub. L. No. 111-291 (Dec. 9, 2010), approving four water rights settlements for seven tribes. Thereafter, on March 15, 2012, the Committee on Indian Affairs held a hearing "promoting the negotiation and implementation of water settlements in Indian Country." Recognizing the challenges and concerns over settling Tribes' water rights, U.S. Senator Hon. Daniel K. Akaka in his opening statement noted a continuing need to review the settlement process. David J. Hayes, Deputy Secretary of the U.S. Department of the Interior, further stated that the water settlements help the United States achieve their promise that reservations serve as permanent homelands and end controversies between tribes and neighboring communities over water. According to Secretary Hayes, "[s]ettlement negotiations foster a holistic, problem-solving approach that contrasts with the zero-sum logic of the courtroom, replacing abstract application of legal rules that may have unintended consequences for communities."

However, other testimony indicated that these settlements do not in all circumstances lead to a fast, less-expensive wet water right. Specifically, there was testimony indicating that while the settlement process has been termed "more flexible to collaboration," this flexibility is limited given the United States position that legislation "ties its hands" in preserving pre-existing federally reserved rights to water on reservations. Additionally, concerns over deadlines imposed by confirming legislation generate apprehension about dwindling federal funding. Given the shortage of water supply to many Indian communities, what is the best course of action? Should a tribe negotiate a water settlement that may take years to realize due to limited funding? Testimony also indicated that in some circumstances it is difficult for some tribes to get the federal government to the negotiating table, especially where the interests cross more than one state's boundaries.

For a thorough and insightful treatment of Indian water rights settlements, see BONNIE G. COLBY, JOHN E. THORSON & SARAH BRITTON, NEGOTIATING TRIBAL WATER RIGHTS: FULFILLING PROMISES IN THE ARID WEST (2005). The book outlines the varying goals of parties usually involved in water settlements, including tribes, non-Indian water users, federal governments, state water agencies. Although many of these participants' goals conflict, some may be shared, such as reliable access to water, effective management of water resources, improved community and intergovernmental relations, economic development, conflict resolution, and some measure of stability and ability to plan for the future. Later, the book analyzes and identifies the standard components of water settlements, including finding a source of water to settle tribal claims, securing funds for water development projects, and resolving questions of jurisdiction over water management. The book also explains how these elements have been negotiated, and offers case studies of representative settlements, including the Ak-Chin Water Settlement, the Gila River Settlement, and the Truckee-Carson-Pyramid Lake Water Settlement. Another outstanding treatment of the subject is DANIEL McCOOL, NATIVE WATERS: CONTEMPORARY INDIAN WATER SETTLEMENTS AND THE SECOND TREATY ERA (2002).

TABLE OF CASES

[References are to pages; primary cases in boldface.]

[References are to pages; primary cases in boldface.]

C

[References are to pages; primary cases in boldface.]

[References are to pages; primary cases in boldface.]

E

F

[References are to pages; primary cases in boldface.]

[References are to pages; primary cases in boldface.]

[References are to pages; primary cases in boldface.]

K

L

[References are to pages; primary cases in boldface.]

[References are to pages; primary cases in boldface.]

[References are to pages; primary cases in boldface.]

O

[References are to pages; primary cases in boldface.]

[References are to pages; primary cases in boldface.]

[References are to pages; primary cases in boldface.]

[References are to pages; primary cases in boldface.]

[References are to pages; primary cases in boldface.]

[References are to pages; primary cases in boldface.]

INDEX

[References are to pages.]

[References are to pages.]

[References are to pages.]

[References are to pages.]

[References are to pages.]